NEW YORK PRACTICE

NEW YORK PRACTICE

Third Edition

By

DAVID D. SIEGEL
Distinguished Professor of Law
Albany Law School of Union University

PRACTITIONER TREATISE SERIES®

WEST
GROUP

ST. PAUL, MINN., 1999

COPYRIGHT © 1978, 1991 WEST PUBLISHING CO.
COPYRIGHT © 1999 By WEST GROUP
              610 Opperman Drive
              P.O. Box 64526
              St. Paul, MN 55164–0526
              1–800–328–9352

ISBN 0–314–23933–2

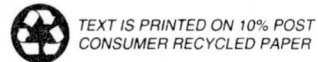
TEXT IS PRINTED ON 10% POST
CONSUMER RECYCLED PAPER

For Rosemarie, Sheela, and Rachel

*

Preface to Third Edition

New York Practice is a scene in motion. Events are frequent, both major and minor, and there have been many developments since the publication of the second edition in 1991.

One is the adoption of the filing system for commencing actions in the supreme and county courts. Another is a set of changes in the disclosure provisions. Earlier changes requiring frequent judicial attention are the adoption of the Uniform Rules that replaced the myriad compilations of individual rules that each of the courts previously had, and the adoption of the Individual Assignment System (IAS) in the supreme and some other courts, replacing the old Master Calendar System. These and other areas of change are sometimes highlighted in this Third Edition by new sections, which bear a letter following the number, like personal service by mail (§ 76A), the IAS (§ 77A), the adjustment of joint liability (§§ 168A–168D), the adoption of sanctions for frivolous conduct (§ 414A), the requirement to supplement prior disclosure responses (§ 352A), and the system for the court-annexed arbitration of claims under specified amounts (§ 585B), to cite a few examples.

More routinely, statutory changes affecting the Civil Practice Law and Rules (CPLR) and other procedural statutes have been numerous, and caselaw, as always, is prolific, sometimes closing gaps but sometimes creating new problems and pitfalls that I have found it important to call attention to. Statutory developments are covered through the first part of the New York Legislature's 1999 session, and caselaw to approximately mid-year in 1999. Numerous recent cases are noted, but cases from the mid 1960s to the mid 1970s, when the main caselaw on the new CPLR was being made, of course remain in large numbers.

I have again included in this edition the federal chapter (Chapter 23) that I devised for the second edition, summarizing the civil jurisdiction and practice of the federal courts and comparing and contrasting it with New York Practice in a number of particulars. It has turned out to be the biggest chapter in the book, and one of the most rewarding I've had the pleasure to construct. I have taught Federal Jurisdiction and Practice alongside New York Practice from the outset, and in my mind the two subjects have evolved into an intertwined series of comparisons and contrasts, automatically recalling, whenever I deal with a procedure in one practice, the counterpart procedure in the other. With Conflict of Laws as the third member of my trio of subjects, my disposition to compare has taken on all the vigor of an instinct. Comparing and contrasting is a sure way to avoid pitfalls, and pitfall-avoidance was my principal aim as I put together the federal chapter. Much of the chapter's materials first emerged in seminars on federal practice that I've participated in with national groups, and the book's longest single section, enumerating the factors to consider in deciding which forum to choose when there is a choice between a federal and a state forum (§ 616), originated in seminars conducted through the New York State Bar Association.

I undertook the editorship of the Association's New York State Law Digest at just about the time the first edition of this book came out. The Law Digest goes monthly to all the Association's members. On its pages I have made many forays into procedural problems in and about the litigation process, especially on matters in which a wrong step can breed harsh consequences, a subject that always absorbs me. Most of these extended procedural treatments were in the form of a lead note with which I customarily began each edition of the Digest. I have referred to these Digest lead notes often in this book, since what they do is expand on my thinking on a procedural subject that I necessarily have to deal with in more summary form in a one-volume text.

For reasons of space, the Law Digest had to discontinue those procedural treatments in 1993. To fill the gap, in April of 1993 I began Siegel's Practice Review, also published monthly, in essence doing two four-page newsletters each month: the New York State Law Digest as a Court of Appeals reporter and Siegel's Practice Review as a reporter on general developments in civil practice. More than 80 issues of the Practice Review are in print as of this writing. They are cited at various points in the book for what are often more expanded treatments of matters necessarily set forth in more abbreviated form here.

The same thing holds true for the Practice Commentaries that I have been writing for McKinney's Consolidated Laws of New York. These go back not just to 1978, when the first edition of this book came out, but to 1963, when the New York Civil Practice Law and Rules came out. The availability of both the Commentaries and Practice Review for cross-citation has enabled me to include in this text a number of points that could otherwise not be encompassed in a single-volume work at all. The form of citation to Siegel's Practice Review is by issue number and page, separated by a colon: "SPR 79:4", for example, refers to page 4 of Issue 79 of the Review. Subscription information about the Practice Review appears at the end of each issue.

This Third Edition is done in two forms. The Practitioner's Edition is in hard cover, with a pocket part in the back for the supplements that will update it annually. The abridged Student Edition, in soft cover, omits the chapters on federal practice and on arbitration, which have their own courses in law school, and the materials on landlord-tenant proceedings and small claims, which are often incidents of other courses, like real estate transactions and consumer rights.

Sometimes a section will note a point elaborated earlier, and perhaps just a section or two earlier. This is done because I nevertheless deem the point a necessary building block for the present section as well. To the student reading several sections through, or a whole chapter at a time, this may seem repetitive. The student should bear in mind that this is done to assure that the book remain an effective tool for the practitioner, who will likely have less time for research and homework. A brief restatement of a point in the section consulted makes it unnecessary for the busy lawyer to hunt it out elsewhere. I think it makes the book a better tool for the lawyer or judge who has to consult it in the tighter time frame of practice. (After joining the practicing bar, the student may register a nunc pro tunc appreciation of the system.)

Several of my former students have checked out the manuscript or proofs of the Third Edition. For this I am grateful to Joanne M. Gaboriault, Jonathan P. Whalen, Daniel R. Ryan, Matthew F. Jones, and Christopher C. O'Brien. Special thanks go to Matthew J. Sava, who obliged me, on short notice, by reading the final pageproofs from beginning to end.

Because it is no less on my mind now, with the Third Edition, than it was when I wrote the first one decades ago, I repeat and even stress what I said then: for his influence on the chain of events that have led me to this point, I have a profound debt to Dean Harold F. McNiece of St. John's University School of Law, deceased for many years now, but not in my memory. My professional life has been a progression through doors he opened to me, and, for good measure, it was he who first introduced me to Rosemarie, my wife now of 30 years.

DAVID D. SIEGEL

Albany, New York
June 1999

*

WESTLAW® Overview

New York Practice, Third Edition, by David D. Siegel, offers a detailed and comprehensive treatment of basic rules, principles and issues relating to New York practice. To supplement the information contained in this book, you can access Westlaw, a computer-assisted legal research service of West Group. Westlaw contains a broad array of legal resources, including case law, statutes, rules, expert commentary, current developments and various other types of information.

Learning how to use these materials effectively will enhance your legal research abilities. To help you coordinate the information in the book with your Westlaw research, this volume contains an appendix listing Westlaw databases, search techniques and sample problems.

THE PUBLISHER

*

Summary of Contents

———

*

Table of Contents

C. FORUM NON CONVENIENS

D. OTHER RESTRICTIONS ON JURISDICTION

E. CONDITIONS PRECEDENT TO SUIT

CHAPTER THREE.   THE STATUTE OF LIMITATIONS

A. INTRODUCTORY

B. THE APPLICABLE PERIODS

C. ALTERING THE PERIOD

D. ACCRUAL

E. INTERPOSITION

F. EXTENSIONS AND TOLLS

K. SUBSTITUTION

L. POOR PERSONS

M. INFANTS AND INCOMPETENTS

CHAPTER EIGHT. PAPERS

CHAPTER NINE. PLEADINGS

A. BASIC RULES OF PLEADING

B. SPECIFIC ITEMS

C. DEMAND FOR RELIEF

D. ELECTION OF REMEDIES

E. SPLITTING

F. THE ANSWER

G. COUNTERCLAIMS

H. CROSS–CLAIMS

I. THE REPLY

J. CORRECTIVE MOTIONS

K. SERVICE OF PLEADINGS

L. VERIFICATION

M. AMENDMENT OF PLEADINGS

C. SUMMARY JUDGMENT

D. SUMMARY JUDGMENT IN LIEU OF COMPLAINT

E. DEFAULT JUDGMENT

F. VOLUNTARY DISCONTINUANCE

G. CONFESSION OF JUDGMENT

H. TENDERS AND OFFERS

I. ACTION ON SUBMITTED FACTS

CHAPTER TWELVE. PROVISIONAL REMEDIES

A. INTRODUCTORY

B. ARREST

C. ATTACHMENT

D. INJUNCTION

E. RECEIVERSHIP

F. NOTICE OF PENDENCY

G. SEIZURE OF CHATTEL

CHAPTER THIRTEEN. DISCLOSURE

A. GENERALLY

D. LAXNESS DISMISSALS

E. MODE OF TRIAL

F. SUBPOENAS AND OATHS

CHAPTER FIFTEEN. THE TRIAL

A. INTRODUCTORY

B. SELECTING A JURY

C. THE TRIAL PROPER

D. THE VERDICT

E. TRIAL MOTIONS

CHAPTER SIXTEEN. THE JUDGMENT

A. CONTENTS OF JUDGMENT

B. INTEREST

C. FEES, COSTS AND DISBURSEMENTS

D. RECORDING THE JUDGMENT

E. RECORDING SATISFACTION

F. VACATING JUDGMENTS AND ORDERS

G. RENEWAL OF JUDGMENT

H. DECLARATORY JUDGMENT

CHAPTER SEVENTEEN. RES JUDICATA

A. INTRODUCTORY

B. GENERAL REQUISITES

C. COMPARISON WITH OTHER DOCTRINES

D. RES JUDICATA IN PARTICULAR SITUATIONS

E. COLLATERAL ESTOPPEL

F. IDENTITY OF PARTIES

G. IDENTIFYING THE ISSUE

H. MULTIPARTY SITUATIONS

I. DIFFERENT COURTS

J. PROCEDURAL INCIDENTS

CHAPTER EIGHTEEN. ENFORCEMENT OF JUDGMENTS

INTRODUCTORY

PART I. ENFORCEMENT OF NON–MONEY JUDGMENTS

A. JUDGMENTS INVOLVING A CHATTEL OR REALTY

B. ENFORCEMENT BY CONTEMPT

PART II. ENFORCEMENT OF MONEY JUDGMENTS

A. IN GENERAL

B. PROPERTY SUBJECT TO ENFORCEMENT

C.   DEVICES IN PERSPECTIVE

D.   PROPERTY EXECUTIONS

E.   INCOME EXECUTION

F.   THE "SUPPLEMENTARY PROCEEDINGS"

G.   INCIDENTAL MATTERS

H.   PRIORITIES AND LIENS

I.   PROTECTION AGAINST ABUSE

J.   CONTEMPT AS BACK–UP DEVICE

CHAPTER NINETEEN. APPEALS

A. INTRODUCTORY

B. APPEALABILITY

C. REVIEWABILITY

D. TAKING THE APPEAL

E. PERFECTING THE APPEAL

F. INCIDENTAL APPELLATE PRACTICE

G. CONCLUDING THE APPEAL

CHAPTER TWENTY. SPECIAL PROCEEDINGS

PART I. THE SPECIAL PROCEEDING, IN GENERAL

CHAPTER TWENTY–ONE.   SMALL CLAIMS

CHAPTER TWENTY–TWO.   ARBITRATION

A.   IN GENERAL

B.   THRESHOLD QUESTIONS

C.   COURT APPLICATIONS

D.   THE ARBITRATION

E.   CONVERTING AWARD INTO JUDGMENT

F.   RELATED PROCEDURES COMPARED

CHAPTER TWENTY–THREE. FEDERAL PRACTICE REVIEWED AND COMPARED: PARALLELS AND PITFALLS

A. FEDERAL PRACTICE, INTRODUCTORY

B. SUBJECT MATTER JURISDICTION

C. CHOOSING THE FORUM

D. FORMS

E. COMMENCEMENT AND PERSONAL JURISDICTION

F. PARTIES, PLEADINGS, AND PAPERS

G. MOTIONS

NEW YORK PRACTICE

*

Chapter One

INTRODUCTION

§ 1. Purpose of this Book

This book has been designed as a basic text on civil practice and procedure in the New York courts. It seeks to afford a broad perspective in each subject, setting forth the basics and stressing the problem areas that appear most often. It also endeavors to correspond as much as possible to actual practice, going heavily into things regularly met by lawyers and judges and more lightly—or not at all—into matters seldom if ever encountered, no matter what the quantity of verbiage a statute or rule may devote to them. For the practicing lawyer, it highlights pitfalls in practice, warning of their whereabouts and suggesting ways around them. For the judge, it addresses not only matters already governed by a statute or rule or covered by caselaw, but problems likely to arise; it suggests avenues of resolution and collateral matters to be alert to in the process.

The book's awareness of the law student is reflected in the fact that every topic starts from scratch, building rather than assuming. By so doing, it also seeks to offer both the lawyer and the judge a quick refresher in an area they may have been away from for a while. The hope is to reduce to nil the "gap" one often hears described between what a student learns in law school and what the new lawyer actually meets afterwards in practice. There should not be such a gap.

Much effort has been made to avoid what this writer has sometimes perceived to be a fault in law books. They start off with great energy, devoting much time and attention to subjects met early in the study, but then grow weary, or concerned about space, and for that reason allow later subjects—equally and perhaps even more important—to fall by the way, inadequately covered or not covered at all. It is no accident that the chapter on the enforcement of money judgments in this book, Chapter 18, rivals both in coverage and in size the earlier chapters on personal jurisdiction, Chapter 4, and parties, Chapter 7. The rationale is hardly a subtle one: to what avail, for example, a spring of jurisdiction when one knows nothing about realizing on a judgment that comes out of it? The book also lays needed stress, in Chapter 13, on disclosure, that mass of devices whereby an attorney prepares to meet an adversary's case in court. There is much of the conceptual in the study of subjects like jurisdiction and parties, grand stuff for the give and take of a classroom. Disclosure and enforcement, on the other hand, involve less of the conceptual and much of the practical. The text feels an equal commitment to all of them.

There are independent chapters, towards the end of the book, on appeals and special proceedings, the latter including a separate treatment of both the Article 78 proceeding and the ubiquitous Summary Proceeding ("Landlord–Tenant") to Recover the Possession of Real Property. These are designed at least in part to supply practitioners some recourse to these important topics if they want a perspective or a review of them. The same is true of Small Claims, a subject of much moment to the average citizen; it has a short but independent chapter of its own.

1

There is a chapter on arbitration, Chapter 22. Arbitration is expanding in great strides, and so, therefore, is the body of caselaw surrounding it. Since this is the next-to-last chapter in the book, much effort has been made to assure it its place in the skyline: an imposing structure next to the courthouse and not some shack off to the rear.

The last chapter, Chapter 23, on federal jurisdiction and practice, is a special one devised to emphasize contrasts with New York practice and to point out special pitfalls for New York lawyers stepping into the federal courts without the same familiarity with federal practice that they have with New York practice. It also performs the reverse function of cluing lawyers with primarily a federal practice into major points of difference with state practice.

To facilitate access to the wide range of subjects that fall under the heading of civil practice, they have been subdivided into as many separate sections as feasible. Their captions appear in the table of contents at the front of the book, and are repeated under the boldface headings used within each chapter. These headings, under which related sections are gathered, offer a quick reference point for review of a given area. Cross-references have been generously sprinkled about to connect one subject with another without unnecessary repetition.

"SPR" references appear frequently. They refer to Siegel's Practice Review, a monthly newsletter reporting on developments in New York civil practice. Because this textbook is updated annually while the SPR, which is also authored by this writer, is published monthly, the SPR serves as a kind of interim monthly updater between the regular annual supplements. Conversely, this text often serves as background for the special notes and summaries that appear in the SPR. Because the SPR treatments are of course more extensive than space allows in a single-volume work or its annual supplements, an effort has been made to include these SPR references whenever the

subject or case under discussion has received an SPR treatment.

The form of an SPR citation is by Issue number and page, separated by a colon. The citation "SPR 58:4", for example, refers to page 4 of Issue 58 of Siegel's Practice Review.

The accessibility of the Practice Review through these citations has also made it possible to inject tersely a number of additional points that would otherwise be beyond the range of a one-volume text.

§ 2. The CPLR

The Civil Practice Law and Rules, officially citable as CPLR,[1] is the major tool in New York civil practice. It governs in all courts of civil jurisdiction except to the extent that an inconsistent statute governs. The purpose of this deference by the CPLR is to make it the generally applicable body of procedural law while also enabling more specific statutes to govern in special situations or in courts with particularized functions.

The CPLR became effective on September 1, 1963, replacing the Civil Practice Act of 1921, which superseded the Code of Civil Procedure—known as the Throop Code after Montgomery Throop—of the 1870's. That in turn replaced the famous Field Code—after David Dudley Field—of 1848. The Field Code was a major American step forward in the modernization of civil procedure and a national inspiration that is still felt in many other states and in the Federal Rules of Civil Procedure.

The CPLR is largely the product of the Advisory Committee on Practice and Procedure, appointed in 1955 to modernize practice. The committee was appointed by the Temporary Commission on the Courts, whose other major effort was the reorganization of the New York courts that became effective September 1, 1962. The committee wrote a number of reports, which are valuable references in practice and are cited from time to time in the book.

There are slots for 100 articles in the CPLR, not all of them filled. Gaps appear wherever

§ 2

1. CPLR 101.

the legislature thought it wise to keep openings for future use. The first numbered CPLR provision is 101, the last 10005. This system enables each number to identify the article in which the provision appears as well as the provision's position within the article. Dropping the last two digits leaves the article number: § 101 is in Article 1 (drop the 01), § 10005 is in Article 100 (drop the 05), etc.

Within a given article the numbering of provisions is usually consecutive, but there are sometimes gaps. These, too, represent a legislative judgment about where room should be left for future activity. In Article 32, for example, the first numbered provision is 3201 and the next 3211, while in Article 3 the initial provisions are numbered consecutively.

It will also be noticed that some CPLR provisions are preceded by a section designation (§) and others by the word "Rule". The former are strictly statutes and can be altered only by the legislature. Originally, those designated "Rule" could be altered by either the legislature or the Judicial Conference (now superseded by the Office of Court Administration). So provided § 229(e)(3) of the Judiciary Law, but it was repealed in 1978 in conjunction with the overhaul of judicial administration[2] without being addressed in the superseding legislation. It thus appears that even the alteration of a mere "rule" is now reserved to the legislature alone.[3]

Both the statutes and the rules in the CPLR are law as long as they do not conflict. If they do conflict, presumably the statute controls. It isn't possible to guess which CPLR provisions are statutes and which are rules. The designations are often arbitrary. Which one a given provision is can be learned only by looking it up. CPLR 101 authorizes the citation of CPLR provisions without indicating whether the provision cited is a statute or rule, and that manner of citation has become the common practice.

A definitions section, CPLR 105, singles out a number of commonly used words and phrases and gives them a specific meaning for CPLR use. They will be mentioned from time to time as context requires.

§ 3. Other Procedural Tools

The supreme court in New York, which as will be seen is a court of primarily original, not appellate, jurisdiction, is governed directly by the CPLR. It does not have an individual court act. Neither do the county courts, whose civil practice also comes directly from the CPLR. But each of the other courts of original jurisdiction in the state has a "court act".

A court act prescribes the court's jurisdiction and regulates selected procedures in varying degrees. Each court is governed first by its own court act, but as long as there is no conflict between the court act and the CPLR, civil practice in the court is governed by the CPLR as well. In some courts having their own court acts, in fact, the CPLR is relevant far more often than the court act itself is because the latter addresses only a handful of selected procedures thought to need special treatment in the court.

This is especially the case in the courts governed by the so-called "uniform acts", which govern the lower courts of civil jurisdiction. These acts are largely uniform among themselves, right down to the numbering system. Four were considered necessary because of certain differences among the lower courts in jurisdiction and to some extent in procedure as well. The four are the New York City Civil Court Act, which governs the civil court in New York City; the Uniform District Court Act, modeled on the New York City Civil Court Act and governing civil practice in the Nassau and Suffolk county district courts (those are the only two counties that presently have district courts); the Uniform City Court Act, modeled on the Uniform District Court Act and governing civil practice in all city courts (61 of them) outside New York City; and finally the Uniform Justice Court Act, modeled on the

---

2. See § 5 below.

3. This applies only to a "Rule" appearing in the CPLR and should not be confused with the individual rules of particular courts or categories of courts. Those

rules, including the Uniform Rules for the New York State Trial Courts, are adopted and regulated by the Chief Administrator of the Courts. See §§ 3 and 5, below.

Uniform City Court Act and governing civil practice in all of the town and village courts of the state. The jurisdiction of those courts will be treated later.

Article 2 in each of the uniform acts sets forth the subject matter jurisdiction of the courts governed by the particular act. The remainder of each act singles out certain procedures in order to simplify them, recognizing that these courts service the smaller cases.

The surrogate's court has its own court act, called the Surrogate's Court Procedure Act, or SCPA. So has the family court, governed by the Family Court Act. Since those courts handle business substantially different from the ordinary run of civil litigation, their court acts are more profuse on procedure and the need to rely on the CPLR is consequently reduced. But the CPLR is still applicable when consistent.[1]

The court of claims is governed by the Court of Claims Act, which sets forth the court's jurisdiction. It has only a handful of procedural provisions, with the result—intended—that the CPLR is more frequently used there.

The Real Property Actions and Proceedings Law (RPAPL) contains a number of special provisions relevant only in certain categories of actions affecting realty. These provisions are additional to the CPLR, which is still the major tool in those actions.[2] The CPLR is also the major tool in matrimonial actions, although the Domestic Relations Law contains some special procedural instruction, which will be referred to from time to time.

Some of the consolidated laws have important procedural provisions. These, too, will be cited and discussed as they arise. Among the better known are the Business Corporation Law sections that deal with process service,[3] and the non-resident motorist statute.[4]

Superimposed on all of this are the rules of court. Prior to January 6, 1986, there were

numerous sets of rules, each court having its own. These were rescinded on that date and a few sets of "Uniform Rules" promulgated in their place. Each category of court has its own set of uniform rules, as follows:

Part 200: Uniform Rules for Courts Exercising Criminal Jurisdiction

Part 202: Uniform Civil Rules for the Supreme Court and the County Court

Part 205: Uniform Rules for the Family Court

Part 206: Uniform Rules for the Court of Claims

Part 207: Uniform Rules for the Surrogate's Court

Part 208: Uniform Civil Rules for the New York City Civil Court

Part 210: Uniform Civil Rules for the City Courts Outside of the City of New York

Part 212: Uniform Civil Rules for the District Courts

Part 214: Uniform Civil Rules for the Justice Courts

There is additionally a Part 125, entitled "Uniform Rules for the Engagement of Counsel", of interest to every trial lawyer in the state. It has instructions for the resolution of "conflicting engagements", a perennial friction in practice when lawyers find their presence demanded in two or more courts at the same time.

The Uniform Rules, notably Part 202 (which governs in the supreme court), will often be cited in this book, especially when fundamental procedures (not mere incidents) are affected. Among the fundamentals that come from the uniform rules are those governing certain aspects of motion practice and those governing the "note of issue" and "certificate of readiness", the papers whose filing puts the case on the court's trial calendar.[5]

---

§ 3

1. SCPA 102; Fam.Ct.Act § 165. For discussion of the application of the CPLR in the Family Court, see Schwartz v. Schwartz, 23 A.D.2d 204, 259 N.Y.S.2d 751 (1st Dep't 1965).

2. Further discussion of the interplay of the RPAPL and CPLR is in § 571, below (Practitioner's Edition), in the treatment of the summary proceeding.

3. Bus.Corp.L. §§ 304–307.

4. Veh. & Traf.L. § 253.

5. These are discussed in §§ 369 and 370. A "calendar" is just a list of cases awaiting trial or other disposi-

A given court governed by an assigned set of uniform rules may also have individual rules. In a court system with a mission as extensive and as varied as New York's, uniformity is sometimes elusive if not altogether illusory.

The rules are also the source of the compulsory arbitration procedure for claims of $6000 or less, officially called the "Alternative Method of Dispute Resolution by Arbitration".[6]

§ 4. One Form of Action

Law and equity have long been merged in New York and the old common law forms of action have long been abandoned. The distinctions between law and equity are officially abolished,[1] but linger. They are still relevant, for example, in determining the right to trial by jury. They persist also in that claims sounding in what was once equity, and which appeal to the conscience of the court, are still subject to certain equitable defenses, such as laches and clean hands, to which law claims are not.

The CPLR governs in both actions and special proceedings. The reader who knows what a motion is can quickly learn what a special proceeding is. An action is the plenary prosecution of a right, seeking a final judgment. A motion is generally an application made within an action for some item of incidental relief, usually involving some step in the processing of the action. The procedures of a motion, to be met in detail in a later chapter,[2] are quick and expeditious. The movant picks a motion day—a day on which the court or the individual judge assigned to the case hears motions—and notifies the court and the other parties of the relief sought. The motion comes on at the appointed time for hearing, and for disposition shortly thereafter.

A special proceeding is as plenary as an action in that it seeks the vindication of a right in a final judgment,[3] but it is brought on with the procedure and speed of a motion.[4] With so expeditious a path, the special proceeding is of course preferable to an action whenever it is available, but it is available only when a statute specifically prescribes it;[5] otherwise the usual procedures of a plenary action must be followed. Examples of authorized special proceedings are many. Some are contained in the CPLR itself, such as the Article 78 proceeding, whose primary mission is to review administrative decisions, and the special proceedings authorized by Article 75 to test whether a given dispute is arbitrable. Among the most highly specialized (and frequently brought) of special proceedings is the Summary Proceeding to Recover Possession of Real Property, used to settle landlord-tenant disputes quickly. It is governed in detail by Article 7 of the Real Property Actions and Proceedings Law. Special proceedings are treated in depth in Chapter 20.

In the CPLR, the word "action" includes a special proceeding.[6] This enables procedures that are applicable in terms to an "action" to govern in special proceedings as well, whenever appropriate,[7] without having constantly to repeat the words "special proceeding". Sometimes a lawyer will assume that a special proceeding lies in a given situation when in fact it does not. Sometimes it can be a close question. In older practice, the bringing of a special proceeding when an action was appropriate, or vice versa, resulted in dismissal. Dismissal is no longer permitted in that situation. Under CPLR 103(c), as long as jurisdiction over the parties has been obtained, the court today must convert the case to proper form.[8] The defect is nothing more than a "mischaracteri-

tion. See § 368.

6. The governing provisions are in Part 28 of the Rules of the Chief Judge—available in the annually recompiled McKinney's N.Y. Rules of Court softcover—promulgated on the authority of CPLR 3405. See § 585B below (Practitioner's Edition).

§ 4

1. CPLR 103(a).

2. Chapter 10 below.

3. CPLR 411.

4. Compare CPLR 403 (special proceeding) with CPLR 2214 (motion).

5. CPLR 103(b).

6. CPLR 105.

7. For discussion of those procedures that are unique to the special proceeding, see § 550 et seq., below.

8. CPLR 103(c) came into New York practice as part of the original CPLR, which went into effect on Sept. 1, 1963. It had no forebear.

zation",[9] and the conversion entails nothing more than an order reciting that the pleadings in the special proceeding are to be deemed the pleadings in an action and directing that the case proceed henceforth as if it were an action in which the answer has just been served.[10] Similarly, a party may sometimes make a mere motion for relief that technically requires a special proceeding. If no prejudice is demonstrated, a like conversion may be allowed, this time from motion to special proceeding.[11] And a proceeding mistakenly captioned under one statute can be treated as having been brought under the proper one.[12] CPLR 103(c) has even been invoked to treat a special proceeding as an appeal.[13]

§ 5. Administration of the Courts

The authority and responsibility for administrative supervision of the courts is in the chief judge of the court of appeals, who shall, says the state constitution, "after consultation with the administrative board, ... establish standards and administrative policies for general application throughout the state", and submit them to the court of appeals. The policies are "promulgated", however, only after "approval" by the court.[1] Thus the court of appeals has the ultimate authority over the "standards" and "policies" of judicial administration, which practically speaking amounts to a kind of veto power.

The chief judge has the initiative of administration. This she exercises through a chief administrator whom she appoints and through deputy administrators and "administrative judges" of the various courts, whom the chief administrator in turn appoints. The appoint-

ment of the chief administrator by the chief judge is made "with the advice and consent of the administrative board". The chief administrator serves at the "pleasure" of the chief judge, in whose behalf he carries out the day-to-day administration of the court system.[2]

The administrative board is a five-judge body consisting of the presiding justice of each of the four appellate divisions, and the chief judge, who acts as chair.[3] The chief judge's administrative functions are carried out in periodic "consultation" with the board. There is also a "judicial conference", representative of all of the state's courts.[4]

The Judiciary Law elaborates the functions of each of the components in this administrative hierarchy, the functions of:

—the chief judge and the court of appeals, in Judiciary Law § 211;

—the chief administrator, in § 212;

—the administrative board, in § 213;

—the judicial conference, in § 214–a.

The Office of Court Administration (OCA) is the physical base of judicial administration in New York.[5] Administrative and related directives are channeled through the Office of Court Administration to the various courts, either directly or through designated local administrators and administrative judges.[6] OCA is also the statistical repository of the court system.

Through an advisory committee on civil practice, appointed by the chief judge and consisting of lawyers, judges, and professors, OCA watches over the CPLR and tries to keep it up to date with the procedural needs of litigation.

---

9. Altona Citizens Committee, Inc. v. Town of Altona, 77 A.D.2d 954, 430 N.Y.S.2d 894 (3d Dep't 1980), aff'd 54 N.Y.2d 908, 445 N.Y.S.2d 131, 429 N.E.2d 809 (1981).

10. See Phalen v. Theatrical Protective Union No. 1, 22 N.Y.2d 34, 290 N.Y.S.2d 881, 238 N.E.2d 295, cert.den. 393 U.S. 1000, 89 S.Ct. 486, 21 L.Ed.2d 465 (1968).

11. See, e.g., Empire Mutual Ins. Co. v. Palladino, 54 A.D.2d 863, 388 N.Y.S.2d 601 (1st Dep't 1976).

12. See, e.g., Malatestinic v. Board of Educ. of City of N.Y., 132 A.D.2d 661, 518 N.Y.S.2d 34 (2d Dep't 1987), treating a proceeding brought under Article 78 of the CPLR (relating to administrative action) as one brought under Article 75 (relating to arbitration).

13. See Carroll v. Gammerman, 193 A.D.2d 202, 602 N.Y.S.2d 841 (1st Dep't 1993), noted in SPR 19:2.

§ 5

1. Const. Art.VI, § 28(c); Jud.L. § 211(2).

2. Const. Art.VI, § 28(a),(b); Jud.L. § 210(3).

3. Const. Art.VI, § 28(a); Jud.L. § 210(2).

4. Jud.L. § 214.

5. The Office of Court Administration has its principal offices at 25 Beaver Street, New York, New York 10004.

6. See Bellacosa, Judicial Administration, New York State Bar Journal, July 1986, p.6.

OCA also conducts procedural studies, which may be found along with judicial statistics in its published annual reports. OCA reports annually to the legislature with its recommendations for procedural changes and updating.

§ 6. Liberal Construction

The direction contained in the CPLR about how it shall be construed is in CPLR 104:

> Construction. The civil practice law and rules shall be liberally construed to secure the just, speedy and inexpensive determination of every civil judicial proceeding.

"Civil judicial proceeding" means actions and special proceedings collectively. It includes everything but a criminal action.[1]

CPLR 104 is modeled on Rule 1 of the Federal Rules of Civil Procedure, which makes the federal caselaw available by analogy should a point arise that has not been addressed by a case in New York. A sound approach to CPLR 104 would be this: when a provision is met and differing applications are suggested for it, its intent should be determined and its language subordinated to what is known to be its intent. In other words, find the direction in which the provision aims, and when two constructions are equally permissible apply the one that will send it farther in its intended direction.

There are two provisions in the CPLR of such pervasive relevance to all of procedure—and to the "liberal" construction that CPLR 104 espouses—that they should be noted at the outset of any study of New York practice. They are CPLR 2001 and 2004.

CPLR 2001, governing mistakes and omissions in general, reads as follows:

> At any stage of an action, the court may permit a mistake, omission, defect or irregularity to be corrected, upon such terms as may be just, or, if a substantial right of a party is not prejudiced, the mistake, omis-

sion, defect or irregularity shall be disregarded.

That statement should be treated as part of the liberal construction edict. It puts procedure into perspective by reminding bench and bar that procedure is a means, not an end. Even if some CPLR requirement is violated, the possibility of avoiding prejudice to other parties by mere correction of the mistake mandates that the correction be allowed. If the error prejudices no one, the court can merely direct that it be ignored, even relieving the errant party of the trouble of correcting it. This provision is of great value in practice. As long as the mistake does not affect jurisdiction, it qualifies as an irregularity at worst.[2] Only when the defect touches jurisdiction does the need arise to distinguish between mere irregularities (which CPLR 2001 can correct or disregard) and jurisdictional defects (which it cannot). This matter is elaborated elsewhere.[3] When jurisdiction is not involved, CPLR 2001 is a faithful standby, preventing procedure from becoming an end in itself. It recognizes the margin of human error and gives the court a margin to remedy or forgive it.

CPLR 2004, the provision governing extensions of time, is another fundamental of practice. It reads as follows:

> Except where otherwise expressly prescribed by law, the court may extend the time fixed by any statute, rule or order for doing any act, upon such terms as may be just and upon good cause shown, whether the application for extension is made before or after the expiration of the time fixed.

Considering the large number of time periods met in civil practice (and to be considered in this book), it is nice to know at the outset that occasional tardiness need not be fatal. But this early notification about the courts' generosity in extending time periods is not offered as reassurance to the tardy: good practice re-

§ 6

1. CPLR 105.

2. Patrician Plastic Corp. v. Bernadel Realty Corp., 25 N.Y.2d 599, 307 N.Y.S.2d 868, 256 N.E.2d 180 (1970).

3. See § 64, below, which discusses jurisdictional defects versus mere irregularities in conjunction with sum-

mons service. The provisional remedies, treated in Chapter 12, are the major exception to the rule of liberal construction in CPLR 104. They are considered to be drastic in nature and are given a tighter construction. See § 306 below.

quires prompt responses to time-limited demands, or at minimum a stipulation with one's adversary extending the time (which would ordinarily obviate an application to the court for an extension). The statute is intended more as an admonition to practitioners who would hold their opponents too rigidly to time requirements. CPLR 2004 is in the wings and can be put on stage by mere motion. The courts are not patient with lawyers who make too much of timeliness when jurisdiction is not involved. The courts resent that their own time "should have been expended in a matter that properly should have been disposed of by the exercise of simple courtesy between attorneys",[4] and they expect this mutual courtesy to supply reasonable time extensions when requested.[5]

There are two statutory exceptions to the power of CPLR 2004 to extend time. One is the statute of limitations itself, i.e., the time in which an action has to be commenced. It is not subject to discretionary extensions.[6] The second is the time in which to take an appeal.[7] Occasionally some other time period is unexpectedly treated as a statute of limitations, with the result that it, too, becomes unextendable under CPLR 2004,[8] but the exceptions are few and the uses of CPLR 2004 many.

§ 7. Forms

CPLR 107 authorizes the chief administrator of the courts to promulgate forms for civil practice. When he does so the forms become official forms, and they "shall", says the statute, "be sufficient ... [to] illustrate the simplicity and brevity of statement" that the CPLR is looking for. A number of forms have been promulgated under this provision. Several of them are set forth in this text at relevant junctures.

All the other myriad forms available through law publishers for civil practice in general and for pleadings in particular are helpful, but not official. They merely represent what some lawyer, retained by the publisher to do a little form work, deems satisfactory in a given instance. Often the form used is one that got by without objection in an actual case. The lawyer should not be unduly impressed with printed forms. They are suitable for guidance, but the lawyer should not hesitate to make whatever variation is needed for the case. There is no magic in print and, indeed, some printed forms used repeatedly have suddenly been rejected by the courts because of intervening changes in the law or in constitutional attitudes, among other reasons.[1] The warning, therefore, is not to use privately published form books mindlessly. With a small injection of imagination, however, they can be excellent guides.

An official form has this much advantage, anyway: when it is used in its appropriate context, it is "sufficient as a matter of law".[2]

---

4. Bermudez v. City of New York, 22 A.D.2d 865, 254 N.Y.S.2d 420, 421 (1st Dep't 1964).

5. For a brief time during the early 1980s, courtesy between lawyers in the granting of extensions of time to plead disappeared almost entirely because of a short-lived caselaw rule that denied the courts discretion to consider "law office failures"—the cause of most pleading delays—as excuses. This led to a refusal of pleading (and even other) time extensions between lawyers in the hope of obtaining an irrevocable default against the other side. A statute, CPLR 2005, was added in 1983 to overrule the case that started it all—Barasch v. Micucci, 49 N.Y.2d 594, 427 N.Y.S.2d 732 (1980)—and restore judicial discretion. In the process, it restored courtesy between lawyers as well. See § 231.

6. CPLR 201.

7. CPLR 5514(c).

8. This happened with the period in which to test whether an issue is arbitrable under CPLR 7503(c). See § 593 (Practitioner's Edition).

§ 7

1. See, e.g., Long Island City Sav. and Loan Ass'n v. Suggs, 78 Misc.2d 16, 355 N.Y.S.2d 550 (Sup.Ct., Nassau County, 1974).

2. Pritzker v. Falk, 58 Misc.2d 989, 990, 297 N.Y.S.2d 622, 625 (Sup.Ct., Queens County, 1969).

Chapter Two

THE COURTS AND THEIR JURISDICTION

Analysis

A. THE COURT SYSTEM

Table of Sections

§ 8. Kinds of Jurisdiction

There are many ways to subdivide "jurisdiction". Initially a distinction should be made between "subject matter" jurisdiction and "personal" jurisdiction. Personal jurisdiction has to do with the court's authority to bind a particular party to its judgment. A plaintiff submits to that authority by bringing an action in the court; the defendant is subjected to it when she is served with the court's process under circumstances that require her to defend the action—i.e., when a jurisdictional basis exists against her, a topic explored in a later chapter.[1] An objection in this category of jurisdiction is waivable, and one way a defendant waives it is by contesting on the merits without raising it.

The various kinds of "rem" jurisdiction are really subcategories of personal jurisdiction, usually turned to only when personal jurisdiction is lacking. They are subject to the same kind of waiver. With "rem" jurisdiction, the court has obtained actual or constructive custody of some property of the defendant, so that it is able, even without personal jurisdiction, to render a judgment effective at least to the extent of divesting the defendant of any interest in that property.[2]

Subject matter jurisdiction is a more rigid concept. It concerns the court's competence to entertain a given kind of case. A court gets its subject matter jurisdiction from the constitution and laws of the sovereign it serves. If the jurisdiction is not so conferred, the court lacks

---

§ 8

1. Chapter 4. The discussion of bases for personal jurisdiction is in § 59 and § 80 et seq., below

2. Rem jurisdiction is discussed beginning in § 101.

"subject matter" jurisdiction. This defect is generally not curable by waiver, consent, estoppel, laches, or anything else.

Jurisdiction of the subject matter cannot be conferred on the court by any consent or stipulation of the parties. The objection may be taken at any stage of the action, and the court may, on its own motion whenever its attention is called to the facts, refuse to proceed further, and dismiss the action.[3]

If a court lacks subject matter jurisdiction, its judgment is void, which generally means that the judgment is subject to collateral attack, i.e., that it can be resisted when the question of its validity arises in another forum later on.[4] Thus, for example, if a city court, which lacks matrimonial jurisdiction, purports to divorce the parties, the judgment would be of no effect. Fortunately, problems of subject matter jurisdiction are relatively infrequent in the New York courts, in contrast with the federal courts.[5]

One aspect of this contrast between the federal and New York courts highlights the difference between "general" and "limited" jurisdiction. Federal courts sitting within the states are all courts of limited jurisdiction; they can hear only such cases as Congress has authorized by statute. If the case is not within a jurisdiction-giving Act of Congress, a United States district court is incompetent to entertain it. All of the courts in the New York state system, original and appellate both, are also courts of limited jurisdiction, but with the important exception of the New York Supreme Court, the state's sole court of "general" jurisdiction. "General" jurisdiction implies all the jurisdiction that a court of original instance can have. Since used in contradistinction to "limited", the word "general" is sometimes taken to mean "unlimited". That goes too far. But while there are some exceptions, to be discussed under supreme court jurisdiction later,[6] "general" comes pretty close to meaning "unlimited".

The jurisdiction of a court of general jurisdiction is presumed; that of a court of limited jurisdiction must, whenever questioned, be specifically demonstrated, i.e., it must be shown that the particular claim is within some law or constitutional provision conferring subject matter jurisdiction.

It is important not to confuse "limited" with "impotent". In the phraseology of subject matter jurisdiction, "limited" signifies only that the categories of cases the court may hear are restricted. Several strictures narrow the appellate path to the New York Court of Appeals, for example, but when a case has accurately negotiated them and the court's jurisdiction is properly exercised in the case, the court's powers are potent, indeed. On all matters of New York law, it is the court of last resort. In this sense, the U.S. Supreme Court, the highest court in the land, may be said to have the most limited jurisdiction of all.

Other possible pairings of subject matter jurisdiction are self-explanatory: civil and criminal is one set; original and appellate is another. Some courts can have a bit of each. Several in New York are in that category.

Another sorting is into courts of record and courts not of record. This is relatively unimportant in the present age because all courts keep records. Today, whether a court is officially a court "of record" depends entirely on the legislature. If the court is listed in § 2 of the Judiciary Law, it is a court of record; if not, it is not. All of the state's courts are courts of record, because so listed, except the town and village courts.

§ 9. Court System; Geography

New York is divided into four judicial departments, each of which is subdivided into judicial districts consisting of counties. The map appearing below illustrates this. The districts are relevant mainly for the election of supreme court justices and for administration.

---

3. Robinson v. Oceanic Steam Navig. Co., 112 N.Y. 315, 324, 19 N.E. 625, 627 (1889).

4. A "collateral" should be distinguished from a "direct" attack. The prime examples of the direct attack are

the motion to vacate the judgment, made to the court that rendered it, and the appeal.

5. See § 611 below (Practitioner's Edition).

6. See § 12 below.

The role of the counties in civil practice is a greater one. Venue in supreme court actions, for example, is based on a county nexus.

A chart of the court system, appearing after the map, illustrates a number of differences among the courts, each of which, and its jurisdiction, will be discussed in ensuing sections.

The court of appeals is the state's court of last resort. Below it are the main intermediate appellate courts—the appellate divisions—one in each of the four judicial departments. The main court of original jurisdiction is the supreme court, whose place on the chart is larger and higher than that of the other trial-level courts to recognize that the supreme court has general jurisdiction, while all the others have limited jurisdiction. On the next level are the family court, the court of claims, the surrogate's court, and the county court. They have been put on that level because the state constitution gives their process territorial scope equal to that of the supreme court: it may be served in any part of the state.[1]

Below those courts are six more. The three on the next level down are the New York City civil and criminal courts and the district courts. The legislature may permit their process to be served statewide.[2] The city, town, and village courts are on the last level because their process cannot be served beyond an adjoining county. The constitution has thus put them in a niche below the others.[3] The box for the city courts has been made larger than that assigned to the town and village courts merely to flag the fact that judges of the city courts— and of all of the other courts on the chart— must be lawyers, while the justices of the town and village courts need not be.[4]

The supreme court box has an appellate term inserted at the bottom. The appellate term is a court that exists only if the appellate division of the particular department creates it. An appellate term can hear appeals from the county courts and from the courts on the bottom two levels.

The lines indicate appellate paths. Broken lines indicate that whether the appeal follows that path depends on either of two factors: the kind of case (capital cases, for example, go directly to the court of appeals from the trial court), or whether the particular appellate division has created an appellate term and directed lower court appeals to it (the First and Second departments have, the others have not).

Direct appeal to the court of appeals, bypassing intermediate appellate courts, also lies in certain cases involving constitutional issues.[5] Lines so indicating have been omitted; they would run from most of the courts on the chart.

§ 9

1. Const. Art. VI, § 1(c). As will be seen in the study of personal jurisdiction, process may today be served even beyond the state in many instances. See § 100 below.

2. Const. Art. VI, § 1(c).

3. Id.

4. Const. Art. VI, § 20(a).

5. See CPLR 5601(b)(2).

JUDICIAL DEPARTMENTS
AND
JUDICIAL DISTRICTS

See
McKINNEY'S JUDICIARY LAW
§§ 70 and 140

1st Judicial Dept. includes Judicial District 1, 12
2nd Judicial Dept. includes Judicial Districts 2, 9, 10, 11
3rd Judicial Dept. includes Judicial Districts 3, 4, 6
4th Judicial Dept. includes Judicial Districts 5, 7, 8

12ᵗʰ – Bronx
1ˢᵗ – N.Y.
2ⁿᵈ – Richmond & Kings
11ᵗʰ – Queens

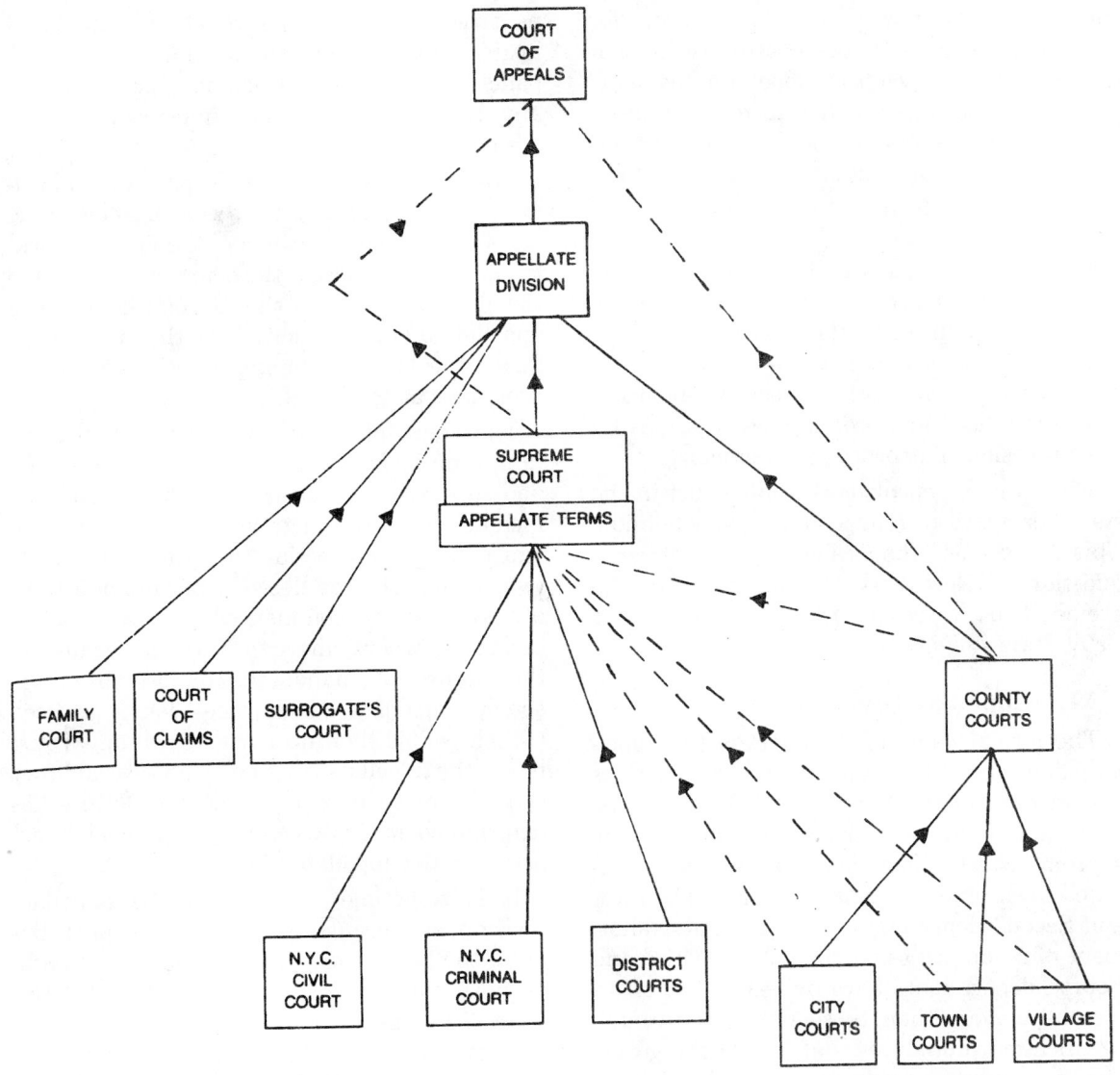

§ 10. Court of Appeals

The highest court of the state is the New York Court of Appeals. It has jurisdiction in both criminal and civil matters, but appellate only. The court consists of a chief judge and six associate judges who are appointed by the governor for 14–year terms from a list recommended by a judicial nominating commission. The appointments are subject to senate ratification. Five judges are needed for a quorum, four for a decision.[1] The Constitution itself limits the jurisdiction of the Court of Appeals, which may be said to be a court of very limited jurisdiction.

The court reviews only questions of law, except in two instances in which it reviews the facts.[2] One is on an appeal from a criminal judgment imposing the death penalty; the other from an appellate division decision reversing or modifying a judgment, finding new facts, and directing that a final judgment be

§ 10

1. Const. Art. VI, § 2(a).

2. The jurisdiction of the Court of Appeals is treated in detail in §§ 527 and 528, below.

entered on the new facts.[3] The reason for reviewing the facts in the death case is that the appeal bypasses the appellate division,[4] and it is New York's policy to allow at least one appellate review of the facts, which also explains the second situation: the new facts found by the appellate division have not yet had appellate review.

Most of the appeals to the court are from the appellate division. In certain narrow instances, in addition to the death case, direct appeal from a lower court is allowed.[5] The court also appoints and oversees the Board of Law Examiners[6] and promulgates the rules for the admission of attorneys to practice.[7]

The court of appeals is the only court in the state permitted to render an advisory opinion. This it may do when called on to answer a question of New York law by the U.S. Supreme Court, a federal court of appeals, or a sister state's highest court.[8]

§ 11.   Appellate Division

The formal name of the court is the appellate division of the supreme court. There is one in each of the four judicial departments. The justices are duly elected members of the supreme court whom the governor has designated to sit on the appellate division. The First and Second departments have a regular allotment of seven justices each, and the Third and Fourth departments have five each, but all in fact have more than those numbers through certification procedures that enable the governor to appoint more justices as judicial busi-

ness requires. Whatever the total number of justices assigned to an appellate division, a panel for a given case cannot exceed five in any department. Four is a quorum and three are needed for a decision.[1]

The court's jurisdiction is primarily appellate.[2] It hears appeals from the supreme court and from the county courts,[3] the family court,[4] the surrogate's court,[5] the court of claims,[6] and the appellate terms of the supreme court.[7] The appellate division reviews both the law and the facts,[8] the latter including exercises of discretion made at trial level.

The court also has some original jurisdiction, prominent among which is the admission and supervision of attorneys.[9] Other instances include where the facts are not in dispute, in which event an action on submitted facts (which requires the decision of only questions of law) may be commenced in the appellate division;[10] where an Article 78 proceeding in the nature of mandamus or prohibition is sought against a supreme court justice[11] (which would be incongruous in any court below the appellate division); and several other special proceedings that the legislature has determined to expedite by giving them direct access to the appellate division.[12]

It is sometimes noted that the appellate division, as a branch of the supreme court, has all of the latter's original jurisdiction;[13] at other times doubt is expressed about that.[14] But even if the assumption is that the appellate division has it all, it has been held that "as a matter of administrative convenience, it will

---

3.   Const. Art. VI, § 3(a).

4.   Const. Art. VI, § 3(b).

5.   Const. Art. VI, § 3(b)(2); CPLR 5601(b)(2).

6.   Jud.L. §§ 56, 461, 462.

7.   Jud.L. § 53.

8.   Const. Art. VI, § 3(b)(9). See § 528A below.

§ 11

1.   Const. Art. VI, § 4(b).

2.   The jurisdiction of the appellate divisions is treated in detail in § 526, below.

3.   CPLR 5701. County court appeals may be directed instead to an appellate term if a given department has established one. Const. Art. VI, § 8(d).

4.   Fam.Ct.Act § 1111.

5.   SCPA 2701, CPLR 5701.

6.   Ct.Cl.Act § 24.

7.   CPLR 5703(a).

8.   CPLR 5501(c).

9.   Jud.L. § 90, CPLR 9401.

10.   CPLR 3222(b)(3). See § 304 below.

11.   CPLR 506(b)(1).

12.   See, e.g., Tax Law § 2016, the proceeding to review a determination of the Tax Appeals Tribunal affecting a capital gains tax on a real property transfer.

13.   See, e.g., Merritt Hill Vineyards, Inc. v. Windy Heights Vineyard, Inc., 61 N.Y.2d 106, 472 N.Y.S.2d 592, 460 N.E.2d 1077 (1984).

14.   See, e.g., Waldo v. Schmidt, 200 N.Y. 199, 93 N.E. 477 (1910).

ordinarily decline to take original jurisdiction" though it "may do so whenever it sees fit."[15] It rarely sees fit.[16] Practically speaking, the only matters of which the appellate division regularly assumes original jurisdiction are the few expressly conferred.

§ 12. Supreme Court

The supreme court is a single court of statewide jurisdiction, with a branch in each county. Its process may be served anywhere in the state[1] and in some instances, to be studied later, beyond. Justices are elected to the court from judicial districts, for 14–year terms.[2]

The "supreme" court is a misnomer. It is not "supreme". It is two rungs below the state's court of last resort, which is the court of appeals. It is, however, the state's only court of "general" jurisdiction. This refers to original jurisdiction and means that the court has almost all of the jurisdiction the state can confer. The word "almost" is used because a qualification is necessary. Although usually juxtaposed with "limited", "general" in this context does not mean "unlimited". There are two broad categories of original jurisdiction that the supreme court lacks: cases of which exclusive jurisdiction has been conferred by Congress on the federal courts,[3] and actions against the state, of which the New York Legislature has conferred exclusive jurisdiction on the court of claims.[4]

With those exceptions, perhaps expanded to include the few instances in which the appellate division exercises original jurisdiction, the supreme court has all the rest of original juris-

diction. It is the superseder of all the jurisdiction, civil and criminal, exercised by the English law courts and court of chancery. When law and equity merged in the 1846 New York Constitution, the supreme court got the equity jurisdiction, too.[5]

There are many other courts of original jurisdiction in New York, and it is the policy of the state to have these other courts handle matters of which they have jurisdiction even though the supreme court has it, too. The supreme court can probate a will, for example, even though that is the primary business of the surrogate's court,[6] and it has jurisdiction, for another example, of a summary proceeding even though it is the state's policy to have the summary proceeding (landlord-tenant business) tried in the lower courts.[7] In these instances of concurrent jurisdiction, when a case is brought in the supreme court that could have been brought in some other court, the supreme court will usually transfer it to the appropriate other court even while acknowledging that it—the supreme court—has jurisdiction of the matter.[8] It will make that acknowledgement even in the face of a statute purporting to give another court "exclusive" jurisdiction.[9] How can such a statute be disregarded? The reason is this:

The intention to secure the supreme court's general jurisdiction is in the constitution itself. It is even provided that when new classes of actions are created, the supreme court "shall have jurisdiction" over them even though another court may receive the jurisdiction as

---

15. In re Association of the Bar of the City of New York, 222 A.D. 580, 585, 227 N.Y.S. 1, 6 (1st Dep't 1928).

16. Even where original jurisdiction is expressly conferred on the appellate division by statute, the court may sometimes exert itself to resist it. See, e.g., In re Willmark Serv. System, 21 A.D.2d 478, 251 N.Y.S.2d 267 (1st Dep't 1964).

§ 12

1. Const. Art. VI, § 1(a),(c).

2. Const. Art. VI, § 6(c).

3. The supremacy clause of the federal constitution accounts for this. U.S.Const. Art. VI. Examples of exclusive federal jurisdiction are bankruptcy matters, 28 U.S.C.A. § 1334, and patent and copyright infringement suits, 28 U.S.C.A. § 1338(a), among many others.

4. This limitation on supreme court jurisdiction results from the fact that suit against the state requires a waiver of sovereign immunity and the state, in making the waiver, has conditioned it on the court of claims having exclusive jurisdiction. See Ct.Cl.Act §§ 8, 9.

5. In re Steinway, 159 N.Y. 250, 53 N.E. 1103 (1899).

6. In re Malloy, 278 N.Y. 429, 17 N.E.2d 108 (1938).

7. See Antique & Period Furn. Co. v. Lassandro, 40 Misc.2d 635, 243 N.Y.S.2d 711 (Sup.Ct., N.Y. County, 1963).

8. 3505 Realty Corp. v. Weinberger, 41 Misc.2d 254, 245 N.Y.S.2d 150 (Sup.Ct., Bronx County, 1963).

9. See, e.g., People v. Davis, 27 A.D.2d 299, 278 N.Y.S.2d 750 (1st Dep't 1967).

well.[10] This means that the supreme court gets the jurisdiction from the new law automatically, even if only some other court is named in the jurisdiction-conferring statute.[11]

It is also the state's policy to have a money action brought in the lowest court jurisdictionally competent to entertain it. To this end there are costs punishments for cases brought in the supreme court when, whatever the amount sought, the judgment ends up below a stated sum.[12] But if the reason for bringing the case in the supreme instead of a lower court is that the latter's summons could not reach the defendant for want of territorial jurisdiction, or that the lower court would otherwise lack jurisdiction, the costs punishment does not apply.[13]

The supreme court also has some appellate jurisdiction, discussed in the treatment of the appellate term in the next section.

Appeals from the supreme court go in almost all instances to the local appellate division.[14]

The CPLR is of course the main source of procedure in the supreme court, but Part 202 of the Uniform Rules provides further procedural detail for practice in the supreme court (along with the county courts) and will be referred to at a number of places in this book.

§ 13. Appellate Term

This court exists at the pleasure of the appellate division of the particular department.

At present only the First and Second departments have appellate terms. The court consists of three to five (usually three) supreme court justices assigned to hear appeals from certain lower courts.[1] In both the First and Second departments, appellate terms hear appeals from the New York City Civil and Criminal courts.[2] In the Second Department an appellate term also hears appeals from the district, city, town, and village courts in all cases, and from the county courts in civil cases and in certain criminal cases.[3]

No more than three justices may sit as a panel; two make a quorum and two are also needed for a decision.[4]

Appeals from the appellate term go to the appellate division.[5]

§ 14. County Courts

There is a county court in each county outside New York City. Its judges are elected for 10–year terms.[1] It has criminal jurisdiction, including the felonies, and substantial civil jurisdiction.[2]

The court does not have a separate court act for its civil practice. The CPLR applies directly, and Part 202 of the Uniform Rules supplies further procedure for the supreme and county courts together. The only need for a separate statute is to elaborate the subject matter jurisdiction of the court—the basics of which are constitutionally supplied[3]—and this is done in

---

10. Const. Art. VI, § 7(b).

11. Kagen v. Kagen, 21 N.Y.2d 532, 289 N.Y.S.2d 195, 236 N.E.2d 475 (1968). The case establishes that even grants of jurisdiction to other courts made prior to the effective date of the new judiciary article (Const. Art. VI, eff. September 1, 1962) are to be deemed within supreme court jurisdiction.

12. CPLR 8102. In New York City, costs are denied the plaintiff who brings the action in the supreme court and recovers less than $6000. Subd. 1. Outside New York City, a recovery of less than $500 in the supreme court brings about the denial of costs. Subd. 2.

13. See, e.g., Friedman v. Great A. & P. Tea Co., 174 Misc. 185, 20 N.Y.S.2d 392 (Sup.Ct., Schenectady County), decided in 1940 when the county court lacked jurisdiction of a foreign corporation (an impediment removed in 1971 by amendments of §§ 190 and 190–a of the Judiciary Law).

14. CPLR 5701.

§ 13

1. Const. Art. VI, § 8.

2. 22 NYCRR §§ 640.1, 730.1(b). The abbreviation is for the New York Code of Rules and Regulations, whose chapter 22 contains the numerous court rules, which may also be found in the annually recompiled rules pamphlet accompanying McKinney's Consolidated Laws of New York. The appellate term is created by rule or order of the appellate division.

3. 22 NYCRR § 730.1(d).

4. Const. Art. VI, § 8(c).

5. CPLR 5703(a).

§ 14

1. Const. Art. VI, § 10.

2. Const. Art. VI, § 11(a).

3. Id.

the Judiciary Law, primarily in §§ 190 and 190–a.

Unlike the supreme court, which is a single statewide court, the county court is treated as distinct to each county. It has jurisdiction of money actions up to $25,000,[4] raised to that in 1984 from the previously applicable $6000.

There is an additional jurisdictional requirement in money actions. The defendant, or all of the defendants if there are more than one, must either reside or have a business office in the county at the time the action is commenced; and if a business office instead of a residence is relied on, it must also be shown that the claim arose in the county. These are statutory requirements,[5] and since they are jurisdictional, the action is dismissed if they are not met.[6] But while they appear to concern subject matter jurisdiction, which would make them unwaivable objections, they are treated as going to personal jurisdiction, with the result that they can be waived if not timely interposed.[7]

Prior distinctions between foreign and domestic corporations in money actions in the county court[8] were largely abandoned in 1971 and today the county court can entertain a money claim, within the applicable monetary figure, against either kind of corporation as long as it has an office or facility in the county.[9]

The court can hear certain of the real property actions if the land is in the county, and here there is no monetary limitation.[10] It has replevin jurisdiction if the chattel is in the county and does not exceed in value the court's monetary jurisdiction.[11] It also has jurisdiction of incompetency proceedings affecting county residents or realty[12] and of summary proceedings to recover real property in the county.[13]

Appeals go to the appellate division,[14] except in the Second Department where appeals (in all but felony cases) go to the appellate term.[15]

The county court itself acts as an appellate court for certain lower court decisions. In the Third and Fourth departments, it hears appeals from city courts[16] and from town and village courts.[17]

If the summons and complaint are served together in a county court action brought for more than the court's monetary jurisdiction, the court has been held to lack even the jurisdiction needed to allow an amendment to reduce the demand to fit the money maximum.[18] But since the county court is today empowered by the constitution to transfer such a case to the court that does have the needed jurisdiction,[19] the court should by analogy have the power to permit an amendment that would retain the case.

On a money counterclaim (as opposed to main claim) the constitution itself specifies that the county court has jurisdiction without limit as to amount, and it authorizes the legislature to give the county court whatever equity jurisdiction it wishes.[20] The equity jurisdiction so far conferred under this power is primarily in the realty actions already mentioned.

The court's process may be served anywhere

---

4. Jud.L. § 190(3).

5. Id.

6. Bonk v. Hodgkins, 68 Misc.2d 148, 326 N.Y.S.2d 140 (Schenectady County Court 1971).

7. Meyers v. American Loc. Co., 201 N.Y. 163, 94 N.E. 605 (1911).

8. See Wachtel v. Diamond State Eng'g Corp., 215 A.D. 15, 213 N.Y.S. 77 (2d Dep't 1925).

9. Jud.L. § 190–a as amended in 1971. A corporation having such a facility is the equivalent of a resident for this purpose.

10. Jud.L. § 190(1). Among the realty actions are the typical ones of partition, mortgage foreclosure, specific performance, deed rescission, reformation, etc.

11. Jud.L. § 190(3).

12. Jud.L. § 190(4).

13. RPAPL § 701(1).

14. CPLR 5701.

15. 22 NYCRR § 730.1(d). There are no county courts in the First Department.

16. Unif.City Ct.Act § 1701.

17. Unif.Just.Ct.Act § 1701.

18. Heffron v. Jennings, 66 A.D. 443, 73 N.Y.S. 410 (4th Dep't 1901).

19. Const. Art. VI, § 19(b).

20. Const. Art. VI, § 11(b).

in the state[21] and in some instances beyond.[22]

The practitioner should inquire about which categories of jurisdiction the county court in a particular county customarily exercises. It may be found that in a given county the court is used primarily as the felony court, while civil matters are brought in the supreme court. These are administrative variations one meets notwithstanding that the court may technically have jurisdiction over a range of things.

It is permissible, if statute so directs, for one person to perform simultaneously the function of county judge, surrogate, and family court judge, or any combination of the three.[23] This wearing of several judicial hats is found in the more rural counties.

§ 15. Surrogate's Court

There is a surrogate's court in each county of the state. Each has at least one judge, called a surrogate; New York County has two. Election is by county. In the New York City counties the term is 14 years; elsewhere, 10.[1]

The surrogate's court handles all matters concerning decedents' estates. Its basic grant of jurisdiction is contained in § 12(d) of Article VI of the state constitution and in § 201 of the Surrogate's Court Procedure Act (SCPA). The SCPA is profuse with procedural detail; thus, although the CPLR applies in the court,[2] it is less needed there than in the courts that try the usual civil actions. Further details of procedure for the surrogate's court are found in Part 207 of the Uniform Rules.

As long as "affairs of decedents" is the subject, the court's jurisdiction is secured whether it involves law or equity.[3] This includes all the jurisdiction needed to entertain matters involving both testamentary and, as of 1980, "lifetime" inter-vivos trusts.[4]

The court's process is servable anywhere in the state[5] and in some circumstances beyond.[6] Appeals go to the appellate division.[7]

§ 16. Family Court

There is a family court in each county of the state. There is at least one judge on each family court, and as many more as statute provides.[1] The term is 10 years, elective outside New York City, appointive (by the mayor) within.[2]

The court's jurisdiction covers almost the complete range of family matters, whether in other contexts they would qualify as criminal or civil.[3] Officially the terminology of "criminal" court is avoided. It is generally regarded as a civil court[4] but has been termed "a unique court, completely dissimilar to any other.... [and] is primarily a social court designed to handle the complex problems of family life."[5] Its jurisdiction includes neglect, support, and paternity proceedings; adoption, guardianship and custody; juvenile delinquency and persons in need of supervision; family offenses; and conciliation proceedings. The jurisdiction is supplied by the Family Court Act (FCA). The court's procedure is supplied by that act and by Part 205 of the Uniform Rules. Procedure is necessarily less formal than in other courts. Process is servable statewide.[6] Appeals go to

21. Const. Art. VI, § 1(c).

22. CPLR 313, to be studied later. See § 100.

23. Const. Art. VI, § 14.

§ 15

1. Const. Art. VI, § 12(a), (c); Jud.L. § 179.

2. SCPA 102; CPLR 101.

3. SCPA 201(2), (3). See the Commentary on McKinney's SCPA 201.

4. SCPA 209(6). See the Commentary on McKinney's SCPA 201.

5. Const. Art. VI, § 1(c).

6. SCPA 210, 211.

7. SCPA 2701, CPLR 5701.

§ 16

1. Family Court Act (FCA) § 131.

2. Const. Art. VI, § 13(a).

3. The family and criminal courts have concurrent jurisdiction over a number of acts involving family members, many of which would be strictly criminal if family were not involved. See FCA § 812.

4. In re Lang, 44 Misc.2d 900, 255 N.Y.S.2d 987 (Family Ct., N.Y.County, 1965).

5. In re Anonymous, 37 Misc.2d 827, 831, 238 N.Y.S.2d 792, 796 (Family Ct., Nassau County, 1962).

6. Const. Art. VI, § 1(c). CPLR 302(b) and 313 apply in the family court, FCA § 165, CPLR 101, and authorize service outside the state in support proceedings. FCA § 154(b) goes further, allowing extrastate service in pro-

the appellate division.[7]

The item that the lay person and even the general practitioner perhaps most associate with a "family" court is the matrimonial action (divorce, annulment, separation). Ironically, the family court lacks jurisdiction of it. The matrimonial action is in the exclusive jurisdiction of the supreme court,[8] although the family court may entertain certain custody and support incidentals of such actions if the supreme court refers them to the family court.[9]

Adoption proceedings[10] are in the concurrent jurisdiction of the family and surrogate's courts.[11]

§ 17. Court of Claims

The court of claims has jurisdiction "to hear and determine claims against the state or by the state against the claimant".[1] Its jurisdiction is set forth in detail in the Court of Claims Act.[2] In a landmark decision in 1996[3] the Court of Appeals expanded the court's jurisdiction by adopting the "constitutional tort". It held that the state of New York is liable in damages for violations of the equal protection and search and seizure clauses of the state constitution, and that the court of claims has jurisdiction to hear the claims.[4]

The Court of Claims Act also governs procedure in the court, but the act's provisions are few and the CPLR, which is applicable in the court pursuant to its own terms as well as under a direction from the Court of Claims Act

itself,[5] is used there more frequently than in the surrogates' or family courts.[6] Administrative matters and details of court of claims procedure are found in Part 206 of the Uniform Rules.

Judges are appointed by the governor by and with the advice and consent of the senate; the term is nine years.[7]

The court is statewide but divided into districts for administrative purposes.[8] Appeals are to the appellate division.[9] Process is servable statewide.[10]

Multi-party occurrences involving the state pose special problems. If the state is one of several tortfeasors, for example, it can be sued only in the court of claims; the other tortfeasors must be sued in other courts. The state employees responsible for the tort must also be sued in the supreme or some lower court of ordinary civil jurisdiction; they may not be sued in the court of claims even if the state would have to indemnify them.[11] The possibility of inconsistent verdicts because of these restrictions is well recognized.[12] Apportionment problems in tort cases are especially confused, and the courts ambivalent, mainly because a divestiture of the right to trial by jury can result if a person is compelled to seek relief in a court of claims action (where there is no jury), or if a judgment as to one of the court of claims parties is held to bind that party elsewhere.[13] Nor may the state itself, the

---

ceedings "to establish paternity or to seek support" when the required New York contacts are satisfied.

7. FCA § 1111.

8. Infanto v. Infanto, 66 Misc.2d 699, 321 N.Y.S.2d 928 (Family Ct., Queens County, 1971).

9. Const. Art. VI, § 13(c). If not incidental to a matrimonial action, the family court does have jurisdiction of these proceedings.

10. Dom.Rel.L. Art.7.

11. FCA § 641.

§ 17

1. Const. Art. VI, § 9.

2. Ct.Cl.Act § 9.

3. Brown v. State of New York, 89 N.Y.2d 172, 652 N.Y.S.2d 223 (1996).

4. The case is the subject of the lead note in New York State Law Digest No. 444.

5. CPLR 101; Ct.Cl.Act § 9(9).

6. See McNamara, The Court of Claims: Its Development and Present Role in The Unified Court System, 40 St. John's L. Rev. 1 (1965).

7. Const. Art. VI, § 9.

8. Uniform Rule 206.4. Part 206 of the Uniform Rules governs in the court of claims.

9. Ct.Cl.Act § 24.

10. Const. Art. VI, § 1(c).

11. Morell v. Balasubramanian, 70 N.Y.2d 297, 520 N.Y.S.2d 530, 514 N.E.2d 1101 (1987).

12. Braun v. State, 203 Misc. 563, 117 N.Y.S.2d 601 (Ct.Cl. 1952).

13. See Tierney v. State, 55 A.D.2d 158, 389 N.Y.S.2d 709 (4th Dep't 1976), overruling Bartlett v. State, 40 A.D.2d 267, 340 N.Y.S.2d 63 (4th Dep't 1973), and agreeing with Valentino v. State, 44 A.D.2d 338, 355 N.Y.S.2d 212 (3d Dep't 1974), which was at odds with Bartlett. Discussion of res judicata and collateral estoppel problems defendant in the court of claims, implead a potential indemnitor or contributor.[14] If the state brings suit as a plaintiff in some other court, moreover, which the state of course can do, the defendant there cannot counterclaim.[15] In the court of claims itself, however, where the state is the defendant, counterclaims are allowed.[16]

Because the state is so often involved in multi-party occurrences and transactions, it would of course be helpful to merge the court of claims into the supreme court. That was one of the proposals of a court reorganization referendum that got a start at the 1986 legislative session, but it never made it through the following session, as required to start a constitutional referendum. The merger continues to be the subject of discussion, as does the simplification of the whole court system, but it has not yet passed the study stage.

The court of claims may have jurisdiction over certain state agencies as well as over the state itself.[17] It depends on whether the agency is considered an arm of the state, which is often a hard question[18] (and another reason for the court's merger into the supreme court).

§ 18. New York City Criminal Court

This court exists only in New York City and has only criminal jurisdiction. It is mentioned here only as part of a perspective on the court system.

It handles the misdemeanors and lesser offenses. (Felonies in New York City are tried in the supreme court.) Its judges are appointed by the mayor for 10–year terms.[1] Procedure in the court is governed by the New York City Criminal Court Act and by the Criminal Procedure Law. Appeals go to an appellate term.[2]

§ 19. New York City Civil Court

This court is one of the biggest in the world. It has only civil jurisdiction and functions only in the City of New York. It has monetary jurisdiction up to $25,000, including replevin when the value of the chattel does not exceed that amount.[1] It also has jurisdiction of the real property actions, analogous to those of which the county court has jurisdiction but with the important difference that the monetary limit of $25,000, inapplicable in the county court in these cases, does apply in the civil court.[2]

The civil court has jurisdiction of the summary proceeding, in which, in addition to a judgment of dispossession, judgment for rent may be rendered in any sum, unlimited by the usual $25,000 restriction that governs in the conventional civil action.[3] It also has jurisdiction of interpleader claims within the $25,000 figure.[4] The monetary limit does not apply to counterclaims but it has been held applicable to cross-claims.[5] The court's equity jurisdiction is generally limited by statute to the real prop-

---

involving the court of claims, including instances in which its judgment can affect a later jury case, appears in § 470, below.

14. See Horoch v. State, 286 A.D. 303, 143 N.Y.S.2d 327 (3d Dep't 1955), noting, however, that while impleader is precluded, interpleader is allowed. (For the difference between those devices, see §§ 148 and 155, below.) If, without impleader, rights can be adjusted among those already parties, that is permissible. See General Foods Corp. v. State, 18 Misc.2d 293, 188 N.Y.S.2d 635 (Ct.Cl. 1959).

15. In re Hicka, 180 Misc. 173, 40 N.Y.S.2d 267 (Sup. Ct., N.Y.County, 1943).

16. Ct.Cl.Act § 9(3).

17. See Easley v. New York State Thruway Auth., 1 N.Y.2d 374, 153 N.Y.S.2d 28, 135 N.E.2d 572 (1956).

18. See Belscher v. N. Y. State Teachers' Ret. Sys., 45 A.D.2d 206, 357 N.Y.S.2d 241 (4th Dep't 1974).

§ 18

1. Const. Art. VI, § 15(a).

2. See 22 NYCRR §§ 640.1 (First Department) and 730.1(b)(2) (Second Department).

§ 19

1. Const. Art. VI, § 15(b); New York City Civil Court Act (NYCCCA) § 202.

2. See NYCCCA § 203, which also sets forth the methods by which to gauge whether the monetary limitation is met.

3. NYCCCA § 204.

4. NYCCCA § 205.

5. Const. Art. VI, § 15(b); NYCCCA § 208(b); 125 Church St. Devel. Co. v. Grassfield, 170 Misc.2d 31, 648 N.Y.S.2d 515 (Civ. Ct., N.Y.County, 1996), noted in SPR 64:4.

erty actions and to actions to rescind or reform contracts not involving more than $25,000,[6] but a 1972 amendment addressed to residential housing problems in New York City widely expands equity jurisdiction in housing cases.[7]

In New York City the so-called Small Claims "court" is part of the New York City Civil Court, entertaining money cases up to $3000.[8] Distinct from cases brought as small claims is the procedure, authorized by CPLR 3405 and elaborated in Part 28 of the Rules of the Chief Judge, for the arbitration of claims of $10,000 or under. Arbitration in that instance is compulsory.[9]

Judges of the court are elected and serve 10–year terms.[10]

Procedure is governed by the New York City Civil Court Act (NYCCCA), the prototype of the uniform acts governing practice in the state's lower courts, and by Part 208 of the Uniform Rules. Article 2 of the court act sets forth the court's jurisdiction; the rest of it aims to simplify certain procedures and make them less expensive. As long as it is not inconsistent with the relatively few things governed by the court act, the CPLR applies in the court.[11]

Process is servable anywhere in New York City and in certain instances beyond.[12] Appeals are to the appellate term.[13] The city marshals as well as the sheriff are the court's enforcement officers.[14]

§ 20. District Courts

There are two district courts in the state, one covering Nassau County and the other the western part of Suffolk County. They are unrelated to and shouldn't be confused with the United States District Court. Their civil jurisdiction and practice is governed by the Uniform District Court Act (UDCA),[1] with further procedural detail supplied by Part 212 of the Uniform Rules. The district court has criminal jurisdiction of misdemeanors and lesser offenses as determined and governed by the Criminal Procedure Law.

The court's civil jurisdiction in money and replevin actions goes up to $15,000.[2] It also has jurisdiction of the summary proceeding, in which judgment for rent is not limited in amount.[3] As with the county courts and the New York City Civil Court, counterclaim jurisdiction is also without monetary limitation.[4] The district court has little equity jurisdiction, although it can entertain interpleader claims within the $15,000 limit.[5] In Nassau and western Suffolk, the Small Claims part is to be found in the district court. Small Claims jurisdiction goes up to $3000.[6] Cases for $6000 and under may be sent to compulsory arbitration as authorized by CPLR 3405 and implemented by Part 28 of the Rules of the Chief Judge.[7]

Process is limited to the county except in certain instances.[8] Appeals go to the county court unless an appellate term has been established for such appeals.[9] Judges are elected to

---

6. See NYCCCA §§ 208(c), 213.

7. NYCCCA § 110.

8. NYCCCA Article 18. Small claims, though often called a "court", is not one. It is merely a simplified procedure—invoked at the option of the claimant—set up in some of the lower court acts. Small Claims procedure is the subject of Chapter 21, below (Practitioner's Edition).

9. See § 585B (Practitioner's Edition). Do not confuse this category of arbitration with the well-known voluntary arbitration governed by Article 75 of the CPLR, discussed in § 586 et seq. (Practitioner's Edition).

10. Const. Art. VI, § 15(a).

11. CPLR 101; NYCCCA § 2102.

12. See NYCCCA Art. 4.

13. NYCCCA § 1701. See the appellate term rules in 22 NYCRR §§ 640.1 (First Department) and 730.1(b)(1) (Second Department).

14. NYCCCA § 701.

§ 20

1. The UDCA is modeled on the New York City Civil Court Act, right down to the numbering system. The differences are mainly in those areas in which the constitution or legislative preference has varied jurisdiction or practice.

2. Const. Art. VI, § 16(d); UDCA § 202.

3. UDCA § 204.

4. UDCA § 208(b).

5. UDCA § 205.

6. UDCA Article 18.

7. See § 585B below (Practitioner's Edition).

8. UDCA Article 4.

9. UDCA § 1701. An appellate term has been established. See the appellate term rules in 22 NYCRR § 730.1(d).

six-year terms.[10] District courts can be adopted elsewhere (the purpose would ordinarily be to supersede the justice courts), but only by local referendum.[11]

The CPLR governs in the court as long as it is not inconsistent with the UDCA.[12]

§ 21.   City Courts

There is a city court in each of the 61 cities outside New York City. Most go by the formal name of "city court", but other names are occasionally used. Whatever the names, their civil jurisdiction and practice is governed by the Uniform City Court Act (UCCA),[1] with further procedural detail supplied by Part 210 of the Uniform Rules. Monetary jurisdiction was set for a long time at a $6000 maximum. A statute raised it to $10,000 as of July 1, 1988, and to $15,000 as of July 1, 1991.[2] The CPLR applies to the extent that it is consistent with the UCCA.[3] It usually is.

In addition to money and replevin claims, which are also subject to the applicable money limit, the city court entertains the summary proceeding. A rent judgment in a summary proceeding and a counterclaim in any case have no monetary limitations.[4] Interpleader jurisdiction exists within the applicable money limit.[5] The court has little equity jurisdiction. In city court money actions, certain local contacts have to be shown, akin to those already met in the county court but not identical.[6] No such requirements are imposed in the civil court or in the district courts.

Process is servable anywhere in the county and in some instances in an adjoining county,[7]

but the constitution prevents it from going farther.[8] The city courts also have criminal jurisdiction of misdemeanors and below as supplied and regulated by the Criminal Procedure Law.

Appeals go to the county court unless the local appellate division has set up an appellate term to hear them.[9]

In the cities outside New York City it is the city court that has the Small Claims part, entertaining through its informal procedures money claims not exceeding $3000.[10] And on the authority of CPLR 3405, implemented by Part 28 of the Rules of the Chief Judge, cases for $6000 and under can be sent to compulsory arbitration.[11]

§ 22.   Town and Village Courts

Each county in the state outside New York City is divided into towns. Within these towns, villages are sprinkled around the state by the score. Most of these towns and villages have courts serviced respectively by town justices and village justices. The town court is also known as the "justice of the peace", and the village court as the "village police justice". Collectively they are known as the justice courts,[1] the easiest terminology to use here.

The courts have criminal jurisdiction of misdemeanors and below, as set forth and regulated in the Criminal Procedure Law.

Civil jurisdiction and practice in each town and village court is governed by the Uniform Justice Court Act (UJCA), the last of the quar-

---

10. Const. Art. VI, § 16(h).

11. Const. Art. VI, § 16(b & c).

12. CPLR 101; UDCA § 2102.

§ 21

1. UCCA § 102. The UCCA is modeled on the UDCA much as the UDCA is modeled on the NYCCCA, making for a uniformity among the acts and helping the practitioner to step from one court's practice to another's without undue difficulty.

2. See L.1988, c.397, amending UCCA § 202. The jurisdiction of the city courts may not exceed that of the district courts. Const. Art. VI, §§ 17(a), 16(d).

3. CPLR 101; UCCA § 2102.

4. UCCA §§ 204, 208(b).

5. UCCA § 205.

6. UCCA § 213. See the Commentary on McKinney's UCCA § 213 (Vol. 29A, Part 3).

7. UCCA Article 4.

8. Const. Art. VI, § 1(c).

9. UCCA § 1701. See the Second Department's appellate term rules, 22 NYCRR § 730.1(d). There are no city courts in the First Department.

10. UCCA Article 18.

11. See § 585B below (Practitioner's Edition).

§ 22

1. See the definitions contained in § 2101 of the Uniform Justice Court Act.

tet of uniform acts,[2] with procedural detail furnished by Part 214 of the Uniform Rules. The justice courts have monetary and replevin jurisdiction up to $3000, and unlike the other civil courts this limitation also applies to counterclaims.[3] The court has jurisdiction of the summary proceeding, in which a judgment for rent is not limited in amount.[4]

It also has the Small Claims part, which also has a ceiling of $3000 at the present time,[5] the practical result of which is that all money claims brought in a town or village court qualify as Small Claims and can be pursued as such by the plaintiff. Even before the Small Claims jurisdiction was raised to the same level as the courts' regular monetary jurisdiction, many would have argued that even in cases invoking the latter, the great informality made the case hard if not impossible to distinguish from an outright Small Claim.

Lawyers must also be alert to inquire whether the compulsory arbitration procedures authorized by CPLR 3405 and implemented by Part 28 of the Rules of the Chief Judge[6] have been made applicable in a given justice court.

The justice courts have no significant equity jurisdiction. They are the only courts in the state whose judges need not be lawyers,[7] and most are not. The summons, servable in the home county,[8] cannot constitutionally be permitted to go beyond an adjoining county.[9]

As with the city courts under the Uniform City Court Act, a special provision appears in the UJCA requiring local contacts to be demonstrated as an additional jurisdictional prerequisite in money actions.[10]

Appeals are to the county court[11] unless an appellate term has been set up to hear them.[12]

§ 23. Aggregating or Reducing Claims

Suppose a plaintiff interposes several claims in a lower court action, or that several plaintiffs join their claims in a lower court—as they may do when the claims have common origins.[1] If each separate cause of action fits within the court's original jurisdiction when independently measured, all the claims may be joined and are deemed within the court's jurisdiction even though their total may exceed it. This is accomplished by § 211 in each of the lower court acts[2] and is thus the clear rule in the civil, district, city, town, and village courts. Some cases had apparently sustained such aggregation in the county court, too,[3] but the Second Department, within which they were decided, later distinguished or overruled them and rejected aggregation in county courts.[4] The county court has no counterpart of the lower court acts' § 211, but by analogy to that section—which after all reflects a broad legislative intent about how lower court jurisdictional problems are to be handled—the aggregation ought to be allowed.

Suppose that a single cause of action is brought in one of the lower courts for a sum in excess of its jurisdiction. As will be seen short-

---

2. UJCA § 2300(b)(1), (2). The UJCA is modeled on the Uniform City Court Act and thus traces back through the Uniform District Court Act to the original New York City Civil Court Act. All four acts were originally designed for maximum uniformity but have lost much of it because of piecemeal and uncoordinated amendments since the middle of the 1960's.

3. UJCA § 208. Interposition of a counterclaim for more than $3000 waives the balance. See the Commentary on § 208 in McKinney's UJCA (Vol. 29A, Part 2).

4. UJCA § 204.

5. UJCA Article 18. Small Claims and their procedures are the subject of Chapter 21, below.

6. See § 585B below (Practitioner's Edition).

7. Const. Art. VI, § 20(a),(c).

8. UJCA § 403.

9. Const. Art. VI, § 1(c).

10. See UJCA § 213 and its Commentary in McKinney's UJCA.

11. UJCA § 1701.

12. See the Second Department's appellate term rule, 22 NYCRR § 730.1. There are no town or village courts in the First Department.

§ 23

1. See CPLR 1002(a).

2. The New York City Civil Court Act and the Uniform District, City, and Justice court acts, McKinney's Vol. 29A, Parts 2 and 3.

3. Baron v. Bobroy, 11 A.D.2d 766, 205 N.Y.S.2d 173 (2d Dep't 1960); Weber v. Kowalski, 85 Misc.2d 349, 358 n. 2, 376 N.Y.S.2d 996, 1007 n. 2 (Sup.Ct., Dutchess County, 1975).

4. Mandel v. Kent, 70 A.D.2d 903, 417 N.Y.S.2d 306 (1979).

ly, the case can be transferred to a court having adequate jurisdiction.[5] But if the plaintiff is willing to reduce the demand to bring it within the subject matter jurisdiction of the lower court, may the plaintiff do that and thus have the case retained there? Old caselaw indicated that this amendment is permissible only when the summons is served alone, but not when the summons and complaint are served together.[6] The theory was that the complaint, by identifying a claim beyond the lower court's jurisdiction, put it beyond the court's jurisdiction even to entertain a reduction in the amount demanded.

Although one still sees this rule applied occasionally,[7] it is too technical by today's lights. Given the broad powers of transfer now authorized or at least contemplated by the constitution,[8] every court of civil jurisdiction should today be conceded the power to entertain a plaintiff's offer to reduce the demand so as to keep the case where it is, and some recent cases so hold.[9] This should be so whether or not the complaint accompanied the summons.[10]

It has been held that in a bifurcated trial in a tort case—in which issues of liability are tried before damages[11]—the plaintiff's share of the damages under the comparative negligence rule[12] can be excluded in determining the court's monetary jurisdiction, thus preserving jurisdiction even if the plaintiff's share, added in, would exceed it.[13]

---

5. See § 24 below.

6. See Heffron v. Jennings, 66 A.D. 443, 73 N.Y.S. 410 (4th Dep't 1901).

7. E.g., Silverman v. Abdul, 85 Misc.2d 11, 379 N.Y.S.2d 671 (Rockland County Ct. 1976).

8. Const. Art. VI, § 19, treated in § 24, below.

9. See, e.g., B & R Textiles Corp. v. Empire Bias Binding Co., 126 Misc.2d 965, 484 N.Y.S.2d 487 (N.Y.C.Civ.Ct. 1985). Contra: Mend–Foley v. Spencer Mgmt. Corp., 158 Misc.2d 471, 601 N.Y.S.2d 553 (City Court of New Rochelle, 1993).

10. In most of the lower courts it is mandatory that the complaint accompany the summons. See § 902 in the N.Y.C.Civ.Ct.Act and in the Uniform District, City, and Justice court acts, McKinney's Vol. 29A, Parts 2 and 3. In the county courts, which are governed directly by CPLR 305(b) and 3012(a), serving a complaint with the summons is optional, but if a complaint is not initially served, the summons must contain or have appended at least a brief notice of the object of the action. CPLR 305(b). See § 231 below.

B. TRANSFERS BETWEEN COURTS

Table of Sections

§ 24. Mistake in Choice of Court

If an action is initially brought in a court that lacks subject matter jurisdiction of it—the "wrong court", to give it a simple handle—it need not be dismissed; it should be transferred to the court that does have jurisdiction. One way to accomplish this is to ask the supreme court, by motion, to transfer the case from the wrong to the right court, a power conferred on the supreme court by CPLR 325(a).

Another is to ask the wrong court itself to transfer the case to the right court, but this can be done only if the wrong court has been given such transfer power. The state constitution directly authorizes certain courts to transfer out of themselves, and to the proper court, actions of which they lack subject matter jurisdiction. The courts so authorized are the county courts,[1] the surrogate's court,[2] the family court,[3] and the New York City civil and criminal courts.[4] When such power exists in the

---

11. See § 130 below.

12. CPLR 1411. See § 168E below.

13. Azzopardi v. St. Vincent's Medical Center, 132 Misc.2d 412, 503 N.Y.S.2d 700 (N.Y.C.Civ.Ct., Richmond County, 1986).

§ 24

1. Const. Art. VI, § 19, subd.b.

2. Id., subd.d.

3. Id., subd.e.

4. Id., subd.f. Since these courts are empowered to correct jurisdictional defects by transferring a case out, they should by analogy be able to entertain such amendments as the plaintiff may request to enable the case to remain where it is. Thus, if a case initially seeks more than the court can give but the plaintiff is willing to amend to bring the case within the court's jurisdiction, the court should itself be able to allow the amendment and keep the case. Older cases to the contrary, such as Heffron v. Jennings, 66 A.D. 443, 73 N.Y.S. 410 (4th Dep't 1901), wrong court, the parties have the choice of making the transfer motion in that court under the appropriate constitutional provision, or in the supreme court under CPLR 325(a).

So, for example, if an action is brought in the civil court for $50,000, the transfer to the supreme court may be made by motion to the supreme court under CPLR 325(a) or by motion to the civil court under the constitutional provision.

Courts still lower than those listed can be given such transfer powers by statute,[5] but until that happens, CPLR 325(a) will have to do the job: when one of those courts is involved, the transfer motion will have to be made to the supreme court.

Procedure in conjunction with a transfer motion under CPLR 325 is governed by CPLR 326, which, while not explicitly applicable to transfers made directly under the constitution, would be an appropriate guidepost there, too.

A special provision for transferring cases between lower courts, subdivision (g) of CPLR 325, applies to all district, city, town, and village courts. It governs not when there has been a mistake in choice of court, but when all the judges of any one of those courts are for any reason incapable of acting in the case, or if a jury cannot be formed. It permits a judge of the county court in which the lower court is located, on motion, to transfer the case to any other of those four categories of court in either the same county or an adjoining county, as long as the transferee court has the requisite subject matter and personal jurisdiction.

While CPLR 325(a), authorizing a transfer from the wrong to the right court, is generally thought of as applying to transfers among trial courts, it has also been held applicable to permit a transfer to the appellate division when the latter is the right court (as when the proceeding involved is within the appellate division's original jurisdiction).[6]

§ 25. Transfer Up for More Relief

When an action is brought in a court that does have jurisdiction of it, but the plaintiff now wants more or different relief than the court can grant, the governing provision is CPLR 325(b) and the procedure is to make the transfer motion in the court to which the transfer is sought. That would be the next highest court locally available for the case. This usually happens when the plaintiff wants to raise the monetary demand in a money (usually a tort) action beyond the limits of the original court.

Distinguish this situation from that involved under CPLR 325(a), treated in the prior section. There the assumption is that the action has been brought in the wrong court to begin with, and there the statute authorizes only the supreme court to transfer the case.

An example under CPLR 325(b) would be an action commenced in the Nassau County district court for $5000 (which is within its jurisdiction) but in which the damages later appear to be $20,000 (which is not). The case may be transferred to the local county court, which has $25,000 jurisdiction. The motion for the transfer is made to the county court on those facts, not to the supreme court.

The motion also includes a request for leave to amend the complaint to demand the greater relief. Whether to allow the amendment and order the transfer is in the court's discretion.[1] It will turn on how convincingly the plaintiff justifies the greater relief and excuses the delay in obtaining the evidence that supports it.

A transfer up under CPLR 325(b) can be granted even in a case that was previously transferred down under other provisions, such as subdivision (c) or (d) of CPLR 325. It turns, again, on how convincing the new proof of damages is.[2]

§ 25

1. See Kornfeld v. Wagner, 12 N.Y.2d 348, 239 N.Y.S.2d 668, 190 N.E.2d 15 (1963).

2. See, e.g., Hornung v. Mucci, 52 A.D.2d 904, 383 N.Y.S.2d 379 (2d Dep't 1976).

ought to be discarded in light of the approach taken by Article VI of the constitution, and especially its § 19.

5. Id., subd.i.

6. See Hopper v. Comm'r of Taxation and Finance, 224 A.D.2d 733, 637 N.Y.S.2d 494 (3d Dep't 1996), noted in SPR 49:4.

In the event a jury has been waived in the lower court, the waiver becomes inoperative after it is transferred up under CPLR 325(b), thus reopening the door for a jury demand.

§ 26. Transfer Down on Consent

CPLR 325(c) offers yet a further variation on the transfer theme. Here, as in 325(b), the action has been brought in the right court, but in this instance the plaintiff later determines that the need for damages is less than he thought and the case can therefore fit the jurisdiction of a local lower court. In this instance the motion is made to the court in which the action is pending. It seeks leave to amend the complaint to reduce the damages demand to a figure within the lower court's jurisdiction, and to transfer the case down to that court.

If the defendant has counterclaimed, her consent to the transfer is needed. And if the action could not have been brought in the proposed transferee court because of limitations on personal jurisdiction, such as where the defendant could not have been reached with the court's process because of territorial limits, the transfer is precluded.

Sometimes a plaintiff who fails to appreciate the small worth of the case is helped to that realization by an enthusiastic judge during a pretrial conference of some kind, with the defendant helping the judge help the plaintiff see the light. This is primarily a phenomenon of the personal injury case. The practice varies administratively from place to place, but it boils down to a preliminary review, by a judge with experience in tort cases, of the medical evidence to see if the case can reasonably sustain a verdict in a sum sufficient to justify keeping it in the original court. That is usually the supreme court, so we will use that as the example. If the judge thinks the case can earn such damages, it gets what is popularly known

as a "general preference" and stays in the supreme court. Otherwise, a little gentle arm-twisting takes place to get the plaintiff to invoke CPLR 325(c) and permit the case to go down to a lower court voluntarily.

If the plaintiff refuses, the practice under CPLR 325(c) is merely to deny the case a "general preference" in the supreme court, which means it goes at the bottom of the calendar with the privilege of remaining there indefinitely.[1] A plaintiff in that posture must either appeal the order denying the general preference, or reduce the demand and let the case go down under CPLR 325(c).

If there is no barrier to begin with, as where the relief initially sought would have been within the lower court's jurisdiction all the while and no reduction in damages is needed, a transfer can be made without consent and apparently without complications.[2] From time to time one even sees the supreme court making a transfer down without the plaintiff's consent in a case beyond the lower court's monetary limits, and with those limits remaining, but cases so holding[3] have been discredited.[4] One possible theory to justify such a transfer is that the supreme court has rendered a limited summary judgment in the case—to the effect that as a matter of law the facts pleaded cannot justify a verdict in excess of the lower court's jurisdiction—but even for that the general view is that legislative authorization is needed, and there is none.

If granted, a transfer down under CPLR 325(c) invalidates any existing jury waiver, setting the stage for a jury demand in the transferee court.

In the next section we treat the non-consensual transfer down under CPLR 325(d), which has much reduced dependence on the "general" preference tool used in connection with 325(c).

---

§ 26

1. For a treatment of preferences, and the differences between a "general" and "special" preference, see §§ 372 and 373, below.

2. See Frankel Assocs., Inc. v. Dun & Bradstreet, Inc., 45 Misc.2d 607, 257 N.Y.S.2d 555 (Sup.Ct., N.Y. County, 1965).

3. E.g., Haas v. Scholl, 68 Misc.2d 197, 325 N.Y.S.2d 844 (Sup.Ct., Westchester County, 1971).

4. See Frydman v. Arcure, 75 A.D.2d 863, 427 N.Y.S.2d 888 (2d Dep't 1980).

Once a case has been transferred down, the transferee court should not transfer it back. It would likely be deemed an attempt by the lower court to do the unseemly: review a higher court's order.[5] If the plaintiff is aggrieved, the appropriate step is to appeal the order transferring the case down.

§ 27. Transfer Down Without Consent

The denial of a general preference, as discussed in the preceding section, used to be the primary if not the sole remedy against a plaintiff who would not reduce the complaint's monetary demand. The court could not transfer the case down without the voluntary reduction, although occasionally a case would run against the tide and try.[1]

Onto that scene arrived an overhauled judiciary article of the state constitution in 1962. Part of it was a little noticed provision, subdivision k of § 19 of Article VI, which authorized the legislature to dispense with monetary limitations in transferred cases, i.e., the legislature could allow a transferee lower court to disregard its usual monetary limitations (even those set elsewhere in the constitution), but only in a case transferred to the lower court (not one commenced in it). Subdivision k requires legislature exploitation, however. That came in the form of CPLR 325(d), a 1968 addition, but 325(d) merely passed the buck farther, delegating to the appellate divisions the power to invoke this monetary dispensation by rule.[2]

The upstate departments invoked CPLR 325(d) promptly, the downstate departments somewhat later, all in separate rules. Those were abrogated on January 6, 1986, when the Uniform Rules took effect. Today, CPLR 325(d) transfers are prescribed by one rule, UR 202.13, but not uniformly:

The supreme court can make a CPLR 325(d) transfer to the civil court in New York City.[3] In the Third and Fourth departments and in the five counties of the 9th District (immediately north of New York City), the supreme court can make the transfer to either a county or city court,[4] but in Nassau and Suffolk counties only to the county court.[5] Only the supreme court has this transfer power, except in a handful of counties in which the county court has also been given it.[6]

The rules should be periodically checked for any changes in the implementation of CPLR 325(d)'s transfer provision. In 1998, for example, the rule authorizing a CPLR 325(d) transfer down from the supreme to the New York City Civil Court was amended to permit the transfer only if it can be administratively established that the civil court will be able to try the case within 30 days after the preliminary conference at which the issue about transferring the case arises.[7]

Cases whose need of supreme court jurisdiction is doubtful—doubtfulness is supposed to be the criterion, anyway—can thus get transferred down without consent in many parts of the state today, the lower court getting the case, and, in the bargain, jurisdiction to award all the money originally demanded.

The lower court judges are often chagrined by these transfers.[8] It appears that it is not only the "doubtful" supreme court case that gets transferred down under CPLR 325(d). There have been instances of wrongful death cases being so transferred, and almost every such case has a potential for greater damages

---

5. See, e.g., Unterberg v. Scarsdale Improvement Corp., 128 Misc.2d 873, 491 N.Y.S.2d 571 (Sup.Ct., Westchester County, 1985).

§ 27

1. See notes 3 (Haas) and 4 (Frydman) in § 26, above.

2. The power presumably resides today in the chief administrator, as a constitutional matter, see § 5, above, not in the appellate divisions. But when an issue like that arises—caused by the legislature's overlooking a few of the numerous statutes that required conforming amendments when the power of judicial administration was altered in a 1977 amendment of the state constitution (Art.VI, § 28)—

the chief administrator usually avoids the problem by eliciting the approval of the appellate divisions for the proposed change.

3. UR 202.13(a).

4. UR 202.13(b), (d), and (e).

5. UR 202.13(c).

6. See the last few subdivisions of UR 202.13.

7. See the discussion in SPR 74:1.

8. See, e.g., Denner v. Katz, 75 Misc.2d 51, 347 N.Y.S.2d 365 (N.Y.C.Civ.Ct.), affirmed as modified 77 Misc.2d 53, 351 N.Y.S.2d 308 (App.Term, 1st Dep't, 1973).

than any lower court can award. Civil court judges report verdicts—sustainable verdicts—in transferred cases many times in excess of the civil court's basic jurisdiction,[9] although it was not the intention of the constitution to authorize indiscriminate transfers of this kind; the provision was intended for cases near the monetary border, or at least visible from it.

Indiscriminate transfer has resulted in other abuses. In Kings County, for example, plaintiffs were bringing in the supreme court cases unlikely to justify a recovery in excess of $10,000, the civil court's basic limit at the time, and therefore likely to be transferred down, which was apparently just what the plaintiffs expected. Their aim was to keep open the possibility of getting more money—the very fact that the transfer was predicated on CPLR 325(d) meant that the transferee court was not bound by its usual monetary limitations—while also securing an early trial, the civil court being up to date with its calendars while the supreme court was behind. The courts answered this problem, at least for a while, by holding that cases patently below a $10,000 potential would be transferred down, as plaintiffs expected, but without dispensing with transferee limits.[10]

Although the money limits of a transferee court expand on a CPLR 325(d) transfer, they expand only up to the amount demanded in the plaintiff's complaint in the court in which the action was commenced. Suppose it appears later, after a transfer down, that the damages are even greater. May the lower (the transferee) court entertain an application under subdivision (b) of CPLR 325[11] to send the case back? At least one court has said no, holding that the motion to increase and transfer back must be made to the original transferor, the supreme court.[12]

After a transfer back up to the original court under CPLR 325(b), however, the case would presumably become ripe once again for another transfer down under 325(d), so perhaps the supreme court, entertaining the 325(b) motion to increase and transfer up in a case previously transferred down under 325(d), can with just another breath grant only the increase part, and let the case stay right where it is—in the lower court.

Discussion up to now has addressed the usual money action. What about other relief? When equitable relief is demanded in a supreme court action, even if a money demand is also included, it has been held that CPLR 325(d) does not permit a transfer down to a lower court.[13]

And what about personal jurisdiction? Before a case is sent down under CPLR 325(d), it must be shown that the case would have been within the personal jurisdiction of the lower court had it been initially commenced there. Suppose it would not have been. Assume, for example, that the supreme court has sent down to the New York City Civil Court a case in which the summons had been served in Westchester County. That would give jurisdiction of the defendant in the supreme court, whose process is statewide, but the process of the civil court does not extend beyond New York City unless the claim itself has contacts with the city,[14] and assume that it has not.

Spinnell v. Doris L. Sassower, P.C. was such a case.[15] The transferee lower court held itself without the power to return the case to the supreme court, but also held that it nevertheless lacked jurisdiction to hear the case and could not go ahead with it. It dismissed the action, which of course poses a dilemma for the plaintiff.[16]

---

9. See, e.g., Roy v. Hartogs, 85 Misc.2d 891, 381 N.Y.S.2d 587 (App.T., 1st Dep't, 1976).

10. See, e.g., Offner v. Rothschild, 87 Misc.2d 565, 386 N.Y.S.2d 188 (Sup.Ct., Kings County 1976). Offner relied on the Haas case, note 3 in § 26, above, as authority for such an involuntary transfer, but the authority has since been undermined. Id., note 4.

11. See § 25 above.

12. Huston v. Rao, 74 A.D.2d 127, 427 N.Y.S.2d 36 (2d Dep't 1980).

13. Chung v. Kim, 170 A.D.2d 232, 565 N.Y.S.2d 510 (1st Dep't 1991).

14. See § 404 of the N.Y.C. Civil Court Act and the Commentary on it.

15. 155 Misc.2d 147, 589 N.Y.S.2d 230 (N.Y.C.Civ.Ct. 1992).

16. See the discussion in SPR 3:4.

C. FORUM NON CONVENIENS

Table of Sections

§ 28. Forum Non Conveniens

The doctrine of forum non conveniens, or inconvenient forum, is largely the product of caselaw. It is a body of rules designed to keep out of the New York courts cases in which jurisdiction technically exists both of the subject matter and of the person, but in which there are no significant New York contacts to warrant entertainment of the case. If, for example, P is a nonresident and brings a $50,000 foreign claim against D in the supreme court, nonresident D being served with process while passing through New York, the court secures jurisdiction of D. But if the case has nothing to do with New York, it should not be the burden of the New York court system and the New York taxpayer who supports it.

New York, recognizing its own status as an international commercial center, has over the years been liberal about making its courts available for foreign actions. The rule has traditionally been that its courts will entertain jurisdiction of foreign-arising claims involving nonresidents if shown a "special circumstance" for doing so.[1]

In one major case the plaintiffs were Canadian residents (defendant of Brazil) seeking to impress a trust on assets allegedly belonging to plaintiffs and located in many parts of the world. Some of the assets were in New York and one of the alleged conduits in the transfer of the assets was a New York corporation. The court held that these circumstances warranted entertainment of the suit, that New York was as appropriate a forum as any, and that the conveniens doctrine is relevant not only in tort cases (as had been thought), but in contract and property cases as well.[2]

Until 1972 there was a generally recognized rule that if any party to the action was a New York resident or a domestic corporation, the court would have to entertain the case; that the conveniens doctrine would not apply.[3] That was changed by Silver v. Great American Insurance Co.,[4] in which the Court of Appeals held that the doctrine "should turn on considerations of justice, fairness and convenience and not solely on the residence of one of the parties".[5] In *Silver*, the plaintiff was a physician resident in Hawaii who alleged that the defendant (a New York corporation) had defamed him in both Hawaii and New York. On remand from the Court of Appeals, the appellate division, free now to apply its discretion even though one of the parties was a resident, dismissed for inconvenient forum,[6] finding Hawaii more appropriate.

The conveniens doctrine, including the *Silver* contribution, was codified in 1972. Embodied today in subdivision (a) of CPLR 327, it reads:

> When the court finds that in the interest of substantial justice the action should be heard in another forum, the court, on the motion of any party, may stay or dismiss the action in whole or in part on any conditions that may be just. The domicile or residence in this state of any party to the action shall not preclude the court from staying or dismissing the action.

CPLR 327(a) is only a codification, confirmatory rather than innovative.

If the plaintiff is a New York resident, a conveniens dismissal, although permissible, is less likely than when the defendant is the New York resident. The obvious reason is that the New York courts are primarily for the use of New Yorkers. But the Court of Appeals has said that a conveniens dismissal can visit even

---

§ 28

1. Taylor v. Interstate Motor Freight Sys., 309 N.Y. 633, 132 N.E.2d 878 (1956).

2. Bata v. Bata, 304 N.Y. 51, 105 N.E.2d 623 (1952).

3. De la Bouillerie v. De Vienne, 300 N.Y. 60, 89 N.E.2d 15 (1949).

4. 29 N.Y.2d 356, 328 N.Y.S.2d 398, 278 N.E.2d 619 (1972).

5. Id. at 361, 328 N.Y.S.2d at 402, 278 N.E.2d at 622.

6. 38 A.D.2d 932, 330 N.Y.S.2d 156 (1st Dep't 1972).

a case in which all parties are New York residents,[7] a result that should be rare, indeed, reserved solely for a case in which all of the other contacts—situs of the transaction, performance, witnesses, documents, physical evidence, etc.—are elsewhere.

The conveniens doctrine is one of judicial discretion "to be exercised by reviewing and evaluating all the pertinent competing considerations", which include among other things the burden on the court, the hardship to the defendant that an action here would entail, and the availability elsewhere of a reputable forum.[8] If the "elsewhere" is a foreign country rather than a sister state, a conveniens dismissal is permissible but somewhat less likely. It depends on how much confidence we have in the jurisprudence of the foreign nation.[9] It is mandatory in all cases, however, that all relevant considerations be weighed by the court.

How does an "ouster" agreement figure on the forum non conveniens scene? An "ouster" agreement is a provision in a contract purporting to confer exclusive jurisdiction of a given dispute on a court in a given jurisdiction, thereby presuming to put it beyond the jurisdiction of all other courts. Such an agreement was once regarded in New York as void on public policy grounds. Today an agreement that purports to oust New York of jurisdiction by stipulating to exclusive jurisdiction elsewhere, while not by itself decisive, gets added to the list of things a New York court will consider on a forum non conveniens balanc-

ing.[10] Quite in contrast to an ouster agreement that seeks to strip New York of jurisdiction is the reverse kind: the one that seeks to confer jurisdiction on the New York courts exclusively. A 1984 amendment that added subdivision (b) to CPLR 327[11] provides that in a commercial transaction involving "not less than one million dollars" and in which the parties have stipulated in their contract to both a choice of New York law substantively and the jurisdiction of the New York courts exclusively, the conveniens doctrine is superseded and the New York courts must entertain the case.[12]

A related situation is one that involves a "service of suit" clause in a contract, requiring one side, when asked to by the other side, to submit to the jurisdiction of a court in a particular place. This will accomplish the submission to the selected court's jurisdiction, but it won't guarantee that the court there will exercise the jurisdiction. The court selected can still apply its own forum non conveniens doctrine and dismiss the case if it finds that foreign contacts predominate and that there's no special reason for the court to entertain the case.[13]

When successfully invoked, the New York forum non conveniens doctrine usually dismisses the action, but a stay is sometimes used instead. CPLR 327(a) permits either. This contrasts with federal practice, where the doctrine usually does no more than transfer the case to a more appropriate federal district,[14] and

7. Westwood Assocs. v. Deluxe General, Inc., 53 N.Y.2d 618, 438 N.Y.S.2d 774, 420 N.E.2d 966, aff'g 73 A.D.2d 572, 422 N.Y.S.2d 1014 (1st Dep't 1979).

8. Varkonyi v. S.A. Empresa de Viacao A.R.G., 22 N.Y.2d 333, 337–8, 292 N.Y.S.2d 670, 673, 239 N.E.2d 542, 544 (1968).

9. In one case, more amusing than consequential because of its unique facts, the foreign sovereign itself was the plaintiff seeking the aid of the New York courts to get at assets allegedly stolen by its former monarch. Its own courts were clearly the most appropriate for the suit, but it appeared that the world had little confidence in them and that their judgments would not be recognized and enforced in other nations. Holding that the plaintiff had only itself to blame for that, the Court of Appeals ordered the suit dismissed under the conveniens doctrine. Islamic Republic of Iran v. Pahlavi, 62 N.Y.2d 474, 478 N.Y.S.2d 597, 467 N.E.2d 245 (1984).

10. Export Ins. Co. v. Mitsui Steamship Co., 26 A.D.2d 436, 274 N.Y.S.2d 977 (1st Dep't 1966).

11. The original contents of CPLR 327 were designated as subdivision (a) by this amendment.

12. See CPLR 327(b), referring to Gen.Oblig.L. § 5–1402, which in turn refers to § 5–1401. The three statutes together, sought by New York City to propitiate commercial interests, effect this result. See the memorandum of the city's legislative representative at page A–689 of McKinney's 1984 Session Law News. A federal court in New York would not be bound by such a contract, however. See item #8 on the list of choice of forum factors in § 616 below (Practitioner's Edition).

13. A "conveniens" dismissal in that setting was the result in Brooke Group Ltd. v. JCH Syndicate 488, 87 N.Y.2d 530, 640 N.Y.S.2d 479 (1996), a New York action against a Lloyd's insurance syndicate based in London.

14. 28 U.S.C.A. § 1404(a).

where dismissal is the exception rather than the rule.

The dismissal or stay may be conditional. The court can, for example, dismiss on condition that the moving defendant stipulate to accept service in a designated forum elsewhere, thus easing the plaintiff's jurisdictional path there,[15] or require the defendant to stipulate to waive the defense of the statute of limitations when sued elsewhere.[16] Interesting issues arise when the defendant does so stipulate, and then violates the stipulation.[17]

The conveniens doctrine is not restricted to personam cases; it may also be applied in actions based on rem jurisdiction.[18]

The way to raise the conveniens objection is by a simple motion on notice. It is expressly authorized by CPLR 327(a); under prior law, the objection, although not the same as subject matter jurisdiction, fell into that category for the purpose of authorizing a dismissal motion under CPLR 3211(a)(2).[19]

It takes a motion by a party to invoke the conveniens doctrine. The court cannot invoke it sua sponte. A court would occasionally raise the objection on its own, on the ground that it might otherwise be imposed on unduly merely because the lawyers on both sides wanted to use the court even for cases lacking reasonable contacts with the forum,[20] but the Court of Appeals appears to have put an end to that:

> The Appellate Division acted outside of its authority in *sua sponte* dismissing the complaint on forum non conveniens grounds. Under CPLR 327(a) a court may stay or dismiss an action in whole or in part on forum non conveniens grounds only upon the motion of a party; a court does not have

the authority to invoke the doctrine on its own motion.[21]

There is no stated time limit on when the motion can be made, but a defendant bent on avoiding inconvenience should make the motion before answering. Since the conveniens ground has sometimes been treated as synonymous with subject matter jurisdiction, however—a matter elaborated in the next section—it might be thought permissible to make the motion at any time, because a subject matter objection lies at any time. The assumption is unsound. If a defendant has subjected itself to the inconvenience of a trial, and lost on the merits, a court should not accept its inconvenience argument if saved till then. It should simply hold that the defendant has waived it. This does not mean that a rigid time period must be singled out to govern the conveniens motion; it merely suggests that a motion that claims inconvenience to the defendant should not be delayed until it has seriously inconvenienced the plaintiff (who, because the objection was saved, has gone on to prepare for trial). This reasoning applies as well to the conveniens objection in an action against a foreign corporation, discussed in the next section.

While primarily a feature of supreme court practice, the conveniens doctrine is occasionally seen in one of the lower courts. It was the subject of conflicting decisions in the New York City Civil Court in the same county (Queens). One applied the doctrine to dismiss a case that was thought more appropriate to another county,[22] while the other refused a conveniens dismissal on the facts while ex-

15. See Barry v. American Home Assur. Co., 38 A.D.2d 928, 329 N.Y.S.2d 911 (1st Dep't), aff'd 31 N.Y.2d 684, 337 N.Y.S.2d 259, 289 N.E.2d 180 (1972).

16. Ginsburg v. Hearst Pub. Co., 5 A.D.2d 200, 170 N.Y.S.2d 691 (1st Dep't 1958), aff'd 5 N.Y.2d 894, 183 N.Y.S.2d 77, 156 N.E.2d 708 (1959).

17. See Cesar v. United Technology of New York, 148 Misc.2d 918, 562 N.Y.S.2d 903 (Sup.Ct., N.Y. County, 1990), aff'd 173 A.D.2d 394, 570 N.Y.S.2d 25 (1st Dep't 1991), discussed in the lead note in New York State Law Digest No. 380.

18. Vaage v. Lewis, 29 A.D.2d 315, 288 N.Y.S.2d 521 (2d Dep't 1968). A special forum non conveniens provision,

Dom.Rel.L. § 75–h, governs in child custody cases, which can involve personam or rem jurisdiction or a combination of both. See Dom.Rel.L. § 75–d.

19. See Commentary C3211:12 on McKinney's CPLR 3211.

20. See, e.g., Roseman v. McAvoy, 92 Misc.2d 1063, 401 N.Y.S.2d 988 (N.Y.C.Civ.Ct. 1978).

21. VSL Corp. v. Dunes Hotels and Casinos, Inc., 70 N.Y.2d 948, 524 N.Y.S.2d 671, 519 N.E.2d 617 (1988).

22. Neuro Rehab. Health Care v. N.Y. Central Mut. Fire Ins. Co., N.Y. Law Journal, Feb. 4, 1997, p.29, col.3 (Weiss, J.).

pressing doubt about whether the civil court could entertain such a dismissal on any facts.[23]

§ 29. Forum Non Conveniens and Corporations

Business Corporation Law § 1314, on the scene long before CPLR 327 arrived, applies to certain cases involving defendant foreign corporations. If the plaintiff is a New York resident or domestic corporation, BCL § 1314(a) states unequivocally that the action "may be maintained". This implies that the court must entertain the suit against the foreign corporation. It has not yet been resolved whether CPLR 327(a), which authorizes dismissal if otherwise warranted even though one of the parties is a New Yorker, will change this rigid requirement of BCL § 1314(a) and permit a dismissal in such a case. It should. CPLR 327, as the later statute, can be deemed to make a pro rata dent in § 1314(a).

When the plaintiff is a nonresident or a foreign corporation suing a foreign corporation, § 1314(b) applies. It authorizes entertainment of the action only if at least one of the following five requirements is met:

(1) The action is for damages for breach of a contract made or to be performed in New York or relates to property that was in New York when the contract was made.

(2) The "subject matter" of the case, presumably meaning some kind of identifiable property, is in New York.

(3) The claim arose in New York (unless it seeks to affect the title to foreign realty).

(4) The defendant would be subject to jurisdiction under CPLR 302 (this is "longarm" jurisdiction, to be met later[1]).

(5) The defendant is authorized to do or is doing business in New York.

If the only item satisfied is number 5 on the list—that the corporation is doing business in New York—caselaw imposes the additional requirement that a special circumstance be shown before the action will be entertained.[2] The reason is that so many foreign corporations have a New York presence that some leverage is needed to exclude cases having nothing to do with the corporation's New York activities and in which no other factor is present to make New York an appropriate forum.[3]

If one of the first four items on the BCL § 1314(b) list is satisfied, however, it presumably suffices by itself to require entertainment of the suit. Here a clash with CPLR 327(a), which in general terms authorizes conveniens dismissals without getting into the kinds of specifics that § 1314(b) contains, is less likely because meeting one of the specific requirements of § 1314(b) would in most cases qualify as the kind of discretionary factor that would also warrant retention of the suit under CPLR 327(a).

The test for determining whether the corporation is "doing business" under § 1314(b)(5) is essentially the same as the one that determines amenability to personal jurisdiction under CPLR 301,[4] treated later.[5]

Section 1314 should be deemed a forum non conveniens statute,[6] although it has sometimes been referred to as going to subject matter jurisdiction.[7] The conveniens doctrine is often discussed as if it were the same as subject matter jurisdiction, but it is not the same, either technically or practically. The more cur-

23. Suffolk Chiropractic Center v. Geico Ins. Co., 171 Misc.2d 855, 656 N.Y.S.2d 107 (Civ.Ct., Queens County, 1997). See the discussion of this and the Neuro case in SPR 54:3 and 55:3.

§ 29

1. See § 84 below.

2. Yesuvida v. Pennsylvania R.R., 200 Misc. 815, 111 N.Y.S.2d 417 (Sup.Ct., Kings County, 1951).

3. If the case falls under subdivision (b) of CPLR 327, however, which makes the exercise of jurisdiction mandatory in certain commercial cases (see § 28, note 12, and text at that point, above), this special circumstance rule

would presumably give way and jurisdiction would have to be entertained.

4. Fremay, Inc. v. Modern Plastic Mach. Corp., 15 A.D.2d 235, 240, 222 N.Y.S.2d 694, 699–700 (1st Dep't 1961).

5. See § 82 below.

6. See Abkco Industries, Inc. v. Lennon, 85 Misc.2d 465, 377 N.Y.S.2d 362 (Sup.Ct., N.Y.County, 1975), mod'd in part and aff'd 52 A.D.2d 435, 384 N.Y.S.2d 781 (1st Dep't 1976).

7. Robinson v. Oceanic Steam Nav. Co., 112 N.Y. 315, 19 N.E. 625 (1889).

rent thinking of the Court of Appeals is that "when a court, on the ground of forum non conveniens, dismisses an action which it could entertain, it is exercising a discretionary power".[8] One need only add that there is nothing discretionary about subject matter jurisdiction.

Even the rule that a court will not allow itself to become embroiled in the "internal affairs" of a foreign corporation—corporate structure, stock and bond set-ups, rights of shareholders inter se, etc.—once thought to go rigidly to subject matter jurisdiction, has more recently been placed in the more flexible category of forum non conveniens.[9]

D.   OTHER RESTRICTIONS ON JURISDICTION

Table of Sections

§ 30.   Unlicensed Plaintiff Corporation

Business Corporation Law § 1312 precludes a foreign corporation doing business in New York from maintaining a New York action without having duly licensed itself and paid all required fees and taxes. This is a revenue measure, designed to place foreign corporations on the same footing with domestic ones. Its purpose is therefore fulfilled when the foreign corporation complies and the state gets the money. Thus, if the plaintiff corporation is in breach of the statute when it begins an action but duly (and retroactively) complies while the action is pending, the action is validated ab initio and may proceed unhindered.[1]

But nothing less than full compliance will suffice; the mere payment of security for costs, which a different statute exacts of nonresident plaintiffs, is not sufficient.[2]

Section 1312 should not be confused with § 1314 of the BCL. The latter is a forum non conveniens statute concerned mainly with defendant foreign corporations while § 1312 is a money measure aimed at plaintiff foreign corporations.

Section 1312 is not jurisdictional,[3] which means that the defendant had best make an objection under it affirmatively, by motion or answer, despite indications that the plaintiff should plead compliance as a condition precedent to suit.[4] It should be so administered, however, as to preclude a plaintiff in violation of it from realizing any benefits from an action until compliance is had.

The statute applies in a federal court in New York as well as in the state courts, at least when the basis of federal subject matter jurisdiction is diversity of citizenship.[5]

What constitutes "doing business" sufficient to invoke § 1312 is apparently tested by the same yardstick used to determine a corporation's amenability to personal jurisdiction under CPLR 301,[6] but there are periodic statements to the effect that the tests are not the same.[7]

The statute does not apply if the commerce that the corporation is engaged in is exclusively interstate.[8]

§ 31.   Interference with Interstate Commerce

Another category of objection to the entertainment of jurisdiction, analogous to forum

---

8. Bata v. Bata, 304 N.Y. 51, 55, 105 N.E.2d 623, 625 (1952).

9. Broida v. Bancroft, 103 A.D.2d 88, 478 N.Y.S.2d 333 (2d Dep't 1984).

§ 30

1. Oxford Paper Co. v. S. M. Liquidation Co., 45 Misc.2d 612, 257 N.Y.S.2d 395 (Sup.Ct., N.Y. County, 1965).

2. CPLR 8501(a). See Dixie Dinettes, Inc. v. Schaller's Furn. Inc., 71 Misc.2d 102, 335 N.Y.S.2d 632 (N.Y.C.Civ. Ct. 1972).

3. Hot Roll Mfg. Co. v. Cerone Eqpt. Co., 38 A.D.2d 339, 329 N.Y.S.2d 466 (3d Dep't 1972).

4. Oxford Paper Co. v. S. M. Liquidation Co., note 1, above.

5. Woods v. Interstate Realty Co., 337 U.S. 535, 69 S.Ct. 1235, 93 L.Ed. 1524 (1949). Cf. Grand Bahama Petroleum Co. v. Asiatic Petroleum Corp., 550 F.2d 1320 (2d Cir.1977).

6. See § 83 below.

7. E.g., Von Arx, A.G. v. Breitenstein, 52 A.D.2d 1049, 384 N.Y.S.2d 895 (4th Dep't 1976), aff'd 41 N.Y.2d 958, 394 N.Y.S.2d 876, 363 N.E.2d 582 (1977).

8. International Text-Book Co. v. Tone, 220 N.Y. 313, 115 N.E. 914 (1917).

non conveniens but occupying a separate niche and occasioning separate inquiry because based on the federal constitution, is that the maintenance of the suit will constitute an undue burden on the defendant's interstate commerce. This is an objection that has fallen into disuse in recent years, apparently because of the rapidity of transportation today and because New York's reasonable forum non conveniens rules are likely to dispose of the case before the commerce objection is reached: an action likely to interfere unreasonably with the defendant's interstate commerce is also likely to run afoul of New York's own conveniens' rules and be shown the door by that route alone.

The common carrier was the primary beneficiary of this interstate commerce rule, as illustrated in Baltimore Mail S.S. Co. v. Fawcett,[1] where a steamship company was sued on a claim arising in Virginia. It was held that the action could not be entertained because the need to defend a suit far from the place of the occurrence and the main centers of its business would constitute an unreasonable burden on the defendant's transportation business.

All lawsuits are a burden. To succeed with the commerce objection, the defendant must show on the facts of the particular case that it would be an "oppressive and unreasonable" burden,[2] a difficult showing at best in a state with sound conveniens rules. The objection does not often succeed today.[3]

It is perhaps ironic that a carrier, which would usually have the readiest facilities to transfer records pertaining to a foreign lawsuit, should have been the chief beneficiary of the commerce rule. It is clear today, however,

that the rule also applies to other categories of defendant.[4]

E. CONDITIONS PRECEDENT TO SUIT

Table of Sections

Sec.
32. Conditions Precedent to Suit; Notice of Claim; Leave to Sue.

§ 32. Conditions Precedent to Suit; Notice of Claim; Leave to Sue

In a few instances a condition precedent may have to be met before suit is allowed. The most common of these is the notice of claim, a requirement that the potential defendant be notified of the existence of the claim within a given period after the claim arises. This requirement may come from a contract[1]—of which the insurance policy is the prime example—or from a statute. Various requirements, with short time periods, are imposed for filing claims against the state in the court of claims, for example. These are governed by § 10 of the Court of Claims Act, which should be the first thing consulted by one with a claim against the state.

The most notable—or, to plaintiffs' lawyers, notorious—notice of claim provision is that of § 50-e of the General Municipal Law. It applies to tort claims against a public corporation, which includes among other things a city, county, town, village, fire district, and school district.[2] The notice of claim must ordinarily be served on the entity within 90 days after the claim arises, i.e., the accident occurs.[3] The 90-day period moves fast; some lawyers, ama-

---

§ 31

1. 269 N.Y. 379, 199 N.E. 628, cert. den. 298 U.S. 675, 56 S.Ct. 939, 80 L.Ed. 1396 (1936).

2. International Milling Co. v. Columbia Transp. Co., 292 U.S. 511, 520, 54 S.Ct. 797, 800, 78 L.Ed. 1396 (1934).

3. See, e.g., Ceravit Corp. v. Black Diamond S. S. Corp., 46 Misc.2d 979, 260 N.Y.S.2d 848 (App.T., 1st Dep't, 1965).

4. Banque de France v. Supreme Court, 287 N.Y. 483, 41 N.E.2d 65, cert. den. 316 U.S. 646, 62 S.Ct. 1279, 86 L.Ed. 1730 (1942). The commerce objection did not succeed and the action in New York was sustained, the main reason being that the plaintiff would otherwise have had to bring its action in a Nazi-occupied country. That alter-

native made the New York suit reasonable. The case incidentally shows the similarity between the elements that go into the New York forum non conveniens doctrine and those that count under the federally inspired interference-with-commerce test.

§ 32

1. E.g., Cuzdey v. American Motorists Ins. Co., 45 A.D.2d 134, 357 N.Y.S.2d 143 (3d Dep't 1974), aff'd 37 N.Y.S.2d 939, 380 N.Y.S.2d 648, 343 N.E.2d 287 (1975).

2. See Gen.Constr.L. § 66.

3. Gen.Mun.L. § 50-e(1)(a).

teur relativity theorists, swear it runs faster than other 90–day periods. If the client retains the lawyer with time still left in which to get the notice of claim served, and it is not served, the lawyer is open to a malpractice charge.

The purpose of the notice of claim is to enable the public corporation to investigate claims and obtain evidence promptly.[4] Drawing and serving the notice is a simple step to carry out. It is a sworn-to writing naming the claimant and attorney and describing the nature of the claim, the when, where, and how of its arising, and the injuries claimed insofar as now discernible.[5] It is served on the would-be defendant by personal delivery or by registered or certified mail to one upon whom a summons could be served in the defendant's behalf, or, if the defendant has a "regularly engaged" attorney, to the attorney.[6]

If the notice is served on time, but in an improper manner, the defect is waived if the defendant demands an examination of the plaintiff (to which the defendant is entitled under the statute). Defects in manner of service are also waived if it is shown that the defendant actually received the notice within the required time, unless the notice of claim is returned to the plaintiff within 30 days after being received, with a statement specifying the alleged defect.[7] If the defendant does that, the plaintiff then has 10 days in which to serve a new notice, curing the defect,[8] which of course takes the profit out of the defendant's attempt to exploit mere defects in method of service. That's the purpose of this provision.

Ordinary mail is an improper method. Hence, if it is used, it must actually be received within the 90 days (which opens the door to issues of fact connected with service). The mere posting of ordinary mail within the 90 days does not suffice, as it does when the registered or certified mail expressly prescribed by § 50–e is used.[9] Using one of the prescribed methods, which produces a post office receipt, also assures the claimant better proof against the possibility that the defendant will deny service.

Defects in the contents of the notice, not shown to prejudice the defendant, such as an omission of how the claim arose or the items of damage, have also been held curable or disregardable,[10] but the courts are not consistent. In one case, for example, in which the accident site was misdescribed, the court voided the notice even though the defendant municipality's own police department had on record a proper site description.[11] The lesson is that if the plaintiff's attorney needs a little outlet for carelessness, the notice of claim is not the place for it.

Defects in manner of service or in the content of the notice of claim have been a continuous source of grief for plaintiffs, but by no means the main one. That spot is reserved for timeliness. Before September 1, 1976, the grounds on which the late service of a notice of claim might be allowed were narrow, and narrowly construed. The case annotations under § 50–e in McKinney's General Municipal Law were literally a graveyard of meritorious claims barred by lateness.[12] The court had no general discretion to allow a late filing. This changed with the 1976 amendment of the section,[13] but if the continuing annotations are

---

4. State v. Waverly Cent. Sch. Dist., 28 A.D.2d 628–629, 280 N.Y.S.2d 505, 507 (3d Dep't 1967).

5. Gen.Mun.L. § 50–e(2).

6. Gen.Mun.L. § 50–e(3)(a).

7. Gen.Mun.L. § 50–e(3)(c).

8. Gen.Mun.L. § 50–e(3)(d).

9. Adkins v. City of New York, 43 N.Y.2d 346, 401 N.Y.S.2d 469, 372 N.E.2d 311 (1977).

10. Gen.Mun.L. § 50–e(6). See, e.g., Montana v. Incorporated Village of Lynbrook, 23 A.D.2d 585, 256 N.Y.S.2d 651 (2d Dep't 1965).

11. Caselli v. City of New York, 105 A.D.2d 251, 483 N.Y.S.2d 401 (2d Dep't 1984).

12. To spare federal civil rights claims a similar interment, the U.S. Supreme Court has held that the 90–day notice of claim requirement does not apply in a case predicated on 42 U.S.C.A. § 1983. Felder v. Casey, 487 U.S. 131, 108 S.Ct. 2302, 101 L.Ed.2d 123 (1988). The New York Court of Appeals had previously held to the contrary in 423 South Salina Street, Inc. v. City of Syracuse, 68 N.Y.2d 474, 510 N.Y.S.2d 507, 503 N.E.2d 63 (1986).

13. The amendment was drafted by Professor Paul S. Graziano at the behest of the New York State Judicial Conference, in a study set forth in its entirety in 21st Jud.Conf.Rep.Leg.Doc. (1976) No.90, p.362. The study offers a devastating picture of the quagmire built over the years around the notice of claim requirement.

any indication, the turn-around has not proved as complete as would-be plaintiffs might wish.

A major accomplishment of the amendment is the expansion of judicial discretion to allow late service,[14] but with a cutoff: the court cannot extend the time to serve a notice of claim longer than the applicable statute of limitations, i.e., the time in which to start an action. The statute of limitations on a tort claim against a public corporation is one year and 90 days, as provided by § 50–i of the General Municipal Law. The court can stretch the 90–day notice of claim period of § 50–e up to the year and 90 days of § 50–i. And if a tolling provision extends the statute of limitations,[15] such as for the plaintiff's infancy, it will also stretch the time for the court's discretionary grant of leave to file a late notice.[16]

An application to serve a late notice of claim or to cure some other defect is made to the supreme or county court of the appropriate county, and can even be made after an action has been commenced on the claim.[17] But while it may be made after the action has been commenced, it must be made within the year and 90 days, unless, of course, a toll applies. Absent a toll, "the application for the extension may be made before or after the commencement of the action but not more than one year and 90 days after the cause of action accrued".[18] This also means—when a motion for leave to file late is made after the year and 90 days—that a complaint served within that time, even though it contains everything a

notice of claim is supposed to contain, cannot merely be "deemed" a notice of claim and allowed to serve as such.[19]

An application for leave to serve a late notice of claim is likely to be made when no jurisdiction has yet been obtained over the would-be defendant. If that's the case, the papers bringing on the motion for leave should be served in the same manner as a summons in order to assure that jurisdiction is acquired. The best thing to do is bring the application on as a special proceeding.[20] That would secure the procedural guidance of Article 4 of the CPLR, which includes a provision, CPLR 403(c), requiring that the initiatory papers be served in the same manner as a summons.

In determining whether to grant a late filing, the court is expressly empowered to take into consideration whether the defendant or his attorney or insurance carrier had actual knowledge of the facts constituting the claim within the 90–day period "or within a reasonable time thereafter". Other relevant factors are the would-be plaintiff's death during the 90–day period, the disabilities of mental or physical incapacity, and the disability of infancy mentioned above.[21]

The court may also consider whether the plaintiff withheld service of a notice of claim in "justifiable reliance" on settlement negotiations, and whether there was any confusion in identifying precisely which public corporation was liable for the particular accident.[22] Also an

---

14. Gen.Mun.L. § 50–e(5).

15. Limitations' tolls are treated beginning in § 50, below.

16. Cohen v. Pearl River Union Free School Dist., 51 N.Y.2d 256, 434 N.Y.S.2d 138, 414 N.E.2d 639 (1980).

17. Gen.Mun.L. § 50–e(5), (7).

18. Pierson v. City of New York, 56 N.Y.2d 950, 954, 453 N.Y.S.2d 615, 617, 439 N.E.2d 331, 332 (1982).

19. See Tarquinio v. City of New York, 84 A.D.2d 265, 445 N.Y.S.2d 732 (1st Dep't 1982), affirmed by the Court of Appeals along with the Pierson opinion, above. The logic of that proposition is hard to defend.

20. In Lewin v. County of Suffolk, 239 A.D.2d 345, 657 N.Y.S.2d 734 (2d Dep't 1997), the court suggests that the special proceeding is the only proper vehicle; that a motion is improper. The court in Lewin did treat the motion as a special proceeding, however, an appropriate application of CPLR 103(c).

21. Of the few grounds accepted under prior law to excuse a late filing, infancy was the most successful. See Murray v. City of New York, 30 N.Y.2d 113, 331 N.Y.S.2d 9, 282 N.E.2d 103 (1972); Crume v. Clarence Cent. School Dist. No. 1, 43 A.D.2d 492, 353 N.Y.S.2d 579 (4th Dep't 1974).

22. See, e.g., Bender v. New York City Health and Hospitals Corp., 38 N.Y.2d 662, 382 N.Y.S.2d 18, 345 N.E.2d 561 (1976). The public authority, of which there are a number in New York, has been a special offender in this regard. See the Graziano study, 21st Jud.Conf.Rep. (1976) 362, 375; Reinhart v. Troy Parking Auth., 36 A.D.2d 654, 318 N.Y.S.2d 852 (3d Dep't 1971); Conroy v. L. I. R. R., 31 A.D.2d 834, 298 N.Y.S.2d 105 (2d Dep't 1969). Indeed, the statute of limitations itself, applicable to a given public authority, may be construed to be a "condition precedent" to the claim rather than an ordinary statute of limitations—see § 34, below, for the difference—with the usual disastrous consequence of a dismissal of the claim. See, e.g., Savino v. Demiglia, 128 A.D.2d influential factor, of course, is whether the defendant was "substantially prejudiced" by the delay.[23]

Under no circumstances should an attorney rely on settlement negotiations to the extent of letting the time for serving a notice of claim expire. If negotiations are pending, the attorney can serve the notice of claim accompanied by a polite letter advising that it is only a precaution. Even if the court buys the "settlement talks" argument and extends the time, the lawyer will leave the courthouse with a red face and a trail of laughter.

It is always uncomfortable to have to seek leave to file a late notice of claim. And while the grant of late filing permission is clearly more liberal under the present § 50–e than it was before—although, as already noted, not as liberal as some hoped—the lawyer must note that its generosity is restricted to cases in which the defendant is a municipal corporation or other entity governed by § 50–e. It does not necessarily apply, for example, to a notice of claim requirement "with respect to the state or a state agency", where the notice of claim requirement may still be considered "jurisdictional".[24] For actions against public authorities, however, § 2980 of the Public Authorities Law, enacted in 1990, does adopt § 50–e for uniform use in wrongful death actions, but in other categories, like the personal injury action, whether § 50–e governs depends on the statute governing the particular authority.[25]

When a notice of claim requirement is statutorily imposed it is usually deemed an element of the substantive cause of action and as such its satisfaction must be pleaded in the complaint.[26] The defendant can raise the defect either as a defense in the answer or by motion to dismiss for failure to state a cause of action.

When the claim against a governmental entity is on some ground other than tort, a notice of claim requirement may still obtain and yet not be found in a relatively uniform provision like the one that § 50–e supplies for tort cases. The lawyer should make inquiry forthwith. Contract actions, for example, may be governed by separate statutes for different municipalities.[27]

Lawyers should never be self-indulgent in analyzing a given claim against a government unit. If there is any doubt whatever about whether a notice of claim provision is applicable, apply it and carry out its requirements to the letter. Suppose, for example, that a municipality has withheld money or property of X even after the dismissal of a criminal action in which the property was seized. X wants it back and sues for it. This is not a typical personal injury or property damage claim of the kind usually associated with § 50–e, but notice of claim is required, at least for any claims based on state law, and X can't avoid it by trying to cast the claim for relief in some other form, such as a proceeding under Article 78 of the CPLR against the property's custodian.[28]

Although the notice of claim is the foremost illustration of a condition precedent to suit, there are some others. In a few rare instances, for example, such as an action against the committee of an incompetent, it has been held that leave to sue must be secured from the

858, 513 N.Y.S.2d 776, substituted opinion on reargument 133 A.D.2d 389, 519 N.Y.S.2d 384 (2d Dep't 1987), and its summary in New York State Law Digest No. 332.

23. Gen.Mun.L. § 50–e(5).

24. Luciano v. Fanberg Realty Co., 102 A.D.2d 94, 475 N.Y.S.2d 854 (1st Dep't 1984).

25. See Chapter 804 of the Laws of 1990, which enacts a set of uniform provisions governing public authorities in wrongful death actions, Pub.Auth.L. §§ 2980–2982, but continues to retain separate provisions for other categories. Chapter 804 contains that mass of provisions, some of which adopt § 50–e, but not all do, so it remains imperative to check out each authority's applicable statute individually. This is true of the notice of claim as well as the

statute of limitations itself, the subject of the next chapter.

26. See Gen.Mun.L. § 50–i(1). When it is imposed by contract instead of by statute, the plaintiff need not plead its satisfaction but will have to prove it if the defendant should raise the issue. See CPLR 3015(a).

27. See, e.g., CPLR 9802 (governing villages); Town L. § 65(3). As to counties, see Meed v. Nassau County Police Dep't, 70 Misc.2d 274, 332 N.Y.S.2d 679 (Sup.Ct., Nassau County, 1972).

28. See Neumark v. N.Y.C. Police Property Clerk, 122 A.D.2d 210, 504 N.Y.S.2d 744 (2d Dep't 1986). For what an Article 78 proceeding is, see § 557, below.

court in advance.[29] This is true also of an action against a receiver. It has been held, however, that the failure to obtain such ad-vance permission is not jurisdictional and can therefore be cured with a nunc pro tunc order after the action has been commenced.[30]

29.　Matter of Boruk, 21 Misc.2d 875, 195 N.Y.S.2d 468 (Sup.Ct., Queens County, 1959).

30.　Copeland v. Salomon, 56 N.Y.2d 222, 451 N.Y.S.2d 682, 436 N.E.2d 1284 (1982) (receiver).

Chapter Three

THE STATUTE OF LIMITATIONS

Analysis

A. INTRODUCTORY

Table of Sections

§ 33. Statute of Limitations, Generally

"At common law there was no fixed time for the bringing of an action. Personal actions were merely confined to the joint lifetimes of the parties. The Statute of Limitations was enacted to afford protection to defendants against defending stale claims after a reasonable period of time had elapsed during which a person of ordinary diligence would bring an action. The statutes embody an important policy of giving repose to human affairs."[1]

The periods enacted are arbitrary; they represent what the legislature deems a sufficient period in a particular kind of case. There are explicit provisions prescribing how time periods are computed.[2]

Although the statute of limitations is generally deemed "procedural", there is little else in the law that can destroy a case so quickly, and

from the defendant's point of view so conveniently. What better gift for a defendant than a victory without even having to address the merits? The impact is in a real sense "substantive" and the plaintiff's lawyer should abandon all other pursuits when a case first comes to the office and determine, by the most conservative estimates, the latest possible day for commencing the action. A notation should then be made on that day in a long-term diary, and an additional warning notation should be made—that the last day is coming up—a week earlier, a month earlier, and several months earlier. Six or eight months earlier, we think.

A recurring theme in this book is that as a general rule it is wise to commence actions, if at all possible, with at least six or eight months to spare on the statute of limitations. The reason is that things can happen during the early stages of a case, often unexpectedly, with or without fault on the lawyer's part, that can dismiss an action without reaching the merits. When one of these things does occur, like a jurisdictional objection based on something as paltry as a technical defect in the summons, it is nice to know that the time is

---

§ 33

1. Flanagan v. Mount Eden Gen. Hosp., 24 N.Y.2d 427, 429, 301 N.Y.S.2d 23, 25, 248 N.E.2d 871, 872 (1969).

2. See §§ 20, 24, 25, and 25–a of the General Construction Law. See also § 34, below, and more particularly § 202 on the service of papers generally.

still open for a new action. It can probably be shown by facts and figures that the lawyer who has made it a habit to leave time under the statute of limitations for a new action will also end up with a longer life expectancy on the actuarial charts.[3] We have devoted a special section, § 231A, below, entitled "Leave Time for Trouble", to demonstrating how an unanticipated contingency that brings about a mild inconvenience at worst when time for trouble has been reserved can impose capital punishment when it has not. We urge all readers, especially the infrequent litigator, to peruse that section carefully.

The reason that the statute of limitations is so uncompromising and so violent is not hard to trace. CPLR 2004 gives the courts broad discretion to extend periods of time contained in the CPLR for doing a myriad of things, "[e]xcept where otherwise expressly prescribed by law". The statute of limitations is one of those exceptions. CPLR 201 provides that "[n]o court shall extend the time limited by law for the commencement of an action".[4] The result is that although it is subject to a variety of statutory tolls and extensions, to be met later, the statute of limitations is not subject to a discretionary judicial extension of time no matter how good the reason for the delay may be.

§ 34.   Theory, "Suspension of Remedy"; Reckoning

The theory of the statute of limitations generally followed in New York is that the passing of the applicable period does not wipe out the substantive right; it merely suspends the remedy.[1] But the application of the statute of limitations usually dismisses the action as permanently as a final judgment on the merits, at least insofar as further suit in New York is

concerned. Clients told that they've lost only their remedies, not their rights, have not been known to embrace their attorneys in tearful gratitude.

One of the practical consequences of this theory is that it makes the statute of limitations an affirmative defense to be pleaded and proved by the defendant. The statute of limitations must be raised either by a motion to dismiss or as a defense in the answer;[2] a defendant who does neither waives it.[3]

Most of the periods of limitation supplied by New York law, in or out of the CPLR, are of this suspend-the-remedy type. Occasionally one meets the other kind, often referred to as a "condition precedent", in which the passing of the stipulated period abolishes the underlying right. It is seldom a happy meeting for the plaintiff, appearing more often than not when a foreign cause of action is involved, but a few survive in New York law, too.[4] Probably the most common criterion applied by the courts when they conclude that a time period is of the condition precedent kind is where a cause of action unknown to the common law is created by statute and a time period is included in the very statute that creates the claim.[5] Paradoxically, the quintessential illustration of that standard, the wrongful death cause of action, has a statute of limitations—two years[6]—that has been construed to be of the ordinary suspend-the-remedy kind.[7]

In the exceptional instance of the abolish-the-right kind of period, the complaint must plead and the plaintiff has the burden of proving that the claim was brought on time. It is a condition precedent and deemed a substantive part of the plaintiff's cause of action. In the more usual case, in which the burden of raising the timeliness issue is on the defendant, the plaintiff need not even refer to the time

---

3. Attempts at summons service on the last day of the statute of limitations is probably the principal cause of high blood pressure among litigation lawyers.

4. Another major exception is the time in which to take an appeal. See § 533 below.

§ 34

1. Hulbert v. Clark, 128 N.Y. 295, 28 N.E. 638 (1891).

2. CPLR 3018(b), 3211(a)(5).

3. CPLR 3211(e).

4. See, e.g., Savino v. Demiglia, 128 A.D.2d 858, 513 N.Y.S.2d 776 (2d Dep't 1987), substituted opinion on reargument 133 A.D.2d 389, 519 N.Y.S.2d 384 (2d Dep't 1987), involving a statute of limitations against a public authority.

5. E.g., Romano v. Romano, 19 N.Y.2d 444, 280 N.Y.S.2d 570, 227 N.E.2d 389 (1967) (annulment action).

6. EPTL § 5–4.1.

7. Sharrow v. Inland Lines, Ltd., 214 N.Y. 101, 108 N.E. 217 (1915).

element in the complaint.[8] The most signifi-cant consequence of the condition precedent category of time period is that it is not subject to the tolling provisions.[9] Applied to an ordi-nary statute of limitations, a tolling provision operates to extend the period.[10]

When the United States brings a claim, it is subject to neither the statute of limitations nor the doctrine of laches, except to the extent that it agrees to be.[11] When the State of New York sues, however, a statute provides that it is as subject to these defenses as a private litigant.[12]

In reckoning a statute of limitations, the day of accrual is excluded and the count begins the next day.[13] With a limitation period measured in years, this makes the event's anniversary date in the last year the last day for the bringing of the action.[14] Thus, if an accident occurs on July 8, 1999, the last day on which to bring a personal injury action, which is subject to a three-year period, is July 8, 2002.[15]

When the last day of the period falls on a Saturday, Sunday, or public holiday, the time for commencing the action is extended to "the next succeeding business day".[16] In our adver-sary system, the plaintiff's lawyer who plays the statute of limitations that close is asking for trouble, and the defendant's lawyer owes it to the defendant to take advantage of the plaintiff's tardiness.

B.　THE APPLICABLE PERIODS

8.　See Romano v. Romano, note 5, above.

9.　See, e.g., Kahn v. TWA, Inc., 82 A.D.2d 696, 443 N.Y.S.2d 79 (2d Dep't 1981), involving the two-year period applicable to a claim against an air carrier under the Warsaw Convention.

10.　For treatment of New York's tolling provisions, see § 50 et seq., below.

11.　United States v. Summerlin, 310 U.S. 414, 60 S.Ct. 1019, 84 L.Ed. 1283 (1940); In re Feinberg, 18 N.Y.2d 499, 277 N.Y.S.2d 249, 223 N.E.2d 780 (1966). See 28 U.S.C.A. § 2415, and the discussion in Cracco v. Cox, 66 A.D.2d 447, 414 N.Y.S.2d 404 (4th Dep't 1979). Laches is dis-cussed in § 36, below.

12.　CPLR 201; State v. Waverly Cent. Sch. Dist., 28 A.D.2d 628, 280 N.Y.S.2d 505 (3d Dep't 1967).

§ 35.　The Various Time Periods

The various time periods are generally keyed to the kind of claim being brought. Most are in the CPLR on lists contained in CPLR 211 through CPLR 217; some are in other laws. It is not necessary to repeat all of the lists here but it would be worthwhile to stress certain items.

CPLR 211 lists the claims subject to a 20–year period, the longest period supplied by the CPLR. A major one here is the action on an already rendered judgment. Because of the language of CPLR 211(b), the passing of the 20–year period has been held to create a conclusive presumption of payment and an absolute bar to suit. This means that it is construed to be of the abolish-the-right (or "condition precedent") rather than the more common suspend-the-remedy kind,[1] a situa-tion the legislature has seen fit to preserve.[2]

The major claim subject to the 10–year peri-od of CPLR 212 is the one based on 10 years of possession of realty, commonly known as a claim of adverse possession.[3] This is a change from the 15–year period previously applicable.[4]

The claims subject to a six-year period are listed in CPLR 213. The most notable of these is the claim in contract, express or implied.[5] It includes a cause of action for indemnification whether it arises expressly or by operation of

13.　See Gen.Constr.L. § 20, which prescribes how time periods are counted. See also § 202, below, on the service of papers generally.

14.　Evans v. Hawker–Siddeley Aviation, Ltd., 482 F.Supp. 547 (S.D.N.Y.1979).

15.　See Rush v. Bauerle, 49 Misc.2d 595, 268 N.Y.S.2d 67 (Sup.Ct., Orange County, 1966).

16.　Gen.Constr.L. § 25–a. The list of public holidays that New York recognizes is in § 24 of that law.

§ 35

1.　See § 34 above.

2.　5th Rep.Leg.Doc.(1961) No.15, p.50.

3.　CPLR 212(a).

4.　Civ.Prac.Act § 34, superseded Sept.1, 1963.

5.　CPLR 213(2).

law. Thus, where P sues D for personal injuries based on negligence (or any other theory) at the very last moment and D, after the negligence period has expired, seeks to implead X for indemnification or contribution on the ground that X's conduct is responsible in some degree for the tort, the impleader claim is timely because D's claim against X sounds in indemnity rather than in negligence or whatever other theory (e.g., warranty, strict products liability, etc.) may underlie the main claim.[6]

In installment-contract situations the six-year period may be deemed to commence separately on each installment as it accrues.[7]

Sales contracts subject to the Uniform Commercial Code, which covers the sale of nearly everything except realty and services,[8] are governed by the 4–year period of UCC § 2–725, to which the CPLR defers. The breach of warranty in conjunction with the sale of a product (including a personal injury claim so predicated) is a common category of breach of contract met under the UCC and is therefore governed by this 4–year provision. The sale of realty or services continues to be subject to the CPLR six-year period. In some cases it may be difficult to determine the category. It has been held that if services is the principal item sold and a chattel that is part of the sale is merely incidental, the six-year period governs, as in the sale of funeral services including a casket.[9]

The breach of a warranty contained in the lease of a chattel, as opposed to its sale, has been given the six-year rather than the four-year period.[10]

The residual or "catch-all" period of six years is also in CPLR 213. It is subdivision one and is treated in the next section, on equity actions.

The three-year claims are in CPLR 214. They are in the main the unintentional torts. The personal injury claim, whether predicated on negligence or the more recent "strict tort liability" or "strict products liability" theory, is here in subdivision 5. This three-year period is also the one applicable to a federal civil rights action brought in either a federal or state court in New York under 42 U.S.C.A. § 1983.[11]

A three-year period also governs a claim for an "injury to property",[12] which covers not only property damage in a negligence case but a wide range of harms—including conversion—under the broad definition of "injury to property" applicable in New York practice.[13] Replevin also gets a three-year period under CPLR 214.[14]

Another frequently invoked three-year period under CPLR 214 is the one applicable to "an action to recover upon a liability, penalty or forfeiture created or imposed by statute".[15]

---

6. Hansen v. City of New York, 43 Misc.2d 1048, 252 N.Y.S.2d 695 (Sup.Ct., Kings County, 1964). This matter is elaborated in § 162.

7. See Walsh v. Andorn, 33 N.Y.2d 503, 355 N.Y.S.2d 329, 311 N.E.2d 476 (1974).

8. UCC §§ 2–102, 2–105.

9. Joseph P. Suchy, Inc. v. Stuerzel, 82 Misc.2d 40, 370 N.Y.S.2d 316 (App.T., 1st Dep't, 1975).

10. Owens v. Patent Scaffolding Co., 50 A.D.2d 866, 376 N.Y.S.2d 948 (2d Dep't 1975).

11. Wilson v. Garcia, 471 U.S. 261, 105 S.Ct. 1938, 85 L.Ed.2d 254 (1985). Having been supplied no time period by federal law, a § 1983 claim borrows the period applicable to the most nearly analogous state cause of action, and the Wilson case finds the personal injury claim to be the most analogous. See Commentary C4–41 on Fed.R.Civ.P. Rule 4 in 28 USCA. The period of a year and 90 days applicable to tort claims against municipalities under Gen. Mun.L. § 50–i (discussed further on in this section) is superseded by this three-year period in § 1983 cases, and the 90–day notice of claim requirement of Gen.Mun.L. § 50–e, generally applicable to tort claims against munici-

palities (see § 32 above), does not apply in a § 1983 case. See Felder v. Casey, 487 U.S. 131, 108 S.Ct. 2302, 101 L.Ed.2d 123 (1988), in effect overruling 423 South Salina Street, Inc. v. City of Syracuse, 68 N.Y.2d 474, 510 N.Y.S.2d 507, 503 N.E.2d 63 (1986), which had concluded the other way.

12. CPLR 214(4).

13. Gen.Constr.L. § 25–b defines an injury to property as any "actionable act, whereby the estate of another is lessened, other than a personal injury, or the breach of a contract". Any case involving a property loss and not otherwise supplied a time period is therefore subject to the three-year period of CPLR 214(4).

14. CPLR 214(3).

15. CPLR 214(2). This had been a six-year period under § 48(2) of the old Civil Practice Act, but was reduced to three with the adoption of the CPLR in order to coordinate it with the three years applicable to personal injury and property damage claims predicated on negligence, which often involve an additional count based on the breach of a statutory duty.

Thus, when a cause of action unknown to the common law is created by statute and a specific period is not enacted to accompany it, CPLR 214(2) governs and the period is three years.

A malpractice claim, which is in essence a claim of negligence against a professional, gets three years in non-medical cases, such as against lawyers and architects,[16] but a claim for medical, dental, or podiatric malpractice gets only 2-1/2 years.[17] This shorter period applies only to "medical" misconduct, however. While a hospital and nurse as well as a physician enjoy the shorter period for activities qualifying as "medical" treatment, they don't for other conduct, such as failing to supply competent personnel or to establish proper emergency room rules, where the usual negligence three-year period applies.[18] And the services of a psychologist, while of course professional, have also been held to be beyond the "medical" category, making the 3–year rather than 2 1/2–year period applicable.[19]

The one-year claims are in CPLR 215. The most significant here are the intentional torts, like assault, defamation, and the violation of the right of privacy.[20] One year is also the period in which to confirm an arbitration award.[21]

The proceeding under CPLR Article 78, which replaces the old writs of certiorari to review and mandamus, must be brought within four months from the time the determination becomes "final and binding" (certiorari) or a demand to perform a duty is refused (mandamus).[22] Article 78 also replaces the writ of prohibition, but since that writ is used mainly to test whether an officer or judge has jurisdiction, there is usually no time limitation on it.[23] The four-month period has also been held to apply to disputes involving the assessment of real property even if the gist of the attack is on the validity of the rate schedule that grounds the assessment, the kind of constitutional issue that in other contexts might earn a longer period by being brought in the form of a declaratory judgment.[24]

Some of the more important time periods supplied by statutes other than the CPLR are the five-year period for divorce or separation on some (but not all) grounds[25] and the already mentioned four-year period governing breaches of sales contracts (including the breach of warranty) under the UCC.[26] The EPTL supplies a two-year period for the wrongful death claim.[27] The periods applicable to claims against the state are in § 10 of the Court of Claims Act. Usually shorter than the CPLR periods, they can be expanded to CPLR length by the court, on motion, if special requirements are met.[28] In the unusual case, in which the period provided in the Court of Claims Act proves longer than the period applicable gener-

---

16. CPLR 214(6). For a while, the malpractice period against nonmedical professionals was stretched to six years under a Court of Appeals decision, Santulli v. Englert, Reilly & McHugh, 78 N.Y.2d 700, 579 N.Y.S.2d 324, 586 N.E.2d 1014 (1992), which held that because there is also a contractual relationship between the parties in these situations, the plaintiff has the option of relying on the contractual six years of CPLR 213(2) as an alternative. An amendment of CPLR 214(6) that took effect September 4, 1996, overruled Santulli and restored the three years exclusively. See SPR 48:2. The three-year period may sometimes be extended under a kind of "continuous treatment" theory, analogous to and adopted from that applicable in medical malpractice cases. See § 42 at notes 11 to 15 below.

In 1996 and 1997, the present CPLR 214–d appeared, governing actions against architects, engineers, and land surveyors for design defects in buildings. Its purpose is to impose a 10–year cut-off period in favor of such defendants. See the discussion in SPR 51:2.

17. CPLR 214–a.

18. Bleiler v. Bodnar, 65 N.Y.2d 65, 489 N.Y.S.2d 885, 479 N.E.2d 230 (1985).

19. Karasek v. LaJoie, 92 N.Y.2d 171, 677 N.Y.S.2d 265 (1998).

20. CPLR 215(3).

21. CPLR 215(5). See CPLR 7510, 7514(a).

22. CPLR 217(1).

23. See § 566 below.

24. See Press v. County of Monroe, 50 N.Y.2d 695, 431 N.Y.S.2d 394, 409 N.E.2d 870 (1980), treated in the lead note in New York State Law Digest No. 252. Press holds that the application of the shorter period is indispensable to the continuity of government, which depends on the tax collection process.

25. See Dom.Rel.L. § 210.

26. UCC § 2–725.

27. EPTL § 5–4.1.

28. Ct.Cl.Act § 10(6). See L.F. O'Connell Assocs. v. State, 176 Misc.2d 697, 674 N.Y.S.2d 900 (Ct.Cl.1998), noted in SPR 75:4.

ally, as on a defamation claim for which CPLR 215 supplies only a one-year period, the state has been held entitled to the benefit of the shorter period.[29]

A tort action against a municipality must be brought within one year and 90 days under General Municipal Law § 50–i, which, as a statute of limitations, should not be confused with the 90–day notice of claim period of § 50–e, also applicable in such cases.[30]

§ 36. Equity Actions; Laches

There is no time period addressed to the "equity" action as such. It falls under CPLR 213(1) and gets six years as "an action for which no limitation is specifically prescribed by law". (Some equity actions, as will be seen in a moment, are additionally subject to an application of the laches doctrine.) The six-year period of CPLR 213(1) is often referred to as the "residual" or "catch-all" provision. It applies in such equity cases as accounting,[1] injunction,[2] and reformation of contract.[3]

The substantive law rule that equity will not intercede unless the plaintiff has no adequate remedy at law has a limitations' counterpart, too. If the plaintiff does have an adequate legal remedy but sues for equitable relief instead, the equitable claim, even if the court is disposed to entertain it under less rigid modern concepts, will be measured by the period of limitations—usually shorter—applicable to the law claim. This made more of a difference under prior law when the residual (equity) period was 10 years.[4] When P sued for an accounting (equity), for example, in a case in which simple breach of contract (law) was found to be just as effective, the equity claim was held subject to the legal six-year period.[5] Today, with the old residual of 10 now reduced to six, the point in the cited example would be academic.

There is indeed a nonsequitur in this approach. Presumably, even today, equitable relief is entertainable only when no legal remedy is adequate, so that law's adequacy in a given situation would preclude the equitable claim on that ground alone, avoiding the problem of deciding which statute of limitations to apply. That the problem exists, and has been addressed in the cases, suggests that the courts today will entertain equitable relief in some cases even though there is an adequate remedy at law, while at the same time insisting that the period applicable to the law claim, at least when shorter, govern the equitable one. There is an internal contradiction in that. The lesson to the lawyer who would retain control of the time element is never to let the "law" period lapse in reliance on getting the longer "equitable" period applied.

If the legal alternative is inadequate—this makes more sense—the plaintiff who sues in

---

29. See Kilbourne v. State, 111 Misc.2d 161, 443 N.Y.S.2d 538 (Ct.Cl.1980), whose rationale was adopted in Trayer v. State, 90 A.D.2d 263, 458 N.Y.S.2d 262 (3d Dep't 1982).

30. For treatment of the notice of claim of § 50–e, see § 32, above. The one year and 90 days of § 50–i has been held to supersede other time periods that might otherwise seem applicable to a municipality, whether the other is longer or shorter. Szerlip v. Finnegan, 77 Misc.2d 655, 354 N.Y.S.2d 555 (Sup.Ct., Orange County, 1974), aff'd 47 A.D.2d 603, 365 N.Y.S.2d 1016 (2d Dep't 1975). By analogy to the Kilbourne case and its discussion of the Court of Claims Act, note 29 above, it might be urged that a municipality, like the state, should have the benefit of the shorter period in such cases. But the analogy wouldn't hold in a wrongful death case, anyway, because of a 1981 amendment of Gen.Mun.L. § 50–i, which provides specifically that the wrongful death two-year period remains applicable even in actions against municipalities. And an intent is sometimes found in a given statute to allow more rather than less time. See Tharps v. City of New York, 59 N.Y.S.2d 1023, 466 N.Y.S.2d 960, 453 N.E.2d 1249 (1983) (New York City Transit Authority).

If a municipality is required to indemnify the employee responsible for the act that created the liability, as it is, for example, when the employee operates a municipal vehicle in the scope of employment (Gen.Mun.L. § 50–b), the year and 90 days also applies to an action against the employee. And a condition precedent to the employee action is that the usual 90–day notice of claim of Gen. Mun.L. § 50–e have been served on the municipality. See Fitzgerald v. Lyons, 39 A.D.2d 473, 336 N.Y.S.2d 940 (4th Dep't 1972).

§ 36

1. La Russo v. Paladino, 109 N.Y.S.2d 627 (Sup.Ct., Kings County, 1951), aff'd 280 App.Div. 988, 116 N.Y.S.2d 617 (2d Dep't 1952).

2. Petnel v. American Tel. & Tel. Co., 280 App.Div. 706, 117 N.Y.S.2d 294 (3d Dep't 1952).

3. Hanover Fire Ins. Co. v. Morse Dry Dock and Repair Co., 270 N.Y. 86, 200 N.E. 589 (1936).

4. Civ.Prac.Act § 53.

5. Keys v. Leopold, 241 N.Y. 189, 149 N.E. 828 (1925).

equity is not beholden to the law period. Suppose, for example, that P is a judgment creditor and that judgment debtor D has fraudulently transferred assets to frustrate collection of the judgment. P can disregard the transfers and just issue execution on the judgment, i.e., proceed at law. But it is recognized that such a procedure is impractical because the property sought stands in the name of others: sheriffs will balk and further proceedings will be necessary. Thus, the plaintiff who seeks in equity to set aside the transfers is entitled to the equity period because the legal relief is inadequate.[6] But if P does seek legal relief, such as by a subsequent action for damages for fraud, the law period will apply.[7] The reason for this is that the inadequate-remedy-at-law rule has no converse: a plaintiff suing at law is not to be denied legal relief (nor is the equity period to be applied to the claim) merely because an equitable remedy happens to be available.

In those equity actions in which relief lies in the discretion of the court, such as an action for the specific performance of a contract or for an injunction, the doctrine of laches applies. And it applies in addition to but independent of the statute of limitations.[8] The bringing of the action within the six-year period of CPLR 213(1) is mandatory, but if the defendant can show (1) that the plaintiff has been guilty of undue delay and (2) that the delay has been prejudicial (both showings are needed to support the defense of laches), the court can dismiss the action even though it was brought within the applicable statute of limitations.[9]

Whether the delay was so unreasonable as to invoke the laches doctrine is a sui generis inquiry.[10]

An analogous approach is taken in the declaratory judgment action. If declaratory judgment is the only effective remedy the plaintiff has, it will get the six-year residual period of CPLR 213(1).[11] But if another adequate remedy is available, with a shorter period, the shorter period applies.[12] This point is discussed in more detail in the chapter that includes the declaratory judgment.[13]

§ 37. Multiple Theories

From but a single wrong, a plaintiff may have many possible theories of recovery. The plaintiff should as a rule interpose them all in her action. A common example today is the personal injury caused by a defective product. It may give rise to several theories of recovery: negligence, which gets a three-year period under the "personal injury" provision of CPLR 214(5); "strict products liability",[1] which is also a tort and is governed by the same provision—and as with negligence the period starts to run from the injury;[2] and breach of warranty, which gets a four-year period under UCC § 2–725. With warranty the period starts from the sale of the defective item rather than from the time of injury.[3]

In such a case, where the plaintiff has suffered but one harm, she has but a single cause of action and each of the available supporting theories is merely a different count in support of the single claim.[4] In a sense, it is technically

---

6. Hearn 45 St. Corp. v. Jano, 283 N.Y. 139, 27 N.E.2d 814 (1940).

7. Nasaba Corp. v. Harfred Realty Corp., 287 N.Y. 290, 39 N.E.2d 243 (1942).

8. Groesbeck v. Morgan, 206 N.Y. 385, 99 N.E. 1046 (1912).

9. Feldman v. Metropolitan Life Ins. Co., 259 App.Div. 123, 18 N.Y.S.2d 285 (1st Dep't 1940).

10. Herrick v. Watters, 50 A.D.2d 627, 374 N.Y.S.2d 745 (3d Dep't 1975).

11. See Gambold v. MacLean, 126 Misc. 820, 215 N.Y.S. 607 (Sup.Ct., Kings County, 1926).

12. Calder v. Teachers' Retirement Bd., 4 Misc.2d 166, 156 N.Y.S.2d 494 (Sup.Ct., N.Y.County, 1956) (four-month period of CPLR 217 applied where Article 78 proceeding would lie for the relief sought in the declaratory action).

13. See § 438 below.

§ 37

1. See Velez v. Craine & Clark Lumber Corp., 33 N.Y.2d 117, 350 N.Y.S.2d 617, 305 N.E.2d 750 (1973).

2. Victorson v. Bock Laundry Machine Co., 37 N.Y.2d 395, 373 N.Y.S.2d 39, 335 N.E.2d 275 (1975).

3. See § 41 below.

4. The official language of the CPLR is "cause of action", CPLR 3211(a)(7), while the federal language is "claim", FRCP Rule 12(b)(6). While the two are sometimes said to differ, see, e.g., Garcia v. Hilton Hotels Int'l, Inc., 97 F.Supp. 5 (D.Puerto Rico 1951), the differences are not satisfactorily explained. Since both require a cognizable substantive basis for relief, there is little to pick between them. This text prefers "claim" because it is shorter, but uses the word interchangeably with the phrase "cause of action".

inaccurate to say that a plaintiff so situated has multiple causes of action or multiple claims. Since the plaintiff can have but one recovery for the wrong, regardless of the multiple theories available and even though each may carry a different period of limitations, the plaintiff has in the ultimate sense but a single claim.

The strict liability ground has in common with the warranty ground that both dispense with proof of negligence. For that reason, and because strict liability was a relative latecomer, it was thought for a while that strict liability had pushed warranty off the personal injury scene altogether.[5] That notion was dispelled by a 1975 amendment of UCC § 2–318, the warranty statute,[6] and the Court of Appeals now upholds the view that warranty is still an available alternative.[7] Since the statute of limitations is the principal element affected—warranty offering four years from sale as an alternative to the three years from injury that applies to strict products liability—the plaintiff does no harm throwing warranty in as an extra count. But for safety's sake the plaintiff should bring the case within three years of the injury to assure that no inadvertent time omission will bar the negligence and strict liability grounds.[8]

It had been thought in some quarters that in a product-caused tort, the warranty and strict liability grounds are—except for the statute of limitations—substantively identical. The Court of Appeals rejected that idea in 1995 in Denny v. Ford Motor Co.,[9] finding a distinction between them and sustaining a verdict that had found a breach of warranty while rejecting a claim of strict liability. Strict liability requires a "weighing" of the product's dangers against its advantages, the court said; marketing the product, with its dangers, might be held acceptable by the jury should it find that reasonable alternatives were not available to the manufacturer. But that won't necessarily insulate against a warranty claim, the court concluded.[10]

The warranty versus strict products liability example manifests how one count in support of a claim can offer substantial advantages or support remedies not available on the other. The four-year warranty period can preserve a personal injury claim sued on after the three-year tort period—which governs both the negligence and strict liability counts—has expired. (And, paradoxically, the tort three may sometimes prove longer than the warranty four! The three run from injury; the four from the sale. If the injury occurs long after the sale, a tort ground may still be alive when the warranty claim is already dead.)

In one case the plaintiff pleaded five counts in support of a claim for injury caused by the inhalation of dust years earlier: negligence, nuisance, breach of contract, fraud, and breach of a statutory duty. The plaintiff was seeking a longer period than the negligence three years, which had lapsed. The court held that the first four counts, however denominated, all required proof of negligence and so were in effect only negligence claims and were barred by the three-year statute. But the fifth count, alleging violation of a statute and requiring no proof of negligence, was held to qualify as a statutory claim entitled to a six-year measure[11] and was sustained.[12]

The same conduct will sometimes constitute both a breach of contract and the tort of conversion. The conversion claim has only a three-year period;[13] adding a count in contract may secure the application of the longer con-

5. See Martin v. Julius Dierck Equipment Co., 43 N.Y.2d 583, 403 N.Y.S.2d 185, 374 N.E.2d 97 (1978).

6. See Singer v. Federated Department Stores, Inc., 112 Misc.2d 781, 447 N.Y.S.2d 582 (Sup.Ct., N.Y.County, 1981).

7. Heller v. U.S. Suzuki Motor Corp., 64 N.Y.2d 407, 488 N.Y.S.2d 132, 477 N.E.2d 434 (1985).

8. See § 41, below, and the lead note in New York State Law Digest No. 268.

9. 87 N.Y.2d 248, 639 N.Y.S.2d 250, 662 N.E.2d 730.

10. The case is the subject of the lead note in New York State Law Digest No. 435.

11. The statutory claim today gets three years. CPLR 214(2).

12. Schmidt v. Merchants Despatch Transp. Co., 270 N.Y. 287, 200 N.E. 824 (1936). In another respect, dealing with when a tort claim accrues when based on exposure to a dangerous substance, the Schmidt case is overruled by the 1986 adoption of CPLR 214–c. See § 40 below.

13. CPLR 214(4).

tract period[14] if it should be needed. But in other contract and tort situations the courts have been ambivalent, suspecting subterfuges conjured up by tardy plaintiffs to avoid a lapsed claim. In one case, for example, a plaintiff's contract claim, on which the time period ran from the breach, had expired. The plaintiff tried to plead a claim in fraud, whose time starts at discovery and would have been alive, but the Court of Appeals held the claim barred.[15] The court said that "in applying the Statute of Limitations we look for the reality, and the essence of the action and not its mere name."[16] If a plaintiff makes out the elements of a fraud claim, however, why shouldn't the plaintiff have the benefit of it, including its postponed-until-discovery accrual? The *Brick* case seems to reward a fraud merely because it also happens to be a breach of contract, which tends to teach a wrongdoer that sometimes two wrongs make a right.

A later decision addresses the plaintiff's use of alternative contract and tort theories in a case against architects. In Sears, Roebuck & Co. v. Enco Associates, Inc.,[17] the defendant was an architectural firm that allegedly misdesigned ramps leading to the plaintiff's store. The plaintiff sought various items of property damage. Suit was brought more than three but less than six years after the ramp was completed, and this, on a technical measure, meant that it would be timely if the claim sounded in contract but untimely if it had to rely on tort. The Court of Appeals, noting that the essence of the relationship between the parties was a contractual one, held that the statute of limitations is not concerned with the theory but with the remedy. It sustained the action as timely, but with the proviso that the only damages that could be recovered were those associated with contract. The limitations barri-

er would be applied to bar only those damages associated exclusively with tort. As we shall see, however, in a case like *Sears* there's really no difference in the damages.

The *Sears* lesson would seem to be that if the plaintiff sues within the time applicable to all available grounds, the plaintiff does get them all—tort, contract, whatever—and with all the damages associated with any of them.[18]

A later Court of Appeals case that relied on *Sears*, Video Corp. of America v. Frederick Flatto Associates,[19] involved a defendant insurance broker's failure to obtain adequate insurance for the plaintiff. The plaintiff alleged among other things that the defendant failed to use due care, which is tort language. But since the wrong had its genesis in contract, the court held the claim timely even though brought after the three years applicable to tort.

The Second Department in Baratta v. Kozlowski[20] saw *Video* as "portentous" for implicitly extending the rationale of *Sears*. *Sears* involved a formal written contract, the court pointed out, while *Video* extended it to less formal contract-based arrangements as well. As *Baratta* anticipated, this ultimately led to the Court of Appeals 1992 decision in Santulli v. Englert, Reilly & McHugh,[21] holding that claims against lawyers, because also contract-based, could also rely on the six years of CPLR 213(2) instead of being restricted to the malpractice three of CPLR 214(6). *Santulli* was overruled in a 1996 amendment, however.[22]

While the damages associated with tort would be precluded if a given action, using the *Sears/Santulli* rule, fell within the contract six years but beyond the tort three, this would rarely if ever make a difference in malpractice-type cases brought against lawyers or accoun-

14. CPLR 213(2); UCC § 2–725(1).

15. Brick v. Cohn–Hall–Marx Co., 276 N.Y. 259, 11 N.E.2d 902 (1937).

16. Id. at 264, 11 N.E.2d at 904.

17. 43 N.Y.2d 389, 401 N.Y.S.2d 767, 372 N.E.2d 555 (1977).

18. The Court of Appeals has had difficulty on other fronts, however, in deciding when to permit a tort theory to emerge from a contract-based relationship. See, for example, Board of Education of the Hudson City School

District v. Sargent, Webster, Crenshaw & Folley, 71 N.Y.2d 21, 523 N.Y.S.2d 475, 517 N.E.2d 1360 (1987), dealing with contribution among tortfeasors, and the discussion of the case in New York State Law Digest No. 340.

19. 58 N.Y.2d 1026, 462 N.Y.S.2d 439, 448 N.E.2d 1350 (1983).

20. 94 A.D.2d 454, 464 N.Y.S.2d 803 (2d Dep't 1983).

21. 78 N.Y.2d 700, 579 N.Y.S.2d 324, 586 N.E.2d 1014.

22. See § 35, note 16.

tants or the like, because such actions as a rule seek only economic damages. In personal injury cases, on the other hand, as *Baratta* shows, there is a great difference in that situation: the pain and suffering element, which is associated exclusively with tort, would be lost. But while pain and suffering is a major element in a malpractice action against a physician, it is not an element in the property damage category into which most frequently fall non-medical[23] malpractice cases like those against lawyers and accountants and sometimes architects and engineers and the like.

After the *Santulli*-overruling 1996 amendment of CPLR 214(6), it will once again become necessary to determine precisely whether a given claim sounds in malpractice, because, if it does, it must presumably be restricted to the three years of CPLR 214(6) and can't rely on the contractual six years of CPLR 213(2). Still an open question, moreover, is the extent to which the 1996 amendment overrules *Sears* itself. *Sears* was against architects, architects are professionals, misfeasance by a professional is malpractice, and under CPLR 214(6) the malpractice statute of limitations is three years "whether the underlying theory is based in contract or tort". By that yardstick, would all contract-based claims against an architect be ousted now in favor of "malpractice" exclusively, and its three-year period?

While there are some complications about what damages are available with which claim, and which claim gets what period, the one point that emerges clearly from all of the foregoing discussion is that the plaintiff who timely joins everything, and does so within the shortest of the applicable statutes of limitation, is in the best position to get it all.

---

23. Medical malpractice has its own statute of limitations. See CPLR 214–a, discussed in § 42 below.

§ 38

1. Stewart v. Keyes, 295 U.S. 403, 55 S.Ct. 807, 79 L.Ed. 1507 (1935).

2. Campbell v. Holt, 115 U.S. 620, 6 S.Ct. 209, 29 L.Ed. 483 (1885). This distinction is difficult to defend: a substantial money claim may be a much greater threat to a defendant in a given case than a claim that seeks a tangible property of less economic value.

3. Const.Art I, § 6.

C. ALTERING THE PERIOD

Table of Sections

§ 38. Statutory Alterations

Constitutional considerations intervene when the legislature attempts to revive an expired period or curtail an existing one.

If the passage of the period has as a practical matter resulted in the vesting of an interest in tangible property, real or personal, the federal due process clause has been held to preclude its revival.[1] If the claim is a mere chose in action, however, such as a money action on a contract, the federal constitution is apparently no barrier to revival[2] but the state constitution may be. The state constitution's due process clause[3] has been construed to require all revivor statutes to be demonstrably reasonable.[4] The question is sui generis and it is of course the courts that have the ultimate say on reasonableness. In one leading case in which the claim had expired while its owner had disappeared in a Nazi-occupied country, a revivor statute, afterwards made a permanent part of New York law,[5] was sustained as reasonable under the circumstances.[6] Revivor legislation is considered drastic and the intent to revive must be clear.[7]

The most significant "revival" undertaking in recent years appeared in a tort reform package.[8] One part of it enacted CPLR 214–c, adopting a "discovery" rule for future exposure cases—cases involving personal injury or property damage caused by exposure to a dele-

---

4. Robinson v. Robins Dry Dock and Repair Co., 238 N.Y. 271, 144 N.E. 579 (1924), app. dism'd 271 U.S. 649, 46 S.Ct. 636, 70 L.Ed. 1131 (1926).

5. CPLR 209(c).

6. Gallewski v. Hentz & Co., 301 N.Y. 164, 93 N.E.2d 620 (1950).

7. Hopkins v. Lincoln Trust Co., 233 N.Y. 213, 135 N.E. 267 (1922).

8. Chapter 682 of the Laws of 1986.

terious substance.[9] The other revived previously dead "exposure" cases, but only for exposure to any of five named substances,[10] and permitted an action at any time up to July 30, 1987 (the end of the one-year period following the effective date of the enactment).

An abridgement statute—one curtailing an existing period—poses a problem only as to claims existing when it becomes operative. It is constitutionally required that the plaintiff be allowed at least a reasonable time in which to sue, measured from the abridgement statute's effective date.[11] As long as the plaintiff has at least a reasonable time, which is initially for the legislature but ultimately for the courts to determine sui generis,[12] it makes no difference that the unexpired period of the superseded statute would have been much longer. The 1996 curtailment to three years of the non-medical malpractice statute of limitations, which had been set at six years by caselaw,[13] is the most recent example of an abridgement statute that posed constitutional issues.[14]

§ 39. Agreements to Shorten or Lengthen the Period

CPLR 201 allows the parties to provide by contract for a shorter time limitation than the law supplies, but the court must be satisfied that the period agreed to is reasonable.[1] If it is found unreasonable it is disregarded. This, too, is a sui generis inquiry. A three-month limit in a bill of lading has been held reasonable[2] while a two-month limit in a steamship ticket has been found unreasonable.[3] The steamship ticket was an adhesion contract and the court's scrutiny is closer there. If the period is cut back into mere days, it is likely to be held unreasonable as a matter of law, as happened in one case with a 15-day period.[4] Sales contracts governed by the UCC may also be shortened, but there an arbitrary limit is imposed: the period cannot be cut back to less than a year.[5]

An agreement to lengthen the statute of limitations is invalid if made before the cause of action accrues but will be honored if made afterwards, with the proviso that the agreement be in writing and signed; if it is, it needs no consideration.[6] Such a post-accrual agreement will start the applicable period running all over again unless it stipulates a shorter period.

Those are the rules for contract cases. There is no statutory rule for extension agreements in tort and other non-contract cases.[7] If such an agreement is made in a non-contract case, however, it should be a basis on which to estop the defendant from pleading the statute of

---

9. See § 40 below.

10. Diethylstilbestrol (DES), tungsten carbide, asbestos, chlordane, and polyvinyl chloride (PVC). The revivor provision should be cited merely as § 4 of Chapter 682 of the Laws of 1986; it has no codified niche. It is discussed in the lead note in New York State Law Digest No. 321.

11. Gilbert v. Ackerman, 159 N.Y. 118, 53 N.E. 753 (1899); see Wilson v. Iseminger, 185 U.S. 55, 22 S.Ct. 573, 46 L.Ed. 804 (1902).

12. See Parmenter v. State, 135 N.Y. 154, 31 N.E. 1035 (1892).

13. See § 37 above.

14. The question was whether the amended statute, CPLR 214(6), was retroactive—the enactment did not address the issue—and, if so, whether the plaintiff should have at least a reasonable time from the amendment's effective date (Sept. 4, 1996) in which to bring suit. The matter was controversial and the courts divided. See the tracking of the issue in SPR 48:2, 53:2, 55:2, 56:2, and 58:2.

§ 39

1. Planet Constr. Corp. v. Board of Educ., 7 N.Y.2d 381, 198 N.Y.S.2d 68, 165 N.E.2d 758 (1960).

2. North British & Mercantile Ins. Co. v. Central Vermont R.R. Co., 9 App.Div. 4, 40 N.Y.S. 1113 (3d Dep't 1896), aff'd 158 N.Y. 726, 53 N.E. 1128 (1899).

3. Kemelhor v. Furness, Withy & Co., 139 Misc. 64, 248 N.Y.S. 659 (N.Y.C.Mun.Ct. 1931).

4. Brown & Guenther v. North Queensview Homes, Inc., 18 A.D.2d 327, 239 N.Y.S.2d 482 (1st Dep't 1963).

5. UCC § 2–725(1).

6. Gen.Oblig.L. § 17–103(1). UCC § 2–725(1), governing sales transactions, also precludes an extension agreement in the original contract.

7. It was the Law Revision Commission that recommended G.O.L. § 17–103, and the Commission addressed only the contract case. One of its aims was to preclude an extension agreement made before a claim accrues, which is relevant in contract but not tort cases. See the text of the Commission's study and report in McKinney's 1961 N.Y. Session Laws, p.1869.

limitations.[8] Any other view would seem to tell parties who think that with a little more time they can resolve their dispute that when the deadline nears they can't buy the time with a mutually agreed-to extension. That would force onto the courts' calendars a lawsuit that might otherwise be avoided, which would be at war with the state's policy of encouraging settlements.

D. ACCRUAL

§ 40. "Accrual" of the Claim

The statute of limitations starts to run when the claim "accrues",[1] and while in most cases it is not hard to determine the moment of accrual, a few situations present problems.

In the personal injury case predicated on negligence, the applicable three-year period starts at the moment of injury. The majority of automobile, airplane, construction, sidewalk, etc., accidents are in that category. But this time-of-injury rule worked to the plaintiff's detriment when the cause of the injury was more subtle. In Schmidt v. Merchants Despatch Transp. Co.,[2] the cause was the inhalation of dust more than three years before the

suit. The resulting injury did not appear for many years after the inhalation, but the court nonetheless held that the period began when the dust was inhaled because the injury was suffered at that time even though not discerned until much later. The plaintiff, said the court, could have sued immediately and shown such damages as "would result" from the inhalation. In other words, the plaintiff should sue promptly upon the inhalation and convince a jury that a carcinoma will appear several years later. That unrealistic view prevailed for half a century. There were many efforts to overrule it. None succeeded, until 1986.

In 1986, with the enactment of CPLR 214–c, the legislature at last adopted a "discovery" rule for personal injury and property damage cases based on "exposure" to a foreign substance.[3] Under subdivision 2 of the statute, the three-year time period in such cases begins to run not from the exposure itself, as in *Schmidt*, but from the later time when the plaintiff discovers or with reasonable diligence should have discovered the injury. And there is no outer time limit. As long as the claim is brought within three years from discovery—and as long as the discovery occurred after the 1986 enactment of CPLR 214(c)—it makes no difference when the exposure first came about; it could have been decades earlier. In Rothstein v. Tennessee Gas Pipeline Co.,[4] for example, the exposure had been to a substance given the plaintiff 40 years earlier to facilitate an x-ray.[5]

---

8. Subdivision 4(b) of G.O.L. § 17–103 provides that the statute "does not affect" the court's estoppel powers. Estoppel to plead the statute of limitations is treated in § 56, below.

§ 40

1. CPLR 203(a).

2. 270 N.Y. 287, 200 N.E. 824 (1936).

3. Exposure is defined by subdivision 1 of the statute to include "direct or indirect . . . absorption, contact, ingestion, inhalation, implantation or injection" of any substance harmful to the body. These cases are sometimes collectively referred to as the "toxic torts". "Implantation" was added in 1992 to overcome Martin v. Edwards Laboratories and Lindsey v. A.H. Robins Co., 60 N.Y.2d 417, 469 N.Y.S.2d 923, 457 N.E.2d 1150 (1983), which had held that malfunctioning devices like a prosthesis or contraceptive, "intended to have a continuing function", are governed by the usual time-of-injury rule. See Alexander, 1992 Commentary C214–c:1 on McKinney's CPLR 214–c.

4. 87 N.Y.2d 90, 637 N.Y.S.2d 674, 661 N.E.2d 146 (1995). The Rothstein case is treated in New York State Law Digest No. 433. A month before Rothstein, in Consorti v. Owens–Corning, 86 N.Y.2d 449, 634 N.Y.S.2d 18, 657 N.E.2d 1301 (1995), also addressing an exposure case, the Court of Appeals had held that a "discovery" rule doesn't apply to a spouse's loss of consortium claim even though neither injured person nor spouse discovered the injury until after 1986, and even though suit was brought within the requisite time after discovery. Whether *Rothstein* overrules *Consorti* is discussed in the lead note in New York State Law Digest No. 434.

5. CPLR 214–c took effect on July 30, 1986. In a subdivision 6, it addresses how it is to be applied in transition cases. A distinct but related provision, not to be confused with CPLR 214–c and its application in future cases, revived all previously dead "exposure" cases, but for only a limited time and for only certain substances. See § 38 above. Both provisions are discussed in the lead note

The assumption, of course, is that the plaintiff knows what caused the injury. If the plaintiff does not know, but discovers the cause (and can therefore attribute it to the defendant) within five years after discovering the injury, subdivision 4 of CPLR 214–c permits the plaintiff, as an alternative, to bring suit within one year from the discovery of the cause. The burden on the plaintiff is heavy; the plaintiff must show that the scientific information from which to draw conclusions about cause was not available within the five-year period. And the state of technical and scientific knowledge that the statute is referring to is the general knowledge of the scientific community, not the particular plaintiff's own actual knowledge.[6]

The delayed-accrual rules of CPLR 214–c also apply to the service of a notice of claim.[7] They do not apply in medical or dental malpractice actions, however,[8] where the more limited "discovery" accrual rule of CPLR 214–a continues to govern.

CPLR 203(g), treated in more detail below,[9] purports to reduce to two years any longer period measured from discovery. It probably should not apply to CPLR 214–c, not only because 214–c is a later enactment silent as to the effect of 203(g), but because, in enacting postponed discovery, subdivision 2 of 214–c specifically says that it is "the three-year period" that "shall be computed from the date of discovery". But just in case the courts hold otherwise, a plaintiff is safer by suing within two years of the discovery of the injury.

The claim of repetitive stress injury (RSI) by a keyboard user alleging an improperly designed computer keyboard, a claim frequently seen today, has been held to accrue at the onset of symptoms or the last use of the keyboard, whichever is earlier.[10]

In certain instances a demand may be necessary before a claim accrues, as where a depositor seeks a withdrawal from an ordinary bank account and the bank denies liability,[11] or where one from whom property has been taken seeks to recover it from the innocent third person who may now have possession of it.[12] In cases in which a demand would otherwise seem necessary, it ceases to be, and the period begins to run without it, if on the facts it appears that a demand would be futile.[13]

The one-year period applicable in defamation cases[14] begins to run from the moment that the actionable words are published. But in the case of a mass-circulated publication such as a book or magazine or Sunday newspaper supplement, which often reaches the public before the day scheduled for formal distribution, the formal distribution is nonetheless the moment of accrual[15]—else many a defamer could escape liability by letting a segment of the public see the words a year before the general public does.

in New York State Law Digest No. 321, which also includes treatment of how this "exposure" provision, logically enough applied in a personal injury case, can be applied in a property damage case. The application of CPLR 214–c in wrongful death cases is discussed in § 44 below.

6. Wetherill v. Eli Lilly & Co., 89 N.Y.2d 506, 655 N.Y.S.2d 862, 678 N.E.2d 474 (1997), noted in New York State Law Digest No. 448.

7. CPLR 214–c(3) so provides for governmental units and Court of Claims Act § 10(7) so provides for the state itself. For what a notice of claim is, see § 32, above.

8. CPLR 214–c(5). We should assume podiatric actions are similarly excluded. The legislature has almost everywhere indicated an intention to lump the podiatric case with the medical and dental ones, see, e.g., CPLR 214–a, 3406(a), and probably omitted reference to it here only by oversight.

9. See § 43.

10. See Blanco v. American Telephone and Telegraph Co., 90 N.Y.2d 757, 666 N.Y.S.2d 536 (1997), treated in the lead note of New York State Law Digest No. 459.

11. CPLR 206(a)(2). In the law of commercial paper the period of limitations on a demand instrument begins to run "upon its date or, if no date is stated, on the date of issue", i.e., immediately (and without awaiting a demand). UCC § 3–122(1)(b). A claim against an indorser on any instrument accrues "upon demand following dishonor". UCC § 3–122(3).

12. See Menzel v. List, 49 Misc.2d 300, 267 N.Y.S.2d 804 (Sup.Ct., N.Y.County, 1966), mod. on other grounds 28 A.D.2d 516, 279 N.Y.S.2d 608 (1st Dep't 1967), mod. rev'd 24 N.Y.2d 91, 298 N.Y.S.2d 979, 246 N.E.2d 742 (1969).

13. See Tillman v. Guaranty Trust Co., 253 N.Y. 295, 171 N.E. 61 (1930).

14. CPLR 215(3).

15. Sorge v. Parade Publications, Inc., 20 A.D.2d 338, 247 N.Y.S.2d 317 (1st Dep't 1964).

The desultory distribution of additional copies of books or magazines from stock after initial publication will not start the year running anew, but a general re-publication will. In Rinaldi v. Viking Penguin, Inc.,[16] for example, several thousand copies of a text not originally bound in hardcover and another several thousand of the hardcovers that had not been sold were used in a softcover issue (the hard covers coming off in the process). This was held to be a general re-issuance of the book, starting the one-year statute of limitations afresh.

Continuing wrongs, such as a continuous trespass, were at one time held to avoid the barrier of the statute of limitations altogether by being deemed to accrue constantly.[17] In 1993, however, in Jensen v. General Electric Co.,[18] a divided Court of Appeals held that this was changed by the 1986 enactment of CPLR 214–c. In an unexpected application of the statute to the trespass scene, the court held that a damages claim for trespass accrues when the plaintiff first learns of it. When shown that this would mean an unlimited license to trespass if the defendant can just get past the original statute of limitations, the majority responded that its holding applies only to a claim for money damages; that there would be no statute of limitations barrier against the plaintiff's seeking an injunction against the trespass at any time. But if this means that no damages at all can be recovered for this injury to the plaintiff's property if the action is brought more than three years after the discovery of the trespass—not even the damages suffered during the three-year period immediately preceding the lawsuit—it would seem to tell the continuing trespasser that while he may one day have to stop, he'll never have to pay, and there is no evidence that the

sponsors of CPLR 214–c intended anything like that.

Special limitations issues arise in warranty, malpractice, and wrongful death cases, which get separate treatment in ensuing sections. The limitations' aspects of an indemnity claim, especially when asserted by a defendant by way of impleader, are treated in the chapter on third-party practice.[19]

§ 41. Accrual in Warranty Cases

A breach of warranty claim in connection with a product accrues upon "tender of delivery"[1]—roughly speaking from the day of sale—and not when the wrong is discovered or an injury occurs. This poses problems when a warranty has allegedly been given for a period longer than the four years applicable to a warranty claim under UCC § 2–725. If the warranty's breach is not discovered until, say, seven years later, i.e., the product's defect does not appear until then, this can lead to some unpalatable results. In one case some equipment allegedly under a 30–year warranty proved defective more than the then-applicable six years after the sale. No matter, held the court: the warranty claim still accrued at the sale and had lapsed.[2] The result is still possible today. The way to avoid it is to follow the advice of the UCC and see to it that in the sales contract itself the warranty "explicitly extends to future performance". If that is done, "the cause of action accrues when the breach is or should have been discovered."[3]

The advantage of having express warranty commitments instead of having to rely on implied warranties is illustrated even in cases governed by pre-UCC law. In Bulova Watch Co. v. Celotex Corp.,[4] for example, a roofer's express promise to repair a "bonded" roof for a 20–year period after the sale of the roofing

---

16. 52 N.Y.2d 422, 438 N.Y.S.2d 496, 420 N.E.2d 377 (1981).

17. See 509 Sixth Avenue Corp. v. N. Y. C. Trans. Auth., 15 N.Y.2d 48, 255 N.Y.S.2d 89, 203 N.E.2d 486 (1964).

18. 82 N.Y.2d 77, 603 N.Y.S.2d 420, 623 N.E.2d 547.

19. See § 162 below.

§ 41

1. UCC § 2–725(2).

2. Citizens Utilities Co. v. American Loc. Co., 11 N.Y.2d 409, 230 N.Y.S.2d 194, 184 N.E.2d 171 (1962).

3. UCC § 2–725(2); see Mittasch v. Seal Lock Burial Vault, Inc., 42 A.D.2d 573, 344 N.Y.S.2d 101 (2d Dep't 1973).

4. 46 N.Y.2d 606, 415 N.Y.S.2d 817, 389 N.E.2d 130 (1979).

materials was held to give the plaintiff-customer a separate claim, and a fresh accrual for limitations purposes, for each breach. Hence, as long as each claim of breach (of the repair obligation) arising within the 20–year period in such a case is sued on within the period as measured from that particular breach, the claim is timely.

If an explicit warranty extending to future performance is not used, the four-year UCC warranty will run from the sale itself even in personal injury cases, and this has produced some bizarre law in New York. In Mendel v. Pittsburgh Plate Glass Co.,[5] D sold plate glass in 1958 to B, a bank. In 1965, P was hurt by the glass. Alleging breach of warranty, P sued D within three years after the injury. The Court of Appeals, on a 4–3 vote, held that the warranty claim accrued in 1958 and was barred by 1962, years before the plaintiff was hurt. The dissent in *Mendel* urged that there existed, quite apart from warranty, the theory of strict liability in tort, and that the *Mendel* claim could be kept alive on that ground (which gets a three-year tort period running from the injury).

What the majority in *Mendel* brought about, therefore—but only for a while, as it turned out—was the substantive divestiture of a "strict liability" theory, which, because it dispenses with proof of negligence, is something like a warranty claim with the added benefit of a tort limitations' accrual. The *Mendel* case was later restricted to warranty, and the "strict liability" ground was substantively reinstated,[6] accompanied by a time-of-injury accrual. This was confirmed by the Court of Appeals in Victorson v. Bock Laundry Machine Co.[7] It supports the conclusion that although the *Mendel* case still dictates the limitations' rules on a warranty claim—four years, but with accrual at sale—their severity can usually be avoided by turning instead to the theory of strict products liability. It ordinarily offers the injured person an equivalent prospect of recovery but with the benefit of tort limitations' rules (three years, but with accrual at injury).

The lawyer should also remember that warranty itself may in some instances offer a limitations' advantage: when the injury occurs close in time to the sale, for example, the four years measured from the sale are likely to give the plaintiff a longer time than three years measured from the injury.

In 1985, in Heller v. U.S. Suzuki Motor Corp.,[8] the Court of Appeals resolved an important question on accrual in warranty cases that had been open for a long time. It was often thought that suit against a warranty defendant was timely as long as the plaintiff sued within four years after the purchase of the damage-causing product from a retailer; that the time of sale by a defendant other than the retailer, such as a manufacturer or distributor, was irrelevant. Not so, held *Heller*. Each defendant along the line of manufacture and distribution is entitled to a separate accrual date based on its own sale of the product and can't be kept exposed to a warranty suit indefinitely merely because (e.g.) a retailer or intermediate jobber has kept a manufacturer's product on its shelves for an inordinate time.

§ 42. Accrual in Malpractice Cases

On a claim for medical malpractice (including dental and podiatric malpractice), which today has a 2 1/2 year statute of limitations under CPLR 214–a, several points about accrual must be noted. In general the period runs from "the act, omission or failure complained of or last treatment where there is continuous treatment for the same illness, injury or condition".[1] The basic rule, therefore, is that the time starts from the wrong itself, whether the plaintiff is aware of wrongdoing or not.[2]

---

5. 25 N.Y.2d 340, 305 N.Y.S.2d 490, 253 N.E.2d 207 (1969).

6. See Codling v. Paglia, 32 N.Y.2d 330, 345 N.Y.S.2d 461, 298 N.E.2d 622 (1973); Velez v. Craine & Clark Lumber Corp., 33 N.Y.2d 117, 350 N.Y.S.2d 617, 305 N.E.2d 750 (1973).

7. 37 N.Y.2d 395, 373 N.Y.S.2d 39, 335 N.E.2d 275 (1975).

8. 64 N.Y.2d 407, 488 N.Y.S.2d 132, 477 N.E.2d 434.

§ 42

1. CPLR 214–a.

2. An exception to this rule is the fetus injured by medical malpractice while in the womb. If the fetus is later born alive, its malpractice claim starts at birth. LaBello v.

The time-of-injury rule gave rise to injustice in a number of situations under prior law, and to a number of efforts to circumvent it.

Among the most successful of these efforts was and remains the "continuous treatment" theory, which postpones the start of the statute of limitations until treatment in respect of the particular ailment is concluded. First adopted by caselaw,[3] the continuous treatment postponement is now codified, as the foregoing quotation from CPLR 214–a manifests. If the treatment has in effect been concluded, however, and a further examination is undertaken at the plaintiff's request "for the sole purpose of ascertaining . . . the patient's condition", the examination does not qualify as a continuous treatment so as to start the period anew. The same is true even if it is the doctor who initiates the new contact, as long as the prior course of treatment had been terminated.[4]

The treatment must be continuous rather than merely intermittent,[5] and termination of treatment is deemed to occur not upon the patient's last actual visit to the doctor, but upon the last scheduled one, if it is later.[6]

The continuous treatment doctrine has been visited several times by the Court of Appeals. In its 1991 decision in Daniel J. v. New York City Health and Hospitals Corp.,[7] the court determined more specifically how the continuous treatment doctrine operates. Before *Daniel J.*, it had been understood as merely postponing the moment of "accrual" until the last treatment. Looking at the matter more closely, the court decided that instead of operating to postpone "accrual" of the claim, the doctrine functions merely as a "toll", suspending the running of the statute during the period of continuous treatment. Hence the claim does "accrue" at the time of the original injury, but

is in effect immediately suspended until treatment is concluded. This may seem like the same thing, but it has impact on another toll, that of CPLR 208, applicable to the plaintiff's infancy. The latter toll is subject to a 10–year cut-off in medical malpractice actions.[8] *Daniel J.* requires the 10–year cut-off period to be measured from the original "accrual"—the time of the original injury—and not from the later point to which the continuous-treatment doctrine in effect postpones the start of the statute of limitations.

In Nykorchuck v. Henriques,[9] the court split on what constitutes a "continuous treatment". A lump in the plaintiff's breast, ultimately diagnosed as cancer and requiring surgery, was first brought to the doctor's attention in 1979, when he said he'd have to "keep an eye on it". The plaintiff made subsequent visits to the doctor over the next several years. If these other visits could be called "treatment" in respect of the lump condition, the action would have been timely. A 5–2 majority held that the visits were not related to the original lump condition; that this was at most a continuing diagnosis ("isolated breast examinations") and that "[i]n the absence of continuing efforts by a doctor to treat a particular condition", the policy behind the continuous treatment doctrine is not on the line—the policy of enabling the physician to complete treatment of a disorder before the patient starts thinking about a malpractice action.

The court has also held that a patient unaware of a misdiagnosis gets no postponed accrual because here, too, the policy of the continuous treatment doctrine is not implicated.[10]

The continuous treatment doctrine doesn't apply against a hospital when the later treat-

Albany Medical Ctr. Hosp., 85 N.Y.2d 701, 628 N.Y.S.2d 40, 651 N.E.2d 908 (1995).

3. See Borgia v. City of New York, 12 N.Y.2d 151, 237 N.Y.S.2d 319, 187 N.E.2d 777 (1962).

4. See Rizk v. Cohen, 73 N.Y.2d 98, 538 N.Y.S.2d 229, 535 N.E.2d 282 (1989).

5. Davis v. City of New York, 38 N.Y.2d 257, 379 N.Y.S.2d 721, 342 N.E.2d 516 (1975).

6. Richardson v. Orentreich, 64 N.Y.2d 896, 487 N.Y.S.2d 731, 477 N.E.2d 210 (1985).

7. 77 N.Y.2d 630, 569 N.Y.S.2d 396, 571 N.E.2d 704 (1991).

8. See § 54 below.

9. 78 N.Y.2d 255, 573 N.Y.S.2d 434, 577 N.E.2d 1026 (1991).

10. See Young v. N.Y.C. Health & Hosps. Corp., 91 N.Y.2d 291, 670 N.Y.S.2d 169 (1998).

ment was at a different hospital, even though both hospitals have the same owner.[11]

The considerations underlying the continuous treatment theory are also inapplicable to a laboratory that misdiagnoses cancer by misreading tissue slides. Hence the statute of limitations extension that the theory may earn against a physician won't be available against a lab.[12] But a kind of continuous treatment theory, with equivalent limitations benefits, has been applied to suits against other professionals, including lawyers,[13] accountants,[14] and architects,[15] where the applicable period is three years.[16] But there, too, an ongoing professional relationship in respect of the subject matter of the claim must be shown.

Muller v. Sturman[17] can illustrate. A client exploiting the theory against a lawyer, holds *Muller*, must show continuous representation by the lawyer on the same matter on which the lawyer is accused of malpractice. The malpractice in *Muller* was alleged to be the lawyer's failure to sue on a certain note, but the court found for the attorney. There was not "an ongoing, continuous, developing and dependent relationship", said the court, "marked with trust and confidence". There had been a drifting apart, and the client did not try to press for suit on the note.

Foreign Object Cases

The most prominent injustice in the medical malpractice field was in surgery cases in which a foreign object was left inside the plaintiff.[18] Periodically urged to adopt a "discovery" accrual in these instances, the legislature regularly refused, until the Court of Appeals took the step itself in 1969 in Flanagan v. Mt. Eden

Gen. Hosp.[19] The legislature then addressed the matter in 1975 with the adoption of CPLR 214–a, which, in "foreign object" cases only, allows the action within one year from the date the plaintiff discovered the wrong or facts that would reasonably lead to its discovery, "whichever is earlier". The one-year period is apparently an alternative, the action still being timely if brought within two and a half years after the wrongful act regardless of when the injury was discovered.

Cases prior to 1975 did not insist that something be left inside the patient, however; they applied the discovery rule, as it came from the *Flanagan* case, even to injuries inflicted on internal organs during an operation notwithstanding that nothing foreign was left in.[20] The Court of Appeals subsequently adopted a view of the "discovery" rule more restrictive than that. Holding in Rodriguez v. Manhattan Medical Group,[21] for example, involving an intrauterine device, that a failure to find and remove the device is not a "foreign object" case and doesn't earn a "discovery" accrual for limitations purposes, the court said that the "foreign object" referred to in CPLR 214–a can't apply to what amounts to a misdiagnosis situation. The failure to detect a device implanted earlier, and by a different physician, is described as "involving misdiagnosis—a category from which the benefits of the 'foreign object' discovery rule have routinely been denied". A mere misdiagnosis is still subject to the usual time-of-wrong accrual.[22]

CPLR 214–a excludes from the "foreign object" category any "chemical compound, fixation device or prosthetic aid or device", i.e.,

---

11. See Allende v. New York City Health and Hosps. Corp., 90 N.Y.2d 333, 660 N.Y.S.2d 695 (1997).

12. McDermott v. Torre, 56 N.Y.2d 399, 452 N.Y.S.2d 351, 437 N.E.2d 1108 (1982).

13. Siegel v. Kranis, 29 A.D.2d 477, 288 N.Y.S.2d 831 (2d Dep't 1968).

14. Wilkin v. Dana R. Pickup & Co., 74 Misc.2d 1025, 347 N.Y.S.2d 122 (Sup.Ct., Allegany County, 1973).

15. County of Broome v. Vincent J. Smith, Inc., 78 Misc.2d 889, 358 N.Y.S.2d 998 (Sup.Ct., Broome County, 1974).

16. CPLR 214(6).

17. 79 A.D.2d 482, 437 N.Y.S.2d 205 (4th Dep't 1981).

18. See, e.g., Conklin v. Draper, 229 App.Div. 227, 241 N.Y.S. 529 (1st Dep't 1930), aff'd 254 N.Y. 620, 173 N.E. 892 (1930).

19. 24 N.Y.2d 427, 301 N.Y.S.2d 23, 248 N.E.2d 871.

20. See, e.g., Dobbins v. Clifford, 39 A.D.2d 1, 4, 330 N.Y.S.2d 743, 747 (4th Dep't 1972). The court noted that "professional diagnostic judgment" was not involved, thus minimizing false claims and satisfying the Flanagan standards.

21. 77 N.Y.2d 217, 566 N.Y.S.2d 193, 567 N.E.2d 235 (1990).

22. Schiffman v. Hospital for Joint Diseases, 36 A.D.2d 31, 319 N.Y.S.2d 674 (2d Dep't 1971).

anything intentionally left in the patient's body as part of the medical procedure. There would thus be no discovery accrual in those instances. "It is now clear", said one court, "that intentionally implanted devices ... cannot be considered 'foreign objects' within the meaning of CPLR 214–a".[23] A suture inserted into the wrong organ during surgery has been held a "fixation device", not a "foreign object", and hence does not get the benefit of the "foreign object" rule.[24] It has even been held that a surgeon's failure to remove a "stent" that the surgeon inserted with the very intention of removing it at a later time is not a "foreign object" case.[25] Shouldn't such an object be deemed a "foreign" one as of the time of the procedure that failed to take it out?

It might cross the reader's mind that fixation devices and other objects could qualify as harmful "substances" under CPLR 214–c, the so-called "exposure" statute,[26] and earn a postponed accrual under that statute. That crossed some other minds as well: CPLR 214–c(5) states explicitly that CPLR 214–c does not apply in medical malpractice actions.

§ 43. "Discovery" Accruals

In several instances the applicable period of time starts to run from the plaintiff's "discovery" of the wrong. CPLR 203(g)[1] is a legislative change of mind about these. It concludes that as measured from the wrong's discovery, the maximum the plaintiff ought to have is two years.[2] In most instances of "discovery" accruals, therefore, CPLR 203(g) superimposes itself and provides that the claim can keep its stated period, but measured only from the wrong itself; that insofar as measured from discovery, it will get only two years. The result

is that in each of these "discovery" cases there are actually two measurements: (1) the stated period running from the wrong itself, and (2) the two-year period running from its discovery. The plaintiff can use whichever is longer.

Fraud is one of the most common claims whose period, which is six years, has a discovery accrual.[3] The operation of CPLR 203(g) on it gives the plaintiff either six years from the fraud or two years from the discovery of the fraud, whichever is longer. If actual fraud underlies the claim, this discovery rule is applicable even when the plaintiff is seeking equitable relief, such as in a creditor's action to set aside a fraudulent conveyance.[4]

CPLR 203(g) also provides that if the plaintiff "could with reasonable diligence" have discovered the wrong earlier than actual discovery, the earlier moment is the starting time. Plaintiffs are not permitted to disregard factors that might put them on notice.

Expressly excepted from the operation of CPLR 203(g) is the four-year warranty period of UCC § 2–725, which has a discovery accrual in certain instances (it is not cut back to two years), and the "foreign object" claim in medical malpractice cases, which is preempted by CPLR 214–a, discussed in the prior section. Apparently the three-year period applicable in the so-called "exposure" cases, for which a discovery rule was enacted in 1986, is also immune from the 203(g) reduction.[5]

Another period running from discovery is the breach of warranty of authority,[6] the claim a victim has against one who falsely represents his capacity to act as agent for another. This is a category of contract and has a six-year period,[7] which would be reduced to two under CPLR 203(g) insofar as measured from discov-

---

23. Provenzano v. Becall, 138 A.D.2d 585, 526 N.Y.S.2d 167 (2d Dep't 1988).

24. See Rockefeller v. Moront, 81 N.Y.2d 560, 601 N.Y.S.2d 86, 618 N.E.2d 119 (1993).

25. LaBarbera v. N.Y. Eye and Ear Infirmary, 91 N.Y.2d 207, 668 N.Y.S.2d 546 (1998).

26. See § 40, at note 3.

§ 43

1. Until 1992, the designation of this provision was subdivision (f); a 1992 amendment changed it to (g). In conducting research, especially when using a tool like

WESTLAW, keep in mind that the many pre–1992 cases that deal with it cite it as (f).

2. See McLaughlin, The Discovery Provisions of Article Two, 10th Jud.Conf.Rep.Leg.Doc. (1965) No. 90, p.96.

3. CPLR 213(8).

4. See Quadrozzi Concrete Corp. v. Mastroianni, 56 A.D.2d 353, 392 N.Y.S.2d 687 (2d Dep't 1977).

5. See § 40 above.

6. CPLR 206(b).

7. CPLR 213(2).

ery. It is not clear what the starting point of the alternative six-years-from-wrong would be in that case. Apparently the six years would start sometime after the agent makes her last representation of authority,[8] and the plaintiff would have either that period, or two years from discovery of the misrepresentation, whichever is longer.

The Court of Appeals is asked periodically to adopt a "discovery" rule of accrual for actions against professionals, but has declined.[9]

§ 44. Wrongful Death Cases

The wrongful death statute of limitations is supplied by EPTL 5–4.1. It is two years and runs from the moment of death. But the statute also provides that the action lies only if the defendant "would have been liable to the decedent" for the wrong had death not ensued. This has been construed to require that the day of death be looked at to determine if, on that day, the decedent had a timely claim against the wrongdoer for the injuries from which the death resulted. If, for example, the basis of liability is negligence, which carries a three-year period, and on the date of death the three years for the negligence action had not yet expired, this condition precedent is met and the action would lie. There are thus two statutes of limitation to be investigated in a death case. The first is the two-year period measured from death—the claim must in any event be brought within that time—and the second is the period applicable to whatever the decedent's underlying cause of action is (three years for negligence, four years for warranty, one year for assault, etc.). On the day of death the relevant statute of limitations for the underlying personal injury claim must still be alive.[1] Take this example.

P is injured in an accident involving D's car on May 1, 1994, and has a negligence claim. P

dies of his injuries on June 3, 1997 without having brought suit. A wrongful death claim, even if brought within two years after death, is barred: the statute of limitations on the underlying claim had expired before P died. Had P in the example died on or before May 1, 1997, the wrongful death claim would lie; although P had not in fact sued for the personal injury, he could have done so timely. Of course, if timely suit had been begun by P prior to his death and was still pending at that time, the condition precedent is met even if the statute of limitations applicable to the underlying claim has now long since expired. The timely bringing of the suit and its pendency at the moment of death give the plaintiff a viable claim against the defendant at that time, which is what EPTL § 5–4.1 insists on.

The pre-death settlement of the underlying claim, however, or the pre-death satisfaction of a judgment recovered on it, destroys the necessary condition precedent and bars the death claim.[2] This can obviously pose a delicate problem for the plaintiff's lawyer to whom a substantial personal injury settlement is tendered by the tortfeasor while the client is in extremis. Acceptance of the settlement bars any wrongful death claim that might otherwise accrue to the client's dependents.

A point should be made about the availability of a wrongful death claim in the so-called "exposure" case—a case in which CPLR 214–c postpones the running of the statute of limitations until the plaintiff has discovered the injury. CPLR 214–c specifically refers only to personal injury and property damage cases, which might lead to the hasty assumption that the "discovery" rule of CPLR 214–c doesn't apply in wrongful death cases. It does apply, but its application requires no explicit reference. Its relevance is in measuring whether the decedent had a valid personal injury claim

8. Moore v. Maddock, 251 N.Y. 420, 167 N.E. 572 (1929). CPLR 206(b) was intended to clarify Moore, but confusion persists under the impact of CPLR 203(g).

9. See, e.g., Ackerman v. Price Waterhouse, 84 N.Y.2d 535, 620 N.Y.S.2d 318, 644 N.E.2d 1009 (1994) (malpractice action against accountant). Some courts have applied a kind of continuous treatment theory in nonmedical as well as medical malpractice actions, however, and this also

has the effect of extending the time for such actions. See § 42 above.

§ 44

1. Kelliher v. New York Cent. and Hudson R.R. Co., 212 N.Y. 207, 105 N.E. 824 (1914).

2. Fontheim v. Third Ave. Ry. Co., 257 App.Div. 147, 12 N.Y.S.2d 90 (1st Dep't 1939).

on the date of death. The incidents of CPLR 214–c about postponed accrual based on discovery of injury and discovery of cause[3] are applicable in that measure.

E. INTERPOSITION

Table of Sections

§ 45. "Interposition" of the Claim; "United in Interest"

The plaintiff must "interpose" the claim within the applicable period.[1]

In New York practice, it had long been the rule that the service of the summons marked the commencement of the action and therefore the moment that "interposes" the claim, in contrast with federal practice where the filing of the complaint does so regardless of when the summons is ultimately served.[2] That is still the rule in the state's lower courts—the New York City Civil and the district, city, town, and village courts—but in 1992 the legislature changed the rule in the supreme and county courts.[3] In the supreme and county courts, it is the filing of the initiatory papers that constitutes "commencement" of the action (which includes a special proceeding) and marks the key moment at which to measure whether the statute of limitations has been satisfied.

3. CPLR 214–c and its incidents are discussed in § 40, above.

§ 45

1. CPLR 203(a).

2. FRCP Rule 3. If subject matter jurisdiction in the federal action is based on diversity of citizenship, however, the moment that a claim is deemed "interposed" for statute of limitations purposes is governed by state law, not by Rule 3. See § 625 below (Practitioner's Edition).

3. L.1992, c.216. The change affects the surrogates' courts, too, for which see the Commentary on § 301 of McKinney's SCPA and the note in SPR 35:4.

4. CPLR 304. This "notice" alternative is allowed by CPLR 305(b). See § 60 below.

The papers that must be filed in an action in the supreme and county courts are the summons and complaint, or the summons along with a brief notice of what the claim is about.[4] In a special proceeding, the papers that must be filed are the notice of petition (or order to show cause, when that method is used to start the proceeding[5]) and the petition.[6] Service must be made within a specified period of time afterwards.[7]

Effecting a filing should rarely prove difficult, but if it does, and time is running out, the plaintiff may seek an ex parte order from a judge directing that the filing take place within five days after the judge signs the order. The mere signing of such an order marks the moment of "interposition"—and commencement—for a statute of limitations measure.[8] A plaintiff who plans to mail the initiatory papers to the clerk, which is permissible, should remember that commencement doesn't occur until the clerk receives the papers; it is not deemed to occur on mere posting.[9]

Allowing a mere notice to accompany the summons instead of requiring a complaint is somewhat unique to New York practice,[10] and, for various reasons, often a bad way to start things off. Using a complaint at the very outset is the better practice.[11] When the notice method is used, the complaint comes later after a demand is made.[12] The option of serving the summons without a complaint is not available in the lower courts, where the complaint must be served with the summons pursuant to their own court acts but where the

5. CPLR 403(d). Detailed discussion of how to commence a special proceeding and the time elements that apply to it are in §§ 550 and 553 below.

6. CPLR 304.

7. The time periods, which differ between actions and special proceedings, are discussed in § 63 below.

8. CPLR 203(c)(2), 304.

9. See Enos v. City of Rochester, 206 A.D.2d 159, 619 N.Y.S.2d 459 (4th Dep't 1994), noted in SPR 26:2.

10. In federal practice the complaint must accompany the summons. See § 623 below (Practitioner's Edition).

11. See § 60 below.

12. CPLR 305(b), 3012(b).

complaint itself may be a simple "indorse-ment".[13]

When two acts of service are necessary, as with the "affix and mail" requirements of CPLR 308(4), both steps must be accomplished within the applicable period. Thus, where the affixing takes place within the period but the mail is posted a day later, the action has been held barred.[14]

If there are several defendants and they are "united in interest", commencement as to one—whether by filing, as in the supreme or county court, or service, as in the lower courts—will preserve the action as against the others,[15] even though the others will of course have to be served before the court gets juris-diction of them. Essentially what this provi-sion does is permit summons service to be made on the others after the statute of limita-tions has expired, as long as there has been timely commencement as to one. To qualify as "united" under this rule, however, the defen-dants' interests must be without mutual hos-tility. Where P sought to rescind an insurance policy, for example, the beneficiary and the insured were both "united" in their wish to preserve the policy and service on the benefi-ciary within the applicable period therefore preserved the claim as against the insured as well.[16]

On the other hand it has been held that unity of interest does not exist for this purpose between a blood center that provides blood and the hospital that administers the blood.[17] And while a doctor and the professional ser-vice corporation of which he is a member may be united in interest under this rule, the unity does not exist between member doctors[18] be-cause while the corporation is liable for the acts of Dr. A as a matter of substantive law, Dr. B is not. The "united in interest" provi-sion follows the substantive law for this limita-tions' purpose.

The test is pragmatic. Joint tortfeasors own-ing or driving different cars in an accident that injures the plaintiff are not united in interest. Each is hostile to the other and would gladly lay liability at the other's door. But if the joint tortfeasors are the owner and driver of the same car, with the owner only derivatively responsible for the driver, both have been held united in interest against the plaintiff and commencement as to one preserves the claim against the other.[19] Even that conclusion can be debated, however,[20] and it is best to assume hostility among tortfeasors of any kind and to see to it that proper commencement is effected as to each before the statute expires.[21]

§ 46. Provisional Remedy as Interposi-tion

There are four provisional remedies in New York practice, each having a CPLR article of its own. They are attachment (Article 62), injunction (63), receivership (64), and notice of pendency (65). They are studied later[1] but must be mentioned now because of their rele-vance to the statute of limitations. As will be seen more fully in the later study, some of the provisional remedies, all of which need a court order except the notice of pendency (which is merely filed in a clerk's office), may be sought and granted prior to commencement of the action. When that happens, the granting of the order for the provisional remedy constitutes

---

13. See § 902(a)(1) in each of the New York City Civil, Uniform District, Uniform City, and Uniform Justice court acts, and Commentary C3012:3 on McKinney's CPLR 3012.

14. Furey v. Milgrom, 44 A.D.2d 91, 353 N.Y.S.2d 508 (2d Dep't 1974). The same conclusion should obtain for the dual "deliver and mail" service of CPLR 308(2). These substituted service methods are treated in §§ 72 and 74 below.

15. CPLR 203(b), (c).

16. Prudential Ins. Co. v. Stone, 270 N.Y. 154, 200 N.E. 679 (1936).

17. Mondello v. New York Blood Center, 80 N.Y.2d 219, 590 N.Y.S.2d 19, 604 N.E.2d 81 (1992).

18. Connell v. Hayden, 83 A.D.2d 30, 443 N.Y.S.2d 383 (2d Dep't 1981).

19. Jordan v. Westhill Cent. School Dist., 42 A.D.2d 1043, 348 N.Y.S.2d 620 (4th Dep't 1973).

20. See Halucha v. Jockey Club, 31 Misc.2d 186, 220 N.Y.S.2d 567 (Sup.Ct., N.Y.County, 1961).

21. The Connell case, note 18 above, offers a review of the relationships that satisfy the united in interest stan-dard.

§ 46

1. Section 306 et seq.

commencement of the action for limitations' purposes, provided that the summons is actually served within 30 days thereafter[2] (60 days when attachment is the remedy involved[3]). With the notice of pendency—commonly known as a "lis pendens" and used in realty actions—the mere filing of the notice constitutes commencement under this rule.[4]

This provision applies only in the lower courts, the courts in which service marks commencement. It does not apply in the supreme or county courts, where filing marks it. In the latter two, an application for a provisional remedy is made with or after the filing of the summons and complaint that commences the action and there is therefore no need to have the provisional remedy deemed the moment of commencement.

In the lower courts, where the provision applies, it works this way. Assume that the last day on which to commence an action against a nonresident defendant is July 1, 1997. On that day the plaintiff secures an order of attachment against the defendant.[5] It is levied a few days later and service of the summons is then made on August 12, 1997. The action is timely because it was deemed commenced on July 1 and service was made during the 60 days following. If service were made after the 60 days, the service would not relate back and the action would be subject to dismissal for untimeliness.

§ 47. Delivery to Sheriff or Clerk

An important provision on the statute of limitations—and a favorite of lawyers who wait for the last minute to commence actions—is CPLR 203(b)(5). It used to apply in all courts of the state, but the 1992 legislation that adopted the filing system for commencing actions in the supreme and county courts made it inapplicable in those courts because, under the filing system, it is not needed.

CPLR 203(b)(5) is often needed, however, and is most valuable, in the lower courts of the state, in which the service of the summons marks commencement. The plaintiff gets from this statute an automatic 60-day extension of the time for commencing the action with nothing more than a delivery of the summons to the sheriff or a filing of the summons with the county clerk. Whether it's to be the sheriff or the county clerk depends on where "the defendant resides, is employed or is doing business". If the defendant has those contacts with a county in New York City, filing with the county clerk of that county is the proper step; if with a county outside New York City, delivery to a sheriff of that county is the proper step. The plaintiff should mark this carefully. A mixing-up of the procedures as between New York City and upstate, as by delivering to the sheriff when a filing with the clerk is called for, can be fatal; it does not earn the 60-day extension.[1]

Thus, if July 1, 1997 is the last day on which suit may be brought, a delivery of the summons to the proper sheriff or a filing of it with the proper clerk on that day will give the plaintiff another 60 days in which to effect service. Technically, the 60 days are tacked on to the end of whatever period otherwise remains, so that a delivery or filing five months before the applicable statute is due to expire presumably adds the 60 days to the five months. Despite the statutory language, a safer assumption is that the statute gives only an alternative 60 days measured from delivery to the sheriff or clerk.

Service during the 60-day extended period need not be made by the sheriff or clerk, however. Any process server will do. This is just an extension statute.[2] Indeed, the lawyer

---

2. CPLR 203(b)(3). If service by publication is used, the first publication must take place within the 30 days.

3. CPLR 203(b)(4), adopting the provisions of CPLR 6213.

4. King v. Quinn, 23 A.D.2d 615, 256 N.Y.S.2d 823 (3d Dep't 1965).

5. CPLR 6201(1).

§ 47

1. Dominquez v. DeTiberus, 53 N.Y.2d 778, 439 N.Y.S.2d 918, 422 N.E.2d 578 (1981), aff'g 78 A.D.2d 848, 432 N.Y.S.2d 724 (2d Dep't 1980).

2. Reliable Constr. Corp. v. Relide Realty Corp., 6 Misc.2d 857, 162 N.Y.S.2d 550 (Sup.Ct., N.Y.County, 1957).

may not want the sheriff to serve the summons, using the sheriff only to obtain the 60–day extension. The lawyer should instruct the sheriff accordingly.

If the plaintiff, after "reasonable inquiry", does not know of a county with which the defendant has the requisite contact, then the county the defendant was last known to have had it with, or the county in which the cause of action arose, qualifies. The plaintiff who does not know those things either should not rely on this provision.

"Residence" under this statute means just that, not "domicile". This has been held to mean that if the defendant has several residences, the county of any one of them qualifies.[3]

With a corporate defendant the proper county is any "in which [the corporation] may be served or in which the cause of action arose", which may afford a number of options. It has been held that a county in which the corporation "may be served" means a county "in which one of the officers, directors, employees or agents of the corporation enumerated in subdivision 1 of CPLR 311(a) either has his dwelling or place of business".[4]

The corporation need not be a domestic one. As long as the claim arose in New York, making the county in which it arose available for CPLR 203(b)(5) use, a foreign corporation having no place of business in the state at all is subject to the statute.[5]

If the defendant's contacts are with a New York City county, so that a filing with a county clerk is the proper step, the county clerk's office is to be the filing repository, not the office of the court's own clerk.

The complaint, even if only an indorsed complaint as used in lower court practice,[6] must accompany the summons or the 60–day toll won't be awarded.[7]

If the last day has arrived, and the delivery or service is made by mail on that day, the mere posting of the papers has been held sufficient even though the mail is not actually received until later.[8] Since the statute of limitations is involved, delivery in person may be a better idea, just to avoid any possible argument about when the posting occurred.

It may happen that the plaintiff tenders the summons to the proper sheriff, who refuses it on the mistaken assumption that some other county is the right one. The tender itself has been held sufficient to earn the 60 days in that situation.[9]

The 60–day provision applies even in the town and village courts, where, however, the delivery is made to the court's own enforcement officer rather than to a sheriff.[10]

When the statute of limitations applicable in the action is not of the ordinary "suspend the remedy" kind, but one of the "condition precedent" variety,[11] there is no 60–day extension available from CPLR 203(b)(5), as the occasional luckless plaintiff learns.[12]

Plaintiffs who have been given a 60–day reprieve by this provision should not press their luck too far, perhaps hoping to string together a series of extensions. It has been held that a plaintiff who has gotten one CPLR 203(b) extension must make service on the defendant within the time as extended; that he

---

3. Kleila v. Miller, 1 A.D.2d 697, 147 N.Y.S.2d 589 (2d Dep't 1955).

4. Arce v. Sybron Corp., 82 A.D.2d 308, 441 N.Y.S.2d 498 (2d Dep't 1981).

5. Hartford Ins. Co. v. Universal Elec. Co., 97 A.D.2d 498, 468 N.Y.S.2d 15 (2d Dep't 1983), distinguishing the Arce case cited in note 4, above.

6. See § 902 in each of the New York City Civil, Uniform District, Uniform City, and Uniform Justice court acts.

7. Frerk v. Mercy Hospital, 63 N.Y.2d 635, 479 N.Y.S.2d 519, 468 N.E.2d 701, aff'g 99 A.D.2d 504, 470 N.Y.S.2d 673 (2d Dep't 1984).

8. See Sanford v. Garvey, 81 A.D.2d 748, 438 N.Y.S.2d 410 (4th Dep't 1981), and Dowling v. Hillcrest General

Hospital, 89 A.D.2d 435, 455 N.Y.S.2d 628 (1st Dep't 1982) (citing other departments).

9. Filardi v. Bronxville Obstetrical and Gynecological Group, P.C., 67 A.D.2d 997, 413 N.Y.S.2d 729 (2d Dep't 1979).

10. CPLR 203(b)(6).

11. See § 34 above.

12. See Savino v. Demiglia, 128 A.D.2d 858, 513 N.Y.S.2d 776, substituted opinion on reargument 133 A.D.2d 389, 519 N.Y.S.2d 384 (2d Dep't 1987), involving the one-year statute of limitations applicable against the Port Authority of New York and New Jersey.

can't then invoke another, such as by securing a provisional remedy, which would ordinarily offer its own extension (as treated in the prior section).[13]

§ 48. Counterclaims

A counterclaim is contained in the defendant's answer, but it has the advantage of being deemed interposed, for statute of limitations purposes, as of the moment the claim in the complaint was interposed.[1] This means that a counterclaim in a supreme or county court action—courts in which filing constitutes commencement—is deemed interposed when the plaintiff filed the main action.[2] In the lower courts—where service marks commencement[3]—the counterclaim is deemed interposed as of the time of the plaintiff's service of the summons and complaint. In either instance the measure is an advantage to the defendant, and this rule applies whether or not the counterclaim is related to the plaintiff's claim.[4]

Suppose, for example, that in a supreme court action the statute of limitations on D's counterclaim expires on July 11, 1997. P files the action on July 10, 1997, and the answer containing D's counterclaim is served in due course on July 25, 1997. The counterclaim is in all respects timely.[5] If the same action were in a city court, the defendant could have the same kind of relation back for the counterclaim, but only if the summons and complaint were served on or before July 11.

Assume now that the counterclaim is untimely even if measured by the moment of the main action's commencement. All is not necessarily lost. If D's claim arises from the same

transaction or occurrence as P's claim, it may be interposed regardless of timeliness, but in this situation it will suffice only to neutralize or set off P's claim; D will not be allowed to take an affirmative judgment against P for any balance that might be due in D's favor.[6]

This is the limitations aspect of a doctrine known as "equitable recoupment". For example: P, a physician who treated D, sues D for his fee within the six-year contract period applicable to it.[7] D counterclaims for malpractice, which has a 2–1/2 year period,[8] contending that he was injured by the treatment. Assume that even as measured by the moment of the main action's commencement, the counterclaim is too late. Because it arises out of the transaction on which P sues, it may still be entertained, but only to the extent, and no further, of cancelling out what P is owed.[9] Nor need the counterclaim be of the same theory as the main claim in order to invoke this recoupment doctrine. The malpractice counterclaim sounds in tort in the example, while the main claim is in contract. This is permissible.

D can't exploit the recoupment theory merely by showing some general relationship between counterclaim and main claim. The Court of Appeals has indicated that only an outright "recoupment" earns this treatment, i.e., a claim for recovery by D based on something "growing out" of P's claim. Thus, where P's claim was to recover for rent overcharges based on a wrongful computation of increases, and D, the landlord, sought by counterclaim to reform the lease, the reformation claim was held not to arise "out of" P's claim, and was

---

13. Oliver v. Basle, 55 A.D.2d 975, 390 N.Y.S.2d 466 (3d Dep't 1977).

§ 48

1. CPLR 203(d). Subdivision (d) was lettered (c) before a 1992 amendment gave it its present designation. Because it is frequently cited in the caselaw, lawyers must keep this relettering in mind, especially when using a research tool like WESTLAW. Punching in the wrong letter can produce either nothing, or a mass of irrelevant cases.

2. CPLR 304.

3. See § 400 in each of the New York City Civil, Uniform District, Uniform City, and Uniform Justice court acts.

4. See Chevron Oil Co. v. Atlas Oil Co. of Utica, Inc., 28 A.D.2d 644, 280 N.Y.S.2d 731 (4th Dep't 1967).

5. See Styles v. Gibson, 27 A.D.2d 784, 277 N.Y.S.2d 245 (3d Dep't 1967).

6. See Title Guarantee & Trust Co. v. Hicks, 283 App.Div. 723, 127 N.Y.S.2d 340 (2d Dep't 1954).

7. CPLR 213(2).

8. CPLR 214–a.

9. In this regard CPLR 203(d) apparently overrules Fish v. Conley, 221 App.Div. 609, 225 N.Y.S. 27 (3d Dep't 1927). See Advisory Committee 2d Rep.Leg.Doc. (1958) No. 13, pp. 50, 494–5.

denied the limitations advantage.[10]

A counterclaim barred by time by all measures but interposed as a recoupment because it arises out of the complaint's transaction is being used in effect as a defense. Same difference: CPLR 203(d) applies to defenses as well as counterclaims.

The structure of CPLR 203(d) is misleading. It has a brief first sentence and an extended second one, suggesting that the first is the general rule and the second its exception. In point of the number of situations affected, it's the other way around. The first sentence states that a counterclaim is deemed interposed "when a pleading containing it is served", which would mean the service of the answer. But most counterclaims are asserted in D's original answer, and these are deemed interposed, pursuant to the second sentence of CPLR 203(d), as of the time of commencement of the main action.

Then when would the first sentence apply? If D later in the case should get leave to amend the answer to include a counterclaim having no relationship to P's claim or to anything contained in D's original answer, the counterclaim would be deemed interposed only as of the service of the amended answer. That would give the first sentence of CPLR 203(d) something to operate on.[11]

CPLR 203(d) applies to cross-claims as well as counterclaims. In one case, for example,[12] P sued D and X for personal injury. D interposed an answer containing a cross-claim against codefendant X for contribution in respect of P's

injuries and another for D's own property damage. For the contribution part, which amounts in essence to an indemnification claim, there are special limitations advantages[13] and there was thus no time problem. But there was a potential problem for the property damage cross-claim. The answer containing it was served more than the applicable three years after the accident, and hence the cross-claim could be sustained as timely only if allowed a relation back to the original commencement of the action. It was allowed it.

What about the situation in which P has sued D and D has impleaded X, and in which X counterclaims against D? Does the counterclaim relate back, for a timeliness measure, to the time of commencement of P's original action against D, or only to D's service of the third-party complaint on X? It should be the latter. Here X, the third-party defendant, is the one claiming the limitations advantage, and for CPLR 203(d) purposes the relation back is to the pleading interposed against the one so claiming.[14]

§ 49. Claim in Amended Pleading

Section 203(f) is the CPLR's principal "relation back" statute.[1] It provides that for limitations' purposes a claim in an amended pleading will be deemed to relate back to the time the claim in the original pleading was interposed as long as the original one gives notice of the transaction or occurrence out of which the claim in the amended pleading arises.[2]

---

10. SCM Corp. v. Fisher Park Lane Co., 40 N.Y.S.2d 788, 792, 390 N.Y.S.2d 398, 402, 358 N.E.2d 1024, 1027 (1976).

11. Cf. Werner Spitz Constr. Co. v. Vanderlinde Elec. Corp., 64 Misc.2d 157, 314 N.Y.S.2d 567 (Monroe County Ct. 1970).

12. Colichio v. Bailey, 77 A.D.2d 694, 429 N.Y.S.2d 504 (3d Dep't 1980).

13. See § 162 below.

14. See Goldberg v. Sitomer, Sitomer & Porges, 97 A.D.2d 114, 469 N.Y.S.2d 81 (1st Dep't 1983), aff'd 63 N.Y.2d 831, 482 N.Y.S.2d 268, 472 N.E.2d 44 (1984). Compare the case in which X counterclaims against P. See text at notes 26 and 27 in § 49 below.

§ 49

1. The 1992 legislation that adopted the "filing" system for commencing actions in the supreme and county

courts relettered most of the subdivisions of CPLR 203. Subdivision (f) of the current CPLR 203 had previously been subdivision (e). Researchers must keep this change in mind. This is a key statute of limitations provision and old subdivision (e) was cited in many cases. In relearning it as subdivision (f)—especially in something like a WESTLAW search—keep in mind that its old letter was (e).

2. CPLR 203(f) is the counterpart of the often invoked Rule 15(c) of the Federal Rules of Civil Procedure, which is similar to but not the same as CPLR 203(f). There have been disputes about which to choose in a federal action predicated on diversity of citizenship jurisdiction. See § 615 below (Practitioner's Edition).

If such notice is not given by the original pleading, the new claim will be measured for timeliness by service of the amended pleading that contains it. If the amendment is one for which leave of court is necessary, which requires a motion,[3] it has been held that the claim can be deemed interposed as of the service of the motion papers containing the proposed amendment instead of the later time when the motion is granted.[4] This of course assumes a grant of the motion. A denial of the motion makes the matter academic.

A simple example of a relation back is where the amendment adds an assault claim arising out of the same incident as the negligence claim contained in the original complaint.[5] Since the original complaint's claim is deemed interposed as of the original filing of the action (in the supreme or county court) or as of the service of the summons and complaint (in a lower court),[6] the assault claim asserted by amendment gets the double advantage of relating right back to the original commencement of the action.

This rule is sometimes operative even if the amendment's claim technically belongs to a different plaintiff, as long as the defendant has the requisite notice. A wrongful death claim in an amended complaint, for example, which belongs to dependents of the decedent and not to the decedent himself, was held by the Court of Appeals in Caffaro v. Trayna[7] to relate back to the original complaint, which pleaded only the decedent's claim for personal injury (from which the death later resulted).[8]

Some subsequent decisions seem inconsistent with *Caffaro*. In Laudico v. Sears, Roebuck and Co., for example,[9] it was held that a wife's loss of services claim could not be related back to her husband's damages claim, from which it derived. But isn't it a kind of derivative claim in behalf of another, the very scenario *Caffaro* operates on? Disagreeing with the *Laudico* case and other cases to the same effect, Anderson v. Carney[10] holds that a spouse's derivative claim, sought to be interposed through an amended pleading, does relate back to the time of the interposition of the personal injury claim from which it derives.

With a counterclaim, a triple relation back can be seen. If an amended answer adds a counterclaim arising out of an occurrence mentioned in the original answer, it relates back to the original answer;[11] the original answer then relates back to the complaint's claim;[12] and the complaint relates back to the commencement of the action.[13]

CPLR 203(f) is usually invoked to add an additional claim the plaintiff has against a defendant already a party. What about a new defendant whom the plaintiff wants to add as a party? Brock v. Bua[14] sets forth the rules for applying CPLR 203(f) in that situation.

P in *Brock* sued A but did not initially join B. Then P, with a supplemental summons and

---

3. For the difference between an amendment that a party can make as of right and one that requires leave, see §§ 236 and 237, below.

4. Vastola v. Maer, 48 A.D.2d 561, 370 N.Y.S.2d 955 (2d Dep't 1975), aff'd 39 N.Y.2d 1019, 387 N.Y.S.2d 246, 355 N.E.2d 300 (1976).

5. See Watso v. City of New York, 39 A.D.2d 960, 333 N.Y.S.2d 492 (2d Dep't 1972).

6. CPLR 203(b),(c). See § 45 above.

7. 35 N.Y.2d 245, 360 N.Y.S.2d 847, 319 N.E.2d 174 (1974).

8. Caffaro holds that it makes no difference that the wrongful death claim technically did not exist when the original complaint was served, and only arose afterwards. The notice purpose of CPLR 203(e) is still fulfilled. See Commentary C3025:12 on McKinney's CPLR 3025. Caffaro is distinguished in Goldberg v. Camp Mikan–Recro, 42 N.Y.2d 1029, 398 N.Y.S.2d 1008, 369 N.E.2d 8 (1977), which held that there can be no relation back when the

true plaintiff is dead at the time of suit and the person who brought the suit has not been duly appointed personal representative. But a different statute, CPLR 205(a), treated in § 52 below, was later held to offer a statute of limitations extension for a new action in such a case, Carrick v. Central Gen. Hosp., 51 N.Y.2d 242, 434 N.Y.S.2d 130, 414 N.E.2d 632 (1980). Goldberg therefore ends up as an inconvenience at worst—it requires a new action, but without statute of limitations consequences—and is even regarded in some quarters as overruled. See Snay v. Cohoes Mem. Hosp., 110 A.D.2d 1021, 487 N.Y.S.2d 899 (3d Dep't 1985).

9. 125 A.D.2d 960, 510 N.Y.S.2d 787 (4th Dep't 1986).

10. 161 A.D.2d 1002, 557 N.Y.S.2d 575 (3d Dep't 1990).

11. CPLR 203(f).

12. CPLR 203(d).

13. CPLR 203(b)(1), (c)(1).

14. 83 A.D.2d 61, 443 N.Y.S.2d 407 (2d Dep't 1981).

complaint (for which leave was duly obtained), added B as a defendant, but the statute of limitations had by this time expired and the only way to preserve the claim against B was to have it measured by the original commencement of the action against A. That would require a relation back through use of CPLR 203(f), or a combination of 203(f) plus either 203(b) or 203(c).[15] For such an application, *Brock* held that the plaintiff must show:

1. that the same event underlies the claims against both A and B;

2. that there is such a unity of interest between A and B that the service on A amounts to notice to B, thus warning B to prepare his case; and

3. that B knew or should have known that the action would have been brought against him as well as against A, but for the excusable mistake of the plaintiff in identifying the parties.

In the *Brock* case, P met the first two tests but failed the third and was denied a relation back. B in *Brock* was a corporation and A its president. The libel on which the suit was based was in a letter written by A on B's own stationery, from which P would have notice of B's involvement. P's mistake in initially omitting B was therefore not excusable, and timely suit against A thus did not save the claim against B.[16]

The *Brock* test was adopted by the Court of Appeals in Mondello v. New York Blood Center,[17] where the test was applied to the "united in interest" provision,[18] the provision the Court of Appeals deems relevant when P seeks to add a new party, with subdivision (f) apparently deemed applicable only when P seeks to add a new claim against a person already a party.[19] Then, in a follow-up to *Mondello*, the court held that when the as-yet-unjoined B had notice of the claim within the applicable statute of limitations, from whatever source, thus divesting B of any claim of prejudice, the plaintiff does not have to show that the mistake in failing to join B at the outset was "excusable", i.e., need not satisfy the third requirement of the three-part *Brock* test.[20]

The use of an "amendment" to assert the claim against one not already a party is in essence an effort to add that person as a party. That's why the issue so often becomes bound up with the statute of limitations. The proper procedure to add as a party a person not originally named and joined is by use of a supplemental summons on that person. Until 1996, the formal addition of the new party through use of a supplemental summons required court leave. A 1996 amendment of CPLR 1003 allows it by other means as well. One is by stipulation of all parties who have appeared in the action. Another dispenses even with a stipulation if the plaintiff acts early enough in the litigation.[21]

If the links that would satisfy the *Brock* standard exist, it has been held permissible to relate back to the original commencement of the action not only a claim the plaintiff seeks to add in the same action, but even one sought to be added to a separate but connected action.[22]

A related situation that has arisen a number of times concerns a claim that a plaintiff wants to assert against a third-party defendant who has been impleaded. P has sued D on time, and D has impleaded X. If all D seeks of X is

15. These are the "united in interest" provisions that enable commencement as to A to be deemed commencement as to the later-joined B as long as both are "united in interest". See § 45 above. They are involved in the Mondello case cited in note 17 below.

16. Brock relies, incidentally, on the test assumed to apply under the analogous FRCP Rule 15(c), but that rule was amended effective December 1, 1991, and the amendment would probably lead to a different result if applied to facts like those of the Brock case.

17. 80 N.Y.2d 219, 590 N.Y.S.2d 19, 604 N.E.2d 81 (1992).

18. CPLR 203(b) and (c). See § 45 above.

19. See the discussion in SPR 17:2.

20. Buran v. Coupal, 87 N.Y.2d 173, 638 N.Y.S.2d 405 (1995), treated in the lead note in New York State Law Digest No. 436.

21. See § 138, below, and SPR 43:1.

22. See Town of Guilderland v. Texaco Refining and Marketing, Inc., 159 A.D.2d 829, 552 N.Y.S.2d 704 (3d Dep't 1990).

contribution or indemnity to cover P's main claim against D, D's claim against X is timely because of the special limitations' advantages applicable to third-party claims.[23] But what if P amends her complaint after D impleads X, as P may do as a matter of right,[24] and asserts a claim directly against X? How shall the statute of limitations be applied to that? Resolving a conflict among the cases, the Court of Appeals held in Duffy v. Horton Memorial Hospital[25] that as long as D's impleader of X took place within the original period applicable to P's claim, P's later amendment to assert that claim directly against X is timely: it may be deemed to relate back at least to the impleader moment.

And what about a counterclaim by X, the third-party defendant, directly against P?[26] It has been held that even that can be related back to the original action's commencement as long as the notice elements on which the statute is based are present.[27]

F. EXTENSIONS AND TOLLS

Table of Sections

23. See § 162 below.

24. See CPLR 1009.

25. 66 N.Y.2d 473, 497 N.Y.S.2d 890, 488 N.E.2d 820 (1985).

26. The rights of an impleaded third party include the right to counterclaim against the main plaintiff. CPLR 1008.

27. T.R. America Chemicals, Inc. v. Seaboard Surety Co., 116 Misc.2d 874, 456 N.Y.S.2d 608 (Sup.Ct., N.Y. County, 1982).

§ 50

1. CPLR 201, 2004.

2. Balzano v. Port of New York Auth., 232 N.Y.S.2d 776 (Sup.Ct., Kings County, 1962), aff'd 23 A.D.2d 573, 256 N.Y.S.2d 495 (2d Dep't 1965). See § 34 above.

3. Gen.Oblig.L. § 17–101.

§ 50. Extensions and Tolls, Generally

Although the court cannot in its discretion extend the statute of limitations,[1] there are a handful of statutory provisions and a few case-law doctrines that can, and do. These are generally known as tolling provisions and they can take various forms. They may suspend the running of the statute during a stated period, or start it all over again as of a given moment, or offer an alternative period. (These tolling provisions are not as a rule applicable to those relatively uncommon "condition precedent" periods.[2])

A written and signed acknowledgment of a debt or other obligation starts the statute of limitations running anew.[3] This applies to contract claims, not torts.[4] A letter can satisfy.[5] But whatever form the writing takes, it must imply a promise to pay. "It should contain nothing inconsistent with an intention on the part of the debtor to pay it".[6] So if D does acknowledge the debt, but in a writing claiming that P owes D even more than D owes P, there is no implied promise to pay and the writing will not start the statute anew.[7]

Wholly apart from any written acknowledgment, an actual payment made by D under circumstances establishing that it is intended as a part payment towards a larger debt starts the period running anew on the balance.[8] The effect will be the same even if the payment is made after the period has expired; the period will start up all over again as of the part payment.[9] It does not matter how P (the creditor) applies the payment; it is entirely a mat-

4. Maryland Cas. Co. v. Byrne, 172 Misc. 152, 15 N.Y.S.2d 68 (N.Y.City Ct.1939).

5. Lorenzo v. Bussin, 7 A.D.2d 731, 180 N.Y.S.2d 625 (2d Dep't 1958), aff'd 7 N.Y.2d 1039, 200 N.Y.S.2d 423, 167 N.E.2d 73 (1960).

6. Manchester v. Braender, 107 N.Y. 346, 349, 14 N.E. 405, 406 (1887).

7. Curtiss–Wright Corp. v. Intercontinent Corp., 277 App.Div. 13, 97 N.Y.S.2d 678 (1st Dep't 1950).

8. See P. H. Carlyon, Inc. v. Roberts, 188 Misc. 569, 64 N.Y.S.2d 792 (Chautauqua County Ct. 1946), aff'd 271 App.Div. 1060, 70 N.Y.S.2d 133 (4th Dep't 1947).

9. Brooklyn Bank v. Barnaby, 197 N.Y. 210, 90 N.E. 834 (1910).

ter of how the debtor intended that it be applied. So held Crow v. Gleason,[10] a leading case in which P had let horses to D over a period of time, each time making a debit on D's account. P did not bill D periodically for the total balance, however, but he did bill individual lettings. P claimed that a payment D had made was a part payment toward the whole balance, but the proof was just as consistent with D's claim that the last payment he made was for only the most recent letting and not towards any claimed balance. The payment was at best ambiguous and from it, therefore, no unequivocal intent to pay the balance could be drawn. On such facts, the statute could not begin anew.

In the case of joint debtors, it is each one for herself. Payment by one does not renew the period as to the other. The same is true between principal and surety.[11]

The so-called "mutual" account should be distinguished from the situation discussed above. It is one in which two parties have agreed to a course of dealings in which each periodically furnishes something to the other, each keeping a running account of credits and debits in the expectation that the party in whose favor a balance exists will send the other a bill from time to time. This kind of account is governed by CPLR 206(d), and, if it is found to exist, only the last entry (on either side) need be alive (under the statute of limitations) to preserve the whole balance.[12]

As a general rule, in the absence of any indication to the contrary, the tolling provisions apply in both actions and special proceedings.[13]

§ 51. Toll Where Action Stayed

If the commencement of an action is put off or otherwise stayed by court order or by statute, the period of the stay is not part of the running of the applicable period.[1] Where, for example, a federal court enjoined P from suing D, the period of the injunction was not part of the running of the statute of limitations.[2]

Suit against a municipality for tort cannot be brought until 30 days have passed after a notice of claim has been served.[3] It has been held, however, that that stay does not get the benefit of the CPLR 204(a) toll for the reason that the legislature has expressly compensated for it by adding 90 days to the previously applicable one-year period of limitations.[4] That accounts for the year and 90 days that constitutes the applicable tort period in such cases today.[5] But if an application is made under Gen.Mun.L. § 50–e(5) for leave to file a late notice of claim, the period of the application's pendency is not part of the period for commencing an action. So held the Court of Appeals in Giblin v. Nassau County Medical Center.[6] While the relevant statutes don't "specifically proscribe the prosecution of an action", said the court, they have the same effect because an action does not properly lie until it can be shown that a notice of claim was duly served.

The toll applies only to a statutory or court-ordered stay, not to one agreed to by contract. But in such a case the agreement would likely work an estoppel against the defendant and accomplish the same end by that route.[7]

The period during which the arbitrability of a claim is being determined by the courts, measured from the initial demand for arbitration until a final judicial determination that

10. 141 N.Y. 489, 36 N.E. 497 (1894).

11. Peoples Trust Co. v. O'Neil, 273 N.Y. 312, 7 N.E.2d 244 (1937).

12. See Green v. Disbrow, 79 N.Y. 1 (1879).

13. CPLR 103(b), 105(b). See Elliot v. Green Bus Lines, Inc., 58 N.Y. 76, 459 N.Y.S.2d 419 (1983).

§ 51

1. CPLR 204(a).

2. Chance v. Guaranty Trust Co., 164 Misc. 346, 298 N.Y.S. 17 (Sup.Ct., Kings County, 1937), aff'd 251 App. Div. 855, 297 N.Y.S. 293 (2d Dep't 1937).

3. Gen.Mun.L. § 50–i(1)(b).

4. See Joiner v. City of New York, 26 A.D.2d 840, 274 N.Y.S.2d 362 (2d Dep't 1966).

5. Gen.Mun.L. § 50–i.

6. 61 N.Y.2d 67, 471 N.Y.S.2d 563, 459 N.E.2d 856 (1984).

7. See Robinson v. City of New York, 24 A.D.2d 260, 265 N.Y.S.2d 566 (1st Dep't 1965).

arbitration is not required,[8] if that should be the holding, is expressly removed from the running of the statute of limitations, another example of a statutory toll.[9]

When the statute of limitations expires on a claim while suit on it is stayed because of federal bankruptcy proceedings against the debtor, the federal law[10] offers the creditor (the would-be plaintiff) a fresh period of 30 days for suit, measured from the termination of the bankruptcy stay. But that's just a minimum. If state law offers the creditor more, as CPLR 204(a) does by holding the statute of limitations tolled for the whole period of the stay, it has been held that the creditor is entitled to rely on the longer state period.[11]

§ 52. Termination of Prior Action

If an action is brought within the applicable period and is terminated not on the merits but on a basis that keeps the claim alive and enables a later suit to be brought on it, CPLR 205(a) gives the plaintiff six months from that termination in which to sue anew even though the original statute of limitations has now expired. Thus, where the suit was dismissed because P had not submitted to an appraisal procedure on which P and D had agreed in a contract, the dismissal was based only on the action's prematurity and the six months in which to sue afresh was applicable.[1]

At one time the statute said that the second suit had to be for the "same cause of action" as the first, but it was construed liberally: the second action need merely have arisen out of the same transaction as the first. A breach of warranty claim meeting that requirement in round two was held to earn the extension, for example, even though the claim dismissed in round one was for fraud.[2] Just so there would

be no mistake about that, a 1978 amendment of CPLR 205 removed the phrase "cause of action" and substituted broader language intended to assure the six months to a later claim arising out of the same "transaction or occurrence or series of transactions or occurrences" as the earlier one.

A further amendment of CPLR 205(a) in 1978 added the requirement that in order for the second action to be timely, it must be shown that the claim would have been timely had it been interposed in the first action. The implication that CPLR 205(a) might be applied to revive a claim that had already expired when the earlier action was brought is thus avoided.

Sometimes—and it's difficult to predict when because of inconsistencies in the cases— a key inquiry is whether the defendant had notice within the applicable period of limitation. If the defendant did, even a dismissal based on a defect in parties on the plaintiff's side has been held to secure the extension. CPLR 205(a) has been applied, for example, to a personal injury claim that had been dismissed because brought after the death of the injured person, which is not permissible without the appointment of a personal representative. That was in George v. Mt. Sinai Hospital,[3] where the attorney did not know that his personal injury client had died. A second action, with a proper personal representative as plaintiff, was then begun within six months after the dismissal and was sustained.

The Court in *George* distinguished Goldberg v. Camp Mikan–Recro,[4] where on similar facts an attempted relation back (within the original action) under CPLR 203(f) was not allowed. It then undertook to reconcile both cases in Carrick v. Central Gen. Hosp.,[5] where

---

8. CPLR 7502, 7503.

9. CPLR 204(b).

10. 11 USCA § 108(c).

11. Zuckerman v. 234–6 W. 22 St. Corp., 167 Misc.2d 198, 645 N.Y.S.2d 967 (Sup.Ct., N.Y. County, 1996). It is of course assumed that the claim has survived the bankruptcy proceedings, which the claim in Zuckerman (mortgage foreclosure) did.

§ 52

1. Buchholz v. U. S. Fire Ins. Co., 269 App.Div. 49, 53 N.Y.S.2d 608 (1st Dep't 1945).

2. Titus v. Poole, 145 N.Y. 414, 40 N.E. 228 (1895).

3. 47 N.Y.2d 170, 417 N.Y.S.2d 231, 390 N.E.2d 1156 (1979).

4. 42 N.Y.2d 1029, 398 N.Y.S.2d 1008, 369 N.E.2d 8 (1977).

5. 51 N.Y.2d 242, 434 N.Y.S.2d 130, 414 N.E.2d 632 (1980). Carrick is treated in the lead note in New York State Law Digest No. 254.

the plaintiff wife had not yet obtained letters of administration when she brought a claim for the wrongful death of her husband, and the action was therefore dismissed. Obtaining proper letters, she brought a new action within six months after the dismissal and it was sustained under CPLR 205(a).

It is welcome news that substantive forfeiture of the claim need not be the consequence of an omission to obtain letters earlier, but the distinction that *Carrick* makes of the *Goldberg* case is unfortunate. *Goldberg* involved essentially the same defect as *Carrick* but sought to preserve the action with a relation-back amendment under CPLR 203(f). It was not allowed. But *Carrick* does allow an altogether new action on the claim, with the award of the CPLR 205(a) six months.[6] The bottom line is that a plaintiff who sues without first obtaining the requisite letters will at minimum be put to the burden of a new action to cure the defect; the device of a mere amendment to preserve the original action under CPLR 203(f) won't work.

There are four statutory exceptions to the six-months rule of CPLR 205(a). If the prior action was terminated by (1) voluntary discontinuance, (2) want of personal jurisdiction over the defendant, (3) dismissal for neglect to prosecute, or (4) final judgment on the merits, the six months is not given.

Number (4) need not detain us because in that instance the second suit would usually be met by the res judicata defense and be disposed of that way. Number (1) is straightforward enough, the procedures for a voluntary discontinuance being clearly outlined in CPLR 3217.[7] Number (3), the neglect to prosecute ground, has from time to time been a disaster

area for plaintiffs. The main neglect to prosecute procedure is governed by CPLR 3216, and if and when a dismissal is made under that provision, it is squarely within the exception of CPLR 205(a) and does not get the six months. It is this consequence that makes the want-of-prosecution dismissal so disastrous to plaintiffs.[8] Plaintiffs must be warned here that CPLR 3216 is not the only source of a dismissal that falls within the CPLR 205(a) "neglect to prosecute" exception. A dismissal for failure to serve a complaint, answer a calendar call, or submit to pretrial disclosure[9] may also qualify as "neglect to prosecute" under CPLR 205(a) and thus not get the six months for a new action.[10]

We've saved number (2) on the list—the dismissal for want of jurisdiction—for treatment at this point because it's had an involved history and needs a more extended discussion. Only in 1992 was it made an explicit exception in CPLR 205(a). Before that, it was a caselaw exception. (The 1992 addition is really only a codification of the caselaw.) Whether through caselaw or statute, however, this exception is bad news for plaintiffs. If the earlier action was dismissed for lack of personal jurisdiction of the defendant, the six months do not append.[11] And many an action is dismissed for some defect going to personal jurisdiction. Some caselaw held for a time that this use of CPLR 205(a) would be denied only if the defendant did not have notice of the action within the period of limitation, but that if the defendant did have notice, and the dismissal, albeit for personal jurisdiction, was based on a mere technical flaw such as service beyond the court's territory, the six months would be given and a second action thereby preserved.[12]

---

6. See note 7 in § 49, above, where this conflict is also noted in conjunction with the Caffaro case and its treatment of CPLR 203(e), the relation back statute.

7. See §§ 297, 298, below.

8. CPLR 3216 and its history is treated in § 375, below.

9. For a while there was a conflict about whether a dismissal for failure to make a required disclosure would qualify as a CPLR 205(a) neglect to prosecute. See Ivory v. Ekstrom, 98 A.D.2d 763, 469 N.Y.S.2d 478 (2d Dep't 1983). The conflict appears to have been resolved in Carven Assocs. v. American Home Assur. Corp., 84 N.Y.2d

927, 620 N.Y.S.2d 812, 644 N.E.2d 1368 (1994), holding that this category of dismissal does amount to a want of prosecution, at least when the prior dismissal was for the plaintiff's "willful and repeated refusal to obey court-ordered disclosure". (Those are usually the circumstances that produce a CPLR 3126 dismissal.)

10. See Commentary C3216:33 on McKinney's CPLR 3216.

11. Erickson v. Macy, 236 N.Y. 412, 140 N.E. 938 (1923).

12. Amato v. Svedi, 35 A.D.2d 672, 315 N.Y.S.2d 63 (2d Dep't 1970).

This salvation for plaintiffs was short-lived, erased by the Court of Appeals in 1984 in Markoff v. South Nassau Community Hospital.[13] In holding in *Markoff* that there is no CPLR 205(a) extension after a dismissal for want of personal jurisdiction, the court made no allowance for differences between defects. Hence, whether the earlier jurisdictional dismissal was for want of proper summons service (despite good basis), or for want of basis (despite good service), or anything else going to personal jurisdiction, the action today, under the 1992 codification of the *Markoff* holding, is as good as dead if its only hope is CPLR 205(a).

Another 1984 Court of Appeals case, Parker v. Mack,[14] has equally bleak news for plaintiffs at another point on the same front. For a long time in New York practice an action could be commenced with the service of a bare summons. As noted in § 60, below, CPLR changes that took effect in 1979 cancelled that option. In all but matrimonial actions,[15] the summons today must be served with either a regular complaint or at least the little default notice allowed by CPLR 305(b). It was clear from the notes on the amendment, and decisional law made it clearer still, that a defect on this score—serving a bare summons—would be a jurisdictional one, requiring dismissal. But an open question was whether at least the CPLR 205(a) six-month period could be tacked on to the dismissal. It can't be, held *Parker*. The dismissal is in the category of personal jurisdiction and can't qualify for the six months of CPLR 205(a).

Between them, the *Markoff* and *Parker* cases guarantee that a defect in connection with the summons or its service will continue to be fatal in New York practice whenever the dismissal it produces occurs, as it most often

does, when the original statute of limitations has expired.[16] Plaintiffs who wait until they are down to the wire and then wax careless about jurisdiction as they near it are plaintiffs for whom the bell tolls, not the statute of limitations.

For a short period of time—from 1992 to the end of 1997—the plaintiff got something of a break from another statute, CPLR 306–b(b), when the dismissal was based on improper service: the plaintiff was given 120 days by that statute, measured from the dismissal, in which to commence a new action, even if the statute of limitations had long since expired.[17] It applied only to dismissals for improper service, however, which is only one category of defect that goes to personal jurisdiction. To other such categories the 120–day gift did not apply, and it was removed even from the improper service dismissal when a 1997 amendment repealed the original CPLR 306–b and enacted a new one that did not include it.[18]

Defendants often include the boilerplate defense of improper service in their answers without having the slightest idea whether it has any basis, making it necessary for plaintiffs to move to strike the defense just to get it adjudicated early and be able to determine whether to bring a new action, if need be, before the statute of limitations expires. Or plaintiffs would just commence a second action anyway, as a precaution. During the brief reign of the 120–day "sleeper" provision, the plaintiff did not have to worry about the improper service objection; with its repeal, careful attention must once again be paid to it.[19] A partial compensation to plaintiffs for this loss appears in an amendment of another statute,[20] which shortens the life of an improper service objection that has been taken as a defense in the answer.

---

13. 61 N.Y.2d 283, 473 N.Y.S.2d 766, 461 N.E.2d 1253.

14. 61 N.Y.2d 114, 472 N.Y.S.2d 882, 460 N.E.2d 1316.

15. For the practice in matrimonial actions, see § 76 below.

16. The cases are the subject of the lead note in New York State Law Digest No. 292.

17. This has been referred to as something of a "sleeper" (see New York State Law Digest No. 391, page 5, and SPR 50:3–4 and 64:2) because it was buried in the middle

of provisions that had primarily bad news for plaintiffs in the rigid requirements they were otherwise imposing on the commencement of actions in the supreme and county courts.

18. See SPR 62:1. CPLR 306–b, a key statute on commencing cases in the supreme and county courts, is treated at length in § 63 below.

19. See § 274 below

20. CPLR 3211(e), eff. January 1, 1997. See SPR 50:3.

The commencement ritual in a court of claims action is governed by § 11 of the Court of Claims Act, and involves both a filing and a serving. If the action is dismissed for an omission of either act, it has been held that CPLR 205(a) does not apply to offer its six months for a new action.[21]

A dismissal for want of subject matter jurisdiction does get the six months.[22] Presumably the glue for these several entries is that as long as D has been notified of the action, a basic statute of limitations purpose has been fulfilled and the benefits of CPLR 205(a) can append. But that doesn't jibe with *Markoff's* denial of the six months to the dismissal based on a mere technical defect in the method of service, so there is indeed a contradiction here.

Contradiction or no, the fact that the six months applies to dismissals for subject matter jurisdiction is especially good news for federal plaintiffs. If the federal action is dismissed on that ground, such as where the plaintiff thought the claim arose under federal law but the court disagreed, or where the plaintiff depended on diversity of citizenship and it turned out that diversity was lacking, the six months will append to the dismissal and preserve a new action in state court.[23]

The prior action must have been brought in a court in New York. That includes, as noted, a federal court, but it has been held that the six-months extension period will not append to an action brought in either a state or federal court outside New York.[24]

While the period supplied by CPLR 205(a) will be measured from an appellate determination if the earlier action went through an appellate stage, this applies only where an appeal was available and was in fact taken. If the appeal required leave and leave was not granted, the six months will not be measured from the denial of leave, or, analogously, from a denial of certiorari by the U.S. Supreme Court.[25] Since the statute of limitations is involved, it is important to draw that lesson sharply: if there is any doubt about whether the application for leave to appeal (or for certiorari) will be acted on in time to commence a new action should the leave be denied, and there is yet time to act, the practitioner should commence the new action as a safeguard. It can be discontinued (see CPLR 3217) if it should prove unneeded.

§ 53. Defendant's Absence

If the defendant is outside New York when a claim accrues against her, the statute of limitations does not start until she comes back. If she is in New York when it accrues but leaves afterwards, she must remain out for at least four months in order for her absence to be a toll, in which event the whole of the absence (not just the excess beyond four months) is a tolling period. This absence toll is from CPLR 207, which goes on to state this exception:

If the defendant is subject to the jurisdiction of the New York courts without being personally served in the state, the toll for absence does not apply. So, when a basis of jurisdiction exists, such as under CPLR 301 or 302, on which service outside New York is authorized by CPLR 313, the toll of CPLR 207 does not apply,[1] and this means that CPLR 207 and its absence toll does not apply in most cases. The advent of longarm jurisdiction,[2] which is what CPLR 302 supplies, has reduced the utility of CPLR 207. Under prior law, when extrastate service was allowed only in a few narrow instances, plaintiffs had more occasion to depend

21. So held a divided Court of Appeals in Dreger v. N.Y. State Thruway Authority, 81 N.Y.2d 721, 593 N.Y.S.2d 758, 609 N.E.2d 111 (1992), treated in the lead note in New York State Law Digest No. 397.

22. Gaines v. City of New York, 215 N.Y. 533, 109 N.E. 594 (1915).

23. Dyer v. Cahan, 150 A.D.2d 172, 540 N.Y.S.2d 785 (1st Dep't 1989).

24. Baker v. Commercial Travelers Mutual Accident Ass'n, 3 A.D.2d 265, 161 N.Y.S.2d 332 (4th Dep't 1957).

25. Cohoes Housing Auth. v. Ippolito–Lutz, Inc., 65 A.D.2d 666, 409 N.Y.S.2d 811 (3d Dep't 1978), aff'd 49 N.Y.2d 961, 428 N.Y.S.2d 948, 406 N.E.2d 803 (1980).

§ 53

1. Yarusso v. Arbotowicz, 41 N.Y.2d 516, 393 N.Y.S.2d 968, 362 N.E.2d 600 (1977). There are actually three listed exceptions in CPLR 207, but the first two will be found to be embraced by the broad language of the third.

2. See § 84 et seq. below.

on a limitations' toll for the defendant's absence.

It has been held that as long as service beyond the state is permissible, the absence toll is inapplicable even if service is difficult and the plaintiff has to move for an order for service as a last resort.[3] If the defendant is regularly in New York, moreover, so that a diligent process server could get at him—as where the defendant was a New Jersey resident but worked in New York and was here daily—the purpose of this absence provision is not at hand and the toll does not apply.[4]

If, unknown to the plaintiff, the defendant is residing in the state under an alias, the period of such residence is also one in which the statute of limitations is suspended under CPLR 207. But with the numerous ways constitutional service can still be made under the flexible provisions of CPLR 308, despite inability to find the defendant,[5] a plaintiff who postpones suit in reliance on this provision is today taking some risk.

§ 54. Disabilities as Tolls

Infancy and insanity are disabilities resulting in tolls under CPLR 208. Imprisonment used to be but was dropped in 1973 and no longer tolls the statute.

If the applicable statute of limitations is less than three years, the entire period of disability is a tolling period, i.e., the statute of limitations does not run during it. If the applicable period is three years or longer, the plaintiff will have at least three years for suit from the time the disability ceases, but only if he needs it. If the time left on the original statute exceeds three years when the disability ends,

in other words, the extension is not needed and CPLR 208 does not give it.

There are yet further qualifications in the statute, but they are self-explanatory. The statute itself is more an exercise in arithmetic than in law, but several matters deserve highlighting.

CPLR 208 applies only when it is the plaintiff who is under the disability. The defendant can be both an infant and insane—a crazy kid—but there is no toll.

In a wrongful death case it is the duly appointed personal representative who has title to the claim, and he of course must be of age, so there is ordinarily no toll even if some of the beneficiaries of the potential wrongful death recovery are infants.[1] But if the sole distributee of the decedent is an infant, and the decedent dies intestate, it has been held that the statute of limitations on the wrongful death claim will toll until either a guardian is appointed for the infant or the infant comes of age.[2] Should the decedent leave a will, however, and the will appoints an adult as executrix and as guardian of the infant children, the adult/executrix is the person "entitled to commence [the] action" within the meaning of CPLR 208, and the infancy of the beneficiaries in that situation will not count.[3]

In a controversial decision, the Second Department Appellate Division held in 1998 in Henry v. City of New York,[4] that when the parents retain a lawyer for the infant, the toll stops, reasoning that under CPLR 208 the disability must be "because" of infancy and that the retention of counsel effectively cancels the infancy as a disabling factor. There is even confusion, under *Henry*, about whether the

---

3. Goodemote v. McClain, 40 A.D.2d 22, 337 N.Y.S.2d 79 (4th Dep't 1972). The provision authorizing court-ordered service is CPLR 308(5).

4. Mack v. Mendels, 249 N.Y. 356, 164 N.E. 248 (1928).

5. CPLR 308(5) and the power it gives the court to devise a service method may prove especially helpful when the defendant cannot be found. See § 75 below.

§ 54

1. Mossip v. F. H. Clement & Co., 283 N.Y. 554, 27 N.E.2d 279 (1940), aff'g 256 App.Div. 469, 10 N.Y.S.2d 592 (4th Dep't 1939).

2. Hernandez v. New York City Health and Hospitals Corp., 78 N.Y.2d 687, 578 N.Y.S.2d 510, 585 N.E.2d 822 (1991).

3. Baez v. New York City Health and Hospitals Corp., 80 N.Y.2d 571, 592 N.Y.S.2d 640, 607 N.E.2d 787 (1992).

4. 244 A.D.2d 93, 676 N.Y.S.2d 616 (2d Dep't 1998).

formal retention of a lawyer is needed to suspend the toll, i.e., perhaps just the presence of a parent acting for the child would do it.[5] The First Department held to the contrary hardly a month before *Henry*, in Rosado v. Langsam Property Serv. Corp.,[6] adhering to the traditional view that "[a]n infant should not be penalized for the failures or neglect of his guardian or attorney".[7]

Until the status of the *Henry* case is clarified, attorneys for infants should assume the worst: that they will not be awarded a toll, at least not as of the time of their hiring to represent the infant.

The disability must exist when the cause of action accrues. If it accrues afterwards, there is no toll. This is significant only when insanity is the ground. (There is no reported case in New York in which a plaintiff of age when the claim accrued became an infant afterwards.)

Insanity resulting from the very injury involved in the action does invoke the toll, even though the insanity does not appear until later,[8] but the Court of Appeals has held that the toll must be "narrowly interpreted" and won't cover, for example, "the temporary effects of medications administered in the treatment of physical injuries".[9] Nor will an alleged post-accident "neurosis" qualify as a toll as long as the plaintiff can still manage his affairs.[10]

The insanity need not have been formally adjudicated at accrual time.[11]

Since inability to protect one's affairs is often assumed to be the criterion for an "insanity" toll,[12] it should invoke the toll not only for a plaintiff under the outright incompetency status that "insanity" usually implies, but also for a plaintiff under mere "conservatorship" status, as it was once called (and still is in the CPLR[13]), which, with less stigma, is designed for an individual not necessarily insane but nevertheless unable to manage his affairs. CPLR 208 specifies only insanity, however, and the plaintiff should not assume that it will be applied to a lesser status until the point is fully settled.

CPLR references to such terms as "conservator", "conservatee", "committee", and "incompetent" are now archaic, incidentally. A 1992 statute prescribes that they be replaced by "guardian" and "incapacitated person", and contains an instruction that the older terms be deemed to include the new ones.[14]

The insanity ground cannot result in an extension beyond 10 years from accrual of the claim. The infancy ground can, however, except in an action for medical malpractice (including dental and podiatric malpractice), where the 10–year cut-off does apply even to infants.

Neither disability precludes suit from being brought in the plaintiff's behalf during the disability. Indeed, given the variety of persons who can sue in behalf of an incapacitated plaintiff,[15] relatively few claims by those under CPLR 208 disabilities are postponed so long that they have to invoke a CPLR 208 toll.

The disability toll applies only to the claim of the incapacitated person. A derivative claim by one who is not under a disability, such as that of a parent for loss of the infant's services, does not get the toll.[16]

---

5. See the treatments of the Henry case and its fallout in SPR 74:2, 76:3, 77:2, 78:3, and 81:2.

6. 251 A.D.2d 258, 675 N.Y.S.2d 53 (1st Dep't 1998).

7. When there was a conflict of interest between the parents and the infant, the toll was held to continue even by a lower court in the Second Department. See Wright v. Area Bus Corp., Sup.Ct., Kings County, Dec. 11, 1998, 1998 WL 956742 (1998), treated in the lead note in SPR 79.

8. Chartener v. Kice, 270 F.Supp. 432 (E.D.N.Y.1967).

9. Eisenbach v. Metropolitan Transp. Auth., 62 N.Y.2d 973, 479 N.Y.S.2d 338, 468 N.E.2d 293 (1984).

10. McCarthy v. Volkswagen of America, Inc., 55 N.Y.2d 543, 450 N.Y.S.2d 457, 435 N.E.2d 1072 (1982).

11. Hammer v. Rosen, 7 N.Y.2d 376, 198 N.Y.S.2d 65, 165 N.E.2d 756 (1960).

12. See Hurd v. Allegany County, 39 A.D.2d 499, 336 N.Y.S.2d 952 (4th Dep't 1972).

13. See, e.g., CPLR 1201.

14. L.1992, c.698. See § 194 below. All prior proceedings taken under the old terminology are of course preserved until set aside or modified by a judge under the new law. See SPR 5:4.

15. See CPLR 1201.

16. Lewis v. N.Y.C. Transit Auth., 100 A.D.2d 896, 474 N.Y.S.2d 555 (2d Dep't 1984).

Another disability toll is that for military service. This one comes not from the CPLR but from the Military Law[17] and differs from the CPLR 208 tolls in that (1) it applies whether it is the plaintiff or the defendant who is in military service and (2) the period of service is a tolling period no matter when the claim accrued, i.e., the disability of military service does not have to exist when the claim accrues, as is required of the infancy and insanity disabilities.

Other disabilities emanating from war are recognized and treated in CPLR 209.

§ 55. Tolling for Death

The death of a potential party after the statute of limitations expires has no effect on a claim not yet sued on—the claim is barred— but death before expiration has. What the effect is depends on who died.

If the would-be plaintiff dies, her personal representative has at least a year from death in which to sue.[1] This is an alternative period, not an extension, and is used only if needed. If at the moment of death more than a year remains on the original period, this provision adds nothing.[2] And whatever remains is usable; the time left is not cut back to a year.[3]

A case showing the limitations' interplay between the decedent's personal injury claim and his next of kin's wrongful death claim is Brandt v. Hashinsky.[4] There the personal representative joined both claims in one action, which was brought a year and a half after death. At the moment of death, there were only a few months to go on the personal injury claim, which therefore needed, and got, the one-year death alternative. But the suit was not brought within the year and that barred

the personal injury claim. The wrongful death claim, however, was alive; it was brought within two years of death and its condition precedent (that the deceased's underlying claim be alive at the time of death[5]) was fulfilled.

When the would-be defendant dies before suit, there is an 18–month toll.[6] It is easier to remember it this way: 18 months are tacked on to whatever period remains. This is an addition and not, as where the potential plaintiff dies, a mere alternative.[7] Suit in such case must be brought against the decedent's personal representative. If none is appointed at the behest of his family—an omission that may be aimed at frustrating the suit—the plaintiff is herself authorized to apply to the surrogate's court for the appointment.[8]

A claim that does not accrue to P until after D's death exists not against D, but against D's estate, and gets no death extension. To this an important exception has been carved out when both parties die in a common disaster, as happened in Gibson v. Meehan,[9] in which D died immediately and P a few days later. The claim for P's wrongful death thus arose after D had died, which would ordinarily have precluded a toll for D's death, but the court rejected the technical construction in this situation and added the 18 months to the two-year wrongful death period.

§ 56. Estopping Defendant from Pleading Limitation

"Our courts have long had the power, both at law and equity, to bar the assertion of the affirmative defense of the Statute of Limitations where it is the defendant's affirmative wrongdoing ... which produced the long delay" in bringing suit. Thus spoke the Court of Appeals in General Stencils, Inc. v. Chiappa,[1] a

---

17. N.Y.Mil.L. § 308.

§ 55

1. CPLR 210(a).

2. Ruping v. Great A. & P. Tea Co., 279 App.Div. 322, 109 N.Y.S.2d 286 (3d Dep't 1952).

3. Tamburello v. Mooney, 51 Misc.2d 1093, 274 N.Y.S.2d 437 (Sup.Ct., Albany County 1966).

4. 16 Misc.2d 564, 177 N.Y.S.2d 648 (Sup.Ct., Kings County, 1958).

5. See § 44 above.

6. CPLR 210(b).

7. Schwartz v. Public Adm'r, 27 A.D.2d 913, 278 N.Y.S.2d 968 (1st Dep't 1967).

8. SCPA 1002(1).

9. 7 N.Y.2d 93, 195 N.Y.S.2d 649, 163 N.E.2d 874 (1959).

§ 56

1. 18 N.Y.2d 125, 128, 272 N.Y.S.2d 337, 340, 219 N.E.2d 169, 171 (1966).

conversion claim against an embezzling book-keeper, but the lawyer should not take the case as a general authority for liberal use of the estoppel doctrine. In that case there was an inherent secrecy in the very nature of the defendant's actionable conduct.

The estoppel doctrine is in fact applied sparingly and may not be used by a naive plaintiff who lets the claim lapse on a general understanding (or hope?) that it will be settled.

An actual agreement between P and D reasonably leading to postponement of suit can and should work an estoppel,[2] but anything less than that should not be depended on. It is easy enough to start the action amicably—perhaps the plaintiff should even tell the defendant that suit is being commenced just as a precaution—and continue settlement talks afterwards.

The estoppel doctrine is one of caselaw, today acknowledged by statute;[3] even so, if there is still time to sue and the defendant will not agree in writing to an extension, the plaintiff is better off assuming that the doctrine does not exist.

In the ordinary run of litigation, like damage claims in tort or breach of contract, there is rarely to be found anything like the stealth involved in embezzlement. If the facts that give rise to the claim are open enough (they were not in the *General Stencils* case), so that the plaintiff knows she has a cause of action, she acts at her peril by delaying suit based on what the defendant says or does afterwards.

This is not to say that estoppel can't work in something as ordinary as a negligence case. In Croop v. Odette,[4] for example, it was sustained, but it is interesting to note that the sustaining was at the pleading stage; the plaintiff had yet to prove that his reliance on the defendant's representations was justification for letting the statute of limitations pass.

If there is a fiduciary or other special relationship between the parties, estoppel may have easier sailing. In Simcuski v. Saeli,[5] for example, the defendant was the plaintiff's physician. The doctor damaged a nerve in the plaintiff's neck while performing an operation. When the plaintiff lost sensation in her right side and brought this to the doctor's attention, he assured her that it was only temporary and would correct itself in time. Relying on this advice, the plaintiff refrained from seeking other help, although timely attention, as she later learned, could have corrected or cured her condition, which became permanent. The doctor's representations had the direct effect of getting the plaintiff to forego suit and on these facts (as pleaded) the plaintiff could reasonably rely on the representations. Thus, in a malpractice action brought after the expiration of the applicable period, enough was spelled out to work an estoppel against the doctor and prevent him from invoking the time bar.

G. FOREIGN CLAIMS

Table of Sections

§ 57. Foreign Claims; the "Borrowing" Statute

In the conflict of laws arena, CPLR 202 is known as a "borrowing" statute. It is designed to apply when a foreign cause of action is sued on; it determines whether the foreign or local statute of limitations applies.

CPLR 202 first provides that when the cause of action accrues outside New York to one who was at the time a New York resident, only the New York statute of limitations applies; the foreign one is disregarded. For a time "resident" here was construed to mean "domiciliary",[1] but the Court of Appeals rejected that construction in Antone v. General Motors

---

2. Robinson v. City of New York, 24 A.D.2d 260, 265 N.Y.S.2d 566 (1st Dep't 1965).

3. Gen.Oblig.L. § 17–103(4)(b).

4. 29 Misc.2d 606, 219 N.Y.S.2d 805 (Sup.Ct., Oneida County, 1961), aff'd 14 A.D.2d 724, 218 N.Y.S.2d 532 (4th Dep't 1961).

5. 44 N.Y.2d 442, 406 N.Y.S.2d 259, 377 N.E.2d 713 (1978).

§ 57

1. See, e.g., Jones v. Greyhound Bus Lines, 73 Misc.2d 109, 341 N.Y.S.2d 159 (Sup.Ct., Orange County, 1973).

Corp.,[2] holding that it means just what it says: resident. Hence the *Antone* plaintiff, who technically had a New York domicile when he was injured in a Pennsylvania accident, but was residing in Pennsylvania at the time, could not rely solely on the New York statute of limitations.[3]

If a claim that originally accrued to a New York resident is paid by the New Yorker's foreign insurer and it's the insurer that's suing on the claim as subrogated plaintiff, the insurer has been held to stand in the insured's shoes and can rely exclusively on the New York period.[4]

The "borrowing" takes place only when the foreign claim accrues to a nonresident, which includes a foreign corporation.[5] The New York period is looked to on the one hand, and, on the other, the period applicable under the laws of the place "where the cause of action accrued". The two are then compared and the *shorter* of the two is the one applied. If the claim has expired under either the New York or foreign period, in other words, it is barred. Note that there is not necessarily a "borrowing", therefore; the statute really dictates a comparison, with a "borrowing" of the foreign period only it if is the shorter one.[6]

The two periods that are compared are the "net" periods. That is, the New York period, with all relevant New York extensions and tolls integrated, is one prong of the comparison, and the foreign period, with the foreign tolls and extensions integrated, is the other.

The New York tolls are not superimposed on the foreign period, or vice versa.[7]

The question of where the cause of action "accrued" can be a sticky one, especially in this age of more sophisticated choice of law principles. The doctrine of Babcock v. Jackson[8] —adopting what has become known as the "most significant contacts" test to determine which state's substantive law governs a given issue in a case with foreign elements—is also likely to have an effect on "where" a cause of action accrues under CPLR 202. But the New York Court of Appeals has not yet resolved the matter and until it does there will necessarily be some guesswork.

It is the federal bench that has been most involved with these issues. In diversity cases the federal courts are required to apply state choice of law principles,[9] and they have tried to predict how the New York Court of Appeals would want CPLR 202 construed. One Second Circuit case, Sack v. Low,[10] in which the claim might have accrued in part in each of two other states, holds that CPLR 202 should be construed to bar the claim if the laws of either of those foreign states would bar it. In this writer's view the action should be barred if it is shown to be barred by the law of any foreign jurisdiction having contacts with the case at least as significant as New York's.[11] The obvious purpose of CPLR 202 is to bar from imposing on the New York courts any case that has an equal or greater claim on the attention of a foreign forum. If there are several such forums

---

2. 64 N.Y.2d 20, 484 N.Y.S.2d 514, 473 N.E.2d 742 (1984).

3. His claim was put through the borrowing process and subjected to the shorter Pennsylvania statute of limitations, which barred it.

4. United States Fidelity & Guaranty Co. v. E. W. Smith Co., 46 N.Y.2d 498, 414 N.Y.S.2d 672, 387 N.E.2d 604 (1979).

5. American Lumbermens Mut. Cas. Co. v. Cochrane, 309 N.Y. 1017, 133 N.E.2d 461 (1956), aff'g 284 App.Div. 884, 134 N.Y.S.2d 473 (1st Dep't), aff'g 129 N.Y.S.2d 489 (Sup.Ct., N.Y.County, 1954).

6. See Kirsch v. Lubin, 248 N.Y. 645, 162 N.E. 559 (1928).

7. Cellura v. Cellura, 24 A.D.2d 59, 263 N.Y.S.2d 843 (4th Dep't 1965). The Court of Appeals in the Antone case, note 2 above, incidentally confirms this use of "net" periods.

8. 12 N.Y.2d 473, 240 N.Y.S.2d 743, 191 N.E.2d 279 (1963). See Neumeier v. Kuehner, 31 N.Y.2d 121, 335 N.Y.S.2d 64, 286 N.E.2d 454 (1972), for a review of the Babcock influence on the decade following it.

9. Erie R.R. Co. v. Tompkins, 304 U.S. 64, 58 S.Ct. 817, 82 L.Ed. 1188 (1938); Klaxon Co. v. Stentor Elec. Mfg. Co., 313 U.S. 487, 61 S.Ct. 1020, 85 L.Ed. 1477(1941). A "diversity" case is one in which federal jurisdiction is based on the fact that the parties are citizens of different states. See 28 U.S.C.A. § 1332.

10. 478 F.2d 360 (2d Cir.1973).

11. Cf. George v. Douglas Aircraft Co., 332 F.2d 73 (2d Cir. 1964). See generally the discussions in Gegan, Where Does a Personal Injury Action Accrue under the New York Borrowing Statute?, 47 St. John's L. Rev. 62 (1972), and Gartner, New York's Borrowing Statute and Problems in "Place of Accrual" Analysis, 6 Journal of the Suffolk Academy of Law (1989) 63.

that would be just as appropriate for suit as New York, and any one of them bars the claim, the intent underlying CPLR 202 is that it should be barred in New York, too.

Securities fraud accounts for a significant segment of federal judicial business. Citing the *Sack* case, the Second Circuit has held that in securities fraud litigation

> the cause of action for purposes of New York's borrowing statute ... accrues in the state where the loss resulting from the misrepresentation was sustained. The New York courts are in accord.[12]

In a prognostication of what it thought the New York Court of Appeals would say, the Second Circuit held in 1981 that if a given defendant would not be subject to jurisdiction in a particular state, the claim could not be deemed to arise in that state under CPLR 202 and its statute of limitations would therefore not be borrowed with respect to that defendant.[13] The prediction proved wrong as the New York Court of Appeals held to the contrary in 1997 in Insurance Co. of North America v. ABB Power Generation Inc.[14]

The *ABB* case was a contract claim with which California—with a four-year statute of limitations (New York's is six)—had almost all the contacts. In a dispute involving the breakdown of a multi-million dollar generating plant, the victim's insurer paid the loss and then, subrogated, sued ABB, the alleged wrongdoer, in New York. A contract between the parties called for arbitration in New York, which was how New York got involved in this essentially California dispute in the first place. Piercing through the complications, the issue boiled down to whether New York, under CPLR 202, would borrow the shorter period of a foreign state even as against a party who could not be sued in that state for want of jurisdictional contacts. New York would, the court responded, because "the purposes underlying the borrowing statute do not require that amenability to suit be demonstrated before an action can be said to accrue in a particular jurisdiction".[15]

The question of when the claim is "interposed" (i.e., whether by filing or service or sheriff delivery or the like), as against what period applies, is a New York matter in all cases and does not involve any borrowing.[16]

---

12. Industrial Consultants, Inc. v. H.S. Equities, Inc., 646 F.2d 746 (2d Cir.1981).

13. Stafford v. International Harvester Co., 668 F.2d 142 (1981).

14. 91 N.Y.2d 180, 668 N.Y.S.2d 143 (1997).

15. The case is the subject of the lead note in New York State Law Digest No. 456.

16. Drummy v. Oxman, 280 App.Div. 800, 113 N.Y.S.2d 224 (2d Dep't 1952).

Chapter Four

PERSONAL JURISDICTION

Analysis

A. INTRODUCTORY

Table of Sections

Sec.
58. Personal Jurisdiction, Introduction.

§ 58. Personal Jurisdiction, Introduction

In this chapter we examine how the court gets jurisdiction to bind the parties to its determination. The plaintiff submits to the court's jurisdiction when she invokes it by suing. Other parties must be brought within it, and the steps that accomplish this are the stuff of this chapter, entitled "personal jurisdiction". A subcategory of it is "rem" jurisdiction, which is usually turned to only as an alternative when personal jurisdiction is lacking. The rem materials come towards the end of the chapter.[1]

Exercising personal jurisdiction always requires homage to the due process clause, the principal constitutional restraint on potential excesses of state judicial power. The traditional requirements of that clause are (1) notice and (2) opportunity to be heard,[2] a team so pervasively publicized that the lawyer may be prone to overlook that the team is really a trio, not a duet. There is a third member, often even louder than the other two:

Suppose a two-car accident in New York between drivers N and F. N is a New Yorker, F a Floridian. A few months later N is served in New York with a Florida summons advising him of a personal injury action F has brought in Florida, and with a complaint stating a claim arising from the New York accident and advising N that he has 30 days in which to appear and answer. Has N been given due notice and an opportunity to be heard? He has been given both. But has the New York service given the Florida court jurisdiction? It has not. And the barrier is the due process clause. It requires not just notice and an opportunity to be heard. It has a third requirement—jurisdictional basis—and that's what Florida lacked here. A state cannot subject a nondomiciliary to its jurisdiction without a thread of some kind, often referred to as a "nexus", connecting the state, the defendant, and the case. Those threads are the "bases" of personal jurisdiction.

In the example put above, New York could have subjected F to its jurisdiction if suit had

---

§ 58

1. Section 101 et seq.

2. Mullane v. Central Hanover Bank & Trust Co., 339 U.S. 306, 70 S.Ct. 652, 94 L.Ed. 865 (1950).

been brought in New York and F was served in Florida. The fact that the accident occurred in New York would have given New York the jurisdictional basis that Florida lacked. The basis in this case is called "longarm" jurisdiction; it involves a claim arising out of the defendant's activity within the state.

Jurisdictional basis on the one hand and the requirement of notice on the other, although both are products of due process and each is essential to jurisdiction, are best investigated separately. A failure to separate them can breed confusion.[3]

The CPLR begins its jurisdictional article, Article 3, by treating jurisdictional basis. That's what CPLR 301 and 302 are all about. Only later on, with 307 and 308 et seq., does the article get into the question of how to make service, and only with CPLR 313 are we told when service outside New York can be made. The provisions overlap, and treatment of one often entails a preliminary reference to another. Our treatment will stress methods of service first, concentrating at the outset on service in New York in cases in which all the defendants are in the state.

The reader would do well to read CPLR 301, 302, and 313 at the outset. It will show that everything studied about service within the state will apply with equal force to service outside the state when CPLR 313 is finally reached. The only impact, in fact, of such celebrated provisions as CPLR 302, the "longarm" statute, is that its applicability invokes CPLR 313 and permits service on the defendant, with full personam effect, anywhere in the world. And yet CPLR 313 does nothing more than dissolve state lines; as far as method of service is concerned, method still comes from CPLR 308 and the other sections concerned with the mechanics of service. When it applies, CPLR 313 just changes the words

"within the state", wherever they appear in the method statutes, into "anywhere".

B. THE SUMMONS

Table of Sections

§ 59. Summons Service in New York as Jurisdictional Basis

If the summons is personally delivered to the defendant in New York, the several requirements of due process are fulfilled simultaneously. The reason is that local service is its own basis for jurisdiction. If service is made outside New York, no matter how perfectly, it must be separately demonstrated that there is some basis—some New York connection—justifying the extraterritorial service. Delivery of the summons to the defendant while the defendant is physically in the state is therefore the only instance in which the separate demands of due process—basis on the one hand, notice and opportunity to be heard on the other—overlap.

This is the residuum of the capias ad respondendum, the writ which at common law commanded the sheriff to bring the defendant physically before the court. That was how a law action was begun. The writ has long since given way to mere local service of the summons on the defendant,[1] and for a long time

---

3. See, e.g., Doughney v. Fauset, 9 Misc.2d 759, 170 N.Y.S.2d 419 (Sup.Ct., N.Y.County), decided in 1958 before the CPLR was enacted. The case involved an estate. X, one of its executors, was sued both as an individual and as executor, and was served outside New York. The court assumed that the service was good against X as an individual, but not necessarily against the estate. No stress was laid on the fact that the plaintiff's claim, which was for personal injury, arose in New York. Today that fact would

be not merely relevant, but decisive, under CPLR 302(a)(2) and 313, which together give jurisdiction against any tortfeasor, or his executor, served anywhere if the tort occurred in New York.

§ 59

1. International Shoe Co. v. Washington, 326 U.S. 310, 66 S.Ct. 154, 90 L.Ed. 95 (1945).

service within the state was the only way to get personal jurisdiction of an unwilling defendant. So declared Pennoyer v. Neff[2] in 1877, and *Pennoyer* reigned well into the 20th century. The demands of commerce and the increasing ease of communication and movement ultimately made their mark: jurisdictional notions were generously expanded, and *Pennoyer*'s restrictive attitude abandoned.

To this day, however, personal delivery of the summons to the defendant within the state, no matter how transient the defendant's presence, will still give personal jurisdiction, and in that way the old capias hangs on. This jurisdiction lies regardless of the nature of the claim—it can be wholly foreign—and regardless of the defendant's domicile or residence. The doctrine of forum non conveniens can dismiss such a case, of course,[3] but that does not change the fact that the court obtained jurisdiction for the sole reason that the defendant was served in New York. Under present concepts, this ancient idea would doubtless have demanded reconsideration a long time ago if the conveniens doctrine had not been available as a kind of insulation, casting out cases in which appropriate New York contacts were lacking even though the defendant may have been in the state at the moment of service.

While on the state side any pressure under the state constitution to reexamine this transient service rule is abated by the accessibility of the conveniens doctrine, on the federal side there is no constitutional pressure at all after the U.S. Supreme Court 1990 decision in Burnham v. Superior Court,[4] which affirmed the constitutionality of transient service as a jurisdictional basis. Service on a nonresident individual within the state even on a claim unrelated to the state thus continues to give full personam jurisdiction.

Because summons service in the state is its own jurisdictional basis as well as the act that gives the defendant notice of the action and an opportunity to be heard, it is a good starting point in our treatment.

§ 60. Issuance of Summons; Accompanying Papers

The plaintiff's attorney issues and signs the summons in New York, and under nothing more than the attorney's signature the summons is deemed official process of the court. This is in contrast to federal practice, where the clerk issues the summons.[1] Sufficient copies of the summons should be issued so that a separate one can be served on each party. This is a good precaution whatever their interests may be. Even married defendants have been held entitled to individual summonses.[2]

In New York practice, the moment that an action is deemed commenced depends on the court in which the action is being brought. In the supreme and county courts, the filing of the summons and complaint constitutes commencement;[3] in the lower courts—the New York City Civil Court and the district, city, town, and village courts—service of the summons and complaint marks commencement.[4] These are important points to keep in mind because they involve the statute of limitations. If today is the last day for suit, for example, and the plaintiff takes a step that does not mark commencement in the court in which the action is brought, the action will be subject to a dismissal for untimeliness even though the step taken may have been the right one in some other court.[5]

---

2. 95 U.S. 714, 24 L.Ed. 565.

3. See § 28 above.

4. 495 U.S. 604, 110 S.Ct. 2105, 109 L.Ed.2d 631.

§ 60

1. FRCP Rule 4(b). See § 621 below (Practitioner's Edition).

2. McCormack v. Gomez, 137 A.D.2d 504, 524 N.Y.S.2d 247 (2d Dep't 1988).

3. CPLR 304. For practice in the surrogate's court, see SCPA 301.

4. See § 400 in each of the four lower court acts—the New York City Civil and the Uniform District, City, and Justice (town and village) court acts, which provide that the filing system applicable in the supreme and county courts does not apply in the lower courts.

5. Coleman v. Vansteen, 227 A.D.2d 919, 643 N.Y.S.2d 264 (4th Dep't 1996). For the problems met when a case intended for a "filing" court is mistakenly brought instead in a "service" court, see SPR 52:2.

The filing practice, applicable in the supreme and county courts, is similar to federal practice, where the first step is the filing of the complaint[6] and where service on the defendant comes afterwards.[7] But the incidents of service differ substantially between federal and state practice and attorneys must be alert to this.[8] (The Individual Assignment System used in New York practice, and the Request for Judicial Intervention [RJI] procedure for getting a judge assigned to a case, are treated later.[9])

In supreme and county court practice under the CPLR, the summons may be served with either the complaint or a brief notice (as described below), at plaintiff's option.[10] This is one of the differences from federal practice, in which the summons and complaint are served together.[11] In the lower courts in New York, in which service marks commencement, the complaint does accompany the summons, but it often takes the form of a brief "indorsement" on the summons.[12]

Leaving lower court practice to the prescriptions of the lower court acts, we concentrate henceforth on supreme and county court practice.

When the summons is served with the complaint, it notifies the defendant to answer the complaint within a specified time. The period is 20 or 30 days, depending on the place and method of service. If the service is by personal delivery to the defendant in New York, the period is 20 days; if the service is by a different means in New York, or by any method at all outside New York, the period is 30 days.[13] Although the summons in such an instance commands the defendant to answer the complaint, the defendant has the option of instead moving to dismiss the complaint or compel its amendment.[14] There is an official form for this summons, promulgated as Official Form 1 by the Office of Court Administration. It is reprinted in the next section.

When the summons is served without a complaint,[15] it must be accompanied by a brief notice, commonly called a "default notice", as provided by CPLR 305(b). The notice must briefly state the object of the action and the relief sought, including the sum of money being sought if the claim is for money.[16]

The notice can be set forth on the summons itself or can accompany the summons as a separate paper. There is also an official form (Form 3) for a summons served with this notice. It is reprinted two sections hence.

Prior to 1979, a third option was available. A bare summons could be used to start things off, accompanied by neither a complaint nor a notice. This option was eliminated in 1979 in amendments made in CPLR 305(b) and 3012(b). The use of a bare summons is now a jurisdictional defect and results in a dismissal for want of personal jurisdiction. Worse than that, should the statute of limitations now have expired, is that the dismissal does not get the six months of CPLR 205(a) for a new action.[17] It has been held that the defendant's service of a notice of appearance and demand for the complaint will waive an objection to the plaintiff's service of a naked summons,[18] but serving a bare summons is not authorized and the plaintiff who uses it is asking for trouble.[19]

---

6. FRCP Rule 3.

7. Rule 4(m).

8. The incidents and details of summons service following commencement in supreme and county court practice are treated in § 63 below.

9. See §§ 77A and 77B below.

10. CPLR 305(b), 3012(a).

11. FRCP Rule 4(c)(1).

12. See § 902(a)(1) in each of the New York City Civil, Uniform District, Uniform City, and Uniform Justice court acts, McKinney's Vol. 29A, Parts 2 and 3.

13. CPLR 3012(a),(c).

14. CPLR 3211(e), 3024(c).

15. When this happens the complaint is served later under the demand procedure prescribed in CPLR 3012(b). See § 231 below.

16. In a medical malpractice action, no monetary sum is stated. See also in this regard CPLR 3017(c), which bars the complaint's reference to a specific sum in certain cases. See § 217.

17. See the discussion of the Parker case in § 52, above.

18. Bal v. Court Employment Project, Inc., 73 A.D.2d 69, 424 N.Y.S.2d 715 (1st Dep't 1980); Aversano v. Town of Brookhaven, 77 A.D.2d 641, 430 N.Y.S.2d 133 (2d Dep't 1980).

19. See LeConte v. City of New York, 129 Misc.2d 719, 493 N.Y.S.2d 745 (Sup.Ct., Queens County, 1985).

It may not even be safe to use the notice itself. It is better as a general rule to serve a regular complaint with the summons. How much need one include in a "notice" to be sure it's sufficient, for example? When service of a bare summons was an available option, the consequence of including too little in a notice was harmless; it was the same as serving a bare summons, which was acceptable. But today, with the bare summons option eliminated, an insufficient notice is likely to result in dismissal. Add to that a statute of limitations problem and the peril of relying on CPLR 305(b) should be plain enough.[20]

Caselaw suggests, perhaps too reassuringly, that not much is needed to qualify as a CPLR 305(b) notice. There are indications from the appellate divisions that statements like "damages for breach of contract", "libel", "legal services", "motor vehicle negligence", "automobile negligence", and even simple "negligence", suffice,[21] but the Court of Appeals has not yet spoken to the point and the service of a complaint is the better precaution until it has.

If the statute of limitations is so close that there is no time to draft a good complaint, perhaps the lawyer can just draft a bad one, which requires little talent. Ironically, a bad complaint can usually be amended as a matter of right,[22] with the action preserved, while an inadequate notice can't be amended and can therefore result in a jurisdictional dismissal. Even a bad complaint should contain at least enough verbiage to satisfy as a notice and avoid a dismissal.[23]

If the CPLR 305(b) notice is adequate, it is a sufficient predicate for a default judgment if the defendant fails to appear.[24]

When the complaint does not accompany it, the summons, instead of requiring the defendant to answer the complaint, requires the defendant to appear in the action, which the defendant does by serving a notice of appearance on the plaintiff's attorney. The time in which to appear is, again, either 20 or 30 days, depending on the place and method of service.[25] It is customary in New York practice to accompany the appearance with a demand for the complaint[26] and in fact the two things are often done in the same paper. No jurisdictional objection is waived by the service of such an appearance.[27]

While the use of a notice in lieu of a complaint will permit a default judgment if the defendant does not appear, a complaint will still have to be served if he does. The demand procedures that then become necessary[28] cost time and can delay the plaintiff's action by weeks or months, suggesting that unless the plaintiff is expecting a default he should for this additional reason make it a practice to effect service of the summons and complaint together.

Defendants' lawyers entertaining the possibility of removing a state action to a federal court if there should be some federal basis on which to do so must be aware of the time limits applicable to removal and alert to the fact that the time may run from the service of a CPLR 305(b) notice and not necessarily from the later service of the complaint.[29]

---

20. See Commentary C3012:1 on McKinney's CPLR 3012.

21. See Rowell v. Gould, Inc., 124 A.D.2d 995, 508 N.Y.S.2d 794 (4th Dep't 1986) and Viscosi v. Merritt, 125 A.D.2d 814, 510 N.Y.S.2d 30 (3d Dep't 1986), and the treatment in the lead note in New York State Law Digest No. 330. Omission of only a monetary demand in an ordinary money action may not be a jurisdictional defect— see the discussion in Hollander v. Lensky, 124 Misc.2d 683, 477 N.Y.S.2d 284 (Sup.Ct., Tompkins County, 1984)—but that, too, is a generous supposition not certain to prevail.

22. CPLR 3025(a).

23. The lesson about making it a habit to use a complaint instead of a notice is well taught in Scaringi v. Elizabeth Broome Realty Corp., 154 Misc.2d 786, 586

N.Y.S.2d 472 (Sup.Ct., N.Y.County, 1991), aff'd 191 A.D.2d 223, 594 N.Y.S.2d 242 (1st Dep't 1993), which is the subject of the lead note in New York State Law Digest No. 394.

24. CPLR 3215(f). See § 295 below.

25. CPLR 320(a).

26. CPLR 3012(b). The complaint must then be served within 20 days after the demand, and the defendant then has 20 days after service of the complaint in which to answer or move. See § 231, below, and Commentary C3012:10 on McKinney's CPLR 3012.

27. See § 111 below.

28. CPLR 3012(a),(b).

29. See § 619 below (Practitioner's Edition).

§ 61. Form of Summons Served with Complaint

SUPREME COURT OF THE STATE OF NEW YORK
COUNTY OF NEW YORK

A.B., Plaintiff,

      against   **Summons**

C.D., Defendant.

    To the above-named defendant:

    You are hereby summoned and required to serve upon plaintiff's attorney an answer to the complaint in this action within twenty days after the service of this summons, exclusive of the day of service, or within thirty days after service is complete if this summons is not personally delivered to you within the State of New York. In case of your failure to answer, judgment will be taken against you by default for the relief demanded in the complaint.

    The basis of the venue designated is [specify basis, as: the residence of plaintiff, which is (set forth address)].

Dated:

                                                __[Print name]__
                                                Attorney for Plaintiff
                                                  Address:
                                                Telephone Number:

[F7296]

The above is Form 1 of the Official Forms promulgated by what is now the Office of Court Administration. The basis of the venue is required by CPLR 305(a). As shown in the form, it is satisfied by the simple addition of a sentence. Venue is met in Chapter 6.

§ 62. Form of Summons Served with 305(b) Default Notice

**SUPREME COURT OF THE STATE OF NEW YORK
COUNTY OF NEW YORK**

A.B., Plaintiff,

     against   **Summons with Notice**

C.D., Defendant.

    To the above-named defendant:

    You are hereby summoned to appear in this action by serving a notice of appearance on plaintiff's attorney within twenty days after the service of this summons, exclusive of the day of service, or within thirty days after service is complete if this summons is not personally delivered to you within the State of New York.

    Take notice that the nature of this action and the relief sought is to recover damages for breach of contract, and that in case of your failure to appear judgment will be taken against you by default for the sum of twenty thousand dollars with interest from June 1, 1966, plus the costs and disbursements of this action.

    The basis of the venue designated is [specify basis, as: the residence of plaintiff, which is (set forth address)].

Dated:

                                       [Print name]

                                     Attorney for Plaintiff
                                     Address:
                                     Telephone Number:

[F7297]

IM–991

The above is Form 3 of the Official Forms, but with the "nature" of the action substituted for the "object" of the action that the official form still has. The change reflects an amendment of CPLR 305(b) effective in 1979, an incident of several amendments whose main mission was to withdraw the option of serving a bare summons.

How much of a statement is necessary to satisfy as a description of the "nature" of the action? According to the form itself, a mere naming of the action ("damages for breach of contract"), plus a statement of the amount sought, suffices, but the plaintiff's lawyer may want to include somewhat more. The problem of including an inadequate description today is that it is the equivalent of serving a bare summons, which is no longer permissible and which brings about a jurisdictional dismissal and possibly the barrier of the statute of limitations. Until the Court of Appeals clarifies how much is necessary to satisfy the CPLR 305(b) requirement, the cautious practitioner does best by starting every action with the service of a summons and complaint together.

These matters are discussed in § 60, above.

§ 63. Commencement of Action; When and by Whom Summons Served

In the earlier editions of this book, the caption of this section was simply "When and by Whom Summons Served". The moment of commencement in the New York courts at that time was marked by the service of the summons, not its filing. While that remains the rule in the lower courts of the state—the New York City Civil Court and the district, city, town, and village courts—it changed for the supreme and county courts in the early 1990s, when filing was made the moment of commencement. Because many complications were introduced with the new system, the caption of this section has been changed in this edition to add "Commencement of Action".

Service of a summons can be made on any day except Sunday. Service on a holiday is allowed, but service of the summons on a Sunday in civil cases is permitted only when accompanied by an injunction needed to avoid irreparable injury.[1] Otherwise Sunday service is void,[2] impermissible even if service is made outside the state in a jurisdiction that permits it on Sunday.[3] A plaintiff whose summons was served on Sunday was even allowed to recognize its invalidity himself and reject an answer tendered by a defendant who was apparently willing to overlook the defect.[4] If both parties disregard the defect and proceed on the merits to judgment, however, one wonders whether the statute[5] will still insist that the service is so "absolutely void" as to permit the defendant—or for that matter even the plaintiff—to undo the judgment at that stage.

Service on a Saturday is made a misdemeanor if made "maliciously" on one who actually celebrates Saturday as the sabbath,[6] and case-law permits the service to be invalidated on motion if that showing is made.[7]

The summons may be served by any person 18 or over and not a party.[8] The plaintiff's attorney, or a member of the plaintiff's family, may serve it. Even the guardian ad litem of an infant plaintiff[9] or a director or officer of a corporate plaintiff may serve it.[10] They are not the parties. And even if a party does serve it, the defect must be raised promptly or it is deemed waived,[11] a rule harder to apply today because the defect is a jurisdictional objection and can be taken as a defense in the answer instead of by motion, at the defendant's option.[12] If taken by answer and the plaintiff wants it disposed of promptly, the plaintiff can test the defense's validity by moving to strike it under CPLR 3211(b).

Even in federal practice today, service may be made by any person 18 or over and not a party.[13] Before 1983 the marshals were the main summons servers in federal practice, but an amendment effective in 1983 took them out of summons service almost entirely.[14]

The "Filing" System for Commencing Actions

Effective July 1, 1992, the "filing" method of starting actions in the supreme and county courts was adopted in New York. As noted above, the "service" system was retained in the lower courts, but in the supreme and county courts the filing of the summons and complaint, or summons and CPLR 305(b) default notice—in a special proceeding the filing of the notice of petition and petition—was made the key statute of limitations moment.[15]

§ 63

1. Jud.L. § 5. A writ of habeas corpus may of course be served on any day. CPLR 7005.

2. Gen.Bus.L. § 11.

3. Eisenberg v. Citation–Langley Corp., 99 A.D.2d 700, 471 N.Y.S.2d 595 (1st Dep't 1984).

4. Scott Shoe–Machinery Co. v. Dancel, 63 A.D. 172, 71 N.Y.S. 263 (1st Dep't 1901).

5. Gen.Bus.L. § 11.

6. Gen.Bus.L. § 13.

7. Jewish Center of Baldwin v. Winer, 216 N.Y.S.2d 153 (Sup.Ct., Nassau County, 1961).

8. CPLR 2103(a). When the service by mail method of CPLR 312–a is used, not even a process server is necessary. See § 76A below.

9. Donnelly v. Donnelly, 29 Misc.2d 469, 217 N.Y.S.2d 850 (Sup.Ct., Queens County, 1961).

10. Outdoor Supply Co. v. Westhome Sec. Corp., 140 Misc. 48, 249 N.Y.S. 571 (App.Term, 1st Dep't, 1931).

11. Myers v. Overton, 2 Abb.Pr. 344 (N.Y.Cmn.Pleas 1855).

12. CPLR 3211(e).

13. FRCP Rule 4(c).

14. This and a number of other changes effected by the 1983 amendment are treated in the Commentaries on Federal Rule 4 in 28 U.S.C.A. See § 624 below (Practitioner's Edition).

15. The filing system also applies in the appellate division in the infrequent situations in which an action or proceeding may be initially commenced there. See Spodek v. New York State Commissioner of Taxation and Finance, 85 N.Y.2d 760, 628 N.Y.S.2d 256, 651 N.E.2d 1275 (1995). A 1996 amendment of CPLR 8022(b) requires that the appellate divisions collect a fee for such original proceed-

All of the ensuing discussion concerns the supreme and county courts, not the lower courts. And the discussion concerns an action, not a special proceeding, which is separately discussed elsewhere.[16]

The reader will find in the filing procedures some similarities to federal practice, but there are some significant differences; lawyers familiar in any measure with federal practice can be led astray by assuming that the two practices are identical. The differences were much more pronounced when comparing the original 1992 filing system, especially CPLR 306–b, one of its cornerstones, but a key amendment that took effect on January 1, 1998, altered CPLR 306–b, simplified the procedure, and reduced the differences. To the extent that differences remain, we will note them. The treatment here is of the current system—the one that went into effect on January 1, 1998. The system it superseded was something of a disaster area. We do have to mention the old system from time to time, however, because many points of research that may be undertaken under the current statute will cross paths with cases under the superseded statute (which proliferated), and these cases can be incomprehensible without knowing what was driving them.

The first step is for the plaintiff to file the summons and complaint or summons and notice—we'll henceforth assume that "complaint" comprehends a notice as well if the notice method is being used—with the clerk of the court. CPLR 306–b then allows 120 days after the filing in which to effect service on the defendant. (The 120–day idea comes from subdivision (m) of Rule 4 of the Federal Rules of Civil Procedure.[17]) As long as service is made within that period, or within the period as extended by the court, the service relates back to the filing, and as long as the filing was within the applicable statute of limitations, the

action is timely. So, if the last day of the statute is June 1st, and the filing takes place on that day, service made at any time within 120 days thereafter is okay.[18]

Note that in a "service" court, i.e., a New York lower court, the filing in the example would have been inconsequential and the service made after June 1st too late. The case would have been subject to a dismissal motion based on the statute of limitations. The plaintiff's lawyer must therefore be careful not to confuse courts, as by inadvertently using in the supreme court a form of summons devised for a lower court, or vice versa. This kind of thing has happened, and can have serious consequences.[19]

Note also that when the plaintiff is using a provisional remedy,[20] like an attachment or lis pendens, there may be other and shorter time limits for making service.[21] These may impinge on the 120–day time period that CPLR 306–b would otherwise allow for service, but that's the price the plaintiff may have to pay when seeking one of the special advantages offered by the provisional remedies.

If service can't be made within the 120 days despite the plaintiff's diligent efforts, the plaintiff can move for an extension of time, just as under Federal Rule 4(m). And there is no arbitrary limit on how long an extension the court can grant. It can grant whatever it believes the facts call for, and can do so in a series of extensions, if need be, when genuine difficulties are being experienced in effecting service.[22]

The plaintiff should be able to show "good cause" for the extension, but CPLR 306–b also allows the court to grant it without good cause, "in the interest of justice". This poses the anomaly of inviting a court to allow an enlargement of time in its discretion when the plaintiff can show no good cause for invoking

---

ings. See SPR 47:1. For practice in the surrogate's court, see SCPA 301 and the Commentaries on it in McKinney's SCPA.

16. See § 550 below.

17. It was subdivision (j) prior to an amendment of Federal Rule 4 that went into effect on Dec. 1, 1993.

18. If the last day is drawing near and for any reason the courthouse is inaccessible for a filing, the plaintiff can

seek an ex parte order from a judge extending the filing time for up to five days. See § 45 above.

19. See SPR 52:2, 65:1.

20. The provisional remedies are treated in § 306 et seq., below.

21. See §§ 319 and 335 below; SPR 65:2.

22. See SPR 61:2–3.

that discretion. An equivalent peculiarity exists under Federal Rule 4(m), however, and the cases have grappled with it.[23]

The extension can be granted even after the expiration of the 120 days, as has often happened under the federal rule when the plaintiff's application for a time enlargement has taken the form of a cross-motion in opposition to the defendant's motion to dismiss for lack of timely service. But a plaintiff does well to seek the extension within the 120 days. Doing so may itself serve as some indication of diligence.

When service is being made by publication, which has to be effected in a series of publishings within a prescribed time period,[24] the availability of a time extension may prove more than helpful; it may prove indispensable.[25]

There may be a special need for a time extension when service is being made in a foreign country, especially one with primitive procedures or an indifferent bureaucracy. Rule 4(m) factors this in by making the 120-day time limit altogether inapplicable when service is being made in a foreign nation. CPLR 306-b doesn't except foreign country service, but the situation would be one with a special appeal to the court's time-extending powers.[26]

If service in any case is attempted, but fails, and a dismissal on that ground occurs within the 120-day period (an unlikely contingency), or if the plaintiff has developed apprehensions about whether the service is good and in order to take no chances prefers to disregard the first service and make a second one within the remaining time (a likelier contingency), the plaintiff can do that.[27]

If the plaintiff is getting down to the wire and can't make service because (e.g.) the plaintiff doesn't know where the defendant resides and hence cannot use such substituted service

provisions as paragraphs 2 or 4 of CPLR 308, the plaintiff can consider moving for an ex parte order under CPLR 308(5), under which the court can invent a method of service for the plaintiff.[28]

A dismissal for failure to make service within the 120-day period may be made only on the defendant's motion. The court can't do it sua sponte.[29] This is consistent with the rule that a defect of personal jurisdiction is for the defendant to plead and prove,[30] and as the *Fry* case (treated below) establishes, filing system defects go to personal, not subject matter jurisdiction.

Contrasting the Former CPLR 306-b

The vice of the original 1992 version of CPLR 306-b was its uncompromising rigidity. Not only did service have to be made within 120 days; the plaintiff also had to secure and file proof of service within that time. The failure to file such proof within the 120 days—even if service was timely and properly made—resulted in the action's being "deemed dismissed". The dismissal occurred automatically, calling for neither a direction of a judge nor even an entry by the clerk. The court had no discretion whatever to extend the time period no matter how diligent the plaintiff's efforts.

This ill-advised (and now happily superseded) procedure resulted in innumerable dismissals even in cases in which the plaintiff was proceeding with diligence but was experiencing difficulties beyond her control.

There was one favor conferred on the plaintiff under the 1992 system. If a "deemed" dismissal occurred on the 120th day, the plaintiff then had a second 120-day period in which to commence a new action—with a new fee—and the second action was then allowed to relate back to the moment that the first was commenced, so that if the first action was filed within the statute of limitations, the second

---

23. See, e.g., the discussion in Boley v. Kaymark, 123 F.3d 756 (3d Cir.1997), cert.den. 118 S.Ct. 1038, 140 L.Ed.2d 104 (1998), and in SPR 63:2.

24. See § 107 below.

25. See SPR 63:2.

26. See SPR 61:2.

27. See SPR 62:2.

28. See § 75 below. Court ordered service of this kind is available today even against a corporation. See CPLR 311(b).

29. In federal practice a sua sponte dismissal of this kind is explicitly authorized by Federal Rule 4(m).

30. See CPLR 3211(a)(8), (e). See § 274 below.

action would also be deemed timely. This seemed generous enough, but it, too, was undone by its inflexibility. As generous as 240 days may seem, there are situations in which it won't suffice. The original CPLR 306–b did not care about that. The court had no power to let the plaintiff go beyond the 240th day.

Horror stories under the "deemed dismissal" procedure abounded.[31] With the court once again empowered to intervene with the flexible tool of the time extension offered by the 1998 CPLR 306–b, these stories will hopefully be at an end. At the very least, the deserving plaintiff can be given some relief.

Further Points under Current Law

Because a filing of one set of the papers takes place up front, followed by the service of another set, the papers served should be the same as those filed. It's a bad idea to make changes in the papers after their filing and before their service, lest, for statute of limitations purposes, the needed link to the moment of filing be impaired.[32] Even if the plaintiff detects some omission in the papers after their filing, it may be best not to chance an amendment until the defendant has appeared.[33]

It is always a bad idea to wait for the last day of the 120–day period before acting, because at that point seemingly innocent oversights can turn lethal. A classic case of fatal lastminutism is Fornino v. Campola,[34] in which P waited until the last day of the service period and on that day did serve and file the papers, but that was the wrong sequence. The action was dismissed because the filing had to come first; the service, when made, had no

pending action to give it context and was held a nullity.[35]

Lest a case like *Fornino* be deemed too technical, let the reader take note of Gershel v. Porr,[36] in which the Court of Appeals opts for a strict construction of the filing system's requirements.[37]

While *Gershel* takes the strict construction path, the Court of Appeals held a few months later, in Fry v. Village of Tarrytown,[38] that the defendant or respondent can waive the plaintiff's (or petitioner's) failure to fulfill these requirements, and does so by appearing and defending without raising the objection. The requirements are held to fall in effect under the caption of "personal" as opposed to "subject matter" jurisdiction, making them waivable under the provisions of CPLR 3211(e). To deem them requirements of subject matter jurisdiction, the court pointed out, would jeopardize judgments indefinitely in cases that were fully and fairly litigated, despite the responding party's failure to interpose any procedural objections.

Because these requirements don't go to subject matter jurisdiction, they may be waived through inaction of the defendant, holds *Fry*; the court may not raise them on its own motion, as the trial judge had tried to do in the case.[39]

The combination of *Gershel* and *Fry* is a Court of Appeals balancing of conflicting policies. Plaintiffs and petitioners are deterred from casualness by being put on notice that the technical requirements will be strictly construed, while defendants and respondents are warned that if they want to capitalize on technicalities they must mind their own proce-

---

31. These are chronicled in what became almost a regular department in this writer's monthly Practice Review, usually under a caption devoted to "The Filing System". Commencing with Issue 1 in April 1993, cases and situations falling under that caption went into dozens of SPR issues.

32. This writer has stressed this point many times. See SPR 5:2, 15:3, 17:3, 19:2, 35:2, and 59:2.

33. See the discussion in SPR 67:3–4.

34. Sup.Ct., Oneida County, Feb. 12, 1996 (Index No. 95–02508, RJI No. 32–95–1656; Grow, J.), noted in SPR 41:2.

35. In Fornino, which was decided under the old CPLR 306–b, the proceedings took place on the last day of the

second 120–day period then allowed, literally on the 240th day after the filing of the action. The case remains a stark lesson, however, because the same result would ensue under the current CPLR 306–b if the events occurred on the 120th day.

36. 89 N.Y.2d 327, 653 N.Y.S.2d 82 (1996).

37. Gershel is discussed in the lead note in New York State Law Digest No. 446.

38. 89 N.Y.2d 714, 658 N.Y.S.2d 205 (1997).

39. Fry is the subject of the lead note in New York State Law Digest No. 448.

dures. The court will not allow a "subject matter jurisdiction" label to be affixed to these requirements, because it could needlessly imperil judgments.

Some cases have held minor omissions of other kinds correctable without requiring a dismissal, such as an omission to specify the date of filing on the summons, or to include on the summons an index number timely bought and paid for.[40] Other courts have held that the omission of both things—the filing date and the index number—is a jurisdictional defect.[41] Still others have held that the double omission is not jurisdictional, at least when the statute of limitations is not a factor.[42] Given the strict construction rule afterwards adopted by the Court of Appeals in its *Gershel* decision, a plaintiff would be foolish to omit any of these requirements.

Problems under the filing system will also arise when trying to add new parties to an action before all the original parties have been duly served. The plaintiff would likely attempt this through something like an amendment, and we've already noted that the better practice is not to try to amend the papers after filing but before service because it violates what appears to be the rule that the papers served should be identical to the papers filed.[43]

Difficulties have arisen in urban and suburban courts in which the "clerk's" office has many subdivisions. With which clerk must the initial filing of the summons and complaint be made? And what papers get filed in what places when the action is brought under CPLR 3213, entailing the initial use of motion papers

at the outset instead of the usual summons and complaint, thereby involving the motion part of the court? Before 1996 it took caselaw to resolve some of these issues.[44] A statutory resolution was offered in 1996 when references to the "clerk of the court" in CPLR 203(c)(1) and 306–a(a) were omitted and CPLR 304 was amended to clarify that the filing is to be deemed made when the proper initiatory papers are delivered to the clerk of the court "or any other person designated by the clerk of the court for that purpose". The designation should be satisfactory even if not embodied in a formal writing.[45] All problems of service were compounded for plaintiffs' attorneys when—quite by coincidence and not at all a product or by-product of the filing system—the Court of Appeals held in Kleeman v. Rheingold[46] that the plaintiff's attorney is responsible for the activities of the process server and cannot escape the responsibility by relying on the theory that the process server is an independent contractor. Hence a foul-up by a process server that brings about a dismissal of the action too late for a new one under the statute of limitations will be laid at the door of the attorney who retained the process server and will make the attorney liable to the client for legal malpractice.[47]

Special note should be taken of cases in which service is made under paragraph 2 or 4 of CPLR 308, each of which requires that proof of service be filed within 20 days after service[48] and provides that service is not "complete" until the filing. The moment service is "complete" under those statutes affects only

40. See, e.g., Nussinow v. AMW Ventures, Inc., Sup. Ct., Suffolk County, Oct. 15, 1993 (Index No. 93/14977, Oshrin, J.), noted in SPR 13:3.

41. See, e.g., Federal Deposit Ins. Corp. v. Eckman, N.Y. Law Journal, Oct. 17, 1994, p.27, col.4 (Sup.Ct., New York County, Davis, J.), noted in SPR 25:3.

42. See, e.g., Lee Crossley & Assocs. v. Batlle, 167 Misc.2d 183, 638 N.Y.S.2d 274 (Sup.Ct., Onondaga County, 1995). These conflicts are discussed in SPR 40:2.

43. See discussion above at the points of note 32 and 33.

44. See, e.g., Federal Deposit Ins. Corp. v. Goodman, N.Y. Law Journal, July 13, 1994, p.25, col.5 (Sup.Ct., N.Y. County, Schackman, J.), discussed in the lead note in SPR 21.

45. See SPR 49:3–4.

46. 81 N.Y.2d 270, 598 N.Y.S.2d 149, 614 N.E.2d 712 (1993).

47. The Kleeman case is treated in the lead note of New York State Law Digest No. 402. A concern of lawyers after Kleeman is just how far this liability goes. If a presumably independent process server is the attorney's agent for the purpose of imposing a respondeat superior liability on the attorney, are others hired by the lawyer also to fit that mold, such as an expert witness? Is the attorney responsible for the expert's actions? Ituarte v. Kolbrener, N.Y. Law Journal, Dec. 9, 1993, p.27, col.4–5 (Sup.Ct., Nassau County, McCaffrey, J.), treated in SPR 12:4, says no.

48. These are the so-called "substituted service" statutes, treated at greater length in §§ 72 and 74 below.

the defendant's answering time. For purposes of satisfying the 120–day period of CPLR 306–b, only the service itself—both steps (paragraph 2 of CPLR 308 requires a delivery plus a mailing, paragraph 4, an affixing and a mailing) need take place within the 120–day period. The filing of the proof of service for which these CPLR 308 paragraphs call can take place after its expiration.

§ 64. Amendment of the Summons

The court may at any time "allow any summons . . . to be amended, if a substantial right" of the defendant is not violated.[1] Insubstantial defects are mere irregularities and are thus subject to this kind of amendment, but if there is a violation of a substantial right, the defect is jurisdictional and an amendment is precluded. The courts are not of one mind about where to draw the line, however, which suggests that the drafting of the summons—or the filling out of a printed form if one is used—is another place that errors should be kept out of. The omission from the summons of the court and county, for example, was held to be a jurisdictional defect in Tamburo v. P & C Food Markets, Inc.,[2] while a similar defect in Tobia v. Town of Rockland[3] was held, we think correctly, to be a mere correctable irregularity. *Tobia* cited the fact that even before the service the parties were notified of the omission, but that distinction hardly seems enough to dictate the difference between salvation and dismissal.

A mere defect in naming a defendant who has been duly served and who knows from all of the papers served that he is the intended defendant is a mere amendable irregularity. Where, for example, the proper defendant was served but was designated as Emma Stockton instead of the correct Mary Stockton, a name

change by amendment was allowed. The action was for mortgage foreclosure; the complaint was served with the summons (always helpful because it identifies the claim for the defendant); and the defendant was not misled.[4]

The so-called idem sonans cases, in which there are only minor spelling defects, such as Rus–Kap for Russ–Kap or Schutz for Schultz, always present mere amendable irregularities as long as the right person has been served.[5]

It has been acknowledged that "[n]o rule or measure has ever been devised by which we may determine in every case, with definite certainty, whether a defect is jurisdictional or is a mere irregularity,"[6] for which reason many of the cases in this area seem irreconcilable. The rule of prejudice is as close to a rule of thumb as we have, even though there continues to be some judicial disagreement on what is and what is not prejudicial.

What about the "d/b/a" cases, in which a corporation or individual "doing business as" something or other is sued in its doing-business name instead of its technically correct name? Commenting on how little there is about that in the cases, the court in Victor Auto Parts, Inc. v. Cuva[7] sustained a "d/b/a" action even at the post-judgment stage. It is of course risky at best for a plaintiff to let things go that far; the proper name should be substituted at the plaintiff's earliest opportunity. And a required showing in any event is that service was made on the proper person whatever the name used in the papers.

When a claim is brought in a court of limited jurisdiction in an amount beyond its monetary limit, the summons can ordinarily be amended to reduce the sum demanded to bring it under the court's ceiling, a matter taken up

§ 64

1. CPLR 305(c).

2. 36 A.D.2d 1017, 321 N.Y.S.2d 487 (4th Dep't 1971).

3. 106 A.D.2d 827, 484 N.Y.S.2d 226 (3d Dep't 1984).

4. Stuyvesant v. Weil, 167 N.Y. 421, 60 N.E. 738 (1901).

5. Russ–Kap, Inc. v. Connolly, 197 Misc. 464, 95 N.Y.S.2d 887 (Sup.Ct., Nassau County, 1950).

6. Valz v. Sheepshead Bay Bungalow Corp., 249 N.Y. 122, 134, 163 N.E. 124, 128 (1928).

7. 148 Misc.2d 349, 560 N.Y.S.2d 269 (Sup.Ct., Monroe County, 1990). The court retained intact an income execution and even made it operative on past as well as future payments. (This is more frequently an issue met in Small Claims procedure—see §§ 1813 and 1814 in the New York City Civil and in the Uniform District, City, and Justice court acts—with which the Victor result is consistent.)

in an earlier chapter.[8] In that instance it may technically be the complaint rather than the summons that is being amended, the "complaint" quite often taking the form of just a sentence or two (called an "indorsement") written on the face of the summons.[9]

Note that while a pleading can sometimes be amended by a party as of right, without judicial permission,[10] the amendment of a summons requires a court order.

§ 65. Amending Summons to Change Parties; Supplemental Summons

When the plaintiff draws the initial summons, she can name any defendants she wants to and effect service on them all to make them parties. Joining additional parties afterwards is more involved. Until 1996, the rule was that the plaintiff could not add more parties without court leave, even if all existing parties were willing to stipulate to it.

That changed with a 1996 amendment of both CPLR 305(a) and 1003. If the plaintiff acts no later than the 20th day after the defendant's service of the answer, the plaintiff may add additional parties without leave,[1] and does so by filing with the clerk a supplemental summons along with the complaint that the new defendant is required to answer, and then serving both on the new party.[2] While the cited provisions don't say so, it is a good idea to serve copies of the supplemental summons on all existing parties who have appeared so as to assure that all are aware of the new joinder.[3] It is also a good idea for the plaintiff to see to it that the supplemental summons and amended complaint are served on the new party within 120 days after their filing, just as required with respect to initially joined defendants.[4]

The amendments also allow the addition of new parties if all existing parties who have appeared so stipulate. In the absence of stipulation, and if the time for the additional joinder as of right has expired, the plaintiff must get court leave for the joinder.

It is important to keep in mind that these amendments were not drawn with the statute of limitations in mind.[5] How the statute of limitations fares in joinder cases therefore remains unchanged by the amendments. This gets all embroiled in the so-called "relation-back" doctrine, in which, if the original statute of limitations has already expired when a new party is joined, it may still be possible to preserve the claim against the new party if the claim can be deemed to "relate back" to the time of the interposition of the original claim.

The relation back doctrine that applies in amendment cases is treated in the statute of limitations chapter.[6] Amendment of the complaint on the one hand and the additional joinder of a party on the other are really separate subjects, but they sometimes overlap, and one of the overlaps is in the delicate area of the statute of limitations. When the statute of limitations has expired as against the party whom the plaintiff now wants to add, a supplemental summons, even if allowed, is likely to be too late. The 1996 amendments may facilitate the joinder, but don't guarantee its timeliness.

Suppose, however, that the problem is just some kind of misdescription of the defendant, rather than a matter of adding an entirely new defendant. In that situation, the plaintiff may be able to convince the court to allow a mere "change of title", redesignating the defendant as named to the defendant as it should have

---

8. See § 23 above.

9. See § 902(a)(1) in the New York City Civil Court Act and in the Uniform District, City, and Justice court acts, McKinney's Vol. 29A, Parts 2 and 3.

10. CPLR 3025(a).

§ 65

1. CPLR 1003. If there are multiple defendants, it has been held that the 20 days for joining an additional party run from the service of the last answer to come in. Dynaire Corp. v. Germano, N.Y. Law Journal, Aug. 1, 1996, p.22, col.1 (Sup.Ct., N.Y. County; Friedman, J.).

2. CPLR 305(a).

3. See CPLR 2103(e).

4. See § 63 above.

5. Statute of limitations and other issues in conjunction with joining additional parties under the 1996 amendments are explored in more detail in the lead note in SPR 43.

6. See § 49.

been named. This is done by an amendment, but it can be done only if the court is persuaded that the error is one of mere misdescription, thus negating prejudice.

Two things must be shown for an amendment of this kind. First, it must be clear from all the papers served (such as the complaint if it accompanied the summons) that the defendant now sought to be added (or "redesignated") should have known that it was the intended defendant. Second, it must be shown that the summons was served on a person authorized by law to be served in behalf of the intended defendant. That's what happened, for example, in a case in which the plaintiff sought to sue the Pierce Brake Service Center, Inc. but named it as Pierce Muffler Shops. The latter was in fact a different corporation, but the same personnel controlled both and service was made on X, who was an officer of both and hence servable in behalf of either.[7] Because of the nature of the claim sued on, moreover, the papers made clear which defendant was intended. An amendment was allowed.[8] The effect of an amendment of this kind is to dispense with a supplemental summons and to allow the original moment of commencement against the misnamed defendant to be deemed the moment of commencement as against the redesignated defendant, thereby saving the plaintiff's claim from the limitations' barrier.

If no such amendment and relation back is permissible on the facts, the interposition of the claim against the newly joined party, through the filing or service—depending on which court the case is in[9]—will be deemed the key moment for a statute of limitations measure.

Sometimes the problem arises when the plaintiff has named the defendant as a corporation and it turns out to be a partnership, or vice versa. The same dual test applies. If the plaintiff designates the defendant as a corpora-

tion and has the summons served on X thinking X is a corporate officer (servable in the corporation's behalf), the plaintiff is in luck if, when it turns out that the defendant is a partnership, X turns out to be one of the partners (servable in the partnership's behalf).[10] That satisfies one of the requirements. The other is that the papers make clear who the intended defendant is. If both requirements are met, an amendment is allowed to redesignate the corporation as a partnership and limitations problems are avoided.[11] Conversely, where it is sought to redesignate a partnership as a corporation, the one presumably served as a partner had best turn out to be someone on the list of those who may be served in behalf of the corporation.[12] If the person served is not on the list, the amendment is precluded.[13]

If a motion is made to add an additional party, those who are already parties need only be given notice of the motion through the ordinary mail channels applicable to motions made within actions.[14] This applies even when the plaintiff seeks to add the new person as an additional plaintiff instead of as a defendant. Where P sued and served X and Y, for example, and then sought to add A as an additional plaintiff, defendants X and Y were not entitled to be served with the summons anew notwithstanding that the new plaintiff was now adding its claim.[15] As a rule, it is only the party to be added who must be served with the supplemental summons, and even service on that party is dispensed with if he consents to jurisdiction, as the new plaintiff did in the example.

C. THE METHODS OF SERVICE

Table of Sections

7. CPLR 311(a)(1).

8. Luce v. Pierce Muffler Shops, 51 Misc.2d 256, 272 N.Y.S.2d 845 (Sup.Ct., Onondaga County, 1966), aff'd 28 A.D.2d 826, 282 N.Y.S.2d 724 (4th Dep't 1967).

9. See § 45 above.

10. CPLR 310.

11. De Witt v. Abraham Bros. Horse & Mule Co., 170 A.D. 610, 156 N.Y.S. 658 (1st Dep't 1915).

12. CPLR 311(a)(1).

13. See Grant v. Miles Shoes, 205 Misc. 554, 127 N.Y.S.2d 743 (Sup.Ct., Schenectady County, 1954).

14. CPLR 2103(b).

15. Patrician Plastic Corp. v. Bernadel Realty Corp., 25 N.Y.2d 599, 307 N.Y.S.2d 868, 256 N.E.2d 180 (1970).

§ 66. Personal Delivery of Summons under CPLR 308(1)

CPLR 308 dictates the mechanics of service. It consists of five subdivisions. The first is the age-old method of personal delivery of the summons to the defendant within the state.[1] The second is known as "deliver and mail" and is treated later.[2] Either of these first two can be used at the outset. No effort need be made at personal delivery under CPLR 308(1) prior to use of the deliver-and-mail method of CPLR 308(2). (Nor need CPLR 308 be resorted to at all in first instance. Personal service by mail is available as an alternative under CPLR 312–a treated below.[3])

We concentrate here on what satisfies as personal delivery under 308(1).

All the process server has to do is tender the summons to the defendant. The summons need not be and in fact should not be in any container or envelope. Any effort to conceal the fact that it is a summons will vitiate service. In one case, for example, a husband saw his wife off on a sea trip and bid her bon voyage by having his associate give her a present for her mother and an instruction not to open it until she finished her journey. She followed his instructions and found the gift to be a summons in a divorce action. When she finally worked her way back to New York she easily got the service and all subsequent proceedings vacated.[4]

It is even helpful to have the summons exposed to view when tendered. The tender can be in silence, although it is customary to announce that it is a summons. The normal reaction of anyone to whom a paper is tendered, except in certain parts of Manhattan, is to extend a hand to receive it. But if the defendant does not do that, the process server need only leave the summons on a table or other item nearby, or on the floor in front of the defendant (or behind him as he walks away).

In one case the defendant deliberately ran off to his car, locked all the windows and sat staring straight ahead as the process server showed the summons through a window. Off drove the car with the summons stuck in the space between door and window. Service was sustained.[5]

Once confronted, a defendant had best accept the service. Indeed, lawyers should ordinarily advise clients expecting suit to accept service of a summons. If personal delivery is refused, other methods will be resorted to, equally valid but less likely to give notice, and the defendant may even end up paying, by way of disbursements if the plaintiff wins, whatever additional costs are incurred for such service. The only exception in which avoidance may perhaps bring tactical advantage is where the defendant stands a chance of having the statute of limitations expire—an unlikely prospect with the alternatives available to a diligent plaintiff today.

The act of service should be unambiguous. If there is reasonable basis for the defendant to doubt that service of process was intended as such, it will be set aside. Where the defendant was an elderly woman in a nursing home, for example, and the process server, after asking her about her son's whereabouts, left the sum-

---

§ 66

1. CPLR 308 also dictates the methods of out-of-state service when CPLR 313 authorizes it, a point we return to when CPLR 313 is met later. See § 100 below.

2. See § 72 below.

3. See § 76A below.

4. Bulkley v. Bulkley, 6 Abb.Pr. 307 (Sup.Ct., 7th Dist., 1858).

5. Levine v. National Transp. Co., 204 Misc. 202, 125 N.Y.S.2d 679 (Sup.Ct., Queens County), aff'd 282 A.D. 720, 122 N.Y.S.2d 901 (2d Dep't 1953).

mons on a nightstand in an envelope marked with the son's name, the court held that the act of service was not unconditional and clear and the service was set aside.[6]

The so-called "redelivery" scenario is important. Redelivery refers to the situation in which the process server serves not the right person, but someone else who immediately or later the same day or the next day (in any event close in time) gives it to the right person. A number of older cases sustained this kind of service on the theory that the intermediary, retained or not by the plaintiff, in effect acted as the process server, but a more stringent requirement was imposed by the Court of Appeals in 1968 in McDonald v. Ames Supply Co.[7]

The defendant in McDonald was a corporation and the server went to the building in which the corporation had its office and gave the summons to a receptionist who later that same day gave it to the appropriate corporate official. The server had apparently made no effort to see if he could serve the right person or even to determine who that person was. He just served the receptionist who, as it turned out, was not even employed by the corporation. The court felt that to sustain the service would encourage carelessness on the part of process servers. To avoid that, it pronounced the "due diligence" test: only if it is demonstrated that a diligent effort was made to find and serve the right person will service on the intermediary (with his prompt redelivery to the right person) be allowed. Subsequent cases have looked for diligence on a sui generis basis and have deemed the McDonald standard satisfied when they found it. Earlier cases should survive only if on their facts they meet that standard.

In McDonald, the person served was not an employee of the corporation. When the person

was, and represented that she was authorized to accept process, the service was upheld.[8]

The reader should take note of yet another point tacitly made in McDonald and like cases. The subject treated here is personal delivery under paragraph one of CPLR 308, and CPLR 308 is captioned "personal service upon a natural person". Where do corporations, which are governed by CPLR 311(a)(1), fit in? Or, for that matter, how do we fit in any other category of defendant covered in some provision other than CPLR 308, such as a partner governed by CPLR 310? The answer is that those other provisions are at root only lists of persons on whom the summons may be served in behalf of defendants of various categories. The method of "delivering" the summons to one of the listed persons, however, is governed as a practical matter by CPLR 308(1) and its caselaw. CPLR 311, moreover, which lists servable corporate agents, also speaks of "delivering" the summons, and for that reason involves the same principles. McDonald actually construed and applied CPLR 311(1), but the case is an equally influential lesson on CPLR 308(1).[9]

Members of the defendant's family who answer the door when the process server knocks are often cast in a redeliverer's role. Earlier caselaw held that when the defendant from a few feet away sees the process server (and vice versa) and hears him announce that he has a summons, delivery of the summons to the door answerer with subsequent redelivery by that person to the defendant is satisfactory,[10] but that if server and defendant do not see each other, it is not.[11] These cases have lost importance in view of the adoption of CPLR 308(2), in which the delivery of the summons to the door answerer (whatever that person thereafter does with it) is good service on the defendant provided that it is followed by the second

6. In re Bonesteel, 16 A.D.2d 324, 228 N.Y.S.2d 301 (3d Dep't 1962).

7. 22 N.Y.2d 111, 291 N.Y.S.2d 328, 238 N.E.2d 726.

8. Fashion Page, Ltd. v. Zurich Ins. Co., 50 N.Y.2d 265, 428 N.Y.S.2d 890, 406 N.E.2d 747 (1980). The person served was the secretary of a corporate officer.

9. Some of the other provisions, such as CPLR 309 (infants and incompetents) and 310 (partnerships), do not

even offer an instruction as specific as "delivering" the summons; they just speak of "serving" it and tacitly leave to CPLR 308(1) and its caselaw all the mechanics.

10. Buscher v. Ehrich, 12 A.D.2d 887, 209 N.Y.S.2d 941 (4th Dep't 1961).

11. Ives v. Darling, 210 A.D. 521, 206 N.Y.S. 493 (3d Dep't 1924).

step of mailing provided for in that statute.[12] CPLR 308(1) becomes academic in such a case.

A major case on CPLR 308(2), in fact, Bossuk v. Steinberg,[13] treated in § 72, below, should have impact on 308(1) as well. One part of 308(2)'s two-part service method is a delivery of the summons to a person of suitable age at the defendant's premises. *Bossuk* holds that when that person won't open the door to receive it, leaving the summons outside the door is an adequate delivery. That should apply under CPLR 308(1), too, when it is the defendant himself standing behind the door and refusing to open it. As long as it is established that the person is in fact the defendant, the logic of *Bossuk* should apply to CPLR 308(1) and sustain as an adequate personal delivery a service made by leaving the summons outside the door, announcing the fact, and leaving.

Bossuk has apparently proved helpful in serving apartment house defendants. In Spector v. Berman,[14] for example, the server went to the apartment house and rang the defendant's downstairs doorbell. The defendant answered on the intercom and he and the server identified themselves, but the defendant would not come down to meet the server or allow him into the building to go upstairs to the apartment. So the server said he was putting the summons into the mail slot, and did. The service was upheld. In *Bossuk*, the server and deliveree had been separated by only a door; in *Spector*, they were separated by two doors and a few flights of stairs. A distinction without a difference, held the *Spector* panel. "The defendant did not acquire an immunity from the *Bossuk* principle simply because there were two doors and some steps involved."

When it is not clear that the person served is the defendant himself, however, it is obvious

that the precaution of mailing an additional copy of the summons, as CPLR 308(2) requires, and thereby satisfying that provision, can't hurt. The additional step of mailing, in other words, takes the importance out of whether the deliveree is the defendant or just some person found at his home or office. Without the mailing, paragraph 1 is relied on, and paragraph 1 is just not safe to depend on in these "redelivery" cases, even when the deliveree is (e.g.) the defendant's son and even though the son promptly gives the papers to his father.[15] (The personal service by mail provision of CPLR 312–a, already mentioned, in which mail by itself suffices, may make some of these points about CPLR 308 academic.[16])

In almost all of these cases in which service is attacked, the attack takes the form of a prompt motion to dismiss for lack of jurisdiction.[17] The plaintiff in answering such a motion is often tempted to argue (and the reader to conclude) that the service must have been good or the defendant would not have had sufficient notice to be in court attacking it. The argument doesn't work. It would "negate the statutory procedure for setting aside a defectively served summons",[18] which is ordinarily a prompt motion to dismiss, and would perhaps encourage defendants to suffer defaults and instead move later, after the lapse of a respectable period, to vacate the judgment based on the service defect. That postpones disposition of the jurisdictional question, however, which is often detrimental to both sides.

§ 67. Enticement into Jurisdiction

The use of false pretenses to entice a defendant from beyond the court's territorial jurisdiction to within it, so as to serve him with

---

12. CPLR 308(2) is treated in § 72, below.

13. 58 N.Y.2d 916, 460 N.Y.S.2d 509, 447 N.E.2d 56 (1983).

14. 119 A.D.2d 565, 500 N.Y.S.2d 735 (2d Dep't 1986).

15. See Macchia v. Russo, 67 N.Y.2d 592, 505 N.Y.S.2d 591, 496 N.E.2d 680 (1986).

16. See § 76A below.

17. CPLR 3211(a)(8), (e). An alternative is to include the objection as a defense in the answer, a ploy the defendant used to indulge regularly in the hope of post-

poning an adjudication of the issue until he could be sure that, should the defense be upheld at some later point, the plaintiff would by then be clearly out of time. A 1996 amendment of CPLR 3211(e) takes much of the profit out of that by requiring a defendant who pleads the objection of improper service as a defense to move for judgment on the defense within 60 days, or waive it. See § 274, below, and SPR 50:3.

18. McDonald v. Ames Supply Co., note 7, above, 22 N.Y.2d at 115, 291 N.Y.S.2d at 331, 238 N.E.2d at 728.

process, is ground for upsetting the service.[1] But a phony representation that prompts only a short move by the defendant from one place to another within the state is not. So held Gumperz v. Hofmann,[2] where the process server just telephoned defendant's hotel room from the lobby and asked him to come down to receive a letter. Down came the defendant and was served with process instead, hardly an inconvenience worth taking judicial notice of.

The lawyer should still be wary, however, of substantially inconveniencing a defendant even if the false pretext doesn't bring about a crossing of jurisdictional lines. It is not hard to imagine the court vitiating service if the defendant is enticed from Buffalo to Brooklyn, for example—a trip of several hundred miles—just to make it easier to serve him in a supreme court action, even though the service could have been made with equal effect in Buffalo. In the age of longarm jurisdiction, moreover, when CPLR 313 often permits service to be made anywhere in the world, an enticement from Hawaii (or Tibet) to New York might not, territorially speaking, make a shred of jurisdictional difference, but it is not the kind of thing the courts would want to encourage. Setting aside service in such a case may be the only lawful deterrent, lest the outraged defendant gratify himself with a little violence.

A sincere invitation to a would-be defendant to come into the state for settlement talks will not be deemed an enticement if the talks break down and service is made at that time,[3] but cases like that are all sui generis and require difficult probing into subjective intentions. A plaintiff who would preserve his action should steer clear of any misconstruable invitations, and defendants can be notorious misconstruers.

§ 68. Immunity from Service

We have briefly met the doctrine of sovereign immunity, which New York has waived to the extent of allowing itself to be sued in the court of claims.[1] Foreign sovereigns also get immunity from New York process in their governmental but not necessarily other capacities. In tort actions, for example, the general rule is that the immunity does not apply if the occurrence causing the damage was incidental to a "proprietary", as opposed to a "governmental", function. Thus, where Missouri set up a commission to arrange for the state's participation in a fair, the purpose was primarily to amuse visitors and there was no immunity.[2] Similarly, when one of the cars involved in a New York accident was on the business of South Carolina, the state was held subject to New York jurisdiction on a tort claim arising out of the accident.[3]

Diplomatic immunity is an offspring of sovereign immunity. It protects individuals representing foreign sovereigns. But while it protects ambassadors and their staffs, even in private, non-governmental litigation,[4] it has been held inapplicable to private suits against foreign consuls, consular officials being considered commercial rather than diplomatic representatives of their governments.[5] Doubts about diplomatic or consular status are often resolved by reference to documents secured by a party from the U.S. Department of State.[6] Even if mere consular status is shown, the New York courts may avoid decision of the immunity question today on the ground of

§ 67

1. Garabettian v. Garabettian, 206 A.D. 502, 201 N.Y.S. 548 (1st Dep't 1923).

2. 245 A.D. 622, 283 N.Y.S. 823 (1st Dep't 1935), aff'd 271 N.Y. 544, 2 N.E.2d 687 (1936).

3. See, e.g., Waljohn Waterstop, Inc. v. Webster, 37 Misc.2d 96, 232 N.Y.S.2d 665 (Sup.Ct., Kings County, 1962).

§ 68

1. See § 17 above.

2. Tiernan v. Missouri N. Y. World's Fair Comm'n, 48 Misc.2d 376, 264 N.Y.S.2d 834 (Sup.Ct., N.Y.County,

1965). Analogously, the immunity of foreign nations is governed by federal statutes—applicable in federal and state courts alike—whose main aim is to immunize governmental but not commercial activity. See 28 U.S.C.A. §§ 1604–1607.

3. Morrison v. Budget Rent A Car Systems, Inc., 230 A.D.2d 253, 657 N.Y.S.2d 721 (2d Dep't 1997), treated in the lead note in SPR 57.

4. See Carrera v. Carrera, 174 F.2d 496 (D.C.Cir.1949).

5. Id.; see also Ohio ex rel. Popovici v. Agler, 280 U.S. 379, 50 S.Ct. 154, 74 L.Ed. 489 (1930).

6. See French v. Banco Nacional de Cuba, 23 N.Y.2d 46, 295 N.Y.S.2d 433, 242 N.E.2d 704 (1968).

exclusive federal jurisdiction. A federal statute provides that "all civil actions and proceedings against . . . consuls or vice-consuls" are under the exclusive jurisdiction of the U.S. district courts.[7]

The defense of sovereign immunity is waivable. It was held to be waived, for example, when the defendant—the instrumentality of a foreign government—answered, counterclaimed, and participated in several years of litigation maneuvering before finally seeking to assert the immunity defense.[8]

An entirely separate immunity doctrine protects nondomiciliaries of New York from civil process while they are voluntarily in the state to participate in legal proceedings of any kind, whether as parties or as mere witnesses. To win this immunity the participation must be voluntary; it will not apply to one here under the compulsion of a subpoena or an arrest.[9] But if D voluntarily entered the state for judicial proceedings in first instance, and was then served with a subpoena or then gave bail, so that his later return might be said to be under compulsion, the fact that his original appearance was voluntary is the key factor and the immunity therefore applies to his subsequent appearance.[10]

New York has been generous with the doctrine. The original proceeding for which D voluntarily comes into the state can be civil or criminal, and in federal or state court. The doctrine applies to participation in pretrial proceedings[11] and even to appellate argument,[12] where the client's presence is hardly necessary. It does not apply to a nonresident lawyer who is here for the proceeding, however, because the lawyer is here in pursuit of his business and not just to facilitate New York litigation.[13] But it does apply to a nonresident plaintiff here to take part in his own action.[14] In fact, New York allows the immunity not only in judicial proceedings, but in arbitral, legislative, and administrative hearings as well.[15]

The immunity applies to any civil action brought against the voluntary participant whether or not the action is related to the matter for which he is in the state. But if it is a related matter, there is likely to be a basis for subjecting that person to jurisdiction through service outside New York, and that may dissolve the immunity because of an important exception that has evolved:

Whenever it is shown that the action sought to be commenced against the visitor is one in which full personam jurisdiction could be obtained over him without service in New York, such as where CPLR 302 and 313 authorize service outside New York or a designation of a state agent for service is in effect in the case,[16] the purpose of the immunity falls and with it falls the immunity itself.[17]

To take advantage of the immunity the person should show that she came to New York solely for the proceeding. The person who has a dual purpose will probably lose the immunity. The immunity covers a reasonable period before the proceeding, in order to prepare for it, and a reasonable period afterwards for return home.[18] The question of reasonableness naturally depends on the facts of each case.

7. 28 U.S.C.A. § 1351.

8. Aboujdid v. Singapore Airlines, Ltd., 67 N.Y.2d 450, 503 N.Y.S.2d 555, 494 N.E.2d 1055 (1986).

9. See Glendon v. Glendon, 45 Misc.2d 855, 258 N.Y.S.2d 20 (Sup.Ct., Kings County, 1964), mod'd 24 A.D.2d 492, 261 N.Y.S.2d 443 (2d Dep't 1965).

10. Thermoid Co. v. Fabel, 4 N.Y.2d 494, 176 N.Y.S.2d 331, 151 N.E.2d 883 (1958).

11. New England Industries v. Margiotti, 270 A.D. 488, 60 N.Y.S.2d 430 (1st Dep't), aff'd 296 N.Y. 722, 70 N.E.2d 540 (1946).

12. Chase Nat'l Bank v. Turner, 269 N.Y. 397, 199 N.E. 636 (1936).

13. Kutner v. Hodnett, 59 Misc. 21, 109 N.Y.S. 1068 (Sup.Ct., N.Y.County, 1908).

14. Petrova v. Roberts, 245 N.Y. 518, 157 N.E. 841 (1927). The way to proceed against such a plaintiff so as to make him a defendant in a separate action is to use CPLR 303 and serve his attorney. See § 96 below.

15. Thorp v. Adams, 11 N.Y.S. 479 (Sup.Ct., 1st Dep't, 1890); Stern v. Worth, 167 Misc. 605, 4 N.Y.S.2d 392 (N.Y.City Ct.1938).

16. See Chauvin v. Dayon, 14 A.D.2d 146, 217 N.Y.S.2d 795 (3d Dep't 1961).

17. Merigone v. Seaboard Capital Corp., 85 Misc.2d 965, 381 N.Y.S.2d 749 (Sup.Ct., Nassau County, 1976).

18. See Robinson v. Stichman, 18 A.D.2d 449, 240 N.Y.S.2d 82 (1st Dep't 1963).

This immunity, too, is waivable, and is waived like any objection to personal jurisdiction: by not raising it either in a motion to dismiss or in the answer.[19]

Another point relevant to immunity is that presence within a federal military installation in New York will not insulate the defendant from New York jurisdiction.[20]

Finally, under the broad "immunity" caption, a word should be said about whether there is any rule against serving a defendant in the courthouse. Although the courts frown on such endeavors, wary of a breach of the peace, such service has been sustained when a breach was not threatened.[21] There have apparently been a growing number of courthouse service attempts, often in connection with a proceeding trying to quash a prior attempt at service. The issue became important enough in one court to generate the consolidation of five such endeavors, producing a consolidated opinion. In each of the five cases, the original service was by other than personal delivery and was contested, thus necessitating a second service. In three of them the second service was "in the courtroom or its vicinity" and in another the service was made "while the respondent was actually testifying". The court criticized but sustained the service.[22]

§ 69. Whom to Serve in Behalf of Various Defendants

For various categories of defendants there are lists of persons who may be served in the defendant's behalf. It will be helpful to review some of these provisions. (Corporations are separately treated in the next section.)

a. Infants. An infant is anyone who has not yet reached the age of 18.[1] Suit against an infant requires no prior court leave, but service has to be made on someone listed in CPLR 309(a). Various persons are listed: a parent or guardian having legal custody (service on the parent is the most common method) or, if the infant is married and living with a spouse who is of age, on the spouse. If no such person is in the state, service may be made on any adult with whom the infant resides or on the infant's employer. The infant herself must also be served if she is 14 or over, which means two services in that case. If two are necessary and only one is made, the defect is jurisdictional,[2] and it will not do to show that the infant hired an attorney who appeared for her. Such an appearance cannot cure the jurisdictional defect for the reason that an infant cannot hire her own attorney; someone authorized to appear for the infant must do the hiring.[3]

If a basis for extraterritorial service exists in the case, state lines disappear under CPLR 313 and either or both of the persons on whom service has to be made may be served outside New York.[4] Absent such basis, the unavailability in New York of one of the two people required to be served vitiates jurisdiction.[5] The question of who may be served in an action against an infant should not be confused with who may appear for the infant, which is the subject of Article 12 of the CPLR and is treated later.[6] The service by mail method of CPLR 312–a[7] is not available against an infant.

---

19. CPLR 3211(e).

20. See Reybold v. Reybold, 45 A.D.2d 263, 357 N.Y.S.2d 231 (4th Dep't 1974).

21. See Baumgartner v. Baumgartner, 273 A.D. 411, 77 N.Y.S.2d 668 (1st Dep't 1948).

22. Department of Housing Preservation & Development v. Koenigsberg, 133 Misc.2d 893, 509 N.Y.S.2d 270 (N.Y.C. Civ. Ct., 1986). The procedure entailed the service of an order to show cause and a petition, but the holding is relevant to ordinary summons service, too.

§ 69

1. CPLR 105. The age of majority in New York was reduced in 1974 from 21 to 18.

2. Randall v. Randall, 12 Misc.2d 468, 172 N.Y.S.2d 985 (Sup.Ct., Bronx County, 1958). If the nonresident

motorist statute, Veh. & Traf.L. § 253, is used against the infant, which is permissible, it has been held that its methods apply to the exclusion of CPLR 309(a), thus dispensing with the dual service on which the latter insists. Nelson v. Fraboni, 38 A.D.2d 633, 326 N.Y.S.2d 934 (3d Dep't 1971).

3. See § 193 below.

4. See Fox v. Gower, 48 Misc.2d 1043, 266 N.Y.S.2d 658 (Sup.Ct., Monroe County, 1966).

5. See Higgins v. Blauvelt, 49 Misc.2d 327, 267 N.Y.S.2d 461 (Sup.Ct., N.Y.County, 1966).

6. See § 193 below.

7. See § 76A below.

b. Incompetents and Conservatees: "Incapacitated Persons". CPLR references to such terms as "conservator", "conservatee", "committee", and "incompetent", still contained in CPLR 309(b) and 309(c) and yet other CPLR provisions, are archaic. In 1993, a new Article 81 of the Mental Hygiene Law took effect. Recognizing varying kinds and degrees of dependency, it abolishes the older language and substitutes for all of it the term "incapacitated person" for the dependent person and "guardian" for the person appointed to look after the dependent person's needs. It also instructs that the older terms be deemed to include the new ones.[8] Although the CPLR continues the older terminology in several places, we will try to use the newer language in this text. Doing so will incidentally offer the convenience of a single set of terms—"incapacitated person" and "guardian"—to describe relationships that had several different descriptions prior to the enactment of Article 81 of the Mental Hygiene Law. All prior proceedings taken under the old terminology are in any event preserved until set aside or modified by a judge under the new law.[9]

If the defendant is an incapacitated person for whom a guardian has been appointed, CPLR 309(b) and 309(c) provide that service must be made on the guardian as well as on the incapacitated person. The court can by order dispense with service on the incapacitated person. The plaintiff would apply for such an order when, for example, the defendant is confined or dangerous. Unless an order of dispensation is secured, the plaintiff proceeds at his peril by failing to have the incapacitated person served. Incapacitated persons and infants are wards of the court and procedural defects innocent and disregardable in other contexts can become decisive and jurisdictional when a ward is concerned. In one especially harsh case in which the guardian was served but the incapacitated person was not (and no

order dispensing with service had been sought), the jurisdictional defect resulted in a dismissal of a mortgage foreclosure action too late for a new one, with the effect of forfeiting a mortgage loan.[10]

The motion for the order dispensing with service on the incapacitated person is presumably ex parte. If the court in a given case wants someone notified of the motion (the incapacitated person included), the court can reject the ex parte application, treat it as an order to show cause—which enables the court to prescribe the details of the motion procedure[11]—and dispose of it accordingly. As wards of the court, incapacitated persons are entitled to its extra protective powers.

If the defendant has not been declared an incapacitated person but just seems that way to the plaintiff, the plaintiff starts the action in the usual way be merely serving the defendant. Jurisdiction is thereby secured and whatever other protection is necessary for the defendant is provided by Article 12, dealing with appearances.[12] If no attorney appears for the defendant, the plaintiff can call to the court's attention any debility he perceives in the defendant and let the court decide whether it is necessary to appoint someone to protect the defendant's interests.[13]

As with an infant, the mail service provision of CPLR 312–a[14] is inapplicable to an incapacitated person.

c. Partnerships. In New York, a partnership can be a plaintiff or a defendant in its own name without all the partners being named.[15] When the partnership is the defendant it should be named as such; then, to get jurisdiction of it, service need only be made on one of the general partners.[16] Service should not be made on a limited partner, who is neither a necessary nor even a proper party to an action involving a limited partnership, un-

---

8.   See § 194 below.

9.   See L.1992, c.698, § 4.

10.   Sinley v. Estco, Inc., 25 Misc.2d 172, 200 N.Y.S.2d 939 (Sup.Ct., Nassau County, 1960). Ward or not, one must question the need for so rigid an approach when the service omission is so innocent.

11.   See § 248 below.

12.   See § 194 below.

13.   CPLR 1201, 1202.

14.   See § 76A below.

15.   CPLR 1025.

16.   CPLR 310(a).

less the action specifically involves the rights of limited partners as such.[17] Some caselaw indicates otherwise, upholding service on a limited partner,[18] but until the point is definitively resolved a plaintiff does best to seek out a general partner for service.

Naming the partnership and serving any general partner enables the plaintiff to secure a judgment good against assets held by the partnership. If the plaintiff would have the judgment good against the personal assets of any individual partner, he must see to it that that partner is also named in the caption and is individually served. Otherwise, the words "not summoned" are written next to the names of unsummoned partners when the judgment is docketed,[19] which means that their individual property is unavailable to satisfy the judgment. Where a person had a malpractice claim against her lawyers, for example, who were operating as a professional service corporation (P.C.), and interposed the claim only against the P.C. but not against any individual attorney, the judgment was held inoperable against the individuals.[20] While there may be ways to cure the omission with subsequent proceedings, such as a separate action to charge the individuals with that part of the judgment that could not be satisfied out of partnership assets,[21] there are problems with that course of action[22] that are avoided by initially naming and securing jurisdiction over the individual partners whose property is, or merely may be, sought for application to a judgment.[23]

Unlike the situation that obtains with a corporation, each partner, or in any event

each general partner, carries the partnership about for jurisdictional purposes, so that personal delivery of the summons in New York to a general partner by itself gives jurisdiction of the partnership without regard to the partnership's whereabouts or the nature of the claim.[24] Lest this notion suggest too broad an exercise of jurisdiction, the lawyer should remember the availability of the forum non conveniens doctrine,[25] which precludes the entertainment of actions having no business imposing on the New York courts.

The mechanics of serving a partnership has been the subject of some dispute. While an individual being sued and served as such is subject to the substituted service methods of paragraphs 2 and 4 of CPLR 308, there was doubt about whether those methods could be used when the individual was a partner being served in behalf of the partnership. To address the matter, and presumably to make dependence on CPLR 308 unnecessary when serving a partner in the partnership behalf, subdivisions (b) through (e) were added to CPLR 310 in 1991. These contain their own prescriptions, but the First Department, reviewing them in Bell v. Bell, Kalnick et al.,[26] said they added nothing to the options that existed before the amendment (and continue to). In *Bell*, the court sustained service under CPLR 308(2)—deliver and mail[27]—on a receptionist at the office of an individually named partner, with mail the following day to that partner in an unmarked envelope. (A mere receptionist suffices for service under CPLR 308(2) while only a "managing agent" would do under CPLR 310.[28])

---

17. See Partnership Law § 115.

18. See, e.g., Micheli Contracting Corp. v. Fairwood Associates, 73 A.D.2d 774, 423 N.Y.S.2d 533 (3d Dep't 1979), which does not cite Partnership Law § 115.

19. CPLR 5018(a).

20. See Somer & Wand, P.C. v. Rotondi, 219 A.D.2d 340, 642 N.Y.S.2d 937 (2d Dep't 1996).

21. See CPLR 1502.

22. One problem, for example, is that the earlier judgment is not res judicata in the subsequent action, thus requiring the relitigation of the issues, with the prospect of an inconsistent result. Procedural issues like these are by-products of the common law's indecision about the nature of the partners' substantive liabilities. See Werner,

Shared Liability: An Alternative to the Confusion of Joint, Several, and Joint and Several Obligations, 42 Alb. L. Rev. 1 (1977).

23. See the discussion of the Somer case in SPR 51:4.

24. Rait v. Jacobs Bros., 49 Misc.2d 903, 268 N.Y.S.2d 750 (Sup.Ct., Nassau County, 1966). There the general partner who was served resided in New York, but the result would apparently be the same if, although residing elsewhere, he was served in New York.

25. See § 28 above.

26. 246 A.D.2d 442, 668 N.Y.S.2d 177 (1998).

27. See § 72 below.

28. See the discussion of Bell in the lead note in SPR 71:1.

When corporation C is a partner in partnership X, which is in turn a partner in partnership Y, service on a corporate officer of C under CPLR 311(a)(1) (the corporate service statute[29]) constitutes service on both partnerships and satisfies CPLR 310.[30]

If the plaintiff is suing the partner individually and the partnership as well, both being named in the summons, and the named partner is served in both his own and the partnership's behalf, it has been held that there still need be only one copy served on the partner.[31] The same rule applies to a corporation being sued along with a corporate officer.[32] In an action against an infant, however, where the parent may be served for the infant, additional service must be made on the infant if the infant is 14 or over.[33] When an infant in that age range is being served pursuant to CPLR 308(2), and the parent is the person of suitable age to whom a delivery of the summons is being made in behalf of the infant under that provision, two summonses must be presented to the parent.[34] We see no logical way to distinguish these situations and would advise plaintiffs to use two summonses in all of them.[35]

d. *Associations.* The unincorporated association is amenable to jurisdiction under New York law without naming or serving all of its members, who may in some cases number in the thousands. Suit by or against the association may be brought in the name of its president or treasurer.[36] When the association is the defendant, naming and serving that official gives jurisdiction of the association. As with a partnership, such an officer is held to carry the association about with her, so that service on that officer while she is present in New York, whatever her mission and whatever the nature of the claim, gives jurisdiction of the association.[37] Were the conveniens doctrine[38] not available to insulate inappropriate cases from this loose jurisdictional concept, its use would present constitutional issues.

e. *Estates and Trusts.* Assuming jurisdictional basis, the question of whom to serve in an action against an estate or trust is merely a matter of identifying the real party in interest. In the case of the estate, the real party in interest is the personal representative (executor or administrator); in the case of an express trust, the trustee.[39] Such person is the proper defendant and is the one to be served. But unlike the association and partnership, these fiduciaries do not necessarily carry their estates and trusts with them. Thus, a foreign personal representative in New York on only personal business unrelated to the estate or trust is not amenable to jurisdiction in her fiduciary capacity merely because she is served in New York.[40]

f. *Foreign Nations and Agencies.* Service on a foreign nation or agency is governed not by New York but by federal law, applicable in federal and state courts alike. There is one set of service methods when the defendant is the foreign nation itself or one of its political subdivisions,[41] and a separate set when the defendant is an "agency or instrumentality" of the foreign nation.[42] The footnoted statutes address even such details as the time service is deemed made, the time in which to answer, and the requirements applicable to a default judgment;[43] counterpart New York provisions would of course have to defer to these federal

---

29. See § 70 below.

30. 885 W.E. Residents Corp. v. Coronet Props. Co., 220 A.D.2d 305, 632 N.Y.S.2d 556 (1st Dep't 1995).

31. Brown v. Sagamore Hotel, 184 A.D.2d 47, 590 N.Y.S.2d 934 (3d Dep't 1992).

32. See § 70 below.

33. CPLR 309(a).

34. See § 72 below.

35. See the discussion of this matter in the treatment of the Brown case in SPR 11:4.

36. CPLR 1025. A "labor organization" can be served via service on any of its major officers. See Gen.Assoc.L. § 13.

37. Gross v. Cross, 28 Misc.2d 375, 211 N.Y.S.2d 279 (Sup.Ct., N.Y.County, 1961).

38. See § 28 above.

39. CPLR 1004.

40. Cf. Doughney v. Fauset, 9 Misc.2d 759, 170 N.Y.S.2d 419 (Sup.Ct., N.Y.County, 1958).

41. 28 U.S.C.A. § 1608(a).

42. 28 U.S.C.A. § 1608(b).

43. Id., subdivisions (c), (d), & (e).

directions in any instance of conflict. All of this assumes that the defendant is amenable to jurisdiction, i.e., that some exception to what would otherwise be its sovereign immunity is applicable. That, too, is governed by federal law.[44]

§ 70. Service on a Corporation

Those who may be served in behalf of a corporation—domestic or foreign, no distinction is made—are listed in CPLR 311(a)(1). They are an officer, director, managing or general agent, cashier or assistant cashier, or "any other agent authorized by appointment or by law to receive service". By cashier is meant someone at a high level who has charge of the corporation's funds. The person who gives out shoes in a bowling alley doesn't qualify.[1]

Most frequently met in the caselaw is the question of who qualifies as a "managing or general agent". Those words are liberally construed and even include someone in charge of only a corporate branch office.[2] If there are a handful of employees at a corporate office, the person who appears to be in charge qualifies as a managing agent for service and needs no formal title indicating high position.[3] Someone holding himself out as "a person of responsibility" at the corporate office qualifies,[4] but a mere office boy, such as a stand-in for the usual freight agent at a railroad station, has been held not to qualify even though he forwards the summons promptly to the right person.[5] The test is not whether the summons was in fact forwarded, but whether the one served bears such a relationship to the corpo-

ration as to compel the inference that it will be.[6]

If the officer served, X, is also being sued individually—both the corporation and individual being named in the caption—a single service on X satisfies as commencement against both.[7] But when the service on X is made in behalf of the corporation and in behalf of A, another individual (corporate connected or not), such as where A works at the corporate office and delivery is being made to X as a person of suitable age and discretion at A's place of business under CPLR 308(2),[8] two copies of the summons must be served on X, one for each.[9]

When the defendant is a domestic corporation, or a licensed foreign one, it will have designated the secretary of state as its agent for service on any claim.[10] Service on the secretary in such an instance is always available as an alternative to service under the CPLR. The method of service in that case is governed by § 306(b) of the Business Corporation Law, which consists of delivering to the secretary or to his deputy or designee in Albany two copies of the summons. The secretary retains one for his files and sends the other by certified mail to the corporation at its office address as it appears in those files. The jurisdictional act is the delivery of the two copies to the secretary. The latter's failure to forward one to the corporation does not void the service.[11]

While service on a licensed corporation can be carried out pursuant to BCL 306, service on an unlicensed corporation is governed by BCL 307. The methods under the two statutes dif-

---

44. See 28 U.S.C.A. §§ 1605–1607.

§ 70

1. Oustecky v. Farmingdale Lanes, Inc., 41 Misc.2d 979, 246 N.Y.S.2d 859 (Sup.Ct., Nassau County, 1964).

2. Green v. Morningside Heights Hsg. Corp., 13 Misc.2d 124, 177 N.Y.S.2d 760 (Sup.Ct., N.Y.County), aff'd 7 A.D.2d 708, 180 N.Y.S.2d 104 (1st Dep't 1958).

3. See Municipal Mortgage Co. v. 461 Eighth Ave. Co., 195 A.D. 370, 186 N.Y.S. 322 (1st Dep't 1921).

4. Buckner v. D & E Motors, Inc., 53 Misc.2d 382, 278 N.Y.S.2d 932 (Sup.Ct., Erie County, 1967).

5. Isaf v. Pennsylvania R.R., 32 A.D.2d 578, 299 N.Y.S.2d 231 (3d Dep't 1969).

6. Mastan v. Desormeau Dairy–Vend Serv., 11 A.D.2d 860, 203 N.Y.S.2d 343 (3d Dep't 1960).

7. Port Chester Elec. Co. v. Ronbed Corp., 28 A.D.2d 1008, 284 N.Y.S.2d 9 (2d Dep't 1967).

8. CPLR 308(2) is treated in § 72, below.

9. Raschel v. Rish, 120 A.D.2d 945, 502 N.Y.S.2d 852 (4th Dep't), aff'd 69 N.Y.2d 694, 512 N.Y.S.2d 22, 504 N.E.2d 389 (1986).

10. Bus.Corp.L. § 304.

11. Micarelli v. Regal Apparel, Ltd., 52 A.D.2d 524, 381 N.Y.S.2d 511 (1st Dep't 1976). See Farrell, Survey of New York Practice, 28 Syracuse L.Rev. 379, 405–6 (1977).

fer and using the 307 method in a case in which 306 governs may void the service.[12]

In an action against an insurance company doing business in New York, an alternative is to serve the superintendent of insurance, whom all such insurers must designate as an agent for service.[13]

CPLR 311(a), in paragraphs 2 through 8, also lists those to be served in behalf of various governmental corporations. Keeping the paragraph numbers just as they appear in CPLR 311, service is made on those corporations as follows:

2. New York City: serve the corporation counsel or his filed-in-New–York–County designee;

3. any other city: the mayor, comptroller, treasurer, counsel, or clerk or, if none, whoever carries out an equivalent function;

4. a county: the chairman or clerk of the board of supervisors, clerk, attorney, or treasurer;

5. a town: the supervisor or the clerk;

6. a village: the mayor, clerk, or any trustee;

7. a school district: a school officer;[14]

8. a park, sewage, or other district: the clerk, any trustee, or any member of the board.

It is apparently not sufficient that the plaintiff follow these service provisions to the letter. If there happens to be some extra requirement lurking in a local law that requires someone other than a person on the above list to be served, the CPLR service may not suffice. It did not suffice, for example, in Horowitz v. Inc'd Village of Roslyn,[15] where a plaintiff suing a county effected service on the county clerk as explicitly authorized by CPLR 311(a)(4) but failed to serve the county executive or county attorney as stipulated by the

Nassau County Administrative Code. Even though the clerk promptly turned the summons over to the county attorney, the action was dismissed.

In Yung v. County of Nassau,[16] the Court of Appeals indicates implicitly that the *Horowitz* result was wrong, but for a reason that perpetuates the problem. While the customary rule is that a special provision will govern over a general one, the court held that the general one will prevail over the special one if the general one—the CPLR provision here—is the more recent enactment, which was the case in *Horowitz*. This of course leaves the door open to the problem—of having the CPLR directing service on one set of individuals and the local law on another set—when it is the general law that gets adopted first.

It is submitted that when two provisions offer different methods of service, a better way to reach the same result is to conclude that the two merely supply alternatives, making each of the people listed in either law a proper servee. That would entail a finding that the two laws are consistent, however, and the plaintiff in *Yung*, perhaps too obligingly, conceded that they were not. A good rule is to serve in accordance with both provisions, which is good for the paper industry, anyway. The best rule, of course, and perhaps the only one that can protect against hidden traps of this kind, is to leave plenty of time for trouble.[17] A plaintiff with a few months left over on the statute of limitations when the defendant springs that kind of objection may grumble a bit, but will keep breathing.

Service on the state itself is governed by CPLR 307, which is rarely used because as a rule the state can be sued only in the court of claims and the Court of Claims Act[18] governs commencement of suit there. Service on a court, board, or commission is governed by CPLR 312.

The "public authority" is not on the CPLR 311 list, or covered anywhere else in the

12. See § 95 below.

13. Insurance Law § 1212.

14. See Educ.L. § 2.

15. 144 A.D.2d 639, 535 N.Y.S.2d 79 (2d Dep't 1988).

16. 77 N.Y.2d 568, 569 N.Y.S.2d 361, 571 N.E.2d 669 (1991).

17. See § 231A below.

18. See Ct.Cl.Act § 11.

CPLR—an indefensible omission that needlessly expends the time and energy of plaintiffs. Sometimes the plaintiff can't find even in the "Public Authorities Law" a statute that governs service on the particular authority she wishes to sue. In such an instance the public authority has been likened to an ordinary business corporation and service permitted on someone listed in CPLR 311(a)(1),[19] but the lesson to a plaintiff planning suit against any kind of "authority" is, once again, to leave some time for homework. If quick research doesn't resolve all questions, call the authority, ask for counsel, and put the question to counsel. Realize, however, that this is the enemy and ask, ever so politely, for citations in support. Another source that may help is punching the authority's name and a few key words—summons, process, service, etc.—into WESTLAW to see if scanning a few cases answers the question.

In each instance, service should be made by personal delivery to one of the persons listed. CPLR 311(a) specifically directs the "delivering" of the summons, and thus seems to make CPLR 311 pre-emptive of method of service, requiring delivery only and precluding use of the various substituted service methods offered by CPLR 308. Other provisions, such as CPLR 309 governing infants and incompetents, speak of "serving" the persons listed, which offers ground for making all of the methods of CPLR 308—whose caption is personal "service"—available for service in those instances, including the deliver and mail method of 308(2) and the affix and mail method of 308(4). Caselaw indicates that those methods are not available against corporations, however;[20] that CPLR 308 is for individuals and CPLR 311 is for corporations, and that the two don't mix.

A helpful provision in serving individual defendants is CPLR 308(5),[21] which allows the

court to invent a method of service when the prescribed methods prove impracticable. A similar authorization was adopted for use against corporations with the addition of subdivision (b) to CPLR 311, allowing the court to invent a method upon a showing that the plaintiff can't make timely service on the corporation by the prescribed methods.[22]

Keep in mind that discussion in this section is directed only to method of service—whom to serve in the corporate behalf—not amenability to jurisdiction. If the corporation is a foreign one, therefore, not licensed to do and not doing business in New York, and there is no other basis for jurisdiction against it, the mere fact that service is made on a corporate official in New York does not give jurisdiction of the corporation. The corporation being a creature distinct from its personnel, those personnel do not—as do those to be served for a partnership or association[23]—carry the corporation around with them. This circumstance has led to the famous "corporate presence" or "doing business" test, by which a corporation's amenability to local jurisdiction is measured by the aggregate of its local activities. That test is concerned with jurisdictional basis rather than mere method of service, however, and is treated later.[24]

§ 71. "Sewer Service"; the Amendment of CPLR 308

When a process server swears to service in an affidavit duly returned to the plaintiff, but the server did not in fact make the service, the perjury usually results in a default judgment taken against the unnotified defendant. Such a situation, commonly referred to as "sewer service", reached epidemic proportions in the 1960s, especially in the civil court in New York City. The problem led to the 1973 enactment of a provision[1] authorizing, through adminis-

---

19. See Ware v. Manhattan & Bronx Surface Transit Op. Auth., 49 Misc.2d 704, 268 N.Y.S.2d 519 (Sup.Ct., N.Y. County, 1965).

20. Lakeside Concrete Corp. v. Pine Hollow Building Corp., 104 A.D.2d 551, 479 N.Y.S.2d 256, aff'd 65 N.Y.2d 865, 493 N.Y.S.2d 309, 482 N.E.2d 1225 (1985).

21. See § 75 below.

22. See the discussion of the 1998 amendment of CPLR 311(b) in SPR 74:2.

23. See § 69, paragraph c, above.

24. See § 82 below.

§ 71

1. Originally § 217–a of the Judiciary Law, now subdivision (c) of CPLR 5015.

trative channels, an en masse vacatur of fraudulently secured default judgments,[2] sparing each defendant victimized by the practice the burden of making an individual motion in each case. Prior to January 1, 1990, when CPLR 312–a took effect to allow personal service by simple, first-class mail,[3] the major step undertaken to discourage sewer service was an amendment of CPLR 308 in 1970 to make service easier.

As originally enacted, CPLR 308 had four subdivisions. The third was popularly known as "substituted service". It was a two-part requirement: a mailing plus either a delivery to some person or an affixing at some premises. But it was usable only if with due diligence service could not be made under CPLR 308(1), the personal delivery method. The 1970 amendment's chief purpose was to allow some kind of substituted service to be used in first instance as an alternative to personal delivery without the condition precedent of a "diligence" requirement.[4]

The amendment divided the original "substituted service" provision into two parts, one the deliver-and-mail procedure now in CPLR 308(2) and the other the affix-and-mail procedure now in CPLR 308(4). The latter continues to be available only if with due diligence the other methods don't work. But the deliver-and-mail method of the recast CPLR 308(2) became and remains available in first instance: no prior effort need be made at personal delivery under CPLR 308(1). The change eased service requirements and reduced instances of "sewer service" even if it did not abolish them entirely.

Prior to the amendment, the words "substituted service" described what was then CPLR 308(3). When that was broken down into present subdivisions two and four of CPLR 308, "substituted service" lost some focus. The phrase can today mislead to either subdivision

two or four and should be avoided in favor of the numerical CPLR citation or the respective phrases "deliver and mail" for CPLR 308(2) and "affix and mail" for CPLR 308(4). Further confusing matters, the phrase "substituted service" is sometimes used to refer to any method of summons service other than personal delivery. The lawyer should be sensitive to inquire into precisely how the phrase is being used in a given context.

As part of the 1970 amendment, the former CPLR 308(2), dealing with service on a CPLR 318 agent,[5] became CPLR 308(3), and the court ordered service of the former 308(4) became 308(5). The personal delivery method of CPLR 308(1) remained unchanged. Paragraph 6, added to CPLR 308 in a still later amendment, is treated in § 72 below.

In researching a process-service problem, the lawyer may meet pre–1970 cases using the older numbers. The 1970 reshuffling should be recalled and references in older cases adjusted accordingly.

§ 72. Deliver-and-Mail Service under CPLR 308(2)

This is a two-fold requirement whose advantage is that it is an alternative to personal delivery under CPLR 308(1) and can be employed without any prior effort to use that provision. Nor does it require a court order.[1] It has some complications, however, and has to be negotiated carefully. Since jurisdiction turns on it, it is not a good place for mistakes, especially if the statute of limitations is closing in.

The first requirement is a delivery "to a person of suitable age and discretion" at certain premises; the second is a mailing either to the defendant's "last known residence" or to his actual (presently used) place of business. Both the delivery and the mailing are required

---

2. It codifies a practice initiated earlier in the New York City Civil Court by its Administrative Judge at the time, Edward Thompson, and is therefore sometimes called "Thompson's Law". See Commentary C5015:13 on McKinney's CPLR 5015.

3. See § 76A below.

4. See 16th Jud.Conf.Rep.Leg.Doc. (1971) No.90, p. A38.

5. See § 73 below.

§ 72

1. The exception, in which a court order is required, is the matrimonial action.

for jurisdiction, and both steps must be taken within 20 days of each other.[2]

The person of suitable age need not be an adult. A responsible teenager, for example, will do. The criterion should be whether the person can be expected to advise the defendant of the service. This requirement is modeled on Rule 4(e)(2) of the Federal Rules of Civil Procedure and caselaw on that provision is some guidepost, at least as far as age is concerned.[3] But it must be noted that although modeled on the federal provision, CPLR 308(2) is by no means identical. Under the federal rule, for example, the deliveree must be someone "residing" at the premises, which is not a New York requirement. An apartment house doorman has been held to qualify under CPLR 308(2), for example, at least when access to the defendant's own apartment has been refused.[4] It is submitted that the doorman should also qualify if, although access is allowed, no one is at home.

The delivery can be made "at the actual place of business, dwelling house or usual place of abode" of the defendant. Underscore "actual"; it means that the place is presently being used by the defendant. If an outright, presently-used residence of the defendant is known, it satisfies for both prongs of the CPLR 308(2) requirement. But the provision does not use the word "residence". The precise meaning of the phrases used has yet to be discerned, but it is rather clear that something less than an outright "residence" can satisfy as a "dwelling house"[5] or "place of abode".[6]

An important point about the delivery aspect of CPLR 308(2) is addressed in Bossuk v.

Steinberg.[7] If the "suitable age and discretion" person comes to the door but won't open it, as when the delivery is being made to the defendant's house, *Bossuk* holds that the process server's merely leaving the summons outside the door will qualify as an adequate delivering.[8]

A serious problem may arise when the plaintiff is relying on a delivery of the summons to a person of suitable age at what is assumed to be the defendant's presently used residence, and the assumption proves false. The problem comes from Feinstein v. Bergner.[9] It involves CPLR 308(4), the affix-and-mail requirement, treated later,[10] but has important bearing on CPLR 308(2) as well. (Under paragraph 4, the affixing is made at the same premises to which a delivery is made when paragraph 2 is being used.)

In *Feinstein*, the residence at which the affixing was made under paragraph 4 had been the defendant's when he lived with his parents—and it was the address he had furnished at the scene of the accident involved in the action—but it was no longer his residence at the time of suit, although his parents still lived there. The Court of Appeals upset the service, and it was now too late for the plaintiff to start over under the statute of limitations.

The *Feinstein* facts seemed to be tailor-made for an estoppel against the defendant, and an estoppel was in fact invoked on similar if not identical facts in McNeil v. Tomlin,[11] but the practitioner does well to note *Feinstein* and to take steps to avoid falling into its trap.[12]

---

2. CPLR 308(2).

3. See De George v. Mandata Poultry Co., 196 F.Supp. 192 (E.D.Pa.1961).

4. Braun v. St. Vincent's Hospital and Medical Center, 57 N.Y.2d 909, 456 N.Y.S.2d 763, 442 N.E.2d 1274 (1982); F.I. Dupont, Glore Forgan & Co. v. Chen, 41 N.Y.2d 794, 396 N.Y.S.2d 343, 364 N.E.2d 1115 (1977).

5. Karlin v. Avis, 326 F.Supp. 1325 (E.D.N.Y.1971), sustained as a "dwelling house" a New York apartment that was one of four places where the defendant divided his time. It holds that the defendant need not be a New York "resident" in order for a New York apartment to qualify as a dwelling house.

6. See Rich Products Corp. v. Diamond, 51 Misc.2d 675, 273 N.Y.S.2d 687 (Sup.Ct., Erie County, 1966).

7. 58 N.Y.2d 916, 460 N.Y.S.2d 509, 447 N.E.2d 56 (1983).

8. The bearing the Bossuk case has on the most common service method of all—personal delivery to the defendant under paragraph 1 of CPLR 308—is discussed in § 66, above.

9. 48 N.Y.2d 234, 422 N.Y.S.2d 356, 397 N.E.2d 1161 (1979).

10. See § 74 below.

11. 82 A.D.2d 825, 439 N.Y.S.2d 430 (2d Dep't 1981). McNeil gives the Feinstein case only a "cf".

12. Feinstein is further discussed in § 74, below.

The mailing requirement can be carried out either at a "last known residence", or at an actual, i.e., presently used (not "last known") place of business. Ordinary first class mail is used. Neither registered nor certified mail is required, and, while it is probably permissible, many lawyers deliberately avoid registered and certified mail when it is not explicitly required, fearing the complications caused when postal officials can't find the defendant or other proper person to sign the required receipt. If postal evidence of a mailing is sought, a simple certificate of first-class mailing can be secured from the post office when the mail is posted.[13]

The mail that constitutes one of the two service steps under CPLR 308(2) must of course be distinguished from the outright mail service allowed by CPLR 312–a.[14]

If the mailing is to the place of business, the envelope must be labeled "personal and confidential" and not bear any indication that it comes from a lawyer or relates to a law suit, requirements that don't apply to a mailing made to a last known residence. Because these requirements are designed to spare the defendant embarrassment, their violation has been held to void jurisdiction and bring about a dismissal.[15]

The mere fact that a physician has a relationship with a hospital and performs operations there does not make the hospital a place of business at which a delivery of the summons may be made to a person of suitable age (etc.) in behalf of the physician under CPLR 308(2), at least not when the physician has an office elsewhere and bills from there.[16]

A paragraph numbered 6 was added to CPLR 308 in 1994. It expands the meaning of the "place of business" referred to in paragraphs 2 and 4 of CPLR 308. CPLR 308(6) provides that

[f]or purposes of this section, "actual place of business" shall include any location that the defendant, through regular solicitation or advertisement, has held out as its place of business.

This was designed to make a simple letter drop address, being used for business purposes, a proper address at which to carry out both steps of the service requirements of paragraph 2 (the deliver and mail provision) or paragraph 4 (the affix and mail provision). A number of problems arise under this statute, however, not least of which is that CPLR 308 has been held unavailable for use against corporations—which, ironically, are the entities that the 1994 change was primarily aimed at. There are also issues about whether the claim sued on must have arisen out of business done from the mail drop address and whether the address has to be shown to be an active one at the time of service.[17] Because of this, careful lawyers have been hesitant to trust this provision, especially where there's a potential statute of limitations problem in the case.

If either of the two CPLR 308(2) requirements is to be carried out outside New York State, it will be necessary to establish a basis for extraterritorial jurisdiction under CPLR 313. If the case has no contacts with New York, for example, a personal delivery to the defendant in New York under CPLR 308(1) will give jurisdiction but a delivery to some suitable-age person in New York under CPLR 308(2) coupled with a mailing to the defendant's residence outside New York will not.[18]

In an action against an infant, the parent may be served, but if the infant is 14 or over the infant must be separately served as well.[19] When the infant is being served pursuant to CPLR 308(2), and the father is the person of suitable age to whom a delivery is being made in behalf of the infant, two summonses must be presented to the father: one for himself and

---

13. This certificate, signed by the postal official at the point of sending, is to be distinguished from certified mail in that it requires no signed paper, even by a postal official, at the other end.

14. See § 76A below.

15. Mastropierro v. Bennett, 233 A.D.2d 483, 650 N.Y.S.2d 287 (2d Dep't 1996).

16. Glasser v. Keller, 149 Misc.2d 875, 567 N.Y.S.2d 981 (Sup.Ct., Queens County, 1991).

17. See the extended treatment of CPLR 308(6) in the lead notes in SPR 26 and 27.

18. See Durgom v. Durgom, 47 Misc.2d 513, 262 N.Y.S.2d 874 (N.Y.C. Civ.Ct. 1965).

19. CPLR 309(a). See § 69 above.

one for the infant.[20] Contrast this with corporate service, where it has been held that a single summons served on a corporate officer satisfies as service on the officer individually and on the corporation too.[21] We suggest the use of two summonses in all of these instances.[22]

When CPLR 308(2) is used, the filing of proof of service is required. It must be made within 20 days after the delivery or mailing, "whichever is effected later". Service then becomes "complete" 10 days after proof of service is filed, which means only that the defendant's responding time will not start until then. The responding time is 30 days.[23] Integrating the 10-day period, the easiest way to remember this point is that when CPLR 308(2) is used, the defendant actually has 40 days in which to respond, measured from the filing of proof of service.

The "completion" of service under CPLR 308(2) has nothing to do with the statute of limitations, incidentally, which is satisfied if the service acts are carried out within the applicable period even though service may not be deemed "complete" until after the statute has run.[24] In the lower courts, which are "service" courts,[25] both the delivery and the mailing must be carried out within the statute of limitations; in the supreme and county courts, which are "filing" courts, both the delivery and the mailing must be carried out within the 120-day period for service that follows the filing of the action.[26] Delivery within the applicable period but mailing a day later has been held unsatisfactory.[27] If the mail is posted within the period it will satisfy, however, even

though not received until after.[28] It is imprudent, to say the least, to play things that close.

While the failure to file proof of service under this statute is not jurisdictional,[29] and does not affect the statute of limitations, the time periods of CPLR 308(2) can become intertwined with the 120-day period allowed for service in supreme and county court actions under the filing system.[30] The interplay of these provisions and how to treat their sometimes overlapping time periods is elaborated elsewhere.[31]

CPLR 308(2) should not be used against a corporate defendant.[32] Because other alternatives are often available against a corporation,[33] the statute should not be missed there.

§ 73. Service on Rule 318 Agent under CPLR 308(3)

CPLR 318 authorizes a person or entity to designate a person to act as agent for service of process. It is done in an acknowledged writing on which the agent endorses consent. The writing is then filed with the county clerk of the county in which the designor "resides or has its principal office". It is effective for three years. CPLR 308(3) allows service of process to be made on that agent in behalf of that principal.

CPLR 308(3) and its CPLR 318 companion count for little in New York practice. Theoretically, the designation makes it easier for a plaintiff to effect service on a defendant, but the easing of the plaintiff's path is never the defendant's purpose. The practical accomplishment of the designation is to prevent the statute of limitations from tolling if the defendant

---

20. Giving the father only one was held insufficient service in Kolodzinski v. Ferreiras, 168 A.D.2d 431, 562 N.Y.S.2d 554 (2d Dep't 1990).

21. T.E.A. Marine Automotive Corp. v. Scaduto, 181 A.D.2d 776, 581 N.Y.S.2d 370 (2d Dep't 1992).

22. On this point, see also the discussion of partnerships in § 69 above.

23. CPLR 320(a), and 3012(a), (c).

24. William Iser, Inc. v. Garnett, 46 Misc.2d 450, 259 N.Y.S.2d 996 (Sup.Ct., Nassau County, 1965). Proof of service is treated in more detail later. See § 79 below.

25. See § 45 above.

26. See § 52 above.

27. Furey v. Milgrom, 44 A.D.2d 91, 353 N.Y.S.2d 508 (2d Dep't 1974). Furey concerned CPLR 308(4), but its conclusions govern CPLR 308(2) as well. The posting was made a day after the statute of limitations expired.

28. Weill v. Erickson, 49 A.D.2d 895, 373 N.Y.S.2d 370 (2d Dep't), aff'd 37 N.Y.2d 851, 378 N.Y.S.2d 39, 340 N.E.2d 473 (1975).

29. See, e.g., Weininger v. Sassower, 204 A.D.2d 715, 612 N.Y.S.2d 249 (2d Dep't 1994), discussed in SPR 32:3.

30. See CPLR 306-b.

31. See § 63, above, at the point of footnote 48.

32. See § 70 above.

33. See § 70, above, and § 95, below.

should leave the state.[1] That was also its effect under prior law.[2] But under prior law it was more important because there were few other things that could prevent a tolling for the defendant's absence. Under the CPLR, on the other hand, the mere fact that there exists an in personam basis for jurisdiction authorizing extraterritorial service, such as under CPLR 302 and 313,[3] denies the plaintiff a limitations' toll for the defendant's absence[4] and vastly reduces the significance of CPLR 318 and its agency. Hence it is rarely used.

No attempt need be made to discover a CPLR 318 agency as a condition for using some other service provision. CPLR 308(4), for example, the affix-and-mail method, requires a prior effort to use paragraphs 1 and 2 of CPLR 308 but not paragraph 3. The reason is that a plaintiff can't be sure where such an agency may be on file. Suppose the defendant has several residences, for example. Or suppose the defendant has several offices. Which is the "principal" one, at which the filing of the designation is required? Realizing that a wrong guess, and a search of the clerk's records in the wrong county, can have jurisdictional consequences, the legislature has isolated CPLR 308(3). It is sometimes suggested that these agencies be centralized in a state office, such as the secretary of state's. That would help, but it is not likely to divest CPLR 308(3) and 318 of their wide reputation for unimportance.

§ 74. Affix-and-Mail Service under CPLR 308(4)

Service under this provision is similar to the steps required under paragraph 2 of CPLR 308, in a number of details. For those provi-

sions that are parallel the reader is referred to the treatment of paragraph 2 in § 72, above.[1]

There are really only two major differences between paragraph 2 and paragraph 4 that require treatment here. The first is that under paragraph 4 an affixing to the premises replaces the delivery requirement of paragraph 2. The second is that paragraph 4 may not be used unless service under paragraphs 1 and 2 "cannot be made with due diligence".[2]

Because of this due diligence requirement, service under paragraph 4 requires a more detailed affidavit of service. The affidavit must set forth the particular steps taken in attempting service under the other provisions. This enables the court to determine whether due diligence was used. Form affidavits in this kind of case are usually inadequate and have been rejected.[3]

As to what constitutes "due diligence", it is a sui generis test. The courts don't like to count service attempts,[4] but a single visit to the premises, when no one is at home, will not suffice. A few visits on different occasions and at different times to both residence and place of business, if known, will.[5]

A mere showing of many visits will not automatically do. If the server deposes that for five straight business days he went to the defendant's residence at 10 a.m. and found no one home, he is more likely to be credited with obtuseness than with diligence. He should vary the time of his visits. At least for purposes of satisfying the diligence requirement of CPLR 308(4), it should be shown that the process server made genuine inquiries about the defendant's whereabouts and places of employment.[6]

---

§ 73

1. See CPLR 207(1).
2. Civ.Prac.Act §§ 19, 227.
3. See §§ 84, 100.
4. CPLR 207(3). See § 53 above.

§ 74

1. Section 72 should also be consulted for the relevance of CPLR 308(6), which defines the "actual place of business", as used in paragraph 4, to include a mail drop address. The several problems connected with paragraph 6 are discussed in § 72.

2. As noted in § 73, above, an attempt at service on an agent under paragraph 3 of CPLR 308 is not a condition precedent to service under paragraph 4.

3. See, e.g., Blatz v. Benschine, 53 Misc.2d 352, 278 N.Y.S.2d 533 (Sup.Ct., Queens County, 1967).

4. See Huntington Util. Fuel Corp. v. McLoughlin, 45 Misc.2d 79, 255 N.Y.S.2d 679 (Sup.Ct., Suffolk County, 1965).

5. O'Connor v. O'Connor, 52 Misc.2d 950, 277 N.Y.S.2d 424 (Sup.Ct., Suffolk County, 1967).

If it is known that the premises are no longer used by the defendant, such as where the defendant has permanently left a former residence, an attempt to execute the two requirements of CPLR 308(4) at that place will fail.[7]

While a "last known residence" suffices for the mailing requirement, it does not suffice for the affixing requirement, as the plaintiff learned to her chagrin in Feinstein v. Bergner,[8] a case with an important lesson for all plaintiffs using either paragraph 2 or 4 of CPLR 308.

Feinstein involved an automobile accident in which P was injured and her husband killed. D at the accident scene revealed his proper address—D then lived with his parents—but when P got around to service several years later D no longer resided there, although his parents still did. After two unsuccessful attempts to deliver the summons at that address under paragraph 2 of CPLR 308, the process server turned to paragraph 4 for an affixing.[9]

The mailing to D at the parental address, which requires only a "last known residence", was okay, but the affixing requires a presently used premises (business or residential) and since the parental address no longer qualified as that, an affixing to those premises was found unacceptable and resulted in a jurisdictional dismissal of the action—too late to start a new one.

As expanded in the dissenting opinion in *Feinstein*, the facts indicate that D left no forwarding address with the post office. The result was that the post office delivered the mailed summons to his parents' address, and D's father, receiving it at that address, mailed it on to D. But if the address was one still thought by the post office to be D's present residence, shouldn't P be entitled to make the same assumption for a CPLR 308(4) affixing?

It does not appear whether D notified his insurance carrier or the motor vehicle bureau of his change of address, as it is incumbent on him to do under the Court of Appeals decision in Dobkin v. Chapman,[10] or whether P checked with those sources. Hence the *Feinstein* decision should not be deemed to annul the obligation of a person involved in a vehicle tort to supply prompt and accurate address changes to his insurer and to the motor vehicle bureau, if not to the injured person directly (which *Dobkin* allows as an alternative).

The *Dobkin* case does not suggest that the defendant leave a forwarding address with the post office, but since that seems the most obvious step for any person to take to keep everyone apprised of an address change, the omission of such a suggestion was probably a mere inadvertence in *Dobkin*. In the *Feinstein* case, in any event, the very fact that the mailing went through to the parental address, which was the one originally furnished by D to P, is an element that should support an estoppel against D and sustain jurisdiction. The classic lines of an estoppel would seem to be spelled out in that D represented at the accident scene that the parental address was his; he ratified that representation by failing to leave a forwarding address with the post office, thus causing the mailing to reach him via the original address; P, perceiving as much, was entitled to conclude that the address was still D's; and P would be seriously damaged if D should be allowed to prevail.

A practical lesson for the plaintiff's lawyer is to make full inquiry of both the motor vehicle bureau and D's insurer. The failure to apprise

---

6. Smith v. Wilson, 130 A.D.2d 821, 515 N.Y.S.2d 146 (3d Dep't 1987).

7. Polansky v. Paugh, 23 A.D.2d 643, 256 N.Y.S.2d 961 (1st Dep't 1965).

8. 48 N.Y.2d 234, 422 N.Y.S.2d 356, 397 N.E.2d 1161 (1979). The case is the subject of the lead note in New York State Law Digest No. 239.

9. An incidental but important point, and one helpful to plaintiffs, is that the two visits under paragraph 2 were found by the lower courts to satisfy the "due diligence"

requirement, which must be met before service can be made under paragraph 4. On this point the Court of Appeals was "unprepared to say that the finding was erroneous as a matter of law".

10. 21 N.Y.2d 490, 289 N.Y.S.2d 161, 236 N.E.2d 451 (1968). Dobkin is treated at length in § 75, below. It concerns court ordered service under paragraph 5 of CPLR 308, but what it says about a defendant's obligations in regard to changes of address should apply regardless of the provision the defendant is being served under.

the bureau of an address change worked an estoppel against D in that instance would seem inevitable.

How should the "affixing" be carried out? It must be done in such a way as to avoid damage. A railroad spike is too much. A tack should do nicely. So should a reasonably secure taping. Wrapping the summons around the doorknob with a rubber band has been sustained.[13] A method should be used that ensures "a genuine adherence"; wedging the summons between door and door jamb has been held insufficient.[14] When the defendant lives in an apartment to which the server can't gain access, there is some suggestion that the affixing may be to the main lobby door of the apartment house.[15]

Proof and "completion" of service and the defendant's responding time are the same under this provision as under CPLR 308(2).[16]

A contrast should be made between CPLR 308(4) and § 735 of the Real Property Actions and Proceedings Law. The latter governs in the summary proceeding to recover possession of realty (the so-called "landlord-tenant" case),[17] and requires, in addition to a mailing, an affixing to a "conspicuous" part of the premises.[18] It has been held that if only that provision is satisfied, a default by the tenant will justify only an eviction judgment, but that if the service also satisfies the "due diligence" requirements of CPLR 308(4), the landlord will also be entitled to a money judgment for rent arrears.[19]

§ 75. Court–Ordered Service under CPLR 308(5)

This provision was born with the CPLR. It may be invoked whenever service proves "im-

---

After *Feinstein*, plaintiffs in a similar situation must apparently be prepared to turn to CPLR 308(5), i.e., to make an ex parte motion to have the court direct service. Perhaps it would be appropriate for P to do so not only when P knows that D's previously furnished address is no longer used, but also when P does not know whether it is or not. P would seem to be able to set a proper foundation for a CPLR 308(5) application by making inquiries about D's present address of the vehicle bureau, D's insurer, the post office, and perhaps D's family at the original address (with an ordinary letter). The job is not all that big; it entails several pieces of correspondence and a waiting period for responses. Of course, the plaintiff who has waited to the last minute for suit obviously can't spare the time. The luxury of an opportunity to make those inquiries is reserved only to plaintiffs who leave ample time for trouble.[12]

Should the responses all indicate that there has been no change of address, although in fact there has been, it is quite possible that the court on a CPLR 308(5) application would take the position that it should offer no aid because service is available under CPLR 308(4). But that poses an interesting question. If the court does take that position, and P turns of necessity to paragraph 4, P is likely to be met with the same dismissal motion that D made in *Feinstein*, and on the same grounds. An estop-

---

11. 82 A.D.2d 825, 439 N.Y.S.2d 430 (2d Dep't 1981).

12. See § 231A below.

13. Merchandise Nat'l Bank v. Lister, 5 A.D.2d 653, 174 N.Y.S.2d 102 (1st Dep't 1958).

14. PacAmOr Bearings, Inc. v. Foley, 92 A.D.2d 959, 460 N.Y.S.2d 662 (3d Dep't 1983).

15. See Mittelman v. Mittelman, 45 Misc.2d 445, 257 N.Y.S.2d 86 (Sup.Ct., Queens County, 1965).

16. See § 72 above. Proof of service is more fully treated in § 79, below.

17. The summary proceeding is treated in § 571 et seq., below (Practitioner's Edition).

18. Because the word "conspicuous" appears in the affixing requirement of RPAPL § 735, the phrase "conspicuous service" is often used in connection with summary proceedings; but because the consequences differ, as the text shows, the phrase should not be used to describe service under CPLR 308(4).

19. See 1405 Realty Corp. v. Napier, 68 Misc.2d 793, 328 N.Y.S.2d 44 (N.Y.C.Civ.Ct. 1971). Since the money judgment sought in the summary proceeding is for rent for use of the very premises at which service is made, it is difficult to countenance this kind of distinction between what suffices for eviction and what suffices for a rent judgment. Service good for one would seem to be adequate for both.

practicable" under the earlier paragraphs of CPLR 308.[1] Under paragraph 5, all the plaintiff has to do is make an ex parte motion—a motion without notice to any other potential party—requesting the court to devise a method of service. The court can by order direct any kind of service it wishes, restricted only by the basic demands of due process, the facts of the particular case, and the judge's imagination.

One early case involved a defendant domiciled in Spain but subject to New York long-arm jurisdiction under CPLR 302(a)(1). The court on a CPLR 308(5) motion, assisted by the plaintiff's showing of the defendant's relationship with people in New York, made an order directing that the summons be delivered in the defendant's behalf to the defendant's New York literary agent, even though the agent was not involved in the transaction sued on. That was done, and the service was sustained.[2]

When is service under the earlier paragraphs sufficiently "impracticable" to invoke paragraph 5? It is clear that service need not prove "impossible" under those paragraphs. The same due diligence required under paragraphs 1 and 2 as a prelude to the use of the affix-and-mail method of paragraph 4 should also set the stage for the use of paragraph 5, necessitating only the additional showing that paragraph 4 will not work either. If, for example, the plaintiff has diligently tried to find the defendant's New York place of business or dwelling house or place of abode, and failed, the paragraph 5 stage should be set.

It has been held, in fact, that the "impracticable" standard of paragraph 5 is not as demanding as the "due diligence" standard of paragraph 4, but that a plaintiff applying under paragraph 5 must still "make some showing" that other CPLR 308 methods won't work.[3] If it is simply want of a proper effort on the plaintiff's part that creates the service problem, even in situations in which there are numerous defendants, the plaintiff will not be allowed help from CPLR 308(5).[4]

Apparently, for paragraph 5 purposes, the plaintiff need not actually try one of the previously listed CPLR 308 methods; she must just be prepared to show that it would have been futile for some adequate reason: the defendant can't be found, there are no known premises at which to carry out the requirements of paragraphs 2 or 4, etc.

The situation is not the same as that obtaining under the "due diligence" standard of paragraph 4, because that standard applies chiefly to assure that efforts have been made to deliver the summons (under paragraph 2) to an appropriate person at an already identified premises. Identifying those premises for the delivery purpose of paragraph 2 clarifies their availability for the affixing purpose of paragraph 4. Hence the requirement that actual and bona fide efforts be made to find someone at the premises for a delivery under paragraph 2 before turning to the less dependable expedient of an affixing under paragraph 4.

Caselaw also indicates that the plaintiff need not attempt service in a foreign country as a condition precedent to the use of paragraph 5, i.e., that inability to effect service within New York suffices for a paragraph 5 application,[5] but that may be going a bit far. If without undue trouble or expense such service can be arranged for outside the state, or, in the case of paragraphs 2 or 4, can be made by executing one of the two requirements within the state and the other outside, the plaintiff should take those steps. The court may of course deny a paragraph 5 motion if a prescribed method appears feasible, remitting the plaintiff to try that method, without prejudice to a further

---

§ 75

1. CPLR 308(3), providing for service on a Rule 318 agent, is excepted; no effort to use it need precede an application under paragraph 5. See § 73 above.

2. Totero v. World Telegram Corp., 41 Misc.2d 594, 245 N.Y.S.2d 870 (Sup.Ct., N.Y.County, 1963).

3. Markoff v. South Nassau Community Hospital, 91 A.D.2d 1064, 458 N.Y.S.2d 672 (2d Dep't 1983), aff'd 61 N.Y.2d 283, 473 N.Y.S.2d 766, 461 N.E.2d 1253 (1984). In Markoff, the plaintiff didn't make that showing.

4. See Horner v. Waste Management of New York, Inc., Sup.Ct., Oneida County, Dec. 13, 1995 (Index No. 94–12613; Tenney, J.), discussed in SPR 39:3.

5. This point seems implicit in the Totero case, note 2, above.

paragraph 5 application if the method does prove futile.

If service under one of the earlier paragraphs would be unduly expensive, the expense has been held to be a factor tending to make the service sufficiently "impracticable" to invoke paragraph 5.[6]

The leading New York authority on methods that can suffice under paragraph 5 and the factors to be considered by the court in devising the method is known as the *Dobkin* trilogy. The Court of Appeals decided three cases together—Dobkin v. Chapman, Sellars v. Raye, and Keller v. Rappoport—delivering a consolidated opinion and setting forth guidelines for the use of CPLR 308(5).[7] In each of the three cases there had been an accident in New York, thus invoking longarm jurisdiction under CPLR 302(a)(2) and allowing service outside the state, if necessary, under CPLR 313. There was, in other words, no problem of jurisdictional basis. It was strictly a question of notice. The problem in each case was how to make service.

In *Dobkin*, D at the scene of the accident had furnished P a Pennsylvania address. Ordinary mail to that address was not returned but registered mail was. In *Sellars* and in *Keller*, D gave P his apparently correct New York address but D afterwards moved. Registered mail in *Sellars* was returned "Moved—Left No Address".[8] In *Keller*, inquiries of D's former neighbors, of the New York Motor Vehicle Bureau, and of D's former employer did not reveal D's present whereabouts.

In each of the three cases an order was made under paragraph 5, as follows:

a. in *Dobkin*, an order was made directing service on D by ordinary mail at the address D had given P;

b. in *Sellars*, there were two orders, one directing service pursuant to Vehicle and Traffic Law § 253, which requires service on the secretary of state[9] along with a mailing, and a second directing service by publication when the mail was returned;

c. in *Keller*, the order directed two steps, a mailing to D at the address D furnished plus a delivery of the summons to D's insurance carrier.

In all three cases the Court of Appeals sustained the methods used, even though it was far from certain that the methods would assure notice to the defendants. Due process does not guarantee notice, the court said; it requires only that the plaintiff do under the circumstances what is reasonably calculated to give the defendant notice. The court stressed that if the defendant failed to get notice, it would have been his own fault, observing that in accident cases the plaintiff's needs must also be taken into account. And the court laid down the rule that it is the defendant's duty in such cases to make information about his whereabouts available, either by keeping his address current with state licensing authorities, or with his insurance carrier, or with the injured person by direct communication. Although the court doesn't specify it, perhaps equally acceptable would be for the defendant to leave an accurate and active forwarding address with the post office.

---

6. See Dolgow v. Anderson, 43 F.R.D. 21 (E.D.N.Y. 1967). The cost would have been $120 to make service in Missouri.

7. 21 N.Y.2d 490, 289 N.Y.S.2d 161, 236 N.E.2d 451 (1968).

8. In § 97, below, is discussion of the nonresident motorist statute, Veh. & Traf.Law § 253, which prescribes its own method of service and is available as an alternative in automobile tort cases. The unsuccess of registered or certified mail under § 253 has been held to vitiate the service. This rigidity in treating the mail aspect of § 253 should perhaps be reconsidered and abated under the reasoning of the Dobkin case. A mailing constitutional under one statute, CPLR 308(5), should not be unconstitutional under another, Veh. & Traf.Law § 253, in the very same case. The fact that under the former the mailing

results from a court order while under the latter it is directly required by statute should not make a constitutional difference. But see National Eqpt. Rental, Ltd. v. Szukhent, 375 U.S. 311, 84 S.Ct. 411, 11 L.Ed.2d 354 (1964), and its distinguishing of Wuchter v. Pizzutti, 276 U.S. 13, 48 S.Ct. 259, 72 L.Ed. 446 (1928). Under a 1978 amendment of § 253, a procedure is set up for using ordinary mail if the registered or certified mail is returned "unclaimed". It is not clear just how far this will go to overrule earlier cases involving the "moved, left no address" situation. The plaintiff's lawyer might do better to seek an order of service under CPLR 308(5) than to rely on § 253 in a doubtful situation.

9. See § 97 below.

The court was influenced by the fact that the three cases in *Dobkin* were tort cases involving plaintiffs with personal injuries, and that in some of the cases the defendant's insurer was known. It also stressed that in the event of a default—because the defendant might really not get notice—New York's default-vacating provisions are available and are generously applied.[10]

There is some authority that with a nunc pro tunc order the court can validate under CPLR 308(5) a method of service undertaken by the plaintiff without prior court leave,[11] but such a procedure is perilous and should be avoided.[12]

In tort cases in which the plaintiff knows who the defendant's insurer is, service on the insurer in behalf of the insured is a common step.[13] It is sometimes suggested that a liability insurer that does not itself know the insured's whereabouts will disclaim liability and thus deny the plaintiff a solvent source of recovery. But that point did not detain the court in the *Keller* case, and, indeed, a disclaimer merely because the insured has not kept in touch with the insurer is not easy in New York, where the injured person's interest in the insurance policy is also recognized.[14]

Methods under paragraph 5 should always be trimmed to fit the case. In one instance in which demonstrators had taken over a building and blocked its entry, the posting of a temporary restraining order in the vicinity of the building and the announcement of its injunctive edict through a bullhorn were sustained by analogy to CPLR 308(5).[15] And in a federal action also involving a court's broad discretionary powers, service in a hostile foreign nation was ordered by telex, the airspace functioning as the process server.[16]

The plaintiff's affidavits on the ex parte motion, in addition to showing the prescribed methods to be impracticable, should set forth all facts that can aid the court in deciding on a potential method of service. The plaintiff's lawyer should also be prepared to recommend a few feasible methods to the court.

The subject of court-ordered service under paragraph 5 in matrimonial actions is separately treated.[17]

There is a curiosity about CPLR 308(5) indicating that an appellate court should be hesitant to overturn a lower court order directing service under CPLR 308(5), unless the plaintiff can be shown to be at fault in some way in the evidence laid before the court. If the plaintiff sets forth all of the facts accurately, and suggests several methods of service, and the nisi prius judge selects a method she deems satisfactory to due process and directs its use, the overturning of that method on appeal can mean the end of the plaintiff's case, as where the statute of limitations has expired and a new action would now be barred. It would be an unusual example of a party's being made to pay the price of a judge's error. Hence an appellate court should give every deference to the discretion exercised below, saving a reversal for only that case in which the court sees no alternative as a matter of law.

Service under paragraph 5 of CPLR 308 may not be directed against a corporation.[18] But a 1996 amendment enacting CPLR 311(b) allows court ordered service on a corporation in some circumstances.[19]

---

10. CPLR 317, 5015(a)(1).

11. See Rodgers v. Rodgers, 32 A.D.2d 558, 300 N.Y.S.2d 275 (2d Dep't 1969).

12. See Giordano v. McMurtry, 79 A.D.2d 548, 433 N.Y.S.2d 583 (1st Dep't 1980), aff'd 53 N.Y.2d 962, 441 N.Y.S.2d 688, 424 N.E.2d 555 (1981), later appeal 90 A.D.2d 451, 454 N.Y.S.2d 537 (1982), aff'd 58 N.Y.2d 872, 460 N.Y.S.2d 492, 447 N.E.2d 40 (1983).

13. See, e.g., Lerman v. Church, 54 Misc.2d 402, 282 N.Y.S.2d 622 (Sup.Ct., N.Y.County, 1967).

14. See Thrasher v. United States Liab. Ins. Co., 19 N.Y.2d 159, 278 N.Y.S.2d 793, 225 N.E.2d 503 (1967).

15. Cornell Univ. v. Livingston, 69 Misc.2d 965, 332 N.Y.S.2d 843 (Sup.Ct., Tompkins County, 1972).

16. New England Merchants National Bank v. Iran Power Generation and Transmission Co., 495 F.Supp. 73 (S.D.N.Y.1980).

17. See § 76 below.

18. CPLR 311 governs corporations and does not admit of a CPLR 308(5) application. See LTD Trading Enterprises v. Vignatelli, 176 A.D.2d 571, 574 N.Y.S.2d 745 (1st Dep't 1991).

19. See § 70 above.

§ 76. Service in Matrimonial Actions

The matrimonial actions, including divorce, annulment, and separation, have special provisions governing commencement and an interesting history leading up to them. The key provision is 232 of the Domestic Relations Law. The developments about to be noted evolved when service rather than filing marked commencement of a matrimonial action.

Prior to 1974, DRL 232 provided for service by the usual personal delivery method, but if that proved unfeasible the only other method allowed was service by publication. Paragraphs 2, 3, and 4 of CPLR 308 contained clauses expressly precluding their use in matrimonial actions, and, because DRL 232 was deemed preemptive, resort to court-ordered service under CPLR 308(5) was also held by some courts to be precluded.

Then came Boddie v. Connecticut,[1] in which the U.S. Supreme Court held that due process prevents a state from denying a divorce plaintiff access to its courts solely because of inability to pay costs and fees. Service by publication being required by New York as the only alternative to personal delivery, and being expensive (in addition to being nearly useless as a way of giving notice), ensuing caselaw in New York held that if government required such service, government would have to pay for it for indigent matrimonial plaintiffs. A conflict then arose among departments as to whether local government or the state would have to foot the bill. The Court of Appeals resolved the conflict in Deason v. Deason[2] by holding it to be a local burden: in New York City a city charge and elsewhere a county charge. The court in *Deason* also hinted that court-ordered service under CPLR 308(5) might be available in matrimonial actions, and on remand the trial court took the hint and so held.[3]

DRL 232 was then amended in 1974 to permit service by any of the methods of CPLR 308, with concomitant amendments of paragraphs 2, 3, and 4 of CPLR 308 to recognize the change, which they do with a simple cross-reference to DRL 232. An important qualification, however, is that only the personal delivery method of CPLR 308(1) may be used without court leave in a matrimonial action; the other CPLR 308 methods are available, but all require an order of court in the matrimonial action whereas only service under CPLR 308(5) requires one in other actions.

Service by publication is still available in the matrimonial action as a court-ordered alternative,[4] but should be used only as a last resort.

Because the matrimonial action is in the jurisdiction of the supreme court exclusively, and the supreme court is a "filing" court,[5] the matrimonial action, like all other actions in the supreme court, is commenced today not by the service of the initiatory papers, but by their filing.[6] The same time restrictions that then come into play for service, notably the 120–day period and the requirements applicable to it,[7] apply equally to matrimonial actions.[8]

Pinpointing the moment of commencement is important for several reasons, one of them being that it marks the "interposition" of the claim for statute of limitations purposes. In relatively few instances, however, is there a statute of limitations issue in a matrimonial context.

In an ordinary civil action in the supreme court, the summons is accompanied by either a complaint or by the brief notice prescribed by CPLR 305(b).[9] DRL 232 has its own instructions for matrimonial actions, however, providing that if the complaint does not accompany the summons, the summons itself must con-

§ 76

1. 401 U.S. 371, 91 S.Ct. 780, 28 L.Ed.2d 113 (1971).

2. 32 N.Y.2d 93, 343 N.Y.S.2d 321, 296 N.E.2d 229 (1973).

3. 73 Misc.2d 964, 343 N.Y.S.2d 276 (Sup.Ct., Albany County, 1973).

4. See CPLR 314(1), discussed in § 102 below, and CPLR 315.

5. See § 45 above.

6. DRL 211, CPLR 304.

7. See § 63 above.

8. For detailed treatment of the commencement of matrimonial actions, see the Commentaries by Alan D. Scheinkman on McKinney's DRL §§ 211 and 232.

9. See § 60 above.

tain a notice that the action is for matrimonial relief, specifying its nature—e.g., "Action for a divorce", "Action for a separation", etc. Here a mistake in labeling can have jurisdictional consequences. A "separation" label will not be allowed to support a divorce judgment, for example, especially if there has been a default.[10] Also required, if the complaint does not accompany the summons, is that the summons include a demand for any ancillary relief sought (support, custody, etc.). The omission of the request for ancillary relief is not jurisdictional, however; it just bars the ancillary relief if the defendant should default.[11]

The requirements of labeling the summons to recite that it's for matrimonial relief and of having it specify any ancillary relief sought do not apply if the complaint accompanies the summons at the outset.

§ 76A. Personal Service by Mail

CPLR 312–a, providing for service of the summons by ordinary mail and not even requiring the use of a process server, was enacted in 1989.[1] As will be seen shortly, the procedure requires the defendant's cooperation, and many attorneys have reported that cooperation is so infrequent that some of them don't even bother with CPLR 312–a. Service by mail undertaken timely and used carefully, however, can avoid some of the problems associated with the more traditional service methods. The idea of trying it should not be rejected out of hand, at least where the end of the statute of limitations is nowhere in sight.

Mail service is available as an immediate initial option. No effort has to be made to make service by any other means before using the mail method of CPLR 312–a. And anyone at all, even the plaintiff herself, can be the mailer. The method is available against all categories of defendants—individuals, corporations and other entities, partnerships, governmental agencies, the state itself, etc.—with the exception of infants and incapacitated persons.[2] The method used is ordinary, first-class mail.

The summons is accompanied by the notice or complaint (whichever the plaintiff is opting for[3]), by two copies of a "statement of service by mail and acknowledgment of receipt", and by a postpaid envelope addressed to the sender.[4] The form of this statement and acknowledgment is explicitly prescribed in the statute.[5] The defendant's obligation is to subscribe and "affirm"[6] the acknowledgment[7] and return one copy of it in the envelope supplied. If it is not returned, the plaintiff will have to issue the summons to a process server and have it served by some other method.

The penalty to the defendant for not acknowledging, thus making service by another method necessary, is that the court may assess against the defendant the "reasonable expense" of the other service.[8] The statement and acknowledgment include a notice to that effect.

Service by another method after abortive mail service must indicate that an attempt was

10. See Fishman v. Fishman, 42 N.Y.2d 856, 397 N.Y.S.2d 774, 366 N.E.2d 862 (1977).

11. See Rosen v. Rosen, 161 Misc.2d 795, 614 N.Y.S.2d 1018 (Sup.Ct., Queens County, 1994), noted in SPR 33:3.

§ 76A

1. CPLR 312–a was modeled on the federal rule, Rule 4(c)(2)(C)(ii) of the Federal Rules of Civil Procedure, as it was at the time of the enactment of CPLR 312–a. Ironically, the federal procedure of service by mail was abrogated shortly afterwards under an amendment of Rule 4 that went into effect on December 1, 1993. Adopted in place of service by mail under the 1993 federal amendment is a formal procedure whereby the plaintiff can seek from the defendant a waiver of service. See Federal Rule 4(d) and Commentaries C4–15 to C4–18 on Rule 4 in 28 U.S.C.A., and § 623, below (Practitioner's Edition). No comparable waiver procedure exists in New York practice.

2. For discussion of what an "incapacitated person" is, see caption b in § 69 above.

3. See § 60 above.

4. CPLR 312–a(a).

5. CPLR 312–a(d).

6. This is apparently intended to adopt the form of affirmation attorneys and other professionals are permitted to make in lieu of an affidavit. See CPLR 2106; § 205 below.

7. CPLR 312–a(c). The returned acknowledgment is proof of service, the equivalent of the affidavit of service used when service is made by other means.

8. CPLR 312–a(f).

made to serve by mail under this provision.[9] Perhaps just an additional clause can be included in the summons to satisfy this requirement, or an additional paper served with the summons.

Because a voluntary acknowledgment by the defendant is required in order to give this method validity, it is not important what address the plaintiff directs the mail to: residence, business, vacation home, etc. Any address the plaintiff thinks the defendant can be reached at can be used.

The defendant has 30 days in which to return the acknowledgment.[10] If the complaint is served with the summons, an answer has to be served within 20 days after the defendant returns the acknowledgment. If a notice instead of a complaint is served with the summons, the statute is less clear. Presumably the acknowledgment acts as the equivalent of a demand for the complaint and starts the plaintiff's 20-day period for serving the complaint.[11]

If the defendant is a corporation or other entity, or in any instance in which someone other than the named defendant signs the acknowledgment, the signer must indicate his authority or his relationship to the defendant.

Because only the "reasonable expense" of the other service is assessed (when service by some other means is made necessary because of the defendant's failure to acknowledge), it may make the sum so inconsequential that defendants may feel no qualms at all about refusing to acknowledge, especially if there is any chance of putting the plaintiff out of time altogether with a little delay. The prospect of also having to pay an attorney's fee for the extra time that may be entailed when the plaintiff's attorney has to arrange for other service would give the defendant more incen-

tive to acknowledge voluntarily, but such a fee is apparently not included in the assessment.

Putting the plaintiff out of time always refers to the statute of limitations, and on that front plaintiffs who use mail service must be extremely wary:

In the supreme and county courts, where the filing of the summons and complaint mark commencement for limitations purposes, the plaintiff has 120 days in which to make service and file proof of service.[12] The time for making service by mail, the time for the defendant to ponder whether to acknowledge it (the defendant has at least 30 days), and the time for the return of the acknowledgment even if the defendant does decide to return it, all comes out of the 120-day period. When the plaintiff using mail service finally determines that the defendant is not going to return the acknowledgment, there may be precious little of the 120 days left in which to make service by some other means. It is for reasons like this that many plaintiffs, or in any event those at the tail end of the statute of limitations, stay away from mail service altogether.

What about the lower courts, in which service rather than filing signifies the commencement of the action for statute of limitations purposes? Under the mailing procedure of CPLR 312–a, "commencement" should be deemed to occur in "service" courts when, under CPLR 312–a(b)(1), "the signed acknowledgment of receipt is mailed or delivered to the sender".[13] Plaintiffs in these courts must be even more wary of mail service than plaintiffs in the "filing" courts when near the deadline of the statute of limitations. Service is not deemed made until the defendant returns the acknowledgement, which may enable the de-

---

9. CPLR 312–a(e).

10. CPLR 312–a(b).

11. See § 231 below.

12. See § 63 above.

13. As originally drafted, CPLR 312–a(b)(1) said explicitly that commencement would be deemed to occur at this moment. The reference to "commencement" was eliminated in the 1992 legislation that adopted the filing system for the supreme and county courts, so as to enable the moment of "filing" rather than service to mark commencement in those courts, even when the mail method of

CPLR 312–a was being used. The statute provided at that time, and still does after the amendment, that mail service is deemed "complete on the date the signed acknowledgment of receipt is mailed or delivered to the sender". The apparent intention was to have this moment of completion of service continue to constitute commencement for statute of limitations purposes in the lower ("service") courts. Note in this respect, however, that in other contexts, such as substituted service under CPLR 308(2) and 308(4), the moment that service is "complete" is not the moment that marks commencement. See § 72 above.

fendant to maneuver the plaintiff out of time. Plaintiffs who are anywhere near the expiration of the statute of limitations when they undertake service should be hesitant indeed to try mail service. They should get the summons into the hands of a process server and see to it that service is effected promptly.

The statute explicitly authorizes mail service in a special proceeding as well as in an action, but it is probably a bad idea to try it in a special proceeding.[14] The special proceeding, like a motion, requires the setting of a specific return day for a hearing, which can be as close as a few weeks after the service of the papers.[15] How can a petitioner who serves the initiatory papers on (e.g.) July 1st confidently make them returnable on July 15th when the validity of the service depends on the respondent's voluntary acceptance of the service and the respondent need not even decide whether to accept it until July 31st or later? And if a short statute of limitations applies to the special proceeding—like the four-month period of CPLR 217 that applies to the common Article 78 proceeding[16]—reliance on CPLR 312–a is even more hazardous. For the time being, plaintiffs would do best to restrict their use of CPLR 312–a to plenary actions.

D. GETTING INTO THE COURTHOUSE

Table of Sections

14. For what a special proceeding is, see § 547 below.

15. See § 550 below.

16. See § 557 et seq., below

§ 77

1. See § 45 above.

2. Federal Rules of Civil Procedure, Rule 3. The summons need not be filed with the complaint in federal practice, but usually is. See Commentary C4:12 on Federal Rule 4 in 28 USCA.

§ 77. General Filing Requirements; Federal Practice Compared

Before we conclude this discussion about how an action is commenced, note should be taken of the procedure for opening a file of the case in the clerk's office, and several connected matters. To the student or young lawyer trying to keep everything in perspective, the intervention of these and the several ensuing sections—about opening a case, getting an index number, filing papers, the individual assignment system (IAS), the request for judicial intervention (RJI), the preliminary conference, and proof of service—may seem to burst out of nowhere. We've put them under the caption "Getting into the Courthouse", because there is no obvious, single juncture in litigation at which to address them. They can become relevant at any of a number of points.

In the supreme and county courts, where the "filing" system of commencing actions was inaugurated in 1992, the step that initiates an action is of course the filing of the summons and complaint,[1] so in those courts, as of 1992, a filing takes place right at the outset, with the case getting an index number right off and having its place identified in the clerk's files. This is akin to federal practice, where the filing of the complaint commences the action.[2] But in the lower courts in New York—the New York City Civil Court and the district, city, town, and village courts—the service of the summons and complaint, not their filing, continues to mark commencement.[3] While there are requirements in lower court practice for filing the summons after its service,[4] these

3. See § 400 in each of the New York City Civil, Uniform District, Uniform City, and Uniform Justice court acts.

4. See N.Y.C.Civ.Ct.Act § 409, Unif.Dist.Ct.Act § 409, and Unif.Justice Ct.Act § 409 (town and village courts). Even there it is a filing required within a specified period after the summons is served, not, as the supreme and county courts and in federal practice, before. And it applies only to the summons, not generally to other papers. In the city courts, whether or not filing is to be required is left to court rule. See Unif.City Ct.Act § 409.

requirements do not go to jurisdiction,[5] so it is possible in the state's lower courts, as it was for a long time in the supreme and county courts before the 1992 introduction of the filing system, for a case to come and go—such as by settlement—without the court having any record of the case at all. That phenomenon, which no longer obtains in the supreme and county courts but continues to in the lower courts, comes as quite a surprise to the lawyer weaned on federal practice or the practice of any of most other states.

While an initial filing of the summons and complaint now takes place at the outset in the supreme and county courts, which opens a file of the case and secures an index number, the full mandatory filing system as used in federal practice has not been adopted in New York, either in the lower courts or in the supreme and county courts.

In federal practice there is a general requirement that any paper served on any party "be filed with the court within a reasonable time after service".[6] This is sometimes called the mandatory filing system. It has no counterpart in civil practice in New York. The requirement in the supreme and county courts in New York is to file the initial summons and complaint. While additional filings of one sort or another may be required for a few specific things in litigation practice, and in both the higher and lower courts—such as for motion papers[7] and for the note of issue[8]—there is nothing like the across-the-board federal practice of requiring the filing of everything that is served between the parties. In New York practice this frees many papers from any filing requirement, including answers, replies, amended and supplemental pleadings, notices in disclosure proceedings, demands for bills of particulars, etc.

Under the 1992 adoption of the filing system, it will at least be true that whatever post-commencement filing of a paper takes place in a supreme or county court action, including

any kind of application to the court, it will have an existing file to refer to. But in the lower courts, the "service" courts, that will not necessarily be the case. There may indeed be no existing file of the case when a paper has to be filed or an application of some kind made. In that instance the party seeking to file the paper or make the application will have to pay the fee that opens the file, and that will not necessarily be the plaintiff. One common instance in which the plaintiff does get the file-opening duty is where the defendant has defaulted and the plaintiff seeks a default judgment.[9]

If no file yet exists for the case, a file can be voluntarily opened by any party at any time, but if it isn't done voluntarily—again a phenomenon today primarily of lower court practice because in the supreme and county courts a file will have been opened at the outset—the first step that will require the opening of a file will be the first step that requires the attention of a judge. A judge has to be requested at that time. The procedure for requesting one is the filing of a Request for Judicial Intervention (RJI).[10] That will necessitate the opening of a file if nothing else has.

There are some situations in which things go the other way, with a file started even before commencement of an action, but these are few. One is where an application is made under CPLR 308(5) for court-ordered service. Another is where the plaintiff applies for a provisional remedy, such as an order of attachment, before commencing the action.[11] Yet another may be where a would-be plaintiff is applying for leave to file a late notice of claim.[12] If any of these applications is being made in a supreme or county court action, however, and the summons and complaint accompanies the application when the papers are presented for filing, as will sometimes be the case, the presence of the summons and complaint among the filed papers will ordinarily

---

5. See the Commentary on § 409 in McKinney's N.Y.C. Civ. Ct. Act, Vol.29A, Part 3.

6. FRCP Rule 5(d).

7. CPLR 2214(c).

8. CPLR 3402(a).

9. See § 293 et seq., below.

10. See § 77B below.

11. See § 46 above.

12. See § 32 above.

denote the action's formal commencement, which means that the accompanying application will be occurring simultaneously with commencement rather than, as in lower court practice, before commencement. The point for present purposes is that the application will then have that concurrently-opened file to refer to.

In one instance—the medical (including dental and podiatric) malpractice action—a special filing requirement has been imposed by the CPLR for all courts, although most germane in the supreme court, where most medical malpractice actions are brought. CPLR 3406, added in 1985, requires that in any such action the plaintiff file a notice describing the action within 60 days.[13] The point that starts the 60 days is not the commencement of the action, however, but the joinder of issue (the moment when the defendant serves an answer).[14] The notice is designed to trigger the scheduling of a pretrial conference that will expedite the action. The Court of Appeals has held that the plaintiff's omission to serve a timely notice under CPLR 3406(a) can be punished with money sanctions, but not a dismissal. Dismissal can ensue, however, for a failure to carry out the requirements of an order emanating from the pretrial conference.[15] The notice is usually easy to carry out. A plaintiff failing for any reason to serve it timely should seek a

time extension under CPLR 2004 as promptly as possible.

§ 77A. The Individual Assignment System (IAS)

Prior to January 6, 1986, an action in a New York court was not assigned to a given judge, and might eventually occupy the time of many judges. If a motion had to be made, for example, it would come before whatever judge happened to be assigned to the court's motion part at the time. Several motions often meant that several different judges had to become familiar with the background of the case, only to have yet another judge preside at the trial. This system, known as the "master calendar" system, was felt in many quarters to be duplicative and wasteful. Under an "individual" calendar system, as long used in the local federal courts, a case gets assigned to but a single judge, to whom it then belongs from cradle to grave: all motions and applications go to that judge, who presides at the trial as well.

Effective January 6, 1986, that kind of system, or something close to it, officially denominated the "Individual Assignment System", or IAS, took effect in New York as part of the Uniform Rules that also became effective on that day. The IAS is implemented by these provisions:

For	Uniform Rule
Supreme and County courts	202.3
Family Court	205.3
Court of Claims	206.3
City courts outside New York City	210.3

For the time being the IAS is not being used in the New York City Civil Court or in the Nassau or Suffolk district courts.[1] And the system is apparently deemed unnecessary in the surrogates' courts—each of which (except New York County) has but one surrogate—and in the town and village courts.

While most cases fall into the system and end up in the hands of a single judge, there are some exceptions. Under the IAS rules applicable in the supreme court, which we will henceforth use for illustration, special "parts" can be set up for particular categories of cases, such as matrimonial actions, condemnation cases, tax assessment reviews, cases against a

---

13. See Uniform Rule 202.56, a detailed implementation of CPLR 3406.

14. A form for the notice is prescribed in Uniform Rule 202.56, and further procedures are elaborated there.

15. Tewari v. Tsoutsouras, 75 N.Y.2d 1, 550 N.Y.S.2d 572 (1989).

§ 77A

1. See UR 208.3, 212.3.

municipality, commercial cases, etc.[2]

If such parts are established, judges will be specially assigned to them, perhaps being exempted from regular caseloads in the process. The rule also says that if several judges are assigned to any such part, the assignment of cases to those judges "shall be at random" within the part.

Some judges can be kept in "reserve" to try cases in "exceptional" circumstances. Other judges may be directed to hear matters when the assigned judge is not available. And in a provision that may hold the cure for periodic ailments that can from time to time appear in any individual assignment system, a transfer can be ordered, administratively, "of any action or proceeding ... from one judge to another in accordance with the needs of the court".[3] What these exceptions consist of and where they can be found are matters of local regulation—despite the "uniform" in the Uniform Rules—and must therefore be checked out on a local basis.

The chief administrator is empowered to permit a given court, or a court in a given district or county, to inaugurate what is called a "dual track system of assignment". This is really a modified individual assignment system. Under the dual track system a case gets assigned to one judge for all pretrial proceedings, but to a different judge for the trial itself.[4] A similar system—if it's not, indeed, the same one under a different name—is the "trial assignment part" or "TAP" system, under which trial-ready cases get transferred to a "calendar" judge who first tries to settle the case and then transfers it to a standby judge for trial if it doesn't settle. Whether the dual track or TAP procedure is applicable locally must also be ascertained by local inquiry.

One of the options considered before the IAS system was adopted was the adoption of the federal system of having a judge assigned to the case as soon as the action was commenced. The federal option was rejected. Instead, a judge is assigned only upon the first step taken in the action that requires one—which the mere commencement of the action ordinarily does not. Hence no judge is automatically assigned at the outset, but only at that later point when one is needed. When and how a case is assigned to a judge involves a paper known as a Request for Judicial Intervention, or "RJI", discussed in a separate section.[5] Practice in a special proceeding, which does require the assignment of a judge at the very outset, is also the subject of a separate section.[6]

Critics of the IAS among the bar have argued that the IAS works well only when the assigned judge is a good one. The system's proponents counter that if any judge is not doing his job, the IAS will be more prone to expose him. In any event, they conclude, there are tools within the system—some of them already noted—for meeting problems as they arise. There is also the factor that most intermediate (nonfinal) orders are appealable of right in New York practice,[7] in contrast with the federal system where precious few are.[8] The immediate appealability of just about any order serves as a safeguard against abuses by a judge under the IAS,[9] or, for that matter, under any system.

§ 77B. Getting a Judge Assigned: Request for Judicial Intervention (RJI)

Implementing the Individual Assignment System entails the early assignment of the case to a judge. How early? If a case is to be assigned to a single judge, one might expect a procedure whereby a judge is assigned to the case at its very commencement, as in the federal courts.[1]

---

2. See, e.g., UR 202.3(c)(2).
3. UR 202.3(c)(5).
4. UR 202.3(c)(6).
5. Section 77B below.
6. Section § 550 below.
7. See CPLR 5701(a)(2), discussed in § 526, below.
8. See § 642 below (Practitioner's Edition).

9. See, e.g., Goldheart International Ltd. v. Vulcan Constr. Corp., 124 A.D.2d 507, 508 N.Y.S.2d 182 (1st Dep't 1986), precluding judges from requiring a party to obtain permission before making a motion.

§ 77B

1. See the discussion in § 77, above.

Adoption of such a procedure for the New York courts was considered and rejected. The way a case gets assigned to a judge under the IAS is through the filing of a paper known as a Request for Judicial Intervention, or RJI. In the supreme court, to which discussion will be directed here, the governing provision is Uniform Rule 202.6, and appended to the rule is an official form of RJI, which is reprinted below in § 77C.

The filing of the RJI activates the IAS machinery and gets the case assigned to a judge, who is designated the "assigned judge"[2] and who then has the case till the end, subject to some exceptions built into the IAS.[3] But when is an RJI filed?

The first need of judicial attention is the occasion for the filing of an RJI. Hence UR 202.6 requires that if a judge has not already been assigned to the case, an RJI, in duplicate, must accompany any of the following:

—a notice of motion

—an order to show cause

—an application for an ex parte order

—a notice of petition

—a note of issue

—a notice of medical, dental, or podiatric malpractice action[4]

—a statement of net worth in matrimonial actions[5] or

—a request for a preliminary conference.

The "preliminary conference", treated in more detail below in § 77D, is a procedure prescribed by UR 202.12.[6]

Note that if judicial attention is not yet needed, there is no authorization for filing an RJI.

The assignment of an index number to a case occurs upon the filing of the first paper in the action (at which time the filing fee is paid),[7] but not even in the supreme and county courts, where the filing of the summons and complaint constitutes the commencement of the action, does the filing necessarily trigger the assignment of a judge. The paper filed will occasion such an assignment only if it is one of those listed above, i.e., a paper that an RJI must accompany. If the paper filed is merely proof of service, for example, an RJI does not go along with it unless other papers that accompany the proof of service—such as papers moving for a default judgment against the defendant—fall into one of the categories on the above list and call for an RJI.

If the filing of the RJI is occasioned by the filing of a paper that is the first filed in the action, and therefore occasions the opening of a file and the assignment of an index number, the rule in point, UR 202.5, requires that the person filing the paper notify all other parties, in writing, of the index number. Necessary to superimpose on that requirement is the fact that under the filing system for commencing actions in the supreme and county courts, the filing of the summons and complaint itself secures an index number, and those papers must bear the number when served on the defendant. That service should be deemed to satisfy this rule requirement about giving notice of the index number.

It may sometimes be difficult to effect a filing of the summons and complaint in supreme and county court practice, as necessary to satisfy the statute of limitations, and time may be short. The plaintiff in that situation may apply to a judge for an order directing filing within five days, which amounts to a five-day alternative if there are fewer than five days to go on the statute of limitations.[8] This is a variety of ex parte order, which is one of the events that requires the filing of an RJI.

---

2. UR 202.3(b).

3. The "dual track" system may have been put into operation locally, for example, entailing an assignment to one judge for pretrial purposes but to another for the trial. Or special parts may have been set up in the court to hear particular categories of cases. See § 77A above.

4. A special mandatory filing requirement applies in these cases. See CPLR 3406 and UR 202.56.

5. See UR 202.16, implementing this requirement as imposed by Dom.Rel.L. § 236.

6. The "preliminary" conference should not be confused with the "pretrial" conference of UR 202.26, treated in § 374, below.

7. Getting an index number is the subject of § 78, below.

8. CPLR 203(c), 304. See § 45 above.

Presumably, therefore, an application for such an order should be accompanied by an RJI. This seems a paltry event to occasion the permanent assignment of a judge, and it has other peculiarities.[9]

If and when a judge is assigned, notice of the assignment will presumably be given to all parties by the clerk. If not, whichever party is notified of the assignment would do well to identify the assigned judge to the other parties. Here again, inquiry into local practice should be made. Try as any "uniform" compilation may, distinct local variations inevitably evolve, like regional accents on the Queen's English.

---

9. See captions 9 and 12 in the lead note in New York State Law Digest No. 391.

§ 77C.　Form of Request for Judicial Intervention (RJI)

The following is the official form of RJI used in the supreme court, as drafted and promulgated by the Office of Court Administration and as reprinted from the annually recompiled "McKinney's New York Rules of Court".

<u>REQUEST FOR JUDICIAL INTERVENTION</u>

SUPREME (COUNTY) COURT, _____ COUNTY

INDEX #: _____ DATE PURCHASED _____

PLAINTIFF(S):

DEFENDANT(S):

IAS ENTRY DATE

JUDGE ASSIGNED

R J I DATE

Date issue joined: _____ Bill of particulars served: [Yes] [No]

NATURE OF JUDICIAL INTERVENTION (check ONE box only AND enter information)
- [ ] Request for preliminary conference
- [ ] Note of issue and/or certificate of readiness
- [ ] Notice of motion (return date _____)　　Relief sought _____
- [ ] Order to show cause (clerk enter return date _____)　　Relief sought _____
- [ ] Other ex parte application (specify _____)
- [ ] Notice of petition (return date _____)　　Relief sought _____
- [ ] Notice of medical or dental malpractice action (specify _____)
- [ ] Statement of net worth
- [ ] Writ of habeas corpus
- [ ] Other (specify _____)

NATURE OF ACTION OR PROCEEDING (check ONE box only)

MATRIMONIAL		
[ ] Contested	— CM	
[ ] Uncontested	— UM	

COMMERCIAL		
[ ] Contract	— CONT	
[ ] Corporate	— CORP	
[ ] Insurance (where insurer is a party, except arbitration)	— INS	
[ ] UCC (including sales, negotiable instruments)	— UCC	
[ ] * Other Commercial	— OC	

REAL PROPERTY		
[ ] Tax Certiorari	— TAX	
[ ] Foreclosure	— FOR	
[ ] Condemnation	— COND	
[ ] Landlord/Tenant	— LT	
[ ] * Other Real Property	— ORP	

TORTS		
Malpractice		
[ ] Medical/Podiatric	— MM	
[ ] Dental	— DM	
[ ] * Other Professional	— OPM	
[ ] Motor Vehicle	— MV	
[ ] * Products Liability	— PL	
[ ] Environmental	— EN	
[ ] Asbestos	— ASB	
[ ] Breast Implant	— BI	
[ ] * Other Negligence	— OTN	
[ ] * Other Tort (including intentional)	— OT	

SPECIAL PROCEEDINGS		
[ ] Art. 75 (Arbitration)	— ART 75	
[ ] Art. 77 (Trusts)	— ART 77	
[ ] Art. 78	— ART 78	
[ ] Election Law	— ELEC	
[ ] Guardianship (MHL Art. 81)	— GUARD 81	
[ ] * Other Mental Hygiene	— MHYG	

[ ] * Other Special Proceeding   — OSP

OTHER MATTERS

[ ] * _____ — OTH

Check "YES" or "NO" for each of the following questions. Is this action/proceeding against a:

YES   NO   YES   NO
[ ]   [ ]   Municipality: specify _____   [ ]   [ ]   Public Authority: specify ____

YES   NO
[ ]   [ ]   Does this action/proceeding seek equitable relief?
[ ]   [ ]   Does this action/proceeding seek recovery for personal injury?
[ ]   [ ]   Does this action/proceeding seek recovery for property damage?

All Cases Except Contested Matrimonials:

Estimated time period for case to be ready for trial (from filing of RJI to filing of Note of Issue):

              ☐ 0–12 months   ☐ 12–15 months

Contested Matrimonial Cases Only: (Check and give date)

    Has summons been served?   ☐ No ☐ Yes, Date _____
    Was a Notice of No Necessity filed?   ☐ No ☐ Yes, Date _____

ATTORNEY(S) FOR PLAINTIFF(S):

NAME   ADDRESS   PHONE NO.

ATTORNEY(S) FOR DEFENDANT(S):

NAME   ADDRESS   PHONE NO.

Parties appearing _pro se_ (without attorney) should enter information in space provided above for attorneys.

INSURANCE CARRIERS:

RELATED CASES: (IF NONE, write "NONE" below)

Title   Index #   Court   Nature of Relationship

    I affirm under penalty of perjury that, to my knowledge, other than as noted above, there are and have been no related actions or proceedings, nor has a request for judicial intervention previously been filed in this action or proceeding.

Dated: _____

                            (Signature)

                            _____

                            (Print or type name)

                            _____

                            Attorney for

          Attach rider sheet if necessary to provide required information

* If asterisk used, please specify further.

§ 77D. The Preliminary Conference

    With the adoption of the Uniform Rules in 1986, the practice of a "preliminary conference" was introduced, governed by § 202.12 of the Uniform Rules. It was at first mandatory in all but a few cases, but was found to be unnecessary or unwanted in many cases and was therefore made optional in the supreme and county courts, to take place at a party's request.[1]

The Uniform Rules in fact provide for two conferences. The "preliminary conference" that we treat here is a pre-note of issue discussion.[2] It takes place early. The other is the "pretrial conference",[3] which occurs after a note of issue is filed.[4] The function of a "pretrial" conference is to administer the finishing touches to an already prepared case before it goes to trial. The "preliminary" conference that we take up here, if it doesn't bring about a settlement of the case, is designed to get the case ready in the first place by lining it up for the customary preparatory procedures, mainly the disclosure devices of Article 31 of the CPLR.[5]

Officially, the preliminary conference is an early meeting between lawyers and judge designed (1) to simplify the issues, (2) to establish a timetable for using and completing the disclosure devices, (3) to add other parties if necessary, and (4) to discuss settlement and other things the court deems appropriate.[6] Despite the uniformity at which the conference rule aims, however, what the conference turns out to be depends in large measure on the individual judge. It thus behooves each lawyer, whatever she may cull from the specific instruction of the applicable rule, to determine the practice of the assigned judge.

A request for a preliminary conference may be made only after issue is joined and after bill of particulars practice, which takes place after the pleadings are served, has been concluded,[7] the premise being that the conference will be more meaningful if the pleadings are in and a bill of particulars is in with them. The conference ordinarily precedes use of the disclosure devices.

Any party may request the conference. If nothing has occurred earlier to occasion the assignment of a judge to the case with an RJI,[8] an RJI must accompany the request for the conference.

The contents of the request are prescribed in the rule. If the request procedure is properly followed, the court orders the conference, fixes its date and time—which as a rule must be within 45 days from the time the RJI is filed[9]—and notifies the parties.

If the parties are able to agree to a disclosure schedule on their own, they may do so in a stipulation submitted to the court before the date set for the conference. The court must approve the stipulation, and does so by affixing its "so ordered" to it. If the court gives the stipulation the "so ordered", the conference is cancelled.[10]

The rule adds the time-worn requirement, previously articulated only in some local provisions, that all attorneys attending the conference be "thoroughly familiar with the action and authorized to act" on the client's behalf.[11]

The making of motions after the conference is scheduled but before it has been conducted is discouraged. The motion "may be denied unless there is shown good cause" why relief is needed before the conference can come on.[12] The date of the preliminary conference can be advanced upon application of a party showing "special circumstances", and the court can, in its discretion, hold additional conferences.[13]

In matrimonial actions, medical malpractice actions, and, in New York City, tax certiorari proceedings, the preliminary conference is per-

---

§ 77D

1. The preliminary conference as used in the supreme and county courts is the subject here. Other courts may have preliminary conference rules, but they are likely to be cast in general terms, with much less detail. See, e.g., UR 206.10 (court of claims) and UR 210.10 (city courts).

2. See § 369 below.

3. The pretrial conference, prescribed and governed by UR 202.26, is discussed in § 374, below.

4. Note of issue practice is the subject of § 369 below.

5. The disclosure devices are studied in § 343 et seq., below.

6. UR 202.12(c).

7. UR 202.12(a).

8. Request for Judicial Intervention. See § 77B above.

9. UR 202.12(b).

10. Id.

11. Id.

12. UR 202.12(h).

13. UR 202.12(g),(j).

mitted only to the extent consistent with other rules that govern those things in more detail.[14]

At the conclusion of the conference, the judge is required to make a written order embodying any directions she has made at the conference.[15] If the case is not settled and disclosure directions are included in the order, the order must establish a timetable directing that disclosure proceedings be completed within 12 months, "unless otherwise shortened or extended by the court".[16] The "unless" clause is needed to acknowledge unusual circumstances that may in a given case require more than the usual allotment of time, but that is supposed to be the exception; the general rule is that a year is to be the outer limit for pretrial preparation. To carry out its own end of the bargain, the court should be ready for trial when the case is, but that, too, is an ideal, not a guarantee.

Instead of an order, the judge's directions can be taken down by a reporter and transcribed, the parties to share the cost and the transcript to be filed by the plaintiff.[17] When a note of issue is later filed, one of the things its accompanying certificate of readiness must attest to[18] is compliance with the preliminary conference's order or transcript.[19]

§ 78. Getting an Index Number

In the supreme and county courts, where the filing of the summons and complaint constitutes the commencement of the action,[1] the filing occasions the payment of a filing fee, the assignment of an index number, and the opening of a file on the case.[2] In the lower courts of the state—the New York City Civil Court and the district, city, town, and village courts—in which service rather than filing marks commencement, a file of the case will not necessarily be opened at the outset. In those courts, the occasion that starts a case is the filing of the first paper in the action, which may be any of a variety of papers: proof of service, an application by the plaintiff for a default judgment, a motion of any kind by either party, etc. At that time a filing fee will be paid, a file opened, and an index number assigned. If nothing else has happened to open a file in a lower court, the event that will trigger it—if the case is expected to go to trial—is the filing of a notice of trial,[3] the lower court equivalent of the note of issue used in the supreme and county courts.[4] The clerk will not accept any paper for filing unless it has an indexed file to refer to.

It is also permissible for any party to apply for an index number (and the opening of a file) voluntarily, at any time, a rare practice today in the supreme and county courts, however, in view of the compulsory filing that commences the action. But even in those courts there may be occasion to apply for judicial relief in advance of commencement, such as with an application for pre-action discovery,[5] or for leave to file a late notice of claim,[6] or for a court order directing service,[7] etc. In those instances the case may get a file and index number before commencement.

Whoever does the initial filing, and whatever the occasion that generates it, the index number once assigned adheres to the case permanently. The party who obtains the number must communicate it in writing to all other

14. See UR 202.12(k).

15. UR 202.12(d).

16. UR 202.12(c)(2). This is for "standard" cases, a word used to distinguish them from "complex" cases, which have a 15–month outer time limit. What case is "complex" is determined administratively.

17. UR 202.12(d).

18. See § 370, below, for certificate of readiness practice.

19. UR 202.12(e).

§ 78

1. See § 45 above. For commencement procedure in special proceedings, see §§ 550 and 553, below.

2. For the fees applicable in the supreme and county courts, see CPLR 8018(a).

3. See § 1301 in the New York City Civil, Uniform District, and Uniform City court acts. Procedure in the town and village courts is less formal. See Uniform Justice Court Act § 1301.

4. See § 369, below, for note of issue practice.

5. CPLR 3102(c). See § 352 below.

6. See § 32 above.

7. CPLR 308(5), 311(b). See §§ 70, 75, above.

parties.[8] If the defendant has had to pay the filing fee in a supreme or county court action—an unusual situation for the reason that there is no case pending until the plaintiff files the action, which requires the payment of the fee—a peculiar statute enables the defendant to get reimbursed by the plaintiff through an application to the clerk, and even authorizes the *clerk* to order a dismissal of the action if the plaintiff does not pay.[9] This appears to confer on the clerk what seems in every sense a judicial power, which has to cast it into constitutional jeopardy. Judging is for judges, not clerks, however great their talents. There are several problems with this uninspired statute.[10]

§ 79. Proof of Service

CPLR 306 governs proof of service. With service by mail under CPLR 312-a, proof of service consists of the defendant's signed acknowledgment of receipt and requires nothing more than that.[1] With other methods, proof takes the form of a certificate if service is made by a sheriff or other enforcement officer of the court. If made by some other person, that person's affidavit is proof of service.[2] The person served can admit service in writing,[3] which would then dispense with other kinds of proof, but admissions of that kind, more common for interlocutory papers served back and forth between attorneys after the action is begun, are not common for summons service.

The certificate or affidavit specifies the papers served, the person on whom service was made, the when and how of the service, and facts showing that the process server was a proper person, i.e., 18 or over and not a party.[4] It must also include a description of the person

to whom the summons was delivered—including sex, color of skin and hair, approximate age, weight, and height, and other identifying features.[5] These requirements were enacted to help discourage sewer service[6] but they can prove impracticable for even the most upright process server, who often has only the briefest glance at the person served. The defendant doesn't often invite the process server in for a cup of tea and then pose for him under a bright light. Fortunately, the courts have approached these requirements pragmatically, holding them satisfied as long as the person served proves to be the person intended. In that event, defects in proof of service are played down.[7] Other evidence can also be included in the server's affidavit to establish the identity of the person served, such as correspondence—seen by the process server—addressed to that person.[8]

This approach evinces judicial sensitivity to the process server's problems. It makes defects in these regards significant only when there is doubt about the identity of the person to whom process was delivered.

When service is made under paragraph 4 of CPLR 308—the affix-and-mail provision, which requires a showing that service under prior paragraphs is unworkable—the affidavit of service must detail the "dates, addresses and the times of attempted service" under those earlier paragraphs.[9]

Until the 1992 adoption of the filing system for commencing actions in the supreme and county courts, there was no general requirement that proof of service be filed in those courts, although some of the methods of service imposed a filing requirement, and still do, like paragraph 2 (the deliver-and-mail method)

---

8. See, e.g., UR 202.5.

9. CPLR 306–a(b).

10. See the extensive treatment of CPLR 306–a(b) in Caption 4 of the lead note in New York State Law Digest No. 390.

§ 79

1. CPLR 312–a(b), 306(d).

2. CPLR 306(d).

3. CPLR 306(e).

4. CPLR 306(a).

5. CPLR 306(b). In matrimonial actions, there is the additional requirement, when the defendant spouse is served directly, that the process server set forth how he knew that the person served was the defendant. Dom. Rel.L. § 232(b).

6. See § 71 above.

7. See Mrwik v. Mrwik, 49 A.D.2d 750, 372 N.Y.S.2d 693 (2d Dep't 1975).

8. Coutain v. Coutain, 76 Misc.2d 982, 353 N.Y.S.2d 294 (Sup.Ct., Kings County, 1974).

9. CPLR 306(c).

and paragraph 4 (the affix-and-mail method) of CPLR 308.[10] The failure to file proof of service even under those provisions did not vitiate jurisdiction, however.

Under CPLR 306–b, a key part of the 1992 legislation, the filing of proof of service became for a while not only a jurisdictional requirement, but a rigid and malevolent one, mandating the filing of proof of service within 120 days after the filing of the summons and complaint and visiting a dismissal on the case if the deadline was missed. This got the filing of proof of service enmeshed in the commencement of the action and the follow-up of service of process. It was cured in a 1998 amendment, as noted in an earlier section.[11]

The failure to file proof of service under statutes like CPLR 308(2) and 308(4) is a mere correctable irregularity.[12] It presumably requires court leave, but if the plaintiff files late without court leave and the defendant doesn't take issue with it, the filing should stand. The main consequence of a late filing under those provisions is that it extends the defendant's responding time.[13]

Service under paragraphs 2 or 4 of CPLR 308 is not "complete" until 10 days after the filing of proof of service, which means only that the defendant's responding time doesn't start until the expiration of that period.

There is no express requirement for the filing of proof of service when service is made by court order under paragraph 5 of CPLR 308. The court can, if it wishes, include directions on that matter in the order.

Proof of service loses its importance under these provisions if the defendant makes a timely appearance and defends without contesting jurisdiction. But it is a key item if the defendant defaults; it then becomes an indispensable part of the papers that must be filed for a default judgment.[14] It also becomes important if the defendant disputes jurisdiction. If, for example, the defendant moves to dismiss based on non-service, the affidavit of service will be the plaintiff's chief item in opposition.

If a testimonial hearing is ordered on the issue of service, which occurs when the court is unable to resolve the issue on papers alone, there is some dispute as to whether the process server's affidavit may be taken in evidence. Some courts say that it may not; that if the dispute goes to viva voce hearing, the process server himself must be called as a witness.[15] Other courts hold that the affidavit, while not decisive, may be received in evidence.[16] Although in the context of a testimonial hearing an affidavit is usually unacceptable hearsay, perhaps an exception is warranted for such as the process server's affidavit when service is contested, at least when the server is unavailable to give testimony. A rigid rule excluding the affidavit in testimonial hearings could result in a jurisdictional dismissal whenever the defendant merely says he was not served—simply because the one who served him is not there in person to say otherwise. The problem is recognized in Denning v. Lettenty,[17] where the process server died before the hearing. The court held that the affidavit makes out a prima facie case of service and that the defendant then has the burden of refuting it, which he does not do merely by saying that he did not see or find the summons.

A federal statute,[18] applicable in state as well as federal courts, requires that when the defendant defaults and the plaintiff applies for a default judgment, the plaintiff must include in the application an affidavit that the defendant is not in military service. The papers and problems connected with that requirement,

10. See §§ 72 and 74 above.

11. Section 63 above.

12. Lopez v. Quickset Printers, 70 Misc.2d 732, 334 N.Y.S.2d 808 (Sup.Ct., Nassau County, 1972).

13. William Iser, Inc. v. Garnett, 46 Misc.2d 450, 259 N.Y.S.2d 996 (Sup.Ct., Nassau County, 1965).

14. See CPLR 3215(f), discussed in § 295 below.

15. Prudential Property and Casualty Ins. Co. v. Holtzman, 135 A.D.2d 696, 522 N.Y.S.2d 595 (2d Dep't 1987).

16. See, e.g., Otto v. Royal Palm Bar, Inc., 86 N.Y.S.2d 307 (App.T., 1st Dep't, 1949).

17. 48 Misc.2d 185, 264 N.Y.S.2d 619 (Sup.Ct., N.Y.County, 1965).

18. 50 U.S.C.A. App. § 520.

seen more often in the lower courts, is discussed in New York City Housing Authority v. Smithson.[19]

E. THE JURISDICTIONAL BASES

Table of Sections

§ 80. Basis for Jurisdiction; CPLR 301

Having completed treatment of the service of the summons—the "notice" aspect of due process—we can turn to the "basis" part of it.

Whenever the summons is served on the defendant outside the state, or even within the state by some substituted method (since as a general rule it is only personal delivery within the state that simultaneously serves as its own jurisdictional basis[1]), due process requires that the court have some foundation for jurisdiction. Any of several things can satisfy as a "jurisdictional basis", including the defendant's New York domicile,[2] or, in the case of a corporate defendant, its doing business in New York.[3] The designation by the defendant of an agent for New York service, either express or implied, can be the basis;[4] or the defendant's agreement to submit to New York jurisdiction in a contract.[5]

To one degree or another, all of these things were recognized as jurisdictional bases prior to the adoption of the CPLR on September 1, 1963. It is the terse but potent mission of CPLR 301 to carry forth for use under the CPLR all of those prior law bases. It says that the courts "may exercise such jurisdiction over persons, property, or status as might have been exercised heretofore." The "property or status" refer to rem jurisdictional bases and are met later.[6] The "persons" part accomplishes the carry-over of anything that previously supported personam jurisdiction.

CPLR 301 having brought forward everything prior law offered as a jurisdictional basis, CPLR 302, the so-called "longarm" statute, then goes on to establish additional bases for extraterritorial jurisdiction of nondomiciliaries, not exploited under prior law. It does this so successfully that today longarm jurisdiction, in which the claim arises from an activity conducted by the defendant within the state, accounts for a substantial part of the courts' civil calendars.

A coordinate note is that whenever either CPLR 301 or 302 supplies a jurisdictional predicate, CPLR 313 immediately becomes ap-

---

19. 119 Misc.2d 721, 464 N.Y.S.2d 672 (N.Y.C.Civ.Ct. 1983).

§ 80

1. See § 59 above.
2. See § 81 below.
3. See § 82 below.
4. See § 95 below.

5. See § 98 below.

6. See § 101 et seq., below. Quasi in rem jurisdiction, one of the rem categories exploited by New York extensively prior to the CPLR and for a long time after it, was vastly reduced by the U.S. Supreme Court in 1977 and thus, despite CPLR 301, is not available to the extent it was under prior law. See § 104 below.

plicable to permit summons service to be made outside New York as well as within.

All of these matters are the subject of the ensuing sections.

§ 81. Domicile as Basis

A defendant who is a New York domiciliary is amenable to the jurisdiction of the New York courts no matter where served with process. This is a basis constitutionally recognized by the U.S. Supreme Court[1] and exploited by statute in New York. CPLR 313 subjects a New York domiciliary to service of process outside New York on any cause of action. Of course, the fact of New York domicile will usually mean that the defendant is physically available for service within the state, but since domicile is not synonymous with residence, that is not always so. "Domicile" implies physical presence coupled with an intention to remain indefinitely, i.e., to make the state one's "home", while residence entails mere physical presence not necessarily accompanied by that intention.[2]

If the defendant is merely en route to a new domicile but has not yet reached it, the rule is that she has failed to achieve the new domicile and therefore retains the old one.[3]

The key time to look to in this instance is the commencement of the action; as a general rule, it is at that moment that the defendant must be a domiciliary in order for the plaintiff to exploit this basis.

The question arises whether the defendant's residence in New York, without domicile, would also constitute a jurisdictional basis. The Court of Appeals said in Dobkin v. Chapman that "[r]esidence itself may provide a foundation for the exercise of personal jurisdiction over an absent defendant by means of substituted service",[4] but did not elaborate. If the defendant, although technically domiciled

elsewhere, maintains a regular New York residence, it would not be unreasonable to conclude that he thereby establishes a relationship with New York and that the state may exploit it jurisdictionally. Perhaps that is what the *Dobkin* dictum implies. The fact is, however, that all three cases disposed of in *Dobkin* involved New York accidents and therefore had longarm bases for jurisdiction, which made dependence on other bases unnecessary.[5]

The Restatement takes the position that residence is a good jurisdictional basis "unless the individual's relationship to the state is so attenuated as to make the exercise of such jurisdiction unreasonable."[6]

§ 82. The Corporate "Presence" Doctrine

We have seen that the oldest and easiest way to get personal jurisdiction of a natural person defendant is to deliver the summons to him personally while he is physically present in New York. With the natural person, "presence" is spelled out by determining where the legs and feet are planted.

No such facile determination can be made of a corporation's presence because it is an intangible creature distinct from the humans who run it. One who happens to be a corporate director or officer or like person does not necessarily carry the corporation about with her. If, for example, such officer is in New York on private rather than corporate business when served, jurisdiction of the corporation does not necessarily result. The question is not whether a corporate officer is in New York, but whether the corporation is.

For the purpose of analogizing the corporation to the individual so as to determine whether the corporation is physically "present" in the state, decisional law has invented the "doing business" test. The corporation

---

§ 81

1. Milliken v. Meyer, 311 U.S. 457, 61 S.Ct. 339, 85 L.Ed. 278 (1940); Restatement, 2d, Conflict of Laws, § 29.

2. See Rawstorne v. Maguire, 265 N.Y. 204, 192 N.E. 294 (1934).

3. See Alvord & Alvord v. Patenotre, 196 Misc. 524, 92 N.Y.S.2d 514 (Sup.Ct., N.Y.County, 1949).

4. Dobkin v. Chapman, 21 N.Y.2d 490, 506, 289 N.Y.S.2d 161, 174, 236 N.E.2d 451, 460 (1968), citing Fishman v. Sanders, 15 N.Y.2d 298, 258 N.Y.S.2d 380, 206 N.E.2d 326 (1965).

5. The Dobkin trilogy of cases and the service methods used in each are treated in § 75 above.

6. Restatement, 2d, Conflict of Laws, § 30.

carries on its business through its employees and agents and the "doing business" test looks at the aggregate of the activities conducted in the state on that business. If those activities are found to be conducted on a regular day-to-day basis, the corporation is deemed "present" in the state and, by analogy to the natural person found here physically, it renders the corporation amenable to the jurisdiction of the New York courts on any claim at all (whether or not related to the state).

The finding of such presence under the doing business test is one of the bases of jurisdiction carried over by CPLR 301, which means that it invokes CPLR 313, which in turn means that service may be made on the corporation outside the state if need be.[1] The basis here is not the nature of the claim or its New York contacts; it is the physical presence of the corporation in New York.

This basis of judicial jurisdiction has long been recognized by the U.S. Supreme Court,[2] but its most popular and often quoted articulation is that of Judge Cardozo writing for the New York Court of Appeals in Tauza v. Susquehanna Coal Co.:[3] if the corporation "is here, not occasionally or casually, but with a fair measure of permanence and continuity, then, whether its business is interstate or local, it is within the jurisdiction of our courts."[4]

The thing to do, then, is look at the aggregate of activities carried on for the corporation in New York. In Bryant v. Finnish National Airline,[5] the Court of Appeals said that the doing business test "is and should be a simple pragmatic one". The plaintiff in Bryant was a New Yorker injured in Paris when a gust of air from the defendant's aircraft blew a baggage cart against her. She sued in New York, claiming that the defendant was doing business here. All the defendant had in New York was a one-and-a-half room office with three full-time and four part-time employees whose function was to receive and transmit, for confirmation in Europe, reservations from other carriers and from travel agencies. The defendant's local bank account was only for paying the employees' salaries and the rent and maintenance of the New York office. The court nevertheless found these activities sufficient and held the corporation "present" and amenable to jurisdiction. Bryant is regarded as liberalizing the doing business test,[6] although the "simple pragmatic" test it contemplates is possible only on simple pragmatic facts. As we shall see, some cases refuse to cooperate.

It is often said that the "mere solicitation" of business by the corporation will not suffice for a corporate presence, but that solicitation coupled with some additional activities will.[7] Apparently all the corporation was doing in the Bryant case was soliciting, but it had an office and a small staff with which to do so and those were the extras that gave jurisdiction.[8] There is "no precise measure of the nature or extent of local ... activities" that will make for a corporate presence,[9] but when those activities are carried on in New York by natural

---

§ 82

1. Whatever the basis of jurisdiction may be against the corporation, service on it is made in the usual way, i.e., by serving one of the individuals listed in CPLR 311(a)(1). If the corporation is an unlicensed foreign one found to be doing business in New York, Bus.Corp.L. § 307 authorizes service on the secretary of state as an alternative. In that instance the secretary is an implied-in-law agent, in contrast to his actual designation as agent for the domestic and licensed foreign corporation. See § 95 below.

2. See, e.g., International Harvester Co. v. Kentucky, 234 U.S. 579, 34 S.Ct. 944, 58 L.Ed. 1479 (1914). Shaffer v. Heitner, 433 U.S. 186, 97 S.Ct. 2569, 53 L.Ed.2d 683 (1977), which banned the use of quasi in rem jurisdiction in all but a few instances (see § 104, below), includes a footnote that seems designed to preserve the corporate presence basis of jurisdiction, or at least to prevent the Shaffer decision from being construed as undoing it. See 433 U.S. at 204, n.19, 97 S.Ct. at 2580, n.19.

3. 220 N.Y. 259, 115 N.E. 915 (1917).

4. Id. at 267, 115 N.E. at 917.

5. 15 N.Y.2d 426, 260 N.Y.S.2d 625, 208 N.E.2d 439 (1965).

6. See Central Sch. Dist. No. 2 v. C. R. Evans Corp., 49 Misc.2d 924, 268 N.Y.S.2d 800 (Sup.Ct., Chemung County, 1966).

7. See, e.g., Elish v. St. Louis S.W. Ry. Co., 305 N.Y. 267, 112 N.E.2d 842 (1953).

8. In the Tauza case, a corporate presence was spelled out upon a showing that the defendant maintained a New York office with a sales agent, eight salesmen, and clerical assistance, and that it regularly solicited business with that staff.

9. Sterling Novelty Corp. v. Frank & Hirsch Distrib. Co., 299 N.Y. 208, 210, 86 N.E.2d 564, 565 (1949).

persons directly employed by the corporation, the *Bryant* case seems to facilitate the inquiry.

When the activities are carried out not by employees of D Corporation, but through X, an independent person or entity, the solicitation rule may protect D, but it won't insulate X. Hence where X was a New Jersey company whose business was soliciting for its customers, and it carried out this business through "persons in its employ and present in New York", jurisdiction over X was upheld.[10]

A new dimension is added when it is alleged that Corporation X, acting for Corporation D in New York, is not independent, but in effect a mere employee or department of D. Assume that X Corporation, for example, is concededly doing business or even licensed to do business in New York. It is alleged that X is acting for D and that under the law of agency the aggregate of X's New York activities in behalf of D constitute D present in the state. This is indeed a possibility. Some major New York cases involve that situation, further complicated (or facilitated?) by interlocking ownership or directorship.

The rules that govern these inquiries are essentially rules of agency. One corporation can be acting as another's agent so pervasively as to constitute the principal "present" in New York even though ownership and directorship of the two corporations are entirely separate. As a result of the Court of Appeals decisions in Taca International Airlines, S.A. v. Rolls–Royce of England, Ltd.,[11] and Frummer v. Hilton Hotels International, Inc.,[12] however, the fact of interlocking ownership has taken on an influential role.

In *Taca*, the corporation that the plaintiff wanted to get at was E, the parent Rolls–Royce corporation, an English company. E owned all the stock of C, the Canadian Rolls Royce corporation, which in turn owned all the

stock of N, a Delaware corporation licensed to do business and concededly present in New York. It was alleged that E was doing regular business in New York through N. It was shown that there were some directors in common; that the business of N was solely to sell E's products; that the employees of N got their training from E in England; that it was E's warranties that accompanied N's sales of E's cars but that N performed on E's aero engines the requirements of those warranties; that key employees were exchanged both ways between N and E; and that all of N's income went to C and appeared on C's balance sheet and ultimately on E's. These and yet other factors suggested agency. The question was whether N was an independent entity or a mere department of E. The court held that N, for all the facade of separateness, was at root a mere department of E, and that E was therefore present in New York through N.

In *Frummer*, which involved the Hilton Hotel chain, the corporations seem to have maintained an even more punctilious separateness, but the interlocking ownership was apparent, and complex. The defendant was L, the London Hilton, an English corporation. Clearly present in New York was R, the Hilton Reservation Service. A different foreign corporation in the Hilton setup owned L and, together with still another one, owned R. R took and confirmed reservations in New York for L (and for other hotels in and out of the Hilton chain). Jurisdiction was sustained on a 4–3 vote, the majority finding that R was doing all the business in New York that L "could do were it here by its own officials."[13] The dissent took issue; it found the majority sustaining jurisdiction "over a foreign corporation simply because of its relationship with subsidiary or affiliated corporations".

10. Laufer v. Ostrow, 55 N.Y.2d 305, 449 N.Y.S.2d 456, 434 N.E.2d 692 (1982).

11. 15 N.Y.2d 97, 256 N.Y.S.2d 129, 204 N.E.2d 329 (1965).

12. 19 N.Y.2d 533, 281 N.Y.S.2d 41, 227 N.E.2d 851 (1967).

13. This statement in Frummer had impact, and perhaps undue impact, on the later case of Gelfand v. Tanner Motor Tours, 385 F.2d 116 (2d Cir.1967), in which the

corporation was held to be doing business in New York through an entirely independent representative because it would otherwise have had to go to New York to perform the service for itself. The service was the taking of reservations for the defendant's sightseeing bus business and the court stressed the large number of bookings that originated in New York and the high percentage of the defendant's overall tour business generated in New York.

Perhaps the meat of the *Frummer* decision is in the general aura created by the fact of interlocking ownership. The question of the New York presence of the parent through the local activities of its subsidiary will turn on rules of agency, suggest the majority, "and the fact that the two are commonly owned is significant only because it gives rise to a valid inference as to the broad scope of the agency".[14] In other words, we do go by principles of agency, but once agency is indicated by the facts, the additional fact of the parent-subsidiary relationship can intercede to stretch the agency into an outright parental "presence".

It is instructive to distinguish yet another case in which a local service took reservations for hotels outside New York. In Miller v. Surf Properties, Inc.,[15] the local service in New York took reservations for Florida hotels, but that did not result in the hotels' corporate presence in New York. A major distinction is that the service in *Miller* was an independently-owned profit-making organization, which enabled the court to regard it as an independent contractor. In *Frummer* the service was not independently owned and was not a profit-maker; it was run (so the majority found) for the benefit of the Hilton chain.

We can apply these principles instructively to two other major international corporations, the German Volkswagen Corporation and the Japanese Toyota Corporation.

Volkswagen escaped New York "presence" jurisdiction in Delagi v. Volkswagenwerk AG.[16] It owned all the stock of the New Jersey corporation that imports Volkswagens into this country, but the cars get into New York through a franchisee owned by American investors independent of the German and New Jersey companies. The franchisee picks the cars up at various delivery points, none of them in New York. Various devices by which the German corporation exercised ultimate control over the activities of the New York franchisee were shown, but these did not confer jurisdiction. The Court of Appeals said that it "has never held a foreign corporation present on the basis of control, unless there was in existence at least a parent-subsidiary relationship."[17]

That statement appears to confirm what the dissent contended in *Frummer*: that the interlocking aspect of ownership was being given a decisive role jurisdictionally. Indeed, it was the failure of the Japanese Toyota Corporation to mind these Ps and Qs that resulted in their being held to a New York presence in Sunrise Toyota, Ltd. v. Toyota Motor Co.:[18] the California corporation doing business in New York was wholly owned by the Japanese parents.

It may come as a surprise to learn that a company like the German Volkswagen Corporation, despite its thousands of cars on the New York highways, is not "present" in the state. But the "mere sales of a manufacturer's product in New York," said the court in *Volkswagen*, "however substantial, have never made the foreign corporation manufacturer amenable to suit in this jurisdiction."[19]

These various entries, and yet others, are not entirely reconcilable, but we can note two helpful facts:

First, a need to measure corporate "presence" is confronted only when the cause of action itself has no New York roots, because, if it has, the case gets longarm jurisdiction under CPLR 302 and does not need any corporate "presence" help from CPLR 301. In *Taca*, for example, the suit was for Nicaraguan property damage; in *Frummer*, for an injury in London; in *Delagi*, for an accident in Germany. Had those occurrences taken place in New York, CPLR 302 would have given jurisdiction and made a corporate "presence" inquiry unnecessary.

14. 19 N.Y.2d at 538, 281 N.Y.S.2d at 45, 227 N.E.2d at 854.

15. 4 N.Y.2d 475, 176 N.Y.S.2d 318, 151 N.E.2d 874 (1958).

16. 29 N.Y.2d 426, 328 N.Y.S.2d 653, 278 N.E.2d 895 (1972).

17. Id. at 432, 328 N.Y.S.2d at 657, 278 N.E.2d at 897. See Birnbaum, 1972 Survey of New York Law, Civil Practice, 24 Syracuse L.Rev. 447, 457–58 (1973).

18. 55 F.R.D. 519 (S.D.N.Y.1972).

19. 29 N.Y.2d at 433, 328 N.Y.S.2d at 657, 278 N.E.2d at 898.

Second, even if the claim has no CPLR 302 contacts and something else is needed as a basis for personal jurisdiction of a corporate defendant, that basis automatically appears if the corporation is either a domestic one or a duly licensed foreign one because both categories are required to designate the secretary of state as agent for service.[20] That designation is good no matter where the claim arises. Service can be made in that instance on the secretary[21] or, as an alternative, on any of the designees listed in CPLR 311(a)(1).

The need to use the "presence" doctrine thus arises only when (1) the defendant is an unlicensed foreign corporation, and (2) the cause of action does not arise out of an activity conducted in New York.[22]

While designed historically to determine the amenability of a corporation to local service, it has been held that the "doing business" test extends also to a nonresident individual working in New York, permitting extrastate service on the individual although the claim did not arise out of New York activities.[23]

§ 83. Comparing Corporate "Doing Business" Tests

The "doing business" test examined in the prior section determines whether a corporation is amenable to New York jurisdiction. It's a test carried forward by CPLR 301 and for convenience we can call it the CPLR 301 test.

We have also met two other doing business tests. One arises under § 1314(b)(5) of the Business Corporation Law, a kind of forum non conveniens provision that requires a showing in certain cases that a defendant corporation is doing business in New York before the court is authorized to entertain the case. We can call this one the BCL 1314 test.[1]

The third arises under § 1312 of the Business Corporation Law, which precludes a plaintiff foreign corporation from maintaining a New York action if it is doing business in New York without having duly licensed itself to do so.[2] We will refer to that one as the BCL 1312 test.

Are these tests the same? As a practical matter they ought to be. One should be able to take all of the cases just reviewed under the CPLR 301 test and apply them under the other provisions as well. It seems idle to go through this exercise afresh for the other provisions, using different tests, especially because there is no convincing evidence that the policies underlying the three tests necessarily diverge. But while the CPLR 301 and BCL 1314 tests are said by caselaw to be the same,[3] the CPLR 301 and BCL 1312 tests are said by caselaw to differ.[4] The extent of the difference is not clear, but more appears to be demanded for the BCL 1312 test because of its penal effect in precluding suit by a foreign corporation.

Section 1301(b) of the Business Corporation Law lists certain corporate activities and provides that these by themselves shall not constitute "doing business" for BCL purposes, and this applies to both the 1312 and 1314 tests. The activities listed include bringing or de-

---

20. Bus.Corp.L. § 304(a), (b).

21. Bus.Corp.L. § 306(b).

22. It has been suggested that big "multinational" corporations should be deemed amenable to local jurisdiction merely because of their deliberate commercial exploitation of a local market, with no other test required, see Bulova Watch Co. v. K. Hattori & Co., 508 F.Supp. 1322 (E.D.N.Y.1981), but New York has not adopted such a test. Jurisdiction in Bulova, moreover, was apparently available under either CPLR 301 (the corporate presence doctrine that is the subject of this section) or CPLR 302 (longarm jurisdiction, the subject of § 84 et seq.).

23. See FCNB Spiegel Inc. v. Dimmick, 163 Misc.2d 152, 619 N.Y.S.2d 935 (Civ.Ct., N.Y.County, 1994), citing ABKCO Industries, Inc. v. Lennon, 52 A.D.2d 435, 384 N.Y.S.2d 781 (1st Dep't 1976), treated in § 83, below.

§ 83

1. See § 29 above.

2. See § 30 above.

3. Fremay, Inc. v. Modern Plastic Machine Corp., 15 A.D.2d 235, 222 N.Y.S.2d 694 (1st Dep't 1961); see also Simonson v. International Bank, 16 A.D.2d 55, 225 N.Y.S.2d 392 (1st Dep't 1962), aff'd with opinion 14 N.Y.2d 281, 251 N.Y.S.2d 433, 200 N.E.2d 427 (1964).

4. Beja v. Jahangiri, 453 F.2d 959 (2d Cir.1972); William L. Bonnell Co. v. Katz, 23 Misc.2d 1028, 196 N.Y.S.2d 763 (Sup.Ct., N.Y.County, 1960). The difference is rooted in fears for the constitutionality of BCL 1312's predecessors and has to do with possible interference with interstate commerce, at least as that prospect was conceived in an earlier era. See International Text-Book Co. v. Tone, 220 N.Y. 313, 115 N.E. 914 (1917).

fending a proceeding, holding directors' or shareholders' meetings, maintaining bank accounts or maintaining offices or agencies for securities activities. Doing only those things does not establish a corporate presence.

By listing activities that may not alone be taken to satisfy the 1312 or 1314 doing business tests, however, BCL 1301 evinces an intention that whatever tests do apply to those provisions should be the same. If that is so— and caselaw has yet to meet this matter full face—then the BCL 1314 test has the unique distinction of being the same as two other tests that differ. This suggests that the three tests are all the same, or that someone has had too much wine.

The doing business test that subjects a defendant to jurisdiction under CPLR 301 was traditionally restricted to the corporate defendant, but was extended to nondomiciliary individuals as well, and in language to suggest that it can also be used against foreign partnerships and associations.[5] When so applied, it enables any claim to be asserted against the defendant, whether or not the claim arises out of the business done in New York. The test is apparently to be an alternative; jurisdiction can still rest, instead, on local service on a partner or on the association's president or treasurer.[6]

§ 84. "Longarm" Jurisdiction, Background

In 1945, in the landmark case of International Shoe Co. v. Washington,[1] the U.S. Supreme Court said that if the claims sued on "arise out of or are connected with ... activities within the state", the state can exercise personal jurisdiction of the defendant in respect of those claims no matter where the

defendant is served with process. This came to be known as "longarm" jurisdiction. It allows the state to exercise extraterritorial jurisdiction of a nondomiciliary defendant based on contacts the defendant had with the state if— and this is the key "longarm" factor—the claim arises out of those contacts. Operations within the state, if the claim is a product of those very operations, "make it reasonable and just according to our traditional conception of fair play and substantial justice" to subject the one conducting those operations to extraterritorial jurisdiction.[2]

Even cases prior to *International Shoe* had begun to escape the strictures of Pennoyer v. Neff,[3] which regarded personal jurisdiction as permissible only when the defendant was personally served within the state. The nonresident motorist statutes, for example, under which an implied designation of a state official as an agent for service automatically results if a claim arises from in-state driving,[4] were sustained as constitutional.[5] But those and like statutes still paid lip service to *Pennoyer* by regarding the within-the-state service on the state official as the jurisdiction-getting act. In 1940, however, outright extrastate service, with personam effect, was sustained in Milliken v. Meyer[6] on the basis that the defendant was a domiciliary of the forum.

The facts of *International Shoe* show that the state in that case was still looking for a local "agent" on which to effect service, but as a matter of historical perspective it is nonetheless the *International Shoe* case that takes the credit for abandoning *Pennoyer* and allowing the states to extend their summons beyond their borders, as long as it is limited to instances in which the claim arises from those

---

5. See ABKCO Industries, Inc. v. Lennon, 52 A.D.2d 435, 384 N.Y.S.2d 781 (1st Dep't 1976).

6. See § 69 above.

§ 84

1. 326 U.S. 310, 66 S.Ct. 154, 90 L.Ed. 95.

2. Id. at 320, 66 S.Ct. at 160. The International Shoe facts suggest that the activities of the defendant corporation in the state might have been regular enough to constitute a corporate "presence" under the doing-business test, which would have allowed jurisdiction against it

on any claim (see § 82 above), but the court took it as the occasion to pronounce the elements of the "longarm" category of jurisdiction, and it is that category for which International Shoe stands as the historical precedent.

3. 95 U.S. 714, 24 L.Ed. 565 (1877).

4. Veh. & Traf.L. § 253. See § 97 below.

5. Hess v. Pawloski, 274 U.S. 352, 47 S.Ct. 632, 71 L.Ed. 1091 (1927).

6. 311 U.S. 457, 61 S.Ct. 339, 85 L.Ed. 278.

"minimum contacts" a defendant must have with the forum in order to satisfy due process.

It is the due process clause of the 14th Amendment that oversees exercises of state jurisdiction, and it is the U.S. Supreme Court that oversees the clause, thus accounting for the Supreme Court's key role in the area of longarm jurisdiction. The court in *International Shoe* indicates that whether there is longarm jurisdiction in any given case is a sui generis inquiry:

> Whether due process is satisfied must depend rather upon the quality and nature of the activity in relation to the fair and orderly administration of the laws which it was the purpose of the due process clause to insure.[7]

For a while there wasn't much guidance from the Supreme Court, especially in tort cases. *International Shoe* of 1945 involved the collection of state taxes. The next U.S. Supreme Court address to longarm jurisdiction was in 1957 in McGee v. International Life Ins. Co.,[8] an action on an insurance policy. And a year later, in 1958, came Hanson v. Denckla,[9] a complicated wills-trust case.[10] Those three cases were all the Supreme Court had to say about longarm jurisdiction until 1980—a 35-year period as measured from *International Shoe*'s 1945 beginning—and not one was a tort case. For all the hundreds and perhaps thousands of longarm tort cases in the interim, from both state and federal courts, it was not until 1980, in World–Wide Volkswagen Corp. v. Woodson,[11] that the tort case was addressed, and with more restrictive notions about how far a state may go than had

been assumed under some state statutes, including New York's.[12]

It is by statute or rule that longarm jurisdiction is exploited. Some states responded to *International Shoe*'s invitation more quickly than others, and some limited their longarm statutes to specific activities while others went all the way by enacting a general statute authorizing jurisdiction whenever it would be compatible with due process.[13] Illinois was one of the quicker responders but chose to restrict its longarm jurisdiction to claims arising out of designated activities.[14] New York got around to general longarm jurisdiction on September 1, 1963, when the CPLR took effect containing New York's first general longarm statute, CPLR 302, which was originally modeled on the Illinois statute.[15] CPLR 302 does not go as far as due process permits. It delineates only certain categories. But although these do not go all the way,[16] they go far, as will be seen.

"Longarm" and like categories, in which jurisdiction is predicated not on the defendant's regular presence in the state but on the claim's arising out of some in-state event for which the defendant is responsible, is sometimes called "specific jurisdiction", with the term "general jurisdiction" used to describe the "presence" category, which supports jurisdiction of all claims against the defendant, related or not to the state.[17]

§ 85. Longarm   Jurisdiction   under CPLR 302, Generally

CPLR 302(a) opens with the language that "[a]s to a cause of action arising from any of the acts enumerated in this section, a court

---

7.   326 U.S. at 319, 66 S.Ct. at 160.

8.   355 U.S. 220, 78 S.Ct. 199, 2 L.Ed.2d 223.

9.   357 U.S. 235, 78 S.Ct. 1228, 2 L.Ed.2d 1283 (1958).

10.   In Hanson, Florida tried to exercise personal jurisdiction over Delaware trustees and over property in Delaware on the basis that if the transactions which sent the property to Delaware were stricken down the property would revert to a Florida estate. Jurisdiction was rejected. The court noted the liberal trend set by the McGee case of the prior year but added that "it is a mistake to assume that this trend heralds the eventual demise of all restrictions on the personal jurisdiction of state courts." Id. at 251, 78 S.Ct. at 1238.

11.   444 U.S. 286, 100 S.Ct. 559, 62 L.Ed.2d 490.

12.   This matter is elaborated in § 88, below, in treating one of New York's longarm tort statutes.

13.   E.g., Cal.Code Civ.Pro. § 410.10: "A court of this state may exercise jurisdiction on any basis not inconsistent with the Constitution of this state or of the United States."

14.   Ill.Ann.Stat., ch. 735, § 5/2–209.

15.   See 2d Rpt.Leg.Doc. (1958) No. 13, p.39.

16.   New York also has one of those all-the-way longarm statutes, but it is applicable only in the surrogate's court. See SCPA 210.

17.   See Burger King Corp. v. Rudzewicz, 471 U.S. 462, 105 S.Ct. 2174, 85 L.Ed.2d 528 (1985).

may exercise personal jurisdiction over any nondomiciliary, or his executor or administrator, who in person or through an agent" does any of the things listed. Before turning to seriatim treatment of the listed activities, several general observations should be made about the statute as a whole.

CPLR 302(a) is applicable to all categories of defendants. It speaks of a "nondomiciliary", but that includes a corporation, association, partnership, trustee of a trust—any person or entity capable of being made a defendant in a lawsuit—as well as a natural person. And it applies whether the listed activities were carried on by the defendant in person or through an agent.

If the would-be 302 defendant dies before the action is commenced, it may be commenced against his personal representative, who is just as amenable to jurisdiction in a longarm case as the decedent himself would have been.[1] And if a duly served 302 defendant dies during the lawsuit, his foreign personal representative need only be substituted in his place. This requires no new action; it entails only that the representative be served with the papers that bring on the motion to substitute,[2] and those papers are servable outside New York with personam effect under CPLR 302(a) and 313.[3]

Longarm jurisdiction under CPLR 302 is available in the federal courts in New York; state extraterritorial bases of personal jurisdiction have been adopted by the Federal Rules of Civil Procedure without regard to the basis on which federal subject matter jurisdiction may rest in the case (diversity of citizenship, federal question, etc.).[4] Some of the state's lower courts have their own longarm statutes and these, when applicable, permit service outside the area serviced by the particular court just as CPLR 302 and 313 dispense with state lines in the supreme court.[5]

Longarm jurisdiction is usable against any person sought to be made a party to an action. It can be used in third-party practice, for example,[6] such as by D when impleading X for contribution or indemnification in respect of the claim on which P is suing D, as long as local contacts are demonstrated in respect of the third-party claim itself. The court does not get extraterritorial jurisdiction of the alleged indemnitor (X in the example) merely because it has jurisdiction of the party claiming indemnification (D in the example).[7]

The statute is also available against one who was a domiciliary at the time of the alleged 302 acts. In several cases it appeared that the defendant had moved from New York after the acts but before suit. He then ingeniously alleged that he could not be amenable to jurisdiction under CPLR 302(a) because that statute applies only to nondomiciliaries; and that he could not be subjected to extrastate service as a domiciliary because that requires domicile at the time of suit and he had left the state by that time. A few lower court judges bought the argument but the Court of Appeals finally held that there is no such "gap" in jurisdiction and that CPLR 302(a) may also be applied to defendants domiciled here at the time of the acts.[8]

---

§ 85

1. Such a rule had earlier been applied and constitutionally sustained under the nonresident motorist statute, (now) Veh. & Traf.L. § 253, in Leighton v. Roper, 300 N.Y. 434, 91 N.E.2d 876 (1950).

2. CPLR 1015 authorizes the substitution in case of death and CPLR 1021 supplies the procedure, which is a mere motion.

3. See Rosenfeld v. Hotel Corp. of America, 20 N.Y.2d 25, 281 N.Y.S.2d 308, 228 N.E.2d 374 (1967), which also sustains the constitutionality of CPLR 302 and 313 in this respect.

4. FRCP Rule 4(k)(1)(A). See § 626 below (Practitioner's Edition).

5. See § 404 in the New York City Civil Court Act and in the Uniform District and City Court Acts, McKinney's Vol. 29A, Part 3.

6. Moss v. Frost Hempstead Corp., 43 Misc.2d 357, 251 N.Y.S.2d 194 (Sup.Ct., Nassau County, 1964). Third-party practice is treated in § 155 et seq., below.

7. Media Corp. of America v. Motif Mfg. Co., 524 F.Supp. 86 (S.D.N.Y.1981). The case is discussed, and suggestions made about how the indemnitee might try to protect itself, in the lead note in New York State Law Digest No. 269.

8. State v. Davies, 24 A.D.2d 240, 265 N.Y.S.2d 358 (3d Dep't 1965), aff'd 18 N.Y.2d 950, 277 N.Y.S.2d 146, 223 N.E.2d 570 (1966). The same rule applies to a foreign corporation that was "present" at the time of the acts but

A nondomiciliary or nonresident plaintiff may use CPLR 302. It is not restricted to the use of New York plaintiffs. But the doctrine of forum non conveniens[9] can of course intervene to dismiss the case if, notwithstanding jurisdiction, New York involvement is too tenuous to impose the case on the New York courts.

Note that CPLR 302(a) does not require that the cause of action arise in New York. It requires only that it arise "from" the acts listed in the section. The claim can therefore arise elsewhere and still give New York jurisdiction as long as there are adequate New York acts "from" which it arises.

§ 86. "Transacts Any Business" under CPLR 302(a)(1)

If the defendant transacts business in New York and the claim arises from it, jurisdiction is conferred by the first clause of CPLR 302(a)(1), "transacts any business within the state",[1] and the defendant is subject to service outside New York under CPLR 313. This provision is invoked regularly; the question is invariably whether what the defendant did in New York constitutes a sufficient "transaction" to satisfy the statute: the inquiry is sui generis, the annotations on CPLR 302(a)(1) are many, and the lawyer bent on securing longarm jurisdiction should consult them straightaway. The cases are so numerous that despite extensive factual variations, the lawyer will often find a case fairly close to her own. Our mission is to set forth illustrative cases, especially from the appellate courts, to establish the general principles, and to illustrate a few of the more common situations.

The leading cases, as might be expected, are for the most part the early ones. Among the first from the New York Court of Appeals was Longines–Wittnauer Watch Co. v. Barnes & Reinecke, Inc.,[2] in which D was a foreign corporation with its principal place of business in Illinois. P was a New York corporation that bought $118,000 worth of complicated machinery from D, which D shipped f.o.b. Chicago. Some preliminary negotiations had taken place in New York but the original contract was executed in Chicago. Most significantly, D sent several of its employees, including two engineers, into New York for several months to help install the machinery. When P later sued D for breach of warranty, jurisdiction under CPLR 302(a)(1) was sustained. The Court of Appeals would not determine whether any one of the New York contacts sufficed; it indicated that the test is not quantitative but qualitative and that the inquiry should determine whether "defendant has engaged in some purposeful activity in this State in connection with the matter in suit."[3] In Longines, defendant did engage in such purposeful activity, and was subject to longarm jurisdiction. The case also clarifies that for a contract action to be sustainable under CPLR 302(a)(1), the contract need not have been made in New York.

A case in which the Court of Appeals rejected jurisdiction shortly afterwards is Kramer v. Vogl.[4] There D was an Austrian leather manufacturer which, by an agreement made in Europe, made P its exclusive American distributor. All of D's contacts with P in New York were by mail. P bought the leather from D outright and it was shipped f.o.b. European ports.[5] P sued D for fraud, alleging that D gave

---

left the state afterwards. Sharp Export, Ltd. v. Mulco Products, Inc., 50 Misc.2d 611, 270 N.Y.S.2d 787 (Sup.Ct. Nassau County, 1966).

9. See §§ 28 and 29 above.

§ 86

1. The "contracts anywhere" clause, the second segment of CPLR 302(a)(1), is separately treated in § 86A, below.

2. 15 N.Y.2d 443, 261 N.Y.S.2d 8, 209 N.E.2d 68 (1965).

3. Id. at 457, 261 N.Y.S.2d at 18, 209 N.E.2d at 75. The court relied on the U. S. Supreme Court's requirement, in Hanson v. Denckla, 357 U.S. 235, 253, 78 S.Ct.

1228, 1240, 2 L.Ed.2d 1283 (1958), that the defendant be shown to have "purposefully avail[ed] itself of the privilege of conducting activities" within the state and thus "invok[ed] the benefits and protections of its laws."

4. 17 N.Y.2d 27, 267 N.Y.S.2d 900, 215 N.E.2d 159 (1966).

5. The f.o.b. feature frequently appears in these cases. Its influence, when the defendant is the seller of goods, apparently consists in the fact that an f.o.b. shipment cuts off the seller's obligations, and therefore its contacts, at the f.o.b. point. The f.o.b. aspect was played down in Galgay v. Bulletin Company, Inc., 504 F.2d 1062 (2d Cir.1974), where the plaintiff was the seller. For an explanation of "f.o.b.", see UCC § 2–319.

distribution rights to others in violation of the agreement. The court held that D had not transacted any business in New York. Selling and sending goods into New York pursuant to orders sent from New York does not by itself give longarm jurisdiction.

Longines and *Kramer* sometimes act as poles between which yet other cases are set to see which one the new case will gravitate towards. McKee Electric Co. v. Rauland–Borg Corp.[6] was such a case. D manufactured sound equipment in Illinois and shipped it f.o.b. Chicago to P in New York. P was one of D's distributors and the distribution contract was made in New York. The goods proved defective and P sustained losses for which it now sued D in breach of contract and conspiracy. The case thus far seems much like *Kramer*. But when difficulties arose D sent one of its employees, a trouble-shooter, into New York to confer with P. He did so for about a day. Although that tended to push the case closer to *Longines*, a majority of the court held that it did not push hard enough, that this contact was "so infinitesimal" as to make no difference. *Kramer* governed, and jurisdiction was turned down.

One reconciliation is that the crew sent into New York in *Longines* was indispensable to the agreement; if they were not sent, no agreement would have been made. The sending of the trouble-shooter in *McKee* can be contrasted as a mere gesture to P, rather than as an understood part of the bargain. A minority of three would not draw that contrast and voted to sustain jurisdiction.

In Singer v. Walker,[7] a case decided in a consolidated opinion with *Longines*, jurisdiction was sustained under CPLR 302(a)(1) for the tort of personal injury, establishing that this paragraph about transacting business is not limited to contract or other commercial actions but can apply to torts as well if they arise from the transaction. In *Singer*, neither the negligent act nor the resulting injury oc-

curred in New York, but jurisdiction was still sustained. D was a foreign manufacturer and made, among other things, what it labeled "unbreakable" geological hammers. These were shipped in substantial quantities into New York and P's aunt bought one in New York from a dealer and gave it to P, an infant, who was injured while using it on a Connecticut trip. Jurisdiction was upheld as arising out of D's transaction of business in New York under CPLR 302(a)(1).

Singer is somewhat of a maverick. It apparently holds, or at least the *Kramer* court thought so, that if a foreign seller, otherwise beyond 302(a)(1) jurisdiction, "solicits business in this State by means of catalogue, advertisements or other promotional material circulated here"[8] (D did those things in *Singer*), it can be subjected to jurisdiction for causes of action connected with local purchase of its products. Those promotional activities in *Singer* would then appear to be the jurisdiction-giving factor that distinguishes the jurisdiction-rejecting *Kramer* case. It may also be significant that *Singer* involved personal injury and *Kramer* only a property right, but the courts do not say outright that that makes a jurisdictional difference.

CPLR 302(a) has two paragraphs devoted to torts, paragraphs 2 and 3, but they both exclude defamation. Perhaps ironically, paragraph 1 has been held available for a defamation claim if it can be shown to arise out of the defendant's transaction of business in New York.[9] That this is so makes longarm jurisdiction a New York possibility in defamation cases, and makes relevant in turn two major U.S. Supreme Court cases on the subject, involving national publications: Calder v. Jones[10] (involving the National Enquirer) and Keeton v. Hustler Magazine,[11] both decided in 1984. Not only the publication itself, but also the individuals writing and editing it, were found to be within the jurisdiction of the forum,

---

6. 20 N.Y.2d 377, 283 N.Y.S.2d 34, 229 N.E.2d 604 (1967) (4–3 decision).

7. 15 N.Y.2d 443, 261 N.Y.S.2d 8, 209 N.E.2d 68, cert.denied sub nom. Estwing Mfg. Co. v. Singer, 382 U.S. 905, 86 S.Ct. 241, 15 L.Ed.2d 158 (1965).

8. Kramer v. Vogl, note 3, above, 17 N.Y.2d at 31, 267 N.Y.S.2d at 903, 217 N.E.2d at 161.

9. See § 87 below.

10. 465 U.S. 783, 104 S.Ct. 1482, 79 L.Ed.2d 804.

11. 465 U.S. 770, 104 S.Ct. 1473, 79 L.Ed.2d 790.

which in each case was one of many states in which the publications were sold and circulated but not one in which any of the writing or editing was done. The generous reach allowed the longarm statutes involved in these libel cases (California's and New Hampshire's) suggest that the Supreme Court views differently, and more expansively, longarm efforts aimed at intentional as against unintentional torts.[12]

When the defendant is a corporation, it is necessary to distinguish between "doing business", which constitutes a corporation "present" in the state under CPLR 301,[13] and "transacts any business", the standard applicable under CPLR 302(a)(1). For "presence", the corporation's activities in New York must be regular; if they are, the corporation is amenable to suit in the state on any claim, arising or not arising out of the New York acts. If the activity is not regular, but it is shown that the claim arises out of whatever the local activity was, the activity can qualify as a "transaction of business" within the intendment of CPLR 302(a)(1). In these senses, "transacts" is narrow and "doing" is broad, but these are merely the special uses to which the terms are put in this jurisdictional realm of New York law. They are not to be taken as the literal meaning of the terms, nor may they necessarily be exported for equivalent use in other contexts.

Under neither category is jurisdiction present against a foreign hotel or like entity which does no more than maintain a listing in a New York telephone directory, even if a toll-free number is furnished. A number of hotels do this, and the courts have apparently decided that this activity, without more, will not confer jurisdiction either under CPLR 301 or 302(a)(1).[14]

Two classic buy-and-sell situations should be highlighted, for in each of them longarm jurisdiction has been refused under the "transacts"

clause of CPLR 302 (although it might be accepted under the "contracts" clause treated in the next section). One, already seen in *Kramer*, is where P is a New York buyer who orders goods from D, a foreign seller. The mere shipment of goods to New York on an order sent by P from New York does not give longarm jurisdiction against the foreign seller, such as for breach of warranty. Conversely, if P is a New York seller and D the foreign buyer who simply sends an order to P in New York, by telephone or otherwise, pursuant to which P ships the goods f.o.b. New York, there is no longarm jurisdiction against the foreign buyer, such as for the price of the goods.[15] Additional contacts might mean jurisdiction, but those bare facts alone do not. If, for example, the foreign buyer came to New York in addition to conducting negotiations by telephone and mail, longarm jurisdiction for the purchase price of the goods can result,[16] but it won't if the trip to New York was on an unrelated transaction.[17]

In Galgay v. Bulletin Co.,[18] D was a Pennsylvania publisher that ordered more than a million dollars in special machinery from P, a manufacturer located in New York. The goods were made pursuant to the contract and shipped f.o.b. New York, an agent of D coming to New York to pick up the equipment. The contract also stipulated to the application of New York substantive law. The Second Circuit analogized the case, a contract claim for the balance due, to the simple situation in which a foreign buyer orders goods from a New York seller, and rejected jurisdiction. The analogy might be appropriate if the goods ordered were stock items, whatever the quantity ordered, but it is submitted that when the order is for the manufacture of special, expensive, and sophisticated machinery, especially when combined with the several other contacts manifest

---

12. The cases are discussed in the lead note in New York State Law Digest No. 297.

13. See § 82, above, treating the doing-business or "presence" test.

14. See, e.g. Ziperman v. Frontier Hotel of Las Vegas, 50 A.D.2d 581, 374 N.Y.S.2d 697 (2d Dep't 1975).

15. M. Katz & Son Billiard Products, Inc. v. G. Correale & Sons, Inc., 20 N.Y.2d 903, 285 N.Y.S.2d 871, 232

N.E.2d 864 (1967), affirming 26 A.D.2d 52, 270 N.Y.S.2d 672 (1st Dep't 1966).

16. See Harry Winston, Inc. v. Waldfogel, 292 F.Supp. 473 (S.D.N.Y.1968).

17. Pacamor Bearings, Inc. v. Molon Motors & Coil, Inc., 102 A.D.2d 355, 477 N.Y.S.2d 856 (3d Dep't 1984).

18. 504 F.2d 1062 (2d Cir.1974).

on the *Galgay* facts, longarm jurisdiction should exist. When a nondomiciliary arranges for a company to manufacture in New York a substantial quantity of made-to-order equipment, the mission of longarm jurisdiction would seem at hand. Subsequent cases have nevertheless placed *Galgay* in the simple category of a sale "by telephone or mail from a New York plaintiff" and insulated the buyer from New York jurisdiction.[19]

The fact that a contract has been made in New York does not by itself guarantee jurisdiction if other contacts are lacking,[20] although it is always a factor to be considered.[21] But if the contract contemplates an ongoing relationship between a New Yorker and the nondomiciliary, rather than a random or single transaction, its negotiation and execution in New York will likely tip the scales in favor of jurisdiction, as it did in George Reiner and Co. v. Schwartz.[22]

The defendant in *George Reiner* was a Massachusetts resident who responded to an ad placed by the plaintiff, a New York corporation, in the Boston Globe. The defendant then came to New York at plaintiff's expense and after a day's discussions and negotiations[23] made a contract to be the plaintiff's New England salesman. For four years that relationship continued, the defendant working out of his Massachusetts home. The plaintiff then sued for the excess of defendant's drawings over earned commissions and longarm jurisdiction was sustained under CPLR 302(a)(1). Quoting and stressing the language of the U.S. Supreme Court in Hanson v. Denckla,[24] that jurisdiction is authorized when "the defendant purposefully avails itself of the privilege of conducting activities within the forum State, thus invoking the benefits and protection of its

laws", the Court of Appeals held that the defendant's physical presence in New York when he made the contract, coupled with its contemplation of a continuing relationship between the parties, constituted such conduct and satisfied as a 302(a)(1) "transaction". The casual New York visit of the trouble-shooter in *McKee*, discussed earlier in this section, was distinguished; it was not at all the source, as the *George Reiner* visit was, of the parties' contract and continuing arrangement.

The court did note, however, that the panel in *McKee* did not weigh the possible New York execution of the original distributorship contract, hinting that perhaps jurisdiction could have been sustained if it had; that the *McKee* court chose instead to rely on the aggregate of activities, as *Longines* had, finding the aggregate inadequate in *McKee*, however sufficient it may have been in *Longines*.

Some of the *George Reiner* language might be read to suggest that the mere making of the contract in New York is by itself sufficient to support CPLR 302(a)(1) longarm jurisdiction. But the Court of Appeals said in Presidential Realty Corp. v. Michael Square West, Ltd.,[25] shortly after the *George Reiner* decision, that if the formal execution of the contract takes place in New York only because the parties happen to be physically in the state at the moment of execution, longarm jurisdiction will not attach under CPLR 302(a)(1). That was the situation in *Presidential*, where the agreement had been negotiated in three southern cities and it was only because the plaintiff wanted further talks, which took place at its New York office, that the formal execution of the contract took place in the state.

---

19. See, e.g., Concrete Pipe & Products Corp. v. Modern Building Materials, Inc., 213 A.D.2d 1023, 624 N.Y.S.2d 496 (4th Dep't 1995), holding that the principle applies to a nondomiciliary who leases as well as to one who buys.

20. McNellis v. American Box Board Co., 53 Misc.2d 479, 278 N.Y.S.2d 771 (Sup.Ct., Onondaga County, 1967).

21. See the review of "transaction" cases in Standard Wine & Liquor Co. v. Bombay Spirits Co., 20 N.Y.2d 13, 281 N.Y.S.2d 299, 228 N.E.2d 367 (1967).

22. 41 N.Y.2d 648, 394 N.Y.S.2d 844, 363 N.E.2d 551 (1977).

23. For treatment of how negotiations conducted in New York figure in determining "transacts" jurisdiction, especially when the contract itself is technically executed outside the state, see Moser v. Boatman, 392 F.Supp. 270 (E.D.N.Y.1975).

24. 357 U.S. 235, 253, 78 S.Ct. 1228, 1240, 2 L.Ed.2d 1283 (1958).

25. 44 N.Y.2d 672, 405 N.Y.S.2d 37, 376 N.E.2d 198 (1978).

Note how the *Longines* case manifests the converse proposition: that the making of the contract outside New York will not preclude "transaction" jurisdiction if other contacts are present.

The case of Parke–Bernet Galleries v. Franklin[26] is an important one. It involves the agency aspect of CPLR 302(a). P was an auction gallery and D a Californian who wanted to participate in P's New York auction without coming to New York. P let one of its employees hold an open telephone line to D in California during the auction. Through this employee, D put in his bids, won a few, and then refused to pay. Longarm jurisdiction was sustained on the ground that the employee, although on P's payroll, had actually been made an agent by D, a kind of borrowed servant.

An intriguing line of cases involves a New York plaintiff who has in one way or another been retained to act in New York for the foreign defendant, and where the plaintiff himself brings suit against the defendant for something connected with their arrangement. To get longarm jurisdiction in this kind of case, the plaintiff tries to impute his own New York acts to the defendant, as, for example, when P is a New York lawyer hired to act for D and who now sues D for his fee. The Court of Appeals has held that there is no longarm jurisdiction in such a case; that New York acts performed by P for D cannot be jurisdictionally imputed to D in a suit by P.[27]

Conversely, out-of-state lawyers acting for a New York plaintiff don't automatically confront New York longarm jurisdiction if the New Yorker is unhappy with their services. California lawyers acting for a New York plaintiff, but acting only in California without coming into New York, escaped longarm jurisdiction in a malpractice action brought in federal court in New York in Mayes v. Leipziger.[28] The lawyers' services had been solicited in California. The court distinguishes the Parke–Bernet case, discussed above.

Perhaps there are some instances in which P's overall New York activities can be imputed to D.[29] If, for example, P's New York activities are solely in behalf of D—P performs services for no one else—they may support an imputation and support jurisdiction.[30] It seems equally clear, however, that if P acts for D and others, such as where P is an independent broker, his New York activities will not be ascribed to D and therefore will not support longarm jurisdiction of his suit against D.[31] These agent-against-own-principal situations, in which jurisdiction is refused, should not be confused with the case in which a third person is suing the principal after having dealt with the principal through the agent. In that instance there is, of course, an imputation of the agent's acts to the principal under CPLR 302(a).[32]

The refusal to impute agency activities to the principal when the agent is the plaintiff is also the rationale used to protect the New York courts from what might otherwise be a deluge of litigation emanating from ordinary stock transactions. Assume that P is a national brokerage house. D visits an office of P outside New York with a sell order, which P processes through its own channels back to New York, where the order is executed on a national exchange. D now refuses to turn over the stock, which P has to replace. In an action by P for the replacement cost, is there longarm jurisdiction? Caselaw has said no. This is at root just another illustration of suit by agent against principal where the agent is trying to bring off a jurisdictional imputation of its own

26. 26 N.Y.2d 13, 308 N.Y.S.2d 337, 256 N.E.2d 506 (1970).

27. Haar v. Armendoris Corp., 31 N.Y.2d 1040, 342 N.Y.S.2d 70, 294 N.E.2d 855 (1973), reversing on the dissenting opinion in 40 A.D.2d 769, 337 N.Y.S.2d 285 (1st Dep't 1972).

28. 674 F.2d 178 (2d Cir.1982).

29. See the caselaw review in Amins v. Life Support Med. Eqpt. Corp., 373 F.Supp. 654 (E.D.N.Y.1974).

30. See A. Millner Co. v. Noudar, Lda., 24 A.D.2d 326, 266 N.Y.S.2d 289 (1st Dep't 1966).

31. Glassman v. Hyder, 23 N.Y.2d 354, 296 N.Y.S.2d 783, 244 N.E.2d 259 (1968).

32. Orient Mid–East Lines, Inc. v. Albert E. Bowen, Inc., 297 F.Supp. 1149 (S.D.N.Y.1969).

acts to the principal.[33] Whatever the rationale, a different rule would in effect lend New York longarm jurisdiction to any transaction that ultimately results in a purchase or sale on one of New York's national exchanges.

The defendant is apparently protected in these stock transactions only when he engages in them on his own turf. If, for example, the defendant is a customer who deals directly with the broker's New York office by phone or mail in a number of transactions instead of dealing with the broker at the broker's local office outside New York, longarm jurisdiction may be upheld.[34]

In what may be regarded as one category of typical textile industry transaction, an important segment of New York commerce, longarm jurisdiction was rejected in Dero Enterprises, Inc. v. Georgia Girl Fashions, Inc.[35] W was a New York clothing wholesaler and R a Georgia retailer that occasionally used A, a New York company, as a purchasing agent. When W approached A looking for buyers, A produced R, telling R about W's line. R bought, but the clothes were alleged to be defective and R wouldn't pay. W sued. The court said there was no jurisdiction, stressing that it was W that initiated the contact with R. There might have been jurisdiction if R had been the initiator.

Another conclusion that has spared the New York courts what might otherwise be an undue category of longarm cases is that making a piece of commercial paper payable in New York does not by itself constitute a "transaction" sufficient to confer jurisdiction of an action on the paper, such as a promissory note.[36]

Just as CPLR 302(a)(1) may be used on a tort claim, so may it be used for a contract of a non-commercial nature. It has been held that the statute may be applied to the obligations arising under a separation agreement made in New York.[37] This "transaction" jurisdiction under CPLR 302(a)(1) should not be confused with anything offered by CPLR 302(b), which applies only in the context of an outright matrimonial action—a separation agreement can be the subject of a simple contract action—or family court proceeding.

When longarm jurisdiction is asserted against an individual corporate officer or employee as well as against the corporation, can the individual avoid jurisdiction by alleging that he was acting only in behalf of the corporation and that he is therefore insulated from individual jurisdiction, just as he is insulated from personal liability as a matter of substantive law? This is the "fiduciary shield" doctrine, and the Court of Appeals appeared to reject it in 1988 in Kreutter v. McFadden Oil Corp.[38]

New Yorker P gave $70,000 to a company present in New York to invest in a certain oil-related venture through Texas companies. He got back not even an acknowledgment. He sued, naming several corporate defendants and one X, a power behind some of the corporations and a nondomiciliary of New York. X tried to invoke the shield doctrine, but the court found the "transacts any business" clause satisfied as against X on sustainable allegations that those who conducted New York activities in this matter did so in part as X's own agent. X contended that he was acting only in the corporations' behalf and that he could not be personally bound unless there were a piercing of the corporate veil. But that, answered the court, relates to substantive liability, and what the substantive liability may come to is not relevant to the jurisdictional matter. "Liability may be considered only after

---

33. Hertz, Newmark & Warner v. Fischman, 53 Misc.2d 418, 279 N.Y.S.2d 97 (N.Y.C.Civ.Ct. 1967).

34. See L.F. Rothschild, Unterberg, Towbin v. Thompson, 78 A.D.2d 795, 433 N.Y.S.2d 6 (1st Dep't 1980).

35. 598 F.Supp. 318 (S.D.N.Y.1984).

36. American Recreation Group, Inc. v. Woznicki, 87 A.D.2d 600, 448 N.Y.S.2d 51 (2d Dep't 1982); Hubbard, Westervelt & Mottelay, Inc. v. Harsh Bldg. Co., 28 A.D.2d 295, 284 N.Y.S.2d 879 (1st Dep't 1967).

37. Kochenthal v. Kochenthal, 28 A.D.2d 117, 282 N.Y.S.2d 36 (2d Dep't 1967). Whitaker v. Whitaker, 32 A.D.2d 595, 299 N.Y.S.2d 482 (3d Dep't 1969), appears to take a contrary position but it actually viewed itself only as a matrimonial action, not a contract action on a separation agreement.

38. 71 N.Y.2d 460, 527 N.Y.S.2d 195, 522 N.E.2d 40.

it is decided ... that the defendant is subject to ... jurisdiction.... ''

This conclusion about irrelevancy may become a troublesome point in a strictly contract case, which *Kreutter*, however, was not. The claims asserted in *Kreutter* included tort claims (fraud and conversion) along with contract claims, and as long as tort is part of the package, it is reasonably clear that there is no shield for an individual to hide behind.[39] Perhaps, from the point of view of a plaintiff seeking jurisdiction of the individual as well as the corporation, it would be a good idea to see whether there isn't some tort theory that can be added to the complaint. The fact that there were tort claims present in *Kreutter* seemed to lead to a sustaining of longarm jurisdiction that a complaint couched only in contract might not have achieved. If this kind of obscuration can bring a plaintiff jurisdiction while a straight contract claim would not, we must note that it doesn't take much for an imaginative plaintiff's lawyer to inject a tort claim into a commercial setting.

Longarm inquiries go on and on. The foregoing treatment, perhaps too long as it is, sets forth only a few essentials about what constitutes a "transaction of business" under CPLR 302(a)(1). The matter is of great moment in any case in which it is even arguably applicable, because the very issue of jurisdiction depends on it. The plaintiff who makes out a "transaction" gets New York jurisdiction and need not sue elsewhere. But important as these sui generis longarm investigations may be, the candid negotiator with CPLR 302(a)(1) will confess that they are tedious—and sometimes even the cause of low blood pressure among the judges. One federal judge opened an opinion with the cheerless lament that his case requires yet "another decision in the interminable line of cases applying the New York long-arm statute, CPLR § 302."[40]

Interminable or not, CPLR 302 makes up in importance for what it causes in tedium. It is no small gift for a plaintiff to be able to choose the forum, and CPLR 302 is a key factor in the choice.

§ 86A. "Contracts Anywhere" under CPLR 302(a)(1)

A 1979 amendment of paragraph 1 of CPLR 302(a) expanded longarm jurisdiction to reach a defendant who "contracts anywhere to supply goods or services in the state", a jurisdictional category distinct from the "transacts any business" of the first clause and a study in itself. Hence this separate section.

In commercial transactions, which are what the "contracts anywhere" clause principally aims at, the U.S. Supreme Court has taken a generous view of longarm jurisdiction. *Burger King Corp. v. Rudzewicz*[1] is the major indicator. Burger King, the fast food giant, has its base in Florida. Under a Florida longarm statute purporting to assert jurisdiction of anyone who "[b]reach[es] a contract in this state by failing to perform acts required by the contract to be performed in this state", Burger King was allowed to obtain Florida jurisdiction over a Michigan franchisee who never set foot in Florida. Among the obligations the franchisee undertook in Michigan, however, where it had its operation, was to send periodic payments under the franchise agreement to Florida. The court held this a major ingredient in satisfying due process.[2]

Relying on *Burger King*, the Second Circuit sustained New York jurisdiction over two California individuals in another franchise case,[3] holding that with contacts even greater than those that sufficed in *Burger King*, they "reached into New York to obtain the benefits of selling seven franchises [computer software stores] to be operated in the state". Misrepresentations and omissions in behalf of the now bankrupt corporation for which the defendants

---

39. See the discussion of the CPC case in § 87, below.

40. Orient Mid–East Lines, Inc. v. Albert E. Bowen, Inc., 297 F.Supp. 1149, 1150 (1969).

§ 86A

1. 471 U.S. 462, 105 S.Ct. 2174, 85 L.Ed.2d 528 (1985).

2. The case is the subject of a lead note in New York State Law Digest No. 308.

3. Retail Software Services, Inc. v. Lashlee, 854 F.2d 18 (2d Cir.1988).

purportedly acted were claimed. The main negotiations had apparently been made at a California meeting and in telephone calls to New York, but the statements were also allegedly contained in franchise registrations and ads in New York.

This generous view of longarm jurisdiction in cases of intentional conduct, like *Burger King* (a commercial case) and the *Calder* and *Keeton* cases (involving intentional torts[4]), may be contrasted with the more restrictive view taken when accidents are involved.[5]

The utility of the "contracts anywhere" clause is plain in the vast realm of the mail order catalog and in mail solicitations generally. Every time a New Yorker orders something by mail and the seller at the other end sends it on, he has apparently contracted "to supply goods" in the state and on the face of CPLR 302(a)(1) that would mean jurisdiction. But the lawyer has to be circumspect about using the "contracts anywhere" clause of CPLR 302(a)(1) in small cases. Suppose, for example, that a New Yorker orders a $1500 computer from a Chicago store. It is sent but does not work right. Will the statute require the store to defend an action for breach of warranty in New York? Same example, but with a $150 radio from a department store in St. Louis, or a $15 music box ordered by mail from a small notions shop that the plaintiff remembered from a visit to Tucson, Arizona? Does the exercise of longarm jurisdiction in such small cases satisfy the constitution?[6]

On the constitutional front, there have been cases in New York, involving relatively modest transactions, in which the New York courts have refused recognition to a sister-state judgment because it was found to be predicated on a jurisdictional foundation that violated due process because the rendering state had insufficient contacts with the defendant (a New Yorker), when the very same contacts, in converse circumstances, would satisfy the "con-

tracts anywhere" clause of CPLR 302(a)(1) to the letter.[7]

And even if a given exercise of the "contracts anywhere" clause would satisfy constitutional standards, the time and trouble of invoking the statute in a small case must be weighed against the stakes involved. In this connection there are several points to make about the lower courts.

They have longarm statutes. Section 404 in the New York City Civil Court Act and in the Uniform District and Uniform City court acts[8] is modeled on CPLR 302 so as to reach defendants outside the lower court's territory when the transaction or event has local contacts. Only the Civil Court Act was amended to add the "contracts anywhere" clause,[9] requiring, of course, that the contacts be with New York City rather than with the state in general. The district and city court acts were not so amended, and remain without this far-reaching clause.

This means that within New York City small cases that depend on the contracts-anywhere language can be brought in the civil court, but that outside New York City they have to be brought in the supreme court. In this respect, however, note that the costs statute that would otherwise punish the bringing of such cases in the supreme court, CPLR 8102, does not apply to cases that depend for jurisdiction on the "contracts anywhere" clause. CPLR 8102 visits its sanction only on a case in which jurisdiction could have been obtained over the defendant in a lower court. In this category of cases—those brought in the supreme court outside New York City—jurisdiction can't be obtained over the defendant in the lower court because its longarm statute doesn't contain the contracts-anywhere clause. Thus, even the smallest cases falling under the new language of CPLR 302(a)(1) can be brought in the supreme court outside New York City without facing the CPLR 8102 costs deterrent.

---

4. See § 86 above.

5. See § 88 below.

6. Note the "bigness" point mentioned in § 88, below.

7. See, e.g., Pinna v. Davis, 67 A.D.2d 967, 413 N.Y.S.2d 460 (2d Dep't 1979).

8. McKinney's Vol. 29A, Part 3.

9. The amendment was made in 1983, four years after the 1979 amendment that added the "contracts anywhere" clause to CPLR 302.

The plaintiff shouldn't bother with the clause in small cases, however, unless convinced that the defendant will voluntarily pay a judgment or has assets in New York against which the judgment can be easily enforced. Otherwise the judgment will have to be taken to the defendant's jurisdiction and made the subject of an action there to convert it into a judgment of that place. Only then could it proceed to make use of enforcement devices likely to reach the defendant's assets. The cost of these steps may make their attempted use uneconomical in small cases. The point must in any event be discussed with the client, lest the client get a satisfaction of judgment accompanied by a fee bill from her own attorney that exceeds it.

Sending an employee into the state to repair a piece of machinery has been held to be the furnishing of services in New York and thus to support jurisdiction of a claim connected with the service. In Island Wholesale Wood Supplies, Inc. v. Blanchard Industries, Inc.,[10] the court examined the language of the 1979 amendment, held that the legislature intended it "to extend jurisdiction to the limits of due process", and concluded that it must therefore be given "a broad construction".

Does the new clause alter the significance of the "f.o.b." shipment that often insulated the seller from jurisdiction under the "transacts any business" clause?[11] The court in Blanchard described this as a "difficult question" but found it unnecessary to decide it. Perhaps the court decided it implicitly, anyway. The "broad construction" the court finds the statute calling for is certainly not consistent with the idea that a seller can insulate himself merely by shipping goods f.o.b. its own jurisdiction. Practitioners should be aware that some of the cases in which jurisdiction was rejected under the original "transacts any business" clause of CPLR 302(a)(1), including several cited in the Law Revision Commission's report, involve fact patterns that would today fall under the new contracts-anywhere language. If research produces "transacts any business" cases that

reject jurisdiction, they should be reviewed to see if they fit under the "contracts anywhere" description. Two cases that might be successfully refitted in that way are the Kramer and McKee cases previously reviewed under the "transacts" clause.[12]

In treating that clause in § 86, two "classic buy-and-sell situations" (as we labeled them) are discussed, in each of which jurisdiction is rejected. One of these, involving a New York plaintiff's purchase from a nondomiciliary seller, would seem to fall under the new contracts-anywhere phrase. The Kramer case, involving a continuing sales arrangement, is a prime example, but the new language, literally applied, would also reach one-shot sales and transactions involving small and even paltry sums. (The Kramer sales were substantial.)

What of stock exchange transactions? D, the owner of a few nationally traded shares, lives in Oregon. He goes to the local office of a national broker to sell, and the order goes through the broker's channels to its New York office, where the sale is made on one of the New York exchanges. D does not turn over the shares. He says he has good reason. Will suit in New York obtain jurisdiction of D? Are the shares "goods" so that D can be said to have contracted "to supply goods" in New York? It could mean quite an additional burden for the New York courts were they deemed jurisdictionally competent to reach all the sellers of any stock traded on one of New York's national exchanges. Even if the shares are "goods", moreover, in the example given the defendant could be deemed to have contracted to furnish the shares not in New York, but in Oregon, the defendant's home, so that it is the plaintiff broker, not the defendant seller, who is responsible for the trip the shares make to New York.

In a similar situation, in which the out-of-state defendant (D) was the buyer instead of the seller and ordered the shares merely by telephoning the New York broker (P) on a single transaction, D was held not subject to longarm jurisdiction in an action by P on the

---

10. 101 A.D.2d 878, 476 N.Y.S.2d 192 (2d Dep't 1984).

11. See § 86 above.

12. See § 86 above.

agreement for the reason that D did not conduct "sufficient purposeful activity" for jurisdiction.[13]

Ironically, some situations in which jurisdiction seems quite fair to exercise remain beyond the language of the new clause. One example is the *Galgay* case.[14] The Pennsylvania publisher in *Galgay* ordered more than a million dollars in special machinery from the New York plaintiff, which the plaintiff made and shipped. Jurisdiction of a claim for a balance due was nevertheless rejected. Unless the money that the publisher contracted to pay can qualify as "goods" under the contracts-anywhere clause, an unlikely conclusion,[15] the publisher has not contracted to furnish either "goods" or "services" in New York and so remains beyond jurisdiction.[16]

What about making a promissory note calling for payment in New York? Such doing is analogous in that it implicitly poses the question of whether agreeing to pay money in New York may be considered an agreement to furnish goods in New York within the intendment of the contracts-anywhere clause. The question arose in American Recreation Group, Inc. v. Woznicki.[17] The court held that making a promissory note payable in New York cannot by itself subject the maker to longarm jurisdiction if all the rest of the defendant's contacts with the case are outside New York.

The Court of Appeals has held that the furnishing of a drug to a New York patient outside the state, by a Massachusetts physician to whom the plaintiff went for treatment, even if the intent was that the plaintiff take the drug home, does not support jurisdiction under the "contracts anywhere" clause.[18] The court said that in enacting this provision the legislature "was not concerned with limited provision of supplies incident to medical treatment".

Cases on similarly worded sister-state statutes can also offer guidance on the scope and application of the "contracts anywhere" clause of CPLR 302(a)(1).[19]

§ 87. "Tortious Act" under CPLR 302(a)(2)

This provision clearly applies to something like an assault committed in New York, and to any tort, intentional or unintentional, in which the actionable conduct takes place in New York. It does not apply when the tortious conduct takes place outside New York, even though it causes injury within New York. This is the result of Feathers v. McLucas,[1] decided in 1965. In that case K was a Kansas corporation that manufactured tanks in Kansas. It sold one of these to M, a Missouri corporation. M mounted it on a wheelbase and sold it to C, a Pennsylvania corporation and an interstate carrier. After the tank was filled with propane

---

13. L.F. Rothschild, Unterberg, Towbin v. McTamney, 59 N.Y.2d 651, 463 N.Y.S.2d 197, 449 N.E.2d 1275 (1983), affirming on the appellate division opinion in 89 A.D.2d 540, 452 N.Y.S.2d 630 (1st Dep't 1982).

14. Section 86 above.

15. But compare in this respect the language of the Florida statute in the Burger King case, above, which was held to embrace mere payments of money required to be sent to the state.

16. It is not certain, however, that the New York Court of Appeals would agree with the Galgay court's release of the defendant from the "transacts any business" clause were a similar fact pattern to arise today.

17. 87 A.D.2d 600, 448 N.Y.S.2d 51 (2d Dep't 1982).

18. Etra v. Matta, 61 N.Y.2d 455, 474 N.Y.S.2d 687, 463 N.E.2d 3 (1984).

19. Several are cited by the Law Revision Commission, the amendment's sponsor, in its 1979 report, reprinted at page A–57 of McKinney's 1979 New York Session Law News. Massachusetts, for example, has a "contracting to

supply services or things" provision, Massachusetts Annotated Laws, C.223A, § 3(b), which got a broad construction in Sarno v. Florida East Coast Ry. Co., 327 F.Supp. 506 (D.Mass.1971), a services case. The uniform act, Unif. Interstate and Int'l Proceed. Act § 1.03(a)(2), 13 U.L.A. 361 (1986), settles on a similar provision, but more by adoption than innovation. Other statutes the reader can consult are those that go all the way with longarm jurisdiction, i.e., assume jurisdiction whenever due process permits it. California has such a statute, for example. See § 84 above.

§ 87

1. 15 N.Y.2d 443, 261 N.Y.S.2d 8, 209 N.E.2d 68, cert.den. sub nom. Estwing Mfg. Co., v. Singer, 382 U.S. 905, 86 S.Ct. 241, 15 L.Ed.2d 158 (1965). Feathers is the third of three cases the Court of Appeals consolidated into a single opinion that played a key role in the development of longarm jurisdiction early in the life of the CPLR. The other two are the Longines and Singer cases, treated in § 86, above, which sustained jurisdiction under CPLR 302(a)(1).

gas and sent on its way to Vermont, it exploded while passing through New York and injured P. P sued K and served K in Kansas. The court dismissed the case for lack of jurisdiction.

This is the jurisdictional phase of the so-called "products liability" area. Jurisdiction was rejected because, said the Court of Appeals, under CPLR 302(a)(2) it is the tortious "act" that must take place in New York. The occurrence of only the injury in New York does not satisfy. Whatever "act" K was guilty of in *Feathers* had been performed outside New York.

Feathers came as a surprise. Since CPLR 302 was modeled on the Illinois statute and a major Illinois case[2] had sustained jurisdiction on similar facts, it was widely assumed that it would also be sustained in New York. But it was not. The major result of *Feathers* was the prompt amendment of CPLR 302(a) to add what is now paragraph 3, the subject of the next section. *Feathers* remains the lord of paragraph 2, however, which continues to require that the wrongful "act" take place in New York. Thus, where P bought pills in Germany and brought them back to New York, and the pills resulted in deformities to later born children, paragraph 2 did not give jurisdiction because the pills were manufactured outside New York.[3]

The statute has also been held inapplicable to a paternity claim, on the ground that the act involved is voluntary rather than tortious.[4] No matter. While subdivision (a)(2) of CPLR 302 may exclude the paternity suit, the plaintiff can turn to subdivision (b), added and altered afterwards, for longarm jurisdiction on a paternity claim today.[5]

Defamation is expressly excepted from the "tort" parts of CPLR 302(a), i.e., paragraphs 2 and 3, because it was feared that national and international libels and slanders could too easily find their way into New York and impose unduly on its courts. But jurisdiction of a defamation arising out of the defendant's transaction of New York business has been sustained under paragraph 1, which does not have a defamation exclusion.[6]

In many of the instances in which CPLR 302(a)(2) confers jurisdiction, it will be found that some other statute also confers it. If, for example, negligent driving in New York results in an accident, the injured party can invoke either CPLR 302(a)(2) or the nonresident motorist statute,[7] or both.

What about longarm jurisdiction over an individual who was on a corporate mission at the time of the tort? When an individual is acting solely in behalf of a corporation on a strictly commercial matter, like the negotiation of a contract, the individual has no personal liability for it as a substantive matter, and this would presumably insulate the individual from longarm jurisdiction on it as a procedural matter as well. This is the "fiduciary shield" doctrine, and even in the commercial realm today there is doubt about whether it applies. In the tort sphere, however, it is clear that it does not apply at all.[8] The corporate employee is individually liable for any tort he commits, whether or not the corporation is derivatively liable as well, and when subjected to longarm jurisdiction under one of the tort provisions, the individual cannot erect the "fiduciary shield"—i.e., plead that he was only acting in behalf of the corporation—as a defense to jurisdiction. After some conflict on the point among lower courts, the Court of Appeals held in *CPC International, Inc. v.*

---

2. Gray v. American Radiator & Standard Sanitary Corp., 176 N.E.2d 761 (Ill.1961). See 2d Rep.Leg.Doc. (1958) No. 13, p.39.

3. Harvey v. Chemie Grunenthal, G.m.b.H., 354 F.2d 428 (2d Cir.1965), cert.denied 384 U.S. 1001, 86 S.Ct. 1923, 16 L.Ed.2d 1015 (1966). Jurisdiction might today be sustained under CPLR 302(a)(3).

4. Anonymous v. Anonymous, 49 Misc.2d 675, 268 N.Y.S.2d 710 (Fam.Ct., Queens County, 1966). Longarm statutes elsewhere, albeit different in terminology, have

been stretched to offer jurisdiction in similar instances. See, e.g., Neill v. Ridner, 286 N.E.2d 427 (Ind.Ct.App. 1972).

5. See § 90 below.

6. Legros v. Irving, 38 A.D.2d 53, 327 N.Y.S.2d 371 (1st Dep't 1971). See § 86 above.

7. Veh. & Traf.L. § 253, treated in § 97, below.

8. See the discussion of the Kreutter case in § 86, above.

McKesson Corp.,[9] that in a tort case under paragraph 2 of CPLR 302(a) the so-called "fiduciary shield" doctrine does not apply and the individual is therefore subject to longarm jurisdiction for the tort.

Perhaps jurisdiction in this regard is just following the substantive law, the individual being subject to jurisdiction for the corporate act only when he is substantively liable for the corporate act.[10] With tort, unlike contract, an individual purporting to act for another does not escape personal liability under some kind of innocent agency theory.

The *CPC* case concerned the purchase by P of the stock of the Mueller Corporation (the pasta giant) from its corporate parent, McKesson Corp. Various defendants, including two individuals associated with the companies, were charged with deliberately creating fictitious projections of Mueller's financial prospects after Mueller's own executives had predicted "a sharp decline" in a report to parent McKesson, all in order to raise the purchase price (by an excess of some $61 million, according to the plaintiff). The tort claimed was common law fraud, and the individuals were also held subject to CPLR 302(a)(2) jurisdiction on it—i.e., were denied the "fiduciary shield".

Because of the *Feathers* strictures, CPLR 302(a)(2) is used only in the relatively clear-cut situation of a tort actually committed in New York. It generates less caselaw than the situations in which conduct outside results in injury inside New York, a jurisdictional niche filled by CPLR 302(a)(3), treated in the next section.

§ 88. Act Without/Injury Within New York under CPLR 302(a)(3)

Paragraph 3 of CPLR 302(a) was added in 1966 in response to the restrictive interpreta-

tion the Court of Appeals made of CPLR 302(a)(2) in the *Feathers* case.[1] It was the product of a study conducted by the Judicial Conference.[2] Like paragraph 2, paragraph 3 applies to personal injury as well as property damage cases.

In all instances under paragraph 3 it must be shown (1) that the defendant committed a tortious act outside New York and (2) that the act caused injury within New York. Those two requirements must be met in all cases, but the plaintiff must also satisfy either one of the two subparagraphs of paragraph 3. One additional showing is necessary if subparagraph (i) is used, which makes a total of three showings needed for 302(a)(3)(i) jurisdiction; two additional showings are necessary if subparagraph (ii) is relied on, for a total of four.

The two subparagraphs of paragraph 3 are the principal sources of dispute, but there has also been activity on the introductory clause, which contains the omnibus pair of requirements applicable to both provisions. When co-conspirators are involved, for example, there have been some apparently conflicting decisions on whether the tortious activity of one can be imputed to the other as a "tortious act" for longarm jurisdiction.[3]

To satisfy subparagraph (i), the plaintiff is required to show that the defendant

regularly does or solicits business, or engages in any other persistent course of conduct, or derives substantial revenue from goods used or consumed or services rendered, in the state.

This subparagraph requires at root a showing that the defendant has some overall contact with New York, or derives some substantial commercial benefit from New York. The cause of action sued on need not be related to

---

9. 70 N.Y.2d 268, 519 N.Y.S.2d 804, 514 N.E.2d 116 (1987).

10. It is submitted that this ought to be the rule, but it is not at all clear that it is. See the discussion of this point and of the CPC case generally in the lead note in New York State Law Digest No. 336.

§ 88

1. See § 87 above.

2. The background study by Professor Willis L.M. Reese is published in the 11th Annual Report (1966) of the Judicial Conference, p.132.

3. See Lehigh Valley Industries, Inc. v. Birenbaum, 389 F.Supp. 798 (S.D.N.Y.), affirmed in 527 F.2d 87 (2d Cir.1975) and distinguished in Hargrave v. Oki Nursery, Inc., 636 F.2d 897 (2d Cir.1980).

those New York activities, however. Requiring those activities is designed to assure only that the defendant's overall contact with New York is substantial enough to make it reasonable to subject the defendant to jurisdiction here.

If the defendant is a corporation regularly "doing business" in New York, it is of course subject to "presence" jurisdiction under CPLR 301 and no help is needed from CPLR 302. In this connection note that the "does business" requirement of CPLR 302(a)(3)(i) was not intended to require as much activity as the CPLR 301 "doing business" test requires.[4]

Of the several items listed in subparagraph (i), the one most often relied on is the defendant's derivation of substantial revenue from goods sold in New York. A uniformly dependable yardstick for what is or is not "substantial" has not yet been devised but a proportion test is one measure, comparing the defendant's overall income with its New York portion. Such a test has been used,[5] but there is no rigid rule about what percentage suffices.

A quantity test can be used in the alternative. The amount of revenue the defendant derives from New York may be great, for example, and yet constitute only a small percentage of the defendant's overall business. That was the situation in Allen v. Canadian General Electric Co.[6] In Allen, the $9 million of New York income was only 1% of the defendant's overall business. The defendant contended that the small percentage meant that the $9 million was not "substantial revenue". The contention was rejected, and jurisdiction sustained, but the defendant got an award for keeping a straight face throughout the proceedings.

Gross and net income are looked at,[7] but whether the sums involved are "substantial" requires a factual inquiry in each case.

If the plaintiff is depending on subparagraph (ii), the requirements differ. Here the plaintiff must show that the defendant

expects or should reasonably expect the act to have consequences in the state and derives substantial revenue[8] from interstate or international commerce.

As far as the statute is concerned, the commerce need not take in the state of New York. It can be interstate commerce on the West Coast only, for example. This aspect of subparagraph (ii) can be called the "bigness" requirement. It is imposed not to guarantee an overall contact with New York, as subparagraph (i) is designed to do, but to assure that the defendant is economically big enough to be able to defend a New York law suit without undue hardship. It is the foreseeability aspect of subparagraph (ii) that is supposed to tie the case to New York and satisfy due process.

The foreseeability requirement is a general one. The defendant need not foresee the specific injury-producing event in New York. In the case of a product, for example, it is sufficient if the defendant knew that it was likely to end up in New York and, if defective, to do injury.[9]

That the commerce showing need not take in New York state and that the foreseeability aspect suffices to give New York the requisite due process nexus are the assumptions underlying subparagraph (ii), but they are too rosy a set of conclusions today. The same may be said of subparagraph (i)'s contentment with a simple showing that the defendant "derives substantial revenue from goods used or consumed" in New York. In a major pronouncement on longarm jurisdiction in 1980, years after the 1966 enactment of CPLR 302(a)(3), the U.S. Supreme Court took a considerably more restrictive view about longarm jurisdiction in World–Wide Volkswagen Corp. v.

---

4. 12th Jud.Conf.Rep. (1967) 343. The doing business test is treated in § 82, above.

5. See Gillmore v. J.S. Inskip, Inc., 54 Misc.2d 218, 282 N.Y.S.2d 127 (Sup.Ct., Nassau County, 1967).

6. 65 A.D.2d 39, 410 N.Y.S.2d 707 (3d Dep't 1978), aff'd 50 N.Y.2d 935, 431 N.Y.S.2d 526, 409 N.E.2d 998 (1980).

7. See Allen v. Auto Specialties Mfg. Co., 45 A.D.2d 331, 357 N.Y.S.2d 547 (3d Dep't 1974).

8. The test for what constitutes "substantial" revenue should be similar to that used under subparagraph (i).

9. Gonzales v. Harris Calorific Co., 64 Misc.2d 287, 315 N.Y.S.2d 51 (Sup.Ct., Queens County), aff'd 35 A.D.2d 720, 315 N.Y.S.2d 815 (2d Dep't 1970).

Woodson,[10] its first address to longarm jurisdiction in a tort case. The due process standard under *World-Wide* is more restrictive of state options in accident cases than had been assumed under many of the state statutes— including CPLR 302(a)(3)—and it is likely that many jurisdiction–sustaining cases under them, reexamined in the light of *World-Wide*, would not pass the jurisdictional test today.

In New York, it is paragraph 3 of CPLR 302(a) that most feels the brunt of the *World-Wide* case. It would be instructive, after reviewing the facts and highlighting key parts of the *World-Wide* opinion, to treat a few of New York's older cases to see how they fare under it. Elements satisfactory to the New York statute will sometimes be seen as failing the supervening due process test.

The plaintiffs in *World-Wide* were New Yorkers when they bought an Audi automobile from a retailer (R) in an upstate New York village. The regional distributor of the car (W, for wholesaler) operated in New York, New Jersey, and Connecticut. Both R and W were New York corporations. The plaintiffs were on their way to Arizona in the car when it was involved in an accident in Oklahoma, the state whose jurisdictional statute was involved—and found unconstitutional—in *World-Wide*. Alleging personal injuries caused by the defective design of the car, the plaintiffs sued four defendants. In addition to R and W, they joined in the Oklahoma action M, the foreign manufacturer, and N, the importer and national distributor of Audi cars.

The Oklahoma statute on which jurisdiction was predicated is akin to subparagraph (i) of New York CPLR 302(a)(3), the subparagraph that seeks to exercise jurisdiction whenever a tortious act outside the state causes injury within the state if (among other things) the particular defendant "derives substantial revenue from goods used or consumed ... in this state".

In respect of defendants R and W, the U.S. Supreme Court found "a total absence of those affiliating circumstances that are a necessary predicate to any exercise of state-court juris-

diction." Those defendants "carry on no activity ... close no sales ... perform no services ... avail themselves of none of the privileges and benefits of Oklahoma law ... [and] solicit no business there". Hence, in respect of R and W, the due process clause barred Oklahoma from assuming jurisdiction.

R's activities were centered around its upstate New York village and W's activities, although they crossed state lines, did so only to enter the two adjoining states of New Jersey and Connecticut, not Oklahoma. But W's activities were nevertheless interstate if not national, and in this regard the *World-Wide* case can be viewed as a restriction not only on subparagraph (i) of CPLR 302(a)(3), but also on subparagraph (ii). The latter's jurisdictional predicate is that the defendant derives substantial revenue from interstate commerce even if New York is not included in that commerce, but the fact that W in the *World-Wide* case was involved in interstate commerce didn't help.

While the *World-Wide* decision seems on its face to have bad jurisdictional news for tort plaintiffs—including a refusal by the Supreme Court to accord an automobile any unique jurisdictional status on a "dangerous instrumentality" theory, as had often been relied on—a bit of probing beneath the surface may reveal a more optimistic message for tort plaintiffs. Both M, the manufacturer, and N, the national distributor, remained parties to the litigation, not having brought any jurisdictional objection before the Supreme Court. And even if they had, there is language in the court's opinion suggesting that as to them the jurisdictional objections would not have succeeded and Oklahoma jurisdiction would have been sustained. That would give the plaintiffs jurisdiction over the two final links in the chain of purchase, and solvent sources for any sum awarded as damages, so that in many cases it would be unimportant that the immediate seller and the regional distributor are jurisdictionally unavailable. Indeed, Justice Blackmun in a dissenting opinion in *World-Wide* expresses puzzlement at why the plain-

10. 444 U.S. 286, 100 S.Ct. 559, 62 L.Ed.2d 490.

tiffs should be so insistent on jurisdiction over the retailer and wholesaler when the obviously solvent manufacturer and national distributor did not challenge Oklahoma jurisdiction.

The *World-Wide* case was a 6–3 decision. A statement by the majority designed to show that minimal jurisdictional contacts were lacking with respect to the retailer and regional distributor seems to show the requisite contacts present, and supporting jurisdiction, as applied to the manufacturer and national distributor. "The forum State", says the court, "does not exceed its powers under the Due Process Clause if it asserts personal jurisdiction over a corporation that delivers its products into the stream of commerce with the expectation that they will be purchased by consumers in the forum State."

The court afterwards came close to rejecting the "stream of commerce" test in 1987 in Asahi Metal Industry Co. v. Superior Court,[11] however, in which a motorcycle accident in California was allegedly caused by a defective tire tube and its valve. While jurisdiction over the tube manufacturer, a Taiwanese company selling its product by the thousands in California, was present there, jurisdiction over the Japanese valve manufacturer, from which the Taiwanese company bought the valve assemblies and which it tried to implead, was rejected.

Jurisdiction with respect to only an indemnification claim between the two companies was at issue in *Asahi*, and a majority of the court stresses that point. Would a different view prevail if the injured plaintiff were the one seeking jurisdiction of the valve manufacturer? For the moment the possibility is not entirely foreclosed.

It may of course happen in a given case that fault is traceable to something that the retailer or regional distributor did—something that does not implicate the national distributor or manufacturer. In a case like *World-Wide*, that would mean no jurisdiction. But a case of that nature would seem the exception rather than the rule. Defective design or manufacture is more often likely to be the liability predicate, and with warranty or strict products liability available as liability theories against the manufacturer and national distributor, who are available jurisdictionally, the regional distributor may not be missed.

The foreseeability element, a key one under the jurisdictional requirements of subparagraph (ii) of CPLR 302(a)(3), gets much attention in the *World-Wide* case and is given much less effect than the New York statute envisioned. Foreseeability will therefore prove less helpful as a jurisdictional link in the future. In this respect, Erlanger Mills, Inc. v. Cohoes Fibre Mills, Inc.,[12] decided in 1956, is noteworthy. The Fourth Circuit in *Erlanger* took a negative view of a mere foreseeability connection. *Erlanger* appeared to lose currency with each passing year, however; in the context of later cases it seemed a maverick, a doddering old curmudgeon sputtering mild epithets about these upstart longarm statutes and where they all lead. The senile old thing, barely tolerated by the successor generation, appears to be transformed into something of an oracle by the *World-Wide* case. *Erlanger* is favorably cited in the case to show what the U.S. Supreme Court obviously deems the mischief of a broad "foreseeability" criterion.

In Helicopteros Nacionales de Colombia, S.A. v. Hall,[13] decided only a few years after *World-Wide*, the Supreme Court adhered to this restrictive attitude about longarm jurisdiction in unintentional tort cases. In *Helicopteros*, plaintiffs in Texas tried unsuccessfully for longarm jursdiction against a Colombian company providing a helicopter service in South America, where one of its craft crashed in Peru, killing several U.S. citizens. Jurisdiction was rejected despite Texas contacts in the negotiation and purchase of the helicopters and the Texas situs of training in their use.[14]

---

11. 480 U.S. 102, 107 S.Ct. 1026, 94 L.Ed.2d 92 (1987).

12. 239 F.2d 502 (4th Cir.).

13. 466 U.S. 408, 104 S.Ct. 1868, 80 L.Ed.2d 404 (1984).

14. Helicopteros is discussed in the lead note in New York State Law Digest No. 297.

Taking note that *World-Wide* and *Helicopteros* involved unintentional torts, and contrasting the two national libel cases treated earlier—the *Calder* and *Keeton* cases[15]—in which jurisdiction was sustained, it appears that the U.S. Supreme Court takes a more generous view of longarm jurisdiction when the tort involved is an intentional one.

The *World-Wide* case and its *Helicopteros* follow-up have impact on longarm jurisdiction generally, so that their jurisdictional precepts will be guideposts regardless of the particular statute being used. It is sometimes possible, for example, to fit under CPLR 302(a)(1), as a "transaction of business", a fact pattern that may also fit the statutory language of paragraphs 2 or 3 of CPLR 302(a), the tortious-act provisions. An attempted jurisdictional exercise that runs afoul of constitutional restrictions, however, as occurred in *World-Wide*, would fail whether predicated on the particular language of the statute the court has before it—in *World-Wide*, the Oklahoma statute akin to New York's CPLR 302(a)(3)(i)—or any other provision.

A case that found *World-Wide*'s jurisdictional requirements satisfied is Darienzo v. Wise Shoe Stores, Inc.,[16] in which D manufactured shoes in New Hampshire, selling all of them in New Hampshire to a co-owned company, X. It was X that sold them into interstate commerce. A batch of them ultimately reached the shelves of a Brooklyn retailer, from whom the plaintiff bought. While the plaintiff was wearing a pair of the shoes in New York, one of them broke and she fell and sustained injuries. D was held to New York jurisdiction under CPLR 302(a)(3)(ii). The factor at issue under that provision was whether D derived substantial revenue from interstate commerce. D's "corporate existence was entirely dependent" on interstate commerce, said the court, distinguishing the local and regional companies of

which jurisdiction was rejected in *World-Wide*. We may analogize D in *Darienzo* to the manufacturer and national distributor in *World-Wide*. The national market was their commercial aim, and so was D's in *Darienzo*; and as for deriving revenue from it, it made no jurisdictional difference that the revenue came indirectly through X.

Now for a look at some cases decided before *World-Wide* to see whether their fact patterns can survive a reexamination. Would the case that occasioned the adoption of CPLR 302(a)(3), for example, the *Feathers* case,[17] itself be a casualty of the tightened standards?[18] To whom do we analogize the Kansas tank manufacturer involved in the *Feathers* case? If to the car manufacturer in *World-Wide*, jurisdiction would be upheld. Did the tank manufacturer in *Feathers* intend to blanket the country with its tanks as the Volkswagen Company intended to blanket the country with its cars in *World-Wide*? That would be a key inquiry. Each prior case requires a similar scrutiny under the principles of the *World-Wide* decision.

Another illustration of subparagraph (ii) in operation in a case decided before *World-Wide* is Brown v. Erie–Lackawanna Railroad Co.[19] There the defendant was a foreign railroad engaged in interstate commerce. It leased a car to X, which used it in New York where it came loose, went wild, and killed the plaintiff's intestate. All four CPLR (a)(3)(ii) elements were met and jurisdiction was sustained: (1) act outside New York (negligent maintenance), (2) injury within New York, (3) foreseeability that the car would be used in New York and could do damage here, and (4) derivation of substantial revenue from interstate commerce. But would the case pass muster under *World-Wide*?

---

15. See § 86 above.

16. 74 A.D.2d 342, 427 N.Y.S.2d 831 (2d Dep't 1980).

17. See § 87 above.

18. As far as the statutory overruling of the Feathers case is concerned (which occurred long before the World-Wide case came down from the U.S. Supreme Court), CPLR 302(a)(3)(ii) did its job well. The Feathers litigation,

dismissed under paragraph 2 of CPLR 302(a), see § 87, above, was promptly re-commenced after paragraph 3 was added a year or so later. Defendant's counsel advised this writer that jurisdiction was then conceded and the case settled.

19. 54 Misc.2d 225, 282 N.Y.S.2d 335 (Sup.Ct., Oneida County, 1967).

The facts of each such pre–1980 case have to be reinvestigated along lines that would meet current due process requirements, and often there may not be sufficient facts visible on the face of the opinion to make the reappraisal.

There are several other things worth stressing under the statute. With respect to both subparagraphs (i) and (ii), it has been held that the original injury must occur in New York. If the injury occurs outside New York and just becomes manifest in New York, or has its greatest consequences in New York, or results in loss of earnings in New York, the statute is not satisfied.[20]

Longarm jurisdiction was tried, unsuccessfully, against a physician practicing in his own state, to whom a New York physician sent a New York patient who lived near the Vermont border. She later died of cancers the defendant allegedly failed to notice. On these facts, a divided Court of Appeals held that the physician was not involved in "interstate commerce" because all of his treatment of the patient occurred outside New York.[21]

The Court also held in a commercial setting that injuries do not have a New York situs merely because the plaintiff has a New York domicile. In Fantis Foods, Inc. v. Standard Importing Co.,[22] plaintiff P and defendant D were competitors in wholesaling imported cheese. D was a New York corporation. D impleaded X, a nondomiciliary importer, alleging conversion, but it was shown that the goods at issue were shipped f.o.b. Greece and were addressed to Chicago. Apparently all D could show was consequential damage to itself in New York. This did not suffice for jurisdiction of X. The original injury must occur in New York, and in Fantis it was not established that it did.

That CPLR 302(a)(3) applies to commercial as well as personal torts is perhaps best illustrated in Sybron Corp. v. Wetzel,[23] where the Court of Appeals applied it to sustain longarm jurisdiction for injunctive relief against a New Jersey defendant, D, about to retain the services of X, one of P's former employees in possession of P's trade secrets. D had no New York office or employees and could therefore be reached only through longarm jurisdiction, if at all. He was.

Other important points in Sybron are that no tort had as yet been committed, and the action was for an injunction, not damages. The court held that the longarm statute is available for injunctive relief, and for mere "anticipatory" relief at that—as long as the requisite longarm elements are demonstrated. Those of subparagraph ii of CPLR 302(a)(3) were held satisfied in Sybron, with stress on the fact that P would suffer great injury in New York through loss of customers if its trade secrets were to get out.

Nor does the statute confine itself to claims sounding directly in tort. It may be used for any claim "arising" from a tortious act.[24] It applies to warranty claims, for example.[25]

Cases have begun to appear in New York on how far the statute will reach to take jurisdiction of nondomiciliary defendants who have carried on activity on a website on the Internet. In Bensusan Restaurant Corp. v. King,[26] for example, in which a New York jazz club tried to sue a club in a moderate sized Missouri town for using the plaintiff's name and violating its trademark, the Second Circuit held that the New York Court of Appeals would not uphold jurisdiction of the Missouri defendant.[27]

If the defendant is a bigger enterprise with operations through the Internet that reach

20. Black v. Oberle Rentals, Inc., 55 Misc.2d 398, 285 N.Y.S.2d 226 (Sup.Ct., Onondaga County, 1967).

21. Ingraham v. Carroll, 90 N.Y.2d 592, 665 N.Y.S.2d 10 (1997). The case is the subject of the lead note in New York State Law Digest No. 455.

22. 49 N.Y.2d 317, 425 N.Y.S.2d 783, 402 N.E.2d 122 (1980).

23. 46 N.Y.2d 197, 413 N.Y.S.2d 127, 385 N.E.2d 1055 (1978).

24. Garbellotto v. Montelindo Compagnie Navegacion, S.A., 294 F.Supp. 487 (S.D.N.Y.1969).

25. Naples v. City of New York, 34 A.D.2d 577, 309 N.Y.S.2d 663 (2d Dep't 1970).

26. 126 F.3d 25 (1997).

27. The Internet subject is discussed in SPR 62:3.

well beyond its own bailiwick, other courts have sustained longarm jurisdiction.[28] In an extensive review in Hearst Corp. v. Goldberger,[29] however, a magistrate in New York's Southern District declined to follow cases upholding what it described as "Internet Personal Jurisdiction".

CPLR 302(a)(3) is obviously not perfect.[30] In view of recent U.S. Supreme Court cases, it is not even entirely constitutional. But it still poses numerous jurisdictional opportunities if constitutional strictures are kept in mind. If there is doubt in a given case, it may be worth a try to get jurisdiction in the New York courts, but the lawyer must keep a careful eye on statute of limitations requirements applicable in the state or states to which the plaintiff would have to turn for jurisdiction should New York's jurisdiction not be sustained.

§ 89. Real Property Longarm Cases under CPLR 302(a)(4)

This paragraph has generated few cases. It subjects the defendant to longarm jurisdiction on a claim arising out of the ownership, use, or possession of New York real property. It has been applied to a claim to compel D to convey the realty to P or pay damages in the alternative.[1] That kind of case arises from D's ownership of the property. An early one that arose from the possession of the property was a suit by a landlord against a dentist who leased premises and then reneged on the lease and moved to Maine. Jurisdiction was upheld for unpaid rent, reletting charges, incidental charges, and attorney's fees.[2]

When B is not a domiciliary or resident of New York and never enters the state, but contracts to buy New York land by negotiating

for it from outside the state and then fails to make the required payments and complete the transaction, it was held in Black River Associates v. Newman[3] that B is subject to the personal jurisdiction of the New York courts in a specific performance suit by the seller.[4]

Suppose now that a loan is transacted outside New York between nonresidents and a mortgage on New York realty is given to secure it, with the mortgage, in form satisfactory to New York law, being sent to New York for recording but without any of the parties entering the state. There would be no difficulty about later getting New York jurisdiction to foreclose the mortgage, because mere rem jurisdiction would suffice for that, but suppose a deficiency arises, the land not bringing in enough to pay the debt. Under the reasoning of the Black River case, CPLR 302(a)(4) should supply jurisdiction to support a deficiency judgment, even though the deficiency arises on the bond, and even though the bond itself, when viewed apart from the mortgage, did not have New York contacts. Since the mortgage, which did have the requisite New York contacts, was given as security for the bond, the foreclosure action should fall under New York jurisdiction in all its incidents.

It is permissible for the cause of action to accrue after the land has been disposed of. If the claim arises from the ownership, use, or possession of the land and can be traced to just that, it should make no difference that at the moment of its arising the defendant no longer has an interest in the land.[5] If the defendant is substantively liable for something arising out of the ownership, use, or possession of land, and that liability exists even though the defen-

---

28. See, e.g., Inset Systems, Inc. v. Instruction Set, Inc., 937 F.Supp. 161 (D.Conn.1996).

29. 1997 WL 97097 (1997).

30. Drawing a specific and yet perfect statute is impossible because of the numerous potential factual variations. The Conference study, note 2, above, concedes this and leaves it implicitly to caselaw, armed with the due process clause, to watch the outer fringes of these longarm exercises.

§ 89

1. Tebedo v. Nye, 45 Misc.2d 222, 256 N.Y.S.2d 235 (Sup.Ct., Onondaga County, 1965).

2. Hempstead Medical Arts Co. v. Willie, N.Y. Law Journal, December 9, 1963, p.18, col. 6 (Sup.Ct., Nassau County, Farley, J.).

3. 218 A.D.2d 273, 637 N.Y.S.2d 880 (4th Dep't 1996).

4. The Black River case is the subject of the lead note in SPR 41.

5. See Karrat v. Merhib, 62 Misc.2d 72, 307 N.Y.S.2d 915 (Sup.Ct., Oneida County, 1970).

dant no longer has that interest in the land, jurisdiction should exist under CPLR 302(a)(4).

§ 90. Longarm Jurisdiction for Support and Other Relief under CPLR 302(b)

CPLR 302(b) gives the court longarm personal jurisdiction in certain family actions. It applies in the matrimonial action[1] in the supreme court and in any family court proceeding in which support is claimed. At first it offered longarm jurisdiction only for "support or alimony". With subsequent amendments, however, designed to recognize all of the property categories applicable after the 1980 adoption of the equitable distribution system in matrimonial actions,[2] it offers longarm jurisdiction for "support, alimony, maintenance, distributive awards or special relief in matrimonial actions".

CPLR 302(b) applies to either spouse. While it is usually the husband or father against whom money is sought and who is liable for it in family matters, the wife or mother may also face this liability today.[3] Whenever the particular defendant (respondent in a family court proceeding) is substantively liable for the money or property demanded, CPLR 302(b) offers longarm jurisdiction to assist in getting it.

The statute has several other requirements. The party against whom the demand is made need not be a domiciliary or resident of New York, but the party making the demand must be such when the demand is made—which is ordinarily when the suit is brought. It must also be shown that:

(1) New York was the matrimonial domicile of the parties before their estrangement; or

(2) "the defendant abandoned the plaintiff" in New York; or

(3) the claim for the relief "accrued under the laws" of New York or "under an agreement executed" in New York.

The first requirement, about matrimonial domicile, was construed by the Second Department in Lieb v. Lieb[4] to require that the matrimonial domicile be shown to have existed immediately prior to the estrangement, not at some more distant time in the past. But in Paparella v. Paparella,[5] in which the parties' departure from the state was recent, the state was their matrimonial domicile for many years, and the plaintiff had resumed a New York domicile at action time, the Fourth Department held the statute satisfied. *Paparella* distinguishes the *Lieb* case as involving "attenuated" New York contacts.

Disagreeing with *Lieb* as "unnecessarily restrictive" and taking note of the other departments' views, the Third Department sustains the use of CPLR 302(b) in a case in which New York had been the matrimonial domicile of the parties years earlier, but had long since ceased to be when they separated.[6]

An attempt to use CPLR 302(b) as a predicate for support jurisdiction in a paternity suit was rejected in 1981 in Nilsa v. Blackwell.[7] At the time, the language of requirement number 3 on the above list was that "the obligation to pay" must have accrued under New York law. The court held that no such obligation "accrues" until a filiation order is entered, i.e., that the "obligation" means one already embodied in a judicial direction. The legislature responded with an amendment of CPLR 302(b) in 1982, striking out the "obligation to pay" and substituting the "claim for" language set forth above. The statute should therefore be available for support jurisdiction in a paternity suit today on a showing that the

---

§ 90

1. The matrimonial action is defined by CPLR 105 to include divorce, separation, annulment, and several actions declaring on the validity of the marriage or a purported foreign divorce.

2. Dom.Rel.L. § 236. See Scheinkman, Introductory Commentary on McKinney's DRL 236.

3. See Dom.Rel.L. §§ 236 and 240.

4. 86 Misc.2d 75, 381 N.Y.S.2d 757 (Sup.Ct., Queens County), aff'd 53 A.D.2d 67, 385 N.Y.S.2d 569 (2d Dep't 1976).

5. 74 A.D.2d 106, 426 N.Y.S.2d 610 (4th Dep't 1980).

6. See Levy v. Levy, 185 A.D.2d 15, 592 N.Y.S.2d 480 (1993), noted in SPR 1:3.

7. 84 A.D.2d 295, 445 N.Y.S.2d 579 (2d Dep't 1981).

child was born in New York, or perhaps merely conceived in New York though born elsewhere.[8] Given the benevolent purpose of this provision, the claim should be deemed to "accrue" under New York law under either showing.

When the statute applies, it invokes CPLR 313 and permits service without regard to state lines.

CPLR 302(b) may not be used to support matrimonial relief, i.e., a divorce, separation, etc. But if the plaintiff spouse is a New York domiciliary, the marriage itself is deemed to have a New York presence and qualifies as a res supporting rem jurisdiction for matrimonial relief under CPLR 314(1).

Nor does CPLR 302(b) supply jurisdiction to award custody of a child. Section 75–d of the Domestic Relations Law supplies the jurisdictional bases for custody awards. Both matrimonial and custody jurisdiction are discussed elsewhere.[9]

Note, however, that a single action can of course involve all three jurisdictional statutes and satisfy all of them: CPLR 302(b) for support, CPLR 314(1) for matrimonial relief, and Domestic Relations Law § 75–d for custody.

§ 91. The Restricted Appearance under CPLR 302(c)

It is the state's policy to encourage longarm defendants to submit to New York jurisdiction without contesting it. As an incentive, CPLR 302(c) guarantees defendants that if they do appear in the action, the appearance may not be exploited by the plaintiff to add non-longarm claims against them. If, for example, the plaintiff in a case predicated on longarm jurisdiction should seek to amend the complaint to add an additional claim, that claim would also have to fall within the longarm standards of CPLR 302. If the new claim does not, it may

not be interposed in the action through amendment or otherwise.

This has come to be known as the "restricted appearance",[1] to distinguish it from other kinds of appearances met later.[2] It is applicable only when jurisdiction is based "solely" on CPLR 302. If any other jurisdictional basis is used, CPLR 302(c) does not apply, although some other statute may apply and offer analogous protection.[3]

§ 92. Jurisdiction Versus the Merits

Suppose P sues nondomiciliary D for an assault allegedly committed in New York, serving D outside the state. P bases jurisdiction on CPLR 302(a)(2), defendant's commission of a "tortious act" in New York. D moves to dismiss for lack of jurisdiction, contending that he did not commit such tortious act. The court denies the motion and sustains jurisdiction. To do this, the court has to find that D committed the "tortious act": it is the jurisdictional prerequisite of CPLR 302(a)(2). But if the court does, isn't it also finding for the plaintiff on the merits, since the tort is precisely what P is suing for? Is P entitled at that moment to have liability determined in his favor and the case set down merely for an assessment of damages?

The question looks challenging because of this curious overlap of jurisdictional and merits requirements, but the courts have come up with practical solutions and the challenge is theoretical only. Distilling a single conclusion from a number of cases in the area, we may say this: the jurisdictional and merits questions, no matter how similar, are separate. A holding for jurisdictional purposes does not dictate how the case must be decided on the merits.

Conversely, a merits determination will not go back and undo a jurisdictional finding. In

---

8. See Shirley D. v. Carl D., 224 A.D.2d 60, 648 N.Y.S.2d 650 (2d Dep't 1996), applying Fam.Ct.Act § 154.

9. See § 102 below.

§ 91

1. See Homburger and Laufer, Appearance and Jurisdictional Motions in New York, 14 Buff.L.Rev. 374, 388 (1964).

2. See §§ 109 and 112 below.

3. See §§ 113 and 114, below, which discuss the limited and qualified appearances.

the example given, suppose that jurisdiction is sustained, that the case goes through the usual pretrial preparation, and that at the main trial on the merits the jury finds that D did not commit a tort. Will the dismissal of P's case at that stage be on the merits, or merely for lack of jurisdiction because a jurisdictional fact has now been found wanting?

It will be on the merits. The jurisdictional line having long since been crossed, the case will not retreat to it again no matter how inconsistent the two determinations may seem. This is a simple fact of life when jurisdiction depends in some measure on the merits, as longarm jurisdiction often does. The practical and theoretical justifications for these conclusions are ample, however, so they aren't really so contradictory after all.

To sustain longarm jurisdiction, P has to show facts that, assuming they are actionable, would give rise to longarm jurisdiction under CPLR 302. P's conclusion that the acts are "tortious" is generally accepted at the jurisdictional stage. If the defendant was the performer of acts and the complaint "adequately frames a cause of action in tort arising from those acts", the jurisdictional requirement is met.[1]

§ 93.　Burden of Proving Jurisdiction

A jurisdictional question can arise in any case, but it is more challenging in the longarm case and is therefore best treated in that context.

It is often said that the plaintiff has the burden of proving jurisdiction whenever the issue is raised,[1] but it would seem that that conclusion is either taken a bit lightly in longarm cases, or else amounts to a bout with semantics. If, for example, D moves to dismiss and a factual dispute arises between P and D as to whether D performed longarm acts, a

judge with some doubts might be inclined to sustain jurisdiction and let the case go to trial on the merits. Technically, however, if each side makes out an equally convincing case, the party with the burden of proof is supposed to lose, and a longarm plaintiff seldom loses on a close jurisdictional point. A judge can avoid the issue, and sustain jurisdiction, just by finding that the two sides are not "equally" convincing; that the plaintiff's showing is a mite stronger—just strong enough to discharge this "burden" of proof on the jurisdictional question. What is actually happening, however, is that the plaintiff is being given the benefit of the doubt on the jurisdictional point, a result theoretically at war with the notion that the burden of proof of jurisdiction is on the plaintiff.

Whoever may have this "burden", the degree of proof needed to sustain jurisdiction is not as heavy as that needed to sustain a recovery on the merits.[2] In other words, the plaintiff may have the "burden", but it's a burden that discharges more easily than other burdens.

In Peterson v. Spartan Industries, Inc.,[3] a dispute arose over facts on which longarm jurisdiction depended. P needed to use the disclosure devices against D to help develop the jurisdictional facts. The court held that P is entitled to compel D to submit to disclosure in such an instance without first making out even a "prima facie showing of jurisdiction"; that P makes a "sufficient start" just by showing that his position is not "frivolous".[4] Apparently, the mere fact that the defendant has moved to dismiss sets up a sufficient nexus for the court to take the limited step, not of sustaining jurisdiction, but of making the defendant submit to an examination on the facts on which jurisdiction depends. How else would the court get the limited jurisdiction it needs

---

§ 92

1. Evans v. Planned Parenthood of Broome County, Inc., 43 A.D.2d 996, 997, 352 N.Y.S.2d 257, 259 (3d Dep't 1974).

§ 93

1. See, e.g., Unicon Mgmt. Corp. v. Koppers Co., 250 F.Supp. 850 (S.D.N.Y.1966).

2. Buckley v. Redi–Bolt, Inc., 49 Misc.2d 864, 268 N.Y.S.2d 653 (Sup.Ct., Rensselaer County, 1966).

3. 33 N.Y.2d 463, 354 N.Y.S.2d 905, 310 N.E.2d 513 (1974).

4. Id. at 467, 354 N.Y.S.2d at 908, 310 N.E.2d at 515.

to let P even examine D on the jurisdictional question?[5]

If the jurisdictional facts are so in dispute that they cannot be resolved from affidavits and other submissions on the dismissal motion, a hearing may be required. A fast resolution of the jurisdictional question is usually preferred. The court does have the option to refrain from deciding the jurisdictional objection and direct the defendant to use it instead as a defense in the answer,[6] the idea being to postpone its resolution until the main trial, but the alternative is unattractive because if the later decision is against jurisdiction, all the intervening effort preparing for trial will have been wasted. And for plaintiffs, postponement of the issue can be more than just a waste of time; because of statute of limitations considerations, it can destroy the case.

When one hears, therefore, that courts do not favor viva voce hearings for only a jurisdictional question, with the calling of witnesses and the usual testimonial proof, it is usually a federal source that's doing the talking.[7] In New York practice, such hearings are all too frequent, especially if the statute of limitations would now be dead on a new action should the present one be dismissed. The dismissal would be for want of personal jurisdiction, a category of dismissal that does not get the six months that CPLR 205(a) offers for a new action.[8] In practical terms, therefore, the prospect is that the disposition of this mere "jurisdictional" question can mean the death of the case substantively, motivating the court to dispose of the question immediately for the obvious reason that if the decision is against jurisdiction, it will save the time and trouble of a lengthy trial on the merits.

Hence jurisdictional objections by defendants and immediate trials of fact issues connected with them proliferate in New York. Indeed, as a common usage, the term "traverse" in New York practice has come to be applied almost exclusively to the trial of an issue of fact arising on a motion to dismiss for want of personal jurisdiction—most often for some defect in the manner of service but sometimes just to determine whether there are sufficient longarm contacts for extraterritorial jurisdiction.

If such a trial seems necessary, and the situation is one in which jurisdictional and merits requirements overlap,[9] the parties might stipulate that the result of the jurisdictional trial be deemed binding on the merits as well. That would at least expedite the case, but that phenomenon, too, is seen more often in federal than New York state practice.[10]

§ 94. Overlap of Longarm Bases

It will sometimes happen that several different provisions offer a predicate for jurisdiction. They may be different statutes altogether, or different subdivisions of the same statute. Two and sometimes even three of CPLR 302(a)'s paragraphs can apply in the same case, for example, as where D is a nondomiciliary in the business of owning and operating New York City apartment houses. If D's negligence in the maintenance of a common hallway injures P, P may base jurisdiction against D on paragraph 1 of CPLR 302(a) (transacting business), paragraph 2 (tortious act), or paragraph 4 (claim arising out of the ownership of realty).

There are other statutes on the books that will overlap CPLR 302 from time to time. A notable example is the nonresident motorist

---

5. When the federal courts meet the question of whether they have enough jurisdiction to decide issues on which that very jurisdiction depends, they have developed the theory of "jurisdiction to determine jurisdiction". See United States v. United Mine Workers, 330 U.S. 258, 67 S.Ct. 677, 91 L.Ed. 884 (1947). At least where the parties are before the court, even if only to pose a jurisdictional question, the court gets at least as much jurisdiction as it needs to determine the jurisdictional question. These doings under the New York longarm statute are analogous and could also benefit from an application of the doctrine of "jurisdiction to determine jurisdiction".

6. CPLR 3211(d).

7. See, e.g., Unicon Mgmt. Corp. v. Koppers Co., 38 F.R.D. 474 (S.D.N.Y.1965).

8. See the discussion of the Markoff case in § 52, above.

9. See § 92 above.

10. See, e.g., United States v. Montreal Trust Co., 35 F.R.D. 216 (S.D.N.Y.1964).

statute,[1] separately treated later.[2] If it applies, service may be made on the secretary of state as the implied-in-law agent of the nondomiciliary defendant. Through this "agency", jurisdiction is secured on service technically made in New York, but at root it is a kind of longarm jurisdiction since it gives jurisdiction of a nondomiciliary notified outside the state. The statute will more often than not overlap CPLR 302(a)(2). When it does, the plaintiff can predicate jurisdiction on either statute and use the service of process provisions of the one chosen.

Other statutes that use the "agency" theory in one form or another, requiring that a person or corporation actually designate a local agent for service, or merely deeming such agent to be appointed automatically, also have a longarm mission that can overlap CPLR 302. These are discussed under the separate category of "agency as jurisdictional basis".[3] They, too, are alternatives to CPLR 302 when an overlap exists.

§ 95. Agency as Jurisdictional Basis

The court can get personal jurisdiction of the defendant by service on someone whom the defendant has designated as agent for service, either in connection with the particular claim or with claims generally. The agency can be express or implied.

One express agency already met is under CPLR 318, which allows a defendant to designate any person of choice as an agent for service.[1] That one is voluntary. Other kinds may be mandatory, like the designation of the secretary of state by licensed corporations and the superintendent of insurance by insurance companies.[2] These designees may be used for any claim against the defendant. Still another is the designation of the surrogate's court

clerk that an estate fiduciary is required to make before letters are granted.[3]

An express designation voluntarily made by a would-be defendant can be as broad or as narrow as the parties stipulate. It can be limited to only certain claims. An example of a limited one would be a contract that designates an agent for service as to claims arising under the contract. The designation of an agent for service as authorized by CPLR 318 is not an exclusive method and therefore does not preclude contractual designations of a less formal kind.

There are several implied agencies on the books. An implied agency is a designation, usually of a state official, that results not from an actual designation by the would-be defendant, but as the automatic consequence of some act the defendant commits or is responsible for in New York. The classic illustration is the nonresident motorist statute,[4] and such statutes exist today for boats[5] and planes[6] as well as ground vehicles.

A broad implied agency, the superintendent of insurance being the agent, exists against unauthorized insurers under § 1213 of the Insurance Law on a variety of insurance contacts so extensive that it has been said to go to the "very perimeters" of due process.[7] This separate and comprehensive treatment of what amounts to longarm jurisdiction in insurance matters is the reason why CPLR 302(a), the state's general longarm statute, has no separate insurance category, although its Illinois model[8] had.

These and like statutes will often be found to overlap some part of CPLR 302. When that happens, the plaintiff can base jurisdiction on CPLR 302 and make service under the usual CPLR provisions or rely instead on the special

§ 94
1. Veh. & Traf.L. § 253.
2. See § 97 below.
3. See § 95 below.

§ 95
1. See § 73 above.
2. Bus.Corp.L. § 304, Insurance Law § 1212, treated in § 70, above.

3. SCPA 708.
4. Veh. & Traf.L. § 253, treated in § 97, below.
5. Navig.L. § 74.
6. Gen.Bus.L. § 250.
7. Ford v. Unity Hospital, 32 N.Y.2d 464, 470–71, 346 N.Y.S.2d 238, 242, 299 N.E.2d 659, 663 (1973).
8. Ill.Ann.Stat., ch.110, § 5/2–209.

statute and make service as that statute provides.[9]

When the corporation is a domestic or licensed foreign corporation, the designation of the secretary of state as agent for service is express and the governing provision on service is BCL 306, treated earlier.[10] In this connection, note yet another provision: BCL 307, which contains an implied designation of the secretary of state as agent of any *unlicensed* foreign corporation that is subject to jurisdiction under any part of Article 3 of the CPLR. Since a corporation subject to CPLR jurisdiction is also subject to CPLR service, § 307 simply offers the alternative of serving the secretary of state in these instances, just as BCL 306 does for licensed corporations. But while both 306 and 307 involve designations of the secretary of state as agent for service, the methods of service differ and the difference can have jurisdictional consequences.

Under BCL 306 the designation is an actual one and the secretary of state has a current listing of the corporation's address on her records, while under BCL 307 the designation is an implied one, spelled out only from the corporation's activity in New York, and the secretary has no such record. That's what generates a difference in the methods of service. Under BCL 306, two copies of the summons are delivered to the secretary of state, with the secretary mailing one to the corporation, while under BCL 307 the secretary is served with only one copy and it is the plaintiff who must mail another to the corporation. The Court of Appeals held in Flick v. Stewart–Warner Corp.,[11] that when BCL 306 instead of 307 is mistakenly used for service on an unlicensed corporation, jurisdiction will not obtain even if the secretary, gratuitously, manages to mail a copy of the summons to the corporation and the corporation gets it.

The Court adhered to this rigid construction of BCL 307 a few years later in Stewart v. Volkswagen of America, Inc.[12] The statute has a progression of options in which each becomes available only if the preceding one can't be satisfied. The court called it a "menu" and held that a plaintiff can't choose from it at random, but must go in sequence in order to secure jurisdiction.

§ 96. Attorney as Agent under CPLR 303

If nondomiciliary P sues D in the supreme court, D can interpose any claim as a counterclaim because the supreme court has general jurisdiction. But if P sues D in some other court, whose subject matter jurisdiction of counterclaims is limited and does not embrace D's claim, D will have to sue on her claim separately in a court that has the requisite jurisdiction. When D tries to effect service on P in that separate action, however, she may find that P himself is outside the state, or in New York in connection with the P v. D suit and therefore immune from summons service for that reason.[1]

The answer to D's dilemma in that situation is to effect service of the summons on the attorney who is representing P in the P v. D action. CPLR 303 authorizes this. (The clerk becomes the person to serve if P is appearing pro se.) This automatic designation is available only on behalf of D in the P v. D action. A stranger can't exploit it.

This designation is good only during the pendency of P's action, and it terminates with final judgment.[2] It has also been held that it applies only when P commences a court action or proceeding; that commencement of a New York arbitration, for example, will not invoke CPLR 303.[3]

---

9. See § 94 above.

10. Section 70 above.

11. 76 N.Y.2d 50, 556 N.Y.S.2d 510, 555 N.E.2d 907 (1990).

12. 81 N.Y.2d 203, 597 N.Y.S.2d 612, 613 N.E.2d 518 (1993). The case is the subject of the lead note in New York State Law Digest No. 406.

§ 96

1. See § 68 above.

2. Banco do Brasil v. Madison Steamship Corp., 61 Misc.2d 1028, 307 N.Y.S.2d 341 (Sup.Ct., N.Y.County, 1970).

3. Gillespie & Co. of New York, Inc. v. Coleport Fabrics, Inc., 48 Misc.2d 333, 264 N.Y.S.2d 653 (Sup.Ct., N.Y.County, 1965).

It may seem a bit odd to immunize P from service while allowing service on his attorney. It would be more palatable simply to deprive nondomiciliaries of immunity from service when they themselves use the New York courts. But why tempt fate? CPLR 303 works in this situation and should be used.

Since CPLR 303 applies only to a suit in New York "by a person not subject to personal jurisdiction", it should not apply when, in whatever suit D wants to bring against P, P would be amenable to extraterritorial service. So, for example, if D's claim has a longarm jurisdictional basis against P under CPLR 302, D may not use CPLR 303 to make service on P's attorney.

§ 97. The Nonresident Motorist Statute

Section 253 of the Vehicle and Traffic Law is the best known of the provisions that imply the designation of a state official for service, and there is enough caselaw on it to merit separate treatment. Section 253 is sometimes confused with § 388 of the Vehicle and Traffic Law, but its mission is quite different. Section 253 is just a jurisdiction giver. Section 388 is a substantive liability creator, imputing to the owner of a vehicle the conduct of one driving with the owner's permission, so as to make the owner, and her insurance policy, available to pay the damages of an injured third person.

Under § 253, a nonresident driving in New York or owning a vehicle being driven in New York with permission is "deemed equivalent" to the appointment of the secretary of state for service of process with respect to any claim emanating from an accident or collision growing out of the "use or operation" of the vehicle in New York. The statute then supplies in detail the method of service, which requires a mailing of a copy of the summons to the secretary in Albany (or a personal delivery of a copy to one of his branch offices) plus a mailing of summons, complaint, and notice to the defendant by registered or certified mail, return receipt requested, with a provision for ordi-

nary mail if the registered mail should be refused. Note that here, where the secretary's designation is implied, only one copy of the summons is served on the secretary, and it is the plaintiff who mails another copy to the defendant. When the designation is express, as with the domestic or licensed foreign corporation under the Business Corporation Law, two copies of the summons are served on the secretary of state and it is she who mails one out to the defendant.[1] The reason for the difference is that when the designation is express, the address of the defendant is on file with the secretary, which is not so when the secretary is merely an implied designee.

The implied designation exploited in the nonresident motorist statute is really an ingenious way around the strictures of Pennoyer v. Neff.[2] The statute is at root just a "longarm" statute whose underlying theory is the same as CPLR 302. But *Pennoyer* precluded extrastate service, regardless of local contacts, thus forcing state legislatures to some substitute. The substitute here was the "deemed" designation of a local state official who could then be served within the state in the defendant's behalf with personam effect. The "jurisdictional" service was the one made in New York on the secretary of state; the mailing of a copy to the defendant outside New York gave the defendant the notice that due process also requires but was not the "jurisdictional" act and hence did not have to occur in New York.

Section 253 details the follow-up procedures, including filing of the receipt along with the other papers after the receipt comes back. Service is complete upon the filing.[3] An alternative to the mailing is personal delivery to the defendant outside New York.

There will often be an overlap between V&TL 253 and CPLR 302(a)(2), which supplies longarm jurisdiction for a tortious act committed in New York. When both provisions apply, the plaintiff can choose either, using the ordinary service methods of the CPLR if CPLR 302 is chosen. If both statutes were always

§ 97

1. Bus.Corp.L. § 306(b), treated in § 70, above.
2. 95 U.S. 714, 24 L.Ed. 565 (1877).

3. See § 72, above, for the significance of when service is "complete".

certain to apply to the same situations, the plaintiff's choice would be based only on which one's service provisions would be easier on the facts of the case. But that's the question: are the two statutes so similar that one always applies when the other does? Probably not, but it isn't clear. CPLR 302(a)(2) bases its jurisdiction on the defendant's alleged "tortious act" in New York. All § 253 requires is that the claim emanate from an accident arising out of the "use or operation" of the vehicle in New York. Although § 253 does not predicate jurisdiction on a showing of a "tort", it is tort that the plaintiff invariably claims when suing under § 253, thus tending to make the two provisions parallel. The lawyer in any event does well to note some of the situations to which § 253 has been extended.

Where the vehicle was left unattended, with motor idling, and it rolled forward and tipped over a stove, resulting in the burning of P's property, P's suit for property damage was held to arise out of the "operation" of the vehicle.[4] And where D negligently allowed a slippery condition to exist on the floor of a truck while it was being unloaded, this was held a "use" of the truck and gave jurisdiction when P fell.[5] Similarly, where P slipped on an oil accumulation on a boat, the oil coming from a defective hose leading to the boat from D's truck, the accident was held to arise from the truck's "use".[6]

In another case D took his mother's car without permission and then let his friend drive it while D sat in the passenger seat. An accident occurred. D, although neither the owner nor the driver of the car, was held to be "using" the vehicle and was subject to jurisdiction under § 253.[7]

Would each of the above situations also satisfy CPLR 302(a)(2) as involving a "tortious act" by D? It is nice to know that the inquiry may not be necessary as long as V&TL 253 stands on the books as an alternative.

Turning now to the service part of § 253, we should stress that present caselaw is prone to void the service entirely in some situations (and frustrate use of § 253 altogether) if the mailing does not work out right. If D voluntarily gives P an incorrect address, D may be estopped from pleading non-compliance and jurisdiction will result,[8] but if the address given by D was correct and he merely moves, with the result that the certified mail is returned "moved, left no address", the follow-up ordinary mail has been disallowed, service held invalid, and jurisdiction denied.[9]

The Court of Appeals has held that when service is made by court order under CPLR 308(5), the order can direct mail to an address D furnished even though D later moved and left no forwarding address; that jurisdiction will be upheld in such an instance on the ground that a would-be defendant involved in an accident is under a duty to see to it that persons hurt in the accident have continuing access to data about the defendant's whereabouts.[10] Such a rule should logically apply to like situations under § 253 and would mean an overruling of cases that void the § 253 service even though it was D's own failure to leave a forwarding address that accounted for his not getting notice. The analogy is tempting, but whether the courts will buy it remains to be seen. Indeed, the Court of Appeals itself, in a case on paragraph 4 of CPLR 308 (the affix-and-mail method of service), later cast doubt on whether the defendant is under a

4. Raspante v. Trans. Supply & Mgmt., Inc., 214 N.Y.S.2d 583 (Sup.Ct., Oneida County), aff'd sub nom. Frank Bonomo and Co. v. Trans. Supply & Mgmt., Inc., 11 A.D.2d 1090, 207 N.Y.S.2d 447 (4th Dep't 1960).

5. Aranzullo v. Collins Packing Co., 14 N.Y.2d 578, 248 N.Y.S.2d 874, 198 N.E.2d 255 (1964), aff'g 18 A.D.2d 1068, 239 N.Y.S.2d 398 (1st Dep't 1963). The appellate division opinion points out that the addition of the word "use" was intended to give jurisdiction even with respect to accidents occurring when the vehicle is not moving.

6. Landolphi v. Wilhelmsen, 39 Misc.2d 950, 241 N.Y.S.2d 942 (Sup.Ct., Kings County, 1963).

7. Wahler v. Thompson, 36 Misc.2d 847, 234 N.Y.S.2d 105 (Sup.Ct., Onondaga County, 1962), rev'd on other grounds 26 A.D.2d 895, 274 N.Y.S.2d 862 (4th Dep't 1966).

8. Greenwood v. White, 25 A.D.2d 73, 266 N.Y.S.2d 1012 (3d Dep't 1966).

9. Bauman v. Fisher, 12 A.D.2d 32, 208 N.Y.S.2d 317 (3d Dep't 1960).

10. See § 75 above. The Dobkin trilogy, treated in the cited section, holds such mail service to be constitutional when the defendant moves without advising of it.

duty to keep advice current about his where-abouts.[11]

The best the practitioner can do is be aware of these things and use whatever scheme has proved tried-and-truest on the particular facts.

What about a return marked "unclaimed"? Caselaw had held that it voids the service,[12] but a 1978 amendment of § 253 overruled the caselaw to allow a follow-up procedure by ordinary mail when the registered or certified mail is returned unclaimed. The amendment does not address the "moved, left no address" situation, however, and there is therefore some peril in treating it the same as an "unclaimed" delivery. The lawyer may prefer here, too, therefore, if CPLR 302(a)(2) is applicable as an alternative jurisdictional basis and there is any doubt about the procedures to be followed under § 253, to avoid § 253 and apply instead for a court order of service under paragraph 5 of CPLR 308. The practitioner who uses V& TL 253 should note all of its procedural incidents, including filing of proof of service and the time when service is deemed complete.

Lawyers will find the working out of these problems comfortable only if they have left plenty of time for trouble should the statute of limitations be anywhere around. If the statute is closing in, an oversight can prove fatal.[13]

§ 98. Jurisdiction by Written Agreement

A court can derive its jurisdiction from a party's written contract, in which the party simply stipulates that the New York courts will have jurisdiction to hear any dispute, or a given dispute, arising under the agreement. The constitutionality of this basis was sustained in National Equipment Rental, Ltd. v. Szukhent,[1] and the basis is exploited by the

New York courts. Sometimes, as in *Szukhent* itself, the contract also contains the designation of an agent for service, in which event the "agency" may be deemed the jurisdictional basis. But other cases involve agreements containing the jurisdictional submission without an agency designation,[2] and these illustrate how the contractual submission can serve simply as a jurisdictional basis.

If the agreement provides for jurisdiction but says nothing about service, service would be made as usual under the CPLR. And since caselaw made use of this jurisdictional basis prior to the adoption of the CPLR,[3] CPLR 301 should be deemed to carry it forth for present use, thus invoking CPLR 313. This in turn means that service may be made within or without the state when consent jurisdiction of this kind is involved.

The agreement providing for New York jurisdiction may also provide for a non-CPLR method of service. If the agreed method is reasonable, it will be allowed to supersede CPLR methods. Where, for example, the contract provided for certified mail, service by that means was sustained.[4]

No particular form of language is necessary. It can be as "refreshingly simple and brief" as a letter, and merely say that as to any (or a given) dispute arising under the agreement, the parties "consent to the jurisdiction of any court within the State of New York."[5]

The agreement involved in the *Szukhent* case came close to being upset as an adhesion contract. There were four dissenters in the U.S. Supreme Court and the adhesion factor played a role. A later lower court case in New York refused a submission under circum-

---

11. See the discussion of the Feinstein case in § 74, above.

12. Grandison v. College Truck Renting Corp., 26 A.D.2d 260, 273 N.Y.S.2d 567 (1st Dep't 1966).

13. See § 231A below.

§ 98

1. 375 U.S. 311, 84 S.Ct. 411, 11 L.Ed.2d 354 (1964).

2. See, e.g., National Eqpt. Rental, Ltd. v. Dec–Wood Corp., 51 Misc.2d 999, 274 N.Y.S.2d 280 (App.T., 2d Dep't, 1966).

3. See, e.g., National Eqpt. Rental, Ltd. v. Graphic Art Designers, Inc., 36 Misc.2d 442, 234 N.Y.S.2d 61 (Sup.Ct., Nassau County, 1962).

4. National Eqpt. Rental, Ltd. v. Dec–Wood, note 2, above.

5. Albert Levine Assocs., Inc. v. Hudson, 43 F.R.D. 392, 393 (S.D.N.Y.1967).

stances it found "unconscionable".[6] But perhaps this apprehension is unwarranted. If the dispute has New York contacts, it will likely have a longarm basis for jurisdiction under CPLR 302 and the contractual submission in such an event would be superfluous. If, on the other hand, the controversy lacks significant New York contacts, the forum non conveniens doctrine[7] should intercede to dismiss it. The contract may supply jurisdiction to the court, but if the case lacks reasonable New York contacts the contract can't ordinarily compel the court to exercise the jurisdiction.

A contractual agreement as the source of a court's jurisdiction is not common in New York. (The availability of generous longarm jurisdiction is apparently what accounts for this.) It is very common, however, as the source of an arbitrator's jurisdiction,[8] and there is some interplay between the two realms.

When there is an agreement to arbitrate, the courts' involvement is limited. The courts decide, if asked, only whether the dispute is arbitrable and whether the arbitration was timely sought.[9] If it is found arbitrable and goes to arbitration, the courts' only further involvement is in determining whether the arbitrators' award is enforcible and in confirming it into a judgment.[10] But even for that limited involvement, the courts must have some source of their own jurisdiction over the parties. The same agreement that authorized the arbitration in New York may be deemed to authorize the New York courts to entertain whatever personal jurisdiction they need to carry out the narrow judicial involvement in the arbitral process. Indeed, even the means of

service needed to commence the connected judicial proceedings may be drawn from or through the agreement to arbitrate. Where, for example, the parties agreed to arbitrate according to a certain body of rules, and among those rules was one authorizing service on a party's attorney in any connected court proceeding, the court's jurisdiction and the facilitated service were both sustained.[11]

§ 99. Continuing Jurisdiction

In a matrimonial action in which alimony is awarded or in a family court proceeding in which support is ordered,[1] the judgment or order may provide for payments to be made in periodic installments. It may become necessary later on to enter an arrears judgment on accrued installments, or to move the court to modify the amounts up or down based on changed circumstances. Suppose, however, that the defendant or respondent, clearly within the in personam jurisdiction of the court at the outset, has since left the state. Is he still subject to the personal jurisdiction of the court on an application to affect the judgment in some way, even if served with the motion papers outside New York?

If the judgment to be affected is that of the supreme court in a matrimonial action in which the defendant was originally within the court's personam jurisdiction, continuing jurisdiction of that kind exists.[2] If it arose in a family court proceeding there is some debate, even though there was personam jurisdiction at the outset. An appellate division case says that continuing jurisdiction in the family court applies only to subject matter, not personal, jurisdiction.[3] A later family court case in the

---

6. Paragon Homes, Inc., v. Carter, 56 Misc.2d 463, 288 N.Y.S.2d 817 (Sup.Ct., Nassau County), aff'd 30 A.D.2d 1052, 295 N.Y.S.2d 606 (2d Dep't 1968). The plaintiff was a New York assignee of a contract entirely between non-residents and a simple forum non conveniens dismissal was at that time precluded because of the plaintiff's New York residence.

7. See § 28 above.

8. CPLR 7501.

9. CPLR 7502, 7503. See § 589 below (Practitioner's Edition).

10. CPLR 7510, 7511, 7514. See §§ 601, 602 below (Practitioner's Edition).

11. Board of Ed. of Half Hollow Hills Cent. Sch. Dist. v. Half Hollow Hills Teachers Ass'n, Inc., 79 Misc.2d 223, 358 N.Y.S.2d 285 (Sup.Ct., Suffolk County, 1974). These matters are more fully explored in Chapter 22 below (Practitioner's Edition).

§ 99

1. Dom.Rel.L. § 236; Fam.Ct.Act §§ 442, 443.

2. See Schneidman v. Schneidman, 188 Misc. 765, 65 N.Y.S.2d 876 (Sup.Ct., Kings County, 1946).

3. Wasserman v. Wasserman, 43 A.D.2d 951, 352 N.Y.S.2d 207 (2d Dep't 1974).

same department, apparently unaware of the appellate division decision of a few months earlier, holds that there is a continuation of personal jurisdiction as well.[4]

The constitutionality of continuing jurisdiction has been upheld where the personal representative of an estate subsequently left the state of appointment. The personal representative was held subject to continuing personal jurisdiction in a proceeding to remove him and require him to account.[5] New York exploits this constitutional permission indirectly by having the personal representative designate the clerk of the surrogate's court as agent for service.[6]

Continuing jurisdiction has been applied in New York after judgment was rendered in favor of a plaintiff against tortfeasors A and B, with full jurisdiction, to enable A to get a contribution judgment against B even though B had since moved from the state.[7] It should make no difference whether the subsequent contribution proceeding is processed by motion captioned in the original action or by a separate action.

By analogy, once judgment has been rendered against a defendant with jurisdiction, that jurisdiction ought to continue, at least as against the defendant himself, for all steps necessary to enforce the judgment. Exploitation of the continuing jurisdiction doctrine would allow the extrastate service of papers in connection with appropriate enforcement devices,[8] but New York has not yet taken that broad a position. One of the devices most helpful in the enforcement of a judgment, for example, is a subpoena used to make the defendant reveal data about his assets. Such a

subpoena is authorized by CPLR 5224 and should be servable, with personam effect, even on a defendant who moved from the state after judgment. But other provisions have been construed—unfortunately, it is submitted—to preclude extraterritorial subpoena service,[9] thereby depriving the enforcement realm of the helpful and reasonable device of continuing jurisdiction when subpoenas are the weapon used.

The Restatement regards jurisdiction as continuing "throughout all subsequent proceedings which arise out of the original cause of action", as long as there was jurisdiction to begin with and notice of subsequent steps is given.[10]

F. SERVICE OUTSIDE NEW YORK

Table of Sections

§ 100. Service Outside New York under CPLR 313

As has been noted many times already, CPLR 313 permits service outside the state whenever the defendant is a New York domiciliary or there exists a basis for jurisdiction against the defendant under either CPLR 301 or 302.

The 301 bases that authorize this extrastate service include corporate presence in New York under the "doing business" test.[1] Of course, the very fact that the corporation is doing business in New York would usually assure that an appropriate corporate agent is

---

4. Iannone v. Iannone, 78 Misc.2d 294, 355 N.Y.S.2d 992 (Fam.Ct., Suffolk County, 1974).

5. Michigan Trust Co. v. Ferry, 228 U.S. 346, 33 S.Ct. 550, 57 L.Ed. 867 (1913).

6. SCPA 708(1).

7. Ohlquist v. Nordstrom, 143 Misc. 502, 257 N.Y.S. 711 (Sup.Ct., Chautauqua County, 1932), aff'd 238 A.D. 766, 261 N.Y.S. 1039 (4th Dep't), aff'd 262 N.Y. 696, 188 N.E. 125 (1933).

8. CPLR Article 52 supplies these devices, some of which are mere motion procedures, e.g., CPLR 5226, which would be easier to implement if extrastate service of notice is permitted.

9. See DuPont v. Bronston, 46 A.D.2d 369, 362 N.Y.S.2d 471 (1st Dep't 1974). It may be that DuPont is no longer followed. See AABCO Sheet Metal Co. v. Lincoln Center, 249 A.D.2d 39, 670 N.Y.S.2d 494 (1st Dep't 1998), but see also DeLeonardis v. Subway Sandwich Shops, Inc., N.Y.L.J. March 20, 1998, p.28, col.3 (Sup.Ct., N.Y. County, Tompkins, J.).

10. Restatement, 2d, Conflict of Laws, § 26.

§ 100

1. See § 82 above.

available for service in New York. But whether that is so or not, extrastate service on the corporation under CPLR 313 is permissible.[2]

Another CPLR 301 basis on which extrastate service may be predicated is where the defendant has agreed by contract to submit to New York jurisdiction.[3]

CPLR 313 does not supply any of the mechanical methods of service. These it adopts from the service statutes in Article 3. Thus, as soon as CPLR 313 is activated in a case in which an individual is the defendant, the lawyer must then turn back to CPLR 308 for the methods, the practical impact of CPLR 313 merely being to translate the words "within the state", wherever found in CPLR 308, into "within or without the state". The net result of a successful invocation of CPLR 313, therefore, is simply to remove state lines as an impediment to process.

All of the paragraphs of CPLR 308 are available for service outside the state, and with the same conditions.[4] Thus, for example, service outside could be initially made under paragraphs 1 or 2 of CPLR 308, but, before paragraphs 4 or 5 could be used, their conditions precedent would have to be satisfied, as with a showing of an attempt to make service under paragraph 1 or 2 before paragraph 4 could be used.

If CPLR 313 applies, it is even permissible, under such two-step service requirements as the deliver-and-mail method of paragraph 2 and the affix-and-mail method of paragraph 4, to execute one step within the state and the other outside. CPLR 313 being applicable, state lines lose significance. But one of the bases of jurisdiction on which CPLR 313 relies would have to be present. Without such a

basis, service may not be "split" in this fashion and would have to take place entirely within the state because there would be no authority for carrying out either step outside the state.[5]

If service is made outside the country, the plaintiff must be alert to the Hague Convention, a treaty to which the United States subscribes,[6] which requires that any conditions imposed on service by the nation in which the service takes place must be fulfilled, such as that service shall not be made by mail, or that a translation must accompany the papers served, etc.[7] The convention and its requirements apply only when the defendant has to be served in the foreign country. If the defendant, as is often the case, is amenable to service anywhere in the United States, the convention does not apply.[8]

Any New York resident over 18 and not a party may make the out-of-state service. But so may anyone authorized to make service under the laws of the place of service, even though such person could not make service under New York law. Any person duly qualified as a lawyer in the place of service is also authorized by CPLR 313 to act as process server. It turns out, therefore, that those who may serve New York process outside New York make up a longer list than those authorized to serve it within.

The New York rule against serving process on Sunday[9] applies to extrastate service, and it makes no difference that the place where service is made allows Sunday service.[10]

CPLR 313 permits service to be made on the defendant's personal representative if the would-be defendant dies before suit, which raises an old issue about what happens when

2. Decisionware, Inc. v. Systems Equipment Lessors, Inc., 45 A.D.2d 971, 359 N.Y.S.2d 586 (2d Dep't 1974).

3. See § 98 above.

4. Service on a Rule 318 agent under CPLR 308(3) would probably be an exception, since that agent, designated in papers filed with New York clerks, would usually not be amenable to service outside the state. But if he were, apparently even CPLR 308(3) could be used for extrastate service.

5. See Durgom v. Durgom, 47 Misc.2d 513, 262 N.Y.S.2d 874 (N.Y.C.Civ.Ct. 1965).

6. The convention is reprinted following Rule 4 in 28 USCA.

7. See Chase, Serving Summons Abroad, N.Y. Law Journal, June 28, 1983, p.1, col.1.

8. Volkswagenwerk A.G. v. Schlunk, 486 U.S. 694, 108 S.Ct. 2104, 100 L.Ed.2d 722 (1988). See § 624 below (Practitioner's Edition).

9. See § 63 above.

10. Eisenberg v. Citation–Langley Corp., 99 A.D.2d 700, 471 N.Y.S.2d 595 (1st Dep't 1984).

the defendant dies during the action instead of before it. The appropriate step is of course to substitute the personal representative in place of the defendant, but the question arises whether the representative is subject to extrastate service of the papers that bring on the substitution.

It is clear today that if the original jurisdiction against the decedent was based on long-arm contacts or on some other basis authorizing out-of-state service, the representative is also subject to out-of-state service for the purpose of substitution.[11] But if the only predicate of jurisdiction over the decedent was that he was personally served in New York, older case-law, not explicitly overruled, holds that the court has no jurisdiction whereby to substitute his nondomiciliary representative,[12] i.e., there is no authority to serve the substitution papers on the representative outside New York.

It would seem, however, through a combination of CPLR 301 and 313, that this old case-law is overruled and that substitution, through extrastate service on the personal representative, would today be permitted in either situation. CPLR 313 says that if the "person", apparently meaning the original defendant, was subject to jurisdiction under CPLR 301, then so is his personal representative. Since personal delivery within New York to D himself is the oldest of jurisdictional bases and is carried over by CPLR 301, one may conclude that CPLR 313 covers it. It should make no difference that the representative is being substituted rather than initially sued, or that in one instance initial jurisdiction was through local service, a CPLR 301 basis, while in another it was founded on longarm jurisdiction, a CPLR 302 basis, because both bases are specified in CPLR 313.

Territorial service in New York as an automatic jurisdictional predicate, while subject to legitimate criticism, was recently reaffirmed by the U.S. Supreme Court.[13] As long as it exists there seems scant reason to say that a defendant served here during his lifetime, and thus brought within New York jurisdiction, can frustrate the jurisdiction just by dying.

G. REM JURISDICTION

Table of Sections

§ 101. Rem Jurisdiction, Generally

Rem jurisdiction turns on the presence within the state of a res—a thing—of some kind. It is generally turned to only when personam jurisdiction of D is unavailable. It enables the court to give P a judgment against D good to the extent of D's interest in the res. Rem jurisdiction can be subdivided into several categories, and it helps to do that for analysis. For convenience of reference, we can break it down into three parts and call them:

1. strictly in rem;

2. in rem; and

3. quasi in rem.

Categories 1 and 2 have this in common: they both involve an action in which P is after the particular thing. Rather than seeking a general money judgment, P wants possession of the particular item of property, or wants to establish his ownership or other interest in it, or to exclude D from an interest in it.

The difference between 1 and 2 is that with "strictly in rem" jurisdiction, the action is brought against the thing but binds everyone in the world, whether named or not and whether notified or not in the action. The action in rem against a ship under admiralty jurisdiction is the most common example of

---

11. Rosenfeld v. Hotel Corp. of America, 20 N.Y.2d 25, 281 N.Y.S.2d 308, 228 N.E.2d 374 (1967). See § 85 above.

12. McMaster v. Gould, 240 N.Y. 379, 148 N.E. 556 (1925); Helme v. Buckelew, 229 N.Y. 363, 128 N.E. 216 (1920).

13. See § 59 above.

this, but that category of action is not seen in the New York courts because it is exclusively federal.[1] There is at least one item of "strictly in rem" jurisdiction of which the New York courts do have jurisdiction, however: the proceeding to register land title under Article 12 of the Real Property Law.[2] It is rarely seen today, however, and should not be confused with any other action affecting an interest in land. Practically speaking, therefore, "strictly in rem" jurisdiction is not a significant part of New York practice.

But the second item on the list, "in rem" jurisdiction, is, at least theoretically. Also brought to affect an interest in a particular and identifiable property of some kind, an action in this "in rem" category of action produces a judgment binding only on those who have been named as parties and duly notified. In this category are many actions familiar to the lawyer, including foreclosure of a mortgage or other lien on real or personal property in the state, replevin, ejectment, an action to quiet title, etc. There is no need to draw out the list. As long as the property is in the state and all P is seeking is to affect interests in it, this category of jurisdiction does the job.[3]

The third category, which we have labeled "quasi in rem" jurisdiction, differs from the first two in that it does not seek to affect interests in any particular property. Here all P wants is money. P wants to bring an ordinary money action against D but cannot get personal jurisdiction of D. Through the use of appropriate judicial process, quasi in rem jurisdiction purports to let P actually or constructively seize any property D may have in the state, thus assuring P that any money judgment P may get in the action will be enforcible at least to the extent of the property seized. In New York, the device used for this purpose in the ordinary money action is called "attachment". As will be seen three sections hence, this category of rem jurisdiction has been severely circumscribed by the U.S. Supreme Court.

The reader should take careful note that the three rem subdivisions used above are for reference purposes only. In fact, the Restatement uses the words "in rem" to describe item 1 on the list, the strictly in rem jurisdiction, and applies "quasi in rem" to categories 2 and 3 together.[4] Characterization is of secondary importance, however. The three-part division used above, although not as accurate historically, is more helpful for analysis and reference. When all three categories are to be referred to collectively, we can simply call them "rem" jurisdiction, without any qualifying word.

Rem jurisdiction can also support a matrimonial action, ingeniously theorizing that the "marital res" is present in the state if the plaintiff spouse is domiciled there, even though the defendant spouse is not. This makes rem jurisdiction over the marital status sufficient to support matrimonial relief (divorce, separation, etc.) against an absent spouse.[5]

CPLR 314 exploits all of the available rem bases of jurisdiction. Its several parts are studied in the ensuing sections. Whenever CPLR 314 applies, service may be made on the defendant inside or outside New York. But unless

---

§ 101

1. 28 U.S.C.A. § 1333(1). Admiralty and maritime actions that may be brought in state courts under the "saving to suitors" clause contained in § 1333(1) do not include the strictly in rem action against the vessel. Such an action was not known to the common law, and only items of relief recognized at common law, such as maritime suits seeking only money (as most do), may at the plaintiff's option go into state court through the saving to suitors clause.

2. See Real Prop.L. § 391.

3. The concept has been advanced that in rem jurisdiction even over property located outside the state may be exercised by a court if it can be shown that the other state

or nation, where the property is located, is cooperating in the venture. See United States v. All Funds, 63 F.3d 148 (2d Cir.1995), noted in SPR 40:4.

4. See Introductory Note on Topic 2 of Chapter 3, Restatement, 2d, Conflict of Laws. Noting this categorization, the U.S. Supreme Court, in circumscribing quasi in rem jurisdiction in Shaffer v. Heitner, 433 U.S. 186, 97 S.Ct. 2569, 53 L.Ed.2d 683 (1977), was at pains to note that in the Restatement's terminology it was only the second type of "quasi in rem" jurisdiction that was being restricted—the category 3 "quasi in rem" jurisdiction we use in the above text. See § 104 below.

5. See § 102 below.

there happens to be some personam basis coincidentally applicable, only rem jurisdiction results.

§ 102. Rem Jurisdiction of Marital Status

CPLR 314(1) authorizes the use of rem jurisdiction in a matrimonial action. The marriage, sometimes termed the "marital res" or "matrimonial res" or "marital status", is deemed present within the state as long as one of the spouses is a domiciliary (not a mere resident) of the state. (It is usually the plaintiff spouse who is the domiciliary when this category of jurisdiction is relied on.) The presence of the marital res allows the court, along rem jurisdictional lines, to affect the marriage, such as by divorce or separation.[1] The action is brought in the usual way, and the defendant may be served anywhere. If he or she defaults, the resulting judgment of (e.g.) divorce is valid and must be recognized by all other American jurisdictions under the full faith and credit clause.[2]

In some instances, New York, as an internal matter, requires that the plaintiff show not just that he or she is a domiciliary at the time of commencement of the action, but has been so for a year, or in some cases two years, prior to suit.[3]

If there is personam jurisdiction of the defendant spouse, this rem category of jurisdiction of course becomes academic. It is needed and hence is used only when personam jurisdiction of the defendant is lacking.

Distinguish CPLR 302(b), which offers personam jurisdiction for monetary relief in marital and family disputes in certain circumstances. CPLR 302(b) applies only to monetary relief, however, not to the matrimonial remedy itself. In a given case, of course, the court may have rem jurisdiction to affect the marriage under CPLR 314(1) as well as personam jurisdiction sufficient to affect the parties' monetary rights under CPLR 302(b), but the matrimonial relief (divorce, separation, etc.) does not get longarm personam jurisdiction under CPLR 302 and must rely on rem jurisdiction under CPLR 314(1) if some other personam basis is lacking.

Nor does the presence of rem matrimonial jurisdiction afford basis to affect the custody of a child. For custody, the rule was that the court needed personam jurisdiction of the parent whose custody right was to be affected, or else personam jurisdiction of the child. In the latter instance, a kind of rem jurisdiction was working: having the child before it, the court could affect the absent parent's right to the custody of the child.[4] The adoption of Article 5–A of the Domestic Relations Law, which took effect in 1978, made some changes in custody matters. The article, an adoption of the Uniform Child Custody Jurisdiction Act,[5] has an extensive set of jurisdictional bases on which custody jurisdiction can be predicated,[6] exploiting a mixture of both personam and rem jurisdiction conceptually akin to the "longarm" jurisdiction underlying CPLR 302 as well as the rem jurisdiction found in CPLR 314. Under the Custody Act, the physical presence of the child is a jurisdictional predicate only if certain other requirements are met.[7]

Rem jurisdiction in the matrimonial context is really in a class by itself. If it had to be fitted into one of the three categories we devised in the preceding section, it would come somewhere between the first two. A judgment in a matrimonial action comes close to binding

§ 102

1. Geary v. Geary, 272 N.Y. 390, 6 N.E.2d 67 (1936).

2. Williams v. North Carolina [Williams I], 317 U.S. 287, 63 S.Ct. 207, 87 L.Ed. 279 (1942). A footnote in the U.S. Supreme Court's opinion in Shaffer v. Heitner seems designed to assure that this "status" category of rem jurisdiction is not undone by the strictures Shaffer places on quasi in rem jurisdiction. See note 30 at 433 U.S. 186, 208, 97 S.Ct. 2569, 2582, 53 L.Ed.2d 683 (1977).

3. Dom.Rel.L. § 230. The statute speaks in terms of "residence" but has been construed to mean "domicile".

Usher v. Usher, 41 A.D.2d 368, 343 N.Y.S.2d 212 (3d Dep't 1973).

4. See Levitt v. Kinori, 80 Misc.2d 557, 363 N.Y.S.2d 707 (Sup.Ct., Suffolk County, 1974), aff'd 47 A.D.2d 598, 365 N.Y.S.2d 785 (2d Dep't 1975).

5. It consists of §§ 75–a through 75–z of the Domestic Relations Law.

6. These are listed in Dom.Rel.L. § 75–d.

7. See subdivisions 1(c), (d), and 2 of Dom.Rel.L. § 75–d.

the whole world, so it is not in category 2, which is the "in rem" jurisdiction binding only on notified persons. On the other hand, the judgment may be attackable by some nonparties,[8] which keeps it out of the "strictly in rem" category of number 1 on the list.

The "matrimonial action", in which rem jurisdiction is authorized by CPLR 314, is defined in CPLR 105. It includes not just divorce, annulment, and separation, but also actions that seek a declaratory judgment affecting the marriage or a purported divorce of it.[9]

If P brings a declaratory action seeking to affect only P's own marriage with D, P can sometimes use this rem category of jurisdiction even though the judgment may affect the marriage of a nonparty, as occurred, for example, in Sacks v. Sacks.[10] W–1 sued H to declare invalid a Mexican divorce H purportedly obtained from W–1. W–1's New York domicile was held to give jurisdiction of the declaratory action even though a judgment for W–1, invalidating the Mexican divorce, could indirectly undo H's marriage with W–2. W–2 was held bound by the rem judgment as long as duly notified (i.e., named as a party and served, even if only outside the state).

In the *Sacks* case, New York had substantial contacts with the parties to be affected by the judgment. Later developments indicate that such New York contacts may be indispensable to justify even this in rem exercise of jurisdiction. The Court of Appeals held in Carr v. Carr[11] that where H had no New York marital domicile with either W–1 or W–2 at any time, W–2 had no New York contacts of any kind, and W–1 did not attempt to bring a New York action until after H had died, New York had no jurisdiction to entertain the action. After H died, W–1 had moved to New York and brought a declaratory judgment action to undo a divorce H had obtained from W–1 in a for-

eign country. The court dismissed the action, saying that this rem theory, which uses the plaintiff's local domicile as its jurisdictional touchstone, "however useful and appropriate it may be during the joint lives of the husband and wife, ceases to have any vitality or legal substance after the death of either".

Even if H were still alive when W–1 brought the declaratory action in New York, the impression one draws from *Carr* is that since a voiding of the divorce, which is what W–1 sought in the action, would have incidentally destroyed W–2's marriage with H, such a doing could not be tolerated at a place lacking contacts with either W–2 or the first marriage.

§ 103. In Rem Jurisdiction Under CPLR 314(2)

CPLR 314(2) supplies the New York courts with the whole range of in rem actions brought to affect interests in specific and identifiable property found in New York. Whether real or personal, if the property is in New York and all P wants to do is affect D's interest in it—no matter what the merits of the action may require by way of proof to sustain the relief sought—the fact that the property is in the state gives the court all the jurisdiction it needs.

The courts have sometimes overlooked this simple fact of life with in rem jurisdiction, erroneously mixing jurisdiction and the merits together. In one case, for example, Morgenstern v. Freudenberg,[1] in which P was seeking an interest in an item of property concededly in the state—which is the only requirement for in rem jurisdiction—the court said that it needed personam jurisdiction of D because P could have no right to the property until a P–D agreement was first rescinded. That proposition is questionable.[2] As long as the resulting judgment is limited to affecting interests in

8. See Johnson v. Muelberger, 340 U.S. 581, 71 S.Ct. 474, 95 L.Ed. 552 (1951).

9. Chittenden v. Chittenden, 46 Misc.2d 347, 259 N.Y.S.2d 738 (Sup.Ct., Monroe County, 1965).

10. 47 Misc.2d 1050, 263 N.Y.S.2d 891 (Sup.Ct., N.Y. County, 1965).

11. 46 N.Y.2d 270, 413 N.Y.S.2d 305, 385 N.E.2d 1234 (1978).

§ 103

1. 7 Misc.2d 273, 165 N.Y.S.2d 934 (Sup.Ct., N.Y.County, 1957).

2. The Morgenstern case finds dubious support in what is at best an unfortunate dictum in Jackson v. Jackson, 290 N.Y. 512, 517, 49 N.E.2d 988, 990–91 (1943).

property in New York, the court can, on an in rem foundation, do anything at all with regard to the merits. Not only can it rescind a contract; it can declare D a witch or a vagabond, as long as the resulting judgment does no more than exclude D from an interest in the New York property.

Dependence on this in rem category of jurisdiction has been much reduced under the CPLR for the reason that longarm jurisdiction almost always applies today under CPLR 302 to give personam jurisdiction in cases that had to depend on in rem jurisdiction in earlier times. Some major New York in rem cases of yesteryear can illustrate this.

In a case involving a contract to sell New York realty, it was always possible for buyer B to get in rem jurisdiction sufficient to compel the nondomiciliary seller S to convey the property, as in a specific performance action, because since all B wanted from S was the realty, its New York situs made in rem jurisdiction effectual.[3] But when S was seeking specific performance from B, a nondomiciliary buyer, in rem jurisdiction did not suffice because what S wanted from B was money, and that needed personam jurisdiction. It still does, but today CPLR 302(a)(4) is likely to supply it. When a nondomiciliary buyer contracts to buy New York land, he may be said to be making a "use" of that land under the cited provision. Alternatively, such a contract may qualify as a transaction of New York business and thereby face personam jurisdiction under CPLR 302(a)(1).

In another old New York case, mortgagor R, a nondomiciliary, gave mortgagee E a mortgage on some New York realty. E later had to foreclose the mortgage in New York and did so, but the realty was not enough to pay the debt and a deficiency judgment resulted. Treating that deficiency just as if it were a personam judgment, E then tried to levy execution on the judgment against a different parcel R happened to own in New York. E

could not do that.[4] The foreclosure was good against only the mortgaged property, and the action, lacking personam jurisdiction, could not support any other relief. Today, of course, personam jurisdiction could arise in such a foreclosure action. As with the prior specific performance example, the mortgage transaction could be seen as a New York transaction of business under CPLR 302(a)(1) or as arising out of the ownership, use, or possession of New York realty under CPLR 302(a)(4), either of which would support personam jurisdiction. That would validate a deficiency judgment and permit a levy of execution on it against any other property of R found in New York.

The lesson to the lawyer, if the issue arises today, is to look carefully at pre–1963 (the year of the CPLR) in rem cases, the category formulated as number 2 on the list in § 101. See if the fact pattern can invoke one of today's longarm jurisdictional bases. If it can— and it apparently can so often today that this ordinary category of in rem jurisdiction is now rarely used—personam jurisdiction is at hand and the availability of in rem jurisdiction is academic.

One interesting recent example of the utility of in rem jurisdiction is in a domestic dispute involving equitable distribution. The Court of Appeals ruled that if the property that is the subject of the dispute between spouses or former spouses is in New York, in rem jurisdiction can be invoked to support the action even if neither of the parties is a New Yorker, i.e., personam jurisdiction is not indispensable for an equitable distribution.[5]

When "in rem" jurisdiction is used, i.e., when the action seeks to affect interests in specific property, there is no rule, as there is with attachment in quasi in rem actions to be discussed in the next section, that judicial process of some kind must issue in advance of the action so as to bring the property into the court's actual or constructive possession before

3. Garfein v. McInnis, 248 N.Y. 261, 162 N.E. 73 (1928). If S is ordered to make a deed to B and refuses, the sheriff may be directed to make it in S's behalf. CPLR 5107. The effect is the same.

4. Schwinger v. Hickok, 53 N.Y. 280 (1873).

5. See McCasland v. McCasland, 68 N.Y.2d 748, 506 N.Y.S.2d 329, 497 N.E.2d 696 (1986), reversing 110 A.D.2d 318, 494 N.Y.S.2d 534 (3d Dep't 1985), in which a divided panel had held personam jurisdiction necessary.

jurisdiction is exercised. The fact that the property is in New York usually suffices without such a step. A statutory exception is the replevin action. When an action to recover a chattel (replevin) rests on an in rem foundation, and personam jurisdiction of the defendant is lacking, the chattel must be seized before service of process can be made.[6]

Notice is not dispensed with merely because an action rests on rem rather than personam jurisdiction,[7] as was sometimes supposed in the past. New York requires that the intended defendants be named and served in the action in the usual way. The only advantage is that CPLR 314 allows the service to be made outside New York. The methods of service are for the most part the same as when CPLR 313 applies to allow extrastate service in a personam action, i.e., CPLR 308 applies, but with its words "within the state" now read as "within or without the state". Another possible method of service in the rem categories of action is publication, to be discussed later.[8]

The category of rem jurisdiction we have been discussing, in which the property involved is the very subject of the claim in suit, is not affected by the U.S. Supreme Court's decision in Shaffer v. Heitner.[9] The restrictions pronounced by that case affect quasi in rem jurisdiction, as treated in the following section.

§ 104. Quasi in Rem Jurisdiction

If P seeks a mere money judgment against D but can't get personam jurisdiction of D, the doctrine of quasi in rem jurisdiction allows P to attach any property D happens to have in New York and use it as a jurisdictional basis. Even if D is served outside New York and defaults, the doctrine assures P that a resulting judgment will be good at least to the extent of the seized property. Very active in New York until 1977, this doctrine was greatly

restricted by the U.S. Supreme Court in Shaffer v. Heitner[1] during that year. There are a few situations in which the *Shaffer* case still permits quasi in rem jurisdiction, but these are narrowly confined. We will return to them later.

The objection of the *Shaffer* case was that in this category of jurisdiction, the coincidental local presence of a nondomiciliary's property was being used to force the nondomiciliary to submit to the court's jurisdiction to litigate a claim having no relationship to the forum, contrary to the demands of due process. While perhaps justified during an earlier era, when strictures on personal jurisdiction prompted the exploitation of rem concepts in order to move jurisdiction forward, the doctrine could no longer be tolerated in the current era in which personam jurisdiction had been released from its earlier confinement. The major case accounting for the personam expansion was International Shoe Co. v. Washington,[2] the founding father of longarm jurisdiction and the subject of study earlier.[3] In *International Shoe*, the U.S. Supreme Court held that a forum can entertain personal jurisdiction over a nondomiciliary served outside the state as long as she has had such minimal contacts with the forum, in respect of the claim, that the forum's entertainment of the suit would not offend the basic concepts of fairness underlying due process. In *Shaffer*, the court extends the same or in any event a similar minimal contacts test to quasi in rem jurisdiction, the category in which, among the three devised in § 101 earlier, the property attached is unrelated to the claim sued on. The court holds that "the relationship among the defendant, the forum, and the litigation" must be the center of the inquiry.[4]

On *Shaffer*'s facts, the relationship was not demonstrated and jurisdiction failed. The suit was a corporate derivative action brought in

---

6. This requirement is imposed by CPLR 314(3). The seizure is effected by the sheriff pursuant to a court order secured under CPLR Article 71.

7. See Griffin v. Griffin, 327 U.S. 220, 66 S.Ct. 556, 90 L.Ed. 635 (1946).

8. See § 107 below.

9. 433 U.S. 186, 97 S.Ct. 2569, 53 L.Ed.2d 683 (1977).

§ 104

1. 433 U.S. 186, 97 S.Ct. 2569, 53 L.Ed.2d 683 (1977).

2. 326 U.S. 310, 66 S.Ct. 154, 90 L.Ed. 95 (1945).

3. See § 84 above.

4. 433 U.S. at 204, 97 S.Ct. at 2580.

Delaware. Jurisdiction over certain directors and officers was based on the seizure of stock they held in the corporation.[5] Neither the individuals nor the claim had any relationship to Delaware.

The highest point to which the U.S. Supreme Court had ever carried quasi in rem jurisdiction was in Harris v. Balk.[6] It came down in 1905, during the restrictive reign of Pennoyer v. Neff,[7] which allowed personal jurisdiction only if D were served within the state. *Harris* was an endeavor, enlightened for its age, to circumvent *Pennoyer's* personam restrictions by expanding rem jurisdiction. *Harris* allowed a court that lacked personam jurisdiction of D to attach a debt owed to D by G by the service on G of an attachment order while G was in the state.

P in *Harris* lived in Maryland and had a money claim against D, who lived in North Carolina and of whom personam jurisdiction was unavailable in Maryland. G was also a North Carolinian concededly in debt to D. G happened through Maryland one day and P had G served with a Maryland attachment purporting to seize the G-to-D debt. G paid the debt to the Maryland sheriff and it was credited to the P v. D claim. When D later tried to sue G on the debt in North Carolina, G's payment on the Maryland attachment was allowed as a complete defense.[8]

The *Shaffer* case overrules *Harris* and like decisions[9] that purport to rest jurisdiction of a money claim on the coincidental local presence of some property belonging to the defendant.

Perhaps it would be better, in view of *Harris's* thoughtful endeavor to move forward without wounding *Pennoyer's* pride, to say that the *Shaffer* case gives *Harris* honorable retirement after yeoman's service. It's kinder than the brush-off that a mere overruling implies. And the retirement of *Harris* is only a partial one at that:

It must be stressed that *Shaffer* addresses and affects only the quasi in rem jurisdictional use to which the *Harris* case put the attached property. In other respects, *Harris* is probably still good law. Its manner of theorizing the situs of a debt, for example—finding it present in the forum when the debtor is present in the forum—does not appear to be undone by *Shaffer*. If an attaching creditor seeks seizure of the debt not for jurisdictional but for mere security purposes—personam jurisdiction being present—*Harris* should still be available to theorize the situs of the debt through the presence of the debtor. The same should be true when the debt is sought to satisfy a valid in personam judgment already rendered against the person to whom the debt is owed.[10]

The question outstanding, then, is the extent to which quasi in rem jurisdiction survives at all after *Shaffer*. When may a defendant's local property be attached, not merely as security when jurisdiction in personam exists, but to *supply* a limited jurisdiction to adjudicate a claim when personam jurisdiction is lacking and when the property has no relationship to the claim?[11] *Shaffer* appears to permit this in several situations:

---

5. Under Delaware law, the situs of shares in a Delaware corporation is always in Delaware, apparently without regard to where the certificates representing the shares may be. It is possible that Delaware would have been allowed to exercise personam longarm jurisdiction on the facts of Shaffer, predicated on Delaware's interest in the directorial and managerial activities of its corporations, but Delaware chose to lay jurisdiction entirely on the quasi in rem basis and Shaffer disposed of the constitutional issues on that basis.

6. 198 U.S. 215, 25 S.Ct. 625, 49 L.Ed. 1023 (1905).

7. 95 U.S. 714, 24 L.Ed. 565 (1877).

8. The fact that G in Harris conceded his debt to D simplified matters. Had G disputed that he owed the debt, and had a Maryland court assumed to adjudicate whether he did or not, personam jurisdiction of D would have been required before an adjudication that G did not owe D the

debt could be jurisdictionally upheld. See and compare New York Life Ins. Co. v. Dunlevy, 241 U.S. 518, 36 S.Ct. 613, 60 L.Ed. 1140 (1916).

9. See, e.g., Pennington v. Fourth Nat. Bank, 243 U.S. 269, 37 S.Ct. 282, 61 L.Ed. 713 (1917).

10. Fixing the situs of an intangible, towards which Harris makes a substantial and probably still viable contribution, is reserved for general treatment in the enforcement of judgments chapter. See §§ 489 and 491, below. Harris should also remain good law for the purpose of protecting a garnishee who has paid a debt over to a sheriff pursuant to a valid attachment or execution. See § 326 below.

11. The Shaffer case makes plain that the strictly in rem and in rem classes of jurisdiction, categories 1 and 2 on the list formulated in § 101, above, remain valid, or are at least unaffected by Shaffer.

1. Minimal Contacts.

Shaffer authorizes quasi in rem jurisdiction when the forum has the requisite minimal contacts in the *International Shoe* sense. An initial New York reaction to this would be that the presence of such contacts would authorize outright personam ("longarm") jurisdiction under CPLR 302, making quasi in rem jurisdiction superfluous. But that is not necessarily so. As indicated during the earlier discussion of longarm jurisdiction, CPLR 302 does not go the constitutional limit.[12] Should a case arise in which the defendant's contacts with the forum in respect of the subject claim are sufficient to permit New York jurisdiction under due process but technically beyond the contacts statutorily required by CPLR 302, a "gap" would arise. If the defendant in a case falling within that gap should happen to have property in New York, *Shaffer* would seem to authorize quasi in rem jurisdiction. In this instance, the action would be restricted to rem jurisdiction, not because of constitutional strictures, but because of the failure of New York law to go as far on the personam track as due process permits.

And even in situations in which New York would choose to go the limit, there is obviously a gap within the due process clause itself—as *Shaffer* reads it—between what is needed for outright personam jurisdiction and what will satisfy for the less demanding purposes of quasi in rem jurisdiction. Some cases have appeared manifesting what the courts have considered contacts just sufficient for the rem measure but just short on the personam scale. For example:

An early case following *Shaffer* is the Second Circuit decision in Intermeat, Inc. v. American Poultry, Inc.[13] P was a New York corporation that sold meat to D, an Ohio corporation without a New York office and presumably without the New York activities that would mean either "presence" jurisdiction of D under CPLR 301 or longarm jurisdiction of D under CPLR 302. D sold much of its own product to New York buyers, however, and one of these, the A & P, owed D money. That debt is what P attached. Analyzing how D bought the meat from P, including paper work and deliveries, and how and to whom D sold the meat, the court found some $7 million annually (about 30%) of D's business to involve New York. It sustained the quasi in rem jurisdiction, holding that the test is "narrower" for that than for personam jurisdiction.

Another case is Banco Ambrosiano S.P.A. v. Artoc Bank & Trust Ltd.,[14] involving a loan between foreign banks. The loan had no connection with New York except that it called for initial deposit and subsequent repayment in New York banks, which were the correspondent banks of the two foreign banks concerned. D's sole contact with the state was the account it maintained with the New York bank, but since that was "the very account through which [D] effectuated the transaction at issue", the account was held attachable and gave quasi in rem jurisdiction in the action even though there wasn't enough for personam jurisdiction.[15]

Majique Fashions, Ltd. v. Warwick & Co.[16] is still another example. D was to inspect goods for P in Asia. Alleging a failure to inspect and/or negligent inspection, P brought a New York action against D, but D had no New York office. It did have several New York accounts, however, in one of which P was to make the deposit required by the P–D contract. Noting additionally that D could foresee that its behavior could result in harm to P in New York, i.e., introducing a foreseeability element by a kind of tacit analogy to CPLR 302(a)(3)(ii), the court held the *Shaffer* trio of elements satisfied.

Dependence on analogizing the foreseeability element to CPLR 302(a)(3)(ii) may be risky today because of the rejection of foreseeability as a longarm factor by the U.S. Supreme Court in World–Wide Volkswagen Corp. v. Woodson,

---

12. See § 84 et seq., above.

13. 575 F.2d 1017 (2d Cir.1978).

14. 62 N.Y.2d 65, 476 N.Y.S.2d 64, 464 N.E.2d 432 (1984).

15. The subject is treated in the lead note in New York State Law Digest No. 295.

16. 67 A.D.2d 321, 414 N.Y.S.2d 916 (1st Dep't 1979).

decided in 1980, after the *Majique* case was decided. But a distinction from *World-Wide*, an unintentional tort case,[17] can be made in that in *Majique* and like cases the contact that the defendant had with New York, whatever it consisted of, was intentional. The U.S. Supreme Court appears to be allowing longarm jurisdiction greater scope in cases involving deliberate as opposed to accidental conduct,[18] and in this respect foreseeability may still count as an influential factor if the defendant's conduct was intentional, as it invariably is in contract cases.

Yet a further application of quasi in rem jurisdiction occurred in a situation in which longarm personal jurisdiction is usually rejected. This has to do with agency. In the earlier discussion of longarm jurisdiction,[19] it is shown that in an agency situation in which P claims that its own acts in New York should be imputed to D for jurisdictional purposes because they were performed as agent of D, New York will not ordinarily make the imputation. It has been held that such an imputation can be made, however, in a case involving mere quasi in rem jurisdiction.[20] This would be another illustration of where activities insufficient to support personal jurisdiction may nonetheless satisfy the apparently less demanding standards of quasi in rem jurisdiction. Some lower courts tend in that direction, in any event.

Stipulations in a contract for the arbitration of a controversy in New York, or for the application of New York commercial law to govern the transaction substantively, have also been cited as significant New York contacts in cases sustaining quasi in rem jurisdiction under *Shaffer*.[21]

The above are mere illustrations. There are others. One commentator has suggested that a sampling of post-*Shaffer* cases "does not indicate any slackening in the use of the [quasi in rem] device, or any inclination on the part of the courts to take [*Shaffer*] seriously", seeing *Shaffer* as being treated too lightly if not, indeed, being "brushed aside" altogether.[22]

2. All Property in New York.

Suppose the defendant has moved all of his property to New York. The *Shaffer* case holds that even in that situation, the state may not adjudicate a claim against the defendant if the claim and the defendant have no nexus with the state. But the case does say that an attachment of the property may be allowed in that situation as security for a judgment being sought on the claim in an appropriate forum.[23] This suggests that if New York is the property state, it can allow an attachment before the foreign action has gone to judgment. There is at present no statutory authority in New York for an attachment in that situation, however. The closest New York comes is the allowance of an attachment after the foreign action has gone to judgment, in conjunction with a New York action now being brought on that judgment.[24]

3. No Other Forum.

Shaffer leaves the door open to quasi in rem jurisdiction in an unrelated forum if it should be shown that there is no other and presumably more appropriate forum to litigate the claim.[25] That would not be a common situation, except perhaps in wartime, or in any event a state of severely strained relations between the domestic and the would-be for-

---

17. The case is treated at length in § 88, above.

18. See §§ 86, 86A, and 88, above.

19. See § 86 above, the "transacts any business" provision of CPLR 302.

20. Drexel Burnham Lambert, Inc. v. D'Angelo, 453 F.Supp. 1294 (S.D.N.Y.1978).

21. See, e.g., ACLI Int'l, Inc. v. E.D. & F. Man (Coffee) Ltd., 76 A.D.2d 635, 430 N.Y.S.2d 858 (2d Dep't 1980).

22. See Barker, New York Practice, N.Y. Law Journal, Dec. 28, 1987, p. 1, col.1.

23. 433 U.S. at 210, 97 S.Ct. at 2583.

24. CPLR 6201, paragraph 5. Paragraph 3 of CPLR 6201, which authorizes an attachment when the defendant disposes of or secretes property with the intent to defraud creditors, contemplates a New York action, not a foreign one, on the underlying claim. If the New York courts were to permit an anticipatory action, i.e., one brought here in anticipation of a judgment yet to be obtained elsewhere, the provisions of CPLR 6201(3) might be stretched to support an attachment if New York were the state to which, rather than from which—as is usually contemplated—the defendant has transferred property.

25. See note 37 at 433 U.S. 211, 97 S.Ct. 2584.

eign forum. If the defendant should happen to have property in the domestic forum in that situation, but not be amenable to its personal jurisdiction, the quasi in rem seizure of the property could evidently be allowed. This also supposes that it would not otherwise be unfair to proceed against the absent defendant. It would be, for example, if the defendant were interned on enemy soil.

Quasi in Rem Procedure

Since quasi in rem jurisdiction, although curtailed, still exists in the foregoing situations and has proved itself tenacious in the years that have passed since *Shaffer* came down, its procedural requisites should be reviewed.

CPLR 314(3) is the statute that exploits this category of jurisdiction, ordinarily using the order of attachment as the expedient for the seizure of the property. In deference to the lingering requirement of Pennoyer v. Neff, it requires that the attachment be secured and levied before the summons is served.[26] The procedure is simple. Subject to detailed study later,[27] we can note briefly that P gets the order of attachment from the court by ex parte application[28] and delivers it to the sheriff. The sheriff must levy on it before the summons is served. In the case of realty, the sheriff levies by filing a notice of attachment with the clerk of the realty county.[29] To levy against personal property, the sheriff merely serves a copy of the order of attachment on the garnishee.[30] (A garnishee in New York practice is any person who has possession of property belonging to D

or who owes a debt to D.[31]) As soon as the sheriff files (in the case of realty) or serves the garnishee (in the case of personalty), there has been a "levy" sufficient to permit commencement of the action.[32] CPLR 314(3) insists that this levy precede summons service. If it does not, the property will not be attached and jurisdiction will not obtain.[33] In supreme and county court practice, where the filing of the summons and complaint marks commencement of the action, the filing may precede the levy as long as service follows it.[34]

Service in this quasi in rem category may be made outside New York on the express authority of CPLR 314. If D should default, and P's claim is not completely satisfied out of the previously attached property, P has a subsisting claim against D for the balance and can sue on it without facing any charge of having "split" the claim. The judgment will not be binding on any issue in the subsequent action, however, for the obvious reason that the court's jurisdiction existed only as to the property attached and could not affect D's personal rights beyond that.[35]

This category of jurisdiction works not only on tangible property of D found in New York, but on any intangible property for which a New York situs can be fixed. If, for example, D maintains an account at a New York bank, the account can be attached for quasi in rem purposes. The sheriff merely serves a copy of the order of attachment on the bank, which in this instance is the garnishee.

---

26. 95 U.S. 714, 24 L.Ed. 565 (1877). The requirement that for quasi in rem jurisdiction the constructive seizure must precede service may be the most significant part of Pennoyer that still remains in force in New York.

27. See § 316 et seq., below.

28. CPLR 6201, 6211, 6212.

29. CPLR 6216.

30. CPLR 6214(a).

31. CPLR 105.

32. As will be seen later in the study of attachment, § 319, below, the summons must be served within 60 days after the order of attachment is granted or it loses its validity under CPLR 6213. Thus, the levy must precede the service and both must occur within the 60 days. This sequence is mandatory, however, only where, as here, attachment is being used for its quasi in rem jurisdictional function. When used for mere security, i.e., when there is

personam jurisdiction in the action, the levy need not necessarily precede the service of the summons.

33. Nemetsky v. Banque de Developpement de la Republique du Niger, 48 N.Y.2d 962, 425 N.Y.S.2d 277, 401 N.E.2d 388 (1979); Dimmerling v. Andrews, 236 N.Y. 43, 139 N.E. 774 (1923).

34. CPLR 306–b ordinarily allows 120 days for service after filing. A plaintiff securing an attachment for quasi in rem use, however, must make service within 60 days after the granting of the order. CPLR 314(3), 6213. So, in a supreme or county court action, service within the 120 days but after the 60 may preserve the action but will forfeit the attachment.

35. Benadon v. Antonio, 10 A.D.2d 40, 197 N.Y.S.2d 1 (1st Dep't 1960).

Fixing the situs of an intangible can sometimes be a problem, so the CPLR tries to establish a situs for some of the more significant intangibles. A negotiable instrument, for example, has its situs wherever the instrument is, as does a certificate of stock representing interests in a corporation, and in each instance the person holding the instrument or certificate is the proper garnishee on whom to serve a copy of the attachment.[36] If P wants to levy against an interest D has in an estate, the personal representative of the estate is the appropriate garnishee.[37]

Before Harris v. Balk[38] was for the most part retired by *Shaffer*, New York made a remarkable exploitation of what the Court of Appeals perceived to be *Harris*'s quasi in rem jurisdictional opportunities. This it did with the doctrine of Seider v. Roth,[39] an intriguing entry in American jurisprudence born in 1966 in Albany and interred at the tender age of 14 in Washington, D.C. *Seider* needs the privacy of a separate section. It follows.

§ 105.   The Doctrine of Seider v. Roth

P was a New Yorker injured in a Vermont collision with D, a Canadian. D's car was covered by a liability policy issued in Canada by G, a Connecticut insurer. P clearly had no personam basis on which to sue D in New York, nor did D have in New York any tangible or even intangible property of a traditionally recognizable kind, such as a bank account. But it was shown that G, the Connecticut insurer, was doing business in New York and hence had a New York presence. In effect exploiting the Harris v. Balk doctrine, discussed in the prior section, P claimed that G owed to D the obligations to defend and indemnify any claim that might be brought against D within the policy; that these obligations constituted attachable "property" under New York law; and that they had a New York situs because G, the "ower" of the obligations, was doing business in New York. On a 4–3 vote, the New York Court of Appeals accepted that rationale in Seider v. Roth[1] and sustained a quasi in rem attachment of these peculiar obligations in New York.

The doctrine threw open the doors of the New York courts to all New Yorkers injured anywhere in the country—or the world—as long as it could be shown that the alleged tortfeasor's insurer happened to maintain an office in New York. The doctrine was exploited heavily for 14 years, until 1980, when the U.S. Supreme Court overruled it in Rush v. Savchuk.[2] Actually involved in *Rush* was Minnesota's short-lived adoption of the doctrine. For the 14 years of *Seider's* New York life, the U.S. Supreme Court never accepted a New York *Seider*-based case for review. But upon Minnesota's adoption of the doctrine almost a decade and a half later, the court reviewed and overturned it promptly, finding it a deprivation of the insurer's property without due process by subjecting it to jurisdiction in a state with which neither its insurance policy nor its insured had sufficient contact.

The overruling took place on January 21, 1980. Under due process, held the Supreme Court, a *Seider*-based case lacks the requisite contacts even for quasi in rem jurisdiction. Thus ended a bizarre jurisdictional saga.

Since the *Seider* basis for jurisdiction can no longer be used, almost all discussion of it is of historical interest only. *Seider* was widely relied on, however, and was cited often at many different procedural stages of numerous actions in both the state and federal courts, so that it still crops up in the course of researching procedural issues. When it does, it sometimes adds a difficult twist to the issue or poses some special peculiarity understandable only if one is familiar with *Seider*. We therefore include here a synopsis of the doctrine

---

36. CPLR 5201(c)(4).

37. CPLR 5201(c)(2). See § 491, below, for further discussion of who the proper garnishee is in diverse situations.

38. Note 6 above.

39. 17 N.Y.2d 111, 269 N.Y.S.2d 99, 216 N.E.2d 312 (1966).

§ 105

1. 17 N.Y.2d 111, 269 N.Y.S.2d 99, 216 N.E.2d 312 (1966).

2. 444 U.S. 320, 100 S.Ct. 571, 62 L.Ed.2d 516.

and its doings from its pronouncement in the mid 1960's through its demise in 1980.

Immediately upon its pronouncement, *Seider* posed both theoretical and practical problems. While P had previously been allowed to attach insurance proceeds to which D was entitled, the insurance in those instances was burglary or fire or casualty, or insurance of some similar kind, in which D had a direct interest and which existed as an attachable property independently of the main action, for which it was to be used as a jurisdictional crutch.[3] The G-to-D debt in such cases had an economic viability of its own and could be used for quasi in rem jurisdictional support by one of D's creditors (P).[4]

In *Seider*, the "obligations" attached were a liability insurer's obligation to defend and indemnify a tortfeasor, and it was argued that neither of these obligations could even be said to exist until an action was brought by P against D with jurisdiction. How could two obligations that don't exist until there is jurisdiction, supply the jurisdiction in the first place? It was like trying to pull oneself up by the bootstraps,[5] and this posed theoretical difficulties. When the property of D that P is pursuing is an intangible "debt" of some kind, CPLR 5201(a) allows its seizure only if the debt is either past due or certain to become due. The "debts" involved in *Seider* were neither. CPLR 5201(a) sought to avoid the kinds of problems *Seider* presented, but the statute was nevertheless construed to allow the attachment and *Seider* was on its way.

On the practical side, there were equivalent difficulties. If the defendant, D, duly notified,

defaulted, for example, the CPLR requirement was (and remains) that the attached property must be sold at public auction.[6] Who bids at a sheriff's auction on an insurer's obligation to defend or indemnify? That and a number of other problems were never addressed by the courts. Some were avoided, others ignored.

The history of *Seider* is fascinating. Its highlights are these:

1. The cases, both state and federal,[7] in which *Seider's* theory was exploited for jurisdiction began to proliferate. One of them, Simpson v. Loehmann,[8] brought to the New York Court of Appeals the question of *Seider's* federal constitutionality, an issue, curiously, that the *Seider* case itself had not raised. It was contended that *Seider* went beyond the permissible limits of due process. The New York Court of Appeals in *Simpson* rejected that argument and sustained *Seider's* constitutionality, but in a set of opinions that manifested that if the Court of Appeals had the case to decide all over again—this in 1967, just a year after *Seider* came down—it would reject *Seider* as a matter of New York law without even reaching the constitutional issue.[9]

2. Lower court judges in New York would of course deem themselves bound by the New York Court of Appeals view of *Seider's* constitutionality, but federal judges are not so deferential. At the time, CPLR 320(c) insisted that an attachment defendant submit to personam jurisdiction if she wanted to defend the action, or else default and forfeit whatever of her property was attached. Citing this obviously unfair "leverage" aspect of the attachment, a

---

3. See, e.g., Baumgold Bros. v. Schwarzschild Bros., 276 A.D. 158, 93 N.Y.S.2d 658 (1st Dep't 1949), aff'd 302 N.Y. 628, 97 N.E.2d 357 (1951).

4. See the concurring opinion of Breitel, J., in Simpson v. Loehmann, 21 N.Y.2d 305, 314, 287 N.Y.S.2d 633, 640, 234 N.E.2d 669, 674 (1967). G, who is the insurer in the text's examples, stands for garnishee.

5. Seider v. Roth, 17 N.Y.2d 111, 115, 269 N.Y.S.2d 99, 103, 216 N.E.2d 312, 315 (1966) (dissenting opinion).

6. Such are the directions of CPLR 5230(a), 5232 and 5233, for enforcement of a judgment in an action predicated on attachment.

7. The federal courts make use of the forum state's quasi in rem attachment procedures and essentially follow

the state rules governing them. FRCP Rule 4(n)(2). See § 627 (Practitioner's Edition).

8. 21 N.Y.2d 305, 287 N.Y.S.2d 633, 234 N.E.2d 669 (1967).

9. One of the judges in the *Seider* majority of four had in the interim retired and Judge Charles D. Breitel, no friend of the *Seider* doctrine, was appointed to the vacancy. As a matter of New York internal law, Judge Breitel voted to support *Seider* only because he did not think that the mere coincidence of a change in judicial personnel on the Court of Appeals should undo a recent and important statutory interpretation. Id. at 314, 287 N.Y.S.2d at 640, 234 N.E.2d at 674.

federal court in Podolsky v. Devinney[10] declared *Seider* unconstitutional, the New York Court of Appeals' view to the contrary notwithstanding. Such coercive use of rem jurisdiction to exact a personam appearance seemed to be an unanswerable constitutional point. In *Seider* context it would mean that a defendant driving his own car in his own state would have to submit to the personam jurisdiction of a New York court—and the reputed generosity of a New York jury—which would mean in turn that if liability were assessed at a sum beyond his insurance coverage, unlikely though such a prospect might be if the defendant were sued at home or where the accident occurred, he would have to pay the difference out of pocket.

3. There now followed a kind of miracle. A motion had been made in the New York Court of Appeals to reargue the *Simpson* case. The Court of Appeals took that occasion, not to do battle with *Podolsky's* reasoning, but to reconstrue CPLR 320(c) to divest it of its coercive effect in *Seider*-based cases. After setting forth certain conclusions, the court said that "[t]his, it is hardly necessary to add, means that there may not be any recovery against the defendant . . . in an amount greater than the face value" of the insurance policy. In other words, the court was, by construction, divesting CPLR 320(c) of its "leverage" use and inviting the defendant to appear and defend without facing personam judgment.[11] It was good that the court added the clarification, "hardly necessary" though the court thought it was, because few would have perceived it otherwise.

That was only part of the miracle. The court further concluded, again without setting forth

its reasoning, that the things attached in *Seider* were not the obligations to defend or indemnify, but the face amount of the insurance policy.[12] The *Simpson* reargument opinion was an unsigned per curiam with the distinction of being unanimous. The court had manifested in earlier opinions that it could not reach consensus on the *Seider* components and apparently decided that it would be best to reach as many conclusions as need be to offer guidance to the lower courts and preserve *Seider's* validity, but the less said about reasons the better. Perhaps it is commendable that the judges made so concerted an effort at consensus, albeit in the humbling forum of a per curiam denial of a motion to reargue. But *Seider* compensated in impact for what it lacked in grace.

4. The *Simpson* reargument opinion, compelled in essence by the *Podolsky* case, took what was then deemed to be the major constitutional objection out of *Seider*: the coercive use of an attachment to squeeze an in personam submission out of a nondomiciliary defendant who had no contacts with New York. With that, the *Seider* doctrine was sustained as constitutional by a divided Second Circuit in Minichiello v. Rosenberg, and certiorari was denied.[13]

5. The use of *Seider* by nonresident plaintiffs was foreclosed on forum non conveniens grounds,[14] but in a discretionary disposition that left the door open to keeping jurisdiction in such cases in special circumstances. The door was then closed and locked by the Court of Appeals in Donawitz v. Danek,[15] a medical malpractice action based on a foreign injury but with at least some medical treatment in New York. Although special circumstances

---

10. 281 F.Supp. 488 (S.D.N.Y.1968).

11. Simpson v. Loehmann, opinion denying reargument, 21 N.Y.2d 990, 991, 290 N.Y.S.2d 914, 916, 238 N.E.2d 319, 320 (1968). CPLR 320(c) was later amended to add paragraph (1), codifying this result and authorizing a limited appearance in all instances (not just Seider cases) in which attachment is the sole predicate of jurisdiction. That stands as the law today. See § 113 below.

12. The Simpson reargument opinion purports to quote the "court's opinion" with respect to the main argument, which was not the court's opinion at all in the original Simpson decision but only that of Chief Judge Fuld with one other judge concurring, 21 N.Y.2d 305, 307, 287 N.Y.S.2d 633, 634, 234 N.E.2d 669, 671. The unani-

mous per curiam opinion on reargument in effect adopts whatever parts of Judge Fuld's earlier opinion it quotes.

13. 410 F.2d 106 (1968), upheld en banc at page 117 (1969), cert.denied 396 U.S. 844, 90 S.Ct. 69, 24 L.Ed.2d 94 (1969). The court took the unusual step of suggesting that the New York Court of Appeals reexamine the Seider doctrine, reissuing the invitation several years later in Beja v. Jahangiri, 453 F.2d 959 (1972). The invitations were not accepted.

14. Vaage v. Lewis, 29 A.D.2d 315, 288 N.Y.S.2d 521 (2d Dep't 1968).

15. 42 N.Y.2d 138, 397 N.Y.S.2d 592, 366 N.E.2d 253 (1977).

were apparently present in *Donawitz* because several of the defendants were New Yorkers and within personam jurisdiction, the action was nonetheless dismissed as against a New Jersey physician on the ground that the duty to defend and indemnify "is not of sufficient substance to support quasi in rem jurisdiction where the plaintiff is a nonresident."[16]

6. *Seider* involved a liability insurance policy applicable to a vehicle, but it was cited as authority for attaching other liability policies, including a homeowner's policy[17] and a medical malpractice policy (which the *Donawitz* case involved).

7. Courts in other states, asked to adopt *Seider's* approach, almost uniformly refused.[18] Only one or two went along.[19] One of these, New Hampshire, made a kind of retaliatory adoption of *Seider*, stressing that a New Hampshire seizure of an insurance policy in connection with a foreign accident is, because of *Seider*, peculiarly appropriate when the defendant is a New Yorker.[20]

8. Numerous problems arose as *Seider* wended its way through jurisprudence. Questions appeared about whether there was jurisdiction to impose disclosure obligations on a mere "quasi in rem defendant", on the res judicata and collateral estoppel impact of a quasi in rem judgment in subsequent actions, on disclaimers of coverage by the insurer, on federal jurisdiction, on choice of law, on statute of limitations, on preferences, and on many other matters of which treatment proliferated.[21]

9. *Seider* went onto the books as a kind of indirect direct action against a liability insurer.[22] At root it regards the insurer as the real party in interest, and circumvents New York's rule against direct actions. With the "limited appearance" read into *Seider* by the *Simpson* reargument opinion, *Seider* had the major merit of giving a New York plaintiff a New York forum, which was of course the purpose of the *Seider* doctrine, but without the unpalatable attempt to subject the nondomiciliary insured to personal liability.

Seider's demerit was not its result, which made an insurer come to a plaintiff rather than making the plaintiff hunt out the insurer, but its lawlessness. CPLR 5201(a) said that inchoate rights not sure to ripen into reality were not leviable; *Seider*, by ignoring the statute, held that they were. CPLR 320(c) said there was to be no limited appearance; *Seider*, assisted by its offspring, the *Simpson* reargument opinion, said there was. Insurance Law § 167(7)[23] said there was to be no direct action against a liability insurer; *Seider* said in effect that there was.

---

16. Id. at 142, 397 N.Y.S.2d at 595, 366 N.E.2d at 256. It is difficult to understand how the presence in New York of the insurer's obligations can be made to depend on where the plaintiff lives, a point made in both the concurring and dissenting opinions in Donawitz.

17. See Flemming v. Williams, 30 A.D.2d 834, 293 N.Y.S.2d 45 (2d Dep't 1968) (Connecticut homeowner's policy on Connecticut accident).

18. See, e.g., Javorek v. Superior Court of Monterey County, 17 Cal.3d 629, 552 P.2d 728, 131 Cal.Rptr. 768 (1976); Howard v. Allen, 254 S.C. 455, 176 S.E.2d 127 (1970); Ricker v. Lajoie, 314 F.Supp. 401 (D.Vt.1970); De Rentiis v. Lewis, 106 R.I. 240, 258 A.2d 464 (1969).

19. See, e.g., Rintala v. Shoemaker, 362 F.Supp. 1044 (D.Minn.1973).

20. Forbes v. Boynton, 113 N.H. 617, 313 A.2d 129 (1973). Chief Judge Friendly, writing for the en banc majority in Minichiello, had warned that Seider might be taken up "defensively" in this way. 410 F.2d at 119.

21. See, e.g., Stein, Jurisdiction by Attachment of Liability Insurance, 43 N.Y.U.L.Rev. 1075 (1968), and the sources cited in the panel and en banc opinions in the Minichiello case, note 13, above.

22. New York does not allow a direct action, requiring that the insured first be sued. Only after securing judgment against the insured can the policy be looked to. The Judicial Conference, based upon a study by Professor Maurice Rosenberg, recommended that a direct action be allowed (in conjunction with which Seider would be legislatively overturned), see 16th Jud.Conf.Rep. (1971), pp. 289 (proposed statute) and 264 (study), but it was never adopted. It was hoped, by supporters of the Seider rule, that the fact that the insurer in a Seider case is the real party in interest and that the Seider attachment is available only at the behest of a New York plaintiff, would save Seider by giving the case a New York nexus sufficient to meet the requirements of Shaffer v. Heitner. (Shaffer is the 1977 U.S. Supreme Court decision requiring a relationship between the defendant, the claim, and the forum. See § 104, above.) If the insurer could be regarded as the defendant, and if its doing business in the forum could be deemed to invoke that forum's interest in protecting its residents from injuries inflicted by tortfeasors insured with that insurer no matter where the conduct occurs, Seider could sneak under the Shaffer fence. As things turned out, of course, it didn't work.

23. Now Ins.L. § 3420.

10. The Court of Appeals wearied of *Seider* but felt constrained to stand by it as a precedent. Neuman v. Dunham[24] is one indication. The plaintiff was a New York resident injured in a Pennsylvania accident. When the New York *Seider*-based action was brought, the Pennsylvania two-year statute of limitations had expired, but the New York three-year period was alive. CPLR 202 provides that when a foreign claim accrues to a New Yorker, only the New York period governs. The defendant pointed out, however, that, but for *Seider*, the action could not have been brought in New York at all; that insult should not be added to injury by subjecting the defendant to the longer New York period after subjecting him to such flimsy New York jurisdiction. Evincing a mixture of institutional loyalty and professional impatience, the court applied CPLR 202 and sustained the action "on the ground of *stare decisis* alone". A year later, acknowledging *Seider's* bad press, a majority of the court voted to retain *Seider* based on "considerations of institutional stability and the mandates of *stare decisis*" and because "it would be scandalous for us to abandon it at this time".[25]

11. There were yet other statutes destined to be "deconstrued", had *Seider* not been overturned. CPLR 6214(b), for example, "freezes" attached property, requiring that it be held to the credit of the attaching plaintiff. CPLR 5234(b) gives the plaintiff an outright lien on the attached property. With that in mind, look at this situation:

There are 10 persons injured in a State X accident. Two are New Yorkers who return to New York and attach the policy under *Seider* in a New York action. The other eight sue in State X, their domicile, and get judgments against the insured, seeking now to satisfy their judgments out of the insurance policy, as

they are surely entitled to do, but the insurer refuses to pay the judgments, pleading that the policy has been attached in New York and can be used only for the claims of the two New York plaintiffs. That is precisely what CPLR 6214(b) and 5234(b) say, but their literal application in such an instance would have been patently unconstitutional, a deprivation of the property rights of the eight State X plaintiffs. Had *Seider* not been overturned when it was, those two statutes, too, would have eventually joined CPLR 5201(a), old CPLR 320(c), and former Insurance Law § 167(7), in that special purgatory *Seider* reserved for statutes that got in its way.

§ 106. Sequestration in Matrimonial Actions

Even if the defendant/spouse in a matrimonial action is not subject to the court's personam jurisdiction, his or her property may be sequestered and used for the support of the family.[1] Just as with attachment, which is not available in matrimonial actions[2] for the reason that sequestration has been made available instead, any property interest that the defendant has in the state can be sequestered. The procedure is by motion. If the motion is granted the court appoints a sequestrator, who can be the plaintiff spouse, to seize the defendant's property and dispose of it pursuant to court direction. The motion can initially be ex parte and the seizure can be made before the defendant has notice. But notice must be given at some time before the property is actually used.[3]

Caselaw authorizes the use of this sequestration device for quasi in rem jurisdiction, i.e., to secure property of the support debtor out of which monetary awards can be satisfied even though he or she is beyond personam jurisdic-

24. 39 N.Y.2d 999, 387 N.Y.S.2d 240 (1976), aff'g 49 A.D.2d 733, 374 N.Y.S.2d 296 (1st Dep't 1975).

25. Donawitz v. Danek, 42 N.Y.2d 138, 142, 397 N.Y.S.2d 592, 595, 366 N.E.2d 253, 255 (1977).

§ 106

1. Dom.Rel.L. § 233. We are here concerned with sequestration only for quasi in rem jurisdictional use. Its other use, governed by Dom.Rel.L. § 243, is as an enforce-

ment (rather than jurisdictional) device to implement support and alimony orders and judgments. Property sequestered for jurisdictional use under § 233 may afterwards be applied for enforcement under § 243.

2. CPLR 6201.

3. Matthews v. Matthews, 240 N.Y. 28, 147 N.E. 237 (1925).

tion.[4] In this respect, one must of course ask today whether this kind of jurisdiction can continue in matrimonial actions in view of the general ban on quasi in rem jurisdiction pronounced by the U.S. Supreme Court in Shaffer v. Heitner.[5]

Shaffer requires a showing that the defendant and the case have some relationship to the forum. It should be possible to satisfy the court of that relationship in most matrimonial actions. Even if the defendant support debtor is not a New York domiciliary, the fact that his or her family is domiciled in New York—a general condition precedent to the exercise of any kind of matrimonial jurisdiction under § 230 of the Domestic Relations Law—combined with the fact that the defendant has property in New York, should, in respect of a support obligation, afford the kind of nexus *Shaffer* contemplates.

These conclusions should obtain even in view of the U.S. Supreme Court decision in Kulko v. Superior Court of California,[6] which holds that a mere showing of a child's presence in a state is not by itself an adequate jurisdictional basis for a support award in favor of the child against its nonresident father. But *Kulko* involved personam jurisdiction and in this section we are addressing only quasi in rem jurisdiction. An additional showing that the defendant/parent has property in New York should supply nexus enough for quasi in rem jurisdiction under the criteria of the *Shaffer* case. The additional "contact" that the presence of the property constitutes, although inadequate to satisfy personam jurisdiction, should support the more limited quasi in rem jurisdiction.[7]

Unlike attachment, which is statutorily required to precede the service of process in an action when the attachment is used for quasi

in rem jurisdiction,[8] sequestration need not precede service. It can come after, and can be sought at any time up to judgment. If personam jurisdiction of the defendant is not obtained during the action, the monetary award in the judgment will of course be enforcible only out of sequestered property.

Pennoyer v. Neff,[9] whence clearly comes the requirement that quasi in rem seizure precede judgment, is a bit ambiguous as to whether it even has to precede the service of process in the action. New York in effect reads *Pennoyer* both ways. When used for jurisdictional purposes, an order of attachment in an ordinary money action must precede service[10] while an order of sequestration in a matrimonial action has been allowed to follow it.[11] Following it is not mandatory, however. The sequestration can precede the service of process. If it does, however, service must be made within a reasonable time afterwards.[12]

The need for sequestration as a quasi in rem jurisdictional substitute for personam jurisdiction in matrimonial actions was much reduced by the addition of CPLR 302(b) in 1974. CPLR 302(b) offers personam jurisdiction for money claims in matrimonial actions and in family court matters based on certain prescribed longarm contacts that the case has with the state.[13]

For equitable distribution, too, quasi in rem jurisdiction can be invoked if the property affected is in New York.[14]

§ 107. Service by Publication

We've saved this method of service for last because as a matter of due process it is "the method of notice least calculated to bring to a potential defendant's attention the pendency

---

4.   Geary v. Geary, 272 N.Y. 390, 6 N.E.2d 67 (1936).

5.   433 U.S. 186, 97 S.Ct. 2569, 53 L.Ed.2d 683 (1977). The Shaffer case is discussed more fully in § 104, above.

6.   436 U.S. 84, 98 S.Ct. 1690, 56 L.Ed.2d 132 (1978).

7.   The Kulko case is the subject of the lead note in New York State Law Digest No. 223.

8.   CPLR 314(3).

9.   95 U.S. 714, 24 L.Ed. 565 (1877).

10.   CPLR 314(3), 6213.

11.   Matthews v. Matthews (2d appeal), 247 N.Y. 32, 159 N.E. 713 (1928).

12.   Matthews v. Matthews (1st appeal), note 3, above. Note that there is no arbitrary period for service, such as there is for attachment (60 days under CPLR 6213).

13.   See § 90 above.

14.   McCasland v. McCasland, 68 N.Y.2d 748, 506 N.Y.S.2d 329, 497 N.E.2d 696 (1986).

of judicial proceedings".[1] Service by publication amounts only to a gesture and "when notice is a person's due, process which is a mere gesture is not due process".[2] In a case with many defendants, all of whom have a common interest, such as a proceeding to settle a trust fund with many beneficiaries, a reasonable effort to give personal notice to each may justify a general service by publication if some can't be personally notified after reasonable effort. The mass reached can be expected to protect the interests of the few not reached.[3] But because of supervening due process demands, the use of service by publication in an ordinary one-on-one personam action is risky at best and should be avoided.

In one case in which New York City had condemnation rights to upstate waterways, the city notified certain riparian owners by two methods: by publication and by posting notice on nearby trees—a boon to the tree-reading public. This was all done pursuant to a then-applicable statute and the service was sustained by the New York courts. The U.S. Supreme Court summarily and unanimously reversed, held the methods unconstitutional, and suggested that all the plaintiff had to do to satisfy due process was send each of the riparian owners a letter.[4]

The scheme of the CPLR in regard to service by publication satisfies due process requirements. CPLR 315 is the governing statute. First of all, it permits service by publication only in the rem actions, i.e., those listed in CPLR 314. Then it provides that even in those cases, publication can be ordered only "if service cannot be made by another prescribed method with due diligence", which includes, among other things, any and all of the usual service methods contained in CPLR 308. Where, for example, the plaintiff/wife in a matrimonial action[5] had a military address for the defendant/husband, a retired soldier living in Germany, but made no effort to contact him or to learn of his whereabouts through that address, a divorce predicated on service by publication was vacated.[6] Service by publication, said the court, "should be utilized only as a last resort where all other methods are unavailable", and the unavailability of other methods had not been established.

With CPLR 308(5) on the books as the ultimate alternative—authorizing the court to invent a method of service if nothing else works—the need for publication even in the rem case should be reduced to near the vanishing point.

Technically, service by publication can still be found even in the personam case, despite its being restricted by CPLR 315 to rem cases. A court may order service by publication on a CPLR 308(5) application in a personam action, for example, but it is obviously a last resort even there. If it is done, it should at least be accompanied by some other method.

The mechanics of publication, in the relatively rare instances when it is ordered—and publication can come about only by court order—are contained in CPLR 316. The publication is to be in two newspapers, designated by the judge, and is to run at least once in each of four consecutive weeks. For the matrimonial action, where service by publication is permissible but less likely today,[7] publication need be in only one newspaper once in each of three consecutive weeks.[8] The statute also requires—but only in the matrimonial action—

---

§ 107

1. Boddie v. Connecticut, 401 U.S. 371, 382, 91 S.Ct. 780, 788, 28 L.Ed.2d 113 (1971).

2. Mullane v. Central Hanover Bank & Trust Co., 339 U.S. 306, 315, 70 S.Ct. 652, 657, 94 L.Ed. 865 (1950).

3. Id. at 319, 70 S.Ct. at 659.

4. Schroeder v. City of New York, 371 U.S. 208, 83 S.Ct. 279, 9 L.Ed.2d 255 (1962). As a matter of fact, it would probably be a lot faster and cheaper for the plaintiff to use the newspapers and the trees. The extensive search of county records needed to identify all riparian interests

along a waterway costs time and poses pitfalls, but due process requires whatever effort it takes to identify those whose property is sought in eminent domain.

5. The matrimonial action is a category in which in rem jurisdiction of the "marital res" can support jurisdiction (see § 102 above) and in which service by publication under CPLR 315 can therefore become available.

6. Caban v. Caban, 116 A.D.2d 783, 497 N.Y.S.2d 175 (3d Dep't 1986).

7. See § 76 above.

8. CPLR 316(a).

that the summons be mailed to the defendant.[9]

First publication of the summons must be made within 30 days after the order for service by publication is granted. This is strict, and it has been held that even a short delay will void the service.[10] Service is complete on the 21st day after first publication in a matrimonial action, and on the 28th day in all other actions.

When an order of attachment has been obtained in what starts out to be a quasi in rem action,[11] the summons is served on the defendant only after the attachment has been levied. If it is served by publication and it turns out that the defendant is a New Yorker, does the service by publication give personam jurisdiction? For a long time under the old Civil Practice Act (CPA), the question remained unanswered. After the CPA became history, Fishman v. Sanders[12] answered the question and said yes, personam jurisdiction results, but specified that the question was being answered only under the CPA, not under the CPLR. A definitive answer under the CPLR will apparently have to wait until it is superseded sometime in the 21st Century by something else, but no one is holding any breath.[13]

H. VACATING DEFAULTS

Table of Sections

Sec.
108. Vacating Default Judgment.

§ 108. Vacating Default Judgment

A duly served defendant who does not appear and against whom a default judgment is

taken may move to vacate the judgment within a year. Two CPLR provisions authorize this: CPLR 317 and CPLR 5015(a)(1).[1] CPLR 317 applies when service was made by a method other than personal delivery to the defendant under CPLR 308(1) or the defendant's Rule 318 agent under CPLR 308(3). CPLR 5015(a)(1) gives the court discretion to vacate a judgment for "excusable default" regardless of the method of service. Hence a defendant to whom CPLR 317 is unavailable because she was personally served may move to vacate under CPLR 5015(a).[2]

We are assuming here that the court has jurisdiction, both of the subject matter and of the defendant's person, and that all the defendant wants to do is have the default opened and be allowed to defend on the merits. The situation is not to be confused with the one in which jurisdiction is contested, such as where the defendant contends that service was never made, or where the court lacks jurisdiction for any other reason.[3] In a lack-of-jurisdiction case, the defendant wants the default judgment vacated and the action dismissed. In the present discussion jurisdiction is assumed and all the defendant is asking is a vacatur of the judgment coupled with an opening of the default so that the defendant can defend the action.

If the defendant believes jurisdiction is lacking but is apprehensive that the court will not agree, which happens often enough, the defendant's step is to request relief in the alternative: move to vacate the judgment and either dismiss the action or, if jurisdiction is sus-

---

9. CPLR 316(b).

10. Caton v. Caton, 72 Misc.2d 544, 339 N.Y.S.2d 92 (Sup.Ct., Monroe County, 1972).

11. See § 104 above.

12. 15 N.Y.2d 298, 258 N.Y.S.2d 380, 206 N.E.2d 326 (1965).

13. Service by publication is not likely to be ordered on such a defendant under the CPLR. Given the broad discretion of the court under CPLR 308(5), limited only by judicial imagination, the occasion to order service by publication should be rare indeed today. And given a basis for extraterritorial jurisdiction, as there was in Fishman (the defendant was a tortfeasor involved in a New York accident as well as a domiciliary), the procedure today is to get a service order under CPLR 308(5), such as by mail to the defendant's last known address, which will give personam

jurisdiction even if D no longer lives there. See § 75, above, treating CPLR 308(5).

§ 108

1. CPLR 5015(a)(1) is broader, applying to the vacatur of any kind of default, not just a default for failure to appear, but both statutes are discussed here only as applied to the default based on nonappearance, i.e., the default that follows the defendant's failure to respond to the summons.

2. See Commentary on McKinney's CPLR 5015.

3. E.g., lack of jurisdictional basis for extraterritorial service, even though service was made by a proper method.

tained, open the default and allow a defense on the merits.

Each of the two provisions purports to require that the motion to vacate the default be made within a year, but each starts the year at a different time. CPLR 317 starts the year from the time the defendant "obtains knowledge of entry of the judgment", apparently without regard to the source through which the defendant got the knowledge. CPLR 5015(a)(1) starts its year from the time the defendant is formally served with "written notice" of the entry of the judgment, apparently without regard to whether she knew about it before then or not. If that formal service is never made, the one year never starts.[4]

CPLR 317 has a maximum five-year cut-off, which means that the motion under 317 does not lie if more than five years have elapsed since the entry of judgment. No such limitation inhibits CPLR 5015(a)(1).

The differences between the two provisions might appear to require the drawing of a sharp line between them in situations in which either may be invoked—which would be whenever service is made by a method other than personal delivery—so as to clarify just which one governs what. That might be helpful, but it isn't necessary for the reason that the one-year period is not a statute of limitations[5] and is therefore not rigid. The court has inherent discretionary power to vacate a default in the interests of justice and retains this power even though the allotted year has expired.[6] This is true of CPLR 317[7] as well as CPLR 5015(a)(1).[8] Then to what avail the one-year requirement? It is not clear, but if the year has expired the excuse for the default had best be all the more compelling.

The foregoing should evince how liberal the New York courts are about vacating defaults. It is in the broad discretion of the court. Given a reasonable excuse, the court is likely to grant the vacatur. There are even instances of deliberate defaults being vacated, usually with a stiff costs penalty,[9] but a defendant had best have analyzed things quite closely before suffering a default intentionally. The more usual vacatur basis is a showing that as a practical matter circumstances disabled the defendant from protecting her interests.[10]

The New York rule of thumb is that a motion to vacate a default requires two showings: (1) an excuse for the default and (2) an "affidavit of merits", as it is commonly called, in which the defendant is required to satisfy the court that she has a meritorious defense.[11] This offers assurance that vacating the default will not be a wasted effort; that the defendant does have a reasonable position on the merits and is not just wasting time. (If the defendant has no defense on the merits, the rule's theory is that a default judgment is as good as any to close things out.)

The affidavit should be made by the defendant herself or by someone else with first-hand knowledge of the facts. An affidavit of merits made by one without such knowledge will be ignored as having no probative force, which means that the default-vacating papers will be deficient and that the motion to vacate will be denied. Quite often in the reported cases the affidavit of merits submitted is that of the defendant's lawyer, but unless the lawyer happens to have been involved in the transactions between the parties, which occasionally happens in a commercial or realty case but virtually never in a tort action, even the affidavit of merits of the lawyer is worthless. And if the lawyer did have an involvement and consequently knows the facts, it is still better to have the client furnish the affidavit of merits; an attorney's affidavit of merits arouses judicial suspicion readily.

---

4. Redfield v. Critchley, 277 N.Y. 336, 14 N.E.2d 377 (1938).

5. Ladd v. Stevenson, 112 N.Y. 325, 19 N.E. 842 (1889).

6. Machnick Builders, Ltd. v. Grand Union Co., 52 A.D.2d 655, 381 N.Y.S.2d 551 (3d Dep't 1976).

7. 2d Rep.Leg.Doc. (1958) No.13, p.169.

8. 3d Rep.Leg.Doc. (1959) No.17, p.204.

9. See, e.g., Hensey Properties, Inc. v. Lamagna, 23 A.D.2d 742, 258 N.Y.S.2d 495 (1st Dep't 1965).

10. Benadon v. Antonio, 10 A.D.2d 40, 197 N.Y.S.2d 1 (1960).

11. Id.

Caselaw construing the predecessor of CPLR 317 held that a motion to vacate a default needs the usual affidavit of merits, in common with what CPLR 5015(a)(1) requires, but that it does not need an excuse for the default.[12] The present structure of CPLR 317, requiring the defendant to show that he did not get notice "in time to defend", should suggest that this is no longer so and that an excuse for the default is just as necessary on a CPLR 317 as on a 5015(a)(1) motion.[13] Caselaw continues to hold, however, that the CPLR 317 applicant does not have to excuse the default; that she just has to show that she didn't receive notice in time to defend, even if the reason for not receiving notice was her own fault.[14]

Many of the reported cases on default-opening motions involve a corporate defendant served through the secretary of state's office.[15] A common scenario is that the defendant failed to get notice because it failed to keep its address current on the secretary's books, as it is required to do by law, and that the secretary therefore mailed the summons to an old address and the corporation never got it. The omission ought to be laid at the defendant's door, generating at least a money sanction as a condition to a vacatur, but some courts nevertheless continue to forgive the omission and grant vacaturs by such corporate applicants almost as a matter of course. The defendant does best to cite CPLR 317 on its default-vacating motion, however. CPLR 5015(a)(1), since it requires a decent excuse for the default, doesn't work in this situation,[16] but it has been held that if the defendant makes the default vacatur application under 5015, it can be treated as having been made under the more advantageous 317.[17]

This generous attitude towards corporations may have prompted some of them to take too much for granted, even when there has been no address change, such as by letting certified mail sent to a present address remain unclaimed. It has been held that if the corporation does know about the mail—and it is of course Post Office policy to see that it does—leaving the mail unclaimed will produce a default judgment that will not be vacated under CPLR 317 or anything else.[18] It has also been held that if the corporation, once having had a default vacated on wrong-address grounds, still doesn't get its address corrected, the next default will stick.[19]

In the early 1980s, there was a great to-do about defaults predicated on what are known as "law office failures"—omissions on the part of the attorney or someone connected with the attorney's office. It started in 1980 with the Court of Appeals decision in Barasch v. Micucci,[20] which held categorically that "law office failures" may not be accepted as excuses for the plaintiff's late service or nonservice of a complaint under CPLR 3012(b). Then, in Eaton v. Equitable Life Assurance Society of the U.S.[21] in 1982, the holding was extended to defendants' defaults in answering, the most typical category of default and the one addressed in the present section. Thenceforth referred to as the *Barasch/Eaton* rule to denote its application to pleading defaults on either side, it had the parties lying in ambush for each other, hoping for a default and jumping in for it as soon as things were ripe.

Barasch/Eaton was overruled by the legislature in 1983 with the addition of § 2005 to the CPLR and the addition of subdivision (d) to

---

12. Carpenter v. Weatherwax, 277 A.D. 264, 98 N.Y.S.2d 673 (3d Dep't 1950).

13. If the reason the defendant defaulted is that he did not get notice in time because of the method of service, that itself may satisfy as an excuse.

14. See Wharton v. 241 Corp., 99 A.D.2d 979, 473 N.Y.S.2d 17 (1st Dep't 1984), citing and relying on Taieb v. Hilton Hotels Corp., 60 N.Y.2d 725, 469 N.Y.S.2d 74, 456 N.E.2d 1197 (1983).

15. Bus.Corp.L. § 306. See § 70 above.

16. The lead note in New York State Law Digest No. 290 addresses this subject.

17. DiLorenzo v. A.C. Dutton Lumber Co., 67 N.Y.2d 138, 501 N.Y.S.2d 8, 492 N.E.2d 116 (1986).

18. See Rifenburg v. Liffiton Homes, Inc., 107 A.D.2d 1015, 486 N.Y.S.2d 529 (4th Dep't, 1985). The court in Rifenburg remanded the case to determine whether the corporation had notice of the certified mail, the vacatur to be denied if it had.

19. Paul Conte Cadillac, Inc. v. C.A.R.S. Purchasing Serv., Inc., 126 A.D.2d 621, 511 N.Y.S.2d 58 (2d Dep't 1987).

20. 49 N.Y.2d 594, 427 N.Y.S.2d 732, 404 N.E.2d 1275.

21. 56 N.Y.2d 900, 453 N.Y.S.2d 404, 438 N.E.2d 1119.

CPLR 3012. Discretion to consider law office failures along with other excuses reverted to approximately where it was before the *Barasch/Eaton* era. It must be stressed, however, that the legislation merely restores judicial discretion; it does not assure a defaulter that all will be forgiven. Costs sanctions, including hefty attorney's fees, are a frequent alternative now for the excusing of a default.[22]

---

22. The 1983 amendments and more on the Barasch/Eaton background are discussed in § 231, below. The hectic few years before the overruling of Barasch/Eaton are chronicled in lead notes on the subject in the New York State Law Digest editions of July 1982 (No.271), after Eaton came down, and June 1983 (No.282), when the overruling legislation took effect. The latter (Digest 282) enumerates earlier Digest treatments.

Chapter Five

APPEARANCE

§ 109. Appearance, Generally

An appearance is a participation of some kind in an action. It comes in several varieties and lawyers should spare themselves the idle pursuit of trying to give it a precise definition. It is at root a way of submitting to the court's jurisdiction, either for a particular purpose or for all purposes.

Under prior law, there existed a "special" appearance. A special appearance was used by the defendant for the sole purpose of objecting to the court's jurisdiction of his person, and prior law was strict about it. The only way the jurisdictional objection could be raised was by motion with the "special appearance" label, and jurisdiction had to be the only objection stated. If accompanied by any merits objection the jurisdictional objection was ipso facto waived.[1]

The CPLR abolished the "special" appearance, and since the "general" appearance was used only to differentiate it from the special

one, both categories have disappeared under the CPLR. The main provision in point is CPLR 320(a), and it speaks only of an "appearance". Under the CPLR lawyers have to know (1) what constitutes an "appearance" and (2) how to make and preserve a jurisdictional objection, and they should absorb the two topics independently before negotiating the interplay between them. The two are no longer wedded, as they were under prior law.

Some unique categories of appearance do exist under present law, such as the so-called "restricted" and "limited" and perhaps even "qualified" appearance; these will be treated shortly.[2] There also remains an "informal" appearance.[3] But the "special" and "general" appearances are gone.

§ 110. How and When to Appear

A plaintiff appears in an action merely by bringing it. A defendant can appear in any of the three ways listed in CPLR 320(a):

1. by serving a notice of appearance; or

2. by serving an answer; or

3. by making a motion that has the "effect" of extending the answering time.

Two motions have that automatic "effect": the motion to correct a pleading of CPLR 3024,[1] seen infrequently, and the dismissal motion of CPLR 3211,[2] seen all the time. The making of either kind of motion is therefore an appearance in the action.

---

§ 109

1. Civ.Prac.Act § 237–a. The statute and the background of New York appearances under prior law are treated in Frumer & Graziano, Jurisdictional Dilemma of the Nonresident Defendant in New York—A Proposed Solution, 19 Ford.L.Rev. 125 (1950).

2. See §§ 113 and 114 below.

3. See § 112 below.

§ 110

1. See CPLR 3024(c).

2. See CPLR 3211(f).

If the summons is served with the notice permitted by CPLR 305(b)[3] instead of with a complaint, the defendant responds by serving a notice of appearance[4] and a demand for the complaint.[5] These are usually incorporated into one paper, which can read as simply as: "Take notice that the defendant, through the undersigned as attorney, hereby appears in the action and demands a copy of the complaint."

By serving such a paper the defendant formally "appears" in the action, but the appearance does not constitute a waiver of any jurisdictional objection, which can be made later.[6]

The time in which to take this responsive step to the summons depends on the place and method of its service. If the summons is served by personal delivery to the defendant in New York, the responding period is 20 days; if it is served by any other means in New York, or by any means at all (including personal delivery) outside New York, the responding period is 30 days after service is complete.[7] If service by publication is used and the defendant appears during the period of publication, the defendant's appearance itself completes the service[8] and dispenses with further publications.

§ 111. Making and Preserving a Jurisdictional Objection

An objection to jurisdiction of the subject matter may be taken at any time and in just about any form,[1] but the rules about the objection to personal—including rem—jurisdiction are more demanding[2] and run as follows:

Before the 1963 adoption of the CPLR, an objection to personal jurisdiction could be taken only by a motion made in conjunction with a special appearance.[3] The CPLR abolishes the special appearance—an appearance made for the sole purpose of objecting to jurisdiction—and permits the objection to be taken in either of two ways, at the defendant's option: by a motion to dismiss under CPLR 3211[4] or as a defense in the answer.[5] Thus, as long as the time to answer is still open, the right to make a jurisdictional objection is still alive. The fact that the defendant may have appeared earlier does not mean that the jurisdictional objection was waived. Where, for example, the summons is served with only a CPLR 305(b) notice and the defendant responds by serving a notice of appearance and demand for the complaint, the response is an appearance in the action. But since the defendant's answering time is still open, and in fact will not even begin to run until the plaintiff responds to the demand by serving the complaint, the defendant's jurisdictional objection is preserved.

When the complaint is finally served in that situation, the defendant may now assert the jurisdictional objection either by moving or answering. If the defendant chooses the motion route, which is usually the preferable method because it disposes of the objection early, the defendant may join in the motion any other grounds for dismissal listed in CPLR 3211(a).[6] (Under prior law and its special appearance, the addition of other grounds brought a waiver of the jurisdictional objection.)

Technical defects in carrying out the various requirements of the filing system, used for commencing actions and proceedings in the supreme and county courts, have also been

---

3. See § 60 above.

4. CPLR 320(a).

5. CPLR 3012(b). Procedure when the complaint is served with the summons is treated in § 231, below.

6. Although the notice of appearance is of course an appearance under CPLR 320(a), the demand for the complaint under CPLR 3012(b) by itself is not—an anomaly resulting from lack of legislative coordination between the two provisions. The matter is of little moment. Even though the demand, when accompanied by a notice of appearance, constitutes an "appearance" under CPLR 320(a), it does not waive jurisdictional objections, see § 111, below, the factor that divests the inconsistency of its significance.

7. CPLR 320(a).

8. CPLR 320(d).

§ 111

1. CPLR 3211(a)(2), (e). See Commentary C3211:11 on McKinney's CPLR 3211.

2. See Homburger & Laufer, Appearance and Jurisdictional Motions in New York, 14 Buffalo L.Rev. 374 (1965).

3. Civ.Prac.Act § 237–a.

4. CPLR 3211(a)(8) (personam objection) or (9) (rem objection).

5. CPLR 3211(e), 320(b), 320(c)(2).

6. See CPLR 3211(e).

held waived if the defendant or respondent proceeds with the merits without raising the objection either by motion or answer; the court may not raise the objection on its own motion.[7]

If the jurisdictional objection is one that comes into being only after the time for making a CPLR 3211 motion or serving an answer has expired, the waiver rule does not apply and the objection may be asserted when it arises. Where, for example, the defect is a failure to perfect an initially valid order of attachment in a case based on quasi in rem jurisdiction—a failure that voids the levy and the quasi in rem jurisdiction along with it[8]— the objection may be asserted in a motion for summary judgment.[9]

If the defendant has defaulted and a judgment has been entered in a case in which the defendant believes jurisdiction was lacking, the jurisdictional objection may be taken by a motion to vacate the default judgment. And if the defendant has any other objections such as would have been joinable on a CPLR 3211 motion had there been no default, these, too, may be joined on the motion to vacate.[10] They may be joined in the alternative. The defendant can seek vacation of the judgment plus either (1) dismissal of the action for want of jurisdiction or, should jurisdiction be sustained, (2) an opening of the default with leave to defend on the merits. The court would ordinarily pass first on the jurisdictional objection. Only if it finds jurisdiction present would it go on to rule on the request to open the default. That's the obvious order in which to dispose of the alternative objections, but a court sometimes overlooks this and reverses the sequence.[11]

Although most of the objections on the CPLR 3211(a) list may be taken either by motion or by answer, at the defendant's option, the objections to personal jurisdiction under paragraph 8 and to rem jurisdiction under paragraph 9 have a special requirement. If no CPLR 3211 motion is made at all, those objections may be included as defenses in the answer. But if the defendant does make a CPLR 3211 motion, on any ground at all, and omits from it the personal or rem jurisdictional objections, those objections are waived and may not be included in any later answer.[12] This is to discourage the making of a 3211 motion unless it includes those fundamental jurisdictional objections, objections so basic that the court should have a chance to dispose of them before being burdened with having to address anything else.

If the objection is taken as a defense in the answer instead of by motion, it evinces the defendant's preference to defer determination of the objection until later, perhaps until the trial itself. The plaintiff, however, may bring the issue to prompt adjudication by moving to dismiss the defense pursuant to CPLR 3211(b). Indeed, if there is a statute of limitations problem in the case, the plaintiff will be glad to have that tool.[13]

The objection of improper service invokes another special rule. If the defendant asserts the objection in the answer, the defendant must then move for judgment on it within 60 days thereafter or the objection is waived.[14]

Since the CPLR allows D to take the jurisdictional objection by motion or by answer, it has been held that when the answer method is used, the pleading of a counterclaim—which is also contained in the answer—does not waive

7. Fry v. Village of Tarrytown, 89 N.Y.2d 714, 658 N.Y.S.2d 205 (1997). In this sense, the defects fall under the category of personal, not subject matter, jurisdiction. See the discussion of the Fry case in § 63, above, and in the lead note in New York State Law Digest No. 448.

8. See § 104, above, and § 321, below.

9. See Rich v. Rich, 103 Misc.2d 723, 426 N.Y.S.2d 936 (Sup.Ct., N.Y.County, 1980).

10. Mutual Home Dealers Corp. v. Alves, 23 A.D.2d 791, 258 N.Y.S.2d 786 (2d Dep't 1965).

11. Id.

12. CPLR 3211(e); Dominion of Canada Gen. Ins. Co. v. Pierson, 27 A.D.2d 484, 280 N.Y.S.2d 296 (3d Dep't 1967).

13. Always relevant to the plaintiff, when the defendant has interposed a jurisdictional objection, is the timing of its adjudication. In New York State Law Digests 274–276 are a three-part series of lead notes on the urgency of that timing when the statute of limitations is close at hand.

14. CPLR 3211(e). This product of a 1996 amendment is discussed in SPR 50:3.

the jurisdictional objection if the counterclaim is related to the plaintiff's claim.[15] To hold otherwise would nullify the CPLR permission to plead rather than move on a jurisdictional objection. But it has been held that the pleading of an unrelated counterclaim does waive an objection to jurisdiction.[16]

To determine relatedness in this situation, the Court of Appeals has adopted a collateral estoppel test. If there are common issues between the main claim and the counterclaim, such that the resolution of any common issue in the course of adjudicating the main claim would also be dispositive of the issue when it arises on the counterclaim, "relatedness" is established and the risk of waiving the objection to jurisdiction merely by pleading the counterclaim is avoided.[17]

While these rules presumably apply as well to a cross-claim,[18] D's impleader of a third-party defendant is not necessarily inconsistent with D's preservation of a jurisdictional objection and therefore does not waive it.[19]

The spectacle has arisen of a defendant serving an answer and objecting to jurisdiction in an action in which he has not even been served with process. Although not served, D was named as a defendant along with others. The fact that D is named, held the court, gives D a sufficient nexus with the case to support his application to dismiss for want of jurisdiction. Until a court rules on jurisdiction, D's position is insecure—perhaps service was attempted but D was unaware of it, for example—and as a named party, served or not, D may, if he fancies himself entitled to a jurisdic-

tional dismissal, interpose the objection and ask for it.[20]

If the defendant moves to dismiss for want of personal jurisdiction in an ordinary in personam action, she had best stay on and defend on the merits if the motion is denied. If the defendant leaves the action after the denial, a default judgment will result and will be binding in personam. The defendant therefore derives no advantage at all by attempting to withdraw after losing a jurisdictional objection in a personam action, although withdrawal may offer a benefit in certain rem cases.[21] Under New York law, an immediate appeal may be taken from an order denying a motion to dismiss for lack of jurisdiction,[22] even though it is of course not final, i.e., does not terminate the case. But the defendant has the alternative, little used with jurisdictional objections, of foregoing an immediate appeal and instead seeking appellate review of the order as part of a later appeal from the final judgment on the merits, should it be adverse.[23] At whatever stage the jurisdictional point is appealed, an appellate determination that jurisdiction was lacking will result in a dismissal, incidentally cancelling out a trial on the merits if one has already taken place.

The rule in American jurisprudence is that each defendant is entitled to one day in court on a jurisdictional question. If the defendant asserts the objection by motion or answer in the original action, she uses up that day in court at that time and is bound by the court's holding on the issue. In fact, if she appears in the action and defends on the merits even without raising a jurisdictional objection, the rule is that, by appearing, she had the oppor-

---

15. Goodman v. Solow, 27 A.D.2d 920, 279 N.Y.S.2d 377 (1st Dep't 1967).

16. Liebling v. Yankwitt, 109 A.D.2d 780, 486 N.Y.S.2d 292 (2d Dep't 1985).

17. Textile Tech. Exch., Inc. v. Davis, 81 N.Y.2d 56, 595 N.Y.S.2d 729, 611 N.E.2d 768 (1993). The various tactical considerations confronted by the defendant in this situation are discussed in a lead note on the *Textile* case in SPR 4.

18. See Commentary C3211:60 on McKinney's CPLR 3211. Counterclaims and cross-claims may be interposed in New York practice even though unrelated to any other claim in the case. CPLR 3019(a), (b). See §§ 224 and 227, below.

19. Italian Colony Restaurant, Inc. v. Wershals, 45 A.D.2d 841, 358 N.Y.S.2d 448 (2d Dep't 1974).

20. Colbert v. International Sec. Bureau Inc., 79 A.D.2d 448, 437 N.Y.S.2d 360 (2d Dep't 1981).

21. See § 113 below.

22. CPLR 5701(a)(2)(v).

23. CPLR 5501(a)(1). Compare Dorfman v. Hassett, 187 Misc. 1048, 66 N.Y.S.2d 591 (Broome County Ct. 1946), which was decided in the now expired era of the special appearance but whose conclusions, allowing deferral of appellate review of jurisdictional objections until later appeal on the merits, should still obtain under CPLR 5501. See § 530 below.

tunity to raise it, that her silence forfeited it, and that this is the equivalent of a day in court on the issue and precludes any other American court, under the full faith and credit clause, from later questioning the first court's jurisdiction.[24] Even if the defendant did not appear in the first court at the outset, but made her jurisdictional objection to that court by a motion to vacate a default judgment after such was entered against her, the post-judgment motion constitutes the day in court under this rule, so that an adverse decision on the motion, sustaining jurisdiction, seals it and precludes collateral attack on it later in any other court.[25]

§ 112. Informal Appearance

In addition to the formal appearances listed in CPLR 320(a),[1] the law continues to recognize the so-called "informal" appearance. It comes about when the defendant, although not having taken any of the steps officially treated as an appearance under CPLR 320(a), nevertheless participates in the case in some way relating to the merits. Thus, where the defendant's lawyer showed up at the trial and questioned witnesses on the merits, the defendant was held to have appeared in the action and thereby submitted himself to jurisdiction.[2]

Participation at the pre-trial stage of proceedings can also bring about an informal appearance, such as where the defendant submits to the taking of his deposition or seeks to take the plaintiff's deposition on any matter touching the merits of the case.[3]

The occasion for this kind of appearance, an infrequent thing, may be a case in which there are multiple defendants, some of whom have appeared and are defending. This affords a context in which another defendant, duly named in the summons but perhaps not served, hears about the action from the other defendants. Taking no step that would constitute a formal appearance, he nevertheless participates and addresses the merits in some way, as in the above examples.

An informal appearance can also occur if the defendant participates in the trial of a damages issue after a judgment by default has been rendered establishing liability.[4]

A defendant who has and would preserve any kind of jurisdictional objection had best not appear informally. The consequence of the informal appearance is that while it is a full submission to jurisdiction, and in fact perfects a jurisdiction otherwise lacking, it is also a waiver of any jurisdictional objection the defendant might otherwise have had. A jurisdictional objection, as has been seen,[5] can be interposed only by motion or answer, and if no motion was made and the time to answer has expired, as where the defendant was served and let the time pass without a responsive step, an informal appearance at a later point forfeits the only opportunity a defendant is allowed to assert the jurisdictional objection.

§ 113. Appearance in "Rem" Actions; "Limited" Appearance

A few special points have to be made about appearances and the making of jurisdictional objections in the rem categories of actions, rare as they are today. The method of taking the objection is the same as in the personam action, i.e., by motion to dismiss or as a defense in the answer, but the appearance itself can have different consequences in certain actions or at certain stages. The following discussion assumes that there is no personam jurisdiction in the action, and that only rem jurisdiction is claimed.

If the sole basis of jurisdiction is the attachment of the defendant's local property,[1] New

24. Sherrer v. Sherrer, 334 U.S. 343, 68 S.Ct. 1087, 92 L.Ed. 1429 (1948).

25. Vander v. Casperson, 12 N.Y.2d 56, 236 N.Y.S.2d 33, 187 N.E.2d 109 (1962).

§ 112

1. See § 110 above.

2. Henderson v. Henderson, 247 N.Y. 428, 160 N.E. 775 (1928).

3. McGowan v. Bellanger, 32 A.D.2d 293, 301 N.Y.S.2d 712 (3d Dep't 1969).

4. The default concedes liability but not damages. See § 293 below.

5. See § 111 above.

§ 113

1. This is the quasi in rem jurisdiction treated in § 104, above. As discussed in that section, this category of jurisdiction was much curtailed by the U.S. Supreme

York allows the defendant what has become known as a "limited" appearance. In this kind of action, and only in this one, the defendant is permitted to appear and defend without facing any personam consequences. Whether he defaults, or defends and loses, the resulting judgment is effective only to the extent of—and execution on the judgment can be levied only against—the property previously attached. This is the gift of CPLR 320(c)(1),[2] a provision added in a 1969 amendment. The amendment codifies the result of the reargument opinion in Simpson v. Loehmann, which interpolated a limited appearance into the pre-amendment version of CPLR 320(c). The *Simpson* case did that in a *Seider* situation, i.e., where the property attached was the defendant's liability insurance policy,[3] but the amendment allows the limited appearance in any case in which attachment is the sole basis for jurisdiction.

If the defendant exploits the limited appearance and defends on the merits, the action follows the usual procedures. The only consequence is that a judgment for the plaintiff will have limited effect. In the realization that even a victory may afford the plaintiff only partial satisfaction of the claim, i.e., satisfaction only to the extent of the attached property, thus necessitating yet another action later to collect the balance, the plaintiff sometimes seeks a special preference for the attachment-based case so as to get it tried early. The courts are not ordinarily receptive to this. They reason that the plaintiff could have sued for everything at once in a court with personam jurisdiction and spared everyone the extra action.[4]

If the defendant contends that even quasi in rem jurisdiction is lacking for some reason—insufficient service, defective attachment, etc.—she can move to dismiss for want of rem jurisdiction under CPLR 3211(a)(9). If that motion is not successful, the defendant loses nothing by staying in and defending on the merits. Doing so does not result in personam jurisdiction. The limited appearance still insures that the judgment will be valid only as against the attached property.

That is not so, however, with any other category of rem jurisdiction, such as the usual "in rem" category described in § 103. These others are governed by CPLR 320(c)(2), and here an appearance confers personal jurisdiction even though there was no personal jurisdiction to start with. If the defendant maintains that even the rem jurisdiction was lacking at the outset, he may make the dismissal motion under CPLR 3211(a)(9). If the defendant wins on that motion, all is dismissed and he can go home. But if the motion is denied, the defendant now faces a choice: he must either withdraw from the litigation, thus allowing a default judgment to be entered against him—which forfeits without contest whatever interest he has in the property involved in the case—or he may remain in the action and defend on the merits. By remaining, however, he submits himself to personam jurisdiction and a judgment in the action is not restricted to the defendant's interest in the property.

It is to be seen, therefore, that except in the attachment case where the defendant is allowed a limited appearance, in all other rem actions in New York an appearance subjects the defendant to a kind of leverage in which the defendant must either submit to personam jurisdiction (by appearing and defending) or forfeit his interest in the property (by defaulting). In some cases this can pose the same kind of constitutional objection that resulted in the caselaw adoption of the limited appearance in the *Seider* situation discussed earlier.[5] But given the expanded modern bases for personam jurisdiction, today's diminished reliance on rem jurisdiction[6] makes the issue largely if not entirely academic.

Court in Shaffer v. Heitner, 433 U.S. 186, 97 S.Ct. 2569, 53 L.Ed.2d 683 (1977), but subsists in several situations.

2. See also CPLR 5230(a).

3. See § 105 above.

4. See Tjepkema v. Kenney, 59 Misc.2d 670, 299 N.Y.S.2d 943 (Sup.Ct., N.Y.County, 1969), an action based on the since-overruled Seider doctrine (see § 105).

5. See the paragraphs numbered 2 and 3 in the discussion of Seider v. Roth in § 105, above.

6. See § 103 above.

Suppose the defendant does not know precisely what kind of jurisdiction the plaintiff is asserting—personam or rem or quasi in rem—and that she has some jurisdictional objections. Even the plaintiff may be unsure of what kind of jurisdiction exists.[7] The objection to personal jurisdiction is made under paragraph 8 of CPLR 3211(a), the rem objection under paragraph 9. The unsure defendant should base the dismissal motion on both paragraphs and should in the moving papers request that the court specify, in the order deciding the motion, what kind of jurisdiction, if any, exists. Since different consequences append to later steps in the case, depending on the kind of jurisdiction sustained, a judicial determination sustaining any kind should clarify what kind it is.

As with the objection to personam jurisdiction, an order denying a motion to dismiss for want of rem jurisdiction may be appealed immediately or deferred for appellate review until later appeal of an adverse judgment on the merits.[8] In either instance, the appellate court will be the final judge of jurisdiction. Under CPLR 320(c)(2), if the defendant has stayed in the action and defended after her jurisdictional motion was denied, thus submitting to personam jurisdiction, a later appellate finding that the court lacked rem jurisdiction—and that the jurisdictional motion should have been granted—will result in a dismissal, incidentally cancelling the trial, if already had, and with it the personam "submission" that the trial court had exacted of the defendant.

§ 114. Adding Claims in Various Appearance Situations

Assume that a nondomiciliary defendant is temporarily in the state and is served with a summons and CPLR 305(b) notice, the latter setting forth a contract claim. Assume no long-arm or other basis for extraterritorial service exists. The defendant serves a notice of appearance and a demand for the complaint. Is the complaint that the plaintiff now serves confined to the contract claim of which the CPLR 305(b) notice advised the defendant, or may the complaint put in additional claims not referred to in the notice? The New York Court of Appeals held in Everitt v. Everitt,[1] that the complaint is not confined to the claim described in the notice, which was a contract claim for $46,900 in *Everitt*, and may as a matter of right plead any other claim the plaintiff may have. The *Everitt* plaintiff added a tort claim for $350,000.

The justification for this result is that when the defendant is personally served in New York, the service is a good jurisdictional predicate for any claim.

By way of dictum, the court added in *Everitt* that had the action been commenced by service of the summons and complaint together, "[i]t may well be that ... the complaint cannot be amended by adding new causes of action after the defendant has left the State".[2] That presumably means that the defendant has "left the State" without further participation in the action, i.e., without even putting in an appearance, because when the defendant does appear in that kind of case the plaintiff has been held entitled to add, in an amended complaint, even claims of which the original complaint gave no notice. The appellate division held in Mendoza v. Mendoza[3] that in an amendment as of course—an amendment a party is entitled to make without court leave[4]—the plaintiff can as a matter of right add whatever she wishes in the amended complaint, whether the original complaint gave notice of the matter or not. *Mendoza* allowed an amendment to add a fraud claim to an original complaint that had pleaded only a cause of action to annul a marriage.

7. See Kelly v. Stanmar, Inc., 51 Misc.2d 378, 273 N.Y.S.2d 276 (Sup.Ct., Albany County, 1966).

8. See § 111 above.

§ 114

1. 4 N.Y.2d 13, 171 N.Y.S.2d 836, 148 N.E.2d 891 (1958).

2. Id. at 16, 171 N.Y.S.2d at 838, 148 N.E.2d at 893.

3. 4 Misc.2d 1060, 77 N.Y.S.2d 169, (Sup.Ct., N.Y. County, 1947), aff'd 273 App.Div. 877, 77 N.Y.S.2d 264 (1st Dep't 1948).

4. CPLR 3025(a); see § 236 below.

If the amendment is sought by court leave,[5] which is necessary when the of-right amendment is used up or the time for it has expired, whether or not to allow new or additional claims is in the court's discretion.[6]

The Court of Appeals in Matter of Einstoss[7] introduced the possibility of what might be called a "qualified" appearance when it refused to recognize an Alaskan judgment that had failed to honor a condition the defendant had stipulated when he appeared. P had sued D in an Alaska court to foreclose a mortgage. In that action, D was served outside Alaska and the court got no personam jurisdiction.[8] The State of Alaska was a co-defendant. D agreed to appear in the action, thereby facilitating P's proceedings, but only on the understanding that P would not seek a personam judgment against D. The co-defendant State of Alaska ignored that P–D understanding, however, interposed a cross-claim jurisdictionally dependent on D's appearance, and took a default judgment against D. There were further complications that contributed to the Court of Appeals refusal to recognize the judgment on the cross-claim, but apparently the main ground was that since the judgment had depended jurisdictionally on the appearance, it could not at the same time violate the condition that had legitimately qualified the appearance.

Whether such a "qualified" appearance will be permissible in internal New York practice has yet to be elaborated, but if the defendant would attempt it he had best do no more than D did in *Einstoss*: put in the appearance, duly qualified, and then participate no further. But in that case why appear at all? One advantage is that the defendant who appears but does not defend is entitled to notice of subsequent proceedings,[9] whereas the outright defaulter is not.

The still nebulous "qualified" appearance should not be confused with the already discussed "restricted" and "limited" appearances. The "restricted" one is authorized by CPLR 302(c) and applies to preclude a plaintiff from adding against a CPLR 302 defendant any additional claims not also having an extraterritorial jurisdictional basis under 302.[10] The "limited" appearance is permitted by CPLR 320(c)(1) in the case in which jurisdiction rests solely on the local attachment of the defendant's assets.[11] Even if the defendant appears in the attachment case, incidentally, the amendment of the complaint to add claims should not matter because, whatever is added, a judgment in the action will still be enforcible only against the attached property.

With these restricted and limited appearances, the defendant is actually defending the case on the merits. Hence, except for the special advantage built into the particular kind of appearance, such a defendant is subject to the usual procedural rules. He must, for example, submit to deposition taking and other pretrial proceedings.[12]

§ 115. Representation by Attorney

Adult natural persons may prosecute or defend an action in person, but a corporation and association may do so only through an attorney.[1] It has been held, however, that the assignee of a corporation may sue in person.[2] Infants and incapacitated persons—incompetents, conservatees, etc.[3]—can neither appear

---

5. CPLR 3025(b).

6. Alkalaj v. Alkalaj, 190 Misc. 326, 73 N.Y.S.2d 678, (Sup.Ct., N.Y. County, 1947).

7. 26 N.Y.2d 181, 309 N.Y.S.2d 184, 257 N.E.2d 637 (1970).

8. There is no indication in the report that Alaska had a longarm or like statute for extraterritorial jurisdiction. It would seem that if it had, the Alaskan judgment would have been entitled to full faith and credit because of the personal jurisdiction that would have resulted based on the apparent contacts Alaska had with the claim.

9. See CPLR 3215(g)(1).

10. See § 91 above.

11. See § 113 above.

12. See Gazerwitz v. Adrian, 28 A.D.2d 556, 280 N.Y.S.2d 233 (2d Dep't 1967).

§ 115

1. CPLR 321(a).

2. Kamp v. In Sportswear Inc., 39 A.D.2d 869, 332 N.Y.S.2d 983 (1st Dep't 1972), rev'g on dissenting opinion below, 70 Misc.2d 898, 335 N.Y.S.2d 306 (App.Term 1972).

3. The terminology of "incapacitated person" is used today in place of incompetent and conservatee, and "guardian" in place of committee and conservator. See § 69 above, paragraph (b).

for themselves nor hire lawyers. Appearance in their behalf must be made by persons authorized by CPLR 1201. The common practice is for the appropriate CPLR 1201 person to retain an attorney to act in behalf of the ward.

Exceptions apply in the Small Claims parts of the lower courts. A corporation can appear without a lawyer in the "commercial" Small Claims part of the New York City Civil Court and of the district and city courts,[4] and in the usual Small Claims part of those courts and of the town and village courts. In the usual (non-"commercial") part, the corporation is allowed only to defend (not prosecute) a small claim.[5]

An appearance by an attorney in purported behalf of a nondomiciliary, but without the latter's authority, confers no jurisdiction and any judgment based on it will be vacated on motion.[6] An unauthorized appearance in behalf of a New Yorker was upheld by the old case of Denton v. Noyes,[7] but the holding was roundly criticized[8] and appears to have been abandoned.[9] An unauthorized appearance even for a New York resident would thus seem to be void.

CPLR 321(b) authorizes a change of attorney by merely filing with the clerk a consent signed by the retiring attorney, and both signed and acknowledged by the party. Notice of the change must then be given to all other parties. Absent consent, the court can effect a change of attorneys upon motion,[10] the general rule being that a party can change attorneys at any time. If because of death or any other reason a party's attorney becomes unable to act before judgment, leave of court is needed before any further step may be taken against that party unless she is given at least 30 days notice to appoint a new attorney.[11]

What happens when a party purports to discharge his lawyer without following the authorized procedure, such as with a mere letter, and then by himself negotiates a settlement with the opposing party, who has a lawyer? The Second Department in Moustakas v. Bouloukos[12] allowed the party so doing to rescind the settlement. The Third Department, however, probably better reflecting the consensus on this point, disagreed and held that a party is bound by what he does on his own after deliberately discharging his lawyer and electing to proceed pro se.[13]

An interesting problem about representation sometimes arises in a case involving liability insurance. In Chemprene, Inc. v. X–Tyal International Corp.,[14] for example, P, through an attorney, sued D. D interposed a counterclaim against P. P carried insurance on the liability asserted in the counterclaim and was entitled to have the insurer defend it. Must P choose but a single lawyer to prosecute the main claim and defend on the counterclaim? Not necessarily, ruled the Court of Appeals, especially when there is a "possibility of diverse interests and a need for two attorneys". The matter is for the trial court to determine on the facts of the particular case, in its discretion. In *Chemprene*, the trial court did not require the plaintiff to choose and the Court of Appeals upheld the trial court.

---

4. See Article 18–A in the New York City Civil Court Act and in the Uniform District and City court acts, and the Commentaries on them in McKinney's Vol. 29A, Part 3. Article 18–A took effect in the district and city courts on January 1, 1989; its effective date in the civil court was January 1, 1991.

5. See § 1809(2) in the three acts cited above and in the Uniform Justice Court Act (McKinney's Vol. 29A, Part 2). A 1987 amendment (eff. January 1, 1988) adding § 501 to the Uniform Justice Court Act appears to permit a corporation to appear in town and village courts without a lawyer in any category of action, not just a small claim. See the Commentary on McKinney's UJCA § 501.

6. Vilas v. Plattsburgh & M. R. Co., 123 N.Y. 440, 25 N.E. 941 (1890).

7. 6 Johns. 296 (N.Y.1810).

8. See, e.g., Note, Unauthorized Appearance, 25 St. John's L.Rev. 325 (1951).

9. The Third Department held in Wickham v. Liberty Mut. Ins. Co., 73 A.D.2d 742, 423 N.Y.S.2d 273 (3d Dep't 1979), that Denton and like cases "have no present-day validity". The Second Department agreed in Skyline Agency, Inc. v. Ambrose Coppotelli, Inc., 117 A.D.2d 135, 502 N.Y.S.2d 479 (1986).

10. The motion is usually brought on by order to show cause. See CPLR 321(b)(2).

11. CPLR 321(c).

12. 112 A.D.2d 981, 492 N.Y.S.2d 793 (1985).

13. Imor v. Imor, 119 A.D.2d 913, 501 N.Y.S.2d 195 (1986).

14. 55 N.Y.2d 900, 449 N.Y.S.2d 23, 433 N.E.2d 1271 (1982).

When an attorney is discharged, or a substitution is made, an issue often arises about whether, and on what, the attorney may have a lien. A distinction must be made between a "retaining" lien, which attaches to any papers or property of the client in the lawyer's possession, and a "charging" lien, which applies only to the proceeds of a given action.[15]

15. See Justice Lazer's instructive discourse in Kaplan v. Reuss, 113 A.D.2d 184, 495 N.Y.S.2d 404 (2d Dep't 1985), which is the subject of the lead note in New York State Law Digest No. 318.

Chapter Six

VENUE

Analysis

A. INTRODUCTORY

Table of Sections

§ 116. Venue, Generally

Venue means the geographical subdivision in which an action may be brought. The supreme court, for example, has statewide jurisdiction, but the suit can't be brought anywhere merely at the plaintiff's whim. For venue purposes, the supreme court is subdivided into counties, and the venue rules of Article 5 of the CPLR determine which of the counties is proper for the particular supreme court action.

There is little occasion to apply Article 5, and especially § 503 (the main venue-choosing provision of the CPLR), in any other but the supreme court. Venue rules are needed only for courts with territorial subdivisions. The county courts, for example, have none. Each is an independent entity in the particular county and whether or not to sue in a county court is

a question of jurisdiction, not venue. The venue-fixing provisions of Article 5 therefore do not apply in the county courts. Nor do they apply in the lower courts. Like the county court, each of the city, town, and village courts is independent in its municipality and therefore needs no "venue" provisions as such.[1] The New York City Civil Court and the district courts in Nassau and Suffolk counties, on the other hand, do have subdivisions—the civil court consists of the five New York City counties and the district courts of districts into which the county is divided—but they have their own venue provisions[2] and are thus not governed by the venue-laying provisions of the CPLR.[3]

Venue presupposes that the court already has both subject matter and personal jurisdiction, because an absence of either would produce a jurisdictional dismissal and make a venue question academic. Venue even assumes that there is no forum non conveniens objection in the case, because that, too, would be a dismissal ground. A mere defect of venue, on the other hand, is not a dismissal ground in

§ 116

1. A provision analogous to a venue provision applies in the city courts (UCCA § 213) and in the town and village courts (UJCA § 213). It keeps out of those courts cases that don't belong there for want of municipal contacts. See the Commentaries on those provisions in McKinney's Vol.29A, Parts 2 and 3.

2. Article 3 in each of the New York City Civil (CCA) and Uniform District (UDCA) court acts, McKinney's Vol. 29A, Part 3, supplies the venue rules in those courts.

3. The family court, established in each county of the state, also comes in for occasional treatment as a "statewide" court so as to permit the transfer of a case from one county to another. See Prospero v. Prospero, 39 A.D.2d 634, 331 N.Y.S.2d 318 (4th Dep't 1972).

New York practice.[4]

This is in contrast with federal practice. If suit in a U.S. district court is brought in the wrong district, a federal statute permits dismissal.[5] If suit in the New York supreme court is brought in the wrong county, the New York statute precludes dismissal; the court is required to entertain the case unless the venue is changed to a proper county on motion.[6] Curiously, just the reverse occurs between the two court systems on a forum non conveniens objection. Successful application of the conveniens doctrine in New York dismisses the action,[7] while in the federal courts it usually results in a mere transfer to the more convenient district.[8]

A judgment is valid even though rendered by the supreme court in an improper county of venue. Hence the worst that can happen to an improperly venued supreme court action is a change of venue to a proper county.[9]

It is also true of supreme court practice that as long as the case can get by jurisdictional and conveniens objections, there will always be some proper county of venue.[10]

When specific real or personal property is involved in the action, venue can be based on the situs of the property. If it is, the action is called a "local" one for venue purposes.[11] All other actions qualify as "transitory" (the popular but unofficial term), and these, which include the ordinary money actions, are by far the more numerous. In the transitory action, venue is keyed to residence.[12] If there are multiple parties and claims, or even an ordinary P v. D suit with several claims, venue

proper as to any one of the claims satisfies for the whole action, including the claims that would have demanded different venue if sued on alone.[13]

Venue is measured by the plaintiff's claim; it is not ordinarily affected by a counterclaim.[14] The defendant who interposes a counterclaim therefore submits it to the venue the plaintiff has selected.

A change of venue requires a motion. That the change cannot be made by the court sua sponte is an old rule,[15] generally still followed,[16] but under more modern administrative standards the notion may have to give way. Else a given county could, by simple agreement among opposing lawyers, become unduly burdened with cases not locally germane. The court does have the power to change venue, although not specifically requested to do so, in conjunction with a motion to consolidate under CPLR 602[17] or a motion under CPLR 3211(a)(4) to dismiss an action because of a duplicative action already pending elsewhere.

§ 117. Agreement to Fix Venue

CPLR 501 permits the parties to fix venue by contract. They can even choose a county that would not otherwise be proper under CPLR Article 5. It is said that it is "mandatory" to uphold the contract choice,[1] but there is also authority that the agreement need not be upheld if "public policy" is violated, as where the county selected is the residence of neither party nor otherwise connected with the subject

---

4. Compare CPLR 513, applicable in a consumer credit transaction (as defined in CPLR 105). It requires the clerk to refuse to file the summons if it appears on its face that the venue is improper.

5. 28 U.S.C.A. § 1406(a). See § 617 (Practitioner's Edition).

6. CPLR 509.

7. See § 28 above.

8. 28 U.S.C.A. § 1404(a). See § 618 (Practitioner's Edition).

9. Benson v. Eastern Bldg. & Loan Assn., 174 N.Y. 83, 66 N.E. 627 (1903).

10. CPLR 503(a), 502.

11. CPLR 507, 508, treated in § 121, below.

12. CPLR 503, treated in § 118, below.

13. CPLR 502.

14. Taconic Inn Corp. v. Holsapple, 188 Misc. 322, 65 N.Y.S.2d 262 (Sup.Ct., N.Y.County, 1946).

15. CPLR 509. See Phillips v. Tietjen, 108 A.D. 9, 95 N.Y.S. 469 (2d Dep't 1905).

16. See Kelson v. Nedicks Stores, Inc., 104 A.D.2d 315, 478 N.Y.S.2d 648 (1st Dep't 1984).

17. Smith v. Witteman Co., 10 A.D.2d 793, 197 N.Y.S.2d 877 (4th Dep't 1960).

§ 117

1. Harvey v. Colonial Home Improvement Co., 57 Misc.2d 196, 291 N.Y.S.2d 755 (Sup.Ct., Oneida County, 1965).

of the suit.[2] Another court held that the contract choice can't be said to violate public policy because statute expressly authorizes it, but the parties in that case chose a county without a heavy calendar.[3] If the parties opt for an unrelated county that does have a substantial backlog, the public policy argument surely offers a distinction. The problem is whether the distinction can make a difference in the face of a statute as unambiguous as CPLR 501.[4]

The only ground expressly recognized by CPLR 501 for rejecting a contract-selected venue is a finding that an impartial trial can't be had in the selected county. When the ground is merely that the convenience of witnesses will be better served elsewhere, there is a dispute about whether the agreement can be overridden.[5]

As with any case of improper venue, the remedy when an action is brought in other than the county agreed on is a change of venue to the stipulated county, not a dismissal.[6]

B. VENUE IN PARTICULAR ACTIONS

Table of Sections

§ 118. Venue in Transitory Actions

Section 503 is the main venue-setting provision of the CPLR. It is captioned "venue based on residence". The word "transitory" is popularly used to describe an action in which venue is keyed to residence. The majority of actions, including money actions, are in this "transitory" category.

The general New York rule is that the plaintiff may bring the action in any county in which any one of the parties, on the plaintiff's or on the defendant's side, resides. The choice is the plaintiff's, at least initially. The plaintiff makes the choice based on a number of considerations, including calendar congestion, convenience of witnesses, convenience to the plaintiff and his attorney, and, alas, inconvenience to the defendant. The plaintiff more often than not chooses to sue at home.

In recent years Bronx County has become such a favored venue of plaintiffs with personal injury claims that some plaintiffs' attorneys have had their clients move to the Bronx—or purport to—in situations in which the Bronx had nothing to do with the case and would otherwise not qualify as proper venue. In several reported cases the ploy didn't work.[1]

If no party is a resident—which assumes that the case has managed to get by a forum non conveniens objection—the plaintiff may bring the action in any county she wishes. It is this aspect of CPLR 503(a) that establishes that no action in the supreme court will ever want for proper venue.

In determining where "residence" is, the moment of commencement of the action is looked to under CPLR 503(a), which also acknowledges that a party can have more than one residence. If the party has several, any of

2. See Syracuse Plaster Co. v. Agostini Bros. Bldg. Corp., 169 Misc. 564, 7 N.Y.S.2d 897 (Sup.Ct., Onondaga County, 1938).

3. Callanan Indus. Inc. v. Sovereign Const. Co., 44 A.D.2d 292, 354 N.Y.S.2d 486 (3d Dep't 1974).

4. By analogy, motion (as opposed to action) venue laid in a busy urban county has been rejected even when it was a permissible choice under the applicable rules. See the discussion of the Cordero case in § 245.

5. Gardner & North Roofing and Siding Corp. v. Demko, 82 Misc.2d 922, 370 N.Y.S.2d 294 (Sup.Ct., Oneida County, 1974), holds that it can't be. Kenron Awning & Window Corp. v. Abbott, 43 Misc.2d 552, 251 N.Y.S.2d 593

(Sup.Ct. Onondaga County, 1964), holds that it can. The "convenience" ground is one of the discretionary ones treated in § 124, below.

6. See Graziano v. Indem. Ins. Co. 1 N.Y.2d 817, 153 N.Y.S.2d 74, 135 N.E.2d 604 (1956), aff'g 286 A.D. 867, 142 N.Y.S.2d 44 (2d Dep't 1955).

§ 118

1. See Koschak v. Gates Constr. Corp., 225 A.D.2d 315, 639 N.Y.S.2d 10 (1st Dep't 1996), and Brown v. Doxsee Sea Clam Co., Sup.Ct., Bronx County, Nov. 12, 1997 (Index No. 18388/92, Salman, J.). See the "Ode to the Bronx" in SPR 47:4 and its reprise in SPR 67:4.

them is proper venue, thus expanding the plaintiff's choices.

While multiple residences are permissible, a party can as a rule have only one "domicile". Domicile is the place a person calls home, however many residences she may maintain. "Residence" as used in the venue provisions means just that, not domicile.[2] This is in contrast to the statutes governing matrimonial actions, where "residence" is usually construed to mean domicile.[3]

Although residence does not require the continuity that domicile does, it still requires "more stability than occasional stopovers at a hotel". Even when P maintained a year-round room at the hotel, a showing that his presence there was sporadic and only business-connected prevented it from qualifying as a residence for venue purposes.[4] But if the party, while residing most of the year in County X, regularly maintains a residence in County Y even if only for vacation purposes, there is indication that County Y can also serve as proper venue.[5]

A trailer to which the party regularly returns, blocked up on a rented site, is a residence.[6] So is the place of a party's prolonged hospitalization, at least when the party evinces an intention to remain there.[7]

The assignee of a claim cannot, in a transitory action, sue in his own county unless it is also the assignor's or some other party's.[8] This prevents an assignment from securing venue advantages. Assignees for the benefit of creditors and the holders of negotiable instruments

are exempted from this limitation and can sue at home.

Fiduciaries who sue and are sued in their own name are deemed residents of the county of their appointment as well as of the county where they actually reside, thus expanding venue choices in cases involving them.[9] These fiduciaries are the executor, administrator, trustee, committee, conservator, guardian,[10] and receiver. The theory of this provision is that the fiduciary, rather than the estate or person represented, is the proper party to the litigation.

§ 119.   Venue for Corporations and Other Private Creatures

The domestic and licensed foreign corporation is deemed a resident for venue purposes. Its residence is the county in which its certificate, as filed with the secretary of state, officially lists its office: that county has been held to be the "principal office" of the corporation under CPLR 503(c) regardless of where the actual "principal" office may be.[1] An unlicensed foreign corporation is not a resident, with the result that suit by or against it must be brought in some other party's county. A derivative action may be brought in the residence county of one of the shareholder plaintiffs,[2] even though the action is brought in the right of the corporation.

In addition to the usual venue choices, suit by or against a common carrier, such as a railroad, may be brought alternatively in the county where the claim arose.

---

2. For treatment of the differences between domicile and residence, see Matter of Newcomb, 192 N.Y. 238, 84 N.E. 950 (1908).

3. See, e.g., Usher v. Usher, 41 A.D.2d 368, 343 N.Y.S.2d 212 (3d Dep't 1973).

4. Hammerman v. Louis Watch Co., 7 A.D.2d 817, 818, 181 N.Y.S.2d 65, 67 (3d Dep't 1958). If that county were the party's principal business office, it would today qualify as proper venue. See § 119 below.

5. See Fromkin v. Loehmann's Hewlett, Inc., 16 Misc.2d 117, 184 N.Y.S.2d 63 (Sup.Ct., Queens County, 1959).

6. Vrooman v. Vrooman, 183 Misc. 233, 50 N.Y.S.2d 694 (Sup.Ct., Otsego County, 1944).

7. Bradley v. Plaisted, 277 A.D. 620, 102 N.Y.S.2d 295 (3d Dep't 1951).

8. CPLR 503(e).

9. CPLR 503(b).

10. The guardian meant here is a general or testamentary guardian. Not included is the mere guardian ad litem—who is appointed solely for the purpose of a particular litigation, see § 196, below—whose residence county is irrelevant.

§ 119

1. General Precision, Inc. v. Ametek, Inc., 24 A.D.2d 757, 263 N.Y.S.2d 470 (2d Dep't 1965).

2. Feldmeier, v. Webster, 208 Misc. 996, 145 N.Y.S.2d 365 (Sup.Ct., Onondaga County, 1955), aff'd 1 A.D.2d 938, 150 N.Y.S.2d 581 (4th Dep't 1956).

If the corporation is of a kind not required to designate an office in its filed papers, it may be deemed a resident of the county in which it actually maintains an office.[3]

It has been seen that the unincorporated association may sue or be sued through its president or treasurer.[4] The residence of that person—whichever one is suing or being sued in the particular case—is a proper venue, but the suit may be brought alternatively in the county of the association's principal office.[5]

Similarly with a partnership, as plaintiff or defendant. The partnership's principal office is a proper residence for venue. So is the actual residence of the partner "suing or being sued"—language of CPLR 503(d) that has been construed to permit venue in the partner's residence county "only where that partner is himself a plaintiff or defendant".[6] So, if a given partner's own county is to be made the venue, he should be named as a party in the summons along with the partnership in its own name and should be individually served with process.[7]

CPLR 503(d) also treats an "individually-owned business" as a partnership for this purpose. The effect is to add as a permissible venue the county of the individual's principal office, but only as to claims arising out of the business.[8] A professional like a doctor or lawyer is deemed an individually owned business under this provision, because "when we offer our services to the public, we are engaged in a business".[9]

In all of these situations, the "principal office" county is just an alternative. The cases are essentially transitory ones in which venue may of course be based on the residence of any of the natural-person parties.

§ 120. Venue for Governmental Entities

An action against a county must be brought in that county,[1] and one against a city, town, village, school district, or district corporation must be brought in the county of the defendant's location.[2] An action against the City of New York is brought in the county where the claim arose, or in New York County (Manhattan) if the claim did not arise in the city.[3] These venue requirements supersede anything to the contrary contained in the particular unit's charter, thus assuring the practitioner proper venue by reference to the CPLR alone, but they apply only when the unit is a defendant. When the unit is the plaintiff, the usual venue rules apply and the case may be brought in the defendant's or in the plaintiff's county. If one of these units sues another, such as city against city, CPLR 504 should apply and limit suit to the defendant's county.

Venue in an action involving a public authority is where its principal office is "or where it has facilities involved in the action". This is the governing rule whether the authority is a plaintiff or defendant.[4]

All of these rules apply to plenary actions involving these governmental entities and should not be confused with a special proceeding, such as the Article 78 proceeding brought against a governmental agency or unit. The special proceeding has a special venue provision.[5]

---

3. See General Acc. Fire & Life Assur. Corp. v. Allcity Ins. Co., 53 Misc.2d 596, 279 N.Y.S.2d 422 (Sup.Ct., Nassau County, 1967).

4. See § 69, paragraph d, above.

5. If the particular unincorporated creature has filed a certificate with a state office, which an association may do, see Gen.Ass'n.L. § 18, the office listed in that paper should, by analogy to the Ametek case on corporations (note 1, above), be deemed its residence. Otherwise the office that qualifies as the "principal" one will have to be decided as an issue of fact.

6. Bensaull v. Fanwood Estates, 128 Misc.2d 110, 488 N.Y.S.2d 944 (Sup.Ct., N.Y. County, 1984).

7. See § 69, paragraph c, above.

8. Friedman v. Law, 60 A.D.2d 832, 400 N.Y.S.2d 562 (2d Dep't 1978).

9. Harrington v. Cramer, 129 Misc.2d 489, 493 N.Y.S.2d 390 (Sup.Ct., N.Y. County, 1985).

§ 120

1. CPLR 504(1).

2. CPLR 504(2). This also applies to actions against the "officers, boards or departments" of these governmental units.

3. CPLR 504(3). The New York City Transit Authority is treated the same way for venue purposes. CPLR 505(b).

4. CPLR 505(a).

5. CPLR 506(b), treatment of which is deferred to § 565, below, in the chapter on special proceedings.

It has been held that a municipality may be impleaded into an action pending in a county other than the one in which an original suit against the municipality would have to be brought; that the best the municipality can do in a case like that is seek a change of venue back to its own county, and whether to do that lies in the court's discretion.[6]

§ 121. Venue in Local Actions

While most actions are of the "transitory" kind in which venue is based on residence, the action that "would affect the title to, or the possession, use or enjoyment of, real property" qualifies as a local action and must be brought in the county of the realty.[1] It is not sufficient that the action merely involves realty; it must be shown to "affect" it in some way before coming under this venue provision. It has been held, for example, that an action to recover commissions on the sale of realty does not "affect" it, however much it may involve it, and is not a local action.[2] The courts have not been consistent here. A mere trespass action, for example, which may involve the realty but does not really "affect" it, has been held, albeit reluctantly, a local one.[3]

An action to rescind a land sale contract is a local one whether the contract is executory or already executed.[4] Some old caselaw had distinguished the two situations by holding only the case of the executed contract to be a local one.[5]

While there is as yet no definitive appellate ruling on venue in cases involving a cooperative apartment, there is caselaw at trial level analyzing the purpose of having a realty action deemed local—the purpose is the centralization and certainty of realty records—and concluding that an action for the specific perfor-

mance of a contract to sell cooperative shares is not a local action and need not be brought in the cooperative's county.[6]

The action to recover a chattel may be treated as either local, and brought where the chattel is, or as transitory, with venue based on residence.[7] (The realty action is not allowed the option of being treated as transitory.)

§ 122. Special Venue Requirements in Consumer Credit Cases

To remedy certain abuses in a "consumer credit transaction", CPLR 503(f) requires that the action be brought in the defendant's (the consumer's) county or in the county where the transaction occurred. The net result of this is to preclude the plaintiff from suing in its own county unless it also happens to satisfy as the defendant's or the transaction's. If the defendant is a nonresident and the transaction occurred outside New York, the usual residence options of CPLR 503(a) apply.

The "consumer credit transaction" (CCT) is defined by CPLR 105 as one "wherein credit is extended to an individual and the money, property or service which is the subject of the transaction is primarily for personal, family or household purposes". Whether the transaction qualifies as a CCT in a given case is obviously a question of fact. The plaintiff who would avoid trouble had best give the defendant the benefit of the doubt, treat the transaction as a CCT, and sue where the defendant resides or the transaction took place.

The summons must state the basis of venue in all New York actions, and must identify the case as a CCT if it is one.[1] In a CCT the clerk is required to reject (refuse to file) a summons which "upon its face" shows that venue has

6. Holmes v. Greenlife Landscaping, Inc., 171 A.D.2d 916, 567 N.Y.S.2d 193 (3d Dep't 1991).

§ 121

1. CPLR 507.

2. McNamara Realty v. Hutchinson, 54 Misc.2d 810, 283 N.Y.S.2d 422 (Sup.Ct., Albany County, 1967).

3. Geidel v. Niagara Mohawk Power Corp., 46 Misc.2d 990, 261 N.Y.S.2d 379 (Sup.Ct., Nassau County, 1965).

4. Merrill Realty Co. v. Harris, 44 A.D.2d 629, 353 N.Y.S.2d 570 (3d Dep't 1974).

5. See Birmingham v. Squires, 139 A.D. 129, 123 N.Y.S. 906 (1st Dep't 1910).

6. Suddin v. Lynbrook Gardens Co., 127 Misc.2d 406, 486 N.Y.S.2d 155 (Sup.Ct., N.Y. County, 1985).

7. CPLR 508.

§ 122

1. CPLR 305(a).

been laid in the wrong county.[2] A clerk rejecting the summons must so indicate on it and name the counties that would be proper.[3] The plaintiff must then file the summons in a proper county along with proof of its service on the defendant and further proof that the defendant has additionally been served—in this instance by registered or certified mail—with a notice telling the defendant what occurred and about her extended answering time. In this situation the defendant's answering time does not begin to run until 10 days after the summons is filed in the proper county.[4]

C. CHANGE OF VENUE

Table of Sections

§ 123. Change of Venue from Improper to Proper County; "Demand" Procedure

When D contends that P has laid venue in an improper county and D seeks to change it to a proper county as a matter of right, D must follow the special "demand" procedure of CPLR 511(b).

With or before the answer,[1] D must serve on P a written demand that venue be changed to the county D specifies as proper.[2] Within five days after service of the demand, P must do one of two things:

1. serve on D a written consent agreeing to the change; or

2. serve on D an affidavit showing either that the county chosen by P is proper or that the one to which D seeks transfer is not.

If P takes step 1, the consent is filed pursuant to CPLR 511(d) and the change D wants is effected. If P takes step 2, it is now incumbent on D to move to change the venue, the court to decide whether the change is in order. If P takes neither step within the five days, D is allowed to make the motion in the county to which she seeks transfer.[3] This can be a tactical advantage. But it is the only advantage conferred by P's failure to respond within the five days. P's failure does not automatically entitle D to the venue change; it merely gives D a broader option on where to move for it. Nor does P, by omitting to respond, forfeit the right to resist the motion. Wherever D moves, P may still oppose the motion and show that his chosen county is proper (or that D's is not).[4]

P's affidavit (responding to the demand) must at least purport to justify P's choice or negate D's. An affidavit that purports to do neither has been deemed no affidavit at all, thus permitting D to move in the proposed transferee county.[5]

If P has several choices (such as counties X and Y) available, but lays venue in an improper county (Z), P's right of first choice will be forfeited to D. So if P, opposing D's motion, urges that the change be to X, while D wants Y, Y will be the county to which the venue is ordered changed.[6] The point is that P may lose

---

2. CPLR 513(a).

3. CPLR 513(b).

4. CPLR 513(c). Here there is indication that the statute was drafted for lower court rather than supreme court practice. It speaks of the time within which an answer is to be "filed", there being no such requirement in supreme court practice (the requirement is that the answer merely be served on the plaintiff's lawyer). The drafters apparently had in mind § 902(a)(2) of (e.g.) the New York City Civil Court Act, in which the defendant answers to the clerk rather than to the plaintiff's lawyer directly.

§ 123

1. CPLR 511(a).

2. D may apply under CPLR 2004 to extend the time to make the demand. Levkovich v. Vivian Hotel Corp., 27 A.D.2d 754, 279 N.Y.S.2d 1018 (2d Dep't 1967).

3. This means that D may make the motion either in the county in which P has laid venue or in the proposed transferee county, and it may even include a variety of other venue options under CPLR 2212(a), depending on local rules adopted under CPLR 2212(d). See § 245 below.

4. McDermott v. McDermott, 267 A.D. 171, 45 N.Y.S.2d 321 (1st Dep't 1943).

5. Payne v. Civil Serv. Employees Ass'n, 15 A.D.2d 265, 222 N.Y.S.2d 725 (3d Dep't 1961).

6. Kelson v. Nedicks Stores, Inc., 104 A.D.2d 315, 478 N.Y.S.2d 648 (1st Dep't 1984).

first choice to D by laying venue in an altogether improper county.

If D has followed the demand procedure and P has served an appropriate affidavit within the allotted five days, D must move for the venue change within 15 days from the time she served the demand. Since five of those days have already expired awaiting P's response, D must move promptly for the change. If the motion is made within the 15 days, and it establishes that P's county is improper while the one D wants is proper, D generally gets the change as a matter of right—unless the court directs that the action be retained where it is or transferred to yet another county on one of the discretionary change of venue grounds, such as the convenience of witnesses,[7] discussed in the next section.

If D does not so move within the 15 days, she is no longer entitled to a change of venue as of right. She may still make the motion, however, any time before trial, but because of its tardiness it now becomes one for the court to grant or deny in its discretion. If there is strong reason to prefer the proper county, such as where realty records are involved in what qualifies as a local action, the court's discretion is likely to favor the change, tardy as the motion may be.[8]

The demand procedure for a change of venue from an improper to the proper county may also be invoked by a third-party defendant, who should serve the demand for the change with its answer.[9]

§ 124. Discretionary Grounds for Change of Venue

CPLR 510, in addition to authorizing a change of venue from an improper to a proper county,[1] offers two other grounds for a change of venue: (1) that there is reason to believe that an impartial trial can't be had in a proper county[2] or (2) that the convenience of material witnesses and the ends of justice will be promoted by a change.[3]

These discretionary grounds can be applied even though the venue selected by the plaintiff is proper, and can even bring about a change to a county that would not be a proper one under the initial venue-fixing rules.

The demand procedure set up by CPLR 511(b) for the change from an improper to a proper county has no application to a change of venue sought on these discretionary grounds.[4] Here the change is sought by direct motion made "within a reasonable time after commencement".[5] What's "reasonable" is of course sui generis. Five months has been held reasonable when no prejudice traceable to the delay could be shown.[6]

Since change on a discretionary ground does not follow the demand procedure, the motion for such a change may not be made in the proposed transferee county. Nor will the court in that county, if the motion to change venue is made there on the improper-to-proper ground, entertain any of the discretionary grounds should the movant try to throw them in for good measure.[7]

The defendant is not the only one permitted to move for a venue change on these discretionary grounds. The plaintiff can,[8] and so can a third-party defendant.[9]

The impartial trial ground does not appear often. An example of it was an action by a Kings County judge who in his own court sued a doctor for malpractice. The case was trans-

---

7. Windhurst v. Town of Thompson, 78 A.D.2d 930, 433 N.Y.S.2d 516 (3d Dep't 1980).

8. Reichenbach v. Corn Exch. Bank Trust Co., 249 A.D. 539, 292 N.Y.S. 732 (1st Dep't 1937).

9. See Kearns v. Johnson, 238 A.D.2d 121, 655 N.Y.S.2d 498 (1st Dep't 1997), noted in SPR 57:3.

§ 124

1. CPLR 510(1).

2. CPLR 510(2).

3. CPLR 510(3).

4. Baker v. Julius Pollak & Sons, 277 A.D. 11, 97 N.Y.S.2d 694 (1st Dep't 1950).

5. CPLR 511(a).

6. Ryan v. Great A. & P. Tea Co., 30 A.D.2d 549, 290 N.Y.S.2d 849 (2d Dep't 1968).

7. See Nevelson v. Piesner, 272 A.D. 555, 74 N.Y.S.2d 105 (4th Dep't 1947).

8. Kenford Co. v. Erie County, 38 A.D.2d 781, 328 N.Y.S.2d 69 (4th Dep't 1972).

9. Champlain Creameries v. Hovey, Stanter & Co., 141 N.Y.S.2d 271 (Sup.Ct., N.Y.County, 1955).

ferred to another county to avoid the "unconscious bias" of his colleagues.[10] In a similar case in which the surrogate of a county brought a private law suit in the supreme court of that county, the defendant's motion to change venue was denied because the court found nothing to suggest that there could not be an impartial trial.[11] A change of venue is probably advisable in all such cases, even from the point of view of the party—the judge, in these examples—who is presumably the beneficiary of "unconscious bias": he can find himself the victim, instead, when his colleagues bend over backward to avoid even the appearance of prejudice.

Juror prejudice is more sensitive still. When a power company brought suit locally to recover some $62,000,000 of alleged over-charges from a fuel company—costs that are of course passed along to the consumer—the action was transferred out of the county whose consumers were directly affected.[12]

Perhaps the most frequent ground for a change of venue is the convenience of witnesses. The witnesses whose convenience counts here are the "material" ones: those who can testify to the facts of the occurrence or transaction involved in the case. And the convenience of witnesses testifying on issues of liability is "entitled to greater weight" than that of witnesses testifying only on damages.[13]

Expert witnesses will not ordinarily be considered, but this applies only to those who are to be called solely for opinion. If they can testify to material facts, their convenience is a factor.[14]

A witness who is employed by a party or otherwise under the party's control carries little weight on a change of venue scale.[15]

Indeed, the general rule is that the convenience of the parties and their employees is not to be considered on the motion.[16]

P's choice of forum will not be disturbed unless there is a clear balance in favor of D's witnesses.[17] It has also been held that where, on a change of venue motion, the convenience of witnesses is fairly evenly balanced between sides, a "transitory action should be tried in the county where the cause of action arose."[18]

The motion for a change of venue based on the convenience of witnesses requires a detailed affidavit from the moving party setting forth "what he expects to prove by the alleged witnesses, and that he cannot safely proceed to trial without the testimony of such witnesses, as he is advised by his counsel".[19] Even more ideal, although not essential, are affidavits secured from the potential witnesses themselves.

§ 125. Effecting the Change of Venue

If a change of venue is ordered, or if P has served on D a written consent to the change under the demand procedure, CPLR 511(d) directs that the order be entered, or the consent filed, with the clerk in the original county. The latter is then required to deliver all papers in the action, including certified copies of any minutes that may already have been taken, to the clerk of the transferee court. That clerk must now make them part of her records as if the case had originally been brought there. Subsequent proceedings then follow on the same assumption, unless otherwise directed by the court. To avoid confusion as to where an appeal may be taken from the order granting the change, it is specifically required that it be in the department in which

10. Arkwright v. Steinbugler, 283 A.D. 397, 128 N.Y.S.2d 823 (2d Dep't 1954).

11. Midonick v. Peppertree Hill Dev. Corp., 49 A.D.2d 721, 373 N.Y.S.2d 2 (1st Dep't 1975).

12. Long Island Lighting Co. v. New England Petroleum Corp., 80 Misc.2d 183, 362 N.Y.S.2d 350 (Sup.Ct., Queens County, 1974).

13. Katz v. Goodyear Tire and Rubber Co., 116 A.D.2d 506, 497 N.Y.S.2d 376 (1st Dep't 1986).

14. See Delair v. T. Southworth Tractor & Machine Co., 142 N.Y.S.2d 449 (Sup.Ct., Franklin County, 1955).

15. Hoffman v. Boston & Maine R.R., 259 A.D. 958, 20 N.Y.S.2d 460 (3d Dep't 1940).

16. Katz v. Goodyear Tire and Rubber Co., note 13, above.

17. Cf. Marzello v. Kiamesha Concord, Inc., 26 A.D.2d 986, 274 N.Y.S.2d 1002 (3d Dep't 1966).

18. Katz v. Goodyear Tire and Rubber Co., note 13, above; Strosberg v. Kiamesha Concord, Inc., 26 A.D.2d 723, 271 N.Y.S.2d 767, 769 (3d Dep't 1966).

19. Dairymen's League Co-op. Ass'n v. Brundo, 131 Misc. 548, 549, 227 N.Y.S. 203, 206 (Sup.Ct., Oneida County, 1927).

the motion for the change was made and decided.

If a stay of proceedings has been applied for in conjunction with the change, the court is precluded from granting the stay "unless it appears from the papers that the change is sought with due diligence".[1] The lesson to a defendant who wants the proceedings suspended while the change is sought is to seek a stay promptly.

§ 125

1. CPLR 511(c).

Chapter Seven

PARTIES

Analysis

A. JOINDER OF CLAIMS AND ACTIONS

Table of Sections

Sec.
126. Joinder of Claims.
127. Consolidation, Joint Trial, Severance, and Separate Trial, Defined.
128. Consolidation and Joint Trial.
129. Severance and Separate Trial.
130. Bifurcated Trial.

§ 126. Joinder of Claims

A plaintiff may join in a single action as many claims as the plaintiff has against the defendant, whether the claims are related or not.[1] The idea is to get everything over with at once. If the claims are totally unrelated and would confuse a jury, or unduly influence it in some way, the remedy is a severance.[2] Even that can be avoided. The court can, in its discretion, have each claim tried to the same jury, consecutively but separately, thus enabling the claims to remain in one action and sparing the court's calendar an additional case, which is what a severance produces.[3]

This liberal permission to interpose any claims at all includes a defendant putting in counterclaims or cross-claims, as long as all those initially made parties have been made so in satisfaction of the joinder-of-parties rules. The generosity of CPLR 601(a), allowing the interposition of any claims at all "when there are multiple parties", assumes that those parties are in the suit on the authority of one of the provisions of Article 10 of the CPLR. If, for example, A and B are both injured in the same accident, they may join as plaintiffs in a single action against D for their respective injuries. CPLR 1002(a), the statute on permissive joinder of parties, allows this.[4] A and B, as legiti-

---

§ 126

1. CPLR 601(a).

2. See Sporn v. Hudson Transit Lines, 265 A.D. 360, 38 N.Y.S.2d 512 (1st Dep't 1942). Severance is treated in § 129 below.

3. See § 129, below, on severance and separate trial.

4. Permissive joinder is treated in § 134 below.

mate co-parties under that provision, may now exploit the join-any-claim permission of CPLR 601(a). That would permit A, for example, to add against D yet another claim not arising out of the accident and not having any link at all with B.

§ 127. Consolidation, Joint Trial, Severance, and Separate Trial, Defined

These four items make up a kind of set determining when actions may be merged or separated. They need some definition before being treated individually.

Consolidation and severance are diametrical opposites. Consolidation takes two or more actions and fuses them into one; severance takes one action and separates it into two or more.

Joint trial and consolidation are much the same in accomplishment, but differ in mechanics. Joint trial, like consolidation, puts two or more actions together, but with joint trial the actions maintain their separate identities. With consolidation, there is a total fusion of the actions. They take on one caption and culminate in one judgment—which pronounces on the rights of all parties involved—and in but a single bill of costs. With joint trial, the actions keep their separate captions and go to separate verdicts, although perhaps delivered by the jury at the same time, and to separate judgments and bills of costs. Consolidation fuses them organically, while joint trial, available by the same criteria as consolidation under CPLR 602, offers the same advantages without the additional paper work that consolidation entails.[1]

If one party would find herself on both sides of the versus sign if the cases were merged, then joint trial is probably preferable to consolidation just to avoid confusing the jury.[2] It should be preferable for other reasons as well. Since joint trial usually secures the same advantages as consolidation without the latter's drawbacks, the thoughtful attorney ought to prefer it more often than the older caselaw indicates. The reason that consolidation has been sought more often than mere joint trial may be the bar's unawareness of the difference.[3]

Whether the one or the other prevails in a given case, the pair is favored by the courts, rising even to the level of "public policy". This can be seen when a contract presumes to bar consolidation or joint trial of designated claims. While there is no absolute prohibition against such a contract provision, it will be scanned closely to see if it treads unduly on the court's prerogative and will be disregarded if it does. Disregarding it in a lease case, the court stressed that the device can even be invoked by the court sua sponte.[4]

The relationship between severance and separate trials is analogous to that between consolidation and joint trials. While the severance cleaves the action in two and sends each claim off as a distinct case for all purposes (separate judgments, etc.), the separate trial can often accomplish the same thing without the cleavage. Two unrelated claims in a single action, for example, need not be severed to avoid jury confusion. The court can merely have one tried first, right through to a verdict, before the second is touched. This is all in the court's discretion. Severance is not a favored device today because of the additional burden it imposes on judicial calendars—one action becomes two. The separate trial is usually a satisfactory alternative.

Consolidation and joint trial are authorized by CPLR 602, while severance and separate trials are governed by CPLR 603. Individual treatment of them follows.

§ 128. Consolidation and Joint Trial

When two or more actions are pending before a court and they involve "a common ques-

---

§ 127

1. See Vidal v. Sheffield Farms Co., 208 Misc. 438, 141 N.Y.S.2d 82 (Sup.Ct., Bronx County, 1955).

2. See Padilla v. Greyhound Lines, Inc., 29 A.D.2d 495, 288 N.Y.S.2d 641 (1st Dep't 1968).

3. Id.

4. Ultrashmere House, Ltd. v. 38 Town Assocs., 123 Misc.2d 102, 473 N.Y.S.2d 120 (Sup.Ct., N.Y. County, 1984).

tion of law or fact", CPLR 602(a) permits the court, on motion, to consolidate them or order them jointly tried. If they are pending in different divisions of the court, such as where they are both in the supreme court but in different counties, the order would also have to include a change of venue for one or several of them. If they are pending in different courts altogether, it would also entail a removal from one court to another. If so, the removal is from the lower to the higher court, not vice versa.

While any court can consolidate or jointly try cases pending before itself, only two courts in the state have the power to remove cases from other courts in conjunction with these devices. The county court has the power, but only over district, city, town, and village courts in the same county. The supreme court has the power over all courts. It is the only court that can reach within or beyond its county and bring to itself for consolidation or joint trial actions pending in any other court of original jurisdiction.[1] In order for the supreme court or the county court to effect a removal and consolidation,[2] at least one of the actions to be affected has to be pending in the removing court. Where, for example, two actions are pending in two different lower courts and no related case is in the supreme court, the supreme court may not reach down to put the two together.[3]

Unless a New York state court action is duly removed to a U.S. district court,[4] where it can then be consolidated with other federal actions under federal procedure,[5] neither a federal nor a state court can consolidate one of its own actions with one pending in the other's system. But the parties to separate federal and state actions can, if they wish, stipulate to

consolidate their disclosure proceedings and other pretrial steps.[6]

Consolidation and joint trial are today preferred remedies because they reduce calendar congestion and economize legal and judicial effort. When consolidation is proposed, the burden today is on the resisting party to show that it would prejudice him,[7] and the mere fact that his case may be somewhat delayed by the consolidation will not suffice to bar it.

There is no stated time limit on a motion to consolidate, but it can't as a rule be made before issue has been joined in the several actions affected, because not until then would the court know whether the actions present common issues. Since the motion lies in the court's discretion, the applicant should move promptly. Laches, determined on a sui generis basis, can be an enemy.

Consolidation is even more liberal than the permissive joinder of parties is today, and that is liberal indeed. For the initial joinder of different parties in one action, CPLR 1002 requires not only that the several claims have a question of law or fact in common, but also that they be shown to emanate from the same transaction or occurrence or series of them.[8] The latter showing is not required for consolidation, which requires only the common question of law or fact.

The court's discretion guards against fusing separate actions that technically meet this requirement but which on balance should not be put together. Because of the greater requirement for permissive joinder under CPLR 1002, a showing that the parties in two separate actions could have sued, or been sued, in but a single action a fortiori satisfies the requirement for consolidation.[9] This applies only to the standard governing the joinder of parties,

---

§ 128

1. CPLR 602(b). Excepted, of course, is the court of claims case, which is not removable to the supreme court.

2. Since the standards for consolidation and joint trial are the same and what differences exist between them are covered in the prior section, everything said henceforth about consolidation will also apply to the joint trial, unless otherwise indicated.

3. Curriere v. Roeill, 55 Misc.2d 1049, 287 N.Y.S.2d 747 (Sup.Ct., Nassau County, 1967).

4. See 28 U.S.C.A. §§ 1441, 1446, 1447.

5. See Rule 42(a) of the Federal Rules of Civil Procedure.

6. See General Aniline & Film Corp. v. Photo–Marker Corp., 28 A.D.2d 990, 284 N.Y.S.2d 106 (1st Dep't 1967).

7. Vigo S. S. Corp. v. Marship Corp., 26 N.Y.2d 157, 309 N.Y.S.2d 165, 257 N.E.2d 624.

8. See § 134 below.

9. See Tanbro Fabrics Corp. v. Beaunit Mills, Inc., 4 A.D.2d 519, 167 N.Y.S.2d 387 (1st Dep't 1957).

however, and not necessarily to the standard that governs the joinder of claims by the same party. Where, for example, P has two separate but unrelated claims against D and joins them in one action, as he may do under CPLR 601, his bringing them as separate actions does not authorize their consolidation because they have no common question of law or fact.[10]

Two actions can be consolidated despite the fact that one is a law claim (triable by jury) and the other an equitable one (triable by the court), but the consolidation does not divest the right to the jury on the law claim.[11] The point is not unique to consolidation. It can arise in a single action in which the plaintiff has joined the two different categories of claims, or in which the defendant meets the plaintiff's law claim with an equitable counterclaim, or vice versa. Issues of who tries what are recognized and resolved by CPLR 4102(c).[12]

It is also permissible today to consolidate an action with a special proceeding,[13] and even with a summary proceeding to recover the possession of realty, the so-called landlord-tenant case.[14] But in the latter situation it should require some very special circumstance indeed before the summary proceeding is divested of its "summary" nature and subjected to the delay common to an action.[15]

So popular is consolidation today that attorneys often make little effort to resist it when it's moved for, trying instead to secure certain incidental rights. The major of these is the right to open and close to the jury.[16] The plaintiff ordinarily has this right, which gives her the first statement to the jury as the case starts and the last word before the jury retires.

The latter especially is a grand advantage. What wouldn't Brutus give in retrospect for the last word?

When separate actions are consolidated and involve different plaintiffs, both want the right to open and close. The rule is that other things being equal, the right belongs to the plaintiff whose action was commenced first. And it makes no difference that the earlier action may have been in a lower court. This race is generally to the swift regardless of which court the swift sued in.[17] If three actions are consolidated, the plaintiff in the earliest one will open first and sum up last, the plaintiff in the second-commenced action will open second and sum up next-to-last, etc. It is usual for the judge who orders consolidation to determine, in the order, who has this open-and-close right, but when joint trial is ordered it is more the custom to leave the matter to the trial judge.[18]

When the actions to be consolidated are supreme court actions in different counties, the parties now vie to secure the most favorable venue for the consolidated action. The same rule applies: other things being equal, the county that gets the consolidated action is the one where the earliest of the actions was venued.[19]

One phenomenon that can undo the "other things being equal" assumption (and venue the merged action elsewhere) is a showing that one of the counties involved has a light calendar while the other's is backlogged. The fact that one can offer a speedier trial is a factor,[20] although not necessarily a decisive one. There is also some preference to have a consolidated

---

10. Gibbons v. Groat, 22 A.D.2d 996, 254 N.Y.S.2d 843 (3d Dep't 1964).

11. Philip Shlansky & Bro. v. Grossman, 273 A.D. 544, 78 N.Y.S.2d 127 (1st Dep't 1948).

12. See § 378 below.

13. In re Elias, 29 A.D.2d 118, 286 N.Y.S.2d 371 (2d Dep't 1967).

14. Notarius v. Hess Oil & Chem. Corp., 30 A.D.2d 663, 292 N.Y.S.2d 1 (2d Dep't 1968).

15. See Hotel New Yorker Pharmacy, Inc., v. New Yorker Hotel Corp., 40 A.D.2d 967, 968, 338 N.Y.S.2d 697, 699 (1st Dep't 1972) (dissenting opinion).

16. CPLR 4016.

17. Brink's Express Co. v. Burns, 230 A.D. 559, 245 N.Y.S. 649 (4th Dep't 1930). The case also says that the party otherwise entitled to the opening and closing right in the consolidated action waives it if he is the one who moves for the consolidation, but that notion has long since been abandoned in New York.

18. Rockaway Blvd. Wrecking & Lumber Co. v. Raylite Elec. Corp., 25 A.D.2d 842, 270 N.Y.S. 1 (1st Dep't 1966).

19. Rae v. Hotel Governor Clinton, Inc., 23 A.D.2d 564, 256 N.Y.S.2d 741 (2d Dep't 1965).

20. See Poly Const. Corp. v. Oxford Hall Contracting Corp., 24 A.D.2d 637, 262 N.Y.S.2d 206 (2d Dep't 1965).

action tried where the claim arose,[21] a standard justified by the fact that it is the place most likely to conduce to the witnesses' convenience, another matter the court considers.

If the several actions are pending in the supreme court in different counties, the consolidation motion may be made in any one of them,[22] and should be made on notice to all parties to all of the actions affected.[23]

Under the Individual Assignment System,[24] a consolidation order can of course entail removing a case not merely from another court, but specifically from another judge of coordinate jurisdiction. Indeed, it may even entail sending the consolidated cases *to* another judge, as where the latter sits in the venue chosen for the consolidated action. It might therefore be a good idea for the judge entertaining the consolidation motion to consult with the other judges concerned. Friction may otherwise result and require administrative resolution.

§ 129. Severance and Separate Trial

The severance is the ubiquitous device for lopping off claims and making separate actions of them. Because there are no stated statutory criteria for a severance, it is available from its main niche in CPLR 603 in any instance in which a sound exercise of judicial discretion suggests it. There are other listings for it in the CPLR, probably unnecessary because of CPLR 603, but these are overlaps at worst. One is CPLR 3212(e) in conjunction with partial summary judgment; another is CPLR

3215(a) for default judgments; and yet another is CPLR 5012 in connection with judgments generally.

The occasions for the use of a severance are many and will be treated in this book as their contexts appear. One common application is where the liberal joinder rule of CPLR 601 has resulted in the interposing of claims so unrelated that the jury would be confused by them.[1] Another is where a party's retention in a particular context would unduly prejudice it, as where a disclaiming liability insurer has been impleaded by its insured in an ordinary negligence action. The Court of Appeals requires a severance of the impleader claim as a matter of law in that instance.[2]

Despite the court's broad powers of severance under CPLR 603, severance cannot be ordered once consolidation of those very claims has previously been ordered by another judge.[3] In that situation the severance is barred by the doctrine of the law of the case.[4]

No time limit is placed on the motion to sever or separately try. As with the consolidation motion, it should not be made before issue is joined because not until then can the issues be seen.[5] Laches can of course be considered.

The power to order separate trials co-exists with the severance power in CPLR 603. Often if not always a direction for separate trials can be used instead of a severance. Where, for example, unrelated claims have been joined and their trial together will confuse the jury,

---

21. Braff v. Par–Du Leasing, Inc., 25 A.D.2d 897, 269 N.Y.S.2d 222 (3d Dep't 1966).

22. Velasquez v. Pine Grove Resort Ranch, Inc., 77 Misc.2d 329, 354 N.Y.S.2d 65 (Sup.Ct., Ulster County, 1974).

23. Barch v. Avco Corp., 30 A.D.2d 241, 291 N.Y.S.2d 422 (4th Dep't 1968), indicated that if actions are pending in counties X and Y and a consolidation motion is made in X, the parties to the Y action need not respond to the X motion. This overlooks that CPLR 602 is itself authority for the making of the motion in any of the counties involved, and that venue of the motion is not in this instance dictated exclusively by CPLR 2212(a), which is treated in § 245, below. Commentary C3211:19 on McKinney's CPLR 3211 suggests alternatives for the parties if Barch remains law. See also Kent Development Co. v. Liccione, 37 N.Y.2d 899, 378 N.Y.S.2d 377, 340 N.E.2d 740 (1975), and § 262, below.

24. See § 77A above.

§ 129

1. See, e.g., Pierce v. Int'l Harvester Co., 65 A.D.2d 254, 411 N.Y.S.2d 456 (4th Dep't 1978).

2. Kelly v. Yannotti, 4 N.Y.2d 603, 176 N.Y.S.2d 637, 152 N.E.2d 69 (1958). The common method to test the validity of the disclaimer, so as to determine whether the insurer is obliged to defend the pending suit against the insured, is a separate declaratory judgment action. See § 437 below.

3. Dain & Dill, Inc. v. Betterton, 39 A.D.2d 939, 333 N.Y.S.2d 237 (2d Dep't 1972).

4. This is an intra-action res judicata doctrine. See § 448 below.

5. See Hamm v. Richards, 12 A.D.2d 953, 210 N.Y.S.2d 871 (2d Dep't 1961).

they can be tried in succession. One can be disposed of in its entirety before the other is even touched, and without the need of a severance. This really concerns the sequence of trial, in this regard overlapping CPLR 4011, which allows the court broad discretion in determining "the sequence in which the issues shall be tried". Perhaps one difference between the two provisions is that under CPLR 4011 the trial judge controls the sequence, whereas CPLR 603 apparently contemplates a pretrial order directing the separate trial of certain claims or issues. The CPLR 603 motion can be denied, however, without prejudice to a later application to the trial judge for similar relief. In view of this power to order separate trials and avoid jury confusion that way, perhaps the principal justification today for an outright pretrial severance of multiple claims is where they should not be kept together even for the pretrial remedies, such as depositions and other disclosure devices, although those items, too, can be separately managed within the framework of the same case.

If claims are related they should ordinarily be tried together. Separate trials in such an instance would require some special reason.[6]

§ 130. Bifurcated Trial

The ordinary definition of bifurcate is to divide into two parts. In New York practice, bifurcation has come to mean the trial of the liability issue in a personal injury or wrongful death case separately from and prior to trial of the damages question. The advantage of doing this is that if the liability issue is determined in the defendant's favor, there is no need to try the damages question, which can be an involved one entailing expensive expert witnesses and other proof. The plaintiff often

resists an attempt to bifurcate, especially when the liability issue is a close one, because he understandably wants to exploit the sympathy factor and have the jurors aware of the injuries and damages when they deliberate liability. The defendant for the opposite reason often prefers bifurcation.

The Uniform Rules state that judges are "encouraged" to order a bifurcated trial in personal injury cases, not directing when it should be ordered but merely prescribing some procedure when it is.[1] Even under the rules, therefore, bifurcation is in the court's discretion.

Whether to bifurcate depends on whether the two issues are wholly distinct and whether there is a substantial saving that can result. Bifurcation was seldom used under prior law.[2] It came into vogue in the mid–1960s and has achieved wide judicial acceptance as the "authorized and accepted practice".[3] An incisive treatment of the subject is in Mercado v. City of New York,[4] which ordered a retrial of only a damages question in a case in which damages were deemed excessive but liability was clearly established. Where, however, the nature of the plaintiff's injuries have a direct bearing on the question of liability, as when there is a serious question of whether the defendant's conduct was the proximate cause of the particular injury, the jury should consider the two items simultaneously and bifurcation is not appropriate.[5]

If bifurcation is ordered and the liability trial produces a verdict for the plaintiff, the damages trial goes forward. Its precise time is of course fixed by the court. The judge may direct that the damages trial proceed forthwith and before the same jury, which the rules prefer because the main advantage of the split trial is otherwise lost.[6] But if the parties have

---

6. See Greenberg v. City of Yonkers, 45 A.D.2d 314, 358 N.Y.S.2d 453 (2d Dep't 1974), aff'd 37 N.Y.2d 907, 378 N.Y.S.2d 382, 340 N.E.2d 744 (1975).

§ 130

1. In the supreme court and in the county courts, the applicable rule is UR 202.42. Other courts may have similar rules. See, for example, UR 208.35, applicable in the civil court, and UR 206.19, applicable in the court of claims.

2. See Hacker v. City of New York, 25 A.D.2d 35, 266 N.Y.S.2d 194 (1st Dep't 1966).

3. Williams v. City of New York, 36 A.D.2d 620, 318 N.Y.S.2d 536, 537 (2d Dep't 1971).

4. 25 A.D.2d 75, 265 N.Y.S.2d 834 (1st Dep't 1966).

5. Culley v. City of New York, 25 A.D.2d 519, 267 N.Y.S.2d 282 (1st Dep't 1966).

6. See Trimboli v. Scarpaci Funeral Home, 37 A.D.2d 386, 326 N.Y.S.2d 227 (2d Dep't 1971), aff'd 30 N.Y.2d 687, 332 N.Y.S.2d 637, 283 N.E.2d 614 (1972).

to go through further preparation for the damages trial, such as the calling of busy expert witnesses, it may be tried before the same jury after a brief adjournment or before a new jury if the delay is prolonged. The rules allow for that, too, provided the judge states "in the record" why it's necessary.[7] The delay between trials may even be occasioned by the defendant's appeal of the liability judgment and his securing of a stay of further proceedings in conjunction with it.[8]

There is a general policy against allowing appeal from a liability finding before damages are tried, however, and it has been held that such an appeal lies only when an interlocutory judgment has been permitted by the court on the liability finding.[9] Whether to permit it is in the court's discretion.[10]

While the economizing aims of bifurcation are generally realized by having liability tried before damages, and the rules prescribe that as the norm[11], it will occasionally happen that economy is better served by reversing the order and trying damages first, as when an issue of wilful misconduct, which goes to liability, does not become relevant unless damages are shown to exceed a certain figure.[12] The rules cover that, too.[13]

Bifurcation can give way to what might be called trifurcation in certain cases, such as the multi-defendant tort case involving apportionment of culpability under the doctrine of Dole v. Dow Chemical Co.[14] The three separable issues would be (1) whether there is any liability at all, and if so (2) what are the parties' respective shares of it, and (3) what are the plaintiff's damages. As a rule, little is gained by keeping (1) and (2) separate. The responsibilities of defendants to the plaintiff as well as

to themselves are best determined by the jury at one time. Indeed, the Court of Appeals frowns on "trifurcation" if it subdivides the liability phase.[15] It should be even less justifiable under the comparative negligence rule adopted in New York in 1975,[16] since that rule entails an allotting of actual fault among all the parties, including the plaintiff, and it would be awkward to apportion percentages, supposed to total 100%, in segments totaling less.

B. NECESSARY JOINDER OF PARTIES

Table of Sections

§ 131. Necessary Joinder of Parties, Background

A plaintiff ordinarily has little trouble determining the parties to sue. She knows who the defendants should be and simply names them, serves them, and gets an action going. One does not often find a "necessary joinder" problem in practice.

In many situations, P has a claim not only against X, but against X and Y jointly, or jointly and severally. She may have it absolutely or contingently. She may own it herself, or share it with A, or with A and B, and the sharing may be outright, or on some condition. Perhaps the liability P asserts is not "joint" in the substantive law sense, but the relief P wants is such that X, or X and A, or X and Y, or Y and A, or any of a myriad of others, can

---

7. See the rules cited in note 1, above.

8. The Trimboli case, above, shows the additional interest the defendant may have to pay if the defendant is responsible for this further delay in the damages trial.

9. See Jack Parker Constr. Corp. v. Williams, 35 A.D.2d 839, 317 N.Y.S.2d 911 (2d Dep't 1970).

10. A treatment of this question appears in Bank of N.Y. v. Ansonia Assocs., 172 Misc.2d 70, 656 N.Y.S.2d 813 (Sup.Ct., N.Y.County, 1997), noted in SPR 69:3. See the discussion in § 526 below.

11. See note 1 above.

12. See Harari–Raful v. T.W.A., Inc., 41 A.D.2d 753, 341 N.Y.S.2d 655 (2d Dep't 1973), involving the Warsaw Convention.

13. Uniform Rule 202.42, for example, while prescribing liability and then damages as the sequence, permits the court to order "otherwise".

14. 30 N.Y.2d 143, 331 N.Y.S.2d 382, 282 N.E.2d 288 (1972). See § 171 below.

15. See Greenberg v. City of Yonkers, 37 N.Y.2d 907, 378 N.Y.S.2d 382, 340 N.E.2d 744 (1975).

16. CPLR 1411. See § 168E below.

in some way be affected. Must these others be made parties to the action? If so, which of them? And shall they be plaintiffs or defendants? May they sometimes be joined and at other times omitted? These questions are the crux of the subject known as "necessary joinder".

Prior law endeavored to formulate criteria whereby some persons in some situations were to be deemed "indispensable" parties without whom the action could not continue and whose lack of joinder would force a dismissal. Others were to be only "conditionally necessary", and their joinder was desirable but the action could nonetheless continue without them if they were beyond jurisdiction.[1] This approach proved futile. The Advisory Committee candidly noted that the subject of necessary joinder "defies definitive statement" and must rest in each instance in the sound discretion of the court.[2]

Acknowledging that in a given case a particular person could prove "indispensable" in the sense that it would not be effectual to proceed in her absence, the committee decided that the matter "should be determined in the light of all the factors and interests involved including those of the court". Stressing that "there is no single certain criterion" that would prove airtight by itself,[3] the committee therefore adopted an approach of maximum flexibility, leaving the matter to be determined by the court on a case by case basis and with an abundance of discretion. This approach is embodied in CPLR 1001.

§ 132. Necessary Joinder of Parties, CPLR Approach

CPLR 1001(a) provides that

§ 131

1. See § 193 of the old Civil Practice Act.
2. 1st Rep.Leg.Doc. (1957) No. 6(b), p.29.
3. Id. at 30.

§ 132

1. See § 458 below.
2. An illustration of this practical approach appears in City of New York v. Long Island Airports Limousine Serv. Corp., 48 N.Y.2d 469, 423 N.Y.S.2d 651, 399 N.E.2d 538 (1979). See and compare Rule 19(a) of the Federal Rules of Civil Procedure.

Persons who ought to be parties if complete relief is to be accorded between the persons who are parties to the action or who might be inequitably affected by a judgment in the action shall be made plaintiffs or defendants.

The phrase "persons who ought to be parties" is used with the aim of escaping from the rigorous caselaw built up around the word "indispensable" that prior law used. CPLR 1001 omits it. The joinder of an ought-to-be-party person is directed whenever either of the following is indicated:

     1. his joinder would make the relief between those already parties more complete; or

     2. the judgment may in some way inequitably affect him.

The second item does not require a showing that the judgment would be entitled to res judicata or collateral estoppel effect against such person; indeed, if he has not been joined, it probably couldn't be.[1] The possibility that a judgment rendered without him could have an adverse practical effect on him is enough to indicate joinder.[2]

The problem is usually avoided if the plaintiff (P) merely resolves doubts in favor of joinder. If the person has an interest in any way adverse to P, she should be made a defendant. If she has some share in P's claim and ought to be a co-plaintiff, P should consult her, for she might consent to join with P in bringing the action. If she resists, P can make her a defendant[3]—the main aim is to get her into the case—and the court will render judgment as need be regardless of who is on what side of the "versus" sign.[4]

3. CPLR 1001(a) specifically provides for this.
4. Adding someone as a party plaintiff is of course easier when he consents, see Abschagen v. Goldfarb, 8 A.D.2d 750, 185 N.Y.S.2d 339 (3d Dep't 1959), but if he should be a plaintiff and will not consent he can be made a defendant. The federal approach sometimes allows him to be made an "involuntary plaintiff", FRCP Rule 19(a), a distinction perhaps important for federal jurisdictional purposes (measuring whether there is diversity of citizenship between the parties, for example) but carrying little difference in New York practice.

A serious problem arises, therefore, in but a single situation: when the person who "ought to be joined" is not subject to the personal jurisdiction of the court and will not submit to it voluntarily. If X ought to be joined and is subject to jurisdiction, CPLR 1001(a) directs that she be named and joined now. Hence the underlying premise of the joinder statute is that there is no occasion to determine if X is "indispensable" as long as jurisdiction of X can be obtained. X simply gets joined and the problem is done with. The point sometimes seems to be overlooked by the courts, but as long as the statute of limitations is still alive for an action that joins the needed party, the harm is minimal.[5] Of course, if the plaintiff has had ample opportunity to join the needed parties and fails to, dismissal may result.[6]

It's when jurisdiction is not obtainable that the problem reaches its peak. The next section treats it.

§ 133. Avoiding Dismissal for Nonjoinder

The Advisory Committee's resolution of the necessary joinder problem is in CPLR 1001(b). The assumption throughout the ensuing treatment of it is that the ought-to-be-joined person is not subject to personal jurisdiction.

Dismissal of the action for nonjoinder of a given person is a possibility under the CPLR,[1] but it is only a last resort. Before reaching that point, the court should stretch its judicial imagination to see if it can devise some way of allowing the action to proceed without that person's joinder. CPLR 1001(b) gives the court plenary power to keep the action alive without that person "when justice requires", and to aid the court in making that determination the statute lists five things the court "shall" consider:

1. whether the plaintiff has another effective remedy in case the action is dismissed on account of the nonjoinder;

2. the prejudice that may accrue from the nonjoinder to the defendant or to the person not joined;

3. whether and by whom prejudice might have been avoided or may in the future be avoided;

4. the feasibility of a protective provision by order or in the judgment; and

5. whether an effective judgment can be rendered in the absence of the person who is not joined.

The list is not exhaustive but it covers most of the possibilities that come to mind. It makes no distinction between law and equity actions. It is a challenge to the judge as well as to the lawyers who must inform her, and it requires both imagination and energy. It implicitly instructs that a determination of "indispensability" is to be reached only after the list has been thoughtfully negotiated and found to offer no alternative. A few examples will illustrate.

a. P and X were joint lessors of Chicago realty leased to D. P sued D in New York for money due under the lease. X, an Illinoisian, would not join in the action and was not subject to New York jurisdiction. The court held that P could maintain the action without X but would of course have to account to X for his share of the proceeds.[2] The same result can be reached today under CPLR 1001(b), especially paragraph 4 (authorizing a protective provision in the judgment requiring P to account to X). Ironically, however, even a dismissal may be appropriate in that kind of case today. Perhaps P sued in New York because he could not get jurisdiction over D in the sister state where the realty was. If it were shown that jurisdiction could be had in that state

---

5. See, e.g., Storrs v. Holcomb, 245 A.D.2d 943, 666 N.Y.S.2d 835 (3d Dep't 1997).

6. See Llana v. Town of Pittstown, 245 A.D.2d 968, 667 N.Y.S.2d 112 (3d Dep't 1997).

§ 133

1. CPLR 1003, 3211(a)(10).

2. Keene v. Chambers, 271 N.Y. 326, 3 N.E.2d 443 (1936). The Keene case should cast some doubt on cases that automatically conclude that a co-obligee is indispensable to the litigation, such as Natter v. Isaac H. Blanchard Co., 153 A.D. 814, 138 N.Y.S. 969 (1st Dep't 1912), especially in view of present CPLR 1001(b).

today under a longarm statute akin to CPLR 302(a)(4), then CPLR 1001(b)(1) might be applied to dismiss the action without prejudice to suit in Illinois, where personal jurisdiction would be available against both X and D. Forum non conveniens[3] is another basis on which such a dismissal might rest.

b.   Husband H and Wife W are joint buyers of realty. D is the seller. H sued D to recover the down payment, but without joining W, from whom H had separated. The court dismissed the action for nonjoinder of W, the court apparently finding nothing in CPLR 1001(b) that could preserve the action.[4] But if New York realty were involved, CPLR 302(a)(4), the longarm statute, might have offered jurisdiction over W, wherever she might have to be served. If so, W should simply have been ordered joined. It does not appear that counsel raised that possibility. If the realty were elsewhere, and the other jurisdiction had an equivalent longarm statute, this could have been called to the court's attention and the action dismissed on that basis under CPLR 1001(b)(1), remitting the parties to suit in the realty state. If those possibilities did not exist, however, dismissal may have been the only fair thing from D's point of view. Suppose, for example, that W had wanted specific performance as a remedy instead of the damages that H sued for? If a situation like that should occur, one course that might be followed today is for the court to dismiss the New York action on condition that D submit to jurisdiction wherever W would be subject to it, thus assuring H a forum with jurisdiction over everyone.

c.   The Federal Rules of Civil Procedure have grappled with this problem, producing some caselaw pertinent to CPLR 1001(b). Consider the following example involving a shareholders' derivative action in behalf of a corporation (New York having at one time held the corporation indispensable in that kind of case[5]).

Shareholder P brought an action to compel the declaration of a dividend. P could not get jurisdiction over all or even a majority of the corporation's directors and was able to serve only three out of 12. The court held that the absent directors were not necessary parties.[6] It noted that it had jurisdiction of the corporation and that it had all of the tools that any court of equity needs to effectuate a judgment. If the declaration of a dividend were directed by the court, rare though that may be substantively, the court could see to it that the corporation paid it, levying against local property of the corporation if necessary. Under CPLR 1001(b)(5), the New York courts would have equal power in a similar situation, assuming that the case could survive an application of the forum non conveniens doctrine.

d.   The nonjoinder problem has appeared in an insurance controversy. P insured X's life and afterwards sued the beneficiaries to rescind the policy. One of them moved to dismiss for P's failure to join the estate of X, who had since died. The court denied the motion and held that the insured, in this case the estate of X, was not an indispensable party.[7] It held that if P could gain rescission against those whom P did join (the beneficiaries), P would have a meaningful judgment even though it might not bind X's estate. Should X's estate later sue the insurer, and the insurer be required to relitigate the case between itself and X, that would be no skin off the beneficiaries' necks. They will have their day in court now and can't avoid it merely because subsequent relitigation between insurer and insured is possible later. If anyone were to be inconvenienced by that relitigation prospect it would be P, and P is not complaining.

Now suppose that suit is brought by beneficiary B against I, the insurer, to collect on the policy. I moves to dismiss for the nonjoinder of X, the insured, who is beyond jurisdiction. Is the situation the same? It differs significantly. If B collects from I, and I is afterwards sued by

---

3.   See § 28 above.

4.   Mechta v. Scaretta, 52 Misc.2d 696, 276 N.Y.S.2d 652 (Sup.Ct., Queens County, 1967).

5.   See the pre-CPLR case of Carruthers v. Jack Waite Mining Co., 306 N.Y. 136, 116 N.E.2d 286 (1953).

6.   Kroese v. General Steel Castings Corp., 179 F.2d 760 (3d Cir.1950).

7.   New England Mut. Life Ins. Co. v. Brandenburg, 8 F.R.D. 151 (S.D.N.Y.1948).

X in a separate action, the prior judgment may not bind X, who can therefore collect all over again from I—as where the factfinders in the second suit disagree with those in the first. In this situation, dismissal for nonjoinder may be justified but, again, it should be so conditioned as to maneuver the parties into some other court that has or would get (through a protective provision in the New York disposition) jurisdiction over everyone.

In circumstances like these, the insurer can of course turn to its interpleader remedies,[8] but even the need of interpleader as a cure has diminished in this age of expanded extraterritorial jurisdiction. Cases in which an ought-to-be-joined person is not amenable to jurisdiction have become increasingly rare.

A prime possibility when such a case does crop up, already alluded to several times, is for the court to see whether any sister state or reasonably accessible (and trusted) foreign court would have jurisdiction over all of the interested persons if New York hasn't. P's action could then be dismissed on condition that within a stated period D stipulate to submit to jurisdiction in the other court, where the absent X would be subject to suit. Such a disposition would be a combined exercise under paragraphs 1 and 4 of CPLR 1001(b). It is in effect a leverage use of whatever jurisdiction the court has: if D wants the action dismissed for nonjoinder of a third person, D may have the dismissal only by consenting to jurisdiction in a court in which the third person can be joined as a party.[9]

Rule 19 of the Federal Rules of Civil Procedure was recast in 1966 to meet the same kind of problem CPLR 1001(b) addresses. This enables us to take note of the U.S. Supreme Court's first and so far major decision on the

revised rule, which noted that "a court does not know whether a particular person is 'indispensable' until it has examined the situation to determine whether it can proceed without him",[10] the very premise on which CPLR 1001 is bottomed.

This subject sometimes overlaps the less serious "misnomer" cases discussed earlier, in which a proper party was served but under a technically incorrect name in the summons.[11]

C. PERMISSIVE JOINDER OF PARTIES

Table of Sections

§ 134. Permissive Joinder of Parties

The CPLR is generous about the joinder of multiple parties. Parties with separate and distinct claims may join, and those against whom the claims exist may be joined, in a single action if the several claims (1) arise out of "the same transaction[s], occurrence[s], or series of transactions or occurrences" and (2) have in common any "question of law or fact".[1] These standards apply to the voluntary joinder of claims by multiple plaintiffs as well as to the joinder of multiple defendants by one or more plaintiffs.

A simple example of plaintiffs' joinder is where several plaintiffs injured in the same accident join their separate claims for personal injuries or property damage (or both) in a single action. As long as a common thread ties all of the claims together, enabling the court to say that they all arise out of a common series of transactions or occurrences, the first criteri-

---

8. Interpleader (see § 148 et seq., below) is the device whereby a stakeholder can avoid double liability by bringing conflicting claimants to court, thereby subjecting them to a judgment that protects the stakeholder from later suit by any of them.

9. A brief memorandum in Cushing–Murray v. Adams, 49 A.D.2d 874, 373 N.Y.S.2d 191 (2d Dep't 1975), states that the dismissal may not be conditioned on the defendant's stipulating to submit to jurisdiction elsewhere. This is a needlessly broad restriction. One of the court's options is "a protective provision by order of the court", under CPLR 1001(b)(4). An order conditioning dismissal on a

submission to jurisdiction in a more appropriate forum seems well within the possibilities contemplated.

10. Provident Tradesmens Bank & Tr. Co. v. Patterson, 390 U.S. 102, 119, 88 S.Ct. 733, 743, 19 L.Ed.2d 936 (1968).

11. See § 64 above.

§ 134

1. CPLR 1002(a) (for plaintiffs) and (b) (for defendants).

on is met. In Akely v. Kinnicutt,[2] for example, where D circulated a fraudulent prospectus in connection with a stock floater and 193 different persons relied on it, all were permitted to join their fraud claims in a single action even though the claim of each was distinct and in no way dependent on any other's. The second requirement, that there be a common question of law or fact, was also met. The question of whether or not the prospectus was false was one such common question.

Note that the existence of separate questions, distinct to each plaintiff, does not defeat the joinder as long as there is some common question, too. In *Akely*, there were several questions unique to each plaintiff, among them the issues of whether that particular plaintiff relied on the prospectus and what his damages were. *Akely* also establishes that the fact that the diverse claims arise at different times does not defeat the joinder; the transactions can still constitute a "series". The defendant's argument that he should be allowed a separate jury on each claim is given short shrift by the court.

The word "transaction" in CPLR 1002 connotes a consensual dealing. "Occurrence" includes non-consensual happenings, such as tort claims. It was added to expand the scope of permissive joinder.[3]

The statute works the same way on the defendant's side. Where P was insured with two companies, for example, each insuring a separate part of the same loss—thus giving rise to separate and independent claims against the two when a burglary loss occurred—the insured was permitted to join both companies in a single action.[4] The common questions were the fact of the burglary and the value of the insured merchandise.

CPLR 1002(c) provides that "[i]t shall not be necessary that each plaintiff be interested in obtaining, or each defendant ... in defending against, all the relief demanded or as to every claim included in an action". As long as

the threads of "series of transactions" and "common question of law or fact" run through the several claims, the absence of an interest by each litigant in the claims asserted by or against the others offers no barrier to joinder. Of course, despite their valid joinder, the distinctness of the claims may in some instances make it impractical or infeasible to hear them all together, but for that CPLR 1002(c) has a flexible remedy. It provides that the court "may order separate trials or make other orders to prevent prejudice", among which would be an order severing some of the claims and sending them off as separate actions.[5] The remedy of a severance would be particularly appropriate where, because of the broadness of joinder, a person finds herself involved in a case with an "adverse" party with whom she has no argument.

In short, the CPLR sets broad boundaries for permissive joinder and simply invites the court to curtail them when the exigencies of a given case indicate.

While joinder by different plaintiffs against one defendant ordinarily requires, under CPLR 1002(a), that the claims arise out of a single transaction or series of transactions, an exception is carved out for consumer credit transactions[6] by CPLR 601(b),[7] which provides that five separate consumer credit transactions may now be joined in a single action provided that all are against the same defendant and that all the plaintiffs are represented by the same attorney.

In the lower courts, which have monetary limitations on their jurisdiction, the CPLR provisions on permissive joinder are equally applicable. As long as each of the claims falls within the court's monetary jurisdiction when independently measured, the court may entertain them all in one action. There is even permission for a single judgment to be rendered for more than the court's monetary jur-

2. 238 N.Y. 466, 144 N.E. 682 (1924).

3. 15 Jud.Council Rep. (1949) 211, 216.

4. Bossak v. National Surety Co., 205 A.D. 707, 200 N.Y.S. 148 (1st Dep't 1923).

5. CPLR 603, 1003.

6. See the definition in CPLR 105.

7. Subdivision (b) was added to CPLR 601 in a 1996 amendment. The amendment is treated in SPR 52:2–3.

isdiction, as long as none of the claims exceeds the jurisdiction individually.[8]

§ 135. Joinder in the Alternative

Particularly helpful to plaintiffs is the permission of CPLR 1002(b) to join defendants "in the alternative", so that when P has a claim but does not know who, as between X and Y, is liable on it, P can sue them both. A typical situation is where goods left P's possession, went through the hands of several others (carrier, dyer, cutter, packer, warehouseman, return carrier, etc.), and then came back into P's possession with some of the goods missing or damaged, but with all of the handlers denying it was their fault. P may sue them all, establishing the condition of the goods when they left P, the condition in which they were returned, and the fact that each of the defendants handled the goods somewhere in between. This is enough to throw onto the defendants the burden of coming forward with proof of their due care, thus helping to fix liability as among themselves.[1] P's showing satisfies as a prima facie case in this kind of situation, and a defendant's silence in the face of such proof can therefore be taken by the factfinder as an admission of liability. What generally occurs is that each defendant tries, if she can, to pin liability on some other, with the plaintiff ending up the beneficiary rather than the victim.

The final judgment can be based on any proof in the record regardless of who introduced it. A statute explicitly so providing under prior law[2] was omitted from the CPLR (probably inadvertently), but no matter; the same conclusion has been reached under the CPLR[3] and no other would be appropriate. Thus, if the evidence that implicates defendant

X is introduced by defendant Y, P has full use of it.

Joinder in the alternative is available on even more remote contingencies. In one case P's agent, A, was supposed to have brought timely suit in P's behalf against D. It was questionable whether he did. P sued A and D in the alternative, asserting primary liability against D but pleading for judgment against A in the event that the statute of limitations now barred P's claim against D. The suit was allowed in that form.[4] The "common question" was whether the statute of limitations had expired on P's claim against D.

A concomitant of joinder in the alternative is pleading in the alternative, which is also invited by the CPLR.[5]

Suit in the alternative generally involves alternative defendants, but it can apply to plaintiffs. A situation can arise, for example, in which two or more persons do not know who as between them should sue as plaintiff. In that situation today, suit by the plaintiffs in the alternative should be allowed. It was allowed in the past,[6] but not when the claim of each was clearly exclusive. Where, for example, both maker and payee sued a bank on a check, the court held the two misjoined as plaintiffs because the claim of each destroyed the other's.[7] CPLR 1002(a) should permit joinder even in that kind of case today.

D. PROPER PARTIES

Table of Sections

---

8. See § 23 above.

§ 135

1. S. & C. Clothing Co. v. United States Trucking Corp., 216 A.D. 482, 215 N.Y.S. 349 (1st Dep't 1926).

2. Civ.Prac.Act § 212(1).

3. Shaw v. Lewis, 55 Misc.2d 664, 286 N.Y.S.2d 758 (N.Y.C.Civ.Ct.1968), aff'd 58 Misc.2d 1072, 299 N.Y.S.2d 615 (App.Term, 1st Dep't, 1968).

4. Great N. Tel. Co. v. Yokohama Specie Bank, 297 N.Y. 135, 76 N.E.2d 117 (1947).

5. CPLR 3014. See Tanbro Fabrics Corp. v. Beaunit Mills, 4 A.D.2d 519, 167 N.Y.S.2d 387 (1st Dep't 1957), discussing the interplay between the joinder and pleading provisions.

6. See, e.g., Roecklein v. American Sugar Ref. Co., 222 A.D. 540, 226 N.Y.S. 375 (2d Dep't 1928).

7. See Olsen v. Bankers' Trust Co., 205 A.D. 669, 199 N.Y.S. 700 (1st Dep't 1923).

§ 136.   Standing to Sue

Questions of proper parties generally focus on who must be made defendants. Less frequent is the question of who should be the plaintiff. One category that occasionally raises the issue is known as "standing to sue".

It is the law's policy to allow only an aggrieved person to bring a lawsuit. One not affected by anything a would-be defendant has done or threatens to do ordinarily has no business suing, and a suit of that kind can be dismissed at the threshold for want of jurisdiction without reaching the merits. When one without the requisite grievance does bring suit, and it's dismissed, the plaintiff is described as lacking "standing to sue" and the dismissal as one for lack of subject matter jurisdiction. A want of "standing to sue", in other words, is just another way of saying that this particular plaintiff is not involved in a genuine controversy, and a simple syllogism takes us from there to a "jurisdictional" dismissal: (1) the courts have jurisdiction only over controversies; (2) a plaintiff found to lack "standing" is not involved in a controversy; and (3) the courts therefore have no jurisdiction of the case when such a plaintiff purports to bring it.

Although a question of "standing" is not common in New York, its infrequent appearance is likely to be where administrative action is involved. A good example is Dairylea Cooperative, Inc. v. Walkley,[1] in which the Commissioner of Agriculture and Markets granted L, a milk dealer, a license to distribute milk in an area already serviced by P. P sought to annul the determination,[2] which had been made without a hearing, and the question was whether P as a mere competitor had standing to bring the suit. The court concluded that P had the requisite standing because P was able to show: (1) that the administrative action would harm P and (2) that P's interest

was "arguably" within the "zone of interest" to be protected by the statute involved—in the *Dairylea* case, a licensing statute. The court said that "[o]nly where there is a clear legislative intent negating review . . . or lack of injury in fact will standing be denied."[3] The test today is a liberal one, according to *Dairylea*, and the right to challenge administrative action, articulated under the "standing" caption, is an expanding one.

While the public interest was involved in *Dairylea*, the crux of the case was a private argument between commercial competitors. This facilitated a finding of direct aggrievement at least sufficient to conclude that one competitor had the capacity to contest official activity that benefitted the other. In awarding standing to sue, the court was hardly deciding a matter of urgent public policy.

Economic interest in the outcome of a case will not assure a plaintiff standing to sue if the plaintiff's claim is based on a statute that seeks to implement non-economic interests, as was the case in Society of the Plastics Industry, Inc. v. County of Suffolk,[4] where the court barred a plastics maker from making an attack on a county's "plastics law" under the State Environmental Quality Review Act. The court found that the attackers were motivated by economic interests, while standing under the act is available only to those with noneconomic (environmental, aesthetic, etc.) interests.[5]

A singular involvement of the standing doctrine in the economics sphere has been in the so-called "taxpayer" suit, an action brought by a citizen-taxpayer, with a minimal personal stake, to test the constitutionality of an expenditure of state money. New York was among the few states to preclude such an action; it found the plaintiff's interest either lacking or so infinitesimal as to be in effect lacking, and thus adjudged the plaintiff to be without

§ 136

1. 38 N.Y.2d 6, 377 N.Y.S.2d 451, 339 N.E.2d 865 (1975).

2. He brought an Article 78 proceeding (see § 557 et seq., below), the New York procedure for contesting administrative action.

3. 38 N.Y.2d at 11, 377 N.Y.S.2d at 455, 339 N.E.2d at 868.

4. 77 N.Y.2d 761, 570 N.Y.S.2d 778, 573 N.E.2d 1034 (1991),

5. The Plastics case is discussed in the lead note in New York State Law Digest No. 379.

"standing".[6]

What was involved was really a policy determination that the validity of legislative expenditures should not be broadly supervised by the courts. This was a fundamental decision about the separation of powers, and one of great moment, and yet the closing of the judicial door was attributed, with a strained effort, to a lack of "standing". There has since been, incidentally, a total change of heart in New York on the taxpayer suit, which is now allowed to challenge state expenditures just as it has for years been allowed to challenge municipal expenditures.[7] The Court of Appeals made the change in Boryszewski v. Brydges,[8] noting the expanding attitude towards "standing". The legislature made the same change almost simultaneously with the enactment of Article 7–A of the State Finance Law,[9] elaborating procedure and imposing certain conditions.

These developments suggest that neither the legislature nor the Court of Appeals is about to allow the "standing to sue" category to become the controversial battleground in New York practice that it has become in the federal courts. There, in addition to serving as the door-closer for taxpayer suits seeking to test federal spending measures,[10] it has also come to mirror the prevalent views of the U.S. Supreme Court on the scope and reach of federal judicial jurisdiction. When a majority of the Supreme Court was of an expansive mind, "standing" was generously accorded taxpayers to test legislative enactments and administrative action.[11] In one case, the court seemed almost to be interring the "standing" barrier

and laying out a red carpet for a variety of suits previously thought insulated by restrictive notions of "standing".[12] When through personnel changes the Supreme Court then retrenched to a more restrained view of the federal judicial function, it was the "standing" doctrine that got trotted out to rebuild the wall.[13]

In federal practice, one also finds under the "standing" caption, or related to it, a number of other headings under which a court may refuse to entertain a case: justiciability, advisory opinion, political question, ripeness, mootness, etc.[14] Their significance in New York State practice is discussed by the New York Court of Appeals in New York State Inspection, Security and Law Enforcement Employees v. Cuomo,[15] an unsuccessful attempt by correction personnel to stop the closing of a correctional facility. The issues involved were found "political" (i.e., of a kind that must be left to the other branches of government) instead of "justiciable" (of a kind that the courts can entertain).[16]

As for the "advisory opinion", the New York courts can't entertain one. An actual controversy is required, with one notable exception. A 1985 constitutional amendment[17] empowers the New York Court of Appeals, and only that court, to entertain requests for advisory opinions on New York law submitted by the U.S. Supreme Court, a federal Court of Appeals, or a sister state's highest court.[18]

While the expanded use of the class action in

6. See St. Clair v. Yonkers Raceway, Inc., 13 N.Y.2d 72, 242 N.Y.S.2d 43, 192 N.E.2d 15 (1963).

7. See Gen.Mun.L. § 51.

8. 37 N.Y.2d 361, 372 N.Y.S.2d 623, 334 N.E.2d 579 (1975).

9. Sections 123 to 123(j), L.1975, c.827.

10. Massachusetts v. Mellon, 262 U.S. 447, 43 S.Ct. 597, 67 L.Ed. 1078 (1923).

11. See, e.g., Flast v. Cohen, 392 U.S. 83, 88 S.Ct. 1942, 20 L.Ed.2d 947 (1968); U.S. v. SCRAP, 412 U.S. 669, 93 S.Ct. 2405, 37 L.Ed.2d 254 (1973).

12. See Association of Data Processing Service Organizations, Inc. v. Camp, 397 U.S. 150, 151, 90 S.Ct. 827, 829, 25 L.Ed.2d 184 (1970), reciting that "[g]eneralizations about standing to sue are largely worthless as such".

13. See U.S. v. Richardson, 418 U.S. 166, 94 S.Ct. 2940, 41 L.Ed.2d 678 (1974).

14. See § 612 below (Practitioner's Edition).

15. 64 N.Y.2d 233, 485 N.Y.S.2d 719, 475 N.E.2d 90 (1984).

16. These and related doctrines are discussed in the lead note in New York State Law Digest No. 305.

17. The amendment added paragraph 9 to section 3(b) of Article VI of the state constitution.

18. A Court of Appeals rule, Rule 500.17, implements the new procedure, whose first invoking—there have been many since—appears to have occurred in Kidney v. Kolmar Labs., Inc., 68 N.Y.2d 343, 509 N.Y.S.2d 491, 502 N.E.2d 168 (1986). The procedure is discussed in the lead note in New York State Law Digest No. 329.

New York[19] may increase the occasions for determining standing and like questions touching also on matters of policy, we can still conclude, and with some relief, that "standing" is not now and is not likely to become the arena it constitutes in federal practice. With the taxpayer suit having been expressly adopted in New York, and with the Court of Appeals having acknowledged that in general "standing" is to be measured generously, the occasion for closing the court's doors to a plaintiff by finding that his interest is not even sufficient to let him address the merits, which is what a "standing" dismissal means, should be infrequent. Ordinarily only the most officious interloper should be ousted for want of standing.

§ 137. "Real Party in Interest"

Under § 210 of the old Civil Practice Act every action was required to be prosecuted "in the name of the real party in interest", except in certain enumerated circumstances. The successor provision, CPLR 1004, omits that statement as obvious on the one hand (who else would bring the action?), misleading on the other (does it require in a trust case that the beneficiaries rather than the trustee bring suit?), and "an inept statement of . . . substantive law" in any event.[1] Low praise, indeed.

We thus have an acknowledgment that the questions of who may bring suit and against whom it may be brought are really questions of substantive rather than procedural law and must be answered as such. Who owns the cause of action? Whose right has been interfered with? Who interfered with it?

CPLR 1004 confines its specific references to a few basic legal relationships, mostly of a fiduciary character, by providing that suit may be brought by or against these representatives instead of the person represented:

1. an executor or administrator of a decedent's estate;

2. a guardian of an infant's property;

3. a committee of a declared incompetent;

4. a conservator of a conservatee;

5. a trustee of an express trust;

6. an insured to whom the insurer has become subrogated; and

7. the intermediary in a third-party beneficiary situation.

Number 2 on the list does not include the mere guardian ad litem, whose brief tenure in the infant's life is only to act as a representative in litigation. Nor does it include the parent of the infant, even though the parent may be served in the infant's behalf under CPLR 309(a). CPLR 309(a) requires among other things that the infant be served as well as the parent when the infant is over 14, a requirement that can't be circumvented by naming only the parent as the party. It is apparently only the formally appointed "guardian of the property" of an infant,[2] a person met only rarely, who may be designated the party in place of the infant.[3]

With respect to numbers 3 and 4 on the list, note the archaic terminology. The committee/incompetent and conservator/conservatee descriptions have both been officially replaced by guardian/incapacitated person.[4]

For number 5 it should be noted that in an ordinary action between the trust and a stranger, the trustee is of course the proper party and the beneficiaries do not belong in the case. But the beneficiaries should be joined if the action or proceeding affects the validity of the trust itself,[5] or if there is a dispute between trustee and beneficiaries.

Number 6 on the list concerns the situation in which the insurer has paid the loss to its insured and stepped into the shoes of the insured for the purpose of making a claim against, and suing if need be, the third person who caused the loss. The action may still be

19. See § 139 et seq., below.

§ 137

1. 1st Rep.Leg.Doc. (1957) No. 6b, p.33.

2. See § 196 for the distinctions among "guardians".

3. See Cramer v. Henderson, 123 Misc.2d 159, 473 N.Y.S.2d 672 (Sup.Ct., Yates County, 1984).

4. See § 69, paragraph (b), above.

5. McKnight v. Bank of N. Y. & Trust Co., 254 N.Y. 417, 173 N.E. 568 (1930).

maintained in the insured's name. The insured may have given the insurer a "subrogation receipt", but CPLR 1004 makes clear that the right of subrogation does not depend on the title of the document that confers the right. It can be any "agreement" evincing a purpose to give over to the insurer all or part of the insured's claim. The aim is to prevent the jury from knowing that the claim was covered by insurance,[6] and in all but name the action is prosecuted and paid for by the insurer. If the insured has been paid only part of the claim, this device enables the action to be maintained in the insured's name for the entirety of the claim but with the portion already paid going back to the insurer out of the proceeds.

Number 7 on the list, while presumably governing in the third-party beneficiary situations encountered in contract law, is most often met in agency cases, particularly when the persons involved, although acting as agents, have acted throughout in their own names.[7]

CPLR 1004 is phrased permissively ("may") so that, under categories 6 and 7 anyway, the insurer (rather than the insured) and the third-party beneficiary (rather than the benefactor) should have the option of bringing the action in its own name.

The opening language of CPLR 1004, "[e]xcept where otherwise prescribed by order of the court", enables the court to intercede in any of the listed situations so as to require the joinder of the various behind-the-scenes persons who would not otherwise have to be joined.

E. PROCEDURE FOR JOINDER PROBLEMS

Table of Sections

6. Leone v. Lohmaier, 205 Misc. 467, 128 N.Y.S.2d 618 (Sup.Ct., Monroe County, 1954).

7. See Watts v. Phillips–Jones Corp., 211 A.D. 523, 207 N.Y.S. 493 (2d Dep't 1925), aff'd 242 N.Y. 557, 152 N.E. 425 (1926).

§ 138

1. See Rosenblatt v. Birnbaum, 20 A.D.2d 556, 245 N.Y.S.2d 72 (2d Dep't 1963), aff'd 16 N.Y.2d 212, 264 N.Y.S.2d 521, 212 N.E.2d 37 (1965).

§ 138. Motion to Add or Drop Parties; Procedure

CPLR 1003 supplies the procedure for defects of joinder. It provides that parties may be added or dropped by the court, on motion of any party or on its own initiative, at any stage of the action and upon such terms as may be just.

The court may thus act on its own without waiting for a motion, and will do so whenever a hint of need appears. Where, for example, an argument ensued between parents as to how money was being expended for the children, the children's guardian ad litem was ordered joined by the court so as to assure a representation unfettered by the emotions to which the parents were necessarily subject.[1]

The court may take this sua sponte action at any time and may make its orders conditional.

A formal motion to add or drop parties, whether made by P or D, must be made on notice to all who are already parties, but notice need not be given to the person sought to be added. If that person does not come into the action voluntarily, he must be duly served with a "supplemental summons",[2] which must specify the pleading he is required to answer. The court can adjust the procedure in the order directing joinder, but in the absence of court direction the new party should have a 20–or 30–day answering time, just as any original defendant would, depending on the time and manner of service.[3]

Under CPLR 1003, the "[m]isjoinder of parties is not a ground for dismissal of an action". The remedy to cure a misjoinder is simply to drop the improperly joined party. If an action has been tried with an improper party present and judgment has been rendered as to all

2. CPLR 305(a).

3. CPLR 320(a), 3012(c).

parties, the improper party can be dropped and the judgment preserved as to the others.[4]

Laches will be considered by the court. If the litigation has proceeded to the point where X, a defendant, has appeared and answered, P has no absolute right to drop X and X may resist the attempt, especially if P could sue X all over again later. P's endeavor to "drop" X in that situation is just a "discontinuance" in disguise and will be treated as such.[5] This means that the court need not permit it if P has any ulterior motive, e.g., if P doesn't like the way the case has been going and simply wants to start again.[6]

As previously discussed,[7] the ultimate remedy for nonjoinder of a necessary party is a dismissal, but it is only a last resort. If the needed person is subject to jurisdiction, the court merely orders her joined; if she is not subject to jurisdiction, the court should go through the CPLR 1001(b) list to find some possible alternative, because only the complete absence of alternatives is the predicate for considering whether the absent person is indispensable (so as to dismiss the action if she is). Prior law had a futile "dual motion" procedure, in which on D's first motion the court would order P to try to serve X even if it was clear that X could not be served or otherwise brought within jurisdiction. Only after some time passed during which P was supposed to make that attempt could D then move for dismissal for X's nonjoinder. This requirement of two motions has been abandoned.[8] Dismissal can be ordered on D's initial motion if X proves to be indispensable and if the CPLR 1001(b) list offers no alternative. The rub is that with a bit of imagination an alternative is likely to be found and a dismissal—at least an

unconditional one—therefore avoided in just about all cases.

When S is in the position of a stakeholder with two claimants, C–1 and C–2, making conflicting claims against him, he can, as will be seen, interplead them.[9] If C–1 sues S, S can defensively interplead C–2.[10] If S can't get jurisdiction of C–2 in the latter situation, he would of course like to have the action dismissed for the nonjoinder of C–2. Pre–CPLR caselaw suggested that there can be no dismissal for nonjoinder in such a case.[11] Today, however, the devices of CPLR 1001(b) should be available to help the stakeholder so that he is not faced with the prospect of double liability if there is anything the court can do to avoid it, such as dismiss the action on the condition that C–1 submit to jurisdiction in a place where jurisdiction is available over C–2.[12] Occasionally the courts have treated a situation that smacks of the interpleader problem as if it were only a joinder question,[13] a flexibility that CPLR 1001(b) should encourage.

Before 1996, the plaintiff could not, after the action was commenced, alter the line-up of defendants without court leave. After the initial papers set the roster of defendants, the addition of a new defendant required permission of the court. A 1996 amendment of CPLR 1003 changed that. While a court order is still a permissible way to add a party, the joinder is also allowed by stipulation of all parties who have appeared in the action. If the plaintiff acts early in the case, moreover, not even a stipulation is required. Drawing on CPLR 3025(a), the statute that allows each party one amendment of its pleading as a matter of course (i.e., without leave or stipulation),[14] CPLR 1003 allows the plaintiff one opportunity to join an additional party as a matter of

---

4. Kosiba v. City of Syracuse, 287 N.Y. 283, 39 N.E.2d 240 (1942).

5. In re Cowles' Will, 22 A.D.2d 365, 255 N.Y.S.2d 160 (1st Dep't 1965), aff'd 17 N.Y.2d 567, 268 N.Y.S.2d 327, 215 N.E.2d 509 (1966).

6. See Commentary C3217:12 on McKinney's CPLR 3217. Discontinuance is the subject of §§ 297 and 298, below.

7. See § 133 above.

8. See Blumenthal v. Allen, 46 Misc.2d 688, 260 N.Y.S.2d 363 (Sup.Ct., N.Y. County, 1965).

9. CPLR 1006(a). See § 148 below.

10. CPLR 1006(b).

11. See Petrogradsky Mejdunarodny K. B. v. National City Bank, 253 N.Y. 23, 170 N.E. 479 (1930).

12. See the examples in § 133 above.

13. See and compare Cohen v. Douglas L. Elliman & Co., 279 A.D. 161, 108 N.Y.S.2d 386 (1st Dep't 1951).

14. See § 236 below.

right as long as the plaintiff acts within any of three time periods:

within 20 days after service of the original summons;

at any time before the time for responding to the summons expires; or

within 20 days after the service of a pleading responding to the summons.

Some questions can arise under the statute, especially when a party other than the plaintiff seeks to add parties, as on a counterclaim or cross-claim, or when several defendants named in the original summons were served at different times. The plaintiff is best off assuming that the time periods are measured from the earliest service, responding time, etc.,[15] but it has been held, to the plaintiff's advantage, that in multiple defendant cases the 20 days run from the service of the answer of the last defendant to answer.[16]

A supplemental summons is used to join the new party.[17]

The time between the making of a motion to add X as a party and the entry of an order granting the motion is a period during which the statute of limitations against X is tolled,[18] but incidental questions arise here that should make the lawyer watchful.[19] The motion should in any event include a proposed supplemental summons and amended complaint.

F. CLASS ACTIONS

Table of Sections

§ 139. Class Actions, Background

A unique remedy afforded by procedural law is the "class action", a device whereby a few persons get together and bring an action in behalf of themselves and an entire category or "class" of persons. The class is described as such but its other members, who may be numerous indeed, are not joined. The few who take the initiative and bring the action are called the representatives. The device can also operate on the defendant's side, the plaintiff naming and joining only a few of the members of the class but designating the whole class as a defendant.[1]

The class action is a major exception to the general rule of law that only those individually brought within the jurisdiction of the court can be bound by its judgment. When the class action is properly used it operates as res judicata for or against all members of the class,[2] although the extent of this binding effect is "not precisely defined by judicial opinion".[3] The res judicata aspect accounts for much but by no means all of the judicial ambivalence manifested towards the class action over the years. The energetic opposition of the would-be opponents of the class, often powerful corporate interests, contributes. One must also cite the fact that a class action involves the

---

15. See the extended discussion in SPR 43:1.

16. Dynaire Corp. v. Germano, N.Y. Law Journal, Aug. 1, 1996, p.22, col.1 (Sup.Ct., N.Y. County; Friedman, J.).

17. CPLR 305(a). In the supreme or a county court, the supplemental summons should be filed and then served on the new party. It has been held that no additional fee is required when a new party is added. Kheyfets v. El Amari, Inc., 231 A.D.2d 684, 647 N.Y.S.2d 982 (2d Dep't 1996), noted in SPR 50:4.

18. Perez v. Paramount Communications, Inc., 92 N.Y.2d 749, 1999 WL 76927 (1999).

19. See the discussion in New York State Law Digest No. 471 and in SPR 77:2.

§ 139

1. See § 146 below.

2. Supreme Tribe of Ben–Hur v. Cauble, 255 U.S. 356, 41 S.Ct. 338, 65 L.Ed. 673 (1921); Graham v. Board of Supervisors, 25 A.D.2d 250, 269 N.Y.S.2d 477 (4th Dep't 1966). For the res judicata effect of federal class judgments, see Berry Petroleum Co. v. Adams & Peck, 518 F.2d 402, 411–413 (2d Cir.1975).

3. Hansberry v. Lee, 311 U.S. 32, 41, 61 S.Ct. 115, 118, 85 L.Ed. 22 (1940).

courts in a much more active managerial role than they have been accustomed to in our adversary system, and some judges aren't very much turned on by that.

When it works, the class action enables numerous persons with small stakes to litigate related claims that would be prohibitively expensive for any one or a few of them to prosecute alone, with the prospect, therefore, that without a device like the class action they would refrain from suit and literally make the wrongdoer the beneficiary of the very massiveness of its own wrong. The class action is a spur to the vindication of rights that simple economics would otherwise deter.[4]

There are two key years in the development of the class action in New York. The first is 1849, a year after the original Field Code. By an 1849 amendment of that code, the class action took the form it was to have for well over a century.[5] It kept that form, even becoming a national model, right through the CPLR of 1963, where it was carried forth as CPLR 1005. Subdivisions (b) and (c) of CPLR 1005 were traceable to then-recent Judicial Council recommendations;[6] subdivision (a) was merely a restatement of prior law,[7] and prior law meant the Field Code provision.[8]

The second historic year for the class action in New York was 1975, when the ferment of the previous decade, whose prime agent was Rule 23 of the Federal Rules of Civil Procedure and the great activity spawned around it, finally distilled some new spirits in New York. In 1975, CPLR 1005 was repealed and a new Article 9 enacted, consisting of CPLR 901–909. The new article, explored in detail in ensuing sections, is an enlightened and powerful one, in some respects more ambitious than Federal Rule 23, on which it was largely (but not entirely) based. Article 9 will be easier to negotiate if at least the immediate background from which it emerged is looked at first.

The amended Federal Rule 23, giving the class action the active role it afterwards achieved in the federal courts, took effect in 1966. It quickly became the enthusiastic expedient for bringing into court some of the major substantive issues of the age,[9] involving, to cite just a few examples, the rights of African-Americans,[10] migratory workers,[11] prisoners,[12] demonstrators,[13] and soldiers.[14] It also became an activist model for class action reform in other states. In those states, and in others in which no new statute was enacted but the old one was more expansively construed, consumer rights found a new friend. California, for example, applied its old statute to sustain some imaginative consumer actions.[15]

But while these other states, either with new statutes or with a re-construction of older ones, were forging new ground with the class action device, New York was marking time. CPLR 1005 continued to be narrowly construed. The Court of Appeals would from time to time prod the legislature to replace the statute with a more modern one,[16] but the

---

4. See Weinstein, Revision of Procedure: Some Problems in Class Actions, 9 Buffalo L.Rev. 433, 435 (1960).

5. The code provision was itself devised from pre-existing chancery practice. See 1st Rep.Leg.Doc.(1957) No. 6(b), p.35.

6. See 18th Jud.Council Rep.(1952) 217. The cited report is a major study of the class action by Professor Adolf Homburger.

7. Civ.Prac.Act § 195.

8. A different subdivision (a) proposed by the CPLR's draftsmen, containing the substance of the 1952 Judicial Council recommendation, see 1st Rep.Leg.Doc.(1957) No. 6b, p.34, was rejected and the Field Code provision restored in 1962 and carried forward. See 6th Rep.Leg. Doc.(1962) No. 8, p.153.

9. See Meyer, Social Utility of Class Action, 42 Brooklyn L.Rev. 189 (1976).

10. E.g., Cypress v. Newport News Gen. & Nonsectarian Hosp. Assn., 375 F.2d 648 (4th Cir.1967) (en banc).

11. E.g., Petersen v. Talisman Sugar Corp., 478 F.2d 73 (5th Cir.1973).

12. E.g., Wallace v. McDonald, 369 F.Supp. 180 (E.D.N.Y.1973).

13. E.g., Sullivan v. Murphy, 478 F.2d 938 (D.C.Cir. 1973).

14. E.g., Committee for G. I. Rights v. Callaway, 370 F.Supp. 934 (D.D.C.1974), rev'd on other grounds 518 F.2d 466 (D.C.Cir.1975).

15. See, e.g., Daar v. Yellow Cab Co., 67 Cal.2d 695, 433 P.2d 732, 63 Cal.Rptr. 724 (1967); Vasquez v. Superior Court, 4 Cal.3d 800, 484 P.2d 964, 94 Cal.Rptr. 796 (1971). But see City of San Jose v. Superior Court, 12 Cal.3d 447, 525 P.2d 701, 115 Cal.Rptr. 797 (1974).

16. See Moore v. Metropolitan Life Ins. Co., 33 N.Y.2d 304, 352 N.Y.S.2d 433, 307 N.E.2d 554 (1973).

court would not undertake, through the construction route, to break new ground itself. In Hall v. Coburn Corp.,[17] for example, a consumer action, the court rejected use of the class action in an opinion that left no doubt that it regards suits like this as an indirect procedural way of altering substantive rights, a legislative function the court said it would not usurp.

The court afterwards withdrew at least to some extent from that view. In Ray v. Marine Midland Grace Trust Co.,[18] it said that "there has been a continuing development and definition of the appropriate sphere of class actions", and indicated that it would be inappropriate to regard CPLR 1005 as intending to keep the class action static. This was as encouraging a suggestion of upcoming judicial relief in this area as had ever been tendered in New York, but it served more as a legislative spur than as a herald of future Court of Appeals action.

In 1975, just a year after the *Ray* case, Article 9 was enacted and CPLR 1005 laid to rest. It is just as well that the legislature acted. Had the Court of Appeals tried to extend the "continuing development" it spoke of in the *Ray* case, it would have been hard pressed to collate and reconcile the massive and conflicting caselaw handed down on the New York class action statute over the years, cases that Professor Adolf Homburger, long a champion of the class action, said "defy logical analysis" and lose sight of the purpose of the class action.[19]

The drive for an expanded New York class action accelerated when the U.S. Supreme Court curtailed the jurisdictional scope of the federal class action, thereby creating a gap which, were it to be filled at all, could be filled only by a generous state class action provision, which New York did not have. The federal curtailment occurred as follows.

Federal Rule 23 with its procedural authorization for a class action is generous, but it may be used only when there is some basis for federal subject matter jurisdiction. Rule 23 regulates procedure only; it can't expand the subject matter jurisdiction of the federal courts,[20] authorization for which must be found in some federal statute. When a case invokes a statute conferring federal jurisdiction based on the cause of action arising under federal law, there is no minimal monetary requirement[21] and the federal class action confronts no jurisdictional barrier on that count. But when the cause of action does not arise under federal law and the sole basis on which federal jurisdiction rests is the diversity of citizenship of the parties, there is a problem.

The diversity statute is 28 U.S.C.A. § 1332, and it requires complete diversity: the citizenship of each plaintiff must differ from that of each defendant.[22] On the citizenship aspect, the Supreme Court has treated the class action generously: for diversity purposes, only the representatives' citizenship need differ from those of the other side; the citizenships of unjoined class members need not be considered.[23]

But § 1332 also has a monetary requirement; a case based on diversity must involve more than $75,000. On that aspect, the court has been less generous. It held that the claim of each of the representatives must meet the monetary minimum independently; that the interests of the representatives can't be aggregated to reach it.[24]

Advocates of the class action then argued that if at least one or a few of the representatives could meet the monetary requirement individually, the claims of the others (including those of the members of the class) ought to be sustained under recognized federal doc-

---

17. 26 N.Y.2d 396, 311 N.Y.S.2d 281, 259 N.E.2d 720 (1970).

18. 35 N.Y.2d 147, 151, 359 N.Y.S.2d 28, 31, 316 N.E.2d 320, 322 (1974).

19. 18th Jud.Council Rep.(1952) 223–24.

20. See Rule 82 of the Federal Rules of Civil Procedure.

21. See 28 U.S.C.A. § 1331, the so-called "general" federal question statute.

22. Strawbridge v. Curtiss, 3 Cranch (7 U.S.) 267, 2 L.Ed. 435 (1806).

23. Supreme Tribe of Ben–Hur v. Cauble, 255 U.S. 356, 41 S.Ct. 338, 65 L.Ed. 673 (1921).

24. Snyder v. Harris, 394 U.S. 332, 89 S.Ct. 1053, 22 L.Ed.2d 319 (1969).

trines of "pendent" or "ancillary" jurisdiction so as to permit the federal court to entertain the whole class suit. In Zahn v. International Paper Co.,[25] the Supreme Court rejected that alternative, too, thus effectively sounding the death knell of the federal class action in diversity cases—or at least those in which the class consists of numerous persons with relatively small individual money claims. People in that category, however, are the class action's major dependents.[26]

With the federal arena practically closed to the huge diversity of citizenship category, the class action would have to look to state hospitality. In New York it did so in vain—until 1975. The New York problem before 1975 was that the class action was well received only when the relief sought was something like an injunction or a declaratory judgment. There, with one judgment, the court could satisfy the whole class and be done with the case. But when more was at stake, like the separate monetary interests of all of the members of the class, judicial hackles were up and the class action was out. Professor Homburger documents this in his 1971 study of the class action, a study done almost two decades after his earlier one[27] and from which comes the new Article 9. He concludes that:

in the absence of a limited fund or a substantive relationship of some sort among the members of the class, the New York courts [would] not countenance class actions for separate and distinct relief of individual members of the class even if the basic issues of law or fact around which the controversy [revolved were] common to all.[28]

The new Article 9 not only countenanced such class actions; it offered them a red carpet, or so its sponsors intended. The carpet did not prove as posh as planned, however. The judicial reception was mixed, as will be seen.

§ 140. Prerequisites to Class Action; the Old Law Reviewed

The old New York criterion for the class action, the one embodied in subdivision (a) of the repealed CPLR 1005 (which had been carried over with little change from the Field Code amendment of 1849), read as follows:

Where the question is one of a common or general interest of many persons or where the persons who might be made parties are very numerous and it may be impracticable to bring them all before the court, one or more may sue or defend for the benefit of all.

The number that would satisfy as "many persons" or as "very numerous" was decided on a case-by-case basis.[1] Most of the attention of the cases was directed at what would satisfy as "a common or general interest". The straitjacket that the class action found itself in was woven of the courts' insistence that the interests of the class members be so uniform that each could be said to wish the same relief, or a substantial part of it. In Brenner v. Title Guarantee & Trust Co.,[2] for example, D sold shares in a bond secured by a mortgage. Many bought. Alleging that the sales were induced by fraudulent representations, three buyers sued in behalf of all to recover the purchase prices. The court would not allow it in class

---

25. 414 U.S. 291, 94 S.Ct. 505, 38 L.Ed.2d 511 (1973).

26. There is currently a dispute about whether the 1990 adoption of 28 U.S.C.A. § 1367, the statute on "supplemental" jurisdiction that codifies the federal caselaw doctrines of "pendent" and "ancillary" jurisdiction, was intended to overrule the Zahn case. See the discussion in § 630 below (Practitioner's Edition).

27. The earlier one is the 1952 study for the Judicial Council, cited in note 19, above.

28. Homburger, State Class Actions and the Federal Rule, 17th Jud.Conf.Rep.(1972) 242, 250. The study is republished in that report with the permission of the Columbia Law Review, where it first appeared in 71 Col.L.Rev. 609, 619 (1971). See also Weinstein, Revision of Procedure: Some Problems in Class Actions, 9 Buffalo

L.Rev. 433 (1960). The Homburger and Weinstein articles are good bibliographical starting points for the student who would read more deeply on the class action. So is the advisory committee note on Federal Rule 23 (which may be found in the 28 U.S.C.A. volume covering that rule). Another series of general lessons on the class action and some of its difficulties may be found in the majority and dissenting opinions in Eisen v. Carlisle & Jacquelin, 417 U.S. 156, 94 S.Ct. 2140, 40 L.Ed.2d 732 (1974).

§ 140

1. See pp.226–29 of the Homburger study in the 18th Jud.Council Rep.(1952).

2. 276 N.Y. 230, 11 N.E.2d 890 (1937).

form, but did allow it as an ordinary action.[3] Although there were common issues, the court found that there were not common interests. The fact that each of the buyers had a separate and distinct cause of action was not by itself the deterrent, because that is often so of class actions. The major rejecting factor in *Brenner* was that it could not be said that each of the buyers wanted the same relief. Some might want back the purchase price, others might prefer a formal rescission in equity, still others a tort action for fraud damages. There might even be a group not deeming themselves defrauded at all, and who, aware of the facts, would have wished to preserve the transaction. Under the criteria applicable under CPLR Article 9 today, a case like *Brenner* ought to pass the class action test without difficulty.

Brenner is prototypical of where class status would be denied under prior law: the case in which the court would have to award money judgments in different sums to a large number of people. While that wasn't an absolute deterrent,[4] it was almost one. If the money claims could be satisfied only out of a limited fund, class action status was more generously awarded, such as where the plaintiffs were looking to the bond of a surety company to make good on losses caused by a defalcation.[5] On close examination, one might even find cases in which class form was permitted for money claims not limited to a fund,[6] but in context these could almost be called accidents. With the exception of the "fund" cases, the judicial restriction of class form to where only injunctive or declaratory relief was sought was carried virtually to the point of exclusiveness, and that was no gift at all to the "class action" concept. There was little more for the court to do in that kind of case than in an ordinary action. The presence of the "class" was reduced to a mere esthetic formality. The final

judgment would just enjoin or declare, and as far as time and trouble were concerned, it was the same to the court whether the injunction or declaration was at the behest of a single plaintiff or a mob.

Kovarsky v. Brooklyn Union Gas Co.[7] is a good illustration. There the court allowed the class action for a declaration that a certain service charge by a public utility was unlawful, and an injunction restraining its collection in future, but the court would not order an accounting, which would have led to a huge number of individual money judgments, in nominal sums, returning prior charges. Whether the new class action provision will invite new remedies in a situation like that, such as by using what has become known as the "fluid recovery",[8] still remains to be seen.

This almost total barrier to the use of class actions for money was legislatively removed with the adoption of CPLR Article 9 in 1975. A few of the old anti-money cases will be reexamined under the new article to see how they would fare today.

§ 141. Prerequisites to Class Action; Present Law

Subdivision (a) of CPLR 901 sets forth the basic conditions for a class action. It says that "[o]ne or more members of a class may sue or be sued as representative parties on behalf of all if:

1. the class is so numerous that joinder of all members, whether otherwise required or permitted, is impracticable;

2. there are questions of law or fact common to the class which predominate over any questions affecting only individual members;

---

3. Actual joinder is permitted in a case like this because the claims arise out of a related series of transactions and involve common questions. CPLR 1002(a). Akely v. Kinnicutt, 238 N.Y. 466, 144 N.E. 682 (1924), is an example. See § 134 above. Actual joinder should not be confused with class form, in which the injured persons are represented rather than joined.

4. See, e.g., Lichtyger v. Franchard Corp., 18 N.Y.2d 528, 277 N.Y.S.2d 377, 223 N.E.2d 869 (1966).

5. See Guffanti v. National Sur. Co., 196 N.Y. 452, 90 N.E. 174 (1909).

6. See, e.g., Case v. Indian Motorcycle Co., 300 N.Y. 513, 89 N.E.2d 246 (1949).

7. 279 N.Y. 304, 18 N.E.2d 287 (1938).

8. See § 145 below.

3.   the claims or defenses of the representative parties are typical of the claims or defenses of the class;

4.   the representative parties will fairly and adequately protect the interests of the class; and

5.   a class action is superior to other available methods for the fair and efficient adjudication of the controversy."

The drafters believe this formulation to be more uniform than the federal rule, which they find "overlapping and more complex".[1] The first four items have counterparts in subdivision (a) of Federal Rule 23. The requirements of paragraph 2, about common questions predominating, and paragraph 5, about the class action being superior to other available methods, have counterparts in Federal Rule 23(b)(3), but while they are stated only as alternative requirements in the federal provision, they are made uniform prerequisites for all class actions under CPLR 901(a).

Since CPLR 901(a) is intentionally phrased "in pragmatic and functional terms avoiding any reference to the abstract nature of the substantive rights involved",[2] it contains no limitation based on the kind of substantive claim asserted. It has no stated preference for one kind of claim against another, presumably making itself available to any as long as CPLR 901(a) requirements are met. Nor is the 901(a) list exclusive. As will be seen in a later section discussing CPLR 902 and the procedure whereby the court by order determines whether the action may proceed in class form,[3] there are a number of other matters that must also be considered by the court before determining whether to allow a class action.

All of these requirements—the basics from 901(a) and the several additional from 902— must be examined individually in each case to see if the case passes muster in class form. Each case is sui generis, but with the obvious support that Article 9 gives the class action,

the courts' examination of the prerequisites in each individual case should at least be divested of its pre–1975 hostility. The New York case-law on Article 9 has been developing, and the lawyer also has the innumerable cases on Federal Rule 23 to turn to for ideas and guidance,[4] but given the highly individual nature of each case requesting class form, the emanations of the cases offer only general aid.

While it is more usual for a handful of representatives to get together for the suit, even one can bring it. So provides CPLR 901(a), in common with its federal counterpart in Rule 23(a). The caselaw condones a single representative if the representative is a good one. The court is not concerned so much with the number of representatives as with the quality of their lawyers.[5] Because of the high degree of judicial management required in a class action, and the great numbers affected by the result, the court is especially sensitive to assure quality representation. If one person brings the action, but with a lawyer of repute and ability, the court will be more content than if several sue with a staff of lawyers about whom the court has doubts. These doubts are seldom expressed, to be sure, but they result in more intense judicial scrutiny of the proceedings.

When several attorneys are on the scene to represent the class, and come from different firms, there may occasionally arise some dispute as to who will control the litigation on the class's side (subject, of course, to judicial superintendence). This can be resolved by the court, by motion or sua sponte; it can assign control of the case to lawyer X but with instruction that she consult with lawyers Y and Z before taking designated steps. Application to the court can be made if agreement on a given point can't be achieved.

There is no set quantity that will make the membership so "numerous" under CPLR 901(a)(1) as to make actual joinder "impracti-

§ 141

1. 20th Jud.Conf.Rep.(1975) 206–7.

2. Id.

3. See § 142 below.

4. See, e.g., Huebner v. Caldwell & Cook, Inc., 139 Misc.2d 288, 526 N.Y.S.2d 356 (Sup.Ct. Monroe County, 1988).

5. See, e.g., Hohmann v. Packard Instrument Co., 399 F.2d 711 (7th Cir.1968).

cable". As under prior law, the number can vary from case to case. Even for such initial requisites, the court's discretion controls. The requirement must be weighed in context.

The class action is especially appropriate when a fraud, such as that contained in a stock prospectus, has harmed a large number.[6] It is also fitting in the kind of situation met in the *Kovarsky* case,[7] in which all the utility users in a large municipality were unlawfully charged for a certain service. In that case, it will be recalled, the class device was sustained for injunctive and declaratory relief but not for the return of the improperly collected money. Under CPLR 901(a) it should be sustainable for the money, too, whatever the logistics of getting the money back into proper hands. No longer should one hear the frequent insistence of old caselaw that the class action is usable for money recoveries only when a limited fund is involved. Under CPLR 901(a), most of the non-"fund" cases in which prior law rejected the class action[8] should be overruled and the class action allowed. CPLR 901(a) should also, of course, continue to permit a class action in cases in which old CPLR 1005 did, and that means continued utility of the class weapon when an injunction or declaration is the principal aim, a conclusion buttressed by CPLR 904(a).[9]

The class need not have a common interest in all of the issues. CPLR 901(a)(2) makes this clear when it requires that common issues "predominate" rather than preempt. If it appears that there are several common issues but one predominates for one part of the class and another for a different part, the class can be divided into "subclasses and each subclass treated as a class".[10] So, for example, if a defendant, in furtherance of a commercial scheme, issues two fraudulent documents (e.g., prospectuses), large numbers relying on each

to their detriment, a class action need not be disallowed merely because two issues (the fraud with respect to each document) predominate. The court can order a severance, making separate class actions of the two groups, or merely keep the case but with "subclass" treatment within it.

It is not of great moment that damages differ individually among the various members of the class, numerous though they be. In Vickers v. Home Federal Savings & Loan Assoc.,[11] for example, allowing a class action under federal truth-in-lending provisions, the court held that the fact that the representatives seek damages in different amounts than the class members or even a different category of remedy altogether does not bar a class action or necessarily impair the representatives' capacity to act fairly for all. The court can allow class status for the purpose of trying the common issue and then, through various discretionary alternatives, set up a mechanism whereby each class member can individually prove his damages.[12] Indeed, there is explicit authority to bring the class action to try only a particular issue[13] rather than all issues. So, for example, a class action can be brought to establish only the fraudulence of a document relied on by many, the many then being left to bring separate actions to test the individual elements of reliance and damages if the class action establishes the fraud. In those later actions, the fraud issue will then be the subject of a collateral estoppel and the class action will have served its purpose well.

Disputes about whether common issues predominate over individual issues often engenders disagreement among the judges. Rosenfeld v. A. H. Robins Co.[14] illustrates. The action was brought in behalf of all women injured by an allegedly defective intrauterine

---

6. See and compare Brenner v. Title Guarantee & Trust Co., 276 N.Y. 230, 11 N.E.2d 890 (1937).

7. 279 N.Y. 304, 18 N.E.2d 287 (1938), discussed in § 140, above.

8. E.g., Society Milion Athena, Inc. v. National Bank of Greece, 281 N.Y. 282, 22 N.E.2d 374 (1939).

9. CPLR 904(a), discussed in § 143, below, dispenses with initial notice to the class when injunctive or declaratory relief is the main object of the action.

10. CPLR 906(2).

11. 56 A.D.2d 62, 390 N.Y.S.2d 747 (4th Dep't 1977).

12. See, e.g., Nix v. Grand Lodge of Int'l Ass'n. of Machinists and Aerospace Workers, 479 F.2d 382 (5th Cir.1973).

13. CPLR 906(1).

14. 63 A.D.2d 11, 407 N.Y.S.2d 196 (2d Dep't 1978).

device. Despite the numerousness of the class and the majority's concession that there were at least several issues in the case that would lend themselves to class treatment, the court rejected class form. Not only would damages be individual to each class member's case, stressed the majority, but causality and reliance (on the manufacturer's representations) would be individual as well. The dissent accented, instead, the common issues and notably the common opportunity to obtain disclosure, which in *Rosenfeld*, by the defendant's own concession, would involve some 100,000 documents—obviously beyond the economic ability of each class member to pursue on her own.

The *Rosenfeld* case illustrates how much of the class action's future depends on the attitude of the judges. The factors that must be considered before determining whether to permit an action in class form are so flexible that equally reasonable minds can flex them either way.

Another factor is whether the court finds the class action "superior" to other kinds of action, an element listed in CPLR 901(a)(5). The New York courts apparently don't find the class action superior when its main purpose is just to establish a legal principle of importance to many. They find adequate in that situation the doctrine of stare decisis: whether the plaintiffs are few or many, the courts postulate, the precedent set by the case will be available statewide. This want of enthusiasm for the class action is especially apparent when governmental obligations are involved, such as in an action to determine entitlement to public assistance.[15]

That coin has a flip side, however. Governmental obligations were involved in Beekman v. City of New York,[16] for example, where the court nevertheless sustained a class action in behalf of all New York City firemen denied terminal leave and vacation prior to a certain day. Although each member of the class was seeking individual damages—the factor that

often turns the courts off rather than on to a class action—separate suits by all of them were deemed virtually certain to follow if class form were denied. The court indicated that although the class was large, it was nevertheless "defined and limited" and hence the action was more manageable than one in behalf of "indefinite numbers". Perhaps a lesson for advocates of class form is that they will help their cause if they can convince the court that far from being an encumbrance, the class action will spare the court numerous separate actions; that the interest of each class member is sufficient to spur a separate action by each if the court refuses to allow them to proceed as a class.

When a case involves more than just a legal principle, in other words, manifesting as well that there are throngs out there who are up in arms about the wrong and will sue on their own if not allowed their day in court within the framework of the class action, the courts are less likely to reject the action by pointing to the stare decisis doctrine.

In this connection, consider again the *Brenner* case discussed in the prior section. Under the old New York statute, *Brenner* refused class status to an action brought to recover the purchase price of shares in a mortgage-secured bond. Shouldn't class status now be allowed in a case like that under CPLR 901(a)? The action was based on fraud and the class device, since it would enable that issue to be adjudicated in one instead of numerous actions, ought to be deemed "superior" to other methods to protect the class.[17] Any device that would allow one action to do a job that would otherwise have to be done by many should be considered "superior". Were all the potential class members to bring separate actions, the common issue would permit consolidation of all of them[18] and the courts would be almost certain to grant such a consolidation. This is not to say that class status is permissible whenever, were each class member to bring

---

15. See, e.g., Gaillard v. Lavine, 51 A.D.2d 181, 380 N.Y.S.2d 7 (1st Dep't 1976).

16. 65 A.D.2d 317, 411 N.Y.S.2d 620 (1st Dep't 1979).

17. See, e.g., Dolgow v. Anderson, 43 F.R.D. 472 (E.D.N.Y.1968), rev'd on other grounds 438 F.2d 825 (2d Cir.1970).

18. CPLR 602(a).

separate suit, consolidation could ensue. It is only to stress that as far as CPLR 901(a)(5) is concerned, New York does deem a single action a "superior" way to adjudicate multiple claims. To that extent the analogy is compelling.

A probing self-examination into the old and to some degree continuing judicial resistance to the class action appears in the Second Department case of Friar v. Vanguard Holding Corp.[19] *Friar* sustained in class form an action in behalf of all persons who sold realty to buyers for whom defendant D was acting as mortgage lender. D allegedly forced the sellers to pay a certain tax at the closings, in violation of law. *Friar* is a convincing decision, and yet not unanimous. A First Department case subscribing to *Friar's* more generous attitude toward the class action is Brandon v. Chefetz,[20] which allowed class status to numerous minority shareholders against two of the major ones for obtaining special breaks for themselves in a corporate take-over situation.[21]

The use of the class action in multi-party personal injury cases is discussed in a later section.[22]

An action to recover a statutory penalty is expressly barred from class form unless the statute imposing the penalty specifically says otherwise.[23]

§ 142. Order Allowing Class Action

No court permission is needed in advance of a class action. The representatives simply bring it. But CPLR 902 requires the plaintiffs, shortly after the action is begun, to move for an order permitting maintenance of the class action, thus promptly affording the court in each class action an opportunity to determine whether the requirements of class form are met. The time within which the plaintiff must make this motion is 60 days after the defendant's answering time has expired. This policy of requiring early court attention to class-action appropriateness is borrowed from the federal class action rule, but while federal rule requires only that the adjudication be made "as soon as practicable",[1] the New York provision imposes a stated time limit and thus offers greater assurance of prompt disposition of the matter.

The court on this motion, in addition to determining whether the stated requirements of CPLR 901 are met, must also consider the factors listed in CPLR 902. Five are listed:

1. the interest of members of the class in individually controlling the prosecution or defense of separate actions;

2. the impracticability or inefficiency of prosecuting or defending separate actions;

3. the extent and nature of any litigation concerning the controversy already commenced by or against members of the class;

4. the desirability or undesirability of concentrating the litigation of the claim in the particular forum;[2] and

5. the difficulties likely to be encountered in the management of a class action.[3]

The list is illustrative, not exhaustive. Any other factors the court deems relevant may

---

19. 78 A.D.2d 83, 434 N.Y.S.2d 698 (1980). The case is the subject of a more extended treatment in New York State Law Digest No. 255.

20. 106 A.D.2d 162, 485 N.Y.S.2d 55 (1985).

21. The court sustained class status only in respect of New York shareholders, however. The power to exercise jurisdiction over nonresident class members was unclear at the time, but was shortly afterwards approved by the U.S. Supreme Court. See the Phillips case discussed in § 144 below.

22. See § 142 below.

23. CPLR 901(b). This exception was added by the legislature; it was not part of the Judicial Conference draft. See 20th Jud.Conf.Rep. (1975) 206–07. Penalty provisions under federal truth-in-lending statutes were held to authorize a class action in terms satisfactory to CPLR 901(b), and such a class action was sustained in Vickers v.

Home Fed. Sav. & Loan Ass'n, 56 A.D.2d 62, 390 N.Y.S.2d 747 (4th Dep't 1977). The sustaining may have avoided some constitutional issues under the supremacy clause. See Homburger, The 1975 New York Judicial Conference Package: Class Actions and Comparative Negligence, 25 Buffalo L.Rev. 415, 423–24 (1976).

§ 142

1. FRCP Rule 23(c)(1).

2. See Bloom v. Cunard Line, Ltd., 76 A.D.2d 237, 430 N.Y.S.2d 607 (1st Dep't 1980). This is just a kind of forum non conveniens rule specifically articulated for the class action.

3. See Homburger, State Class Actions and the Federal Rule, 71 Columbia L.Rev. 609, 652 (1971).

also be considered. The apparent merits of the class claim may be looked at,[4] for example, but this is likely only when merit (or lack of merit) appears to be plain at the outset.

The listed factors are to be considered in all class actions, and not, as under the federal rule, in only some of them.[5] The second listed item, about the impracticability of separate actions,[6] has no counterpart in the federal rule (although it is of course a matter the federal judge can and often does consider); the other four items on the list do have federal counterparts.[7]

If the court after considering all of the required factors finds favorably on them, and finds all of the CPLR 901 prerequisites satisfied as well, it will make an order permitting the class action. If it does, the order must describe the class.[8] The order can be conditional, and it may be amended, either on motion of a party or on the court's own motion, at any time before the case is decided on the merits.[9]

CPLR 902 is a key section, perhaps every bit as much so as CPLR 901. The matters to be considered by the court in deciding whether class form is warranted, which are essentially discretionary, can be used to implement or frustrate the broad purposes of the legislature, depending entirely on the attitude of the judges. A given factor in a case can be viewed in a negative light, and that illumination can easily be allowed to obscure positive beams emanating from other factors, thus defeating the class action at the threshold.

Until the various factors are put into some sequence of stress and dominance, individual cases may be uncomfortably dependent on the predilections of individual judges. Lawyers considering or involved in class actions should

therefore keep a running check on caselaw on a departmental basis. While the ultimate destiny of the class action in New York under the current Article 9 would seem to depend on the Court of Appeals, the facts of the daily life of the class action indicate that the Court of Appeals may have little occasion to address the matter. The custodians of the issue seem to be the appellate divisions, for the following reasons:

The Court of Appeals is a law court. It doesn't review exercises of discretion unless they rise to the level of an "abuse", which not many do. Since "[c]lass action certification is a question vested in the sound discretion of the court",[10] and for exercises of discretion the appellate division is in effect the court of last resort, it may be the fate of the class action to run hot and cold depending on the temperature in the local appellate division.[11] The Court of Appeals may be called on from time to time to answer a question of law connected with the class action, but the big question in almost every attempted class action is whether the particular action qualifies for class status. Since the Court of Appeals, perhaps ironically, ends up with little role on that point, it turns out to have little role in the class action in New York. When it has before it a case in which class status was acted on below—one way or the other—and there was basis for going either way, the Court of Appeals sees little option but to affirm, even if the appellate division was itself closely divided.

An example is Harris v. Shearson Hayden Stone, Inc.,[12] a case seemingly tailor-made for class relief but rejected for it by a closely divided (3–2) appellate division. Here was an intriguing battle between the class action of Article 9 on one side and the Article 75 re-

---

4. See 20th Jud.Conf.Rep.(1975) 607–8.

5. Compare paragraph (3) of FRCP Rule 23(b), which is alternative to the rule's paragraphs (1) and (2).

6. This is an important factor in small claimants' consumer actions. See Homburger, State Class Actions and the Federal Rule, 71 Columbia L. Rev. 609, 637 (1971).

7. See subparagraphs A–D in FRCP Rule 23(b)(3) and compare (b)(1).

8. CPLR 903.

9. CPLR 902.

10. Askey v. Occidental Chemical Corp., 102 A.D.2d 130, 137, 477 N.Y.S.2d 242, 247 (4th Dep't 1984).

11. See Weinberg v. Hertz Corp., 116 A.D.2d 1, 499 N.Y.S.2d 693 (1986), aff'd 69 N.Y.2d 979, 516 N.Y.S.2d 652, 509 N.E.2d 347 (1987), and the year-end review of the class action by Thomas A. Dickerson in the New York Law Journal of December 30, 1987.

12. 82 A.D.2d 87, 441 N.Y.S.2d 70 (1st Dep't 1981), aff'd 56 N.Y.2d 627, 450 N.Y.S.2d 482, 435 N.E.2d 1097 (1982).

quirement of arbitration on the other. A major brokerage house "floated" remittances to commodities customers, i.e., drew checks on distant banks to prolong collection (thereby prolonging as well the broker's retention of the high interest the money was earning in the meantime), and aggrieved customers brought a class action against the practice. Class status was rejected because all of the customers had signed contracts containing arbitration agreements. Having consented to arbitration, they were held to have waived the right to sue in court and with it the right to use the class action. The dissenting justices, with what would seem the better of the argument if the intentions underlying the 1975 enactment of Article 9 are made the guide, note the adhesion nature of the contract and that customers could not have opened accounts without signing it. A suggestion of the dissent was to hold the arbitration commitment in abeyance to see whether the requisites of a class action were met. If they were, litigation in class form could proceed; if they were not, arbitration could go forward.[13]

The practice of "floating" can be debated as an issue of law. But when the broker relies on an arbitration commitment contained in a take-it-or-leave-it contract to bar a judicial test altogether (all the while evincing no inclination to accept the holding of any one customer's arbitration as a warrant to discontinue the floating practice as to others), it is not unreasonable to assess the issue in ethical terms. That would make a court test appropriate as a matter of public policy and easily, under these lights, subordinate the arbitration aims of CPLR Article 75 to the class action purposes of Article 9.

Well into the third decade of Article 9, a definitive answer is still awaited to the question of whether the class action will be allowed in multi-party accident cases, at least for the liability issue: will it be allowed in the massive plane or train tragedy in which numerous persons are injured or killed? The Federal Advisory Committee, thorough and even committed though they may have been in other regards, hedged on this one. They said that the "mass accident . . . is ordinarily not appropriate for a class action", citing the prospect of varying defenses "affecting the individuals in different ways".[14] But such a delicate approach to the "mass accident", at least on the ground cited, may be unwarranted. What part, after all, do "defenses" play when 100 people on a plane or 200 on a train were reading magazines or sleeping or conversing when they were suddenly subjected to injury or death? Can contributory or even comparative negligence be expected to play any realistic role at all in these occurrences?

Two important factors suggest that the question of using the class action in mass accident cases may have been tabled, indefinitely if not permanently. Expanded application of the collateral estoppel (issue preclusion) doctrine[15] is one contributing factor. The New York Court of Appeals held in 1984, almost a decade after the 1975 enactment of Article 9, that once one victim has successfully sued a tortfeasor other victims of the same tort may be allowed, in their individual lawsuits, a free estoppel ride on the liability finding.[16] That accomplishes in many instances what the class action would. It enables a nonparty to make use of the doctrine against one who was a party to the first action and thus fully heard on the issue. The doctrine does not work against the nonparty, however,[17] so that a victory by the tortfeasor against the plaintiff in one action could not be invoked against a different plaintiff in another. This means that the estoppel doctrine is only a partial resolution.

The second factor, and perhaps a fuller answer to the question of using the class action

---

13. Nothing in federal sources was cited to void the arbitration obligation as involuntary, but in this respect the case of Ames v. Merrill Lynch, 567 F.2d 1174 (2d Cir.1977), should be consulted.

14. See Advisory Committee notes to amended (1966) FRCP Rule 23 in 28 U.S.C.A.

15. The doctrine is treated in § 457 et seq., below.

16. See Koch v. Consolidated Edison Co. of N.Y., 62 N.Y.2d 548, 479 N.Y.S.2d 163 (1984), discussed in § 467, below, and the lead note in New York State Law Digest No. 309.

17. See § 458 below.

in the mass tort case, is the opting-out procedure, treated below.[18] The first factor listed for consideration in CPLR 902 is "the interest of members of the class in individually controlling the prosecution ... of separate actions". In personal injury actions plaintiffs usually prefer to retain their own lawyers, choose their own venues (those reputed to offer the highest verdicts), and make their own settlements. The potential recovery in most personal injury suits makes such an independent prosecution economically worthwhile. Hence an attempt to use a class action for victims of a mass tort would probably result in many if not most of them invoking the "opting out" procedure, frustrating the class suit by that route.

Perhaps the class action would have better sailing, therefore, in a mass accident case in which individual damages to most victims are modest. It may then be economical to them to have the liability issue presented in one trial, damages then to be resolved individually, either as follow-ups in the same (the class) action or in separate actions. The point is that at least in some mass accident cases, the class action can be of value. The door should be left open to it.

The venue rules as they apply in class actions are reviewed in Mazzocki v. State Farm Fire & Cas. Co.,[19] which holds that venue in a class action must be based on the residence of an actual party, not a mere class member.

§ 143. Notice of Class Action

There was no requirement under prior law that the members of the class be notified of an action brought in their behalf. There still is none in a class action "brought primarily for injunctive or declaratory relief", although the court may in its discretion require notice if it is deemed necessary to protect the class and the cost of the notice will not deter pursuit.[1] But in any other kind of class action today, including the one that seeks money, "reasonable notice of the commencement of a class action shall be given to the class in such manner as the court directs."[2] The giving of notice is thus mandatory in other than injunctive and declaratory cases,[3] but its method has been left to the discretion of the court. There is therefore room to allow in a given case notice by publication or by some other collective method,[4] thus saving the great expense that can attend individual notification, but the method chosen will of course have to be tailored to the facts. The court can authorize publication, for example, but also order actual notice, by mail or otherwise, to designated class members or groups of them, or to a certain number of class members selected at random or as the court directs. In determining the method of notice, CPLR 904(c) requires the court to consider:

1. the cost of giving notice by the various possible methods;[5]

2. the resources of the parties; and

3. the stake of each class member and the likelihood that significant numbers of them might wish to be excluded from the class, and thus not be bound by the judgment.[6]

---

18. See § 144 below.

19. 170 Misc.2d 70, 649 N.Y.S.2d 656 (Sup.Ct., N.Y.County, 1996). If a change of venue is sought promptly, the court says that it should be resolved before the class action is certified by the court. In this case, D was an insurer resident in Saratoga County and P, of Orange County, apparently chose New York County for the lawyer's convenience. D's prompt effort to change the venue to Saratoga succeeded.

§ 143

1. CPLR 904(a).

2. CPLR 904(b).

3. The Judicial Conference wanted notice to be optional even in these cases, but the legislature made it mandatory. See 20th Jud.Conf.Rep.(1975) 208.

4. Cf. FRCP Rule 23(c)(2) and Eisen v. Carlisle & Jacquelin, 417 U.S. 156, 94 S.Ct. 2140, 40 L.Ed.2d 732 (1974).

5. In this connection the Judicial Conference called attention to the situation in which the class consists of corporate shareholders and the corporation is also a party, where the notification can be as competent and inexpensive as merely ordering the corporation to enclose the notice in its next mailing to shareholders. See 20th Jud.Conf.Rep.(1975) 209, citing Dolgow v. Anderson, 43 F.R.D. 472, 500 (E.D.N.Y.1968), rev'd on other grounds 438 F.2d 825 (2d Cir.1970).

6. This list is the formulation of the legislature. The Judicial Conference proposal was more general but did mention several of these considerations in its notes. See id. at 208–09.

The court can assist itself in determining this likelihood (under the third item) by having notice sent to a random sampling of the class.[7]

The content of the notice must be approved by the court,[8] and this is so whether the requirement of notice is a discretionary matter, as in an injunction or declaratory judgment action, or mandatory, as in a money action.[9] The plaintiff can seek the court's directions and approval by motion, which should be on notice to adverse parties. If need be, the motion can be brought on by order to show cause in which the court can determine what notice the adverse parties shall be given. It will be recalled that under CPLR 902 the plaintiff must move for an order allowing the action in class form. Perhaps that requirement can be combined with the CPLR 904 requirements in regard to notifying the class and having the court approve the notice's content. It would seem permissible for the plaintiff, by a single motion, to seek (1) court leave to prosecute the action in class form as required by 902, (2) (if leave is granted) court determination of the method by which the class is to be notified of the action's pendency, and (3) court approval of the contents of the notice.

The CPLR is specific about the expense of notification and who must bear it, thus avoiding the dispute that arose in this regard under the federal rule.[10] Unless the court says otherwise, the plaintiff must bear the expense of notifying the class. That can be costly and sometimes prohibitively costly if individual notice is required, as opposed to the collective notice offered by something like publication. But the court is empowered, "if justice requires", to make the defendant pay all or part of the notice expense. The court can investigate the potential merits of the case to inform its determination. The court may even conduct a preliminary hearing to determine how notice costs should be apportioned.[11]

A hearing on any of the ingredients that go into a class action certification, including a preliminary look at the merits, is sometimes called a "mini-hearing".[12]

§ 144. Opting Out

CPLR 903 provides in part that "[w]hen appropriate the court may limit the class to those members who do not request exclusion from the class within a specified time after notice". This contemplates that the notice served on the class members, advising them of the pendency of the action and its purpose, will also offer each member an opportunity to notify the court that she does not wish to be part of the class or subject to the judgment. This procedure is popularly known as "opting out". When and how it is used is left to the discretion of the court under CPLR 903.[1] Under the federal counterpart, on which it's modeled, the opting out offering is mandatory in certain cases.[2] As contemplated by the Judicial Conference, the opting out procedure would be used:

   i. when representation of the entire class is not needed for a just disposition of the controversy;

   ii. when the class members have a significant practical interest in individually controlling the litigation; and

   iii. when individual notice is feasible without imposing a prohibitive economic or administrative burden on the parties.[3]

---

7. CPLR 904(c)(III).

8. CPLR 904(c).

9. An example of a notice approved by the court in a class action seeking money damages appears as an appendix to Vickers v. Home Federal Savings & Loan Assoc., 56 A.D.2d 62, 390 N.Y.S.2d 747 (4th Dep't 1977).

10. See Eisen v. Carlisle & Jacquelin, note 4, above. Eisen interprets only FRCP Rule 23, however, not the constitution, thus leaving it open to the states to fashion their own procedures.

11. CPLR 904(d).

12. See Chimenti v. American Express Co., 97 A.D.2d 351, 467 N.Y.S.2d 357 (1st Dep't 1983).

§ 144

1. The opting-out procedure was ordered in Vickers v. Home Fed. Sav. & Loan Ass'n, 56 A.D.2d 62, 390 N.Y.S.2d 747 (4th Dep't 1977), and a copy of the notice implementing it, called an "Exclusion Request", is appended to the opinion.

2. See FRCP Rule 23(c)(2).

3. 20th Jud.Conf.Rep. (1975) 208. A special and more specific opting-out provision, contained in Gen.Bus.L.

With the opting out procedure available, the New York courts may perhaps be less hesitant about allowing a class action in personal injury cases. As mentioned two sections earlier, a factor that can be cited against the use of class form in personal injury cases is that the plaintiffs, for tactical reasons, often have great interest in individually controlling their own cases.[4] Those who do can opt out; class form can still be retained for the rest and still result in a substantial benefit to the class (and to the court's calendars).

Item iii on the list concerns notice of the action's pendency. Since notice is not required when the relief sought is injunctive or declaratory (although it remains a court option),[5] the fact that the opting out procedure is initiated in the notice means that its primary use would be in other categories of class action, categories in which notice is mandatory.[6] Even when notice is mandatory, however, the method of notice is still left to judicial discretion. Since the opting out procedure confers an important right, it would be inappropriate to offer it in a collective form of notice, such as by publication or by posting in public places. It is therefore contemplated that the court will order opting out steps only when it has also decided to require individual notice, and that the court will order individual notice only when the "economic or administrative burden" of giving such notice is not "prohibitive".[7] Whether it is depends in large measure on the numbers involved. If the class has many thousands, the burdens are real.

In actions in which the class members would have different remedies to choose from—as opposed to those in which each class member would clearly be seeking money and nothing else—and in circumstances indicating that there might be conflict among them as to the remedy pursued, the use of the opting out procedure may be decisive of whether the court will allow a class action at all. Whether opting out is workable may also depend on the number of class members and the feasibility of identifying them. Gaynor v. Rockefeller,[8] for example, was an action under the old class action statute by African–Americans alleged to have been denied admission to certain unions. They sued for declaratory and injunctive relief. Pointing out that some of the class members might prefer a complaint to the Human Rights Commission or an action for money damages, and that the claim of each class member would turn on its own particular facts, the court disallowed class form. It said that

> a class action may not be maintained where the wrongs asserted are individual to the different persons involved and each of the persons aggrieved "may determine for himself the remedy which he will seek" and may be subject to "a defense not available against others".[9]

The categorical rejection of class form for actions meeting that description is no longer valid, but such problems will still influence judicial discretion about whether to allow a class action on a case by case basis. Using the *Gaynor* facts, for example, one question would be whether the individual class members are identifiable. If they are, an opting out notice can be sent to each of them and each can determine whether he wants the collective remedy proposed (in which case he can stay in) or some other remedy (in which case he can opt out and follow his own course). The appropriateness of different remedies, the relevance of different options, and the existence of individual defenses, are of course factors that must be initially considered before class form is sustained under the basic requirements of CPLR 901, but the availability of the opting

---

§ 342–b, applies to governmental entities being represented as a "class" by the attorney general suing for damages caused by monopolistic practices (see Gen.Bus.L. § 340) or violations of the federal antitrust laws.

4. This is one of the factors to be considered in determining whether to allow a class action. CPLR 902(1).

5. CPLR 904(a).

6. CPLR 904(b).

7. 20th Jud.Conf.Rep. (1975) 208.

8. 15 N.Y.2d 120, 256 N.Y.S.2d 584, 204 N.E.2d 627 (1965).

9. 15 N.Y.2d at 129, 256 N.Y.S.2d at 590, 204 N.E.2d at 631. The court was quoting from its own prior decision in Society Milion Athena, Inc. v. National Bank of Greece, 281 N.Y. 282, 292, 22 N.E.2d 374, 377 (1939).

out procedure is germane to the court's thinking when it negotiates those factors.

If a given member does opt out, he is excluded from the class and a judgment unfavorable to the class doesn't bind him. But what if the judgment is in favor of the class? There is some dispute about whether one who opted out may make collateral estoppel use of the judgment in an individual action later.[10] Because a class action carries res judicata consequences only when the several requirements applicable to it have been faithfully met, it has even been urged that a class member who has not opted out (although offered the opportunity) may still seek to be relieved of the effects of the judgment by showing that the prerequisites of a class action were not met.[11]

There should also be room within the structure of Article 9 to use a kind of "opting in" procedure. When the class is very numerous, for example, and all or most of its members can't be identified and there is a likelihood of diversity in their choice of remedies even if they could be, the court should be able to order a collective notice given, such as by publication in an appropriate periodical, in which the proposed class relief is stated and the members of the class are offered the right to opt in. Under such a procedure, only those specifically responding would be included in the class and permitted to share in its fruits. That would not preclude separate actions by those not responding, but it could substantially curtail the total number of actions by enabling the class action to dispose of many if not all of the potential claims.

When the remedy sought is one that redounds to the whole class automatically, opting out will seldom if ever be appropriate. Here again the injunctive and declaratory actions are the examples—the same ones that found welcome even under prior law. Greer v. Smith[12] is typical. The defendant operated a fat-rendering plant in the city of Rye. Refuse from it was emptied into a pond which in turn

polluted a local brook, spreading obnoxious odors through the neighborhood. A few local residents brought a class suit for an injunction and it was allowed. The court noted that "the tortious act [nuisance] in its entirety operates on all".[13] And all that was before the court was the request for an injunction, which meant that in one thrust the wish of all could be satisfied. Also noted by the court was the fact that each member of the class could, in his own right, have brought the action for the same relief without doing so in class form or otherwise involving any other class member. Each had, in other words, a private right to the same relief individually, which is true of most class actions.

Dissent among the class as to the remedies to be pursued is seldom in prospect when it is an injunction or mere declaration that is sought, but, as the *Gaynor* case shows, it may be. Whether potential dissent should preclude class form altogether, or allow it but invoke the opting out procedure, has to be approached practically. Class form should not be denied and the opting out procedure should not be invoked if choice of a different remedy is just a fanciful or remote possibility; both alternatives should be reserved for cases in which it is reasonable and perhaps even likely that a substantial number of class members would not go along with the relief asked for by the representatives who brought the suit. In such instances, the formation of subclasses may be a way out of the dilemma.

If the courts were to take an approach any more rigid than that, the class action could not exist. When the class is large, it can perhaps always be demonstrated that at least one or two among the class do not want the relief sought. Suppose, for example, that several of the Rye residents in the *Greer* case found the odors innocuous, or even pleasant; or, indeed, that they were employed at the offending plant. Should they be allowed to bar the suit in class form? The larger the group, the greater

10. See Homburger, State Class Actions and the Federal Rule, 71 Columbia L.Rev. 609, 647, republished in 17th Jud.Conf.Rep. (1972) 242, 270.

11. Id., 71 Columbia L.Rev. at 646, 17th Jud.Conf.Rep. at 269–70.

12. 155 A.D. 420, 140 N.Y.S. 43 (2d Dep't 1913).

13. Id. at 423, 140 N.Y.S. at 45.

the prospect that it will include a few mavericks or iconoclasts of unique taste and preference. What must govern here is not the remote possibility that one or a handful of the members of a large class might personally prefer to resist the suit. The courts must look to cultural realities—to a prevailing norm of human behavior. If by that standard it can be said that all but a few loners are going along with the relief, the potential dissent of the reclusive few should not be a barrier. The facts of Onofrio v. Playboy Club of New York[14] can serve as an example:

Five out of 50,000 members of the class (club members) sought in behalf of the class damages of over a million dollars for the club's failure to fulfill its agreement to operate and maintain a private club. An individual money judgment (or series of judgments) was sought returning the membership fee of $25 to each member of the class. Class form was denied in this old law case and one of the bases for the denial was that the remedy desired by some class members might differ from the monetary one sought. Class form should be sustainable under Article 9 today in a case like Onofrio, but should possible preferences for different remedies prompt utilization of the opting out procedure? What other remedies might class members seek? An injunction requiring maintenance of the club? Will equity undertake that, entailing as it does the management of an involved project and a running check on the good faith of its operators? A declaratory judgment that the club should be opened? Is that not even less effectual than an injunction? Is there a real and reasonable prospect that individual class members could show money damages in excess of the $25 they paid for membership? Factors like these must all be considered, but if alternative choices of remedy prove in context to be unfeasible or unreasonable, then perhaps not even the opting out step should be required.

The availability of the opting-out procedure turned out to be the factor that answered a long-outstanding question: can a court entertain jurisdiction over nonresident members of the class. The issue was a major one in class action practice and was finally resolved by the U.S. Supreme Court in Phillips Petroleum Co. v. Shutts,[15] involving the plaintiffs' side as the class (the usual scenario) under a sister state's class action statute.

Rarely has a court any occasion to address how it gets jurisdiction of a plaintiff. It is jurisdiction over the defendant that produces battle, and acres of caselaw. But the class action is an exception. If the members of the plaintiff class come from many places, by what right does a court in a state other than a given class member's domicile presume to entertain jurisdiction of her? Shall we apply to a plaintiff something like the "minimum contacts" test that we apply to measure extraterritorial jurisdiction of a defendant?[16] The U.S. Supreme Court in *Phillips* said no, sustaining Kansas jurisdiction over a huge class of plaintiffs even though only a bare fraction of them had Kansas contacts. It was the opting out device, which Kansas had and properly used in *Phillips*, that was held to satisfy the demands of due process. The members were notified of the suit and if they didn't want to be bound by the Kansas proceedings they had only to say so in response to the opting out notice. Many did.[17] Those who didn't would be bound by the judgment.

Addressing the jurisdiction-over-nonresidents issue in Matter of Colt Indus. Shareholder Litigation,[18] the New York Court of Appeals held that while the opting-out procedure would be mandatory when it is damages that the nonresident is seeking, it does not apply to a class action's demand for equitable or collective relief, such as an injunction or a declaratory judgment.

14. 15 N.Y.2d 740, 257 N.Y.S.2d 171, 205 N.E.2d 308 (1965), reversing on dissenting opinion below, 20 A.D.2d 3, 6, 244 N.Y.S.2d 485, 488 (1st Dep't 1963).

15. 472 U.S. 797, 105 S.Ct. 2965, 86 L.Ed.2d 628 (1985).

16. See § 84 above.

17. The case is discussed in the lead note in New York State Law Digest No. 311.

18. 77 N.Y.2d 185, 565 N.Y.S.2d 755, 566 N.E.2d 1160 (1991). The case is summarized in New York State Law Digest No. 375.

§ 145. "Fluid Recovery"

In *Onofrio*, discussed in the prior section, the possibility of different choices of remedy among the class members was cited as a major reason for refusing class form to the action. But the real explanation lay in the prospect that at one point or another the court might have to render 50,000 individual money judgments, or one massive judgment awarding $25 plus incidental sums to each of 50,000 different persons, each of whom would have to be identified and ultimately named. That kind of prospect was a sotto voce but influential deterrent in many old law cases. Without expanding the topic unduly, we should mention what has become known nationally as the "fluid recovery", which may supply a compromise but fair solution in cases like *Onofrio*.

The fluid recovery contemplates a judgment against the defendant in a sum sufficient to divest it of all the fruits of its wrong, but the beneficiaries are the class to which the past victims belong rather than the specific victims themselves.[1] Fluid recovery can be accomplished, for example, by requiring the seller of a product or a service regulated by law to reduce its price not just to the maximum, but below it, and to maintain it there for a period of time sufficient to repay, to the general body of users of the product or service, what was previously overcharged.[2] That promises a remedy if the monetary wrong is so massive that it is impracticable if not impossible to reimburse the actual victims, and almost any remedy is better than letting the wrongdoer get away with it.

The part of the fluid recovery concept that divests the wrongdoer of illicit gains has already gained judicial support even when there was nothing to do with an unclaimed part of the recovery but turn it over to the state. In a later phase of Friar v. Vanguard Holding Corp., the facts of which were noted earlier,[3] the wrongdoer was required to disgorge its wrongful charges but not all of the overcharged victims could be found. Some $14,000 was left over and the defendant sought to get it back. Nothing doing, held the court: "permitting reversion of the unclaimed funds to this defendant would be equivalent to awarding it the benefit of its own wrongdoing, a result which should not be sanctioned". The court directed the money to be turned over to the state as abandoned property.[4] That, too, is a "fluid recovery".

§ 146. Defendant's Side as Class

A suit against a defendant class is permitted by CPLR 901 but is seen less frequently than one by a plaintiff class and is approached even more cautiously by the courts. The sensitive nerve here is an attempt by the plaintiffs, who initially designate those who are to be the defendant-class's representatives, to pick out weak ones. The court can check into that and will doubtless be diligent in doing so. If the action otherwise satisfies class form but the court is uncomfortable about those who have been designated the representatives of the defendant class, the court can designate others, additionally or alternatively. An example of a defendant-as-class action which passed muster even under prior law is Northwestern Telegraph Co. v. Western Union Telegraph Co.,[1] in which the defendants were the shareholders of the plaintiff corporation in a dispute involving whether certain moneys paid by a third person should go to the shareholders directly or to the corporation itself.

---

§ 145

1. See Homburger, Private Suits in the Public Interest in the United States of America, 23 Buffalo L.Rev. 343, 371–73 (1973); Malina, Fluid Class Recovery as a Consumer Remedy in Anti–Trust Cases, 47 N.Y.U.L.Rev. 477 (1972); Comment, Due Process and Fluid Class Recovery, 53 Oregon L.Rev. 225 (1975). The New York statutes neither invite nor prohibit a fluid recovery, leaving the matter to the courts on a case-by-case basis. See Homburger, The 1975 New York Judicial Conference Package: Class Actions and Comparative Negligence, 25 Buffalo L.Rev. 415, 429–30 (1976).

2. See Comment, Manageability of Notice and Damage Calculation in Consumer Class Actions, 70 Mich.L.Rev. 338, 363–73 (1971).

3. See § 141 above.

4. 125 A.D.2d 444, 509 N.Y.S.2d 374 (2d Dep't 1986).

§ 146

1. 197 Misc. 1075, 99 N.Y.S.2d 331 (Sup.Ct., N.Y.County, 1950).

A situation like that should not be confused with the well known derivative action in which shareholders sue in the right of the corporation. The derivative action, a species of class action (in which the class is usually on the plaintiffs' side), is subject to more detailed statutory regulation.[2]

Dudley v. Kerwick[3] is an unusual example of class status being conferred on both sides. Some 88% of the landowners of a town got themselves ordained as "ministers" of the "Universal Life Church" through a simple mail application procedure that apparently did not involve the inconvenience of seminary training. So ordained, they then got tax exemptions on religious grounds. The unordained 12% thereupon inherited the town's entire tax bill. They ungratefully renounced the inheritance and brought suit to lift the exemptions.[4] It was allowed in class form on both sides.

§ 147. Pervasive Court Discretion in Class Action; Settlement and Judgment

Recognizing how the class action eludes precise statutory direction, the CPLR gives the court broad discretion in the management of the class action and the protection of the class. Old CPLR 1005(b) did this in general terms by allowing the court to "impose . . . terms" to protect the class at any stage of the action. CPLR 907 offers at least as much discretion to the court "in the conduct of class actions", but contains a more detailed list illustrating the kinds of protective orders the court can make. CPLR 907 allows the court to make an order:

1. determining the course of proceedings or prescribing measures to prevent undue repetition or complication in the presentation of evidence or argument;

2. requiring, for the protection of the members of the class, or otherwise for the fair conduct of the action, that notice be given in such manner as the court may direct to some or all of the members of any step in the action, or of the proposed extent of the judgment, or of the opportunity of members to signify whether they consider the representation fair and adequate, or to appear and present claims or defenses, or otherwise to come into the action;

3. imposing conditions on the representative parties or on intervenors;

4. requiring that the pleadings be amended to eliminate therefrom allegations as to representation of absent persons;

5. directing that a money judgment favorable to the class be paid either in one sum, whether forthwith or within such period as the court may fix, or in such installments as the court may specify; and/or

6. dealing with similar procedural matters.

The last item, number 6 on the list, manifests that the list is illustrative rather than exclusive. The first four items have counterparts in the same numbered paragraphs of Rule 23(d) of the Federal Rules of Civil Procedure. The fifth, which addresses the terms of payment of a money judgment rendered in behalf of the class, lacks a federal analog; it is an indulgence felt by the Judicial Conference to be due the defendant "so as to avoid harsh economic and social consequences".[1] Under its general power over "similar procedural matters" (the sixth item), there should still be room for the court in an appropriate case to direct the "fluid recovery" discussed earlier.[2]

Protection of the opponent of the class is just as much an aim of CPLR 907 as is protection of the class. The gubernatorial message approving Article 9 stressed the presence of powers whereby the court can "prevent abuse of the class action device" and thus assure respect for "the rights of the class as well as those of its opponent."[3]

---

2. See Bus.Corp.L. § 626.

3. 84 A.D.2d 884, 444 N.Y.S.2d 965 (3d Dep't 1981).

4. The case is discussed in the lead note in New York State Law Digest No. 261.

§ 147

1. See 20th Jud.Conf.Rep. (1975) 210.

2. See § 145 above.

3. McKinney's Sess.L. of N.Y. (1975), p.1748.

Under item 2, the court can permit class members to appear and participate without a formal motion to intervene.[4] The motion of course remains an alternative available to any class member who wants in.[5]

CPLR 907 explicitly states that orders for the conduct of class actions "may be altered or amended as may be desirable from time to time". All of these CPLR 907 orders, original or amending, may be sought by motion of a party or made by the court sua sponte.

CPLR 908 provides that a class action may not be dismissed, discontinued, or compromised without the court's approval, and even provides that if any such step is proposed, notice of it "shall be given to all members of the class in such manner as the court directs." The notice is mandatory, but again, its method lies in the court's discretion.[6] By requiring court leave for a compromise or settlement, CPLR 908 makes it harder for the defendants to buy the plaintiffs off with a settlement advantageous to the representatives but not necessarily to the class itself. That was the famous "strike suit" phenomenon, most visible in the corporate derivative actions of yesteryear, which was easier to bring off before the reins of the class action were taken from the parties and turned over to the court. By placing control in the court, CPLR 908 seeks not only to bar the plaintiffs from being bought, but also to prevent the defendants from getting off too cheaply in the bargain. Professional ethics are an especially sensitive matter in the class action.[7]

CPLR 908's notice requirement applies even when the settlement is sought before class status has been awarded.[8] It would otherwise be possible, by foreclosing the members of the class from a hearing on the subject, for the representatives to make a private settlement beneficial to themselves, a possibility the notice requirements are designed to foreclose.

While notice of a settlement, or of a dismissal or discontinuance, must be given to the class under the terms of CPLR 908, notice of judgment on the merits is not mandatory. It is left to judicial discretion under CPLR 907.

The merits judgment in a class action, whether for or against the class, must "include and describe those whom the court finds to be members of the class."[9] Under the federal rule, the use of the word "describe" follows the language of the first but not the second sentence of Federal Rule 23(c)(3); under the second sentence, a federal court can require that the judgment "specify" the class members. Significance should be attached to the New York use of "describe" and its exclusion of "specify". It means that a mere description of the class suffices. The naming of the individual members of the class is not a general requirement, although the court must of course have discretion to require such naming in given instances, especially if the opting out procedure has been used[10] (where the judgment may have to recite that it is not binding on certain persons).

According to the Judicial Conference, the issue of the res judicata or collateral estoppel effect of the judgment on one who is a member of the class but who neither appeared nor opted out can be determined only in a subsequent action in which that member is a party.[11]

The class action is one of the rare exceptions to the American rule that attorneys' fees may not be awarded to the winner against the loser. CPLR 909 expressly provides that if the class prevails, the court has discretion to award a fee to the representatives' attorneys based on the "reasonable value" of the legal services rendered, and to impose this sum on the class's opponent. This controversial provision was not recommended by the Judicial

---

4. See 20th Jud.Conf.Rep. (1975) 210.

5. CPLR 1012(a)(2), 1013.

6. Notice of settlement was optional with the court under the prior law counterpart, the old CPLR 1005(b)(1).

7. See Homburger, Private Suits in the Public Interest in the United States of America, 23 Buffalo L.Rev. 343, 373–75 (1973).

8. Avena v. Ford Motor Co., 85 A.D.2d 149, 447 N.Y.S.2d 278 (1st Dep't 1982).

9. CPLR 905.

10. Compare Federal Rule 23(c)(3) (last sentence).

11. See 20th Jud.Conf.Rep. (1975) 209.

Conference only because it was felt that it would have rough going in the legislature. It was therefore omitted from the Conference's 1975 proposals, although contained in the CPLR Committee's original 1972 recommendations.[12] Paradoxically, legislative hands reinserted the provision and included it in the initial enactment of Article 9. Attorneys' fees were not expressly authorized by statute under prior law, but caselaw allowed them.[13]

The *Friar* case, cited several times already for other matters,[14] treats the method of computing attorneys' fees in class actions, including use of the so-called "lodestar" fee.

G.   INTERPLEADER

Table of Sections

§ 148. Interpleader, Generally

Interpleader is the situation in which someone faces a possible multiple liability at the hands of conflicting claimants. It allows that person, who in interpleader context is known as a "stakeholder", to bring all the claimants into court to fight it out, producing a judgment binding on all the claimants and, under the doctrine of res judicata, forever protecting the stakeholder, S, from further suit at the behest of any of them.

S can take the initiative and simply bring an action of interpleader, making all of the claimants defendants.[1] Or, if one of the claimants (C–1) brings an action against S, S can interplead the other claimants (C–2 etc.) from her position as defendant. The latter procedure is called "defensive" interpleader.[2]

S commences an action of interpleader as he would any other, describing the situation in the complaint and pleading that the defendants be made to put in their claims. In defensive interpleader, in addition to serving a summons and interpleader complaint on the other claimants (the ones to be added), S must serve copies of all prior pleadings already served in the action.[3] Failure to serve the other pleadings is not a jurisdictional defect, however, so that the omission does not impair jurisdiction and a default judgment can follow if the person interpleaded fails to respond.[4]

A liability insurer can presumably pay off judgments rendered against the insured in the sequence in which the judgments are presented to the insurer, but the interpleader device is also available to the insurer and one insurer that used it was commended by the court for doing so,[5] apparently based on the justice of having all claims pro rated rather than encouraging a race.[6]

No court order is necessary for either an action of interpleader or defensive interpleader. Whether as plaintiff or defendant, S simply does it. Most of the old requirements that once severely circumscribed the interpleader remedy are no longer applicable. CPLR 1006(d) addresses the point by stating that

It is not ground for objection to interpleader that the claims of the several claimants or the titles on which their claims depend do

---

12. See 18th Jud.Conf.Rep. (1973) A27, A41.

13. Cf. Runcie v. Bankers Tr. Co., 16 N.Y.S.2d 917 (Sup.Ct., Nassau County, 1939).

14. See §§ 141 and 145 above.

§ 148

1. CPLR 1006(a).

2. CPLR 1006(b).

3. Id. The interpleader summons and complaint must be filed with the court, for defensive as well as original interpleader, and a filing fee paid in either instance. See SPR 22:1.

4. Donas v. European American Bank and Trust Co., 106 Misc.2d 437, 431 N.Y.S.2d 873 (Sup.Ct., N.Y.County, 1980).

5. See Boris v. Flaherty, 242 A.D.2d 9, 672 N.Y.S.2d 177 (4th Dep't 1998).

6. See the discussion in the lead note in SPR 75. In a similar situation in which one insured tried to intervene in the other's personal injury action to avoid the latter preempting the insurance proceeds, intervention was denied. See David v. Bauman, 24 Misc.2d 67, 71, 196 N.Y.S.2d 746, 750 (Sup.Ct., Nassau County, 1960), discussed in § 181 above.

not have a common origin or are not identical but are adverse to and independent of one another . . . .

It was once otherwise.[7] Today the only real criterion is whether S "is or may be" subject to conflicting claims. C–1 may be claiming the proceeds of an insurance policy as its named beneficiary, C–2 the same proceeds under an alleged contract with the insured, C–3 the same through the insured's estate, etc. It makes no difference. As long as it appears that the claims are or simply "may be" mutually exclusive, i.e., that only one of the claimants should prevail, the interpleader device is available. S can use it unless the alleged conflicting claim "is so patently without substance that [S] can reject it without risk that . . . an independent action . . . may be able to establish a right" to the fund or property.[8]

Interpleader is also available in the lower courts of civil jurisdiction as long as the money or property involved is within the court's subject-matter jurisdiction.[9]

§ 149. Liberal Use; Discharge of Stakeholder

CPLR 1006(f) sets up a procedure whereby the stakeholder can move to be discharged. This can be done only when it is established that the stakeholder is no more than that, and that the sole battle is between the claimants. If a discharge is allowed, the stakeholder leaves the action fully protected: the claimants will be left to fight things out and will be bound by the judgment afterwards reached on the merits. The procedure for the discharge is a motion, on affidavits or any other proof, and

it can be made at any time after the pleading time of all the parties has expired. If a discharge is granted, the court can order the money or property paid into court, delivered to a designated person, or retained by the stakeholder pending further order of court. The order of discharge makes appropriate provision for "expenses, costs and disbursements" and these "may be charged against the subject matter of the action",[1] i.e., are payable out of the money or property interpleaded. Interpleader is also one of the few instances in which an attorney's fee may be allowed.[2]

The stakeholder does not have an automatic right to be discharged. The law is liberal about the use of the interpleader device to get into court any dispute in which conflicting liability is merely possible, but discharging the stakeholder before a trial on the merits is another matter entirely. It is clear today, for example, that S may use interpleader even if his position is that he is not liable to any of the claimants.[3] In making interpleader available when S "is or may be" liable to two or more claimants, CPLR 1006(a) recognizes its utility even if the merits ultimately show that S is liable to no one, or liable to all the claimants, or to some but not all. It is the existence of the last possibility that makes interpleader available procedurally, and the resulting judgment is valid whatever the merits turn out to be.

Suppose, for example, that C–1 sues S, who defensively interpleads C–2, and that the court sustains the interpleader but the merits then resolve that S is independently liable to both C–1 and C–2. Each will take judgment against S.[4] The interpleader device, which enabled S to

---

7. See Frumer, On Revising the New York Interpleader Statutes, 25 N.Y.U.L.Rev. 737 (1950). The main revision was in 1954, amending the old Civil Practice Act (see C.P.A. § 285 et seq.) at the instigation of the Judicial Council. See 20 N.Y.Jud.Council Rep. 271, 319 (1954).

8. Boden v. Arnstein, 293 N.Y. 99, 103, 56 N.E.2d 65, 67 (1944).

9. See § 205 in each of the New York City Civil, Uniform District, and Uniform City court acts. There is no § 205 in the Uniform Justice Court Act; the town and village courts lack interpleader jurisdiction.

§ 149

1. Under CPLR 1006(f), the interest rate applicable to the claim, absent agreement to the contrary, is that set by the Federal Reserve Bank of New York for member banks.

2. See Metropolitan Life Ins. Co. v. Brody, 35 Misc.2d 384, 228 N.Y.S.2d 312 (Sup.Ct., Albany County, 1962).

3. CPLR 1006(d).

4. An example of where S would incur such a multiple liability is where S is a seller of realty who has given, inadvertently or otherwise, an exclusive sales right to several brokers if they produce a buyer on given terms, and several produce.

bring C–2 into the C–1 action and get both sides of his liability resolved, has in that instance filled a gap which would otherwise have needed other devices, such as consolidation[5] or impleader,[6] but it is not a guarantee to S that she will end up with but a single liability.

To be discharged, so as not to have to stay on for the trial, S has to convince the court, as a matter of law, that she is liable to only one or a designated number but not to all the claimants, i.e., that this is a fight between the claimants in which S is really just a bystander. The proof offered by S to support a discharge should be as weighty on the single-liability issue as the proof needed to support any summary judgment motion under CPLR 3212. The effect of an order of discharge is essentially the same as the grant of summary judgment: it is the equivalent of a trial. If the court has any doubt about whether S is just a stakeholder, or for any reason feels that S should remain in the action as a party, it will deny S's motion to be discharged.[7]

If S does get the discharge, the resulting judgment between the claimants protects S from further suit by any of them—winners or losers.

§ 150. Mode of Trial

If the case is one of genuine interpleader, one in which two or more claimants are battling for the same money or property and the stakeholder is indifferent as between them, or, indeed, has made a deposit into court and been discharged, the case sounds in equity, through which interpleader evolved, and is presumably not triable by jury.[1] But if the nature of the dispute is such that it would have been jury triable had it not made its appearance in an interpleader context, the right to a jury re-

mains. An example is Geddes v. Rosen,[2] in which C–1 sued S to recover an escrow fund and S defensively interpleaded C–2. It appeared that if a certain sale were not consummated, C–1 would have a claim directly against C–2 rather than against S. The parties were held entitled to jury trial. Apparently the way to test this sometimes difficult issue[3] is to inquire whether, without the interpleader remedy, there would be an adequate remedy at law to litigate the underlying dispute. If there would be, the right to jury trial remains despite the fact that the issue has come into court in an interpleader vehicle.

§ 151. Discretionary Tools

A wide range of discretionary tools is available to handle problems in interpleader cases. CPLR 1006(c) sees to this by empowering the court to make such "order as may be just".

One situation contemplated by CPLR 1006(c) is where S as defendant wants to interplead C–2, but another action is pending between them on the same dispute. If the other action is in a New York court, it can be consolidated or ordered to joint trial with the interpleader case.[1] Or one can be dismissed or stayed in deference to the other.[2]

The consolidation (or joint trial) remedy is the most cohesive of the several supplied by the CPLR because it enables the several actions to be united, with a broad range of advantages. Only a single common question of law or fact is needed for consolidation or joint trial,[3] and either device can avoid expense and embarrassment. Where, for example, C–1 has two possible grounds of recovery, only one of them involving other potentially conflicting claimants, it is advantageous to C–1 to be able

---

5. CPLR 602. Consolidation would come into play, for example, when C–1 and C–2 sue S separately. See § 128 above.

6. Given the broader approach to impleader today, S could probably even have impleaded C–2 into the C–1 action under CPLR 1007. See § 157 below.

7. See Nelson v. Cross & Brown Co., 9 A.D.2d 140, 192 N.Y.S.2d 335 (1st Dep't 1959).

§ 150

1. Clark v. Mosher, 107 N.Y. 118, 14 N.E. l96 (1887).

2. 22 A.D.2d 394, 255 N.Y.S.2d 585 (1st Dep't), aff'd 16 N.Y.2d 816, 263 N.Y.S.2d 10, 210 N.E.2d 362 (1965).

3. See the dissenting opinion of Breitel, J., in the Geddes case, above, 22 A.D.2d at 400, 255 N.Y.S.2d at 591.

§ 151

1. As to which court can effect the consolidation or joint trial, see § 128, above.

2. CPLR 3211(a)(4). See § 262 below.

3. CPLR 602.

to litigate both grounds in one action, even though only one involves an interpleadable controversy.[4] Were they pending in separate actions, consolidation could fuse them.

Within the action, whether the action is the product of consolidation, interpleader, or initial joinder, the court has available the severance and separate trial devices[5] and general control of the sequence of trial[6] to aid its hearing and disposition of the issues.

§ 152. The Stakeholder's Jurisdictional Dilemma

If S, either by an action of interpleader or by defensive interpleader, can bring all conflicting claimants under the roof of but a single court, she will get her protection from double liability because the judgment of that court will bind all claimants. But when, for lack of jurisdiction over all claimants, S cannot maneuver them all before a single court, she meets her most serious problem. The New York legislature has tried to remedy the problem in two ways, neither very effective. One is the attempted use of rem jurisdiction for a mere money claim, the subject of the next section. The other is the procedure now found in CPLR 216.

The CPLR 216 procedure applies where C–1 has brought an action against S in New York in which S cannot interplead C–2 because C–2 is a nondomiciliary and not otherwise subject to extraterritorial service. Under CPLR 216, S gets an order from the court authorizing S to serve on C–2, by registered mail at C–2's last known address, a notice of the pending action accompanied by a summons and complaint and

a copy of the order.[1] S then shows the court that he has made such service, whereupon the court stays the pending C–1 v. S action for one year.[2] The hope is that during the year C–2 will either intervene in C–1's action or else commence a separate action in New York,[3] which could then be consolidated with C–1's.

If C–2 takes neither step within the year, the only effect of all this CPLR 216 business is that an action by C–2 against S after the year expires will be met by the bar of the statute of limitations (which is why the stuff of CPLR 216 appears in Article 2 of the CPLR). The whole impact of this provision is to abbreviate to one year the period of limitation otherwise applicable to C–2's claim.[4] This is all quite effective against any endeavor by C–2 to sue S in New York after the allotted year. The trouble is that it does not prevent C–2 from catching and suing S in some other state, or country, which need not recognize or apply the New York statute of limitations.[5] S thus remains subject to double liability, and the CPLR 216 procedure proves well intentioned but ineffective.[6]

An obvious question is this: if S cannot get C–2 before the same court, why doesn't she just move to dismiss C–1's action for failure to join a necessary party?[7] The trouble on that score is some old caselaw indicating that a stakeholder's inability to interplead the other claimant is not a defense to C–1's suit. The main decision in point is Petrogradsky Mejdunarodny K.B. v. National City Bank,[8] but perhaps the case should not be read as absolutely precluding such a defense today. First, *Petro-*

---

4. See American Motorists Ins. Co. v. Oakley, 172 Misc. 319, 14 N.Y.S.2d 883 (Sup.Ct., Broome County, 1939), discussed in 20 N.Y.Jud.Council Rep. 271, 276 (1954).

5. CPLR 603.

6. CPLR 4011.

§ 152

1. CPLR 216(a)(2). The procedure applies where the money is payable under a contract and involves more than $50.

2. CPLR 216(a)(3).

3. See Solicitor for the Affairs of His Majesty's Treasury v. Bankers Trust Co., 304 N.Y. 282, 107 N.E.2d 448 (1952).

4. CPLR 216(a)(1). When the year passes and the case resumes, S may defend on the merits against C–1. The use of the CPLR 216 procedure does not waive S's rights. See the Solicitor case, id.

5. Warner v. Buffalo Drydock Co., 67 F.2d 540 (2d Cir.1933).

6. The procedure also applies when the conflict is as to specific property within the state instead of mere money, CPLR 216(b), but the need for it in that situation is questionable because rem jurisdiction under CPLR 314 will usually afford the stakeholder all the jurisdiction required. See § 153 below.

7. The motion lies under CPLR 3211(a)(10).

8. 253 N.Y. 23, 170 N.E. 479 (1930).

gradsky involved the unique problem of Russian assets in the United States before our recognition of the then Soviet Union. Second, procedural developments since then offer the court significant and perhaps even decisive alternatives. One is CPLR 1001(b). Recast in the CPLR (from what it had been in the old Civil Practice Act), it now permits the court a broad range of discretion in shaping relief when someone who ought to be a party has not been joined.[9] If, for example, there is any other forum before which C–2 can reasonably be brought, the New York court might just dismiss C–1's action without prejudice to an action in such other forum, even exacting from S a stipulation to submit to that other forum's jurisdiction. Such a step would avoid the problem at which the ineffective CPLR 216 aims, and with less strain.

Due process might even be found today to mandate the pursuit of other available courses. Due process is offended when a court compels a litigant to relinquish property without the assurance that he will not confront liability again in another forum.[10] A court risks offending the constitution in that way if, with alternatives available, it disregards them and insists on continuing with C–1's case in C–2's absence, thus exposing S to a double liability unnecessarily.

Another barrier to dismissal of a C–1 v. S action under prior law was where either party was a New York resident. The residency would have precluded a forum non conveniens dismissal. Today, however, if "in the interest of substantial justice the action should be heard in another forum ... [t]he domicile or residence in this state of any party ... shall not preclude the court from staying or dismissing the action."[11]

Also relevant is the advent of longarm jurisdiction under CPLR 302 and like statutes.

CPLR 302 authorizes personam jurisdiction against nondomiciliaries when the case has New York contacts—which many such interpleader cases have—making CPLR 216 superfluous for that reason, too. Indeed, the national omnipresence of longarm jurisdiction may have resolved just about all of the stakeholder's jurisdictional problems. If the subject matter of the interpleader dispute has roots anywhere in the United States, it is almost certain that the state involved will have a longarm statute ready to reach out and assume personal jurisdiction of all claimants. And, of course, there is the statute that seeks to "reify" a sum of money so as to bind claimants under a rem jurisdictional theory, the next topic.

§ 153. Rem Jurisdiction as Interpleader Basis

If the dispute concerns specific property instead of money, and the property is located in New York, rem jurisdiction will usually suffice even in an interpleader situation to secure for S a judgment binding even on claimants served outside New York and not amenable to the state's personal jurisdiction.[1] That will be so whenever S wants only to affect the claimants' right in the subject property. But will rem jurisdiction avail when the subject obligation involves no specific property, nor even a trust or other limited fund, but a mere money obligation?

A naked attempt to convert mere money into "property" so as to exploit rem jurisdiction, as CPLR 1006(g) purports to allow, has been held unconstitutional both by the New York Court of Appeals[2] and the U.S. Supreme Court,[3] a combination that would normally discourage the most tenacious advocate. But CPLR 1006(g) is not easily dissuaded. It still authorizes the court, upon S's motion, to permit a sum of money to be paid into court[4] and

---

9. See § 133 above.

10. See Western Union Tel. Co. v. Pennsylvania, 368 U.S. 71, 82 S.Ct. 199, 7 L.Ed.2d 139 (1961).

11. CPLR 327. See Silver v. Great Amer. Ins. Co., 29 N.Y.2d 356, 328 N.Y.S.2d 398, 278 N.E.2d 619 (1972).

§ 153

1. CPLR 314(2).

2. Hanna v. Stedman, 230 N.Y. 326, 130 N.E. 566 (1921).

3. New York Life Ins. Co. v. Dunlevy, 241 U.S. 518, 36 S.Ct. 613, 60 L.Ed. 1140 (1916).

4. Alternatively, the court can order the money paid to a designated person or retained by the stakeholder to the credit of the action.

thereby deemed a "res" so as to invoke the rem jurisdiction offered by CPLR 314(2). That enables service on the claimants to be made outside the state and purports to bind them to the judgment to the extent of their "interest" in the money—that is, if it works.

It should work, despite the older caselaw, for the reason that CPLR 1006(g) does not authorize this procedure as to any money at all. It allows it only when the money is "payable in the state pursuant to a contract or claimed as damages for unlawful retention of specific real or personal property in the state". So limited—and this factor seems to have been overlooked by the courts[5]—CPLR 1006(g) can be treated as a kind of longarm statute, analogous to CPLR 302. If the particular interpleader situation involves substantial New York contacts—which it may ordinarily be expected to do when the requirements of CPLR 1006(g) are met—the case satisfies federal constitutional criteria evolved after the earlier restrictive cases[6] and should be jurisdictionally sustainable on an outright personam basis. If that is so, then CPLR 1006(g), far from going too far, doesn't even go as far as it can. CPLR 1006(g) is not a blunderbuss effort to convert money into a res. It is really a kind of longarm statute requiring the usual contacts analysis called for in that category of jurisdiction.[7]

§ 154. Interpleader in the Federal Courts

Perhaps the most meaningful resolution of the stakeholder's jurisdictional problem before the arrival of general longarm jurisdiction was the procedure Congress authorized in the federal courts, commonly known as federal statutory interpleader.[1] It was designed for cases in which federal jurisdiction is based on diversity of citizenship. Still exploited when the need arises, it offers four distinct advantages:

First, it measures subject matter jurisdiction by the citizenship of the claimants, disregarding the citizenship of the stakeholder and sustaining jurisdiction as long as any two of the claimants are of diverse citizenship.[2] Thus, if there are a dozen adverse claimants, all of them citizens of State X except one, who is a citizen of State Y, the diversity requirement is met. This is known as "minimal" diversity and its constitutionality has been sustained.[3]

Second, while the usual diversity case requires that the amount in controversy exceed $75,000, the minimum is set at only $500 in statutory interpleader cases.[4]

Third, while the general rule in federal actions is that in the absence of special statutory authority service of process may not cross state lines, i.e., that the district court's personal jurisdiction is limited to those reachable by process within the state in which the particular federal court sits,[5] process service in statu-

---

5. See, e.g., Cordner v. Metropolitan Life Ins. Co., 234 F.Supp. 765 (S.D.N.Y.1964).

6. The potentate of general longarm jurisdiction is International Shoe Co. v. Washington, 326 U.S. 310, 66 S.Ct. 154, 90 L.Ed. 95, decided in 1945, long after the U.S. Supreme Court's Dunlevy case of 1916, note 3, above, and the New York Court of Appeals' Hanna Case of 1921, note 2, above. See also Shaffer v. Heitner, 433 U.S. 186, 97 S.Ct. 2569, 53 L.Ed.2d 683 (1977), discussed in § 104, above.

7. See § 84, above, discussing longarm jurisdiction in general. A contacts analysis of this kind occurred in Atkinson v. Superior Court, 49 Cal.2d 338, 316 P.2d 960 (1957) (Traynor, J.), app. dism'd sub nom. Columbia Broadcasting System, Inc. v. Atkinson, 357 U.S. 569, 78 S.Ct. 1381, 2 L.Ed.2d 1546 (1958), where the court went as far as it thought it could based on local contacts while rejecting any arbitrary conclusions about whether money could be converted into a res.

§ 154

1. There is also "rule" interpleader in the federal courts. Rule 22 of the Federal Rules of Civil Procedure authorizes interpleader but does not give it the special

advantages of subject-matter jurisdiction, personal jurisdiction, and venue accorded to "statutory" interpleader.

2. 28 U.S.C.A. § 1335(a)(1).

3. State Farm Fire & Cas. Co. v. Tashire, 386 U.S. 523, 87 S.Ct. 1199, 18 L.Ed.2d 270 (1967). In contrast with § 1335, the general diversity of citizenship statute, 28 U.S.C.A. § 1332, requires complete diversity, Strawbridge v. Curtiss, 7 U.S. (3 Cranch) 267, 2 L.Ed. 435 (1806), which means that the citizenship of each plaintiff must differ from that of each defendant. For who qualifies as a "citizen" of a state in diversity parlance, see § 611 (Practitioner's Edition).

4. 28 U.S.C.A. § 1335(a).

5. FRCP Rule 4(k). See § 626 below (Practitioner's Edition) and Commentaries C4:29 et seq. on Rule 4 in 28 U.S.C.A.

tory interpleader cases is nationwide.[6]

Fourth, the venue requirements are relaxed; the stakeholder may bring the action in any district in which any claimant resides.[7]

This generous quartet will often serve the stakeholder at least as well, if not better, than the New York remedies. But if the stakeholder cannot satisfy even the relaxed jurisdictional requirements of federal statutory interpleader—as where there is no diversity of citizenship at all or the amount in controversy is less than $500—she must turn to the state remedies, such as they are. Worth noting again is that with general longarm jurisdiction available under statutes like CPLR 302, the state interpleader remedies treated in the prior two sections are needed less and less, and the federal one treated in this section is turned to more because of limitations on subject matter than personal jurisdiction.

H. IMPLEADER

Table of Sections

§ 155. Third–Party Practice, or "Impleader", Generally

Officially it is called "third-party practice";[1] popularly it is known as "impleader", the name this text will most often use. When P sues D, and D claims that X will be, or merely may be, liable to D for all or part of that which P may recover of D, impleader enables D to bring X into the P v. D action and have the D v. X dispute resolved at the same time. In this procedure, D is denominated the "third-party plaintiff" and X the "third-party defendant". For ease of reference in our examples, D will remain D and X will represent the impleaded third-party defendant.

The advantages of impleader are many. It avoids multiplicity of suits, since without impleader D would have to bring a separate later action against X. (D may still do that. Impleader is not compulsory.) It saves time, money, and effort. And it reduces the prospect of inconsistent verdicts. If a separate action were used, the court or jury in that action could ignore the result of the P v. D action—assume it was determined in favor of P against D—and determine that D should not have been held liable to P, leaving X with no liability to D despite the P v. D victory (which could not bind nonparty X).[2]

The third-party claim is also known as a "claim over", especially when D is seeking straight indemnity from X to cover D's liability to P.

§ 155

1. CPLR 1007.

2. For the background and historical development of impleader, see 11 N.Y.Jud.Council Rep. 370, 375 (1945).

6. See 28 U.S.C.A. § 2361, which also authorizes the interpleader court to enjoin the claimants from maintaining conflicting suits in state or other federal courts.

7. 28 U.S.C.A. § 1397. The general venue requirements in a diversity case, found in 28 U.S.C.A. § 1391(a), are not quite as generous. See § 617 below (Practitioner's Edition).

When an issue arises concerning impleader it more often than not touches on the basic question of whether impleader lies rather than the procedure for its use. Whether it lies depends on the substantive law applicable to D's claim against X. If X as a matter of substantive law, as applied to the facts that D pleads against X, would be required to reimburse D for all or part of P's recovery against D, impleader lies.[3] The source of X's obligation is secondary. It may come from an express contract or it may be implied in law. Here are a few common examples.

(a). O owns some property and hires K, a contractor, to repair the sidewalk. K repairs it negligently and P trips and is injured. P sues O, who bears liability for the defect. O can implead K.[4]

(b). A and B are joint venturers involved in a commercial project. They agree to split expenses and liabilities 50–50. P sues A on one of the enterprise's projects. A may implead B to make B share the liability.[5]

(c). P sues G, a general contractor, for breach of an agreement to build a house. The defect is in the plumbing, done by S, a plumbing subcontractor hired by G. G may implead S.[6]

(d). P sues O, the owner of a car, for injuries P suffered when the car, driven by X, struck P. Since the fault is X's driving, O may implead X.[7]

(e). P is injured in a two-car accident. The drivers are D–1 and D–2. If P sues only one driver, the one sued can implead the other.[8]

(f). P is injured by tortfeasor D. X is a hospital or a physician or like person who then negligently treats P, aggravating the injury. P sues D for all the damages P suffered in the accident, because D is substantively liable for the original as well as the aggravated damages. D may implead X, however, who must indemnify D for such part of the damages as X caused.[9]

(g). P is an employee injured on a construction job and sues D, the owner or general contractor, who bears liability for the tort. Maintaining that the fault belongs in whole or in part to X, P's employer, against whom P cannot bring a direct action because of the exclusivity of workers' compensation, D may implead X for indemnity or contribution. A qualification since the enactment of the so-called Omnibus Workers' Compensation Reform Act of 1996[10] is that D may do this only if it is shown that P suffered a "grave" injury in the accident.[11]

§ 156. Basic Procedure for Impleader

Impleader requires no court leave under the CPLR. D merely files a summons and third-party complaint and serves those papers on X along with copies of all prior pleadings in the action.[1] The methods of service are the same as apply to the initial commencement of an

---

3. This assumes that D has an outright indemnity claim against X. Today, impleader extends even beyond that. See § 157 below.

4. See Koerner, Modern Third–Party Practice—Substantive or Procedural?, 3 N.Y.L.Forum 159, 166–68 (1957).

5. McCabe v. Queensboro Farm Products, Inc., 22 N.Y.2d 204, 292 N.Y.S.2d 400, 239 N.E.2d 340 (1968).

6. See Comment, Third–Party Practice in New York, 37 Cornell L.Q. 721, 744–45 (1952).

7. See Traub v. Dinzler, 309 N.Y. 395, 131 N.E.2d 564 (1955). Be careful to distinguish O's personal rights in this situation from those of O's insurer. If X, the driver, is an additional insured under O's liability policy, as X usually is, O's insurer, who is conducting O's defense, may not implead X. But if the amount demanded by P of O exceeds the policy, O may implead X to make good the excess. See Beck v. Renahan, 46 Misc.2d 252, 259 N.Y.S.2d 768 (Sup. Ct., Nassau County, 1965), aff'd 26 A.D.2d 990, 275 N.Y.S.2d 1010 (2d Dep't 1966).

8. This involves contribution among tortfeasors, for which see § 169 et seq., below. The impleader device is used to implement contribution just as it is outright indemnification.

9. See Musco v. Conte, 22 A.D.2d 121, 254 N.Y.S.2d 589 (2d Dep't 1964).

10. Chapter 635 of the Laws of 1996.

11. The "grave injury" qualification is discussed more fully in § 171 below.

§ 156

1. CPLR 1007. A separate filing fee must be paid for this, but no separate index number is assigned; the index number of the main action remains applicable. The omission to serve the prior pleadings is sometimes held a jurisdictional defect, but the better view is that it is at worst a correctible irregularity. See Wings & Wheels Express Inc. v. Sisak, 73 Misc.2d 846, 342 N.Y.S.2d 891 (Sup.Ct., Queens County, 1973).

action, i.e., they are governed by Article 3 of the CPLR. X must answer the third-party complaint.[2] The answering time is determined by the place and method of service, just as if X were a defendant initially sued.[3]

D is also required to serve a copy of the third-party complaint on P's attorney, which must be done "simultaneously" with the "issuance for service" of the third-party complaint.[4] This enables P to keep abreast of any impleader introduced into the action.

The same bases for extraterritorial jurisdiction available against an original defendant are available against a third-party defendant. Thus, whenever the requirements of CPLR 313 are met as to the third-party claim, service of process may be made on the third-party defendant without regard to state lines. It has been held, however, that local contacts must be demonstrated in respect of the third-party claim itself; that a forum does not get extraterritorial jurisdiction of X, an alleged indemnitor, merely because D, the alleged indemnitee, purports to implead X into the action in which D has been sued by P on the underlying obligation.[5]

The only CPLR statement about the time for impleader is that D must not undertake it until D has served an answer to the main complaint.[6] It is permissible any time afterwards, but D must be wary of laches. If D has unduly delayed the impleader, the court can in its discretion dismiss or sever it,[7] thus remitting D to a separate later action against X. Whether there has been such undue delay as to warrant a dismissal or severance is of course sui generis. The courts recognize that since D would still have the right to bring a separate action against X, an impleader claim should not ordinarily be dismissed for tardi-

ness unless the delay has been palpably prejudicial.[8]

An example of such prejudice is Pierce v. International Harvester Co.[9] The case had gone to trial and went to both judgment and appeal without any attempt to implead. Only after the appellate court had reversed (on a point not touching the impleader issues) and remanded the case for a new trial was an impleader finally undertaken by D. Too late, held the court; the delay was in years and P's case was sharpened and ready for the retrial. It would not be fair to P to subject the case to the delays that so belated an impleader would entail.

While D can later sue X, the would-be third party defendant, after paying out on such judgment as P might obtain, and without statute of limitations problems,[10] this is not an ideal alternative for D. Lost to D would be the advantage of having the same jury that found D liable to P also determine whether D is to be made whole by X.

D should make it a rule to implead X as early as possible for the additional reason that it avoids duplication of effort. Much of the preparation will be the same as that required for the main claim, including use of the disclosure devices. The best rule of thumb for D is to implead X right after the service of the answer to the main complaint.

When X, the impleaded person, is a municipality or other governmental entity against which initial suit would not ordinarily lie unless it has first been served with a notice of claim, the notice of claim requirement is dispensed with. The notice of claim requirement applies only when the governmental entity is an original defendant, not a third-party defendant.[11]

---

2. CPLR 1008.

3. See CPLR 3012.

4. CPLR 1007.

5. Media Corp. of America v. Motif Mfg. Co., 524 F.Supp. 86 (S.D.N.Y.1981). The case is discussed, and suggestions made about how the indemnitee might try to protect itself, in the lead note in New York State Law Digest No. 269.

6. CPLR 1007.

7. CPLR 1010.

8. See Manganaro v. Estwing Mfg. Co., 27 A.D.2d 711, 276 N.Y.S.2d 891 (1st Dep't 1967).

9. 65 A.D.2d 254, 411 N.Y.S.2d 456 (4th Dep't 1978).

10. See § 162 below.

11. Valstrey Serv. Corp. v. Board of Elections, 2 N.Y.2d 413, 161 N.Y.S.2d 52, 141 N.E.2d 565 (1957).

If P has already joined D and X as co-defendants in the original action, there will of course be no need for D to implead X in order to assert a claim over; in that situation, D may assert the claim as a mere cross-claim in D's answer, which need not be accompanied by a summons and which can be served by mere mail.[12] A difference between the devices of cross-claim and impleader is that a cross-claim may be asserted by one defendant against another for any cause of action at all,[13] whether or not related to the main claim. An indemnity claim is only one of the things a cross-claim can include, while impleader under the CPLR is usually found to embrace only the indemnity-type claim, although its use has been expanded in recent years, as the next section discusses.

§ 157. Indemnification as Impleader Basis; Other Bases

It is tempting to think of impleader as being used only when D has an out-and-out "indemnification" claim against X. That's its primary function, and if we include contribution, which is a variety of indemnification, it accounts for the great majority of third-party claims. If D's claim is for "indemnification" or "contribution", it means that X is liable to D only if D is liable to P, and that if D can get off P's hook, X avoids liability to D automatically.

Although it accounts for most impleaders, a formal, substantive "indemnity" or "indemnification" or "contribution" claim is not indispensable to the use of impleader today. An older case in point is B.M.C. Mfg. Corp. v. Tarshis,[1] in which P contracted to buy steel from D and D turned around and made a contract to buy the steel from X. The contracts were independent and a breach of the D-X contract would have permitted suit by D against X without regard to whether D would be liable to P. Thus D's claim against X was

not for "indemnification", but when P sued D, D was nevertheless allowed to implead X. It was held sufficient that X, by breaching the contract with D, had "exposed" D to all or part of the liability P was asserting.

Under a liberal approach, impleader should lie whenever the link between the P–D and D–X claims is such as to suggest the practical soundness of having them heard together. There is no requirement under the CPLR that the two claims be related by a common question of law or fact, although of course in most cases they are. That point was made in Norman Co. v. County of Nassau,[2] which stated that the true test today "is simply whether the third-party defendant may be liable to defendant-third-party plaintiff, for whatever reason, for the damages for which the latter may be liable to plaintiff."[3] Norman was a liberal reading of the impleader statutes, and yet it still looked for an indemnity link of some kind.

While usually present, and always a strong glue for impleader, the indemnity link was largely abandoned as an impleader requirement in George Cohen Agency, Inc. v. Donald S. Perlman Agency, Inc.,[4] a major pronouncement on the impleader device. The court held that impleader is no longer to be limited solely to claims of indemnity or contribution. "[I]t has grown beyond its early limitations", said the court, "and should now be seen primarily as a tool for economical resolution of interrelated lawsuits."

P in the George Cohen case sold an insurance portfolio to D and took back notes in payment. When D defaulted and P sued, D claimed that he was fraudulently induced to buy the portfolio by both D and X. He sought to implead X, who maintained that the impleader would not lie because it was not exclusively to indemnify D for what P was claiming. The court upheld D in his contention that

---

12. See § 202 below.

13. CPLR 3019(b).

§ 157

1. 278 A.D. 266, 104 N.Y.S.2d 254 (3d Dep't 1951).

2. 63 Misc.2d 965, 314 N.Y.S.2d 44 (Sup.Ct., Nassau County, 1970).

3. 63 Misc.2d at 969, 314 N.Y.S.2d at 50. Quoting the Norman case, the appellate division adopted this expansive view of impleader in Holloway v. Brooklyn Union Gas Co., 50 A.D.2d 603, 375 N.Y.S.2d 396 (2d Dep't 1975).

4. 51 N.Y.2d 358, 434 N.Y.S.2d 189, 414 N.E.2d 689 (1980), discussed in the lead note in New York State Law Digest No. 253.

impleader should lie for any claims related to P's main claim, including any that D might have against P and X jointly. The argument that D should just bring separate actions and then move to consolidate them with P's action (CPLR 602) is rejected by the court as "a needless procedural dance".

If any claims impleaded under the generous *George Cohen* view would unduly impede the litigation in any way, the court has plenty of room for a cure with the severance and separate trial tools of CPLR 603.

George Cohen is a commercial case, but its expansive view of impleader will help in the tort area as well. Suppose, for example, that A and B in their separate cars collide and injure P, who sues only A. A impleads B. Both before and after the *George Cohen* case, A could assert against the impleaded B an indemnification or contribution claim in respect of P's main claim. But before the case, A could not (or it was in any event debatable) add against B a claim for A's own personal injuries or property damage suffered in the accident. It is now clear that A can add such claims.

A concomitant of this key decision is that no longer is a defendant's money demand against the impleaded third-party defendant limited to the sum the original plaintiff has demanded in the main complaint.

The *George Cohen* case should be deemed to overrule older cases that barred impleader in a variety of situations in which factual links were present to make impleader useful but an outright indemnity claim was missing. Take *Horn v. Ketchum*,[5] for example, in which P sued D for realty commissions. D impleaded X, to whom D had apparently paid the commissions in error. Noting that D could bring an action against X to recover the commissions regardless of P's claim against D, the court disallowed the impleader. Today it should be allowed.

A relevant consideration under the *George Cohen* approach is that in a case like *Horn* the common questions would have enabled the two disputes, had they been brought as separate actions, to be consolidated.[6] The court has broad discretion in the handling of an impleader claim,[7] and can treat the claim as a separate action and merely order it consolidated with the main claim,[8] thus enabling the two to be heard together by that route.[9] When it is shown that the consolidation route would be available were D's claim brought separately, the *George Cohen* case indicates that D should be allowed to get the claim in with the impleader device.

Courts still occasionally speak of the need for "some minimal jural relationship, aside from possible common questions of fact or law [which is all consolidation requires], between the liability of the defendant asserted in the main action and the liability over claim in the third-party complaint",[10] suggesting that an impleader without that link would be error. If so, it is submitted that the error is harmless as long as a common question of fact or law exists; that the court should ask whether it would order consolidation if the claim were brought separately and consolidation were moved for; and that if the court answers the question yes, it should sustain the impleader with nothing more than a citation of CPLR 2001, the statute about ignoring unprejudicial errors. If under that test it appears that a consolidation would not be ordered, the court can simply sever the impleaded claim and send it off as a separate action.

When the impleader claim is based on a contract, the contract's terms will of course govern the claim. If it is a straight indemnity agreement, the claim over may seek judgment for all of the main claim. If it is an agreement only to share the loss, the impleader can be used to secure whatever portion the contract

5. 27 A.D.2d 759, 277 N.Y.S.2d 177 (3d Dep't 1967). Compare Cleveland v. Farber, 46 A.D.2d 733, 361 N.Y.S.2d 99 (4th Dep't 1974).

6. CPLR 602.

7. CPLR 1010.

8. Ellenberg v. Sydharv Realty Corp., 41 Misc.2d 1078, 247 N.Y.S.2d 226 (Sup.Ct., Kings County, 1964).

9. See § 161 below.

10. Zurich Ins. Co. v. White, 129 A.D.2d 388, 518 N.Y.S.2d 469 (3d Dep't 1987).

covers.[11]

Another major source of indemnification is an obligation to indemnify implied by law. A leading example here is the tort case in which tortfeasor X, derivatively liable for the tort of Y, seeks to implead Y. (At one time X in this situation would be denominated the "passive" tortfeasor and Y the "active" one.[12]) Also during an earlier era, an indemnity contract would not be deemed to cover the indemnitee's "active" negligence unless it did so expressly,[13] but today such an obligation can arise by implication if the particular contract lends itself to it,[14] constituting a kind of mixed express-implied indemnification agreement.

The impleader claim, especially after the liberalizing edict of the *George Cohen* case, need not rest on the same underlying ground or theory as the main claim, which was yet another notion of an earlier time. The main claim, for example, may be in tort and the claim over in contract, or vice versa.[15] The main claim may be based on warranty and the claim over on negligence.[16] The test is simply whether what X has done has exposed D in any measure to the liability P is asserting. Indeed, as has already been stressed, impleader may even be used today when the claim over is independent of the main claim and only common questions of law or fact offer a nexus for it.

What about attorneys' fees? If D is entitled to have X cover D for D's liability to P, does X also have to pay D's attorneys' fees? The mat-

ter was considered in Chapel v. Mitchell,[17] in which the Court of Appeals held that when D's indemnification claim against X prevails, X must pay D's attorneys' fees for defending P's suit but is not liable for D's attorneys' fees in prosecuting the impleader claim. Issues necessarily arise under this rule about how to apportion the efforts of D's attorneys between the defense of P's claim and the pursuit of the impleader claim, and apportionment may be even more contentious when the indemnification sought by the impleader claim is for only part of the main claim, such as in a contribution instead of outright indemnification situation.[18]

§ 158. Effect if Impleader Complaint Negates Main Claim

If D's impleader complaint against X pleads a state of facts that would, if proved, relieve D of all liability to P, it has been held that impleader does not lie and that the impleader complaint must be dismissed. Thus, where P sued D for injuries caused by D's manufacture of defective goods, and D pleaded that X's alterations of the goods were the cause of P's injuries, the impleader was barred. The court said that "a claim over for indemnity is insufficient where its allegations would, if established, preclude liability on the part of the one asserting it."[1]

Cases of that kind usually involve tort claims and the old active-passive dichotomy that used to determine impleader rights.[2] With

---

11. See McCabe v. Queensboro Farm Products, Inc., 22 N.Y.2d 204, 292 N.Y.S.2d 400, 239 N.E.2d 340 (1968).

12. See § 170 below. Related to this is "contribution", a separate topic, for which the impleader device also supplies the procedure. See the treatment of contribution in § 169 et seq., below.

13. Thompson–Starrett Co. v. Otis Elevator Co., 271 N.Y. 36, 2 N.E.2d 35 (1936).

14. See Levine v. Shell Oil Co., 28 N.Y.2d 205, 321 N.Y.S.2d 81, 269 N.E.2d 799 (1971).

15. See Sol Lenzner Corp. v. Aetna Cas. & Sur. Co., 20 A.D.2d 305, 246 N.Y.S.2d 950 (4th Dep't 1964).

16. In tort cases today, especially the action for a personal injury caused by a product, many theories are used: negligence, breach of warranty, strict liability in tort, and sometimes even the breach of a statutory duty. Their allotment between main claim and impleader

claim—if each claim does not list all possible theories, as they can usually be trusted to do—is not decisive of the question of allowing impleader as long as each wrong listed is a possible factor in the plaintiff's injury.

17. 84 N.Y.2d 345, 618 N.Y.S.2d 626, 642 N.E.2d 1082 (1994).

18. See the discussion of the Chapel case in the lead note in New York State Law Digest No. 420. The court in Chapel addressed only the common law indemnity claim, i.e., the one arising by implication of law instead of by express contract, distinguishing the contractual situation.

§ 158

1. Beckerman v. Walter J. Munro, Inc., 25 A.D.2d 448, 449, 266 N.Y.S.2d 996, 998 (2d Dep't 1966).

2. See, e.g., LaRosa v. Edward J. Furhmann & Co., 34 A.D.2d 881, 311 N.Y.S.2d 948 (4th Dep't 1970), and the discussion of the active/passive rule in § 170 below.

the arrival of the *Dole* case,[3] however, and its subsequent codification in Article 14 of the CPLR, allowing the sued tortfeasor to implead other alleged participants in the tort, impleader by D should be sustainable today even if there is a possibility that the fault will be found to belong entirely to X and relieve D of liability altogether.

The logical relationship of the claims should determine, and the capacity of one claim to negate the other is itself a factor establishing such a relationship. The Court of Appeals decision in the 1980 *George Cohen* case[4] is relevant on this point with its approval of the appellate division statement that "it is the logical relationship of the claims which should determine whether third-party practice is appropriate, not the mechanistic approach of the past."[5]

§ 159.   Impleader as Premature Suit

Impleader is one of the rare instances in which the law permits what amounts to a premature action. That is so, in any event, when the impleader is used for straight indemnity, because should P lose on the claim against D there will be nothing for which X has to indemnify D. In fact, the statute of limitations on D's cause of action for indemnity does not even begin to run until D has paid P's judgment.[1] Yet impleader permits the D v. X dispute to be set in motion even before P has had judgment entered against D. Impleader "does not vitiate the requirement of a showing of actual loss before there may be recovery, but does permit an indemnitee to obtain a conditional judgment fixing the potential liability without the need for payment until it is shown that the judgment in the principal action has been satisfied in whole or part."[2]

Ordinarily, however, the D v. X suit does not mature to the point of being litigable until P has at least sued D. Thus, if P has merely made a claim against D without actually putting it into litigation, it has been held that the D v. X suit for indemnity does not yet lie.[3] But as long as the underlying P v. D action is pending, even if pending outside New York, a separate D v. X suit for what amounts to indemnity has been permitted. It was allowed in W.T. Grant Co. v. Uneeda Doll Co.,[4] for example, an early case on pleading under the CPLR.[5] Since the impleader of X into the P v. D action is almost always preferable to a separate indemnity action by D against X afterwards, it would seem that one of the few instances in which D would be justified in bringing a separate action would be where personal jurisdiction of X is not available in the state where the P v. D action is pending, which may have been the problem in *Grant*.

§ 160.   Impleader in Insurance Situations

When an insurer is so positioned as to be liable to D for all or part of what P is claiming of D, the insurer as a general rule is just as subject to impleader as any other person or entity. But there is a notable exception with liability insurance.

The usual liability policy provides that when the insured (D) is sued for a covered tort, the insurer will supply the attorney, handle the defense, and pay any resulting judgment. There is therefore no need to implead an insurer if it fulfills these obligations. If the insurer should disclaim coverage, however, and D does implead it, the impleader will likely be a waste of time when the insurance involved is liability insurance because the insurer is enti-

---

3. Dole v. Dow Chemical Co., 30 N.Y.2d 143, 331 N.Y.S.2d 382, 282 N.E.2d 288 (1972). See § 171 below.

4. Section § 157 above.

5. 69 A.D.2d 725, 734, 419 N.Y.S.2d 584, 589 (1979).

§ 159

1. See § 162 below.

2. McCabe v. Queensboro Farm Products, Inc., 22 N.Y.2d 204, 208, 292 N.Y.S.2d 400, 403, 239 N.E.2d 340, 342 (1968). McCabe actually involved a separate D v. X action (because it had been severed from the P v. D

action), but even as a separate action it was allowed to go forward. For enforcement of judgment problems, see § 165 below.

3. Lasker–Goldman Corp. v. Delma Eng'g Corp., 32 A.D.2d 513, 298 N.Y.S.2d 747 (1st Dep't 1969).

4. 19 A.D.2d 361, 243 N.Y.S.2d 428 (1st Dep't 1963), aff'd 15 N.Y.2d 571, 254 N.Y.S.2d 834, 203 N.E.2d 299 (1964).

5. See the discussion in Commentary C3014:8 on McKinney's CPLR 3014.

tled to a severance of the third-party claim on demand.[1] The purpose is to avoid prejudice to the insurer at the hands of a jury, because a jury in New York—a land of compulsory automobile liability insurance—is assumed not to know that D is insured. If a jury has perchance been waived, however, the severance may be refused.[2]

If D is the owner of a car driven by X, and D but not X is sued, the insurer may not ordinarily implead X if X is an additional insured under the policy, as X usually is.[3]

When an insurer is the named defendant on a cause of action brought by the plaintiff insured, whatever the kind of insurance involved, the insurer ordinarily may implead a third person who is responsible for the insured loss even though the insurer's right of subrogation does not technically accrue until it has paid its insured under the policy.[4] But there is an exception to that rule when automobile collision coverage is the insurance involved.[5] Third-party practice by the insurer is barred there to spare the insured the impeding of the presumably modest property damage suit.[6]

§ 161. Discretionary Powers of Dismissal, Severance, and Like Steps

CPLR 1010 expressly authorizes the dismissal or separate trial of the impleader claim, and its further permission for the court to make "such other order as may be just" covers several other discretionary possibilities, such as severance, consolidation, joint trial, etc. The rule requires the court to consider "whether the controversy between the third-party plaintiff and the third-party defendant will unduly delay the determination of the main action or prejudice the substantial rights of any party". When prejudice does appear, it is usually because of delay, although other possibilities exist.[1]

Since one of the major advantages of impleader is having the same jury that passes on D's liability to P then determine X's liability to D, an impleader claim with an arguable basis should rarely be dismissed. If D's claim against X is a genuine indemnity one, every effort should be made to have it tried to the same jury. (There may be more justification for dismissal or severance when the impleader claim is not for outright indemnity.[2]) If the problem is that the simultaneous trial of the impleader claim will create undue complications for the jury, the appropriate remedy is a separate trial. This enables the main claim to be tried to a verdict, with the impleader claim to be tried immediately afterwards to the same jury.

If the impleader claim has a question of law or fact in common with the main claim but does not appear to be for straight indemnity, a remedy is to treat the impleader claim as if brought separately and order it, or just deem it, consolidated or jointly triable with the main claim.[3]

§ 162. Statute of Limitations on Impleader Claims

When the claim over is a formal indemnity cause of action, whether based on an express agreement or implied in law, it gets two important benefits for purposes of the statute of limitations. The first is that the period that applies to it is the six years applicable to contract;[1] the second is that the period does

§ 160

1. Kelly v. Yannotti, 4 N.Y.2d 603, 176 N.Y.S.2d 637, 152 N.E.2d 69 (1958).

2. See Koolery v. Lindemann, 91 N.Y.S.2d 505 (Sup. Ct., Kings County, 1949).

3. See § 155 above.

4. Krause v. American Guar. & Liab. Ins. Co., 22 N.Y.2d 147, 292 N.Y.S.2d 67, 239 N.E.2d 175 (1968).

5. Ross v. Pawtucket Mut. Ins. Co., 13 N.Y.2d 233, 246 N.Y.S.2d 213, 195 N.E.2d 892 (1963). See 38 St. John's L.Rev. 406, 421 (1964).

6. See the distinction offered in the Krause case, note 4 above, 22 N.Y.2d at 156, 292 N.Y.S.2d at 73–4, 239 N.E.2d at 180.

§ 161

1. One example is the prejudice that may result to a liability insurer if retained in the same action in which its insured is being sued. See § 160 above.

2. See Norman Co. v. County of Nassau, 63 Misc.2d 965, 314 N.Y.S.2d 44 (Sup.Ct., Nassau County, 1970).

3. CPLR 602. See Ellenberg v. Sydharv Realty Corp., 41 Misc.2d 1078, 247 N.Y.S.2d 226 (Sup.Ct., Kings County, 1964), and the discussion in § 157 above.

§ 162

1. CPLR 213(2).

not start running until the underlying claim is paid.[2] This is so even if the basis of the indemnity claim is tort, such as where one tortfeasor seeks partial indemnification from another. So held Musco v. Conte[3] in 1964, during the age of restricted contribution among tortfeasors. The restrictions were lifted in 1972 in Dole v. Dow Chemical Co.,[4] and since contribution is just a form of indemnification, the Court of Appeals then held in Bay Ridge Air Rights, Inc. v. State of New York[5] that the same statute of limitations rules govern contribution. *Bay Ridge* concerned the time requirements applicable to a tortfeasor's contribution suit against the state (a co-tortfeasor) in the court of claims, the tortfeasor having been previously sued in another court.

The postponed accrual rule relieves the tortfeasor of any pressure to bring a contribution suit until at least after the underlying action has given rise to a judgment and the judgment has been paid. It is especially helpful when barriers of subject matter jurisdiction preclude impleader—impleader is usually the best course if it's available—such as when a tortfeasor is sued in the supreme court and wants to implead the state as a co-tortfeasor but can't because the state can be sued only in the court of claims. A separate action in the court of claims is necessary in that situation, and it's nice to know it doesn't face time problems.

There had been some difficulty under prior law when warranty was the basis underlying the impleader claim. Assume that P sued D for personal injuries and that D impleaded X for indemnity or contribution. If the underlying basis of D's impleader claim was X's negligence, the law treated the claim as a formal indemnity cause of action and gave it the limitations' benefits. If its basis was warranty, however, some cases[6] continued to treat it as a formal "warranty" cause of action even in third-party context, and denied it the limitations' advantages. They held in that situation that even though D sought only indemnification from X for whatever D might have to pay P, the D v. X claim would not get the indemnity six years, but rather only the warranty four,[7] and that the period would run not from a payment by D to P, but from the sale of the warranted item by X to D. The effect of such a holding appears in the following hypothetical:

X is a manufacturer and sells an item to D, a retailer, in 1975. In 1976, P buys the item from D and is injured by it in 1979. P brings a warranty suit against D in 1980, timely because within four years of the D-to-P sale. D promptly impleads X on the ground that X's breach of warranty is the real underlying cause of P's injury, and let us assume that it is. The impleader claim was held barred because its period was held to be four years and the four years were measured from X's 1975 sale to D, not D's 1976 sale to P, while had the claim over been in negligence the law would have stamped an official "indemnity" caption on it and given it both the six-year period and the postponed—until payment by D to P—accrual.

The different treatment when the impleader claim was rooted in warranty was an unjustifiable enigma in New York,[8] and it was abandoned with the Court of Appeals decision in 1980 in McDermott v. City of New York,[9] overruling the earlier caselaw. Today it should make no difference in a tort case whether the claim over sounds in negligence, strict liability, warranty, or something else. Whatever its underlying theory of wrong, the claim over is officially one for "indemnity" and gets the statute of limitations advantages applicable to it.

§ 163. Rights of Third–Party Defendant

The third-party defendant, X, may assert any defenses she has to the third-party claim.

2. Bunker v. Bunker, 80 A.D.2d 817, 437 N.Y.S.2d 326 (1st Dep't 1981).

3. 22 A.D.2d 121, 254 N.Y.S.2d 589 (2d Dep't).

4. See §§ 169–171, below.

5. 44 N.Y.2d 49, 404 N.Y.S.2d 73, 375 N.E.2d 29 (1978).

6. E.g., C.K.S., Inc. v. Helen Borgenicht Sportswear, Inc., 22 A.D.2d 650, 253 N.Y.S.2d 56 (1st Dep't 1964).

7. UCC § 2–725.

8. See Siegel, Procedure Catches Up—and Makes Trouble, 45 St. John's L.Rev. 63, 69–70 (1970).

9. 50 N.Y.2d 211, 428 N.Y.S.2d 643, 406 N.E.2d 460.

X is also given "the rights of a party adverse to the other parties in the action, including the right to counter-claim, cross-claim and appeal".[1] There is some doubt as to whether this broad right allows X to interpose unrelated claims that X may happen to have. CPLR 1008 might be read to admit unrelated claims but an easy remedy in any event would be for the court to sever the unrelated ones pursuant to CPLR 603 and let them pend as separate actions.

Perhaps most importantly, CPLR 1008 also permits X to assert any defenses D may have against P's main claim. This recognizes that X's liability is usually contingent upon D's, and that whatever can defeat P's claim against D will ipso facto destroy D's claim over against X. It also acknowledges that if X is solvent and D is reasonably sure of getting an indemnity judgment over, D's kinship or friendship with P may prompt D to be lax in his own defense on the theory that X will have to make everything good to D anyway. CPLR 1008 in effect permits X to prosecute D's case against P if D should prove remiss, and caselaw warns D that if D gets lazy about his own rights he may end up with a liability to P unindemnified by X. On interposing a defense omitted by D, in other words, X may be let off the hook while D stays on. For example:

P neglected prosecution of his claim against D, and D could have moved to dismiss it on that ground.[2] D did not so move, but X did in D's behalf. The court dismissed the main action, but only insofar as X was concerned, leaving D to face liability to P with no further prospect of indemnity from X.[3] We may formally denominate this a disappointment to D,

and if D was remiss out of some relationship with P—family and friend relationships are not uncommon between P and D in tort actions, for example—D may wish he had another chance.[4]

Such a D-against-P defense may be used by X even if the defense has since become barred to D because of some omission on his part. Thus, where it appeared that D had been so lax that he would not even be able to assert his defense against P in an amended pleading, the diligent X was still permitted to use the defense, and with the same unhappy consequences for D.[5]

The rule permitting X to interpose one of D's defenses against P does not necessarily permit X to use a defense he might himself have against P if P were to try to sue X directly. Thus, where X is P's employer and direct suit by P against X would be barred by the exclusivity of workers' compensation relief, X is not permitted to use that defense when X is impleaded by D, another person involved in the occurrence who has been sued by P.[6]

The right of X to use defenses available to D can have some impact on appeal, too. Suppose, for example, that P has won against D and D has won a judgment over against X. X appeals, but D does not. If X shows on the appeal that P should not have had judgment against D, the appellate court can reverse and dismiss D's judgment against X while leaving the P v. D judgment intact for D's failure to appeal.[7] Some older cases had held that the appellate court does have discretion to reverse the main P v. D judgment "in the interest of justice" in that situation,[8] but the Court of Appeals after-

§ 163

1. CPLR 1008.

2. For neglect to prosecute dismissals today, see CPLR 3216, treated later in § 375.

3. Lewis v. Borg–Warner Corp., 64 Misc.2d 454, 315 N.Y.S.2d 56 (Sup.Ct., Orange County, 1968), mod'd 37 A.D.2d 609, 325 N.Y.S.2d 314 (2d Dep't 1971).

4. It is not clear whether the result would be the same today. In Sharrow v. Dick Corp., 86 N.Y.2d 54, 629 N.Y.S.2d 980, 653 N.E.2d 1150 (1995), for example, a nonappealing defendant was allowed the advantage of an appellate victory won by a third-party defendant. As mani-

fest from the discussion further on in this section, in respect to appeals, the cases are in conflict on this issue and have yet to be reconciled.

5. See Marrone v. John A. Johnson & Sons, Inc., 283 A.D. 1114, 131 N.Y.S.2d 853 (2d Dep't 1954) (involving defense of statute of limitations).

6. Bellefeuille v. City and County Sav. Bank, 43 A.D.2d 335, 351 N.Y.S.2d 738 (3d Dep't 1974).

7. Frankel v. Berman, 10 A.D.2d 838, 199 N.Y.S.2d 261 (1st Dep't 1960).

8. See, e.g., Rome Cable Corp. v. Tanney, 21 A.D.2d 342, 250 N.Y.S.2d 304 (4th Dep't 1964).

wards said no.[9] Not appealing in such an instance is a perilous course for D in any event. D should cover all contingencies by taking his own appeal, at least when his indemnitor, X, has appealed.[10]

X's right to stand in D's shoes applies even to steps at the trial itself. Where, for example, it had been stipulated that the claim over would be tried to the court although P's main claim against D was tried to a jury, X had to be given a chance to sum up to the jury on the main claim.[11]

§ 164. Additional Claims Among the Parties

The main plaintiff, P, may assert directly against the third-party defendant, X, any claim P may have against X,[1] doing so merely by amending the complaint to add the claim. P has 20 days in which to do this, measured from the service on P of X's answer to the third-party complaint. While CPLR 1008 requires X to serve the answer to the third-party complaint only on the main defendant, D, CPLR 2103(e) requires that any paper served on any party be served on every other party.[2] Hence X must serve a copy of the answer on P as well. P's time to amend so as to assert a direct claim against X will not start to run until P is so served.

If P makes the amendment within the required 20 days, P needs no court leave; after the 20 days, P does. When the amended complaint is served on X, no summons need accompany it because X is already a party.[3]

There is still some doubt about whether D, the main defendant who impleaded X, can assert against X claims unrelated to P's claim. Unrelated claims were not allowed under prior law.[4] While the Court of Appeals has more recently held that impleader is no longer to be restricted to indemnity and contribution claims, and that D may use the device to assert any claims D may have against X that bear any relationship to P's main claim against D, including D's own claim for damages against X,[5] there is still some doubt about whether a claim wholly unrelated to anything in the transaction or event underlying P's main claim would be permissible.

Several things point to permitting it. CPLR 601 as a general matter allows broad joinder of claims "when there are multiple parties", and there is specific authority in CPLR 1008 for the interposition of claims among impleaded parties.[6]

On all of these questions the soundest conclusion would be to allow the free interposition of claims between and among all parties legitimately joined at the outset or subsequently impleaded, leaving judicial discretion to keep order with an ad hoc application of such remedies as an order for a separate trial or severance or even a discretionary dismissal, all of which are available to the court.[7]

Assuming that a claim by D against X is relevant enough to remain, the *George Cohen*[8] case holds that D's demand against X can exceed the sum P is seeking of D on the main claim. (When impleader was strictly limited to

---

9. See Hecht v. City of New York, 60 N.Y.2d 57, 467 N.Y.S.2d 187, 454 N.E.2d 527 (1983), discussed in the lead note in New York State Law Digest No. 285.

10. See the discussion of the Hecht and other cases in § 543, below.

11. Phillips v. Chevrolet Tonawanda Div., 43 A.D.2d 891, 352 N.Y.S.2d 73 (4th Dep't 1974).

§ 164

1. CPLR 1009. The kinship that P's several claims must have under CPLR 1002(b) for the initial joinder of a defendant does not apply to P's claims against X under CPLR 1009.

2. See § 203 below.

3. See Harlem River Consumers Coop., Inc. v. Manufacturers Hanover Trust Co., 68 Misc.2d 608, 327 N.Y.S.2d 903 (N.Y.C.Civ.Ct. 1972).

4. See, e.g., Otto v. Wegner, 11 Misc.2d 499, 172 N.Y.S.2d 115 (App.T., 1st Dep't, 1958).

5. George Cohen Agency, Inc. v. Donald S. Perlman Agency, Inc., 51 N.Y.2d 358, 434 N.Y.S.2d 189, 414 N.E.2d 689 (1980). See § 157 above.

6. CPLR 1008 authorizes third-party defendants to counterclaim and cross-claim. See Bellefeuille v. City and County Sav. Bank, 43 A.D.2d 335, 351 N.Y.S.2d 738 (3d Dep't 1974).

7. CPLR 1010, 603. See § 161 above. If a party would have a statute of limitations problem if a new action would now have to be brought on a dismissed claim, severance instead of dismissal would be the more appropriate step.

8. See note 5 above.

indemnity claims, a corollary was that the impleader claim could not exceed the sum demanded on the main claim.)

§ 165. Enforcement of Third–Party Judgment

Since an impleader judgment is in most cases one to make X indemnify D for all or part of what P recovers of D, it cannot be allowed to go to actual enforcement until D has paid something to P. It may go to judgment before payment of the underlying obligation, and the judgment may even be formally entered, but it will necessarily be only "a conditional judgment fixing the potential liability" until there is some proof of "payment of the main judgment".[1] If D should seek to enforce its judgment against X before paying any part of P's judgment, X will be entitled to cancellation of the enforcement step.[2]

If the main defendant, D, is unable for any reason to pay P on the main judgment, this circumstance will ordinarily redound to the benefit of any person against whom D has an impleader judgment but against whom P has not been awarded a direct judgment. If X is such a person, D cannot compel X to pay P directly, nor can P collect from X directly. This arises in contribution more often than indemnity context and is elaborated later, with some discussion of a possible way for P to circumvent this barrier.[3]

The court can work out any needed details in arranging for enforcement. It may even require that D's judgment over be articulated in conditional terms, with leave to D to apply to strike the condition and make the judgment enforcible upon proof of a designated kind (such as an affidavit) presented to the court or the clerk, attesting to (e.g.) the datum that D has paid P on the main judgment.

If there is a default by X on the third-party claim, D faces an apparent dilemma: D really can't have judgment against X unless and until something is adjudicated in favor of P against D, and the contested P v. D suit may be a long way from trial. The dilemma never materialized. Caselaw held that the requirement of CPLR 3215(c), that a default judgment be entered within a year after the default occurs, does not apply to third-party defaults. The year in that instance commences only upon entry of judgment in favor of P against D on the main claim, whenever that may be.[4]

§ 166. Successive Impleaders

The third-party defendant—X in our examples—may also do some impleading. X may bring in any person who "is or may be liable to him for all or part of the third-party claim."[1] And that person may do the same against yet another. The parties to such later impleaders are sometimes called fourth-party plaintiffs and defendants, fifth-party ones, etc.[2]

When a counterclaim is asserted against the plaintiff, the plaintiff has the same impleader rights vis-a-vis the counterclaim as an original defendant has on the main claim.[3]

The usual discretionary tools—dismissal, severance, separate trial—remain available to prevent things from getting out of hand.

§ 167. Impleader in Various Courts and Proceedings

Impleader is applicable to all New York courts of original civil jurisdiction except the court of claims.[1] It has limited use in courts of special jurisdiction, such as the surrogates'

§ 165

1. McCabe v. Queensboro Farm Products, Inc., 22 N.Y.2d 204, 208, 292 N.Y.S.2d 400, 403, 239 N.E.2d 340, 342 (1968).

2. See CPLR 5240. Enforcement occurs under Article 52 of the CPLR, met and treated in Chapter 18, below.

3. See § 175 below.

4. Multari v. Glalin Arms Corp., 28 A.D.2d 122, 282 N.Y.S.2d 782 (2d Dep't 1967). See Commentary C3215:13 on McKinney's CPLR 3215.

§ 166

1. CPLR 1011.

2. See Sheftman v. Balfour Housing Corp., 37 Misc.2d 468, 234 N.Y.S.2d 791 (Sup.Ct., Queens County, 1962).

3. CPLR 1011.

§ 167

1. See Patti v. State, 47 Misc.2d 622, 263 N.Y.S.2d 158 (Ct.Cl. 1965).

and family courts, but it is important in the lower courts of civil jurisdiction. It is of course limited to the subject matter jurisdiction of the particular court.

In regard to personal jurisdiction, some lower court provisions are designed to assist impleader by allowing service of process on a third-party defendant beyond the area to which the court's summons is ordinarily restricted.[2]

While impleader requires no permission in an action, it is available in a special proceeding only by leave of court.[3] The summary proceeding to recover the possession of real property under Article 7 of the Real Property Actions and Proceedings Law is one kind of special proceeding. Because of its summary nature,[4] the use of impleader is perhaps even less appropriate there than in any other kind of special proceeding. It is nevertheless tried from time to time, and there are at present conflicting decisions on whether it is permissible. One occasional context of its appearance has been a proceeding brought by the landlord against the tenant for the nonpayment of rent, with the tenant seeking to implead the local welfare official allegedly responsible for the rent payment.[5]

§ 168. Vouching–In

The device known as "vouching-in" is the "common-law counterpart and antecedent of statutory impleader",[1] and while with the growth of impleader it has fallen into disuse, it is still permitted under caselaw and still puts in an occasional appearance.

Where X bears an indemnification relationship to D, who has been sued by P, D can "vouch in" X by merely giving X notice of the pending action and offering X control of the

defense.[2] The notice need not be formal; it has even been held that it can be oral.[3] D would be wise to make the notice as formal as possible, of course; such expedient as a certified mailing would make proof of the notice, if needed, easier later on. The notice does not make X a party, but X may seek to intervene as such.

If P does get judgment against D, the judgment does not operate directly against X. Whether or not X has participated, it will still be necessary for D to bring a separate action against X for indemnification. The vouching-in notice will have accomplished this much, however: in the later action, X will not be permitted to relitigate the issues resolved between P and D in the prior suit. D's burden in the indemnity action against X will therefore be to prove only the indemnification relationship, the fact of the prior judgment, and that a vouching-in notice was duly given to X. Were X not vouched in, X could in the indemnity suit relitigate the P–D dispute, perhaps convincing the fact trier, to the obvious detriment of D, that P should not have prevailed. In short, the vouching-in device makes the P v. D judgment res judicata against X.

Because outright impleader is more effectual in that it makes X a party to the P–D action, and, if P wins, enables D to get a simultaneous indemnity judgment against X, it is of course preferable to the more cumbersome vouching-in device. But if, for one reason or another, D can't implead X, the vouching-in notice may offer some help. It would seem, however, that whenever vouching-in would lie, so would outright impleader. We do know that for D to implead X, D needs a basis for jurisdiction.[4] If X is outside the state and there is no basis for extraterritorial jurisdiction, impleader will be unavailable. It is sometimes urged that vouch-

---

2. See N.Y.C.Civ.Ct.Act § 408, removing city lines for purposes of process service; Unif.Dist.Ct.Act § 408, removing county lines; and Unif.City Ct.Act § 408, allowing service in adjoining counties. All three acts are in McKinney's Vol.29A, Part 3.

3. CPLR 401.

4. See § 571 below (Practitioner's Edition), discussing in general the function of the summary proceeding.

5. See § 577 below (Practitioner's Edition).

§ 168

1. Glens Falls Ins. Co. v. Wood, 8 N.Y.2d 409, 412, 208 N.Y.S.2d 978, 980, 171 N.E.2d 321, 322 (1960).

2. Hartford Acc. & Indem. Co. v. First Nat. Bank & Trust Co., 281 N.Y. 162, 22 N.E.2d 324 (1939).

3. Bouleris v. Cherry–Burrell Corp., 45 Misc.2d 318, 256 N.Y.S.2d 537 (Sup.Ct., Albany County, 1964).

4. See, e.g., Ferrante Eqpt. Co. v. Lasker–Goldman Corp., 26 N.Y.2d 280, 309 N.Y.S.2d 913, 258 N.E.2d 202 (1970). See § 156 above.

ing-in will serve in such a case, but the notion supposes that a vouching-in notice has a jurisdictional reach broader than impleader. Indeed, the Uniform Commercial Code seems to assume just that, without comment.[5] Since the vouching-in device has the effect of binding X to the result of the P v. D action, however, its jurisdictional support should be no less than that which supports outright impleader. Hence, if impleader is jurisdictionally barred, vouching-in would appear to be barred as well.[6]

In Castignoli v. Van Guard,[7] after an impleader claim against X was dismissed for want of personal jurisdiction, D served a vouching-in notice on X, which the trial court refused to vacate. On appeal the decision was reversed, but only on the ground that the notice was served late (some four months after the filing of the note of issue), thus appearing to preserve the lower court decision as some authority giving vouching-in a broader jurisdictional reach than impleader itself has.[8]

It would be of obvious benefit to X, as soon as X is purportedly vouched in, to be able to use something like a motion to strike the notice so as test the validity of the device in the particular action, i.e., secure a determination of whether X bears an indemnification relationship to D and is therefore required to assume the defense. It has been held that the court in the P v. D action has no general authority to strike the notice, even on X's motion,[9] but the conclusion is questionable. It's premised on the distinction between outright impleader and a mere vouching-in notice, as if the latter has no significant impact. But it has: use of vouching-in can make the underlying issues in the main action res judicata against the person vouched-in, which is impact enough. Although the issue of X's obligation to indemnify would of course be open in D's later suit against X if not earlier determined, X should not be compelled to wait until then to have the issue decided. It would mean having to pick up the burden of D's defense just as a precaution, and that would seem an unreasonable burden to impose on X if X can summarily establish the absence of any possible indemnification relationship to D.

Vacatur of the vouching-in notice on the basis of its untimely service is apparently permissible,[10] and it would be useful to permit a vacatur motion on the validity ground as well. If X is impleaded outright, X may move to dismiss;[11] when X is instead vouched in, a motion to strike the vouching-in notice is nothing more than the equivalent of impleader's dismissal motion.

§ 168A. "Joint" Tort Liability Adjustment; Background

At this point, impleader having been completed and contribution to follow, we inject Article 16 of the CPLR, enacted in 1986, which makes adjustments in the liability of tortfeasors. This section is background.

The rule of "joint and several" liability has long been the rule in tort cases, meaning that each tortfeasor is responsible not only for the share of plaintiff P's damages that she herself caused ("several" liability), but also for the shares attributable to the other culpable tortfeasors ("joint" liability). The practical impact of this rule is that as long as any one of the tortfeasors—call her S—is solvent, able to pay the whole judgment though in point of fault accountable for just a small part of it, P can collect all from S. S can then turn around and seek recompense from the other tortfeasors based on their shares. That's what "contribution" is all about under Article 14 of the

---

5. See U.C.C. § 3–803.

6. See and compare Glens Falls Ins. Co. v. Wood, note 1, above, and Comment, Constitutional Limitations on Vouching, 118 U.Pa.L.Rev. 237 (1969). For D's right to recover from X the cost of defending P's suit, see Clarke v. Fidelity & Cas. Co., 55 Misc.2d 327, 285 N.Y.S.2d 503 (Sup.Ct., N.Y.County, 1967).

7. Sup.Ct., Nassau County (Index No. 34415/94, Jan. 30, 1996, Collins, J.), rev'd 242 A.D.2d 357, 661 N.Y.S.2d 280 (2d Dep't 1997).

8. See the discussion in the lead note in SPR 70:1.

9. Bouleris v. Cherry–Burrell Corp., note 3, above; Urbach v. City of New York, 46 Misc.2d 503, 259 N.Y.S.2d 975 (Sup.Ct., Kings County, 1965).

10. See Cole v. Long Island Lighting Co., 14 A.D.2d 922, 222 N.Y.S.2d 293 (2d Dep't 1961).

11. CPLR 1010.

CPLR.[1] But if the others can't pay, S ends up with the whole bill.

The rule of "joint and several" liability thus assures that if there is to be a loser in the pack, it won't be P, the injured person; it will be the solvent tortfeasor, whom the argot calls the "deep pocket". Until 1986, apportionments among tortfeasors affected only an adjustment of their rights among themselves after P had been paid by any able-to-pay source among them.

The injustice of the traditional rule of joint and several liability is that a tortfeasor guilty of only the smallest share of wrongdoing will sometimes end up having to pay all or most of P's damages, at best receiving in return a contribution judgment against the other tortfeasors, who may be insolvent. What good is a juicy judgment against a juiceless debtor?

The paying tortfeasor, S, always complained when that happened, but for a variety of reasons no cure was offered. Probably the chief reason was that the plaint was really that of S's insurer, and as long as the cycle of increasing premiums made sure that the insurer would ultimately recoup, the pressure just never rose to the point of legislative reaction. It finally reached that point in 1986, with the enactment of Article 16 of the CPLR (§§ 1600–1603). Among the major forces advocating the enactment were the state's municipalities.

A municipality is often the "deep pocket" in a multi-party tort case, exposed to liability for something like a pothole, an unmarked intersection, a defective traffic light, an overhanging tree limb, etc., but just as often under circumstances to suggest that this played only a small role in causing the accident, a few percentage points at most; that the real culprit, at fault even in a jury's eyes for perhaps 90% or 95% of the tragedy, was (e.g.) a drunk driver, a wild teenager, etc. The culprit's insurer might have to pay the injured person its whole policy, but that might be only the mini-

mum sum called for by the state's compulsory insurance rule, which always falls short of the damages sustained in a serious injury case. Hence a $1 million judgment for which the municipality was at most a few thousand dollars responsible might end up costing it the whole million. And there was also, and there continues to be, the problem of the wholly uninsured motorist.

Municipal officials complained that insurance premiums had been burgeoning to the point that insurance was in effect unavailable. So did many others, but the municipal voices were apparently strongest, and were heard. (A municipality will usually have the ear of a legislator.) Although the municipalities were the medium, many tortfeasors, not just the municipalities, ended up the beneficiaries.

Albeit with a myriad of exceptions and conditions, the legislative answer to the "joint" liability issue is the undistinguished piece of statutory prose known as Article 16, enacted as part of Chapter 682 of the Laws of 1986 and applicable to "all actions commenced . . . on or after" July 30, 1986, the statute's effective date.[2]

Article 16 makes an adjustment in "joint" liability, but only in part, and with many exceptions. First, the adjustment affects only "non-economic" damages.[3] (There is no change in the rule of joint and several liability in respect of economic damages: loss of earnings, hospital and medical expenses, etc.) Pain and suffering, mental anguish, and loss of consortium are the major "non-economic" elements that the rule works on.

Second, only a "personal injury" claim is affected.[4] Tortfeasor liability on property damage and wrongful death claims remains joint and several in respect of all damages. This is consistent: damages on those claims are economic in nature and are therefore beyond the "non-economic" category aimed at by Article 16. If property damage and wrongful death

§ 168A

1. The treatment of contribution begins in § 169 et seq., below.

2. Chapter 682 is a concession to defendants, but not without exacting a quid pro quo for plaintiffs: Chapter 682 is also the chapter that enacted CPLR 214–c, the provision

that at last adopted a "discovery" rule for the statute of limitations in "exposure" cases. See § 40 above.

3. CPLR 1600.

4. CPLR 1601.

claims are joined with a personal injury claim in the action, as they may be and often are, the old rules apply to them and there will be the need to adjust figures and judgments accordingly. Article 16 operates only on the personal injury claim and only on its non-economic damages segment.

We treat the subject here because it is one that should be covered before getting into the "contribution" topic. Contribution adjusts rights among tortfeasors but does not affect their exposure to the plaintiff. Article 16 does affect tortfeasors' exposure to the plaintiff, and when it does it diminishes the need for contribution. (Rights of indemnity and contribution, incidentally, remain intact under Article 16.[5])

§ 168B.   "Joint" Tort Liability Adjustment: The 50%-Or-Less Tortfeasor

To earn the benefit of the new law and be rid of "joint" liability—securing what we might call "several-only" status—a tortfeasor must be found to have "fifty percent or less of the total liability assigned to all persons liable". So provides CPLR 1601(1). If found 51% or more at fault, the tortfeasor's liability remains joint. Example:

P brings a personal injury claim against T1 and T2 and gets a verdict of which $100,000 represents non-economic damages.[1] T1 is found 60% culpable, T2 40%. T2 is responsible to P for only $40,000. T2 is a beneficiary of the new law. T1 remains responsible to P for the full $100,000. If T1 pays that to P, T1 can of course seek contribution of $40,000 from T2. But if T2 can't pay, T1 is the loser. If T2 pays P T2's own $40,000 share, on the other hand, T2 would obviously not get contribution from T1 because T2 has paid P only what T2 is individually responsible for. P in that situation can of course collect the balance of $60,000 from T1, or try to.

If in the above example the whole verdict were $150,000, the additional $50,000 being for economic damages (e.g., loss of earnings and medical costs), T2 would be severally liable for her own $40,000 segment of the $100,000, the non-economic portion, but both jointly and severally liable, along with T1, for the whole of the $50,000, the economic portion.

If T1 is only derivatively liable for the tort of T2, as in an employer-employee context, and T2 is 100% responsible for the accident, T1 may have 0% culpability but retains 100% liability. CPLR 1602(2)(iv) makes this clear by providing that liabilities arising under the "respondeat superior" doctrine are not altered by Article 16. T1 is of course entitled to indemnification from T2 if T1 pays P all in this situation.

If employee T2 is 40% at fault and a separate tortfeasor, T3, is 60% at fault, employer T1 is responsible for T2's 40% but T1 and T2 are both relieved of joint liability for T3's 60% share; they are beneficiaries of the 50%-or-less test. T3, on the other hand, fails that test and is jointly liable to P for the whole verdict, including the T1/T2 40% share.[2]

Is the plaintiff's share of fault factored in?

The comparative negligence rule of Article 14-A of the CPLR, which enables a plaintiff responsible in some measure for her own damages to recover from the defendants nevertheless, but with damages—both economic and non-economic, there's no distinction in this instance—diminished by the percentage of culpability the jury has ascribed to the plaintiff, remains intact under Article 16.[3] But how will the plaintiff's percentage of fault figure in determining the Article 16 liabilities of the defendants?

Take a sidewalk-fall case in which P's non-economic damages are found to be $100,000, with P found 40% at fault while T1 (who

---

5. See §§ 168B and 168C, below.

§ 168B

1. Remember that in this and all examples, unless otherwise noted, damage sums refer to only the non-economic segment of the verdict, the only segment that Article 16 operates on. See § 168A above.

2. Rights of contribution and indemnification under these and other circumstances are, as already noted, discussed in § 169 et seq., below.

3. CPLR 1602(2)(iii).

supposedly fixed the sidewalk) is found 40% at fault and T2 (the property owner) 20% at fault. If P's 40% share counts in calculating whether either T1 or T2 is entitled to a several-only judgment, then both are entitled to it; neither has joint liability for the other's share because each is less than 50% at fault. But if P is factored out, and the 40% and 20% shares of the defendants are extrapolated to 100%, then T1 becomes 66 2/3% responsible and T2 33 1/3% responsible. That still means the benefit of the new law for T2, but not for T1, who now goes on the hook for T2's share. If T2 is insolvent, then the factoring out of P means that T1 pays T2's $20,000 share, while if P is factored in, P is the loser to the extent of the $20,000.

Which shall it be? Article 16 does not address the point, a fundamental one. CPLR 1601 speaks in one breath of the "total liability assigned to all persons liable" and in another of "the relative culpability of each person causing or contributing to the total liability for non-economic loss". The word "culpability" is comparative negligence language as used in Article 14–A and suggests that P's share is considered. The word "liability", on the other hand, suggests to most ears the shares of those who will have to pay a judgment, which would mean defendants only.

There are arguable points on both sides. Probably more consistent with the overall structure of Article 16 is that P's share should not be considered. The extensive narrowing-down of the new rule of CPLR 1601 through the numerous exceptions contained in CPLR 1602 favors the view that had the legislature considered the point, it would have excluded P's own share of fault from the joint versus joint-and-several tabulation. When P turns to the defendants, moreover, it is only for the sum left over after P's share of the damages has come off the top, which is the way the comparative negligence rule operates. With respect to that left-over sum—$60,000 in the above sidewalk-fall example, after subtracting P's share of $40,000 from the $100,000 total—

the shares of T1 and T2 are indeed the extrapolated 66 2/3% and 33 1/3%.

If we assume that T2 can't pay, however, a curious mockery can appear if such an extrapolation is used (i.e., if P's share is excluded from consideration). In the above example, where P is 40% at fault, P collects $60,000, T1 picking up T2's share. But if the percentages are instead assessed at P 20% and T1 and T2 40% each, P recovers only $40,000, because, even with extrapolation, T1 and T2 end up with 50% shares and a 50% share for T1 means that T1 does not face joint liability and does not have to pick up the insolvent T2's $40,000 share. The rule of "extrapolation" in these examples, in other words, gives more money to the less deserving plaintiff: $60,000 to the 40%-at-fault plaintiff and only $40,000 to the 20%-at-fault plaintiff. Defendants, opposing an "extrapolation" construction, have quite an argument on that point.

It took a while, but caselaw addressing the issue has begun to appear. In Robinson v. June,[4] for example, drunk rowdies X and Y assaulted P outside T's tavern. The jury found X and Y together responsible for 45% of P's injuries and the tavern 50% responsible under the Dram Shop Act. The other 5% was P's share. Because X and Y were guilty of intentional conduct, they retain joint liability under an exception to the rule (met later[5]). The tavern, which with 50% fault would presumably get the benefit of "several" liability, ended up with joint liability when the extrapolation brought the 50% to 52.63%.[6]

§ 168C. "Joint" Tort Liability Adjustment; Provisos and Exceptions

There are a number of qualifications and exceptions in Article 16, all of them apparently pro-plaintiff, the result of intense legislative trading that required a lot of small steps back after the agreement had been made in the back rooms to take the main pro-defendant step forward.[1]

4. 167 Misc.2d 483, 637 N.Y.S.2d 1018 (Sup.Ct., Tompkins County, 1996).

5. CPLR 1602(5). See § 168C below.

6. The case is discussed in SPR 40:1.

Share of Nonparty Tortfeasor Not Considered

CPLR 1601(1) states that in determining shares of fault, "the culpable conduct of any person not a party to the action shall not be considered . . . if the claimant proves that with due diligence he or she was unable to obtain jurisdiction over such person". The idea is that if P can get jurisdiction of T1 but not T2, that's T1's bad luck: T1 must carry T2's share.

T1, the tortfeasor joined in the action, should look about to be sure that all other tortfeasors are there with T1. The only time T1 can accept the absence of another tortfeasor, whom we can call T2, is where T1 knows that T2 has settled the case and is insulated from suit by the settlement statute.[2] But absence because of settlement is not what CPLR 1601 means; the absence that Article 16 is concerned with is where T2 is not subject to "jurisdiction". Personal, not subject matter, jurisdiction is meant by this, and if personal jurisdiction is lacking over T2, it should be because T2 is a not a domiciliary of New York and no basis for extraterritorial (i.e., longarm) jurisdiction is available against T2. Problems of process service, as long as there is some basis for service outside the state, should not be a barrier to jurisdiction or an excuse for the plaintiff's failure to join T2. If worse comes to worst, the plaintiff can seek court-ordered service.[3]

Nor should T1 wait for P to join T2. P may for a variety of reasons drag his heels. T1 should make every effort to implead T2, and, if that succeeds, it will alone prove T2 amenable to jurisdiction and assure the injection of T2's share into the case, increasing T1's chance of getting down to a 50% or less exposure. It is not even necessary that T2 be actually made a party in order for T2's share of fault to be injected into the case. All that has to be shown is that T2 is subject to jurisdiction, whether P has actually joined T2 or not.

These standards also apply when the state is one of the tortfeasors and the court of claims is one of the courts involved. When the injured person sues the state in the court of claims and the state wants to show the fault of the other tortfeasors—the others of course beyond court of claims jurisdiction but at least shown to be subject to the personal jurisdiction of some other New York court—statute allows the state to have the court of claims consider the fault of the absent tortfeasors to the end of possibly reducing the state's share to 50% or below.

In the converse situation there's no statute in point, but some caselaw has filled in. It was held in Rezucha v. Garlock Mechanical Packing Co., for example,[4] that when tortfeasor A is sued in the supreme court, A may show the share of fault of S, the state, a co-tortfeasor but not a co-party in the supreme court (because the state may be sued only in the court of claims), again to the end of bringing A's share of fault to 50% or below.

For the purposes of applying this provision, a bankrupt tortfeasor has been held to be beyond the court's jurisdiction, thus excluding the bankrupt's share from an Article 16 calculus.[5]

There is a paradox in this provision about not considering the share of fault of a tortfeasor beyond the court's jurisdiction. T2 will be beyond jurisdiction mainly if not exclusively when the claim accrued outside New York. (It is on that kind of claim that longarm jurisdiction won't avail to get other tortfeasors into the action.) But if the claim accrued in another place, why does this statute assume that New York law with its Article 16 can even be ap-

---

§ 168C

1. Much of the text here is excerpted from this writer's lead notes in editions 322–324 of the New York State Law Digest, but the notes are more extensive and parts will merely be footnoted as they become relevant.

2. The settlement statute is § 15–108 of the General Obligations Law, for which see § 176 below.

3. See CPLR 308(5) and 311(b).

4. 159 Misc.2d 855, 606 N.Y.S.2d 969 (Sup.Ct., Broome County, 1993).

5. Brooklyn Navy Yard Asbestos Litigation, 971 F.2d 831 (2d Cir.1992). An analogous situation arises and a similar rule is applied under the settlement statute, Gen. Oblig.L. § 15–108. See § 176 below.

plied to the case?[6]

Effect of Settlement under Gen.Oblig.L. § 15–108

No analysis was made by the legislature of the effect that a settlement between (e.g.) P and T1 but not T2 might have on Article 16. But just to be sure that the settlement statute, § 15–108 of the General Obligations Law,[7] is not in any way undermined by Article 16, subdivision (2) of CPLR 1601 provides that "[n]othing in this section shall be construed to affect or impair any right of a tortfeasor under section 15–108". The section appears to be compatible with Article 16 in most situations.[8]

Contribution and Indemnification Rules Intact

Subdivision 1 of CPLR 1602, which is directed to rights of contribution and indemnification, seems to be superfluous in that it seeks to retain contribution and indemnification rights intact. It wasn't needed for that.[9]

"Non–Delegable" Duty Exception

A tortfeasor shown to have violated what the law denominates a "non-delegable duty" gets no several-only status.[10] Perhaps the most common examples of this under our law are in construction cases under Article 10 of the Labor Law,[11] which includes the well known Labor Law §§ 240 and 241 and the quasi "absolute" liabilities they impose on owners and contractors at construction sites. A tortfeasor running afoul of such a provision, even though found responsible for (e.g.) only 30% of the accident, remains 100% accountable to the plaintiff for all damages if that 30% is predicated on a "non-delegable duty" provision like the cited Labor Law statutes.

An example of a defendant being denied an Article 16 reduction for having breached a non-delegable duty is where the defendant violated a statutory duty to remove lead paint from a premises.[12]

In what must be a surprise to the state's municipalities, who championed Article 16 and are generally regarded as having spurred its adoption, a municipality was denied the benefits of Article 16 under the "non-delegable duty" provision in Rubinfeld v. City of New York,[13] where the court found non-delegable a city's duty to maintain traffic signals. The impact of the "non-delegable duty" exception, which was apparently inserted towards the end of the frantic behind-the-scenes maneuverings that produced Article 16, may not have been appreciated at the time: total liability for something like a traffic light failure, when a jury ascribes only a small percentage of the fault to it, was the kind of thing from which Article 16 was designed to insulate municipalities.

Special Rule When Plaintiff's Employer Impleaded

An odd situation results from subdivision 4 of CPLR 1602. The subdivision concerns the well known situation in which employee E is injured on the job in part by the fault of employer R, but can't sue R because of the exclusivity of the remedy of workers' compensation against an employer. E can sue any other person, however, such as T, responsible in part for E's injury, and T is then allowed to implead R for contribution in this anomalous but frequent New York scenario. As originally drafted, CPLR 1602(4) denied an Article 16 adjustment to the defendant who impleaded the employer, but apparently allowed the adjustment to the defendant who did not implead the employer but did prove fault on the part of the absent employer.

---

6. See the lead note in New York State Law Digest No. 322, p.3.

7. Section 176 below.

8. See the lead note in New York State Law Digest No. 323, p. 2, and the examples cited there.

9. Illustrations of contribution and indemnification in this context appear in the first few paragraphs of § 168B above.

10. CPLR 1602(2)(iv).

11. The reference is repeated, perhaps redundantly, by subdivision 8 of CPLR 1602.

12. Cortes v. Riverbridge Realty Co., 227 A.D.2d 430, 642 N.Y.S.2d 692 (2d Dep't 1996).

13. 170 Misc.2d 868, 652 N.Y.S.2d 688 (Sup.Ct., Kings County, 1996). The case is noted in SPR 59:3.

Those distinctions are apparently eliminated by a 1996 amendment of CPLR 1602(4), made as part of the Omnibus Workers' Compensation Reform Act of 1996.[14] An important part of the act is that it precludes the defendant's impleader of the plaintiff's employer unless it is shown that the employee sustained a "grave injury", as defined by statute.[15] The amendment applies to the situation in which grave injury to the plaintiff does exist, but it is not clear what is supposed to happen. To the extent of the employer's share, the defendant is apparently not entitled to an Article 16 adjustment. If that is so, the defendant would be responsible to the plaintiff for the employer's share even if the defendant's own share comes to 50% or less, but would of course be entitled to a contribution judgment against the employer for whatever of the employer's share the defendant pays.[16]

Intentional Conduct and "Reckless Disregard" Cases Excepted

At two junctures the point is made that a tortfeasor found guilty of intentional conduct gets no Article 16 benefit, whatever the percentage of fault allotted to him. He remains a joint tortfeasor with all the others. Subdivisions 5 and 11 of CPLR 1602 so provide, the latter requiring a showing that the defendant acted "in concert" with another.

Subdivision 5 removes the benefits of the new rule from any action "requiring proof of intent". To whatever extent they might otherwise be placed in the "personal injury" category, therefore, torts like assault and fraud, which have intent elements, remain wholly in the joint and several class.

An interesting problem arises in the case that involves both categories of defendant. In Siler v. 146 Montague Assocs., for example,[17] which had to balance an intentional against an unintentional tortfeasor, the court split on how to apply the apportionment rules.[18] In another case in which police officers were the

unintentional tortfeasors (failing to protect a woman from her husband's violence), they were allowed an Article 16 adjustment for the husband's intentional conduct.[19]

Subdivision 7 adds that a tortfeasor acting "with reckless disregard for the safety of others" is also to be denied several-only status. This of course induces the plaintiff to inject the "reckless disregard" issue into as many cases as possible.

One might at first assume that a tortfeasor found guilty of "reckless disregard" conduct is not likely to be found less than 50% at fault by a jury. But it can happen. If there are several causes of P's injury, for example, and T1's act is 70% responsible while T2's is only 30% responsible, a finding, nevertheless, that T2's conduct was the result of T2's "reckless disregard for the safety of others" would make T2 liable to P for 100%. If T1 were unable to pay the judgment, the "reckless disregard" finding against T2 would assure P's collection of the whole judgment against T2, a party less than 50% at fault.

The Motor Vehicle Exception

Reading the initial parts of Article 16 and seeking to summon up examples, the uninitiated are apt to use perhaps the most common source of all personal injuries: the motor vehicle accident. This makes the exception contained in subdivision 6 of CPLR 1602 all the more influential, and interesting. It says that the several-only advantage conferred by Article 16 does not apply to any person held liable by reason of his use, operation, or ownership of a motor vehicle or motorcycle, as those terms are defined respectively in §§ 311 and 125 of the vehicle and traffic law.

Example. P sues T1 and T2, drivers of two cars who injured pedestrian P. P's non-economic damages are $100,000, with T1 found 60% at fault and T2 40%. Each is liable to P for the full $100,000. T2, although less than

---

14. See § 155 above.

15. See § 171 below.

16. If grave injury to the plaintiff is not shown, the Omnibus Act bars the employer's impleader altogether.

17. 228 A.D.2d 33, 652 N.Y.S.2d 315 (2d Dep't 1997).

18. See the discussion in the lead note in SPR 53.

19. Morales v. County of Nassau, ___ A.D.2d ___, 683 N.Y.S.2d 127 (2d Dep't 1998).

50% at fault, gets no several-only status. He was a driver and drivers are not beneficiaries of Article 16. That would also be true if T2 were sued as owner of the car. But it would not be true, and T2 would be allowed several-only status, if T2 were the manufacturer of the car, or its designer, or some other tortfeasor involved with the car in a capacity other than "use, operation, or ownership".

And there are exceptions to this exception. The definitions referred to in the statute exclude police and fire vehicles from the "vehicle" exclusion, for example, so that drivers and owners of those vehicles, most notably municipalities, do get the benefits of Article 16's several-only exposure. This is consistent with one of the prime motives known to underlie Article 16: the protection of municipal entities, the usual owners and operators of fire and police vehicles. But it is not a consistent consistency because other municipal vehicles are not excepted and do generate joint liability. Garbage trucks would be an example. Shall we describe them as exceptions to the exception of the exception that CPLR 1602(6) constitutes?

Take an example. Four vehicles collide, injuring pedestrian P, who sues six defendants: O1, the owner of car 1 (for the negligence of the driver for whom O1 is derivatively liable under New York law); G1, a garage that negligently repaired the brakes of car 1; D2, the driver of car 2; M2, the manufacturer of car 2 (for negligent clutch design); V3, the village that owns vehicle 3, a police car on duty at the time; and C4, a city that owns vehicle 4, a garbage truck that was in the village at the time to dump some garbage under a city-village contract.

The jury finds P's noneconomic damages to be $100,000 and finds all defendants in some degree at fault: 20% for O1 for the ownership of the negligently driven vehicle, 20% for G1 for negligent brake repair, 30% for D2 for negligent driving, 10% for M2 for negligent car design, 15% for V3 for negligent driving, and 5% for C4 for negligent driving. Integrating just how each defendant qualifies under the interlocking exceptions noted, P is entitled to judgment against

O1 for $100,000 (the private car owner falls under the exception and so loses the several-only status);

G1 for $20,000 (a garage is not under the exception, so it gets the status);

D2 for $100,000 (a private car driver falls under the exception and so loses the status);

M2 for $10,000 (a manufacturer is not under the exception, so it gets the status);

V3 for $15,000 (a police car owner falls under the exception to the exception and so gets the status);

C4 for $100,000 (a garbage truck owned by a city falls beyond the exception to the exception, so the city loses the status).

It's not hard, just involved.

Medical Malpractice and "Successive Tortfeasor" Cases

We've said nothing up to now about how Article 16 figures in medical malpractice actions, or when tortfeasors are not "concurrent" and "joint" ones but "independent" and "successive" ones.

Article 16 applies in medical malpractice actions, of course, to the extent it can find a situation in which tortfeasors would be "jointly" liable there. If, for example, two doctors worked on P concurrently, and the jury assigns MD1 60% responsibility and MD2 40% responsibility, MD2 would presumably have several-only standing while MD1 would have joint responsibility for MD2's share.

More typical, though, and clearly more challenging under Article 16, is the accident-plus-malpractice situation, which brings us into the "successive tortfeasors" arena.

The operation of Article 16 should be carefully analyzed in a situation in which a successive rather than concurrent liability is involved. The classic example is where P is hurt at the hands of tortfeasor T (a driver, contractor, sidewalk owner, etc.) and is then treated for her injury by MD, whose malpractice aggravates the injury. Under existing tort law, before even considering Article 16, T has joint and several liability and is responsible for both his own and MD's share, but MD's liability is several only. MD is responsible to P for only MD's own share, not T's. With respect to MD, therefore, Article 16 offers no gift because MD already has several-only status.

Suppose the jury finds that only 20% of P's damages were caused by the conduct of T in bringing about the accident and that MD's negligent medical treatment accounts for the other 80%? MD is still accountable for only his own 80%, not T's 20%. MD has several-only status from prior law, independent of Article 16, and keeps it without regard to Article 16's 50% threshold.

But what of T? Does T's 20% invoke Article 16 and relieve him of MD's 80% share? It would appear that T retains 100% exposure to P, including MD's share, for several reasons. One is that CPLR 1601(1) operates only when there are two or more tortfeasors "jointly liable". T and MD in this common context are not "jointly liable"; they are successive, not concurrent, tortfeasors. While T is liable for MD's share, MD is not liable for T's.

Another reason is the policy ground behind the original rule refusing to declare T and MD "joint" tortfeasors. Its theory is that T was the evil one whose conduct brought about P's injury, while MD was the benevolent one who at least tried to put things right. Hence the law differentiates between the initial group, the tortfeasor or tortfeasors accountable in varying measures for the infliction of P's original injury, and the subsequent or "successive" group, the medical profession that gets involved only as a consequence.

While there is obvious evidence in Article 16 of a wish to adjust liabilities among the first group so as to relieve of "joint" liability those among them with light involvement, and while we can also find an intention to retain an initial tortfeasor's liability for all of the ensuing medical malpractice, things become murky, and a good deal more interesting, when there are several members of the original tortfeasor group and the question is whether responsibility should be placed on all of them for all of the subsequent medical malpractice, without regard to their percentages of fault for the original tort. Example:

Passenger P is hurt in a car designed by M and driven by D over a road maintained by Town T. P is taken for treatment to MD, whose treatment aggravates P's injury. P sues all four. The jury sets P's non-economic damages at $100,000. It finds that the original accident caused 40% of P's damages, the other 60% being caused by MD. For the original accident the assigned responsibility is M 10%, D 70%, and T 20%. How do we resolve that case under Article 16?

For the $40,000 of P's damages caused by the original accident, M and T, each with less than a 50% share, should be severally liable for only their own shares, which would be $4000 for M and $8000 for T. D, whose 70% passes the Article 16 threshold, should be accountable to P for the whole $40,000.

But what about the responsibility of M, D, and T for MD's $60,000 share? Is each of them responsible for the whole $60,000 regardless of the shares assessed against them for the initial $40,000? An argument can be made to that effect. Since each contributed in some measure to the original accident that occasioned the medical treatment, they could each be made jointly accountable for the whole of MD's share. That would make this their total exposure to P: M $64,000, T $68,000, and D $100,000. MD's exposure to P continues, as under prior law, to be for only his own $60,000 share of P's damages.

In this example, M and T, with only 10% and 20% culpability for the accident, which is itself accountable for only 40% of P's damages, are made to bear full responsibility to P for MD's 60% share of those damages.

Perhaps, in a "successive" tort situation, it would be more consistent with Article 16 (and its wish to insulate the less-than–50% tortfeasors from joint liability) to hold each of the original tortfeasors responsible for the MD-caused damages only in the percentage they are found accountable for the initial damages. Of the $60,000 assigned to MD, that would make M jointly liable for $6000 and T jointly liable for $12,000. D, on the other hand, having failed Article 16's 50% threshold test initially, would continue to bear joint liability for the whole of the $60,000.

These situations involving a physician should not be frequent. They would arise only when the damages involved in phase two, the medical treatment, are not paid, and they imply an ability to pay on the part of the original tortfeasors greater than the ability to pay of the "successive" group. But there can be "successive" tort situations in which the second-round injury is not caused by medical treatment, but by (e.g.) a second collision and the like. Inability of the second-round tortfeasor to pay in that situation may be more frequent, and the above illustrations consequently less academic.

§ 168D. "Joint" Tort Liability Adjustment; Burdens of Proof

A tortfeasor seeking to obtain several-only status under Article 16 has the burden of proving it was 50% or less at fault. So provides CPLR 1603. It amounts to a defense that should be pleaded as such in the answer. It can be pleaded hypothetically: "If I am liable at all, I am 50% or less so". This burden is consistent with the defendant's wish to lay as much fault as possible at the door of co-tortfeasors so as to maximize his own contribution rights against them under Article 14 of the CPLR,[1] and with his wish to establish some culpability on the part of the plaintiff, too, so as to obtain a comparative negligence reduction under Article 14–A of the CPLR. For the latter, incidentally, CPLR 1412 specifically imposes the burden of proof on the defendant.

When an Article 16 issue is present, the difficulty of determining who has the burden of proof has generated a conflict among the appellate divisions about whether D is obliged upon demand to serve a bill of particulars on the plaintiff. The Fourth Department held in Ryan v. Beavers[2] that reliance on Article 16 is a defense and that the defendant must particularize it on demand, but a divided Second Department afterwards held otherwise in Marsala v. Weinraub.[3] Defendants' attorneys who want to be on the safe side should follow the suggestions in Justice Ritter's concurrence in Marsala: plead Article 16 as a defense and be prepared to particularize it.[4]

For a number of reasons, Article 16's demands among them, the defendant is usually best off including in its answer allegations placing at least some blame on others if others may be in any way involved in the tort. By so doing the defendant may preserve rights under Article 16, and under the tort settlement statute,[5] that it may not even have thought about yet.[6]

Whatever the defendant may do in this regard, however, it behooves the plaintiff, in the course of bill of particulars or pretrial disclosure practice, to inquire into whether the defendant seeks to hold anyone else accountable for the plaintiff's claim. It has been held that the defendant is under no duty to volunteer names of persons it may hold accountable under Article 16, so that a plaintiff failing to specifically inquire into the subject in pretrial practice can't complain if the defendant at the trial unexpectedly places some blame on a third person not identified earlier.[7]

If one of CPLR 1602's many exceptions is claimed, such as would cancel out the several-only advantage that Article 16 might otherwise confer on a given defendant, the burden of pleading and proof is now on the plaintiff, the one claiming that the exception governs. Where would the plaintiff plead this? It's premature before the answer is served, so the complaint wouldn't seem the place. And without a court order a reply can't be served unless there's a counterclaim in the answer.[8] Does CPLR 1603 implicitly authorize a reply? If not, perhaps P should just serve one despite the seeming want of authority. A savvy defendant would hardly be bothered opposing it. Technically, an argument could be made that P need

§ 168D

1. See § 169 et seq., below.
2. 170 A.D.2d 1045, 566 N.Y.S.2d 112 (1991).
3. 208 A.D.2d 689, 617 N.Y.S.2d 809 (1994).
4. See the discussion in the lead note in SPR 29.
5. Gen.Oblig.L. § 15–108.

6. See the treatment of this subject in the lead note in SPR 30.

7. See Rodi v. Landau, 170 Misc.2d 180, 650 N.Y.S.2d 514 (Sup.Ct., Rockland County, 1996).

8. CPLR 3011.

not plead the exception at all (though of course having to prove it at the trial): CPLR 3018(a) provides that when the answer calls for no responsive pleading, its affirmative allegations "are deemed denied or avoided". The court shouldn't let any consequence append to a mere pleading omission on this point, anyway, since CPLR 1603 in effect puts P into the awkward position of having to interpose a defense to a defense.

A defendant who would preserve her Article 16 rights against a co-defendant should be alert against any step that might take the co-defendant out of the picture. In one case, for example, in which P sued A and B and in which A successfully moved for summary judgment against P, B did not oppose the motion. The court held that because of this B forfeited the right to implicate A at the trial, thus diminishing B's own chances of avoiding joint liability by having A's liability remain an issue in the case.[9]

§ 168E. The Comparative Negligence Rule of CPLR Article 14–A

This is an appropriate point to say a word about New York's comparative negligence rule, lest confusion between it and the contributory negligence rule (which it replaced) add unnecessary complications to the discussion of contribution that begins in the next section.

Prior to 1975, New York applied a rule of "contributory negligence" in tort cases. Under it, a plaintiff (P) guilty of contributing in any measure at all to her own injuries would recover nothing. Technically applied, this meant (for example) that a defendant 95% at fault in causing an accident would get off the hook completely. The 5% culpability that P had would bar any recovery at all. The rule often disposed juries to disregard contributory fault altogether in order to preserve a recovery for a seriously hurt plaintiff. Many lawyers urged

adoption of a "comparative" negligence rule, under which a plaintiff guilty of culpable conduct does recover, but with her damages diminished by the percentage of her own culpability. "To keep the jury honest", they argued.

Article 14–A of the CPLR, consisting of §§ 1411–1413, adopts such a rule. It was enacted in 1975 and made applicable to all causes of action accruing on or after September 1, 1975.[1] (Claims accruing before continued to be governed by the contributory negligence rule.)

The rule is one of "pure" comparative negligence, which enables a plaintiff to recover even if responsible for more than 50% of her own damages, the damages just being reduced by whatever percentage the fact finder, usually a jury, finds to be the plaintiff's own fault.

The rule bases the reduction not on allotments of culpability contributing to the accident or occurrence—this is an important point—but to the plaintiff's damages,[2] which is broader. In an automobile accident case, for example, it permits a comparative fault deduction based on the extent to which the plaintiff's damages were caused by her failure to wear a seat belt, an omission that may have played no role at all in causing the accident.[3]

The burden of pleading and proving the plaintiff's comparative culpability is on the defendant. It has been made an affirmative defense,[4] and a defendant should make sure to plead it as such in the answer.[5] (Under the old contributory negligence rule, the plaintiff had the burden of the issue, required both to plead in the complaint and to prove at the trial that she was not guilty of any contributory fault.)

Like the contribution and apportionment rules of the *Dole* case and its CPLR Article 14 codification, which concern adjustments of liability among the tortfeasors and are taken up beginning in the next section, the comparative negligence rule of Article 14–A is essentially a

---

9. See Drooker v. South Nassau Comm. Hosp., 175 Misc.2d 181, 669 N.Y.S.2d 169 (Sup.Ct., Nassau County, 1998), noted in SPR 72:3. For the same reasons, B should consider opposing any effort by the plaintiff to discontinue the action against A. See SPR 77:3.

§ 168E

1. CPLR 1413.

2. CPLR 1411.

3. It can sometimes play a role even in causation of the accident. See Curry v. Moser, 89 A.D.2d 1, 454 N.Y.S.2d 311 (2d Dep't 1982).

4. CPLR 1412.

5. See § 223 below.

rule of substantive law. But it, too, is a CPLR product and is often bound up with matters of procedure.

We introduce it here, between two batches of sections concerned with the defendants' rights and obligations, for several reasons. One is that in charging the jury about where the defendants stand under the law, the judge has to fit in at the same time what the plaintiff's rights and duties are and how they affect the defendants' liabilities. Another reason is that what the plaintiff gets from the defendants may be very much affected by the adjustment in joint and several liability made by Article 16 of the CPLR, treated in the preceding sections, while what the defendants' liabilities may be among themselves, as taken up in the ensuing sections under the "contribution" caption, are very much affected by both the Article 16 adjustment and the comparative culpability adjustment treated here.

The interplay of culpabilities, responsibilities, obligations, faults, rights, duties, etc., under all of these various provisions, including those on contribution yet to be negotiated, can be challenging, even gnarled, sometimes creating both conceptual problems substantively and practical problems procedurally. An example is Caiazzo v. Volkswagenwerk, A.G.[6], treated later.[7]

A derivative claim, like one for loss of consortium, is diminished under the comparative negligence rule by the same percentage that diminishes the claim of the injured person from whom the claim derives. Thus, if a woman is found responsible for 30% of her own injuries, her husband's loss of services claim is also diminished by 30%.[8]

The role that the assumption of risk doctrine plays within the framework of the comparative negligence rule, which has occasioned some difficulty in recent years, comes in for an extended treatment by the Court of Appeals in a quartet of cases decided together.[9] In the first three, the assumption of risk doctrine is applied to bar the claim on summary judgment at the very threshold of the action; in the fourth, the doctrine is found insufficient by itself to bar the action, necessitating a trial.[10]

I. CONTRIBUTION

Table of Sections

§ 169.　Contribution, Introductory

Contribution is the right of a wrongdoer who has paid the injured person's damages to make other wrongdoers contribute to what has been paid. It has always been a phenomenon primarily of the tort realm, arising automatically when certain factors are present and not requiring any kind of agreement between or among the wrongdoers. After the 1987 Court of Appeals decision in the *Hudson* case,[1] it will apparently have to be regarded as exclusively a tort phenomenon. The *Hudson* case holds that contribution does not apply when the one from whom it is sought is liable only in contract.[2]

6.　647 F.2d 241 (2d Cir.1981), rev'g 468 F.Supp. 593 (E.D.N.Y.1979).

7.　See § 175 below.

8.　Maidman v. Stagg, 82 A.D.2d 299, 441 N.Y.S.2d 711 (2d Dep't 1981).

9.　Morgan v. State, Beck v. Scimeca, Chimerine v. World Champion John Chung etc., and Siegel v. City of New York, 90 N.Y.2d 471, 662 N.Y.S.2d 421 (1997).

10.　The cases are the subject of the lead note in New York State Law Digest No. 454.

§ 169

1.　Board of Educ. of the Hudson City Sch. Dist. v. Sargent, Webster, Crenshaw & Folley, 71 N.Y.2d 21, 523 N.Y.S.2d 475, 517 N.E.2d 1360.

2.　The case and its problems are discussed in Barker, The Badly Performed Contract, N.Y. Law Journal, Nov. 28, 1988, p.3, and in the lead note in New York State Law Digest No. 340.

"Contribution" differs from "indemnity" in that it "is not founded on nor does it arise from contract and only ratable or proportional reimbursement is sought", while indemnity "springs from a contract, express or implied, and full, not partial, reimbursement is sought."[3]

Actually, the matter of terminology is more historical than accurate. When A seeks to make B "contribute" to tort damages paid by A to the injured person, A may also be said to be seeking to make B "indemnify" A for that portion of the hurt that was B's fault. In practical effect, contribution can be described as partial indemnity and indemnity can be described as total contribution. It is nonetheless convenient to separate the two items along the lines suggested above, using "indemnity" to describe a situation in which B should reimburse everything A has paid and "contribution" to describe B's obligation to pay only part.

With the 1974 enactment of a new Article 14 of the CPLR, in essence codifying the important Court of Appeals decision in Dole v. Dow Chemical Co.,[4] a tortfeasor sued alone in a multi-party tort case is allowed to bring in the other tortfeasors and make them share—"contribute" to—the injured person's damages. It had previously been A's fate, if made the sole defendant, to bear all the damages alone with no right to bring in or otherwise pursue the other tortfeasors to make them share the load.

§ 170. The Picture Before Dole v. Dow Chemical Co.

The Dole case[1] burst onto the scene suddenly and it is helpful to set the scene.

At common law the injured person, P, could pick from among the tortfeasors, singling out any one or any combination of them to pay P's damages. P could, for example, sue only tort-

feasor A, and if P did, A had no recourse against any other tortfeasor. In these multi-party tort cases, B and C and all of the others were off the hook at P's whim. The common law had various reasons for this. One was that the law should not lend its hand to adjust rights among wrongdoers.[2] Another was that the rule would discourage torts by warning each tortfeasor that there is no safety in numbers; that if P should sue A alone, A would have no recourse against the other tortfeasors, so that P could therefore single A out and make A pay all of P's damages alone.[3]

Those motivations may have been relevant as applied to the intentional tort, but the restrictive rule they created was imported without critical analysis to govern in the era of the unintentional tort, where the rule's application was irrational. Before Dole, only a few developments took place to abate the rigors of the rule, and the abatement was only partial.

One was the creation of a statutory right of contribution. This was itself limited. It still depended on P's voluntarily joining more than one tortfeasor, and so it still left A to face liability alone when P chose to sue A without B. It was a step, but a grudging one.[4]

Another development was the caselaw creation of the so-called "passive-active" dichotomy. If A, the sued tortfeasor, could show that A was merely "passive" in conduct while the real culprit was B, whose conduct was "active", A would be allowed to implead B. It was usually a case of all or nothing. If A was merely "passive" and B "active", B would be required not merely to contribute to what A paid the injured person, but to indemnify A for all of it. It was in effect a "contribution" label sewn into what was really an "indemnity" garment.

The passive-active standard was easy enough to apply in cases of straight derivative

---

3. McFall v. Compagnie Maritime Belge, 304 N.Y. 314, 327–8, 107 N.E.2d 463, 470–1 (1952).

4. 30 N.Y.2d 143, 331 N.Y.S.2d 382, 282 N.E.2d 288 (1972).

§ 170

1. Dole v. Dow Chem. Co., 30 N.Y.2d 143, 331 N.Y.S.2d 382, 282 N.E.2d 288 (1972).

2. Id. at 147, 331 N.Y.S.2d at 386, 282 N.E.2d at 291.

3. See Developments in New York Practice, Dole v. Dow Chemical Co.: A Revolution in New York Law, 47 St. John's L.Rev. 185 (1972).

4. See § 174, below, comparing the old CPLR 1401 with the new Article 14.

or automatic liability. If, for example, P sued O, the owner of a building, for injuries sustained in P's fall on a defective sidewalk, O could implead G, the general contractor whose negligent repair caused the defective condition. In a situation like that, O was rather clearly "passive" in conduct and G "active". Similarly with a master, M, sued for the tortious wrong of a servant, S. M was only derivatively liable, which qualified as passive, and M could therefore implead S. And a car owner, O, sued for injuries caused by the driving of D, could implead D.[5]

The endeavor to apply the passive-active criterion in other situations, however, was hard and sometimes theoretically unacceptable. In many cases the same conduct on the part of a tortfeasor could be phrased by an able lawyer in either passive or active terms. If P pleaded against A "actively", A was ipso facto barred from impleading B. Illustrative cases were numerous. The problem was well illustrated and discussed by Justice (later Chief Judge) Charles Breitel in Bush Terminal Buildings Co. v. Luckenbach Steamship Co.[6] The *Bush* case demonstrated how allegations of commission versus omission could be used in an attempt to parallel active versus passive conduct and how erratic that attempt could be, and how P's choice of words would nonetheless be allowed to control so substantial a right as whether A could secure contribution from B. Cases involving the so-called "nondelegable" duty were notorious examples of unfairness; the person with the statutory "nondelegable" duty was deemed guilty of "active" negligence and thereby automatically precluded, no matter how innocent, from impleading any other person, no matter how guilty.[7] And throughout the era, P's complaint controlled the defendant's impleader right. The impleader was allowed if P alleged "passive" conduct by D but

was precluded if P pleaded "active" behavior,[8] even though these matters concerned only the rights of the tortfeasors inter se, as to which P was usually indifferent. These misfortunes are largely swept away by the *Dole* decision.

As sound as the *Bush* analysis was—it pressed for the adoption, more than two decades before *Dole*, of an approach that would determine primary and secondary grades of culpability rather than the artificially denominated "active" and "passive" classes—the decision was reversed by the Court of Appeals[9] along the old lines. Its lessons came in due course to prevail in the Court of Appeals with the 1972 *Dole* decision, and in the legislature with the 1974 adoption of CPLR Article 14.

§ 171. The Arrival of Dole

The active-passive lines on the caselaw front and old CPLR 1401 and its limited right of contribution on the statutory front continued to stand until March 22, 1972, when the Court of Appeals in *Dole* abruptly abandoned the active-passive restriction and gave the sued tortfeasor the right to interpose a contribution claim against any other tortfeasor alleged to have participated in the tort, joining the other as a party if necessary. The relative percentages of the several tortfeasors' culpabilities were henceforth to be gauged by the jury and their relative liabilities apportioned accordingly.

The rights of P, the injured person, remained the same, however. After 1975, with the adoption of the comparative negligence rule in Article 14–A of the CPLR,[1] there would of course be a reduction of P's damages for P's own percentage of culpable conduct, but even under *Dole* P would still take judgment for the balance against each of the defendant tortfea-

---

5. See Farrell and Wilner, Dole v. Dow Chemical Co.: A Leading Decision—But Where?, 39 Brooklyn L.Rev. 330 (1972).

6. 11 A.D.2d 220, 202 N.Y.S.2d 172 (1st Dep't 1960).

7. See, e.g., Milne v. Chandler and Hatlee, 45 Misc.2d 593, 257 N.Y.S.2d 476 (Sup.Ct., Schenectady County, 1964), aff'd 23 A.D.2d 711, 257 N.Y.S.2d 460 (3d Dep't 1965).

8. Kennedy v. Bethlehem Steel Co., 282 A.D. 1001, 125 N.Y.S.2d 552 (4th Dep't 1953), aff'd 307 N.Y. 875, 122 N.E.2d 753 (1954).

9. 9 N.Y.2d 426, 214 N.Y.S.2d 428, 174 N.E.2d 516 (1961), with Chief Judge Desmond and Judge (later Chief Judge) Fuld dissenting.

§ 171

1. See § 168E above.

sors, jointly and severally.[2] If P joined A and B as defendants and P's damages were assessed at $20,000 and P's own fault at 25%, the $20,000 would be reduced to $15,000 but P would take a full $15,000 judgment against A and B and could collect it all from either one. Under *Dole*, whatever proportions of fault were found in A and B respectively governed only contribution between them. If P sued only A, who impleaded B, P's judgment would run only against A, but A would get a judgment over against B for whatever the jury found B's share to be.[3]

The apportionment rule of *Dole* applies in all unintentional tort situations,[4] not solely in vehicle cases. *Dole* in fact involved no cars at all. P was sent by his employer, R, to clean out an enclosure that had been sprayed with D's product but had not yet been adequately defumigated. P inhaled poisonous fumes and died. His widow sued D. D impleaded R. Before *Dole*, the impleader would have been precluded because D was accused of acts—labeling and circulating a poison product—which would have qualified as "active" negligence. *Dole* abandoned that standard and allowed the impleader.

The involvement in *Dole* of the employee/employer relationship requires a word of explanation here. The widow in *Dole* could not sue R directly because as against R, the employer, workers' compensation was (and remains) the exclusive remedy.[5] But when suit by or in behalf of the employee is brought against some other person liable for the tort, the latter may turn around and implead the employer. The theory is that such a third-party claim is one for indemnity, a variety of contract, not for tort, and is therefore not precluded by the exclusivity of the workers'

compensation remedy. *Dole* is a typical illustration of this phenomenon in New York, which subjects the employer indirectly (via having to make good as a third-party defendant) to the common law tort liability for which suit by the employee may not be brought against the employer directly. It also accounts for the monumental effort some lawyers make, when a tort case involving an employee marches into the office, to uncover some person other than the employer on whom liability might be pinned. That opens the door to common law tort damages, without which the more modest workers' compensation sums would be all the employee or the employee's family could obtain.

Before *Dole*, the defendant could implead a third party (employer or otherwise) only for indemnification—full coverage for the defendant's exposure to the plaintiff. The passive-active dichotomy held sway and impleader was available only for indemnity, not mere contribution. *Dole* allowed the impleader device of CPLR 1007 to be used to bring in tortfeasors merely for contribution purposes.

We may remark that the *Dole* case (and the statutory package of Article 14 that codifies it[6]) pronounces in essence a rule of substantive law. *Dole* creates a right of contribution where none existed before, as substantive a doing as the law can manage. The CPLR was chosen as the site of its codification because it affects procedure in so many ways. *Dole* can be viewed as a kind of comparative negligence rule applicable only among tortfeasors, and the case can in fact be given some of the credit for accelerating New York's 1975 adoption of a full comparative negligence rule,[7] which applies to the plaintiff in replacement of the

---

2. Kelly v. Long Island Lighting Co., 31 N.Y.2d 25, 334 N.Y.S.2d 851, 286 N.E.2d 241 (1972).

3. Until 1986, when Article 16 was adopted adjusting the "joint and several liability" rule in tort cases (see §§ 168A through 168D above), the courts of course had to assume that insofar as defendants were "joint" tortfeasors—as opposed to "successive" or "independent" tortfeasors, for example—each defendant was accountable to P for all of P's damages regardless of the defendant's own allotted proportion, which counted only in determining contribution rights among the defendants. Under Article 16, and subject to its many exceptions, treated in § 168C,

a tortfeasor whose culpability is assessed at 50% or less is no longer responsible to the plaintiff for the shares of other tortfeasors.

4. CPLR 1411, embodying the comparative negligence rule enacted after Dole was decided, does not purport to restrict itself to unintentional conduct.

5. Work.Comp.L. § 11.

6. Article 14 is discussed in § 172 below.

7. CPLR 1411. See § 168E above.

contributory negligence rule that was in effect when *Dole* came down in 1972.

On the subject of the employee/employer relationship and its status in the indemnity/contribution realm, incidental notice should be taken of the enactment of the Omnibus Workers' Compensation Reform Act of 1996,[8] which permits a defendant sued by an employee to implead the employer only when it is shown that the employee has suffered a "grave injury" as defined by statute.[9]

§ 172. Contribution Under CPLR Article 14

Article 14 of the CPLR, enacted in 1974, codifies the basics of the *Dole* case. It creates a right of contribution for a tortfeasor regardless of whether the other tortfeasors have been sued by P, the injured person.[1] If P joins them initially, the contribution can be sought within the action. If P doesn't, the sued tortfeasor can implead those P has omitted.[2]

The amount of contribution to which a tortfeasor is entitled is the "excess" she pays beyond her own "equitable share" of the injured person's judgment. But the one from whom the contribution is sought need not pay more than his own share; he can't be made to recompense the paying tortfeasor for yet another tortfeasor's share. (This may mean that tortfeasor A, from whom P has collected all, can get only B's share from B but can't make B contribute part of the share of insolvent tortfeasor C, which A then has to absorb alone.

This is an injustice that Article 14 apparently perpetuates.)

The "equitable share" of each tortfeasor is his "relative culpability" as found by the jury or other fact trier.[3] When Article 14 was first enacted, a plaintiff suing two or more tortfeasors and winning against all would take judgment against all of them in the full amount of the verdict. Under Article 16 of the CPLR, adopted in 1986, P takes judgment in the full sum—less, of course, the plaintiff's share of comparative fault if any has been found—only against tortfeasors found responsible for more than 50% of the liability; those with 50% or less are on P's hook for only their own percentage.[4] To whatever extent a given tortfeasor in the more-than–50% category (whom we can designate M) pays out on what is really the share of a 50%-or-less tortfeasor (L), M has a contribution claim against L. (L would at no point have a contribution claim against M because, being liable to P for only L's own share, L would at no point be paying P any part of M's share.)

It if appears that the relationship between any tortfeasors is such that one is entitled to outright indemnification from the other, the right remains unimpaired.[5] Suppose, for example, that P sues E (employee) and R (employer) for E's negligent tort, for which R bears only derivative liability. While of course liable to P for the whole of P's damages, R is entitled to full indemnification from E rather than mere contribution.

---

8. Chapter 635 of the Laws of 1996.

9. See § 11 of the Workers' Compensation Law. The Omnibus Act and its effect on the liability of employers is discussed at length in SPR 48 and 49. Particularly controversial during the year or two after the act was adopted was whether it was retroactive in respect of its provisions governing the impleader of employers, a number of cases addressing the issue. (These are tracked in SPR 48:4, 49:3, 56:1, 59:2, 62:3, and 63:3.) The Court of Appeals resolved the matter in Majewski v. Broadalbin–Perth Cent. Sch. Dist., 91 N.Y.2d 577, 673 N.Y.S.2d 966 (1998), the subject of the lead note in New York State Law Digest No. 461. The provisions are not retroactive, held the court; they should be applied only prospectively, to actions filed by employees "after the effective date of the relevant provisions" (which was September 10, 1996).

§ 172

1. CPLR 1401. Article 14 was adopted on the recommendation of the Judicial Conference and was based on a study by Professor M.E. Occhialino which appears in the 19th Annual (1974) Report of the Judicial Conference at page 217.

2. CPLR 1403.

3. CPLR 1402.

4. This applies only to the "non-economic" segment of the damages; for economic damages Article 16 retains full joint liability for all tortfeasors. See §§ 168A through 168D, above.

5. CPLR 1404(b). See Logan v. Esterly, 34 N.Y.2d 648, 355 N.Y.S.2d 381, 311 N.E.2d 512 (1974). CPLR 1404(b) also preserves subrogation rights, such as the right of A's insurer, after paying the judgment P got against A, to seek contribution from the other tortfeasor, B.

If two causes concur to cause the tort, both contribution and indemnification can be sought in the same action.[6] For example:

P alights from a bus and has one foot on a defective part of the sidewalk. At that moment the bus takes off and P is injured. Both the premature takeoff and the defective sidewalk combine to produce the injury. P sues B, the bus company, O, the owner of the land, and K, the contractor who had purportedly fixed the sidewalk (and who would be responsible to O if the sidewalk was not properly fixed). The jury finds for P against all, further finding that the driving was 60% responsible and the sidewalk condition 40% responsible for P's damages. P obtains judgment for all of P's damages against B (B retains joint liability under CPLR Article 16), and for all of P's economic damages against O and K, but for only 40% of P's "non-economic" damages against O and K (who are relieved of joint liability under Article 16 for the non-economic segment). Assume that B pays the whole judgment. B is entitled to 40% contribution from O and/or K. Should O pay any part of that, however, O would be entitled to recover back from K whatever O pays because between them there is an indemnification relationship.[7]

Liability for the same personal injury, injury to property, or wrongful death is the factor that allows contribution under CPLR 1401. It applies not only to joint tortfeasors, but also to concurrent, successive, independent, alternative, and even intentional tortfeasors.

It has had some interesting applications. In one case A, an attorney, failed to sue in time, relying on D's settlement promises. P, the client, then sued D for fraud. D impleaded A for having also contributed to the lapse of P's claim. The court sustained the impleader.[8] Both A and D contributed to P's loss, notwithstanding the distinct sources of their liability—fraud by D, negligence by A.

In another case on contribution between attorneys, the wife's first lawyer was apparently responsible for her losing out on alimony because after she had obtained a default judgment for it against her husband, the judgment was vacated because of the attorney's mistakes. She sued him for malpractice. He then impleaded the wife's second lawyer, who, he said, was also responsible in some measure for the alimony loss because he failed to take such steps, after his retainer, as would have at least reduced the amount of the loss. Since both lawyers might be shown to have a role in the alimony loss for which the wife had sued the first lawyer, the links needed for contribution were present and the first lawyer was allowed to seek it with an impleader of the second.[9]

Each party's responsibility will be apportioned according to the party's "equitable share" and "relative culpability",[10] regardless of theory, the mixture of theories, or the consistency of theories either among the apportionment claims or between them and the main claim. The contribution claim can thus be based on negligence, breach of warranty, breach of statutory duty, strict products liability, or any other, as long as it contributed to the damages suffered by the person to whom the party seeking contribution has been found liable.[11]

Another bus accident case, Zuckerman v. City of New York,[12] can illustrate. P in the Zuckerman case fell when about to enter a bus. She alleged that the sole cause of her injury was a defective sidewalk, for which C (the city) and T (the transit company) were both responsible. She sued both, and C, seek-

---

6. If an express contract of indemnification is involved, it will govern; neither Dole nor the new Article 14 changes that. CPLR 1404(b). See Williams v. D.A.H. Constr. Corp., 42 A.D.2d 877, 346 N.Y.S.2d 862 (2d Dep't 1973).

7. See and compare Bundy v. City of New York, 23 A.D.2d 392, 261 N.Y.S.2d 221 (1st Dep't 1965), decided under CPLR 1401 prior to the 1974 amendment.

8. Taft v. Shaffer Trucking, Inc., 52 A.D.2d 255, 383 N.Y.S.2d 744 (4th Dep't 1976).

9. Schauer v. Joyce, 54 N.Y.2d 1, 444 N.Y.S.2d 564, 429 N.E.2d 83 (1981).

10. CPLR 1402.

11. Doundoulakis v. Town of Hempstead, 51 A.D.2d 302, 381 N.Y.S.2d 287 (2d Dep't 1976), rev'd on other grounds 42 N.Y.2d 440, 398 N.Y.S.2d 401, 368 N.E.2d 24 (1977).

12. 66 A.D.2d 248, 413 N.Y.S.2d 657 (1st Dep't 1979, 3–2 decision). The case was reversed by the Court of Appeals on a different point. See note 13 below.

ing contribution from T, added as a ground T's negligent operation of the bus. The added theory was held permissible. The case manifests that tortfeasors seeking contribution among themselves are not bound by the theories introduced by the plaintiff.

This would appear to be a natural corollary of the *Dole* rule itself, which is designed to take out of the plaintiff's hands the power to sue fewer than all tortfeasors and by so doing deny the ones sued any recourse against the others. Since *Dole* enables the sued tortfeasor to implead the others for contribution, it should follow that the impleading tortfeasor should not be bound by the theories on which the plaintiff relies; that just as a tortfeasor sued alone may implead another for contribution, so may she add against the other a ground of liability at least arguably supportable on the facts, whether depended on by the plaintiff or not.[13]

"Dram Shop" cases often involve the right of contribution. The New York Dram Shop Act[14] creates a cause of action against one who sells liquor to an already drunk person, in behalf of any person injured by reason of that person's drunkenness. When such a liability is asserted against the seller, it has been held that the seller can seek contribution from the drunk person.[15]

§ 173. Methods of Seeking Contribution

If P has initially joined tortfeasors A and B, each can seek contribution from the other with a mere cross-claim. If only A is joined, A can implead B for contribution. If the contribution is sought from a plaintiff, a counterclaim may be used.[1]

A separate action is still permitted, in lieu of impleader, at the tortfeasor's option—A, without attempting to implead B, can simply pay P's judgment and then sue B for contribution—but this is a decidedly poor alternative. If impleader is possible, it should be used.

Notice of claim requirements, such as might be applicable to a municipality when initially sued by the injured person, do not apply to contribution claims, whether asserted by a pleading within the original action, by impleader, or in a separate action later.[2]

If the tortfeasors are in the action initially, each should assert its contribution claim as an affirmative cause of action, usually a cross-claim. If that is done—and it can be deemed mandatory under CPLR 1403—there should be no need to ask or answer whether there is any other way that contribution rights can be injected into the case, or whether the judge can inject them sua sponte. If there is no undue prejudice to the other side, a pleader omitting a contribution claim from its original pleading can be permitted to assert it in an amended one.[3] If all parties omit contribution claims, they may be found to have waived them, although it is difficult to reach that conclusion in view of the fact that even a separate action is a permissible way of seeking contribution.[4]

§ 174. The Old Contribution Rules Contrasted; Judgment Limited to Excess

The lawyer conducting research into the contribution area may meet pre–1974 cases

---

13. In 49 N.Y.2d 557, 427 N.Y.S.2d 595, 404 N.E.2d 718 (1980), the Court of Appeals reversed Zuckerman, but on a ground that apparently leaves these principles intact. (The reversal ground was that the new theory was introduced into the case in unacceptable form.)

14. Gen.Oblig.L. § 11–101.

15. Zona v. Oatka Restaurant, 68 N.Y.2d 824, 507 N.Y.S.2d 615, 499 N.E.2d 869 (1986). For further discussion of contribution rights in dram shop cases, see Weinheimer v. Hoffman, 97 A.D.2d 314, 470 N.Y.S.2d 804 (3d Dep't 1983).

§ 173

1. CPLR 1403. An example of a counterclaim so used would be where A, driving with her son S as passenger, collides with B. If A sues B in behalf of herself and S, B's contribution claim against A, in respect of S's claim, may be used as a counterclaim.

2. See Zillman v. Meadowbrook Hosp. Co., 45 A.D.2d 267, 358 N.Y.S.2d 466 (2d Dep't 1974).

3. CPLR 3025(b), discussed in § 237, below, permits liberal amendment of pleadings.

4. CPLR 1403. Compare Caucci v. Fesko, 76 Misc.2d 614, 349 N.Y.S.2d 886 (Sup.Ct., Westchester County, 1973), which held apportionment rights waived in a transition case under Dole. The court remitted the tortfeasors to straight 50%–50% contribution, a choice not expressly offered by the subsequent Article 14 codification but nonetheless a result that might remain appropriate if several tortfeasors have been found liable but the jury has not made an apportionment.

built around the old contribution law. To adjust those cases to the present Article 14 of the CPLR, it is helpful to contrast prior law.

Four things had to concur under the pre-1974 version of CPLR 1401 before the right of contribution among tortfeasors arose. The first three requirements have been abandoned. Only the fourth remains: it limits the paying tortfeasor to a contribution judgment for only the excess he actually pays beyond his own share. These are the four requirements of prior law, with the result under present law juxtaposed:

First. The injured person (P) had to name two or more tortfeasors in her initial summons and complaint. Article 14 doesn't require that now. It permits tortfeasor A, if sued alone, to implead B and any other tortfeasors. Contribution rights are no longer contingent on P's election to join several tortfeasors as original defendants.

Second. P had to secure jurisdiction over two or more of the tortfeasors. If she got jurisdiction over A but not over B—because B was not served or for any other reason—A's contribution right against B died right there. The new law makes those considerations irrelevant by enabling A to implead B.[1]

Third. P had to obtain a joint judgment against A and B. If the jury found against A but in favor of B, A's right of contribution would not arise. If A paid the judgment, A could not even prosecute an appeal against B either in its own or in P's right. Under the new law no joint judgment is needed. If A or B are joined but the verdict goes only against A, A can today take an appeal in an endeavor to obtain a reversal and hold B in for contribution. If P sues only A, A can implead B or bring a separate later action against B.

Fourth. Under prior law, A could have a contribution judgment against B only if A paid P's judgment and only for the excess beyond

A's own share. And the contribution judgment could not exceed B's share. This part of prior law continues. The paying A is still restricted to recovering only the excess A pays beyond her own share; A cannot recover from B more than B's share. This can produce some unfair results. For example:

Assume that in an accident involving the driving of three private cars,[2] one of the passengers, P, is injured. Judgment for P has been rendered for $60,000 with the tortfeasors' shares found to be $30,000 for A, $20,000 for B, and $10,000 for C. A pays the whole judgment. A may not collect more than $20,000 from B. This means that if C should be insolvent and have no available insurance coverage, A, the paying tortfeasor, ends up with C's whole share of the judgment.[3] This is an apparent inequity of both the old and the new law.

When the right of contribution did arise under prior law, its proportions were based on the number of concurring causes and not the "relative culpability" now provided by CPLR 1402. If, for example, P had sued two drivers, A and B, the ultimate contribution between them would have been 50%–50%; if three drivers, 33 1/3% each. Those percentages were automatic and were applied by the court; the jury did not pass on them. Today the jury decides actual percentages of fault, and contribution rights are adjusted accordingly.

§ 175. Some Problem Areas in Contribution

A few situations pose unique questions in the contribution area.

a. Non-supervision of child.

Assume a two-car collision involving drivers A and B. A's child, C, is a passenger and is injured. A, in behalf of C, sues B. B may counterclaim against A for contribution in respect of C's injuries. The case presents no

---

§ 174

1. CPLR 1403.

2. There is no adjustment of liability under Article 16 of the CPLR in this situation, so the liability of each tortfeasor to the plaintiff remains joint and several. See § 168C above.

3. CPLR 1402. An analogous problem occurs when P, who has a judgment against D, cannot collect from D. Even if D should have a judgment-over against X, and X is solvent, it may not avail P. D's inability to pay can become a shield for X. See paragraph d in § 175, below.

unique difficulty. But now assume that instead of a two-car collision, C runs out into the street while playing and is hit by B's car. Parent A, in behalf of C, sues B. B counterclaims A for contribution, this time on the ground that it was A's non-supervision of C that contributed to the accident. After much litigation and a number of lower court decisions and opinions, the Court of Appeals held in Holodook v. Spencer[1] that the counterclaim in the second situation does not lie as a matter of substantive law; that the infant itself has no direct tort claim against its parent for non-supervision; and that since a non-supervision claim does not exist directly against a parent in favor of the infant it cannot be asserted against the parent by a third person seeking contribution, i.e., the third person's right is in a sense derivative of the infant.

This rationale enabled the courts to avoid imposing personal liability on the parent for what is usually an uninsured liability. In the first example, in which A is charged with A's own negligent driving, A's liability is covered by insurance, which is compulsory in New York at least to certain limits.[2] In the second instance, it is unlikely that parent A will carry insurance coverage for a "non-supervision" claim, with the result that A would have to pay any contribution judgment out of A's own pocket. It is appealing at first blush to conclude that if A's non-supervision, as found by the jury, accounts for such-and-such a percent of the accident, it is only fair that A pay that percent. But countervailing considerations are that if A knows he will have to make good out of his own pocket a part of his child's recovery,[3] he will be less diligent in prosecuting the claim (if he prosecutes it at all), and that if a contribution judgment should bankrupt A or

otherwise press him too hard, C himself will suffer as an infant member of the family.[4]

Although insurance seems to be a decisive factor between the lines, it is rarely recited by the courts to differentiate the cases. The judiciary has preferred to bar the non-supervision claim as a simple matter of substantive law. The difficulty is that this approach is only a partial answer. In the first situation discussed above, in which parent A was a driver, he does face a contribution counterclaim by B. Yet A's insurance policy can be as low as the current insurance minimum prescribed by law. If B's contribution claim is sustained for more than that, the excess will have to come out of A's pocket, posing the same problem mentioned above but without a "non-supervision" door to close on it.

An interesting and important distinction was made of the *Holodook* case in Nolechek v. Gesuale.[5] A partially blind infant was allowed by his parent to use a motorcycle. Doing so, he rode onto the defendant's land, did not see a cable that closed off a road, and was killed. In a wrongful death case brought by the parent, the defendant counterclaimed for contribution. The Court of Appeals allowed the counterclaim, but not on the "non-supervision" ground, which *Holodook* foreclosed. Rather, the court found that the parent had entrusted a "dangerous instrument" (the motorcycle) to the infant, in whose hands it damaged the defendant. The departure that this theory makes from the conventional "dangerous instrument" cases is that here the damages sought by the contribution-claiming defendant were not for a personal injury, but rather for monetary exposure "resulting from potential liability" in a lawsuit.

§ 175

1. 36 N.Y.2d 35, 364 N.Y.S.2d 859, 324 N.E.2d 338 (1974).

2. See Veh. & Traf.L. §§ 311, 312.

3. The child's recovery is ordinarily unavailable to the use of the parent. See CPLR 1206, 1210.

4. It has been observed that allowing such a cause of action would adversely affect family unity by creating a direct conflict between parent and child. Lastowski v. Norge Coin–O–Matic, Inc., 44 A.D.2d 127, 133, 355

N.Y.S.2d 432, 439 (2d Dep't 1974). The case of Gelbman v. Gelbman, 23 N.Y.2d 434, 297 N.Y.S.2d 529, 245 N.E.2d 192 (1969), which removed the immunity barrier that had previously barred a tort suit between parent and child, is distinguished on the ground that it exposed pre-existing tort liabilities but did not create any new ones, and that the non-supervision claim did not pre-exist. See Holodook v. Spencer, note 1, above.

5. 46 N.Y.2d 332, 413 N.Y.S.2d 340, 385 N.E.2d 1268 (1978).

Reasonable minds may obviously differ about this rationale. *Holodook* purported to bar such claims altogether, as falling under the "non-supervision" category. The *Nolechek* court was in fact divided, but only one judge dissented (on the ground that the decision undermines the *Holodook* barrier).

The same rules that the *Holodook* case applies to non-supervision by a parent apply as well to non-supervision by a sibling. Sister S took her younger brother B next door to D's place, where D's dog bit B. B sued D, and D sought to implead S on the ground that S did not properly supervise B. The impleader claim was not allowed.[6]

b. *Applicability of insurance to impleaded spouse.*

Section 3420(g) of the Insurance Law, formerly § 167(3),[7] provides that no liability insurance policy shall be deemed to cover damages suffered by the insured's spouse unless it covers them expressly. (It usually doesn't cover them expressly.) Thus, when the insured, H, is driving and his wife, W, is injured, the insurance policy does not cover an action by W against H and the insurer need not defend it.

But now assume that H, with W a passenger, is driving his car when it collides with a car driven by X. W sues X, who impleads H with a contribution claim based on H's negligent driving. Does H's insurance policy cover him in that third-party context? The Court of Appeals had held in State Farm Mut. Auto. Ins. Co. v. Westlake[8] that it does not; that even if the prospect of collusion, which it was the statute's purpose to avoid, is not present in the impleader situation—where both H and W would want to impose liability only on X rather than on their own insurer—the statute is explicit and can be changed only by the legislature. The legislature accepted the invitation in 1976, overruling *State Farm* and amending the

statute to provide that coverage is excluded "only where the injured spouse, to be entitled to recover, must prove the culpable conduct of the insured spouse". Since W, when suing X, levies all of her proof against X and none against H, and it is only X who is trying to implicate the impleaded H, the insurance policy in this contribution situation does cover H, who is therefore entitled under the amendment to both defense and indemnity from his insurer.

c. *Imputation of control to owner present in car.*

Suppose that the owner of car one, O–1, is a passenger in it while D–1 is driving, and there is a collision with D–2's car. O–1 sues D–2 for O–1's damages. The old case of Gochee v. Wagner[9] held that in such a situation O–1 could not recover if D–1 was also guilty of negligence; that if O–1 was present in the car, he was presumed to have control of D–1; and that the driver's negligence was therefore to be imputed to the owner.[10]

Recognizing that it was incongruous to retain so arbitrary a fault-imputing rule in light of the *Dole* case, the Court of Appeals in Kalechman v. Drew Auto Rental, Inc.,[11] overruled *Gochee*. The result is that an owner, or any other person with control of the car, such as a borrower who lets yet another person drive, can today be held accountable, when suing for her own damages, only for her own demonstrable culpability, if any. The driver's negligence will not be imputed to her automatically.

The lawyer should not confuse this situation, in which the owner is a plaintiff, with that in which the owner is a defendant being sued by an injured third person. In that case the driver's negligence is indeed imputed to the owner.[12]

---

6. Smith v. Sapienza, 52 N.Y.2d 82, 436 N.Y.S.2d 236, 417 N.E.2d 530 (1981).

7. It was renumbered in a 1984 amendment.

8. 35 N.Y.2d 587, 364 N.Y.S.2d 482, 324 N.E.2d 137 (1974).

9. 257 N.Y. 344, 178 N.E. 553 (1931).

10. New York at this time had a rule of contributory negligence, which barred a plaintiff from all recovery if plaintiff was to blame at all, a result afterwards changed with the adoption of the comparative negligence rule. See § 168E above.

11. 33 N.Y.2d 397, 353 N.Y.S.2d 414, 308 N.E.2d 886 (1973).

d. P's attempt to bypass D and collect from third-party X.

P can seek satisfaction of her judgment only against those whom she has joined and kept as defendants, or against those she has pleaded against after their impleader.[13] If P cannot collect her judgment from one of those persons, she will not be able to collect from a person against whom only an impleader (third-party) judgment stands. Example:

P sues D, and D impleads R, P's employer (whom P could not sue directly because of the exclusivity of workers' compensation[14]). P gets a $50,000 judgment against D and D gets a contribution judgment of (say) $30,000 against R. If D is insolvent and cannot pay P's judgment, P still cannot "jump over" D and collect directly from R. R in that situation escapes payment. Such is the result of the Court of Appeals ruling in Klinger v. Dudley,[15] which involved an even more unpalatable loss to P.

P in *Klinger* had sued A and B, but a summary judgment of dismissal had been awarded to B based on the taking effect of a preclusion order that B had secured against P for P's failure to serve a bill of particulars.[16] B did remain in the action, however, but only with respect to A's contribution cross-claim against him.

In due course P had judgment against A, and A had judgment over against B. A was unable to pay a good part of P's judgment. The question was whether B could be made to pay any part of B's own contributory share before A, the only party with a judgment against B, had paid more than his own pro rata share to P. The court held that B had no such obligation; that B's duty was to contribute only

upon A's payment, not upon A's mere exposure to liability.

There was lively colloquy for a while among bench and bar about whether there would be any way whereby P, with a judgment against an insolvent D, could collect directly or indirectly from a solvent cross-claim defendant like B or third-party defendant, X, against whom D had a contribution judgment.[17] In due course, a lending scheme to accomplish just such a circumvention was sustained by the Court of Appeals in Feldman v. New York City Health & Hospitals Corp.[18]

P in *Feldman* was injured in D's car and was treated at H hospital. P sued D but did not join H; D impleaded H. P obtained judgment for $835,000 but of course it did not run against H, which was nevertheless found to have 54% responsibility for the damages and against which D had the usual inchoate judgment-over for contribution. D was able to pay only $25,000 (D's insurance coverage). The rest of the case is an elaborate agreement among P, D, and one L, whereby L lent D the money to pay P, thus setting the stage for D to collect from H on the judgment over. The money was carefully escrowed so that L would not lose control of it while the court test pended. The arrangement gave L 25% of the recovery.

The fact that in *Feldman* an outside lender came off with 25% of the recovery for a no-risk loan suggests that the *Klinger* case, which makes these circumventions necessary, needs reexamining.[19]

The third-party defendant in the *Feldman* case was not the plaintiff's employer. To give some effect to the policies of the Workers' Compensation Law that insulates an employer from common law liability to its employee, the

---

12. Veh. & Traf.L. § 388.

13. CPLR 1009.

14. See § 171 above.

15. 41 N.Y.2d 362, 393 N.Y.S.2d 323, 361 N.E.2d 974 (1977).

16. See § 241, below, for discussion of preclusion orders. A in Klinger had also impleaded another tortfeasor, X, who was also found responsible for a percentage of the accident, but X is not needed in the present illustration.

17. Commentary C5230:4 on McKinney's CPLR 5230 goes into some of the suggestions that were advanced as possibilities for P.

18. 56 N.Y.2d 1011, 453 N.Y.S.2d 683, 439 N.E.2d 398 (1982), adopting the nisi prius opinion of Justice Aronin, 107 Misc.2d 145, 437 N.Y.S.2d 491 (Sup.Ct., Kings County, 1981).

19. The Feldman case and its lending scheme are treated in the lead note in New York State Law Digest No. 273.

Court of Appeals later held in Reich v. Manhattan Boiler & Equip. Corp.[20] that a *Feldman*-type loan will not be recognized when the third-party defendant is the employer of the plaintiff.[21]

e. Difficulties in dividing fault.

As noted earlier,[22] the interplay of the plaintiff's duty to himself (implicating the comparative negligence rule of CPLR Article 14–A), the defendants' rights and duties vis-a-vis the plaintiff (implicating the joint and several liability rules of CPLR Article 16), and the defendants' rights and duties among themselves (implicating the contribution rules of Article 14), can sometimes create both conceptual problems substantively and practical problems procedurally. An example arising even before Article 16 was on the scene is Caiazzo v. Volkswagenwerk, A.G.[23]

The case involves a multi-party problem. P was injured when he was thrown from his car as a result of D's negligence in driving his car into P's, which was not moving. P did nothing to cause the accident. It was caused solely by D. But P added to his own injuries by failing to wear a seat belt. Clearly P's damages had to be diminished by the proportion in which P's seatbelt omission might be found by the jury to have contributed to P's injuries. An added complication, however, was that P's being thrown from the car was allegedly contributed to by yet another cause: the negligent design or manufacture of the car door, implicating manufacturer M. D was responsible for all of P's damages save those caused by the seat-belt omission, which was a defense for D to prove. This meant that D would also be accountable for M's contributory share, for which D was responsible for having caused the accident. M was not liable for D's share, however, because M was implicated only in the door design, which contributed to P's injuries but not to the causation of the accident.

The court met the issues by stressing burdens of proof, in essence leaving the apportionment of damages dilemma to the jury and apparently prepared to accept the jury's verdict as long as its allotments appeared rational. *Caiazzo* was an early entry onto a field destined to present many such skirmishes, especially because of the later (1986) addition of Article 16, modifying the rules of joint and several liability applicable to tortfeasors.[24]

§ 176. Effect of Settlement with Fewer than all Tortfeasors

A settlement with one tortfeasor does not bar the injured person's suit against any other tortfeasor, but special rules govern the effect that the settlement is to have. Throughout the ensuing discussion P will stand for the injured person, S for the settling tortfeasor, and N for the non-settling tortfeasor. The applicable rules come from § 15–108 of the General Obligations Law.

If S settles in good faith with P, and is released by P, P may still sue N. If P does, N will be allowed to inject the issue of S's culpability into the case even though S is not a party. In that action, the jury will make findings of the relative shares of fault of parties P and N as well as nonparty S. If the jury brings in a verdict against N, and also finds S at fault, the court will reduce the verdict against N by whichever of the following three figures is the highest:

1. the amount stipulated in the release;

2. the consideration paid for the release;[1] or

3. the settling tortfeasor's equitable share of the damages as found by the jury (or other fact-trier).

The reduction is made by the court in the

---

20. 91 N.Y.2d 772, 676 N.Y.S.2d 110 (1998).

21. See the discussion of the Reich case in the lead note in New York State Law Digest No. 464.

22. See § 168E above.

23. 647 F.2d 241 (2d Cir.1981), rev'g 468 F.Supp. 593 (E.D.N.Y.1979).

24. See §§ 168A—168D, above.

§ 176

1. This figure is usually the same as that stipulated in the release, so that items 1 and 2 are generally the same and will be assumed to be the same in the examples used in this section.

absence of the jury,[2] and the judgment that P takes against N is for only what remains.

The impact of this is that if S's share of the verdict is found in the P v. N action to be more than S settled for, the difference is P's loss, while if S's share is found to be less than the settlement—not a frequent occurrence—the difference is S's loss. Take these examples.

P and S settle an automobile accident case for $10,000. The jury in P's action against N finds P's damages to be $100,000 with N and S each responsible for half. S's equitable share is $50,000; that amount is subtracted from the verdict—because it is higher than the $10,000 settled for—leaving P with a $50,000 judgment against N. With a $50,000 judgment against N and the $10,000 settlement with S, P ends up with $60,000. The difference between that and the $100,000 that the jury found to be P's damages is $40,000. That $40,000 is P's loss.

Again assume that P and S settle for $10,-000, but now the jury in P's action against N brings in a verdict of $12,000 for P, with S found 40% responsible and N 60%. S's equitable share comes to $4800, which is less than his settlement figure of $10,000. Since the $10,000 is the higher, the $10,000 is the figure deducted from P's verdict. This leaves N to pay a $2000 judgment, although N's equitable 60% share of P's $12,000 damages would otherwise have come to $7200. The $5200 difference between N's equitable share and the judgment that P actually takes against N is windfall for N, and S's loss.

A possibility like that might appear to discourage settlement by S, but a settlement that turns out to be greater than a jury actually determines the settler's share to be was apparently deemed too uncommon to warrant a different approach. And it will still be true that the big gift to S when S settles is that S will no longer be subject to the predilections of a jury, while the non-settling N is still taking his chances.

Having settled with P, S cannot afterwards seek contribution in respect of P's injuries from any other tortfeasor.[3] But by the same token the settlement immunizes S from any contribution claim *by* any other tortfeasor in respect of P's injuries:[4] when P settles with S and then sues N, N can't implead S.

If the settlement does not occur until after P, having sued both S and N, has had judgment against S on the main claim and S has had a contribution judgment against N, S's contribution claim against N is not wiped out by the settlement. So held the Court of Appeals in Rock v. Reed–Prentice Div. of Pkg. Machinery Co.[5] At this post-judgment stage, the settlement by S with P in a sum less than the judgment is clearly advantageous to N because it automatically reduces the contribution judgment S has against N (the contributory share of N now being applied to the settlement figure instead of to the judgment figure). A post-judgment settlement like that is compatible with the purpose of § 15–108, held the court, which is to foster settlements.

The rule of the *Rock* case, allowing post-judgment settlements without the parties' forfeiting the advantages of § 15–108, is especially helpful when the state is one of the tortfeasors and the restrictions on court of claims jurisdiction enter the picture. It has been held that if the state is cast in judgment in a court of claims action, in which the co-tortfeasor could of course not be joined because of jurisdictional restrictions,[6] and the state settles with the claimant after the judgment has been rendered, the settlement at that post-judgment point does not bar the state from bringing a contribution claim in the supreme court against the other tortfeasor, based on the settlement figure.[7]

But while a post-judgment settlement may preserve contribution rights, a pre-trial settlement won't, even if the settlement in terms

---

2. CPLR 4533–b.

3. Gen.Oblig.L. § 15–108(c).

4. Gen.Oblig.L. § 15–108(b).

5. 39 N.Y.2d 34, 382 N.Y.S.2d 720, 346 N.E.2d 520 (1976).

6. See § 17 above.

7. State of New York v. County of Sullivan, 43 N.Y.2d 815, 402 N.Y.S.2d 397, 373 N.E.2d 291 (1977), rev'g on the dissenting opinion of Presiding Justice Koreman in 54 A.D.2d 29 at 33, 386 N.Y.S.2d 253 at 256 (3d Dep't 1976).

tries to. Lettiere v. Martin Elevator Co.[8] illustrates. P sued S, who impleaded R (P's employer, who was immune from direct suit by P because of the exclusivity of workers' compensation). S was willing to settle but wanted a jury to decide R's share so as to support a judgment for S against R for contribution. S settled with P before the trial for $250,000, with the stipulation that the trial proceed to determine R's contributory share (which percentage would then be applied to the settlement figure, with S to have judgment against R accordingly). The scheme didn't work and S ended up with no contribution at all. The *Rock* case is distinguished for the point within the litigation at which the settlement occurred, and perhaps even more importantly because in *Rock* it was the judgment that determined P's damages while in *Lettiere* the settlement did, thereby invoking § 15–108 in *Lettiere* and barring the contribution claim.

In a later case in the Court of Appeals, Gonzales v. Armac Indus., Ltd.,[9] the settlement was made in a percentage figure instead of a monetary figure, but brought about the same result. It was a typical P v. D case in which D impleaded R, P's employer. The P–D settlement provided for an admission by D of 2% fault, the 2% to be applied to anything the jury might award. This is just *Lettiere* in disguise, held the court, trying to do with percentages what *Lettiere* tried to do with a dollar amount, but both are the same in that they are pre-trial settlements that invoke the settlement statute and let the impleaded third person (in this case the employer) out entirely.

An unusual situation in which a pretrial settlement did immunize the settling tortfeasor from contribution even though the settlement depended in some measure on the verdict appears in Reynolds v. Morka Enterprises, Inc.[10] The only matter between the settling

parties that depended on the outcome of the action was an additional $50,000 in damages. S paid P $100,000 and agreed to pay up to $50,000 more unless P recovered at least that much from N. The purpose was to assure P at least $150,000 in all. In making the computations called for by Gen.Oblig.L. § 15–108, N would have the benefit of having the settlement figure of $150,000 applied in reduction of the verdict (N to be liable to P only if the verdict exceeded $150,000). For this reason, the settlement condition was found to contain no prejudice to N, and S was therefore permitted the benefits of § 15–108: immunity from a contribution claim by N.

What about a conventional bifurcated trial situation—with none of the unusual *Reynolds* elements to contend with—in which the settlement occurs right in the middle of things: after a liability finding but before damages are determined? It was held in Makeun v. State of New York[11] that § 15–108 does apply and bars contribution by S against N. The *Rock* case[12] is distinguished because in *Rock* the judgment determined the damages and the settlement came after, while in *Makeun* the settlement determined the damages.

Since a settlement by S under § 15–108 does not prevent N from injecting S's fault into a P v. N action even though S is not a party, the question arises whether N is entitled to have the jury know of the settlement, as reflecting, for example, on S's motivation, interest, and credibility. An interesting "gang-up" case, Meleo v. Rochester Gas & Elec. Corp.,[13] holds that at least in some circumstances a jury's being kept in ignorance of the settlement may so prejudice the non-settling N as to require the overturning of a verdict against him.

Meleo was a gas explosion case. All defendants except N settled, but the settling ones

8. 62 A.D.2d 810, 406 N.Y.S.2d 510 (2d Dep't 1978), aff'd 48 N.Y.2d 662, 421 N.Y.S.2d 879, 397 N.E.2d 390 (1979).

9. 81 N.Y.2d 1, 595 N.Y.S.2d 360, 611 N.E.2d 261 (1993). The case is the subject of the lead note in New York State Law Digest No. 401.

10. 82 A.D.2d 199, 442 N.Y.S.2d 664 (3d Dep't 1981). The case, a complicated one with a number of parties, is summarized in New York State Law Digest No. 262.

11. 98 A.D.2d 583, 471 N.Y.S.2d 293 (2d Dep't 1984).

12. Note 5 above.

13. 72 A.D.2d 83, 423 N.Y.S.2d 343 (4th Dep't 1979). The case is the subject of the lead note in New York State Law Digest No. 244.

were allowed—rightly or wrongly—to remain in the case for apportionment purposes. They turned all their guns on N, and, with P's sights similarly oriented, it was no surprise that N was found exclusively at fault. Allowing the settling tortfeasors to remain in the action while at the same time preventing the jury from knowing about the settlement stacked the deck, held the court. It granted a new trial.

Often in a tort case two claims are interposed, one for the personal injury suffered by the decedent and one for the wrongful death in which it culminated. The claims belong to different persons—the first to the decedent's estate, the second to statutory designees—and must therefore be kept distinct. If S settles both claims with P (the decedent's personal representative who is prosecuting both of them), but in one sum, who determines how that sum shall be divided and allocated for the purpose of applying § 15–108 in an action by P against N? It has been held that the allocation is to be decided by the fact trier in the P v. N action; that the allocations purportedly made by P and S can't bind N.[14]

It was held in Didner v. Keene Corp.,[15] that a formal release is not necessary to establish that there has been a settlement as long as the circumstances of the settlement make clear that it's a binding one.

Didner also resolved the issue of how settlement credits are to be allotted in multi-party cases in which some tortfeasors settle and some don't. If there are a number of settlors, and the verdict in the action against the non-settlors—which assesses the shares of responsibility of both the settling and nonsettling ones—indicates that for some of the settlors the settlement figure is higher than their pro rata share of the verdict, and for others the opposite, should the court consider each settlor separately and reduce the verdict by the higher of the two figures for each, or should it

aggregate all of the settlors' pro rata shares on one side, and all their settlements on the other, and reduce the verdict by the higher of the two aggregated figures?

Didner adopts the "aggregate" rule, rejecting the alternative, which it describes as the "pick-and-choose" method. The court acknowledges that § 15–108(a) does not supply a direct answer to the question, but holds that the "aggregate" rule more closely comports with the overall purpose of the settlement statute, which is to encourage settlements. Doing the opposite—allowing a reduction for the higher of the settlement versus the apportioned share of each settlor separately—would give the holdout defendant the best of both worlds with respect to every settling tortfeasor, which would not serve to encourage settlements.

Suppose that after a settlement has been reached with some tortfeasors, the others, who remain in the action, fail to inject into the trial the issue of the shares of the settling ones, with the result that there are no jury-apportioned figures applicable to the settlors to juxtapose with their settlement figures. The problem arose and is resolved in Williams v. Niske,[16] another and more complicated Court of Appeals decision on § 15–108.

In *Williams*, the fault of some of the settling tortfeasors was not injected into the trial. That may have been inadvertent. A better test of the effect of such an omission occurred in the later Court of Appeals decision in Whalen v. Kawasaki Motors Corp.,[17] in which N deliberately refrained from injecting S's fault into the trial and in which an added factor was the contributory fault of P. S settled for $1.6 million. The verdict at trial was $2,415,000, with N 8% at fault and P 92% contributorily at fault. P argued that N was entitled to no deduction at all for S's settlement because N did not introduce S's fault into the trial. That

---

14. Casey v. State, 119 A.D.2d 363, 507 N.Y.S.2d 159 (2d Dep't 1986). The facts of the case and the practical reasons for its conclusion are summarized in New York State Law Digest No. 327.

15. 82 N.Y.2d 342, 604 N.Y.S.2d 884, 624 N.E.2d 979 (1993). See the lead note in New York State Law Digest No. 408.

16. 81 N.Y.2d 437, 599 N.Y.S.2d 519, 615 N.E.2d 1003 (1993), treated at length in the lead note in New York State Law Digest No. 405.

17. 92 N.Y.2d 288, 680 N.Y.S.2d 435 (1998).

would have given P a $193,000 judgment against N (the verdict reduced by P's own 92%). N argued that its $193,000 share should be reduced to nothing by crediting against it S's settlement. The Court rejected both arguments, holding that the settlement does count even without a jury-found share of fault for S against which to juxtapose it, but it is applied first, to reduce the verdict, in this case down to $815,000, and then P's 92% share is applied to reduce that. The result was a judgment for P against N for $65,000.[18]

The effect of the bankruptcy of some of the tortfeasors is addressed in In re New York City Asbestos Litigation.[19] Shall some appropriate ratio be found whereby to allot a portion of the bankrupts' shares to the settlors and a portion to the nonsettlors? The court in the *Asbestos* case says no, holding that all must be allocated to the nonsettlors. Gen. Oblig.L § 15–108 contemplates adjusting what a plaintiff recovers from a nonsettlor by deducting something for what a settlor paid. Tortfeasors who have paid the plaintiff nothing can't qualify as settlors under the statute, and the nonsettlors can't expect any diminution of the verdict to reflect the shares of the nonpayers, which would violate the usual tort rule of joint and several liability.[20]

The Riviello Problem: "Indemnification" versus "Contribution"

A line of cases culminating in the Court of Appeals decision in Riviello v. Waldron[21] holds § 15–108 of the General Obligations Law inapplicable to indemnification situations. Hence when S, the settling tortfeasor, is solely at fault, and N, the non-settling tortfeasor against whom an action is brought, bears a liability entirely derivative of S's, the arithmetic of § 15–108 does not apply, P will be allowed judgment against N undiminished by the proportion of responsibility found by the jury to belong to S (in *Riviello* it was 100%),

and S can be impleaded into the action and made to indemnify N in full.

S in *Riviello* was a tavern employee who injured P while tossing a knife. S settled with P and now P sued N, the employer/tavern. The court held that the relationship between S and N involved total indemnification, not contribution, and was therefore not governed by Gen. Oblig.L. § 15–108, which applies exclusively to the contribution situation. Hence N is not entitled to a credit for the pro rata share of the fault that a jury might impute to S—it would be likely to impute 100%—because that's a mandate of the settlement statute and the statute doesn't apply. Nor is S insulated from impleader by N to make good on whatever N has to pay out to P, because that insulation, too, is a product of the statute. This means in turn that the law prior to the adoption of § 15–108 applies, which credits N with only the actual amount of the settlement and subjects S to impleader and full exposure after all—in the process discouraging settlements in the future in all cases in which indemnification instead of contribution might prove to be the relationship involved.

It takes all incentive away from a primary wrongdoer, like S in *Riviello*, to settle a claim unless P is also willing to release all who derive liability from S. *Riviello* therefore has the unfortunate effect of subverting the intent of the settlement statute, which the Court of Appeals, as evidenced by a number of the cases already noted in this section, has otherwise been sensitive to avoid. The ultimate contradiction of *Riviello* is that the person from whom the law should be most enthusiastic about extracting a settlement in multi-party cases—the culprit solely at fault in the accident—is the one deterred from settling.

There were interesting follow-ups on *Riviello*. In McDermott v. City of New York,[22] the

---

18. See the treatment of the Whalen case in the lead note in New York State Law Digest No. 466.

19. 82 N.Y.2d 821, 605 N.Y.S.2d 3, 625 N.E.2d 588 (1993), affirming "for reasons stated in the opinion by Justice Israel Rubin at the Appellate Division", 188 A.D.2d 214, 593 N.Y.S.2d 43 (1st Dep't 1993).

20. Apparently these cases were not governed by Article 16 of the CPLR, enacted in 1986, which might have required some adjustment in the joint and several liability rule. See §§ 168A through 168D above.

21. 47 N.Y.2d 297, 418 N.Y.S.2d 300, 391 N.E.2d 1278 (1979).

22. 50 N.Y.2d 211, 428 N.Y.S.2d 643, 406 N.E.2d 460

facts were the converse of *Riviello* in that S was apparently the party with only the derivative liability and N presumably the true culprit. P was an employee of S, the City of New York, and sued S for an injury caused by a sanitation truck malfunction.[23] S impleaded the truck's manufacturer, N. Now came the settlement by S with P, and N maintained that this invoked § 15–108 and required dismissal of the impleader claim seeking contribution. The court said no; that what S was seeking here was indemnification, not contribution, and that § 15–108 therefore did not apply.

If the fact trier in a case like *McDermott* should find that N, the manufacturer, is not exclusively at fault, however, and that S, the employer, bears some culpability, be it ever so little, the case would be magically transmuted into a "contribution" claim, which would invoke § 15–108 and require the dismissal of S's impleader claim against N, which shows once again the unsoundness of the *Riviello* construction. It generates litigation that § 15–108 sought to avoid, sometimes forcing a judicial hearing or even a jury trial just to determine whether the situation involves contribution, which would invoke the protections of § 15–108, or indemnification, which would not.[24]

A more graphic illustration of how *Riviello* is doing this is the hold-harmless agreement treated at the appellate division stage of *D'Ambrosio v. City of New York*.[25] P was hurt by something sticking up out of a sidewalk and sued the City (N) which impleaded the owner (S). At this point, P settled with S for $22,500, and in an interesting wrinkle gave S an indemnity agreement to the effect that should S ever have to pay out more on P's claim, P would

make it good to S. The jury found for P for $100,000, and found fault against both N and S, apportioning it at 65% for N and 35% for S.[26] The appellate division, deeming the case one in indemnity rather than contribution under the *Riviello* rule, held N to have only a derivative liability, S being solely at fault.[27] On this matter-of-law "indemnity" premise the appellate division held § 15–108 to be inapplicable, thus sustaining N's impleader of S and requiring S to recompense N for anything that N might have to pay P.

But now look at the impact of the voluntary hold-harmless agreement that P gave S when the case was settled. Whatever S pays N, S gets back from P. This results in a round robin in which P collects from N, N from S, and S back from P, the "obvious effect" of which, notes the appellate division dissent, is that P ends up with only the amount of the original settlement S agreed to anyway.[28] One lesson is that if S wants to settle but is apprehensive about losing the advantages of § 15–108 because of the *Riviello* holding, S will derive at least some benefit if S can get a hold-harmless agreement from P in the settlement.

Another variation on the dissonant themes forced into the settlement realm by *Riviello* is what to do when there are tortfeasor "units", with a "contribution" obligation existing among the units (each unit responsible for a distinct part of the tort) and an "indemnification" obligation existing among the members of one of the units (as where one member's liability is entirely derivative of another member's conduct). A leading case in point is Mead v. Bloom.[29]

(1980).

23. Workers' compensation would presumably have been a complete defense to the city, but the defense does not appear to have been raised.

24. For an example of the "harsh consequences" that can attend a characterizing of a case as "indemnification" instead of "contribution", and vice versa, see Flood v. Re Lou Location Engr., 487 F.Supp. 364 (E.D.N.Y.), aff'd 636 F.2d 1201 (2d Cir.1980).

25. 79 A.D.2d 965, 438 N.Y.S.2d 224 (1981), afterwards reversed by the Court of Appeals on a different point in 55 N.Y.2d 454, 450 N.Y.S.2d 149, 435 N.E.2d 366 (1982).

26. The 1986–adopted Article 16 of the CPLR, affecting joint liability (see § 168A et seq., above), was of course not applicable at the time.

27. It was in this respect that the Court of Appeals reversed, holding that henceforth in these "special benefit" sidewalk situations, an apportionment of fault will be required between municipality and abutting owner instead of a full recovery over. See the summary of the McDermott case in New York State Law Digest No. 245.

28. See the summary of the appellate division D'Ambrosio opinion in New York State Law Digest No. 256.

29. 62 N.Y.2d 788, 477 N.Y.S.2d 326, 465 N.E.2d 1262 (1984), affirming on Justice Boomer's opinion in the appellate division, 94 A.D.2d 423, 464 N.Y.S.2d 904 (4th Dep't 1983).

The accident was allegedly caused by the bad driving of D (of a car owned by O and being driven on the business of R), bad brake repair by B, and bad car design by GM. R, a member of the "unit" responsible for the bad driving and who had an "indemnification" relationship with D, settled. It was held that B was entitled to the benefits of the § 15–108 arithmetic for R's settlement, i.e., that R's "indemnification" relationship with a member of his own unit would not invoke *Riviello* (and cancel out the statutory benefits of § 15–108) as between R and a member of a different unit, there clearly being a "contribution" relationship between units.[30]

Nonsettling tortfeasors, otherwise immune from contribution suit by tortfeasor S after he settles, can waive that immunity and were held to have done so in Mitchell v. New York Hospital.[31] A whole bunch of alleged tortfeasors stipulated in writing that one of their number, S, could pay P all, with S thereafter entitled to proceed against the others to have his contribution rights determined. S paid all and proceeded against the others, who promptly tried to violate their stipulation by moving to dismiss S's contribution claim. Their motion was denied and they were sent to bed without dinner.

Article 16 of the CPLR, adopted in 1986, which alleviates the "joint" liability of certain tortfeasors,[32] specifically provides that it is not to be construed to impair settlements under Gen.Oblig.L. § 15–108.[33]

§ 177. Discretionary Tools in Handling Contribution Claims; Sequence of Trial

Ordinarily it will pose no undue difficulty for either court or jury to have the contribution claims tried right along with the other liability issues. But the court can vary the steps as need be. It can have P's claim against tortfeasors A and B tried first to a verdict, and then, if the verdict is for P against both, have A and B try their contribution claims to the same jury. That will usually be unnecessary. In most cases it would be an outright waste. A preferable step, if any at all should be needed, is to try all of the issues together but feed them to the jury in spurts. That is, the court can charge the jury to pass only on P's rights against A and B, and then, if the verdict comes in against both, charge the jury to go out again and this time find their relative culpabilities.

It is usually best to have all issues of liability tried together, especially now, with CPLR Article 16 on the books. Article 16 adjusts the rules about joint and several liability as they bear on the tortfeasors' exposure to the plaintiff,[1] an exposure that would in any event have to be part of the initial liability hearing, so there is even more reason now than before to have contribution rights among the tortfeasors heard and determined simultaneously. All these things concern percentages of culpability of all of the parties: of the tortfeasors to P on the one hand (involving Article 16 and adjusted tort liability), among the tortfeasors inter se on the other hand (Article 14 and contribution rights among tortfeasors), and of course P's own contributory fault under Article 14–A (if we may be allowed a third hand, which this subject can surely use). Except in unusual circumstances, all three things should be heard and determined together.

The use of a special verdict will clarify the jury's conclusions.[2]

Enforcement questions, such as the form a contribution judgment should take and the moment when the judgment becomes enforci-

---

30. These points are elaborated in the lead note in New York State Law Digest No. 293.

31. 61 N.Y.2d 208, 473 N.Y.S.2d 148, 461 N.E.2d 285 (1984).

32. See §§ 168A through 168D above. The article has already been referred to in this section. See notes 18 and 24 above.

33. CPLR 1601(2). Some examples of the interplay of Article 16 problems and settlement problems appear in the lead note in New York State Law Digest No. 323.

§ 177

1. See § 168A et seq., above.

2. A general verdict merely announces the jury's conclusion without revealing any particular ground or answering any particular question. The special verdict, a list of questions that the jury answers specifically, is more revealing of jury deliberations and is the preferred tool today. See § 399 below.

ble, can be guided by the rules applicable to impleader judgments.[3]

J.   INTERVENTION

Table of Sections

§ 178.   Intervention, Generally

Intervention is a procedure whereby an outsider can become a party to a pending action on her own initiative. It is sometimes available as of right,[1] sometimes only in the court's discretion,[2] but it must be sought by motion in all instances.[3] The courts are liberal in its allowance today—a relatively recent development[4]—and distinctions between intervention of right and discretionary intervention are not sharply applied.[5]

The applicant can seek to intervene on either side of the case, plaintiff's or defendant's. Once let in, the intervenor becomes a party for all purposes.[6]

Intervention is available in a special proceeding, but, as in an action, it requires court leave.[7] Sometimes a special provision authorizing intervention harmlessly overlaps the more general provisions.[8]

§ 179.   Intervention of Right Under Special Statutes

The first basis recognized for intervention as of right under CPLR 1012(a) is when a statute confers "an absolute right to intervene".[1] This is of course superfluous in that if some special statute confers the right, it doesn't need additional permission from the CPLR. The provision can be taken as a simple reminder of the existence of such statutes.

Two such others are in CPLR 1012 itself. Subdivision (b) requires that the court give notice to the attorney-general whenever the constitutionality of a state statute is involved in a case to which the state is not a party. The attorney-general is then given an absolute right to intervene, should he choose to, "in support" of the statute's constitutionality. Subdivision (c) gives the court a similar notice obligation, this time to notify the state comptroller, if not already a party, of any action involving the retirement benefits of public employees. The comptroller so disposed has an absolute right to intervene in the action.

Statutes authorizing intervention of right are found elsewhere in the state's consolidated laws. One well known example gives the corespondent in an adultery-based divorce action the right to defend.[2]

§ 180.   Intervention of Right Where Representation Inadequate

CPLR 1012(a)(2) permits a nonparty to intervene in an action of right

[w]hen the representation of the person's interest by the parties is or may be inadequate and the person is or may be bound by the judgment....

The most notable example of this is the class action, one of the few instances in our law in

---

3.   See § 165 above.

§ 178

1.   CPLR 1012, discussed in §§ 179 and 181, below.

2.   CPLR 1013, discussed in § 182, below.

3.   The procedure for intervention is in § 183 below.

4.   For a brief history of intervention as a procedural device, see 1st Rep.Leg.Doc. (1957) No. 6b, p.46, and 11th Jud. Council Rep. (1945), p.396.

5.   See Raymond v. Honeywell, 58 Misc.2d 903, 297 N.Y.S.2d 66 (Sup.Ct., Dutchess County, 1968).

6.   See Incorporated Vill. of Island Park v. Island Park–Long Beach, Inc., 81 N.Y.S.2d 407 (Sup.Ct., Nassau Coun-

ty 1948), aff'd 274 A.D. 930, 83 N.Y.S.2d 542 (2d Dep't 1948).

7.   CPLR 401.

8.   See, e.g., CPLR 7802(d), authorizing intervention in an Article 78 proceeding. When a specific provision like that exists for a given special proceeding, it preempts the general provisions. CPLR 103(b).

§ 179

1.   CPLR 1012(a)(1).

2.   Dom.Rel.L. § 172(1).

which nonparties may be directly bound by the result of a litigation.[1] Another example is where the proposed intervenors are supposedly represented by a governmental entity already a party.[2] There have even been cases in which the activities of one governmental agency or municipality are taken in behalf of, or have a direct effect on, another. When that happens the latter may intervene as of right, too.[3]

The showing required under CPLR 1012(a)(2) is that the representation "may be" inadequate and that the proposed intervenor "may be" bound by the judgment. It is the possibility rather than the certainty that governs. Well-reasoned caselaw holds that the movant should be given the benefit of the doubt.[4] The potentially binding nature of the judgment on the proposed intervenor is the factor that invokes this provision, even if the law that purports to do the binding is foreign rather than New York law.[5]

Whether the movant will be "bound" by the judgment has reference to the res judicata family of doctrines.[6] "The *stare decisis* effect of the judgment is not enough",[7] although it may be relevant for permissive intervention, which can be sought under CPLR 1013 when the intervenor's claim or defense has a question of law in common with the pending action.[8]

It has been held that even with regard to the of-right provisions, the courts have some discretion.[9] This appears to contradict the seemingly mandatory nature of CPLR 1012, but the statute does say that the intervention must be "timely". Timeliness itself is a factor that var-

ies from case to case and the court of course has some discretion in applying it.

CPLR 1012 may be analogized to Rule 24(a) of the Federal Rules of Civil Procedure, especially since the pre–1966 version of the federal provision was the model for CPLR 1012 and its predecessors.[10] Rule 24(a) was amended in 1966 to broaden intervention of right in the federal courts. All the movant need show under it is that he has an interest in the subject matter of the action and that the situation is such that the pending action "may as a practical matter impair or impede his ability to protect" that interest. The New York statute does not go as far, but with CPLR 1013 standing in the wings offering discretionary intervention in almost every situation in which the applicant falls technically short of CPLR 1012's of-right intervention, the accomplishments of the present Rule 24(a) can pretty well be extracted from the present CPLR 1012.

The subject of intervention lacked sparkle until late in the 1990s, when a controversy erupted concerning the efforts of health insurers to intervene as plaintiffs in their insureds' personal injury actions. It involved the so-called "collateral source" rule,[11] which allows a defendant tortfeasor to show that items of damages claimed by the plaintiff are duplicated by payments the plaintiff has received from outside ("collateral") sources, like health insurance, and allows the court to reduce the recovery by the sums so collected.

Health and like insurers belatedly took notice that they should be getting the payments back out of any recovery realized by its in-

---

§ 180

1. See § 139 above.

2. See Village of Spring Valley v. Village of Spring Valley Hous. Auth., 33 A.D.2d 1037, 308 N.Y.S.2d 736 (2d Dep't 1970).

3. Teleprompter Manhattan CATV Corp. v. State Bd. of Equalization and Assessment, 34 A.D.2d 1033, 311 N.Y.S.2d 46 (3d Dep't 1970). The court suggests that whenever the party to the suit is not "the real party in interest", the real one may intervene. That can happen in representative cases, see CPLR 1004, although a better remedy, if the representative's representation is inadequate, is to take appropriate steps to oust that one and substitute a better one.

4. See Unitarian Universalist Church v. Shorten, 64 Misc.2d 851, 315 N.Y.S.2d 506 (Sup.Ct., Nassau County,

1970), vacated on other grounds 64 Misc.2d 1027, 316 N.Y.S.2d 837.

5. Nardone v. Morris A. Fierberg Co., 40 A.D.2d 60, 337 N.Y.S.2d 884 (3d Dep't 1972).

6. See § 443 below.

7. Unitarian Universalist Church v. Shorten, note 4, above, 64 Misc.2d at 854, 315 N.Y.S.2d at 511. The distinction between the res judicata and stare decisis doctrines is discussed in § 449, below.

8. See § 182 below.

9. E.g., Reurs v. Carlson, 66 Misc.2d 968, 323 N.Y.S.2d 370 (Sup.Ct., Westchester County, 1971).

10. See 1st Rep.Leg.Doc. (1967) No. 6b, p.46.

11. CPLR 4545.

sured against the tortfeasor, instead of the tortfeasor getting credit for the items under the collateral source rule, so they began to include in the insurance contracts subrogation clauses and clauses making the insurance payments a lien on any recovery the insured might get against the tortfeasor.

The next happening was that the insurers came to distrust the way their insureds were prosecuting some tort actions. Indifferent to the insured items for the very reason that insurance covered them, the insureds were accused of orienting their proof of damages away from the items that the insurance covered and over to items, like the pain and suffering element, that the insurance did not cover. To give the insured items a fair shake in the proof, the insurers began to make motions to intervene as plaintiffs so as to handle that aspect of the proof themselves.

The courts divided on whether the intervention is allowable. The Second Department held in Humbach v. Goldstein[12] that it is not, citing the tortfeasor/defendant's collateral source rights under CPLR 4545. It held that the health insurer stands in P's shoes, and that if P is subject to a collateral source reduction, then so is P's health insurer. It distinguished the Court of Appeals decision in Teichman v. Community Hosp.,[13] a medical malpractice action in which an infant's claim was settled for a large sum but without any indication of the components of the settlement. An insurer that had made medical payments to the infant, who was severely injured during birth and required ongoing medical care, sought reimbursement for these payments out of the settlement. Because the settlement's components were not revealed, the court in Teichman noted the possibility that the settlement included some medical expenses and held that the insurer should be allowed to explore the matter. It upheld the insurer's right to intervene for this purpose, in this case in the infant's compromise proceeding that sought approval of the settlement.

The court in Humbach said that because intervention in Teichman was sought only after settlement and the insurer there had no lien, while in Humbach it had a lien and could assert it against any items of recovery "identified as amounts paid for health care", intervention in Humbach would be denied. The insurer of course countered that identifying such amounts is the very reason it was seeking to intervene; that the insured could not be trusted to make a fair effort on that score.

A major decision going the other way was Berry v. St. Peter's Hosp. from the supreme court of Albany County,[14] but it was reversed by a unanimous Third Department,[15] which agreed essentially with the Second Department's Humbach decision. Berry involved a medical malpractice claim by P against several defendants. P settled with the hospital defendant, and all of the settlement was designated to be for "pain and suffering", so P's insurer got nothing out of it.[16] Now P proceeded against other tortfeasors and P's insurers (one via his employer, the state, and one via his wife's policy) wanted to intervene to make sure health benefit expenses got attention. The court said that to allow the intervention would place the insurer in direct conflict with its insured, violating a public policy the court found to outweigh that underlying the intervention statutes.[17]

We have reported this conflict here, in the treatment of intervention of right instead of intervention by permission,[18] because it seems to fall so perfectly under CPLR 1012(a)(2), which invites intervention when representation by the existing parties "is or may be inadequate and the [proposed intervenor] is or may be bound by the judgment".

12. 229 A.D.2d 64, 653 N.Y.S.2d 950 (2d Dep't 1997).

13. 87 N.Y.2d 514, 640 N.Y.S.2d 472 (1996).

14. 173 Misc.2d 214, 660 N.Y.S.2d 795 (1997).

15. Berry v. St. Peter's Hosp., 250 A.D.2d 63, 678 N.Y.S.2d 674 (1998).

16. It was assumed that the settlement's allotment absolutely bound the insurer, a proposition that can stand

some reexamination. Compare Casey v. State, 119 A.D.2d 363, 507 N.Y.S.2d 159 (2d Dep't 1986), summarized in New York State Law Digest 327.

17. See the discussion of the decision in SPR 76:1.

18. Permissive intervention is treated in § 182 below.

Where does the collateral source rule now stand in this competition? Humbach cites it to conclude that the health insurer is not prejudiced by being denied intervention because the items affected would have to be credited to the tortfeasor anyway; Berry says the rule in essence "shifts the costs of medical expenses from liability carriers to health insurers" and that any further adjustment here is for the legislature.[19]

§ 181. Intervention of Right in Property Cases

Paragraph 3 of CPLR 1012(a) confers the right to intervene when the action involves the disposition or distribution of, or the title or a claim for damages for injury to, property and the person may be affected adversely by the judgment.

The paragraph is primarily concerned with the case in which some tangible property, real or personal, or identifiable intangibles, such as stocks or bonds, or even a limited money fund, is the subject of the action. It seeks to assure the right to intervene to anyone with an interest in the subject property. Unlike paragraph 2, it does not require a showing that the intervenor may be bound by the judgment, only that she "may be affected adversely" by it. For example:

L (landlord) leases land to T (tenant). P claims title to the land and sues to evict T. L, who also claims title, may intervene as of right even though she would not be bound by a P v. T judgment rendered in her absence.

The courts are especially prone to authorize intervention when it appears needed to assure an adversary proceeding. In Mann v. Compania Petrolera Trans–Cuba, S.A.,[1] for example, X was a shareholder in a nationalized Cuban corporation and brought an action in New York to preserve the corporation's local assets. The Cuban government appointed S to appear in behalf of the corporation but O, the corpora-

tion's president and an opponent of the Cuban government, also asserted that right. After hearing argument on the point, the court found for O and authorized O's lawyer to represent the corporation. Now S moved to intervene, not necessarily as the corporation's factotum but as the person whom the Cuban government recognized as its spokesman. The difficulty was that the same issues posed on that intervention application were previously disposed of, adversely to S, on the hearing to determine who should represent the corporation. The court held that the earlier determination nevertheless did not control, and allowed S to intervene. An influential factor was that O and X seemed to be allied on the merits, leaving no one to plead the other side.

In New York at present, the notion prevails that when plaintiffs injured in a single accident bring separate suits against the tortfeasor in separate courts, the race to the coverage offered by the tortfeasor's liability insurance policy is to the swift; that whoever gets judgment first is entitled to first crack at the insurance proceeds even if the judgment would exhaust the proceeds and leave nothing for the other injured persons whose suits are still pending. One set of plaintiffs in such a position sought in one case to intervene in the other set's lawsuit when it appeared that judgment in the latter was imminent. They were denied leave to intervene. The main objection was untimeliness, the court said, citing its obligation under CPLR 1013 (permissive intervention) to consider whether the parties to the pending action would be prejudiced by the application.[2] It is submitted that in a case like that the insurance proceeds should be deemed "property" under CPLR 1012(a)(3) and intervention authorized as of right. Timeliness would still be a factor, of course, but of diminished importance.

Another possibility is for the insurer to interplead the insurance proceeds, giving all

---

19. See note 6 at the end of the Berry decision (note 15 above).

§ 181

1. 17 A.D.2d 193, 234 N.Y.S.2d 1001 (1st Dep't 1962).

2. David v. Bauman, 24 Misc.2d 67, 71, 196 N.Y.S.2d 746, 750 (Sup.Ct., Nassau County, 1960). The motion by the plaintiff in the second action was made only after the plaintiff in the first action had won summary judgment on liability. This made untimeliness a factor, and perhaps the decisive one.

claimants a pro rata bite of the apple. An insurer that brought that kind of interpleader action was commended by the court for doing so.[3]

§ 182. Permissive Intervention

When the proposed intervenor's claim or defense has any question in common with a claim or defense involved in the action, intervention is permitted under CPLR 1013 "in the discretion of the court". It is so easy to establish such a common question that the courts have had to be circumspect about exercising this discretion.[1]

When the common question relied on is one of law, the endeavor to intervene is analogous to an application to an appellate court for leave to file a brief amicus curiae, and the disposition is governed by similar factors. Are both sides of the legal issue already well represented in the action? If they are, adding parties may merely make the case more cumbersome. If they are not, the intervention motion of course enables the court to strengthen the existing representation.

The court has to be wary of numbers. If, for example, the legality of rent control or some phase of it is involved in a case, literally tens of thousands of tenants and landlords have sufficient interests in the outcome to apply to intervene. The discretion of the court is the dike against this potential flood. An appropriate step would be to admit one or a few groups or associations shown to be strongly representative of their side. If the interests pressing for intervention are concentrated among a manageable few, the numbers difficulty does not appear and the few can be allowed to intervene.

Since intervention under CPLR 1013 is permissive, the court can of course impose conditions upon its allowance.[2]

One appropriate grant of a discretionary application under CPLR 1013 would be where there's a question in the case about whether intervention exists as of right under CPLR 1012, and the question is a close one.[3]

Intervention by permission under CPLR 1013 can be compared with consolidation under CPLR 602, which is allowed whenever two or more actions involve a common question of law or fact. Consolidation is a favored remedy today[4] because it fuses separate actions into one and relieves judicial calendars accordingly.

On a CPLR 1013 application, the court must consider whether the intervention (1) "will unduly delay the determination of the action" or (2) "prejudice the substantial rights of any party". The two factors listed are not exclusive, however. Another that the court can consider is whether, if intervention is refused, the applicant is likely to bring a separate action and then a motion for consolidation, and how that motion would likely be disposed of. If consolidation is perceived as inevitable, the court may as well permit intervention.

§ 183. Procedure for Intervention

The procedure for intervention, whether of right under CPLR 1012 or in the court's discretion under CPLR 1013, is a mere motion, which should be on notice to all parties to the pending action. A copy of a proposed pleading setting forth the claim or defense on which the movant bases the intervention request must accompany the motion.[1] It has been held that omission of the pleading is jurisdictional; that in its absence the court has "no power" to entertain the motion.[2] That may be an unnec-

---

3. See Boris v. Flaherty, 242 A.D.2d 9, 672 N.Y.S.2d 177 (4th Dep't 1998), and the discussion in the lead note in SPR 75.

§ 182

1. CPLR 1013 is modeled on Rule 24(b) of the Federal Rules of Civil Procedure. See 1st Rep.Leg.Doc. (1957) No. 6b, p.46.

2. See City of Buffalo v. State Bd. of Equalization and Assessment, 44 Misc.2d 716, 254 N.Y.S.2d 699 (Sup.Ct., Albany County, 1964).

3. Cf. United Svcs. Auto. Ass'n v. Graham, 21 A.D.2d 657, 249 N.Y.S.2d 788 (1st Dep't 1964).

4. See § 128 above.

§ 183

1. CPLR 1014.

2. Carriage Hill, Inc. v. Lane, 20 A.D.2d 914, 249 N.Y.S.2d 455 (2d Dep't 1964).

essarily rigid conclusion, but it's a warning to aspiring intervenors to see that the pleading is included.[3] The court should have "power" at least to hold the motion in abeyance while it allows the movant to supply the missing pleading.

The intervenor gets no rights as a party unless and until the motion to intervene is granted,[4] at which time she gets them all, including the right to counterclaim, cross-claim, implead, appeal, etc.

Whether made under CPLR 1012 or 1013, the application must be "timely". That question is always sui generis. The movant should of course apply as early as possible, but intervention has been allowed in appropriate circumstances even for the purpose of permitting the intervenor to appeal.[5] Indeed, it has been granted to enable the intervenor to move to vacate a default judgment taken against the original defendant.[6] But intervention at that stage will not be allowed merely to permit the intervenor to accomplish now what it could have done as of right but deliberately omitted to do earlier. So, for example, where a liability insurer, relying on an untested disclaimer, refused to defend its insured in a tort case and the unrepresented defendant defaulted, the insurer was now denied leave to intervene—so as to vacate the default judgment—and the judgment stood.[7]

K. SUBSTITUTION

Table of Sections

§ 184. Substitution of Parties

Whenever an occurrence during an action logically indicates that an interest in the case has passed from one of the parties to an outsider, the outsider may as a rule be substituted for the party. There are a number of provisions on the subject, covering CPLR 1015 through 1020, but the foregoing general statement summarizes the lot of them. More specifically:

Death of a party during an action is the most common cause of substitution. If the claim does not abate upon death—and most claims do not[1]—the action will nonetheless be suspended, at least as to the decedent, until substitution is made.[2] The same is true on appeal; all is suspended until proper substitution is made.[3] The CPLR says that upon the death of a party, the court "shall" order substitution.[4] The substitute in the case of a decedent is of course the decedent's personal representative. In the ordinary action, the death of a party in effect divests the court of jurisdiction until proper substitution has been made,[5] so that any step taken without it may be deemed void, including even an appellate decision.[6]

---

3. See Ryder v. Travelers Ins. Co., 37 A.D.2d 797, 324 N.Y.S.2d 804 (4th Dep't 1971).

4. See Brown v. Waryas, 45 Misc.2d 77, 255 N.Y.S.2d 724 (Sup.Ct., Dutchess County, 1965), holding that the moment at which the intervenor becomes a party is the entry of the order granting intervention.

5. See, e.g., Unitarian Universalist Church v. Shorten, 64 Misc.2d 851, 315 N.Y.S.2d 506 (Sup.Ct., Nassau County), vacated on other grounds 64 Misc.2d 1027, 316 N.Y.S.2d 837 (1970).

6. Gonzalez v. Industrial Bank, 13 A.D.2d 770, 215 N.Y.S.2d 632 (1st Dep't 1961).

7. See Krenitsky v. Ludlow Motor Co., 276 A.D. 511, 96 N.Y.S.2d 102 (3d Dep't 1950). This kind of case appears less frequently today because of the expanded use of the declaratory judgment action to test the disclaimer's validity. See § 437 below. The declaratory action should be brought while the main tort action pends and before any default is taken. A stay can be sought in the tort action until the declaratory action is concluded.

§ 184

1. See § 185 below.

2. Matter of Einstoss, 26 N.Y.2d 181, 309 N.Y.S.2d 184, 257 N.E.2d 637 (1970). For death before judgment but after verdict or decision, see CPLR 5016(d).

3. Price v. Booth, 21 A.D.2d 680, 249 N.Y.S.2d 1007 (2d Dep't 1964).

4. CPLR 1015(a).

5. Moore v. Washington, 34 A.D.2d 903, 311 N.Y.S.2d 310 (1st Dep't 1970).

6. Thompson v. Raymond Kramer, Inc., 23 A.D.2d 746, 258 N.Y.S.2d 671 (1st Dep't 1965).

If it is the plaintiff who dies, those interested in the plaintiff's estate had best have a personal representative appointed and substituted or the action will not proceed.[7] If the defendant dies, and the defendant's estate is insubstantial, the plaintiff may find the defendant's family singularly unenthusiastic about having a personal representative appointed and substituted—they have little motive to expedite the plaintiff's suit—and yet the action can't proceed until that is done. The plaintiff in that situation can make the application to have a representative appointed and substituted for the deceased defendant.[8] It may even happen that a defendant will have to seek the appointment of a representative in behalf of a deceased plaintiff if the defendant wants to take some further step in the case.[9]

In multi-party cases, there may be no need for substitution when one of the parties dies. Where, for example, the plaintiff is suing several tortfeasors, the death of one doesn't preclude the action from continuing against the others. In that instance the court need merely note the death on the record.[10] Of course, if the plaintiff wants a judgment in the action to bind the decedent's estate, the plaintiff does have to assure that a proper substitution is made for the decedent.

Other events that permit substitution under explicit statutes are an adjudication of a party's incompetency (the committee is substituted) or conservatorship (the conservator is substituted),[11] and the appointment of a receiver for a party (the receiver is substituted).[12]

Any "transfer of interest" during the action, such as by assignment of the claim by the plaintiff, is also permissible ground for substitution of the transferee, but in this instance the court has discretion to permit the action to proceed with the original parties.[13] The above list is not exhaustive of events permitting substitution.[14] Common sense appears to be the major criterion.

§ 185. Abatement of Claims

Whether a claim abates upon the death of a party, or survives it, is a matter of substance, not procedure, but a brief discussion of abatement is helpful in conjunction with the substitution of parties. Most claims survive the death of either or both parties. Abatement of a claim upon the death of a person is rare today.

A rule of non-abatement had long been applied in contract and property cases, precluding abatement on the death of either the plaintiff or defendant (or both) and thus permitting an action to be commenced by or against (or between) their personal representatives. But abatement continued in personal injury cases. It took legislation, enacted in 1935, to preserve the personal injury claim for post-death suit.[1] Earlier, the macabre notion had lingered that if one could but direct the course of his negligence it might be economically preferable to kill rather than merely injure a person.

Today it is clear that neither a personal injury claim nor a property damage claim[2]

---

7. The appointment is sought from and made by the appropriate surrogate's court. The supreme court has jurisdiction to make the appointment but will exercise it only in pressing circumstances. Castrovinci v. Edwards, 59 Misc.2d 696, 299 N.Y.S.2d 1017 (Sup.Ct., Westchester County, 1969).

8. See SCPA 1002.

9. See De Rijdt v. Robert Straile Co., 58 Misc.2d 543, 296 N.Y.S.2d 601 (Sup.Ct., Queens County, 1968).

10. CPLR 1015(b).

11. CPLR 1016. Although the terms incompetent/committee and conservatee/conservator continue to be used in the CPLR and other statutes, the term incapacitated person/guardian is the technically correct phrase today and the other terms should be deemed changed accordingly. See § 54 above.

12. CPLR 1017.

13. CPLR 1018.

14. See, for example, Lazar v. Merchant's Nat. Properties, Inc., 22 A.D.2d 253, 254 N.Y.S.2d 712 (1st Dep't 1964), allowing an initially balky corporation in a derivative action to change its mind and be substituted as plaintiff, i.e., switched from the defendant's side to replace the shareholder plaintiff on whose initiative the action was initially brought.

§ 185

1. See the 1935 Report of the New York Law Revision Commission, Leg.Doc. No. 60, pp.157–225, and the historical discussion contained in Holmes v. City of New York, 269 A.D. 95, 54 N.Y.S.2d 289 (2d Dep't), aff'd 295 N.Y. 615, 64 N.E.2d 449 (1945).

2. Section 37–a of the General Construction Law defines "personal injury" to include "libel, slander and malicious prosecution; also an assault, battery, false imprisonment, or other actionable injury to the person either of the plaintiff, or of another." Injury to property is also broadly abates upon the death of either the injured or the injuring person.[3]

The major category in which abatement still occurs upon death is the matrimonial suit.[4] Since the action is entirely personal, the death of either party before its conclusion by judgment abates the claim—substantively dissolves it. This applies even in mere separation actions.[5] In some situations, however, a statute evinces an intent to preserve even a matrimonial cause of action. Section 140(e) of the Domestic Relations Law, for example, allows an annulment action predicated on fraud to be maintained by the parent or guardian of the innocent spouse. This was held to confer the cause of action substantively on that person, with the result that when the innocent spouse sued, but died before final judgment, the claim was held to survive and substitution of the parent or guardian was held permissible.[6] Section 140(c) of the same law similarly evinces an intent to preclude abatement in certain annulment actions based on mental retardation or illness.

Often in the reported cases the spouse's death occurred during the three-month period after the rendition of "interlocutory" judgment but before the entry of "final" judgment (a procedure no longer used). In Cornell v. Cornell,[7] an interlocutory divorce was granted but plaintiff P didn't have final judgment entered on it. She nevertheless remarried. Eight years later her first husband, the presumably divorced one, died. Years after that, her second husband died and P sought to elect against the second husband's estate. Her election was resisted on the ground that she was still married

to the first husband and that the second marriage was therefore void. The court granted a nunc pro tunc order permitting entry of a final judgment on the years-old interlocutory divorce, holding that P's failure to enter a timely final judgment was a mere ministerial omission, correctable retroactively. With that, clarifying that the first marriage had been dissolved, P had a wife's standing with respect to her second husband's estate.

Problems of this kind are largely swept away by the abolition of the interlocutory period following a matrimonial judgment.[8] Applying the rule of the *Cornell* case today should enable a nunc pro tunc order to effect retroactive entry of a matrimonial judgment in any instance where the case has been decided on its merits and only the ministerial act of entering the judgment is needed.[9] CPLR 5016(d) appears to support this view by providing that as long as the case has been decided, whether by jury verdict or court decision, the subsequent death of a party before the formal entry of judgment does not require a substitution of parties. Entry can be made in the name of the original parties. This evidences an intent to prevent substantive consequences from appending to a delayed entry of judgment after the merits of a case have been fully, and clearly, decided. With the abolition of the interlocutory period in matrimonial actions, this general aim of CPLR 5016(d) should also be given effect in those actions.

Few categories other than the matrimonial action involve an abatement. It has been held that a claim for the invasion of the right of privacy abates upon the death of the one

---

defined in the General Construction Law. See § 35, note 13, above.

3. EPTL § 11–3.2.

4. See In re Crandall's Estate, 196 N.Y. 127, 89 N.E. 578 (1909). The interlocutory three-month period following initial judgment, during which the matrimonial decree was not final and so not yet effective, was involved in Crandall but, as noted shortly in the text, has since been abolished (L.1968, ch. 645). Today, a matrimonial decree becomes final immediately upon rendition and entry.

5. Hoff v. Dugan, 266 A.D. 790, 41 N.Y.S.2d 691 (2d Dep't 1943).

6. Matter of Haney, 14 A.D.2d 121, 217 N.Y.S.2d 324 (4th Dep't 1961). The rule of non-abatement applies when it is the innocent spouse who dies. This enables the

litigation to continue, dissolving the marriage and preventing the wrongdoing spouse from sharing in the innocent one's estate. Abatement does occur, however, when it is the wrongdoing spouse who dies, see Sampson v. Lancaster, 39 Misc.2d 467, 240 N.Y.S.2d 659 (Sup.Ct., N.Y.County, 1963), thus preserving the marriage and enabling the innocent spouse to share in the wrongdoer's estate.

7. 7 N.Y.2d 164, 196 N.Y.S.2d 98, 164 N.E.2d 395 (1959).

8. See note 4 above.

9. See and compare Figueroa v. Figueroa, 53 Misc.2d 1028, 281 N.Y.S.2d 392 (Sup.Ct., Kings County, 1967).

whose right was purportedly invaded,[10] and that a claim for a penalty will abate upon the death of the one entitled to it.[11]

The abatement of claims discussed here fits under the legal caption of "survival" of claims; it is generally viewed, as already noted, as a question of substantive law. The "revival" of a claim, on the other hand, such as by legislative enactments affecting the statute of limitations,[12] is a separate but sometimes overlapping topic. As a rule it falls into the "procedural" category.[13]

§ 186. Procedure for Substitution

Whatever the event mandating or suggesting substitution, the procedure for it comes from CPLR 1021. The procedure is a motion, which should be on notice to all parties. If the event requiring substitution is a party's death and the motion is made by other than the decedent's side, notice of it can't be served on the decedent's attorney because the attorney's authority dissolves when the client dies.[1] In that case, the notice should be served on the would-be representative, and, since he is not already a party, there is some indication that the motion papers should be served in the same manner as a summons.[2] If guidance is needed about whom to serve, the motion can be brought on by order to show cause.[3] The motion may be made by any party or by the successor to the deceased party. If the one who should be substituted doesn't appear voluntarily, she may be made a defendant.

If the substitution-requiring event occurs before judgment, substitution must be made "within a reasonable time" or the action may be dismissed as to the party for whom substitution is needed. But what a "reasonable" time is will always depend on the facts of the particular case.[4] There may even have to be a substitution before determining whether the delay was unreasonable, since without substitution that side can't be heard on the issue.[5]

If the substitution-requiring event occurs after judgment, the motion should be made within four months. If an appeal has been or could be taken, the substitution motion may be made to the original or appellate court,[6] but unless the substitution is made within the four-month period, only the appellate court holds the remedy, and one of the things it can do is dismiss the appeal, outright or conditionally.

When death is the substitution-requiring event, those interested in the decedent's estate must be given an opportunity "to show cause why the action or appeal should not be dismissed".[7] This requirement contemplates the case in which the decedent was the plaintiff, or the appellant on appeal, i.e., the one who would want the action continued or the appeal prosecuted. If the decedent is the defendant, however, her family is not likely to show cause why the action should be continued. In practical terms, the requirement is designed to assure a hearing to the decedent's side, whichever side that may be, before permitting any step detrimental to that side.

If the time within which to take any procedural step in the case is running when the substitution-requiring event occurs, the time "is extended as to all parties until fifteen days

---

10. See Rome Sentinel Co. v. Boustedt, 43 Misc.2d 598, 252 N.Y.S.2d 10 (Sup.Ct., Oneida County, 1964).

11. Brackett v. Griswold, 103 N.Y. 425, 9 N.E. 438 (1886).

12. See § 38 above.

13. Cf. Baltimore & Ohio R.R. Co. v. Joy, 173 U.S. 226, 19 S.Ct. 387, 43 L.Ed. 677 (1899).

§ 186

1. See Friedlander v. Roxy Theatre, Inc., 204 Misc. 740, 127 N.Y.S.2d 765 (Sup.Ct., Bronx County, 1953), aff'd 283 A.D. 860, 129 N.Y.S.2d 896 (1st Dep't 1954).

2. See Lewis v. Lewis, 43 Misc.2d 349, 250 N.Y.S.2d 984 (Sup.Ct., Nassau County, 1964).

3. See § 248 below.

4. It has been held that the period of two years, for example, is not an unreasonable period as a matter of law. Rosenfeld v. Hotel Corp. of America, 20 N.Y.2d 25, 281 N.Y.S.2d 308, 228 N.E.2d 374 (1967).

5. De Rijdt v. Robert Straile Co., 58 Misc.2d 543, 296 N.Y.S.2d 601 (Sup.Ct., Queens County, 1968).

6. If the case is on its way from one appellate court to another, the motion can be made in either one or in the trial court. CPLR 1021.

7. This is the actual language used by CPLR 1021.

after substitution is made".[8] This can amount to quite an extension, and in this instance it applies explicitly even to the rarely extendable period in which to appeal.[9]

§ 187. Public Body or Officer as Party

Whenever suit is brought by or against "a public officer, body, board, commission or other public agency" in its official capacity, only the title of the office or agency need be used in the action. The name of the office's incumbent doesn't have to be added unless the court requires it.[1] The office or agency is the real party and the incumbent's name is not needed.[2]

A plaintiff may save some bother later by designating the office rather than the incumbent now. If there should be a change in office, as by election or appointment, there would then be no need to amend the papers in the action: statute dispenses with substitution when the office and not its occupant has been named, while indicating that substitution is necessary if the individual's name has been added.[3] In practice substitution even in the latter instance is often ignored (harmlessly, it would seem). If substitution is sought, it is by motion on notice to both the successor and predecessor. The court can dispense with service on the latter.

A special statute, CPLR 1026, governs the question of proper parties in suits involving judicial administration. It applies to determinations of the Court of Appeals, and to those of the Chief Judge and the Administrative Board of the Courts made in their administrative rather than judicial capacities, i.e., determinations made pursuant to Article 7–A of the Judiciary Law, the article that governs judicial administration. To avoid even the facial impression that the Chief Judge or the Court of Appeals or any other judge is being sued as such, the statute requires that all actions and proceedings brought to review such determinations name only "the chief administrator of the courts, in his representative capacity" as the adverse party.

§ 188. Unknown Parties

CPLR 1024 provides that when suit is brought against someone whose "name or identity" is unknown, the plaintiff may bring the action against that person "by designating so much of his name and identity as is known". The use of a fictitious name, with a description added, is not required. Indeed, its use can be misleading. If it is used, it should be of the clearly fictitious variety: Mary Doe, Richard Roe, etc.

The description is the important thing in this situation. It should be complete enough to identify the defendant so as to afford notice and an opportunity to defend. As long as it does that it satisfies due process and "the form of description . . . is immaterial".[1]

A diligent effort to learn the party's name is a condition precedent to the use of CPLR 1024,[2] which should therefore be turned to only as a last resort. Even if it suffices for jurisdiction, use of a description, with or without a fictitious name, is likely to create trouble at the enforcement of judgment stage later on.[3] The correct name should be ascertained and inserted before then.

As soon as the person's name becomes known, all later proceedings must be taken under the correct name "and all prior proceed-

8. CPLR 1022.
9. See CPLR 5514(c).

§ 187
1. CPLR 1023.
2. See Heslin v. Schechter, 3 Misc.2d 42, 148 N.Y.S.2d 625 (Sup.Ct., N.Y.County, 1956).
3. CPLR 1019.

§ 188
1. City of Mt. Vernon v. Best Dev. Co., 268 N.Y. 327, 330, 197 N.E. 299, 300 (1935).

2. See Porter v. Kingsbrook OB/GYN Assocs., 209 A.D.2d 497, 618 N.Y.S.2d 837 (2d Dep't 1994).

3. See Kiamesha Concord v. Pullman, 52 Misc.2d 210, 274 N.Y.S.2d 431 (Sup.Ct., N.Y.County, 1966). If execution on the judgment is sought through the sheriff's office, the sheriff can be expected to insist on insertion of the party's proper name before levying.

ings shall be deemed amended accordingly".[4] The plaintiff does not need court leave to amend the papers to insert the name of the party sued fictitiously, once the name is determined.[5] If there's any confusion in fixing the point at which prior papers in the action are to be "deemed" amended to reflect the defendant's true name, a court order can be obtained containing a formal recitation.

To use this designation-by-description, the plaintiff must have a cause of action. It can't be used just to enable the plaintiff to conduct a fishing expedition, perhaps with the idea of later amending the papers to specify the defendant on a cause of action thereby uncovered.[6] But if the plaintiff does have a cause of action, and the defendant is merely being evasive about furnishing its proper name, which the plaintiff through reasonable efforts can't determine precisely, the plaintiff may find CPLR 1024 helpful indeed—especially if the statute of limitations is closing in. The plaintiff in that case should commence the action with an appropriate description, effect timely service and thus secure jurisdiction of the misnamed or unnamed defendant, use the disclosure devices[7] to seek to determine the defendant's right name promptly,[8] and then amend the caption to insert it.

It has been held that in the supreme and county courts, in which filing constitutes commencement of the action—as opposed to service (which marks commencement in the lower courts)—the plaintiff can file papers with a fictitious designation of the defendant but must then learn the name of the party within the 120–day service period so as to be able to effect service with papers that properly name the defendant.[9]

It may also happen, of course, that the plaintiff will not be able to determine the defendant's right name in time for service. That will not be fatal as long as the proper person has been served, albeit under a fictitious name. If for want of the defendant's right name the plaintiff is unable to make service by a prescribed method, service may be sought under CPLR 308(5),[10] under which the court can invent a service method for the plaintiff.

All discussion so far has addressed only the situation in which the defendant is being named fictitiously. What about hiding the plaintiff's name? It has been held that in a proper case—one in which there's a good reason for a plaintiff to seek public anonymity—the plaintiff may use a fictitious name in court papers even for herself as long as she properly identifies herself to the other side.[11]

§ 189. The Unincorporated Association

Procedure can take the substantive law only as it finds it. With the unincorporated association it finds it unclear. The question of when the entire membership is liable for the act of the association is for the substantive law to answer.[1] We will assume here for our proce-

---

4. CPLR 1024.

5. Woodburn Court Assocs. I v. Wingate Mgmt. Co., 663 N.Y.S.2d 445 (3d Dep't 1997). See the discussion of the procedure for suing unknown parties and avoiding statute of limitations problems in SPR 72:4.

6. See Matthews v. Schusheim, 42 Misc.2d 176, 247 N.Y.S.2d 285 (Sup.Ct., Nassau County, 1964).

7. These are in Article 31 and are studied in Chapter 13. The plaintiff should ordinarily wait for the defendant's answer before turning to disclosure, since the defendant may appear through an attorney who may be willing to volunteer the client's right name.

8. Statute of limitations problems may otherwise confront the plaintiff. See Piccinich v. Forest City Tech Place Assocs., 234 A.D.2d 528, 651 N.Y.S.2d 203 (2d Dep't 1996).

9. See Luckern v. Lyonsdale Energy, 229 A.D.2d 249, 654 N.Y.S.2d 543 (4th Dep't 1997). The court draws an analogy to CPLR 203(b)(5), under which, in "service" courts, a delivery of the summons and complaint to the sheriff secures a 60–day extension of the time for service.

10. See § 75 above.

11. See E.K. v. New York Hosp., 158 Misc.2d 334, 600 N.Y.S.2d 993 (Sup.Ct., Orange County, 1992), noted in SPR 19:4, in which the plaintiff did not want it revealed that she had been under care for mental illness. The action was in fact against a hospital and its employee for wrongfully disclosing the datum.

§ 189

1. The caselaw is not consistent. See 76 Harv.L.Rev. 983 (1963). Substantively, it would seem that the association and all of its membership should be subjected to liability for any act (tortious, contractual, or otherwise) performed or committed in its behalf or in the course of its business under simple principles of agency. The courts may be moving in that direction, see Madden v. Atkins, 4 N.Y.2d 283, 174 N.Y.S.2d 633, 151 N.E.2d 73 (1958), but the issue remains unresolved, as will be manifest when one reads in the Madden case the distinction sought to be made of Martin v. Curran, 303 N.Y. 276, 101 N.E.2d 683

dural purpose that the liability being asserted is one for which the entire membership must ultimately answer.

Procedurally, an action may be brought by or against an unincorporated association in New York merely by naming its president or treasurer,[2] and, when the association is the defendant, by serving the one named. This obviates naming and serving all of the members, a requirement that would as a practical matter impede if not prohibit suit whenever the association has a large membership, as it often has.

If suit against the association goes to judgment, it is enforcible only against association property, i.e., property owned jointly by all of the members.[3] If, however, an execution on the judgment is returned in any part unsatisfied, suit may be brought against the members "or, in a proper case . . . any of them".[4]

The plaintiff does have the option to forego suit against the association collectively and bring it instead against the members directly,[5] but rarely pursues that alternative for obvious practical reasons.

Suit by or against the members of an association may be maintained in the form of a class action if class action requirements[6] are otherwise met.[7]

L. POOR PERSONS

Table of Sections

(1951). The Madden case seems to be applying agency principles, which ought to govern association liability just as they do partnership liability.

2. CPLR 1025; Gen.Assoc.L. § 13.

3. Gen.Assoc.L. § 15. The judgment is not good against the individual assets of the president or treasurer through whom the association litigated.

4. Gen.Assoc.L. § 16. The quoted language, "in a proper case", is an acknowledgement that the legislature, too, is uncertain about when substantive liability exists against the entire membership.

5. Gen.Assoc.L. § 17. See Mandell v. Moses, 209 A.D. 531, 205 N.Y.S. 254 (3d Dep't), aff'd 239 N.Y. 555, 147 N.E. 192 (1924).

§ 190. Poor Person Status

A person "unable to pay the costs, fees and expenses necessary to prosecute or defend" an action or appeal may apply for poor person status.[1] The status can be sought by any party at any stage of the action on affidavit proof of such inability. The seeker need no longer show, as was once required, that he is not worth $300 in cash or available property; the Advisory Committee rejected that standard as too rigid.[2]

The applicant is required to set forth in the affidavit the amount and sources of her income and a list of her property and its value. This broad look into resources is the necessary basis for the court's determination of whether to grant the application, which lies in the court's discretion. It has been held that eligibility for public assistance or legal aid under other statutes and standards, though germane, does not conclusively entitle the litigant to poor person status under Article 11 of the CPLR.[3]

The applicant's motives may also be investigated, because if leave is granted it is the public that pays his way.[4]

In addition to stating inability to pay and listing income and assets, the affidavit must state the nature of the action and include a statement of facts sufficient to enable the court to determine whether there is any merit to the applicant's claim or defense. Finally, it must assert whether any other person is interested in the recovery sought and whether such other person is able to pay for the litigation. This was designed primarily to enable the

6. See §§ 141–142 above.

7. House v. Schwartz, 18 Misc.2d 21, 37–8, 188 N.Y.S.2d 308, 324–5 (Sup.Ct., N.Y.County, 1959).

§ 190

1. CPLR 1101(a).

2. 2d Rep.Leg.Doc. (1958) No.13, p.389.

3. Lancer v. Lancer, 70 Misc.2d 1045, 335 N.Y.S.2d 138 (Sup.Ct., Nassau County, 1972).

4. 2d Rep.Leg.Doc. (1958) No. 13 at 388.

court to determine whether a plaintiff applicant has an attorney working on a contingent fee basis, in which event poor person status will not be granted.[5]

§ 191. Procedure to Secure Poor Person Status

The usual procedure for securing poor person status is by motion to the court of original instance. When the status is sought for purposes of an appeal, however, the motion may be made to the original or appellate court.[1] It had been held preferable even in that instance to make it to the original court: the appellate court would often deny the application without prejudice to renewal below,[2] or perhaps just transfer the application to let the lower court handle it, but a 1987 amendment requires the appellate court itself to entertain the application if made before it.[3]

If an action has already been commenced, notice of the motion must be given to all parties. Notice is also required to be given to the corporation counsel if the action is in New York City and to the county attorney in actions outside the city, because it is the municipality that has to pay for transcripts later on.[4] This notice is apparently required whether the application is made before or after commencement of the action. The court may require the movant to append to her application an attorney's certificate stating that the attorney has examined the action and finds merit in the applicant's contentions.[5]

In the supreme and county courts, in which the filing of the summons and complaint marks commencement of the action, a more elaborate procedure is spelled out, designed to enable the applicant to apply for poor person status before paying any filing fee. The plaintiff seeking poor person status can file the summons and complaint along with an affidavit of inability to pay costs and fees,[6] and upon doing so will be assigned an index number

without paying a fee. The application will then be referred to a judge. If the judge approves the application, the plaintiff will be notified by a written order that fees are waived. If the application is disapproved, the written order will instruct the plaintiff that the action will be dismissed if the fee is not paid within 120 days, measured from "the date of the order".[7] That presumably means the time of the order's service on the plaintiff, but it might be construed more rigidly to mean that the time runs from the date of the order's entry, whatever the delay in its service on the plaintiff, so the plaintiff intent on pursuing the claim should pay the fee expeditiously if the application is denied.

Meanwhile, nothing is said in CPLR 1101(d) about giving the plaintiff any different time— than that provided in the new CPLR 306–b (a 120–day period)—for effecting service of the summons after the filing, whatever the status may be of the plaintiff's poor-person application to the court. The plaintiff has gotten the index number promptly under this provision, so it is expected that the plaintiff will proceed to service promptly, bound by the 120–day provisions of CPLR 306–b. If it turns out that the plaintiff's application for poor person status is denied, the plaintiff will have to pay the filing fee within 120 days of the order of denial whether service has already been effected or not.

Poor person applicants should not confuse the 120 days for service (which is governed by CPLR 306–b and starts from the initial filing) with the 120 days for paying the fee (which is governed by CPLR 1101[d] and starts from the court order denying the poor person application).

If the plaintiff is represented by a "legal aid society or ... other nonprofit organization ... furnishing ... legal services to indigent persons", or by a lawyer working for such a

5. Id. at 390.

§ 191

1. CPLR 1101(a).

2. See, e.g., Jenks v. Murphy, 21 A.D.2d 346, 250 N.Y.S.2d 848 (4th Dep't 1964).

3. L.1987, c.312, amending CPLR 1101(a).

4. CPLR 1101(c).

5. CPLR 1101(b).

6. CPLR 1101(a).

7. CPLR 1101(d).

group, and the group or lawyer certifies that the plaintiff meets the poor person standards, the fee is waived without application to the court.[8]

§ 192. What Poor Person Designation Accomplishes

The privileges conferred on one who qualifies as a poor person are listed in CPLR 1102. A major one is that the court may assign an attorney.[1] There is no absolute right to assigned counsel in civil litigation, however. The Court of Appeals held in Matter of Smiley[2] that whether to make the assignment in a given case is in the discretion of the court.

The applicant may already have an attorney, often appearing in court through a lawyer previously assigned by one of the governmental, quasi-governmental, or even private organizations that offer legal assistance generally or in special situations. It may even be the attorney who is bringing the poor person application.

If the court does appoint a lawyer, is the lawyer entitled to compensation? There had been some dispute about whether the lawyer is entitled to be paid out of public funds. The *Smiley* case then held that the lawyer is not; that it is for the legislature and not the courts to appropriate money for this purpose. There is a general expectation among judges that lawyers will accept unpaid assignments for indigent litigants from time to time, as a professional obligation.[3] While not abating that traditional responsibility,[4] *Smiley* acknowledges that the lawyer's own constitutional

rights may be infringed by judicial resort to the involuntary assignment too often.[5]

Once the status is granted, the poor person is not liable for any costs or fees in the action. But if the poor person recovers a judgment, some or all of those items as well as a reasonable sum for the assigned attorney may be ordered paid out of the recovery, as may anything the municipality has paid for a transcript.[6] CPLR 1102(b) entitles the poor person to two free copies of the transcript (one copy is filed with the court). These are a municipal charge. But it has been held that the free copy covers only the main trial or hearing and not necessarily pretrial depositions,[7] even though these can be expensive and play an important and sometimes even decisive role in litigation.

This statutory allowance of a transcript and suspension of court costs and fees has avoided a clash with the federal constitution, whose supervening requirements have been felt on related fronts. Out-of-court expenses, for example, are not necessarily dispensed with when poor person status is allowed under CPLR Article 11. Notorious among these expenses had been the cost of service by publication in matrimonial actions. The U.S. Supreme Court then held this to be a governmental expense if government, as was the case in New York, insisted on imposing a method of service that incurs a substantial expense.[8] New York responded to the problem in Deason v. Deason,[9] making the cost of service by publication a government expense but imposing it on the municipality rather than the state. Confirmatory legislation followed.[10]

8. CPLR 1101(e).

§ 192

1. CPLR 1102(a).

2. 36 N.Y.2d 433, 369 N.Y.S.2d 87, 330 N.E.2d 53 (1975). For the position of the U.S. Supreme Court on the requirement to assign counsel under the due process clause and for the difference between criminal and civil actions in this respect, see Lassiter v. Dep't of Social Services, 452 U.S. 18, 101 S.Ct. 2153, 68 L.Ed.2d 640 (1981).

3. See Jacox v. Jacox, 43 A.D.2d 716, 350 N.Y.S.2d 435 (2d Dep't 1973).

4. See Yearwood v. Yearwood, 54 A.D.2d 626, 387 N.Y.S.2d 433 (1976).

5. See also Menin v. Menin, 79 Misc.2d 285, 359 N.Y.S.2d 721 (Sup.Ct., Westchester County, 1974), aff'd 48 A.D.2d 904, 372 N.Y.S.2d 985 (2d Dep't 1975).

6. CPLR 1102(d).

7. Lester v. Lester, 69 Misc.2d 528, 330 N.Y.S.2d 190 (Sup.Ct., Sullivan County, 1972).

8. Boddie v. Connecticut, 401 U.S. 371, 91 S.Ct. 780, 28 L.Ed.2d 113 (1971).

9. 32 N.Y.2d 93, 343 N.Y.S.2d 321, 296 N.E.2d 229 (1973).

10. The matter is discussed in the section on service in matrimonial actions. See § 76 above.

If an appeal is involved, a party who has been granted poor person status need submit only typed briefs and appendices to the appellate court, "furnishing one legible copy for each appellate justice".[11] Distinct from a motion for poor-person status, an appellant can move the appellate court for leave to appeal on a typed transcript and typed briefs in a minimum number of copies, which accomplishes the more limited but still substantial benefit of eliminating the need to print, offset, or otherwise machine-reproduce those papers. That kind of motion accomplishes only what the appellate court prescribes. An order granting such leave, for example, does not automatically entitle the applicant to go back to the lower court and insist on a free transcript,[12] while an order granting full poor-person status does.

M. INFANTS AND INCOMPETENTS

Table of Sections

§ 193. Representation of Infant

An infant, who is any person not yet 18 years old,[1] can't appear in its own behalf or by an attorney of its own hiring. An infant must appear through one of the persons listed in CPLR 1201, and if it is to appear by attorney, the attorney must be retained by the appropriate listed person. The first person on the list is a formally (judicially) designated guardian of the property—not to be confused with a mere guardian ad litem[2]—if the infant should have one, which it rarely does. Absent such guardian, the infant may be represented by the parent having legal custody. Statistically, it is most often the parent who does the representing. If no parent has custody of the infant, an appearance may be made in behalf of the infant "by another person or agency having legal custody". This has been held to mean custody determined by judicial decree, so that a longstanding but informal custody will not suffice.[3] Finally, if the infant is married to and resides with an adult spouse, the spouse may appear for the infant.

There is no longer a requirement that an infant appear by a guardian ad litem, i.e., a guardian appointed solely for the purpose of representing the infant in a particular litigation. Such a guardian may of course be appointed by the court if no one on the CPLR 1201 list is available or willing to represent the infant, and the court may also appoint a guardian ad litem, despite the availability of a listed person, upon a finding of conflict of interest or any other cause.[4] Because the infant is a ward of the court, it takes little "other cause" to prompt appointment of a guardian ad litem. In a suit by a father, for example, to make the mother account for money paid to her for the child's support under a separation agreement, with each parent claiming to represent the child's best interests, the court held that it would be best for a guardian ad litem to be appointed,[5] for the reason that the parents could not prevent their own interests from becoming confused with the child's.

§ 194. Representation of Incapacitated Person

CPLR 1201 and other parts of the CPLR and other laws still use the terminology of

---

11. CPLR 1102(c). For further details on matters like this, the lawyer should consult the individual rules of the particular appellate court.

12. Moriarity v. Butler Bin Co., 21 A.D.2d 865, 251 N.Y.S.2d 44 (1st Dep't 1964), aff'd 15 N.Y.2d 901, 258 N.Y.S.2d 429, 206 N.E.2d 361 (1965).

§ 193

1. CPLR 105.

2. See § 196 below.

3. Villafane v. Banner, 87 Misc.2d 1037, 387 N.Y.S.2d 183 (Sup.Ct., N.Y.County, 1976).

4. CPLR 1201.

5. Rosenblatt v. Birnbaum, 20 A.D.2d 556, 245 N.Y.S.2d 72 (2d Dep't 1963), aff'd 16 N.Y.2d 212, 264 N.Y.S.2d 521, 212 N.E.2d 37 (1965).

"incompetent", for whom a "committee" has been appointed, and "conservatee", for whom a "conservator" has been appointed, but all four phrases have been officially replaced by two: "incapacitated person", for whom a "guardian" has been appointed. The replacement terminology comes from Article 81 of the Mental Hygiene Law, which superseded Articles 77 and 78, and a brief instruction in § 4 of the enacting bill[1] directs that

> [w]herever a statute uses the terms conservators or committees, such statute shall be construed to include the term guardian notwithstanding the provisions of this article unless the context otherwise requires.[2]

The appointment of a "conservator" was a lighter step than the appointment of a committee. The situation was one in which a person was subject to an infirmity that disabled the person from caring for property or discharging obligations to dependents but did not call for the more drastic, and stigmatic, "incompetency" determination. CPLR 1201 requires that an adjudicated incompetent appear in litigation through its committee and that a person adjudicated a conservatee appear through its conservator. To parallel CPLR 1201, we will use its terminology when it's necessary to distinguish between the two categories of disability, otherwise using the new terms. If, as with infants, there is any conflict of interest between the pair,[3] or if for "other cause" the court deems it best, it may appoint a guardian ad litem.

If the person has not been adjudicated an incapacitated person, but appears to be "incapable of adequately prosecuting or defending his rights", a guardian ad litem may be appointed.

It is not a good idea for one party to proceed against another knowing the other to be incap-

able of looking after her rights, despite the absence of a formal adjudication to that effect. Thus, where P knew that D had been institutionalized but nonetheless sued and took a default judgment against D, the court, analogizing the situation to where an improperly represented infant has been proceeded against without a guardian ad litem, held the judgment jurisdictionally void, vacated it, and opened the default.[4] So, when D's ability to look after his interests is doubtful, it may even be politic for P to make sure that D is properly represented. The thing for P to do in D's behalf, if no one else steps in to do it first, is move to have a guardian ad litem appointed for D. Without such a guardian, a judgment against D may be in jeopardy even if D purported to appear by an attorney of her own choosing,[5] apparently on the theory that D lacked even the competence to choose.

Suit against an incompetent for whom a committee has been appointed requires leave of court,[6] a rule that can be viewed as applicable to suit against a conservator, too. The matter is not of great moment as long as a failure to secure advance leave is not treated as jurisdictional, and caselaw indicates that it is not.[7]

§ 195. Representation Distinguished from Service

When the infant or incapacitated person is the defendant, a distinction must be drawn between service of process, which is made pursuant to CPLR 309, and appearance, which is governed by CPLR 1201. Service on an incapacitated person is made by serving both him and the guardian, unless service on the incapacitated person is dispensed with.[1]

For service on an infant, CPLR 309(a) governs and contains a list of people who may be

§ 194

1. L.1992, Chapter 698.

2. All prior proceedings taken under the old terminology are of course preserved until set aside or modified by a judge under the new article. See SPR 5:4.

3. See Matter of Berman, 24 A.D.2d 432, 260 N.Y.S.2d 736 (1st Dep't 1965).

4. Oneida Nat. Bank & Trust Co. v. Unczur, 37 A.D.2d 480, 326 N.Y.S.2d 458 (4th Dep't 1971).

5. See Rand v. Lockwood, 65 Misc.2d 182, 316 N.Y.S.2d 950 (Sup.Ct., Nassau County, 1970).

6. Sinley v. Estco, Inc., 25 Misc.2d 172, 200 N.Y.S.2d 939 (Sup.Ct., Nassau County, 1960).

7. Van Vooren v. Cook, 191 Misc. 794, 77 N.Y.S.2d 173 (Sup.Ct., Ontario County), aff'd 274 A.D. 966, 85 N.Y.S.2d 526 (4th Dep't 1948).

§ 195

1. CPLR 309(b), (c). See § 69 above.

served in the infant's behalf,[2] but the lawyer should not confuse the CPLR 309(a) list of servees with the CPLR 1201 list of appearers. They are similar but not the same. The CPLR 1201 list sets up rigid priorities concerning who may appear; the CPLR 309(a) roster of servees is more an offering of alternatives.

The plaintiff about to sue an infant or incapacitated person need not concern herself initially with CPLR 1201. She should merely effect service pursuant to CPLR 309. Doing so secures jurisdiction.[3] Ordinarily it is only then that CPLR 1201 becomes relevant, now determining who may appear for the defendant. Presumably, someone on the defendant's side will see to it that a proper person appears and defends. Only if that does not happen need the plaintiff take the initiative to assure that an appropriate guardian is appointed for the defendant.[4]

If an infant has a "guardian of the property", whichever of the guardianships that may be deemed to refer to,[5] CPLR 1004 permits the guardian instead of the infant to be named as the party.[6] It is better not to rely on that authorization and to see to it that the infant is named, too. The authorization applies, in any event, only when a formally appointed "guardian of the property" is present; it does not apply to some other person, such as a parent, through whom the infant usually appears. Nor can the requirement of CPLR 309(a), that the parent and infant both be served to start the action, be circumvented by theorizing that the parent qualifies as a "guardian" in the CPLR 1004 sense so as to dispense with both the naming and serving of the infant.[7]

§ 196. Guardian Ad Litem Distinguished from Other Guardianships

A guardian ad litem is appointed only to represent someone in litigation, which is what "ad litem" means. The phrase "special guardian" is no longer used in civil practice.[1]

The guardian ad litem should not be confused with more permanent guardianships for infants. CPLR 1210 supplies one of them, just called a "guardian", who is as a rule appointed when the child's parents are dead or disabled or when there is friction between them. It is sometimes used to resolve custody disputes.[2] Those disputes are more likely to arise in matrimonial litigation, however, where the court can make directions as to custody, which is in effect guardianship, through regular orders and judgments. These often include money directions (maintenance, support, etc.) as well.[3] Habeas corpus, and alternatively a mere petition and order to show cause, are also recognized as ways to secure custody of a child.[4] Those devices are plenary in themselves; they need not be connected to a matrimonial action. They secure guardianship (without calling it that) as effectively as would a direct application for it. They doubtless contribute to the disuse into which the CPLR 1210 guardianship has fallen.

The surrogate's court can appoint a guardian of the infant's person and/or property even if both parents are alive.[5] The county court has some analogous jurisdiction of infants,[6] the family court shares that authority with both courts,[7] and of course the supreme court has it

---

2. See § 69 above.

3. If the defendant is an incapacitated person, leave to sue should be secured in advance. See § 194, note 6, above.

4. See § 197 below.

5. See § 196, below, for the distinction between a guardian ad litem and other guardianships.

6. See § 137 above.

7. See Cramer v. Henderson, 123 Misc.2d 159, 473 N.Y.S.2d 672 (Sup.Ct., Yates County, 1984).

§ 196

1. See Matter of Becan, 26 A.D.2d 44, 270 N.Y.S.2d 923 (1st Dep't 1966).

2. See and compare Matter of Brown, 17 N.Y.S.2d 188 (Sup.Ct., Nassau County, 1939).

3. See Dom.Rel.L. §§ 236, 240.

4. Dom.Rel.L. § 240.

5. SCPA 1701. See also SCPA § 1750 et seq., authorizing guardianships for mentally retarded persons.

6. Jud.L. § 190(4).

7. Fam.Ct.Act § 661.

concurrently with all of them.[8] A surviving parent can appoint a guardian for the person or property, or both, of the children, by inter-vivos instrument or by will.[9] If by will, the appointee is known as a "testamentary" guardian.

Any of these guardians should ordinarily qualify as the "property" guardian authorized by CPLR 1201 to appear for an infant in litigation, and all should be distinguished from the mere guardian ad litem. The latter is appointed only for an action or special proceeding, and the appointment will ordinarily be made only when the infant does not have one of the other formally decreed or recognized guardians or custodians or when its parents and other potential CPLR 1201 appearers are dead, disabled, or in conflict of interest.

§ 197. Procedure for Appointment of Guardian Ad Litem

CPLR 1202 supplies the procedure for the appointment of a guardian ad litem. It is a motion made in the court in which the action has been or is about to be brought. The motion may be made at any time and may be made by a party or by the court sua sponte. It is ordinarily made by someone on the side of the infant or incapacitated person, such as "a relative, friend or a guardian, committee of the property, or conservator".[1] In the case of an infant over 14, the infant itself can make the application.[2] Since the infant and incapacitated person are wards of the court, the question of who calls to the court's attention the need for a guardian ad litem is not important.

If the defendant is the ward, the plaintiff should be sensitive that the person who shows up to represent the defendant is one duly authorized by CPLR 1201. A defect here can jeopardize any judgment the plaintiff may recover. If the plaintiff has serious doubt about the qualifications of the person purporting to represent the defendant and no one on the defendant's side moves the appointment of a guardian ad litem within 10 days after service of the summons is complete, the plaintiff may make the motion herself.[3]

If the ward has a duly appointed guardian, notice of the motion to appoint a guardian ad litem must be served on that person. If the ward has not, notice is served on the one with whom the ward resides. If the ward is over 14, the ward must also be served with notice of the motion, but an adjudicated incapacitated person apparently need not be.[4] If the court does appoint a guardian ad litem, the designation will not take effect until the appointee submits to the court a written consent accompanied by proof of financial ability to answer for any potential negligence or misconduct.[5]

In an action against an infant, as has been indicated, the plaintiff merely effects service pursuant to CPLR 309 without any preliminary court order or application. There is no authority for the court to appoint a guardian ad litem for the defendant in advance of commencement of the action so as to enable summons service itself to be made on the guardian. In an ordinary action, in fact, the court is without power to appoint a guardian ad litem for the defendant until jurisdiction is secured, and it is service under CPLR 309 that secures jurisdiction.[6] A special proceeding, however, may be commenced either by service in the usual way, i.e., pursuant to CPLR 309 in the case of an infant or incapacitated person,[7] or by an order to show cause.[8]

If the order to show cause is used, the court can determine the method of service in the order itself. Early in the life of the CPLR, some caselaw held that this would also authorize the court, in advance of service, to both appoint a guardian ad litem for the prospective

8. Const. Art. VI, § 7(b); Kagen v. Kagen, 21 N.Y.2d 532, 289 N.Y.S.2d 195, 236 N.E.2d 475 (1968).

9. Dom.Rel.L. § 81.

§ 197

1. CPLR 1202(a)(2)

2. CPLR 1202(a)(1).

3. CPLR 1202(a)(3).

4. CPLR 1202(b).

5. CPLR 1202(c).

6. Soto v. Soto, 30 A.D.2d 651, 291 N.Y.S.2d 37 (1st Dep't 1968).

7. CPLR 403(c).

8. CPLR 403(d). See § 553 below.

respondents and direct service on the appointee in their behalf,[9] but that procedure did not catch on and does not appear to be used today.[10] The alternative is in any event unavailable in an ordinary action because an order to show cause is not available as an alternative to start an action.

§ 198. Qualifications, Rights and Authority of Guardian Ad Litem

Any adult person who is capable of protecting the interests of the ward and has no conflict of interest may be appointed guardian ad litem.[1] The person need not be a lawyer.[2]

The court is authorized to permit the guardian ad litem "a reasonable compensation" for its services, which may be ordered paid by an adverse party, from the ward's recovery (if any), or from other of the ward's property.[3] It has been noted that such guardians are often required "to accept most moderate compensation for their services". The compensation will of course depend on the nature of the services rendered,[4] and the value of a nonlegal service performed by a guardian who happens to be a lawyer is not "enhanced just because an attorney does it".[5]

The authority of a guardian ad litem terminates when the infant reaches majority,[6] if it has not been terminated by the court before. If the attorney appearing for the ward before majority is to continue after it, the appearance must now be with the ward's consent, not just

the guardian's. If an infant has been appearing all the while without acceptable representation, such as where she instead of her parent or guardian retained the attorney, the infant's continued appearance after reaching majority has been held to validate all of the proceedings nunc pro tunc.[7]

§ 199. Risks If No Proper Representative Present

Prior to the 1963 adoption of the CPLR, an infant could appear only by a guardian ad litem. A by-product was that the absence of the guardian could carry severe consequences, not for the ward, but for the adverse party. Indeed, even where a guardian ad litem had been duly appointed, evidence of improper representation could result in the setting aside of any proceedings taken against the ward,[1] while there was a concomitant tendency, if the proceedings went the ward's way, to uphold them regardless of defects in the representation.[2]

Although there is no requirement that a guardian ad litem do the representing today, the infant and incapacitated person are still wards of the court. Evidence of improper representation, no matter by whom, can still imperil whatever an adverse party may otherwise accomplish in the case. Prior caselaw will therefore continue to have much to say. The counseling point for the adverse party, whether as plaintiff or defendant, is to take no joy from evidence of weak representation of the ward's interest. A victory in such an instance

---

9. In re Beyer, 21 A.D.2d 152, 249 N.Y.S.2d 320 (1st Dep't 1964).

10. See Matter of Pugach, 29 A.D.2d 518, 285 N.Y.S.2d 258 (1st Dep't 1967), aff'd 23 N.Y.2d 901, 298 N.Y.S.2d 306, 246 N.E.2d 160 (1969). The holding of the Beyer case, id., the main decision that authorized precommencement appointment of a guardian ad litem for a respondent in a special proceeding, was in any event restricted to cases in which the ordinary procedure "would constitute a danger to the infant's interest", Matter of Bank of New York, 25 A.D.2d 727, 268 N.Y.S.2d 911 (1st Dep't 1966), at best a remote contingency.

§ 198

1. Specific direction to this effect in prior law was omitted from the CPLR as "self-evident". See 2d Rep.Leg. Doc. (1958) No.13, p. 372.

2. In the surrogate's court, a guardian ad litem must be a New York attorney. SCPA 404. Bolsinger v. Bolsinger, 144 A.D.2d 320, 533 N.Y.S.2d 934 (2d Dep't 1988).

3. CPLR 1204.

4. See Matter of Becan, 26 A.D.2d 44, 270 N.Y.S.2d 923 (1st Dep't 1966).

5. Bolsinger v. Bolsinger, note 2 above.

6. Matter of Fassig, 58 Misc.2d 252, 295 N.Y.S.2d 146 (Surr.Ct., Nassau County, 1968).

7. See Petker v. Rudolph, 168 Misc. 909, 6 N.Y.S.2d 296 (Sup.Ct., Bronx County, 1938), aff'd 258 A.D. 1040, 17 N.Y.S.2d 1020 (1st Dep't 1940).

§ 199

1. See and compare Glogowski v. Rapson, 20 Misc.2d 96, 198 N.Y.S.2d 87 (Sup.Ct., Monroe County, 1959).

2. See, e.g., Rima v. Rossie Iron–Works, 120 N.Y. 433, 24 N.E. 940 (1890).

may be short-lived.[3] The adverse party in such a situation would therefore do well to assume the initiative of getting a guardian ad litem appointed for the ward.[4]

The ward status retained by infants and incompetents also accounts for the provision precluding default judgments against them until proper representation has been secured,[5] and for the requirement of a court order before a controversy involving a ward can be submitted to out-of-court arbitration.[6]

§ 200. Settlement of Infant's or Incapacitated Person's Claim

The settlement of the claim of an infant or incapacitated person requires court approval, which is applied for with a motion or special proceeding. If an action has been brought, there is a pending litigation that furnishes a context and a motion is the procedure. If no action has been brought, context is lacking and a special proceeding is used, brought in the court in which, based on the amount of the settlement, an action for that sum would have been brought. Whether the motion or special proceeding is the appropriate device, it should be brought on by order to show cause.[1] If the motion procedure is used, an approval of the settlement results in an order and the order has the effect of a judgment.

CPLR 1208 prescribes the papers to be submitted and the incidental procedure to be followed, and the rules elaborate.[2] These requirements should be carried out to the letter. On the hearing of the settlement application the applicant, the ward, and the ward's attorney must attend before the court "unless attendance is excused for good cause".[3] The ward and representative must be consulted about the settlement—often referred to in practice as a "compromise"—and it can't ordinarily be effected by their attorney without consultation.[4] But even though consultation is necessary, the court can approve the settlement over the ward's objection[5] and even over the objection of the representative,[6] unlikely though that may be.[7] Sometimes the ward's representative, deeming a settlement at a given figure a fair one and of a mind to encourage the defendant to pay it quickly, may try to push the settlement by purporting to give the defendant an agreement indemnifying the defendant for anything that a court may later award beyond the settlement sum. To discourage this, such agreements have been declared invalid.[8] They of course don't bind the ward, but neither may they be enforced against the representative. The voiding of such agreements has been deemed necessary to prevent the representative, perhaps motivated by selfish interest, from relaxing diligence in behalf of the ward.

---

3. See Oneida Nat. Bank & Trust Co. v. Unczur, 37 A.D.2d 480, 326 N.Y.S.2d 458 (4th Dep't 1971); Anderson v. Anderson, 164 A.D. 812, 150 N.Y.S. 359 (1st Dep't 1914).

4. CPLR 1202(a)(3).

5. CPLR 1203. A default taken in violation of this requirement will be vacated. State Bank of Albany v. Murray, 27 A.D.2d 627, 275 N.Y.S.2d 985 (3d Dep't 1966). CPLR 1203 was not amended in 1981 to add the conservatee when the surrounding provisions in Article 12 were (L.1981, c.115), but it is best read as applying to a conservatee as well. The court's general power to vacate default judgments would cover the situation in any event.

6. CPLR 1209. The statute makes an exception for uninsured and underinsured motorist cases, where court permission for arbitration of the infant's claim is not required.

§ 200

1. CPLR 1207, by providing that "[n]otice of the motion or petition shall be given as directed by the court", means to require use of the show cause procedure. See § 248 below.

2. Uniform Rule 202.67, applicable in the supreme and county courts, supplies detailed procedure for the settlement application. Uniform Rules of other courts then adopt that rule by reference, e.g., 208.36 (N.Y.C. Civil Court), 212.36 (district courts), and 210.36 (city courts).

3. CPLR 1208(d). Bittner v. M.V.A.I.C., 45 Misc.2d 584, 257 N.Y.S.2d 521 (Sup.Ct., N.Y.County, 1965), demonstrates the strictness of the court's approach to CPLR 1208. The provision applies even when the settling party is a governmental entity or is otherwise involved in the public interest (as the MVAIC is).

4. See Fasano v. City of New York, 22 A.D.2d 799, 254 N.Y.S.2d 133 (2d Dep't 1964).

5. Armour v. Broadman, 283 A.D. 351, 128 N.Y.S.2d 281 (1st Dep't), aff'd 307 N.Y. 896, 123 N.E.2d 90 (1954).

6. Glogowski v. Rapson, 20 Misc.2d 96, 198 N.Y.S.2d 87 (Sup.Ct., Monroe County, 1959).

7. See Lee v. Gucker, 27 A.D.2d 722, 279 N.Y.S.2d 697 (1st Dep't 1967).

8. Valdimer v. Mt. Vernon Hebrew Camps, Inc., 9 N.Y.2d 21, 210 N.Y.S.2d 520, 172 N.E.2d 283 (1961).

The disposition of the proceeds of an infant's claim is prescribed by statute,[9] as is the procedure for applying an infant's property towards the infant's support and maintenance.[10]

The court's approval of an infant's settlement does not necessarily bar an action for legal malpractice against the lawyer who negotiated the settlement for the infant. While the settlement acts like a judgment and (absent fraud or the like) forever protects the opposing party from the claim, it has been held that it offers no such insulation to the infant's lawyer, against whom malpractice may be established on the basis of simple professional negligence or incompetence in negotiating the settlement.[11]

9. CPLR 1206.
10. CPLR 1211.

11. See Fletcher v. Hatch, 197 A.D.2d 775, 602 N.Y.S.2d 718 (3d Dep't 1993).

Chapter Eight

PAPERS

§ 201. Form of Papers

CPLR 2101 governs the form of papers in New York practice, with further elaboration in the rules.[1] All papers are to be of letter size, 11 x 8½ inches,[2] with the exception of summonses, subpoenas, notices of appearance, notes of issue, and exhibits.[3] Exhibits can be of any size. The other excepted papers are usually printed forms that have traditionally been short and which continue to be acceptable in reduced size. Use of the short paper even in those few instances is optional; when the needs of the case require it the usual letter size may be used. Where, for example, the action involves so many parties that the usual short-form summons can't contain them, a regular letter-size paper can be used. And it can be typed.

There is no mystique in print and the CPLR does not require printing. It requires only that "the writing shall be legible and in black ink".[4] Printed forms are acceptable whenever they do the job. The mere fact that they are in print guarantees nothing, of course, else anyone with a little printing press could claim the earth.

Except for the summons, print size must be at least 10–point type. For the summons, the minimum required is 12–point type.[5] It has been held that using smaller than 12–point is not jurisdictional,[6] but the lawyer should not take chances with as key a document as a summons.[7] Litigation backs may continue to use smaller type.[8]

Each paper used in the case should have a caption. This consists of the name of the court and the venue of the action, its title, and, to the right of the title, what the paper is—complaint, answer, notice of motion, demand for change of venue, etc. Also to the right of the title the case's index number should appear if the case has already been assigned one,[9] and in courts using the Individual Assignment

---

§ 201

1. Rule 202.5 of the Uniform Rules, governing papers filed in the supreme and county courts, contains several instructions on form, in effect codifying a number of practices, like requiring the cover and the first page of each paper to state the action's venue and a brief description of what the paper is. There are equivalent Uniform Rules for the filing of papers in other courts: 205.7 (family court); 206.5 (Court of Claims); 207.4 (surrogate's court); 208.4 (N.Y.C. Civil Court); 212.4 (district courts); and 210.4 (city courts).

2. The old legal size was abandoned by amendment of CPLR 2101 in 1973, effective in 1974. The appellate courts apparently didn't deem themselves bound by the new 11 x 8½ rule and some continued to use the longer legal size. By early 1988, the Court of Appeals and three of the four appellate divisions had gone over to 11 x 8½ voluntarily, the Second Department holding out for a while but finally

going along as well. These momentous events were duly noted in New York State Law Digests Nos. 339 and 347.

3. CPLR 2101(a).

4. Id.

5. Id.

6. See United States Fid. & Guar. Co. v. King Van, Sup.Ct., Nassau County, Dec. 12, 1995 (Index No. 8196/95; Ain, J.), noted in SPR 40:3.

7. See the discussion in SPR 28.

8. A memorandum circulated to the clerks by the Office of Court Administration so provides, noting that the various notices, verifications, certifications, and the like that appear on litigation backs are just "secondary or ancillary material peripheral to the case".

9. CPLR 2101(c).

System, or IAS,[10] such as the supreme court, the name of the judge should also be set forth if one has been assigned.[11]

The only three papers required to name all parties are the summons, complaint, and judgment. All others need only name the first party on each side, with an "et al." or the like to indicate that there are more.[12]

Each paper served or filed must bear the name, address, and telephone number of the lawyer for the party serving or filing it, or of the party herself if she is appearing pro se.[13] It was for a long time sufficient if the attorney's name was typed or printed; an actual subscription was not required.[14] That was changed as of March 1, 1998, when an amendment of the sanctions rule, Rule 130–1 of the Rules of the Chief Administrator, took effect. It requires the actual subscription, by an attorney, to all papers "served on another party or filed or submitted to the court",[15] and that includes pleadings, motions, and any other paper that has traditionally born the printed or typed name of the lawyer.

The signature automatically constitutes the attorney's certification, without any formal attestation or certification language being required, of the integrity of the paper to the best of the attorney's knowledge. The language of the rule is that merely "[b]y signing a paper, an attorney ... certifies".[16] The bar had many questions about the signing requirement and its implications,[17] including how far the lawyer has to go in checking into the facts supplied by the client before in effect certifying the paper with a signature. While answers to these more substantive issues will have to await judicial

resolution,[18] early caselaw addressed to some procedural incidentals held that in the absence of prejudice to the other side the inadvertent omission of a signature is curable by supplying it late,[19] and that this applies even to the summons.[20]

Lawyers must note that a significant violation of the signature requirement, as by signing a paper the lawyer knows or should know contains false or misleading data, amounts to a frivolous litigation practice and can result in heavy sanctions.[21]

A typing or printing of the name must appear beneath the signature[22] to assure that it can be read.

The CPLR is generally content to have copies rather than originals used, whether for service or filing.[23] It is common practice to save the "original" for the court, serving mere copies on parties. In this technological age it may be hard in many cases to distinguish between them. (Filing or serving by electronic means, incidentally, is barely at an experimental stage in New York at the present time.)

If a copy of some paper is required to be formally "certified"—distinguish this from the automatic certification implied by a lawyer's signature—the certification need not be made by the clerk with whom the paper is on file; it can be made by the attorney.[24]

CPLR 2101(f) provides that any defect in mere form, if no one is prejudiced by it, shall be disregarded or at worst corrected. This provision overlaps CPLR 2001, the CPLR's general statute about forgiving or amending harm-

---

10. See § 77A above.

11. See Uniform Rule 202.5(a).

12. CPLR 2101(c).

13. CPLR 2101(d).

14. 2d Rep.Leg.Doc. (1958) No.13, p.174.

15. Rule 130–1.1–a.

16. Rule 130–1.1–a(b).

17. See the three-part treatment in SPR 66–68.

18. Federal caselaw on Rule 11 of the Federal Rules of Civil Procedure, on which the 1998 amendment of Rule 130–1 was modeled, can supply some guidance in the interim.

19. Di Russo v. Hendrick, Sup.Ct., Westchester County, March 9, 1998 (Index No. 2033/97, Lefkowitz, J.), treated in SPR 69:2.

20. See SPR 70:1.

21. Sanctions are treated in § 414A below.

22. CPLR 2101(a).

23. CPLR 2101(e).

24. CPLR 2105. The thing certified is that the paper has been compared with the original and "found to be a true and complete copy." That is all a certification is. At one time it was necessary for the certifier to compare the original and the copy line by line and word by word—visions of a clerk on a high stool in a Dickens setting. Today xerography does the job.

less mistakes,[25] but it is even less tolerant of nit-picking. When the defect is one of mere form, the one served with the paper must, in order to preserve the objection, return the paper within two days with "a statement of particular objections". If the defect is truly one of mere form, the complaining party will even then be disappointed, because the best he can expect is an amendment to correct the form.

Papers served or filed are often stapled into a "back" of some kind, variously known as a "blue-back" or "litigation-back", or the like, but there is no official color or name, nor even requirement, for it. It is available through legal stationers and has a number of handy printed forms on it, such as verifications (for use with pleadings), affidavits of service, notices of entry or settlement, admissions of service, and the like, to use in conjunction with the particular paper enclosed. Firms with heavy litigation practices order stocks of these forms with the firm name, address, and telephone number printed on them. Unless there is a need to use one of the form boxes included on the back, in which event the use of the back may spare the use of a separate paper for the needed form (like an affidavit, notice of entry, etc.), it may be idle as well as environmentally inappropriate to use a back.

§ 202. Service of Papers; Method and Time Computation

The only kind of service studied so far is service of the summons, which is governed by CPLR 308. CPLR 308 allows various methods but nothing as simple as mere mailing. (CPLR 312-a allows mailing, but not a "mere" mailing; it sets up a special procedure, as noted in § 76A.) For the service and filing of almost all the rest of the mass of papers that fly back

and forth in litigation, ordinary first-class mailing is the common method of service.

CPLR 308 and its punctilious demands apply to the service of jurisdiction-getting papers. The summons is the main one, securing jurisdiction of the defendant in an action. Another is the notice of petition, securing jurisdiction of a respondent in a special proceeding.[1] The subpoena is also considered a jurisdiction-getting paper, in this instance securing jurisdiction of a witness. Those papers must therefore be served in the same manner as a summons,[2] and so it falls to CPLR 308 to govern them.

But for almost all other papers served and filed in litigation after jurisdiction has been secured—papers sometimes called "interlocutory" or "intermediary" papers—CPLR 2103 governs. Its subdivision (a) is the source of the permission for any nonparty over 18 to serve papers in New York practice.[3] Subdivision (b) then supplies the rules about how intra-action papers are to be served, which makes it one of the busier provisions of the CPLR.

It is profitable to spend a preliminary moment on how time periods are computed in New York practice,[4] since many if not most papers in litigation have to be served on or before a particular day. The day from which a time period runs is excluded in the computation.[5] If a plaintiff has 20 days to reply to a counterclaim, for example, and the answer containing the counterclaim is served on April 1, the last day for serving the answer is April 21. The count starts on April 2 and counting 20 days with April 2 as the first day makes the last day the 21st. If the last day falls on a Saturday, Sunday, or legal holiday,[6] the time is extended until "the next succeeding business

---

25. See § 6, above, which discusses CPLR 2001.

§ 202

1. See § 553 below.

2. CPLR 403(c) (special proceedings); CPLR 2303 (subpoenas). CPLR 308 would also govern in any other instance in which service is directed to be made in the same manner as a summons, as required, for example, by CPLR 5231(c) and (d) for an income execution.

3. This provision also governs summons service. There is no CPLR rule that summons servers be licensed, but there may be a local requirement to that effect, as there is

in New York City for those serving more than a certain number of summonses a year. See NYC Administrative Code §§ 20–403 to 20–409.

4. Passing mention was made of the applicable General Construction Law statutes in §§ 33 and 34, above, on the statute of limitations, where inaccurate time reckoning can of course have its most serious consequences.

5. See, e.g., Gen.Constr.L. § 20.

6. The list of legal holidays is in Gen.Constr.L. § 24.

day".[7] The time extensions when a paper is served by mail or by an overnight service, to be discussed below, must be factored in accordingly.

Perhaps the most significant aspect of CPLR 2103(b) is its requirement that interlocutory papers be served on the attorney rather than the party. Only if the party is appearing without an attorney, or if the attorney is unservable, may the service be made on the party directly.[8] Hence, as soon as it is perceived that a party is appearing by attorney, all further contacts with that party by the opposing attorney, including the service of papers, must be made through that party's attorney.

The attorney may of course be served by personal delivery,[9] but that method is generally used only when there is some special hurry or when lawyers' offices are in close proximity. The most common method is ordinary first-class mail to the lawyer's office address,[10] as set forth on the last paper served by that lawyer in the action. The paper must be enclosed in a properly stamped envelope,[11] and it is deemed served—i.e., service is deemed complete—when it is merely dropped into the letter box or mail chute or other official post office gadget or postal official's hand.[12] The receptacle or office must be in New York State, however, or the paper will not be deemed served when posted.[13] A mailing from outside the state does not invoke the rule,[14] and the service will be deemed complete only upon receipt, not posting. This can have serious consequences when a paper must be served within a stated time, such as a notice of appeal, whose untimely service is not curable with a simple time extension.

Delivery through an overnight delivery service, like Federal Express or the U.S. Post Office's own "Express Mail", which is also permitted, is deemed complete when the paper is delivered into the custody of the particular service prior to the latest time it requires in order to assure overnight delivery.[15] Service by "electronic means", such as facsimile ("fax") machine, is also permitted for interlocutory papers. (It is not yet authorized for summons service.[16]) When fax service is used, it is also necessary to mail a copy of the paper to the fax recipient.[17]

Fax service, even of mere interlocutory papers, requires the consent of the recipient. Including a fax number on a paper served in the action (such as a litigation back containing a pleading, motion, etc.), signifies such consent, but it has been held that its inclusion only on an office letterhead does not.[18] The point is somewhat mooted by the rule that permission to use fax, even if granted, can be withdrawn at any time merely by serving a

---

7. See Gen.Constr.L. §§ 25 (for periods set by contract) and 25–a (for periods set by statute), which also contain instructions for when a particular hour is specified. If no hour is specified, and it rarely is, service can be made at any time on the last day.

8. CPLR 2103(c). If neither the party nor his attorney is servable, the paper can simply be filed with the clerk. CPLR 2103(d).

9. CPLR 2103(b)(1).

10. CPLR 2103(b)(2). Paragraph 3 of CPLR 2103(b) allows service on the attorney by delivering it to the person in charge of the attorney's office or inserting it into the office letter drop. Paragraph 4 allows service at the lawyer's residence, but only if service can't be made at the office.

11. If the postage is insufficient but the adverse party pays the difference and accepts the paper, all is in order and the recipient can't later reject or return it. Jack London Products, Inc. v. Edkiss, 17 Misc.2d 453, 187 N.Y.S.2d 671 (Sup.Ct., N.Y.County, 1959). The rule might be otherwise if the addressee refuses to pay the postage due, if, indeed, the post office should undertake delivery without sufficient postage.

12. CPLR 2103(b)(2).

13. See CPLR 2103(f)(1).

14. See National Org. for Women v. Met. Life Ins. Co., 70 N.Y.2d 939, 524 N.Y.S.2d 672, 519 N.E.2d 618 (1988), discussed in a note in New York State Law Digest No. 384.

15. CPLR 2103(b)(6).

16. The attempted filing of a court of claims case by fax was rejected in Espinal v. State, Ct.Cl., Claim No. 86418, Motion No. M–54289, Jan. 21, 1997 (Mega, J.), and the claim dismissed.

17. CPLR 2103(b)(5). The fax statute speaks of "mailing" an additional copy of the faxed paper, but this would apparently include the alternative of the overnight delivery service provided for in CPLR 2103(b)(6).

18. See Levin v. Levin, 160 Misc.2d 388, 609 N.Y.S.2d 547 (Sup.Ct., Nassau County, 1994). The case involved an order to show cause, which can be deemed a category of process, and, as noted in the text, there's no present authority for serving a summons or other process by fax. Perhaps papers of a more obviously interlocutory nature can be sent by fax based only on a letterhead fax number.

notice on the would-be user.[19]

Fax service is complete "upon the receipt by the sender of a signal from the equipment of the attorney served indicating that the transmission was received, and the mailing of a copy of the paper to that attorney".

Although service by ordinary mail is deemed complete upon the mere posting, a showing that the paper was never received will usually prompt the court to undo any default predicated on the absence of a response. A mere denial of receipt, however, especially when set forth in unconvincing affidavits, will not suffice to raise an issue of service.[20] Common courtesy among members of the bar should prompt the serving attorney to inquire into the reason for an adversary's lack of response, and when that comity is extended these problems don't arise.

A lost argument about the mailing or receipt of a mailed paper can sometimes have serious consequences. It is to the credit of the bar that there are so few disputes—at least relatively few—about whether or not a mailed paper was received, and to the credit of the bench that so few of these few get as far as the "contest" stage. But occasionally the contest comes on, and has telling effect. It did in Engel v. Lichterman,[21] for example, and went all the way to the Court of Appeals. It was a dispute about whether a conditional order allowing P a new period in which to serve a bill of particulars[22] was received by P. D said he mailed it, and won the argument when P could only protest that he didn't receive it. The court apparently did not believe P, and D ended up with summary judgment. P had been lax in earlier phases of the case, whose lesson is the negative effect dilatory conduct can have on the procrastinator's credibility,[23] even on so seemingly picayune a point as whether a mailed paper was received.[24]

The one who mails the paper, usually a secretary or someone else in the lawyer's employ, should fill out an affidavit of mail service. This may be done on the litigation back encasing the original, or on a separate sheet, which is retained as proof of service for ultimate filing in court.

To secure a piece of more objective evidence that a paper was mailed, some lawyers sometimes use certified or even registered mail. While permissible,[25] it is not necessary,[26] and it will sometimes bring on delays, as when the post office does not deliver the envelope because it cannot obtain a signature of receipt. The lawyer who wants some post office evidence of a mailing can simply obtain from the post office a "Certificate of First–Class Mailing", not to be confused with either "certified" or "registered" mail. Its cost is nominal. It recites that a piece of first-class mail was posted, and involves no signature-seeking activities.

We meet at this point the provisions about the additional days the recipient gets for responding to a paper when it is served by mail or by an overnight delivery service. The additional time is 5 days when the paper is served by mail, but only 1 day if it is served through an overnight delivery service.

CPLR 2103(b)(2) provides that whenever a period of time is measured from the service of a paper and the paper is served by mail, the party required to take the responsive step gets 5 additional days.[27] This recognizes that the service was deemed complete upon posting and it compensates for the delay in mail delivery. This 5–day addition has ubiquitous application and in fact has to be superimposed on a number of time periods we have already met. Where, for example, D serves on P a demand for a change of venue, P has 5 days in which to

---

19. CPLR 2103(b)(5).

20. See 14 Second Avenue Realty Corp. v. Szalay, 16 A.D.2d 919, 229 N.Y.S.2d 722 (1st Dep't 1962).

21. 62 N.Y.2d 943, 479 N.Y.S.2d 188, 468 N.E.2d 26 (1984).

22. Bill of particulars practice is taken up in § 238 et seq., below.

23. See § 231A below.

24. The Engel case is treated in a lead note in New York State Law Digest No. 300.

25. See Cohen v. Shure, 153 A.D.2d 35, 548 N.Y.S.2d 696 (2d Dep't 1989).

26. Registered mail is especially gratuitous because it's more expensive, designed as it is primarily for the shipment of valuables.

27. Before 1983 it was 3 days. Many cases involving the issue refer to the 3–day period.

respond to it.[28] If the demand was served by mail, however, which is usually the procedure, the 5 days become 10. The 5 days are added to the stated period when any mail-served paper requires a responsive step within a stated period. The CPLR has a big array of these periods.

Note that the 5–day mail extension does not apply in administrative proceedings.[29] Note also that it will not apply even in litigation when a particular statute specifically provides that the *receipt* of the paper starts the time for responding to it, as occurs, for example, with the 90–day demand procedure that must precede a motion to dismiss for neglect to prosecute.[30]

When an overnight delivery service is used, the 5–day addition is reduced to a mere 1–day addition.[31] No additional time for responding is prescribed when fax service is used, but since fax service must also be accompanied by a mailing of the faxed paper, it can be argued that the time addition applicable to the mailing or overnight delivery (whichever is used to back-up the fax service) will be applicable. Otherwise, because a fax transmission is immediate, there would presumably be no time extension, a situation an attorney can avoid for the present by withholding permission for fax service.

If any confusion should arise in a given situation about just how long a responding period is, whether because of the additional day or days or otherwise, the one expecting the response should not be too hasty to treat the other side as in default. Attorneys must bear in mind the court's broad power under CPLR 2004 to extend time periods, and to do so even after the applicable period has expired.[32] That power is likely to be invoked with lightning swiftness to preclude major confrontations over minor time omissions traceable to the

impact of the 5–day mail extension, or to disagreements about what kind of time extension attends what kind of service, at least in situations when the time provision involved does not have jurisdictional impact. (Here again the notice of appeal comes forth as the example of a procedure in which the time element does affect jurisdiction.)

The additional time is added to responding periods not only when it is a statute or rule that sets the responding time, but also when a court order does,[33] as illustrated in the *Engel* case discussed above.

It must always be kept in mind that the 5–day or 1–day add-ons apply only to papers served within an already commenced and pending litigation. They do not apply—as already noted—at least not by their own force from their niche in CPLR 2103(b), to papers served in an administrative or other out-of-court proceeding, even if the particular paper is the final step in the proceeding and its service starts the statute of limitations applicable to a court action to review the determination.[34] Indeed, it is especially in that situation that a party must avoid thinking there is extra time. Some cases below Court of Appeals level hold or assume that the extensions do apply in those situations,[35] and lawyers who put all their eggs into that basket are likely to lose the eggs.

The provision requiring service on the attorney applies as soon as a party appears by one. (The plaintiff appears by attorney as soon as a summons bearing the lawyer's name is served on the defendant.) This covers the whole of the litigation, and can even go beyond. A notice of appeal, for example, must still be served on the would-be respondent's attorney. And for the purpose of authorizing a judgment

---

28. CPLR 511(b). See § 123 above.

29. See De Milt v. Tax Appeals Tribunal, 232 A.D.2d 824, 649 N.Y.S.2d 66 (3d Dep't 1996), noted in SPR 70:3. .

30. CPLR 3216(b)(3). Public Serv. Mut. Ins. Co. v. Zucker, 225 A.D.2d 308, 639 N.Y.S.2d 5 (1st Dep't 1996). The dismissal for neglect to prosecute is treated in § 375 below.

31. CPLR 2103(b)(6), added in 1989. Before that, the 5–day addition for responding was held to apply even when express mail, with a guaranteed next-day delivery,

was used. See Application of Rolm Corp., 127 Misc.2d 662, 487 N.Y.S.2d 309 (Sup.Ct., Queens County, 1985).

32. See § 6, above, in which CPLR 2004 is discussed.

33. Corradetti v. Dales Used Cars, 102 A.D.2d 272, 477 N.Y.S.2d 779 (3d Dep't 1984).

34. Fiedelman v. N.Y. State Dep't of Health, 58 N.Y.2d 80, 459 N.Y.S.2d 420 (1983).

35. See, e.g., Miller v. General Electric Co., 102 A.D.2d 966, 477 N.Y.S.2d 834 (3d Dep't 1984).

creditor's attorney to execute a satisfaction of judgment, the attorney's authority extends 10 years beyond the judgment's entry.[36]

CPLR 2103(b) authorizes the court to determine whom to serve in doubtful situations. A judge's aid can be obtained by resorting to an order to show cause.[37]

The filing of all papers with the court, as opposed to their service on other parties, is not a general requirement of New York law, as has already been noted.[38] Filing is required in some instances[39] and permissible in just about all instances. Whether required or volunteered, the filing takes place with the clerk of the court in which the action has been brought.[40]

§ 203. Service on All Parties

Lawyers sometimes wonder whether they are required to serve a given set of papers on all parties, or only on adverse parties or those affected by the particular papers. CPLR 2103(e) does not leave them guessing. It requires that each paper be served "on every other party who has appeared". Thus, attorneys must make it their practice to draw papers in sufficient copies to enable one to be served on each of the other parties to the action, no matter whose side they are on, and without regard to any notions about who is or isn't interested in the particular paper. All the parties will make that judgment for themselves.

Parties who have not appeared ordinarily need not be served. If the particular party's time to appear has not yet expired, the one seeking to serve some paper on that party should wait for its expiration before assuming the party is in default, so as not to have to serve him. If a new or additional claim is being asserted against a party who has not appeared, however, even if that party is long in default, it must not only be served on her: it must be served on her in the same manner as a summons.[1] This is to prevent a default from being taken against the non-appearing party on some claim of which he did not have due notice, and it therefore applies whether or not the original responding time has expired.[2]

If the party—ordinarily a defendant—who wants to serve some paper does not know who has or has not appeared, so as to assess her duties under CPLR 2103(e), she may demand a list of the appearers from the plaintiff's attorney, who knows who they are because they appear by serving their papers on him.[3] The plaintiff must furnish the list, and must include in it the names and addresses of the parties' attorneys. A defendant who wants to cross-claim co-defendants, for example, may have to depend on a list furnished by the plaintiff under this provision.

The aim of CPLR 2103(e) is to keep all parties posted of all steps taken in the action. Those who fail to appear are deemed to waive being kept posted. One who does appear but then defaults at some later stage of the proceedings is not held to this waiver, however, and therefore retains the right to be served with all papers, and an important right this can be. A party may wish, for example, to concede liability but contest at the damages trial,[4] or to keep track of foreclosure proceedings against her so as to assure that the sale of her property fulfills applicable requirements,[5] or, in a multi-party case, to see what co-defendants are doing so as to ascertain whether he might be the beneficiary of some defense they

---

36. CPLR 5020(b).

37. Show cause orders are treated in § 248, below.

38. See § 77 above

39. A prime example is the note of issue, CPLR 3402(a), without whose filing the case doesn't get on the calendar. It is discussed in § 369 below.

40. CPLR 2102.

§ 203

1. CPLR 3012(a).

2. First Nat. City Bank v. Elsky, 62 Misc.2d 880, 312 N.Y.S.2d 325 (N.Y.C.Civ.Ct. 1970).

3. See § 110, above, for what constitutes an appearance.

4. An appearing but later defaulting defendant automatically gets the right to be notified of when the damages trial is to take place. A non-appearing defendant can assure himself this notice merely by serving the plaintiff with a demand pursuant to CPLR 3215(g)(2).

5. Even an appearance not made until after the entry of judgment entitles the appearer to notice of all subsequent steps. See and compare Jamaica Sav. Bank v. Spiro, 206 Misc. 897, 135 N.Y.S.2d 728 (Nassau County Ct., 1954).

put in. The party who has appeared is entitled to service of all later papers, which keeps that party apprised of all later proceedings notwithstanding a post-appearance default.

Even a tardy notice of appearance or answer should suffice to require that all further papers be served on the one interposing the appearance or answer, since both qualify as an "appearance" under CPLR 320(a) whether timely or not.[6]

§ 204. Stipulations

The parties can stipulate to almost anything in an action. The litigation is theirs and they can pretty much dispose of their rights any way they want to. But if they contemplate the need of any judicial aid in carrying out their stipulation, they must have it in writing. CPLR 2104 requires that all stipulations be written and subscribed by those to be bound, unless made in open court.[1] If made in open court, the stipulation should be taken down by the stenographer.[2] The purpose is to assure irrefutable proof of the agreement. It has also been held that the "personal notes" of a judge don't qualify as an "open court" stipulation.[3]

CPLR 2104 applies to stipulations of settlement as well as to stipulations affecting the management and incidentals of the case.[4] Attorneys purporting to represent their clients at settlement talks are assumed to be acting with authority. The Court of Appeals has even invoked the doctrine of apparent authority to prevent a party from reneging on a settlement by claiming that his attorney acted without his permission.[5]

Unless "reduced to the form of an order and entered", says CPLR 2104, the stipulation must be "subscribed" by the party to be bound by it, but it has been held that the party who prepared the stipulation is bound by it without an actual subscription.[6] Oral stipulations would be absolutely taboo if CPLR 2104 were applied rigidly, but they are nevertheless used by lawyers, especially for incidental matters like an extension of time for responding to some paper. To the bar's credit, an oral stipulation is not often reneged on. Even when it is, the courts have from time to time accepted it anyway, as when "there is no dispute" that the parties entered it.[7] It has been said that "a party is precluded from invoking CPLR 2104 to avoid an oral stipulation if it appears that the stipulation was made".[8] But if one side chooses to deny it, how can the other always be confident of proving it? It is risky to rely on oral stipulations, and especially risky to make it a habit. In some of the more generous cases upholding oral stipulations, it will be found that reliance on the stipulation led to some kind of default, and that the court could simply have invoked its broad default-vacating powers[9] without even addressing the stipulation.[10]

It is also worth noting that whether to vacate a default is a matter of discretion, that in

6. The court in the Jamaica case suggests that a late answer is by itself an insufficient appearance to require notice of further steps, a doubtful conclusion when made and even more doubtful today. Involved in the case was a foreclosure sale that would have been undone had the court held otherwise.

§ 204

1. It has been held that an arbitration panel qualifies as the equivalent of a court for this purpose. Central New York Regional Market Auth. v. John B. Pike, Inc., 120 A.D.2d 958, 503 N.Y.S.2d 462 (4th Dep't 1986).

2. Gonyea v. Avis Rent A Car System, Inc., 82 A.D.2d 1011, 442 N.Y.S.2d 177 (3d Dep't 1981).

3. Estate of Janis, 210 A.D.2d 101, 620 N.Y.S.2d 342 (1st Dep't 1994), noted in SPR 34:3.

4. In re Dolgin Eldert Corp., 31 N.Y.2d 1, 334 N.Y.S.2d 833, 286 N.E.2d 228 (1972). There is some indication in Dolgin that a stipulation in the judge's chambers would not satisfy as one made in "open court", but an important factor is that the substance of the alleged stipulation in

Dolgin was disputed. The test should be whether the stipulation, if not otherwise in writing, was taken down by a stenographer.

5. Hallock v. State of New York, 64 N.Y.2d 224, 485 N.Y.S.2d 510, 474 N.E.2d 1178 (1984). A loss of consortium claim has been held to be an adjunct of the injured spouse's personal injury claim for settlement purposes, so that the settlement of the injured party's claim, whether it mentions the consortium claim or not, automatically releases it. Buckley v. National Freight, Inc., 90 N.Y.2d 210, 659 N.Y.S.2d 841 (1997).

6. Stefaniw v. Cerrone, 130 A.D.2d 483, 515 N.Y.S.2d 66 (2d Dep't 1987).

7. Rhulen Agency, Inc. v. Gramercy Brokerage, Inc., 106 A.D.2d 725, 484 N.Y.S.2d 156 (3d Dep't 1984).

8. La Marque v. North Shore Univ. Hosp., 120 A.D.2d 572, 573, 502 N.Y.S.2d 219, 220 (2d Dep't 1986).

9. See § 427 below.

10. See the discussion in the La Marque case, note 8 above.

matters of discretion the appellate divisions are in effect the courts of last resort, and that discretion can take different turns in different courts and even among different panels of the same court. All in all, it is bad business to rely on oral stipulations.

The stipulation must be clear and all matters claimed to be covered by it must be set out; the court "cannot be asked to divine what was in counsel's mind or to seek the intent from other evidence".[11]

The party who consents to stipulate away some right, however minor, may of course condition it. D ordinarily has the option, for example, of using the answering time to either answer or move to dismiss.[12] But if P stipulates to extend D's time, P can limit the extension to the service of the defendant's answer, refusing to extend it for the making of a motion.[13] A stipulation extending the answering time without that qualification would be deemed to extend the moving time as well.[14]

The answering time is one of the most common periods extended, and the stipulation extending it is often oral. But even this frequent and pro forma extension must technically be in writing. It is sound practice for one of the parties to draw up the stipulation promptly and forward it to the other already signed (as where the one allowing the time extension prepares the stipulation), or for signing and return (as where the one seeking the extension prepares it). Some offices, when they seek the stipulation, draw it and send it to the other side's attorney with a stamped, self-addressed envelope for convenience.

The court can of course enforce the terms of any valid stipulation and will usually do so on motion.[15] The court also has the power to permit a stipulation to be withdrawn, but will exercise it only for good cause, such as where its purpose has been frustrated or where a condition that it contemplated has not materialized.[16] Fraud, collusion, mistake, accident, and the like may be grounds for setting aside the stipulation, especially if the status quo is restorable.[17] The remedy is a motion to vacate the stipulation, made to the court in which the action is pending, or to the court in which the stipulation was entered if there is no action pending.[18] If the stipulation had the effect of discontinuing or dismissing the action, however—such as can happen with a stipulation of settlement—some older cases hold that a plenary action would be necessary to undo the stipulation,[19] or even to enforce it.[20] The Court of Appeals cast doubt on those cases when it more recently held that even in that situation a mere motion can do the job, captioned in the presumably settled action.[21] A motion ought to suffice, just as it suffices to vacate a judgment on a myriad of grounds.[22]

§ 205. Affidavits

An affidavit is a sworn statement. Its utility at the trial itself, where live testimony from cross-examinable witnesses is the primary source of proof, is limited if not altogether absent. But it is the foremost source of proof on motions. The affidavit ordinarily begins with its venue (the state, county, and city in which it is made), contains an opening statement such as, "Mary Jones, being duly sworn, says", and then marches into a recitation of whatever it is that Mary Jones wants to say. At the end is her signature, subscribed and sworn to before a person authorized to admin-

11. Columbia Broadcasting Sys. v. Roskin Distribs., Inc., 31 A.D.2d 22, 24, 294 N.Y.S.2d 804, 806 (1st Dep't 1968), aff'd 28 N.Y.2d 559, 319 N.Y.S.2d 449, 268 N.E.2d 128 (1971).

12. CPLR 3211(e).

13. Venizelos v. Venizelos, 30 A.D.2d 856, 293 N.Y.S.2d 20 (2d Dep't 1968).

14. See CPLR 3211(e).

15. Allard v. Allard, 27 A.D.2d 776, 277 N.Y.S.2d 50 (3d Dep't 1967).

16. Central Valley Concrete Corp. v. Montgomery Ward & Co., 34 A.D.2d 860, 310 N.Y.S.2d 925 (3d Dep't 1970).

17. Matter of Frutiger, 29 N.Y.2d 143, 324 N.Y.S.2d 36, 272 N.E.2d 543 (1971).

18. Matter of Horton, 51 A.D.2d 856, 379 N.Y.S.2d 569 (4th Dep't 1976).

19. E.g., Schweber v. Berger, 27 A.D.2d 840, 277 N.Y.S.2d 855 (2d Dep't 1967).

20. Yonkers Fur Dressing Co. v. Royal Ins. Co., 247 N.Y. 435, 160 N.E. 778 (1928).

21. Teitelbaum Holdings, Ltd. v. Gold, 48 N.Y.2d 51, 421 N.Y.S.2d 556, 396 N.E.2d 1029 (1979).

22. See § 426 et seq., below, treating CPLR 5015.

ister oaths, usually a notary public, who then attests with his own signature that the affidavit was "Sworn to before me this 19th day of May, 1998." This is followed by the notary's stamp, including his number, or by the number written in.

It has been held that an affidavit properly signed and in other respects proper is sufficient even if it omits the statement that the affiant was duly sworn.[1]

Certain professionals have been authorized by CPLR 2106 to make written statements by mere affirmation by including words to the effect that their averments are "true under the penalties of perjury."[2] Such statements are the equivalent of affidavits without the need of a swearing ceremony or a notary's signature. The persons allowed merely to affirm in this way are New York attorneys, doctors, and dentists who are not parties to the action. One using this provision must actually subscribe the affirmation.[3]

A notary who continues to notarize documents after her commission has expired may be subject to both civil and criminal liability, but parties to lawsuits in which the documents so notarized are used apparently need not worry. The documents' validity is preserved by § 142–a of the Executive Law, a statute intended to let the public continue relying on "the presumption of validity" attending a notarized document.[4]

§ 206. Undertakings

Various provisions in the CPLR impose the requirement that an undertaking be furnished

in conjunction with a particular procedure. These are common with the provisional remedies, for example, where undertakings may be required by law[1] or by the court in its discretion.[2] In some instances, the furnishing of an undertaking may be optional, such as where it is given to stay the execution of a judgment pending an appeal.[3]

Wherever in the CPLR an undertaking, often referred to as a bond, may be statutorily or judicially mandated or voluntarily furnished by the party, the detailed rules governing it will be found centralized in Article 25 of the CPLR. While the lawyer usually understands an undertaking to be an obligation assumed by a surety to pay a sum of money on a stated contingency, and that is of course one recognized definition of the term,[4] the CPLR permits the one who is required to furnish an undertaking in a stated sum to deposit, instead, cash or United States or New York bonds in that sum.[5]

Acknowledging the scarcity of caselaw on Article 25, the court in City of New York v. Britestarr Homes, Inc.[6] treats how excepting to sureties under CPLR 2506 and justifying sureties under CPLR 2507 interplay, and how a motion under CPLR 2508 for a new or additional undertaking, which is permissible at any time, can cover an omission to make prompt use of the other provisions.

More will be said about undertakings in particular situations as those situations are met.[7]

§ 205

1. Collins v. AA Trucking Renting Corp., 209 A.D.2d 363, 618 N.Y.S.2d 801 (1st Dep't 1994). It has also been held that a notary's failure to sign the jurat is not a jurisdictional defect. See SPR 26:2–3.

2. False swearing in either an affidavit or CPLR 2106 affirmation constitutes perjury under Chapter 210 of the Penal Law.

3. Sandymark Realty Corp. v. Creswell, 67 Misc.2d 630, 324 N.Y.S.2d 504 (N.Y.C.Civ.Ct. 1971).

4. Parks v. Leahey & Johnson, 81 N.Y.2d 161, 597 N.Y.S.2d 278, 613 N.E.2d 153 (1993).

§ 206

1. E.g., in conjunction with an attachment, CPLR 6212(b), preliminary injunction, CPLR 6312(b), or receivership, CPLR 6403.

2. E.g., in conjunction with a temporary restraining order, CPLR 6313(c), or notice of pendency ("lis pendens"), CPLR 6515.

3. See CPLR 5519(a)(2).

4. CPLR 2501(1).

5. CPLR 2501(2).

6. 150 Misc.2d 820, 570 N.Y.S.2d 882 (Sup.Ct., Bronx County, 1991).

7. See, e.g., § 325 below.

Chapter Nine

PLEADINGS

Analysis

A. BASIC RULES OF PLEADING

Table of Sections

§ 207. Pleadings, Background

The liberalization of pleadings is one of the major accomplishments of the CPLR. The common law hoped that by requiring the parties to trade pleadings back and forth, the whole controversy could shortly be reduced to but a single succinct issue, or just a few clearly defined ones. The hope was forlorn, its offshoot was the exaltation of form over substance, its heritage was a set of forms of action into which all civil claims of whatever variety had to be squeezed, and the squeezing gave rise to the extended use of fictions. The Advisory Committee tackled the pleadings problem in its first report, where it offers both a background study[1] and a helpful bibliography.[2]

Under the old Civil Practice Act, the pleader had to set forth the "facts" relied on "but not the evidence" by which they would be proved.[3] The requirement to plead "facts" precluded the pleading of a conclusion of law. In the construction process, the cases carried this so far that it was apparently taboo to plead "negligence" in a negligence case because it was too conclusory.[4] But to furnish too much detail, on the other hand, made the pleading too

§ 207
1. 1st Rep.Leg.Doc. (1957) No.6(b), p.261.
2. Id. at 266.

3. Civ.Prac. Act § 241.
4. See Newell v. Woodward, 241 A.D. 786, 270 N.Y.S. 258 (3d Dep't 1934).

evidentiary. The pleader thus walked a tight-rope with an abyss on either side—one ready to consume him if the pleading was so summary that it amounted to a conclusion of law, and the other just as hungry if the pleading contained too much evidence. This rigidity was found to be too demanding without being productive, and was abandoned. The major culprit, around which the caselaw had built these rigid requirements, was the word "facts". The Advisory Committee therefore abandoned the word and with it fell the cases. If a pleading today otherwise satisfies the new pleading requirements—to be taken up shortly—its inclusion of a legal theory is permissible.[5] Nor is there any specific barrier in the CPLR against the inclusion of "evidence". It doesn't belong in the pleading, and including it is a burden assumed by the pleader gratuitously, but the inclusion does not by itself invalidate the pleading.

The decline in the importance of pleadings has its counterpart in the ascent of the disclosure devices.[6] Today those devices enable the parties to probe their adversaries' positions more incisively than pleadings ever could, and the free availability of the disclosure devices more than fills any gap left by the relaxation of the old pleadings requirements.

§ 208. The Basic Pleading Requirement

CPLR 3013 provides that

> Statements in a pleading shall be sufficiently particular to give the court and parties notice of the transactions, occurrences, or series of transactions or occurrences, intended to be proved and the material elements of each cause of action or defense.

Those few words are the theme of pleadings under the CPLR. The word "statements" in-

stead of "facts" is used mainly to eliminate the caselaw previously built around "facts". Averments in pleadings are still, of course, primarily factual.[1] The main mission of an affirmative pleading—as opposed to the defensive pleading taken up beginning in § 221 below—whether it is the main claim in the complaint, or a counterclaim or cross-claim in the answer, etc., is to give "notice" of the event out of which the grievance arises. If the pleading can be said to give that notice, the first pleading requirement is satisfied. If the allegations also cover the substantive material elements that make up the particular cause of action relied on, the second requirement is met and the pleading satisfies the CPLR. The major challenge to an affirmative pleading is a motion under CPLR 3211(a)(7) to dismiss it for failure to state a cause of action; a pleading that meets the two stated requirements successfully defeats that motion.[2]

All pleadings must be liberally construed. Draftsmanship is secondary. Under the CPLR, if a cause of action can be spelled out from the four corners of the pleading, a cause of action is stated and no motion lies under CPLR 3211(a)(7). The pleading can be pathetically drawn; it can reek of miserable draftsmanship. That is not the inquiry. We want only to know whether it states a cause of action—any cause of action. If it does, it is an acceptable CPLR pleading.[3]

The CPLR intention to make pleadings less rigid and to measure the validity of complaints solely by whether they state a cause of action was given a decisive judicial boost when, only half a year after the CPLR took effect, the case of Foley v. D'Agostino[4] was handed down. It sustained as adequately pleaded several derivative causes of action and in the course of

---

5. 1st Rep.Leg.Doc. at 63.

6. Article 31 of the CPLR supplies the disclosure devices. They are studied in Chapter 13.

§ 208

1. See Commentary C3013:4 on McKinney's CPLR 3013.

2. See Siegel, A Perspective on Pleading Under the CPLR: A Motion Yardstick, 38 St. John's L.Rev. 190, 198 (1963).

3. This is not to encourage sloppy pleading. If the pleading, although it states a cause of action and satisfies CPLR 3013, is so jumbled or disorderly that it can't be answered, the defendant can move to compel a more definite statement. That motion lies under CPLR 3024(a), studied in § 230 below, but that's a matter distinct from whether the pleading states a cause of action, and whether the pleading states a cause of action is the sole inquiry on a motion under CPLR 3211(a)(7).

4. 21 A.D.2d 60, 248 N.Y.S.2d 121 (1st Dep't 1964).

doing so sent the word out that the CPLR drafters' intention to relieve pleadings of their formalism was going to get not mere lip service, but full judicial cooperation, a view afterwards consistently approved by the Court of Appeals.[5]

It is not necessary that the claim pleaded be given any particular name. It can even be named wrong.[6] It is sufficient if the pleading alleges any cause of action that the law recognizes and on which it offers relief.[7] Its substance prevails over its articulateness.[8] Giving notice is the key. It has sometimes even been held under the CPLR that if the other party has gotten the requisite notice from some other source in the case, such as statements written on the summons itself, the notice requirement may be deemed satisfied.[9]

The several elements that make up the substantive claim must of course be covered by the allegations, but even in that fundamental regard an omission that appears to be remediable by a mere amendment will be remedied by just that, and not a dismissal. One of the substantive elements that make up a fraud claim, for example, is a showing that P relied on D's misrepresentation. When reliance is not alleged, the complaint violates CPLR 3013, but it has been held that a simple amendment can add the allegation and cure the defect.[10]

So successful was the *Foley* case in setting the tone for liberal pleadings that some practitioners may have gone a bit too far, and the same court, the First Department, had to remind the bar a few months later in another case that "it is still essential ... that the pleading enable the defendant to determine the nature of the plaintiff's grievances and the relief he seeks in consequence of the alleged wrongs".[11] Missing in that case were some

material elements, a clear violation of CPLR 3013, but the plaintiff was still allowed to replead.

It is only a want of notice or the absence of a material element that violates CPLR 3013. The lack of either prejudices the defendant because she can't prepare her case. Thus, a defendant who can show that CPLR 3013 has been violated can show prejudice. A showing of prejudice is the indispensable condition precedent to any application to the court for a remedy against an allegedly defective pleading.

CPLR 3026 says that pleadings shall be liberally construed. Even more significantly, it adds that "[d]efects shall be ignored if a substantial right of a party is not prejudiced". As will be seen, there are other pleading requirements besides those in CPLR 3013, applicable generally or in particular situations, but when CPLR 3013 has been fulfilled the likelihood is much reduced that some other defect will breed the prejudice needed to justify judicial intervention. Taking note of some of these other provisions, such as CPLR 3015 and 3016,[12] which impose special pleading requirements in designated situations, the court in *Foley* said that these, too, must be subordinated to CPLR 3013,[13] i.e., that a pleading satisfying CPLR 3013 is not likely to prejudice the other side even if some other provision is technically violated. When one of these others is violated in such a way as to prejudice the other party, moreover, the breach is likely to offend CPLR 3013 as well. The theme, in other words, is set by CPLR 3013, and everything else among the pleadings' requirements must be in harmony with it.

Two sections hence, when we look at some of the official forms of pleadings, illustrations will give color and body to these conclusions,

---

5. See, e.g., Guggenheimer v. Ginzburg, 43 N.Y.2d 268, 401 N.Y.S.2d 182, 372 N.E.2d 17 (1977).

6. Barrick v. Barrick, 24 A.D.2d 895, 264 N.Y.S.2d 888 (2d Dep't 1965).

7. CPLR 3017(a) governs the relief clause and is treated in § 217, below.

8. Dulberg v. Mock, 1 N.Y.2d 54, 150 N.Y.S.2d 180, 133 N.E.2d 695 (1956), so held even under prior law.

9. See Lederman v. McLean Trucking Co., 41 A.D.2d 5, 342 N.Y.S.2d 570 (2d Dep't 1973). This is not to encourage

the pleading to omit notice in reliance on its being given elsewhere. It just helps set the tenor for the liberalization of pleadings.

10. Brickner v. Linden City Realty, Inc., 23 A.D.2d 560, 256 N.Y.S.2d 533 (2d Dep't 1965).

11. Shapolsky v. Shapolsky, 22 A.D.2d 91, 253 N.Y.S.2d 816, 817 (1964).

12. CPLR 3015 is discussed in § 215, below; CPLR 3016, in § 216.

13. 21 A.D.2d at 63–64, 248 N.Y.S.2d at 125–26.

which at this stage are still the sterile products of introductory discourse.

§ 209. Theory of the Pleadings Rule Abolished

At various stages of prior law, a rule was applied to the effect that plaintiffs had to prove and recover on the very theory on which they pleaded. Where, for example, P pleaded in tort but was able to prove only a contract claim, P was denied a judgment.[1] This was known as the "theory of the pleadings" rule, and the CPLR has abandoned it.[2] It is today permissible, although of course not advisable, to prove a theory different from that pleaded, as long as the pleading gives notice of the transaction out of which the proved claim arises and covers its material elements. If no prejudice is shown, CPLR 3017(a) allows the court to grant "any type of relief . . . appropriate to the proof whether or not demanded", and CPLR 3025(c) permits an amendment to conform the pleadings to the proof. As long as the pleading embraces the elements of the proved claim, the fact that it theorizes it as something else is immaterial.[3]

Even before the CPLR, the Court of Appeals indicated that a plaintiff would not be bound by the theory pleaded if the theory proved was adequately embraced in the transactions of which the pleading gave notice and if no prejudice could be shown by the variance. In the well known case of Diemer v. Diemer,[4] the plaintiff husband sued for separation because his wife would not submit to sexual relations with him. His theory was that this was cruel and inhuman treatment. The Court of Appeals held that it was not, but proceeded to sustain the separation on the unpleaded and unargued theory of abandonment: it held that the wife's conduct amounted to an abandonment, if not to cruel treatment, and that either was a permissible ground for separation. Whatever criticism may be directed at such a conclusion— the parties were not even offered an opportunity to brief and argue the point—it surely inters all lingering notions about the existence of a theory-of-the-pleadings rule.

With the demise of that rule, and the substitution of a rule based on notice and prejudice, the only remaining problem concerns trial by jury. If, for example, P pleads an equitable claim, which does not get tried by jury,[5] but ends up proving a legal one, which does, an award of judgment would divest D of her right to jury trial. The converse is no problem, and apparently never was. When P sues at law, and a jury is present, but ends up proving an equity theory, judgment on the equity ground is permissible.[6] The judge, presiding at the trial all the while, can decide the facts and the jury's presence can be treated as superfluous. But when the case is pleaded in equity, and no jury is present to try it, the establishment of a mere law claim may not ground judgment if the defendant objects.[7]

The courts remain sensitive to preserving the right to trial by jury. Even when the case is denominated one in equity, the courts will allow its trial by jury if they believe it to be in essence a law case.[8] As a practical matter, the claim's sufficiency for pleading purposes is irrelevant to whether relief flowing from it is legal or equitable;[9] the only problem to be resolved in these situations, therefore, is how to preserve the right to trial by jury.

The problem is addressed by CPLR 4103. Although the plaintiff waives the right to trial

---

§ 209

1. Barnes v. Quigley, 59 N.Y. 265 (1874).

2. Lane v. Mercury Record Corp., 21 A.D.2d 602, 252 N.Y.S.2d 1011 (1st Dep't 1964), aff'd 18 N.Y.2d 889, 276 N.Y.S.2d 626, 223 N.E.2d 35 (1966).

3. See McGinnis v. Bankers Life Co., 39 A.D.2d 393, 334 N.Y.S.2d 270 (2d Dep't 1972).

4. 8 N.Y.2d 206, 203 N.Y.S.2d 829, 168 N.E.2d 654 (1960).

5. As to what claims are triable by jury in New York, see § 377 below.

6. Emery v. Pease, 20 N.Y. 62 (1859).

7. Jackson v. Strong, 222 N.Y. 149, 118 N.E. 512 (1917).

8. See, e.g., City of Syracuse v. Hogan, 234 N.Y. 457, 138 N.E. 406 (1923), in which an action asking for the equitable relief of injunction to remove an encroachment and to reform a deed was found to be at root an ejectment claim to test title (a law action) and thus required to be tried by jury.

9. Advance Music Corp. v. American Tobacco Co., 296 N.Y. 79, 70 N.E.2d 401 (1946).

by jury by pleading in equity, the defendant doesn't. In that situation the defendant must be given an opportunity to demand a jury. If the defendant does demand it, a new trial will be required, which will nullify the one just had before the judge. It's a high price to pay, but in the legislature's view a reasonable price to protect the right of trial by jury.

A similar problem arises when the plaintiff pleads both equitable and legal claims. When both kinds are pleaded in respect of the same transaction, the plaintiff waives jury trial on the legal claim, but, again, the defendant doesn't.[10] The defendant must specifically demand jury trial on the legal claim, however, or he, too, will be held to waive it.[11]

Yet another situation in which this problem of jury trial arises is where P sues in equity but D counterclaims with a legal cause of action. That happened in DiMenna v. Cooper & Evans Co.,[12] where P sued to foreclose a mechanic's lien (equity and no jury) and D counterclaimed for damages (law and jury trial) regarding the same transaction. The problem in a case like this is that the judge (the fact-finder on the equity claim) and the jury (the fact-finder on the law claim) can disagree on who breached the contract—or on some other fact that both claims have in common—in such a way as to create an irreconcilable conflict. That prospect was avoided in *DiMenna*, in which the jury's verdict was held to bind all parties on all claims, because D had apparently not insisted in time that the judge determine the facts on P's equity claim. But even if the judge had, the court could avoid the problem, and still can today, by treating the jury,

impaneled as of right to hear the law claim, as an "advisory" jury[13] to hear the equitable claim. Although the court can reject a mere advisory verdict, it ought to treat such a unique case as one triable of right by jury. When the U.S. Supreme Court, in an analogous situation, had before it several related maritime claims, some jury triable and some not, it held that the presence of one that was jury triable required all of the claims to be submitted to the jury and the verdict to be treated as binding.[14]

§ 210. Some Official Forms

There are a few handfuls of official forms of pleadings.[1] These are designed to offer the practitioner samples of "the simplicity and brevity of statement" contemplated by the CPLR.[2] Official Form 6, to illustrate, is a complaint in an action for goods sold and accepted. Its body, exclusive of the "wherefore" (the relief) clause, has only a few lines and reads:

Defendant owes plaintiff $20,000 for goods sold to, and accepted by, defendant between June 1, 1966 and December 1, 1966.

It fully satisfies CPLR 3013. The money lent complaint, Official Form 9, is even shorter:

Defendant owes plaintiff $20,000 for money lent by plaintiff to defendant on June 1, 1965.

Even the presumably involved tort case has its official illustration. Official Form 12 is a complaint in the so-called "pedestrian knockdown" case and has only three paragraphs:

1. On June 1, 1966, in a public highway called Broadway in New York City, defen-

---

10. CPLR 4102(c). If the claims arise out of separate transactions, the plaintiff does not waive jury trial of the law claim by joining the two. DiMenna v. Cooper & Evans Co., note 12, below.

11. I.H.P. Corp. v. 210 Central Park South Corp., 12 N.Y.2d 329, 239 N.Y.S.2d 547, 189 N.E.2d 812 (1963).

12. 220 N.Y. 391, 115 N.E. 993 (1917). Today, too, the interposition of a legal counterclaim where the plaintiff has brought an equitable claim does not waive jury trial of the counterclaim, CPLR 4102(c), but a specific demand for jury trial is still required and without it a waiver does result. CPLR 4102(a). These matters are elaborated in § 378, below.

13. In any case in which the court is to be the fact finder, the judge has the power to give the question to an

advisory jury, CPLR 4212, but in that case the verdict does not bind and the judge can disregard it and find the facts contra. See § 381 below.

14. Fitzgerald v. United States Lines Co., 374 U.S. 16, 83 S.Ct. 1646, 10 L.Ed.2d 720 (1963).

§ 210

1. They were promulgated in the 1960s by the Judicial Conference. Today, the power to promulgate forms is in the Chief Administrator of the Courts. CPLR 107. See §§ 5 and 7, above.

2. The language is that of CPLR 107, which confers the power to promulgate forms. See § 7 above.

dant C.D. negligently drove a motor vehicle against plaintiff who was then crossing the highway.

2. That motor vehicle was then owned by defendant E.F. and driven by defendant C.D. with defendant E.F.'s permission.

3. Solely as a result of defendant C.D.'s negligence, plaintiff was personally injured, lost earnings and incurred expenses for [e.g., care and treatment, etc.].

In several regards the form is archaic, and yet it still shows the simplicity aimed for. The last paragraph reflects the contributory negligence rule, applicable when the form was drafted. (The form hasn't yet been amended and updated.) Claims accruing on or after September 1, 1975, are governed by the comparative negligence rule,[3] which makes any culpable conduct of the plaintiff an affirmative defense for the defendant to plead,[4] which in turn makes it unnecessary for the plaintiff to plead that the defendant was "solely" to account for the occurrence.[5] There should also be added to the form an allegation that the case does not fall under the no-fault law and is therefore proper for a court action, another requirement adopted after the form was promulgated.[6]

In each instance, a "wherefore" clause concludes the complaint, setting forth the demand for relief.

These are fairly simple cases. More involved ones will naturally entail more extended pleading, but the brevity the forms are designed to illustrate comes across. Official Form 15, for example, a specific performance claim to convey land, has only five brief paragraphs. All of these forms, which bear the imprimatur of the court system itself, are generally terser by far than those in the commercial form books, and they are presumptively satisfactory as well.

The lawyer should not hesitate to adjust any form she consults, official or otherwise, to the needs of the case. For example, Official Form 12, above, is technically inadequate at the moment because it does not contain an allegation showing that the case satisfies the requirements applicable under the no-fault law for a fault suit.[7] The lawyer should merely add a paragraph containing the necessary allegations.

The lawyer who fears pleading error most often chooses to err on the side of too much rather than too little. It is interesting, therefore, to note that there may sometimes be just as much danger in pleading too much. In one case, for example, the complaint on a promissory note had 30 paragraphs. The court compared it with Official Form 5, which has only three. It held the complaint "inordinate" and unacceptable.[8]

§ 211. Pleading in the Federal and Lower Courts Compared

The federal pleading requirement comes from Rule 8 of the Federal Rules of Civil Procedure, which requires "a short and plain statement of the claim showing that the pleader is entitled to relief". The federal "claim" is for all practical purposes the same as the New York "cause of action",[1] and the measure of whether the pleading passes muster should be the same under both Federal Rule 8 and CPLR 3013. Pleading under the Federal Rules is at least as liberal as under the CPLR. In the well known federal case of Dioguardi v. Durning,[2] for example, decided early in the life of the Federal Rules, a plaintiff conversant with neither the law nor the English language appeared and pleaded pro se. He babbled on— even his spelling illustrated his accent—but the Court of Appeals for the Second Circuit sustained his complaint as stating not one but

3. CPLR 1413.

4. CPLR 1412.

5. See § 171 above.

6. CPLR 3016(g). See § 216 below.

7. CPLR 3016(g), added in 1974, for which see § 216 below.

8. Domestic Finance Corp. v. Milner, 59 Misc.2d 867, 868, 300 N.Y.S.2d 636, 637 (Sup.Ct., Onondaga County, 1969).

§ 211

1. Occasionally a case tries to distinguish the two terms, e.g., Garcia v. Hilton Hotels Int'l, Inc., 97 F.Supp. 5 (D.Puerto Rico 1951), but without much success.

2. 139 F.2d 774 (2d Cir.1944).

two claims. The lesson is not to encourage poor pleading, but to deter technical attacks on sufficient pleading.

As liberal as pleadings are under the CPLR, they are even more so in the lower courts in New York under the uniform court acts. In the New York City Civil Court and in the district, city, town, and village courts, pleading by mere "indorsement" is permitted in money actions. An indorsement is a brief statement of "the nature and substance of the cause of action". It can be appended to the summons or merely written or typed on it.[3] In other than money actions, a formal pleading is generally required in those courts, and there may be provisions in the rules of a particular court requiring formal pleadings even in enumerated money actions,[4] or, to the contrary, dispensing with formal pleading altogether in all actions under stated circumstances, such as where the plaintiff appears pro se.[5]

An indorsement pleading need not satisfy even the modest requirements of the CPLR,[6] which probably means that an indorsement can be little more than a short name or description of the cause of action.[7] If a formal complaint is required in one of the lower courts in a given case, whether by statute or rule, and an indorsement is used instead, the defect should be an amendable irregularity and a formal complaint should be permitted nunc pro tunc.[8] If only a bare summons is served, however, with neither a formal complaint nor an indorsement accompanying it, the defect has been held jurisdictional, resulting in a dismissal.[9] As a result of amendments effective in 1979, the service of a bare sum-

mons was eliminated as an option even in supreme and county court practice, and with the same result for a violation: dismissal of the action.[10]

§ 212. Separate Statement and Numbering

If CPLR 3013 can be considered the commanding general of pleadings, then CPLR 3014 should be deemed its chief of staff. CPLR 3014 contains, among other things, the instructions about numbering and stating allegations. Its preference is that every pleading "consist of plain and concise statements in consecutively numbered paragraphs"—already illustrated in Official Form 12 as set forth two sections back—and that each paragraph "contain, as far as practicable, a single allegation".

As a general rule, the assignment of a separately numbered paragraph to each factual allegation aids clarity and facilitates responsive pleading. (Admissions and denials in the answer thereby secure clearer reference points.) But this numbering requirement is governed by the "practicable" standard. If presentation is facilitated by including a few facts in a single paragraph, it is permissible, and many parts of even the official forms do that. Paragraph two of Official Form 12, for example, reads that the "motor vehicle was then owned by defendant E.F. and driven by defendant C.D. with defendant E.F.'s permission". There are three factual averments in that paragraph—ownership, operation, and permission—and yet it is not only good pleading, but official pleading. Breaking the statement down

---

3. See § 902(a) in the New York City Civil Court Act and in the Uniform District, City, and Justice court acts, McKinney's Vol. 29A, Parts 2 and 3.

4. See, e.g., Uniform Rule 212.7, applicable in the district courts.

5. See, e.g., Uniform Rule 208.7, applicable in the New York City Civil Court.

6. See § 903 in each of the lower court acts, note 3, above.

7. See the Commentary on § 903 in the New York City Civil Court Act. Since indorsement pleading is permissive rather than mandatory in the lower courts, lawyers there often elect the more formal pleading, but under the CPLR today the "formal" pleading itself is hardly a burdensome thing.

8. Creative Woodworking Co. v. Bohn, 44 Misc.2d 369, 253 N.Y.S.2d 711 (N.Y.C.Civ.Ct. 1964). Compare Knauer v. Long Island Airports Limousine Serv. Corp., 53 Misc.2d 1017, 280 N.Y.S.2d 343 (App.T., 1st Dep't, 1967). It has been held that if the rules authorize the court with an ex parte order to permit an indorsement complaint, the order can be granted nunc pro tunc. Onorati v. National Automatic Laundry & Cleaning Council, Inc., 85 Misc.2d 236, 379 N.Y.S.2d 295 (N.Y.C.Civ.Ct. 1976).

9. Paskus, Gordon & Hyman v. Peck, 41 Misc.2d 1004, 246 N.Y.S.2d 874 (N.Y.C.Civ.Ct. 1964).

10. In the supreme and county courts, the summons may be accompanied by a notice under CPLR 305(b) at the outset, instead of a complaint, the complaint to follow later under a demand procedure. See § 60 above.

into three separately numbered paragraphs is of course permissible, but would be awkward and verbose.

An adverse party who feels prejudiced by the pleader's failure to separately state and number can make a motion to compel it.[1]

Since factual averments within a single cause of action must be separately numbered, of course separate causes of action must also be separately stated and numbered. This sometimes necessitates the unrewarding search for a definition of a "cause of action"— a phrase of "shifting meanings" which "may mean one thing for one purpose and something different for another".[2] It is one of the most "theory-ridden of legal concepts" and cannot be defined except in its particular context.[3] Usually, the ultimate test of whether the plaintiff has one or several causes of action is resolved by applying the double recovery test: ask whether, if the plaintiff were to get a satisfied judgment on theory A, she could then turn around and seek more in a suit on theory B. It is usually easier to put and answer that question than to define a "cause of action", and yet the answer often supplies the needed definition. If the second recovery is permissible, the pleader has in fact two separate causes of action; if it is not, the pleader has but one cause of action, perhaps sustainable on several theories or grounds or counts. Where, for example, the plaintiff sustains one injury but it is actionable under the common law as well as under a statute, a frequent occurrence today, the plaintiff has but one cause of action.[4] Perhaps the most frequently met of this species today is the personal injury caused by a product. It usually supports three theories—negligence, breach of warranty, and strict liability—but it is only one cause of action.

The plaintiff who has separate grounds to support a single cause of action is entitled to the damages offered by the most generous of them. Not all of the counts or grounds will necessarily offer the same quantum of damages. A medical injury, for example, may support both a malpractice and a breach of contract claim. The contract claim does not support an award for pain and suffering,[5] while the malpractice claim does. The plaintiff who joins and prevails on both grounds of course recovers for pain and suffering, even though it pertains to but one ground. But the damage elements common to both counts, such as for further medical treatment, can't be duplicated. No matter how many counts support them, the plaintiff can recover for them only once.

How does this translate into our present purpose, which is to determine separate numbering requirements? Technically, if there's but one cause of action, its various possible theories or counts need not be separately stated and numbered as such. The facts needed to cover them all can be consecutively numbered, but introduced as only one claim: "Cause of action number one", or (favorite terminology among the more ancient members of the bar) "As and for a first cause of action". Quite often separate theories in support of but a single claim are separately numbered, harmlessly enough, as if they were distinct causes of action. The plaintiff who has only one claim— one ultimate "cause of action"—will still be entitled to be recompensed for each item of damages only once. The availability of separate theories does not occasion a windfall for the plaintiff.

Errors of mere verbalization either way— stating separate claims as one or dividing one into two or more—should at worst be correctible by amendment and if unprejudicial should be ignored.[6]

As a general rule, all items of damage emanating from but a single occurrence, event, or transaction and due at the time of suit are deemed parts of but a single cause of action

§ 212

1. See § 230, below, on the corrective motions.

2. United States v. Memphis Cotton Oil Co., 288 U.S. 62, 67–68, 53 S.Ct. 278, 280, 77 L.Ed. 619 (1933).

3. United States v. Dickinson, 331 U.S. 745, 748, 67 S.Ct. 1382, 1385, 91 L.Ed. 1789 (1947).

4. Payne v. New York, S. & W. R. R. Co., 201 N.Y. 436, 95 N.E. 19 (1911).

5. Robins v. Finestone, 308 N.Y. 543, 127 N.E.2d 330 (1955).

6. CPLR 3026.

and should all be joined. Omitting an item of damages risks waiver under the "splitting" rule.[7] But in regard to a tort New York takes the position that its property damage and personal injury aspects are separate causes of action and may be sued on as such;[8] or, if they are sued on together (the more appropriate and more frequent step), they should be separately numbered. Today, moreover, unless the property damage part of the tort claim is small enough to go into the Small Claims part of one of the lower courts, an action on it and a separate action on the personal injury claim may result in consolidation of both on motion of the defendant.

§ 213. Statements Deemed Repeated; Writings

The prior section, on the separate numbering requirement, treated the case in which a pleading sets forth several distinct causes of action, or several different counts or theories in support of the same cause of action. In such cases it is often necessary, at a later point in the pleading, to rely again on something alleged earlier. CPLR 3014 provides that prior statements are "deemed repeated or adopted subsequently in the same pleading", thus dispensing with repetition or even further reference and automatically summoning forth the earlier allegations to support the later claim or count.

If needed for a "clear presentation", however, CPLR 3014 does encourage repetition of the earlier statements, but even there it allows the repetition to be made merely by referring to the numbers of the earlier paragraphs, dispensing with the duplication of their substance. When, for example, a second count or claim is pleaded in a complaint, introduced by language like "Second cause of action [count, claim, ground, theory, etc.]", and most of its

elements are the same as those of the first claim and have already been pleaded, the next numbered paragraph can simply say "Plaintiff repeats the allegations of paragraphs two, four, and five". Further paragraphs can then add the new allegations distinct to the second claim or count.

The allegations are cumulative for all purposes. Even those of a defense stated in an answer, for example, are deemed repeated for purposes of a counterclaim to follow.[1] Allegations in a pleading in a prior litigation, however, are not deemed repeated and may not be incorporated by reference. They must be set forth independently.[2]

The pleader who wishes to make a writing a part of the pleading need merely attach a copy of it. CPLR 3014 then makes it a part of the pleading "for all purposes". It is usual to make some reference to the writing in the body of the pleading. If a conflict arises between the writing itself and allegations made in the pleading, the writing prevails.[3]

§ 214. Various Techniques of Pleading

CPLR 3014 recognizes and approves several special techniques of pleading.

Inconsistency is expressly permitted, either among claims or among defenses. This is done to recognize the unpredictability of litigation. A plaintiff can in one cause of action ask for rescission of a contract and in a second ask for its specific performance, all in the same complaint. A defendant can plead in one defense that she never made the contract and in a second that the contract is illegal. A party can't predict what the fact finding will be and is entitled at the pleading stage to introduce into the case everything she's got. Thus, a cause of action is not dismissible merely because it "contradicts the underlying theory" of one already pleaded.[1] The defense of workers'

---

7. Splitting is treated in § 220 below.

8. Reilly v. Sicilian Asphalt Paving Co., 170 N.Y. 40, 62 N.E. 772 (1902).

§ 213

1. Nussenblatt v. Nussenblatt, 62 Misc.2d 792, 309 N.Y.S.2d 397 (Sup.Ct., Queens County, 1970).

2. Card v. Budini, 29 A.D.2d 35, 285 N.Y.S.2d 734 (3d Dep't 1967).

3. 805 Third Ave. Co. v. M.W. Realty Associates, 58 N.Y.2d 447, 461 N.Y.S.2d 778, 448 N.E.2d 445 (1983).

§ 214

1. Cohn v. Lionel Corp., 21 N.Y.2d 559, 563, 289 N.Y.S.2d 404, 408, 236 N.E.2d 634, 637 (1968).

compensation coverage, for example, is not precluded by an earlier defense denying that the plaintiff was even an employee.[2]

While allowed to plead inconsistent claims, a party can't be allowed an inconsistent judgment. The doctrine of election of remedies, treated later,[3] sees to that. If the claims or theories are consistent, a judgment can of course embody both or all of them. In a personal injury action, for example, the doctrine of res ipsa loquitur, at one time deemed inconsistent with proof of specific acts of negligence, is no longer considered inconsistent;[4] both grounds can go to the jury (and to judgment) together.

Alternative pleading is also recognized and invited by CPLR 3014. This is the pleading counterpart of CPLR 1002, which allows the joinder of parties in the alternative. The example given earlier in the book, of joinder in the alternative,[5] in which P, unable to determine who as among various handlers of his goods was responsible for damage, sues them in the alternative, is also an example of a complaint that pleads in the alternative: the plaintiff pleads facts indicating that at least one of the defendants must be responsible and this establishes a sufficient prima facie case to require each of the defendants to come forward with proof in self-exoneration. The proof offered by any defendant may be used against any other;[6] the jury will decide who (if anyone) is responsible.

A common example of pleading in the alternative is an injured pedestrian's complaint in a negligence case involving two cars. He alleges formally that both cars were responsible, a sufficient pleading basis on which the jury can find either responsible. Official Form 13 is a complaint in a pedestrian injury case in which the plaintiff does not know which of two cars

hit him. It is another example of alternative pleading.

Hypothetical pleading is another technique authorized by CPLR 3014. Whenever an hypothesis, with or without an "if" or "when" or similar clause, would aid presentation of a pleader's case, the pleader can use it. P pleads, for example, for the specific performance of a contract, but pleads also that if the court in its discretion refuses the relief of specific performance—which as an equitable remedy lies in the discretion of the court—then P wants damages for breach of contract. (Damages are a law claim in which judicial discretion plays no role.) In an assault case, for another example, D pleads that he never touched P (defense of mistaken identity) but that if D did, then P had it coming (defense of justification). These hypothetical techniques, among their other possible functions, are one way of interjecting inconsistent claims or defenses.

A few months before Foley v. D'Agostino[7] offered the First Department Appellate Division the full opportunity it had been seeking to implement the CPLR's purpose of divesting pleadings of their rigidity,[8] the court used the case of W.T. Grant Co. v. Uneeda Doll Co.[9] as a kind of herald and in the bargain gave an expansive tone to the use of hypotheses. Retailer R in *Uneeda* bought dolls from manufacturer M and sold one of these to customer C. C was injured by the product and sued R in Connecticut. Before the suit went to judgment R sued M in New York for indemnification, for whatever C might recover of R, on the ground that it was all M's responsibility. M moved to dismiss on the ground that R's claim was premature, but the court sustained R's claim as a hypothetical pleading: "if" C recovers of R "then" R is entitled to recover from M.

In a situation of that kind, stays, continuances, and like remedies can be used in the

---

2. George v. Sparwood Realty Corp., 34 A.D.2d 768, 311 N.Y.S.2d 422 (1st Dep't 1970).

3. See § 219 below.

4. Abbott v. Page Airways, Inc., 23 N.Y.2d 502, 297 N.Y.S.2d 713, 245 N.E.2d 388 (1969).

5. See § 135 above.

6. Shaw v. Lewis, 55 Misc.2d 664, 286 N.Y.S.2d 758 (N.Y.C.Civ.Ct.), aff'd 58 Misc.2d 1072, 299 N.Y.S.2d 615 (App.T., 1st Dep't, 1968).

7. 21 A.D.2d 60, 248 N.Y.S.2d 121 (1st Dep't 1964); see § 208, note 4, above.

8. See § 208 above.

9. 19 A.D.2d 361, 243 N.Y.S.2d 428 (1963), aff'd 15 N.Y.2d 571, 254 N.Y.S.2d 834, 203 N.E.2d 299 (1964).

New York action to await the result of C's Connecticut suit, on which any judgment in the New York indemnification action would of course depend. Whether there was some barrier in the *Uneeda* case to R's impleading M into the Connecticut action, which would have been the ideal step for R to take, does not appear. Perhaps it was a jurisdictional problem.[10] When jurisdiction is not a problem, as where the underlying action is pending in a New York court and impleader of M is clearly available, a separate indemnification action before the thing to be indemnified has been adjudicated will likely be disallowed.[11]

B. SPECIFIC ITEMS

Table of Sections

§ 215. Pleading Certain Specific Matters; CPLR 3015

CPLR 3015 requires particularity in pleading in regard to certain items. Before its several subdivisions are treated, a few related points should be made.

There is no requirement in New York practice that jurisdiction be pleaded. Even with the lower courts, whose subject matter jurisdiction is limited, there is no statutory requirement, as there is in federal practice,[1] that subject matter jurisdiction be pleaded. Whether there is subject matter jurisdiction is technically an affirmative defense for the defendant to raise by motion or answer,[2] and the plaintiff can, when the defense is raised, establish the court's subject matter jurisdiction whether the complaint has mentioned it or not. The same

is true of personal jurisdiction: the complaint need not say anything about it. If personal jurisdiction is lacking, the defendant must raise the objection by motion or answer,[3] and the plaintiff can, in response, adduce whatever is needed to show that personal jurisdiction exists.

Some cases nevertheless held for a time, at least in lower court actions in which process had been served beyond the lines of the municipality serviced by the court, that the complaint had to allege the basis for personal jurisdiction.[4] It was even held that in the absence of the jurisdictional allegation, not even enough jurisdiction is obtained to support an amendment of the complaint to add it.[5] Carried to its logical end, this kind of reasoning would mean that the court would lack even the jurisdiction to declare jurisdiction absent, which in turn should void its decision as a precedent—for want of jurisdiction! The appellate division afterwards righted things in Fishman v. Pocono Ski Rental Inc.,[6] overruling that line of cases. "There is no requirement . . . that the complaint allege the basis for personal jurisdiction", said the court; "lack of personal jurisdiction is an affirmative defense" for the defendant to raise.

It should be unnecessary to plead in the complaint any item that needs an affirmative defense to inject it into the case. Allegations of when a claim accrued, for example, are not an integral part of the claim itself and should therefore need no statement in the complaint: the statute of limitations, to which such allegations pertain, is an affirmative defense for the defendant to plead and prove.[7] Some pre-CPLR caselaw nevertheless indicated that the pleadings themselves should offer the facts about timeliness,[8] and by embodying time allegations some of the official forms under the CPLR

---

10. See Commentary C3014:8 on McKinney's CPLR 3014.

11. See Morey v. Sealright Co., 41 Misc.2d 1068, 247 N.Y.S.2d 306 (Sup.Ct., Onondaga County, 1964).

§ 215

1. Federal Rules of Civil Procedure, Rule 8(a).

2. CPLR 3211(a)(2), (e).

3. CPLR 3211(a)(8), (e).

4. E.g., All–State Credit Corp. v. Riess, 61 Misc.2d 677, 306 N.Y.S.2d 596 (App.T. 9th & 10th Dists., 1970), criti-

cized but followed in Henry Sash and Door Co. v. Medi–Complex Ltd., 69 Misc.2d 269, 329 N.Y.S.2d 892 (Dist.Ct., Suffolk County, 1972).

5. See the All–State case, above.

6. 82 A.D.2d 906, 907, 440 N.Y.S.2d 700, 701 (2d Dep't 1981).

7. CPLR 3018(b), 3211(a)(5), (e).

8. See, e.g., Roth v. Atex Products, Inc., 35 Misc.2d 136, 229 N.Y.S.2d 916 (Sup.Ct., Nassau County, 1962); Manacher v. Central Coal Co., 2 A.D.2d 667, 152 N.Y.S.2d 983 (1st Dep't 1956).

tacitly suggest the same thing.[9] The same conclusions apply to the statute of frauds, also an affirmative defense.[10] Caselaw has held that the complaint should plead whether the contract was oral or written.[11] Some official forms so plead[12]—again suggesting by implication that it is a good thing to do. Although a bill of particulars[13] seems the more appropriate place for such things, it is certainly no burden to include the allegations in the pleading itself, even if they are not part of the substantive claim. Their omission, however, should never be deemed to invalidate the claim or ground a dismissal.

When a given matter, while not ordinarily deemed an integral part of a substantive cause of action, happens to be considered such in a given instance, it must of course be pleaded. Special damages, for example, is not required to give substance to most claims, but it is for some. When it is, as it is for tort claims not having a common law origin, for example, it must of course be pleaded.[14]

The various subdivisions of CPLR 3015 add particularity requirements for only a few things. Subdivision (a) makes it unnecessary for a plaintiff to plead satisfaction of a contractual condition precedent. The pleading burden here is on the defendant to specifically raise the issue of the plaintiff's non-performance of the condition, but if the defendant does plead it, the plaintiff then has the burden of proving that she satisfied the condition. It has been held that if the plaintiff voluntarily pleads on the issue, although not required to by CPLR 3015(a), the plaintiff injects the issue into the case and thereby relieves the defendant from having to raise it in the answer.[15]

While relieved of pleading her own performance under a contract, the plaintiff must still, of course, plead the facts constituting the defendant's alleged breach.[16] It should also be noted that CPLR 3015(a) applies only to a condition precedent imposed by a contract. When it is imposed by a statute, like § 50–e of General Municipal Law (the notice of claim requirement in tort cases[17]), the plaintiff retains the burden both of pleading and of proving the condition's fulfillment.

A tender back of benefits received from a transaction is no longer a condition precedent to an action to void the transaction; the court can adjust the equities in the judgment.[18] Since there is no omnibus requirement of a tender back as a substantive condition to relief, there is of course no requirement to plead such a tender.

If any party to the action is known to be a corporation, that fact must be alleged, along with a specification of the place of incorporation.[19] There is no analogous requirement in regard to non-corporate parties, although a plaintiff who picks his own county of residence as the venue of a supreme court action must specify his residence address on the summons.[20] Having corporate status pleaded is helpful for several purposes, such as a motion to dismiss an action when it appears that it has been brought by a corporate plaintiff doing business in New York without authority.[21] This requirement to plead corporate status has nothing of the importance it can have in federal practice, however, where it may reflect on subject matter jurisdiction in a case based on diversity of citizenship.[22]

Whenever it is appropriate in a pleading to refer to a previously rendered judgment or decision of any court or board or other tribunal, it may be referred to without pleading

---

9. See, e.g., the forms quoted in § 210 above.

10. CPLR 3018(b), CPLR 3211(a)(5), (e).

11. Hanson v. Hanson, 203 Misc. 396, 119 N.Y.S.2d 11 (Sup.Ct., N.Y.County, 1953).

12. E.g., Official Form 15, ¶ 1.

13. The bill of particulars is treated later. See § 238 et seq.

14. Zausner v. Fotochrome, Inc., 18 A.D.2d 649, 235 N.Y.S.2d 698 (1st Dep't 1962).

15. Allis–Chalmers Mfg. Co. v. Malan Constr. Co., 30 N.Y.2d 225, 331 N.Y.S.2d 636, 282 N.E.2d 600 (1972).

16. Baby Show Exhibition Co. v. Crowell Publ'g Co., 174 A.D. 368, 161 N.Y.S. 205 (1st Dep't 1916).

17. See § 32 above.

18. CPLR 3004.

19. CPLR 3015(b).

20. CPLR 305(a).

21. Bus.Corp.L. § 1312. See § 30 above.

22. 28 U.S.C.A. § 1332(c), FRCP Rule 8(a). See § 611 below (Practitioner's Edition).

facts showing the rendering tribunal's jurisdiction.[23]

A signature on a negotiable instrument is admitted unless the opponent's pleading specifically denies it.[24] The same is true of signatures on commercial paper in general under Articles 3[25] and investment securities under Article 8[26] of the Uniform Commercial Code. If the signature is specifically denied, the burden of proving the instrument's validity shifts back to the party claiming under it.

A special provision, CPLR 3015(e), governs business plaintiffs who are required to be licensed by the consumer affairs departments of New York City or certain of the suburban counties around it.[27] When they sue a consumer on a business claim, they have to plead the license. The statute's reference to an "after-acquired license" would seem to suggest that a contractor unlicensed at the time of the work can cure the defect merely by securing a license afterwards, and before suit, but the Court of Appeals rejected that construction in B & F Bldg. Corp. v. Liebig[28] and held that such a claim is valid only if there was a license in effect at the time the work was done.

Because CPLR 3015(e) is a consumer protection measure, it has been held that it does not apply to an unlicensed contractor who furnishes materials not to a "consumer", but to a company. There, suit is maintainable against the company free of the CPLR 3015(e) barrier.[29]

§ 216. Particularity in Specific Actions; CPLR 3016

For most causes of action there are no special pleading requirements. CPLR 3013 and 3014 do the job alone. But for a handful of actions CPLR 3016 introduces a few specific requirements. Before these are negotiated, we should again note the admonition contained in Foley v. D'Agostino:[1] that the theme is still set by CPLR 3013 and that CPLR 3016 is merely the exaction of additional detail in a few selected instances. Omission of such detail, moreover, should be curable by mere amendment or, if a bill of particulars is a likely place for it, the detail can be left to the bill.[2] Treatment (not verbatim statement) of the subdivisions of CPLR 3016 follows:

(a) *Defamation.* In a libel or slander case the defamatory words must be quoted verbatim. This is strictly enforced and any paraphrasing or use of qualifying words makes the complaint defective.[3] The words' applicability to the plaintiff, however, may be stated generally. If extrinsic facts are relied on to give defamatory import to the words, or if the persons to whom the words were uttered had special knowledge that gave the words their defamatory impact, those facts should be pleaded.[4] A bill of particulars is available if the defendant needs more detail.[5]

(b) *Fraud, etc.* Detail of the wrong is required in actions based on misrepresentation, fraud, mistake, wilful default, breach of trust, or undue influence. This is the subdivision that the *Foley* case specifically subordinates to CPLR 3013, noting that satisfaction of CPLR 3013, which imposes the fundamental requirement that notice of the transaction be given and the material elements of the claim be set forth, will usually satisfy CPLR 3016(b) as

---

23. CPLR 3015(c). See Commentary C3015:4 on McKinney's CPLR 3015.

24. CPLR 3015(d).

25. UCC § 3–307(1), overruling Hoffstaedter v. Lichtenstein, 203 A.D. 494, 196 N.Y.S. 577 (1st Dep't 1922).

26. UCC § 8–105(3).

27. The counties presently on the list are Nassau, Suffolk, Westchester, Rockland, and Putnam.

28. 76 N.Y.2d 689, 563 N.Y.S.2d 40, 564 N.E.2d 650 (1990).

29. Bayonne Block Co. v. Porco, 171 Misc.2d 684, 654 N.Y.S.2d 961 (Civ.Ct., Bronx County, 1996).

---

§ 216

1. 21 A.D.2d 60, 248 N.Y.S.2d 121 (1st Dep't 1964).

2. See Pernet v. Peabody Eng'g Corp., 20 A.D.2d 781, 248 N.Y.S.2d 132 (1st Dep't 1964).

3. Gardner v. Alexander Rent–A–Car, Inc., 28 A.D.2d 667, 280 N.Y.S.2d 595 (1st Dep't 1967). An amendment may of course allow the verbatim words to be inserted.

4. Danko v. F.W. Woolworth Co., 29 A.D.2d 855, 288 N.Y.S.2d 509 (1st Dep't 1968).

5. Pappalardo v. Westchester Rockland Newspapers, Inc., 101 A.D.2d 830, 475 N.Y.S.2d 487 (2d Dep't 1984), aff'd 64 N.Y.2d 862, 487 N.Y.S.2d 325, 476 N.E.2d 651 (1985).

well. The consequence of a violation of CPLR 3016(b) is in any event a mere amendment[6] as long as the facts that the statute calls for exist and merely need pleading. If the case is dismissed outright, the explanation will usually lie not in the failure to plead detail, but in the court's being convinced from everything pleaded that there was no fraud or similar misconduct.

The Court of Appeals has said that CPLR 3016(b)

requires only that the misconduct complained of be set forth in sufficient detail to clearly inform defendant with respect to the incidents complained of and is not to be interpreted so strictly as to prevent an otherwise valid cause of action in situations where it may be 'impossible to state in detail the circumstances constituting a fraud'.[7]

The court stressed that the failure to allege "a necessary element of the cause of action" is not to be confused with what it plainly views as the less serious defect of omitting some detail. Should the detail be unavailable at the pleading stage, but the complaint, notwithstanding an absence of detail, satisfactorily state a basic claim in fraud, the complaint can be sustained and the needed detail left to abide pretrial disclosure or, if need be, the trial itself. The court has recognized that it's difficult for the plaintiff to cite detail, since the wrong is often "peculiarly" in the defendant's knowledge.[8]

CPLR 3016(b) wouldn't be on the New York books at all but for the fact that it's in the Federal Rules,[9] which New York's Advisory Committee followed in this respect.[10] It has more justification in federal civil practice, which lacks a bill of particulars to furnish detail unrevealed by a complaint, while New York practice retains the bill for the kind of detail CPLR 3016(b) calls for.[11]

(c) Separation or divorce. In a separation or divorce action the time, place, and circumstances of each act the defendant is accused of must be specified. This provision has been rigidly applied. Even the bill of particulars has been held to be an inappropriate alternative source.[12] The need for this kind of provision—a product of pre-CPLR thinking—derived from the unavailability of free disclosure in matrimonial actions whereby to give the defendant needed detail. Disclosure is more available in those actions under the CPLR,[13] which ought at least to make CPLR 3016(c) flexible.

(d) Judgment. In suit on a judgment, the complaint must state the extent to which the judgment has been satisfied. This is to guard against a possible double recovery. It contemplates, among other things, the situation in which the earlier judgment was predicated on quasi in rem jurisdiction and the instant one is for the balance still due on the claim because the property seized in the first action (because of its quasi in rem jurisdictional base) did not suffice to satisfy the judgment. If the earlier quasi in rem judgment came from a New York court, it would recite on its face that it is enforcible only to the extent of duly attached property,[14] and the fear underlying CPLR 3016(d) would be unwarranted.[15]

(e) Foreign law. Federal and sister-state law must be given judicial notice without even being requested by a party,[16] but foreign law does not get such notice automatically. CPLR 3016(e) requires that each party relying on foreign-country law set forth the substance of

---

6. See Marcucilli v. Alicon Corp., 41 A.D.2d 932, 343 N.Y.S.2d 367 (2d Dep't 1973).

7. Lanzi v. Brooks, 43 N.Y.2d 778, 780, 402 N.Y.S.2d 384, 385, 373 N.E.2d 278, 279 (1977) (quoting Jered Contracting Corp. v. N.Y.C. Transit Auth., 22 N.Y.2d 187, 292 N.Y.S.2d 98, 239 N.E.2d 197 [1968]).

8. Jered Contracting Corp. v. N.Y.C. Transit Auth., 22 N.Y.2d 187, 292 N.Y.S.2d 98, 239 N.E.2d 197 (1968).

9. Federal Rules of Civil Procedure, Rule 9(b).

10. See 1st Rep.Leg.Doc. (1957) No.6(b), pp.67–8.

11. See § 238 below.

12. Pustilnik v. Pustilnik, 24 A.D.2d 868, 264 N.Y.S.2d 400 (2d Dep't 1965).

13. See Commentary C3101:15 on McKinney's CPLR 3101.

14. Benadon v. Antonio, 10 A.D.2d 40, 197 N.Y.S.2d 1 (1st Dep't 1960).

15. These matters are elaborated in Commentaries C3016:6 and 7 on McKinney's CPLR 3016. For discussion of the present (and much diminished) status of quasi in rem jurisdiction, see § 104 above.

16. CPLR 4511(a).

that law in her pleading. Doing so will probably produce the fringe benefit, incidentally, of mandating judicial notice pursuant to CPLR 4511(b). CPLR 4511(b) says that if the party relying on foreign law (1) requests judicial notice for it, (2) shows the court what the foreign law is, and (3) notifies other parties of reliance on the foreign law, the court "shall" take judicial notice. Including the substance of the foreign law in the pleading comes close, by itself, to fulfilling all three of those requirements.

(f) Schedule of goods or services. Whenever the plaintiff's claim involves the furnishing of goods, materials, or services in a significant quantity, the plaintiff can make use of CPLR 3016(f) and include in the complaint a schedule of the various items with agreed price, date of sale or performance, etc. Using such a detailed schedule has the effect of requiring the defendant to address in the answer and deny specifically whatever item in the schedule he disputes. A general denial in this instance is inadequate to contest any individual item in the schedule.[17] But if the defendant's position is that it had no dealings with the plaintiff at all—e.g., that the sales were to a different person—or if the defendant assumes any other posture going to the entirety of the claim and not just disputing individual components, the specific denials stipulated by CPLR 3016(f) are not required.[18]

When the CPLR 3016(f) schedule is used, the complaint must be verified, which in turn requires verification of the answer.

(g) No-fault requirement. Because the no-fault law, which took effect in 1974, precludes ordinary tort suit in personal injury vehicle cases in New York unless certain criteria are met, CPLR 3016(g) commands that the complaint in every such action allege satisfaction of the requirement. Either "serious injury"[19]

or "economic loss greater than basic economic loss"[20] can be shown. Satisfaction of the requirement need merely be "stated". What detail is needed is the province of the bill of particulars.

(h) Not-for-profit entities. CPLR 3106(h) is the concomitant of § 720–a of the Not–For–Profit Corporation Law, which is designed to expand the immunities of uncompensated officials of not-for-profit organizations by excluding suit against them except for acts of gross negligence or for conduct intended to cause harm. Subdivision (h) requires the complaint in such an action to be verified and to allege whether it is based on such conduct.

C. DEMAND FOR RELIEF

Table of Sections

Sec.
217.   Demand for Relief; "Wherefore" Clause.

§ 217. Demand for Relief; "Wherefore" Clause

Every pleading containing a cause of action, which of course includes the complaint, "shall contain a demand for the relief to which the pleader deems himself entitled".[1] It is common in money actions, even those involving the unliquidated tort claim, to include a demand for a specific sum.[2] Especially if the plaintiff expects to take a default judgment against the defendant, the complaint or CPLR 305(b) notice served with the summons must specify the amount claimed.[3]

There are two exceptions to this general rule. One is the action for medical malpractice, the other a money action (for medical malpractice or anything else) against a municipal corporation (county, town, village, or city). In those actions a special provision governs, CPLR 3017(c), and prohibits the plaintiff (the defendant on a counterclaim, etc.) from pleading any money figure unless the adverse party

---

17.   Duban v. Platt, 23 A.D.2d 660, 257 N.Y.S.2d 109 (2d Dep't 1965), aff'd 17 N.Y.2d 526, 267 N.Y.S.2d 907, 215 N.E.2d 164 (1966).

18.   Edwin F. Guth Co. v. Gurland, 246 A.D. 67, 284 N.Y.S. 333 (1st Dep't 1935).

19.   This is defined in Ins.L. § 5102(d).

20.   This is defined in Ins.L. § 5102(a).

§ 217

1.   CPLR 3017(a).

2.   It has been held that this is not indispensable in all situations. See Silvestris v. Silvestris, 24 A.D.2d 247, 265 N.Y.S.2d 173 (1st Dep't 1965); Commentary C3017:1 on McKinney's CPLR 3017.

3.   CPLR 3215(b).

requests it.[4] (It sets up a procedure for the request.) If the action is in the supreme court, however, the plaintiff must state that the amount sought exceeds the jurisdiction of all lower courts that might otherwise have had jurisdiction.[5]

It has been held that when there are multiple claims and any is for medical malpractice, none should contain a money demand, the court suggesting that the same rule should apply when a municipality is a defendant: there should be no money demand in the complaint even if there are other defendants.[6] It has been held that a violation of this rule can apparently be cured with a mere amendment striking the reference to the demand,[7] but the imposition of a money sanction in an appropriate sum might better implement this aspect of CPLR 3017(c). Especially in the case of physicians, a major purpose of this exception is to spare the defendant the embarrassment of local press headlines based on nothing more than the unbinding and perhaps not even influential demand clause of a plaintiff's self-serving complaint.[8]

With only the medical malpractice and municipality exceptions, it is common practice to include a specific money demand in the complaint's relief clause. The issue has even arisen as to whether a failure to include the demand in a CPLR 305(b) notice, when the notice is used at the outset instead of a complaint, makes the notice jurisdictionally defective. It has been held that the defect is not jurisdictional and can be cured by amendment.[9]

The relief clause, which appears at the end of the pleading, is often called the "wherefore" clause; in the money action it is popularly called the "ad damnum".

The relief clause does not count in determining whether a cause of action is stated,[10] except perhaps in those cases in which a showing of damage is a substantive element of the claim. Even a prayer for the wrong relief does not vitiate the pleading as long as the pleading otherwise states a cause of action known to the law. Relief of different kinds may be asked, a natural corollary of the permission that CPLR 3014 offers to plead inconsistent claims. Relief may also be asked for in the alternative, another parallel with CPLR 3014. The ultimate choice between legal and equitable relief, if both are involved in a case, is with the court.[11]

CPLR 3017(a) also authorizes the court to grant "any type of relief within its jurisdiction appropriate to the proof whether or not demanded, imposing such terms as may be just". The only stated exception is where the defendant defaults. There, as previously mentioned, the only relief that can be had against the defendant in a default judgment is that of which she had due notice prior to the default.[12]

This authorization to grant even undemanded relief if the proof supports it is generous. It can be cited to justify legal relief where equitable relief was asked for, and vice-versa—even relief of a different kind or category than that originally demanded—as long as the pleading

---

4. The notice of claim provision applicable to municipalities, § 50–e of the General Municipal Law, has a similar bar (except in New York City): the notice of claim is not to contain a damages demand, at least not until the municipality asks for it. The fact that the amendment of § 50–e (which applies to tort claims) and the amendment that injected the municipality exception into CPLR 3017(c) were made in the same act (L.1980, c.686) suggests that the tort claim was the only one aimed at, but since the language used in CPLR 3017(c) is not limited to tort claims, it can be taken to apply as well to contract and other claims when a municipality is the defendant. See Commentary C3017:12 on McKinney's CPLR 3017.

5. The purpose is to implement the state's policy of having a money claim brought in the lowest court that can entertain it. See § 12 above.

6. Vigo v. New York Hospital, 113 Misc.2d 972, 450 N.Y.S.2d 256 (Sup.Ct., N.Y.County, 1981).

7. See Twitchell v. MacKay, 78 A.D.2d 125, 434 N.Y.S.2d 516 (4th Dep't 1980).

8. See 1981 Commentary C3017:11 on McKinney's CPLR 3017. There is a dispute about whether it would be more consistent with CPLR 3017(c) in medical malpractice actions even to bar mention of a monetary amount in summation to the jury. Bechard v. Eisinger, 105 A.D.2d 939, 481 N.Y.S.2d 906 (3d Dep't 1984), says it would be and bars the mention. Braun v. Ahmed, 127 A.D.2d 418, 515 N.Y.S.2d 473 (2d Dep't 1987), goes the other way.

9. Premo v. Cornell, 71 A.D.2d 223, 423 N.Y.S.2d 64 (3d Dep't 1979).

10. Lehmann v. Kingston Plaza, Inc., 44 Misc.2d 63, 252 N.Y.S.2d 964 (Sup.Ct., Ulster County, 1964).

11. Ungewitter v. Toch, 31 A.D.2d 583, 294 N.Y.S.2d 1013 (3d Dep't 1968), aff'd 26 N.Y.2d 687, 308 N.E.2d 858, 257 N.E.2d 40 (1970).

12. CPLR 3215(b).

gave notice of the underlying transaction and covered the elements of the cause of action (thus precluding the adverse party from claiming prejudice).[13]

For a while it was held that a verdict in a money action could not exceed the amount demanded in the complaint. In one well known case, Naujokas v. H. Frank Carey High School,[14] the jury, apparently unaware that the complaint demanded only $50,000,[15] brought in a verdict for $250,000. The appellate division would not permit judgment for more than the $50,000.[16]

Naujokas and similar cases were overruled by the New York Court of Appeals in Loomis v. Civetta Corinno Constr. Corp.,[17] where the court held that the plaintiff may be allowed to keep a verdict that exceeds the amount demanded in the complaint as long as there is no prejudice to the defendant.[18] An example of prejudice would be the case in which the original demand is within the defendant's insurance coverage—assuring that the defendant would face no personal liability no matter how poor the defense put in for her by her company-assigned lawyer—while the verdict exceeds the coverage. The defendant would have lost her chance to appear through a lawyer of her own choosing to defend against personal liability.[19]

The New York lesson under *Naujokas* and similar cases was that the tort race was to the greedy; that an endeavor to assess a tort claim realistically could hurt the client, while the addition of nothing—one small zero—in the demand clause would supply a figure that,

however voracious, would cover all possible contingencies. Indeed, because of cases like *Naujokas*, inflated demands were as much the product of caution as greed. Though it should not abate caution, the *Loomis* case should at least remove the fear that sent monetary demands in tort cases into outer space.

An amendment to raise the ad damnum in advance of the trial, and even at the trial itself but in advance of the verdict, while not granted for the mere asking, is less controversial. As long as prejudice remains absent, the amendment is permissible,[20] and prejudice at this stage is less likely than at the post-verdict stage.

CPLR 3017(a) can't be used to force on a pleader relief the pleader doesn't want. In Ross v. Ross,[21] for example, W sued H for a separation and found herself awarded a divorce she didn't ask for. Her proof would have supported a divorce but it was H who asked for it. H wanted to remarry, but abandonment was the ground and H was the abandoner, so he wasn't entitled to a divorce. Only W was, but she didn't want it. Reversing, the appellate division vacated the divorce that W earned but did not want and H wanted but did not earn.[22] The case supports the theory that when a movable object is displaced by a resistible force, the plaintiff appeals.

D.   ELECTION OF REMEDIES

Table of Sections

---

13. See Commentaries C3017:4–6 on McKinney's CPLR 3017.

14. 33 A.D.2d 703, 306 N.Y.S.2d 195 (2d Dep't 1969).

15. There was at the time no uniform rule in New York about whether a jury could be told the amount demanded in the complaint. See Williams v. Long Island R.R., 41 A.D.2d 940, 343 N.Y.S.2d 700 (2d Dep't 1973); Commentary C3017:1 on McKinney's CPLR 3017. The Court of Appeals afterwards held in Tate v. Colabello, 58 N.Y.2d 84, 459 N.Y.S.2d 422, 445 N.E.2d 1101 (1983), that amounts could be suggested to the jury during summation.

16. The same conclusion, but involving smaller figures, was reached in Wyman v. Morone, 33 A.D.2d 168, 306 N.Y.S.2d 115 (3d Dep't 1969). Support for the result was found in the Advisory Committee's notes, 1st Rep.Leg.Doc. (1957) No.6(b), p.68, but it flew in the face of the plain language of CPLR 3017(a).

17. 54 N.Y.2d 18, 444 N.Y.S.2d 571, 429 N.E.2d 90 (1981).

18. See the lead note in New York State Law Digest No. 265. A motion to amend to conform the pleadings to the proof under CPLR 3025(c)—in this case to conform to both the proof and the verdict—would be the procedural step for the plaintiff to take in this situation.

19. See Commentary C3017:7 on McKinney's CPLR 3017.

20. See § 237 below.

21. 84 A.D.2d 569, 443 N.Y.S.2d 419 (2d Dep't 1981), aff'd 55 N.Y.2d 999, 449 N.Y.S.2d 481, 434 N.E.2d 717 (1982).

22. This is somewhat akin to the brief life enjoyed by the "reverse summary judgment" in matrimonial actions, for which see § 278.

§ 218. Election of Remedies; Separate Actions

The doctrine of the election of remedies is related to res judicata, but more by affinity than by blood. Res judicata requires a final judgment on the merits.[1] The election of remedies doesn't. The doctrine becomes relevant, although today not necessarily operative, when a plaintiff with two or more remedies to choose from in respect of the same wrong sues on only one. The remedy sued on is deemed the one elected, and technically speaking the election of the one bars later suit on the others. When the doctrine was rigidly applied, the election was deemed made as soon as the complaint was served. But there is little occasion today to treat the doctrine technically. It is "a harsh and arbitrary principle designed only to prevent vexatious litigation",[2] and the courts have held that it should not be extended.[3]

If a plaintiff with theories A and B available to support a claim sues only on theory A, and the case is disposed of on its merits, it is the doctrine of res judicata that bars later suit on theory B. This is because res judicata—in this regard now known as "claim preclusion"—is conclusive "not only as to any matters actually litigated ... but also as to any that might have been ... litigated".[4] Since theory B could also have been litigated in the first action, final judgment on the merits in that action, albeit only with regard to theory A, invokes res judicata itself to preclude later suit on theory B. But res judicata is not on the scene when no final judgment has been rendered on the merits, and that's where the election of remedies doctrine may become relevant.

The general rule is that not just any final judgment invokes res judicata, only a final judgment on the merits. This led to some election of remedies cases difficult to square with res judicata, mainly because of the occa-sional difficulty one meets in determining precisely what a "merits" result is. Judge Cardozo wrote that

> An election of remedies presupposes a right to elect.... If in truth there is but one remedy, and not a choice between two, a fruitless recourse to a remedy withheld does not bar recourse thereafter to the remedy allowed.[5]

That would presumably mean that if the plaintiff didn't really have theory A available, even though she thought she did, a dismissal on ground A would not, under the election doctrine, preclude later suit on ground B. But shouldn't the res judicata doctrine do the precluding in that case? That was the conflict. *Fitzgerald v. Title Guar. & Trust Co.*[6] and *Smith v. Kirkpatrick*[7] illustrate.

In *Fitzgerald*, P's first suit had been in contract and was held barred by the statute of limitations. So P turned around and brought a second action for the same relief but grounded it on fraud, a fraud claim being alive under the accrual-at-discovery rule.[8] The court sustained the claim, holding that it couldn't be barred by the election of remedies doctrine because since P had no live contract claim when he first sued, he couldn't have "elected" the non-existent remedy.

Similarly in *Kirkpatrick*, where P's first action in contract was dismissed because the contract was oral and was barred by the statute of frauds. A second suit in quantum meruit was allowed, the court holding that all the former action determined was that a contract could not be proved, not that no services were rendered or goods delivered. The *Kirkpatrick* case does endeavor to square the result with the doctrine of res judicata by finding the "causes of action" different, but in the ultimate sense P in *Kirkpatrick* had but one cause

§ 218

1. See § 443 below.

2. Strong v. Reeves, 280 A.D. 301, 305, 114 N.Y.S.2d 97, 101 (3d Dep't 1952), aff'd 306 N.Y. 666, 116 N.E.2d 497 (1953).

3. Smith v. Kirkpatrick, 305 N.Y. 66, 111 N.E.2d 209 (1953).

4. Schuylkill Fuel Corp. v. B. & C. Nieberg Realty Corp., 250 N.Y. 304, 306–7, 165 N.E. 456, 457 (1929). See § 447 below.

5. Schenck v. State Line Tel. Co., 238 N.Y. 308, 311, 144 N.E. 592, 593 (1924).

6. 290 N.Y. 376, 49 N.E.2d 489 (1943).

7. Note 3 above.

8. CPLR 213(8), 203(g).

of action for services rendered whether based on contract or quantum meruit.

The Court of Appeals had second thoughts about cases like *Fitzgerald* and *Kirkpatrick* and appears to have overruled them, closing this gap between the election and res judicata doctrines in a pair of cases handed down on the same day: O'Brien v. City of Syracuse[9] and Smith v. Russell Sage College.[10]

In *O'Brien*, P had brought an action involving a public taking of property but lost it when he couldn't establish the taking. P then brought the second action in trespass. The court held that any claim based on a trespass arising out of the acts involved in the earlier action would be barred under the doctrine of res judicata.

Russell Sage involved a statute of limitations point analogous to that in *Fitzgerald*. But in *Russell Sage* P did have, during the first action, knowledge of the facts on which he sought to predicate the second action. What P should have done, said the *Russell Sage* court, was move to amend the complaint during the first action to add the additional claim there.

One lesson from these two cases is that if there is yet time to amend in action number one, as when knowledge of the additional facts comes to the plaintiff during the pretrial stage, the plaintiff should seek the amendment forthwith and will forfeit the claim if she doesn't. A corollary, however, is that if knowledge of the additional facts does not reach the plaintiff in time, a second action on the new count should be permissible.[11]

The main lesson to the lawyer is that the omission of a count or ground or theory today, whether or not amounting to a forfeiture under an "election of remedies" label, amounts to a forfeiture under the res judicata banner and hurts just as much. In every suit on an oral contract (the *Kirkpatrick* situation), the plaintiff should therefore consider joining a quantum meruit count if goods have been delivered or services rendered. And in any action on any claim, the plaintiff should sift all possible bases and—unless she has some well considered tactical reason in mind—join them all to be sure that a statute of limitations advantage available with any one of them (the *Fitzgerald* situation) is not omitted.

The *Kirkpatrick* and *Fitzgerald* cases applied the election doctrine too generously, doing so in apparent fidelity to the legislature's wish to avoid the harshness of the doctrine, a harshness manifest in a number of old cases. The legislature overruled those old cases one by one over the years. Each involved a special situation and the aggregate of the statutes doing the overruling are now gathered up in CPLR 3002,[12] which is simply a list of a few prime instances of legislative relief. Treating CPLR 3002 in more detail and footnoting the cases overruled, its subdivisions run this way:

(a) *Action against several persons.* If P has a claim against both X and Y jointly and severally, suit and even rendition of judgment against X does not bar later suit against Y.[13] Satisfaction of the X judgment will bar the Y suit, of course, because the law does not allow duplicate recoveries. The initial joinder of both X and Y, which is of course permissible,[14] would avoid such issues.

(b) *Agent and undisclosed principal.* This involves the agency area and assumes that substantively both the agent and the undisclosed (but later revealed) principal are liable to P. P's suit and unsatisfied judgment against one will not bar later suit against the other.[15] Again, satisfaction of the first judgment does bar the second suit.

(c) *Conversion and contract.* Theft from P gives P a conversion claim against the thief,

---

9. 54 N.Y.2d 353, 445 N.Y.S.2d 687, 429 N.E.2d 1158 (1981).

10. 54 N.Y.2d 185, 445 N.Y.S.2d 68, 429 N.E.2d 746 (1981).

11. The O'Brien and Russell Sage cases are further treated in § 447 below. They are also the subject of a lead note in New York State Law Digest No. 267.

12. See the discussion in the Kirkpatrick case, 305 N.Y. at 74, 111 N.E.2d at 214.

13. CPLR 3002(a), overruling Fowler v. Bowery Sav. Bank, 113 N.Y. 450, 21 N.E. 172 (1889).

14. CPLR 1002(b).

15. CPLR 3002(b), overruling Georgi v. Texas Co., 225 N.Y. 410, 122 N.E. 238 (1919).

but in that situation New York law also allows P in effect to "ratify" the conversion and sue instead in contract on the theory of an implied obligation to repay the loss.[16] This can supply a statute of limitations advantage because while the conversion ground is an injury to property and gets only three years,[17] the contract ground gets six.[18] When P's claim exists against several persons, CPLR 3002(c) becomes operative. It provides that if P sues one of the liable persons and recovers judgment on either ground, and the judgment is not satisfied, later suit against any of the others is still permissible on either or both grounds.[19] Again, satisfaction of a judgment, meaning that P has been recompensed for his damages, bars further suit by P against anyone. Note, however, that if the first judgment is unsatisfied, CPLR 3002(c) applies to permit the second suit only against the previously unsued persons. It does not authorize a second suit against X on the conversion ground after rendition of judgment against him on the contract ground, or vice-versa. Sound initial practice would avoid all of these questions: the attorney should make it a general rule to join all liable persons and all possible theories in one action.[20]

(d) On contract and to reform. If P sues D on a written contract and does not recover, he may afterwards sue to reform that contract and then sue on it as reformed.[21] Without this provision several doctrines might bar the later reformation action, including the election of remedies and res judicata doctrines. If P sues on a contract and does recover, he may not ordinarily sue later for a reformation.

(e) Damages plus rescission. The old case of Weigel v. Cook[22] held that in an action to rescind an agreement, the plaintiff could not also seek damages. It overlooked that rescission alone might not be enough because of D's conduct; that damages might also be necessary

to restore P to status quo and that the refusal to allow damages plus rescission could be a windfall to the wrongdoer. The legislature recognized this and with CPLR 3002(e) and its predecessor overruled the *Weigel* case. Thus, where D's fraud induced the contract, entitling P to rescind it but also causing P monetary injury, which rescission alone would not requite, P may seek (and get) both in one action. They are not to be deemed inconsistent remedies.

(f) Vendee's lien. The lien a buyer gets when she buys realty was at one time deemed forfeit if the contract of sale was rescinded. CPLR 3002(f) provides that the buyer's suit to rescind or otherwise disaffirm the agreement does not automatically forfeit the lien. Old caselaw[23] had made the lien wholly contingent on the contract, and disaffirmance of the contract was held to carry with it destruction of the lien. CPLR 3002(f) overrules that.

We can conclude this discussion with the lesson taught by Hahl v. Sugo,[24] in which P brought and won an ejectment action based on the encroachment of D's wall on P's land. An ejectment judgment is enforcible by an execution delivered to the sheriff,[25] but the sheriff in *Hahl* had returned it unsatisfied because he found it "impracticable" to enforce. P then brought a new action seeking equitable relief, which, had it succeeded, would have earned P a judgment directing D to remove the encroachment himself under penalty of contempt. The equitable action was held barred because of P's earlier election of the ejectment count.

The lesson is that it is easy enough to ask for the equitable relief to begin with. If D tries to defeat the equitable relief by pleading the adequacy of the legal (the ejectment) remedy, P should cite the *Hahl* case. The warning,

---

16. Dentist's Supply Co. v. Cornelius, 281 A.D. 306, 119 N.Y.S.2d 570 (1st Dep't), aff'd 306 N.Y. 624, 116 N.E.2d 238 (1953).

17. CPLR 214(4).

18. CPLR 213(2).

19. CPLR 3002(c), overruling Terry v. Munger, 121 N.Y. 161, 24 N.E. 272 (1890).

20. Compare Hahl v. Sugo, note 24, below.

21. CPLR 3002(d), overruling Steinbach v. Relief Fire Ins. Co., 77 N.Y. 498 (1879).

22. 237 N.Y. 136, 142 N.E. 444 (1923).

23. Davis v. Rosenzweig Realty Operating Co., 192 N.Y. 128, 84 N.E. 943 (1908).

24. 169 N.Y. 109, 62 N.E. 135 (1901).

25. CPLR 5102.

once again, is to make it a rule to join in the very first action brought all counts, grounds, and theories that support one's claim.[26]

It will be noted that all of the discussion in this section has concerned the situation in which the plaintiff did not bring suit on all possible grounds, or against all of the arguably liable persons. When the plaintiff does join all claims and defendants in one action, a different and much easier election of remedies problem arises, if it arises at all. It's discussed in the next section.

§ 219. Election of Remedies; Within an Action

The prior section discussed the more serious election of remedies situation: that in which not everything was interposed in the first action, thereby necessitating a second one. Here we deal with the case in which everything has been joined—all claims, grounds, theories, counts, and persons potentially liable. If the several counts asserted are consistent, no election of remedies problem should arise at all. If, for example, P sues D for injuries sustained in an accident, and P can show that D was negligent, breached a warranty, and violated a statutory duty, P can interpose all of those bases of liability. At no time will she have to elect among them; the remedies are consistent.

The sensitive situation, therefore, is one in which the several theories or demands for relief are inconsistent. There is explicit CPLR authority for an inconsistent pleading,[1] but not for an inconsistent judgment. If the remedies sought are mutually exclusive, the plaintiff will have to elect from among them at some point in the case. If the plaintiff does not voluntarily elect, the trial judge will determine what that point is.[2] Probably the only safe conclusion one can reach is that the election

will have to be made before judgment. The judgment should not ordinarily embody inconsistent items of relief, although one occasionally encounters such a judgment.[3] But the election can be reasonably postponed right up to the point of judgment.

Suppose, for example, that P is suing D to rescind a contract for fraud, or for specific performance in the alternative in the event that the fraud claim is not sustained. Rescission and specific performance are about as inconsistent as demands can be. Yet the trial judge can postpone the election until after the trial. The trial, in fact, may manifest that the plaintiff has no election after all. It may find, for example, that the defendant is not guilty of fraud, which would mean that rescission is barred and leave only the plaintiff's alternative demand, the demand for specific performance. The fact-finding process, in other words, can be allowed to precede the election whenever there is any doubt about what the plaintiff has to elect from. And if the facts found do sustain both items of relief, the election can be compelled after trial but before judgment. The election of remedies within an action is left almost entirely to judicial discretion.

A plaintiff who makes it a practice to join all available theories and grounds may realize a fringe benefit and become the beneficiary of an unanticipated advantage. Conversely, the plaintiff may become the victim of an unsuspected detriment when some grounds are omitted. Galich v. Sibley, Lindsay & Curr Co.[4] can illustrate. P sued in contract for goods delivered and won, getting a money judgment against D. But because it was based only on contract, it was afterwards discharged in D's bankruptcy. Had it been based on fraud it would have survived the discharge. The omis-

---

26. Another illustration of why all possible grounds should be joined at the outset appears in Galich v. Sibley, Lindsay & Curr Co., 59 Misc.2d 836, 300 N.Y.S.2d 670 (Monroe Count Ct. 1969), where omission of a fraud count in deference to a contract claim apparently resulted in a later forfeit of the judgment when the defendant went bankrupt.

§ 219

1. CPLR 3014. See § 214 above.

2. Baratta v. Kozlowski, 94 A.D.2d 454, 464 N.Y.S.2d 803 (2d Dep't 1983).

3. A replevin judgment, for example, recites the money value of the chattel so that the sheriff can enforce it like a money judgment if the chattel can't be found, CPLR 7108(a), 5102, although of course a recovery of the chattel itself is inconsistent with a money award for its value.

4. 59 Misc.2d 836, 300 N.Y.S.2d 670 (Monroe County Ct. 1969).

sion of the fraud ground resulted in the demise of a judgment that might otherwise have remained good.

E. SPLITTING

Table of Sections

Sec.
220. Splitting.

§ 220. Splitting

The splitting doctrine is related to the election of remedies. While the election doctrine generally deals with a claim having different theories or counts, the splitting doctrine is usually concerned with a money claim sued on in spurts instead of at one time.[1] If P has a money claim against D and sues for only part of what is presently due, P forfeits the rest under the splitting rule. A simple example is where a landlord sues a monthly tenant for rent for only one month although several months rent is due at the time. An action like that splits the claim and forfeits the part due but not joined at the time of suit.[2] This is the law's approach to all installment contracts: suit must join all installments due at suit time. Amounts not due at suit time but accruing later, albeit under the same agreement, of course cannot be joined at that time and so are not deemed split off and can ground a later action.[3] If additional installments fall due while the action is pending, it is usually a better idea to move to amend the complaint to include them.

The main question to ask, in order to resolve a splitting problem, is the old one about whether the plaintiff has but one cause of action, or several. If several—and P is sure of it!—P may safely sue on them separately, or in any event omit from suit on one the amounts due on the other. Thus, where P's two claims

against D arise out of two entirely separate contracts, P's suit on one is not a splitting and therefore not a waiver of the other.[4] Of course, a wrong guess about whether P has one or several causes of action can result in a splitting, which suggests that P make it a practice to resolve all doubt in favor of joining all sums due from D even if they probably emanate from separate transactions and constitute separate causes of action. Even if separate and distinct, the joinder is permissible,[5] and obviously preferable to the inadvertent forfeiture that the splitting rule threatens.

If P sues D on a quasi in rem jurisdictional foundation, attaching D's property but getting no personam jurisdiction, P's judgment will be effective only to the extent of the property attached.[6] And if the property does not suffice to pay P's whole claim, P may bring later suit for the balance. In this situation the earlier judgment is not deemed a splitting or given any other kind of res judicata treatment in the second action.[7]

Since the splitting doctrine was designed to prevent unreasonable harassment, it will not be applied when good reason is shown for omitting part of the claim from an earlier action. Where, for example, a judgment was duly obtained and paid in an action to enforce shareholders' liability against A and B based on their ownership of a certain number of shares, and it was later learned that A and B in fact owned more shares, a second suit, based on ownership of the additional shares, was allowed. Tracing the ownership had been made difficult by A and B themselves because of complicated assignments and bookkeeping entries. Finding that if the defendants were vexed by the second suit it was not in this instance an unreasonable vexing, the court

---

§ 220

1. The distinction is a handy one, but not sharp. The Restatement, for example, also describes as a "splitting" an attempted use, in a second action, of "grounds or theories" omitted from the first. See Rst.2d, Judgments § 25 (1982).

2. Maloney v. McMillan Book Co., 52 Misc.2d 1006, 277 N.Y.S.2d 499 (Syracuse City Ct. 1967).

3. See Industrial Dev. Foundation, Inc. v. U. S. Hoffman Mach. Corp., 16 A.D.2d 600, 229 N.Y.S.2d 857 (4th Dep't 1962).

4. Secor v. Sturgis, 16 N.Y. 548 (1858).

5. CPLR 601.

6. See §§ 104 and 113 above.

7. Benadon v. Antonio, 10 A.D.2d 40, 197 N.Y.S.2d 1 (1st Dep't 1960).

held that the reason for the splitting rule, and hence the rule itself, was inapplicable.[8]

The splitting rule will also be set aside when a duality of actions can be explained by the presence of different parties in interest, even though it might apply were there but a single party in interest. Where, for example, an insured is paid for part of a loss by an insurer, and then sues the person responsible for the loss for only the uninsured part, a later suit by the insurer to recover the part that it paid will not be deemed a splitting, even if prosecuted nominally in the name of the insured.[9]

The benefit of the splitting doctrine is subject to waiver. A good illustration would be where D objects to the court's hearing a certain part of P's claim for the reason that that part is the subject of a separate action: D waives the doctrine and can't assert it in that other action.[10] A waiver has also been held to result when the defendant acquiesces in multiple suits. Since the purpose of the rule is "to protect defendants from being vexed by multiple suits, it stands to reason that acquiescence by the defendant will work a waiver", as it did in a case in which P brought two actions against D arising out of the same transaction and D went along with this, making no motion to consolidate the two or dismiss one based on the pendency of the other.[11]

F. THE ANSWER

Table of Sections

§ 221. The Answer; Denials

The answer is the defendant's pleading. It has several chores to perform.[1] The first is found in CPLR 3018(a), which requires the defendant to respond to the complaint with denials or admissions.

There are three kinds of denials:

1. If the defendant knows at first hand that the allegation is false, the denial is outright, without any qualifying language: "Defendant denies the allegations of paragraphs 2 and 3 of the complaint."

2. If the defendant does not know at first hand but has information (and believes it) suggesting the falsity of an allegation, the denial is on information and belief: "Upon information and belief, defendant denies the allegations of paragraphs 5 and 6 of the complaint."

3. If the defendant has no knowledge one way or the other and can't say whether the allegation is true or false, the denial is of knowledge or information sufficient to form a belief: "Defendant denies knowledge or information sufficient to form a belief of the allegations of paragraphs 7 and 8 of the complaint."

Silence in a responsive pleading is an admission. In the above example, paragraphs 1 and 4 of the complaint, not having been addressed by the answer, are deemed admitted.

Whichever form of denial is used, the plaintiff has the burden of proving the matter denied. And under a denial, whatever its form, the defendant is entitled at the trial to disprove any fact the plaintiff is required to prove.

Denials should of course be made in good faith. A denial of knowledge or information sufficient to form a belief of something the defendant must know one way or the other can lead to trouble for the defendant, although the consequences are not clear-cut. If the denials lend an aura of sham to the whole of the defendant's posture in the litigation, they may be deemed to go to the crux of his case and

---

8. White v. Adler, 289 N.Y. 34, 43 N.E.2d 798 (1942).

9. See Clarcq v. Chamberlain Mobile Home Transport, Inc., 58 Misc.2d 227, 294 N.Y.S.2d 550 (Sup.Ct., Monroe County, 1968).

10. Stoner v. Culligan, Inc., 32 A.D.2d 170, 300 N.Y.S.2d 966 (3d Dep't 1969).

11. Brown v. Lockwood, 76 A.D.2d 721, 740, 432 N.Y.S.2d 186, 199 (2d Dep't 1980).

§ 221

1. The rules to be discussed in this section apply not only to the defendant's answer to the complaint, but to all responsive pleadings, like a plaintiff's reply to a counterclaim, a co-defendant's answer to a cross-claim when an answer is demanded, etc. For purposes of this treatment, all responsive pleading steps are discussed in terms of the defendant answering the complaint.

lead to summary judgment. That's what happened in effect in Dahlstrom v. Gemunder,[2] where P sued an agent whose defense was that his principal had paid P. In a reply, P denied knowledge or information about the payment. The court held that P may not just "close his eyes and ears for the purpose of avoiding knowledge and information"[3], and P in *Dahlstrom* paid a price for doing so. If P is genuinely in the dark, as where she is an executrix who had no personal part in the transaction involving her decedent, her denials of knowledge would not suggest bad faith and would not invoke such consequences.

If the subject of a given allegation of a complaint is only presumptively in D's knowledge, the denial-of-knowledge form is permissible to meet the allegation. If some of the denials in that situation are good while some are bad and some borderline, there is not likely to be enough to support a summary judgment against the responsive pleader.[4] And there is no motion available under the CPLR to strike denials.[5] One risk the bad faith denier runs, however, is that the matter purportedly denied may be deemed admitted. It is not a common result, nor something the other side can assume unless and until the court so holds, but even a denial made upon information and belief, type 2 on the list, may be deemed ineffective and the matter addressed deemed admitted if the court is convinced that the denier had to know the fact at first hand one way or the other.[6]

Certain other denial techniques are frowned on and can get the denier in trouble. One of these is the inconsistent-version denial. Here the responsive pleader does not deny a fact directly, but sets forth a different version in the expectation that the reader will imply or infer a denial. This technique should not be

used; it has been held inadequate to deny the fact[7] and may therefore result in its admission.

Another unacceptable ploy, related to the inconsistent-version denial, is the so-called "negative pregnant"—a negation pregnant with an admission. "The defect known as negative pregnant usually arises where the answer denies immaterial allegations of the complaint, which relate to time and place merely."[8] P pleads, for example, that at 10:29 a.m. on May 20, 1998, D drove a car against P at the corner of Holland and Delaware Avenues in Albany, New York, and D responds that "D denies that at 10:29 a.m. on May 20, 1998 D drove a car against P at the corner of Holland and Delaware Avenues in Albany, New York". This is a negative pregnant. Perhaps the accident occurred at 10:50 a.m. instead, or on May 19, or not at the very corner, etc. D is hiding behind an incident, hoping to evade the crux of the allegation because some inconsequential phase of it is not entirely accurate.

A "general denial", as it is popularly known, is usually a terse but total denial of everything contained in the complaint: "Defendant denies all the allegations of the complaint." If intended in good faith, it is acceptable, and if the complaint is terse it may be quite appropriate. But the more precise and detailed the complaint is, the less appropriate the general denial becomes. If used against a complaint containing extended allegations, it may create the same aura of frivolity or sham that the wrong kind of specific allegation, as previously discussed, can amount to. The courts frown on general denials in such instances, but unless the judge is convinced that it is patently phony, there is not likely to be any serious consequence appended to it,[9] except perhaps an

---

2. 198 N.Y. 449, 92 N.E. 106 (1910). The Dahlstrom case involved a judgment on the pleadings, a remedy superseded under the CPLR by summary judgment under CPLR 3212.

3. 198 N.Y. at 454, 92 N.E. at 108.

4. See Kirschbaum v. Eschmann, 205 N.Y. 127, 98 N.E. 328 (1912).

5. See Commentary C3018:4 on McKinney's CPLR 3018.

6. See City of Rochester v. Diksu Corp., 47 Misc.2d 407, 262 N.Y.S.2d 690 (Sup.Ct., Monroe County, 1965).

7. Smith v. Coe, 170 N.Y. 162, 63 N.E. 57 (1902).

8. Kellogg v. Freeland, 195 N.Y.S. 912, 913 (Sup.Ct., Erie County, 1922).

9. See Doyle v. Buturlinsky, 26 A.D.2d 717, 271 N.Y.S.2d 349 (3d Dep't 1966).

award of costs.[10] If the context suggests that the general denial is frivolous, it can result today in the imposition of a more serious money sanction.[11]

A good faith general denial enables the defendant to adduce evidence in respect of any matter of which the plaintiff has the burden of proof.[12]

In some instances a general denial is explicitly forbidden. If a schedule of goods or services is used under CPLR 3016(f), for example,[13] the defendant must address specifically any enumerated item that she wants to refute. Signatures and contractual conditions precedent must also be specifically denied.[14]

Although silence in response to a given allegation is an admission, admissions may also be made expressly: "D admits the allegation of paragraph 11 of the complaint." Silence is probably better. As a general rule, the only time a responsive pleader should make an admission expressly is when the allegation addressed also contains some matter that has to be denied. D should in that instance deny the allegations of the subject paragraph "except that D admits thus-and-so". In other words, single out the fact to be admitted and deny the rest. Don't do the reverse, singling out the matter to be denied and admitting the rest. That only increases the chance of an inadvertent admission.[15]

When a pleading requires no response—examples would be a reply, or an answer containing no affirmative claims—all of it, including any affirmative defenses it may contain, is deemed denied.[16]

If convenient and clear, a single numbered paragraph can contain D's responses to several paragraphs of the complaint. This does not violate the separate numbering requirement of CPLR 3014.[17]

§ 222. Marked Pleadings

A marked pleading is one that states an affirmative cause of action and whose numbered allegations each bear, usually in the left margin, some indication of what the adverse party's response is. Using the complaint and answer as the illustration, each paragraph of the complaint would have a "D" pencilled in if the allegation is denied outright, "I & B" or "DI & B" if it's denied on information and belief, "DKI" if it's something of which knowledge or information is denied, and "A" if admitted. If a paragraph has several allegations, some of which are denied in one form, some in another, some admitted, etc., any set of markings clearly showing the response would satisfy.

Marked pleadings must be submitted to the trial judge. CPLR 4012 requires that they be furnished by the party who files the note of issue in the case (either party can file it under CPLR 3402). The court's rules may require marked pleadings on other occasions in connection with motions, pre-trial conferences, etc.

§ 223. Affirmative Defenses

Under a denial, a defendant can disprove anything the plaintiff is required to prove. But a number of matters are not the plaintiff's burden to prove as part of the cause of action and are thus the defendant's burden to broach in the answer and sustain at the trial, i.e., to plead and to prove. These are the "affirmative defenses"; they are defined, and the main ones listed, in CPLR 3018(b).

Most of the affirmative defenses are well known and the attorney does not have to stop to figure out what they are. The well known ones are the several listed in CPLR 3018(b):

arbitration and award
collateral estoppel

---

10. See Rouse v. Champion Home Builders Co., 47 A.D.2d 584, 363 N.Y.S.2d 167 (4th Dep't 1975).

11. See § 414A below.

12. Hoffstaedter v. Lichtenstein, 203 A.D. 494, 196 N.Y.S. 577 (1st Dep't 1922).

13. See § 216 above.

14. CPLR 3015(d), (a).

15. See Commentary C3018:8 on McKinney's CPLR 3018.

16. CPLR 3018(a).

17. See paragraph one of Official Form 17, which includes all of D's responses on fewer than half a dozen lines.

culpable conduct of the plaintiff under the
    comparative negligence rule

discharge in bankruptcy

illegality

fraud

infancy or other disability of the defendant

payment

release

res judicata

statute of frauds

statute of limitations

The list is not exhaustive. Other things may
qualify as affirmative defenses, and will if they
meet either of these two descriptions: (1) the
matter is one that would be likely to surprise
the plaintiff; or (2) the matter raises fact issues not appearing on the face of the complaint.[1]

The "surprise" standard is not very helpful
for determining whether a given item must be
raised by way of defense. Few things in the
parties' dealings are likely to "surprise" the
plaintiff. Should P be surprised to learn that
he sued too late, or that his contract is oral, or
that his claim was previously adjudicated?
More meaningful is the second standard: that
the matter raises issues not introduced by the
complaint.

Other matters than those listed have also
been held to be affirmative defenses, such as
truth in a defamation action,[2] adverse possession,[3] qualified privilege,[4] and standing to sue,[5]
to name but a few. Another comes from Article
16 of the CPLR, the article added in 1986 to

relieve of "joint" liability tort defendants with
culpability of 50% or less. Defendants in that
category bear "several-only" liability, meaning
that they are responsible to the plaintiff for
only their own shares of the plaintiff's "non-
economic" damages.[6] The burden of proof on
this score is on the defendant.[7] It amounts to
an affirmative defense and should be pleaded
as such.[8] The defendant's attorney should consider it an additional item on the list contained
in CPLR 3018(b).

A few points should be made about the
culpable conduct defense embodied in the comparative negligence rule. There have been
some decisions in automobile tort cases on the
need to plead as a separate defense the plaintiff's failure to wear a seat belt. At least one
case has held that the seat belt defense must
be separately pleaded; that it would not be
deemed embraced by a general defense alleging the plaintiff's negligence.[9] The general defense of the plaintiff's culpable conduct has
been held to cover the seat belt defense as
well,[10] but a later statutory change appears to
mandate the pleading of the seat belt defense
distinctly,[11]

The cautious lawyer will conclude that it
does no harm to articulate the seat belt defense as a separately numbered one, and that's
probably the best course as long as the answer
does not appear to put all the eggs in that
basket. The defendant should keep in mind
that being too specific with defenses in a
pleading can sometimes have a restricting effect at the trial.[12] If the seat belt omission is

---

§ 223

1. These are the definitions of CPLR 3018(b). The text
uses the example of a defendant answering a complaint,
but the obligation to plead affirmative defenses applies
equally to any party required to respond to an affirmative
claim, such as a plaintiff replying to a counterclaim, a co-
defendant answering a cross-claim, a third-party defendant answering an impleader claim, etc.

2. Bounds v. Mutual of Omaha Ins. Co., 37 A.D.2d
1008, 325 N.Y.S.2d 573 (3d Dep't 1971).

3. Brink v. Central School Dist. No. 1, 63 Misc.2d 293,
311 N.Y.S.2d 424 (Sup.Ct., Dutchess County, 1970), aff'd
36 A.D.2d 796, 320 N.Y.S.2d 896 (2d Dep't 1971).

4. Chiappinelli–Marx, Inc. v. Pacitto, 46 Misc.2d 611,
260 N.Y.S.2d 355 (Sup.Ct., Westchester County, 1965),
aff'd 25 A.D.2d 619, 267 N.Y.S.2d 1018 (2d Dep't 1966).

5. Fossella v. Dinkins, 66 N.Y.2d 162, 495 N.Y.S.2d
352, 485 N.E.2d 1017 (1985).

6. See § 168A above.

7. CPLR 1603.

8. See § 168D above.

9. Brodvin v. Hertz Corp., 487 F.Supp. 1336 (S.D.N.Y.
1980).

10. Fernandez v. Vukosa, 108 Misc.2d 48, 436 N.Y.S.2d
919 (N.Y.C.Civ.Ct. 1980).

11. See V. & T.L.§ 1229–c(8) and Costanza v. City of
N.Y., 147 Misc.2d 94, 553 N.Y.S.2d 616 (N.Y.C. Civ. Ct.
1990).

12. See the discussion of the Linton case at the point
of note 22 below.

not the only culpable conduct the defendant plans to show against the plaintiff, words should be chosen to make that clear in the answer.

The defendant's rule of thumb should be to treat as an affirmative defense—pleading it and being prepared to prove it—anything she is not sure of being able to introduce pursuant to her denials.[13] The defendant may thereby be assuming a "burden" of pleading and perhaps even of proof that she might otherwise not have had, but that's more a theoretical than a practical element.[14] Assuming a doubtful burden more than offsets the alternative prospect: that of forfeiting a defense for not having realized that it was one. It has been held, moreover, that the defendant does not even assume the burden in such an instance; that the burden remains the plaintiff's despite the defendant's gratuitous "defense".[15]

In tort actions involving multiple tortfeasors, it is almost always advisable for each defendant to include in its answer an allegation placing at least some blame on the others, whether the others are named in the main action or not. By so doing, the defendant preserves its rights under at least two statutes that may prove germane later even if the defendant is not thinking about them now.[16] One is Article 16 of the CPLR and the insulation it offers defendants from joint liability in certain circumstances.[17] The other is General Obligations Law § 15–108, which reduces a nonsettling defendant's exposure based on settlements the injured person has reached with other tortfeasors.[18]

If the plaintiff introduces in the complaint a matter that would ordinarily be an affirmative

defense for the defendant to plead, the defendant's omission to plead it should not be held a forfeiture. So holds Green Bus Lines, Inc. v. Consolidated Mut. Ins. Co.,[19] where the issue was whether certain insurance coverage was excluded, a matter for the defendant to plead and prove. But while the defendant was relieved of the burden of pleading on the issue—because the plaintiff had assumed it—it was nevertheless held to retain the burden of proof.

Defenses can be complete or partial. They are subject to the usual pleading rules and get the usual pleading advantages. Under CPLR 3014, they can be inconsistent and may be pleaded in the alternative or hypothetically.

As the official forms illustrate,[20] brevity is not only permissible, but encouraged. The Court of Appeals has held that the "statute of limitations" is a sufficient pleading of that defense.[21] Sometimes terseness may even be safer. In Linton v. Unexcelled Fire Works Co.,[22] for example, P sued D for wrongful discharge. D set up the defense of justification, setting forth many specific instances. Then at the trial D tried to prove even further instances. He was precluded from doing so on the ground that P was entitled to rely on the list of instances D had volunteered in the answer. The court hinted that if D had pleaded justification in general terms, he might have been able to prove any specific instances of it, because the plaintiff would not then have been misled.[23]

Another example, a century later, of what we might call "over pleading" appears in Hatch v. Tran,[24] in which a defendant who pleaded that the complaint wasn't "properly

---

13. See Northway Eng'g, Inc. v. Felix Indus., Inc., 77 N.Y.2d 332, 567 N.Y.S.2d 634, 569 N.E.2d 437 (1991), where the defendant pleaded as a defense, gratuitously, something it could have preserved through a mere denial. The case is discussed in a note in New York State Law Digest No. 378.

14. See Commentary C3018:16 on McKinney's CPLR 3018.

15. Beece v. Guardian Life Ins. Co., 110 A.D.2d 865, 488 N.Y.S.2d 422 (2d Dep't 1985). See 1985 Commentary C3018:16 on McKinney's CPLR 3018.

16. See Ward v. City of Schenectady, 204 A.D.2d 779, 611 N.Y.S.2d 932 (3d Dep't 1994), and the lead note in SPR 30.

17. See §§ 168A through 168D above.

18. See § 176 above.

19. 74 A.D.2d 136, 426 N.Y.S.2d 981 (2d Dep't 1980).

20. See § 228, below, showing Official Form 17.

21. Immediate v. St. John's Queens Hospital, 48 N.Y.2d 671, 421 N.Y.S.2d 875, 397 N.E.2d 385 (1979).

22. 124 N.Y. 533, 27 N.E. 406 (1891).

23. Id. at 537, 27 N.E. at 407.

24. 170 A.D.2d 649, 567 N.Y.S.2d 72 (2d Dep't 1991).

served" (which concerns the method of service) was precluded from afterwards contending that there was no jurisdictional basis (which concerns only the place of service). Both objections are embraced within the category of want of personal jurisdiction set forth in CPLR 3211(a)(8), and the defendant would probably have preserved both just by asserting the general defense of want of personal jurisdiction.[25]

Many of the affirmative defenses may at the defendant's option be raised by a motion to dismiss instead of being pleaded in the answer. It depends on whether the particular defense is among the motion grounds listed in CPLR 3211(a). A comparison of that provision and CPLR 3018(b) made later in the book[26] shows which of the defenses are available for motion use.

The defense should be included in the defendant's initial answer, but it has been held that if it is not, it is still permissible for the defendant to include it in an amended answer made as of course.[27] That amendment is made pursuant to CPLR 3025(a). If the time for making the of-course amendment has expired,[28] the defendant must then seek leave of court under CPLR 3025(b) in order to amend and add the defense. Whether to grant leave lies in the discretion of the court and usually turns on whether the other side would be unreasonably prejudiced.[29]

In a given case a defense may be preserved through conduct even though not included in the answer. It has been held, for example, that D's omission of a defense from the answer becomes unprejudicial and can even be made the basis of a summary judgment or dismissal motion when the subject matter of the defense

is explored through the disclosure devices and the element of surprise is thereby removed from the case.[30] That won't often happen. It is always best that the defendant plead the defense and not take chances.

G. COUNTERCLAIMS

Table of Sections

§ 224. Counterclaims, Generally

A counterclaim is a claim the defendant (D) interposes against the plaintiff (P). It is contained in the answer, following the denials and defenses. The CPLR permits D to use as a counterclaim any claim D has against P, related or not to P's action.[1] If it is unrelated and would unduly confuse the jury, it can be severed or ordered separately tried; but it can't be dismissed, as at one time it could,[2] merely because it is inconvenient or unrelated. The usual pleading rules applicable to a plaintiff's statement of a claim in the complaint apply to counterclaims as well.[3]

When P invokes the court's jurisdiction by bringing suit, P also subjects herself to the court's jurisdiction in respect of the defendant's counterclaims. Hence no process service need be made on P for counterclaim jurisdiction. And it has been held that once having served a summons on D, P can't avoid the court's counterclaim jurisdiction by trying to abandon the action without serving a complaint.[4]

---

25. This is in contrast with federal practice, which, in Rule 12(b) of the Federal Rules of Civil Procedure, lists the defects separately and requires the defendant to specify the one relied on. See § 635 in this Supplement (Practitioner's Ed.) below.

26. See § 263 below.

27. Solarino v. Noble, 55 Misc.2d 429, 286 N.Y.S.2d 71 (Sup.Ct., N.Y. County, 1967).

28. The time for an amendment as of course is limited to the early stages of the action. See § 236 below.

29. See Commentary C3211:62 on McKinney's CPLR 3211.

30. See Rogoff v. San Juan Racing Ass'n, Inc., 77 A.D.2d 831, 431 N.Y.S.2d 16 (1st Dep't 1980), aff'd 54 N.Y.2d 883, 444 N.Y.S.2d 911, 429 N.E.2d 418 (1981).

§ 224

1. CPLR 3019(a).

2. See § 262 of the old Civil Practice Act.

3. CPLR 3019(d).

4. See Edelman v. Edelman, 88 Misc.2d 156, 386 N.Y.S.2d 331 (Sup.Ct., Nassau County, 1976).

All counterclaims are permissive in New York: D can use his claim as a counterclaim or save it and sue on it separately. D may save it for separate suit even when it is a related counterclaim, i.e., when it arises out of the same transaction or occurrence as P's claim. Batavia Kill Watershed Dist. v. Charles O. Desch, Inc.[5] can illustrate.

Owner O retained contractor G on a project. G sued O for breach of the agreement. O had a damages claim against G arising out of the transaction but did not interpose it as a counterclaim, successfully defending and defeating G's suit and only afterwards bringing an action against G for O's own damages. The trial court held that O waived the right to bring the separate action against G. Its reason was that O had told the jury in G's action that O had suffered damage at G's hands, but made no affirmative claim against G for relief, thus possibly misleading the jury into thinking that O was absorbing its damages and thereby making the jury all the more sympathetic to O. The appellate division nevertheless reversed and not only allowed O to bring the separate action, but on the merits applied the collateral estoppel (issue preclusion) doctrine in favor of O against G.[6]

In federal practice such a related claim would be denominated "compulsory"[7] and the failure to use it as a counterclaim would waive it;[8] only unrelated counterclaims in the federal courts are permissive.[9]

Things worked out well for O in the *Batavia* case and furnished a classic example of the permissive nature of New York's counterclaim rule even as applied to related counterclaims. But the notion that a defendant with a related claim can safely withhold it and sue on it later can be misleading and perilous. The reason is that any fact adjudicated or legal conclusion reached in the P v. D action will be conclusive and binding if it should become germane—as it became in *Batavia*—in D's later action against P,[10] and not always with such happy results for D. Had O, who was the defendant in the *Batavia* setting, lost in the first action, for example, it being established that O and not G was the breacher of the contract, the estoppel would have gone against O and brought about a dismissal of the second action.[11] This suggests that unless a defendant with a related counterclaim has some special tactical reason for saving it (and taking a chance on losing it through the estoppel route), he should use it as a counterclaim in the plaintiff's original action and not depend on the notion that all counterclaims are "permissive". O swam against the tide in *Batavia* and had a victory that a similarly situated defendant might not enjoy the next time around.

D will likely want to use his claim at least as a defense to P's action, if not as an outright counterclaim, but in one case in which D did so he was held to have waived the right to sue on the same subject matter afterwards. In *Musco v. Lupi*,[12] P sued D for money due under a contract. D defended and won on the ground that P, and not D, had breached the contract. D's later suit against P for damages for breach of that same contract was held barred, a holding not at all at home with an ostensibly "permissive" counterclaim rule. *Batavia* could be read as overruling *Musco*, but the appellate division in *Batavia* purports merely to distinguish it on the ground that in *Musco* the court in the first action had specifi-

---

5. 57 N.Y.2d 796, 455 N.Y.S.2d 597, 441 N.E.2d 1115 (1982), affirming on the appellate division opinion reported in 83 A.D.2d 97, 444 N.Y.S.2d 958 (3d Dep't 1981).

6. The Batavia case is the subject of a lead note in New York State Law Digest No. 258. The reversing appellate division case is summarized in Digest No. 267 and the Court of Appeals affirmance in Digest No. 276.

7. Federal Rules of Civil Procedure, Rule 13(a).

8. See Cummings v. Dresher, 18 N.Y.2d 105, 108, 271 N.Y.S.2d 976, 978, 218 N.E.2d 688, 690 (1966) (concurring opinion of Fuld, J.).

9. FRCP Rule 13(b).

10. See Pace v. Perk, 81 A.D.2d 444, 440 N.Y.S.2d 710 (2d Dep't 1981).

11. The doctrine of collateral estoppel is studied in Chapter 17. See § 457 et seq., below.

12. 6 Misc.2d 930, 164 N.Y.S.2d 84 (Sup.Ct., Orange County, 1957).

cally invited D to amend and assert a counter-claim and D didn't accept it. That seems a tenuous distinction; D had the right to assert a counterclaim and the judicial invitation, how-ever cordial, was hardly relevant. The trial court in *Batavia* cited an even better reason for holding D to a waiver—D had led the jury to think that D was generously absorbing the loss caused it by P—but the appellate division still reversed and said there was no waiver.

If P's claim is brought in a lower court, and D prefers the supreme court for D's claim (or must turn to the supreme court because the lower court lacks subject matter jurisdiction of D's claim), an alternative open to D is to commence prompt separate suit on his claim in the supreme court and then make a motion to remove and consolidate P's action.[13]

A counterclaim needs a reply.[14] If D pleads something that is in effect a counterclaim but not formally denominated one, P need not reply to it,[15] although from P's point of view it may be wiser to.[16]

If D has a claim against P and some other person, X, who is not a party, the CPLR allows D to interpose the claim against P while simul-taneously joining X as an adverse party on the claim. D just serves the answer containing the counterclaim on both P and X, but with the service on X accompanied by a summons and made by the usual methods of summons ser-vice.[17] To take advantage of this permission to add X, the counterclaim should exist at least in part against P. A common example is where the plaintiff bringing suit against D is an

assignee of the claim, rather than the person to whom the claim originally accrued, and where D counterclaims on something due from the assignor and adds the assignor as a party.[18]

A few points should be noted about counter-claims in some of the lower courts. The subject matter jurisdiction of the New York City Civil Court and of the district, city, town, and vil-lage courts in respect of a counterclaim is always at least as broad as that governing the main claim, but in some instances counter-claim jurisdiction is even broader. Jurisdiction of money counterclaims, for example, although subject in the town and village courts to the same monetary limitation that govern the main claim,[19] is unlimited in the New York City Civil Court and in the district and city courts.[20] Those courts also have jurisdiction of a counterclaim to rescind or reform the trans-action out of which the main claim arises.[21]

§ 225. Counterclaims; Parties with Several Capacities

If a party has several capacities, a counter-claim involving that party may be used only in respect of the capacity in which she appears in the action.[1] Where T is a trustee, for example, and brings an action in behalf of the trust, the defendant can interpose as a counterclaim any claim existing against T in T's trust capacity, or against the whole body of beneficiaries of the trust, but not a claim existing against T personally and having no relationship to the trust.[2] The same rule applies when the plain-tiff is a trustee in effect though not in name.[3]

---

13. CPLR 602(b).

14. CPLR 3011.

15. Fromm v. Glueck, 161 Misc. 502, 293 N.Y.S. 530 (Sup.Ct., Greene County, 1937).

16. See Commentary C3011:9 on McKinney's CPLR 3011.

17. A preliminary filing and fee paying must be made for this joinder of X as an additional party. See CPLR 3019(d) and the discussion in SPR 22:2–3.

18. See § 226 below.

19. Unif.Just.Ct.Act § 208, McKinney's Vol. 29A, Part 2.

20. See § 208 in the New York City Civil, Uniform District, and Uniform City court acts, McKinney's Vol. 29A, Part 3.

21. Id. The Civil Court also has jurisdiction to order a partnership accounting by way of counterclaim in certain instances. N.Y.C.Civ.Ct.Act, § 208(c)(2).

§ 225

1. Corcoran v. National Union Fire Ins. Co. of Pitts-burgh, Pa., 143 A.D.2d 309, 532 N.Y.S.2d 376 (1st Dep't 1988).

2. CPLR 3019(c). See Commentary C3019:16 on McKinney's CPLR 3019.

3. See, e.g., Helman v. Dixon, 71 Misc.2d 1057, 338 N.Y.S.2d 139 (N.Y.C.Civ.Ct. 1972).

If P sues a partnership (consisting of X, Y, and Z) on a partnership liability, the partnership may of course interpose any claim it has against P even though not all the partners were served.[4] If the partnership were to interpose against P a claim owned personally by partner X, however, it would have to be with X's permission because it amounts to an assignment by X to the partnership of an asset owned individually by X.

When the partnership is the plaintiff, only a claim existing against the partnership collectively, or against the partners together, may be used as a counterclaim. If the claim exists against partner X personally, but not against the partnership or partners Y or Z, the defendant may not use it.[5]

CPLR 3019(a) is rather broadly phrased in regard to representative situations and might even be read as permitting D, sued by P for (e.g.) assault, to counterclaim for money due to D from a decedent for whom P just happens to be the executor. It must therefore be stressed that CPLR 3019(a) was "not intended to alter the well-settled rule requiring a counterclaim to be a claim against the plaintiff in the capacity in which [the plaintiff] sues".[6]

An exception is where there is a complete merger of the party's several capacities. If P sues as administrator of an estate of which he is the sole heir, for example, D may in some instances use as a counterclaim a claim existing against P personally.[7] Similarly, where the merger of capacities is on D's side—where D is sued individually, for example, but happens to be the sole shareholder of a corporation which has a claim against P—D can use that claim as a counterclaim.[8]

The remedy against a counterclaim interposed in violation of this "capacities" rule is a motion under CPLR 3211(a)(6) to dismiss the counterclaim.

§ 226. Counterclaim Against Assignee-Plaintiff

When P is the assignee of a cause of action and sues D on it, D may of course interpose against P any claim D has directly against P. But to what extent, if at all, may D interpose against P a claim that D has only against R, the assignor who originally owned the assigned claim now owned by P? Different rules apply, depending on whether the would-be counterclaim has a relationship to the assigned claim.

When the counterclaim arises out of the same transaction or occurrence as that out of which the assigned claim arises, i.e., when it is a related counterclaim, it may be used as an offset by D. That is, it may be interposed as a counterclaim but only to the extent of neutralizing P's claim. Should a balance be due in D's favor, D may not have affirmative judgment against P for it. This is an example of the doctrine of equitable recoupment, and it applies even if the counterclaim was not yet in existence or owned by D when R assigned the main claim to P. Where P sued for the balance due for fans sold by R to D, for example, and D counterclaimed against P for commissions earned on the sale of those fans and for certain freight charges on them, the counterclaims were held good for offset purposes even though they may have technically accrued after the assignment and presumably even after D was notified of the assignment.[1]

When the counterclaim that D would interpose against P is unrelated to the assigned claim, the time that D is notified of the assignment becomes a key moment. The law's policy is to preserve such claims as D may legitimately have against R, and to preclude R, through the simple expedient of an assignment, from divesting D of use of those claims as counterclaims. Thus, any claim D already has against R when D learns of the assignment is usable against P, the assignee—again, only to the extent of an offset—even if it has no relation-

---

4. Fox Chase Knitting Mills, Inc. v. Handal, 232 A.D. 498, 250 N.Y.S. 416 (1st Dep't 1931).

5. Ruzicka v. Rager, 305 N.Y. 191, 111 N.E.2d 878 (1953).

6. 1st Rep.Leg.Doc. (1957) No. 6(b), p. 71.

7. Anderson v. Carlson, 201 A.D. 260, 194 N.Y.S. 112 (2d Dep't 1922).

8. Conant v. Schnall, 33 A.D.2d 326, 307 N.Y.S.2d 902 (3d Dep't 1970).

§ 226

1. James Talcott, Inc. v. Winco Sales Corp., 14 N.Y.2d 227, 250 N.Y.S.2d 416, 199 N.E.2d 499 (1964).

ship to the assigned claim.[2] But any claim against R that comes into D's ownership afterwards is not usable against P. This is to prevent D, after getting such notice, from deliberately acquiring someone else's claim against R, perhaps at a discount, so as to use it against P. A lesson to P in this situation is to give prompt notice to D of any claim assigned to P by R.

In any situation in which D is allowed to interpose against P the claim D has against R, whether it is a related counterclaim (and interposable regardless of when D got it) or an unrelated one (but already in D's hands when notified of the assignment), D can join R as an additional party on the counterclaim,[3] which would enable D to get an affirmative judgment against R for anything that might be left over after the claim has been used as an offset against P.

If P is not merely the assignee of a cause of action, but the complete successor of R and of R's liabilities, as in a merger of two corporations, these qualifications become irrelevant and P faces the counterclaim in full.

With some exceptions, the law recognizes an agreement whereby D consents not to use against the assignee, P, a claim D has against R, but the agreement had best be drawn carefully because it has been severely circumscribed by statute[4] and is distrusted by the courts. In an adhesion contract, its likelihood of success is remote.[5]

Throughout this discussion we have assumed that the thing assigned by R to P is a mature cause of action. If it is something close but really something else, these rules may be irrelevant and D's claim may be altogether unusable as a counterclaim. Suppose, for example, that R sells a building to P, after which, while P is owner, rent falls due from a tenant, D. When sued by P for rent, D may not counterclaim P for something due from R. It was P, now the owner, who furnished the consideration for which P now sues, and D's claim against R doesn't belong in the action at all.[6]

H.   CROSS–CLAIMS

Table of Sections

§ 227. Cross–Claims

A cross-claim is a claim by one defendant against another; in New York it can be for any claim at all, whether or not related to the plaintiff's claim.[1] This is a contrast to federal practice, where a cross-claim is interposable only if related to some other claim in the case.[2] If, for reasons of relevancy or otherwise, a cross-claim should prove unnecessarily burdensome in a given case, it can be severed or ordered separately tried.[3]

One of the popular uses of a cross-claim by defendant A is for indemnification or contribution from co-defendant B in respect of a tort claim for which the injured person, P, is suing both of them. This is only one of the uses of a cross-claim, however. The cross-claim can be a claim by A against B for A's own injuries suffered in the accident, or a claim on a promissory note, or, theoretically, a claim for divorce if A and B happen to be married. Here we can distinguish the cross-claim from the

2. Gen.Oblig.L. § 13–105; UCC §§ 3–306, 9–318(1)(b).

3. CPLR 3019(d); D.P.C. Corp. v. Jobson, 15 A.D.2d 861, 224 N.Y.S.2d 772 (4th Dep't 1962).

4. Section 302(9) of the Personal Property Law bars from any "retail installment contract" any provision by which the buyer agrees not to assert defenses against the seller's assignee. Coordinately, Pers.Prop.L. § 403(5) subjects the assignee to all such defenses. Both statutes limit these defenses to offset use, however, insulating the assignee from any affirmative judgment for a balance that the buyer may claim. Section 9–206(1) of the UCC, which validates defense-renouncing agreements in some situations, excepts the transaction involving "consumer goods"

and thus appears to defer to the Personal Property Law provision when such goods are involved.

5. See B.W. Acceptance Corp. v. Richmond, 46 Misc.2d 447, 259 N.Y.S.2d 965 (Sup.Ct., N.Y.County, 1965).

6. See Stafford Security Co. v. Kremer, 258 N.Y. 1, 179 N.E. 32 (1931).

§ 227

1. CPLR 3019(b).

2. Federal Rules of Civil Procedure, Rule 13(g). See § 632 below (Practitioner's Edition).

3. See CPLR 603.

impleader (third-party claim) of CPLR 1007. A third-party claim is designed primarily for an indemnity or indemnity-like claim, including a contribution claim,[4] whereas a cross-claim can interpose those or any other claims. Another distinction is that a third-party claim entails summons service because it joins someone not yet a party, while a cross-claim, addressing someone already in the action, does not. The cross-claim is a popular expedient for interposing apportionment claims in tort cases under CPLR 1401 and 1403.[5] Such claims are virtually pro forma in multi-defendant tort actions.

The cross-claim is pleaded in the defendant's answer[6] and is subject to the usual rules for pleading a cause of action. As with a counterclaim, it is also interposable against a nonparty along with the co-defendant. The non-party is joined by filing a copy of the answer containing the cross-claim along with a summons, and paying a filing fee, and then serving the answer and summons on the nonparty being joined.[7] Suppose, for example, that P, injured in an accident involving tortfeasors A, B, and C, sues only A and B. A in his answer can cross-claim both B and C for contribution, but, since C is not a party, C would have to be served with a summons accompanying the answer containing the cross-claim, while B would be served with only the answer and the service would be by mere mail to his attorney.[8]

A cross-claim requires an answer only if the pleading containing the cross-claim demands one. In the absence of a demand, the allegations of the cross-claim are deemed denied.[9] While this applies to all cross-claims, it was designed primarily to dispense with answers to contribution cross-claims, which are interposed almost automatically between joint tortfeasors in personal injury and wrongful death cases. Answers in that situation are straight denials and recriminations and were found to

add nothing to the case but paper. A better remedy might have been to dispense with answers only to contribution cross-claims, but the legislature left with the cross-claimant in all cases the option of demanding an answer.

In the situation mentioned above, in which a nonparty is being joined as an additional adverse party on a cross-claim, it would be preferable for the new party to answer the cross-claim whether or not an answer is demanded, so that the new party's posture in the case can be discerned. Under the terms of CPLR 3011, however, apparently even such a new party need answer only when an answer is demanded. The court can in any event require an answer in its discretion. If an answer is to be made, it should be served within 20 days after service of the pleading containing the cross-claim.[10] When the cross-claim is being served on a nonparty, such as C in the example used above, the answering time would be a 20–or 30–day period under the usual rules governing summons service.[11]

Since the defendant's answer is the place for the cross-claim, the cross-claim would presumably have to be asserted within the cross-claiming defendant's original answering time. But the co-defendant against whom the cross-claim is to be used may not yet have been served in the main action and thus subjected to the jurisdiction of the court. The courts, recognizing such problems, are not strict about the time for cross-claiming if no prejudice is shown.[12] Furthermore, there is always the ubiquitous CPLR 2004 to authorize an extension of time or forgive short lapses of time if needed. If defendant A would cross-claim co-defendants but does not know whether they have yet appeared—if they have, service need only be made by mail to their attorneys[13]—A

---

4. CPLR 1007. Its use was expanded by the Court of Appeals in 1980. See § 157 above.

5. See § 173 above.

6. CPLR 3011.

7. CPLR 3019(b), (d).

8. CPLR 2103(b)(2). See § 202 above. Of course an alternative and more common way for A to join C is by impleader under CPLR 1007.

9. This is the result of a 1977 amendment of CPLR 3011. Previously, all cross-claims required answers.

10. CPLR 3012(a).

11. CPLR 3012(c). See § 231 below.

12. See Manganaro v. Estwing Mfg. Co., 27 A.D.2d 711, 276 N.Y.S.2d 891 (1st Dep't 1967).

13. CPLR 2103(b)(2).

can demand of the plaintiff a list of the appearers.[14]

§ 228. Form of Answer

The following is Form 17 of the Official Forms. It illustrates denials (¶ 1), affirmative defenses (¶ ¶ 2–5), and the proper positions of counterclaims and cross-claims. The first paragraph of the counterclaim would be numbered 6, picking up after the last allegation of the affirmative defenses. Note that the wherefore clause first asks dismissal of the complaint— which is the relief sought by the defendant based on the denials and defenses—and then affirmative relief on the counterclaim and cross-claim.

---

14. CPLR 2103(e). For discussion of service on a non-appearing co-defendant, see Commentary C3012:7 on

McKinney's CPLR 3012.

SUPREME COURT OF THE STATE OF NEW YORK
COUNTY OF NEW YORK

A.B., Plaintiff,

against

C.D. and E.F., Defendants.

Answer

Index No. _____

1. Defendant C.D. admits the allegations in paragraphs 1 and 4 of the complaint; states that he lacks knowledge or information sufficient to form a belief as to the truth of the allegations in paragraph 2 of the complaint; and denies each and every other allegation in the complaint.

First Affirmative Defense

2. The cause of action set forth in the complaint did not accrue within six years next before the commencement of this action.

Second Affirmative Defense

3. Defendant C.D. entered into the contract annexed to the complaint as Exhibit A in reliance upon the truth of the oral statements made by plaintiff to defendant C.D. on or about July 1, 1966, that [specify alleged misrepresentation].

4. Plaintiff made those statements in order to induce defendant C.D. to enter into the contract and with the intention that defendant C.D. rely upon plaintiff's statements.

5. In fact and to the knowledge of plaintiff at the time he made those statements they were false in that [state facts].

Counterclaim

[Here set forth any cause of action as a counterclaim in the manner in which a claim is pleaded in a complaint].

Cross-Claim Against Defendant E.F.

[Here set forth any cause of action as a cross-claim against defendant E.F. in the manner in which a claim is pleaded in a complaint].

Wherefore defendant C.D. demands judgment (1) against plaintiff dismissing the complaint, (2) against plaintiff on the counterclaim in the sum of _____ dollars, plus interest, (3) against defendant E.F. on the cross-claim in the sum of _____ dollars, plus interest, and (4) against plaintiff and defendant E.F. for costs and disbursements.

_____
[Print name]
Attorney for Defendant C.D.
Address:
Telephone Number:

[F7296]

I. THE REPLY

Table of Sections

Sec.
229. The Reply; Further Pleadings.

§ 229. The Reply; Further Pleadings

CPLR 3011 lists the few pleadings used in New York practice. The plaintiff's initial pleading is of course the complaint and the defendant's is the answer. The only other one listed is the plaintiff's reply.

A main purpose of CPLR 3011 is to state the instances in which a responsive pleading is required. The defendant's answer to the complaint is of course mandatory. But a reply by the plaintiff, as will be elaborated shortly, is required only when the answer contains a counterclaim. A third-party (impleader) complaint requires an answer; so does an interpleader complaint. Prior to a 1977 amendment of CPLR 3011, every cross-claim also required an answer, but this was found to be generating too much superfluous paper in tort cases, as described in a prior section.[1] Under the amendment, a cross-claim requires an answer only when the cross-claimant demands one, which she can do with appropriate language in the answer containing the cross-claim, perhaps in an additional paragraph. The amendment is not limited to the tort case, however; it requires a demand before any cross-claim need be answered. In the absence of a demand, the allegations of the cross-claim are deemed denied.

An auxiliary function of CPLR 3011 is to give all claims and pleadings a label, but any CPLR provision authorizing the assertion of a claim in any context should be given effect without regard to whether CPLR 3011 has an apt label for it. "The rights of parties are not ultimately determined by the names given their pleadings".[2] If that approach is not taken, labels take over and substance becomes lost in the shuffle.[3]

A reply is the plaintiff's response to an answer. It is required when the answer contains a counterclaim[4] and, indeed, the failure to reply in that situation amounts to a default on the counterclaim.

Sometimes the same matter will lend itself to use either as a defense or a counterclaim. If the defendant has used it as a counterclaim, the plaintiff who withholds a reply on the assumption that it is only a defense risks a default. Usury, for example, can be treated as a mere defense, negating the plaintiff's claim, or as an outright counterclaim seeking affirmative relief, such as rescission. A plaintiff who failed to reply to a usury allegation when it was denominated a counterclaim was held to be in default.[5] A plaintiff in doubt does best to serve a reply. If the plaintiff, in doing so, has guessed wrong, and the defendant moves to dismiss the reply, it amounts to a concession that the defendant is seeking no affirmative relief. The plaintiff can live with that.

If there is no counterclaim in the answer, not only need the plaintiff not reply; he may not even do so voluntarily. Absent a counterclaim, a reply is permissible only by court order.[6] Either party can move for the order. Affirmative defenses contained in an answer having no counterclaim (and therefore requiring no reply) are deemed denied.[7]

Whether to order a reply to a non-counterclaiming answer is in the court's discretion. A reply will not be ordered unless the court is convinced that it will serve some useful purpose.[8] It is sometimes ordered when the an-

---

§ 229

1. See § 227 above.

2. Axelrod & Co. v. Telsey, 77 Misc.2d 1035, 1038, 353 N.Y.S.2d 596, 599 (Sup.Ct., N.Y.County, 1973).

3. See the discussion at notes 14–17 below.

4. CPLR 3011. As to whether a reply that is required because the answer contains a counterclaim may also respond to defenses, see Commentary C3011:10 on McKinney's CPLR 3011.

5. Loew v. McInerney, 159 A.D. 513, 144 N.Y.S. 546 (2d Dep't 1913). Defaults are vacatable, however, and

vacatur of a default in this situation would likely be granted for the mere asking if sought expeditiously. See § 108 above.

6. CPLR 3011.

7. CPLR 3018(a).

8. See Olsen & Chapman Constr. Co. v. Village of Cazenovia, 30 A.D.2d 738, 291 N.Y.S.2d 388 (3d Dep't 1968).

swer has something like a statute of frauds defense, so as to compel the plaintiff by reply to say whether the contract was oral; or a statute of limitations defense, to compel the plaintiff to set forth relevant dates.[9] An alternative might be to require the plaintiff to state such facts in the complaint,[10] but since they are matters of defense the complaint should not have to reflect on them at all. The courts are not disposed to make any pleading do that kind of extra bidding today; the bill of particulars and the disclosure devices are more likely to get the assignment.

A reply should not be used by the plaintiff to amend the complaint or to set forth new matter.[11] Nor should a reply ordinarily state an affirmative cause of action. The plaintiff who wants at that stage to add another claim should amend the complaint, obtaining leave to do so if necessary.[12] If the reply does state a claim, however, and in the context of the particular case it seems an appropriate thing to do, it has been held permissible. Thus, if there are two defendants, and defendant A counterclaims plaintiff P for damage to A's car, and P maintains that defendant B is the one responsible for that damage, P may, in the same reply that responds to the counterclaim, include a "cross-claim" against defendant B for contribution or indemnification in respect of the counterclaim.[13] This is sound. The pressing of recriminations and apportionment claims back and forth among parties to a tort suit is frequent and in a context like the one supposed the reply is often not merely an appropriate but even an obvious place for such claims.

In a case decided before the *Dole* case,[14] defendant X interposed a counterclaim against P for which P maintained that defendant Y was required to indemnify P. Had Y not been a

party, P could have impleaded Y for the indemnification.[15] But Y was a party, so P simply included the indemnity claim against Y (calling it a "cross-complaint") in the same reply that responded to the counterclaim, a seemingly sound procedural step. The court disallowed it,[16] apparently remitting P to implead Y into an action in which Y was already a party. The "cross-complaint", under that or any other label, should have been allowed. In the face of a clear legislative intent to allow the indemnity claim, the label appended to the pleading interposing it should have been subordinate.[17]

The reply is ordinarily the final pleading because "[t]here shall be no other pleading unless the court orders otherwise".[18] Suppose, however, that P's reply to a counterclaim contains the defense of the statute of limitations. The court could order D to cross-reply to that defense with the relevant dates. Under old law it sometimes did.[19] But such a step is largely wasteful in view of the availability, as already noted, of the bill of particulars and the disclosure devices to do the job.

J. CORRECTIVE MOTIONS

Table of Sections

§ 230. Motions to Correct Pleadings; CPLR 3024

There are two statutorily recognized corrective motions—motions that seek to compel an amendment of a pleading rather than its dismissal. Both are in CPLR 3024.

Subdivision (a) of CPLR 3024 is the motion for a more definite statement. It's available only to a party required to respond to the

---

9. See, e.g., Barker v. O'Grady, 98 Misc. 42, 162 N.Y.S. 262 (Sup.Ct., Monroe County, 1916).

10. See § 215 above.

11. Eidlitz v. Rothschild, 87 Hun. 243, 33 N.Y.S. 1047 (Gen.Term., 1st Dep't, 1895).

12. CPLR 3025(a), (b); Habiby v. Habiby, 23 A.D.2d 558, 256 N.Y.S.2d 634 (1st Dep't 1965).

13. De Mato v. County of Suffolk, 79 Misc.2d 484, 360 N.Y.S.2d 570 (Sup.Ct., Suffolk County, 1974).

14. See §§ 170 and 171 above.

15. CPLR 1011.

16. Chambland v. Brewer, 51 Misc.2d 231, 272 N.Y.S.2d 903 (Sup.Ct., Queens County, 1966).

17. Axelrod & Co. v. Telsey, 77 Misc.2d 1035, 353 N.Y.S.2d 596 (Sup.Ct., N.Y.County, 1973).

18. CPLR 3011.

19. See, e.g., Rosner v. Globe Valve Corp., 276 A.D. 462, 95 N.Y.S.2d 531 (1st Dep't 1950).

objectionable pleading. It may be used by the defendant against the complaint and by the plaintiff against a counterclaim, for example, but it is unavailable to the plaintiff if the answer contains no counterclaim because in that case the plaintiff doesn't have to respond to the answer. The movant's burden is to show that the pleading, whether it states a claim or not, is so jumbled or disorderly that she "cannot reasonably be required to frame a response". If the pleading is answerable and what the movant is really seeking is an amplification of it, the motion for a more definite statement will be denied and the movant will be remitted to a bill of particulars.[1]

Subdivision (b) of CPLR 3024 contains the only motion the CPLR recognizes for striking objectionable matter from a pleading.[2] It permits a motion to strike out "scandalous or prejudicial matter unnecessarily inserted in a pleading". Mere repetitiveness is not a ground for a motion to strike.[3] Nor is a mere showing that irrelevant matter is included in the pleading.[4] Corrective motions had been allowed on those grounds under prior law.[5] Nor does an allegation of scandalousness by itself suffice. An allegation of mayhem in an assault claim is scandalous, for example, but belongs in the pleading, as does a charge of adultery in a divorce case. "Prejudice" by itself has little meaning here because most of what a party pleads is intended to prejudice the other side. The key words are "unnecessarily inserted", and they have to do with relevancy.

Matter directly relevant to the claim stays in. If something is prejudicial or scandalous while only indirectly relevant at best, it has been held that it may be stricken out even if it can be made to appear sufficiently relevant at

the trial to be admitted into evidence.[6] In Guiliana v. Chiropractic Institute of New York,[7] for example, where P sued a chiropractic facility for letting an inexperienced student treat P, allegations that D allowed other unready students to work on other unwary patients were stricken out—"though possibly pertinent as proof"—because not a necessary part of P's claim. The *Guiliana* case is best treated as one in which the objectionable matter was only indirectly relevant. It should not be read as authority to strike out anything not needed for the statement of the claim. Reading it so would needlessly encourage corrective motions of this kind in a vast range of cases simply because so little is needed today to state a cause of action. Relevancy is still the best key to whether the matter is "unnecessarily" pleaded, and the best key to relevancy is whether it would be admissible in evidence at the trail.

In addition to the explicit corrective motions of subdivisions (a) and (b) of CPLR 3024, there is also the motion to separately state and number, which arises by implication from CPLR 3014.[8] This is akin to the motion for a more definite statement in that the need of it is usually felt only by a party required to respond to the objectionable pleading. The motion would be appropriate, for example, if a more accurate numbering of allegations would better enable one of several defendants to determine which of the allegations are meant for him.[9]

There is some dispute between departments as to whether an order on a separate numbering motion is appealable only by permission, like an order on either of the expressly listed corrective motions of CPLR 3024,[10] or as of

§ 230

1. State v. New York Movers Tariff Bureau, Inc., 48 Misc.2d 225, 254, 264 N.Y.S.2d 931, 963 (Sup.Ct., N.Y.County, 1965).

2. Koos v. Ludwig, 22 A.D.2d 666, 253 N.Y.S.2d 380 (1st Dep't 1964).

3. See Hewitt v. Maass, 41 Misc.2d 894, 246 N.Y.S.2d 670 (Sup.Ct., Suffolk County, 1964).

4. In re Emberger's Estate, 24 A.D.2d 864, 264 N.Y.S.2d 277 (2d Dep't 1965).

5. Rule 103 of the old (pre 1963) Rules of Civil Procedure.

6. See Schachter v. Massachusetts Protective Ass'n, 30 A.D.2d 540, 291 N.Y.S.2d 128 (2d Dep't 1968).

7. 45 Misc.2d 429, 430, 256 N.Y.S.2d 967, 968 (Sup.Ct., Kings County, 1965).

8. See Wolf v. Wolf, 22 A.D.2d 678, 253 N.Y.S.2d 509 (1st Dep't 1964).

9. See Shapolsky v. Shapolsky, 22 A.D.2d 91, 253 N.Y.S.2d 816 (1st Dep't 1964).

10. See CPLR 5701(b)(2), (3).

right,[11] because not set forth expressly in CPLR 3024. The Second Department holds that it is appealable as of right;[12] the First, that permission is needed.[13]

The time to make a corrective motion is within 20 days after the objectionable pleading is served.[14] This is so even though there may be a 30–day period applicable to the answering time.[15] The time limit applicable to the expressly listed motions of CPLR 3024 should apply as well to the separate numbering motion.

The service of an answer waives the motion for a more definite statement and the motion for separate numbering,[16] since answering establishes answerability, which both motions are designed to assure. But it does not necessarily waive the motion to strike objectionable matter. If the matter is scandalous and irrelevant, for example, it is just as much so before as after answering. This has prompted the courts to be less rigid with the time requirements for the motion to strike.[17]

The mere making of a corrective motion extends D's answering time. If the motion is denied, D may serve the answer within 10 days after being served with notice of entry of the order denying the motion. If the motion is granted, P is required to serve an amended complaint[18] within 10 days after notice of entry of the order granting the motion.[19] D then has 20 days to answer the amended complaint.[20]

K. SERVICE OF PLEADINGS

Table of Sections

§ 231. Service of Pleadings; Responding Time

Response to the summons is made within either a 20– or 30–day period, depending on the place and method of service. If the summons is served by personal delivery in New York, the responding period is 20 days; if served by any other means, or by any means at all outside New York, the period is 30 days. CPLR 320(a) so provides when the complaint does not accompany the summons; CPLR 3012(c) so provides when it does.[1] (In certain malpractice actions a special certificate of merit must accompany the complaint.[2]) The defendant's responsive step when the summons is served without a complaint is to appear and demand a copy of the complaint.[3] The defendant's responsive step when the summons and complaint are served together is to serve an answer or make a motion.[4]

CPLR 320(a), governing the time to appear when the complaint is not served with the summons, and CPLR 3012(b), allowing the defendant to demand a copy of the complaint, should be read together. Since the demand is a

---

11. See CPLR 5701(a)(2)(v), discussed in § 526 in the appeals chapter, below.

12. Weicker v. Weicker, 26 A.D.2d 39, 270 N.Y.S.2d 640 (1966).

13. Consolidated Airborne Systems, Inc. v. Silverman, 23 A.D.2d 695, 257 N.Y.S.2d 827 (1965).

14. CPLR 3024(c).

15. CPLR 3012(c).

16. Albemarle Theatre, Inc. v. Bayberry Realty Corp., 27 A.D.2d 172, 277 N.Y.S.2d 505 (1st Dep't 1967).

17. See Szolosi v. Long Island R.R. Co., 52 Misc.2d 1081, 277 N.Y.S.2d 587 (Sup.Ct., Suffolk County, 1967).

18. All of this discussion of the corrective motions has assumed the defendant to be the moving party and an objectionable complaint to be the pleading moved against. Any party against whom a pleading is interposed may of course make equivalent use of these corrective motions.

19. CPLR 3024(c).

20. CPLR 3012(a).

§ 231

1. If P should serve D by two methods, each having a different answering time, such as where a corporate defendant is served via the secretary of state, which affords a 30–day period, as well as by personal delivery to an officer, which offers 20 days, CPLR 320(a), 3012(a), (c), D may take advantage of the longer period and is not in default when the shorter one expires. Olson v. Jordan, 181 Misc. 942, 43 N.Y.S.2d 348 (Sup.Ct., N.Y.County, 1943).

2. CPLR 3012–a requires that in medical, dental, and podiatric malpractice actions, the complaint, whenever served, must have with it the certificate of the plaintiff's lawyer attesting that she consulted with an appropriate expert and believes, based on the consultation, that there is a "reasonable basis" for the action. For the sanction applied for a violation of this requirement, see the McKinney's Commentaries on CPLR 3012–a.

3. CPLR 320(a), 3012(b).

4. CPLR 3011, 3211(e).

step taken in response to the summons, it should be made within the period for appearing as offered by CPLR 320(a). Before CPLR 3012(b) was amended in 1978, some old caselaw suggested that when a complaint was not served with the summons, the defendant could stymie the plaintiff altogether by just doing nothing; that the plaintiff could not then serve a complaint voluntarily.[5] Some later caselaw disagreed.[6] The amended CPLR 3012(b) not only permits but requires the plaintiff to serve a complaint if the defendant appears in the action, even if the defendant does not serve a demand.

If the defendant does not respond at all after being served with a summons, whether the summons has with it a complaint or CPLR 305(b) notice, the plaintiff can apply for a default judgment under CPLR 3215.[7] If the defendant needs or just wants additional answering time, he should get a written stipulation from the plaintiff, or a court order, extending the time.[8]

If the summons was served "bare", accompanied by neither a complaint nor a notice, the defendant can move to dismiss the action on the ground that the defect is jurisdictional.[9] That would be an appropriate tactic for the defendant if the statute of limitations would now bar a new action by the plaintiff. But if the statute is still alive, and a dismissal would just result in a new and timely service by the plaintiff, with proper papers, the defendant should consider whether a motion to dismiss is worth bothering with.[10]

(It has also been held in lower court practice that if no complaint of any kind accompanies the summons, the defect is jurisdictional and

the action can be dismissed on the defendant's motion.[11] In most of the lower courts, the summons and complaint are served together, but the complaint can be a mere "indorsement" on the face of the summons.[12])

The common procedure when only a CPLR 305(b) notice is served with the summons is for the defendant to serve on the plaintiff a single paper embodying both a notice of appearance and a demand for the complaint. CPLR 3012(b) states explicitly that the demand by itself is not an appearance, but, even if it is, the point has lost its significance under the CPLR. It had to do with preserving a jurisdictional objection and was significant during the old era of the special appearance, which required that a jurisdictional objection be made immediately and by itself.[13] Under old law, therefore, any kind of appearance before objecting to jurisdiction ran the risk of waiving the objection altogether. Hence, as an assurance to the defendant, it was decided that a demand alone would not be considered an appearance and would run no risk of waiver.[14] Under the CPLR the defendant doesn't need that assurance. A notice of appearance today will not waive any jurisdictional objection, which can be taken by motion or answer after the complaint is served later on.[15] A notice of appearance may thus accompany the demand without waiving a jurisdictional objection.

After the summons has been served, as noted earlier,[16] other papers in the action—and this includes all later pleadings as well—become "interlocutory" or "intermediate" papers and may be served by mail on the party's attorney. When the complaint accompanies the summons, the methods of service applicable to

---

5. See Gluckselig v. H. Michaelyan, Inc., 132 Misc. 783, 230 N.Y.S. 593 (Sup.Ct., N.Y.County), aff'd 225 A.D. 666, 231 N.Y.S. 757 (1st Dep't 1928).

6. E.g., Keyes v. McLaughlin, 49 A.D.2d 974, 373 N.Y.S.2d 891 (3d Dep't 1975).

7. See § 295 below.

8. See § 204 above.

9. See § 60 above.

10. Some of the unsuspected implications of the 1978 change that bars the service of a naked summons appear in the 1978 Commentary C3012:1 on McKinney's CPLR 3012.

11. See Paskus, Gordon & Hyman v. Peck, 41 Misc.2d 1004, 246 N.Y.S.2d 874 (N.Y.C.Civ.Ct. 1964).

12. See § 902 in the N.Y.C.Civ.Ct.Act and in the Uniform District, City, and Justice court acts, McKinney's Vol. 29A, Parts 2 and 3. The indorsement is somewhat akin to the CPLR 305(b) notice applicable in supreme and county court practice.

13. See § 237–a in the old Civil Practice Act.

14. See, e.g., Muslusky v. Lehigh Valley Coal Co., 225 N.Y. 584, 122 N.E. 461 (1919).

15. CPLR 3211(a)(8),(9), (e); 320(b), (c).

16. See § 202 above.

the summons of course govern. When it does not, but is served later pursuant to the defendant's demand, the complaint qualifies as an intermediate paper and may be served on the defendant's attorney by ordinary mail.

It is common practice, and deemed common courtesy among attorneys, to allow one another reasonable extensions of time to plead. While often oral, these are in every sense stipulations and, routine though stipulations to extend a pleading time may be, they should be in writing.[17] The Court of Appeals spoke to this in a case in which a plaintiff, asked by the defendant for an extension of time to answer, wanted to qualify the extension to exact of the defendant a waiver of jurisdictional defenses as a quid pro quo. The court held that the plaintiff must have the defendant sign the stipulation as qualified or the qualification won't bind and the defendant's jurisdictional objection will be preserved.[18]

The party who needs an extension but can't get it from the other side can move the court for it pursuant to CPLR 2004. And if the other side threatens to take a default before the motion can come on for a hearing, the motion can be accelerated by the procedure of an order to show cause.[19]

Neither party, when under the gun with an obligation to plead, should be casual about time limits, perhaps a bit too serene in the assumption—usually sound enough—that the court will be generous about vacating a default judgment even if the other side should obtain one. Omissions of a few days and perhaps even a few weeks have been forgiven, but attorneys have been notoriously remiss in this matter with little heed of the consequences. Delays of months and years have been recorded,[20] bringing on dismissals, and every such dismissal qualifies as a neglect to prosecute within the meaning of CPLR 205(a),[21] which means that

no additional time for a new action will be awarded if the original statute of limitations has expired (as it usually has).

The problem of pleading defaults became an epidemic for a while after the Court of Appeals handed down Barasch v. Micucci[22] in 1980, dealing with pleading defaults based on "law office failures". The epidemic subsided under 1983 legislation, but it left behind some scars. It also left behind some good lessons, and to preserve them we've made the brief but painful history of *Barasch* an independent subtopic, following.

The Era of Barasch and "Law Office Failure": March 25, 1980 to June 21, 1983

Barasch came down with an audible thud on March 25, 1980. From that day until June 21, 1983, when amendments overruling the case took effect—principally the amendments adding CPLR 2005 and subdivision (d) of CPLR 3012—New York practice was a chaotic arena. Each side would pounce on the other with a default application for just about any delay at all in the service of a pleading.

Barasch held—as a matter of law, and unanimously—that law office failure is not an acceptable excuse for the late service or nonservice of a pleading. "Law office failure" is a caption that embraces most of the reasons tendered over the years to excuse defaults: the attorney confused folder numbers in the office, misplaced the file, misplaced a secretary, became ill, was on trial in Elmira, was on Elba deposing a retired general, was indisposed for personal reasons, relied on an inexperienced associate, moved offices, changed partners, went dancing, ad infinitum.[23] Applied in *Barasch* to a plaintiff's delay in serving a complaint, the holding was afterwards extended to

---

17. CPLR 2104. See § 204 above.

18. See Klein v. Mount Sinai Hospital, 61 N.Y.2d 865, 474 N.Y.S.2d 462, 462 N.E.2d 1180 (1984).

19. See § 248 below.

20. See, e.g., Kahn v. Samson Management Corp., 44 A.D.2d 571, 353 N.Y.S.2d 227 (2d Dep't 1974).

21. Wright v. Farlin, 42 A.D.2d 141, 346 N.Y.S.2d 11 (3d Dep't 1973). See § 52 above.

22. 49 N.Y.2d 594, 427 N.Y.S.2d 732, 404 N.E.2d 1275. The case is the subject of the lead note in New York State Law Digest No. 247.

23. With apologies to the adage about the candle and the darkness, it is better to serve a timely complaint than to define a law office failure.

a defendant's default in serving an answer, this time by a closely divided (4–3) Court of Appeals in Eaton v. Equitable Life Assurance Society,[24] handed down on June 15, 1982. At one point or another during *Barasch's* more than three-year reign, moreover, the summary rejection of law office failure as an excuse was extended to delays affecting bills of particulars, failures to prosecute within the action (after the pleading stage), failures to show up at a calendar call, etc.

While the question of whether to allow the late service of a pleading or bill of particulars or to excuse a calendar failure had been traditionally regarded as a matter of judicial discretion to be exercised on a case-by-case basis, the effect of *Barasch* was to withdraw all discretion and virtually mandate a default judgment for the omission. Said the *Barasch* court:

> [T]hose excuses which may be roughly categorized under the heading of "law office failures" cannot properly serve as a basis for defeating a motion to dismiss under CPLR 3012 (subd b). . . .

Barasch described itself as a "rare" instance in which a dismissal was required as a matter of law. But the case was more typical than rare, and it was therefore not hard to predict that *Barasch* would have the impact it in fact ended up with. The impact was great. The cases were often described by the lawyers concerned as horror stories (meritorious claims lost, meritorious defenses barred, all for relatively innocent omissions).[25] The overruling of *Barasch* was effected by the enactment of CPLR 2005, explicitly permitting the court to consider "law office failure" as an excuse for a pleading delay, and CPLR 3012(d), permitting the court, in excusing a pleading default, to impose "such terms as may be just".

The lawyer must remember that the overruling of *Barasch* and its progeny is not a guarantee that all pleading defaults will be forgiven upon the presentation of any excuse at all, law-office connected or not. All the overruling does is restore discretion to the court to consider law office failure alongside any other excuses in determining whether to forgive the late service of a pleading or some other default. If the delay has been long, or the reasons are particularly weak, or for any other combination of factors judicial discretion is not impressed with the showing, the court can reject the party's request to be relieved of the default, and let it stand. In more than a few cases after the *Barasch* overruling the courts did just that.[26]

By and large, the preference of the judges, with *Barasch* no longer pressuring them, was (and remains) to excuse defaults upon the condition that the defaulter pay the other side costs (including an attorney's fee) in a sum the judge deems appropriate to the delay and to the excuse offered.[27] There is ample authority for that under the "such terms as may be just" provision of CPLR 3012(d).

The accused defaulter must be sure to include among his motion papers, along with his excuses, an affidavit of merits. In a case involving a plaintiff's lateness in serving a complaint, the Court of Appeals held—even after *Barasch*—that the absence of the affidavit from the plaintiff's opposing papers still mandates an unconditional dismissal "as a matter of law".[28]

The affidavit of merits had best be that of the party; rarely will the lawyer's affidavit or affirmation do the job because the lawyer has no first-hand knowledge of the claim. And the affidavit should be included in the original papers. It has been held that it is no abuse of discretion for a court to reject the late filing of a party's affidavit after the prior (and useless)

---

24. 56 N.Y.2d 900, 453 N.Y.S.2d 404, 438 N.E.2d 1119. The case is the subject of the lead note in New York State Law Digest No. 271.

25. These cases may be found in the various installments of the New York State Law Digest, enumerated in the lead note in Digest 282 (June 1983).

26. See, e.g., Bernard v. City Sch. Dist. of Albany, 96 A.D.2d 995, 465 N.Y.S.2d 793 (3d Dep't 1983).

27. See Commentary C3012:19 on McKinney's CPLR 3012. The commentary also treats defects other than pleading omissions that can turn delays into fatal defaults.

28. Kel Management Corp. v. Rogers & Wells, 64 N.Y.2d 904, 488 N.Y.S.2d 156 (1985).

submission by the lawyer of his own.[29]

§ 231A. Leave Time for Trouble

A default caused by a failure to take a step within a prescribed time, or by a defect in the taking, can occur in a variety of contexts in litigation, and at every stage of it. A treatment designed to warn about the consequences of leaving insufficient time to remedy a mistake or omission, and the unsuspecting ways in which it can destroy a claim or defense, has no obvious chronological niche in a practice text. It is nevertheless helpful to centralize a set of warnings under one heading, which requires a more or less arbitrary choice of a place. The place we choose for this treatment is a separate section right here, following the *Barasch* era of pleading defaults. It could as well appear following the study of the dismissal for neglect to prosecute more than 100 sections further on,[1] or at the very beginning of the chapter on the statute of limitations some 100 sections back,[2] or at any assortment of other places.

Choice of place is secondary. What is important is that every student of practice in the courts, novice and veteran alike, make at least some effort to coordinate and review the subject in one sitting and try to settle deep in mind the often unappreciated advantage of doing all things, whenever possible, with time to spare.

That an action has to be started within the applicable statute of limitations, or that a pleading has to be served by a stated date to avoid a default, may be obvious enough. But there are a number of less obvious steps in litigation whose misdoing can carry dire consequences only *because* of the time element. Things like that crop up insidiously in the course of daily litigation practice, in both the New York and federal courts, and quite often the only thing prominent about them is the consequence: a dismissal or default of some

kind too late to allow for a redoing, and with the consequent forfeiture of a claim or defense, and, not unlikely, a malpractice claim against the lawyer.

An inadequate notice served with a summons under CPLR 305(b), for example, might be assumed to be amendable. It is not, however,[3] and when the plaintiff who doesn't know that finds it out, it will be only the time element that dictates the consequence: if there is time for a new action, the defect is minor; if there is not, the defect is fatal. The inadequacy of the notice may be the apparent offender here, but the real culprit is time: the bringing of the action so near the expiration of the statute of limitations that when the defect arises—even one that arises as early in the case as this one does—there is no time left for a new action.

Simply put, the plaintiff in these situations has failed to leave time for trouble, and the statute of limitations was waiting in the wings. It waits like that with a mass of things whose misdoing may seem innocent enough on the surface. If time was left for trouble, the case stays on the surface and the litigant can correct the defect. But if a time margin has not been left, the case will sink dead away. This has happened time and again, at many junctures of litigation. The mission of this section is to set forth at least an illustrative list of them.

1. The Statute of Limitations.

We begin with the obvious. Starting cases too late under the statute of limitations is a good way to lose both cases and clients. If litigation is inevitable—and lawyers should not develop the habit of judging inevitability solely by the approach of the statute of limitations—it is wise as a rule of thumb to start the action with six or eight months to spare under the applicable period, if there is any choice in the matter. The case should be diaried with con-

---

29. Foitl v. G.A.F. Corp., 64 N.Y.2d 911, 488 N.Y.S.2d 377 (1985).

§ 231A

1. The neglect to prosecute dismissal is the subject of § 375, below.

2. The statute of limitations treatment begins with § 33, above.

3. See § 60, and the discussion of the Parker case in § 52, above.

servative rather than rosy assumptions.[4] Unexpected threshold problems can arise and bring dismissal. These are illustrated in the next few paragraphs.

2. Inadequate Notice under CPLR 305(b).

This is the example referred to above. As was shown earlier, in the treatment of the CPLR 305(b) notice, there is no safe formula for determining how much suffices to satisfy as a proper "notice". If the notice is found improper, by only a word or phrase, the result is a dismissal, the dismissal is jurisdictional, and there is no time extension offered by CPLR 205(a) for a new action.[5] Had the action been brought with several months to go, any objection to the adequacy of the CPLR 305(b) notice would have had to be raised by the defendant by way of motion or answer, which would have called the defect to the plaintiff's attention and permitted the bringing of a new action before the statute of limitations expired.

3. Defect in Summons Service.

Among lawyers representing defendants in litigation, notably tort litigation, there has been almost a tradition of raising an objection to service of process. The reward of a dismissal on so facile a ground is such a temptation that few can resist it even if the prospect is only a remote one. Some attorneys include the defense in the answer without even having ascertained the facts from the client. If the statute of limitations is closing in, and the objection should be sustained, the sustaining will work a dismissal when it is too late to start over. CPLR 205(a) does not offer its six months for a new action when the earlier action was dismissed for want of proper service.[6]

One of the best examples of this kind of trouble, which even a relatively blameless plaintiff can get into by waiting to the last minute for suit, is Feinstein v. Bergner,[7] in-

volving service under paragraph 4 of CPLR 308. Paragraph 4 is the affix-and-mail requirement,[8] and the affixing must be made to a premises presently used by the defendant. In *Feinstein*, the place at which the affixing was made under paragraph 4 had been the defendant's residence earlier, but it was no longer such when the action was commenced. His parents still lived there, though, and the mailing, the second required step, did get through to the defendant. No matter, held the Court of Appeals. Service was no good, and it was now too late for the plaintiff to start over.[9]

Almost any plaintiff could have made a mistake like that, but the only plaintiff that gets a second chance is the one who has left time for trouble. Suing with enough time for a new action when a jurisdictional defect is raised may even be a way for the plaintiff to find out about the defendant's present whereabouts within the action itself, when the defendant spills the beans on a motion to dismiss. What a delight for the plaintiff when an education accompanies the dismissal, and there is still time to do things right!

Service under the recently enacted CPLR 312–a is by ordinary mail, and requires a signed acknowledgment.[10] There is no caselaw on this point yet, but suppose the acknowledgment is forged, or, simply, that it is made by one without authority to act for the defendant. That and similar issues can arise under CPLR 312–a, and should the action be dismissed for want of jurisdiction it will be reassuring to the plaintiff to know that there is still time to make the service afresh.

Not even court-ordered service under CPLR 308(5) can be considered airtight. An appellate court can disagree and hold the method approved by the lower court invalid.[11] Again, the only thing that can save the plaintiff is that there is still a bit of time to start a new action.

---

4. See § 33 above.

5. See § 60 above. Serving no notice or complaint at all with the summons is also, of course, a jurisdictional defect.

6. See the treatment of the Markoff case in § 52 above.

7. 48 N.Y.2d 234, 422 N.Y.S.2d 356, 397 N.E.2d 1161 (1979).

8. See § 74 above.

9. The case has equal bearing on service under paragraph 2 of CPLR 308, the deliver-and-mail requirement.

10. See § 76A above.

11. See § 75 above.

4. Serving the Wrong Person.

It can also be an innocent plaintiff who is victimized by a jurisdictional quirk involving service on someone who is technically the wrong person, or only one of several persons who must be served in behalf of a given entity. This point is illustrated in Horowitz v. Inc'd Village of Roslyn,[12] treated earlier.[13] The suit was against a county and the plaintiff served the county clerk as authorized by CPLR 311(4). But unknown to the plaintiff, there was also a service provision in the Nassau County Administrative Code, requiring service on the county executive or county attorney. The clerk turned the summons over to the county attorney, but the action was dismissed just the same.

Unless the plaintiff is virtually clairvoyant, the only way to protect against a hidden trap like this is to sue with plenty of time for a new action. Defects of this kind arise early in the litigation, or can in any event be flushed out of the defendant by an alert plaintiff early in the litigation, so that the plaintiff can take remedial steps as needed, and on time. A motion by the defendant will raise a jurisdictional objection promptly and enable the plaintiff to start a new action just as promptly, if one is necessary. If the defendant raises the objection by way of defense in the answer instead of by motion, which is the defendant's option,[14] the plaintiff can test the defense quickly with a motion to strike it under CPLR 3211(b).[15] If the defendant's first step is to ask the plaintiff for an extension of time to plead, a frequent first step, the plaintiff should exact from the defendant in return either a stipulation waiving jurisdictional defenses or at least a conversation about whether the defendant has any. If the defendant hesitates, the plaintiff should refuse the extension and insist on a timely answer, which will show whether or not the objection exists.[16]

Analogous to serving the wrong person is naming the wrong person in the first place. The Court of Appeals has held that when the designated defendant is "a nonexistent entity", the person served is not a proper person to serve in behalf of the intended entity, and the intended entity does eventually get notice of the action but only after the expiration of the statute of limitations, the plaintiff has lost it all.[17] Just allowing some extra time could have enabled the plaintiff to fix things up.[18]

5. Other Jurisdictional Defects.

A dismissal for a defect of personal jurisdiction based not on flawed service, but on want of a jurisdictional basis, such as where long-arm jurisdiction is lacking,[19] is even more serious, because here a proper service will not cure the defect. A new action will have to be brought in some other place, and the statute of limitations of that place will be the one applicable. It is wise to have checked it out before commencing the New York action, so that time enough is left for a new action in the other place, under *its* statute of limitations, should the New York action fail. This involves a lot of research and a lot of timing, but the reward will be the ability to start afresh for having left time for trouble.[20]

6. Dispensing with Reliance on Relation–Back Doctrine.

All of the tension connected with the so-called "relation-back" doctrine, embodied in CPLR 203(f)[21] for New York practice and in Rule 15(c) of the Federal Rules of Civil Procedure for federal practice[22] is tension created by the time element. The plaintiff who has omitted a claim and wants to add it now can do so

---

12. 144 A.D.2d 639, 535 N.Y.S.2d 79 (2d Dep't 1988).

13. See § 70 above.

14. See § 111 above.

15. See § 269 below.

16. See the series of lead notes in New York State Law Digest Nos. 274–276 on the timing of jurisdictional objections.

17. Maldonado v. Maryland Rail Commuter Serv. Admin., 91 N.Y.2d 467, 672 N.Y.S.2d 831 (1998).

18. See the discussion of the Maldonado case in New York State Law Digest No.461.

19. See § 80 above.

20. See the trio of New York State Law Digest lead notes cited in note 16, above.

21. See § 49 above.

22. See § 615 below (Practitioner's Edition).

only if the statute of limitations on it is still alive. If it is not alive at amendment time, the plaintiff's hope is that it can be "related back" to the time of the original commencement of the action, which requires a showing that the new claim arises out of the same transaction that the original one does. If it can't be related back, the claim is lost. A showing that the original statute of limitations is still alive will make a relation back unnecessary, but the statute will be alive only for plaintiffs who have left time for trouble.

7. Need to Add New Parties.

Something in the early stages of litigation, usually something coming out of one of the disclosure devices,[23] may suggest that the plaintiff needs to join someone as an additional party, which requires the service of a supplemental summons;[24] or, indeed, that the plaintiff has joined the wrong party to begin with and must now go out and get the right one. If the original statute is still alive, that should be no problem. If it is dead, it is a problem that may have no solution.

8. Procrastinator's Credibility Affected.

It was also noted earlier that the lawyer who procrastinates at one point in litigation may find his credibility impaired at a later point,[25] and that it may cost the client the case. That appears to be what happened in Engel v. Lichterman,[26] a dispute about whether a conditional order allowing P a new period in which to serve a bill of particulars was received by P. D said he mailed the bill. P protested that he didn't receive it, but the court did not believe P, who had been lax in earlier phases of the action. D ended up with summary judgment. The case teaches what a negative effect dilatory conduct can have on an attorney's credibility, even on so seemingly picayune a point as whether a mailed paper was received.

23. These are studied beginning with § 343 below.

24. See § 65 above.

25. See § 202 above.

26. 62 N.Y.2d 943, 479 N.Y.S.2d 188, 468 N.E.2d 26 (1984).

27. See § 375 below.

A more impressive lesson still is that the timely commencement of an action, and with jurisdiction perfected, is no guarantee against meeting up with the statute of limitations later. Failing to do things timely within the action can bring on a dismissal, such as for neglect to prosecute the case diligently,[27] and a new action after a dismissal at this later stage is all the more likely to meet the statute of limitations barrier. One might guess that since a dismissal of this kind is not for want of jurisdiction, it will get the six months of CPLR 205(a) for a new action. It will not. Lack of prosecution is another item on the list of things to which CPLR 205(a) will not accord a six-month statute of limitations extension.[28]

The courts have often warned that procrastination even after the proper commencement of an action can invoke the policies of repose underlying the statute of limitations.[29]

9. Similar Problems on the Federal Side.

Similar problems can arise in the federal courts, which have in addition a prize problem not often met in the New York courts: it is often difficult in a federal action predicated on a federal question (as opposed to diversity of citizenship) to determine what statute of limitations applies to the case in the first place.[30]

* * *

In all practices, there is a bonus for the litigant who leaves time for trouble.

L. VERIFICATION

Table of Sections

28. See § 52 above.

29. See Sortino v. Fisher, 20 A.D.2d 25, 245 N.Y.S.2d 186 (1st Dep't), treated in § 375, below.

30. See § 615 below (Practitioner's Edition).

§ 232. Verification of Pleadings, Generally

A verification is an affidavit swearing to the truth of a pleading.[1] Verification is largely optional under the CPLR and would for the most part have been abandoned if the Advisory Committee had had its way. The committee recognized that the pleading, although technically the statement of the party, is really the product of the lawyer. It proposed to have the lawyer certify instead of having the party verify.[2] The legislature rejected the proposal and restored verification in pretty much the same form it had under old law.

The requirement of verification is supposed to encourage honesty in pleading. A false verification is technically a perjury,[3] but district attorneys seldom become involved, excusing themselves on the ground of more pressing problems. Earlier in our legal history the requirement of swearing may have been underwritten by a genuine fear of hell, but hell has had little impact on New York practice. Quite the contrary. Verification, in a word, has nothing more to recommend it than the legislature.

With a legislative imprimatur, but with almost all of its teeth gone, verification still smiles grotesquely from the pages of the CPLR, which requires us to give it at least a few pages of homage.

In only a few instances is verification mandatory. All pleadings must be verified in a matrimonial action, except the part of a responsive pleading that responds to a charge of adultery (because—not to upset the reader unduly—adultery is a crime and pleading with respect to it invokes privilege).[4] In a summary proceeding to recover the possession of real property (the usual landlord-tenant vehicle), the petition must be verified.[5] Among the CPLR instances of mandatory verification of a complaint are where it contains or has appended the schedule of goods and services available for optional use under CPLR 3016(f),[6] or where it seeks to charge an obligor with an amount still unsatisfied after prior suit by the obligee against a co-obligor.[7] The pleadings in an Article 78 proceeding also require verification.[8]

To continue this stimulating saga, we note that in a few instances an answer must be verified even if the complaint is not. If the complaint charges the defendant with fraud, a statute requires the answer to be verified.[9] Such conduct is likely to amount to a criminal charge, however, which would invoke the privilege against self-incrimination and dispense with verification altogether,[10] but these are mere constitutional requirements and must not be allowed to impede the jolly meandering of the law of verification. Another instance of required verification of the answer is that of a corporate defendant being sued on a promissory note,[11] a requirement so trivial that it lacks the minuscule electric charge needed to adhere to some portion of the brain.[12] There is also a requirement in the CPLR that a defense be verified if it "does not involve the merits".[13] This would embrace such defenses as lack of jurisdiction, lack of capacity, other action pending, failure to join a party, and a number of others. Court files are filled, however, with unverified answers embracing such defenses, and there is mounting evidence that no one cares. The fact that no one cares speaks well of bench and bar.

§ 232

1. CPLR 3020(a).

2. See 1st Rep.Leg.Doc.(1957) No. 6(b), pp. 73–74.

3. See, e.g., Penal Law §§ 210.10, 210.15.

4. Dom.Rel.L. § 211. Penal Law § 255.17 still makes adultery a criminal act.

5. RPAPL 741.

6. See § 216 above.

7. CPLR 1502.

8. CPLR 7804(d).

9. CPLR 3020(b)(1).

10. Kellogg v. Match Supply Co., 165 A.D. 885, 151 N.Y.S. 361 (3d Dep't 1915), recognized this problem two practice acts ago. See Commentary C3020:5 on McKinney's CPLR 3020.

11. CPLR 3020(b)(2).

12. The provision is archaic. If the suit is based on a promissory note, it would probably not be brought as an ordinary action at all; it would likely be brought under CPLR 3213, which dispenses with pleadings altogether. See § 288 et seq., below, and Commentary C3020:5 on McKinney's CPLR 3020.

13. CPLR 3020(c).

With the few exceptions above and a few others in which verification is mandatory, verification is optional. When opted for, it requires that all subsequent pleadings (including those of adverse parties) also be verified.[14] But if any matter in a responsive pleading would be privileged under any of the rules of evidence, the pleader need not verify as to the privileged portion of the responsive pleading (although he must verify as to the rest).[15] If the privilege is that against self-incrimination, every doubt is resolved in favor of the responsive pleader, who will be excused from verifying if the matter can have any incriminatory tendency whatever.[16]

The answer of an infant need not be verified, whether the complaint is or not.[17] It is one of the unsuspected advantages of youth and would probably inspire George Bernard Shaw if only he could be revived and offered the information. Subsequent claims, such as counterclaims or cross-claims or third-party claims, may be verified even if the complaint is not.[18] Pleadings responding to those claims would then need verification.

It is the lawyer who manages the entire pleading phase of the action, and the meaningful deterrent to false pleading is not verification, but the threat of disciplinary proceedings against the lawyer who, knowing the facts, falsifies them. That threat presumably obtains whether the pleading is verified or not. Today, moreover, there hangs over all deliberately false pleading the threat that it will be denominated a frivolous practice and will invoke a money sanction against lawyer or client or both.[19] That, too, applies whether the pleading is verified or not.

§ 233. Who May Verify

The general rule is that the party and not the lawyer makes the verification.[1] The practitioner does well to leave verification to the client. Seldom does the lawyer know the facts at first hand and it takes little effort to have the client make the affidavit of verification.

If there are multiple parties "united in interest", one who has knowledge of the facts may verify for all.[2] Here joint tortfeasors have been held united in interest.[3] An infant has been held competent to verify.[4] Any officer can verify in behalf of a domestic corporation,[5] and anyone acquainted with the facts can verify in behalf of a governmental unit or agency.[6]

CPLR 3020(d)(3), which is the provision most often involved when cases on verification appear, reads as follows:

[I]f the party is a foreign corporation, or is not in the county where the attorney has his office, or if there are two or more parties united in interest and pleading together and none of them acquainted with the facts is within that county, or if the action or defense is founded upon a written instrument for the payment of money only which is in the possession of an agent or the attorney, or if all the material allegations of the pleading are within the personal knowledge of an agent or the attorney, the verification may be made by such agent or attorney.

It is this paragraph that permits an agent or attorney to verify in place of the party.[7] An

14. CPLR 3020(a). A pleading mandatorily verified will also, of course, require verification of subsequent pleadings.

15. CPLR 3020(a). Knight v. Maybee, 44 Misc.2d 152, 253 N.Y.S.2d 59 (Sup.Ct., Erie County, 1964).

16. Travelers' Ins. Co. v. Mulligan, 231 A.D. 222, 247 N.Y.S. 85 (1st Dep't 1931).

17. CPLR 3020(a).

18. Id.

19. See § 414A below.

§ 233

1. CPLR 3020(d).

2. Id.

3. Finn Hannevig & Co. v. Frankel, 207 A.D. 180, 201 N.Y.S. 762 (1st Dep't 1923). This is somewhat in contrast

with what "united in interest" means under CPLR 203(b), where its purpose is to determine when an action is deemed commenced under the statute of limitations. There, joint tortfeasors have been held not to be united in interest. See § 45 above.

4. Serani v. Rowe, 43 Misc.2d 307, 250 N.Y.S.2d 918 (Sup.Ct., Suffolk County, 1964). Serani involved a 19-year-old. Today infancy stops at 18, de jure if not de facto. CPLR 105.

5. CPLR 3020(d)(1).

6. CPLR 3020(d)(2).

7. When the verification is the attorney's, it may of course be made by mere affirmation, CPLR 2106, rather than by formal affidavit. See § 205 above.

attorney or agent who has "personal knowledge" of the facts can apparently verify in behalf of a party of any kind (individual, corporate, etc.). But the attorney who lacks such knowledge, and has to verify on second-hand information, must satisfy one of the other grounds listed in the excerpt quoted above. Perhaps the most frequently invoked ground is where the client "is not in the county where the attorney has his office".[8] In metropolitan centers it is this provision that enables the lawyer to verify when the client lives in one of the suburban counties. In New York City it accounts for the quantity of attorney verifications coming out of Manhattan (New York County). The attorney permitted to verify is not only the attorney of record, but any associated with that attorney,[9] which would of course embrace partners.

§ 234. Form of Verification

The form of verification is governed by CPLR 3021. There are some official forms to illustrate. The following is Official Form 20, the verification by a party; the "Jurat" at the lower left is a notary's statement to the effect, "Sworn to before me this _____ day of _____, [year] ", followed by the notary's signature and, usually on a rubber stamp, the notary's identifying number and other data.

STATE OF NEW YORK
CITY OF BUFFALO
COUNTY OF ERIE

A.B., being duly sworn, states that he is the plaintiff in this action and that the foregoing complaint is true to his own knowledge, except as to matters therein stated to be alleged on information and belief and as to those matters he believes it to be true.

_____
[Print signer's name below signature]

[Jurat]

[F7295]

The form set forth just above follows the letter of the first sentence of CPLR 3021, which allows the party to state summarily his belief in those matters alleged "on information and belief", i.e., those allegations of which he lacks direct knowledge. With neither category of allegation need it be stated how the information was come by. This is in contrast with the verification made by someone other than the party, as illustrated by Official Form 21, the verification by the party's attorney:

---

8. At one time it had to be shown, before an attorney would be allowed to verify, that the client was not in the attorney's residence, not mere office, county, see Treen Motors Corp. v. Van Pelt, 106 Misc. 357, 174 N.Y.S. 500 (Sup.Ct., Kings County, 1919), but the office county is now the relevant one under CPLR 3020(d)(3).

9. Teichman v. Ker, 60 Misc.2d 789, 303 N.Y.S.2d 985 (Sup.Ct., Nassau County, 1969).

STATE OF NEW YORK
CITY OF NEW YORK
COUNTY OF NEW YORK

J.K., being duly sworn, states that he is the attorney for plaintiff in this action and that the foregoing complaint is true to his own knowledge, except as to matters therein stated on information and belief and as to those matters he believes it to be true; that the grounds of his belief as to all matters not stated upon his knowledge are correspondence and other writings furnished to him by plaintiff and interviews with officers and employees of plaintiff; and that the reason why the verification is not made by plaintiff is that [e. g., plaintiff is a foreign corporation].

_____

[Print signer's name below signature]

[Jurat]

IM-394

There are two major differences between the above and the prior (the party's) form. First, as to matters alleged in the pleading only upon information and belief, the nonparty verifier must state the grounds of her belief. The party verifier doesn't have to. As the attorney form shows, however, brief references to such things as correspondence, writings, and interviews are deemed sufficient. Second, there must appear a statement of why the party is not doing the verifying.[1] Anything contained in CPLR 3020(d) that authorizes the verification to be made by other than the party need merely be referred to in the verification itself to satisfy this requirement.

If a nonparty verifier fails to specify the grounds for information-and-belief allegations, the verification is defective. If the defect is in the purported verification of a complaint, the answer then need not be verified.[2]

Forms of verification, both individual and corporate (including an affirmation for use by an attorney), are usually contained on the litigation backs available at legal stationers[3]

and need merely be filled in and executed to meet verification requirements.

The practitioner should note a peculiarity about verification. Usually, when papers in litigation are being prepared and served, originals are saved for the court's file and copies are served on parties and retained by the server. The copies seldom have signatures executed. Though there are no rigid rules about this, execution usually takes place on the original only—to the extent that an original can be distinguished from a copy in this technical age[4]—with the copies merely conformed. Some caselaw has held, however, that adverse parties are entitled to fully executed copies of verifications, i.e., the notary's signature must appear on the copy served on the opposing party; that service of anything less entitles the recipient to treat the pleading as unverified.[5] More recent cases reject that, holding that service of a mere conformed copy suffices.[6] Perhaps the cautious lawyer does best to have the notary subscribe the original, destined for the court's file, as well as each copy to be served on another party.

§ 234

1. CPLR 3021.

2. Bowery Sav. Bank v. Ward, 188 A.D. 593, 177 N.Y.S. 219 (1st Dep't 1919).

3. See § 201 above.

4. Id.

5. See Crimmins v. Polhemus, 189 Misc. 183, 68 N.Y.S.2d 819 (Syracuse Mun.Ct. 1947).

6. Scaringe v. Kinley, 154 A.D.2d 836, 546 N.Y.S.2d 702 (3d Dep't 1989).

§ 235. Remedy for Defective Verification

If P voluntarily verifies the complaint but the verification is defective, D may treat it as unverified[1] and serve an unverified answer to it. If P refuses the answer, insisting that it be verified, D can move to compel P's acceptance of it.[2]

The remedy for defects when verification is mandatory, whether because mandated by statute or because a pleading being responded to is verified, is more involved. The recipient of an unverified or defectively verified pleading may, if he is entitled to a verified one, "treat it as a nullity" provided he gives the serving attorney notice "with due diligence" that he is so treating it.[3] Due diligence here has been held by some courts to mean "within twenty-four hours"[4]—an admonition to the nit-picker to pick quickly. The notice must also specify the particular reasons for deeming the verification defective, such as that the verification was made by a nonparty without first-hand knowledge.[5] If the particulars are not specified, the notice is inadequate. In Treen Motors Corp. v. Van Pelt,[6] P returned D's answer because of a defective verification but failed to specify what the defect consisted of. The result was held to be the same as if P had retained the answer and the default judgment P hoped for didn't materialize. If P, entitled to a verified answer, had returned it to D with a proper statement of reasons, P could then have applied for a default judgment.[7] For good measure, the Treen case added that "pleaders insisting upon strict compliance with the rules of practice must follow the same themselves."[8] The Treen case is of 1919 vintage, and if judicial impatience with the carping and captious verificationist was so manifest then, it should be even greater now.

CPLR 3026, the provision that mandates disregarding all pleading defects if no substantial right is prejudiced, has been given a role in verification. The verification provisions are part of the pleadings article and are therefore subject to CPLR 3026. There is so scant an advantage emanating from verification that the party who deems herself entitled to a verified pleading can be deemed unprejudiced if she doesn't get it. These considerations have prompted at least one court, citing CPLR 3026, to hold that even where a complaint is required to be verified, no prejudice can result if it is not.[9]

M. AMENDMENT OF PLEADINGS

Table of Sections

§ 236. Amendment as of Course

The CPLR allows each party to amend its pleading once without leave of court.[1] This is commonly known as an amendment as of course. Since it must be made early in the case, it is at root just a final version of the original pleading. The pleader may make the

---

§ 235

1. CPLR 3022.

2. See Commentary C3022:1 on McKinney's CPLR 3022.

3. CPLR 3022.

4. E.g., Lentlie v. Egan, 94 A.D.2d 839, 463 N.Y.S.2d 542 (3d Dep't 1983), aff'd 61 N.Y.2d 874, 474 N.Y.S.2d 467, 462 N.E.2d 1185 (1984).

5. See, e.g., Lefrak v. Robinson, 115 Misc.2d 256, 454 N.Y.S.2d 571 (Mount Vernon City Court 1982), voiding a petition in a summary proceeding governed by § 741 of the Real Property Actions and Proceedings Law (which adopts the relevant CPLR provisions) but preserving the proceeding so as to permit new service.

6. 106 Misc. 357, 174 N.Y.S. 500 (Sup.Ct., Kings County, 1919).

7. See State v. McMahon, 78 Misc.2d 388, 356 N.Y.S.2d 933 (Sup.Ct., Albany County, 1974).

8. 106 Misc. at 361, 174 N.Y.S. at 503.

9. Capital Newspapers Div.—Hearst Corp. v. Vanderbilt, 44 Misc.2d 542, 254 N.Y.S.2d 309 (Sup.Ct., Albany County, 1964). There were special considerations in the Capital case, which was a labor dispute in need of prompt resolution on the merits. That may deprive the case of status as a general anti-verification precedent. For further discussion of remedies for defects when verification is required, see Commentary C3022:2 on McKinney's CPLR 3022.

§ 236

1. CPLR 3025(a).

amendment as of course within any of three time periods:

    1. within 20 days after the pleading has been served; or

    2. within the period that the adverse party has for responding to it (so that when the defendant has a 30–day answering period, for example, the plaintiff may amend the complaint within that period); or

    3. within 20 days after a responsive pleading is served.[2]

The last period is probably the most meaningful, since it enables a plaintiff to remedy some defect in the complaint to which attention has been called in the answer. Any other party pleading a cause of action, such as a defendant with a cross-claim or counterclaim, should also keep that in mind. Upon realizing, before a responsive pleading is in, that there's some defect in the complaint (counterclaim, etc.), the pleader should consider waiting until the response is served before using up its one as-of-course amendment. If saved until that time, it can cure the error or omission initially realized as well as any pointed out by the responsive pleading.

The second and third alternative time periods listed are available only when the pleading to be amended requires a response. If it doesn't require one, like an answer containing no counterclaim, the only period for the of-course amendment is the first one listed: within 20 days after its own service.

If the pleading to be amended does require a response—take the complaint as an example—and the defendant, instead of answering, moves to dismiss the complaint under CPLR 3211 or to correct it under CPLR 3024, the making of either kind of motion automatically extends the defendant's responding time,[3] and

by so doing extends as well the time in which the plaintiff may amend the complaint as of course. This enables the plaintiff, even before the motion is heard, to amend the complaint and perhaps even correct the defect at which the defendant's motion was aimed.[4]

The of-course amendment can include anything that could have been included in the original pleading. It can add separate and distinct causes of action or substitute a different one for the original.[5] Similarly, when a summons is served with only a CPLR 305(b) notice at the outset and the defendant demands the complaint in due course, the complaint can also include matter not referred to in the 305(b) notice.[6] This naturally assumes that no other impediment is present. Where, for example, jurisdiction of the claim is based on CPLR 302's longarm contacts, a special statute provides that no non–302 claims may be added after the defendant appears.[7]

When the pleading being amended is a responsive one, the responder can sometimes end up with two of course amendments. Suppose, for example, that D amends the answer. That's D's first of-course amendment. P then amends the complaint and D answers the amended complaint, as D must.[8] D may then amend that answer as of course, and that's D's second one.[9] The reason for this is that P's service of an amended complaint restarts the cycle.

As will be seen, the many important objections listed in CPLR 3211(a) may be taken either by motion to dismiss under CPLR 3211 or by way of defense in the answer,[10] but they are waived if taken by neither.[11] If one of those objections is not taken by motion and is also omitted from the original answer, it has been held that the waiver can still be avoided by

---

    2. Id.

    3. CPLR 3211(f), 3024(c).

    4. As to whether an amendment that purports to cure the moved-against defect abates the motion, see Commentary C3211:65 on McKinney's CPLR 3211.

    5. Mendoza v. Mendoza, 4 Misc.2d 1060, 77 N.Y.S.2d 169 (Sup.Ct., N.Y.County, 1947), aff'd 273 A.D. 877, 77 N.Y.S.2d 264 (1st Dep't 1948).

    6. Everitt v. Everitt, 4 N.Y.2d 13, 171 N.Y.S.2d 836, 148 N.E.2d 891 (1958). See Commentary C3025:3 on McKinney's CPLR 3025.

    7. CPLR 302(c). See § 91 above.

    8. CPLR 3025(d).

    9. Brooks Bros. v. Tiffany, 117 A.D. 470, 102 N.Y.S. 626 (1st Dep't 1907).

    10. See § 274 below.

    11. CPLR 3211(e).

including the objection in an amended answer made as of course.[12]

An amendment without leave of court is sometimes authorized by some other provision. Where, for example, X has been impleaded into the P v. D action, P is given 20 days, measured from the service on P of X's answer to the third-party complaint, in which to amend the main complaint to add a claim directly against X.[13]

If the pleading being amended required a responsive pleading, so does the amended one. Where P amends the complaint, D must serve an answer to it even though D has already troubled to answer the original complaint. The period within which to serve the responsive pleading is 20 days after service of the amended one.[14] If the amendment as of course has been used up, or the period for making it has expired, the pleader who would now amend must either obtain the other parties' stipulation or get a court order under CPLR 3025(b).[15] The latter is the amendment by leave, treated in the next section.

§ 237. Amendment by Leave

CPLR 3025(b) provides that

A party may amend his pleading, or supplement it by setting forth additional or subsequent transactions or occurrences, at any time by leave of court or by stipulation of all parties. Leave shall be freely given upon such terms as may be just including the granting of costs and continuances.

This is one of the most important and often used provisions in practice. It assures flexibility throughout the action and adjusts the pleadings to the substantive rights involved

whenever it can be done without prejudice. If there is no prejudice to the other side, leave to amend must be freely given. The courts stress this time and again.[1] There is no stated time limit for the amendment by leave under subdivision (b), as there is for the amendment of course under subdivision (a) of CPLR 3025. Nor is there a stated limit on the number of by-leave amendments a party may have. (It is not common to seek more than one.)

The CPLR 3025(b) amendment lies in the discretion of the court and may be denied on such discretionary grounds as laches, undue advantage, etc.[2]

CPLR 3025(b) governs both the amendment and the supplement of a pleading. By grouping them together, it downplays the difference between them.[3] Technically, a "supplement" to a pleading adds something that has only come into existence since the earlier pleading—such as an additional installment falling due in a contract action or an additional claim becoming actionable in the interim—while an "amendment" is any change in a pleading without regard to whether the relevant facts existed at the time of the initial pleading. By combining the amendment and the supplement and directing that leave be "freely given" for both, CPLR 3025(b) rejects the old practice, applicable in law cases, restricting the action to facts in existence when it was first brought, and instead adopts for all actions the equity practice of allowing the case to take cognizance of facts arising right up to the time of the trial.[4]

Causes of action can be added or subtracted by amendment, whether they involve changes of fact or changes of theory. If the theory alone

---

12. Solarino v. Noble, 55 Misc.2d 429, 286 N.Y.S.2d 71 (Sup.Ct., N.Y.County, 1967). See Commentary C3211:62 on McKinney's CPLR 3211. DeFilippis v. Perez, 148 A.D.2d 490, 539 N.Y.S.2d 22 (2d Dep't 1989), may on its face be taken as suggesting that Solarino is no longer law, but there is a substantial distinction between the two cases on their facts. See the summary of DeFilippis in New York State Law Digest No. 355.

13. CPLR 1009.

14. CPLR 3025(d).

15. Orlik v. National Carbon Co., 176 A.D. 600, 163 N.Y.S. 768 (1st Dep't 1917).

§ 237

1. See Thompson v. Alleva, 76 A.D.2d 1022, 429 N.Y.S.2d 481 (3d Dep't 1980).

2. Leutloff v. Leutloff, 47 Misc.2d 458, 262 N.Y.S.2d 736 (Sup.Ct., Onondaga County, 1965).

3. Town Bd. of Town of Fallsburgh v. National Surety Corp., 53 Misc.2d 23, 277 N.Y.S.2d 872 (Sup.Ct., Sullivan County, 1967), aff'd 29 A.D.2d 726, 286 N.Y.S.2d 122 (3d Dep't 1968).

4. See Renwick v. Town of Allegany, 18 A.D.2d 877, 879, 236 N.Y.S.2d 902, 905 (4th Dep't 1963) (concurring opinion).

is changed, but the facts remain as originally pleaded, a problem should not often be met because there is little the other party would now have to do by way of new preparation.[5] Conceptual rather than factual changes are always easier. Inadvertent omissions are also curable with the of-leave amendment, as where a denial[6] or even a defense[7] has been left out of an answer through mere oversight. Objections listed in CPLR 3211(a)—CPLR 3211(a) objections must be taken either by motion or answer[8]—may be added in an amended answer if omitted from the original one, but while this has been held to be automatically permissible for an amendment as of course under CPLR 3025(a),[9] it will be allowed in an amendment by leave under 3025(b) only if there is no prejudice to the plaintiff.[10] It is up to the plaintiff to show prejudice in that situation.[11]

What does prejudice, sufficient to defeat an amendment, consist of? It must obviously be a showing of prejudice traceable not simply to the new matter sought to be added, but also to the fact that it is only being added now.[12] Almost everything parties seek to add to their pleadings is designed to prejudice the other side. That's what litigation is all about. So, the showing of prejudice that will defeat the amendment must be traced right back to the omission from the original pleading of whatever it is that the amended pleading wants to add—some special right lost in the interim, some change of position or some significant trouble or expense that could have been avoided had the original pleading contained what the amended one now wants to add.[13]

For example: D answered a personal injury action with only a general denial and a year later wanted to amend the answer to add the defense that P was an employee of D and that workers' compensation was therefore the exclusive remedy. The time in which to seek such compensation had meanwhile expired. The court denied the motion to amend: had the amendment been allowed, it would have meant the substantive loss of all claims.[14] In a similar case in which the time to apply for compensation was still alive, however, the late defense was allowed.[15] If P had notice from other sources of D's intention to rely on the defense, prejudice can be deemed avoided by that route, and an amendment allowed, perhaps with a money sanction against the dilatory defendant.[16]

Another example: D answered with denials only, and P prepared his whole case accordingly. On the eve of trial D wanted to add defenses that could readily have been pleaded earlier. The amendment to add them was denied.[17] Here the prejudice was the loss of the time and effort expended in preparing a case against a pleading from which significant material had been needlessly withheld. The emerging tactical lesson is that if the plaintiff, half expecting the answer to contain a defense like lack of jurisdiction, statute of limitations, or the like, sees the answer come in without the defense and with the time to amend as of course now expired, the plaintiff should promptly take preparatory steps: draw and serve a bill of particulars if one has been demanded, immediately initiate use of the disclosure devices, respond

---

5. Rife v. Union College, 30 A.D.2d 504, 294 N.Y.S.2d 460 (3d Dep't 1968).

6. LaBate v. Meyerbank Elec. Co., 23 A.D.2d 503, 256 N.Y.S.2d 420 (2d Dep't 1965).

7. Ciunci v. Wella Corp., 23 A.D.2d 754, 258 N.Y.S.2d 994 (1st Dep't 1965).

8. CPLR 3211(e).

9. See Solarino v. Noble, 55 Misc.2d 429, 286 N.Y.S.2d 71 (Sup.Ct., N.Y.County, 1967), and the discussion in § 236 at note 12, above.

10. See Commentary C3025:7 on McKinney's CPLR 3025.

11. See Lermit Plastics Co. v. C.W. Lauman & Co., 40 A.D.2d 680, 336 N.Y.S.2d 187 (2d Dep't 1972).

12. Edenwald Contracting Co. v. City of New York, 60 N.Y.2d 957, 471 N.Y.S.2d 55, 459 N.E.2d 164 (1983).

13. Fulford v. Baker Perkins, Inc., 100 A.D.2d 861, 474 N.Y.S.2d 114 (2d Dep't 1984); A.J. Pegno Constr. Corp. v. City of New York, 95 A.D.2d 655, 463 N.Y.S.2d 214 (1st Dep't 1983).

14. Ciccone v. Glenwood Holding Corp., 44 Misc.2d 273, 253 N.Y.S.2d 576 (N.Y.C.Civ.Ct. 1964).

15. Murray v. City of New York, 43 N.Y.2d 400, 401 N.Y.S.2d 773, 372 N.E.2d 560 (1977).

16. See, e.g., Godell v. Greyhound Rent A Car, Inc., 24 A.D.2d 568, 262 N.Y.S.2d 318 (2d Dep't 1965).

17. See James–Smith v. Rottenberg, 32 A.D.2d 792, 302 N.Y.S.2d 355 (2d Dep't 1969).

promptly to any disclosure demands the defendant has made,[18] etc. The plaintiff is then prepared to cite those steps—taken on the strength of an answer barren of defenses—if the defendant seeks leave to add a defense later.

Yet another example of prejudice would be where the allowance of a late defense by the present defendant would deprive the plaintiff of recourse against some other person because of the lapse of time.[19]

Liberal though they are directed to be by CPLR 3025(b), the courts are more hesitant to grant amendment motions when the facts on which they are based were known to the movant from the beginning and could have been pleaded without trouble earlier.[20] As a rule, mere lateness is not a barrier to the amendment, but lateness coupled with significant prejudice is. Those are the classic elements of the laches doctrine, the major obstacle to the CPLR 3025(b) amendment. Where, for example, D wanted to amend its answer to add a counterclaim but waited a year after the joinder of issue and only after P had moved for a trial preference, the amendment was rejected. The court pointed to all the pretrial procedures that would now have to attend the belated claim, such as dismissal motions, bill of particulars procedures, disclosure devices, and even appeals from those steps, and held it prejudicial to hinder the plaintiff with those new things at this late stage.[21]

The amendment may be allowed conditionally, and the conditions can affect time and money, among other things. If the amendment is sought close in time to the trial, for example, but the court is disposed to grant it, the court can adjourn the trial to enable the adverse party to prepare to meet the new matter. Costs, too, may be imposed as a condition to a grant. There are indications that tardy amendments which in the past would have been refused outright may be allowed today with a costs assessment imposed instead.[22] In a case involving an inexcusable lateness in seeking an amendment to add defenses, for example, the court allowed the amendment but only on the condition that D pay P a stated sum, including an attorney's fee, to cover the cost of preparing to meet the new defense.[23]

While not a usual part of a costs award in New York, an attorney's fee can be awarded whenever a court, in granting relief, is permitted to grant it conditionally. It's a shorter and kinder step than the outright denial of the relief, in this case the amendment of a pleading, to which the court might have been otherwise disposed. Other examples of this will be seen in practice on the bill of particulars[24] and disclosure.[25]

On a motion to amend, the court will not ordinarily consider the merits of the proposed new matter unless it is so obviously lacking in merit as to have no chance of success whatever, in which case the motion will indeed be denied on that ground.[26] Some courts have even said that a grant of the motion without looking at the merits may only necessitate a later motion to test the merits. Labeling that procedure wasteful, they hold that at least the prima facie merit of the new matter should be considered on the amendment motion.[27]

A common motion to amend under CPLR 3025(b) is one to raise the demand in the wherefore clause (the so-called "ad damnum") in a money action. The courts have mixed emotions about this. The Third Department at one point took the position that such a motion will be granted almost for the asking, and even

---

18. Disclosure is the subject of Chapter 13, below.

19. See Pace v. Perk, 81 A.D.2d 444, 440 N.Y.S.2d 710 (2d Dep't 1981).

20. See, e.g., L.B. Foster Co. v. Terry Contr'g Inc., 25 A.D.2d 721, 268 N.Y.S.2d 618 (1st Dep't 1966).

21. O'Hara v. Tidewater Oil Co., 23 A.D.2d 870, 259 N.Y.S.2d 263 (2d Dep't 1965).

22. See Armstrong v. Peat, Marwick, Mitchell & Co., 150 A.D.2d 189, 540 N.Y.S.2d 799 (1st Dep't 1989).

23. Mirabella v. Banco Industrial de la Republica Argentina, 34 A.D.2d 630, 309 N.Y.S.2d 400 (1st Dep't 1970).

24. See § 241 below.

25. See § 367 below.

26. B v. B, 78 Misc.2d 112, 355 N.Y.S.2d 712 (Sup.Ct., Kings County, 1974). A totally groundless motion may also risk a sanction as a frivolous practice. See § 414A below.

27. See, e.g., East Asiatic Co. v. Corash, 34 A.D.2d 432, 312 N.Y.S.2d 311 (1st Dep't 1970).

on the eve of trial,[28] only to retreat afterwards and cite as authority the stricter standards of the First Department.[29] Ironically, the First Department, for a time the sternest on this motion,[30] did just the opposite: relaxed its rigorous approach and cited as authority the Third Department's leniency.[31] This institutional ambivalence is often the result of changes in the court's judicial personnel. The lesson to the lawyer, and a very key one, is that because amendments under CPLR 3025(b) are almost entirely discretionary, posing no issue of law, the appellate division is for all practical purposes the court of last resort on them.

A showing that should meet the standards of any department would be one that presents in detail the facts on which the additional sum is based, the reason why that sum was not sought at the outset, a strong affidavit of merits (strong affidavits should support all amendment motions), and an assurance to the court that the application is being made promptly upon the uncovering of the new facts.[32] Those new facts should be in affidavits made by those with first hand knowledge. Attorneys' affidavits carry little weight here.[33]

The motion to raise the ad damnum is most common in the personal injury case. There the moving papers should include a physician's affidavit detailing the injuries alleged to justify the increased damages.[34] If the additional damages are a mere updating of items of damages included in the original bill of particulars,

CPLR 3043(b) permits a supplement of the bill of particulars to do the updating as a matter of right up to 30 days before the trial, but the money demand in the complaint would still have to suffice to cover the updated damages or the amendment of the complaint would still be necessary to raise the demand. This kind of problem can usually be avoided by seeing to it that the original demand asks enough to cover all contingencies.

If this sounds a bit familiar, it's because we've already had at least one round with this problem in its more difficult phase: the motion to increase the ad damnum after a verdict has come in for more than the sum demanded in the complaint.[35] That post-verdict motion is made under subdivision (c) of CPLR 3025, the motion to conform the pleadings to the proof,[36] while the instant motion, which is made before the trial, is made under subdivision (b).

For purposes of the statute of limitations, matter in an amended pleading is deemed to relate back to the earlier one as long as the earlier one gave notice of the transaction or occurrence out of which the new matter arises.[37] This has been generously applied by the Court of Appeals. For a while there had been some debate, for example, as to whether a wrongful death claim sought to be added by amendment could be allowed to relate back to the original complaint, which pleaded only the claim for personal injury (from which the death later ensued).[38] An argument was made that such a relation back was conceptually

---

28. Ryan v. Collins, 33 A.D.2d 966, 306 N.Y.S.2d 777 (1970).

29. See Boehm Development Corp. v. State, 42 A.D.2d 1018, 348 N.Y.S.2d 251 (3d Dep't 1973), citing and relying on Osborne v. Miller, 38 A.D.2d 298, 328 N.Y.S.2d 769 (1st Dep't 1972), in which a new trial was ordered unless the plaintiff stipulate to reduce the verdict from $800,000 to $300,000. The rigor of the result in Osborne is abated when it is noted that the court denied the amendment not merely because it was late, but because the court found anything more than $300,000 to be excessive. Eight New York Supplements (less than a year) later, in the Hrusko case, note 32, below, the same court took a much gentler line and only the dissent cited Osborne.

30. See Jimenez v. Seickel & Sons, 22 A.D.2d 643, 252 N.Y.S.2d 891 (1st Dep't 1964).

31. Hrusko v. Public Serv. Coordinated Transport Corp., 40 A.D.2d 659, 336 N.Y.S.2d 544 (1st Dep't 1972).

32. See Koi v. P.S. & M. Catering Corp., 15 A.D.2d 775, 224 N.Y.S.2d 774 (1st Dep't 1962). While so thorough a showing should do the job in all departments, it may be overkill in some of them. In Wagner v. Huntington Hosp., 65 A.D.2d 771, 410 N.Y.S.2d 121, for example, the Second Department indicated, at least for a time, that absent prejudice a mere "re-evaluation of the damages" sufficed to justify the ad damnum amendment.

33. See Ryan v. Collins, 33 A.D.2d 966, 306 N.Y.S.2d 777 (3d Dep't 1970).

34. Jimenez v. Seickel & Sons, note 31, above.

35. See § 217 above.

36. That motion is treated in § 404 below.

37. CPLR 203(f). The relation-back doctrine of CPLR 203(f) is more fully discussed in § 49 above.

38. See Commentary C3025:12 on McKinney's CPLR 3025.

untenable because the wrongful death claim did not exist at the earlier time and because it does not belong to the same owner.[39] Those arguments were rejected and the relation back allowed in Caffaro v. Trayna,[40] a Court of Appeals decision inviting a pragmatic rather than a technical approach to the relation-back provision.

If the amendment is allowed, the amended pleading must be served on the other parties. The court usually provides in the order for how much time the amender has to serve it. If it requires a responsive pleading—as it will if the original pleading did—the response must be served within 20 days.[41]

N. BILL OF PARTICULARS

Table of Sections

§ 238. Bill of Particulars, Generally

A "bill of particulars" in civil practice is an amplification of a pleading. It supplies more detail and therefore affords the adverse party a more detailed picture of the claim or defense being particularized. It is designed to limit the proof and prevent surprise at the trial.[1]

The bill of particulars is tied in with the burden of proof. Parties are required to particularize only that of which they have the burden of proof.[2] Upon demand—a bill of particu-lars is as a rule served only when demanded[3]—plaintiffs must particularize their claims, de-fendants their defenses, counterclaims, cross-claims, and third-party claims, etc. But the defendant need not particularize denials con-tained in the answer because the matters in-volved are the plaintiff's burden to prove, not the defendant's.[4] This is in contrast with the disclosure devices of CPLR Article 31, where burden of proof is irrelevant.[5]

It is the general rule that a bill of particu-lars is not usable to obtain evidence.[6] The supplying of evidentiary material is not the bill's office.[7] The bill is supposed to offer a more expansive statement of the pleader's con-tentions rather than the evidentiary basis on which they rest. Thus, where P sued D for breach of a contract for P to do a musical score for D, which P said he did, D was not entitled to a copy of the score as part of a bill of particulars.[8]

D would be able to get it, however, by using the discovery device of CPLR 3120(a).[9] The court should be able to treat a bill of particu-lars demand, should the matter reach it on a motion of some kind, as a discovery demand as well, and direct that a relevant item be fur-nished. The disclosure devices are probably the most important in litigation. Although often expensive, they are worth their expense in substantial cases. But the disclosure devices can quickly prove too expensive, even though needed just as much, in smaller cases.

Some thoughtful decisions have suggested that the bill of particulars be allowed a disclo-sure function in actions with relatively small

---

39. The personal injury claim belongs to the injured person and goes to that person's estate upon death, while the wrongful death claim itself belongs to the deceased's dependents, EPTL § 5–4.4, not the estate.

40. 35 N.Y.2d 245, 360 N.Y.S.2d 847, 319 N.E.2d 174 (1974).

41. CPLR 3025(d).

§ 238

1. State of New York v. Horsemen's Benevolent and Protective Ass'n, 34 A.D.2d 769, 311 N.Y.S.2d 511 (1st Dep't 1970).

2. Hydromatics, Inc. v. County National Bank, 23 A.D.2d 576, 256 N.Y.S.2d 438 (2d Dep't 1965).

3. CPLR 3041, the basic statute on the bill of particu-lars, provides that a party "may require" the other to serve a bill.

4. L.F. Dommerich & Co. v. Diener & Dorskind, Inc., 31 A.D.2d 516, 294 N.Y.S.2d 613 (1st Dep't 1968).

5. CPLR 3101(a). See § 344 below.

6. Yardarm Club Hotel, Inc. v. Morgan, 22 A.D.2d 700, 253 N.Y.S.2d 920 (2d Dep't 1964).

7. State of New York v. Horsemen's Benevolent and Protective Ass'n, note 1, above.

8. Elman v. Ziegfeld, 200 A.D. 494, 193 N.Y.S. 133 (1st Dep't 1922).

9. See § 362 below, in the chapter on the disclosure devices.

stakes,[10] and the First Department sided with that view in Twiddy v. Standard Marine Transp. Services, Inc.,[11] holding that while it is not the mission of the bill of particulars to secure materials more appropriately left to the disclosure devices of Article 31 of the CPLR, "the rule is not an inflexible one". If the party on whom the demand is served makes no showing of prejudice, the demand for the bill can be allowed to serve as a disclosure notice as well, and was allowed to in *Twiddy*. "A rigid adherence to the purpose behind a bill of particulars in this case", the court said, "would only result in additional meaningless time-consuming motion practice."

The Advisory Committee had planned to abolish the bill of particulars altogether (it has been abolished in federal civil practice), but the legislature restored it in substantially the same form it had under prior law.[12] The committee's idea was to have the disclosure devices fill the gap. With that history, it would not be amiss to give the bill a reasonable disclosure function in smaller cases if doing so would save the parties substantial expense.

Technically a bill of particulars is not a pleading, but just an expansion of its contents. The extent to which it can be treated as a pleading has met some judicial ambivalence. If a pleading is complained of because it lacks adequate detail, for example, the courts are likely to sustain the pleading and just remit the complainer to a bill of particulars or to the disclosure devices or to both.[13] This suggests that if in a given case some item that arguably belongs in the pleading can instead be gotten through the bill, the bill can for that purpose be treated as the pleading itself. Some courts had held that a pleading omission could not be

remedied by the bill,[14] but the Court of Appeals later said that in considering the sufficiency of a pleaded cause of action the bill may be looked to as well.[15] Things appear to end up this way: if the bill is being used in the case, or the court on some motion can direct a bill, the bill can be made to carry out some of the pleading's function. Since the adverse party has both items, it should make no difference.

What a party may demand in a bill—and the demand, as long as it is reasonable, determines the bill's contents—is necessarily personal to the particular case. Whatever the pleading pleads, the bill must particularize. With the exception of the personal injury action, where the items that may be demanded have been codified,[16] the things that may be demanded and thus must be particularized are a sui generis inquiry. An eminent New York surrogate learned this when he had occasion to research the matter. He came out of the books aghast at the mass of cases—literally hundreds—each establishing only what had to be particularized in the given case. These cases, he noted, had no general utility, "no application to cases presenting divergent states of fact". So declared Surrogate Wingate in 1935.[17] The decades since then have added more cases, but not more utility.

"In furnishing the particulars requested, a bill should follow the designation of the items set forth in the demand and each item of the demand must be answered separately and categorically under its own number and subdivision".[18] Laws relied on as well as facts alleged have to be particularized,[19] especially when the laws relied on are foreign.[20] While special damages are the proper subject of a bill,[21] general

10. See, e.g., Block v. Fairbairn, 68 Misc.2d 931, 328 N.Y.S.2d 497 (Sup.Ct., Ulster County, 1972).

11. 162 A.D.2d 264, 556 N.Y.S.2d 622 (1990).

12. See Commentary C3041:1 on McKinney's CPLR 3041.

13. See, e.g., Pernet v. Peabody Eng'g Corp., 20 A.D.2d 781, 248 N.Y.S.2d 132 (1st Dep't 1964).

14. E.g., Melino v. Tougher Heating & Plumbing Co., 23 A.D.2d 616, 256 N.Y.S.2d 885 (3d Dep't 1965).

15. Nader v. General Motors Corp., 25 N.Y.2d 560, 565, 307 N.Y.S.2d 647, 650, 255 N.E.2d 765, 767 (1970).

16. CPLR 3043(a), set out later on in this section.

17. In re Herle's Estate, 157 Misc. 352, 356, 283 N.Y.S. 588, 592 (Kings County 1935).

18. Coonradt v. Walco, 55 Misc.2d 557, 560, 285 N.Y.S.2d 421, 425 (Sup.Ct., Rensselaer County, 1967).

19. Sacks v. Town of Thompson, 33 A.D.2d 627, 304 N.Y.S.2d 729 (3d Dep't 1969).

20. Haines v. Cook Electric Co., 20 A.D.2d 517, 244 N.Y.S.2d 483 (1st Dep't 1963).

21. Penn–Ohio Steel Corp. v. Allis–Chalmers Mfg. Co., 9 A.D.2d 620, 191 N.Y.S.2d 65 (1st Dep't 1959).

damages—those presumed to flow from the harms disclosed—need not be particularized.[22]

In a personal injury action, the items to be particularized are enumerated in a statutory list. This is designed to reduce arguments and the need for court applications in this most numerous category of litigation. The list is in CPLR 3043(a). In addition to supplying the personal injury items specifically, the statute gives some idea of how a bill of particulars demand functions generally. CPLR 3043(a) provides (verbatim) that in actions for personal injuries the following particulars may be required:

(1) The date and approximate time of day of the occurrence;

(2) Its approximate location;

(3) General statement of the acts or omissions constituting the negligence claimed;

(4) Where notice of condition is a prerequisite, whether actual or constructive notice is claimed;

(5) If actual notice is claimed, a statement of when and to whom it was given;

(6) Statement of the injuries and description of those claimed to be permanent, and in an action designated in [Ins.L. § 5104(a)] for personal injuries arising out of negligence in the use or operation of a motor vehicle in this state, in what respect plaintiff has sustained a serious injury, as defined in [Ins.L. § 5102(d)], or economic loss greater than basic economic loss, as defined in [Ins.L. § 5102(a)];

(7) Length of time confined to bed and to house;

(8) Length of time incapacitated from employment; and

(9) Total amounts claimed as special damages for physicians' services and medical supplies; loss of earnings, with name and address of the employer; hospital expenses; nurses' services.

The court can add to or subtract from the above list in a given case,[23] but the list is of course the standard for the profession in these cases and the court seldom has occasion to vary it. Note that item 6 involves the no-fault law, requiring elaboration of the facts on which the plaintiff relies to take the case out of the no-fault realm and permit it to be brought as an ordinary fault action. CPLR 3016(g) requires the pleading of those facts, but while the pleading need merely allege them in conclusory form, the bill must elaborate them.

At one time it was thought inconsistent in a negligence case for the plaintiff to rely both on the doctrine of res ipsa loquitur as well as on specific acts of negligence. Upon reexamination, the Court of Appeals determined that the two things are not necessarily inconsistent and held that both may be relied on in a given case.[24] When they are, the specific acts of negligence claimed must be particularized, as item 3 on the CPLR 3043(a) list manifests.[25]

If an account is pleaded, the adverse party is entitled to demand a copy of the items of the account. CPLR 3041 in fact defines "bill of particulars" to include "items of an account" when an account is involved.

If a pleading is verified, any bill of particulars in respect of it or copy of the items of an account alleged in it must also be verified. But in the negligence case, the bill must be verified whether or not the pleading is.[26] The reason for this is known to few living organisms.

§ 239. Procedure for Bill of Particulars

The procedure governing the bill of particulars is in CPLR 3042, which was overhauled in 1994, effective January 1, 1995. The old procedures will be noted only when a contrast seems especially helpful.[1]

---

22. Arett Sales Corp. v. Island Garden Center, Queens, Inc., 25 A.D.2d 546, 267 N.Y.S.2d 623 (2d Dep't 1966).

23. CPLR 3043(c).

24. Abbott v. Page Airways, Inc., 23 N.Y.2d 502, 297 N.Y.S.2d 713, 245 N.E.2d 388 (1969).

25. See Fizette v. Riverview Plaza, Inc., 40 Misc.2d 1, 242 N.Y.S.2d 594 (Sup.Ct., Seneca County, 1963).

26. CPLR 3044.

§ 239

1. An extensive treatment comparing and contrasting the new and old procedures appears in a three-part series of notes in SPR 23–25.

A mere demand starts things off. The party seeking the bill of particulars serves a "written demand" on the other side stating the items with respect to which particulars are desired. In this treatment the party who serves the demand will be S (for seeker) and the party on whom the demand is served R (for recipient).

There is no stated time for when the demand may be served, but ordinarily it should not be served before joinder of issue. The common practice for the defendant is to serve the demand with or after the answer. If the plaintiff wants a bill in respect of defenses in the answer, the plaintiff can demand it any time after the answer is served; if the answer contains a counterclaim, a demand for a bill of particulars in respect of the counterclaim may be served with or after the reply.

Under the CPLR, the service of a bill is not a condition precedent to the opening of disclosure proceedings, but the court can make it so if it finds reason to in a given case.[2]

R has 30 days in which to respond to the demand. R must review the demand promptly and decide which particulars she is willing to furnish and which particulars she objects to. R must answer the unobjectionable ones and, in the same response, include a statement of reasons for not responding to the others. Each objection must be stated "with reasonable particularity".[3]

R's response within the 30 days must therefore cover everything. Objecting to one or more items is not ground for withholding or even delaying a response to the unobjectionable items, nor is there any delay or extension of time allowed.[4]

If S has any objections to the bill that R furnishes, or, indeed, where R has altogether

failed to serve a bill, S's remedy is a motion to compel compliance, which is governed by subdivision (c) of CPLR 3042. If R's failure is deemed willful, the motion can include a request for penalties. For irresponsible behavior on either side, subdivisions (d) and (e) provide penalties.[5]

§ 240. Amending and Supplementing the Bill

CPLR 3042(b) allows the particularizer one amendment of the bill as of right, provided the amendment is made prior to the filing of the note of issue.[1] Presumably this amendment can make any change in the bill, just as an amendment as of course can make any change in a pleading under CPLR 3025(a). But the latter is restricted in time to the outset of the action while CPLR 3042(b) keeps the bill's amendment time open during the whole prenote of issue period. Should the amended bill introduce a substantial change, however, the other side can still resort to the disclosure devices to prepare to meet it. That's one of the purposes of making the note of issue the cutoff.[2]

What does the recipient do who has received a valid demand but who does not yet know all of the details needed to draw the bill of particulars? The recipient should draw the bill as completely as then able to, and candidly note the present inability to go any further, setting forth an explanation.[3] This can occur, for example, when the recipient needs to conduct a deposition of the demander in order to secure the necessary data. A more common situation along this line is the personal injury action in which the permanency of the injuries and damages is not yet known when the demand is

---

2. See, e.g., Rochester Radio Supply Co. v. State, 43 A.D.2d 897, 351 N.Y.S.2d 234 (4th Dep't 1974).

3. CPLR 3042(a).

4. Note the similarity of this change to the one made a year earlier, effective January 1, 1994, with respect to the disclosure devices of the interrogatory, the discovery notice, and the notice of physical and mental examination. See §§ 361 and 362 below.

5. See § 241 below.

§ 240

1. For note of issue practice, see § 369 below.

2. Disclosure proceedings must ordinarily be concluded before the note of issue is filed, the note of issue having to be accompanied by a statement of readiness attesting to the completion of disclosure proceedings, among other things. See § 370 below for statement of readiness practice.

3. Afrecan v. Caledonian Hospital, 29 A.D.2d 544, 285 N.Y.S.2d 912 (2d Dep't 1967).

served.[4] That used to be a dilemma, but isn't any longer. The plaintiff can obviously use the of-right amendment to update damages, but if the amendment has been used up, or the note of issue has already been filed (cutting off the right to amend without court leave), the personal injury plaintiff can turn to yet another device enacted to meet this updating problem: the supplemental bill.

CPLR 3043(b) allows the plaintiff in a personal injury case to serve a supplemental bill of particulars, also as a matter of right (no court leave needed), but only "with respect to claims of continuing special damages and disabilities". The supplemental bill permits the plaintiff to expand on the extent of the injuries and damages[5]—an especially helpful opportunity in the personal injury case in which the permanency of injuries was not known earlier in the action—and it may be served even after the note of issue is filed, as long as it is served at least 30 days before the trial.[6] It can't be used to add new grounds or theories, however, as an of-right amendment can.

If the note of issue has been filed, cutting off an amendment as of right, or if the of-right amendment has already been used up even though the note of issue has not yet been filed, or if the time for the of-right supplement of the damages claims in a personal injury case has expired, court leave will be required for any change in the bill.[7] The standard used by the courts in considering whether to allow the amendment is generally that applicable to the pleading itself under CPLR 3025(b).[8] In the absence of prejudice the motion should be freely granted.[9] In fact, the absence of prejudice,

such as where the party had knowledge all the while of just what it is that her adversary wants to add to the bill, may make it an abuse of discretion to refuse the amendment.[10] After the filing of the statement of readiness, however, which is designed to assure that the case is ready for trial before being added to the calendar,[11] motions of this kind will be entertained only when unanticipated circumstances are shown.[12]

§ 241. Remedies in Connection with Bill of Particulars

If the party receiving the demand for a bill of particulars (R) serves a bill that the seeker (S) deems inadequate, S may not return it; that's not the remedy.[1] Under subdivision (c) of CPLR 3042, S's remedy for that as well as for R's failure to serve a bill at all is to move to compel compliance, or, if such failure is willful, for the imposition of penalties pursuant to subdivision (d) of this rule.

This is intended to replace the prior procedure under which S could do nothing more than make a motion to preclude, which was almost invariably granted conditionally (giving R a second chance as a matter of right). The old procedure did not contemplate penalties right away. Only if R disobeyed the court order could S seek penalties, which of course entailed a second trip to court. Under CPLR 3042(c), the court is not limited to a simple conditional preclusion order. If R's behavior is found "willful", sanctions can be applied on the initial motion to compel compliance.

---

4. See, e.g., Marshall v. Zimmerly's Express, 30 A.D.2d 929, 294 N.Y.S.2d 85 (2d Dep't 1968).

5. Tate v. Colabello, 58 N.Y.2d 84, 459 N.Y.S.2d 422, 445 N.E.2d 1101 (1983).

6. An extensive discussion of this "supplement" provision, including its interplay with the "amendment" provision discussed above, is in Commentary C3043:2 on McKinney's CPLR 3043.

7. Stipulation in lieu of motion can of course accomplish these things, and the courts are usually delighted with the substitute. The lawyer should always try to adjust these items with the other side before running to the judge with a motion.

8. Maloney v. Union Free School Dist. No. 7, 46 A.D.2d 789, 360 N.Y.S.2d 699 (2d Dep't 1974).

9. Kerlin v. Green, 36 A.D.2d 892, 320 N.Y.S.2d 200 (4th Dep't 1971).

10. Ackerman v. City of New York, 22 A.D.2d 790, 253 N.Y.S.2d 775 (2d Dep't 1964).

11. See § 370 below.

12. Hernandez v. Ezrow, 24 A.D.2d 730, 263 N.Y.S.2d 372 (4th Dep't 1965). See Commentary C3042:9 on McKinney's CPLR 3042.

§ 241

1. See Lutza v. Bollacker, 36 A.D.2d 789, 319 N.Y.S.2d 371 (3d Dep't 1971).

What constitutes willful conduct under this new provision remains to be seen. If R does not respond in any way at all within the 30–day period, a start may already have been made towards a finding of willfulness. If R needs more time, R should contact S and seek an extension of time by stipulation. If the stipulation is refused, R may move the court for a time extension.

S will likely be wasting S's own time as well as R's by making a compliance motion without first trying to work things out with R. Unless there is something on the scene to show R's omission willful, so that the result of S's motion will be not merely a compliance order but a sanction to go with it, S may end up with a court order carrying no meat, just setting the stage for yet a further court application should the order now be disobeyed.

Prior to the 1995 amendment that overhauled bill of particulars practice, the courts were not quick to find conduct willful and impose sanctions. They should not be as hesitant under the present statute. Manifestly indifferent conduct by R should qualify as willful. The purpose of the amendment, in the words of the committee that drafted it, is to

> curtail pronounced and widespread abuses which have arisen under present law ... [where] [i]nitial requests for bills of particulars routinely are ignored. Some attorneys routinely serve demands that are so prolix and burdensome demands [that] ... harass opponents ... [and] [s]till other attorneys routinely serve patently defective bills.[2]

The penalties sword of course cuts two ways, slashing at whichever side is at fault: R, covered by subdivision (d) of CPLR 3042, and S, covered by subdivision (e).

Subdivision (d) says that if R, the recipient of the demand for the bill,

> willfully fails to provide particulars which the court finds ought to have been provided ... , the court may make such final or conditional order with regard to the failure

or refusal as is just, including such relief as is set forth in [CPLR 3126].

CPLR 3126 is the statute that provides the penalties for a failure to make disclosure under Article 31. Its penalties move in degrees, from an order establishing the relevant facts against the recalcitrant party, to a preclusion order, to the ultimate civil penalty of finding the party in default. The listed penalties are not exclusive. Under CPLR 3126, the court can make any orders that it finds "just", and a popular one is an order giving the wrongdoer another chance but only on condition that it pay a stated sum to cover the other side's costs and attorneys' fees associated with the misconduct.[3]

The reference to CPLR 3126 makes all of these remedies available as well for bill of particulars omissions, including the money assessment, but just as the remedies that CPLR 3126 contains are not exhaustive of the court's options there, the entirety of the CPLR 3126 package is not exhaustive of the court's options here, with the bill of particulars. The court can dip into the CPLR 3126 pot if it finds it appropriate, but doesn't have to. It can, independently of CPLR 3126, make its own "just" order under CPLR 3042(d).

The phrase "final or conditional" in subdivision (d) enables the court to include, with whatever penalty it chooses, a qualification, such as suspending the penalty "unless" compliance is forthcoming within a set time. "Unless" dispositions have been common in bill of particulars practice. The word "final" in subdivision (d) would seem to make it permissible, however, for the court to visit the ultimate sanction of a default on the wrongdoing party.

If the remedy selected by the court is a conditional preclusion order, and the condition has been violated, what is the next step? The ultimate remedy is summary judgment against R on the simple (and obvious) premise that since R is precluded from putting in a case, there is no reason for prolonging the agony of the litigation. Although delays even beyond the time offered by a conditional preclusion

---

2. See the memorandum of the Office of Court Administration at p.3304 of McKinney's 1994 Session Laws.

3. See § 367 below.

order can be forgiven, and for good cause will be,[4] summary judgment is exactly what awaits the recalcitrant party who presses his luck too far and who has no good reason for the delay.[5] When a plaintiff does that, the court may even specify that the judgment is "on the merits", or "with prejudice",[6] clarifying that any attempted new action will be met by the defense of res judicata. The continued disregard of court orders in bill of particulars practice has been held to warrant the appending of such a fatal qualification to the dismissal.[7]

Penalties Against S, the Demanding Party

Subdivision (e) is the tool that R, the recipient of the demand, may be able to use against S, the party who is seeking the particulars, but it may be invoked only if the court finds that S's demand is "improper or unduly burdensome". Demanding things not relevant to the case would be "improper", for example; demanding things that may be technically relevant but of a nature or quantity disproportionate in context would invoke the "unduly burdensome" standard.

Here the court may impose a sanction in addition to vacating or modifying the demand. Presumably the sanction would be monetary, but one can conjure up a situation in which it could be worse. Under subdivision (e) there is no explicit invitation to apply CPLR 3126, as there is in subdivision (d) in dealing with remedies against the party from whom the bill is demanded, but in the general language of subdivision (e) that permits "such order as is

just" is an independent routing to CPLR 3126, should the court choose to use it.[8]

Under subdivision (e), the only conduct on the part of S, the demanding party, that can invoke a sanction is the service of an improper or excessive demand. Other conduct by S that would seem appropriate for a sanction but which does not come down to an improper or excessive demand is not subject to a penalty under subdivision (e). If S's conduct rises to the level of "frivolous", however, it can be made the subject of a sanction under Rule 130–1.[9] That happened in First Nat'l Bank v. Volpe,[10] for example, where the demanding party moved to preclude before the bill of particulars was even due.

In both subdivisions (d) and (e) the court's remedial powers are summed up in the phrase permitting the court to make such order "as is just", thus leaving the matter almost entirely in the court's hands.[11]

Any and all motions affecting the bill of particulars, whether made by the party demanding it or by the party required to serve it, must include an affirmation by the moving party's lawyer "that counsel has conferred with counsel for the opposing party in a good faith effort to resolve the issues raised by the motion".[12]

§ 242. Variances

Variances between the bill of particulars and the pleading on one side, and the proof at trial on the other, are usually resolved today by giving the proof the upper hand and allowing the pleading and the bill to be amended to conform to the actual evidence, at least when

---

4. See, e.g., Abramowitz v. Berger, 20 A.D.2d 903, 248 N.Y.S.2d 936 (2d Dep't 1964).

5. See, e.g., McCraith v. Wehrung, 42 A.D.2d 825, 345 N.Y.S.2d 803 (4th Dep't 1973); Vandoros v. Kovacevic, 79 Misc.2d 238, 360 N.Y.S.2d 367 (App.T., 2d Dep't, 1974); Jansen's Bottled Gas Serv., Inc. v. Warren Petroleum Corp., 47 Misc.2d 461, 262 N.Y.S.2d 768 (Sup.Ct., Albany County, 1965). Cases in the First Department suggesting that summary judgment is not an appropriate remedy were decided when summary judgment was available only in certain actions, see Commentary C3042:12 on McKinney's CPLR 3042, and are not authority today, when summary judgment is no longer so restricted. See § 280 below.

6. See Palmer v. Fox, 28 A.D.2d 968, 283 N.Y.S.2d 216 (4th Dep't 1967), aff'd 22 N.Y.2d 667, 291 N.Y.S.2d 361, 238 N.E.2d 751 (1968).

7. See Mitchell v. Kiamesha Concord, Inc., 94 A.D.2d 914, 463 N.Y.S.2d 626 (3d Dep't 1983).

8. See SPR 25:1–2.

9. Rule 130–1, the sanctions rule applicable in civil actions, is treated in § 414A below.

10. 219 A.D.2d 867, 632 N.Y.S.2d 732 (4th Dep't 1995).

11. A similar deference to the court's judgment appears in several other procedural provisions that may provide additional guidance by analogy. See SPR 25:2.

12. See Uniform Rule 202.7(a).

no prejudice is shown.[1] And if the proof is within the purview of the pleading but not in conformity with the bill, the variance may be held inconsequential.[2] It is therefore difficult today to say just what the consequence of a variance will be. If the other side can't convince the court that it was misled by the variance, the court is not likely to penalize it. The bill of particulars, in other words, appears to have lost some of its purpose in narrowing the issues.[3] It's an amplification and therefore an adjunct of the pleading and as such enjoys the same liberal rules of construction that prevent pleadings from being handled too rigidly.

Practically speaking, the other side will not be heard to complain unless (1) the bill of particulars has actually misled it and (2) it is prejudiced as a result. This is not common today, but when it occurs it can be painful. The lawyer would do well to absorb the lesson of Mammarella v. Consolidated Edison Co.,[4]

for example. It was a wrongful death action and D demanded of P particulars as to the deceased's employment and loss of earnings, among other things. P responded to that portion of the demand with a pithy "not applicable", indicating that no damages were being claimed for those things. D therefore didn't prepare to address them. P was nevertheless allowed at the trial to prove such losses and when a verdict of $55,000 came in for P, it was discernible that $35,000 of the total was imputable to the very things P had so casually denominated "not applicable". The appellate division, tacitly holding D to have been unfairly misled, reduced the verdict from $55,000 to $20,000 and ordered P to take that or a whole new trial—together with the risk that a new jury might find liability lacking and that P would end up with nothing. That's the kind of consequence that awaits a party who takes too much for granted in bill of particulars practice.

§ 242

1. CPLR 3025(c) (see § 404 below); Sharkey v. Locust Valley Marine, Inc., 96 A.D.2d 1093, 467 N.Y.S.2d 61 (2d Dep't 1983).

2. See, e.g., Pogor v. Cue Taxi Serv., Inc., 43 Misc.2d 487, 251 N.Y.S.2d 635 (N.Y.C.Civ.Ct. 1964), aff'd 45 Misc.2d 933, 258 N.Y.S.2d 60 (App.Term 1st Dep't, 1965).

3. See Commentary C3042:10 on McKinney's CPLR 3042. The advent of liberal disclosure under Article 31 of the CPLR, see Chapter 13, below, probably accounts for this.

4. 44 A.D.2d 571, 353 N.Y.S.2d 38 (2d Dep't 1974).

Chapter Ten

MOTION PRACTICE

§ 243. Motion Practice, Generally

A motion is an application for an order.[1] It is usually made within the framework of an existing action or proceeding and is ordinarily made on notice, but some motions may be made without notice. One without notice is called an ex parte motion.

Orders are the devices whereby the courts manage litigation and resolve various disputes between the parties, and motions are the expedients for securing the orders. Most motions concern only incidents, i.e., they seek orders processing some housekeeping phase of the case, such as the pleadings or the disclosure devices; others seek relief that is actually or in effect final, such as motions to dismiss or for summary judgment.

As to who may move for what, there is one grand rule of thumb: any order the court can make, an interested party may move for. Some orders may be granted by the court on its own motion, but the great majority of orders result from motions made at the initiative of a party.

A motion on notice is deemed made when the motion papers are served.[2] When they are served by mail, which is the usual method, the moment of service occurs when the stamped and properly addressed envelope containing the papers is dropped in the letter box.[3] Thus, when the envelope leaves the fingers and drops into the box, the movant has "made" the motion even though the motion is not returnable in court until a number of days later and even though it will be several days before the motion papers are received. It is necessary to pinpoint the moment of service because many motions have to be made within a specified time and the mere posting within that time usually satisfies the requirement. A motion by the defendant for a more definite statement, for example,[4] must be made within 20 days after the complaint is served.[5] Posting the motion papers on the 20th day fulfills that requirement.

An ex parte motion is "made" when the motion papers and proposed order are submitted to the court.[6]

Most motions are made on written papers. The ensuing sections will discuss the various steps in making, scheduling, and disposing of motions. At the trial itself oral motions are common, especially for the purpose of resolving evidentiary disputes. The court has sometimes entertained an oral motion—i.e., one not made by a formal written notice of motion—in

---

§ 243

1. CPLR 2211.
2. Id.
3. CPLR 2103(b)(2).

4. CPLR 3024(a).
5. CPLR 3024(c).
6. 2d Rep.Leg.Doc. (1958) No. 13, p. 181.

other contexts when the parties were before it and when it appeared that no prejudice would result from the informal procedure. Thus, where P brought a special proceeding against D and both were before the court on the return day of the proceeding, D's oral motion to dismiss for lack of jurisdiction (based on defective service of the initiatory papers) was entertained. Prejudice to P was avoided in that the court held its decision off until P could submit opposing affidavits, which the court reviewed when it got them. The procedure was upheld.[7]

The fact that the court may occasionally entertain an oral motion in a context that ordinarily calls for the conventional written one is not something a lawyer should depend on. It should on no account be taken as an invitation to withhold papers in the hope that an oral request during a court hearing will do the job.

The subject of motion practice is much affected by the adoption of the Individual Assignment System (IAS) that went into effect on January 6, 1986[8] as part of the Uniform Rules (UR). Almost everything said about motion practice today—and this has to be kept in mind in consulting the ensuing sections that review the CPLR's diverse requirements on motion practice—has to be qualified to note that if the case is in the hands of a single judge, that judge's preferences have to be negotiated with respect to a good deal of motion procedure. Some judges have drawn and published their own individual rules, sometimes called "information sheets", instructing on diverse procedures, such as the day and time the judge hears motions, whether an appearance is required, whether oral argument is allowed, deadlines for the filing of motion papers or requests for adjournment, etc.

Despite the uniformity at which the Uniform Rules aim, when it comes to motions the IAS brings about less rather than more uniformity. The lawyer with any question at all about a motion after consulting the UR, and of course the particular judge's rules if there are any, would seem to have no alternative but to call the judge's chambers and find out specifically how the judge wants things done.

Restricting discussion here to the supreme and county courts, the Uniform Rules have not one but two rules on motion practice, 202.7 on calendaring and 202.8 on other procedural aspects.[9] But study as one may what the Uniform Rules purport to prescribe, it is still not safe to take a step without inquiring into what the assigned judge wants.

If no judge has yet been assigned when a motion is first made, the lawyer should consult UR 202.8(b), which has a procedural prescription for that situation. But even there, it doesn't hurt for the lawyer in doubt to ask about local trimmings in a call to the clerk in the county of venue.[10] Also in that situation—where no judge has yet been assigned—the motion papers must be accompanied by a Request for Judicial Intervention, the "RJI" discussed earlier.[11]

Some judges early in the life of the IAS, following the controversial practice of some federal judges, required that their permission be obtained before a motion could be made in one of their assigned cases. The appellate division rejected that restriction, holding in Goldheart International, Ltd. v. Vulcan Constr. Corp.[12] that a judge can't refuse to entertain a properly made motion. Other judges have required a kind of "conference" before a formal motion is made, hoping to resolve the dispute that might otherwise entail a motion. If this is seen as just a back door to requiring pre-motion permission, it may also meet appellate division disapproval. But if it doesn't add to the burdens of the lawyers and is seen as a device for resolving in a telephone

7. Shanty Hollow Corp. v. Poladian, 23 A.D.2d 132, 259 N.Y.S.2d 541 (3d Dep't 1965), aff'd 17 N.Y.2d 536, 267 N.Y.S.2d 912, 215 N.E.2d 168 (1966).

8. See § 77A above.

9. These are reviewed in the lead note in New York State Law Digest 313.

10. Motion venue, too, is affected by the IAS, for which see § 245 below.

11. See § 77C above.

12. 124 A.D.2d 507, 508 N.Y.S.2d 182 (1st Dep't 1986). The Second Circuit also curtailed the get-permission-first rule used by some federal district judges. See Richardson Greenshields Securities, Inc. v. Lau, 825 F.2d 647 (1987).

call or in a brief visit to chambers that which might otherwise require the time, effort, and expense of a formal motion, it should be upheld.

Because some judges continued the practice of requiring prior leave for motions, the First Department returned to the matter with an even more definitive statement in Hochberg v. Davis.[13] In an Article 78 proceeding against a judge by an aggrieved party, the court set aside a judge's rule exacting such permission and this time added the admonition that the "information sheets" used by some judges as the equivalent of rules are not valid unless filed with the Chief Administrator. In so doing, the court therefore made another point the bar had wanted clarified: that a preliminary leave requirement for motions can't be tolerated from "information sheets" any more than from outright "rules". To the extent that a permission requirement is felt to be a way of avoiding frivolous motions, the court pointed out that the answer to a frivolous motion is a frivolity sanction.[14]

New York allows an appeal from non-final (interlocutory) dispositions.[15] That plus the further availability of a mandamus-type proceeding against a judge to compel the exercise of mandatory duties serve as checks on possible IAS abuses. In a proceeding brought against one supreme court justice, for example, it was held that upon the request of an aggrieved party, a judge must sign an order reflecting a motion's outcome or otherwise make a written record on which an appeal can be predicated.[16]

The Uniform Rules has governing provisions for motion practice in other courts, too, including the Court of Claims,[17] the New York City Civil Court,[18] the district courts,[19] and the city courts.[20] The Individual Assignment System is not operative in all of them.[21]

§ 244. Ex Parte Motions

Although New York statutory law is not explicit on the point, the general rule from the cases is that motions must be made on notice. Practically speaking, the only time a party should attempt to move ex parte is when a statute or rule explicitly authorizes it. Only a few statutes do this. One is the motion for an order devising a method of summons service.[1] Another is the motion for an order in the supreme or county courts extending the plaintiff's time to file an action—the court can grant an extension of up to five days—when the statute of limitations is about to expire, and here the mere signing of the order marks the commencement of the claim for limitations purposes.[2] Others are found among the provisional remedies.[3]

Some caselaw holds that a motion may be made ex parte even without statutory authority if the other side would not be "prejudiced or affected in the least" by the relief sought[4]—a difficult notion to accept because the very issue of whether a party is affected by a motion is an issue on which that party should be heard.[5] Cases upholding ex parte applications made without statutory sanction are happily infrequent, and there is a widespread and healthy judicial distaste for such attempts.[6] Lawyers should make it their business to make all motions on notice unless there is an unambiguous statute or rule at hand authoriz-

---

13. 171 A.D.2d 192, 575 N.Y.S.2d 311 (1st Dep't 1991).

14. See Rule 130-1, treated in § 414A below.

15. See § 526 below.

16. Grisi v. Shainswit, 119 A.D.2d 418, 507 N.Y.S.2d 155 (1st Dep't 1986). There is of course a general requirement that orders be in writing. See CPLR 2219(a), discussed in § 250 below.

17. UR 206.8, 206.9.

18. UR 208.10, 208.11.

19. UR 212.10, 212.11.

20. UR 210.8, 210.9.

21. See § 77A above.

---

§ 244

1. CPLR 308(5), 311(b).

2. See CPLR 203(c)(2) and 304. See § 45 above.

3. See, e.g., CPLR 6211, 6313.

4. See, e.g., Matter of Salmon, 34 Misc. 251, 253, 69 N.Y.S. 215, 216 (Sup.Ct., Monroe County, 1901).

5. See Fosmire v. Nicoleau, 144 A.D.2d 8, 536 N.Y.S.2d 492 (2d Dep't 1989).

6. See Lohne v. City of New York, 25 A.D.2d 440, 266 N.Y.S.2d 909 (2d Dep't 1966); Cooke v. Wozen Equities, Inc., 143 Misc.2d 578, 540 N.Y.S.2d 629 (Sup.Ct. N.Y.County 1988).

ing the particular motion to be made ex parte. If there is difficulty in determining whom to serve with notice, or any other difficulty impeding the flow of an ordinary motion on notice, the order to show cause procedure can be used (in which the judge can resolve the difficulty).[7]

There is an important rule the lawyer should remember on all ex parte motions. All of them. There is a strong policy against having one judge overrule another of coordinate jurisdiction, or putting a judge into the embarrassing position of doing so inadvertently, or even confronting a judge with the possibility of overruling herself because she has forgotten some earlier ruling she made in the case. Recognizing that on an ex parte motion there is no adverse party to offset the movant's one-sided presentation, it is required that the moving papers on every ex parte application include an affidavit attesting to whether this or any similar relief has been moved for previously and, if so, what new facts justify this new application.[8] The affidavit should describe precisely what occurred on the earlier application.

The Individual Assignment System (IAS), under which a case goes to a single judge and stays there throughout, might be thought to reduce the need for this attestation of prior activity because the prior activity in the case would presumably have been before the same judge. But that notion gives too much credit to judicial memory, especially when the judge may have hundreds of cases to track, and there are in any event exceptions from place to place under the IAS in which the system is not operative and in which the case does get exposed to different judges.

An order on an ex parte application is not appealable.[9] If the adverse party wants the order vacated, he should move for the vacatur on notice; the order granting or denying the

vacatur will then be appealable. He may alternatively seek vacatur of the order by an ex parte application made to the judge who granted it,[10] but if that application is denied the order of denial will not be appealable. The party has yet another alternative: to move, ex parte, to have the appellate court or one of its judges vacate the order. CPLR 5704 expressly authorizes this, and even authorizes a movant whose ex parte motion below has been denied to seek its grant from the appellate court.[11] CPLR 5704 contemplates a simple, ex parte motion procedure before the appellate court, not an appeal procedure with its attendant time, trouble, and expense. The First Department declared in 1964 that it would not entertain such applications,[12] remitting the movant to repeating the motion before the lower court, this time on notice—so that the resulting order would be appealable—but this hostility to CPLR 5704 did not spread to other departments and, indeed, the indications are that it is no longer present even in the First Department.

Under the IAS,[13] all motions, the ex parte ones included, must as a rule be made to the assigned judge. If an ex parte motion is made in a case in which a judge has not yet been assigned, the papers must be accompanied by a Request for Judicial Intervention. It is this "RJI" that occasions the assigning.[14] If there is a time pressure that can't await the usual local assignment machinery, an inquiry about any special procedure should be made promptly of the clerk. There may be a judge on "stand by" for such an exigency. In populous counties there may even be a regularly assigned "stand by" judge, the equivalent of the judge presiding at what used to be widely known as "Special Term, Part II" in some counties, to handle such emergency applications. (The fact that the order to show cause, the prime servant of

---

7. See § 248, below, treating the order to show cause.

8. CPLR 2217(b).

9. CPLR 5701(a)(2).

10. CPLR 2221(a)(2).

11. The appellate division has these ex parte powers only in respect of the lower courts of which it has appellate jurisdiction. CPLR 5704(a). In the First and Second departments, the appellate term and its justices have like

powers for their lower courts, which include the New York City Civil Court, the district courts, etc. CPLR 5704(b).

12. See In re Willmark Service System, Inc., 21 A.D.2d 478, 251 N.Y.S.2d 267 (1st Dep't 1964).

13. See § 77A above.

14. See § 77B above.

an emergency, also falls into the "ex parte" category gives this subject extra importance.[15])

A stand-by judge may be available under local procedure even for emergency applications in cases in which a judicial assignment is already in effect, as where the assigned judge is indisposed, or off on circuit to a distant part of the district. Uniformity on these matters is illusive, and a call to the clerk reassuring.

As will be seen more fully in the treatment of the venue of motions,[16] each supreme court justice carries the ex parte powers of the court around wherever he or she may be and can be approached for ex parte relief in any part of the state,[17] presumably without regard to where the action is venued or who the assigned judge is. But the Uniform Rules qualify this to require the judge approached to refer the ex parte application to the appropriate county or judge "unless . . . the urgency of the motion requires immediate determination".[18]

More on motion venue below.[19]

§ 245. Where Motion Made (Venue of Motions)

The question of where a motion may be made, i.e., what counties are proper venue for the motion, arises mainly in supreme court actions. Since supreme is a statewide court with local subdivisions, its jurisdiction is statewide. Proper venue for supreme court motions therefore needs pinpointing. The county court, on the other hand, is independent in each county that has one—all except the counties in New York City have one—and all motions in one of its actions are made returnable in that county except under special circumstances.[1]

A motion on notice in a supreme court action has a broad choice of venues, although,

because of the Individual Assignment System (IAS), under which a case goes to a single judge and remains with that judge for all purposes,[2] the "choice" may be illusory today in many instances. An effort was made to reconcile the statutes on motion practice, embodied for the most part in Article 22 of the CPLR, with the IAS-implementing Uniform Rules, but the "reconciliation" did not rework the statutes to coordinate with the rules; it merely added language at key points subordinating the statutes to such rules as the chief administrator might adopt.[3] The rules adopted pursuant to those authorizations may be uniform, as where something in the Uniform Rules themselves addresses the matter, or just local. Given practices, whether by adoption in a rule or by direction by administrative order or otherwise, may be prescribed for application only in a given district or court or county.

The lesson to the lawyer is to check things out on a local basis—indeed, with the individual assigned judge if there is one—if there is any doubt whatever about procedures followed locally.

The main venue statute[4] offers a choice of counties, or shall we say *purports* to offer a choice of counties, in which to make a motion in a supreme court action. The motion may be noticed to be heard, i.e., made returnable, in the county in which the action is pending (the most common choice), or in any other county in the same judicial district, or in any county physically adjoining the pendency county even if not in the same district.[5] The original and legitimate purpose of this surprisingly broad choice was to recognize the frequent unavailability of motion terms and permanently assigned justices in the more rural counties, a problem not met in the urban counties (where

---

15. The order to show cause is the subject of § 248 below.

16. See § 245 below.

17. CPLR 2212(b).

18. Uniform Rule 202.7(e).

19. See § 245 below.

§ 245

1. See CPLR 2213. As to the venue of motions in the lower courts, see Commentary C2212:6 on McKinney's CPLR 2212.

2. See § 77A above.

3. See CPLR 2212(d), 2213(c), 2217(d), 2221(b).

4. CPLR 2212.

5. CPLR 2212(a).

alternatives to the pendency county were therefore less frequently used for motions). Whatever the motivations, the provision, at least until the advent of IAS, continued to make for a lot of judge shopping.

These generous venue alternatives of CPLR 2212(a) can't comfortably co-exist with a system that insists that all motions in a case go to but a single judge. Subdivision (d) of CPLR 2212 therefore confers on the chief administrator the power to withdraw the 2212(a) alternatives. The power is supposed to be exercised "by rule", but whether an administrative "rule" or "order" or perhaps just a local practice is in effect in a given area must, once again, be inquired into locally. In a case in which a judge has already been assigned, motions will presumably be following the judge thenceforth, wherever the judge may be at the time.

Following the judge about can of course be a problem in upstate districts covering large areas because the judge may be on assignment to a distant county. At least for emergency applications, such as ex parte applications that can't wait, there will presumably be some more expeditious alternative set up in the county in which the action was commenced and in which the assigned judge is ordinarily resident.[6]

Assuming that once a judge has been assigned, the CPLR 2212(a) venue options dissolve and the motion must be made to the assigned judge, that still leaves the situation in which a motion is made before a judge has been assigned to the case. There, at least, it would seem that the movant could exercise his CPLR 2212(a) options and make the motion in a county other than the main action's venue. Rule 202.8(b) of the Uniform Rules addresses the point, however, and appears to discourage

the exercising of these 2212(a) choices. It sets up a procedure for getting a judge assigned— whichever county has initially been made the motion venue—re-noticing the motion in accordance with the assigned judge's calendar, and notifying the parties when all this is done.

The IAS does seem to sound the death knell of that favorite old use of the CPLR 2212(a) motion options: judge shopping. And if it's not the death knell, then it's at least some early tolling. An attempt to invoke the CPLR 2212(a) venue alternatives by making a motion in the Bronx in an action pending in Westchester was rejected in Sullivan & Donovan, LLP v. Bond,[7] denying the motion without prejudice to its renewal in Westchester. The court held in effect that the statute does not apply when the alternative venue imposes on an urban county.[8] Even before the IAS came in, the use of the venue options had been excluded from some counties by caselaw.[9]

Although a county may have no resident supreme court justice, each county outside New York City usually has a sitting county court judge. Recognizing this, the CPLR allows the rules to permit supreme court motions to be made to the county judge in certain circumstances.[10] The lawyer should find out if such a rule is applicable in the particular county, at least in the Second, Third, and Fourth departments.[11]

If a supreme court motion is made returnable in an altogether wrong county, the result should be nothing more serious than a change of venue back to a proper county, as happens when the action itself has been improperly venued.[12] It has even been observed that the parties can stipulate to a venue for their motion,[13] which suggests that motion venue is not jurisdictional. Some caselaw has indicated that

---

6. See § 244 above.

7. 175 Misc.2d 386, 669 N.Y.S.2d 131 (Sup.Ct., Bronx County, 1997).

8. See the discussion in SPR 63:4.

9. In Cordero v. Grant, 95 Misc.2d 153, 407 N.Y.S.2d 383 (Sup.Ct., N.Y.County, 1978), for example, New York County, which has one of the heaviest calendars in the state, was held to be unavailable as a motion venue for actions pending in other counties. The case is discussed in Commentary C2212:1 on McKinney's CPLR 2212. CPLR

2212(d), incidentally, in permitting administrative withdrawal of the 2212(a) venue options, requires that "the practice in counties within the city of New York shall be uniform".

10. CPLR 2212(c).

11. There are no county courts in the First Department.

12. See CPLR 509–511. See § 123 above.

13. See 2d Rep.Leg.Doc. (1958) No. 13, 183.

it is, but upon closer reflection courts so indicating have come round to the view that it is not.[14] Even the consequence of holding the matter jurisdictional should not often be serious, however: instead of a transfer, it merely results in a denial of the motion, or perhaps to its mere "dismissal", without prejudice to its being made anew in a proper county. Pressed too far, the treatment of a venue defect as jurisdictional can do unnecessary damage.

If the supreme court on a wrongly venued motion (to which no one objects) passes on its merits, the order on the motion should be deemed valid.[15]

CPLR 2212(b) provides that an ex parte supreme court motion may be made at a motion term duly prescribed for such motions or—take note—to any justice of the court anywhere in the state, but here, too, the rules can take away what the statute gives. One of the Uniform Rules does a little of this taking away. It provides that an ex parte motion made to a judge outside the action's venue county "shall be referred to the appropriate court in the county of venue", but it also leaves an important power intact by adding the qualification, "unless the judge [to whom the ex parte application was presented] determines that the urgency of the motion requires immediate determination".[16] Hence the rules do preserve each judge's power to act ex parte when an emergency is at hand, even in a case not the judge's own.

Where does a judge get such power? The answer is that each justice of the supreme court carries the ex parte powers of the court around with her. The judge can be approached at any time or place (in or out of court) with an ex parte motion. If the motion is made far from the action-pending county, and to a wholly inappropriate justice (one not even in the same judicial district), the reason had best be good. The consequence, otherwise, is that the motion may be denied without even reaching the merits, leaving the movant to repeat it before the assigned judge or at least in a more appropriate place. This statewide authority in connection with ex parte motions is designed to help the litigants and their lawyers in emergencies, and if there is no emergency, and no special reason for the far-from-home motion, the justice applied to need merely refuse the requested order.[17] Indeed, under the Uniform Rules the judge is required to refuse it unless there's "urgency".

Perhaps the prime beneficiary of this statewide authority is the order to show cause, the litigant's truest friend in a tight situation. The show cause order starts off ex parte and it is no small advantage to be able to present it to any available justice if there's an emergency at hand.[18]

§ 246. The Motion Papers

The moving papers consist of a notice of motion and such supporting papers as the movant relies on. The notice of motion specifies the time and place of the hearing,[1] the supporting papers, the relief demanded, and the grounds for the relief. It can seek relief "in the alternative or of several different types".[2] Whatever motion remedies one party fancies herself entitled to against another at any given time, in other words, may all be joined in one motion if the movant is so disposed.

The main supporting papers on a motion are affidavits, but any relevant exhibits, documents, depositions, etc., are also includible. The supporting papers should be referred to in the notice of motion, as illustrated in the form contained in § 252. Opposing papers are also made up principally of affidavits.

---

14. Compare Newell v. Huston, 35 A.D.2d 908, 317 N.Y.S.2d 66 (4th Dep't 1970), with Cwick v. City of Rochester, 54 A.D.2d 1078, 388 N.Y.S.2d 753 (4th Dep't 1976). The latter warns, however, that counsel's contriving a wrong motion venue for its own convenience will not be countenanced.

15. See Commentary C2212:7 on McKinney's CPLR 2212.

16. Uniform Rule 202.7(e).

17. See Commentary C2212:9 on McKinney's CPLR 2212.

18. See § 248, below, for discussion of the order to show cause.

§ 246

1. See § 247, below, for the applicable time requirements.

2. CPLR 2214(a).

The moving papers should not be served until they're ready. In one case where the lawyer served deficient moving papers accompanied by a statement that later "a further more detailed affirmation will be furnished"— a kind of "stay tuned to this station" announcement—the court denied the motion with $100 costs and a $500 sanction.[3] It said that it is "unheard of" that a party should deliberately make a motion with inadequate supporting papers and then just supplement them at some future time. In the absence of an agreement between the parties—and sometimes even when there is one, as where the motion has already been submitted—leave is required before motion papers already served can be supplemented.

If the motion concerns either the bill of particulars or disclosure, an affirmation must also be included in the moving papers to the effect that the movant's lawyer has consulted with the other side in a good faith effort to resolve the dispute, but without success.[4]

Each party furnishes to the court all papers served by him. Any other papers needed by the court are to be supplied by the moving party. If a needed item is in the possession of the other party, the moving party can, in the notice of motion, require that it be produced at the hearing. Only papers duly served on other parties and furnished to the court in accordance with these instructions are to be considered, unless for good cause the court otherwise directs.[5]

Before the adoption of the Uniform Rules, there was no omnibus requirement about serving on the other side a memorandum or brief used on a motion. The Uniform Rules today require the movant to include in her moving papers any brief she intends to use on the motion, and the opposing party to include a responding brief in the answering papers.[6] Rule or no, common courtesy insists that no lawyer spring a memorandum or brief on his adversary without giving her some chance to peruse it before the return day and to draw her own in rebuttal.[7]

If the motion is the first thing in the action to require judicial attention, no judge having yet been assigned, the motion papers have to be accompanied by a Request for Judicial Intervention (RJI).[8]

§ 247. Making the Motion; Notice Requirements

The moving party determines when a motion on notice shall be heard, but she has to consult the court's or judge's calendar practice first. The movant picks out a "return day" sufficiently far off to assure that the notice requirements of CPLR 2214(b) can be met, making sure as well that the day picked is a motion day on which the assigned judge hears motions.

Under the practice used before adoption of the Individual Assignment System (IAS), the motion was made returnable to the court rather than the judge. There was usually a motion term in session on every business day in urban and most suburban counties, but in a rural county there might be only one every few weeks or even months. In the larger counties the movant would also have to determine the "part" before which the motion was to be returnable, local rules prescribing these things. Most contested motions were returnable before a single part, usually called "Special Term, Part I" in metropolitan counties. But a given motion might be of a kind directed to a special part (matrimonial, condemnation, tax assessment, etc.).

Under the IAS, it is the practice of the individual judge that has to be noted, and it should be noted in all respects: the day or days on which the judge hears motions, the place of the hearing, the time of day, whether oral

---

3. Rosenman Colin Freund Lewis & Cohen v. Edelman, 165 A.D.2d 533, 568 N.Y.S.2d 590 (1st Dep't 1991).

4. Uniform Rule 202.7.

5. CPLR 2214(c).

6. Uniform Rule 202.8(c). The rule prescribes when the papers have to be filed with the court. It also reminds us that affidavits are for the facts and briefs for the law. In clean and crisp practice, the two missions are kept distinct.

7. See Commentary C2214:20 on McKinney's CPLR 2214.

8. See § 77B above.

argument is allowed, etc. The Uniform Rules have the details, requiring that all papers be filed on or before the return date and addressing also the filing of answering and reply papers, the setting up of oral argument, adjournments of the return date, and the holding of a preliminary conference in conjunction with a motion affecting disclosure or a bill of particulars.[1] As the time elements in the making of motions are discussed in this section, the reader should keep in mind the need to consult the Uniform Rules as well as the particular judge's own rules. The judge may call these "information sheets". Under whatever name, they should be consulted. If a clear path can still not be discerned, the judge's chambers should be consulted.

"All motions shall be returnable before the assigned judge",[2] and while guidance on procedure may sometimes have to be sought from the judge's chambers, the judge's advance permission is not required in order to make a motion.[3]

CPLR 2214(b), designed as it is to assure reasonable notice periods for moving papers, answering papers, cross-motions, etc., remains applicable under the Uniform Rules and the IAS. It requires that the movant give all other parties at least 8 days notice of the motion, which becomes 13 if the motion papers are served by mail, as they usually are.[4] When that minimum is used, however, the adverse party can mail her answering papers to the movant as late as two days before the motion is to be heard, which usually means that the movant will not receive them in time to respond to them at the hearing.[5]

To assure receipt of the answering papers earlier than that, the movant can use the 12–7–1 option also offered by CPLR 2214(b), which means that if the movant gives at least 12 days notice of the motion instead of 8 (17 instead of 13 if mail is used), she can require the adverse party to serve answering papers no later than 7 days before the return day. Even if those papers are mailed on the 7th day prior to the return day, the movant will still get them several days before and will be able to prepare to meet them. A statement requiring such 7–days-before answering papers should be included in the notice of motion.[6]

When picking out a motion day satisfactory to the notice requirements, the movant should recognize that various delays may occur before the moving papers can actually be served, and that the notice requirement is measured not from the day the papers are prepared or dated, but—when mail is the method used—from the moment of posting. If the movant adds a few days to the notice period, picking out a motion day more than the minimum number of days away, this will automatically compensate for any delays encountered in gathering up the moving affidavits and other supporting papers and will assure that the return day will satisfy the minimum notice requirements, even if the mailing of the papers is delayed.

It is therefore good practice to make motions returnable at least three weeks away from the planned date of mailing, and to include, automatically, the requirement that the other side serve answering papers at least 7 days before the return day. This enables the motion to be served by mail, gives sufficient notice to support the 7–day answering requirement, and leaves a few days for a late mailing if some snag prevents posting on the day planned.

If speed is needed, the shorter notice time can be used, forfeiting the right to 7–day answering papers, but the difference of the few days is usually insignificant. If speed is really

---

§ 247

1. See, e.g., Uniform Rule 202.8, applicable in the supreme and county courts. See the discussion in SPR 3:3.

2. Uniform Rule 202.8(a).

3. The judge can, however, require that the dispute be "conferenced" before being made the subject of a motion. See § 243 above.

4. CPLR 2103(b)(2). See § 202 above.

5. The add–5–days-for-mail provision does not apply to the service of answering papers. It applies only to a paper whose service measures another party's obligation. The original notice of motion does that, setting the return day and thus determining when answering papers are due, but the service of the answering papers does not; hence, no 5–day addition applies.

6. CPLR 2214(b). See the last paragraph in the form of notice of motion contained in § 252.

the aim, the order to show cause is the remedy.[7]

A reply affidavit in this 12–7 situation need only be served (which means mailed) one day before the return day. If delayed until that time, however, it will arrive in the opposing side's hands too late—probably after the motion day has come and gone. The CPLR does not resolve that problem, although the rules require that "all" papers be filed with the court no later than the return day,[8] and that should also include reply papers. The problem usually arises only between lawyers denying one another the professional courtesies. Judges usually resolve lateness disputes with some pragmatic response, such as offering the parties more time, requiring the trading of as-yet-unreceived papers in the courthouse corridor, adjourning the motion, etc. Judges do not like arguments about these things—or the lawyers who make them necessary. Each attorney should defer literal compliance with these service rules to practical compliance, seeing to it that the other side has timely receipt of all needed papers.

While CPLR 2214(b) provides for minimum notice time on motions, it sets no arbitrary outer limit. Theoretically, therefore, a moving party may make a motion returnable way off into the future. But the absence of an outer time limit has a reason: the infrequency of motion terms in some parts of the state.[9] Since many motions have to be "made" within a specified period, making them would be impossible if they had to be made returnable no later than a certain day and if there were no available motion term prior to or on that day.[10]

The absence of the outer limit can lead to abuse. An example of this is where a movant may want the automatic stay that results upon the making of certain motions, like a motion to dismiss under CPLR 3211, whose mere making automatically stays disclosure.[11] If a movant under a court direction to make disclosure seeks to avoid the direction by making a CPLR 3211 motion with a far out return day just before the disclosure is due, the court, upon being advised of this, is likely to foil the plot.[12] And if the conduct really strikes the court as frivolous,[13] moreover, the court can even apply a money sanction against the abuser.

It is sound practice to hold off preparing the notice of motion until all required affidavits and other proof have been gathered up and legal memoranda drawn. This enables a return day to be picked out with more precision because the movant knows that the motion papers are all at hand and ready for posting.

The original of the motion papers—it used to be called the "ribbon copy" before the word processor replaced the typewriter and the duplicating machine replaced carbon paper—is usually filed with the court. Copies are served on the other parties. If there are many parties, each is entitled to be served with a copy of the motion papers whether that party is on the same side or an opposing side and whether the movant fancies that party to be interested in the motion or not.[14] The time by which the moving papers have to be filed with the court is a matter usually regulated by rule.[15] Upon receiving the papers, the clerk or judge's assistant will simply add the motion to the motion calendar for the return day specified in the notice of motion. Again, individual judges' rules have to be consulted on this.

If the motion is the first step in the action that requires judicial attention, no judge having yet been assigned to the case, the motion papers must include a Request for Judicial Intervention (RJI),[16] which brings about the

---

7. See § 248 below.

8. See Uniform Rule 202.8(a).

9. See 2d Rep.Leg.Doc. (1958) No. 13, p. 181.

10. See Commentary C2214:11 on McKinney's CPLR 2214.

11. See CPLR 3214(b).

12. See Town of Southampton v. Salten, 186 A.D.2d 796, 589 N.Y.S.2d 355 (2d Dep't 1992), Commentary C2214:11 on McKinney's CPLR 2214, and SPR 13:4.

13. See § 414A below.

14. CPLR 2103(e).

15. See Uniform Rule 202.8 and any applicable local rules or orders. If they don't answer, call the judge's chambers or the clerk.

16. See § 77B above.

assignment of a judge. A special rule prescribes procedure in that situation.[17]

To the court's set of motion papers should be appended an affidavit of service, attesting that copies of the motion papers have been duly served on all other parties. This affidavit, filled in on the printed form appearing on the litigation back containing the papers when a back of this kind is used, may be made by whoever mailed the papers—the attorney, a secretary, etc.

Opinion is divided on the effect of giving inadequate notice, that is, making the motion returnable too early. Some courts have held it jurisdictional, at least when there has been no appearance by the other side,[18] and deny the motion without prejudice (or "dismiss" it, which is the same thing). Others hold that it's not jurisdictional "unless there is substantial prejudice", and that there is no prejudice when the opposing party prepared a response and in fact submitted it to the court,[19] although the court of course has discretion to give the adverse party more time, even adjourning the motion for that purpose.[20] Responding on the merits amounts to a waiver of insufficient notice.[21]

The failure to give any notice at all, in an instance where notice is required and where the unnotified party is not before the court, should invalidate the motion altogether.[22] It would be equivalent to making the motion ex parte, which is ordinarily permissible only when explicitly authorized by statute.[23] If the motion has been the subject of voluntary ad-

journment by the parties and the adjournments have added enough time to compensate for the short notice, the initial defect should be disregarded.[24] The rules prefer that stipulations of adjournment be in writing, as, indeed, all stipulations are supposed to be,[25] and be submitted to the judge.[26]

Ordinarily a motion may be withdrawn by its maker at any time before it is submitted,[27] but the judge or clerk and the other parties should be notified,[28] if not consulted. After submission, the motion may not ordinarily be withdrawn, even if the judge has not yet decided it, except upon the judge's order or upon consent of all the parties (to which the judge is not likely to object). The "submission" ordinarily occurs when the oral argument of the motion is concluded or, if it is to be submitted on papers alone without argument, on the return day.[29]

Whether oral argument of the motion is required, or even permissible, is, as noted, up to the individual judge. If oral argument is desired, the movant asks for it in the moving papers, the other party on the top page of the answering papers.[30]

§ 248. Order to Show Cause

An order to show cause is basically only a substitute for a notice of motion. It has several features, among them that it can shorten the notice time.[1] An ordinary notice of motion can't be brought on for hearing earlier than the eighth day after the motion papers are

17. Uniform Rule 202.8(b).

18. See, e.g., Thrasher v. U. S. Liab. Ins. Co., 45 Misc.2d 681, 257 N.Y.S.2d 360 (Sup.Ct., N.Y.County, 1965).

19. National Microtech, Inc. v. Satellite Video Services, Inc., 107 A.D.2d 860, 861, 484 N.Y.S.2d 303, 304 (3d Dep't 1985).

20. Motion relief may of course be granted by default. Even the movant can be guilty of a default, resulting in the denial of the motion, as when he fails to appear on the return day.

21. Todd v. Gull Contracting Co., 22 A.D.2d 904, 255 N.Y.S.2d 452 (2d Dep't 1964).

22. Burstin v. Public Service Mut. Ins. Co., 98 A.D.2d 928, 471 N.Y.S.2d 33 (3d Dep't 1983). See Commentary C2211:7 on McKinney's CPLR 2211.

23. See § 244 above.

24. See Coonradt v. Walco, 55 Misc.2d 557, 285 N.Y.S.2d 421 (Sup.Ct., Rensselaer County, 1967).

25. See § 204 above.

26. See Rule 202.8(e).

27. Oshrin v. Celanese Corp., 37 N.Y.S.2d 548 (Sup. Ct., N.Y.County), aff'd 265 A.D. 923, 39 N.Y.S.2d 984 (1st Dep't 1942), aff'd 291 N.Y. 170, 51 N.E.2d 694 (1943).

28. See Commentary C2211:9 on McKinney's CPLR 2211.

29. See Wallace v. Ford, 44 Misc.2d 313, 253 N.Y.S.2d 608 (Sup.Ct., Erie County, 1964).

30. Uniform Rule 202.8(d).

§ 248

1. CPLR 2214(d).

served.[2] With an order to show cause the hearing can be brought on at any time the court directs, which can be fewer than eight days, or as close as the next day. If the court is convinced there is a real emergency, it can schedule the hearing for a few hours later, or, in the direst case, "forthwith" the service of the order to show cause.

An ordinary notice of motion merely notifies the recipient that a motion is being made for specified relief. The burden of proof is on the movant. Although in most cases it is just as innocent as an ordinary notice of motion, the order to show cause gets its name by directing the recipient to "show cause" why the particular relief being asked for should not be granted. It sounds as if the burden of proof is being shifted to the recipient, but it isn't; it specifies the time and place of the hearing on the application and, when the hearing comes on, the burden of proof is where it always is on a motion: on the movant.

If the order to "show cause" is served on the lawyer, it holds no terror; the lawyer knows it for what it is. But if it is directed to the client or some other lay person, as it often is, it sounds to the recipient as if some monster with sharp fangs is pointing a crooked and threatening finger. It's all bluster—no more or less malevolent than an ordinary notice of motion.

The order to show cause is presented to the court ex parte. It has these advantages:

(1) The court determines the time of its return, as already mentioned, and the place as well.

(2) The court determines whom to serve with the order. Usually, of course, this is the other side's attorney, but if any difficulty should arise about who the attorney is, or if there is doubt about whether the attorney's authority subsists,[3] the procedure of order to show cause resolves the dilemma by having the court decide the matter.[4]

(3) The court determines the method by which the order is to be served. It will usually direct a method consistent with the time element. If the order is not returnable too soon, mail may be sufficient. If it is to come on for hearing fast, the court will direct personal delivery or any other quick and effective method consistent with the needs of the case. An order to show cause directing "personal service" has been held to invoke CPLR 308, thereby authorizing deliver-and-mail service under 308(2), for example, rather than only personal delivery under 308(1).[5]

(4) The court can include in the order a provision staying designated proceedings or enjoining specified out-of-court conduct, thus retaining the status quo until a hearing is had. Although the order to show cause can contain any kind of stay the court has the power to grant,[6] the most important one is the temporary restraining order, the device that holds the status quo pending a hearing for a preliminary injunction.[7] The temporary restraining order is popularly called a "TRO" by the bar. The order to show cause is its traditional vehicle.

All four of the above items are illustrated in the form of order to show cause contained in § 252.

The CPLR says nothing more about an order to show cause than that it may be used "in a proper case",[8] which leaves it entirely to the judge's discretion to determine what a proper case is.[9] Any fact suggesting a problem as to

---

2. CPLR 2214(b).

3. When a motion is made long after a judgment has been rendered, for example, such as one to vacate the judgment pursuant to CPLR 5015, there may be doubt as to whether the former attorney still represents the client.

4. An order to show cause bringing on a motion against a state body must also be served on an assistant attorney general under the terms of CPLR 2214(d), for which see Commentary C2214:30 on McKinney's CPLR 2214.

5. Weill v. Erickson, 49 A.D.2d 895, 373 N.Y.S.2d 370 (2d Dep't 1975).

6. See the discussion of stays in § 255 below.

7. CPLR 6313. For the distinction between the temporary restraining order and the preliminary injunction, see § 330 below.

8. CPLR 2214(d).

9. Mallory v. Mallory, 113 Misc.2d 912, 450 N.Y.S.2d 272 (Sup.Ct., Nassau County, 1982).

any of the items listed above would be sufficient to invoke judicial discretion and justify the show cause procedure, which is in fact liberally used.

If the order is signed after its ex parte presentation, it is then returned to the movant for service according to its terms. When served, it becomes the true equivalent of a notice of motion, albeit with the force of an injunction if it should contain a stay or TRO.

A judge cannot be compelled to sign an order to show cause, such as with a proceeding under Article 78 of the CPLR.[10] Because the order to show cause is in first instance a species of ex parte order, if the judge refuses to sign it an application for it can be made to the appellate court under CPLR 5704.[11]

It is the time of the service of the order, not the date the court signs it, that counts as the "making" of the motion. The point becomes a key one whenever there is a time limit on the motion involved, as illustrated in Property Clerk v. Chevers,[12] where the validity of a counterclaim depended on a showing that it had been duly preceded by the timely service of a notice of claim.[13] No notice was served and time was running out even on the period in which the defendant could move to extend the notice of claim period. On the last day to move, the defendant applied for and got an order to show cause, but did not serve it on that day. The motion was held too late.

Since the order to show cause is initially sought ex parte, it is always necessary on a show cause application to include an affidavit attesting to whether this or similar relief has previously been applied for and what new

facts, if any, have appeared to justify the new motion, etc.[14]

Under the Individual Assignment System (IAS), an order to show cause has to be made to the assigned judge. If made to some other judge, or outside the county of the action's venue, as CPLR 2212(b) allows,[15] the rules require that it be referred back to the proper county—and under the IAS that means back to the assigned judge if there is one—"unless ... the urgency of the motion requires immediate determination".[16] The "unless" clause covers the emergency situation, about which other applicable procedures should be consulted locally. If the assigned judge is unavailable, for example, there may be some other judges on "stand by" in the county of the action's venue.[17]

If a show cause application is the first judge-needing step taken in an action, it must be accompanied by a Request for Judicial Intervention.[18]

In a few instances, the show cause procedure to bring on a motion has been made mandatory.[19] And whenever a given statute requires a motion to be brought on in such manner as the court may direct, or requires that the motion papers be served on such persons as the court may designate, or by such notice as the court may determine, it contemplates that the procedure of order to show cause will be used.[20] If show cause procedure is required in a given instance, and an ordinary notice of motion is used instead, the defect has sometimes been held jurisdictional, precluding the court from passing on the motion's merits even

10. Greenhaus v. Milano, 242 A.D.2d 383, 661 N.Y.S.2d 664 (2d Dep't 1997). The Article 78 proceeding is taken up in § 557 et seq., below.

11. See § 244 above.

12. Sup.Ct., N.Y.County (Cahn, J.), Index No. 41097/90, March 1, 1991.

13. See § 50–e of the General Municipal Law, treated in § 32 above.

14. CPLR 2217(b). See § 244 above.

15. As a species of ex parte application, the order to show cause falls under CPLR 2212(b), applicable in the supreme court, and may be presented to any judge of the court anywhere in the state.

16. Uniform Rule 202.7. Under CPLR 2212(d), the rules are allowed to supersede the statutory venue requirements of the other parts of CPLR 2212.

17. See § 244 above.

18. Uniform Rule 202.6. See § 77B above.

19. Prior to 1977, the procedure for punishing a civil contempt was required to be by order to show cause under Jud.L. § 757, as it then was. Amendments in 1977 made an ordinary notice of motion acceptable, Jud.L. § 756, Dom.Rel.L. § 245, the show cause procedure thereupon becoming only an alternative, as it is with motions in general. See § 484 below.

20. See, e.g., CPLR 5015(a).

though good notice resulted.[21] The better view, however, is that the defect should be ignored as harmless and the merits treated.[22] The movant can avoid the problem by using the show cause procedure whenever it seems to be called for.

§ 249. Cross–Motion

After a motion has been made, some other party, on the opposing side or even on the same side—the notice of motion has to be served on all parties under CPLR 2103(e)—may also want some motion relief. That party can of course make an independent motion, setting up a different return day, but she can instead make what is known as a "cross-motion". A cross-motion is made returnable at the same time and place as the pending motion. Its advantage is that it requires less notice time: the notice demanding cross-relief may be served as late as the third day before the return day set by the original motion papers, which presumably means that merely dropping the papers in a letter box on or before the third day before the return day constitutes adequate notice of cross motion.

Some caselaw has held, however, that the three days for making a cross-motion become eight when mail is used, invoking the five-day mail addition prescribed in CPLR 2103(b)(2) and requiring that a mailed cross-motion be dropped in the mail no later than the eighth day before the return day.[1] An argument may be made against this construction,[2] but the holding is a good one simply in that it assures that the cross-motion will reach the other side in time to permit a meaningful response to it.

Any kind of relief can be demanded on a cross-motion, just as on any motion, and it need not be responsive or even related to the relief demanded on the main motion.[3] Supporting affidavits and other papers may of course be used on a cross-motion, but they are optional; if, for example, all the proof relied on by the cross-movant is already before the court in the papers used pro and con on the main motion, the same proof may be exploited by the cross-motion, which requires only a notice.

Under CPLR 2215, the cross-moving party must serve an explicit "notice of cross-motion",[4] a requirement added by a 1980 amendment designed to overcome the problem, complained about by moving parties and judges, of a demand for cross-relief being mentioned only in the middle of the opposing papers instead of in a formal notice appearing at the very top of those papers. The proper practice under the amendment, when the opposing party wants both to oppose the main motion as well as obtain affirmative relief of her own, is to include a notice of cross-motion as the lead-off paper, with accompanying affidavits in support. Those affidavits can offer proof against the main motion as well as in support of the cross-motion, but they should not be the housing for the demand for cross-relief.[5] Before the 1980 amendment, even an opposing affidavit asking for cross-relief was held acceptable.[6] It is not acceptable today, however, and it is surely "not enough to request such relief orally on the return date of the movant's motion".[7]

What about the time the original movant has for serving answering papers to the cross-motion? CPLR 2215 says nothing about this and the law on the subject can be said to be, if not altogether absent, altogether unsatisfactory. The judges manage the matter on a case by case basis. In one case, for example, D de-

---

21. See, e.g., Papadakos v. Papadakos, Supreme Court, Suffolk County, N.Y.Law Journal, January 29, 1968, p. 20, col. 5.

22. Hornok v. Hornok, 121 A.D.2d 937, 504 N.Y.S.2d 660 (1st Dep't 1986).

§ 249

1. See, e.g., Perez v. Perez, 131 A.D.2d 451, 516 N.Y.S.2d 236 (2d Dep't 1987); Porcelli v. Ozcoz, Sup.Ct., Rockland County (Lefkowitz, J.), N.Y. Law Journal, April 9, 1992, p.28, col.5.

2. See the note in SPR 4:3.

3. CPLR 2215.

4. Estate of Briger, 95 A.D.2d 887, 464 N.Y.S.2d 31 (3d Dep't 1983).

5. See Commentary C2215:3 on McKinney's CPLR 2215.

6. Plateis v. Flax, 54 A.D.2d 813, 388 N.Y.S.2d 245 (3d Dep't 1976).

7. Guggenheim v. Guggenheim, 109 A.D.2d 1012, 1013, 486 N.Y.S.2d 489, 490 (3d Dep't 1985).

manded answering papers to his cross-motion at least two days before the return day, which is of course the same return day as the main motion. The last day for that service was a Saturday, so the court held that P had until the following Monday to serve answering papers, but that *was* the return day. It was held error—as it usually is in these unguided situations—for the motion court to refuse the papers.[8]

§ 250. Deciding the Motion; Drawing and Entering the Order

The court has 60 days from the submission of the motion (20 days in the case of a motion relating to a provisional remedy[1]) in which to decide it.[2] The period is precatory rather than jurisdictional, however: a decision made after the required time is valid and a party who tries to attack a late decision only after he learns that it has gone against him will meet an estoppel.[3] An Article 78 proceeding[4] is available to compel a judge to render an overdue decision,[5] but is rarely used for that purpose. Attorneys are apprehensive that it will not merely get them a decision, but also enable them to predict what the decision will be.

A motion culminates in an order, which must be reduced to a writing, and the written order must conform strictly to the decision. In the event of conflict the decision of course controls.[6] It is the common practice for the winner on the motion to draw the order and see to its entry, unless the court or clerk does it, as happens with some boiler-plate orders, or the judge states in the decision that the decision will also constitute the order, a point we return to below.

The requirement that the order be in writing is explicit in CPLR 2219(a). Practitioners nevertheless report instances in which oral directions are issued by judges, such as in the course of conferences or proceedings in chambers, or even by telephone, which amount to orders but are not reduced to a writing or otherwise recorded (as when no stenographer is present). This of course impedes appellate review should an aggrieved party seek it. A 1996 amendment of CPLR 2219(a) responded to the situation by requiring that any such "order or ruling" made by a judge "be reduced to writing or otherwise recorded" if any party requests it. This is not an invitation to the entry of separate orders based on mere rulings made in the course of a trial. There, objections are merely noted in the record, as usual, with appellate review of the rulings to abide the final judgment that concludes the trial.[7]

If the order as drawn is deemed incorrect by the other side, i.e., not a correct reflection of the court's decision, the way to correct things is by a motion to resettle the order. This is usually done, of course, by application to the motion judge, but a correction of this kind has even been made on an appeal.[8] "Resettlement", which connotes the revising of the order to make it reflect the decision more accurately, "is a procedure designed solely to correct errors or omissions as to form, or for clarification. It may not be used to effect a substantive change in or to amplify the prior decision of the court".[9]

As the example form of court order in § 252 illustrates, the order is to be dated and is to bear the judge's signature or initials. It should recite, in addition to the decision, the papers on which it is based.[10] It is required that the

---

8. Dimovich v. Talev, 248 A.D.2d 951, 670 N.Y.S.2d 290 (4th Dep't 1998). See the note, "The Perennial Arguments Over Late Service of Papers in Motion Practice", in SPR 78.

§ 250

1. The provisional remedies are listed in CPLR 6001 and are separately provided for in Articles 62–65. They are treated in Chapter 12, beginning with § 306 below.

2. CPLR 2219(a).

3. Kaminsky v. Abrams, 51 Misc.2d 5, 272 N.Y.S.2d 530 (Sup.Ct., N.Y.County, 1965).

4. See CPLR 7802(a), 7803(1).

5. See, e.g., Rothman v. Thurston, 67 Misc.2d 543, 324 N.Y.S.2d 331 (Sup.Ct., N.Y.County, 1971).

6. Di Prospero v. Ford Motor Co., 105 A.D.2d 479, 480 N.Y.S.2d 784 (3d Dep't 1984).

7. See SPR 43:2.

8. See Rowlee v. Dietrich, 88 A.D.2d 751, 451 N.Y.S.2d 467 (4th Dep't 1982).

9. Foley v. Roche, 68 A.D.2d 558, 566, 418 N.Y.S.2d 588, 593 (1st Dep't 1979).

10. CPLR 2219(a).

order be filed with the clerk of the court where the action is pending.[11] If the motion has been brought and decided in some other county, as it sometimes may be in supreme court practice,[12] the winner of the motion should also see to its filing in the action-pending county.[13] If the order directs the payment of money, it may be docketed like a judgment,[14] and enforced in the same manner.[15]

The winning party should see to it that the order is entered and then served on the losing party with notice of entry. More detailed treatment of the procedures follows below, but the point should be stressed right up front that, generally speaking, an order is not enforcible until it has been entered, and perhaps not even until it has been served on the loser with notice of entry. A First Department case[16] in which a pharmacist had been penalized with an administrative exclusion from Medicaid participation zeroes in on this point.

On the pharmacist's petition, the trial court overturned the agency decision. The appellate division then reversed the trial court and upheld the agency in a decision published in the New York Law Journal on February 28, 1991, but no notice in writing was given the petitioner until a letter dated March 12, 1991. The court held that the Law Journal publication was not the moment at which the order took effect; the written notice to the petitioner or his lawyer was the moment. There was approximately a two-week hiatus between the two events, and during that time, held the court, the lower court decision held sway and the petitioner remained a Medicaid participant and was entitled to reimbursements for that period.

The court acknowledges that while there is no statutory requirement that an order be served before it is effective, caselaw so holds, and if the party has an attorney, service on the attorney is an "all but universally codified" requirement.

The usual procedure is for the winning party to draw the order and get it entered by the clerk. But if it is a standard kind of motion giving rise to a simple and standard order, it may be the practice in some courts for the clerk to draw the order—which usually entails nothing more than the filling out of a printed form—and enter it, notifying the parties of so doing. This kind of order is sometimes known as a "short-form" order, an informal rather than official terminology.

A court rule provides that "[u]nless the circumstances require settlement of an order, a judge shall incorporate into the decision an order effecting the relief specified in the decision".[17] This is designed to save the parties the need to draft and submit an order by making the decision itself serve also as the order whenever possible.

What does "settle" mean? What does "submit" mean? The lawyer should be familiar with these terms, so often met in motion practice. If the decision on the motion concludes with "order filed", or words to that effect, this usually signifies that the judge or clerk has drawn and entered the order and that it is already in the file. The winning party in that instance should have copies made of the order and serve them on the other parties with notice of entry, which is merely a notice that the order was entered on such-and-such date and place.

If the decision ends with "submit order" or similar words, this signifies that the winning party is to draw the order and submit it to the clerk for entry, and it usually means that the adverse party need not be consulted in advance. If the order does not conform to the decision (the clerk can usually be trusted to see that it does), the adverse party can make a motion to resettle it after it is served on him following entry.

---

11. CPLR 2220.

12. CPLR 2212(a).

13. See Commentary C2220:2 on McKinney's CPLR 2220.

14. CPLR 2222, 5018.

15. The devices for enforcing money judgments are in Article 52 of the CPLR. See § 485 et seq., below.

16. Raes Pharmacy, Inc. v. Perales, 181 A.D.2d 58, 586 N.Y.S.2d 579 (1st Dep't 1992).

17. See Uniform Rule 202.8(g), applicable in the supreme and county courts.

If the decision says "settle order", an alternative used for more complicated relief, the court is signifying that it wants the winning party to draft the order and to work out the proposed draft with the adverse party so that the latter can determine whether it also fits her understanding of the motion's decision. If the parties can agree, the order can be entered without trouble. If they can't, a motion to settle must be made. Procedure for the motion to settle, including the time periods applicable to it, is governed by rule.[18] On such a motion the court determines the form and content of the order.

If the phrase used in the decision does not clearly connote the procedure the judge wants followed with respect to the drawing and entry of the order, or, indeed, if the decision contains no direction at all, a clarification should be obtained from the clerk or the judge's chambers. The Court of Appeals in Funk v. Barry,[19] discusses the differences between the "submit" and "settle" instructions.[20]

Now to a key question. Just how much time does the winner have in which to get an order drawn and entered on the decision? Before 1986 there was no uniform time limit. A case would occasionally come along to invoke the laches doctrine against a long-delayed entry,[21] but that was rare. The law relied on the winner's incentive of getting the loser's appeal time running and over with as soon as possible. Getting the order entered and serving it on the losing party is the act that starts the time to appeal in New York practice.[22]

The Uniform Rule closed that procedural gap. Uniform Rule 202.48(a) requires that the order be settled or submitted for signature "within 60 days after the signing and filing of the decision".[23] The rule applies to the entry of a judgment as well as an order, and failure to submit on time "shall be deemed an abandonment of the motion or action". With this limit on the victor's time to translate the victory into an order and submit it for signing and entry, the winner can no longer dally.

The lawyer should not confuse the 60-day period the court has for deciding a motion, which comes from CPLR 2219(a) and is anything but rigid, with the 60-day period the winner of the motion has for getting it filed, entered, and served under Rule 202.48, which can lead to trouble.

The courts do have the power to excuse a delay in honoring the 60-day rule "for good cause shown",[24] and to permit late entry of the order, but they have indicated that the delay will not be excused just for the asking. In what was probably the first case on the 60-day limit, a defendant who got a complaint dismissed found it reinstated, and the plaintiff's action preserved, by letting some five months elapse after the decision without reducing the victory to an order and getting it entered.[25]

For a while, some courts held that the 60-day time period for getting an order entered after a motion, or a judgment entered after a decision in a court-tried case, applied also to the entry of a judgment following a jury verdict. The Court of Appeals rejected that idea in the *Funk* case, referred to earlier, adopting in effect the position taken by the First Department in Helfant v. Sobkowski:[26] the 60-day rule applies only to orders and judgments that have to be submitted to the court for signa-

---

18. See, e.g., Uniform Rule 202.48(c), applicable in the supreme and county courts. The losing party may tender his own suggested form of order. This is called a counter order. The rule also addresses that.

19. 89 N.Y.2d 364, 653 N.Y.S.2d 247 (1996).

20. See the note on "Muddling the Distinction Between 'Submit Judgment' and 'Settle Judgment' and Abandoning a Victory as a Result", in SPR 52:3.

21. See. e.g., Vickery v. Village of Saugerties, 106 A.D.2d 721, 483 N.Y.S.2d 765 (3d Dep't 1984), aff'd 64 N.Y.2d 1161, 490 N.Y.S.2d 735, 480 N.E.2d 349 (1985), involving a judgment in an Article 78 proceeding. Orders and judgments are generally treated alike for time-for-entry purposes.

22. See CPLR 5513.

23. UR 202.48 applies in the supreme and county courts. Similar rules address similar matters in other courts, including the surrogate's court (UR 207.37), the N.Y.C. Civil Court (UR 208.33), the district courts (UR 212.33), and the city courts (UR 210.33).

24. UR 202.48(b).

25. Urena v. N.Y.C. Health and Hospitals Corp., Sup. Ct., N.Y. County, Index No. 6549/86 (April 24, 1987, per Sklar, J.).

26. 174 A.D.2d 340, 570 N.Y.S.2d 552 (1991).

ture, which is not the procedure on a verdict, so that the 60–day rule does not apply to verdicts.

Funk, the leading decision on the 60–day entry rule, held that the time limit does not apply to a trial or to a motion unless the court's decision explicitly calls for the submission or settlement of an order or judgment. Hence a decision that contains no instructions about the drawing of the dispositive order will not produce "abandonment" consequences for the prevailing party. In that situation, the main spur to the winning party's securing entry of the order and serving a copy of it on the other side with notice of entry is the continuing rule that the losing party's time to appeal will not run until that is done.[27]

Ordinarily, an order is filed and entered at the same time, a practice so common that some lawyers think of the two steps as contemporaneous and consider all of them embraced under "entry". Occasions will arise, however, when the order is signed but for one reason or another is not promptly entered and filed with the clerk. It has been held that such a filing must also occur within the 60–day period after signing, and an order that the defendant got signed but did not also get filed (entered) within the rule's 60–day period was deemed abandoned under the rule.[28] Under the Court of Appeals *Funk* case noted above, however, a result like this would be supportable today only if the court explicitly required the further activity and the party failed to perform it.

Practices will differ on these procedural details. In some places the judges may themselves see to the entry of their orders; in others it may be the convention for the judges to leave the securing of the entry to the winning party. At least one case has held that in this age of the photocopy machine, the clerk's stamp "Filed" on a copy of the order will itself connote entry,[29] and this would presumably be

so for purposes of the 60–day "abandonment" rule as well. And we note again a 1993 amendment of the rules designed to encourage the judge to include sufficient instruction in her decision so that the decision itself can serve as the dispositive order, and to have the decision recite as much, thereby making a separate order unnecessary.[30]

The practice pursued, as long as not plainly offensive to the rules, may depend on the kind of order, on the judicial department, on the size of the court, on the geographical distribution of the judges, on the predilection of the particular judge, simply on local habit, or on yet other factors. Whatever it is, significant consequences can attend these otherwise incidental "details".

The court can extend the 60–days or excuse their passing, but only "for good cause shown".[31] If good cause is not shown, and the worst does happen—the motion victory is deemed abandoned—the impact of the abandonment can pose a dilemma.

In Feldman v. New York City Transit Auth.,[32] for example, the defendant won on its motion for summary judgment but then abandoned the motion by failing to secure entry. Holding that to allow the defendant to keep its victory, perhaps with only a monetary slap on the wrists for the delay, was not sufficient, the First Department held that the abandonment sticks, remanding the case but without further instructions. Should such a case now be tried, even though it has been judicially determined that there is nothing to try? Does the abandonment mean to turn things around 180 degrees, so as to declare summary judgment for the plaintiff?[33]

The peculiarity of the situation prompted the Second Department to take a different view of the matter in a similar summary judg-

---

27. Funk is treated at length in the lead note in New York State Law Digest No. 445.

28. See Simmons v. Mercer, Sup.Ct., Albany County, March 15, 1990 (Index No. 11624–86, Doran, J.).

29. Resource Funding Co. v. McNamara, 150 Misc.2d 1041, 570 N.Y.S.2d 762 (Sup.Ct., N.Y. County, 1990).

30. See the lead note in SPR 5.

31. See Uniform Rule 202.48(b).

32. 171 A.D.2d 473, 567 N.Y.S.2d 228 (1st Dep't 1991).

33. See the discussion in the lead note in New York State Law Digest No. 382.

ment situation in Russo v. City of New York.[34] Holding that a court should not be burdened with a "demonstrably meritless action", it imposed motion costs on the defendant but let it keep the summary judgment.

In an analogous situation the same court let a defendant keep its judgment with a nunc pro tunc order. The trial court had directed judgment for D after P's proof was in and directed D to settle the judgment. D didn't, and had no good cause, so the trial court deemed D's victory abandoned and restored the case to the calendar. Reversing, the appellate division said that a nunc pro tunc order should have been used; that the trial court's disposition would not bring the "repose" to judicial proceedings that the rule contemplates.[35]

Suppose that D gets a forum non conveniens dismissal of P's claim but then abandons it by not entering a timely order. May D move again for the same relief? Must the court entertain the case now, with its own—not just the parties'—convenience now at stake?[36]

If the 60–day entry issue has not been raised, and an order has been entered on the decision more than 60 days later, the order is fully valid.[37]

The consequence of "abandonment" is obviously aimed at a movant who has won on the motion. In the situation, just as common, in which the motion has been denied, making the one moved against the winner, it has been held that the 60–day period does not apply.[38] Perhaps the rule is intentionally aimed only at the winning movant and does not intend to prescribe so dire a result as "abandonment" when the other side prevails and the motion is denied. That party, too, however, should not dally in getting the order entered. Digging into

the facts of some involved cases may reveal that the 60–day abandonment rule was indeed applied against the victorious opponent of the motion, as in Aetna Cas. & Sur. Co. v. F & F Maintenance, Inc.[39]

P in *Aetna* moved for a default judgment against D. The motion was denied, so D won on that, but didn't get an order entered. P moved for the default again, and now the court held that D abandoned its prior victory; it granted P a default (with an inquest ordered to determine damages). So, at least indirectly, the court seemed to be saying that a nonmovant who wins when the motion is denied also faces abandonment consequences for not securing entry. Again, however, such a result would be permissible today, under the Court of Appeals *Funk* case, only if the court's instructions about entry are explicit and are disobeyed.

In all instances the winner on a motion—movant or opponent—should see to it, after the order is entered, that a copy of it with notice of entry is formally served on the loser; as noted above, it is this service that starts the loser's appeal time running.[40]

It is a general principle, as already noted,[41] that service of the order on the adverse party may even be necessary to give it validity.[42] It has been held, however, that with respect to the winning party the order is valid without service. This becomes especially important if the victory was conditional: the failure to fulfill the condition may not only undermine the victory on the motion, but undo the winner's case altogether. That happened to a plaintiff who defeated the defendant's motion to dismiss and on a cross-motion even got leave to serve a late reply, but on the condition that he serve the reply within X days. He didn't, and

---

34. 206 A.D.2d 355, 614 N.Y.S.2d 55 (2d Dep't 1994).

35. See Meany v. Supermarkets Gen. Corp., 239 A.D.2d 393, 658 N.Y.S.2d 338 (2d Dep't 1997), and the discussion in SPR 79:4.

36. See Persaud v. Goriah, 143 Misc.2d 225, 539 N.Y.S.2d 872 (Sup.Ct., Bronx County, 1989), and the discussion in the lead note in New York State Law Digest No. 358.

37. See Alexander v. C.P. Craska, Inc., Sup.Ct., Bronx County, Feb. 3, 1992 (Index No. 13273/90, per Friedman, J.), in which the order directed an attorney to turn over a

file. It was disobeyed and the disobedience was punished as a contempt.

38. See Estate of Germain, 138 A.D.2d 918, 526 N.Y.S.2d 662 (3d Dep't 1988), treated in the lead note in New York State Law Digest No. 326.

39. 168 A.D.2d 876, 564 N.Y.S.2d 550 (3d Dep't 1990).

40. CPLR 5513.

41. See note 16, above, and the text at that point.

42. See also McCormick v. Mars Associates, Inc., 25 A.D.2d 433, 265 N.Y.S.2d 1004 (2d Dep't 1966).

the action was dismissed for want of prosecution.[43]

Obviously, the prevailing party can't undertake her chores of drawing the order, securing its entry, serving it on the other side with notice of entry, etc., without being aware that the motion has been decided. It therefore behooves the lawyer to find out about the decision promptly. The method whereby a party may learn of the decision varies from place to place. In the New York City metropolitan area, the New York Law Journal announces decisions. Elsewhere local legal publications may do so, or the clerk may advise the parties by mail or perhaps even by phone, or the parties may simply be expected to keep in touch with the clerk's office. In some places a party wanting notice of the court's decision, or a copy of it, may be asked to furnish the judge or clerk a stamped and self-addressed envelope. Again an inquiry into local practice is a good idea for the uninitiated, especially the visiting lawyer whose base is elsewhere.

There is a provision in the motion article for the enforcement of mandates,[44] but that subject is best deferred until the chapter on the enforcement of judgments.[45]

§ 251.   Trial of Issue of Fact Arising on Motion

CPLR 2218 authorizes a separate trial of an issue of fact arising on a motion. It applies to all motions except the motion for summary judgment under CPLR 3212, which has its own, and very restrictive, provision on the subject.[1] The main motion on which a fact issue is likely to warrant a separate preliminary trial is the motion to dismiss under CPLR 3211. That rule also has its own provision authorizing such a trial, however, so that CPLR 2218, even if also applicable there, is not needed.[2] As a general principle, no issue of fact arising on any motion should be ordered to immediate trial unless there is some compelling reason for it—such as when jurisdiction depends on it, or when it is a succinct issue whose resolution might avoid a trial by bringing about a dismissal or stay of the action. If the hearing needed to resolve the issue is likely to be a lengthy one, that factor militates against ordering the separate trial.[3] Further investigation of this matter is reserved for the treatment of CPLR 3211.[4]

§ 252.   Some Forms

It will be helpful to illustrate a few papers connected with motion practice. For some things there are official forms. For most things there are not.

(a) Form of notice of motion. Official Form 23 among the official forms is a sample notice of motion. Apart from that is the form of notice of motion prescribed in the rules of the various courts. Since the rules are the more recent expression of preference by the Office of Court Administration, we set forth as a sample here the form prescribed by Uniform Rule 202.7, applicable in the supreme and county courts:

---

43. Lyons v. Butler, 134 A.D.2d 576, 521 N.Y.S.2d 477 (2d Dep't 1987).

44. CPLR 2223.

45. Chapter 18 below.

§ 251

1. See § 284 below.

2. CPLR 3211(c).

3. Stowell v. Berstyn, 26 A.D.2d 828, 274 N.Y.S.2d 120 (2d Dep't 1966).

4. See § 271 below.

_____ COURT OF THE STATE OF NEW YORK,
COUNTY OF _____

A.B.,
 	
                 Plaintiff
C.D.,
     -against-
 	
Defendant. _____
	) Notice of Motion
	) Index No.
	) _____
	) Name of Assigned Judge
	) _____
	) Oral argument is requested
	) ☐
	) (check box if applicable)

Upon the affidavit of _____, sworn to on _____, [year] and upon (list supporting papers if any), the _____ will move this court (in Room __) at the _____ Courthouse, _____, _____, New York, on the __ day of _____, [year], at __ (a.m.) (p.m.) for an order (briefly indicate relief requested).

The above-entitled action is for (briefly state nature of action, _e.g.,_ personal injury, medical malpractice, divorce, etc.).

This is a motion for or related to interim maintenance or child support ☐. (check box if applicable)

An affirmation that a good faith effort has been made to resolve the issues raised in this motion is annexed hereto. (required only where the motion relates to disclosure or to a bill of particulars)

Pursuant to CPLR 2214(b), answering affidavits, if any, are required to be served upon the undersigned at least seven days before the return date of this motion ☐. (check box if applicable)

Dated:

                                     _____
                                       (Print Name)
                               Attorney[1] (or Attorney in charge of case if law firm) for moving party

                               Address:
                               Telephone number:

TO: _____ (Print Name) _____
      Attorney[1] for (other party)
      Address:
      Telephone number:
           (Print Name)
      Attorney[1] for (other party)
      Address:
      Telephone number:

(b) Form of order to show cause. The following is a form (not an official form) of order to show cause to vacate an execution and default judgment and dismiss an action:

SUPREME COURT OF THE STATE OF NEW YORK
COUNTY OF NEW YORK

A.B., Plaintiff,   )
    against   ) Order to Show Cause
C.D., Defendant.   ) Index No. _____

Upon the affidavits of C.D. and his attorney, J.R., sworn to on April 21, 1999, and upon the default judgment entered in the office of the clerk of this court on March 18, 1999, and upon a copy of an execution issued to the Sheriff of the City of New York in this action and bearing receipt date of April 13, 1999, and upon all prior papers and proceedings in this cause, it is hereby

ORDERED, that the plaintiff show cause before this court, at IAS Part 27, to be held at the Courthouse at 60 Centre Street in the City and County of New York, at 9:30 a.m. on April 30, 1999, why an order should not be entered in this action vacating the execution and the judgment in this action in its entirety for lack of jurisdiction and for total lack of service of process of any kind, or granting such other and further relief as may seem just and proper to the court; and it is further

ORDERED, that until further order of this court and pending the hearing and determination of this application, the plaintiff and his attorney and all purporting to act in his behalf, and the Sheriff of the City of New York, are hereby stayed from taking any further step to levy the execution or otherwise enforce the judgment.

LET SERVICE of a copy of this order and of the papers on which it is based, by personal delivery to the plaintiff's attorney, or to a person of suitable age and discretion at his office, and to the Sheriff of the City of New York, or to a deputy sheriff in the County of New York, on or before April 23, 1999, be deemed sufficient service thereof.

This order has been signed by me this 21st day of April, 1999, and shall upon presentation be entered in the office of the clerk.

Carlo Buti
Justice, Supreme Court,
New York County

(c) *Form of court order.* CPLR 2219(a) provides that there is to be no difference between a court order and a judge's order made out of court (such as on an ex parte motion). The following is Official Form 27, an order on a motion, made on notice, to dismiss the complaint:

SUPREME COURT OF THE STATE OF NEW YORK
COUNTY OF NEW YORK

A.B., Plaintiff,	) Order
against	) Index No.
C.D., Defendant.	) ————

Upon defendant's notice of motion dated December 1, 1966, for a dismissal of the complaint and for dismissal of the first, second and third causes of action therein, and upon the complaint, the affidavit of C.D. sworn to December 1, 1966, and the affidavit of A.B. sworn to December 8, 1966, and [plaintiff having appeared in opposition] [or] [there being no appearance in opposition], it is ordered that:

1. The first cause of action is dismissed. The plaintiff may upon application to the court, within ___ days from service of a copy of this order with notice of entry thereof, submit evidence to the court to justify the granting of leave to plead again.

2. The motion to dismiss the second cause of action is denied, with leave to assert the statute of limitations as a defense in defendant's answer.

3. All further proceedings on the third cause of action are stayed, except upon leave of this court, until the final determination of the action entitled A.B., Plaintiff against X.Y.Z., Inc., Defendant, presently pending in the Superior Court of New Jersey (Index No. ————), on condition that defendant file a stipulation, within ———— days from service of a copy of this order with notice of entry thereof, that all discovery proceedings in the action in the Superior Court of New Jersey shall be usable in this action with the same force and effect as though originally taken herein.

4. In all other respects the motion of the defendant is denied.

New York, New York, December 20, 1966

[Print name to be signed or initialed]
Justice, Supreme Court
New York County

---

§ 253. Motion Affecting Prior Order

CPLR 2221 and to a lesser extent CPLR 2217 address the situation in which one judge may be asked in a case to do something another judge refused to do, or to undo something the other judge did. The situation is less frequent under the Individual Assignment System,[1] in which one judge gets the case from cradle to grave and no other touches it, but it still happens.

It can happen, for example, when the assigned judge is unavailable, for any of a variety of reasons. It can arise in those areas of the state following the so-called "dual track" system, in which the assigned judge leaves the case as of the filing of the note of issue and another takes over for the trial: the trial judge may be asked to take a step inconsistent with the previous judge's order. It can arise in courts in which the IAS is not in effect at all. Even in courts that have the IAS it can arise

§ 253

1. See Rosenshein v. Rosenshein, 158 A.D.2d 268, 550 N.Y.S.2d 670 (1st Dep't 1990).

in special categories of cases that have been exempted from IAS treatment and which are handled in special "parts".[2]

Whenever the situation is at hand, the concerns of CPLR 2221 and to some degree CPLR 2217 are at hand. Both were amended in 1986 to empower the chief administrator by rule to exclude the application of either provision from any given department, district, or county. This means that local practice may vary and that a local inquiry will sometimes be necessary. If no such implementing rule is found, the cited CPLR provisions govern.

CPLR 2221, the main provision in point, provides that any motion affecting a prior order shall be made only to the judge who made that order unless she is unable to hear it. Excepted from such a requirement is the order rendered by default; since nothing was judicially passed on in that instance, the later motion can be made to any judge of the court but must be made on notice. If the earlier order was made ex parte, the later motion affecting it may be made ex parte to the same judge or on notice to any other judge.

Again the reminder that these instructions give way when the IAS is strictly applicable. There, everything must go to the assigned judge.

Under CPLR 2221, a motion made to the wrong judge must be transferred to the right one. The design of the rule is to prevent a second judge of the same court from sitting in effect as an appellate court over a colleague—a procedure the appellate courts have long frowned on.[3] It has even been held that when the prior order was made by a judge sitting only temporarily in the court by administrative assignment, the transfer of the second motion may be made to that judge even after the assignment has expired and the judge is back on his own court; the judge's jurisdiction of the matter is deemed to continue.[4]

To fall under CPLR 2221, the second motion must "affect" the earlier order. If it does not affect it at all, but is merely another motion in the same action, that's where CPLR 2217 comes in, making it permissible but not mandatory to refer the motion to the judge who heard the earlier motion.[5] The aim of this CPLR 2217 permission is to conserve judicial energy. The aim of CPLR 2221, on the other hand, is to avoid judicial conflict. It is not necessary, however, in order to invoke CPLR 2221 and *require* application to the same judge, that the second motion be an outright attempt to have the second judge undo what the first judge did. It is sufficient if the second motion merely touches on or influences the first. Where a respondent, for example, in a proceeding to review a tax assessment, had secured an extension of time from Judge X and then a second from Judge Y, the appellate division criticized the procedure and said it would have been more appropriate to seek the second extension from Judge X.[6] Doubt about whether the second motion affects the first should be resolved by assuming that it does, and by moving before the same judge. That judge's inability to hear it should as a rule be the sole ground for moving before a different judge.

Many kinds of motions qualify as motions "affecting" a prior order. Specifically embraced by CPLR 2221 are motions to renew or reargue the prior motion, or to stay, vacate or modify the order entered on it, or to secure leave to appeal the order. Other motions may fall into the CPLR 2221 category even though not explicitly listed, like a motion to resettle the order.

A motion may be transferred to a different judge even if it has no effect whatever on a

---

2. See § 77A, above, for discussion of these points about the Individual Assignment System and its exceptions.

3. See Sloan v. Beard, 125 A.D. 625, 110 N.Y.S. 1 (2d Dep't 1908).

4. Prudential Lines, Inc. v. Firemen's Ins. Co., 109 Misc.2d 281, 440 N.Y.S.2d 155 (Sup.Ct., N.Y.County, 1981).

5. CPLR 2217(a).

6. Lansingburgh Realties, Inc. v. Commissioner of Assessments and Taxation, 42 A.D.2d 646, 345 N.Y.S.2d 152 (3d Dep't 1973).

prior order if the judge to whom the motion is made is "for any reason unable to hear it".[7]

§ 254. Motion to Reargue or Renew

A motion to reargue is based on no new proof; it seeks to convince the court that it was wrong and ought to change its mind. The motion to renew[1] is based on new or additional proof not used the first time around. (Both should be distinguished from the motion to resettle, which just corrects the order to reflect what the decision was or in some other way affects form only.[2]) The new proof need not necessarily be newly discovered,[3] but the motion stands a better chance if it is and a still better chance if good reason is shown why the additional proof was not discovered until now.

An order granting or denying a motion to renew is appealable. An order granting a motion to reargue is appealable even if, after the granting, the prior decision is adhered to. It has even been held that an order granting reargument supersedes the original order.[4] But an order denying a motion to reargue is not appealable; if it were, it would amount to an extension of time in which to appeal the original order. It is not allowed to do that.

A motion to reargue must be made within the time in which an appeal from the original order could have been taken.[5] No such time limit inhibits the motion to renew; the new proof on which the motion is based accounts for that. But any untoward delay in making the motion will necessarily affect the court's discretion when its merits are examined. Gross laches would be ground to deny the motion without even reaching its merits.

Since the motion to reargue may not ordinarily be made after expiration of the time in

which to appeal the original order, not even a change in the law (occurring after that time) may be made the basis of a motion to reargue. The loser, in other words, is stuck with the old decision. "While this result might at times seem harsh, there must be an end to lawsuits and the time to take an appeal cannot forever be extended."[6]

But suppose that the loser did take an appeal from the original order and that the appeal is still pending when, months after the original decision, a different and authoritative case clarifies that the lower court was wrong and that the loser should have won. In that situation, since the appellate court to which the old order is being taken would apply the new law in its decision, the lower court may itself do so on a reargument motion[7] as long as the appeal has not yet been submitted.[8] Here the reargument motion is obviously not being used to secure a new appeal period.

If a motion is based on new proof but is erroneously termed a "reargument" motion, the mislabel will be ignored and the motion will be treated as one to renew.[9] And vice-versa. This is important on the question of appealability. And if an appeal is being planned, or just being considered, the lawyer should be aware of special problems concerning the time in which to take an appeal if orders of reargument or renewal are also loitering about the premises. These problems are discussed in the appeals chapter.[10]

The motion to reargue and the motion to renew are listed in CPLR 2221 and must therefore be made to the judge who made the original order. That instruction, a product of the now-superseded Master Calendar System,

---

7. CPLR 2217(c).

§ 254

1. The motion to renew is sometimes called a motion to "rehear". No consequence appends to the distinction. See Commentary C2221:9 on McKinney's CPLR 2221.

2. See § 250 above.

3. See Webb & Knapp, Inc. v. United Cigar–Whelan Stores Corp., 276 A.D. 583, 96 N.Y.S.2d 359 (1st Dep't 1950).

4. See Dennis v. Stout, 24 A.D.2d 461, 260 N.Y.S.2d 325 (2d Dep't 1965).

5. Liberty National Bank & Trust Co. v. Bero Constr. Corp., 29 A.D.2d 627, 286 N.Y.S.2d 287 (4th Dep't 1967).

6. In re Huie, 20 N.Y.2d 568, 572, 285 N.Y.S.2d 610, 612, 232 N.E.2d 642, 644 (1967).

7. Ferrizz v. Jahelka, 125 A.D.2d 537, 509 N.Y.S.2d 613 (2d Dep't 1986).

8. See Commentary C2221:8 on McKinney's CPLR 2221.

9. Turkel v. I.M.I. Warp Knits, Inc., 50 A.D.2d 543, 375 N.Y.S.2d 333 (1st Dep't 1975).

10. See § 532 below.

is self-evident under its replacement, the Individual Assignment System. It remains relevant in a number of situations even in the IAS era.[11]

§ 255. Stay

A stay is a suspension of the case or some designated step in it. It is a kind of injunction with which a court freezes proceedings at a particular point. It can be used to stop the prosecution of the action altogether, or to hold up only some phase of it. The stay can be granted during the action's pendency or even afterwards during an appellate or enforcement stage (as by staying an execution about to be levied on a judgment).

The word "stay" in New York practice usually connotes a court's suspension of its own proceedings, not those of another court. Although the terminology of "stay" is sometimes applied to the enjoining by one court of an action being brought in another, the latter is more accurately considered an "injunction": it partakes of all of the principles of equity applicable to injunctions and may be sought only of a court with equitable powers adequate to entertain injunctive relief. In New York the main tribunal with equity jurisdiction is of course the supreme court, where a plenary action would be needed to enjoin the prosecution of an action in another forum.[1]

But pursuant to CPLR 2201, any court in New York can stay its own proceedings "in a proper case, upon such terms as may be just". The stay is sought by a mere motion, but it must have good ground to support it. It is left to the courts to determine what a "proper case" is as a matter of discretion, which must be exercised with circumspection.[2] It may be prudent, for example, to stay an action for a brief time if the point of law involved is about to be definitively decided by an appellate court whose decision would bind, but such a decision had best be imminent; the mere pendency of such a case on appeal is not by itself ground on which to stay an action.[3]

One of the most common examples of a stay is that granted to suspend one action because of the pendency elsewhere of another action between the same parties on the same claim. That stay rests more on the authority of CPLR 3211(a)(4), which even authorizes a dismissal in such an instance, than on CPLR 2201.[4] It will be found, in fact, that most of the stays one meets in civil practice are not the product of CPLR 2201, the general stay statute, but of some specific stay-authorizing statute applicable to a particular situation. There are a number of these. Among the more prominent are the stay of a judgment's enforcement during an appeal[5] and the stay of an action brought in violation of an agreement to arbitrate.[6]

If one of the parties is in military service and therefore lacks the freedom of movement that civilians have, a federal statute,[7] also applicable in state courts, requires a stay of the action on the application of the military person unless the court finds that the service does not impair preparation of the case. Where, for example, it appeared that the defendant was in service but intended to put his case in through a third-party witness, the court found that "the defendant's ability to defend ... [was] not materially affected by his military service" and denied the stay.[8]

The willful violation of a stay is a contempt of court and may be punished as such.[9] If the reason for the stay is no longer valid, it may be vacated. The party seeking the vacatur need merely move for it.

---

11. See § 253 above.

§ 255

1. See Indestructible Metal Products Co., Inc. v. Summergrade, 197 A.D. 199, 188 N.Y.S. 642 (1st Dep't 1921).

2. On stays generally, see the Commentaries on McKinney's CPLR 2201.

3. Compare In re Weinbaum's Estate, 51 Misc.2d 538, 273 N.Y.S.2d 461 (Surr.Ct., Nassau County, 1966).

4. See § 262 below.

5. CPLR 5519.

6. CPLR 7503.

7. 50 U.S.C.A. app. § 521.

8. Deacon v. Witham, 131 Misc.2d 217, 219, 499 N.Y.S.2d 317, 319 (Hudson City Court 1985). Deacon was a small claims case, to which the federal statute applies just as it does to any other.

9. Cornell v. T.V. Development Corp., 50 Misc.2d 422, 270 N.Y.S.2d 45 (Sup.Ct., Nassau County, 1966). See also § 481, below, treating the contempt remedy in the enforcement chapter.

Chapter Eleven

ACCELERATED JUDGMENT

Analysis

A. INTRODUCTORY

Table of Sections

Sec.
256. Accelerated Judgment; CPLR Article 32.

§ 256. Accelerated Judgment; CPLR Article 32

Article 32 of the CPLR, entitled "Accelerated Judgment", contains the motion to dismiss,[1] the summary judgment motions,[2] and, among a few other things, the provisions governing the default judgment,[3] the dismissal for want of prosecution,[4] the voluntary discontinuance,[5] the confession of judgment,[6] and the action on submitted facts.[7] All of these devices have one unifying thread: they all contemplate the possibility of disposing of the case or some significant part of it without having to try the merits.

In attempting to follow some kind of logical sequence for these devices—recognizing that no sequence is perfect because variations from case to case are too unpredictable—Article 32 is reasonably accurate in its grouping. Because of an amendment to the want of prosecution rule, CPLR 3216, however, which ties it to the note of issue, that rule will be treated later in calendar practice, where the note of issue is a key item.[8] With that exception, the contents of Article 32 will be treated in this chapter.

B. MOTION TO DISMISS

Table of Sections

Sec.
257. The Motion to Dismiss, CPLR 3211 Generally.
258. The Dismissal Grounds: CPLR 3211(a).
259. Defense Based on "Documentary Evidence"; Paragraph 1.
260. Subject Matter Jurisdiction; Paragraph 2.
261. Lack of Capacity to Sue; Paragraph 3.
262. Other Action Pending; Paragraph 4.
263. Affirmative Defenses Usable on Dismissal Motion; Paragraph 5.

---

§ 256

1. CPLR 3211.
2. CPLR 3212, 3213.
3. CPLR 3215.
4. CPLR 3216.
5. CPLR 3217.

6. CPLR 3218.
7. CPLR 3222.
8. See §§ 369 and 370. The want of prosecution motion is treated in § 375, below.

§ 257. The Motion to Dismiss, CPLR 3211 Generally

CPLR 3211 is the main dismissal motion in New York civil practice. It contains in subdivision (a) the diverse grounds for the dismissal of a cause of action, and in subdivision (b) the motion to dismiss a defense. CPLR 3211 is the mechanical expedient that implements many important realms of procedural law. Earlier chapters in this book that studied topics like subject matter jurisdiction, statute of limitations, and personal jurisdiction—all extensive studies in themselves—each had a singular purpose. One sought to determine whether the court could entertain a given kind of action, another to determine if the action was timely brought, still another to determine if the particular defendant could be subjected to the court's jurisdiction. For these and for many other procedural realms already met, and some yet to come, the whole inquiry is converted into an actual result through the singular expedient of the motion to dismiss supplied by CPLR 3211. It's the bridge that leads the inquiry to its conclusion, one way or the other. Or, to choose another metaphor, it's the waist-line of the hour glass that converts the conclusions housed in the top sphere into the judgment that inhabits the bottom.

CPLR 3211(a) and its dismissal grounds are available for use by any party against whom a cause of action is asserted. It is of course most commonly used by the defendant against the plaintiff, and that situation will supply the context of the examples we will be using. But it is equally available for use by a plaintiff against a counterclaim, a defendant against a co-defendant's cross-claim, a third-party defendant against the third-party claim, etc. And the same is true of the CPLR 3211(b) motion to strike a defense. Although most often seen as the plaintiff's motion to strike one of the defendant's defenses, it is equally the tool of a defendant who wants to move against a defense used by a plaintiff replying to a counterclaim, of a cross-claiming defendant against a defense interposed to the cross-claim, of a third-party plaintiff against the third-party defendant's defenses, etc.

It may be noted in general that CPLR 3211 does not countenance or even recognize any differences among its various grounds as far as evidence is concerned. Affidavits, depositions, documentary proof, admissions, letters, and any other papers or proof having an evidentiary impact in the particular situation may be considered on any CPLR 3211 motion[1] regardless of its ground.[2] This is so whether the motion contends that the pleading is defective on its face, which presumably requires no extrinsic proof, or, though adequate on its face, lacks merit or requires dismissal on some other basis, which obviously does require extrinsic proof. If the contention is that the pleading is facially defective as a matter of law and the movant is even willing to concede the truth of the factual allegations in the attacked pleading, extrinsic proof is of course unnecessary. The point is that even in that situation the proof is permissible.

If the one whose claim or defense is being attacked by a CPLR 3211 motion contends that facts adequate to defeat the motion do

§ 257

1. See CPLR 3211(c), adopting for 3211 the evidentiary rule of CPLR 3212(b), governing summary judgment.

2. An exception, not a very important one, is CPLR 3211(a)(1), treated in § 259 below.

exist but can't then be stated, that party should explain this to the court in the opposing affidavits. CPLR 3211(d) permits the court in a situation like that to deny the motion without passing on its merits and allow the movant to assert the objection, instead, in its responsive pleading. By that means the objection is put off until the trial, by which time the needed evidence will presumably be available. Alternatively, CPLR 3211(d) lets the court retain the motion but postpone its decision—in effect, adjourn the motion—until further affidavits are secured or depositions taken or opportunity otherwise afforded for such other steps as the court may deem appropriate. This provision is applicable even when the additional evidence pertains to a jurisdictional objection.

In Peterson v. Spartan Industries, Inc.,[3] for example, P claimed jurisdiction under CPLR 302(a)(1), the "transaction of business" long-arm statute,[4] and D moved to dismiss under CPLR 3211(a)(8) on the ground that jurisdiction was lacking because D did not transact business in New York. It was contended that until jurisdiction was established by P, there was not even enough basis to allow P to seek disclosure from D related to jurisdiction. Rejecting the contention, the Court of Appeals sustained the use of CPLR 3211(d) even there and permitted P to use the discovery device,[5] one of the disclosure tools, to aid in garnering evidence to oppose D's CPLR 3211 motion. Not even a prima facie showing of jurisdiction is necessary to sustain such use of CPLR 3211(d), the court said. The mere making of the CPLR 3211 motion was apparently basis enough to require the defendant to reveal facts relevant to it.[6]

§ 258. The Dismissal Grounds: CPLR 3211(a)

A motion to dismiss a cause of action may not be made on just any ground at all; it must

find authority somewhere. CPLR 3211(a) is the principal authority, listing the various grounds on which a dismissal motion may be predicated. Its list is almost exclusive, but not quite. There are a handful of other provisions on which a dismissal motion may be based. The more prominent of these are:

(1) CPLR 327, dismissal for forum non conveniens;

(2) CPLR 3012(b), dismissal of the action for failure to serve a duly demanded complaint;

(3) CPLR 3126, dismissal for failure to submit to disclosure; and

(4) CPLR 3216, dismissal for neglect to prosecute.

With the above exceptions and perhaps a few others, CPLR 3211(a) and its list of dismissal grounds is just about it.

The grounds listed in CPLR 3211(a) may be raised by motion, but the motion is optional. They may instead be used as defenses in the answer.[1] As will be seen later, most of them may even be divided up, some raised by motion and, if the motion fails, the rest raised by answer.[2]

It is permissible to use CPLR 3211(a) against all claims pleaded, or against one or a selected few. Indeed, the rule may even be used to dismiss but part of a single cause of action if the part is severable without macerating the whole case.[3] An example is where P sues D for both compensatory and punitive damages in respect of the same wrong. If D can convince the court on a motion under CPLR 3211(a), most likely paragraph 7 (failure to state a cause of action), that the malice needed to sustain the punitive damages claim is plainly wanting, the court can dismiss the

3. 33 N.Y.2d 463, 354 N.Y.S.2d 905, 310 N.E.2d 513 (1974).

4. See §§ 84–86 above.

5. This device, which comes from CPLR 3120, is one of the most popular of Article 31's disclosure weapons. See § 362 below.

6. 33 N.Y.2d at 467, 354 N.Y.S.2d at 908, 310 N.E.2d at 515.

§ 258

1. CPLR 3211(e).

2. See § 274 below.

3. See Forse v. Turner, 55 Misc.2d 810, 286 N.Y.S.2d 538 (Sup.Ct., Broome County, 1968).

punitive damages demand while retaining the rest of the case for trial in respect of compensatory damages. Note that in such a situation the court does not technically "dismiss" the claim or part of it, as CPLR 3211(a) formally articulates; it merely strikes out the part of the complaint containing the rejected matter, in this instance the allegations that reflect only on punitive damages as well as the punitive damages demand in the relief clause. This is all permissible procedure under CPLR 3211.

If D is in doubt as to which of several grounds might apply in a given case, such as where they seem to overlap, D's rule of thumb is to join both or all grounds. It may happen, for example, that P is purporting to sue in behalf of an estate that he has not been duly appointed to represent. That defect would support an objection under paragraph 3, in that P lacks capacity to maintain the action, as well as under paragraph 7, in that P is not stating a cause of action belonging to him. Both paragraphs should ground the motion.

If the wrong ground is designated on the motion, but some other CPLR 3211(a) ground does apply, the court can treat the motion as having specified the right ground, as long as no prejudice can be claimed. In one case where D based his motion on paragraphs 1, 2, and 8, for example, the court granted it on grounds 3 and 7 instead, basing its action on the general relief clause contained in the notice of motion—which all well-drawn motions include[4]— and on the absence of prejudice to P.[5] If P did not have notice of the undesignated grounds from any appropriate source, or if the court

was convinced that if the intended grounds had been properly designated P's opposing proof would have differed, it could of course have denied the motion, stayed it for further affidavits, etc.

Some of the 11 numbered paragraphs of CPLR 3211(a) are self-explanatory, and can be treated succinctly. Others require more extensive comment. With the exception of paragraph 11, which has a narrow mission,[6] the CPLR 3211(a) list is important enough in civil practice to warrant a separate treatment for each entry. The ensuing sections offer that seriatim treatment.

§ 259. Defense Based on "Documentary Evidence"; Paragraph 1

Rather than single out a particular category of objection, as most of the other paragraphs of CPLR 3211(a) do, paragraph 1 permits the dismissal motion whenever the defense is founded on "documentary evidence". This was not a basis for dismissal under pre-CPLR law, and there is not much to tell us what qualifies as "documentary" under this paragraph.

When a mortgage and note unambiguously made the property itself the plaintiffs' sole recourse, barring a personal action, the documents were held to suffice under paragraph 1 to support a dismissal of the personal action.[1] A judgment has also been held to be an acceptable document.[2] Mortgages, deeds, contracts, and the like would also seem to be acceptable.[3] The difficulty is that CPLR 3211(a)(1) contem-

---

4. A general relief clause favored by lawyers for its reassuring prolixity is to ask, after reciting the specific relief sought, for "such other, further, and/or different relief as to the court may seem just and proper". The last clause, too, has the sort of archaic word order and patronizing pomposity that many moving lawyers find moving. Limiting the adjectives and conforming the word order to Modern English Usage are acceptable alternatives, but only in well established law firms.

5. Wolfe v. Bellizzi, 58 Misc.2d 773, 296 N.Y.S.2d 860 (Sup.Ct., Schenectady County, 1969).

6. Paragraph 11 was added in 1986, designed to cover only one situation: that in which an uncompensated official of a not-for-profit organization is the defendant and seeks a dismissal of the action based on the absence of gross negligence or harmful intent. Coordinate legislation immunizes such officials from suit unless either element is

present. All this comes from L.1986, c.220, and is discussed in Commentary C3211:34a on McKinney's CPLR 3211.

§ 259

1. Bronxville Knolls, Inc. v. Webster Town Center Partnership, 221 A.D.2d 248, 634 N.Y.S.2d 62 (1st Dep't 1995).

2. Heaney v. Purdy, 29 N.Y.2d 157, 324 N.Y.S.2d 47, 272 N.E.2d 550 (1971).

3. Subdivision (d) of CPLR 3212 had a provision about the use of documentary evidence in connection with summary judgment in a matrimonial action. The subdivision was repealed in 1978, but those things that qualified as documents under it should still qualify as documentary evidence under CPLR 3211(a)(1). See Brill v. Brill, 10 N.Y.2d 308, 222 N.Y.S.2d 321, 178 N.E.2d 720 (1961).

plates that the defense will be established by the "documentary evidence" alone, because affidavits, which are the most common source of proof on most motions and which are available for use on a CPLR 3211(a) motion grounded on any other paragraph, can't be made the basis for a paragraph 1 motion. Nor can depositions, apparently. If it turns out that documentary evidence is available but that affidavit or deposition support is also necessary and that no other CPLR 3211(a) ground appears to be applicable, an alternative for the defendant is to forget about CPLR 3211, serve an answer, and then promptly move for summary judgment under CPLR 3212 (where the other papers can be included without difficulty).[4]

The Advisory Committee noted that most of the grounds supported by documentary evidence are in paragraph 5 and that paragraph 1 was added only to cover something like a defense based on the terms of a written contract.[5] All in all, CPLR 3211(a)(1) has not been very helpful and can't be deemed very important in practice.

§ 260. Subject Matter Jurisdiction; Paragraph 2

Chapter 2 of this book is occupied at length with the courts and their jurisdiction. Whenever a court lacks jurisdiction of the subject matter of the case, the way to raise the objection is by motion to dismiss under paragraph 2 of CPLR 3211(a). As is true of all the objections listed in CPLR 3211(a), so with this one: it may be taken as a defense in the answer instead of by motion, but the motion is usually the more expeditious route. There is no time limit for moving on this ground, however; the defect is deemed to go to the root of the court's power.[1]

Until 1972, CPLR 3211(a)(2), while phrased in terms of "subject matter" jurisdiction, was also used to raise the objection of forum non conveniens, an objection that also gives rise to a dismissal. Although the two categories of objection are not the same,[2] the subject matter dismissal ground had traditionally served as the motion mechanism to raise the conveniens objection as well.[3] Today, a motion to dismiss on the ground of forum non conveniens is based on CPLR 327.

§ 261. Lack of Capacity to Sue; Paragraph 3

If the party asserting the claim lacks capacity to sue, a motion to dismiss lies under CPLR 3211(a)(3). If an infant, for example, purports to sue pro se or even to retain an attorney—only someone listed in CPLR 1201 can do that for the infant—the infant would lack capacity to sue and this ground of objection would be invoked.

Capacity questions sometimes involve a trustee of one kind or another. If a plaintiff's claim should have been but wasn't listed in his bankruptcy proceeding, for example, the plaintiff can't sue on it because capacity is wanting: the claim now belongs to the trustee in bankruptcy, not the plaintiff.[1]

The paragraph 3 objection can sometimes overlap paragraph 7. A trust situation will illustrate this, too. Where, for example, a plaintiff without even an arguable title or right as a trustee presumes to sue in behalf of the trust, the plaintiff lacks capacity to sue and is subject to the paragraph 3 dismissal. But it would also be true that the complaint, interposed by so irrelevant a person, would fail to state a cause of action, thus invoking the paragraph 7 objection as well. As suggested at

---

4. See Commentary C3211:10 on McKinney's CPLR 3211.

5. 1st Rep.Leg.Doc. (1957) No. 6(b), p. 85.

§ 260

1. See § 272 below.

2. See § 29 above.

3. See, e.g., Rohlsen v. Latin American Airways, Inc., 65 N.Y.S.2d 644 (Sup.Ct., N.Y.County, 1946), in which the action involved regulation and management of the affairs

of a foreign corporation. The court properly noted that it must in its discretion "decline" jurisdiction in such cases—the appropriate phraseology of the conveniens objection—and it did so, but on a motion phrased to dismiss for lack of subject matter jurisdiction.

§ 261

1. Quiros v. Polow, 135 A.D.2d 697, 522 N.Y.S.2d 596 (2d Dep't 1987).

the outset,[2] the defendant in a situation like that should invoke both grounds in the dismissal motion.

If the plaintiff's capacity to sue depends on status, which is disputed, an action brought to clarify that status can't be defeated with the capacity objection. Where, for example, P sued for a declaration that a certain voting trust agreement was valid and that P was its proper trustee, a motion to dismiss on the ground that P lacked capacity to sue as trustee was denied; it was the very matter in issue.[3]

§ 262. Other Action Pending; Paragraph 4

Paragraph 4 of CPLR 3211(a) is designed to avoid duplicative litigation. It's one of the more active paragraphs of CPLR 3211(a) and has a substantial caselaw. It implements its purpose by permitting the court to dismiss the action whenever it is shown that another action between the same parties on the same cause is pending elsewhere. The elsewhere need not be a New York court, moreover; it can be a federal court anywhere in the country, or a court in another state.

The general rule is that for the instant action to be dismissed because of the other's pendency, the other must have been commenced first,[1] but the rule is not rigid. If the other action was technically commenced first because the summons was served earlier, for example, but the summons was served alone while the instant action was begun by summons and complaint and came to issue earlier, it should be permissible to dismiss the other action in deference to the present one by motion duly made in the other.[2]

Most of the cases on this statute were decided before 1992, when service of the summons marked commencement of the action—and still does in lower court actions[3]—but as of 1992 the filing of the summons and complaint marks commencement in the supreme and county courts, so that in those courts the action filed first would be the action commenced first.[4]

To invoke this provision, it should be shown that the two causes are essentially the same. If they aren't, there is no duplication and the purpose of the provision falls. If the only difference between the two actions is that the relief demand differs and it appears that the relief demanded in either action could by amendment be demanded in the other, the motion to dismiss should be granted.[5] If the present suit involves more than the other one does, however, and the other can't be made to do as much, the dismissal should be denied.[6] When the earlier action is quasi in rem, for example, and its judgment will be good only to the extent of attached property, the subsequent in personam suit, which is not subject to such a limitation, will not be dismissed.[7]

If in the earlier action by P against D, D interposes a counterclaim and then commences separate suit (D v. P) on that claim, D's action is dismissible under this provision. The claim in the earlier context can be a counterclaim instead of a main claim if the requirements of paragraph 4 are otherwise met.[8]

Dismissal on this ground does not ordinarily lie before at least the complaint is served in the present action, and the pleadings relevant

---

2. See § 258 above.

3. Kittinger v. Churchill Evangelistic Ass'n, Inc., 239 A.D. 253, 267 N.Y.S. 719 (4th Dep't 1933).

§ 262

1. Izquierdo v. Cities Serv. Oil Co., 47 Misc.2d 1087, 264 N.Y.S.2d 58 (Sup.Ct., Kings County, 1965).

2. Cf. Frank Pompea, Inc. v. Essayan, 36 A.D.2d 745, 320 N.Y.S.2d 441 (2d Dep't 1971).

3. See § 60 above.

4. For discussion of the effect of the filing system on determining which of two competing actions is to be accorded priority on an application under CPLR

3211(a)(4), see Kevorkian v. Harrington, 158 Misc.2d 464, 601 N.Y.S.2d 522 (Sup.Ct., N.Y. County, 1993), and D'Gani v. Dagani, N.Y. Law Journal, May 22, 1995, p.27, col.4 (Sup.Ct., N.Y. County, Silbermann, J.), treated in SPR 9:3 and 39:3.

5. See Stanley Elec. Serv. Inc. v. City of New York, 26 A.D.2d 951, 275 N.Y.S.2d 222 (2d Dep't 1966).

6. See Mann v. Mann, 45 Misc.2d 19, 255 N.Y.S.2d 686 (Sup.Ct., Albany County), aff'd 22 A.D.2d 992, 254 N.Y.S.2d 1010 (3d Dep't 1964).

7. See Tjepkema v. Kenney, 59 Misc.2d 670, 299 N.Y.S.2d 943 (Sup.Ct., N.Y.County, 1969).

8. Frank Pompea, Inc. v. Essayan, note 2, above.

to the inquiry should also have been served in the earlier action because only then can the court determine the identity of the cause. An action in which only a summons and notice are initially served is therefore not likely to be treated, until the complaint is served, as a prior pending action for CPLR 3211(a)(4) purposes.[9] Hence if no complaint has yet been served in the other action, a paragraph 4 motion in the instant action is at best premature.[10]

There should also be a substantial identity of parties.[11] If the present parties are also parties to the prior suit, this requirement would be met, but if there are additional parties in the instant action and it appears that it will thus afford broader relief than the other, it will not be dismissed. If the parties are not the same, even though the two lawsuits have pretty much the same purpose, the courts are loath to apply paragraph 4 and dismiss because it may in effect leave the parties in the dismissed action to depend on whatever representation the other parties have secured in the remaining action. Where stockholder X brought a derivative action in the corporate behalf against certain directors, for example, and stockholder Y brought a similar derivative action, the second action was not dismissed but instead consolidated with the first.[12]

Consolidation is possible instead of dismissal because the court has a broad range of discretion, and as a result a whole bag of other tools, in disposing of a motion under paragraph 4. The paragraph says that "the court need not dismiss ... but may make such order as justice requires". If both actions are pending in New York courts, for example, consolidation or joint trial is permissible and in many instances preferable to dismissal.[13] Consolidation and joint trial ordinarily require a motion by one of

the parties, but as an alternative to dismissal on a paragraph 4 motion the court can order it sua sponte.[14] Neither consolidation nor joint trial should be ordered, however, unless all parties to all actions affected have been notified.[15]

A stay instead of a dismissal is another permissible alternative under the discretion afforded by paragraph 4. A stay can be especially appropriate when the action to which the instant one is asked to defer is pending in another state's court or in a federal court. Since an outright dismissal would surrender or in any event impede the New York court's ability to lend its aid if some unforeseen difficulty should later arise in connection with the other action, a stay may be preferable. When a stay is used, later difficulties can re-secure the context of the New York action and whatever aid may be appropriate from the New York court, through the simple expedient of a motion to vacate the stay.

Since it supplies the courts the general stay power, CPLR 2201 can be viewed as the authority for a stay even under paragraph 4 of CPLR 3211(a), but in paragraph 4 cases it isn't needed because the "such order as justice requires" language of paragraph 4 supports a stay. But when the other action is pending in a court of a foreign country, a situation to which paragraph 4 doesn't apply, CPLR 2201 can be turned to as authority to stay the instant action and defer to the foreign one. That would only be done, of course, when the foreign forum appears by just about all standards to be the more appropriate one, and a stay of the present action would be the most that could be granted. Absent an outright objection of forum non conveniens, there would be no authority, because of the inapplicability of

---

9. John J. Compagna, Jr., Inc., v. Dune Alpin Farm Associates, 81 A.D.2d 633, 438 N.Y.S.2d 132 (2d Dep't 1981).

10. See Louis R. Shapiro, Inc. v. Milspemes Corp., 20 A.D.2d 857, 248 N.Y.S.2d 85 (1st Dep't 1964).

11. Bradford v. Brooklyn Trust Co., 269 A.D. 549, 56 N.Y.S.2d 379 (1st Dep't 1945).

12. Dresdner v. Goldman Sachs Trading Corp., 240 A.D. 242, 269 N.Y.S. 360 (2d Dep't 1934). Statements in the Dresdner case about dismissal being precluded if the

other action is in a federal court or a court in another state are today inapplicable under CPLR 3211(a)(4).

13. See, e.g., Cooperman v. C.O.R. Land Corp., 41 Misc.2d 330, 245 N.Y.S.2d 651 (Sup.Ct., Kings County, 1963). For the distinctions between consolidation and joint trial, see § 127 above.

14. John J. Compagna, Jr., Inc. v. Dune Alpin Farm Associates, note 9, above.

15. Kent Development Co. v. Liccione, 37 N.Y.2d 899, 378 N.Y.S.2d 377, 340 N.E.2d 740 (1975).

paragraph 4, to dismiss the instant action merely because one is pending in a foreign nation.

If both actions are pending in New York courts, yet another alternative is available: an order directing the discontinuance of one of them. In one case it was the first action that was ordered discontinued; the second was allowed to stand, both having been brought in the same court.[16]

Dispositions under this provision can also be conditional. In one case the action was allowed to stand on the condition that the plaintiff stipulate to allow X, a party to the other action but not a party to the present one, to use in the other action whatever collateral estoppel benefits might result from a judgment against the plaintiff in the present action.[17]

If the defendant tries to play games with this provision, he may find the court wanting in team spirit. Suppose, for example, that after D moves to dismiss the first action for lack of jurisdiction over D, and P commences a precautionary second action while the motion is pending, D then moves to dismiss the second action on the ground of the pendency of the first. The motion will be denied,[18] in effect working an estoppel against D, and a sanction may even be imposed on D for what the courts deem duplicitous conduct.[19] Alternatively, the court can stay the present action to see what happens with the jurisdictional motion in the first. If the first is dismissed, the second can then be continued. If the motion to dismiss the first is denied, the second can then be dismissed.

Suppose that the New York action has been brought just as a precautionary back-up to an action elsewhere, lest the statute of limitations or a problem of jurisdiction bar the action there (while not being a problem in the New York action). Will New York allow itself to be used as a kind of holding action in that situation? The Court of Appeals indicated a yes in Flintkote Co. v. Amer. Mut. Liab. Ins. Co.,[20] discussing the use of a stay to keep the New York action alive lest some "unforeseen difficulty should arise in connection with the other [foreign] action". Further indications appeared to similar effect.[21] An extensive address to the issue appears in Rye Psychiatric Hospital Center, Inc. v. State of New York.[22]

Federal practice has no statute precisely the same as paragraph 4 of CPLR 3211(a). Guidance for what a federal court would do when the equivalent of a CPLR 3211(a)(4) motion is made before it—to dismiss or stay the federal action in deference to a state court action, for example—is found principally in caselaw.[23]

§ 263. Affirmative Defenses Usable on Dismissal Motion; Paragraph 5

The objections listed in paragraph 5 are those officially denominated affirmative defenses by CPLR 3018(b) but which, at the defendant's option, may be raised on a CPLR 3211(a) dismissal motion instead of being pleaded as defenses in the answer. The defenses for which the option is offered are:

arbitration and award

collateral estoppel

discharge in bankruptcy

---

16. Cogen Properties, Ltd. v. Griffin, 78 Misc.2d 936, 358 N.Y.S.2d 929 (Sup.Ct., Sullivan County, 1974).

17. Gallo v. Mayer, 50 Misc.2d 385, 270 N.Y.S.2d 295 (Sup.Ct., Nassau County), aff'd 26 A.D.2d 773, 272 N.Y.S.2d 1007 (2d Dep't 1966).

18. Clark v. Bilt–Rite Land Corp., 82 Misc.2d 1026, 372 N.Y.S.2d 466 (Sup.Ct., Orange County, 1975).

19. See Scheichet & Davis v. Sukoff, Sup.Ct., N.Y. County, Aug. 12, 1991 (Index No. 8056/90, per Cohen, J.), finding the defendant's conduct frivolous and imposing a money sanction of $500 on the defendant pursuant to Rule 130–1, for which see § 414A below.

20. 67 N.Y.2d 857, 501 N.Y.S.2d 662, 492 N.E.2d 790 (1986), affirming on the appellate division opinion in 103 A.D.2d 501, 480 N.Y.S.2d 742 (2d Dep't 1984).

21. See Houston v. Trans Union Credit Info. Co., 154 A.D.2d 312, 546 N.Y.S.2d 600 (1st Dep't 1989); Hollendonner v. Kiem, 138 A.D.2d 230, 525 N.Y.S.2d 43 (1st Dep't 1988); and the lead note in New York State Law Digest No. 364.

22. N.Y.Ct.Cl., Motion No. M–42081, July 3, 1990 (Margolis, J.).

23. See, e.g., Moses H. Cone Memorial Hospital v. Mercury Constr. Corp., 460 U.S. 1, 103 S.Ct. 927, 74 L.Ed.2d 765 (1983), and Wilton v. Seven Falls Co., 515 U.S. 277, 115 S.Ct. 2137, 132 L.Ed.2d 214 (1995), major addresses to the issue. The Mercury case and the situation in general is the subject of the lead note in New York State Law Digest No. 281.

infancy or other disability of the moving party

payment

release

res judicata

statute of limitations

statute of frauds

It is CPLR 3018(b) that defines an affirmative defense and which lists, as illustrative, the main defenses. Most of the defenses listed in CPLR 3018(b) are also contained in CPLR 3211(a)(5), which means that the responding party has the option of taking them by dismissal motion or by answer. Only three of the CPLR 3018(b) defenses are not adopted by CPLR 3211(a)(5): the comparative negligence defense (that the plaintiff was guilty of culpable conduct), and the defenses of illegality and fraud. The illegality defense can be squeezed under paragraph 7 of CPLR 3211(a), however. If the claim is illegal, a motion would lie to dismiss it under paragraph 7 for failure to state a cause of action. That leaves the culpable conduct and fraud defenses as the only two on the CPLR 3018(b) list that are not imported for alternative motion use by CPLR 3211(a)(5). The reason for the omission is that the two almost invariably involve issues of fact, making them inappropriate for the matter-of-law treatment that CPLR 3211(a) contemplates.[1]

Other affirmative defenses—besides those listed in CPLR 3018(b), whose list is not exhaustive[2]—may not be used on a dismissal motion under CPLR 3211 unless one of the objections listed in 3211(a) can somehow be made to cover it. That's sometimes possible.

The defense of the election of remedies, for example, essentially a member of the "res judicata" family, can be fitted under that objection.[3]

The "arbitration and award" constituting the first item on the paragraph 5 list requires a showing that arbitration has already been had and gone to award. Only then is a dismissal of the action, presumably brought in disregard of the award, the proper remedy.[4] If a defendant, sued in court on a claim that the defendant says is arbitrable, wants to compel its arbitration, the remedy is not a dismissal motion under CPLR 3211 but a motion to stay the action (and compel arbitration) under CPLR 7503.[5]

The "infancy or other disability" listed in paragraph 5 refers to the defendant's disability; paragraph 3, dealing with "incapacity to sue", is concerned with the plaintiff's disability.

§ 264. Non–Interposable Counterclaim; Paragraph 6

The various grounds listed in CPLR 3211(a) may be used against any affirmatively pleaded cause of action, with the exception of paragraph 6, which is concerned with only a counterclaim. Paragraph 6 is the ground used primarily when a counterclaim has been interposed in violation of the "capacity" rule. A counterclaim may be interposed by or against a party only in the capacity in which that party is present in the case. If the plaintiff is a partnership, for example, the defendant may interpose only a counterclaim that lies against the partnership as such. A claim existing against only one of the part-

---

§ 263

1. Fraud can become the central issue on a CPLR 3211 motion by other routes. If the defendant raises the defense of fraud in the answer, for example, the plaintiff can move to strike the defense under subdivision (b) of CPLR 3211. Fraud can also become the key issue in conjunction with some other objection raised under CPLR 3211(a). D may claim release under paragraph 5, for example, and P may contend that the release was procured by fraud. See Barker v. Conley, 267 N.Y. 43, 195 N.E. 677 (1935). Allowing fraud to become the dispositive issue through those channels is of course inconsistent with the reason for not including the defense of fraud in paragraph 5 in the first place: that it is too subjective an issue for summary

motion disposition and must therefore be left to the fact trier.

2. See § 223 above.

3. Cf. Incorporated Village of Laurel Hollow v. Laverne, Inc., 43 Misc.2d 248, 250 N.Y.S.2d 951 (Sup.Ct., Nassau County, 1964), modified 24 A.D.2d 615, 262 N.Y.S.2d 622 (2d Dep't 1965). See Commentary C3211:35 on McKinney's CPLR 3211.

4. Langemyr v. Campbell, 23 A.D.2d 371, 261 N.Y.S.2d 500 (2d Dep't 1965).

5. See § 592 below.

ners, personally, would not be usable;[1] should the defendant attempt to use it, the plaintiff's remedy would be a motion to dismiss the counterclaim under CPLR 3211(a)(6).

Although a counterclaim that violates the capacities rule may be dismissed under paragraph 6, and any counterclaim in the case is subject to dismissal on any of the other grounds listed in CPLR 3211(a), there is no authority under the CPLR to dismiss an otherwise valid counterclaim merely because it is not convenient to have it present in the case. Such authority did exist under prior law,[2] but the worst that can befall such a counterclaim under the CPLR is a severance, sending it off as a separate case.

§ 265. Failure to State a Cause of Action; Paragraph 7

One of the most important and frequently used dismissal grounds is the failure to state a cause of action of paragraph 7. The motion of course lies if the pleading is defective on its face, and in that respect it's the equivalent of the old common law demurrer (presumably long since abandoned in New York), which conceded the truth of everything pleaded but contended that, even so, the pleading stated nothing actionable under the law.

More important under the CPLR is that the paragraph 7 motion may be made even against a claim perfectly pleaded.[1] At least the way the CPLR's drafters envisioned it, the motion may, upon affidavits and the same kind of other proof usable on any CPLR 3211 motion, go behind the pleading and prove that it lacks merit. And since pleadings have been so successfully informalized by the CPLR,[2] so that it does not take much to "state" a cause of

action, the paragraph 7 motion is used more often today to attack the merits of the cause of action than to attack its articulation. Of course, in order to succeed on the motion, the defendant must convince the court that nothing the plaintiff can reasonably be expected to prove would help; that the plaintiff just doesn't have a claim. The criterion for determining such a motion is akin to that used to decide a motion for summary judgment,[3] for which reason the court may treat the motion as such if the court is so disposed and the proof warrants it.[4]

The utility of the CPLR 3211(a)(7) motion was largely reduced by the Court of Appeals decision in *Rovello v. Orofino Realty Co.*[5] *Rovello* held that as long as the complaint states a claim on its face, the plaintiff need not come forward with affidavits or other proof unless the court does in fact elect to treat the motion as one for summary judgment. This has resulted in holdings that the court cannot even *consider* the defendant's affidavits on a CPLR 3211(a)(7) motion unless and until it has elected to exercise its treat-as-summary-judgment power. This might in turn lead defendants to assume that they should not even bother submitting affidavits, but defendants should make no such assumption unless, of course, it is their intention to test only the face of the complaint.[6]

For purposes of a paragraph 7 motion, especially when it attacks the pleading on its face, the allegations of the pleading are deemed to be true. More than that, the pleading will be deemed to allege whatever may be implied from its statements by reasonable intendment;[7] the pleader is entitled to every favor-

---

§ 264

1. See § 225 above.

2. Civ.Prac.Act § 262. See Jayell Films, Inc. v. A.F.E. Corp., 67 N.Y.S.2d 77 (Sup.Ct., N.Y.County, 1946).

§ 265

1. Kelly v. Bank of Buffalo, 32 A.D.2d 875, 302 N.Y.S.2d 60 (4th Dep't 1969).

2. Foley v. D'Agostino, 21 A.D.2d 60, 248 N.Y.S.2d 121 (1st Dep't 1964). See § 208 above.

3. In some respects the CPLR 3211(a)(7) motion not aimed at only the face of the pleading is like a short-cut to

summary judgment, the motion that CPLR 3212 supplies only after the joinder of issue. (A CPLR 3211 motion doesn't have to wait for that. See § 272 below.)

4. See § 270 below.

5. 40 N.Y.2d 633, 389 N.Y.S.2d 314, 357 N.E.2d 970 (1976).

6. See the discussion in §§ 270 and 275, below, and in the lead note in New York State Law Digest No. 353.

7. Foley v. D'Agostino, note 2, above.

able inference that might be drawn.[8]

While the general rule about the CPLR 3211(a) objections is that any of them can at the defendant's option be used as a defense in the answer instead of being taken by motion under CPLR 3211,[9] there is some doubt about whether this is true of the paragraph 7 objection of failure to state a cause of action. That objection is implicit in the very fact that there's a lawsuit, a tune imbedded in the vocal chords of just about every defendant. Some courts have therefore held that the objection cannot be used as a defense in the answer.[10] The point is not important, though, because pleading it in the answer is superfluous at worst: the objection is so fundamental that the defendant can raise it at any time during the action, whether pleaded as a defense in the answer or not.[11]

The relief clause is of no great consequence on a paragraph 7 motion. As long as the complaint as a whole manifests a cause of action recognizable under the law, it is of no moment that the wrong relief was asked for.[12] It has also been held that if there are several claims alleged, and any one of them is sufficient, a paragraph 7 motion aimed at the whole pleading will be denied in its entirety,[13] a lesson to the attacker to single out the allegedly defective claim and aim the motion directly at it.

For the lawyer who finds federal comparisons helpful, CPLR 3211(a)(7) is the counterpart of Rule 12(b)(6) of the Federal Rules of Civil Procedure. That rule uses the terminology "failure to state a claim upon which relief can be granted"; the CPLR language is "fails to state a cause of action". There is little if any practical difference between the terms,

however,[14] especially when one considers this kind of dismissal motion, for which reason we have been using the word "claim" as synonymous with "cause of action"; it has the great merit of being only one syllable as against the four for the longer-winded "cause of action".

§ 266. Lack of Personal Jurisdiction; Paragraph 8

Whenever it is contended that the court lacks personal jurisdiction of the defendant, a dismissal motion lies under CPLR 3211(a)(8). If the lack of jurisdiction affects the whole complaint, as where the defendant maintains that he was never served with process, the motion seeks dismissal of the entire action; if it affects only a given claim, as where the defendant was served outside New York and one claim has a basis for extraterritorial service under CPLR 302 and 313 but another has not, the motion seeks to strike only the latter.

The motion lies whatever the nature of the defect, as long as the defect goes to personal jurisdiction. It lies if the claim has a basis for extraterritorial jurisdiction but service was improper, or where a summons was served properly but beyond the state without an extraterritorial basis. It applies where the summons is sufficient but its service is inadequate, or where the service is good but the summons is defective.[1] It applies even when the summons is well drawn and served by a proper means within the state, but where the enticement or immunity doctrine applies to divest personal jurisdiction.[2]

If the summons is served without a complaint and the summons itself or its method of service is defective, the paragraph 8 motion

---

8. Westhill Exports, Ltd. v. Pope, 12 N.Y.2d 491, 240 N.Y.S.2d 961, 191 N.E.2d 447 (1963).

9. See § 258 above.

10. See, e.g., Bentivegna v. Meenan Oil Co., 126 A.D.2d 506, 510 N.Y.S.2d 626 (2d Dep't 1987).

11. See § 272 below. The subject is treated in the lead note in New York State Law Digest No. 333.

12. State v. Ole Olsen, Ltd., 65 Misc.2d 366, 317 N.Y.S.2d 538 (Sup.Ct., Westchester County, 1971), aff'd 38 A.D.2d 967, 331 N.Y.S.2d 761 (2d Dep't 1972).

13. See Griefer v. Newman, 22 A.D.2d 696, 253 N.Y.S.2d 791 (2d Dep't 1964); Commentary C3211:26 on McKinney's CPLR 3211.

14. See § 631 below (Practitioner's Edition).

§ 266

1. In this regard CPLR 3211(a)(8) is more comprehensive than its federal counterpart. Rule 12(b) of the Federal Rules of Civil Procedure lists as separate grounds lack of jurisdiction over the person, insufficiency of process, and insufficiency of service of process, all of which fall under the simple "jurisdiction of the person" category of CPLR 3211(a)(8).

2. See §§ 67 and 68 above.

lies before a complaint is served. But if the complaint must be seen in order to determine a jurisdictional defect, such as where the plaintiff bases jurisdiction on a longarm statute and an investigation of the claim is required in order to determine its New York contacts, the motion does not lie until after the complaint has been served.[3]

For tactical reasons, a defendant sometimes prefers to include an objection to personal jurisdiction as a defense in the answer instead of taking it by motion under CPLR 3211(a). If the action was timely commenced, but just barely, postponing the adjudication of the objection can, if it prevails, bring on a dismissal of the action too late for the plaintiff to start over. The plaintiff had best be aware of this.[4]

With the objection of improper service a special rule governs: if the defendant takes the objection as a defense in the answer, the defendant must move for judgment on it within 60 days or the objection is waived.[5] Note that this applies only to the objection of improper service, which is just one of several specific objections that falls under the category of "jurisdiction of the person".

Under the filing system for commencing actions in the supreme and county courts that took effect in 1992, the filing of the summons and complaint is the key moment for statute of limitations purposes. Service of process comes afterwards. If there is any defect in carrying out the system's requirements, the indications are that the defects go only to personal jurisdiction, not subject matter jurisdiction. This suggests that a defendant with such objections can raise them by motion under paragraph 8 of CPLR 3211(a) or as defenses in the answer, and that doing neither waives them.[6]

§ 267. Lack of Rem Jurisdiction; Paragraph 9

Paragraph 9 refers to an objection to jurisdiction in a case in which service was made

under CPLR 314 or 315. The reference means rem jurisdiction, which is governed by those provisions. Whenever rem jurisdiction of any kind is what the pleader is relying on, and the defendant maintains that even that jurisdiction is lacking for some reason (location of the res, failure of an attachment, defect in the summons, lack of summons service, etc.), the motion to dismiss is grounded on paragraph 9 of CPLR 3211(a).

Paragraph 9 can be safely made the sole ground of the motion only when the movant, D, is sure that personal jurisdiction is not even arguably present and that rem jurisdiction is the sole kind claimed. If there is any doubt whatever about the kind of jurisdiction the plaintiff, P, is asserting, D is wise to base the dismissal motion on paragraphs 8 (personal jurisdiction) and 9 together. Even the plaintiff herself may be uncertain about her jurisdictional basis in a given case, which has prompted the courts to be forgiving in such a situation if the defendant, also mistaking it, asserts the wrong ground.[1] The invoking of both grounds is a precaution that should avoid the problem. D should even include in the motion papers a request that, if any jurisdiction is found present, the court specify in its order precisely what kind it is—in rem, quasi in rem, or in personam. Different consequences, involving the law of appearances, append to different conduct of a defendant following disposition of a jurisdictional motion,[2] and since these consequences are tied in with the kind of jurisdiction that exists in the case, the disposition should be clear.

§ 268. Dismissal for Indispensable Party; Paragraph 10

We have already discussed the question of whether a dismissal lies for the plaintiff's fail-

---

3. Fraley v. Desilu Productions, Inc., 23 A.D.2d 79, 258 N.Y.S.2d 294 (1st Dep't 1965).

4. See § 269 below. A three-part series of lead notes on the urgency of timing the adjudication of jurisdictional objections appears in New York State Law Digest Nos. 274–276.

5. CPLR 3211(e). See also § 274, below, and SPR 50:3.

6. See the discussion in § 111 above.

§ 267

1. See Kelly v. Stanmar, Inc., 51 Misc.2d 378, 273 N.Y.S.2d 276 (Sup.Ct., Albany County, 1966).

2. See §§ 111 and 113 above.

ure to join as a party someone who is indispensable to the case.[1] It was pointed out that the conclusion of indispensability is reached only as a last resort today, if it is reached at all. Considering the numerous alternatives available to the court,[2] it is a rare case in which such a dismissal is warranted, and so the mission of CPLR 3211(a)(10) is a curtailed one. But if the issue does arise, as it does from time to time,[3] the defendant can raise the issue by a motion to dismiss under CPLR 3211(a)(10).

Since it is clear from CPLR 1001(b) that conditions may be imposed on a motion to dismiss based on the absence of a party,[4] the dispositive order on such a motion may contain conditions even though the motion is formally made pursuant to CPLR 3211(a)(10), which does not expressly authorize the imposition of conditions.

§ 269. Motion to Dismiss Defense

CPLR 3211(b) provides that a party may move to dismiss one or more defenses on the ground that a defense "is not stated or has no merit". As subdivision (a)(7) does with the motion to dismiss a cause of action, so subdivision (b) does with a defense: it allows the attack to challenge the defense as deficient on its face—i.e., argue that it fails even to articulate a defense—or go behind a perfectly pleaded defense to test its merit. Unlike subdivision (a), which enumerates grounds on which a cause of action may be dismissed, there are no listed grounds on which a defense may be attacked. Any defense may be attacked on any ground.

The test and the rules of construction in disposing of the motion on its merits are also akin to those applied to the (a)(7) motion to dismiss a complaint for failure to state a cause of action. So, when the defense is attacked on its face, the truth of its allegations will be assumed; when the attack goes beyond, and with affidavits and other extrinsic proof aims at the defense's merit, all reasonable inferences are drawn in favor of the defense.

There is a disagreement among the courts about whether the defense of failure to state a cause of action, the ground listed in CPLR 3211(a)(7), may be included in the answer instead of taken by motion. The Second Department has held that it may not be, and that the plaintiff can therefore move to strike such a defense from the answer under CPLR 3211(b).[1] The First Department position is that the inclusion of the defense in the answer is surplusage at worst, and that it isn't necessary for the plaintiff to move to strike it.[2] The latter would seem the sounder position. The defense of failure to state a cause of action is always open to the defendant during the action. It's one of those objections not subject to the rigid time limits that CPLR 3211(e) otherwise imposes on CPLR 3211(a) objections, so it remains viable whether included in the answer or not. The plaintiff's motion to strike, and the court's granting of the motion, would both seem wastes of time.[3]

The motion to dismiss a defense is an especially important tool for the plaintiff who needs an early determination of whether the defense is good. Suppose, for example, that the defendant has an objection to personal jurisdiction. The defendant contends he was never served with process and got notice of the action only by coincidence, or that the service was made by an improper method, or that it was made outside the state without an extraterritorial jurisdictional basis. The defendant opts, as she may,[4] to assert the jurisdictional

---

§ 268

1. See § 133 above.

2. CPLR 1001(b).

3. See, e.g., Storrs v. Holcomb, 245 A.D.2d 943, 666 N.Y.S.2d 835 (3d Dep't 1997).

4. See CPLR 1001(b)(1), (4).

§ 269

1. See, e.g., Bentivegna v. Meenan Oil Co., 126 A.D.2d 506, 510 N.Y.S.2d 626 (2d Dep't 1987).

2. Riland v. Frederick S. Todman & Co., 56 A.D.2d 350, 393 N.Y.S.2d 4 (1st Dep't 1977).

3. See the lead note in New York State Law Digest No. 333.

4. CPLR 320(a), 3211(e).

objection as a defense in the answer rather than by motion to dismiss under CPLR 3211(a)(8). If the adjudication of the defense is postponed until the trial, and the statute of limitations on the claim meanwhile expires, a sustaining of the defense at that later point will result in a jurisdictional dismissal too late to enable the plaintiff to start over.[5] By allowing the plaintiff to move early in the case to dismiss the defense, CPLR 3211(b) enables the plaintiff to test its validity in time to permit a new and timely action if the defense is sustained. If the plaintiff fails to make the CPLR 3211(b) motion, and the jurisdictional adjudication is sustained later, after the applicable statute of limitations has expired, the attitude of the courts is that the plaintiff has only himself to blame.[6] Both sides, in fact, should take note of the tactics in and about the assertion and adjudication of a jurisdictional objection—the plaintiff in order to avoid a dismissal too late to start over, and the defendant in order to see whether she can't maneuver the plaintiff into just that position.[7]

An amendment of CPLR 3211(e) that took effect in 1997 reduces the scope of this problem for the plaintiff when the objection is improper service: it requires a defendant who takes the objection by answer to move for judgment on the defense within 60 days. There is no such restriction on other jurisdictional defenses, however, like a defective summons or a want of basis for extraterritorial service, where the plaintiff's timing problem remains.

A CPLR 3211(b) motion does what is called "searching the record". This means that the court looks not only at the answer whose defense the plaintiff is attacking, but at the pleading to which the answer responds—the complaint—and, if the complaint is defective, it and not the defense gets dismissed, without the defendant's even cross-moving for it.[8] This phenomenon is better known in connection with the summary judgment motion and is discussed more fully there.[9]

§ 270. Treating 3211 Motion as Summary Judgment

Under CPLR 3211(c), the court is empowered to treat any 3211 motion as a summary judgment motion. The effect of doing so will ordinarily mean that the resulting judgment is to be deemed a judgment on the merits, invoking the doctrine of res judicata. As will be seen later,[1] the res judicata effect of a 3211 motion not so treated is more circumscribed.

The summary judgment motion itself, governed by CPLR 3212, does not lie until after issue has been joined.[2] Since that is so, one might assume that a 3211 motion could not be given summary judgment treatment until after joinder of issue. But 3211 motions are almost always made—indeed, most of them have to be made—before the joinder of issue,[3] and subdivision (c) of CPLR 3211 makes it explicit: the joinder of issue is not necessary for summary judgment treatment of a 3211 motion.

Because of its res judicata impact, treating a 3211 motion as one for summary judgment is drastic. Before it can be done, therefore, the court must notify the parties of its intention to make the treatment so as to enable them to submit whatever additional proof they may have to buttress their positions.[4] The nature of the ground on which the 3211 motion was made may not necessarily have elicited all the evidence that might be expected on an out-

---

5. CPLR 205(a) does not offer its six months for a new action when the prior action was dismissed for a want of personal jurisdiction. See § 52 above.

6. Dickinson v. Houston, 97 A.D.2d 665, 469 N.Y.S.2d 207 (3d Dep't 1983).

7. There is a three-part treatment of this subject, with a variety of illustrations, under the caption, "The urgency of timing the adjudication of jurisdictional objections", in the lead notes in Nos. 274–276 of the New York State Law Digest.

8. See Rand v. The Hearst Corporation, 31 A.D.2d 406, 298 N.Y.S.2d 405 (1st Dep't 1969), aff'd 26 N.Y.2d 806, 309 N.Y.S.2d 348, 257 N.E.2d 895 (1970); Hyman v. Hillel-

son, 79 A.D.2d 725, 434 N.Y.S.2d 742 (3d Dep't 1980), aff'd 55 N.Y.2d 624, 446 N.Y.S.2d 251, 430 N.E.2d 1304 (1981).

9. See § 282 below.

§ 270

1. See § 276 below.

2. CPLR 3212(a).

3. See § 272 below.

4. See Mareno v. Kibbe, 32 A.D.2d 825, 302 N.Y.S.2d 324 (2d Dep't 1969).

right summary judgment application. This notice requirement therefore offers the parties
an opportunity to submit everything they've
got.[5] To implement it, the court notifies the
parties that it is considering the treat-as-summary-judgment option, that they have until X
date in which to submit further proof, and
that a determination of the motion will be held
in abeyance until after that date.[6]

There had been some disagreement among
departments about whether the notice to treat
a 3211 motion as one for summary judgment
under 3212 must be given by the court, or can
come from some other source.[7] The Court of
Appeals resolved the conflict in Mihlovan v.
Grozavu:[8] it must come from the court.

No matter what ground the CPLR 3211
motion was made on, any aggregate of proof
before the court that arouses the court's suspicion that this is a one-sided situation on the
merits with no genuine issue of fact is sufficient to invoke this treatment. Realistically
speaking, the grounds most likely to produce a
record thorough enough to give the court this
kind of insight into the case are CPLR
3211(a)(7), the motion to dismiss a claim for
insufficiency,[9] and CPLR 3211(b), the motion
to dismiss a defense.[10] Technically, however,
the court has the power to make the summary
judgment treatment regardless of the specific
ground on which the 3211 motion was originally based.

Defendants planning to make a motion to
dismiss under CPLR 3211(a)(7) might assume,
because of Rovello v. Orofino Realty Co.[11] and

its progeny, that they should not submit any
affidavits at all on the motion unless and until
the court invokes its powers under subdivision
(c) and elects to treat the motion as one for
summary judgment.[12] That would be an unfortunate assumption. If the court does make the
summary judgment treatment, it will only be
because something in the case aroused its suspicion that the plaintiff may have no case at
all. The chief suspicion-arousers are likely to
be the defendant's moving affidavits. Caselaw
holding that the court may not *consider* the
defendant's affidavits on a CPLR 3211(a)(7)
motion[13] does not suggest that the court cannot *read* them, and the court's reading them is
the defendant's best hope of getting the court
to treat the motion as one for summary judgment.[14]

If the treatment is made and the motion is
disposed of as a summary judgment motion,
the order should so state, especially because of
the res judicata impact of the treatment.

§ 271. Immediate Trial of Fact Issue Under CPLR 3211

CPLR 3211(c) allows the court, "when appropriate for the expeditious disposition of the
controversy," to order an immediate trial of an
issue of fact arising on a CPLR 3211 motion.
CPLR 2218 contains such an authorization for
motions generally,[1] but CPLR 3211(c) contains
its own, superfluous as it may be.

The power is broad, but is exercised only
when the immediate trial has some potential
for ending the litigation. It is appropriate, for

5. State Board of Equalization and Assessment v. Kerwick, 72 A.D.2d 292, 425 N.Y.S.2d 640 (3d Dep't 1980),
aff'd 52 N.Y.2d 557, 439 N.Y.S.2d 311, 421 N.E.2d 803
(1981).

6. Lustig v. Congregation B'Nai Israel, 62 Misc.2d 216,
308 N.Y.S.2d 480 (Sup.Ct., Kings County, 1970).

7. See and compare Reed v. Shoratlantic Devel. Co.,
121 A.D.2d 525, 503 N.Y.S.2d 840 (2d Dep't 1986), and
Four Seasons Hotels, Ltd. v. Vinnik, 127 A.D.2d 310, 515
N.Y.S.2d 1 (1st Dep't 1987).

8. 72 N.Y.2d 506, 534 N.Y.S.2d 656, 531 N.E.2d 288
(1988).

9. See Martin v. State Liquor Authority, 43 Misc.2d
682, 252 N.Y.S.2d 365 (Sup.Ct., Albany County, 1964),
aff'd on opinion below 15 N.Y.2d 707, 256 N.Y.S.2d 336,
204 N.E.2d 496 (1965).

10. See Blatz v. Benschine, 53 Misc.2d 352, 278
N.Y.S.2d 533 (Sup.Ct., Queens County, 1967).

11. 40 N.Y.2d 633, 389 N.Y.S.2d 314, 357 N.E.2d 970
(1976).

12. See § 265, above, and § 275, below, for fuller
treatment of the Rovello case.

13. E.g., FYM Clinical Lab., Inc. v. Perales, 147 A.D.2d
840, 537 N.Y.S.2d 998 (3d Dep't 1989). See § 275 below.

14. A defendant who would sidestep the problem altogether can of course ignore CPLR 3211, draft and serve an
answer, and then move directly for summary judgment
under CPLR 3212. Drafting an answer may be a major
undertaking in a given case, however, and therefore one
the defendant would prefer to avoid.

§ 271

1. See § 251 above.

example, on a CPLR 3211(a)(8) motion (to dismiss for lack of jurisdiction) if a genuine issue exists about whether service of process was made or as to any other fact going to jurisdiction,[2] because it is wasteful to preserve a case and put it through all kinds of pretrial processing only to dismiss it for want of jurisdiction later. The trial of an issue of fact on a jurisdictional motion, notably one raising an issue about whether or not the defendant was properly served with process—perhaps the most prolific example of this genre—is commonly called a "traverse" in New York practice, some parts of the state virtually monopolizing the word for that use. The traverse is ordered, however, only when there is a genuine dispute about service, one side swearing unequivocally to one version and the other just as unequivocally to an inconsistent version of the facts. A hedgy or coy affidavit by the defendant, for example, perhaps saying only that he doesn't "remember" being served, won't do to dispute service,[3] which will simply be upheld.

An immediate trial would be even more appropriate to order on a CPLR 3211(b) motion (the motion to strike a defense) if the motion has the potential for ending the case on the merits. Where, for example, D interposed the defense of release and P moved to dismiss it on the ground that the release was procured by fraud, it was held suitable to try the fraud issue immediately because, should D prevail on it (and the release be upheld), P's action would be at an end.[4] It is this case-ending prospect, though of course not its certainty, that governs judicial discretion as to whether to order an immediate trial.

The word "immediate" in CPLR 3211(c) is a relative term, merely indicating that the trial should be given a preference. When the trial actually takes place turns on a number of administrative factors—under the IAS, mainly

on the judge's calendar—but it touches also on whether the trial is to be by jury. Is it to be by jury?

If the claim itself would have been jury triable—assuming jury trial has not been waived[5]—and if the motion whose fact issue is to be tried is one which, if granted, puts an end to the case on the merits, a jury trial must be had of the issue if either party requests it. Thus, where P sued in contract, D moved to dismiss on the statute of frauds, and P then adduced a memo which he said satisfied the statute, an issue of fact as to whether the memo was signed by an agent of D had to be tried by jury.[6]

But if the ground does not preclude a new action for the same relief, the fact issue would not be jury triable even though the main claim itself, were its merits reached, would be. An example here would be the usual "traverse". Assume a simple damages action (ordinarily jury triable) in which D moves under CPLR 3211(a)(8) to dismiss for want of proper service. A CPLR 3211(c) trial of whether service was made would not ordinarily require a jury because P, although dismissed, could turn right around and sue again.[7]

Taking things a step further, however, suppose that the statute of limitations has expired, so that a new action would now be barred if the motion to dismiss for lack of jurisdiction should succeed. Will that make it necessary to try the jurisdictional issue by jury if a party insists? Controversy on this point is apparent in Cerrato v. Thurcon Constr. Corp.,[8] where the First Department held 3–2 that a jury trial is required in such circumstances.[9]

§ 272. Time for 3211 Motion

CPLR 3211(e) provides that the defendant's motion against a claim under CPLR 3211(a) must be made within the responding time. If D

---

2. See Usher v. Usher, 41 A.D.2d 368, 343 N.Y.S.2d 212 (3d Dep't 1973).

3. See Le Fevre v. Cole, 83 A.D.2d 992, 443 N.Y.S.2d 533 (4th Dep't 1981).

4. Barker v. Conley, 267 N.Y. 43, 195 N.E. 677 (1935).

5. For waiver of jury trial, see § 378 below.

6. Herzog v. Brown, 217 A.D. 402, 216 N.Y.S. 134 (1st Dep't), aff'd 243 N.Y. 599, 154 N.E. 622 (1926).

7. See Commentary C3211:48 on McKinney's CPLR 3211.

8. 92 A.D.2d 89, 459 N.Y.S.2d 765 (1st Dep't 1983).

9. The subject is treated in the lead note in New York State Law Digest No. 283.

has 20 days to answer the complaint, and chooses to move under 3211(a) in lieu of answering, she must make the motion within the 20 days; if the responding time is 30 days,[1] or 40 days, or even more,[2] D has that time. If D is bent on moving, it is best for D to make the motion instead of answering. While CPLR 3211(e) technically permits the motion before the answer "is required", so that, for example, D's motion on the 15th day after service would seem permissible even though D answered on the 12th day, it has been held that the service of an answer waives the right to make the motion.[3] The service of an answer before moving is in any event idle: if the motion is granted the action will be dismissed and the answer will have been wasted.

These time limits apply to all of the subdivision (a) grounds except those of paragraphs 2 (subject matter jurisdiction), 7 (insufficiency of the cause of action), and 10 (nonjoinder of a party). That trio is excepted by 3211(e), and as to them the dismissal motion may be made at any time (although it is usually a good idea even with these objections to make the motion before answering).

With those three exceptions, the time to move is keyed to the answering time, and because of that a stipulation extending the answering time will also extend the time to make the CPLR 3211(a) motion. But if the stipulation specifies that the extension is offered only for pleading, not for moving, it should not extend the moving time.[4] The court of course has discretion to extend the time to take either step,[5] but it may be more prone to

grant the extension for the purpose of answering than for moving.[6]

CPLR 3211(a)(6), the motion to dismiss a counterclaim because it is not properly interposed in the action,[7] is also technically subject to the responding-time limit of CPLR 3211(e), but does not lend itself to it readily. If, for example, the counterclaim does not belong in the case because it has been interposed against the plaintiff in a capacity other than that in which the plaintiff is bringing the action,[8] the motion under paragraph 6 to strike it is akin to a paragraph 7 motion for insufficiency and perhaps ought to be allowed, as the paragraph 7 motion is, at any time. An alternative, available throughout the action, is a motion to sever the counterclaim. The motion to sever is governed by CPLR 603, which has no arbitrary time limit.[9]

There is no time limit on a motion under CPLR 3211(b) to dismiss a defense.

§ 273. Single Motion Rule

CPLR 3211(e) allows only one subdivision (a) motion per case. This is designed to avoid duplication because the movant can join in the one motion whatever grounds she has. It has been held, however, that a second motion is permissible if based on paragraph 7 (insufficiency of the claim),[1] but the Court of Appeals seemed to assume otherwise in McLearn v. Cowen & Co.[2] Omitting the insufficiency objection from an initial CPLR 3211 motion will not waive it, in any event. It is just a matter of determining what mechanical device to use for the paragraph 7 objection after the defen-

---

§ 272

1. CPLR 320(a), 3012(c).

2. Under the substituted service methods of CPLR 308(2) and (4), where completion of service depends on filing proof of service, the responding period can be 40 days or longer.

3. Incorporated Village of Laurel Hollow v. Laverne, 43 Misc.2d 248, 250 N.Y.S.2d 951 (Sup.Ct., Nassau County, 1964), modified 24 A.D.2d 615, 262 N.Y.S.2d 622 (2d Dep't 1965).

4. See Santos v. Chappell, 63 Misc.2d 730, 313 N.Y.S.2d 320 (Sup.Ct., Nassau County, 1970).

5. CPLR 2004.

6. See Smith v. Pach, 30 A.D.2d 707, 292 N.Y.S.2d 333 (2d Dep't 1968).

7. See § 264 above.

8. See § 225 above.

9. Compare Jayell Films, Inc. v. A.F.E. Corp., 67 N.Y.S.2d 77 (Sup.Ct., N.Y.County, 1946), which was decided when a counterclaim, legitimately interposed or not, could be dismissed for mere inconvenience. That power does not exist under the CPLR, which prefers the remedy of a severance.

§ 273

1. Higby Enterprises, Inc. v. City of Utica, 54 Misc.2d 405, 282 N.Y.S.2d 583 (Sup.Ct., Oneida County, 1967), aff'd 30 A.D.2d 1052, 295 N.Y.S.2d 428 (4th Dep't 1968).

2. 60 N.Y.2d 686, 468 N.Y.S.2d 461, 455 N.E.2d 1256 (1983).

dant's CPLR 3211 motion has been used up. If CPLR 3211 is unavailable, the defendant can raise the objection just as well with a summary judgment motion under CPLR 3212. It is usually best for the defendant to join the insufficiency ground on any CPLR 3211 motion the defendant chooses to make on any ground, even though it's not obligatory.

Since paragraphs 2, 7, and 10 are treated uniformly for time purposes, the foregoing discussion about the insufficiency objection of paragraph 7 should apply equally to the objection of subject matter jurisdiction under paragraph 2 and the objection of failure to join a party under paragraph 10. Certainly a second motion would have to be entertained on the paragraph 2 ground of lack of subject matter jurisdiction, whatever the motion may be called, and with paragraphs 2, 7, and 10 treated as a package by CPLR 3211(e), it would be awkward to reach any other conclusion for the other objections.

A second motion may be permitted on any of the subdivision (a) grounds if the first motion was premature and it was only because of the prematurity that the motion was not considered on its merits. Where, for example, a paragraph 8 motion (lack of personal jurisdiction) was made before a complaint had been served, and it was necessary to consider the complaint because jurisdiction was based on CPLR 302 and the claim's New York contacts had to be examined, the court denied the motion without prejudice to renewal after service of the complaint.[3]

It is also permissible for a party to make a second CPLR 3211 motion if each aims at a different pleading. In one case, for example, where D moved to dismiss P's claim and then moved to dismiss a co-defendant's cross-claim, both motions were allowed.[4]

If the 3211 motion is used up, motion relief is not yet lost. As long as the subdivision (a) objection has been preserved by being included as a defense in the answer, it can be made the subject of a summary judgment motion under CPLR 3212 after answering.[5] If it is, and the second motion is labeled a 3211 motion, the court may just treat it as if it were properly labeled a summary judgment motion, and dispose of it on its merits.[6]

Suppose that while D's 3211(a) motion against the complaint is pending, P amends the complaint, as P is allowed to do.[7] Will the amendment automatically abate the motion? It should not. Even if the motion attacks the complaint under CPLR 3211(a)(7) for insufficiency on its face, for example, and the complaint as amended remedies the deficiency and the motion does lose its purpose, whether the motion formally "abates" is something that must still be determined by the court if the parties can't work it out voluntarily. The "better rule" holds that the movant has "the option of withdrawing its motion or pressing it with regard to the amended pleading"; that insisting that the motion automatically abates "only invites additional motion practice".[8] The First Department has said that when P amends the complaint while D's dismissal motion is pending, D "has the option to decide whether its motion should be applied to the new pleading".[9] Thus, unless the defendant withdraws the motion, the plaintiff should respond to it on the return day and let the court decide the abatement issue.[10] Many 3211(a) objections, moreover, are not curable by mere amendment of the complaint.

§ 274. Option to Plead Instead of Move; Waiver

If D has available a number of objections listed in subdivision (a) of CPLR 3211, subdivi-

3. Fraley v. Desilu Productions, Inc., 23 A.D.2d 79, 258 N.Y.S.2d 294 (1st Dep't 1965).

4. Nassau Roofing & Sheet Metal Co. v. Celotex Corp., 74 A.D.2d 679, 424 N.Y.S.2d 786 (3d Dep't 1980).

5. See § 283 below.

6. Hertz Corp. v. Luken, 126 A.D.2d 446, 510 N.Y.S.2d 590 (1st Dep't 1987).

7. CPLR 3025(a).

8. Sholom & Zuckerbrot Realty Corp. v. Coldwell Banker Commercial Group, Inc., 138 Misc.2d 799, 801, 525 N.Y.S.2d 541, 542 (Sup.Ct. Queens County, 1988).

9. Sage Realty Corp. v. Proskauer, Rose LLP, 251 A.D.2d 35, 675 N.Y.S.2d 14 (1st Dep't 1998) (noted in SPR 74:2).

10. See Commentary C3211:65 on McKinney's CPLR 3211.

sion (e) allows D to raise them all by a dismissal motion or, instead, plead all of them as defenses in the answer. Or, D may divide them up and take some by motion, and if the motion does not succeed, plead the rest by answer. It is of course preferable as a rule to take them all by motion since an answer will not be needed at all if the motion is granted.

To the above there is an important exception for the objections of personal and rem jurisdiction, the grounds listed in paragraphs 8 and 9 of subdivision (a). These objections are deemed so fundamental that wasting the court's time on a CPLR 3211 motion based on other subdivision (a) objections without including the jurisdictional objections waives the latter.[1] If, for example, D moves to dismiss the complaint based on one of the affirmative defenses listed in CPLR 3211(a)(5) and the motion is denied, the answer that D now serves may not plead the defenses of lack of personal or rem jurisdiction, which are waived, although D may plead as defenses any of the other subdivision (a) objections D may have, which are not waived.[2]

The Court of Appeals has construed this strictly, holding in Addesso v. Shemtob[3] that even in the situation in which P amends the complaint while D's CPLR 3211(a) motion is pending, as P may do, an answer that D afterwards serves to the amended complaint may not include the jurisdictional objection that D omitted from the motion.

It has been held that when the original answer omits the jurisdictional objection but an amendment of the answer made as of course under CPLR 3025(a) includes it, the objection is preserved.[4] This is sound because the amendment as of course, which has to be made early in the case, is really only a final version of the original pleading. The situation can be distinguished from that in *Addesso*

because it involves no motion and hence no imposition on the court's time, as *Addesso* did. Careful practitioners who do not want to test the *Addesso* case in this way should see to the inclusion of the jurisdictional defense in the original answer.

Whether an amendment by leave of court under CPLR 3025(b) will be allowed to raise a 3211(a) objection for the first time should depend on whether the delay in asserting the objection can be shown to have prejudiced the plaintiff.[5]

CPLR 3211(e) singles out the objection of improper service of process and imposes a special additional time limit on asserting it. If the objection is taken by answer instead of by motion, as it may be, the party so asserting it must move for judgment based on the objection within 60 days after serving the answer, or the objection is waived. The motion with which to accomplish this is the motion for summary judgment under CPLR 3212.

Note in this respect that while the objection to improper service is embraced within the category of "jurisdiction of the person" under paragraph 8 on the CPLR 3211(a) list, the other objections that go to personal jurisdiction, such as want of extraterritorial basis for service, defective summons, etc., are not—when taken by answer—subject to this 60–days-to-move-for-judgment requirement.[6]

Caselaw holds that a defendant does not waive a jurisdictional objection by interposing a counterclaim related to the plaintiff's claim or by impleading a third party defendant,[7] either step being deemed a necessary precaution should the jurisdictional objection fail. But the defendant does waive the objection by interposing a counterclaim unrelated to the plaintiff's claim. It makes the defendant the

---

§ 274

1. CPLR 3211(e). Competello v. Giordano, 51 N.Y.2d 904, 434 N.Y.S.2d 976, 415 N.E.2d 965 (1980).

2. Montcalm Pub. Corp. v. Pustorino, 125 A.D.2d 188, 508 N.Y.S.2d 455 (1st Dep't 1986).

3. 70 N.Y.2d 689, 518 N.Y.S.2d 793, 512 N.E.2d 314 (1987).

4. Solarino v. Noble, 55 Misc.2d 429, 286 N.Y.S.2d 71 (Sup.Ct., N.Y.County, 1967).

5. See Commentary C3211:62 on McKinney's CPLR 3211.

6. See the discussion of this provision in SPR 50:3.

7. See Commentaries C3211:60 on McKinney's CPLR 3211.

equivalent of a plaintiff who initially invokes the court's jurisdiction.[8]

The key to determining relatedness for this purpose is the collateral estoppel (issue preclusion) doctrine. When there are issues in common between the counterclaim and the plaintiff's main claim, such that an adjudication of an issue in the course of trying the main claim would necessarily be dispositive of the same issue when it afterwards becomes relevant on the trial of the counterclaim, then the counterclaim is to be deemed a related one and, practically speaking, the defendant really has no choice but to interpose it. Doing so, therefore, does not waive a jurisdictional defense that the defendant may also have.[9]

With the exception of the trio of objections in paragraphs 2, 7, and 10 of subdivision (a), which may be taken at any time, any subdivision (a) objection is waived if it is not taken either by a CPLR 3211 motion or as a defense in the answer,[10] and if no amendment of the answer is allowed to insert the objection belatedly. In this connection it has been held that an appellate court ruling during a prior review in the case, that the omission of a defense from the defendant's answer constituted a waiver, does not necessarily bar the trial court on remand from entertaining the defendant's motion to amend the answer to add the defense and thereby undo the waiver.[11]

§ 275. Leave to Replead

On a motion to dismiss a claim for insufficiency under CPLR 3211(a)(7), or to dismiss a defense for insufficiency under 3211(b), the party whose claim or defense is attacked will likely want a chance to plead over if the motion is granted. The court can and often does grant such leave, but CPLR 3211(e) contains a few instructions about it.

The party moved against should specifically ask for leave to replead in the event the motion is granted. She makes this request in the opposing papers and should include in them whatever evidence she has to convince the court that a claim or defense exists. The evidence should be in the form of affidavits of those with direct knowledge; the affidavit of one lacking knowledge will of course not suffice.[1] The court may require further evidence, but it has been held that the evidentiary requirement for leave to replead is not as stringent as on a motion for summary judgment.[2] According to the rule, the pleader must convince the court that she has a genuine prima facie claim or defense. If the court is convinced, leave to replead is granted.

All of this appears to be relevant today only when the motion is based on the facial deficiency of the claim or defense. It was the aspiration of CPLR 3211(a)(7) and (b) to make the dismissal motion available even when the pleading was sufficient on its face, by letting the opposing party, with affidavits and other proof, go beyond its face and show it devoid of merit. That would in turn suggest that when, for example, the defendant uses such proof on a CPLR 3211(a)(7) motion against the complaint, the plaintiff is under an even greater obligation to come forward with sustaining proof. But the Court of Appeals held in Rovello v. Orofino Realty Co.[3] that as long as the pleading is sufficient on its face, the plaintiff is under no obligation to come forward with sustaining proof unless and until the court elects to treat the motion as one for summary judgment and advises the parties that it is doing so.[4] The result of this has been to restore the CPLR 3211(a)(7) motion to the simple equivalent of the old common law demurrer, in which

8. Liebling v. Yankwitt, 109 A.D.2d 780, 486 N.Y.S.2d 292 (2d Dep't 1985).

9. Textile Technology Exchange, Inc. v. Davis, 81 N.Y.2d 56, 595 N.Y.S.2d 729 (1993). See the discussion in SPR 4:1.

10. CPLR 3211(e). Raoul v. Olde Village Hall, Inc., 76 A.D.2d 319, 430 N.Y.S.2d 214 (2d Dep't 1980).

11. See Marks v. Macchiarola, 221 A.D.2d 217, 634 N.Y.S.2d 56 (1st Dep't 1995) (involving the defense of the statute of frauds).

§ 275

1. See Young v. Nelson, 23 A.D.2d 531, 256 N.Y.S.2d 649 (4th Dep't 1965).

2. Cushman & Wakefield, Inc. v. John David, Inc., 25 A.D.2d 133, 267 N.Y.S.2d 714 (1st Dep't 1966).

3. 40 N.Y.2d 633, 389 N.Y.S.2d 314, 357 N.E.2d 970 (1976).

4. See § 270 above.

the facts as pleaded are assumed to be true and the only question is the law question of whether the facts state a cause of action.[5] Indeed, it has been held, based on *Rovello*, that in the absence of a summary judgment treatment the court may not even consider the defendant's affidavits on a CPLR 3211(a)(7) motion,[6] although, ironically, the courts can and do consider the plaintiff's affidavits in support of the complaint should the plaintiff elect voluntarily to submit such affidavits.[7]

The generosity of the courts in granting leave to the plaintiff to replead is greater than the supposedly strict standards of CPLR 3211(e) would suggest. This is of course manifest in *Rovello* itself and its holding that the plaintiff does not have to come forward with claim-sustaining evidence unless the court elects to treat the motion as one for summary judgment, which it can do under CPLR 3211(c) only after notifying the parties of its intention to do so.[8]

As noted, however, this tends to convert the CPLR 3211(a)(7) motion into a simple demurrer—testing only the facial adequacy of the complaint as a pleading. New York presumably abandoned the demurrer in favor of turning the CPLR 3211(a)(7) motion into the more probing test of whether the plaintiff *has* a cause of action.[9]

Perhaps the plaintiff should not rely too heavily on *Rovello*. A safer practice for the plaintiff faced with a CPLR 3211(a)(7) motion is to come forward, in the responding papers, with as much solid proof as she can muster to show a viable claim. *Rovello* appears to be an aberration that obscures that lesson, adding

unnecessary time and expense to litigation in the bargain.

§ 276. Res Judicata Effect of CPLR 3211 Disposition

A judgment resulting from the grant of a CPLR 3211 motion is not res judicata of the entire merits of the case (unless the motion was treated as one for summary judgment). But it is res judicata of whatever it determined, and that can sometimes have the same effect. Where, for example, the first action is dismissed as barred by the statute of limitations, a second New York action that attempts to duplicate the claim will be dismissed: it is res judicata that the claim is time barred.[1]

If the first-round dismissal was under subdivision (a)(7) for a mere pleading deficiency in the cause of action, a new action with a complaint identical to the first will be barred by res judicata,[2] but a new action with a complaint that remedies the deficiency will be sustained.[3] Investigation must therefore be made to determine precisely what the ground was for the granting of the dismissal.

Until recently, caselaw sometimes invoked the election of remedies doctrine to preserve a claim that should have been barred under res judicata. In one older case, for example, in which the first action was dismissed because the contract on which it was based was oral and unprovable under the statute of frauds, a second action, pleading in quantum meruit instead of contract, was sustained. The court held that the first action did not decide that no services were rendered or goods delivered, only that no contract for those things could be

---

5. See the dissenting opinion of Judge Wachtler in the Rovello case, note 3, above.

6. See, e.g., FYM Clinical Lab., Inc. v. Perales, 147 A.D.2d 840, 537 N.Y.S.2d 998 (3d Dep't 1989).

7. See the discussion in the lead note of New York State Law Digest No. 353.

8. See § 270 above.

9. See § 265 above.

§ 276

1. Spindell v. Brooklyn Jewish Hosp., 35 A.D.2d 962, 317 N.Y.S.2d 963 (2d Dep't 1970), aff'd 29 N.Y.2d 888, 328 N.Y.S.2d 678, 278 N.E.2d 912 (1972).

2. Flynn v. Sinclair Oil Corp., 20 A.D.2d 636, 246 N.Y.S.2d 360 (1st Dep't), aff'd 14 N.Y.2d 853, 251 N.Y.S.2d 967, 200 N.E.2d 633 (1964).

3. See Addeo v. Dairymen's League Co-op. Ass'n, 47 Misc.2d 426, 262 N.Y.S.2d 771 (Sup.Ct., N.Y.County, 1965).

proved.[4] It then added that since the quantum meruit remedy does not depend on contract, an "election" had not been made against it when the plaintiff sued in contract earlier. Taking a broader view under the res judicata doctrine, which deems concluded not only that which was litigated in the earlier action but also that which could have been litigated if it springs from the same event or transaction, the Court of Appeals has overruled that line of cases, which had allowed the election of remedies doctrine to serve as a detour around the res judicata barrier.[5]

Whenever it gives rise to a final judgment, the grant of a CPLR 3211 motion invokes the "res judicata" doctrine outright, whatever its scope may be in the particular case (which of course depends on what the objection was that the court sustained). The reduction of the case to a final judgment is one of the doctrine's major requirements.[6] But a denial of the motion, or a grant that does not give rise to a final judgment (such as where it strikes one cause of action or defense but leaves others intact for trial), does not end in a judgment; it ends in an order denying the motion, or granting it only in part. The effect of the order in those situations is also res judicata, but under a different name. The order invokes a doctrine known as the "law of the case", which is in essence a doctrine of intra-action res judicata.

The law of the case doctrine is fundamental, and powerful in practice. It holds that once an issue is decided, it cannot again be litigated at trial level,[7] although it may of course be reviewed by an appellate court either by immediate appeal or as part of a later appeal from a final judgment in the action.[8] Where, for example, D moves to dismiss P's complaint on one of the objections listed in CPLR 3211(a)(5) and the motion is denied, the denial is a holding that the objection lacks merit and it cannot afterwards be raised as a defense in the answer.[9]

The court may sometimes refrain from passing on the merits of a given CPLR 3211(a) motion and allow the defendant to plead the objection as a defense in the answer instead.[10] No law of the case doctrine would apply in that situation because a determination of the merits of the objection is being deliberately postponed.

§ 277. Motion under CPLR 3211 Extends Responding Time

A defendant moving to dismiss a complaint under CPLR 3211 need not be apprehensive about being in default for failure to answer. Nor need she get an order extending the answering time. As long as the CPLR 3211 motion is itself timely,[1] the mere making of the motion automatically extends the answering time even if the motion is denied. In that instance P, winning on the motion, must serve on D a copy of the order denying the motion with notice of entry. D has 10 days after that in which to answer.[2] So the mere making of the motion not only extends the answering time, but extends it substantially. Depending on when the motion comes on for hearing and how long the judge takes to decide it, the extension can run into months.

If several claims are asserted but only one is moved against, it has been held that the motion extends the answering time as to the entire complaint, including the claims not moved against.[3]

The making of a CPLR 3211 motion also suspends all pending disclosure proceedings

4. Smith v. Kirkpatrick, 305 N.Y. 66, 111 N.E.2d 209 (1953).

5. See § 218 above.

6. See § 444 below.

7. State of New York Higher Educ. Servs. Corp. v. Starr, 158 A.D.2d 771, 551 N.Y.S.2d 363 (3d Dep't 1990).

8. CPLR 5701(a)(1),(2), 5501(a).

9. Masterson v. Valley Nat. Bank of Long Island, 70 Misc.2d 623, 334 N.Y.S.2d 356 (Sup.Ct., Nassau County, 1972).

10. See CPLR 3211(d).

§ 277

1. See § 272 above.

2. CPLR 3211(f), analogous in this respect to CPLR 3024(c) and its answer-extending effect on corrective motions. (CPLR 3211 is a dispositive as opposed to merely corrective motion.)

3. United Equity Services v. First Amer. Title Ins. Co., 75 Misc.2d 254, 347 N.Y.S.2d 377 (Sup.Ct., Nassau County, 1973).

until the motion is determined or the court orders otherwise.[4] An exception is where the objection is for improper service, where no automatic stay of disclosure results unless the court specifically so provides. The defendant who seeks the stay in that situation can bring the motion on by order to show cause.

C. SUMMARY JUDGMENT

Table of Sections

§ 278. Summary Judgment, Generally

CPLR 3212 allows the court on motion to grant summary judgment for a party. The grant means that the court, after going through the papers pro and con on the motion, has found that there is no substantial issue of fact in the case and therefore nothing to try. Summary judgment is often termed a drastic remedy and will not be granted if there is any doubt as to the existence of a triable issue.[1] As the procedural equivalent of a trial,[2] it is used sparingly.[3] When saved for a proper case it is a perfectly constitutional weapon. It does not deny the parties a trial; it merely ascertains that there is nothing to try. Rather than resolve issues, it decides whether issues exist. As is often said of the motion, issue finding rather than issue determination is its function.[4]

If the court on the motion finds genuinely controverted any fact on which liability depends, it cannot grant the motion,[5] but note that this applies only to liability. If liability is summarily established and only damages remain to be proved, the motion may be granted and the damages issues ordered to immediate trial. In a few instances, to be discussed later,[6] immediate trial may be had even on certain issues on which liability depends, but as a general rule the appearance of issues of fact in connection with liability results in the denial of the motion.

If an issue is arguable, trial is needed and the case may not be disposed of summarily.[7] "Where the court entertains any doubt as to whether a triable issue of fact exists, summary judgment should be denied."[8] The same is true when a key issue turns on the credibility of opposing affiants. Only rarely can a credibility issue be resolved as a matter of law.[9]

CPLR 3212(b) draws an analogy between the motion for summary judgment and the motion for a directed verdict made at the trial.[10] The analogy is valid in that in both instances the court is taking the case away from the fact trier by determining that there is nothing to try, but the job on summary judgment is harder because the judge is asked to take this step on papers alone while the trial judge, on a motion for a directed verdict, has

---

4. CPLR 3214(b).

§ 278

1. Moskowitz v. Garlock, 23 A.D.2d 943, 259 N.Y.S.2d 1003 (3d Dep't 1965).

2. Crowley's Milk Co. v. Klein, 24 A.D.2d 920, 264 N.Y.S.2d 680 (3d Dep't 1965).

3. Wanger v. Zeh, 45 Misc.2d 93, 256 N.Y.S.2d 227 (Sup.Ct., Albany County, 1965), aff'd 26 A.D.2d 729 (3d Dep't 1966).

4. Sillman v. Twentieth Century Fox Film Corp., 3 N.Y.2d 395, 404, 165 N.Y.S.2d 498, 505, 144 N.E.2d 387, 392 (1957); Esteve v. Abad, 271 A.D. 725, 727, 68 N.Y.S.2d 322, 324 (1st Dep't 1947).

5. CPLR 3212(b).

6. See § 284 below.

7. Barrett v. Jacobs, 255 N.Y. 520, 175 N.E. 275 (1931).

8. Daliendo v. Johnson, 147 A.D.2d 312, 317, 543 N.Y.S.2d 987, 990 (2d Dep't 1989).

9. Rickert v. Travelers Ins. Co., 159 A.D.2d 758, 551 N.Y.S.2d 985 (3d Dep't 1990).

10. The motion for a directed verdict, although still called that in practice, is officially known as a motion for judgment during trial. See CPLR 4401, § 402 below.

had the advantage of hearing the testimony and seeing the evidence in the flesh.

Whether to grant summary judgment in a given case is another of those inquiries that must always be sui generis. One can go through the reports and find literally hundreds of appellate cases reversing lower court grants of summary judgment. It shows how judges can disagree on the relative strength of the same paper proof.[11] The first lesson to the lawyer is a comforting one: most of this mass of caselaw is largely useless (and therefore largely ignorable) as far as general principles are concerned; each case is a judicial reaction to the particular papers in a particular situation and has little precedential significance. The second lesson confirms that if the papers are such that reasonable minds may disagree on what they lead to, the court's recourse is to deny the motion and remit the parties to the fact trier. If material facts are in dispute, or if different inferences may reasonably be drawn from facts themselves undisputed, the case must go to trial and summary judgment must be denied.[12]

If a main element in the case is a highly subjective one, such as fraud (because of the investigation of intent that it entails), the case is likely to be unsuitable for summary judgment,[13] although, as will be seen a few sections hence, there is no arbitrary restriction on the categories of action in which summary judgment may be sought.[14]

There have been innumerable articulations of standards by which summary judgment should be measured, but when all is said and done the perception of whether or not the papers raise an issue of fact sufficient to ground the judgment is not the product of

book-learned verbalizations of criteria, but of the judge's total experience on the bench, and, before that, at the bar. Many judges will admit that they can't explain a summary judgment situation by a uniform standard but, as Justice Stewart noted about pornography,[15] they know it when they see it.

§ 279. Time to Move for Summary Judgment

The soonest a motion for summary judgment may be made is after the joinder of issue,[1] which occurs when the answer is served in respect of the main claim and when a reply is served in respect of a counterclaim. The summary judgment motion under CPLR 3212 may not be made before the joinder of issue,[2] but a dismissal motion under CPLR 3211, which may of course be made prior to joinder, can be treated as one for summary judgment,[3] so that the likes of a pre-joinder summary judgment can come about that way.

This no-earlier-than requirement has been part of CPLR 3212(a) from the outset. Until 1996 it was the only stated time restriction. Now there are outer limits as well. The court can set an outer time limit in a given case, as long as the court allows the motion until at least the 30th day following the filing of the note of issue.[4] If the court sets no time limit, the statutory limit is the 120th day following the filing of the note of issue. Upon a showing of "good cause", however, the court can allow a late motion in either instance.

The outer time limits were adopted in a 1996 amendment brought about by complaints by many judges and parties about the motion—which can of course dispose of the case early and save much time and trouble for all

---

11. See, e.g., Millerton Agway Coop., Inc. v. Briarcliff Farms, 17 N.Y.2d 57, 268 N.Y.S.2d 18, 215 N.E.2d 341 (1966).

12. Gerard v. Inglese, 11 A.D.2d 381, 206 N.Y.S.2d 879 (2d Dep't 1960).

13. See, e.g., Falk v. Goodman, 7 N.Y.2d 87, 195 N.Y.S.2d 645, 163 N.E.2d 871 (1959).

14. See § 280 below.

15. Jacobellis v. Ohio, 378 U.S. 184, 197, 84 S.Ct. 1676, 1683, 12 L.Ed.2d 793 (1964) (concurring opinion).

§ 279

1. CPLR 3212(a).

2. Milk v. Gottschalk, 29 A.D.2d 698, 286 N.Y.S.2d 39 (3d Dep't 1968).

3. CPLR 3211(c). For a discussion of whether a pre-joinder 3212 motion can be treated as a 3211 motion, which pursuant to 3211(c) can then be re-treated as a summary judgment motion—a series of doings which might sustain an otherwise premature 3212 motion—see Commentary C3212:12 on McKinney's CPLR 3212.

4. For note of issue practice, see §§ 368–369 below.

concerned—being saved for the eve of trial or even the opening of the trial itself.[5]

What will constitute "good cause" for the allowance of a late motion? The Third Department held in Rossi v. Arnot Ogden Med. Cent.,[6] that since rigidity would perpetuate meritless cases, the trial court should have "wide latitude" in allowing a late motion. In *Rossi* it was held that the allowance of a late motion was not an abuse of discretion even though the delay was "inordinate".

If from the motion papers, however late, it does appear that there is no issue of fact and that summary judgment is warranted, it would seem idle to force the case to trial. If the lateness is excused, of course the simple solution is just to entertain the late motion. If it is not, but the papers still manifest that there's no issue to try, perhaps a compromise solution is for the court to entertain the motion, but with a money sanction imposed on the movant for the lateness. Some cases have been rigid on the subject—needlessly, it is submitted—holding that unless there is some excuse for the delay in the making of the motion, all the merit in the world to the motion itself is not sufficient ground for allowing it.[7] The difficulty with such cases, when the motion is meritorious but brought late, is that they don't tell us what's to happen in the case. Is the motion totally and permanently barred? Does the case have to go to trial when there's nothing to try?[8]

The mere making of a summary judgment motion under CPLR 3212 automatically suspends all pending disclosure proceedings until the motion is determined or the court orders otherwise.[9]

It is rare that more than one summary judgment motion should be made in a case, but there is no stated restriction in CPLR 3212. "Multiple summary judgment motions in the same action [are] discouraged in the absence of a showing of newly discovered evidence or other sufficient cause".[10] One situation in which the courts allow a second motion for summary judgment is where "a new, as yet untested defense is permitted to be added by amendment".[11]

§ 280. Actions in Which Summary Judgment Available

Before 1959 there was a list of actions in which summary judgment could be sought. If a given category of action was not on the list, the motion could not be used in it. The list was contained in Rule 113 of the old Rules of Civil Practice. In 1959, the rule was amended to abolish the list and extend the summary judgment tool to all actions except the matrimonial action.[1] In 1978, after the liberalization of New York's divorce laws, even the matrimonial exception was eliminated and today the summary judgment motion has no restrictions at all with respect to category of action.

The main accomplishment of the 1959 amendment was to permit summary judgment in negligence and other personal injury actions, a numerous category of litigation from which summary judgment had previously been excluded. The plaintiff's bar regarded this event with fervor; they hoped it would pave the way to quick judgment in many cases, at least on the issue of liability, obviating a trial. They awaited court tests eagerly. In a couple of key negligence cases summary judgment was granted for the plaintiff, but on fact pat-

---

5. See the discussion in SPR 51:1.

6. 252 A.D.2d 778, 676 N.Y.S.2d 699 (3d Dep't 1998) (noted in SPR 75:3).

7. See, e.g., John v. Bastien, 178 Misc.2d 664, 681 N.Y.S.2d 456 (Civ.Ct., Kings County, 1998).

8. These and other questions are noted in the discussion of the John case in SPR 79:2.

9. See CPLR 3214(b). Note the exception made for the defense of improper service: if the summary judgment motion is based solely on that, the making of the motion does not suspend disclosure.

10. LaFreniere v. Capital District Transp. Auth., 105 A.D.2d 517, 518, 481 N.Y.S.2d 467, 468 (3d Dep't 1984).

11. See Armstrong v. Peat, Marwick, Mitchell & Co., 150 A.D.2d 189, 191, 540 N.Y.S.2d 799, 801 (1st Dep't 1989).

§ 280

1. The reason for the exception of the matrimonial action was the legislature's policy against the so-called "consent" divorce (the fear that the movant's proof on a summary judgment motion might by agreement be left unrefuted).

terns that, as it turned out, were to offer little encouragement for the long-range use of summary judgment in the conventional tort action.

In what was probably the first major test case, Di Sabato v. Soffes,[2] the plaintiffs were waitresses at work behind their counter when the defendant's car came careening into the store, causing equipment to fall and injure them. The driver had double-parked across the intersection and tried to let someone out on the passenger side, but the door stuck. So he went back around and had the passenger sidle along the seat onto the driver's side. During the sidling the car took off and caused the accident. On these facts, the First Department granted summary judgment for the plaintiffs on the issue of the defendant's negligence. But the vote was 3–2, and the dissenting opinion by Justice (later Chief Judge) Breitel pointed to a number of fact questions that had to be tried no matter how tempting it might be to guess that the jury would find them in the plaintiff's favor. The defendant swore, for example, that he set the brake and put the car in neutral. The dissent was of the view that if that were so, negligence as a matter of law was not established.[3] Because of this dissent and despite the majority's grant of judgment, *Di Sabato* over the years became an influence against, not for, summary judgment in a negligence case.

If the facts are not disputed, and the only issue is one of law, summary judgment will of course be granted even in a negligence case;[4] but if the issue is at root one of negligence, it is a question of fact for the jury and summary judgment is barred. Granting summary judgment in a negligence case takes something as unusual as the defendant almost deliberately inculpating herself in her own deposition, as happened in Gerard v. Inglese,[5] an early (1960) Second Department test of the use of summary judgment in the negligence area. The defen-

dant driver deposed that at the time of the accident, while driving at about 45 m.p.h., she took her eyes off the road to light a cigarette and hit the curb. At this point in the deposition the plaintiffs' lawyer probably pinched himself. The plaintiffs, her passengers in the personal injury action, were awarded summary judgment.

A self-inculpating deposition accomplished the same result some years later in the Court of Appeals case of Andre v. Pomeroy.[6] The defendant driver said that the accident occurred just after she looked down to get her compact; she hit the slowed or stopped car in front of her. The plaintiff was the defendant's daughter, and the plaintiff's lawyer was a happy man. A divided Court of Appeals gave the plaintiff summary judgment.

That was a so-called rear-end collision case, which might be thought of as a consistent candidate for summary judgment. But even that case will elude summary judgment if the defendant by affidavit or deposition offers strong opposition to the motion, as where he attests that there was an oil slick on the road, causing skidding, or that the brakes went suddenly and without warning, or that the defendant took suddenly ill at the wheel.[7] The Court of Appeals has acknowledged that "[n]egligence cases by their very nature do not usually lend themselves to summary judgment".[8]

Cases like the pair noted above, in which the defendant literally gives the case away in a deposition, are a dilemma for the insurer, who assigns and pays for the defendant's lawyer. It is often a case in which the defendant (the insured) is being scrupulously honest or deliberately dishonest. If the latter, the reason is usually the collusion of the defendant to assure a recovery to the injured plaintiffs, who are family or friends. One may wonder how enthusiastic the defendant's self-inculpating deposings would be if the sum sought by the

---

2. 9 A.D.2d 297, 193 N.Y.S.2d 184 (1st Dep't 1959).

3. Id. at 306–7, 193 N.Y.S.2d at 195.

4. See, e.g., Farkas v. Cedarhurst Natural Food Shoppe Inc., 51 A.D.2d 793, 380 N.Y.S.2d 287 (2d Dep't 1976), aff'd 41 N.Y.2d 1041, 396 N.Y.S.2d 165, 364 N.E.2d 829 (1977).

5. 11 A.D.2d 381, 206 N.Y.S.2d 879 (2d Dep't 1960).

6. 35 N.Y.2d 361, 362 N.Y.S.2d 131, 320 N.E.2d 853 (1974).

7. See, e.g., Velten v. Kirkbride, 20 A.D.2d 546, 245 N.Y.S.2d 428 (2d Dep't 1963).

8. Ugarriza v. Schmieder, 46 N.Y.2d 471, 474, 414 N.Y.S.2d 304, 305, 386 N.E.2d 1324, 1325 (1979).

plaintiff exceeded the defendant's insurance coverage—a sure way to test friendship, or to see just how thick blood is.

A summary judgment is sometimes entertained on the basis of a defense not formally pleaded, but only when "reliance upon that defense neither surprises nor prejudices the plaintiff", as when the plaintiff knows the score from other sources in the case, such as motion papers.[9] Indeed, summary judgment may even be permissible on a theory not contained in the pleadings,[10] but it is exceedingly rare and can be permitted only when other sources within the action have given the other side adequate notice and an opportunity to prepare.

§ 281. Proof on Summary Judgment Motion

Any form of evidence, documentary or otherwise, may be considered on a motion for summary judgment.[1] Affidavits are the primary source of proof. Depositions and written admissions are specifically mentioned.[2] The fruits of any other of the disclosure devices[3] would also be usable. As has already been seen, depositions are excellent sources of proof. In fact, when summary judgment is granted for the plaintiff in a personal injury case it is likely that the defendant's self-damaging deposition has turned the trick.[4]

Affidavits on any motion should be made only by those with knowledge of the facts, and nowhere is this rule more faithfully applied than on the motion for summary judgment.

The attorney's affidavit, unless the attorney happens to have first-hand knowledge of the facts—which is the exception rather than the rule—has no probative force.[5] The movant for summary judgment may be expected to include in her papers just about everything she has, but the opposing party must not overlook his own burden if the motion is to be defeated. He must avoid mere conclusory allegations and come forward to lay bare his proof;[6] the consequence of failing to do so will lead the court to infer that there is no genuine fact issue to be tried.[7] Failing to respond to a fact attested to in the moving papers, for example, will be deemed to admit it.[8] Nor will pleading ignorance of the fact be a sufficient response, unless it is shown that the ignorance is unavoidable and that with diligent effort the fact could not be ascertained.[9]

The evidence will be construed in a light most favorable to the one moved against,[10] but this normal rule of summary judgment practice will not be applied if the opposition is evasive, indirect, or coy. Offering only part of one's opposing proof on the assumption that it will suffice to defeat the motion, and for tactical purposes holding back the rest for trial use, can backfire. It can be done safely only when the opposer is sure that what he uses will suffice to beat back the motion. A wrong guess will find the opposer on the wrong side of a summary judgment. Although the courts sometimes grant a motion for summary judgment with leave to move to vacate it,[11] it is rare and should not be anticipated.

9. Olean Urban Renewal Agency v. Herman, 101 A.D.2d 712, 713, 475 N.Y.S.2d 955, 957 (4th Dep't 1984).

10. See Dampskibsselskabet Torm v. P.L. Thomas Paper Co., 26 A.D.2d 347, 274 N.Y.S.2d 601 (1st Dep't 1966).

§ 281

1. Wilkinson v. Skinner, 34 N.Y.2d 53, 356 N.Y.S.2d 15, 312 N.E.2d 158 (1974).

2. CPLR 3212(b).

3. The disclosure devices are in Article 31 of the CPLR.

4. See, e.g., Andre v. Pomeroy and Gerard v. Inglese, noted in § 280 above.

5. South Bay Center, Inc. v. Butler, Herrick & Marshall, 43 Misc.2d 269, 250 N.Y.S.2d 863 (Sup.Ct., Nassau County, 1964).

6. Hanson v. Ontario Milk Producers Co-op., Inc., 58 Misc.2d 138, 294 N.Y.S.2d 936 (Sup.Ct., Oswego County, 1968).

7. Banasik v. Reed Prentice Div. of Package Mach. Co., 34 A.D.2d 746, 310 N.Y.S.2d 127 (1st Dep't 1970), aff'd 28 N.Y.2d 770, 321 N.Y.S.2d 376, 269 N.E.2d 918 (1971).

8. Kuehne & Nagel, Inc. v. Baiden, 36 N.Y.2d 539, 369 N.Y.S.2d 667, 330 N.E.2d 624 (1975).

9. Overseas Reliance Tours & Travel Serv., Inc. v. Sarne Co., 17 A.D.2d 578, 237 N.Y.S.2d 416 (1st Dep't 1963).

10. Weiss v. Garfield, 21 A.D.2d 156, 249 N.Y.S.2d 458 (3d Dep't 1964).

11. See Frutos v. Shapiro, 11 A.D.2d 1005, 206 N.Y.S.2d 18 (1st Dep't 1960).

Drawing the line between what the moving party has to show to earn a summary judgment and what the opposing party has to show to defeat the summary judgment is a perennial battle in the courts, both federal and state. And it is a case-by-case battle, manifesting the relatively limited value of general language about who has what burden. A major case in point on the federal side is Celotex Corp. v. Catrett,[12] a 1986 determination of the U.S. Supreme Court suggesting that the resisting party need not come forward with proof to sustain its claim until the moving party has demonstrated something tending to show some basic element missing from the claim. The application of the principle in particular cases generates much argument, and many, many annotations on *Celotex*.

A party relying on a technical application of the *Celotex* standards may perhaps too confidently gauge its own tactics by its view of whether the other side has carried out, or can carry out, its supposed burden, and form a conclusion about that on which the court may disagree. If the mis-gauger is the movant, presumably the worst that can happen is that the motion will be denied. But if the mis-gauger is the resisting party, the consequence may be the grant of summary judgment against it. This suggests that the resister not be too picky in mustering its opposing proof, lest it find itself out the door on summary judgment, and with all further opportunity to put in proof dissolved.

If a key fact in issue is within the exclusive knowledge of the moving party the motion for summary judgment will be denied,[13] a situation that can easily occur, for example, when the opposer is an executor or administrator of a decedent and had no actual part in the trans-

action at issue. Denial of the motion will also result when an important fact is one the opposing party cannot know, as where it turns on the scope of the movant's knowledge of his own agent's act.[14]

If a key fact turns on an item of evidence whose admissibility at the trial is arguable, summary judgment must be denied.[15] Because of the drastic nature of the remedy, a rule has even arisen that occasionally permits the court to consider incompetent evidence, i.e., evidence that would be inadmissible at a trial, but only if it tends to defeat the motion. (It will not be considered in support of the motion.) This rule has been applied when the so-called dead-person statute, now CPLR 4519, was involved. Thus, where P's only opposing evidence was a communication that the statute would exclude at a trial, the evidence was nevertheless entertained and D's summary judgment motion denied on the basis of it. The court did seem to be at some pains, however, to point out that P might have some other way to make out a prima facie case. The court thus appeared to leave the door open to a different result, and to the exclusion of the incompetent evidence, in a case lacking such an alternative.[16]

If the opposing party needs further opportunity to secure affidavits or conduct disclosure or otherwise summon forth evidentiary aid in opposing the motion, the court can make any order it deems appropriate, as long as the party attests in an affidavit that such opposing facts may exist.[17] The court can stay the motion and give the party the needed chance to get the additional data or seek the requisite disclosure, or it can deny the motion outright with similar purpose,[18] without prejudice to renewal later.

---

12. 477 U.S. 317, 106 S.Ct. 2548, 91 L.Ed.2d 265 (1986).

13. Krupp v. Aetna Life & Cas. Co., 103 A.D.2d 252, 479 N.Y.S.2d 992 (2d Dep't 1984). The movant in such a case should be put to her proof so that the opposing party can be afforded an opportunity for cross-examination.

14. See Franklin Nat. Bank v. DiGiacomo, 20 A.D.2d 797, 248 N.Y.S.2d 586 (2d Dep't 1964).

15. Gallo Painting, Inc. v. Aetna Insurance Co., 49 A.D.2d 746, 372 N.Y.S.2d 699 (2d Dep't 1975).

16. Phillips v. Joseph Kantor & Co., 31 N.Y.2d 307, 338 N.Y.S.2d 882, 291 N.E.2d 129 (1972). See also Raybin

v. Raybin, 15 A.D.2d 679, 224 N.Y.S.2d 165 (2d Dep't 1962), and compare Falk v. Goodman, 7 N.Y.2d 87, 195 N.Y.S.2d 645, 163 N.E.2d 871 (1959). Another point stressed in Phillips is that CPLR 4519 excludes the communication with a decedent only when an interested witness offers it "upon the trial", and that the objection may therefore not be asserted or waived until then.

17. CPLR 3212(f), the counterpart of CPLR 3211(d).

18. See, e.g., Kagan v. United States Life Ins. Co., 21 A.D.2d 846, 250 N.Y.S.2d 889 (4th Dep't 1964).

One of the moving affidavits should include a statement attesting to the validity of the movant's claim or defense or to the invalidity of the other party's. This is expressly required by CPLR 3212(b). It is a pro forma part of summary judgment motion papers.

§ 282. Searching the Record

CPLR 3212(b) provides that "[i]f it shall appear that any party other than the moving party is entitled to a summary judgment, the court may grant such judgment without the necessity of a cross-motion". If P moves for summary judgment against D, for example, D can end up getting summary judgment against P without even asking for it. Popularly known to bench and bar as "searching the record", this device is more likely to be remembered by its victim as the doctrine of extreme disappointment. It occurs, as a rule, when the pleading being attacked by the summary judgment motion is a responsive one, as in the example, where P's motion is actually an attack on the answer. A motion in that category requires the court to go behind the answer to examine the sufficiency of the complaint. If the complaint is defective, it and not the answer is dismissed, and the plaintiff, although the movant, becomes the victim. The theory is that a bad answer is good enough for a bad complaint.

There is some indication, even though the language of CPLR 3212 is permissive, that a searching of the record on a summary judgment motion is mandatory.[1] It has even been known to take place on appeal.[2] And it can occur on a motion under CPLR 3211 as well as one under 3212. When P moves under 3211(b) to dismiss a defense, for example, and the cause of action in the complaint turns out to be inadequate, the complaint gets dismissed instead of the defense.[3]

While the court can grant summary judgment for the non-movant by searching the record, there is no general authorization for a court to grant summary judgment sua sponte. A motion is necessary, on papers, so that all sides have an opportunity to muster their proof.[4]

Following the prescription of human nature, the one who moves for summary judgment is the party who wants it for himself. But in matrimonial actions for a while, for tactical reasons unique to that realm, the defendant husband was moving to have summary judgment granted for the plaintiff wife, and it was the wife who was resisting.[5] Earning for itself the name "reverse summary judgment"—a kind of party-initiated cousin of the court-initiated search-the-record phenomenon—the procedure was upheld by the Court of Appeals on the ground that a party who seeks a judgment can't be heard to complain when it is awarded to her summarily.[6] But there were legitimate complaints about this bizarre procedure, and the legislature overturned it with an amendment of CPLR 3212(e).[7]

The amendment bars reverse summary judgment only in matrimonial actions, however, where it had found some use; it is still available in other actions, where it really has none. Hence, if a defendant in a million dollar commercial or tort action wants the plaintiff to have summary judgment, the court will not stand in the way, and the plaintiff can probably be prevailed on to cooperate, too.

§ 283. Summary Judgment Under 3212 Based on 3211 Ground

The usual summary judgment motion is based on the overall merits of the case rather than on an individual defense like the statute of limitations, lack of jurisdiction, other action pending, etc. But it is permissible to base it on

§ 282

1. See Wilkinson v. Skinner, 34 N.Y.2d 53, 356 N.Y.S.2d 15, 312 N.E.2d 158 (1974).

2. See, e.g., Wiseman v. Knaus, 24 A.D.2d 869, 264 N.Y.S.2d 331 (2d Dep't 1965).

3. See § 269 above.

4. Ressis v. Mactye, 98 A.D.2d 836, 470 N.Y.S.2d 502 (3d Dep't 1983).

5. E.g., the husband wanted to remarry quickly, or hoped that the court would drag its heels on the equitable distribution (i.e., the money) aspect of the case if the matrimonial relief were out of the way, etc.

6. Leeds v. Leeds, 60 N.Y.2d 641, 467 N.Y.S.2d 568, 454 N.E.2d 1311 (1983).

7. L.1984, c.827, effective August 5, 1984. See Commentary C3212:29 on McKinney's CPLR 3212.

one of those grounds or any of the other grounds listed in CPLR 3211(a).[1] It will be recalled that the long list of CPLR 3211(a) objections may, under CPLR 3211(e), be taken either by a motion to dismiss or as defenses in the answer. When the latter alternative is used, the objection, duly preserved by inclusion in the answer, may then be made the basis of a summary judgment motion.[2] And if the objection was not included in the original answer but the defendant seeks to include it in an amended answer, the requests to amend to include the defense and for summary judgment based on it may be included in one motion.[3]

This applies not only to a defense that can constitute an effective disposition on the merits, such as the defense of payment or release,[4] but also to a defense that brings on a mere temporary abatement, i.e., dismisses without precluding a new action, such as lack of jurisdiction[5] or the curable incapacity of the plaintiff.[6]

The grant of summary judgment based on one of these "abatement" defenses will not import the full res judicata effect[7] carried by the usual summary judgment aimed at the merits of the case generally. The lesson to the losing party is to see to it that the dispositive order clarifies the particular ground on which the summary judgment is based. If it is based only on the defense of lack of jurisdiction of the defendant, for example, the order should say so; it will clarify that the merits of the claim were not disposed of and that a new action lies if jurisdiction can now be obtained.

§ 284. Immediate Trial of Fact Issue Under CPLR 3212

If liability is summarily established and only damages remain in dispute, CPLR 3212 autho-

rizes summary judgment and the case is set down for an immediate trial of the damages question. But an issue of fact going to liability requires denial of the motion; the issue may not be immediately tried.[1] This makes the summary judgment motion the sole exception to the court's general power, under CPLR 2218, to order the immediate trial of any issue of fact arising on a motion.

Before 1973, this restriction applied to any issue at all not related to damages, and this posed an anomaly. On a dismissal motion under CPLR 3211, the immediate trial of an issue of fact is permissible.[2] And as discussed in the prior section, if the CPLR 3211(a) objection is taken by answer instead of by motion, it can be made the basis of a summary judgment motion under CPLR 3212. If it is, however, and CPLR 3212 were to prohibit the immediate trial of an issue of fact arising on it, the anomaly would result that the same issue of fact that could be ordered to immediate trial if raised by a 3211 motion made on Tuesday could not be ordered immediately tried if raised on a 3212 motion accompanying an answer served on Wednesday. To avoid the anomaly, CPLR 3212(c) was amended in 1973 to allow the immediate trial even of a liability-related fact issue as long as it is shown to arise on a 3212 motion that is grounded on a 3211(a) objection pleaded as a defense.

The court must of course be as circumspect in ordering the immediate trial under 3212 as it would be under 3211. The immediate trial of a liability-affecting issue of fact should be ordered only when it has some prospect of putting an end to the case.[3] If liability is established and only the damages issue needs trial, the trial should as a rule go forward immedi-

§ 283

1. Houston v. Trans Union Credit Info. Co., 154 A.D.2d 312, 546 N.Y.S.2d 600 (1st Dep't 1989).

2. See Commentary C3212:20 on McKinney's CPLR 3212.

3. See Armstrong v. Peat, Marwick, Mitchell & Co., 150 A.D.2d 189, 540 N.Y.S.2d 799 (1st Dep't 1989).

4. CPLR 3211(a)(5).

5. CPLR 3211(a)(2), (8), (9).

6. CPLR 3211(a)(3).

7. Res judicata as applied to summary judgments is treated in § 287 below.

§ 284

1. Stowell v. Berstyn, 26 A.D.2d 828, 274 N.Y.S.2d 120 (2d Dep't 1966).

2. CPLR 3211(c). See § 271 above.

3. See Commentary C3212:22 on McKinney's CPLR 3212, and § 271, above.

ately.[4]

The mode of the damages trial, and notably whether it is to be by jury, depends on the nature of the case itself. If the case would have been triable by jury had there been no summary judgment, and either party insists on jury trial, a jury is required.[5] Under the 1973 amendment authorizing the immediate trial of some liability-related fact issues, the question of whether a jury is required should depend further on whether the ground involved disposes of the case permanently. If it does not, such as where D seeks summary judgment dismissing P's action for lack of personal jurisdiction (the answer having pleaded this as a defense), a trial by jury should not ordinarily be necessary.[6]

§ 285. Partial Summary Judgment; Effect of Counterclaim

CPLR 3212(e) authorizes partial summary judgment. It applies to part of a single cause of action as well as to separate causes of action: summary judgment can be granted as to claim #1 but denied as to claim #2, or it can be granted as to part of claim #1 but denied as to another part of it as long as the part on which summary judgment is granted can be logically separated. Where P pleads two theories in respect of the same wrong, for example, one being summarily attackable but the other not, the court can, with a partial summary judgment, dismiss the one theory while retaining the other even though P has in essence only one cause of action.

Partial summary judgment may be granted "on such terms as may be just". This makes

available for the court's incidental use the usual broad range of procedural tools: severance, stay, separate trial, the imposing of conditions, etc.

Although the provision speaks in terms of partial summary judgment as to one or more "causes of action", it can operate on defenses in the answer as well. Where, for example, one defense is shown to be bad but the other good, the court can grant summary judgment dismissing the bad one. A motion under CPLR 3211(b), to dismiss that defense, would be an alternative route to the same end.

There is a substantial body of law treating the situation in which P's claim is summarily established, but where D has interposed a counterclaim that requires trial. Or vice-versa. What effect does the counterclaim have, if any, on a grant of summary judgment for P? Despite a quantum of caselaw, it all boils down to a simple conclusion: the court can work out whatever seems fair in the particular case.

It is clear that the mere assertion of the counterclaim does not bar an otherwise warranted summary judgment on the main claim.[1] One alternative is that P be given summary judgment for all of the main claim with the entry of it stayed until the counterclaim is tried (to see what effect the counterclaim may have in diminishing P's claim in whole or in part).[2] If the main claim exceeds the counterclaim, P may be given summary judgment for the balance with the right to seek immediate enforcement of it, the rest being held in abeyance for possible offset by whatever D proves on the counterclaim.[3] If the counterclaim in that situation does not then succeed, P can be

---

4. Before the 1973 amendment, the rule said that the court "shall" order the immediate trial of damages if liability is established. The 1973 amendment was intended only to authorize the immediate trial of liability-related fact issues arising on 3211(a) grounds, not to remove the mandatory requirement of an immediate trial of damages issues when liability is established.

5. See Livingston v. Blumenthal, 248 A.D. 138, 289 N.Y.S. 5 (1st Dep't 1936). As to trial by referee, see CPLR 4212, CPLR Article 43, and contrast two Third Department cases, Angelo v. Laramet Corp., 23 A.D.2d 191, 259 N.Y.S.2d 428 (1965), and Keown v. Wright, 89 A.D.2d 932, 454 N.Y.S.2d 49 (1982). Keown shows how the matter of appointing referees is influenced by the caseloads and availability of judges.

6. See § 271, above, which also points up the relative nature of the word "immediate" in the phrase "immediate trial".

§ 285

1. M & S Mercury Air Cond'g Corp. v. Rodolitz, 24 A.D.2d 873, 264 N.Y.S.2d 454 (2d Dep't 1965), aff'd 17 N.Y.2d 909, 272 N.Y.S.2d 132, 218 N.E.2d 898 (1966).

2. CPLR 3212(e)(2); Casten v. Tannenbaum, 42 Misc.2d 118, 246 N.Y.S.2d 954 (Sup.Ct., Queens County, 1964).

3. Atlas Arm Co. v. Smith, 25 A.D.2d 669, 268 N.Y.S.2d 385 (2d Dep't 1966).

given summary judgment for the rest of the main claim at that time.

If D's counterclaim exceeds P's claim and P is given summary judgment on the main claim, the staying of entry or enforcement of the judgment until the counterclaim is adjudicated will protect D. But if there is no prospect of P's insolvency, so that D is assured of payment of any judgment that may be warranted on the counterclaim, the stay would not even be required; P could go to immediate entry and enforcement of the summary judgment.[4]

The solvency of P is probably the main inquiry needed in this situation. It would be unfair, if P were unable to pay D's later judgment on a counterclaim, to let P get and enforce a judgment on the main claim; it would be fairer in that situation to hold P's claim in abeyance to be offset by whatever the counterclaim may establish. But if P is plainly solvent, and the court is convinced that the solvency will not be lost while a counterclaim pends, it can allow the main claim to go to judgment and enforcement—and it will, especially when the counterclaim, though permissibly interposed in the action, has no relationship to the main claim.[5]

The court must be especially circumspect in imposing conditions with respect to one claim when the other has no relationship to it at all. The court has "wide discretion in imposing conditions upon the grant of partial summary judgment so as to avoid possible prejudice to the party against whom that judgment is granted", but the discretion "is not unlimited, and is to be exercised only if there exists some articulable reason for concluding that the failure to impose conditions might result in some prejudice, financial or otherwise ... should that party subsequently prevail on the unsettled claims". So wrote the Court of Appeals in Robert Stigwood Organisation, Inc. v. Devon Co.,[6] adding that this is especially so "where ... counterclaims with respect to which par-

tial summary judgment [is] granted are ... independent of the plaintiff's claim".

Conversely, if there is so intimate a relationship between the main claim and the counterclaim that the latter falls substantively if the main claim prevails, then the counterclaim, despite its apparent validity, must abide the trial and can't go to summary judgment before. The Court of Appeals so held in Created Gemstones, Inc. v. Union Carbide Corp.,[7] in which P was a distributor for D and concededly owed money to D under the contract. But P alleged that D failed to fulfill its obligations under the contract and sued D for damages. D thereupon interposed as a counterclaim a demand for the sum owed by P. It was found that the debt by P to D could be substantively cancelled were P to establish D's breach, and that summary judgment for D was therefore barred on the counterclaim.

Requiring X to post a bond in order to stay the enforcement of Y's summary judgment, the bond conditioned on X's making good whatever Y is still entitled to after X's claim is adjudicated, is a good example of a conditional order.[8]

§ 286. Salvaging Something from Abortive Motion

CPLR 3212(g) provides that if a summary judgment motion is denied or granted only in part, the court may nonetheless determine whether any of the facts involved are established. It is a discretionary thing, and the court may even interrogate counsel to see what facts, if any, are uncontroverted. If the court, with or without such an interrogation, finds any facts to be beyond issue, it need only list those facts in the order denying or partially granting the motion. The facts so listed are then deemed established for all purposes in the case, relieving all parties from preparing proof of them for a trial.

4. Pease & Elliman, Inc. v. 926 Park Ave. Corp., 23 A.D.2d 361, 260 N.Y.S.2d 693 (1st Dep't 1965), aff'd 17 N.Y.2d 890, 271 N.Y.S.2d 992, 218 N.E.2d 700 (1966).

5. Id. at 362–3, 260 N.Y.S.2d at 695–6.

6. 44 N.Y.2d 922, 923, 408 N.Y.S.2d 5, 6, 379 N.E.2d 1136, 1137 (1978).

7. 47 N.Y.2d 250, 417 N.Y.S.2d 905, 391 N.E.2d 987 (1979).

8. See Dalminter, Inc. v. Dalmine, S. p. A., 29 A.D.2d 852, 288 N.Y.S.2d 110 (1st Dep't), aff'd 23 N.Y.2d 653, 295 N.Y.S.2d 337, 242 N.E.2d 488 (1968).

The CPLR abolished the old motion to strike denials,[1] but an order under CPLR 3212(g) can sometimes carry out the same function by determining some of the denied facts to be established.[2]

Perhaps if calendars were less congested and judges had more time for each case, an order under CPLR 3212(g) establishing given facts would be more common. As things stand, however, CPLR 3212(g) appears to be little used.

It can be versatile, too. If a defense is formally pleaded as such, for example, a plaintiff who wants to test it can of course move to dismiss it with a motion under CPLR 3211(b). If the defense is not pleaded, but is injected into the parties' papers on a summary judgment application, the defense can be disposed of with a kind of minuscule declaratory judgment under CPLR 3212(g). That happened in E.B. Metal & Rubber Industries, Inc. v. County of Washington,[3] for example, the court "declaring" that the defense of sovereign immunity was not available to the defendant in a certain property damage suit. "Such a declaration is appropriate ... and salvages something of value from an otherwise aborted CPLR 3212 motion", said the court.

§ 287. Res Judicata Effect of Summary Judgment Motion

The denial of a motion for summary judgment establishes nothing except that summary judgment is not warranted at this time.[1] So if it appears at the trial that judgment is warranted as a matter of law for one side or the other, the trial judge, despite the pretrial denial of a motion for summary judgment, may

direct a verdict or grant judgment notwithstanding the verdict.[2]

The grant of summary judgment, on the other hand, does operate as an adjudication on the merits and is entitled to res judicata treatment.[3] The grant is usually based on a review of the overall merits of the case and so it is of course appropriate to give it such treatment. But it must also be recalled that the grant may be more narrowly based. It may be grounded, for example, on one of the objections listed in CPLR 3211(a).[4] When so based, the summary judgment is of course res judicata only of the point decided. Where, for example, D pleads as a defense lack of personal jurisdiction, and a summary judgment for the defendant is granted on that ground, a later action in which jurisdiction is perfected will of course not be dismissible on res judicata grounds.[5]

D. SUMMARY JUDGMENT IN LIEU OF COMPLAINT

Table of Sections

§ 288. Summary Judgment Motion in Lieu of Complaint; CPLR 3213

CPLR 3213 recognizes that some claims have greater presumptive merit than others and should have easier access to the courts than an ordinary plenary action gets. It singles

---

§ 286

1. See Chicago Dressed Beef Corp. v. Gold Medal Packing Corp., 22 A.D.2d 1010, 254 N.Y.S.2d 717 (4th Dep't 1964).

2. See Commentary C3212:36 on McKinney's CPLR 3212.

3. 102 A.D.2d 599, 479 N.Y.S.2d 794 (3d Dep't 1984). The case and the application of CPLR 3212(g) in general are the subject of a lead note in New York State Law Digest No. 298.

§ 287

1. Puro v. Puro, 79 A.D.2d 925, 434 N.Y.S.2d 424 (1st Dep't 1981).

2. Sackman–Gilliland Corp. v. Senator Holding Corp., 43 A.D.2d 948, 351 N.Y.S.2d 733 (2d Dep't 1974).

3. Eidelberg v. Zellermayer, 5 A.D.2d 658, 174 N.Y.S.2d 300 (1st Dep't 1958), aff'd 6 N.Y.2d 815, 188 N.Y.S.2d 204, 159 N.E.2d 691 (1959).

4. See § 283 above.

5. Of course the plaintiff must be wary of the statute of limitations in a situation like this. While a dismissal for want of personal jurisdiction does not lead to res judicata consequences, it can easily lead to a statute of limitations dismissal of a new action if the original statute has expired. There is no time extension under CPLR 205(a) for a dismissal based on personal jurisdiction. See § 52 above.

out these claims and permits them to be brought on by an initial summary judgment motion. Instead of a complaint accompanying the summons, a set of summary judgment motion papers does. Instead of merely having the defendant answer the complaint at any time within a stated period following service, the motion papers pick out a specific return day and require the defendant to appear and argue the case on that day.[1]

The claims to which this expeditious treatment is afforded are those based on "an instrument for the payment of money only" or on a judgment (for money or anything else). No other category of claim is entitled to use this "motion-action" of CPLR 3213.

Because this procedure is more expeditious than the usual action, many a resourceful plaintiff has tried to use it for items that fall rather short of what CPLR 3213 has in mind. This is so, in any event, on the "instrument" side of CPLR 3213. The "instrument" and "judgment" categories are separately treated in the next two sections.

§ 289. Money Instrument as Basis for CPLR 3213 Motion

It is the instrument for the payment of money only that has created a big body of caselaw under CPLR 3213. The plaintiff waves a paper at the court and insists it's an instrument for "the payment of money only", but it often falls short of the mark. In several cases, for example, a separation agreement was used, the plaintiff claiming that its money clauses satisfied as the equivalent of a money-only instrument. The courts have pretty much re-

jected that contention,[1] principally because the various other rights and obligations under separation agreements interplay with the monetary provisions and prevent the agreement from qualifying as a money-only obligation.

The negotiable instrument for the payment of money of course qualifies for CPLR 3213 use. So does a non-negotiable instrument if for money only.[2]

One helpful standard for what qualifies as a proper CPLR 3213 "instrument" case is that offered by Seaman–Andwall Corp. v. Wright Machine Corp.,[3] which says that a case is made out for CPLR 3213 use if two things are shown: (1) the instrument itself and (2) proof of non-payment pursuant to its terms. The instrument doesn't qualify "if outside proof is needed". So stating in Weissman v. Sinorm Deli, Inc.,[4] the Court of Appeals rejected for CPLR 3213 treatment an indemnification commitment included in a stock agreement.

Presumably any paper requiring the payment of money only and qualifying as a piece of "commercial paper" under the Uniform Commercial Code[5] would satisfy for CPLR 3213 use. And if a given paper, although not formally a money "instrument", contains the requisite (and limited) terms, it will be accepted, as a mere letter was in one case.[6]

Some courts have held an unconditional guarantee to be an instrument for the payment of money only,[7] even when it required, dehors the instrument, a determination of costs, expenses, and attorneys' fees,[8] but going that far afield from the instrument itself hardly comports with the simple standard of the *Seaman* and *Weissman* cases.

---

§ 288

1. CPLR 3213 is very much like a special proceeding, see § 547, below, and in fact could have accomplished its result in fewer words merely by authorizing the use of a special proceeding instead of spelling out a procedure of its own.

§ 289

1. See Orenstein v. Orenstein, 59 Misc.2d 565, 299 N.Y.S.2d 648 (App.T., 2d & 11th Dist. 1969), rev'g 58 Misc.2d 377, 295 N.Y.S.2d 116 (N.Y.C.Civ.Ct. 1968); Wagner v. Cornblum, 36 A.D.2d 427, 321 N.Y.S.2d 156 (4th Dep't 1971).

2. Louis Sherry Ice Cream Co. v. Kroggel, 42 Misc.2d 21, 245 N.Y.S.2d 755 (Sup.Ct., N.Y.County, 1963).

3. 31 A.D.2d 136, 295 N.Y.S.2d 752 (1st Dep't 1968), aff'd 29 N.Y.2d 617, 324 N.Y.S.2d 410, 273 N.E.2d 138 (1971).

4. 88 N.Y.2d 437, 646 N.Y.S.2d 308 (1996), treated in the lead note in New York State Law Digest No. 438.

5. See U.C.C. § 3–104.

6. See Baker v. Gundermann, 52 Misc.2d 639, 276 N.Y.S.2d 495 (Sup.Ct., Nassau County, 1966).

7. European American Bank & Trust Co. v. Schirripa, 108 A.D.2d 684, 485 N.Y.S.2d 763 (1st Dep't 1985).

8. See Chase Manhattan Bank, N.A. v. Marcovitz, 56 A.D.2d 763, 392 N.Y.S.2d 435 (1st Dep't 1977).

If the instrument calls for something in addition to the payment of money, it doesn't qualify.[9] Numerous cases have embroiled bench and bar in the question of whether or not a given piece of paper fits the CPLR 3213 requirement.[10] Each such case takes the attention of all away from the merits and concentrates it instead on whether or not the device of CPLR 3213 is fit to pose the merits. This suggests that the plaintiff should not use CPLR 3213 without a paper that unequivocally qualifies. If the plaintiff instead brings an ordinary action and simply waits until the answer is in, she can then make a conventional summary judgment motion under CPLR 3212. It costs a little more time, but not much,[11] and the reward will be that the court will not be sidetracked and the substantive issues smokescreened by a procedural inquiry about whether or not CPLR 3213 has been properly invoked.

§ 290. Judgment as Basis for CPLR 3213 Motion

It is usually easy enough to apply this provision when a judgment is the basis of the action, because, in contrast with an "instrument", which must be for money only, there is no requirement that the judgment be of a particular kind. Any judgment qualifies to invoke CPLR 3213 and allow the action to be commenced with the motion procedure it supplies, but that is of course no guarantee that the court will grant the motion. That depends entirely on whether the judgment qualifies for recognition and adoption.

Sister state judgments and those of the federal and territorial courts and the District of Columbia, since all are entitled to full faith and credit as long as rendered with jurisdiction of subject matter and parties,[1] are of course entitled to recognition and readily qualify for a CPLR 3213 motion.[2] But, ironically, they don't need CPLR 3213: New York gives those judgments the even more expeditious device of Article 54 of the CPLR, which allows a judgment to be converted into the equivalent of a New York judgment through a mere registration procedure.[3] The only such judgment denied summary registration under Article 54 is one taken in the earlier forum either by default for non-appearance or by confession,[4] and only those, therefore, would normally need to invoke CPLR 3213. Quick as it is, CPLR 3213 still sets up an adversary proceeding before converting the judgment into a New York one, in contrast to the summary registration offered by Article 54.

CPLR 3213 is not restricted to money judgments. It has been held that the statute may be used to convert a sister-state matrimonial decree into a New York judgment, thus enabling it to be enforced here.[5] But there is still some debate about how far New York will go in "adopting" a sister-state decree, replete with its periodic payment awards, and about the other procedures to be followed.[6]

CPLR 3213 should also be available to renew a judgment originally rendered by a New York court. Although not frequent—why would a person who already has a New York

---

9. Dann v. Bernstein, 73 A.D.2d 782, 423 N.Y.S.2d 524 (3d Dep't 1979).

10. See the cases collated in Interman Industrial Products, Ltd. v. R.S.M. Electron Power, Inc., 37 N.Y.2d 151, 371 N.Y.S.2d 675, 332 N.E.2d 859 (1975). Interman rejects for CPLR 3213 use a claim based on an implied account stated.

11. See Commentary C3213:4 on McKinney's CPLR 3213.

§ 290

1. U.S.Const., Art IV, § 1; 28 U.S.C.A. § 1738.

2. More extensive discussion of when the full faith and credit clause applies to mandate recognition is reserved for the chapter on res judicata, since the doctrine is essentially one of compulsory interstate res judicata. See § 471 below.

3. See § 435, below, on Article 54, which is New York's adoption of the Uniform Enforcement of Foreign Judgments Act.

4. CPLR 5401.

5. Mittenthal v. Mittenthal, 99 Misc.2d 778, 417 N.Y.S.2d 175 (Sup.Ct., N.Y.County, 1979).

6. See Blackburn v. Blackburn, 113 Misc.2d 619, 449 N.Y.S.2d 827 (Sup.Ct., Delaware County, 1982), adopting a Georgia divorce judgment. The subject of adopting sister-state marital decrees is treated in the lead note in New York State Law Digest No. 237. For a general discussion of the conversion of a sister-state divorce decree in a family court proceeding, see Pearson v. Pearson, 108 A.D.2d 402, 489 N.Y.S.2d 332 (2d Dep't 1985) (majority and dissenting opinions), aff'd 69 N.Y.2d 919, 516 N.Y.S.2d 629, 509 N.E.2d 324 (1987).

judgment need to renew it?—there are, indeed, occasions when renewal is useful and sometimes even indispensable.[7]

It is really the foreign country judgment that can best exploit CPLR 3213—the judgment that is not entitled to full faith and credit under federal law and which therefore depends on New York's willingness to recognize it, an acquiescence loosely known as "comity". Here Article 53 of the CPLR is relevant, having much to say on which judgments must be recognized and which need not be. Article 53 applies only to money judgments,[8] however. Other kinds are governed by caselaw, but as it happens New York decisional law is quite generous in recognizing foreign judgments. This is also a res judicata topic, reserved for more extensive treatment in a later chapter.[9] Suffice it to note here that when the lawyer is seeking to convert a foreign country's judgment into its New York equivalent, so as to make it enforcible in New York, the best tool is CPLR 3213 whether the judgment is for money or something else and whether it is governed by Article 53 or by common law.

§ 291. Procedure Under CPLR 3213

The plaintiff using CPLR 3213 must pick out a return day just as she would on a motion for summary judgment within an action, but the time and paper requirements vary. While an ordinary motion within an action can be brought on with notice of as few as eight days,[1] the minimal notice period when CPLR 3213 is used—since the motion papers accompany a summons and start the action—is 20 or 30 days, depending on the place and method of service. It is based, in other words, on the time the defendant would have in which to appear under CPLR 320(a) when an ordinary action is brought. If service is to be made by personal delivery in New York, for example, the earliest

return day of the motion would be the 20th day after service and the motion papers should pick out a day accordingly.

The plaintiff is also permitted to add up to 10 days to the notice period. The advantage of doing this is that the plaintiff may require the defendant to serve answering papers as many days in advance of the motion day as the plaintiff has added. If P sets the return day on the 27th day after service, for example, P may require D to serve answering papers on P seven days before the return day.[2]

The defendant's failure to serve answering papers within the required time does not authorize an immediate default, however. The plaintiff who wants a default judgment must ask for it on the return day. And the default may of course be excused by the court for good cause shown.[3]

Methods of summons service are the same as in a plenary action prosecuted in the usual form, i.e., they come from CPLR 308 for individuals, CPLR 311(1) for corporations, etc. But since a specific hearing date is set under CPLR 3213, rather than an open-ended requirement to answer within X days, such as applies in an ordinary action, it may be difficult to work out the additional requirements of paragraphs 2 or 4 of CPLR 308 if the substituted service methods of those provisions are used. They require the filing of proof of service and delay the start of the answering time until 10 days after that filing. This suggests that it is wise to use personal delivery under CPLR 308(1) in CPLR 3213 cases. If the other methods must be resorted to, however, it would be reasonable for the court to adjust or even disregard their requirements about filing proof of service and postponing completion of service. Otherwise it may prove impossible to satisfy both CPLR 3213 and the substituted service provisions of CPLR 308 simultaneously.[4]

---

7. See § 434 below.

8. CPLR 5301(b).

9. See § 472 below.

§ 291

1. CPLR 2214(b).

2. See Commentaries C3213:5,6 on McKinney's CPLR 3213.

3. CPLR 3213; see Commentary C3213:14 on McKinney's CPLR 3213.

4. An analogous problem existed at one time with subpoena service under CPLR 2303. The courts made do with a common sense application of the statute and the legislature finally corrected the problem with an amendment in 1982. See Commentary C2303:2, 4, on McKinney's CPLR 2303.

When there are several defendants, and difficulties arise in meeting the return date because summons service on one of them fails, or because one of them contests service, or because of like problems, the court can set an adjourned date or otherwise defer the motion until the jurisdictional problem is resolved. It can order a trial of an issue of fact as to whether X was served, for example, while a merits disposition is held in abeyance as to Y and Z, a new hearing date to be set as to all parties if jurisdiction against X is sustained.[5]

There are obvious similarities between the motion/action of CPLR 3213 and the special proceeding, for which Article 4 of the CPLR supplies the regulatory detail,[6] but they are not identical and the differences should be noted. Both the special proceeding and the CPLR 3213 action come on to be heard like a motion, for example, and that's a similarity, but the special proceeding, like an ordinary motion, can be brought on by an order to show cause,[7] while the CPLR 3213 application can't be,[8] which makes for a significant difference.

In the supreme and county courts, the filing system for commencing actions applies to both actions and special proceedings, but no specific attention was given to how it applies to the CPLR 3213 procedure. The requirement in those courts is that in an action the summons and complaint must be served within 120 days after they're filed, but the period is only 15 days in a special proceeding.[9] As an action, the CPLR 3213 application should enjoy the 120-day period for service rather than the special proceeding's 15 days. Even if it does, however, the CPLR 3213 papers are likely to require service long before the 120th day, since the papers as filed must specify a return day and a properly set return day can't ordinarily be postponed for so long a time after filing.[10]

As a motion, the CPLR 3213 application must also include a Request for Judicial Intervention (RJI),[11] and some adjustments may have to be made at the outset to assure that the return day set in the papers is satisfactory to the judge assigned. Because a judge is not ordinarily assigned until after the initial papers are filed, this can complicate the initial filing steps on a CPLR 3213 application, as it sometimes does with a special proceeding,[12] but if a CPLR 3213 plaintiff gets all the papers ready, files them with an RJI and gets an index number, makes sure that the assigned judge approves the return date, and then serves the papers expeditiously, things should work out at least well enough to avoid any conflict with the 120-day time requirement. If there are any rough edges, the court should consider the plaintiff's dilemma and smooth things over as well as can be.

§ 292. Effect of Denial; Conversion

If CPLR 3213 is rightly used (e.g., the instrument sued on is a proper one), it obviously doesn't guarantee the plaintiff success on the merits. One might say that a claim under CPLR 3213 is presumptively meritorious, but even that may be technically incorrect because nothing in CPLR 3213 alters the burden of proof otherwise belonging to the plaintiff in an action. However that may be, the defendant may refute the claim, and, if she does, summary judgment may be granted for the defendant instead of the plaintiff. If the refutation is not total, but establishes that genuine issues of fact exist which require trial, the court will deny the motion. In doing so, however, it will not dismiss the action; under CPLR 3213, the court will merely convert the action into an ordinary one, the moving papers becoming the equivalent of a complaint and the answering

---

5. See Lemme v. TME Fashion Exchange, Inc., N.Y. Law Journal, October 13, 1981, page 14, col. 5 (Sup.Ct., N.Y. County, per Stecher, J.).

6. Special proceedings are discussed in § 550 below. The CPLR 3213 plaintiff may find it helpful to consult that section.

7. See CPLR 2214(d) (motion), CPLR 403(d) (special proceeding).

8. Bullard v. Bullard Orchards, Inc., 153 Misc.2d 136, 580 N.Y.S.2d 131 (Sup.Ct., Saratoga County, 1992).

9. CPLR 306–b.

10. On setting the return day of motions, see § 247 above.

11. See § 77B above.

12. See § 553 below.

papers an answer.[1] The case is now the equal of an action brought in conventional form in which a summary judgment motion has just been denied. Whether the issues of fact that resulted in the denial are to be preferred for trial would be governed by the same rules that govern summary judgment motions in general.[2]

Even if the plaintiff has mistaken his remedy altogether, and CPLR 3213 is not usable because the plaintiff's claim is not even arguably within the judgment or instrument requirement of 3213, it has been held that the action should still not be dismissed, but simply converted to ordinary form.[3] If, moreover, the case is unsuitable for CPLR 3213 treatment but the defendant does not point this out, she may be held to waive objection to the use of CPLR 3213 and the court can go right on to the merits.[4]

The question of whether a counterclaim should be entertained in CPLR 3213 context, in view of the statute's intention to get the main claim through to judgment summarily, is an interesting one. The courts are generally reticent about allowing a counterclaim to impede a legitimate CPLR 3213 claim, and while a better case can be made for entertaining a counterclaim if it is related to the plaintiff's claim than if it is not,[5] it has been held that even if a counterclaim arises out of the "same general transaction" as the main claim does, its interposition should not be allowed to impede P's ride to summary judgment on the main claim unless the counterclaim also amounts to a "defense" to the main claim.[6]

Other equities must also be considered, such as whether the plaintiff will be able to pay a counterclaim if it is disallowed here but successfully prosecuted to judgment in a separate action.[7] The simple remedy for an unrelated counterclaim, which really should not be allowed to impede a CPLR 3213 claim at all, is a severance.[8]

E.　DEFAULT JUDGMENT

Table of Sections

§ 293.　Taking Default Judgment

In several situations the defendant's conduct (or non-conduct) amounts to a default and entitles the plaintiff to take a default judgment. The most common situation is where the defendant does not respond to the summons within the requisite time. This amounts to what CPLR 3215, the default statute, calls a failure to appear.

Non-appearance is the most frequent default basis, but not the only one. A defendant who has duly appeared can be guilty of a default at a later stage of the action, such as by failing to show up at the trial at the scheduled time. Failure to plead is also a default basis, and can be distinct from a failure to appear. Where P serves only a summons and notice at the outset, for example, D's step is to demand a copy of the complaint. If P then serves the complaint and D fails to answer it, the failure to plead is a default.

These default bases are listed in CPLR 3215(a), which also acknowledges as grounds for a default judgment any other category of dismissal ordered by the court for a "neglect

---

§ 292

1. Fine v. Di Stanti, 79 A.D.2d 673, 433 N.Y.S.2d 873 (2d Dep't 1980).

2. See § 284 above.

3. CPLR 103(c). See Stern v. Chemical Bank, 83 Misc.2d 508, 372 N.Y.S.2d 913 (N.Y.C.Civ.Ct. 1975).

4. P. Ballantine & Sons v. Boston Celtics Basketball Club, 36 A.D.2d 914, 320 N.Y.S.2d 876 (1st Dep't 1971).

5. Fine v. Di Stanti, note 1, above.

6. See Harris v. Miller, 136 A.D.2d 603, 523 N.Y.S.2d 586 (2d Dep't 1988), where the main claim got summary

judgment and the counterclaims were severed for pleading in a formal answer and for litigation in due course. The main claim in Harris was on a note executed by D to P. The counterclaims were for legal services.

7. See Commentaries C3213:17, 18 on McKinney's CPLR 3213.

8. Wildeb Rest., Inc. v. Jolin Restaurant, Inc., 69 Misc.2d 1012, 331 N.Y.S.2d 575 (Dist.Ct., Suffolk County, 1972).

to proceed".[1]

While a "default" is usually associated with an omission by the defendant, the plaintiff can also be guilty of conduct that constitutes a default. The plaintiff defaults, for example, by not showing up at the trial,[2] or by refusing to submit to pretrial disclosure.[3] Whichever side defaults, the other is entitled to apply for a default judgment. Examples to be used in our discussion will assume the defendant has defaulted, the more common situation.

The application for the default may be made to the court or to the clerk, depending on the claim involved. Application to the clerk is the preferable procedure, because it gives the plaintiff a final judgment on papers alone, a ministerial procedure with nothing to try. Application to the court, on the other hand, needs more, and may even require a testimonial hearing.[4] But application may be made to the clerk only when the plaintiff's claim is for "a sum certain or for a sum which can by computation be made certain".[5] That would apply to liquidated contract claims, such as a claim for the delivery of X number of items at the agreed price of Y dollars each, and to a claim on a money instrument. It also applies to an action on a previously rendered money judgment,[6] even if the claim underlying it was not liquidated.

All of the claims involved in the case must satisfy this "sum certain" criterion in order for the clerk to handle the default entry; if any does not, the default application has to be made to the court.[7] As long as all qualify, the fact that there are multiple defendants and not all of them have defaulted is not necessari-

ly a barrier. The clerk is authorized to enter the judgment against the defaulter and at the same time to enter an order severing (and thus continuing) the claim against the others.[8] The clerk's failure to enter such an order can be corrected nunc pro tunc, and it has been held that the nunc pro tunc order may even be sought ex parte.[9]

Anything that prevents mere arithmetic from reducing the claim to a sum certain requires that the application be made to the court. The Court of Appeals has indicated that only the most liquidated and undisputed of claims can be taken care of by the clerk.[10] This of course means that in that most numerous category, the personal injury action, and for that matter almost all torts, the application must go to the court rather than to the clerk. The difference in procedure is that on the application to the court damages have to be inquired into. The court is authorized to conduct that inquiry with an assessment (popularly called an "inquest") with or without a jury, or to give the question to a referee.[11] If the damages, although unliquidated, can be established by paper alone, and do not require oral testimony—one may draw an analogy here to the standards used on a summary judgment motion[12]—the court can make the assessment without an oral hearing.

A defendant who defaults in appearing concedes only liability. New York holds that a default in a money action does not concede the amount of the plaintiff's damages.[13] The defaulting defendant is therefore permitted to appear and give proof at any damages trial or

§ 293

1. A defendant's refusal to submit to pretrial disclosure, for example, can result in a default judgment. CPLR 3126(3).

2. CPLR 3215(a).

3. CPLR 3126 and its penalties for non-disclosure, see note 1, above, also apply to the plaintiff. On defaults by a plaintiff, see Commentary C3215:5 on McKinney's CPLR 3215.

4. CPLR 3215(a), (b).

5. CPLR 3215(a).

6. Serkey v. Gladstein, 40 Misc.2d 962, 244 N.Y.S.2d 461 (Sup.Ct., N.Y.County, 1963).

7. Geer, DuBois & Co. v. O.M. Scott & Sons Co., 25 A.D.2d 423, 266 N.Y.S.2d 580 (1st Dep't 1966).

8. CPLR 3215(a).

9. Citibank Eastern, N.A. v. Minbiole, 50 A.D.2d 1052, 377 N.Y.S.2d 727 (3d Dep't 1975).

10. Reynolds Securities, Inc. v. Underwriters Bank & Trust Co., 44 N.Y.2d 568, 406 N.Y.S.2d 743, 378 N.E.2d 106 (1978).

11. CPLR 3215(b).

12. See § 278 above.

13. McClelland v. Climax Hosiery Mills, 252 N.Y. 347, 169 N.E. 605 (1930).

hearing.[14] The uniform rules have something to say about this, however. They provide that if the defendant doesn't show up for the damages hearing, the plaintiff may put in affidavits to prove damages. And they go further by providing that even if the defendant does show up, the plaintiff may use "written statements of the witnesses, in narrative or question and answer form, signed and sworn to".[15] This appears to be a watering down of the defendant's confrontation and cross-examination rights at a damages trial, manifesting that while the defaulter may have the right to contest damages, the right will not be as broad as had there been no default. Caselaw prior to the Uniform Rules had held the right to contest at a damages trial to include, even for a defaulting defendant, the pretrial tools of a bill of particulars and the disclosure devices.[16]

Perhaps the practical lesson to a defendant who wants to contest only on damages is not to default at all. The defendant might just serve an answer silent as to the liability allegations of the complaint (thereby admitting them), or admitting liability explicitly but only on the condition that full adversary rights are reserved to the defendant in regard to preparing for a damages trial.

When a trial is necessary, whether and under what circumstances a jury is required is unclear. There appears to be broad discretion to direct a reference instead. If the claim is such that it would in due course have been tried by jury had there been no default, one may reasonably conclude that a defaulting defendant has waived it. But one cannot as simply conclude that the defendant's default can deprive the plaintiff of a jury to hear the damages question if the plaintiff otherwise wants one.[17]

The default judgment can't exceed in amount or differ in kind of relief from that demanded in the complaint or notice served with the summons. A judgment directing the return of a chattel, for example, can't be entered if the complaint asked only damages for its retention.[18] Unlike the situation in which the defendant has appeared, where the plaintiff is usually able to amend the complaint to seek more or different relief than originally asked, the defendant who does not appear can be subjected to a judgment only for that of which she was originally notified.

As was indicated earlier in the book, New York is very liberal about vacating default judgments. The showing needed is (1) an excuse for the default and (2) an affidavit assuring the court of the merits of the defaulter's case.[19]

A default judgment is entitled to res judicata (claim preclusion) treatment.[20] It is also to be remembered that a judgment by default is not appealable. The procedure of the defendant is to move to vacate the default judgment, and, if the motion is denied, to appeal the order of denial.

If a settlement is reached in a pending action, it can provide for the entry of judgment in accord with its terms and the clerk can enter the judgment as if there had been a default.[21]

§ 294.   Time for Default Application

A plaintiff entitled to take a default judgment against a defendant, whatever the nature of the defendant's default, must apply for

---

14. Cf. James v. Powell, 19 N.Y.2d 249, 279 N.Y.S.2d 10, 225 N.E.2d 741 (1967).

15. See Uniform Rule 202.46, applicable in the supreme and county courts.

16. See, e.g., Ayala v. Boss, 120 Misc.2d 430, 466 N.Y.S.2d 128 (Sup.Ct., Bronx County, 1983).

17. See Commentary C3215:7 on McKinney's CPLR 3215.

18. Lape v. Lape, 23 A.D.2d 539, 255 N.Y.S.2d 953 (1st Dep't 1965).

19. See § 108, above, on the vacatur of default judgments. Note also, and distinguish, the procedure authorized today for the en masse vacatur of tainted default

judgments through administrative channels, as in the case of an extensive consumer fraud. The procedure, now codified in CPLR 5015(c), is known as "Thompson's Law", for Edward Thompson, the then Administrative Judge of the New York City Civil Court who first used it. See the Commentary on McKinney's CPLR 5015.

20. The default judgment even gets collateral estoppel ("issue preclusion") effect in New York. See § 451 below.

21. CPLR 3215(1). See Commentaries C3215:21, 22, on McKinney's CPLR 3215.

it within one year after the default occurs.[1] Failure to do it within the year results not only in forfeiture of the default judgment against the defendant, but can also bring about the dismissal of the plaintiff's own complaint "as abandoned".[2] The court can dismiss the complaint on its own motion, moreover, without waiting for the defendant's request. So provides CPLR 3215(c), but it does give the court discretion, for "sufficient cause", to excuse the default and allow the entry of judgment after the year has expired.[3]

If the complaint is dismissed and the statute of limitations has now passed, the dismissal is likely to be the end of things for the plaintiff. The dismissal qualifies as a neglect to prosecute, with the result that CPLR 205(a) will not authorize a new six-month period for a fresh action.[4]

Suppose there are multiple defendants and not all of them default. Under the terms of CPLR 3215(c), the plaintiff must seek a default judgment against the defaulters within a year, and yet it may take more than a year to try the case against the nondefaulters. In that situation, the court, on ex parte application, can order that the inquest against the defaulters take place at the same time as, or even after, the trial against the nondefaulters, without regard to the one-year limit of CPLR 3215(c). The plaintiff must apply for such an order within the one-year period.[5]

The one-year requirement posed a dilemma for a while in third-party actions. If defendant D impleads third-party X, it is usually for indemnification of some kind, and D's entitlement to it depends on whether and what P

recovers from D in the main action. D is thus unable to take judgment against X until P has had judgment against D. If X should default on the third-party claim, a requirement that D take a default judgment against X within a year presupposes that the P v. D action will go to judgment within that time, which may not be the case at all. For this reason, it has been held that the one-year period in which D must apply for a default judgment against X does not start to run until the entry of a P v. D judgment in the main action.[6]

If it is the plaintiff who has defaulted, as by failing to proceed to trial when the case is called, a one-year requirement also applies to the defendant's application for a default judgment.[7]

§ 295. Papers on Default Application

The proof needed on an application for a default judgment is governed by CPLR 3215(f), whose requirements are three:

    1. proof of summons service including a complaint or CPLR 305(b) notice;

    2. proof of the claim, including the amount due if it is a money claim; and

    3. proof of the default.

Note with respect to the first requirement that if the affidavit of service does not reveal that either the complaint or notice went with the summons,[1] the clerk will not accept it for filing and neither court nor clerk will entertain a default application. Proof of service usually takes the form of an affidavit by the process server.[2] Its contents are dictated by

---

§ 294

1. CPLR 3215(a), (c).

2. See Herzbrun v. Levine, 23 A.D.2d 744, 259 N.Y.S.2d 237 (1st Dep't 1965).

3. Charles F. Winson Gems, Inc. v. D. Gumbiner, Inc., 85 A.D.2d 69, 448 N.Y.S.2d 471 (1st Dep't), aff'd 57 N.Y.2d 813, 455 N.Y.S.2d 600, 441 N.E.2d 1118 (1982).

4. Shepard v. St. Agnes Hospital, 86 A.D.2d 628, 446 N.Y.S.2d 350 (2d Dep't 1982). See § 52 above.

5. CPLR 3215(d).

6. Multari v. Glalin Arms Corp., 28 A.D.2d 122, 282 N.Y.S.2d 782 (2d Dep't 1967).

7. CPLR 3215(a).

§ 295

1. If service by publication was used, the affidavit should instead show that the published notice satisfies the requirements of CPLR 316(a). In the lower courts, where an "indorsement" pleading may be used, the indorsement is the equal of a complaint for the purpose of a default application under CPLR 3215(e). See §§ 902 and 1402 in each of the New York City Civil, Uniform District, Uniform City, and Uniform Justice court acts, McKinney's Vol. 29A, Parts 2 and 3.

2. When service is made by mail under CPLR 312–a, the acknowledgment returned by the defendant counts as proof of service. See § 76A above.

CPLR 306, which today requires even a physical description of the person served.[3]

The second requirement, proof of the claim itself, is usually made by the plaintiff's own affidavit, buttressed, if need be, by additional affidavits of others having knowledge. The affidavit of the plaintiff's lawyer, unless the lawyer happens to have complete first-hand knowledge of the claim, should not be used to fulfill this requirement. While it has been held that the use of the lawyer's rather than the client's affidavit as proof of merit on a default application does not necessarily make the default judgment void—the defect can be waived by the other side[4]—it is a bad practice that can make trouble.[5] A verified complaint, for example, if it accompanied the summons, may serve as an affidavit of the claim, but not if the verification was made by the attorney.[6]

At one time there was a special rule in a matrimonial action: mere paper proof of the claim did not suffice; the plaintiff, despite the defendant's default, would have to take the stand and testify to the facts of the claim. The requirement wasted time and effort, was unpopular with judges who resented having to preside mindlessly at what was known in some parts of the state as the "uncontested matrimonial part", and was eliminated with an amendment of the applicable statute[7] in 1978. Default judgments in matrimonial actions, as in any other kind, may now be based on paper proof of the claim. Live courtroom testimony is not required. The point is mentioned just to reassure lawyers whose research brings up pre–1978 cases.[8]

Even at an inquest on damages conducted after the defendant has conceded liability by failing to appear, the plaintiff may put in paper proof of damages; live testimony is not indispensable.[9]

The third requirement is proof of the default. Here the affidavit of the plaintiff's lawyer is not just acceptable, but ideal. A literal reading of CPLR 3215(f) suggests that the affidavit of the plaintiff's attorney may be used to establish the defendant's default only when a verified complaint has been served. In fact, it is almost always the attorney's affidavit that proves the defendant's default, whether a verified complaint is used or not. It is upon the plaintiff's attorney that the defendant's notice of appearance, answer, or motion must be served.[10] The failure to serve such, which constitutes the default, is therefore known at first hand by the plaintiff's lawyer rather than by the plaintiff proper—to whom, indeed, it would be mere hearsay.[11]

Hence a trio of affidavits is the ideal composition of a default application: the server's affidavit of service, the plaintiff's affidavit of merits, and the lawyer's affidavit of the default.

The trio may become a quartet if the defendant is a natural person and the action is one for money due under a contract. In that category of action, CPLR 3215(g)(3) requires that a notice—additional to the notice that service of the summons gives—be mailed to the defendant, and it supplies detailed instructions for it. The mailing must be made at least 20 days before the entry of the default judgment, but may be made as early as the time the summons is first served.[12] An affidavit attesting to

---

3. See § 79 above.

4. Freccia v. Carullo, 93 A.D.2d 281, 462 N.Y.S.2d 38 (2d Dep't 1983).

5. See § 108 above.

6. Joosten v. Gale, 129 A.D.2d 531, 514 N.Y.S.2d 729 (1st Dep't 1987).

7. Section 211 of the Domestic Relations Law.

8. On this score the reader should also keep in mind the general relettering of subdivisions that was made in CPLR 3215 in 1992 to make way for a new subdivision (d). Subdivisions (a) through (c) retained their original lettering but original subdivisions (d) through (h) were relettered (e) through (i). Practitioners should be alert to the

relettering, especially when doing something like a WEST-LAW search.

9. See Uniform Rule 202.46, applicable in the supreme and county courts. A similar rule may apply in other courts. See, e.g., UR 208.32, applicable in the N.Y.C. Civil Court.

10. CPLR 2103(b).

11. See Commentary C3215:16 on McKinney's CPLR 3215.

12. Before 1986, when an amendment moved this provision from CPLR 308 to its present niche in CPLR 3215, it had been the understanding in some places that the notice had to be given at some later time.

the mailing must also be included on the default application.

This extra mailing requirement, while applicable in any kind of contract case (not just to a formal or express contract[13]), is apparently not a jurisdictional one. It has been held that a failure to carry it out will not qualify by itself as a ground for vacating a default judgment; that if the defendant would not otherwise be entitled to vacate it—meaning that the judgment is proper in all other respects—she won't be allowed to vacate it solely because this additional notice wasn't given.[14]

If personam jurisdiction is lacking, and the sole basis of jurisdiction is quasi in rem (grounded on the attachment of the defendant's property), the application should also include an affidavit so stating and describing the property levied on and its value.[15] The judgment in that instance is enforcible only against the attached assets and it has been held that the judgment itself should reflect that fact.[16]

§ 296. Notice of Default Application

CPLR 3215(g)(3), as partially noted in the prior section, requires that in certain cases at least 20 days additional notice by mail be given before a default judgment is taken against an individual on a contract claim for money, or against a corporation served under § 306 of the Business Corporations Law. Those categories are clear and specific.

To those specific exceptions must be added the more general notice requirement contained in paragraph 1 of CPLR 3215(g), applicable whether the application is one that may be made to the clerk or one that has to go before the court. It provides that if the defendant has appeared in the action (so that the default consists of something else, such as not pleading after appearing), she must be given at least

five days notice of the default application. And if the year for the taking of the default has gone by, any defendant, whether having appeared or not, is entitled to the five-day notice.

This makes it plain that the plaintiff who applies for the default after the allotted year has expired is additionally penalized by having to give the defendant notice of it, violating the adage about letting sleeping dogs lie.

When the default consists of the defendant's failure to show up when the case is called for trial, the court is authorized to dispense with the notice. This is designed to enable the court, if it wishes, to go forward with an assessment of damages immediately.

When the notice has to be given to a defaulting defendant in a situation in which there are other defendants who have not defaulted, it has been held that a copy of the notice need not be served on the others.[1] But at least one case has said that it does have to be served on the others if it appears that they may bear an indemnification relationship to the defaulting defendant and thus be entitled to defend in his behalf.[2] If there is any doubt on that score, requiring the notice to be served on all parties appears to be the soundest course.

As long as the application for the default judgment is made within the year, notice is dispensed with, even if the assessment itself does not take place within the year.[3] The plaintiff can't control the court's calendars and hence should not be held responsible for judicial delays in getting around to the assessment.

Even a defendant in default for failure to appear, the most fundamental default category, may nonetheless keep apprised of later proceedings. At any time before the damages hearing, the defendant may simply serve on the plaintiff a demand that notice of the hear-

---

13. Vanderveer v. Magedson, 148 Misc.2d 185, 560 N.Y.S.2d 265 (Sup.Ct., Franklin County, 1990).

14. Kirkman/3hree, Inc. v. Priority AMC/Jeep, Inc., 94 A.D.2d 870, 463 N.Y.S.2d 579 (3d Dep't 1983).

15. CPLR 3215(f).

16. Benadon v. Antonio, 10 A.D.2d 40, 197 N.Y.S.2d 1 (1st Dep't 1960).

§ 296

1. Card v. Polito, 55 A.D.2d 123, 389 N.Y.S.2d 696 (4th Dept 1976).

2. Rivera v. Laporte, 120 Misc.2d 733, 466 N.Y.S.2d 606 (Sup.Ct., N.Y.County, 1983).

3. Q.P.I. Restaurants, Ltd. v. Slevin, 93 A.D.2d 767, 461 N.Y.S.2d 334 (1st Dep't 1983).

ing be served on her. A plaintiff so served must give the defendant five days notice of any reference or jury trial of the damages question.[4] This is a meaningful right for the defendant, who is allowed at the assessment to put in proof in mitigation of damages notwithstanding the default, which concedes only liability.[5] A mere demand for a copy of the complaint, not combined with an appearance, does not qualify as a demand that requires notice of subsequent proceedings.[6]

The CPLR rules about default judgments are generally applicable in the lower civil courts as well as in the supreme court.[7]

F. VOLUNTARY DISCONTINUANCE

Table of Sections

§ 297. Voluntary Discontinuance, Methods

Any party asserting a claim may be allowed to discontinue it. That includes not only the plaintiff, but also the defendant with a counterclaim, cross-claim, or third-party claim. Our examples will assume that the plaintiff seeks to discontinue. There are three ways in which it can be done: (1) notice; (2) stipulation; or (3) order.

(1) Discontinuance by notice. At one time a party could discontinue a claim at any time without any permission from court or adversary.[1] A party still has that power, but only at the very outset of the action. Under CPLR

3217(a)(1), the plaintiff can discontinue the claim merely by serving a notice of discontinuance on the defendant and filing the notice, with proof of service, with the clerk, but must do so within 20 days after serving the complaint or in any event before the defendant has answered. The service of an answer cuts off the plaintiff's right to discontinue by mere notice even if the 20–day period from complaint service is still open.[2] The purpose of this restriction is to prevent the plaintiff from discontinuing at whim after the defendant has troubled to answer, and to require either the defendant's permission (discontinuance by stipulation) or court leave (discontinuance by order). For that reason, too, a plaintiff whose original complaint has been answered should not be allowed, merely by amending the complaint, to get a new chance to discontinue by notice.

(2) Discontinuance by stipulation. Discontinuance is permitted on stipulation by all parties. According to the CPLR,[3] the stipulation can be filed with the court at any time before the case has been submitted to the fact-trier, but under the more stringent demands of the uniform rules, which implement the Individual Assignment System, the requirement is that the stipulation be filed within 20 days of its execution and that the court be notified "immediately".[4]

If any party is an infant or incapacitated person (incompetent or conservatee), the stipulation method is not available; a court order is needed. Nor may a class action be discontinued by mere stipulation.[5]

---

4. CPLR 3215(g)(2). This provision applies only to default applications that have to be made to the court; notice is not necessary when the claim is for a sum certain and goes before the clerk under CPLR 3215(a).

5. See § 293, above, and Commentary C3215:19 on McKinney's CPLR 3215.

6. Simmons v. Mercer, 146 A.D.2d 833, 536 N.Y.S.2d 862 (3d Dep't 1989).

7. See § 1402 in the New York City Civil, Uniform District, Uniform City, and Uniform Justice court acts, McKinney's Volume 29A, Parts 2 and 3.

§ 297

1. See 19th Jud.Council Rep. (1953) 197, 207.

2. Discontinuance when there are several adverse parties is discussed in Commentary C3217:5 on McKinney's CPLR 3217.

3. CPLR 3217(a)(2).

4. See UR 202.28, applicable in the supreme and county courts. A similar rule, UR 210.16, applies in city courts outside New York City. In courts in which the Individual Assignment System (IAS) is not in operation, the notifications are made to the "calendar clerk". See UR 208.16 (N.Y.C. Civil Court), 212.16 (district courts).

5. CPLR 908.

Old caselaw held that once an action was discontinued by stipulation, a later endeavor to vacate the stipulation and revive the case would require a plenary action. That was the holding in Yonkers Fur Dressing Co. v. Royal Ins. Co.,[6] where the discontinuance was part of a stipulation of settlement. *Yonkers* was criticized for requiring a new action when a mere motion could do the job with so much less trouble,[7] and in Teitelbaum Holdings, Ltd. v. Gold[8] the Court of Appeals joined the criticism and allowed a mere motion to enforce a settlement stipulation, which in that case called for money payments by D to P and authorized the offset of a certain debt owed by P to D. The court cited the criticism of *Yonkers*, the expeditiousness of the motion procedure, and, by analogy, the availability of mere motions to undo action-terminating judgments in other contexts, all of which suggests that *Gold* overrules *Yonkers*.

(3) Discontinuance by order. If the plaintiff's time to vacate by notice has expired and if the defendant will not stipulate to discontinue, the plaintiff must turn to the third and last method: a court order. The court can allow discontinuance by order any time before submission of the case to the fact trier. After that submission, the only method of discontinuance recognized by the CPLR is a combination of stipulation and order.[9]

The courts are reasonably liberal about ordering a discontinuance. It has been held that the plaintiff should be allowed to discontinue the action at any time "unless substantial rights have accrued or his adversary's rights would be prejudiced thereby".[10] If the court detects any illegitimate motive in the plaintiff's wish to discontinue, however, it will deny the motion. Where, for example, the plaintiff realized at the trial that things were going

badly and that a loss was imminent, his discontinuance motion was properly regarded by the court as merely an effort "to make another try", and was denied.[11]

If the plaintiff has tactically mistaken his forum, however, a discontinuance has been allowed. A leading case is Schimansky v. Nelson,[12] where P brought a wrongful death action in a state court in a rural county. After the case had reached an advanced stage of preparation, P realized that federal jurisdiction was available—and in a New York City federal court, where damages are reputedly awarded in greater sums. Conditioning its order on P's payment to D of costs and expenses to date, the court allowed P to discontinue so as to start afresh in federal court.

Conditioning the order and imposing such terms as it deems just are expressly authorized by CPLR 3217(b). A money sanction beyond just costs and expenses can be imposed, for example,[13] or the discontinuance can be granted on the condition that a given party be permitted to use, in a different action, the record that had been accumulated in the discontinued one.[14]

§ 298. Effect of Discontinuance

CPLR 3217(c) governs the res judicata effect of a discontinuance. The general rule is that unless the discontinuance itself states otherwise, whether in the notice, stipulation, or order, it is not res judicata so as to bar a new action.

An order of discontinuance can dictate what its res judicata effect is to be. The court can specify, for example, that no later action may be brought on the claim,[1] a result that invokes the res judicata doctrine. So does the shorthand phrase "with prejudice". Whatever

---

6. 247 N.Y. 435, 160 N.E. 778 (1928).

7. See, e.g., Commentary C3217:10 on McKinney's CPLR 3217.

8. 48 N.Y.2d 51, 421 N.Y.S.2d 556, 396 N.E.2d 1029 (1979).

9. CPLR 3217(b).

10. Louis R. Shapiro, Inc. v. Milspemes Corp., 20 A.D.2d 857, 248 N.Y.S.2d 85, 86 (1st Dep't 1964).

11. Getz v. Harry Silverstein, Inc., 205 Misc. 431, 432, 128 N.Y.S.2d 436, 438 (N.Y. City Court, 1954).

12. 50 A.D.2d 634, 374 N.Y.S.2d 771 (3d Dep't 1975).

13. Brockman v. Turin, 130 A.D.2d 616, 515 N.Y.S.2d 545 (2d Dep't 1987).

14. See 1st Rep.Leg.Doc. (1957) No. 6b, p. 104.

§ 298

1. First Rep.Leg.Doc. (1957) No. 6b, p. 104.

phrase is used should make clear the court's intent.

If any action on the same claim was previously discontinued, by any method, in any federal or state court including a New York court, the discontinuance of the second action by the notice method operates as res judicata and bars relitigation.[2] Discontinuance of the second action by the stipulation or order method, however, is not such an automatic bar; the matter in that instance is left to the terms of the stipulation or order.

Giving res judicata effect to a discontinuance-by-notice of a second action is designed to avoid harassment of the defendant. It has therefore been held that when the purpose of the second discontinuance, albeit by notice, involves no harassment, the res judicata rule will not operate and another action will be allowed. Where, for example, P discontinued the second action by notice (after discontinuance of a prior action) because D had moved to dismiss the second action for lack of jurisdiction, P's discontinuance in that instance was simply a concession of D's jurisdictional point and a third action was held permissible.[3]

Keep in mind that all of these conclusions about a later action being permissible concern only the res judicata doctrine, not the statute of limitations. They assume that the original statute of limitations is still alive so that a later action will not meet a time barrier. Here we must refer yet again to the potent CPLR 205(a), which gives a plaintiff six months, from a prior non-merits termination of an action, in which to sue anew notwithstanding the interim expiration of the original period.[4] The lawyer about to discontinue must always remember that a voluntary discontinuance, by any method at all, is an exception to CPLR 205(a) and does not get the six months. A discontinuing plaintiff planning to start over must always make sure either that the original statute of limitations is still alive, or that the plaintiff has in hand an agreement by the

defendant not to interpose the statute of limitations defense in the new action.

G. CONFESSION OF JUDGMENT

Table of Sections

§ 299. Confession of Judgment, Generally

A confession of judgment dispenses with an adversary proceeding and gives the creditor the fruits of a successful one by permitting the creditor merely to file the confessed judgment. It serves as a security device by enabling a creditor to obtain judgment without an action even before a debt is due, although of course it may not be enforced until due. If the debt is already due, the confession of judgment is a concession of liability and still has the advantage of avoiding an action. A confessed judgment is valid only if it conforms to the strict requirements of CPLR 3218. It is a device virtually limited to money claims.

Confession of judgment is available for "money due or to become due" or "to secure the plaintiff against a contingent liability in behalf of the defendant".[1] The latter phrase enables it to be used in a situation where it is not certain that the defendant will ever owe the plaintiff any money. A simple example is where P agrees to act as surety or guarantor for a debt incurred by D to some third person. If D pays the debt, P will never have to, but P is nonetheless allowed to enter a confessed judgment against D to cover P's potential liability in the interim, enforcement of course suspended until P is actually called on to pay all or part of the debt to the third person.

---

2. CPLR 3217(c).

3. Headley v. Noto, 45 Misc.2d 284, 256 N.Y.S.2d 750 (Sup.Ct., Kings County), aff'd 24 A.D.2d 493, 261 N.Y.S.2d 846 (2d Dep't 1965).

4. See § 52 above.

§ 299

1. CPLR 3218(a).

The confession device is used primarily if not exclusively in contract situations. It is not precluded in tort cases,[2] but has little to offer there: a confession is usually sought by the creditor before payment of the debt is due and torts are not known to be negotiated in advance. Its readiest use is in a loan or other credit transaction, but here the attorney must take note of CPLR 3201, which precludes the use of a confessed judgment in transactions of $1500 or less involving installment purchases of personal (as opposed to business) goods. As will be seen,[3] the affidavit of the debtor is a key paper in the confession procedure and in these under-$1500 installment purchases the affidavit is unacceptable if executed prior to default. (In confession situations generally a pre-default affidavit is permissible.)

When joint debtors are involved, not all need confess judgment. Any of them can. The creditor may take confessed judgment against the one who does, retaining the right to bring an ordinary action against those who don't.[4]

§ 300. Affidavit for Confession of Judgment

A confessed judgment may be entered only if accompanied by an affidavit executed by the defendant—the confessor—in conformity with the requirements of CPLR 3218(a). The affidavit must state the sum in which entry is to be permitted and the defendant's residence county (where the entry takes place). If the defendant is a nonresident, the affidavit should specify a county in which entry is authorized.[1]

The most important mission of the affidavit is to state the facts of the transaction on which the confession is based. If it is for a contingent

liability, as in the surety or guarantee example given in the prior section, the affidavit must state the facts constituting the potential liability and manifest that the confessed judgment does not exceed it.[2]

In the more common situation, where the confessed judgment is for money, whether now due or to become due, the affidavit must concisely state "the facts out of which the debt arose" and must show that the debt is a just one.[3] It is here that the careless creditor most often has trouble. The caselaw requires a more exhaustive factual picture than the "concise" statement the statute seems to call for. Even the Advisory Committee contemplated that if the facts stated in the affidavit sufficed to state a cause of action in a pleading, they would satisfy this confession requirement,[4] but the committee had in mind older cases, decided when pleadings were more detailed, and did not anticipate how successful the CPLR would be in liberalizing pleadings.

So little does it take to satisfy the pleading requirements today that the creditor who merely applies the pleading standard to the confession affidavit is likely to miss the mark. County National Bank v. Vogt,[5] in which the court itself apparently overlooked the irony, illustrates. The confession in *Vogt* was for a debt, and the affidavit's statement of the transaction was in perfect conformity not only with the general pleading requirement but also with Official Form 9.[6] The court nonetheless held the affidavit inadequate.

The lesson is clear: the confession affidavit should contain genuine detail, enough to put the confessing debtor in peril of perjury if the statement is false.[7] An affidavit saying only

---

2. Cf. Granville v. Gratzer, 281 A.D. 514, 120 N.Y.S.2d 797 (1st Dep't 1953).

3. See § 300 below.

4. CPLR 3218(d).

§ 300

1. CPLR 3218(a)(1).

2. CPLR 3218(a)(3).

3. CPLR 3218(a)(2).

4. See 1st Rep.Leg.Doc. (1957) No. 6b, p. 108.

5. 28 A.D.2d 793, 280 N.Y.S.2d 1016 (3d Dep't 1967), aff'd 21 N.Y.2d 800, 288 N.Y.S.2d 631, 235 N.E.2d 772 (1968).

6. Official Form 9 authorizes as a pleading in a case for money lent the simple statement that "defendant owes plaintiff $20,000 for money lent by plaintiff to defendant on June 1, 1965". The affidavit in Vogt stated that it was "for a debt justly due to the plaintiff arising from the following facts: Money loaned by Plaintiff to Defendant and not repaid", and was found inadequate (and not because the date was missing). 28 A.D.2d at 793, 280 N.Y.S.2d at 1018.

7. Princeton Bank and Trust Co. v. Berley, 57 A.D.2d 348, 394 N.Y.S.2d 714 (2d Dep't 1977).

that liability was for "legal services rendered" was held inadequate by that standard, and a law firm's judgment against its client therefore vacated at the behest of a competing creditor.[8] The simple conclusory standards that govern pleadings must not be relied on.

The purpose of the affidavit is to protect third persons, not the judgment debtor.[9] An inadequate affidavit therefore can't be availed of by the debtor herself. The affidavit's major aim is to enable other and presumably junior creditors to investigate the claim and determine its validity,[10] because if the claim is not legitimate, and junior can defeat it, junior becomes senior. The statement of facts in the affidavit should be drawn with that in mind.

The affidavit may be amended in the discretion of the court.[11] Discretion apparently turns on the nature of the affidavit's deficiency. Innocent and merely technical omissions are correctible nunc pro tunc,[12] but basic defects in the statement of underlying facts, especially when the rights of other creditors have become involved, are not likely to be correctible by amendment.[13]

The New York confession procedure must be distinguished from the old "cognovit" practice, which no longer obtains in New York but does elsewhere. A cognovit instrument at its worst purports to allow a creditor to designate any attorney to act as the debtor's attorney so as to confess judgment in the debtor's behalf, and allows the judgment to be entered without notice anywhere the creditor chooses. New York held in Atlas Credit Corp. v. Ezrine[14] that such an instrument is so offensive to due process that even a judgment predicated on it in a sister state lacks jurisdiction and is therefore not entitled to full faith and credit, but the

U.S. Supreme Court later held in D.H. Overmyer Co. v. Frick Co.[15] that a cognovit instrument is not per se unconstitutional. It said that the right to notice and hearing guaranteed by due process is waivable and that if a debtor, with knowledge and appreciation of the consequences, signs such an instrument, he waives his rights and will be bound by any judgment rendered on the instrument.

The court in *Overmyer* stressed that the debtor before it, a corporation, was represented by counsel and sophisticated in the preservation of its rights, and hence could be bound by its cognovit commitment. It left the door open to a contrary result, invalidating the cognovit procedure, if the debtor should be shown to have unequal bargaining power or if the contract should be one of adhesion. After that, a New York court bent on refusing recognition to a cognovit-based judgment of a sister state would have to find some such factor present.

Acknowledging this in its later decision in Fiore v. Oakwood Plaza Shopping Ctr., Inc.,[16] the Court of Appeals reviewed its *Atlas* holding in light of the *Overmyer* case, found the defendants before it to have had a sufficiently strong position to intelligently waive notice and hearing, and, so finding, upheld the waiver, overruling *Atlas* and requiring recognition of a cognovit-based sister-state judgment (again, coincidentally, from Pennsylvania). *Fiore* was no adhesion contract, involving a $1 million project for the sale of land for a shopping mall and debtors represented by counsel.

The cognovit practice, although a precursor of confession of judgment, must be distinguished from it.[17] New York's confession rules, both in regard to the affidavit, which must be made by the debtor proper rather than by

8. Baehre v. Rochester Dental Prosthetics, Inc., 112 Misc.2d 270, 446 N.Y.S.2d 901 (Sup.Ct., Erie County, 1982).

9. Giryluk v. Giryluk, 30 A.D.2d 22, 289 N.Y.S.2d 458 (1st Dep't 1968), aff'd 23 N.Y.2d 894, 298 N.Y.S.2d 91, 245 N.E.2d 818 (1969).

10. Baehre v. Rochester Dental Prosthetics, Inc., note 8, above.

11. County National Bank v. Vogt, note 5, above.

12. Princeton Bank and Trust Co. v. Berley, note 7, above.

13. See Commentary C3218:10 on McKinney's CPLR 3218.

14. 25 N.Y.2d 219, 303 N.Y.S.2d 382, 250 N.E.2d 474 (1969).

15. 405 U.S. 174, 92 S.Ct. 775, 31 L.Ed.2d 124 (1972).

16. 78 N.Y.2d 572, 578 N.Y.S.2d 115, 585 N.E.2d 364 (1991).

17. The history of cognovit instruments and the evolution of the more moderate New York confession procedure is traced in the Atlas case, 25 N.Y.2d at 225–6, 303 N.Y.S.2d at 387–8, 250 N.E.2d at 478–9.

some fictional agent, and in regard to the place of entry, which is restricted, are tight and should satisfy constitutional demands. But even here the door must be left open to the invalidation of a confession contained in a particularly one-sided (in bargaining power) adhesion contract, or one that runs afoul of the Uniform Commercial Code's "unconscionability" standards.[18] All confessions of judgment in New York, whatever their source, "are always closely scrutinized ... and in judging them a liberal attitude should be assumed in favor of the judgment debtor".[19]

§ 301. Filing, Enforcement, and Effect of Confessed Judgment

The time within which the affidavit may be filed and the confessed judgment entered is three years from the execution of the affidavit. The filing and entry take place in the county of the defendant's residence, and when the defendant is a nonresident, in the county specified in the affidavit. The clerk enters judgment in the supreme court[1] and it may then be enforced as if duly rendered by that court.[2]

There may be no enforcement until something is due, however. Although the confessed judgment may be filed before a default occurs, no execution or other enforcement step may be taken until that time. Executions may periodically issue for such sums as fall due, but each must specify the amount now due so that the sheriff will not levy for more.[3] Should execution be sought for too much, the levy can be vacated on motion.[4]

Since the clerk must docket the judgment when he enters it,[5] the judgment becomes a lien on the defendant's real property in the county as of that time even though enforcement is not yet permissible.[6]

A confessed judgment in New York is given both res judicata and collateral estoppel effect.[7]

§ 302. Vacating Confessed Judgment

If the judgment has been entered in violation of the terms of the affidavit, it may be vacated. But as far as attacking the affidavit itself is concerned, especially in its statement of the underlying transaction, it must be remembered that the affidavit is for the protection of third persons, not the debtor.[1] A defect in the terms of the affidavit may therefore be exploited by another creditor—even though the underlying transaction is valid—but not by the debtor. If the transaction is good, then as far as the debtor is concerned the affidavit is irrelevant. But the debtor may of course attack the confessed judgment if the underlying transaction is bad, as where it was induced by fraud.

Whenever made by the right person on the right ground, the attack takes the form of an application to vacate the judgment. Whether this requires a plenary action or can be brought on by mere motion also turns on who is seeking the vacatur and the ground for it. If the vacatur is sought by another creditor of the debtor, a mere motion will do.[2] But if the debtor seeks it, she can use the simple motion

---

18. See UCC § 2–302.

19. Rae v. Kestenberg, 23 A.D.2d 565, 566, 256 N.Y.S.2d 737, 739 (2d Dep't), aff'd 16 N.Y.2d 1023, 265 N.Y.S.2d 904, 213 N.E.2d 315 (1965).

§ 301

1. If the amount sought is within the monetary jurisdiction of a lower court, the confessed judgment may be entered there if the affidavit so provides. See § 1403 in each of the New York City Civil, Uniform District, Uniform City, and Uniform Justice court acts, McKinney's Vol.29A, Parts 2 and 3.

2. CPLR 3218(b).

3. CPLR 3218(c).

4. CPLR 5230, 5240.

5. For the difference between entry and docketing, see §§ 418 and 421, below.

6. CPLR 5203. This result was apparently intended, see 1st Rep.Leg.Doc. (1957) No. 6(b) p. 107, but see Commentary C3218:15 on McKinney's CPLR 3218. The judgment becomes a realty lien only when the judgment is entered and docketed in the supreme or county court. For how to make a judgment of a lower court, including a confessed judgment, a lien on real property, see §§ 421–422 below.

7. See § 451 below.

§ 302

1. Mall Commercial Corp. v. Chrisa Restaurant, Inc., 85 Misc.2d 613, 381 N.Y.S.2d 391 (App.T., 1st Dep't, 1976).

2. County National Bank v. Vogt, 28 A.D.2d 793, 280 N.Y.S.2d 1016 (3d Dep't 1967), aff'd 21 N.Y.2d 800, 288 N.Y.S.2d 631, 235 N.E.2d 772 (1968).

procedure only if the judgment has been entered in violation of the affidavit's terms, such as where it states a time that has not arrived or a contingency that has not occurred. If the entry is valid on its face and the debtor's objection is based on some extrinsic factor, like fraud or misrepresentation, it has been held that a plenary action is required to do the vacating; that a mere motion won't do.[3]

H.   TENDERS AND OFFERS

Table of Sections

§ 303.   Tenders and Offers; CPLR 3219–3221

The devices of tender and offer, never to be confused with the tender offers that preoccupy corporate practice and sometimes the federal penitentiaries, make up the trio of CPLR 3219, 3220, and 3221. They have in common that each enables a defendant (or any party against whom a claim is asserted) to make some kind of gesture to the plaintiff in advance of trial that concedes something in the hope of securing some incidental advantage in return. The plaintiff can accept or refuse. A refusal is at the risk of some additional penalty if the thing tendered is ultimately adjudged to have been adequate.

CPLR 3219, entitled "Tender", enables a defendant against whom a contract claim is asserted to deposit in court a sum the defendant deems sufficient to satisfy the claim, thereby requiring the plaintiff to accept the sum in full settlement, or else. The or else is that if the plaintiff rejects the tender and gets no higher sum at the trial, the plaintiff forfeits interest and costs as of the time of the tender. Here the defendant concedes liability but disputes damages.

Under CPLR 3220, entitled "Offer to liquidate damages conditionally", it is mainly liability that the defendant disputes, although

she may dispute damages as well. This offer, like the tender of CPLR 3219, is available only in contract cases, but here the defendant offers to pay a specified sum only if the plaintiff establishes liability at the trial. If the plaintiff accepts, and then wins on the liability issue at trial, the amount offered is the amount he gets; if the plaintiff rejects the offer, and then at the trial gets no greater damages than the defendant offered, the plaintiff must pay the expenses incurred by the defendant in trying damages.

The last member of the trio, CPLR 3221, is not limited to contract cases. It is usable in all but matrimonial actions. It is entitled "Offer to Compromise" and enables a defendant to offer the plaintiff judgment for a specific sum or for specified property. The plaintiff's acceptance results in judgment and closes the case. If the plaintiff rejects the offer and then does no better at the trial, the plaintiff loses costs from the time of the offer and must pay the defendant's costs as of that time.

None of the tenders or offers of CPLR 3219, 3220, or 3221 may be made known to the jury and each of the cited provisions prescribes in detail the procedures to be followed, including time requirements. A chart comparing and contrasting the three provisions was prepared for the McKinney's Commentaries and may be found there.[1]

I.   ACTION ON SUBMITTED FACTS

Table of Sections

§ 304.   Action on Submitted Facts

One of the most useful but unfortunately underused devices in practice today is the action on submitted facts supplied by CPLR 3222. Here the adversaries agree on the facts

---

3. See Scheckter v. Ryan, 161 A.D.2d 344, 555 N.Y.S.2d 99 (1st Dep't 1990). It can be argued that a mere motion should be adequate in this situation, too. See CPLR 5015(a)(3), and § 429 below.

§ 303

1. The chart, prepared by Professor Paul S. Graziano, appears with Commentary C3221:3 on McKinney's CPLR 3221.

and disagree only on their legal implication. They draw up a paper called a "submission of controversy" in which they fully state all the facts relevant to their dispute, acknowledge it before a notary just as they would a deed, and file it with the court. The court applies the law to the submitted facts and renders judgment accordingly. There is no summons, pleading, bill of particulars, disclosure, or delay. Whenever an attorney believes there is agreement with the other side on the facts, she should contact her opposite number and try to work up a submission. Since it will result in a substantial saving for both sides, even the opposing lawyer—the would-be defendant's lawyer—owes it to the client to consider the use of this device.

It can be used in any kind of dispute except a matrimonial action, from which it has been excluded as a possible back door to a consent divorce. All that is needed is agreement on the facts and a mutual willingness to put them into a submission.

The whole controversy must be submitted. It has been held that the court will not take just a piece of it, such as a defense that is part of a pending conventional action.[1]

The CPLR 3222 submission is sometimes confused with the declaratory judgment. It should not be. While the declaratory judgment action can also be used as the litigation vehicle for a variety of disputes, it is ordinarily prosecuted in conventional adversary form—with summons, pleadings, disclosure, trial, etc.— and it can pose issues of fact just like any other action. Its main distinction from other actions is that it seeks declaratory rather than coercive relief. If the parties can agree on the facts, declaratory relief can of course be sought

on a CPLR 3222 submission, and often is. Declaratory judgment is treated later.[2]

The submission should be a direct statement of facts. It should narrate what the facts are rather than recite that X would testify to this and Y would testify to that.[3] It must contain a statement to the effect that "the controversy is real and ... the submission is made in good faith".[4] It may not, in other words, be used to get an advisory opinion or otherwise involve the court in anything short of an actual controversy. Nor will it be entertained if one not a party to it has an apparent interest in the outcome.[5]

The submission is filed with the clerk of the court specified in the agreement, which of course must be a court having jurisdiction of the subject matter. If it is the supreme court, the submission must also specify the county. A special advantage here is that if it is a supreme court submission (it usually is), the parties may stipulate to have it go to the appellate division in first instance.[6] If they do, the submission eliminates one step in the litigation process, for which reason CPLR 3222 submissions more often than not do specify the appellate division.

The provisional remedies of attachment and injunction are unavailable in an action on submitted facts,[7] as are the disclosure devices and other pretrial procedures.[8]

§ 305. Disposition of Submission

The controversy in an action on submitted facts must be determined on the submission.[1] There is to be no live testimony nor even affidavits or other argumentative proof. It is permissible, however, to append a legal instrument (a contract, deed, will, mortgage, etc.) if

§ 304

1. See Braun v. C.E.P.C. Distributors, Inc., 80 A.D.2d 505, 435 N.Y.S.2d 289 (1st Dep't 1981).

2. See § 436 et seq., below.

3. Ciunci v. Wella Corp., 26 A.D.2d 109, 271 N.Y.S.2d 317 (1st Dep't 1966).

4. CPLR 3222(a).

5. See Justino v. Fassi, 15 A.D.2d 676, 224 N.Y.S.2d 173 (2d Dep't 1962).

6. CPLR 3222(b)(3). As an alternative, the stipulation can instead choose a specific judge or referee, subject to that person's consent.

7. CPLR 3222(b)(1); see Commentary C3222:6 on McKinney's CPLR 3222.

8. See Commentary C3222:7 on McKinney's CPLR 3222.

§ 305

1. CPLR 3222(b)(2).

its terms are not disputed and only its legal implications are at issue.

At one time the factual statement had to be so complete that the court was not even required to draw inferences from the facts stated. In one case, for example, a safebox user found money on the floor of a booth at a bank. The controversy concerned whether the user or the bank was entitled to the money. The court dismissed the submission as inadequate because the submission did not state whether the place was a public place or whether a customer or a stranger dropped the money.[2] A fact trier, the court noted, could draw inferences to answer such questions, but the court on a submission could not. The result was unfortunate, and no longer obtains. The court is now explicitly authorized to "find facts by inference from the facts stipulated".[3]

The submission should state what judgment each party is looking for. The disposition will take the form of a judgment, just as if the case had been tried to a conclusion in due course. If the submission is before the appellate division, the court can if need be order that the judgment be entered in the supreme court of a designated county, which would enable the judgment to enjoy the usual rules about lien value and enforcement.[4]

If the submission is found by the court to be inadequate to support a judgment, the court can dismiss it or call for an additional statement.[5] If additional facts are needed and the parties can't agree on them, an additional submission will of course not help and an ordinary plenary action will be needed to resolve the controversy.

2. Cohen v. Manufacturers Safe Dep. Co., 297 N.Y. 266, 78 N.E.2d 604 (1948).

3. CPLR 3222(b)(4).

4. See Commentary C3222:10 on McKinney's CPLR 3222.

5. CPLR 3222(b)(5).

Chapter Twelve

PROVISIONAL REMEDIES

Analysis

A. INTRODUCTORY

Table of Sections

Sec.
306. Provisional Remedies, Generally.
307. Provisional Remedies; Constitutional Requirements.

§ 306. Provisional Remedies, Generally

CPLR 6001 lists the four official provisional remedies,[1] each of which is then given its own article for the law applicable to it. The four are attachment (Article 62), injunction (Article 63), receivership (Article 64), and notice of pendency (Article 65). The notice of pendency is more commonly known as "lis pendens". To these four may be added a few others which, while not actually "provisional", are provisional-like and are traditionally treated as part of the family. They are the order to seize a chattel in a replevin action, procedure for which is in Article 71 of the CPLR, and the order of sequestration in a matrimonial action, supplied by §§ 233 and 243 of the Domestic Relations Law.

The four provisional remedies are "provisional" in the sense that they afford the plaintiff some kind of security or protection while the action is pending, but they operate only as interim devices which, at least theoretically, do not effect any permanent divestiture against the defendant. They may come close, however, and in any event they do inflict deprivations, even if only "provisional". This engendered a series of constitutional determinations that reduced the freedom with which the remedies used to be granted. The constitutional limitations are discussed as an independent topic in the next section and are the subject of brief reminders as they become relevant.

Broadly viewed, and subject to elaboration and detail as each of the remedies is separately treated in ensuing sections, the provisional remedies operate this way:

Attachment seizes the defendant's property and prevents the defendant from using it during the pendency of a money action unless the defendant discharges the attachment with a bond, whereupon the bond substitutes for the attached property and the plaintiff gets just as much security that way.

---

§ 306

1. There were five when the CPLR started out in 1963. The fifth was the order of civil arrest, which was inherited from prior law and which occupied Article 61. It was rarely used and was abolished in 1979 with the repeal of Article 61. The five sections devoted to the civil arrest in the first edition of this book, §§ 308 through 312, are omitted from later editions.

Injunction operates to require the defendant to maintain a specified status quo during the pendency of the action, usually with an instruction not to do a given act (a negative rather than positive direction).

A receiver takes possession of designated property of the defendant and protects it during the pendency of the action, preventing the defendant from selling it, squandering it, or abusing it.

The lis pendens, which is merely a paper the plaintiff files in a county clerk's office, puts the world on notice that the plaintiff has a claim to a described parcel of the defendant's real property and that anyone who buys it or lends money against it or otherwise relies on the defendant's unfettered ownership of it does so subject to whatever the pending action decides to be the plaintiff's right.

The order to seize a chattel, a provisional-like remedy, is available only in a replevin action. It is not officially "provisional" because it can result in the plaintiff's actually getting the chattel before the action goes to judgment. We mention it here—it is taken up more fully later[2]—only to show why the seizure order does not officially qualify as "provisional".

The same may be said of sequestration, a device used to seize property of a spouse or parent in a matrimonial action, thus enabling support and other money obligations to be paid out of the sequestered assets. Since the property seized may actually be expended—sold and reduced to money and the money used to support the family during the action—the sequestration device, too, falls beyond the merely "provisional" frame.[3]

Each of the remedies is available only in certain categories of actions or under designated conditions. For each of the four provisional remedies, the opening section of its CPLR article states those categories and conditions. All the remedies require a court order except the lis pendens, which the plaintiff merely files. The reader should note whether the motion for the order must be on notice, or may be ex parte. Some are available ex parte, and for these the constitution is on close watch.

For two significant purposes the order to seize a chattel is added to the four provisional remedies to make a total of five. One of these has already been met in the chapter on the statute of limitations: the granting of any one of the five remedies is deemed to commence the action for limitations' purposes, provided that the summons is served within 30 days (60 days for attachment) afterwards.[4]

CPLR 6001 provides that the five are also a package for a second purpose: that of requiring the plaintiff to elect from among the remedies in the event the action should qualify for more than one of them.[5] To enable the court to determine whether to require an election, the plaintiff must state, on every motion for a provisional remedy or for an order to seize a chattel, whether any of the other remedies has been sought or secured in the same action.[6] Ordinarily, only ex parte motions have to attest to such facts.[7] With the provisional remedies even motions on notice must.

The provisional remedies are usually sought by the plaintiff against the defendant, but CPLR 6001 also makes them available to a defendant for use against the plaintiff on a counterclaim or against a co-defendant on a cross-claim.

On some of the provisional remedies the plaintiff must furnish a bond whose sureties undertake to pay any damages the defendant suffers if the remedy should prove unwarranted. These will be met in the study of the remedies individually. It should be noted at the outset, however, that even if a given reme-

---

2. See §§ 337–342 below.

3. Sequestration is discussed in § 106, above. It also performs a jurisdictional function, enabling the local assets of the spouse or parent to be seized to make good on support awards even without personal jurisdiction. It is this jurisdictional use that is stressed in § 106. But sequestration is available even when personal jurisdiction exists. Under § 243 of the Domestic Relations Law, for example, it can be used to satisfy a support order in a pending matrimonial action. The procedure, which is the same whether jurisdictional or enforcement use is being made of sequestration, is also discussed in § 106.

4. CPLR 203(b)(3), (4). See § 46 above.

5. See, e.g., Todd–Buick, Inc. v. Smith, 118 Misc. 102, 192 N.Y.S. 459 (Sup.Ct., Essex County), aff'd 202 A.D. 774, 194 N.Y.S. 985 (3d Dep't 1922).

6. CPLR 6001.

7. CPLR 2217(b).

dy has no bonding requirement, the plaintiff may face a personal liability to the defendant if he misuses one of the remedies. It has been held, for example, that the misuse of a lis pendens can give rise to an abuse of process claim.[8]

Because the provisional remedies are drastic—suspending or reducing the defendant's property rights before a final adjudication of the merits—they are subject to rules of strict construction[9] and are therefore an exception to the CPLR's general rule of liberal construction.

All four of the provisional remedies have a security function. Attachment can have a jurisdictional function as well: it is the device used in New York to secure quasi in rem jurisdiction against the defendant in a money action.[10] Sequestration can serve a similar function in a matrimonial action.[11] The seizure of a chattel affords a rem basis on which to adjudicate a replevin claim even without personal jurisdiction of the defendant. Those three devices, then—attachment, sequestration, and seizure of chattel—should also be remembered for their jurisdictional utility.

All of the provisional remedies, along with the seizure of a chattel, are available in the supreme and county courts. The chattel seizure is available in all of the lower courts, too—the New York City Civil Court and the district, city, town, and village courts. Attachment and lis pendens are available in appropriate actions in the civil, district, and city courts, but use of the injunction and receivership is restricted.[12]

§ 307. Provisional Remedies; Constitutional Requirements

The fact that some of the provisional remedies were (and to some degree still are) available by ex parte order before the defendant has been given any hearing whatever subjected them to extensive constitutional (due process) attack. Until 1971, in fact, the seizure of a chattel provided for by Article 71 of New York's CPLR did not even require a court order. The plaintiff's lawyer just drew and delivered to the sheriff a requisition along with a bond and affidavit, and the sheriff, without any court direction, was thereupon required to seize the designated chattel from the defendant, even breaking down a door if necessary to get at it.[1] A constitutional tightening up from the U.S. Supreme Court was not unexpected. It began at the tail end of the 1960s and produced some rudimentary criteria regulating the provisional remedies.

The case that started the constitutional ball rolling was Sniadach v. Family Finance Corp.[2] As is common with cases that break new ground, the facts were one-sided and the statute involved in the case particularly obnoxious. It was a Wisconsin law that allowed a creditor, before suit, to garnish 50% of the debtor's wages, to be put aside to the credit of a potential judgment, the debtor being thus divested of half her income without a hearing. The Supreme Court held that a prejudgment garnishment of that kind "may as a practical matter drive a wage-earning family to the wall"[3] and struck the statute down. It is no answer, held the court, that the wages will be returned to the debtor if she prevails on the merits: due process requires the hearing before, not after, the seizure. Perhaps such a summary procedure might be deemed to meet the requirements of due process in "extraordinary situations", the court suggested, but none such were present in Sniadach.

---

8. Parr Meadows Racing Ass'n v. White, 76 A.D.2d 858, 428 N.Y.S.2d 509 (2d Dep't 1980). See § 336 below.

9. See, e.g., Penoyar v. Kelsey, 150 N.Y. 77, 80, 44 N.E. 788, 789 (1896); Northern Blvd. & 80th Street Corp. v. Siegel, 16 A.D.2d 523, 229 N.Y.S.2d 827 (1st Dep't 1962). Both cases deal with attachment, but the discretionary nature of all the provisional remedies that require a court order—all do except the lis pendens—bring all of them under the same strict construction banner. See Sartwell v. Field, 68 N.Y. 341 (1876).

10. See § 104 above.

11. See § 106 above.

12. See § 209 in each of the lower court acts (McKinney's Vol. 29A, Parts 2 and 3).

§ 307

1. CPLR 7102 and 7110 prior to the 1971 amendments.

2. 395 U.S. 337, 89 S.Ct. 1820, 23 L.Ed.2d 349 (1969).

3. Id. at 341–2, 89 S.Ct. at 1822–3.

New York's counterpart law on wage seizure is called an "income execution". Found in CPLR 5231, it could probably pass muster under *Sniadach* for two reasons. The first is that it operates on only 10%, not 50%, of the debtor's wages, a gap in degree that might be great enough to make a constitutional difference. The second and probably more important reason is that it is available only after judgment, which means that the debtor has already had a hearing on the merits and lost. Before the CPLR, New York law did allow the 10% post-judgment execution to be used for pre-judgment attachment as well,[4] and there is statutory authority that could be read as continuing the practice,[5] but in fact it is no longer so used.[6]

Sniadach therefore had little impact on New York law. The same could not be said of Fuentes v. Shevin,[7] however, which the U.S. Supreme Court handed down in 1972. *Fuentes* upset the summary replevin writs authorized by the law of two other states. It would have done the same to the New York procedure, which at the time allowed a mere "requisition" by the plaintiff's lawyer to activate the sheriff's seizure, but New York had anticipated as much and had already amended its statute to eliminate the objectionable procedure.[8] New York did this in response to an earlier (1970) decision by a three-judge federal district court which had expressly overturned the New York replevin procedure.[9] The New York answer was a cautious one. Recognizing that specific constitutional limitations on replevin procedures were only in the process of being formulated, and might remain unclear for a while, New York abandoned the requisition procedure and substituted in its place a motion-and-order procedure to be carried out "to conform to . . . due process".[10]

The major requirement of *Fuentes* is that a hearing precede any seizure of the defendant's property. The case involved statutes of Pennsylvania and Florida that authorized seizure without a preliminary hearing. Household goods were involved, but the court declared that the kind of property involved doesn't matter. It said that the constitution is satisfied as long as the defendant has an opportunity to be heard in advance of the seizure, and that a duly notified defendant can forfeit the opportunity merely by failing to appear at the hearing. But giving the defendant an opportunity to be heard only after the seizure does not satisfy due process, said the court, except in special instances under narrowly drawn statutes (of which the *Fuentes* two were not examples).

One of the exceptions recognized by the court in a footnote[11] is where the seizure of property is needed to serve as a jurisdictional basis.[12] That exception proved important with attachment, the device New York uses to secure quasi in rem jurisdiction of a nondomiciliary through seizure of his local assets.[13] The other exception *Fuentes* acknowledges as permitting ex parte seizure is where a "public

---

4. Morris Plan Industrial Bank v. Gunning, 295 N.Y. 324, 67 N.E.2d 510 (1946).

5. See CPLR 6202.

6. The New York Court of Appeals sidestepped the question in Glassman v. Hyder, 23 N.Y.2d 354, 296 N.Y.S.2d 783, 244 N.E.2d 259 (1968). See § 323 below. Given that the New York Court of Appeals today finds more protective force in the state constitution's due process clause than the federal clause has been given (see the discussion of the Svendsen case at the point of note 27, below), the allowance of a pre-judgment wage attachment would not likely be approved.

7. 407 U.S. 67, 92 S.Ct. 1983, 32 L.Ed.2d 556 (1972).

8. The statutes amended are CPLR 7102, 7103, 7104, and 7110. The year of the amendments was 1971.

9. Laprease v. Raymours Furniture Co., 315 F.Supp. 716 (N.D.N.Y.1970).

10. CPLR 7102(d)(1), (c)(5). Further and more specific amendment of Article 71 of the CPLR was made in 1978. The current constitutional status of New York's law of chattel seizure is discussed in § 338, below.

11. Footnote 23 at page 91 of 407 U.S., page 1999 of 92 S.Ct., page 576 of 32 L.Ed.2d.

12. The court cited for this proposition Ownbey v. Morgan, 256 U.S. 94, 41 S.Ct. 433, 65 L.Ed. 837 (1921), which sustained a state's rather one-sided attachment statute. We may infer that the court was now not especially enthusiastic about Ownbey, but that it wanted to leave the door open to ex parte seizures for at least some jurisdictional uses. It had second thoughts about that in 1977 in the Shaffer case. See § 104 above.

13. For discussion of the general constitutionality of New York's attachment remedy, using the present treatment as background, see § 315, below.

interest" is involved.[14]

A creditor's or seller's hope of exacting a waiver of these due process rights was dashed in *Fuentes* when the court indicated that a waiver in an adhesion contract, where it would most likely be found, would not be effective.

The court acknowledged that its *Fuentes* holding was going to create inconvenience and increase the expense of chattel seizure (and like procedures), but, it said, due process is a higher consideration to which these other factors would just have to defer.

Fuentes was a catalyst as well as a landmark. In New York, it got the legislature to further review and update the provisional remedy statutes. It also occasioned the New York Court of Appeals' interpretation of the state constitution's due process clause, which was then found to go even farther than its federal counterpart. It is helpful to chart these two post-*Fuentes* paths separately, New York's first and the federal, to some degree academic in New York because of New York's own doings, afterwards.

New York Developments

In 1973, on the basis of the *Fuentes* decision, the New York Court of Appeals in Blye v. Globe–Wernicke Realty Co.[15] voided certain procedures under the New York statute giving an innkeeper a lien on a guest's property.[16] The statute allowed the innkeeper by a mere notice to sell the guest's property to cover an unpaid bill. This was held to constitute state action because it amounted to the enforcement of a lien, a traditional state function.

Then in 1978, in reliance on *Blye*, the court declared unconstitutional the enforcement procedures of the garage owner's lien,[17] again for the reason that they did not offer an advance hearing. This the court did in Sharrock v. Dell Buick–Cadillac, Inc.[18]

By this time the Court of Appeals, in applying the state constitution's due process clause, had gone ahead of the restrictions the U.S. Supreme Court had laid down in interpreting the federal clause. At issue in *Sharrock* was the constitutionality of provisions in the New York Lien Law authorizing the ex parte sale of a chattel to implement a lien, in the *Sharrock* case a garage owner's lien. While concluding that the lien itself was valid, the majority held that an opportunity to be heard must be afforded the car owner before the car is sold to make good the unpaid bill. The requirement comes not from the federal constitution, noted the Court of Appeals in *Sharrock*, because the U.S. Supreme Court had found no such requirement in the federal due process clause in an analogous situation,[19] but from the state constitution, where the absence from the due process clause of language explicitly requiring state action facilitates a more "flexible" approach to what will or will not constitute "state action" sufficient to invoke due process protections.

Using this more flexible standard, the *Sharrock* panel found the Lien Law's relevant provisions, §§ 200, 201, 202, and 204, to constitute state action and held them unconstitutional insofar as they purported to authorize a sale of the chattel without affording the owner a preliminary hearing. A number of liens other than the garage owner's lien are also governed by the cited provisions, and these others were also affected by the decision. Among these others are the liens of the artisan, jeweler, veterinarian, and trucker.

The legislature in 1980 produced a package of amendments[20] to meet the *Sharrock* objections. The heart of the package was the addition of Lien Law § 201–a, which authorizes the owner of the goods to commence a special proceeding against the lienor within 10 days

---

14. Cited for this proposition is Coffin Bros. & Co. v. Bennett, 277 U.S. 29, 48 S.Ct. 422, 72 L.Ed. 768 (1928), which involved a bank failure. According to footnote 23 in Fuentes, it is only "a most basic and important public interest" that justifies the ex parte use of a seizure device.

15. 33 N.Y.2d 15, 347 N.Y.S.2d 170, 300 N.E.2d 710 (1973).

16. Lien Law § 181.

17. Lien Law §§ 200, 201, 202, 204.

18. 45 N.Y.2d 152, 408 N.Y.S.2d 39, 379 N.E.2d 1169 (1978). The case is the subject of the lead note in New York State Law Digest No. 225.

19. See the discussion of the Flagg Brothers case, note 26, below.

20. L.1980, c.715.

after being served with a notice of sale. Although it requires the owner of the goods to take the initiative of bringing the proceeding, it does set up a pre-sale hearing and it imposes on the lienor the burden of notifying the owner about the right to bring the proceeding. The proceeding may be brought in any court of appropriate monetary jurisdiction.[21]

The innkeeper's lien voided by the Court of Appeals in the *Blye* case was cited by the majority in *Sharrock*, but the dissent rejected the analogy, noting that the property seized by an innkeeper for application to an unpaid hotel bill has no direct relationship to the bill, while in the case of the garage owner the lien is asserted against the very property bettered by the repair being sued for. The dissent also noted that the innkeeper's lien involves a seizure of the property while with the garage owner the property is already in the owner's possession.

There appears at the end of the majority opinion in *Sharrock* a footnote[22] in which the Court of Appeals appears to invite the lawyer for such as a garage owner/lienor to arrange things so that the ex parte sale can go forward, just as the Lien Law contemplates it. The lienor can do this by "securing the owner's knowing waiver of his opportunity for a hearing when possession is initially transferred". This probably means that something like a big, bold-faced or red-lettered waiver, prominent on the face of the repair authorization and perhaps additionally called to the customer's attention orally or by an obvious notice posted on the repair shop wall, will permit an ex parte sale to go forward under the Lien Law provisions without a court hearing if the bill is not paid.

The sale procedures called for to implement the garage owner's and like liens, especially as

they existed before the 1980 Lien Law amendments, should be contrasted with the steps used with a mechanic's lien. With the latter, all that is contemplated ex parte is the filing of a paper to note of public record the claim of the mechanic; subsequent steps are necessary—and these on notice—to realize on the lien out of the liened property. This was found to be a distinction with a constitutional difference, and it accounts for the sustaining of the mechanic's lien procedures in Carl A. Morse, Inc. (Diesel Const. Div.) v. Rentar Industrial Devel. Corp.[23]

Morse held that although the filing of the lien diminishes the economic value of the real property, it does not bar its sale or encumbrance and therefore does not deprive the defendant of any significant property interest. The court said that the requirement of a hearing in advance of the filing of the lien would destroy its utility for those who have expended labor or material on the premises.

This stresses the distinction between provisional and provisional-like remedies that involve the mere filing of a paper, and those that involve the seizure of property. The only one of the New York provisional remedies effectuated through a mere filing of a paper is the notice of pendency ("lis pendens") of CPLR Article 65.[24] It puts the world on notice of the plaintiff's potential rights in designated realty of the defendant. It doesn't bar a sale or encumbrance of the realty, but it of course makes those things more difficult. The *Morse* opinion draws an analogy between the mechanic's lien and a lis pendens, thereby suggesting that the lis pendens provisions of Article 65 of the CPLR are constitutionally safe.

Contrasting the self-help provisions of the Uniform Commercial Code—provisions that

---

21. This means that the lower courts can do the job, and it would seem to make it clear that nothing of the formal nature of a "foreclosure" proceeding is needed. (The word "foreclosure" was used at a few points in the Sharrock opinion but not in context to suggest the need of the formal judicial steps of a foreclosure action.) The amendments and the procedures they contemplate are treated in the lead note in New York State Law Digest No. 251.

22. Footnote 7.

23. 56 A.D.2d 30, 391 N.Y.S.2d 425 (2d Dep't 1977). The case was affirmed by the New York Court of Appeals on the appellate division opinion. 43 N.Y.2d 952, 404 N.Y.S.2d 343, 375 N.E.2d 409 (1978). An appeal to the U.S. Supreme Court, sub nom. Rentar Industrial Development Corp. v. Carl A. Morse, Inc., 439 U.S. 804, 99 S.Ct. 59, 58 L.Ed.2d 96 (1978), was then dismissed for want of a substantial federal question.

24. The lis pendens is taken up in § 334, et seq., below.

permit a lienor to sell the liened goods without court leave—manifest the more expansive view of due process taken by the New York Court of Appeals than by the U.S. Supreme Court. The self-help provisions applicable to the Code's warehouser's lien,[25] for example, were sustained by the Supreme Court in Flagg Bros., Inc. v. Brooks,[26] the court holding that they did not amount to state action and therefore did not offend the federal constitution. But the New York Court of Appeals went the other way in Svendsen v. Smith's Moving and Trucking Co.,[27] holding that they do offend the state constitution. *Sharrock* governed, held the court, and while the curative 1980 Lien Law amendments (treated above) addressed the garage owner's lien, they were not applicable to the UCC's warehouser's lien, which therefore remained vulnerable to constitutional attack. This led to amendments of the New York UCC.[28]

That's about where things stand today on the constitutional front, at least in New York. Since it is generally permissible for a state to impose higher standards under its due process clause than the U.S. Supreme Court does under the federal due process clause, the broader range given the New York provision may make academic in New York some of the Supreme Court cases subsequent to *Fuentes*, the catalyst that really started New York's attack along the broad front of the provisional and provisional-like remedies. But just to round out the picture, a bird's eye view of the U.S. Supreme Court's major entries subsequent to *Fuentes*, most of them the product of the 1970s—the era of the revision of the provisional remedies—is pertinent.

Federal Developments

The first of the major post-*Fuentes* cases was Mitchell v. W.T. Grant Co.,[29] in 1974. To the dissent of four justices and to the outright

chagrin of one of them (Justice Stewart), a bare majority in *Mitchell* sustained the Louisiana ex parte replevin statute. *Sniadach* was distinguished because it involved only a money claim underlain by no specific lien on any particular property, whereas in *Mitchell* the plaintiff was after goods on which the plaintiff had a lien. That was one distinction. *Fuentes* was differentiated because the statutes involved there did not require the court to issue the process, while in *Mitchell* the court had to do the issuing—although it was allowed to do so without notice, resulting in the seizure before a hearing. The initial participation of a judge was therefore distinction number two. A third was that the statute in *Mitchell* provided for a prompt hearing after seizure, albeit on the defendant's application. Justice Stewart, who authored the *Fuentes* opinion, could not in his dissent abide these distinctions and insisted that the court was disregarding stare decisis and overruling *Fuentes*.[30] Justice Powell, concurring with the majority, was also of the view that *Fuentes* had been overruled.[31] The others in the majority purported only to distinguish it.

So things stood until about half a year later when the Supreme Court decided North Georgia Finishing, Inc. v. Di–Chem, Inc.[32] With that case, the pendulum seemed to swing back to the debtor, this time to the relief of Justice Stewart, who was moved in concurrence to paraphrase Mark Twain and observe that the rumors (from *Mitchell*) of *Fuentes'* death had been greatly exaggerated.[33]

North Georgia involved, and upset, another garnishment statute, this time used against the bank account of a substantial corporate debtor instead of a poor one, which is the more frequent case. The court again declared that the kind of property involved is not a key consideration. It then cited the following fac-

---

25. UCC § 7–210.

26. 436 U.S. 149, 98 S.Ct. 1729, 56 L.Ed.2d 185 (1978).

27. 54 N.Y.2d 865, 444 N.Y.S.2d 904, 429 N.E.2d 411 (1981).

28. UCC § 7–210 was amended in 1982 to provide notice requirements and § 7–211 was added to supply a special proceeding to test the lien.

29. 416 U.S. 600, 94 S.Ct. 1895, 40 L.Ed.2d 406.

30. Id. at 634–5, 94 S.Ct. at 1913–14, 40 L.Ed.2d at 429–30.

31. Id. at 623, 94 S.Ct. at 1908, 40 L.Ed.2d at 423.

32. 419 U.S. 601, 95 S.Ct. 719, 42 L.Ed.2d 751 (1975).

33. Id. at 608, 95 S.Ct. at 723, 42 L.Ed.2d at 758.

tors as distinguishing *Mitchell*, and, in the eyes of some, reviving *Fuentes*:

   1. the affidavit in *North Georgia* (which supported the application) did not have to be made on knowledge; in *Mitchell* it did;

   2. the *North Georgia* affidavit could depose in conclusory terms; in *Mitchell* it had to set out underlying facts;

   3. the *North Georgia* writ was made by the clerk, no judge participating; in *Mitchell* a judge made the order;

   4. in *North Georgia* there was no provision for an early hearing and only a bond from the defendant could release the property, the bond being held insufficient recourse to substitute for a pre-seizure hearing; in *Mitchell* the court found a requirement for a prompt hearing, albeit post-seizure and albeit on defendant's own motion.[34]

Presumably, if a given provisional remedy is found to satisfy each of the four items listed (which the *North Georgia* statute did not), it would get by.

***

Constitutional issues in provisional remedy context are briefly reviewed later, in the treatment of the order of attachment[35] and the order to seize a chattel.[36]

B. ARREST

Table of Sections

[NOTE: There are no §§ 308 through 312. They concerned the provisional remedy of the order of civil arrest, which was abolished in 1979 with the repeal of Article 61 of the CPLR.]

C. ATTACHMENT

Table of Sections

34. Id. at 607, 95 S.Ct. at 722–3, 42 L.Ed.2d at 757–8.

35. See § 315 below.

36. See § 338 below.

§ 313. Attachment, Generally

An order of attachment is a device whereby a plaintiff effects a seizure of a defendant's property, the sheriff taking constructive and sometimes actual hold of it under the terms of the order. The device in New York practice is supplied by Article 62 of the CPLR. It operates on only the property of the defendant, not on his person.

The order of attachment always serves a security purpose, since the property attached is held by the sheriff, actually or constructively, to apply to the plaintiff's judgment in the action if the plaintiff should win. But it can also serve a jurisdictional purpose. It is the device New York uses to implement the "quasi in rem" category of jurisdiction. Today, of course, that category of jurisdiction is much curtailed, the result of the U.S. Supreme Court decision in Shaffer v. Heitner.[1] The subject is discussed in the chapter on jurisdiction, which listed the surviving instances in which quasi in rem jurisdiction may still be allowed.[2] If one of those cases is at hand, so that quasi in rem jurisdiction is operative, the attachment is the tool for its exploitation: if the defendant is not amenable to personal jurisdiction but has property of any kind in New York, the plaintiff can with an order of attachment confiscate the

§ 313

1. 433 U.S. 186, 97 S.Ct. 2569, 53 L.Ed.2d 683 (1977).

2. See § 104 above.

property, thereby guaranteeing that a judgment in the action will be good at least to the extent of the property attached.

As will be seen, the seizure under an attachment is more often constructive than actual, but just as real in either case because it executes its main mission—that of depriving the defendant of the free use of the property, including the ability to sell or encumber it. It also constitutes a kind of lien on the property, giving the plaintiff first crack at it for his judgment if he wins on the merits.

The "garnishee" plays a major role in the attachment process, so it is well to introduce the garnishee at the outset. A garnishee is any person (which of course includes a corporation) who owes a debt to the defendant or who has in its possession or custody any property in which the defendant has an interest.[3] The garnishee is a key figure when personal rather than real property is being attached, which is most often the case, because a levy against personal property is carried out by service of the order of attachment on the garnishee (while a levy against real property is effected by a mere filing).[4]

§ 314. Grounds for Attachment

There are two requirements to make out a case for an order of attachment. Both are stated in CPLR 6201. First, the plaintiff must be seeking a money judgment from the defendant. Second, the plaintiff must satisfy one of the five numbered paragraphs of CPLR 6201.

The plaintiff need not be seeking only a money judgment. Under prior law that was the case but today other claims, seeking something besides money or otherwise posing an inadequate basis for attachment, may be joined as long as the plaintiff seeks a money judgment among other things and satisfies one of the five numbered requirements.[1] The matrimo-

nial action is excepted; attachment is unavailable there but isn't missed because the sequestration remedy[2] does an equivalent job in the matrimonial category.[3]

The list of five items is for the most part self-explanatory. In addition to the money demand the plaintiff must show that:

1. the defendant is a nondomiciliary residing without the state, or is a foreign corporation not qualified to do business in the state; or

2. the defendant resides or is domiciled in the state but cannot be personally served despite diligent efforts to do so; or

3. the defendant, with intent to defraud creditors or frustrate the enforcement of a judgment that might be rendered in the plaintiff's favor, has assigned, disposed of, encumbered, or secreted property, or removed it from the state, or is about to do any of those acts; or

4. the action is by a crime victim suing the perpetrator for damages caused by the crime; or

5. the cause of action is based on a judgment, decree or order of a court of the United States or of any other court which is entitled to full faith and credit in this state, or on a judgment which qualifies for recognition under the provisions of article 53.

The easiest ground to satisfy, and statistically the most often resorted to in the past, is paragraph 1. If the defendant is an individual, the needed showing under paragraph 1 is that she is neither a domiciliary nor a resident of the state. The defendant's having either a domicile or a residence in New York, even though the other may be elsewhere (in the relatively infrequent instance when an individual's domicile and residence are not the same), makes paragraph 1 inapplicable.[4] The theory is

---

3. CPLR 105, 6202.

4. CPLR 6214–6216. The mechanics of the levy are detailed in § 320 below.

§ 314

1. See Bradford v. Eden, 47 Misc.2d 482, 262 N.Y.S.2d 788 (App.T., 1st Dep't, 1965).

2. For discussion of sequestration, see § 106 above.

3. See Dom.Rel.L. §§ 233, 243.

4. See Zenatello v. Pons, 235 A.D. 221, 256 N.Y.S. 763 (1st Dep't 1932).

that either domicile or residence in New York assures a way to get personal jurisdiction of the defendant and obviates resort to the substitute of quasi in rem jurisdiction, for which paragraph 1 of CPLR 6201 was primarily designed.[5]

When the defendant is a domestic corporation, or a foreign corporation duly qualified to do business in New York, paragraph 1 does not apply. (Personal jurisdiction is available and quasi in rem jurisdiction is not needed.) But it does apply to authorize attachment against an unqualified foreign corporation. There is presently a conflict about whether such a corporation, by getting itself qualified after the attachment has been granted and levied, is entitled to have it vacated. The Second Circuit says it is.[6] The First Department disagrees and holds that it is not; that the attachment should be retained in that situation to serve its security function.[7]

With the ground listed in paragraph 3 of CPLR 6201, it is the security rather than the jurisdictional aspect of the attachment device that is being exploited. With paragraph 3, which authorizes attachment if it can be shown that the defendant is finagling with his property with intent to defraud creditors, allegations raising a mere "suspicion" of fraudulent intent have been held insufficient. "It must appear that such fraudulent intent really existed in the defendant's mind. Furthermore, the mere removal or assignment or other disposition of property is not grounds for attachment".[8]

With paragraph 5, which allows the attachment to aid the conversion into a New York judgment of a judgment already rendered elsewhere, it is apparently both functions of an attachment—jurisdiction and security—that are served. If the judgment debtor has moved all of her assets to New York, for example, but remains beyond New York's personal jurisdiction, there would be at hand one of the cases in which the *Shaffer* case apparently continues to permit the exercise of quasi in rem jurisdiction.[9]

The lawyer should note that before 1977 there were eight grounds listed in CPLR 6201 for attachment, among them showings that the defendant was about to leave the state to defraud creditors,[10] was guilty of fraud in incurring a contractual liability,[11] or converted public funds (peculation),[12] or that the action was for conversion or fraud.[13] Those four categories were abolished by the 1977 legislation[14] that produced the present CPLR 6201, treated at the beginning of this section. These superseded provisions are mentioned only because older cases, bound to crop up during research, may refer to them and it is helpful to be aware of what happened to them.

§ 315. Attachment; Status of Constitutionality

Since the attachment procedure usually begins with an ex parte motion, as will be seen in detail, it has gone through some constitutional testing. In 1974, a three-judge federal district court[1] in Sugar v. Curtis Circulation Co. held certain parts of the New York attachment

---

5. With quasi in rem jurisdiction its main mission, paragraph 1 has a reduced function today as a result of the U.S. Supreme Court's curtailment of this category of jurisdiction in Shaffer v. Heitner, 433 U.S. 186, 97 S.Ct. 2569, 53 L.Ed.2d 683 (1977). See § 104, above, for treatment of the Shaffer case.

6. Brastex Corp. v. Allen Int'l, Inc., 702 F.2d 326 (1983).

7. Elton Leather Corp. v. First General Resources Co., 138 A.D.2d 132, 529 N.Y.S.2d 769 (1988).

8. See Computer Strategies, Inc. v. Commodore Business Machines, Inc., 105 A.D.2d 167, 483 N.Y.S.2d 716 (2d Dep't 1984).

9. See § 104 above. Paragraph 3 of CPLR 6201 might also lend itself to quasi in rem jurisdictional use. See note 24 in § 104.

10. Former paragraph 3 of CPLR 6201.

11. Former paragraph 5 of CPLR 6201.

12. Former paragraph 6 of CPLR 6201.

13. Former paragraph 8 of CPLR 6201.

14. L.1977, c. 860. For further background of the 1977 legislation, see the 1977 Judicial Conference Report to the Legislature, p. 13, and the background study by Professor Donnelly in 21st Jud.Conf.Rep. (1976) 452 et seq.

§ 315

1. For a description of this court, see § 483, note 2, below.

statutes, as they existed prior to 1977, unconstitutional,[2] but its judgment was vacated by the U.S. Supreme Court under the name Carey v. Sugar and the case was remanded to await a definitive construction of the relevant statutes by the New York courts.[3] These matters were briefly alluded to earlier, in the discussion of the constitutionality of the provisional remedies in general,[4] but it will help here to be more specific about attachment.

During this period of constitutional testing, the Judicial Conference's CPLR Committee assigned the attachment article for study.[5] From this came legislation in 1977,[6] responding to virtually all of the constitutional objections raised by the three-judge district court in Sugar. The constitutional objections having been thus addressed by statute, a judicial test of the original provisions was avoided. The main accomplishments of the 1977 legislation can be highlighted here. The rest of them, and each procedure summarized now, will be elaborated in later sections.

The 1977 amendments reduced the attachment grounds of CPLR 6201 from eight to four (now five) paragraphs—those that were found consistent with the purposes of an attachment on the one hand and with the requirements of the constitution on the other.

Subdivision (b) was added to CPLR 6211. It provides that when the attachment order is initially issued ex parte, as it usually is, the plaintiff must, within a specified number of days after the attachment is levied, make a motion on notice to "confirm" the attachment. The motion is usually brought on by order to show cause so as to enable the court to determine how the motion papers should be served. The procedure affords the defendant a prompt opportunity to refute the plaintiff's showing and vacate the attachment, thus protecting her property interest. Before 1977, a "confir-

mation" was not required as a follow-up to an ex parte attachment.

CPLR 6210 was added. It seeks to encourage the plaintiff to apply for the attachment order by a motion on notice in first instance instead of using the ex parte application and follow-up confirmation motion. It does this by authorizing the issuance of a temporary restraining order prohibiting the garnishee's transfer of assets pending further proceedings. If the CPLR 6210 restraint is sought, it is sought by order to show cause or the equivalent, with the restraining order rather than a seizure of the property being the only relief granted ex parte.

CPLR 6212(a) was amended to require the plaintiff to show not only that he has a cause of action against the defendant, but "that it is probable that the plaintiff will succeed on the merits", a showing that was often exacted of the plaintiff as a matter of practice under prior law.

As far as constitutionality is concerned, the attainment-in-chief of the 1977 legislation was the addition of subdivision (b) to CPLR 6223, unequivocally imposing on the plaintiff, at any hearing to vacate, modify, or confirm the attachment, "the burden of establishing the grounds for the attachment, the need for continuing the levy and the probability that he will succeed on the merits."[7] The absence of such a requirement was the major objection of the three-judge district court in the Sugar case. It was not at all clear that the burden of proof would lie with the defendant under New York caselaw,[8] but the 1977 legislation makes the point academic and places the burden of proof squarely on the plaintiff.

A further constitutional safeguard is included in CPLR 6211(b). It permits the court, on granting an attachment ex parte, to prohibit the sheriff from taking actual custody of the

---

2.   383 F.Supp. 643 (S.D.N.Y.1974).

3.   425 U.S. 73, 96 S.Ct. 1208, 47 L.Ed.2d 587 (1976).

4.   See § 307 above. The reader might find it helpful to review those general constitutional considerations at this point.

5.   See 21st Jud.Conf.Rep. (1976) at 452 et seq., containing the study by Professor Samuel J.M. Donnelly of the Syracuse University College of Law.

6.   See the 1977 Judicial Conference Report to the Legislature, p. 13.

7.   CPLR 6211(b), the confirmation provision, adopts the burden of proof provision of CPLR 6223(b).

8.   See, e.g., Regnell v. Page, 82 Misc.2d 506, 369 N.Y.S.2d 936 (Sup.Ct., N.Y. County, 1975), rev'd on other grounds 54 A.D.2d 540, 387 N.Y.S.2d 253 (1st Dep't 1976).

property without further court direction. This was not a major accomplishment; as will be seen, the attachment usually involves only a constructive rather than an actual seizure anyway.[9]

Another stated objection of the three-judge district court was that the only ground New York would entertain on a motion by the defendant to vacate the attachment was a showing that the attachment was not needed for the plaintiff's security. This was an incorrect assumption. While that was the only ground expressly listed in CPLR 6223(a), it was by no means a negation of other possible vacatur grounds: it was included in terms in CPLR 6223 only because it had not been a vacatur ground under prior law.[10] The addition of subdivision (b) to CPLR 6223 moots the point. Under that provision the plaintiff's failure at the hearing to establish an attachment ground, to justify a continuing need for the attachment, or to show a probability of success on the merits, is also ground to vacate the attachment.

§ 316. Applying for the Attachment

An order of attachment can be applied for by motion ex parte or on notice, at the plaintiff's option. Since giving notice at the outset may enable the defendant to remove the property, the ex parte procedure is preferred by plaintiffs.

If the ex parte procedure is used, the plaintiff can obtain the order and have it levied before the defendant is heard, but then the plaintiff must, within a specified number of days after the levy,[1] repeat the motion, this time on notice. This is known as a motion to confirm. The period for moving to confirm is five days after the levy, except when the attachment is based on paragraph 1 of CPLR 6201—the defendant's foreign status—which is the ground relied on when the attachment is

being used for its quasi in rem jurisdictional function. A 10–day period applies in that case.

The plaintiff's obligations become tight when the attachment has a jurisdictional function, as will be seen later,[2] and procedure is adjusted a bit to recognize this. The main adjustment is the stretching from five to 10 days for the post-levy confirmation motion, which the court is also empowered to extend by an additional 10 days.[3] These adjustments are designed to coordinate with the requirement of CPLR 6219, which requires the garnishee through whom the attachment is levied to serve on the sheriff a list of any assets of the defendant that the garnishee holds or any debts the garnishee owes the defendant. The garnishee ordinarily has 10 days from the levy in which to serve that statement,[4] but the information about the defendant's property is needed extra fast when the attachment is being used for its jurisdictional purpose. Hence, when the attachment is based on paragraph 1 of CPLR 6201, the garnishee has only five instead of 10 days in which to serve the statement, and must serve a copy of it on the plaintiff as well as on the sheriff.

If the attachment has been granted ex parte, invoking the confirmation requirement—whatever time period applies to it—the motion to confirm should be made within the required time even if the garnishee, through whom the levy is sought, doesn't have any leviable property of the defendant. The rationale is that to permit the attachment to remain outstanding, without confirmation, while the plaintiff flits from garnishee to garnishee in search of property, would be inconsistent with the defendant's rights.[5]

The confirmation procedure affords the defendant the constitutionally required opportunity to be heard promptly.[6] If the motion on notice procedure is initially used, the plaintiff

---

9. See § 320 below.

10. See 3d Rep.Leg.Doc. (1959) No. 17, pp. 357–8.

§ 316

1. What the levy consists of is discussed in § 320 below.

2. See § 319 et seq., below.

3. CPLR 6211(b).

4. CPLR 6219.

5. See Eisenberg v. Citation–Langley Corp., 92 A.D.2d 795, 459 N.Y.S.2d 788 (1st Dep't 1983).

6. CPLR 6211(b) supplies the confirmation procedure, to which the text returns later.

can obtain, ex parte, a temporary restraining order to be served on the garnishee pending return of the motion, enjoining any transfer of the property by the garnishee in the interim. Although a temporary restraining order is ordinarily contained in an order to show cause,[7] in this instance it apparently need not be. A show cause order is an alternative way of bringing on a notice of motion, and in this instance the motion, for the order of attachment, is being made against the defendant, not against the garnishee. The governing statute, CPLR 6210, apparently contemplates an ex parte application for the restraining order against the garnishee at about the same time the plaintiff serves motion papers giving the defendant notice of the motion for the attachment. The plaintiff should be allowed the restraining order sufficiently in advance of the defendant's actual receipt of the motion papers so as to enable the plaintiff to effect the restraint's service on the garnishee before the defendant tries to get the property from the garnishee.

Application for the attachment can be made before or after service of the summons and at any time before final judgment.[8] If sought after summons service, the attachment is presumably being used solely in its security aspect. When used for quasi in rem jurisdiction, the attachment must be sought and granted before the summons is served. Indeed, in that instance it must even be levied before the summons is served, a requirement imposed by CPLR 314(3).

The plaintiff must furnish an undertaking. It is mandatory on an attachment motion. The court fixes the amount of the undertaking but it can't be less than $500.[9] The undertaking is governed by Article 25 of the CPLR, which determines such matters as who may act as

surety on it.[10] The condition of the undertaking in this instance is that the plaintiff will pay the defendant all costs and damages, including reasonable attorney's fees,[11] that may be sustained if the defendant should win on the merits or if it is otherwise ultimately determined that the plaintiff was not entitled to the attachment.

The main part of the plaintiff's moving papers, on a motion for an attachment as well as on a post-levy motion to confirm, is the proof on which the plaintiff bases the motion. This always includes at least one affidavit, but it may include as many as the plaintiff can muster along with any other written proof available. The proof must establish to the court's satisfaction that the plaintiff has a money cause of action, that it is "probable" that the plaintiff will succeed on the merits, and that at least one of the attachment grounds listed in CPLR 6201 has been satisfied. The plaintiff's affidavit must also attest that the amount the plaintiff is demanding from the defendant exceeds all counterclaims "known" to the plaintiff, an express requirement of the statute[12] but one that the plaintiff can usually satisfy just by listing only those counterclaims she concedes.

The plaintiff has the burden of proof on these issues, not a very difficult burden when the application is ex parte—there is no one to deny anything—but one that becomes quite important on the post-levy motion to confirm or on any motion the defendant may make to vacate or modify the attachment.[13]

If the ex parte procedure is used, the plaintiff's affidavit must also depose as to whether this or a like application has previously been made and, if so, to whom, when, where, what

---

7. See § 330 below.

8. CPLR 6211(a). Although CPLR 6211's caption suggests that it applies only to the attachment sought "without notice", its options about when the attachment may be sought should be deemed to apply to the motion on notice as well.

9. CPLR 6212(b).

10. CPLR 2502.

11. See § 325 below.

12. CPLR 6212(a).

13. CPLR 6223(b). The burden of proof should also belong to the plaintiff on an initial motion on notice if that's the procedure the plaintiff chooses for the attachment, although the statutes in point, CPLR 6210, 6223(b), don't say so expressly. A statute does say so expressly in respect of a confirmation motion, used when the initial attachment application is ex parte. See CPLR 6211(b), adopting CPLR 6223(b) in this respect.

happened, what new facts have come to light, etc.[14]

Each affidavit should be made by a person with first-hand knowledge of the facts sworn to. Affidavits by those whose knowledge is at best indirect will surely weaken the appeal to the court's discretion, to which the attachment is addressed. If an affidavit by one with only second-hand knowledge is necessary, it should at least include an explanation of why it is not being made by one with knowledge.[15]

The affidavit(s) should convince the court of the merits of the plaintiff's claim. When CPLR 6212(a) requires the plaintiff to show that it is "probable" that the action will succeed on the merits, it means that there must be something in the proof stronger than the mere prima facie case that could satisfy in a pleading. The 1977 amendment that added the "probability" language in effect codified caselaw. "What is sufficient for a pleading may be insufficient for attachment", said Judge Cardozo in Zenith Bathing Pavilion, Inc. v. Fair Oaks S.S. Corp.,[16] which well illustrates the point that for an attachment there must be evidentiary detail stronger than the summary and conclusory allegations that suffice in a pleading.

In *Zenith*, the plaintiff was suing for trespass for part of a vessel left on his land. He sued four defendants in the alternative, not being sure which of them was responsible. As a matter of pleading he made out a prima facie case readily enough against all of them, as a kind of suit in the alternative if nothing else, but only against one of the defendants was there the kind of evidentiary showing sufficient to sustain the drastic remedy of attachment. Thus, only against that one was an attachment permissible, and that was so even though it might develop at the trial that another, against whom attachment was initially refused for lack of evidentiary detail, was the real culprit after all.

There is no requirement that the plaintiff submit a copy of the complaint as part of the moving papers. But it is permissible, of course, and if the complaint is verified it can serve as an additional affidavit.[17] The moving papers should include a copy of the proposed order of attachment.

CPLR 6212(a) does not require, as a precondition to an attachment, a showing that the defendant has property in New York, much less its value.[18] Usually the plaintiff will not bother with an attachment unless she knows or at least suspects that the defendant has local property, but the showing is not required on the attachment motion. If the plaintiff ends up with an attachment that can't be levied because the sheriff can't find any property of the defendant, so much the worse for the plaintiff; the attachment order becomes a souvenir. Since the motion is addressed to the court's discretion, however,[19] a showing that the defendant has significant local property can become a contributory element in invoking that discretion.

If the attachment motion is granted, CPLR 6211(a) requires the order to specify the amount that the attachment is to secure, including interest, costs, and sheriff's fees and expenses. The court decides how much the order of attachment will be permitted to secure. It can specify a lower figure than the plaintiff demands when, on the proof submitted, the plaintiff's demand appears to be inflated.

The order, which also includes the name and address of the plaintiff's lawyer, is directed to the sheriff of any county or of New York City and directs the sheriff to levy on any of the defendant's property found within his jurisdiction, up to the amount specified in the order.[20] Quite often the sheriff must gauge the value of the property levied on so as to stop the levy when the amount specified in the order is reached.

14. CPLR 2217(b).

15. See Rubin v. Lesser, 35 Misc.2d 172, 228 N.Y.S.2d 798 (Sup.Ct., N.Y.County, 1962).

16. 240 N.Y. 307, 312, 148 N.E. 532, 534 (1925).

17. See the definition of "verified pleading" in CPLR 105.

18. See ABKCO Industries, Inc. v. Apple Films, Inc., 39 N.Y.2d 670, 385 N.Y.S.2d 511, 350 N.E.2d 899 (1976).

19. See § 317 below.

20. CPLR 6211(a).

Several additional points should be made about the confirmation motion that the plaintiff is required to make when initially obtaining the order ex parte.[21] The confirmation procedure is in CPLR 6211(b) and usually comes about as follows:

The order is delivered to the appropriate sheriff and levied. It will usually take a considerable amount of time before the sheriff effects the levy. Only when the sheriff finally levies, however,[22] does the period begin to run in which the plaintiff must make the motion to confirm. The motion must be made "on such notice as the court shall direct", which means that it is to be made by the procedure of order to show cause or its equivalent—that being the common means whereby to have the court dictate as to method of service. Notice must be given to the defendant, to the garnishee, and to the sheriff.

All the plaintiff has to do is "move" within the applicable period, i.e., serve the motion papers as directed by the court. The return day of the motion need not—and likely will not—be scheduled for within the period. But if the plaintiff fails to at least "make" the motion within it, the order and levy become void and both may be vacated on motion.

If the five-day period for confirmation is applicable, as it is when a ground other than that of paragraph 1 of CPLR 6201 is relied on for the attachment, the five days are not a set period, but a maximum. CPLR 6211(b) directs the court to set the period, and provides only that it is "not to exceed five days after levy". When attachment is based on paragraph 1 of CPLR 6201 and the 10–day confirmation period applies, the period does appear to be a set

one; the court is not invited, as it is with the five-day period, to shorten it.

CPLR 6211(b) also provides that an order of attachment granted ex parte may preclude the sheriff from taking "actual custody" of levied property without further leave of court. This is not terribly important in the average case. Provision is made in Article 62 for levy by actual seizure of the property,[23] but the far more common method of effecting an attachment levy is by the sheriff's mere service, on the garnishee, of a copy of the order of attachment.[24]

§ 317. Attachment Discretionary

Even if the plaintiff makes out a case for attachment under CPLR 6201, its granting is still discretionary with the court. The plaintiff cannot demand it as a matter of right.[1] The Advisory Committee that produced the CPLR acknowledged its discretionary nature,[2] and if the judge should perceive from the papers that the plaintiff does not need an attachment, either for jurisdiction or security, discretion is appropriately exercised against it even though a CPLR 6201 showing has been made. As a practical matter, however, the courts are freer with attachment than they are with other provisional remedies, like injunction and receivership.

As indicated in the introductory section on the provisional remedies,[3] the usual rule of liberal construction applicable to the CPLR at large[4] does not apply to these remedies. It has been noted with attachment, for example, that the remedy is harsh, is in derogation of the common law, and must be construed "strictly in favor of those against whom it may be employed."[5] The lesson to the plaintiff is that

---

21. The confirmation requirement is a codification of the directive of Edward Thompson, who as Administrative Judge of the New York City Civil Court devised it to answer constitutional objections to the ex parte procedure as it then was.

22. The act of the sheriff that constitutes the "levy" is discussed in § 320 below.

23. CPLR 6215.

24. CPLR 6214(a). See § 320 below. Even the "perfection" of the levy, the follow-up steps that must be taken after the delivery of the order of attachment to the garnishee, does not require that the sheriff take actual custo-

dy of the attached property; there are alternatives. See § 321 below.

§ 317

1. Sartwell v. Field, 68 N.Y. 341 (1877).

2. See 3d Rep.Leg.Doc. (1959) No. 17, p. 144.

3. Section 306 above.

4. CPLR 104.

5. Penoyar v. Kelsey, 150 N.Y. 77, 80, 44 N.E. 788, 789 (1896).

an attachment will not be assured merely by eking out a prima facie showing under CPLR 6201. The affidavits should be ample and should add whatever else is both relevant and likely to influence judicial discretion.

Requiring affidavits of that strength should also satisfy constitutional requirements, which, remember, are always on standby when an attachment is sought, especially when it is sought ex parte. In Connecticut v. Doehr,[6] for example, the U.S. Supreme Court struck down a state attachment statute on due process grounds where the plaintiff's claim was just a general money claim in tort, asserted no pre-existing interest in the property attached (real property), and was accompanied by no showing of exigent circumstances such as to justify postponing the defendant's hearing until after levy of the attachment.

§ 318. The Various Time Periods Concerning Attachment

Article 62 of the CPLR sprinkles time periods about abundantly. Some of these carry sudden and stark jurisdictional consequences if overlooked, such as the time under CPLR 6211(b), already discussed, in which to move to confirm an order of attachment initially granted ex parte. At least four other time periods affect the plaintiff's obligations and should be noted in perspective at the outset:

1. A one-day period. After the levy has been made, a procedure to be met shortly,[1] the defendant may serve a written demand on the plaintiff requiring service on the defendant of the papers on which the attachment is based. Within one day after that demand the plaintiff must serve the papers.[2] The consequence of a failure here is not clear, but if the demand is served by mail it should be deemed to add five days to stretch the responding period to six, and the plaintiff should then be able to satisfy the obligation by merely posting the papers within the six-day period.[3]

2. A 10–day period. If the order of attachment is granted, the plaintiff must within 10 days thereafter file it and its underlying papers with the clerk of the court.[4] The 10–day period may be extended, but, if it isn't, the omission to file within the period invalidates the order.[5] Both this and the one-day requirement of the prior paragraph are easy to carry out and it will be assumed through all further discussion of attachment, and of various examples to be used in the course of it, that both have been met.

3. A 60–day period. This applies only when the order of attachment is granted before service of the summons, which means that it always applies when the attachment is being used for its jurisdictional purpose (where, as will be seen, the levy of the attachment must precede commencement).[6] The requirement is that the summons be served within 60 days after the granting of the order; if it is not, the order becomes invalid.[7] This is a fundamental part of the procedure when the attachment is being used for quasi in rem jurisdiction.[8] It should be kept in mind that this 60–day period and the 10–day period mentioned in the prior paragraph run from the granting of the order.

4. A 90–day period. This period is relevant when personal rather than real property is being levied on, which is most of the time. Like the period of CPLR 6211(b) in which to confirm the attachment—the confirmation period can be either five or ten days, depending on the CPLR 6201 ground on which the attachment is predicated[9]—it runs from the moment of levy, which is the moment the sheriff serves a copy of the order of attachment on the garnishee.[10] Within the 90 days the plaintiff must see to it that the levy is "perfected". What perfection consists of will also be a dis-

---

6.   501 U.S. 1, 111 S.Ct. 2105, 115 L.Ed.2d 1 (1991).

§ 318

1.   See § 320 below.
2.   CPLR 6212(d).
3.   CPLR 2103(b)(2).
4.   CPLR 6212(c), CPLR 2102.
5.   CPLR 6212(c).

6.   CPLR 314(3). See §§ 319 and 320 below.
7.   CPLR 6213.
8.   See § 104 above.
9.   See § 316 above.
10.   CPLR 6214(a), (b), (e).

tinct subject later.[11] Note now, though, that the failure to perfect within 90 days can destroy the plaintiff's entire case. Examples will demonstrate how.[12]

The interplay of the 60–day and 90–day provisions will become clear as we treat them in detail. A brief listing has been set forth here for reference purposes. Attachment is one remedy in which time periods often have jurisdictional consequences, which is reason enough to stress them and their interplay. The workings of the confirmation period of CPLR 6211(b) were treated in an earlier section.[13]

§ 319. Summons Service Within 60 Days

If the order of attachment is granted before service of the summons, the summons must be served within 60 days after the granting of the order or the order becomes invalid. If service by publication is being used, as it may be in this instance, only the first publication need be made within the 60 days as long as the rest of the publications are completed in due course.[1] Should the defendant die within the 60 days, the plaintiff has 60 days from whenever a personal representative is duly appointed. Finally, it is permissible for the court to extend the period, but for not more than an additional 60 days. The motion to extend must be made before the expiration of the original 60 days.[2]

As far as Article 62 is concerned, the levy of the attachment, which in the case of personal property consists only of the sheriff's delivering to the garnishee a copy of the order of attachment,[3] need not be made within any particular time. But when jurisdictional as against mere security use is being made of the attachment, the interplay of Articles 3 and 62 of the CPLR puts a time limit on when the levy must be made. CPLR 314(3) requires, for quasi in rem jurisdiction, that the levy of the

attachment precede the service of the summons, while CPLR 6213 requires that the summons be served within 60 days after the attachment order is granted. Putting the two together therefore requires not only that the levy be made within the 60 days, but early enough so that summons service can follow the levy and still be within the 60 days. This is New York statutory homage to the old notions of Pennoyer v. Neff,[4] which indicated that to secure quasi in rem jurisdiction the absent defendant's property has to be constructively seized before commencement of the action. If the summons is served before the levy is made, quasi in rem jurisdiction is not obtained. For example:

P gets an order of attachment against D on July 6, 1998. The summons is served on D (against whom no personam jurisdictional basis exists) in Vermont on August 21, 1998. The sheriff levies the attachment by serving it on G, a New York garnishee (who has property of D), on August 31, 1998. A motion made by D on September 8, 1998, or at any other time after the expiration of 60 days from July 6, 1998, to dismiss the action for lack of jurisdiction will be granted. Although both summons service and attachment levy were made within the 60–day period, the levy did not precede the summons service, as CPLR 314(3) requires.

The summons service within the 60–day period is made in the usual way, i.e., pursuant to CPLR 308 for individual defendants, CPLR 311 for corporate defendants, etc. Service by an unauthorized method will not do and can vitiate the proceedings. Thus, where the garnishee just happened to turn over to the defendant copies of the papers the sheriff delivered to the garnishee (which in this instance included the summons and complaint), this did not constitute due service and the attachment was vacated.[5]

---

11. See § 321 below.

12. See § 322 below.

13. See § 316 above.

§ 319

1. CPLR 315, 314(3). For the number of publications needed, see CPLR 316.

2. CPLR 6213. The application for such an extension should be permissible ex parte.

3. CPLR 6214(a).

4. 95 U.S. 714, 24 L.Ed. 565 (1877).

5. Kieley v. Central Complete Combustion Mfg. Co., 147 N.Y. 620, 42 N.E. 260 (1895).

In the lower courts of the state,[6] in which service of the summons marks commencement of the action, the 60–day period may also play a role in measuring the statute of limitations. In those courts the granting of the provisional remedy of attachment constitutes commencement of the action for purposes of satisfying the statute of limitations, as long as the summons is then served in accordance with CPLR 6213, i.e., within 60 days. So provides CPLR 203(b)(4),[7] which does not apply in the supreme or county courts, however. In those courts, the filing of the summons rather than its service marks commencement of the action and the application for a provisional remedy is made with or after that filing.

Also to be noted when the action is to be brought in the supreme or county court is that the plaintiff who seeks an attachment has two time provisions to satisfy in making service. The service of the summons must occur within 60 days after the granting of the order of attachment, so as to satisfy CPLR 6213, and must also occur within 120 days after the filing of the action itself, in order to satisfy CPLR 306–b. If the plaintiff files the action and then delays the application for an order of attachment for more than two months, for example, the plaintiff may have to effect service within a shorter period than the 60 days allowed by CPLR 6213 in order to satisfy the 120–day period of CPLR 306–b. Conversely, if the plaintiff secures the order of attachment shortly after filing the action, the requirement to make service within 60 days after the granting of the order will curtail the 120 days that CPLR 306–b would otherwise have allowed for service. The plaintiff must coordinate these periods. Prompt steps on all fronts should make that easy enough.

If proper proceedings are had in a case in which the defendant is not subject to personal jurisdiction, and the attachment results in the acquisition of quasi in rem jurisdiction, a judgment rendered in the action will be effective only against the attached property. This is so even if the defendant, served outside New York, appears and defends the action. This is a consequence of the "limited" appearance that New York allows to an attachment defendant.[8]

§ 320. Levy of the Attachment

The plaintiff should deliver the order of attachment to the sheriff of the county in which the property to be levied on is located. In New York City the sheriff's office is city-wide but the delivery should be made to the branch office in the county where the property is. The method whereby the sheriff levies the attachment depends on whether the property levied is real or personal.

A real property levy is simple. The sheriff just files a notice of attachment with the county clerk of the realty county. The notice contains the name and address of the plaintiff's attorney, names the parties to the action, states the amount specified in the order, and describes the realty. The clerk records and indexes the notice like a lis pendens, and it serves a like function: it puts the world on notice of the plaintiff's potential rights so that any later encumbrancer or buyer takes subject to the plaintiff's rights should the plaintiff win in the attachment action.[1] No follow-up step is necessary when realty is levied. The notice of attachment stands of record and warns off potential buyers and lienors. When attachment is being used jurisdictionally, and realty is being levied, this filing of the notice of attachment is all that is needed to satisfy CPLR 314(3) and enable service of the summons to be made.

Levying personal property is more involved and requires follow-up steps not satisfied by the mere filing of a paper. There are two ways in which the sheriff can levy against personal property: (1) by seizing it or (2) by serving the order of attachment on the garnishee.

Levy by seizure is uncommon. It is permissible only when the property is tangible and

---

6. The New York City Civil Court and the district, city, town, and village courts.

7. See § 46 above.

8. CPLR 320(c)(1), discussed in § 113, above.

§ 320

1. See CPLR 6216, in effect adopting CPLR 6501, the lis pendens provision treated in § 334, below.

hence capable of delivery, but even in that instance the sheriff is not required to make a "seizure" unless the plaintiff so directs and—the main discouragement to this method—furnishes the sheriff indemnity, satisfactory to the sheriff or fixed by the court, against such liability as the sheriff may sustain if the proceedings taken in the plaintiff's behalf should prove unwarranted.[2]

By far the most common method of levying against personal property is the second one listed above, supplied by CPLR 6214. Here the sheriff levies merely by serving a copy of the order of attachment on the garnishee—the one who has possession of property belonging to the defendant or who owes a debt to the defendant.[3] The service is the "levy". When the attachment is being used for jurisdiction, the service therefore satisfies CPLR 314(3) and secures quasi in rem jurisdiction and permits summons service within the 60 days supplied by CPLR 6213. As earlier noted, there is no time stated in Article 62 within which a levy must be made, but since CPLR 314(3) requires that the levy precede service of the summons when the attachment is being exploited for jurisdiction, CPLR 314(3) and 6213 read together require that summons service follow the levy and that both occur within 60 days after the granting of the order.

The effect of this levy-by-service is injunctive: it precludes the garnishee from disposing of the defendant's property to anyone but the levying sheriff, unless and until the court says otherwise. This is provided by CPLR 6214(b), which offers detailed guidance as to the garnishee's obligations. The levy applies not only to property of the defendant then in the garnishee's possession, for example, but also to any property of which the garnishee obtains possession thereafter; not only to debts then

due and owing by the garnishee to the defendant, but also to debts coming due later.

When this mode of levy is used—this levy-by-service—the mere service on the garnishee accomplishes the "levy" enough to assure quasi in rem jurisdiction and permit commencement of the action. However, unlike the levy-by-seizure, it requires some follow-up step within 90 days after the levy. Failure to take that step—which is commonly known as "perfecting" the levy—voids everything ab initio. Perfection of the levy is treated in the next section.

If the situation is such that the garnishee may not know that the property belongs to the defendant, such as where it stands of record in the garnishee's possession under some alias of the defendant, or for any other reason, CPLR 6214(b) permits the plaintiff to include with the order a notice, which the sheriff is to serve along with the order, identifying the property specifically. Doing so subjects it to the levy. This is a helpful option for the plaintiff, but it must of course be exercised with caution. If the plaintiff is mistaken, she is liable to the true owner of the property for any interference with the ownership that the attachment may cause. The provisional remedies are not toys.

The sheriff's duties after the levy are governed by CPLR 6218, which manifests the difference between an attachment levy and a levy of execution on a judgment. In the latter instance all of the procedures are devised to enable the sheriff to seize and sell the property, convert it to money, and pay the judgment.[4] With attachment, the sheriff's only duty if and when he gets possession of the property, whether by seizure or by the garnishee's handing it over to him voluntarily after a levy by service, is to "hold and safely keep" the property to answer a possible future judgment.[5]

---

2. See CPLR 6215.

3. CPLR 6214(a). This statute allows the levy to be made by serving the order of attachment on the defendant himself if the property is in the defendant's possession, but, as the reader can guess, the plaintiff's course is easier when there is a separate garnishee to deal with. Since the garnishee is personally liable to the plaintiff for whatever property she permits to slip through the injunctive effect

of the levy, the garnishee is far more likely to cooperate in the procedure than the defendant is.

4. See CPLR 5232, 5233, 5236.

5. CPLR 6218(a). If "urgency" dictates, such as where the property attached consists of perishables, the court can direct sale of the property, converting it to money, the money to be held in place of the property. Any money coming into the sheriff's possession under a levy must be deposited in an interest-bearing account as directed by

Attachment's maximum power is to keep the defendant away from the property or its free use; it does not give the property to the plaintiff.

Within 10 days after service of the order of attachment on the garnishee or such shorter time as the court directs, the garnishee must serve on the sheriff a detailed statement of debts she owes the defendant and of any property in the garnishee's possession in which the defendant has an interest.[6] When the attachment is based on paragraph 1 of CPLR 6201— the foreign status of the defendant—the garnishee has only five days in which to serve this statement and must also serve a copy of it on the plaintiff.[7] If the plaintiff loses out because of the garnishee's default under this provision, as where the statement the garnishee serves is false, the garnishee is liable to the plaintiff for whatever damage is suffered.[8]

§ 321. "Perfecting" the Levy

When a levy is made against real property, there is nothing further to be done; the filing with the county clerk does the whole job under CPLR 6216. The same is true of a levy against personal property when the levy is made by seizure under CPLR 6215. But when a levy is made against personal property by service of the order of attachment on a garnishee under CPLR 6214, the most common situation, some step must be taken within 90 days afterwards or the levy becomes void.[1] It is therefore only the levy-by-service procedure with which we are concerned in this section, for it is only there that the 90–day period for a follow-up step, popularly called "perfection" of the levy, applies.

Any one of three things will constitute "perfection" and satisfy this 90–day requirement:

(1) The garnishee need only deliver the attached property to the sheriff. The sheriff will then hold it to apply to whatever judgment the plaintiff may get in the action. This contemplates that the garnishee will deliver the property voluntarily. That would settle everything. But if the garnishee doesn't, there is also a provision for the sheriff to seize the property. CPLR 6214(c) contemplates the possibility of seizure as a follow-up step after levy-by-service—not to be confused with seizure under CPLR 6215 as an initial method of levy. But the explicit requirement under CPLR 6215 requiring the plaintiff to indemnify the sheriff as a condition to initial levy by seizure has been found by implication to apply also to a seizure used only as a "perfection" step after a levy-by-service,[2] thus discouraging the seizure procedure in both instances. If the garnishee delivers to the sheriff all property then in his possession belonging to the defendant, later property of the defendant coming into the garnishee's custody or possession is not subject to the levy.[3]

If the property is too big to deliver, or is an intangible, such as a debt not yet due, physical delivery by the garnishee is impracticable but the same result is accomplished by the garnishee's serving a paper on the sheriff, agreeing to hold the property as the equivalent of the sheriff's agent. In one case, in which the garnishee just set aside merchandise in response to the levy and so advised the defendant, this was held to suffice as tantamount to an assignment to the sheriff.[4] A simple letter from the garnishee to the sheriff has also been held to do the job.[5]

(2) An alternative step that would constitute a "perfection" of the levy and satisfy the

---

CPLR 6218(a). Property other than money must be inventoried as provided in CPLR 6218(b).

6. CPLR 6219.

7. CPLR 6211(b). See § 316 above.

8. See Leber–Krebs, Inc. v. Capitol Records, 779 F.2d 895 (2d Cir.1985).

§ 321

1. CPLR 6214(e).

2. See Lacharite v. Ducatte, 4 A.D.2d 130, 164 N.Y.S.2d 361 (3d Dep't 1957), aff'd 4 N.Y.2d 945, 175

N.Y.S.2d 820, 151 N.E.2d 617 (1958). The Advisory Committee, in addressing this subject, did not cite the Lacharite case (see 3d Rep.Leg.Doc. (1959) No. 17, p.350), which therefore presumably still governs.

3. CPLR 6214(b).

4. Fantasy Records, Inc. v. Travelers Indemnity Co., 54 Misc.2d 799, 283 N.Y.S.2d 473 (N.Y.C.Civ.Ct. 1967).

5. See Kalman v. Neuman, 80 A.D.2d 116, 438 N.Y.S.2d 109 (2d Dep't 1981).

90–day requirement is for the plaintiff to begin a special proceeding against the garnishee, also giving notice of the proceeding to the parties to the action and to the sheriff. This would be the step taken when the garnishee refuses to deliver to the sheriff either the property or at least a statement acknowledging that the garnishee holds such property or owes a debt to the defendant. The proceeding need only be "commenced" within the 90–day period in order to satisfy this requirement.[6] This means that all the plaintiff has to do is have the notice of petition and petition—the papers that commence a special proceeding[7]—filed and served (if the action was brought in the supreme or county court) or just served (if the action was brought in the lower courts) on the garnishee and other respondents. That accomplishes "perfection" regardless of when the special proceeding is terminated.

The proceeding is designed to make the garnishee turn the money or property over to the sheriff. The garnishee may of course defend the proceeding with anything he might have used against the defendant had the defendant brought suit over the subject property. (The garnishee is not divested of his defenses merely because a creditor of the defendant instead of the defendant herself is seeking the property.) Although the statute authorizing the proceeding states that the plaintiff may bring it against the garnishee,[8] caselaw holds that it may be brought against the defendant if the property sought is in the defendant's possession.[9]

(3) The third and, paradoxically, the easiest alternative whereby to "perfect" the levy, at least so as to remove the onus of the 90–day period and its threat to void the levy, is to have the period extended. The court is empowered to extend the 90 days, and it takes no more than a motion by the plaintiff, on notice

to the defendant, to obtain the extension. The extension motion should be made within the original 90–day period because the statute says that the levy shall be "void" if the period expires without extension.[10] It has been held that the period can be extended even by application made after the period has expired, if no one is prejudiced thereby,[11] but the holding took place in the context of the Seider v. Roth doctrine,[12] which has since been overruled.[13] While the court's language in the cited case[14] indicates that tardy applications may be permissible in any category of attachment action, it is unwise for the plaintiff to proceed on that assumption. The plaintiff should get the extension while the 90–day period is still in effect.

Another bonus is that the extension is not limited to another 90–day period. The court can extend the original 90–day period almost indefinitely. A common disposition is for the court to extend it until 10 days after the entry of such judgment as may be rendered in the main action, which means after trial on the merits. That may be many months and perhaps even years away. In one instance the appellate division extended the time until 30 days after disposition of an appeal to the Court of Appeals.[15]

With so easy a set of options—any one of the three listed items is sufficient to fulfill the 90–day requirement and remove it as a potential destroyer of jurisdiction—there is no excuse for the lawyer to let the 90 days lapse, thereby voiding the levy, which is precisely what happens. Where, for example, all initial steps were properly taken but the 90–day period went by without a perfection step, all was voided: the levy, the order of attachment, and the jurisdiction obtained in the action itself which, when quasi in rem jurisdiction is relied on, depends

---

6. CPLR 6214(e).

7. CPLR 304, 403.

8. CPLR 6214(d).

9. Hom–De–Lite Realty Corp. v. Trimboli, 28 A.D.2d 1127, 284 N.Y.S.2d 141 (2d Dep't 1967).

10. CPLR 6214(e).

11. Seider v. Roth, 28 A.D.2d 698, 280 N.Y.S.2d 1005 (2d Dep't 1967).

12. Seider authorized, in personal injury cases, the attachment of foreign liability insurance policies for quasi in rem jurisdiction against nondomiciliary defendants.

13. See § 105 above.

14. Seider v. Roth, note 11, above.

15. Stines v. Hertz Corp., 22 A.D.2d 1018, 256 N.Y.S.2d 321 (2d Dep't 1964), aff'd 16 N.Y.2d 605, 261 N.Y.S.2d 59, 209 N.E.2d 105 (1965).

on an effectual levy.[16]

It has been held that if the 90 days expire but the order of attachment remains valid, which is the case when the attachment is not being used for jurisdiction, the sheriff can re-levy it and start a new 90 days running[17] as long as no other creditor sneaks in and steals priority in the interim, but the New York Court of Appeals has not yet spoken to the point and until it does the plaintiff should try to avoid the situation. Anything done, including that easiest step of all—the obtaining of a time extension—should be done within the original 90 days.

These New York attachment procedures are also applicable, by adoption, in the federal courts in New York, where they are just as rigid, and plaintiffs in federal actions should therefore be just as wary of them.[18]

§ 322. Examples of Interplay of Attachment Requirements

Illustrations can help in understanding the interplay of some of the attachment procedures. We assume here a jurisdictional use of the attachment, because when the attachment is used for jurisdiction its procedures are at their most rigid and the illustrations their most instructive. Suppose a case in the supreme court in which no personam jurisdiction is available to New Yorker P, who is suing D, a domiciliary of Vermont, where the claim arose. Assume the following 1998 occurrences on the stated dates:

June 15   Summons and complaint filed and order of attachment granted ex parte by the supreme court.

June 22   Levy by service of the order of attachment by the sheriff on garnishee G (a New York bank where D has an account).

June 26   Motion made by P to confirm the attachment.

July 10   Court confirms the attachment in an order.

Aug. 7   Summons service is made on D in Vermont.

Sept. 8   Special proceeding is begun by P against G.

Oct. 5   Motion is made by D to vacate everything.

The motion would be denied because all is in order. The levy preceded the service of the summons; a motion to confirm was made within the required time (10 days in this case) after the levy and was granted; the summons was served within 60 days after the order was granted (satisfying CPLR 6213) and within 120 days after the filing of the action (satisfying CPLR 306–b); and, within 90 days after the levy, the levy was perfected by the commencement of the special proceeding.

Now take all the facts to be the same but omit the September 8 special proceeding and assume that no perfection step of any kind is taken within 90 days following June 22. Under older law,[1] the October 5 motion would be granted, voiding everything. The levy is void under CPLR 6214(e) for lack of perfection within 90 days; the action is dismissed for lack of quasi in rem jurisdiction, which depended on the levy; and the order of attachment is vacated because the action's dismissal means that no action was properly commenced within 60 days after the granting of the order. More recent law suggests that the 90 days can be extended even by motion made after the period has expired,[2] and if that becomes the prevailing view, then P, upon excusing the delay,

---

16. See Sturcke v. Link, 176 Misc. 93, 26 N.Y.S.2d 748 (Sup.Ct., N.Y.County, 1941).

17. Fireman's Fund Ins. Co. v. D'Ambra, 766 F.2d 95 (2d Cir.1985).

18. See Worldwide Carriers Ltd. v. Aris S.S. Co., 312 F.Supp. 172 (S.D.N.Y.1970). For treatment of the provi-

sional remedies in federal actions, see § 640 (Practitioner's Edition).

§ 322

1. See Sturcke v. Link, 176 Misc. 93, 26 N.Y.S.2d 748 (Sup.Ct., N.Y. County, 1941).

2. See § 321, notes 11–13 above.

should be able to have the 90–day period extended by late motion which, if granted, would preserve everything. P is better off by not assuming that this generosity about allowing an extension on motion made after the passing of the 90 days will be upheld by the higher courts; P should make the motion within the initial 90 days.

Take all the facts to be the same as listed, but reverse the levy and summons service: the summons is served on June 22, and the levy is made on August 7. Even assuming the granting of a proper and timely confirmation motion, a defect would subsist in that the levy did not precede service, as it must under CPLR 314(3), which means that quasi in rem jurisdiction was not secured, requiring dismissal of the action. (If personam jurisdiction exists— the attachment being used for mere security rather than for quasi in rem jurisdiction—the proceedings would be valid and no dismissal would be required.)

Take all the facts to be the same as listed, but omit the perfection step of September 8 and have the summons service of August 7 made on D, not in Vermont, but in New York while D is visiting. The October 5 motion, insofar as it seeks vacatur of the levy, would— unless the court allows a late application to extend the 90 days—be granted. The 90–day perfection step is required no matter what kind of jurisdiction may exist in the action, i.e., whether the attachment is being used for jurisdiction or for mere security. But insofar as the October 5 motion seeks dismissal of the action, it would have to be denied: the August 7 service in New York conferred personam jurisdiction over D and made all further questions of rem jurisdiction academic. The failure of the levy, needed for rem but not for personam jurisdiction, would become irrelevant for jurisdiction.

Take all the facts to be the same as listed, except that summons service is made on D in Vermont on August 22 instead of August 7. Here the defect is that the summons has not

been served within 60 days after the granting of the order, which makes the order void under CPLR 6213. This in turn voids the levy, and that in turn defeats the quasi in rem jurisdiction that P was relying on. So here again is a scenario in which the whole edifice crumbles.

§ 323. What Property Attachable?

Article 62 does not specify what property may be attached. CPLR 6202 provides simply that whatever property can be applied to enforce a judgment under CPLR 5201 can be attached before judgment under Article 62. CPLR 5201 is the standard for both, and for this purpose the "judgment debtor" of CPLR 5201 is to be treated as the mere "defendant" that she is at attachment time.

CPLR 5201 defines property broadly. It makes no endeavor to list the innumerable categories of property interests a defendant can have. Such a list would always be incomplete, and thus restrictive despite its best endeavors. With the narrow exception of property explicitly exempted by statute from application to a judgment,[1] CPLR 5201(b) subjects to the judgment (and hence to attachment) any property interest of the defendant that is assignable or transferable. Whatever the interest is, and whether tangible or intangible, it is leviable as long as the defendant can assign or transfer it, which means that almost any property interest of the defendant is reachable. Although further discussion of this matter can abide the chapter on the enforcement of judgments,[2] it is especially useful, when discussing attachment, to refer to subdivision (a) of CPLR 5201, which is purportedly an exception to the broad property criterion of subdivision (b).

Subdivision (a) provides that when the property consists of a "debt" owing to the defendant (D) by the garnishee (G), it can be subjected to levy only if it is presently due or certain to become due in the future, either

§ 323

1. CPLR 5205 and 5206 contain the main (but not the exclusive) lists of property exempted from application to a

judgment and hence from an attachment as well. See § 490 below.

2. See § 486 et seq., below.

upon some inevitable contingency, such as the mere passage of time, or upon demand of D. The purpose of this restriction was to preclude a levy against contingent obligations not certain to ripen into something real, but it was found too inflexible and was much reduced in scope—and the contingent intangible made much more accessible—by the Court of Appeals in its 1976 decision in Abkco Industries, Inc. v. Apple Films.[3] The decision is discussed at length in the enforcement chapter, but since the pre-judgment attachment can find itself in pursuit of an intangible just as often as a post-judgment execution can—*Abkco* in fact involved an attachment—the *Abkco* decision is a key one for an attaching creditor.[4]

When considering what property of the defendant may be levied on, a helpful rule of thumb is what may be called the "step into the shoes" doctrine.[5] The plaintiff generally has no greater standing than the defendant herself has in some item of the defendant's property. But the plaintiff can reach at least the interest that the defendant does have, i.e., stand in the defendant's shoes, and that is what the plaintiff tries to accomplish with the levy. This, too, will be seen in more depth in the enforcement of judgments chapter, but with this difference noted once again: when a levy of execution is made on a judgment, the sheriff's obligation is to convert the property into money (if it is not money itself) and pay the plaintiff's judgment, while with attachment the sheriff just takes possession or custody of the property, actually or constructively, and holds it, thereby keeping it away from the defendant's use but without letting the plaintiff have it either. If the plaintiff wins on the merits, what is contemplated is that the plaintiff will then issue an execution on the judgment to the same sheriff, who will then take the further enforcement steps needed to liquidate the property, convert it into money, and satisfy the plaintiff's judgment.

The fact that on an attachment there is no pressure to get and sell the property makes it much simpler than the levy of execution on a judgment. If, for example, some property or debt is duly attached while in the hands of a garnishee, whether it is a tangible or a debt, and the plaintiff gets the 90–day period of CPLR 6214 extended until after judgment,[6] that simple step suspends everything until that later time when, a judgment now on the scene, it becomes the burden of Article 52 and its enforcement of judgments to convert the property into money. The garnishee fulfills his obligation by keeping the property interest away from the defendant in the meantime, but no one is pressing to have the interest sold or even, perhaps, measured, all of which abides final judgment and a levy of execution on it.

A problem that attachment and execution have in common is that of identifying the proper garnishee. In most situations it is not hard: the garnishee is the person who has physical possession of some piece of the defendant's property or who owes a debt to the defendant.[7] In some instances, especially those involving intangible property interests, such as shares in a corporation or an interest in a decedent's estate, a statute assists by specifically identifying the garnishee.[8]

The plaintiff must see to it that the sheriff directs his efforts to an appropriate garnishee, since address to a wrong one will frustrate the proceedings. Suppose, for example, that D is one of several persons having some beneficial interest in a trust and that the trust owns certain tangible assets. In a suit against D, D's interest in the trust, to whatever extent that interest is subject to levy, is the thing to go after, and the proper garnishee is the trustee. But no particular assets belonging to the trust may be levied on in that situation because those are the property of the trust and not the property of any one of its beneficiaries.[9] A person, other than the trustee, who happens to have possession or custody of such a trust

---

3. 39 N.Y.2d 670, 385 N.Y.S.2d 511, 350 N.E.2d 899.

4. See § 489 below.

5. See § 488 below.

6. See CPLR 6214(e) and its discussion in § 321, above.

7. See the definition of garnishee in CPLR 105.

8. See CPLR 5201(c).

9. See William A. White & Sons v. Scott, 14 A.D.2d 307, 220 N.Y.S.2d 342 (1st Dep't 1961).

asset would therefore not be a proper garnishee.

An analogous question concerns the attachment of partnership property, which arose often enough under prior law to earn special mention from the CPLR's drafters.[10] The only time specific property of a partnership can be attached is when the claim is against the partnership as such.[11] A given partner's individual interest in the partnership is his share of the profits and surplus,[12] and one with a claim against an individual partner attaches that rather than specific property owned by the partnership. The creditor does this either with a levy or with what is known as a charging order.[13] The latter requires a motion; the levy does not, and is therefore the preferable method when priorities among creditors are at stake.[14]

One of the major devices for the enforcement of a judgment is the income execution of CPLR 5231, which enables a judgment creditor to reach 10% of the judgment debtor's income and apply it to the judgment. Under prior law, the case of Morris Plan Industrial Bank v. Gunning[15] held that this post-judgment income levy could be exploited for pre-judgment attachment as well; that it would operate as a continuing levy, requiring, all pursuant to the single attachment, that the employer (the garnishee) deduct 10% every payday and send that amount to the sheriff until the plaintiff's demand was met.[16] The indications are that *Morris Plan* is not followed today; whether the income execution authorized by CPLR 5231 to

enforce a judgment may be exploited for attachment is, as noted earlier,[17] a question expressly reserved by the Court of Appeals in Glassman v. Hyder.[18]

It is tempting to delve further into this property topic, but it would be duplicative of the effort required later[19] in the enforcement of judgments, in deference to which we stop here.

§ 324. Disclosure to Aid Attachment

If help is needed to determine the location or extent of the defendant's assets or even whether such assets exist, CPLR 6220 enables the plaintiff to apply for a court order directing disclosure. This makes available any disclosure device contained in Article 31, the CPLR's disclosure article,[1] if the court finds the device appropriate or helpful to reveal the nature or whereabouts of the defendant's property. Depositions on oral questions,[2] for example, and the discovery and inspection of documents,[3] may be directed.

A significant distinction is that disclosure directly under Article 31 is usually available by mere notices served between parties, while disclosure in aid of attachment under CPLR 6220 requires a court order. Since the motion for the order is required to be on "such notice as the court may direct", it should be brought on by order to show cause.[4] This enables the court to determine the method of notice and whether other parties should be notified, including

---

10. See 3d Rep.Leg.Doc. (1959) No. 17, p. 140.

11. Partnership Law § 51(2)(c).

12. Partnership Law § 52.

13. See Part.L. § 54.

14. See § 520 below.

15. 295 N.Y. 324, 67 N.E.2d 510 (1946).

16. The case allowed a New York attachment of a Pennsylvania defendant's wages, earned in Pennsylvania, despite the fact that Pennsylvania itself exempted such wages. New York theorized that these wages had a New York situs because D's employer, G, happened to be a corporation with a New York office. The court assumed that the obligation underlying the judgment was a Pennsylvania one. New York's attempt to subject to a New York levy wages earned (and exempted from levy) in Pennsylvania puts Morris Plan under a constitutional cloud. It is a question of choice of law and Morris Plan

may have given it the wrong answer. Compare Home Insurance Co. v. Dick, 281 U.S. 397, 50 S.Ct. 338, 74 L.Ed. 926 (1930). Another relevant factor is that the plaintiff in Morris Plan was a New York corporation, a factor which at the time precluded a forum non conveniens dismissal. A conveniens dismissal would be permissible in a like situation today. See §§ 28 and 29 above.

17. See § 307 above.

18. 23 N.Y.2d 354, 296 N.Y.S.2d 783, 244 N.E.2d 259 (1968).

19. See § 486 et seq., below.

§ 324

1. See Chapter 13 below.

2. CPLR 3107.

3. CPLR 3120.

4. CPLR 2214(d).

the one from whom disclosure is sought. It is helpful to have the court direct as to these items because the juncture at which this kind of disclosure is sought—after the granting of the attachment order but before the levy and often before the summons has been served—muddies the rules about the notice of motion.

Any person with data reflecting on the defendant's property may be required to make disclosure under this provision, including the defendant and the garnishee[5] as well as one who is neither, such as a friend or relative of the defendant who does not have the defendant's property but knows something about it.

§ 325. Defendant's Remedies: Vacatur; Discharge; Annulment; Action on Undertaking

The CPLR offers the attachment defendant a number of options, which can be considered seriatim.

1. Vacating or modifying the attachment. The defendant can move at any time before or during the action to vacate or modify the attachment order. CPLR 6223(a) supplies this right,[1] and any ground that affects the validity of the attachment is vacatur ground. Before 1977, the motion to vacate was the principal context for the presentation of the defendant's side of the case: the order of attachment was almost always granted ex parte and there was no standing requirement that the plaintiff afterwards make a motion—on notice—to confirm the attachment. With the 1977 amendment adding CPLR 6211(b), which mandates such a follow-up motion in all instances in which an attachment is granted ex parte, it will likely be on the motion to confirm that the defendant's objections are raised. And since CPLR 6211(b) contemplates that the confirmation motion will be made after the levy, the motion will enable the defendant to pose objections not only to the validity of the order of attachment, but to the validity of the levy as

well. Motions to vacate are therefore less frequent under present practice. Indeed, any issue decided on the contested confirmation motion should be deemed binding on any later motion by the defendant to vacate, under the law of the case doctrine.[2] Motions to vacate or modify should therefore be based on new facts arising after the disposition of the confirmation motion.

The motion to vacate may have more scope in a situation in which the plaintiff has elected to apply for the attachment by motion on notice in the first place. Since the levy would not yet have taken place in that instance, defects connected with the levy would not be raised on the motion, as they might be on a post-levy motion to confirm following an ex parte attachment.

One of the vacatur grounds listed in CPLR 6223(a) is that "the attachment is unnecessary to the security of the plaintiff". The ground was not explicitly set forth under pre-CPLR law and that's the sole reason for its inclusion,[3] a point overlooked by the lower court in Carey v. Sugar, necessitating its reversal by the U.S. Supreme Court,[4] as previously discussed.[5] The lower court had erroneously assumed that the expression of the one ground negated all others, while it was clear under New York law that anything on which the attachment depended—any showing that the plaintiff had to make to obtain the attachment ex parte in the first place—could be negated by the defendant on a motion to vacate.

A vacatur on the ground that the attachment is unnecessary for the plaintiff's security is intended primarily for the case in which the attachment is being used for quasi in rem jurisdiction rather than mere security. This is why CPLR 6223(a) provides that this ground may be invoked only after the defendant has appeared in the action: the assumption is that the attachment is valid and that it has secured jurisdiction. With the reduced use of quasi in

---

5. See Michelsen v. Brush, 233 F.Supp. 868 (E.D.N.Y. 1964).

§ 325

1. The garnishee and any other interested person is also authorized by CPLR 6223(a) to make this motion.

2. See § 448 below.

3. See 3d Rep.Leg.Doc. (1959) No. 17, pp. 357–8.

4. 425 U.S. 73, 96 S.Ct. 1208, 47 L.Ed.2d 587 (1976).

5. See § 315, note 3, above.

rem jurisdiction after Shaffer v. Heitner,[6] attachment for a jurisdictional purpose is not as frequent as under prior law.

On a motion to vacate or modify the attachment, the plaintiff has the burden of establishing the grounds for the attachment—including a sustaining of the particular paragraph of CPLR 6201 depended on as well as a showing of a "probability" of success on the merits—and of convincing the court of the need for continuing the levy.[7] If these issues should arise on a motion to confirm, as they are more likely to do today, the plaintiff retains the burden of proof on them there as well.[8]

The motion to vacate or modify is made on notice to all parties and to the sheriff.[9] The resulting order is appealable.[10]

Modification of the order is a permissible alternative to vacatur. An example of a modification would be where the court on the motion finds that the amount stated in the original order—which is the amount to be secured by the levy—has proved to be inflated and should be reduced.

On the defendant's motion to vacate the attachment, the court may give the plaintiff "a reasonable opportunity to correct any defect".[11] This clearly evinces that not every defect is a jurisdictional one requiring vacatur of the attachment. If the defect consists of a paper omission or error that can be corrected by mere amendment, amendment rather than vacatur is the remedy. Part of the plaintiff's showing is that there is a sufficient cause of action for money, for example, which tends to make the rules about the sufficiency of a pleading relevant to some extent to the plaintiff's affidavits in support of attachment. A primary purpose of this permission to allow defects to be corrected is to prevent the strict and technical old rules about pleadings—no longer applicable to pleadings themselves today—to be used to defeat the attachment.[12]

2. Discharging the attachment. A "discharge" of the attachment involves the substitution, in place of the attached property, of the defendant's undertaking, committing the defendant to pay whatever judgment the plaintiff may recover in the action, limited by the value of the property the defendant wants to get unattached. The discharge is sought by motion under CPLR 6222 and if granted it releases the property and returns it to the defendant's use. When the defendant has no basis for contesting the jurisdictional validity of the attachment and so can't get it vacated, she can turn to the discharge motion, albeit at the expense of whatever the undertaking costs.

Neither a vacatur motion under CPLR 6223 nor a discharge motion under CPLR 6222 constitutes an appearance in the action. This is to assure that a defendant making either kind of motion will not inadvertently submit to an otherwise lacking jurisdiction, a fear that is probably unwarranted under the CPLR since objections to jurisdiction are no longer wedded to the concept of a "special appearance", as they were under prior law.[13]

3. Annulling the attachment. Yet another word, to be distinguished from both the vacatur of the attachment under CPLR 6223 and its discharge under CPLR 6222, is its "annulment" under CPLR 6224. Annulment of the attachment requires no motion; it occurs automatically. If the defendant wins on the merits, for example, the attachment is automatically annulled—although the defendant may have to remind garnishees and sheriffs about it. (If the sheriff should resist, for example, and refuse return of the defendant's property, the defendant's remedy is a motion to compel the return under CPLR 6225.) If the plaintiff wins on the merits, the annulment does not occur until the plaintiff's judgment is fully satisfied. If the action for any reason abates before judgment on the merits, such as by a dismissal

---

6.   433 U.S. 186, 97 S.Ct. 2569, 53 L.Ed.2d 683 (1977). See § 104, above, for discussion of the Shaffer case.

7.   CPLR 6223(b).

8.   CPLR 6211(b), adopting CPLR 6223(b).

9.   CPLR 6223(a).

10.   CPLR 5701(a)(2)(i).

11.   CPLR 6223(a).

12.   See 3d Rep.Leg.Doc. (1959) No. 17, p. 358.

13.   See § 109 above. Take note also of the limited appearance permitted in attachment cases by CPLR 320(c)(1). See § 113 above.

under CPLR 3211 on a non-merits ground,[14] or by a voluntary discontinuance,[15] that also annuls the attachment.

4. Action on plaintiff's undertaking. The undertaking that the plaintiff must furnish for an attachment requires the plaintiff and the sureties on the bond to stand good to the defendant for "all costs and damages, including reasonable attorney's fees, which may be sustained by reason of the attachment if the defendant recovers judgment or if it is finally decided that the plaintiff was not entitled to an attachment".[16] Note, therefore, that all that need occur in order to invoke the condition of the plaintiff's undertaking is for the defendant to win on the merits. And even a merits victory by the plaintiff does not prevent the defendant's suit on the undertaking, as where the attachment depended on a ground involving an extrinsic fact, such as a showing under CPLR 6201(1) that the defendant was neither a domiciliary nor resident of the state, and it turns out that the defendant was indeed a New Yorker.

The undertaking that the defendant (D) must furnish in order to discharge the attachment, the second remedy discussed above, guarantees collection of the plaintiff's judgment, while the undertaking under discussion here, which the plaintiff (P) must supply, covers only damages sustained by D "by reason of the attachment".

Usually the main question in connection with P's undertaking, when its condition is invoked, is whether the defendant's attorneys' fees were incurred solely because of the attachment. Suppose, for example, that D wins on the merits. If D is a nondomiciliary served outside New York and the sole basis for jurisdiction is the attachment of D's New York property (i.e., jurisdiction is quasi in rem only), any defect in the attachment process that would lend itself to a vacatur motion would require that such a motion be made, or that the defendant at least point the defect out by way of opposing the plaintiff's motion to confirm. Defending on the merits—and even winning—without raising the defect means that the defendant went further than he had to. The undertaking would therefore not cover attorneys' fees incurred in defending the action.

But if the attachment is in all technical regards valid, so that the only way for the defendant to protect his property is to defend on the merits, and he does so and wins, the fee of his attorney in defending the action is covered by the undertaking.[17] There the defense on the merits—remember that there was no personam jurisdiction in the case—was necessitated solely by the attachment. But where the defendant is within the court's personam jurisdiction, divesting the attachment of any jurisdictional function, it is the personam jurisdiction, and not the attachment, that requires that the action be defended. The defendant's expense of an attorney in that instance is not traceable to the attachment and is therefore not ordinarily covered by the undertaking.[18]

Even a defendant who was within the court's personam jurisdiction may be allowed to recover attorneys' fees for steps shown to have been induced by the attachment, as where the defendant's commercial viability depended on lifting the attachment.[19]

While the amount of the undertaking necessarily limits the liability of the sureties, it does not limit the liability of the plaintiff himself.[20]

§ 326. Disposition of Property; Disputes; Priorities

The plaintiff's hope is that the garnishee, after the attachment levy, will turn over to the

---

14. E.g., paragraph 3 of CPLR 3211(a), lack of capacity to sue, or paragraph 4, the pendency of a duplicative action.

15. CPLR 3217.

16. CPLR 6212(b).

17. Thropp v. Erb, 255 N.Y. 75, 174 N.E. 67 (1930). The case was codified in 1977 by an amendment of CPLR 6212(b) and the addition of 6212(e).

18. Dinnerstein v. Max's Gas Station, 172 Misc. 27, 13 N.Y.S.2d 1014 (App.T., 2d Dep't, 1939).

19. See A.C. Israel Commodity Co. v. Banco Do Brasil, S.A., 50 Misc.2d 362, 270 N.Y.S.2d 283 (Sup.Ct., N.Y.County, 1966).

20. See CPLR 6212(e), codifying Siegel v. Northern Blvd. & 80th St. Corp., 31 A.D.2d 182, 295 N.Y.S.2d 804 (1st Dep't 1968).

sheriff whatever money the garnishee, G, owes the defendant, D, or whatever property of the defendant the garnishee is holding. Doing so offers the garnishee complete protection. Should D afterwards sue G for the debt or property, G has as a complete defense its payment to the New York sheriff at the behest of one claiming as D's creditor.[1]

If G does not voluntarily hand the property over, the plaintiff, P, can, as we have seen, bring a special proceeding to compel him to.[2] If it has been handed over to the sheriff and the attachment or its levy is then wholly or partly vacated, the court can, on the motion of any interested person—most likely the defendant—direct the sheriff to return the property. This is authorized by CPLR 6225, which gives the court, through the simple expedient of a motion, the power to undo whatever parts of the attachment process require undoing.

Now assume that some outsider, X, is claiming the property that has up to now been assumed to belong to D. Any such adverse claimant to the property may bring a special proceeding against the plaintiff to determine ownership or other interests in the property. Notice of that proceeding must be given to the sheriff and to each of the parties to the action. And although the statute in point[3] does not say so, it would also be appropriate to join the garnishee and any outsiders who are making claim to the property. If issues of fact arise in the proceeding, the court is authorized to try them, thus obviating a plenary action.

A few basic priority problems are addressed by Article 62. Priorities in real property of the defendant are usually easy to measure because

they invariably come about by a filing of papers in the county clerk's office—levy of attachment is made by such a filing[4]—and it is just a matter of determining who filed what first. Personal property is more involved.

The general way to secure a priority in the defendant's personalty, i.e., to secure a kind of lien superior to later ones, is to deliver the order of attachment to "a sheriff".[5] That mere delivery, before any levy has been made, will at least give P a right higher than that of someone to whom D afterwards gratuitously transfers the property. But if D's transfer is made to one who pays fair consideration for the property and who does not know of the attachment, that transferee, even though the transfer comes after the attachment, prevails over the attaching plaintiff.[6]

After a levy is made, it behooves the plaintiff to try to get the property into the hands of the sheriff, for many reasons. One of them is that if the sheriff has not taken possession of the property, then even if a levy has been made (as by his serving a copy of the order of attachment on G), a person who pays fair consideration for the property without knowing of the levy prevails over the plaintiff.[7] If the property is in the possession of a garnishee, this latter situation is less likely to occur because a garnishee who after levy prematurely returns possession of the property to D or his designee faces a personal liability to P. But if D himself has possession, D fears little in the way of additional liability, and P's efforts to get the property out of D's hands and into the sheriff's custody should be all the more diligent.

---

§ 326

1. CPLR 6204. The constitutionality of such as CPLR 6204 has been upheld by the U.S. Supreme Court. Harris v. Balk, 198 U.S. 215, 25 S.Ct. 625, 49 L.Ed. 1023 (1905). Insofar as the Harris case authorizes quasi in rem jurisdiction through the seizure of a debt owed to the debtor, it is largely overruled by Shaffer v. Heitner, 433 U.S. 186, 97 S.Ct. 2569, 53 L.Ed.2d 683 (1977), see § 104, above, but Harris probably remains good law for its fixing of a debt's situs for the purpose of levying execution against it on a judgment and even for its seizure on an attachment being used for mere security rather than for jurisdiction. See § 104 above. It should also remain good law for the purpose for which it is cited here: the protection of a garnishee who has paid the debt over to the sheriff pursu-

ant to a valid levy, whether on a pre-judgment attachment or on a post-judgment levy of execution.

2. CPLR 6214(d).

3. CPLR 6221.

4. CPLR 6216.

5. CPLR 6203. The enforcement officers of the various lower courts of civil jurisdiction of the state, such as the city marshals in the case of the New York City Civil Court, are to be deemed the same as a "sheriff" for these enforcement purposes. See § 701 in each of the New York City Civil, Uniform District, Uniform City, and Uniform Justice court acts, McKinney's Vol. 29A, Parts 2 and 3.

6. CPLR 6203(1).

7. CPLR 6203(2).

Utopia for the attaching plaintiff is to have the garnishee either hold the property away from D, or put it into the sheriff's hands; to have the action go forward to judgment for P against D; to issue an execution on the judgment to the same sheriff who levied the attachment; and to have that sheriff levy now on the execution, which means selling the property[8] and paying the proceeds of the sale over to P to satisfy the judgment. CPLR 6226 contemplates that situation, but it also contemplates further priority fights if there are multiple attachment creditors or other judgment creditors. If there are several attachment creditors dealing through different sheriffs, the one whose attachment gets levied first gets priority; if they have delivered their attachment orders to the same sheriff, priority is in the order of delivery.[9]

D. INJUNCTION

Table of Sections

§ 327. Preliminary Injunction, Grounds

Article 63 of the CPLR supplies the provisional remedies of the preliminary injunction, which keeps status quo while an action is pending, and the temporary restraining order (TRO), which keeps status quo while a motion is brought on for a preliminary injunction. While there are special injunction statutes applicable in particular situations,[1] and these supersede the general CPLR provisions of Article 63,[2] the central and most frequently in-

voked authority for a preliminary injunction is CPLR 6301.

CPLR 6301 authorizes a preliminary injunction in either of two situations:

1. where it appears that the defendant threatens or is about to do, or is doing or procuring or suffering to be done, an act in violation of the plaintiff's rights respecting the subject of the action, and tending to render the judgment ineffectual; or

2. in any action where the plaintiff has demanded and would be entitled to a judgment restraining the defendant from the commission or continuance of an act, which, if committed or continued during the pendency of the action, would produce injury to the plaintiff.[3]

In the first situation, the action[4] is not necessarily brought for a permanent injunction. The plaintiff is seeking some kind of relief with respect to a particular "subject matter", and it is in respect of that very subject matter that the plaintiff needs an injunction lest the defendant do something to make a potential judgment "ineffectual". Where, for example, P sues D to rescind a contract to transport goods for P, and it is shown that D's negotiation of the bill of lading could render a rescission judgment ineffectual, P may be granted a preliminary injunction enjoining D from either negotiating or demanding payment on the bill.[5]

Since this, the first part of CPLR 6301, requires a specific "subject matter", an action for money only does not qualify, and of course a money action does not qualify under the second part of the statute, either, in which the object of the action itself is a permanent injunction. The provisional remedy of injunction

---

8. CPLR 5232, 5233.

9. CPLR 6226. The section evinces an intent that it be read alongside CPLR 5234, to which it refers. When the contest is between attaching creditors on the one side and execution and other judgment creditors on the other, CPLR 5234 is the priority resolver. See § 520 below.

§ 327

1. In labor disputes, for example, there is detailed instruction about injunctions, whether permanent or preliminary. See Labor Law §§ 807, 808.

2. CPLR 101.

3. CPLR 6301 has no numbered subparagraphs. Its content is divided in two here to aid reference.

4. A preliminary injunction may also be sought in a special proceeding if it otherwise satisfies the requirements of CPLR 6301. See City Commission on Human Rights v. Regal Gardens, Inc., 53 Misc.2d 318, 278 N.Y.S.2d 739 (Sup.Ct., Queens County, 1967).

5. Gross v. State Cooperage Export Crating & Shipping Co., 32 A.D.2d 540, 299 N.Y.S.2d 773 (2d Dep't 1969).

is therefore unavailable in that most numerous of all actions, the money action. Although the inclusion of a money demand will not necessarily preclude an injunction if other relief, which would satisfy this provision of CPLR 6301, is also sought, the court will refuse the injunction if convinced that a money judgment is the true object of the action and that all else is incidental. (In a money action, P often fears that D will secrete property during the action's pendency and thus make a money judgment uncollectable. P's remedy there, if P can establish such conduct by D convincingly, is an order of attachment under CPLR 6201[3], not an injunction under Article 63.)

Under this first segment of CPLR 6301, equity actions are not the only ones that qualify. Although the money action, the major specimen of an action at law, is not an acceptable context for an injunction, other law actions may qualify if they involve a specific subject matter, such as an ejectment or replevin action. If the chattel is unique, there is even separate authority for the granting of an injunction in the replevin context,[6] but if it is not unique the authority of the first part of CPLR 6301 can apparently be invoked.[7]

The second part of CPLR 6301 is invoked more frequently than the first. Under the second part, P is bringing an injunction *action* against D, the well known equity action seeking a final judgment of permanent injunction. But even if the action is prima facie sustainable, it will still be a while before a trial on the merits can determine P's right to a permanent injunction. Unless enjoined in the meantime, however, D can do the very thing P has sued to enjoin. This provision of CPLR 6301 authorizes a preliminary injunction to enjoin during the action that which P seeks to enjoin permanently with the final judgment.

One riffling through the annotations on CPLR 6301 will find numerous cases on the preliminary injunction. The standards for the issuance of these injunctions are so well known that most judges don't even bother to cite the source—CPLR 6301—so that even written opinions accompanying preliminary injunction grants often omit citations.

The plethora of cases on the injunction is not as forbidding as the numbers suggest. As far as general principles are concerned, most of the cases play no role at all; they merely illustrate whether, on the facts of a particular case, the injunction is warranted.[8]

Because the substantive equity action of injunction is the context for the seeking of a preliminary injunction when the second part of CPLR 6301 is the ground invoked, one can easily convert an inquiry about a preliminary injunction into a full fledged equity course on injunction actions. That temptation will be resisted here, but the factors to be considered on our inquiry—adequacy of legal remedy, irreparable injury, judicial discretion, etc.—derive from that majestic body of law that falls under the caption of "equity" and necessarily figure even when the injunction being considered is to be only a transient one. One advantage to be drawn from the fact that our standards for preliminary injunctions derive from the rules of equity applicable to permanent injunctions is apparent: whenever it appears that a permanent injunction would not be granted even if the plaintiff establishes at trial the facts alleged in the complaint, it of course follows that a preliminary injunction must also be denied.[9]

While acknowledging the relationship, we should not let it obscure the fact that Article

---

6. CPLR 7109(a). See the discussion of restraints in replevin actions in § 339 below.

7. See, e.g., Carter v. Phillips, 127 Misc. 903, 217 N.Y.S. 621 (Sup.Ct., Lewis County, 1926). If the chattel lacks uniqueness, however, the element of urgency traditionally insisted on for an injunction of any kind would seem to be lacking.

8. The same has already been noted with the bill of particulars, see § 238, and the summary judgment motion, see § 278. Cases in all three areas are for the most part

sui generis dispositions offering little in the way of general guidance.

9. See, e.g., Arpels v. Arpels, 8 N.Y.2d 339, 207 N.Y.S.2d 663, 170 N.E.2d 670 (1960). The court's entire dissertation in Arpels is on equity's traditional reluctance to enjoin a party to a New York action from prosecuting an action elsewhere, and yet the discourse was generated by an appeal from an order disposing of an application for only a preliminary injunction.

63 is concerned not with making or remaking the substantive law of equitable injunctions, but with taking that law as it is and asking, additionally, whether enough has been shown to warrant even a preliminary restraint. The legislature itself sometimes overlooks that Article 63 was set up to govern only the provisional remedy.[10]

The preliminary injunction of Article 63 should be distinguished from a "stay" of proceedings as authorized by CPLR 2201. Technically, a "stay" refers to a court's temporary suspension of its own proceedings, while an endeavor to stop a proceeding in some other court usually involves an outright "injunction" and all of the relevant requirements of equity. If a temporary injunction is sought, it also involves Article 63. The terms of "stay" and "injunction" are sometimes used interchangeably, however, even in statutes.[11]

§ 328. Required Showing; Discretion

The plaintiff's showing on an application for a preliminary injunction must be convincing.[1] The plaintiff must show that the claim falls under either of the two categories listed in CPLR 6301, i.e., that it is either (1) a cause of action having a specific and identifiable subject matter, or (2) a cause of action for a permanent injunction. The plaintiff must also show that the statutorily required peril is in prospect: a potentially ineffectual judgment if the defendant does something during the action that could make the later final judgment futile.

It will not suffice for the plaintiff merely to make out a prima facie possibility of success on the merits of the claim. Standards sufficient for a pleading will not automatically do for an injunction, a point previously made with the attachment remedy[2] but just as true here with injunctions. The plaintiff has the burden of proof and must demonstrate a likelihood of success,[3] which means a strong showing in affidavits and other proof supplying evidentiary detail. The plaintiff should then show "that he would be irreparably damaged if an injunction were not granted before trial",[4] and should demonstrate this factually and convincingly. Mere apprehensions do not suffice; the injunction will issue only upon a showing that the defendant's wrongful acts are occurring or are threatened and reasonably likely to occur.[5] If the defendant, opposing the application, offers substantial proof of defenses tending to negate the plaintiff's claim on the merits, such as laches and unclean hands, the injunction is likely to be denied.[6]

Of course, the defendant's merely serving opposing papers disputing some of the facts on which the plaintiff's application is premised can't by itself be allowed to defeat the injunction. Because it doesn't take much to create an issue of fact, that would put too many aces into the defendant's hand. Some cases had been perceived as adopting such a position, however. Citing two of these,[7] the Advisory Committee recommended that CPLR 6312 be amended and the legislature responded with

---

10. In 1971, for example, it added to the article § 6330, which determines the availability of permanent injunctive relief in obscenity cases. The section is of course designed to recognize the delicacy of prior restraints on First Amendment (free speech) activities, see Gaetano v. Erwin, 46 A.D.2d 735, 360 N.Y.S.2d 741 (4th Dep't 1974), but it has no logical place in Article 63. It would be more appropriately housed in something like the Civil Rights Law. It is concerned only with permanent injunctions—the substantive stuff of equity—and does not even address itself to the temporary injunction, the meat of Article 63. Corroborating that CPLR 6330 does not address the preliminary injunction, the only subject that justifies its appearance in Article 63, is that it took caselaw to establish that an injunction under CPLR 6301 is permissible in a CPLR 6330 case. See Vergari v. Pierre Productions, Inc., 43 A.D.2d 950, 352 N.Y.S.2d 34 (2d Dep't 1974).

11. See, e.g., CPLR 6312(b) and Commentaries C2201:1–4 on McKinney's CPLR 2201.

§ 328

1. Etter v. Littwitz, 47 Misc.2d 473, 262 N.Y.S.2d 924 (Sup.Ct., Monroe County, 1965).

2. See § 316 above.

3. Metz v. People, 73 Misc.2d 219, 341 N.Y.S.2d 940 (Sup.Ct., Nassau County, 1973).

4. De Candido v. Young Stars, Inc., 10 A.D.2d 922, 200 N.Y.S.2d 695, 696 (1st Dep't 1960).

5. Eldre Components, Inc. v. Kliman, 47 Misc.2d 463, 262 N.Y.S.2d 732 (Sup.Ct., Monroe County, 1965).

6. De Candido v. Young Stars, Inc., note 4, above.

7. Price Paper and Twine Co. v. Miller, 182 A.D.2d 748, 582 N.Y.S.2d 746 (2d Dep't 1992); Hart Island Committee v. Koch, 137 Misc.2d 521, 520 N.Y.S.2d 977 (Sup. Ct., N.Y.County, 1987).

an amendment in 1996 that adds a subdivision (c) to CPLR 6312, providing that as long as the plaintiff's papers supply the elements needed for the injunction,

> the presentation by the defendant of evidence sufficient to raise an issue of fact as to any of such elements shall not in itself be grounds for denial of the motion. In such event the court shall make a determination by hearing or otherwise whether each of the elements required for issuance of a preliminary injunction exists.

It remains, in other words, a matter of the court's balancing all the proof, including consideration—but not undue consideration—of issues of fact raised by the defendant. An evidentiary hearing is permissible, but not mandatory. The court may, as it usually does in these situations, continue to determine the application on the papers alone.[8]

As a general rule—again borrowing from the substantive realm of equity—the injunction will not be granted if the plaintiff has an adequate remedy at law. An overly rigid adherence to this old principle, however, would undo some of the benefits wrought by the merger of law and equity. So, practically speaking, the standard has been reworked to require the injunction's denial only when the legal remedy is plain, adequate, and complete, and from a pragmatic viewpoint as efficacious as an injunction. Where the doing of the act could not be readily compensated by money damages, to use a frequent example, the legal remedy is not adequate and an injunction may be allowed.[9]

Perhaps the most instructive point about the preliminary injunction is that its granting is discretionary with the court.[10] This is so even though the plaintiff has made out a minimum showing under CPLR 6301.[11] Of course this discretion can be abused, and the appellate divisions may and do deny injunctions

granted below, and vice-versa. But discretion is still the keynote and there is therefore little need for rigidity when resorting to the broad catalog of equitable principles governing injunctions. Under a judicious application of discretion all manner of factors, whether pointing to or away from the injunction, can be given appropriate weight. Discretion will figure prominently, for example, in calculating the efficacy of an alternative legal remedy: if the alternative is suggested but there is significant doubt as to how completely it would do the job, discretion can be exercised to allow the injunction so as not to remit the plaintiff to an alternative that could prove impotent. Conversely, discretion can be relied on to deny the injunction if it would be futile, as where it seeks to enjoin an act that has already been done and can't be undone, or where the issue has become academic, as where P wants to enjoin an activity that D has long since clearly discontinued.

Perhaps the highest role discretion plays is in determining whether the plaintiff would be "irreparably" injured were the injunction withheld. The adverb is often seen in opinions treating injunctions, and yet were it literally applied few injunctions would issue. Whether the plaintiff's hurt would be "irreparable" turns on many things, all of which can be weighed and balanced by an astute judicial exercise of discretion. If all past cases granting provisional injunctions were collated and analyzed, many if not most would not pass a rigid "irreparable injury" test. The test must be applied commonsensically to give appropriate due to all factors. With a banner of discretion waving over the field of injunctions, pragmatism is the theme. This tends to prevent any single factor, no matter what its individual dictate might be, from rejecting the injunction out of hand despite countervailing considerations. Take this example.

---

8. See the discussion in SPR 43:2. The amendment was applied and even given retroactive effect in Independent Health Ass'n, Inc. v. Murray, 233 A.D.2d 883, 649 N.Y.S.2d 616 (4th Dep't 1996).

9. See, e.g., Republic Aviation Corp. v. Republic Lodge No. 1987, 10 Misc.2d 783, 169 N.Y.S.2d 651 (Sup.Ct., Queens County, 1957).

10. Sartwell v. Field, 68 N.Y. 341 (1877).

11. See Walsh v. New York State Liq. Auth., 45 Misc.2d 827, 257 N.Y.S.2d 971 (Sup.Ct., Suffolk County), modified on other grounds 23 A.D.2d 876, 259 N.Y.S.2d 491 (2d Dep't), aff'd 16 N.Y.2d 781, 262 N.Y.S.2d 502, 209 N.E.2d 821 (1965).

P is the H.J. Heinz Co. It has made a contract with farmer D to get all of the tomatoes grown on D's 25–acre tract. D then threatens to sell the crop to someone else. P sues to enjoin that sale and seeks a preliminary injunction. Should P get it? The literal, to say nothing of the rigid, application of the several traditional requirements applicable to the provisional injunction would preclude its issuance. P has a remedy at law, which is to buy 25 acres of tomatoes somewhere else and sue D for the difference in price. And it would border on the incredible to conclude that the H.J. Heinz Co. could be "irreparably" injured even if it were to lose the 25 acres of tomatoes altogether. The court nonetheless granted the injunction,[12] and rightly so. It took note that no harm would come to the defendant by granting the injunction because (1) it required him to do only that which he said he was going to do anyway (he admitted the 25–acre contract and said he was not violating it) and (2) a bond exacted of the plaintiff would indemnify the defendant for any resulting damages.

The plaintiff Heinz Company had an adequate remedy at law and that, considered alone under a rigid construction, would have precluded the injunction. Nor would the company have been irreparably injured, no matter what the defendant did with the 25 acres of tomatoes, and that, considered alone, would also have precluded the injunction. But they were not considered alone. They were part of a whole picture in which the competition of other factors, less generic in the texts and more individual to the case, prompted discretion to allow the injunction. The lesson is not that the inadequacy-of-legal-remedy and irreparable-injury factors are to be ignored; it is that both must be balanced in context. Everything is relative, even in the law of preliminary injunctions.

The courts generally prefer to couch preliminary injunctions in negative terms, especially if there is any chance that by giving P a mandatory preliminary injunction P will get everything she wants in advance and thus lose incentive to prosecute the claim on the merits. Where, for example, P was suing to be restored to membership in an association, the Court of Appeals said that the preliminary injunction could adequately maintain the status quo by enjoining D from denying P the benefits of membership (negative injunction), but that it should not go so far as to require full reinstatement (mandatory injunction) because that might prompt P, having gotten all he wants on the preliminary injunction, to let the action lapse.[13]

There is no absolute bar to mandatory relief in a preliminary injunction if the facts warrant it, however.[14] In fact, in many instances the line between a mandatory and negative injunction is semantic, and whenever that is so the distinction will likely be academic. What difference is there between requiring the defendant to sell his tomato crop to the plaintiff exclusively (mandatory injunction) and enjoining him from selling it to anyone but the plaintiff (negative injunction), as long as the defendant is bent on sale?

Since a preliminary injunction seeks only to retain status quo until the merits can be duly tried and adjudicated, neither its granting nor its refusal binds the trial court when the main trial comes on. There, the issues will be tried as if no provisional injunction were ever applied for.[15] The granting of a preliminary injunction, in other words, does not invoke the doctrines of res judicata or the law of the case.[16]

§ 329. Applying for the Injunction

The procedure for getting a preliminary injunction is a motion, which must be made on notice. (If the case is urgent, a faster motion and an interim restraint can be secured with a temporary restraining order in an order to

---

12. H.J. Heinz Co. v. Currie, 83 N.Y.S.2d 705 (Sup.Ct., Niagara County, 1948).

13. Bachman v. Harrington, 184 N.Y. 458, 77 N.E. 657 (1906).

14. See, e.g., Graham v. Board of Supervisors, Erie County, 49 Misc.2d 459, 267 N.Y.S.2d 383 (Sup.Ct., Erie County, 1966), modified 25 A.D.2d 250, 269 N.Y.S.2d 477 (4th Dep't 1966).

15. Walker Memorial Baptist Church, Inc. v. Saunders, 285 N.Y. 462, 35 N.E.2d 42 (1941).

16. Law of the case is a doctrine of intra-action res judicata. See § 448 below.

show cause, the subject of the next section.) The notice of motion for the preliminary injunction may be served with or after the summons, or at any time before final judgment.[1] A preliminary injunction is available only in a pending action.

The proof consists of affidavits and any other evidence the plaintiff has. It must show satisfaction of either of the two requirements stated in CPLR 6301.[2] Bearing in mind the discretionary nature of the remedy, the fact that the plaintiff has the burden of proof, and the several equitable considerations discussed in the prior section, such as a showing of irreparable injury, the proof should be clear and convincing.

It should not be necessary to submit the complaint as part of the moving papers because the requisite facts, including those that show a cause of action, can be proved by affidavit.[3] But if a complaint is submitted it will be considered, and if it fails to make out a claim satisfactory to CPLR 6301 it will result in a denial of the injunction.[4] If a verified complaint is submitted, it can be treated as an affidavit.[5]

Before getting a preliminary injunction, the plaintiff will have to submit an undertaking (bond)—this is mandatory—in an amount to be fixed by the court, conditioned that "if it is finally determined that he was not entitled to an injunction", the plaintiff will pay the defen-

dant "all damages and costs which may be sustained by reason of the injunction".[6]

CPLR 6315 provides that the court may ascertain these damages by motion brought on by order to show cause. This is designed to facilitate things by enabling D, with a mere motion procedure, to have the amount of her damages ascertained within the framework of P's action before bringing a separate action on the undertaking to recover judgment for those damages.[7] This procedure is optional; the damages can be ascertained in the separate action.[8] It has also been held that if they are ascertained by motion in P's action, a judgment for them can be awarded without even requiring a separate action.[9]

Assuming that the condition of the bond has been met—and it can be met by so simple a development as D's winning the case on the merits[10]—what are the damages that may be recovered on the bond? Expenses, including attorneys' fees, may be recovered, but ordinarily only for proceedings to vacate the preliminary injunction and for proceedings to assess D's damages. D is not entitled to recover an attorney's fee for the trial of P's action on the merits if it is shown, as it often can be, that the trial would have gone forward whether P had obtained a preliminary injunction or not.[11] By implication, the same should be true of pretrial activities in general, notably disclosure proceedings. Attorneys' fees for them should be recoverable only if incurred as a result of the injunction.[12]

§ 329

1. CPLR 6311(1).

2. CPLR 6312(a).

3. Some courts require submission of the complaint when the application for the preliminary injunction is based on the nature of the action, i.e., where the action seeks a final judgment of injunction under the second part of CPLR 6301 as opposed to an application based on the defendant's acts "respecting the subject of the action" under the first part. See, e.g., Seplow v. Century Operating Co., 56 A.D.2d 515, 391 N.Y.S.2d 124 (1st Dep't 1977).

4. Rodgers v. Rodgers, 30 A.D.2d 548, 290 N.Y.S.2d 608 (2d Dep't 1968).

5. CPLR 105.

6. CPLR 6312(b). Special added conditions are imposed by paragraphs 1 and 2 of the statute for undertakings given for injunctions to stop a party from prosecuting other actions. If P wants to enjoin D's enforcement of a money judgment that D has against P, for example, para-

graph 3 of CPLR 6312(b) requires that P's undertaking be to the effect that it will make good the judgment.

7. Gross v. Shields, 130 Misc.2d 641, 496 N.Y.S.2d 894 (Sup.Ct., N.Y. County, 1985).

8. See 4th Rep.Leg.Doc. (1960) No. 20, p. 233.

9. See, e.g., Carroll v. Kenin, 25 A.D.2d 743, 269 N.Y.S.2d 226 (1st Dep't 1966).

10. Dismissal of P's complaint carries with it an implicit finding that the injunction was unwarranted and supports a damages claim on the bond. Sweets v. Behrens, 118 Misc.2d 1062, 462 N.Y.S.2d 398 (Sup.Ct. Schenectady County, 1983).

11. See Cross Properties, Inc. v. Brook Realty Co., 76 A.D.2d 445, 430 N.Y.S.2d 820 (2d Dep't 1980).

12. See Carroll v. Kenin, note 9, above. For a general discussion of the damages the defendant is entitled to if he prevails on the merits, including attorneys' fees for defending, see Bausch & Lomb Inc. v. Hydron Pacific, Ltd.,

As long as the condition of the undertaking has been satisfied, damages are recoverable even if it is shown that P did not act in bad faith.[13] But the damages are ordinarily limited to the amount of the undertaking.[14] It has been held that there is no common law liability for an improperly issued injunction, so that the undertaking is the very source of the liability.[15]

The effect on the bond of an interim appellate determination of the propriety of the injunction has been addressed by the Court of Appeals. The court held that an interim determination that the injunction is proper does not entitle P to a discharge of the bond; that things can still go against P on the merits, which would entitle D to look to the bond despite the earlier indications that sustained the injunction.[16] But in the converse situation, in which the interim appellate determination is that the preliminary injunction is not proper, D has an immediate right to damages on the bond: the bond covers damages for wrongful *preliminary* injunction no matter how things may later turn out on the merits.[17]

The difference between the bond required for a preliminary injunction under Article 63 and the bond required for an attachment under Article 62 is highlighted in A & M Exports Ltd. v. Meridien Int'l Bank, Ltd.[18] When the condition of the bond is invoked, the applicable statute on an Article 63 bond is CPLR 6315, the court must ascertain the defendant's damages (it can't just award as damages the face amount of the bond), and the amount of the bond constitutes the outer limit on any permissible award made. Under Article 62, on the other hand, the bond defines the surety's liability, but the plaintiff can be subjected to damages in excess of the bond's amount.

The *Meridien* case holds that even the limited temporary restraining order authorized in conjunction with an attachment under CPLR 6210 is to be considered an Article 63 injunction for the purpose of ascertaining damages, making the governing provision CPLR 6315.

Counsel fees are includible in the damages.

§ 330. Temporary Restraining Order

A preliminary injunction, the official name for the device under Article 63 of the CPLR, goes by other popular names. It may variously be referred to as a "temporary" injunction, or an injunction "pendente lite", or even as an "interlocutory" injunction. Whatever the alias, the device is used to enjoin the defendant from doing something while the action is pending and must be distinguished from the "temporary restraining order", whose mission is shorter lived but more urgent. Since a motion for a preliminary injunction may be made only on notice under CPLR 6311, there is a risk that between the time the motion papers are served and the day set for the hearing (the return day) the defendant will do the act the plaintiff wants restrained and make all further proceedings futile. The sole mission of the temporary restraining order (TRO for short) is to effect a restraint against the defendant during that brief interim.

CPLR 6301 allows the TRO only if the plaintiff shows that "immediate and irreparable injury, loss or damage will result unless the defendant is restrained before the hearing [on the preliminary injunction] can be had." A plaintiff who wants a TRO does not use the ordinary motion-on-notice procedure, but rather an order to show cause to bring on the motion for a preliminary injunction. It's the order to show cause that includes the TRO. CPLR 6313(a), the TRO statute, requires that the time for the preliminary injunction be set by the court, and by so doing it makes clear that the show cause procedure is to be used.[1]

---

82 Misc.2d 576, 371 N.Y.S.2d 292 (Sup.Ct., Monroe County, 1975).

13. Sweets v. Behrens, note 10, above.

14. Doran & Associates, Inc. v. Envirogas, Inc., 112 A.D.2d 766, 492 N.Y.S.2d 504 (4th Dep't 1985).

15. Honeywell, Inc. v. Technical Building Svcs., Inc., 103 A.D.2d 433, 480 N.Y.S.2d 627 (3d Dep't 1984).

16. J.A. Preston Corp. v. Fabrication Enterprises, Inc., 68 N.Y.2d 397, 509 N.Y.S.2d 520, 502 N.E.2d 197 (1986).

17. Margolies v. Encounter, Inc., 42 N.Y.2d 475, 398 N.Y.S.2d 877, 368 N.E.2d 1243 (1977). On that basis the J.A. Preston case distinguishes Margolies.

18. 222 A.D.2d 378, 636 N.Y.S.2d 35 (1st Dep't 1995).

§ 330

1. Setting a return time different from the one required by the motion-on-notice statute, CPLR 2214(b), is one of the functions of an order to show cause.

So, the plaintiff who wants a TRO applies for it ex parte by presenting an order to show cause to the court. And since an order to show cause is a species of ex parte application, the plaintiff must inform the court in an affidavit whether this or like relief was previously applied for and what the result was of any such prior application.[2] If the judge signs the order to show cause, the judge will determine in the order itself (1) the time and place of the hearing for the preliminary injunction, (2) who shall be served with the order, (3) how the service shall be made, and (4) the terms of the TRO.[3] After signing by the judge, the order is returned to the plaintiff's attorney, who then effects service of it on the defendant pursuant to its terms.

Several rules apply here. If the court grants a TRO, it must set the hearing for the preliminary injunction for "the earliest possible time",[4] which merely recognizes that an ex parte restraint against a defendant should be as brief as possible.[5] If an order to show cause containing a TRO does not contain directions as to the method of service, then service is to be made in the same manner as a summons. The papers served must include the papers on which the TRO is based.[6]

If the summons has not yet been served, the summons should accompany the order to show cause and be served on the defendant at the same time. Since the order to show cause serves as notice of motion for a preliminary injunction, this procedure will satisfy the requirement of CPLR 6311(1) that notice of the injunction motion be served with or after the summons. In the lower courts, in the relatively rare instances in which an injunction may be entertained, requiring the summons to accompany the order to show cause if the summons has not already been served will mean that the action is being commenced now.[7] Thus, the ex parte granting of the TRO in an order to show cause may be had before commencement of the lower court action, provided that the summons is then served on the defendant when the order is.

In the supreme and county courts, where the filing of the summons and complaint marks the commencement of the action, the usual practice is for the plaintiff to file the summons and complaint when applying for the TRO, so that an action will immediately be pending and give its context to the application. It will also enable the plaintiff to secure an index number and include it on the summons and complaint as well as on the order to show cause.

The courts should recognize, however, that the TRO is an emergency device, and if the emergency is such that the securing of an index number in advance of the service of the order to show cause (and summons) is not practicable, it should be permissible to add the index number later. Since only a "filing" constitutes commencement in a supreme or county court action, this will mean that the order to show cause and TRO (and summons) are being served before commencement of the action, but that does not appear to be of great concern under Article 63 of the CPLR. The time constraints imposed on serving notice of the injunction application are phrased not in terms of commencing the action, but in terms of serving the summons.[8]

It would be a good idea, however, in any situation in which the judge signs an order to show cause (containing the TRO) without a preliminary filing, for the judge to require, in the order itself, a filing with the clerk within a specified time, perhaps with an instruction to the plaintiff to communicate the index number to the defendant when one is assigned or when the defendant is served (whichever occurs later).

An undertaking, mandatory if a preliminary injunction is granted, is discretionary with the

---

2. CPLR 2217(b).

3. See § 248 above.

4. CPLR 6313(a).

5. No TRO may issue under CPLR 6313 in a labor dispute, in which injunctions are governed by Labor Law § 807.

6. CPLR 6313(b).

7. In the lower courts, service of the summons marks commencement of the action. See § 63 above.

8. See CPLR 6311(1).

court when it grants a TRO.[9] This acknowledges that time may be so tight and the situation so urgent that opportunity may not exist even to secure an undertaking. If the court does require an undertaking, its terms are the same as the one required for the preliminary injunction.[10] If there appears to be any difficulty about getting the parties into court for a hearing, so that it looks as if the "earliest possible time" required for the hearing by CPLR 6313(a) is not going to be so early after all, the court should recognize that while it may be granting a TRO in form, it is granting a preliminary injunction in effect, and should therefore require an undertaking.[11]

Whatever showing of urgency is needed to sustain a preliminary injunction, presumably that much more is needed to justify a TRO. That's the conclusion one would ordinarily draw from a reading of CPLR 6301 and 6313(a), both of which reserve for the TRO the most demanding standard articulated by the injunction article—more demanding, in any event, than the requirements verbalized for the preliminary injunction itself. A little logic applied to the situation, however, can lead one to reverse these roles and require less for a TRO than for a preliminary injunction. The injunction, after all, will cover the whole period of litigation, which can be a long one, while the TRO will live for only the few days, and sometimes only the few hours, needed to bring on a hearing for the preliminary injunction. Since the preliminary injunction can ensue only after an adversary hearing, the court can weigh, in at least some leisure, the opposing views of the parties. The air of emergency in that context is therefore not as tense as that surrounding the TRO. On the TRO, by contrast, the court has before it an excited if not frantic applicant pleading for an instant enjoinment lest the defendant do something even

before a hearing can be had. Greater though the stated requirement may be for the issuance of a TRO than for a preliminary injunction, therefore, a judge—contradiction though this may seem—may be more disposed to issue a TRO than a preliminary injunction.

The TRO keeps status quo until the judge can hear both sides. Things work out pretty much that way in practice, anyway, not because the judges are ignoring the applicable standards, but because the TRO comes to the judge on the ex parte papers of the plaintiff and the plaintiff can, without the defendant there to traverse, all the more easily convince the court that the world may come to an end if a TRO is withheld.

As one of the introductory sections of this chapter stressed, the provisional remedies, because of their ex parte nature, are under constitutional scrutiny and some have been severely circumscribed. The preliminary injunction appears to be on safe ground because it requires notice of motion and thus offers the defendant a hearing in advance. The TRO does not give advance notice, but the fact (1) that it is in the court's control, (2) that it requires the court to set an "earliest possible time" hearing for the injunction,[12] and (3) that it can be granted only if the plaintiff shows that irreparable injury will result if any delay at all is allowed, suggest in the aggregate that even the TRO is on a sturdy constitutional track.[13]

Statute prohibits the issuance of a temporary restraining order "against a public officer, board or municipal corporation of the state to restrain the performance of statutory duties",[14] a provision sometimes circumvented by theorizing that it does not apply if the plaintiff can make it appear—and the plaintiff is usually hell bent to make it appear—that

---

9. CPLR 6313(c).

10. These terms come from CPLR 6312(b), discussed in the prior section.

11. Honeywell, Inc. v. Technical Building Svcs., Inc., 103 A.D.2d 433, 480 N.Y.S.2d 627 (3d Dep't 1984).

12. CPLR 6313(a).

13. See the discussion of constitutional requirements in § 307 above. In free speech cases, the U.S. Supreme Court has forbidden a TRO unless it is shown that there is

no possibility whatever of giving reasonable notice. See Carroll v. President and Commissioners of Princess Anne, 393 U.S. 175, 89 S.Ct. 347, 21 L.Ed.2d 325 (1968). New York afterwards adopted CPLR 6330, a statute on obscenity, which acknowledges the policy against prior restraints in such cases by supplying special preferences for their trial.

14. CPLR 6313(a).

the body is acting unlawfully and hence not within its "statutory duties."[15] In any event, this is a restriction only on the TRO, not on the preliminary injunction. If the restriction applies, an order to show cause, although it can't in this instance include a TRO, may still be used to expedite a hearing on the preliminary injunction, which will reduce to a bare minimum the period in which the public officer or body is unrestrained.[16] This can have a positive ecological impact by guarding against an unbridled infestation of unrestrained public officers.

When the plaintiff's action is seeking a judgment of permanent injunction, the offerings of Article 63 show how complete the plaintiff's injunctive protection can be from the earliest moment of perceived need. Assuming the plaintiff prevails at all stages,

1. the TRO puts the defendant under a restraint while a motion for a preliminary injunction is brought on;

2. the preliminary injunction takes over from the TRO and continues the restraint during the entire pendency of the action until final judgment; and

3. the judgment of permanent injunction takes over at that point, covering the future and closing the case.

§ 331. Vacating or Modifying Injunction or TRO

The defendant may move at any time to vacate or modify the preliminary injunction or temporary restraining order. Since the injunction is granted only on notice, the motion to vacate it must also be made on notice. Conversely, since the TRO is granted without notice, the motion to vacate or modify it may be made without notice, but only if made to the

judge who granted it; only in the absence or disability of the granting judge may it be made without notice to another one.

An ex parte order vacating or modifying a TRO, and the papers underlying the order, must be filed with the clerk and served on the plaintiff. The order is not effective unless they are. An order vacating or modifying either an injunction or TRO can be conditioned on the defendant's furnishing an undertaking, in an amount fixed by the court, that the defendant will reimburse the plaintiff any loss occasioned by the order of vacatur or modification.[1]

The violation of either a preliminary injunction or a temporary restraining order is of course a contempt of court and may be punished as such. The procedure for the contempt punishment (which is also the enforcement device for several classes of final judgment), including distinctions between criminal and civil contempt and their applicable sanctions, is treated in the chapter on the enforcement of judgments.[2]

E. RECEIVERSHIP

Table of Sections

§ 332. Temporary Receivership

Article 64 of the CPLR supplies the provisional remedy of receivership. The Article 64 receiver is a person appointed by the court to take control of designated property and see to its care and preservation during litigation. This is only a temporary receivership, functioning to preserve the property during that time,[1] and should therefore be distinguished

---

15. See, e.g., Komyathy v. Board of Education of Wappinger Cent. School Dist., 75 Misc.2d 859, 348 N.Y.S.2d 28 (Sup.Ct., Dutchess County, 1973).

16. CPLR 6311 also has some special requirements for preliminary injunctions against public officers and bodies, restricting the venue of motions seeking such injunctions, CPLR 6311(1), and requiring that notice of the motion be served on the Attorney General as well as on the particular defendants, CPLR 6311(2).

§ 331

1. CPLR 6314. If the defendant is a public body or officer, it may not be subjected to this condition, an exception which to some extent overlaps the more general one in CPLR 2512.

2. See § 481 et seq., below.

§ 332

1. Decker v. Gardner, 124 N.Y. 334, 26 N.E. 814 (1891).

from a permanent receiver, such as one appointed in conjunction with the dissolution of a corporation.[2] It should also be distinguished from two other CPLR receivers, those under CPLR 5106 and 5228. The Article 64 receiver takes control of property during the action. If the plaintiff wins on the merits, a CPLR 5106 receiver may then be appointed to dispose of the property under the judgment. The CPLR 5106 receiver can be considered the post-judgment counterpart of the Article 64 receiver. The same person appointed under Article 64 can later be appointed under CPLR 5106, but the two provisions are independent and the use of one does not require the use of the other.

The CPLR 5228 receiver is one appointed to help enforce a money judgment. Our concentration here will be on only the temporary, or "provisional", receiver of Article 64.

This category of receivership may be sought only in an action having some specific and identifiable "property" as the "subject of the action".[3] The plaintiff must be asserting some right in that specific property, for which reason this kind of receivership is unavailable in an action for money only.[4] It is available, however, if it seeks the money proceeds of specific assets in the context of a fiduciary relationship. It is therefore available in an accounting action in equity, for example,[5] even though money is the ultimate object of the plaintiff's quest in an accounting action.

The temporary receiver is historically an aspect of equity practice, and so it is more often than not an equity action that qualifies for one.

Receivership is one of the rarer of the provisional remedies. Probably its best known context is the action to foreclose a mortgage on a rental or other income-producing property, where a receiver may be appointed to collect the rents and profits and in effect manage the property while the foreclosure steps proceed.

The reason for the relative infrequency of this provisional remedy is that a showing that the action involves specific property is not enough. The plaintiff must also demonstrate that "there is danger that the property will be removed from the state, or lost, materially injured or destroyed".[6] This showing is indispensable, and many actions having specific property as their subject fail to satisfy it. Receivership, in common with the other provisional remedies, is considered a drastic remedy, and it ordinarily lies in the discretion of the court. This discretion will be exercised to deny the receivership unless the court deems it necessary to preserve the property until the action makes clear who has the right to it.[7]

The powers of a temporary receiver, which are more circumscribed than those of a permanent one, are set forth in CPLR 6401(b). The receiver is authorized to take and hold personal or real property and to sue for, collect, and sell debts or claims "upon such conditions and for such purposes as the court shall direct". The lesson is that the receiver should see to it that whatever she does has basis in the appointing order or some subsequent one. No sale of any asset received, for example, should be made without court authorization, or the receiver may end up paying for it out of pocket, i.e., being surcharged.[8] Nor can the receiver retain counsel without explicit court approval,[9] and this approval should be obtained in advance of the retainer. There is some authority, however, "under exigent circumstances", for

---

2. See Bus.Corp.L. Art. 12; Matter of Sheridan Constr. Corp., 22 A.D.2d 390, 256 N.Y.S.2d 210 (4th Dep't), aff'd 16 N.Y.2d 680, 261 N.Y.S.2d 300, 209 N.E.2d 290 (1965).

3. CPLR 6401(a). The Article 64 receivership is available only in the supreme court or a county court under the terms of CPLR 6401(a), but may also be used in certain actions in the New York City Civil Court under § 209(c) of its court act (McKinney's Vol. 29A, Part 3).

4. See Mack v. Stanley, 74 A.D. 145, 77 N.Y.S. 574 (1st Dep't 1902), in which P's action for fraud, a mere money claim, was held to preclude a receivership regardless of the nature of the underlying transaction.

5. See Meurer v. Meurer, 21 A.D.2d 778, 250 N.Y.S.2d 817 (1st Dep't 1964).

6. CPLR 6401(a).

7. See E.H.A. Successor Corp. v. Vogel, 21 A.D.2d 176, 249 N.Y.S.2d 568 (1st Dep't 1964).

8. A good illustration of how the court determines and supervises the receiver's powers is Security Nat. Bank v. Village Mall at Hillcrest, Inc., 79 Misc.2d 1060, 361 N.Y.S.2d 977 (Sup.Ct., Queens County, 1974).

9. CPLR 6401(b).

the court to ratify an appointment of counsel previously retained.[10]

Any person capable of performing a receiver's duties can be appointed as one. Ideally the appointee should be a disinterested person,[11] but a party is sometimes appointed.[12] Occasionally the appointee is disinterested in all but the fee, and the receivership has been known to be a patronage plum. A receiver's compensation is on a commission basis, set by the court that appoints him. The commission can't exceed 5% of sums received and disbursed, but a fee of up to $100 may be allowed if the 5% computation comes to less.[13]

Upon appointment, receivers are required to take an oath[14] and to give an undertaking to perform their duties faithfully. The amount is fixed by the appointing court.[15] They are also required by statute to keep accurate accounts,[16] and as officers of the court they may be removed by the court at any time on the motion of a party or sua sponte.[17]

§ 333. Applying for the Receivership

A temporary receiver is appointed on motion, which may be made by any person having "an apparent interest" in the property to be received. The primary supporting papers are, as usual, affidavits (and any other proof the plaintiff has) making out a cause of action having specific "property" as its subject matter and setting forth facts showing the danger that the property will be removed from New York or otherwise lost, injured, or destroyed,

i.e., that the case comes within the requirements of CPLR 6401(a). Usually the motion is made by the plaintiff who has brought or is about to bring an action, but it can be made in a pending action even by one not a party to it, as where the nonparty movant has an interest in the property involved in the action and fears that it will be removed or destroyed if left in a party's hands. Such a motion by a nonparty makes her a party, i.e., it constitutes an appearance in the action.[1] There is also provision for extending the receivership to another action involving the same property,[2] which would then require the receiver to account to the parties in both actions.

The motion for the appointment of a receiver is made on notice, but if a contract between the parties calls for an ex parte appointment, it is permissible. Mortgages often contain stipulations for ex parte receiverships in foreclosure actions, statute expressly approves of it,[3] and the constitutionality of such no-notice appointments has, at least for the time being, been upheld.[4]

The appointment may be made before or after the service of the summons.[5]

The court can permit the receivership to extend beyond judgment,[6] where it would serve primarily to preserve the property during an appeal.[7] If it is sought to continue the receivership beyond judgment for the purpose of enforcing the judgment, the more appropriate authorizing provision would be CPLR

---

10. See Emigrant Savings Bank v. Elan Mgmt. Corp., 114 Misc.2d 472, 453 N.Y.S.2d 977 (Sup.Ct., Queens County, 1982).

11. Hahn v. Wylie, 54 A.D.2d 622, 387 N.Y.S.2d 255 (1st Dep't 1976).

12. See, e.g., Broder v. Broudarge, 38 N.Y.S.2d 282 (Sup.Ct., Kings County, 1942).

13. CPLR 8004(a). The party who moved the appointment may be required to pay the fees of the receiver and her lawyer (assuming a lawyer has been allowed) if there are no funds in the hands of the receiver out of which fees can be paid. CPLR 8004(b).

14. CPLR 6402.

15. CPLR 6403.

16. CPLR 6404.

17. CPLR 6405.

§ 333

1. CPLR 6401(a).

2. CPLR 6401(b).

3. Real Prop.L. § 254(10).

4. Security Nat. Bank v. Village Mall at Hillcrest, Inc., 79 Misc.2d 1060, 361 N.Y.S.2d 977 (Sup.Ct., Queens County, 1974). The constitutionality of the receivership provisions, especially when invoked ex parte, was under review for a while. See the Judicial Conference's Report to the 1977 Legislature, p.80, and Professor Donnelly's study of the temporary receivership in 21st Jud.Conf.Rep. (1976) p.483.

5. CPLR 6401(a).

6. CPLR 6401(c).

7. The appointment for appeal purposes is expressly authorized by CPLR 6401(a), and in this regard subdivisions (a) and (c) of CPLR 6401 overlap.

5106, under which, as already noted, the 6401 receiver can be continued for that purpose.

As an officer of the court, a receiver should not be sued except by leave of court, but the absence of prior leave is not a jurisdictional defect but can be cured with a nunc pro tunc order and an action brought in violation of this requirement thereby preserved.[8]

F. NOTICE OF PENDENCY

Table of Sections

Sec.
334. Notice of Pendency, Generally.
335. Procedure for Filing.
336. Cancellation of Notice.

§ 334. Notice of Pendency, Generally

A notice of pendency (or "lis pendens" as it is commonly called) is a paper usable in a realty action. The plaintiff files it with the county clerk of the realty county, putting the world on notice of the plaintiff's potential rights in the action and thereby warning all comers that if they then buy the realty or lend on the strength of it or otherwise rely on the defendant's right, they do so subject to whatever the action may establish as the plaintiff's right. The device takes advantage of the immobility of realty and the ease with which the mere filing of a paper can affect interests in it. Where mortgagee E had a lis pendens on file, for example, E prevailed over B even though B bought the land from mortgagor R only after being shown a satisfaction-piece signed by E. The lis pendens still stood of record at the title closing.[1]

It has been held that if the person who files the lis pendens knows of another person's prior interest, the prior interest will prevail even though it is unrecorded.[2]

CPLR 6501 allows the lis pendens to be used only in an action that can "affect the title to, or the possession, use or enjoyment of, real property".[3] The well known realty actions, such as mortgage foreclosure, specific performance, partition, etc., easily fall within the category, but despite the seemingly generous language of the statute (including the phrase "use or enjoyment"), it has been held that the lis pendens can't be used where the plaintiff claims no "right, title, or interest" in the property itself. It was therefore held unavailable in an action in which P sought to prevent D from using D's land in such a way as to create a nuisance. Although P sought an injunction, his grievance was found to be in essence just a tort claim.[4] This is perhaps unduly severe, since it would be useful to a potential buyer to have notice that use of the property may be restricted—the use the buyer sees D making of the land and which the buyer may wish to pursue herself.

In the landlord-tenant arena, when the essence of a dispute is over a month-to-month tenancy, there is at present a dispute among departments about whether a lis pendens may be used.[5]

The Court of Appeals has also said that a lis pendens cannot be used if the realty is owned by a corporation or partnership and the plaintiff's contractual right is not to buy the land directly, but only to buy shares in the owning entity. It so held in 1984 in 5303 Realty Corp. v. O & Y Equity Corp.,[6] a case that may impair some of the purpose of a lis pendens, which is to protect a plaintiff in realty transactions. The defendant/owner, unencumbered by the deterrent that the lis pendens would be to a buyer, can sell unimpeded to one who might not go near the transaction if made aware of— and subject to—the plaintiff's claim. The court

8. Copeland v. Salomon, 56 N.Y.2d 222, 451 N.Y.S.2d 682, 436 N.E.2d 1284 (1982).

§ 334

1. Goldstein v. Gold, 106 A.D.2d 100, 483 N.Y.S.2d 375 (2d Dep't 1984), aff'd 66 N.Y.2d 624, 495 N.Y.S.2d 32, 485 N.E.2d 239 (1985). E was seeking to have the satisfaction-piece canceled based on fraud.

2. LaMarche v. Rosenblum, 50 A.D.2d 636, 374 N.Y.S.2d 443 (3d Dep't 1975).

3. CPLR 6501.

4. Braunston v. Anchorage Woods, Inc., 10 N.Y.2d 302, 222 N.Y.S.2d 316, 178 N.E.2d 717 (1961).

5. See Nadeau v. Tuley, 160 A.D.2d 1130, 553 N.Y.S.2d 912 (3d Dep't 1990).

6. 64 N.Y.2d 313, 486 N.Y.S.2d 877, 476 N.E.2d 276.

said in the *5303* case that the plaintiff can fall back on an attachment or an injunction for protection, but this overlooks that if a conveyance is what a plaintiff wants, an attachment will not do because it is available only in a money action,[7] and an injunction, while a better prospect, depends on the defendant's fear of contempt proceedings and does not put other potential buyers on notice.

Mere money actions of course do not qualify for a lis pendens. Nor may a lis pendens be used if the plaintiff merely *could* state a realty claim, as where he might assert a lien against the premises for goods affixed to it or services rendered on it or money otherwise spent on it. If the complaint asserts in essence only a money claim, the plaintiff forfeits the use of the lis pendens.[8]

The realty action can be pending in a New York court or in a federal court in New York; a lis pendens can be used in connection with either.[9]

The lis pendens must state the names of the parties to the action, state the object of the action, and describe the realty affected. The plaintiff should be as explicit as possible, but as long as the lis pendens contains such data as will at least put potential buyers and encumbrancers on inquiry, they can't claim to be misled and the lis pendens suffices.[10]

The lis pendens is effective for a period of three years measured from the date of its filing. It can be extended for like periods, but each extension must be applied for within the prior three-year period so that any extension order can be filed and indexed before the existing notice expires.[11] This avoids a gap in the constructive notice afforded by the lis pendens

and prevents some third person from slipping in and taking priority. It has been held that if the three-year period passes without extension, the court can't then extend it.[12] But where it appeared that P at least started the extension machinery within the three-year period, as with an order to show cause to bring on the motion to extend, and even filed the order, P was allowed a nunc pro tunc order to retain the continuity of the lis pendens.[13] It ill behooves a plaintiff to so postpone commencing the renewal process.

Generally speaking, the filing of a lis pendens is optional with the plaintiff. In an action to foreclose a mortgage, however, the filing has been made mandatory.[14]

The constitutionality of the lis pendens was alluded to earlier.[15] It has been held that the filing of a lis pendens does not amount to a taking in the due process sense.[16]

§ 335. Procedure for Filing

The lis pendens is the only one of the provisional remedies that does not require a court order. The plaintiff just makes it out and files it with the clerk of the realty county.

If the lis pendens is filed before the summons has been served, the summons must be served within 30 days after the filing of the lis pendens. If the summons has already been served, the lis pendens may be filed at any time up to final judgment. If the complaint has not already been filed, it should be filed with the lis pendens.[1] In an action in the supreme or county courts, both of which have plenary jurisdiction of the real property actions,[2] the soundest procedure for the plaintiff is to start the action itself with the filing of a summons

---

7. CPLR 6201. See § 314 above.

8. Gokey v. Massey, 278 A.D. 630, 102 N.Y.S.2d 581 (4th Dep't 1951).

9. CPLR 6501.

10. Mechanics Exchange Savings Bank v. Chesterfield, 34 A.D.2d 111, 309 N.Y.S.2d 548 (3d Dep't 1970).

11. CPLR 6513.

12. Robbins v. Goldstein, 32 A.D.2d 1047, 303 N.Y.S.2d 822 (2d Dep't 1969).

13. Thelma Sanders & Assocs., Inc. v. Hague Devel. Corp., 131 A.D.2d 462, 516 N.Y.S.2d 93 (2d Dep't 1987).

14. RPAPL § 1331.

15. See the discussion at the point of note 24 in § 307, above.

16. United State v. Rivieccio, 661 F.Supp. 281 (E.D.N.Y.1987).

§ 335

1. CPLR 6511(a).

2. Some limited use of a lis pendens may be allowed in the New York City Civil Court, which has some limited realty jurisdiction. See §§ 203 and 209(d) of the New York City Civil Court Act (McKinney's Vol. 29A, Part 3).

and complaint and at the same time present the lis pendens for filing as well.[3] The plaintiff must then be sure to effect service of the summons within 30 days afterwards, or the lis pendens will become void. That's the requirement of CPLR 6512, whose impact is to deny the plaintiff the full 120–day period that CPLR 306–b would otherwise have allowed for summons service.[4]

If there are several defendants, service on one within the 30–day period satisfies CPLR 6512.[5] And if service is made under either CPLR 308(2) ("deliver and mail") or 308(4) ("affix and mail"), each of which involves two steps and contains provisions about when service is "complete", it is sufficient if the two steps are taken within the 30 days even though the service does not become "complete" until afterwards.[6]

If the clerk maintains what is known as a "block index", which is common in urban counties, the lis pendens must contain the number of the block containing the land affected.[7] A clerk with such an index records the lis pendens against the block and searchers find it there easily. If a block index is not in effect in the county, the clerk records the lis pendens against the names of all defendants named in the action,[8] in whatever alphabetized books the clerk maintains for this purpose.

If the lis pendens is properly filed but the clerk fails to index it, and a purchaser or encumbrancer is damaged because a search fails to uncover it, liability for the omission lies with the state and damages should be sought in a court of claims action.[9]

If the lis pendens has become void, even a person who accepts title with knowledge of the lis pendens takes free of the plaintiff's claim,[10] but the buyer's or mortgagee's lawyer would do better to insist on a court order cancelling the lis pendens rather than merely assume its nullity from facts as yet unadjudicated.

The lis pendens can be amended by court leave if no prejudice would result.[11]

§ 336. Cancellation of Notice

There are several ways to cancel a lis pendens. One is for the plaintiff's attorney to file an affidavit attesting that all the defendants' time to appear has expired and none has appeared, but that of course applies only where all the defendants are in default.[1] If any defendants have appeared, a stipulation of the appearing ones (agreeing to the cancellation)

---

3. When no lis pendens is filed until after the summons has been served, CPLR 6512 would seem to require another service of the summons, this one to be made within 30 days after the filing of the lis pendens. This language is the product of a 1994 amendment of the statute that had a different mission. It was not the drafters' intention to require an additional process service. See the discussion in SPR 22:3.

4. Letting the 30 days pass without service of the summons will not require dismissal of the action—as a passing of the 120–period would—but it will undo the lis pendens.

5. Micheli Contracting Corp. v. Fairwood Associates, 73 A.D.2d 774, 423 N.Y.S.2d 533 (3d Dep't 1979). The plaintiff should serve the others as promptly as possible since a failure to do so can qualify as a want of prosecution and justify a discretionary cancellation of the lis pendens under CPLR 6514(b).

6. See William Iser, Inc. v. Garnett, 46 Misc.2d 450, 259 N.Y.S.2d 996 (Sup.Ct., Nassau County, 1965), holding that the word "completed" in CPLR 6514(a), which authorizes a cancellation of the lis pendens, refers only to service by publication. When that method is used, only the first publication need be made within the 30–day period, CPLR 6512, provided that the remaining publications are carried out in due course.

7. CPLR 6511(b).

8. CPLR 6511(b), (c). In a partition action, it is also recorded against the plaintiff's names if there is no block index.

9. Ashland Equities v. Clerk of New York County, 110 A.D.2d 60, 493 N.Y.S.2d 133 (1st Dep't 1985). It has been held that in the filing and indexing of judgments, the county clerk is a state agent whose negligence supports a court of claims action. See National Westminster Bank, USA v. State of New York, 76 N.Y.2d 507, 561 N.Y.S.2d 541 (1990), and the discussion in the lead note of New York State Law Digest No.372.

10. Skoler v. Rimberg, 20 A.D.2d 580, 246 N.Y.S.2d 147 (2d Dep't 1963).

11. See Lake Louise Marie Community Assoc., Inc. v. Lake Louise Marie Corp., 25 A.D.2d 475, 266 N.Y.S.2d 156 (3d Dep't 1966), which allowed an amendment to describe the property more accurately. The case did not involve any of the jurisdictional difficulties tied in with the 30–day service-of-summons requirement of CPLR 6512.

§ 336

1. CPLR 6514(e).

must accompany the affidavit.[2]

The lis pendens can of course be cancelled by court order. On the motion of any aggrieved person, which is ordinarily brought on by order to show cause, the court is required to cancel the lis pendens in any of several situations. The first, already met, is where the summons has not been served within the 30 days allowed by CPLR 6512. Another is where the action has been settled, discontinued, or abated. Yet another is where the plaintiff loses on the merits and the appeal time has expired, or where, having taken an appeal, the plaintiff does not get a stay of enforcement of the judgment during the appeal's pendency. Each of those things is expressly listed in CPLR 6514(a), and mandates cancellation. Not listed, but just as clearly a ground for mandatory cancellation, is a showing that the plaintiff's action doesn't qualify for a lis pendens under CPLR 6501 in the first place.

The lis pendens is in a sense a privilege that can be lost if abused. In one case, for example, P filed a lis pendens in a county court realty action. It was later cancelled for want of summons service. P then brought the same action in the supreme court and again filed a lis pendens. The lis pendens was cancelled; the court held that having abused the privilege in the first action, the plaintiff was not entitled to it in the second.[3] Note that a second action in such circumstances is not barred by res judicata (the first action not having been disposed of on the merits); it is only the privilege of the lis pendens that the plaintiff forfeits. In a mortgage foreclosure action, however, the cancellation of one lis pendens does not preclude the filing of a second one, because in that category of action a lis pendens is mandatory, not optional.[4] This has led the courts to conclude that in mortgage foreclosure the lis pendens is a right rather than just a privilege.[5]

Then there is the cancellation directed by the court as a matter of discretion. Under CPLR 6514(b), the court can order cancellation of a lis pendens as a discretionary matter, and will if it finds that the plaintiff has not prosecuted the action diligently. This is to recognize that the defendant's rights are suspended for as long as the action pends. Again, the motion to cancel is brought on by order to show cause.

Upon making any order under CPLR 6514 cancelling a lis pendens, the court may direct the plaintiff to pay the defendant such costs and expenses as the filing of the lis pendens may have occasioned.[6] Such expenses are imposed on the plaintiff, and they are not necessarily backed by an undertaking.

Undertakings are not mandatory in lis pendens practice, but they do figure in the cancellation requirements of CPLR 6515, which run as follows. Any person aggrieved by the filing of the lis pendens (presumably the defendant) may volunteer an undertaking for the plaintiff's protection in an amount to be fixed by the court. If the court finds that the undertaking is adequate for the plaintiff's protection, it will order cancellation of the lis pendens.[7] If money alone would not be adequate protection, as where the interest the plaintiff asserts is unique—this is not just an action to foreclose a lien, for example, in which the plaintiff is usually after money and nothing more—cancellation would not be ordered under this provision.

Cancellation might be ordered under another provision, however, a bit baroque in design. Even if an undertaking would not be adequate to protect the plaintiff, the court can still cancel the lis pendens if the defendant offers an undertaking and the plaintiff does not respond with the plaintiff's own undertaking to protect the defendant.[8] It's a kind of lever the defendant can pull to try to make the plaintiff

2. CPLR 6514(d).

3. Israelson v. Bradley, 308 N.Y. 511, 127 N.E.2d 313 (1955). Resort to another provisional remedy, however, such as an injunction, is not necessarily barred in these circumstances. Vincent v. Seaman, 152 A.D.2d 841, 544 N.Y.S.2d 225 (3d Dep't 1989).

4. RPAPL § 1331.

5. Robbins v. Goldstein, 36 A.D.2d 730, 320 N.Y.S.2d 553 (2d Dep't 1971).

6. CPLR 6514(c).

7. CPLR 6515(1).

8. CPLR 6515(2).

furnish an undertaking in return. If the plaintiff does furnish it, its condition is that the plaintiff will indemnify the defendant for damages traceable to the lis pendens, as where the defendant wins on the merits.[9] In an action for the specific performance of a realty contract, a "double bonding", requiring each side to post an undertaking to indemnify the other, has been held to be the "preferred" course.[10]

It might be fairer, and it surely would be simpler, if the legislature were to make an undertaking by P mandatory with the lis pendens, as it is with an order of attachment[11] and a preliminary injunction.[12]

The absence of an undertaking is by no means an insulation from liability for the plaintiff in a lis pendens situation. The plaintiff faces serious penalties, only recently clarified, for abusing the lis pendens device, and this is so even if there is no undertaking in the picture at all. The Second Department held in Parr Meadows Racing Ass'n v. White[13] that the defendant has an abuse of process claim against the wrongdoing plaintiff for misuse of a lis pendens, and remanded the case to have damages determined. The result on remand is a lesson to all would-be abusers of the lis pendens.

O in the *Parr* case had been about to get a favorable mortgage loan on some land when L, a lawyer, sued O on a money claim and in that action, without any basis whatever, filed a lis pendens against the land. In order to lift the lis pendens and free the land for the loan, O settled that suit on unfavorable terms. When all was clear, O turned about and brought an abuse of process suit against L and proved his case. Among the remedies awarded O against L was cancellation of the settlement of L's action, a return of O's payment and a note

given under the settlement, the legal fees it cost O to clear the title report, and a $5000 attorney's fee for having to bring the abuse of process suit.[14]

G.   SEIZURE OF CHATTEL

Table of Sections

§ 337.   Replevin Action, Generally

A "replevin" action today describes an action to recover a chattel. Technically, at least in New York, "replevin" meant the device whereby the sheriff seizes the chattel before judgment,[1] a provisional-like remedy that was, and is, available as an incident of an action to recover a chattel, just as attachment is an incident of a money action. The phrase "order of seizure" is best used to describe this provisional-like remedy today, with "replevin" reserved to describe the substantive action itself.[2]

CPLR 7101 provides that an action may be brought under Article 71 "to try the right to possession of a chattel", and one would think from such an introduction that the whole article is designed to supply the substantive law governing the action. It is not. Common law, as expanded or contracted by statute, governs who has the substantive right to the chattel. Article 71 is concerned with procedural incidents of the action, notably the provisional-like order of seizure by which the chattel can

---

9. Excepted from these undertaking trade-offs of CPLR 6515 are the actions for foreclosure of a mortgage, for partition, and for dower. In none of these will the defendant's furnishing of an undertaking authorize cancellation of the lis pendens. For the elements to be considered in fixing the amounts of the CPLR 6515 undertakings, see Ronga v. Alpern, 45 Misc.2d 1029, 258 N.Y.S.2d 731 (Sup.Ct., Bronx County, 1964).

10. Andesco, Inc. v. Page, 137 A.D.2d 349, 530 N.Y.S.2d 111 (1st Dep't 1988).

11. CPLR 6212(b).

12. CPLR 6312(b).

13. 76 A.D.2d 858, 428 N.Y.S.2d 509 (2d Dep't 1980).

14. N.Y. Law Journal, Aug. 26, 1983, p.15, col.1 (Sup. Ct., Suffolk County, DeLuca, J.). The case is the subject of the lead note in New York State Law Digest No. 288.

§ 337

1. See 4th Rep.Leg.Doc.(1960) No. 20, p. 249.

2. So widespread is its use for this purpose that it is the principal definition of "replevin" found in Black's Law Dictionary (7th ed.).

be taken before or during the action. Concentration in all but the present section will be on the seizure remedy and the other procedural aspects of the replevin action.

The reason for this overlapping of substantive and procedural functions is historical. Predecessor acts had carried forward some of replevin's substantive elements, such as rules about when D could defeat P just by showing that some third person had a higher right than either of them. That defense, known as the jus tertii, was good when it was alleged that the chattel had been wrongfully detained although properly taken at first. But when the charge was that the chattel was wrongfully taken in the first place, the defense could be used by D only if he could connect himself with the third person.[3] These and like distinctions did not have much to commend them and were abandoned by the CPLR's drafters. Today the action lies, substantively speaking, to test "the relative possessory rights of the parties", whatever their source.[4] Also casualties of the modern CPLR approach are the old rules about whether the action lies only if the defendant has possession of the goods now, or lies even if he has not, and about whether the goods were taken from the defendant by legal process, or parted with voluntarily.[5] The CPLR attitude is to allow the action in all these instances and let the final judgment on the merits adjust whatever substantive rights emerge.[6]

Another question often met in the action to recover a chattel is whether the plaintiff must make a demand for its return before suing. This is not a procedural question, but, in certain circumstances, at least historically, a condition precedent to the very existence of the substantive right, as where the defendant secured possession lawfully in first instance. The absence of a demand in a case like that resulted in dismissal under prior law, albeit without prejudice to a new action after a demand had been duly made.[7] Of course, if the facts showed that a demand would be futile, it was dispensed with, as where the defendant was fully aware of the plaintiff's hostile claim to the chattel.[8] The futility rule is a healthy one, and continues, but there is indication that dismissal still threatens a case that shows neither a demand nor facts indicating its futility.[9] It is unusual and perverse for P to sue D for something D would return upon P's mere demand. If P brings an action in a situation like that, and D pouts that upon mere demand he would have returned the chattel or paid its value, D can be afforded that opportunity now: the court can dismiss the action on the condition that D return the chattel or pay its value. If P had no excuse for suing without making the demand, D should be awarded costs. A dismissal without prejudice, contemplating that P will now make the demand but face the burden of bringing yet another action if the demand is not met, is an idle relic of an earlier time, breeds suspicion and disrespect for the law, and should be abandoned.

A further substantive point to make before turning to procedure, which is the main mission of Article 71, is that the action to recover a chattel, a law action, is not necessarily the plaintiff's exclusive remedy to get the chattel back. In certain commercial situations, notably under the Uniform Commercial Code, the plaintiff is permitted to use self-help.[10]

If the chattel is unique, moreover, the plaintiff can seek equitable relief. Thus, for example, where P and D had a contract whereby D agreed to return a specific item to P, a showing that the item was unique and thus irreplaceable by money[11] enabled P to sue in equi-

---

3. Civ.Prac.Act § 1093.

4. See 4th Rep.Leg.Doc. (1960) No. 20, pp. 253–4; Bulman v. Bulman, 57 Misc.2d 320, 292 N.Y.S.2d 572 (Sup.Ct., Rensselaer County, 1968).

5. See, e.g., Sinnott v. Feiock, 165 N.Y. 444, 59 N.E. 265 (1901).

6. See 4th Rep.Leg.Doc. (1960) No. 20 at p. 250.

7. See, e.g., Cohen v. M. Keizer, Inc., 246 A.D. 277, 285 N.Y.S. 488 (1st Dep't 1936).

8. Employers' Fire Ins. Co. v. Cotten, 245 N.Y. 102, 156 N.E. 629 (1927).

9. See, e.g., Agawam Trading Corp. v. Mayer Malbin Co., 37 A.D.2d 946, 325 N.Y.S.2d 757 (1st Dep't 1971).

10. See the discussion at the point of note 11, the Jefferds case, in § 338, below.

11. The ordinary judgment in an action to recover a chattel calls for the return of its possession or for a levy on other property of the defendant to obtain the chattel's money value instead. See § 342 below.

ty for specific performance,[12] which is backed by the contempt remedy.[13] That would still be the case, but the same thing can be accomplished in the law action itself today. An explicit CPLR provision says that if the chattel is unique, the judgment can direct its return under the threat of contempt,[14] which is of course what plaintiffs are relying on when they sue in equity.

§ 338. Constitutionality of Preliminary Seizure

An earlier section discusses constitutional issues concerning the provisional remedies generally, including the pre-judgment seizure of a chattel in a replevin action,[1] but a brief review is in order.

Prior to 1971 in New York, a chattel would be seized by the sheriff on the say-so of the plaintiff's attorney, with no initial court involvement at all. The attorney merely made out and delivered to the sheriff, along with certain other papers, a "requisition", on the basis of which the sheriff was required to seize the chattel forthwith.[2] Because that procedure was declared unconstitutional by a federal court,[3] the legislature in 1971 amended several of Article 71's provisions to replace the requisition with a court order and to impose other requirements designed to satisfy constitutional requirements. Not quite sure what those requirements were at the time, the legislature left the details to the courts with the simple instruction that procedure conform to "due process of law".[4] Then, in 1978, the constitutional demands having become clearer through caselaw, the legislature further amended Article 71, more specifically §§ 7102, 7104, 7108, and 7112, to fulfill constitutional demands in a new set of instructions.[5]

The gist of the constitutional exaction is that notice and an opportunity to be heard precede the issuance of a seizure order. The exception is where an important governmental interest or a need for very prompt action appears.[6]

One situation in which the seizure can be authorized by an ex parte order is where the replevin action is based on rem rather than on personam jurisdiction. If the chattel is in New York, it affords the New York courts an in rem basis on which to adjudicate rights in it, even as against an absent nondomiciliary defendant of whom personal jurisdiction is lacking.[7] It is required, however, that the chattel's seizure precede the commencement of the action as a jurisdictional foundation.[8] By analogy to attachment, where ex parte procedure has been found permissible when attachment is being used for its jurisdictional purpose,[9] a seizure of the chattel by ex parte order should also be allowable in that situation.

In some instances, almost always involving a contract, statutes that permit a plaintiff to seize a chattel with no court order required at all, and without even the intervention of a public official (like a sheriff), have been sustained. The self-help provisions of the Uniform Commercial Code, for example, which allow a secured party to take peaceable possession of the collateral that secures an obligation,[10] have been upheld by the appellate division.[11] If the self-help procedure is otherwise applicable, in fact, it has been held that it can be resorted to even after an order of seizure under Article 71

---

12. Chabert v. Robert & Co., 273 A.D. 237, 76 N.Y.S.2d 400 (1st Dep't 1948).

13. See § 481 below.

14. See CPLR 7109(b), discussed in § 342, below.

§ 338

1. See § 307 above.

2. See the pre–1971 CPLR 7102.

3. Laprease v. Raymours Furniture Co., 315 F.Supp. 716 (N.D.N.Y.1970).

4. See the 1971 amendment of CPLR 7102(d)(1), L.1971, c.1051, § 1.

5. These are treated in §§ 339 and 340, below.

6. Cedar Rapids Engineering Co. v. Haenelt, 39 A.D.2d 275, 333 N.Y.S.2d 953 (3d Dep't 1972).

7. See § 103 above.

8. CPLR 314(3).

9. See § 315 above.

10. See UCC §§ 9–503, 9–504.

11. See Jefferds v. Ellis, 132 A.D.2d 321, 522 N.Y.S.2d 398 (4th Dep't 1987), involving a truck.

has been obtained, instead of going ahead with the order.[12]

§ 339. Applying for the Seizure

The procedure to obtain an order of seizure is a motion. The general rule, or at least the underlying assumption in the structure of CPLR 7102, the main provision in point, is that the motion will be on notice, but the order can be granted without notice (ex parte) if

> in addition to the other prerequisites . . . the court finds that . . . it is probable the chattel will become unavailable for seizure by reason of being transferred, concealed, disposed of, or removed from the state, or will become substantially impaired in value.[1]

It sounds as if the motion on notice would be the common method and the ex parte motion the exception, but if statistics were charted the reverse might prove to be the case. Ex parte applications are not uncommon. They are just more demanding of procedural guidance. Much of CPLR 7102 is designed to furnish it.

The plaintiff's main paper on an application for a seizure order is, as with the provisional remedies generally, an affidavit, whose contents are enumerated in CPLR 7102(c). The affidavit must identify the chattel and show that the plaintiff is entitled to it and that the defendant is wrongfully withholding it. It must also state whether the action has yet been commenced and, if so, its status. And it must set forth the chattel's value.

All of the substantive elements of the replevin claim should be deposed to in the affidavit. If, for example, this is one of those cases in which a demand is a condition precedent,[2] facts showing the demand (or the futility of

making one) should be stated. The plaintiff must also aver that she knows of no defense to the claim.[3]

Accompanying the affidavit must be an undertaking, in not less than twice the chattel's value, to the effect that the chattel will be given to whoever is awarded possession by the final judgment and that the plaintiff will pay any sum of money the judgment may award against him.[4] This undertaking may not be withdrawn until the right to possession is resolved.[5]

If the order of seizure is granted, the plaintiff delivers it to the sheriff along with the undertaking, the papers on which the order was based, and the summons and complaint, which must bear the index number of the case.[6] This of course means that the summons and complaint must be filed before the seizure, and this is so whether or not the filing signals the "commencement" of the action. In the supreme and county court, the "filing" does signal commencement. In the state's lower courts, it does not; service does. Either way, the index number should appear on the summons and complaint that are delivered to the sheriff.[7]

As long as the proceedings in respect of the chattel, including its initial seizure, are completed before the service of the summons, the risk that the defendant will be forewarned of the seizure so as to abscond with the chattel, if the plaintiff is apprehensive about that, can be avoided.

Whether on notice or ex parte, the motion for the order of seizure is ordinarily best made when the action is first filed and an index number assigned. If the plaintiff does make the motion before summons service, the sheriff can serve the summons and complaint on the defendant at or about the time he seizes the

---

12. See GMAC v. Ayanru, 126 Misc.2d 607, 483 N.Y.S.2d 593 (N.Y.C.Civ.Ct. 1984), involving a car under a standard financing agreement.

§ 339

1. CPLR 7102(d)(3).

2. See § 337 above.

3. CPLR 7102(c)(6).

4. CPLR 7102(e).

5. Monte Publishing Co. v. Cohen, 39 A.D.2d 661, 331 N.Y.S.2d 918 (1st Dep't 1972). For a discussion of the undertaking and its surety requirements, see Consolidated Edison Co. v. Alston, 110 Misc.2d 188, 441 N.Y.S.2d 802 (N.Y.C.Civ.Ct. 1981).

6. CPLR 7102(a).

7. See the discussion of the 1994 amendment of CPLR 7102(a), which accounts for these requirements, in SPR 22:3–4.

chattel. Also, in that motion-first-summons-after situation, the rules about the service of motion papers, so clear during the pendency of an action when all parties have appeared through their attorneys, are more difficult, and the plaintiff planning to apply for the seizure order with a motion on notice had best bring the motion on by order to show cause. That will enable the court to determine how and upon whom the motion papers should be served. It also enables the court to set an earlier return day than an ordinary motion requires and, if the plaintiff so requests, to include in the order to show cause a temporary restraining order (TRO) forbidding the defendant from removing or secreting the chattel until further court direction.

The TRO device, supplied by CPLR 7102(d)(2) for use in replevin context, is designed to encourage the plaintiff to tender the defendant a hearing before the seizure. It has the effect of preserving the chattel for subsequent seizure even if the defendant gets preliminary notice of the plaintiff's intent to seize it. When this procedure is used—an order to show cause including a TRO—it is contemplated that a seizure will not occur until a hearing has been afforded the defendant on the return of the order to show cause because the TRO in this situation is presumably the plaintiff's security.

When the ex parte procedure is used without a TRO, the seizure precedes the hearing but the plaintiff is then obliged to make a follow-up motion "confirming" the order of seizure.[8] Assuming that the plaintiff has satisfied the requirement of a pre-hearing seizure, quoted above, the order of seizure is—recapitulating now—signed by the judge, given to the plaintiff, delivered by the plaintiff to the sheriff

with the other required papers, and executed by the sheriff with a seizure of the subject property. Now, after the seizure, the plaintiff must move to confirm the seizure order—in essence make the motion all over again—but this time on notice. It is this confirmation motion that sets up the hearing that the defendant is constitutionally entitled to when the seizure starts off ex parte. It's a requirement of CPLR 7102(d)(4), analogous in this respect to the post-levy confirmation order required in attachment cases when the attachment is granted ex parte.[9]

The motion to confirm must be made no more than five days after the seizure, and the failure to make this motion results in a voiding of all prior proceedings and a return of the chattel to the defendant. It has been held, moreover, that merely presenting a blank order to show cause to the clerk on the last day for making a motion to confirm does not satisfy the five-day confirmation requirement.[10]

In all cases, whether on a pre-seizure motion made ex parte or on a confirmation motion, the burden of establishing the merits of the case is on the plaintiff, and it is not met by a simple showing of a prima facie case. The plaintiff must show that it is "probable" that she will succeed on the merits.[11]

The court can permit the sheriff to break down a door to get the chattel,[12] but the plaintiff who wants such an authorization must include in the affidavit facts justifying it.[13]

As far as identifying the chattel is concerned, the description need only be sufficient to enable the sheriff to single it out and seize it. The chattel need not have any intrinsic monetary value. A package of letters and personal and professional papers in identifiable condition has been held sufficient against a claim that it lacked monetary significance.[14]

---

8. CPLR 7102(d)(4).

9. See § 316 above.

10. See Quality Ford v. Metro Auto Leasing, Inc., 172 Misc.2d 635, 660 N.Y.S.2d 341 (Sup.Ct., Westchester County, 1997), noted in SPR 65:3. The court says that a plaintiff who is having trouble getting the order signed within the required time should notify the clerk, and an effort will be made to accommodate the plaintiff.

11. See CPLR 7102(d)(1) and (4), which place on the plaintiff the burden of establishing all the grounds for the order.

12. CPLR 7102(d)(1), 7110.

13. See CPLR 7102(c)(5). See also Laprease v. Raymours Furniture Co., 315 F.Supp. 716 (N.D.N.Y.1970), which discusses this breaking-in permission in light of the search and seizure clause of the Fourth Amendment.

14. Hipsley v. Hipsley, 186 Misc. 458, 60 N.Y.S.2d 10 (App.T., 1st Dep't, 1946).

The hearing, whether brought on by initial motion on notice or by a confirmation motion following an ex parte seizure, is not the occasion for finally determining the merits of the replevin claim; it is designed only to determine whether a preliminary seizure is proper. The court can ordinarily decide that issue on the papers submitted pro and con and on the oral argument heard on the motion. Live testimony and the calling of witnesses, although the court can permit it, is not required.[15]

The order of seizure directs the sheriff of any county where the chattel may be found to seize it "without delay". Copies of the order, the affidavit and other papers on which the order is based, and the undertaking, all of which, as noted, are delivered to the sheriff of the appropriate county, must be served by the sheriff "upon the person from whose possession the chattel is seized". Copies of those papers must also be served on the defendant— along with the summons and complaint if not already served—and this service must be in the same manner as a summons. If perchance the defendant has already appeared in the action, the service can be by the usual mail or other methods for serving interlocutory papers.[16]

A frequent use of the order to seize a chattel is by a public utility seeking to replevy its meter after non-payment of its bill. A number of abuses in connection with one utility's procedures in such cases were enumerated in Consolidated Edison v. Church of St. Cecelia,[17] extruding a statement of what should be done through a detailed list of what should not.

If at any time the plaintiff needs assistance in locating the chattel, she may seek leave to compel any person with light to shed on the subject to give a deposition on its whereabouts.

The plaintiff may move "upon such notice as the court may direct",[18] i.e., by order to show cause, to have the court order the deposition, or, in fact, any of the disclosure devices of Article 31 of the CPLR that can offer aid for this purpose.[19]

§ 340. The Seizure and Subsequent Proceedings

On receipt of the order, affidavit, and undertaking, the sheriff is required to seize the chattel[1] and then serve copies of those papers on the one from whom possession is taken. Copies are also to be served by the sheriff on each defendant, so that if the defendant herself is not in possession, extra copies of the papers will have to be delivered to the sheriff to enable a set to be served on the possessor as well as on each defendant. Service on the defendants must be in the same manner as a summons.[2] This assumes that the service of the seizure papers is being made before the service of the summons and complaint in the action, as is most often the case, but if that service has already been made and the defendants have appeared, the other papers may be served by mailing them to their attorneys.[3]

After seizing the chattel, the sheriff's obligations depend in some measure on how the seizure order came on. If it was ex parte, the sheriff holds the chattel until served with an order of confirmation. That of course presupposes that the seizure will be confirmed, which may not happen. What is apparently meant is that when the seizure has been made ex parte, the sheriff should hold the chattel until he receives further directions from the court (or perhaps from the replevying plaintiff), whether the directions are embodied in an order of confirmation or any other kind of order. If the plaintiff does not make a confirmation motion

---

15. Long Island Trust Co. v. Porta Aluminum Corp., 44 A.D.2d 118, 354 N.Y.S.2d 134 (2d Dep't 1974).

16. CPLR 7102(b). For service of interlocutory papers, see § 202 above.

17. 125 Misc.2d 744, 480 N.Y.S.2d 284 (N.Y.C.Civ.Ct. 1984).

18. CPLR 7112.

19. See CPLR 3101(a), 3102(c); G.A.C. Commercial Corp. v. La Pardo Bros. Excavating Contractors, Inc., 33 A.D.2d 777, 307 N.Y.S.2d 186 (2d Dep't 1969).

§ 340

1. CPLR 7102(a).

2. CPLR 7102(b). The service is directed to follow CPLR 314, which means that the service methods of CPLR 308 et seq. may be used, within or without the state.

3. CPLR 2103(b)(2).

within the required time, the order loses effect (and can be vacated on motion if need be) and the chattel must be returned "forthwith" to the defendant.[4]

If the order of seizure was granted on notice, the sheriff must hold the chattel for 10 days. This assumes that the sheriff will know whether the granting of the order was ex parte or on notice. The order ought to say. If for some reason it doesn't, and the sheriff doesn't know which it was, the sheriff does best either to retain the chattel until the facts on which he may safely act have been presented to him, or apply to the court for a clarifying direction (especially when the chattel is of substantial value and the consequences of improper procedure are therefore all the greater).

These waiting periods—the 10 days when the seizure was on notice and the until-served-with-a-confirmation-order when the seizure was ex parte—are to give the defendant a chance to do any of three things: (1) except to the sureties on the plaintiff's undertaking; (2) move to impound the chattel or have it returned; or (3) reclaim the chattel.[5] If the defendant does none of those things within the waiting period, the sheriff turns the chattel over to the plaintiff.[6]

It is this last possibility that takes the seizure order out of the "provisional" category. The fact that the plaintiff can end up with the chattel before the case is adjudicated on the merits makes the seizure order a good deal more than a provisional remedy.

Any person claiming the right to possession of the chattel, including of course the defendant, may reclaim it after its initial seizure. The reclaimer procedure, which is governed by CPLR 7103(a) and is carried out during the waiting period, entails the service of a reclaim-er notice, an affidavit showing the reclaimant to be entitled to possession, and an undertaking similar to the one the plaintiff has to furnish on the initial seizure motion.[7] Upon receipt of such reclaimer papers, the sheriff must now hold the chattel for an additional 10-day period. During this time the plaintiff cannot again effect a seizure—that would amount to an endless Alphonse-and-Gaston routine—but he can except to the sureties on the reclaimant's undertaking or move to impound the chattel. If the plaintiff does nothing within that period, the chattel goes to the reclaimant. If more than one person purports to reclaim the chattel, the sheriff may move to have the court determine who gets it.

An impounding order keeps the chattel out of the possession of either party.[8]

If one not already a party to the action takes any of the steps authorized by CPLR 7103, such as by moving to impound or return the chattel or by serving a notice of reclaimer or exception to sureties, that person thereby becomes a party[9] and is bound by any judgment rendered in the action.

The sheriff is entitled to fees and expenses from the party to whom possession is delivered.[10] Within 20 days after that delivery, the sheriff must file a return with the clerk stating what action he's taken.[11] Any perishables among the chattels seized may be ordered sold and the proceeds of the sale deposited in their place.[12]

The plaintiff is personally liable to the defendant if the seizure turns out to be wrongful. The defendant can of course pursue the sureties on the bond, but is not restricted to that remedy. If the order is granted ex parte, moreover, the failure to secure its post-seizure

---

4. CPLR 7102(d)(4).

5. If the seizure was on notice, the likelihood of the defendant's now being able to have the chattel summarily returned is remote. Presumably the defendant has just been heard on the point and didn't prevail. The other remedies, though, the excepting, impounding, or reclaiming, would ordinarily still be open.

6. CPLR 7102(f).

7. A mere lienholder can't reclaim, CPLR 7103(a); the theory is that money alone will satisfy her claim and that

the plaintiff's undertaking therefore gives the lienholder what protection she needs.

8. See CPLR 7103(b). If the chattel is in the category of a necessity, there is a special and additional procedure whereby the defendant can secure its return before final judgment. See CPLR 7103(c).

9. CPLR 7103(d).

10. CPLR 7106(a).

11. CPLR 7107.

12. CPLR 7105.

confirmation makes the plaintiff liable for the defendant's attorneys' fees. The plaintiff's personal liability is not limited, as the sureties' liability is, to the amount of the undertaking.[13]

§ 341. Commencing the Action

It will be recalled that the summons and complaint must also be delivered to the sheriff with the initial seizure papers.[1] CPLR 7102(b) contemplates that the summons and complaint will be among the papers that the sheriff serves after seizing the chattel. No time limit is set as to when that service must be made, but it is contemplated that it will be done soon after the seizure. The law's standby time period, a reasonable time, should be implied. Predecessor statutes were construed as not mandating service of process at all, which enabled a plaintiff to get the chattel through the seizure papers and to forego suit altogether.[2] Such a result is unacceptable. Between subdivisions (a) and (b) of CPLR 7102, it is clear that a pre-action seizure of the chattel must be followed by service of the summons and complaint on each defendant, at least in instances when the summons and complaint have not already been served.[3] In the lower courts, in which service of the summons and complaint marks commencement of the action, the failure to make that service means that the context of the seizure order—a replevin action—has not been set up as contemplated by the statute. In the supreme or county court, the context would be lost if, after the filing of the summons and complaint, they are not served within 120 days thereafter.[4] In either instance, this should result in the vacatur of the seizure order and a direction that the chattel, if taken from the defendant's possession, be returned.[5]

As discussed in the prior section, the defendant can take some step during the waiting period following the initial seizure.[6] Any such step automatically makes the defendant a party.[7] One may therefore be inclined to assume, if the defendant does nothing within the waiting period and the sheriff at the end of it turns the chattel over to the plaintiff, that the defendant is conceding the plaintiff's right on the merits and that it is therefore idle to force the plaintiff to commence the action. But the assumption may be unwarranted. Even if the defendant would like to reclaim the chattel, which is one of the things the defendant can do during the waiting period, she may not be able to afford the undertaking indispensable to a reclaimer. The steps of the waiting period are optional with the defendant, who can take none of them and just insist that the plaintiff commence the action promptly and prove a right on the merits. Although the defendant's inaction will result in the plaintiff's getting the chattel after the waiting period, that does not amount to an adjudication that it is rightfully the plaintiff's. And even if it does, the "adjudication" would not bind the defendant unless she has defaulted in the action proper after being duly served with the summons and complaint. Technically, therefore, the plaintiff who abandons all further proceedings upon getting the chattel at the end of the waiting period risks having to return it. As a matter of common experience, however, plaintiffs who get the chattel after the waiting period will frequently let matters lapse. The case is often one in which the defendant does not have a defense and would only lose to the plaintiff if she contested. With so bleak a chance on the merits, and as a matter of economics, the defendant is deterred from taking steps to void

---

13. CPLR 7108(a).

§ 341

1. CPLR 7102(a).

2. See, e.g., Kurzweil v. Story & Clark Piano Co., 95 Misc. 484, 159 N.Y.S. 231 (N.Y.City Ct.1916).

3. That was the purpose of requiring the summons and complaint to be delivered to the sheriff, CPLR 7102(a), and of requiring the sheriff to serve the defendants, CPLR 7102(b), when seizure precedes commencement. See 4th Rep.Leg.Doc. (1960) No. 20, p. 257.

4. See CPLR 306–b.

5. Cf. Sears Roebuck & Co. v. Austin, 60 Misc.2d 908, 304 N.Y.S.2d 131 (N.Y.C.Civ.Ct. 1969), which dismissed the action and voided the seizure but did not direct return of the chattel.

6. CPLR 7102(f). The waiting period is 10 days following the seizure if the seizure order was granted by motion on notice. If it was granted ex parte, the waiting period is however long it takes for the plaintiff to obtain and serve on the sheriff an order confirming the seizure.

7. CPLR 7103(d).

the proceedings and get back the chattel, with the result that the plaintiff keeps the chattel—and the case, for all practical purposes, is closed.

Still, the plaintiff who would wrap the case up in an airtight legal package after getting possession of the chattel through the seizure device had best let the default consist of the defendant's failure to answer after due service of the summons and complaint rather than the defendant's mere failure to act during the waiting period.

After the defendant has been duly served, the plaintiff should see to the diligent prosecution of the action. A discontinuance or a dismissal, which would include a dismissal for want of prosecution, requires that the chattel be returned to the one from whom it was initially taken.[8]

§ 342. Judgment in Replevin Action

The judgment in an ordinary replevin action awards possession to the winner. If the winner does not already have possession it also fixes the chattel's value,[1] measured as of the time of the trial.[2] Enforcement of an ordinary replevin judgment is through an execution delivered to the sheriff, who seizes the chattel (if he hasn't already obtained possession of it) and turns it over to the party to whom judgment was awarded. If the chattel can't be found, the sheriff levies as if on a money judgment,[3]

which is the reason why the judgment fixes the chattel's value. Since the judgment can also award damages for the wrongful taking or detention of the chattel,[4] the plaintiff would do well to include a claim for such damages in the complaint. If the plaintiff is entitled to both the chattel and damages, the sheriff levies the chattel part by turning the chattel over to the plaintiff and the money part as he would any money judgment.

The remedy of money in place of the chattel is an unacceptable alternative when the chattel is unique and irreplaceable. So, if the chattel is unique, the judgment can additionally direct that the possessor deliver the chattel to the winner. The advantage of such a direction is that disobedience is enforcible as a contempt of court.[5] The general standard for determining whether or not a chattel is unique is whether it can be replaced. An item with sentimental value, a painting, a family heirloom, a pet, a patent; these and like items all qualify as unique.[6]

As noted earlier,[7] the uniqueness of the chattel can in some cases justify the plaintiff's bringing an equitable action instead of a replevin action (which is a law claim), but the availability of contempt as an enforcement remedy in a replevin judgment itself under CPLR 7109(b) will often make the equitable alternative superfluous.

---

8. CPLR 7108(a).

§ 342

1. CPLR 7108(a). In certain circumstances, set forth in CPLR 7108(b), the chattel's value is not fixed in the judgment.

2. Colonial Funding Corp. v. Bon Jour Int'l, Ltd., 148 A.D.2d 654, 539 N.Y.S.2d 405 (2d Dep't 1989).

3. See CPLR 5102.

4. CPLR 7108(a).

5. CPLR 7109(b).

6. See Morse v. Penzimer, 58 Misc.2d 156, 295 N.Y.S.2d 125 (Sup.Ct., Oneida County, 1968).

7. See § 337 above.

Chapter Thirteen

DISCLOSURE

Analysis

A. GENERALLY

Table of Sections

§ 343. Disclosure; Introduction

One of the most important articles in the CPLR is Article 31, entitled "Disclosure". It contains the aggregate of devices, including among others the deposition, discovery, and interrogatory, by which the trial lawyer, well in advance of the trial and in order to be completely prepared for it, probes into the other side's case and into whatever data or material nonparties may have reflecting on the issues. It is the trial lawyer's major preparation tool. Its purpose is to prevent litigation from becoming a game by requiring parties and witnesses to shed their light before the trial so as to prevent surprise at it. Its design is "to advance the function of the trial to ascertain truth and to accelerate the disposition of suits".[1]

Article 31 starts off with the criteria for disclosability. CPLR 3101 supplies those crite-ria and sets the tone for the whole article. The rest of the article supplies the various mechanical devices by which disclosure may be sought and the incidents of their use. The devices will be studied individually. There are fewer than a dozen of them; some are more useful and hence more used than others.

It should be remembered at all times that whatever the device used, the question of whether or not the datum or item sought is a disclosable one is governed by CPLR 3101, the article's opening section and the herald to which all inquiries about disclosability must turn. It should also be remembered that there is no priority of use among the devices. There is in general no sequence in which they must be used, nor any arbitrary limitation on how many may be used or how many times any one of them may be used.[2] As long as the disclosure devices are legitimately sought for data or material open to disclosure under CPLR 3101, the lawyer will find Article 31 and its offering of devices to be largely free of any built-in limitations.

Rather than encumber each device with individual restrictions, Article 31 centralizes in one place, CPLR 3103, a broad judicial power

---

§ 343

1. Rios v. Donovan, 21 A.D.2d 409, 411, 250 N.Y.S.2d 818, 820 (1st Dep't 1964).

2. For further discussion of this priority topic, see § 350, below.

to make what is known as a "protective order". This the court does upon application or even sua sponte in the particular case; the protective order enables the court on an individual basis to take any needful step to prevent abuse of the easily abused disclosure devices. With that power centrally contained and invokable at any time, the rest of the article is free to concentrate on supplying a broad range of disclosure devices and incidents.

The word one most often hears to describe the equivalent devices in federal practice is "discovery", the title of the counterpart article in the Federal Rules of Civil Procedure being "Depositions and Discovery".[3] New York has settled on the word "disclosure". The difference is not significant.[4] The federal rules have influenced New York disclosure, notably in the efforts of the CPLR's drafters and in the generous reception and interpretation given to the CPLR's disclosure article by the New York judiciary.

A revision of pretrial discovery that took effect on January 1, 1994, effected a number of changes in Article 31[5] that had been advocated before New York's Advisory Committee on Civil Practice for more than a decade. There was some pressure for full adoption of federal practice, but a middle ground prevailed: there was no wholesale changeover to the Federal Rules but several things were borrowed from them. An irony is that this partial turn to some federal practices took effect exactly one month after some significant changes in federal disclosure itself took effect. So, just as New York took a few strides towards the federal practice, federal practice vacated its position and stepped into a new one. The resulting gap may be even bigger than the one New York thought it was closing in on.[6]

Article 31 applies in all New York courts of civil jurisdiction. It has a few minor modifications in some of the lower courts,[7] but it applies as is in the surrogates' courts,[8] as it of course does in the supreme and county courts.

A final introductory note is that full and free pretrial disclosure is a comparatively recent development in litigation. It was accomplished in grudging steps away from the common law, where a profusion of traded pleadings were supposed to sharpen the issues. They rarely did. The emergence and growth of pretrial disclosure has been in roughly inverse proportion to the decline in the importance, and certainly in the rigidity, of pleadings. Under the old pleadings rules, the game was for lawyers to keep their cards close to their vests until the trial, where they hoped to surprise their adversaries with a datum too late to meet or counter. The game works less often today, and if Article 31 and its caselaw are faithfully applied, it is not supposed to work at all.

Unfortunately, the very freedom of use that has been accorded the disclosure devices sometimes generates a game of its own, with one side with abundant resources over-using them to the disadvantage of another and less affluent side. Or—the biggest game of all—two well-heeled parties go at each other with the words flying, the papers piling high, and the lawyers' billable hours piling higher. The abuse is worse in the federal than in the New York courts. The cure in both, insofar as the law has evolved any, is the ad hoc protective order.

---

3. See FRCP Rules 26 through 37.

4. "Disclosure" was chosen because it is more comprehensive than the federal title. See 1st Rep.Leg.Doc. (1957) No. 6(b), p. 114.

5. L.1993, c.98. These changes, integrated in this text in the sections to which they pertain, are treated in narrative form in a five-part series of articles in SPR Issues 7–11.

6. The federal changes are briefly noted in § 636 below (Practitioner's Edition).

7. See, for example, Article 11 in the New York City Civil Court Act and in the Uniform District, City, and Justice courts acts, McKinney's Vol. 29A, Parts 2 and 3. It will be found that as a practical matter the lower the court, the less use is made of the disclosure devices. This recognizes that the devices can sometimes be expensive to use and that as a matter of simple economics the justification for their use diminishes as the stakes involved in the case decline.

8. The business of the surrogates' courts is carried on in a series of special proceedings, but CPLR 408, which governs in special proceedings and requires a court order for disclosure, expressly excludes the surrogates' courts and thus leaves Article 31 to govern in them directly.

§ 344. Disclosure Criteria; CPLR 3101(a)

Subdivision (a) of CPLR 3101 sets up the standard for disclosability in New York practice, sounding a generous note and then leaving it to subdivisions (b), (c), and (d) to carve out a few exceptions (to be met later). The opening language of subdivision (a) contains the standard: "There shall be full disclosure of all matter material and necessary in the prosecution or defense of an action.... "

Seemingly, the key words in that statement are "material and necessary", the phrase used in the predecessor provision of the Civil Practice Act.[1] The CPLR's drafters felt that the phrase was too restrictive and sought to abandon it, recommending instead the equivalent of the federal standard. They proposed to require disclosure not just of relevant evidence, but also of all information "reasonably calculated to lead to the discovery of relevant evidence",[2] criteria clearly broader than the "material and necessary" standard. But the legislature rejected the proposal and reverted to the old language, which stands to this day as the verbalization of CPLR 3101(a). If the courts had construed "material and necessary" under the CPLR as they did under its predecessor, which they had every legislative warrant to do since the same language was carried forward, disclosure would not be as generous today as it has in fact become. Determining whether a given datum or item was "material and necessary" under prior law involved inquiry, and hence effort, much beyond what bench and bar are accustomed to today.[3]

The reason we are spared the effort is the gift of the Court of Appeals in Allen v. Crowell–Collier Publishing Co.,[4] which fused the dual requirements of "material and neces-sary" into the single word "relevant". A determination of whether a datum or item is "relevant" to the case is a lot easier than determining whether it is "material" or "necessary", or both. All disputes of basic disclosability can therefore be resolved under the CPLR merely by asking whether what is sought is relevant. The statutory phrase "material and necessary", said the Court of Appeals, must be

> interpreted liberally to require disclosure upon request, of any facts bearing on the controversy which will assist preparation for trial by sharpening the issues and reducing delay and prolixity. The test is one of usefulness and reason.[5]

And so it appears that what the drafters could not accomplish in new statutory language, they accomplished through the Court of Appeals' construction of the old language. Under the *Allen* case, whatever is relevant to the case is for that reason alone "material and necessary" to it.

Another potential problem that the original CPLR 3101(a) posed was that it spoke of "evidence" that is material and necessary, which might have been construed to permit disclosure to elicit only that which would itself qualify as "evidence". It was construed more broadly than that. Well-considered caselaw specifically rejected this "evidence in chief" doctrine, stating that "disclosure extends to all relevant information calculated to lead to relevant evidence",[6] i.e., is the same in effect as the federal standard is in terms. If that statement is correct, and appellate caselaw affirms that it is,[7] then the construction route has even done that part of the drafters' bidding. Corroboration that it is correct lies in the fact that information sought only for rebuttal or for cross-examination is available.[8] With an

---

§ 344

1. Civ.Prac.Act § 288.

2. First Rep.Leg.Doc. (1957) No. 6(b), p. 117. See and compare the federal criteria of FRCP Rule 26(b)(1), discussed in § 637 below (Practitioner's Edition).

3. See 1st Rep., id., at 440–448. A detailed study of pre-CPLR disclosure, of which the cited pages are part, begins at page 429 of the First Report.

4. 21 N.Y.2d 403, 288 N.Y.S.2d 449, 235 N.E.2d 430 (1968).

5. Id. at 406, 288 N.Y.S.2d at 452, 235 N.E.2d at 432.

6. West v. Aetna Casualty and Surety Co., 49 Misc.2d 28, 29, 266 N.Y.S.2d 600, 602 (Sup.Ct., Onondaga County, 1965), mod'd 28 A.D.2d 745, 280 N.Y.S.2d 795 (3d Dep't 1967).

7. See Johnson v. N.Y.C. Health & Hospitals Corp., 49 A.D.2d 234, 374 N.Y.S.2d 343 (2d Dep't 1975).

8. Matter of Genesee Valley Union Trust Co. of Rochester, 21 A.D.2d 843, 250 N.Y.S.2d 753 (4th Dep't 1964).

amendment that took effect on January 1, 1994, changing "evidence" to "matter" in CPLR 3101(a), these attestations to the liberal bent of the courts on the subject of pretrial disclosure were in effect approved by the legislature.

Another strong indication, even before the 1994 amendment, that disclosure under the CPLR embraces information that merely leads to evidence is that a party can be required under the CPLR to reveal the name of a witness to a fact in issue.[9] While a witness's name is hard to consider "evidence" as such, knowledge of the witness's name surely leads to evidence, and a rule that compels the revelation of a witness's name can hardly be at home in a practice that limits disclosure to "evidence" alone.

From all of this we can distill that the CPLR requires the disclosure of all evidence relevant to the case and all information reasonably calculated to lead to relevant evidence.

The burden of proof is immaterial to disclosure. CPLR 3101(a) requires disclosure "regardless of the burden of proof", the purpose being to require the parties to show where they stand on each issue no matter who may have the burden of that issue at the trial. The plaintiff, for example, who has the burden of proof of every substantive element of the claim, is entitled to full disclosure from the defendant of everything relevant to it, and the same right belongs to the defendant seeking disclosure from the plaintiff about an affirmative defense, on which the burden of proof at trial is on the defendant. Each party is entitled to know the other's position on every element.

The reader should not confuse this rule of disclosure with the rule governing the bill of particulars, where the burden of proof does play a role: a party need particularize only that of which she has the burden of proof.[10]

The relevancy standard has itself been evolving. For a dozen years under the CPLR,

and during the reigns of all of its forebears, the defendant's liability insurance policy in a personal injury or other tort action was deemed irrelevant, and hence undisclosable. It was periodically pointed out that knowledge by the plaintiff of the amount and scope of the policy could accelerate a settlement, among other things, but the courts still rejected the disclosure,[11] holding that it would be up to the legislature to effect a change. The legislature, following the federal example,[12] made the change in 1975 by adding subdivision (f) to CPLR 3101. It requires disclosure of both the "existence and contents" of the policy. The policy does not thereby become admissible at the trial or otherwise disclosable to the jury, however.

As far as CPLR 3101(a) indicates, its generous disclosure standard (as construed by the courts) is applicable to all actions without qualification. And given the continuous availability of the protective order,[13] by which abuses can be avoided on a case by case basis, there would seem to be no warrant for judicial interpolation of categorical restrictions. There have nonetheless been some, notably during the early days of the CPLR when the influence of prior law (and its meaner disclosure standard) still held sway. A reference to the few categories of actions in which disclosure was supposed to be restricted appears in Nomako v. Ashton,[14] decided in 1964. The categories (all old law carryovers) in which disclosure is supposedly restricted are the matrimonial action, the shareholders' derivative and other representative actions, and the accounting action. In none of them is disclosure altogether precluded; the difference is embodied in such caselaw-imposed requirements as that a stronger prima facie case, or a need for disclosure beyond simple relevance, be shown. All such categorical restrictions are suspect.

The principal action in which this subject garnered attention under the CPLR is the

9. See § 349 below.

10. See § 238 above.

11. See, e.g., Mosca v. Pensky, 42 A.D.2d 708, 345 N.Y.S.2d 606 (2d Dep't), rev'g 73 Misc.2d 144, 341 N.Y.S.2d 219 (Sup.Ct., Westchester County, 1973). The

Court of Appeals affirmed the Appellate Division in 35 N.Y.2d 764, 362 N.Y.S.2d 148, 320 N.E.2d 864 (1974).

12. See what is now FRCP Rule 26(a)(1)(D).

13. See CPLR 3103, treated in § 353 below.

14. 20 A.D.2d 331, 247 N.Y.S.2d 230 (1st Dep't 1964).

matrimonial action. The reason for restricted disclosure in the matrimonial action under prior law was the fear of exacerbating the relationship and thus diminishing the prospect of reconciliation. Legislation in 1967, however, set up a procedure to require attempts at reconciliation before the action could go forward, thus clarifying that a matrimonial action already under way was one in which reconciliation had been found futile.[15] Even that preliminary reconciliation attempt proved ineffectual and was afterwards abandoned,[16] thus leaving the matrimonial action without a statutory reconciliation procedure either before or after judgment and thereby removing much of the old justification for limiting the use of disclosure. Later cases conceded, as earlier cases had begun to do,[17] that restrictions on disclosure in a matrimonial action should be left to individual protective orders rather than embodied in a categorical prohibition.[18] There is still a conflict, however, about the free availability of disclosure on the merits, i.e., on the issue of fault, in matrimonial actions, tersely summarized by this statement from Nigro v. Nigro, a Third Department case:[19]

> Although the rule in other Departments may be that disclosure on the merits in matrimonial actions is prohibited absent some showing of extraordinary circumstances [citing the Second Department's Ginsberg v. Ginsberg[20] and the First Department's divided court in McMahan v. McMahan[21]], we are of the view that any such restrictions are better left to individual pro-

tective orders to prevent abuse, rather than embodied in a blanket prohibition. . . .

The Fourth Department inclines to the same view as the Third,[22] so the conflict appears to be between downstate and upstate.

It concerns only the fault issue, however. On the subject of the parties' finances, one of the most frequent disclosure topics in a matrimonial action, full disclosure is mandated, and without any requirement that special circumstances be shown.[23] A detailed provision in the rules also governs "financial disclosure in actions and proceedings involving alimony, maintenance, child support and equitable distribution".[24]

The defamation action, also one in which prior law had some general reservations about disclosure, is apparently free of them today.[25]

In proceedings for condemnation, appropriation, or review of tax assessments, a special CPLR provision[26] authorizes the rules to provide for the exchange of appraisal reports (which are relevant in all such cases). Several of the rules so provide.[27]

§ 345. Disclosure from Parties and Nonparties

The only requirement imposed by CPLR 3101(a) on disclosure by one party at the behest of another is that the information or item be relevant.[1] For this purpose, the word "party" includes an "officer, director, member,

---

15. See Commentary C3101:15 on McKinney's CPLR 3101.

16. L.1973, c.1034.

17. E.g., Hochberg v. Hochberg, 63 Misc.2d 77, 310 N.Y.S.2d 737 (Sup.Ct., Nassau County, 1970); Lachoff v. Lachoff, 69 Misc.2d 512, 330 N.Y.S.2d 227 (Sup.Ct., Nassau County, 1972).

18. Lemke v. Lemke, 100 A.D.2d 735, 473 N.Y.S.2d 646 (4th Dep't 1984). See also Schaeffer v. Schaeffer, 70 Misc.2d 1033, 335 N.Y.S.2d 510 (Sup.Ct., Nassau County, 1972).

19. 121 A.D.2d 833, 504 N.Y.S.2d 264 (3d Dep't 1986).

20. 104 A.D.2d 482, 479 N.Y.S.2d 233 (1984).

21. 100 A.D.2d 826, 474 N.Y.S.2d 974 (1984).

22. Lemke v. Lemke, note 18 above.

23. See § 236, the equitable distribution provision in the Domestic Relations Law, enacted in 1980, and

Scheinkman, Practice Commentaries on McKinney's Dom. Rel.Law § 236.

24. Uniform Rule 202.16, applicable in the supreme court, which has exclusive jurisdiction of matrimonial actions. Annexed to the Uniform Rules as Appendix A is an extensive form of "Statement of Net Worth" required in matrimonial actions.

25. See Nomako v. Ashton, 20 A.D.2d 331, 247 N.Y.S.2d 230 (1st Dep't 1964).

26. CPLR 3140.

27. See Uniform Rules 202.59 (tax assessment reviews outside New York City), 202.60 (tax assessment reviews in New York City), and 202.61 (eminent domain proceedings).

§ 345

1. See § 343 above.

agent, or employee of a party"[2]: generally speaking, anyone who is in the control of the party, so that sanctions can be fairly invoked against the party if the disclosure is not forthcoming. Also treated as a party, so as to require disclosure upon a mere showing of relevancy, is any person who previously possessed a claim or defense involved in the case,[3] of whom the prime example is an assignor.

There is today full disclosure among all parties, regardless of the position they hold in the case vis-a-vis one another.[4] The plaintiff of course gets full disclosure from the defendant, and vice versa, and the defendant from a third-party defendant, and vice versa, but these are self-evident conclusions born of the obvious adversary status of those parties. Parties not necessarily in adversary status, or at least not directly so, are also required to make full disclosure one to the other, such as codefendants, and the plaintiff and third-party defendant. Disclosure is even permissible between plaintiffs.[5] To the extent that disclosure between any two parties in a given case appears to be wholly unnecessary, or is shown to be sought for harassment, it can be controlled by individual protective order. It is also permissible for a party to cause her own deposition to be taken. This is done, for example, when the party wants to perpetuate her own testimony for use at the trial if she is apprehensive about surviving it.[6]

When it comes to seeking disclosure from a nonparty, such as a witness or a person who has possession of something related to the case, the requirement of relevancy imposed by CPLR 3101(a) of course applies, but is not alone. For disclosure against a nonparty the seeking party must also satisfy either paragraph 3 or paragraph 4 of CPLR 3101(a), which impose additional requirements. A party relying on paragraph 3 would have to show that the nonparty is

> about to depart from the state, or without the state, or residing at a greater distance from the place of trial than one hundred miles, or so sick or infirm as to afford reasonable grounds of belief that he will not be able to attend the trial....

These items are self-explanatory, and a showing of any one of them satisfies the requirement and justifies the disclosure. A party unable to meet one of the paragraph 3 requirements can turn to paragraph 4, which permits the party to obtain disclosure from a nonparty by merely serving a notice on all other parties and a subpoena on the nonparty, advising of the disclosure[7] and stating "the circumstances or reasons such disclosure is sought or required". This paragraph 4 requirement, the product of a 1984 amendment, eased up on disclosure from nonparties.

Before the amendment, "special circumstances" had to be shown under paragraph 4 for disclosure from a nonparty. That requirement, however, while stringent on its face, had been read generously by the courts. A showing that the nonparty was hostile was held sufficient to justify the disclosure, and the courts demanded less and less to establish "hostility" for that purpose. Any showing of kinship or friendship between the witness and a party did the job. A simple showing that the witness would not voluntarily furnish the seeker an affidavit or other proof needed to prepare for trial was deemed sufficient. Then a still more generous view appeared: the seeking party merely had to show the need of the nonparty's deposition in order to prepare for the trial.[8] Quite liberal was this attitude, and the First Department held in Slabakis v. Drizin[9] that

---

2. CPLR 3101(a)(1).

3. CPLR 3101(a)(2).

4. See Lombardo v. Pecora, 23 A.D.2d 460, 262 N.Y.S.2d 201 (2d Dep't 1965).

5. Rosado v. Valvo, 58 Misc.2d 944, 297 N.Y.S.2d 230 (Sup.Ct., Kings County, 1969).

6. See Lapensky v. Gordon, 41 Misc.2d 958, 246 N.Y.S.2d 442 (Sup.Ct., Kings County, 1964).

7. See § 351, below, and Commentary C3101:23 on McKinney's CPLR 3101.

8. Kenford Company v. County of Erie, 41 A.D.2d 586, 340 N.Y.S.2d 300 (4th Dep't 1973).

9. 107 A.D.2d 45, 485 N.Y.S.2d 270 (1st Dep't 1985). In BAII Banking Corp. v. Northville Industries Corp., 204 A.D.2d 223, 612 N.Y.S.2d 141 (1st Dep't 1994), noted in SPR 30:3, the court adhered to the view that the dropping of the word "special" from the "circumstances" requirement of CPLR 3101(a)(4) was intended to expand the opportunities for disclosure from a nonparty.

the interpretation of the amended paragraph 4 of CPLR 3101 should be at least as liberal. Indeed, since the "circumstances" no longer have to be "special" under paragraph 4, the interpretation should be even more generous, but that view is not universal. Some courts still insist on a showing of some special element before upholding nonparty disclosure, such as that "the information sought ... cannot be obtained from other sources".[10]

Whatever the "circumstances" relied on to satisfy this requirement, they should be stated not only in the notice served on the other parties but also in the subpoena that has to be served on the nonparty.[11]

The federal counterpart of CPLR 3101, Rule 26 of the Federal Rules of Civil Procedure, contains no added requirements for disclosure by a nonparty. This has often been cited as a factor by a plaintiff opting for a federal rather than a New York court when a choice was available and when the testimony of a nonparty was a key element.[12] The generosity of New York caselaw, which played down CPLR 3101(a)(4) by according a broad and liberal scope to what would satisfy as a "special circumstance", was occasionally overlooked or even disregarded by some judges. One would hear laments about the frequent difficulty of deposing nonparty witnesses in New York state courts. With the abolition of the "special circumstance" requirement from CPLR 3101(a)(4), the obtaining of disclosure from nonparties should be easier now than ever before in New York practice.

When medical testimony is required, as is so often the case in tort actions, another part of paragraph 3 of CPLR 3101(a) becomes relevant. It permits a party to obtain disclosure as a matter of right from his own treating physician and from any physician he has duly retained as an expert witness.[13] While P can depose P's own treating physician under this part of paragraph 3, D cannot. But D may depose P's treating physician under some other part of paragraph 3, as where the physician is residing more than 100 miles from the courthouse.[14] When convinced in a given situation of the need for pretrial interrogation, the courts have also required a treating physician (as opposed to an expert) to depose under CPLR 3101(a)(4), of course taking care to see that the deposition does not unduly interfere with the doctor's practice.[15]

While paragraph 3 does not entitle one side to depose the other side's medical experts, some other provisions may authorize it, such as subdivision (d)(1)(ii) of CPLR 3101 or subdivision (b) of CPLR 3121, discussed below.[16]

When a person is a party to a lawsuit in a representative rather than personal capacity, some old caselaw holds that that person can be examined as a party only as to data come by in his representative status; that in respect of anything the party has to say or give in his personal capacity, he must be treated as a nonparty witness and the requirements of either paragraphs 3 or 4 of CPLR 3101(a) must be met.[17] Such an approach is of doubtful validity today, especially under the broad view taken of paragraph 4. The mere fact that the person from whom data is sought individually is also, in his representative capacity, a party to the suit (or vice versa), should in any event automatically establish the kind of hostility that would satisfy paragraph 4, as it did even when paragraph 4 contained the "special circumstance" requirement.[18]

---

10. Dioguardi v. St. John's Riverside Hospital, 144 A.D.2d 333, 533 N.Y.S.2d 915 (2d Dep't 1988).

11. Bigman v. Dime Savings Bank of New York, 138 A.D.2d 438, 526 N.Y.S.2d 17 (2d Dep't 1988). The subpoena requirement comes from CPLR 3106(b). See § 351 below.

12. See item 15 on the list of choice of forum factors in § 616 (Practitioner's Edition).

13. A 1993 amendment clarifies that dentists and podiatrists also fall under this provision.

14. See Roeck v. Columbia–Greene Med. Cent., 248 A.D.2d 921, 670 N.Y.S.2d 269 (3d Dep't 1998).

15. See Villano v. Conde Nast Publications, Inc., 46 A.D.2d 118, 361 N.Y.S.2d 351 (1st Dep't 1974). Compare Johnson v. New York City Health & Hospitals Corp., 49 A.D.2d 234, 374 N.Y.S.2d 343 (2d Dep't 1975), involving a malpractice action in which the plaintiff deposed the defendant as an expert.

16. See §§ 348 and 363 below.

17. See, for example, Pardee v. Mutual Ben. Life Ins. Co., 238 A.D. 294, 265 N.Y.S. 837 (4th Dep't 1933).

18. The Pardee view, id., is not compatible with that of Kenford, note 8 above, decided by the same court four decades later. The Pardee case illustrates the earlier hos-

Disclosure can be obtained from an infant, and under oath, with the proviso, if the matter is contested, that the court conduct "a preliminary examination to determine the competency of the infant".[19]

A party who needs data or material from a corporation but can't single out the particular person in the corporation's employ to whom disclosure papers would be properly directed can direct them to the corporation as such and leave it to the corporation to designate the appropriate deponent, i.e., treat the corporation itself as the witness.[20] In fact, whenever disclosure is sought from a corporation, whether as a party or as a nonparty witness, the choice in first instance of who is to depose in the corporate behalf is with the corporation and not with the examining party.[21] That was the general rule and it would seem to remain so despite the addition of a subdivision (d) to CPLR 3106 in 1984 presuming to change it. The change is illusory. It purports to allow the seeking party to name the "particular officer, director, member or employee" who is to do the deposing—"unless" a notice is served by the corporation's side, at least 10 days before the scheduled deposition, that someone else will be produced instead, identifying that person. If such a notice is used by the corporate side—and there's nothing to it—the matter would still have to be ironed out either through amicable adjustment by the parties or by an application for a protective or like order from the court, and that's just about the way things were before.[22] If the corporation should submit an employee who does not have the requisite knowledge, it can be compelled afterwards, with a protective order, to produce a designated employee who does.[23]

Lawyers seeking disclosure from foreign nationals should be aware of the Hague Evidence Convention.[24] The convention's disclosure procedures were described in Wilson v. Lufthansa German Airlines[25] as "quite costly and cumbersome even in situations where the foreign government has agreed to cooperate". Certainly they are more trouble than the procedures of the New York CPLR or the Federal Rules of Civil Procedure. The party seeking the disclosure would like to side-step the convention whenever possible, and it is apparently possible whenever the foreign national is within the jurisdiction of the court, at least when the claim arose locally, as in the *Wilson* case. In that situation the case holds the convention's use optional, not mandatory.

B.   EXCLUDED MATTERS

Table of Sections

§ 346.   Privileged Matter

Subdivision (b) of CPLR 3101 accords to "privileged matter" an immunity from disclosure. What is and what is not privileged is governed by the same rules of evidence that would apply at a trial. Whatever is privileged there is privileged as well on pretrial disclosure. All privileges are included, whether they come from the constitution directly, such as that against self-incrimination,[1] from evidence statutes like those governing communications

---

tility to disclosure, even grounding its distinction on an unmanageable fiction: that an individual can so compartmentalize her brain as to distinguish readily between facts entering it through her different "capacities".

19. Muscoreil v. Pool Mart, Inc., 107 A.D.2d 1025, 486 N.Y.S.2d 518 (4th Dep't 1985).

20. See Southbridge Finishing Co. v. Golding, 2 A.D.2d 430, 156 N.Y.S.2d 542 (1st Dep't 1956).

21. See Necchi S.P.A. v. Nelco Sewing Machine Co., 23 A.D.2d 543, 256 N.Y.S.2d 347 (1st Dep't 1965).

22. See Commentary C3106:7 on McKinney's CPLR 3106.

23. JMJ Contract Mgmt., Inc. v. Ingersoll–Rand Co., 100 A.D.2d 291, 475 N.Y.S.2d 528 (3d Dep't 1984).

24. Its formal name is the Hague Convention on the Taking of Evidence Abroad in Civil or Commercial Matters. It can be found as an appendix to 28 U.S.C.A. § 1781. It was ratified by the United States in 1972.

25. 108 A.D.2d 393, 489 N.Y.S.2d 575 (2d Dep't 1985).

§ 346

1. U.S.Const. Amends. V, XIV. See also CPLR 4501.

between spouses,[2] attorney and client,[3] physician and patient,[4] clergyman and penitent,[5] and the like, from the law of criminal procedure, such as that governing the secrecy of grand jury proceedings,[6] or, indeed, from case-law, such as the murky one that purports to excuse communications made in the course of governmental activities.[7]

As long as properly objected to, all privileged matter is excluded. The original version of CPLR 3101(b) recognized this in explicit language when the objection was made by a party, but in practice anyone entitled to assert the privilege was entitled to interpose the objection, even if not a party (e.g., a nonparty witness). By eliminating the word "party" and permitting the objection to be made by any "person entitled to assert the privilege", a 1993 amendment of CPLR 3101(b), effective January 1, 1994, confirms that a nonparty may also invoke privilege.

If it appears that not everything involved in an examination will be privileged, the examination can be scheduled as usual but with the deponent's right to decline privileged answers preserved.[8] This applies even to a party's attorney when, because of involvement in the transaction at issue, the attorney has been directed to submit to a deposition.[9] If it appears that all questions would fall into a privileged sphere, however, the examination can be denied in toto.[10]

The Court of Appeals has held that a report by outside counsel giving legal advice to a client doesn't lose its immunity just because it may refer to unprivileged matter, like communications with third persons.[11] Nor need there be any showing that a report was prepared for litigation before it can earn an attorney/client privilege under subdivision (b) of CPLR 3101. The proximity of litigation, basic in determining immunity for material prepared for litigation under CPLR 3101(d)(2),[12] is not a major factor in determining privilege under CPLR 3101(b). Obviously, the attorney/client privilege is not restricted to the litigation scene. If it were, a myriad of other legal specialties that don't involve litigation would suddenly be stripped of any attorney/client confidentiality.

If a paper contains a privileged communication, it may be withheld for that reason.[13] If an issue arises as to whether the privilege obtains and it appears necessary for the court to examine the material in order to resolve the issue, the court can do so in camera before it directs the item to be turned over to the adverse party.[14]

Since the scope of the privilege is a matter of the law of evidence and its resolutions are adopted from that realm, it need not detain us here. The same may not be said, however, for the exclusions contained in subdivisions (c) and (d) of CPLR 3101, which Article 31 creates and is therefore obliged to regulate. The immunity for privileged matter conferred by subdivision (b) is absolute, in common with that conferred on an attorney's work product by subdivision (c). Both are to be contrasted shortly with the exemption for material prepared for litigation, created by subdivision (d)(2), which is conditional only.

---

2. CPLR 4502.

3. CPLR 4503.

4. CPLR 4504.

5. CPLR 4505.

6. See Melendez v. City of New York, 109 A.D.2d 13, 489 N.Y.S.2d 741 (1st Dep't 1985), discussing the circumstances under which grand jury testimony may be disclosed in a civil action.

7. See, e.g., Cirale v. 80 Pine St. Corp., 35 N.Y.2d 113, 359 N.Y.S.2d 1, 316 N.E.2d 301 (1974). The Freedom of Information Law (FOIL) enacted in 1974 and recast in 1977, Public Officers Law §§ 84–90, is relevant here. It and its interplay with CPLR disclosure is discussed in § 348 below.

8. Flanigen v. Mullen and Gunn, Inc., 45 Misc.2d 944, 258 N.Y.S.2d 609 (Sup.Ct., Erie County, 1965).

9. Planned Industrial Centers, Inc. v. Eric Builders, Inc., 51 A.D.2d 586, 378 N.Y.S.2d 760 (2d Dep't 1976).

10. DiFrancesco v. DiFrancesco, 47 Misc.2d 632, 262 N.Y.S.2d 831 (Sup.Ct., Kings County, 1965).

11. Spectrum Systems International Corp. v. Chemical Bank, 78 N.Y.2d 371, 575 N.Y.S.2d 809 (1991). The Spectrum case is the subject of the lead note in New York State Law Digest No. 386.

12. See § 348 below.

13. Falk v. Kalt, 44 Misc.2d 172, 253 N.Y.S.2d 188 (Sup.Ct., Suffolk County, 1964).

14. Cirale v. 80 Pine St. Corp., note 7, above.

§ 347. Attorney's Work Product

Subdivision (c) of CPLR 3101 makes unobtainable the "work product of an attorney"—an ill-defined category whose potential for mischief has been avoided only because the judiciary has accorded it narrow scope. It is a category wholly distinct from the "materials ... prepared in anticipation of litigation" of subdivision (d)(2), treated in the next section. The fact that the (c) immunity is absolute while that of (d)(2) is only conditional is the factor that requires as sharp a line as possible between them.

The drafters of the CPLR did not intend the categories to be separate; they proposed a single subdivision covering both and as to both of them the immunity was to be only conditional, i.e., dissolvable (so as to necessitate disclosure) upon stated contingencies.[1] That would have codified for New York the federal approach as enunciated in Hickman v. Taylor.[2] The *Hickman* case might have occasionally offered some insights into the resolution of problems arising under these New York provisions, but the value of the case on the New York scene is undermined by this subdividing, with one category wholly and the other only conditionally immune.[3]

Although it spoke of the "work product of an attorney", *Hickman* gave it no absolute immunity; the phrase was used in *Hickman* to describe such phenomena as "interviews, statements, memoranda, correspondence, briefs, mental impressions, personal beliefs, and countless other tangible and intangible" things.[4] Whatever those things might amount to in a given case, there would be no absolutes connected with them that would tie the courts' hands and bar case-by-case solutions.

In giving the "work product" of subdivision (c) an absolute immunity, the legislative hands that wrought the change probably assumed that without it there'd be some risk that the privileged lawyer-client communication would be invaded. But protection against that result is what subdivision (b) accomplishes by immunizing—absolutely—"privileged" matter, and for that it needed (and needs) no help from subdivision (c). In one case, for example, the court noted that

> reports of an attorney to his client as to the progress of pending litigation or advice and opinions rendered to a client who is on the brink of litigation should clearly be considered "work product of an attorney" and thus within the protection

of subdivision (c).[5] But wouldn't the attorney-client privilege itself, independently applicable under subdivision (b), insulate those items just as securely? As enacted by the legislature, in other words, and as they remain on the books today, subdivisions (d)(2) (materials prepared for litigation) and (b) (privileged matter) between them accomplish what the legislature stuffed into the "attorney's work product" category of subdivision (c).

The question then is, where does that leave subdivision (c)? What is it that can be categorized as an attorney's work product distinct from both privileged matter on the one side and materials prepared for litigation on the other? The more obvious the items that come to mind, the more absurd it is to think that the legislature wants them immunized from disclosure. What could be more the "work product" of an attorney than a deed, will, contract, mortgage, bond, or the like? Certainly these, if relevant to the litigation, can't be concealed from an adversary's view. *Hickman*, the case from which both categories emerged, offers no support for the idea that items like those just listed are to be excluded (absolutely!) from cases in which, indeed, they may be dispositive of all the substantive rights and obligations asserted.[6]

§ 347

1. See 1st Rep.Leg.Doc. (1957) No. 6(b), p. 119.

2. 329 U.S. 495, 67 S.Ct. 385, 91 L.Ed. 451 (1947).

3. This bifurcation was the work of legislative staff after the drafters had handed over their recommendations. See 5th Rep.Leg.Doc. (1961) No. 15, p. 444.

4. 329 U.S. at 511, 67 S.Ct. at 393.

5. Wickham v. Socony Mobil Oil Co., 45 Misc.2d 311, 312, 256 N.Y.S.2d 342, 344 (Sup.Ct., Albany County, 1965).

6. See Siegel, Disclosure under the CPLR: Taking Stock After Two Years, 11th Jud.Conf.Rpt. (1966) 148 at 151–158.

The judiciary, in large measure tacitly, has recognized this. It has cast precious little under the "work product" category of subdivision (c), preferring instead to fit doubtful items under the "materials ... prepared in anticipation of litigation" banner of subdivision (d)(2), where the immunity can be withdrawn and the matters ordered disclosed when stated conditions are met. It has been held that an item will not even begin to qualify as "work product" merely upon a showing that a lawyer drew it or did it; it must be shown to be something that only a lawyer could do.[7] The fact that a lawyer has taken a statement from a witness, for example, does not transmute the statement into a "work product": a lay person could have taken it.

The general rule is that data received by the attorney from others while investigating in behalf of the client is neither privileged under subdivision (b) nor a "work product" under subdivision (c). This is so even though the material itself, such as a statement or report, may qualify as "prepared in anticipation of litigation" and thus be immunized by subdivision (d)(2). If the client is questioned about the information, his lawyer's knowledge is imputed to him and he must answer the questions.[8]

The dormant state in which the "work product" of subdivision (c) finds itself earns it less of a place in our study. It may have already been given more treatment than it deserves, and it's gotten this much only because in *Hickman* it was the Siamese twin of subdivision (d)(2)'s "materials ... prepared in anticipation of litigation". The surgery that separated them was a botched job; all of the vital organs went to (d), which is as active in New York practice as (c) is quiescent. Perhaps (c)'s only claim to attention, in fact, is the history it shares with (d).

§ 348. Materials Prepared for Litigation

The most exercised exclusionary category is "materials ... prepared in anticipation of litigation", governed by subdivision (d)(2) of CPLR 3101. It gives a conditional immunity to materials otherwise discoverable under the broad criteria of subdivision (a), if it is shown that they were "prepared in anticipation of litigation".[1]

The condition that removes the immunity and makes the materials discoverable is a finding by the court

> that the party seeking discovery has substantial need of the materials in the preparation of the case and is unable without undue hardship to obtain the substantial equivalent of the materials by other means.[2]

The report of an expert is one example of a material prepared for litigation that is subject to the provisions of paragraph 2 of CPLR 3101(d)—not to be confused with the identification or deposing of the expert, which are governed by paragraph 1 and are separately treated later.[3] The expert's report, embodying his opinion, is often a subject of dispute. Probably the medical expert in the personal injury case is the first example to spring to mind because of the proliferation of tort cases in New York, but the provision embraces any expert in any context. Where an engineer at D's behest examines a washing machine al-

---

7. Brunswick Corp. v. Aetna Casualty and Surety Co., 49 Misc.2d 1018, 269 N.Y.S.2d 30 (Sup.Ct., Erie County, 1966), mod'd 27 A.D.2d 182, 278 N.Y.S.2d 459 (4th Dep't 1967).

8. Kenford Co. v. County of Erie, 55 A.D.2d 466, 390 N.Y.S.2d 715 (4th Dep't 1977).

§ 348

1. Before 1985, when subdivision (d) was amended, the counterpart category consisted of "any writing or anything created by or for a party or his agent in preparation for litigation". It generated much caselaw. The new language borrows extensively from the terminology of the counterpart provisions of Rule 26 of the Federal Rules of Civil Procedure, but in so doing makes more a change in language than in substance. Most of the standing legion of caselaw on the old subdivision (d)—especially cases that end up allowing discovery—remain intact under the new language. The more important of those cases will be treated in this section. A treatment of the CPLR 3101(d) amendment appears in Commentary C3101:29 on McKinney's CPLR 3101.

2. The pre–1985 language was that "the court finds that the material can no longer be duplicated because of a change in conditions and that withholding it will result in injustice or undue hardship", which amounts to essentially the same thing and also preserves the great body of caselaw on the predecessor provision.

3. See § 348A below.

leged to have injured P, for example, the engineer's report qualifies as expert and is governed by this provision.[4]

Court rules about the trading of medical reports in the ordinary tort case narrow the operation of subdivision (d)(1) substantially,[5] and in one instance another statute, CPLR 3121(b), does the same thing by directing the exchange of medical reports in certain instances.[6] The reports of appraisers are also the subject of a separate provision, CPLR 3140, which allows the rules to supersede the provisions of CPLR 3101(d) in condemnation and tax review proceedings. Such rules have been adopted.[7] Unless such a special provision exists, however, or the court makes a disposition under its expanded powers under paragraph 1 of CPLR 3101(d),[8] paragraph 2 governs the reports of experts.

Most often seen under paragraph 2 are papers of one sort or another, statements and reports of diverse kinds. Whether or not a given item qualifies for the paragraph 2 immunity as litigation material is usually a sui generis inquiry, resolved on the basis of the pro and con papers submitted on a motion for a protective order.[9] Probably the most common example of an item sought by one side but claimed by the other to be litigation material is a statement given by a witness, a situation once again most often associated with the tort case. These statements ordinarily do qualify for the subdivision (d)(2) immunity, and are hence undisclosable unless the stated conditions are satisfied.

To be distinguished from the statement of a witness is the statement of a party made to someone on the other side. (Such a statement may be given, for example, when a person injured in an accident is approached by the potential defendant's insurance adjuster before the injured person has retained counsel.) Parties are entitled as a matter of right to obtain copies of their own statements pursuant to the explicit authority of subdivision (e) of CPLR 3101; subdivision (d) does not govern it. Photographs are in the same category. A photograph taken of one party by or at the behest of another, at least when the photos are taken with the subject's permission, must therefore be disclosed upon mere demand;[10] subdivision (d) doesn't cover them.

Surveillance tapes have become so commonly embroiled in tort cases (although not limited to them) that a subdivision (i) was added to CPLR 3101(d) to regulate them. This requires some background.

When they suspect a personal injury plaintiff of feigning or exaggerating an injury, defendants may try to make a surveillance videotape of the plaintiff carrying on various activities, hoping through this graphic evidence to prove that the plaintiff's injuries aren't as claimed. The Court of Appeals, resolving a departmental dispute on the issue, held in DiMichel v. South Buffalo Ry. Co,[11] that the plaintiff is entitled to a discovery of the tapes, but that the plaintiff is first required to narrate his injuries in a deposition, the premise being that a malingerer can be exposed by that means.

The Court in *DiMichel* applied its holding only to tapes the defendant intends to use at the trial, but subdivision (i) of CPLR 3101, enacted afterwards,[12] makes all surveillance tapes available for discovery whether the side making the tapes intends to use them at the

---

4. Silberberg v. Hotpoint Div., Gen. Elec. Co., 23 A.D.2d 754, 259 N.Y.S.2d 60 (1st Dep't 1965).

5. See, e.g., Uniform Rule 202.17, the rule applicable in the supreme and county courts. The rule was amended effective April 17, 1998, to make it unnecessary for a party to secure a narrative report from the physician and to make acceptable the briefer notations found in such as insurance and workers' compensation forms. (See Bauman, Letter to the Editor, N.Y. Law Journal, June 1, 1998, p.2.). Similar changes were made in the parallel rules of other courts. See SPR 73:1–2.

6. See § 363 below.

7. See Uniform Rules 202.59—202.61, applicable in the supreme and county courts.

8. See § 348A below.

9. See, e.g., Corona Courts v. Frank G. Shattuck Co., 50 Misc.2d 1066, 272 N.Y.S.2d 217 (Sup.Ct., Monroe County, 1966).

10. Saccente v. Toterhi, 35 A.D.2d 692, 314 N.Y.S.2d 593 (1st Dep't 1970).

11. 80 N.Y.2d 184, 590 N.Y.S.2d 1, 604 N.E.2d 63 (1992).

12. It took effect Sept. 1, 1993.

trial or not. The statute also requires that all "memoranda" of the tapes be furnished. Parts of a memorandum that constitute privileged communications may be redacted, however.[13] There is a conflict at present about whether the enactment of CPLR 3101(i) alters the requirement that the plaintiff submit to a deposition before getting the tapes,[14] but it has in any event been held that the defendant must reveal, before such a deposition is taken, whether such a tape exists.[15]

While paragraph (i) was enacted with the defendant's surreptitious tapes of the plaintiff in mind—and we have made that the assumption of our treatment—its language is broad enough to embrace any tapes made of a party should they prove relevant in the action. In one case, for example, D was allowed a discovery of tapes P had made of her wedding, which took place about a year and a half after her alleged injury on D's train platform. The tape was held relevant because it could depict P "in activity which contrasts with her claims that she is no longer able to exercise regularly".[16]

Leaving the tapes topic and returning to the general subject of material prepared for litigation, note that the party resisting disclosure on the ground that the item falls under subdivision (d)(2) usually has the burden of showing that it does.[17] If the papers before the court don't suffice for resolution of the issue, the court can require that the item be produced for inspection in camera before the item is turned over to the other party.[18] If the court is satisfied that the particular item, report, or statement was drawn up only after consultation with counsel and upon counsel's advice, it will ordinarily get the subdivision (d) immunity as material prepared for litigation.[19]

Although a subdivision (d)(2) inquiry is largely a case-by-case one, there is at least one class of cases that has been carved out for wholesale treatment under the statute, and it's a big one. In the tort case in which the defendant is represented and defended by an attorney retained by the defendant's liability insurer, the insurer's whole file of the case qualifies as litigation material and is conditionally immune. This is popularly known as the *Kandel-Finegold* rule, after the principal cases that pronounced it.[20] Its theory is that this category of insurance is a kind of institutionalized attorney. Other kinds of insurance earn no such treatment,[21] and whether, in cases involving these others, a given item merits the subdivision (d) immunity involves an individual inquiry.[22] The usual items in the liability insurer's file that get the litigation-material immunity are the statements of witnesses and the reports of employees and other personnel.

The *Kandel-Finegold* rule applies only to an action in which the insurer represents the insured, not where the insurer represents itself.[23] Where, for example, the insured is suing

---

13. See Marigliano v. Krumholtz, 159 Misc.2d 596, 603 N.Y.S.2d 1020 (Sup.Ct., Queens County, 1993), noted in SPR 12:4.

14. See, e.g., Boulware v. Triborough Bridge and Tunnel Auth., 161 Misc.2d 435, 613 N.Y.S.2d 580 (Sup.Ct., N.Y. County, 1994) (noted in SPR 21:2–3), holding that the deposition requirement continues; DiNardo v. Koronowski, 252 A.D.2d 69, 684 N.Y.S.2d 736 (4th Dep't 1998), holding that it does not. See the discussion in SPR 79:3.

15. Fronckowiak v. City of Buffalo, 162 Misc.2d 718, 619 N.Y.S.2d 237 (Sup.Ct., Erie County, 1994), noted in SPR 36:3. Other issues may arise, as where the defendant has already deposed the plaintiff before beginning tape surveillance. See the discussion in the lead note in SPR 32.

16. Srok v. L.I.R.R., Sup.Ct., N.Y. County, Aug. 18, 1993 (Index No. 1671/92; Cohen, J.). Such a tape would probably have been discoverable under the general relevancy standard of subdivision (a) of CPLR 3101 even had no subdivision (i) been enacted.

17. Dikun v. N.Y. Cent. R.R., 58 Misc.2d 439, 295 N.Y.S.2d 830 (Sup.Ct., Jefferson County), aff'd 31 A.D.2d 719, 297 N.Y.S.2d 711 (4th Dep't 1968).

18. Haire v. L.I.R.R. Co., 29 A.D.2d 553, 285 N.Y.S.2d 717 (2d Dep't 1967).

19. Albano v. Schwab Bros. Trucking Co., 27 A.D.2d 901, 278 N.Y.S.2d 780 (4th Dep't 1967).

20. Kandel v. Tocher, 22 A.D.2d 513, 256 N.Y.S.2d 898 (1st Dep't 1965); Finegold v. Lewis, 22 A.D.2d 447, 256 N.Y.S.2d 358 (2d Dep't 1965).

21. See Rodolitz v. Greater New York Mutual Ins. Co., 82 Misc.2d 1024, 371 N.Y.S.2d 89 (Sup.Ct., Nassau County, 1975).

22. See Commentary C3101:32 on McKinney's CPLR 3101.

23. See Collins v. Jamestown Mut. Ins. Co., 56 Misc.2d 964, 290 N.Y.S.2d 791 (Sup.Ct., Schoharie County, 1968), mod'd on other grounds 32 A.D.2d 725, 300 N.Y.S.2d 391 (3d Dep't 1969).

the insurer to recover for an "excess" verdict rendered against the insured at the behest of an injured person and alleged to have been caused by the insurer's unreasonable failure to negotiate and settle the earlier action in good faith, the *Kandel-Finegold* rule does not apply and neither, therefore, does the subdivision (d) immunity.[24] The file is open. The insurer's file that gets the insulation, in other words, is the insurer's file accumulated in the present suit, not the file accumulated in a prior and distinct one.[25]

Reports and statements made in the ordinary course of operating a business get no immunity and must therefore be distinguished from those prepared for litigation, a sometimes difficult chore when the item's existence is traceable to mixed motives and litigation is only one of them. A common example is an accident report made by an employee in a restaurant, hotel, or other public place. If someone is injured and sues, the proprietor's lawyer would like to make it appear that the accident report was prepared for litigation so that he will not have to disclose it. One lawyer for a big hotel had his client route such reports directly to him in an effort to make them smack of litigation and nothing else. He didn't succeed. The court noted that the reports serve internal business purposes as well and thus earn no protection from CPLR 3101(d),[26] incidentally establishing a proposition now commonly recognized: that in order to qualify as "litigation" material the item must have been prepared exclusively for litigation. Incidental potential use in litigation, the courts have observed, may also be a function of such reports, but they have at least an equal if not greater mission "to prevent future accidents, discipline careless employees, or, generally, to increase the economy and efficiency of the

operation."[27] Multi-motived reports therefore do not warrant the immunity if litigation is but one of the motives.

Subdivision (g), enacted in 1980, is addressed to "accident reports" specifically. It requires disclosure of "any written report of an accident prepared in the regular course of business operations". There is no condition imposed as to whether it was prepared for litigation, but since the sole exception that it recognizes is a report prepared by a peace officer in connection with a criminal investigation, one is prone to conclude that its apparent purpose is to make a regular course-of-business accident report fully disclosable even if it was prepared for litigation and would otherwise fall under the immunity of subdivision (d). That's the construction given the provision in *Pataki v. Kiseda*,[28] holding the accident report to be disclosable even if it was prepared "exclusively" for litigation. But the contrary has also been suggested: that subdivision (g) is just a codification of prior law,[29] and therefore effects no change.

There appears to be a consensus at least to the effect that the *Kandel-Finegold* rule, which insulates an accident report made by insured to insurer, remains intact under subdivision (g). The Third Department had held to the contrary on the point,[30] but appears to have withdrawn from that position and joined the consensus.[31]

Even if an item comes under subdivision (d)(2) and gets the immunity, it must always be recalled that what it is getting is not absolute, as are the immunities for the attorney's work product of subdivision (c) and the privileged matter of subdivision (b). The (d)(2) immunity is conditional only, and the conditions

---

24. Colbert v. Home Indemnity Co., 45 Misc.2d 1093, 259 N.Y.S.2d 36 (Sup.Ct., Monroe County), aff'd 24 A.D.2d 1080, 265 N.Y.S.2d 893 (4th Dep't 1965).

25. Bennett v. Troy Record Co., 25 A.D.2d 799, 269 N.Y.S.2d 213 (3d Dep't 1966).

26. Weisgold v. Kiamesha Concord, Inc., 51 Misc.2d 456, 273 N.Y.S.2d 279 (Sup.Ct., Sullivan County, 1966).

27. Kandel v. Tocher, 22 A.D.2d 513, 516, 256 N.Y.S.2d 898, 900 (1st Dep't 1965).

28. 80 A.D.2d 100, 437 N.Y.S.2d 692 (2d Dep't 1981).

29. See Harris v. Processed Wood, Inc., 89 A.D.2d 220, 455 N.Y.S.2d 411 (4th Dep't 1982).

30. See Vandenburgh v. Columbia Memorial Hospital, 91 A.D.2d 710, 457 N.Y.S.2d 591 (3d Dep't 1982), and Commentary C3101:33 on McKinney's CPLR 3101. Subdivision (g) is the subject of a lead note in New York State Law Digest No. 279, reviewing the activity of all four departments on this front.

31. See Gavigan v. Otis Elevator Co., 117 A.D.2d 941, 499 N.Y.S.2d 253 (3d Dep't 1986).

that will remove it, thereby exposing the materials to full disclosure, are that the party has "substantial need" of the materials and "is unable without undue hardship to obtain the substantial equivalent of the materials by other means".

If the materials are relevant, they are likely to be needed, satisfying the first condition for that reason alone and making the second condition, inability to get their equivalent elsewhere, the key one. A good example is a photograph taken at an accident scene at or shortly after the event. It is rarely possible to duplicate the scene and the subdivision (d)(2) conditions are easily met, requiring disclosure of the photo.[32] Another example is an item that can no longer be found and on which tests have to be conducted. In Sherman v. M. Lowenstein & Sons, Inc.,[33] for example, a garment had burned and P bought a duplicate to conduct a test on. Because of the lapse of time, D could not later find a duplicate even though D was the manufacturer, and P was required to surrender for testing the duplicate P had bought.

But note that P did not have to furnish a copy of the report made by the expert; the report itself was litigation material under subdivision (d)(2) and the immunity-lifting conditions of that provision had not been met because D could, upon getting the garment, have his own report made. If P could not furnish the garment, however, the court held that P would then have to furnish the report; the absence of the garment would make it impossible for D to duplicate the test and the circumstances of P's report would then satisfy the subdivision (d)(2) conditions.

If the thing to be examined is available for examination by an expert in a party's behalf, the courts are reluctant to order disclosure of a report made by an adversary's expert, especially where no showing has been made of any difficulty in obtaining other expert testimony.[34] This conclusion applies, however, only when

the matter is controlled by CPLR 3101(d)(2). When some other and more specific provision governs, and authorizes the disclosure, such as CPLR 3121(b) does with medical reports and the rules adopted under CPLR 3140 do with appraisal reports, they of course preempt.

The Freedom of Information Law[35] has had an impact on pretrial disclosure generally under the CPLR, and on material prepared for litigation in particular. The purpose of the FOIL is to open to public scrutiny a broad range of governmental records. The key question for litigants concerns the situation in which the criteria of the CPLR would not allow disclosure in a given instance, as with a report prepared for a public agency about to be involved in litigation, but the FOIL provisions would. Can the litigant invoke the FOIL in that instance, thus in effect circumventing the CPLR even though the materials are sought for use in the litigation? The Court of Appeals, surprising bench and bar by overturning the prevalent notion on the matter, answered with an unequivocal yes in M.Farbman & Sons, Inc. v. N.Y.C. Health and Hospitals Corp.[36] The court said that

> we refuse to read into the FOIL the restriction that, once litigation commences, a party forfeits the rights available to all other members of the public and is confined to discovery in accordance with article 31. If the Legislature had intended to exempt agencies involved in litigation from FOIL, it certainly could have so provided.

When a public agency is one of the litigants, this means that it has the distinct disadvantage of having to offer its adversary two routes into its records, while having only one path going the other way. That's the price of open government, the Court of Appeals in effect responds.

The FOIL excludes from its reach, among other things, any information "specifically exempted from disclosure by state or federal

---

32. See Hayward v. Willard Mountain, Inc., 48 Misc.2d 1032, 266 N.Y.S.2d 453 (Sup.Ct., Rensselaer County, 1966).

33. 42 Misc.2d 770, 248 N.Y.S.2d 1000 (Sup.Ct., Queens County, 1964).

34. Gugliano v. Levi, 24 A.D.2d 591, 262 N.Y.S.2d 372 (2d Dep't 1965).

35. Pub.Officers L. §§ 84–90.

36. 62 N.Y.2d 75, 476 N.Y.S.2d 69, 464 N.E.2d 437 (1984).

statute",[37] so that another issue is whether CPLR 3101(d) and its material prepared for litigation is a "specific" exemption within the meaning of that provision. The *M.Farbman* case addresses only the general disclosure standards of the two competitors, the CPLR and FOIL, not their exemption categories. Hence the Court of Appeals saved for another day the question of whether the disclosure would be required if, while it falls within the basic criteria of the FOIL, it also falls under one of the exemption categories of CPLR 3101.[38] In Burke v. Yudelson, meanwhile, which was affirmed by the appellate division,[39] it was held that the CPLR 3101 exclusions of subdivisions (b), (c) and (d) are all general in scope and hence not of the "specific" kind to which the FOIL defers, and that something purportedly exempt by one of the CPLR provisions therefore does face disclosure if embraced as part of public records under the FOIL and not exempted by that statute.

There is also the question of what procedure to use to obtain the disclosure. The CPLR and the FOIL have their own procedures. The FOIL's procedures are more elaborate and usually more time consuming: application must be made by turns to an access officer, an appeals officer, the supreme court in an Article 78 proceeding, an appellate court, etc.[40] CPLR disclosure is more expeditious. Can the CPLR procedures be used to obtain only FOIL-authorized disclosure? It has been held that they cannot.[41]

What about the disclosability of data connected with settlements? A new section added to the evidence article of the CPLR, Article 45,

bars from evidence any indication that something of value was tendered or accepted during compromise negotiations and "any conduct or statement made" during them, whether offered to reflect on liability or on damages. The new statute, CPLR 4548, extends the exclusion beyond just the offers made during the bartering, which have traditionally been excluded, to embrace as well statements made by any of the parties. They can't be let in as admissions, for example.[42]

Other settlement-related matters have occupied the courts. It has been held that defendants are not entitled to a discovery of an agreement made among the plaintiffs about maintaining unity in settling with the defendants. The court saw nothing in such an agreement relevant to the triable issues in the case.[43] Another case held that defendants are not even entitled to data about the plaintiffs' settlements with co-defendants, despite the relevancy of settlements in computing a post-verdict judgment.[44] The court said that the matter doesn't become germane until after the verdict and may therefore not be the subject of pretrial disclosure.[45] There is caselaw permitting pretrial disclosure in respect of "collateral source" payments, however, which are in some ways analogous to settlement payments.[46]

§ 348A. Identification of Experts; Statement of Expected Testimony

The 1985 amendment that repealed and re-enacted subdivision (d) of CPLR 3101 altered the provision on materials prepared for litiga-

---

37. Pub.Officers L. § 87(2)(a).

38. The M.Farbman case and the general subject of FOIL versus CPLR disclosure is treated in the lead note in New York State Law Digest No. 296.

39. 81 Misc.2d 870, 368 N.Y.S.2d 779 (Sup.Ct., Monroe County, 1975), aff'd 51 A.D.2d 673, 378 N.Y.S.2d 165 (4th Dep't 1976). The lower court in Burke endeavors to distinguish what it calls a "perplexing footnote" about the application of the Freedom of Information Law contained in Cirale v. 80 Pine St. Corp., 35 N.Y.2d 113, 359 N.Y.S.2d 1, 316 N.E.2d 301 (1974).

40. See Pub.Officers L. § 89.

41. Moussa v. State, 91 A.D.2d 863, 458 N.Y.S.2d 377 (4th Dep't 1982). This to-each-its-own-procedure rule is also addressed in the M.Farbman decision.

42. Modeled on Rule 408 of the Federal Rules of Evidence, the statute took effect in July 1998. It has some exceptions. See the Advisory Committee note on Federal Rule 408 in 28 U.S.C.A.

43. See Allegretti–Freeman v. Baltis, 205 A.D.2d 859, 613 N.Y.S.2d 449 (3d Dep't 1994), noted in SPR 27:4.

44. See § 276 above.

45. Hulse v. A.B. Dick Co., 162 Misc.2d 263, 616 N.Y.S.2d 424 (Sup.Ct., N.Y.County, 1994), aff'd 222 A.D.2d 381, 635 N.Y.S.2d 641 (1st Dep't 1995).

46. See the discussion of the Hulse case in SPR 29:4. and in the New York Law Journal of March 6, 1995 (p.1, cols.2–3).

tion. The "materials" provision, discussed in the prior section, is in paragraph 2 of subdivision (d), altered by the amendment in language but not substance. The present section, § 348A, treats paragraph 1, an entirely new provision added by the 1985 amendment. Its title is "Experts". It consists of three subparagraphs, (i), (ii), and (iii).

Subparagraph (i) is an innovation in New York. It provides that "upon request" by one side, the other is required to identify "each person whom the party expects to call as an expert witness at the trial" and to disclose

> in reasonable detail the subject matter on which each expert is expected to testify, the substance of the facts and opinions on which each expert is expected to testify, the qualifications of each expert witness and a summary of the grounds for each expert's opinion.

It starts off with this big bang and then tones down considerably. It sets forth no particular time for the making of the request, and no particular time for responding to it, but does provide that the recipient shall not be precluded from using the expert at trial "solely" because the party failed to comply with the request. But if the court can't preclude for noncompliance, then what can it do? Says the statute: "the court may make whatever order may be just". Not exactly a beacon.

If the expert has not yet been decided on when the request is made, caselaw says the request must be considered "to be of a continuing nature", so that the requested party is under a legal duty to respond upon the expert's retention.[1]

And what form shall the request take? Any kind of a paper appropriately captioned and clearly stating the request should do. Some judges have held that the request can be embodied as an additional paragraph in a demand for a bill of particulars.[2] Others say no, because that would confuse bill of particulars remedies with disclosure remedies.[3] The argument can be avoided by putting the request on a separate paper and appending it to and serving it with the bill of particulars demand, if one is used.

The court would seem to have plenary power under the "whatever order may be just" language to invoke whatever sanction it deems appropriate for failing to honor the request, regardless of the form the "request" takes, as long as it is clear. One drastic but appropriate sanction for a deliberate violation of this requirement, as will be seen, is an order barring the expert from testifying.

Caselaw has also held that all the requester is entitled to is a statement of the "substance" of the facts and opinions the expert would testify to. A request that apparently sought a complete statement of the facts and opinions was rejected as "excessively detailed".[4]

The most controversial aspect of this statute is its failure to impose a time limit. While failing to respond to a proper demand for expert data can of course result in a party's being altogether precluded from using the expert at the trial,[5] the absence of any statutory time limit on when the expert data has to be furnished has made it difficult to determine what remedy, if any, applies before the action reaches the trial stage. It has been held that when the case is still "at an early stage", the court should not even set a deadline for the disclosure,[6] but that waiting until the eve of trial can result in preclusion, and with obviously serious consequences if the case requires the use of an expert. Where expert testimony was essential to the plaintiff's case, for example, the plaintiff's unexcused failure to supply the expert data resulted in summary judgment for the defendant.[7]

§ 348A

1. Dunn v. Medina Memorial Hosp., 131 Misc.2d 971, 502 N.Y.S.2d 633 (Sup.Ct., Erie County, 1986). The case notes that there is no requirement that the expert be retained before depositions are taken.

2. E.g., Salander v. Central General Hosp., 130 Misc.2d 311, 496 N.Y.S.2d 638 (Sup.Ct., Nassau County, 1985).

3. E.g., Galtman v. Edelman, 134 Misc.2d 599, 511 N.Y.S.2d 1011 (Sup.Ct., Kings County, 1987).

4. Renucci v. Mercy Hosp., 124 A.D.2d 796, 508 N.Y.S.2d 518 (2d Dep't 1986).

5. See the discussion in SPR 18:4.

6. DiPiano v. Truchly, 221 A.D.2d 182, 633 N.Y.S.2d 156 (1st Dep't 1995).

Judicial ambivalence about how to punish delayed expert disclosure has contributed to misleading attorneys into case-forfeiting conduct.[8]

These rules about expert disclosure apply in all categories of actions, including medical, dental, and podiatric malpractice actions, but with an important exception applicable in those three categories (which we'll collectively refer to as just the "medical" categories). Everything the provision requires must be forthcoming, including a statement of the qualifications of the expert, but in the medical categories the identity of the expert can be withheld. This was designed to avoid peer pressure sometimes brought to discourage the expert from testifying against a fellow professional in the medical categories.

What to do when revelation of the expert's qualifications, which is required, would tend to reveal the expert's identity, too, which could otherwise be withheld? The consensus is that in the medical malpractice categories the judge should hear the arguments of the parties, examine in camera the expert's qualifications, redact such parts of them as would make identification possible, and give only the redacted version to the requester.[9] The Second Department had initially reached a different conclusion,[10] but shortly afterwards also agreed that those qualifications that would allow identification of the expert need not be furnished.[11]

Unless a time period has been set and violated, it has been held permissible for the party

who has not yet furnished the expert data in one of the medical categories to include the affidavit of the expert, with the name redacted, in papers opposing a motion for summary judgment.[12] But redaction is not permissible when the affidavit is being used to support the summary judgment motion. It can't be used, in other words, as a sword.[13] As a guard against the use of such a motion just to flush out the otherwise concealable name of an adversary's expert, the court can inspect the affidavit in camera and direct redactions accordingly.[14]

Subparagraph (ii), applicable only in the medical malpractice categories of action, merely offers a kind of trade-off by a party willing to name and submit to deposition the medical expert that subparagraph (i) otherwise permits the party to withhold. If the other side is amenable, what the offering party gets in return is the other side's agreement to do likewise.

Getting away from these special issues that apply in the medical categories and back to the disclosure of expert data generally, several additional points should be noted. The fact that the substance of the facts and opinions of the expert must be furnished under subparagraph (i) of CPLR 3101(d)(1) does not by itself authorize the deposing of the expert. But "upon a showing of special circumstances", subparagraph (iii) permits the court to order such further disclosure as it deems warranted in the situation, and that would presumably include a deposition of the expert, especially where the party has delayed so long in retaining the expert that the extra disclosure is deemed nec-

7. Grassel v. Albany Med. Ctr. Hosp., 223 A.D.2d 803, 636 N.Y.S.2d 154 (3d Dep't 1996).

8. See the lead note in SPR 42. Different attitudes among the departments are cited and discussed in *Marks v. Solomon*, 174 Misc.2d 752, 667 N.Y.S.2d 194 (Sup.Ct., Westch.County, 1997).

9. See, e.g., McGoldrick v. W.M. Young, Jr. Health Ctr., 135 Misc.2d 200, 514 N.Y.S.2d 872 (Sup.Ct., Albany County, 1987). The subject is treated in the lead note in New York State Law Digest No. 332. Redaction of identifying features can sometimes apply even to the plaintiff's examining physician. If the plaintiff plans to call the examining physician as an expert, for example, P can redact, from the report of that physician that may be required under CPLR 3121(b), the physician's name and identifying data. See Ryan v. Michelsen, 241 A.D.2d 434,

660 N.Y.S.2d 435 (1st Dep't 1997). CPLR 3121(b) is the provision governing the trading of medical reports after a physical examination has been conducted. See § 363 below.

10. Catino v. Kirschbaum, 129 A.D.2d 758, 514 N.Y.S.2d 751 (1987).

11. Jones v. Putnam Hospital Ctr., 133 A.D.2d 447, 519 N.Y.S.2d 665 (1987).

12. See, e.g., Kozlowski v. Alcan Alum. Corp., 209 A.D.2d 930, 621 N.Y.S.2d 240 (4th Dep't 1994), noted in SPR 38:4.

13. Marano v. Mercy Hosp., 241 A.D.2d 48, 670 N.Y.S.2d 570 (2d Dep't 1998).

14. See, e.g., Napierski v. Finn, 229 A.D.2d 869, 646 N.Y.S.2d 415 (3d Dep't 1996), noted in SPR 61:4.

essary to compensate for the delay and facilitate the requester's preparation for trial. A determination of that kind could be supported under either the "special circumstances" language of subparagraph (iii) or the "whatever order may be just" power conferred by subparagraph (i).

Another special circumstance warranting the deposing of the expert is the present unavailability of the physical evidence on which the expert's opinion is based.[15] Under CPLR 3101(a)(3), treated earlier,[16] a party may depose her own treating or expert physician. Subparagraph (iii) acknowledges this right and leaves it intact, lest the requirement of court leave imposed for further disclosure under subparagraph (iii) be construed to divest the deposition right that emanates from CPLR 3101(a)(3).

§ 349. Revelation of Names of Witnesses

The caselaw under the CPLR has confirmed that parties must reveal the names of any persons they know of who witnessed the event at issue.[1] This does not mean that upon demand each party must serve on the other a list of all the witnesses she intends to use at the trial. It doesn't cover, for example, character or expert witnesses, whatever the effect other provisions may have on compelling the disclosure of such witnesses.[2] Its concern is with those ordinary witnesses who can shed light on what happened.[3] If liability occurred all at once, such as in an accident, the witnesses included are not only those who beheld the occurrence, but also those who can reflect on

any fact that can help account for it. It embraces, for example, not just a bystander who saw the crash, but anyone who can reflect on the condition of a traffic light alleged to have played a role, or who can show whether the driver or pedestrian was drunk or sober, such as a bartender or companion, or who can testify about the speed of the vehicle, such as an old man sitting on a bench two blocks away who saw the car careening out of control around the corner, or a mechanic who warned the defendant a day earlier that his brakes were defective, and so on. There is no satisfactory ground for distinguishing between a witness to the accident itself and one who can reflect on some cause of it.[4] All are within this rule and the names of all, if known by a party, must be revealed if asked for.

It had previously been held that the only witnesses a party had to reveal were those learned of at the scene of the accident itself, as opposed to those learned of later by investigation. These latter were deemed litigation material under CPLR 3101(d)(2) and immunized.[5] Earlier still it had been held that the only revealable witnesses were those who participated in the event in some way, as opposed to those who merely saw it.[6] Both these older approaches have been discarded as unworkable and unduly restrictive.[7]

Conflict on the point lingered into the early 1980s, the Third Department continuing to exempt from the disclosure requirement the name of a witness through whom a tort defendant is alleged to have had notice of a dangerous condition that caused an accident, i.e., a

---

15. See Rosario v. General Motors Corp., 148 A.D.2d 108, 543 N.Y.S.2d 974 (1st Dep't 1989).

16. See § 345 above.

§ 349

1. See, e.g., Rios v. Donovan, 21 A.D.2d 409, 250 N.Y.S.2d 818 (1st Dep't 1964), which was an early appellate discussion of the problem.

2. See § 348A above.

3. See, e.g., Sanfilipo v. Baptist Temple, Inc., 52 Misc.2d 767, 276 N.Y.S.2d 936 (Sup.Ct., Monroe County, 1967).

4. Zayas v. Morales, 45 A.D.2d 610, 360 N.Y.S.2d 279 (2d Dep't 1974).

5. See Varner v. Winfield, 33 A.D.2d 807, 307 N.Y.S.2d 3 (2d Dep't 1969).

6. See, e.g., Coleman v. Kirkey, 53 Misc.2d 947, 279 N.Y.S.2d 803 (Sup.Ct., Monroe County, 1967).

7. Hartley v. Ring, 58 Misc.2d 618, 296 N.Y.S.2d 394 (Sup.Ct., Queens County, 1969), rejected the "participant" distinction such as Coleman, id., used, but adopted the learned-of-later distinction, which Varner, above, later approved of. Varner and Hartley were then overruled in Zellman v. Metropolitan Transp. Co., 40 A.D.2d 248, 339 N.Y.S.2d 255 (2d Dep't 1973), which adopts the current rule.

"notice" witness,[8] but the court withdrew the distinction in Bombard v. County of Albany in 1983.[9] The withdrawal, as the court recognized, harmonized the views of all departments on the issue.

Distasteful as it is to lawyers to reveal the names of witnesses harvested through their investigative efforts, the names must be divulged. The lawyer who has gone to any expense learning of them can, on a protective order motion, ask the court to make the seeking side share the bill.

The inquiry into the names of witnesses often occurs at a deposition where in the course of the questioning the party is asked if there were any witnesses and if so who they are. The deponent's lawyer, who would at one time interpose himself promptly at that point and direct the client not to answer the question, must now grin and bear it, or, in any event, bear it. If the question is not answered, the questioning party can take the matter to court and will be sustained.

A discovery notice is another device that can be used to compel the revelation of witnesses, but the deposition is usually more effectual.[10]

Distinguish between the witness's name and a statement the witness may have given. The name is not immunized litigation material under CPLR 3101(d)(2), but the statement may be.[11]

C. DEVICES AND METHODS IN PERSPECTIVE

Table of Sections

8. See the lead note in New York State Law Digest No. 243.

9. 94 A.D.2d 910, 463 N.Y.S.2d 633 (3d Dep't).

10. See Rios v. Donovan, 21 A.D.2d 409, 250 N.Y.S.2d 818 (1st Dep't 1964).

11. See § 348 above.

§ 350. The Disclosure Devices; Priority of Use

CPLR 3102(a) lists the disclosure tools, but each is later allotted a separate provision in Article 31 supplying details on the use of each tool. Following that lead, we will list each tool here and briefly describe how it works, leaving it to later sections to elaborate on the devices individually.

1. Deposition on oral questions.[1] This is one of the most useful and hence frequently used of the devices. It's a session around a table, usually in an attorney's office,[2] with all parties represented by their lawyers. The party or witness being deposed is questioned in depth by all the lawyers in turn while a stenographer, or tape recorder, takes everything down verbatim. All is later reduced to a transcript. It all takes place in front of an officer, usually just a notary public, and just as usually the stenographer has qualified as a notary and carries out both roles.

2. Deposition on written questions.[3] This is also a session around a table, but much rarer than the oral deposition and nowhere near as effectual. The deposition on written questions is wooden and inflexible. It is used mainly for depositions outside the state. Each party furnishes written questions to the officer who is to conduct the deposition, who then goes to where the witness is and puts the written questions verbatim (no variations!), taking down the answers and afterwards reducing all to a transcript. The attorneys are usually not present at the session.

3. Interrogatories.[4] These are questions drawn up by the attorney and sent to an opposing attorney, who drafts verified answers to them as furnished by the client, and just sends them back to the first lawyer. Interrogatories differ from the deposition on written questions in that the deposition is a session

§ 350

1. For elaboration, see § 354 below.

2. For the place of taking the deposition, see § 355 below.

3. For elaboration, see § 359 below.

4. For elaboration, see § 361 below.

around a table while interrogatories and their answers flow back and forth through the mails. For reasons to be seen later, the interrogatory in New York practice has less utility than it has in federal practice and is therefore met less frequently.

4. *Commission or letters rogatory.*[5] These are used to take testimony outside the state and are usually resorted to only when an ordinary deposition will not do the job. The only apparent difference between a "commission" and a deposition on written questions (or perhaps even oral questions if that's what the parties want) is that the "commissioner" carries the court's seal while the officer settled on by the parties does not. The letter rogatory is a different animal. It is a communication addressed by a local judge to a foreign tribunal asking for its aid in the securing of disclosure in the foreign place. The letter is usually carried by some person designated by the requesting court. That person can also be designated a "commissioner".

5. *Demand for address.*[6] Each party is entitled to know the address of any other party, or of its officers and assignors.

6. *Discovery and inspection.*[7] This ranks with the oral deposition in the frequency of its use and its importance in litigation. With the discovery device the seeker is after a thing rather than testimony. The thing is usually a paper or document of some kind, but it can be any tangible item relevant to the case. Through this device, a party can also be required to permit entry onto real property that the party owns or controls for inspections of various kinds.

7. *Physical and mental examinations.*[8] If the physical or mental condition of any party is in controversy, that party can be compelled with this device to submit to an examination by appropriate professionals, whose testimony and reports are important in such cases. In personal injury cases, for example, the physical examination is as important a device as the deposition or discovery. In incompetency proceedings, the key device is the mental examination. In a commercial case, or any other in which a physical or mental condition is not ordinarily implicated, the device plays no role at all.

8. *Request for admission.*[9] With this device a party can require another to admit or deny stated facts or the genuineness of appended documents or photographs, all under oath. It sounds much more useful than it has actually proved in practice, mainly because the sanctions for inadequate responses are unpredictable and often grudgingly applied by the judges, if they are applied at all.

Those are the devices, briefly listed. Note that the bill of particulars is not a disclosure device but rather an incident of pleadings,[10] although it always does tend to disclose something (as, indeed, the pleading itself does). It has been suggested that expanded use of the bill of particulars should be allowed, at least in smaller cases, to perform the task that the more expensive disclosure devices carry out in bigger ones.[11] The suggestion has merit,[12] but it has not achieved great currency; the lawyer should not consider the bill of particulars a disclosure device until the CPLR or the courts do. Nor is there any requirement under the CPLR that a bill of particulars be furnished before resort is made to a disclosure device, although the court can impose that chronology through a protective order in a given case.

There is no priority in the use of the devices. They need not be sought in any particular

---

5. The commission and letters rogatory are not specified on the CPLR 3102(a) list, but appear later in CPLR 3108. They are important devices, especially when disclosure from a foreign source is required. They are elaborated in § 360 below. For a good review of the disclosure devices in general and those used to obtain disclosure from outside the state in particular, see Wiseman v. American Motors Sales Corp., 103 A.D.2d 230, 479 N.Y.S.2d 528 (2d Dep't 1984).

6. See § 365 below.

7. For elaboration, see § 362 below.

8. For elaboration, see § 363 below.

9. For elaboration, see § 364 below.

10. The bill of particulars is the subject of § 238 et seq., above.

11. See Block v. Fairbairn, 68 Misc.2d 931, 328 N.Y.S.2d 497 (Sup.Ct., Ulster County, 1972).

12. See Commentary C3041:11 on McKinney's CPLR 3041.

sequence. The party resorts to whichever device will best do the job needed and in whatever order the job needs doing. Nor is there any arbitrary limit on the number of devices that may be used or, indeed, on the number of times any single device may be used. Any abuses in this regard are handled by the courts on a case by case basis, usually on a motion for a protective order under CPLR 3103. With a protective order the court can prescribe whatever priority or sequence it deems appropriate to the facts (deposition first, discovery next, etc.).[13] If one device proves inadequate, the party can turn to another.[14]

The usual time for disclosure is the pretrial period after the action has been commenced but before the trial. Certificate of readiness rules restrict the period further, requiring that disclosure be concluded before the case is even placed on the calendar.[15] This means that as a practical matter disclosure is conducted within the several months after the action has been begun and the pleadings are in. The general attitude of the CPLR, embodied in its statute authorizing a motion to dismiss for neglect to prosecute, CPLR 3216, is that a plaintiff who lets an action go more than a year without seeing to the completion of whatever the case needs of the disclosure devices begins to face the threat of a dismissal for lack of prosecution.[16]

Disclosure sought at other times than the pretrial period—e.g., before commencement, after calendaring, at the trial, etc.—requires leave of court.[17]

§ 351. Method of Bringing on Disclosure; Stipulation or Notice

CPLR 3102(b) provides that stipulation or notice shall be the ordinary means for bringing on disclosure, whatever the device used. Only in certain instances is a court order initially required. (These are listed in the next section.)

By stipulation is meant agreement among the attorneys for all the parties, usually initiated by telephone after each attorney has checked with her client. It is primarily the deposition that requires this checking: since it requires a session at an appointed time, day, and place, the convenience of the parties and their lawyers must be considered. Technically, the stipulation setting up the deposition should be in writing and subscribed,[1] but quite often it's done orally, or merely confirmed by one lawyer to another in a letter. Alternatively, the lawyer seeking the deposition may first ascertain from his adversary the availability of the proposed deponent, choose a time accordingly, and then serve notices on attorneys for all parties advising of the time and place selected.

It is technically permissible for the seeking attorney just to pick out a day, time, and place[2] for an adverse party's deposition and simply serve notices on all parties advising of it, but that's inviting trouble; if the deponent is legitimately preoccupied at the time set and does not show up, the court is likely to require nothing more than a rescheduling, without any sanction at all. The court will not countenance deliberate discourtesies among attorneys. A refusal to work out the time and place of a deposition is a high form of discourtesy.

Although the deposition is usually the most demanding of the devices in regard to scheduling, others may need some programming, too. A discovery, for example, which requires the producing of a paper or thing or the inspection of a designated item or premises, may also have to be scheduled for a particular time and place, especially when it involves something of which a mere copy can't be made and furnished to the seeker by mail, as when it concerns something more cumbersome, like three file cabinets of records, or a roomful of them, or a swimming pool, or a fire escape or gymnasium contraption, etc. The physical and mental

---

13. See Rios v. Donovan, 21 A.D.2d 409, 250 N.Y.S.2d 818 (1st Dep't 1964).

14. Katz v. Posner, 23 A.D.2d 774, 258 N.Y.S.2d 508 (2d Dep't 1965).

15. This aspect of the readiness rules is discussed in § 370 below.

16. See CPLR 3216 and its discussion in § 375 below.

17. See § 352 below.

§ 351

1. CPLR 2104.

2. The place of the deposition's taking is discussed in § 355 below.

examination is in the same category; it requires the party to appear in person and thus needs the setting of a day, time, and place for the appearance. Other devices, which contemplate the mere mailing of papers back and forth, such as interrogatories and requests to admit, need no designated session and thus impose fewer logistical demands.

If a stipulation is used, it should be the stipulation of all parties, and it is well that the seeking party confirm the stipulation (if it is not already in the form of a subscribed writing) by notices served on all. If notice is used without stipulation, the notice must be served on the attorney for each party, not merely on the deponent's attorney. A deposition may not be used against a person not notified of its taking.[3] An exception is the party who is in default for failure to appear in the action; nothing need be served on that party.[4] The time requirements connected with the giving of notice will be discussed in the later treatments of the devices individually, since they are not uniform for all.

For the deposing of a party, stipulations or notices do the job. But if the deponent is a nonparty witness, the deponent must be served with a subpoena.[5] This recognizes that the usual sanctions available against a party who violates a notice or stipulation—such as a preclusion order or even a default judgment[6]— hold no terror for a nonparty. The use of the subpoena makes available against the nonparty the sanction of contempt for disobedience.

It will be recalled that in order to depose a nonparty witness, relevancy is not the only showing needed; the additional requirements of paragraph 3 or 4 of CPLR 3101(a) must be met. Since only the court can ultimately determine whether they have been, the question arises whether the deposing of a witness requires a preliminary order, in which the court would make that determination, or can proceed by mere stipulation or notice. The latter is the practice. The seeking attorney proceeds in first instance without an order, merely coordinating time and place with the other parties, confirming it in notices served on them, and effecting subpoena service on the witness. If objection is made that the additional "witness" requirements of CPLR 3101(a) are not met, a protective order can be sought by the adverse party or even by the nonparty witness, suppressing the examination.[7] This practice was confirmed in 1984 with an amendment of CPLR 3101(a)(4) dropping out the reference to the determination of "special circumstances" by the court and allowing the disclosure upon the seeking party's service on the other parties of a mere notice "stating the circumstances or reasons such disclosure is sought or required".[8] The caselaw on what satisfied as "special circumstances", which for the most part set a liberal standard, will continue to define the "circumstances" that the amended provision refers to,[9] if, indeed, the new language doesn't invite an even more generous standard.

If a notice or stipulation setting up disclosure is ignored or otherwise violated, the aggrieved party can seek a court order compelling the disclosure,[10] or, if the disobedience is wilful, a penalty against the offender.[11] In some instances, however, an order must be secured before disclosure is permitted at all. These are listed in the next section.

§ 352. Instances Where Order Initially Required

Even in instances in which a mere notice may be and is used to bring on disclosure,

---

3. CPLR 3117(a)(3).

4. CPLR 3105.

5. CPLR 3106(b). An "officer, director, member or employee of a party" equals the party itself for this purpose and thus need not be served with a subpoena. The notice served on the party is deemed adequate to compel that person's deposition.

6. CPLR 3126. The sanctions are treated in § 367.

7. Spector v. Antenna and Radome Research Associates Corp., 25 A.D.2d 569, 267 N.Y.S.2d 843 (2d Dep't 1966).

8. See § 345 above. The subject is treated in the lead note in New York State Law Digest No. 304.

9. Slabakis v. Drizin, 107 A.D.2d 45, 485 N.Y.S.2d 270 (1st Dep't 1985). See Commentary C3101:23 on McKinney's CPLR 3101, where the conflict on this point prior to the 1984 amendment is also noted.

10. CPLR 3124. See § 366 below.

11. CPLR 3126. See § 367 below.

disobedience may ensue and a court order compelling disclosure may be needed. The CPLR provides for such an order,[1] but there the order is sought only as a follow-up. In some instances, the notice method is not available at all and a court order must be sought in first instance. These situations are the following:

1. Before action commenced. If disclosure is sought before an action has been duly commenced, a court order is required. Disclosure at this stage may be obtained "to aid in bringing an action, to preserve information or to aid in arbitration".[2] The last, designed to secure the aid of a court to compel disclosure in connection with an out-of-court arbitration, is frowned on by the courts,[3] although every now and again the courts can be prevailed on to lend a hand when the disclosure is needed to present "a proper case" to the arbitrator.[4] Free use of the disclosure devices would of course be inconsistent with the purposes of arbitration, among which are ease, expedition, and economy. The parties are better off seeking disclosure authorizations from the arbitrators.[5]

The preservation of information—or perpetuation of testimony, as it is better known—was one of the earliest functions of disclosure. It abides, but is not frequently seen. It may be used, for example, when a key witness is in extremis or about to depart the state and there is not even time to commence an action and seek disclosure within it.

Disclosure to aid in "bringing" an action is seen a bit more often. It may not be used to determine whether the plaintiff has a cause of action,[6] but as long as the plaintiff can satisfy the court that there is one, the disclosure can be sought to help determine who the defendants should be or the form that the action should take.[7] If a would-be defendant is under a duty to allow a would-be plaintiff to inspect records, for example, as a hospital is when a patient seeks the inspection, and the defendant violates that obligation, the right to pre-action disclosure is at hand and it has been held that the plaintiff's application for the disclosure does not even require an affidavit of merits.[8] If the disclosure is needed merely to help in the drafting of the complaint, an alternative procedure is to commence the action with only a CPLR 305(b) notice[9] and then seek the disclosure within the action itself. If the complaint can be drawn without the datum that the disclosure seeks, the disclosure will not be allowed at all for this purpose. Where, for example, the plaintiff seeks disclosure for the purpose of pleading the amount of damages in a case in which a damages estimate in the complaint suffices, disclosure will be refused.[10]

2. During or after trial. If disclosure is sought after the trial has begun, it needs a court order.[11] Disclosure at this stage is extremely rare, since disclosure must as a rule be concluded before the case can even be put on the calendar to await trial and its purpose is to aid preparation *for* the trial. But it can arise, for example, where some new element is introduced at the trial of which the pleadings did not give notice.

Disclosure to aid in the enforcement of a judgment, which of course becomes relevant only after judgment has been rendered, is subject to a special set of provisions[12] and is not governed by this one.

---

§ 352

1. CPLR 3124.

2. CPLR 3102(c).

3. See De Sapio v. Kohlmeyer, 35 N.Y.2d 402, 362 N.Y.S.2d 843, 321 N.E.2d 770 (1974).

4. See Hendler & Murray, P.C. v. Lambert, 127 A.D.2d 820, 511 N.Y.S.2d 941 (2d Dep't 1987).

5. See Hooper v. M.V.A.I.C., 42 Misc.2d 446, 248 N.Y.S.2d 255 (Sup.Ct., N.Y.County, 1963). See § 597 below (Practitioner's Edition).

6. Application of Janosik, 71 A.D.2d 1058, 420 N.Y.S.2d 815 (4th Dep't 1979).

7. See In re Pelley, 43 Misc.2d 1082, 252 N.Y.S.2d 944 (Nassau County Ct. 1964).

8. Matter of Taylor, 143 Misc.2d 259, 540 N.Y.S.2d 162 (Sup.Ct. Kings County 1989).

9. See § 60 above.

10. Zakarias v. Radio Patents Corp., 20 A.D.2d 795, 248 N.Y.S.2d 75 (2d Dep't 1964).

11. CPLR 3102(d).

12. CPLR 5223, 5224. See § 509 below.

3. Disclosure to aid foreign action. CPLR 328(b) provides that serving a paper on someone in New York in connection with a foreign proceeding requires no court order, although the aid of a New York court is available pursuant to CPLR 328(a) if it proves necessary. If the paper served requires compliance of some kind, however, the assistance of a New York court is more likely to be needed and the need is felt most when disclosure is sought in New York to aid in the foreign proceeding. CPLR 3102(e) was enacted to fill that need.

CPLR 3102(e) is an adaptation of the Uniform Foreign Depositions Act. It offers the machinery of the New York court system to compel a witness found in New York to give testimony for use in a proceeding pending elsewhere. The one seeking the disclosure, usually acting through a New York attorney retained for the purpose, can apply to the supreme court or to a county court for aid, the court making whatever order is appropriate in the circumstances. The methods and processes to be used are the same as for disclosure sought for local actions. The seeker here can be a commissioner carrying the seal of the foreign court, or the bearer of a foreign letter rogatory,[13] or just an attorney or other person authorized by the foreign law or by the parties in the foreign action as permitted by the foreign law. If an objection of any kind is raised, such as by the person to be examined as a witness, the court need only assure that the examination is relevant to the issues in the foreign action and that the witness's rights are protected. No showing of special circumstances is required to invoke CPLR 3102(e).[14]

If the law of a foreign place, including a sister state, has such a provision, it assists in the converse situation: the securing of disclosure there to aid in a New York action.

4. Disclosure by the state. As a rule, the state can be sued only in the Court of Claims. But it can sue in any court as a plaintiff or voluntarily intervene in any even as a defendant, so the state is therefore seen in other courts and in other postures as well. Disclosure by the state, whatever its posture and whatever the court, was at one time available only by court order. A 1984 amendment of CPLR 3102(f) eliminated that requirement and made the disclosure devices available against the state through the same procedures applicable to any other party.[15]

It has been clarified that the state is also subject to disclosure as a nonparty witness. For that reason, state officials or employees in command of data relevant to a pending action and not otherwise privileged can't resist disclosure by pleading either their state employment or the fact that the state is not a party.[16]

5. Prisoners. Disclosure from a prisoner requires a court order.[17] Prison doors do not open, even temporarily, for a mere notice or stipulation.

6. Discovery against nonparty witness. The discovery device of CPLR 3120, which seeks to compel the production of a paper or thing and which proceeds by mere notice against a party, requires a court order when the item is sought from a nonparty witness.[18] This recognizes, among other things, the possible inconvenience that the item's production may cause the witness and enables the court to assess the need for the discovery and the cost to the witness, providing for reimbursement or even the advance payment of those costs if need be.

7. Disclosure after case on calendar. After the case has been placed on the calendar with the filing of a note of issue[19] accompanied by a

---

13. See, e.g., Application of Levine, 116 Misc.2d 922, 456 N.Y.S.2d 936 (Sup.Ct., N.Y.County, 1982).

14. Brandes v. Harris, 78 A.D.2d 638, 432 N.Y.S.2d 116 (2d Dep't 1980).

15. For a while, two of the devices, the interrogatory and the notice to admit, were not available against the state at all. The reason for these exceptions was unconvincing and in 1993 they were eliminated, putting the state on essentially the same footing as a private litigant with respect to all of the disclosure devices. The change was recommended by the Advisory Committee on Civil

Practice in light of Vista Business Eqpt. Inc. v. State, N.Y.L.J., Jan. 23, 1986, p.12, col.3 (Ct.Cl., Weisberg, J.), which reviewed the legislative history of CPLR 3102(f).

16. Kaplan v. Kaplan, 31 N.Y.2d 63, 334 N.Y.S.2d 879, 286 N.E.2d 260 (1972).

17. CPLR 3106(c).

18. CPLR 3120(b).

19. CPLR 3402. This is a matter of calendar practice and is treated in § 369 below.

statement of readiness, as required under the rules, disclosure is available only upon a showing of "unusual or unanticipated circumstances".[20] It thus requires a motion satisfying the court that the circumstances have been met. This is a court rule rather than CPLR requirement, but one that is strictly enforced.[21]

8. *Special proceedings.* In a special proceeding (as opposed to an ordinary action), all disclosure except the request to admit device must be sought by court order.[22] This does not apply in the surrogates' courts, however, which conduct their business in a series of "proceedings" but where the same methods are used as those in the supreme court—notice, stipulation, etc.[23]

Whenever the disclosure is sought without the context of an action or proceeding, as where it is sought by application before the action has been commenced, there may be some confusion about the procedures for the application: how to make it, whom to serve, etc. It may be helpful to bring the motion on with an order to show cause in which the court can give direction about those things, especially when jurisdictional problems may need resolution.[24] It has been held that a special proceeding may be used to bring the application on,[25] just as it may be for leave to serve a late notice of claim.[26] This is a good idea because using a special proceeding secures the helpful procedural guidance of Article 4 of the CPLR.[27] The initial steps of a special proceeding are essentially the same mechanically as those of a motion, so the use of the proceeding instead of a motion would in any event be harmless error that a court could ignore.[28]

There appears to be a conflict about whether the application has to be on notice. The appel-late division has indicated that the seeking attorney may just use a subpoena in that situation without first seeking a prior CPLR 3102(e) order allowing it.[29] That would presumably be a New York attorney issuing the subpoena out of a New York court under the caption of a CPLR 3102(e) application. It has been held that a subpoena issued by an attorney in the foreign jurisdiction would not do the job.[30]

§ 352A. Requirement to Supplement Prior Responses

Subdivision (h) of CPLR 3101 is known as the supplementation requirement. It requires a party to update prior responses whenever the party obtains information indicating that a prior response was

> incorrect or incomplete when made, or ... though correct and complete when made, no longer is correct and complete, and the circumstances are such that a failure to amend or supplement the response would be materially misleading.

The provision was added in 1993 and took effect January 1, 1994. Its model was Rule 26(e) of the Federal Rules of Civil Procedure, but the New York statute is not identical. Coincidentally, Federal Rule 26(e) was also amended effective December 1, 1993. The New York provision drew on the federal rule as it existed prior to the federal revision as well as on the revision itself, notably in its borrowing of the "incomplete or incorrect" phrase, which was floating around in drafts of what was then merely a proposed federal change.

The purpose of the federal revision is sum-

---

20. See, e.g., Uniform Rule 202.21, the rule applicable in the supreme and county courts.

21. The certificate of readiness rules and their enforcement is discussed in § 370, below.

22. CPLR 408. The request to admit is governed by CPLR 3123, treated in § 364 below.

23. See the Commentary on SCPA 102 in McKinney's Surrogate's Court Procedure Act.

24. See Commentary C3102:6 on McKinney's CPLR 3102.

25. Robinson v. Government of Malaysia, 174 Misc.2d 560, 664 N.Y.S.2d 907 (Sup.Ct., N.Y.County, 1997).

26. See Billone v. Town of Huntington, 188 A.D.2d 526, 591 N.Y.S.2d 437 (2d Dep't 1992).

27. See § 32 above.

28. See Affiliated Distillers Brands Corp. v. Metropolitan Package Stores Assn., 23 A.D.2d 650, 257 N.Y.S.2d 495 (1st Dep't 1965).

29. See Application of Ayliffe and Cos., 166 A.D.2d 223, 564 N.Y.S.2d 297 (1st Dep't 1990).

30. See Matter of Deloitte, Haskins, and Sells, 146 Misc.2d 884, 552 N.Y.S.2d 1003 (Sup.Ct., N.Y. County, 1990).

marized in a federal advisory committee note[1] stating that one of its purposes was to clarify that the supplementation requirement "applies to interrogatories, requests for production, and requests for admissions, but not ordinarily to deposition testimony". The New York provision makes no exception for a deposition; it applies "to all disclosure devices".[2] Hence a response in a deposition, if it falls under the criteria quoted above, is also subject to the supplementation requirement.

If a party was asked to identify its fact witnesses, there was a standing requirement under the prior version of the federal rule[3] to advise the other side of any new fact witnesses the party subsequently learned about. The New York provision does not adopt that requirement in terms, but if a party to a New York action was specifically asked to identify fact witnesses and gave a complete list at the time, the later uncovering of another witness would fall under the general supplementation language used in the New York provision.

Subdivision (h) of CPLR 3101 makes no reference to the disclosure of expert witnesses, which the federal rule does,[4] for the reason that the subject is treated in CPLR 3101(d)(1) in terms that make a separate reference to supplementation unnecessary.

Supplementing is to be made "promptly" upon the party's obtaining the new information.

The language of subdivision (h) indicates some hesitation about whether a failure to supplement should result in preclusion against the party withholding the information. The legislature left the matter to the courts. All there is is a general instruction that the court may make "whatever order may be just". Preclusion is of course a possibility, but the court can turn to other cures. A failure to supple-

ment is also backed by the penalties of CPLR 3126,[5] and it would also seem possible to subject a violator to the money sanctions of Rule 130–1 if the conduct can be found to rise to the level of "frivolous".[6]

If a dispute arises about whether a given discovery or disclosure should have been supplemented, it is not unlikely that it will arise at the trial itself. A finding at that point that the supplementing should have been made can have the effect of denying use of the unrevealed information altogether.[7]

Since the supplementation requirement is intended to apply to all of the disclosure devices—depositions, discoveries, interrogatories, etc.—it should apply no matter what the tool is that brought on the original disclosure, e.g., notice, stipulation, or court order. But what form shall the supplementation take?

The form should follow as closely as possible the form in which the information now being supplemented was originally given. If the information to be updated first came out in a deposition by party P, for example, P can merely send a statement to the other parties advising that the answer she gave in response to the question asked at the top of folio 49 of the deposition now appears to be incorrect, and that based on subsequent information coming to the deponent's attention the answer should be changed to thus-and-so. The statement should be sworn to, just as the original deposition was. The other parties would ordinarily be entitled to this, so that they can make the same use of the supplementary data at the trial as they could have made of the deposition itself. The same considerations apply to the supplementing of interrogatories.

If a discovery is involved, and the document or thing requested was not available earlier but can be furnished by the party now, it

§ 352A

1. See the materials following Rule 26 in the Federal Rules segment of 28 U.S.C.A.

2. See the 1993 Report of the Advisory Committee on Civil Practice to the Chief Administrator of the Courts (Dec. 1992), p.19.

3. See subparagraph (A) of paragraph (1) of the pre–1993 Federal Rule 26(e).

4. The subject was part of Rule 26(e)(1) and remained so after the 1993 revision.

5. See Commentary C3126:1 on McKinney's CPLR 3126.

6. For discussion of the frivolity sanctions, see § 414A below.

7. See the more extended treatment of the supplementation requirement in SPR 8:1 and in Commentary C3101:49 on McKinney's CPLR 3101.

should be furnished now, with an accompanying explanation (in a letter, notice, statement, etc.). Here the supplementing is less formal. Unless some verification is required in connection with the identification of the document or thing, a swearing or affirmation in this instance would not ordinarily be necessary.

The court is likely to be little concerned about form as long as the updating has been carried out with integrity, the form used makes the supplementary material just as usable as the original material, and no party entitled to the supplementation can claim prejudice in how it has been made.

While the statute anticipates automatic supplementation by each party, it has been held that a motion is permissible "to force an amendment or supplementary response".[8]

D. PROTECTION AGAINST ABUSE

Table of Sections

Sec.
353. Protective Order; CPLR 3103.

§ 353. Protective Order; CPLR 3103

The protective order is the court's perpetual guard against disclosure abuses. Addressed always to the particular situation at hand and available on motion or sua sponte whenever needed, it relieves the rest of the disclosure article from having to stop at key junctures to anticipate and arm against harassment. It is well to quote CPLR 3103(a):

The court may at any time on its own initiative, or on motion of any party or of any person from whom discovery is sought, make a protective order denying, limiting, conditioning or regulating the use of any disclosure device. Such order shall be designed to prevent unreasonable annoyance,

expense, embarrassment, disadvantage, or other prejudice to any person or the courts.

The statute recognizes how readily the devices can be abused, and wisely surrenders all attempts to enumerate potential abuses. The cure is an ad hoc order. If advantage is being taken of a given party's attorney, low on either talent or experience, or if the party has no attorney, or if for any other reason the court detects an abuse before a party or witness has complained of it by motion, the court may make the order on its own motion.

When a party seeks the protective order by motion, which is of course the more common situation, the mere making of the motion suspends the scheduled disclosure until the court, disposing of the motion, decides what is to follow.[1] If the disclosure involves a nonparty witness, the moving party must notify the witness that the disclosure is suspended.[2] CPLR 3103(a) permits the witness to seek the protective order, but by contacting the opposing party the witness will often be able to get that party to make the motion in the witness's behalf.

The phrase "any person from whom discovery is sought" includes a nonparty from whom a deposition is sought and the custodian of a paper or thing from whom discovery is sought.[3]

As a general rule, the time is always open to move for a protective order. The best time to move is of course before the disclosure has been had; the motion's mere making, as indicated, stays the disclosure until the court decides whether it is to proceed. But if the disclosure has already gone forward and the testimony or item has already been given, a protective order may still prove useful. Any information improperly or irregularly obtained may be ordered suppressed, i.e., barred from any use at the trial.[4]

---

8. See Green v. Staten Island Univ. Hosp., 161 Misc.2d 976, 615 N.Y.S.2d 856 (Sup.Ct., Richmond County, 1994), aff'd 221 A.D.2d 416, 634 N.Y.S.2d 386 (2d Dep't 1995), noted in SPR 37:3.

§ 353

1. CPLR 3103(b).

2. CPLR 3106(b).

3. An amendment of CPLR 3103(a), effective January 1, 1994, changed the word "witness" to the phrase "person from whom discovery is sought" in order to clarify that the mere custodian of a relevant paper or thing is also included. This change was an adoption of the language of Rule 26(c) of the Federal Rules of Civil Procedure.

The protective order is available no matter what disclosure device is implicated. Early conflict about whether the protective order can be used to test the validity of a request to admit under CPLR 3123 has also been resolved. It can be.[5] In the lower courts the protective order is also available against a bill of particulars if the bill is being used for harassment, although the bill is not officially a disclosure device.[6]

The Advisory Committee, whose draft of CPLR 3103(a) got through the legislature unscathed, set forth a number of matters that the court can regulate on a protective order motion:

1. the time, order, and place of taking depositions;

2. the number and names of persons to be questioned;

3. the time within which the information must be obtained;

4. the number, kinds of questions, or specific questions that may be asked;

5. the disclosure device or combination of devices that may be used; and

6. the matters that may or may not be inquired into.[7]

The enumerated matters are illustrative, not exclusive. There follows in the Advisory Committee's notes a list of examples of protective orders. A perusal of the list will confirm to the lawyer the numerous possibilities and corroborate the drafters' judgment to leave disclosure

rectifications to the courts on a case by case basis.[8] Provision is made to protect against the unnecessary revelation of trade secrets, for example.

The protective order can also balance the situation in which a disparity in the economic resources of the parties is disabling one from participating in the disclosure process or empowering another to take undue advantage of it. The court can order one party to defray initially the costs of another's participation in the disclosure,[9] but this is not a favored step; ordinarily the judicial preference is to have the parties pay their own disclosure way. The later winner on the merits recovers these expenses, or at least a segment of them, from the loser as post-judgment disbursements.[10]

With a protective order, the court can limit the number of disclosure devices that may be used.[11]

It was the imposing of a protective order that occasioned an extensive review of the question of public access to pretrial proceedings, including depositions, the court observing in Lisa C.R. v. William R.[12] that the press has been consistently barred from such proceedings in New York.

The court can assign a given judge or referee to supervise all or part of the disclosure proceedings in a particular case,[13] including a judicial hearing officer.[14] It has been held that this power should be exercised sparingly, however,[15] and it is. An example of a case warranting the appointment of a referee is where a party has a "long history of ... intransigence" in resisting disclosure and a "constantly available

4. CPLR 3103(c). See Juskowitz v. Hahn, 56 Misc.2d 647, 289 N.Y.S.2d 870 (Sup.Ct., Nassau County, 1968).

5. Epstein v. Consolidated Edison Co., 31 A.D.2d 746, 297 N.Y.S.2d 260 (2d Dep't 1969); Nader v. General Motors Corp., 53 Misc.2d 515, 279 N.Y.S.2d 111 (Sup.Ct., N.Y.County), aff'd 29 A.D.2d 632, 286 N.Y.S.2d 209 (1st Dep't 1967).

6. See § 1101 in the New York City Civil, Uniform District, Uniform City, and Uniform Justice court acts, McKinney's Vol. 29A, Parts 2 and 3, and the Commentaries on it.

7. First Rep.Leg.Doc. (1957) No. 6(b), p. 124.

8. The list is from 1st Rep.Leg.Doc. (1957) No. 6(b), p.125, and is printed verbatim following McKinney's CPLR 3103.

9. Buffone v. Aronson, 45 Misc.2d 454, 257 N.Y.S.2d 47 (Sup.Ct., Westchester County, 1965).

10. See Fairchild Camera & Instr. Corp. v. Barletta, 21 A.D.2d 768, 250 N.Y.S.2d 679 (1st Dep't 1964).

11. See, e.g., Estates Roofing Co. v. Savo, 85 Misc.2d 1028, 381 N.Y.S.2d 198 (Suffolk County Dist.Ct. 1976).

12. 166 Misc.2d 817, 635 N.Y.S.2d 449 (Sup.Ct., N.Y. County, 1995) (involving a matrimonial dispute).

13. CPLR 3104(a).

14. CPLR 3104(b). A judicial hearing officer is a retired judge designated as such pursuant to § 850(1) et seq. of the Judiciary Law.

15. National Dairy v. Lawrence A.F.W. Corp., 23 A.D.2d 650, 257 N.Y.S.2d 471 (1965).

supervisor" is needed.[16] A middle step, which doesn't require the appointee to sit in on the disclosure proceedings proper, is to direct that all disclosure applications in a given case be made to a designated judge or referee.[17]

If the parties stipulate, they can name an attorney to act as a referee.[18] The powers of the referee, including a judicial hearing officer and a lawyer appointed by the parties, are set forth in the statute.[19] Review of a referee's determination must be sought before the appointing court. It does not go directly to an appellate court even if the referee is a judicial hearing officer.[20]

Affirmation Requirement on Disclosure Motions

Every motion relating to disclosure must be accompanied by the moving lawyer's affirmation that a good faith effort was first made to resolve the disclosure dispute with the other side.[21] The motion for a protective order is of course one of the motions requiring this affirmation. The affirmation should not be a mere boiler-plate recitation. It has been held that

> [s]ignificant, intelligent and expansive contact and negotiations must be held between counsel to resolve any dispute and such efforts must be adequately detailed in [the] affirmation [and that mere] computer generated form letters or cursory telephone conversations [are not acceptable].[22]

E. THE DEVICES INDIVIDUALLY

Table of Sections

§ 354. Deposition on Oral Questions: The "EBT"

The oral deposition is one of the most probing of the disclosure devices. There are several aspects of it to be negotiated. This section will treat its initial scheduling. Succeeding sections will discuss where and how the deposition is taken and executed and the use that can be made of it at the trial.

At the outset we have a question of terminology. In practice a popular name for the oral deposition is "EBT", standing for examination before trial. The three-letter recitation is deeply ensconced in practice, and generally accurate but not technically so. The usual time for the deposition is after commencement of the action and before the trial, giving currency to the "EBT" description, but depositions can also be scheduled by court order before the action is begun,[1] after the trial is under way,[2] and even after it is over.[3] By avoiding time references and embracing all oral examinations, "deposition" is more accurate. "EBT" by definition embraces the most usual one but is sometimes used casually to describe all of them.

CPLR 3107 contains the basic requirements for setting up a deposition. Ideally, the deposi-

---

16. Baker v. General Mills Fun Group, Inc., 101 Misc.2d 193, 420 N.Y.S.2d 820 (Sup.Ct., N.Y.County, 1979).

17. See In re Dietrich's Will, 65 Misc.2d 811, 318 N.Y.S.2d 72 (Sup.Ct., Erie County, 1970), aff'd 36 A.D.2d 1027, 321 N.Y.S.2d 449 (4th Dep't 1971).

18. CPLR 3104(b).

19. CPLR 3104(c).

20. Crow–Crimmins–Wolff & Munier v. County of Westchester, 110 A.D.2d 871, 488 N.Y.S.2d 429 (2d Dep't 1985).

21. See, e.g., Uniform Rule 202.7, the rule applicable in the supreme and county courts.

22. See Eaton v. Chahal, 146 Misc.2d 977, 553 N.Y.S.2d 642 (Sup.Ct., Renss. County, 1990), a consolidated decision in six cases before the court that rejects as inadequate the affirmations tendered in five of them.

§ 354

1. CPLR 3102(c).

2. CPLR 3102(d).

3. CPLR 5229.

tion is set up by agreement among all parties, so that whatever notices pass among them merely confirm what they have already agreed to. A notice of deposition that picks its own day for the examination without first consulting other parties, including the deponent, must set the day for not earlier than 20 days after the notice is served. This of course means not earlier than 25 days if mail is used.[4] As previously indicated, it may be idle to set a day arbitrarily without first consulting other parties for their convenience. Without that consultation, the court is less likely to visit any penalty on a nonappearance.

The notice must be in writing, state when and where the deposition is to take place, and indicate who is to be deposed. It need not enumerate the matters on which the person is to be examined. It is understood that the examination can delve into anything relevant to the case and any phraseology so indicating will suffice. The deponent's lawyer may schedule for the same time and place a deposition of the noticing (and any other) party, the advantage being that only 10 days notice is needed for that (whereas 20 is the requirement if the examination is scheduled independently).

Ordinarily, the defendant is entitled to examine the plaintiff before the plaintiff gets a turn at the defendant. The theory is that the defendant is blameless until the plaintiff proves otherwise.[5] The CPLR spells out this pro-defendant priority backhandedly. It provides that if a notice of deposition is served by the plaintiff before the defendant's answering time has expired, it requires leave of court, while the defendant's notice served on the plaintiff during that time doesn't.[6] Even this who-goes-first direction can be varied by the court in a protective order. The courts are impatient with priority battles, reasonably believing that counsel can work these things out

without court aid and condemning "the consummate waste of time occasioned by attorneys' picayune and pettifogging contentiousness", especially when it necessitates judicial intervention.[7] The requirement of the uniform rules, that every motion related to disclosure be accompanied by an affirmation of a good faith effort to resolve the dispute without resort to the court,[8] is a by-product of that kind of contentiousness.

A nonparty deponent must be served with a subpoena, which, like the notice when a party is to be examined, must be served at least 20 days before the deposition.[9] The parties are of course entitled to notice of a nonparty's deposition as well as a party's. Common practice is to serve notices on the parties, advising of the witness's deposition, at about the same time the witness is served with the subpoena. One difference is that the notices served on the parties are interlocutory papers which go by mail to the parties' lawyers,[10] while the subpoena must be served on the witness in the same manner as a summons.[11]

Errors in the notice of deposition are waived unless a written objection is served on the noticing party at least three days before the scheduled deposition.[12] Other phases of the deposition cycle may come in for substantial objections, but the initial step of noticing it usually does not.

The expenses of scheduling and taking a deposition are on the party seeking it, unless the court otherwise directs, such as on a motion for a protective order.[13]

A simple form of notice to take a deposition can read as follows:

Please take notice that, pursuant to CPLR Art. 31, the deposition on oral examination of the defendant _____, whose address is _____, will be taken on the _____ day of

4. CPLR 2103(b)(2).

5. Skrill v. Skrill, 42 Misc.2d 22, 247 N.Y.S.2d 207 (Sup.Ct., Nassau County, 1964).

6. CPLR 3106(a). After expiration of the answering time, the one who serves the notice first gets to take the deposition first.

7. Goldberg v. Freedman, 33 A.D.2d 754, 305 N.Y.S.2d 996 (1st Dep't 1969).

8. See, e.g., Uniform Rule 202.7, applicable in the supreme and county courts.

9. CPLR 3106(b).

10. CPLR 2103(b)(2).

11. CPLR 2303. See § 383 below.

12. CPLR 3112.

13. CPLR 3116(d).

_____, 19__, at _____ o'clock at the office of the attorney for the plaintiff at _____.[14]

§ 355. Place of Deposition

The venue of a deposition to be taken in the state is set by CPLR 3110, which lists the proper counties. If the person to be examined is a party, the deposition may be scheduled in the county in which (1) the party resides, or (2) the party has a place of business, or (3) the action is pending.[1] If the person to be examined is a nonparty, the alternative of the action-pending county is unavailable and the venue is limited to the county of the witness's residence or business; and if the witness is not a resident, then to the county of her employment or, simply, the county in which she is served.[2] If the witness can't be served here and has no contacts with the state, her testimony will have to be taken outside the state by devices to be met later.[3]

If a party resides outside New York, the convenience of that party will be considered by the court, especially when the party must travel from a foreign country. While the stated requirements of CPLR 3110 are as applicable to foreign as to domestic parties, a protective order can adjust venue as well as it can any other thing. It can cancel a duly scheduled deposition of the foreign party, even if that party is the plaintiff, on condition, for example, that the party submit to local examination at a later time a stated number of days in advance of the trial.[4] That will enable the party to make but one trip to the state, deferring pretrial disclosure to that occasion when the party would have shortly had to come to New York for the trial anyway. This is sometimes called the "eve of trial" rule, but it's not applied just for the asking.[5]

There is of course less tendency to defer disclosure when the nonresident comes from a sister state, especially a neighboring one.

CPLR 3110 merely prescribes the county of the deposition; it doesn't say where, within the county, the deposition may be held. The most common practice is for the noticing lawyer to arrange the deposition for his office, if the office is in a proper county. Any appropriate place within the county where a table and chairs are available in an atmosphere of decorum should do. In some counties the courthouse has facilities for the taking of depositions. This must be inquired into locally. When available, a deposition set for the courthouse is of course permissible, but not mandatory. It has been held, however, that if an opposing party objects to having a deposition at the noticing attorney's office, the court should on application direct that it be held elsewhere. The courthouse would seem the most appropriate place when relations between counsel have so deteriorated.[6]

When the party to be examined is a public corporation, which includes all of the municipalities (cities, counties, towns, and villages) among other entities,[7] or any of its officers, agents, or employees, the action-pending county is the proper venue and the deposition may be set for the office of one of the public corporation's officers, agents, or employees.[8] The parties can stipulate otherwise, and the court can of course vary this requirement with a protective order.

For purposes of disclosure, New York City is deemed one county, so that if any of its five counties answers to a requirement of CPLR 3110, the deposition can apparently be scheduled in that county or in any of the four other

---

14. This notice is modeled on 2 West's McKinney's Forms, CPLR § 6:154, which also contains caption, signature, and an additional clause used when the deponent is also to be required to produce papers or other things designated for use in conjunction with the examination. See CPLR 3111, discussed in § 362.

§ 355

1. CPLR 3110(1).

2. CPLR 3110(2). The thing with which the nonparty is served is of course a subpoena. CPLR 3106(b).

3. See §§ 359 and 360, below.

4. See Zilken v. Leader, 23 A.D.2d 644, 257 N.Y.S.2d 185 (1st Dep't 1965).

5. See Rakowski v. Irmisch, 46 A.D.2d 826, 361 N.Y.S.2d 68 (3d Dep't 1974).

6. See Ambrose v. Wurlitzer Co., 27 A.D.2d 732, 277 N.Y.S.2d 160 (2d Dep't 1967).

7. See the definitions contained in Gen.Constr.L. § 66.

8. CPLR 3110(3).

counties. The protective order stands by here, too, as a remedy for abuse.

Although CPLR 3110, in setting venue, addresses itself only to the deposition, it should be taken as the guide for any disclosure device that requires a face-to-face session. It is not of moment with something like the request to admit or the interrogatory, because those devices ordinarily move by mail between lawyers' offices. But it may be relevant for the discovery device of CPLR 3120, especially when the person must show up with the item at a stated time and place and can't merely send it on. And absent any contrary direction in a rule, it may be relevant as well to the physical or mental examination allowed by CPLR 3121.[9] Whenever, for any device, a place of in-state disclosure must be singled out and instructions are not found elsewhere, CPLR 3110 is the appropriate guidepost.[10]

§ 356. Taking the Deposition

The deposition is taken before a person authorized to administer oaths, typically a notary public. Often the stenographer hired to record the questions and answers has qualified as a notary and carries out both functions. The party setting up a deposition must see to it that the officer and stenographer attend at the session. Stenography is still the predominant method, but the use of videotape is permitted.[1] An elaborate rule prescribes the procedures when videotape is used.[2] Disqualified from taking a deposition, i.e., from serving as the officer before whom it is taken, are the attorney for a party, the attorney's employees, and anyone who would be disqualified by interest, blood, or affinity from serving as a juror in the case.[3] But an employee of the attorney can operate the tape equipment when tape is used.[4]

Separate provisions list the persons authorized to conduct a deposition elsewhere in the United States and in foreign countries.[5] Objection to the person designated to take the deposition must be made before it is taken or as soon afterwards as the disqualification becomes known.[6] It is also permissible, of course, for a judge or referee,[7] or an attorney if the parties stipulate,[8] to conduct the deposition.

When the session finally gets under way, with the deponents and the lawyers for all parties present along with the officer and stenographer or tape operator, the officer puts the deponent under oath and the noticing attorney starts the questioning, the other attorneys to have their chance in due course. The inquiry may be into anything relevant to the case. It is no longer a defense to cry "fishing expedition". In the parlance of the CPLR, where relevance is the standard under CPLR 3101(a) and the *Allen* case construing it,[9] anything relevant is fair game; the once handy epithet, "fishing expedition", won't defeat it. Realistically, the questioner is indeed fishing— into every posture the deposing party takes on every fact involved in the case.

The testimony, question-and-answer, colloquy and dispute, is recorded verbatim. All objections, whatever their nature (and there are sometimes many at a deposition), are to be noted by the officer and "the deposition shall proceed subject to the right of a person to apply for a protective order". And it shall

---

9. The rule governing medical examinations in the supreme and county courts is Uniform Rule 202.17, which leaves it to the court to adjust venue if the parties can't agree to it.

10. See Cattat v. Alfa Romeo, Inc., 81 Misc.2d 119, 364 N.Y.S.2d 772 (Sup.Ct., Oneida County, 1975).

§ 356

1. CPLR 3113(b) permits the deposition to be recorded by "stenographic or other means".

2. See Uniform Rule 202.15, applicable in the supreme and county courts. Subdivision (j) of the rule applies when only an audio taping is sought. Counterpart rules adopting Rule 202.15 govern in the N.Y.C. Civil Court (UR 208.12), the district courts (212.12), and the city courts (210.12).

The Court of Claims has its own rule on the subject (206.11).

3. CPLR 3113(a). For an enumeration of those so disqualified, see CPLR 4110.

4. Uniform Rule 202.15(c).

5. CPLR 3113(a)(2), (3). See Commentary C3113:1 on McKinney's CPLR 3113.

6. CPLR 3115(c).

7. CPLR 3102(c), 3104(a).

8. CPLR 3104(b). The attorney selected is not likely to be the attorney for either side, but to keep from running afoul of CPLR 3113(a), the court should make sure it isn't.

9. See § 344 above.

proceed, moreover, "without unreasonable adjournments".[10] The purpose is to prevent any objection from cancelling the whole examination if that can possibly be avoided. If the parties disagree on a question and the deponent on counsel's advice declines it, the examination, as CPLR 3113(b) would have it, should continue on other matters until the questioner has exhausted all of her questions, answered or not. Any unanswered ones to which the questioner thinks answers are required may be made the subject of a later motion for a disclosure order. It is also possible, if the deposition is being conducted in the courthouse or close by, to have the judge rule on the legitimacy of questions and the requirement of answers during the course of the deposition.[11]

CPLR 3113(b) also authorizes any party to submit written questions to the officer, to be propounded at the session, without that party's attorney attending. This is not a sound practice, however, unless done by all parties; it leaves the deponent at the mercy of those lawyers who do attend and precludes such permissible objections as might be interposed spontaneously in the client's behalf if her attorney were present.

Examination and cross-examination proceed as at a trial in open court, with a few notable exceptions. If the deposition is taken at the instance of the adverse party, which is most often the case, the deponent may then be cross-examined by his own lawyer. Cross-examination, moreover, is not limited to the subject matter of the main examination, as it ordinarily is at the trial. It can explore new ground.[12] Any party against whom the deposition may later be used[13] is also entitled to cross-examine the deponent.[14]

To encourage every party to be relaxed and open at the deposition, insofar as any law can bring that off, it is provided that no objection is waived by not being made at the session. Later, if and when the particular question is read at the trial, any lawyer can object to it, and the objection at that time will be disposed of under the rules of evidence even though the question was answered without objection at the deposition. If the applicable rule bars the answer, it will be kept from the jury regardless of the fact that the answer stands forth in full flower on the folios of the transcript.[15]

An exception to this rule concerns an objection to the form of the question. Here the theory is that the prompt putting of the objection will enable the questioner to cure it with a mere rephrasing. Mere form objections must therefore be noted at the deposition or are waived.[16]

The trial lawyer is still cautious at the deposition. The fact that substantial objections need not be made does not mean that they cannot be. If they are made, disputes about them are usually resolved—whether by an immediate ruling by the court, if feasible, or on a later motion to compel disclosure—by reference to the rules of evidence just as they would be at the trial. The courts are especially impatient with petty objections at this stage, however. It has been suggested that the lawyer should restrict deposition objections to only those questions that are palpably irrelevant or which violate some legal privilege or constitutional right.[17] Perhaps the rule of thumb for the lawyer seeking an ideal stance is to object to only those questions which, in addition to invoking some exclusionary evidentiary rule, elicit a datum that he does not want the opposing side—not just the jury—to know at all.

When stenography is the recording method, the device used most often is that noiseless little contraption that makes the recording process very quiet and the stenographer very

---

10. CPLR 3113(b).

11. This is discussed in § 366, below, treating CPLR 3124.

12. CPLR 3113(c).

13. The uses of the deposition are treated in § 358, below.

14. Beatty v. Donley, 31 Misc.2d 164, 220 N.Y.S.2d 218 (Sup.Ct., Nassau County, 1961).

15. CPLR 3115(d). See Johnson v. N.Y.C. Health & Hospitals Corp., 49 A.D.2d 234, 374 N.Y.S.2d 343 (2d Dep't 1975).

16. CPLR 3115(b), (d).

17. Freedco Products, Inc. v. New York Telephone Co., 47 A.D.2d 654, 366 N.Y.S.2d 401 (2d Dep't 1975).

prosperous. The use of longhand has been held an imposition and is precluded.[18] As already indicated, tape recording is permissible. For a time it was used only experimentally, with a stenographer present and working as a back-up.[19] While an extensive rule prescribes the procedures when a deposition is taken by videotape, the issue of when the tape method may be used is not resolved in either the CPLR or the rules. It has been held, however, that a party willing to pay for the videotaping may use it without the other side's consent.[20]

Admissibility of the tape at the trial is governed basically by the same rules that apply to stenographic transcripts.[21]

Everything is done in English. If the deponent does not speak the language, the noticing party must supply and pay for a complete translation of questions and answers.[22]

§ 357. Executing the Deposition

When stenography, still the predominant method, is used for the recording of the deposition, the stenographer in due course types up a transcript of the deposition and makes as many copies as the parties order. The expense as a rule belongs to the noticing party,[1] but agreement on this subject is usually reached with other parties if they want their own copies. Absent agreement to the contrary, the noticing party must file the deposition with the clerk,[2] so that parties lacking copies will always have access to the filed deposition.

The deposition transcript is first submitted to the deponent for perusal, usually by merely being sent to the deponent's attorney for forwarding. The deponent may correct it, and must then sign it under oath, so that deponents usually go through two swearing pro-cesses: one at the deposition itself and one on signing the transcript later. Corrections must be made at the end of the deposition,[3] where the appropriate procedure is to refer to the particular question, set forth a corrected answer, and state why the answer as initially recorded is not right. Under no circumstances should the original answer be obliterated.[4] The changes and the reasons for them should be set forth individually. Omnibus reasons set forth in general rather than specific terms will not do.[5]

The time to make corrections is when the witness is reviewing the deposition prior to execution. It has been allowed afterwards, sometimes as late as the eve of trial,[6] but allowance at that late date runs the risk of prejudicing parties who have prepared based on the original answer and requires special reasons.

What happens if the witness fails to sign the deposition? For a while there was a procedure whereby the officer before whom the deposition was taken could sign in the witness's place. That procedure was erased in the course of several amendments of CPLR 3116(a) in the 1990s. Under the current statute, the signature of a balking deponent is simply dispensed with if the deponent does not sign and return the transcript within 60 days, and the unsigned transcript may then be used "as fully as though signed". This of course does not bar the deponent from testifying to the contrary at the trial, but so testifying will, as usual, expose the deponent to the impeachment use of the deposition.[7]

Some lawyers have reported situations in which the side taking the deposition tries to use it on a motion before giving the deponent

---

18. See Gammarata v. Bill's Garage, Inc., 40 Misc.2d 1081, 244 N.Y.S.2d 832 (Dist.Ct., Nassau County, 1963).

19. See, e.g., Rubino v. G.D. Searle & Co., 73 Misc.2d 447, 340 N.Y.S.2d 574 (Sup.Ct., Nassau County, 1973).

20. See Roche v. Udell, 155 Misc.2d 329, 588 N.Y.S.2d 76 (Sup.Ct., Nassau County, 1992), noted in SPR 3:4.

21. Uniform Rule 202.15(i). Bichler v. Eli Lilly & Co., 50 A.D.2d 90, 376 N.Y.S.2d 144 (1st Dep't 1975). These requirements are treated in § 358, below.

22. CPLR 3114.

§ 357

1. CPLR 3116(d).

2. CPLR 3116(b).

3. CPLR 3116(a).

4. See 11th Jud.Conf.Rep. (1966) 148, 206–7.

5. See Marine Trust Co. v. Collins, 19 A.D.2d 857, 243 N.Y.S.2d 993 (4th Dep't 1963).

6. See, e.g., Roberts v. Ausable Chasm Co., 47 A.D.2d 979, 367 N.Y.S.2d 120 (3d Dep't 1975).

7. See the discussion in SPR 46:1.

an opportunity to review and sign it, or in which the side required to execute it tries to use it on a motion before doing so. These are improper practices and can result in the court's rejection of the unexecuted transcript.[8]

The procedure for correcting, editing, certifying, and filing videotaped depositions is in the rules. Parties who want a stenographic transcription made of a taped deposition must make their own arrangements for it. The court in its discretion may require it.[9]

Documentary evidence and exhibits used during the depositions are annexed to and returned with it, absent agreement among the parties to the contrary (agreement is usually present) or a request from the producing party for return of the exhibits (in which event each party is given an opportunity to inspect them first).[10]

§ 358. Use of Deposition

With some of the disclosure devices, there's not much to know about what use can be made of the product. With the discovery device of CPLR 3120, for example, a paper or thing is produced and the party who sought it studies it or tests it, etc., and may then use it according to the usual rules of evidence. With the deposition, however, there is a general state policy against unfettered use at the trial; the preference is to have the deponent appear and respond to questioning in person, if reasonably possible, so that the fact-trier can observe the witness's demeanor, an important aid in appraising credibility. The deposition will of course have served to acquaint the parties with each others' contentions in advance of the trial—itself a most important "use" of the deposition and perhaps ultimately its major use—but an actual reading from the deposition at the trial must satisfy the strictures of CPLR 3117(a), whose instructions run this way:

The deposition of any deponent—party or nonparty—may be used by any party "for the purpose of contradicting or impeaching" the deponent.[1] This assumes that the deponent has taken the stand at the trial and testified to something contrary to what she previously said in the deposition: the deposition is being cited to show the contradiction. In this instance the theory is that the deposition is not being used as "evidence in chief" of the data deposed to, but only to make the deponent out a liar. The hope is that the jury, thinking the deponent dishonest, will disbelieve what the deponent is now saying on the stand. As a practical matter, of course, this will cause the jury to believe the contrary. The contrary is usually what the deponent said in the deposition, however, and the deposition thus ends up getting believed through a kind of back door. To many trial lawyers this is sometimes just as forceful as "evidence in chief"; it therefore matters little to them that it does not officially fall under that caption. Although the rule provides that "any deposition" may be so used "by any party", it has been held that a party may not so use his own deposition, i.e., may not impeach himself with it. Infrequent though this may be, it does happen.[2]

CPLR 3117(a)(2) allows one party's deposition to be used "for any purpose" by any adverse party. Hence the deposition of a party, as opposed to that of a nonparty witness, may be used as evidence in chief (as well as for impeachment) by any adverse party. This means that without any special foundation being laid, the plaintiff can be allowed to read from the defendant's deposition, and vice-versa, as competent evidence of the facts deposed to. For this purpose, "party" includes one who was an officer or agent of the party when the deposition was taken, or an employee of the party "produced by that party", and it is sufficient for this purpose to show that the employer "produced" the employee for the deposition,

---

8. See, e.g., Palumbo v. Innovative Communications Concepts, Inc., 175 Misc.2d 156, 668 N.Y.S.2d 433 (Sup. Ct., N.Y. County, 1997), aff'd 251 A.D.2d 246, 675 N.Y.S.2d 37 (1st Dep't 1998), noted in SPR 69:3–4.

9. See Uniform Rule 202.15.

10. CPLR 3116(c).

§ 358

1. CPLR 3117(a)(1).

2. See Mravlja v. Hoke, 22 A.D.2d 848, 254 N.Y.S.2d 162 (3d Dep't 1964) (clarification in dissenting opinion), aff'd 17 N.Y.2d 822, 271 N.Y.S.2d 271, 218 N.E.2d 314 (1966).

even if the employee is not "produced" by the employer to testify at the trial.[3] The relationship creates a presumption that the deponent was doing the party's bidding and the deposition may therefore be treated, for purposes of its use at the trial, as one by the party proper.

The Court of Appeals held in Feldsberg v. Nitschke[4] that the phrase "for any purpose" in CPLR 3117(a)(2) does not divest the trial court of its usual discretion to determine the points during the trial at which the deposition may be used. At issue in *Feldsberg* was the location of D's vehicle at a certain moment. D's deposition addressed the matter. P called D as a witness but did not use the deposition during D's testimony. D was to return to the stand later on a different matter, however, and, when D did, P then sought to probe into the location issue with the deposition. The court upheld a ruling by the trial court that P had waived this use of the deposition by failing to use it earlier. A convincing three-judge dissent in *Feldsberg* views the case as one in which the trial judge did not exercise discretion in the matter, but rather deemed himself bound as a matter of law, incorrectly, to hold P to a waiver.

Recognizing policy considerations as well as logistical difficulties often met in trying to coordinate the courtroom attendance of physicians, paragraph 4 of CPLR 3117(a), adopted in 1977, permits any party to use a physician's deposition for all purposes, evidence in chief included, without any special justification.[5]

Before the deposition of any other person—party or witness—can be used as evidence in chief, the requirements of CPLR 3117(a)(3) must be met. Satisfying this provision is sometimes popularly called "laying a foundation" for the use of the deposition. The statute's introductory language makes clear that in all instances under (a)(3) the deposition can be used only against a party who was duly notified of the taking of the deposition (whether the party elected to attend or not). It is this requirement that makes it so important that all parties be notified of deposition takings. Indeed, if in advance of a deposition session the court is made aware that not all parties have been duly notified, it can cancel the session altogether,[6] or postpone it until the requisite parties have been given the requisite notice. Assuming proper notice has been given to the party against whom the deposition is now sought to be read, the reading may proceed, but only if there is some special reason for allowing it. The five subparagraphs of CPLR 3117(a)(3) are in effect just a list of special reasons recognized by the law. Verbatim, they allow the reading if the court finds:

(i) that the witness is dead; or

(ii) that the witness is at a greater distance than one hundred miles from the place of trial or is out of the state, unless it appears that the absence of the witness was procured by the party offering the deposition; or

(iii) that the witness is unable to attend or testify because of age, sickness, infirmity, or imprisonment; or

(iv) that the party offering the deposition has been unable to procure the attendance of the witness by diligent efforts; or

(v) upon motion or notice, that such exceptional circumstances exist as to make its use desirable, in the interest of justice and with due regard to the importance of presenting the testimony of witnesses orally in open court.

The last item on the list is seldom met, and with the others there is a necessarily pragmatic interpretation given by the judges. Under subparagraph (iv), for example, a cursory visit to the witness's home without finding him there doesn't satisfy as a "diligent" effort and, without more, does not support use of the

---

3. CPLR 3117(a)(2) (as amended in 1993). The amendment overrules some caselaw that had held to the contrary. See SPR 5:3.

4. 49 N.Y.2d 636, 427 N.Y.S.2d 751, 404 N.E.2d 1293 (1980).

5. See Commentary C3117:8 on McKinney's CPLR 3117.

6. See, e.g., Lake Minnewaska Mountain Houses, Inc. v. Smiley, 62 Misc.2d 311, 307 N.Y.S.2d 739 (Sup.Ct., Ulster County, 1970).

deposition.[7] Similarly, where the plaintiff disappears after giving her deposition and can't be located even by her own lawyer, that lawyer may not put in the plaintiff's case with the deposition unless some satisfactory explanation is made to the court. The disappearance would otherwise be of the plaintiff's own doing,[8] and the plaintiff will not be allowed so casually to flout the law's preference for oral testimony in open court.

If the requirements of CPLR 3117(a)(3) have been met, the party may use the deposition of any "person", which embraces a party as well as a nonparty witness, including the party's own deposition. When a party dies between the deposition and the trial, for example, and his personal representative is duly substituted, it is this provision that admits the decedent's deposition in behalf of the decedent's own case.

Suppose that P has sued both A and B, and that P wants to use A's deposition against B even though A may no longer be a party at the time of the trial. A 1996 amendment of CPLR 3117(a)(2) addresses the situation. If adversity existed between A and B at the time one of them is deposed, but the deponent thereafter drops out (as through a settlement), the deposition may still be used in full by any remaining party.[9]

Subdivision (b) of CPLR 3117 seeks to assure perspective. Recognizing that a party will always try to read in only those passages favorable to itself, it allows the court, upon any reading by any party for any purpose, to permit any other party to read in any other passages "which ought in fairness to be considered in connection with the part read". The court should ordinarily require the other party to await the putting in of her own case before allowing a cross-reading from the deposition, rather than permit it on the heels of the initial

reading during her opponent's case.[10] This is so only when the deposition is being used as evidence in chief, however. It doesn't apply when the deposition is being used for impeachment, which occurs when the witness is on the stand. For all of these matters, the trial judge must be conceded a fair measure of discretion to introduce variations when the peculiar circumstances of the case warrant them.

The effect of using the deposition is governed by CPLR 3117(d), whose chief assurance is that a party does not make a deponent his own witness merely by taking the deposition. And as far as using the deposition is concerned, the only time a party need concern herself about adopting a deponent as her witness is when the deposition is used after a foundation for it has been laid under paragraph 3 of CPLR 3117(a). Using the deposition for contradiction or impeachment under paragraph 1, or a party's using an adverse party's deposition under paragraph 2, does not adopt the deponent.

The last sentence of CPLR 3117(d) says that any party at the trial "may rebut any relevant evidence contained in a deposition, whether introduced by him or by any other party". As applied to a party's deposition, however, the lawyer should not invert that instruction. Subdivision (d) allows a party by testimony at the trial to rebut what she said in a deposition, but it does not permit her with a deposition to rebut what she says at the trial. This is not to recommend the former step either, of course, lest the other side have a picnic with the contradiction during summation.

A party to an action that has been consolidated with another action and who does not want to be bound by depositions already taken in the other should take some initiative, reviewing the depositions and perhaps seeking to

7. See McNerney v. N.Y. Polyclinic Hosp., 18 A.D.2d 210, 238 N.Y.S.2d 729 (1st Dep't 1963).

8. See Jobse v. Connolloy, 60 Misc.2d 69, 302 N.Y.S.2d 35 (N.Y.C.Civ.Ct. 1969).

9. The amendment resolves a conflict on the point. See SPR 46:2. In Nixon v. Beacon Transportation Corp., 239 A.D. 830, 264 N.Y.S. 114 (2d Dep't 1933), the court held that this inter-party use of a party's deposition may be

made only if, when A's deposition was taken, the notice of deposition specified that A was being deposed both as a party and as a nonparty witness. Such a restriction is of doubtful validity today, especially in view of the 1996 amendment.

10. See Villa v. Vetuskey, 50 A.D.2d 1093, 376 N.Y.S.2d 359 (4th Dep't 1975).

depose the same persons himself.[11]

For the use in later actions of depositions taken in earlier actions involving the same parties, there is an explicit provision.[12]

The deposition should be used only after it has been properly executed, or after the time for its review and execution have expired. Otherwise the attempt to use it is likely to be rejected.[13]

§ 359. Deposition on Written Questions

CPLR 3108 provides that a deposition may be taken on written questions "when the examining party and the deponent so stipulate or when the testimony is to be taken without the state". With the stipulation, it can be taken anywhere; without it, it can presumably be taken only outside the state. It is elsewhere provided, however, that when an oral deposition has been duly scheduled, any party may, instead of participating in it, transmit written questions to the officer, who must then propound them to the witness and take down the answers.[1] This, as already pointed out,[2] should not ordinarily be done by one party unless the others do the same because it enables the lawyers who do attend to take advantage, with objectionable questions and conduct, of the party whose lawyer is absent.

Compared with the usual oral deposition, the deposition on written questions is a rare one. If all counsel appear, an examination that starts out on written questions can be readily converted into an ordinary oral one.[3]

There is no rule against taking oral depositions outside the state, but the additional expense for the travel and accommodation of the lawyers are practical impediments except in big cases. With the deposition on written questions, which the lawyers do not ordinarily attend, expense would ordinarily be incurred only for the officer who takes the deposition.

If the testimony is to be taken of a nonparty witness, it may have to take place outside the state if the witness is not amenable to New York process and can't be persuaded to enter the state voluntarily. If the testimony is that of a party, as where a nonresident plaintiff or defendant is to be deposed, the court of course has leverage to make the party come to the state for an ordinary oral examination, but it will often try to reach a middle point accommodating the convenience of all. It may for the time being require the deposition to proceed outside the state on written questions, for example, but require the nonresident party, within X days before the trial, to appear in the state and submit to an oral examination,[4] thereby cutting down on the number of trips the party has to make to New York.

The procedure for the formulation of the written questions, which must of course be devised in advance and delivered to the officer who is to take the deposition, is in CPLR 3109(a). It contemplates a serving of questions back and forth among the parties until the whole set is worked out. The party seeking the examination starts things off with a notice served on all other parties, setting forth the name of the person to be examined, identifying the officer who will do the examining, and containing the proposed questions. Within 15 days after the notice is served, the other parties must serve the questions they propose, called cross-questions. The initiating party then has seven days in which to serve "redirect" questions; the other parties then have five days for "recross" questions. There is some indication that objections to written questions should be raised within the time for otherwise responding to them,[5] but the stated time periods are not rigid and a protective order would in any event be available to re-

---

11. See Bianchi v. Federal Ins. Co., 142 Misc.2d 82, 535 N.Y.S.2d 952 (Sup.Ct., N.Y.County, 1988).

12. CPLR 3117(c).

13. See the discussion in SPR 69:3–4.

§ 359

1. CPLR 3113(b).

2. See § 356 above.

3. See Ryan v. Saunders, 45 Misc.2d 1089, 259 N.Y.S.2d 31 (Sup.Ct., Ontario County, 1964).

4. See Zilken v. Leader, 23 A.D.2d 644, 257 N.Y.S.2d 185 (1st Dep't 1965).

5. See CPLR 3115(e), which applies, however, only to objections of form.

solve disputes that an agreement can't smooth out.

When at last formulated, the questions are delivered by the noticing party to the officer, who must proceed "promptly" to take the deposition.[6] If the deposition is to take place outside New York, the officer must be guided by any rules applicable at that place. If the witness there does not voluntarily submit to being deposed, the officer may have to seek the aid of the courts or other tribunals of that jurisdiction, which may have a statute akin to CPLR 3102(e),[7] designed to lend local judicial aid to the securing of depositions for use elsewhere. These problems must of course be anticipated and researched in advance.

The parties' lawyers may attend the foreign deposition session to assure that all requirements have been complied with,[8] but this does not mean that one side's lawyer, without permission from the others, can simply appear and propound his questions and comments orally.[9] If a given party prefers the oral deposition, and can afford it, the court can with a protective order still bar the oral questions, or allow them only on the condition that that party pay the way of the other lawyers whose clients can't afford the trip.[10]

The deposition on written questions may be used at the trial in the same manner as an oral one.

§ 360. Commission or Letters Rogatory

The second sentence of CPLR 3108 provides that "a commission or letters rogatory may be issued where necessary or convenient for the taking of a deposition outside of the state". These devices are more often resorted to when the disclosure is sought in a foreign country than in a sister state.

The only apparent difference, under the CPLR, between an officer designated by the parties to take testimony elsewhere, and a commissioner appointed to do so, is that the latter, although perhaps the nominee of the parties, bears the court's imprimatur. This can make a difference if and when the officer must apply to a foreign court for disclosure aid. It all depends on the law of the foreign place. The deposition to be taken can be on oral or written questions, as the parties may agree or as the court directs. If on oral questions, it is commonly called an "open" commission;[1] if written, the terminology is that it's a "sealed" one. It can be used to elicit the testimony of either parties or nonparty witnesses, who reside elsewhere. It has been used to take the testimony of a plaintiff residing in a foreign country who did not plan to come to this country even for the trial,[2] although the court can require in person testimony for the trial if circumstances otherwise require it and resources permit it.

The letter rogatory, or as the Federal Rules of Civil Procedure now call it, the letter of request,[3] is a further aid to the taking of foreign testimony. A commissioner who bears the seal of the appointing court has good standing to seek the aid of a foreign tribunal if she should need it, but the bearer of a letter rogatory has even stronger call. The letter is merely a writing addressed by the New York court or its clerk to the foreign tribunal, describing the facts and showing the need for aid in taking testimony, asking that the foreign machinery be made available for that purpose, and usually ending with the amenity that the New York courts will be happy to return the favor. Sometimes the letter is secured and carried by a "commissioner", i.e., the one appointed to take the testimony, so that these devices for extrastate disclosure often overlap

---

6. CPLR 3109(b).

7. See the discussion of CPLR 3102(e) in § 352, paragraph numbered 3, above.

8. See Gorie v. Gorie, 48 Misc.2d 411, 265 N.Y.S.2d 19 (Sup.Ct., N.Y.County, 1965).

9. See Commentary C3109:1 on McKinney's CPLR 3109.

10. See item 5 on the list contained in 1st Rep.Leg. Doc. (1957) No. 6(b), p. 125.

§ 360

1. See Wiseman v. American Motors Sales Corp., 103 A.D.2d 230, 479 N.Y.S.2d 528 (2d Dep't 1984).

2. See Bosurgi v. Chemical Bank New York Trust Co., 30 A.D.2d 950, 294 N.Y.S.2d 45 (1st Dep't 1968).

3. See Rule 28(b).

and even merge. Whether one or two or more, or any combination of them, are needed is for the court to determine if the parties can't agree. There is no prescribed form for a letter rogatory.[4] It is sought by an ordinary motion.

It has been held that the letter rogatory should be resorted to last, after a showing that other devices won't work in the particular case. The reason cited is that the letter rogatory anticipates the use of the foreign tribunal's rules and devices to aid the disclosure, and these are not as certain as our own devices are to implement our domestic values of confrontation and cross-examination of witnesses.[5]

§ 361. Interrogatories

Interrogatories are written questions drawn by one party and served on another, answered by the latter under oath, and sent back. They may be served in the same manner as any other interlocutory paper—mail has been the principal method—and therein lies a major distinction from the deposition: the deposition requires a session at a designated time and place while interrogatories are initiated and responded to by mail.

Interrogatories are used to elicit answers from parties, where they can probe any relevant subject.[1] In matrimonial actions, additionally, they can be used on nonparties to probe the parties' finances.[2]

The interrogatory is a frequently used device in federal practice;[3] it has found less use in New York practice because of certain built-in restrictions (to be discussed) and apparently because of simple tradition as well. Interrogatories came in with the CPLR, but while the drafters planned to make them available in all

actions (as they are in federal practice),[4] a suspicious legislature, fearful that wealthy litigants with a battery of lawyers could bury their poorer adversaries in a blizzard of paper, restricted their use in certain tort actions. The restrictions themselves then went through a metamorphosis.

At the outset, the legislature made the interrogatory unavailable in actions to recover damages "for an injury to property, or a personal injury, resulting from negligence, or wrongful death".[5] This meant that in New York the interrogatory could not be used in many if not most actions since the excluded ones preponderated on judicial calendars. The poorly drafted language of the exclusion made for some hard cases, too. While the interrogatory could not be used in a property damage or personal injury case in which liability was predicated on "negligence", for example, it was held usable if liability was founded on breach of warranty[6] and would presumably be available as well if liability were founded on the then-recently resurrected basis of "strict products liability",[7] since negligence is not an element in those claims. When liability rested on several possible grounds, some involving negligence and others not, some courts permitted the interrogatory, but only to explore the claims that did not.[8]

Because of the context in which the word "negligence" appeared in CPLR 3130, it was held that the word applied to the property damage and personal injury case but not to the wrongful death case. The result was that in the wrongful death case the interrogatory was excluded no matter what basis of liability was relied on.[9] The hostility to the interrogatory in

---

4. For sample forms see 2 McKinney's Forms, 6:162–5.

5. See Matter of Siiderof, N.Y. Law Journal, Feb.18, 1982, p.6, col.6 (Surr.Ct., N.Y.County, per Lambert, S.). The court in Siiderof denied the request for letters rogatory without prejudice to a renewal of the application later, upon a showing that nothing else would do the job.

§ 361

1. CPLR 3130(1).

2. CPLR 3130(2).

3. See FRCP Rule 33.

4. See 1st Rep.Leg.Doc. (1957) No. 6(b), p. 148.

5. CPLR 3130. When first enacted as part of the CPLR, § 3130 had no subdivisions. Those came in 1983.

6. See, e.g., Ford Motor Co. v. O.W. Burke Co., 51 Misc.2d 420, 273 N.Y.S.2d 269 (Sup.Ct., N.Y.County, 1966).

7. See Victorson v. Bock Laundry Machine Co., 37 N.Y.2d 395, 373 N.Y.S.2d 39, 335 N.E.2d 275 (1975); Codling v. Paglia, 32 N.Y.2d 330, 345 N.Y.S.2d 461, 298 N.E.2d 622 (1973).

8. See Rollin v. B.F. Goodrich Co., 55 A.D.2d 985, 390 N.Y.S.2d 683 (3d Dep't 1977).

9. See Allen v. Minskoff, 38 N.Y.2d 506, 381 N.Y.S.2d 454, 344 N.E.2d 386 (1976).

these common tort cases, at least the unintentional torts, meant that the device had its use primarily in commercial and realty cases, and perhaps in matrimonial actions if disclosure was otherwise being allowed there.[10]

The legislature afterwards relaxed the restriction somewhat, or perhaps just changed its nature. In a line of amendments, the applicable provision became what is presently subdivision 1 of CPLR 3130, with the result that the device is now available in all actions, but with some qualifications. The personal injury, injury to property, and wrongful death claims still make up a trio, but now for a different purpose. When negligence is the ground of liability in any of those three, the interrogatory is no longer excluded absolutely, but a party may not resort to both the interrogatory and a deposition without leave of court; she has to choose. (The choice most often made is for the deposition.) When something other than negligence, or in addition to negligence, is the ground, both devices are available and no choice is necessary.

When available, the scope of the disclosure that may be sought with interrogatories is governed, like all the disclosure devices, by CPLR 3101.

According to CPLR 3131 the answers to interrogatories "may be used to the same extent as the depositions of a party", but that may be misleading. It was held in Matter of New York City Asbestos Litig.,[11] for example, that the answer to an interrogatory may be used against the answering party as an admission, but otherwise it's just hearsay. The facts of the case were that P sued D–1 and D–2. D–1, the party that answered the interrogatory, settled out, and at the trial D–2 wanted to use the answer to show more fault by D–1 and

hence less by D–2, giving D–2 a better chance to be assessed 50% or less of the fault and thus, under CPLR Article 16, to escape joint liability. The court would not let D–2 use the answer.[12]

By making the admissibility of depositions the standard for admitting interrogatory answers as well, CPLR 3131 invokes CPLR 3117 and its various conditions. The latter prevents a party from introducing his own answers, for example, unless a proper foundation is laid,[13] while allowing a party to use his adversary's answers without such a foundation.[14]

Interrogatories may also require the furnishing of copies of papers and documents relevant to the answers,[15] but a party intent on securing such items will usually find the discovery device[16] more effective for that purpose. It is interesting, in fact, to ask lawyers the sequence in which they prefer to exploit the disclosure devices. In the federal courts, where the interrogatory is widely used without artificial restrictions, practitioners sometimes report that they like interrogatories first, because the answers they furnish help identify papers and other items relevant to the case; the discovery device second, because it enables them to require production of those items; and then the deposition, because the give-and-take of its questioning is more meaningful when relevant documents and books have been secured and perused in advance. In smaller cases, the expense involved in disclosure may color these priorities and mandate a coupling of the devices, but "[i]n complex commercial cases and when dealing with corporations, the initial use of proper interrogatories is preferred in order to save time and money".[17]

Subdivision 2 of CPLR 3130 is much narrower in aim than subdivision 1. It allows and regulates financial disclosure from nonparties

---

10. The use of disclosure of any kind to probe the fault issues in matrimonial actions still gets a mixed reception in New York. See § 344 above.

11. 173 Misc.2d 121, 660 N.Y.S.2d 803 (Sup.Ct., N.Y.County, 1997).

12. See § 168B above. The court stresses the absence of the opportunity to cross-examine. See the related discussion in United Bank Ltd. v. Cambridge Sporting Goods Corp., 41 N.Y.2d 254, 392 N.Y.S.2d 265 (1976).

13. CPLR 3117(a)(3). A party's attempt to use his own answers in evidence is also likely to violate the hearsay rule. See United Bank Ltd. v. Cambridge Sporting Goods Corp., 41 N.Y.2d 254, 392 N.Y.S.2d 265, 360 N.E.2d 943 (1976).

14. CPLR 3117(a)(2).

15. CPLR 3131.

16. CPLR 3120, treated in § 362, below.

17. Barouh Eaton Allen Corp. v. I.B.M. Corp., 76 A.D.2d 873, 429 N.Y.S.2d 33 (2d Dep't 1980).

in matrimonial actions. Financial disclosure in matrimonials is extensively regulated by a rule.[18]

Because the interrogatory tends to duplicate the function of the bill or particulars, another basic provision of CPLR 3130(1) is that a party can't use both devices against the same party. If D has demanded a bill of particulars of P, in other words, which many a defendant's lawyer does automatically upon serving an answer, she may not afterwards serve interrogatories on P.

Both of CPLR 3130(1)'s you-have-to-choose mandates—the interrogatory versus the bill of particulars in litigation generally and the interrogatory versus the deposition in a negligence-based tort action—refer only to the use of both devices against the same party. It is apparently permissible for party A to use one device against party B and the other device against party C.[19] If several parties seeking the disclosure are represented by the same attorney, however, it has been held that the several qualify as only one party and must elect.[20]

Both the interrogatory and the bill of particulars are available in the matrimonial action,[21] where they have evolved distinct uses, the bill of particulars often used to probe the grounds for the matrimonial relief and the interrogatory to aid financial disclosure.

The procedure for the service and answer of interrogatories is in CPLR 3132–3134. They may be served by one party on another any time after commencement of the action,[22] and, as previously noted, they are usually served by mail.[23] The recipient must respond within 20 days, answering unobjectionable interrogatories and stating "with reasonable particularity" the reasons for not responding to the others.[24] While the requirement that the recip-

ient respond to the unobjectionable interrogatories is clearly the legislature's preference, it is not absolute. It has been held that when the demand is itself "outrageous" in its excessiveness and in the irrelevance of many of its items, the recipient may still, instead of responding to the demand at all, seek to strike it altogether with a motion for a protective order.[25]

Copies of interrogatories and of answers, no matter by which party initiated or to whom directed, must be served on all parties.[26]

Answers must be under oath. If the party is a business entity of some kind, the answers must be furnished by an employee or agent having the requisite data. The answer should follow each question rather than be contained in a separate list,[27] which suggests that the server of the interrogatories should leave adequate room after each question for the information sought. A common practice is for the answerer to retype the question as she answers it, taking such space as is needed. It has been suggested that if both sides are computer-equipped, diskettes can be used (with hard copy attached), which would enable the recipient to use as much space as necessary for each answer right after the question and to coordinate everything into a neat hard copy with just the striking of a few keys.[28]

Once an answer has been made to an interrogatory, an amendment of it requires court leave,[29] except in the situation in which a duty to supplement arises under the general terms of CPLR 3101(h).[30] Because each answer to an interrogatory is carefully formulated under the guidance of counsel before being sent to the adverse party, an amendment is seldom need-

---

18. See Uniform Rule 202.16.

19. See Commentary C3130:3 on McKinney's CPLR 3130.

20. Liemer v. Kings Highway Hospital Center, Inc., 140 Misc.2d 94, 529 N.Y.S.2d 967 (Sup.Ct., Kings County, 1988).

21. CPLR 3130(1).

22. CPLR 3132.

23. CPLR 2103(b)(2).

24. CPLR 3133(a).

25. See Hanover Ins. Co. v. Lama, 164 Misc.2d 843, 629 N.Y.S.2d 945 (App.Term, 9th and 10th Dists., 1995), noted in SPR 33:3.

26. CPLR 3132.

27. CPLR 3133(b).

28. See Vincent v. Seaman, 142 Misc.2d 196, 536 N.Y.S.2d 677 (Greene County Ct., 1989).

29. CPLR 3133(c).

30. See § 352A above.

ed, in contrast with the more frequent need a deponent may feel to correct her deposition.

The remedy for a party's failure to respond to interrogatories is a motion under CPLR 3124 to compel a response, and the motion for a protective order under CPLR 3103 is of course on stand-by to cure abuses. If the court finds in a given case that the interrogatories are "burdensome, oppressive and improper", it will vacate them in toto rather than prune them.[31] When they are "burdensome, oppressive and improper", they are just as much so to the court as to the adverse party.

Priority in the serving of interrogatories parallels that applicable to depositions. A defendant can serve interrogatories on the plaintiff immediately after being served with the complaint, while the plaintiff must wait until the defendant's answering time has expired before being allowed to serve interrogatories on the defendant.[32]

Recipients of interrogatories often charge that there are too many. Efforts to place an arbitrary limit on their number in New York practice have failed.

§ 362.　Discovery and Inspection

CPLR 3120 supplies the device for requiring a person to produce a paper or thing for inspection, testing, photographing, or copying. The caption of the rule begins "discovery and production"; the more popular name in practice is "discovery and inspection". Small matter. The device accomplishes both. Under subdivision (a) of CPLR 3120, discovery is available from a party by mere notice, but

from a nonparty subdivision (b) governs and requires a court order.

The criterion for whether or not the item is disclosable, here as with any of the other devices, comes from CPLR 3101. CPLR 3120 merely supplies the mechanical device to get the item. But many of the cases determining whether an item in a given case is discoverable have been annotated by the publishers under CPLR 3120 instead of 3101 (where they belong) and lawyers should be aware of that in their researches.

The papers and things that may be the subject of a discovery are as variable as litigation itself. One hesitates to offer even a few examples for fear that they may be taken as exhaustive rather than merely illustrative. CPLR 3120 permits a party to get at any tangible thing relevant—the 3101 criterion—to the case, whether made of paper, cloth, metal, gold, silver dust, or anything else. More often than not, the thing sought is a writing, such as a witness's statement,[1] or tax return[2] or business record. Papers of any other kind, including photographs, are equally fair game[3] as long as relevant. Tape recordings can be had,[4] as can any object involved in the event or transaction out of which the case arises, such as, in a tort action, the bolt whose breaking caused the fire escape to fall, the cowboy hat that caught fire, the tin can that contained the infected mushrooms, the soda bottle that exploded, etc. They can be had for examination, or for testing, or for copying, or for whatever else it seems appropriate to do.

When a party takes a deposition in a foreign language, CPLR 3114 requires the examining

---

31. Barouh Eaton Allen Corp. v. I.B.M. Corp., 76 A.D.2d 873, 429 N.Y.S.2d 33 (2d Dep't 1980).

32. CPLR 3132.

§ 362

1. Rios v. Donovan, 21 A.D.2d 409, 250 N.Y.S.2d 818 (1st Dep't 1964).

2. See Altman v. City of New York, 46 Misc.2d 133, 258 N.Y.S.2d 977 (Sup.Ct., N.Y.County, 1965), demonstrating also a substitute procedure for obtaining the tax return when the party doesn't have a copy of it. Parties claiming loss of earnings as an item of damages, as plaintiffs so often do in personal injury actions, waive any right to confidentiality of their income tax returns and must disclose them upon demand. In an action for punitive

damages, wealth is a legitimate topic on which the defendant may be required to make disclosure and that would include the furnishing of copies of tax returns, but it becomes relevant on punitive damages issues only after malice has been established as part of a preliminary finding of liability. See Rupert v. Sellers, 48 A.D.2d 265, 368 N.Y.S.2d 904 (4th Dep't 1975).

3. See Murdick v. Bush, 44 Misc.2d 527, 254 N.Y.S.2d 54 (Sup.Ct., Onondaga County, 1964).

4. A special provision, subdivision (i) of CPLR 3101, clarifies the disclosability of the so-called "surveillance" tapes that defendants often take surreptitiously of plaintiffs in personal injury cases to try to prove malingering.

party to furnish a translation of it.[5] In contrast, a party surrendering a foreign-language document pursuant to a discovery demand is not required to supply a translation with it; it's the seeking party, not the producing party, who must get it translated.[6]

If land is involved in the case, a discovery under CPLR 3120 can require a party to permit entry onto land owned or controlled by that party for "inspecting, measuring, surveying, sampling, testing, photographing or recording by motion pictures or otherwise the property or any specifically designated object or operation thereon."[7] In one case, for example, the permission sought was to take borings, tests, and measurements on the land.[8] In another, a party was allowed to get at poles and wires on another party's land,[9] the discovery device immunizing the seeker from what might otherwise be a trespass charge.

Against a party, discovery requires only a notice, which must specify the time, place, and manner of making the discovery or entry.[10] All of these things should be worked out in advance among the parties concerned so that the mutual convenience of all parties is considered, as is usually done as well with a deposition scheduling. A party should not arbitrarily schedule discoveries without preliminary consultation with the other parties, unless perhaps the discovery involves only the sending of a paper or document through the mails.

During the initial decades of the CPLR, the discovery notice had to identify the paper(s) or item(s) sought very specifically; asking for "any and all" documents of a general description was usually unacceptable. If additional information was needed before the item could be adequately identified, a landmark case, Rios

v. Donovan,[11] said that a deposition should first be used to elicit the identifying data. Of course if the data were at hand, the discovery could proceed without a preliminary deposition,[12] and "any and all" language could be disregarded as mere surplusage as long as the notice could otherwise be seen as directed at "limited and specific subject matter".[13] One might say that when a demand for discovery used words like "all", "all other", or the "any and all", a kind of suspicion arose in New York practice that the specificity required by CPLR 3120 was lacking, even though there was no absolute barrier to the use of such words. This was in contrast with federal practice, a distinction noted as late as 1991 by the First Department in Mendelowitz v. Xerox Corp.[14]

The specificity requirement was relaxed in 1994 in an amendment of CPLR 3120(a) that adopted the federal practice of allowing discovery by "category". The word "specifically" and the phrase "specified with reasonable particularity in the notice", as they were used in paragraph 1(i) of CPLR 3120(a), were dropped, and the word "category" was added in paragraph 2. When "an inspection, copying, testing or photographing" of an item or items is sought, CPLR 3120(a)(2) now requires that the seeking party set them forth

> by individual item or by category, and ... describe each item and category with reasonable particularity.[15]

Even under this new permission to demand by category, however, a demand may still be vacated in its entirety if it is found "unduly burdensome".[16]

In a further address to the subject in 1998, subdivision (c) was added to CPLR 3122, re-

---

5. CPLR 3114.

6. See Rosado v. Mercedes–Benz of North America, 103 A.D.2d 395, 480 N.Y.S.2d 124 (2d Dep't 1984).

7. CPLR 3120(a)(1)(ii).

8. See 1417 Bedford Realty Co. v. Sun Oil Co., 21 A.D.2d 684, 250 N.Y.S.2d 455 (2d Dep't 1964).

9. Parker v. N.Y. Tel. Co., 47 Misc.2d 342, 262 N.Y.S.2d 700 (Sup.Ct., Albany County), aff'd 24 A.D.2d 1067, 265 N.Y.S.2d 740 (3d Dep't 1965).

10. CPLR 3120(a)(2).

11. 21 A.D.2d 409, 250 N.Y.S.2d 818 (1st Dep't 1964).

12. See Huttner v. State, 59 Misc.2d 831, 300 N.Y.S.2d 409 (Ct.Cl. 1969).

13. See Breslauer v. Dan, 150 A.D.2d 324, 540 N.Y.S.2d 854 (2d Dep't 1989).

14. 169 A.D.2d 300, 573 N.Y.S.2d 548.

15. The changes in CPLR 3120 are discussed at length in Commentary C3120:4 on McKinney's CPLR 3120 and in SPR 9:2.

16. See Konrad v. 136 East 64th St. Corp., 209 A.D.2d 228, 618 N.Y.S.2d 632 (1st Dep't 1994).

quiring that the person responding to an order or notice for document discovery produce the documents "as they are kept in the regular course of business or"—note that the conjunction is "or", not "and"—"shall organize and label them to correspond to the categories in the request". The option of which to do is on the responding party, who is likely to favor the first choice, which may perpetuate the kind of overbroad response it was the purpose of CPLR 3122(c) to discourage.[17]

When entry onto land is what is desired, and an inspection of some object or operation on the land is sought, the requirement that the object or operation be "specifically designated" remains.[18]

The only stated time requirements concerning a notice of discovery are that it await commencement of the action[19] and that it give the recipient at least 20 days to respond.[20] Ideal, as usual, is for the parties to come to terms on the point. If a specific place must be chosen for the discovery, as where the examination must take place while all sides are represented (because the item involved can't be surrendered, or because each side must observe the other lest chicanery occur, etc.), the venue rules of CPLR 3110, governing the deposition, should be applied.[21]

Until the early 1990s, a party objecting to a discovery notice was required by CPLR 3122 to state its objections in a motion for a protective order, and to make the motion within 10 days after service of the discovery notice.[22] That procedure was changed in an amendment

of CPLR 3122 that took effect on January 1, 1994, addressed to the physical and mental exam of CPLR 3121 as well as the discovery device of CPLR 3120. We discuss it here in its CPLR 3120 context, but the discussion will also apply, to the extent relevant, to its use with the CPLR 3121 devices, met later.[23]

If R has no objections to the notice, R (the recipient of the notice) should comply within the period specified in the notice, or at least work something out with S (the party that served the notice) to assure that compliance will be forthcoming. What procedure, if R does have objections?

Under subdivision (a) of CPLR 3122, R's procedure is to serve a "response" on S,

> which shall state with reasonable particularity the reasons for each objection. If objection is made to part of an item or category, the part shall be specified.

If R withholds documents that appear to be among those demanded by S, subdivision (b) requires R to explain why and requires the explanation to include the following information with respect to each withheld document:[24]

(1) the type of document;

(2) the general subject matter of the document;

(3) the date of the document; and

(4) such other information as is sufficient to identify the document for a subpoena

---

17. See SPR 75:2.

18. CPLR 3120(a)(1)(ii). This specificity requirement, in the case of land only, was deliberately kept on by the Advisory Committee.

19. CPLR 3120(a)(1). An incidental problem created for CPLR 3120(a) by the adoption of the filing system for commencing actions in the supreme and county courts concerns the time for seeking discovery. The statute says that any party may notice discovery from any other any time after "commencement" of the action. Since mere filing of the summons and complaint now constitutes commencement in those courts, CPLR 3120(a)(1) would appear to give the plaintiff an advantage because the defendant is not likely to be aware of the "commencement" until service is made, which can be as long as 120 days later. (See CPLR 306–b.) It would be more consistent on all sides simply to read the phrase "after commencement of the action" in CPLR 3120(a) to read "after service

of the complaint". See the discussion in SPR 28:2 and 36:3.

20. CPLR 3120(a)(2).

21. See Commentary C3110:2 on McKinney's CPLR 3110, and compare Cattat v. Alfa Romeo, Inc., 81 Misc.2d 119, 364 N.Y.S.2d 772 (Sup.Ct., Oneida County, 1975).

22. CPLR 3122 (before its 1994 amendment).

23. See § 363 below.

24. CPLR 3122 is addressed in general to any CPLR 3120 discovery and any CPLR 3121 physical or mental examination, but subdivision (b) addresses only "documents". If the discovery that S seeks is of things other than documents, and R is disposed to furnish some but not other of the things sought, it would be appropriate for R to follow the procedures of subdivision (b) there, too. R should produce the unobjectionable things and state in a notice the grounds of objection to the things withheld.

duces tecum.[25]

If the inclusion of any of the enumerated information would violate some privilege, R may of course exclude the information, but must state in the notice that it is being withheld on that ground. The reference to "privileged" information is probably intended as a reference to all of the categories excluded from disclosure by CPLR 3101.[26]

If S is dissatisfied with R's response, and feels entitled to more than R is willing to give voluntarily, subdivision (a) of CPLR 3122 makes it incumbent on S to

> move for an order under rule 3124 with respect to any objection to, or other failure to respond to or permit inspection as requested by, the notice or any part thereof.

The hope of the statute is to have the parties iron out the objections among themselves. Only if the parties can't resolve their dispute privately is the court to be imposed on with a motion.

Because the instruction to S, the moving party, is to make the motion "under rule 3124", which provides for a motion that seeks only to have the court direct compliance, there is some doubt about whether S may, as an alternative, base the motion on CPLR 3126, the sanctions provision, i.e., skip CPLR 3124 as an intermediate step and jump right into CPLR 3126 in the hope of getting at least a conditional order directing disclosure backed by a sanction if the order is disobeyed. That was permissible before the amendment.[27] Some

caselaw indicates that a CPLR 3124 stopover is still unnecessary.[28]

If a document within the embrace of a discovery demand is not available when the demand is served, but becomes available later, it will fall under the supplementation requirement of CPLR 3101(h). This means that a copy of the document or thing will have to be furnished to the other side promptly, without awaiting a new demand. Failing to furnish it may bar its use at the trial.[29]

Discussion of CPLR 3120 up to now has concerned subdivision (a), governing discovery from a party. Discovery against a nonparty is governed by subdivision (b). It is essentially the same in scope and accomplishment as one against a party, but it requires a court order,[30] a requirement designed to recognize the inconvenience that may be caused a nonparty in the absence of court supervision. The order is secured by the usual notice of motion to other parties, with the added requirement that the nonparty be served with the notice in the same manner as a summons. The order supplies all the needed details of the discovery, and will ordinarily provide for defraying such expenses as the nonparty may be put to in meeting the order. Payment of those expenses can be deferred until the discovery is completed, especially if their amount can't be ascertained before.[31]

If the seeking party doesn't know who has the paper or thing sought, but an adverse party does, the latter must reveal that person's name.[32] The state qualifies as such a

---

25. The reference to the subpoena duces tecum is just a handy way of assuring that the identification offered would, if included in a subpoena, be sufficient to invoke the contempt penalty if the subpoena were to be disobeyed (assuming, of course, that the document is otherwise legitimately discoverable).

26. The reference in the statute is to allegedly "privileged" information, and it appears in such context as perhaps to suggest that "privilege" is the only ground for the withholding of the document. The word is apparently used, ineptly, as just a shorthand reference to the several categories excluded from disclosure under CPLR 3101, of which "privileged" matter is only one, coming from subdivision (b) of CPLR 3101. The other CPLR 3101 exclusionary categories are also recognized bases for withholding documents, including subdivision (c) (attorney's work product) and subdivision (d)(2) (material prepared for litigation), and there is nothing in the background of the

1994 change in CPLR 3122 to suggest an intention to remove those exclusions.

27. See SPR 10:1.

28. See Matter of T./P. Children, 165 Misc.2d 333, 629 N.Y.S.2d 677 (Fam.Ct., Albany County, 1995), noted in SPR 37:2.

29. See the discussion of the supplementation requirement in § 352A, above.

30. The requirement of a court order was adopted in 1966 in an amendment recommended in this writer's disclosure study conducted for the Judicial Conference. See 11th Jud.Conf.Rep. (1966) 148, 189–192.

31. See In re Stauderman's Will, 56 Misc.2d 580, 289 N.Y.S.2d 703 (Surr.Ct., Nassau County, 1968).

32. Major Chevrolet, Inc. v. Charles Pisacano, Inc., 58 Misc.2d 374, 295 N.Y.S.2d 363 (N.Y.C.Civ.Ct. 1968).

person for the discovery purposes of CPLR 3120(b).[33]

CPLR 3120 should not be confused with CPLR 3111, which provides for a limited kind of discovery, one sought in conjunction with a deposition. It provides that the notice or subpoena (bringing on the deposition) may require the production of papers and things in the custody of the deponent, for use upon the examination. CPLR 3120, on the other hand, supplies a discovery wholly independent of a deposition. If the particular item or items can be identified in the initial notice scheduling the deposition, the notice can require their production and, hopefully, kill two birds with one stone. If not, a preliminary deposition can be set up to identify the items, and the discovery device of CPLR 3120 can then be used to get them. If needed, yet another deposition can be taken, to permit further questions based on the newly revealed materials.[34] Unless the case is one in which the use of interrogatories is restricted,[35] an interrogatory can initially inquire into the nature and whereabouts of the item, too, obviating a deposition at that stage; the discovery device can then be used to get the item and the deposition can then be turned to afterwards, when the item will be at hand to assist it. In fact, an interrogatory can be used as a kind of limited discovery device itself, akin to the function of CPLR 3111.[36]

The line between CPLR 3111 on the one hand, and 3120 on the other, is not sharply defined, and probably needn't be, given the court's power by protective order to do what has to be done without overnice attention to the scope of any one device. CPLR 3111 generally requires that the item sought be in the possession or control of the deponent proper, since the discovery here is in conjunction with a deposition.[37] It is also "well settled that a notice pursuant to CPLR 3111 to produce ma-

terials at an examination before trial need not contain the specificity required for the discovery and inspection of materials sought pursuant to CPLR 3120".[38]

Because CPLR 3111 is an adjunct of a deposition, and notice of the deposition must of course be given all parties, all are also entitled to notice of whatever is being sought of the deponent through CPLR 3111. A nonparty witness who will not submit to a deposition voluntarily must be served with a subpoena.[39] The subpoena can also contain a duces tecum clause, or be accompanied by a distinct subpoena duces tecum, to implement CPLR 3111 and require the witness to produce documents and things at the deposition. It is improper to keep notice of any of these steps from an adverse party. In one much publicized case, a party set up a deposition of a nonparty witness and served a subpoena duces tecum on the witness to elicit key materials under CPLR 3111. The party then cancelled the deposition but, without advising the other side, collected up the materials the subpoena had produced, armed itself with a thorough ex parte review of the materials, and used them tellingly in deposing—and surprising—the other side. An irate appellate division suppressed all of the materials, disqualified the offending law firm, and remitted the matter to the local disciplinary committee for investigation.[40]

What appears to be contemplated by CPLR 3111, and to have been violated in the case just discussed, is that the materials produced will be produced *at* the deposition, or in any event at such time and place as will give access to all parties equally, and simultaneously.

If an item in the possession of a nonparty is needed in conjunction with a different person's deposition (party or nonparty), it would seem permissible either to secure the item in ad-

---

33. Kaplan v. Kaplan, 31 N.Y.2d 63, 334 N.Y.S.2d 879, 286 N.E.2d 260 (1972).

34. See Mayer v. Albany Medical Center Hospital, 56 Misc.2d 239, 288 N.Y.S.2d 771 (Sup.Ct., Albany County, 1968), mod'd 37 A.D.2d 1011, 325 N.Y.S.2d 517 (3d Dep't 1971).

35. See § 361 above.

36. See CPLR 3131.

37. See Western Elevating Ass'n v. Chapman, 238 A.D. 14, 263 N.Y.S. 62 (4th Dep't 1933).

38. Early v. County of Nassau, 98 A.D.2d 789, 469 N.Y.S.2d 809 (2d Dep't 1983).

39. CPLR 3106(b).

40. Beiny v. Wynyard, 129 A.D.2d 126, 517 N.Y.S.2d 474, reargument denied with further opinion 132 A.D.2d 190, 522 N.Y.S.2d 511 (1st Dep't 1987).

vance with an application under CPLR 3120(b) and schedule the deposition only after obtaining it, or to schedule a discovery under CPLR 3120(b) by the nonparty for the same time and place as the deposition, by agreement among the parties if possible or by order of the court if not.

A 1994 amendment of CPLR 3111 added the requirement that when the papers or things are sought from a nonparty deponent, the party seeking the items must defray the nonparty's expenses.[41]

§ 363. Physical and Mental Examinations

CPLR 3121(a) requires that a party whose physical or mental condition, or blood relationship to someone, is "in controversy", must submit to an examination at the behest of another party by "a designated physician". Agents, employees, and others under the party's control confront this examination, too, if their condition is in controversy, but it is mainly the party proper, notably the plaintiff in the ubiquitous personal injury case, who makes the caselaw on this device.

Plaintiffs bringing personal injury actions of course put their physical condition in controversy and must submit to examination, incidentally waiving the doctor-patient privilege that might otherwise insulate these matters.[1] Although most often it is the plaintiff's condition that's in controversy, the defendant may also be required to submit to examination if his own condition is genuinely in controversy in the case, as where impairment of the defendant's vision has become a substantial point of dispute.[2] The party's condition need not actually be "in issue", however; it need only be "in controversy", which the courts regard as a less demanding standard[3] and therefore an easier one on which to require an examination. But the condition must be rationally in dispute. One party's pique at another's posture on the facts will not suffice. A tort defendant's simple statement that he didn't see the plaintiff at an intersection, for example, does not entitle the plaintiff to an eye examination of the defendant.[4]

Although the defendant's condition can be injected into the case by the plaintiff, injection from that source will not cause a waiver of the defendant's doctor-patient privilege: mere denials by the defendant will not deprive the defendant of the privilege no matter how thoroughly the plaintiff has injected the issue.[5] The defendant's levying of the issue himself will result in a waiver, however, as where he injects it with a counterclaim or defense.[6] When dispute arises as to whether a party's condition is in controversy, the burden of showing that it is is on the party seeking the examination.[7] The tendency of the courts is to allow an examination—physical, mental, or blood—if it can be shown to have some practical value in the case.[8] If the examination "presents the possibility of danger to [the] life or health" of the person, it can of course be dispensed with.[9]

While the personal injury action is the one that springs to mind when a medical examination is the topic, the examination may become relevant in a variety of other actions. In the tort sphere, the intentional tort, such as assault, will warrant a physical examination if injuries are claimed. Blood relationship and hence blood examination is invariably involved in a paternity suit, as is mental capacity and

---

41. This does not mean that the seeking party must now resort to the procedure of a motion in order to secure the deposition-associated discovery contemplated by CPLR 3111. See the discussion in SPR 20:2–3.

§ 363

1. See Chester v. Zima, 41 Misc.2d 676, 246 N.Y.S.2d 144 (Sup.Ct., Erie County, 1964).

2. See Constantine v. Diello, 24 A.D.2d 821, 264 N.Y.S.2d 153 (4th Dep't 1965).

3. See Fisher v. Fossett, 45 Misc.2d 757, 257 N.Y.S.2d 821 (Sup.Ct., Erie County, 1965).

4. Courtney v. Olsen, 45 Misc.2d 283, 256 N.Y.S.2d 748 (Sup.Ct., Westchester County, 1965).

5. Dillenbeck v. Hess, 73 N.Y.2d 278, 539 N.Y.S.2d 707, 536 N.E.2d 1126 (1989).

6. Koump v. Smith, 25 N.Y.2d 287, 303 N.Y.S.2d 858, 250 N.E.2d 857 (1969).

7. Ibid.

8. See Carpinelli v. Manhattan Bottling Corp., 21 A.D.2d 792, 250 N.Y.S.2d 756 (2d Dep't 1964), allowing a psychogalvanic skin reaction test.

9. Lefkowitz v. Nassau County Medical Center, 94 A.D.2d 18, 462 N.Y.S.2d 903 (2d Dep't 1983).

hence mental examination in incompetency proceedings. Physical or mental examinations or a combination of them can become relevant in such unsuspected places as a contract, trust, succession, insurance, custody, or matrimonial case in which undue influence, overreaching, duress, capacity, ability, or general or specific condition is injected. Where the plaintiff sued for fraud and breach of a contract concerning a stock transaction and the defendant pleaded that he did not remember receiving or signing the plaintiff's checks, defendant's condition was found to be sufficiently in controversy to support an examination.[10] Recognition of these diverse possibilities is the reason why the statute, CPLR 3121, does not attempt to restrict examinations to any particular category of action.

In any instance in which hospital records are relevant to the party's condition, that party is required upon demand to execute and acknowledge written authorizations allowing the other parties to the action to obtain and make copies of those records. A party who obtains the authorization and then makes copies of the hospital records is required by CPLR 3121 to serve a duplicate copy on the party who furnished the authorization. This has been held to apply, however, only where the examining party actually makes a copy of the record.[11]

Some of the cases construing and applying the statute seem to have become a bit academic today for the reason that rules have been promulgated to cover the subject, and in much detail. On the subject of physical examinations especially, practitioners should first consult the rules to see if there's anything in point. They may find that by doing so they don't have to consult CPLR 3121 at all. That

may well be the case in the personal injury and wrongful death action, where a detailed rule governs examinations and medical reports.[12] Practitioners may sometimes be surprised to find that a procedure prescribed in a rule may seem in some respects at odds with CPLR 3121.[13] Unless the matter is important enough to make an issue of, which it rarely is, it is politic just to follow the rule. Practitioners may also be distressed to note that a rule violation can result in a substantial forfeiture,[14] another good reason for following the rule. There have been cases when a court, on a closer look, has been prevailed on to set aside even one of its own rules as inconsistent with the statutory prescription,[15] but it's a rare event. Unless the thing is worth fussing over, follow the rule.

With that lesson in tow, we can turn to the procedure for the scheduling and conduct of the examination. The title of Uniform Rule 202.17 is "Exchange of medical reports in personal injury and wrongful death actions", but on the personal injury side it also regulates the examination itself, and in much detail. If the rule applied in all cases, consideration of the rule instead of the statute, which is almost completely eclipsed by the rule, might be in order. But since the rule addresses only the personal injury and wrongful death case, the statute remains in force for examinations in all other cases and requires treatment.

Under the statute, a mere notice brings on the examination. It is served by the examining party on the examinee and the other parties, setting forth the time, the place, the conditions, and the scope of the examination. If authorizations to secure hospital records are sought, a demand for them may be included in

---

10. Estabrook & Co. v. Masiello, 75 Misc.2d 784, 348 N.Y.S.2d 879 (Sup.Ct., Westchester County, 1973).

11. See Czekanski v. Hanretta, 42 Misc.2d 115, 247 N.Y.S.2d 352 (Sup.Ct., Erie County, 1964).

12. See Uniform Rule 202.17, applicable in the supreme and county courts. Similar rules apply in the N.Y.C. Civil Court (Uniform Rule 208.13), the district courts (212.13), and the city courts (210.13).

13. If all the rule offers is additional instruction, it passes muster. See Commentaries C3121:4, 5 on McKinney's CPLR 3121.

14. A rule involved in Delgado v. Fogle, 32 A.D.2d 85, 299 N.Y.S.2d 898 (2d Dep't 1969), for example, enabled a party to set up his own physical examination, that is, to notify other parties of his availability for examination at a stated time. The other side then had to show up with its examining physician at the appointed time, which it failed to do in Delgado. The case was one of first impression, so the court forgave the default but put the bar on notice that in future the rule would be strictly enforced.

15. See, e.g., Calhoun v. Pickett, 77 A.D.2d 776, 431 N.Y.S.2d 212 (3d Dep't 1980), aff'd 52 N.Y.2d 605, 439 N.Y.S.2d 831, 422 N.E.2d 491 (1981).

the notice. The general rule is that the examinee's attorney, or a same-sex stand-in, may be present during the examination, but it has been held that a videotaping of the examination may not be allowed except in "special or unusual circumstances".[16]

As far as time is concerned, CPLR 3121(a) requires that at least 20 days notice of the examination be given. Uniform Rule 202.17, for its personal injury and wrongful death actions, requires more notice than that.

Notwithstanding elaboration of the "notice" procedure or any other procedure in either the statutes or the rules, the prevalent notion about disclosure proceedings has stronger application here, with the physical examination, than perhaps anywhere else: work things out with the other side and don't just send off notices with ultimatums in them. With other devices, the time of the parties and their lawyers is on the line; with this one, the time of physicians has to be figured in, too. There should be consultation among the parties in advance to set up a time and place convenient to parties, to counsel, and to the examining physician. The lawyer should not, relying only on the letter of CPLR 3121 or even on a detailed rule in point, just serve a notice arbitrarily setting up the examination.

If the party served with the notice has objections to it, she should serve a response within 20 days, stating the objections "with reasonable particularity". That's the requirement of CPLR 3122(a), which then provides that the server of the notice may make a motion under CPLR 3124 to test the objections and/or compel compliance. CPLR 3122 applies to the CPLR 3120 discovery notice as well as the CPLR 3121 examination notice, but some segments of CPLR 3122 indicate that its thinking is directed primarily to the CPLR 3120 discovery notice. To whatever extent its provisions can fit the CPLR 3121 devices, however, CPLR 3122 applies to them. More detailed treatment of CPLR 3122 appears in § 362 above, in treating its application to the CPLR 3120 discovery notice.[17]

A party who has conducted a physical or mental examination will ordinarily have the examining physician draw up a report. Any other party who wants a copy of that report, and who has, in exchange for it, a medical report of an examination that it has had conducted of the same person's condition, can compel the exchange by tendering a copy of its own report.

Such is the express instruction of subdivision (b) of CPLR 3121. The scope of this statute was addressed by the Court of Appeals in Hoenig v. Westphal,[18] which held that while CPLR 3121(b) is addressed to the exchange of medical reports in general, it applies only to the report of a non-treating physician, i.e., one whose report is made after an examination conducted pursuant to subdivision (a) or otherwise made solely for litigation. The court said that the report of a treating physician is not in that category and may therefore be discovered under the basic disclosure standard of CPLR 3101(a). It is not material prepared exclusively for litigation under CPLR 3101(d) and thus faces no discovery impediment from that statute. Nor may it be deemed the product of an examination conducted pursuant to CPLR 3121(a) and hence it is not subject to the exchange-of-reports requirement of CPLR 3121(b).

In an action for medical, dental, or podiatric malpractice, if the person conducting the CPLR 3121(a) examination is to serve as an expert in the case, the policies of CPLR 3101(d)(1)(ii) are implicated, allowing the redaction of the expert's name and identifying features[19] from the report he furnishes under CPLR 3121(b).[20]

---

16. See Lamendola v. Slocum, 148 A.D.2d 781, 538 N.Y.S.2d 116 (3d Dep't 1989).

17. Most of the caselaw on CPLR 3122 is built around its pre–1994 version, which is substantially different from the present version, which is the product of an amendment that took effect January 1, 1994. The changes are extensively discussed in SPR 10:1–2.

18. 52 N.Y.2d 605, 439 N.Y.S.2d 831, 422 N.E.2d 491 (1981).

19. See § 348A above.

20. See Ryan v. Michelsen, 241 A.D.2d 434, 660 N.Y.S.2d 435 (1st Dep't 1997).

Again, in a given category of case a rule may require the trading of the reports of all physicians, without distinction between treaters and non-treaters.[21] If it does, follow the rule.

It has been held that when a physician bases his report solely on hospital records and not on a personal examination of the party, the report is not subject to the exchange directed by CPLR 3121(b).[22]

A rule that requires the plaintiff, in advance of an examination, to serve on all parties copies of the reports of physicians who previously treated or examined the plaintiff and which at one time required that these include a narrative report rather than the briefer notations found in such as insurance and workers' compensation forms, was amended in 1998 to allow the briefer ones.[23]

The reference in CPLR 3121(a) is to a "physician". The Court of Appeals has held that while this may bar examinations by other professionals under CPLR 3121, non-physician professionals can conduct examinations under the general and broader terms of CPLR 3101(a) whenever relevant.[24]

§ 364. Notice to Admit

CPLR 3123 supplies a disclosure device known as a "notice to admit", whereby one party can require another to admit stated facts, or the genuineness of a paper or document, or the correctness of photographs. Copies of any paper or documents involved accompany the notice unless they have already been furnished. The device is usable only when the seeking party "reasonably believes there can be no substantial dispute" about the matter and when it is within the knowledge of the other party or ascertainable by him "upon reasonable inquiry".[1] The notice does not

work, and even if ignored will invoke no sanction, if the matters as to which admissions are sought are not "attuned to any reasonable belief that they [are] free from substantial dispute."[2]

The purpose of the device is to save a party the trouble and expense of proving a readily admittable fact. It will usually work well enough to compel an admission that the adverse party owned a car of a given description, for example, or was driving it on a stated occasion, or that he was or was not in the vehicle at a stated time, or that the signature that appears on the appended contract is his, or that this is the last deed signed by the party, or that this photograph accurately represents the intersection at which a collision occurred, and numerous other matters of like tenor. But it is not to be used to compel the defendant to admit that she was driving negligently, or that it was she who breached the contract or defrauded, defamed, assaulted, or embezzled from the plaintiff. It may not be used, in other words, for matters "which constitute the very dispute of the lawsuit".[3] Nor may it be used for technical or scientific information such as is ordinarily elicited from an expert.[4]

It may not be used to make a party admit what some other party knows. Demands that party X admit that party Y owned certain premises continuously for a stated period, or that Y admit that certain matters were known to party Z, were held improper in Taylor v. Blair,[5] where the appellate division said this:

The sole function of such a notice is to expedite the trial by eliminating from contention that which is public knowledge or

21. See Uniform Rule 202.17.

22. Edelman v. Holmes Private Ambulances, Inc., 32 A.D.2d 563, 300 N.Y.S.2d 372 (2d Dep't 1969).

23. UR 202.17, as amended effective April 17, 1998. The amendment is discussed in SPR 73:1.

24. See Kavanagh v. Ogden Allied Maintenance Corp., 92 N.Y.2d 952, 683 N.Y.S.2d 156 (1998), allowing examination by a vocational rehabilitation expert. Other cases have allowed exams by other professionals. See the lead note in New York State Law Digest No. 469.

§ 364

1. CPLR 3123(a).

2. Marguess v. City of New York, 30 A.D.2d 782, 291 N.Y.S.2d 956, 957 (1st Dep't 1968), aff'd 28 N.Y.2d 527, 319 N.Y.S.2d 71, 267 N.E.2d 884 (1971).

3. Spawton v. James E. Strates Shows, Inc., 75 Misc.2d 813, 349 N.Y.S.2d 295 (Sup.Ct., Erie County, 1973).

4. Falkowitz v. Kings Highway Hospital, 43 A.D.2d 696, 349 N.Y.S.2d 790 (2d Dep't 1973).

5. 116 A.D.2d 204, 500 N.Y.S.2d 133 (1st Dep't 1986).

easily provable and which the party reasonably believes is not in dispute.

What may have happened in *Taylor* is that the plaintiff drew up all the admission subjects he had listed for any of several defendants and included them in but one notice to admit served on all of them. Even in respect of proper subjects, a separate notice to admit should be drawn for each party so as not to elicit from one something suitable for admission only by another.

Because of its inherent limitations, the notice to admit is under-used. It is also true that the matters to which it lends itself are often admitted by opposing parties in the course of pleadings, depositions or other disclosure devices, or preliminary conferences, or are so easily and inexpensively proved that a party feels no need to avoid the proof by securing the admission.

The usual time for using the notice to admit is after the joinder of issue but before the filing of the note of issue, the usual time frame for pretrial disclosure generally.[6] The certificate of readiness rule requires certification that disclosure is complete before the note of issue (which the certificate accompanies) may be filed, and disclosure after the filing requires a showing of "unusual or unanticipated circumstances".[7] But CPLR 3123 permits use of the notice to admit at any time up to "twenty days before the trial". The First Department held in Hodes v. City of New York[8] that service of a notice to admit up until that time is okay even though the certificate has already been filed because the notice is not truly a disclosure device but just a procedure designed to "crystallize issues".[9]

The recipient of a notice to admit has 20 days to respond. A recipient who wishes to

admit the matter need do nothing; silence is an admission. If the recipient wishes to deny the matter, she must do so in a sworn writing, to be served within the 20–day period. The writing may include qualifications or explanations. Privileged matters and trade secrets can be labeled such, for example, and admission refused on those grounds.[10]

Although it may happen that a given notice to admit will be found so unreasonable that a party ignoring it entirely will face no sanction,[11] its ignoring under ordinary circumstances is perilous. If the recipient would deny the matter, the denial should be made; if the recipient deems the notice unreasonable, she should promptly move for a protective order determining the issue one way or the other. It is clear today that the protective order of CPLR 3103 is available to test the validity of a notice to admit under CPLR 3123;[12] earlier doubts about that in the Second Department were dispelled and the availability of the protective order for this purpose acknowledged.[13] A recipient of a notice to admit who neither denies the matters nor moves to test the validity of the notice is courting trouble. If he guesses wrong, he will be held to the usual rule that silence is an admission. Indeed, the fact admitted may even prove dispositive of the claim. In one case, for example, the impact of an admission-by-silence was to concede that the party learned of a fraud early enough to subject the claim to the bar of the statute of limitations.[14]

An admission under CPLR 3123 is usable in the pending action only. It has been held analogous to a pleading,[15] and therefore binds to the same degree.

With leave of court, an admission can be amended or withdrawn. The leave can be

6.   See § 350 above.

7.   See § 370 below.

8.   165 A.D.2d 168, 566 N.Y.S.2d 611 (1991).

9.   The notice used in Hodes, however, consisting of some 50 pages, was found to be a mere subterfuge to obtain more disclosure by trying to circumvent the readiness requirement with a notice to admit. It was disallowed.

10.   CPLR 3123(a).

11.   See Marguess v. City of New York, note 2, above.

12.   See Nader v. General Motors Corp., 53 Misc.2d 515, 279 N.Y.S.2d 111 (Sup.Ct., N.Y.County), aff'd 29 A.D.2d 632, 286 N.Y.S.2d 209 (1st Dep't 1967).

13.   Epstein v. Consolidated Edison Co., 31 A.D.2d 746, 297 N.Y.S.2d 260 (2d Dep't 1969).

14.   Psaroudis v. Psaroudis, 30 A.D.2d 841, 293 N.Y.S.2d 24 (2d Dep't 1968), aff'd 27 N.Y.2d 527, 312 N.Y.S.2d 998, 261 N.E.2d 108 (1970).

15.   Seidenberg v. Rosen, 114 N.Y.S.2d 279 (Sup.Ct., N.Y.County, 1952).

granted conditionally.[16]

If the recipient of the notice wishes to deny the matter, the denial should be outright. The techniques applicable to denials in a pleading have been held inappropriate to address to a notice to admit. Hence a denial "upon information and belief", or of "knowledge or information sufficient to form a belief", are not countenanced,[17] at least not when the denier has ready access to sources that will enable her either to admit or deny outright. There is some dispute as to whether the attorney can do the denying in behalf of the client;[18] the sounder practice is of course to have the client do it.

The notice to admit device of CPLR 3123 is the only one that has its own built-in penalty for a violation and to which the usual sanctions, to be met shortly in the treatment of CPLR 3126,[19] therefore do not apply. If the party upon whom the notice to admit is served duly responds with a denial, the seeking party will have to prepare to prove the matters denied, amassing witnesses and evidence for the purpose. If she does, and if the matter is proved at the trial, the sole remedy is to move for an order compelling the denying party to pay the costs of the proof. This is one of those rare instances, however, when a reasonable attorney's fee can be included. The costs award can be made even though the prover has lost the case on the merits.

The court is supposed to award the costs unless it finds "that there were good reasons for the denial ... or that the admissions sought were of no substantial importance". All of this is provided by CPLR 3123(c). Attorneys distrust provisos like that, however, and if they are going to keep special tabs on the costs of witnesses and evidence in regard to a certain matter, as well as special track of their own time, they want the effort to pay off with a costs award with more certainty than CPLR 3123 offers. The unless clause is a refuge for judges unenthusiastic about CPLR 3123 costs sanctions. That appears in any event to be a widespread feeling among the bar. It's probably another reason for the relative disuse of CPLR 3123.

The motion for the costs sanction must be made "at or immediately following the trial", since it is only then that the court can determine whether the fact denied has in fact been proved. The motion should be made promptly, perhaps even before the court has adjourned, which means that the lawyer contemplating the motion should have the required proof ready—affidavits and bills and the like—on what is expected to be the trial's final day. It has been held that a CPLR 3123 costs motion made four days after the trial is too late.[20]

§ 365. Demand for Address

There are several situations in which a party may have to know another's address. It may be relevant to determine the propriety of the venue, which is most often based on residence,[1] and parties may sometimes have to be served with papers at their residence.[2] CPLR 3118 provides that upon demand by any party, any other must serve a verified statement of its post office address and residence and that of any "officer or member" of the party or of any assignor to whom a claim or defense in the action once belonged. This is of course a minor disclosure device, but it has its uses. Since it operates only to require that the party reveal its own or an assignor's address, it is not the device used when the address of a nonparty witness, otherwise disclosable, is sought. There the seeker can use other devices, however, such as the discovery notice or the ordinary deposition.[3]

---

16. CPLR 3123(b).

17. Barnes v. Shul Private Car Serv., Inc., 59 Misc.2d 967, 301 N.Y.S.2d 907 (Sup.Ct., Kings County, 1969).

18. See discussion in the Barnes case. Id.

19. Section 367 below.

20. Halligan v. Glazebrook, 59 Misc.2d 712, 299 N.Y.S.2d 951 (Sup.Ct., Suffolk County, 1969). See Commentary C3123:9 on McKinney's CPLR 3123.

§ 365

1. See CPLR 305(a), 503.

2. CPLR 2103(b)(4), (c).

3. For disclosability of witnesses' names, which would also include their addresses, see § 349 above.

By analogy to CPLR 3118, which operates during the action, it has been held that a judgment debtor's attorney, upon being served with a post-judgment disclosure subpoena,[4] must reveal the judgment debtor's address. As a general rule, the address is not a privileged datum.[5]

F. COMPELLING DISCLOSURE

Table of Sections

§ 366. Order Compelling Disclosure; Rulings

Most of the disclosure devices are brought on, if not by stipulation of the parties, then by mere notices served among them. Only in a few instances, treated earlier,[1] is a preliminary court order needed. If the stipulation or notice is ignored, in whole or in part, or if a demanded datum or thing is withheld, or if a party refuses to submit to examination at all, CPLR 3124 authorizes an application to the court for an order compelling the disclosure, whatever the device that was used to seek it.[2]

CPLR 3124, which was amended in 1993 as part of an overhaul of the disclosure article, contemplates a disclosure order without a penalty. If a sanction of some kind is sought, for the disobedience of either a notice or an order, the application is made under CPLR 3126. Caselaw under the original statute held that a CPLR 3126 sanction motion need not necessarily be preceded by a disclosure order under CPLR 3124,[3] which of course made the motion under CPLR 3126 the preferred one. The design was to avoid the two-motion procedure generated by making a party go to CPLR 3124 first and allowing access to CPLR 3126 only as

a follow-up. Under the new 1993 amendments, however, there are at least two instances in which it appears that a bypass of CPLR 3124 in favor of a direct motion under CPLR 3126 may be barred. When the devices involved are the discovery of CPLR 3120 or the physical or mental examination of CPLR 3121, the also-amended CPLR 3122 appears to require that a preliminary CPLR 3124 application be made— for a court order directing disclosure without a sanction—before a sanction can be invoked with a CPLR 3126 motion.[4] The courts will have to resolve that question.[5] The party seeking disclosure would of course prefer the direct route to CPLR 3126. Why seek to compel disclosure under CPLR 3124 when it can be compelled just as well with a motion under CPLR 3126, where the direction can be accompanied with a sanction or at least a threatened sanction?

When the disclosure device being used requires a session, as the ordinary deposition does, and answers to certain questions are refused on various evidentiary grounds, the hope of CPLR 3124 is that the deposition will turn to other things until everything susceptible of resolution between the parties is covered. Its preference is that all unanswered questions be gathered up afterwards in one batch and made the subject of a single, formal, written motion for a disclosure order in which the court can all at once pass on the validity of, and hence the need to respond to, each question.[6]

But there is yet another way of securing court instruction on the validity of individual questions, informally known as the "let's get a ruling" system, sometimes used when the deposition is taking place in the courthouse or near enough to the courthouse to get a judge to issue an informal but nonetheless binding "ruling", usually oral, on whether a given

---

4. See CPLR 5224.

5. See Chemical Bank v. Sinoto, N.Y. Law Journal, December 1, 1981 (Sup.Ct., N.Y.County, per Stecher, J.).

§ 366

1. See § 352 above.

2. Excluded from the list is CPLR 3123, the notice to admit, which has its own built-in procedures. See § 364 above.

3. Wolfson v. Nassau County Medical Center, 141 A.D.2d 815, 530 N.Y.S.2d 27 (2d Dep't 1988).

4. See the discussion in SPR 10:1.

5. At least one court has held that such preliminary resort to CPLR 3124 is not necessary. See § 362, above, and SPR 37:2.

6. See § 356 above.

question need be answered. This procedure, in which the attorneys leave the deposition table and march resolutely to the courthouse, or across the courthouse lobby, or to its staircase or elevators, to find a judge,[7] is, even where available, only an alternative to the use of the single, formal motion made after the session is concluded. Whether or not CPLR 3124 wanted to preserve the let's-get-a-ruling alternative, it was held almost immediately after the CPLR took effect that the system survives.[8] The court's or a given judge's calendars may even be helped by it: it may be more economical to dispose of a key objection with an informal ruling on the propriety of a question than to encourage formal, post-session motions that constitute a disproportionate burden on the motion calendars. Even where the "rulings" system is available, however, it is not mandatory;[9] the parties may opt instead for the formal motion procedure offered.[10]

In those areas where the IAS[11] system is in operation, it must presumably be the assigned judge who makes rulings on deposition issues. Under the old master calendar system, the ruling could be sought in some counties from the judge assigned to one of the motion parts for the day, even though the judge had nothing to do with the case. If it must today be the IAS judge, and the judge is unavailable, the formal, post-session motion may be the only remedy the examining party has.

Since any motion in the case would have to be made to the IAS judge, if the case has one, a formal motion should be returnable before that judge, wherever she may be, or in accord with her directions. If IAS doesn't apply in the court or if for any other reason the motion needs a venue, the motion to compel disclosure under CPLR 3124 may be made in any county otherwise permissible for a contested motion in the action, which is usually the county

where the action is pending. But for this purpose the county in which the disclosure session has been set under the venue rules of CPLR 3110 may be treated as the county in which the action is pending, unless, of course, the rules have removed this option, as they are authorized to do.[12]

A motion to compel disclosure under CPLR 3124, as is true of any kind of motion relating to disclosure, must be accompanied by the moving attorney's affirmation that there has been a good faith consultation with the other side's lawyer in an effort to resolve the dispute, and that it came to nought.[13]

§ 367. Sanctions for Nondisclosure

The sanctions for nondisclosure are provided by CPLR 3126, which reads as follows:

> If any party, or a person who at the time a deposition is taken or an examination or inspection is made, is an officer, director, member, employee or agent of a party or otherwise under a party's control, refuses to obey an order for disclosure or wilfully fails to disclose information which the court finds ought to have been disclosed pursuant to this article, the court may make such orders with regard to the failure or refusal as are just, among them:
>
> 1. an order that the issues to which the information is relevant shall be deemed resolved for purposes of the action in accordance with the claims of the party obtaining the order; or
>
> 2. an order prohibiting the disobedient party from supporting or opposing designated claims or defenses, from producing in evidence designated things or items of testimony, or from introducing any evidence of the physical, mental or blood condition

---

7. Some judges may even entertain such a request by phone during the deposition.

8. See Bustard v. Kedala, Inc., N.Y.Law Journal, September 23, 1963, p. 14, col. 1 (Sup.Ct., Kings County, per Brown, J.).

9. See Cohen v. Heine & Co., 39 A.D.2d 563, 331 N.Y.S.2d 751 (2d Dep't 1972).

10. Since the only appealable items in New York practice are a judgment or an order, the question arises as to

whether a mere "ruling", not reduced to an order, may be appealed. See § 526, below, and Commentary C3124:5 on McKinney's CPLR 3124.

11. This stands for "Individual Assignment System". See § 77A above.

12. CPLR 3125.

13. See, e.g., Uniform Rule 202.7.

sought to be determined, or from using certain witnesses; or

3. an order striking out pleadings or parts thereof, or staying further proceedings until the order is obeyed, or dismissing the action or any part thereof, or rendering a judgment by default against the disobedient party.

It will be noted first that the sanctions apply to nondisclosure by a party, not by a nonparty. "Party" for this purpose includes anyone controlled by a party at the time disclosure is sought; the theory is that the control enables the party to compel the disclosure and that it is therefore fair to penalize the party if the disclosure is not forthcoming. It is not fair, on the other hand, to invoke a sanction against a party for the recalcitrance of a nonparty beyond her control, and for this reason the CPLR requires the use of a subpoena[1] or preliminary court order[2] to compel disclosure from a nonparty: the disobedience of either the subpoena or the order is a contempt of court[3] and the contempt punishment therefore serves as the enforcement remedy.[4] As against a party, however, the meaningful civil sanctions of CPLR 3126 obviate resort to the contempt remedy. There is doubt, for that reason, whether contempt is even available against a party for nondisclosure.[5]

The 3126 sanctions are available not only when an order for disclosure has been disobeyed, but also when the disobedience is of a mere notice. A court order, such as one under CPLR 3124 directing disclosure, is not a condition precedent to the invocation of CPLR 3126.[6] The statute so provides explicitly by applying when the party either disobeys an order "or"

wilfully fails to disclose, and it was so construed even before a 1978 amendment clarified the matter.[7] This accounts for the diminished use made today of CPLR 3124, which contemplates an order directing disclosure without a sanction. CPLR 3126 can direct the disclosure but with a sanction added if the direction should be disobeyed. It can do this, for example, in a conditional order, a popular step among the judges today. The backing of the sanction makes the CPLR 3126 order preferable to the CPLR 3124 order, and the CPLR 3126 motion far more frequent than one under CPLR 3124.

A rule applicable in the supreme and county courts requires that either motion, as a motion affecting disclosure, be accompanied by the moving attorney's affirmation that a good faith effort was made with opposing counsel to resolve the dispute, but that it didn't succeed.[8]

The sanctions are available not just for the disobedience of an order or the disregard of a notice. Under subdivision (h) of CPLR 3101, a party is required to supplement prior responses in certain circumstances, and to do so voluntarily, i.e., without the other side having to serve a new notice, demand, request, interrogatory, or anything else.[9] The CPLR 3126 sanctions are available for a failure to supplement under that provision, even though no order or notice has specifically requested supplementation. The requirement to supplement is automatic.[10]

All of the disclosure devices are backed by the sanctions of CPLR 3126, with the exception of the request to admit, which carries its

---

§ 367

1. CPLR 3106(b).

2. CPLR 3120(b).

3. CPLR 2308, 5104.

4. The procedures for invoking the contempt punishment will be found in the enforcement chapter. See § 481 et seq., below.

5. See Commentary C3126:4 on McKinney's CPLR 3126.

6. See Wolfson v. Nassau County Medical Center, 141 A.D.2d 815, 530 N.Y.S.2d 27 (2d Dep't 1988). With the devices of the discovery of CPLR 3120 and the physical or

mental examination of CPLR 3121, CPLR 3122 appears to require that a preliminary application be made under CPLR 3124 before the stage is properly set for a sanction under CPLR 3126 (see the discussion in SPR 10:1), but some caselaw has held that such a preliminary step is unnecessary. See § 362, above, and SPR 37:2.

7. See Coffey v. Orbachs, Inc., 22 A.D.2d 317, 254 N.Y.S.2d 596 (1st Dep't 1964); Goldner v. Lendor Structures, Inc., 29 A.D.2d 978, 289 N.Y.S.2d 687 (2d Dep't 1968).

8. See Uniform Rule 202.7.

9. See § 352A above.

10. See the discussion in SPR 8:1–2.

own set of consequences.[11] The sanctions of CPLR 3126 can become relevant, moreover, for any phase of a given device. They can be invoked, for example, not just for the failure to attend a deposition, but for the failure to answer appropriate questions propounded during it, or for the failure to execute a transcript of the deposition afterwards.[12]

If a CPLR 3126 sanction motion is addressed to a mere notice to disclose, as opposed to an order, it must be shown that the disobedience was "wilful". One might guess that the cases would be filled with discussion of what is and what is not "wilful" in this sense, but it has not worked out that way. The courts prefer to determine whether the disclosure is required and, if it is, to make an order directing the party to make the disclosure whether the prior refusal was wilful or not. The order is usually a conditional one, applying a sanction unless the disclosure is made within a stated time. With this conditioning, the court relieves itself of the unrewarding inquiry into whether a party's resistance was wilful. The court usually reserves the "wilful" finding for cases where it is convinced not only that the party refused disclosure in the past, but will not make any in the future either. In that situation, which is the exception rather than the rule, the sanction will be imposed outright rather than conditionally.[13] Any unnecessary trouble the seeking party has been caused in this process is usually remedied, as will be seen, by requiring the resisting party, in addition to making the disclosure now, to pay the seeking party an attorney's fee.

The first of the illustrative sanctions is the resolving order, which can be used when the refusal to disclose relates to an isolatable matter. It results in an order deeming the matter to be established as the seeking party claims it to be.[14] The second is also available in that kind of situation. It involves a preclusion order akin to that which punishes a failure to furnish a bill of particulars:[15] it precludes the resisting party from supporting or opposing a given claim, defense, or contention, or from giving evidence on a designated issue or using a particular witness.[16] Where, for example, a defendant refused to produce books reflecting on the value of certain stock, he was precluded from contending that the stock was worth less than X dollars.[17]

A resolving or preclusion order may also be used when the court finds, even if only by negative inference from the party's reaction to disclosure efforts, that the party destroyed evidence reflecting on a specific issue.[18] Suppose that an object in one side's control was lost after it was tested and made the subject of an expert's report, and is therefore unavailable to the other side for testing now. It will not necessarily be precluded from evidence if there is a reasonable way to set things right. In one case, for example, in which the expert was made available for deposition and in which unredacted copies of the expert's report had been made available to the other side, which took advantage of both, preclusion was not directed.[19]

Resolving and preclusion orders are usually feasible only when the refusal to disclose touches on just part of the case. There the court can effectively shape the sanction to the failure—to make the punishment fit the crime—which is what CPLR 3126 is after. But when a party's resistance is total, or involves a matter that goes to the core of the whole case, the sanction has to go just as far. The third paragraph of CPLR 3126 covers that.

11. CPLR 3123. See § 364 above.

12. See Adamo v. Kirsch Beverages, Inc., 80 Misc.2d 369, 363 N.Y.S.2d 58 (Dist.Ct., Suffolk County, 1974). Today, failure to execute a deposition is remedied by allowing its use without execution. See § 357 above.

13. See, e.g., Matter of Porter, 64 Misc.2d 1016, 316 N.Y.S.2d 504 (Surr.Ct., N.Y.County, 1970).

14. CPLR 3126(1).

15. See § 241 above.

16. CPLR 3126(2).

17. Feingold v. Walworth Bros., Inc., 238 N.Y. 446, 144 N.E. 675 (1924).

18. Ferraro v. Koncal Associates, 97 A.D.2d 429, 467 N.Y.S.2d 284 (2d Dep't 1983).

19. See Ashline v. Kestner Eng'rs P.C., 219 A.D.2d 788, 631 N.Y.S.2d 783 (3d Dep't 1995), where there was no proof that the object was deliberately hidden or destroyed, which could of course make a difference, as it did in Hallock v. Bogart, 206 A.D.2d 735, 614 N.Y.S.2d 651 (3d Dep't 1994), noted in SPR 33:3.

Paragraph 3 permits the court to strike the party's pleading, to stay further proceedings by that party, or—the ultimate civil sanction—to default that party in the action. If the resisting party is the plaintiff, this can consist of a dismissal of the action.[20]

If the resisting party is the defendant, the court can hold liability established and set the case down for an assessment of the plaintiff's damages.[21] When the refusal to disclose is based on privilege, such as that against self-incrimination, the availability of a sanction may depend on who is invoking the privilege. If the defendant does, and legitimately, no sanction may be invoked because the privilege is a shield and that's the way the defendant is using it. But when the plaintiff invokes it—the very person who brought the case to court—the invocation amounts to an attempt to use the privilege as a sword. Although the plaintiff can't be precluded from using the privilege, he will face a civil sanction under CPLR 3126 if he does,[22] up to and including the ultimate sanction of a dismissal or default.

This ultimate penalty for nondisclosure is not favored by the courts. They save it for cases of aggravated resistance, where "[l]ess drastic action would only serve to encourage dilatory conduct and reward an obstructionist approach to discovery proceedings".[23]

The spoliation of evidence can bring about a dismissal. In Kirkland v. N.Y.C. Hous. Auth.,[24] for example, the issue was whether the deceased was a suicide or was knocked out of a hi-rise window in D's building by a stove explosion. D impleaded the stove maker (T), but not until six years after being sued, by which time the stove had been destroyed. The court held that this so prejudiced T in the prepara-

tion of its case that the impleader claim had to be dismissed even if the destruction was not intentional.

CPLR 3126 is the remedy turned to when a party has not offered enough. Suppose the reverse: that a party has gotten too much. CPLR 3103, the protective order statute, will offer a cure in that situation. When a plaintiff obtained a defendant's confidential files on the sly, for example, and attempted to exploit them, it was held that the court could apply the ultimate sanction of a default against the plaintiff: a dismissal of the action. What happened was that P found a pile of papers that D inadvertently left on a courtroom table, and, instead of returning them to D, took them home, copied them, absorbed them, and attempted to make use of them against D.[25]

Since CPLR 3126 authorizes "such orders ... as are just", the court is not restricted to the illustrative sanctions contained in the three numbered paragraphs. In fact, the court's tendency is to stay away from the listed sanctions, especially when it is the attorney rather than the client who is responsible for the nondisclosure.[26] The favored device today is the conditional order in which a designated sanction is invoked "unless" the party makes the requisite disclosure within a stated time. The order often contains the added condition that the resister pay to the seeking party costs to date plus an attorney's fee in a designated sum to cover the extra time and expense engendered by the unwarranted resistance. This conditional order together with the added sanction of an attorney's fee was alighted on early as an alternative to the listed sanctions of CPLR 3126,[27] which many judges

20. See Laverne v. Incorporated Vill. of Laurel Hollow, 18 N.Y.2d 635, 272 N.Y.S.2d 780, 219 N.E.2d 294 (1966).

21. See James v. Powell, 26 A.D.2d 525, 270 N.Y.S.2d 789 (1st Dep't 1966), rev'd on other grounds 19 N.Y.2d 249, 279 N.Y.S.2d 10, 225 N.E.2d 741 (1967).

22. See Levine v. Bornstein, 13 Misc.2d 161, 174 N.Y.S.2d 574 (Sup.Ct., Kings County), aff'd 7 A.D.2d 995, 183 N.Y.S.2d 868 (2d Dep't), aff'd 6 N.Y.2d 892, 190 N.Y.S.2d 702, 160 N.E.2d 921 (1959).

23. Sawh v. Bridges, 120 A.D.2d 74, 507 N.Y.S.2d 632 (2d Dep't 1986).

24. 236 A.D.2d 170, 666 N.Y.S.2d 609 (1st Dep't 1997).

25. See Lipin v. Bender, 84 N.Y.2d 562, 620 N.Y.S.2d 744, 644 N.E.2d 1300 (1994), affirming the appellate division decision reported in 193 A.D.2d 424, 597 N.Y.S.2d 340 (1st Dep't 1993). The case is discussed in the lead notes in New York State Law Digest No. 419 and in SPR 6.

26. See, e.g., Page v. Lalor, 24 A.D.2d 883, 264 N.Y.S.2d 599 (2d Dep't 1965); Laurie v. State, 49 Misc.2d 413, 267 N.Y.S.2d 546 (Ct.Cl. 1966).

27. See Nomako v. Ashton, 22 A.D.2d 683, 253 N.Y.S.2d 309 (1st Dep't 1964); DiBartolo v. American & Foreign Ins. Co., 48 Misc.2d 843, 265 N.Y.S.2d 981 (Sup. Ct., Suffolk County), aff'd 26 A.D.2d 992, 275 N.Y.S.2d 805 (2d Dep't 1966).

find too harsh. This authority for a money sanction under CPLR 3126 exists independently of the general sanctions provision,[28] which means that the disclosure misconduct need not rise to level of "frivolous" to support a sanction under CPLR 3126.[29]

The amount of the money sanction is in the court's discretion,[30] and if the court finds that the resistance is the fault of the attorney, it may order the attorney—including one representing a governmental unit, like a member of the attorney general's staff[31]—to pay the sum out of pocket,[32] without reimbursement at any time from the client. The court can of course impose other conditions as well. It can require, for example, that the resister file a bond to secure the seeking party in some phase of the litigation or even to make good the potential recovery on the merits.[33]

Although the conditional order is perhaps most often used when it is a notice that has been disregarded, it can be used as well for the disobedience of a prior order. In other words, the invocation of CPLR 3126 for the violation of a court order rather than of a mere notice does not mean that a sanction must be applied outright. The fact that a court order has already been disobeyed will, however, influence the court's discretion in the choice of a sanction, and a CPLR 3126 penalty applied unconditionally is of course a higher possibility in that situation.

Judicial reluctance to make free use of severe sanctions such as those presently listed in CPLR 3126, which trepidation accounts for the evolution of the conditional order with an attorney's fee as an alternative, is a residuum of the common law hostility to open pretrial disclosure. Some judges may still feel that keeping one's cards close to the vest is part of the game, or at least that the player should not be too gravely punished for trying. This attitude is at war with the CPLR, however, and it as much as anything else accounts for the high number of disclosure applications on the motion calendars. It also accounts for the adoption of the rule in some courts requiring that all disclosure motions include the attorney's affirmation that a good faith effort was first made to resolve the dispute with the other side.[34]

28. Rule 130–1.

29. See Mazarakis v. Bronxville Glen I Ass'n, 229 A.D.2d 661, 644 N.Y.S.2d 793 (3d Dep't 1996). The general sanctions provision, Rule 130–1, penalizes frivolous conduct in litigation. See § 414A below.

30. It was $500, for example, in Warner v. Bumgarner, 49 Misc.2d 488, 267 N.Y.S.2d 825 (Sup.Ct., Monroe County, 1966), a heavy sanction for that time.

31. See Kulers v. State, 141 Misc.2d 1079, 535 N.Y.S.2d 931 (Ct.Cl. 1988).

32. See, e.g., Cotteral v. City of New Rochelle, 33 A.D.2d 791, 307 N.Y.S.2d 568 (2d Dep't 1969).

33. Bredin v. Buchman, 32 A.D.2d 518, 298 N.Y.S.2d 748 (1st Dep't 1969).

34. See, e.g., Uniform Rule 202.7, applicable in the supreme and county courts.

Chapter Fourteen

PRETRIAL INCIDENTS

Analysis

A. CALENDAR PRACTICE

Table of Sections

§ 368. Calendar Practice, Introductory

A "calendar" is a list of cases awaiting treatment of some kind, usually but not always a trial. (There are motion and conference calendars, for example.) But the phrase "calendar practice" is almost always used to refer to trial calendars; it connotes to lawyers the various rules for putting a case on one of the court's trial calendars and keeping it there until its turn for trial is finally reached in due course. The case does its waiting from its calendar position. Whatever the prevalent delay with the particular judge or court may be, it is usually measured not from the time the action is commenced, but from the moment it is placed on the calendar. There will usually be several and sometimes many different calendars used in a given court or area or by a given judge. It is entirely a matter of administration, either with each individual judge, as in the supreme and other courts that the Individual Assignment System (IAS) operates in, or centrally, as in courts that don't have the IAS.[1]

The kinds of calendars there are to be and how a case can attain them is provided for by the rules, to which the CPLR defers. CPLR 3401 in fact mandates that these matters be managed by rule; it provides that "the chief administrator of the courts shall adopt rules regulating the hearing of causes, which may include the filing of notes of issue, the preparation and publication of calendars and the calendar practice for the courts".[2] The courts involved are consulted and frequently their judicial and nonjudicial staffs draft or assist in the drafting of the rules in concert with the administrative judge of the district or court, but the ultimate promulgation of the rules is a matter for the chief administrator.

Illustrative calendars in the supreme court are listed in the rules, from which the court or judge may choose. They include a general cal-

---

§ 368

1. See Uniform Rule 202.22, applicable in the supreme and county courts. There are uniform calendar practice rules in the Court of Claims (UR 206.13 et seq.), the New York City Civil Court (208.14, 208.17 et seq.), the district courts (212.14, 212.17 et seq.), and the city courts (210.14, 210.17 et seq.).

2. It requires that the calendar rules in New York City be uniform "[i]nsofar as practicable".

endar, onto which a case goes when all pretrial procedures (pleading, disclosure, etc.) are completed, and then various follow-up calendars—reserve, ready, military,[3] etc.—each briefly defined in the rule.[4]

The heavier the caseload, the more varied are the calendars. Lawyers accustom themselves quickly to the calendar divisions and practice in the courts they practice in.

The step that puts the case on the trial calendar in a supreme court action is the filing of a paper known as a "note of issue", as will be treated in the next section. Interlocked with the note of issue is the question of the right to trial by jury because if a jury is appropriate to the particular case and the parties want it, it is in the note of issue, or in response to the note of issue, that a jury is demanded.[5] The very first mention of calendaring therefore makes triability by jury a topic. That in turn necessitates treatment of the other modes of trial—court or referee. Those subjects are also part of this chapter. This overlaps the subject of the trial itself only to the extent of determining who the fact-trier shall be. Proceedings at the trial proper, from the picking of the jury right through the verdict and including all the trial motions, are treated in the next chapter.

Also interlocked with the note of issue is a paper known as a "statement [or certificate] of readiness". This is entirely a creature of court rule, the CPLR having nothing about it. Also indispensable in any study directed to calendar practice, it is another matter taken up in this chapter.[6]

In courts in which the IAS is fully operative, a case goes to but one judge at the outset and stays with that judge throughout, including the trial. In what is called a "dual track" system, introduced in an amendment of the applicable rule[7] in 1988, a modification was made. With "dual track", the case stays with one judge from the outset until the filing of the note of issue, at which time it can then be assigned to a different judge for the trial. Whether dual track applies in a given court or area is of course a matter of local practice as prescribed by the chief administrator and must be checked out on a local basis.

§ 369. Note of Issue

A case is placed on the calendar by the filing of a "note of issue", a paper that contains the basic statistics of the case.[1] (Ultimately these notes of issue become a primary source of the statistics published annually about the court system by the Office of Court Administration.) The case is entered on the calendar "as of the date of the filing of the note of issue".[2] Its turn for trial is measured by that filing and not, as is sometimes assumed, by the date of the action's commencement. As far as the CPLR is concerned, the note of issue may be filed any time after issue has been joined or after 40 days have elapsed following the completion of summons service. But it is rarely if ever filed that early. Court rules, which impose many additional demands before a note of issue may be filed, virtually own the note of issue today. It is part and parcel of "calendar practice", control of which is delegated to the chief administrator of the courts,[3] and the time requirements of CPLR 3402(a) defer totally to the rules. The item in the rules that postpones to a much later stage the filing of the note of issue is the "certificate of readiness", often referred to as the "statement of readiness", treated in the next section. The certificate must ordinarily accompany the note of issue.

---

3. A "military" calendar, which plays little role during peacetime, is for cases in which one of the parties or even a witness is in military service and the action can't go forward on mere deposition evidence. The courts try to manage things to accommodate the person in military service. See, e.g., Goot v. Board of Education etc., 82 A.D.2d 985, 440 N.Y.S.2d 403 (3d Dep't 1981).

4. Uniform Rule 202.22. Also listed are some pretrial calendars, including a motion calendar and one for preliminary conferences.

5. The procedure for demanding a jury trial is in § 378.

6. See § 370 below.

7. Uniform Rule 202.3.

§ 369

1. See the form of note of issue contained in § 371, below.

2. CPLR 3402(a).

3. CPLR 3401.

The note of issue and the certificate of readiness are prescribed, with forms, in the rules.[4] A "notice of trial" instead of a note of issue is used in the lower courts, as provided by their court acts,[5] but the implementing rules prescribe a certificate of readiness to accompany the notice of trial.[6] A special rule governs calendar practice in medical (including dental and podiatric) malpractice actions, and also regulates the special notice that CPLR 3406 requires at the outset of those actions.[7]

The filing of the note of issue adds the case at the bottom of what is usually called the "general" calendar.[8] From there its travels depend largely on what calendars the particular court or judge uses, which depends in turn on the kinds and quantity of cases the court or judge has. If nothing happens to cause a case's transfer to some other calendar, it will rise in due course to the top of the general calendar. From there it will usually be transferred to yet another list (every calendar is just a list) still closer to trial but perhaps not quite there. Each transfer is usually from the top of one calendar to the bottom of the next. The closer the particular calendar is to actual trial, the readier must the attorneys and their witnesses be, including expert witnesses, whose time is expensive.

In courts that don't use the Individual Assignment System (IAS), there may be a "calendar part", under that or some other name, whose assigned judge has the job of parceling cases out to "trial parts" and who has to keep cases moving to assure that no judge will be idle for lack of ready cases. It's a frequent source of friction between bench and trial bar. Busy trial lawyers with commitments in many courts ("previous engagement", as the jargon has it), each of which has its own calendar obligations and may require readiness for trial on short notice, find themselves in choppy straits when two courts are suddenly ready for their cases at the same time and neither is too enthusiastic about deferring to the other. Occasionally a judge, idled for a day by the failure of counsel to appear for a trial, will invoke a money sanction against the offender, payable to the other side or perhaps even to the clerk for payment into the public treasury.[9]

In IAS courts, including of course the supreme court, the friction may be greater still as pressure for priority of the lawyers' time comes from individual judges. A special rule was enacted, as part of the uniform rules, addressed to "Engagement of Counsel". It prescribes which cases shall have priority of a given lawyer's time, when adjournments will be granted, and when, without adjournment, substitute counsel will be required.[10]

CPLR 3402(a) allows any party to file the note of issue. Two copies must be filed, and the filing must take place within 10 days after the note of issue is served on the other parties. As may be guessed, it is usually the plaintiff who serves and files the note of issue. The plaintiff, after all, is the one who wants the case to go forward. But the defendant may do it. The filing requires payment of a fee,[11] but the fee qualifies as a disbursement which the merits winner, if she paid it, may recover from the loser.[12]

If the case is triable by jury and the party filing the note of issue wants a jury, he demands it in the note of issue. If any other

---

4. See Uniform Rule 202.21, which requires that a note of issue be used in special proceedings as well as in actions. Its appearance in a special proceeding is rare, apparently contemplated only when the proceeding poses an issue of fact that needs a plenary trial, which is clearly the exception rather than the rule. See § 556 below.

Note of issue practice in the Court of Claims is governed by UR 206.12.

5. See § 1301 of the New York City Civil Court Act and of the Uniform District and City court acts (McKinney's Vol. 29A, Part 3).

6. The applicable rules are UR 208.17 in the N.Y.C. Civil Court, 212.17 in the district courts, and 210.17 in the city courts.

7. See Uniform Rule 202.56.

8. See Uniform Rule 202.22, applicable in the supreme and county courts.

9. The occasion for doing this is usually a motion to restore after the case has been stricken from the calendar for the nonappearance of counsel. See Campbell v. Regency Towers, Inc., 76 Misc.2d 33, 349 N.Y.S.2d 928 (Sup.Ct., N.Y.County, 1973).

10. Uniform Rule 125.1.

11. CPLR 8020.

12. CPLR 8301(a).

party wants the jury and the note of issue does not ask for one, that party must serve a demand for jury within 15 days after the note of issue is served.[13]

Preferences are a topic treated later,[14] but we should note here that if a preference is sought by the party filing the note of issue, that party must ordinarily move for it in a notice of motion accompanying the note of issue; if some other party wants it, she must move for it within 10 days after being served with the note of issue.[15] In an IAS court, the motion is made to the IAS judge, or, if the court or district uses the "dual track" feature of the IAS,[16] to whichever judge or part the rules direct. If the court doesn't use the IAS, the motion for a preference may have to be directed to a special part of the court, as the rules may prescribe.[17]

The filing of the note of issue must of course be made in the county in which venue is laid. It has been held that a filing in any other county is nullity,[18] which means that the case will not secure a calendar position. The same will probably be the case if, under the IAS, the note of issue should be filed with the wrong judge, who is not likely to accord it an enthusiastic welcome.

If a new party should be added after a note of issue has been filed, the party bringing in the new party must serve him with a copy of the note of issue and must serve the clerk and other parties with a statement advising of the addition of the new party.[19] Because under the rules a note of issue is ordinarily not ripe for filing until the case is ready for trial, joinder of an additional party after the filing of the note is relatively rare. But it is possible, and, if it takes place, overlooking this note of issue requirement can have repercussions.[20]

§ 370. Statement of Readiness

The "certificate of readiness", sometimes popularly called the "statement of readiness", is a creature of the rules rather than of the CPLR. It's the almost constant companion of the note of issue today. It attests that the case is ready—that pretrial procedures have been completed or that opportunity for them has come and gone, that the case is ready for trial, and that any preliminary conference order that may have been made in the case has been complied with.[1]

Since the rules are the home of the certificate of readiness, a number of rules and rule subdivisions are going to be cited in the footnotes in this section. The reader is warned that the Uniform Rules are still an unstable compilation, being tested and tried, and that rule changes can come down suddenly. In making changes, rulemakers are notoriously prone to renumber rules and especially subdivisions within rules freely, undermining whatever foothold the prior numbers or letters may have attained in the consciousness of the profession and even in reported cases that are a permanent part of the library. (They don't see this in moral terms, as authors do.) The reader should bear this in mind, always double-checking to make sure a rule's or a subdivision's number has not been casually altered, along with a dozen others, to make way for some little tidbit stuck in between. It's not a good way to do business, but it's been made a fact of life for those who practice law.

The general rule is that the certificate must be served with the note of issue,[2] but there are some exceptions. When a pretrial proceeding can't be completed because of forces beyond the party's control, for example, the party can

---

13. CPLR 4102(a). Jury demands are elaborated in § 378.

14. See §§ 372 and 373 below.

15. CPLR 3403(b).

16. See § 368 above.

17. See Vinal v. New York Central R.R., 48 Misc.2d 362, 264 N.Y.S.2d 824 (Sup.Ct., Albany County, 1965).

18. Holihan v. Regina Corp., 54 Misc.2d 264, 282 N.Y.S.2d 404 (Sup.Ct., Onondaga County, 1967).

19. CPLR 3402(b).

20. See Kaufman v. Clearview Gardens Federal Credit Union, 71 Misc.2d 945, 337 N.Y.S.2d 323 (N.Y.C.Civ.Ct. 1972), involving the "notice of trial", the lower courts' equivalent of the note of issue.

§ 370

1. The preliminary conference is discussed in § 77D above.

2. See Uniform Rule 202.21(a).

move the court for leave to file the note of issue without the certificate of readiness, the court to make provision for its filing later.[3] Medical malpractice actions have a special governing rule.[4] And while the certificate of readiness, just like the note of issue, must be filed in special proceedings as well as in actions, neither is required for an application to settle the claim of an infant, incompetent, or conservatee.[5]

An official form of certificate of readiness, manifesting the certificate's diverse requirements in a checklist of items, is included in the rule.[6] We concentrate here on the application of the certificate of readiness rule in the supreme and county courts. Other courts have their own rules.[7]

Occasional attacks on the certificate of readiness rule, contending that because it requires total preparation before the note of issue can be filed it nullifies the permission of CPLR 3402(a) to file the note of issue any time after issue is joined, were rejected in the past, citing the express authorization that CPLR 3401 gives the chief administrator (previously it was the appellate divisions) to make calendar rules.[8] Such an attack stands even less chance of succeeding today.

The major item the courts want concluded and at rest when the case goes on the calendar is disclosure. The experience before the certificate of readiness was first adopted in the 1950s was that too much attention and effort was spent on motions for disclosure made after the case was on the calendar, engendering numerous adjournments and unnecessary delay as judicial time was spent on unready actions. No matter how needful the disclosure, the courts' general attitude today is that it

should be had before the parties allow the case to go on the calendar under any pretext that the case is ready. That the case is ready is what all parties are held to represent when the certificate is filed without challenge.[9]

If the certificate is disputed and the position of some other party is that it has been prematurely filed, whether for lack of opportunity to complete disclosure proceedings or for any other reason, the remedy of that party is to move to vacate the note of issue. The party has 20 days in which to do that, measured from the service of the certificate of readiness.[10] If, on a timely motion to vacate, the movant can show that disclosure proceedings have not yet had their fair run, the motion will be granted.[11] In the absence of a motion to vacate, further disclosure will simply be deemed waived.[12]

If the note of issue has been vacated and the case stricken from the calendar, it can be reinstated on motion, with affidavit proof that all is now ready.[13]

The policy behind the certificate of readiness rule, the policy of precluding further disclosure or other pretrial proceedings after the filing, is implemented by requiring any party seeking post-filing disclosure to show that "unusual or unanticipated circumstances" developed after the filing.[14] These have to be shown by a motion supported by affidavit. If, without such a court application, a party serves a mere disclosure notice after the note and certificate have been filed, the other side's remedy is to move to vacate the notice.[15]

The courts are not generous about finding these special requirements met, lest an attitude of judicial laxness undermine the purpose of the certificate of readiness rule. Post-filing

---

3. UR 202.21(d).

4. UR 202.56.

5. UR 202.21(a).

6. The form is set forth in § 371 below.

7. In the Court of Claims, Uniform Rule 206.12 applies. The applicable rules in the lower courts are UR 208.17 in the N.Y.C. Civil Court, 212.17 in the district courts, and 210.17 in the city courts.

8. See, e.g., Bedingfield v. Dairymaid Farms, Inc., 46 Misc.2d 146, 259 N.Y.S.2d 292 (Sup.Ct., Suffolk County, 1965).

9. See Jacobs v. Peress, 23 A.D.2d 483, 255 N.Y.S.2d 492 (1st Dep't 1965).

10. UR 202.21(e).

11. See Falk v. Kalt, 44 Misc.2d 172, 253 N.Y.S.2d 188 (Sup.Ct., Suffolk County, 1964).

12. Williams v. N.Y.C. Transit Auth., 23 A.D.2d 590, 256 N.Y.S.2d 708 (2d Dep't 1965).

13. UR 202.21(f).

14. UR 202.21(d).

15. Price v. Brody, 7 A.D.2d 204, 181 N.Y.S.2d 661 (1st Dep't 1959).

disclosure thus requires something unanticipated. Where the plaintiff, for example, content in a relatively small case to await the trial to develop his proof, files the note of issue and is afterwards met with the defendant's summary judgment motion, a showing that the plaintiff needs disclosure from the defendant in order to respond to the motion has been deemed a circumstance justifying post-filing disclosure.[16]

Unexpected complications can also do the job, such as where cases have been consolidated and it appears that disclosure has not been completed in all the actions.[17] That's not a theme on which to end, however, because most often the conditions are not met and disclosure is not allowed. The practitioner's attention is better directed to a prompt motion to vacate a note of issue prematurely filed, which will preserve the right to further disclosure, than

to a post-certificate effort to obtain the disclosure, which will more likely than not be rejected.

An attempt to get on the calendar speedily by attesting in a certificate of readiness that disclosure proceedings were either completed or not desired, with the attesting party then trying to resort to the Freedom of Information Law (FOIL) to obtain the discovery, was held impermissible in John T. Brady & Co. v. City of New York.[18]

§ 371. Form of Note of Issue and Statement of Readiness

Rule 202.21 of the Uniform Rules applicable in the supreme and county courts has official forms for both the note of issue and the certificate of readiness. These are set forth below.

(a) Form of note of issue.

---

16. Connell v. City of New York, 102 Misc.2d 585, 424 N.Y.S.2d 81 (N.Y.C.Civ.Ct. 1979).

17. See Wahrhaftig v. Space Design Group, Inc., 33 A.D.2d 953, 306 N.Y.S.2d 863 (3d Dep't 1970).

18. 84 A.D.2d 113, 445 N.Y.S.2d 724 (1st Dep't 1982). Anything the Brady case suggests about the FOIL not

being available to litigants as an alternative to CPLR disclosure is overruled by the M.Farbman case discussed in § 348, above, but Brady's point about a party's not being entitled to file a certificate of readiness if FOIL disclosure is in fact being pursued for litigation purposes is not necessarily overturned by M.Farbman.

NOTE OF ISSUE

Calendar No. (if any) ....   For use of clerk
Index No. ....
.... Court, ... County
Name of assigned judge ....

Notice for trial

Trial by jury demanded ....
    ... of all issues
    ... of issues specified below
    ... or attached hereto
Trial without jury ...
Filed by attorney for ....
Date summons served ....
Date service completed ....
Date issue joined ....
            Nature of action or
            special proceeding
Tort:
    Motor vehicle negligence   ......
    Medical malpractice   ......
    Other tort   ......
Contract   ......
Contested matrimonial   ......
Uncontested matrimonial   ......

Special preference
claimed under ....
Tax certiorari   ......
    Condemnation   ......
....
    Other (not itemized above)   ......
on the ground that ....
            (specify) ....
....

Attorney(s) for Plaintiff(s)
Office and P.O. Address:
Phone No.
    Indicate if this action is   ......
    brought as a class action

Attorney(s) for Defendant(s)
Office and P.O. Address:
Phone No.

Amount demanded $ ....
Other relief ....
Insurance carrier(s), if known:

NOTE: The clerk will not accept this note of issue unless accompanied by a certificate of readiness.

The above is the body of the note of issue; the usual caption and other accouterments are omitted. Note that the note of issue is required to recite, among other things, whether a preference is claimed for the case. Preferences are the subject of the following sections.

    (b) Form of certificate of readiness.

CERTIFICATE OF READINESS FOR TRIAL (Items 1–7 must be checked)

	Complete	Waived	Not Required
1. All pleadings served	....	....	....
2. Bill of particulars served	....	....	....
3. Physical examinations completed	....	....	....
4. Medical reports exchanged	....	....	....
5. Appraisal reports exchanged	....	....	....
6. Compliance with section 202.16 of the Rules of the Chief Administrator (22 NYCRR 202.16) in matrimonial actions	....	....	....
7. Discovery proceedings now known to be necessary completed	....	....	....

8. There are no outstanding requests for discovery
9. There has been a reasonable opportunity to complete the foregoing proceedings
10. There has been compliance with any order issued pursuant to section 202.12 of the Rules of the Chief Administrator (22 NYCRR 202.12)
11. If a medical malpractice action, there has been compliance with any order issued pursuant to section 202.56 of the Rules of the Chief Administrator (22 NYCRR 202.56)
12. The case is ready for trial

Dated: _____
(Signature) _____
Attorney(s) for: _____
Office and P.O. address: _____

B. PREFERENCES

Table of Sections

§ 372. The "General" Preference

A preference, as the name implies, is an order giving a case a "preferred" position on the calendar. One must be careful in New York practice to distinguish between two kinds of preferences, however. One is commonly known as a "general" preference, entirely a product of court rules. The other, which the bar has come to call a "special" preference, is supplied by CPLR 3403 and is a real preference in every sense.

The general preference is not a preference to the case that gets it; it's a punishment to the case that doesn't. In proper sequence the general preference should be treated first, because a case required to qualify for a general preference and failing to do so is not likely to be allowed a special preference.[1] The special preference will be treated in the next section.

§ 372

1. See Rab v. Colon, 37 A.D.2d 813, 324 N.Y.S.2d 809 (1st Dep't 1971).

The general preference is a device for administering the calendars of the supreme court. It aims primarily at the ubiquitous personal injury and wrongful death actions, the unintentional torts,[2] which are so substantial a part of judicial calendars today. The function of the general preference is to keep out of the supreme court cases in which the injuries (and hence the damages) are not permanent or protracted and which should therefore have been brought for a smaller sum and in a lower court. If the complaint in such a case asks a sum beyond the monetary jurisdiction of the lower court, the plaintiff thereby insisting on remaining in the supreme court, the case will be denied a "general" preference.[3] The impact of the denial is that the case will go onto the calendar at the bottom and stay there; it will not, as will cases that do get the general preference, move up and get tried in due course. Attorneys sometimes facetiously call this the "oblivion" calendar.

In New York City, where the civil court is the one to which a case goes if transferred down by the supreme court, the $25,000 mark (the civil court's maximum jurisdiction) is the one the supreme court is looking at when it determines whether to grant the case a general preference. The court or judge makes this determination in some pretrial context, perhaps a preliminary conference.[4] It is based on the pleadings and bill of particulars and on the medical information accumulated in the case, such as reports of physical examinations and hospital records. This is of course not the occasion for trying the case; the judge's obligation is only to ascertain whether the aggregate of the written medical evidence could, if presented to a jury in testimonial form, support a verdict for more than $25,000. A mere prima facie showing of such a possibility warrants the preference.[5]

The monetary prospect is the crux of general preference practice, but it is recognized that sometimes even cases falling short of the money threshold may for other good reason justify supreme court jurisdiction and hence a general preference. If, for example, territorial restrictions applicable to the lower court but not to the supreme court would have made the defendant unreachable with the lower court's summons, the case is right for the supreme court and gets the preference.[6] Acknowledging that these rules are designed to promote judicial economy, it has been held that in a multi-plaintiff case the preference should ordinarily be awarded the whole case if any plaintiff qualifies for it individually.[7]

A denial of a general preference can as a practical matter keep a supreme court case in limbo indefinitely if not forever, and this prompted a constitutional attack. It failed. The general preference was held to be a reasonable calendar measure and the principle to be one of "ancient and undisputed law that courts have an inherent power over the control of their calendars, and the disposition of business before them, including the order in which disposition will be made of that business."[8] The remedy of a plaintiff aggrieved by the denial of a general preference is either to appeal the order of denial, or else consent to reduce the monetary demand to bring it within the lower court's jurisdiction and permit the case to be transferred down. The topic was treated earlier, when CPLR 325(c) was discussed.[9]

---

2. See, e.g., DiGilio v. William J. Burns Int'l Detective Agency, Inc., 46 A.D.2d 650, 359 N.Y.S.2d 688 (2d Dep't 1974).

3. For an extensive discussion of the general preference rules and their purpose, see Weber v. Kowalski, 85 Misc.2d 349, 376 N.Y.S.2d 996 (Sup.Ct., Dutchess County, 1975). The Weber case was overruled in Mandel v. Kent, 70 A.D.2d 903, 417 N.Y.S.2d 306 (2d Dep't 1979), but not in respect of preferences, on which subject it remains an instructive discourse. The rules involved have now been superseded by the Uniform Rules, which may or may not have the likes of a general preference lurking among their myriad parts.

4. See Uniform Rule 202.12.

5. Freedman v. Black, 23 A.D.2d 770, 258 N.Y.S.2d 563 (2d Dep't 1965).

6. See Chiques v. Sanso, 72 Misc.2d 376, 339 N.Y.S.2d 394 (Sup.Ct., Westchester County, 1972).

7. Martin v. Suarez, 30 A.D.2d 947, 293 N.Y.S.2d 950 (1st Dep't 1968).

8. Plachte v. The Bancroft Inc., 3 A.D.2d 437, 438, 161 N.Y.S.2d 892, 893 (1st Dep't 1957). The case traces in depth the origin of the general preference rules.

9. See § 26 above.

It is CPLR 325(c) that authorizes a plaintiff to reduce the demand and consent to have the case transferred to a lower court. The judge who feels that a case does not warrant the monetary jurisdiction of the supreme court, and who threatens to deny it a general preference for that reason, is actually doing a little arm-twisting to get the plaintiff to reduce the demand and consent to have the case transferred down under CPLR 325(c). CPLR 325(c) is therefore largely regarded as an adjunct of the general preference device. The 1968 enactment of subdivision (d) of CPLR 325, however, and the rules adopted pursuant to it, have dramatically reduced dependence on subdivision (c) and, indeed, on the whole system of "general" preferences.

Under the rules that exploit CPLR 325(d), a transfer down does not have to be accompanied by a reduced demand to meet the lower court's jurisdiction. As discussed earlier,[10] the usual monetary limits of the lower court disappear in a case transferred down under CPLR 325(d).[11] This enables the plaintiff to retain and have tried, in the transferee lower court, whatever sum the complaint originally demanded, and a CPLR 325(d) transfer down therefore requires no consent from the plaintiff. The problem for which the general preference was devised as a cure, therefore—to devote supreme court trial energies to those cases that have only the supreme court to call on—is now met with an obligatory CPLR 325(d) transfer down instead of with a denial of a general preference.

If CPLR 325(d) or its implementing rules should be repealed with respect to any particular district or county, general preference practice of the kind we have been discoursing on in this section may again become, in that place, the only way to discourage the bringing of unworthy cases in the supreme court.

Although the general preference is a serious but apparently not fatal casualty of the era of CPLR 325(d) and its implementing rules, the special preference remains alive and vigorous. It's the next subject.

§ 373. The "Special" Preference

The "general" preference treated in the prior section is just a filter to keep small cases out of the supreme court. The preference set forth in CPLR 3403(a) is the real preference. Its purpose is to single out cases that for some pressing reason deserve to be tried earlier than their calendar position would ordinarily allow. It is popularly called a "special" or "statutory" preference, although CPLR 3403(a) doesn't call it by either name. The bar adopted the general-special dichotomy as a shorthand way of distinguishing between the two kinds. The general preference is presently in a state of eclipse, but the eclipse is not necessarily permanent, as we point out in the prior section. To the extent that it still hangs around, homeless as far as the rules are concerned but capable of materializing out of the shadows in some places, it has to be acknowledged. Also requiring acknowledgment, then, is the proposition, announced when both preferences were an active part of the scene,[1] that a case not qualifying for a general preference is ordinarily in no position to ask for a special one.[2]

The CPLR 3403(a) preference is addressed and expanded on in the uniform rules, which continue to refer to it as a "special" preference.[3]

CPLR 3403(a) provides that "civil cases shall be tried in the order in which notes of

---

10. See § 27 above.

11. CPLR 325(d) is an invoking of Const. Art. VI, § 19, subd. (k)—the ultimate authority for dispensing with the ordinary monetary limitation of a lower court.

§ 373

1. For example, the rule that implements CPLR 325(d) by allowing the mandatory transfer down—Uniform Rule 202.13—for a time excluded the 9th District, which consists of Westchester, Putnam, Dutchess, Rockland, and Orange counties. When that was so, the denial of a general preference was the method of compelling plaintiffs with inadequate cases to reduce their demands and consent to transfer down of their cases.

2. See Rab v. Colon, 37 A.D.2d 813, 324 N.Y.S.2d 809 (1st Dep't 1971).

3. See Uniform Rules 202.24 and 202.25, applicable in the supreme and county courts. There are also uniform rules on the "special" preference in the N.Y.C. Civil Court (UR 208.20, 208.21), the district courts (UR 212.20, 212.21), and the city courts (210.20, 210.21).

issue have been filed, but the following shall be entitled to a preference:

1. an action brought by or against the state, or a political subdivision of the state, or an officer or board of officers of the state or a political subdivision of the state, in his or its official capacity, on the application of the state, the political subdivision, or the officer or board of officers;

2. an action where a preference is provided for by statute;

3. an action in which the interests of justice will be served by an early trial;

4. in any action upon the application of a party who has reached the age of seventy years;

5. an action to recover damages for medical, dental or podiatric malpractice; [and]

6. an action to recover damages for personal injuries where the plaintiff is terminally ill and alleges that such terminal illness is a result of the conduct, culpability or negligence of the defendant."

Several of these paragraphs require some comment. One example of a statutorily preferred action under paragraph 2 is perhaps the most preferred action of all: the election dispute,[4] in which the whole electorate has an interest. Even the Court of Appeals arranges special and expedited calendars for election cases during the pre-voting season, usually in late summer and in autumn.

Local practice, with or without impetus from a rule, may also develop preferences—in effect special ones—in certain situations, as for a case back for a new trial after an appeal.[5]

The preferences authorized by paragraphs 4, 5, and 6 of CPLR 3403(a) were added after the CPLR's original enactment. Paragraph 4 pres-

ently recognizes age 70 as an age at which any party should be entitled to a preference. The applicant is usually the plaintiff reaching that age, of course, but a defendant attaining it would also, under the provision's language, be authorized to move for the preference. The preference is available only at the request of the party attaining that age, not some other party. Hence a plaintiff under 70 was not allowed a preference based on the defendant's having passed that age.[6]

When a party with only a derivative cause of action reaches 70, however, such as a husband with a loss of consortium claim based on his wife's injury, it has been held that a preference can be granted to the whole case even though the main claimant, in this example the wife on the personal injury claim, is under 70.[7]

The paragraph 5 preference for the medical malpractice case, expanded to include dentistry and podiatry, was part of a package of 1975 legislation, affecting many statutes, designed to avert a strike by doctors stung by their burgeoning malpractice insurance premiums.[8]

The preference for terminal illness under paragraph 6 applies only when the plaintiff is suffering the illness, and only when the illness is alleged to be a by-product of the wrong for which the suit is being brought.

It has been held that preferences may not be "stacked". When the plaintiff qualified for two preferences, for example, the one for medical malpractice actions under paragraph 5 and the other for a plaintiff over 70 under paragraph 4, the award of the first was held to preclude the second. The court said that orderly calendaring would be "virtually impossible if multiple preferences were permitted".[9]

Unique situations can of course arise, and as a perusal of the enumerated grounds would

---

4. See Elec.L. § 16–116, which gives the election proceeding "preference over all other causes in all courts". Uniform Rule 202.64 follows through on this with the same instruction.

5. See Bierzynsky v. New York Cent. R.R., 59 Misc.2d 315, 298 N.Y.S.2d 584 (Sup.Ct., Erie County, 1969).

6. Libow v. Brill, 127 Misc.2d 661, 486 N.Y.S.2d 648 (Sup.Ct., Nassau County, 1985).

7. Bobowski v. Toomey, 108 Misc.2d 1061, 439 N.Y.S.2d 239 (Sup.Ct., Albany County, 1981).

8. See L.1975, ch.109, § 8, and the Governor's accompanying message. McKinney's N.Y. Session Laws (1975) p. 1739. An insurance law provision that was part of the same package contains a definition of medical malpractice that may prove helpful under paragraph 5. See Ins.L. § 5501(b).

9. Green v. Vogel, 144 A.D.2d 66, 537 N.Y.S.2d 180 (2d Dep't 1989).

indicate, it is paragraph 3 that enables the court to take them into consideration. Paragraph 3 authorizes a preference when the "interests of justice" will be served by it. This enables a variety of situations to be recognized as deserving special preferences. A plaintiff's terminal illness not arising out of the conduct sued on, for example (which is governed by paragraph 6), can be taken into consideration on a sui generis application under paragraph 3.

Although the paragraph 3 preference may be sought in any kind of case, it is again the personal injury action that supplies much of the caselaw. The preference is not likely to be granted in personal injury cases unless there is a persuasive showing of destitution or probability of death before trial. So the First Department has held,[10] in any event. But when the subject is the special preference, one can't confidently appropriate the holdings of one department for automatic use in another. Despite the fact that CPLR 3403(a) purportedly governs uniformly across the state, there is room, in determining what will satisfy the "interests of justice", for each department to take cognizance of its own calendar conditions, which they do. Rules and practices in one department or part of it may be unwarranted in another department or part of it, and this the courts candidly acknowledge.[11] Much discretion is involved and discretionary matters, because they constitute questions of fact rather than of law—unless an "abuse" of discretion is involved—are not reviewed by the Court of Appeals.[12] As a practical matter, then, this leaves each appellate division the ultimate judge of what will be recognized locally as sufficient for a special preference. In one place, for example, the fact that the plaintiff is destitute enough to be receiving public assistance

may earn an automatic preference,[13] while elsewhere it may not be decisive at all.[14]

Destitution is always an important factor, of course, and there need be no showing that the wrong sued on caused the indigency,[15] although causation is a factor.[16] If local calendar conditions are tight and the attitude towards special preferences consequently sparing, some courts have even been known to take into consideration, in support of denying the preference, the defendant's willingness to pay—while the action is pending—the plaintiff's past and continuing medical and living expenses. The First Department considered that in Martinkovic v. Chrysler Leasing Corp.[17]

The traditional attitude about the special preference was stated in Dodumoff v. Lyons,[18] which held that a special preference "emphatically ... is never to be lightly granted, for the granting of a preference represents a favoring of one case over the many other cases awaiting trial on a calendar heavy with accident injury cases". As a general rule that statement could have validity statewide, but the rigor of its application invariably depends on local conditions. The perennial difficulty when the calendars are heavy is that whatever standards are set for the sui generis inquiry necessitated by paragraph 3 of CPLR 3403(a), there are invariably a huge number of cases that can meet them.

A sensitive treatment of the factors that the court would ideally consider is in Tintner v. Marangi,[19] where an elderly couple avoided imposing on public assistance by sharing a small bedroom with their grandchildren in their son's home. The court stressed the deprivations the couple faced, psychological as well as physical, and held that if the tort recovery they were seeking would restore the plaintiffs

---

10. See Rothschild v. Carolina Coach Co., 23 A.D.2d 729, 258 N.Y.S.2d 49 (1st Dep't 1965).

11. See, e.g., Smith v. Schnabel, 34 A.D.2d 603, 308 N.Y.S.2d 502 (3d Dep't 1970).

12. CPLR 5501(b).

13. See, e.g., Harvin v. Chiusano, 52 Misc.2d 836, 276 N.Y.S.2d 701 (Sup.Ct., Kings County, 1967).

14. See, e.g., Smith v. Schnabel, 34 A.D.2d 603, 308 N.Y.S.2d 502 (3d Dep't 1970).

15. Matheson v. Joy–Kar Taxi, Inc., 32 A.D.2d 544, 299 N.Y.S.2d 660 (2d Dep't 1969).

16. Beltran v. Borstein, 32 A.D.2d 954, 303 N.Y.S.2d 9 (2d Dep't 1969).

17. 29 A.D.2d 636, 286 N.Y.S.2d 195 (1st Dep't 1968).

18. 4 A.D.2d 626, 627, 168 N.Y.S.2d 183, 185 (1st Dep't 1957).

19. 57 Misc.2d 318, 292 N.Y.S.2d 779 (Sup.Ct., Rockland County, 1968).

to living circumstances of dignity and self-respect, they merited the special preference; that the courts should not unduly stress whether the plaintiffs or the calendar will first expire; and that the struggles of an old person to avoid public assistance should be rewarded with a grant of the preference rather than cited as a reason for its denial. It would be nice to report a universal adoption of that approach, but it is not yet to be discerned in the cases. The circumstances of each case can appeal heavily to the judge, but the overall caseload has unfortunately required the drawing of careful lines.

As to what the nature of the preference will be—assuming a case is made out for the grant—that will also depend on geography, calendar conditions, and the exigency of the factors accounting for the preference. The case can be set down for a day certain, or just accelerated to a more advanced calendar. The rules say that if a preference is granted, "the case shall be placed ahead of all non-preferred cases pending as of that date, unless the court otherwise orders".[20]

The special preference is ordinarily sought by motion. The motion papers are served with the note of issue if sought by the party filing it, or within 10 days after the filing if sought by some other party. When the ground is that the applicant has attained age 70, or is terminally ill, the motion may be made when the applicant reaches that age, or any time after the terminal nature of the illness becomes known, even though the note of issue has already been filed.[21] In personal injury and wrongful death cases, the rules impose more detailed requirements for the preference motion, including a showing that the venue of the action is proper.[22]

There are also rules prescribing the steps for opposing a preference application,[23] requiring the court to make sure the preference is justified even if there's no opposition to it,[24] and permitting the court, on its own motion, to withdraw a preference already granted.[25]

We have been discussing preferences in the trial of an action, the subject of CPLR 3403(a). Occasionally a preference is called for on the hearing of a motion, the best known of which is the motion for a preliminary injunction in an instance in which a temporary restraining order is outstanding.[26]

C.   PRETRIAL CONFERENCE

Table of Sections

Sec.
374.   Pretrial Conferences.

§ 374.   Pretrial Conferences

Another creature of the rules rather than the CPLR is the pretrial conference, the second of the conferences provided for by the rules. The first is the preliminary conference of Uniform Rule 202.12, treated earlier.[1] The preliminary conference, a pre-note of issue session that comes early in the action if it comes at all, was mandatory when the uniform rules first took effect on January 6, 1986, but was made optional as of April 1, 1988. The pretrial conference that we address here[2] has been optional from the outset. It's a device designed to get the parties and the judge together on the eve of trial for a variety of purposes, notably to evaluate the case and discuss possible settlement or, failing settlement, to narrow the issues by securing admissions of fact or agreements about documents.[3]

---

20.   Uniform Rule 202.24(d).

21.   CPLR 3403(b).

22.   See Uniform Rule 202.24(b).

23.   UR 202.25(a).

24.   UR 202.25(c).

25.   UR 202.25(b).

26.   See CPLR 6313(a).

§ 374

1.   See § 77D above.

2.   Treatment here is of Uniform Rule 202.26, applicable in the supreme and county courts. The establishment of pretrial conferences in the N.Y.C. Civil Court (UR 208.22) and in the district courts (UR 212.22) is left to the chief administrator to determine by separate rule. In the city courts, conferences are left to each judge to set up "as required by the needs of the court". UR 210.22.

3.   The evolution of the pretrial conference is briefly discussed and some statistics on its effectiveness appear in the Judicial Conference's Second Annual Report (1957) at page 66 et seq.

The pretrial conference occurs after the filing of the note of issue. While the rule in point, Uniform Rule 202.26, says that the judge "shall" order a pretrial conference, it adds in the same clause that the judge can dispense with it. This presumably recognizes that under the Individual Assignment System (IAS) the judge has been on top of the case from the outset, perhaps including an initial review of it in a preliminary conference earlier, so that the judge knows one way or the other whether there would be any utility in going through a "pretrial" conference.

If the pretrial conference is to take place, the rule says that to the extent "practicable" it should be held between 15 and 45 days in advance of the anticipated day of trial.

The attorneys who appear at the conference must be "authorized to make binding stipulations".[4] This is designed to discourage the firms involved from sending down junior lawyers without any authority to take meaningful steps in the case.

Modeled in some measure on the counterpart federal provision,[5] the rule says that the conference can consider

1. simplification of the issues;

2. securing admissions and documents "to avoid unnecessary proof";

3. "disposition" of the action (a euphemism for settlement talks) and its scheduling (if there is no settlement);

4. amendment of pleadings and bill of particulars;

5. limiting the number of expert witnesses;

6. insurance coverage if relevant; and anything else.

Even as late as the pretrial conference, a supreme court justice retains the power to transfer the case down to a lower court under CPLR 325 if—all pretrial proceedings, including disclosure, now having been completed and the view of the case therefore having been brought into better focus—the justice finds that it fits within the monetary jurisdiction of a lower court and doesn't belong in the supreme court.[6] The transfer down can be based on either CPLR 325(c)[7] or CPLR 325(d).[8]

Whatever the stated reasons for a "conference"—any kind of conference—the practical experience of the bar is that with some judges, at least in tort cases, it can turn into an arm-twisting session in which the judge tries hard to get the case settled. Some judges, self-conscious about their "track record", have developed special touches to increase their settlement credits, sending the plaintiff out while the defendant is bargained up and then reversing the audience to bargain the plaintiff down. It's a procedure criticized publicly but applauded privately, especially by court administrators concerned about sagging calendars and overtaxed facilities. At the preliminary conference that occurs early in an action, judges have even been known to attempt—improperly—retributive measures against recalcitrant parties who don't settle on terms the judge deems fair, like the granting of a preference in the case to punish a balky defendant.[9]

D. LAXNESS DISMISSALS

Table of Sections

§ 375. Dismissal for Want of Prosecution; CPLR 3216

In Chapter 11, on the accelerated judgment, we discussed all of Article 32 of the CPLR

---

4. Uniform Rule 202.26(e).

5. Rule 16 of the Federal Rules of Civil Procedure.

6. UR 202.26(g).

7. See § 26 above.

8. See § 27 above. An amendment of the applicable rule in 1998 imposes a restriction on transfers down from the supreme to the New York City Civil Court Act under

CPLR 325(d). It provides that if it is not clear at the pretrial conference that the case would be tried faster in the civil than in the supreme court, there shall be no transfer unless it can be established that the civil court will try the case within 30 days after the conference. See the discussion in SPR 74:1.

9. See § 77D above.

except CPLR 3216[1], which authorizes a dismissal for the plaintiff's want of diligence in the prosecution of the action. This category of dismissal was saved for now because developments in the 1960s tied it to the note of issue, which therefore had to be treated first.

CPLR 3216 permits a want of prosecution dismissal only after the defendant has served on the plaintiff what is known as a 90–day notice (or "demand", as it is popularly referred to), giving the plaintiff a chance to serve and file the note of issue during the 90–day period following the demand. A plaintiff who serves and files the note within that time automatically avoids the dismissal—no matter how much past delay the plaintiff has been guilty of and no matter how inexcusable the delay may have been. This pro-plaintiff provision, which in essence wipes the slate clean of past laxness and gives the plaintiff a new start, is the product of an extraordinary lobbying effort, all in reaction to the 1963 case of Sortino v. Fisher,[2] in which the First Department abruptly overturned decades of judicial leniency and sharpened the teeth of the original CPLR 3216.

The CPLR 3216 enacted as part of the CPLR, which became effective on September 1, 1963, merely reproduced in substance its prior-law counterpart,[3] which in terse and general terms authorized a dismissal upon a showing that the plaintiff neglected to proceed in the action. While there would occasionally be dismissals under that provision, over the years the courts, recognizing the dire consequences attending a want of prosecution dismissal, showed themselves receptive to almost any excuse the plaintiff offered in resisting the motion. It was that list of excuses, grown long with time, that the Sortino case reviewed in depth and rejected almost in toto. It dismissed for want of prosecution a number of cases that the court had put together for purposes of a single, comprehensive opinion. The plaintiffs' bar found it devastating.

The source of the devastation should be noted right off. Although the court can specify that the dismissal is on the merits,[4] which the court would ordinarily do only if the pro and con papers delve into the merits and the court is convinced that the case has none,[5] the papers seldom go that deep and seldom, therefore, does the court designate that the dismissal is "on the merits", or "with prejudice", which is generally used to connote the same thing. The fear that in a future action the defense of res judicata will be interposed is therefore not a significant factor. The problem is the statute of limitations. The neglect to prosecute dismissal is one of the exceptions listed in CPLR 205(a), which means that there is no six-month period, from the dismissal, in which to sue again. If the original statute of limitations is still open, the action can of course be commenced anew without time barriers, but defendants, aware of that, will rarely make the motion until the statute has expired. The consternation of a 3216 dismissal, therefore, is the statute of limitations, and recognition of this dire prospect is what prompted the courts, before Sortino, to be generous in the acceptance of a plaintiff's excuses.

Handed down in December of 1963 when the CPLR was just a few months old, Sortino thrust at the heart of the so-called "negligence" bar: the lawyers representing plaintiffs in the omnipresent personal injury and wrongful death tort cases. Sortino struck a receptive chord in other courts throughout the state and quickly became a statewide authority, and without Court of Appeals involvement—the elements that go into the dismissal are discretionary and are therefore beyond the usual ken of the Court of Appeals. The court in Sortino actually numbered the various excuses

---

§ 375

1. Although CPLR 3216 is a "rule" rather than a statute, it is the product of the 1967 legislature. There is in any event little practical distinction between the two captions today. See § 2 above.

2. 20 A.D.2d 25, 245 N.Y.S.2d 186 (1st Dep't). The date of this key decision was December 10, 1963.

3. Civ.Prac.Act § 181.

4. CPLR 3216(a).

5. The court has discretion, however, to make the dismissal "on the merits" without actually considering the merits. Jones v. Maphey, 50 N.Y.2d 971, 431 N.Y.S.2d 466, 409 N.E.2d 939 (1980). It's an extraordinary thing to do. Fairer sanctions are at hand, as will be discussed.

tendered by plaintiffs over the years, treated them seriatim, and rejected them all. The listed excuses and the factors relevant to their consideration are these:

1. Extent of delay. The court noted that no particular period is required. Mere months may qualify.

2. Law office failures. The court rejected explanations based on the mistakes of the lawyers or their employees, a common source of excuse (overlooked calendars, misread papers, misplaced files, replaced secretaries, displaced associates, and the like). From its vantage point in *Sortino*, "law office failures" became the famous catchphrase of the later Barasch v. Micucci era.[6]

3. Settlement negotiations. That these are continuing ceases to be an excuse shortly after the last communication between the parties.

4. Other continuing pretrial activity, such as disclosure.

5. Statute of limitations. That it has run is no excuse for denying the motion, because the purpose underlying the statute of limitations (preserving evidence and witnesses and memories) can be defeated just as much by delay after commencement as by postponing commencement itself.

6. Defendant's duty. Attempts to blame the defendant for delay are unacceptable because the plaintiff, having brought the suit, is the one obliged to press it.

7. Plaintiff's belated activity. A spurt of activity by the plaintiff only on the eve of the dismissal motion may not be recognized.

8. Disabling circumstances. These may excuse delay (personal catastrophes or the need for foreign disclosure were cited as examples), but none such were adduced in the cases before the court in *Sortino*.

9. Parallel litigation. The need, for practical reasons, to await the outcome of other litigation might be an excuse. No such need in these cases.

10. Affidavit of merits. Since a neglect to prosecute is a kind of default, the court insisted that the plaintiff's papers in response to the motion attest in strong affidavits to the merits of the case, a showing commonly required of one who seeks to undo a default. The court held that a delayed case is suspect on the merits, and the longer the delay the greater the suspicion.

Around the state at the time of *Sortino* were literally hundreds of cases qualifying as neglected under *Sortino's* new guidelines, and at the prompt initiative of defendants—the "insurance" bar, as it is sometimes called—these cases began to get dismissed by the dozens. Cases were being lost, in effect by default, and lawyers were being left to face the possible personal consequences of a malpractice action, to which the dismissal can give rise if the delay is the lawyer's fault,[7] as it usually is. Possible disciplinary proceedings are also in prospect in that situation, which can mean censure,[8] or suspension,[9] or even disbarment.

Prompt efforts by the plaintiffs' bar to amend CPLR 3216 to restrict its use brought forth a 1964 amendment introducing the 90-day demand procedure—actually a 45-day demand procedure at the time but later increased to 90 days—but caselaw gave the amendment a restrictive interpretation and thus made it a virtual nullity.[10] Cases continued to get dismissed in large numbers for delay in prosecution. Intervening steps and

---

6. The Barasch case concerns the consequences of pleading defaults. See § 231 above.

7. See Gladden v. Logan, 28 A.D.2d 1116, 284 N.Y.S.2d 920 (1st Dep't 1967).

8. See Matter of Ribolow, 26 A.D.2d 579, 271 N.Y.S.2d 45 (2d Dep't 1966).

9. See Matter of Higgins, 27 A.D.2d 340, 279 N.Y.S.2d 197 (1st Dep't 1967).

10. The nullification consisted of interpreting the statute to apply only to a 3216 motion based on a failure to file a note of issue, not to one based on the plaintiff's "general" delay, although that was what the legislature meant to reach. The Court of Appeals ultimately upheld that interpretation in Thomas v. Melbert Foods, Inc., 19 N.Y.2d 216, 278 N.Y.S.2d 836, 225 N.E.2d 534 (1967). The result was that after the 1964 amendment, and right up until the 1967 overhaul of 3216, defendants were avoiding the 1964 amendment by simply phrasing their 3216 motions to address "general delay" rather than specifying the plaintiff's failure to file the note of issue.

developments are mainly of historic interest.[11] The next one important to note here is the 1967 statute.

Stung by their experience under the deconstrued 1964 amendment, the plaintiffs' bar pressed for and got a complete repeal of the old CPLR 3216 and the enactment of a new one, which is the one on the books today. It again required the 90–day (then still a 45–day) demand procedure, but now in unequivocal terms it said that no matter what delay the plaintiff may ever have been guilty of, all is forgiven and the action stays in court as long as the plaintiff files the note of issue within the 90 days following the defendant's demand. It even postponed the moment when such a demand could be served.

So construction-proof was the 1967 statute that the only way it could be avoided was to declare it unconstitutional, which is just what the First Department did, holding it to be an interference with the court's inherent power to control its calendars. This time, however, the Court of Appeals disagreed,[12] reversing the very case in which the appellate division so held, Cohn v. Borchard Affiliations.[13] The Court of Appeals held in *Cohn* that the power to regulate court procedure is with the legislature; that a procedure that can result in dismissal cannot, as can one designed merely to regulate the trial sequence of cases, be ascribed to mere calendar practice; and that for better or worse the 1967 statute is valid and its terms must be upheld and applied.

The present CPLR 3216 thus has free reign on its subject, and its requirements are clear. The dismissal can't be made earlier than a year after the joinder of issue and must be preceded by the defendant's service on the plaintiff, by registered or certified mail,[14] of a notice requiring resumption of prosecution and the filing of a note of issue by the plaintiff within 90 days following the notice. The notice must warn the plaintiff that a failure to comply will produce a CPLR 3216 motion.[15]

The interplay of these requirements means that the defendant can't serve the demand on the plaintiff until at least nine months have elapsed since the joinder of issue. Serving the demand at that time and then waiting 90 days, if the plaintiff does not comply, would enable the defendant to make the motion at just about the time that the year, measured from the joinder of issue, expires. CPLR 3216 is saying that as a practical matter a plaintiff has at least nine months from joinder in which to get the case ready before even being reminded about a CPLR 3216 motion, and at least a year from joinder before a motion can be made to dismiss for want of prosecution. These are the technical minimums, and a defendant prone to move under CPLR 3216 as promptly as possible had best take careful note of them. A premature motion may not even be entertained by the court.

If the plaintiff files the note of issue within the 90 days following the demand, the court is not permitted to consider delay preceding the demand, whether measured in months or years.[16] So carefully drawn was the rule that even the court must follow the 90–day demand procedure if it should seek the dismissal on its own motion rather than (as is more usual) await the defendant's.

A plaintiff who lets the 90–day period pass without filing the note of issue or without at least making a manifestly good-faith attempt to get the case moving, becomes subject to the

---

11. All of the developments are traced in Commentary C3216:3 on McKinney's CPLR 3216.

12. This is in contrast to the experience under the 1964 amendment, where the Court of Appeals in the Thomas case, note 10, above, upheld the First Department's restrictive view, which had been elaborated in Brown v. Weissberg, 22 A.D.2d 282, 254 N.Y.S.2d 628 (1964).

13. 25 N.Y.2d 237, 303 N.Y.S.2d 633, 250 N.E.2d 690 (1969), reversing 30 A.D.2d 74, 289 N.Y.S.2d 771 (1st Dep't 1968).

14. The Court of Appeals has held that the use of ordinary mail instead of the required registered or certified mail is not a jurisdictional defect as long as the plaintiff actually receives it. Balancio v. American Optical Corp., 66 N.Y.2d 750, 497 N.Y.S.2d 360, 488 N.E.2d 106 (1985).

15. CPLR 3216(b).

16. CPLR 3216(c), (d).

3216 motion.[17] Not infrequently, even a good faith attempt to file the note of issue within the 90 days may be frustrated by the certificate of readiness rule, which requires completion of disclosure and other pretrial proceedings before a note of issue can be filed.[18] The plaintiff should not be penalized if the readiness rule gets in the way, as long as the plaintiff can satisfy the court that she pressed forward as diligently as possible after being served with the 90–day demand.[19]

The best idea for the plaintiff who is trying to get the note of issue filed within the 90 days but finds that more time than that is needed is to ask the defendant for a stipulation extending the time, or, if the defendant won't stipulate, to make a motion for a time extension under CPLR 2004.[20] The psychological benefit of merely making the extension motion is that it does tend to suggest that the plaintiff is now trying.

A plaintiff near the border of the 90–day period and planning to mail the note of issue to the clerk should keep in mind Stein v. Wainwright's Travel Service, Inc.[21] The case holds that when mail is used, a "filing" with the clerk—which is the requirement that the plaintiff must meet within the 90 days—is not deemed to occur upon the mere posting, as it does when the applicable requirement is service rather than filing. Hence no filing is deemed to occur at that time, and in Stein the later moment when the filing actually took place was too late. The consequence to the plaintiff was a dismissal for want of prosecution. Mailing the note of issue on the 90th day is therefore asking for trouble.

Nor is the plaintiff who files the note of issue after the 90 days rescued by the mere fact that the filing occurs before the defendant makes the CPLR 3216 dismissal motion. The

motion still lies and the case is still subject to dismissal.[22]

The defendant's erroneously offering fewer than the required 90 days, as by erroneously referring in the notice to the 45 days originally enacted, does not invalidate the notice as long as the plaintiff ends up being accorded the required 90 days.[23]

The defendant waives no rights by serving a CPLR 3216 demand, such as the right to conduct disclosure proceedings during the 90–day period that the plaintiff has now been given to get the case ready,[24] but a waiver has been held to result, and by all parties, when the plaintiff complies with the demand by serving the note of issue within the required time.[25] The note of issue, it must be remembered, has to be accompanied by a certificate of readiness, which—if the defendants don't take prompt steps to vacate the note of issue[26]—constitutes a representation by all that the case is ready.

If and when the motion to dismiss for want of prosecution lies, and is made, its disposition on its merits will still be largely dictated by the Sortino case or any of the numerous subsequent decisions that approve and follow Sortino. Thus, while the legislative activity on CPLR 3216 has vastly reduced the number of cases susceptible to the motion, whichever cases do face it face Sortino as well.

One would think, with the tense lessons of the 1960s and the second chance the revised CPLR 3216 gives to plaintiffs, that the motion to dismiss for want of prosecution would virtually disappear from the practice. Hardly. Cases continued to appear all over the state in which the plaintiff bungled the second chance that the CPLR 3216 demand procedure offered, apparently not even trying to file the note of issue after duly receiving the 90–day notice.

---

17. CPLR 3216(e).

18. See § 370 above.

19. See Commentaries C3216:20, 21, 22 on McKinney's CPLR 3216.

20. See Nappi v. St. John's Cemetery, 73 A.D.2d 687, 423 N.Y.S.2d 240 (2d Dep't 1979).

21. 92 A.D.2d 961, 460 N.Y.S.2d 659 (3d Dep't 1983).

22. Scott v. Columbia Memorial Hospital, 134 A.D.2d 792, 522 N.Y.S.2d 257 (3d Dep't 1987).

23. Smith v. City of Troy, 77 A.D.2d 691, 429 N.Y.S.2d 796 (3d Dep't 1980), aff'd 54 N.Y.2d 890, 444 N.Y.S.2d 918, 429 N.E.2d 425 (1981).

24. Baxt v. Cohen, 96 A.D.2d 661, 466 N.Y.S.2d 737 (3d Dep't 1983).

25. Gray v. Crouse–Irving Memorial Hosp., Inc., 107 A.D.2d 1038, 486 N.Y.S.2d 540 (4th Dep't 1985).

26. See § 370 above.

Dismissals, although scaled down, still appeared, and in all departments.[27] They continue to even now, several decades after the 1967 amendment.

But also appearing from time to time afterwards was the assumption in the courts, appellate as well as original, that plaintiffs should not, or at least not always, be penalized for the delays of their attorneys. This prompted what seemed to be a near renunciation of the CPLR 3216 dismissal in some quarters, even if the 90–day demand procedure had been duly followed and the plaintiff had still not acted. One began to see frequently a denial of the motion even in that instance, but conditioned on the plaintiff's attorney paying costs of a specified sum to the defendant, including an attorney's fee, presumably (but not actually) representing the additional expense caused the defendant by having to resort to CPLR 3216.[28] In Neyra y Alba v. Pelham Foods, Inc.,[29] for example, the First Department, which begat and nurtured *Sortino*, was almost casual in denying a CPLR 3216 motion even though acknowledging that the plaintiff's opposing papers were "far from satisfactory". It said that clients should not suffer for the omissions of their lawyers, and required the lawyer personally to pay a stated sum to the defendant. This is not just a reflection of a change in the judicial personnel of the First Department, although that may be a factor; it would appear more to reflect a loss of confidence in a significant segment of lawyers and a pro rata abandonment of the idea that client and lawyer are professionally one.

It would be a mistake, however, for lawyers to be lax about their cases on the assumption that they can preserve them by paying a nominal sum to the defendant—and in this context a few hundred dollars may be nominal, indeed. Neither a possibility nor even a likelihood is a

guarantee, and a plaintiff can still find the case dismissed under CPLR 3216, especially if there is no solid evidence of an intention to keep it going. Even in *Neyra*, the court found that the plaintiff had no intention to abandon the case, thus enabling the case to abide as authority for an outright CPLR 3216 dismissal, rather than the mild alternative of a costs sanction, if the court in a different case is not able to make that finding. And the costs sanction, too, can be more than nominal; it can be measured in the thousands, depending on the nature of the case and the delay in prosecuting it.

Delay prior to the filing of the note of issue—delay that has put off the filing—has been the subject up to now. Laxness after the filing of the note of issue, while more likely to be punished by striking the case from the calendar under CPLR 3404,[30] can also or alternatively bring a dismissal under CPLR 3216, and may do so "irrespective of any compliance (or non-compliance) with a 90–day notice".[31]

The defendant's motion to dismiss the plaintiff's claim is the situation in most of the CPLR 3216 cases. But CPLR 3216 is generic in terminology and can work for a plaintiff moving against a counterclaim, a co-defendant moving against a cross-claim, etc.[32] And if there should be a CPLR 3216 dismissal of the plaintiff's claim, it does not bar the plaintiff from defending against any counterclaim that may remain standing,[33] presumably diligently prosecuted and therefore preserved.

Plaintiffs who would relieve their cases of any threat from CPLR 3216 should serve their pleadings and bills of particulars timely, set up all of their disclosure proceedings promptly, pressure the defendants to do the same—in letters of which copies are inserted in the file for potential future use in resisting CPLR

---

27. See, e.g., Palm v. American Progressive Health Ins. Co., 34 A.D.2d 629, 309 N.Y.S.2d 639 (1st Dep't 1970); Navillus Inc. v. Guggino, 34 A.D.2d 648, 310 N.Y.S.2d 13 (2d Dep't 1970); Beermont Corp. v. Yager, 34 A.D.2d 589, 308 N.Y.S.2d 109 (3d Dep't 1970).

28. See, e.g., Moran v. Rynar, 39 A.D.2d 718, 332 N.Y.S.2d 138 (2d Dep't 1972).

29. 46 A.D.2d 760, 761, 361 N.Y.S.2d 14, 15 (1974).

30. CPLR 3404 is treated in § 376 below.

31. Hillegass v. Duffy, 148 A.D.2d 677, 539 N.Y.S.2d 426 (2d Dep't 1989).

32. It is less likely that these claims, or a third-party claim, will meet want of prosecution objections because they usually depend on the initiative with which the plaintiff is pressing the main claim. See Commentary C3216:9 on McKinney's CPLR 3216.

33. Chin v. Chin, 44 A.D.2d 812, 355 N.Y.S.2d 422 (1st Dep't 1974).

3216 motions—and otherwise fulfill whatever the certificate of readiness requirement mandates. That will clear the path for the filing of the note of issue even if a 90–day demand of CPLR 3216 should appear, and it will remove the spectre of CPLR 3216 from the case.

§ 376. Dismissal of Abandoned Cases; CPLR 3404

Distinct from the dismissal for neglect to prosecute under CPLR 3216 is the dismissal under CPLR 3404. The CPLR 3216 dismissal is aimed primarily at cases so delayed that they have never reached the calendar. CPLR 3404, entitled "Dismissal of abandoned cases", is directed to cases that have reached the calendar but have afterwards been struck from it. The striking, or marking "off", usually results from a party's failure to appear at a duly scheduled "calendar call", whether conducted by a judge or by the clerk; or because a party appeared at the call without being ready to proceed and without good reason for an adjournment; or for still other reasons. Some of these fall under the heading of "Engagement of Counsel", a catch-all phrase and the caption of an important rule that sets up criteria and priorities to guide adjournment of a case in one court based on the engagement of one of the attorneys in some other.[1]

Whatever the reason for the striking, unless the court makes some direction to the contrary, CPLR 3404 requires that the case be restored to the calendar within one year afterwards or it shall be "deemed abandoned and ... dismissed ... for neglect to prosecute". In other words, the plaintiff, whose default is usually the one that invokes CPLR 3404, had best move to restore the case within a year or a dismissal will attend the case. The dismissal is a kind of automatic one, moreover: CPLR 3404 directs that the clerk, without any need

to involve the judge, make "an appropriate entry without the necessity of an order".

Because the dismissal under CPLR 3404 is explicitly labeled as a "neglect to prosecute", the plaintiff will not get from CPLR 205(a) any six-month period in which to sue anew if the original statute of limitations has expired, as it usually has.[2] The dismissal thus gets, in effect, the worst of two worlds: it's a neglect to prosecute in the CPLR 205(a) sense, forfeiting any limitations' extension, yet it's not governed by CPLR 3216—the major neglect to prosecute dismisser—and therefore does not get the protective 90–day demand procedure built into that rule. The practitioner also has to distinguish, for CPLR 205(a) purposes, between a dismissal under CPLR 3404, which gets no new limitations' period, and other kinds of analogous (but not identical) dismissals, which may or may not get it. If, for example, the plaintiff's case is dismissed for failure to select a jury and proceed to trial, it would seem at first blush to be a neglect to prosecute. But that depends on whether the trial judge, who made the dismissal, intended it to be such. A record indicating that that was the intention will mean no new period from CPLR 205(a),[3] while one suggesting that the dismissing judge did not regard the activity as a neglect to prosecute will earn the CPLR 205(a) limitations' extension.[4] These can be close questions, and a plaintiff is wise to assume the worst, taking precautions accordingly. The cautious plaintiff will not merely accept the dismissal and just try to sue over, but will try to get the case restored before dismissal, or, if dismissal there has already been, try to vacate it[5] and restore the case to the calendar.

Whether the motion to restore is made before or after a dismissal, however, the plaintiff must recognize that this is a category of de-

---

§ 376

1. See Part 125 of the Uniform Rules. A violation of this rule can ultimately lead to a default. See Romer v. Middletown School District, 137 Misc.2d 46, 519 N.Y.S.2d 924 (Sup.Ct., Orange County, 1987).

2. Pomerantz v. Cave, 10 A.D.2d 569, 195 N.Y.S.2d 437 (1st Dep't 1960).

3. See Wright v. L.C. Defelice & Son, Inc., 22 A.D.2d 962, 256 N.Y.S.2d 63 (2d Dep't 1964), aff'd 17 N.Y.2d 586, 268 N.Y.S.2d 345, 215 N.E.2d 522 (1966).

4. Schuman v. Hertz Corp., 17 N.Y.2d 604, 268 N.Y.S.2d 563, 215 N.E.2d 683 (1966), rev'g 23 A.D.2d 646, 257 N.Y.S.2d 400 (1st Dep't 1965).

5. The dismissal can be treated as the equivalent of a default and the motion to vacate it may be based on CPLR 5015(a)(1).

fault. The motion should therefore include the usual duet: an excuse for the default and an affidavit of merits.[6] Sometimes the court may also require a showing that the defendant is not prejudiced,[7] which suggests that the mere fact of delay does not give rise to a presumption of prejudice by itself.

The showing needed to restore a case under CPLR 3404 has been likened to that needed to defeat a motion to dismiss for want of prosecution under CPLR 3216.[8]

The rules play a role here, implementing and overlapping CPLR 3404. Uniform Rule 202.27, applicable in the supreme and county courts, applies not only when the call of a "calendar" is not answered, but also when a party does not appear at a duly scheduled "conference".[9] Even under CPLR 3404 itself, before the Uniform Rules arrived on the scene, it was held that CPLR 3404 would apply to the striking of a case from any calendar, even a motion calendar, if the case was on it to await a testimonial hearing of some kind.[10] Hence the rule seems quite compatible with CPLR 3404.

The rule suggests (but doesn't mandate) consequences that the judge may invoke when one side or the other defaults, such as a default judgment and inquest for the plaintiff when the defendant defaults, or a dismissal of the action when the plaintiff defaults. These consequences under the rules have to be coordinated with the consequence of missing a calendar call under CPLR 3404. In courts that are not under the Individual Assignment System (IAS) and in which the clerk still conducts a "calendar call", a case marked "off" is presumably still subject to the "deemed abandoned" impact of CPLR 3404 if not restored within a year. In courts that do have the IAS,

including of course the supreme court, there are less likely to be the kinds of "calendar call" that would invoke CPLR 3404. But if any individual judge should set up such a calendar call, and a case is unanswered and thereupon struck from the calendar, there is nothing to stop the CPLR 3404 consequence from visiting the case if the judge does not intervene with a different prescription.

The court will often today condition a restoration to the calendar on the payment of a sum of money to the defendant, presumably compensating the defendant for the inconvenience that way,[11] and will sometimes stress that the payment must be made by the plaintiff's attorney personally, not to be reimbursed by the client.[12] In counties and among judges with crowded calendars, a judge may even find it necessary to admonish defendants for not being vigorous enough in opposing restoration motions made by plaintiffs, as a judge did in a case that had been on the calendar 68 times![13]

The "shall be deemed abandoned and shall be dismissed" language of CPLR 3404, when the year has passed without restoration after the case was marked off the calendar, has the ring of the absolute to it. But it has been held to create only a presumption of abandonment, and a rebuttable one at that. The key decision is Marco v. Sachs,[14] a case that had been hanging fire in the courts for a quarter of a century—a page out of Dickens. Nonetheless, the Court of Appeals found that at the time of the calendar dismissal other activity connected with the case, including the pendency of three appeals, indicated that there was no intention to abandon it. Taking their cue from the *Marco* case, which enables the motion to restore to be made even after the year has expired (and

---

6. Renne v. Roven, 29 A.D.2d 866, 288 N.Y.S.2d 415 (2d Dep't 1968).

7. See Sal Masonry Contractors, Inc. v. Arkay Constr. Corp., 49 A.D.2d 808, 373 N.Y.S.2d 424 (4th Dep't 1975).

8. Shea v. City of New York, 77 A.D.2d 21, 432 N.Y.S.2d 87 (1st Dep't 1980).

9. The rules have two kinds of conference, one a "preliminary conference", see § 77D, and one a "pretrial conference", see § 374, above.

10. Marine Midland Bank v. Safari Animal Country, Inc., 110 A.D.2d 1024, 488 N.Y.S.2d 312 (3d Dep't 1985).

11. See, e.g., Barrada v. Target Constr. Corp., 31 A.D.2d 810, 299 N.Y.S.2d 708 (2d Dep't 1969).

12. See Schickler v. Seifert, 45 A.D.2d 816, 357 N.Y.S.2d 225 (4th Dep't 1974) (payment of $1000 required).

13. Butter v. Brookdale Hospital, 67 Misc.2d 727, 324 N.Y.S.2d 502 (Sup.Ct., Kings County, 1971).

14. 10 N.Y.2d 542, 226 N.Y.S.2d 353, 181 N.E.2d 392 (1962).

the case has presumably been dismissed), the courts have often permitted the abandonment presumption to be rebutted (and the case to be restored) upon a showing of relatively little activity. Continuing settlement negotiations and a pending motion, for example, have been held sufficient to show that the litigation was still in progress, warranting a restoration.[15] For a while, in fact, it seemed that less and less was qualifying more and more for the restoration as some courts sought to relieve clients of the omissions of their lawyers. A divided First Department restored one case, for example, which was more than 12 years old at restoration time, in which EBTs had been adjourned 24 times, the case adjourned on calendar calls 33 times, and 34 months had elapsed before the plaintiff got around to renewing an earlier restoration motion which had been denied for want of an affidavit of merits.[16] One wonders whether it is even advisable to flag these unusually generous—to plaintiff—cases. Practitioners can't safely depend on them. The courts in their area may, or may at the moment, be less generous, and plaintiffs who assume the worst are more likely to do their best.

A prolonged period after the dismissal, or after the passing of the year that generates the dismissal, without any activity to suggest that the case is alive, will of course cause the court to conclude that the action is dead, i.e., that the presumption of abandonment has become conclusive for want of rebuttal.[17]

As has been seen, the essence of the plaintiff's burden, when the plaintiff moves to restore during the year following the calendar striking, is to excuse the laxness. The plaintiff will thus be adducing proof, as already noted, similar to that used in opposing a motion to dismiss for neglect to prosecute under CPLR 3216, the motion that's made before the case goes on the calendar in the first place. Some-

times, when the plaintiff makes the CPLR 3404 motion to restore, the defendant will counter with a cross-motion to dismiss under CPLR 3216. The defendant does not have to; he can accomplish the same thing merely by opposing the plaintiff's motion. The cross-motion under CPLR 3216 is harmless, however, and its making in these circumstances should not invoke the 90–day notice requirement imposed by CPLR 3216. That requirement applies only when the dismissal motion is made before the filing of the initial note of issue.[18]

It should be remembered that the calendar is just as much the courts' concern as it is the parties'. Hence even if the defendant is willing to stipulate to the restoration of a stricken case, the stipulation is no guarantee under CPLR 3404. The best it will do is count as a factor in the exercise of discretion by the court, but the court has the final word on matters affecting its calendars.[19]

CPLR 3404 is applicable by its own terms to only the supreme and county courts, but lawyers should check into the rules of other courts in which they may find themselves. And whether or not the lower courts' rules refer to CPLR 3404, the provision may still find application in the lower courts through the general provisions of their court acts adopting the CPLR for matters not otherwise addressed.[20]

E.   MODE OF TRIAL

Table of Sections

§ 377.   Triability by Jury

Because different calendars are often kept for jury and nonjury cases, the time when the

15. Tactuk v. Freiberg, 24 A.D.2d 503, 261 N.Y.S.2d 438 (2d Dep't 1965).

16. Cichorek v. Cosgrove, 47 A.D.2d 883, 367 N.Y.S.2d 7 (1st Dep't 1975). The plaintiffs' attorney was directed to pay $350 to the defendant.

17. See Levine v. Levy, 31 A.D.2d 289, 297 N.Y.S.2d 215 (4th Dep't 1969).

18. Travelers Indemnity Co. v. Central Trust Co., 49 A.D.2d 1024, 374 N.Y.S.2d 483 (4th Dep't 1975).

19. See Incorporated Village of Thomaston v. Biener, 84 A.D.2d 781, 443 N.Y.S.2d 887 (2d Dep't 1981).

20. See, e.g., N.Y.C. Civil Court § 2102.

case first goes on the calendar is usually the occasion to determine the mode of trial as well, i.e., whether the facts are to be tried by a jury, the court, or a referee. Even under the Individual Assignment System (IAS), that remains the assumption, because the paper that puts the case on the calendar, the note of issue, is also the paper that includes a jury demand if a jury is desired.[1] That's the requirement of CPLR 4102(a), discussed in the next section. The mission of this one is to discuss which cases are triable by jury.

CPLR 4101 provides for the actions in which jury trial is required. For the most part they are the actions evolved through the common law courts, as opposed to those developed in equity (chancery), which continue to be triable by the court. The most numerous of the law actions is the simple money action, listed in CPLR 4101(1). Causes of action for money only, whether sounding in tort—such as the prolific personal injury, property damage, and wrongful death actions whether based on negligence, warranty, breach of a statutory duty, or strict products liability—or in contract, like the common actions for goods sold and delivered, services rendered, money loaned, damages for breach, etc., are all triable by jury. This of course refers to issues of fact; issues of law are for the court whatever the mode of trial of the facts.

In gauging whether to allow a jury trial, the courts tend to look at the relief being sought, at least if it's responsive to the facts pleaded. In the event of a conflict, the pleaded facts control the demand for relief. Where, for example, P demands only money of D (law), but the complaint manifests that P is entitled to an accounting from D (equity) if he is entitled to anything, the pleaded facts control the demand[2] and a jury would not be allowed.

If the demand for relief is responsive to the facts pleaded and both manifest a claim at law, the court is likely to allow a jury today even though the claim may have been interposed in a form generally regarded as equitable. Where, for example, a shareholder brought a derivative action in behalf of a corporation, joining the corporation as a defendant along with the alleged wrongdoers but without seeking any relief from the corporation, the court allowed trial by jury. It noted that the action sought money only without any equitable demand; that it would have been triable by jury had it been brought (as the plaintiff said it should have been) by the corporation itself; and that the claim's appearance in derivative rather than direct context should therefore not deprive a party of the substantial right to be heard by a jury. The court stressed the language of CPLR 4101(1) which, without addressing contexts, allows a trial by jury in any action "in which a party demands and sets forth facts which would permit a judgment for a sum of money only".[3]

Paragraph 2 of CPLR 4101 makes triable by jury actions for ejectment, dower,[4] waste, abatement of and damages for a nuisance, replevin (an action to recover a chattel), and the action to compel the determination of a claim to real property.[5]

Paragraph 3 is a reminder that a jury will also be allowed in any other actions in which it is either constitutionally guaranteed or afforded as a matter of legislative grace, and the relatively infrequent cases on CPLR 4101 are more likely to involve this paragraph than the first two. The New York Constitution guarantees trial by jury "in all cases in which it has heretofore been guaranteed by constitutional provision",[6] and the Court of Appeals held in Matter of Garfield's Estate[7] that this right cannot be divested by authorizing "a court of

§ 377

1. See the note of issue form contained in § 371 above.

2. See, e.g., Geddes v. Rosen, 22 A.D.2d 394, 255 N.Y.S.2d 585 (1st Dep't), aff'd 16 N.Y.2d 816, 263 N.Y.S.2d 10, 210 N.E.2d 362 (1965).

3. Fedoryszyn v. Weiss, 62 Misc.2d 889, 310 N.Y.S.2d 55 (Sup.Ct., Nassau County, 1970).

4. Dower actions are growing scarcer with the passing years. Dower was abolished in New York except as to

marriages entered into before September 1, 1930. See Real Prop.L. § 190.

5. This action is authorized and governed by Article 15 of the Real Property Actions and Proceedings Law.

6. Const. Art. I, § 2.

7. 14 N.Y.2d 251, 251 N.Y.S.2d 7, 200 N.E.2d 196 (1964).

equity", meaning a court in some other context than a plenary law action, to take jurisdiction of the claim.

The *Garfield* facts, involving the surrogate's court, illustrate. A was an attorney seeking to recover for services rendered to the testator. He made a claim for them by petitioning for an accounting in the surrogate's court.[8] The executrix rejected A's claim, thus necessitating a trial, and demanded a jury. A maintained that since the claim was asserted in an accounting proceeding in the surrogate's court, it took on an equitable air and lost its jury right. The Court of Appeals held that the claim's appearance in this context was not decisive; that the claim itself was one for money only and not governed by any equitable principles; and that it was therefore triable of constitutional right by jury, on the executrix's demand, even in the surrogate's court.[9]

A tracing of the constitutional sources preserving trial by jury starts with New York's first constitution, that of 1777. It guaranteed trial by jury in all cases in which it had "heretofore been used".[10] This was intended to carry forward with constitutional protection jury trial in all cases in which the common law afforded it. Later constitutions, through that of 1894, used similar terminology. The effect was to bestow a constitutional guarantee of trial by jury on all cases in which the legislature, between the 1777 and 1894 constitutions, had offered it only as a matter of legislative grace. Among the actions and proceedings in which that happened, for example, and in which today the right to trial by jury is therefore a constitutional one, is the so-called "discovery proceeding" in the surrogate's court, by which the personal representative can seek data

about assets belonging to the decedent and compel the possessor to hand them over.[11] The 1894 constitution was the last one to use the "heretofore used" language. The 1938 constitution gives the jury guarantee only to cases in which jury trial had been previously "guaranteed by constitutional provision"—language still applicable.[12] The result is that all cases on which the legislature conferred the right of trial by jury after 1894 get it today only from statute, if at all, and not as a constitutional right. If a demand is made for a jury in a case not specified for jury trial in any statute, the judge must determine whether a jury was required at common law or offered by a statute enacted between 1777 and 1894.[13] It is not a frequent inquiry, but as the discourses in *Garfield* and in the more recent Court of Appeals treatment in Motor Vehicle Manufacturers Ass'n v. State of New York[14] indicate, it can be a complex one.

In the *Motor Vehicle* case, which the court handed down early in 1990, the constitutionality of the procedure set up by the New York Lemon Law was at issue. The procedure calls for arbitration of a dispute between a car buyer and the car's manufacturer, but only at the option of the buyer. This, complained the manufacturer, divested it of the right to trial by jury. The court analyzed the remedies offered to the owner by the Lemon Law—either replacement of the vehicle or a refund of the full purchase price—and found both of them equitable in nature. Hence, held the court, there was no divestiture of the right to trial by jury and the Lemon Law procedure was upheld.

There are a number of statutes besides CPLR 4101 that authorize trial by jury. Jury is

---

8. Authorization for making the claim in this mode after it has been rejected by the personal representative is in SCPA 1808.

9. Had A rather than the executrix demanded the jury, a jury would not have been allowed for the reason that A's submission of the claim to the surrogate's court was voluntary. A had the option—which the executrix had not—of bringing the claim as an ordinary money action in some other court after its rejection, see SCPA 1810, in which other court either party could have demanded a jury.

10. Const. 1777, Art. XLI.

11. See Matter of Goldfarb's Estate, 18 Misc.2d 773, 188 N.Y.S.2d 55 (Surr.Ct., N.Y. County, 1959). The discovery proceeding is today governed by SCPA 2103 and 2104, whose predecessors were added by L.1870, ch. 359, 394.

12. See Const. Art. I, § 2.

13. See Matter of Luria's Estate, 63 Misc.2d 675, 313 N.Y.S.2d 12 (Surr.Ct., Kings County, 1970).

14. 75 N.Y.2d 175, 551 N.Y.S.2d 470, 550 N.E.2d 919 (1990).

allowed in divorce cases[15] and in most annulment actions.[16] It is allowed also in the ubiquitous summary proceeding to recover the possession of real property, the common landlord-tenant forum,[17] but valid waiver provisions commonly found in leases make trial by jury in summary proceedings infrequent.[18] CPLR provisions other than 4101 may also offer jury trial.[19] Whether these and similar statutes have constitutional underpinnings is an inquiry needed only if the legislature should by mere statute attempt to rescind the right to trial by jury in the given instance.[20]

The fact that among the actions in which trial by jury is preserved are those in which it was used prior to 1777 accounts for the main surviving distinction between law and equity today, despite the merger of the two systems. In pre–1777 New York, when it was an English colony, jury trial was allowed in law actions but not in chancery (equity) suits.[21] The merger of law and equity has in many respects obscured the differences between the two, and, with the liberalization of practice and procedure, claims previously associated with one context can now arise in different ones. It is the changed-context claim that is likely to account for the relatively few instances in which a traceback of the claim, to determine its pre–1777 antecedents and hence its triability by jury, is needed today. This was so in the *Garfield* case, for example, where a simple money claim (law) appeared in an "accounting" context (presumably equity) in the surrogate's court, the Court of Appeals downgrading the context and awarding the right to a jury based on the relief sought. Similar conclusions explain how a jury is awarded on a simple money claim interposed in a corporation's behalf in a derivative suit.[22]

Perhaps the most interesting case in which to inquire about the necessity for a jury is the

declaratory judgment action, which did not come into being in New York until long after the merger of law and equity. Because the declaratory action is not taken up until later in this book, however, treatment of trial by jury in that category of action is also postponed until then.[23]

Sometimes trial by jury, otherwise required, has been abolished by the constitution, or by a statute with constitutional sanction. A notable illustration here is the worker's compensation claim.[24]

CPLR 4101 declares that "equitable defenses and equitable counterclaims" are to be tried by the court; this applies even though they are interposed in what is otherwise a law action. Where, for example, P sues for money on a contract and D counterclaims for reformation of that contract, the reformation claim is clearly equitable and if tried separately from the main claim, which it may be, does not get a jury. The same would be true even if all the defendant wants to accomplish with the "counterclaim" is to avoid liability on the plaintiff's claim, i.e., where the defendant is in effect using the "counterclaim" as a defense. Under prior law, much effort was spent determining whether a counterclaim was being used as a mere "defense" to the main claim, in which case it would go to a jury if the main claim did, or as a true "counterclaim", in which event the court would try it. CPLR 4101 spares that effort by directing the court to try it without a jury whatever category it falls under.[25]

The nature of this kind of "counterclaim-defense" will be looked at by the court, which will then determine whether a jury is required, even where twice removed from the main claim. Where, for example, P sued for money and D pleaded release as a defense, P in a

---

15. Dom.Rel.L. § 173.

16. Dom.Rel.L. § 143.

17. RPAPL § 745.

18. As to waiver of jury trial, see § 378, below.

19. See, e.g., CPLR 3034(3), treated in § 609, below.

20. See generally 2d Rep.Leg.Doc. (1958) No. 13, pp. 217–8.

21. See Matter of Luria, note 13, above.

22. See Fedoryszyn v. Weiss, note 3, above, and text at that point.

23. See § 439 below.

24. Const. Art. I, § 18.

25. See Menado Corp. v. Indemnity Ins. Co. of N. Amer., 53 Misc.2d 533, 279 N.Y.S.2d 84 (N.Y.C.Civ.Ct. 1967).

reply then sought to rescind the release. Whether regarded as a counterclaim or as a defense, the rescission demand contained in the reply was held equitable and not triable by jury. Furthermore, since everything else in the case depended first on the rescission demand, it was even granted a separate and prior trial.[26]

A counterclaim interposed in its own right rather than just as an offset—by "offset" is meant a mere endeavor to neutralize the plaintiff's claim—will be independently measured for triability by jury, a matter discussed in the next section.

When there are both legal and equitable claims present, the court may have to do some careful analyzing to determine the proper allotment of the fact-finding function, a matter illustrated in Mercantile & General Reinsurance Co. v. Colonial Assur. Co.,[27] in which S was in the business of guaranteeing that capital equipment would have a specific residual value at a stated future date. To make its product more attractive to customers, S secured insurance with X to back up its guarantees. X then reinsured with insurer P. Alleging that misrepresentations had been made by S, P later brought suit against both S and X for a formal rescission of the reinsurance contract. The rescission claim was equitable and triable by the court without a jury. But S counterclaimed against P for money damages in both contract and tort based on S's loss of customers. That claim sounded at law and was jury triable.

A jury was impaneled to hear the case and the judge gave the jury interrogatories covering both the legal and equitable claims. The answers revealed that the jury's verdict was for S: that S had made no misrepresentations and that P breached the contract. The verdict was of course binding in respect of the law claim, but only advisory on the rescission

claim, which, sounding in equity, was for the court to decide. Exercising its prerogative to disregard the advisory segment of the verdict, the trial court set aside the jury's finding that S had made no misrepresentations and found that S did make them. It awarded P judgment rescinding the contract.

The Court of Appeals upheld the trial court's power to do this, even though the upholding of the equitable rescission claim would nullify the verdict the jury had awarded S on its money counterclaim. The court pointed out that the facts in respect of the rescission claim did not overlap any of the facts the jury found on the law claim, observing that

> [t]o find material misrepresentation [which grounds rescission], the court did not need to contradict any of the factual findings the jury made in deciding the factual issues pertinent to the legal claim for breach of contract because a finding of material misrepresentation is not inconsistent with a finding that the parties entered into a contract. To the contrary, the very essence of a rescission action is to set aside a contract that is otherwise valid and binding.[28]

§ 378. Demand and Waiver of Trial by Jury

CPLR 4102 contains the basics about how to demand trial by jury and the ways in which a jury may be waived. (We assume, of course, that the case is one triable by jury.) Trial by jury must as a rule be affirmatively demanded and the place to demand it is in the note of issue. Thus, if the party filing the note of issue (any party may file it[1]) wants a jury trial, she must demand it in the note of issue. This is usually done simply by putting a check mark in the appropriate box on a printed note of

---

26. See Rill v. Darling, 44 Misc.2d 174, 253 N.Y.S.2d 184 (Sup.Ct., Madison County, 1964). For the origin of this problem and the distinction between an equitable and a legal defense, see 2d Rep.Leg.Doc. (1958) No. 13, p. 576.

27. 82 N.Y.2d 248, 604 N.Y.S.2d 492 (1993).

28. The case is the subject of the lead note in New York State Law Digest No. 409. Its impact is explored at

length in Gegan, Turning Back the Clock on the Trial of Equitable Defenses in New York, 68 St. John's L. Rev. 823 (1994).

§ 378

1. CPLR 3402(a).

issue form.[2] If a party served with a note of issue not containing the demand wants a jury trial, his procedure is to file, within 15 days after being served with the note, a "demand" for trial by jury. If no party demands trial by jury in one of these ways, trial by jury is waived.[3] A note of issue silent as to jury is therefore a waiver of it by the one filing the note. The CPLR does allow the chief administrator of the courts to provide by rule for the reverse: that a silent note of issue is deemed to demand the jury;[4] but the note of issue filer, if she wants jury trial, does herself no harm by affirmatively making the demand for it in the note of issue even if such a rule is in force. A party who would rely on such a rule, in any event, had best ascertain that it is currently in force. Trial by jury is a substantial right and it is sometimes easy to overlook rule changes.

Once trial by jury has been duly demanded by a party, the demand can't be withdrawn without the consent of the other parties.[5] This is designed to enable each party to rely on a jury demand made by any other, obviating an additional demand and sparing, in a multi-party case, a plethora of demands. This rule was always dependable enough when the note of issue contained the demand: those on whom the note is served can rely on it and withhold their own demands.[6] The Court of Appeals held in Gonzalez v. Concourse Plaza Syndicates, Inc.,[7] however, that if the note of issue omits the demand, and some other party demands the jury, the demander may later withdraw the demand without the consent of the party who filed the note of issue, but *Gonzalez* was overruled in a 1990 amendment of CPLR 4102(a), explicitly requiring consent of all parties to the withdrawal of a jury demand "regardless of whether another party previously filed a note of issue without a demand for trial by jury".

The one who first demands a jury may specify only certain issues on which trial by jury is sought. Absent such a specification, the demand will be deemed to cover all issues. If the demand is for only some issues, any other party may, within 10 days after service of the limited demand, serve and file a demand for jury trial of some or all of the rest of the issues.[8] In order to save the time and trouble of trial by jury, the rules may express a preference that if only some issues are to be tried by jury, those that are not should be tried first,[9] just in case they prove dispositive and make a jury trial unnecessary.

CPLR 4102(c) provides that a party will also waive trial by jury by failing to appear at the trial, by filing a written waiver with the clerk, or by waiving it orally in open court, and that these things will waive the jury even if that party is the one who previously demanded it. But if such a demand was duly made, any other party may continue to rely on it; that is, an attempted waiver now by the one who demanded the jury will not cancel the jury if any other party still wants it. Thus, once a demand has been made by one party and relied on by the others, some kind of waiver conduct will generally have to be shown against all parties before trial by jury will be cancelled.

In this era of calendar congestion, many judges, recognizing that a trial with a jury is much more demanding and time consuming than one without, welcome jury waivers. Sometimes they may even suggest the waiver. This is permissible only if no undue pressure is brought to bear by the judge. Judicial pressure is often difficult for a lawyer to resist, and if an appellate court finds on the record that the judge overstepped discretion in exacting the waiver, such as where the judge threatened to declare a mistrial and start over unless the case was continued before him without the

---

2. See § 371, above, for the note of issue form.

3. CPLR 4102(a).

4. CPLR 4102(d).

5. CPLR 4102(a).

6. This is not true of practice in the surrogate's court, where each party desiring jury trial must demand it independently and where each demander is entitled to withdraw the demand later without the consent of other par-

ties. SCPA 502(2)(a), (5)(b). See the Commentary on McKinney's SCPA 502.

7. 41 N.Y.2d 414, 393 N.Y.S.2d 362, 361 N.E.2d 1011 (1977), following Downing v. Downing, 32 A.D.2d 350, 302 N.Y.S.2d 334 (1st Dep't 1969).

8. CPLR 4102(b).

9. See, e.g., Uniform Rule 202.40.

jury, it will undo the coerced stipulation of waiver and remand the case for a new trial.[10]

Jury waiver can result in other ways than those recited by CPLR 4102(c). It can be waived in a contract between the parties,[11] and as long as no deceit is shown affecting the waiver of jury clause, a mere unawareness of the clause's existence will not necessarily undo the waiver.[12] There is some dispute about that, however.[13] The waiver should in any event be clear and unequivocal, for it will be strictly construed against the party who drafted the instrument containing it.[14]

Even if the waiver is in an "adhesion" contract, it is apparently valid. They have been held valid, in any event, in one category often qualifying as an adhesion contract: the apartment lease. The lease waiver suffices to cancel jury trial in the summary proceeding, the usual landlord/tenant device designed to collect the rent or dispossess the tenant for nonpayment or for holding over past term,[15] but in actions between landlord and tenant "for personal injury or property damage" the waiver has been made ineffective by statute,[16] thus preserving the right to trial by jury in those categories.[17]

A waiver resulting from a failure to comply with CPLR 4102, such as by omitting to demand a jury by the methods specified, can be relieved by the court "if no undue prejudice to the rights of another party would result".[18] Intentional waivers are not likely to be undone on this authority,[19] but if the waiver was inadvertent, such as where the paper first filed omitted the jury demand but was corrected

shortly afterwards by a refiling with a paper containing the demand, it has been forgiven and the late demand accepted.[20] Needless to say, the party relying on such an amnesty is tempting fate; trial by jury is too precious to let pass as a matter of right and then seek as a matter of discretion—which the court has much of in determining whether to forgive a waiver.

A waiver of trial by jury is itself waivable. If a contract waives trial by jury, for example, but a jury is demanded and no one makes a timely objection to it, trial by jury will proceed.[21]

The joinder of claims, or of different demands for relief in respect of but a single claim, is a sensitive area when jury trial is at stake and should be carefully considered. The rules come from CPLR 4102(c). If a plaintiff has two or more entirely separate claims emanating from separate transactions, the plaintiff can under the rules of joinder sue on them in one action,[22] and if one claim asks legal relief (jury) and the other equitable relief (no jury), the plaintiff will not, by the joinder, forfeit the right to a jury trial on the legal claim. But a plaintiff who joins claims or demands based on the same transaction, asking legal relief on one and equitable relief on the other, or in the alternative, waives trial by jury entirely. Thus, the plaintiff who seeks both money damages (jury) and an injunction (no jury) based on the same transaction will be held to waive trial by jury even on the money claim. But this does not affect the defendant, who can still demand

10. Kay v. Tankel, 16 A.D.2d 96, 225 N.Y.S.2d 642 (1st Dep't 1962).

11. See International Roofing Corp. v. Van Der Veer, 43 Misc.2d 93, 250 N.Y.S.2d 387 (Sup.Ct., Monroe County, 1964).

12. James Talcott, Inc. v. Wilson Hosiery Co., 32 A.D.2d 524, 299 N.Y.S.2d 460 (1st Dep't 1969).

13. See Colgate Construction Corp. v. Hill, 70 Misc.2d 646, 334 N.Y.S.2d 1002 (Mount Vernon City Ct., 1972).

14. Barrow v. Bloomfield, 30 A.D.2d 947, 293 N.Y.S.2d 1007 (1st Dep't 1968).

15. See Belmont Theatre Corp. v. Bunny Cinema Corp., 71 Misc.2d 379, 336 N.Y.S.2d 298 (N.Y.C.Civ.Ct. 1972).

16. Real Prop.L. § 259–c.

17. See Avenue Associates, Inc. v. Buxbaum, 83 Misc.2d 719, 373 N.Y.S.2d 814 (App.T., 1st Dep't 1975), rev'g 83 Misc.2d 134, 371 N.Y.S.2d 736 (N.Y.C.Civ.Ct. 1975).

18. CPLR 4102(e).

19. See Heller v. Hacken, 40 A.D.2d 1012, 338 N.Y.S.2d 943 (2d Dep't 1972).

20. See Matter of Mirsky's Estate, 81 Misc.2d 9, 365 N.Y.S.2d 122 (Surr.Ct., N.Y.County, 1975).

21. See Import Alley of Mid–Island, Inc. v. Mid–Island Shopping Plaza, Inc., 103 A.D.2d 797, 477 N.Y.S.2d 675 (2d Dep't 1984).

22. CPLR 601.

a jury on the money claim.[23]

Similarly, a defendant who interposes a counterclaim, cross-claim, or third-party claim, itself jury triable, in an action in which the main claim is not jury triable, does not waive the jury on the new claim, and that is so even though all of the claims come from the same transaction. This, too, is the assurance of CPLR 4102(c). Thus, where P sues for specific performance (no jury) and D counterclaims for money damages (jury) on the same contract, D is entitled to jury trial of the counterclaim. But when the claims are reversed, and P brings a claim triable by jury and D meets it with a related counterclaim not triable by jury, there is presently a conflict. Some courts hold that D waives trial by jury even on P's law claim in that situation;[24] others say no and preserve D's right to jury trial on the law claim on the theory that a contrary holding would only encourage D to bring his equitable claim separately because by so doing she would preserve the right to demand a jury trial in P's law action.[25]

Suppose that the interposer of the law claim wants a jury trial, is entitled to it, and demands it. What happens if the nonjury claim, interposed by the other party, involves common issues of fact, as is likely to be the case when all the claims arise out of the same transaction? Take the example of P suing for damages for breach of a realty contract (jury triable with a jury duly demanded by P), with D counterclaiming for specific performance (for which there is no jury). Since each contends that the other breached the contract, the facts can ordinarily be determined only one way. The jury will have to try the facts on the damages claim while the court must resolve the same facts on the specific performance claim. If judge and jury disagree, there is an apparent dilemma, which seems to have no theoretical solution. It does have a practical one, however. As will be seen in a later section, the court has the power to convene an "advisory" jury even for cases triable by the court.[26] Exercising that power, the court can treat the jury, impaneled as of right for the damages claim, as an advisory one on the specific performance claim, and merely adopt the jury's findings, if supportable, to dispose of all the claims.[27]

Yet another possibility in this situation might be to have one claim tried before the other, which is usually in the court's discretion to do as a matter of the sequence of trial.[28] The problem this time is that if the nonjury claim is tried first and its results are sought to be given res judicata effect on the jury claim, it can amount to a back-door divestiture of jury trial.[29] When the equitable claim is one to rescind a contract, the Court of Appeals has held that it may be decided by the court even if its effect is to bar jury-triable damages claims based on the same contract and interposed by other parties to the action.[30] The court does not apprehend this as a negation of the right to trial by jury because the right doesn't arise unless there's a contract and the court in the exercise of its equity powers can, by ordering a rescission, determine that there is none.

Another situation that periodically arises is that in which the parties prepare for only one mode of trial, based on a claim initially interposed, only to have it appear at the trial itself that another mode is appropriate. This happens, for example, when P brings an equitable claim and has it processed all the way through to trial on the nonjury calendar. It is now tried by the judge, who finds that P, while not having made out a claim for equitable relief, has established enough to warrant a law recov-

---

23. Heller v. Hacken, note 19, above.

24. See Compact Electra Corp. v. Connell, 46 A.D.2d 649, 359 N.Y.S.2d 686 (2d Dep't 1974).

25. See, e.g., International Playtex, Inc. v. CIS Leasing Corp., 115 A.D.2d 271, 495 N.Y.S.2d 864 (4th Dep't 1985).

26. CPLR 4212. See § 381 below.

27. See Motor Vehicle Manufacturers Ass'n v. State of New York, 75 N.Y.2d 175, 551 N.Y.S.2d 470, 550 N.E.2d 919 (1990), discussed in § 377 above. See also John W.

Cowper Co. v. Buffalo Hotel Development Venture, 99 A.D.2d 19, 471 N.Y.S.2d 913 (4th Dep't 1984).

28. CPLR 4011, 603. See Vinlis Construction Co. v. Roreck, 23 A.D.2d 895, 260 N.Y.S.2d 245 (2d Dep't 1965).

29. See Import Alley of Mid–Island, Inc. v. Mid–Island Shopping Plaza, Inc., note 21, above.

30. This is what occurred in the Motor Vehicle Manufacturers case, note 27, above.

ery.[31] If D objects, on the reasonable ground that he would have been entitled to a jury had the case been processed, as it should have been, as a law claim, D must now be afforded an opportunity to demand a jury trial before the legal relief can ensue.[32] This can entail (after impaneling a jury) a whole new trial. The court may even require an amended complaint, specifying legal relief,[33] and, as a calendar matter, order the case re-noticed for trial on a jury calendar.[34]

The converse of the above, a case starting out at law and therefore being tried by jury only to have it appear at the trial that equitable relief is permissible and is now sought by the plaintiff, is a rarity. And should it arise, it's not a serious problem. The jury can merely be dismissed, and the judge, in attendance all the while, can make the findings of fact bearing on the equitable claim. The court must be sensitive in this instance, however, to permit the defendant to introduce any defenses he may have to the equitable claim that were not relevant to the legal claim, such as the defense of laches, or clean hands.

§ 379. Triability by Referee

The CPLR provides that if the case is triable by neither a jury nor a referee, it is tried by the judge.[1] Triability by jury was the subject of the prior sections; trial by the judge is the subject of the next one. Trial by referee is the subject of this one. When may a referee be the trier?

A referee is a person (usually a lawyer[2]) appointed by the court to conduct a hearing or to perform some court-related function. Also permitted to serve as a "referee" is a "judicial hearing officer", a retired judge who has been duly certified as able to perform judicial duties.[3]

The CPLR recognizes three kinds of references: (1) to determine an issue; (2) to perform an act; and (3) to hear and report on an issue.[4] The reference to determine, category 1, means that the referee hears the case as the court would; the decision is binding. There are several kinds of category 2 references (for the performance of acts), found in and out of the CPLR. One CPLR kind is the assignment of a referee to supervise all disclosure proceedings in a case.[5] A frequently met kind is the referee appointed to mortgage, lease, or sell real property in various contexts.[6] The reference to hear and report, category 3, makes the referee a kind of assistant to the court; the referee conducts a hearing and reports her findings and conclusions back to the court, which can accept or reject them. The report of a referee to report, in other words, is only a recommendation, while the decision of a referee to determine is binding, like the decision of a judge.

The provisions about referees are not in the best order in the CPLR. By its title, "Trial by a Referee", Article 43 would seem to reposit all one needs to know about referees, but while it does supply the general powers and procedures to be followed by referees, it is CPLR 4001 which in broad language invests the court with the power to appoint them. And yet the appointment power in CPLR 4001 lacks specifics. These may be found in Article 43 for the reference to determine,[7] and in Article 42 for the reference to report.[8] Article 42 con-

31. An example would be a claim for specific performance found at the trial to be barred by laches, while a damages claim, which is not subject to the laches doctrine, is alive and sustainable.

32. CPLR 4103.

33. Newman v. Resnick, 38 Misc.2d 94, 238 N.Y.S.2d 119 (Sup.Ct., N.Y.County, 1963).

34. Vinlis Construction Co. v. Roreck, note 28, above.

§ 379

1. CPLR 4211.

2. CPLR 4312(1).

3. See CPLR 105. A 1983 amendment of CPLR 4301 included the judicial hearing officer in the "referee" definition. Related amendments in CPLR 4312, 4313, 4315, and 4321 are discussed in the Commentaries on those provisions in McKinney's CPLR.

4. CPLR 4001. One might consider as a fourth kind a reference to receive and report evidence, see CPLR 4311, which presumably means that the referee will not even suggest tentative conclusions but leave them entirely to the judge.

5. CPLR 3104.

6. See RPAPL § 1611.

7. CPLR 4317.

8. CPLR 4212.

cerns trial by the court; since the reference to report is only a recommendation, the court retaining the power and responsibility of the final decision, Article 42 was deemed the proper place for it.

The reference to determine is authorized by CPLR 4317, which provides in subdivision (a) for the reference by consent of the parties and in subdivision (b) for the reference by court direction regardless of the parties' consent.

CPLR 4317(a) states that when the parties stipulate, "any issue" shall be determined by a referee, and it permits the parties to designate the referee themselves. But in three listed instances a reference to determine, even if desired by all parties, requires leave of court and requires that the court designate the referee: (1) matrimonial actions; (2) certain actions to dissolve a corporation or to receive or distribute its property; and (3) actions in which a defendant is an infant.

The matrimonial exception is designed to prevent the parties from getting themselves a simple consent divorce or other matrimonial relief merely by appointing a referee who will give them what they want without regard to the evidence. The corporate dissolution exception contemplates the proceedings of Article 11 of the Business Corporation Law.[9]

The reference to determine without the parties' consent, which comes from CPLR 4317(b), is commonly known as a "compulsory reference". This category of reference is authorized in "long account" cases or to try damages if they are separately triable and don't require trial by jury. The "long account" case is an old example of the compulsory reference. If the account involved is a "long" one in this sense, it can even take the fact-findings away from a jury, and, over the objections of a

party, give them to a referee to determine, presumably a person of expertise in the subject involved. This is constitutional because New York's first constitution, that of 1777, guaranteed trial by jury only in cases in which it was theretofore used,[10] and the pre–1777 practice was to allow the compulsory reference of a long account.[11]

That a long account is involved, sufficient to invoke this compulsory reference provision, must appear from the plaintiff's statement of the cause of action in the complaint, however. If only a counterclaim manifests a long account, the compulsory reference may not be used unless the counterclaiming defendant in effect concedes the plaintiff's claim—because that's the way things were before 1777.[12] The quantity of items the account involves is not the sole or even the main criterion for determining whether it is a "long" one, justifying the reference. It must be shown that the account is so long and detailed, and its diverse parts so hard to keep in mind, that a jury would find "great trouble" in resolving it.[13] But it need not be a law action that presents the long account and invokes the compulsory reference. An equity action—of which the accounting action itself would be the most relevant example in this context—can do it, too,[14] although the contract action at law is the context from which the compulsory reference arose.[15]

The compulsory reference has been cited by analogy to sustain the special system of appointing "housing judges" to the housing part of the New York City Civil Court pursuant to § 110 of its court act.[16]

The other provision of CPLR 4317(b), authorizing a nonconsensual reference "to deter-

---

9. See Dalminter, Inc. v. Siderexport S.p.A., 23 A.D.2d 749, 258 N.Y.S.2d 954 (1st Dep't 1965). If the action is brought by the Attorney–General, leave of court for the reference is not needed. CPLR 4317(a).

10. The history of jury trial is discussed in § 377 above.

11. The leading case on the point, replete with historical traceback, is Steck v. Colorado Fuel & Iron Co., 142 N.Y. 236, 37 N.E. 1 (1894).

12. See Schaffer v. City Bank Farmers Trust Co., 269 N.Y. 336, 199 N.E. 503 (1936).

13. Longo v. Adirondack Drilling, Inc., 14 A.D.2d 476, 217 N.Y.S.2d 905 (3d Dep't 1961).

14. See Thayer v. McNaughton, 117 N.Y. 111, 22 N.E. 562 (1889).

15. Steck v. Colorado Fuel & Iron Co., note 11, above.

16. See Glass v. Thompson, 51 A.D.2d 69, 379 N.Y.S.2d 427 (2d Dep't 1976). At the outset the housing judges were called "hearing officers".

mine an issue of damages separately triable and not requiring a trial by jury," was added by the CPLR's drafters because, they stated, the same reason justifying the compulsory reference of long account cases—their intricacy and difficulty—applies as well to the trial of complex damages issues.[17] This provision, unlike the provision that governs the long account, retains jury trial if a jury is otherwise required for the damages issue. Damages are "separately triable" in several situations. One is where summary judgment has been granted on liability and only damages remain to be tried.[18] If the case would have gone to trial by jury if there had been no summary judgment, the damages trial must also be by jury if a party insists.[19] CPLR 4317(b) acknowledges this and thereby wards off the risk of being found unconstitutional. An instance in which damages are "separately triable" and where a compulsory reference might be allowed is where a default has conceded liability.[20]

All we have just discussed concerns the reference to determine. The referee to determine has the same powers the court would have in carrying out a like function, except that a referee can't relieve himself of his duties or appoint a successor. He has the power to punish for contempt a witness before him, but no other contempt powers,[21] so he can't enforce a decision through the contempt power, as a judge might do on certain judgments. It has also been held that a referee may not decide to bifurcate[22] a trial, i.e., try liability and damages in separate segments; that since CPLR 4311 says specifically that the order assigning a referee shall direct the referee to determine "the entire action or specific issues", the deci-sion about what the referee is to try "will already have been made".[23]

The reference to report, because it amounts to only a recommendation rather than a final decision, is not quite so delicate. (A reference made just "for hearing", without specifying what kind it is, will ordinarily be assumed to be a reference to hear and report.[24]) Although the parties in a jury-triable case can waive the jury and agree instead to a reference to report (or, for that matter, a reference to determine), this category of reference is mainly associated with court-triable issues. The main source of the reference to report is CPLR 4212, which allows the court to submit "any issue of fact required to be decided by the court" to a referee to report, but only "upon a showing of some exceptional condition requiring it or in matters of account".[25]

The reference to report may be sought under CPLR 4212 on the motion of a party. A motion for trial by a referee should ordinarily be made within 20 days after the note of issue is filed.[26] This presumably applies to the reference to determine as well as to the reference to report, but in either instance the 20 days should be subject to extension.[27] The rule is that an application for a reference should not be made before the note of issue is filed.[28]

The reference to determine may of course be directed by the court sua sponte, but so may a reference to report be made by the court "on its own initiative"[29]—assuming of course that the "exceptional" condition or the account is present. This suggests that the consent of the parties to a reference to report is not needed. That, indeed, is the assumption of much case-law, even including cases that demonstrate

---

17. See 2d Rep.Leg.Doc. (1958) No. 13 at pp. 250–1.

18. CPLR 3212(c).

19. Livingston v. Blumenthal, 248 App.Div. 138, 289 N.Y.S. 5 (1st Dep't 1936). See Commentary C3212:27 on McKinney's CPLR 3212.

20. For the right to jury trial in that situation, see Commentary C3215:7 on McKinney's CPLR 3215.

21. CPLR 4301.

22. On bifurcation, see § 130 above.

23. Dunleavy v. White, 236 A.D.2d 316, 653 N.Y.S.2d 597 (1st Dep't 1997), involving a judicial hearing officer, who is considered a referee by CPLR 4301.

24. See Sternberg v. Sternberg, 88 A.D.2d 950, 451 N.Y.S.2d 187 (2d Dep't 1982).

25. As noted earlier in the text, if the account qualifies as a "long account" within the meaning of CPLR 4317(b), it is of course subject to a reference to determine rather than just a reference to report, and a compulsory one at that.

26. CPLR 4015.

27. CPLR 2004.

28. See Uniform Rule 202.43, applicable to references in the supreme and county courts.

29. CPLR 4212.

hostility to the reference,[30] but the absence of consent is in any event an element to be considered by the court in deciding whether to refer the matter. Other cases indicate that the reference to report is restricted to only that which the parties consent to.[31] A constitutional argument can be urged against a reference to report made over a party's objection: it can be urged that the party has a right to have the case tried before a duly constituted judge of the court,[32] and that this requirement is not met merely by having the judge review the referee's findings.[33] The argument, whichever way it may ultimately be resolved, loses currency if all parties consent to the reference.

Even assuming the court's power to make a reference to report without consent of all parties, the "exceptional condition" requirement of CPLR 4212 must still be met, and it is not met if the issue can be decided by the court "without extraordinary impingement on [its] regular business".[34]

Attitudes about references may be influenced by the condition of judicial calendars, and may vary among departments and even from time to time within a given department. In Angelo v. Laremet Corp.,[35] for example, the Third Department said that as long as judges are available they should try all controverted issues, with or without a jury (as required), notwithstanding a statutory permission to refer them. Circumstances changed in the Third Department after that, judges became scarcer and the departmental attitude more receptive to the use of referees.[36]

These factors are important if the court proposes to refer a matter without the parties' consent. Their import drops considerably and in most cases even disappears if the consent is present. If the parties consent who is there to complain? And it's the consensual reference to report that, practically speaking, commands attention.

A reference to report is a good way to have the case heard by an expert on the particular subject, or to expedite matters when a number of documents have to be analyzed.[37] The referee to report may be analogized in many ways to the old master in chancery, who acted as a kind of assistant to the chancellor in the carrying out of various judicial functions.[38] Vestiges of the master's role appear in Rule 53 of the Federal Rules of Civil Procedure, on which the CPLR's drafters occasionally drew in formulating the CPLR's referee provisions.[39]

As long as the parties consent to the reference, they will ordinarily be allowed to be their own judge of what condition suffices as "exceptional" enough to warrant it. Some very unexceptional situations have been voluntarily submitted to referees. Often an issue of personal jurisdiction is referred, whether complicated (as where a series of alleged longarm acts under CPLR 302 have to be parsed) or simple (as where the question is whether or not the process server properly served the summons on the defendant).

Trial in the usual way will not be deemed waived by implication, so the agreement to refer must be clear and the referee must restrict herself to the matters referred.[40] The order of reference should be specific about the referee's obligations, i.e., whether the referee is to perform an act, hear all or only designated issues, report them, or report only the evidence offered on them, or decide them (if it's a reference to determine), etc. It may limit the referee's powers and fix a time and place

---

30. See Wilder v. Silbert, 5 A.D.2d 1, 168 N.Y.S.2d 1005 (1st Dep't 1957).

31. See L.H. Feder Corp. v. Bozkurtian, 48 A.D.2d 701, 368 N.Y.S.2d 247 (2d Dep't 1975).

32. See, e.g., De Hart v. Hatch, 3 Hun. 375 (Gen.T. 1st Dep't, 1875), which speaks of the court's duty to "entertain" a case as well as determine it.

33. Cf. L.H. Feder Corp. v. Bozkurtian, 48 A.D.2d 701, 368 N.Y.S.2d 247 (2d Dep't 1975).

34. Wilder v. Silbert, 5 A.D.2d 1, 3, 168 N.Y.S.2d 1005, 1007–8 (1st Dep't 1957).

35. 23 A.D.2d 191, 259 N.Y.S.2d 428 (3d Dep't 1965).

36. See Keown v. Wright, 89 A.D.2d 932, 454 N.Y.S.2d 49 (3d Dep't 1982).

37. See Burlington Industries, Inc. v. Eastern Express, Inc., 23 A.D.2d 841, 259 N.Y.S.2d 678 (1st Dep't 1965).

38. See La Buy v. Howes Leather Co., 352 U.S. 249, 77 S.Ct. 309, 1 L.Ed.2d 290 (1957); In re Peterson, 253 U.S. 300, 40 S.Ct. 543, 64 L.Ed. 919 (1920).

39. See 2d Rep.Leg.Doc. (1958) No. 13, p. 244 et seq.

40. L.H. Feder Corp. v. Bozkurtian, 48 A.D.2d 701, 368 N.Y.S.2d 247 (2d Dep't 1975).

for the hearing.[41] Unless the order of reference otherwise prescribes, a referee to report has the power to issue subpoenas, to administer oaths, and to conduct disclosure proceedings as well as the trial,[42] which is conducted in the same manner as a judge trying a nonjury case.[43]

The referee to report has 30 days, after the matter is submitted after the hearing, in which to file the report with the assigning judge,[44] and any party has 15 days after that in which to move to confirm or reject the report.[45] The court can reject the report in whole or in part, take additional testimony, make new findings, or even order a new hearing, but if no issues remain to be tried the court must decide the case and direct judgment accordingly.[46] The referee to determine also has 30 days from submission in which to file, but in this instance the thing filed is a decision rather than a report, and the decision stands as the decision of the court.[47]

If all parties consent, the referee can be a layperson; otherwise the referee must be a duly qualified New York lawyer.[48] Parties can consent, for example, to a layperson who has much expertise in the subject matter involved. In matrimonial actions only a judicial hearing officer or "special referee" so designated by the chief administrator of the courts may be used, and may be designated even if all parties object to the designee.[49] All but the judicial hearing officer and the "special" referee[50] must take an oath before embarking on their duties, unless the oath is waived.[51]

The order of reference, or the stipulation if that's the source of the reference, should determine "the basis and method of computing the referee's fees and provide for their payment", and the court may make an order for the referee's reasonable expenses.[52] In default of such a provision, the statutory rate will apply.[53] That rate is unrealistically low,[54] but absent an order or stipulation directing as to the referee's fees, it applies. The fee can be set at a higher figure by the court.[55] That's best done before the referred matter is heard, but it has been done afterwards.[56] Unless ordered or agreed otherwise, fees or expenses advanced to the referee may be recovered back by a winning party from the loser as part of a bill of

41. CPLR 4311.

42. CPLR 4201.

43. CPLR 4318, 4320(a).

44. CPLR 4320(b). A transcript of testimony and the exhibits must accompany the report unless the parties stipulate otherwise.

45. Uniform Rule 202.44 elaborates the procedure for confirming or rejecting the report, placing the burden of the application on the plaintiff.

46. CPLR 4403.

47. CPLR 4319. In an extensive review of the history of the statutes on references, John Hancock Mut. Life Ins. Co. v. 491–499 Seventh Ave. Assocs., 169 Misc.2d 493, 644 N.Y.S.2d 953 (Sup.Ct., N.Y. County, 1996), concludes that CPLR 4319, on the time for rendering a decision, was not intended to govern a mere reference to report, which is governed instead by CPLR 4320. See the discussion of the John Hancock case in the Commentary on McKinney's CPLR 4319 and in SPR 57:3–4.

48. CPLR 4312(1). Provision is made to have three referees instead of one, but this is rare. If there should be three, proceedings are governed by CPLR 4316. Paragraphs 3 and 4 of CPLR 4312 disqualify as referees certain judicial and nonjudicial personnel and those associated with the lawyers in the case.

49. CPLR 4312(2). This provision is an effort to discourage consent divorces through the device of securing the services of amenable referees. It assumes that the parties, although having no voice in the selection of a referee, have nonetheless consented to a reference.

50. The "special" referee is an amorphous thing. The primary allusion by the CPLR's drafters to a "special" referee, that which now appears in CPLR 4312(2), was deemed to require a "clarification" to indicate that the appellate division was to appoint him, see 5th Rep.Leg. Doc. (1961) No. 15 at p. 537, although it is not clear today whether a referee becomes "special" only when appointed by the appellate division. Apparently a special referee is a "standing" one, such as a retired judge so designated, as opposed to one appointed on an ad hoc basis. The appointer of special referees today, in any event, is not the appellate division, but the chief administrator of the courts, and the adoption of the provisions on judicial hearing officers, who are retired judges (see CPLR 105), would seem to make the office of special referee superfluous.

51. CPLR 4315.

52. CPLR 4321(1). The fees provision doesn't apply when a judicial hearing officer is the referee. CPLR 4321(2).

53. Neuman v. Syosset Hospital Anesthesia Group, P.C., 112 A.D.2d 1029, 493 N.Y.S.2d 26 (2d Dep't 1985).

54. It is presently $50 per day under CPLR 8003.

55. CPLR 8003.

56. See O'Dwyer v. Robson, 103 A.D.2d 1036, 478 N.Y.S.2d 407 (4th Dep't 1984).

costs.[57]

Dispute on these matters will be resolved by the court.[58] The referee should not apply to the parties for money that hasn't been agreed to for the obvious reason that it can compromise his impartiality, or the appearance of it.[59]

The additional expense incurred by the parties when a referee is used has been cited as further reason for limiting the use of referees to where the parties consent to it.[60]

§ 380. Triability by the Court

If the issues are not triable by jury, whether because jury trial is not available in the particular action or because a jury has been waived, and they have not been referred to a referee to determine, they must be decided by the court.[1] This means that the judge must decide fact issues not only when the judge is hearing the case alone, but also when it has been heard by a referee to report or by an advisory jury;[2] the report or verdict in such instance is only a recommendation and the final word lies with the judge.

Although the sequence of trial, i.e., the order in which the various trial steps are taken, is essentially the same whether a jury is present or the court is hearing the case alone,[3] it is less formal when there is no jury. This informality touches especially the rules of evidence, which are applied with less rigidity. While one periodically finds admonitions that even in a judge-tried case "the practice of overly admitting otherwise inadmissible evidence is not to be condoned",[4] such admittings will not often necessitate a new trial. This is for the obvious

reason that since the appellate division in a judge-tried case stands in the position of the trial judge, it can disregard incompetent evidence in determining whether to uphold the decision and can render whatever judgment is appropriate to the proof as purged.

Before the case is finally submitted, the judge must allow the parties an opportunity, if they want it, to submit requests for findings of fact; these should be numbered and so phrased that the court may conveniently pass on them.[5] This has been held to mean that the requests should succinctly state, without being argumentative or repetitious, the ultimate facts on which the case turns, not the evidentiary facts from which they come.[6]

As measured from the final submission of the case, the judge has 60 days in which to render a decision unless the parties extend the time.[7] This is the same time a judge has in which to decide an ordinary motion and, as mentioned in that connection,[8] the period is not jurisdictional and a late decision is not void.[9] Even a delay of 18 months, though found shocking, did not void the decision, especially not on the complaint of a loser who made no objection to the delay until he found out he'd lost.[10] A rule requires the chief administrator of the courts to get periodic accountings from all judges of any matters they have held for more than the maximum 60 days,[11] and this helps to expedite decisions.

"The decision of the court may be oral or in writing and shall state the facts it deems essential." So provides CPLR 4213(b), disposing tersely of the court's obligation in judge-tried cases generally, but it goes on to require the

---

57. CPLR 4321(a).

58. See Davis v. Commercial Metals Co., 54 Misc.2d 729, 283 N.Y.S.2d 366 (N.Y.C.Civ.Ct. 1967).

59. National Bank of North America v. New Paltz Growers, Inc., 89 A.D.2d 647, 453 N.Y.S.2d 124 (3d Dep't 1982).

60. See Wilder v. Silbert, 5 A.D.2d 1, 168 N.Y.S.2d 1005 (1st Dep't 1957).

§ 380

1. CPLR 4211.

2. The advisory jury is the subject of the next section.

3. CPLR 4011. The formalities of the trial stage are reserved for Chapter 15.

4. See, e.g., Dann v. Sands, 38 A.D.2d 661, 327 N.Y.S.2d 222, 223 (3d Dep't 1971).

5. CPLR 4213(a).

6. Charles F. Ryan & Son, Inc. v. Lancaster Homes, Inc., 22 A.D.2d 186, 254 N.Y.S.2d 473 (4th Dep't 1964), aff'd 15 N.Y.2d 812, 257 N.Y.S.2d 934, 205 N.E.2d 859 (1965).

7. CPLR 4213(c).

8. See § 250 above.

9. Kessler v. Hunter, 53 Misc.2d 965, 280 N.Y.S.2d 474 (Sup.Ct., Westchester County, 1967).

10. Mix v. Tarazskiewicz, 24 A.D.2d 808, 263 N.Y.S.2d 784 (3d Dep't 1965).

11. See § 4.1 of the Rules of the Chief Judge.

judge to itemize damages in detail in the principal tort actions and in certain actions against public employers in order to facilitate the application of several other laws whose implementation requires a parsing of the verdict, such as the so-called "collateral source" rule,[12] contribution among tortfeasors,[13] and issues of joint versus several liability.[14] These CPLR 4213(b) requirements in a court-tried case are akin to those imposed by CPLR 4111 in a jury case.[15]

An "oral" decision should be used only when rendered in open court and taken down by the stenographer. A written decision, no matter how terse, is preferable for many reasons, including appellate review, which is one of the main purposes of requiring that the facts found be stated.[16] Without those findings the appellate court can't properly review the decision and may have to reverse and remand it for proper findings.[17] If the record before the appellate court is complete, however, the court can if it chooses make the requisite findings itself and render a decision accordingly. This merely recognizes that in a court-tried case the first-tier appellate court stands in the shoes of the trial judge.[18] Or the appellate court can take the middle step of holding the case while remanding it to the lower court for findings and re-transmittal. This was done in a case that reminds us that the parties' waiver of findings of fact, and of their right to make requests to find, does not relieve the trial judge of the responsibility under CPLR 4213(b) to state the basic facts that support the judgment.[19]

§ 381. Advisory Jury

CPLR 4212 authorizes the court on motion of a party or on its own motion to submit to an "advisory" jury any issue of fact triable by the court. There is no criterion set forth, and the provision applies whether the case is not triable by a jury because of its nature, or because trial by jury in the case has been waived.[1] When a jury is so used, the verdict, like the report of a referee, is only a recommendation that the court can accept or reject as it sees fit—thus the "advisory", which comes from the counterpart federal rule.[2] CPLR 4212 is also the provision that authorizes submission of an issue to a referee to report, but while that requires a showing of some "exceptional condition", no such limitation appends to a submission to an advisory jury. A party who would move such a submission must ordinarily make the motion within 20 days after the filing of the note of issue.[3]

Despite the absence of any stated restriction on its use, or, indeed, of any standard at all, the advisory jury is relatively rare. It amounts to a luxury in an era when the courts in many parts of the state are delayed in supplying even the necessity: the jury of right. One of the most appropriate uses of the advisory jury is in the situation, previously discussed,[4] in which legal and equitable issues in respect of the same transaction arise in the same case. Suppose, for example, that P sues for specific performance of a contract (no jury) and D counterclaims for damages for breach of the same contract (jury). A jury will determine the counterclaim, but the court must decide the facts insofar as they relate to the main claim. The court can treat the jury, present as of right on the counterclaim, as an advisory one to try the main claim, too. Technically, the verdict in respect of the main claim will not

---

12. CPLR 4545.

13. CPLR Article 14.

14. CPLR Article 16.

15. See the Commentaries on McKinney's CPLR 4111 and 4213.

16. Conklin v. State, 22 A.D.2d 481, 256 N.Y.S.2d 477 (3d Dep't 1965).

17. Sager v. Sager, 21 A.D.2d 183, 249 N.Y.S.2d 467 (3d Dep't 1964).

18. See Mellon v. Street, 23 A.D.2d 210, 259 N.Y.S.2d 900 (3d Dep't 1965).

19. Nutone Inc. v. William E. Bouley Co., 38 A.D.2d 670, 327 N.Y.S.2d 256 (4th Dep't 1971).

§ 381

1. See 2d Rep.Leg.Doc. (1958) No. 13, p. 240.

2. FRCP Rule 39(c).

3. CPLR 4015. If the court submits issues to an advisory jury on its own initiative, CPLR 4212, the time limit of CPLR 4015 does not apply. See Wargo v. Wargo, 48 Misc.2d 349, 265 N.Y.S.2d 37 (Sup.Ct., Erie County, 1965).

4. See § 378 above.

bind the court, but if it has support in the record, if it would withstand any effort to overturn it were it the verdict of an of-right jury, and if the court's refusal to confirm it would cause it to conflict with the verdict rendered on the counterclaim—on which the verdict binds—the court would do well, as a matter of the practical if not the technical, to treat it as binding.[5]

A judge may find an advisory jury particularly helpful in a case expected to produce much conflicting testimony. It enables the judge to apply a kind of community experience to the difficult fact-finding task. One judge, for example, called on an advisory jury on his own motion when counsel cautioned, at the outset of a trial of a family dispute over insurance proceeds, that the testimony would be especially conflicting and bitter.[6]

The procedures used in connection with an advisory jury are essentially the same as those used with the usual of-right jury,[7] but the final decision lies with the judge, who can confirm or reject the verdict in whole or in part and make different findings. A party who would move to confirm or reject the verdict should do so within 15 days after it is rendered.[8]

If the case has already been tried without a jury, the court must render a decision; it can't avoid the duty by trying to impanel an advisory jury now to try the case anew. So doing abuses discretion and an Article 78 proceeding can be used to compel the judge to decide the case.[9]

---

5. Cf. Dellefield v. Blockdel Realty Co., 1 F.R.D. 689 (S.D.N.Y.1941). There have been analogous instances in which the verdict of a jury, present in a case as of right for one claim, has been held binding on another claim that would not be jury triable if brought by itself. See Fitzgerald v. United States Lines Co., 374 U.S. 16, 83 S.Ct. 1646, 10 L.Ed.2d 720 (1963).

6. Wargo v. Wargo, note 3, above.

7. CPLR 4212.

8. CPLR 4403.

9. See Matter of Island Improvement, Inc., 231 A.D. 837, 246 N.Y.S. 424 (2d Dep't 1930).

§ 382

1. A third kind, used in connection with the enforcement of money judgments, is called an "information subpoena". It is merely a set of interrogatories served and

---

F. SUBPOENAS AND OATHS

Table of Sections

§ 382. Subpoenas; Issuance

A subpoena is a judicial process whereby a witness is subjected to the jurisdiction of the court and required to give relevant information, "under penalty" (which is what "subpoena" means) of contempt for disobedience. Article 23 of the CPLR governs subpoenas. CPLR 2301 recognizes two basic kinds. The first and most common one secures testimony from the witness. Its formal name is "subpoena ad testificandum", but the CPLR adopts the common practice of just calling it a "subpoena". The second is a subpoena "duces tecum",[1] which seeks a paper or thing rather than testimony. It is served on the person having possession or control of the item and is satisfied if the item is produced at the appointed time and place whether by the person served or by some other person familiar with it.[2] If the issuer wants the testimony of the person served with the subpoena duces tecum as well as the paper or thing, the subpoena should contain both testimonial and duces tecum clauses,[3] or two subpoenas should be served.

The subpoena used in litigation, which is the one we are concerned with here,[4] ordinarily

---

answered by mail. See CPLR 5224(a)(3), discussed in § 509, below.

2. CPLR 2305(b).

3. See the forms contained in § 386.

4. Various tribunals, agencies, committees, and other like creatures besides courts have the subpoena power. Their subpoenas qualify as "non-judicial" and involve the courts—and our attention—only in regard to applications to quash, modify, or enforce the subpoenas, to which reference will be made in ensuing sections.

needs the context of an action or proceeding, whose caption it bears; it is not an independent process.[5]

With only a few exceptions, there is no stated minimum or maximum time for the return of the subpoena. The issuer decides when and where the witness shall appear and the subpoena instructs accordingly.[6] Recognizing, however, that the court will consider all relevant factors in determining whether to punish for contempt if the subpoena is disobeyed, the issuer should afford the witness what in context amounts to a reasonable time.[7] The "forthwith" subpoena is permissible when the exigencies suggest it, but it is best left as the exception.

As a rule, the issuance of a subpoena does not require leave of court,[8] and an array of people have the power to issue it. A subpoena may be issued by the clerk, the judge (especially when there is no clerk[9]), an arbitrator, a referee, or any member of a board or commission empowered to hear or determine a matter requiring the taking of proof. Most importantly, the subpoena may be issued by the attorney of record of any party to an action, administrative proceeding, or arbitration.[10]

It is in fact the attorneys who most often issue subpoenas in New York practice. They do so on their own initiative, based only on the reasonable needs of the proceeding to which the subpoena relates. This has long been the practice in New York (but only recently became so in federal practice[11]). The clerk also has this power, but exercises it less often,

usually at the behest of a party appearing pro se. Whether issued by the clerk, attorney, judge, or any other authorized person, the litigation subpoena stands as process of the court and the contempt remedy stands behind it as the enforcement tool.

The subpoena may provide that the person appear on the date stated "and any recessed or adjourned date" of the trial, and if given reasonable notice of the adjourned time no new subpoena is necessary.[12] Often at the end of a day during a continuing trial, the issuing lawyer will also ask the court to instruct the witness, if still needed, to return on the following day, which the court usually does as a matter of course.

It is appropriate at this juncture to interpose a practical advice. It is always best that the party secure the testimony of a favorable witness amicably, without the coercion of a subpoena. To this end, the party should be prepared to pay voluntarily all of the witness's actual expenses[13] in attending the trial or hearing, including the costs of transportation and lodging as well as reimbursement for any earnings the witness loses in order to give testimony.[14] The use of a subpoena should be reserved for hostile witnesses who will not respond with anything less, in which event the lawyer issuing the subpoena had best have taken that witness's deposition before trial[15] so as not to be surprised by the witness's testimony. The subpoena is also useful for friendly or indifferent witnesses who have to be served with the subpoena for some practical reason, as where they need it to show their employers

---

5. See Matter of Blake, 51 Misc.2d 42, 272 N.Y.S.2d 597 (Surr.Ct., Nassau County, 1966).

6. See Matter of Mullen, 177 Misc. 734, 31 N.Y.S.2d 710 (Queens County Ct. 1941).

7. See McKinney's Commentary C2305:1, which also cites several special subpoena provisions having time minimums.

8. Some do require court leave, such as where the testimony of a prisoner is needed. See CPLR 2302(b).

9. This recognizes that some courts, notably the justice courts in the state's towns and villages, do not have a regular court "clerk" to whom a civil litigant appearing pro se can turn for a subpoena.

10. CPLR 2302(a).

11. FRCP Rule 45(a)(3); see Commentary C45–5 on Rule 45 in 28 U.S.C.A.

12. CPLR 2305(a). An additional fee is required, however, for each additional day. Fees are treated in the next section.

13. The statutory witness fees are nominal, and the mileage (the rate per mile for travel expenses), which the witness also gets in certain instances, is only a bit more substantial. See CPLR 8001.

14. This is so notwithstanding that the sums expended will not necessarily be recoverable as a disbursement, which may be restricted to the statutory fees. See § 415 below.

15. See Commentary C3101:22 on McKinney's CPLR 3101; Kenford Co. v. County of Erie, 41 A.D.2d 586, 340 N.Y.S.2d 300 (4th Dep't 1973).

so as to be let off work, which is frequently the case with governmental employees.

§ 383. Service of Subpoena

CPLR 2303 requires that a subpoena be served in the same manner as a summons, which means that all of the alternatives of CPLR 308 are available. Service by personal delivery under paragraph 1 of CPLR 308 is usually preferable to the other methods, especially when the subpoena has a short return time, because it entails but a single step and gets done quickly. The other methods are available if needed.

For a while there were impediments to the use of the deliver-and-mail and affix-and-mail methods of paragraphs 2 and 4 of CPLR 308 because of the filing of proof of service requirements imposed by those provisions and principally because of their postponed "completion" of service.[1] Using them sometimes undermined the effectiveness of the subpoena by prompting the courts to withhold the contempt remedy when service complications appeared,[2] and the threat of contempt is the thing that gives the subpoena its teeth. The legislature met the problem with an amendment of CPLR 2303 in 1982, dispensing with the filing of proof of service and deeming service complete immediately upon the carrying out of the second of the two service steps that each of paragraphs 2 and 4 of CPLR 308 requires.[3] Similar problems can be met in trying to use the personal service by mail method of CPLR 312–a,[4] suggesting that it may be politic to avoid that provision for subpoena service, especially when the

subpoena is returnable in only a few days or weeks.

The subpoena can be served, as can a summons, by any person over 18 and not a party.[5]

The subpoenaed person must be paid a witness fee and mileage, and these must be "paid or tendered in advance".[6] It is customary to tender these sums along with the subpoena, and to pay them in cash, but a check has been held permissible.[7]

As for the territorial reach of the subpoena, it may generally be served wherever the particular court's summons may be served, but there are some special restrictions in the lower courts.[8] In the supreme, county, surrogate's, and family courts, and in the court of claims, subpoena service is statewide under direct constitutional authority.[9] But a New York subpoena may not be served outside the state regardless of the court involved. Even in situations in which, by analogy to summons service, authority might be spelled out for the service of a subpoena outside New York, the language used in § 2–b of the Judiciary Law, which speaks of subpoenas directed to persons "found in the state", has been applied to preclude extrastate service of a subpoena.[10] This is a needlessly restrictive interpretation,[11] but as long as it stands, a New York subpoena may not reach beyond New York borders whatever the bases or justifications in the particular situation. A party in need of an outsider's testimony must therefore turn to the pretrial disclosure devices,[12] and must preserve the re-

---

§ 383

1. See Commentary C2303:2 on McKinney's CPLR 2303.

2. See, e.g., Garrison Fuel Oil of Long Island, Inc. v. Grippo, 127 Misc.2d 275, 486 N.Y.S.2d 136 (Nassau County Ct. 1985), involving the enforcement-of-judgment subpoena of CPLR 5224.

3. The amendment, in 1982, is discussed in Commentary C2303:2 on McKinney's CPLR 2303.

4. See § 76A above.

5. CPLR 2103(a).

6. CPLR 2303. The sums applicable are found in CPLR 8001.

7. Osborne v. Miller, 67 Misc.2d 824, 325 N.Y.S.2d 150 (Sup.Ct., N.Y.County, 1971).

8. See §§ 1101 and 1201 in each of the New York City Civil, Uniform District, Uniform City, and Uniform Justice court acts (McKinney's Vol. 29A, Parts 2 and 3).

9. Const. Art. VI, § 1(c).

10. See, e.g., Siemens & Halske, GmbH v. Gres, 37 A.D.2d 768, 324 N.Y.S.2d 639 (1st Dep't 1971). It has been held that an information subpoena, used in the enforcement of judgments (see CPLR 5224, treated in § 509 below), may be mailed to the judgment debtor outside the state. See Banco do Estado de Sao Paulo S.A. v. Mendes Junior Int'l Co., N.Y. Law Journal, Nov. 24, 1997, p.29, col.4 (Sup.Ct., N.Y. County; Ramos, J.), discussed in SPR 64:3.

11. See Commentary C2303:6 on McKinney's CPLR 2303.

12. See, e.g., CPLR 3108.

sulting product for use at the trial[13] unless, of course, the witness is willing to come into the state voluntarily.

The Court of Appeals has held that if a corporation is subject to in-state service of the subpoena, thus avoiding the problem of extra-state service, the corporation may be required to produce knowledgeable officers and employees even if they are stationed outside the state.[14] Consistent with this, if testimony is sought from the employee of a corporate party, a subpoena served on the corporation can compel the appearance of the employee even without service on the employee proper, and in this situation no independent basis for jurisdiction of the witness is needed and the degree of the witness's knowledge is held irrelevant.[15]

The provision of CPLR 2303 providing that the "manner" of service be the same as that used for a summons imports as well the list of proper persons to serve in behalf of the entity or unit.[16] Hence, when the subpoena is served on an entity or governmental unit of some kind, the person to be served may ordinarily be any person upon whom a summons could be served in an action brought against the entity or unit.

When records are sought, the subpoena duces tecum should of course be addressed to the person who has custody of them. If the records are with some big entity with a central office in one place and a bunch of branches all around, it has been held that service at the branch that has the records or at the central office will do.[17]

It has been held that a person, or in any event a New Yorker, served in New York with a subpoena issued out of an action or proceeding pending in a sister state need not respond to it.[18] There may be instances, however, in which the contacts of the served individual with the jurisdiction whose subpoena is involved suffice to justify the extraterritorial service and require a response.[19]

§ 384. Motion to Quash Subpoena

If the person served with a subpoena has some objection to it or wishes to test its validity, the remedy is a motion to quash, condition, or modify the subpoena. The motion should be made to the court in which the subpoena is returnable.[1] It should be made promptly, and in any event before the return day. If the time is short, the motion can be brought on by order to show cause, abbreviating the notice time. If the subpoena is not returnable in a court, such as one issued for a deposition scheduled in a lawyer's office[2] or in conjunction with an administrative proceeding, a request to withdraw or modify the subpoena should first be made to the person who issued it. If that does not avail, a motion to quash may be made to the court.

If the subpoena has not issued out of a court, the motion to quash or modify is made to the supreme court.[3] The applicable statute does not supply a venue, but since "[a] motion to quash a nonjudicial subpoena is similar to a CPLR article 78 proceeding",[4] the purpose of which is to review administrative action,[5] the proper venue in which to quash a subpoena issued out of an administrative proceeding

13. See Commentary C2303:7 on McKinney's CPLR 2303.

14. Standard Fruit & Steamship Co. v. Waterfront Comm., 43 N.Y.2d 11, 400 N.Y.S.2d 732, 371 N.E.2d 453 (1977).

15. See 23/23 Communications Corp. v. GM Corp., 172 Misc.2d 821, 660 N.Y.S.2d 296 (Sup.Ct., N.Y. County, 1997), noted in SPR 70:4.

16. See § 69 above.

17. See Application of Bott, 125 Misc.2d 1029, 481 N.Y.S.2d 266 (Monroe County Court 1984), noting the time element that the lawyer has to be conscious of and taking a pragmatic approach to matters of this kind.

18. See Doe v. Roe, 190 A.D.2d 463, 599 N.Y.S.2d 350 (4th Dep't 1993).

19. See the discussion in SPR 26:4.

§ 384

1. CPLR 2304.

2. See CPLR 3106(b); Commentary C3110:4 on McKinney's CPLR 3110.

3. CPLR 2304. See Commentary C2304:4 on McKinney's CPLR 2304.

4. New York Republican State Committee v. New York State Commission on Government Integrity, 138 A.D.2d 884, 526 N.Y.S.2d 264 (3d Dep't 1988).

5. See § 557 et seq., below.

would be a county in which an Article 78 proceeding could be brought against the agency.[6] If the subpoena issued out of an arbitration, the appropriate venue would be that set by statute for other applications in connection with the arbitration.[7]

A motion to quash challenges the validity of the subpoena or the jurisdiction of the issuing authority.[8] These categories can embrace a myriad of defects, however, ranging from the most substantive, such as where the subpoena seeks matter irrelevant to the proceeding,[9] to the most procedural, such as where there was some formal defect in its service. Other grounds, perhaps not technically sufficient to affect "validity" or "jurisdiction", may also be raised. Perhaps the demands of the subpoena are such that the witness can't afford to meet them on the meager fees[10] tendered. The court is empowered, on a motion to quash or modify, to impose any condition the court finds just.[11] One condition the court may resort to is that the issuing party advance to the subpoenaed person, in addition to the nominal statutory fees, the reasonable actual cost of honoring the subpoena, especially when it is a subpoena duces tecum requiring the witness to go to expense to produce the papers or things sought. Conditionings of this kind are not frequent, probably because a party in need of a witness's testimony or materials will ordinarily advance such expenses voluntarily, thereby obviating the motion to condition (and possibly even the subpoena itself) and propitiating the witness.

§ 385. Disobedience of Subpoena

The disobedience of a subpoena issued in conjunction with a court proceeding is punishable as a contempt.[1] It also subjects the recalcitrant person, whether a party or a non-party witness, to the actual damages the disobedience causes the issuer as well as a penalty of up to $50. If the disobeyer is a party, civil penalties may also be imposed, up to and including the striking of the party's pleading.[2]

The disobedience of a non-judicial subpoena, which refers to one issued in an out-of-court proceeding like an administrative hearing or an arbitration, is not directly punishable as a contempt. The issuer or the person in whose behalf the subpoena was issued must first move in the supreme court to compel compliance. If the court then orders compliance, further disobedience is a violation of the order and may now be the subject of contempt proceedings.[3] Like subdivision (a) of CPLR 2308, this provision also allows the court, through the issuance of warrants, to command the sheriff to produce the witness before the appropriate body and to commit the witness if need be until obedience is secured.

§ 386. Form of Subpoena

The following are illustrative forms for the testimonial subpoena and the subpoena duces tecum.

(a) Form of testimonial subpoena.

6. CPLR 506(b). See Matter of Associated Homeowners and Businessmen's Organization, Inc., 85 Misc.2d 676, 381 N.Y.S.2d 191 (Sup.Ct., Kings County, 1976).

7. CPLR 7502(a). See § 591 (Practitioner's Edition).

8. Santangello v. People, 38 N.Y.2d 536, 381 N.Y.S.2d 472, 344 N.E.2d 404 (1976).

9. See, e.g., Temporary State Commission on Living Costs and the Economy v. Bergman, 80 Misc.2d 448, 363 N.Y.S.2d 977 (Sup.Ct., N.Y.County, 1975).

10. See CPLR 8001.

11. CPLR 2304. See 1st Rep.Leg.Doc. (1957) No. 6(b), p. 165.

§ 385

1. The procedures and penalties for punishing contempt are discussed in the enforcement chapter. See § 481 et seq., below.

2. See CPLR 2308(a), which in addition to invoking the general contempt punishment authorizes the court to issue a warrant directing the sheriff to bring the witness to court forcibly and to jail the witness if the contumely continues.

3. CPLR 2308(b). See Dias v. Consolidated Edison Co. of New York, Inc., 116 A.D.2d 453, 496 N.Y.S.2d 686 (1st Dep't 1986).

SUPREME COURT OF THE STATE OF NEW YORK
COUNTY OF NEW YORK

A.B., Plaintiff,
         against   }   Subpoena
C.D., Defendant.   Index No. _____
To E.F.   Name of Assigned Judge _____

Greetings:

You are hereby commanded to appear at a trial before the Hon. Beatrice Shainswit, a Justice of this Court, at [Part or Room Number], to be held at the Courthouse at 60 Centre Street, in the Borough of Manhattan, City of New York, on April 16, 1999, at 9 o'clock in the morning, and at any recessed or adjourned date and time of that trial, to testify and give evidence as a witness on behalf of the defendant in the above-captioned action. For a failure to attend you will be deemed guilty of a contempt of court as well as liable for all damages sustained by the defendant because of your failure and to a penalty of $50 as well.

Dated April 9, 1999,

_____
Attorney for Defendant
Address:
Telephone Number:

(b) Form of subpoena duces tecum. The caption, introductory amenities and signature read the same as in the testimonial subpoena above. "Duces Tecum" is added to "Subpoena" to the right of the caption and the body of the subpoena duces tecum can read:

You are hereby commanded to appear at a trial before the Hon. Beatrice Shainswit, a Justice of this Court, at [Part or Room Number] to be held at the Courthouse at 60 Centre Street, in the Borough of Manhattan, City of New York, on April 16, 1999, at 9 o'clock in the morning, and at any recessed or adjourned date of the trial, and to bring with you and produce at that time and place the following documents and things [describe them here as precisely as possible], of which you have custody or control. For your failure to do so you will be deemed guilty of a contempt of court as well as liable for all damages sustained by the defendant because of your failure and to a penalty of $50 as well.

Although often phrased to require the person served to "appear" or "attend", a statute makes clear that a subpoena with only this general kind of "duces tecum" language is adequately met when any person able to identify the item and attest to its custody shows up at the appointed time and place with the papers or things sought.[1] It is for this reason that the issuer who wants testimony as well as materials from the subpoenaed person should serve that person with the two subpoenas, or in any event with a subpoena having separate-ly delineated testimonial and duces tecum clauses.[2]

§ 387. Notice to Produce

Quite apart from a subpoena, and finding its authority in caselaw rather than statute, is a device known as a "notice to produce". By the use of this notice, which is only a paper served by one attorney on an opposing attorney a reasonable time in advance of the trial, the recipient can be made to produce designated books and documents. This notice is bound up

§ 386

1. CPLR 2305(b).

2. See § 382 above.

with the best evidence rule, since its violation merely precludes the served party from using the items in evidence while permitting the serving party to introduce secondary evidence of the items sought.[1] Reference to the item in a pleading is deemed the equivalent of a notice to produce the item and an adequate basis for secondary evidence if it is not produced.[2] The sanctions of contempt, damages, and money penalties, which stand behind the subpoena, are irrelevant to the notice to produce.

Seeking a paper by such a notice, or even by a discovery notice before trial,[3] does not require the seeking party to use it in evidence after getting it.[4] The seeking party's purpose may have been merely to peruse the item to determine whether it is needed.

If the item is present in the courtroom, even this advance notice is not necessary. The attorney who wants the item can merely ask the court to compel its surrender by the attorney who has it, and if the item is relevant and not immunized by any exclusionary rule of evidence, the court will order it turned over.[5]

The notice to produce is thus a device for use between parties. When an item is sought from a nonparty witness who will not surrender it before trial, the compulsion of a subpoena duces tecum is indicated, as indeed it would be against a party, too, if secondary evidence of the thing sought is not available to warrant use of the relatively weak notice to produce.

§ 388. Oaths and Affirmations

Two basic groups of people are authorized by the CPLR to administer oaths: those authorized to conduct hearings and take evidence and those authorized to take acknowledgements of deeds.[1] The first group embraces judges, arbitrators, administrative hearing officers, and the like. The second is taken by adoption from the Real Property Law's lists of those who may acknowledge deeds.[2] The clerk, for example, one of the leading oathgivers in litigation, is on one of those lists.[3] The notary public is the leading entry on the realty lists[4] and the chief oathgiver outside the courtroom. The affidavit, which is the principal item of proof on an ordinary motion, is usually sworn to before a notary.

Any form of oath is satisfactory as long as "calculated to awaken the conscience and impress the mind of the person taking it in accordance with his religious or ethical beliefs."[5] The ceremony should be "solemn ... an unequivocal act of assent to tell the truth."[6] As long as it is, it will be backed, at least theoretically, by the perjury penalties in the Penal Law, which defines "oath" to include "an affirmation and every other mode authorized by law of attesting" to what is said.[7] This "affirmation", by the way, is a form of oath, duly taken before one qualified to administer an oath, and should not be confused with the "affirmation" authorized by CPLR 2106. The latter, it will be recalled,[8] is authorized for certain professionals in subscribing affidavits: it dispenses with the formal swearing ceremony usually required of affiants. But when those persons, including lawyers and doctors, take the stand in open court they must go through the same swearing ceremony required of all witnesses.

---

§ 387

1. Smith v. Rentz, 131 N.Y. 169, 30 N.E. 54 (1892).

2. Lawson v. Bachman, 81 N.Y. 616 (1880), aff'd 109 U.S. 659, 3 S.Ct. 479, 27 L.Ed. 1067 (1884).

3. CPLR 3111, 3120(a).

4. Smith v. Rentz, note 1, above.

5. See Whelan v. Gorton, 15 Misc. 625, 37 N.Y.S. 344 (N.Y.City Ct.1896).

§ 388

1. CPLR 2309(a). A number of other provisions also grant the power to administer oaths. See 2d Rep.Leg.Doc. (1958) No. 13, pp. 205–208.

2. See Real Prop.L. §§ 298, 299, 301.

3. Real Prop.L. § 298(2)(a). The provision includes clerks of courts "of record". That includes all of the courts of the state except the town and village courts, Jud.L. § 2, but the clerks of those courts get oath-administering powers elsewhere. See § 109 of the Uniform Justice Court Act. Hence the clerks of all New York courts have the power to administer oaths.

4. Real Prop.L. § 298(1)(d).

5. CPLR 2309(b).

6. 2d Rep.Leg.Doc. (1958) No. 13, p. 204.

7. Penal Law § 210.00(1).

8. See § 205 above.

An oath or affirmation taken outside the United States or Canada must, in order to be used in New York proceedings, be accompanied by a certificate of a governmental official of the foreign place authenticating the oathgiver's authority. This requirement comes from CPLR 2309(c), and the certificate is sometimes familiarly called a "flag".[9] The absence of the flag is not jurisdictional, however. It can be secured later and given nunc pro tunc effect,[10] but its omission may cause at least temporary rejection of the document sworn to,[11] entailing, if nothing else, delay while the flag is secured.

9. It comes about by the adoption, by CPLR 2309(c), of whatever is currently required by the Real Property Law for deed acknowledgements. Real Prop.L. § 311 requires a "flag" only for oaths taken outside the United States or Canada.

10. See Raynor v. Raynor, 279 A.D. 671, 108 N.Y.S.2d 20 (2d Dep't 1951).

11. See Majestic Co. v. Wender, 24 Misc.2d 1018, 205 N.Y.S.2d 317 (Sup.Ct., Nassau County, 1960).

Chapter Fifteen

THE TRIAL

Analysis

A. INTRODUCTORY

Table of Sections

Sec.
389. The Trial, Introductory.

§ 389. The Trial, Introductory

With this chapter we arrive at the trial itself, propelled there by the calendar practices discussed in the opening sections of the last chapter. Whatever calendars the case has visited—and this will depend almost entirely on the practice of the particular judge or in the particular part or court—the case has endured to the day of trial, statistically quite an accomplishment today. If both the judge and the case are at last ready together, the case goes to trial, the actual time to be determined by the judge, usually in consultation with the parties. In multi-judge courts that don't use the Individual Assignment System (IAS), this may mean that it will be sent by an "assignment judge" or equivalent person to a "part", i.e., a courtroom to which another judge has been assigned who is ready for another case. At this initial moment, however, the lawyers probably have neither the parties nor the witnesses with them. This is because the case may have to detour on its way to the courtroom so that the lawyers can pick a jury, which they usually do themselves, as we shall see; this may take them to a different section of the courthouse where the jurors are waiting. The parties and witnesses do not as a rule show up until the jury selection process is completed, and that can take some time.

Concentration throughout this chapter will be on trial by jury rather than on trial by the court or by a referee. Stressing trial by jury will offer more thorough insights into the trial process because (1) a number of important procedures that it involves, such as the impaneling of the jury at the outset and the judge's charge to it at the end, are not found at all in the other modes of trial, and (2) those procedures and rules applicable to all modes of trial are more strictly applied when a jury is present, notably in regard to the rules of evidence, to rulings on evidentiary objections, to the summation, and to post-trial motions. One experienced in the process of trial by jury can turn easily to trial by the court or by a referee; the additional points to be absorbed in order to make that conversion are few. Some have already been covered in discussing the mode of trial;[1] the few remaining ones can be unobtru-

---

§ 389

1. See § 379 on triability by referee and § 380 on triability by the court.

sively integrated in this chapter as they become relevant.

Article 40 of the CPLR is entitled "Trial Generally" and contains a few basics applicable to one degree or another in all modes of trial. Some of these, too, are best viewed in jury-trial context and will be treated at appropriate junctures later in this chapter. A few can be noted and disposed of here:

The trial will almost invariably take place at the courthouse, but there is authority, if the parties stipulate, that all or part of it take place elsewhere.[2] This is rarely invoked and should be reserved for unique situations, such as where a key witness can give testimony only from a hospital bedside, and for like exigencies.

CPLR 4014 provides that the trial "shall continue until it is completed", even though the particular term of court at which it began has expired. This of course does not preclude reasonable adjournments of the trial for any of myriad causes. The rule about adjournments is that they are in the discretion of the trial judge and will not be interfered with by an appellate court except in cases of clear abuse.[3]

Recognizing the inevitable problems of scheduling when conflicting demands are made by several courts on the time of one or more of the trial lawyers, an extensive guidepost, Uniform Rule 125.1, endeavors to regulate when and how adjournments based on "engagement of counsel" may be made. The courts' individual rules then require that all such adjournments follow that rule.[4]

Some of the uniform rules require that when a lawyer other than the attorney of record is to try the case, that lawyer be identified in a filed writing within designated time limits.[5] There may also be court rules governing the absence of the attorney during the trial.[6] But the rule of greatest importance in trial practice remains the "engagement of counsel" rule, Part 125 of the Uniform Rules, which governs and sets up the standards for determining when an attorney's actual involvement in some other trial will be allowed to earn an adjournment of the present one. Violating this rule can have serious consequences, including a default judgment against the side violating it.[7]

B. SELECTING A JURY

Table of Sections

§ 390. Impaneling a Jury

Trial by jury in a civil action today is by six persons under a 1972 amendment of CPLR 4104, which had previously offered a choice of six or 12.[1] An elaborate machinery goes to work before those six are selected, however, beginning with the process of aggregating the "array"—the large body of citizens who have been summoned to jury duty for a particular term of court and from which lawyers will ultimately draw a jury for their individual cases. The provisions for the basic qualifications of jurors and for the methods of summoning an array are in Article 16 of the Judiciary Law and in Part 128 of the Uniform Rules for the Jury System. The Judiciary Law provisions had been overhauled in 1977 to bring them up to date and make impanelment procedures more uniform throughout the

---

2. CPLR 4013.

3. See Case's Will v. Donovan, 24 A.D.2d 797, 263 N.Y.S.2d 861 (3d Dep't 1965).

4. See Uniform Rules 202.32 (applicable in the supreme and county courts), 205.13 (family court), 206.17 (court of claims), 207.33 (surrogate's court), 208.25 (N.Y.C. Civil Court), 212.25 (district courts), and 210.25 (city courts).

5. See, e.g., UR 202.31, applicable in the supreme and county courts.

6. See, e.g., UR 202.36, applicable in the supreme and county courts.

7. See, e.g., Romer v. Middletown School District, 137 Misc.2d 46, 519 N.Y.S.2d 924 (Sup.Ct., Orange County, 1987).

§ 390

1. The reduction from 12 to six is authorized by the constitution. N.Y.Const., Art. VI, § 18(a). The number is also six in the lower courts, see § 1305 in each of the New York City Civil, Uniform District, Uniform City, and Uniform Justice court acts (McKinney's Vol. 29A, Parts 2 and 3), in some of which the smaller jury predates the amendment of CPLR 4104.

state, and the uniform rules that went into effect a decade or so later aimed further in the same direction. Parts of the impanelment process are explicitly delegated to the chief administrator of the courts or to the appellate divisions to prescribe by rule or other direction.[2]

The jurors must of course be selected at random, but as long as they meet the basic statutory qualifications[3] they can be selected from any number of sources, including voter registration lists and such other lists of county residents as the chief administrator may specify, including lists of utility subscribers, vehicle owners or operators, taxpayers, and even consent-filing volunteers.[4] Outside New York City, the official charged with carrying out the selection process is the person appointed to serve as the county commissioner of jurors; in the five counties of New York City the county clerk serves as commissioner.[5]

The chief administrator prescribes the mechanical method for drawing jurors.[6] The use of electronic devices can be permitted as an alternative to the old fashioned ballot box, for which the law specifically provided prior to 1977.[7] The ballot box may still be an option, and it can serve as an illustration of a typical way of impaneling the basic array as well as the smaller array from which lawyers pick the jurors who will actually try the case.

The name of each qualified person goes on to a separate ballot, which is placed in a general ballot box with an aperture large enough to admit only a hand.[8] From this box are periodically drawn an array in numbers sufficient to meet the contemplated needs of the particular jury term.[9] The jurors so drawn are notified of when and where to appear, usually by a summons mailed by the commissioner or served by the sheriff at the commissioner's direction.[10] By a similar procedure, the names of the jurors who have appeared and are on hand, not having been for one reason or another excused, are again placed in a ballot box. It is from this one that a sufficient number of names are then drawn to meet the requirements of the waiting case or cases.

All of the names in these boxes are on separate ballots thoroughly mixed so that each has an equal chance of being pulled. An inadvertent and unprejudicial oversight in this connection need not vitiate the selection, however. In one instance, for example, in which the names of jurors returning from one case had been kept clipped together when re-inserted into the ballot box for further call, and thus failed to circulate freely and independently, a jury picked from that box was nonetheless held proper, and its verdict upheld.[11]

A statute that had contained generic lists of employments, statuses, and circumstances that disqualified categories of persons as jurors,[12] and another that contained a substantial list of exemptions,[13] were repealed in 1995. "Postponement and Excusal from Jury Service" is now governed by Part 128.6–a of the Uniform Rules, which today determines the methods whereby a juror may be allowed to postpone service or avoid it entirely. Hence, when the clerk draws names from the ballot box for a waiting case, all named are ordinarily on hand and ready to be questioned by the lawyers to determine whether they are individually fit to try the particular case. This involves an inquiry into their personal attitudes towards the subject matter, their relationship to the parties and lawyers, their unique biases or prejudices, and the like (all of which we take up in more detail two sections hence, where we deal with challenges). This inquiry, commonly known as a "voir dire", is usually the first contact the lawyers have with the jurors, who up to this time have passed through the hands

---

2. See Jud.L. §§ 506, 508, 522.

3. Jud.L. § 510.

4. Jud.L. § 506; Uniform Rule 128.3.

5. Jud.L. § 502; UR 128.0.

6. UR 128.5.

7. See, e.g., § 668 of the Judiciary Law prior to its repeal by L.1977, c. 316.

8. This was the procedure prescribed by the old § 668, ibid.

9. Jud.L. § 508.

10. Jud.L. § 516; UR 128.6.

11. See Chaffee v. Marsh, 2 A.D.2d 934, 156 N.Y.S.2d 376 (3d Dep't 1956).

12. Jud.L. § 511.

13. Jud.L. § 512.

of others: clerks, commissioners, sheriffs, and diverse other nonjudicial personnel connected with the basic impanelment process.

A sufficient number of jurors to constitute at least a petit jury (the jury of six that will try the case) are called for the voir dire, a replacement coming in for each juror excused in the course of the questioning until a fully satisfactory jury of six is assembled.[14] This questioning in New York civil practice is usually conducted by the lawyers themselves, without a judge present,[15] but a judge must attend if a party requests.[16] A judge's failing to attend when duly requested has been held reversible error that can undo a judgment.[17] The lawyers will often agree on which jurors are to be excused; if they can't, and any dispute in need of judicial resolution arises, it can be taken to the judge in chambers or the courtroom.

Jurors must respond candidly and honestly to all questions asked. Concealment of facts suggesting possible bias can vitiate a later verdict;[18] it is in fact one of the few grounds on which a juror may be heard to impeach the verdict of the jury, as where juror A by affidavit attests to a fact revealed to him by juror B but improperly withheld by B on the voir dire.[19]

§ 391. Alternate Jurors

If it is contemplated that the trial will be prolonged, increasing the prospect that the disability of a juror will void all prior proceedings and put all parties to the expense of starting afresh, it will be helpful to have an extra juror available who has heard all of the proceedings and can take the place of the one who may become disabled. CPLR 4106 provides for this by authorizing the impaneling of either one or two extra jurors, along with the basic six, the extra ones to act as "alternate" jurors. When this is done, a panel of seven or eight will hear the whole case, but no alternate will participate in deliberations unless and until one of the regular six jurors is disabled. The first six qualified still constitute the jury.[1] The additional ones are just standbys.

Before 1972 only a judge could order that alternate jurors be drawn. The 1972 amendment that produced the current CPLR 4106 allows either party to have an alternate or two drawn, but empowers the court to order otherwise. The effect is to switch the initiative to the parties while keeping a veto power in the court.

While it was traditionally the contemplated long trial that prompted the selection of alternates, CPLR 4106 states no criteria. For obviously brief issues, an alternate may be a needless public expense and the court can intercede to preclude it.

§ 392. Challenges to Jurors

A challenge is an objection to jurors or, more frequently, to an individual juror. There are several kinds of challenges. The first is a challenge to the array, which is an objection to the whole panel; it can be either substantive, objecting to the basic statutory qualifications or disqualifications of jurors on the ground that they do not make for an array representative of the community, or procedural, objecting to some defect of form or method in the impanelment process. A challenge to the array is uncommon in civil actions; it is more likely to appear in criminal context,[1] but it is infre-

---

14. If one or two alternate jurors are to be used, see § 391, below, they are picked and qualified at the same time. CPLR 4106.

15. Compare the federal practice under FRCP Rule 47(a), which permits the judge to decide whether to conduct the examination or let the lawyers do it.

16. CPLR 4107.

17. See Baginski v. New York Telephone Co., 130 A.D.2d 362, 515 N.Y.S.2d 23 (1st Dep't 1987).

18. See, e.g., Holland v. Blake, 38 A.D.2d 344, 329 N.Y.S.2d 169 (3d Dep't), aff'd 31 N.Y.2d 734, 338 N.Y.S.2d 108, 290 N.E.2d 147 (1972).

19. See McHugh v. Jones, 258 App.Div. 111, 16 N.Y.S.2d 332 (2d Dep't 1939), aff'd 283 N.Y. 534, 29 N.E.2d 76 (1940).

§ 391

1. CPLR 4105.

§ 392

1. See, e.g., People v. Young, 46 Misc.2d 364, 259 N.Y.S.2d 577 (Seneca County Ct. 1965).

quent there, too. Attorneys ordinarily reserve their challenges for individual jurors.

A challenge to an individual juror is known as a challenge to the poll or polls. There are two kinds, the peremptory challenge and the challenge for cause, the latter further subdivided into a challenge for principal cause and a challenge to the favor. Each of these will be discussed in turn after preliminaries are disposed of.

It is upon the voir dire that the questioning of potential jurors proceeds so as to determine whether any is subject to challenge. This questioning, as already noted, is generally conducted by the attorneys without a judge being present. A challenge for cause, if it has any colorable basis, often results in the mutual agreement of counsel to excuse the juror, thereby obviating a ruling by the court on the validity of the objection. If agreement is lacking and a ruling is necessary, the challenge is today tried and determined by the court. This is so whatever the ground of the objection, i.e., whether to the array or to the polls, and whether the issue it poses is one of law or of fact.[2]

Challenges for cause are the subject of CPLR 4110. Subdivision (b) disqualifies persons related within the sixth degree to a party, either by blood or marriage. The related party waives the objection by not raising it before the trial starts; any other party (who would presumably be the prejudiced one) has until six months after the verdict to raise it, although it should of course be raised as promptly as possible. This category of objection is known as one "for principal cause", which means that the existence of the relationship disqualifies the juror as a matter of law.[3]

The most common kind of challenge for cause is known as a challenge "to the favor", the subject of CPLR 4110(a). This one differs from the challenge for principal cause in that it poses an issue of fact rather than an issue of law. The difference rarely has practical significance; what little it has is likely to be felt more

in the scope of review on appeal than at trial level.[4] An experienced attorney is usually reluctant to resist an arguable challenge made by the other side, and the experienced judge equally reluctant to overrule an objection that has a possible basis, for the reason that doing so would tend to confer a tactical advantage on the objector: if she wins on the merits with the objectionable juror present, the objection will expire, but if she loses she may have a trump card to lay before the appellate court. It is rarely necessary, therefore, to draw sharp lines between challenges for principal cause ("law" objections) and challenges to the favor ("fact" objections).

While not ordinarily present at the voir dire, the judge must attend it if requested to by one of the attorneys.[5] Objections not resolvable by stipulation can in any event be brought to the judge for rulings either to chambers or the courtroom.

A challenge to the favor can be based on anything tending to show that the juror can't judge the case indifferently. The factors that can support that showing are infinite.[6] The potential jurors at the voir dire are told about the kind of case it is, and the parties and their lawyers are identified. The questioning of jurors can then touch on anything reflecting on their capacity to maintain objectivity in the case. Fair subjects here are, among other things, any kind of relationship the juror may have to the parties or to their lawyers or to any other persons, such as witnesses, involved in the case, whether the relationship is by blood, marriage, business, friendship, or anything else. Utter candor is the juror's obligation. As has already been indicated, a falsehood on the voir dire is one of the few revelations one juror may make of another after the verdict is in, even if it tends to destroy the verdict.

Any datum tending to show bias by the juror, in whatever direction it may carry the juror's inclination in the case, is a permissible

---

2. CPLR 4108.

3. Butler v. Glens Falls, S.H. & F.E. St. R.R., 121 N.Y. 112, 24 N.E. 187 (1890).

4. Ibid.

5. CPLR 4107.

6. Butler v. Glens Falls, etc., note 3, above.

topic of voir dire examination. This is important to note even before turning to the specific contents of CPLR 4110(a), because the statute is by no means exclusive; it merely lists a few frequently arising grounds and subjects them to challenges to the favor. The juror's employment by a party is listed as a ground for challenge to the favor, for example, while the juror's employment by one of the lawyers or by a close friend or relative of a party is not. Yet it would be equal ground for challenge. Another example: if a party is a corporation, the juror's status of shareholder is a listed objection, but his status as a creditor or debtor of the corporation is not; yet it would still be a factor on which to base a challenge if there is any doubt about its effect on the juror's disinterest.

Since personal injury and wrongful death cases today are a big part of judicial calendars and are almost invariably defended by liability insurers, CPLR 4110(a) permits the jurors to be asked whether any has any position with or interest in such an insurer, and authorizes a challenge to the favor against one who has. This may of course tend to suggest the presence of insurance to the jury, but the question may be asked if done without undue stress or histrionics. While neither the fact nor the sum of applicable insurance may be announced to the jury, its existence, in the compulsory insurance state of New York, has been statutorily recognized at least to the extent of allowing the voir dire question just noted.[7] Although it is probably safest to put the question in the identical terms in which CPLR 4110(a) casts it,[8] it has been held that related matters may also be investigated if done "without undue emphasis"—such as asking whether the jurors have heard through public media about the effect of negligence verdicts on insurance rates,[9] a datum that can prejudice a juror against the plaintiff.

If a municipality (city, village, town, or county) is a party, the fact that a juror is a resident or taxpayer of that municipality is not a ground for challenge to the favor;[10] it would often be difficult, if that were not the rule, to get a jury in cases in which a municipality is a party.[11]

Lawyers usually prefer to address questions to the jurors collectively, pursuing an individual juror with follow-up questions only when that juror's response to the collective question suggests it.

A party learning that a juror has withheld a pertinent datum on the voir dire, to that party's prejudice, should apprise the court promptly; withholding the objection until after a loss on the merits will likely forfeit it.[12]

Up to now we have been discussing challenges for cause. An entirely different kind of challenge needs no ground at all: the peremptory challenge. Originally, CPLR 4109 gave "each party" three peremptories plus one for each alternate juror, taking cognizance of the situation in which there were more parties on one side than another by empowering the court to give additional challenges to the side with the fewer. A 1996 amendment altered this by giving three peremptories to each side rather than to each party, and by allowing one additional peremptory challenge for each two alternates instead of for each one.[13] When there are several parties on a side, the court can allocate the side's peremptories among them.

---

7. As part of pre-trial disclosure, a copy of the defendant's liability policy must be given to the plaintiff upon demand, but may not be made known to the jury. See CPLR 3101(f).

8. Is anyone among you "a shareholder, stockholder, director, officer or employee, or in any manner interested, in any insurance company issuing policies for protection against liability for damages for injury to persons or property"?

9. Graham v. Waite, 23 A.D.2d 628, 257 N.Y.S.2d 629 (4th Dep't 1965).

10. CPLR 4110(a). Nor is a judge disqualified from presiding in a case involving a municipality merely because he is a resident or taxpayer of it. Jud.L. § 15, CPLR 4110–a.

11. See the venue limitations applicable to an action against a municipality. CPLR 504.

12. See Gamell v. Mt. Sinai Hosp., 40 A.D.2d 1010, 339 N.Y.S.2d 31 (2d Dep't 1972).

13. There is an unresolved issue under the 1996 amendment about whether a third-party defendant is entitled to a separate set of peremptory challenges, or must share the allotment that the main defendants get. See the lead note in SPR 50.

Also prior to the 1996 amendment, if the interests on one side were antagonistic, each would get their own batch of peremptory challenges,[14] such as where there were co-defendant drivers of different cars in a personal injury case, each being patently hostile to the other. Whether there is now to be an adjustment for mutual hostility among the members of a given side is another matter awaiting definitive judicial resolution.

As long as a side's peremptory challenges last, the rule until recently was that the side can exercise them as arbitrarily as it pleases, and no reason need be assigned. A lawyer could take a dislike to a potential juror for as infinite a variety of reasons as there are people in the world. It could be based on something in the juror's background, comportment, or appearance which suggested a lack of sympathy with the questioner's cause; it could be a look, a nod, or the lawyer's own paranoia. Whatever it was, it remained a secret as long as the lawyer wished to keep it so.

While that is still largely the rule, an exception has been carved out for the peremptory challenge suspected of violating the equal protection clause. Following the lead of the federal courts, the First Department held in Ancrum v. Eisenberg[15] that the equal protection clause bars the discriminatory use of peremptory challenges against jurors in civil actions. The plaintiffs in the case were black and the defendant used all of his peremptory challenges against black jurors. A verdict for the plaintiff was overturned and the case remanded for a new trial. The court said that in a case like that, the party exercising the peremptory challenge must offer "a race-neutral explanation" that is "not mere pretext", which the defendant in *Ancrum* was unable to do.

The attorney often does best to save her peremptory challenges for last. It is helpful, for example, to have at hand a peremptory challenge to excuse a juror against whom the lawyer has made an unsuccessful challenge for

cause. The juror may have been offended by the effort.

Trial lawyers develop their own preferences for the kinds of jurors they want in a given case or on a given side. Cultivating one's own predilections is one of the by-products of membership in the trial bar.

C. THE TRIAL PROPER

Table of Sections

§ 393. Sequence of Trial

The sequence of proceedings at a jury trial has been standardized by tradition, but if there are any issues in the case that are not jury triable, whether because not so by their nature or because trial by jury as to them has been waived, the preference of the rules is that they be disposed of before any proceedings involving the jury get under way. Indeed, the stated preference is that a jury not even be impaneled until nonjury issues are decided, especially when they may be dispositive of the case.[1]

If the nonjury issues are not dispositive, or if there are none in the case, trial by jury gets under way. After such initial discussions between court and counsel as are needed to familiarize the judge with the case, or perhaps just to refresh the judge's recollection of it, the formal steps in a trial by jury follow this general order: the plaintiff makes an opening statement to the jury; the defendant does the same; the plaintiff calls her witnesses and puts in the case; the defendant does the same (each party cross-examining the other's witnesses); the defendant makes a closing argument ("summation") to the jury; the plaintiff does

---

14. See Heiston v. Taylor, 281 App.Div. 800, 119 N.Y.S.2d 452 (4th Dep't 1953).

15. 206 A.D.2d 324, 615 N.Y.S.2d 14 (1st Dep't 1994). The case is noted in SPR 21:2.

§ 393

1. See Uniform Rule 202.40.

the same; the court charges the jury; and the jury retires, deliberates, and renders its verdict.[2] Through all of this runs the ever-present progression of objections, rulings, and related colloquies, while the stenographer keeps track of it all. More serious discussions of evidentiary matters, or of legal points that hold some potential for prejudice if the jury should hear the dialogue, are taken out of the jury's hearing, either at the bench or in chambers, or by excusing the jury.

At the trial's outset the party who filed the note of issue—ordinarily the plaintiff—must furnish the court a set of marked pleadings.[3] Under the Individual Assignment System (IAS), the trial is not likely to be the judge's first contact with the case unless the "dual-track" system is in effect in the area, under which the case leaves the IAS judge and goes to a different judge for trial after the note of issue is filed.[4] If dual track does apply, however, or if the IAS is not used in the particular court, the marked pleadings may be the trial judge's first contact with the case. Marked pleadings offer a bird's-eye view of the issues. The parties should also hand up any other papers or documents the court ought to have at the outset, such as formal admissions made under CPLR 3123 (which obviate trial of the issues admitted). A copy of any statute a party intends to rely on at the trial must also be submitted.[5] The court can direct the submission of trial memoranda and their exchange among counsel at the trial or even before it.[6]

The trial example we are using is the trial by jury, which enables us to see the trial at its most formal. Trial before a judge or referee is less rigidly structured. At the very outset, for example, a formal "opening" statement might be dispensed with. CPLR 4016 expressly authorizes an opening statement regardless of the mode of trial, but in the absence of a jury the trial judge may just peruse the pleadings, impatiently waive off an opening statement as superfluous, and direct the plaintiff to call his first witness. Since an opening statement is designed to acquaint the fact trier with the issues and with what to look for in the proof, lawyers recognize that an experienced trial judge can discern this from a scanning of the pleadings and will not press their formal right to "open"[7] unless the case is triable by jury, or the judge or referee calls for an opening.

After the openings, the witnesses are called and the evidence starts accumulating, the plaintiff going first. At this point the rules of evidence take over. Objections and their preservation become a prime topic.[8] If the court finds it helpful, it can allow the jury to visit and view a premises relevant to the action.[9] After the evidence is closed, both sides having rested, the parties sum up, in inverse order to their openings.[10] Summation, about which there are a number of points to be made, is a separately treated topic,[11] as is the court's charge to the jury,[12] which in the sequence of the trial follows the summations. The jury then goes to its deliberations and renders its verdict.

Only five of the six jurors are needed for a verdict in a civil action;[13] if five can't agree "after being kept together for as long as is deemed reasonable by the court"—this is popularly known as a hung jury—"the court shall discharge the jury and direct a new trial before

---

2. CPLR 4011, although captioned "sequence of trial", is not intended to vary this traditional progression of events at a common law trial. Its principal mission is to authorize the trial of one issue before another, as elaborated in § 394, below.

3. CPLR 4012. Marked pleadings are described in § 222. This requirement of CPLR 4012 is picked up and expanded on by the Uniform Rules to include other papers. See, e.g., UR 202.35 (applicable in the supreme and county courts).

4. See § 77A above.

5. See, e.g., Uniform Rule 202.35.

6. See, e.g., Uniform Rule 202.35.

7. The right to open and close is treated in § 395 below.

8. Objections and rulings are the subject of § 396 below.

9. CPLR 4110–c. See the Practice Commentary on that section in McKinney's CPLR.

10. CPLR 4016.

11. See § 397 below.

12. See § 398 below.

13. CPLR 4113(a). As to whether the same five jurors have to agree on all the issues in the case, see § 400 below.

another jury".[14] What a "reasonable" time is depends entirely on the facts of the particular case, the length of the trial, and the complexity of the issues.

The verdict will usually be followed by motions by the loser, a motion for judgment notwithstanding the verdict or for a new trial being the foremost examples of post-verdict motions. In the case of a money verdict the plaintiff may seek to raise the sum or the defendant to lower it, which introduces the procedures known as additur and remittitur. These are also separate later topics.[15]

§ 394. Separate Trial of Issues; Bifurcation

CPLR 4011 allows the court to determine "the sequence in which the issues shall be tried and otherwise regulate the conduct of the trial in order to achieve a speedy and unprejudiced disposition of the matters at issue in a setting of proper decorum". It is not the purpose of CPLR 4011, however, although captioned "sequence of trial", to vary the traditional order in which steps are taken at a jury trial, as generally discussed in the prior section. An occasional variation in that order may be appropriate, and CPLR 4011—which is only a confirmation, anyway, of the powers of a common law judge[1]—may perhaps be cited to support it, but the rule's primary aim is to allow the court to direct that one issue be tried before another in a case with several (and separable) issues. Its assumption is that if a case has several issues and the trial of one of them separately from and prior to another will expedite the case, that one ought to be tried first. When there is still outstanding at trial time, for example, a defense like lack of jurisdiction, release, statute of limitations, or the like, which if resolved against the plaintiff can end the case then and there, the court can single it out for trial before the complaint's main issues are addressed.

If there are both jury and nonjury issues in the case, as when a jury trial of fewer than all issues has been demanded, the rules express a clear preference to have the nonjury issues disposed of first.[2]

When the main issues for trial are the liability and damages phases of a personal injury or wrongful death action, and the liability issue is tried first, which is a common practice today, the bench and bar call this "bifurcation". Today, the rules do, too. The rule in point in the supreme and county courts, Uniform Rule 202.42,[3] provides that judges are "encouraged" to order bifurcation. It doesn't say when a bifurcated trial is necessary; it merely provides guidance for such a trial when bifurcation is directed "by law or in the court's discretion". Bifurcation is preferred, with the issue of liability tried first, for the obvious reason that if liability is negated, a damages trial, with all the frills upon it, is unnecessary.

The topic of bifurcation was previously discussed in the study of CPLR 603. That was the more appropriate place for it because an order of bifurcation is often directed in a pretrial order, grounded on CPLR 603 ("severance and separate trials"). If a direction for bifurcation should be made at the trial itself, however, no formal pretrial order having directed it, CPLR 4011 can be cited as the authority, along with the rules. The justifications for bifurcating will generally be similar whether ordained by pretrial order or directed at the trial itself, which makes the several considerations treated earlier[4] relevant here.

§ 395. Right to Open and Close

The right to open and close is jealously guarded in a trial by jury because the party who has it gets both the first and the last word to the jury. The two things are a set: the party who makes opening remarks to the jury first has the right to deliver summation last. (The right to open and close was once before

---

14. CPLR 4113(b).

15. See §§ 405–407 below.

§ 394

1. Martin v. Marshall, 25 A.D.2d 594, 266 N.Y.S.2d 992 (3d Dep't 1966).

2. Uniform Rule 202.40. See § 393 above.

3. Similar rules should be looked for in other courts. See, e.g., UR 208.35, applicable in the N.Y.C. Civil Court.

4. See § 130 above.

touched on, when the subject of consolidation of actions was treated.[1] The topic there was how to adjust the right when there are multiple parties.)

The right is tied in with the burden of proof. It belongs to the plaintiff almost invariably, but not quite. If the plaintiff does not have the affirmative of any issue, and the defendant does, the defendant will get the open-and-close right, but that rare situation must be manifest from the pleadings themselves. If the defendant by answer denies any allegation of the complaint so as to put the plaintiff to the burden of proving the allegation, the plaintiff retains the right to open and close with respect to the whole case. The defendant will not be allowed to appropriate the right to open and close by attempting to concede the plaintiff's case at the trial itself. This is designed to prevent a defendant, for whom the trial is not going well, from usurping at least the psychological advantage of closing to the jury by the simple expedient of conceding all of the plaintiff's case and then addressing only a defense or counterclaim (on which the defendant has the burden of proof).[2]

If, on the other hand, the defendant should have conceded the plaintiff's case in the answer, the plaintiff is not likely to dispute the defendant's right to open and close on a defense or counterclaim at the trial: the plaintiff will likely be there with a summary judgment already in hand, for which the plaintiff should have promptly moved when the answer and its concessions first arrived. Indeed, if the answer that conceded the plaintiff's claim offered only a defense, but no counterclaim, the plaintiff would likely have had the defense disposed of, one way or the other, by a pretrial motion to dismiss the defense under CPLR 3211(b), leaving no issues in the case at all and avoiding a trial altogether.

Contrary to popular misconception, a party is not rigidly bound by her opening statement. The omission of an item requisite to a prima facie case, for example, will not necessarily be fatal; it can be cured during the trial.[3] Judges are realistic about this and ordinarily will not permit even a variance between the pleading and the bill of particulars on the one hand and the opening statement on the other to undermine a case if there is still in prospect an evidentiary possibility of making out a claim.[4] CPLR 4401 does authorize judgment for a party "on the basis of admissions", but, as will be seen,[5] the admissions intended are those that absolutely preclude all possibility of judgment for the admitter rather than those that merely vary (from the papers in the case) some facts or even theories without prejudicing the other side or foreclosing a foundation for a victory on the merits. An "admission" during the opening is prone to be of the latter kind, and it is therefore hardly a basis for judgment.

Sometimes a party can end up as both a plaintiff and a defendant in the same case. In a two-car accident, for example, driver A, with a privately retained lawyer, may be suing driver B in one action, while driver B is suing A in a separate action in which A is represented by a lawyer retained by his insurance company. When the two actions are consolidated, a not infrequent occurrence, a clamor goes up among the parties to win the right to open and close. It has been held that someone in A's position is not entitled to have opening and closing statements made by both his lawyers; that the court retains discretion to determine how that right shall be allotted.[6]

§ 396. Objections and Rulings

After the parties have opened to the jury, the witnesses are called and the evidence begins. The law of evidence takes over during this phase of the trial, but a few essential

---

§ 395

1. See § 128 above.

2. See Lake Ontario Nat. Bank v. Judson, 122 N.Y. 278, 25 N.E. 367 (1890).

3. See Justice Rosenblatt's discussion in De Vito v. Katsch, 157 A.D.2d 413, 556 N.Y.S.2d 649 (2d Dep't 1990), New York's most detailed treatment of the subject to date.

4. See § 404, below, discussing CPLR 3025(c).

5. See § 402 below.

6. See Tomassi v. Town of Union, 58 A.D.2d 670, 395 N.Y.S.2d 747 (3d Dep't 1977).

things can be noted about the making and preservation of objections without undue trespass on the law of evidence, to which the objections will usually relate.

There is no magic word or formula for the making of objections. "Objection" is the most obvious and hence the most popular word, and so it remains the most frequent opening word in the usual counsel-and-court colloquy about the admissibility of a question, datum, or item. When a ruling is requested, the lawyer's obligation is to make known the action she thinks the court should take or her objection to the action already taken or proposed to be taken by the court;[1] the combination of words that so apprises the court is quite secondary.[2] If an evidentiary objection is sustained and an answer or item is consequently excluded, the aggrieved party should make an offer of proof for the sake of the record, describing the nature and purpose of the excluded item so as to enable the appellate court to adjudge its admissibility—its relevancy, competency, materiality, etc. In some instances, depending on the potential prejudice the offer of proof may have if made in front of the jury, the court may insist that it be made at the bench or otherwise beyond the jury's hearing or vision.

The failure to advise the court of an objection will have impact on the appellate process, where it will restrict the scope of review. A "ruling" itself is not appealable; nor are a series of rulings. But the final judgment is appealable, and if appealed will bring up for review a number of things, including evidentiary rulings and remarks of the court. But the review will ordinarily embrace only those rulings and remarks to which objection was made.[3]

If, upon an objection by the other side, the offerer responds with arguments justifying admissibility and the court hears both sides before ruling, the record in regard to that ruling should be adequate to preserve review at the behest of whichever party loses on the point.

But even a lawyer's mere putting of a question, or tender of a document, should bear implicitly a contention of its admissibility, requiring no further objection on the offerer's part if, upon the sustaining of an adversary's objection, the question or item is excluded. If the appellate court is convinced from the record that the court was aware of the appellant's position on the ruling, it will deem an objection to the court's action on the matter to have been both made and preserved. This of course assumes that the matter is one of substance and that the party with the objection did not afterwards acquiesce in the ruling.

There is no requirement today to follow an unfavorable ruling with the word "exception" or any other word or words to indicate displeasure. As long as the loser's position on the point has been made known to the court, the unfavorable ruling is preserved for appellate review without the follow-up utterance of the pouty "exception"[4] at one time in favor—and still used today, unnecessarily but harmlessly, by some lawyers. The word "exception", instead of "objection", is sometimes heard in initial opposition to a question. It is just as effective. The use of either word or neither word or other words will bear no consequence as long as the party's grievance is made known.[5] But words of some kind should be used; a surly look is hard to record on a transcript.

In making an objection, it may be politic to omit any specification of ground at the outset. This is called a "general" objection. If the court sustains it and there is any ground at all to support it, the ruling will be upheld on appeal. If the objection is sustained on a particular ground, however, the appellate court may refuse to entertain any but the cited ground to determine the ruling's validity. If the cited ground is found invalid, the ruling may be overturned notwithstanding the existence of another ground, uncited, that might

---

§ 396

1. CPLR 4017.

2. More punctilio is necessary for the charge to the jury, treated separately in § 398 below.

3. CPLR 5501(a)(3), (4).

4. CPLR 4017.

5. See 2d Rep.Leg.Doc. (1958) No. 13, p. 213.

have supported it.[6] An exception is where the evidence excluded is found by the appellate court to be wholly incompetent by all standards, in which event exclusion will be approved despite the trial court's reliance on a specific but incorrect ground. Conversely, if a general objection is overruled, and the evidence is received, the appellate court will uphold its receipt unless, again, it is by all criteria incompetent.[7] If a sanguine objector, bent on deriving some tactical benefit from this rule, makes an objection generally, the offerer of the evidence, sensing this, should be able to keep the objector honest simply by asking the court to have the objector specify the ground relied on. Unless the evidence is patently incompetent, and the validity of the objection consequently obvious, the court is likely to be receptive to that suggestion.

Objections should be timely from a tactical as well as a technical point of view. If the objection is addressed to a question, it should be made before the question is answered and the answer heard by the jury; if addressed to an item, it should be put when the item is tendered—before it is admitted into evidence and before the jury is made aware of its purpose or contents. If made afterwards, the objection becomes what is known as a motion to strike, i.e., to strike the answer from the record or the item from the evidence. Although called a "motion", it is really only a form of objection—a request for a ruling. It is obviously less effective than a timely objection that prevents the answer or item from emerging in the first place, but it has its niche in trial practice. Sometimes a witness is faster with an answer than the opposing lawyer is with an objection. Sometimes an answer or item depends for its evidentiary validity on something to come later, and is admitted by the court "subject to connection" with the later item, and the later item does not materialize, or emerges much less potently than the court was led to believe. The appropriate remedy in these instances is a motion to strike. It is often

accompanied by a court instruction that the jury disregard the particular question and answer, or the item. Although this may be unrealistic in many cases, it is important, once again, in order to preserve the objection for review on appeal. If the matter admitted is found on appeal to have been so prejudicial that the instruction to disregard it could not work, a new trial will be ordered.

A motion to strike may also be available to a party who, excusably, did not earlier realize that there was a valid evidentiary objection, and it is of course permissible when a perfectly valid question elicits a wholly unresponsive and prejudicial answer. The motion may also be the expedient whereby a judge, now convinced that he was in error in admitting an objectionable answer or item earlier, attempts to remedy the mistake.

The most important note here, which may lend some sense to the motion to strike procedure, which sometimes seems senseless—how does one get a jury to unsee, unhear, or unknow something?—is that as far as the appellate process is concerned, the key word is "prejudice". No error, or even quantum of errors, in the course of evidentiary rulings, whether in response to early objections or to later motions to strike, will overturn the verdict unless the appellate court is convinced that the error materially prejudiced the losing party.

§ 397. Summation

The lawyer's closing statement to the jury is called the "summation", or sometimes the "argument". Summations are made in inverse order to openings: the party who opens first sums up last.[1] The right to the final word has a psychological impact that makes it a forensic prize. However effective a defendant's summation may be, its most telling points may be blunted by an equally able plaintiff's summation. Plaintiffs are comforted throughout their summations by the knowledge that the defen-

---

6. See Bloodgood v. Lynch, 293 N.Y. 308, 56 N.E.2d 718 (1944).

7. See Tooley v. Bacon, 70 N.Y. 34 (1877).

§ 397

1. CPLR 4016. See the discussion of the right to open and close in § 395 above.

dant will not get another chance to address this jury.

It is the right of counsel in summation to comment on every fact relevant to the case and arguably supported by the evidence. Allowed the widest latitude, the attorney will be interrupted by the court only when necessary to prevent prolixity, waste of time, or totally unjustifiable comment,[2] which means making statements on matters not in evidence or indulging arguments having no basis whatever in the proof—including appeals to prejudice or passion.[3] Overstepping those bounds, even if the trial judge does not intervene, can bring reversal on appeal and necessitate retrial.[4] Sometimes an appellate court will grant a new trial because of the cumulative effect of a series of unwarranted comments in summation,[5] even though perhaps none individually would justify it. Irrelevancies and absurdities in quantity will turn the trick, as where in a personal injury case the plaintiff's lawyer leads off by buttering up the judge, pledges his love for the venue, and then offers discourse on his deprived youth and a large cast of unbilled characters ranging from Perry Mason to the immortal bard.[6] In such a case, it's not that the lawyer is pressing for unsupported conclusions. It's that the aggregate of the asininities will so divert the jurors from the issues that the rights of the parties will be lost in the morass. When summation exceeds all reasonable frontiers of propriety, the opposing lawyer need not stand by in silence. He may object during the summation,[7] asking for a court direction that counsel desist and that improper remarks be disregarded.[8] One lawyer should

not, however, interrupt another's summation for anything less than palpably improper conduct or comment. It should be a courtesy among lawyers that each allow the other an unfettered opportunity for argument, which is what a summation is.

If attorneys are abiding by the expected amenities, there may be no need to have the stenographer record the summations. A hint of trouble, however, should prompt a request that they be taken down and it has been held reversible error to refuse such a request.[9] The difficulty of reviewing objectionable comments without a verbatim record may itself require a new trial,[10] or amount to a waiver of the objections.[11]

A frequent topic on summation, and a legitimate one, is the other party's failure to call a given witness, especially if because of relationship the witness's testimony would presumably favor that party and the witness's absence has not been explained, such as where the plaintiff does not call his own physician in a personal injury case or a party does not call his own employee.[12]

Until the early 1980s, there was no uniform practice around the state about allowing the plaintiff in a tort case to state in summation the amount demanded in the complaint, although there was appellate division caselaw allowing it based on the rule that the content of the pleadings may always be revealed to the jury.[13] The money demand (the "ad damnum") in a tort case was usually so unrealistic[14] (and often still is) that a strong argument could be

---

2. Williams v. Brooklyn El. R.R., 126 N.Y. 96, 26 N.E. 1048 (1891).

3. See Cherry Creek National Bank v. Fidelity & Cas. Co. of N.Y., 207 App.Div. 787, 202 N.Y.S. 611 (4th Dep't 1924).

4. See McCabe v. Queensboro Farm Products, Inc., 21 A.D.2d 675, 250 N.Y.S.2d 91 (2d Dep't 1964).

5. See Bishin v. New York Cent. R.R., 20 A.D.2d 921, 249 N.Y.S.2d 778 (2d Dep't 1964).

6. See Laughing v. Utica Steam Engine & Boiler Works, 16 A.D.2d 294, 228 N.Y.S.2d 44 (4th Dep't 1962).

7. Samuel v. Porchia, 40 A.D.2d 697, 336 N.Y.S.2d 387 (2d Dep't 1972).

8. Layton Sales & Rentals, Inc. v. Somat Realty Corp., 39 A.D.2d 640, 331 N.Y.S.2d 164 (4th Dep't 1972).

9. Robinson v. Ferens, 33 A.D.2d 688, 306 N.Y.S.2d 530 (2d Dep't 1969).

10. See Devine v. Keller, 32 A.D.2d 34, 299 N.Y.S.2d 249 (3d Dep't 1969).

11. See Leven v. Marguerite, 52 A.D.2d 970, 383 N.Y.S.2d 120 (3d Dep't 1976).

12. See the extended treatment of this subject in Seligson, Morris & Neuburger v. Fairbanks Whitney Corp., 22 A.D.2d 625, 257 N.Y.S.2d 706 (1st Dep't 1965).

13. See, e.g., Rice v. Ninacs, 34 A.D.2d 388, 312 N.Y.S.2d 246 (4th Dep't 1970).

14. Plaintiffs' lawyers had to keep their demands high because the verdict could not exceed the demand, a restriction afterwards abandoned. See § 217 above.

made against its divulgence to the jury. The point was clarified when the Court of Appeals held in Tate v. Colabello[15] that it is "counsel's privilege" to suggest to the jury the sum counsel believes appropriate as damages in an unliquidated damages case like one involving personal injuries, and in conjunction with that to reveal also the amount demanded in the complaint. An important concomitant is that the jury be charged that the ultimate determination of damages is up to them, an instruction the trial court had properly made in *Tate*.

An exception has been made by at least one court in the medical malpractice action. CPLR 3017(c) bars mention of a monetary amount in the demand clause of the complaint in such an action,[16] and the Third Department has held this to mean that a sum may not be suggested to the jury in summation, either.[17] The Second Department disagrees and holds that it may.[18]

The precursor of CPLR 4016 in the early studies of the CPLR's drafters included a provision expressly authorizing the court to limit the time for opening and closing statements,[19] a provision afterwards omitted, apparently with the intent to leave the time allotment to judicial discretion to be exercised on a case by case basis.[20]

§ 398. The Charge

The charge, which follows the parties' summations, is the court's address to the jury in which it instructs them on the law applicable to the diverse issues in the case. It is made by the judge by direct address in person.[1] The jury are advised that they will determine all issues of fact, and the law charged advises them of the legal impact of their fact-findings. The charge thus enables the jury, as necessary, to convert their conclusions of fact into conclusions of law and render a verdict accordingly. The court should therefore tell the jury not only what the law is, but also what the factual contentions of the parties are with respect to the legal principles charged.[2] It should discuss the evidence and relate it to the rules of law, including a careful delineation for the jury of which party has the burden of proof on each issue and how the discharge of that burden is to be gauged. General or abstract principles of law, no matter how correct, are frowned on because they are not helpful to a jury unless made relevant to the issues of fact that it is the jury's responsibility to resolve.[3]

Elaborate itemization of the verdict is required today in the major tort actions as a result of amendments expanding or creating substantive rights affecting damages. The right of defendants to have "collateral source" payments credited against the verdict,[4] to have contribution rights determined among themselves,[5] to have their "joint" liability cancelled under certain circumstances,[6] and to pay certain parts of the plaintiff's "future" damages in installments instead of in one lump sum (in what is known as a "structured judgment"[7]), all turn in some measure on what the jury finds each individual item of damages to be and the share of fault of each party with respect to it. The statutes enacted or amended to accomplish this itemization task are subdivisions (d) and (f) of CPLR 4111. It is the obligation of the court to assure that the

---

15. 58 N.Y.2d 84, 459 N.Y.S.2d 422, 445 N.E.2d 1101 (1983).

16. See § 217 above.

17. See Bechard v. Eisinger, 105 A.D.2d 939, 481 N.Y.S.2d 906 (3d Dep't 1984).

18. Braun v. Ahmed, 127 A.D.2d 418, 515 N.Y.S.2d 473 (2d Dep't 1987).

19. See 2d Rep.Leg.Doc.(1958) No. 13, p. 212.

20. See 5th Rep.Leg.Doc.(1961) No. 15, p. 517.

§ 398

1. The use of tape, for example, has been held impermissible. See Fogel v. Lenox Hill Hospital, 127 A.D.2d 548, 512 N.Y.S.2d 109 (1st Dep't 1987).

2. Arroyo v. Judena Taxi, Inc., 20 A.D.2d 888, 248 N.Y.S.2d 952 (1st Dep't 1964).

3. Green v. Downs, 27 N.Y.2d 205, 316 N.Y.S.2d 221, 265 N.E.2d 68 (1970).

4. CPLR 4545.

5. CPLR Article 14. See § 172 et seq., above.

6. CPLR Article 16. See § 168A et seq., above.

7. See CPLR Articles 50–A and 50–B.

charge to the jury clarifies the jury's obligation to furnish this detailed itemization.[8]

In New York, several volumes of "Pattern Jury Instructions" ("PJI") are available, which set forth representative charges in a number of different settings. These were drawn by judges and scholars. While they are not binding on trial judges, they represent well-respected authority, have been found of great value by the judiciary generally,[9] and have been favorably cited by the New York Court of Appeals.[10]

Because the charge is a key part of the trial, lawyers must be alert to advise the court thoroughly on the law as each contends it to be. It is the responsibility of every trial advocate to see to it that the judge is made aware of every law relevant to the facts and favorable to the client, and this includes statutes, rules, regulations, ordinances, decisions, and any other sources that may qualify as "law" and govern the rights of the parties. The lawyer does this in what is called a "request to charge", governed today by CPLR 4110–b, which was added to the CPLR in 1973. The section permits any party at the close of the evidence to submit[11] "written requests that the court instruct the jury on the law as set forth in the requests". The court is required to rule on the requests before summation and out of the jury's hearing, so as to enable counsel to adjust their summations accordingly.[12] Before the addition of CPLR 4110–b, practices varied, but probably the most common one was to save requests to charge until after summation, submitting them before the judge's charge or even after it (when they would amount to requests for additional charges or substitutes for objectionable portions of the charge already delivered). That is still done. The submission of requests to charge before summation is something a party "may" do under CPLR 4110–b, which leaves the option to the party. And even

if the option is picked up, it need not preclude further requests after summation or even after the court's main charge.

It will probably take some time before CPLR 4110–b succeeds, if it ever does, in making it a norm for the parties to submit their requests to charge before summation, although much benefit may come of it. It avoids, for example, the occasional fiasco in which a lawyer delivers a fine summation built around an anticipated rule of law that then doesn't materialize in the charge. It tells the lawyer early what the judge sees as the applicable rule of law on each issue, which necessarily teaches the lawyer something about how to construct the argument to the jury. In fact, CPLR 4110–b contemplates such requests to charge not just before summation, but even "at such earlier time during the trial as the court reasonably directs". In potentially long trials, or in trials involving complex issues, for example, it is especially advantageous both to judge and counsel that each understand the other's position on the governing legal principles. It can assist the lawyer in presenting evidence and the court in ruling on its admissibility. Indeed, it is good practice in long or complex trials to submit at the outset, to both court and adversary, a legal memorandum setting out, to the extent tactically appropriate in advance of trial, the submitter's specific postures on the legal issues involved.

While CPLR 4017 governs the making and preservation of objections generally in the course of a trial, CPLR 4110–b has a more specific instruction about objections concerning the court's charge to the jury. It provides that "no party may assign as error the giving or the failure to give an instruction unless he objects thereto before the jury retires to consider its verdict", and the party must specify "the matter to which he objects and the

---

8. Subdivision (e) of CPLR 4111 has a similar but narrower mission, addressed only to actions against certain public employers. There the benefits of the collateral source rule are the subject aimed at.

9. See, e.g., Acerra v. Trippardella, 34 A.D.2d 927, 311 N.Y.S.2d 522 (1st Dep't 1970).

10. Green v. Downs, note 3 above.

11. CPLR 4110–b uses the word "file" rather than "submit", which betrays its federal origin. (The provision is modeled on Rule 51 of the Federal Rules of Civil Procedure.) What the lawyer should do is submit at least one copy to the court and give one to each of the other parties in the action.

12. See the Practice Commentary on McKinney's CPLR 4110–b.

grounds of his objection". The court is directed to afford the objectant an opportunity to make the objection out of the jury's hearing. The technical deadline, then, for the making of an objection affecting the charge, whether the objection is to the court's refusal to charge as requested or to something contained in the court's charge as made, is before the jury retires. But if on the facts counsel has acted with apparent diligence in at least trying to make objections timely, they will be preserved. Thus, where the judge indicated that he wished to have objections heard in chambers, and the chambers conference followed the jury's retirement to deliberate, the objections were deemed timely; the appellate court noted that a prompt recall of the jury at that early moment, for such further instruction as a sustaining of the objection might have called for, would have had scant impact on the jury's deliberative process.[13]

The trial court has broad power to recall a jury for further instructions. It usually does this when it is the jury that requests it, such as where the jury is confused on a point and wants it clarified. But the recall may also be made on the court's initiative,[14] which can be triggered by a party's request.

The main consequence of a failure to make a timely objection to a charge or to the rejection of a request to charge is that the objectant may be held to have waived the objection on appeal. An error in connection with the charge, as is true of trial errors in general, is preserved for appellate review only when duly objected to.[15] In other words, a failure to except to a given instruction may constitute it the "law of the case".[16] There is an important exception, however: if the appellate court finds the error in respect of the charge "fundamen-

tal", it can order a new trial in the interest of justice even though the error was not objected to.[17] This appellate power is not undone by CPLR 4110–b.[18] Of course, even an error properly objected to in the charge will not be ground for reversal unless found to be prejudicial. Harmless error, even in the charge to the jury, is ignored.[19]

D. THE VERDICT

Table of Sections

§ 399. Kinds of Verdict

The verdict is the determination of the jury on the issues submitted. It can be either general or special. A "general" verdict is one in which the jury merely finds in favor of a party; it is pronounced in just that conclusory way and the various component findings that account for it remain unspoken. "We find in favor of the defendant." Or: "We find for the plaintiff in the sum of $175,000." The "special" verdict is a statement by the jury of the facts it has found. What it really is is the jury's answers to questions submitted to it, sometimes very detailed questions. The court then reviews the answers and determines which party is to have judgment.[1]

The general verdict is still in use today, but losing ground to the special verdict, especially in tort cases. With the expansion in the 1970s of contribution rights among tortfeasors,[2] closely followed by the adoption of a rule of comparative negligence applicable to a tort plaintiff to replace the traditional New York

---

13. Meagher v. L.I.R.R., 27 N.Y.2d 39, 313 N.Y.S.2d 378, 261 N.E.2d 384 (1970).

14. See Barreto v. Calderon, 31 A.D.2d 896, 297 N.Y.S.2d 799 (1st Dep't 1969).

15. CPLR 4017, 5501(a)(3).

16. See Olsen v. St. Margaret of Scotland Roman Catholic Church, 21 A.D.2d 827, 251 N.Y.S.2d 512 (2d Dep't 1964). The "law of the case" doctrine is a species of intra-action res judicata. See § 448 below.

17. See, e.g., Jemison v. Goodman, 49 A.D.2d 1011, 373 N.Y.S.2d 926 (4th Dep't 1975).

18. DiGrazia v. Castronova, 48 A.D.2d 249, 251–2, 368 N.Y.S.2d 898, 902 (4th Dep't 1975). The case illustrates what can qualify as so "fundamental" an error as to mandate a new trial.

19. See, e.g., Lieberman v. Washington Square Hotel Corp., 40 A.D.2d 647, 336 N.Y.S.2d 518 (1st Dep't 1972).

§ 399

1. CPLR 4111(a).

2. CPLR 1401–1404. See § 172 above.

rule of contributory negligence,[3] and with the adoption in the 1980s of the collateral source rule[4] and the rule adjusting joint liability among tortfeasors,[5] the need to have the jury reveal its specific findings of percentages of fault in personal injury and wrongful death cases gave the special verdict new vogue. Elaboration by the jury of allotments of fault and items of damages in tort cases was ultimately made mandatory.[6] It has even been held that if there are issues of comparative negligence in a case, it is reversible error for the judge to elicit only a general verdict unless the parties stipulate to it.[7]

The special verdict entails the submission to the jury of written questions susceptible of brief answer, or written forms of the various alternative findings the jury can choose from, or some other equivalent method to elicit written findings. Whichever device is used, the charge must of course clarify the jury's obligations on all of the issues involved. The parties must be alert to assure that all the questions of interest to their side are submitted: if any such issue duly raised by the pleadings or evidence is not among the proposed submissions, the interested party must demand its inclusion before the jury retires. Otherwise, trial by jury of the omitted issue may be waived and a consent implied to the court's determining it; or, in default of an express judicial finding, the issue will be deemed resolved in accordance with the judgment.[8] This is designed, when a special verdict is used, to prevent invalidation of the whole trial through the inadvertent omission of but one issue.[9]

The special verdict is especially appropriate when several different grounds are alleged in support of a claim. Suppose, for example, that a jury renders a general verdict for P on a claim allegedly supported by two grounds. An appellate court finds one of the grounds unsupported by the record but cannot determine whether the jury relied on that one, which would require a reversal,[10] or the valid one, which could bring affirmance. The court has no choice in that situation but to reverse and remand for a new trial.[11] A special verdict, by clarifying whether the supportable ground was sustained by the jury, would avoid that. This has frequently prompted appellate courts, on remanding for a new trial in an instance of multiple theories, to require that a special verdict be used.[12]

The court has yet a third way of submitting the case to the jury. It is known as a general verdict accompanied by answers to interrogatories, a kind of mixture of general and special verdicts. It clarifies the jury's constituent findings, but also enables the jury to draw the conclusion they believe the findings justify. This device comes from CPLR 4111(c),[13] which also provides for the situation in which there is conflict between the conclusion (the general verdict) and one of the answers. As long as the answers are consistent with each other, they will ordinarily prevail over the general verdict. The underlying theory is that the components of the jury's findings are more revealing than its conclusions.[14] But the court retains discretion to send the jury back for further deliberations or to order a new trial. When one of the answers is in conflict with the general verdict and it also appears that the answers are not consistent among themselves, further deliberations or a new trial are the court's only options; judgment in accordance with the answers would be precluded.[15]

3. CPLR 1411. See § 168E above.

4. CPLR 4545, noted in § 180 above.

5. CPLR Article 16. See § 168A et seq. above.

6. See CPLR 4111(d), (e), and (f). See § 398 above. A similar set of requirements applies to the judge in a judge-tried case under CPLR 4213. See the Commentaries on McKinney's CPLR 4111 and 4213.

7. See Russo v. Rifkin, 113 A.D.2d 570, 497 N.Y.S.2d 41 (2d Dep't 1985).

8. CPLR 4111(b).

9. See 2d Rep.Leg.Doc.(1958) No. 13, pp. 234–235. This provision is adapted from Rule 49(a) of the Federal Rules of Civil Procedure.

10. See Blair v. New York Univ. Coll. of Dentistry, 15 A.D.2d 211, 222 N.Y.S.2d 1 (1st Dep't 1961).

11. See Hamilton v. Presbyterian Hosp., 25 A.D.2d 431, 267 N.Y.S.2d 656 (1st Dep't 1965).

12. See, e.g., Corbett v. Brown, 32 A.D.2d 27, 32, 299 N.Y.S.2d 219, 224 (3d Dep't 1969).

13. CPLR 4111(c) is modeled on FRCP Rule 49(b).

14. See and compare Chevalier v. Farrell, 58 Misc.2d 991, 296 N.Y.S.2d 896 (Sup.Ct., Rensselaer County, 1968).

Suppose, for example, that in a tort case governed by New York's comparative negligence rule, P and each of the defendants A and B are found guilty of 40% fault. That would total an impossible 120% and the answers, without even having to consider how they stack up against the general verdict, would necessitate further deliberations or a new trial.

The special verdict by itself is probably a neater tool to discern the jury's intentions, but whether to use it alone or in combination with the general verdict, giving rise to the general verdict accompanied by interrogatories, is left to the court's discretion. The Court of Appeals has observed that the technique of submitting interrogatories to the jury is "especially well suited to cases with multiple parties and legal theories",[16] to which we may add issues of comparative and contributory fault, but no uniform criteria have yet been developed for whether to use the interrogatories with or without a general verdict. Even appellate courts, when remanding cases for new trials, sometimes seem to suggest one or the other indifferently.[17]

As a matter of tactics, plaintiffs' attorneys in tort cases, especially those involving serious injuries but questionable liability, prefer the general verdict alone and put the special verdict at the bottom of their list of options. Their fear is that a jury bent on finding facts without at all times being aware of their legal impact will be more prone to find for the defendant. The fear had more basis under the now-superseded contributory negligence rule, where a finding of any negligence on the plaintiff's part destroyed the case. It lost much of its justification under the superseding rule of comparative negligence,[18] which allows a negligent plaintiff to recover for at least the defendant's proportionate share of the plaintiff's damages.

§ 400. Delivery of the Verdict

When the jury have reached a verdict, they advise the court, which arranges for them to return to the courtroom to make formal delivery of the verdict while all parties are present or represented. Only five of the six jurors need agree on the verdict;[1] unlike a jury's verdict in a criminal action, the civil verdict need not be unanimous. But unless the parties stipulate otherwise, all six must participate in the deliberations. If, without the parties' permission, one juror is absent, for whatever reason, a verdict of the others will be invalidated even though it is a verdict of five.[2] The theory is that the absent juror might have disagreed and persuaded at least one other juror to do likewise, thus precluding a verdict or perhaps even tilting the verdict the other way.

If there's a stipulation to accept a jury of fewer than six, it has been held that all parties must subscribe to it; that if only one does, the verdict is invalid no matter who wins it. In one case, for example, in which one of the six jurors took ill and had to be excused, P consented to five but D would not go along. The court allowed the five to proceed anyway and the five then produced a unanimous verdict for D, who promptly re-examined his conscience, found a jury of five okay after all, and magnanimously offered to accept the verdict. The appellate division looked this gift horse in the mouth and kicked it and the verdict out; it held that a party will not be allowed to exploit such a no-lose situation.[3]

If the case is divisible into segments and the jury must decide each of them, it should not be

---

15. CPLR 4111(c).

16. Marine Midland Bank v. John E. Russo Produce Co., 50 N.Y.2d 31, 427 N.Y.S.2d 961 (1980).

17. Compare Gandy v. Wuster, 25 A.D.2d 478, 266 N.Y.S.2d 544 (4th Dep't 1966) with Corbett v. Brown, note 12, above.

18. CPLR Article 14–A.

§ 400

1. CPLR 4113(a).

2. See Measeck v. Noble, 9 A.D.2d 19, 189 N.Y.S.2d 748 (3d Dep't 1959).

3. Waldman v. Cohen, 125 A.D.2d 116, 512 N.Y.S.2d 205 (2d Dep't 1987). If the trial is likely to be prolonged, the answer to the prospect of an incapacitated juror is an alternate or several alternate jurors. See § 391 above. In the Waldman case, the deliberations were so close to commencing that the alternate jurors had been excused.

necessary for the same five jurors to agree on everything. Where, for example, five of the six agree on the defendant's liability in a personal injury case but a different five then agree on what the plaintiff's damages are—a different one of the six jurors dissenting on each phase—the verdict should stand. At least one case had held otherwise,[4] but its holding seems untenable in a system that recognizes the bifurcated trial,[5] which allows the two phases even to be tried separately, and by separate juries.

While it is not necessarily inconsistent for a juror voting against liability to participate afterwards in the assessment of P's damages, what of the liability phase itself? If liability is at issue between or among defendants, perhaps with the comparative fault of the plaintiff thrown in for good measure, and an apportionment of the shares of fault of all is necessary, is consistency required on the part of each juror? Can the juror who votes P free of fault on the 5–1 vote holding P contributorily negligent, for example, then be one of the majority on another 5–1 vote finding P's precise percentage of fault? The Second Department said yes in Schabe v. Hampton Bays Union Free School District[6] and adopted the "any five" rule. Extensively reviewing the issue in an opinion by Justice Leon Lazer, the court held that while consistency must be maintained from question to question on the special verdict as a whole, "individual juror voting patterns" need not be consistent.

Also part of the *Schabe* holding is that jurors are free to argue on each subsequent issue and can't be "bound" by how they voted on an earlier one. Otherwise the casting of a dissenting vote on any question would reduce the dissenter's influence "to a state of practical impotence", held *Schabe*, and create "a mandate for continued unanimity among the other jurors on the remaining questions".

On yet another key point, *Schabe* held that it is permissible to tell a jury the effect that their answers will have on the outcome of the case, lest they just speculate and possibly end up guessing wrong.[7]

A party can determine whether a given juror supports the verdict by polling the jury after the verdict has been delivered. Conducting such a poll is a party's right.[8] The poll is conducted by asking each juror whether the verdict is his or hers, thus revealing the juror's individual support for, or opposition to, the verdict. A polling question so propounded as to inquire only whether the verdict delivered is the verdict of the *jury* is improper, because even a juror who individually disagreed with it may be misled to answer yes to the question.[9] In a bifurcated tort trial in which liability and damages are being tried separately but to the same jury, a polling of the jury after a finding of liability can be deferred until after trial of the damages phase, after which the jury can be polled on both parts.[10] It would seem appropriate, however, to poll in respect of the liability finding immediately, to determine whether the finding is valid. The damages trial might otherwise prove a waste.

When a five-sixths verdict is rendered sustaining liability in the bifurcated trial situation, and there is some doubt about whether the holdout juror on liability even participated in the deliberations on damages, the juror in question may be asked about that during the polling process.[11] Whichever way the holdout juror may have been disposed to vote on the issue of damages, all parties are entitled to

---

4. Murphy v. Roger Sherman Transfer Co., 62 Misc.2d 960, 310 N.Y.S.2d 891 (App.T., 1st Dep't, 1970).

5. See § 130 above.

6. 103 A.D.2d 418, 480 N.Y.S.2d 328 (1984).

7. The issue arose in Schabe in the common context of a bifurcated trial. The jury, having imputed 41% fault to P during the liability trial, didn't know whether the figure they were producing now, on the damages trial, was the actual amount P would get, or a figure that the 41% would then reduce. Schabe acknowledges conflict on the several points it decides, notably on the "any five" rule, both in

New York and nationally. The case is the subject of the lead note in New York State Law Digest No. 301.

8. Knox v. State Bank of Albany, 260 App.Div. 964, 23 N.Y.S.2d 233 (3d Dep't 1940).

9. See O'Brien v. Mix, 14 A.D.2d 832, 220 N.Y.S.2d 652 (4th Dep't 1961).

10. Pickering v. Freedman, 32 A.D.2d 649, 300 N.Y.S.2d 742 (2d Dep't 1969).

11. See Sharrow v. Dick Corp., 86 N.Y.2d 54, 629 N.Y.S.2d 980, 653 N.E.2d 1150 (1995), discussed in the lead note in New York State Law Digest No. 427.

have all jurors take part in the deliberations and doubt about whether all of them did will vitiate the verdict.

The jury delivers its verdict in the courtroom, usually orally. But an alternative is the sealed verdict, in which the jury writes its verdict down and delivers the writing to a designated court official. It's in the court's discretion to order a sealed verdict, which is used, for example, when the judge or the lawyers can't stand by and be available to return to the courtroom when the verdict is reached. The sealing of the verdict enables the jury to be dispersed. They then reassemble in the courtroom at a later time, designated by the judge, and it is only on that occasion (absent agreement by the parties to the contrary) that the verdict is unsealed and formally delivered. An opening of the sealed verdict is deferred until then primarily to enable polling to proceed. A sealed verdict is otherwise treated the same as an oral one.[12]

If the verdict is improper in form but its substantive content is clearly discernible, the court can correct it to reflect its legal impact. Thus, where the jury in a personal injury case, finding defendants A and B negligent in respective proportions of 70% and 30%, also tried to restrict the liability of each to his own share, the court corrected the verdict to permit entry of judgment against each defendant for 100% of the plaintiff's damages.[13] Percentages of fault among joint tortfeasors dictated their contribution rights among themselves at the time, but the plaintiff was entitled to a joint and several judgment against each defendant.[14]

If the jury can't deliver a verdict because of irreconcilable disagreement among them "after being kept together for as long as is deemed reasonable by the court", they are a hung jury and are discharged. The discharge of a hung jury results in a new trial before a new jury.[15]

Assuming that a valid verdict has been rendered, the next step is its entry. The clerk is required to enter in the minutes the details of the verdict, along with a specification of the time and place of the trial, the names of the jurors and witnesses, and any directions of the court about subsequent proceedings.[16] The "clerk" who does this is usually the nonjudicial employee assigned to the particular courtroom. If that person acts also as the "judgment" clerk, her own minutes will supply whatever data about the verdict is needed to verify the validity of a judgment later presented for entry. (A judgment based on a verdict must refer to the verdict and state the result of it.[17]) In urban areas, where the judgment clerk, with whom the judgment is formally "entered",[18] is a separate official, the common practice is to take to the judgment clerk an extract from the minutes of the clerk who attended in the courtroom, attesting to the verdict.

§ 401. Defective Verdicts; Impeachment

A general rule in New York is that jurors may not be heard to impeach the verdict of their own jury. This means that they can't, with affidavits or testimony or in any other way, adduce anything that would tend to overturn the verdict once it's been delivered. The primary intent of this rule is to keep sacrosanct the processes and deliberations of the jury and to insulate the verdict from later revelations of what went on in the jury room.[1]

12. See the dissenting opinion of Dowling, J., in Wirt v. Reid, 138 App.Div. 760, 779, 123 N.Y.S. 706, 720 (1st Dep't 1910).

13. Gleich v. Volpe, 32 N.Y.2d 517, 346 N.Y.S.2d 806, 300 N.E.2d 148 (1973).

14. Under the later adjustment of joint and several liability with the adoption of Article 16 of the CPLR, defendants who are found 50% or less at fault in some tort actions are freed of joint liability. See § 168A et seq., above.

15. CPLR 4113(b).

16. CPLR 4112.

17. CPLR 5011.

18. See § 418 below.

§ 401

1. Persons other than jurors are not subject to this anti-impeachment rule, but nor are they privy to the jury's deliberations. They thus have scant opportunity to reveal them. Invasion of the secrecy of the jury room is in any event a criminal contempt. See People ex rel. Choate v. Barrett, 56 Hun. 351, 9 N.Y.S. 321, aff'd 121 N.Y. 678, 24 N.E. 1095 (1890).

The rule is not applicable, however, to the prejudicial conduct of a juror outside the jury room even if the conduct is learned of by another juror inside. So, for example, where a juror made an unauthorized visit to the scene of the occurrence at issue in the case, the visit could be revealed by other jurors and the verdict overturned.[2]

The most common exception to this rule of non-impeachment is where a juror has lied or deliberately concealed a material fact on the voir dire. For a long time this has been a basis for entertaining a co-juror's affidavit attesting to the falsehood or concealment, even though learned of in the jury room or courtroom or during some jury recess. A new trial was mandated, for example, where it was shown that a juror concealed an ethnic prejudice against the defendant.[3] It is also permissible for the court to put the offending juror on the stand in such an instance to ascertain the facts in a testimonial hearing.[4]

There is no established rule barring a juror from revealing the jury's deliberations after the trial is over and the jury has been dismissed, but the courts frown on outright post-trial investigations of jurors, probing their deliberations and relationships. It is felt to constitute an undue harassment of jurors and an undermining of the jury process.[5] The primary design of the anti-impeachment rule, in fact, is to divest such fishing expeditions of their most hoped-for reward—the overturning of the verdict—candidly acknowledging that many a verdict could be assailed if jury room deliberations could be revealed and made the basis for post-trial motions to invalidate the verdict.[6]

Efforts to clarify what the verdict in fact is are a wholly different matter. Here affidavits of the jurors are acceptable. In one case, for example, involving a sealed verdict, several jurors had changed their minds—which they

are entitled to do before the verdict is recorded—and tried to communicate as much to the judge before the verdict was opened. Their change of mind had changed the verdict but they could not get through to the judge in time. Their affidavits to show this were entertained. Although it might at first seem an attempt to impeach the verdict, it was in essence quite the contrary: an endeavor to show that the verdict as recorded was not the verdict at all.[7]

There are some well known categories of defective verdict. One of them is the "compromise" verdict, which can be discerned as such merely be looking at it in light of the evidence. It therefore requires no affidavits from jurors. A good illustration of a compromise verdict when New York followed the contributory negligence rule—under which any negligence at all on the part of the plaintiff destroyed the case entirely[8]—would sometimes appear in a tort action involving extensive injuries (and hence damages) but doubtful liability. A verdict for the plaintiff in a grossly inadequate sum would manifest that the jury was sympathetic to the plaintiff but did not really find the defendant at fault, "compromising" by faulting the defendant but underassessing the damages. Such a verdict could not stand.[9] The comparative negligence rule,[10] under which the plaintiff with a share of fault is allowed to recover but with damages reduced by that share, validates that kind of verdict today and removes it from the tainted "compromise" category.

There may be other evidences of irreconcilable compromise. In one case, for example, P sued D for negligence in permitting a certain hair spray to come in contact with P's forehead. D impleaded T, the manufacturer, alleging that the spray itself was defective. Clearly

---

2. Bainton v. Board of Educ. of City of New York, 57 Misc.2d 140, 292 N.Y.S.2d 229 (App.T., 2d Dep't, 1968).

3. People v. Leonti, 262 N.Y. 256, 186 N.E. 693 (1933).

4. Id.

5. See Gamell v. Mt. Sinai Hospital, 40 A.D.2d 1010, 339 N.Y.S.2d 31 (2d Dep't 1972).

6. See the discussion in People v. DeLucia, 20 N.Y.2d 275, 282 N.Y.S.2d 526, 229 N.E.2d 211 (1967).

7. Spielter v. North German Lloyd S.S. Co., 232 A.D. 104, 249 N.Y.S. 358 (1st Dep't 1931).

8. The contributory negligence rule was replaced by the comparative negligence rule, CPLR Article 14–A, as of September 1, 1975.

9. See Lallo v. W.T. Grant Co., 31 A.D.2d 941, 298 N.Y.S.2d 802 (2d Dep't 1969).

10. CPLR 1411, 1413.

D's application of the product would not have caused the injury if the product itself were not defective. A finding that D was liable but that T was not was therefore inconsistent and could not stand.[11]

Another kind of presumably defective verdict is the "quotient" verdict, appearing in tort and other unliquidated damages cases. Each of the jurors jots down the damages figure he or she deems appropriate and these are then added up and divided by the number of jurors. Many a verdict is reached that way. If all jurors stood firm on their own figures, there would never be a verdict, and the courts recognize this.[12] The only thing that makes a "quotient" verdict invalid, therefore, is the jurors' advance agreement to be bound by the quotient no matter what it comes to. If they reach for a quotient with the understanding that they can then deliberate on it before concluding themselves, the verdict is good.[13]

Unlike the "compromise" verdict, whose invalidity appears on its face, proof that the verdict is an invalid "quotient" one must come from a juror. It entails, in other words, divulging the deliberations and therefore runs into the anti-impeachment rule. Rare, therefore, is the money verdict attackable as a "quotient" one.

E.   TRIAL MOTIONS

Table of Sections

11.   Toner v. Constable, 61 Misc.2d 586, 306 N.Y.S.2d 323 (N.Y.C.Civ.Ct. 1968), mod. on other grounds 61 Misc.2d 591, 307 N.Y.S.2d 231 (App.T., 1st Dep't, 1969).

12.   See Hamilton v. Owego Waterworks, 22 A.D. 573, 48 N.Y.S. 106 (3d Dep't 1897), aff'd 163 N.Y. 562, 57 N.E. 1111 (1900).

§ 402.   Motion for Judgment During Trial

CPLR 4401 provides the motion for judgment during trial. It reads:

> Any party may move for judgment with respect to a cause of action or issue upon the ground that the moving party is entitled to judgment as a matter of law, after the close of the evidence presented by an opposing party with respect to such cause of action or issue, or at any time on the basis of admissions. Grounds for the motion shall be specified. The motion does not waive the right to trial by jury or to present further evidence even where it is made by all parties.

The main motion authorized by this provision is better known to the bar as the motion for a "directed verdict". That terminology is still used, but in official CPLR parlance today it is simply a motion for "judgment as a matter of law" under CPLR 4401.

A party may make this motion only after the other side's case is in, so that it is not seen at the outset of the trial unless it is based on "admissions". A motion based on admissions is authorized "at any time".

One might see at the beginning of a trial, however, a CPLR 3211 dismissal motion based on certain grounds, like lack of subject matter jurisdiction, failure to state a cause of action, or failure to join a party, the grounds set forth in paragraphs 2, 7, and 10 of CPLR 3211(a), because those grounds are not governed by the usual time restrictions of CPLR 3211(e) and may therefore be made at any time. While it is technically permissible, a party's withholding a CPLR 3211(a) dismissal motion until the trial is not likely to get a warm reception. Postponement to the trial of a motion that could have avoided a trial is gross laches, whatever the technical permission of CPLR 3211 may be. It would also be a violation of the spirit, if

13.   Honigsberg v. N.Y.C. Transit Auth., 43 Misc.2d 1, 249 N.Y.S.2d 296 (N.Y.C.Civ.Ct. 1964).

not the letter, of the certificate of readiness rule.[1]

A traditionally pretrial motion that the courts did sometimes see at the opening of a trial was the motion for summary judgment under CPLR 3212, which until 1997 had no outer time restriction. It was then given one, however, with the explicit design of barring the practice of saving a summary judgment motion for the trial and forcing any party with a summary judgment aspiration to make the motion either before the filing of the note of issue or within a set number of days after it.[2] Under the amendment, the practice of saving a summary judgment motion for the trial has presumably been dissolved, but one may wonder how this will play out. If the case is truly one for summary judgment, but a motion for it at the outset of the trial is barred, the trial proof itself, pretty soon after it gets under way, should manifest the one-sidedness of the case and readily produce a CPLR 4401 motion for judgment at some point during the trial. But doesn't this amount to the forcing of a trial in a case in which there is really nothing to try?

While a motion for judgment based on admissions is authorized "at any time", one must today be circumspect about what will satisfy as an admission for this purpose. The courts are justifiably reticent about putting an abrupt end to a case—after it has survived all the pretrial stages and at last arrived at trial—before the parties have put in their evidence. The motion for judgment based on admissions will therefore be granted only when counsel "deliberately and intentionally states or admits some fact that in any view of the case is fatal to the action",[3] and counsel obviously does not make a habit of something like that. The admissions should be of a kind intended as the virtual equivalent of a pleading rather than some mere evidentiary statement that

the party is not precluded from contradicting with other evidence.[4] A formal admission made under CPLR 3123, if sufficient to warrant judgment against the admitter as a matter of law, should suffice, but it is tactically unlikely that the opposing party would have saved such a motion for the trial when she could have used the same admission to ground a summary judgment motion under CPLR 3212 long before.

Much of the caselaw on this phase of CPLR 4401 involves the plaintiff's opening to the jury and whether counsel made some fatal admission during it. The complaint will not be dismissed on the opening statement, however, unless it plainly appears that there is really no issue of fact holding the case up; that taking as true every fact the plaintiff alleges and resolving in the plaintiff's favor every fact the defendant disputes, the plaintiff has no case.[5] An admission in the opening that amounts to nothing more than an immaterial variance from the complaint or bill of particulars, or even from a deposition, will not ground a dismissal. Where, for example, the complaint and bill of particulars in a tort case alleging a failure of supervision by school officials charged that unauthorized hard balls were used in a certain game, and on the opening to the jury counsel said instead that soft balls were used, this was no judgment-grounding admission: a prima facie case was made out on the opening regardless of discrepancies in the size or texture of the ball.[6]

Practically speaking, if the trial looks to be a short one (not more than a day or two), if both sides are at hand with their witnesses, and if there is nothing in the plaintiff's case so summarily defective that it would have lent itself to a dismissal with some pretrial device like a motion to dismiss or for summary judgment, a dismissal on the plaintiff's opening is best

---

§ 402

1. See § 370 above.

2. See CPLR 3212(a) (as amended effective January 1, 1997), discussed in § 279 above.

3. Hoffman House v. Foote, 172 N.Y. 348, 351, 65 N.E. 169 (1902).

4. See Martin Fireproofing Corp. v. Maryland Casualty Co., 45 Misc.2d 354, 257 N.Y.S.2d 100 (Sup.Ct., Erie

County, 1965), aff'd 26 A.D.2d 910, 275 N.Y.S.2d 375 (4th Dep't 1966).

5. Runkel v. City of New York, 282 App.Div. 173, 123 N.Y.S.2d 485 (2d Dep't 1953).

6. Rivera v. Board of Educ. of City of N. Y., 11 A.D.2d 7, 201 N.Y.S.2d 372 (1st Dep't 1960).

avoided even by a judge with serious doubts. There is no harm in waiting until the plaintiff has called witnesses and put in his case.

In an authoritative decision on this matter in De Vito v. Katsch,[7] the court said that a dismissal based on the plaintiff's opening to the jury has to be reserved for a most unique case, and a strong general rule deemed to exist against so narrowly based a dismissal. The court must give the plaintiff the benefit of every doubt, examining the pleadings to determine whether there is anything in them that amounts to a conceding away by the plaintiff of an element indispensable to the plaintiff's case. In De Vito, the trial court had dismissed an action after the plaintiff said on her opening that she would not be calling any first-hand witnesses. The appellate division reversed, holding that the plaintiff had to be given a chance to establish her case by circumstantial evidence.

It is after the evidence is in, either on the plaintiff's side or on both sides, that the meaty motion of CPLR 4401—what bench and bar will probably always call the motion for a directed verdict[8]—makes its appearance. It is not based on anything as flighty as indecisive statements in opening statements; it is based on the evidence itself. To see that this evidentiary foundation is complete enough for a court-directed judgment, CPLR 4401 authorizes the motion for judgment only after the movant's adversary has completed her case.

The only stated criterion is that the movant is entitled to judgment "as a matter of law". The standard has been phrased in these general terms to recognize the limitless variety of fact situations that can invoke it. The judge may grant the motion, which of course takes the case out of the jury's hands, only when convinced that the jury could not find for the other party by any rational process;[9] when, in support of the party against whom it proposes to order judgment, the court can find "no evidence and no substantial inferences";[10] when reasonable minds reacting to the evidence could not differ and would have to conclude just one way.[11] The court must accept as true all of the evidence offered by the party against whom the motion for judgment aims, and must even resolve in that party's favor all questions relating to the credibility of witnesses.[12] There are many word combinations one may summon to describe a situation appropriate to a motion for judgment, but it is essentially a matter of an experienced reaction to a given fact pattern. Piling up a lot of generalizations doesn't really help.[13]

Since the essence of the movant's posture when judgment is sought under CPLR 4401 is that there is no fact issue to be tried, the very making of the motion was at one time deemed a concession that no fact issue existed. This meant that even if the motion was denied, the movant by its mere making was held to waive all further right to trial by jury. That is no longer the case. CPLR 4401 in express language assures the movant that the making of an unsuccessful motion for judgment does not waive trial by jury or the right to present further evidence. The movant need not even "reserve" those rights when he makes the

7. 157 A.D.2d 413, 556 N.Y.S.2d 649 (2d Dep't 1990).

8. A "directed verdict" does not contemplate, and has not for a long time, that the jury will actually retire and then come back with the verdict the court has directed. In today's practice the old terminology is just shorthand for the situation in which the judge during the trial takes the case away from the jury and directs judgment as a matter of law.

9. Prince v. City of New York, 21 A.D.2d 668, 250 N.Y.S.2d 107 (1st Dep't 1964).

10. African Metals Corp. v. Bullowa, 288 N.Y. 78, 81, 41 N.E.2d 466, 468 (1942).

11. Cesario v. Chiapparine, 21 A.D.2d 272, 250 N.Y.S.2d 584 (2d Dep't 1964). In one situation, a special

statute mandates dismissal after the plaintiff's case is in: in an action for medical malpractice based on lack of informed consent, the plaintiff is required to produce expert medical testimony on the issue and a failure to do so requires dismissal, CPLR 4401-a, notwithstanding that other proof may support the plaintiff's claim.

12. Hurder v. Samuel Kosoff & Sons, Inc., 23 A.D.2d 804, 258 N.Y.S.2d 1 (4th Dep't 1965).

13. See § 408, above, comparing the CPLR 4401 motion for judgment during trial with the CPLR 3212 motion for judgment before trial and the CPLR 4404 motion for judgment after trial. Note also that the motion for judgment under CPLR 4401 is not the occasion for "weighing" the evidence, which is a post-trial phenomenon governed by CPLR 4404, treated later. See § 406.

motion,[14] and these assurances obtain even when all parties move for judgment under CPLR 4401.[15]

The requirement that each party await the conclusion of the other's case before moving for judgment is designed to afford all parties a day in court. The general assumption is that the party has offered everything he has and if his case is still legally inadequate an end may as well be put to it now. But if it appears that some deficiency in one party's case can possibly be remedied when some other party, even an adverse party, puts in her evidence, the court will deny the motion and let the case go on. If P sues A and B in tort, for example, and it appears that some defect in P's case may be filled in by A or B, who are hostile to each other, the court should not grant judgment against P at the close of P's proof.[16]

There is a tie-in between CPLR 4401 and CPLR 5013. The latter provides that a dismissal against a plaintiff before the close of the plaintiff's evidence is not on the merits (which means that a dismissal made at that point will not bar a fresh suit), while a dismissal after the close of the plaintiff's evidence does qualify as a merits determination (which would subject a new action to the defense of res judicata).[17] The juncture at which CPLR 4401 authorizes its main motion for judgment is therefore a juncture at which, if the motion is granted, the movant will ordinarily draw the added advantage of res judicata.

The court does have power to provide otherwise, however, i.e., to give res judicata effect to a dismissal made before the close of the plaintiff's evidence or to deprive of res judicata

effect a dismissal made after it.[18] Whether the court will exercise this discretionary power depends on the state of the evidence. If the dismissal is based, for example, on a failure of proof that the plaintiff may yet be able to come up with, the dismissal after the close of plaintiff's case should be without prejudice, i.e., not on the merits.[19] But if there is no indication that curative proof exists, the dismissal at that stage should not be qualified and should thus be left to stand as a judgment on the merits.[20]

The appending of a qualification may also occur through pretrial motion practice, serving a punitive purpose when the plaintiff has been guilty of neglecting the case. An order entered on the plaintiff's default in failing to serve a bill of particulars pursuant to a conditional preclusion order, for example, dismissing the complaint "upon the merits" or "with prejudice", has been held to bar a second action. The court said that while the power to qualify a dismissal made before the plaintiff's case has been put in is "sparingly exercised", it is appropriate to exercise it when "the only purpose of new litigation is to circumvent the preclusion decree".[21] The "continual disregard" of court orders in bill of particulars practice is seen as one of those "exceptional circumstances" that warrant the appending of a fatal qualification to the dismissal.[22]

If the dismissal has not been specified to be without prejudice, and there is nothing in the record to corroborate that it was intended to be, even the judge who ordered the dismissal may be precluded from later amending it to

---

14. Woodard v. M.V.A.I.C., 23 A.D.2d 215, 259 N.Y.S.2d 918 (3d Dep't 1965).

15. Application of LaManna, 23 A.D.2d 957, 259 N.Y.S.2d 987 (4th Dep't 1965).

16. See, e.g., Simon v. Lowenthal, 169 Misc. 718, 8 N.Y.S.2d 484 (N.Y.C.Mun.Ct. 1938).

17. CPLR 5013 refers to the "proponent" of the evidence, thus imposing its res judicata consequences on counterclaims, cross-claims, and the like, as well as on the plaintiff's main claim. The latter is used in our examples. A CPLR 4401 judgment against a plaintiff counts as the "judgment dismissing a cause of action" referred to in CPLR 5013.

18. CPLR 5013.

19. See Harsco Corp. v. Rodolitz Realty Corp., 61 Misc.2d 644, 307 N.Y.S.2d 531 (Sup.Ct., Queens County, 1969). An alternative to a dismissal in this instance, of course, especially when the witness or document needed to remedy the failure of proof is close at hand, is a mere adjournment.

20. Hansen v. City of New York, 274 App.Div. 196, 80 N.Y.S.2d 249 (1st Dep't 1948), aff'd 299 N.Y. 136, 85 N.E.2d 905 (1949).

21. Palmer v. Fox, 28 A.D.2d 968, 283 N.Y.S.2d 216 (4th Dep't 1967), aff'd 22 N.Y.2d 667, 291 N.Y.S.2d 361, 238 N.E.2d 751 (1968).

22. Mitchell v. Kiamesha Concord, Inc., 94 A.D.2d 914, 463 N.Y.S.2d 626 (3d Dep't 1983). See the discussion in § 241 above.

add the qualification; it may amount to the judge's sitting as an appellate court over himself.[23] But if the record does support that this was the court's initial intention and the omission of the qualification was inadvertent, a nunc pro tunc amendment should be permissible.[24]

As a general and salutary rule, the courts prefer to deny CPLR 4401 motions during the trial in deference to the CPLR 4404 motion after it. The reasons for this are discussed later.[25]

§ 403. Motion for Mistrial

The motion for a mistrial is a device to cancel or discontinue a trial in order to start it afresh before a new jury or continue it at a later time before the same one. It used to be known as a motion "to withdraw a juror",[1] which resulted in an incomplete jury and a breakdown of the trial. It was the device alighted on as a good way to remedy certain prejudicial defects in the course of a trial by jury. It is commonly known today as a simple "mistrial" motion, but the CPLR does not even use that terminology. The governing provision is CPLR 4402, whose caption is "motion for continuance or new trial during trial". Its substance is one sentence:

> At any time during the trial, the court, on motion of any party, may order a continuance or a new trial in the interest of justice on such terms as may be just.

The statute offers the alternatives of a mere continuance (i.e., adjournment) or an outright new trial, before a new jury if necessary. Which if any step to take depends on the defect to be remedied and perhaps even on whether it was inadvertent or contrived. Inad-

vertent and unobtrusive mentions of the existence of insurance in a personal injury case, for example, may be cured by a mere instruction, while a deliberate attempt by the plaintiff to show that insurance exists[2] or by the defendant to show that it does not[3] will necessitate a new trial before a new jury.

Misconduct that may necessitate a new trial is not restricted to that of a party or lawyer. The intemperate comments or conduct of a judge, for example, suggesting the judge's prejudice against a party or cause, will require a new trial and may even occasion an appellate reprimand.[4] The misconduct of a juror will do the same, as where a juror walks the plaintiff home during the trial and assures her that everything will be okay.[5] There are no arbitrary limits on the trial judge's power to declare a mistrial. Whatever the source of the prejudicial conduct, if it deprives an innocent party of a fair trial the court can make it the basis of a mistrial.

If the defect is something that does not induce jury bias and is curable by a mere adjournment, a new trial is not necessary under CPLR 4402 and a mere continuance will be ordered. This is appropriate where, for example, a key witness has not appeared in time, or has taken temporarily ill and cannot show up for a few days, or where some surprise element has arisen at the trial and a party needs some time to secure evidence to meet it. A refusal to order an adjournment when it is reasonable to do so will meet appellate censure, as in one case where the judge would not wait half an hour for the imminent arrival of medical experts.[6] Even an adjournment of several weeks may be appropriate in order to

---

23. Id. If the application is prompted by newly discovered evidence not known about during the earlier trial, the applicant's remedy is to make a motion to vacate the judgment and for a new trial under CPLR 5015(a)(2).

24. CPLR 5019(a).

25. See § 405.

§ 403

1. See Schultze v. Huttlinger, 150 App.Div. 489, 135 N.Y.S. 70 (1st Dep't 1912).

2. See the discussion in Ismail v. City of New York, 18 Misc.2d 818, 181 N.Y.S.2d 848 (Sup.Ct., Queens County, 1959).

3. Rendo v. Schermerhorn, 24 A.D.2d 773, 263 N.Y.S.2d 743 (3d Dep't 1965).

4. See, e.g., Habenicht v. R.K.O. Theatres, Inc., 23 A.D.2d 378, 260 N.Y.S.2d 890 (1st Dep't 1965).

5. See Campbell v. Tower, 46 Misc.2d 891, 261 N.Y.S.2d 458 (Sup.Ct., Kings County, 1965).

6. Murphy v. City of New York, 273 App.Div. 492, 78 N.Y.S.2d 191 (1st Dep't 1948).

secure the testimony of a key witness.[7]

A party who deems himself irrevocably prejudiced by some piece of conduct during the trial should move for a mistrial promptly upon learning of it. He cannot hold the datum as a trump card, speculating on a favorable verdict and moving the mistrial only if he does not get it.[8]

The use of the words "on motion of any party" in CPLR 4402 indicates that a mistrial may not be granted by the court sua sponte. Instances exist, however, in which the court has done that,[9] and as a practical matter there is no cure for it if it is done before the verdict is rendered: there is no verdict to reinstate and a new trial is necessary anyway. A judge bent on granting a mistrial because of something prejudicial occurring during the trial, whether through his own conduct or another person's, should advise the presumably prejudiced party of her willingness to entertain a mistrial motion. Under the rule discussed in the prior paragraph, a party failing to respond to that invitation may be held to have waived a mistrial.

If a mistrial is declared, the case should be rescheduled for trial. A specific rule may even require it.[10]

§ 404. Motion to Conform the Pleadings to the Proof

CPLR 3025(c) provides that "the court may permit pleadings to be amended before or after judgment to conform them to the evidence, upon such terms as may be just including the granting of costs and continuances". This is really an adjunct of the liberalization of pleadings. Its purpose is to have the final judgment dictated by what the evidence actually reveals at the trial rather than by what the pleadings and bill of particulars alleged it would be.

The courts are today quite free with the amendment as long as no party can claim prejudice because of it. Prejudice is the key, and legitimate surprise is the key to whether there's prejudice. As long as the papers in the case advised the other side sufficiently of the transaction, occurrence, or event out of which the claim or defense arises—to such an extent that a diligent lawyer could be deemed to have been on notice that the matter now sought to be changed or added by amendment could reasonably have been expected to arise at the trial—the purpose of the rule is fulfilled and the amendment permissible.

The amendment is not available to add a new substantive claim, otherwise barred by the statute of limitations and clearly beyond what the other side could have expected,[1] but mere changes in theory are permissible. A classic instance of this in New York is the case of Diemer v. Diemer.[2] A husband's separation complaint had pleaded cruel and inhuman treatment as its ground. On appeal the court substituted, and sustained, the ground of abandonment, holding that the proved underlying wrong, which was the wife's refusal to have sexual relations with her husband, constituted abandonment as a matter of law. As long as it is clear that the responsive proof would have been the same whichever conclusory theory or ground had been pleaded, permitting such an amendment is sound modern practice. But if there is any reasonable possibility that the other party would have prepared different proof with which to respond to the altered ground—a party in this position should show the court that this is so—the amendment should be denied or, at worst, an adjournment had to permit the gathering of such proof.

The amendment is always good for mere technical defects, such as to amend an equity

---

7. See Bruce v. Hospital for Special Surgery, 34 A.D.2d 963, 312 N.Y.S.2d 765 (2d Dep't 1970).

8. Schein v. Chest Serv. Co., 38 A.D.2d 929, 330 N.Y.S.2d 147 (1st Dep't 1972).

9. See, e.g., Jaworski v. New Cassel Fuel Corp., 21 A.D.2d 753, 251 N.Y.S.2d 929 (2d Dep't 1964).

10. See, e.g., Uniform Rule 202.45, applicable in the Supreme and County courts.

§ 404

1. McGough v. State of New York, 41 Misc.2d 78, 244 N.Y.S.2d 1007 (Ct.Cl. 1963).

2. 8 N.Y.2d 206, 203 N.Y.S.2d 829, 168 N.E.2d 654 (1960). An amendment had not even been formally moved for in the Diemer case.

complaint to include an inadvertently omitted allegation that there is no adequate remedy at law.[3]

One of the main functions of the amendment is to divest of impact unprejudicial variances between pleadings and proof. Pleadings for this purpose include the bill of particulars. A CPLR 3025(c) amendment can give effect to trial evidence that varies from both the pleading and the bill as long as there is no prejudice. Where, for example, a deposition or other pretrial disclosure device puts the other party on notice of what later emerges at the trial, the claim of prejudice dissolves and the amendment lies.[4] Trial proof within the purview of the complaint may ground the amendment even if the bill of particulars does not embrace the matter, as where the bill alleges only that the defendant passed a stop sign and the trial proof shows there was no stop sign but reveals other grounds of negligence embraced in the complaint.[5] The trial itself is the usual scene for an amendment under CPLR 3025(c). It becomes relevant when the proof establishes something arguably omitted from, or at variance with, the papers in the case. The motion is usually oral and is made right in the courtroom to the trial judge. It need not await an adversary's objection (to the effect, e.g., that the new matter is incompetent or irrelevant because not embraced by the pleading or bill of particulars), but often does. It can be made as a formal written motion, but that is usually unnecessary. Whether oral or written, the motion should in any event be made only to the trial judge, as is true of trial and post-trial motions generally.[6]

An actual "amendment" of the pleadings under CPLR 3025(c) is not necessary. The court, if it grants the motion, can merely recite in the order that the pleadings are "deemed" amended to conform to the evidence and, indeed, even an "order" for this purpose is not required. Since the motion and its surrounding colloquy ordinarily takes place at the trial, the stenographer takes it all down and the transcript then evinces everything needed. Should a party aggrieved by the court's action on the motion wish to appeal it, she can do so as part of an appeal from the final judgment.[7] A party wishing to appeal it independently might try to secure the entry of a formal order on the court's ruling and appeal that.[8]

An appellate court as well as the trial court can conform the pleadings to the proof,[9] and can even do so sua sponte.[10] It has been done even in the Court of Appeals: the *Diemer* case discussed above is an example of it.

CPLR 3025(c) allows the amendment to be made conditional. The conditions include the granting of costs and continuances. These are not often needed but they may be useful. Suppose, for example, that a party does wish at the trial to change an allegation or add an item, and that an arguable claim of surprise is made against it. The objector convinces the court that he is unprepared, not unreasonably, to meet the new matter, but the court is equally convinced that a short adjournment is all that is needed to enable that party to secure the witness or proof required. The court can permit the amendment and give the objector that chance, continuing the case and even requiring the party who moved for the amendment to pay the objector the costs of securing the belated proof. This is of course cutting things close, even with so generous a rule as CPLR 3025(c): an amendment at the trial stage that requires an adversary to get new proof to meet it is not always remediable

3. See American–Russian Aid Ass'n v. City of Glen Cove, 41 Misc.2d 622, 246 N.Y.S.2d 123 (Sup.Ct., Nassau County 1964), aff'd 23 A.D.2d 966, 260 N.Y.S.2d 589 (2d Dep't 1965).

4. DiBenedetto v. Lasker–Goldman Corp., 46 A.D.2d 909, 363 N.Y.S.2d 5 (2d Dep't 1974).

5. Pogor v. Cue Taxi Service, Inc., 43 Misc.2d 487, 251 N.Y.S.2d 635 (N.Y.C.Civ.Ct. 1964), aff'd 45 Misc.2d 933, 258 N.Y.S.2d 60 (App.T., 1st Dep't, 1965).

6. CPLR 4405. Note also the 15–day time limit in that provision. See § 405 below.

7. CPLR 5501(a).

8. CPLR 5701(a)(2)(iv), (v). Unless reduced to an order, a disposition qualifying as a mere "ruling" will not be appealable separately. See § 526 below.

9. Dampskibsselskabet Torm A/S v. P.L. Thomas Paper Co., 26 A.D.2d 347, 274 N.Y.S.2d 601 (1st Dep't 1966).

10. Harbor Associates, Inc. v. Asheroff, 35 A.D.2d 667, 317 N.Y.S.2d 897 (2d Dep't 1970).

by mere conditions and is therefore not granted for the asking.

Twice before we have seen a motion to amend a complaint to increase the "ad damnum"—the amount demanded in the wherefore clause of a money complaint. An attempt to secure this amendment after trial and verdict was one instance, evolving from what seemed an absolute No for a while to at least a conditional Yes.[11] The other was an attempt to secure the amendment by motion under CPLR 3025(b), in advance of the trial. That one, as we saw, has a better chance, but is still not granted for the mere asking.[12] What of an endeavor to get an ad damnum amendment not before or after the trial, but during it? A motion for an increased ad damnum made at the trial under CPLR 3025(c) may involve elements applicable to either or both of the previously treated motions. If, for example, the standard for a pretrial amendment requires a showing that the need to increase the damages demand was only just discerned, and that the motion to amend is made on the heels of the new discovery, such a showing is likely to be required as well when the motion is made at the trial. Attitudes may vary from department to department on these essentially discretionary matters.[13] It will also be remembered that judicial rejection of the motion, when delayed until after the verdict, may be predicated on the insurance factor: that if the figure to which the increase is now sought exceeds the defendant's insurance coverage, it will be too late for the defendant to secure counsel of his own choice and the verdict, to the extent of the difference, will have to be paid out of his personal assets as a fait accompli.[14] The same is true (if the ad damnum is to jump from within to beyond coverage) when the motion is made during the trial, albeit before the verdict: it is still too late for the defendant to get an attorney of her private choosing. The at-

trial ad damnum amendment therefore does not always have clear sailing.

§ 405. Post-Trial Motion for Judgment

The post-trial motion comes from CPLR 4404, subdivision (a) governing in jury trials and subdivision (b) in nonjury trials. The motion comes after the verdict or decision; a motion for judgment before that time belongs technically under CPLR 4401, as a motion "during" the trial, even though it may be made after both sides have rested.

CPLR 4404(a) provides that after a verdict is rendered the court can set it aside and either (1) grant judgment to whichever party is entitled to it as a matter of law or (2) order a new trial on the ground that the verdict is "contrary to the weight of the evidence". The first item is by this time a familiar one: the "matter of law" standard is the same as that used for judgment during the trial under CPLR 4401. There the bar knows it as a motion for a "directed verdict"; here, since it entails discarding a verdict already rendered, it becomes the equally well known "judgment notwithstanding the verdict", or judgment "n.o.v."[1] Both have criteria in common with the pretrial motion for summary judgment.[2]

The "weight of the evidence" phenomenon is quite different and will be returned to in a moment.

Because the standards for judgment as a "matter of law" are largely the same whether the motion is made before the verdict under CPLR 4401 or after it under CPLR 4404(a), the court can grant it at either time but ordinarily prefers to await the verdict. This is especially so when the motion for judgment is made at the end of all the evidence. If made before that time, as where the defendant moves for judgment under CPLR 4401 at the

---

11. See § 217 above.

12. See § 237 above.

13. See, for example, Natale v. Pepsi–Cola Co., 7 A.D.2d 282, 182 N.Y.S.2d 404 (1959), a First Department case taking a rigid position that afterwards seemed to relax, while the more relaxed attitude of the Third Department seemed to grow stricter. See Commentary C3025:14 on McKinney's CPLR 3025. Movements of this kind have

been known to reverse themselves, however, and the lawyer must keep track of current local attitudes.

14. See § 217 above.

§ 405

1. This stands for non obstante veredicto, Latin for "notwithstanding the verdict".

2. All three are compared in § 408 below.

end of the plaintiff's case, its grant at least spares further trial. But when a motion for judgment is made after both sides have rested, there is nothing left to try and there is thus little to gain and much to lose by granting the motion at that time rather than after submitting the case to the jury and awaiting its verdict.

The reason is obvious: the judge is authorized to grant judgment as a "matter of law" only when she believes that on this record reasonable minds could not differ and there is therefore only one way a jury can go. The difficulty is that reasonable minds may differ about whether reasonable minds may differ, and among them may be the reasonable minds that inhabit the appellate court. If the trial judge grants judgment for a side under CPLR 4401 without letting a jury pass on the issues, an appellate court that disagrees with her action has no verdict to reinstate and must therefore order a new trial, wasting the earlier one. But if the trial judge waits until a verdict is in, saving her action for CPLR 4404 and granting judgment notwithstanding the verdict (should the jury have found the other way), a disagreeing appellate court has a verdict to reinstate. This is no small economy, and it accounts for the widespread practice among judges of letting a fully tried case go to the jury before ruling on a motion for judgment.[3]

There is also the possibility, of course, and perhaps even the probability, that the jury will react to the evidence just as the judge did, finding for the party whom the judge also finds entitled to judgment. That would make it unnecessary for the judge to act at all. Hence, "[u]nless it appears that the defendant's case will consume an inordinate amount of the trial court's time, the better practice is to submit the case to the jury".[4]

If the court finds the verdict to be against the "weight of the evidence", it orders a new trial rather than directing judgment for the opposing party. This is a long recognized alternative for the court when it sets aside a verdict on a post-trial motion under CPLR 4404(a). The elusive criteria for "weighing" the evidence are treated in the next section. A party may make a CPLR 4404 motion after the trial even though he made no CPLR 4401 motion during it, or move for judgment n.o.v. after the verdict without having moved for judgment before it. One is not a condition precedent to the other. Still, a party who loses the verdict and wants judgment n.o.v. is in a more consistent position if she can show that she moved for judgment as a matter of law before the jury retired.[5]

Each party does well to make a motion, even if it is only pro forma, for judgment under CPLR 4401 at the close of the evidence, on which the court may rule or instead reserve decision until after the jury renders a verdict. At one time the judge could not act on her own motion to grant judgment after the verdict unless an earlier motion had been made for a directed verdict and the judge had reserved decision on it. That requirement, too, has been abandoned: CPLR 4404 authorizes the post-trial motion by either a party or by the court sua sponte.

If there are separable issues in the case, a post-trial motion under CPLR 4404 can address them individually, and this is so even if they are all part of but one cause of action. A common example of this is where the court sustains a jury finding of liability in a personal injury case but directs a new trial on the issue of damages. This involves procedures known

---

3. See, for example, Muszynski v. City of Buffalo, 49 Misc.2d 957, 268 N.Y.S.2d 753 (Sup.Ct., Erie County, 1966), which discusses the matter and where subsequent appellate steps illustrate it. The trial court did not grant a motion to dismiss the complaint after the close of the evidence, waiting for the verdict, which was for the plaintiff. The appellate division then reversed and reinstated the verdict, 33 A.D.2d 648, 305 N.Y.S.2d 163 (4th Dep't 1969), and was affirmed by the Court of Appeals in 29 N.Y.2d 810, 327 N.Y.S.2d 368, 277 N.E.2d 414 (1971).

4. Rosario v. City of New York, 157 A.D.2d 467, 549 N.Y.S.2d 661 (1st Dep't 1990).

5. In federal practice, this is a requirement imposed by the Federal Rules of Civil Procedure, Rule 50(b) allowing a party who moved for judgment before the verdict to "renew" the motion after it. The federal purpose is to assure the other side an opportunity to fill any gaps in its proof before the case goes to the jury. See the Advisory Committee's notes on the 1991 amendment of Rule 50.

as "additur" and "remittitur", which are discussed later.[6]

The post-trial motion is usually made promptly upon the delivery of the verdict, and orally, in the courtroom. In addition to such an oral application, however, each party aggrieved by the verdict is entitled to make one formal, written motion under CPLR 4404. For the written motion, the several requirements of CPLR 4405 and 4406 must be met. The motion may be made only to the judge who presided at the trial and must be made within 15 days after the verdict.[7] If a judgment has been entered in the interim, the granting of the motion can incidentally vacate the judgment.[8]

The taking of an appeal from a final judgment in the case will not cut off the trial court's power to grant a post-trial motion under CPLR 4404.[9] Argument or submission of the appeal will cut it off, but given the short time limit for the making of a CPLR 4404 motion, the idea that an appeal will have advanced to that stage while the trial court's time to act on a CPLR 4404 motion is still open is a fantasy.

Only one formal post-trial motion under CPLR 4404 is allowed, and if any party against whom the motion is made would himself make a CPLR 4404 application, that party must now do so by the expedient of a cross-motion.[10] The 15–day period in which to make a CPLR 4404 motion is not a period of limitations and is presumably subject to discretionary extension by the court under CPLR 2004, but since the plain purpose of the time restriction is to put an expeditious end to the case, a delay will not be kindly received.

There is some interplay between CPLR 4404 and CPLR 5015(a), the statute that authorizes vacatur of judgments on certain grounds. The losing party who finds the CPLR 4404 door closed may find relief under CPLR 5015(a).[11]

In a nonjury, or "bench", trial, the post-trial motion is governed by CPLR 4404(b). The technical rules, such as the time for the making of the motion—measured now from "decision" instead of "verdict"—are the same as govern the trial by jury, but the court's powers are of course more extensive. In a court-tried case, the judge on the post-trial motion can make new findings and conclusions, take additional testimony if need be, and render a new and entirely different decision, while on a jury trial the judge's powers are necessarily more restricted.

On an appeal, the appellate court stands in the same position as the trial court. In a judge-tried case it can therefore make whatever findings it determines the trial court should have made and render judgment itself.[12]

§ 406. Motion for New Trial on the "Weight of the Evidence"

When the court sets aside a verdict on a post-trial motion under CPLR 4404(a), it has the alternative of granting a new trial instead of awarding outright judgment to the other side. The new trial is the route the court takes when, while not confident that any party is entitled to judgment as a matter of law, it nonetheless finds the verdict contrary to the "weight of the evidence". Here CPLR 4404(a) allows a new trial "in the interest of justice", but neither of the quoted phrases is very informative. Precision about what is meant is elusive if not impossible: the "weight" of the evidence involves the judge's viscera as much as her intellect. There are really three different situations to be distinguished, among which the new trial based on the weight of the evidence is the middle one:

The first situation requires the court to keep hands off, merely confirming the verdict and directing that judgment be entered on it: there are issues of fact that can be resolved either way and it is for the jury to resolve them. If the facts give rise to conflicting inferences, for

---

6. See § 407 below.

7. CPLR 4405. The reference in CPLR 4405 to "this article" is meant to be a reference to only the post-trial motion of CPLR 4404.

8. CPLR 4404(a).

9. CPLR 4405.

10. CPLR 4406.

11. See § 428 below.

12. See, e.g., Mellon v. Street, 23 A.D.2d 210, 259 N.Y.S.2d 900 (3d Dep't 1965).

example, it is for the jury to draw the inferences.[1] If the issue is one of credibility, it is for the jury to determine who is telling the truth.[2] If reasonable minds may differ, in short, it is for the jury to determine who prevails.[3] Most verdicts fall into this category.

The third category is the matter-of-law situation. This one involves more than the mere "weight" of the evidence;[4] this is the situation in which—in the judge's thinking—reasonable minds could not differ and the judgment can go only one way.

In between the two, without sharp lines on either side, is the elusive but often visited "weight of the evidence" terrain. Here the court is dissatisfied with the verdict, enough to reject it but not quite enough to direct judgment notwithstanding it. The key is the judge's common sense reaction to the evidence,[5] because there can of course be no precise standard by which to "weigh" it. The scale is in the court's exclusive keeping and not every judge will read it the same way. A lawyer inexperienced in trial practice may even be surprised to learn that the weighing of the evidence is left entirely to the court's discretion, and that this discretion may be exercised to set aside the verdict even where the evidence may be technically sufficient to sustain it.[6]

Since the plaintiff has the burden of proof, it has been held that a verdict for the defendant can be set aside only when the evidence preponderates greatly in the plaintiff's favor,[7] i.e., that the scale must tip sharply in order for the judge to set aside a defendant's verdict while it perhaps need tilt only moderately to set aside a plaintiff's verdict.

A setting aside of a verdict as against the weight of the evidence produces only a new trial; it does not authorize a judgment for a different party.

The court finds the verdict against the weight of evidence when there is something about the case that arouses its suspicions and makes it uncomfortable, although it cannot say clearly that the result can go in only one direction. It may be some testimony that strikes the court as incredible, or a story it finds morally improbable.[8] It may be some misconduct on the part of counsel that the judge thinks may have influenced the verdict.[9] It may be any of a number of other factors manifest in a plethora of cases over the years, because this power to set aside a verdict and grant a new trial is an inherent one. CPLR 4404(a) is merely a codification of it.[10]

The point at which a judge concludes that a new trial is required is not fixed on the caprice of judicial individualism; it is rather arrived at by a synthesis of all the experience that the judge has had; in the beginning as a law student, in the later controversies of law practice, in the hearing of cases and the writing of decisions, in the sum of all that he has absorbed in the courtroom and in the library.[11]

It is another of those moments, in other words, that a judge can recognize but cannot always describe, which is why one may observe that it is as much visceral as intellectual. Since the new trial may be granted even where the

§ 406

1. Rosen v. M.V.A.I.C., 22 A.D.2d 671, 253 N.Y.S.2d 297 (1st Dep't 1964).

2. Sherman v. Smith, 23 A.D.2d 642, 256 N.Y.S.2d 947 (1st Dep't 1965).

3. McDonald v. Metropolitan St. Ry., 167 N.Y. 66, 60 N.E. 282 (1901).

4. Lakin v. M.V.A.I.C., 23 A.D.2d 488, 255 N.Y.S.2d 678 (1st Dep't 1965).

5. Micallef v. Miehle Co., Division of Miehle–Goss Dexter, Inc., 39 N.Y.2d 376, 384 N.Y.S.2d 115, 348 N.E.2d 571 (1976).

6. See Cohen v. Hallmark Cards, Inc., 45 N.Y.2d 493, 410 N.Y.S.2d 282 (1978), and the extended discussion in McDonald v. Metropolitan St. Ry., note 3 above.

7. Tannenbaum v. Mandell, 51 A.D.2d 593, 378 N.Y.S.2d 468 (2d Dep't 1976).

8. See, e.g., Bottalico v. City of New York, 281 App. Div. 339, 119 N.Y.S.2d 704 (1st Dep't 1953).

9. See, e.g., Robinson v. Klein, 21 A.D.2d 778, 250 N.Y.S.2d 977 (1st Dep't 1964).

10. McCarthy v. Port of New York Authority, 21 A.D.2d 125, 248 N.Y.S.2d 713 (1st Dep't 1964). To illustrate the broad range of grounds on which the power to order a new trial may be based, the McCarthy case cites the indexes of annotations following CPLR 4404 and CPLR 5015 in McKinney's CPLR. A hung jury is also, of course, ground for a new trial. CPLR 4113(b), 4404(a).

11. Mann v. Hunt, 283 App.Div. 140, 141, 126 N.Y.S.2d 823, 824 (3d Dep't 1953).

evidence is sufficient to support the verdict,[12] it may be argued that the grant deprives the winning party of trial by jury. From one standpoint that may be so, but it is so only to the extent that the case goes to a new jury, not to final judgment. It is a kind of compromise with which the law has long since made peace.

Since the motion for a new trial on the weight of the evidence is governed by CPLR 4404(a), it is subject to the several requirements of CPLR 4405 and 4406, discussed in the last section. It can be made as a written motion, for example, in addition to having been made the subject of an oral motion in the courtroom. If it is made in writing, it must be made within 15 days after the verdict is delivered. In either form it must be directed to the judge who presided at the trial; it is only that judge who holds the scale on which the evidence in the case may be "weighed".

§ 407. Additur and Remittitur

If the verdict for damages in a money action is inadequate or excessive, the court can try to raise or lower the figure by the devices of additur and remittitur.[1] As a general rule the court cannot raise or lower the sum directly, at least not in personal injury and like cases involving unliquidated damages, because the setting of damages is strictly a jury function.[2] But the court can grant a new trial "unless" the defendant stipulates to a higher sum ("additur") or the plaintiff stipulates to a lower one ("remittitur"). This is really a kind of "weight of the evidence" phenomenon,[3] and it is a step frequently taken at either trial or appellate level. It will sometimes happen, in fact, that after the trial judge has exacted one

reduction (or increase) the appellate court will exact yet another.[4]

The figure set by the court, and the one to which the party is required to stipulate or face a new trial, represents the minimum (in the case of additur) or the maximum (in the case of remittitur) found by the court to be permissible on the facts. Each of those terminals, in other words, is treated in effect as a matter-of-law terminal, whether it is technically that or not. That would insulate the procedure from the accusation that it unconstitutionally denies a party trial by jury. The Court of Appeals considers it an exercise of the trial and intermediate appellate courts' inherent constitutional powers,[5] a matter "committed to the discretion of the trial court and the Appellate Division" and hence beyond the Court of Appeals' review powers.[6]

Of course, if each terminal is deemed the legal bottom or top of the case—and they are treated that way—the trial or intermediate appellate court should be able to set the outside figure directly and order judgment accordingly, in which event the requirement of a stipulation would be superfluous. However that may be, it is well established in unliquidated damage cases that the court may not affect the figure by such direct action; that it can at best order a new trial unless the party affected stipulates to the court-set figure.

The figure used by the judge in these situations is, once again, the product of her whole experience brought to bear on the facts that have been tried before her.[7] What is maximum or minimum to one judge is not necessarily so to another, of course, and, as already noted, appellate judges will disagree, too. This ac-

---

12. McDonald v. Metropolitan St. Ry., note 3 above. See Recommendations with Respect to Motions for Directed Verdicts and Similar Practice Motions, 15th Jud.Council Rep. (1949) 241, including discussion of the McDonald case at p. 276.

§ 407

1. The word "remittitur" also defines the sending back of a case from an appellate to a lower court for the entry of judgment or further proceedings, but that is not the definition that concerns us here.

2. Kupitz v. Elliott, 42 A.D.2d 898, 347 N.Y.S.2d 705 (1st Dep't 1973); Ferro v. Maline, 31 A.D.2d 779, 296 N.Y.S.2d 967 (4th Dep't 1969).

3. CPLR 4404(a). See § 406 above.

4. See, e.g., Saltzberg v. Kiamesha Concord, Inc., 24 A.D.2d 876, 264 N.Y.S.2d 428 (2d Dep't 1965), aff'd 17 N.Y.2d 847, 271 N.Y.S.2d 283, 218 N.E.2d 323 (1966).

5. See O'Connor v. Papertsian, 309 N.Y. 465, 131 N.E.2d 883 (1956).

6. Tate v. Colabello, 58 N.Y.2d 84, 459 N.Y.S.2d 422, 445 N.E.2d 1101 (1983).

7. See Mann v. Hunt, 283 App.Div. 140, 126 N.Y.S.2d 823 (3d Dep't 1953).

counts for the many varied illustrations of additur and remittitur that roam through the cases. A remittitur can reduce the verdict to a fraction of what the jury has set,[8] and an additur can multiply it several fold.[9] A verdict of X dollars set by the jury can be remitted down to Z dollars by the trial court and then readjusted up to Y dollars, yet a third figure, by an appellate court.[10]

The traditional standard for altering the verdict is that its sum is so great or so small that the court finds that it "shocks the conscience".[11] That standard was relaxed in 1986 in tort actions, including the common personal injury and wrongful death actions in which additur and remittitur are most often seen,[12] when an amendment of CPLR 5501(c) permitted the alteration of the verdict on the lighter finding that the award "deviates materially from what would be reasonable compensation", but the amendment authorized this only for the appellate division. For a while it appeared that the trial court would still be limited to the "shocks the conscience" standard, but the futility of having the trial court apply a standard different from that applicable on appellate review prompted the courts to hold that the "deviates materially" standard, while applicable in terms only to the appellate division under CPLR 5501(c), must be applied in the trial courts as well, superseding the "shocks the conscience" criterion.[13] The "deviates materially" standard is also applicable in a federal action in which subject matter jurisdiction is based on diversity of citizenship and New York law is applicable.[14]

The new trial that results if the stipulation exacted on an additur or remittitur is not forthcoming is usually limited to damages only, but it can be for liability as well if in the particular case liability is intertwined with damages, as where there are difficult questions of impact or causation in a personal injury case.

A party confronted with an additur or remittitur order can (1) accept the new trial by refusing the stipulation, (2) accept the court-set figure by giving the stipulation, or (3) appeal the order.[15] It should also be noted that the other party may be dissatisfied with the court-set figure as well as with the verdict. Thus, even if the stipulation is accepted and final judgment is entered in the changed figure, the other side can still appeal it.[16]

Whether a party will accept the additur or remittitur and give the stipulation will of course depend on how that party appraises the chances of doing any better on a new trial. If the substituted figure is not too far from the supposed mark, the party may be prone to offer the stipulation rather than risk the vagaries of a second trial. In one case, for example, a plaintiff with a $75,000 verdict refused to remit it to $30,000, preferring a new trial. The new trial brought the plaintiff a verdict of only $16,000, and the court upheld it.[17] Nor would there be any way for such a plaintiff, after the new trial, to appeal the old remittitur order, even were the time to do so still alive (which is unlikely): by giving the stipulation the party ceases to be aggrieved by the order and thereby forfeits the right to appeal it.[18] Appeal is allowed, of course, if the stipulation is not

8. See, e.g., Rivera v. Monticello Central School Dist., 51 A.D.2d 616, 377 N.Y.S.2d 822 (3d Dep't 1976), sustaining a remittitur from $602,345 to $39,845.

9. See, e.g., Mollitor v. Smith, 24 A.D.2d 497, 261 N.Y.S.2d 204 (2d Dep't 1965).

10. See, e.g., Williams v. Sterling Estates, Inc., 26 A.D.2d 841, 274 N.Y.S.2d 407 (2d Dep't 1966).

11. See the legislative policy statement in § 1 of Chapter 266 of the Laws of 1986.

12. The actions affected are those in which an itemized verdict is required under CPLR 4111.

13. See Wendell v. Supermarkets General Corp., 189 A.D.2d 1063, 592 N.Y.S.2d 895 (3d Dep't 1993); Prunty v. YMCA of Lockport, 206 A.D.2d 911, 616 N.Y.S.2d 117 (4th Dep't 1994).

14. See Gasperini v. Center for Humanities, Inc., 518 U.S. 415, 116 S.Ct. 2211, 135 L.Ed.2d 659 (1996).

15. Mormon v. Serkanic, 25 A.D.2d 526, 267 N.Y.S.2d 661 (2d Dep't 1966).

16. Saltzberg v. Kiamesha Concord, Inc., 24 A.D.2d 876, 264 N.Y.S.2d 428 (2d Dep't 1965), aff'd 17 N.Y.2d 847, 271 N.Y.S.2d 283, 218 N.E.2d 323 (1966). See CPLR 5501(a)(5).

17. See Reinertsen v. George W. Rogers Constr. Corp., 519 F.2d 531 (2d Cir.1975).

18. See Borgia v. City of New York, 12 N.Y.2d 151, 237 N.Y.S.2d 319, 187 N.E.2d 777 (1962).

given,[19] which shows some of the delicate prognosis required of a party in these situations.[20]

§ 408. Motions for "Judgment", Compared

We have seen at this stage no fewer than three motions for a merits "judgment", each of which takes the case out of the jury's hands and has the court determining which party wins. The first was the motion for summary judgment under CPLR 3212, which is made before the trial; the second the motion under CPLR 4401 for judgment during the trial; and the third the motion under CPLR 4404 for judgment after the trial. What relationship do they have, if any?

Every motion for judgment that takes the case away from the jury assumes that there is no material issue of fact to be tried and is necessarily sui generis. It turns on the experience of the judge and his ability to discern when there is something to try and when there is not. Hence the criteria must be stated generally. The CPLR 4401 and 4404 motions are at least built on testimony and evidence at the trial. The CPLR 3212 motion, on the other hand, is not, and is perhaps the more difficult because the judge can depend only on affidavits and other writings, not having the courtroom advantage of hearing the testimony and observing the demeanor and credibility of the witnesses. And yet the root criterion of all of these motions for judgment is the same: that the movant is entitled to judgment as a matter of law.

Judges can identify these situations far more readily than they can articulate them, and both judiciary and legislature have even defined one in terms of the other, as if one of them could draw sharp definition by analogy to another no sharper. The justification for granting a motion for summary judgment before trial under CPLR 3212, for example, depends on whether the showing is such as would warrant the granting of a CPLR 4401 motion for judgment during the trial.[1] The grant of the CPLR 4401 motion depends in turn on whether, if the case were to go to the jury and the jury were to find the other way, the judge would have to grant judgment notwithstanding the verdict under CPLR 4404.[2]

The practical teaching of this interplay is that the verbalization of when judgment is due as a matter of law is an exercise in semantics if not futility. Each of these motions may draw eclectically on the experience of the others, but "experience" is likely to be the only building material. When a court proposes to put a summary and permanent seal on a case, a few words in a book are no substitute for a few years in the courtroom.

19. See Mormon v. Serkanic, note 15 above. Such an appellate alternative is not so readily available in federal practice, as the Reinertsen case in note 17 demonstrates.

20. Special problems arise in attempting to determine what constitutes a "final" disposition in additur and remittitur cases for the purpose of determining when a case becomes ripe for an appeal to the Court of Appeals. Recognizing the variations, and complications, that additur and remittitur dispositions can engender for the appellate process, the court offers some guideposts to the bar in Whitfield v. City of New York, 90 N.Y.2d 777, 666 N.Y.S.2d 545 (1997). See § 527 below.

§ 408

1. CPLR 3212(b).

2. See Tirschwell v. Dolan, 21 A.D.2d 923, 251 N.Y.S.2d 91 (3d Dep't 1964).

Chapter Sixteen

THE JUDGMENT

Analysis

A. CONTENTS OF JUDGMENT

Table of Sections

§ 409. Content of Judgment

A judgment is the resolution of the dispute and the note on which the action or proceeding ends. It is the embodiment of the verdict or decision, to which it must refer, and if it is the result of a default it must refer to that. All actions and proceedings in the usual courts of civil jurisdiction today end in a "judgment".[1] The "final order" that used to end a special proceeding before the CPLR arrived in 1963 is no longer used[2] and the "decree" that once terminated an equity action action had given way to a simple "judgment" long before that (when law and equity merged).[3]

There is no rigid form for a judgment. It varies according to the needs of the particular case. The money judgment, the most common in litigation, is the most familiar and probably as close as we come to a "standard" judgment.[4] A money judgment is rendered in dollars and cents, unless based on a claim "denominated in a currency other than [that] of the United States", in which event the court is to render judgment in the foreign currency, with a conversion into U.S. currency at the rate of exchange applicable at the time of entry.[5]

At one time, and in fact until quite recently, it could be said that the only item needing change on the bottom line of a money judgment from one case to another was the amount involved. That changed in the mid 1980's when the legislature prescribed use of a "periodic payment" judgment[6] in the unintentional tort actions, designed to spread out over a period of years, instead of awarding as an

---

§ 409

1. CPLR 5011.

2. See CPLR 411, RPAPL 747.

3. An exception is the surrogate's court, whose proceedings continue to end in what is denominated a "decree", see SCPA 602, which is still nothing more than a "judgment".

4. A common form of money judgment is contained in § 417.

5. Jud.L. § 27(b).

6. It is sometimes popularly referred to as a "structured judgment", after the "structured settlement" terminology that had evolved earlier when the parties were able to agree on it.

immediate lump sum, a portion of the projected future damages found to have been sustained by the plaintiff.[7]

At the other end of the spectrum is the judgment of injunction, which must carefully address the facts of the particular case and delineate the defendant's obligations with respect to them. Here an omission can seriously undermine enforcement of the judgment, which has to depend on contempt proceedings.

Today the verdict or decision, which the judgment merely reflects, establishes the rights of the parties regardless of the source from which the supporting evidence comes. It is no longer necessary that it be the plaintiff's proof that implicates the defendant, or the defendant's that defeats the plaintiff. Where P's case against defendant A has a gap, for example, it can be filled by proof put in by defendant B.[8] Likewise in third-party context: proof adduced by X, the third-party defendant, can defeat P's claim against D, the main defendant, even though D stands mute.[9] The judgment will be determined by the whole of the evidence, without regard to the channel through which it came.

CPLR 5011 provides that the judgment "may be either interlocutory or final". A "final" judgment is the one we have been talking about, and the one to which almost all talk about judgments relates. (Interlocutory judgment is the subject of the next section.) Except for appeal of the judgment and for the few narrow grounds on which a judgment can be set aside,[10] the final judgment terminates the controversy and sets the stage for enforcement.

A judgment can determine the whole case or only part of it. It can determine one cause of action and leave others for later. It can even decide part of but a single cause of action, or give judgment as to some but not all parties.[11] The needs of the particular case will dictate, and to the extent that part but not all of the case is sent to judgment, the court has several tools to help it make the division. The first and most obvious is the severance, available at any appropriate juncture of an action[12] or special proceeding.[13] Where, for example, on a motion to dismiss under CPLR 3211 or for summary judgment under CPLR 3212 only one cause of action is disposed of but others remain to be tried, the order of disposition will include a severance of the concluded claim and leave the undecided claims to be tried.

A single judgment can dispose of the entire case no matter how many claims or parties are involved. It will merely go through its recitations in some logical sequence until the rights of all parties with respect to all claims are clarified. If in the court's discretion claims or parties are so profuse that the embodiment of all of their rights in a single paper is unduly confusing, the court can, with or without a severance, direct that separate papers reflect the rights involved, cross-referencing one paper to another if need arises. It is flexibility that the general language of CPLR 5011 aims for.

Also to be included in the judgment are costs and disbursements. If the judgment is for money, interest may also have to be added. These things are discussed in later sections.[14]

§ 410. Interlocutory Judgment

CPLR 5011 provides that the judgment may be interlocutory or final. When used alone, "judgment" usually means a final judgment. An interlocutory judgment, which is not common today, is one lacking finality in some

---

7. See CPLR Article 50–A, enacted in 1985, governing medical, dental, and podiatric malpractice actions, and CPLR Article 50–B, governing in the rest of the personal injury, injury to property, and wrongful death actions. The two articles are virtually identical and could easily have been enacted as one. See the Commentary on Article 50–B in McKinney's CPLR.

8. See Simon v. Lowenthal, 169 Misc. 718, 8 N.Y.S.2d 484 (N.Y.C.Mun.Ct. 1938). There used to be a statute so providing expressly: § 212(2) of the old Civil Practice Act. A counterpart does not appear in the CPLR. The matter is

apparently deemed implicit in sound modern practice without need of statutory statement.

9. CPLR 1008.

10. CPLR 5015(a).

11. CPLR 5012.

12. CPLR 603.

13. CPLR 407.

14. See §§ 411–415 below.

respect. It decides part but not all of the case,[1] or it decides all of it but postpones conclusiveness for a designated time or until a designated event. Until 1968, the latter use was the most frequent in an interlocutory judgment in New York. It was used in matrimonial actions where an annulment or divorce would first go to interlocutory judgment and not become "final" until three months later. The three months were a cooling-off period during which the parties would, so the legislature hoped, reunite, preserve the marriage, and make the entry of a final judgment unnecessary. The statutes so providing[2] were repealed in 1968 in conjunction with the liberalization of New York's divorce laws, and today divorce and annulment judgments become final immediately, permitting remarriage without a waiting period.

The interlocutory judgment remains available to the court whenever it has some appropriate aid to offer. It is sometimes used in the bifurcated personal injury or wrongful death action to reflect that liability has been found, and if the liability finding is to be separately appealed before damages are tried, the entry of an interlocutory judgment becomes mandatory. The trial judge determines whether to authorize such a judgment, which in effect gives the court the say as to whether to allow an immediate appeal of the liability determination.[3]

A major treatment of the subject appears in Bank of N.Y. v. Ansonia Assocs.,[4] in which a jury found gross negligence in a ceiling fall case, grounding punitive damages, which set the stage for discovery proceedings with respect to the defendants' net worth. The defendants were denied the interlocutory judgment that would have permitted an immediate appeal of the liability finding, which required the trial to continue through the damages phase.

The use of an interlocutory judgment in those contexts, money actions at law, are analogous to its more traditional use in the accounting action in equity. It was (and may still be) used there to reflect whether there is a *right* to an accounting, i.e., whether the conditions precedent to that equitable right have been met (such as the existence of a fiduciary relationship between the parties[5]), before the accounting itself is allowed. In neither instance is it indispensable, however. The finding on the first phase (liability) need not, except in connection with the appellate process discussed, be reduced to interlocutory judgment in order for the case to proceed into the second phase (damages). The requisite finding can just be held in abeyance, reduced neither to an order nor a judgment, while the rest of the case proceeds.

By the general language of CPLR 5011, it is today open to the court to direct the use of an interlocutory judgment whenever in the court's view it has a useful function to serve. In Rupert v. Sellers,[6] for example, P sued D for punitive damages and sought disclosure as to D's wealth. The court held that D's wealth is relevant on a punitive damages assessment, since the money to be awarded has to be enough to make a dent in D's assets, but that the subject is not ripe unless and until D is found guilty of malice, a prerequisite to the imposition of punitive damages. The court held that disclosure on the wealth topic must therefore abide a special verdict establishing malice. Once rendered, the court can reflect such a verdict in an interlocutory judgment, thus setting the stage for both disclosure and trial on the subject of D's wealth. But here, again, it is a mere option for the court; if the court finds it unnecessary, as where no immediate appeal is sought and no other right is asserted that can be shown to depend on the entry of an interlocutory judgment, it need not be used.

---

§ 410

1. See Moza v. Sun Mut. Ins. Co., 13 Abb.Prac. 304, 22 H.P. 60 (N.Y.Superior Ct. 1861).

2. Dom.Rel.L. §§ 241, 242.

3. See Jack Parker Constr. Corp. v. Williams, 35 A.D.2d 839, 317 N.Y.S.2d 911 (2d Dep't 1970).

4. 172 Misc.2d 70, 656 N.Y.S.2d 813 (Sup.Ct., N.Y. County, 1997) (noted in SPR 69:3).

5. See Kaminsky v. Kahn, 23 A.D.2d 231, 259 N.Y.S.2d 716 (1st Dep't 1965), rev'd (in effect) on other grounds 20 N.Y.2d 573, 285 N.Y.S.2d 833, 232 N.E.2d 837 (1967).

6. 48 A.D.2d 265, 368 N.Y.S.2d 904 (4th Dep't 1975).

If the court does direct an interlocutory judgment, and the later moment arrives when the case becomes ripe for a final one, the party entitled to the final judgment can move for it.[7] If by the terms of the interlocutory judgment the right to a final one becomes automatic with the mere passage of time or the mere occurrence of some readily proved condition, even a motion should not be necessary; the clerk upon appropriate proof should be able to enter the final judgment.

B. INTEREST

Table of Sections

Sec.
411. Allowance of Interest.
412. Rate of Interest.

§ 411. Allowance of Interest

Interest is the cost of the use of money and the CPLR provides for it on litigated obligations. There are three distinct periods to be considered, governed respectively by CPLR 5001, 5002 and 5003:

1. Interest on the cause of action from its accrual until the verdict (or the decision, if the case is tried by the court);

2. Interest on the verdict or decision until judgment is entered; and

3. Interest on the judgment from entry until payment.

Interest in categories 2 and 3 attaches uniformly to all money obligations once reduced to verdict or judgment, including money awards incidental to equitable relief. This is not so of category 1, where there are a number of points to note.

All actions for money seeking in essence to recover for property loss, whether sounding in contract or tort, get interest as a matter of right in category 1. This is so if the action is one at law, in any event, which means that it

is so in most categories of money actions, almost all of which sound at law. If the money demand is incidental to an equitable claim, however, whether to allow category 1 interest is left to the court's discretion. (In categories 2 and 3 the interest lies as a matter of right on money claims without regard to their legal or equitable auspices.)

The main exceptions to category 1 are the personal injury and punitive damages claims, neither of which carries interest from accrual to verdict (although both carry interest in categories 2 and 3). Denial of interest on the personal injury claim, which includes not just the negligent torts but some of the intentional ones as well,[1] of course means that one of the most common claims in litigation does not draw interest until a verdict or decision is rendered in court. The Advisory Committee considered altering this but decided against it because it involves "difficult policy considerations" and entails speculative assessments of potential future losses, especially in regard to the element of pain and suffering which is such a key part of these cases.[2]

Even when the personal injury has a contract ground to rest on, as it frequently does today when a product has caused the injury and the theory of breach of warranty supports the claim, it will not draw interest from accrual, i.e., interest in category 1.[3] The wrongful death claim, governed by a special statute,[4] gets interest from the time of death until the verdict or decision, at which time CPLR categories 2 and 3 take over. When a property damage or wrongful death claim, each of which does get interest from accrual, is joined with a personal injury claim, which does not, the plaintiff had best ask the court to instruct the jury to bring back separate verdicts on each claim so that the interest-bearing portion can be given its category 1 allotment. A failure to request the separate verdicts will waive the

---

7. CPLR 5016(e).

§ 411

1. Such as defamation. Rupert v. Sellers, 50 N.Y.2d 881, 430 N.Y.S.2d 263 (1980).

2. See 3d Rep.Leg.Doc.(1959) No. 17, p. 88.

3. Gillespie v. Great A & P Tea Co., 26 A.D.2d 953, 276 N.Y.S.2d 372 (2d Dep't 1966), aff'd 21 N.Y.2d 823, 288 N.Y.S.2d 907, 235 N.E.2d 911 (1968).

4. EPTL § 5–4.3.

interest.[5] In this age of the special verdict,[6] which when properly used reveals the details of the jury's determination, an inadvertent merging of the personal injury and property damage elements is less likely than it once was.

Since interest is designed to compensate for the loss of use of money, money to be awarded as punitive damages (which requires a showing of the defendant's malice) is denied category 1 interest on the theory that these damages are not designed to compensate but rather to punish.[7] Once reduced to verdict, in any event, which establishes the plaintiff's entitlement to the money, the category 2 interest does attach to punitive damages, as the category 3 interest also does when judgment is entered.

In determining when the cause of action accrued for purposes of category 1 interest, it will often be satisfactory to adopt and apply the same accrual moment applicable under CPLR 203(a) in determining the start of the statute of limitations. But CPLR 5001(b) recognizes that this will not always be so and permits the court to handle the interest problem flexibly. Interest is to be computed "from the earliest ascertainable date the cause of action existed".

When items of damage, all incidents of a single claim, accrue at different times, a separate interest computation is made for each, measured from its own accrual, if the fact can be discerned. Otherwise "a single reasonable intermediate date" can be set, with interest on the aggregate of the damages measured from that time.[8] Where, in a contract case, for example, the date of breach was clear but money payable under the contract fell due at different times and the record was not clear about when, the court picked out a point midway between the breach and the contract's expiration date and measured interest from then.[9] In other instances, in which discerning the appropriate dates is difficult, as in an action for unfair competition where pinpointing the moment of damage accrual involves conjecture, the category 1 interest may be held to start only upon commencement of the action.[10]

The accrual moment in this first category is often just a question of fact. If the point is in doubt, the facts should be litigated and the matter left to the jury or other fact trier. If the case is being tried to a jury and the jury is discharged without its having fixed the interest-starting date, the plaintiff may be in trouble. The clerk may be able to fix the interest on an affidavit if the facts on which interest depends have been incidentally determined and are clear on the record, and there have even been special instances in which an appellate court has awarded interest for the first time,[11] but if interest depends on facts that the plaintiff neglected to litigate, the result can be a substantial forfeiture. In one case, for example, inattention to the facts on which interest depended resulted in a forfeiture of some $88,000.[12] With dates in hand, the clerk makes the actual computation of interest and adds it to the basic damages for inclusion in the verdict or decision.[13] The total then bears interest as part of category 2.

Category 2, which is governed by CPLR 5002, is as a general rule the least important category of interest and therefore often ignored by lawyers. It contemplates that the whole of the verdict or decision, including the category 1 interest awarded, will be added together, and that category 2 interest will then run on that sum until a judgment is formally entered, at which point category 3 takes over.

---

5. See Helman v. Markoff, 255 A.D. 991, 8 N.Y.S.2d 448 (2d Dep't 1938), aff'd 280 N.Y. 641, 20 N.E.2d 1012 (1939).

6. See § 399 above.

7. See 3d Rep.Leg.Doc.(1959) No. 17, p. 88; Delulio v. 320–57 Corp., 99 A.D.2d 253, 472 N.Y.S.2d 379 (1st Dep't 1984).

8. CPLR 5001(b).

9. Zimmer v. Wells Management Corp., 366 F.Supp. 215 (S.D.N.Y.1973).

10. Delong Corp. v. Morrison–Knudsen Co., 20 A.D.2d 104, 244 N.Y.S.2d 859 (1st Dep't 1963), the point discussed here being afterwards affirmed in 14 N.Y.2d 346, 251 N.Y.S.2d 657, 200 N.E.2d 557 (1964).

11. See, e.g., Newburger, Loeb & Co. v. Gross, 611 F.2d 423 (2d Cir.1979).

12. See Lee v. Joseph E. Seagram & Sons, Inc., 592 F.2d 39 (2d Cir.1979), a federal case in which interest was governed by New York law, so that CPLR 5001 applied.

13. CPLR 5001(c).

But since the time between rendition of the verdict and the formal entry of judgment is usually brief (a diligent lawyer will seldom let more than a few days elapse before getting judgment entered[14]), interest here is likely to be negligible. Sometimes when entering judgment the clerk will just measure interest on the claim (category 1 interest) until the moment of entry of judgment, thus in effect disregarding category 2.

The only difference is one of compounding: if the category 1 interest is included in the sum on which category 2 interest is computed, the plaintiff will earn interest on interest between verdict and judgment, whereas deferring the addition of interest until judgment is entered skips that step.[15]

In some instances, however, the category 2 interest can take on independent importance. That will be so whenever there is a long period between verdict and judgment—as can happen, for example, in a bifurcated trial of a personal injury claim in which a verdict of liability on phase one is reduced to an interlocutory judgment and is separately appealed before damages are tried. It has been held that if the appeal fails, thus upholding liability, whatever damages are then assessed will be held to run from the original liability verdict.[16]

The matter becomes significant in a personal injury case for the obvious reason that since category 1 interest is not allowed in that kind of case, interest gets its start only from the verdict, i.e., in category 2. This should at least prompt second thoughts by a defendant before taking a separate appeal from the liability finding in a bifurcated trial. Delay in settlement, which category 1 in effect rewards by withholding interest on a personal injury claim, will not necessarily carry advantages once a liability verdict is in, even though damages have yet to be tried.

Similar questions arise in this situation:

Suppose that a personal injury judgment, including damages, is appealed, and the appellate court orders a new trial. Will a new verdict for the plaintiff, and whatever its damage award may be, carry category 2 interest from the old (the reversed) verdict? It has been held that it will, at least where the defendant is found to have unreasonably prolonged the appellate process.[17] But absent a finding of unreasonable delay, the court may hold that the interest will run only from the new verdict. These are not academic points; in one case, for example, in which category 2 interest upon a new trial was held to run from the new rather than the old verdict, the difference in interest amounted to more than $6500.[18]

The Court of Appeals, addressing the issue of category 2 interest in Love v. State[19] and allowing interest to relate back to an earlier liability finding, rejects the suggestion that the interest should be given a relation back only when the defendant is found to have caused delay in the trial of the damages issue.

The award of an arbitrator has been held the equivalent of a court decision so as to carry category 2 interest under CPLR 5002.[20]

---

14. The act of "entry" of the judgment is discussed in § 418.

15. Suppose, for example, that on October 18 the plaintiff is awarded a verdict of $20,000 on a property damage claim accruing exactly three years earlier. At 9% per year, interest on that sum would be $5400, and the verdict should then be treated as one for $25,400. Assume judgment is entered three days later, on October 21. If category 2 interest is distinctly treated, the sum of $25,400 would bear three days interest, amounting to about $18.79, for a total of $25,418.79, to go in as the initial judgment figure. If category 2 is skipped, and interest on $20,000 is computed for three years and three days, the total comes to about $25,414.79. The difference is only about $4.00, which accounts for the frequent bypassing of the second category.

16. Trimboli v. Scarpaci Funeral Home, 37 A.D.2d 386, 326 N.Y.S.2d 227 (2d Dep't 1971), aff'd 30 N.Y.2d 687, 332

N.Y.S.2d 637, 283 N.E.2d 614 (1972). Even the state is subject to interest from the time of the verdict when it unsuccessfully appeals a liability finding in a bifurcated trial. Gunnarson v. State, 70 N.Y.2d 923, 524 N.Y.S.2d 396, 519 N.E.2d 307 (1987).

17. See Beyer v. Murray, 33 A.D.2d 246, 306 N.Y.S.2d 619 (4th Dep't 1970).

18. See Lindwall v. Talent Cab Corp., 51 Misc.2d 381, 273 N.Y.S.2d 261 (Sup.Ct., N.Y.County), aff'd 27 A.D.2d 647, 276 N.Y.S.2d 565 (1st Dep't 1966).

19. 78 N.Y.2d 540, 577 N.Y.S.2d 359, 583 N.E.2d 1296 (1991). The case and the issue are discussed in the lead note in New York State Law Digest No. 384.

20. Kavares v. M.V.A.I.C., 29 A.D.2d 68, 285 N.Y.S.2d 983 (1st Dep't 1967), aff'd 28 A.D.2d 939, 323 N.Y.S.2d 431, 271 N.E.2d 915 (1971).

The award will be computed accordingly when confirmed into a judgment through the procedures of CPLR 7510 and 7514, met later.[21]

Category 3 interest runs on the judgment until it is satisfied. The judgment should technically include all interest awarded under categories 1 and 2 but, as noted, the second category is sometimes disregarded. The moment from which category 3 interest runs is the "entry" of the judgment. For this purpose, an order directing the payment of money may be entered as if it were a judgment[22] and will draw category 3 interest accordingly.[23]

While in category 3 (as in category 2) the plaintiff is entitled to interest as a matter of right, the right may be waived, or the plaintiff may be estopped from asserting it, as occurred, for example, in Juracka v. Ferrara.[24] After settling the action, the plaintiff apparently had second thoughts and used diverse tactics to avoid the settlement while the defendant was at all times willing to pay it. The estoppel doctrine was invoked against the plaintiff.

Before 1992, there was no stated time limit within which the sum agreed to in the settlement of an action had to be paid. With the 1992 enactment of CPLR 5003–a, a time limit was imposed. When the action is settled, it is the plaintiff's obligation under the statute to draw up a release and serve a copy of it on the settling defendant along with a copy of a stipulation discontinuing the action. If the settlement requires judicial approval, as it does, for example, when the claim is that of an infant, a copy of the order approving the settlement must also be included. Within 21 days from the tender of those papers, the defendant must pay the amount of the settlement.[25]

If the settlement isn't paid on time, the plaintiff may seek the entry of a judgment against the defendant for the amount of the settlement, plus costs, disbursements, and interest on the amount of the settlement, measured from the date of the tender. The consequence of not paying the stated amount of the settlement on time, in other words, is that costs and disbursements will now be added to it, along with interest.[26]

In wrongful death cases that involve both past (pre-verdict) and future (post-verdict) losses, the Court of Appeals has prescribed how to compute interest.[27]

It is not clear how interest is to be figured under the "periodic payment" provisions governing judgments in tort cases that involve an award of future damages.[28] The court can be applied to for instructions if the parties can't agree about interest. When a periodic payment judgment has been rendered, and the problem is the debtor's failure to make payment pursuant to it, the matter of interest is left to the court explicitly.[29]

It has already been noted that money obligations emerging in equitable context draw interest as a matter of right in categories 2 and 3, but not category 1. In that category, whether to award interest at all—and the date from which it is to run if awarded—is in the court's discretion on an equitable claim. Argument sometimes arises, therefore, as to whether a given claim is equitable or legal. In this connection an action brought on a separation agreement has been held to draw category 1 interest as of right because it amounts to claim at law, while a money claim arising out of a matrimonial action or out of an equitable action involving the monetary rights of the family may have to depend on judicial discretion

---

21. See §§ 601 and 605, below (Practitioner's Edition).

22. CPLR 2222.

23. CPLR 5003. The statute refers to the "docketing" of the order as a judgment, but the word would be better read as "entered" if it is to govern the lower as well as the supreme and county courts. See § 421 below.

24. 120 A.D.2d 822, 501 N.Y.S.2d 936 (3d Dep't 1986).

25. Governmental defendants are allowed 90 days.

26. It was held in O'Meara v. A & P, Inc., 169 Misc.2d 697, 647 N.Y.S.2d 424 (Sup.Ct., Westchester County,

1996), that while interest in this situation runs only from the time of the plaintiff's tender of the settlement papers, the costs and disbursements awarded will be for the entirety of the action.

27. See Milbrandt v. A.P. Green Refractories Co., 79 N.Y.2d 26, 580 N.Y.S.2d 147, 588 N.E.2d 45 (1992), summarized in New York State Law Digest No. 386.

28. Articles 50–A and 50–B of the CPLR, §§ 5031–5039 and 5041–5049.

29. CPLR 5034, 5044.

for this class of interest.[30]

Whichever of the three categories is involved, all matters relating to interest should be resolved within the action, if need be by a motion to amend, to resettle, or to modify the judgment. Interest may not ordinarily be sought in a separate action.[31]

Except when computing category 2 interest on a verdict that includes category 1 interest, or computing category 3 interest on a judgment that includes interest under either of the first two categories, there is no compounding of interest under the CPLR. If a judgment for $10,000 is outstanding for five years, for example, at 9% a year,[32] the interest to be computed at this moment would be $4500, which is a straight $900 a year for five years.

§ 412. Rate of Interest

Sections 5001 through 5003 provide only for when interest is to be allowed; the rate of interest is left to CPLR 5004.[1] Prior to 1972, CPLR 5004 adopted and applied the so-called "legal" rate, i.e., the prevalent rate applicable to ordinary commercial loans. That rate was supplied by § 5–501 of the General Obligations Law, commonly known as the usury statute. In later years that statute did not set a straight rate for interest, leaving it instead to the State Banking Board to set from time to time in response to current economic conditions.[2] For a time before 1972, therefore, the rate applicable to litigated obligations, as supplied through adoption by CPLR 5004, was the prevalent loan rate applicable during the period that the particular obligation was outstanding. If there were several different rates applicable during its life, because of periodic statutory or Banking Board changes, several computations would be made so as to use the

applicable rate for the applicable period. It posed no serious problems and had the merit of keeping the litigation rate the same as the current "legal" rate, thus offering neither benefit nor detriment to one defaulting on a loan: the defaulter would ordinarily pay the same rate after default (governed by CPLR 5004) as it had contracted to pay before it.

In 1972, however, CPLR 5004 was amended to supply a straight 6% rate, later raised to 9% (in 1981), where it is now, and to discontinue the practice of adopting the current legal rate. The amendment's assumption was apparently that there would be no serious commercial disadvantage in applying a different rate in litigation than had been contracted for before it. It is at least theoretically incongruous, however, to reward a defaulting debtor, who has borrowed money on a promise to pay (for example) 12% interest, by charging him 3% less for the money after he defaults. That is how things work out, though, with perhaps one important exception:

In categories 2 and 3 (as we drew those categories at the beginning of the prior section), the 9% rate of CPLR 5004 applies without variation, and does so on all money claims once reduced to a verdict or decision,[3] or to a judgment.[4] In those categories, the 9% governs whether the money claim arose at law or in equity, in contract or in tort. In category 1, however, some variations must be noted. If the money claim arose in equity (few do),[5] interest from accrual until verdict, if allowed at all, will be at whatever rate the court's discretion dictates.[6] The nice question that arises in category 1 involves the law action consisting of a money claim based on contract.

Can the contract itself fix a higher rate than the 9% allowed by CPLR 5004? An important

---

30. See Sinclair v. Wieder, 48 A.D.2d 866, 369 N.Y.S.2d 18 (2d Dep't 1975).

31. See Ferguson v. City of New York, 67 Misc.2d 812, 324 N.Y.S.2d 894 (Sup.Ct., Orange County, 1971), modified 39 A.D.2d 569, 331 N.Y.S.2d 735 (2d Dep't 1972).

32. The rate of interest is the subject of a separate section, § 412 below.

§ 412

1. An exception is the money claim arising in equity, in which the rate from default until decision is fixed by the

court in its discretion, CPLR 5001(a); after decision, interest is at the CPLR 5004 rate.

2. See Banking Law § 14–a.

3. CPLR 5002.

4. CPLR 5003.

5. An example would be a judgment awarding specific performance of a contract to convey land, with incidental damages caused by the delay in conveying.

6. CPLR 5001(a).

appellate division case, Astoria Federal Savings and Loan Association v. Rambalakos,[7] held that it can. The case involved a bond and mortgage specifying that interest would be at the rate of 8½% "until the principal is fully paid". The court held that this requires the interest computation in category 1, from default until verdict or decision,[8] to be at the contract rate rather than the CPLR 5004 rate of 9%. A lender's draftsman should use similar language in the contract—the *Astoria* formula would be good to follow but other formulations may also do the job[9]—if the point is open to negotiation, but should of course stipulate a rate no greater than the current usury rate so as to insulate the transaction from a charge of usury. Doing so will at least secure to the plaintiff the higher interest rate set by the contract. Failing to can bring about a substantial forfeiture of interest, as it did in one case in which the interest lost came to $17,000.[10]

This is all relevant only to interest in category 1, however; once reduced to verdict or decision (category 2), or to judgment (category 3), the 9% rate of CPLR 5004 takes over.

There is an indication that the contract can arrange for a higher rate in the latter categories, too. It is principally a matter of how to draft the contract.[11]

What interest rate applies to a foreign judgment after it has been converted into a New York judgment, the New York 9% or the rate the foreign law prescribes? In an 1887 decision, Wells Fargo & Co. v. Davis,[12] the Court of Appeals held for the New York rate, but Hospital Service Plan of New Jersey v. Warehouse Production & Sales Employees Union[13] more recently held for the foreign rate. Other cases then joined the fray and the issue is now in conflict.[14]

The "except" clause in CPLR 5004 is a reminder that if a different rate of interest is set in any particular kind of case or situation, CPLR 5004 defers to it. A low rate of interest is set on certain judgments against municipalities, for example.[15]

A number of these other statutes, whether providing for 9%, as CPLR 5004 presently does, or a lower rate, do not simply prescribe the rate, but provide that the interest awarded "shall not exceed" the stated rate. For a long while, the courts appeared to be disregarding the qualification and just applying the stated rate outright. This practice was overturned by the Court of Appeals in 1997 in Rodriguez v. New York City Hous. Auth.[16] in a case involving the 9% rate specified in § 157(5) of the Public Housing Law, governing housing authorities. Holding that the 9% in that situation is just a maximum, the court remanded the case for the trial court to determine what an appropriate rate would be within that maximum.

Because a number of similar statutes stipulating a rate for other entities do so in the same "shall not exceed" language that § 157(5) does, like § 3–a of the General Municipal Law for municipalities in general and § 16 of the State Finance Law for the state itself, each stipulating 9% but with the "shall not exceed" qualification, the issue became a controversial one. Some of the "shall not exceed" statutes have maximums even less than 9%, some as low as 3% or 4%. Under *Rodriguez*, an application of any of these statutes now requires a determination, apparently on a case-by-case basis, of an appropriate rate within the stated maximum.

Efforts are under way to resolve the matter with legislation. It will take either that, or a

---

7. 49 A.D.2d 715, 372 N.Y.S.2d 689 (2d Dep't 1975).

8. The court refers to the period after maturity and before "judgment", but probably means "verdict or decision", at which point CPLR 5002 supersedes CPLR 5001. It is another example of the small role CPLR 5002 plays, see § 411, when the time lapse between the verdict (or decision) and the judgment is not great.

9. See, e.g., Citibank, N.A. v. Liebowitz, 110 A.D.2d 615, 487 N.Y.S.2d 368 (2d Dep't 1985).

10. See Chipetine v. McEvoy, 238 A.D.2d 536, 657 N.Y.S.2d 88 (2d Dep't 1997), noted in SPR 78:4.

11. See Marine Mgmt., Inc. v. Seco Mgmt., Inc., 176 A.D.2d 252, 574 N.Y.S.2d 207 (2d Dep't 1991), aff'd 80 N.Y.2d 886, 587 N.Y.S.2d 900, 600 N.E.2d 627 (1992).

12. 105 N.Y. 670, 12 N.E. 42 (1887).

13. 76 A.D.2d 882, 429 N.Y.S.2d 31 (2d Dep't 1980).

14. See the summary in SPR 21:3.

15. See Gen.Mun.L. § 3–a; 3d Rep.Leg.Doc. (1959) No. 17, p. 92.

16. 91 N.Y.2d 76, 666 N.Y.S.2d 1009, 689 N.E.2d 903.

definitive appellate adoption of a standard formula, in order to save the many hours of time otherwise likely to be spent by lawyers, clerks, and judges in figuring interest on a case by case basis.[17]

C. FEES, COSTS AND DISBURSEMENTS

Table of Sections

§ 413. Fees, Costs, and Disbursements, Generally

Fees are sums fixed by statute for the taking of various steps in litigation. They are usually payable to a court or court-related officer for the taking of some official step, but the article that provides for them, Article 80 of the CPLR, sets up a fee schedule for a variety of other things as well. A perusal of the article, vast and varied though it is, will offer a quick perspective of it. When it is the business of the person to whom the fee is payable to collect it, such as the clerk of the court, the sheriff, a stenographer, etc., that official can be trusted to advise the party of precisely what the fee is—while it may be better to give than to receive, the receivable is easier to remember. When the recipient is someone less knowledgeable, the party may have to be a little more punctilious about checking about fees. A subpoenaed witness must be paid a fee,[1] for example, and many a witness is not initially aware of this. If the witness learns of it later, however, and before the subpoena's return day, his non-appearance is less likely to be punished for contempt if the fees were not duly tendered to him.

The fees of the clerk for the performance of various acts are among those covered by Article 80. The initial fee for the assignment of an index number to the case, for example, is in CPLR 8018(a); for placing a case on the calendar, in CPLR 8020(a); for demanding jury trial, in CPLR 8020(c); etc. Fees for doing identical acts may differ between and among counties, especially between urban and rural ones, under either some CPLR provision or under a local law. A constitutional attack on geographical discrepancies of this kind in New York, based on both due process and equal protection grounds, was rejected and the differences held permissible.[2] Courts that have their own court acts (all courts of original jurisdiction do except the supreme and county courts) may have their own fee schedules.[3] These prevail over the fee schedules of Article 80 of the CPLR to the extent of any inconsistency.[4]

Costs and disbursements differ from "fees". Briefly, costs are an arbitrary statutory sum that the winner gets from the loser. Disbursements are the winner's out-of-pocket expenses (as a general rule not including an attorney's fee), which the winner also gets from the loser. Ensuing sections elaborate.

§ 414. Costs

"Costs" under the CPLR are an arbitrary figure generally allowed the winner against the loser. They are designed as solace to the winner for the trouble and expense of litigation, theoretically engendered by her adversary's failure to deal with her fairly. They are not, as is sometimes thought, a substitute for an attorney's fee or even a theoretical equivalent.[1] Attorneys' fees, the major expense of a

---

17. The matter is discussed in SPR 69:4 and periodically tracked in later issues, e.g., SPR 70:2.

§ 413

1. CPLR 8001.

2. See Manes v. Goldin, 400 F.Supp. 23 (E.D.N.Y.1975) (3–Judge District Court), aff'd 423 U.S. 1068, 96 S.Ct. 851, 47 L.Ed.2d 80 (1976).

3. See, for example, § 1911 in each of the New York City Civil, Uniform District, Uniform City, and Uniform Justice court acts, McKinney's Vol. 29A, Parts 2 and 3.

4. CPLR 101.

§ 414

1. See Harlan v. Weiner, 80 Misc.2d 723, 364 N.Y.S.2d 270 (N.Y.C.Civ.Ct. 1974).

litigant, are not generally recoverable in American jurisprudence, and New York follows the mainstream. Attorneys' fees may be awarded, along with other sanctions,[2] for frivolous conduct in litigation, but this should not be confused with an award of attorneys' fees merely as a part of the winner's recovery.

In a few selected categories of action, however, the legislature has varied the general rule and allowed an attorney's fee, such as in class actions[3] and in certain actions against the state or its agencies under the "Equal Access to Justice Act".[4] A notable example of Congress's authorizing attorneys' fees is in federal civil rights litigation,[5] jurisdiction of which is concurrent in both federal and state courts.[6]

The failure to make it a general rule to include an attorney's fee in the winner's recovery is often criticized but seldom addressed. A study by the Judicial Conference dug into the issue once again and came up with ameliorative recommendations, but got nowhere. It justly criticized "costs" in this country, and in New York, as "a monumental absurdity".[7] When we see a bit later the amount of those costs, we can accept the epithet.

We should first discuss when costs are allowed, which is the mission of Article 81 of the CPLR, and then discuss their amount, as separately supplied by Article 82.

The party who wins the judgment gets costs against the loser unless statute says otherwise or the court determines that on the facts of the particular case it would not be fair to allow costs.[8] That's the rule applicable at trial level when the case is disposed of, and a similar rule governs costs on an appeal.[9] Costs on a motion are discretionary with the court.[10]

The court can deny costs to the winner, either at trial or appellate level, and can do so on any ground that touches discretion, such as where a brief is found inadequate on the one hand[11] or too long on the other.[12] If the court finds warrant for it on the facts, it can not only deny costs to the winner, but make the winner pay costs to the loser.[13]

The common procedure is for the winner to make up a bill of costs and submit it to the clerk, who peruses it for accuracy and includes the sum in the judgment if it passes muster. This procedure is known as "taxing" costs.[14]

If P's claim against D fails without reaching the merits, as where it has been dismissed for want of jurisdiction, and costs are awarded D against P in conjunction with that dismissal, a later action by P against D on the same claim will be stayed until the costs are paid.[15]

If D has interposed a counterclaim and lost on it while P has lost on the main claim, both parties being losers, D is ordinarily deemed the prevailing party so as to get costs, but the court can vary that, too, if need be.[16] If P sues A and B and prevails against A but not B, P ordinarily gets costs against A while B gets them against P.[17]

Article 81 also has the provision that denies costs to the winner in a money action if the damages awarded show that the claim was sued on in too high a court and could have

---

2. See § 414A below.

3. CPLR 909.

4. CPLR Article 86. A fee will not be awarded if the state's position is found "substantially justified" or "special circumstances make an award unjust". CPLR 8601. See Fried, Attorneys' Fees Against the State: The Equal Access to Justice Act, N.Y. Law Journal, April 2, 1990, p.1.

5. See 28 U.S.C.A. § 1988.

6. See 28 U.S.C.A. § 1983.

7. Crane, Adequacy of Costs Allowable in Litigation, 16th Jud.Conf.Rep. (1971) 246 at 247. The Judicial Conference is now the Office of Court Administration. See § 5 above.

8. CPLR 8101.

9. CPLR 8107.

10. CPLR 8106.

11. Tsomis v. Benenson, 23 A.D.2d 654, 257 N.Y.S.2d 894 (1st Dep't 1965).

12. Tri–State Pipe Lines Corp. v. Sinclair Refining Co., 24 A.D.2d 756, 264 N.Y.S.2d 138 (1st Dep't 1965).

13. See, e.g., Schiff v. Loomer, 23 A.D.2d 481, 255 N.Y.S.2d 482 (1st Dep't 1965).

14. Taxation of costs and the procedure for having the court review the costs is discussed in § 416.

15. See, e.g., Prudential Oil Corp. v. Phillips Petroleum Co., 83 A.D.2d 453, 445 N.Y.S.2d 438 (1st Dep't 1981), where the earlier costs award to D was in a federal court.

16. See Graybill v. VanDyne, 67 Misc.2d 228, 324 N.Y.S.2d 291 (Sup.Ct., Monroe County, 1971).

17. Montague v. Hunt, 50 Misc.2d 442, 270 N.Y.S.2d 771 (Sup.Ct., Greene County, 1966).

been brought in a lower one. To get costs in a supreme court action, for example, P must recover at least $6000 if the case was brought in any county in New York City,[18] the theory being that if P does not recover at least that much, the case should have been brought in the New York City Civil Court. Outside New York City, where there is generally a wider variety of lower courts to pick from, the recovery minimum in order for the winner to get costs in a supreme court action is $500.[19]

It should be noted that an award of costs in an appellate court does not mean costs in all courts, unless the appellate court so provides in the particular case.[20] A litigant in doubt in this regard should secure a clarification from the appellate court, such as with a motion to clarify or resettle the dispositive order.

The amount of costs is supplied by Article 82 of the CPLR. Perusing the sums allowed confirms that while they are not as nominal as they used to be,[21] they have no relationship at all to the actual cost of litigation. In an action in the supreme court, for example, costs are $200 if the case terminates before the note of issue is filed, an additional $200 if it terminates after that but before the trial, and an additional $300, for a grand total of $700, if the case has gone to trial.[22] In the lower courts there may be different costs schedules, just as there may be different fee schedules.[23]

Motion costs if awarded may not exceed $100.[24]

The costs provisions applicable to an action also apply to a special proceeding.[25]

Another phenomenon distinct from costs, but relevant to them, is known as "security for costs". This is a device ordinarily used against a nonresident plaintiff to make sure that if the nonresident loses the case he will not return home and leave the defendant with a costs judgment that can be enforced only in the plaintiff's home state. Security for costs is provided for by Article 85 of the CPLR. The defendant ordinarily seeks it by ex parte motion,[26] which if granted requires the plaintiff to furnish a $500 bond in New York City ($250 elsewhere).[27] The initial penalty for not furnishing the bond is a stay of the plaintiff's action, but it can ripen into an outright dismissal.[28] There is no time limit on when a defendant can move for security for costs.[29]

§ 414A. "Frivolity" Sanctions

The sanction of an attorney's fee and other costs and expenses and even a punitive money penalty for a frivolous litigation practice became a vigorous and controversial topic in the mid–1980s with the adoption of CPLR 8303–a and afterwards Rule 130–1 of the Rules of the Chief Administrator.

Before that the most common and most visible source of an award of attorneys' fees seen in New York practice was the penalty imposed against a party as a condition for getting out from under a default.[1] The situation there is that a party has been guilty of so serious a default that the court, on motion of the other side, has clear power to make the default stick. Doing so, however, exacts a forfeiture of the party's claim or defense and is often viewed by the judges as too severe, a draconian requisi-

---

18. CPLR 8102(1).

19. CPLR 8102(2).

20. See Barton Realty Corp. v. Mangan, 25 A.D.2d 730, 268 N.Y.S.2d 869 (1st Dep't 1966).

21. They were increased in 1989.

22. CPLR 8201.

23. See, e.g., Article 19 in the New York City Civil Court Act and in the Uniform District, City, and Justice court acts, McKinney's Vol. 29A, Parts 2 and 3.

24. CPLR 8202. Appellate costs are provided in CPLR 8203–4.

25. City of Buffalo v. George Irish Paper Co., 31 A.D.2d 470, 299 N.Y.S.2d 8 (4th Dep't 1969), aff'd 26 N.Y.2d 869, 309 N.Y.S.2d 606, 258 N.E.2d 100 (1970).

26. CPLR 8501(a).

27. CPLR 8503.

28. CPLR 8502.

29. See Green v. Roosevelt Hotel, Inc., 47 Misc.2d 177, 261 N.Y.S.2d 942 (Sup.Ct., N.Y.County, 1965).

§ 414A

1. As noted in § 414, above, attorneys' fees are not generally recoverable in New York practice, except in a few special categories. In those categories they are assessed by the court as part of the victory. The attorneys' fees that are the subject of the present section are imposed after special findings of misconduct by the lawyer or client in connection with the litigation itself.

tion that penalizes the client for what is most often the fault of the lawyer. The judicial predilection in this category has therefore been to excuse the default, but only on the condition that the defaulter's lawyer pay the other side (or some worthy outside source like the Lawyers' Fund for Client Protection[2]) a sum of money commensurate with the defaulter's delay and his proffered excuse. The court may require the lawyer to pay this out of pocket, not to be reimbursed by the client, or may allot it between client and lawyer.

Pleading defaults have been the most common illustration of this,[3] but they are not the only ones. Defaults in connection with a bill of particulars under CPLR 3042,[4] disclosure under CPLR 3126,[5] a failure to prosecute under CPLR 3216,[6] and calendar calls under CPLR 3404,[7] are other examples. The money sanction in this category is a penalty imposed on the offender almost as a favor—a slap on the wrist offered in lieu of capital punishment. Considering that a malpractice action and disciplinary proceedings can confront the lawyer if the default sticks, this appraisal is no exaggeration. The offense has reached the stage, in other words, at which the court has clear statutory power to impose a full default, and implicit in that ultimate power is the power to do something less. The something less is the attorney's fee imposed as a condition for excusing the default. (The defaulter can always refuse the condition and accept the default!)

These sources of attorneys' fees remain intact, and active. Quite another source today is the attorney's fee imposed for a "frivolous" litigation practice. The defaults just enumerated can often themselves qualify as frivolous conduct, of course, but separate and apart

from them, and standing on its own, is what the bar has come to know outright as the "frivolity" sanction of Rule 130–1 and CPLR 8303–a.

After the Second Department Appellate Division handed down two cases in 1985, holding that the courts have "inherent" power to impose the sanction of an attorney's fee for a "frivolous" litigation practice,[8] the Court of Appeals rejected the conclusion as premature. It held in A.G. Ship Maintenance Corp. v. Lezak[9] that it was not yet necessary to decide whether courts have "inherent" power to impose frivolity sanctions because it perceived the courts as having such authority through rule-making powers delegated by the legislature.[10] It also held that whatever the source of such a power, it should not be exercised on an "ad hoc" basis, but only by a "plenary rule" containing guideposts and standards.

Meanwhile, in 1985 the legislature enacted and in 1986 amended and expanded CPLR 8303–a, a statute that unequivocally authorizes attorneys' fees in the "frivolity" category in designated tort actions—the usual unintentional torts: personal injury, property damage, and wrongful death cases, including those based on medical malpractice. CPLR 8303–a permits a court to award "costs and reasonable attorneys' fees" of up to $10,000 against any party found to have interposed a frivolous claim or defense in such an action. CPLR 8303–a did not (and still does not) apply to other categories of action, however, such as contract, corporate, commercial, property, and matrimonial actions, or to special proceedings. Part 130–1 of the Rules was designed to remedy that.

Part 130–1[11] was first circulated by the Office of Court Administration in July of 1987,

---

2. See, e.g., McLoughlin v. Henke, 130 Misc.2d 1091, 499 N.Y.S.2d 332 (Sup.Ct., Queens County, 1986), one of the first cases to designate the fund the recipient of a "default" sanction.

3. See § 231.

4. See § 241.

5. See § 367.

6. See § 375.

7. See § 376.

8. Gabrelian v. Gabrelian, 108 A.D.2d 445, 489 N.Y.S.2d 914 (2d Dep't 1985), so held of courts of original

jurisdiction for the bringing of frivolous actions, and LTown Limited Partnership v. Sire Plan Inc., 108 A.D.2d 435, 489 N.Y.S.2d 567 (2d Dep't 1985), mod'd 69 N.Y.2d 670, 511 N.Y.S.2d 840, 503 N.E.2d 1377 (1986), so held of appellate courts with respect to frivolous appeals.

9. 69 N.Y.2d 1, 511 N.Y.S.2d 216, 503 N.E.2d 681 (1986).

10. The court cited Article VI, § 30, of the state constitution and § 211(1)(b) of the Judiciary Law as the source.

11. It was originally numbered Part 130, but renumbered Part 130–1 afterwards. A number of decisions cite it as 130. It can simply be read as the 130–1 as cited in those calling for comment from bench and bar. Among the responders were some legislators who asked OCA to hold up on the rule until the legislature had a chance to look into it. OCA obliged, and the originally proposed effective date of January 1, 1988, was put off. When the 1988 legislative session passed with no action, OCA returned to the rule, redrafted it after considering the comments the initial circulation had elicited, and promulgated it with a January 1, 1989, effective date. It took effect on that day and has been doing its work ever since.

Much of the agitation over CPLR 8303–a, which was a controversial subject from the outset, gave way to greater agitation when Part 130–1 entered the scene, a tumult akin to that enveloping Rule 11 of the Federal Rules of Civil Procedure, on which, indeed, important parts of Part 130–1 are modeled.[12]

A number of points must be made about Rule 130–1, in the course of which we will coordinate it with CPLR 8303–a.

1. The rule authorizes two distinct categories of money punishment for frivolous conduct. The first, generally referred to as "costs", awards costs and reasonable attorneys' fees that reimburse actual expenses incurred by the other side because of the frivolous conduct. The second, which is the one that gets the name "sanction", is a separate money assessment imposed as a punishment for the frivolous conduct. At the outset, a $10,000 cap applied to both categories together.[13] An amendment that took effect March 1,

1998, retains the cap on the punitive sanction but removes it from the compensatory award.

2. The "costs" go to the person—party or lawyer—who sustained the expense. The "sanction" has a different destination: if the money is assessed against the party, it goes to the clerk for deposit into the public treasury; if it is assessed against the lawyer, it goes to the Lawyers' Fund for Client Protection, the fund set up to recompense the victims of dishonest lawyers.

3. The assessment may be made against either the party, the attorney, or both, wherever the court finds the fault to lie. When it is made against the attorney, the rule provides that

it may be against the attorney personally or upon a partnership, firm, corporation, government agency, prosecutor's office, legal aid society or public defender's office with which the attorney is associated. . . .

4. Note the inclusion of the "government agency". That includes not only those agencies that have their own legal staffs, but also those that the Attorney–General's office represents in court.[14]

5. On the "sanctions" segment of the new rule there is yet a further consideration. If it is strictly punitive, as it appears to be, there may be difficulty about applying it not only against the state, but even against municipalities,[15] although its application to the individual lawyers who represent the state or municipality is apparently permissible.

decisions and other places (articles, digests, commentaries, etc.).

12. See Chase, Sanctions in State Courts, N.Y. Law Journal, October 22, 1987, p.1, in which the view is expressed that "the disadvantages of judicial sanctions are likely to outweigh the advantages" and that "the federal experience [on which the New York rule is built] is not comforting".

13. An early case imposing the full $10,000 is Winters v. Gould, 143 Misc.2d 44, 539 N.Y.S.2d 686 (Sup.Ct., N.Y. County, 1989), applying it against a tricky character who used the delays of the court system to live rent free off several landlords.

14. There is some doubt about whether the rule applies to the state itself, as when the state is sued for money in an ordinary court of claims action. In authorizing costs and sanctions, Rule 130.1 says the rule applies "except where prohibited by law". Section 27 of the Court

of Claims Act bars costs and attorneys' fees in a court of claims suit. So clear was this barrier in legislative thinking, in fact, that it took an amendment of § 27 in 1987 to refer to CPLR 8303–a explicitly. It was thought that without the amendment, § 27 would be a barrier to the application of CPLR 8303–a in the court of claims. It would seem to follow that if an unamended § 27 would have barred the sanctions contained in a statute, it would a fortiori bar those promulgated in a mere rule like Part 130–1. And the language of § 27 would seem to erect the barrier in both directions, i.e., preclude an assessment against any party to the court of claims suit, not just the state.

15. See and compare the 1982 Court of Appeals decision in Sharapata v. Town of Islip, 56 N.Y.2d 332, 452 N.Y.S.2d 347, 437 N.E.2d 1104.

6. The rule's target of any "frivolous conduct" at all in litigation means that it includes not just a frivolous claim or defense, but a frivolous motion, appeal, or any other piece of conduct that can earn the ignominious "frivolity" label. In this regard, which can prove to be an important one, it differs from CPLR 8303–a. Coordinating 8303–a with the new Part 130–1 poses some questions.

7. Under CPLR 8303–a, sanctions are imposable only for a frivolous claim or defense. In tort cases governed by CPLR 8303–a, there was some doubt at the outset whether Rule 130–1 would also apply, so that a sanction would be available for (e.g.) a frivolous motion or other conduct. Subdivision 5 of Part 130–1 says that the new rule "shall not apply to requests for costs or attorney's fees subject to the provisions of CPLR 8303–a". At first glance that seems to say that the new rule doesn't apply in the tort cases at all, so that nothing but a frivolous claim or defense would do the job in those cases. But the exception[16] says that what the rule doesn't apply to is a "request" subject to CPLR 8303–a, and the only "request" subject to that provision is one relating to a claim or defense. Since a request relating to something like a motion or appeal or other step is not subject to CPLR 8303–a, one may conclude that the new rule is free to operate on it even in a tort case. Since many cases in which Rule 130–1 sanctions have been applied are tort cases that would also fall under CPLR 8303–a, the expansive interpretation suggested is apparently the interpretation followed, and this is no small matter.

8. Whatever definitive answer the courts may give the question in tort cases, the courts clearly have the power to address any kind of frivolous conduct in other actions (contract, commercial, property, matrimonial, etc.), where there is no CPLR 8303–a to confuse matters.

9. There are some other exceptions to take note of. The rule does not apply in the small claims parts[17] or to certain proceedings in the family court.[18]

10. The fact that a "proceeding" as well as an action is included means that special proceedings are included. That embraces Article 78 proceedings against administrative action, where a finding that a determination was "arbitrary and capricious" is among the grounds for overturning a determination.[19] It's interesting to speculate whether there is any appreciable difference between "arbitrary and capricious" on the one hand and "frivolous" on the other? If there isn't, the agency or its lawyer would be sanctionable whenever the determination is rejected as arbitrary and capricious. Needless to say, that hasn't been the conclusion reached, but the idea does lend a light note to break up this dark discourse on sanctions.

11. The summary proceeding (the landlord-tenant device) is a category of special proceeding and is included in Part 130–1.[20] Summary proceedings are brought in the hundreds of thousands annually. Especially when based on non-payment of rent, they often meet defenses that can qualify as frivolous—the obvious product of desperation as a tenant, simply unable to pay, interposes anything the imagination can conjure up to keep a roof over the family for the time being, but:

12. All awards under the new rule lie in the court's discretion. That discretion may have a special role to play in summary and other proceedings that often involve disadvantaged parties.

13. The first-tier appellate court retains the power of plenary review of any sanction imposed, as to both the facts, the law, and the court's discretion. The often vilified interlocu-

---

16. Rule 130–1.5.

17. There are small claims parts in the New York City Civil Court and in each of the district and city courts. See §§ 581–583 below. In the town and village courts, which also have small claims parts, the rule does not apply at all—to the small claims or any other part. (Most of the judges of those courts are not lawyers.)

18. Rule 130–1.1.

19. CPLR 7803(3). See § 561 below.

20. Indeed, Rule 130–1.4 makes sure that the powers conferred by the new rule belong also to the judges of the Housing Part of the New York City Civil Court.

tory appeal[21] may prove to be a hero on this scene, standing by with its red carpet to facilitate review of an individual judge's action under the new rule should it be perceived as excessive in a given case. In this regard, it is noteworthy that:

14. Neither costs nor sanctions can be the product of a moment's judicial whim or bad temper. Rule 130–1.2 permits the award

> only upon a written decision setting forth the conduct ..., the reasons why the court found the conduct to be frivolous, and the reasons why the court found the amount awarded or imposed to be appropriate.

15. The rule requires that the sum granted be entered as a judgment, which would seem to allow—if, indeed, it does not require—that it be a judgment separate from the judgment on the merits.

16. There must be "a reasonable opportunity to be heard" on the issue of a Rule 130–1 award. So provides Rule 130–1.1(d), but it says that the form of the hearing "shall depend upon the nature of the conduct and the circumstances of the case". This is a hedge. It avoids dictating any specific place or point as more appropriate to a hearing than any other. Presumably the court can order an immediate hearing on a costs or sanctions application, suspending further attention to the merits of the case while the hearing goes forward, or postpone it to some later point, perhaps depending on what the allegedly frivolous conduct affected (the whole case? just a defense? some incidental step like a motion? etc.). A discussion of what kind of hearing is required appears in Bruckner v. Jaitor Apartments Co.,[22] where the court said that if a motion is made for sanctions, the return day of the motion is the hearing. Reviewing earlier cases, the court also noted that when the offense occurs right in front of the judge, no further hearing is necessary.

17. The award can be sought either by motion, or by cross-motion, or by the court on its own motion.

18. A key question throughout, of course, is what constitutes "frivolous" conduct. Rule 130–1.1(c) defines frivolity to include conduct that is "completely without merit in law and cannot be supported by a reasonable argument for an extension, modification or reversal of existing law", language borrowed from Federal Rule 11. It also includes conduct taken "to delay ... harass or maliciously injure another", an idea borrowed from Rule 11, and the assertion of "material factual statements that are false".

19. Lest it occur to a party to try to use Rule 130–1 to harass the other side, another part of Rule 130–1.1(c) includes as frivolous conduct the making of an unjustified frivolity motion under Rule 130–1. The drafters don't want to encourage some of the so-called "satellite" litigation that was generated by the federal provision.

20. Yet another part of Rule 130–1.1(c) requires the court to see whether "the conduct was continued when its lack of legal or factual basis was apparent, or was brought to the attention of counsel or the party". Thus a lawyer who was in any measure hoodwinked by the client, believing the claim, defense, motion (or whatever) meritorious at first and only later learning otherwise, is given a chance to discontinue the frivolous pursuit at that time. Doing so avoids the rule; failing to invokes it.

Is Rule 130–1 an end run around the holding of Drago v. Buonagurio,[23] in which the Court of Appeals held in 1978 that even when a defendant is sued without any ground whatever, the defendant can't recover damages against the plaintiff's lawyer? The court said that no existing theory of law would support such a claim, rejecting negligence, abuse of process, malicious prosecution, and "prima facie tort" theories, and rejecting as well an invitation to fashion a new theory to support the claim. The court said that this would have to be done through legislation. Rule 130–1 has in effect adopted, through judicial regulation,

---

21. See § 526 below. An interlocutory appeal implies the appeal of an order that disposes of some intermediate step in the case, short of a final judgment.

22. 147 Misc.2d 796, 555 N.Y.S.2d 563 (Civ.Ct., Queens County, 1990).

23. 46 N.Y.2d 778, 413 N.Y.S.2d 910, 386 N.E.2d 821.

the "wrongful suit" claim that *Drago* rejected, and this appears to be all the more accurate a conclusion now, under the 1998 amendment, which removed the $10,000 cap from the compensatory assessment that the rule allows.

***

There has been a steady accumulation of cases applying Rule 130–1 sanctions.

The Court of Appeals' first review of the rule occurred in Minister, Elders & Deacons v. 198 Broadway, Inc.,[24] where the court imposed a $2500 sanction for a frivolous appeal and dilatory conduct. After that, in Intercontinental Credit Corp. v. Roth,[25] the court imposed a $5000 sanction for a frivolous motion to reargue.

In the lower courts the imposition of sanctions has ranged wide. A "vendetta" against the defendant occasioned a sanction of $2000 in Jones v. Camar Realty Corp.,[26] where the court acted sua sponte in exacting $2000 from the plaintiff's lawyer, whom it found to be on a vendetta not only against the defendant landlord, but also, "it would seem, the courts". The occasion was the denial of a motion seeking reargument of a previously denied motion for leave to appeal an appellate term order. The lawyer threatened to prosecute unmeritorious claims against the landlord and make him spend lots of money defending them. The case was an early warning to parties and lawyers who may once have felt insulated in uttering threats about so exploiting the courts.

If the motive for interposing a claim is found to be malicious, the claimant has been held subject to the sanction of Rule 130–1 even if the claim is found to have some colorable basis.[27]

Sexist comments directed against a female attorney in the course of a deposition brought a $1000 sanction against the offender in Principe v. Assay Partners,[28] half being a compensatory assessment to cover the cost of the sanctions motion and the other half a punitive measure.

It has been held frivolous, and made the subject of a sanction, to take evasive steps to try to avoid the judge who has been assigned to the case. Such an attempt was made in International 800 Telecom Corp. v. Kramer, Levin, Nessen, Kamin & Frankel,[29] where a company was sued in New York County, and lost. In an effort to undo the result (which was presumably destined to failure under the res judicata doctrine anyway), the company then brought another action, and, to avoid assignment to the same judge, brought it in Rockland County. The opposing parties then moved before the original judge in New York County to declare the Rockland action a related one and have it transferred to that judge in New York. The motion was granted and a sanction imposed.

Under the separate Rule 130–2, a costs or punitive sanction may be imposed for failing to show up, or for showing up late, at a scheduled court appearance. Under Rule 130–2, however, the maximum is $2500, and it caps both categories: costs and a punitive sanction together can't exceed $2500.[30]

Cases on Rule 130–1 sanctions proliferate. The above is a mere sampling.

The requirement that the actual signature of an attorney appear on "[e]very pleading, written motion, and other paper, served on another party or filed or submitted to the court", is also part of Rule 130–1, where it appears in subdivision (a) of § 130–1.1–a.[31]

24. 76 N.Y.2d 411, 559 N.Y.S.2d 866, 559 N.E.2d 429 (1990). The case is treated in a lead note in New York State Law Digest No. 367.

25. 78 N.Y.2d 306, 574 N.Y.S.2d 528, 579 N.E.2d 688 (1991).

26. 167 A.D.2d 285, 561 N.Y.S.2d 916 (1st Dep't 1990).

27. See Gordon v. Marrone, 202 A.D.2d 104, 616 N.Y.S.2d 98 (2d Dep't 1994), noted in SPR 29:3.

28. 154 Misc.2d 702, 586 N.Y.S.2d 182 (Sup.Ct., N.Y.County, 1992).

29. 155 Misc.2d 975, 591 N.Y.S.2d 313 (Sup.Ct., N.Y.County, 1992). The case is noted in SPR 2:3–4.

30. See SPR 35:1 and 67:2.

31. The numbering system used for Rule 130–1 is sometimes misleading, but all of the provisions are at hand under "Part 130" of the rules, occupying just a little more than a page in the annually recompiled "McKinney's New York Rules of Court".

Subdivision (b) then provides that the signature constitutes an automatic certification by the signer "that, to the best of that person's knowledge, information and belief, formed after an inquiry reasonable under the circumstances, the presentation of the paper or the contentions therein are not frivolous". No actual certification form or ritual is required. The signing itself constitutes the certification, and a false certification of course grounds a sanction. That's why the signing requirement is contained in the sanctions rule itself: to stress the individual responsibility of the lawyer to make a reasonable effort to ascertain the truth or accuracy of the content of the paper signed.

The signing aspect of the rule is separately treated in the chapter on papers, met earlier.[32]

§ 415. Disbursements

In contrast with "costs", which under the CPLR are arbitrary sums awarded to the winner, disbursements are the winner's out-of-pocket expenditures. The winner also gets these back from the loser. The rule is that the party to whom costs are awarded also recovers disbursements.[1] It is not rigid, however; the court can allow disbursements to a party not awarded costs, and if the winner has won judgment of at least $50 he must be allowed disbursements even if costs are denied him by the court for one reason or another.[2] The disbursements recoverable, however, are those listed in Article 83 of the CPLR, and as a perusal of the main list in CPLR 8301(a) quickly shows, not every expenditure that a party makes is recoverable. Indeed, one of the most significant expenses in litigation, the deposition, is limited to a disbursement of $250 even though the actual expenditure is likely to be well beyond that.[3]

After listing specific recoverable disbursements in its earlier paragraphs, CPLR 8301(a) then allows in paragraph 12 "such other reasonable and necessary expenses as are taxable according to the course and practice of the court, by express provision of law or by order of the court". This paragraph produces most of the caselaw on disbursements. The provision has been held applicable only to the expenses of a party, not those of a nonparty witness,[4] who is limited to the set (and modest) witness fees of CPLR 8001. As far as disbursements are concerned, this is also true of the expert witness, whatever extra the party who retains the expert may be willing to pay out of pocket.[5] This merely means that the party who wants to use the expert must defray the expert's expenses and actual fee without expecting to recover these sums as disbursements.

There is some flexibility in the "reasonable and necessary" phrase of CPLR 8301(a)(12), and a judicial push can send it one way or another on a given claim of disbursement. Some courts, advocating uniformity, suggest that rules of court should provide a more detailed treatment of what items may be considered taxable disbursements and that until there are such rules the matter is left to the discretion of the individual judge.[6] Others take a restrictive view of the disbursement statute, holding that any expansion of the list should await legislative action.[7] A party unclear on local practice should inquire of the clerk and of local practitioners. Because a given expenditure, although disputed, may be insufficient to warrant a judicial contest, the establishment of a uniform list more thorough than that of CPLR 8301(a) is not likely to emerge through the cumbersome common law method. It will more likely require a legislative or regulatory effort, perhaps by the Office of Court Administration.

---

32. See § 201 above.

§ 415

1. CPLR 8301(a).

2. CPLR 8301(c).

3. CPLR 8301(a)(9).

4. Davis Sportswear, Inc. v. Parker, Duryee, Benjamin, Zunino & Malone, 49 Misc.2d 77, 266 N.Y.S.2d 573 (Sup. Ct., N.Y.County, 1966). The court suggests that the wit-

ness may recover those expenses in a plenary action if worth the witness's while.

5. Van Patten v. Sylvia, 76 Misc.2d 899, 352 N.Y.S.2d 565 (Sup.Ct., Schenectady County, 1974).

6. See Muffoletto v. Rivera, 54 Misc.2d 114, 281 N.Y.S.2d 549 (Sup.Ct., Erie County, 1967).

7. See Kiev v. Seligman & Latz of Binghamton, Inc., 47 Misc.2d 364, 262 N.Y.S.2d 766 (Broome County Ct. 1965).

The printing of a record on appeal, because it does involve substantial expenditure, comes in for occasional dispute in disbursement context. It has been held, for example, that the cost of printing a record when a less expensive method than printing is available will not be allowed as a disbursement.[8] In one case, a third-party defendant went to a printing expense of $800 to appeal a $450 judgment. The expense was termed "profligate" and disallowed, and a figure applicable to an alternative and cheaper method was substituted.[9]

The fees statutorily exacted of a party under Article 80 of the CPLR are usually recoverable as disbursements, but not all are. Poundage, for example, which is a percentage of property levied on by a sheriff, is a statutory expense under Article 80[10] but not a taxable disbursement under Article 83. Instead, the sheriff collects the poundage out of the property levied on.[11] Thus the poundage, which can be a very substantial sum indeed and can slip into the picture almost surreptitiously against a debtor able and willing to pay but just a bit too dilatory about doing so,[12] is the debtor's burden. Poundage in the thousands of dollars can become due the sheriff for doing little more than serving a paper.[13]

In certain categories of action, notably those affecting realty, additional allowances may be made to the winner.[14] And in any kind of contested action in which the winner can convince the court that the case was "difficult or extraordinary" (the court is not easily convinced), it can award up to $3000 as an "additional allowance".[15]

§ 416. Taxation of Costs and Disbursements

The practice is for the winning party to get up a bill of costs, including all disbursements she deems herself entitled to, and to present it to the clerk when presenting the judgment for entry. The bill of costs should be supported by affidavits. The clerk is required to review it without waiting for a party's objection. The procedure bears the imposing name of "taxation" of costs, but it has nothing to do with taxation as the term is generally understood. If satisfied that the expenses claimed are permissible, the clerk inserts their total in the judgment as costs and disbursements.[1]

The step is usually taken without notice to the other side. In that case, however, when the winner gets his costs taxed as requested and included in the judgment, he must immediately serve a copy of the bill of costs on the adverse party. He can just include the bill of costs with a copy of the judgment when he serves it with notice of entry. The adverse party then has five days within which to move to "retax" the costs.[2] Alternatively, the party seeking costs can initially give notice of their taxation,[3] thus compelling the other side to put in, at the specified return time, any objections she may have.

Any party dissatisfied with an item taxed (or refused taxation) by the clerk may have the court, by motion or notice, review the item.[4]

The procedure for taxing costs and disbursements is extensively reviewed in East 13th St. Community Ass'n v. New York State Urban Devel. Corp.[5]

8.   See CPLR 8301(a)(6); Lew Morris Demolition Co. v. Bd. of Educ. of the City of New York, 80 Misc.2d 944, 365 N.Y.S.2d 109 (N.Y.C.Civ.Ct. 1974). See also CPLR 5529(a)(1).

9.   Society of the New York Hospital v. Mogensen, 81 Misc.2d 1089, 370 N.Y.S.2d 354 (App.T., 1st Dep't, 1975). As might be expected, it was a government agency that got the "profligate" label: in this case, ironically, the New York City Commissioner of Social Services.

10.   CPLR 8012(b).

11.   DeLia v. DeLia, 32 A.D.2d 987, 302 N.Y.S.2d 5 (3d Dep't 1969).

12.   See Thornton v. Montefiore Hospital, 117 A.D.2d 552, 498 N.Y.S.2d 828 (1st Dep't 1986).

13.   See, e.g., Considine v. Pichler, 72 A.D.2d 103, 422 N.Y.S.2d 429 (1st Dep't 1979).

14.   See CPLR 8302, 8303.

15.   CPLR 8303(a)(2).

§ 416

1.   CPLR 8401.

2.   CPLR 8403.

3.   CPLR 8402.

4.   CPLR 8404.

5.   164 Misc.2d 589, 625 N.Y.S.2d 418 (Sup.Ct., N.Y. County, 1995). The case is treated in the lead note in SPR 38.

§ 417. Form of Judgment

The following is a sample form of judgment as used in an ordinary money action (damages for breach of contract) tried by jury.

SUPREME COURT OF THE STATE OF NEW YORK
COUNTY OF NEW YORK

A.B., Plaintiff,
        against   Judgment
C.D., Defendant.   Index No. _____

The issues in this action having duly been tried before Mr. Justice Xavier C. Riccobono and a jury at Trial Term, Part XIV of this court, held at the courthouse at 60 Centre Street on April 19, 1999, and the plaintiff and defendant having appeared by their respective attorneys, Roland Garrulous and Vera Voluble, and the jury on April 19, 1999, having rendered a verdict for plaintiff against defendant for damages of $40,000, with interest thereon from Dec. 23, 1996, and the plaintiff's costs and disbursements having been duly taxed by the clerk in the sum of $_____,

Now, on motion of Roland Garrulous, plaintiff's attorney, it is

ORDERED, ADJUDGED AND DECREED, that plaintiff A.B., recover of defendant C.D., the sum of $40,000, with interest thereon from Dec. 23, 1996, amounting to $_____, together with costs and disbursements as taxed in the sum of $_____, making in all the sum of $_____, and that the plaintiff have execution therefor.

Judgment signed April 26, 1999.

                                              _____
                                              Clerk

A few comments on the form. The blanks are filled in by the clerk, who computes the interest based on the appropriate dates. The form used here, which is typical, shows how interest from verdict until judgment, as authorized by CPLR 5002, is often omitted as a separate step.[1]

D. RECORDING THE JUDGMENT

Table of Sections

§ 417

1. See § 411 above.

§ 418

1. CPLR 5016(a). The "judgment-roll", discussed in the next section, is presented to the clerk at the same time the judgment is tendered for entry.

§ 418. Entry of Judgment

The judgment, which is usually drafted by the winner, is brought to the clerk for signing and entry. The CPLR provides that formal "entry" occurs when, after the judgment "has been signed by the clerk, it is filed by him."[1] The fact of entry is recorded by the clerk in what is officially denominated a "judgment-book", which court clerks are required to maintain.[2] Once the judgment is entered, the

2. CPLR 9702(1).

winner should serve on the loser a copy of the judgment with notice of entry; it is this service that starts the loser's appeal time.[3] If the judgment contemplates enforcement, as it usually does when the plaintiff is the winner, it is entry that marks the moment that enforcement may be sought.

"Entry" should not be confused with "docketing", although it often is. Technically, the "docketing" of the judgment is its recording in a set of alphabetized books; it is the step that makes the judgment a lien on the defendant's real property. Docketing a judgment is thus a step distinct from its entry, although both steps are almost simultaneous in the supreme and county courts[4] because the county clerk, in whose office the realty docket books are maintained, is ex officio the clerk of both courts.[5] In lower courts, however, there is no such "docketing"; when used in those courts, the term usually intends to connote mere "entry". This topic (including the realty lien) is elaborated in the later treatment of docketing.[6]

When the judgment is based on the general verdict of a jury, the clerk can enter it without specific instruction from the court. The procedure in that situation, especially in the more populous counties (where the "clerk's" office has many personnel), is to secure from the clerk in attendance during the trial a statement describing the verdict—this is sometimes called an "extract" from the clerk's minutes—which the winner takes to the "judgment" clerk along with the draft of the judgment. The extract establishes the fact of the verdict and suffices to permit entry of judgment. If a special verdict was used, i.e., a list of questions submitted to the jury, which has become a much more common practice today, the judge must translate the jury's answers into the appropriate result and direct judgment accordingly.[7] When there is no jury, the decision of

the judge determines the judgment to be entered.[8]

Until recently, there was no time limit on how long the winner had to get judgment entered. The deterrent to delay was the appellate point already made: that the loser's appeal time remains open until the winner serves a copy of the judgment on the loser with notice of entry. Occasionally laches was applied to exact a forfeiture against the dilatory submitter,[9] but that was rare. With the adoption of the Uniform Rules in 1986, a 60–day period was imposed as a time limit for the entry of a judgment or order. The starting point of this 60–day period is ambiguous, however, at least in the case of judgments, because it appears to contemplate a "decision" specifically directing a settlement or submission of the judgment,[10] and, indeed, the Court of Appeals has held that the 60–day period won't start unless the decision has explicitly called for settlement or submission.[11]

Sometimes there will be no so such direction. It is in general a good idea to see to it that all judgments are drawn and entered promptly, and certainly within 60 days after the earliest discernible time of the winner's victory. "Abandonment" of the victory is the explicit consequence imposed by the rule for letting the 60 days pass.

A money judgment has a form well-recognized by lawyers. The judgment in non-money actions can be more complicated. If dispute on the form arises, the court will resolve it on motion.

There are a few points to be noted about the situation in which a party dies before judgment is entered. If the verdict or decision has already been rendered before a party dies, the entry of judgment is allowed, either for or against the deceased, and may even be made in the names of the original parties. But no verdict or decision may be rendered against a

---

3. CPLR 5513(a).
4. CPLR 5018(a).
5. County Law §§ 525, 909.
6. See § 421 below.
7. CPLR 5016(b).
8. CPLR 5016(c).

9. See, e.g., Vickery v. Village of Saugerties, 106 A.D.2d 721, 483 N.Y.S.2d 765 (3d Dep't 1984), aff'd 64 N.Y.2d 1161, 490 N.Y.S.2d 735, 480 N.E.2d 349 (1985).

10. See Uniform Rule 202.48, the rule that applies in the supreme and county courts.

11. See § 250 above.

party who has died.[12] In that instance the decedent's personal representative must be substituted before the case can proceed. If substitution does not take place within a reasonable time, the action may be dismissed as against the side needing substitution.[13]

When entering judgment in a case involving multiple defendants, the plaintiff must bear a few points in mind. If the defendants' liability is joint and several, as is often the case with joint tortfeasors, the entry of judgment against one—if the plaintiff should be entitled to judgment against that one but not against the others[14]—should pose no problem. Each bears an individual liability in that instance, not irrevocably linked with the others. The plaintiff in that situation should see to it, however, that an order of severance is also entered, or that a severance direction is included in the judgment or order being entered, so as to separate and leave for independent adjudication the claims not now going to judgment. The severance direction is easy to secure and should be asked for when applying to enter judgment.[15] Sometimes the clerk will enter a severance order without direction.[16]

If the liability is joint only, however, such as the liability of partners on a contract claim against the partnership,[17] rather than joint and several (statistically the more frequent liability among joined defendants), and through one event or another the plaintiff deems herself entitled to a judgment against one defendant but not all of them, the plaintiff must be cautious about entering a separate judgment against the one. It is safe to do so

when the one has confessed judgment, because in that situation a statute states expressly that such entry does not bar the continued pursuit of the others.[18] But if one but not all of the defendants should default, it has been held that the intentional entry of judgment against the defaulting one will merge (and thus destroy) the claim against the others.[19] Such are the rigors of this "joint" liability. The theory is that any one of the nondefaulters, if successful on the merits, would succeed for all (thus making her cohort's earlier default academic). A plaintiff unaware of these consequences, who enters judgment against a defaulting joint-only debtor, should move to vacate it promptly upon discovery of the mistake,[20] and the court should be receptive to such a vacatur motion, considering the substantive disaster—forfeiture of the plaintiff's claim against the others—to be visited upon so minor a procedural oversight. The Court of Appeals has held that this rule about joint debtors should not apply unless the plaintiff, in entering judgment against one, intentionally waives his rights against the others.[21] A plaintiff entering judgment against only one debtor cannot be said to have intentionally waived his rights against the others if the one does not pay.

§ 419. The Judgment–Roll

The party at whose instance judgment is entered prepares a "judgment-roll", which is submitted with the judgment and which the clerk files when entering the judgment.[1] The judgment-roll consists of the basic papers in

---

12. CPLR 5016(d).

13. CPLR 1021. See § 184 et seq., above, for discussion of the procedure for substitution and connected problems.

14. This can happen, for example, where some but not all of the defendants default or confess judgment.

15. See CPLR 5012.

16. The clerk does this, for example, when entering a default judgment against fewer than all defendants. See CPLR 3215(a).

17. Part.L. § 26(2).

18. CPLR 3218(d).

19. See Salem v. Seigel, 126 N.Y.S.2d 214 (Sup.Ct., N.Y. County, 1953), in which the partner who suffered a default judgment proved to be insolvent. These procedural

peculiarities are the trappings of the common law's distinction between "joint" and "joint and several" liabilities, an anachronism that has been justly criticized. See Werner, Shared Liability: An Alternative to the Confusion of Joint, Several, and Joint and Several Obligations, 42 Albany L.Rev. 1 (1977). Inroads into "joint and several liability" were made with the enactment of Article 16 of the CPLR effective in 1986. See §§ 168a—168d, above.

20. The right to move to vacate a default judgment is available not only to the defendant against whom it was taken, but also to the plaintiff who took it. See § 427 below.

21. United States Printing & Litho. Co. v. Powers, 233 N.Y. 143, 135 N.E. 225 (1922).

§ 419

1. CPLR 5017(a).

the case. It contains the summons, pleadings, judgment, orders "involving the merits or necessarily affecting the final judgment", and any admissions that may have been made in the action (the presence of which would have dispensed with proof of the matters admitted).[2] These contents are specified in CPLR 5017(b), which then goes on to list additional contents of the judgment-roll in specific instances, e.g., in a contested action, or on a default, or upon judgment by confession, etc.[3] If there is doubt as to whether a given paper belongs in the judgment-roll, it is usually best to include it.

Gathering together the judgment-roll is a light task. Quite often the papers required are already in the court's file of the case, which enables the clerk to put the judgment-roll together without further papers from the party.[4] The party need only determine which papers, required as part of the judgment-roll, are not already on file, bringing these along when submitting the judgment for entry and extracting the other needed papers from the file. These should then be put together into a judgment-roll and handed over to the clerk, who will usually put it right back into the file, immediately or ultimately. The file is its permanent repository, where it may be inspected as a public record.

Usually the original of each paper or document is included in the judgment-roll, but this is more a matter of practice than mandate: unless otherwise expressly required, copies instead of originals are appropriate either for service (on a party) or filing (with the clerk).[5]

§ 420. Correcting the Judgment; Nunc Pro Tunc Changes

CPLR 5019(a) provides that "a judgment or order shall not be stayed, impaired or affected by any mistake, defect or irregularity in the papers or procedures in the action not affect-

ing a substantial right of a party", and provides express permission for either the trial or appellate court to cure the mistake. Even errors of substance are correctible under this provision, as where the defendant was found to have title but the plaintiff secured entry of a judgment that recited it to be in himself,[1] as long as the record offers clear support for what was intended. In another case with sufficient record support, the Court of Appeals allowed a county, several years after judgment, an amendment to reflect the special municipal interest rate that the clerk had mistakenly entered at the higher regular rate.[2]

An absence of record support for the change will find the court reluctant to make it, however. No change will be allowed by an appellate court, for example, if the context suggests that the trial court is simply changing its mind on a matter already decided. The trial judge may not sit as an appellate court over herself. The Court of Appeals has said that

> [t]he rule has long been settled and inflexibly applied that the trial court has no revisory or appellate jurisdiction to correct by amendment error in substance affecting the judgment. It cannot, by amendment, change the judgment ... to meet some supposed equity subsequently called to its attention. ... It cannot correct judicial errors either of commission or omission. ... Clerical errors or a mistake in the entry of the judgment or the omission of a right or relief to which a party is entitled as a matter of course may alone be corrected ... through an amendment.[3]

The kinds of mistakes contemplated for correction here are mere ministerial ones, not those involving new exercises of discretion or a further turn of the fact-finding wheel. The rule permits the correction of clerical errors,

---

2. The main source of admissions is CPLR 3123. See § 364 above.

3. In the procedure known as the Simplified Procedure for Court Determination of Disputes, a kind of judicial arbitration, see § 609 below (Practitioner's Edition), the content of the judgment-roll is specified in CPLR 3036(7).

4. See CPLR 5017(a).

5. CPLR 2101(e).

§ 420

1. Stormville Mountain Homes, Inc. v. Zurhorst, 35 A.D.2d 562, 313 N.Y.S.2d 178 (2d Dep't 1970).

2. See Kiker v. Nassau County, 85 N.Y.2d 879, 626 N.Y.S.2d 55, 649 N.E.2d 1199 (1995).

3. Herpe v. Herpe, 225 N.Y. 323, 327, 122 N.E. 204, 205 (1919).

such as where the judgment included interest the clerk was not permitted to insert,[4] but it does not countenance belated judicial steps, such as allowing an expansion of a money demand after a party has already pursued the claim to judgment.[5] A decision permissible when the contest is on, in other words, may not be sought in the guise of an amendment or a resettlement when the contest is over. A judgment dismissing an action "with prejudice", for example, may not be resettled to substitute "without prejudice" if the record does not confirm that "without prejudice" was the court's unambiguous intention.[6] But if there is support in the record, as where the stenographer's minutes plainly record it, even so momentous a change can be considered part of the mere "ministerial" category and thereby permitted by simple amendment under CPLR 5019(a).

It is only an "amendment" that this rule bars from effecting substantial changes unsupported in the record. Substantial changes may indeed be permissible, but they must be sought either through the appellate process or by an outright motion to vacate the judgment,[7] such as on the basis of newly discovered evidence. The procedure to "vacate" the judgment, however, contemplating a fresh judgment embodying the change sought, is simply a motion,[8] so if it can be shown that the opposing party has had full notice of the nature of the change being sought and a fair opportunity to meet it, perhaps the court can just treat the motion to "amend" as one to "vacate".[9]

There must be notice. In one case, for example, where the trial court effected a substantial change in a judgment on its own motion, with neither side advised, the appellate court held the change improper.[10] A formal motion by one side on notice to the other would probably have supported the change.

A closely analogous problem here involves the so-called nunc pro tunc order. Here the party is seeking not only to amend or alter a judgment or order, or to secure its belated entry, but to have the alteration reflect that it is being given retroactive effect as of a stated earlier time. This is permissible only "when a ruling has in fact been made but is improperly evidenced by a defective mandate". An order or judgment may then be made to reflect what was done and to give it effect as of its earlier doing.[11] That is what is known as a nunc pro tunc (now for then) order. It is sought when for one reason or another the party must make the judgment effective as of an earlier date.

The most common instance of this need was the divorce action when the judgment had first to be interlocutory and remain so for three months (during which the marriage subsisted) before final judgment could be entered: death during that period, or merely failing to secure the final judgment when the period expired, posed substantial nunc pro tunc questions. Earlier treatment of them, when abatement of claims was discussed,[12] spares us further discourse here, except to note once again that the interlocutory judgment requirement has been abolished and a divorce judgment today becomes final immediately, like any other judgment.

That development on the divorce front reduced the nunc pro tunc order's arena considerably, but not entirely. Even without the requirement of interlocutory judgment, the divorce action remains one of the few that abate on the death of a party. It is hence a fertile and continuing source of nunc pro tunc questions when death intervenes. A key

---

4. See Dowling v. Stephan, 206 Misc. 518, 133 N.Y.S.2d 667 (Sup.Ct., Kings County, 1954).

5. See the review of permissible and impermissible amendments under CPLR 5019(a) in First National City Bank v. Elsky, 62 Misc.2d 880, 312 N.Y.S.2d 325 (N.Y.C.Civ.Ct. 1970).

6. See, e.g., Dependable Printed Circuit Corp. v. Mnemotron Corp., 22 A.D.2d 911, 255 N.Y.S.2d 638 (2d Dep't 1964).

7. See Herpe v. Herpe, note 3 above.

8. See CPLR 5015(a)(2); §§ 426, 428 below.

9. See, e.g, Horan v. Town of Brookhaven, 29 A.D.2d 563, 286 N.Y.S.2d 450 (2d Dep't 1967).

10. Baum v. Baum, 40 A.D.2d 1000, 347 N.Y.S.2d 960 (2d Dep't 1972).

11. Merrick v. Merrick, 266 N.Y. 120, 122, 194 N.E. 55, 56 (1934).

12. See § 185.

factor is whether a decision granting a divorce was definitively made before the party died, even if not yet reduced to a formal judgment. If it was, the nunc pro tunc order is permissible even though substantial rights turn on it. In one case, for example, the children of H's first marriage sought a nunc pro tunc judgment on a clearly made decision divorcing his second marriage (he died before judgment was entered), in the hope of denying widowhood to the second wife and thus increasing their own Social Security allotment. The lower court refused the order on the ground that the second wife's property rights would be divested; it relied technically on the fact that the divorce did not exist at the earlier time, despite the then existing right to enter the judgment securing it. The appellate court reversed and allowed the nunc pro tunc judgment, holding that "[n]o vested rights of either party will be impaired by the entry of the judgment *nunc pro tunc*".[13] One may even argue that refusing the nunc pro tunc order would itself have qualified as the divestiture of vested rights: the rights won when the divorce decision was rendered.

CPLR 5016(d) contains perhaps the law's strongest clue to what the legislature wishes to be the rule when death occurs after a decision has been made but before the decision has been reduced to judgment. The statute regards the decision as the key element and the judgment an adjunct of it, permitting and perhaps even mandating (judgment "shall" be entered) that judgment ensue. With such a spur, a nunc pro tunc order should be permissible for any judgment when the right sought to be retroactivated was a right at the earlier time, duly decided and unambiguously apparent, and when all that is now sought is a paper—a judgment or order—saying so. That a substantial right may be affected by giving the judgment nunc pro tunc effect is better cited to

support than to oppose the step. Litigation is designed to affect substantial rights.

§ 421. Docketing the Judgment

Quite apart from the "entry" of the judgment is its "docketing", which makes the judgment a realty lien. The docketing of the judgment is significant only when it takes place in the office of the county clerk; it is there that the docketing makes the judgment a lien on the defendant's real property within the county.[1] (Liens on personal property are a different matter.[2]) Since the county clerk is ex officio the clerk of both the supreme court and the county court in the county,[3] a docketing of a judgment of either court with its "clerk" refers to the county clerk and, accordingly, the "docketing" accomplishes the lien. With other courts, however, such as the New York City Civil Court and the district, city, town, and village courts, a "docketing" of a judgment with the court's clerk brings about no lien whatever; in fact, the use of the word "docketing" in those courts is usually a misnomer for "entry". To make a judgment of one of those other courts a realty lien, a transcripting procedure, elaborated in the next section, is used.

Keeping in mind that we are now talking only about money judgments in the supreme and county courts, we can examine the docketing procedure:

For each year or for a period of years, the clerk maintains alphabetized docket books. When the clerk files the judgment-roll upon entering the judgment,[4] she must also docket the judgment.[5] She does this by recording in the docket books, under the surname of the judgment debtor, the various data about the judgment.[6] Any searcher can then find, under an individual's name, whether there is any judgment outstanding against him in the county, whether it is still a timely lien against his realty, and any other datum concerning the

---

13. Jayson v. Jayson, 54 A.D.2d 687, 387 N.Y.S.2d 274 (2d Dep't 1976), reversing 83 Misc.2d 417, 373 N.Y.S.2d 497 (Sup.Ct., Nassau County, 1975).

§ 421

1. CPLR 5203(a). For further discussion of the judgment as a lien on realty, see § 517 below.

2. See §§ 518, 519, and 520, below.

3. County Law §§ 525, 909.

4. CPLR 5017(a).

5. CPLR 5018(a).

6. See CPLR 5018(c), listing the information the docket is to contain.

judgment that may afterwards have been recorded on the docket. This docketing procedure is required for all money judgments, but if requested by the judgment creditor it is also available for judgments in actions directly affecting real property.[7] If the clerk maintains what is known as a "block index"—a set of records listing all realty in the county by section and lot—the judgment involving realty can be "docketed" there instead of in the alphabetized dockets. The block-index alternative is not available for money judgments, however.[8]

If there are two or more judgment debtors on the judgment, the docketing is made separately in the surname of each but the details of the judgment need be recorded only under the name of the first debtor listed in the judgment; under the others goes a cross-reference to the first one and the searcher is put in touch with the relevant facts that way.[9] If the action was brought against a number of named parties, but not all were served with a summons and thus subjected to personal jurisdiction, the words "not summoned" must be written next to the name of the unserved ones to clarify that the judgment is not effective against them.[10] Ordinarily no entry at all should be made in the name of an unserved defendant, since the judgment is void as to her personally; there should thus be no occasion for having to write "not summoned" next to her name.[11] Even in the case of a joint liability, such as that of a partnership on a contract, the

service of the summons on Partner A but not Partner B makes the judgment so ineffective against B that when a subsequent action is brought against him—as it may be to seek from him whatever remains unpaid on a judgment against the partnership itself or Partner A—the earlier judgment is not even res judicata of the facts. Partner B may therefore interpose defenses that could have been raised in the earlier action.[12]

Changes affecting the judgment or its impact as a lien can be reflected on the docket as they arise, thus enabling all searchers to find, centralized in the county of rendition, the judgment's subsequent history.

§ 422. Transcripting Judgments Between Courts and Counties

When a judgment is entered in a court other than the supreme or county court, it is not a lien on real property anywhere. Nor is a judgment docketed in one county a lien in any other. How can it be made so? The procedure to make it so is known as "transcripting" the judgment. A transcript is a paper containing the essentials of the judgment,[1] certified by the clerk with whom the judgment is filed or docketed. To achieve uniformity in its content, there is a statutory form of transcript.[2]

A judgment creditor with a judgment from a lower court who would make it a lien on realty must apply to the clerk of the lower court for a transcript,[3] and then file the transcript with

---

7. The provisional remedy of notice of pendency of Article 65 of the CPLR, also available in actions directly affecting realty, will carry out the function of giving notice to potential buyers and encumbrancers before and during realty actions. Because it is available as a notice-giver even in advance of judgment, it should be considered for use in such actions.

8. CPLR 5018(a).

9. CPLR 5018(c).

10. CPLR 5018(a).

11. Apparently CPLR 1501 is the culprit that accounts for an entry being made next to the name of an unserved debtor, thus necessitating this "not summoned" addendum for CPLR 5018(a). CPLR 1501, applicable to cases of joint liability, authorizes judgment to be taken even against an unserved defendant, apparently theorizing that only by so doing will a collective liability be spelled out (such as will enable partnership assets to be reached on a judgment good as against the partnership on the basis that at least one partner was summoned, see CPLR 310).

Because the partnership and like creatures have no identity apart from their members, there is ordinarily no separate set of books to reflect their liabilities; these can be reflected only by making an entry next to the name of each member, even if a "not summoned" qualification is needed to insulate an unserved member from personal liability. This procedure may overlook that today a partnership can be named and sued in its partnership name without naming any individual partner at all. CPLR 1025.

12. CPLR 1502.

§ 422

1. An order directing the payment of money may be treated as a judgment, CPLR 2222, and therefore transcripted and docketed under these provisions.

2. Jud.L. § 255–c.

3. See § 1502 in the New York City Civil, Uniform District, Uniform City, and Uniform Justice court acts, McKinney's Vol. 29A, Parts 2 and 3. For surrogate's court the county clerk of the home county, who must thereupon docket the judgment in the usual alphabetical docket books. That gives the judgment the same effect as one entered and docketed in an original supreme court action in that county,[4] which accomplishes two things: it makes the judgment a lien on the defendant's realty in that county and it enables the judgment to be enforced as if it were a supreme court judgment.[5] Similar steps can be taken, and with the same accomplishments, for a federal, sister state, or foreign country judgment, as follows:

Federal judgment: For a federal judgment on file in any federal court in New York, a transcript of the judgment can be secured from the clerk of the federal court and may be filed with the county clerk of any county. The filing requires the docketing of the judgment by the clerk, makes the judgment a realty lien in the county of docketing, and enables the judgment to be enforced as if rendered by the New York Supreme Court.[6]

Note that this docketing is permissible only for federal judgments filed in New York federal courts. To accomplish the same thing for a federal judgment rendered outside New York, a simple additional step, authorized by federal law, must be taken. A certified copy of the federal judgment is secured from the rendering court and is then filed with the clerk of a New York federal court, which gives it the "same effect" as if the latter rendered it.[7] Having such effect, a transcript of it, given now by the New York federal court, may be filed with any county clerk in the state.[8]

Sister-state judgment: The judgment of a court of another state[9] must first be converted into a New York judgment before being enforcible in New York. This can be accomplished by mere registration in most cases;[10] or, in any case, by a motion-action seeking quick summary judgment;[11] or through an ordinary plenary action based on the sister-state judgment. In whatever court this is done, the sister-state judgment becomes a judgment of that court; further transcripting steps are taken accordingly.[12]

Foreign-country judgment: The judgment, again, must first be converted into a New York judgment, either by a motion-action[13] or by a plenary action.[14] It then becomes a judgment of the New York court in which the action or motion-action was successfully brought, the transcripting procedures now to follow accordingly.

Thus may the judgments of various courts be made into New York judgments and docketed with a county clerk. All such judgments, however, including an original New York one, will stand as a lien only on the defendant's real property in the county of docketing. In order to make the judgment a lien in other

---

decrees and orders, see SCPA 603. For family court support orders, see FCA § 475.

4. CPLR 5018(a).

5. Some of the various devices of CPLR Article 52 for the enforcement of a money judgment may then be captioned and made returnable in the supreme court instead of in the lower court where the judgment was rendered. This becomes important for enforcing judgments of certain lower courts, in which some of these devices may not be available. See § 493 below.

6. CPLR 5018(b).

7. 28 U.S.C.A. § 1963. See the Commentary on the 1988 revision of that section in the U.S.C.A. Alternatively, a federal judgment rendered outside New York can skip the § 1963 procedure and seek direct registration in New York under CPLR Article 54. See § 435 below.

8. The federal judgment's docketing also makes available for it the New York enforcement devices, CPLR Article 52, and these will even bear the caption of a New York Supreme Court judgment and make use of the New York sheriff (rather than the federal marshal). See Knapp v. McFarland, 462 F.2d 935 (2d Cir.1972). Even protective

measures, available for the judgment debtor under the New York procedure, become applicable to a transcripted federal judgment. See Wandschneider v. Bekeny, 75 Misc.2d 32, 346 N.Y.S.2d 925 (Sup.Ct., Westchester County, 1973).

9. This would embrace the courts of the District of Columbia and of the territories of the United States as well, which are the equivalent of state courts for full faith and credit purposes. See U.S.Const. Art.IV; 28 U.S.C.A. § 1738.

10. CPLR Article 54. See § 435 below.

11. CPLR 3213. See § 288 et seq., above.

12. If the procedure used is the Article 54 registration, the judgment becomes the equivalent of a supreme court judgment. CPLR 5402(b).

13. CPLR 3213, which may also be used for foreign-country judgments.

14. The filing and registration procedures of CPLR Article 54 are not available for the judgments of foreign countries.

counties, a transcript is secured from the county clerk of the home county, which may then be filed with the county clerk of any other county, whereupon the judgment gets docketed[15] and becomes a lien there. A judgment creditor can get as many transcripts from the home county clerk as she requests,[16] for filing in as many counties as she pleases. The judgment becomes a lien in each. It is a common practice in some metropolitan areas for attorneys who do a lot of collection work (enforcement of money judgments) to secure a handful of transcripts for each judgment rendered, filing them in the home and surrounding counties on the premise that the judgment debtor may have, presently unknown to the creditor, some realty nearby.

The foregoing shows that for the purpose of docketing the judgment in other counties, the home county serves as a kind of clearing house, not only for supreme court and county court judgments originally docketed there, but also for lower court judgments and even foreign judgments docketed there by transcript.[17] For example, to make a New York City Civil Court judgment rendered in Kings County a lien on the defendant's realty in Erie County, a transcript must be secured from the civil court clerk and filed with the county clerk in Kings, and yet another transcript obtained from the latter. It is this one that may be filed with the county clerk of Erie County.

At one time there was no way of knowing in what other counties or courts a given judgment had been docketed by transcript. It is now required, however, that whenever a county clerk dockets a judgment by transcript, he must notify the issuing clerk by mail, who is then required to note on the main docket the other place or places of docketing.[18] If, for example, the county clerk of the home county has issued a dozen transcripts and these have been filed in a dozen different counties, the

procedure described will show this on the home county clerk's records and offer the peruser all needed information about where the judgment has been docketed and become a realty lien. It is of course important to know this in order to record a satisfaction of the judgment and other changes in its status on all dockets that reflect it.

This whole transcripting procedure, whether from lower court to county clerk's office or from one county clerk's office to another, touches only the enforcement of the judgment and its effect as a lien. Only for those purposes does it have the effect of a supreme court judgment. For any other purpose it must continue to be treated only as a judgment of the court that originally rendered it. A motion to vacate the judgment, for example, must be made to the original court; the transcripting procedure does not authorize entertainment of such a motion by any other court or in any other county.[19]

§ 423. Changes Affecting Judgments and Dockets

Any number of things can occur to affect a judgment after it has been docketed with the home county clerk or, through a transcript, elsewhere. It may be desirable and perhaps even necessary to have these changes reflected on some or all of these dockets. A subsequent judgment or order may have reversed, vacated, or modified the judgment, for example, or the judgment may have been assigned by the judgment creditor to another. The judgment creditor may have died and his personal representative succeeded to his interest. Or, through one device or another, the judgment may have been wholly or partly satisfied.

When any change occurs in the judgment, such as by reversal, vacatur or modification, the change should first be made on the records of the clerk of the court that rendered the

---

15. CPLR 5018(a).

16. A fee is paid for each. See CPLR 8016(a).

17. This clearing house function of the county clerk's office was the result of 1959 legislation, L.1959, cc. 238, 631. See Study, Proposed Uniform Procedure Relating to Judgments and Their Enforcement, 4th Jud.Conf.Rep. (1959) 130.

18. CPLR 5018(a). The transcript has a stub to facilitate this and to help the issuing clerk to identify the judgment. See Uniform Rule 202.47.

19. Wood v. Ford, 78 A.D.2d 585, 432 N.Y.S.2d 572 (4th Dep't 1980).

judgment. If it is a lower court, such as a city court, and its judgment has previously been transcripted into the county clerk's office, a certificate[1] can then be secured from the lower court clerk attesting to the change. That certificate can be filed with the home county clerk, who then records the change on her docket. Alternatively, instead of the certificate, a certified copy of the judgment or order making the change can be filed with the home county clerk.[2]

Once the change has been recorded on the dockets of the home county clerk, whether directly (because the judgment or order making the change is one by the supreme or county court) or indirectly (through the certificate of a lower court clerk or a certified copy of a lower court judgment or order), it is the certificate of the home county clerk that will thereafter be procured in order to reflect the change on the dockets of any other county clerk with whom the judgment has previously been transcripted, once again making the home county clerk's office the central clearing house for all outside-county activities involving inside-county judgments.[3] When the certificate of the home county clerk is filed with any other county clerk whose docket contains the judgment, an entry must be made by the latter to reflect the change.

The same path is followed when, by judgment, order, or written instrument, the ownership of the judgment changes, such as through an order substituting a personal representative in place of a deceased judgment creditor or through an instrument assigning the judgment to another. (If an order, the order should be certified; if an instrument, the instrument should be acknowledged.) Upon the filing of the paper reflecting the change, the clerk notes the change on the docket,[4] and the path for indicating the change on the dockets of the other clerks is again the same, with the home

county clerk's office acting as the clearing house.[5]

Persons who come into an interest in a judgment should make sure the judgment debtor knows about it. The person to whom a judgment creditor has assigned a judgment, for example, should notify the judgment debtor promptly. The mere filing of the assignment, whatever notice it may give the world at large, does not put the judgment debtor herself on notice, so that a debtor who then pays the judgment as if the original creditor still owned it—as where she pays it to a sheriff levying execution on a judgment obtained by the judgment creditor's own judgment creditor—is fully protected. The debtor need not search county records every time she makes a payment on a judgment.[6]

E.　RECORDING SATISFACTION

Table of Sections

§ 424.　Satisfaction–Piece

A satisfaction-piece is an acknowledged instrument attesting to the complete or partial satisfaction of a judgment. It is the instrument used when the judgment debtor voluntarily pays the judgment. Today it is the judgment creditor's obligation not only to execute the satisfaction-piece when the judgment is paid, but also to see to its filing with the appropriate clerk so that the judgment may be reflected as paid on the court's records. The appropriate clerk is the one who originally entered the judgment or, in the case of a lower court judgment which has been docketed in the county clerk's office by transcript, the county clerk. The satisfaction-piece recites the book and page where the judgment is docketed and upon its filing the clerk must enter the

---

§ 423

1. The certificate is essentially the same in form as a transcript and has been made uniform by statute. Jud.L. § 255–c.

2. CPLR 5019(b).

3. CPLR 5019(d).

4. CPLR 5019(c).

5. CPLR 5019(d).

6. See Tri City Roofers, Inc. v. Northeastern Industrial Park, 61 N.Y.2d 779, 473 N.Y.S.2d 161, 461 N.E.2d 298 (1984).

satisfaction on his dockets.[1] Within 10 days after the filing, the judgment creditor must mail a copy of the satisfaction-piece to the judgment debtor.[2]

If the judgment has been docketed in yet other counties, the judgment creditor is also responsible for having the satisfaction reflected on their dockets. The creditor must obtain certificates from the home county clerk, now indicating the satisfaction, and file one in each of the other counties in which docketing has taken place.[3] This requirement applies, however, only when the satisfaction is complete; if it is only partial, the requirement for certificating the satisfaction into other counties does not apply,[4] although the requirement for filing it in the home county does.[5] A judgment creditor who fails to make the required filings within 20 days after getting full satisfaction is subject to a $100 penalty, which the judgment debtor can seek either in a plenary action or in a small claims proceeding.[6]

The judgment creditor's attorney of record may execute the satisfaction-piece, but only during the 10–year period following entry of the judgment.[7] After that the law assumes that the attorney's authority has expired, and the paying judgment debtor had best pay the judgment creditor directly, or secure new evidence of the attorney's continuing authority. It is good practice for the judgment debtor to draw a check to the judgment creditor and her attorney jointly,[8] or to have both sign a receipt for a cash payment, thus insulating the judgment debtor from any lawyer's-lien disputes

that may arise between the creditor and the creditor's lawyer.

The judgment debtor is not helpless if he is not given a satisfaction-piece after satisfying the judgment in whole or in part. He can obtain a court order directing that an entry of satisfaction be made on the dockets. The order is sought upon motion, which should be made by order to show cause.[9]

There is also a remedy for a judgment debtor ready and willing to pay the judgment but unable to locate the judgment creditor so as to pay and obtain a satisfaction-piece. CPLR 5020–a sets up a procedure that culminates in the debtor's merely depositing with the clerk a certified check in the amount of the judgment.[10]

§ 425. Entry of Satisfaction

As the prior section discusses, a voluntary payment of the judgment usually results in the filing of a satisfaction-piece in the appropriate clerk's office, which then requires that an entry of the satisfaction be made on the docket of the judgment.[1] Whenever a judgment has been satisfied in whole or in part, the judgment debtor is entitled to have it mirrored on the record. If she cannot secure a satisfaction-piece, or if for any other reason or omission the home dockets have not yet been made to reflect a satisfaction in fact made, whether in whole or in part and whether made voluntarily or not, the judgment debtor need only move the court, by order to show cause, for an order directing that an appropriate entry of satisfaction be made.[2] Upon proof of the satisfaction

---

§ 424

1. CPLR 5021(a)(1).

2. CPLR 5020(a).

3. The home county clerk's dockets will list the other counties in which docketing has occurred. See § 422 above.

4. CPLR 5020(d).

5. CPLR 5020(a).

6. CPLR 5020(c). The courts in whose small claims part the penalty can be sought are the New York City Civil Court and the district and city courts. It should also be permissible in the small claims part of the town and village courts, which got a small claims part in 1975, see Article 18 of the Uniform Justice Court Act, McKinney's Vol. 29A, Part 2, but they are not listed in the earlier

amended (1974) CPLR 5020(c). If New York City is the judgment creditor, the judgment debtor must serve on it a demand that the satisfaction-piece be executed and filed, and the penalty will apply only if 20 days then expire without compliance; other creditors are not entitled to such demands.

7. CPLR 5020(b).

8. See Hafter v. Farkas, 498 F.2d 587 (2d Cir.1974).

9. CPLR 5021(a)(2). See § 425 below.

10. For the purpose and impact of this statute, see the Commentary on 5020–a in McKinney's CPLR.

§ 425

1. CPLR 5021(a)(1).

2. CPLR 5021(a)(2).

he is entitled to that order, and the dockets will get entries accordingly.

If the judgment creditor should refuse a tender of complete or partial satisfaction, an infrequent but occasional phenomenon, the judgment debtor may seek an order permitting him to deposit the money into court. This motion, too, is brought on by order to show cause, which enables the court to determine who should be notified of it. A deposit so made entitles the debtor to an entry of satisfaction. When the judgment debtor makes such a motion, he must satisfy the court that there are no outstanding executions on the judgment on which a sheriff's fee may be due.[3] This prevents the debtor from evading the additional charges that might be due the sheriff on the execution by seeking to deposit the money into court instead of paying it over to the sheriff. In this lies a special lesson to the dallying judgment debtor who plans to pay the judgment but who does not pay it promptly, or bond it during an appeal, or make some other arrangement with the judgment creditor before the sheriff levies. The levy may cost the judgment debtor dear. In one case, for example, it cost a debtor fully able to pay the judgment an extra $30,000.[4]

The deposit into court under this provision will stop the running of interest, but the deposit procedure should not be used without good reason (because it entails a possibly needless court application). Good reason would be an inability to locate the creditor. It has been held that if the creditor is available, a tender to him is a condition precedent to a deposit of the money into court.[5]

Another step, entailing a deposit into court but not calling for a motion, may help the judgment debtor who cannot locate the creditor.[6] It does not bring about a recording of satisfaction,[7] but it saves the debtor continuing enforcement expenses.[8]

The execution referred to earlier is one of the devices for enforcing a money judgment under Article 52 of the CPLR. It is a paper issued to the sheriff requiring the sheriff to seek property of the judgment debtor to sell towards payment of the judgment. The details of its procedures come later,[9] but some discussion of the "return" of the execution is appropriate now.

The return is the sheriff's statement of his proceedings on the execution, including whether it brought about any satisfaction of the judgment. The sheriff makes this return to the clerk of the court out of which the execution issued,[10] and if it shows satisfaction of the judgment to any extent, the clerk must reflect it on her records.[11] When a payment is made pursuant to the execution, the sheriff is also required upon request to give the judgment debtor a certified copy of the execution and the return showing the satisfaction.[12] The judgment debtor can file this with the clerk of the county in which the execution was levied, who must docket the satisfaction accordingly. This contemplates a situation in which, for example, a supreme court judgment of county X is enforced in county Y. The execution bears the caption of the home county, county X, and it is

---

3. CPLR 5021(a)(3).

4. See Thornton v. Montefiore Hospital, 117 A.D.2d 552, 498 N.Y.S.2d 828 (1st Dep't 1986).

5. Meilak v. Atlantic Cement Co., 30 A.D.2d 254, 291 N.Y.S.2d 639 (3d Dep't 1968).

6. CPLR 5020–a.

7. To accomplish a recording of satisfaction, a motion under CPLR 5021 would be necessary.

8. See the Commentary on McKinney's CPLR 5020–a.

9. See § 494 et seq., below, discussing CPLR 5230, the source of the execution. We refer here to an ordinary execution against property as opposed to the "income execution" of CPLR 5231, which is a levy against the debtor's wages or other income, treated in § 502 below.

10. CPLR 5230(c).

11. CPLR 5021(b). The statute says "docket", having in mind the county clerk, whose dockets manifest the realty liens. But the provision applies by adoption to the lower courts as well, where "records" would be a more appropriate term than "dockets", although the terms are often carelessly interchanged. See § 701(c) in each of the New York City Civil, Uniform District, Uniform City, and Uniform Justice court acts, McKinney's Vol. 29A, Parts 2 and 3. The cited section in these court acts should be consulted whenever a CPLR enforcement device involving the sheriff is involved; it clarifies the device's use in the lower court and provides for necessary adjustments, including references to the enforcement officers of the lower court.

12. Id.

to the clerk of that county that a return will be sent. But the execution may be delivered for levy to the sheriff of any county.[13] If delivered to the sheriff of Y, who finds property of the debtor there and successfully levies, the Y sheriff must still make his return to the X clerk. That return will assure reflection of the satisfaction on the home dockets in X, but if the judgment has been transcripted into Y it may still remain of record there notwithstanding the successful levy in that very county. The requirement of the certified copy, delivered by sheriff to debtor, immediately offers the debtor a document that he can file locally in Y to evince the satisfaction.[14]

Executions must generally be returned, satisfied or not, within 60 days after issuance.[15] Perhaps overlooking that requirement, or perhaps because the requirement is sometimes disregarded when there has been no satisfaction at all, a more specific instruction to the sheriff has been enacted for small claims judgments.[16]

If the judgment has been docketed outside the home county, via transcripts, a home county satisfaction resulting from any of the methods discussed—voluntary satisfaction, court order, court deposit on order, or satisfied execution—can be certificated onto other-county dockets by the same route. The home county clerk, on whose dockets the satisfaction is recorded, issues the certificates, which other county clerks must file, recording the satisfaction on their dockets accordingly.[17] If the initial satisfaction is recorded on the records of a lower court, a certificate of the latter's clerk, so indicating, can be filed with the home county clerk to get the datum onto his dockets, after which the latter's certificates will be used to reach dockets in other counties.

---

13. CPLR 5230(b).

14. Alternatively, the debtor can wait until the return is recorded on the county X dockets and then get a certificate of satisfaction from the X clerk for filing in Y. CPLR 5021(c).

15. CPLR 5230(c).

16. CPLR 5021(b). Expressly stating that a return of execution is necessary even if unsatisfied, CPLR 5021(b) requires it on small claims judgments within 90 days after the sheriff has received the "judgment", meaning the execution. ("Sheriff" here includes whoever the enforce-

F. VACATING JUDGMENTS AND ORDERS

Table of Sections

§ 426. Motion to Vacate Judgment or Order, Generally

CPLR 5015(a) is a frequently invoked provision in New York practice. It lists the principal grounds on which a judgment or order may be vacated. It provides that "[t]he court which rendered a judgment or order may relieve a party from it upon such terms as may be just, on motion of any interested person with such notice as the court may direct, upon the ground of:

1. excusable default, if such motion is made within one year after service of a copy of the judgment or order with written notice of its entry upon the moving party, or, if the moving party has entered the judgment or order, within one year after such entry; or

2. newly-discovered evidence which, if introduced at the trial, would probably have produced a different result and which could not have been discovered in time to move for a new trial under section 4404; or

3. fraud, misrepresentation, or other misconduct of an adverse party; or

---

ment officer of the particular lower court may be, see § 701 in the lower court acts, note 11, above.) This was done to expedite identification of deadbeat judgment debtors in small claims actions and to facilitate punitive damage suits against them when it is shown that they can pay but have refused to. See § 1812 in the New York City Civil, Uniform District, Uniform City, and Uniform Justice court acts, McKinney's Vol. 29A, Parts 2 and 3. For enforcement of a small claims judgment, see § 583 below.

17. CPLR 5021(c). For elaboration of the transcript route, see § 422 above.

4. lack of jurisdiction to render the judgment or order; or

5. reversal, modification or vacatur of a prior judgment or order upon which it is based."

The five enumerated categories cover just about all possible grounds on which a vacatur might be sought. Should a ground arise not expressly listed, and not susceptible, even with a little push, of being lodged under a listed ground—most are susceptible—the lawyer can take note that thorough as the list may seem, it is not exhaustive. The court has inherent discretionary power to vacate its judgments and orders for good cause shown, not limited by the CPLR 5015(a) list.[1] The Advisory Committee stressed this.[2]

The procedure for seeking the vacatur—vacatur is what CPLR 5015(a) has primarily in mind when it speaks of allowing a court to "relieve" a party of a judgment or order—is a motion made to the court that rendered it. That a transcript of a lower court judgment may have been filed in the county clerk's office, or a transcript of any court's judgment filed in another county, does not authorize any other than the court that rendered the judgment, or courts along its appellate path, to vacate it. The supreme court, for example, cannot vacate a New York City Civil Court judgment merely because the latter has been docketed in the county clerk's office by transcript. The transcript procedure is only an aid to enforcement, not a substitution of tribunals for redoing the merits.[3] The same is true of a supreme court judgment rendered in county X, afterwards transcripted into county Y: ordinarily only X can entertain a vacatur motion.[4]

The requirement that the vacatur motion be made "with such notice as the court may direct" means that it should be brought on by order to show cause. This recognizes that applications of this kind can take place long after the judgment was rendered and that uncertainties can arise concerning, for example, the continued authority of the other side's lawyer. The court in the order to show cause can take cognizance of the applicable facts, including lapse of time, and direct accordingly about whom and how to serve.

While it is of course the losing party who usually moves to vacate a judgment, under CPLR 5015 a party may move to vacate her own judgment. A plaintiff may be allowed to vacate a default judgment she obtained against the defendant, for example, so as to add a fraud claim based on newly discovered evidence.[5]

It is not even indispensable that the person moving the vacatur have been a party to the action. One who was not a party may be allowed to move to vacate the judgment if he demonstrates a legitimate interest in doing so. In one case, for example, P, in taking a default judgment against D Corporation, concealed certain facts, and this concealment gave P more of a judgment than he was entitled to. When D proved insolvent and could not pay the judgment, P thereupon sued X on a charge that X looted D. The claim against X depended on the validity of the judgment P had against D. This was held to give X a sufficient interest to move the vacatur of the P v. D judgment, which X did on the ground of fraud or misconduct, the ground set forth in paragraph 3 of CPLR 5015(a).[6]

§ 426

1. McMahon v. City of New York, 105 A.D.2d 101, 483 N.Y.S.2d 228 (1st Dep't 1984).

2. See 3d Rep.Leg.Doc. (1959) No. 17, p. 204. Rule 60(b) of the Federal Rules of Civil Procedure, on which CPLR 5015(a) is based, has a paragraph 6 which, after earlier paragraphs enumerate specific grounds, authorizes vacatur of a judgment or order for "any other reason justifying relief". The New York provision omits that as superfluous in view of New York caselaw that reaches the same conclusion. See Ladd v. Stevenson, 112 N.Y. 325, 19 N.E. 842 (1889).

3. See § 422 above.

4. See Brenner v. Arterial Plaza, Inc., 29 A.D.2d 815, 287 N.Y.S.2d 308 (3d Dep't 1968).

5. Cooke v. Wozen Equities, Inc., 143 Misc.2d 578, 540 N.Y.S.2d 629 (Sup.Ct., N.Y.County, 1988). See also the Soltys case in § 427, note 6.

6. Oppenheimer v. Westcott, 47 N.Y.2d 595, 419 N.Y.S.2d 908, 393 N.E.2d 982 (1979). Another point made in Oppenheimer is that the availability to X of a plenary action to vacate the judgment does not preclude the use of the CPLR 5015(a) motion as an alternative.

Ensuing sections will treat each listed category of CPLR 5015(a) separately.

§ 427. Excusable Default

The first category of vacatur ground listed in CPLR 5015(a) is excusable default, a ground that in some measure overlaps that supplied by CPLR 317. Both provisions were compared and contrasted earlier.[1] The reader may find it helpful to review that discussion before continuing here; it clarifies, among other things, that the one-year period purporting to restrict this ground of vacatur is not a period of limitation and is therefore not rigidly applied, and that a motion to vacate a default in New York practice, whether based on CPLR 317 or 5015(a)(1), should be accompanied by (1) an excuse for the default and (2) an affidavit of merits.[2]

The courts are liberal in vacating default judgments. They want disputes resolved on the merits and are therefore inclined, practically speaking, to accept a generous range of excuses, sometimes even vacating deliberate defaults,[3] but there is a limit to their patience and from time to time a warning is issued to potential defaulters. One defendant, for example, who apparently suffered the default because he deemed himself execution-proof, moving the vacatur only when it appeared that the plaintiff had discovered a way to get at his property, found his motion denied.[4] If the default is beyond all excusing, it has been said that masses of neither "contriteness nor penitence" will help the defendant,[5] but that view is not universal. Other courts may open the

default and allow the defaulter to repent under a hefty money sanction.

One ordinarily thinks of the defendant as the party making a motion to vacate a default judgment, which is of course the more common situation, but CPLR 5015(a)(1) contemplates that for good cause shown a plaintiff may move to vacate a default judgment entered in his favor. Where it appeared, for example, that a default judgment based only on a loan would have been dischargeable in the defendant's bankruptcy, the plaintiff was allowed to open the judgment so as to add and litigate a fraud ground (substantiating it in his papers), which would survive bankruptcy.[6]

The court can vacate the default in whole or in part. If it deems liability to be inadequately contested in the defendant's moving affidavit of merits, for example, but finds a genuine issue raised in regard to damages, it can vacate the default judgment only to the extent of permitting a damages assessment.[7]

The defaults contemplated by CPLR 317 and 5015(a)(1) are defaults on which a judgment has been rendered or an order made. A party should also be able to undo a default before it has been formally entered in an order or judgment, if disposed to do so: that these provisions allow the default to be opened after entry affords authority a fortiori for the court's entertaining the application before entry.

An assumption under these provisions is that the defaulting party had no hearing in respect of the matter defaulted, which is usually the case when the default consists of a failure to appear in the action. But keep in

---

§ 427

1. See § 108.

2. The assumption in the present section is that the court obtained jurisdiction and the defendant is seeking to open the default only to be allowed to defend on the merits, a matter in the court's discretion. When the motion is based exclusively on lack of jurisdiction, the governing paragraph of CPLR 5015(a) is 4, not 1, involves no discretion, and requires no affidavit of merits, as discussed more fully in § 430 below.

3. See, e. g., Hensey Properties, Inc. v. Lamagna, 23 A.D.2d 742, 258 N.Y.S.2d 495 (1st Dep't 1965). The vacatur of a deliberate default, if allowed at all, should be accompanied by a substantial costs assessment against the defendant, as happened in Hensey.

4. Murphy v. Hall, 24 A.D.2d 892, 264 N.Y.S.2d 782 (2d Dep't 1965).

5. Beetz v. City of New York, 73 A.D.2d 925, 423 N.Y.S.2d 503 (2d Dep't 1980).

6. See Manufacturers Nat. Bank of Troy v. Soltys, 49 Misc.2d 261, 267 N.Y.S.2d 237 (Montgomery County Ct. 1966). See also the Cooke case in § 426, note 5. It would be difficult for a plaintiff to do this kind of thing today unless the plaintiff can show that he had no notice of the fraud in time to include a claim based on it in the earlier action. See the discussion of the "transactional analysis" test in § 747, below in the res judicata chapter.

7. See Schutzer v. Berger, 40 A.D.2d 725, 337 N.Y.S.2d 71 (2d Dep't 1972).

mind that a "default" can be imposed for other behavior than failing to make an initial response to process, such as for repeated failures to make disclosure despite opportunities to do so. In the latter situation, the recalcitrant party has had his hearing and CPLR 5015(a)(1) does not support a motion to vacate the "default".[8] The procedure in that situation is for the defaulter to appeal the judgment, not move to vacate it.[9]

A motion to vacate a default judgment must of course be addressed to the court, whether based on CPLR 317 or 5015(a)(1). But if all parties stipulate to the vacatur, the clerk can do the vacating upon the filing of the stipulation.[10] It has been held, however, that not even a stipulation between the parties—whatever other rights it may affect between them—will undo a sheriff's execution sale already conducted in enforcement of the default judgment.[11]

The motion to vacate a default judgment is ordinarily made on the initiative of a party to the particular action. But a series of abuses in the consumer area, coming to the fore in the 1960s and 1970s, resulted in the enactment of a provision[12] authorizing the en masse vacatur of default judgments found to have been the product of consistent abuse at the hands of a given plaintiff or plaintiffs.[13] This category of collective default vacatur is initiated by the administrative head of the particular court when evidence exists of extended abuse; it is a category apart and should not be confused with the ordinary motion to vacate a default judgment under CPLR 5015(a)(1).

§ 428. Newly Discovered Evidence

The key word in paragraph 2 of CPLR 5015(a) is "probably". Newly discovered evidence will not suffice to open the judgment and permit retrial of the merits unless the court is convinced that the new evidence would "probably" change the result. A mere showing of possibility is insufficient. So is a showing that the new evidence is merely cumulative, or relevant only to a witness's credibility. Perhaps the best known illustration of this motion, while by no means the only one, is the post-judgment appearance of a key witness to the event, unknown-of or unlocatable earlier in spite of diligent effort.[1]

There is no stated time limit for a motion to vacate based on newly discovered evidence. The law implies a reasonable time,[2] and what is reasonable is determined sui generis.

Newly discovered matter such as would reopen the judgment must as a rule be competent evidence, although occasionally even incompetent evidence may be allowed to do it if it tends "dramatically" to undermine the original judgment, as where H discovered, after W was granted a separation from him, that W at the time of the trial was pregnant by another man.[3] Entertaining presumably incompetent evidence for this purpose, however minds may disagree about its utility, has analogy in the summary judgment area, where incompetent evidence has sometimes been entertained to defeat summary judgment.[4]

A further requirement for a motion under CPLR 5015(a)(2) is that the newly discovered evidence could not have been discovered in

---

8. See Champion v. Wilsey, 150 A.D.2d 833, 540 N.Y.S.2d 594 (3d Dep't 1989).

9. See Achampong v. Weigelt, 240 A.D.2d 247, 658 N.Y.S.2d 606 (1st Dep't 1997), noted in SPR 61:4, and Pinapati v. Pagadala, 244 A.D.2d 676, 664 N.Y.S.2d 161 (3d Dep't 1997).

10. CPLR 5015(b).

11. Roosevelt Hardware v. Green, 72 A.D.2d 261, 424 N.Y.S.2d 276 (2d Dep't 1980).

12. Originally Jud.L. § 217–a, now subdivision (c) of CPLR 5015.

13. Fraud, misrepresentation, illegality, unconscionability, lack of adequate service and other "violations of law" are listed as the abuses sufficient to trigger this

procedure. CPLR 5015(c). The provision is sometimes called "Thompson's Law", after Justice Edward Thompson, whose default-vacatur activities as administrative chief of the New York City Civil Court paved the way for this codification.

§ 428

1. See Cizler v. Cizler, 19 A.D.2d 819, 243 N.Y.S.2d 614 (1st Dep't 1963).

2. See 3d Rep.Leg.Doc. (1959) No. 17, p. 205.

3. See Delagi v. Delagi, 34 A.D.2d 1005, 313 N.Y.S.2d 265 (2d Dep't 1970). The source of the alleged incompetence of the evidence in the Delagi case was the doctor-patient privilege.

4. See § 281 above.

time to move for a new trial under CPLR 4404. Since a motion under CPLR 4404 must be made within 15 days after the decision or verdict,[5] the discovery of the new evidence before the expiration of that 15–day period would presumably fit that motion and therefore preclude this one. This is playing things a bit close, and the courts are justifiably reluctant to deny newly discovered evidence motions, otherwise meritorious, that are near these time lines, even if on the wrong side of them. If, for example, the evidence is discovered towards the end of the 15–day period, but nonetheless in time to move under CPLR 4404, a failure to make that motion would technically forfeit the objection altogether, the CPLR 4404 motion being too late and the CPLR 5015(a)(2) motion being unavailable. The courts have tried various ways around this potential injustice,[6] but the shortest answer is that the 15–day period purporting to restrict the CPLR 4404 motion is presumably subject to discretionary extension by the court.[7] In that light, a motion based on CPLR 5015(a)(2) which could have been made just a little earlier under CPLR 4404 can be treated as a late—but excusably late—CPLR 4404 motion.

§ 429. Fraud or Misconduct

"Fraud, misrepresentation, or other misconduct of an adverse party" is ground for vacating the judgment under paragraph 3 of CPLR 5015(a).[1] Of course, the court must be convinced that the conduct complained of is something that could have affected the outcome.

The fraud involved can qualify as either "intrinsic" or "extrinsic". The main point of deciding which it is has to do with where the motion may be made. If the fraud is "intrinsic", it can as a rule be acted on only by direct attack, which means on direct appeal or by a motion to vacate the judgment made to the court that rendered it. If it is "extrinsic", it can also be the basis of a collateral attack, i.e., a separate action to enjoin its enforcement, or a refusal by some other court to recognize it when its validity arises in some context before that court.

An effort to draw a sharp line between the two categories of fraud is not rewarding. Extrinsic fraud is generally considered to be that conduct which deprives a party of a full trial, or has the effect of preventing a party from fully presenting her case. Examples would be where there have been false representations that the action has been discontinued, or will be dropped, or that judgment will be taken only for X relief—prompting a default—with Y relief then being applied for and granted in violation of the understanding.[2] A judgment based on a fraudulent instrument, on the other hand, or perjured testimony, or any other item presented to and acted on by the court, whatever its fraudulent component, is just an intrinsic fraud and may hence be acted on only through direct attack.[3] Airtight distinctions are probably impossible, but perhaps a reasonably accurate general statement is that conduct which precludes a hearing is extrinsic while conduct that injects fraud into the hearing is intrinsic.

In line with the commanding position of the full faith and credit clause,[4] governing state judgments, which requires State 2 to recognize any judgment of State 1 rendered with jurisdiction regardless of any error that the court may have made on the merits,[5] it would be helpful to characterize as "extrinsic" only that fraud which divests State 1 of jurisdiction. Only then would full faith and credit authorize a collateral attack on the judgment. But while that may seem like a good answer, it merely puts the question in different terms: what

---

5. CPLR 4405.

6. See, e.g., Tollin v. Elleby, 77 Misc.2d 708, 354 N.Y.S.2d 856 (N.Y.C.Civ.Ct. 1974).

7. See CPLR 2004.

§ 429

1. Paragraph 3 is modeled on Rule 60(b)(3) of the Federal Rules of Civil Procedure.

2. See the extended treatment in Tamimi v. Tamimi, 38 A.D.2d 197, 328 N.Y.S.2d 447 (2d Dep't 1972).

3. See Crouse v. McVickar, 207 N.Y. 213, 100 N.E. 697 (1912).

4. U.S.Const. Art. IV, § 1.

5. Fauntleroy v. Lum, 210 U.S. 230, 28 S.Ct. 641, 52 L.Ed. 1039 (1908).

fraud will deprive State 1 of jurisdiction? If the party seeking to undo the judgment will seek the undoing by a motion to vacate made to the rendering court, which can entertain the fraud ground whatever its category, a collateral reward will be that there will be no need to determine which "trinsic" it is.

A paragraph 3 objection often overlaps some other paragraph of CPLR 5015(a). The fraud ground, for example, even if only of the "intrinsic" variety, is likely to overlap paragraph 2 of CPLR 5015(a), since the fraudulent conduct now uncovered is likely to qualify as "newly-discovered evidence" as well. If an overlap there be, so much the better for the movant, who should join all grounds. Where, for example, post-judgment motion pictures taken of a personal injury plaintiff who presented a sad physical picture during the trial show a sudden recovery afterwards—better known to fraud than to science—the new data would constitute newly discovered evidence as well as showing fraud. The fraud in that case would probably be an "intrinsic" fraud, but, whatever its category, it would invoke paragraph 2 as well as paragraph 3 of CPLR 5015(a).[6]

Facts that establish an "extrinsic" fraud, on the other hand, which can be seen as affecting the court's jurisdiction, may also invoke the jurisdictional ground of paragraph 4, discussed in the next section. Again, the movant should join both grounds when that is so.

If the fraud does get stamped "extrinsic", it technically dispenses with an affidavit of merits as part of the moving papers because it is deemed to go to jurisdiction.[7] But here the movant may be too easily misled. Since it is often difficult if not impossible to predict in advance which "trinsic" describes the case, the inclusion of a strong affidavit of merits can do no harm.

The Advisory Committee intended the "fraud" of paragraph 3 to have broad meaning, citing Ladd v. Stevenson,[8] a major New York case on the power of a court to vacate its judgments in the interest of justice.[9] Under the *Ladd* case, the power of the court to relieve a party from a judgment taken through mistake, inadvertence, surprise, or excusable neglect "does not depend on any statute, but is inherent".[10]

On the question of time, the rule is the same as for the newly-discovered evidence motion of paragraph 2. There being no stated time, a reasonable time will govern the motion to vacate on the ground of fraud or misconduct, with the court determining reasonableness on a sui generis basis.

§ 430. Lack of Jurisdiction

If the court lacked jurisdiction to render the judgment or order, the motion to vacate is based on paragraph 4 of CPLR 5015(a). Frequent are such vacatur motions, based on lack of subject matter or, far more frequently, personal jurisdiction, but seldom is this provision cited on the motion. The reason is that lack of jurisdiction is so deep a defect, and so obviously a basis for vacatur, that a statute authorizing the vacatur on this ground is like the proverbial fifth wheel. For the same reason, the jurisdictional defect permits the motion without a time limit: the judgment in this instance is theoretically void and the order sought under CPLR 5015(a)(4) is not designed to make it so, but merely to say that it is so, and to cancel of record a judgment that has had the presumption to stand on the books without a jurisdictional invitation.[1]

There is a substantial difference in purpose between this motion and those under the earlier paragraphs of CPLR 5015(a). The others, such as the default opener of paragraph 1 and the newly-discovered evidence ground of paragraph 2, seek to vacate the judgment so as to

---

6. See, e.g., Cohen v. Crimenti, 24 A.D.2d 587, 262 N.Y.S.2d 364 (2d Dep't 1965).

7. Shaw v. Shaw, 97 A.D.2d 403, 467 N.Y.S.2d 231 (2d Dep't 1983). See § 430 below.

8. 112 N.Y. 325, 19 N.E. 842 (1889).

9. See 3d Rep.Leg.Doc. (1959) No. 17, p. 204.

10. 112 N.Y. at 332, 19 N.E. at 844.

§ 430

1. The counterpart provision in the Federal Rules of Civil Procedure is Rule 60(b)(4), whose ground is simply that "the judgment is void".

clear the way for a trial, or for a new trial, while the motion under paragraph 4 seeks to vacate the judgment and dismiss the underlying action altogether. Often when the alleged want of jurisdiction has led the defendant to default, she will join paragraphs 4 and 1 in the alternative: move to vacate the judgment and dismiss the action under paragraph 4 or, if jurisdiction should be found present, to open the default and defend on the merits under paragraph 1.[2]

If the motion is based on paragraph 4 alone—want of jurisdiction—no affidavit of merits is necessary because "[s]uch a judgment is a nullity, irrespective of the question of merit".[3] Indeed, it would not even be proper to make the vacatur of the judgment conditional, such as by requiring the defendant to appear and defend the case on the merits or to waive a defense, such as the statute of limitations. The court in such an instance is "without authority to take any action other than to dismiss".[4]

As already noted, it is generally a good idea for the defendant to hedge his bets, however, and make the motion in the alternative—to vacate the judgment and (1) dismiss for want of jurisdiction or, if the court finds jurisdiction present, (2) to open the default and let the defendant defend on the merits. Since the second alternative requires the affidavit of merits even if the first does not, the affidavit of merits should be included not as an adjunct of the first part, but of the second. The bottom line is that it should be included. To omit it because the first part doesn't require it is to forfeit the second part altogether: the defendant would have to prevail on the jurisdictional point or lose everything, including the very

substantial right to a hearing on the merits. That would be too many eggs in one basket.

If the defect is one of subject matter jurisdiction, it is as a rule unwaivable. But if it goes to personal jurisdiction it is subject to waiver. A waiver can occur, for example, where a defendant makes payments on the judgment for a considerable time after its rendition.[5]

Some objections occasionally thought of as "jurisdictional" are not so, in either the subject matter or personal sense. In matrimonial actions, for example, it is often necessary to show that at least one of the parties was a resident of the state for a minimum of a year prior to the commencement of the action;[6] it is a condition precedent to the maintenance of the matrimonial action, a substantive element of the cause of action itself. But it is not a requirement of "jurisdiction" within the meaning of CPLR 5015(a)(4). Thus, an error in this respect by the trial court, entertaining the action despite the absence of residence, does not void the judgment and subject it to attack indefinitely.[7] If it did, the judgment would be undependable, a particularly dire prospect in the matrimonial realm.

§ 431. Reversal of Underlying Judgment

If the judgment or order is based on some other judgment or order, and the latter is in some way undermined, as by reversal, modification, or vacatur, the dependent judgment can similarly be cancelled or adjusted by motion under CPLR 5015(a)(5). The most likely context for this happening is where a sister-state or foreign country judgment has been converted into a New York one,[1] only to be

---

2. The consequence of specifying only the jurisdictional ground in this situation is illustrated in City of Albany Indus. Devel. Agency v. Hampton Investors, 175 A.D.2d 466, 572 N.Y.S.2d 747 (3d Dep't 1991).

3. Shaw v. Shaw, 97 A.D.2d 403, 467 N.Y.S.2d 231 (2d Dep't 1983). The U.S. Supreme Court has so held as a matter of federal constitutional law. See Peralta v. Heights Medical Center, Inc., 485 U.S. 80, 108 S.Ct. 896, 99 L.Ed.2d 75 (1988).

4. Community State Bank v. Haakonson, 94 A.D.2d 838, 463 N.Y.S.2d 105 (3d Dep't 1983).

5. See, e.g., Star Credit Corp. v. Ingram, 71 Misc.2d 787, 337 N.Y.S.2d 245 (N.Y.C.Civ.Ct. 1972).

6. Dom.Rel.L. § 230. "Residence" here is usually construed to mean "domicile". See Usher v. Usher, 41 A.D.2d 368, 343 N.Y.S.2d 212 (3d Dep't 1973).

7. See Lacks v. Lacks, 41 N.Y.2d 71, 390 N.Y.S.2d 875, 359 N.E.2d 384 (1976).

§ 431

1. This conversion can take place either through an ordinary plenary action, a motion-action under CPLR 3213, or, in the case of judgments entitled to full faith and credit, by the simple registration procedure of Article 54 of the CPLR.

afterwards undone in some way at home. The provision has also been applied, however, to original New York judgments, such as in this situation:

P sued D, who impleaded X—an ordinary indemnity situation—but D won against P, which naturally gave X judgment against D on the third-party claim because there was nothing to indemnify. Only P appealed, but he succeeded, and the judgment for D was reversed. On motion by D under CPLR 5015(a)(5) after remand from the appellate court, X's automatic judgment dismissing D's indemnity claim was also vacated. The court held that the revival of P's claim against D reinstated D's indemnity claim against X.[2]

The counterpart federal provision, in addition to contemplating the vacatur motion when the underlying judgment has been reversed or vacated, also allows it when the underlying judgment has been "satisfied, released, or discharged".[3] New York does not necessarily require a motion to vacate in that instance, contemplating instead the making of appropriate entries on the dockets to reflect the satisfaction. If the judgment debtor can secure from the creditor a satisfaction-piece in respect of the underlying judgment, even if foreign, duly acknowledged and otherwise in conformity with New York requirements,[4] it can be filed with the county clerk of the New York county with whom the foreign judgment was first docketed, resulting in an entry of satisfaction and thereby a cancellation of the judgment as a lien.[5] If the debtor has paid the underlying judgment and cannot secure the required satisfaction piece, she need only make a motion to the New York court, proving the satisfaction, and the court will order that it be entered of record and the docket adjusted accordingly.[6]

There is no stated time limit on a vacatur motion under CPLR 5015(a)(5). A reasonable time is therefore the standard, with the court to gauge reasonableness on the facts of the particular case.

§ 432. Conditioning the Vacatur

There is express authority in CPLR 5015(a) for the court to allow the vacatur "upon such terms as may be just". The conditions can include the granting of costs and disbursements for the trial or appellate levels or both, an attorney's fee, and such other sums as would defray actual expenses to which the other side has been put.[1] If the vacating of the judgment contemplates further proceedings, as where a default is opened and a trial on the merits is directed, or where a retrial results from newly discovered evidence, the judgment can be made to stand as security for the plaintiff pending the trial's outcome,[2] or the defendant can be required to post a bond in the amount of all or part of the judgment.[3]

There are no arbitrary limits on the court's discretion in fixing terms under CPLR 5015(a), as long as the ground relied on imports discretion. The ground of paragraph 4, want of jurisdiction, for example, does not. Hence, when the defendant moves to vacate the judgment solely on the ground of want of jurisdiction, the court cannot impose a condition, like exacting an appearance from the defendant or requiring the waiver of some defense.[4]

§ 433. Restitution

If the judgment or order to be vacated or modified has already been paid in whole or in

2. Feldberg v. Howard Fulton St. Inc., 44 Misc.2d 218, 253 N.Y.S.2d 291 (Sup.Ct., Kings County, 1964), aff'd 24 A.D.2d 704, 261 N.Y.S.2d 1012 (2d Dep't 1965). Contrast this with the situation in which P wins against D and D wins against X, but only X appeals, earning a reversal on the basis that P had no claim against X. See § 163 at note 6, above.

3. FRCP Rule 60(b)(5).

4. See CPLR 5020.

5. CPLR 5021(a)(1).

6. CPLR 5021(a)(2).

§ 432

1. See, e.g., Hensey Properties, Inc. v. Lamagna, 23 A.D.2d 742, 258 N.Y.S.2d 495 (1st Dep't 1965).

2. See, e.g., Treitel v. Arnold Chait, Ltd., 20 A.D.2d 711, 247 N.Y.S.2d 373 (2d Dep't 1964).

3. See, e.g., E. Tetz & Sons v. Carriage Hill Apt. Co., 48 A.D.2d 875, 369 N.Y.S.2d 192 (2d Dep't 1975).

4. Community State Bank v. Haakonson, 94 A.D.2d 838, 463 N.Y.S.2d 105 (3d Dep't 1983). See § 430 above.

part, whether voluntarily or by execution or some other device for the enforcement of a money judgment, the judgment debtor may be entitled to have the money repaid. CPLR 5015(d) covers this by authorizing the court to direct the judgment creditor to make restitution. It adopts for this purpose the provision that authorizes restitution after an appeal has undone some part of a judgment.[1]

The restitution can be directed in the order granting the vacatur or modification, or by a later order. The important point is that the allowance of this relief by order clarifies that the judgment debtor will not be put to the burden of a separate plenary action to recover what has already been paid. The remedy is a mere motion. The lower courts, including the New York City Civil Court and the district, city, town, and village courts, also have this restitution power in respect of their own judgments.[2]

An order directing restitution is the equivalent of an ordinary money judgment and may be docketed and enforced as such,[3] which makes the usual enforcement devices of Article 52 of the CPLR available. But despite its being an "order" to pay the money back, it is not ordinarily enforcible through the contempt punishment.[4]

The restitution requirement can have especially serious consequences in tort cases. When a tort defendant appeals a money judgment, the common practice is for the defendant (usually through its liability insurer) to secure a stay of enforcement by bonding the judgment.[5] It's unusual for the insurer to pay the judgment in the meantime instead, but that's what was done in Polipo v. Sanders,[6] the plaintiff

collecting $500,000 while the case was on appeal. Reversal resulted, and now the insurer sought restitution. Rejecting the plaintiff's contentions that he had changed his life style after getting the money and that the payment amounted in any event to a waiver, the court ordered the restitution.[7]

The insurer's purpose was to save the interest that it would have had to pay had it lost on the appeal. Weighing that against the prospect that the plaintiff would squander the money and make it unavailable for restitution, however, suggests that this kind of gamble is not always a wise one for the insurer.

G. RENEWAL OF JUDGMENT

Table of Sections

§ 434. Renewal of New York Judgment

A plaintiff with a foreign judgment—a judgment rendered by a court in a sister state or foreign country—must, in order to enforce the judgment in New York, first take some step to convert it into a New York judgment. If the judgment is one of a foreign country, an action will have to be brought on the judgment, either in conventional form or by use of the summary judgment device of CPLR 3213;[1] if the judgment is one of a sister state or other American jurisdiction entitled to full faith and credit,[2] it has the even better option of the simple registration procedure of Article 54, treated in the next section.

---

§ 433

1. See CPLR 5523.

2. See § 212 in the New York City Civil, Uniform District, Uniform City, and Uniform Justice court acts, McKinney's Vol. 29A, Parts 2 and 3, and CPLR 101.

3. CPLR 2222.

4. See Marlee, Inc. v. Bittar, 257 N.Y. 240, 177 N.E. 434 (1931). Cf. CPLR 5105.

5. See CPLR 5519(a)(2).

6. 170 Misc.2d 833, 650 N.Y.S.2d 941 (Sup.Ct., Bronx County, 1996), aff'd 245 A.D.2d 2, 666 N.Y.S.2d 406 (1st Dep't 1997).

7. The segment of the interim recovery that went to the lawyer as a contingent fee must also be returned. See Abrahami v. UPC Constr. Co., 248 A.D.2d 272, 670 N.Y.S.2d 457 (1st Dep't 1998), noted in SPR 78:3.

§ 434

1. See §§ 288 and 290, above. As the cited sections manifest, the CPLR 3213 motion device is ordinarily preferable to the ordinary plenary action.

2. See § 471 in the chapter on res judicata, Chapter 17, for a discussion of which judgments get full faith and credit.

A creditor with a New York judgment need not bother with any further proceedings on it: the judgment is ripe for enforcement and the creditor need only go about exploiting the enforcement devices. It would be idle to bring a new action on the judgment because a new one would ordinarily be no better than the old one. A New York action on a New York judgment is therefore precluded—except in a few instances. CPLR 5014 recognizes three such instances.

The first is where the realty lien of the original judgment has expired. Although a New York money judgment has a life of 20 years,[3] it is a lien against realty for only 10.[4] After the 10 years have expired without satisfaction of the judgment, the creditor is permitted to sue on it afresh so as to get a new judgment and hence a new 10–year lien.[5] The original 10–year period is measured from the filing of the judgment-roll in the original rendering court, which means that no new 10–year period will start at some later docketing, such as through the filing of a transcript of the judgment in some other county.[6]

The second exception involves certain default judgments. If a defendant who has failed to appear in a New York action was not served with the summons by personal delivery, and a default judgment was entered, the defendant may move to open the default under CPLR 317. The courts, liberal to begin with in vacating defaults, are especially so when a secondary method of service was used.[7] The plaintiff's default judgment in that situation is therefore insecure, which CPLR 5014(2) recognizes by allowing the plaintiff, if able to effect a personal delivery of the summons in a second action,

to sue on the earlier judgment[8] and secure a second and more secure one. It is an option left with the plaintiff, and it is not exercised very often.

The last part of CPLR 5014, paragraph 3, is an omnibus provision enabling the court to authorize an action on a New York judgment in any situation that appeals to judicial discretion. Under this paragraph leave of court is necessary, which requires a motion;[9] under paragraphs 1 and 2 leave is not required.

Suppose that a judgment creditor, still unable to enforce the judgment and mindful that its 10–year lien on the defendant's real property is about to expire, brings an action under CPLR 5014(a) several months before the 10–year lien of the first judgment expires. Is that permissible? Some caselaw had held such an action premature.[10] But if a new action is not commenced until after the expiration of the original 10–year lien period, whatever time it takes to secure a new judgment would be a period in which there is no lien, which would enable another of the debtor's creditors to jump in with priority.[11] Recognizing this, the legislature amended CPLR 5014 in 1986 to overrule the caselaw and permit the renewal action as early as one year prior to the expiration of the initial 10–year lien period. The new judgment is designated a "renewal judgment" and its 10–year lien begins when the first judgment's lien expires, thereby closing any gap in the continuity of the lien.

If the second action is permissible, whether of right under the first two paragraphs or by leave under the third, it should be able to qualify as an action on a judgment and thus be

---

3.   CPLR 211(b).

4.   CPLR 5203(a).

5.   CPLR 5014(1).

6.   See CPLR 5203(a). The "first docketing" mentioned in CPLR 5014(1) should, for the sake of uniformity, be construed as also referring to the filing of the judgment-roll. It might otherwise give a lower court judgment, docketed by transcript with a county clerk several years after the judgment was rendered, a longer lien period than intended.

7.   See § 108 above. Service on a CPLR 318 agent is the same as personal delivery to the defendant for this purpose, thus precluding a renewal suit under CPLR 5014(2).

8.   An endeavor to base such second action directly on the underlying claim in disregard of the first judgment would probably face the defense of res judicata. See § 450 below.

9.   The motion must be on notice to such persons as the court directs, which means that it should be brought on by order to show cause in which the court can include those directions.

10.   See, e.g., Brookhaven Mem. Hosp. v. Hoppe, 65 Misc.2d 1000, 319 N.Y.S.2d 564 (Suffolk County Dist.Ct. 1971).

11.   See the Practice Commentary on CPLR 5014 in McKinney's CPLR.

entitled to the expedited procedures of CPLR 3213, which means that it can be brought on by service of a summons with summary judgment motion papers instead of a complaint.[12] Perhaps the judgment would even qualify for the summary filing procedures of Article 54, which offers sister-state judgments a registration device that obviates a plenary action altogether. Although Article 54 aims at a "foreign" judgment, it would be consistent with the article's purpose to apply it as well to a New York judgment ripe for renewal under CPLR 5014.[13]

A plaintiff who has a claim against several persons, jointly or severally, and who sues and gets a judgment against only one of them, is not precluded by CPLR 5014 from bringing suit on the judgment against the others if the judgment has not been satisfied.[14] But while the second suit in that situation may be technically "based" on the original judgment, it is really a new suit on the same underlying liability: the new defendant, because not a party to the earlier action, may not be visited with any res judicata or collateral estoppel consequences coming out of it.[15]

§ 435.   Registration of Full Faith and Credit Judgment

Article 54 of the CPLR sets up a procedure for the simple New York registration of an out-of-state judgment, obviating an action on the judgment and even the motion-action of CPLR 3213. It applies, however, only to judg-

ments entitled to full faith and credit,[1] which means the judgments of sister states, the federal courts, the United States territorial courts, and the courts of the District of Columbia.[2] It does not apply to the judgment of a foreign country, which must therefore rely on the conventional action or the CPLR 3213 motion/action.[3]

Article 54 is the adoption, somewhat modified, of the Uniform Enforcement of Foreign Judgments Act.[4] It differs from Article 53, the Uniform Foreign Country Money-Judgments Recognition Act,[5] in two important respects. First, Article 53 is addressed only to foreign country judgments, while Article 54 is addressed to judgments of domestic courts. Second, Article 53 is not concerned with procedure, but rather with the substantive question of what foreign judgments are entitled to recognition. Article 54 leaves to federal statutory and decisional law the question of whether substantive recognition of a given American judgment is called for;[6] it assumes entitlement and simply sets up an expeditious registration procedure.

A "judgment", as we use the word in this chapter, includes a mere order as well, as long as it has sufficient finality where rendered to make it enforcible there. The phrase used by CPLR 5401, in fact, is "judgment, decree, or order".

Generally speaking, all judgments rendered by American courts with jurisdiction must be accorded full faith and credit. Since Article 54

---

12.   See §§ 288 and 290, above.

13.   Registration would seem appropriate when all the plaintiff wants is a renewal of the lien and is relying on paragraph 1 of CPLR 5014. It would not be wise to use it when paragraph 2 of CPLR 5014 is being invoked, for the obvious reason that what the plaintiff wants under paragraph 2 is to secure unequivocal personal jurisdiction over the defendant because of doubt about whether there was jurisdictional support for the first judgment. The registration procedure, as will be seen in the next section, assumes jurisdiction and does not contemplate the jurisdiction-getting act of summons service. A judgment creditor relying on paragraph 2 should therefore bring a plenary action or use CPLR 3213, each of which offers a clear jurisdiction-getting opportunity.

14.   That is what CPLR 5014 intends to convey by its reference to Gen.Oblig.L. § 15–102. Nor, if the judgment is unsatisfied, is such an action against one debtor an election of a remedy against the others. See CPLR 3002(a).

15.   See CPLR 1502.

§ 435

1.   CPLR 5401.

2.   See § 471, below, for further discussion of full faith and credit.

3.   Those routes remain as options for the full faith and credit judgment, too, CPLR 5406, but in view of the great facility of the registration procedure they would ordinarily not be used.

4.   CPLR 5408. See Kulzer, The Uniform Enforcement of Foreign Judgments Act, 13th Jud.Conf.Rep. (1968) 248, the background study of the uniform acts from which Article 54 of the CPLR emerged.

5.   CPLR 5309.

6.   See § 471 below.

assumes that such a judgment is at hand, we make the same assumption here and leave to the later Res Judicata chapter the details of when full faith and credit is mandated.[7]

The only two categories of full faith and credit judgment that the statute explicitly bars from use of the registration procedure are (1) the judgment rendered in F-1 (the first forum) on the defendant's default in appearing,[8] and (2) the judgment by confession.[9] Those judgments, even if valid and entitled to full faith and credit, must seek conversion in a conventional action or with a CPLR 3213 motion.

The "confession of judgment" to which CPLR 5401 denies registration is narrowly construed. Consent judgments in general do qualify for Article 54 registration. It has been held, for example, that an order entered in the foreign action "upon notice and consent of both parties" is entitled to registration.[10] Only the device commonly known as the formal "confession" of judgment, and especially, of course, the "cognovit" judgment, is barred from CPLR 5401 use.[11]

It has been held that a support award contained in a foreign judgment calling for periodic payments but not yet reduced to a final arrears judgment—a common situation in matrimonial and family court litigation—may not use the registration procedures of Article 54.[12] What the creditor really wants in that situation is to have the New York court "adopt" the foreign judgment as its own so as to make the New York judicial machinery available for an application for an arrears

judgment. Whether New York will allow that is treated elsewhere.[13]

The procedure for registration is for the judgment creditor to get the judgment authenticated[14] and, within 90 days afterwards, to file it with the county clerk of any county in the state.[15] Also filed is an affidavit attesting that the judgment was not rendered by default or confession and that its enforcement has not been stayed. The affidavit must also state the sum still remaining unpaid on the judgment— this would of course apply only if the judgment is one for money, as most are[16]—and the name and last known address of the judgment debtor. The clerk's obligation upon that filing is to treat the judgment the same as if rendered by the New York Supreme Court, which makes it fully enforcible as such.[17] The applicant upon the filing must pay the appropriate fee,[18] whereupon the clerk assigns the judgment its own file and index number.[19] That index number should then appear on all enforcement papers, which should be captioned in the New York Supreme Court.

CPLR 5402(b) states that the filing converts the judgment into one of the New York Supreme Court even to the extent that "the same procedures, defenses and proceedings for opening, vacating or staying" a supreme court judgment apply to it. This is misleading and should be treated circumspectly by the courts. The only ground on which New York can refuse recognition to a full faith and credit judgment is lack of jurisdiction in the first court. No quantum of error on the merits or anything else not going to the jurisdiction of the first court is an excuse for refusing recog-

---

7. Id.

8. If the defendant did appear but defaulted at some later stage of the proceedings, the resulting judgment does qualify for registration. See L & W Air Conditioning Co., Inc. v. Varsity Inn of Rochester, Inc., 82 Misc.2d 937, 371 N.Y.S.2d 997 (Sup.Ct., Monroe County, 1975), affirmed on the opinion below in 56 A.D.2d 735, 392 N.Y.S.2d 853 (4th Dep't 1977).

9. CPLR 5401.

10. Mallan v. Samowich, 94 A.D.2d 249, 464 N.Y.S.2d 122 (1st Dep't 1983).

11. See § 299 et seq., above.

12. Glotzer v. Glotzer, 112 Misc.2d 851, 447 N.Y.S.2d 603 (Sup.Ct., N.Y.County, 1982).

13. See § 290 above.

14. For authentication, see CPLR 4540.

15. Although any county is permissible, the judgment creditor would do well, for general convenience, to choose a county where the judgment debtor has property.

16. CPLR 5402(a). A separate statute authorizes the New York filing of another state's child custody decree and gives the decree so filed the effect of a New York custody decree for enforcement purposes. See Dom.Rel.L. § 75–p(1).

17. CPLR 5402(b).

18. See CPLR 8018(a).

19. CPLR 5405.

nition,[20] unless it is shown that the original rendering court itself would permit attack on its judgment on the particular ground. A showing, for example, that an item of newly discovered evidence—such as finding a new witness not earlier known about—would not be allowed to upset the judgment under the law of the rendering court would also preclude New York from refusing recognition on that ground, notwithstanding the contrary assumption of CPLR 5402(b) and even though New York may allow vacatur of its own judgments on that ground.[21] CPLR 5402(b) should be taken in this respect to mean only that New York must make its procedures available to present the grounds, not as suggesting that New York law dictates what grounds will suffice.

Caselaw on just what features of New York law apply to a registered judgment is still developing. In respect of enforcement, there are indications that New York law will govern even in particulars that give the registered judgment wider impact than it would have had at home. It has been held, for example, that a Pennsylvania judgment duly registered under Article 54 is entitled to enforcement against 10% of the defendant's wages, as authorized by New York law,[22] even though Pennsylvania allows no levy against wages at all.[23] Interest on the judgment, on the other hand, has been held to run at the rate prescribed by the law of the place of the judgment's rendition, not by New York law.[24]

Within 30 days after the filing, the judgment creditor must mail notice of the filing to the judgment debtor at its last known address. If any enforcement device should within that time have proceeded to such a degree that there are proceeds to turn over—an optimistic assumption by any measure—they cannot be distributed until 30 days have expired, measured from the creditor's filing of proof of service of the notice.[25] The notice and waiting period are designed to give the judgment debtor a chance to move to vacate the judgment or otherwise attack the registration, as where the judgment was rendered by default or confession in the first forum (and may therefore not exploit the registration procedure of Article 54).

Although any defect in the first forum's jurisdiction can of course be made the basis for vacating the registered judgment, the presence of first-forum jurisdiction is apparently *all* that is needed to justify registration. The background of Article 54 suggests that there is no need to demonstrate New York's jurisdiction. The assumption appears to be that the defendant got full due process in the first court and that there now remains only the need to enforce the judgment, which can proceed wherever the judgment debtor's property may be found and with no demonstration of jurisdiction in that place. Indeed, the state-to-state registration procedure of Article 54 has been viewed as equivalent to the county-to-county transcripting of an internal supreme court judgment under CPLR 5018(a).[26] The notice requirement of CPLR 5403 is not necessarily for the purpose of inviting the judgment debtor to test New York (the second forum) jurisdiction, but to enable her to get the judgment vacated if she can show, for example, that the judgment has been paid.[27]

If the underlying judgment has been stayed in the first forum, because of an appeal or a motion to vacate or the like, the judgment debtor can move to stay the overlaid New York judgment as well, but only upon a showing that if the first forum required security as a

20. See Fauntleroy v. Lum, 210 U.S. 230, 28 S.Ct. 641, 52 L.Ed. 1039 (1908).

21. See CPLR 5015(a)(2).

22. See CPLR 5231.

23. See People's National Bank v. Hitchcock, 104 Misc.2d 647, 428 N.Y.S.2d 850 (Sup.Ct., Broome County, 1980).

24. Hospital Service Plan of New Jersey v. Warehouse Production & Sales Employees Union, 76 A.D.2d 882, 429

N.Y.S.2d 31 (2d Dep't 1980). There appears to be a conflict on this point. See the discussion in § 412 above.

25. CPLR 5403.

26. See the Judicial Conference CPLR Report to the 1969 Legislature, Feb. 1, 1969, p. 46.

27. See the Judicial Conference CPLR Report to the 1970 Legislature, Jan. 2, 1970, p. 27.

condition, the security there has been given.[28] Also, if the judgment debtor can demonstrate a ground that would, under New York law, entitle a domestic judgment to be stayed, he can move to stay the registered judgment on a like ground.[29] This would invoke CPLR 5240, for example, the provision authorizing a court to make protective orders in conjunction with the enforcement of a money judgment,[30] but, as discussed earlier, it would not allow an attack on a validly rendered judgment if the ground of the attack, although recognized by New York law, is not recognized by the law of the place where the judgment was rendered. If there is some doubt about whether a given vacatur ground would be entertained by the first forum, the New York court can stay local enforcement for just long enough to enable the judgment debtor to make the motion to vacate in the other jurisdiction and have the court there, rather than the New York court, determine the issue.

The registration procedure has a respected forebear in federal court practice, where statute[31] has for a long time authorized the registration of federal judgments between and among districts anywhere in the federal system. The availability of this federal registration procedure was even cited by the Second Circuit in a dictum suggesting that the Article 54 procedure does not apply to federal judgments,[32] but after further consideration the court held that it does,[33] pointing out significant differences between the two procedures.[34]

The federal alternative remains, however. The federal route converts any federal judgment into the equivalent of one rendered by a federal court in New York, and New York treats the latter the same as a New York judgment by allowing it to be transcripted into and throughout the state system. It was in the discussion of transcripting, in fact, that the

federal registration statute was met and treated earlier.[35]

H.   DECLARATORY JUDGMENT

Table of Sections

§ 436. Declaratory Judgment, Generally

The declaratory judgment action is primarily a creature of the 20th century; hence it is without direct ancestors either at law or in equity. It is not a difficult thing, but its few elements can touch any of several junctures of a litigation and make it a bit difficult to niche chronologically in a text treatment. We have put it here, at the end of the treatment of judgments, because the foundation it requires needs a few building blocks from among matters already treated. If its sudden appearance in present context seems abrupt, perhaps that explanation will soften the transition.

A declaratory action is like any other, except that it contemplates a judgment that will merely declare the rights of the parties in respect of the matter in controversy and let things go at that. It differs from all of the traditional forms of action, inherited from the courts of common law and chancery, whose judgments go to enforcement either by execution or contempt. The main distinguishing factor of the declaratory action, therefore, is the absence of coercive enforcement. As a rule, the declaratory action can be brought by any person involved in a genuine civil controversy

---

28.   CPLR 5404(a).

29.   CPLR 5404(b).

30.   See § 522 below.

31.   28 U.S.C.A. § 1963.

32.   See Knapp v. McFarland, 462 F.2d 935 (2d Cir. 1972).

33.   See Keeton v. Hustler Magazine, Inc., 815 F.2d 857 (1987), discussed in the lead note in New York State Law Digest No. 334.

34.   See Commentary C5402:3 on McKinney's CPLR 5402.

35.   See § 422 above.

who feels that a mere judicial declaration of rights vis-a-vis the other side will do the job.

"The general purpose of the declaratory judgment is to serve some practical end in quieting or stabilizing an uncertain or disputed jural relation either as to present or prospective obligations."[1]

The declaratory judgment formally entered New York practice with the Civil Practice Act in 1921,[2] although the likes of it had been around for a time.[3] It is a useful and now well ensconced device with a variety of functions, as the next section will demonstrate. It is so much an accepted part of practice today that one must wonder why it had to be so cautiously approached during its early years.

There are only two basic provisions about the declaratory judgment in the CPLR, both of them brief and general. The first is CPLR 3001, which supplies the remedy:

> The supreme court may render a declaratory judgment having the effect of a final judgment as to the rights and other legal relations of the parties to a justiciable controversy whether or not further relief is or could be claimed. If the court declines to render such a judgment it shall state its grounds.

The second provision is CPLR 3017(b), which concerns the relief clause:

> In an action for a declaratory judgment, the demand for relief in the complaint shall specify the rights and other legal relations on which a declaration is requested and state whether further or consequential relief

is or could be claimed and the nature and extent of any such relief which is claimed.

Just about everything the CPLR wants to say about the declaratory judgment is said in those two statutes; the rest is caselaw.

A genuine dispute—or "actual controversy" as it is called in the later adopted federal declaratory judgment provision[4]—is necessary for a declaratory judgment action. In common with an action in the federal courts, no New York action may be used to secure a mere advisory opinion, and this is as true of the declaratory action as of any other.[5] CPLR 3001 also says that the controversy must be "justiciable", but in this context the word is apparently used only to confirm that there must be an actual controversy.[6]

It is sometimes thought that a declaratory action may be brought only when the facts are conceded and only the law is disputed. This unfortunate mistake probably comes from confusing the declaratory action with the action on submitted facts of CPLR 3222.[7] Although a case that poses only law questions may make it ideal for a declaratory judgment,[8] there may indeed be fact issues in the action—and there usually are.[9] Indeed, if the parties do agree on the facts they can draw up a CPLR 3222 submission and with it seek a declaratory judgment, which simply shows that the declaratory action can use the same broad range of procedural tools as any other action.

As a newcomer on the scene—a scene occupied by judges and lawyers trained in the

---

§ 436

1. James v. Alderton Dock Yards, 256 N.Y. 298, 305, 176 N.E. 401, 404 (1931).

2. Civ.Prac.Act § 473.

3. See Commentary C3001:2 on McKinney's CPLR 3001.

4. 28 U.S.C.A. § 2201.

5. See In re Workmen's Compensation Fund, 224 N.Y. 13, 119 N.E. 1027 (1918). An exception to this rule today is the New York Court of Appeals' certification procedure, under which the court answers questions of New York law for federal and sister-state courts. See § 528A below.

6. See, e.g., Jacob Goodman & Co. v. N. Y. Telephone Co., 309 N.Y. 258, 128 N.E.2d 406 (1955), cited on the "justiciable controversy" point in 3d Rep.Leg.Doc.(1959) No. 17, p. 48. In what is probably its most common

context, the separation of powers among the three branches of government, "justiciability" is used to describe issues appropriate to judicial resolution as opposed to those that belong in the legislative or executive branches. See New York State Inspection, Security and Law Enforcement Employees v. Cuomo, 64 N.Y.2d 233, 485 N.Y.S.2d 719, 475 N.E.2d 90 (1984), discussed in the lead note in New York State Law Digest No. 305. "Justiciability" problems met in the federal courts are more involved with the separation of powers problem than they are with the absence of a genuine controversy. See, e.g., Flast v. Cohen, 392 U.S. 83, 88 S.Ct. 1942, 20 L.Ed.2d 947 (1968).

7. The action on submitted facts is discussed in § 304 above.

8. See, e.g., Dun & Bradstreet v. City of New York, 276 N.Y. 198, 11 N.E.2d 728 (1937).

9. See, e.g., Rockland Power & Light Co. v. City of New York, 289 N.Y. 45, 43 N.E.2d 803 (1942).

common law and its respect for precedent—the declaratory action was at first approached with suspicion. The idea took root that declaratory relief is "usually unnecessary where a full and adequate remedy is already provided by another well-known form of action".[10] One may occasionally hear echoes of that approach, but it has in large measure been abandoned. Underlying it may have been the fear that the right of trial by jury could be infringed, or a statute of limitations circumvented, by allowing a declaratory action where one with the right to trial by jury or with a short limitations' period might otherwise have to be resorted to. Those are legitimate apprehensions, but they are met head on today, resolving questions of mode of trial[11] and statute of limitations[12] by direct address without necessarily denying the declaratory form of relief.

It is in fact a paradox to insist that P pursue D by coercive means when all P wants is a judicial statement resolving their dispute. It's like ordering a person to threaten a neighbor with a stick when all he wants to do is have the neighbor sit down to table and reason quietly.

CPLR 3017(b) makes clear that declaratory relief need not be sought by itself, but can be joined with a demand for more traditional relief, and it usually is. A demand for a declaratory judgment is often joined with a demand for an injunction, or for money damages, and there is no bar to either, or to the joinder of any other category of legal or equitable relief to which the plaintiff fancies himself entitled, along with the declaration.

A plaintiff who makes a mistake of form, moreover, and brings a declaratory action when the relief desired must be sought in other guise, should still not face a dismissal as

long as the complaint states any recognizable claim under the law. The worst that can happen is that the declaratory action will be converted to the more appropriate form.[13] It can even be converted into a special proceeding, such as one under Article 78 of the CPLR, if the relief sought is the stuff of that article.[14] The converse is also true, and many an Article 78 proceeding has been treated as a declaratory action.[15]

§ 437. Uses of Declaratory Judgment

One hesitates to set forth examples of declaratory actions, lest the examples used be taken as in any way exhaustive. There is no arbitrary restriction on the kind or character of claim that may be brought in declaratory form. A few prominent categories have found the declaratory action unusually helpful, however, and have used it prodigiously. These should be highlighted, but with the warning that they should not be taken as suggesting in any way the exclusion of the device from other contexts.

The matrimonial area is perhaps the leading beneficiary of the declaratory action. Doubts about the validity of a divorce, for example, especially a foreign one purporting to rest on a rem foundation (the so-called "ex parte" divorce), can be resolved in a declaratory action. This can be brought either by the proponent of the divorce, to declare it valid, or by the other side, to declare it void. Or the action can declare on the validity of the marriage itself, whether or not tied in with a divorce or with any other category of matrimonial action.[1] There must of course be a genuine dispute about the marital status. W was denied a judgment declaring that she was married to H, for

---

10. See James v. Alderton Dock Yards, 256 N.Y. 298, 176 N.E. 401 (1931). The court in James was apprehensive that the declaratory judgment was being sought as a means of securing a premature lien, for which the plaintiff might otherwise have had to wait. It is submitted that if, but for that, declaratory relief would help, the declaration can be granted but the lien denied or postponed.

11. On trial by jury in declaratory actions, see § 439 below.

12. On statute of limitations in declaratory actions, see § 438, below.

13. See CPLR 103(c).

14. See, e.g., Verbanic v. Nyquist, 41 A.D.2d 466, 344 N.Y.S.2d 406 (3d Dep't 1973). The Article 78 proceeding is treated in § 557 et seq., below.

15. E.g., Lakeland Water Dist. v. Onondaga County Water Auth., 24 N.Y.2d 400, 301 N.Y.S.2d 1, 248 N.E.2d 855 (1969).

§ 437

1. See Long v. Long, 281 A.D. 254, 119 N.Y.S.2d 341 (1st Dep't 1953).

example, when despite a showing that H and his girl friend were living together openly and having children, there was no colorable record of a marriage between them and hence no basis on which W would need a declaration.[2]

Insurance disputes have also lent themselves well to declaratory treatment. In ordinary casualty, disability, burglary, and fire insurance cases, for example, especially when the insurer seeks the declaration—if the insured sues it is usually a money action for the policy sum—the action can determine such things as whether a loss was sustained and whether the policy was in effect at the time of the allegedly insured event.

In the liability insurance area, in view of the dominance of tort claims on court calendars today, the declaratory action has been a unique aid. Whenever there is a dispute about whether a liability policy covers a particular case, a declaratory action can make the determination and can usually do it promptly. The principal appearance of this example is where the insurer has disclaimed coverage, or wishes to, whether by reason of the policy's alleged lapse, the inapplicability of its terms, a failure of notice, the insured's want of cooperation, or for any other reason. The first manifestation of the dispute is usually when the insurer, having been duly forwarded a summons and complaint served on its insured, the defendant in a pending tort action, refuses to defend. Both sides confront a dilemma. If the refusal continues, the insured must hire and pay for other counsel, while the insurer, should the disclaimer ultimately be found invalid, may find itself liable on a claim already gone to judgment and with the right to defend it on the merits with counsel of its choice forfeited. Resolution of whether the insurer must under-

take the defense of the tort action, i.e., whether the policy is in force and applicable to the claim, may be resolved in a separate declaratory action brought while the tort action pends. It may be brought by either insurer against insured, or vice-versa, or, recognizing that the person most interested in this dispute is the injured person, some courts allow it to be brought by the injured person against both.[3] If the fact on which coverage depends is one that would have to be resolved in the tort action itself, however, such as whether a driver had permission to use a vehicle (on which finding the owner's liability as well as the applicability of the policy would depend), the insurer will be required to defend and a declaratory action will be rejected[4] or a declaration made that a defense is required.

The action is often used to test the validity, on constitutional or other grounds, or the scope, of a contested statute, ordinance, rule, regulation, or other law. It must of course present a genuine controversy. Although nothing stops this kind of action from presenting issues of fact, if it does pose only questions of law it may be that much more attractive for a declaration.[5]

Use of a declaratory action to test the validity of a statute is available in the administrative area, among others, but if the plaintiff's attack is not on the validity of the applicable law, but only on the propriety of the proceedings taken under it, the plaintiff must ordinarily pursue administrative channels before going to court. This is the well known doctrine of the exhaustion of administrative remedies, a precondition to judicial action, and when the dispute finally goes to court it is usually in a proceeding under Article 78 of the CPLR rath-

---

2. See Somberg v. Somberg, 263 N.Y. 1, 188 N.E. 137 (1933). For criticism of this case, see Commentary C3001:9 on McKinney's CPLR 3001.

3. There's a conflict about that. See Watson v. Aetna Cas. & Sur. Co., 246 A.D.2d 57, 675 N.Y.S.2d 367 (2d Dep't 1998). The injured person may seek to intervene in a pending declaratory action between insured and insurer, but must do so timely. Where the intervention was sought only after the insurer won summary judgment in the declaratory action, and the insured did not appeal, intervention by the injured person was held barred as too late. B.U.D. Sheetmetal Inc. v. Mass. Bay Ins. Co., 248 A.D.2d

856, 670 N.Y.S.2d 228 (3d Dep't 1998) (noted in SPR 76:3).

4. See Nationwide Mut. Ins. Co. v. Dennis, 14 A.D.2d 188, 217 N.Y.S.2d 680 (3d Dep't 1961). A separate declaratory action will be allowed, however, if for some unique reason the decisive issue is removed from the tort action. See Aetna Casualty and Surety Co. v. Lauria, 54 A.D.2d 183, 388 N.Y.S.2d 432 (4th Dep't 1976), where the insured admitted permission.

5. See, e.g., Bunis v. Conway, 17 A.D.2d 207, 234 N.Y.S.2d 435 (4th Dep't 1962).

er than a declaratory action.[6] The line between what is properly the function of Article 78 and what is properly the function of a declaratory action is in fact one of the more obscure borders in litigation, often resulting in a rejection of the one brought because the other is found to be proper. But that is a defect in form only, and under the CPLR the worst that happens in that situation is a conversion from improper to proper form, with jurisdiction retained.[7]

The which-shall-it-be contest with Article 78 also illustrates how the plaintiff can end up with some incidental procedural advantage should an action in declaratory form be sustained. The venue of an Article 78 proceeding is restricted to the choices offered by CPLR 506(b), for example, while venue in a declaratory action is governed by CPLR 503–505, which may offer a preferable venue allotment in a given case.[8]

A declaratory action will not be allowed to evade a criminal prosecution. It will therefore not be entertained when it appears to be an endeavor, by a plaintiff whose activities may be running afoul of the penal law, to force out of a civil action findings that would otherwise have to be made in an outright criminal prosecution.

Reed v. Littleton[9] is a major case in point. P sued in the supreme court for a declaration that stated activities were "not in violation" of certain penal law provisions. The court refused to entertain the case, noting that even if it found a violation to exist, its holding would not be binding in a later criminal action because of the different burdens of proof: "a fair preponderance of the evidence" in the declaratory action (the usual civil burden) as against "beyond a reasonable doubt" (the criminal standard).

The courts are especially sensitive to prevent the declaratory action from affecting a criminal action already pending. There appears to be less hesitancy when the effect is on future prosecutions only. In Morgenthau v. Erlbaum,[10] for example, a criminal court judge, finding unconstitutional a statute dispensing with jury trial in certain cases, was about to use a jury. A district attorney brought a declaratory action in the supreme court to determine that the statute was valid and a jury unnecessary. The Court of Appeals allowed the action, but made the declaration applicable only to future cases, not to the specific criminal case that triggered the declaratory action.

If the facts are not in dispute, it has been held that the declaratory action may be used to determine whether conceded conduct comes within a penal law.[11]

Another advantage of the declaratory action is the initiative it will sometimes offer a person who is involved in a dispute but unable to find among the traditional kinds of action one that will enable her to bring it to court. In one case, for example, P was a composer who wanted a document construed as giving no rights in his compositions to D. It appeared, however, that P had no action at law—he maintained that the document was not a contract and hence that a contract did not exist—and none in equity either, such as for rescission or injunction. P might have waited, and brought the dispute to court with an injunction or damages claim after D actually pirated the property on the strength of this paper, but it was held that P did not have to wait. He was allowed a declaratory action.[12]

Similarly, where P does have other remedies but the others would be defensive only—P could do no better in existing modes than wait to be sued and then put his case in by way of

---

6. See, e.g., Slater v. Gallman, 38 N.Y.2d 1, 377 N.Y.S.2d 448, 339 N.E.2d 863 (1975). For treatment of Article 78, see § 557 et seq., below.

7. CPLR 103(c). See § 563 below.

8. See, e.g., W.T. Wang, Inc. v. New York State Dep't of Taxation and Finance, 108 Misc.2d 641, 438 N.Y.S.2d 453 (Sup.Ct., N.Y. County, 1981). A statute of limitations difference is not so easily avoided, however. See § 438 below.

9. 275 N.Y. 150, 9 N.E.2d 814 (1937).

10. 59 N.Y.2d 143, 464 N.Y.S.2d 392, 451 N.E.2d 150 (1983).

11. See New York Foreign Trade Zone Operators v. State Liquor Auth., 285 N.Y. 272, 34 N.E.2d 316 (1941), and the distinction it makes of the Reed case.

12. Kalman v. Shubert, 270 N.Y. 375, 1 N.E.2d 470 (1936).

defense—declaratory action lies and offers P a way to take the initiative.[13]

§ 438. Procedure in Declaratory Action; Limitations of Time

There is very little that is special about the procedure in a declaratory action. The remedy is generally restricted to the supreme court,[1] but its procedures follow those of any other action: summons, pleadings, bill of particulars, parties, disclosure, venue, trial, etc. The same rules of both personal and rem jurisdiction apply. If there are issues of fact, a trial is necessary. If not, summary judgment is permissible. Whether a trial must be by jury is discussed later.[2]

It has been held that a declaratory judgment may be rendered in a special proceeding.[3] This does not mean that a plaintiff may bring a special proceeding whenever declaratory relief is sought, however; it merely means that if the special proceeding has been authorized by statute in the particular kind of case,[4] relief in it can be demanded in declaratory form.

Earlier discussion touched on the problem of the statute of limitations in declaratory actions.[5] The "problem" is an attempt by a tardy plaintiff to circumvent an expired statute with the declaratory device. Since the declaratory action has no ancestor at law, it comes under none of the periods devised by Article 2 of the CPLR for law actions and therefore falls under the six-year "residual" period of CPLR 213(1), which governs equity actions and all other actions for which no limitation is otherwise prescribed.

The six years is a relatively generous period, however, and the plaintiff does not get it auto-matically just by seeking declaratory relief. That would make it too easy for a plaintiff to evade the shorter period prescribed for an alternative remedy that might be just as effective in the particular case. To guard against this, the Court of Appeals adopted in Solnick v. Whalen[6] what may be described as a kind of next-nearest-context standard: the period applicable to the declaratory action is the shorter one that governs the action or proceeding that would have been brought if the declaratory action had not been invented. The Court said in *Solnick* that

> [a] salutary result of the application of the limitation period appropriate to the other form of judicial proceeding will be to preclude resort by a dilatory litigant to the declaratory remedy for the purpose of escaping a bar of time which has outlawed the other procedure....

Solnick concerned the health commissioner's disallowance of a medicaid reimbursement. An Article 78 proceeding, governed by the four-month limitation period of CPLR 217(1), would have been the usual procedure to contest the commissioner's action. The plaintiff, too late under that measure, got no longer period by suing for a declaration.[7]

It is especially important to note this next-nearest-context rule in a proceeding to contest a real estate assessment. The proceeding is usually governed by a short period, one measured in terms of days or months, and yet it would not be difficult to contest the assessment in terms of a declaratory judgment, such as with an attack on the constitutionality of the rate schedule on which the assessment is

---

13. New York Foreign Trade Zone Operators v. State Liquor Auth., note 11, above.

§ 438

1. CPLR 3001. Under § 212–a of the New York City Civil Court Act, that court has jurisdiction of a declaratory action to test the validity of an insurance disclaimer. We may also note parenthetically that CPLR 3001 is concerned with declaratory judgments only by the courts. An administrative agency can issue a "declaratory ruling" on statutes and rules that are within its enforcement obligations. The statute that authorizes it, § 204 of the State Administrative Procedure Act, was broadly construed in Power Authority of the State of New York v. New York State Department of Environmental Conservation, 58

N.Y.2d 427, 461 N.Y.S.2d 769, 448 N.E.2d 436 (1983). See Commentary C3001:20 on McKinney's CPLR 3001.

2. See § 439.

3. State Division of Human Rights v. State, 77 Misc.2d 597, 354 N.Y.S.2d 287 (Sup.Ct., Rensselaer County, 1973).

4. See CPLR 103(b).

5. See § 36 above.

6. 49 N.Y.2d 224, 425 N.Y.S.2d 68, 401 N.E.2d 190 (1980).

7. Solnick is the subject of the lead note in No. 246 of the New York State Law Digest.

based (which involves no issue unique to the particular case). But if the taxpayer expects to get more time by resorting to the declaratory action, the plan won't work. Emphasizing that municipal funding depends on the prompt disposition of all assessment disputes, the Court of Appeals has held that the shorter period applicable to the usual review proceeding will apply in assessment contests even if the specific issue raised is appropriate to a declaratory action.[8]

Although difficult, because of its youth, to characterize as either wholly legal or wholly equitable, the declaratory action "is governed by equitable principles". Thus spoke the Court of Appeals in Krieger v. Krieger,[9] proceeding to apply the laches doctrine, an equitable defense, to the declaration sought there. H had waited until 12 years after W divorced him, and until after W had remarried, before bringing an action to declare the divorce void. The court held the action barred by laches. Thus, if the declaration is sought in what amounts to equitable context, as in the *Krieger* case, it may get the benefit of the six-year period of CPLR 213(1)[10] only to be undone by the laches doctrine, which can be applied even to bar a claim timely under the applicable statute of limitations.[11]

§ 439. Trial by Jury in Declaratory Action

Since the declaratory judgment action did not arrive on the New York scene until almost a century after the 1840s merger of law and equity and a century and a half after New York's 1777 Constitution—which marks the state's original moment of inheritance of the distinctions between common law and chancery—it is impossible to award the declaratory action to either law or equity. Inability to

niche it poses problems in several areas, some already touched on. Some kind of determination of the "equitable" or "legal" nature of the relief sought may be necessary, for example, to discern the applicable statute of limitations in a declaratory action.[1]

It was also seen that if the particular dispute involved in the case strikes the court as essentially "equitable" in nature, defenses traditionally associated with equity, such as laches, will be allowed despite prosecution of the claim in declaratory form.[2] In such instances, notwithstanding that the passkey to whether the claim is legal or equitable is usually the relief being sought, the court is looking beyond the relief—which, as "declaratory" in nature, will offer no key at all—to the underlying nature of the claim asserted. It is applying a kind of next-nearest-context rule, asking, in effect, what kind of action would most likely have been used to present this claim had the declaratory judgment not been created?

This kind of next-nearest-context rule should also be applied to determine whether the action is in essence equitable, and therefore triable by the court, or legal, and therefore triable by jury. It was applied by the Second Department in Independent Church v. Board of Assessors of Nassau County,[3] involving a challenge to a tax assessment. The most likely judicial context to raise such an issue before the declaratory judgment arrived on the scene was found to be an action to vacate the assessment as a lien, an equitable action. Hence, no jury.

The federal courts had faced the issue earlier. In its major pronouncement, Simler v. Conner,[4] the U.S. Supreme Court took the same approach. A client's suit against his lawyer for a declaration of how much of a fee was due

---

8. Press v. County of Monroe, 50 N.Y.2d 695, 431 N.Y.S.2d 394, 409 N.E.2d 870 (1980). The case is discussed in the lead note in New York State Law Digest No. 252.

9. 25 N.Y.2d 364, 306 N.Y.S.2d 441, 254 N.E.2d 750 (1969).

10. Most of the equity actions also lack specific niches in Article 2 and hence fall into the six-year catch-all provision, as the declaratory judgment does when standing on its own.

11. In Krieger, the statute of limitations was itself no bar because a void judgment, which the divorce was alleged to be, is not subject to the bar of the statute.

§ 439

1. See § 438 above.

2. See Krieger v. Krieger, note 9 in § 438, and text at that point.

3. 72 A.D.2d 554, 420 N.Y.S.2d 765 (2d Dep't 1979).

4. 372 U.S. 221, 83 S.Ct. 609, 9 L.Ed.2d 691 (1963).

was held to be in essence a law action and therefore triable by jury. Had no declaratory action been available, the next-nearest-context to put the question would have been an action by the lawyer against the client for the fee—a simple money action triable by jury. It apparently makes no difference, in applying the next-nearest-context approach, that the more conventional plaintiff-defendant roles are reversed. And it should not. The right to trial by jury, as long as it remains available for use in civil actions, is too important a right to hold forfeit through the artifice of a simple declaration.

§ 440. Judgment in Declaratory Action

If a plaintiff in an ordinary action loses on the merits, the result is a dismissal of the complaint. In a declaratory action, "the court should make a declaration, even though the plaintiff is not entitled to the declaration he seeks".[1] A mere dismissal is not appropriate.[2] The court must determine the rights of the parties in respect of the dispute involved and, if the defendant prevails, the declaration should simply go her way.[3] If the defendant should move to "dismiss" the complaint for failure to state a cause of action, under CPLR 3211(a)(7), the motion in the declaratory context should be taken as a motion for a declaration in the defendant's favor and treated accordingly.

As is true of any judgment in any action, the court can shape its judgment in a declaratory action to suit the needs of the occasion.[4] If the court denies a declaration altogether it must state its grounds.[5]

It will be recalled that the declaration need not be sought alone, but can be joined with any other relief the plaintiff is entitled to, legal or equitable.[6] If the proof sustains a right to such other relief, the judgment should include it along with the declaration.

A duly rendered declaratory judgment is entitled to the full benefits of the res judicata and collateral estoppel doctrines,[7] which means that it is also entitled to full faith and credit from other American jurisdictions.[8]

§ 441. Need for Follow-Up Relief

Since CPLR 3017(b) expressly permits the complaint in a declaratory action to include any other relief the plaintiff has a right to, there is no reason for the plaintiff's withholding any relief due at the time. Indeed, the courts prefer that everything connected with the dispute be resolved at once so that a second action will not be necessary.[1] But if a declaratory judgment is forthcoming, and the plaintiff's rights as declared are afterwards violated, the plaintiff may bring a second action for the necessary subsequent relief. If, for example, the first judgment's violation causes the plaintiff money damages, the plaintiff can seek the damages in a new action.[2]

While it is clear that such follow-up relief, if the need for it is the consequence of the declaration's flouting, may be pursued in a second plenary action, a plaintiff would ordinarily prefer to seek the relief by mere motion, instead, such as one to reopen or modify the original judgment to insert the additional relief. The motion would bear the caption of the original declaratory action and require no new ritual of

§ 440

1. Hirsch v. Lindor Realty Corp., 63 N.Y.2d 878, 483 N.Y.S.2d 196, 472 N.E.2d 1024 (1984).

2. Medical World Publishing Co. v. Kaufman, 29 A.D.2d 859, 288 N.Y.S.2d 548 (1st Dep't 1968).

3. See Justice Court Mut. Housing Co-op., Inc. v. Sandow, 50 Misc.2d 541, 270 N.Y.S.2d 829 (Sup.Ct., Queens County, 1966).

4. First National Stores v. Yellowstone Shopping Center, 21 N.Y.2d 630, 290 N.Y.S.2d 721, 237 N.E.2d 868 (1968).

5. CPLR 3001.

6. CPLR 3017(b).

7. See Rockland Power & Light Co. v. City of New York, 289 N.Y. 45, 43 N.E.2d 803 (1942).

8. Spadaro v. Newark Ins. Co., 21 A.D.2d 226, 249 N.Y.S.2d 753 (4th Dep't 1964), aff'd 15 N.Y.2d 1000, 260 N.Y.S.2d 16, 207 N.E.2d 611 (1965).

§ 441

1. See Silverstein v. Continental Cas. Co., 23 A.D.2d 801, 258 N.Y.S.2d 485 (4th Dep't 1965), aff'd 17 N.Y.2d 845, 271 N.Y.S.2d 282, 218 N.E.2d 323 (1966).

2. Dale Renting Corp. v. Bard, 39 Misc.2d 266, 240 N.Y.S.2d 488 (Sup.Ct., Kings County), aff'd 19 A.D.2d 799, 243 N.Y.S.2d 420 (2d Dep't 1963). See Commentary C3001:5 on McKinney's CPLR 3001.

summons service or pleadings. Fact issues, should they arise on the motion, could be expeditiously tried,[3] and fairness would be better served by sparing the plaintiff a second plenary action after the apparently frustrated victory in the first one. This writer has on several occasions advocated the allowance of a simple motion for follow-up relief,[4] and there may be tacit authority for such a procedure from the Court of Appeals. In Berlitz Publica-

tions, Inc. v. Berlitz,[5] the plaintiff sought to enforce the provisions of an earlier declaratory judgment by an application "at the foot of the judgment", in essence a motion for follow-up relief. The Court denied the relief on the merits, but presumably it would not have reached the merits if the motion method had been found inadequate to introduce them. Trial courts have so read the *Berlitz* case and allowed a simple motion for follow-up relief.[6]

3. CPLR 2218.

4. See Commentaries C3001:6 on McKinney's CPLR 3001, where an analogy is made to practice in connection with the enforcement devices.

5. 37 N.Y.2d 878, 378 N.Y.S.2d 363, 340 N.E.2d 730 (1975).

6. See, e.g., Auer v. Dyson, 125 Misc.2d 274, 479 N.Y.S.2d 102 (Sup.Ct., Oneida County, 1984), aff'd on opinion below 112 A.D.2d 803, 491 N.Y.S.2d 1022 (4th Dep't 1985).

Chapter Seventeen

RES JUDICATA

Analysis

A. INTRODUCTORY

Table of Sections

§ 442. Res Judicata, Introductory

The doctrine of res judicata is designed to put an end to a matter once duly decided. It forbids relitigation of the matter as an unjustifiable duplication, an unwarranted burden on the courts as well as on opposing parties. Its main predicate is that the party against whom it is being invoked has already had a day in court, and, if it was not satisfactory, the proper course was to appeal the unsatisfactory result rather than ignore it and attempt its relitigation in a separate action.

The phrase "res judicata" has taken on several meanings. In its technical sense, res judicata is applicable only when a party is at-

tempting to relitigate her whole cause of action; it intervenes in that instance to foreclose not only matters litigated, but also those which might have been litigated.[1] This has come to be called "claim preclusion", to be distinguished from the doctrine of collateral estoppel, which the Restatement denominates "issue preclusion",[2] terminology that the New York courts have been using increasingly.[3] The differences between them will be seen more clearly in subsequent sections as these and related doctrines, such as the election of remedies and the law of the case, are compared and contrasted.

The other use of "res judicata", and the one more commonly met in practice, is really a shorthand term that takes in all of these doctrines. There is a tendency, harmless enough when taken generally rather than strictly, to denominate as "res judicata" any situation in which a party is foreclosed from something in

§ 442

1. Schuylkill Fuel Corp. v. B. & C. Nieberg Realty Corp., 250 N.Y. 304, 165 N.E. 456 (1929).

2. Restatement of Judgments, 2d, § 27.

3. See, e.g., Koch v. Consolidated Edison Co. of N.Y., 62 N.Y.2d 548, 479 N.Y.S.2d 163, 468 N.E.2d 1 (1984),

cert. den. 469 U.S. 1210, 105 S.Ct. 1177, 84 L.Ed.2d 326 (1985). The courts began to use the new terms as early as the tentative drafts of the Second Restatement. See, e.g., Pace v. Perk, 81 A.D.2d 444, 440 N.Y.S.2d 710 (2d Dep't 1981).

a later action because of something that happened or failed to happen in an earlier one. In this more popular sense "res judicata" is not so much a doctrine as it is a policy—the policy of avoiding duplication when there is no good reason for duplicating. The thread that ties all the related doctrines together is their common aim of implementing some phase of that policy. If one keeps that broad purpose always in mind, the great pliability of "res judicata" itself as well as of all its family members will not take the lawyer by surprise. As long as the attorney is properly forewarned, the myriad of conditions and exceptions and qualifications with which the topic—and therefore this chapter—is replete will all fall into place as appropriate servants of an important and flexible policy, rather as unruly offspring of a rigid doctrine. There is nothing rigid about res judicata. And there is nothing rigid about any of its family, either. Each case must be decided on its own facts. There are a host of cases on res judicata, but only a small fraction of them contain the guideposts by which to judge future cases. In common with caselaw on such things as the bill of particulars and summary judgment, the majority of res judicata decisions are mere illustrations of a result appropriate to the singular facts of the case.

Guideposts for res judicata are almost exclusively the products of caselaw. In the realm of New York practice, that makes the subject unique: statutes play no major role here. There are, to be sure, occasional statutes or rules that touch the doctrine, in effect if not in terms, but these are few and they address specific situations. CPLR 3216, for example, provides that a dismissal for neglect to prosecute is "not on the merits",[4] and CPLR 3217(c) has instructions about when a voluntary discontinuance is "without prejudice" or "on the merits".[5] Perhaps the most significant CPLR dictate about when a result is "on the merits"—a shorthand description often used to invoke res judicata—is that of CPLR 5013. It governs a dismissal of a claim during the trial and provides that the dismissal is "on the merits" if made after the plaintiff's whole case

is in but not if made before.[6] In the overall context of res judicata, however, these and a few other statutes and rules, dispositive as they may be in a given case, play a small role. Recognizing how dependent each case is on its own peculiar facts, the legislature has maintained a hands-off policy: res judicata is and continues to be a common law doctrine. This makes it one of the few areas of New York practice that can turn for help to the American Law Institute's Restatement. The one relevant here is the ALI's Second Restatement of Judgments.

§ 443. Members of the Res Judicata Family

It will be helpful at this early juncture to list and briefly define a number of doctrines often thought of as members or close friends of the res judicata family. Later sections will elaborate with finer distinctions and with citations, but as popularly used in New York practice the coterie's respective functions run this way:

(1) Res Judicata. This one is the parent and in popular usage it often lends its name to the others, a handy title to describe the whole clan. As indicated in the prior section, the res judicata doctrine in its technical sense is concerned with an endeavor to relitigate a whole claim rather than only parts of it. In this sense it has given way to the term "claim preclusion".

(2) Collateral Estoppel. This is the most influential member of the family. More often than not a judge or lawyer saying "res judicata" really means collateral estoppel. Each doctrine is usable only against a party who had a day in court on the relevant issue in the first action, but while res judicata is looking for an attempt to duplicate the whole case, collateral estoppel is looking for less. Collateral estoppel scans the first action and takes note of each issue decided in it. Then if the second action, although based on a different cause of action, attempts to reintroduce the same issue, collateral estoppel intervenes to preclude its relit-

---

4. CPLR 3216(a). See § 375 above.

5. See § 298 above.

6. See § 402 above.

igation and to bind the party, against whom the doctrine is being invoked, to the way the issue was decided in the first action. "Issue preclusion" is the newer terminology, but collateral estoppel still hangs on. The two phrases are usually used to mean the same thing, and we use the terms in this book interchangeably.

Judge Cardozo's famous *Schuylkill* case[1] can illustrate the collateral estoppel—"issue preclusion"—doctrine. P contracted to supply coal to five defendants. They did not pay for a delivery and P sued them for it. They claimed their liability was several only, while P claimed it was joint (making each defendant liable for coal delivered to any one of the others). P won on the point and the defendants' liability under the contract was found joint. P then made another delivery under the same contract and again had to sue for it. The defendants again pleaded that their liability was several. Since it was based on a later delivery, the second action presented a separate cause of action and could not be foreclosed by the res judicata ("claim preclusion") doctrine itself. But since the issue of the nature of the defendants' liability under this very contract had been litigated in the first action, collateral estoppel bound the defendants to the earlier holding on that issue and established for all purposes in the second action that the defendants' liability was joint.

We should note that although the collateral estoppel doctrine operates on a smaller item—an "issue" decided in the first action rather than the whole claim—it operates on a broader plain and hence with more influence. It will rear its head whenever the same issue appears, while res judicata will not show up unless it is convinced that the cause of action is the same. As caselaw manifests, the reappearance of an "issue" is much more frequent than the reappearance of the whole "claim", which makes collateral estoppel the star performer on this stage—and incidentally shows

why "claim preclusion" and "issue preclusion" are handier terms.[2]

(3) Election of Remedies. Res judicata and collateral estoppel generally require a final judgment on the merits. The election of remedies doctrine does not, intervening (or trying to) whenever a plaintiff with a choice of two or more remedies sues on fewer than all of them. The plaintiff is deemed to have "elected" the one sued on, which results in a waiver of the rest. The election doctrine has been severely restricted by both caselaw and statute. Since it often becomes relevant at the pleading stage of an action, it was treated at that point—including contrasts with res judicata—which spares duplication here.[3]

(4) Splitting. This is another member of the res judicata family, and a sibling, if not a twin, of the election of remedies doctrine. The splitting doctrine in New York is largely confined to instances in which a plaintiff with a single money claim omits part of what is due when she sues. The part omitted is waived. This was also the subject of earlier treatment.[4]

(5) Law of the Case. This doctrine recognizes that res judicata, strictly speaking, operates only when there has been a final judgment on the merits. It endeavors to accomplish similar results within an action before judgment is reached. It thus provides that once a point has been decided, it cannot be relitigated even within the action, although it may be raised on appeal. The doctrine was met previously during discussion of the effect of orders disposing of motions under CPLR 3211, the motion to dismiss, and CPLR 3212, the summary judgment motion,[5] and will be returned to in greater depth in this chapter.[6]

(6) Direct Estoppel. This is not a terribly useful term and seldom appears in New York cases, but it may be helpful to note its technical meaning and function. Its area of operation is where a prior action has been dismissed on a

§ 443

1. Schuylkill Fuel Corp. v. B. & C. Nieberg Realty Corp., 250 N.Y. 304, 165 N.E. 456 (1929).

2. The study of collateral estoppel as distinct from res judicata begins in § 457, below.

3. See § 218 above.

4. See § 220.

5. See §§ 276 and 287, above.

6. See § 448 below.

ground that did not reach the merits (and thus does not preclude a second action) but nonetheless disposed of an issue that may arise in a later action on the same claim. The Second Restatement gives this example:

Relying on longarm jurisdiction, P sues D, a nonresident, for injuries suffered when P was hit by a car driven in the state by X on what P claims was D's behalf. D pleads want of permission in X and is upheld, the action being dismissed for lack of jurisdiction, which depends on permission. But suppose that the substantive liability of D also depends on permission. When P sues D (and gets jurisdiction) in a second action, D may plead the want of permission, found only in regard to jurisdiction in the first action, as dispositive of the merits in the second, because the issue is the same. Or so the Restatement concludes by way of illustrating what is sometimes called "direct estoppel".[7] It is not certain in New York practice, however, that an issue disposed of on a jurisdictional dismissal in the first action will be given merits impact in the second.[8]

(7) Full Faith and Credit. This doctrine is one of federal constitutional law.[9] It requires that the judgments of American courts rendered with jurisdiction be given recognition by all other American courts. It is a kind of mandatory, interstate res judicata. It is the subject of distinct treatment near the end of this chapter.[10]

(8) Comity. The judgments of foreign countries, unlike those of American courts, are not within the full faith and credit clause and the states are therefore free to formulate their own rules of recognition. If the state does recognize the judgment, it is giving that judgment "comity". In the realm of the conflict of laws, "comity" has come to describe, casually but helpfully, the whole topic of the recognition of the judgments of foreign nations.[11]

* * *

From among this stately procession of related doctrines at least one can usually be found to preclude relitigation of an issue when relitigation is really inexcusable, but still others may be summoned or fitted out for the maverick case which, while unjustifiably attempting relitigation, slyly evades all of the res judicata family members. Suppose, for example, that D has made a motion to dismiss an action for want of jurisdiction, and before the motion is heard P brings a second action, which D promptly moves to dismiss based on the pendency of the first. D is talking out of both sides of his mouth here, and yet he nicely sidesteps all of the existing doctrines. The court in such a case can invoke a simple *equitable estoppel* against D, or find that with his jurisdictional motion in #1 he has *waived* the right to claim its pendency in #2, or has *consented* to the second suit.[12] Although perhaps not within any of the blood line of res judicata, a situation like this poses the same kind of inconsistency of position that the res judicata family was born to battle.

The equitable estoppel doctrine serves as a kind of general backup whenever the facts elude one of the more standard doctrines. In one case, for example, P contracted to sell certain plants to D, which D contracted to furnish to X for use on a building project. When X postponed the order, D sued X and won, pleading that the plants were ready and in accord with specifications. Then, in a later suit by P against D, D tried to show that the plants did not satisfy specifications. Issue preclusion might have been invoked against D, but issue preclusion is designed for use against a party who lost in the first action, while here D won in that action. No matter, held the court in one case; the doctrine of "estoppel against inconsistent positions" is available to do the job.[13]

---

7. See Restatement 2d, Judgments, § 27, Illustration 3.

8. See § 92 above.

9. U.S.Const. Art. IV, § 1.

10. See § 471.

11. See § 472.

12. See Commentary C3211:16 on McKinney's CPLR 3211 and Ferrandino v. Cartelli, 12 A.D.2d 604, 208 N.Y.S.2d 750 (1st Dep't 1960).

13. Environmental Concern, Inc. v. Larchwood Const. Corp., 101 A.D.2d 591, 476 N.Y.S.2d 175 (2d Dep't 1984).

The caselaw consistently serves the theme of the res judicata tribe, manifesting that a resourceful judge will not suffer a blatant disregard of the family's policy merely because a case dropped by when no one was at home.

Sometimes the visitor may find the premises occupied by a friend while the family is away, and with the friend quite ready to do the family's bidding. The doctrine of stare decisis is such an ally and it can take hold of a case just as it is about to slip away from the premises. This is illustrated in a later section, where stare decisis and the role it plays alongside res judicata is treated.[14]

The concepts of "merger" and "bar" are merely different ways of describing res judicata in different contexts; they also occupy a separate section.[15]

B.   GENERAL REQUISITES

Table of Sections

§ 444.   Necessity of Final Judgment

As a general rule the res judicata doctrine—collateral estoppel included for this purpose—requires a final judgment on the merits.[1] It has been said, therefore, that a verdict or decision not reduced to judgment will not do.[2] The purpose of this rule is to assure finality, however, and if finality is clear, the source of it should be secondary. Indeed, the CPLR provides that if the ministerial act of entering judgment is all that is necessary after the

merits have been duly determined in a verdict or decision, judgment may follow even if the losing party dies in the interim.[3] This can be taken as establishing the CPLR's view that a showing of finality is more important than the name of the paper that embodies it. The key is whether the adjudication is "sufficiently firm", as the Restatement puts it,[4] and a firm one should qualify as a "final judgment", whatever its name.

A settlement made without an action having been brought does not get res judicata effect, but it will often get its equivalent if the claim is sued on in violation of the settlement. The defense of release,[5] for example, can be interposed against the claim and will usually do the job, at least where the action attempts to interpose the whole of the settled claim. A settlement within an action can provide for the entry of a judgment embodying its terms. This is a consent judgment, and it does get res judicata treatment.[6] That would meet the matter head on.

If a judgment for which preclusive effect is sought is itself based on an earlier judgment, domestic or foreign, and the earlier one has been vacated or reversed or otherwise undone, it is of course divested of its finality and the remedy to cancel the second judgment is a motion to vacate it on the ground of the undoing of the first.[7] Until that is done the second one will stand, however. Indeed, there is authority that a second judgment will even prevail over an earlier one involving the same claim if there should be an inconsistency between them.[8]

If it becomes necessary to pinpoint the moment of a judgment's "finality", the general rule is that it becomes final as of the date it is "rendered", as the Restatement has it,[9] or, in

---

14.   See § 449.

15.   See § 450 below.

§ 444

1.   Today a special proceeding culminates in a "judgment," just as an action does. CPLR 411. It used to end in a "final order", but as the equivalent of a judgment that also got full res judicata effect. See Bannon v. Bannon, 270 N.Y. 484, 1 N.E.2d 975 (1936).

2.   Rudd v. Cornell, 171 N.Y. 114, 63 N.E. 823 (1902); Mandracchia v. Russo, 53 Misc.2d 1018, 280 N.Y.S.2d 429 (App.T., 2d Dep't, 1967).

3.   CPLR 5016(d).

4.   Restatement 2d, Judgments, § 13.

5.   CPLR 3018(b), 3211(a)(5).

6.   See § 451 below.

7.   See CPLR 5015(a)(5).

8.   See § 471 below.

9.   See Restatement 2d, Judgments, § 13.

New York Practice, at least as of its formal moment of "entry".[10] The fact that the time in which to appeal the judgment is still open, or even that an appeal has in fact been taken and is pending, does not divest the judgment of its finality in New York.[11] The judgment is still entitled to its res judicata effect, but the fact of the appeal's pendency may be made the basis of a stay application in the second action—the action in which the res judicata doctrine is being pleaded—to await the outcome of the appeal.[12]

If, after a final judgment is rendered, all of the parties settle in a stipulation that prescribes that no judgment shall be entered, or that a judgment already entered shall be vacated, must the courts enforce the agreement, thereby canceling the judgment and depriving it of collateral estoppel effect? The U.S. Supreme Court held in U.S. Bancorp Mortgage Co. v. Bonner Mall Partnership that courts need not honor such a stipulation; that equitable principles govern and that, by settling, the loser forfeits the equitable right of vacatur.[13] The matter has yet to be resolved by the New York Court of Appeals, but *Bancorp* is favorably cited by the appellate division in Paramount Communications v. Gibraltar Cas. Co.,[14] where the court adopts a similar rule for New York, holding that the parties can't get a judgment vacated merely by settling the action and including vacatur as a term of the settlement. To the argument that settlement would be encouraged by permitting such an automatic vacatur, the court answers that the practice could in some ways, on the contrary, discourage settlements.

Perhaps those who seek most often to erase judgments with settlements are manufacturers who face numerous lawsuits because of a defective product, their obvious aim being to deny others, and perhaps numerous others, a free ride on the issue of liability. The impact of such judgments as precedents is mentioned briefly but strongly in the *Bancorp* case.[15]

§ 445. Res Judicata for Order

Since the res judicata doctrine is so frequently mentioned as requiring a "final judgment", it will be helpful if we break in briefly at this point to discuss the extent to which the doctrine can apply to an adjudication embodied in a mere "order".

In New York an order entered on a motion is ordinarily entitled to the same res judicata and collateral estoppel treatment that a judgment gets, as long as the other requisites of those doctrines—finality, opportunity to contest, identity of issue, etc.—are met.[1] This is especially significant when the order made on the motion is dispositive rather than interlocutory or intermediate. An order granting a motion for summary judgment, for example, should get res judicata treatment in an attempted second action.

Questions like this are usually avoided by getting a formal "judgment" entered on the order, but a failure to do that should not be controlling. Even in some phases of the appeal process today New York plays down the difference between a judgment and an order: if one is appealed when the other should have been, the omission is disregarded as long as a copy of the proper paper is ultimately furnished to the appellate court.[2] Of course, if it is unclear whether a particular issue was passed on in the course of deciding a motion—this is more relevant to collateral estoppel (issue preclusion) than to res judicata (claim preclusion)—

---

10. CPLR 5016.

11. See Parkhurst v. Berdell, 110 N.Y. 386, 18 N.E. 123 (1888).

12. CPLR 2201. Compare Commentary C2201:11 on McKinney's CPLR 2201.

13. 513 U.S. 18, 115 S.Ct. 386, 130 L.Ed.2d 233 (1994).

14. 212 A.D.2d 490, 623 N.Y.S.2d 850 (1st Dep't 1995) (noted in SPR 35:3).

15. Where parties to an arbitration agreement stipulate that no award made in the arbitration will have

estoppel impact, the courts have upheld the agreement and denied the estoppel. See, e.g., Kerins v. Prudential Property & Casualty, 185 A.D.2d 403, 585 N.Y.S.2d 637 (3d Dep't 1992), noted in SPR 21:3.

§ 445

1. Vavolizza v. Krieger, 33 N.Y.2d 351, 352 N.Y.S.2d 919, 308 N.E.2d 439 (1974).

2. CPLR 5512(a). See also CPLR 5501(c).

the doctrine will not apply.[3]

In applying the preclusion doctrines to an order, one must of course be mindful of the ground on which the order rests. An order granting a motion for summary judgment based on the overall merits of the case will get full claim preclusion treatment, for example, while one based on a narrower ground, such as want of jurisdiction or incapacity of a party, will be dispositive only of the particular objection and will not preclude a new action that meets and overcomes it.[4]

Motions within actions that result in orders denying them are usually interlocutory rather than final, in the sense that the action continues. While they do not get res judicata treatment as such, they get the equivalent under a doctrine known as "the law of the case", separately discussed below.[5]

§ 446. Necessity for Disposition on "Merits"

The general rule is that the earlier judgment must be on the "merits" in order to invoke the preclusion doctrines[1]. But "merits" in this sense is taken today as meaning only that the earlier disposition can have no greater effect in the second action than it was intended to be given when made in the first. On a straight application of res judicata, or claim preclusion—such as an attempt at relitigation by a plaintiff who lost on the merits after a full trial in the first action—no doubt should arise: the earlier judgment disposed of the merits once and for all and unless it is directly overturned it will preclude a new action. But in other situations the earlier disposition must be subjected to closer scrutiny, especially when the earlier result was a dismissal of the claim on a motion of some kind. The key question is, what kind? A general summary judgment motion, as noted in the prior section, or a CPLR

3211 motion treated as one for summary judgment,[2] is intended to dispose of the whole case and will invoke full claim preclusion if a new action is brought on the same cause of action. But the dismissal of an earlier action on some lesser ground, touching on some curable defect clearly not intended to foreclose the merits, keeps the merits open for a second round.

Examples of this would be a dismissal for lack of prosecution, or a voluntary discontinuance, which do not ordinarily constitute adjudications on the merits,[3] although a second action may well face the bar of the statute of limitations.[4] A number of the objections listed as dismissal grounds in CPLR 3211(a) also come in for only limited res judicata application; they are deemed an adjudication of only the narrow ground predicating the dismissal even though the dismissal is embodied in a formal judgment. Illustrations here would be dismissals based on lack of jurisdiction (subject matter, personal, or rem[5]), the plaintiff's lack of capacity to sue at the time of the earlier action (e.g., the plaintiff was an infant and tried to bring suit pro se),[6] and the failure to join a necessary party (omitted in the earlier action but joined now in the present one).[7] Res judicata applies, but it operates only on the ground on which the earlier adjudication rests and in these situations the ground was not one disposing of the merits of the claim. The doctrinal element in this context is a kind of hybrid between claim preclusion and issue preclusion: the thing dismissed in round one was the "claim", but the dismissal was predicated on what might be considered a single and not-finally-dispositive "issue".

Of course, if a given ground is the common sense equivalent of a general merits disposition, it will be given res judicata effect if relitigation is attempted. Examples here would

3. See Royal Business Funds Corporation v. Ehrlich, 78 Misc.2d 305, 356 N.Y.S.2d 407 (Sup.Ct., N.Y. County), aff'd 45 A.D.2d 823, 356 N.Y.S.2d 1015 (1st Dep't 1974).

4. See § 287 above.

5. See § 448.

§ 446

1. See, e.g., Rudd v. Cornell, 171 N.Y. 114, 63 N.E. 823 (1902).

2. CPLR 3211(c) authorizes this treatment.

3. See CPLR 3216(a), 3217(c).

4. See CPLR 205(a).

5. CPLR 3211(a)(2), (8), (9).

6. CPLR 3211(a)(3).

7. CPLR 3211(a)(10).

be where the earlier action was dismissed on such grounds as release or payment or, indeed, where the earlier action was itself dismissed based on res judicata or collateral estoppel emanating from a still earlier action.[8]

It will be noted that in this last batch of examples the earlier disposition resulted from a motion rather than after trial, but the disposition was—or in any event should have been—embodied in a "judgment" closing out the first action. Suppose the dismissal motion in the earlier action was denied, the denial being embodied in an order and the action continuing because of the denial. Can the matter determined then be raised again *within* the action, i.e., is res judicata unavailable because the disposition is not on the "merits", or "final"? The "law of the case" doctrine, treated two sections hence, will be found to preclude relitigation in this situation, so that if "res judicata" itself proves unwilling, it will also find itself unneeded.

§ 447. Preclusion for "Might Have Been Litigated" Items

Res judicata in its strict sense operates to bar not only matters that were actually put in issue in the prior action, but also those that might have been. The classic statement of the rule is this language of Judge Cardozo in the *Schuylkill* case:[1]

> A judgment in one action is conclusive in a later one, not only as to any matters actually litigated therein, but also as to any that might have been so litigated, when the two causes of action have such a measure of identity that a different judgment in the second would destroy or impair rights or interests established by the first.[2]

The purpose of this rule is to prevent a party from seeking in a later action to inject matters (theories, grounds, counts, defenses,

etc.) that could and should have been used in the first action but were not. This is the claim preclusion doctrine in operation—res judicata in its technical sense (as opposed to collateral estoppel or issue preclusion)—and so it requires a determination of whether the second action involves the same "cause of action".

The best general standard for determining this is the Second Restatement's, which deems the causes the same if they arise out of the same transaction or series of connected transactions.[3] If, for example, P sues D in ejectment because of an encroachment and wins judgment, but cannot enforce the judgment because of a recalcitrant sheriff, P cannot thereafter sue for equitable relief (hoping for a judgment that would make the defendant remove the encroachment himself).[4] P had but one cause of action and could not break it down into segments and bring separate suit on each. In the example, the plaintiff won the first suit on the merits. The same rule would apply when the plaintiff loses the first action on the merits, as where P with a personal injury sues D only in negligence and the jury finds for D: P cannot thereafter sue D for the same injury on counts of breach of warranty or strict products liability or any other that P could have included but omitted in the first action.

Until 1981, this rule was shackled with unusual exceptions when the plaintiff lost based on some threshold objection, like the statute of frauds or the statute of limitations. A judgment of dismissal based on one of those grounds was held to bar a second action based on the same ground but not to foreclose a second action on a different ground even though the cause of action was the same. A second action was allowed on a quantum meruit claim, for example, when the earlier suit in contract was dismissed under the statute of

---

8. See CPLR 3211(a)(5).

§ 447

1. Schuylkill Fuel Corp. v. B. & C. Nieberg Realty Corp., 250 N.Y. 304, 165 N.E. 456 (1929).

2. 250 N.Y. at 306–307, 165 N.E. at 457.

3. Restatement 2d, Judgments, § 24(1). Section 24(2) suggests that a "transaction" or related "series" of them

must be determined "pragmatically", weighing such considerations as time, place, origin, and motivation, and treating also the parties' understanding and expectations.

4. See Hahl v. Sugo, 169 N.Y. 109, 62 N.E. 135 (1901). This overlaps with the election of remedies doctrine, a subject returned to below. Hahl was also met in § 218 above.

frauds for want of a writing.[5] And a second suit based on fraud, for another example, timely under its unique limitations' measure, was allowed even though the first action, in contract, was dismissed as time barred.[6] The reason for this was the courts' endeavor to abate the harsh consequences of the election of remedies doctrine as it was applied at common law,[7] but in so doing the courts seriously undermined the res judicata (claim preclusion) doctrine, most particularly the "might have been litigated" standard that is part of it. These matters were explored in more detail in the treatment of the election of remedies doctrine earlier[8] and need no repetition here, except to cite again the two Court of Appeals cases that overruled the older cases in 1981 and restored the claim preclusion doctrine to its predominant role.

The cases are O'Brien v. City of Syracuse,[9] and Smith v. Russell Sage College.[10] Under them, a plaintiff omitting a count or ground from the earlier action will pay the price of a res judicata forfeiture; no longer can the affixation of an "election of remedies" label circumvent it. The res judicata rule is designed to encourage a plaintiff to put in everything relative to the claim. The *O'Brien* and *Smith* cases implement that rule.[11] In *O'Brien*, the plaintiff was barred from bringing a second action against a city on a trespass count after the first action, based on a wrongful taking, failed: the trespass count could have been joined in the first action. In *Smith*, the plaintiff brought a second action on a ground still timely under the statute of limitations after the earlier action on a different count and with a different time measure was dismissed as too late: the second ground could have been joined in the

first action. The plaintiff had notice of the second ground in time to join it, through the process of amendment if no other way. Only if the plaintiff legitimately and excusably lacked knowledge of the second ground in time to join it in the first action would the tightened claim preclusion doctrine—the Court of Appeals calls it the "transactional analysis" approach—permit a second action. "Transactional analysis" bars all claims arising out of a given transaction, occurrence, or event once any of the claims is litigated.

The "might have been litigated" rule does not apply when the consequences of an earlier criminal action are sought to be used in a later civil one;[12] only the points actually decided in the criminal action may be exploited for civil use.[13] The criminal defendant can therefore conduct his defense without having to pay any attention to the civil impact that omitted matters would otherwise be thought to have.

Nor will the "might have been litigated" rule apply to multiple taxpayer suits; there, an estoppel in the second action will attend only matters actually litigated in the first. So held the Court of Appeals in Murphy v. Erie County,[14] and in a context to suggest that this should also be the result in class actions generally, so as not to conclude the class members with anything but issues actually litigated and decided in the class suit.[15]

Some recent cases have been applying a stronger dose of the "might have been litigated" rule to matrimonial litigation, affecting financial claims between the parties in divorce and like actions. The court clearly has power, for example, to determine an issue between the spouses concerning title to real property,

---

5. Smith v. Kirkpatrick, 305 N.Y. 66, 111 N.E.2d 209 (1953).

6. Fitzgerald v. Title Guarantee & Trust Co., 290 N.Y. 376, 49 N.E.2d 489 (1943).

7. See Strong v. Reeves, 280 A.D. 301, 114 N.Y.S.2d 97 (3d Dep't 1952), aff'd 306 N.Y. 666, 116 N.E.2d 497 (1953).

8. See § 218 above.

9. 54 N.Y.2d 353, 445 N.Y.S.2d 687, 429 N.E.2d 1158 (1981).

10. 54 N.Y.2d 185, 445 N.Y.S.2d 68, 429 N.E.2d 746 (1981).

11. The cases are the subject of the lead note in New York State Law Digest No. 267.

12. For general discussion of civil use of criminal findings, see § 453 below.

13. See Vavolizza v. Krieger, 33 N.Y.2d 351, 352 N.Y.S.2d 919, 308 N.E.2d 439 (1974).

14. 28 N.Y.2d 80, 320 N.Y.S.2d 29, 268 N.E.2d 771 (1971). As to what a "taxpayer" suit is, see § 136 above.

15. Res judicata as applied to class actions and other representative actions is treated in § 454 below.

but injection of the issue was once thought to be permissive rather than mandatory. It is now deemed mandatory, so that a failure to inject the title issue into a matrimonial action is held to waive it.[16]

C. COMPARISON WITH OTHER DOCTRINES

Table of Sections

§ 448. Law of the Case

Since the doctrine of res judicata technically requires a final judgment on the merits in one action and an attempted relitigation in a second, it has no application within an action. The doctrine of the "law of the case" was devised to close that gap. It applies to various stages of the same action or proceeding;[1] its purpose is to avoid the retrial of issues already determined within it.[2] For practical purposes, the doctrine of the law of the case can be considered a kind of intra-action res judicata. It has already been met in this book, with examples, in discussing the res judicata effect of an order disposing of a motion to dismiss under CPLR 3211.[3]

Once a point is decided within a case, the doctrine of the law of the case makes it binding not only on the parties, but on the court as well: no other judge of coordinate jurisdiction may undo the decision.[4] The order embodying the finding is of course open to appellate review, but it may not be negated by any other judge of the same court.[5] Indeed, if a later application is seen to affect a prior order, the preference of the CPLR is that the later appli-

cation be made to the same judge who disposed of the prior one,[6] a point that has become academic in most instances under the Individual Assignment System inaugurated in 1986 (under which a case goes to but a single judge at the outset and remains with that judge[7]).

The res judicata doctrine (including claim preclusion and issue preclusion for this purpose), and the doctrine of the law of the case, between them assure finality for judicial dispositions whether made in a final judgment ending an action or in an intermediate order within the action. This can be seen just by contrasting the grant and denial of a dismissal motion under CPLR 3211, which offers the best illustration. Suppose, for example, that D moves to dismiss a money claim on the ground of payment under CPLR 3211(a)(5). The court grants the motion. This establishes that the claim has been paid and contemplates a final judgment dismissing the case; an endeavor to dispute the point again in a future case will be foreclosed either by res judicata (claim preclusion) itself, as where the identical claim is sued on again, or collateral estoppel (issue preclusion), as where the claim is a different one but whether this particular debt was paid becomes a relevant issue. If the court denies the motion, however, this establishes that payment has not been made, but it contemplates only an order denying the motion. The case goes on, but the doctrine of the law of the case will prevent the defendant from again trying to show that the claim was paid.

A disposition claiming to be the law of the case will usually be found to be embodied in a court order, but that is not indispensable. If one judge's decision on a point is clear, it concludes other coordinate judges whether em-

---

16. See Boronow v. Boronow, 71 N.Y.2d 284, 525 N.Y.S.2d 179, 519 N.E.2d 1375 (1988).

§ 448

1. McGrath v. Gold, 36 N.Y.2d 406, 369 N.Y.S.2d 62, 330 N.E.2d 35 (1975).

2. Fadden v. Cambridge Mut. Fire Ins. Co., 51 Misc.2d 858, 274 N.Y.S.2d 235 (Sup.Ct., Albany County, 1966), aff'd 27 A.D.2d 487, 280 N.Y.S.2d 209 (3d Dep't 1967).

3. See § 276 above.

4. State of New York Higher Educ. Svcs. Corp. v. Starr, 158 A.D.2d 771, 551 N.Y.S.2d 363 (3d Dep't 1990).

5. See George W. Collins, Inc. v. Olsker–McLain Ind., Inc., 22 A.D.2d 485, 257 N.Y.S.2d 201 (4th Dep't 1965), holding that the doctrine applies even to prevent Judge 2 from granting a consolidation motion denied by Judge 1.

6. CPLR 2221. See § 253 above.

7. See § 77A, above, for a discussion of the IAS and its exceptions.

bodied in a formal order or not.[8]

In some situations in which special circumstances suggest the need for speedy resolution of temporary matters, findings made for the temporary purpose will not bind the judge who has to decide the merits of the case later. So, for example, the findings of a judge on a motion for a preliminary injunction will not conclude the trial judge who later has to decide whether to grant a permanent injunction. The preliminary injunction is only a status quo retainer and it would be unseemly to let the findings made in its granting—and made expeditiously just to keep things intact while the merits are investigated—dictate those merits. The same is true of applications for temporary support in matrimonial and other family law contexts. Public policy requires that such applications be disposed of expeditiously lest the needs of a family go wanting, and yet certain findings may be required even before such temporary orders can be made, such as the extent of the family's needs or a spouse's or parent's resources, or even with respect to the validity of the marriage or of a divorce purporting to dissolve it.

Findings on any of those or similar issues made for the purpose of awarding temporary relief do not bind the court when it later makes a final judgment. Indeed, to encourage the trial bench at judgment time to reach findings on these matters independently of the presumably hastier findings made earlier, the appellate courts virtually insist that judicial thinking not be impeded by the earlier doings.[9] This is so even if the temporary findings were the product of a testimonial hearing rather than just motion papers and affidavits, which are the more usual basis.[10]

The justifying rationale in these special situations is sometimes said to be that since the earlier findings were made on only a motion, they cannot under res judicata conclude the action,[11] but since the law of the case doctrine designs to give conclusive effect even to motions within actions, it is perhaps sounder to

consider this temporary support situation as merely an exception to the doctrine, and a reasonable one.

§ 449. Relation to Stare Decisis

The doctrine of stare decisis, which makes the common law what it is by giving judicial precedents the effect of law—binding if from direct appellate level and at least persuasive if from some other source—differs from res judicata in that it applies only to issues of law, while the res judicata family touches both issues of law and issues of fact.

Stare decisis is also more flexible. This is not to say that res judicata and its progeny are rigid—ensuing sections will demonstrate the contrary—but they are not quite as pliable as stare decisis. If a claim or an issue between the same parties is found to be identical with one previously adjudicated between them, even though there is much judgment to be exercised in making such a finding of identity, the res judicata doctrine must be applied and relitigation foreclosed. The doctrine is operating on only one claim, or one issue, and between the same parties. The mission of stare decisis is broader: to set precedents for cases generally. To determine whether to apply a precedent from an earlier case to a legal issue in a later one involving a similar or identical claim, much else comes into play. From what court does the precedent come? When was it decided? Have there been intervening changes in the law itself, from statute or later caselaw, or from changing times and diverging attitudes? Stare decisis and its elasticity enable the judge to consider factors like these before invoking the doctrine, while they play a smaller role, if they play one at all, in the realm of res judicata.

Stare decisis often acts as a good backup when the need for flexibility makes res judicata itself inappropriate despite the presence of its several ingredients. This is notably the case with the periodic assessments of real property.

8. See George W. Collins, Inc. v. Olsker–McLain Ind., Inc., note 5 above.

9. See, e.g., Haber v. Haber, 20 A.D.2d 858, 248 N.Y.S.2d 83 (1st Dep't 1964).

10. Bannon v. Bannon, 270 N.Y. 484, 1 N.E.2d 975 (1936).

11. Id.

If from the time of an earlier assessment there has been no change in either the facts concerning the land and its surroundings or in the rules of law applicable to the assessment, the case would seem to be tailor made for res judicata. But the doctrine does not apply. Public policy dictates that in the interest of the whole community, a finding for an earlier period not bind for a later one, lest, for example, error at an earlier time with respect to a given taxpayer do continuing damage to that one or, indeed, to others, who might have to pick up the first one's share of the tax load. A leading case so holding points out that if all things are the same as they were before, stare decisis can be turned to for aid,[1] nicely compromising the need for flexibility on the one hand with the need for consistency on the other.

A point that often arises in connection with stare decisis in New York is the extent to which—when the Court of Appeals has not yet spoken—an appellate division precedent in one department binds in another. It has been held that trial courts in one department should follow an appellate division precedent set in another until the local appellate division addresses the matter, but that among the appellate divisions themselves the holding of one is persuasive but not binding.[2]

§ 450. "Merger" and "Bar"

These are two theoretical subdivisions of the res judicata doctrine. If the plaintiff is the winner, the cause of action "merges" in the judgment, which technically means that the judgment supersedes the underlying cause of action to such an extent that it disappears.[1] If the defendant wins, the judgment "bars" any later action by the plaintiff on the underlying claim.[2] This dichotomy has doubtful practical significance today; if used at all, it should be used carefully, especially the "merger" doc-

trine, which can do more harm than good when rigidly applied.

The merger doctrine merely seeks to prevent suit from being duplicated on the claim, preferring to regard the judgment as its superseder. This is usually just fine with the plaintiff who, other things being equal, would prefer a judgment any time. But make one of those other things unequal, and merger rigidly applied does needless damage. If there is anything about the underlying claim that offers the plaintiff some advantage, it should retain its identity and peer right through the judgment to make itself felt. If the original claim gave the plaintiff some kind of lien, for example, surely a judgment on it should not destroy the lien.[3] New York subscribes to the healthy view that the merger doctrine will not be allowed to undermine benefits inhering in the claim merely because it has gone to judgment. If, for example, the question is whether a judgment survives the later bankruptcy of the judgment debtor, and the answer depends on the judgment's underlying cause of action, the court will readily pierce the "merger" technicality and look right through to the cause.[4] The essential nature of the primary claim is not necessarily lost when judgment ensues.[5] Indeed, when a claim has been fully litigated, courts should be sensitive to see to it that the judgment is a reward rather than a deprivation.

Exceptions to merger will be spelled out whenever necessary, even to assure just a procedural right associated with the original claim. P had judgment against D in a Massachusetts court, for example, and then sued on it in New York. D, a corporation, had by that time surrendered its authority to do business in New York and pleaded lack of jurisdiction. P countered that under New York law D had

---

§ 449

1. People ex rel. Watchtower Bible & Tract Society, Inc. v. Haring, 286 A.D. 676, 146 N.Y.S.2d 151 (3d Dep't 1955).

2. Mountain View Coach Lines, Inc. v. Storms, 102 A.D.2d 663, 476 N.Y.S.2d 918 (2d Dep't 1984).

§ 450

1. See Restatement 2d, Judgments, § 18.

2. Id., § 19.

3. See Comment g on § 18 of Restatement 2d, Judgments.

4. See In re Williams, 208 N.Y. 32, 101 N.E. 853 (1913) (involving alimony).

5. See State of Wisconsin v. Pelican Ins. Co., 127 U.S. 265, 8 S.Ct. 1370, 32 L.Ed. 239 (1888).

agreed to continuing New York jurisdiction if the liability sued on was, as it was here, incurred in New York. D answered that the Massachusetts judgment merged that liability and that the New York court could not consider it. The court did consider it, however, sustaining jurisdiction and holding that merger will be carried no further than the ends of justice require.[6] A judgment against a defendant is not to be turned into a sword for the defendant to use against the plaintiff, in other words, as a strict use of "merger" would sometimes seem to have it.

When a court is asked for a provisional remedy in an action based on a judgment already rendered, it should be permissible, if the availability of the remedy depends on the nature of the underlying claim, for the court to pierce the judgment and look at the claim. A provisional remedy often involved with this question was the order of attachment, because at one time several of the grounds for allowing it turned on the nature of the claim asserted.[7] Some caselaw had earlier held that the piercing could not take place for this purpose; that the merger would obscure the claim and leave visible only a cause of action on a "judgment".[8] A later amendment of the attachment statute, however, makes suit on a judgment an independent ground for attachment[9] and thus makes the prior caselaw academic, at least in respect of attachment. Should a different remedy, provisional or otherwise, be sought in an action on a judgment, however, the question of merger would subsist and should be resolved along the lines indicated above.

The "bar" doctrine, applicable when the defendant in the first action is the winner, has not posed equivalent problems in New York. Whether an earlier judgment will in fact preclude ("bar") the plaintiff from a second suit on the same claim will of course depend on the

ground of the first action's dismissal. A jurisdictional or like disposition, which contemplates and allows a new action if the earlier objection can be cured, of course does not act as a "bar".[10]

D. RES JUDICATA IN PARTICULAR SITUATIONS

Table of Sections

§ 451. Application to Default and Consent Judgments

A judgment by default or on consent must be given claim preclusion effect,[1] precluding new suit on the same claim. The judgment would not be much good otherwise. The more difficult question is whether a judgment of this kind should be given the more influential effects of collateral estoppel (issue preclusion) as well. As a general rule, New York does give default and consent judgments that effect.

A collateral estoppel lies for any issue duly pleaded in and legitimately a part of the action in which a default was suffered. Reich v. Cochran[2] so held even of the summary proceeding to recover the possession of realty, finding that a default judgment established the validity of the lease and precluded a collateral attempt in a later proceeding to cancel it. A consent judgment was given similar effect in Canfield v.

---

6. Jay's Stores, Inc. v. Ann Lewis Shops, Inc., 15 N.Y.2d 141, 256 N.Y.S.2d 600, 204 N.E.2d 638 (1965).

7. Those grounds were contained in subdivisions 5, 6, and 8 of CPLR 6201, which were repealed in 1977.

8. See, e.g., McCormick v. American Press Publications, Inc., 52 Misc.2d 297, 275 N.Y.S.2d 429 (Sup.Ct., N.Y. County, 1966).

9. Subdivision 4 of CPLR 6201, added as subdivision 7 in 1970 and then renumbered 4 in 1977.

10. See § 276 above.

§ 451

1. Walston & Co. v. Klein, 44 Misc.2d 607, 254 N.Y.S.2d 734 (Sup.Ct., N.Y. County, 1964), aff'd 24 A.D.2d 559, 260 N.Y.S.2d 831 (1st Dep't 1965).

2. 151 N.Y. 122, 45 N.E. 367 (1896).

Elmer E. Harris & Co.,[3] where the judgment consented to had been entered in an earlier action involving D's status as a holdover tenant. When P consented to judgment for D,[4] everything underlying the judgment was deemed resolved in D's favor, including the fact that D was not a holdover tenant, and P was bound by that finding in a subsequent proceeding involving the same issue.

Hence an actual contest is not necessary for collateral estoppel; the only required showing is that the issues were necessary to the determination, contested or not. This is true in New York of both the default judgment[5] and the consent judgment,[6] but not without argument. While few dispute that claim preclusion—res judicata itself in its technical sense—must attend default and consent judgments, there is criticism of New York's giving them issue preclusion effect as well.[7] The main objections are that this gives small judgments too much influence, requires clairvoyance of defendants, penalizing them for not foreseeing how a light (or absent) defense in one case can come back to haunt them collaterally in another, and deters settlements. Even an offer to compromise under CPLR 3221, which is just a category of consent judgment, has been given estoppel effect, binding a defendant who so compromised in P's property damage action and holding D concluded as well in P's later—and possibly unexpected but much more substantial—personal injury action.[8] Although consistent with the overall New York view, a result like that does tend to discourage compromise offers and was not the intention of CPLR 3221.

Perhaps the criticisms, including this writer's,[9] can today be met with more recent suggestions from the Court of Appeals. In a series of important later decisions, notably the *De-Witt* and *Schwartz* cases,[10] a number of sui generis factors have been set up as a kind of check list for a judge to go over before according an earlier judgment issue preclusion impact in a later suit. Those factors, listed and discussed in a later section,[11] are as relevant to default and consent judgments as they are to contested ones and ought to be considered in all of them. By applying them, almost on a sui generis basis, a flexibility is introduced sufficient to deny issue preclusion effect to earlier default and consent judgments whenever one of the listed components suggests it—such as the smallness of the earlier claim and, as a result, the laxity of the defense made against it. The result of such a fresh approach will be the overturning of some earlier precedents that gave default and consent judgments collateral estoppel fruits arbitrarily, without attention to such individual factors as the Court of Appeals requires treatment of today.

That's the way things are going. Two cases separated by three decades can illustrate. In the first,[12] a default judgment of $79.16 in an action by P against D for property damage was held under collateral estoppel to require dismissal of D's later suit against P for personal injury. In the second, a default judgment on a $750 fee claim by a physician against a patient was denied estoppel effect in the patient's later action against the physician for medical malpractice.[13]

---

3. 252 N.Y. 502, 170 N.E. 121 (1930).

4. The consent in this instance was not an outright judgment by confession, such as that authorized by CPLR 3218, but rather a commitment as a stipulation for judgment absolute used in appellate practice, see § 527 below, which amounts to a consent judgment and was so treated by the Court of Appeals in the Canfield case.

5. Trecot v. Taxter, 69 Misc.2d 248, 329 N.Y.S.2d 139 (Sup.Ct., Nassau County, 1972).

6. In re DeChiaro's Estate, 35 Misc.2d 485, 230 N.Y.S.2d 604 (Sup.Ct., Nassau County, 1962).

7. See, e.g., Rosenberg, Collateral Estoppel in New York, 44 St. John's L.Rev. 165, 173–181.

8. Card v. Budini, 29 A.D.2d 35, 285 N.Y.S.2d 734 (3d Dep't 1967).

9. See Commentary C3221:2 on McKinney's CPLR 3221.

10. B.R. DeWitt, Inc. v. Hall, 19 N.Y.2d 141, 278 N.Y.S.2d 596, 225 N.E.2d 195 (1967), and Schwartz v. Public Administrator, 24 N.Y.2d 65, 298 N.Y.S.2d 955, 246 N.E.2d 725 (1969), discussed in §§ 466 and 467, below.

11. See § 467.

12. Roberts v. Strauss, 108 N.Y.S.2d 733 (Sup.Ct., N.Y.County, 1951).

13. Kossover v. Trattler, 82 A.D.2d 610, 442 N.Y.S.2d 554 (2d Dep't 1981). See the discussion in the concurring opinion of Justice Gibbons.

Independent evaluation of each case is the only practical solution to an attempt to give issue preclusion effect to a default or consent judgment. It seems a fair response to the problem, and a complete one to the critics.

§ 452. Application to Counterclaims

Res judicata ordinarily applies in full measure to claims interposed by way of counterclaim, cross-claim, third-party claim, and the like, as long as there was sufficient jurisdiction in the first action to dispose of the claim.[1] In this connection it is important to recall that New York does not have, as the federal system has,[2] a compulsory counterclaim rule; that is, a rule that makes a counterclaim "compulsory" and forces its interposition (under the threat of waiver) if it arises out of the same transaction or event that grounds the plaintiff's main claim. All counterclaims are supposed to be permissive in New York, but we have already seen how misleading that notion can be; how the doctrine of collateral estoppel (issue preclusion) can invade a second action, brought now on the previously withheld counterclaim, and, with findings from the earlier action, dictate its result. That prior discussion during treatment of counterclaims in the pleadings chapter[3] also showed how a defendant's interposition of certain matter as a mere defense in the first action can have the same effect as if it had been used as a counterclaim, barring it from use as a separate claim later. This is a kind of waiver doctrine, and it is an erratic and perilous thing in a practice that presumes to label all counterclaims permissive. Its illustration is best seen in the case of Musco v. Lupi,[4] also met and discussed during that earlier treatment, which the reader would do well to review here.[5]

§ 453. Civil Use of Criminal Findings

It often happens that a single occurrence will give rise to both civil and criminal proceedings. A simple example is an assault. It is clear that a civil judgment against a party cannot be used against that party in a later criminal prosecution for the reason that the burden of proof differs: the civil assault finding rests on a "fair preponderance of the evidence", while the prosecutor in the criminal action has the heavier burden of satisfying the jury "beyond a reasonable doubt". To import the civil finding into, and make it dictate the result of, the criminal action would violate the criminal law standard.

But in the reverse situation that is not a problem. It should be theoretically as well as practically palatable to permit a plaintiff suing a defendant for the civil consequences of his act to make use of a prior criminal conviction of the defendant for the same act. The wrongful act having been proved in the earlier criminal action "beyond a reasonable doubt", that would more than amply cover the "fair preponderance", which is the plaintiff's burden in a civil suit. Notwithstanding this, the courts for a long time did not permit the criminal result to bind the defendant in the civil action, allowing the criminal conviction to qualify at most as only prima facie evidence for the fact trier to consider in the civil case.[1] This was based on the "mutuality" doctrine,[2] whose later rejection[3] set the stage for its abandonment in the criminal-to-civil situation as well.

The abandonment took place in S.T. Grand, Inc. v. City of New York,[4] which required the civil action to import and be bound by the criminal conviction. In *Grand*, bribery in connection with a contract was involved and X was duly convicted of the crime. When X later brought civil suit to recover on the same con-

---

§ 452

1. In respect of counterclaims, see Restatement 2d, Judgments, §§ 21–23.

2. FRCP Rule 13(a).

3. Section 224 above.

4. 6 Misc.2d 930, 164 N.Y.S.2d 84 (Sup.Ct., Orange County, 1957).

5. See § 224 above.

---

§ 453

1. See Schindler v. Royal Ins. Co., 258 N.Y. 310, 179 N.E. 711 (1932).

2. For discussion of this doctrine, see § 460 below.

3. Mutuality was interred in B.R. DeWitt, Inc. v. Hall, 19 N.Y.2d 141, 278 N.Y.S.2d 596, 225 N.E.2d 195 (1967), discussed below in §§ 466 and 467.

4. 32 N.Y.2d 300, 344 N.Y.S.2d 938, 298 N.E.2d 105 (1973).

tract, the defendant was allowed to use the conviction as conclusive proof that the contract was illegal, barring X's civil recovery. The usual requirements that the issue be the same and that X be shown to have had a full opportunity to litigate the earlier (in this case the criminal) proceeding were held to be the governing criteria and the Court of Appeals confirmed this again in Vavolizza v. Krieger.[5]

Both *Grand* and *Vavolizza* involved only the "shield" use of res judicata and collateral estoppel, i.e., the plaintiff in the later civil action was the previously convicted person, and the civil defendant was the one seeking to use the estoppel as a defense. But what of the situation in which the civil plaintiff is the victim, and the civil defendant the convict? May the victim make "sword" use of the conviction, and march off with an affirmative victory in the civil case based on the conviction of the same defendant in the earlier criminal action? It has been held that the victim may; that whether the use to which the estoppel is put in the civil action is affirmative or defensive should make no difference as long as the estopped issue is the same and the civil tribunal is satisfied that there was a full opportunity for the defendant in the criminal action to litigate the issue.[6]

The "full opportunity" is the key. In one leading case, for example, Gilberg v. Barbieri,[7] a city court conviction for harassment—a petty offense not qualifying even as a misdemeanor—was denied estoppel effect in a civil suit by the victim against the same defendant for assault. The Court of Appeals described the criminal action as a "relatively minor" one that the defendant could not be expected to defend "with the same vigor" he would a regular criminal action. "The brisk, often in-

formal, way in which these matters must be tried," said the court, "as well as the relative insignificance of the outcome, afford the party neither opportunity nor incentive to litigate thoroughly."

Gilberg is an example of the full and fair opportunity test in action. The test plays a dominant role in the res judicata domain today. It requires case-by-case analysis of a number of factors, elaborated below.[8]

§ 454. Res Judicata in Representative and Class Situations

In the usual representative situations that one encounters in the courts, res judicata has full operation. Once the representative has litigated the matter, the represented person is fully bound. So it is with the fiduciary (executor, administrator, guardian, etc.) of a person or estate, or the trustee of a trust: the beneficiaries, or represented persons whatever their designation, are bound by the judgment that binds the representative.[1]

This rule also applies to the well-known "class action".[2] The fact that all of the class members are—and constitutionally may be—bound by the judgment[3] is among the reasons why the courts keep such close control of the class action. When res judicata is invoked for a prior class judgment, the court must look carefully into a number of factors, including the adequacy of the representation and of course whether there was truly an identity of interest between the representatives who conducted the class action and the individual class members now sought to be bound.[4]

The rule that res judicata precludes litigation of matters that "might have been litigat-

---

5. 33 N.Y.2d 351, 352 N.Y.S.2d 919, 308 N.E.2d 439 (1974).

6. Read v. Sacco, 49 A.D.2d 471, 375 N.Y.S.2d 371 (2d Dep't 1975).

7. 53 N.Y.2d 285, 441 N.Y.S.2d 49, 423 N.E.2d 807 (1981).

8. See § 467.

§ 454

1. In re Sullivan's Will, 123 N.Y.S.2d 159 (Surr.Ct., Kings County, 1953).

2. The class action is treated in §§ 139–147 above.

3. See Hansberry v. Lee, 311 U.S. 32, 61 S.Ct. 115, 85 L.Ed. 22 (1940). Even members of the plaintiff class who are not residents of the forum state can be bound by the judgment. See § 144 above.

4. See Restatement 2d, Judgments, § 41, Comment e.

ed", as discussed in an earlier section,[5] does not apply rigidly to class actions. The Court of Appeals has so held of taxpayer actions, for example,[6] a variety of class action. As a rule, therefore, the class action judgment will bind only as to matters actually litigated and not necessarily those that merely might have been.

§ 455. Res Judicata for Jurisdictional Issues

Jurisdictional determinations get res judicata treatment, ordinarily limited, of course, to the jurisdictional point itself.[1] Issues of personal jurisdiction support this conclusion readily. Where, for example, D appears in the first action and moves to dismiss it on the ground that notice was inadequate or that the court lacked jurisdictional basis, a determination against D on that motion binds him. If D should afterwards default, or even contest and lose on the merits, res judicata will foreclose in another forum relitigation of the question of the first forum's jurisdiction to the same extent that it will foreclose the merits.[2] The same is true when D does not appear during the action and a default judgment is entered against D. If D then moves to vacate the default on the basis of the jurisdictional objection, an adverse decision on the motion confirms the jurisdiction and res judicata seals the confirmation.[3]

Appearing in the first action, in other words, marks the voluntary submission of the jurisdictional question to the first court. A second court before whom the issue of the first court's jurisdiction arises must discontinue its inquiry into the first court's jurisdiction as soon as it is demonstrated that D appeared in the first

action and raised and lost on the jurisdictional question.[4] The second court cannot, in the guise of re-adjudicating jurisdictional facts, subvert the recognition due the first judgment on the merits.[5]

The answer is different if D did not appear in the first action. In that case the second court may litigate the first one's jurisdiction. Each defendant is entitled to a day in court on the question of jurisdiction just as on any other issue. The law is that D can seek that day in the second court as long as he did not appear and use it up in the first. In that instance, when the second court may and is looking into the first one's jurisdiction, it must cease its inquiry and award recognition to the judgment upon being shown that the first court did have jurisdiction. Conversely, if it is shown, on proper proof, that the first did not have jurisdiction, the judgment may be denied recognition.[6] If this discourse sounds more like one on the federal full faith and credit clause than it does on New York internal law, it is because the issues are similar in both but the caselaw more profuse on the full faith and credit subject.[7]

Rem jurisdictional determinations get res judicata treatment, too, but only to the extent that the judgment affects the res on which jurisdiction was based. The second court may look into the question of whether the first had any rem jurisdiction at all, at least where D did not appear in the first action, but upon being satisfied that rem jurisdiction was present it must treat that issue as res judicata. The judgment will have no impact beyond the subject res, however; it cannot touch D's personal liability.[8] So, for example, if the only

---

5. See § 447 above.

6. See Murphy v. Erie County, 28 N.Y.2d 80, 320 N.Y.S.2d 29, 268 N.E.2d 771 (1971).

§ 455

1. Johnson v. Muelberger, 340 U.S. 581, 71 S.Ct. 474, 95 L.Ed. 552 (1951).

2. Baldwin v. Iowa State Traveling Men's Ass'n, 283 U.S. 522, 51 S.Ct. 517, 75 L.Ed. 1244 (1931).

3. Vander v. Casperson, 12 N.Y.2d 56, 236 N.Y.S.2d 33, 187 N.E.2d 109 (1962).

4. Davis v. Davis, 305 U.S. 32, 59 S.Ct. 3, 83 L.Ed. 26 (1938).

5. Coe v. Coe, 334 U.S. 378, 68 S.Ct. 1094, 92 L.Ed. 1451 (1948).

6. Williams v. North Carolina, 325 U.S. 226, 65 S.Ct. 1092, 89 L.Ed. 1577 (1945). This is the second of the Williams' cases, the first being 317 U.S. 287, 63 S.Ct. 207, 87 L.Ed. 279 (1942); the second makes the point that occupies us here.

7. Full faith and credit as such is separately treated in § 471, below, where several of these matters are seen again.

8. Restatement 2d, Judgments, § 30(2).

jurisdiction the first forum had as against D was quasi in rem based on the attachment of D's property, its judgment is effective only to the extent of the property attached and cannot conclude D if and when D is later sued in personam for a part of the claim still due—as where the attached assets did not suffice to cover it all. The earlier judgment is not res judicata in that situation,[9] even if it involved the identical issues. Not even the "splitting" doctrine will be applied here, because of the first forum's obvious jurisdictional limitations.[10]

It is this rule that accounts for the so-called "divisible divorce" doctrine in the matrimonial area. An example of this is where a husband, H, has gotten a valid ex parte divorce—ex parte in this context means that personam jurisdiction over the defendant spouse was lacking in the divorce court—from his wife, W, in the first forum. The basis of the first court's divorce jurisdiction was that the "matrimonial res" was present there through H's domicile.[11] In a second action, this one in personam, W sues H for alimony and support. H there contends (1) that he is not W's husband because of the earlier divorce judgment and (2) that the earlier judgment also extinguished W's monetary rights. The first contention is correct because the first court had rem jurisdiction of the marital status and that sufficed for the divorce. But the second is wrong because in order to affect W's monetary rights the first court needed personam jurisdiction of W, which it lacked. The "divisible" item is the relief sought: the status and money phases are segregated and the earlier judgment allowed res judicata effect only on the jurisdictionally secure item, the status. Since there was no personam jurisdiction in the first forum to support a monetary adjudication, however, a second action may be brought for that.[12]

The res judicata treatment of jurisdictional issues is not hard to conceptualize when personam or rem jurisdiction is the topic. Since those categories of jurisdictional objection are in any event waivable, even a holding of jurisdiction by a court that does not have it, as long as D appeared and raised the issue, can be accepted on any of several theories, e.g., that D with the appearance consented to have the first court decide the question, or waived the objection by not appealing an adverse determination of it, or is estopped from now contending that jurisdiction was absent after having submitted the issue to the first court. But suppose that the issue is one of subject matter rather than of personal or rem jurisdiction. Unlike the latter two, subject matter jurisdiction cannot be conferred by consent, waiver, estoppel, laches, or anything else.[13] Suppose that the first court's subject matter jurisdiction is called in issue and the court holds, upon D's due appearance and submission of the question, that it has jurisdiction. Does the holding get res judicata treatment? Difficult though the concept may be—how can a court that lacks basic power over a case literally "talk itself" into it?—it usually does. Even issues of subject matter jurisdiction must be laid to rest sooner or later. Based on this need, the U.S. Supreme Court has several times applied res judicata to issues of subject matter jurisdiction, or in any event to issues contended or assumed to involve subject matter jurisdiction. It has done so, for example, in real property[14] and matrimonial[15] cases.

When more than one state is involved, the full faith and credit clause is implicated[16] and the requirements imposed by the U.S. Supreme Court must be met. But when no supervening federal requirement is present, New York's view is that a determination by a court that it has subject matter jurisdiction will be

---

9. See Benadon v. Antonio, 10 A.D.2d 40, 197 N.Y.S.2d 1 (1st Dep't 1960).

10. See § 220 above.

11. See § 102 above.

12. Vanderbilt v. Vanderbilt, 354 U.S. 416, 77 S.Ct. 1360, 1 L.Ed.2d 1456 (1957); Estin v. Estin, 334 U.S. 541, 68 S.Ct. 1213, 92 L.Ed. 1561 (1948).

13. See § 8 above.

14. See Durfee v. Duke, 375 U.S. 106, 84 S.Ct. 242, 11 L.Ed.2d 186 (1963).

15. See Sherrer v. Sherrer, 334 U.S. 343, 68 S.Ct. 1087, 92 L.Ed. 1429 (1948). For further treatment of Sherrer, which appears to require res judicata treatment for adjudications of subject matter and personal jurisdiction alike, see § 471 below.

16. U.S.Const., Art. IV, § 1.

binding—assuming of course that the bound party appeared—only when it turns on an issue of fact rather than an issue of law. If the first court's holding that it has subject matter jurisdiction amounts only to a legal conclusion, the facts not being in dispute, collateral attack is open, i.e., a second court may determine the first's subject matter jurisdiction afresh, no matter what the first may have said about it. So held the New York Court of Appeals in Friedman v. State,[17] an unusual situation involving a removed judge and his right to collect his salary.

A better way to illustrate this distinction is with a federal example:

Suppose that P sues D in a federal district court based on diversity of citizenship.[18] P is a citizen of New York and contends that D is a citizen of Vermont, D insisting, however, that he, too, is a New Yorker. D's citizenship, which is roughly the equivalent of "domicile" in this context,[19] is a question of fact, but its resolution will dictate whether or not there is diversity—clearly a question of subject matter jurisdiction in federal practice. If D moves to dismiss the federal action for want of diversity and loses, the court finding him a citizen of Vermont, that issue of fact gets res judicata effect even though subject matter jurisdiction turns on it.

The Second Restatement takes the position that adjudications of subject matter jurisdiction are entitled to res judicata treatment unless the doctrine's underlying policy (finality) is outweighed by the need to prevent the first court in a given case from expanding its own sphere of competence. Several factors are listed for consideration, including whether the case was "plainly beyond" the first court's subject matter jurisdiction.[20] This is healthy hedging in a tough area. Retaining such flexible standards would at least prevent a city court judge from giving away title to the Gen-

eral Electric Company, or a justice of the peace from rendering a divorce.

The Court of Appeals' holding in the *Friedman* case, that the second court's inquiry into the first's subject matter jurisdiction is always open when it turns only on a legal conclusion rather than on a determination of fact, would cover situations like the foregoing and thus give the second court leeway, at least in clearcut instances, to determine for itself whether the first court had subject matter jurisdiction, unbound by what the first court may have had to say on the point.

§ 456. Res Judicata for Administrative and Arbitral Decisions

It is becoming increasingly clear that parties to an administrative proceeding must bear in mind that the results of what they are participating in may have consequences beyond the proceeding. The Court of Appeals has been giving administrative determinations what appears to be increasing collateral estoppel (issue preclusion) effect. Developments on this front have been intense in recent years, traceable mainly to Ryan v. N.Y. Telephone Co.,[1] decided in 1984. Arbitration awards, too, have come in for some collateral estoppel treatment, as manifest in Matter of Ranni,[2] among other cases. The ensuing discussion may overlap topics not treated in detail until later, such as collateral estoppel[3] and identity of parties.[4] This is a by-product of accelerating developments in res judicata in the area of administrative and arbitral determinations in recent years. It should not be necessary, but some readers may be more comfortable scanning the footnoted sections before undertaking the present one.

It stands to reason that even determinations of tribunals other than courts must be given claim preclusion treatment, or they would have little value. Hence the general rule is that the determination of any tribunal vested

17.   24 N.Y.2d 528, 301 N.Y.S.2d 484, 249 N.E.2d 369 (1969).

  18.   28 U.S.C.A. § 1332.

  19.   See § 611 below (Practitioner's Edition).

  20.   Restatement of Judgments, Second, § 12(1).

§ 456

  1.   62 N.Y.2d 494, 478 N.Y.S.2d 823, 467 N.E.2d 487.

  2.   58 N.Y.2d 715, 458 N.Y.S.2d 910, 444 N.E.2d 1328 (1982).

  3.   See § 457 below.

  4.   See §§ 458–461 below.

with the power to conduct a hearing and decide an issue, whether a board, commission, agency, or the like, is entitled to the same claim preclusion treatment as a duly rendered judicial judgment.[5]

The administrative agency, which proliferates in this bureaucratic age, is the primary beneficiary of this rule. Res judicata appends to its quasi-judicial decisions,[6] as long as the agency is acting within its jurisdiction. Indeed, if it is, and the determination is given res judicata effect by the state it serves, it must also be given binding effect in other American jurisdictions to whatever extent the home jurisdiction dictates.[7]

It is not the claim preclusion aspect of the determination of a nonjudicial tribunal that has made waves in recent years, but the collateral estoppel (issue preclusion) aspect. Staying with the administrative determination for the moment (returning to the arbitration award later), we can take note of the major development, the *Ryan* case.

Ryan involved a misconduct finding made against a claimant in an administrative proceeding, which finding resulted in a denial of the unemployment benefits the claimant was seeking. The claimant then brought an action in court, trying to establish false arrest and like claims against his employer. The claims failed when the administrative finding of misconduct (theft from the employer) was allowed preclusion use against the claimant. The Court of Appeals applied the full and fair opportunity test that had evolved only a few years earlier[8] and found it satisfied in the hearing conducted before the agency, which in *Ryan* was the department of labor.

The case was controversial, for several reasons. One was that the employee had only a union official to represent him before the agency, not a lawyer. The Court of Appeals responded that this was the employee's choice; that he could have used a lawyer if he wanted to. The rejoinder from lawyers practicing before administrative agencies is that employees of modest means do not have so potentially expensive an option.

More important still is the argument that an administrative proceeding cannot be said to satisfy the "full and fair opportunity" requirement for a variety of reasons. The pretrial disclosure devices of Article 31 of the CPLR, for example, vaunted as the treasured source of truth-seeking and trial preparation in the courts, are unavailable before agencies. And the rules of evidence do not apply strictly in administrative proceedings. To some lawyers, *Ryan* means that procedural rights like these, jealously guarded in direct litigation, are being de-sanctified through the indirect format of the collateral estoppel doctrine applied to agency proceedings.[9]

The Court of Appeals appears nevertheless to be adhering to the basic view that the procedural weaknesses of the administrative process do not by themselves mean that a full and fair opportunity was lacking. Citing *Ryan* and applying the full opportunity test several years later in Allied Chemical v. Niagara Mohawk Power Corp.,[10] the court applied estoppel to an administrative determination, but it handed down on the same day two other cases in which estoppel was denied in a similar context.[11] The indication was that while the

---

5. Jones v. Young, 257 A.D. 563, 14 N.Y.S.2d 84 (3d Dep't 1939).

6. See Evans v. Monaghan, 306 N.Y. 312, 118 N.E.2d 452 (1954). By quasi-judicial is meant a decision following an administrative hearing, as opposed to such administrative functions as rule-making, investigation, etc.

7. See Magnolia Petroleum Co. v. Hunt, 320 U.S. 430, 64 S.Ct. 208, 88 L.Ed. 149 (1943). Thomas v. Washington Gas Light Co., 448 U.S. 261, 100 S.Ct. 2647, 65 L.Ed.2d 757 (1980), comes close to overruling the Magnolia case, but doesn't quite muster the votes for it. It does show, however, that Magnolia stands in some disrepute for requiring blind deference by a court in State Two to an administrative determination in State One, in apparent

disregard of State Two's own substantial interest in the resolution of the matters at issue.

8. See § 467 below.

9. A lead note in N.Y. State Law Digest No. 310 discusses the expanding uses of collateral estoppel in administrative contexts, including Ryan.

10. 72 N.Y.2d 271, 532 N.Y.S.2d 230, 528 N.E.2d 153 (1988).

11. Staatsburg Water Co. v. Staatsburg Fire District, 72 N.Y.2d 147, 531 N.Y.S.2d 876, 527 N.E.2d 754, and Halyalkar v. Board of Regents of the State of New York, 72 N.Y.2d 261, 532 N.Y.S.2d 85, 527 N.E.2d 1222, both decided on July 7, 1988, the same day as the Allied case.

basic rule of issue preclusion will apply to an administrative determination, it will apply only if the determination survives the scrutiny of the full opportunity test.[12]

An interesting historical note is that criticism of the *Ryan* case proved powerful enough to produce an amendment of Labor Law § 623, overruling the case in its unemployment insurance setting. Perhaps ironically, the amendment overrules the *Ryan* result only in the specific *Ryan* context: the unemployment insurance proceeding. The fact is, however, that the *Ryan* decision has impact far beyond that. The Court of Appeals used the *Ryan* facts as just a base, taking off from there into the general proposition that credits an administrative hearing as the virtual equal of a court hearing for estoppel purposes. In view of the legislative closing of the base, one might have expected the courts to ground some of the other craft that took off from it, but that does not appear to have happened. Or, to use another metaphor, the seed may have been tainted, but there was no recall of the seedlings.

Turning to the arbitration award, we may note that the claim preclusion doctrine clearly applies to it. The award gets res judicata treatment,[13] including even the award of a panel in a foreign nation if the parties have duly bound themselves to arbitrate there and the procedures followed comport with domestic notions of due process.[14] Any other conclusion would undermine the important and expanding arbitration process,[15] which has done much to prevent the total collapse of the overworked judicial process by drawing a good part of the dispute resolution business to itself.

The claim preclusion effect of arbitral awards made under hit-and-run coverage needs special consideration by lawyers if they

plan any kind of conventional common law action based on a vehicle accident. Should a vehicle other than the hit-and-run vehicle also be involved in the accident, for example, and an arguable claim of fault can be made against it (so as to permit a conventional action), the claim will be lost if the plaintiff applies for and gets an award under the hit-and-run coverage of any applicable insurance policy. So held a divided Court of Appeals in Velazquez v. Water Taxi, Inc.[16]

Applying the issue preclusion rule (the collateral estoppel doctrine) to an arbitration award is a more difficult matter than applying claim preclusion—more difficult even than with the administrative decision because the arbitration process has even fewer safeguards than the administrative process has. The substantive law, applicable in administrative proceedings, ordinarily does not apply in arbitration, and neither does the bulk of the state's procedural law, including the rules of evidence.[17] Nevertheless, the Court of Appeals has indicated that even an arbitration award may come in for issue preclusion treatment.

That appears to be the thrust of the *Ranni* case mentioned at the outset, in which an arbitration award, approving an employee's discharge, had found him insubordinate. The award was held to bind in a later administrative proceeding in which the employee sought unemployment benefits.[18] Benefits would fail if the employee was guilty of misconduct, and the insubordination finding imported from the arbitration was allowed to establish just that, and deny benefits.

Awards emanating from no-fault insurance arbitrations have also been making some of the law on this front. In one case, for example, a plaintiff involved in a vehicle accident sought

---

12. See the lead note in New York State Law Digest No. 344, comparing the three cases.

13. Bird v. Meadow Gold Products Corp., 60 Misc.2d 212, 302 N.Y.S.2d 701 (Sup.Ct., Kings County, 1969).

14. See Gilbert v. Burnstine, 255 N.Y. 348, 174 N.E. 706 (1931). While earning res judicata treatment, an arbitral award does not count as a precedent under the stare decisis doctrine because arbitrators are not bound by the rules of substantive law. See SCM Corp. v. Fisher Park Lane Co., 40 N.Y.2d 788, 390 N.Y.S.2d 398, 358 N.E.2d 1024 (1976).

15. Arbitration is the subject of Article 75 of the CPLR and is treated beginning in § 586 below.

16. 49 N.Y.2d 762, 426 N.Y.S.2d 467, 403 N.E.2d 172 (1980).

17. See § 586 below.

18. It would appear to make no difference that the award was being applied in an administrative proceeding instead of in a court. If the award has collateral estoppel effect in one direction it would presumably have it in the other as well.

no-fault benefits from her insurer for certain injuries but the arbitrator found that she did not sustain them. That finding was held to bind her when she then sought to recover in court for the same injuries from the other vehicle involved in the accident.[19]

That the Court of Appeals intends to retain issue preclusion effect for arbitral determinations is manifest in Clemens v. Apple,[20] in which, in a brief memorandum, the court cited and analogized to the *Ryan* case, as if there were nothing to differentiate arbitral from administrative proceedings. It stressed in *Clemens*, however, that the one against whom the estoppel worked was the party who chose arbitration as a forum, the implication being that an award would not bind a party, in the issue preclusion sense, if that party had no say in whether the claim would go to arbitration, as happens in the compulsory and quasi-compulsory arbitrations (of which no fault-arbitration is a variety) appearing in increasing numbers today.[21]

On the commercial side of arbitration, collateral estoppel was applied in Guard–Life Corp. v. S. Parker Hardware Mfg. Corp.[22] to allow one party in a court action, who was not a party to the arbitration, to make estoppel use of an arbitration finding against a person who was a party to both. P got an arbitration award against X for $75,000 for breach of contract, but was apparently unable to collect it. P then brought a court suit against D for inducing X's breach. D was allowed an estoppel in the action to the extent of limiting the amount of P's damages to $75,000. Thus was D, who was not a party to the arbitration, allowed to make use of its damages findings against P, who was. And the best of it from D's viewpoint is that because D was not part of the arbitration, he is himself not bound by the $75,000 damages figure and is hence free in the action to prove that P's damages are less.

This situation, which gives someone like D the best of both worlds, is not a rare phenomenon on the res judicata scene today.[23] Its counterpart for the other side, the one who was a party to both proceedings, is the worst of both worlds: being subject to estoppel use of negative aspects of the first proceeding while being barred from using its positive elements vis-a-vis one not a party to that proceeding. In Baldwin v. Brooks, for example,[24] another no-fault case in the tort area, P was hit by O's car (driven by D) and brought a no-fault arbitration against O's insurer and won on a causation issue. Then P brought a regular tort action against O and D and wanted an estoppel against them on that issue. The court held that P may not have it because O and D were not parties to the first action; their insurer was the party. Unlike ordinary liability coverage, where insurer and insured are in privity, in no-fault the insurer's obligation runs directly to the injured person and there is no link between insured and insurer sufficient to bind one to an adverse finding made in a proceeding involving the other. But the court observes (citing other decisions) that because P is a party to both proceedings, arbitral findings adverse to P may be used by a party to a later action who was not a party to the no-fault proceeding.

A point of special interest to attorneys involves the arbitration of fee disputes with clients. When lawyer and client agree to arbitrate their dispute about the lawyer's fee before a committee of a bar association, and the lawyer prevails in the arbitration, it has been held that the victory insulates the lawyer from an action for legal malpractice.[25]

E. COLLATERAL ESTOPPEL

Table of Sections

---

19. Kilduff v. Donna Oil Corp., 74 A.D.2d 562, 424 N.Y.S.2d 282 (2d Dep't 1980).

20. 65 N.Y.2d 746, 492 N.Y.S.2d 20, 481 N.E.2d 560 (1985).

21. See § 603 below.

22. 50 N.Y.2d 183, 428 N.Y.S.2d 628, 406 N.E.2d 445 (1980).

23. See § 460 below.

24. 83 A.D.2d 85, 443 N.Y.S.2d 906 (4th Dep't 1981).

25. See Altamore v. Friedman, 193 A.D.2d 240, 602 N.Y.S.2d 894 (2d Dep't 1993), noted in SPR 24:3.

§ 457. Collateral Estoppel, Introductory

The doctrine of collateral estoppel was at one time used principally in cases involving an indemnity relationship of some kind, often in conjunction with a vouching-in notice,[1] to assure that the indemnitor would be bound by the same findings that bound the indemnitee and to avoid what has been termed the "absurd result of having the indemnitor exonerated, while the indemnitee was held liable".[2] Today it has far broader range, no longer limited to indemnity or any other category; its expanded mission today is to implement in substantially all situations "the sound principle that, where it can be fairly said that a party has had a full opportunity to litigate a particular issue, he cannot reasonably demand a second one".[3] Unlike res judicata itself, which applies only when the same cause of action is repeated—and for which reason it often goes under the name of "claim preclusion" today—collateral estoppel applies when the second cause of action is distinct or different, and it applies to issues rather than to whole claims or defenses.[4] The Second Restatement calls it "issue preclusion" and notes that it applies alike to issues of fact and issues of law.[5]

On several previous occasions[6] mention was made of Schuylkill Fuel Corp. v. B. & C. Nieberg Realty Corp.,[7] an opinion by Judge Cardozo that is probably the most quoted on the distinction between res judicata and collateral estoppel. The part that succinctly states the difference is this:

A judgment in one action is conclusive in a later one, not only as to any matters actually litigated therein, but also as to any that might have been so litigated, when the two causes of action have such a measure of identity that a different judgment in the second would destroy or impair rights or interests established by the first.... It is not conclusive, however, to the same extent when the two causes of action are different, not in form only ... , but in the rights and interests affected. The estoppel is limited in such circumstances to the point actually determined....[8]

The first quoted sentence is the doctrine of res judicata, or claim preclusion; the next two are the doctrine of collateral estoppel, or issue preclusion. The estoppel inquiry is whether an issue involved here was disposed of there, and whether the party sought to be bound with it here was a party there, had a fair chance to have the issue determined in her favor there, and failed.[9]

F. IDENTITY OF PARTIES

Table of Sections

§ 458. Identity of Estopped Party

Collateral estoppel, or "issue preclusion", can often be used today by one who was not a party to the first action. An earlier rule known as "mutuality of estoppel" had held otherwise but has since been abandoned.[1] But the law is adamant that the doctrine may not be used against one who was not a party to the first action because that would deny that person a hearing[2] and raise issues of due process. So, for

---

§ 457

1. See § 168, above, for discussion of the vouching-in procedure.

2. Schwartz v. Public Administrator, 24 N.Y.2d 65, 69, 298 N.Y.S.2d 955, 958, 246 N.E.2d 725, 728 (1969).

3. Id.

4. Bonde v. General Security Ins. Co. of Canada, 55 Misc.2d 588, 285 N.Y.S.2d 675 (Sup.Ct., Albany County, 1967).

5. Restatement 2d, Judgments, § 27.

6. E.g., § 447, above.

7. 250 N.Y. 304, 165 N.E. 456 (1929).

8. 250 N.Y. at 306–307, 165 N.E. at 457.

9. Zabriskie v. Zoloto, 22 A.D.2d 620, 257 N.Y.S.2d 965 (1st Dep't 1965).

§ 458

1. On mutuality of estoppel, see § 460 below.

2. Cases in which a party may not have been joined individually but who had a representative as a stand-in are exceptions, the class action being one example of this. See § 454 above.

example, when a car and bus collide and the car driver sues the bus company in tort, is found innocent of contributory fault, and wins, the driver still cannot defend with that victory a later action brought against him by a bus passenger. The passenger was not a party to the earlier suit.[3] This means that the jury in the second action may, disagreeing with the jury in the first, find the car driver at fault.

It may, indeed. Inconsistencies like that are always a possibility when not all claims arising from an occurrence are tried together. Consolidation and joint trial can reduce the likelihood of such separate actions, but even those devices can work only when all claims are pending in the same court system. When several different courts are involved—federal and state courts, courts in different states, etc.— the prospects of inconsistency increase.

If the party to be estopped in action two was not a party to action one, she must at least be shown to be in "strict privity" with the party who lost in the first action.[4] Privity as used in this sense means a relationship of a kind that enables the court to be perfectly comfortable in visiting the consequences of the first action on the party to the second one. Some of these situations are obvious, such as decedent/representative, trustee/beneficiary, guardian/ward, committee/incompetent, and the like: clearly a judgment rendered in an action involving the representative is binding in a later action on the person represented.[5]

Even less obvious situations may be found to involve at base a relationship sufficient to invoke this "privity" concept, or whatever else one would call it. Control of the earlier litigation is the key feature. The Second Restatement holds bound one who, although not a party to the earlier action, "controls or substantially participates in the control" of the case presented by a party to the first action.[6] Whether the participation or control is ample

enough to generate the estoppel is at root a sui generis question and will be decided as such. Where an executor in the second action, for example, was found to have in fact controlled the first action, although not technically a party to it, he was bound by the judgment.[7] Control therefore satisfies as "privity" in the collateral estoppel sense.

So does a merger of interests. A corporation in the second action, for example, may be held bound by the results of the earlier action if a party to the earlier one was the sole or main shareholder of the corporation and the court is convinced on the facts that the one can be said to have been doing the bidding of the other.[8]

If two parties share interests in some respect but are not in privity in all respects necessary to satisfy the court of the fairness of applying the estoppel doctrine, it will not be applied. This is so even if the same person is nominally the party in both actions, a not infrequent occurrence in the insurance area when subrogation is involved. Suppose, for example, in a vehicle accident situation, that P collects from her own insurer for property damage and that the insurer, now subrogated to P, brings a proceeding in P's name to collect from the other car. The latter's win in that proceeding will not conclude P in P's separately brought personal injury action arising out of the same accident. P lacked control of the property damage claim, which was in the complete dominion of the insurer, and this divests the case of the needed "privity" or "control" or "participation" or whatever other word one wants to use when the court, on an analysis of the fairness factors, finds it unfair to work an estoppel.[9]

Being merely a witness in the first action, and even coming in with a lawyer and having the lawyer examine other witnesses during the trial, will not necessarily establish the needed

---

3. See Neenan v. Woodside Astoria Transp. Co., 261 N.Y. 159, 184 N.E. 744 (1933).

4. People v. LoCicero, 14 N.Y.2d 374, 251 N.Y.S.2d 953, 200 N.E.2d 622 (1964).

5. See Restatement 2d, Judgments, § 41; as to assignors and assignees, § 55.

6. Id. § 39.

7. Watts v. Swiss Bank Corp., 27 N.Y.2d 270, 317 N.Y.S.2d 315, 265 N.E.2d 739 (1970).

8. Warren v. County of Monroe, 51 Misc.2d 292, 273 N.Y.S.2d 107 (Sup.Ct., Monroe County, 1966).

9. See Anderson v. Snyder Tank Corp., 44 A.D.2d 761, 354 N.Y.S.2d 241 (4th Dep't 1974).

control to invoke this privity concept. So, where the driver of a car was not a party to the first action, although the owner and the other car's people were, the driver could not be bound by a judgment against the owner even though the driver was a witness in the earlier action and, more significantly still, even though the owner's liability was derivative of the driver's.[10]

If it is shown that a party's representation in the first action was inadequate and the circumstances are such as to suggest that the party was not responsible for this, she will not be bound. This does not mean that the party gets out from under merely because he had a poor lawyer; it takes a more unique circumstance than that. An example would be a tort situation in which the same driver is a defendant in one action and a plaintiff in another. As a defendant he will likely be represented by an attorney assigned by his insurance carrier; as a plaintiff, he will have his own lawyer. If the insurance policy substantially limits the insurer's liability and the defense falls short on effort, such as by "throwing in" the policy and foregoing appeal after an unfavorable verdict so as to avoid further expense, the court may refuse to hold the result binding in the second action, where the former defendant is now the plaintiff pursuing his own claim with his own lawyer. It may even happen that such separate actions will be consolidated, further obscuring things; the court can still cut through the morass, determine whether the representation was adequate, and withhold the estoppel if it was not.[11]

Analogously, a patient's lawsuit against a dentist for malpractice is not concluded by the dentist's exoneration of wrongdoing in a disciplinary proceeding. While the patient had filed the grievance that initiated the proceeding and testified at the hearing, where she appeared with her attorney, her participation was as a witness only: she was allowed no participation at all as the case went through administrative appeal steps. Under such circumstances the patient cannot be said to have had the kind of full and fair opportunity against the dentist that could estop her from pressing her case against him in the law action.[12]

When one person's claim is wholly derivative of another's, it has been held that a determination that the latter has no claim binds the would-be deriver whether or not she is a party to the determination. So, where a husband sued X for personal injuries and a jury found for X, his wife, although not a party, was bound by that determination and could not maintain a subsequent action against X for such derivative claims as the loss of her husband's services and consortium.[13]

§ 459. Different Capacities

If a person has several capacities, a judgment against that person in an action involving one capacity will not necessarily bind her in a second one involving the other. So, for example, if a person appears as a personal representative—executrix or administratrix—in action one, the judgment will not be binding when she pursues her rights as an individual in action two, and vice versa.[1] The assumption underlying this rule is that a proper job of representation necessarily entails a setting aside of one's individual interest, and vice versa, so that neither the fruits nor the consequences of a judgment rendered in the one capacity should bind in the other.[2] If the person appears in both capacities, however, interposing both individual and represented claims, such as a father suing for his child's personal injuries (a representative claim) as well as for the father's own medical expenditures or for

---

10. See, e.g., Willsey v. Strawway, 44 Misc.2d 601, 255 N.Y.S.2d 224 (Sup.Ct., Chemung County, 1963), aff'd 22 A.D.2d 973, 254 N.Y.S.2d 830 (3d Dep't 1964).

11. See, e.g., Huston v. DeLeonardis, 44 A.D.2d 110, 353 N.Y.S.2d 771 (1st Dep't 1974).

12. David v. Biondo, 92 N.Y.2d 318, 680 N.Y.S.2d 450 (1998). The case is the subject of the lead note in New York State Law Digest No. 468.

13. Fischbach v. Auto Boys, 106 N.Y.S.2d 416 (Sup.Ct., Kings County, 1951), rev'd on other grounds 279 A.D. 1035, 112 N.Y.S.2d 283 (2d Dep't 1952).

§ 459

1. Hellstern v. Hellstern, 279 N.Y. 327, 18 N.E.2d 296 (1938).

2. See Restatement 2d, Judgments, § 36, and its accompanying illustrations.

the loss of services of the child (individual claims), he will of course be bound in both capacities.

§ 460. Identity of Estopping Party; "Mutuality" of Estoppel

At one time, even though X had had a full day in court on a particular issue in the first action and lost on it, Y could not have a collateral estoppel on that issue against X in a second action if Y had not himself been a party to the first one. This was known as the doctrine of "mutuality of estoppel", and its predicate was that since X, had he won in the first action, could not have made any later estoppel use of his victory as against Y for the simple reason that Y has not yet been heard and thus could not be bound by the judgment, then Y should not be able to make any estoppel use of the judgment against X if X should lose. The mutuality doctrine was upheld by the Court of Appeals,[1] and was adhered to even when some rethinking appeared to be in order,[2] but it steadily lost credit until the Court of Appeals finally abandoned it entirely, declaring it a "dead letter" in B.R. DeWitt, Inc. v. Hall[3] in 1967. It is a dead letter today.

In *DeWitt*, a truck and jeep collided. The truck driver sued the jeep owner for personal injuries and won. The truck owner then sued the jeep owner for property damage and sought to make estoppel use of the truck driver's earlier victory. He was allowed it, notwithstanding that had the jeep owner won the earlier action he could not have used that victory against the truck owner because the truck owner was not a party to the first action.

The Court of Appeals said the test applied should be the identity of issue test[4] despite the absence of a total identity of parties, citing Israel v. Wood Dolson Co.,[5] a 1956 pronouncement of the court and a major development

along this line. *Israel* held that there is no need to show that the party seeking to use the estoppel was a party to the first action; that it is necessary to show only that the party against whom it is used in the second was a party to the first and thus had a full day in court on the issue there. In the first action in *Israel*, P had sued D for breach of contract and lost, no breach being proved. In the second action P sued X for inducing D's breach of the same contract. Although X was not a party to the first action, he was allowed an estoppel to establish that this contract had not been breached. A showing of a breach being an indispensable element to P's success in the second action, P lost the action because of the estoppel. *Israel* holds that it is not necessary for a party to have had a day in court against a particular litigant; it is sufficient that he had it on the identical issue.

Unbound by any adverse finding in the first action because not a party to it, while able to make use of a favorable finding emanating from it because for that purpose she does not have to be a party to it, a second-round party can today get for herself in some situations the best of two worlds. Where, for example, there are several parties involved in the first action, the nonparty can use collateral estoppel against a first-action loser while being immune to any use of it by a first-action winner.

Given the enthusiastic judicial use of devices like consolidation and joint trial if separate actions arising out of the same occurrence should be brought today, this best-of-both-worlds phenomenon should not be very frequent, but it can and does occur. Suppose, for example, that passenger A in car one is injured in a two-car collision and sues both drivers, winning only against the first driver. Then passenger B sues the same drivers. B can have an estoppel against the first driver, who lost in the first action, but the second driver, who

---

§ 460

1. See Haverhill v. International Ry. Co., 244 N.Y. 582, 155 N.E. 905 (1927), aff'g 217 A.D. 521, 217 N.Y.S. 522 (4th Dep't 1926).

2. See Elder v. New York & Pennsylvania M. Exp., 284 N.Y. 350, 31 N.E.2d 188 (1940). The Elder facts will be treated in the course of some tort examples later. See § 466.

3. 19 N.Y.2d 141, 278 N.Y.S.2d 596, 225 N.E.2d 195 (1967).

4. The identity of issue test is discussed in § 462 below.

5. 1 N.Y.2d 116, 151 N.Y.S.2d 1, 134 N.E.2d 97 (1956).

won in the first action, cannot have an estoppel against B.[6] B is therefore entitled to litigate afresh the second driver's liability, which of course opens the door to a conflicting determination.

One of the more frequent sources of separate actions, and potential conflicts, is the accident involving the liability of both the state, which can be sued only in the court of claims, and a private person, who must be sued in some other court.[7]

Mutuality's abandonment can create such anomalies, but they are easier to live with than a rule that arbitrarily mandates relitigation whenever parties are not totally parallel. The law today looks at the first action's loser and asks whether that person had a full hearing on the dispositive issue; if she had, it is of secondary importance that a nonparty may want to make use of it.

§ 461. "Privity"

Also necessary to put into perspective in a collateral estoppel (issue preclusion) discussion is the loose-limbed doctrine called "privity", which has wiggled in and out of the cases. Unlike "mutuality", which seemed easy to understand (agree with it or not), "privity" in collateral estoppel context was always muddy. When applied to the second-action party against whom the estoppel is sought to be used, "privity", as we have seen, has a clear enough meaning.[1] There, it takes on its traditional meaning, requiring a legal relationship of a kind that would allow the loss of the first action (or of an issue in it) by X to be justly visited upon Y in the second action. X as decedent and Y as X's personal representative would be an example. These are clear instances of what we know as "privity".

The murky area is where X in the second action is the one who wants to use the collateral estoppel. May X do so only if she has some

connection, some "privity", with a winner in the first action? The First Restatement said that before a person in the second action can be either the victim or the beneficiary of the first action's result, she must be shown to have been either a party to the first action or else "in privity" with a party.[2] The Second Restatement abandons that statement; it contains no counterpart for the "privity" rule,[3] at least insofar as it concerns the user of collateral estoppel.

New York joined early in the abandonment of the privity requirement when the estoppel was used only defensively in the second action, but the doctrine still hovered about when offensive use was sought. In Cummings v. Dresher,[4] for example, the driver of car one and his passenger sued the driver[5] of the second car for personal injuries. The passenger won but the first-car driver, found guilty of contributory negligence—at a time when any contributory negligence on the part of a plaintiff would bar the claim entirely—did not. In a subsequent action by the driver of the second car (the first action's defendant) against the driver and owner of the first car, the first-car owner, although not a party to the first action, was allowed a defensive estoppel against the second-car driver: the affirmative negligence found against the second-car driver in the first action was held to constitute contributory negligence against him in his posture as plaintiff in the second action, foreclosing his recovery. While a legal link of a kind that might be called "privity" could be found to exist between the owner and driver of the first car, that would not avail the owner in *Cummings* because the driver lost the first action. It was the passenger who won, and whose victory the owner was allowed to use. That had to mean either that there is "privity" between a car's owner and one who is a mere passenger in it,

6. See Jacobs v. Del Guercio, 67 Misc.2d 606, 324 N.Y.S.2d 773 (Sup.Ct., N.Y. County, 1971).

7. See § 470 below.

§ 461

1. See § 458 above.

2. Restatement 1st, Judgments § 83.

3. See also the Reporter's Memorandum at p. xii of Tentative Draft No. 2 of the Second Restatement.

4. 18 N.Y.2d 105, 271 N.Y.S.2d 976, 218 N.E.2d 688 (1966).

5. Both actions also involved the second car's owner, but the driver suffices for the example.

or, as seems more likely,[6] that "privity" is just not required, at least for an estoppel used defensively.

Despite that indication, the Court of Appeals in the later case of B.R. DeWitt, Inc. v. Hall,[7] in which estoppel was used offensively, still listed a kind of "privity" as a significant factor. A truck owner, suing a jeep owner for property damage in a collision, was allowed estoppel use of the truck driver's previous victory against the same defendant for personal injuries. When recapitulating the factors deemed significant in allowing the estoppel, the court in *DeWitt* mentioned that the truck owner "derived" his right from the driver, thus giving that link some significance even though adding that the owner and driver "do not technically stand in ... privity".[8]

The New York bar awaited further word. Was that kind of liaison, or something like it, whether labeled "privity" or something else, to remain a requirement for estoppel, or was it to expire at last? Its death knell, or at least a major tug at the bell, came in the Court of Appeals statement in Schwartz v. Public Administrator,[9] citing both *Cummings* and *DeWitt*, that the court has "already discarded, as irrelevant ... the fact that there may or may not have been any significant jural relationship between the party seeking to invoke the doctrine and the prior victor".[10] The final round, and the apparent interment of the privity doctrine, awaited the mid–1980s, when the Court of Appeals permitted the use of collateral estoppel by different victims of a multiparty accident. Until then, the privity concept had been one of the stalwarts in avoiding the problem of whether to allow (e.g.) a victory by passenger one to be used by the hundred other passengers involved in the same train or plane accident.[11]

It was not a vehicle accident case that finally met the issue head on, however; it was a blackout in New York City. After one citizen suffering damages in the blackout recovered a judgment against the grossly negligent electric utility, other citizens damaged by the same event were allowed a free estoppel ride on the liability issue. And shortly after that, a cancer-causing drug case added yet another nail to the privity coffin. When a woman damaged by her mother's earlier ingestion of a dangerous drug recovered a judgment from the drug's manufacturer, other women so damaged by the same drug were allowed to invoke the first one's victory on liability issues through the estoppel route. The blackout case is Koch v. Consolidated Edison Co. of New York.[12] The drug case is Kaufman v. Eli Lilly and Co.[13] Together they appeared to have written finis to the privity requirement.[14]

The "privity" concept in this context had no more relevance or utility than the "mutuality" doctrine had. If the New York courts have indeed abandoned it, they have done well. Insofar as it purports to require a link between a first action winner and a second action estoppel user, the privity notion under present lights is unnecessary. The identity of issue test, to which we next turn, seems able to offer the needed protection without help from "privity".

There remain cases, however, in which a link between the second-action user and the first-action winner, whether referred to as privity or anything else, continues to play an important role. In one interesting case, for example, an assaulted person was found to be in privity with the assaulter.

6. See the dissenting opinion in the Cummings case, 18 N.Y.2d at 110, 271 N.Y.S.2d at 979, 218 N.E.2d at 691.

7. 19 N.Y.2d 141, 278 N.Y.S.2d 596, 225 N.E.2d 195 (1967).

8. 19 N.Y.2d at 148, 278 N.Y.S.2d at 602, 225 N.E.2d at 189.

9. 24 N.Y.2d 65, 298 N.Y.S.2d 955, 246 N.E.2d 725 (1969). The Schwartz case is discussed more fully in § 467 below.

10. Id., 24 N.Y.2d at 70, 298 N.Y.S.2d at 958–9, 246 N.E.2d at 728.

11. See Example K in § 468 below.

12. 62 N.Y.2d 548, 479 N.Y.S.2d 163, 468 N.E.2d 1 (1984).

13. 65 N.Y.2d 449, 492 N.Y.S.2d 584, 482 N.E.2d 63 (1985).

14. The cases are treated in more detail later, in the discussion of the full and fair opportunity test. See § 467 below.

P was a shopkeeper shot by D. In a prosecution in which P testified for the state, D was convicted of the crime, including a finding that D was guilty of an intent to injure P. Then P brought a civil suit against D for damages for the assault and got a big default judgment against D. D resided with his parents, who had a homeowner's policy that covered D as an insured, and now P sued the insurer to have it make good on the judgment. The insurer disclaimed on the ground that the policy explicitly excluded coverage of an injury "intended by the Insured". The court sustained the disclaimer, holding that the criminal judgment established the insured's intent to injure and that the finding bound P, the court indicating that even if P had not testified at the criminal trial, P would have been estopped because P was in "privity" with D in respect of the insurance issue.[15]

In a later case, the court held that a patient's lawsuit against a dentist for malpractice was not concluded by the dentist's exoneration of wrongdoing by a disciplinary panel. While the patient had filed the grievance that initiated the disciplinary proceeding and testified at the hearing before the five-member panel, she was not allowed any other participation. The court said that the patient could not be said to have had the kind of full and fair opportunity against the dentist that could estop her from pressing her case against him in the law action.[16]

Can the cases be distinguished in that in the latter, the victim's contention at the administrative hearing (that the dentist was a malpractitioner) was consistent with her position in the court action, while in the first case the victim's testimony at the criminal trial indicated the wrongdoer's intent to harm, not at all consistent with the victim's later endeavor, in trying to get at the policy proceeds, to show that the wrongdoer had no such intent?[17]

---

15. D'Arata v. N.Y. Cent. Mut. Fire Ins. Co., 76 N.Y.2d 659, 563 N.Y.S.2d 24, 564 N.E.2d 634 (1990).

16. David v. Biondo, 92 N.Y.2d 318, 680 N.Y.S.2d 450 (1998), treated in the lead note in New York State Law Digest 468.

17. See the discussion of these cases in the lead note in New York State Law Digest No. 468.

G. IDENTIFYING THE ISSUE

Table of Sections

§ 462. Identity of Issue Test

If the first inquiry in any attempt to use collateral estoppel is whether it is being used only against one who has already had a day in court, then the second would have to be whether the issue on which the estoppel is sought was passed upon during that earlier court day. This is the identity of issue test, and two of its chief proponents are Israel v. Wood Dolson Co.[1] and Schwartz v. Public Administrator.[2]

In *Israel*, a commercial setting, an earlier holding that a plaintiff-defendant contract was not breached collaterally estopped the same plaintiff from contending in a second action that a breach was induced by one X. In *Schwartz*, a tort case, a passenger's recovery from both his own and the other car's drivers, establishing the negligence of both, estopped one driver from afterwards suing the other by importing as contributory negligence in the second action—at a time when the rule was that any contributory negligence on the part of the plaintiff barred the claim altogether—the affirmative negligence established in the first. In each instance the court carefully examined the issue on which estoppel was sought and satisfied itself that it was the same as the one passed upon earlier.

Examples today are numerous. P had a claim against the state because of an alleged trespass by a state contractor. P first sued the contractor in the supreme court, but the contractor won. P then sued the state in the court

---

§ 462

1. 1 N.Y.2d 116, 151 N.Y.S.2d 1, 134 N.E.2d 97 (1956).

2. 24 N.Y.2d 65, 298 N.Y.S.2d 955, 246 N.E.2d 725 (1969).

of claims. The state's liability was found to be derivative of the contractor's and since the contractor had none, then under collateral estoppel neither did the state.[3]

Sometimes it will happen that a dismissal on a seemingly jurisdictional ground will be found upon closer scrutiny to dispose of a piece of the merits as well—perhaps even enough to work an estoppel when the merits are met in another court later. Suppose, for example, that P sues D in a federal court alleging a federal constitutional violation. The basis of federal subject matter jurisdiction is that a federal question is involved. Assume that the federal court, looking into the matter, dismisses the action for want of a substantial federal question, as sometimes happens. It is presumably only a jurisdictional dismissal, but if the federal issue was found inadequate even for mere jurisdiction, how could a later court, which has secured jurisdiction, uphold the issue on its merits? The earlier judgment in that situation, whether purporting to be a mere jurisdictional dismissal or not, may well be given conclusive effect on the merits when the merits are reached in the second action.[4]

An inquiry into the nature of the issue must be a careful one. Sometimes a single statute or part of it can be the source of several kinds of dismissal, only some of which carry final estoppel consequences. A good example is the motion to dismiss for failure to state a cause of action under CPLR 3211(a)(7). The motion can be based either on the pleading's failure to verbalize a good claim (i.e., the pleading is defective on its face), or it can be based on the claim's lack of substantive merit, summarily established by affidavits and other proof even though the pleading on its face is fine. The first kind of dismissal will work an estoppel if the complaint in the second action is "virtually identical" to the complaint in the first,[5] but there will be no estoppel if the earlier pleading defect is remedied.[6] If the dismissal was of the second variety, establishing not just that the pleading was poor but that the plaintiff has no claim, it of course does get estoppel effect.[7] Today, under the Court of Appeals decision in Rovello v. Orofino Realty Co.,[8] this latter category of disposition is likely only if the court elected to treat the CPLR 3211(a)(7) motion as one for summary judgment.[9]

The burden of showing that the issue on which collateral estoppel is sought is the same as one disposed of in the earlier action is on the party who wants the estoppel. But if the resisting party, the one against whom the estoppel is sought, has anything to show to avoid the estoppel, such as that she did not have a full opportunity to contest the issue in the earlier action, the resister has the burden on that score and must go forward with it. So holds the *Schwartz* case,[10] a leading one in New York. *Schwartz* lists a number of factors for the court to consider in determining whether to award an estoppel—these will be explored when the multi-party tort cases are treated later[11]—and when one of these is cited by the party resisting the estoppel to get out from under it, that party carries the burden. Caselaw suggests with good reason that in the final analysis collateral estoppel is sui generis, that its "crowning consideration" is fairness, that rigidity has no place in its application, and that "all the circumstances" of the prior action must be examined to determine whether the estoppel is to be allowed.[12]

If the earlier judgment could have proceeded on any of several distinct facts or theories and it is unclear which of them actually accounts

---

3. Bronxville Palmer, Ltd. v. State of New York, 18 N.Y.2d 560, 277 N.Y.S.2d 402, 223 N.E.2d 887 (1966).

4. See Becker v. Levitt, 81 Misc.2d 664, 366 N.Y.S.2d 940 (Sup.Ct., Nassau County, 1975).

5. See McKinney v. City of New York, 78 A.D.2d 884, 433 N.Y.S.2d 193 (2d Dep't 1980).

6. See Allston v. Incorporated Village of Rockville Centre, 25 A.D.2d 545, 267 N.Y.S.2d 564 (2d Dep't 1966), which was an action. The same rule applies to a dismissed special proceeding. Searles v. Main Tavern, Inc., 28 A.D.2d 1136, 284 N.Y.S.2d 652 (2d Dep't 1967).

7. See § 276, above, and Commentaries C3211:67 and 68 on McKinney's CPLR 3211.

8. 40 N.Y.2d 633, 389 N.Y.S.2d 314, 357 N.E.2d 970 (1976).

9. See § 270 above.

10. Note 2 above.

11. See § 467 below.

12. Read v. Sacco, 49 A.D.2d 471, 375 N.Y.S.2d 371 (2d Dep't 1975).

for it, there can be no estoppel and the matter is open for litigation anew. If, for example, an earlier decision concerning a lease can be accounted for either by a finding that no such lease was made, or that it was made but its ostensible maker had no authority to make it, and the earlier record does not clarify which ground was used, neither can support an estoppel in the second action.[13]

An even more common source of this kind of problem has been the multi-party tort case in which use of estoppel in the second action is frustrated by the fact that a general verdict in the first action obscured the grounds that produced it. Suppose, for example, that P sues a car owner for personal injuries sustained in an accident, and two issues are litigated: whether the driver was negligent and whether the driver had permission to drive (which would be necessary in order to hold in the owner). The jury brings back a general verdict for the owner. The resulting judgment cannot be the source of a later estoppel on either of the two issues because it did not clarify precisely what the jury found on each: a finding in the owner's favor on either of the issues could adequately account for the judgment, depriving it of its clarity and hence its estoppel use.[14]

A special verdict embodying all of the jury's findings in the form of answers to questions would clarify the findings and expedite their use for estoppel purposes in later actions.[15] In this connection, the advent of New York's comparative negligence rule (replacing the contributory negligence rule), applicable to claims arising on or after September 1, 1975,[16] along with a number of other developments,[17] has diminished this kind of estoppel problem by increasing the use of special verdicts. The special verdict always supports issue preclusions better than a general verdict.

§ 463. Law and Fact, Ultimate and Evidentiary

When the whole of an issue arising in a second action was disposed of in the first one, and the lines of the issue in both contexts are identical, the estoppel doctrine applies with no difficulty. This is so whether the issue can be characterized as a legal one or a factual one, because collateral estoppel (issue preclusion) as a general rule applies to both kinds. Indeed, it would be untenable to permit the doctrine and its policies to be evaded merely by stamping the issue one of law rather than one of fact. The line between the two is often blurred.[1]

When the lines of the issue are not entirely parallel, and when there are some strands connected to it in the first action that do not adhere to it in the second, a closer scrutiny may be necessary to determine whether to invoke the doctrine. A good illustration of this problem and of its pragmatic resolution is Hinchey v. Sellers.[2] Simplifying the facts for purposes of illustration: X was a passenger in a car driven by D and owned by O. It went off the road in New York and X was killed. P was X's administrator and because D was a New Hampshire resident, P brought a wrongful death suit against D in a New Hampshire court. O was not a party there but it was claimed that O's insurance covered the accident. The insurer disclaimed, however, on the ground that D was driving without O's permission within the meaning of the policy. The issue was tested in a declaratory action in New Hampshire, involving P, D, and the insurer, and resolved in favor of the insurer: it was found that D did not have permission to drive the car and hence that the insurance did not cover.

In a later action in New York, P sued O on the same cause of action, O's liability being

---

13. Lewis v. Ocean Navigation and Pier Co., 125 N.Y. 341, 26 N.E. 301 (1890).

14. See Manard v. Hardware Mutual Casualty Co., 12 A.D.2d 29, 207 N.Y.S.2d 807 (4th Dep't 1960).

15. See Kret v. Brookdale Hospital Medical Center, 93 A.D.2d 449, 462 N.Y.S.2d 896 (2d Dep't 1983), aff'd 61 N.Y.2d 861, 473 N.Y.S.2d 970, 462 N.E.2d 147 (1984).

16. CPLR §§ 1411–1413.

17. See § 399 above.

§ 463

1. See Restatement 2d, Judgments, § 28, Comment b.

2. 7 N.Y.2d 287, 197 N.Y.S.2d 129, 165 N.E.2d 156 (1959).

predicated on New York's statute[3] imputing the driver's conduct to the owner when the car is driven with permission. O invoked collateral estoppel on that point, however, claiming that the lack of permission established in the New Hampshire action was conclusive upon P in this action as well. P countered that the issue was not the same; that while perhaps called "permission" in both instances, its scope and content was different in each: in the New Hampshire action the issue was permission under the insurance policy while in the instant action it was permission under the New York statute, and the "ultimate legal issue" was not necessarily the same.

The Court of Appeals agreed that the "ultimate legal issue" was not the same in both cases, but, digging into the detailed evidentiary findings on which the issue was resolved in the first action, the court found enough in its foundation to support an estoppel in the second action. Comparing the findings on which "permission" was found to be lacking under the insurance policy, in other words, with the findings necessary to establish want of "permission" under the New York statute, the court found the necessary parallels and upheld the estoppel. The "ultimate" issue was concededly not the same, because what would satisfy as "permission" under the insurance contract would not necessarily satisfy as "permission" under the statute. But this merely meant that the estoppel would not be automatic, that it would instead entail an examination of all the fact findings—the "evidentiary" details—on which the New Hampshire conclusion of non-permission was based, to see whether any one or a combination of them should happen to parallel one of the New York statute's constituents as well. The particular finding that did the job in *Hinchey* was New Hampshire's determination, one of many, that when O lent the car, the permission was conditioned on the borrower's not letting D into the car at all and that D was allowed into the car

in disregard of that stipulation. That destroyed "permission" under the insurance policy; upon independent later examination by the New York courts, it was found that such a violation would also undo "permission" under the New York statute. In that lay the parallel, and down came the estoppel.

The lesson is that an issue need not qualify as "ultimate" to invoke the estoppel. The doctrine will not be undone by a label. If an examination of the record, going into as much detail as need be, reveals that enough was determined—and fairly determined—in the first action to conclude an issue in the second, it is of secondary importance that the fact found to do the job is an "ultimate" fact or something less. Indeed, if we may draw an analogy to pleadings, the pre-CPLR distinction made between "ultimate" and "evidentiary" facts was found to be a useless pursuit and, with much profit, was abandoned.[4] A court can well point to that in the estoppel realm as well.[5] The disposition must be governed by the reality rather than the caption.

§ 464. Underlying Facts Bind, Litigated or Not

The concept usually met, and generally valid, in collateral estoppel ("issue preclusion") is that it will attach only to matters actually litigated, as opposed to claim preclusion (res judicata itself in its stricter sense), which will also foreclose matters that could have been litigated.[1] But now a qualification: the estoppel or issue preclusion doctrine will apply not only to matters actually litigated, but also to all that are necessarily established by the earlier judgment, litigated or not. Where a judgment of a particular kind can be accounted for legally only by the existence of a certain combination of findings, each of those findings will be deemed established by the judgment. A judgment of separation, for example, necessarily establishes that there was a valid marriage because without a valid marriage there is

---

3. Now § 388 of the Vehicle and Traffic Law.

4. See § 207 above.

5. The Second Restatement rejects the attempt to draw a line between ultimate and evidentiary facts, suggesting that the more appropriate question to ask is whether, whatever the label, the parties and fact trier recognized the issue as important and necessary and tried

and determined it accordingly. See Restatement 2d, Judgments, § 27, Comment j.

§ 464

1. Schuylkill Fuel Corp. v. B & C. Nieberg Realty Corp., 250 N.Y. 304, 165 N.E. 456 (1929).

nothing to separate. So, where H sued W for separation and won, and in a later action W sued H for annulment (which action seeks to establish that the marriage was not valid), the first judgment was deemed to establish the marriage's validity and W was estopped from claiming otherwise. The annulment action therefore failed.[2]

Similarly, P's judgment against D for negligent personal injury under the old rule of contributory negligence (which barred P from all recovery if found guilty of any negligence at all) necessarily established (1) that D was negligent and (2) that P was not. The estoppel could thereafter be exploited accordingly. The estoppel would attach to such a judgment even if it had been based only on a general verdict that did not expressly report its underlying findings, for the reason that no other combination of findings could legally explain the judgment. Note, however, that a contrary general verdict under the old contributory negligence rule—one in favor of D against P—would not lend itself to an estoppel because any of several sets of findings could explain it and the set actually used would not be known. (P was negligent and D was not; both were negligent; neither was. Any of these could account for a defendant's general verdict under a contributory negligence rule.[3])

A key lesson emerging from the foregoing is that when a given finding necessarily underlies a judgment, and the judgment's very existence can be explained only by assuming the fact to be thus and so, the fact may become the basis of an estoppel even if it was not litigated in the earlier action. Estoppel does not invariably demand that the point be shown to have been disputed in the first action. "Whatever is necessarily implied in the former decision, is

for the purpose of the estoppel deemed to have been actually decided", as are also "conclusions of law or fact, which necessarily flow from a judgment, although not expressly found."[4]

This phase of the estoppel rule can be summed up as a basic rule thus: any finding essential to the judgment constitutes a component of that judgment and lends itself to an estoppel.[5]

The estoppel can of course be met and offset today with a showing by the other side that the earlier action did not offer a "full and fair opportunity" to litigate the issue, such as for want of a stake big enough to make a vigorous defense worthwhile.[6] In Kossover v. Trattler,[7] for example, a judgment for a physician on a $750 claim against a patient for a fee was denied estoppel effect in the patient's later action against the physician for medical malpractice, even though recovery of the fee necessarily presumed the legitimacy of the medical service rendered. The first judgment in *Kossover* had been rendered by default.[8] In Chisholm–Ryder Co. v. Sommer & Sommer,[9] in contrast, the earlier adjudication occurred in a contested action by attorneys seeking a fee for their services. They were granted summary judgment for the fee and the judgment was given estoppel effect in a later action by the client, who was now attempting to show malpractice in the rendition of those services. The court said that "the prior action between these parties necessarily determined that services were performed by the attorneys for the client and that compensation was due them".[10]

§ 465. Gratuitous Findings

In the prior section we met the rule that a fact or conclusion that is a necessary part of a

---

2. Statter v. Statter, 2 N.Y.2d 668, 163 N.Y.S.2d 13, 143 N.E.2d 10 (1957). In Statter, it was alleged that newly discovered evidence undermined a fact found in the earlier action. That is not ordinarily an excuse to deny an estoppel. The remedy in that situation is a motion, made and captioned in the first action itself, to vacate the first judgment and reopen the case for a new trial. See CPLR 5015(a)(2); § 428 above.

3. The use of a special verdict avoids this problem by announcing all findings expressly. See the discussion towards the end of § 462.

4. Pray v. Hegeman, 98 N.Y. 351, 358 (1885).

5. Hinchey v. Sellers, 7 N.Y.2d 287, 197 N.Y.S.2d 129, 165 N.E.2d 156 (1959).

6. See § 467, below, and more particularly items 2 and 4 on the list of factors enumerated there.

7. 82 A.D.2d 610, 442 N.Y.S.2d 554 (2d Dep't 1981).

8. See the discussion of this point in the concurring opinion of Justice Gibbons in Kossover, id.

9. 78 A.D.2d 143, 434 N.Y.S.2d 70 (4th Dep't 1980).

10. When lawyer and client agree to arbitrate their dispute about the lawyer's fee before a committee of a bar association, and the lawyer prevails in the arbitration, it judgment will be entitled to an estoppel even if it was not actually litigated. We now meet the converse: even an issue actually litigated may be denied the estoppel if it was not necessary to the judgment.

To earn an estoppel, a fact must be shown to be material and relevant to the resolution of the legal issue involved in the first action.[1] Gratuitous findings will not support an estoppel. Where, for example, W sued H for abandonment but did not make out a ground, judgment for H became appropriate dismissing the abandonment charge without further ado. When the court went further, therefore, and found affirmatively that it was W who abandoned H, the finding was deemed gratuitous and barred from estoppel use.[2] One basis for this rule is that once enough has been found to justify a judgment, further findings lose their decisiveness and hence do not invite the responsibility, care, and attention that all judicial findings deserve. Estoppel, in other words, does not apply to unessential facts, and this is so even though they may be put in issue by the pleadings and directly decided.[3]

While that would appear to be the general rule, an exception may have to be carved out today if on the facts of a given case a finding may have been technically "gratuitous", but is found to have been the product of much "care and attention" by the trial judge. The apprehensions underlying the "gratuitous finding" rule—the fear that deliberation will be lax because the result lacks impact—are apparently not at hand in that situation. So indicates Malloy v. Trombley,[4] unless the case is to be put down as strictly sui generis.

A and B in *Malloy*, claimants in different cars involved in the same accident, sued the state in the court of claims but made out no case. When the judge dismissed as against the state, he then found, gratuitously, that both A and B were contributorily negligent. The record indicated such careful deliberation in his doing so, however, that the finding was allowed estoppel use in a supreme court action between A and B, where, under the rule of contributory negligence applicable at the time, it resulted in a dismissal.[5]

Shortly after *Malloy*, the Court of Appeals distinguished it in O'Connor v. G & R Packing Co.[6] on the basis that in *O'Connor* a finding of fault on the part of P was just a general statement made by the court on dismissing at the end of P's case. Thus a different defendant, now sued by P in respect of the same accident, could not invoke the earlier judgment against P.

Sometimes the rule against awarding an estoppel to what the court deems "unnecessary" findings will be invoked even when the finding seems relevant and material to the first action. This is especially so when the issue was resolved against the party who won the first action. The case of Karameros v. Luther[7] will illustrate. W sued H for separation but lost when the court found that a separation ground was not made out. The court also found that there was a valid marriage between the parties. Then H sued W for annulment on the ground that W lacked capacity to marry (because she already had an undivorced husband). W defended on the ground that the earlier action had found that her marriage with H was valid and that this estopped H from plead-

---

has been held that the arbitration victory insulates the lawyer from an action for legal malpractice. See Altamore v. Friedman, 193 A.D.2d 240, 602 N.Y.S.2d 894 (2d Dep't 1993), noted in SPR 24:3.

§ 465

1. Zabriskie v. Zoloto, 22 A.D.2d 620, 257 N.Y.S.2d 965 (1st Dep't 1965).

2. Silberstein v. Silberstein, 218 N.Y. 525, 113 N.E. 495 (1916).

3. Id., and cases there cited.

4. 50 N.Y.2d 46, 427 N.Y.S.2d 969, 405 N.E.2d 213 (1980).

5. Today, under the comparative negligence rule, a dismissal would not be the result unless perhaps the finding was of 100% fault of the party who is plaintiff in the supreme court. But should the court of claims allot precise percentages of fault between A and B, or among A, B, and the state, the allotment between A and B might be available for estoppel use in the supreme court action by extrapolation.

6. 53 N.Y.2d 278, 440 N.Y.S.2d 920, 423 N.E.2d 397 (1981).

7. 279 N.Y. 87, 17 N.E.2d 779 (1938).

ing now that it was not. The court held that H was not estopped; it found that although the validity of the marriage may be an indispensable part of a judgment that grants a separation,[8] in the context of the earlier judgment here, which denied the separation, it was an unnecessary finding.

How can one justify this? A finding on the validity of a marriage is hardly an irrelevant item in a separation action, whichever way the case may go. Is there some magic order in which issues must be tried? There is not, but the result in *Karameros* can be defended on a different ground. In *Karameros*, it was W, the loser in the first action, who in the second action wanted an estoppel on the marriage issue against H, the earlier winner. Suppose, however, that while H was the winner of the first action, H seriously disputed the finding of the marriage's validity, contending throughout the first action that the marriage was invalid. What could H do after the court had found against him on the issue and held the marriage good? H presumably could not appeal, because final judgment nonetheless went in his favor (for W's failure to spell out a ground for separation). As the winner, H would lack aggrieved status sufficient to take an appeal, with the result that the adverse finding on the marriage issue would stand against him without his being able to secure appellate review.

A full day in court in New York practice includes the appellate process if the loser wants it, and a situation in which an appeal is foreclosed can thus be regarded as an inadequate day in court. The Restatement takes that position, too, holding that the estoppel will not apply against a person who could not have obtained appellate review of the earlier judgment.[9]

H. MULTIPARTY SITUATIONS

Table of Sections

§ 466. Multiparty Situations; a Perspective

The extent to which one not a party to the first action may make estoppel use of something coming out of it has already been discussed. The topic of "mutuality" covered it.[1] And the topic of "privity" treated whether such an aspiring user would have to show at least some kind of relationship to the person who prevailed in the first action.[2] Framing those subjects, as it does just about everything in the realm of collateral estoppel, or "issue preclusion", is the rule that the issue sought to be foreclosed must be shown to be the same in both actions. That also had its own section.[3] The ensuing treatment of multiparty situations will involve those topics and will review them, but the reader turning to the present section may find it helpful to review those earlier sections to strengthen perspective for this one. Although by no means unique to tort—multiparty problems of course arise in commercial and property and other settings as well—the tort area, with its calendar-dominating vehicle cases, has in recent decades been the most active and even volatile area of collateral estoppel in New York practice. And so it ends up with the lion's share of our attention.

For a while the courts drew a distinction between what they regarded as "defensive" versus "offensive" use of collateral estoppel, allowing the estoppel in the first category in certain situations but not in the second. Good Health Dairy Products Corp. v. Emery,[4] a 1937 Court of Appeals decision, allowed an estoppel to a vehicle owner, the defendant in action two, based on a victory his driver had against the other vehicle in the first action. The own-

---

8. See Statter v. Statter, 2 N.Y.2d 668, 163 N.Y.S.2d 13, 143 N.E.2d 10 (1957); § 464, above.

9. Restatement 2d, Judgments, § 28(1).

§ 466

1. See § 460 above.

2. See § 461 above.

3. See § 462 above.

4. 275 N.Y. 14, 9 N.E.2d 758.

er, who was not a party to the first action, was using estoppel "defensively", i.e., to escape liability as a defendant. Shortly afterwards, the Court of Appeals in Elder v. New York & Pennsylvania Motor Express, Inc.,[5] refused to allow "offensive" use of an estoppel in a similar context. It was another collision case. The owner of vehicle one sued the owner of vehicle two for property damage and won. The driver of vehicle one, not a party to the first action, then sued ("offensive" use) the same defendant for personal injuries and sought an estoppel based on the owner's victory in the first action. The Court denied the estoppel, distinguishing the *Good Health* case because there the estoppel was used as a shield while in *Elder* the driver was trying to use it as a sword. While the Court of Appeals had been willing to carve out an exception to the mutuality rule so as to allow defensive use of estoppel by a first-action nonparty, it was not willing to make a similar exception for offensive use, so mutuality ruled the roost in *Elder* and estoppel was refused.

Not until 1967, when B.R. DeWitt, Inc. v. Hall[6] finally interred the mutuality doctrine, did the Court of Appeals firmly align itself behind even offensive use of estoppel by those not parties to the first action. The driver of car one sued the driver of car two for personal injuries and won. The owner of car one then sought to use that victory to establish the same defendant's liability in a later action for property damage. Removing the barrier of mutuality, the court allowed the estoppel. The immediate question that came to the fore was whether *Elder* was overruled.[7] It was not, and for yet other reasons it is not at all clear that *Elder* is passe. In *Elder*, the first action was by the vehicle owner for property damage and the second action by the driver for personal injuries; in *DeWitt*, it was the other way around. The dissent in *DeWitt*[8] stressed this distinction, warning that while it might be permissible to bind a defendant to the result of a substantial personal injury action—when it is the first one brought, as it was in *DeWitt*—it does not at all follow that the defendant should be similarly bound by the result of a property damage action if that is the initial suit, as it was in *Elder*. The stakes are different, for one thing. It may be more provident to interpose against a modest property damage claim an equally modest defense, and to let the office novice try the case for the experience rather than bring out the senior trial lawyers, whose fees would be disproportionate to the damages claimed. To bestow an estoppel on the result, however, when the much higher stakes of a personal injury claim are later involved, would be unfair, although it may be quite fair in reverse circumstances—where the first action was on a substantial personal injury claim and was vigorously defended—to allow an estoppel from that one to bind the later and presumably more nominal property damage claim.

In a given case even those ideas can reverse themselves, suggesting an estoppel for a property damage claim involving a solid gold sports car and a fortune in damages so as to make it bind a later personal injury claim amounting to less money. There are a myriad of individual factors to consider on a case by case basis, in other words, before a court can make a sound judgment on whether to work an estoppel, and this is the warning of the three-judge dissent in *DeWitt*. The majority of four take this warning to heart, for at the end of the majority opinion in *DeWitt* are a number of individual factors that the court carefully lists and finds satisfied.

Those factors amount to what is in essence a checklist for the judges to consult and apply in every analogous estoppel case. The list will be parsed and its items treated individually in the next section, entitled "the full and fair opportunity test". Stretched with additional items

---

5. 284 N.Y. 350, 31 N.E.2d 188 (1940).

6. 19 N.Y.2d 141, 278 N.Y.S.2d 596, 225 N.E.2d 195 (1967).

7. A case clearly overruled by DeWitt is Haverhill v. Int'l Ry. Co., 244 N.Y. 582, 155 N.E. 905 (1927), whose result was dictated entirely by want of mutuality.

8. 19 N.Y.2d at 148, 278 N.Y.S.2d at 602, 225 N.E.2d at 199.

from Schwartz v. Public Administrator[9] and further expanded with items from yet other cases and from the Restatement, the list is today the essence of collateral estoppel, or "issue preclusion", in multiparty situations. It is a sui generis consulting table designed to avoid arbitrary conclusions and enable an intelligent judgment to be made only after weighing the factors present in the particular case. It will necessarily require a more thoughtful effort by advocates and a more sensitive analysis by judges than was required earlier, but that is a small price to pay to be rid of such arbitrary and often irrelevant dogmas as "mutuality" and "privity", "offensive use" and "defensive use", and other like notions that were once allowed to block a thoughtful application of the collateral estoppel doctrine.

§ 467. The Full and Fair Opportunity Test; Factors to Consider

When seeking to apply collateral estoppel (issue preclusion) in multiparty cases, lawyers and judges must keep at hand today a long list of factors to consider on a case by case basis. The components, while not restricted to multiparty cases, are especially relevant to them, so all are listed here even though they may have bearing as well in other instances not involving multiple parties. The components are principally drawn from B. R. DeWitt, Inc. v. Hall,[1] from Schwartz v. Public Administrator,[2] from the factors listed in the Second Restatement,[3] and from other cases suggesting elements warranting individual treatment. For convenience and for later reference, it will be helpful to number the items treated. And to the end that as many factors as possible may be listed, we will risk some overlapping by making the list profuse.

1. *Sameness of issue*. It will always be necessary to determine that the issue is the same in both actions. The majority in *DeWitt* stressed this, finding that the issues as framed by the pleadings in that case were the same as those in the earlier action.

The *Schwartz* case offers a good illustration here. In *Schwartz*, a passenger in one vehicle sued the drivers of both vehicles and won against both. The contributory negligence rule, barring all recovery by a plaintiff guilty of any negligence at all, was applicable at the time, and so, in the second action, when driver one sued driver two, the latter sought to import and establish as contributory negligence against driver one in the second action the affirmative negligence found against both drivers in the first action. The courts had said no to this for years,[4] suspicious that the issues were not necessarily the same; that the negligence of the drivers vis-a-vis a passenger was not necessarily negligence as to one another. Satisfying themselves that the negligence issue was the same in both actions, i.e., that the negligence of both drivers as against the passenger was also negligence as against one another, the court in *Schwartz* overruled earlier caselaw and allowed the estoppel.[5]

The door is always open to a showing that the issues differ, however, no matter how alike they may seem on the surface. Suppose, for example, that G is a teenage girl driving a car with P, a passenger. The car is chased by F, G's father, on a disciplinary mission but at so high a rate of speed that an accident occurs, killing P. P's estate sues both G and F and recovers judgment against both. Then G sues F, her father, who pleads that the negligence established in P's favor against both F and G in the earlier action constitutes contributory negligence—the contributory negligence rule

9. 24 N.Y.2d 65, 298 N.Y.S.2d 955, 246 N.E.2d 725 (1969).

§ 467

1. 19 N.Y.2d 141, 278 N.Y.S.2d 596, 225 N.E.2d 195 (1967).

2. 24 N.Y.2d 65, 298 N.Y.S.2d 955, 246 N.E.2d 725 (1969).

3. Rst., 2d, §§ 28 and 29.
4. See, e.g., Glaser v. Huette, 232 A.D. 119, 249 N.Y.S. 374 (1st Dep't), aff'd 256 N.Y. 686, 177 N.E. 193 (1931).
5. A thoughtful dissent by Judge Bergan in the Schwartz case, 24 N.Y.2d at 76, 298 N.Y.S.2d at 964, 246 N.E.2d at 732, suggests that still other factors must be considered, especially in regard to jury sympathy based on the differing contexts of the two actions. See the discussion under item 10 later in this section.

was still at work in this case—against G in the context of the second action, barring it.

Does it bar the second action? The court can well find on facts like these that the negligence issues are not the same; that the duty owed by G to P may have been found breached in respects not applicable to the duties existing between G and F; that it may have been reasonable for G to run for her life from F, but negligent to take P with her, a ground that might explain P's victory against G in the first action but which might count in G's favor when interposed between G and F in the second. In short, the issues of duty and breach can be deemed different and, if they are, there is no estoppel.[6] Issue sameness is one of the primary colors in the estoppel spectrum.

2. *Vigor of defense in first action.* This is on the *DeWitt* list. The court there notes that the earlier action was in fact defended with full vigor. (We may add that in *DeWitt* there was every reason to put in a strong defense because the earlier action was the personal injury claim, the one with the higher stakes.) The door must be kept open to a showing that the defense in the earlier action was not vigorous, presumably with a citation of some reason (e.g., small stakes) to justify the laxity. A harassment conviction in a city court, for example, was denied estoppel effect in a later civil action for damages against the same defendant for the reason that the earlier action was a "relatively minor" nonjury case and the defendant could not have been expected to defend it vigorously.[7]

Another example may be where X as a defendant in an earlier action was represented by a lawyer assigned by X's insurer, as happens in tort litigation, while in the present action X is a plaintiff appearing through a lawyer of her own choice. The mere fact of different lawyers will not ipso facto avoid an estoppel, but if any laxity or patent indiffer-

ence or incompetence on the part of X's lawyer in the first action can be demonstrated, the court would lend an ear to that when considering whether to allow an estoppel in the second.

3. *Link between #2 user and #1 winner.* This is the old "privity" business in its most disorderly sense. The *DeWitt* majority gave it at least passing mention,[8] but it has apparently left the scene almost entirely since then. For a long time it appeared to be the main barrier to the use of collateral estoppel in mass accident cases. Where, for example, 50 bus passengers are injured in an accident and passenger one sues and wins on the issue of the carrier's fault, the want of a link to the winner would have precluded use of estoppel by the 49 other passengers. Then, following *DeWitt*, the Court of Appeals said in the *Schwartz* case itself that it has "discarded, as irrelevant to a proper consideration of the issues in this area, the fact that there may or may not have been any significant jural relationship between the party seeking to invoke the doctrine and the prior victor".[9] Then in the 1980s came the *Koch*[10] and *Kaufman*[11] cases, mentioned earlier,[12] stressing the identity of issue and full opportunity tests and dispensing with any "privity" or other link between the first action winner and the second action user. Both cases involved mass torts.

Koch involved the vast New York City blackout of 1977. A grocer afterwards sued for food spoilage and, winning, established the gross negligence of the defendant, the electric utility. The Court of Appeals held in *Koch* that all others damaged by the blackout may, in their own suits, make estoppel use of the liability issue against the utility. The court reviewed the elements of the full and fair opportunity test and found them met, notably in the fact that the utility knew of the collateral estoppel potential and had every incentive to defend the grocer's suit "fully and vigorously".

6. See Terwilliger v. Terwilliger, 52 Misc.2d 404, 276 N.Y.S.2d 8 (Sup.Ct., Tompkins County, 1966).

7. Gilberg v. Barbieri, 53 N.Y.2d 285, 441 N.Y.S.2d 49, 423 N.E.2d 807 (1981).

8. See § 461 above.

9. Note 2, above, 24 N.Y.2d at 70, 298 N.Y.S.2d at 958–9, 246 N.E.2d at 728.

10. Koch v. Consolidated Edison Co. of N.Y., 62 N.Y.2d 548, 479 N.Y.S.2d 163, 468 N.E.2d 1 (1984).

11. Kaufman v. Eli Lilly and Co., 65 N.Y.2d 449, 492 N.Y.S.2d 584, 482 N.E.2d 63 (1985).

12. See § 461 above.

In the *Kaufman* case, another major statement by the Court of Appeals on the "offensive" use of collateral estoppel by nonparties to the first action, the Court of Appeals indicated that the plaintiff, who claimed to have developed a cancerous condition because of her mother's ingestion years earlier of the drug DES, could be permitted estoppel use of a prior plaintiff's victory against the same defendant (a drug company) on a similar claim.[13]

4. *Size of claim*. This was mentioned in the second item listed above, but we give it independent mention here because it is expressly listed as a factor in the *Schwartz* case. It connotes, simply, that if the earlier claim was a small one, the court is free to determine whether it was too small to earn an estoppel treatment for its result.

5. *Forum of prior litigation*. *Schwartz* lists this. The fact that the earlier adjudication comes from a different court, however, or even from a different court system—federal, sister-state, or foreign country—will not often be a factor against estoppel, but it must be kept open to investigation. If, for example, an adjudication for a substantial sum comes from a court in which procedure is lax and informality the norm (even the town and village courts, which are staffed mainly by nonlawyers, have up to $3000 civil jurisdiction today), a court in the second action should be allowed to weigh that fact before giving the judgment scope beyond its own contemplation.[14] Similarly, if a judgment comes from a court system of a foreign country about whose procedures we know little[15] or whose jurisprudence is at all suspect, a more trenchant investigation is in order. This factor expressly authorizes the investigation. Several later sections treat more specific problems met when different courts are involved.[16]

6. *Use of initiative*. This is on the *Schwartz* list. It overlaps size of claim (the fourth item above), since size of claim will often affect initiative, and vigor of defense (the second

item above). Whatever factor the party against whom the estoppel is sought can show to justify a want of initiative in the earlier action, the door is open to the showing. This has perhaps extra importance in New York, where a default judgment has also been held entitled to collateral estoppel use.[17] While the general rule may be to that effect, a showing that the earlier judgment was rendered by default can be a weighty factor in convincing the second court to deny it estoppel effect.[18]

7. *Extent of the litigation*. This is another item from the *Schwartz* list, and again it overlaps previously listed items. This one can be deemed to take in a hitherto unmentioned element: the context from which the issue, sought to be precluded, emerges in the first action. If the issue had its own clear niche there, meriting and getting appropriate attention, it may earn an estoppel. If on the other hand it was obscured by a mass of other issues in a complicated or prolonged litigation, the court would be free to find it too inadequately considered to deserve estoppel treatment.

8. *Competence and experience of counsel*. The *Schwartz* list recognizes this factor, which must have special bearing in the situation mentioned in item two, above: where the party is appearing with a lawyer of her own choice in the second action while having been represented by a lawyer assigned by her insurance company in the first. An example would be where a passenger sues driver one and wins when driver one is found to be at fault. Then driver one sues driver two, also involved in the accident, who pleads estoppel. Driver one shows that the lawyer assigned to defend her in the earlier action by the passenger was inexperienced and ineffective. On such a showing, the estoppel may be denied.

9. *Availability of new evidence*. This item from the *Schwartz* list confirms that it may sometimes be permissible to deny an estoppel to a previously decided issue on the ground

---

13.   Kaufman posed a different problem, which precluded a simple estoppel. See the discussion under #16, below.

14.   See Restatement 2d, Judgments, § 29(2).

15.   See Restatement 2d, Judgments, § 28(3).

16.   See §§ 469, 470, and 471, below.

17.   See § 451 above.

18.   See the concurring opinion in Kossover v. Trattler, 82 A.D.2d 610, 442 N.Y.S.2d 554 (2d Dep't 1981).

that new evidence has since come to the fore in the interim, which could have changed the result. In an earlier case by X against D, for example, D may have been found liable for damages caused by a certain drug. By the time Y brings suit against D for damages caused by the same drug, a new test may have been devised establishing the drug as harmless. Collateral estoppel will not preclude the new evidence.[19] This basis for refusing an estoppel will usually be restricted to multiparty situations. Contrast the situation in which the parties involved are the same in both actions, in which event the courts prefer that the new evidence be made the basis for a motion to vacate the first judgment (and have the earlier action retried) rather than used to ground a refusal, in a second action, to accord the earlier judgment an estoppel.[20]

10. *Indication of compromise verdict.* If it appears that there was some ingredient in the earlier verdict to suggest that it was a compromise—based, for example, on sympathy or prejudice rather than strictly responsive to the law as applied to the evidence—the *Schwartz* case says that this can be considered by the court in determining whether to award an estoppel.[21] Relevant here is a point made by the dissent in the *Schwartz* case, where a passenger in car one first sued the drivers of both vehicles and won against both. Then, when one of the drivers sued the other, the majority allowed an estoppel to establish the plaintiff driver as contributorily negligent and to bar his recovery. His injuries were serious, the dissent pragmatically noted, and if he had been able to sue the other driver without having been first sued by a passenger, he would likely have won before the jury. He was thus being penalized by the coincidence that there happened to be a passenger, in whose action against both drivers the jury's sympathy would tend to favor the passenger.[22] This

does not suggest a compromise verdict, but rather a verdict influenced by sympathy. Indeed, in the view of the *Schwartz* dissent, the problem was perhaps just the opposite: sympathy such as might have favorably disposed the jury towards the driver was allowed too small rather than too large a role in the earlier action, in which the driver's injuries were not in issue. Whatever it was, it is obvious that it did not persuade the majority of the Court of Appeals in *Schwartz*.

The major appearances of the compromise and sympathy factors in tort litigation were found during the reign of the old rule of contributory negligence. They have less significance under New York's current rule of comparative negligence, which is built on compromise: each side sustaining its share of fault and damages being adjusted accordingly.

11. *Differences in applicable law.* Suppose that injured persons come from several states, and actions have been brought in two of them. Assume further that each state has a different rule, one a rule of comparative and the other a rule of contributory negligence, and that each, under choice of law principles applicable in the conflict of laws, is free to apply its own rule and chooses to. Suppose that the earlier action from which the estoppel is sought was tried under a contributory negligence rule, which allowed the jury to find for the plaintiff only by finding the plaintiff altogether free from fault. That may have encouraged the jury to impose fault on the defendant for the whole of the occurrence, while a jury allowed to apply a comparative negligence rule might at least have made a pro rata reduction in the share of fault allotted to the defendant. It might then be unfair to allow other plaintiffs suing the same defendant to claim an estoppel imposing total fault on the defendant if a comparative

---

19. See Vincent v. Thompson, 50 A.D.2d 211, 377 N.Y.S.2d 118 (2d Dep't 1975).

20. CPLR 5015(a)(2). See Statter v. Statter, 2 N.Y.2d 668, 163 N.Y.S.2d 13, 143 N.E.2d 10 (1957); § 464, above.

21. An argument that the verdict in the earlier action was a compromise verdict was attempted in the Kaufman case, note 11 above, but did not work. See the discussion

of Kaufman in the lead note in New York State Law Digest No. 309.

22. The Restatement might include these phenomena in what it describes as "imperfections in the adjudicative process", and would allow their consideration so as not to extend them unduly by allowing them to dictate in the second action as well as the first. See Restatement 2d, Judgments, § 29, Comment g.

negligence rule is applicable in the later case. This would illustrate what *Schwartz* calls "differences in the applicable law".

An intervening change in the law, such as to suggest a different result under the rule now applicable than that reached under the prior rule, is also a ground on which to deny an estoppel.[23]

12. *Foreseeability of future litigation*. This last item on the *Schwartz* list is also on the Restatement's, which terms the situation possible but considers lack of foreseeability "rare".[24] Lack of foreseeability should therefore be a significant factor only when the context is such that the court can readily accept a party's claim of surprise, e.g., when a reasonably attentive lawyer diligently going about her business could not be expected to contemplate that what is being done here now can have repercussions there later. When many have been damaged by a tort, the tortfeasor usually knows it. In the *Koch* case, for example,[25] in which a utility was held bound by a finding of liability for blackout damages suffered by a grocer, the court stressed the fact that the utility knew of the collateral estoppel potential of the earlier action and had every incentive to defend the grocer's suit "fully and vigorously".

13. *Different burdens of proof*. Passenger P sues drivers A and B and wins against A but not B. It may be that the jury did not find by a fair preponderance of the evidence that B was free of negligence, but merely that the evidence was evenly divided;[26] and that, because P had the burden of proof on the issue of B's negligence, P simply failed to sustain it. Now B sues A and seeks an offensive estoppel. It would be permissible to allow it to B to the extent of establishing A's affirmative negligence, a commodity reasonably importable

from the first action, but should B have it on the issue of B's own negligence as well (exonerating B from any charge of fault and precluding A from showing otherwise)? No fair preponderance of the evidence having yet established whether and in what degree B was negligent, it would remain an open issue in the second action, requiring litigation.[27]

14. *Avoidance of prejudice by joinder*. The Restatement lists for consideration the availability of joinder-of-party devices in the first action.[28] It mentions intervention,[29] for example, but there is little indication from New York caselaw that one not a party to the first action should be denied estoppel use of its result merely because he might have intervened in that action.[30] This item has so far been given little weight in New York estoppel law.

15. *Inconsistency of prior determinations*. The Restatement suggests that consideration be given to whether the determination sought to be made binding here was itself inconsistent with a still earlier determination.[31] This can become relevant in mass accident cases involving, for example, a number of train passengers. One sues and loses; a second sues and wins. Now the others sue and of course want to play up the second one's victory. The fact that there were two prior actions with inconsistent results diminishes the force that might otherwise propel estoppel.

16. *Tactical oversight in prior action*. When the result of an action is sought to affect a myriad of others, the Court of Appeals has indicated that the action had best show a strong, foible-free record. If a tactical oversight taints that record, the court is disinclined to give the judgment the broad impact that collateral estoppel has, however binding (and

---

23. See Restatement 2d, Judgments, § 28(2).

24. Restatement 2d, Judgments, § 28(5), Comment i.

25. See item #3 above.

26. See Restatement 2d, Judgments, § 28(4).

27. See Nesbitt v. Nimmich, 34 A.D.2d 958, 312 N.Y.S.2d 766 (2d Dep't 1970), aff'd 30 N.Y.2d 622, 331 N.Y.S.2d 438, 282 N.E.2d 328 (1972).

28. Restatement 2d, Judgments, § 29(3).

29. Id., Comment e.

30. Indeed, CPLR 1013 makes intervention so available in these common accident situations that a failure to move to intervene, or perhaps to move for consolidation under CPLR 602 where separate actions have been brought, could all too often be used to defeat the estoppel doctrine. There is no significant indication in New York law that these omissions will be allowed so to undermine the estoppel doctrine.

31. Restatement 2d, Judgments, § 29(4).

damaging) the oversight may have been in the earlier action itself.

The court sends this message by pointing to the earlier litigation from which the plaintiff in the *Kaufman* case[32] sought to derive an estoppel. A "concerted action theory" had been submitted to the jury in the earlier action as a basis on which to establish liability against the several drug companies producing the drug DES. Legal acceptance of the theory was in dispute at the time,[33] and it might not have been submitted to the jury if the defendant had properly challenged it. But the defendant failed to make that challenge, and the verdict went for the plaintiff in the first action. Because of that, the court would not allow the plaintiff in the second action an estoppel based on "concerted action". This concededly waters down collateral estoppel somewhat, the court acknowledged, but "policy reasons ... outweigh" simple use of the estoppel doctrine in cases of "mass tort liability".

* * *

The list can be expanded further—it is not exhaustive—but enough has been listed above to alert the reader to the sui generis nature of the inquiry and the numerous factors that go into it. For good measure, the Second Restatement leaves the door open to any "other compelling circumstances" that might be shown to suggest that an estoppel should be withheld.[34]

§ 468. Multiparty Vehicle Tort Examples

Building upon the factors listed in the prior sections and some of the cases cited there, we can review the rules applicable in multiparty vehicle negligence situations through a series of examples using abbreviations to facilitate reference. Assume throughout that there are several vehicles involved in an accident, and a progression of owners, drivers, and passengers. D–1 will indicate the driver of the first vehicle; O–2 the owner of the second vehicle; P–3 a passenger in the third vehicle; and so forth. The assumption will be that each action is for personal injuries; if it is instead for property damage the letters PD will be used. In each example the line-up of the parties in the first action will be given, putting the winner in parenthesis; then the line-up of the parties in the second action, underlining the party seeking the estoppel. That will afford a perspective of the whole situation at just a glance. We will make the examples as profuse as possible, starting with just a two-party situation and then expanding. So that this excursion can serve as a review of the whole multiparty area, all but a few of the examples will be used to make only one major point. In deference to that purpose, incidental matters that could be extracted from each example will not necessarily be treated.

A.   #1   (D–1) v. D–2

#2   D–2 v. <u>D–1</u>

Assuming the applicable rule to be one of contributory negligence,[1] in which any fault on the part of a party precludes that party's recovery, D–1 in the above example is entitled to a full estoppel against D–2 in the second action. The first judgment established D–2's negligence as well as D–1's freedom from negligence, either of which, imported into the second action, would support an estoppel.

B.   #1   D–1 v. (D–2)

#2   <u>D–2</u> v. <u>D–1</u>

Unless in the above example there was a special verdict in the first action clarifying the

---

32. Note 11 above.

33. The dispute was afterwards addressed by the Court of Appeals in Hymowitz v. Eli Lilly and Co., 73 N.Y.2d 487, 541 N.Y.S.2d 941, 539 N.E.2d 1069 (1989).

34. Restatement 2d, Judgments, § 29(8).

§ 468

1. That will be the assumption in these examples unless otherwise indicated. Much of the law in this area was

made during the reign of the contributory negligence rule and the cases involving it continue to offer strong guidance on collateral estoppel in general. A comparative negligence illustration appears later, as Example L, with its different elements noted. The comparative negligence rule is concerned with relative responsibility for the damages rather than for just the occurrence, which can of course have a bearing on estoppel questions.

precise basis on which D–2 won, there can be no estoppel in the second action for either side. A general verdict would not reveal enough to support an estoppel.[2]

C.   #1   (D–1) v.   D–2

     #2   P–1 v. $\underline{\underline{\text{D–1}}}$
                  $\underline{\text{D–2}}$

Neither defendant in the second action can estop P–1. D–1 cannot, even though he won the first action, because P–1 was not a party to the first action and cannot be visited with any negative consequence coming out of it.[3] D–2 will be denied the estoppel for that reason and for the additional reason, of course, that he lost in the first action.

D.   #1   (D–1) v.   D–2

     #2   D–2 v. $\underline{\text{D–1}}$
                  $\underline{\text{O–1}}$

Both defendants in the second action are entitled to an estoppel against D–2. D–1, the first action winner, is of course entitled to it. The additional point made here is that O–1, although not a party to the first action, may also make use of the estoppel—in this case defensively. Want of mutuality is no longer a barrier.[4]

E.   #1   (O–1) v.   O–2   PD
                      D–2

     #2   O–2 v. $\underline{\text{D–1}}$ PD
                  $\underline{\text{O–1}}$

No estoppel for any side in the second action. The issues are different. This introduces the point of Mills v. Gabriel,[5] which holds that a driver's affirmative negligence is imputed to the owner under New York law[6] only when the owner is sued as a defendant—the statutory

2.   See the discussion in § 462 above.

3.   See § 458 above.

4.   See §§ 460 and 466 above.

5.   259 A.D. 60, 18 N.Y.S.2d 78 (2d Dep't), aff'd 284 N.Y. 755, 31 N.E.2d 512 (1940).

6.   See Vehicle & Traffic Law § 388.

7.   It is assumed that the car is not being operated on the owner's business, which can alter the Mills v. Gabriel conclusion. Some courts cast doubt on the continued vitality of the Mills case in light of the Court of Appeals' more

purpose being to increase the likelihood of a solvent source of recovery for an injured person—but not when that owner is suing as a plaintiff for his own property damage.[7] In the above example, therefore, the issue in the first action was D–2's affirmative negligence, which was imputed to O–2 under the New York statute. When O–2 became plaintiff in the second action, however, D–2's negligence in operation became irrelevant because now it would not be imputed to O–2. But what of O–1's responsibility? Could the first action not be deemed to establish that O–1 was free of fault and thus entitled to an estoppel on that issue in the second action? The answer is again no, and for the same reason. When O–1 sued as plaintiff in the first action, D–1's negligence was not in issue because it could not be imputed to O–1. But with O–1 as defendant in the second action an imputation is in order, and hence D–1's negligence in operation of the vehicle must be tried. In the second action, in other words, D–2's negligence, although adjudicated in the first action, is not in issue, but D–1's negligence, not adjudicated in the first action, is.

F.   #1   (P–1) v.   D–2
                      O–2

     #2   O–2 v. $\underline{\text{D–1}}$ PD

No estoppel will be allowed D–1 in the second action for the same reasons assigned in the prior example. While D–2's negligence was at issue in the first action and was imputed there to O–2, it is not in issue in the second action. Therefore nothing coming out of the first action could estop O–2 in the second. D–1's negligence was not in issue in the first action, but it is in the second and must be tried. If it could be shown that in the first action O–2 was held to account not just for his

recent decision in Schwartz v. Public Administrator (§ 467, above). See, e.g., Donato v. Cataffo, 69 Misc.2d 705, 330 N.Y.S.2d 536 (Sup.Ct., Kings County, 1972). But it is submitted that unless the courts wish to reconsider Mills' underlying policy reasons—that of imputing negligence when the owner is a defendant so as to improve the injured plaintiff's chance to satisfy a judgment while freeing the owner from the imputation when he is himself a property damage plaintiff—the Mills holding is not incompatible with present estoppel law.

driver's negligent operation of the car but for something for which O–2 was individually at fault, an estoppel could result. If the first action establishes, for example, that O–2 was found liable for knowingly allowing the car to be driven with defective brakes, which contributed to the accident, this would constitute an independent basis of fault on O–2's part, importable from the first action so as to establish O–2 as contributorily negligent in the second and to bar his recovery under the contributory negligence rule that we are assuming governs these examples.

> G.　#1　(D–1) v.　D–2
>
> 　　#2　　O–1　v.　D–2　PD

O–1 is entitled to an estoppel establishing D–2's affirmative negligence in the second action. This is in essence the *DeWitt* case.[8] The dimension it adds is the allowance of offensive use of estoppel to one not a party to the first action. Presumably there is no issue of O–1's contributory negligence, but if there were, such as where O–1 is charged with some independent act of negligence not raised or litigated in the first action, it would have to be litigated in the second.

> H.　#1　(O–1) v.　D–2　PD
>
> 　　#2　　D–1　v.　D–2

At first blush this would seem to lend itself to the same conclusions as the prior example, in which estoppel was allowed. The distinction is that the positions of D–1 with a personal injury claim and O–1 with a property damage claim are reversed in order of time, and this is apparently a distinction with a difference. This fact pattern is in essence the *Elder* case,[9] which refused the estoppel. Even after *DeWitt*, which allowed the estoppel when the personal injury claim was the first tried, the question whether there should be an estoppel when the sequence is reversed is still open. This has already been discussed,[10] and it is by no means

certain that an estoppel will obtain. A sui generis inquiry will be necessary to determine whether to allow the fruits of a property damage case, presumably involving a modest sum, to govern a later personal injury claim for a lot more. All of the factors listed in the prior section would have to be carefully negotiated.

> I.　#1　(P–1) v.　D–1
> 　　　　　　　　　　D–2
>
> 　　#2　　D–1　v.　D–2

Unless something is affirmatively demonstrated to suggest that the negligence issues are not the same—i.e., that the context is such that negligence by both of the drivers against the passenger would not necessarily constitute negligence between themselves—estoppel applies and D–2 is entitled to a dismissal of the second action. (Remember that these examples assume the applicability of the contributory rather than comparative negligence rule.) This is the *Schwartz* situation, previously discussed.[11] Usually the negligence issues are the same in these situations and an estoppel will apply. An example of where it would not apply, however, was also previously cited: a case in which D–1's conduct might be found reasonable as against D–2 while being found tortious as against P–1.[12]

> J.　#1　P–1　v.　O–1 ⎤　P–1 wins
> 　　　　　　　　　　D–1 ⎬　against O–1
> 　　　　　　　　　　D–2 ⎦　and D–1, but
> 　　　　　　　　　　　　　the O–1 ver-
> 　　　　　　　　　　　　　dict exoner-
> 　　　　　　　　　　　　　ates D–2.
>
> 　　#2　　O–2　v.　D–1　PD
> 　　　　　　　　　　O–1

This fact pattern, invoking a number of principles, is a challenging review. O–2 can probably have an estoppel. The fact that O–2 was not a party to the first action is no barrier because that involves the mutuality doctrine, which the *DeWitt* case abandoned.[13] The same case also confirms that such a first-action non-

8. B.R. DeWitt, Inc. v. Hall, 19 N.Y.2d 141, 278 N.Y.S.2d 596, 225 N.E.2d 195 (1967). See § 466 above.

9. Elder v. New York & Pennsylvania Motor Express, 284 N.Y. 350, 31 N.E.2d 188 (1940).

10. See § 466.

11. See Item 1, sameness of issue, in § 467.

12. See text at note 6 in § 467, above.

13. See § 466 above.

party can make offensive, not just defensive, use of the estoppel. The fact that the findings against D–1 and O–1, which are sought for use in the second action, accrued in favor of someone in the first action (P–1) with whom O–2 lacked "privity" also has no bearing today.[14] The next and last matter is whether the negligence issues are the same: would the fact that D–1 and O–1 were found culpable in this accident vis-a-vis P–1 also establish their culpability with respect to O–2's car? If the answer is yes, O–2 should have an estoppel; if not, he should not. This is in essence the *Schwartz* case, the subject of example I, above, and unless something is shown to satisfy the court that the negligence issues in the two contexts differ, the estoppel applies. Nothing in this example having been shown to suggest a difference in the issues, there ought to be an estoppel.

K. #1 (P–1) v. O–1

#2 P–2 v. O–1

This ostensibly simple situation was for a long time the major open question in the estoppel realm. It involves the mass accident, such as 100 people killed or injured in (e.g.) a plane crash. A passenger sues the owner, driver, or manufacturer of any vehicle involved, and wins. Are all the other 99 passengers to get a free estoppel ride on the coattails of the first successful passenger? The courts' long insistence on a showing of "privity" or a like link between the #2 user and the #1 winner[15] was the barrier to the estoppel ride. That barrier was only recently lifted, and with its lifting the estoppel train took off. Other things being equal, P–2 in the above example is entitled to estoppel against O–1 on the issue of liability.[16] Damages issues are of course unique to each injured person and have to be litigated individually.

L. #1 (P–1) v. D–1
D–2

14. See § 461 above.

15. See, e.g., Cobbs v. Thomas, 55 Misc.2d 800, 286 N.Y.S.2d 943 (Sup.Ct., Dutchess County), aff'd 31 A.D.2d 719, 296 N.Y.S.2d 557 (2d Dep't 1968).

16. See § 461 and item #3 on the list in § 467 above.

#2 P–2 v. D–1
D–2

In this example we assume that the comparative negligence rule applies.[17] It applies in New York to all accidents occurring on or after September 1, 1975. The rule introduced new elements into the estoppel picture. Assume in the above example (in addition to assuming, of course, that there is no barrier to one passenger using another's victory, the stuff of the last example), that P–1, duly seat-belted, is found in the first action to have no fault at all. D–1 and D–2 are found equally responsible (50%–50%) for the accident. As long as nothing is shown in the second action to indicate that any fault on P–2's part contributed to his own injury, P–2 should have a straight estoppel establishing the defendants' fault, leaving only the measure of P–2's damages to be tried. Even the drivers' 50% shares as found in the first action would be a basis for estoppel in the second. Here would be an instance in which responsibility for the occurrence and for the injuries is the same. But note that under the comparative negligence rule, the culpable conduct involved is not that which caused the accident, but rather the "damages".[18] If it can be shown, therefore, that the damages-causing conduct in P–1's action is not the same as in P–2's, the issue would not be deemed disposed of by the first action and would require litigation in the second.

Suppose, for instance, that P–1 was not wearing a seat belt, although it was readily at hand, and that in the first action this failure accounted for 90% of P–1's injuries,[19] even though each defendant driver was found 50% responsible for the occurrence. Estoppel must be imported accordingly. To the extent that in the second action the issue arises out of the drivers' responsibility for the occurrence, an estoppel could establish that each was 50% at fault. But when the ratio of accountability for P–2's injuries arises in the second action, as it

17. CPLR Article 14–A.

18. CPLR 1411.

19. See Spier v. Barker, 35 N.Y.2d 444, 363 N.Y.S.2d 916, 323 N.E.2d 164 (1974).

necessarily will, the matter will be open to litigation, enjoying no estoppel from the first action.

If, for example, P–2 is found by the second jury to have worn a seat belt, the drivers' respective shares of fault in causing the accident may be found applicable to P–2's damages as well. But if P–2 was not wearing a seat belt, or was guilty of any other act or omission contributing to his own injuries, such as engaging in horseplay in the car or sitting perched on the sun roof while the car was at high speed, the ratios of responsibility for P–2's damages could not be dictated by the findings in respect of P–1 in the first action and would need trial.

Under the comparative negligence rule, in other words, whenever the first-round plaintiff is found to have contributed in any measure to his own injuries, an estoppel in respect of responsibility for P–2's injuries in the second action will not result. This is so notwithstanding that any proportions of fault in causing the occurrence—the accident itself—may be an estoppel basis if they become relevant in the second action. If it should be found in the second action, for example, that P–2 suffered total damages of $100,000 and that P–2 was 60% responsible for his own injuries, and the drivers between them accountable for 40% of those injuries, the first-action finding that each driver had 50% responsibility for the occurrence could then be applied to their collective 40% responsibility in the second action, resulting there in respective contributive shares of 20%. That would produce a joint and several judgment for P–2 against the drivers for $40,000, with their contributive shares $20,000 each.

Note also that while P–2 can use the 50%–50% shares of D–1 and D–2 in causing the accident, as found in the first action, P–2, not bound by that finding because not a party to the first action, can instead insist on relitigating those shares in the second action, perhaps

in an endeavor to assign a greater share to the more solvent of the two drivers.

I. DIFFERENT COURTS

Table of Sections

§ 469. Effect When Different Courts Involved

If a court decides an issue clearly within its range of subject matter jurisdiction, there is usually no reason for refusing its judgment estoppel treatment merely because the court is one of limited or inferior jurisdiction. Any other rule would make the dispositions of such courts insecure, and a court system like New York's, with a profusion of lower and special courts, could ill afford that. But the distribution of judicial business among the various courts does occasionally account for a few estoppel dilemmas. These usually occur when a court, in the course of adjudicating a case properly before it, is required, perhaps only as an incident, to pass on something that is really the plenary business of some other court. Often the incidental item arises as part of a defense. The general rule in New York today is that limitations on subject matter jurisdiction apply only to affirmative claims, not to defenses; that a court may entertain—and, indeed, a defendant may not be precluded from interposing—any defense she has to a claim, whether the defense is legal or equitable and regardless of the court in which the claim appears. Statute in some of the lower court acts confirms this expressly,[1] rejecting all prior efforts to deprive a defendant of a legitimate defense under the guise of subject matter jurisdiction.

§ 469

1. See § 905 in the New York City Civil Court Act and in the Uniform District, Uniform City, and Uniform Justice court acts (McKinney's Vol. 29A, Parts 2 and 3).

One proceeding with a potential for this kind of dilemma is the summary proceeding to recover possession of real property (the so-called "landlord-tenant" device brought for nonpayment of rent or holding over after the expiration of the lease). It is within the jurisdiction of all of the state's lower courts,[2] but its function is to determine only the immediate right to possession of the premises; it is not designed to try title.[3] In the great majority of cases no title question arises; the respondent tenant does not dispute title. But every now and again the respondent does: he injects into the middle of a summary proceeding the defense that he has title, or that the petitioner-landlord has not. The court is obliged to reach a determination of the right to possession, and a defense of want of title may well be an effective answer to that claim of right.

So it is that a lower court entertaining a summary proceeding will occasionally have to pass, expressly or tacitly, on a title question. If a court without jurisdiction to adjudicate title questions, such as a town, village, city, or district court, does so, is the adjudication binding in a higher court in a later plenary test of title? The answer is apparently no. Recognizing that the summary proceeding is almost invariably the product of a court of limited jurisdiction, a statute provides that the judgment in it shall not preclude an action "for affirmative equitable relief" barred from the summary proceeding because of the court's limited jurisdiction, if the action is commenced within 60 days after the judgment's entry.[4] Indeed, the statute provides that the judgment shall not even bar "an action to recover the possession of real property", which can be taken to suggest that not even the possessory right adjudicated in the summary proceeding is binding in a plenary action presenting the

same issues later. It should not be so taken, however; issues legitimately a part of a summary proceeding are entitled to issue preclusion effect.[5] But title is not such an issue, so as far as title is concerned the judgment in the summary proceeding is no bar, a view supported by caselaw old[6] and young.[7]

It is permissible, however, for a stipulation to resolve a title question, even if given within a summary proceeding, on the theory that it is the parties' agreement that resolves the issue in that case and that the level of court from which the agreement-embodying judgment comes is secondary.[8]

Practical advice to a summary-proceeding respondent who has a genuine defense of title is to immediately institute a separate action, such as one for a declaratory judgment or other title-testing procedure in the supreme court, and move in that action to remove and consolidate the summary proceeding.

An analogous problem arises when a family court, legitimately passing on a proper piece of its business such as a support proceeding, incidentally passes on the validity of a marriage, or of a divorce purporting to dissolve the marriage, issues that the respondent may have raised as defenses. They are relevant defenses and the family court respondent is entitled to have them heard, but the Court of Appeals has held that determinations on those issues do not bind in later plenary tests of the marriage in the supreme court, which has exclusive jurisdiction of marital actions. Thus a family court holding that a marriage does not exist because a disputed divorce is found good,[9] or, conversely, that a marriage does exist because the divorce is found invalid,[10] does not get estoppel treatment in the supreme court even

---

2. See §§ 19, 20, 21, and 22, above.

3. The summary proceeding is treated in §§ 571–580 below.

4. RPAPL § 747(2).

5. See Reich v. Cochran, 151 N.Y. 122, 45 N.E. 367 (1896), discussed in its other aspects in § 451 above.

6. Willis v. McKinnon, 37 Misc. 386, 75 N.Y.S. 770 (Sup.Ct., Delaware County, 1902), aff'd 79 A.D. 249, 79 N.Y.S. 936 (3d Dep't 1903), aff'd 178 N.Y. 451, 70 N.E. 962 (1904).

7. See O'Frias v. Melton, 32 A.D.2d 1046, 303 N.Y.S.2d 785 (2d Dep't 1969), aff'd 27 N.Y.2d 638, 313 N.Y.S.2d 765, 261 N.E.2d 670 (1970).

8. The Court of Appeals affirmance in the O'Frias case, id., stressed the presence of a stipulation there.

9. See Loomis v. Loomis, 288 N.Y. 222, 42 N.E.2d 495 (1942).

10. See Tcholakian v. Tcholakian, 29 A.D.2d 848, 287 N.Y.S.2d 920 (1st Dep't 1968).

though it may be dispositive of the main issues involved in the family court proceeding.[11]

We may also note parenthetically that a court with subject matter jurisdiction of a claim is not divested of it by anything contained in a defense,[12] whatever the estoppel impact may be of an adjudication made in respect of the defense. A different rule would be tantamount to giving a defendant a veto power over the plaintiff's choice of forum: the mere interposition of the defense would divest the court of its jurisdiction.

The lower the court making an adjudication, the more likely is an estoppel problem of this nature to arise. At the lowest rung of the judicial ladder, the small claim, there is a statutory restriction on the res judicata doctrine. The statute is treated in the small claims chapter,[13] but we may note here that it is the collateral estoppel doctrine (issue preclusion) and not res judicata in its technical sense (claim preclusion) that the statute withholds from a small claims judgment.[14]

In other areas, which lack statutory guidance but in which policy suggests strictures on incidental findings made in lower court or special court proceedings, the New York courts seem ready enough to implement the policy, but they lack a clear set of guideposts. Relevant decisions seem murky and evasive. A cure would be to recognize that the limited or special nature of the court from which the issue seeking the estoppel comes, or the issue's relatively incidental status in its lower court context, are themselves items that must be weighed into the balance before a determination is made of whether the issue has earned an estoppel. Treat this factor, in other words, as one of the sui generis items to be considered in applying the full and fair opportunity test.[15]

An approach of that kind would also hold the key to a still more embarrassing situation:

that in which a state court finding on an exclusively federal issue seeks recognition in a federal court. In prior examples the courts were at least arms of the same sovereign. Here we have courts of two different sovereigns. Suppose, for example, that in a contract action in a state court a defendant interposes as a defense the invalidity of a patent involved in the contract. Were that issue the subject of a direct action (such as one for patent infringement), it would be a matter of exclusively federal jurisdiction.[16] Will the state court's adjudication of the patent issue in defense context be binding in a later federal action involving the same issue? It depends on a number of factors, but it is by no means automatically binding.[17]

The federal doctrine of "pendent [now called supplemental] jurisdiction" occasionally presents some sticky res judicata problems in state courts. The doctrine permits a federal court to entertain a state claim of which it would otherwise lack subject matter jurisdiction when it is joined with a related federal claim, the two arising out of the same event or connected series of events. The federal claim acts as the equivalent of a jurisdictional crutch. The res judicata problem arises when the federal claim is dismissed on its merits early in the federal litigation. If the disposition clearly addresses the merits of the pendent state claim as well, it will of course be entitled to res judicata effect in a state court later. But when the disposition of the state claim is unclear, and the plaintiff, believing that the state claim was not a merits dismissal, commences a new state-court action on it, how shall the state court determine the issue? The point was the subject of address in two phases of McLearn v. Cowen & Co., one from the New York Court of Appeals[18] and the other from the federal Sec-

11. See Restatement 2d, Judgments, § 31(3).

12. See Mohar Realty Co. v. Smith, 46 Misc.2d 849, 260 N.Y.S.2d 685 (App.T., 2d Dep't, 1965).

13. Chapter 21 (Practitioner's Edition), § 581 et seq.

14. See § 585 below (Practitioner's Edition).

15. The test and its list of factors is in § 467, above. Note item 5 on the list. The Restatement also lists differ-

ences in courts as one of the factors warranting individual consideration. See Restatement 2d, Judgments, § 28(3).

16. See 28 U.S.C.A. § 1338.

17. See the Reporter's Note on § 28 in the Second Restatement, note 15, above.

18. 48 N.Y.2d 696, 422 N.Y.S.2d 60, 397 N.E.2d 750 (1979).

ond Circuit.[19]

The case began as a federal district court action. It was based on federal securities violations and a connected state claim was included. The federal claims were dismissed in what amounted to a merits disposition. The plaintiff then brought a state action on the state claim. A divided New York Court of Appeals, perusing the federal record, found the dismissal to be a merits disposition of the state claim as well. Three judges dissented; finding the federal dismissal equivocal at best, they would have entertained the state action. The plaintiff then went back to the federal court with a motion to clarify that the federal dismissal did not reach the merits of the state claim. This led to the Second Circuit decision, which, disagreeing with the New York Court of Appeals, held that the federal *McLearn* dismissal was not a merits termination of the state claim. The Second Circuit was also divided on the point, and even the two majority judges had different rationales.[20]

Meriting separate treatment is the case in which an estoppel is asked for a prior New York Court of Claims judgment. It poses the difficulty of according estoppel in a jury case to an adjudication made in a nonjury case, and is the subject of the next section.

§ 470. Nonjury Determinations; Court of Claims Problems

An additional question that collateral estoppel sometimes poses is whether the doctrine may foreclose in a jury case an issue decided in a nonjury case. It has been held that an issue found in a jury-tried case can be the basis of an estoppel in a case in which no jury trial is permitted,[1] which confirms the usability of a jury-tried law judgment to foreclose issues in a court-tried equity action. But what of the converse situation, most often involving the court of claims, in which there is no jury trial?[2]

A claimant who loses in a court of claims action is usually subject to the estoppel consequences of the loss even though it entails application of the estoppel in a later jury case in some other court. The claimant has been held to subject herself to this merely by bringing suit in the court of claims, or at least by suing there first.[3] So, for example, where P had a negligence claim against both the state and D, and sued the state in the court of claims (he could not and still cannot sue D, a private person, there) and lost upon being found guilty of contributory negligence—at a time when contributory negligence barred a plaintiff's claim entirely—D was allowed to use that loss against P in a later P v. D suit in the supreme court.[4] The theory sometimes cited is that the claimant could have had a jury pass on the issues by bringing the supreme court action first.[5] In this age of the crowded calendar and the delayed trial, however, such an approach can be faulted for overlooking the statute of limitations. Especially when the second action would have to be brought in the court of claims, which has for the state a shorter statute than applies against other defendants,[6] the plaintiff who sues first in some other court and then waits patiently for a determination may find his patience rewarded with a statute of limitations dismissal of a court of claims suit attempted later.

Other problems arise from the separateness of the court of claims. Had P sued the state

19. 660 F.2d 845 (1981).

20. The cases are treated in more detail in editions 240 (lead note) and 265 of the New York State Law Digest.

§ 470

1. Albero v. State, 31 A.D.2d 694, 295 N.Y.S.2d 965 (3d Dep't 1968), aff'd 26 N.Y.2d 630, 307 N.Y.S.2d 469, 255 N.E.2d 724 (1970).

2. It has been held that if the first action could have been tried by jury but the jury was waived, the estoppel can visit the second action without impediment. See, e.g., Vincent v. Thompson, 79 Misc.2d 1029, 361 N.Y.S.2d 282 (Sup.Ct., Nassau County, 1974), rev'd on other grounds 50 A.D.2d 211, 377 N.Y.S.2d 118 (2d Dep't 1975).

3. See Planty v. Potter–DeWitt Corp., 27 A.D.2d 401, 279 N.Y.S.2d 938 (3d Dep't 1967).

4. Chaffee v. Lawrence, 282 A.D. 875, 124 N.Y.S.2d 425 (2d Dep't 1953); Hires v. New York Cent. R. R., 24 A.D.2d 1075, 265 N.Y.S.2d 895 (4th Dep't 1965). On the federal side, the U.S. Supreme Court held a nonjury result binding in a later jury-triable action in Parklane Hosiery Co. v. Shore, 439 U.S. 322, 99 S.Ct. 645, 58 L.Ed.2d 552 (1979), offering a review of the subject.

5. See Jones v. Young, 257 A.D. 563, 14 N.Y.S.2d 84 (3d Dep't 1939).

6. See Ct.Cl.Act § 10.

first and the state wished to implead D, the private person, as an indemnifying or contributing tortfeasor, it would be precluded from doing so because impleader does not lie in the court of claims.[7] A victory for P in the court of claims is thus barred from estoppel use against D for the obvious reason that D was not a party to the court of claims action. Hence these court of claims barriers to impleader and other joinder devices usually make it impossible for the dispute to touch others involved in the occurrence, and with this unhappy denouement for the claimant: if he loses in the court of claims, the loss can be used against him by others, but if he wins in the court of claims he cannot make use of his victory against anyone else who was not a party to the court of claims action.

This has posed special problems in the apportioning of damages among tortfeasors,[8] as we can illustrate with a case that involved the application of the comparative negligence rule and in which the supreme court suit came first. P, a passenger injured while in D's car when it slid on some ice, a condition for which the state was responsible, sued D in the supreme court, established some fault on the part of D, and won a $40,000 verdict against D. Now D sued the state for contribution in the court of claims, which found the state responsible for 40% of P's damages, but it applied the 40% to the $40,000 figure, and this it could not do, at least not yet. It might hold, by way of estoppel, that P's damages could not now be found to *exceed* $40,000, because D was a party to the earlier action and can be estopped from seeking contribution from the state based on anything higher than the $40,000 figure the supreme court action produced, but since the state was not a party to that action it was now free to try to establish that P's damages were less than that.[9]

§ 471. Recognition of Domestic Judgments; Full Faith and Credit

The full faith and credit clause of the federal constitution,[1] combined with Congress' implementation and expansion of it in the full faith and credit statute,[2] requires that all American courts recognize each others' judgments. While the constitutional provision itself refers only to the states, the statute goes further and by language or construction includes in addition to the state courts the territorial courts, the courts of the District of Columbia, and all of the federal courts. Each of these courts must recognize the validly rendered judgments of the others and give them essentially the same preclusive effect the rendering jurisdiction intends for the judgment.[3] The term "American" courts can for convenience be used to describe them collectively. The courts of foreign nations are not under the full faith and credit umbrella; their judgments can at best ask for "comity", a doctrine to be looked at in the next section.

As applied to an American judgment, the full faith and credit doctrine is in essence only res judicata applied interstate and made mandatory. As long as the judgment in the first American forum (F–1) was validly rendered, full faith and credit applies and the judgment is deemed valid as long as F–1 had jurisdiction. Jurisdiction is in almost all cases the sole inquiry. As soon as the second forum (F–2) ascertains that F–1 had jurisdiction, the F–2 inquiry must end and the F–1 judgment must be recognized on its merits. That is so no matter what error there may have been on F–1's part in reaching the merits: as long as F–1 had jurisdiction, any error that F–1 made on the merits must be reviewed by direct attack in F–1[4] and not by collateral attack in F–2.[5]

---

7. People v. Delaware & Hudson R. Corp., 42 A.D.2d 618, 344 N.Y.S.2d 488 (3d Dep't 1973).

8. See Rezucha v. Garlock Mechanical Packing Co., cited in § 168C, above, and the extended note on the case in SPR 13:4.

9. See La Buda v. State, 86 A.D.2d 692, 446 N.Y.S.2d 534 (3d Dep't 1982).

§ 471

1. U.S.Const. Art.IV, § 1.

2. 28 U.S.C.A. § 1738.

3. See, e.g., Gargiul v. Tompkins, 790 F.2d 265 (2d Cir.1986).

4. By direct attack is meant either an appeal in F–1, or a motion to the F–1 court itself to vacate the judgment.

5. Fauntleroy v. Lum, 210 U.S. 230, 28 S.Ct. 641, 52 L.Ed. 1039 (1908).

F–2 may of course look into the question of whether F–1 had jurisdiction. If the defendant did not appear in the F–1 proceeding, F–2 may decide the question of F–1's jurisdiction for itself—looking into the usual jurisdictional items of basis, notice, and opportunity to be heard. Although F–2 must give "proper weight" to what F–1 may have held as to its own jurisdiction, F–2 is not bound by the F–1 holding and may, upon appropriate proof, determine that F–1 did not have jurisdiction even in the teeth of F–1's own determination that it did.[6] The theory is that the F–1 defendant is entitled to a day in court on the question of F–1's jurisdiction and that she must be allowed that day in F–2 as long as she did not appear in F–1. It is in fact this phenomenon of federal constitutional law that lends jeopardy to the so-called "ex parte" divorce, the divorce rendered in F–1 with no personal jurisdiction of the defendant spouse.[7] It is always open to the defendant, if the F–1 divorce should be questioned in F–2, to show that F–1 had no jurisdiction at all, not even the "rem" jurisdiction that might have obtained if the plaintiff spouse were found an F–1 domiciliary—the very fact question on which F–1's jurisdiction in this instance depends and which F–2 can decide for itself by virtue of the defendant's nonappearance in F–1. The question of F–1's jurisdiction remains open, in other words, and any person remarrying on the strength of such an ex parte divorce runs the risk of having F–2 reject the divorce upon determining that F–1 lacked jurisdiction. All this, when the defendant does not appear in the F–1 proceeding.

If the defendant does appear in F–1, the full faith and credit doctrine takes on some added magic: it forecloses reinvestigation of, and binds F–2 to recognize, not just the merits, but the fact of F–1's jurisdiction as well. Here the theory is that by appearing in F–1 the defendant had a direct opportunity to raise and litigate the jurisdictional question. If he did litigate it and lost on it, the holding of F–1's jurisdiction of course binds him.[8] But even if he appeared in the F–1 action without raising a jurisdictional issue, he is foreclosed on it just the same because the opportunity to litigate it was there, whether used or not.[9] This rule applies whether the jurisdictional issue goes to personal or to subject matter jurisdiction.[10] A sister-state divorce rendered on the defendant spouse's appearance, whether in person or through an attorney, invokes this rule of jurisdictional foreclosure. In common parlance this type of divorce is called "bilateral". Just as the ex parte sister-state divorce is insecure, at least until F–2 confirms F–1's jurisdiction, so the bilateral one is airtight for the very reason that the federal constitution bars F–2 from even questioning F–1's jurisdiction.

The foregoing applies only to American judgments. Those of foreign countries, not coming in for full faith and credit and therefore able to rely on comity at best, are separately treated in the next section.

Once it is determined to recognize the F–1 judgment, whether via full faith and credit because it comes from an American court or through comity when it comes from a foreign country, the rest is usually just a matter of applying the rules of res judicata and collateral estoppel, just as those doctrines would apply if all of the courts involved were New York courts. If there is some difference between the law of F–1 and F–2 on the scope to be given the F–1 judgment, F–2 will ordinarily apply the F–1 rules on the theory that to do otherwise would be according less than full credit or comity to the F–1 judgment.[11]

---

6. Williams v. North Carolina, 325 U.S. 226, 65 S.Ct. 1092, 89 L.Ed. 1577 (1945).

7. This is the category of divorce that depends on "rem" jurisdiction of the marital status. F–1 gets this rem jurisdiction if the plaintiff is a domiciliary of F–1. See § 102 above.

8. Baldwin v. Iowa State Traveling Men's Assoc., 283 U.S. 522, 51 S.Ct. 517, 75 L.Ed. 1244 (1931).

9. See Johnson v. Muelberger, 340 U.S. 581, 71 S.Ct. 474, 95 L.Ed. 552 (1951) and Cook v. Cook, 342 U.S. 126, 72 S.Ct. 157, 96 L.Ed. 146 (1951).

10. Sherrer v. Sherrer, 334 U.S. 343, 68 S.Ct. 1087, 92 L.Ed. 1429 (1948).

11. See Magnolia Petroleum Co. v. Hunt, 320 U.S. 430, 64 S.Ct. 208, 88 L.Ed. 149 (1943). Although not directly overruled, the Magnolia case is undermined by the Thomas case, cited in note 7 in § 456, above. See also Johnson

Suppose that F–2 is obliged to recognize an F–1 judgment but fails to, rendering judgment for X although Y, the F–1 winner, should have prevailed. If the validity of both judgments now arises before F–3, which earlier judgment prevails? If has been held that the F–2 judgment prevails; that if F–2 failed to recognize the F–1 judgment, the failure was error which should have been reviewed by appeal in F–2.[12] But if two actions are riding to judgment at the same time, the one arriving at judgment first is the one ordinarily entitled to res judicata treatment even if the other action was commenced first. For res judicata purposes, the moment of judgment and not the moment of commencement is ordinarily the key time.

Special problems have always attended the recognition of child custody decrees. As a matter of federal constitutional law, the U.S. Supreme Court never applied the full faith and credit clause to custody decrees,[13] and New York took the position that the clause was not operative in the custody sphere at all.[14] Implementing a uniform act, New York ultimately adopted a special statute[15] to govern the recognition of child custody adjudications made by other American courts, resting recognition on whether the jurisdictional basis on which the other court purported to ground custody is analogous to one that New York authorizes.[16] This was in effect a voluntary undertaking by the state legislature, but Congress itself intervened and made recognition mandatory in many instances with a statute, § 1738A of Title 28 of the U.S. Code, set right next to the main full faith and credit statute, which is § 1738. In stated situations the statute applies

the full faith and credit clause to custody determinations. It encourages inter-court communication on custody problems, a practice on which New York had embarked under its own statutes even before the federal mandate took effect.[17]

§ 472. Recognition of Foreign–Country Judgments; "Comity"

In the prior section only American judgments were discussed, because only they get full faith and credit. The judgments of foreign countries are not within the full faith and credit requirement, and as long as there is nothing else to require recognition, such as a treaty between the United States and the particular nation,[1] the best that the foreign country judgment can hope for is what is termed "comity". Loosely, this means courtesy, respect, or mutual accommodation;[2] practically, it means that each sovereign, including the State of New York, can decide for itself which foreign country judgments it will recognize and which it will not.

New York's position is stated mainly but not exclusively in Article 53 of the CPLR, which adopts in essence the Uniform Foreign Country Money–Judgments Recognition Act.[3] The act dictates in some detail which foreign money judgments (it does not apply to other kinds of judgment[4]) must be recognized[5] and which need not be.[6]

Article 53, which became law in 1970, was not added because of any special need New York had for guidance in this respect. The state has always been generous in recognizing

v. Muelberger, 340 U.S. 581, 71 S.Ct. 474, 95 L.Ed. 552 (1951).

12. Treinies v. Sunshine Mining Co., 308 U.S. 66, 60 S.Ct. 44, 84 L.Ed. 85 (1939).

13. See the concurrence of Justice Frankfurter in May v. Anderson, 345 U.S. 528, 73 S.Ct. 840, 97 L.Ed. 1221 (1953).

14. See, e.g., Bachman v. Mejias, 1 N.Y.2d 575, 154 N.Y.S.2d 903, 136 N.E.2d 866 (1956).

15. See § 75–n of the Domestic Relations Law.

16. See § 75–d of the Domestic Relations Law.

17. See, e.g., Vanneck v. Vanneck, 49 N.Y.2d 602, 427 N.Y.S.2d 735, 404 N.E.2d 1278 (1980).

§ 472

1. Treaties play an insignificant role in the area of foreign judgments at the moment, but an important international convention, to which the United States is a signatory, does govern international arbitration awards and thus dictates to the states on their recognition. Chapter 2 of Title 9 of the U.S.C.A. contains Congress' implementing provisions for this treaty.

2. See Franzen v. Zimmer, 90 Hun. 103, 35 N.Y.S. 612 (1895).

3. See CPLR 5309.

4. CPLR 5301(b).

5. CPLR 5303.

6. CPLR 5304.

foreign country judgments even without statutory or constitutional pressures, insisting on nothing more, essentially, than that the judgment be shown to have been based on principles of jurisdiction and due process analogous to our own, thus comporting with our own sense of fairness.[7] This attitude continues. Comity under New York caselaw should therefore assure recognition to any money judgment that would have gotten it before Article 53 was adopted. It has even been said that the article is merely a codification of caselaw.[8] And comity would of course continue to be given to nonmoney judgments that would have earned it before, because to them Article 53 is not applicable at all.[9]

The principal motive, in fact, behind the New York adoption of Article 53 was not to prescribe what New York has to do for foreign judgments, but with what the mere existence of Article 53 on the New York statute books would accomplish for New York judgments seeking recognition elsewhere. It was felt that foreign tribunals, especially those that insist on reciprocity, would be more likely to recognize a New York judgment if shown a New York statutory scheme manifesting a ready willingness to reciprocate, especially one based on a uniform act that has achieved some currency domestically and some familiarity overseas.[10] To judges in civil law nations, as opposed to common law nations, it is apparently insufficient, for ready recognition of a New York judgment, to show reciprocal generosity in New York caselaw. A statute is what they want to see, and Article 53 is the New York showpiece. Probably for the reason that New York caselaw has been at least as liberal as Article 53 in acknowledging foreign judg-

ments,[11] the article and its progenitors and counterparts have received "scant judicial attention".[12]

The article must be perused, however, in conjunction with any issue involving recognition of a foreign country money judgment, especially when an outright adoption of that judgment is sought, whether by plenary action or by the motion-action of CPLR 3213, the latter being of course the more expeditious and hence the preferable tool.[13]

The same "last-in-time" rule that governs the recognition of inconsistent sister-state judgments under the full faith and credit clause[14] has also been applied by New York under its comity doctrine. Hence, if two foreign judgments are inconsistent, the later of the two will be the one that New York recognizes.[15]

J. PROCEDURAL INCIDENTS

Table of Sections

§ 473. Evidentiary Sources to Establish Matters Estopped

In resolving any issue of res judicata or collateral estoppel, any competent source can be considered to determine what matters were disposed of in the earlier action. Hopefully the judgment itself will reveal what is needed. Perhaps the judgment will require a juxtaposition with the pleadings to determine the issues

---

7. See Cowans v. Ticonderoga Pulp & Paper Co., 246 N.Y. 603, 159 N.E. 669, aff'g on opinion in 219 A.D. 120, 219 N.Y.S. 284 (3d Dep't 1927).

8. See Island Territory of Curacao v. Solitron Devices, Inc., 489 F.2d 1313 (2d Cir.1973).

9. See CPLR 5307.

10. See Kulzer, The Uniform Foreign Money Judgments Recognition Act, 13th Ann.Jud.Conf.Rep. (1968), p. 194 at 195. Professor Kulzer's study offers extensive background on what later became in essence Article 53 of the CPLR.

11. See, e.g., Von Engelbrechten v. Galvanoni & Nevy Bros., Inc., 59 Misc.2d 721, 300 N.Y.S.2d 239 (N.Y.C.Civ.

Ct. 1969), aff'd 61 Misc.2d 959, 307 N.Y.S.2d 381 (App.T., 1st Dep't, 1970), extending recognition farther than a treaty in the case appeared to require but did not preclude.

12. See Overmyer v. Eliot Realty, 83 Misc.2d 694 at 701, 371 N.Y.S.2d 246 at 255 (Sup.Ct., Westchester County, 1975).

13. See §§ 288 and 290 above.

14. See the discussion in § 471 above.

15. See Ackerman v. Ackerman, 517 F.Supp. 614 (S.D.N.Y.1981), aff'd 676 F.2d 898 (2d Cir.1982).

raised and decided. The pleadings may of course be looked to. A transcript of the earlier proceedings may also be examined, including the charge to the jury, which is a likely source to resolve what the issues were. Indeed, the trial itself may not have followed the pleadings; issues outside the pleadings may have been raised and disposed of, and as a general rule these are also entitled to estoppel treatment.[1]

If the aggregate of the papers in the earlier action, including a trial transcript, do not reveal with clarity the issues disposed of, extrinsic evidence may be received. It may even be received to show that the record in the prior action does *not* accurately reflect what issues were determined.[2]

§ 474. Estoppel Only for Given Issue

Collateral estoppel works on individual issues and not necessarily on the whole case. This has already been noted at several points but it is worth stressing. If the issue precluded is at the crux of the case, it will of course be wholly dispositive. So, for example, where P sues D for inducing X to breach a P–X contract, and an earlier action involving P established that there was no contract, the estoppel attaching to that issue destroys P's whole case against D, entitling D to summary judgment.[1]

If the estoppel visits only a given issue without disposing of the whole case, however, the unprecluded issues must stand for trial. So, to cite a frequent example, where P–1, injured in an accident, recovers a judgment for personal injuries against D after D is found to have caused the accident and P–1 found free of contributory fault, a second person, P–2, suing D for personal injuries incurred in the same accident, may have an estoppel establishing D's fault but will have to litigate any issue

raised about P–2's own contributory negligence. And of course the issue of P–2's damages, not relevant to the first action, will have to be resolved in the second one. In that situation, P–2, although not entitled to summary judgment on her whole case, will be entitled to have it summarily determined, whether through an order or otherwise, that D was at fault in causing the accident.[2] There must of course be a genuine issue as to the unprecluded matter; mere unfounded allegations of such an issue will not suffice, as may sometimes be seen in a tort case involving a passenger against whom not even a colorable accusation of contributory negligence can be made.[3]

In all tort situations involving a second-action plaintiff different from the one who succeeded in the first action, damages will have to be tried even though there may be a full estoppel on issues going to liability. In that situation summary judgment may be granted as to liability and an immediate trial ordered of damages.[4] Conversely, however, if it is the same plaintiff who is suing for the same injuries in both actions—a different defendant being sued in each, as commonly happens in New York when the state itself is one of the defendants and can be sued only in the court of claims—collateral estoppel may even alight upon the amount found as damages in the first action and entitle the second-action defendant to a holding that whatever may be found as to that defendant's liability in the second action, the plaintiff's damages may not be allowed to exceed the sum they were set at in the earlier action.[5] Indeed, whatever the first defendant may have paid in satisfaction of that first judgment will have to be credited against whatever judgment the plaintiff may recover for the same wrong against the second defendant.[6] Any other conclusion would authorize a

---

§ 473

1. See Bronxville Palmer, Ltd. v. State, 18 N.Y.2d 560, 277 N.Y.S.2d 402, 223 N.E.2d 887 (1966).

2. See Restatement 2d, Judgments, § 27, Comment f.

§ 474

1. See Israel v. Wood Dolson Co., 1 N.Y.2d 116, 151 N.Y.S.2d 1, 134 N.E.2d 97 (1956).

2. See Quick v. O'Connell, 53 Misc.2d 1091, 281 N.Y.S.2d 120 (Sup.Ct., Jefferson County, 1967).

3. See, e.g., Jacobs v. Del Guercio, 67 Misc.2d 606, 324 N.Y.S.2d 773 (Sup.Ct., N.Y.County, 1971).

4. CPLR 3212(c).

5. See La Buda v. State, 86 A.D.2d 692, 446 N.Y.S.2d 534 (3d Dep't 1982); § 470, above.

6. As to all of these matters, see Goines v. Pennsylvania R. R., 6 A.D.2d 531, 179 N.Y.S.2d 960 (1st Dep't 1958).

double recovery, and nothing about res judicata or collateral estoppel supports that.

§ 475. Raising the Issue; Burden of Proof

The doctrines of res judicata and collateral estoppel are affirmative defenses for the defendant to plead and prove.[1] They can be taken as affirmative defenses in the answer or, at the defendant's option, may be raised by a motion to dismiss instead.[2] If taken by answer, they can then be made the basis of a motion for summary judgment.[3] If the defense becomes available only after the action has been pending for a while, and the responding time has already expired—as where the action from which the estoppel emerges has only just gone to judgment—the remedy is a motion to amend the responsive pleading[4] to insert the defense, joined, if appropriate, with a demand for summary judgment based on the new defense.

Note that while the official descriptions of these doctrines, in both the pleading[5] and motion[6] provisions, are "res judicata" and "collateral estoppel", they cover the whole family of res judicata doctrines, by whatever name any one of them may go by—claim preclusion, issue preclusion, merger, bar, election of remedies, splitting, etc.[7] As a general rule the pleading-or-motion option is available for all of them.

The burden is on the party relying on the estoppel to show identity of issue and to establish that the issue was necessarily decided in the earlier action. If the party against whom the doctrine is invoked then has anything to show to indicate that he did not have a full and fair opportunity on the issue in the earlier action,[8] the burden of that showing is on him.[9]

---

§ 475

1. CPLR 3018(b).
2. CPLR 3211(a)(5), (e).
3. CPLR 3212.
4. CPLR 3025(b).
5. CPLR 3018(b).
6. CPLR 3211(a)(5).

7. See §§ 443 and 450 above.

8. The ingredients that go into the full and fair opportunity test are set forth in § 467 above.

9. Schwartz v. Public Administrator, 24 N.Y.2d 65, 298 N.Y.S.2d 955, 246 N.E.2d 725 (1969). The distribution of burden of proof was noted earlier during treatment of the identity of issue test. See § 462.

Chapter Eighteen

ENFORCEMENT OF JUDGMENTS

Analysis

INTRODUCTORY

Table of Sections

§ 476.   Enforcement of Judgments, Generally

In many respects this topic gives law its ultimate test. We learn that law is divided into substantive and procedural segments. The whole of the substantive law determines whether the plaintiff has a right and the whole of the procedural law, at considerable expense to the plaintiff, hears everyone out, determines whether the plaintiff has a claim, and gives the plaintiff a judgment if she has. If that judg-ment can't be enforced, law is bound to fall several notches in the esteem of the plaintiff, which makes the enforcement of judgments a key moment in a test of the system.

The traditional division of judgments for enforcement purposes was into law and equity, law judgments enforcible by execution and eq-uity judgments by contempt. Much of the tra-dition survives, but in applying the experience of the years, which has shown the money judgment to pose more enforcement problems than all other categories of judgment com-bined, the legislature has reordered its division into (1) non-money judgments and (2) money judgments. To that we may add yet a third category, the declaratory judgment, which as a

769

creature of the present century has no direct ancestors either at law or in equity.

The first two categories involve what is sometimes called "coercive" relief, some kind of pressure on the defendant or a taking of the defendant's property, while the declaratory judgment involves no coercive step at all. In a manner of speaking the declaratory judgment has no enforcement stage. It merely declares the rights of the parties between or among themselves; the context is such that the declaration alone, embodied in a judgment, resolves the dispute. We speak here of the declaratory judgment in its pure form. The plaintiff who seeks it can of course join demands for other relief,[1] and if other relief is awarded, the judgment on the other relief will pursue the usual coercive enforcement channels. The few words to be said about the enforcement stage of the declaration itself were said when the device was studied,[2] and need no repetition.

The first category, the non-money judgment, includes equity decrees for such as injunction and specific performance. These are backed by the contempt punishment, as they always were. But also in the non-money grouping are ejectment and replevin, two categories of law judgment, which as a rule are not enforced by contempt but rather by execution. Article 51 of the CPLR governs the enforcement of non-money judgments, supplying the few devices needed to enforce them.

One of these, the receivership "to carry the judgment into effect," applies alike to equity and law judgments having specific property as their "subject".[3] It is merely the post-judgment or enforcement counterpart of the provisional receivership supplied by Article 64 of the CPLR[4] and is in fact governed by the several provisions of that article, which was treated earlier.[5] Receivership therefore needs no further discussion, but it should be counted among the small stockpile of devices—the rest to be treated in Part I of this chapter—for the enforcement of a non-money judgment.

Part II will treat the money judgment, whose enforcement arsenal is far more extensive. Article 52 governs the enforcement of money judgments[6] which, as the most common kind rendered by the courts, is our major study. For sheer quantity of governing statute as well as caselaw, the money judgment is the bull of the enforcement market.

§ 476

1. See § 436 above.
2. See §§ 436 and 440 above.
3. CPLR 5106.
4. See CPLR 6401.
5. See §§ 332 and 333.
6. See CPLR 5101.

Part I

ENFORCEMENT OF NON–MONEY JUDGMENTS

A. JUDGMENTS INVOLVING A CHATTEL OR REALTY

Table of Sections

§ 477. Judgment Awarding Possession of Chattel

This is the last stage of a replevin action, whose final judgment is governed by CPLR 7108, part of the article on the provisional-like remedy of seizure of a chattel studied earlier.[1] It will be recalled that if the plaintiff has won in a replevin action, the judgment awards the plaintiff possession of the chattel. If the plaintiff does not already have the chattel (she might have gotten it through the order of seizure[2]), the judgment must also fix the value of the chattel.[3] This enables the sheriff to enforce the judgment like an ordinary money judgment if the sheriff should be unable to locate the chattel and restore its possession to the plaintiff. The value of the chattel is fixed as of the time of the trial. It has been held that fixing it as of some earlier time, such as the commencement of the action, is reversible error that may require a new trial.[4]

The method of enforcement of the judgment is an execution, a paper drawn by the plaintiff's attorney and delivered to the sheriff of the county where the chattel is. It basically follows the requirements applicable to an execution on a money judgment,[5] except that it first directs the sheriff to restore the chattel's possession to the plaintiff, instructing the sheriff to levy as if on a money judgment only if the chattel can't be located in the county.[6]

This is an effective remedy, even if the plaintiff ends up with the monetary value of the chattel instead of the chattel itself, but only if there is nothing unique about it. Money will of course not make amends for the loss of a unique chattel, for which reason, when uniqueness has been demonstrated, the replevin article expressly authorizes a judgment directing the defendant to hand the chattel over under the penalty of contempt. The uniqueness of the chattel authorizes a judgment in alternative form, enforcible either by the usual remedy of execution or by the equitable device of contempt, as the plaintiff chooses.[7]

§ 478. Judgment Awarding Possession of Realty

The main situation in which a possessory dispute over real property arises today involves the landlord-tenant relationship, where the procedure for recovering possession is the summary proceeding of Article 7 of the Real Property Actions and Proceedings Law.[1] Summary proceedings, which number in the hundreds of thousands each year in New York, are usually based on non-payment of rent or holding over after the expiration of a lease, and if the landlord wins in the proceeding and is awarded possession the enforcement procedures are to be found not in the CPLR, but in

---

§ 477

1. See § 337 et seq.
2. See § 340 above.
3. CPLR 7108(a). See § 342 above.
4. Colonial Funding Corp. v. Bon Jour International, Ltd., 148 A.D.2d 654, 539 N.Y.S.2d 405 (2d Dep't 1989).

5. CPLR 5230. See § 494 et seq., below.
6. CPLR 5102.
7. CPLR 7109(b). See § 342.

§ 478

1. See RPAPL 701, 711.

the Real Property Actions and Proceedings Law in the same article that governs the rest of the summary proceeding.[2] The advent of the summary proceeding reduced other forms of action to recover possession of land to what amounts by comparison to an infinitesimal number, including the ancient ejectment action.

If the relationship between disputants does not fall within the reach of the summary proceeding,[3] resort may still be had, of course, to the plenary ejectment or a like action.[4] These may be used, for example, against squatters, interlopers, trespassers, encroachers, etc., and even against outright tenants if based on something besides non-payment of rent, holding over, or one of the other enumerated summary proceeding grounds.[5] When it is used, ejectment still qualifies traditionally as a law action, which has two major consequences: it is constitutionally triable by jury,[6] and the process of enforcement for a resulting judgment is still an execution.[7]

The execution is drawn by the plaintiff's lawyer and delivered to the sheriff of the realty county. It directs the sheriff to do what must be done to restore the plaintiff to possession. In other respects it follows CPLR 5230, which supplies the detail and procedure of the ordinary execution on a money judgment.[8] Execution is a satisfactory remedy if enforcement is a straightforward and trouble-free prospect, as where some portable object has to be removed from the land or a few trespassers put off. Theoretically, however, the sheriff is required to restore possession in any case at all if the execution so directs, whether this entails the removal of a pebble or a skyscraper, an undersized squatter or an army. But theory and practice diverge here. Hahl v. Sugo[9] stands as a mighty illustration of the frustration of

the execution remedy when the sheriff deems the job too big.

The *Hahl* execution entailed the removal of a wall and the sheriff returned the execution as "impracticable" to levy. Perhaps an Article 78 proceeding in the nature of mandamus would lie to compel the sheriff to perform the duty, with the sheriff hiring such people or equipment as may be required. (The plaintiff may be required to pay, in advance, all connected expenses, which may later be recouped from the defendant if recoupment is worth the effort.) With the proper people and equipment the sheriff can do just about any job, but pragmatic lawyers try to avoid this fatiguing course. In a situation at all likely to involve difficulties of enforcement, they bring, instead of ejectment, an equitable claim against the defendant, one that tries the identical facts but results in a judgment directing the defendant to remove the encroachment himself, under threat of contempt. The law usually allows this. The very existence of Hahl v. Sugo and like cases manifests the inadequacy of the legal remedy and thus supplies a traditional element needed to invoke the court's equity jurisdiction.

This lesson must be applied not at the end of an action, however, when seeking enforcement, but at the beginning, when determining what remedy to choose. The best idea when enforcement looms as a problem is to sue in equity, or at minimum to add an equitable count to the complaint. If the claim succeeds on its merits, responsibility for removing the encroachment or otherwise troubling to return possession to the plaintiff will fall on the defendant itself.[10]

We are concerned here only with the enforcement stage of a realty action. Nothing

---

2. See RPAPL 749.

3. The summary proceeding is treated in Part III of Chapter 20, below (Practitioner's Edition), commencing with § 571.

4. Since the forms of action have been abolished, CPLR 103(a), it is not necessary to give the action any name at all.

5. See RPAPL 711.

6. See N.Y.Const., Art.I, § 2; CPLR 4101(2). The right to jury trial is also given in a summary proceeding,

RPAPL 745, but the lease between the parties usually waives it. See §§ 377 and 378 above.

7. CPLR 5102. "Judgment" includes "order" for this purpose, should it happen to be an order that returns possession. See, e. g., Dom.Rel.L. § 234.

8. See § 494 et seq., below.

9. 169 N.Y. 109, 62 N.E. 135 (1901).

10. This is an election of remedies problem. For that aspect of the Hahl case, see § 218 above.

said above should be taken as suggesting a fine line between an action that tries the right to possession of realty and one that tries title to it. As long as a plenary action is used—a summary proceeding tries only the right to possession—and the court in which it is brought has jurisdiction of real property actions, the abolition of the forms of action permits adjudication of both ownership and possessory rights, whatever procedural differences may attend the enforcement steps afterwards.

§ 479. Judgment Directing Sale of Realty

Most of the actions likely to end in a sale of real property, such as partition and mortgage foreclosure, are addressed and governed by the Real Property Actions and Proceedings Law, including the incidents of the sale.[1] The CPLR thus has little to say about the sale. Its concern is to see that the sale takes place in the county of the realty. This and its few other directions appear in CPLR 5103.

The venue provisions of Article 5 of the CPLR will usually assure that an action involving real property is tried only in the county in which it is situated.[2] But it will sometimes happen that it is tried elsewhere, as where the parties waived venue,[3] or where the real property claim was joined with another claim as to which a different county was permissible venue, in which event a county proper for any of the claims becomes a proper one for all of them.[4] If it should happen that a judgment (or order) directing the sale of the realty is rendered in other than the realty county, a certified copy of the judgment or order must be filed with the county clerk of the realty county, who must then enter it. This is to assure that the county clerk's office in the county of the real property will always remain

a dependable repository of records concerning local real estate. Indeed, the buyer at the sale is not required to pay the purchase money or accept a deed until appropriate entry has been made on home county records.[5]

The sale itself must take place in the realty county, conducted either by the sheriff of that county or by a referee, as the court designates. If the property is situated in more than one county the court can order it sold in either one of them, or, if feasible, the property can be divided into parcels with each parcel sold in its own county.[6]

§ 480. Judgment Directing Conveyance of Realty

If the judgment directs the defendant to convey title to the plaintiff, or any party to convey title to another, such as in the common action for specific performance of a contract to sell real property, there are several modes of enforcement. If the property is not in the state, which assumes that the action has been able to get by a forum non conveniens objection, the court cannot act directly against the property and so can do no more than direct the defendant, under penalty of contempt, to make a deed to the plaintiff in form satisfactory to the realty jurisdiction. A failure would then require contempt proceedings, the subject of later sections.

Contempt is theoretically available in that kind of case even if the real property is in New York, as long as personal jurisdiction has been secured over the defendant, but when the property is in the state the court has the alternative of simply directing the sheriff to make the conveyance in the recalcitrant party's behalf.[1] The court will usually prefer this alternative, which lets the judgment act in

---

§ 479

1. For partition, see RPAPL Article 9; for foreclosure, RPAPL Articles 13 and 14.
2. See CPLR 507.
3. See CPLR 509.
4. CPLR 502.
5. CPLR 5103(a).
6. CPLR 5103(b). Cf. Bridgehampton Nat. Bank v. White, 63 Misc.2d 853, 313 N.Y.S.2d 258 (Suffolk County Ct. 1970). Distinguish this situation, in which specific real

property is the subject of the action and the judgment itself is directing its sale, from the sale of realty on execution pursuant to an ordinary money judgment. The latter also takes place in the realty county but is governed in detail by CPLR 5236. See § 500 below.

§ 480

1. See CPLR 5107.

rem.[2] The deed should be made by the sheriff of the realty county. When properly executed, the deed enters county records as if fully executed by the party and accomplishes a total conveyance. This is also approximately what occurs when a money judgment is enforced by the levy of execution against real property: it is also the sheriff who deeds the property to the buyer at the sale.[3]

B. ENFORCEMENT BY CONTEMPT

Table of Sections

§ 481. Enforcement by Contempt; Grounds

CPLR 5104 provides that if any judgment or order, interlocutory or final, is not enforcible under Article 52 or pursuant to CPLR 5102, it is enforcible by contempt. The categories thereby excluded are the money judgment, for which Article 52 lays out the array of enforcement tools, and the judgment awarding possession of either real or personal property, for which CPLR 5102 supplies execution as the enforcement device.[1] For other judgments the remedy is a contempt proceeding.

The usual equity judgments come under this category, notably the injunction, but special statutes have also made some money judgments directly enforcible by contempt.[2] Directions for the payment of alimony or support contained in a matrimonial decree, for example, are so enforcible,[3] as is a judgment directing the payment of money into court.[4]

If a trustee or other fiduciary is directed to pay money because of a wilful breach of trust, the direction is enforcible by contempt.[5] The fiduciaries who fit into that category include a trustee, a personal representative of a decedent, a committee or conservator, a guardian, and in a given set of circumstances the category can embrace still others, such as an escrowee[6] and even corporate officials.[7] A plaintiff who would invoke the contempt penalty in these instances had best be sure that the judgment itself recites the facts manifesting that the dereliction arises out of the required fiduciary connection.[8]

Even a replevin judgment, ordinarily enforcible only by an execution directing the sheriff to seize the chattel and return it to the plaintiff, can be converted into one enforcible by contempt if the chattel is unique and the judgment specifically instructs the defendant to return it.[9]

Insofar as a "judgment" of a given kind or category is enforcible by contempt, so is a court "order" of the same kind or category if it is otherwise properly made. There is no distinction between a judgment and an order in this regard.[10]

The disobedience of a subpoena is also a

---

2. See Garfein v. McInnis, 248 N.Y. 261, 162 N.E. 73 (1928).

3. CPLR 5236(f). See § 500 below.

§ 481

1. See §§ 477 and 478, above, for treatment of the judgments awarding possession of property, and Part II of this chapter, § 485 et seq., below, for the enforcement of money judgments.

2. Although it is not directly available to enforce an ordinary money judgment, the contempt remedy stands behind several of the devices that are, and thus becomes at least an indirect enforcement tool with money judgments. See § 523 below.

3. Dom.Rel.L. § 245.

4. CPLR 5105(1).

5. CPLR 5105(2).

6. Avalon East, Inc. v. Monaghan, 43 Misc.2d 401, 251 N.Y.S.2d 290 (Sup.Ct., N.Y.County, 1964).

7. Gould v. Jacobs, 44 Misc.2d 990, 256 N.Y.S.2d 20 (Sup.Ct., N.Y.County, 1964), aff'd 24 A.D.2d 934, 263 N.Y.S.2d 1004 (1st Dep't 1965).

8. Id. For general discussion of what it takes to satisfy CPLR 5105(2) as a "fiduciary" relationship, see the dissenting opinion in National Sur. Corp. v. Silver, 23 A.D.2d 398 at 402, 261 N.Y.S.2d 511 at 515 (1st Dep't), adopted by the Court of Appeals in 17 N.Y.2d 477, 266 N.Y.S.2d 983, 214 N.E.2d 162 (1965).

9. CPLR 7109(b). See § 342 above.

10. CPLR 5104. The Advisory Committee intended this identity of treatment. See 3d Rep.Leg.Doc. (1959) No. 17, pp. 223, 230.

contempt of court,[11] and sometimes even the disobedience of a mere notice may be.[12]

The process of contempt is sometimes used in other phases of the litigation process. It is not necessarily limited to final judgments and orders. The provisional remedy of preliminary injunction, for example, and its short-lived offspring, the temporary restraining order,[13] are devices wholly dependent on the contempt remedy for enforcement. And without the threat of contempt to hold over a subpoenaed person, the subpoena would lose much of its effect, especially when addressed to nonparty witnesses against whom the threat of civil sanctions within the action, such as preclusion orders and defaults, would be meaningless. Even the device of an internal stay of proceedings, authorized by the CPLR in general terms[14] and having numerous functions, may have to depend on the ogre of contempt to deter violations.[15]

The present study, therefore, consisting of this and the next three sections, which constitute something like a mini-chapter on the contempt remedy, is relevant not exclusively to the enforcement of judgments, although the remedy does serve as the enforcement device for certain judgments; it is germane to all of the judicial processes that have to turn to contempt for implementation. While the contempt punishment may therefore be relevant at many stages of litigation, we have placed its study here, in the enforcement chapter, as the most logical repository. Appropriate references at its other points of relevancy lead back to this one.

In whatever instance the contempt remedy is invoked, the fact of the contempt must be established to the satisfaction of the court, and this requires a motion or proceeding of some

kind. (We are not concerned here with that other variety of contempt, the one committed in the "immediate view and presence" of the court, such as insolent conduct, which is summarily punishable.[16]) The motion or proceeding that brings on the contempt application itself is taken up three sections hence. One of its key inquiries will be whether the alleged contemnor had adequate notice of the direction he was required to obey, which depends heavily on whether he was properly served with the papers containing the direction, a matter we look into now.

Whenever the disobedience of a given direction is punishable as a contempt, the party who wishes to keep the remedy available should follow closely any instructions about service of the paper that contains the direction. A subpoena, for example, must be served in the same manner as a summons.[17] A restraining notice in connection with the enforcement of a money judgment must be served in the same manner as a summons or by registered or certified mail.[18] An order to show cause containing a temporary restraining order must be served as the order itself dictates. In each of these instances, where there is a specific direction about service, it should be followed to the letter. Some categories of judgments and orders enforcible by contempt have special service instructions. A matrimonial judgment or order directing alimony or support, for instance, must be personally served in order to lay a contempt foundation.[19]

If there is no special provision in point, CPLR 5104 governs. It requires that the judgment or order to be obeyed be certified[20] and that the certified copy be served on the person from whom compliance is sought.

---

11. Jud.L. § 753(A)(5).

12. The restraining notice of CPLR 5222, one of the devices for the enforcement of a money judgment, is an example. It requires no judicial permission. See § 508 below. For the broad lists of behavior punishable as a contempt of court, see Jud.L. §§ 750, 753.

13. See §§ 327 and 330 above.

14. See CPLR 2201, treated in § 255 above.

15. See, e.g., Hunter v. National Transp. Co., Inc., 273 A.D. 487, 78 N.Y.S.2d 225 (1st Dep't 1948).

16. This is known as summary contempt and usually falls under the criminal contempt category. See Jud.L.

§ 750(A)(1) and Katz v. Murtagh, 28 N.Y.2d 234, 321 N.Y.S.2d 104, 269 N.E.2d 816 (1971). Civil and criminal contempts are distinguished in § 482 below.

17. CPLR 2303.

18. CPLR 5222(a).

19. Dom.Rel.L. § 245.

20. Certification is not a problem today. It no longer has to be made by the clerk. The attorney can make it. CPLR 2105.

Will defects in service of the paper to be obeyed preclude contempt punishment if the party to be served knew of the direction, from whatever source, and disobeyed it anyway? The New York cases are not in the tidiest state in this area, but the Court of Appeals has said that even the absence of service—let alone technical defects in it—is no excuse for disobedience if there was knowledge of the direction,[21] and has indicated that the knowledge can come about even by telephone.[22] Even those not parties to the action out of which an injunction arises are therefore punishable for contempt if, although aware of the injunction, they act with or under the enjoined party and disobey it.[23] Nor can an enjoined person evade contempt by procuring another to do the proscribed thing, or by resorting to subterfuge, such as by forming a corporation to do it. Upon proof that such person is behind the scenes calling the shots, the contempt will reach him.[24]

The reader should be aware that there is also authority to the contrary: cases that take a more rigid line about service of the paper to be obeyed and that withhold the contempt punishment if service is not carried out to the letter, notwithstanding that the contemnor had knowledge.[25] As the footnote indicates, some courts sway back and forth on the point, but any holding disregarding knowledge and letting the contemnor off because he was not perfectly served not only conflicts with clear pronouncements of the Court of Appeals, but also encourages evasion of judicial process. The function of the contempt remedy is to uphold judicial process and the reasonable expectations of those who turn to it. Distinctions that disregard actual knowledge and turn on overly nice procedural points are not in harmony with that purpose.

§ 482. Criminal and Civil Contempt Distinguished; Punishment

For several purposes it is necessary to draw a line between criminal and civil contempt.

Criminal contempt is an offense against public justice. It is designed to vindicate and uphold the authority of the judiciary and the penalty for it is punitive. If the penalty is a fine, the money goes into the public treasury. Civil contempt is for the violation of a private right. The penalty imposed for it is designed to compensate or otherwise further the right of the party in whose favor the judicial direction was made,[1] and if the penalty is a monetary assessment it goes to the aggrieved party. The penalty for civil contempt is therefore calculated to redress a party's right, while the penalty for criminal contempt is designed to punish the contemnor so that he will stop treading, and not tread again, on the dignity of the judicial arm of the sovereign.[2]

21. See, e.g., Daly v. Amberg, 126 N.Y. 490, 27 N.E. 1038 (1891).

22. See McCormick v. Axelrod, 59 N.Y.2d 574, 466 N.Y.S.2d 279, 453 N.E.2d 508 (1983).

23. People ex rel. Stearns v. Marr, 181 N.Y. 463, 74 N.E. 431 (1905). Stearns says that there is no distinction between criminal and civil contempt insofar as service of the paper to be obeyed is concerned, and that for civil contempt not even actual knowledge of the direction is needed—although it would be for criminal contempt, where the element of intent is a key factor. The differences between these contempts are discussed in § 482 below.

24. See Mead Johnson & Co. v. Rosen, 16 A.D.2d 337, 228 N.Y.S.2d 204 (1st Dep't 1962).

25. See, e.g., R.C. Gluck & Co. v. Tankel, 12 A.D.2d 339, 211 N.Y.S.2d 602 (1st Dep't 1961), which said that service on the attorney instead of the party is inadequate. For that proposition it cited Shakun v. Shakun, 17 Misc.2d 935, 936, 187 N.Y.S.2d 439, 440 (Sup.Ct., Kings County, 1959), which squarely held that the requirement for serving a certified copy of the judgment must be strictly obeyed and that if the service is not carried out just so, "knowledge of the judgment is immaterial". A later phase of that same (Skakun) case went to the appellate division, however, which said just the opposite: that actual knowledge is adequate for contempt even if service was not made. 11 A.D.2d 724, 204 N.Y.S.2d 694 (2d Dep't 1960). In 1964, after the CPLR took effect, the same court, now treating § 245 of the Domestic Relations Law (regarding money in matrimonial actions), said that under that provision personal service on the husband "would appear to be a prerequisite to holding him in contempt". Kohn v. Kohn, 21 A.D.2d 881, 251 N.Y.S.2d 781, 783 (2d Dep't). A decade later the court backtracked and said that service is not needed for contempt; knowledge suffices. Yorktown Cent. School Dist. No. 2 v. Yorktown Congress of Teachers, 42 A.D.2d 422, 348 N.Y.S.2d 367 (2d Dep't 1973). A distinction could perhaps be made on the ground that different subject matter and different statutes were involved from case to case, but the more candid conclusion is that the cases are just in conflict.

§ 482

1. King v. Barnes, 113 N.Y. 476, 21 N.E. 182 (1889).

The same act can be both a criminal and civil contempt,[3] and often is. It is sometimes hard to tell which one it is;[4] more accurately, it is often hard to tell at what point a contempt becomes a criminal one. Any disobedience of a judicial mandate that is punishable by contempt and which injures the party on whose behalf the mandate issued is forthwith a civil contempt, but it does not become a criminal one until it reaches such a stage that it threatens the dignity of the court itself.[5] That is where the murky line appears.

Whether behavior has attained that level is an inquiry individual to the particular case. The reason for the distinction is historical and, today, statutory. The Judiciary Law perpetuates the distinction and appends different punishments to each class of contempt. One may criticize the distinction as overlooking the obvious—that any disobedience of a judicial mandate is an affront to the court and a threat to the system—but arguments of that kind must at this late stage be saved for the legislature. Justified or not, the differences are real.

Another difference, fostered by the U.S. Supreme Court in regard to federal mandates and influential with the New York courts on state mandates, is that punishment for criminal contempt is imposable even though it is ultimately determined that the mandate (judgment, order, etc.) should not have issued because it was improper or even beyond jurisdiction.[6] Punishment for civil contempt is cancelled upon such a determination,[7] but a party advised that an order is beyond jurisdiction disobeys it at risk because he can still be visited with a criminal contempt. In New York, unfortunately, that prospect often lacks in terrorem impact because of the weakness of the penalties imposable for criminal contempt, as we shall shortly see.

The main catalog of conduct that qualifies as a criminal contempt in New York is contained in § 750 of the Judiciary Law. The civil contempt roster is in § 753 of that law, in CPLR 5104, and in diverse other places.[8]

Presumably the criminal contempt—the variety of contempt that at least sounds more serious—would carry the more severe punishment. Not so in New York. Criminal contempt against an individual is in almost all instances punishable by a fine of not more than $1000 or by jail for not more than 30 days, or both[9]—an astounding situation. It confronts a criminal contemnor with a price he can usually afford and at worst the prospect of a month's confinement. The civil contempt penalty—ironically—has sharper teeth, and supplies the higher incentive to obey New York judicial process.

---

2. People ex rel. Munsell v. Court of Oyer and Terminer, 101 N.Y. 245, 4 N.E. 259 (1886).

3. See, e.g., Beth–El Hosp., Inc. v. Davis, 231 N.Y.S.2d 635 (Sup.Ct., Kings County, 1962), aff'd 18 A.D.2d 1138, 239 N.Y.S.2d 535 (2d Dep't 1963).

4. See, e.g., State of New York v. New York Movers Tariff Bur., Inc., 48 Misc.2d 225, 264 N.Y.S.2d 931 (Sup. Ct., N.Y.County, 1965).

5. People ex rel. Stearns v. Marr, 181 N.Y. 463, 74 N.E. 431 (1905).

6. The major federal case is United States v. United Mine Workers, 330 U.S. 258, 67 S.Ct. 677, 91 L.Ed. 884 (1947), admitting as the singular exception (where even criminal contempt would be cancelled) only the case in which the power to make the mandate is not even arguably within the lower court's power. For the New York law, see Mount Sinai Hosp., Inc. v. Davis, 8 A.D.2d 361, 188 N.Y.S.2d 298 (1st Dep't 1959). It is obviously only an appellate court that can determine that lower court jurisdiction was lacking; the party therefore must, at the risk of criminal contempt, obey the mandate at least until an appellate court so determines.

7. Bachman v. Harrington, 184 N.Y. 458, 77 N.E. 657 (1906).

8. CPLR 5251, for example, imposes contempt as the remedy for the disobedience of several of the devices of Article 52 for the enforcement of money judgments.

9. Jud.L. § 751(1). Fines in the case of contumacious unions or hospitals (as opposed to individuals) are not arbitrarily limited and can be substantial. Jud.L. § 751(2), (3). Criminal contempt of the kind under discussion here is also a crime and may be prosecuted as such, Penal Law §§ 215.50, 215.51, leading to more prolonged imprisonment and greater fines, see, e.g., Penal Law §§ 70.00, 70.15, 80.05, 80.10, but prosecutions of this kind are obviously more cumbersome than the proceedings authorized by the Judiciary Law, are not frequent, and are hence not a robust deterrent to criminal contempt of court. Penal Law § 215.54 provides that an adjudication of criminal contempt under Jud.L. § 750(A) does not bar a Penal Law prosecution for it, but that the previous punishment shall be considered by the court before sentence. Such a second proceeding might be barred on grounds of double jeopardy.

Civil contempt carries as a fine any sum that will indemnify the injured party for the actual loss caused by the contempt.[10] The fine must be measured by the injury caused to the contempt's victims and not by the nature of the contempt. It must be formulated "not to punish an offender, but solely to compensate or indemnify private complainants".[11] Damages must be proved by the injured party, and can include an attorney's fee.[12] Absent proof of damages, the party gets only costs plus an arbitrary $250.[13] The nature and extent of the punishment necessarily depends on the facts of the individual case and rests largely in the court's discretion.[14] The punishment in the case of a civil contempt can also include jail, and the term of it is not limited if the mandate calls for the doing of an act which the contemnor still has the power to do. He can be jailed until he does it.[15] Where, for example, a woman wilfully refused to obey a court order directing that she stop concealing a child and produce him in court, she was kept in jail a year and even more while her refusal persisted.[16]

Confinement in that situation is coercive rather than punitive. When the jailing is for a contempt for the doing of a forbidden act which now can't be undone, or for some other past recalcitrance, it is punitive and is limited to six months.[17] Here, too, the jailing is not necessarily alternative, but can be additional to a compensatory assessment.

The imposition of a jail sentence as a punitive rather than coercive measure for a civil contempt poses constitutional issues. Must the proof on the contempt application be established beyond a reasonable doubt, for example, the criminal standard? The courts have been troubled by this.[18] The application often seeks punishment for both categories of contempt, however, and insofar as a punitive jailing may be called for, the criminal aspect of the application, properly processed, supports it and enables the court to sidestep the issue in its civil aspect.[19]

All jailings for contempt must be reviewed at intervals of not more than 90 days.[20]

§ 483. Constitutionality of Contempt Procedure

The next section will discuss the procedure for invoking the contempt punishment, but in order to avoid encumbering it with constitutional issues we address the constitutional points in this section and leave the next one to do its job uncluttered.

Because contempt proceedings can lead to fines and jailings, they must meet minimal constitutional standards analogous to those met and discussed in the provisional remedies.[1] As they stood before 1977, the New York contempt procedures, which are contained in Article 19 of the Judiciary Law, did not on their face meet those standards, or so a three-judge federal district court[2] held in Vail v.

---

10. Jud.L. § 773.

11. State of New York v. Unique Ideas Inc., 44 N.Y.2d 345, 405 N.Y.S.2d 656, 376 N.E.2d 1301 (1978).

12. Quantum Heating Services Inc. v. Austern, 121 A.D.2d 437, 503 N.Y.S.2d 137 (2d Dep't 1986).

13. Jud.L. § 773. See Levine v. 97 Realty Corp., 21 A.D.2d 655, 249 N.Y.S.2d 715 (1st Dep't 1964).

14. In re Hildreth, 28 A.D.2d 290, 284 N.Y.S.2d 755 (1st Dep't 1967).

15. Jud.L. § 774(1).

16. People ex rel. Feldman v. Warden, 46 A.D.2d 256, 362 N.Y.S.2d 171 (1st Dep't 1974), aff'd 36 N.Y.2d 846, 370 N.Y.S.2d 913, 331 N.E.2d 691 (1975).

17. Jud.L. § 774(1).

18. See the majority and dissenting opinions in N.A. Development Co. Ltd. v. Jones, 99 A.D.2d 238, 472 N.Y.S.2d 363 (1st Dep't 1984). A discussion of the constitutionality of the contempt procedure when a warrant has

issued for the seizure of the contemnor appears in § 483 below.

19. This happened in the Jones case, id., in which the dissenting justices complain with good reason that the Judiciary Law's contempt provisions "are long overdue for legislative review and revision".

20. See Jud.L. § 774(2), CPLR 2308(c). Provision is made for notice to other parties to the action out of which the contempt arose. For the moment when each 90-day period starts to run, see People ex rel. Oppenheimer v. Rosoff, 82 Misc.2d 199, 368 N.Y.S.2d 969 (Sup.Ct., N.Y. County, 1975).

§ 483

1. See §§ 307, 315, and 338, above.

2. A "three-judge district court" was a special ad hoc panel set up to hear (among other things) an action to enjoin the enforcement of a state statute on grounds of repugnancy to the federal constitution. Congress in 1976

Quinlan.[3] Under the name of Juidice v. Vail, that decision was reversed by the U.S. Supreme Court, however,[4] with instructions that the district court on remand not entertain the case, i.e., that it "abstain" under the doctrine of Younger v. Harris.[5]

The *Younger* doctrine requires, in the interests of federalism and comity, that the federal courts not interfere unduly with the states' administration of their laws when the area is one of sensitive state interest and when there is an adequate opportunity for a prompt and thorough airing of all the issues in the state courts. Review of federal issues by the U.S. Supreme Court is preserved in that instance by letting the case go through the state system to the highest state court, from which review can be sought from the U.S. Supreme Court.[6]

The major objection voiced by the district court was that one of the possibilities under the New York contempt procedures was that at some point or another an alleged contemnor could be arrested by the sheriff and incarcerated without a hearing.[7] The district court indicated that if the seizure of the contemnor were solely for the purpose of bringing him to court for a hearing, before incarceration, the procedures might pass muster. Tacit in the U.S. Supreme Court's reversal of the district court was that, even assuming it is constitutionally mandated, such a requirement might be interpolated by the state courts if given a chance to review the matter. Indeed, the New York courts proved ready to do just that,[8] and interpolation in this fashion had in the past been recognized as a way of avoiding due process objections.[9]

The problem was in any event abated in 1977 legislation which provides that when an arrest is made pursuant to a warrant issued in a contempt proceeding, the warrant must command the sheriff to bring the defendant "forthwith" before the court.[10]

In many cases the contemnor had been given opportunities for a hearing, and adequate notice in connection with all of them, but disregarded them all. The district court attitude in *Vail* was: no matter, due process requires an actual hearing before imprisonment, not just an opportunity. The U.S. Supreme Court, in reversing, appeared to be at some pains to refute that contention. It stressed the many opportunities the contemnor in *Vail* had already had for a hearing, but had ignored: he was given notice of the underlying action itself, a minor money claim against him, and defaulted; after a default judgment was entered and a subpoena served on him to elicit data about his assets[11] he ignored the subpoena, which was his second default; when contempt proceedings were thereupon instituted for disobedience of the subpoena, by an order to show cause offering him yet another hearing opportunity, he ignored that as well, and that was default number three. Only afterwards did the next step, the warrant of arrest, issue. By observing that the contemnor "had ignored for a period of nine months every stage of the state court proceedings"[12] and forfeited one opportunity after another for a hearing, the U.S. Supreme Court, although concluding only to direct the district court to abstain and let the state courts have a go at

---

abolished the three-judge court system in all but a few instances, leaving these matters to the usual one-judge district court. See Pub.L. 94–381, Aug. 12, 1976, 90 Stat. 1119, repealing 28 U.S.C.A. §§ 2281 and 2282 and amending 2284.

3. 406 F.Supp. 951 (S.D.N.Y.1976).

4. 430 U.S. 327, 97 S.Ct. 1211, 51 L.Ed.2d 376 (1977).

5. 401 U.S. 37, 91 S.Ct. 746, 27 L.Ed.2d 669 (1971). The federal abstention doctrines in general are treated in § 613 below (Practitioner's Edition).

6. See 28 U.S.C.A § 1257.

7. Section 757 of the Judiciary Law, as then constituted, authorized the court, upon issuance of a warrant, to direct the sheriff to arrest the defendant and bring him before the court "either" forthwith or at a later time.

8. See, e.g., Walker v. Walker, 51 A.D.2d 1029, 381 N.Y.S.2d 310 (2d Dep't 1976).

9. See National Eqpt. Rental, Ltd. v. Szukhent, 375 U.S. 311, 84 S.Ct. 411, 11 L.Ed.2d 354 (1964), distinguishing but seeming more to overrule Wuchter v. Pizzutti, 276 U.S. 13, 48 S.Ct. 259, 72 L.Ed. 446 (1928). See also Agur v. Wilson, 498 F.2d 961 (2d Cir.1974), cert. den. 419 U.S. 1072, 95 S.Ct. 661, 42 L.Ed.2d 669 (1974).

10. L.1977, c. 437, amending Jud.L. §§ 772, 773.

11. The subpoena was issued pursuant to CPLR 5224. See § 509 below.

12. 430 U.S. at 330, 97 S.Ct. at 1214.

the issues, was hinting as closely as it could, without actually deciding, that the New York statutes even as then constituted were not offensive to due process.

Therein lies the important constitutional lesson of the *Vail* case: a general admonition that an opportunity for a hearing, rather than an actual one, may be all that due process requires here. There may still be occasions for testing that proposition under New York law, but it is not likely to be in the contempt area. The 1977 contempt legislation appears to contemplate that even when arrest results—previous hearing opportunities having been ignored or not—the next stop must generally be the courthouse if there has not already been a hearing. Jail is to follow only if the judge, having heard the contemnor, orders it, and that satisfies the demands of due process.

§ 484. Procedure to Punish for Contempt

If the alleged contemnor was not a party to the action out of which the contempt arises, it has been held that the application to punish for contempt must take the form of a special proceeding.[1] If the alleged contemnor was a party, the more usual situation, the procedure to punish for contempt is a motion,[2] which may be brought on by the usual notice of motion or by the alternative of an order to show cause.[3] As a mere motion, it should bear the caption of the action or proceeding out of which the contempt arises and should ordinarily be sought from the court in the county in which that action or proceeding was brought.[4]

Specifically designated a motion, the application should not, as long as the contemnor was a party, be deemed a separate special proceeding, unless perhaps it seeks to punish a contempt emanating from a non-judicial proceeding, such as one before an administrative agency. In that instance there would be no pending court action or proceeding to supply the context for a motion. If denominated a motion in such an instance, and it is found that a special proceeding would have been the proper form (and of course assuming that jurisdiction over the alleged contemnor has been secured), the motion should simply be deemed a proceeding, and vice-versa.[5]

If an ordinary notice of motion is used, the motion must be made on no fewer than 10 and no more than 30 days notice. The notice must also contain on its face, in at least eight-point boldface type in capital letters, this admonition: WARNING: YOUR FAILURE TO APPEAR IN COURT MAY RESULT IN YOUR IMMEDIATE ARREST AND IMPRISONMENT FOR CONTEMPT OF COURT.[6] The papers must be served on the contemnor himself, unless the court directs service on his attorney (which would suggest that an order to show cause is being used).[7] Actually the applicant probably does best to serve copies of the motion papers on attorney and client both.

How shall the papers be served? All the applicable statute[8] says is that the papers bringing on a contempt motion "shall be served" on the party. This has been held to mean that ordinary mail service will do; that personal delivery is not required.[9] At least that is so of civil contempt.[10] With criminal

---

§ 484

1. Long Island Trust Co. v. Rosenberg, 82 A.D.2d 591, 442 N.Y.S.2d 563 (2d Dep't 1981). The procedure in special proceedings is governed by Article 4 of the CPLR, treated in § 547 et seq., below.

2. Jud.L. § 756.

3. Before 1977, the show cause procedure had to be used exclusively. Jud.L. § 757 and Dom.Rel.L. § 245 so required. Amendments of those statutes in L.1977, c.437, made the show cause procedure a mere alternative, as it is for motions generally.

4. See Shapiro v. Shapiro, 60 Misc.2d 622, 303 N.Y.S.2d 565 (Sup.Ct., Queens County, 1969).

5. See CPLR 103(c) and the the last part of § 4 above.

6. Jud.L. § 756.

7. Jud.L. § 761.

8. Id.

9. New York Higher Educ. Assistance Corp. v. Cooper, 65 A.D.2d 906, 410 N.Y.S.2d 687 (3d Dep't 1978).

10. See the discussion in Department of Housing Preservation v. Arick, 131 Misc.2d 950, 503 N.Y.S.2d 489 (N.Y.C.Civ.Ct. 1986), cited approvingly in Department of Housing Preservation v. 24 West 132 Equities, Inc., 137 Misc.2d 459, 524 N.Y.S.2d 324 (App.Trm., 1st Dep't, 1987), before being reversed on just a timeliness point in 137 Misc.2d 1079, 526 N.Y.S.2d 51 (App.Trm., 1st Dep't, 1988).

contempt, some courts require personal service.[11] The lawyer who wants to tie up all loose ends should, in any doubtful situation, use the personal service alternative. It is worth remembering that the judges are not anxious to impose the contempt punishment and that procedural defects that may be deemed harmless in other contexts can prove destructive in this one: a convenient hook for a hesitant judge to hang his hat on.

Upon the motion's return, recognizing that a fine or imprisonment may be imposed, statute requires the judge to advise the contemnor that she has the right to counsel. If the contemnor cannot afford counsel, the court may in its discretion assign counsel.[12]

The court must determine whether the alleged contemnor is guilty of the contempt charged and, if he is, what kind of contempt it is and what the punishment will be. If there is a factual dispute as to D's conduct unresolvable from the papers on the motion, a hearing will be necessary and will investigate all relevant factors. The statute requires a hearing,[13] and the right to a hearing would in any event be implied.[14]

An issue of fact requiring a trial does not necessarily require a trial by jury. The general rule, in fact, has been held to be that neither category of contempt, civil or criminal, requires trial by jury for historical reasons,[15] and the Court of Appeals has confirmed that even for criminal contempt a trial by jury is not mandatory because the potential imprisonment upon conviction (30 days) falls into the

"petty" category under applicable U.S. Supreme Court standards.[16]

If the contempt arises in connection with a procedure under the CPLR for the enforcement of a judgment,[17] a showing that the contemnor—the judgment debtor in this instance—has not the means to comply requires a denial of the application to punish. The denial is of course without prejudice to renewal upon proof that the debtor's financial condition has changed.[18]

An order adjudging a person in contempt may be made conditional, i.e., "unless" the contemnor does a particular thing or makes a specified payment within a stated time.[19] This affords the contemnor a chance to purge the contempt.

When the contempt arises out of a procedure for the enforcement of a judgment, including a direction for the payment of money under a matrimonial judgment or order, a special purging procedure is offered even if the contemnor does not respond to the contempt motion. The court in that case is required to make a conditional commitment order, the condition being that the contemnor purge the contempt within 10 days after being personally served with the order. If the 10–day period lapses without performance, as proved by an affidavit furnished to the court, a warrant may now be issued by the court directing the arrest of the contemnor. Upon that arrest, in fulfillment of constitutional requirements, the contemnor will be brought forthwith to court to be heard.[20] If the punishment includes a fine, a similar 10–day conditional purging order is permissible, and

---

11. See, e.g., Lu v. Betancourt, 116 A.D.2d 492, 496 N.Y.S.2d 754 (1st Dep't 1986). A detailed treatment of the subject, noting departmental differences, appears in the Arick case, id.

12. Jud.L. § 770.

13. Jud.L. § 772. See CPLR 2218, made applicable to the contempt application by Jud.L. § 772's adoption of general motion practice. CPLR 2218 authorizes the immediate trial of any issues of fact arising on the motion.

14. See Agur v. Wilson, 498 F.2d 961 (2d Cir.), cert. den. 419 U.S. 1072, 95 S.Ct. 661, 42 L.Ed.2d 669 (1974).

15. See Department of Housing Preservation v. Chance Equities, Inc., 135 Misc.2d 375, 515 N.Y.S.2d 709 (Civ.Ct., N.Y.County, 1987).

16. See Rankin v. Shanker, 23 N.Y.2d 111, 295 N.Y.S.2d 625, 242 N.E.2d 802 (1968), and Morgenthau v.

Erlbaum, 59 N.Y.2d 143, 464 N.Y.S.2d 392, 451 N.E.2d 150 (1983), discussing the applicable constitutional requirements and how New York procedures fare under them.

17. These procedures arise under Article 52 of the CPLR, governing the enforcement of money judgments. Some of the devices supplied by Article 52 are enforced by the contempt penalty under CPLR 5251. See § 523 below.

18. Jud.L. § 770. Reference to the offender's financial condition implies applicability only to money judgments. Other judgments are also backed by the contempt penalty, however. See CPLR 5104; § 481, above.

19. See, e.g., Denberg v. Denberg, 21 A.D.2d 863, 251 N.Y.S.2d 90 (1st Dep't 1964).

20. Jud.L. § 772.

the court may in its discretion include a provision requiring the contemnor to supply an undertaking conditioned upon his paying the fine and performing any act required by the judgment or order.[21]

If the contemnor appears on the return day of the original contempt motion, and the facts are thereupon determined and establish the contempt to the satisfaction of the court, the punishment imposed need not be conditional.

All of the foregoing should be taken to apply whether the contempt involved is of the civil or criminal variety. The statutes supplying the procedural instruction, despite their 1977 amendment and improvement, seem to assume their applicability only to civil contempt,[22] but they would appear to apply to criminal contempt as well. Since the distinctions between civil and criminal contempt are based on the conduct that constitutes the contempt and the nature of the punishment to be imposed for it, there should be little difference in the procedural steps by which the contemptuous conduct is proved and the punishment imposed.[23] Perhaps we may be allowed to pause here to observe that the need constantly to deduce and infer and extrapolate to make sense of the Judiciary Law's contempt provisions gives credence to the observation made in N.A. Development Co. Ltd. v. Jones:[24] that the Judiciary

Law's contempt provisions "are long overdue for legislative review and revision".

Although the mechanics for invoking the punishment should be the same whether the offense involved is civil or criminal or both,[25] the contempt proceeding itself has been held to be of a civil nature. To make this point clear, the Court of Appeals has used words to the effect that criminal contempt arising out of a civil action "constitutes a civil special proceeding".[26] The intent was to require that rules of civil rather than criminal procedure govern the criminal contempt application; it was not intended to require that the application be treated as an independent special proceeding—as opposed to a mere motion—but some courts have been led to that conclusion.[27] If the clerk treats it as a separate proceeding, he may insist on a separate index number and filing fee. Even so, it has been held that the failure to secure the number in advance is curable nunc pro tunc without loss of jurisdiction.[28] Ordinarily the application should not be treated as a distinct proceeding; at least as against one who was a party to the underlying action or proceeding, it should be considered a mere motion arising out of that action or proceeding. This is what § 756 of the Judiciary Law obviously intends by authorizing the motion procedure. Having the context of the original action or proceeding, the motion should need no new file number (or filing fee).

---

21. Jud.L. § 773.

22. See, e.g., Jud.L. §§ 756, 761.

23. See Jud.L. § 751(1), which clearly applies only to criminal contempt. Section 754 provides that any contempt other than one committed in the immediate view and presence of the court (which is what is commonly known as "summary" contempt) may be punished only after the party charged is notified and given a reasonable opportunity to defend. The procedures supplied in this and subsequent sections of the Judiciary Law, which have grounded discussion up to this point, are the most obvious as well as the most convenient source of procedural guidance for the criminal contempt application notwithstanding their reference to civil contempt.

24. 99 A.D.2d 238, 472 N.Y.S.2d 363 (1st Dep't 1984) (dissenting opinion).

25. See People ex rel. Stearns v. Marr, 181 N.Y. 463, 74 N.E. 431 (1905).

26. See Douglas v. Adel, 269 N.Y. 144, 146, 199 N.E. 35, 36 (1935).

27. See, e.g., Board of Educ. of New Rochelle v. Zeluck, 60 Misc.2d 1090, 304 N.Y.S.2d 697 (Sup.Ct., Westchester County, 1969).

28. See Matter of Lakeland Federation of Teachers, 65 Misc.2d 397, 317 N.Y.S.2d 902 (Sup.Ct., Westchester County, 1971).

Part II

ENFORCEMENT OF MONEY JUDGMENTS

A. IN GENERAL

§ 485. Enforcement of Money Judgments, Introductory

The money judgment dominates the area of "enforcement of judgments". This is so for two reasons. The first, as we saw in Part I of this chapter, is that the enforcement of the non-money judgment is a less complicated affair, usually involving but a single device, while the money judgment can involve many. Even when contempt is sought, which can entail the issuance of a warrant and the arresting and jailing of the defendant, the enforcement road of a non-money judgment is seldom a long one. The second reason is that there are many more money judgments seeking enforcement than there are other kinds. Article 52 governs the enforcement of the money judgment.

Ironically, in what is probably the most numerous category of money action today, the personal injury tort, enforcement is less frequently an issue. Since the defendant's liability is most often backed by insurance, the plaintiff's quest is to get the judgment; the insurer sooner or later makes it good, of course limited by the amount of the insurance policy, and this obviates enforcement. But in commercial, property, and matrimonial cases and, indeed, uninsured tort cases or those in which damages exceed the defendant's insurance coverage, enforcement is a frequent problem.

The structure of Article 52 resembles that of Article 31, the CPLR's disclosure article. The opening section, CPLR 5201, tells us what

property of the defendant may be applied to the judgment, just as CPLR 3101 lists the basic disclosure criteria. It also carves out some exceptions, which 3101 does, too. Most of the rest of Article 52 is devoted to supplying a series of devices to aid enforcement, as Article 31 supplies a series of devices to aid disclosure, along with such other items as the ordering of liens and priorities. The two articles even have in common a "protective order". CPLR 5240 does for Article 52 and the enforcement devices what CPLR 3103 does for Article 31 and the disclosure devices: it sets forth in one place an omnibus judicial power to intervene in the use of any device so as to prevent, on a case by case basis, any unjustified harassment or oppression. This frees Article 52 to supply each device without having to incorporate protective or punitive provisions at every turn.

Lawyers bent on familiarizing themselves with the enforcement of judgments should make a general study of each of the devices and its particular function. Only by knowing the function of all of them can they make an intelligent choice of which one to use in a given situation, and the situations are endlessly variable.

If the judgment debtor has no assets whatever, and no job or other income source, Article 52 offers no comfort; it draws no blood from a stone. But if the debtor does have leviable property or income, however ingeniously he has tried to conceal it, imagination and effort brought to bear by the lawyer should be able with Article 52's aid to identify and get through to the property. The legislature has tried in Article 52 to produce a series of devices designed, alone or in combination, to cover the field. There are ways to reach possessory interests when title is lacking, and ownership when the right to possession is lacking; to get at tangibles hands can touch, and intangibles as incorporeal as a cause of action; to obtain property in plain view so that a sheriff can levy, and property concealed so that it must first be sought out and then the debtor made to produce it. There is a tool to reach income to a limited percentage, and a tool to reach more of the income when it is clear that the debtor can afford more. The fact that there is income may be plain, or deducible from a state of facts. There are devices for property that needs to be retained and managed in order to be valuable, and property whose value can be realized only through sale; for property with worth that a public auction can exploit, and property that requires a private sale; for property that can be seized immediately, and property that can be reached only later; for property the debtor has himself, and property that is his but is held by another; and on and on. Further, the creditor may know nothing at all about the debtor's assets and finances to begin with and may need assistance to find out about them, or a third person who controls the asset sought may be about to sell it, or give it back to the debtor, before the creditor can take hold of it. For all of these situations Article 52, through one or a mixture of its devices, has aid to give. By having a general picture of all of the devices—briefly listed in a later section[1] and then treated individually—the lawyer can quickly identify the situations appropriate to each of them.

The moment as of which the judgment becomes enforcible is the moment of its entry. As a general rule, the judgment creditor may then dive into Article 52 and extract whichever devices suit her particular purpose. There is no priority in the use of the devices. No device is a condition precedent to the use of any other; the sequence of their use is for the judgment creditor to decide. Nor is there any general limit on the number of times a single device may be used. If abuse arises, the cure is an ad hoc protective order under CPLR 5240.

To the general rule that a judgment creditor is entitled to seek enforcement of a money judgment immediately upon entry, and for its full sum, is an important exception enacted in the mid–1980s for the periodic rather than lump sum payment of portions of certain tort judgments. Popularly known as the "structured judgment", it is embodied in two articles of the CPLR, Article 50–A for medical, dental, and podiatric malpractice actions and Article 50–B for all other personal injury, injury to property, and wrongful death actions.[2] Damages awards in those categories of action often include an award for the plaintiff's projected future damages. The articles provide that the first $250,000 of those future damages continues to be awardable, and enforcible, in a lump sum, but the amount in excess of $250,000 is to be paid out over the period of future time that the fact trier estimates those damages will be experienced, not exceeding 10 years.[3] It is a kind of annuity arrangement, but only in respect of the "future" segment of the damages found, and only to the extent that they exceed $250,000.

Caselaw on the articles, which present a number of issues, is in its infancy.[4] The first treatment of them by the Court of Appeals appears in Rohring v. City of Niagara Falls,[5] in which the court addresses two issues arising under the articles, one concerning a deduction the article requires for attorneys' fees and the other concerning the computation of interest.[6]

The main limitation on the use of the enforcement devices to aid the collection of a

<hr/>

§ 485

1. See § 492 below.

2. Article 50–A appeared in 1985. Article 50–B, which followed in 1986 and is almost identical to Article 50–A, could easily have been integrated with Article 50–A instead of being made a separate article. The two are compared and the few paltry differences between them noted in the Commentaries on McKinney's CPLR Articles 50–A and 50–B.

3. See Barker, New York Practice, N.Y. Law Journal, October 26, 1987, page 1.

4. For a thoughtful early exercise in the detailed construction of a periodic judgment, see Ursini v. Sussman, 143 Misc.2d 727, 541 N.Y.S.2d 916 (Sup.Ct., N.Y.County, 1989).

5. 84 N.Y.2d 60, 614 N.Y.S.2d 714, 638 N.E.2d 62 (1994).

6. The case is treated at length in a lead note in New York State Law Digest No. 415. See also Schultz v. Harrison Radiator Div. General Motors Corp., 90 N.Y.2d 311, 660 N.Y.S.2d 685 (1997), summarized in New York State Law Digest No. 453.

money judgment is, as one might suspect, money. Some of the devices involve substantial lawyering time, which means they will be costly to the judgment creditor. Depositions to aid disclosure, motions seeking orders of one kind or another, dealings with the enforcement officer, and other steps in pursuit of an elusive judgment debtor can be expensive. If their cost is disproportionate to the amount of the judgment being enforced, the creditor may have to abandon enforcement for reasons of simple economics. This is a misfortune to the judgment creditor and an unflattering comment on the system, but it is really only the enforcement phase of a more serious problem needing legislative attention: ready and reasonably priced access to court and counsel by all. If the judgment creditor emerges from a strenuous enforcement effort without having satisfied the judgment, and the judgment debtor does have assets that might have been applied to the judgment, the fault will not lie with Article 52 for having failed to supply appropriate aids; it will likely be attributable to the economic unfeasibility of pursuing these aids any further. If the stakes are high enough, though, and the hope of realizing on the judgment is real, Article 52 will not be found wanting.

Just as economics may dictate whether a significant effort may be made to pursue the debtor at all, so will it also dictate how far a creditor wants the pursuit to go. From one point of view, the enforcement of judgments is the place to which most other law topics ultimately lead. The assumption is that if the plaintiff has a right and the right is pursued to judgment, it only remains to get the judgment enforced. But there are several subjects, which follow rather than precede the enforcement of judgments, that the judgment creditor should have in mind even during the enforcement journey. A judgment creditor may find that she is not alone in pursuit of the debtor, who may be in such financial extremis that his creditors are legion. At this point the topic becomes what law school curricula often denominate "creditors' rights", a battleground that determines priorities in the assets of a declining debtor. If the progression continues, the law and the law schools also have a name

for the next topic: "bankruptcy". The "enforcement" topic can lead to these other two, which are studies in themselves and beyond the scope of Article 52, but that they lurk just around the corner warns the judgment creditor to be sensitive about the debtor's economic status; pressing the judgment debtor too far, especially when others are also pressing, can result in the creditor's collecting a good deal less than a little patience earlier on might have earned, or nothing at all. Sometimes accepting less than the law technically authorizes, or letting the judgment debtor stretch payments over a longer period than the law requires, is the more provident course. The enforcement of judgments is ruled by pragmatists. Theoreticians have no fun at this party.

The main groupings in the ensuing study will be property subject to enforcement, the devices available to get at the property, liens and priorities in the property, and protective orders. With other incidents integrated at appropriate junctures, that will be the progression.

B.   PROPERTY SUBJECT TO ENFORCEMENT

Table of Sections

§ 486.   Property Applicable to the Judgment, Introductory

The general rule under the CPLR is that any property interest of a judgment debtor, which by law the debtor may assign or transfer, may be sought for application to the judgment. The rule, embodied in subdivision (b) of CPLR 5201, recognizes the futility of trying to list specifically all of a person's possible property interests in an age when "property" takes on so many varied and often sophisticated forms. This standard is a decided improvement over the old Civil Practice Act, which, in trying to supply such a list, found itself on a quest without end.[1] Property rights and interests are as variable as the human engagements that create them, and just as extensive. The CPLR wisely abandons any effort to identify them all and says instead that any property interest the judgment debtor has, other than that rare sort that the law has made unassignable, may be appropriated and applied to the judgment, no matter how difficult the steps needed to accomplish the application. Problems in getting through to the property and realizing on it are the reason for the CPLR's broad variety of enforcement devices. These, with some imagination and initiative, will usually be found to supply what is needed. Property real and property personal; property tangible and property intangible; debts owed and debts claimed; present interests and future interests—for all of these there are ways and means available. For the moment we ask only what property is worth pursuing. The mechanics of the pursuit come later.

Most property interests are assignable. The most significant interest that is not is a cause of action the judgment debtor has against a third person for personal injuries,[2] as where the judgment debtor has been involved in an accident and has not yet recovered on a claim for damages arising out of it. But the courts have made a distinction between the transfer of the personal injury claim itself, which is not permitted, and the transfer of the potential proceeds of the claim, which are.[3] The judgment creditor may therefore pursue the proceeds,[4] which become leviable when the judgment debtor wins judgment or obtains a settlement in the personal injury suit.

A second inquiry the judgment creditor must make is whether the particular property is exempt from seizure. Some property, mainly the basics of domestic life, is statutorily insulated from the owner's creditors. We will come back to this later with a treatment of the CPLR's exemption lists.[5]

A third inquiry must be made in the event the property interest to be pursued is a "debt" allegedly owed to the judgment debtor, or a cause of action the debtor has against a third person. Interests in this category, which are of course intangible, are made leviable only if "past due or ... yet to become due, certainly or upon demand".[6] This is designed to avoid judicial involvement with intangibles that may never ripen into a significant property right, as where they depend on a contingency that may never occur. This category of excluded property has been a problem for the New York courts.[7]

Examples of property rights, both obvious and subtle, that are pursuable (as a matter of law) and worth pursuing (as a matter of economics) will appear in the course of the next few sections.

There is an interplay here between attachment and execution. Any property interest applicable to satisfaction of a judgment is also applicable to a pre-judgment order of attachment.[8] But rather than list separately the property on which the provisional remedy of attachment may be levied, the CPLR concentrates all attention—and avoids needless duplication—on post-judgment enforcement, afterwards making the fruits of the whole project available for attachment as well in a simply worded statute, CPLR 6202, providing that "[a]ny debt or property against which a money judgment may be enforced as provided in section 5201 is subject to attachment". The main difference between the two is that the purpose of the attachment is to keep the property out

§ 486

1. See, e.g., §§ 687, 687–a, and 688 of the Civil Practice Act, repealed eff. September 1, 1963.

2. Gen.Oblig.L. § 13–101.

3. See Grossman v. Schlosser, 19 A.D.2d 893, 244 N.Y.S.2d 749 (2d Dep't 1963). For a more extended discussion of the general differences between assignment of a claim and assignment of its proceeds, see Stathos v. Murphy, 26 A.D.2d 500, 276 N.Y.S.2d 727 (1st Dep't 1966),

aff'd 19 N.Y.2d 883, 281 N.Y.S.2d 81, 227 N.E.2d 880 (1967).

4. Iguanti v. Kronish, 52 Misc.2d 306, 276 N.Y.S.2d 130 (Sup.Ct., Bronx County, 1966).

5. See § 490.

6. CPLR 5201(a).

7. See § 489 below.

8. The provisional remedy of attachment was treated in an earlier chapter. See § 313 et seq., above.

of the debtor's hands, not to convert it to money for payment over to the plaintiff, while conversion and payment are very much the purpose of the post-judgment enforcement devices.

Recognizing that under the CPLR the same property interests lend themselves to pre-judgment attachment and post-judgment enforcement indifferently, cases involving either are cited interchangeably throughout the chapter. In this connection, it should be remembered that the category of quasi in rem jurisdiction—the category in which a plaintiff finding New York property of a nondomiciliary defendant uses it as a jurisdictional basis for a foreign claim against the defendant to secure a judgment good to the extent of the property even without personam jurisdiction—was vastly reduced by the U.S. Supreme Court in Shaffer v. Heitner[9] in 1977. Many of the cases clarifying property interests of one kind or another involved this jurisdictional use of the attachment.[10] These cases are still good law on the subject of leviable property, but, irony though this be, their future utility for jurisdictional attachments—the very realm that produced them—is much curtailed.

§ 487. Examples of Leviable Property Rights

Tangible real or personal property owned outright by the defendant and not within any of the exemption provisions can of course be applied to the judgment, but so can a myriad of other interests. Title to the property is reachable even if the right of possession has been partly divested; the encumbered right of title can be sold for whatever a buyer is willing to pay for it. Conversely, a present right of possession may be levied on even if a right of repossession or outright title lies elsewhere,[1]

as long as the right, however limited, has anything of economic value that might entice a buyer. If it lacks at least that value, it will be useless to the judgment creditor not as a matter of law but as a matter of economics. Indeed, appraisal of the particular interest is an important preliminary for the judgment creditor, lest she go to needless expense in pursuit of what turns out to be an unwelcome duet: leviable but worthless.

Intangible interests, including money belonging to or owed to the judgment debtor, are subject to levy and are infinite in their variety. Some of these incorporeal interests have economic value so real and so direct that a judgment creditor would prefer them to any kind of tangible property. Others are more remote and take greater effort to reduce to money. Others are so contingent that they may never amount to a thing and not even be worth an effort.

An example of a popular intangible that probably qualifies as the judgment creditor's favorite find, if the creditor is lucky enough to find it, is a bank account the debtor has in New York. Even though the bank may have numerous branches, it is best as a rule to pursue enforcement of the account, such as with a levy of execution or the service of a restraining notice—devices to be met in due course—only at the branch where the account is actually maintained.[2] Because of modern communications media that enable a bank served at any office to make almost instant entries on the records of all of them, it has been held that service at the main office of a bank with such a system operates even on an account maintained at the branch.[3] But noting that not all banks have such a "modern centralized and computerized" system, the Second Department held in Therm–X–Chemical & Oil

---

9. 433 U.S. 186, 97 S.Ct. 2569, 53 L.Ed.2d 683 (1977). The Shaffer case, including the few instances in which it still allows quasi in rem use of an attachment, is treated in § 104 above.

10. See, e.g., ABKCO Industries, Inc. v. Apple Films, Inc., 39 N.Y.2d 670, 385 N.Y.S.2d 511, 350 N.E.2d 899 (1976). The ABKCO case is discussed at length in § 489, below, which is concerned with contingent intangible interests of a judgment debtor and their availability to creditors.

§ 487

1. See General Motors Acceptance Corp. v. Maloney, 46 Misc.2d 251, 259 N.Y.S.2d 211 (Sup.Ct., Queens County, 1965).

2. See National Shipping & Trading Corp. v. Weeks Stevedoring Co., 252 F.Supp. 275 (S.D.N.Y.1966).

3. Digitrex, Inc. v. Johnson, 491 F.Supp. 66 (S.D.N.Y. 1980).

Corp. v. Extebank,[4] that the general rule in New York remains "that in order to reach a particular bank account the judgment creditor must serve the office of the bank where the account is maintained". The creditor in *Therm-X* did not do that, relying on service at the main office, and it cost him: the bank was not computerized and the restraining notice was therefore ineffective to reach the branch account. It thus appears the safer course to stick to the branch. When a branch account is involved, service at the branch is certain to accomplish its task; service at the main office is at best chancy.

As long as the deposited money is the debtor's, the creditor can reach the account with ease. It has been held that even a deposit made by the debtor in his own name but in trust for another—the so-called "Totten Trust"[5]—is money belonging to the depositor until his death and may be reached by his creditors.[6]

If the judgment debtor, D, has a joint bank account with another, A, the judgment creditor can pursue it: there is a presumption that each joint tenant is entitled to all of the account. The presumption is rebuttable, however, with the burden on the joint owners to rebut it. If they do rebut it, as by showing that the money was all put in by A, with D added as a party only for A's convenience, the pursuit may bear less fruit, or none at all because the levy is good only to the extent of D's "actual interest", which is subject to proof.[7] Until the presumption of D's interest is rebutted, the quest is usually worthwhile. A bank will sometimes refuse to release funds in a joint account until satisfied of the part belonging to the judgment debtor, putting the credi-

tor to the burden of a court application to resolve the matter.[8]

The interest of a judgment debtor as a beneficiary under a decedent's estate may be reached by her creditor.[9] If it appears that such a beneficiary would not get the use of the money or property, as where she is in a country that would not let her have it, it can be directed into a kind of impoundage deposit;[10] if it is, the deposit can be reached by the beneficiary's creditors, as can almost any funds in custodia legis in which the debtor has a present interest,[11] at least to the extent that the debtor herself could reach the funds if there were no foreign fetters on her.

In the commercial area, assets worth pursuing against a judgment debtor include all variety of debts evidenced by commercial paper or accounts receivable.[12] If an account has been encumbered, the debtor may still retain an equity in it. Any equity of redemption the debtor may have in it or in any other property he may have pledged or otherwise given to another for some security purpose may be levied.[13]

The several varieties of tenancy ownership in real property may be reached by the creditor to the extent of the tenant's interest. In this sphere the most troublesome has always been the tenancy by the entirety, in which spouses have coequal rights in the property. It has been held that the creditor of only one spouse can reach that spouse's interest, but judges have had trouble in determining just what it is that gets reached. If the property produces income, the creditor can be allowed the debtor-spouse's share of it, but the courts are loath to allow the creditor to share possession of the asset with the non-debtor spouse. In a few cases the courts have made this

---

4. 84 A.D.2d 787, 444 N.Y.S.2d 26 (2d Dep't 1981).

5. See Matter of Totten, 179 N.Y. 112, 71 N.E. 748 (1904).

6. Abraham & Straus, Inc. v. Feynman, 71 Misc.2d 928, 337 N.Y.S.2d 654 (Dist.Ct., Suffolk County, 1972).

7. See Viggiano v. Viggiano, 136 A.D.2d 630, 523 N.Y.S.2d 874 (2d Dep't 1988).

8. See, e.g., Household Finance Corp. v. Rochester Community Sav. Bank, 143 Misc.2d 436, 541 N.Y.S.2d 160 (Rochester City Court 1989).

9. Matter of Pallonetti's Estate, 48 Misc.2d 814, 265 N.Y.S.2d 976 (Surr.Ct., Kings County, 1965).

10. See SCPA 2218.

11. See Matter of Leikind, 22 N.Y.2d 346, 292 N.Y.S.2d 681, 239 N.E.2d 550 (1968).

12. See International Ribbon Mills, Ltd. v. Arjan Ribbons, Inc., 36 N.Y.2d 121, 365 N.Y.S.2d 808, 325 N.E.2d 137 (1975).

13. Fitchburg Yarn Co. v. Wall & Co., 46 A.D.2d 763, 361 N.Y.S.2d 170 (1st Dep't 1974).

category of property interest unavailable as a practical matter when the asset involved was the family residence, declaring either that the right of possession is not reachable as a matter of law,[14] or that, whether theoretically reachable or not, it should be insulated with an ad hoc protective order under CPLR 5240.[15] This may mean that all the creditor takes here is a kind of lien against the property, to become fully leviable only if and when the non-debtor spouse predeceases the debtor spouse (who would thereupon succeed to the whole of the property), or to lapse into nothingness if the non-debtor spouse is the survivor. Or, if divorce should undo the marriage and convert the tenancy by the entirety into a tenancy in common, the debtor-spouse's creditor will now be able to levy because the debtor's interest will be transferable to a buyer.[16]

Real property in all of its diverse modern forms of ownership may be sought for application to a judgment, including cooperatives, condominiums, and mobile homes, subject, of course, to the applicable exemption if the property is the debtor's principal residence. Here it is important to note that a judgment debtor's interest in a cooperative apartment, at one time thought to be real property for all purposes and therefore lienable by the mere docketing of the judgment in the county of the apartment's location,[17] was held by the Court of Appeals in State Tax Comm. v. Shor to be personal property for enforcement purposes.[18] Liens on personal property do not arise on the mere docketing of a judgment, with the result in *Shor* that the creditor lost all priority, and some $100,000, for relying on the property's

assumed status as realty. This means that a judgment creditor in pursuit of the judgment debtor's interest in a cooperative apartment must make the greater effort needed to lien personal property,[19] even though for other purposes, such as the residential exemption, the cooperative apartment remains classified as real property.[20] The condominium differs from the cooperative in that the law requires the condominium to be treated as real property for all purposes.[21]

A legitimate arrangement between a judgment debtor and those with whom he deals will be honored, even though it may have the effect of curtailing the value that the property right involved might otherwise have to a judgment creditor. If the debtor's title is subject to a third person's right of possession, for example, or if the debtor's right of possession is subject to a third person's title, what the judgment debtor is left with is necessarily less valuable than if she had the whole interest outright. Still, the creditor can reach nothing more than the debtor has.[22] The law will not tolerate an arbitrary attempt, however, in an arrangement between the debtor and some third person, to put an otherwise leviable asset beyond the reach of the debtor's creditors. If, for example, G owes D money evidenced by paper, the paper cannot without some special and commercially legitimate reason place the debt it represents beyond the reach of D's creditors.[23] A legitimate reason ought to earn judicial recognition, however, as where G leases to D a delicate and expensive instrument which D is equipped to handle but which the

---

14. See Berlin v. Herbert, 48 Misc.2d 393, 265 N.Y.S.2d 25 (Dist.Ct., Nassau County, 1965).

15. See Gilchrist v. Commercial Credit Corp., 66 Misc.2d 791, 322 N.Y.S.2d 200 (Sup.Ct., Nassau County, 1971).

16. See Hohenrath v. Wallach, 37 A.D.2d 248, 323 N.Y.S.2d 560 (2d Dep't 1971). Entirety problems are further discussed in § 522, below, dealing with protective orders.

17. See § 421 above.

18. 43 N.Y.2d 151, 400 N.Y.S.2d 805, 371 N.E.2d 523 (1977).

19. See §§ 518–520 below. The problem of obtaining a lien on a judgment debtor's personal property is the subject of a lead note in New York State Law Digest No. 216.

20. CPLR 5206(a)(2). See § 490 below.

21. Section 339–g of the Real Property Law.

22. See § 488 following.

23. See Oppenheimer v. Dresdner Bank A.G., 50 A.D.2d 434, 377 N.Y.S.2d 625 (2d Dep't 1975), aff'd 41 N.Y.2d 949, 394 N.Y.S.2d 634, 363 N.E.2d 358 (1977). Note also in this connection U.C.C. § 9–311, concerning a debtor's rights in collateral furnished in conjunction with a secured transaction. The provision authorizes a transfer of the debtor's interest in the collateral, voluntarily or involuntarily (including a levy of attachment or execution against the debtor), "notwithstanding a provision in the security agreement prohibiting any transfer or making the transfer constitute a default".

world at large is not: if the arrangement provides for reversion of the asset if taken from D, or if a taking is merely threatened, and the provision is in its nature reasonable, it should be upheld. Here it would be a legitimate protection to the third person, not a calculated evasion designed to "judgment-proof" the debtor.

When dealing with an intangible property interest, it is often important to fix its situs, since it can be dealt with by a New York court only if found to have in some sense a New York situs. If D, the judgment debtor, in turn has a debtor (G), for example, what is the situs to be affixed to the debt that G owes D so that a New York judgment creditor of D can seize it? In Harris v. Balk,[24] it was held that the situs of the debt in that situation is wherever G is, and that if G happens into the state of someone who has a claim or judgment against D, that creditor can seize the debt by serving G with appropriate process,[25] thereby requiring G to pay the debt not to D, but to the creditor.

Although the intangible's situs in the situation just discussed has been fixed, the same intangible may not have the same situs in other contexts. The situs of an intangible, said Judge Cardozo, is a legal fiction and varies from one context to another, being fixed by "a common sense appraisal of the requirements of justice and convenience in particular conditions".[26] A leasehold interest, for example, has been held to be where the real property is rather than where the tenant is,[27] a contrast to the mobility ascribed to the debt in *Harris*.[28]

If a debt—the intangible we have been alluding to—is to be seized, the seizure must be effected through the "garnishee", the person whom the CPLR defines as one who, among other things, owes a debt to the judgment debtor.[29] Determining the proper garnishee is therefore often just another way of fixing the "situs" of the debt itself.[30]

Further illustrations of property interests subject to levy and the extent to which the levy may proceed when the debtor's interest is less than whole are in the next section, which demonstrates how the creditor's standing in an asset depends on the debtor's own standing in it.

§ 488.   Creditor Stands in Debtor's Shoes

When the asset or interest that the judgment creditor wants to apply to the judgment belongs to the judgment debtor only in part, it is only that part that is subject to enforcement. Any right or interest lodged legitimately in a third person remains there, and a levy can proceed only on the debtor's right as is. So, for example, in the common situation in which the judgment debtor is a mortgagor and has deposited with the mortgagee escrow moneys to cover taxes and assessments on the realty, those moneys are for the mortgagee's security and can't be reached by the mortgagor's creditors without the mortgagee's leave.[1] The judgment creditor stands in the shoes of the judgment debtor, and if a given property, asset, interest, or deposit is unavailable to the debtor, it is unavailable to the creditor. If in the hands of the debtor the asset is available but encumbered, it can be levied, but only as encumbered. We can call this the stand-in-the-

---

24.   198 U.S. 215, 25 S.Ct. 625, 49 L.Ed. 1023 (1905). Harris is cited here only for its reflections on the situs of an intangible. The aspect of the Harris case that affects quasi in rem jurisdictional use of a debt has been largely overruled. See § 104 above.

25.   In New York, the process is an order of attachment if the seizure is before judgment, CPLR 6214(a), or an execution if after. CPLR 5232(a).

26.   Severnoe Securities Corp. v. London & Lancashire Ins. Co., 255 N.Y. 120, 124, 174 N.E. 299, 300 (1931).

27.   See Glassman v. Hyder, 23 N.Y.2d 354, 296 N.Y.S.2d 783, 244 N.E.2d 259 (1968); ABKCO Industries, Inc. v. Apple Films, Inc., 39 N.Y.2d 670, 385 N.Y.S.2d 511, 350 N.E.2d 899 (1976).

28.   Further discussion of these matters is in § 489 below.

29.   CPLR 105.

30.   Determining the proper garnishee is the subject of § 491 below.

§ 488

1.   Valerio v. College Point Sav. Bank, 48 Misc.2d 91, 264 N.Y.S.2d 343 (Sup.Ct., Suffolk County, 1965). The addition of subdivision (g) to CPLR 5205 in 1978 specifically exempts from the reach of creditors such money as the debtor may have deposited as security for a lease of realty or in connection with utility services.

shoes rule, and it can resolve many problems and answer many questions.

Applied to an escrow fund, this rule of vicarious standing will intervene to allow the judgment creditor to reach the fund upon a showing that the judgment debtor could do so himself. In the foregoing example of the mortgage escrow, the debtor could not, and so neither could his creditor. But when escrow money in different context was sufficiently in the debtor's control to be reached by him, his judgment creditor was allowed to reach it.[2]

The rule can serve in many instances, whether involving a tangible or intangible interest or property. Where the judgment debtor has pledged stock as collateral for a loan, for example, the judgment creditor will be allowed to levy on the collateral only to the extent of its value over and above the interest of the pledgee. If, allowing for as much of the stock as is necessary to secure the balance still due on the loan, there is something left, that is what the creditor can levy on.[3] If, on the other hand, the collateral is less than the obligation it secures, it leaves nothing for the debtor to touch, which means there is nothing for the creditor to touch either.[4]

Similarly, if the judgment debtor has possession of chattels under a valid conditional sales contract allowing repossession by the conditional seller if default should occur in the contract's terms, a judicial sale of the debtor's possessory right will convey subject to the conditional seller's repossessory right, which the latter can pursue no matter where the chattels may end up.[5] If the right of possession in such a situation has value, it is worth pursuing; otherwise it is not.

The foregoing are situations in which the judgment debtor owns or is using property of some kind on which another has a lien or equivalent encumbrance. But now look at the lien or encumbrance itself. It, too, is property, and may be reached by the judgment creditor of the one who holds the lien. A mortgagee on an ordinary real property mortgage makes a good judgment debtor, for example: her judgment creditor can levy on the mortgage and the buyer at the judicial sale will then become entitled to the mortgage payments as they become due and to all other rights conferred on the mortgagee by the terms of the mortgage.

The mortgage is one of the most common of liens, but less familiar ones are also reachable, whatever mechanical adjustments may be needed to facilitate the reaching. Suppose, for example, that the debtor, D, is an artisan who has done work for G; that G owes her money for it; and that D has possession of some property of G against which the law allows D to assert an artisan's lien. The debt owed by G to D may be levied on by D's judgment creditor, and the one who comes into ownership of it at a judicial sale will be entitled to the liened property as well, and to sell the property to satisfy the debt.[6] Those were the rights of D, the judgment debtor, and those will therefore be the rights of the person who buys in at the execution sale upon the levy by D's creditor.

If the judgment debtor has no right to the money or property, then neither has the judgment creditor, even though the money may be due in conjunction with a transaction in which the judgment debtor was much involved, and perhaps even the key figure. Where, for example, hospital services are furnished to the judgment debtor or his family and payments are due from X to the hospital under an insurance arrangement, the stand-in-the-shoes rule will clarify that the debtor's judgment creditor may make no levy: since the money is due the

---

2. See Koroleski v. Badler, 32 A.D.2d 810, 303 N.Y.S.2d 221 (2d Dep't 1969), in which the debtor's "control" of the fund was found ample enough to support a levy.

3. See U.R.C. Inc. v. Applied Images, Inc., 106 Misc.2d 1034, 431 N.Y.S.2d 859 (Sup.Ct., Nassau County, 1980). See also Cohen v. First Nat. City Bank, 49 Misc.2d 141, 267 N.Y.S.2d 146 (N.Y.C.Civ.Ct. 1966), which suggests several routes whereby to effect the seizure mechanically.

4. See Key Lease Corp. v. Manufacturers Hanover Trust Co., 117 A.D.2d 560, 499 N.Y.S.2d 66 (1st Dep't 1986).

5. See Intermediate Credit Corp. v. Overseas Nat. Airways, Inc., 41 Misc.2d 522, 245 N.Y.S.2d 749 (Sup.Ct., Queens County, 1963).

6. See United States Extrusions Corp. v. Strahs Alum. Corp., 71 Misc.2d 1016, 337 N.Y.S.2d 780 (Sup.Ct., Nassau County, 1972).

hospital rather than the judgment debtor, the debtor has no right to it and so neither, derivatively, has his judgment creditor.[7]

Even a special and seemingly personal right, like the cause of action an insured person has against his liability insurer for unreasonably failing to settle a tort claim made against the insured—a so-called "bad faith" claim by insured against insurer—may be pursued under the step-into-the-shoes principle. Hence, when injured persons recovered a judgment against the insured which was not fully paid, they were allowed the appointment of a receiver to bring suit in the insured's behalf against the insurer on the bad faith claim.[8]

To all of the foregoing conclusions we must append the assumption that the judgment debtor's transactions have been lawful and fraud-free. Indeed, an attempt by a debtor to insulate his property from his creditors by conveying it or encumbering it without fair consideration will be presumed fraudulent, without regard to actual intent, if the debtor is at the time insolvent or will be made so by the transfer.[9] The creditors may pursue the property into the hands of the gratuitous transferee.[10] Moreover, if the gratuitous transfer occurs while the transferor is a defendant in a money action which the plaintiff later wins, the transfer is presumed fraudulent against that plaintiff (now judgment creditor) merely upon a showing that the defendant (now judgment debtor) has not paid the judgment, and without regard to the defendant's solvency.[11]

But assuming fair consideration for the judgment debtor's various undertakings, and their basic bona fides, all existing encum-

brances, restrictions, and qualifications on the debtor's property rights will as a rule modify accordingly the rights of the judgment creditor as well. The creditor who steps into the debtor's shoes may walk only on terrain open to the debtor himself.

§ 489. Contingent Intangibles

CPLR 5201(b), which sets a broad measure for "property" applicable to a judgment, includes intangible property rights and interests as well as the tangible. We have even seen that some categories of intangible, such as a bank account, are favored by creditors for the ease with which they can be levied on. But now attention must be directed to the troublesome subdivision (a) of CPLR 5201, which singles out one category of intangible interest—a "debt" allegedly owed to the judgment debtor—and provides that the debt may be subjected to levy only if it is "past due or ... yet to become due, certainly or upon demand of the judgment debtor.... " Its apparent purpose is to preclude enforcement against a debt—or a cause of action, which it also includes[1]—if the debt depends on a contingency that may never occur. It was adopted almost verbatim from the old Civil Practice Act,[2] but it could have used a little rethinking.

There are some interests that depend on contingencies too remote for the law to bother with. An obligation to pay the debtor only if A survives B and C moves to Budapest should not waste the court's or even the debtor's time. But there are other debts and claims that are less remote, or, despite remoteness, that have economic value sufficient to entice a buyer at a judicial sale. One with a value of

---

7. See Security Nat. Bank v. Associated Hosp. Serv., 63 Misc.2d 731, 313 N.Y.S.2d 561 (Sup.Ct., N.Y.County, 1970).

8. Oppel v. DeGangi, 84 A.D.2d 549, 443 N.Y.S.2d 177 (2d Dep't 1981).

9. Debtor & Creditor Law § 273.

10. Debtor & Creditor Law § 278. The statute offers several remedies. One is to disregard the transfer and try to levy on the transferred property. Blue Giant Eqpt. Corp. v. Tec-Ser, Inc., 92 A.D.2d 630, 459 N.Y.S.2d 948 (3d Dep't 1983). This may prove an impractical course, however, because the sheriff will usually refuse to levy against property not standing plainly in the judgment debtor's name and right. Another, more burdensome to

the judgment creditor but more productive, is a separate action or proceeding against the gratuitous transferee to set aside the transfer. See Crete Concrete Corp. v. Josephs, 66 Misc.2d 837, 322 N.Y.S.2d 935 (Sup.Ct., Rockland County, 1971), modified on other grounds, 39 A.D.2d 543, 332 N.Y.S.2d 601 (2d Dep't 1972).

11. Debtor & Creditor Law § 273–a.

§ 489

1. The line between a "debt" and "cause of action" is often imperceptible, a matter returned to at the end of this section.

2. Civ.Prac.Act § 687(a)(1). See 3d Rep.Leg.Doc. (1959) No. 17, p. 101.

that kind ought to be leviable whether contingent or not, but the present provision would seemingly bar enforcement against all debts contingent on anything more than the mere passage of time or the mere demand of the judgment debtor.

The courts have manifested impatience about this. In the famous case of Seider v. Roth,[3] the Court of Appeals disregarded CPLR 5201(a) and held leviable the obligations of a liability insurer to "defend" and to "indemnify" its insured under a liability insurance policy—obligations which, at a judicial sale, would net nothing.[4] Were *Seider* to be allowed precedential scope, subdivision (a) of CPLR 5201 would disappear altogether: the obligations in nearly every other case even arguably within subdivision (a) were, whatever the nature of their contingencies, less contingent than those in *Seider*. The case of Glassman v. Hyder,[5] for example, involved rents due under a lease of realty in another state. The one who leased the property had a New York presence, just as the insurance company (which "owed" the obligations to defend and indemnify) had in *Seider*, and certainly the obligation to pay rent under the lease was no more contingent than the *Seider* obligation to defend or to indemnify under the insurance policy. Nonetheless, the Court of Appeals in the *Glassman* case held the rents to be unleviable contingencies within the meaning of subdivision (a). The theory was apparently that something might occur, before a rent payment came due, to cancel the lease and with it the obligation to pay.[6] *Seider* and its progeny were distinguished for failing to

make any effort "to classify contractual duties as between debt and property".[7]

It was not clear what would be accomplished by stressing this distinction between "debt" and "property". Was this some kind of hint that an interest of a given kind might be treated as either—leviable if treated as "property" under subdivision (b) of CPLR 5201 although barred from levy as too contingent if treated as a "debt" under subdivision (a)? That is apparently what the Court of Appeals meant, as it later clarified in ABKCO Industries, Inc. v. Apple Films, Inc.,[8] a case that may yet prove to be the most illuminating and helpful in this difficult arena.

In *ABKCO*, a nondomiciliary (D) made a contract with a New York corporation (G), licensing G to show a certain film and obligating G to pay D a certain percentage of the profits. Nothing was yet due to D under that contract when the action was brought; indeed, under the D–G arrangement a balance was owing by D to G at the time, rather than the vice versa needed for a levy. The court said that the right that D had against G could be treated *either* as a "debt" under CPLR 5201(a) *or* as "property" under 5201(b), and held that the levy would be allowed if it passed muster under either. Since the "property" criterion of 5201(b) is satisfied upon a simple showing that the right asserted is assignable, without regard to its contingent nature, the contractual obligation, clearly an assignable one in *ABKCO*, was held leviable despite the fact that it was a

---

3. 17 N.Y.2d 111, 269 N.Y.S.2d 99, 216 N.E.2d 312 (1966). The history of the Seider case, which was overruled by the U.S. Supreme Court on federal constitutional grounds in Rush v. Savchuk after 14 controversial years of life, is treated in detail in § 105 above.

4. So incapable were these obligations of conversion into any kind of pecuniary consequence, that the court later discarded them and held instead that the thing attached in these Seider-based cases is the face amount of the policy itself. See § 105 above.

5. 23 N.Y.2d 354, 296 N.Y.S.2d 783, 244 N.E.2d 259 (1968).

6. There is indication that rents already due may be levied. See Mobil Oil Corp. v. Lovotro, 65 Misc.2d 729, 318 N.Y.S.2d 989 (Monroe County Ct. 1971).

7. 23 N.Y.2d at 359, 296 N.Y.S.2d at 786, 244 N.E.2d at 261.

8. 39 N.Y.2d 670, 385 N.Y.S.2d 511, 350 N.E.2d 899 (1976). Although it concerned the quasi in rem jurisdictional use of an attachment, a category of jurisdiction much reduced if not abolished by Shaffer v. Heitner, 433 U.S. 186, 97 S.Ct. 2569, 53 L.Ed.2d 683 (1977), see § 104, above, the ABKCO case is not at all undone by the Shaffer case. ABKCO is concerned only with defining what a leviable contingent interest is. The use that may be made of that kind of interest in the future is a different question, with which ABKCO is not concerned. The interest ABKCO involves, for example, will be fully available for attachment, but perhaps only when the attachment is being used for mere security rather than for jurisdiction, and it is in any event pursuable by judgment creditors during the post-judgment enforcement stage of a case. Lawyers should keep these factors in mind as they peruse the ABKCO decision, lest they fail to appreciate its utility.

contingency that would have been barred from levy if held up to measure under 5201(a).

This is a sound rule. When left to subdivision (b) as "property", economic reality rather than legal technicality becomes the standard, as it ought to. If a right allegedly held by D against G is levied in behalf of P, a judgment creditor of D, its economic significance and hence its utility as an enforcement asset is measured by what a buyer would be willing to pay for this "right" at a public auction, which is the method used for converting property into money under an execution.[9] In the *ABKCO* case a buyer would likely have offered a tidy sum: the right was to a percentage of profits under the D–G contract and the contract involved a film starring the Beatles, a young English quartet who were an international synonym for money during their heyday beginning in the 1960s. An asset of that value, or of any significant value, is surely one that ought to be leviable by its owner's judgment creditors. When the defendant protested that the obligation depended on a contingency that might never occur—the film might fail—the creditor asked for an opportunity just to wait and see. The Court of Appeals obliged by characterizing the contractual obligation as "property" under subdivision (b), thereby freeing it of the strictures imposed on a "debt" by subdivision (a), and making it leviable.

To be eligible for "property" treatment under subdivision (b), all that need be shown is that the property is assignable and that it has a New York situs. It was on the situs element, in fact, that the *ABKCO* case distinguished *Glassman*. The rents in *Glassman*, both before and after *ABKCO*, would be barred as a "debt" under subdivision (a) because of their contingency, but why would they not qualify as "property" so as to be leviable under subdivision (b)? The Court in *ABKCO* answered this by noting that the "property" in *Glassman* was a leasehold interest; that a leasehold has

its situs where the realty is; and that the situs was not New York in the *Glassman* case. So the *Glassman* rents were leviable neither under subdivision (a), because contingent, nor (b), because not geographically reachable in New York. Had the rents been due on New York property, they would have been leviable under this standard.[10]

An important difference between *Seider* and *ABKCO* is that the contractual obligations in *Seider* lacked economic value of any kind that might invite a significant bid at an auction. In the words of Judge (later Chief Judge) Breitel, "before any intangible right has practical significance as an asset to be levied upon or attached, it must give promise of being translatable into an economically valuable tangible".[11] In *ABKCO*, it had that promise; and in stark contrast to *Seider*, which offered for sale an insurer's obligation to defend and indemnify a tort case, a queue of bidders for the potential profits of the Beatles film involved in *ABKCO* would have circled the globe several times over. It surely helps enforcement that the courts take practical realities like this into consideration. The Court of Appeals in *ABKCO*, incidentally, which is now the ruling precedent in this realm, did not even accord *Seider* the courtesy of mention.

Translatability into something of economic value can also distinguish (and justify) levies against other kinds of insurance rights than the obligations arising under the liability policy involved in *Seider*. Where D has sustained a burglary loss, for example, and has a claim against his insurer (G), a seizure of that claim by one of D's creditors is permissible,[12] and economically worth a try. A bidder may be willing to pay something substantial for the right to pursue the claim.

The distillation of the foregoing is that as long as a New York situs can be spelled out for the intangible at issue, it can be given "prop-

---

9. CPLR 5232–3. Details about levying against personal property, including intangibles, are met later. See §§ 496, 497, and 498, below.

10. In that event, of course, the real property itself would have been leviable, relegating the rents question to the academic.

11. Simpson v. Loehmann, 21 N.Y.2d 305, 315, 287 N.Y.S.2d 633, 641, 234 N.E.2d 669, 674–5 (concurring opinion).

12. See Baumgold Bros., Inc. v. Schwartzschild Bros., Inc., 276 A.D. 158, 93 N.Y.S.2d 658 (1st Dep't 1949), aff'd 302 N.Y. 628, 97 N.E.2d 357 (1951).

erty" treatment under CPLR 5201(b) and subjected to levy. The Court of Appeals' attitude is that the levy can be tried, in any event. If there is anything contingent about the item levied, it may be reflected in what a judicial sale of it attracts, and in that sense a CPLR 5201(b) treatment may be chancy. The new theme, however, is that it ought to be the judgment creditor who is allowed to determine whether the chance is worth taking.

Even before *ABKCO*, courts sometimes allowed a contingent debt or obligation to be treated as leviable property under subdivision (b) if it was perceived as having some economic substance that could make the levy worthwhile.[13] Cases forbidding levy by literal application of the "contingency" rule, on the other hand, notwithstanding that the obligation involved did have real economic potential, imposed a needless restriction on the judgment creditor.[14] Those cases are apparently overruled by the *ABKCO* decision, at least if a New York situs can be found for the obligation or right involved.

Wages or salary to be earned by a judgment debtor, or trust income to become due, could easily be placed under the contingent-debt category and barred from levy by CPLR 5201(a) if not made exceptions to it. But exceptions they are, and hence eminently leviable: wages and trust income may be levied to the extent of 10% under the income execution provision of CPLR 5231,[15] and the judgment debtor can be directed to pay an even higher percentage under an installment payment order.[16]

One final matter. CPLR 5201(a) defines a "debt" as including a "cause of action" that the judgment debtor may have against a third person (a "garnishee"). The line between an outright "debt" on the one hand and a mere "cause of action" on the other is at best a shaky one. If G concedes the obligation, it would be a "debt" G owes to D. If G denies it, or merely denies part of it, it would be a "cause of action" that D has against G. For purposes of determining leviability under CPLR 5201, there should be no need to stress the distinction, which touches the mechanics of perfecting the levy more than it does the initial levy itself.[17] Whichever category the given right is deemed to fall into, its leviability should be adjudged by the *ABKCO* standards, and an assignable "cause of action" with an economic potential should be just as leviable under CPLR 5201(b) as an outright "debt" is. To whatever extent a "debt", unleviable under subdivision (a) of CPLR 5201, can be levied as "property" under subdivision (b), so should a "cause of action".

§ 490. Exemptions

A number of items of personal property as well as certain realty are exempt from application to a judgment. The main exemption sections are CPLR 5205 for personal property and 5206 for real property. These are old sections, inherited with only a few adjustments from prior law because the revisors felt that any extensive changes were beyond their function. A perusal of both sections will manifest their age. Old or not, the items they list may not be sought for enforcement. In general they are what the legislature deems to be the necessities of life, which not even a person's judgment creditors should be allowed to reach.

The CPLR lists are not exhaustive. A number of other provisions in the consolidated laws contain exemptions.[1]

---

13. See, e.g., M.F.Hickey Co. v. Port of N. Y. Auth., 23 A.D.2d 739, 258 N.Y.S.2d 129 (1st Dep't 1965).

14. See, e.g., Fredrick v. Chicago Bearing Metal Co., 221 A.D. 588, 224 N.Y.S. 629 (1st Dep't 1927).

15. See § 502 et seq. The counterpart of the 10% levy is in CPLR 5205(d), which exempts 90% of this income.

16. CPLR 5226. See § 511 below.

17. "Perfecting" the levy is a popular term to describe the follow-up steps that must be taken to convert levied property into money to pay the judgment. These subsequent steps may prove more difficult when one is pursuing

a "cause of action" that G resists, entailing the equivalent of a plenary suit by the judgment creditor, standing in D's position, against G, and a regular trial. Perfection is of course easier when G concedes the "debt" and just pays it over to the sheriff to the credit of the judgment that the sheriff is levying on. The distinction between the levy and its perfection is discussed in detail later. See § 496.

§ 490

1. Many of these are enumerated in the Advisory Committee's Third Report. See Leg.Doc. (1959) No. 17, p. 93.

CPLR 5205(a) exempts the basic household goods: basic appliances, some books, domestic animals, wearing apparel, household furniture, and basic tools used by the judgment debtor at work. In 1976 a television set was added,[2] a legislative indication that it is one of the necessities of the modern age. Indeed, without television there might be a return to reading, which can have unduly propitious effects on education.

The listing of an item of personal property as exempt under CPLR 5205 does not prevent the owner from using the property as security for a loan. Specifically liening it in that fashion is not barred by CPLR 5205.[3]

While CPLR 5205(c) exempts the principal of a trust created for the judgment debtor, the exemption does not apply to any remainder interest the debtor may have in the trust.[4] Income from the trust, moreover, is only 90% exempt. This trust income exemption is contained in the first paragraph of CPLR 5205(d), whose second paragraph makes the well known 90% exemption for wages. The net result is that as a rule only 10% of either trust income or wages is applicable to the judgment. The device used to secure the 10% is the income execution of CPLR 5231.[5]

Note the opening language of CPLR 5205(d), which permits more than 10% to be levied if a court finds, after examining into the needs of the judgment debtor's family, that the debtor can afford more. Those findings are made on a motion for what is known as an installment payment order,[6] met and discussed later.[7] Caselaw has also held that since the 90% ex-

emption is designed to preserve that segment for the judgment debtor's family, the exemption ceases to apply when it is the family that is seeking the money, such as for support[8], thus enabling a court to direct payment of whatever is needed without a percentage limitation.

Any income paid or payable to someone on public welfare is altogether exempt from levy,[9] as is the welfare payment itself.[10] Alimony payments to a wife and support payments to a child under a matrimonial judgment, when the recipient is the judgment debtor, are also immune in full (rather than just to the extent of 90%), but only presumptively; if the court finds that some part can be spared for the judgment creditor it can order payment of that part.[11]

There is frequent controversy about the extent to which federal law insulates from levy a debtor's pension or welfare plan that falls under ERISA (the Employee Retirement Income Security Act),[12] a federal law designed to preserve retirement plans for workers who have been promised a pension. It has been involved in much litigation and several key questions under it are the subject of conflicting decisions around the country. The New York Court of Appeals has held that federal law is not totally preemptive; that there are some situations in which the creditor can reach a pension plan, including one in which it is shown that the plan's "very creation" is fraudulent.[13]

The major points to note about CPLR 5206, which contains the realty exemptions, concern

---

2. CPLR 5205(a)(5).

3. State of New York v. Avco Financial Svc., 50 N.Y.2d 383, 429 N.Y.S.2d 181, 406 N.E.2d 1075 (1980). The unconscionability of the underlying transaction may be a bar, but the issue was not timely injected in Avco.

4. See Sherman v. Kirshman, 261 F.Supp. 858 (S.D.N.Y.1966).

5. See § 502 et seq., below.

6. CPLR 5226.

7. See § 511.

8. See Fordyce v. Fordyce, 80 Misc.2d 909, 365 N.Y.S.2d 323 (Sup.Ct., Nassau County, 1974).

9. Social Services Law § 137–a. See, however, Prior v. Cunningham, 33 A.D.2d 853, 306 N.Y.S.2d 22 (3d Dep't

1969), aff'd 27 N.Y.2d 502, 312 N.Y.S.2d 677, 260 N.E.2d 871 (1970), which holds that while the exemption applies to the expressly listed "wages, salary, commissions, or other compensation" paid to a public welfare recipient, it does not go beyond that. The case is unclear about what other kinds of leviable income the debtor may have, and about why, if he has other income from which payments on the judgment could be directed, he is receiving public assistance.

10. Social Services Law § 137.

11. CPLR 5205(d)(3).

12. 29 U.S.C. § 1001 et seq.

13. See Planned Consumer Marketing, Inc. v. Coats and Clark, Inc., 71 N.Y.2d 442, 527 N.Y.S.2d 185, 522 N.E.2d 30 (1988), treated in the lead note in New York State Law Digest No. 345.

the $10,000 residential, or "homestead", exemption contained in subdivision (a). That amount is exempt whether the residence consists of land and building, shares in a cooperative apartment, units in a condominium, or a mobile home. The place must be a "principal residence" in order to qualify for the exemption; a mere vacation retreat, for example, will not do.[14] If the debtor's equity exceeds $10,000, the balance may be reached by the judgment creditor, but it takes a special proceeding under CPLR 5206(e) to compel the sale. When the residence is a cooperative apartment, which is real property for purposes of the exemption but may be treated as personal property in other respects,[15] the source of the special proceeding to accomplish this may be ambiguous,[16] and may be found in other statutes.[17] When the real property is sold, the first $10,000 goes to the judgment debtor, in whose hands it is exempt for a year thereafter.[18]

The Fourth Department Case of *Wyoming County Bank & Trust Co. v. Kiley*[19] presented the issue of whether the landowner is entitled to assert the $10,000 exemption against a foreclosing mortgagee. Under the terms of CPLR 5206(a), the exemption does not apply against a purchase money mortgagee. The *Wyoming* case holds that it does not apply against any other kind of mortgagee either. The exemption is usable only against a creditor trying to enforce an ordinary money judgment; a mortgage foreclosure judgment is not such.[20] Nor is the foreclosure of a mechanic's lien.[21]

It was held in *First Federal Sav. & Loan Ass'n of Rochester v. Brown*[22] that should there be a mortgage foreclosure, and a surplus left after the mortgage is satisfied, the surplus will not enjoy the $10,000 exemption even if an ordinary judgment creditor is the one pursuing it. The $10,000 exemption lasts only while the premises are occupied by the family, said the court, and the surplus is personal property, while the exemption applies only to real property.

The exemption applies only to the satisfaction of a civil money judgment, moreover. It has no application to a fine imposed by a criminal court.[23]

There is a constitutional requirement to advise the judgment debtor about the possibly exempt status of her property when enforcement steps are taken.[24]

The realty exemption has an important role on the bankruptcy scene. As authorized by federal law, New York has enacted statutes[25] that opt out of the federal bankruptcy exemptions scheme and make New York exemptions exclusive. Under them, each spouse, when both file in bankruptcy, may claim a realty exemption under CPLR 5206. When both file, therefore, the exemption doubles, to $20,000.[26]

§ 491. Proper Garnishee

Since a "garnishee" is defined as anyone who has possession of property belonging to the judgment debtor or in which the debtor

14. See Matter of Galcia, 59 Misc.2d 511, 299 N.Y.S.2d 723 (Surr.Ct., N.Y.County, 1969).

15. See § 487 above.

16. See Swatzburg v. Swatzburg, 137 Misc.2d 1042, 523 N.Y.S.2d 399 (Sup.Ct., N.Y. County, 1987).

17. See, e.g., CPLR 5225, 5227, and the summary of the Swatzburg case, id., in New York State Law Digest No. 344.

18. CPLR 5206(e). See also, Sailors' Snug Harbor v. Tax Commission, 26 N.Y.2d 444, 311 N.Y.S.2d 486, 259 N.E.2d 910 (1970).

19. 75 A.D.2d 477, 430 N.Y.S.2d 900 (4th Dep't 1980).

20. Other departments subscribe to the Wyoming view. See First National Bank of Glens Falls v. G.F. Clear, Inc., 103 A.D.2d 951, 479 N.Y.S.2d 802 (3d Dep't 1984); Citibank, N.A. v. Cambel, 119 A.D.2d 720, 501 N.Y.S.2d 133 (2d Dep't 1986).

21. See Robert S. Moore, Inc. v. Whittaker, 142 Misc.2d 708, 538 N.Y.S.2d 415 (County Ct., Schoharie County, 1989).

22. 78 A.D.2d 119, 434 N.Y.S.2d 306 (4th Dep't 1980).

23. See People v. McArdle, 55 N.Y.2d 639, 446 N.Y.S.2d 256, 430 N.E.2d 1309 (1981), involving a conviction for welfare fraud.

24. This requirement occasioned amendments of several statutes, CPLR 5222, 5232, and 5234, in 1982. See § 508, below, and Commentary C5222:11 on McKinney's CPLR 5222.

25. See §§ 282–284 of the Debtor and Creditor Law, added in 1982.

26. See John T. Mather Memorial Hospital of Port Jefferson, Inc. v. Pearl, 723 F.2d 193 (2d Cir.1983). "The purpose of the New York legislation was clearly to provide joint debtors the opportunity to make a 'fresh start' with a $20,000 homestead exemption."

has an interest, or who owes a debt to the debtor,[1] identifying the proper person to treat as a garnishee is an important step. It is often through a garnishee that enforcement is carried out. In most instances there is no difficulty. If the property is a bank account, the garnishee is the bank. If it is a chattel, the garnishee is the one who has custody of it; if a debt, the one who owes it; if a cause of action, the one against whom it lies. These are common situations. Subdivision (c) of CPLR 5201, in listing the proper garnishee in a few instances, has merely selected some special situations in which it was felt that some statutory instruction about proper garnishee would be helpful.

When the judgment debtor has an interest in an estate or trust, the proper garnishee is the fiduciary—the executor or administrator of the estate, the trustee or equivalent of the trust, etc.[2] When the debtor has an interest in a partnership, any other partner is the proper garnishee.[3] This works even when the judgment is between the partners. Where, for example, in a three-person partnership, partner A has a judgment against partners B and C, B and C each qualify as a garnishee with respect to the judgment that lies against the other.[4]

Special note should be made of the situation in which the pursued asset is a debt represented by some piece of commercial paper. If the paper is negotiable, the paper itself is the asset, deemed property "capable of delivery"; the proper garnishee is not necessarily the person owing the debt, but the person who has custody of the paper.[5] This is so not only of a negotiable instrument for the payment of money, but also of a negotiable document of title under Article 7 of the Uniform Commercial Code.[6]

If the paper representing the interest is non-negotiable, the paper is not deemed the asset; the proper garnishee in that case is the one who owes the debt or the one who has possession of the property.

A similar distinction is made when the asset sought to be reached is the judgment debtor's shares in a corporation or other share-issuing association. If the shares are represented by duly issued and outstanding certificates, these are deemed the property and the person who has them is the garnishee.[7] If none are outstanding, the garnishee is the corporation or association itself.[8]

It is only the judgment debtor's property that the judgment creditor may pursue in the hands of the garnishee, not the garnishee's own property. If, for example, the garnishee owes a debt to the debtor, the creditor may, through appropriate devices, require payment of the debt to him instead of to the debtor. The creditor may not, however, go after any other property belonging to the garnishee,[9] at least not until appropriate follow-up proceedings have been taken and these have produced a judgment in favor of the judgment creditor directly against the garnishee.[10]

§ 491

1. CPLR 105.

2. CPLR 5201(c)(2).

3. CPLR 5201(c)(3). The judgment creditor may not levy against any particular asset of the partnership, because each such asset is collectively the partnership's and does not belong to any given partner. The creditor's remedy here is to levy execution, or to get what is called a "charging order" under § 54 of the Partnership Law, against the debtor partner's interest in the partnership. If a priority is sought, as in a race with another creditor, the levy is preferable to the charging order. See § 520 below. Only if the judgment is rendered against the partnership itself may the partnership's assets be pursued. See CPLR 5201(b) (2d sentence).

4. See Jones v. Palermo, 105 Misc.2d 405, 432 N.Y.S.2d 288 (Sup.Ct., N.Y.County, 1980).

5. CPLR 5201(c)(4). For discussion of what property is "capable of delivery", see § 497 below.

6. This is in conformity with what the Code itself provides on the subject. See UCC § 7–602. It is designed to protect the bailee by authorizing him to reject a levy on goods in his possession unless the negotiable document is surrendered to him.

7. CPLR 5201(c)(4).

8. CPLR 5201(c)(1).

9. See Smith v. Amherst Acres, Inc., 43 A.D.2d 792, 350 N.Y.S.2d 236 (4th Dep't 1973).

10. This can happen, for example, if a garnishee resists the levy. The judgment creditor can bring a special proceeding against the garnishee, in which a money judgment can be rendered for the creditor directly against the garnishee. This judgment may then be enforced against property of the garnishee, who in this situation has become a judgment debtor. See §§ 496 and 510 below.

A fringe benefit emerges from taking note of who the proper garnishee is in these several situations. As noted in the section on "contingent intangibles",[11] almost any kind of assignable interest is leviable today if a New York situs can be found for it. Finding the garnishee is just another way of finding the asset's "situs": if the garnishee has a New York presence, the debtor's asset in the garnishee's hands probably has a New York situs, too. Where, for example, the garnishee owes the judgment debtor a debt, not represented by a negotiable instrument, the garnishee's physical presence in New York fixes New York as the situs of the debt.[12] Where the asset being pursued is a claim that the judgment debtor has against the garnishee, the garnishee's New York presence enables suit on the claim to be brought in New York and thus, again, gives the claim a New York situs. Even in the case of a negotiable instrument, which itself is deemed the property and the proper garnishee is its custodian, one can treat the interest as having a New York situs as long as the garnishee is in New York, even though the instrument or document is in the garnishee's custody at an out-of-state location.

Such a construction would be appropriate, considering that we are enforcing here a duly rendered (and with full jurisdiction) New York judgment: a construction that aids enforcement should, as between competing possibilities, be the one selected. A leasehold interest in realty, however, as mentioned during the earlier discussion of the *Glassman* and *ABKCO* cases,[13] has been held to be where the realty is, putting rents beyond levy when the property is outside New York, notwithstanding that the lessee, i.e., the rent payer, also has a New York presence (such as where it is a corporation doing business in many places, including New York).

Although the state is not subject to the enforcement procedures of Article 52 when it is the judgment debtor, it may be and often is a garnishee and is in general subject to the provisions of Article 52 affecting garnishees.[14] Without statutory authorization, however, the federal government and its agencies may not be compelled to serve as garnishees on New York process, even when a federal employee is the judgment debtor and only her salary is sought to be garnished.[15] The procedure in that situation is to pursue the money only after it reaches the judgment debtor's hands, such as with an installment payment order under CPLR 5226, one of the most versatile of the enforcement devices.[16]

C. DEVICES IN PERSPECTIVE

Table of Sections

§ 492. The Enforcement Devices, Introductory

There are eight enforcement devices in Article 52; nine if we include contempt, which aids enforcement only indirectly. The following is the list, with the CPLR provisions that supply and implement the particular device.

1.	Property execution	CPLR 5230.
	Levy and sale of personalty	CPLR 5232–3.
	Levy and sale of realty	CPLR 5235–6.
2.	Income executions	CPLR 5231, 5241–2.
*3.	Restraining notice	CPLR 5222.
*4.	Disclosure in aid of enforcement	CPLR 5223–4.
*5.	Delivery order or judgment	CPLR 5225, 5227.
*6.	Installment payment order	CPLR 5226.
7.	Receivership	CPLR 5228.
8.	Arrest	CPLR 5250.
9.	Contempt	CPLR 5251.

* The asterisked devices are the ones that rely for implementation on the contempt punishment.

---

11. See § 489 above.

12. See Harris v. Balk, 198 U.S. 215, 25 S.Ct. 625, 49 L.Ed. 1023 (1905), and the discussion in § 487 above.

13. See § 489 above.

14. CPLR 5207. An example of the garnishment contemplated would be the salary of a state employee who is the judgment debtor. By statute, however, tax refunds or credits due the judgment debtor as a taxpayer are not garnishable. Tax L. § 7.

15. A statutory example of where the United States can be a garnishee in a state court proceeding is where it concerns a support or alimony obligation of a federal employee. See, e.g., Diaz v. Diaz, 568 F.2d 1061 (4th Cir.1977).

16. See § 511 below.

The list follows the order in which the devices appear in Article 52, except for the two categories of execution. These have been taken out of their CPLR sequence and listed first mainly because all courts have jurisdiction of them, whereas not all courts have jurisdiction of the others, a matter to be elaborated in the next section. The others, numbers 3 through 9, are collectively known to the bar as the "supplementary proceedings", a terminology borrowed from prior law. Technically the term is not accurate today because the devices in the main are not "proceedings" in the sense of separate special proceedings.[1] They are for the most part just enforcement devices captioned in the very action that produced the judgment, usually entailing nothing more than a motion, and some do not require even that. There are, however, a few special proceedings expressly authorized, such as to require garnishees and other third persons to honor enforcement devices they have not honored voluntarily. These will be met in the course of the individual treatment given each device in subsequent portions of the chapter.

Later sections will also go into some detail about which of the devices give their user a priority or lien on the defendant's personal property,[2] but for the present bird's eye view we can note that the devices that do this are the property execution, number 1 on the above list, and the delivery and receivership orders, numbers 5 and 7.[3] The restraining notice, number 3 on the list, does not give priority under the CPLR, a fact that some lawyers have overlooked to their detriment.[4]

As to the sequence in which the devices must be used, there is none. The judgment creditor can use whichever ones suit the particular purpose at hand, beginning with any one of them and finishing with any other, with no particular progression except that which the judgment creditor has decided suits the case best. The CPLR has no direction about it, preferring for this, as it prefers for enforcement generally, to leave the correction and avoidance of all abuses to individual protective orders under CPLR 5240.[5]

None of the enforcement devices is available against the state when it is a judgment debtor, but the state and its agencies do remain subject to all of the Article 52 devices when the state is a garnishee.[6] And if a genuine dispute arises as to whether the state as garnishee is in fact indebted to the judgment debtor, the guise of an enforcement proceeding will not be able to resolve it, as it could resolve it with a private garnishee, because it would usurp the jurisdiction of the court of claims, which has exclusive power to hear claims against the state.

Under Rule 69(a) of the Federal Rules of Civil Procedure, state practices and procedures are in large measure adopted for enforcement of the judgments of local federal courts, thus making these New York devices, which in the language of the federal rule are "proceedings supplementary to and in aid of a judgment", available to the federal courts situated in New York.[7]

§ 493. Courts in Which Enforcement Devices Available

Courts that have civil jurisdiction usually have jurisdiction of the two execution devices: the property execution and the income execution, the first two devices on the prior section's list. All of the state's lower courts have, including the New York City Civil Court, the

---

§ 492

1. The details of the procedures in special proceedings are met in a later chapter. See § 547 et seq., below.

2. A lien on real property is accomplished by mere docketing. See § 517 below.

3. See §§ 519 and 520 below. An income execution, number 2 on the list, also earns priority, but only with respect to income and only as against other income execution users. See § 504 below.

4. See §§ 508 and 520.

5. The protective order is treated in § 522 below.

6. CPLR 5207. See Bankers Trust Co. v. State Dept. of Audit and Control, 28 A.D.2d 272, 284 N.Y.S.2d 594 (3d Dep't 1967).

7. See § 641 below (Practitioner's Edition).

district and city courts,[1] and even the town and village courts.[2] But devices 3 through 9 on the list, collectively known as the supplementary proceedings, are beyond the jurisdiction of some of the lower courts and must be sought, when a judgment of one of those courts is involved, in the supreme court or in a county court. Which courts have and which courts lack this jurisdiction is determined by CPLR 5221.

In subdivision (a), CPLR 5221 lists the courts that have the necessary jurisdiction. In terms, the subdivision simply lists the courts in which a "special proceeding" authorized by Article 52 may be brought, and the enforcement devices of Article 52 are for the most part not special proceedings; they are mere adjuncts of the original action that gave rise to the judgment. But subdivision (b) of CPLR 5221, by listing the implements whereby the other enforcement devices are exploited, restricts them to only the courts listed in subdivision (a). Thus the two subdivisions between them account for restricting jurisdiction of the so-called "supplementary proceedings" to the courts listed in subdivision (a).

The supreme court and the county courts entertain all of the enforcement devices.[3] So do the New York City Civil Court[4] and the district courts,[5] and even the city courts, but with respect to city court judgments the county court is made an alternative forum for enforcement.[6] The town and village courts lack juris-

diction of the "supplementary proceeding" devices; when one of them is used to enforce a judgment of a town or village court, it is captioned in and seeks the aid of either the supreme court or a county court.[7] Nor do the surrogates' courts entertain these devices.[8] CPLR 5221 also supplies venue for most of the Article 52 devices.[9]

To the extent that any judicial aid is needed, the aim of CPLR 5221 is to require the judgment creditor to seek it only in a place convenient to the person against whom the device is used. A lower court, for example, even if it can entertain all of the enforcement devices, will be allowed to do so only if the person involved resides or works in the county in which the lower court is located, or, in the case of the New York City Civil Court, in New York City. If the person lives and works elsewhere, but within the state, court applications should be addressed to the supreme court or county court of the county of that person's residence or work. If she neither lives nor works in the state, the applications go to the supreme court or county court of the county in which the person is served with the necessary papers or the county in which judgment was rendered.[10] If the needed court is not in session in the right county, the proceeding may be brought in an adjoining county or any other county in the same judicial district.[11] These rules apply whether the person against whom the device

§ 493

1. See Article 15 of the New York City Civil Court Act and of the Uniform District and Uniform City court acts, McKinney's Vol. 29A, Part 3. Execution against realty, however, does not issue out of those courts; a transcripting procedure is invoked and the supreme court is used. See § 1505 in each of the cited acts.

2. See Article 15 of the Uniform Justice Court Act, McKinney's Vol. 29A, Part 2. Again, as mentioned in the prior note, the court's execution may not be levied against real property; the supreme court is used for that after the judgment has been transcribed. See UJCA § 1505. A surrogate's court entertains none of the ordinary money judgment enforcement devices, not even the executions; the supreme court has been designated as its enforcement arm. See SCPA 605. But the surrogate's court does handle the contempt punishment for equity and certain other of its own judgments. See SCPA 606, 607.

3. CPLR 5221(a)(4).

4. CPLR 5221(a)(3).

5. CPLR 5221(a)(2).

6. CPLR 5221(a)(1).

7. CPLR 5221(a)(4). An outright conversion of a lower court judgment into one of the supreme court for enforcement purposes can occur if the lower court judgment is docketed with the county clerk of the home county. See CPLR 5018(a). When that is done, the judgment creditor has the option, for CPLR 5221 purposes, of treating the judgment as one of either the lower court that rendered it or the supreme court.

8. SCPA 605. See note 2 above.

9. It is sometimes necessary to bring a special proceeding to aid in the perfection of an execution, see, e.g., CPLR 5232(a), 5225, 5227. When it is, the court and venue restrictions of CPLR 5221(a) apply, even though the particular lower court can otherwise entertain its own executions.

10. CPLR 5221(a)(4).

11. CPLR 5221(a)(5).

or proceeding is aimed is the judgment debtor proper, a garnishee, or some other third person.[12] They sound more complicated than they actually are. This phase of the rules is just a "where to do" reference chart, which can be consulted as needed when the lawyer is about to use a given device or initiate a special proceeding.

Defects in the use of CPLR 5221 will usually be mere venue errors, correctible with a change of venue or disregardable under the waiver doctrine, but they can sometimes be jurisdictional. An example of a mere venue mistake is where, on a supreme court judgment, an enforcement proceeding has been brought in the wrong county. The respondent's failure to object to it will constitute a waiver of the wrong venue,[13] and even a timely objection should result in nothing worse than a change of venue to the right county.[14] But if enforcement is sought from a court without any jurisdiction at all under the varied terms of CPLR 5221(a), as where it is sought from a county court to enforce a district court judgment, the defect has been held jurisdictional.[15] It should not be serious even in that instance, however: a judgment has a 20–year life,[16] which should without any time strictures enable the judgment creditor to pivot right about and bring the device or proceeding afresh in the right court. A dismissal (and thus a new start) may not even be necessary; transfer may be an alternative, by analogy to the transfer powers that courts have in connection with actions initially brought in wrong courts.[17]

One of the reasons for allowing most judgments to seek full enforcement in their courts of rendition while requiring those of the town and village courts to invoke aid from higher courts is that the town and village courts usually lack the facilities and staff needed to process the supplementary devices, which often require much judicial attention. There are, moreover, a number of incidental equitable powers connected with these devices, including injunctions and orders enforcible by contempt, which the legislature has seen fit to withhold from those courts, whose judges need not even be lawyers and most aren't.

It should be remembered, also, that CPLR 5221 and its offering of various courts designs only to aid enforcement. Only for the enforcement purpose, therefore, may a lower court judgment sometimes be deemed a judgment of a higher or different court. That does not give the latter any power to trifle with the merits of another court's judgment. A motion to vacate the judgment, for example,[18] would have to be made to the rendering court, as would any other kind of motion to modify, correct, or resettle it, or otherwise touch its merits.

It was noted earlier that a judgment of a lower court or of a federal court can be made the equivalent of a supreme court judgment through the simple procedure of docketing the judgment, with a transcript, in a county clerk's office.[19] Either the supreme court or a county court may then be used for enforcement of the judgment so docketed,[20] but it should be remembered that the person against whom enforcement is sought, including the judgment debtor himself, may not yet have been brought within the jurisdiction of the court being used. If the device involved requires an actual application to the court, it may therefore be necessary to use a method of service that secures personal jurisdiction. Where a federal judgment has been so docketed, for example, and an application to punish for contempt has to be made after (e.g.) an enforcement subpoena has been disobeyed, a mere motion served by ordinary mail may not

---

12. An exception is the deposition taken of the judgment debtor (as opposed to some third person), where the county in which the action is pending is made a proper deposition venue even if the debtor neither lives nor works there. See CPLR 5224(c), adopting the venue provision of CPLR 3110(1). It is treated in § 509 below.

13. See Silbert v. Silbert, 25 A.D.2d 570, 267 N.Y.S.2d 744 (2d Dep't 1966).

14. CPLR 511, 103(b).

15. See Garrison Fuel Oil of Long Island, Inc. v. Grippo, 127 Misc.2d 275, 486 N.Y.S.2d 136 (Nassau County Ct. 1985).

16. CPLR 211(b).

17. See § 24 in the chapter on subject matter jurisdiction.

18. See CPLR 5015.

19. See § 422 above.

20. See CPLR 5221(a)(4).

suffice to secure the needed jurisdiction of the contemnor; a special proceeding, brought on by service of the initiatory papers in the same manner as a summons,[21] may be required.[22]

A counseling point about terminology: various devices to be met in this chapter may sometimes be described as issuing "out of" a given court. This merely means that its caption bears the name of that court and that its issuance is upon the authority of that court; it does not necessarily mean that a judge issued it. Several devices do not need court leave, such as the restraining notice of CPLR 5222 and the subpoenas of CPLR 5224. They bear the signature of the judgment creditor's lawyer and are valid process just that way. They are nonetheless deemed to issue "out of" the court whose name their captions carry.

D. PROPERTY EXECUTIONS

Table of Sections

§ 494. The Executions, Generally

There are two categories of execution. The first is the property execution authorized by CPLR 5230. It can be levied against personal property under CPLR 5232 and 5233 or against real property under CPLR 5235 and 5236. The second is the income execution, supplied for money judgments in general by CPLR 5231, which operates against 10% of the judgment debtor's income, and for family support money by CPLR 5241, which allows a

greater percentage. There is no priority of use among any of the executions. One can be used before or instead of the other. There is no requirement that a property execution be tried first.[1] Nor, in the case of the property execution, is there any priority between real and personal property: either class of property can be levied in whatever sequence the judgment creditor and sheriff work out, subject of course to variation by the court with a protective order under CPLR 5240. A preliminary court order is not required for either execution; it is just issued by the judgment creditor's lawyer and sent to the sheriff of the proper county. All of this will appear in more detail as the executions are taken up separately in ensuing sections.

An execution can be issued at any time during the 20–year period of the judgment's life,[2] until the judgment is satisfied.

A sheriff or other court officer charged with carrying out an execution and failing to is subject to the compulsion of an Article 78 proceeding in the nature of mandamus.[3] The sheriff derelict in his duties also faces personal liability to the judgment creditor.[4]

§ 495. Property Execution, Issuance and Contents

The main provision on the property execution is CPLR 5230, which, by its address to the "sheriff" as the enforcement officer, manifests its preoccupation with the supreme court and the county courts, for both of which the sheriff acts as the enforcement official. But CPLR 5230 also serves in the lower courts, with a little help from the lower court acts. These provide that when these enforcement provisions are applied in the lower courts, the word "sheriff" shall be deemed a reference to the court's own enforcement officer, should it be

---

21. CPLR 403(c). See § 553 below.

22. See Federal Deposit Insurance Corp. v. Richman, 98 A.D.2d 790, 470 N.Y.S.2d 19 (2d Dep't 1983).

§ 494

1. Compare § 684 of the old Civil Practice Act.

2. CPLR 211(b). Under CPLR 5014 the judgment can be renewed; if it is, it will get a new 20–year period. See § 434 above.

---

3. Liggett v. Pichler, 142 A.D.2d 206, 534 N.Y.S.2d 973 (1st Dep't 1988). Article 78 proceedings are studied beginning with § 557 below.

4. In Wang v. Bartel, 163 Misc.2d 600, 624 N.Y.S.2d 735 (App.Term, 2d & 11th Dists. 1994), for example, noted in SPR 45:4, the court sustained a damages action by a creditor with a money judgment suing a deputy sheriff for alleged disregard of his duties.

someone other than the sheriff.[1] In the New York City Civil Court, for example, the city marshals and the New York City sheriff both serve as enforcement officers and either may be used by the judgment creditor.[2] With these major adjustments, CPLR 5230 is the uniform guidepost for property executions in the state's courts.

As a result of legislation in 1997 and 1998, executions on supreme court judgments that are to be levied in New York City may be directed to a city marshal as an alternative to the sheriff.[3]

The execution may be issued by the clerk of the court or, the more common practice, by the judgment creditor's lawyer. No leave is needed. It may be directed to the sheriff of any county, and should of course be delivered to one in a county where the judgment debtor has property.[4] For this purpose, no filing of a transcript is needed in the county in which enforcement is sought. Transcripting[5] is not ordinarily a condition precedent to enforcement, at least not when a supreme court or county court judgment rendered in one county is being levied in another: enforcement can proceed in the latter even though the judgment has not been docketed there.[6] But if a lower court judgment is being enforced in other than the lower court itself, it must have been docketed, by transcript, with the home county clerk, and in that situation the execution must specify the date of the transcript's filing.

§ 495

This last is a requirement of CPLR 5230(a), which also specifies the basics of what an execution must contain. Every execution must specify the court in which the judgment was entered, the date of its entry, the original amount of the judgment as well as the sum still due, and of course the names of the judgment creditor and judgment debtor. The lawyer should also, as a practical matter, accompany the execution with a note of some kind describing and locating the judgment debtor's property so that the sheriff can levy on it. The assumption that the sheriff will search for property himself is a bit too optimistic. That can be a demanding task, and even with the best intentioned sheriff other duties ordinarily impede such searches.[7] The statement about property is not mandatory, however. Indeed, the plaintiff may be using the execution just to secure priority in the distribution of the judgment debtor's assets, since the mere delivery of the execution makes it a lien on the debtor's personal property.[8] Because of this automatic lien effect, the failure of a sheriff to accept and receipt an execution only because it is not accompanied by a statement about the defendant's property can result in a liability for the sheriff.[9]

If the execution does specify property, a garnishee is entitled to rely on it. If the sheriff levies against the specified property, therefore, and it turns out that the property does not belong to the judgment debtor, "it is the creditor and not the garnishee who is liable for damages to the actual owner".[10]

1. See § 701(b) in the New York City Civil Court Act and in the Uniform District, City, and Justice court acts, McKinney's Vol. 29A, Parts 2 and 3. As used in this chapter, "sheriff" includes the particular lower court's enforcement officers. To the extent that any further adjustments are needed to make the CPLR's execution provisions workable in a given lower court, these can be found in Article 15 of the cited court acts.

2. New York City Civil Court Act § 701(a).

3. See SPR 61:3, 75:2, and the Commentaries on § 1609 of the New York City Civil Court Act. Reference to a sheriff will henceforth be deemed to include the city marshals when the execution is delivered in New York City.

4. CPLR 5230(b).

5. The transcripting procedure is described in § 422 above.

6. Of course, if it has not been docketed it will not be a lien on real property in that county, see § 517, below, which suggests that when it is real property that the judgment creditor is after, a transcripting would be wise in order to prevent another creditor from inadvertently securing a priority.

7. Some caselaw suggests that it is mandatory to append such instructions to the execution. See, e.g., Princeton Bank and Trust Co. v. Berley, 57 A.D.2d 348, 394 N.Y.S.2d 714 (2d Dep't 1977).

8. For liens and priorities, see § 518 et seq., below.

9. See the discussion in SPR 31:2.

10. Chin Sung Yu v. Riggs Nat. Bank, 248 A.D.2d 235, 670 N.Y.S.2d 187 (1st Dep't 1998).

If jurisdiction in the action that produced the judgment was based solely on the attachment of the judgment debtor's local assets, there being no personal jurisdiction of the debtor, the judgment may be enforced only against the previously attached assets. In that case the execution must state this limitation and direct that only the attached assets be levied.[11]

There is also a special limitation when the judgment is for a debt for which a mortgage was given as security. The policy of the law is to have the mortgagee bring a regular foreclosure action if there is a default, a procedure that preserves the mortgagor's right of redemption.[12] So, while the mortgagee can, if it chooses, ignore the mortgage and just bring an ordinary money action on the underlying debt (the note or bond), the mortgagee will find that at the enforcement stage the one property against which it will not be allowed to levy its money judgment is the mortgaged property itself, lest the important right of redemption be circumvented. Accordingly, the execution in that instance must identify the mortgage by the book and page of its recording, describe (locate) the mortgaged property, and direct that no levy be made against it.[13]

A judgment debtor must be advised about the possibly exempt status of his property.[14] If a notice has previously been served on the judgment debtor advising to that effect[15], the execution should say so.[16] If the execution does not contain the statement, the sheriff can include an appropriate notice about exempt property when he levies. It is the obligation of the judgment creditor to assure that this notice is given.[17]

In the case of a third-party (impleader) judgment, the rule is that there can be no enforcement of the judgment by way of execution or any other device unless and until the defendant has made some payment to the plaintiff on the main judgment. The rule recognizes that a third-party judgment is designed to indemnify the defendant for whatever she may have had to pay the plaintiff on the main judgment.

A violation of this rule with an effort to collect the third-party judgment before collection is ripe can be remedied by an application for a protective order under CPLR 5240, quashing or limiting the execution. In rare instances, notably those involving a personal injury defendant who has been subjected to extra liability because her liability insurer has unreasonably failed to defend or indemnify her in the main action, or to negotiate a settlement in good faith, execution has been allowed before actual payment of the main claim. Indeed, even a separate indemnity suit by insured against insurer for such an "excess"— the amount by which the liability imposed on the insured exceeds the insurance coverage— has been sustained before the insured has paid it out.[18] This recognizes the injustice of requiring an unfairly treated insured person to liquidate her assets only to discharge a liability for which the insurer would have to indemnify her anyway.[19]

---

11. CPLR 5230(a). This occurs only in the quasi in rem category of jurisdiction, which was much reduced by the U.S. Supreme Court in Shaffer v. Heitner, 433 U.S. 186, 97 S.Ct. 2569, 53 L.Ed.2d 683 (1977), discussed in § 104, above, but still has some residual use.

12. See RPAPL § 1352.

13. CPLR 5230(a).

14. Exemptions are discussed in § 490 above.

15. Such an advice must be furnished, for example, when a restraining notice is used under CPLR 5222(e).

16. This is a requirement spelled out indirectly from subdivision (c) of CPLR 5232, added in 1982 to meet constitutional objections directed at several of the CPLR's enforcement devices. See § 508 below.

17. See the 1982 Commentaries C5222:11 and C5232:5 on McKinney's CPLR 5222 and 5232. The requirement is statutory, and the statutes implement constitutional demands, so there are in fact two bases for upsetting enforcement steps that fail to fulfill this notice requirement.

18. See Henegan v. Merchants Mut. Ins. Co., 31 A.D.2d 12, 294 N.Y.S.2d 547 (1st Dep't 1968), and compare Colpan Realty Corp. v. Great Amer. Ins. Co., 83 Misc.2d 730, 373 N.Y.S.2d 802 (Sup.Ct., Westchester County, 1975).

19. On rare occasions the courts have allowed a recovery over of this kind before payment of the main judgment even in non-insurance cases. See, e.g., Bonwit–Teller v. Rosenstiel, 75 Misc.2d 108, 347 N.Y.S.2d 753 (N.Y.C.Civ. Ct. 1968). Except in the insured-versus-insurer example used in the text, however, a pre-payment recovery from a third-party defendant is not permitted. See § 175 above.

Before we turn to the levy of the execution in the following sections, a note of warning to the judgment debtor is appropriate. If the debtor does plan to pay the judgment, or in any event to appeal it and seek a stay of enforcement during the appeal, the debtor should take the appropriate step promptly. Delaying it, so that a levy goes forward, even if it can now be stopped in its tracks, may incur substantial poundage fees to the sheriff that could have easily been avoided. One defendant who delayed bonding a judgment in connection with an appeal, for example, had to pay $30,-000 in otherwise avoidable poundage.[20]

§ 496. Levy on Personal Property

The execution can be levied on personal property in either of two ways. If the property is capable of delivery, and is not in the possession of one who has a superior right to its possession under a pledge or lease, the sheriff levies on it by taking it into his custody. When he does, the sheriff serves a copy of the execution on the person from whom the property is taken. This is levy by seizure under subdivision (b) of CPLR 5232.[1] The sheriff's next duty is to sell the property.[2] Execution in this instance is subject to the requirement that it be returned by the sheriff within 60 days after issuance, unless the judgment creditor gives the sheriff an additional 60 days. This requirement comes from subdivision (c) of CPLR

5230. It recognizes that since the execution gives its issuer priority in the debtor's personal property,[3] it should be levied and perfected expeditiously so as not to delay other judgment creditors unfairly. If there are no other creditors, however, the judgment creditor can continue to give the sheriff 60–day extensions.[4]

If the property is not capable of delivery, the method of levy is for the sheriff to serve a copy of the execution on the garnishee,[5] which must be made in the same manner as a summons. This is known as levy by service and is governed by subdivision (a) of CPLR 5232.[6] When levy is by service instead of by seizure in the first instance, the 60–day limitation on the return time does not apply.[7]

Whatever the method of levy, the sheriff must be certain not to interfere with the rights of third persons. Trespassing on those rights can bring personal liability to the sheriff and his sureties. "Innocent mistake will not exculpate him, nor erroneous direction by the judgment creditor.... If in doubt, [the sheriff] would have the right to secure indemnification from the party seeking to have him act before proceeding to make levy".[8]

Notice must be given to the judgment debtor. CPLR 5232 was one of the statutes declared unconstitutional in the early 1980s for not requiring that notice be given to the judgment debtor about the possibly exempt status

---

20. Thornton v. Montefiore Hospital, 117 A.D.2d 552, 498 N.Y.S.2d 828 (1st Dep't 1986). After convincing the judgment creditor, P, to hold off execution to give D time to bond the judgment while D appealed, D delayed until P finally had the execution levied. D was a hospital and the levy held up D's payroll. D then got P to withdraw the levy, but the sheriff would not waive poundage. Of course, if the judgment should then be reversed on appeal, D would be able to recover the amount of the poundage from the plaintiff as a disbursement. Herbert H. Levess & Co. v. Celebrity Knitwear, Inc., 130 Misc.2d 1055, 498 N.Y.S.2d 974 (Sup.Ct., N.Y. County, 1986).

§ 496

1. The question periodically arises about whether the sheriff can break down the outer door of a residence—there is usually no problem about other places—to get at the property. On this subject see the annotation in 57 ALR 210.

2. CPLR 5233, treated in § 498 below.

3. See §§ 519 and 520 below.

4. CPLR 5230(c).

5. Contrast these levy alternatives with a levy of an attachment. Attachment, designed as it is to serve as security rather than enforcement, is ordinarily levied by delivery of a copy of the order of attachment to the garnishee regardless of the nature of the property, CPLR 6214(a), levy by seizure being required only if the plaintiff indemnifies the sheriff. CPLR 6215. With an execution, the initial levy is required to be by seizure if the property is capable of delivery, and may initially be by mere service only if the property is not deliverable.

6. A CPLR 318 agent of the garnishee may be served with the execution in the garnishee's behalf, but no other agent (such as the secretary of state in the case of a corporation) may be. If the state is the garnishee, service instructions are contained in CPLR 5231(h), which CPLR 5232(a) adopts.

7. Kennis v. Sherwood, 82 A.D.2d 847, 439 N.Y.S.2d 962 (2d Dep't 1981).

8. See Meritum Corp. v. Pichler, Sup.Ct., N.Y. County, (Gammerman, J.), N.Y. Law Journal, Sept. 10, 1980, page 7, col.2.; § 520 below.

of the property that is being pursued for enforcement. It was amended in 1982 to add a subdivision (c) to meet the objection.[9] The requirement is that if a proper notice[10] has not already been served on the judgment debtor, the sheriff must serve it on the debtor along with a copy of the execution. This service, which may be made by the sheriff by either personal delivery or by ordinary first class mail, must be made within four days after the sheriff has served the execution on the garnishee.[11]

The choice of the initial method of levy depends on whether the property involved is "capable of delivery". If it is, levy is by seizure under subdivision (b) of CPLR 5232; otherwise, by service under subdivision (a), where it then requires careful follow-up steps needed to preserve it. These steps are commonly known as "perfecting" the levy.

For the sake of illustrating the perfection steps, it will be assumed that the property is not "capable of delivery".[12] The assumption will be that the levy is being made against (e.g.) a debt owed by the garnishee to the judgment debtor, not represented by an instrument and thus not amenable to a summary "seizure" by the sheriff in first instance. That will do as an example.

In order for this levy-by-service to be effective, the garnishee must, at the time he is served with the execution, either owe a debt to the judgment debtor or have possession of some property in which the judgment debtor has an interest. As long as either is the fact at levy time, the levy applies not just to that debt or property but also to any other property of the defendant that may afterwards come into the garnishee's possession. This includes any debts the garnishee owes to the debtor that may later fall due.[13] If the property is the

judgment debtor's but stands in the name of another, or if for any other reason there is some possibility that the garnishee may not know that some property of which he has possession belongs to the judgment debtor, the judgment creditor can describe and identify that property in a notice accompanying the execution, whereupon the levy applies to it. But the creditor had best be sure about this; the creditor is liable in damages if, using such a notice, he turns out to be mistaken and the mistake has injured the true owner.[14]

The obligation of the garnishee is to transfer the levied property to the sheriff and to pay to the sheriff rather than to the judgment debtor all matured debts owed to the debtor, executing such documents as may be needed to effect the transfer—a kind of attornment. As soon as the garnishee has made such a transfer, turning over to the sheriff everything he has belonging to the judgment debtor, the levy loses effect and applies to no other property coming into the garnishee's possession thereafter.[15]

This transfer should be made within 90 days after the levy, the levy being the moment that the garnishee is served with a copy of the execution. An outright transfer to the sheriff perfects and concludes the levy, now requiring only a sale by the sheriff of the personal property that has come into his possession. The levy must be perfected one way or another during that 90–day period,[16] however, and if the garnishee has not made a voluntary transfer to the sheriff within that time the judgment creditor is going to have to take some other "perfection" step before the 90 days expire.[17] Two other steps are available, either of which will perfect the levy, at least to the extent of satisfying the 90–day requirement. One is for the judgment creditor to commence a special proceeding against the uncooperative

9. The amendment and its requirements are discussed in Commentary C5232:5 on McKinney's CPLR 5232.

10. The notice is prescribed by subdivisions (d) and (e) of CPLR 5222, where it is part of the enforcement device known as the restraining notice. See § 508 below.

11. CPLR 5232(c).

12. What "capable of delivery" means is taken up in the next section.

13. The requirement that the garnishee possess something of the debtor's at levy time in order to preserve validity has a counterpart in the restraining notice provision of CPLR 5222(b). See § 508 below.

14. CPLR 5232(a).

15. Id.

16. Here is another analogy to the attachment device. See § 321 above.

17. CPLR 5232(a).

garnishee,[18] and its mere commencement within the 90 days satisfies the requirement; the proceeding need not be heard or determined within that time. The second alternative, and often the simplest one, is for the creditor to secure an extension of the 90–day period. This the creditor can do by motion, and the extension will be whatever time the court allows, not necessarily limited to 90–day spurts.[19]

During the 90 days, or whatever extended period the court allows, the garnishee is required to preserve the levied property, allowing no one but the sheriff at it unless the court directs otherwise. A garnishee who violates this prohibition, although not subject to the contempt punishment,[20] bears personal liability to the judgment creditor for any resulting damages, which the creditor can recover in the special proceeding noted earlier. If none of the steps discussed above is taken within the 90 days, the levy becomes void and its injunctive effect dissolves.[21] It is unwise, therefore, for the judgment creditor to let the 90 days pass without seeing to it that some appropriate protective step is taken. In one case, for example, in which a garnishee bank had sent a check in fulfillment of the levy but the check was lost, the bank asked the creditor's lawyer to make out a lost check form. The lawyer passed the buck by saying it was the sheriff who should make out the lost check form, and while the buck passed so did the 90 days, and the levy failed.[22] A simple motion to extend the 90 days, made before the period expired, would probably have sufficed to preserve the levy.

The 90–day period is not relevant when the initial levy is by seizure under subdivision (b). It is designed to recognize the need for extra time when the property is not amenable to simple seizure, the scenario contemplated by subdivision (a). The subdivision (b) seizure is governed by the 60–day period of CPLR 5230(c), which requires that the execution be completed and returned within that time. The 60 days run from the issuance of the execution while the 90 days applicable under 5232(a) run from the levy. In each instance the time allowed is felt to be adequate for expeditious enforcement in the particular instance; other judgment creditors may be waiting in line and should not be put off any longer than necessary.[23]

§ 497. Property "Capable of Delivery"

This is an apt juncture at which to address the phrase "capable of delivery" as used in CPLR 5232 and elsewhere in the CPLR.[1] Parts of the upcoming discourse will touch on a few items, like priorities and liens, that are not treated until later, but the phrase is too fundamental a part of the levying of executions to be put off. Anticipatory references will be just brief enough to understand the role that priorities and liens play in making the "capable of delivery" phrase loom larger today than it did under prior law.

Since whether or not a given property is "capable of delivery" will determine whether it is to be levied by initial seizure under CPLR 5232(b) or by initial service under CPLR 5232(a) (with subsequent steps to perfect the levy), we must analyze it carefully in this context. Nowhere in the CPLR is there a comprehensive description of what makes property "capable of delivery", although a few property interests otherwise unlikely to fit without a little push have been brought within the standard. A property interest consisting of a debt represented by a negotiable instrument, for example, has been strictly categorized as a "capable of delivery" property: the instrument itself is deemed the property and the one hold-

---

18. The proceeding contemplated is governed by CPLR 5225 or 5227. See § 510 below. The garnishee in that proceeding can assert her defenses or otherwise explain why the property was not handed over.

19. CPLR 5232(a). An extension is not to be had just for the asking, however. The court is aware that other judgment creditors are waiting and should be satisfied that the judgment creditor is proceeding with diligence.

20. See CPLR 5251.

21. CPLR 5232(a).

22. Wordie v. Chase Manhattan Bank, N.A., 140 A.D.2d 435, 529 N.Y.S.2d 1 (2d Dep't 1988).

23. See Vance Boiler Works, Inc. v. Co–Operative Feed Dealers, Inc., 46 Misc.2d 654, 260 N.Y.S.2d 303 (Sup.Ct., Wayne County, 1965).

§ 497

1. See, e.g., CPLR 6215.

ing the instrument rather than the one owing the debt is deemed the garnishee through whom enforcement is pursued.[2]

We may reasonably deduce that any intangible obligation, whether debt or cause of action or otherwise, not represented by a negotiable instrument, is property "not capable of delivery" and is to be treated as such for enforcement.[3] The question is, is that the only thing that falls beyond the standard? Is everything else, including all interests in a tangible chattel, to be deemed "capable of delivery" without regard to anything else?

Common sense suggests that a pragmatic definition is needed for "capable of delivery" as used in Article 52. It is submitted that any situation in which the sheriff cannot readily lay hands on the property interest involved, and by some means take immediate actual or at least constructive custody of it, should be deemed to involve property "not capable of delivery" and therefore to permit levy by service under subdivision (a) of CPLR 5232 instead of being restricted to levy be seizure under subdivision (b). To say otherwise would often frustrate the levy of an execution when there is no need to.[4] Several prominent illustrations come to mind.

Assume a debt represented by a negotiable instrument. The CPLR clearly deems the instrument "capable of delivery". Now suppose the garnishee who has custody of the instrument will not surrender it, or even tell the sheriff where it is. Is execution to fail completely? Is levy by service under subdivision (a), which would work nicely in that situation, to be precluded because the property is technically "capable of delivery" and thus subject to levy only by seizure under subdivision (b), even though seizure is impossible? That showing should trigger CPLR 5232(a), enabling levy to be made just by serving the garnishee and leaving to the subsequent perfection process such steps as are needed to persuade the garnishee to deliver the instrument. If the gar-

nishee refuses, the judgment creditor may bring a special proceeding against the garnishee as a perfection step under CPLR 5232(a), and this will likely persuade the garnishee to hand over the instrument under pain of facing a direct judgment for its sum. CPLR 5232(a) would thus serve well, while CPLR 5232(b), by insisting on an initial seizure when none is possible, would not work at all.

Another example would be where the property is a chattel of some kind that the garnishee has in her residence or some other place inaccessible to the sheriff.[5] The sheriff can't readily seize it and, were subdivision (b) to preempt, no levy would be possible. This practical impediment should by itself translate the property from capable to incapable of seizure and thereby authorize levy by service under subdivision (a).

Yet another illustration would be where the garnishee has the property, and the sheriff can easily lay hands on it, but when it is under pledge or lease to the garnishee, who therefore has a right to its continued possession. CPLR 5232(b) itself precludes seizure in that case, and by implication authorizes levy by service under subdivision (a), which is meaningful: the service of the execution on the garnishee will warn her that when her possessory right terminates she must give the chattel to the sheriff rather than to the judgment debtor, thus protecting the judgment creditor's interest. Here is a piece of pragmatism built right into CPLR 5232 itself, and it can be cited as inviting a pragmatic approach to the other levy situations.

If reasonable means exist for the sheriff to effect an immediate seizure, even if it entails only constructive custody—as by chaining and locking the working parts of a big piece of machinery so as to make it inoperable, or designating some person on the premises as the sheriff's custodian—the case can be deemed one for subdivision (b) and levy by seizure can be required. But if no such reason-

---

2. CPLR 5201(c)(4). See § 491 above.

3. See 3d Rep.Leg.Doc. (1959) No. 17, p. 296.

4. The situation would be all the more lamentable because sometimes it is only the levy itself, rather than the mere delivery of the execution, that affords the judg-

ment creditor a priority in the property interest involved. See §§ 519 and 520 below.

5. See § 496 above.

able means exist, whether because the property is concealed, or inaccessible, or is for any other reason unseizable even constructively, a levy by service should be permissible under subdivision (a).

The argument may be heard that if the property is not capable of immediate seizure, the judgment creditor need not bother about the execution device at all; that the creditor can just turn to one of the other devices, such as a delivery application under CPLR 5225(b) or 5227. The trouble with that, as we shall see, is that these other devices do not give the judgment creditor a lien on the affected property until the order or judgment sought is actually granted and entered, which can be a long way off, while an execution will afford the judgment creditor a lien directly upon levy by the sheriff, and sometimes even upon mere delivery of the execution to the sheriff.[6] The prior law counterparts of today's restraining notice[7] and disclosure subpoena[8] did create liens for their user,[9] but today neither does.[10] If they did, either would serve as a lien-giver just as effectively as an execution, because either is promptly servable without court leave, just as an execution is. This change from prior to present law makes fast access to the execution all the more important today for the lien it instantly secures.[11] Echoing CPLR 5232(b), old caselaw holds that if property is "capable of delivery" it must be levied by seizure and that if there is no seizure there is no levy.[12] This is not inconsistent with what is urged here, which suggests only that the phrase be interpreted pragmatically.[13]

It is always preferable, especially from the judgment creditor's point of view, to have the

levy made by immediate seizure, and the sheriff remains under obligation to seize whenever it is feasible. If a seizure can be readily effected, a sheriff turning instead to a levy by service under CPLR 5232(a) would be effecting no levy at all, which can well damage the judgment creditor should some competitor achieve priority as a result. For that the sheriff is liable to the creditor,[14] which suggests that the sheriff himself would prefer to turn to levy by service under subdivision (a) only when not reasonably able to effect levy by seizure under subdivision (b). A practical definition of what "capable of delivery" means thus need not be apprehended as inviting laxity on the part of enforcement officers. In fact, increasing the use of levy by service gives the judgment creditor closer control of enforcement proceedings: the execution and/or levy gives the creditor priority, at least for a time, which protects the creditor while he now turns to other devices for enforcement aid without undue concern about whether or not they are also lien-givers.

§ 498. Selling the Personal Property

Any levied personal property that comes into the sheriff's possession and which is not itself money (legal tender) must be sold by the sheriff at public auction pursuant to CPLR 5233. In fact, the sheriff is required to sell not only property that comes to him through an execution, but also that which he gets through any other Article 52 device, such as a delivery order.[1] The sheriff must give notice of the sale[2] and is authorized to sell the property, tangible or intangible, as a unit, in lots, or in such other form as in his judgment will best attract

---

6. See the discussion of liens in §§ 519 and 520 below.

7. CPLR 5222.

8. CPLR 5224.

9. See Civil Practice Act § 781; Wickwire Spencer Steel Co. v. Kemkit Scientific Corp., 292 N.Y. 139, 54 N.E.2d 336 (1944).

10. See City of New York v. Panzirer, 23 A.D.2d 158, 259 N.Y.S.2d 284 (1st Dep't 1965).

11. Graze v. Bankers Trust Co., 45 Misc.2d 610, 257 N.Y.S.2d 483 (Sup.Ct., N.Y.County, 1965), illustrates how one who diligently makes a CPLR 5225 application as well as serves both a 5222 restraining notice and a 5224

subpoena still loses out to another judgment creditor in whose behalf a simple execution levy is made.

12. See, e.g., Pach v. Gilbert, 124 N.Y. 612, 27 N.E. 391 (1891).

13. The interpretation suggested would also appear to be the only one permissible under the liberal construction edict of CPLR 104.

14. See § 520 below.

§ 498

1. CPLR 5225. See § 510 below.

2. CPLR 5233(b) provides for the notice methods.

bidders.[3] If the situation poses any urgency, the court can order immediate sale or other disposition, dispensing with the formal auction requirements.[4] It will exercise that power, for example, in the case of perishables, or where the property involved has only momentary value, such as a news article or film clip on a topic of current interest.

If an issue arises about whether particular property is saleable, such as contraband, the sheriff can apply to the court for instructions.[5]

From whatever is realized at the sale, the sheriff deducts his fees and expenses and any taxes that may be due, paying the balance to the judgment creditor towards satisfaction of the judgment; if anything remains, it goes to the judgment debtor.[6]

§ 499. Levy on Real Property

A levy on real property is easier in its first stage than one on personal property, mainly because it initially involves neither a "seizure" nor even the service of the execution on the garnishee—the methods whereby personalty is levied.[1] With the sale of the real property, it is the second stage, treated in the next section, that becomes more involved, mainly because of CPLR 5236 and its demanding set of statutory requirements for the sale.

The first thing the judgment creditor should see to when she has an eye to the debtor's realty is that the judgment has been docketed in the county clerk's office of the realty county. It is the docketing that makes the judgment a lien on the real property and prevents others from slipping in with a priority while its sale is being carried out.[2]

The initial lien of the judgment is only 10 years, however,[3] while the life of the judgment is 20.[4] This means that if the judgment is more

than 10 years old when the levy is sought (the levy being permissible any time during the life of the judgment), the enforcement will be going forward at a time when the judgment has lost its lien value. For that situation, CPLR 5235 has a special procedure whereby the judgment can once again be made a lien, at least for a long enough time to enable the sheriff to sell the property. The judgment creditor delivers an execution to the sheriff of the realty county and has the sheriff file with its county clerk a "notice of levy", which describes the judgment, the execution, and the property. This is then indexed in the same manner as a notice of pendency.[5] The judgment thereupon becomes a lien once again and remains a lien until the execution is returned by the sheriff,[6] which will not occur until the sale has been completed. The sheriff now goes ahead with the sale.

During the first 10 years of the judgment, when—as long as the judgment has been duly docketed in the realty county—it retains its original lien value, this filing of a notice of levy is unnecessary. If the sheriff has received an execution from the judgment creditor, he simply proceeds with the sale. If the judgment creditor wants to avoid a priority gap, as when the levy occurs near the tail end of the 10–year lien period, she can, during the last year of that period, commence an action to renew the judgment and secure a fresh 10–year lien.[7]

The CPLR has no requirement, incidentally, that a levy on personal property be attempted before the defendant's real property is turned to. The judgment creditor can go after realty directly, subject to an ad hoc protective order varying the progression if the court sees fit.[8]

§ 500. Selling the Real Property

The requirements for the sale of real property under an execution are more profuse and

---

3. CPLR 5233(a).

4. CPLR 5233(c).

5. Subdivision (d), added to CPLR 5233 in a 1979 amendment, so authorizes.

6. CPLR 5234(a).

§ 499

1. CPLR 5232 contains the methods for levying against personal property.

2. For treatment of the docketing of judgments between and among courts, see §§ 421 and 422 above.

3. CPLR 5203(a). See § 517 below.

4. CPLR 211(b).

5. For the methods of indexing a notice of pendency, see § 335 above.

6. CPLR 5203(a).

7. CPLR 5014. See § 434 above.

8. CPLR 5240. See § 522 below.

detailed than those for personal property. The statute in point, CPLR 5236, has come in for a number of amendments, several resulting from a study conducted during the early years of the CPLR.[1] Although its ultimate impact is on the creditor and debtor, the statute is of more immediate moment to the sheriff, who must conduct the sale, and to the title companies, which will end up paying the bill if some oversight causes a title to fail. The title companies, in fact, have been the principal overseers of CPLR 5236 and the advocates of most of its amendments.

The sale of the real property is, as with personal property, by public auction, but with a more elaborate set of notice requirements. The sheriff must post notice of the sale in at least three public places in the town or city in which the realty is located and publish the notice in a newspaper in the realty's county. These exactions and their time instructions are in CPLR 5236(c), which also requires the sheriff to notify the judgment debtor and all others who are shown of record to have any lien on or interest in the realty as of a certain day, fixed with reference to the projected date of sale. The judgment creditor must furnish the sheriff a list of these other lienholders. The requirement that they be notified is to enable them to take such steps as they feel necessary to protect their interests. The auction at which the sale is conducted takes place, unless duly postponed, between the 8th and 9th week following the first publication of the notice of sale.[2]

Among those included on the creditors' list will be other judgment creditors of the same debtor, if their judgments have been made

liens against the property. Upon getting notice from the sheriff, they must deliver their own executions to him, which entitles them to take their proper place in line for the sale's proceeds.[3] Even a creditor whose judgment lien is senior to that of the levied judgment must, upon being notified, deliver an execution. A failure to do so forfeits the lien.[4] If the senior creditor does deliver it, however, he will have first crack at the proceeds of the sale, even though it is at another judgment creditor's initiative that the sale is taking place. Proceeds must be distributed by the sheriff in the order of lien priority of the judgments on which he has received executions.[5] A junior judgment creditor can only hope (as can, indeed, the levying judgment creditor himself if he has confronted senior judgment liens) that there will be enough proceeds for all.

Other categories of senior lienholder, such as a mortgagee, retain their liens, to which the buyer at the sale takes subject, but junior lienors are wiped out by the sale. For that reason, a mortgagee or other lienor junior to the judgment being levied on is also allowed to share in any surplus that an execution sale on that judgment may produce.[6]

Whatever is left over from the sale's proceeds after payment of all fees, expenses, and taxes, in that order, and execution issuers and junior lienors, in the order of seniority among them, goes to the judgment debtor.[7] Other provisions govern the sheriff's conveyance to the buyer at the sale,[8] and issues arising if the buyer's title should for some reason fail.[9] Any party with an objection to the sheriff's proceedings may raise it by a motion to the court

---

§ 500

1. See Sale of Real Property Pursuant to an Execution under the CPLR, 10th Jud.Conf.Rep. (1965) 120.

2. CPLR 5236(a), (d).

3. CPLR 5236(g).

4. CPLR 5236(e); Meadow Brook Nat. Bank v. Goodkin, 53 Misc.2d 1099, 280 N.Y.S.2d 978 (Sup.Ct., Nassau County, 1966), aff'd 28 A.D.2d 648, 282 N.Y.S.2d 441 (2d Dep't 1967).

5. CPLR 5236(g)(1). For priorities and liens with respect to real property, see § 517 below.

6. Bank Leumi Trust Co. of N.Y. v. Liggett, 115 A.D.2d 378, 496 N.Y.S.2d 14 (1st Dep't 1985).

7. CPLR 5236(g)(2). If the property was the judgment debtor's principal residence, $10,000 is of course an exemption, CPLR 5206(a), and goes to the judgment debtor; the creditors share only what is left after the $10,000 is subtracted. See § 490 above.

8. CPLR 5236(f).

9. CPLR 5237. Innocent purchasers are usually protected when their dispute is with one whose lien is junior to that of the levying judgment creditor (through whom they take). See, e.g., First Fed. Sav. and Loan Ass'n v. McKee, 61 Misc.2d 693, 305 N.Y.S.2d 589 (Sup.Ct., Nassau County, 1969).

either under CPLR 5238, a special provision concerned with property levies, or CPLR 5240, the omnibus protective order provision applicable to all of Article 52.

If the judgment is for a mortgage debt on the subject real property and was entered in a money action on the debt instead of in an action to foreclose the mortgage that secures the debt, the real property cannot be levied on pursuant to that judgment because it would circumvent the right of redemption as it exists in mortgage foreclosure context.[10]

Since the realty will be sold to the highest bidder under CPLR 5236, without reference to whether or not the bid equals the judgment debtor's actual equity in the property, unhappy situations arise when the discrepancy is substantial. This is especially the case when the realty is a residence. There have been instances of the family home being sold for substantially less than the family's equity. The sale has nevertheless been upheld when the proceedings were regular and especially when the bidder was a stranger to them.[11]

The problem is the worse because there is no right of redemption here as there is in mortgage foreclosure: the right within a stated time to get up the money to pay off the debt, cancel the proceedings, and get back the property. That is, there is no right of redemption explicitly set forth. With a protective order under CPLR 5240, however, the court can give the judgment debtor more time to seek the money to pay the judgment, postponing the sale for that purpose, and this amounts to a de facto right of redemption. Also, if it appears that a private sale of the property, through the usual channels of advertisement or brokers, will get a substantially better price than the public auction of an execution sale is likely to produce, the court on motion can appoint a receiver to make such a sale.[12] The courts are

sympathetic to judgment debtors faced with the loss of their residential equity for less than its worth. In one memorable case, in which an equity of $13,000 was about to go for $197.25, and to someone in apparent privity with the judgment creditor—who may of course join the bidders but whose presence makes the court all the more suspicious—the court set aside the sale despite the fact that it fulfilled all applicable requirements.[13]

What sum will be credited against the judgment after the sale: the bid price or the actual market value of the property, should it be higher? In the mortgage foreclosure realm, a statute requires that the higher market value price be credited.[14] There is no such direction with respect to the levy of execution on a judgment, and the bid price is therefore the one ordinarily used to determine the sum by which the judgment shall be reduced after the sale. There is authority, however, at least when the judgment creditor is the winning bidder, for borrowing from the mortgage foreclosure realm the rule crediting the debtor with the market value. That was the position taken by the supreme court in Wandschneider v. Bekeny[15] in 1973, and it was adopted and followed by the appellate division in Yellow Creek Hunting Club, Inc. v. Todd Supply, Inc.[16] in 1988. While this will not restore the property, it will at least credit the owner with its true value in reduction of the debt. Without that crediting, the debt will be reduced based only on the bid, and an inadequate bid will mean that the debtor has lost her property without even being able to reduce her obligation by the property's worth.

Judicial intervention of this kind shows that the law has at least some remedies for avoiding injustices, as long as they (and the situations needing remedy) are called to the court's

---

10. CPLR 5236(b). See § 495 above.

11. See, e.g., Matter of Bachner, 82 Misc.2d 107, 368 N.Y.S.2d 749 (Sup.Ct., Nassau County, 1975), where the bid was claimed to be only 41% of the equity's market value.

12. CPLR 5228. See § 512 below.

13. Community Capital Corp. v. Lee, 58 Misc.2d 34, 294 N.Y.S.2d 336 (Sup.Ct., Nassau County, 1968).

14. RPAPL 1371(2).

15. 75 Misc.2d 32, 346 N.Y.S.2d 925 (Sup.Ct., Westchester County).

16. 145 A.D.2d 679, 535 N.Y.S.2d 222 (3d Dep't 1988). The Yellow Creek case is discussed in the lead note in New York State Law Digest No. 351.

attention.[17] What is mainly needed to avoid abuse is ready access to competent counsel by all, regardless of economic station, a matter of great urgency that has not yet earned a fair share of governmental attention.

§ 501. Sheriff's Return

A return is a statement of the sheriff's doings in connection with the execution and of any success the sheriff has had on the levy. The sheriff makes the return to the clerk of the court out of which the execution issued. If the judgment has in any measure been satisfied, the clerk must record as much on the dockets.[1] The general rule is that the property execution must be returned within 60 days after issuance.[2] As a rule, this is feasible only on a personal property levy, and, even there, only when the levy is made by seizure under subdivision (b) of CPLR 5232 rather than by service under subdivision (a), which has its own time provisions.[3] The 60–day period may be extended by the judgment creditor's attorney, but only once as a matter of right; recognizing that other judgment creditors may be waiting, the statute permits further extensions only if none of these others has an execution outstanding in the hands of the same sheriff.[4]

As will be seen, a judgment creditor's delivery of an execution to a sheriff secures for that creditor a lien on the judgment debtor's personal property.[5] That lien is lost when the execution is returned unsatisfied.[6]

The 60–day limitation on return of the execution must also be deemed inapplicable when real property is being levied. The time required for a realty sale under CPLR 5236 goes well beyond 60 days. The docketing of the judgment, moreover, is the step that gives a

judgment its realty lien, which therefore does not, as a personal property lien does, depend on the moment that an execution is delivered to the sheriff. Since the moment of delivery does not have that significance in a realty situation, there is less need for rigidity about when a return is needed; the parties should instead concentrate on the sale procedures of CPLR 5236 and see that they are fulfilled with reasonable diligence. Any problems arising in connection with the sheriff's proceedings can be resolved by the court on motion.[7]

The sheriff is required to keep a complete set of execution records, which must include the date of the execution's issuance, the date and time of its delivery to the sheriff (these to be endorsed on the execution itself and all the more important because they determine priorities), the date of the execution's return, the amount due at delivery time, and anything still due at return time.[8]

E. INCOME EXECUTION

Table of Sections

§ 502. Income Execution, Contents and Service

An income execution operates on the judgment debtor's income from wages and like earnings, and from a trust.[1] It operates on 10%

---

17. Further examples of judicial intervention to prevent injustice appear in § 522, below, where the protective order is treated.

§ 501

1. CPLR 5021(b).

2. CPLR 5230(c).

3. See §§ 496 and 497 above.

4. CPLR 5230(c).

5. See §§ 519 and 520 below.

6. International Ribbon Mills Ltd. v. Arjan Ribbons, Inc., 36 N.Y.2d 121, 365 N.Y.S.2d 808, 325 N.E.2d 137

(1975). This does not preclude issuance of a second execution, but the time between the return of the old and the issuance of the new may enable another judgment creditor to slip in with priority.

7. See CPLR 5238.

8. CPLR 5230(d).

§ 502

1. The implication that only earnings are aimed at by CPLR 5231 was removed by a 1990 amendment, clarifying that trust and like income is included as well. Because earnings are by far the most common income source that of the income, requiring payment of that percentage to the sheriff on each due date. It acts as a continuing levy, unlike an ordinary property execution, which loses validity when the garnishee hands over whatever he presently has belonging to the judgment debtor.[2] It also constitutes an exception to CPLR 5201(a), which precludes levy against contingent intangibles: the income execution operates on income as it comes due even though its effectiveness is premised on continuing services.

The income execution for money judgments in general is supplied and governed by CPLR 5231, the subject that we take up here and in the several sections following. (There is a special income execution for support in family matters, CPLR 5241, which is treated as a distinct subject afterwards.[3]) By allowing levy on 10%, CPLR 5231 is the counterpart of CPLR 5205(d), the provision that exempts 90% of income. By force of habit, the income execution under CPLR 5231 is also what bench and bar usually have in mind when they use the word "garnishment". The income execution is of course only one kind of garnishment; any levy on a debtor's assets in the hands of a third person, including a levy under an ordinary property execution, is also a category of "garnishment".[4]

The income execution is drawn by the lawyer and delivered directly to the sheriff. Its form is largely prescribed by statute.[5] It requires no court order or other preliminary permission, as it once did; nor is an attempt at any other device a condition precedent to use of the income execution, as was the case under old law.[6] It can be the first enforcement device used; in fact, if the creditor knows that income is the debtor's only asset, it is likely to be the first, last, and only device used. It is probably

the most commonly relied on enforcement device and in a sense it is the last refuge of the judgment creditor who has a modest judgment against an unpropertied judgment debtor. Hence there is much caselaw on the income execution.

In addition to the contents generally prescribed for executions by CPLR 5230, the income execution contains the name and address of the employer—or other person (such as a trustee), but the employer will do for our examples—from whom the debtor is receiving money, the frequency of the payments and their amount, and the amount to be deducted. It is delivered to the sheriff, who first serves it on the judgment debtor himself—*before* any turn is made to the employer for payment. The debtor must be allowed at least 20 days to start deducting and paying over the 10%—a CPLR innovation designed to spare the debtor the embarrassment, or worse, of having the income execution served on his employer, and to spare the latter the bother. The income execution must therefore contain a notice to the judgment debtor advising him of his obligation and warning that default will result in service on the employer.[7] Because the income execution is to be served first on the judgment debtor, it is to the sheriff of the debtor's county (if that is not the same as his employer's) that the attorney must initially deliver it. Only if the judgment debtor is a nonresident of the state may it be delivered straight to the sheriff of the employer's county.[8] The sheriff serves it on the judgment debtor in the same manner as a summons or by certified mail with return receipt requested. If the certified mail method is used, additional copies must then be sent to the debtor by regular mail both to his residence and to his last known place of

---

CPLR 5231 is used on, the treatment of the income execution in this and the ensuing sections will assume that the levied item is earnings and that the payer is an employer, but the terms are intended to include as an "employer" any trustee or other garnishee required to make the payments, and as "wages" or "earnings" all forms of compensation for personal services as well as trust income.

Most of the subdivisions of CPLR 5231 were relettered as part of an extensive 1987 amendment of the statute. Because many pre–1987 cases refer to the old lettering, a chart coordinating the subdivisions before and after the

amendment appears in a footnote at the end of § 503 below.

2. CPLR 5232(a).

3. See § 507A.

4. See the definition of "garnishee" in CPLR 105.

5. CPLR 5231(g).

6. See § 684 of the old Civil Practice Act.

7. CPLR 5231(a).

8. CPLR 5231(b).

employment. The sheriff must serve the debtor within 20 days after receiving the execution, a requirement designed to require expeditious treatment of this heavily depended-on device.[9]

Twenty days also measures the judgment debtor's chance to make the deductions himself. If the debtor fails within that time to pay an installment—here the 20 days run from the service of the execution on the debtor—the sheriff is then empowered to serve the employer.[10] There must be flexibility, however. The debtor's salary may be paid monthly, for example, with the first payment due more than 20 days after he has been served. The sheriff will usually supply such additional time as is reasonable in these situations. A judgment debtor proceeding in good faith usually need only contact the sheriff's office to secure the additional time. (Permitting this is also to the creditor's advantage.)

If the debtor defaults on this opportunity to start making payments on the income execution himself (sheriffs report that most do), or if the sheriff is unable to serve the debtor within 20 days after delivery of the execution, the sheriff may now serve the employer.[11]

If the employer is in the same county, it will be the same sheriff who now serves the employer. The sheriff need only serve another copy of the income execution, for which reason it may be helpful to deliver several copies to the sheriff. If the employer is in a different county, however, the likelihood is that the first sheriff will just return the execution, unsatisfied, to the attorney for the judgment creditor, who will now have to deliver another copy to the sheriff of the employer's county. This should also be done within 20 days after the first sheriff's return, because the execution will otherwise lose the priority that the first delivery secured.[12] The sheriff's method of

serving the employer is, again, by personal delivery or by certified mail with return receipt requested.[13]

There is a question, today, about whether an income execution is available if the judgment debtor neither resides nor works in New York, as where the New York judgment against her was based on longarm jurisdiction. Under the old Civil Practice Act, the mere fact that the employer was present in New York, even though the defendant lived and worked for this employer elsewhere, was sufficient not only for post-judgment income execution, but (by adoption) even for pre-judgment attachment. So held Morris Plan Industrial Bank v. Gunning,[14] but the viability of the case today is doubtful. Whatever the merits of an income levy for pre-judgment attachment, however, a good case can be made out for a post-judgment income execution against a nonresident judgment debtor whose employer has a New York presence. As long as the New York judgment itself is shown to have a sturdy jurisdictional foundation, regardless that the debtor neither lives nor works in the state, his obligation to pay a New York judgment is good ground for arguing that the coincidental New York presence of his employer may be reasonably exploited to satisfy the judgment. But is it permissible under CPLR 5231, which as a whole seems to contemplate that the judgment debtor either lives or works in New York?

The courts are in disagreement. Some hold that income execution is not permitted in this instance;[15] others, that it is, and at least one of these has said that the part requiring preliminary service on the debtor before the employer may be served can be met by delivering the execution to an enforcement officer in the foreign state and having him serve the judgment

---

9. CPLR 5231(d).

10. CPLR 5231(e).

11. Id.

12. CPLR 5231(j). Priorities are discussed in § 504 below.

13. CPLR 5231(e). A CPLR 318 agent can be served if the employer has one, but no other designated agent, such as the secretary of state in the case of a corporate employer, is servable in this instance. Special requirements con-

cerning service and its incidents applicable to certain governmental units as employers, including municipalities and the state itself (which is a permissible garnishee under CPLR 5207), are contained in CPLR 5231(h).

14. 295 N.Y. 324, 67 N.E.2d 510 (1946).

15. E.g., Brown v. Arabian American Oil Co., 53 Misc.2d 182, 278 N.Y.S.2d 256 (Sup.Ct., Suffolk County, 1967); Kaplan v. Supak & Sons Mfg. Co., 46 Misc.2d 574, 260 N.Y.S.2d 374 (N.Y.C.Civ.Ct. 1965).

debtor,[16] a procedure that can meet stiff resistance from the foreign official. The matter still awaits definitive resolution.

§ 503. Income Execution; Computing the 10%

The standards for computing exactly how much has to be deducted on the income execution are in subdivision (b) of CPLR 5231, and even more informative is the actual form, supplied by subdivision (g), which has to be included in the income execution itself. The percentage of the deduction is 10%, which is the maximum that New York law allows under CPLR 5231, but federal law[1] exempts part of the debtor's earnings altogether and restricts the computation base, on which the 10% is to be computed, to only what is left over.[2]

A key figure under the federal standard is the current hourly minimum wage multiplied by 30, and a key phrase is "disposable earnings". "Disposable earnings" means the debtor's net income after deductions for sums that the law requires to be withheld: taxes, social security, unemployment insurance, and the like, but not including deductions for voluntary withholdings like union dues or insurance plan payments. The debtor's weekly "disposable earnings" must be at least 30 times the current minimum hourly wage before the income execution becomes operative; that basic sum is deemed essential for the debtor's family needs.

If the earnings do not exceed that figure, there can be no income deduction at all. If they do exceed it, the 10% works only on the excess. The basic sum, in other words, is exempt.[3]

Further restrictions apply when deductions are already being made from the debtor's income for support and related family purposes. If those deductions are 25% or more of the debtor's disposable earnings, there can be no income levy at all on a CPLR 5231 execution.[4] If they do not exceed 25%, a levy is allowed, but the 10% authorized by CPLR 5231 plus the sum being deducted for support cannot together exceed 25% of disposable earnings. To the extent of the excess, it is the CPLR 5231 execution that has to be reduced. It was argued in one case, in which a support order was already garnishing more than 25% and this exhausted the earnings segment that would otherwise have been available for an ordinary judgment creditor, that the 25% is really just the coordinate of a 75% reserve for family

---

16. Oystermen's Bank & Trust Co. v. Manning, 59 Misc.2d 144, 298 N.Y.S.2d 355 (Sup.Ct., N.Y.County, 1969).

§ 503

1. 15 U.S.C.A. §§ 1671–1677.

2. These federal standards were explicitly incorporated into CPLR 5231 in an amendment in 1987 after the prior CPLR 5231 scheme had been invalidated in Follette v. Vitanza, 658 F.Supp. 492 (N.D.N.Y.1987), in part for failing to take the federal statutory requirements into consideration. Other reasons cited for the invalidation were that the New York provisions failed to advise the judgment debtor about the possibly exempt status of her income or about remedies she might pursue to protect her rights. The amendment answers those objections as well, but before it could be drafted and put through the cumbersome legislative process a subsequent order had to be issued by the court to preserve existing income executions, which numbered in the thousands. The order directed remedial steps in the interim. Follette v. Cooper, 658 F.Supp. 514 (1987). These matters, and the flurry of activity that surrounded the two Follette decisions, are described in the lead note in New York State Law Digest No. 328.

3. This is in contrast with the way New York computed the 10% before 1987, when a basic weekly $85 was the key figure, and it was a gross rather than net measure—

no withholding at all could be considered. Nor was it an exemption. It was just a threshold, and once the $85 was reached, the whole $85 became subject to levy: a debtor earning $84 a week, for example, was immune from income levy while one earning $86 had $8.60 deducted. Caselaw confirmed those methods of computation—see, e.g., County Trust Co. v. Berg, 65 Misc.2d 533, 318 N.Y.S.2d 154 (Sup.Ct., Kings County, 1971); Slocum–Dickson Medical Group v. General Electric Co., 66 Misc.2d 363, 320 N.Y.S.2d 883 (Oneida County Ct. 1971)—although an occasional voice in the wilderness, guided by logic because of having inadvertently overlooked the statute's stubborn history, held that take-home pay (after legally required deductions) should be the computation base, e.g., County Trust Co. v. Duerr, 52 Misc.2d 411, 275 N.Y.S.2d 910 (Sup.Ct., Westchester County, 1966). The general background of the income execution under its pre–1987 standards is treated in a series of articles by this writer appearing in the New York Law Journal editions of May 18–20, 1971.

4. A special income execution, CPLR 5241, itself designed to aid in the collection of support money, does not encounter this restriction. A clause in the form supplied by CPLR 5231(g) explicitly advises that nothing in CPLR 5231 limits income deductions for support purposes.

needs, and that the support order should be deemed to come out of the 75%, leaving the 25% available to income execution leviers. The Second Circuit rejected the argument, finding no Congressional intent "to protect the rights of creditors", only a purpose "to limit the ills" that come from unrestricted garnishment.[5]

Mandatory support deductions already being made against a support debtor under CPLR 5241 and 5242, the special support income execution statutes, are applied to reduce a CPLR 5231 levy,[6] but it has been held, unfortunately, that payments conscientiously made by the support debtor pursuant to the terms of a divorce judgment do not reduce the CPLR 5231 levy.[7]

A supervening factor is that all the earnings of one who is getting public assistance are exempt from income levy under New York law,[8] as are the public assistance payments themselves.[9] These exemptions apply whether the money is still in the hands of the disbursing agency or has already reached the hands of the judgment debtor, or, indeed, his bank account, if the money on deposit is shown to be welfare receipts.[10]

All income based on personal services qualifies for income execution, "whether denominated as wages, salary, commission, bonus, or otherwise, and includes periodic payments pursuant to a pension or retirement program".[11] The label is secondary. Even "irregular" payments are to be reached.[12] If the payments are other than weekly, such as monthly or quarterly or even less regular than that, they are to be averaged out to what they amount to by the week, and to face income execution if by that measure they meet the current standards.[13] The judgment debtor should think twice before starting any arguments about whether the payments, however irregular, are for personal services and therefore subject to the income execution. It is to his advantage to have it assumed that they are. A contrary holding, which frees the earnings from the 10% levy, will subject them instead to a 100% levy. In his haste to be rid of the 10% levy, in other words, a debtor may overlook that it is the counterpart of a 90% exemption.

As applied to sums earned before the income execution is delivered to the sheriff, the limitations attach only to earnings for services rendered within the preceding 60 days.[14] Earnings more than 60 days old are subject to total levy, not just 10%.[15] A threatened hardship in a particular case, were a full levy to proceed as authorized, can be met through an individual protective order applied for under either CPLR 5231(i), allowing modification of income executions in particular, or CPLR 5240, the general protective order provision.[16] Conversely, future earnings, all of them presumably 90% exempt, can theoretically be allowed to accumulate beyond the needs of the debtor's family. Here the judgment creditor's remedy is an installment payment order under CPLR 5226, where the court addresses the facts of the individual case and is empowered to direct payment of more than 10% if the debtor can afford it.[17] Until a court directs otherwise, however, even bank

---

5. Long Island Trust Co. v. United States Postal Serv., 647 F.2d 336 (2d Cir.1981), decided when the federal standards were applicable but before they had been included in CPLR 5231 explicitly.

6. CPLR 5231(b)(iii).

7. See Tilden Financial Corp. v. Corwin, 149 Misc.2d 544, 566 N.Y.S.2d 457 (Sup.Ct., N.Y.County, 1990). Tilden acknowledges that it is only the "scoundrel" who benefits from this, but says that the legislature must correct the problem. Criticizing Tilden, but not to the extent of just honoring outright these other support payments being made by the judgment debtor, American Express Centurion v. Melia, 155 Misc.2d 587, 589 N.Y.S.2d 290 (Civ. Court, Kings County, 1992), says that what the court should do is hold a hearing, modifying the CPLR 5231 payments with a protective order if necessary.

8. Social Services Law § 137–a.

9. Id., § 137.

10. Consumer Credit Corp. v. Lewis, 63 Misc.2d 928, 313 N.Y.S.2d 879 (Dist.Ct., Nassau County, 1970).

11. CPLR 5231(c)(i).

12. See 6th Rep.Leg.Doc. (1962) No. 8, p. 496.

13. In re Ostergren's Will, 49 Misc.2d 894, 268 N.Y.S.2d 906 (Surr.Ct., Kings County, 1966).

14. CPLR 5205(d)(2).

15. A good treatment of these matters appears in Girard Trust Bank v. Gotham Football Club, 31 A.D.2d 142, 295 N.Y.S.2d 741 (1st Dep't 1968).

16. See § 522 below.

17. See § 511 below.

account money shown to be recent earnings may be levied only to the extent of 10%.[18]

Complications can also arise when the employer has made advances of salary payments to the employee—advances that the employer would ordinarily be entitled to deduct from further earnings. It has been held that the employer can apply post-execution earnings against legitimate pre-execution advances, thus taking that segment of them out of the category of the debtor's "earnings" and putting it beyond reach of the income execution. The theory is that it is the employer's money, not the debtor's, until all is paid back. Post-execution advances will not be allowed to impede the levying creditor, however,[19] lest collusion be encouraged between a debtor and an unduly cooperative employer. Employers have to be careful about such things. A perusal of the footnoted case suggests that the law is not as clear as it might be. The situation might even be analogized to where the employer itself is a judgment creditor of its employee, one of several judgment creditors, and the employer tries to take advantage of its dual creditor/garnishee role to give itself an advantage. One such person who tried to do that, not adhering strictly to the income execution procedures, ended up not only losing priority, which it had initially achieved by proper procedure, but with personal liability to another creditor who played strictly according to the book.[20]

CPLR 5231 is an important part of New York practice, and as the discussion indicates, the 1987 amendment of CPLR 5231 was a fundamental one. Part of the amendment was a relettering of most of the subdivisions of CPLR 5231, throwing out of kilter references to them made in numerous pre–1987 cases. A chart coordinating the subdivisions before and after the amendment, which may be helpful for reference, is set forth in the footnote.[21]

§ 504. Priorities Among Income Executions

The scheme of priorities governing personal property in general[1] does not apply to the income execution, which has its own system in CPLR 5231(j). Priority among different creditors, when several have judgments against the same debtor, is in the order in which they deliver income executions to the sheriff or other enforcement officer in the county or smaller unit—city or town, relevant when lower court judgments are being enforced by local marshals or constables—in which the judgment debtor resides. The 10% levy operates on only one judgment at a time, at least until a court directs otherwise, such as on a motion for an installment payment order,[2] and continues until the judgment with priority is fully paid. Number two on the priority line does not come in for anything until that time. Number three then awaits satisfaction of number two,

---

18. See Power v. Loonam, 49 Misc.2d 127, 266 N.Y.S.2d 865 (Sup.Ct., Nassau County, 1966).

19. See Larry Goldwater, Inc. v. C. B. Snyder Nat. Realty Co., 48 Misc.2d 669, 265 N.Y.S.2d 542 (N.Y.C.Civ. Ct. 1965).

20. See Franklin Nat. Bank v. Rayno Distributors, 43 Misc.2d 651, 252 N.Y.S.2d 123 (App.T., 2d Dep't, 1964). By reimbursing itself directly rather than through an income execution, the employer was apparently trying to avoid poundage, a percentage the sheriff gets for collecting money on an execution. See CPLR 8012(b).

21. The following charts the 1987 reordering of CPLR 5231:

Pre–1987 Subdivision	Result of 1987 Amendment
(a)	Remained (a)
(b)	Remained (b) but amended to defer to federal maximums
	New subd.(c) added, defining earnings
(c)	Relettered (d)
(d)	Relettered (e)
(e)	Relettered (f) and amended with minor conformity change
	New subd.(g) added, prescribing form of notice to be given debtor
(f)	Relettered (h)
(g)	Relettered (i)
(h)	Relettered (j)
(i)	Relettered (k)

§ 504

1. CPLR 5234, treated in § 518 et seq., below.

2. See § 511 below.

etc. This shows how important priority is. By beating out others even by just a day, a judgment creditor may monopolize the 10% income levy against a debtor for years.

If the judgment debtor balks or cannot be found by the sheriff, necessitating service on the employer, the priority earned by initial delivery will remain while the sheriff now serves the employer. If the latter is in a different county, requiring issuance of another execution to that county's sheriff, the initial delivery to the first sheriff will still determine priority provided that the delivery to the second sheriff is made within 20 days after the execution's return by the first one. The lesson to the judgment creditor's lawyer is to act fast in these situations. When the first delivery is to an enforcement officer other than a sheriff, such as a New York City marshal, and the second one goes to a sheriff—which happens mainly when a lower court judgment is involved—there is some question about whether the initial delivery to the lower-court enforcement officer can qualify as a priority-giver that adheres through the sheriff's proceedings. Caselaw is divided,[3] but it is more compatible with the lower court acts, which equate all enforcement officers with the sheriff,[4] to uphold the continuity of priority in that situation.

If the priority battle is between an ordinary judgment creditor using CPLR 5231 and a support creditor (wife, child, etc.) using CPLR

5241,[5] the support creditor prevails, and without regard to which came first.[6] Other interests, such as a governmental unit with a tax lien, may also compete for the debtor's wages, and may be allowed a kind of simultaneous enforcement.[7] Again, hardship in these instances can be alleviated on a case by case basis through protective order activity by the court.

A judgment creditor may be persuaded to voluntarily accept less than 10% by agreement with the employer. This has been held acceptable as long as there is no competing judgment creditor waiting in the wings. The service on the employer of #2's income execution mandates cancellation of the agreement made with #1 and the full resumption of the 10% levy on #1 as of that moment, to the end that #1's income execution be satisfied as soon as possible to make way for #2.[8]

§ 505. Employer's Obligations on Income Execution

When served with the execution, the employer or other garnishee must withhold 10% each payday and turn it over to the sheriff. If the employment is terminated, so is the employer's obligation on the execution, unless the employment resumes within 90 days, in which event whatever falls due after resumption faces the 10% levy.[1]

If the employer fails to make each appropriate deduction and pay it to the sheriff, the

---

3. Republic Associates v. McRae, 46 Misc.2d 1098, 261 N.Y.S.2d 777 (Sup.Ct., Westchester County, 1965), for example, holds that the priority remains, while Schleimer v. Gross, 46 Misc.2d 931, 261 N.Y.S.2d 670 (Sup.Ct., Nassau County, 1965), holds that it is lost.

4. See § 701 in the New York City Civil Court Act and in the Uniform District, City, and Justice court acts, McKinney's Vol. 29A, Parts 2 and 3.

5. See § 507A below.

6. CPLR 5241(h), 5242(c). Before the so-called "payroll deduction order" of § 49–b of the Personal Property Law was replaced by CPLR 5242, there was a conflict as to the effect to be given a payroll deduction order competing with an income execution. Some courts held that the deduction order got priority, even holding that its mere issuance works an automatic suspension of any outstanding income execution, at least until a court reinstated the execution. See, e. g., Beahm v. Beahm, 47 Misc.2d 900, 263 N.Y.S.2d 533 (Fam.Ct., Richmond County, 1965). Others held that both work simultaneously until a court intervenes. E.g.,

Costa v. Chevrolet–Tonawanda Div. of Gen. Motors Corp., 53 Misc.2d 252, 278 N.Y.S.2d 275 (Buffalo City Court 1963), ultimately approved by the Appellate Division in 24 A.D.2d 732, 263 N.Y.S.2d 319 (4th Dep't 1965). The conflict was noted in Lincoln National Bank v. Colgan, 71 Misc.2d 908, 337 N.Y.S.2d 412 (Syracuse City Court 1972). But there was in any event agreement that whatever the initial rule locally followed, the court on motion could always vary it with an individually tailored protective order.

7. See, e.g., Royal Business Funds Corp. v. Rooster Plastics, Inc., 53 Misc.2d 181, 278 N.Y.S.2d 350 (Sup.Ct., N.Y.County, 1967).

8. See Spatz Furniture Corp. v. Lee Letter Serv., 52 Misc.2d 291, 276 N.Y.S.2d 219 (N.Y.C.Civ.Ct. 1966), aff'd 54 Misc.2d 359, 282 N.Y.S.2d 624 (App.T., 1st Dep't, 1967).

§ 505

1. CPLR 5231(f).

judgment creditor may bring a special proceeding against the employer to compel it, and to collect accrued installments. If the income execution issued out of a lower court not listed in CPLR 5221(a),[2] it has been held that the proceeding must be brought in the supreme court or a county court.[3] If it is found in the proceeding that the income execution is valid, and that the employer failed without justification to make the required 10% deduction, the employer (or other garnishee) is personally liable to the judgment creditor for all that should have been withheld, up to the amount due on the judgment.[4]

An employer is forbidden to discharge an employee on the sole ground that her wages are being subjected to an income execution or series of them, or, indeed, to refuse to hire a person in the first place because of a history of income levies elsewhere. Both damages and reinstatement can be directed against an employer who violates this rule.[5]

§ 506. Sheriff's Obligation on Income Execution

The sheriff must serve the income execution within the stated time limits.[1] Since personal delivery is no longer indispensable, certified mail having been made an alternative, there is no reason for delay if the sheriff has been given the appropriate names and addresses.

The sheriff should compute the interest due on the judgment from the time of its entry to the time it is satisfied, and see to it that the interest is regularly added to the principal sum of the judgment on his records and that the employer/garnishee is kept abreast of the running total. The sheriff must continue to levy until the whole judgment, with interest included, is collected. If the garnishee is not advised of interest due, and pays out until the principal sum is satisfied, the judgment creditor has no further claim against the garnishee.[2]

With an ordinary property execution, the sheriff is sometimes required to make a return within 60 days after issuance. That period does not apply to an income execution,[3] where the sheriff's principal obligation is to accumulate the regularly received payments and to account and pay over to the judgment creditor periodically—at least once every 90 days.[4] The sheriff's "return" in this instance can apparently await the moment when the judgment has been fully paid, or such earlier moment when the execution loses effect, such as where the employment or trust terminates. Should any earlier need arise to reflect on the clerk's dockets the satisfaction made of the judgment to date, the sheriff can be asked to make a partial return earlier.[5] Alternatively, the judgment creditor can be asked for a partial satisfaction piece,[6] which the judgment debtor can file, or the court on motion can order entry of whatever satisfaction has been made.[7]

§ 507. Modifying the Income Execution

Either judgment creditor or judgment debtor can move at any time to modify an income execution pursuant to CPLR 5231(i). As with a special proceeding, it has been held that the motion may not be made in a court not listed

---

2. See § 493 above.

3. CPLR 5221(a)(4). See First Westchester National Bank v. Lewis, 42 Misc.2d 1007, 249 N.Y.S.2d 537 (Westchester County Court 1964), so holding for an enforcement motion, which would a fortiori apply to a special proceeding. See CPLR 5221(b).

4. Franklin Nat. Bank v. Brita Homes Corp., 35 A.D.2d 550, 313 N.Y.S.2d 248 (2d Dep't 1970). In the Franklin case the judgment creditor brought a plenary action against the employer to collect this money, but under CPLR 5231(e) a special proceeding suffices and is of course cheaper and faster. See § 547 below.

5. See CPLR 5252, another part of which, discussed in Commentary C5252:1 on McKinney's CPLR 5252, adds contempt as a remedy.

§ 506

1. CPLR 5231(d), (e).

2. National Surety Corp. v. R.H. Macy & Co., 116 Misc.2d 780, 455 N.Y.S.2d 1007 (Sup.Ct., N.Y. County, 1982). The implication is that the judgment creditor must seek his remedy against the sheriff. Perhaps nothing prevents the creditor from issuing a new income execution to collect the interest still unpaid, but if some other creditor has since come into priority there may be quite a delay in collection.

3. See CPLR 5230(c).

4. CPLR 5231(k).

5. See CPLR 5021(b).

6. CPLR 5020.

7. CPLR 5021(a)(2).

in CPLR 5221(a),[1] which means that in the case of income executions issued out of a town or village court, the motion to modify must be made in the supreme or a county court.[2]

This motion to "modify" is at root only a specialized kind of protective order, and the general protective order provision itself, CPLR 5240, would supply all needed modification authority without any special help from CPLR 5231(i). Whichever provision is used, the motion for the modification is generally brought on by order to show cause. Examples of protective modifications, including adjustments needed when an income execution and an installment payment order compete against the same judgment debtor, are met in later sections.[3]

§ 507A. Special Income Execution for Support

CPLR 5241, supplying a more generous, expansive, and self-executing income execution than 5231 offers, was added to the CPLR in 1985 to aid in the enforcement of a support obligation. The support obligation can come from a judgment, decree, or order of a court, temporary or final, or even from a mere "agreement or stipulation incorporated by reference" in the court paper.[1] CPLR 5241 is available for support obligations only. Among the advantages of the 5241 execution are that it reaches higher percentages than the 10% to which CPLR 5231 is restricted, that the sheriff's or other enforcement officer's office does not have to be used (as it must under CPLR 5231), and that a judgment for accumulated "arrears" is not a necessary preliminary to the enforcement of a 5241 execution.

In addition to the persons who can issue any execution—the sheriff or other enforcement official, the clerk, or the creditor's lawyer—a

"support collection unit" or other agency responsible for support collection can issue a CPLR 5241 execution.[2] A copy of the execution must be served on the debtor,[3] who then has 15 days in which to apply to the court with his defense, which, as will be shown, is limited to a "mistake of fact". When the execution has been issued by a support collection unit, the debtor's defense takes the form of a "submission" to the unit instead of to the court. If the unit rejects the submission, it notifies the debtor and advises that the income execution will now be served on his employer.[4]

The sheriff's office is not used. The creditor can effect the levy just by serving the execution on the employer, and while the service may be made in the same manner as a summons, it is also allowed by the simple alternative of "regular mail".[5]

The amount of the deduction that has to be made from income under CPLR 5241 varies between 50% and 65%, depending on whether the debtor is also supporting a spouse or child other than the creditor and on how long the debtor has been in arrears.[6] The computations are based on the debtor's "disposable earnings", the standard also used on an ordinary income execution under CPLR 5231.[7]

The contents of the CPLR 5241 execution, more detailed than those for other executions, are explicitly laid out in the statute.[8] It takes priority "over any other assignment, levy or process",[9] which of course includes an ordinary income execution issued in behalf of some other judgment creditor under CPLR 5231, even if the latter preceded the CPLR 5241 execution.[10]

Simultaneously enacted with CPLR 5241 was CPLR 5242, supplying an "income deduc-

§ 507

1. See § 505 above.

2. CPLR 5221(b), (a)(4).

3. See §§ 511 and 522 below.

§ 507A

1. CPLR 5241(a)(1).

2. See CPLR 5241(a)(9), (b).

3. CPLR 5241(d).

4. CPLR 5241(e).

5. CPLR 5241(f).

6. See CPLR 5241(g).

7. See § 503 above.

8. CPLR 5241(c).

9. CPLR 5241(h).

10. CPLR 5241(h).

tion order for support enforcement" in replacement of the payroll deduction order that had previously been used for this purpose.[11] Resort to the court for an order under CPLR 5242 is discouraged in the hope that the CPLR 5241 execution will be used instead,[12] but the question of how tightly locked the courthouse door will be is a question that may take some litigating. It has been held that no 5242 application may be made until a 5241 execution has at least been attempted.[13]

The aspiration of CPLR 5241 is to expedite the collection of support money and to deter dilatory conduct by the support debtor by restricting the debtor's defenses to one only: where there has been a "mistake of fact".[14] The courts have had trouble with the phrase, which is defined to include a computation error, a mistake in identifying the debtor, or a showing that the support order does not exist or was vacated.[15] It is the debtor's burden to show that he is not in default in making the required payments,[16] and the courts have noted this,[17] but they have occasionally upheld defenses on bases other than a mistake of fact. In one case, for example, husband H showed that wife W had twice before altered bills and checks upwards, that H had held up several checks in the past only because W had moved without advising him of her change of address, and that some 18 previous checks sent to W had not been cashed. Noting that there had been no problem for almost a decade, during which H apparently fulfilled his obligations under a separation decree, and citing due process requirements, the court granted H's motion to vacate a CPLR 5241 income execution.[18]

F. THE "SUPPLEMENTARY PROCEEDINGS"

Table of Sections

§ 508. Restraining Notice

With the restraining notice of CPLR 5222 we begin the series of devices that bench and bar know collectively as the "supplementary proceedings".[1] The notice is issued by the judgment creditor's attorney (the court clerk is also authorized to issue it), may be served on the judgment debtor or a garnishee, and enjoins the person served from giving over the defendant's property except to the sheriff or pursuant to a court order. It is in every sense an injunction, and acts as such under the signature of the lawyer without a court order or other preliminary leave. It is not a special proceeding, but a mere post-judgment adjunct of the action itself, bearing its caption. Disobedience of a restraining notice is punishable as a contempt of court.[2]

If the judgment creditor has any suspicions about who may have possession of some of the debtor's property, the restraining notice is a good thing to serve promptly, after the entry of judgment, on any suspected persons. It acts as a kind of freeze on such of the debtor's assets as the served person may have, during which the judgment creditor can use other devices, such as an execution, to try to have the property turned over. It buys time, in

---

11. Pers.Prop.L. § 49–b, repealed when CPLR 5242 took over.

12. CPLR 5241 and 5242 are discussed in the McKinney's Commentaries on CPLR 5241 and 5242.

13. Scarey v. Scarey, 131 Misc.2d 252, 499 N.Y.S.2d 866 (Sup.Ct., Schoharie County, 1986).

14. CPLR 5241(c)(4).

15. CPLR 5241(a)(8).

16. "Default" is defined as a failure to make three payments, or allowing arrears to accumulate beyond a month's worth. CPLR 5241(a)(7).

17. Blackman v. Blackman, 131 A.D.2d 801, 517 N.Y.S.2d 167 (2d Dep't 1987).

18. Shutt v. Shutt, 133 Misc.2d 81, 506 N.Y.S.2d 611 (Sup.Ct., Oneida County, 1986).

§ 508

1. See § 492 above.

2. CPLR 5251.

other words. It may be served on any garnishee, with the exception of the judgment debtor's employer.[3]

The restraining notice must name all of the parties to the action, specify those for and against whom the judgment was rendered, the court and date of rendition, the amount of the judgment, and the amount of it still unsatisfied. It is then required to set forth subdivision (b) of CPLR 5222, which contains the injunctive language, and to advise that disobedience will constitute a contempt of court. The notice is served either in the same manner as a summons or by registered or certified mail with return receipt requested.[4] Any nonparty over the age of 18 may effect the service; it need not be the sheriff.

When a state unit is the garnishee, service of the restraining notice must be made on the head of the unit and also on the state department of audit and control.[5] This double-service requirement is not just a pro forma thing; it has been held that the failure to serve the department makes the notice invalid.[6]

CPLR 5222(a) requires that the copy of the restraining notice being served "contain an original signature or copy of the original signature" of the issuer. The statement of such a requirement in CPLR 5222, the product of a 1991 amendment, is now probably superfluous in light of the later amendment of the sanctions rule, Rule 130–1, to require, as of March 1, 1998, the actual signing of all papers served in litigation.[7]

CPLR 5222 was one of several enforcement devices declared unconstitutional in 1982 for failure to require notice to the judgment debtor about the possibly exempt status of her property and to advise the debtor about procedures to protect the exemptions.[8] The legislature promptly amended three of the provisions—CPLR 5222, 5232, and 5234—to meet the objection, with CPLR 5222 selected to do the bulk of the job. The core amendment was the addition of subdivisions (d) and (e) to CPLR 5222, requiring such a notice and setting forth the specific form to be used for it.[9] Doubts were expressed at first about whether the amendments adequately met the constitutional objections, but it was later held that they do.[10]

A failure to give the notice that CPLR 5222 requires has been held to void the restraining notice and any follow-up enforcement steps that depend on it.[11] The failure can also give rise to a damages claim. That was held to be so even under the pre-amendment status of the enforcement devices,[12] but on that point there is some dispute.[13]

While the restraining notice is most effective when served on a garnishee, it may be used against the judgment debtor himself. When served on the judgment debtor, it lasts the life of the judgment or until the judgment is satisfied. It purports to preclude the debtor from in any way divesting himself of unexempt property except by instruction of the sheriff or the court. The restraining notice has a better potential when served on a third-person—a garnishee—who, because of obvious personal risks, will not go quite as far out on a limb to protect the judgment debtor as the debtor is

---

3. CPLR 5222(a). The employer is excepted only in respect of wages, where the income execution of CPLR 5231 is deemed adequate.

4. CPLR 5222(a), which also contains some special instructions for serving state agencies with restraints. Subdivision (g) of CPLR 5222, added in 1994, permits the restraining notice to be served in the form of a magnetic tape instead of a signed paper, but with several provisos. See SPR 20:2.

5. CPLR 5222(a).

6. Remo Drug Corp. v. State, 145 Misc.2d 300, 546 N.Y.S.2d 529 (Ct.Cl. 1989).

7. See § 414A above. Before the adoption of this requirement, conformed rather than actually signed papers could be served in most instances.

8. See Deary v. Guardian Loan Co., 534 F.Supp. 1178 (S.D.N.Y.1982), and the lead note in New York State Law Digest No. 270.

9. The amendments are discussed in Commentary C5222:11 on McKinney's CPLR 5222.

10. McCahey v. L.P. Investors, 774 F.2d 543 (2d Cir. 1985).

11. Weinstein v. Gitters, 119 Misc.2d 122, 462 N.Y.S.2d 553 (Sup.Ct., Suffolk County, 1983).

12. See Warren v. Delaney, 98 A.D.2d 799, 469 N.Y.S.2d 975 (2d Dep't 1983).

13. See Cais v. Pichler, 123 Misc.2d 275, 473 N.Y.S.2d 719 (N.Y.C.Civ.Ct. 1984).

wont to do for himself (such as by secreting assets in violation of the notice).

A restraining notice served on a garnishee is effective only if, when served, the garnishee owes a debt to or has property belonging to the judgment debtor. If the garnishee has such debt or property at that moment, the restraint will apply to that property as well as to all other property "thereafter coming into" the garnishee's possession.[14] If the garnishee lacks any such property or obligation at the moment of service, the restraint never takes effect at all. The restraint precludes the garnishee from selling, assigning, transferring or otherwise disposing of the obligation or property to anyone but the sheriff, unless the sheriff or court directs otherwise.[15] Even a transfer to the judgment debtor's assignee for the benefit of creditors has been held to violate the restraint.[16] In the case of a garnishee, the restraint retains its injunctive effect for only a year after its service (in contrast with the life-of-the-judgment run it gets when served on the judgment debtor), unless extended by protective order under CPLR 5240.

The garnishee may be unaware that property it has possession of belongs to the judgment debtor, or it may think that a debt it owes is due not to the judgment debtor but to someone else. The garnishee is subject to the restraint only if it "knows or has reason to believe" of the judgment debtor's interest; any ambiguity in this respect jeopardizes the restraint. The judgment creditor is therefore authorized to identify, in the restraining notice itself, the debt or property aimed at. If the creditor does that, the property identified falls under the restraint regardless of who the garnishee thinks the owner may be. But a judg-

ment creditor must be reasonably sure about this; a wrong guess makes the creditor liable to the rightful owner for any damages caused by the wrongful restraint.[17] The garnishee who honors the process is not liable if the property designation is incorrect.[18]

The restraint is usually operative against all the debtor's property in the possession of the garnishee, regardless of the amount of the judgment. The restraining notice is not the occasion for measuring the value of the property (if other than outright money) held by the garnishee. But if the garnishee does owe just a monetary debt to the judgment debtor it can, by withholding twice the amount of the judgment, free all other money and property from the restraint.[19]

Once having served the restraint on the garnishee, the judgment creditor is expected to take prompt proceedings through other devices to get hold of the property, and to resolve such disputes as may arise about whom the property belongs to. That's the reason for giving the restraint only a year of life. Nor can the judgment creditor, for these same reasons, let the year pass and just serve a second restraint. A second one needs court leave.[20]

As is true of all of the enforcement devices other than the executions, the restraining notice may issue only out of the courts listed in CPLR 5221(a), which excludes it from the town and village courts. A restraint in respect of the judgments of those courts is permissible, but it must issue out of the supreme court or a county court.[21]

The restraining notice does not secure a lien to its user. This is important to note. While the notice requires no court application or

---

14. CPLR 5222(b). See Laborers Union Local 1298 v. Frank L. Lyon & Sons, Inc., 66 Misc.2d 1042, 323 N.Y.S.2d 229 (Sup.Ct., Nassau County, 1971).

15. It has been held that although the sheriff is the one to whom the property is delivered, its direct delivery to the judgment creditor will not be penalized if no damage is shown. Matter of Wooton, 79 Misc.2d 673, 361 N.Y.S.2d 137 (Surr.Ct., Schenectady County, 1974).

16. International Ribbon Mills, Ltd. v. Arjan Ribbons, Inc., 36 N.Y.2d 121, 365 N.Y.S.2d 808, 325 N.E.2d 137 (1975). Involved there was a transfer by the judgment debtor; the rule would be the same if the transfer were by a garnishee.

17. CPLR 5222(b).

18. See, by analogy, Chin Sung Yu v. Riggs Nat. Bank, 248 A.D.2d 235, 670 N.Y.S.2d 187 (1st Dep't 1998) (noted in SPR 76:2), so holding in respect of an execution. The garnishee is entitled to rely on the property identifications made in the execution.

19. Id.

20. CPLR 5222(c).

21. CPLR 5221(b), (a)(4). See § 493 above.

sheriff assistance and can for that reason be quickly served by the judgment creditor so as to effect an immediate restraint, it had best be followed with expeditious steps using one of the lien-giving devices. In this connection we return to an advantage earlier attributed to the restraining notice. We said that it buys time. We now qualify that to note that it does so only when no other judgment creditor is pursuing the same judgment debtor. If there is another, and that creditor secures a lien through one of the other devices that give one, she will prevail against the creditor who served the restraining notice notwithstanding a showing that the latter was more diligent overall.[22] A general stay of enforcement of the judgment, not accompanied by any bond or other security protecting the judgment creditor, does not cancel the restraint, although it does suspend any further steps, such as payment over of the property to the sheriff.[23]

The contempt punishment, which backs the restraining notice, may be invoked even against one not served with the notice but who knows of its service on someone else and wilfully participates in its violation.[24] And while contempt is the statutorily stated remedy,[25] it is not the exclusive one. The violator is also liable in damages to the judgment creditor, who may seek the damages in an action or even in a special proceeding, such as the one brought to compel a garnishee to honor an execution.[26]

Suppose, for example, that P effects a restraint on D's bank account by duly serving it on the branch where D keeps his account. Negligently overlooking the restraint, the bank (garnishee) lets D withdraw the money through one of its other offices or branches. That happened in one case, for example,[27] and when P sued the bank for its omission, one of

the defenses was that the bank's conduct was not wilful but, at worst, only negligent. Holding that negligence is all it takes for liability, the court held the bank liable to P for the amount D was allowed to withdraw.

It was held in Zemo Leasing Corp. v. Bank of New York,[28] that a bank should have until the close of business of the day following its receipt of a restraining notice in which to effectuate the notice against a depositor's account. In *Zemo*, where the judgment debtor withdrew funds after the bank had received a mailed restraint earlier in the day, the court held that the bank was not liable for the withdrawal; that it needed time to process the restraint and didn't have enough time in this case. Practitioners advising banks may want to be more cautious. Effectuating the restraint forthwith is the best advice.

While a showing of wilfulness is not necessary in order to hold the garnishee to the consequences of a violation, it must be shown that the garnishee had knowledge of the restraining notice, which of course depends on proper service. In one case, for example,[29] the garnishee did not know of the notice and paid the money to the judgment debtor. The notice had been served by mail and was received and signed for by a laborer who had worked for the garnishee for only one day and who did not turn the notice over to an appropriate official. The judgment creditor did not succeed against the garnishee. The case seems to make the creditor responsible for those who receive the garnishee's mail. Perhaps a more constructive lesson to the judgment creditor is not to sit back after a restraining notice has been served—by whatever means—but to contact the garnishee shortly afterwards to inquire

---

22. The lawyer should take careful note of these lien factors, which are treated in § 518 et seq., below.

23. See Nardone v. Long Island Tr. Co., 40 A.D.2d 697, 336 N.Y.S.2d 325 (2d Dep't 1972).

24. Ivor B. Clark Co. v. Hogan, 296 F.Supp. 407 (S.D.N.Y.1969).

25. CPLR 5251. The procedure to punish for contempt is treated in § 481 et seq., above.

26. See CPLR 5232(a).

27. Mazzuka v. Bank of North America, 53 Misc.2d 1053, 280 N.Y.S.2d 495 (N.Y.C.Civ.Ct.1967). Mazzuka involved a plenary action, which today is not necessary. A special proceeding under CPLR 5227, which is faster and cheaper, can do the job. See the Nardone case, note 23 above, and § 510 below.

28. 158 Misc.2d 991, 602 N.Y.S.2d 503 (Sup.Ct., Rockland County, 1993), noted in SPR 10:3.

29. Security Trust Co. of Rochester v. Magar Homes, 92 A.D.2d 714, 461 N.Y.S.2d 103 (4th Dep't 1983).

whether it was received and whether it is being honored.

Although contempt or a damages action may be available against a garnishee who violates the restraint, a transferee who pays fair consideration for the property will prevail over the judgment creditor even though the transferee takes through the violator. A gratuitous transferee, based merely on the equities, may be subordinated to the interests of the judgment creditor whose restraint was disobeyed,[30] but since even a lien-getting judgment creditor may have to defer to a transferee who pays fair consideration,[31] a fortiori a judgment creditor who relies on the restraint of CPLR 5222, which does not even give a lien, would also have to defer to such a transferee.

§ 509. Disclosure in Aid of Enforcement

In the discussion of the enforcement devices up to now, the tacit assumption has been that the judgment creditor knows what and where the judgment debtor's assets are. As likely as not, however, the creditor will know nothing about them. CPLR 5223 and 5224 offer aid on that front. They authorize disclosure and supply subpoenas to implement it.

CPLR 5223 provides that any time before the judgment is satisfied or vacated, the judgment creditor may compel disclosure of "all matter relevant to the satisfaction of the judgment", a broad criterion authorizing investigation through any person shown to have any light to shed on the subject of the judgment debtor's assets or their whereabouts. The creditor can effect service of a subpoena on that person, who may be the judgment debtor himself, a friend or relative who may have information on the subject, a garnishee or one reasonably thought to be a garnishee, including the debtor's bank, accountant, broker, employer, etc. Even the judgment debtor's attorney may have to reveal data about the debtor's finances.[1]

Service of a CPLR 5224 subpoena does not commence a special proceeding. Like the pretrial disclosure subpoena and the trial subpoena, it is merely captioned in the action itself— even though the action has already gone to judgment—and is deemed an adjunct of it. It can be used before, with, or after any other enforcement device. It is common, for example, and often wise, to serve with the subpoena a CPLR 5222 restraining notice. Since neither the subpoena nor the notice requires court leave, because each constitutes judicial process under the signature of the creditor's attorney who acts as an officer of the court, both can be drawn and served promptly. Like the restraining notice, the subpoena of CPLR 5224 is one of the so-called "supplementary proceedings" and may issue only out of courts listed in CPLR 5221(a), which means that when sought in respect of the judgment of a town or village court the subpoena must bear the caption of the supreme court or a county court and seek in that court whatever implementation or enforcement is needed.[2]

In addition to describing the usual obligation of its recipient—requiring attendance at a designated time and place, production of an item, response to questions, etc.—the subpoena must name all of the parties to the action, state the court in which the judgment was rendered, the date and amount of the judgment, and the amount still outstanding. And it must of course advise that a failure to comply will be a contempt of court.

CPLR 5224 does not adopt for enforcement disclosure the whole gamut of pretrial disclosure devices offered by Article 31 of the CPLR during the pretrial phase of an action. It deems adequate an offering of subpoenas, and makes three kinds available:

(1) The usual testimonial subpoena. This produces a deposition. It requires attendance for examination at a designated time and place. The examination may be on oral or

---

30. See International Ribbon Mills, Ltd. v. Arjan Ribbons, Inc., 36 N.Y.2d 121, 365 N.Y.S.2d 808, 325 N.E.2d 137 (1975), note 13 above, and the discussion of priorities in § 518 et seq., below.

31. See CPLR 5202, discussed in § 519 below.

§ 509

1. See Lang, Aids to Collecting After Judgment, N.Y.S. Bar Journal, February 1987, p.38.

2. See § 493 above.

written questions,[3] and is analogous to the pretrial depositions supplied by Article 31.[4] This subpoena must be served in the same manner as a summons.[5] When the deposition is of a third party, it has been held that the judgment debtor has no absolute right to attend it.[6]

(2) The subpoena duces tecum. This requires the production of books and records and other papers at a designated time and place,[7] just as it does for the trial itself. It is the approximate equivalent of the pretrial discovery device of CPLR 3120, but here it is brought on by subpoena instead of by a notice or court order. This subpoena is also served in the same manner as a summons, and, limited only by the "relevant" standard of CPLR 5223, it can pursue any item reflecting on the debtor's assets. It can, for example, require production of a joint tax return filed by debtor and spouse, and their accountant can be subpoenaed for her copy if they do not have one.[8] It has been held that these subpoenas may not be served outside the state, even though they are but the enforcement phase of a New York judgment rendered with all needed jurisdiction and even though there is ample basis for extraterritorial service against the judgment debtor or other person sought to be served.[9]

(3) The information subpoena. This is a third kind of subpoena, not used as such in pretrial or trial practice but explicitly offered for enforcement purposes by CPLR 5224(a)(3). All it really is, though, is a set of interrogatories sent and answered by mail, and for that

reason it does have a counterpart among the pretrial disclosure devices.[10] Service of the information subpoena, unlike the first two subpoenas, need not be in the same manner as a summons. It may be served by registered or certified mail with return receipt requested.[11] Accompanying the subpoena are the original and a copy of the questions with a prepaid and self-addressed return envelope.

The recipient must serve a sworn response to all questions within seven days after being served. If the recipient does not respond within the required time, and the judgment creditor can show that the knowledge that the recipient could have imparted would have enabled the creditor to lay hands on the debtor's property through one of the other Article 52 devices, is the recipient liable to the creditor for the loss? Several cases say no,[12] but if the proof is strong that the judgment creditor's loss can be traced to the recipient's delay in the furnishing of the required data, it is suggested that other courts may not let the recipient off so lightly.[13] In Corpuel v. Galasso,[14] where a fine of $1 1/2 million dollars was imposed on the debtor's wife for not cooperating in the enforcement of the judgment against her husband, the root of the contempt was the ignoring of a subpoena. Even with third persons having no relationship to the judgment debtor, attorneys must ask themselves how they would advise a client showing up with an information subpoena and asking how to respond. The advice should be to respond in full and on time. By no means should

---

3. CPLR 5224(a)(1).

4. See §§ 354 and 359 above.

5. CPLR 2303, CPLR 308. See Commentaries on McKinney's CPLR 2303.

6. See ITT Commercial Finance Corp. v. Bailey, 166 Misc.2d 24, 631 N.Y.S.2d 225 (Sup.Ct., Chautauqua County, 1995), noted in SPR 36:2. But nor is there any standing rule to bar the debtor's attendance. In excluding the debtor in the ITT case, the court invoked CPLR 5240, the protective order provision, citing as a reason the debtor's prior efforts to favor other creditors.

7. CPLR 5224(a)(2).

8. See Siemens & Halske GmbH v. Gres, 77 Misc.2d 745, 354 N.Y.S.2d 762 (Sup.Ct., N.Y.County, 1973).

9. See, e.g., Israel Discount Bank Ltd. v. P. S. Products Corp., 65 Misc.2d 1002, 319 N.Y.S.2d 554 (Sup.Ct., N.Y.County, 1971), applying Jud.Law § 2–b with, it is

submitted, needless rigidity. See Commentary C2303:6 on McKinney's CPLR 2303. There are proposals afoot to allow extrastate subpoena service, at least on the judgment debtor proper. See § 383 above.

10. CPLR 3130 et seq.

11. CPLR 5224(a)(3).

12. See, e.g., Syndicate Bldg. Corp. v. City Univ. of N.Y., 159 Misc.2d 898, 607 N.Y.S.2d 551 (Ct.Cl. 1993); and Miller v. Saretsky, 171 Misc.2d 404, 654 N.Y.S.2d 970 (Sup.Ct., Suffolk County, 1996).

13. The disobedience, unless excused, is in any event a contempt of court. How the contempt punishment interplays with issues of the recipient's personal liability to the judgment creditor is discussed in SPR 56:3.

14. 240 A.D.2d 531, 659 N.Y.S.2d 65 (2d Dep't 1997) (noted in SPR 71:2).

the attorney offer any assurance that the client won't face liability for disregarding or even just unreasonably delaying a response to the notice.

A deposition brought on with a CPLR 5224 subpoena is set up on at least 10 days notice unless the court directs less—which would require a preliminary court application. The provision in point, CPLR 5224(c), contemplates a formal session not only for the deposition, but also for the discovery brought on by the subpoena duces tecum. The discovery need not entail a session, however; if the parties can agree on some other procedure, such as the creditor's attorney just visiting the subpoenaed person's office to inspect or copy the papers or records sought, that would of course be acceptable.

The venue of the deposition session is taken from CPLR 3110. The proper county for it is therefore the deponent's residence or business county, or, if the debtor is the deponent, the county in which the judgment was rendered.[15] The caselaw on CPLR 3110 should also be deemed to govern the question of where, within the county, the deposition may be held.[16] The mechanics and incidents of conducting the examination are in CPLR 5224(d). Those for preparing and signing the deposition are in CPLR 5224(e). Both have close parallels in Article 31, which by adoption in CPLR 5224(c) also prescribes the officers empowered to conduct the examination.[17]

A judgment debtor served with a subpoena gets no fees, but any other person served does. In the case of the testimonial subpoena and the subpoena duces tecum, the sums are one day's witness fee plus mileage.[18] The fees here are no more more realistic than they are in the case of pretrial or trial subpoenas, and here

they even have a ludicrous follow-up: a second examination of the judgment debtor (who gets no fee) within a year after a prior examination needs court leave; a second examination of some other person does not,[19] on the ground that the requirement to pay witnesses' fees is deemed a sufficient safeguard against abuse! A second examination can in any event be cancelled by individual protective order under CPLR 5240 if it is found useless or abusive.

The one-year restriction on follow-up examinations of the judgment debtor does not apply if the second deposition is occasioned by the debtor's unjustified refusal to answer questions at the first examination. Even if it did apply, the court in such an instance would be expected to grant leave for a second examination anyway.[20]

Disclosure is not precluded merely because the assets that the judgment creditor is trying to get at are assets held by the judgment debtor outside the state. The judgment debtor is himself within the court's jurisdiction, and that enables the court to direct that the debtor make disclosure here about assets there.[21]

§ 510. Delivery Order or Judgment

CPLR 5225 and 5227 supply the device commonly known as a delivery or payment order. It is also called a "turnover" order, but in fact it takes the form of an order only when it runs against the judgment debtor himself. When it runs against a garnishee or other third person, as indeed it may, it is not an order at all, but an outright judgment. This results because the procedure for seeking the delivery from the judgment debtor is a mere motion bearing the caption of the main action,[1] while the proce-

---

15. CPLR 3110(1), (2). The alternative of the county in which the judgment was rendered would not necessarily be available if venue were governed by CPLR 5221(a), which governs most other enforcement steps.

16. See Commentary C3110:4 on McKinney's CPLR 3110.

17. See CPLR 3113, 3114, and 3116.

18. See CPLR 8001. For the information subpoena the fee used to be fifty cents, but it was dispensed with in a

1994 amendment of CPLR 5224(b) that was shown to have little effect on world stock markets.

19. CPLR 5224(f).

20. See City of New York v. Marchese, 74 Misc.2d 367, 343 N.Y.S.2d 547 (Sup.Ct., Queens County, 1973).

21. Raji v. Bank Sepah–Iran, 139 Misc.2d 1026, 529 N.Y.S.2d 420 (Sup.Ct., N.Y. County, 1988).

§ 510

1. CPLR 5225(a).

dure for seeking it from a third person is a special proceeding. [2]

CPLR 5225 applies if it is property or money that is being sought; CPLR 5227, when it is a debt owed to the judgment debtor. Because the line between "money" and a "debt" is in many situations difficult or impossible to draw, lawyers often base their applications on both provisions together, an acceptable step because procedurally they are just about the same. The only significant difference between 5225 and 5227, in fact, is that the latter contemplates only a special proceeding because it always aims at a third person (the garnishee who owes the judgment debtor a debt), while CPLR 5225, concerned with personal property, contemplates either a special proceeding or a motion, depending on who has the property. If a third person (garnishee) has it, a special proceeding is used; if the judgment debtor has it, motion practice is used. CPLR 5225 thus has a double mission, involved when either debtor or garnishee has possession of the property, and it supplies a motion or special proceeding, accordingly. Procedural steps properly taken but under the label of the wrong provision can be treated as rightly denominated, and the error can be disregarded.

One situation appropriate for a CPLR 5225 delivery order is where the property or money is located in the judgment debtor's residence, which as a rule effectively places it beyond a sheriff's reach under an execution. [3] Upon proof that the judgment debtor has property applicable to enforcement, whether in her residence or elsewhere, the court on motion can make an order directly instructing the judgment debtor to deliver it or pay it over. It can do this for a painting in the debtor's living room, shares of stock in a desk drawer, a negotiable instrument in a safe, money in a mattress, ad infinitum.

As long as the debtor is subject to the court's personal jurisdiction, a delivery order can be effective even when the property sought is outside the state. [4]

As the reader may guess, the main problem here is securing the proof that will convince the court that the judgment debtor has such money or property. The proof is decidedly difficult in most situations, but no CPLR 5225 order will be made without it. Quite often the judgment creditor must exploit the disclosure tools of CPLR 5224 before being equipped for a CPLR 5225 motion, which manifests a second drawback: an application under CPLR 5225, requiring investigatory proof as well as the close attention of a lawyer, is often so expensive as to be practicable only for big judgments, or those held by wealthy creditors. Otherwise the cost of the procedure may be disproportionate to the judgment being enforced. Assuming that the judgment belongs to a modest creditor like a small contractor or storekeeper or salesman—public attention often forgets the humble status of many creditors as it concentrates on the needs of the debtor—these factors are but another example of how economics can limit access to the courts.

Assuming that the proof is at hand and a CPLR 5225 application worthwhile, we can turn to its mechanics and to its other features.

The motion is made on notice, but the moving papers must be served either in the same manner as a summons or by registered or certified mail with return receipt requested. If the applicant's proof is firm and the court is convinced, it will order the debtor to make the appropriate delivery. If money is involved, the debtor will be directed to pay it to the creditor towards satisfaction of the judgment; if property is involved, the direction will be to deliver it to the sheriff, who will then sell it at public auction, [5] just as the sheriff would sell property levied on an execution. [6] Disobedience of the

---

2. CPLR 5225(b), 5227. A special proceeding ends in a judgment, CPLR 411, not an order.

3. See § 496 above.

4. See Starbare II Partners v. Sloan, 216 A.D.2d 238, 629 N.Y.S.2d 23 (1st Dep't 1995) (noted in SPR 40:3), involving artwork in New Jersey.

5. CPLR 5233.

6. CPLR 5225(a).

order by the judgment debtor is a contempt of court and punishable as such.[7]

A special proceeding, to which we now turn our attention, is required when the property is held or a debt owed by a garnishee or other third person. The reasons for this are that the garnishee was not a party to the main action, is not part of its caption, and has yet to be subjected to the court's jurisdiction. While a motion is only an application in the context of an action, a special proceeding is an independent application and hence more appropriate when addressed to a person being brought within the court's jurisdiction for the first time. The judgment creditor brings the proceeding as petitioner, whether under CPLR 5225 or 5227 (we regard them as interchangeable in this treatment), against the garnishee as respondent, and the procedures that govern it come from Article 4 of the CPLR. Service of the initiatory papers[8] are made in the same manner as a summons unless an order to show cause is used and directs otherwise.[9] Failure to join the garnishee in the proceeding will of course mean that the garnishee cannot be bound by what the proceeding decides.[10]

An additional requirement imposed by CPLR 5225(b) and 5227 is that the judgment debtor, who is not necessarily a named party in the proceeding, be advised of it in a notice served either in the same manner as a summons or by registered or certified mail with return receipt requested. The debtor can be allowed to intervene in the proceeding. For various reasons it is often a good idea for the creditor/petitioner to name the judgment debtor as an actual party. In some instances it may even be indispensable, as when the property entails a special processing of some kind and the judgment debtor appears to be an essential part of it. In Sochor v. IBM Corp., for example, a 1983 Court of Appeals case,[11] the property

that the judgment creditor was seeking enforcement against was a pension plan established by the debtor's employer, and the plan's activation required the debtor to make an election from among various options available under it. The court held that the debtor had to be within the jurisdiction of the court in the proceeding, either to make the required election himself or to enable the court to make it for him. If there should be some kind of jurisdictional problem in locating the debtor for service, as was apparently the problem in the Sochor case, the answer is not to omit the debtor as a party, but to exploit some special method of service of process, like service by a court-invented means under CPLR 308(5).[12]

If there are any other claimants to the property or money involved, they can be allowed to intervene, if, indeed, the judgment creditor has not already joined them in the first place, or the garnishee interpleaded them. Interpleader may be especially appropriate here if conflicting claims are being made to the property or debt, but its use in this context will usually require court leave.[13] The special proceeding, in short, can be converted into a full-fledged test of precisely whom the disputed property or debt belongs to, which is all CPLR 5225(b) and 5227 mean by their cross-references to CPLR 5239.[14]

When interests in it are disputed, the property cannot be applied to the satisfaction of the judgment unless and until the special proceeding resolves that it belongs to the judgment debtor. If the proceeding finds that it belongs to someone else, this enforcement step, as far as this judgment creditor is concerned, fails. But the special proceeding is plenary and can try any fact issues arising between and among all those properly before the court; an ordinary plenary action is not necessary.[15] If the particular dispute would in

7. CPLR 5251. See § 523 below.

8. These are a petition and notice of petition. CPLR 402, 403(a), (b).

9. CPLR 403(c), (d). The special proceeding and its procedures are met later. See § 547 et seq., below.

10. Kennis v. Sherwood, 82 A.D.2d 847, 439 N.Y.S.2d 962 (2d Dep't 1981).

11. 60 N.Y.2d 254, 469 N.Y.S.2d 591, 457 N.E.2d 696.

12. See Commentary C5225:5 on McKinney's CPLR 5225.

13. CPLR 401.

14. See § 521, below, for discussion of the versatility of CPLR 5239.

15. See Ruvolo v. Long Island R. R. Co., 45 Misc.2d 136, 256 N.Y.S.2d 279 (Sup.Ct., Queens County, 1965); First Small Business Investment Corp. v. Zaretsky, 46

more conventional context be jury triable, the right to trial by jury remains, and, if demanded, a jury will be impaneled in the special proceeding itself.[16]

The proceeding may also be used by the judgment creditor to collect damages caused by a garnishee who did not properly carry out the requirements of a restraining notice or an execution. There, too, a plenary action, although permissible,[17] is no longer necessary.[18]

The special proceeding of CPLR 5225 is available not only against a garnishee legitimately holding property or money of the judgment debtor, such as a bank or warehouse, but against a "transferee" of the judgment debtor as well. This would mean any transferee against whom the judgment creditor has (or may possibly have) a higher right, such as a gratuitous transferee.[19] This touches on the realm of the fraudulent transfer made by a debtor to frustrate creditors. A person who has a judgment against that debtor is entitled to set aside such a transfer,[20] but at one time had to bring a regular plenary action to accomplish this. Today, once again, the special proceeding under CPLR 5225 or 5227 can be used.[21]

If the property or money is found to be the debtor's, or if the rights of the judgment creditor are found superior to those of the transferee, the court will direct the respondent (garnishee or transferee) to pay to the judgment creditor enough money to satisfy the judgment, and if the money paid does not suffice, to deliver to the sheriff enough of the debtor's other personal property (the sheriff will sell it) to pay the rest.[22] These directions against the respondent are embodied in a final judgment. If money is involved, the judgment will usually take the form of a money judgment running against the respondent, who would then be subject to the Article 52 enforcement devices directly, just like any judgment debtor. It has been held, moreover, that the judgment may take the form of a direction to the respondent to hand over the money or to deliver designated property to the sheriff, disobedience of which can even subject the respondent to the contempt punishment.[23]

The special proceedings of CPLR 5225 or 5227 are also the ones contemplated as a "perfection" step when a garnishee fails to respond to a levy of execution.[24]

If a document of any kind is needed to effect a payment or delivery of the subject money or property, and it is within the power of the person against whom a CPLR 5225 or 5227 motion or special proceeding has been brought to make or deliver the document, that person can be required to.[25] This would embrace the making, indorsement, or negotiation of any kind of commercial paper, including a bill or note or withdrawal slip for money, a bond or share of stock or other evidence of ownership, a document of title or the like—whatever piece of paper, in short, will facilitate realization of the property interest involved.[26] When the interest aimed at is a debt not yet due, a situation contemplated by CPLR 5227, the paper the respondent may be directed to make would

---

Misc.2d 328, 259 N.Y.S.2d 700 (Sup.Ct., Queens County, 1965).

16. See 1965 Commentary on McKinney's CPLR 5225; Leedpak, Inc. v. Julian, 78 Misc.2d 519, 356 N.Y.S.2d 1011 (Sup.Ct., N.Y.County, 1974).

17. See Mazzuka v. Bank of North America, 53 Misc.2d 1053, 280 N.Y.S.2d 495 (N.Y.C.Civ.Ct. 1967).

18. See Nardone v. Long Island Tr. Co., 40 A.D.2d 697, 336 N.Y.S.2d 325 (2d Dep't 1972).

19. See § 519 below.

20. See American Sur. Co. v. Conner, 251 N.Y. 1, 166 N.E. 783 (1929).

21. See Siemens & Halske GmbH. v. Gres, 32 A.D.2d 624, 299 N.Y.S.2d 908 (1st Dep't 1969).

22. If a receiver has been duly appointed under CPLR 5228, see § 512 below, the court will direct delivery of the property to the receiver instead of to the sheriff for sale.

23. See Carl B. Nusbaum, Inc. v. Calale, 45 Misc.2d 903, 258 N.Y.S.2d 8 (Orange County Ct. 1965). The court apparently deems a judgment under CPLR 5225 or 5227 the equivalent of the "order" for which contempt is authorized by CPLR 5251. Contempt can be justified on the alternative theory that the judgment is simply an equitable one, acting in personam on the respondent and just as susceptible of contempt enforcement as any judgment emanating from an equity action. See CPLR 103(b).

24. CPLR 5232(a). See § 496 above.

25. CPLR 5225(c), 5227.

26. See Jack London Productions, Inc. v. Samuel Bronston Productions, Inc., 22 A.D.2d 870, 254 N.Y.S.2d 397 (1st Dep't 1964).

be an attornment or some similar kind of commitment to pay the debt to the judgment creditor when it falls due, instead of to the judgment debtor. The court can even render a judgment against the respondent for the debt, but, if the debt is not yet due, this would require a stay of either entry or execution until the due date.

A garnishee or other third person who has paid or given to the judgment creditor or sheriff money or property of the judgment debtor, pursuant to regular Article 52 procedures in enforcement of the judgment, is relieved of the obligation to the judgment debtor and may use such payment or delivery as a complete defense if afterwards sued by the judgment debtor.[27] An order under CPLR 5225(a), which should be deemed to include a judgment under CPLR 5225(b) or 5227, gives the judgment creditor who gets it a lien on the subject personal property as of the moment of entry of the judgment or order.[28]

Only the courts listed in CPLR 5221(a) may entertain motions or special proceedings under CPLR 5225 or 5227, thus excluding the town and village courts from entertaining them. When sought in respect of a judgment of one of those courts, the application is made to the supreme court or to a county court.[29]

§ 511. Installment Payment Order

A very useful device against a judgment debtor trying to conceal income and in a variety of other situations is the installment payment order of CPLR 5226. It is brought on by mere motion, captioned in the original action. The motion papers are served on the judgment debtor in the same manner as a summons or by registered or certified mail with return receipt requested. The court on the motion can direct the debtor to make regular payments to the judgment creditor in any sum it finds the debtor able to afford, not limited by the 10% that restricts the income execution of CPLR 5231. The 10% is the corollary of CPLR 5205(d), which exempts 90% of income, but it

will be recalled that the exemption is not absolute; the court can invade any part of the 90% that it finds "unnecessary for the reasonable requirements of the judgment debtor and his dependents", and it is the installment payment motion of CPLR 5226 that usually supplies the occasion for the court to make those findings. It is always a sui generis inquiry, for which reason it requires strong proof, often through diligent use of enforcement disclosure under CPLR 5223 and 5224.

The application can therefore generate much expense in time, effort, and money, which makes the device—akin in this regard to the delivery order of CPLR 5225—practicable only when the judgment is a big one or the judgment creditor well off.

The court on the motion must consider all of the usual family obligations of the debtor. The needs of the debtor's dependents will be reviewed, as well as her obligations to other creditors, especially judgment creditors, including any who have issued income executions or secured wage assignments. Items not falling within family requirements are not likely to earn consideration, as one bachelor debtor found out when he unsuccessfully attempted to have the court factor in his expenses for dating, a credit card, the New York Athletic Club, a golf club, and a wine and food society—everything, in other words, short of maid service on a yacht.[1] No single factor is decisive; all relevant ingredients figure, and the court will simply direct the judgment debtor to pay, at designated intervals, whatever in overall context the court thinks she can afford. That these findings are made on notice, and only after a careful analysis of the debtor's needs, insulates the installment payment device from any blunderbuss due process attack.

The rendering of services without adequate compensation is one of the evasions explicitly addressed by CPLR 5226. Thus, where the debtor worked for a corporation whose assets were owned mainly by his wife, and claimed he

---

27. CPLR 5209. See § 515 below.

28. CPLR 5234(c), 5016(a). See § 518 et seq., below.

29. See § 493 above.

§ 511

1. Yamamoto v. Costello, 73 Misc.2d 592, 342 N.Y.S.2d 33 (Sup.Ct., Nassau County, 1973).

did so gratis, the court fixed the reasonable value of his services and from that sum directed that the debtor pay a designated sum to the judgment creditor every month.[2]

Where the judgment debtor was receiving regular income from her son, who said he would stop payments if any part of them were allowed her creditor, the court nonetheless directed her to pay a stipulated sum per month based on what she had been receiving, saying that the payments would have to continue only as long as income from her son continued, in effect daring the son to cut her off.[3]

The invisible means of support is another evasion that a well-prepared CPLR 5226 motion can pierce. A judgment debtor was shown, for example, to be managing to get on quite well with $700 in monthly living expenses— this in 1963—but, he swore, no salary. Where was he getting the money? Loans, he said. He was apparently employed by someone, and a hearing was ordered to determine what his talents were and what his services were worth.[4] With temerity enough to tell a court that he was living off monthly loans, his services were probably worth a good deal.

A simple situation for an installment order is where the judgment debtor is guilty of no concealment, but is shown to be earning enough to pay his judgment creditor more than the 10% to which an income execution is restricted. The debtor's income may be found ample enough, in fact, to pay one judgment creditor on the 10% execution and another an additional sum ordered under CPLR 5226.[5] When a series of income executions were outstanding against the same debtor, each waiting its proper turn since only one goes forward at a time,[6] another enterprising judgment creditor was able to convince the court, on a CPLR

5226 motion, that the debtor could afford more than 10% and ended up getting the affordable balance while the queued-up income executioners gaped.[7]

It is feasible enough for the court to make a CPLR 5226 order even after a CPLR 5231 income execution has taken hold, because the order factors in the income execution and directs payment of only what the debtor can afford. Difficulty is in store for the debtor when things are the other way around—when, while the installment order of one creditor is being paid, another comes along with an income execution, peremptorily demanding 10%. If the debtor can't afford both, the remedy is a motion under CPLR 5231(g) to modify or abate the income execution in deference to the installment order, or a motion under CPLR 5240 for a protective order abating either.

The installment order is also the tool of the creditor whose debtor's income derives from sources not reachable with an income execution. Where, for example, the debtor works for a federal agency (which is not ordinarily amenable to income execution[8]), and he does not voluntarily make 10% deductions himself, he can be subjected to an installment payment order. Once the wages come into his hands they lose whatever federal exemption they had before disbursement.[9] The 5226 order would do like service when the employer is an out-of-state or foreign one beyond New York jurisdiction, but where the judgment debtor remains within jurisdiction. One may even urge that the order be entertained even if the judgment debtor, too, is now outside New York, under a kind of "continuing jurisdiction" theory. If the judgment itself is good, personam jurisdiction having fully obtained in the action proper, it ought to be deemed to continue for enforcement purposes even if the judgment debtor moves from the state after judgment or was

2. Frooks v. Clurman, 76 N.Y.S.2d 187 (Sup.Ct., Kings County, 1942), aff'd 266 A.D. 859, 43 N.Y.S.2d 861 (2d Dep't 1943).

3. Lewshap Realty Co. v. Shubert, 182 Misc. 343, 44 N.Y.S.2d 65 (N.Y.City Ct.1943).

4. See Kosow v. Greenberg, N.Y.L.J. Sept. 20, 1963, p. 12, col. 6 (Sup.Ct., Nassau County, per Albert, J.).

5. See, e.g., Widder Bros. Inc. v. Kaffee, 19 A.D.2d 817, 243 N.Y.S.2d 601 (1st Dep't 1963).

6. CPLR 5231(h).

7. Schwartz v. Goldberg, 58 Misc.2d 308, 295 N.Y.S.2d 245 (Sup.Ct., Bronx County, 1968).

8. See Reeves v. Crownshield, 274 N.Y. 74, 8 N.E.2d 283 (1937).

9. Erenerol v. McCarthy, 20 A.D.2d 798, 248 N.Y.S.2d 464 (2d Dep't 1964).

never a domiciliary to begin with—as where longarm jurisdiction was used to secure jurisdiction in the underlying action. Continuing jurisdiction theories have constitutional support in a sufficient number of analogous situations[10] to suggest that an extension of it to the enforcement of ordinary money judgments would find equal footing.[11]

The installment payment order is backed by the contempt punishment.[12] It is another of the devices that cannot be entertained by town or village courts. To be used with a judgment of one of those courts, the installment payment order must be sought from the supreme court or a county court.[13]

§ 512. Receivership

We have already met two kinds of CPLR receivership: first the provisional remedy of Article 64 of the CPLR, under which a receiver is appointed to take charge of specific property that is the subject of an action and who functions to preserve the property during the action's pendency,[1] and then a post-judgment receivership designed to carry out a judgment rendered in an action of that kind.[2] The receivership of CPLR 5228, which we take up now, is also a post-judgment variety, but it is designed to aid enforcement of an ordinary money judgment and may therefore operate on any property belonging to the judgment debtor that is applicable to enforcement. Under CPLR 5228, in common with just about all receiverships, the receiver can be authorized to manage and preserve designated property, but unlike some of the others, notably the provisional receivership of Article 64, the CPLR 5228 receiver can be authorized to sell the property— that may indeed be the main purpose of this category of receivership—so as to convert it to money to pay the judgment. The order of appointment specifies the receiver's powers as well as the property to be received.

The receivership is sought by motion brought on by order to show cause, in which the court determines the notice steps. As far as practicable, says CPLR 5228(a), the court should direct that notice be given to the judgment debtor and to other judgment creditors; any of the others can then ask that the receiver be designated to act both for them and for the original movant. If a receiver has already been appointed in behalf of one judgment creditor, another may simply move to extend the receivership to her judgment as well.[3]

The provisions of CPLR 6402 through 6405, which are the parts of the provisional remedy article that govern a receiver's oath, bond, accounts, and removal, are made applicable by adoption to the CPLR 5228 receivership, too.

The receivership is one of the less used of the enforcement devices. One of its prime uses is where it is shown that a private sale of some item of the debtor's property, real or personal, will likely bring a substantially higher price than would the public auction that a sheriff is required to conduct when levying an execution. This is especially the case when the debtor's residence is involved: a receiver can use the usual channels of newspaper advertisements, brokers, etc.

A receivership to sell is not limited to real property, however. It can be used for personal property, too, such as shares in a corporation.[4] A receivership has been held especially appropriate when the property interest involved is intangible, lacks a ready market, and presents nothing that a sheriff can work with at an auction, such as the interest of a psychia-

10. See, e.g., Michigan Trust Co. v. Ferry, 228 U.S. 346, 33 S.Ct. 550, 57 L.Ed. 867 (1913) (removal of estate fiduciary); Ohlquist v. Nordstrom, 143 Misc. 502, 257 N.Y.S. 711 (Sup.Ct., Chautauqua County, 1932), aff'd 238 A.D. 766, 261 N.Y.S. 1039 (4th Dep't), aff'd 262 N.Y. 696, 188 N.E. 125 (1933) (application for contribution judgment from joint tortfeasor); Schneidman v. Schneidman, 188 Misc. 765, 65 N.Y.S.2d 876 (Sup.Ct., Kings County, 1946) (alimony modification in divorce judgment).

11. See Kaplan v. Supak & Sons, 46 Misc.2d 574, 260 N.Y.S.2d 374 (N.Y.Civ.Ct. 1965), and the discussion in Commentary C5226:5 on McKinney's CPLR 5226.

12. CPLR 5251.

13. CPLR 5221. See § 493 above.

§ 512

1. See § 332 above.

2. CPLR 5106. See § 476 above.

3. CPLR 5228(b).

4. See Matter of Myer, 273 A.D. 387, 77 N.Y.S.2d 660 (1st Dep't 1948).

trist/judgment debtor in a professional corporation of which he is a member.[5]

Another good use of this device is where the interest sought is a cause of action the judgment debtor has against a third person (garnishee). Knowing that anything he recovers may be quickly gobbled up by his waiting creditor, a judgment debtor may lack incentive to pursue the claim. A receiver can be appointed to bring the suit. A receivership for this purpose is even allowable to a creditor with a personal injuries judgment when it can be shown that the judgment debtor's insurer unreasonably failed to negotiate and the verdict exceeds the debtor/insured's coverage. The debtor has in that instance what the bar calls an "excess" claim against the insurer. The judgment creditor does not own the claim; it belongs technically to the debtor-insured. But it is deemed a property right of the debtor susceptible of receivership, and a receiver can be appointed at the creditor's behest to sue the insurer on the claim,[6] with the proceeds of course to go towards the judgment.

It is also permissible to have a receiver appointed to manage a property—instead of sell it—collecting profits and making payments on the judgment out of them. This is not a favored use, however. It prolongs enforcement and involves the court, which acts as the receiver's overseer, on a long-term basis. Sale of the whole property and quick conversion to money is preferred, so that a receivership-to-manage would likely be allowed only when the situation is one in which continued management is clearly the only way to realize on the property's value.

A bank can be appointed receiver.[7] So, for that matter, can the judgment creditor himself. But a judgment creditor so appointed is not entitled to compensation, while a receiver other than the judgment creditor is, getting both expenses and such commissions (on the moneys received and disbursed by him) as the appointing court allows, not to exceed 5%.[8]

After deducting for expenses, compensation, and any taxes involved in the proceedings, the receiver must pay over the balance of the receipts to the judgment creditor towards satisfaction of the judgment. Should there be anything left over after that, it of course goes back to the judgment debtor.[9] If a delivery order for personal property is made under CPLR 5225 while a receivership is outstanding, the property is delivered for sale to the receiver instead of the sheriff.[10]

The CPLR 5228 receivership is another of the enforcement devices excluded from use in the town and village courts. Should one be sought in respect of a judgment of one of those courts, it must be applied for to the supreme court or to a county court.[11]

The receivership does have lien value: the judgment creditor securing the receivership gets a lien on the property ordered received as of the entry of the order.[12]

§ 513. Arrest

If it is shown that the judgment debtor is hiding in or is about to leave the state with unexempt property, CPLR 5250 provides that the court on ex parte motion can issue a warrant directing the sheriff to seize the debtor and bring him before the court. The court may then order the debtor to furnish an undertaking that he will appear for an examination about his assets and that he will obey any restraining notice directed against him.

This is a rarely used provision. Body execution as a tool for the enforcement of a money judgment was abolished by the CPLR, and the provisional remedy of civil arrest that was carried into the CPLR as Article 61 was repealed in 1979. The instant arrest is a narrowly tailored cousin of those devices designed mainly to enable the judgment creditor to ar-

---

5. Udel v. Udel, 82 Misc.2d 882, 370 N.Y.S.2d 426 (N.Y.C.Civ.Ct. 1975).

6. See Oppel v. DeGangi, 84 A.D.2d 549, 443 N.Y.S.2d 177 (2d Dep't 1981).

7. Franklin Nat. Bank v. Hall, 51 Misc.2d 736, 273 N.Y.S.2d 810 (N.Y.C.Civ.Ct. 1966).

8. CPLR 5228(a).

9. CPLR 5234(a).

10. CPLR 5228(a).

11. CPLR 5221(a). See § 493 above.

12. CPLR 5234(c). See § 518 et seq., below.

range for an examination of a debtor whose evasiveness has frustrated subpoena service. The theory is that if the debtor could be served with a subpoena, the contempt proceedings that buttress it—these can end in arrest and jailing—would do the job and make arrest under CPLR 5250 unnecessary.[1]

If the judgment debtor is not shown to be hiding in or about to leave New York, no quantity of property in his possession will justify an arrest under CPLR 5250. Nor would it be necessary: the judgment debtor and his property would be available for the whole run of Article 52's other enforcement devices.

Arguments about constitutionality can be made about this device, but it is too rarely used (if it is used at all) to generate much caselaw or to warrant further attention.

G. INCIDENTAL MATTERS

Table of Sections

§ 514. Death of Judgment Debtor

Generally speaking, the death of the judgment debtor prevents further efforts at enforcement from proceeding through the court that rendered the judgment and requires that payment be sought in the surrogate's court that will be administering the debtor's estate. CPLR 5208, the main provision in point, bars all further enforcement steps except upon leave of the surrogate. The main reason for this is that the judgment must now line up with all of the other obligations of the decedent, seeking its priority pursuant to § 1811 of the Surrogate's Court Procedure Act, which

§ 513

1. See 3d Rep.Leg.Doc.(1959) No. 17, p. 315.

§ 514

1. SCPA 1811(2). See the Commentaries on McKinney's SCPA 1811.

2. See § 517 below.

3. Oysterman's Bank & Trust Co. v. Weeks, 35 A.D.2d 580, 313 N.Y.S.2d 535 (2d Dep't 1970).

gives preference to certain other items, mainly taxes.[1]

Even an execution already issued and in the sheriff's hands when the debtor dies, fails, at least insofar as the debtor's personal property is concerned, remitting its issuer to the surrogate's court. But if a levy has already been made, it can apparently proceed to perfection and sale. In the case of real property on which the judgment has been made a lien through docketing in the county clerk's office—a lien against realty does not depend on delivery of executions or their levy[2]—it has been held that the debtor's death does not preclude levy and sale afterwards; that the sheriff can proceed with the sale as long as the execution was issued before the debtor's death.[3] Based on that authority, it was then held that a restraining notice issued and served before death retains its effect,[4] but there is some doubt about what that should be. The court's rationale was that while the debtor's death precludes new enforcement steps from being initiated without leave of the surrogate, it does not nullify such steps as have already been taken.

In some regards it does, however. Priorities, for example, secured by judgment creditors before death can, upon death, be superseded by those of SCPA 1811.[5] And if the surrogate's court under the SCPA can reorder priorities, it should logically also have jurisdiction to take hold of the property against which the priorities are being asserted. It would therefore seem that a restraining notice (which does not even earn a priority for its user under the CPLR[6]) cannot bar the surrogate from control of the affected property, or SCPA 1811 from its say as to who shall have it.

The reason why issues like this do not often arise is that they are ultimately a problem only when the estate is insolvent. As long as

4. Plaza Hotel Associates v. Wellington Associates, Inc., 84 Misc.2d 777, 378 N.Y.S.2d 859 (Sup.Ct., N.Y. County, 1975).

5. See the extensive treatment in 3d Rep.Leg.Doc. (1959) No. 17, p.126. Although as a group judgment creditors may be subordinated to other creditors of the decedent, they at least retain their competitive lien positions among themselves. SCPA 1811(2)(c).

6. See § 520 below.

the estate can pay all of its debts, the worst its creditors confront is some delay; as long as the creditor gets paid, it is ordinarily of small moment whether the payment comes from liquidation of a given estate asset on which the creditor may earlier have had a lien, or from some other asset in which she had no special right at all.

Recognizing the time element, and that an indefinite delay in the surrogate's proceedings can unfairly impede the judgment creditor, the CPLR provides that if no executor or administrator is appointed for the decedent within 18 months after his death, enforcement can proceed through the original court without leave of the surrogate. The procedure for the judgment creditor to use in that situation is to move the original court for leave to continue enforcement, doing so by order to show cause (in which the court can determine how and upon whom notice shall be served).[7]

If the judgment debtor died a domiciliary of a state other than New York, so that it is the probate or like court of that state that is taking on the main administration of the decedent's estate, CPLR 5208 can still be given scope and effect. (Ancillary letters[8] may ultimately be necessary. If they are, they are sought from the New York Surrogate's Court insofar as any local assets of the decedent are affected.) Proceedings in this nondomiciliary situation are not entirely clear, especially when the local creditors' claims have been reduced to judgment. The singular theme of the SCPA in this situation, however, is that local assets should not be let out of the state unless and until local creditors have been paid their just claims, the property to act in effect as security. That theme is sounded for the protection of all local creditors,[9] and it should

a fortiori guide proceedings for those who have achieved the even higher status of judgment creditor.

CPLR 5208 is concerned only with a judgment rendered against the decedent before she died. This must be distinguished from a judgment rendered against the representative of the estate in some action or proceeding afterwards. Although enforcement in that situation, too, requires leave of the surrogate,[10] it is not governed by CPLR 5208.

§ 515. Protecting the Garnishee

In several situations under Article 52, a garnishee who has property of the judgment debtor or who owes a debt to the judgment debtor may be required to deliver or pay it to the judgment creditor instead, or to the sheriff. The garnishee may be obliged to do so on an execution or on some category of Article 52 order or judgment, such as a delivery or "turnover" order under CPLR 5225. Whenever, pursuant to an execution or order, the garnishee makes the required payment or delivery, the garnishee is discharged from any further obligation to the judgment debtor to the extent of it.[1] Thus, if the judgment debtor should afterwards bring suit against the garnishee on the same obligation, the garnishee's prior payment or delivery pursuant to an enforcement device duly issued at the behest of the judgment debtor's judgment creditor will be a good defense, and will be entitled to full faith and credit if the suit is brought in another American jurisdiction.[2]

One thing the garnishee should make sure of in the New York enforcement proceedings is that the property or debt belongs to or is owed to the judgment debtor and not to some third person, especially if the execution has identi-

---

7. CPLR 5208.

8. Ancillary letters are those that appoint someone as fiduciary to administer the local assets of one who died domiciled, and whose main estate is being administered, elsewhere. See SCPA 1604, 1607, 1608.

9. See SCPA 1610(2).

10. See EPTL 11–4.6.

§ 515

1. CPLR 5209. An order as used in this provision should be deemed to embrace a judgment as well, since a

delivery direction against a garnishee under CPLR 5225(b) or 5227 will often emanate from a special proceeding, which ends in a judgment rather than an order. CPLR 411.

2. Harris v. Balk, 198 U.S. 215, 25 S.Ct. 625, 49 L.Ed. 1023 (1905).

fied the judgment debtor but no specific property. If there is any doubt, the garnishee should withhold the property or debt until a court, with jurisdiction of the third person (who would then be bound by all findings), determines the property to be the judgment debtor's. At that point the garnishee may safely pay it over. Doing so without that determination subjects the garnishee to double liability: the third person, in a later suit against the garnishee, would not be bound by any earlier proceedings purporting to adjudicate, or merely to assume, that the property belonged to the judgment debtor.

If an execution has specifically designated property, however, the garnishee who complies is protected; in that situation "it is the creditor and not the garnishee who is liable for damages to the actual owner".[3]

If, because of any risk perceived, the garnishee does refuse to turn over money or property in violation of an execution, the garnishee can expect a special proceeding from the judgment creditor to force the turn-over.[4] But that is just what the doctor orders here. The garnishee can use that proceeding to secure the protective determination needed. If the judgment creditor has voluntarily joined the other claimants in that proceeding, as she is likely to do if the garnishee has pointed to them as the reason for withholding payment over, judgment in that proceeding will bind them. If they have not been initially joined, the garnishee as respondent in that proceeding can move to interplead them,[5] thus converting the proceeding into the equivalent of defensive interpleader.[6] The garnishee can initiate the proceeding,[7] but it is usually more comfortable to leave the initiative on that to the judgment creditor who, because collection of the judgment is meanwhile suspended, can be expected to seize it.

§ 516. Pre-Judgment Enforcement

The moment that permits enforcement to go forward is the entry of the judgment, so that practically speaking all enforcement is a post-judgment procedure. But CPLR 5229 allows two of the enforcement devices to be used during the brief interval after rendition of the verdict or decision but before the formal entry of judgment. These are the examination in regard to assets (otherwise governed by CPLR 5223 and 5224 in post-judgment use) and the restraint against divestiture of those assets (governed after judgment by CPLR 5222). When sought at this pre-judgment moment, however, a court order is required, and it is sought by motion to the trial judge. For that reason it can probably be an oral motion, made right after the decision or verdict comes in, but whether oral or written it is rarely used, probably because the full panoply of enforcement devices will become available as soon as a judgment is formally entered and that usually need not cost even a day.

One situation in which CPLR 5229 has special utility is where an interlocutory judgment establishes liability but where a final judgment must still abide a trial of damages. A restraint in the interim can prevent the defendant from selling off his property and frustrating collection of the ultimate judgment. It is not ordinarily germane in a bifurcated trial in a personal injury case, because in that instance an insurer will usually be paying the ultimate judgment anyway. But it would be helpful in an accounting action, for example, in which liability has gone to interlocutory judgment and where there is some apprehension about the defendant's divestiture of assets before the damages phase can be tried.[1]

Under CPLR 5229, the defendant can apparently be directed by the court to submit to immediate questioning about his assets by the plaintiff's lawyer, but that also presupposes

---

3. Chin Sung Yu v. Riggs Nat. Bank, 248 A.D.2d 235, 670 N.Y.S.2d 187 (1st Dep't 1998) (noted in SPR 76:2).

4. See CPLR 5232(a), 5225(b), 5227.

5. CPLR 401.

6. See CPLR 1006(b).

7. See CPLR 5239, treated in § 521 below.

§ 516

1. See Kaminsky v. Kahn, 46 Misc.2d 131, 258 N.Y.S.2d 1000 (Sup.Ct., N.Y.County), mod'd on other grounds 23 A.D.2d 231, 259 N.Y.S.2d 716 (1st Dep't 1965).

that the lawyer has prepared the questioning, which is usually not the case.

All in all CPLR 5229 is benevolent, but not popular. It may come in handy from time to time though, and the practitioner should keep it in the arsenal. It is not restricted, as are the more popular supplementary proceedings, to the courts listed in CPLR 5221(a);[2] it makes its examination and restraint available in any court with jurisdiction to render a civil judgment.

Indeed, CPLR 5229 applies in federal practice, too, and it is in fact a federal case that gives the statute its most extensive treatment.[3]

H. PRIORITIES AND LIENS

Table of Sections

§ 517. Priorities and Liens on Real Property

Obtaining a lien on the judgment debtor's real property is an easy affair mechanically, at least when contrasted with personal property. It is simply a matter of getting the judgment docketed with the county clerk of the county where the realty is. That docketing, which is an entry under the debtor's name in a set of alphabetized books or an entry on a block index if one is maintained,[1] makes the judgment a lien with nothing more required. But it is only a lien on realty in that county. To make it a realty lien elsewhere, a transcript of the judgment is secured from the home county clerk and filed with the county clerk of the other county, whereupon the latter dockets the judgment and the judgment becomes a lien on realty in that county. Docketing of a judgment is practically automatic when rendered in the supreme court or a county court, because the county clerk is ex officio the clerk of those courts and anything she does as court clerk she does as county clerk as well. So, when a judgment in an action in one of those courts is entered and docketed, and the judgment-roll is filed, events that occur at just about the same time,[2] the judgment immediately becomes a lien on the judgment debtor's local real property. If the judgment was rendered in a lower court, however, a transcript of the judgment must be secured from that court's clerk and filed with the county clerk before a realty lien is realized. The procedures for transcripting judgments between and among courts was the subject of earlier treatment, which the reader may find it convenient to review at this point.[3]

The lien lasts 10 years—measured not from the time of docketing, but from the filing of the judgment-roll,[4] which is essentially the moment the judgment was entered.[5] As indicated, that moment and the moment of docketing is the same in a supreme court or county court action, but it is not the same in the case of a lower court judgment, such as one of a city court. There the lien will not take effect until docketing by transcript with the county clerk, but the 10 years will nonetheless have started when the judgment was entered in the lower court. Where, for example, judgment in an Albany City Court action is entered in 1988 but not docketed with the Albany county clerk until 1990, the lien will have only eight years left at docketing time. The first two years will have been lost as lien time.

CPLR 5203(a) determines the effect of the lien. It provides that no transfer by the judgment debtor of any interest in the liened realty is effective against the judgment creditor after the lien takes effect. It then carves out a set of six exceptions, as follows:

---

2. See § 493 above.

3. See Sequa Capital Corp. v. Nave, 921 F.Supp. 1072 (S.D.N.Y.1996), noted in SPR 45:4.

§ 517

1. CPLR 5018(a).

2. Id.

3. See §§ 421 and 422.

4. CPLR 5203(a).

5. CPLR 5017(a).

1. The lien of course defers to senior judgment liens, so that a buyer at a sale on an execution being levied on a judgment with a senior lien takes free of the junior judgment, and the proceeds of the sale go first to satisfy the senior judgment creditor.[6]

2. If the judgment debtor gave back a purchase money mortgage when he bought the property, that mortgagee prevails over the judgment creditor even if the judgment stood of record when the debtor bought.[7] This situation can arise when a judgment debtor buys the land after judgment against him has been docketed, which suggests that the judgment creditor may have been lax in pursuit of the judgment debtor or he would have uncovered the money that the debtor later used towards purchase of the property.

3. Any purchaser at a judicial sale takes free of judgment liens, including those senior to the judgment being levied.[8] The reason for this is that when realty is sold on execution, the sheriff notifies all the other judgment creditors, senior and junior alike,[9] who must then issue their own executions. The proceeds of the sale are then distributed in the order in which each judgment became a lien on the realty.[10] Seniority is thus recognized by that route and all judgment creditors lose their liens on that realty although they of course retain their other rights against the judgment debtor to the extent that the proceeds of the sale do not satisfy their judgments.[11]

4. If the judgment was entered after the death of the judgment debtor, it does not get a lien,[12] at least not in the technical way it otherwise would. The judgment creditor must

in that case turn to the surrogate's court for satisfaction of the judgment.[13]

5. A judgment against the state or its agencies or against a municipal corporation does not become a lien against real property.[14]

6. If the judgment was rendered against an executor or administrator in his or her representative capacity,[15] the judgment does not become a lien against real property. This enables the fiduciary to pass title to a buyer without the encumbrance of a judgment standing against the land.[16] The judgment creditor's security in this instance is the overall assets of the estate—if there are any—or the bond of the fiduciary, if one was given.

It was noted in number 4 on the list that if the judgment was entered after the death of the judgment debtor, it gets no lien. If it was entered and became a lien before the judgment debtor's death, however, it retains its competitive position as against other judgment creditors, but satisfaction must now be sought through the surrogate's court.[17] In fact, if there was less than two years left on the judgment lien when the judgment debtor died, the lien is extended to two years from death,[18] a provision designed to give the judgment creditor, frustrated in enforcement by the death of the debtor, some time to put the claim before the estate representative or surrogate without losing the lien.

The seniority of liens applies essentially to where the judgment debtor was the owner of the realty when the liens arose. A pro-rata sharing rule applies for after-acquired realty, i.e., realty the judgment debtor comes into after the docketing of the judgment. If the judgment debtor gets the realty by inheri-

---

6. CPLR 5203(a)(1).

7. CPLR 5203(a)(2).

8. CPLR 5203(a)(3).

9. CPLR 5236(c).

10. CPLR 5236(g)(1).

11. CPLR 5236(e). See § 500 above.

12. CPLR 5203(a)(4).

13. CPLR 5208. See § 514 above.

14. CPLR 5203(a)(5).

15. This is to be distinguished from where the judgment was rendered against the decedent, as contemplated by #4 on the list. In the present situation, the judgment

runs directly against the fiduciary, albeit for something in his or her representative capacity.

16. CPLR 5203(a)(6).

17. CPLR 5208. See also SCPA 1811, which clarifies that although the lien progression continues to dictate priorities among judgment creditors, 1811(2)(c), they may as a group become subordinated to other interests, notably those of the sovereign for taxes and other obligations. SCPA 1811(2)(a), (b). These matters are further discussed in § 514 above.

18. CPLR 5208 (last sentence).

tance, for example, after several judgments have been docketed and would stand as realty liens against her if she had any, one does not take priority over another; all share pro rata.[19]

The lien of a judgment can be lifted by court order if, in conjunction with an appeal, the judgment debtor has given an undertaking sufficient to secure the judgment creditor.[20]

We have previously discussed the interplay between the life of a judgment, which is 20 years, and its life as a lien against real property, which is only 10. Since execution can be made at any time during the life of the judgment, it is possible that when it is sought during the second decade of the judgment's life, it will be made while the judgment is not a lien, raising the possibility that some other creditor's lien may intervene. One remedy for that situation is CPLR 5235, which permits a "notice of levy" to be used, offering a brief renewal of the lien for the time it takes to complete an execution sale of the realty.[21] Another is for the judgment creditor to move to extend the original 10-year period to cover the time necessary to conduct the execution sale, but this is less helpful than CPLR 5235 because it is permissible only if the creditor duly delivered an execution to the sheriff before the 10 years expired. The court is also empowered by order to stretch the 10 years by whatever time enforcement of the judgment was stayed, such as in conjunction with an appeal or a motion to vacate the judgment.[22]

The best remedy, however, available only since CPLR 5014 was amended in 1986 to allow it, is for the judgment creditor to act during the year preceding the expiration of the 10-year lien, by bringing an action to renew the judgment. That produces a new 10-year lien and avoids the gap that would otherwise occur between the expiration of the original 10-year lien and the time of actual sale of the realty during the period following.[23]

§ 518. Rights in Personal Property, Introductory

With real property, a filing with the county clerk puts the world on notice of the interest claimed in the filed paper. It accomplishes this so thoroughly that the simple expedient of a filing has been made almost the exclusive method for determining rights and interests in real property. The mobility of personal property, which includes everything from multi-ton tangibles to mere choses in action with no corporeal substance at all, prevents a mere filing from doing so perfect a job.

Only for orders secured under Article 52 has the legislature decided on the moment of filing as the determining point for priorities in personal property; it was felt that with orders, the time of filing is as good as any other. And here the moment of filing that counts is that of the filing of the enforcement order, not of the original judgment. For executions, priority arrives in some instances with delivery to the sheriff, in others only with actual levy. Determining priorities in personal property is the mission of CPLR 5202 when the judgment creditor is vying with a transferee of the judgment debtor, and of CPLR 5234 when judgment creditors are competing among themselves. Each gets separate treatment in the sections following.[1]

The only liens created by the CPLR are judgment liens, and it is therefore only in

---

19. Hulbert v. Hulbert, 216 N.Y. 430, 111 N.E. 70 (1916).

20. CPLR 5204.

21. See the discussion in § 499 above.

22. CPLR 5203(b).

23. See § 434 above.

§ 518

1. The Advisory Committee had initially decided on a scheme of priorities in personal property based on filing with the county clerk or, in the case of a nonresident

debtor, with the secretary of state, see 2d Rep.Leg.Doc. (1959) No. 17, p. 101, but this was afterwards rejected by the legislature. The present schemes of priority contained in CPLR 5202 and 5234 are not the Advisory Committee's work. To the extent that they carry forward prior law, which in significant degree they do, they are criticized by the committee as "extremely uncertain, unnecessarily complex and virtually devoid of rational justification...." Id. at 103. The legislature, apparently assuming that provisions invoking so enthusiastic a criticism can't be all bad, kept them on.

respect of judgment creditors that the CPLR resolves priorities. The CPLR does not in any way purport to resolve all of the limitless disputes that can arise among an equally limitless variety of other interests, and situations involving other interests are by no means rare. A judgment creditor pursuing a debtor will often find that she is not alone. She may recognize a few judgment creditors among her rivals, but be taken aback by the myriad of others with liens emanating from mortgages or pledges, the rendering of services, the sale of goods, the undertaking of a venture, the imposition of taxes, and many more. In a race like that, the CPLR does not dictate the winner; it declares only the lien moment of the judgment creditor, not of other creditors. Nor does any other single source, statutory or otherwise, array all of the others. Some may get their liens from statutes, some from common law. When all come together, therefore, nothing plain dictates the line of march. They are an undisciplined mob and the judge may have a big job sorting them all out.

But if the CPLR does not order the race, it at least supplies the track. With CPLR 5239, whose later treatment will cite a few examples of these lien battles,[2] the CPLR offers a special proceeding whereby any one of the competitors can bring all of the others to court for a test of priorities. When competition gets to that stage, however, it goes beyond the subject of the "enforcement of judgments" and expands into what a law school curriculum sometimes describes as "creditors' rights". And if things cannot be worked out in proceedings involving the various creditors' rights, the next step will lead to yet another subject: bankruptcy. Those are topics beyond the CPLR, but in the ensuing sections we will go at least as far as the CPLR does.

2. See § 521 below.

§ 519

1. See 6th Rep.Leg.Doc.(1962) No. 8, p.456.

2. Civ.Prac.Act § 679(1).

3. CPLR 5202(a)(1). "Fair consideration" for all purposes of CPLR 5202 is as defined by § 272 of the Debtor and Creditor Law. It includes an antecedent debt, see

§ 519. Rights in Personal Property; Judgment Creditor Versus Transferee

A distinction is made between the judgment creditor who uses an execution and one who uses an Article 52 device that gives rise to an order. The execution will be treated first.

CPLR 5202(a) provides that a creditor using an execution gets priority in the judgment debtor's personal property as of the moment he delivers the execution to the sheriff. The priority affects debts and other intangible interests as well as tangible property.

The statute does not require that the sheriff to whom the delivery is made be the sheriff of the county where the property has its situs, but that would be a very sound idea. There is even room for a finding that this is the only sheriff to whom a delivery of the execution will secure the judgment creditor a priority. The legislature indicated that it was essentially adopting prior law in this instance,[1] and prior law specified that the proper sheriff was the one with jurisdiction to levy,[2] which could only be the sheriff of a county in which the property itself could be found or a proper garnishee subjected to jurisdiction.

Assuming that the execution has been delivered to the right sheriff, it gives the judgment creditor a higher right than a later transferee of the judgment debtor, with two stated exceptions:

1. A transfer after the execution is delivered but before it is levied gives the transferee a right superior to the creditor's as long as the transferee is shown to have paid fair consideration for the property.[3]

2. A transfer after the levy (but obviously before payment or delivery of the proceeds to the levying creditor) for fair consideration also gives the transferee a right superior to the judgment creditor's, but in this instance only if it is shown that the transferee had no

International Ribbon Mills, Ltd. v. Arjan Ribbons, Inc., 36 N.Y.2d 121, 365 N.Y.S.2d 808, 325 N.E.2d 137 (1975), including an antecedent mortgage, Ruppert v. Community Nat. Bank, 22 A.D.2d 165, 254 N.Y.S.2d 341 (1st Dep't 1964), aff'd 16 N.Y.2d 589, 261 N.Y.S.2d 52, 209 N.E.2d 100 (1965), or similar obligation, thus protecting a transferee to whom the transfer has been made in fulfillment of the earlier obligation.

knowledge of the levy,[4] which is necessarily a question of fact in each case.

A further distinction between the two exceptions is that the second one applies only when the debt or property is not "capable of delivery", a term investigated in an earlier section[5] in conjunction with a levy of execution. In general, the definition suggested in that section would probably do here as well. If the property is "capable of delivery", the sheriff is required to levy an execution by seizing the property itself;[6] and if the sheriff does that, the property would be in the sheriff's hands and could not afterwards be transferred by the judgment debtor or garnishee. If, on the other hand, the property is not capable of delivery, it would have to be levied on by the mere service of the execution.[7] Whatever the property is, it would remain in the hands of the debtor or garnishee in that situation until later steps bring it into the sheriff's custody, even though the levy itself was technically effected by the sheriff's service of the execution. A transferee can be unaware of a levy by service, and, relying on the fact that no sheriff has taken the property, part with fair consideration for it. Thus, although the transfer takes place after the levy has theoretically been accomplished, the transferee can still be allowed to prevail, but only if she shows that she took in ignorance of the levy. If she knew of the levy, she will lose out to the judgment creditor.

The approach is not perfect. There are a number of situations one can conjure up in which a proposed transferee should be put to the burden of making inquiries that would lead to knowledge of the levy, but this is one of those areas in which the legislature apparently felt that the factual variations are too extensive to admit of qualifications and that a set rule, even if not ideal, would be better. The moral to the judgment creditor is to get the levy perfected both by pressure on the sheriff as well as through his own steps, such as an

application for a delivery order under CPLR 5225 or 5227. Only when the property interest pursued is effectively taken into the sheriff's hands, such as a debt finally paid over to the sheriff or an attornment or other commitment made by the garnishee to pay the debt to the judgment creditor or sheriff at some later time, is the door to a lien-robbing transfer closed.

Besides an execution, the other Article 52 lien-givers are orders that the article authorizes, such as the delivery order under CPLR 5225 and the receivership order under CPLR 5228; each specifies the property involved, and it is that property to which the lien attaches. A judgment creditor who has "secured" such an order[8]—this should be taken to mean the moment the order is filed[9]—prevails over a later transferee of the judgment debtor except one who pays fair consideration for the property and had no notice of the order. For this purpose an "order" should be deemed to include a "judgment" as well, a judgment being what a judgment creditor gets who brings a special proceeding against a garnishee under CPLR 5225(b) or 5227, two of the lien-giving devices of Article 52. The same risks of transfer faced by an execution-using creditor under subdivision (a) of CPLR 5202, as described above, can also be met by an order-securing creditor under subdivision (b). The judgment creditor should close the door to transfers as soon as possible by keeping up the pressure to get possession of the subject property.

The transfer adequate to defeat the judgment creditor must in any event be for fair consideration. If it is not, it qualifies as fraudulent and can be set aside by the judgment creditor in either a separate plenary action or, better, in a special proceeding under CPLR 5225(b), 5227, or 5239.[10]

A judgment creditor who takes no step to secure a lien with some lien-giving device of

---

4. CPLR 5202(a)(2).

5. See § 497.

6. CPLR 5232(b).

7. CPLR 5232(a).

8. CPLR 5202(b).

9. One can deduce this by analogy to CPLR 5234(c), which expressly says "filing"; in both instances this should be deemed to mean "entry" as defined in CPLR 5016(a).

10. Debtor and Creditor Law § 273–a. See § 510 above.

Article 52, i.e., who issues no execution and secures no Article 52 order, leaves the door wide open to transfers that can readily frustrate collection of the judgment.[11]

§ 520. Rights in Personal Property; Judgment Creditors Among Themselves

When it comes to the rights of judgment creditors among themselves, CPLR 5234 governs priorities and liens in the judgment debtor's personal property: subdivision (b) when all the competing creditors are using executions and subdivision (c) when some are using Article 52 devices implemented by court orders.

When two or more executions[1] are issued in behalf of different judgment creditors against the same judgment debtor and are delivered to the same enforcement officer,[2] priority in the proceeds of the execution sale is determined by the order of delivery of the executions.[3] What was said about the proper sheriff in the prior section applies here, too: although this part of the statute does not expressly require that the sheriff used be the sheriff of the county in which the property has its situs, the situs sheriff was probably intended, and is the logical choice in any event. The second sentence of CPLR 5234(b), moreover, does specify that sheriff, and in context to suggest that the sheriff of the situs county—or of one of the situs counties if the property has a multiple situs—is the one intended in all CPLR 5234 situations.

The mission of the second sentence is to dictate priorities when executions have been

delivered to different enforcement officers and all have jurisdiction to levy. This can happen, for example, when judgment creditor A delivers a supreme court execution to the New York City sheriff and judgment creditor B delivers a New York City Civil Court execution to a city marshal, both concerning an asset with a New York City situs. Here the moment of delivery is not the key time, but rather the moment of levy. When there are but two executions involved, the levier gets first crack at the proceeds and the other gets the balance, provided that the non-levying officer makes a demand for such balance on the levying officer. When three or more executions are involved, the levying officer collects the proceeds and his judgment creditor gets first priority in them; the other officers must make a demand on that sheriff to share in the proceeds; they get priority for their judgment creditors in the order in which they make their demands. One whose execution is returned before the levy is made does not share in the proceeds,[4] which is also true, of course, of those whose delivery of an execution does not take place until after the proceeds have been distributed.

The officer who unreasonably fails to levy and returns execution unsatisfied while another officer levies successfully, thus denying the judgment creditor what would otherwise have been his proper share of the proceeds, may be sued for the damages caused by the dereliction. It is not a popular remedy in the courts—sheriffs and other enforcement officers are not big fans either—but it is ancient law that dereliction in respect of judicial process renders the enforcement officer fully liable for

---

11. See, e.g., County Nat. Bank v. Inter–County Farmers Co-op. Ass'n, 65 Misc.2d 446, 317 N.Y.S.2d 790 (Sup. Ct., Sullivan County, 1970).

§ 520

1. Since a pre-judgment order of attachment can seize property to the credit of the attaching plaintiff, a timely attachment will prevail over later levies of post-judgment execution, even on judgments rendered in actions commenced long before the action in which the attachment issued. For this reason, orders of attachment are treated the same as executions in CPLR 5234(b) and (c). The word "execution" is used in this section of the text as including an attachment, and the words "judgment creditor" as including the attaching plaintiff.

2. The words "enforcement officer" include whoever services the particular court: the sheriff for the supreme court and the county courts, the sheriff and city marshals together for the New York City Civil Court (see § 701 of its court act, McKinney's Vol. 29A, Part 3), marshals or constables for the justice courts (see UJCA § 110, McKinney's Vol. 29A, Part 2), etc.

3. This part of CPLR 5234 is analogous to the priorities scheme set up for income executions by CPLR 5231(j). Having its own priority statute, the income execution is not governed by CPLR 5234.

4. See International Ribbon Mills, Ltd. v. Arjan Ribbons, Inc., 36 N.Y.2d 121, 365 N.Y.S.2d 808, 325 N.E.2d 137 (1975).

whatever damages he causes.[5] Damage suits against sheriffs, while not frequent, do appear from time to time.[6] Their infrequency should not prompt enforcement officers to lose sight of their liabilities, bonded or not.

The present assumption is that the sheriff has not gone far enough. Another example of a sheriff's liability is when the sheriff goes too far and becomes subject to liability to a third party.[7] Where, for example, the sheriff levies in behalf of creditor C against property of debtor D which the sheriff knows to be subject to a security agreement that D had previously made in favor of S, the sheriff and his sureties are liable to S.[8]

When the competing judgment creditors have all used orders under Article 52 instead of executions, such as delivery orders under CPLR 5225 or 5227 or receivership orders under CPLR 5228, the time of the filing of those orders[9] determines priority among them.[10] If some creditors are using executions and others rely on orders, the execution creditors have their priorities set in the order of levy, the others as of the time their orders are filed. Here an additional limitation is imposed on the judgment creditor who has secured and filed an order: she must see to it that the transfer it requires, whether to herself, to the sheriff, or to a receiver, is completed within 60 days after the filing, unless the order specifies otherwise or an extension order is secured and filed within those 60 days. Else that creditor loses priority.[11] If she contemplates trouble in securing actual transfer, the judgment creditor should ask, when originally applying for a delivery order under CPLR 5225 or 5227 or a receivership order under CPLR 5228, that an

appropriate extended time period be included in the order.

A garnishee may come under pressure from a number of creditors claiming priorities. A garnishee who is not clear on its obligations should await court action and see to it, whatever form the court procedure takes, that all of the claimants are made parties. In one case, for example, a debt owed by G to D had been duly assigned by D to A. Afterwards J, a judgment creditor of D, issued an execution, which was levied by service on G. G paid the debt to J and because of that was held liable to A for the amount paid.[12]

If the use of some enforcement device has secured a lien and an appeal has been or is now taken from the judgment, the lien can be released by the judgment debtor (appellant) furnishing an undertaking on the appeal adequate to secure the judgment creditor.[13]

It is important for the judgment creditor to remember that under the CPLR, the only devices that give liens are the executions and the orders. There is no priority secured by the service of either a restraining notice under CPLR 5222 or a subpoena under CPLR 5224, whatever those devices can otherwise accomplish and notwithstanding that they gave liens under prior law. Some practitioners, weaned on the old law or absorbing it from epic sagas of the old folks around the campfire, have overlooked this and consequently lost priority for their clients.[14] Nor is it a question of diligence. A diligent judgment creditor who goes to the trouble of serving both a restraining notice and a subpoena and even making an application under CPLR 5225 for a delivery order will still lose out to another creditor who merely has a sheriff levy execution in the

---

5. See Root v. Wagner, 30 N.Y. 9 (1864).

6. Wang v. Bartel, 163 Misc.2d 600, 624 N.Y.S.2d 735 (App.Term, 2d & 11th Dists. 1994), for example, noted in SPR 45:4, sustained a damages action by a judgment creditor suing a deputy sheriff for alleged disregard of his obligations.

7. See § 496 above.

8. See Meritum Corp. v. Pichler, Sup.Ct. N.Y. County, (Gammerman, J.), N.Y. Law Journal, Sept. 10, 1980, page 7, col.2.

9. Filing and entry are virtually synonymous. See CPLR 5016(a).

10. An "order" in this sense must be deemed to include a "judgment" rendered against a garnishee in a special proceeding brought under CPLR 5225(b) or 5227.

11. CPLR 5234(c).

12. See Lincoln Rochester Trust Co. v. S. C. Marasco Steel, Inc., 66 Misc.2d 295, 320 N.Y.S.2d 864 (Monroe County Ct. 1971).

13. CPLR 5204.

14. See City of New York v. Panzirer, 23 A.D.2d 158, 259 N.Y.S.2d 284 (1st Dep't 1965).

interim.[15] The levy is a lien-giver. The restraining notice and the subpoena are not. Nor is the mere application for an order, unless and until the application is granted and the order is filed.

When the judgment debtor happens to be a member of a partnership, a common device for pursuing his interest in the partnership is a charging order under § 54 of the Partnership Law. An application under that provision may also result in an order appointing a receiver of the debtor partner's interest. But neither order will afford a lien until it is filed, so that even in that situation the judgment creditor does better by issuing an execution to the sheriff and having the sheriff levy on the debtor-partner's interest.[16] The charging order contemplated by § 54 is not an exclusive remedy. An ordinary levy of execution is permissible, and, when priorities are involved, preferable because of the lien it promptly secures.[17]

When none of the competing creditors has taken a lien-giving step under CPLR 5234, the latter can be deemed inapplicable, leaving the individual equities of the case to determine who should be awarded priority. In one case, for example, a judgment creditor issued a CPLR 5222 restraining notice to the judgment debtor, after which the debtor, violating the notice, made an assignment for the benefit of creditors. While conceding that the 5222 notice gave no lien, the court held that a creditor who has been diligent enough to convert his claim to judgment should on equitable principles prevail over other creditors who have not.[18]

§ 521. Proceeding to Determine Adverse Claims

As mentioned earlier, the only liens created by the CPLR are judgment liens, and they are therefore the only ones among which the CPLR purports to set priorities. The situation will often arise, however, in which creditors of various stripes and with diverse claims of lien will be competing with judgment creditors to get at the assets of the judgment debtor. Neither the CPLR nor any other single statute purports to enumerate all of these interests or to set down a comprehensive list of how priorities are to be determined among them.[1] The CPLR's only offering, in these multi-creditor pursuits, is a special proceeding designed to enable the claims of all of them to be expeditiously brought to court, however their substantive priorities may be adjudicated after they get there. CPLR 5239 supplies this special proceeding, which may be brought by "any interested person" against "the judgment creditor or other person" with whom a priority dispute exists. Between this proceeding and the special proceedings authorized by CPLR 5225(b) and 5227, the judgment creditor has a selection of priority-determining proceedings to choose from.

If the competitors are both judgment creditors, and one has a CPLR lien superior to the other's, the superior one will of course win. If neither has secured a lien, however, the governing principles will be drawn from outside the CPLR, from statute, caselaw, or equity. In one such case, for example, in which the competition was between the State Tax Commission and a bank, the commission prevailed under the rule that other things being equal, the sovereign and its agencies come first.[2]

When creditors with other than judgment liens are among the competitors, CPLR 5239 is equally available; there have been a number of cases that illustrate how it paves the way to the courthouse even though the CPLR will not have the sole say as to who wins after they enter. Many other statutes purporting to confer liens may have to be considered, along with the judgment liens of the CPLR and cases announcing other equities. Properly perfected

---

15. See Graze v. Bankers Trust Co., 45 Misc.2d 610, 257 N.Y.S.2d 483 (Sup.Ct., N.Y.County, 1965).

16. CPLR 5201(c)(3).

17. See Princeton Bank and Trust Co. v. Berley, 57 A.D.2d 348, 394 N.Y.S.2d 714 (2d Dep't 1977). Unless the judgment is against the partnership itself, no partnership asset can be reached directly. See § 491 above.

18. Matter of City of N.Y. (Nassau Expressway), 56 Misc.2d 602, 289 N.Y.S.2d 680 (Sup.Ct., Queens County, 1968), cited with approval in the Arjan case, note 4, above.

§ 521

1. See § 518 above.

2. See Matter of Robbins' Estate, 74 Misc.2d 793, 346 N.Y.S.2d 86 (Surr.Ct., Suffolk County, 1973).

liens under the Uniform Commercial Code, for example, such as those of a factor in inventory and accounts receivable, are often found in competition with judgment creditors in CPLR 5239 proceedings.[3] So are liens under the Workers' Compensation Law, Social Services Law, Tax Law, etc., in addition to the myriad that come out of the Lien Law itself.[4]

The basic difference between the CPLR 5239 proceeding and those under CPLR 5225(b) or 5227 is that the latter two are brought by the judgment creditor while the 5239 proceeding may be brought by any interested person (judgment creditor included). Any interested persons, including adverse claimants, may be joined as respondents in any of them. If the language of CPLR 5225(b) and 5227 seems narrower than that, the proceeding can instead be based on CPLR 5239,[5] or, better still, on all of them together, gaining maximum scope for itself that way. The only stated time limitation for the CPLR 5239 proceeding is that it be brought before the property involved has actually been applied (i.e., the proceeds distributed) towards satisfaction of a judgment. It is that requirement, in fact, from which we infer that CPLR 5239 can be exploited only when at least one of the competitors, even if only one of a dozen, is a judgment creditor. Intervention is also expressly authorized by CPLR 5239, so that any claimant not already joined can move to be let in.

The proceeding is initiated by serving on the respondents (claimant, sheriff, receiver, etc.[6]) a notice of petition, "in the same manner as a notice of motion". That kind of service, which may be by mere mail to the respondent's lawyer,[7] would be satisfactory only if the particular respondent had been a party to the main action. If he was not, it is safer to make service in the same manner as a summons, recognizing that this respondent has yet to be subjected to the court's jurisdiction.[8] The proceeding will be governed generally in its procedures by Article 4 of the CPLR,[9] and for that reason a petition should accompany the notice of petition.[10] If an execution levy is among the things involved, the proceeding may be brought in the county of levy. It can in any event be brought in a county authorized by CPLR 5221(a), which, as applied here, would mean in any county in which any of the respondents either lives or works.[11] If on balance the county chosen turns out to be inconvenient, a change of venue would be permissible on motion.[12]

The proceeding can try any fact question arising in respect of any of the claims. It is no longer necessary that a plenary action be brought if an issue of fact appears.[13] If a jury would otherwise be required to try the fact, it can be demanded and would have to be al-

---

3. See, e.g., Wm. Iselin & Co. v. Burgess & Leigh Ltd., 52 Misc.2d 821, 276 N.Y.S.2d 659 (Sup.Ct., N.Y.County, 1967).

4. See, e.g., Lacaille v. Feldman, 44 Misc.2d 370, 253 N.Y.S.2d 937 (Sup.Ct., N.Y.County, 1964), and Neilson Realty Corp. v. M.V.A.I.C., 47 Misc.2d 260, 262 N.Y.S.2d 652 (Sup.Ct., Queens County, 1965). The Neilson case also illustrates the overlapping between and among CPLR 5225(b), 5227, and 5239. The proceeding was captioned under CPLR 5227 but was essentially a lien battle of the kind primarily contemplated by CPLR 5239. Any proceeding brought under one of those provisions should be treatable as the equivalent of any of the others, as long as all interested parties are before the court and have had an opportunity for a full hearing.

5. CPLR 5239 was amended to expand its utility as a tool for or against competing claimants. See 10th Jud. Conf.Rep.(1965) 120, 144–5, 151–2.

6. Although not expressly required, it is often a good idea to serve notice of the proceeding on the judgment debtor, D, as well. Certainly that is so if D's rights may be affected beyond the impact of the judgment itself. If, for example, the judgment creditor claims that G owes a debt

to D, and tries to levy it, X may claim that the money is owed to him, X. If G then brings a proceeding against the judgment creditor and X, but without joining D, and the court determines that the money is owed to X, that determination would probably not bind D, and G may therefore confront a double liability later.

7. CPLR 2103(b).

8. See the Commentary on McKinney's CPLR 5239. Cf. Joseph Durst Corp. v. Leader, 51 Misc.2d 72, 272 N.Y.S.2d 448 (Sup.Ct., N.Y.County, 1966).

9. Article 4 and its handful of provisions, which govern in special proceedings, are treated in § 550 et seq., below.

10. See CPLR 403(b). The petition is the pleading in a special proceeding; the notice of petition is the initiatory process.

11. See § 493 above.

12. CPLR 5240, 511, 103(b).

13. See, e.g., First Small Business Investment Corp. v. Zaretsky, 46 Misc.2d 328, 259 N.Y.S.2d 700 (Sup.Ct., Queens County, 1965).

lowed.[14] When ordering a trial, the court can determine who shall hold the disputed property in the meantime and whether such person will have to furnish a protective bond.

The court can render judgment in the proceeding for whatever is warranted after the issues have been resolved. The court's ultimate goal is to determine who shall finally have the disputed property and in conjunction with that it can declare the priority of all claimed liens and incidentally vacate any order, execution, or levy. It can award damages to any party establishing a legal right to them. The proceeding can even be used as a vehicle to set aside a fraudulent conveyance if the fraudulent transferee is a party—something that used to require a separate plenary action.

If the court in the proceeding finds that any claim interposed is fraudulent, it can require the claimant to pay to any other party the damages caused, including attorneys' fees incurred in the proceeding.[15]

I. PROTECTION AGAINST ABUSE

Table of Sections

Sec.
522. Protective Order.

§ 522. Protective Order

CPLR 5240, the statute on protective orders in the enforcement of judgments, provides that

the court may at any time, on its own initiative or the motion of any interested person, and upon such notice as it may require, make an order denying, limiting, conditioning, regulating, extending or modifying the use of any enforcement procedure. Section 3104 is applicable to procedures under this article.

By centering in one place this pervasive judicial power to right any wrong in connection with any of the numerous Article 52 procedures on a case by case basis, the statute frees all of them to go about their missions without each of them having to contemplate and cure abuses. CPLR 5240 is to Article 52, in fact, what the protective order of CPLR 3103 is to the disclosure article, Article 31.[1] Even the provision of the disclosure article that authorizes the designation of a judge or the appointment of a referee to supervise a given procedure, CPLR 3104, is adopted for Article 52 use by CPLR 5240.

The protective order can be granted by the court sua sponte, but it is more often sought on motion of the judgment debtor or other interested person. An order to show cause is the procedure, which is what CPLR 5240 contemplates by directing the court to determine upon whom and how to make service, but an ordinary notice of motion duly served on all needed parties should also be acceptable.

Examples of the uses of a protective order abound. It has been used to vary the sale time of realty otherwise dictated by CPLR 5236,[2] for example, and to vacate an income execution issued after an installment payment order was entered against the judgment debtor.[3] When addressed to an income execution, CPLR 5240 shares power with CPLR 5231(i), which explicitly authorizes the court to modify an income execution. Any protective step affecting an income execution, such as one reducing it from 10% to 5% upon a showing that the debtor can afford no more,[4] can find authority in either provision. Further ideas for what a protective order can accomplish—it can go as far as to preclude use of a given device altogether if the court finds it to be vain or unnecessarily abusive, or remit a seeker from one device to another—can be found by checking the examples contained in the legislative notes on the

14. See the discussion of this matter in § 510 above.
15. CPLR 5239.

§ 522

1. See § 353 above.
2. See Olsen v. Robaey, 45 Misc.2d 33, 256 N.Y.S.2d 103 (Sup.Ct., Suffolk County, 1965).

3. See Rush v. Rush, New York Law Journal, Nov. 26, 1963, p. 15, col. 5 (Westchester County Ct. 1963).

4. See First Westchester Nat. Bank v. Lewis, 42 Misc.2d 1007, 249 N.Y.S.2d 537 (Westchester County Ct. 1964).

analogous CPLR 3103[5] and in cases on that provision as well as on CPLR 5240.

While it has been said that CPLR 5240 does not countenance radical departures from the framework of Article 52,[6] the statute has indeed come in for some liberal if not radical applications. In the case of Wandschneider v. Bekeny,[7] for example, the court used CPLR 5240 to borrow from the mortgage foreclosure realm and apply to execution sales the rule that the underlying debt will be credited with the market value of the realty sold on the execution, thus reducing the judgment debtor's debt by his actual market equity in the levied premises even though the sale's winning bid was for substantially less.[8]

In cases involving a judgment debtor's tenancy by the entirety of the family residence, applications of CPLR 5240 have been generous, and frequent. In one case, for example, the court held that the judgment creditor could presently do nothing against such premises; that the judgment would be deemed a mere lien against the premises, to be denied any effectuation unless and until the judgment debtor is shown to have outlived his or her spouse, at which point the debtor would take full title and be subject to levy; or the spouses voluntarily sell the property, at which point the judgment could be applied against the debtor spouse's share of the proceeds.[9] In another such case citing CPLR 5240 and the family's needs, the court simply precluded levy against the residence, at least for a time, but on the condition that the judgment debtor pay a specified (and modest) sum monthly towards the judgment.[10] In yet another case, the court precluded levy for a year, directing the judg-

ment creditor to try other enforcement devices in the interim, with leave to seek court permission to re-levy if the others did not work.[11] All of these are judicial acknowledgments that any levy against the family home at the behest of the creditor of only one of the spouses would be an intolerable interference with family life. Cases that take this position (not all do) are in effect creating a de facto exemption for the residence in these situations.

While the courts are sympathetic to situations in which a residence is being levied on, their powers under CPLR 5240 are not unlimited. In one case with much appeal to conscience, for example, in which the judgment debtor was an elderly man with his abandoned 7-year-old granddaughter in his charge, the court noted the age of the judgment (some 9 years) and that no part of it had been paid. It did not cancel the levy against the residence, but stayed it for six months to enable the judgment debtor to find new quarters, with the proviso that $750 per month be paid towards the judgment in the interim.[12]

Other examples of protective orders connected with the execution sale of real property appeared earlier.[13]

After the judgment debtor's property has been duly sold to a bona fide purchaser at an execution sale, the protective order provision of CPLR 5240 may not be used to undo the sale.[14]

The protective order shield has been found to have two sides, occasionally flipping over and protecting the judgment creditor from the judgment debtor's spouse playing fast and loose in a tenancy by the entirety case. In one such case the judgment was for $900 against

5. The notes follow McKinney's CPLR 3103.

6. See Kaplan v. Supak & Sons Mfg. Co., 46 Misc.2d 574, 260 N.Y.S.2d 374 (N.Y.C.Civ.Ct. 1965).

7. 75 Misc.2d 32, 346 N.Y.S.2d 925 (Sup.Ct., Westchester County, 1973).

8. The Third Department has also adopted this position. See § 500 above.

9. See Hammond v. Econo–Car of North Shore, Inc., 71 Misc.2d 546, 336 N.Y.S.2d 493 (Sup.Ct., Nassau County, 1972).

10. Holmes v. W. T. Grant, Inc., 71 Misc.2d 486, 336 N.Y.S.2d 601 (Sup.Ct., Nassau County, 1972).

11. Gilchrist v. Commercial Credit Corp., 66 Misc.2d 791, 322 N.Y.S.2d 200 (Sup.Ct., Nassau County, 1971). Nassau County has had a disproportionate share of prob-

lems with residential properties sold pursuant to small judgments, accounting for a number of cases with protective order steps designed to guard against abuse.

12. Federal Deposit Insurance Co. v. Lapadula, 137 Misc.2d 559, 521 N.Y.S.2d 391 (Sup.Ct., Nassau County, 1987).

13. See § 500.

14. Guardian Loan Co. v. Early, 47 N.Y.2d 515, 419 N.Y.S.2d 56, 392 N.E.2d 1240 (1979). The court stressed the absence of any special equities in the case and added that "mere inadequacy of price" is not by itself ground to set aside the sale.

husband H, which wife W could have altogether removed from even lien effect against the property just by paying the judgment. But she did not. She instead bid $1,000 at the sale but was outbid by X who, when H and W later divorced, became a tenant in common with W, enabling X to bring a partition action against W, which he did. Now W moved, under CPLR 5240, to vacate the old execution sale, pleading unsophistication in legal matters. A tempting plea; she did, after all, bid $1000 at the sale when for $100 less she could have paid off the judgment and avoided the sale altogether. But what she was looking to do was win at the sale, in which case she would have (1) won 100% of the residence and (2) wiped out the liens of all other judgment creditors of H as well.[15] The tacit reaction of the court was that if she was as unsophisticated as she claimed, then the naive shall inherit the earth. The court held that even if CPLR 5240 could go this far, which it doubted, W did not present the equities to deserve it; it denied her motion to undo the sale.[16]

There is also caselaw manifesting that a protective order will not protect a judgment debtor from her own deliberate folly. A spectacular lesson on that front is House v. Lalor.[17] P had a $350 small claims judgment against D, which D, a wealthy woman who despised P, flatly refused to pay. The judgment finally went to enforcement through an execution against a cooperative apartment that D owned, and D ended up losing an equity of $185,000 in the apartment. The big winners were the bidder at the auction and future defendants who could take the *House* case as a warning about what the court described as the "obstinacy" of the defendant in resisting enforcement.

J. CONTEMPT AS BACK–UP DEVICE

Table of Sections

Sec.
523.   Contempt Enforcement of Certain Devices.

15.   CPLR 5236(c), (e), (g). See § 500 above.

16.   Murphy v. Grid Realty Corp., 73 Misc.2d 1071, 343 N.Y.S.2d 670 (Sup.Ct., Nassau County, 1973).

17.   119 Misc.2d 193, 462 N.Y.S.2d 772 (Sup.Ct., N.Y.County, 1983), summarized in New York State Law Digest No. 286.

§ 523. Contempt Enforcement of Certain Devices

Contempt is not available as a direct tool for enforcing the ordinary money judgment. But it does serve as the remedy that gives force to a number of the Article 52 enforcement devices and in so doing becomes by indirection an enforcement remedy for money judgments. CPLR 5251 provides that the following behavior constitutes contempt of court:

1.   Wilful disobedience of one of the CPLR 5224 disclosure subpoenas or false swearing at any examination or in response to any questions;

2.   Wilful disobedience of a CPLR 5222 restraining notice;

3.   Wilfully defacing or removing notices of upcoming sales of property, such as in conjunction with levies and sales of personal property[1] or real property;[2]

4.   Wilful disobedience of any order issued under Article 52, among which would be:

    a.   a delivery order under CPLR 5225 or 5227;

    b.   an installment payment order under CPLR 5226;

    c.   an order directing that property be surrendered to a receiver appointed under CPLR 5228;

    d.   pre-judgment orders directing an examination or restraint under CPLR 5229; and

    e.   a protective order under CPLR 5240.

When an application under CPLR 5225(a) is brought against a judgment debtor, it contemplates an order brought on by motion and the disregard of the order would clearly invoke the contempt penalty under CPLR 5251. A nicer question is whether contempt is available

§ 523

1.   CPLR 5233(b).

2.   CPLR 5236(c).

against a garnishee in connection with a delivery proceeding brought under CPLR 5225(b) or 5227. Against a garnishee or other third person, the delivery device is not a motion culminating in an order, but a special proceeding that culminates in a "judgment".[3] Shall the "order" listed in CPLR 5251 be deemed to embrace the "judgment", so as to subject a recalcitrant garnishee to contempt for a failure to obey a delivery judgment rendered in the special proceeding? Or, indeed, shall these provisions be construed to allow an "order" to be entered against the garnishee, instead of a judgment, and invoke CPLR 5251 that way? The matter is not free from doubt. If the court in the special proceeding renders an ordinary money judgment in favor of the judgment creditor against the garnishee, the judgment will then qualify for all of the Article 52 devices, including those that invoke the contempt remedy. But the court in that proceeding is not restricted to a money judgment alone; sitting as a court of equity, it can apparently make a judgment directing the garnishee to turn over specific property. Disobedience in that case will be a contempt, if not under CPLR 5251, then under the basic contempt provisions of the Judiciary Law.[4] There is authority for holding a garnishee for contempt in conjunction with directions issued under CPLR 5225 and 5227.[5]

Even when clearly available, contempt is not necessarily the exclusive remedy. A judgment creditor suffering damages caused by the disregard of an Article 52 device may in some instances bring a money claim against the one who caused the damages, such as a garnishee bank that permits the judgment debtor to draw from an account in disregard of a restraining notice.[6]

CPLR 5251 merely lists the conduct that will be deemed contemptuous. The procedures for determining and punishing the contempt are to be found, as with any contempt, in the Judiciary Law.[7] Their essentials are set forth in Part I of this chapter,[8] in conjunction with the enforcement of non-money judgments. Contempt is the principal enforcement tool for equitable judgments, for example, and whenever it is properly invoked, whether directly, as for equity judgments, or indirectly, as for the devices enumerated in CPLR 5251 in aid of a money judgment, the same Judiciary Law instructions must be followed. Everything contained in the subchapter on contempt in Part I, therefore, has parallel application here.[9]

Only the courts listed in CPLR 5221(a) have the power to punish for contempt, since those are the courts that can entertain the Article 52 devices listed in CPLR 5251.[10] This excludes the town and village courts. Contempt proceedings in respect of Article 52 devices connected with judgments rendered in those courts should be brought in the supreme court or a county court.[11]

---

3. CPLR 411.

4. See Jud.L. § 753(A)(3).

5. See Carl B. Nusbaum, Inc. v. Calale, 45 Misc.2d 903, 258 N.Y.S.2d 8 (Orange County Ct. 1965). See § 510 above.

6. See Mazzuka v. Bank of North America, 53 Misc.2d 1053, 280 N.Y.S.2d 495 (N.Y.C.Civ.Ct. 1967), and § 508 above.

7. Article 19, §§ 750–781.

8. See § 484 above.

9. See § 481 et seq.

10. See CPLR 5221(b).

11. See § 493 above. With respect to pre-judgment enforcement under CPLR 5229, however, which is authorized for use in all courts (see § 516 above), even these lower courts can be deemed to have the contempt power.

Chapter Nineteen

APPEALS

Analysis

A. INTRODUCTORY

Table of Sections

§ 524. Appeals, Introductory

Three articles of the CPLR govern appeals. Article 57 governs appealability to the appellate division and Article 56 appealability to the Court of Appeals, while Article 55, entitled "Appeals Generally", supplies the procedure and incidentals of the appellate process and determines the scope of review. Especially in appellate practice, however, practitioners can never rely exclusively on the CPLR: it is indispensable that they consult the rules of the particular appellate court concerned. The rules will likely have more to say, at least in regard to the mechanics of the appeal, than the CPLR. Indeed, at several key junctures, after making a rather detailed instruction about procedure, the CPLR casually announces that the appellate divisions can change all of this for their own departments if they wish. We will take note of when they do, and references to court rules in this chapter will be more frequent than encountered elsewhere in our study.

The rules can differ from department to department and from court to court, not only in detail, but also in topic selected for address, thus warning even the practitioner who has troubled to learn well the rules of one court that she cannot safely apply them in another. There are no so-called "Uniform Rules" for the appellate courts, as there are for the trial courts. Lawyers taking an appeal to a court they are not yet familiar with are best advised, not just to check out specific matters as they arise, but to read the court's rules through. It will flag a number of things that may not otherwise come to mind. Once tackled, the rules prove much less forbidding than they seem when first approached.

The rules may be found in the state's Official Compilation of Codes, Rules and Regulations, where they constitute Title 22. They will be cited here either with that identification, abbreviated to NYCRR, or simply as Rule so-and-so. They are found more conveniently in McKinney's "New York Rules of Court" pamphlet, a single soft-cover volume recompiled annually. Our citations will be to the rules of the Court of Appeals and the four appellate divisions, or to illustrative ones among them.

There are other appellate courts of which one must take account, however, when dealing with the lower of the trial courts. In the First and Second departments there are appellate terms, to which go appeals from the New York City Civil Court and the district, city, town, and village courts,[1] and in the Second Department even appeals from the county courts in civil matters.[2] In the Third and Fourth departments the county courts sit as appellate courts over city, town, and village courts. When the appeal is from any of these lower courts, the practitioner's first look should be at Article 17 of the Uniform Court Acts.[3] It will be a brief consultation, but it will advise of what is appealable and where the appeal goes: Article 17 in the lower court acts supplies only a few variants from the ordinary appellate practice contained in Article 55 of the CPLR, which it then adopts in full,[4] so that lawyers will find themselves directed right back to the CPLR and to the rules of court for most of what they need even for the lower reaches of the appellate process. In this connection the lawyer should note that the appellate terms have their own rules,[5] which must be consulted by anyone on the way to one of them.

In the study of appeals, among the first questions to ask is what court the appeal goes to, which is just another way of asking about the subject matter jurisdiction of the appellate courts. We met that in Chapter 2; as each trial court's jurisdiction was studied, reference was included to the appellate path of its judgments and orders. The chart of the court system found there should quickly refresh recollection about which court a given appeal goes to.[6]

The next question to ask is one of venue, which overlaps jurisdiction but which in any

event has a brief answer. If appeal is to the county court, it is of course to that of the lower court's county. If appeal is to an appellate term, the appellate term rules determine which one to go to.[7] Supreme court appeals go to the appellate division of the department in which the judgment or order was entered.[8] It is permissible, however, for that appellate division to send the appeal to another department in furtherance of justice, as when their own rules or administrative orders are being contested in the case and the court wishes to avoid even the appearance of prejudice.[9] This amounts to the court's disqualifying itself. It is not a frequent occurrence.[10]

If an appeal is taken to the wrong court altogether, as where it has been taken to the Court of Appeals when it should have gone to an appellate division, it is simply transferred to the right court.[11] The court to which the appeal is erroneously taken can even effect the transfer sua sponte.[12]

The next question is, what may be appealed? This comes under the heading of "appealability" and is the first major topic to be studied. Asking what may or may not be appealed is just another way of inquiring into the subject matter jurisdiction of the appellate court: when an appellate tribunal dismisses an appeal because the particular judgment or order is not "appealable", it is only announcing that it lacks jurisdiction of the subject matter of the appeal.

We start with study of the first level of appeal, principally appeal from the supreme

---

§ 524

1. Rules 640.1, 730.

2. Rule 730.1.

3. These are the New York City Civil Court Act and the Uniform District, Uniform City, and Uniform Justice (town and village) court acts, found in McKinney's Volume 29A.

4. See § 1703 in each of the four acts, ibid.

5. 22 NYCRR, Parts 640 (First Department), 731 (Second and Eleventh Districts in Second Department), and 732 (Ninth and Tenth Districts in Second Department).

6. See § 9 above.

7. See Rules 640.1 (First Department) and 730.1 (Second Department).

8. An exception is the order changing venue in a supreme court action, where appeal is to the department

in which the motion was heard and determined despite the entry of the order in the transferee county. CPLR 511(d).

9. CPLR 5711.

10. To relieve congestion in the appellate division of the overworked Second Department, some of the appeals to it may be sent to other departments. See "Outside Counsel", New York Law Journal, April 23, 1990, page 1, noting the choice of law issues that can arise in transferred cases. Whether such a detour applies in a given case at a given time is a matter of current practice for which inquiry can be made of the clerk.

11. N.Y.Const.Art. VI, § 5(b).

12. See, e.g., Biggs v. Town of Huntington, 35 N.Y.2d 904, 364 N.Y.S.2d 895 (1974).

court to the appellate division, in the course of which we readily integrate appeals from lower courts to their appropriate appellate courts because by adoption in the lower court acts, appealability has been made parallel with that of supreme court judgments and orders. Here the lawyer will note how much broader appealability is in the New York system than in the federal courts. We then take up the appeal to the New York Court of Appeals, which is narrower than the appellate division appeal not only as to what may be appealed, "appealability", but also as to what the court may review. "Reviewability", or "scope of review", is the next topic in line, followed by the mechanics of taking, perfecting, concluding, and implementing the appeal and its determination.

In New York, the general rule is that the only thing that may be appealed is a "judgment" or an "order".[13] There may be no appeal from a decision, verdict, report, opinion, ruling, or anything else but a "judgment" or an "order", which admonishes the lawyer to have whatever it is that aggrieves her reduced to either the one or the other, as may be appropriate.[14] Nor will it avail to label as a judgment or order something not formally that, such as a judge's memorandum.[15] If a court rule makes a given disposition the equivalent of an order, however, it may be appealed, as has been held, for example, with the transcript of a preliminary conference.[16]

Appeal from a court of original instance is of course from the judgment or order entered with its clerk. Appeal from an appellate court is from the appellate court's order, entered in the office of its clerk, not from any judgment or order that the lower court may ministerially enter on the appellate order afterwards upon remand, a requirement that clarifies the obligation of the appellant and avoids confusion about which paper gets appealed. Mistakes in this regard are supposedly remediable, anyway.[17]

As a general rule, an appeal cannot be taken before the appealable paper has been formally entered.[18] An appeal taken before entry, although otherwise ripe, is at worst premature, and the defect is one that the appellate court can ignore.[19] It can treat the notice of appeal from a decision "as a premature notice of appeal from an order", but the court should be convinced that the interests of justice warrant this generosity.[20] It is ordinarily so simple to get an order entered on a decision already made that some special reason should be cited to the court to invoke this power. If any difficulty should arise, a motion can be made to either the original or the appellate court to compel both entry and the filing of the papers on which the order was based.[21] This may become necessary for an ex parte order, for example, one made out of court and whose papers have not yet been channeled back to the courthouse.

An ex parte order cannot be appealed directly; the procedure for the aggrieved party is to move on notice to vacate the order and then, if the motion is denied, appeal the order of denial. But even for that purpose it may be neces-

---

13. CPLR 5512(a).

14. In a few narrow instances, statutes purport to allow an appeal to be taken from the "determination" of an administrative agency or the "award" of an arbitration panel, but this should not be confused with the more common path of judicial review of agency action, which starts with an Article 78 proceeding in the supreme court, see § 557 et seq., culminating in a fully appealable "judgment", CPLR 7806, or with the more limited review of an arbitration award. The statutes that purport to make such a "determination" or "award" appealable to the Court of Appeals—CPLR 5601(d), 5602(a)(1)(ii), and 5602(b)(2)(ii)—are also of questionable constitutional validity, since there appears to be nothing in the relevant part of the state constitution, § 3 of Article VI, to support such an appeal.

15. See Matter of Lynn's Estate, 22 A.D.2d 810, 254 N.Y.S.2d 771 (2d Dep't 1964).

16. See, e.g., Herbert v. City of New York, 126 A.D.2d 404, 510 N.Y.S.2d 112 (1st Dep't 1987).

17. See CPLR 5512(a). Timeliness, however, is measured from the appellate order, not the lower court one, and CPLR 5512(a) in this regard may be something of a trap. See § 553 below.

18. The time in which to appeal, which generally runs not from entry but from the later moment when the appellant is served with notice of the entry, CPLR 5513, is treated in detail later. See § 533.

19. CPLR 5520(c).

20. See, e.g., Scott v. Vassar Brothers Hospital, 133 A.D.2d 76, 518 N.Y.S.2d 422 (2d Dep't 1987).

21. CPLR 5512(b).

sary to get the ex parte order onto the clerk's records and its underlying papers into the court's files.

§ 525. "Aggrieved" Party

Only an "aggrieved" party, or one duly substituted in place of an aggrieved party,[1] may appeal the judgment or order.[2] The word has posed problems, but the revisors retained it for inability to find a better one, leaving its resolution to caselaw.[3] Its basic purpose, of course, is to assure that no one with a mere academic interest in the outcome, or with no interest at all, will be allowed status to appeal.

One must be aggrieved in some real sense in order to be an appellant. Where, for example, an original answer has been superseded by an amended one, an order directed to the original one becomes irrelevant and an appeal from it will be disallowed[4] because no one can be aggrieved by an irrelevancy. The issue can become a good deal more complex, however, and an attorney with any doubt about the client's aggrievement in this appellate sense would do well to check the annotations under CPLR 5511, the statute that requires the aggrieved status.

Lack of aggrievement is what precludes appeal from a judgment or order entered upon a default. The party does not become aggrieved until she has moved to vacate the default and the motion has been denied, and it is therefore the order on that motion that becomes the appealable paper. If there has been a contest on the question of damages, however, even though liability has been established through a default, appeal does lie from the contested damages result (the inquest),[5] which is consistent with the prevalent rule that it takes a contest to generate aggrievement.

One agreeing to a judgment cannot be aggrieved by it, for which reason a consent judgment is also a nonappealable one.[6] But again, accepting a judgment that includes a favorable determination on an issue of liability will not preclude the victorious plaintiff from securing review of the sum awarded if he contends that he was entitled to more; nor will appeal be precluded even by his accepting payment of the lower sum as long as objections to it have been duly preserved.[7] This is merely an example of where a party, although winning the case, has not prevailed on every part of it. If the part with respect to which the otherwise victorious party lost can in a practical sense be regarded as affecting a substantial right, the party can be accorded "aggrieved" status notwithstanding that the overall victory in the case was his. That happens from time to time not only in regard to the damages element, but as to liability as well, as in the matrimonial area when important rights may depend on the particular ground on which a divorce or separation is granted.[8]

A prevailing party should be alert to such a situation. Having won below, her reasonable expectation is that if anyone appeals it should be the loser. But if the loser does appeal, the winner's further assumption may be that she can accomplish whatever she has to just by opposing the loser's appeal. That is often the case, but not always so. If the respondent, the overall winner who is opposing the appeal,[9] asked for any kind of affirmative relief below and was denied it, she should herself consider taking an appeal or a cross-appeal in respect of the denial.

Suppose, for example, that P and D each allege that the other breached the same contract and each seeks damages, D by way of counterclaim. If the judgment denies both of

§ 525

1. See § 184 et seq., above.

2. CPLR 5511.

3. See 2d Rep.Leg.Doc. (1958) No. 13, p. 321.

4. See, e.g., Oceancrest Homes, Inc. v. Golfbay Country Club, Inc., 2 A.D.2d 756, 153 N.Y.S.2d 331 (2d Dep't 1956).

5. James v. Powell, 19 N.Y.2d 249, 279 N.Y.S.2d 10, 225 N.E.2d 741 (1967).

6. See City Bank Farmers Trust Co. v. Macfadden, 13 A.D.2d 395, 216 N.Y.S.2d 215 (1st Dep't 1961), aff'd 12 N.Y.2d 1035, 239 N.Y.S.2d 680, 190 N.E.2d 24, cert. den. 375 U.S. 823, 84 S.Ct. 63, 11 L.Ed.2d 56 (1963).

7. See Cornell v. T. V. Dev. Corp., 17 N.Y.2d 69, 268 N.Y.S.2d 29, 215 N.E.2d 349 (1966).

8. See, e.g., Becker v. Becker, 36 N.Y.2d 787, 369 N.Y.S.2d 697, 330 N.E.2d 646 (1975).

9. CPLR 5511.

them damages, D's opposition to P's appeal, although it will entitle him to show everything relevant to support a denial of damages to P, will not necessarily earn D appellate review of the denial of the damages D sought on the counterclaim. That would be affirmative relief, and the party who seeks it should, notwithstanding that it was his adversary's initiative that produced the appeal, independently appeal the judgment or order, or the aspect of it that denied the affirmative relief sought.[10] This does not mean two appeals or two records or double expense. It usually means only serving a notice of cross-appeal after receiving the other side's notice of appeal, the record to contain copies of both, and the briefs to address both issues.[11]

A controversy may become moot or academic while the case is pending on appeal, such as where the time for the implementation of the particular appellant's right has now passed or the status from which her interest springs has changed, or for any of a number of other reasons. New York takes a realistic view of whether to allow the appeal to proceed in such a situation, allowing it when "the controversy is of a character which is likely to recur not only with respect to the parties before the court but with respect to others as well."[12] The precedential impact of a decision, in other words, may be a reason for letting the appeal go through. If the appellant or some other party has lost interest, and refrains from strong advocacy or from any at all, this is something to be considered. But in cases of public interest it often happens that others have applied for and been granted leave to file briefs amicus curiae.[13] If the court feels that these adequately assure adversary representation on the appeal, it can continue the appeal regardless of the original party's lost enthusiasm.

B. APPEALABILITY

Table of Sections

§ 526.   Appeals to Appellate Division

CPLR 5701 is the key section here, determining which judgments and orders of the supreme court or county courts may be appealed,[1] which are appealable as of right, and which need permission. Few need permission. By adoption, CPLR 5701 also determines what may be appealed from a surrogate's court to an appellate division,[2] and from the New York City Civil Court and the district, city, town, and village courts to their respective appellate courts.[3] Court of claims appeals go to the local appellate division.[4] Appeals from the family court are governed by the Family Court Act.[5]

---

10.   See, e.g., City of Rye v. Public Serv. Mut. Ins. Co., 34 N.Y.2d 470, 358 N.Y.S.2d 391, 315 N.E.2d 458 (1974).

11.   CPLR 5513(b). See § 533 below.

12.   East Meadow Community Concerts Ass'n v. Board of Education of Union Free School District No. 3, 18 N.Y.2d 129, 135, 272 N.Y.S.2d 341, 346, 219 N.E.2d 172, 175 (1966).

13.   Amicus curiae means friend of the court and denotes the situation in which a nonparty with an interest in the case wishes to argue and support a particular side. The nonparty moves the appellate court for leave to file a brief amicus curiae. Whether to grant it is in the court's discretion, and usually depends on how much additional education the court believes it can draw from the amici. If the court feels that all sides are already represented in full, it will deny leave.

§ 526

1.   Appeals from the county courts in civil matters in the Second Department go to an appellate term instead of the appellate division. N.Y.Const., Art. VI, § 8(d); 22 NYCRR § 730.1. Elsewhere they go to the appellate division.

2.   See SCPA 2701, also providing that the "decree" of a surrogate is to be deemed a "judgment" for appellate purposes.

3.   Section 1702 in the New York City Civil Court Act and in the Uniform District, City, and Justice (town and village) court acts is just a tailored version of CPLR 5701, mildly altered to fit the lower courts.

4.   See Ct.Cl.Act § 24. Before 1978, the Third Department processed court of claims appeals arising in the First and Second departments (a calendar management and distribution measure).

5.   See Fam.Ct.Act Article 11.

CPLR 5701 has a number of parts, which should be taken up seriatim.

First, the appealability of judgments. Paragraph 1 of subdivision (a) of CPLR 5701 makes all judgments appealable, whether final or interlocutory, unless the judgment is only a ministerial one being entered on an appellate order that has already disposed of all issues in the action.[6] What judgments are "final" for appeal purposes is a question more often met on appeal to the Court of Appeals and is discussed there.[7]

An example of an interlocutory judgment would be one entered upon a finding of liability in a split ("bifurcated") personal injury trial, damages issues having been held in abeyance for separate trial later, if warranted.[8] By appellate invitation, in fact, trial judges have been using the interlocutory judgment as a kind of appeal-control tool: the liability phase is separately appealable only if the trial judge authorizes the entry of an interlocutory judgment on it. If the judge finds no reason for delay and wants the damages phase to go forward immediately, the judge merely refuses to permit entry of an interlocutory judgment and thereby forecloses a separate appeal.[9]

The appealability of orders, as opposed to judgments, is governed by paragraph 2 of subdivision (a). It is here that New York is unique in its generosity, making a broad range of nonfinal—or "intermediate" or "interlocutory"—orders immediately appealable without waiting for final judgment. Many need not be appealed immediately, but can be saved and later reviewed as part of an appeal from the final judgment.[10] But if the appellate calendars are any gauge, this waiting alternative is little exploited and does not in significant measure discourage immediate and separate appeals from intermediate orders. These are a significant part of appellate division calendars and place New York at the opposite end of the spectrum from federal practice. Although federal practice, like New York's, allows appeal from final dispositions,[11] an appeal from an interlocutory order in federal practice is rarely allowed, in contrast with the unusually generous New York attitude. In the federal courts, precious few nonfinal orders can be appealed as a matter of right,[12] most notable among them applications connected with injunctions;[13] in the New York courts precious few cannot be. Setting the New York statute down verbatim will manifest the provisions that account for this broad appealability. CPLR 5701(a)(2) provides that an order in New York is appealable if it:

(i) grants, refuses, continues, or modifies a provisional remedy; or

(ii) settles, grants or refuses an application to resettle a transcript or statement on appeal; or

(iii) grants or refuses a new trial; except where specific questions of fact arising upon the issues in an action triable by the court have been tried by a jury, pursuant to an order for that purpose, and the order grants or refuses a new trial upon the merits; or

(iv) involves some part of the merits; or

(v) affects a substantial right; or

(vi) in effect determines the action and prevents a judgment from which an appeal might be taken; or

---

6. Further appeal, if sought in that instance, is taken from the appellate order rather than from a judgment entered on it in the lower court on remand. See CPLR 5611.

7. See § 527 below. The question of finality is quite unimportant at the first level of appeal (to the appellate division, an appellate term, or a county court) because even if the determination is not final, as will be seen shortly, the order embodying it is likely to be appealable anyway, final or not, which is not so at Court of Appeals level.

8. The bifurcated trial is the subject of § 130 above.

9. See Jack Parker Constr. Corp. v. Williams, 35 A.D.2d 839, 317 N.Y.S.2d 911 (2d Dep't 1970). A major

treatment of when and whether to allow such an interlocutory judgment appears in Bank of N.Y. v. Ansonia Assocs., 172 Misc.2d 70, 656 N.Y.S.2d 813 (Sup.Ct., N.Y.County, 1997), noted in SPR 69:3.

10. See § 530, below, on scope of review.

11. See 28 U.S.C.A. § 1291.

12. See § 642 below (Practitioner's Edition).

13. See 28 U.S.C.A. § 1292(a). Subdivision (b) of that section sets up a procedure whereby the district judge can set the stage for interlocutory appeal of other orders in certain instances. Rule 54(b) of the Federal Rules of Civil Procedure has a like mission in cases involving multiple claims or parties. See § 642 below (Practitioner's Edition).

(vii) determines a statutory provision of the state to be unconstitutional, and the determination appears from the reasons given for the decision or is necessarily implied in the decision. . . .

The culprits are obviously subparagraphs (iv) and (v) on this list, which authorize appeal if the order involves any part of the "merits", or even if it does not involve the merits at all but just affects some "substantial right". These two act like enormous magnets, overlapping the other listed grounds, making some if not all of them superfluous, and drawing in so much that it is futile even to start a list of orders included. It is easier to set forth a few that have been found to escape these bountiful standards, and in the relatively uncommon instance when such an escapee is identified we have the anomaly of a party troubling to appeal an order only to be told by the appellate court that his "right", which has prompted the appeal, is not "substantial".

The courts have held that these standards, open-hearted though they are, do not include an order continuing an examination before trial,[14] or rulings in connection with questions at the examination itself, even if reduced to an order.[15] The same is true, of course, of mere "rulings" during the trial.[16] It was said in Brown v. Micheletti[17] that

> Generally, decisions made by the court during the course of a trial of an action are deemed trial rulings, not orders, whether or not they are reduced to a writing in the form specified for orders. . . .[18]

An order denying a motion to resettle a prior order has been held unappealable.[19] So have orders directing the immediate trial of an issue of fact arising on a motion[20] or referring the issue of fact to a referee to hear and report.[21] But the rule is not invariable: when the issues were found "serious" and in need of a "lengthy hearing", appeal from the reference order was allowed.[22] Are any of these rights insubstantial?

It has been held that an order granting or denying a motion to dismiss a complaint at or after trial, or for judgment at that time, is not appealable,[23] perhaps because the motion was oral or perhaps because it embodies a mere "ruling". Sometimes the holding of non-appealability is even accompanied by the statement that no "substantial right" is involved.[24] If the situation is one in which the court's "ruling" would set the stage for a final judgment, as where it denies a motion to overturn a verdict or dismiss a complaint after the plaintiff has just won, the judgment can be promptly entered and appealed and there is no reason why time need be wasted on entering a mere "order" to embody the ruling. But if that's not the case, it is difficult to understand why an order granting or denying a motion to dismiss a complaint, or a motion for judgment, does not involve a "substantial right", especially in light of how many less significant orders have been held to.

The holdings that deny appealability are at best erratic, perhaps describable as just an occasional effort by the appellate courts to protect their calendars from the pair of vul-

---

14. See Alterman v. Maimonides Hosp., 25 A.D.2d 864, 270 N.Y.S.2d 134 (2d Dep't 1966).

15. See Kaplan v. State of New York, 36 A.D.2d 655, 318 N.Y.S.2d 127 (3d Dep't 1971).

16. See Matter of Leo T., 87 A.D.2d 297, 451 N.Y.S.2d 147 (1st Dep't 1982).

17. 97 A.D.2d 529, 468 N.Y.S.2d 160 (2d Dep't 1983).

18. This has been held to apply to pretrial evidentiary rulings as well. "It is well settled", said Maguire v. Rebaglia, 232 A.D.2d 380, 648 N.Y.S.2d 142 (2d Dep't 1996), in dismissing an appeal, "that no appeal lies from an order adjudicating [even] in advance of trial the admissibility of evidence."

19. Balboa Ins. Co. v. Herbin, 50 A.D.2d 526, 375 N.Y.S.2d 7 (1st Dep't 1975). The appealability of orders on

motions to reargue or renew was discussed earlier. See § 254.

20. Bagdy v. Progresso Foods Corp., 86 A.D.2d 589, 446 N.Y.S.2d 137 (2d Dep't 1982).

21. Stern v. Stern, 24 A.D.2d 489, 260 N.Y.S.2d 810 (2d Dep't 1965).

22. See Stowell v. Berstyn, 26 A.D.2d 828, 274 N.Y.S.2d 120 (2d Dep't 1966).

23. Tribolati v. Lippman, 24 A.D.2d 769, 264 N.Y.S.2d 6 (2d Dep't 1965).

24. See, e.g., Covell v. H. R. H. Constr. Corp., 24 A.D.2d 566, 262 N.Y.S.2d 370 (2d Dep't 1965), aff'd 17 N.Y.2d 709, 269 N.Y.S.2d 718, 216 N.E.2d 710 (1966).

tures that occupy subparagraphs (iv) and (v) of CPLR 5701(a)(2).

Appeals from temporary alimony orders in matrimonial actions, while allowable, are not encouraged; the courts prefer that the case be tried promptly.[25] At least part of the rationale for this is that appellate review of merely temporary findings is idle since the temporary findings, with or without an appellate imprimatur, do not bind the trial judge who must later make permanent findings.[26]

All of the appealable orders generously embraced in paragraph 2 of CPLR 5701(a) are the result of motions made on notice. When the order results from a motion made without notice, it is not appealable under paragraph 2. In that instance paragraph 3 of CPLR 5701(a) governs. It contemplates that the party aggrieved by the ex parte order will move, on notice, to vacate or modify it, and it allows an appeal from the order disposing of that motion.[27] This is no problem as long as there is an adverse party—someone on whom to serve the notice to vacate or modify. But what happens when there is none, when the proceeding at trial level is one of those rare ones that involve no adverse party and envision only an ex parte application for the particular relief?

A change of name proceeding is an example.[28] It has no adverse party. The appealability problem of course becomes academic as long as the court grants the relief sought (in the present example, a change of name). But if the court refuses and review is sought from an appellate court, the petitioner bumps into the two-sided problem that (1) no appeal lies from an ex parte determination and (2) there is no one to serve with a notice of motion to vacate

the ex parte disposition so as to produce an appealable order. There may still be some routes up, but the courts are presently in conflict about where they lie.[29]

Subdivision (c) of CPLR 5701 provides that any order not appealable as of right may be appealed by permission of the judge who made the order, or, if the judge refuses, by a judge or justice of the appellate court. The latter may also be applied to directly, without application to the judge who made the order.[30] Orders expressly falling into the permission-needed category are those made in the course of an Article 78 proceeding[31] and those granting or denying corrective motions made against pleadings under CPLR 3024, like the motion for a more definite statement and the motion to strike scandalous or prejudicial matter.[32] Were these few not specified, one would be hard pressed to find gainful employment for subdivision (c).

The subdivision allows a motion for leave to appeal from any order not appealable of right under subdivision (a). But before the stage is set for this motion, the order must be shown to be one that neither involves the merits nor affects a substantial right—else it would be appealable as a matter of right—and what chance has an order like that to get the court to exercise its discretion and turn on the appellate machinery voluntarily? It's like asking a judge to allow an appeal because of the established unimportance of the issue. Subdivision (c) was originally devised to accompany a scheme that was planned to be more restrictive of appeals as of right, which would have left a handsome residuum of orders for which it would be worthwhile to seek leave.[33] But

---

25. See, e.g., Goldstein v. Goldstein, 35 A.D.2d 777, 317 N.Y.S.2d 77 (4th Dep't 1970).

26. See § 448, above, in the Res Judicata chapter.

27. These appellate steps should not be confused with the procedure whereby an ex parte motion may be made directly to the appellate court, and sometimes to but one of its judges, for ex parte relief in certain instances under CPLR 5704. That direct procedure, usually more expeditious and less expensive than an appeal, is discussed in the earlier chapter on motion practice. See § 244 above.

28. See Civil Rights Law § 60 et seq.

29. See Matter of Joint Diseases North General Hospital, 148 A.D.2d 873, 539 N.Y.S.2d 511 (3d Dep't 1989). The

problem is the subject of a two-part treatment in the lead notes in New York State Law Digests Nos. 356 and 357.

30. Section 1702(c) of the New York City Civil Court Act and of the Uniform District, City, and Justice court acts, McKinney's Vol. 29A, Parts 2 and 3, is to the same effect.

31. CPLR 5701(b)(1). Article 78 is studied later. See § 557 et seq.

32. CPLR 5701(b)(2), (3). These motions are treated in § 230 above.

33. See 2d Rep.Leg.Doc. (1958) No. 13, pp. 117–19.

that proposal was rejected and appealability as of right was restored in full measure, leaving subdivision (c), which was not recast, with little role.

Appeal by permission, in fact, is an altogether rare procedure at the first appellate level, i.e., on appeal from a court of original jurisdiction. It becomes a frequent and important device at the second level. Appeal to the Court of Appeals, for example, requires leave not in just a few instances, but in most instances, a subject we get to in the next section. And an appeal to the appellate division from another appellate court sometimes requires leave, as when the appeal is sought from an order of an appellate term. The leave in that instance is sought from the appellate term or, if refused there, from the appellate division.[34]

When the appeal is from an order of a county court sitting as an appellate tribunal, such as on an appeal from a city, town, or village court disposition,[35] subdivision (b) of CPLR 5703 governs and the appeal to the appellate division may be taken of right.[36] This provision has given rise to some bizarre caselaw, generated by too literal a construction of the statutory language. The statute is addressed to an appeal of a county court order rendered after reviewing a lower court "judgment". The Third and Fourth departments—the only ones that exploit this appellate aspect of county court jurisdiction (the other two use appellate terms)—agree that "judgment" does not include "order". This means that when the county court has reviewed a mere order of the lower court, further appeal of right to the appellate division is barred. The Third Department allows a motion for leave to appeal in that situation, however,[37] while the Fourth Department bars even that.[38] This led to an anomaly, and a patent injustice, in Ellingsworth v. City of Watertown,[39] causing CPLR 5703(b) to do what it was never intended to: make the county court a court of last resort.

P in *Ellingsworth* sued D in a city court, which denied D's dismissal motion in an order that was of course not final. It was appealable to the county court, however, and D took the appeal. The county court reversed and dismissed the action, producing an order that now amounted to a final disposition. That county court order should have been appealable to the appellate division because it was in every sense final, putting an end to the case. But it was held not to be appealable because what it disposed of was a city court *order*, not a city court *judgment*.[40]

When permission is required, the criteria for determining whether to grant it are left to the discretion of the tribunal applied to. Influential ingredients that help tilt that discretion include the precedential impact of the point involved, the public nature of the case, the newness of the issue, and the fact that the decision below may be in conflict with decisions of other lower courts.[41] The grant of leave may be conditional. It can require, for example, that a moving defendant post security to pay the judgment in the event of an affirmance.[42]

§ 527. Appeals to Court of Appeals as of Right

Appealability to the Court of Appeals is narrower and more complex than to the appellate division. Finality plays a larger role, and so does the appeal by permission. There are conditions and qualifications, especially on appeals by permission, which sometimes require several references back and forth between

34. So provides subdivision (a) of CPLR 5703. This provision also requires a stipulation for judgment absolute in certain cases, a procedure more often met in conjunction with an appeal to the Court of Appeals and reserved for treatment there. See § 527.

35. See Unif.Justice Ct. Act § 1701.

36. The same is provided when a Special Term sits as an appellate court today, which it rarely does.

37. Cammarota v. Bella Vista Development Corp., 88 A.D.2d 703, 451 N.Y.S.2d 309 (3d Dep't 1982).

38. Gastel v. Bridges, 110 A.D.2d 146, 493 N.Y.S.2d 674 (1985).

39. 113 A.D.2d 1013, 494 N.Y.S.2d 587 (4th Dep't 1985).

40. These results are further discussed in the Commentaries on McKinney's CPLR 5703.

41. See Handy v. Butler, 183 App.Div. 359, 169 N.Y.S. 770 (2d Dep't 1918).

42. Rosenberg v. Rosenberg, 24 A.D.2d 26, 263 N.Y.S.2d 586 (1st Dep't 1965).

CPLR sections; lawyers may feel themselves running out of fingers as they try to mark places while flipping pages.

Some of the restrictions are built into the constitution itself.[1] It will be best to study the applicable provisions in the order of their CPLR appearance, promptly making whatever cross-references are needed and explaining what they accomplish. For this reason the reader in search of a quick perspective on Court of Appeals jurisdiction, which is governed by Article 56 of the CPLR, may find it helpful to have a copy of the CPLR handy during the ensuing treatment.

CPLR 5601 governs appeals as of right— appeals that involve no preliminary leave of any court. Subdivision (a) controls when an order of the appellate division finally determines an action originating in the supreme court, a county court, surrogate's court, family court, court of claims, or administrative agency. The order is appealable as of right to the Court of Appeals only "where there is a dissent by at least two justices on a question of law" in favor of the appellant. This is all that is left after a 1985 amendment of subdivision (a). Before the amendment, appeal of right was allowed when only one justice dissented, and, even when the decision was unanimous, it was allowed whenever the decision itself was one of reversal or modification. Generally speaking, a unanimous affirmance by the appellate division was the only disposition not appealable of right under subdivision (a). Now no unanimous decision is. It requires permission, as we shall see in the next section. An exception is where a construction of the New York or federal constitution is directly involved, in which case even a unanimous decision is appealable of right.[2]

The mere existence of a 3–2 disagreement among the appellate division on an undecisive issue, or even the presence of an opinion concurred in by two justices and formally denominated a "dissent", does not assure an appeal of right under subdivision (a). The posture of the dissent must be such as would turn the case the appellant's way. Suppose, for example, that an action has been dismissed on two grounds. On appeal, the appellate division affirms with two dissenters who disagree about ground one but who support the dismissal on ground two. Since they would also dismiss, their dissent would not be "in favor of" the appellant and hence would not support an appeal of right.[3] In this situation, although they may style their position a "dissent", they are in essence concurring in the result.

Cases originating in courts other than those listed in CPLR 5601(a), as enumerated above, do not reach the Court of Appeals as of right. Their first-tier appeals go to appellate courts below the appellate division, presently to either an appellate term or to a county court, and only a further appeal goes to the appellate division.[4] If the case is then to go to the Court of Appeals, which would mean a third appellate step, it needs leave from the appellate division.[5] If it doesn't get leave, that's usually the end of the line. It means in effect that for most of the state's lower courts the appellate division serves as the court of last resort.

Superseding the above is the appeal from a trial-level final judgment if the appeal presents only the question of the validity of a New York or federal statute under the New York or federal constitution. Here the appeal not only lies of right; it also by-passes all intermediate appellate courts and goes directly to the Court of Appeals from the court of original jurisdiction.[6] An example is the case that determined the constitutionality of New York's no-fault statute, which went directly from the supreme

§ 527

1. Court of Appeals jurisdiction is covered by N.Y.Const. Art. VI, § 3.

2. See CPLR 5601(b)(1).

3. See Christavao v. Unisul–Uniao de Coop. Transf. de Tomate Do Sul Do Tejo, S.C.R.L., 41 N.Y.2d 338, 392 N.Y.S.2d 609, 360 N.E.2d 1309 (1977).

4. CPLR 5703. Subdivision (a) of CPLR 5703 governs appeals from an appellate term, which require leave. Sub-

division (b) governs appeals from other appellate courts, mainly a county court sitting as such, but there an appeal to the appellate division lies as of right.

5. CPLR 5602(b)(2).

6. CPLR 5601(b)(2). The statute applies only to a court "of record", an arbitrary distinction today that excludes only the town and village courts. See Jud.L. § 2.

court to the Court of Appeals.[7] To take advantage of this direct appeal route, the constitutional question must be "substantial",[8] the Court of Appeals of course being the ultimate judge of that. And it must be the only question presented on the appeal; the Court of Appeals cannot consider anything else.[9] If the issue is insubstantial, or if the appeal adds any other question, it does not lie to the Court of Appeals at all and if taken there it will be transferred to where it belongs.[10]

A word is in order about what "final" means. It has usually been given a pragmatic interpretation, meaning a judgment or order that puts an end to the case, or to a logically separable part of it, and leaves nothing else in respect of it to be decided. We will cite a few examples, but a practitioner with any doubt should check the annotations.

An appellate division order granting summary judgment on only one of several claims is final as to that one, allowing appeal as to it but not as to the other claims still left standing.[11] Similarly, the dismissal of a counterclaim is final even if the main claim remains to be tried, and in instances like these the dismissed claim, if not actually severed, may be deemed so in order to set the stage for its appeal.

This is sometimes known as the doctrine of implied severance, but it should be relied on only when the counterclaim is completely independent of the main claim.[12] Earlier indications of a less stringent attitude[13] are inappropriate to rely on today, especially after the Court of Appeals decision in Burke v. Crosson,[14] which reviews and adjusts the "implied severance" rule to make it depend entirely on the relatedness of the claims involved. When

some but not all claims are resolved, holds *Burke*, an implied severance will be deemed to occur

> only if the causes of action [that are resolved] do not arise out of the same transaction or continuum of facts or out of the same legal relationship as the unresolved causes of action.

If they do arise out of the same transaction, an implied severance will presumably not occur, barring an appeal until the unresolved matters also go to final judgment.[15]

An order denying a stay of arbitration, in effect compelling arbitration and thus taking the dispute out of the court system, is, as far as the courts are concerned, final and may be treated as such for appellate purposes.[16] Indeed, even a disposition denying arbitration and thus retaining the case in court may be final enough for this appellate purpose if the disposition about arbitrability is made in a special proceeding, as most such dispositions are, instead of in the context of an action.[17] The special proceeding is an independent one, and its disposition, whether for or against arbitration, is usually embodied in a judgment terminating the proceeding and therefore "final" in that context.[18]

When finality is required for the appeal, as it is in the instances discussed so far, the paper that disposes of the issues is the one to be appealed. Thus, when an order of the appellate division is the final one and leaves nothing further to be decided below, the appeal should be taken from the appellate division order and not from any judgment or order afterwards entered on it in the original court. So provides CPLR 5611, which also recognizes that the

7. Montgomery v. Daniels, 38 N.Y.2d 41, 378 N.Y.S.2d 1, 340 N.E.2d 444 (1975).

8. See, e.g., Gerzof v. Gulotta, 40 N.Y.2d 825, 387 N.Y.S.2d 568, 355 N.E.2d 797 (1976).

9. N.Y.Const. Art. VI, § 3(b)(2).

10. See Merced v. Fisher, 38 N.Y.2d 557, 381 N.Y.S.2d 817, 345 N.E.2d 288 (1976).

11. See Northern Operating Corp. v. Town of Ramapo, 26 N.Y.2d 404, 311 N.Y.S.2d 286, 259 N.E.2d 723 (1970).

12. See Lizza Industries, Inc. v. Long Island Lighting Co., 36 N.Y.2d 754, 368 N.Y.S.2d 830, 329 N.E.2d 664 (1975).

13. See Sirlin Plumbing Co. v. Maple Hill Homes, Inc., 20 N.Y.2d 401, 283 N.Y.S.2d 489, 230 N.E.2d 394 (1967).

14. 85 N.Y.2d 10, 623 N.Y.S.2d 524, 647 N.E.2d 736 (1995).

15. The Burke case is treated in the lead note in New York State Law Digest No. 424.

16. Wilaka Constr. Co. v. New York City Housing Auth., 17 N.Y.2d 195, 269 N.Y.S.2d 697, 216 N.E.2d 696 (1966).

17. See § 591 below.

18. CPLR 411. Special proceedings are treated in detail in Chapter 20 below.

order may be final but with a condition imposed whereby finality can be defeated, such as an order dismissing a complaint with leave to replead within a specified time. In such an instance, the order is not to be deemed "final" until the time for doing the conditional act passes without the act's being done. Doing the act, of course, such as by repleading in the example, divests the order of its finality.

In additur and remittitur situations—situations in which the court below has raised or lowered a verdict in response to a party's contention that the amount awarded was either too little (additur) or too much (remittitur)[19]—a variety of steps may follow, involving the parties, the trial court, and the appellate division. These variations can seriously complicate the issue of what follow-up event is the "final" one that can set the stage for Court of Appeals review. Recognizing these difficulties in Whitfield v. City of New York,[20] the Court outlines several scenarios and endeavors to pinpoint in each of them the step that constitutes the "final" one needed for an appeal (or a motion for leave when leave is required) to the Court of Appeals. Despite the court's best efforts at clarification in *Whitfield*, however, there may still be confusion about which disposition is the properly appealable one in a given situation. Perhaps the only safe rule for a party bent on appealing to follow in these and yet other multi-paper situations in appellate practice generally and Court of Appeals practice especially is to appeal everything in sight as often as need be.[21]

A few nonfinal dispositions are appealable as of right to the Court of Appeals. The most infamous and deadly of these is the often misunderstood "stipulation for judgment absolute" supplied by CPLR 5601(c). It is relevant when the appellate division grants a new trial, or affirms an order granting a new trial, in a case originating in any of the five courts listed earlier in this section (supreme, county, surrogate's and family courts, and the court of claims) or in an administrative agency. The

party who won the judgment at trial wants to keep it, and would therefore like to overturn the appellate division order that grants the new trial. But such an order is not final and thus not appealable as of right. It has been made so, however, by CPLR 5601(c), but with the proviso that the appellant stipulate that in the event of affirmance, "judgment absolute shall be entered against him". This means that if the Court of Appeals finds the appellate division to be within its powers in granting a new trial, and hence affirms the order granting it, it will not mean a new trial at all; it will mean that the appellant has lost everything: the trial court judgment that the appellant wanted to reinstate as well as the second chance (the new trial) that the appellate division had offered.

This is a dangerous procedure which an appellant should not use unless the appeal presents only questions of law and not a breath of appellate division discretion, and few appellants of such a mind can be sure the Court of Appeals will see the case in the same light. Since appellate division discretion in ordering a new trial is vast, an appellant should not test it with CPLR 5601(c), which is a CPLR version of Russian Roulette. All the Court of Appeals has to do is find that the appellate division has acted anywhere within the nearly unlimited confines of its discretion in granting a new trial, and the lightning will strike.

Appellate lawyers who have made the mistake of using this device, or who (more likely) have been frantically retained of counsel by others, should consider asking opposing counsel to stipulate to withdraw the appeal altogether. Absent cooperation from the other side, the appellant can move the Court of Appeals to let it withdraw the stipulation (in effect asking that its own appeal be dismissed, and with good riddance). The motion will likely be granted, but the Court may impose costs as a condition.[22] It is also advisable to make

---

19. Additur and remittitur are the subject of § 407 above.

20. 90 N.Y.2d 777, 666 N.Y.S.2d 545 (1997).

21. This is the conclusion reached in the extensive lead note on Whitfield in New York State Law Digest No. 458.

22. See Rattray v. Raynor, 10 N.Y.2d 494, 225 N.Y.S.2d 39, 180 N.E.2d 429 (1962).

the motion before oral argument. The Court of Appeals has indicated that it will not entertain the motion once the appeal has been argued,[23] and it is not wise to hope for an exception.

If the stipulation is given, it must be one that will, in the event of affirmance, dispose of everything, because the purpose of this small opening in the wall of finality is to create at least the possibility of a final determination. Stipulating to judgment absolute solely on the issue of liability therefore doesn't suffice and an appeal based on such a conditional stipulation won't be entertained for the reason that an affirmance would not put an end to the case: there would still have to be a trial of the damages issues.[24]

A similar judgment absolute procedure is set up for an appellate term order granting a new trial, if it is to be appealed to the appellate division.[25] It has no less peril than the one we have been discussing.

Another instance in which an appeal of right lies to the Court of Appeals is under CPLR 5601(d). In that situation, there has been an earlier appeal to the appellate division and its order on that occasion could not be appealed because it was not final; the case was remanded to the lower court for further proceedings. Now those proceedings have been concluded in a final judgment and the case is ready to go up again. If the appellant seeks review of only those points previously decided by the appellate division—it would be idle to take them back to the same court again—she can appeal the judgment directly to the Court of Appeals, skipping the appellate division. It's optional. She can, if she wishes, go back to the appellate division, but should do that only if she seeks review of new matters not covered on the earlier appeal, thereupon setting the stage for a total review by the Court of Appeals afterwards, of both the old and new issues.

Suppose, for example, that the trial court on D's motion dismisses P's claim for failure to serve a notice of claim. P appeals and the appellate division reverses, finding the notice properly served and remanding for a trial of the merits. P wins on that trial and D wants to appeal the judgment. If the only point D wants reviewed is the one concerning the notice of claim, D can take a direct appeal to the Court of Appeals, but D will be limited to that issue alone and may not raise any others that the appellate division has not yet had a go at.

Two additional showings are required for this kind of appeal. One is that the prior appellate order "necessarily affects" the later judgment (the order in the notice of claim example of course does that, since a judgment for P would fall if the notice of claim were no good), and the other is that the absence of finality was the only thing that prevented the prior order from reaching the Court of Appeals. The prior order, in other words, must be shown to satisfy the other ingredients, besides finality, needed for an appeal of right to the Court of Appeals.[26] Today, as noted at the outset, the only surviving ingredient in subdivision (a) is a showing that two justices dissented. The prior order in the notice of claim example satisfied one of the requirements of the pre–1985 version of subdivision (a), viz., that the appellate division disposition was one of reversal, but today that by itself would not do. A two-justice dissent would be required. When CPLR 5601(d) is satisfied in all respects but this last one, appeal as of right still being barred for want of a two-justice dissent, direct appeal will still lie, but only by permission.[27] Appeal by permission is the subject of the next section.

When direct appeal to the Court of Appeals is available under this provision, the appellant must elect whether to invoke it or to appeal

23. See Shtekla v. Topping, 18 N.Y.2d 961, 277 N.Y.S.2d 694, 224 N.E.2d 116 (1967).

24. See Lusenskas v. Axelrod, 81 N.Y.2d 300, 598 N.Y.S.2d 166, 614 N.E.2d 729 (1993).

25. See CPLR 5703(a), where the appeal, even with the stipulation, lies only by permission. There is yet another stipulation instance, in CPLR 5602(b)(2)(iii), which also requires leave.

26. See Buffalo Electric Co. v. State, 14 N.Y.2d 453, 253 N.Y.S.2d 537, 201 N.E.2d 869 (1964).

27. Such a case will fall under CPLR 5602(a)(1)(ii) if it involves one of the higher trial courts (any of the five listed earlier in this treatment), or under CPLR 5602(b)(2)(ii) if it involves one of the lower courts.

instead to the intermediate appellate court, where the new matters can also be reviewed. Choosing the direct appeal waives review of the new matters.[28]

Finally, on CPLR 5601(d), an administrative determination or an arbitration award may be directly appealed to the Court of Appeals, but only where (1) it was to an agency or an arbitrator rather than to a court that the appellate division remitted the proceedings after the earlier appeal; (2) where the agency or arbitrator has now followed through and produced a "final" determination or award; and (3) where the other requirements of CPLR 5601(d) as discussed above have been met. This aspect of CPLR 5601(d) poses constitutional issues.[29]

§ 528. Appeals to Court of Appeals by Permission

The governing provision on appeals to the Court of Appeals by permission is CPLR 5602, divided into two categories. Subdivision (a) provides for cases in which the permission may be granted either by the appellate division or by the Court of Appeals. Subdivision (b) provides for cases in which only the appellate division can grant the permission. Subdivision (a) is further divided. Paragraph 1 is directed to an action originating in any of the five higher courts (supreme, county, surrogate's and family courts, or the court of claims) or in an administrative agency. An appellate division order finally determining such an action and not appealable of right under CPLR 5601 may be appealed by permission under subparagraph (i) of CPLR 5602(a)(1).

Subparagraph (ii) of CPLR 5602(a)(1), authorizing a direct appeal to the Court of Appeals, is the counterpart of CPLR 5601(d), treated earlier.[1]

When permission to appeal is sought under subdivision (a), the one seeking it may first move the appellate division and, if unsuccessful, then move the Court of Appeals, or simply move the latter directly. The procedure is by the basic steps of a motion, but with special additional requirements, usually coming from the rules of the appellate court, to be met later.[2]

When the application is made to the appellate division, the court decides for itself what vote it will require inter se for a grant of leave. But when the application is made to the Court of Appeals, a court rule requires that it be granted if any two judges vote for it.[3] As in the U.S. Supreme Court with a denial of certiorari, so with the New York Court of Appeals: "denial of a motion for leave to appeal is not equivalent to an affirmance and has no precedential value".[4]

Subdivision (b), which authorizes only the appellate division to grant leave to appeal to the Court of Appeals, has two paragraphs. Paragraph 1 authorizes the grant of leave from an appellate division order that does not finally determine an action.[5] Paragraph 2 is concerned with actions originating in the lower courts, which would include the New York City Civil Court and the district, city, town, and village courts, and is broken down into three subparagraphs, which should be treated independently.

---

28. See Parker v. Rogerson, 35 N.Y.2d 751, 361 N.Y.S.2d 916, 320 N.E.2d 650 (1974).

29. There appears to be no constitutional support for an appeal from a "determination" or "award". See § 524 above.

§ 528

1. See § 527 above, at the point of note 27 in the text. For the background of CPLR 5602(a)(2), concerning proceedings involving public officers, boards, and agencies in certain instances, see 2d Rep.Leg.Doc. (1958) No. 13, p. 110, and F.J. Zeronda, Inc. v. Town Bd. of the Town of Halfmoon, 37 N.Y.2d 198, 371 N.Y.S.2d 872, 333 N.E.2d 154 (1975).

2. See § 541 below.

3. Rule 500.11 contains this requirement, continuing a practice the court has long pursued voluntarily, but there

is also now a statute purporting to codify the requirement of such a two-vote rule. It was inserted in an amendment of subdivision (a) of CPLR 5602 as part of 1985 legislation that curtailed the appeal of right.

4. Brooklyn Hospital v. Lennon, 45 N.Y.2d 820, 409 N.Y.S.2d 210, 381 N.E.2d 608 (1978).

5. An exception here is the order granting a new trial or hearing, which is left to the procedure of the stipulation for judgment absolute. CPLR 5602(b)(1) accomplishes this by cross-referencing CPLR 5601(c) and 5602(b)(2)(iii)—the provisions containing the stipulation requirement. (The stipulation for judgment absolute procedure is discussed in § 527 above.) Another exception involves the situation of CPLR 5602(a)(2), mentioned in note 1, above.

If the case gets to the appellate division, and that court's order finally determines it, the order would be appealable to the Court of Appeals as of right if it involved a construction of the state or federal constitution;[6] when the constitutional construction is absent, the mission of subparagraph (i) of CPLR 5602(b)(2) is to require appellate division permission before the case can go any higher.

Subparagraph (ii) of CPLR 5602(b)(2), like CPLR 5602(a)(1)(ii) mentioned at the outset, is also a counterpart of CPLR 5601(d), authorizing direct appeal to the Court of Appeals by leave when CPLR 5601(d) does not offer it as a matter of right. It was also noted towards the end of the last section and has better context for understanding there.[7]

Finally, subparagraph (iii) of CPLR 5602(b)(2) is another stipulation for judgment absolute situation. It differs from the main one, found in CPLR 5601(c), in two ways. First, it applies to actions originating in the state's lower courts while the main one applies to those originating in the higher courts. Second, it requires appellate division leave to go to the Court of Appeals while under the main one the appeal lies as a matter of right. With that differentiation, the two are parallel. They apply when the appellate division has ordered a new trial. Before being allowed to appeal that order, the would-be appellant must stipulate that if the order is affirmed by the Court of Appeals, judgment absolute will be entered against him. It is a perilous course and must be traveled with caution.[8]

A uniform requirement when the appellate division grants leave to appeal to the Court of Appeals, whether under subdivision (a) of CPLR 5602, where it shares with the Court of Appeals itself the power to grant such leave, or under subdivision (b), where it holds the power alone, is that the appellate division state in the order granting leave that in its opinion questions of law have arisen which ought to be reviewed.

When the order being appealed is not final, such as one upholding jurisdiction at the threshold, the order granting leave must also indicate whether lower court fact findings have been affirmed, reversed, modified, or not considered, specifying those that are reversed or modified and setting forth any new findings of fact.[9] All of this has bearing on the scope of review to which the order can be subjected in the Court of Appeals, whose power to review facts is severely circumscribed.[10] It is also in this situation—the order granting leave to appeal from a nonfinal order—that the appellate division certifies the question of law deemed decisive of its determination.[11] If the question certified turns out to be one that the Court of Appeals cannot review—and the Court of Appeals is of course the final judge of that—it will dismiss the appeal.[12]

§ 528A. Certification to Court of Appeals by Other Courts

The New York courts, including the Court of Appeals, must decide issues only in the context of an actual controversy. Advisory opinions, in which an answer to a law question is supplied but resolution of the dispute is left to some other court system to resolve, are as a rule impermissible. A narrow exception has been carved out exclusively for the Court of Appeals.

At the request of the U.S. Supreme Court, a federal Court of Appeals, or the highest court of a sister state, the New York Court of Appeals can now supply the answer to a question of New York law, i.e., render the previously taboo advisory opinion. The authorization, which required a constitutional referendum in the mid–1980s,[1] was designed to recognize the frequency with which, in our mobile federal

---

6. See CPLR 5601(b)(1), treated in § 527.

7. See note 27 in § 527 above.

8. See § 527 above.

9. CPLR 5713.

10. See § 529 below.

11. Const. Art. VI, § 3(b)(4); CPLR 5713.

12. See Rosemont Enterprises, Inc. v. Irving, 41 N.Y.2d 829, 393 N.Y.S.2d 392, 361 N.E.2d 1040 (1977); Arthur Young & Co. v. Leong, 40 N.Y.2d 984, 390 N.Y.S.2d 927, 359 N.E.2d 435 (1976).

§ 528A

1. It added a paragraph 9 to § 3(b) of Article VI of the New York Constitution.

society, questions of New York law arise in other forums from which no direct route is available to the New York Court of Appeals, the only court that can supply definitive answers to questions of New York law.

Implementation of the procedure, which is commonly known as the "certification" procedure because it requires the requesting court to "certify" the issue of law it wants answered, required a rule of court, which the Court of Appeals promptly adopted.[2] The rule supplies the guideposts and procedures for invoking the new procedure and makes clear that even when the certification request is made by a proper court, whether to accept and act on the request is still left to the discretion of the Court of Appeals. Entertaining the request on its merits is not mandatory, no matter which court puts the question.

The first invocation of the new procedure, and a successful one, was at the behest of the U.S. Court of Appeals for the Second Circuit in Kidney v. Kolmar Laboratories, Inc., in which the New York Court of Appeals answered the certified question in a per curiam opinion.[3] The Second Circuit then acted on it by applying the response and closing out the case,[4] also taking the occasion to express its pleasure at having available this new and direct route by which to resolve issues of New York law, which appear so frequently before the court, principally when the basis for federal subject matter jurisdiction is the diversity of citizenship of the parties.

In order "to enhance understanding . . . and to provide an illustration of a form of Certificate that evidently complies with the certification procedure of the New York Court of Appeals", the Second Circuit set forth in full in its *Kidney* opinion a copy of the certificate that it used.

Whether the Court of Appeals accepts and acts on a given certificate is a sui generis determination. The court retains control of all issues, from the basic one of whether to accept the certificate in the first place right down to the details of how the case should be presented, briefed, and argued, if accept it does.

While the *Kidney* case got the certification procedure off to a good start,[5] it did not become quite the herald that the Second Circuit had hoped it would. Several Second Circuit requests for certification were turned down for one reason or another afterwards. An early illustration of a rejected request is Rufino v. United States,[6] in which the New York Court of Appeals noted that the same questions were pending in a case presently before the appellate division and that it would be "unquestionably preferable . . . to secure the benefit afforded by our normal process—the considered deliberation and writing of our intermediate appellate court". Another is Retail Software Services, Inc. v. Lashlee,[7] in which the Second Circuit, having before it a question of whether extraterritorial jurisdiction would be permissible in the case under an as-yet-unconstrued New York statute, asked the Court of Appeals for an answer. Rejecting the request, the court said that the issue "does not comport with our rules" in that "it does not satisfy the requirement of a showing that the court's answer 'may be determinative' of the pending action".

The rule in point[8] requires a showing that the issue "may be determinative", but it does not say determinative of what. Can the Court of Appeals mean that the answer it furnishes must have the potential to determine the whole federal action, or that if a federal constitutional issue is connected to the state-law issue, the constitutional issue must also be submitted to the state court for resolution?[9]

A failure to respond to a certification request can lead to conflict and embarrassment. In the *Rufino* case, for example, the Second

---

2. Rule 500.17.

3. 68 N.Y.2d 343, 509 N.Y.S.2d 491, 502 N.E.2d 168 (1986).

4. 808 F.2d 955 (2d Cir.1987).

5. See the lead note in New York State Law Digest No. 329.

6. 69 N.Y.2d 310, 514 N.Y.S.2d 200, 506 N.E.2d 910 (1987).

7. 71 N.Y.2d 788, 530 N.Y.S.2d 91, 525 N.E.2d 737 (1988).

8. Rule 500.17.

9. See the discussion in the lead note in New York State Law Digest No. 346.

Circuit asked the Court of Appeals to answer a key issue of damages in a tort case—whether New York recognizes the "loss of enjoyment of life" as a damages element distinct from the standard element of pain and suffering. When the Court of Appeals rejected the certification, the Second Circuit, forced to prognosticate how the New York Court of Appeals would respond on the merits, predicted that it would hold the "enjoyment of life" element to be distinct from pain and suffering. But when the issue finally arrived before the Court of Appeals, which it did in McDougald v. Garber,[10] the court went the other way; it held the element to be just another one to be factored in under "suffering".

These reactions apparently cooled the enthusiasm with which the Second Circuit originally greeted the certification procedure. Certifications from the Second Circuit, the most obvious source of such certifications, slowed down for a while after the McDougald case.

C. REVIEWABILITY

Table of Sections

Sec.
529. Reviewability in Particular Courts.
530. Scope of Review from Final Judgment.

§ 529. Reviewability in Particular Courts

The fact that the losing party can appeal the judgment or order does not guarantee an appellate review of the point that aggrieves her. Reviewability and appealability are not the same.

Scope of review is governed by CPLR 5501 and should be considered as posing two questions. The first, which we treat in this section, is what powers of review does the particular appellate court have? The second, which we turn to in the next section, is how much of the case is open to review when a final judgment is appealed?

The appellate division reviews both questions of law and questions of fact,[1] the latter including exercises of discretion. An appellate term has similar review powers,[2] as does also a county court when sitting in an appellate capacity.[3]

This pervasive review power allows the appellate court at the first tier of appeal to stand in the place of the nisi prius judge and do whatever she should have done.[4] It must of course respect a jury verdict, and is bound by it to the same extent the trial judge is. But to the extent that supreme court, for example, can set aside a verdict and grant judgment notwithstanding it, or order a new trial on the ground that the verdict is contrary to the weight of the evidence, or order an "additur" or "remittitur" raising or lowering the damages found by the jury, or otherwise affect the verdict, so can the appellate division.[5] In matters like that, however, which depend on a judicial reaction to what amounts to the whole record, the appellate court is not quick to substitute itself for the trial judge, recognizing the latter's advantage in having observed the demeanor of the witnesses and otherwise having enjoyed the vivid perceptions offered at the trial itself. But it has the power to.[6]

On appeals in court-tried cases (bench trials), the trial judge's powers being broader, so are the appellate court's. If the record is adequate, the court on reversing need not send the case back for retrial, or for the trial judge to act, but can render whatever judgment the

---

10. 73 N.Y.2d 246, 538 N.Y.S.2d 937, 536 N.E.2d 372 (1989).

§ 529

1. CPLR 5501(c).
2. CPLR 5501(d).
3. See §§ 1701 and 1702(d) in the Uniform City and Uniform Justice court acts, McKinney's Vol. 29A, Parts 2 and 3. Section 1702(d) is designed to assure that an exercise of discretion will also be reviewable lest the power to review the facts not be deemed to embrace it (which it does).

4. For reviewability purposes, reference hereafter will be to the appellate division, but with the understanding that scope of review in the other first-tier appeal courts— the appellate terms and county courts—is essentially the same.

5. Thompson v. City of New York, 60 N.Y.2d 948, 471 N.Y.S.2d 50, 459 N.E.2d 159 (1983).

6. Northern Westchester Professional Park Associates v. Town of Bedford, 60 N.Y.2d 492, 470 N.Y.S.2d 350, 458 N.E.2d 809 (1983).

trial judge should have rendered.[7] Hence, one does not often hear arguments in conjunction with review in the appellate division over whether a given question is one of law or one of fact, because in that court it makes little difference.

It makes a great deal of difference, however, in the Court of Appeals, because that court is authorized to review only questions of law. The exception, in which the court can review the facts, is where the appellate division has reversed or modified a judgment and in doing so has found new facts and ordered a final judgment based on them. The exception recognizes that it is New York policy to offer one appellate review of the facts, and the Court of Appeals is the only court positioned to conduct that review when the appellate division is the first fact finder.[8]

For the most part, it is not difficult to distinguish between a question of law and a question of fact; we can at least say that each realm has a galaxy of recognizable occupants. But given the number of issues and questions that arise in the course of litigation, there are always more than enough entries in the gray area in between to manufacture problems and caselaw. The interpretation and construction of documents, for example, such as contracts and trust instruments and the like, while often involving subjective intent (which strikes the senses as touching the facts rather than the law), are treated as law matters and are therefore reviewable by the Court of Appeals.[9]

Whether a given court has power to do a particular thing, or entertain a particular item or relief, is clearly a law question and thus within the ken of the Court of Appeals.[10] This, indeed, is how the Court occasionally gets involved with exercises of discretion.

An exercise of discretion on a given matter, which can run the gamut from whether to allow the amendment of a pleading or an extension of time to serve a bill of particulars or take any other of a hundred steps in litigation, to such heavier issues as whether to allow the late service of a complaint or to dismiss an action for want of prosecution, and including an army of other things that proliferate in litigation and which no few pages can hope to list, qualifies as an issue of fact that the Court of Appeals cannot and will not review.

"Discretion" may be of several different categories. One, for example, "is the familiar scope of choice in the resolution of questions of fact"; another, the discretion "to grant or to withhold a remedy prayed for".[11] Whatever the category, the basic rule is the same. As long as what the lower court has done can find solid ground anywhere within the generous outer limits of the extensive range "discretion" occupies, the Court of Appeals will not substitute its discretion for the lower court's even if, had it been the lower court, it would have alighted on a different part of the range.

But when those outer limits are passed— and only the Court of Appeals can be the ultimate judge of where the limits lie—the lower court's doing exceeds its powers and constitutes an "abuse of discretion", which magically transforms an unreviewable question of fact into a reviewable question of law.[12] And if it is alleged that the lower court, in exercising discretion, has failed to take account of any factor entitled to consideration, that also poses a reviewable law question.[13]

The adequacy, inadequacy, or even over-adequacy, of the record in respect of a given finding can convert what seems to be an issue of fact into one of law. It is clear that an appellate division affirmance of a trial court's finding of fact poses no law question and can-

---

7. See, e.g., Society of New York Hosp. v. Burstein, 22 A.D.2d 768, 253 N.Y.S.2d 753 (1st Dep't 1964).

8. CPLR 5501(b). See Da Silva v. Musso, 53 N.Y.2d 543, 444 N.Y.S.2d 50, 428 N.E.2d 382 (1981). An exception in the criminal area, in which the Court of Appeals reviews the facts, is when the judgment is of death. Const. Art. VI, § 3.

9. See, e.g., Gitelson v. DuPont, 17 N.Y.2d 46, 268 N.Y.S.2d 11, 215 N.E.2d 336 (1966).

10. Dittmar Explosives, Inc. v. A. E. Ottaviano, Inc., 20 N.Y.2d 498, 285 N.Y.S.2d 55, 231 N.E.2d 756 (1967).

11. Patron v. Patron, 40 N.Y.2d 582, 583–4, 388 N.Y.S.2d 890, 891, 357 N.E.2d 361, 362 (1976).

12. Id.

13. See Irrigation & Ind. Dev. Corp. v. Indag S. A., 37 N.Y.2d 522, 375 N.Y.S.2d 296, 337 N.E.2d 749 (1975).

not be reviewed by the Court of Appeals,[14] but that of course assumes there is evidence in the record adequate to support the finding. An issue of whether the record contains such supportive evidence—and here again the Court of Appeals will be the ultimate judge—is one of law and can be reviewed by the Court of Appeals.[15] Conversely, a record may point so compellingly to a given fact that a failure to find it can be regarded as an error of law and set the stage for review by the Court of Appeals.[16] It is at the fringes of normalcy, in other words, that the record tips beyond the realm of fact and falls into the category of law: on the one side too deficient to admit the finding and on the other too ample to exclude it.

If there is no specific issue of law in the case, as where the Court of Appeals reads the record to present only issues of fact and in its judgment the facts found below are supported by the record, the court has nothing to do but affirm. The court has often noted that a given determination, "although appealable, is beyond the scope of our review".[17]

With the diminution in the appeal of right, however, and the concomitant expansion of the appeal by permission, discrepancies between appealability and reviewability must inevitably diminish. The court will presumably withhold permission if it sees in a case no significant point of law that warrants review, and the narrowing of the channel for the appeal of right,[18] presumably a more likely source of cases that have a way to get up but little to posit for review when they get there,[19] has already cut off much of the traffic.

Also shown in earlier sections treating appealability to the Court of Appeals was that an appeal may sometimes be taken there directly from a court of original jurisdiction. One example is where there has been an earlier appeal to the appellate division, whose disposition on that occasion was not final—thus precluding further appeal at that time—because it contemplated further proceedings in the trial court. The judgment resulting upon the later completion of those trial-court proceedings is the one that can be appealed directly to the Court of Appeals.[20] The point we make now is that if this direct-appeal route is used, the only matters that the Court of Appeals can review are those encompassed by the prior nonfinal determination of the appellate division, not any new matters raised by the trial court's later judgment.[21] So limited, this simply amounts to a postponed appeal of matters the appellate division has already passed on. If the appellant would have the new matter reviewed as well, the second appeal must also be taken to the appellate division, with further appeal from everything to abide that court's disposition of the new matter.[22]

§ 530. Scope of Review from Final Judgment

The issue to be reviewed upon an appeal from an intermediate order is ordinarily narrow; the order has usually disposed of just one issue and that's the only one to be looked into by the appellate court. But an appeal from the final judgment in the case opens the door wider, and the loser, and for some purposes even the winner, will try to squeeze through it with all manner of grievances and objections touching many parts of the case. Subdivision (a) of CPLR 5501 determines just how much is opened for review upon an appeal from a final judgment, and for this purpose an order that amounts to the equivalent of a judgment in

---

14. See, e.g., Farr v. Newman, 14 N.Y.2d 183, 250 N.Y.S.2d 272, 199 N.E.2d 369 (1964).

15. See Joseph E. Seagram & Sons, Inc. v. Tax Commission, 14 N.Y.2d 314, 251 N.Y.S.2d 460, 200 N.E.2d 447 (1964).

16. See, e.g., Lazarus v. Bowery Savings Bank, 16 N.Y.2d 793, 262 N.Y.S.2d 717, 209 N.E.2d 889 (1965).

17. See, e.g., Vadala v. Carroll, 59 N.Y.2d 751, 463 N.Y.S.2d 432, 450 N.E.2d 238 (1983).

18. See § 527 above.

19. The Vadala case in note 17, for example, got to the Court of Appeals merely on the basis that the appellate division had reversed the trial court. Under CPLR 5601(a), that was but is no longer a basis for an appeal of right. See § 527 above.

20. CPLR 5601(d), 5602(a)(1)(ii), (b)(2)(ii).

21. CPLR 5501(b).

22. See the discussion of CPLR 5601(d) in § 527 above.

that it disposes of the whole case will also qualify as a judgment and earn the same scope of review.[1] That it may have been labeled an "order" is not decisive,[2] and this includes as well an order of the appellate division that finally determines the action and contemplates nothing more than the ministerial entry of a judgment on it.[3]

Subdivision (a) of CPLR 5501 provides that an appeal from a final judgment brings up for review:

1. any nonfinal judgment or order which necessarily affects the final judgment, including any which was adverse to the respondent on the appeal from the final judgment and which, if reversed, would entitle the respondent to prevail in whole or in part on that appeal, provided that such nonfinal judgment or order has not previously been reviewed by the court to which the appeal is taken;

2. any order denying a new trial or hearing which has not previously been reviewed by the court to which the appeal is taken;

3. any ruling to which the appellant objected or had no opportunity to object or which was a refusal or failure to act as requested by the appellant, and any charge to the jury, or failure or refusal to charge as requested by the appellant, to which he objected;

4. any remark made by the judge to which the appellant objected; and

5. a verdict after a trial by jury as of right, when the final judgment was entered in a different amount pursuant to the respondent's stipulation on a motion to set aside the verdict as excessive or inadequate; the appellate court may increase such judgment to a sum not exceeding the verdict or reduce it to a sum not less than the verdict.

Number 1 on the list raises a number of points. It introduces the sometimes difficult inquiry of what intermediate order or interlocutory judgment "necessarily affects" the final judgment, for it is only such a one that may be reviewed under this provision. One test, not perfect but helpful, is to ask this question: assuming that the nonfinal order or judgment is erroneous, would its reversal overturn the judgment? If it would, it is a reviewable item; if it would not, and the judgment can stand despite it, it is not reviewable. A few examples will help:

An order directing temporary alimony may not be reviewed as part of a later final judgment in a matrimonial action because its reversal would not undermine the judgment's foundation: the ingredients of the order, however similar they may be on some matters to the ingredients of the judgment, are wholly independent of it.[4] Equally independent, whatever its individual importance, is an order granting or denying a preliminary injunction, so that an appeal from a later final judgment will not bring it up for review: whether the final judgment—including such permanent injunctive relief as it may contain—is supported by the record does not turn one way or the other on whether a case was made out for a temporary injunction earlier.[5]

While this test is some guide, it is not a sure one. There is, in fact, no airtight way to determine whether an order "necessarily affects" the final judgment so as to assure review. Some cases have held, for example, that an order denying a pretrial deposition[6] or a bill of particulars[7] does not necessarily affect the final judgment and, strictly speaking, this is so: there is no assurance that, if the deposition or bill had been allowed, the judgment would "necessarily" have gone the other way. Yet it

§ 530

1. See Hurd v. Lis, 126 A.D.2d 163, 513 N.Y.S.2d 278 (3d Dep't 1987).

2. See State v. Wolowitz, 96 A.D.2d 47, 468 N.Y.S.2d 131 (2d Dep't 1983).

3. See De Long Corp. v. Morrison–Knudsen Co., 14 N.Y.2d 346, 251 N.Y.S.2d 657, 200 N.E.2d 557 (1964).

4. See, e.g., Caplin v. Caplin, 33 A.D.2d 908, 307 N.Y.S.2d 486 (2d Dep't 1970).

5. Cinerama, Inc. v. Equitable Life Assur. Soc., 38 A.D.2d 698, 328 N.Y.S.2d 160 (1st Dep't 1972).

6. See Dulber v. Dulber, 37 A.D.2d 566, 322 N.Y.S.2d 862 (2d Dep't 1971), aff'd 29 N.Y.2d 408, 328 N.Y.S.2d 641, 278 N.E.2d 886 (1972).

7. See Collins v. McWilliams, 185 App.Div. 712, 173 N.Y.S. 850 (1st Dep't 1919).

is clear that CPLR 5501(a)(1) does not invariably require such a showing. In Matter of Aho,[8] for example, the Court of Appeals held that an order denying a change of venue does affect the final judgment and may be reviewed as part of its appeal, and yet there is no guarantee there, either, that had the venue been changed the judgment would "necessarily" have differed. The intangibles that distinguish one county from another, however, whether measurable or not, are formidable, and a trial lawyer would corroborate that if the venue order does not "necessarily" affect the judgment, it comes close enough to justify review within the intendment of CPLR 5501. But then, trial lawyers may be heard to plead the same thing for the order denying them a deposition or doing anything else that affects preparation for the courtroom.

The more generous approach manifest in the Aho case can be justified, not because it expands review upon appeal from a final judgment, but because it may have the salutary effect—by assuring later review of borderline "necessarily affects" orders—of sparing separate and immediate appeals from them. With the broad appealability New York allows of intermediate orders, that may be a worthwhile saving. Under a less generous reviewability standard, a lawyer bent on getting the order reviewed would be obliged to appeal it independently.

Some orders by their very nature "necessarily" affect the judgment and are assured review as part of an appeal from a final judgment. Included here are those which, had they gone the other way, would have dismissed the case at the threshold and thereby blocked the judgment altogether. A prime example is the order denying a motion to dismiss the complaint for failure to state a cause of action,[9] since a judgment for the plaintiff would not have come on had the action earlier been dismissed.

Failure to state a cause of action is today only one of many grounds for dismissal offered by CPLR 3211(a), and if a denial of a dismissal on the one ground "necessarily affects" the judgment, so should a denial on any of the other 3211(a) grounds. Thus, an order denying a motion to dismiss based on lack of personal jurisdiction[10]—the ubiquitous vehicle for testing, among other things, whether there is longarm jurisdiction under CPLR 302 or proper service under CPLR 308—necessarily affects the judgment and is preserved for review. Indeed, dismissals denied under provisions other than CPLR 3211 should also qualify for review, such as an order denying a dismissal for failure to serve a complaint under CPLR 3012, for failure to make disclosure under CPLR 3126, or for want of prosecution under CPLR 3216.

The probable reason why one does not run into this point more often is the free availability of the interlocutory appeal—the separate and immediate appeal from a nonfinal order—under CPLR 5701(a)(2).[11] That route is apparently preferred by New York practitioners, for objectionable nonfinal orders in general and for those affecting jurisdiction in particular. Why should a defendant burden itself, the assumption goes, with defending on the merits by postponing review of an order sustaining jurisdiction if the order can, as it can in New York, be appealed immediately?

A suggestion emerging from all that has been said, if we press for one, is that if there is any doubt at all about whether a final judgment would preserve a given kind of order for review, and the order is one the loser definitely wants reviewed, she should opt for the immediate appeal route and spare herself the guesswork.

If the loser does that, however, and the appeal is still pending undetermined when later final judgment comes on and is itself appealed, the earlier appeal will be dismissed: the entry of final judgment precludes the con-

8. 39 N.Y.2d 241, 383 N.Y.S.2d 285, 347 N.E.2d 647 (1976).

9. Schamber Chem. Co. v. Ross & Kominsky Plumbing & Heating Co., 259 App.Div. 784, 18 N.Y.S.2d 368 (4th Dep't 1940).

10. CPLR 3211(a)(8).

11. See § 526 above.

tinuance of an appeal from a nonfinal order.[12] But if the order does qualify as one that "necessarily affects" the final judgment, it will get its review as part of the now appealed final judgment notwithstanding the dismissal of its own earlier interlocutory appeal.[13]

A party who has won the final judgment will not ordinarily appeal it,[14] but if the loser does, the winner may want review of other things that occurred during the action. The winner would be the respondent on the appeal, but some of these other things may have gone against him and one of them, if reversed in his favor, might itself support the judgment even if the court were otherwise disposed to uphold the appellant's position and overturn it. Any nonfinal order with this judgment-supporting potential may, at the respondent's behest, be reviewed on the appeal, which is what CPLR 5501(a)(1) means to allow by sweeping under scope of review such orders as were "adverse to the respondent".

Take this example. D makes a pretrial motion under CPLR 3211(a)(5) to dismiss P's money claim on the ground of release. The court finds the release invalid and denies the motion. No immediate appeal is taken. The case goes to trial and the jury brings in a verdict for D, on which judgment is rendered. P appeals the judgment, alleging various errors in evidentiary rulings. D, the respondent, is entitled to have the appellate court review the pretrial order that held the release invalid. If the release is good, it would uphold the final judgment—"entitle the respondent [D] to prevail"—even though P, having established that there was prejudicial error in rulings at the trial, might otherwise be entitled to a reversal. It just establishes that the appellant's day in the appellate court is to be respondent's, too.

It must be stressed that only a prior "nonfinal" order can get reviewed as part of the appeal from the final judgment. If the prior order qualifies as "final" in its own right, it does not fall under 5501(a)(1) and is not preserved for later review,[15] which is a warning to the aggrieved person who wants such an order reviewed to take an appeal from it forthwith.

Finally, on paragraph 1 of CPLR 5501(a)—all said so far is the discharge of that one provision—is the assurance the CPLR offers that orders reviewable under it need not be specified in the notice of appeal, as was once required.[16] These "necessarily affects" orders are automatically reviewable as long as the final judgment has been properly appealed.

There is no coordinate provision expanding the scope of review of a mere order—unless it qualifies on the facts of a particular case as the equivalent of a final judgment,[17] not a common occurrence. The ordinary intermediate (nonfinal) order is narrower than a judgment, usually disposing of just one issue, and an appeal from that order will review just that one issue. But should there be several matters disposed of in the order, with review sought of all of them, it is best to follow the practice followed with judgments and appeal "from each and every part" of the order. It has been held that "[a]n appeal from only part of an order constitutes a waiver of the right to appeal from the other parts of that order".[18]

If a given order disposes of several things, therefore, the appellant should be careful not to phrase the notice of appeal too narrowly. If all the issues disposed of aggrieve the appellant, the appellant should see to it that the notice of appeal covers them all. Picking and choosing can be perilous, as it proved to be in

---

12. See Matter of Aho, note 8 above.

13. Austrian Lance & Stewart, P. C. v. Jackson, 50 A.D.2d 735, 375 N.Y.S.2d 868 (1st Dep't 1975).

14. A winner may occasionally be accorded "aggrieved" status sufficient to appeal a judgment in his own favor, as where one of the important grounds on which he relied, and which may carry future consequences, was decided against him (other grounds having been present to support the judgment). See § 525 above.

15. Crystal v. Manes, 130 A.D.2d 979, 516 N.Y.S.2d 823 (4th Dep't 1987). P's complaint in Crystal had five

claims. An order dismissed four of them in 1986, which P did not appeal. The fifth and last claim was dismissed in 1987. P did appeal that dismissal and as part of it wanted the 1986 order reviewed. The review was held unavailable; the prior order was final as to the four claims it dismissed.

16. See § 580 of the old Civil Practice Act, repealed effective September 1, 1963.

17. See the Hurd and Wolowitz cases in notes 1 and 2, above, and the text at those points.

18. Royal v. Brooklyn Union Gas Co., 122 A.D.2d 132, 504 N.Y.S.2d 519 (2d Dep't 1986).

City of Mt. Vernon v. Mt. Vernon Hous. Auth.[19]

The order had granted D's cross-motion to dismiss P's complaint while also denying P's motion for leave to amend the complaint. P appealed from "that part of the order" that denied the motion to amend the complaint, but not from the part that granted the dismissal. When P later asked the appellate division for leave to amend the notice of appeal to assert that it was also an appeal from the dismissal part, the court denied the motion, holding that the failure to appeal the dismissal part was a jurisdictional defect.

Paragraphs 3 and 4 of CPLR 5501(a) are the passageways through which come up for review any alleged errors made by the trial court in any of its myriad rulings, made on points of evidence or otherwise, and any prejudicial remarks the judge may have made. A proviso here is that the record manifest that the appellant duly made known the objection to the ruling or remark if there was opportunity to do so, whether by using the word "objection" or "exception" or any other language. The key is that the grievance was made known to the judge; the words used to convey it are secondary.

There is a broad and general rule that the court will not review on appeal any points not raised in the court below, a wholesome requirement designed to avoid waste.[20] Its principal rationale is that if the matter had been duly raised below, it might have prevailed there and the grievance been avoided. The rule is not absolute, however, and the appellate division, exercising its broad discretion to grant a new trial in the interests of justice, may be influenced by something not technically presented and preserved below. There is even indication that the Court of Appeals may sometimes consider something of that nature if special circumstances exist. The court has also confirmed that it may entertain matter raised in the trial court but skipped at appellate division level, although it is rare for it to do so and there is usually good reason when it does.[21]

An exception to the rule that the appellate court will not consider matters outside the record exists when the particular matter involves something undeniable, or which in any event would not generate factual issues needing trial-level resolution, such as the existence and content of the rules of a certain entity.[22] This is analogous to the doctrine of judicial notice, if it is not the doctrine itself. But no lawyer should assume that unpreserved matters have a decent chance of creeping up for appellate review. It is better to leave this subject with the warning that dependence on appellate willingness to entertain something outside the record, which it was both appropriate and feasible to put into the record, is unwise.

Paragraph 5 of CPLR 5501(a) assures review of the amount of the verdict in instances in which, through the use of the additur or remittitur devices,[23] the judgment ends up in a different sum. So, for example, if the verdict is for $100,000, and the court on D's motion orders a new trial unless P stipulates to take $40,000 instead (remittitur), which P accepts, D's appeal from the judgment enables P, without bothering to cross-appeal, to bring up for review the propriety of the reduction and permits the appellate court to restore any part of the sum remitted.

D. TAKING THE APPEAL

Table of Sections

19.   235 A.D.2d 516, 652 N.Y.S.2d 771 (2d Dep't 1997).

20.   See Kolmer–Marcus, Inc. v. Winer, 32 A.D.2d 763, 300 N.Y.S.2d 952 (1st Dep't 1969), aff'd 26 N.Y.2d 795, 309 N.Y.S.2d 220, 257 N.E.2d 664 (1970).

21.   See Telaro v. Telaro, 25 N.Y.2d 433, 306 N.Y.S.2d 920, 255 N.E.2d 158 (1969).

22.   See, e.g., Crawford v. Merrill Lynch, Pierce, Fenner & Smith, Inc., 35 N.Y.2d 291, 361 N.Y.S.2d 140, 319 N.E.2d 408 (1974).

23.   For discussion of these devices, see § 407 above.

§ 531. Taking an Appeal; How

A distinction must be made between "taking" an appeal and what the bar loosely refers to as "perfecting" it. The perfection steps are the involved and expensive ones, consisting of securing the transcript, drawing the record, writing the briefs, getting the whole business printed or otherwise reproduced, serving and filing everything in the required number of copies, getting onto the appellate court's calendar and, finally, arguing or submitting the appeal. The "taking" of the appeal, in contrast, although it confronts a rigid time limitation, is probably the easiest step in civil practice. It is just the service and filing of a paper, or at worst several papers.

CPLR 5515(1) provides that an appeal is taken "by serving on the adverse party a notice of appeal and filing it in the office where the judgment or order of the court of original instance is entered. . . ." Although the statute says "the adverse party", it is best to serve a copy on each of the other parties, whether adverse or not and whether they are deemed affected by the appeal or not. (Let them judge that for themselves.) Note that the copy to be filed is filed with the clerk of the court of original instance, not with the clerk of the appellate court. This is so even when the appeal is being taken from an intermediate appellate court to a higher one. The court to which the appeal is taken gets notice of it through other means, which we will come back to in a moment.

The notice of appeal contains the caption of the action and it specifies the party who is appealing, the judgment or order or part of it being appealed, and the court to which the appeal is being taken.[1] Its contents are standard and straightforward. The whole body of an ordinary notice of appeal from a final judgment can read:

Please take notice that the defendant Jones hereby appeals to the Appellate Division of the Third Department from a judgment of this court [the court having been specified in the caption] in favor of plaintiff Smith for $35,000, entered with the clerk on June 28, 1989, and from every part thereof.

The appeal, since it is in this case from a final judgment, will bring up for review all of the nonfinal dispositions specified in CPLR 5501(a), discussed earlier,[2] and will do so automatically, i.e., without their being specified in the notice of appeal.[3]

The notice of appeal need not be served by personal delivery or by any other service-of-summons prescription. Like any other intra-action paper, it is served pursuant to CPLR 2103. This means that it is served on the other party's attorney, and that it may be served by ordinary mail.[4] Some attorneys prefer registered or certified mail, which is not required. Dispute over whether service was made is rare, but the precaution of registration or certification can do no harm. The filing with the clerk can also be effected by a mere mailing.

The appeal is "taken" when the duly addressed and stamped envelopes containing the notices of appeal are dropped into the letter box.[5]

The foregoing is the procedure when the appeal is being taken as of right. When leave is required, no formal notice of appeal is used. The would-be appellant merely makes the motion for leave to appeal, doing so within the time a notice of appeal would have to be served in an of-right case, and, if the motion is granted, the entry of the order granting the motion is deemed the taking of the appeal.[6]

When the appeal is being taken to the Court of Appeals, a statute requires that the clerk of the original court, with whom the notice of appeal is filed, forthwith send a copy of it to

§ 531

1. CPLR 5515(1).

2. See § 530 above.

3. The record must contain the relevant supporting papers, of course, and the briefs must direct attention to any nonfinal disposition of which review is sought. See

Austrian Lance & Stewart, P.C. v. Jackson, 50 A.D.2d 735, 375 N.Y.S.2d 868 (1st Dep't 1975).

4. The time requirements for doing these things are treated in § 533 below.

5. CPLR 2103(b)(2).

6. CPLR 5515(1).

the clerk of the Court of Appeals.[7] When appeal to that court is being allowed by leave of the appellate division, the latter's clerk sends to the clerk of the Court of Appeals a copy of the order granting permission.[8] By those means the Court of Appeals is promptly apprised of the appeal and can track its business more closely. These requirements are not imposed by statute when the appeal is to the appellate division, but the latter's rules may have similar exactions.[9]

An additional requirement the practitioner should note when the appeal is to the Court of Appeals is that within 10 days after the service of the notice of appeal (or entry of an order granting leave), the appellant must file a jurisdictional statement with the clerk, accompanied by several other papers.[10] This facilitates the court's review of its jurisdiction in the case. Court of Appeals jurisdiction is narrow, and the court often reviews its jurisdiction without waiting for a request by a party.[11]

§ 532. Subsequent Orders

When an order is being appealed, what effect shall be given to a later motion to reargue or renew the motion that gave rise to that order, or to a motion to resettle that order? This has been a matter troublesome enough to earn some special statutory attention. It also takes us back to the discussion of some of these follow-up motions in the chapter on Motion Practice.[1]

The prime lesson to the would-be appellant aggrieved by the original order is to appeal it—the *original* order. If the subsequent motion, whether made by the appellant or by any other party, is made so promptly that the time to appeal the original order is still open, it must still be remembered that the judge is likely to take some time before deciding the new motion. The appellant should not await the outcome of the new motion before taking an appeal from the original order. If the appellant intended to appeal the original, but waited to see what happens with the later application, she may find that she has forfeited an appeal altogether.

CPLR 5517(a) lists several subsequent activities that it specifically says shall not affect the appeal from the original order, thus assuring that the appeal will not be mooted or otherwise cancelled by these later doings. It is useful to treat items not on the list as well as the listed ones, to assume that a timely appeal has been taken from the original order, and to ask what if any effect the later activity will have on the original order.

First, a motion to reargue. If the motion is denied it has no effect at all on the appeal. And the order denying a motion to reargue is not itself appealable, so the appellant had better have taken an appeal from the original order. If the motion to reargue has been duly and timely made by the appellant, and has been granted, and the appellant has obtained in that grant just what he would have wanted from the appeal, he naturally has no further cause to prosecute the appeal. He can discontinue or withdraw it.[2] If the motion has been granted but has essentially adhered to the original determination, it has no effect on a pending appeal from the original,[3] which goes right on through.

Next, a motion to resettle the original order. A denial of that motion has no effect on the appeal. Since as a rule an order denying a motion to resettle may not be appealed,[4] it is again important to appeal the original order.

---

7. CPLR 5515(2).

8. CPLR 5515(3).

9. See, e.g., Rules 600.17 and 670.2(e), the respective rules of the First and Second departments. Absent such a rule, the first notice the appellate court gets of the case may be later on, when the record is filed, or perhaps when a motion is made. Compare the more uniform method statutorily provided in criminal cases. See CPLR 460.10(1)(e).

10. Rule 500.2, part of the Court of Appeals rules.

11. See Rule 500.3.

§ 532

1. See § 254 above.

2. The other side, now aggrieved by the change made by the order granting the motion to reargue, can take an appeal from it. An order granting reargument, in contrast with one denying it, is appealable.

3. CPLR 5517(a)(1).

4. See In re Reed, 230 App.Div. 764, 244 N.Y.S. 217 (2d Dep't 1930).

The granting of a motion to resettle has no effect on the original appeal,[5] but here we must again look at what the resettlement order does. If it makes so substantial a change in the order—this is not likely, but it is possible—that it has dissolved the appellant's grievance, it is once again a situation in which the appellant may wish to withdraw the appeal.[6]

It is especially perilous for an appellant to refrain from taking an appeal from the original order on the assumption that the original is defective in some way and that the defect bars its appeal. The appellant may think that the order must first be resettled before being appealable. There would be no harm, however, in taking an appeal from the original order as a precaution—a resettlement motion can be made while the appeal from the original order is pending, and it would be chancy indeed to wait and appeal only from the order on the resettlement motion. This is true even if the order is resettled in exactly the way the appellant wishes. One of the requirements applicable to an order, for example, is that it "recite the papers used on the motion".[7] It has been held, however, that the failure of the order to recite the papers does not bar an appeal from it, and that an appellant who does not appeal the order on time, waiting instead for the outcome of a motion to resettle the order (to include a recitation of the papers) and appealing only the resettled order instead, forfeits the appeal altogether.[8] If the matter on which resettlement is granted, in other words, would not have affected the appealability of the original order and the respect in which it aggrieved the appellant, the appeal is gone. The resettled matter in the new order would pose nothing the appellant needs reviewed—it is not, after all, the order's failure to recite the papers that the appellant would want an appellate review of—and the appellant who guesses that the

time in which to appeal the original order is automatically extended by the granting of a resettled one is guessing wrong.

Then there is the motion to renew. In contrast with the motion to reargue, the motion to renew is based on new or additional proof. A denial of the motion does not have an effect on the appeal,[9] but by implication an order granting the motion does. This contemplates that the grant will affect the original order in some substantial way, perhaps even abating the original appeal. It would be a happy abatement for the appellant if the order granting the renewal motion actually gives the appellant what he wants. An order either granting or denying a motion to renew is appealable, however, so that, whatever the disposition of the motion is, if it does not give the appellant everything and he still retains a grievance worth appealing, he should take an appeal from the order disposing of the renewal motion.

The jurisdiction of a trial-level judge to entertain one of these follow-up motions—the motion to reargue, renew, resettle, etc.—is not cut off by the fact that an appeal from the original order has been taken and is pending. As a general rule, it is only the submission of the appeal that is generally viewed as cutting off the lower court's jurisdiction.[10]

Several of the orders discussed above are themselves appealable, whether they affect the original appeal or not. In addition to orders granting or denying renewal motions, an order granting reargument is appealable; even an order granting resettlement is if it makes a substantial change,[11] unlike the example in the prior paragraph in which the only change made was the insertion into the order of a list of the papers on which it was based. To secure review of any of these, the appellant who has duly appealed the original order need not take

---

5. CPLR 5517(a)(2).

6. In this situation again, as with the substantial change made by the grant of a motion to reargue illustrated at note 2, above, the very fact that the change divests the appellant of her grievance should aggrieve the adverse party and permit that party, if so disposed, to appeal the order granting resettlement.

7. CPLR 2219(a).

8. Singer v. Board of Education of City of N.Y., 97 A.D.2d 507, 468 N.Y.S.2d 25 (2d Dep't 1983).

9. CPLR 5517(a)(3).

10. William H. Van Vleck, Inc. v. Klein, 50 Misc.2d 622, 271 N.Y.S.2d 64 (Sup.Ct., Kings County, 1966). See § 254 above.

11. Kaehler v. Phoenix Ins. Co., 38 A.D.2d 683, 327 N.Y.S.2d 254 (4th Dep't 1971).

a separate appeal. CPLR 5517(b) provides that the appellate court, on that main appeal, may also review any of the subsequent orders we have been discussing.[12] The appellant need only include in the record a copy of the subsequent order and the papers it is based on, and speak to it in his brief.

The independent appealability of some of these subsequent orders would seem to be relevant, then, only for one who has not appealed the original order.

While CPLR 5517 is helpful, it is still not a source of total security for the careful lawyer. The latter's course, when she is bent on appeal and wants to keep all loose ends tucked in, is to appeal everything in sight: the original order as well as any subsequent one having bearing on the original and not clearly unappealable by itself (such as an order denying reargument). This does not mean multiple records and great additional expense; it merely means the service and filing of an additional notice of appeal from each of the later orders, the inclusion in the record—a single record serves for all—of copies of the later orders, their underlying papers, and the notices of appeal from them, and, of course, whatever attention the party wants to give the later doings in his brief. If any one of the appealed orders proves unappealable, the appellate court will dismiss the appeal from that one. But that is no problem. As long as any of the items appealed is the properly appealable order, the whole appeal will go through to conclusion through its good offices. One sees from time to time an appellate decision reviewing everything through the one order that it has found appealable while dismissing appeals taken from the others as "superfluous".[13] The appellate court, after all, has the final say on what the appealable paper is.

Although CPLR 5517 directs itself only to an appeal from an order, its lessons can by analogy be applied to an appeal from a judgment, especially the lesson of the last paragraph. A judgment, too, is subject to subsequent motions. If not a motion to reargue or renew, then in any event to a motion to resettle or modify or the like. If one who would appeal the judgment is aggrieved as well by a later resettlement order, and has any doubt as to whether an appeal from the one preserves review of the other, he does well to appeal both.

Of course a party who is aggrieved only by the subsequent order, and not by the original—such as the winner on the original motion who has been deprived of his victory by an order granting reargument or renewal and overturning the original, as several times mentioned in footnotes[14]—should appeal only the subsequent order.

An analogous situation in which a would-be appellant can become confused about which paper to appeal involves the granting of a motion to dismiss or for summary judgment. The winner may first get an order entered to reflect the disposition, and it of course behooves the loser to appeal from that. But while that appeal is pending, the winner may then get a judgment entered on the order. Cautious appellants appealed from the judgment as well, especially after the Court of Appeals decision in Matter of Aho,[15] which said that in this situation the mere entry of the judgment terminates the appeal from the order.

An amendment of CPLR 5501(c)[16] obviated the second appeal by providing that the notice of appeal from an order dismissing or granting summary judgment

> shall be deemed to specify a judgment upon said order entered after service of the notice of appeal and before entry of the order of the appellate court....

Some attorneys may choose to take an appeal from the judgment anyway.[17] In these multi-paper situations, the cautious appellate

---

12. See, e.g., Rever v. Nelson, 23 A.D.2d 505, 256 N.Y.S.2d 368 (2d Dep't 1965).

13. See, e.g., Matter of Bingham's Will, 7 N.Y.2d 1, 25, 194 N.Y.S.2d 465, 483, 163 N.E.2d 301, 314 (1959) (clarification in dissenting opinion).

14. See notes 2 and 6 above.

15. 39 N.Y.2d 241, 383 N.Y.S.2d 285 (1976).

16. L.1997, c.474.

17. See the discussion in SPR 60:3.

lawyer is prone to appeal everything in sight, as often as need be.[18]

§ 533. Time to Appeal or Move for Leave

An appeal as of right must be taken within 30 days after the appellant has been served with a copy of the judgment or order to be appealed, with notice of its entry.[1] Not until that service will the 30 days start to run, and it makes no difference that the appellant knows of the entry from other sources. The point is illustrated in Dobess Realty Corp. v. City of New York,[2] where the city was one of several defendants and had earned a dismissal. The other defendants remained in and went to trial, judgment ultimately going against them. Proper service of the judgment with notice of entry was made on those defendants, starting their appeal time running, but the city never made such service and hence the time of the plaintiffs to appeal the old dismissal order made in favor of the city was still alive. The court mentioned that the earlier judgment referred to the city's victory in its recital but not decretal paragraph, perhaps suggesting that mention in both paragraphs might have made a difference. It is not a point worth challenging. One in that position should draw, obtain entry of, and serve a copy of the judgment with notice of entry, and do it all promptly. Whatever is done should be done thoughtfully, and not be allowed to loiter for want of attention. And the rule that imposes a time limit on submitting orders and judgments for entry should be kept in mind.[3]

As a rule, the winning party should serve the judgment or order (with notice of entry) on the loser. Cases have appeared, however, in which the service was made by the court or clerk, and that service was held to start the appellant's appeal time running. An amendment of CPLR 5513 in 1996 overrules those cases and provides that the loser's appeal time won't start until a party does the serving.[4]

A subsisting exception to the rule that the winner's service on the loser starts the appeal time is where the loser herself serves the judgment or order and notice of entry. Either side can get the paper entered and effect service of it on the other side, but it is usually the potential respondent who does so—having won below, the respondent is the one with the incentive. But the would-be appellant can effect the entry if so disposed, and serve the paper with notice of entry on the respondent. If she does, however, her 30 days to appeal run from that time.[5]

The court cannot vary these rules; it cannot, for example, curtail the appellant's appeal time by striking from the order or judgment a requirement that notice of entry be given.[6] Conversely, the court cannot, nor can even the parties by stipulation, extend the time to appeal beyond the statutory allotment.[7] What few extension possibilities exist are discussed in the next section.

If the order or judgment to be appealed is served by mail, five days are added to the 30–day appeal time, making it 35 days.[8] Clearly that's the case when the winner serves the judgment or order. But when the loser does, and makes the service by mail, does the loser's appeal time also get the five-day stretch from 30 to 35 days? There's a conflict on the point,[9]

---

18. See the discussion of the Whitfield case in § 527 above.

§ 533

1. CPLR 5513(a).

2. 79 A.D.2d 348, 436 N.Y.S.2d 296 (1st Dep't 1981).

3. See § 418 above.

4. When leave is required, the same rule applies to the time in which to move for leave to appeal. See the discussion in SPR 47:2.

5. CPLR 5513(a).

6. See Matter of Martz' Will, 16 N.Y.2d 939, 264 N.Y.S.2d 925, 212 N.E.2d 441 (1965).

7. See Ocean Acc. & Guar. Corp. v. Otis Elevator Co., 291 N.Y. 254, 52 N.E.2d 421 (1943).

8. See Messner v. Messner, 42 A.D.2d 889, 347 N.Y.S.2d 589 (1st Dep't 1973), decided when the add-on period was 3 instead of 5 days. It is now 5. See CPLR 2103(b)(2).

9. The Fourth Department in Oliver v. Alcog, 155 A.D.2d 1001, 548 N.Y.S.2d 132 (1989), says yes; the First Department in O'Connor v. Lansdown Entertainment Corp., 231 A.D.2d 970, 648 N.Y.S.2d 489 (1996), indicates no. See the discussion in SPR 49:4.

and the loser does best not to rely on a five-day extension.

In situations in which an order sometimes precedes a judgment, with the judgment being entered "on" the order, a failure to timely appeal the order will not necessarily bar an appeal from the judgment. "It has been repeatedly held", for example, "that a party may appeal from a judgment entered based upon an order granting a motion for summary judgment, despite the fact that the time in which to appeal from the underlying order has elapsed".[10] If the order itself has been appealed, on the other hand, it will also be deemed an appeal from a later judgment entered "on" the order, obviating a separate appeal from the judgment.[11] The cautious practitioner should not refrain from appealing the order on the assumption that he can just appeal the overlaying judgment when it comes in later, at least not when they dispose of the very same thing.

For the winner of a dispositive motion like this, a better and more economical practice is to get the order and judgment entered simultaneously—both embodied in one paper if the clerk will accept it—and serve both, or the consolidated one, on the loser with notice of entry.

When an appeal is taken from an appellate court, the appealable paper is the order of the latter rather than any judgment or order that the trial court may enter on it on remand. CPLR 5512(a) so provides, but then, in a seemingly generous gesture, it adds that if a "timely" appeal is taken from the wrong paper in such an instance, it can simply be deemed taken from the right paper and the defect ignored. This may be more of a trap than a reassurance, however, because, whichever paper the appeal is formally taken from, the timeliness of the appeal will apparently be measured from the service of notice of entry of the *appellate* order.[12] And if that is so, the only mistake CPLR 5512(a) forgives is an erroneous reference, in the notice of appeal, to the overlaying lower court judgment or order rather than to the appellate order itself—a piddling gift.

The same rules of timeliness apply when the appeal is not as of right, but needs permission. The difference is that within the applicable period the aspiring appellant, instead of serving a notice of appeal, must make the motion for leave to appeal, i.e., serve the motion papers that bring on the motion.[13] The mailing of the motion papers within the applicable time satisfies this requirement, even though the motion may not be heard or disposed of until after the period expires. When the situation is one in which leave can be sought from either of two courts (e.g., from the appellate division or, if it refuses leave, then from the Court of Appeals),[14] the 30 days in which to move for the second court's permission is computed from the service of the first court's order denying leave with notice of entry, again with the exception that if the would-be appellant is the one who has done the serving, it is his own service that starts the time running.[15]

The party moving for permission to appeal must make the motion returnable at least 8 days but not more than 15 days after service of the notice of the motion.[16] He must ascertain what the motion days are in the court to which the motion is being made[17] and should then pick the first motion day available following the 8th day after the notice of motion is served. Failing to serve the supporting papers and brief at least 8 days prior to the return day can result in a dismissal of the motion.[18]

The judgment or order served on the appellant should be an exact copy of the original in the clerk's file. It has been held that the service of an incorrect copy of the judgment or

---

10. Flynn v. City of Long Beach, 108 A.D.2d 840, 485 N.Y.S.2d 565 (2d Dep't 1985).

11. A 1997 amendment of CPLR 5501(c) so provides. See the discussion at the end of § 532 above.

12. See Rodolitz v. Neptune Paper Products, Inc., 22 N.Y.2d 383, 292 N.Y.S.2d 878, 239 N.E.2d 628 (1968).

13. CPLR 5513(b).

14. See CPLR 5602(a), 5703(a).

15. CPLR 5513(b).

16. CPLR 5516.

17. See § 541 below.

18. See Dellaratta v. International House of Pancakes, 46 N.Y.2d 936, 415 N.Y.S.2d 211, 388 N.E.2d 348 (1979).

order to be appealed, "containing . . . a substantial alteration of the original", won't start the appellant's appeal time running.[19] It is probably best as a rule of thumb to serve only a photostatic copy of the original, which will automatically pick up hand-written changes, cross-outs, initials, and everything else.

If any issue of timeliness arises, it is ordinarily raised by a motion to dismiss the appeal based on affidavits stating the facts relevant to service.[20] The motion is made to the court to which the appeal is being taken and not to the lower court, since it really has to do with the former's jurisdiction.[21]

It may happen that more than one party will want to appeal, or move for leave to appeal. If party X serves a notice of appeal, or motion papers for leave where leave is required, before party Y does, Y need only serve his own notice of appeal, or motion papers for leave, in response. Y may even get a time extension in that situation. Y may use whatever is left of the original 30-day period, and will in any event get 10 days from the service of X's notice of appeal or motion papers regardless of where the original 30-day period may now be. This is known as a cross-appeal.[22] It does not entail two records or sets of briefs; one serves for both and the record contains whatever is needful to either.

To be on the safe side, each party prevailing on an order or judgment should serve its own notice of entry on the loser rather than depending on a co-party's service, unless several parties are united in interest enough to jointly sign such a notice of entry. The risk, otherwise, is that the loser's time to appeal may be open indefinitely against a winner who fails to serve a notice of entry even after the period has long since run against another winner who did make such service.[23]

Extensions of time are the subject of the next section.

§ 534. Omissions, Defects, and Time Extensions

Various omissions and defects can appear in conjunction with an appeal, but those appearing at the "taking" as opposed to the "perfection" stage are the ones that make the most trouble. They hold the potential for forfeiture of the appeal and are the best ones to avoid. An attempt is sometimes made to divide defects into those that concern the time element and those that do not, but it is a superficial effort. On deeper analysis, almost all of the serious defects can be shown to involve time, because if time were not a barrier the whole step could be taken over and done right.

CPLR 2004 recognizes that there are numerous time periods in the CPLR for the doing of many things. It allows the court to extend any of them for good cause shown "except where otherwise expressly prescribed by law". The time in which to take an appeal is one of the exceptions, and it is rigid. CPLR 5514(c) precludes any extension of time in which to take an appeal, or move for leave to appeal, with only a few narrow exceptions:

If the appellant makes a mistake as to method, taking an appeal of right in a case in which leave is required, or seeking leave when an appeal lies of right, the time in which to take the right step may be recomputed. The time will run anew from the dismissal of the appeal, as where the appellant appeals of right in a case that requires leave, or—vice versa—from the denial of an application for leave when leave is unnecessary because the appeal lies of right. Caselaw has given the mistaken appellant another leg-up in this situation. Although the statute says the new time runs from the dismissal or denial itself,[1] it has been construed by the Court of Appeals to start from the usual service of the order (in this case the one dismissing the appeal or denying the mo-

---

19. Masters, Inc. v. White House Discounts, Inc., 119 A.D.2d 639, 500 N.Y.S.2d 790 (2d Dep't 1986).

20. See Nancy C. v. John J. O'C., 50 A.D.2d 800, 375 N.Y.S.2d 630 (2d Dep't 1975).

21. Runkel v. Homelsky, 137 N.Y.S.2d 870 (Sup.Ct., Kings County, 1955).

22. See CPLR 5513(c).

23. A note on this point, built around Blank v. Schafrann, 206 A.D.2d 771, 615 N.Y.S.2d 107 (3d Dep't 1994), appears in SPR 27:3.

§ 534

1. CPLR 5514(a).

tion for leave) with notice of entry, so as to conform it to what attorneys generally understand of appellate practice and to avoid a needless additional trap.[2] It is also provided that if an appeal has been taken by permission, i.e., permission was granted, only to have it discovered later that permission was not necessary, the appeal shall not be dismissed as long as the motion for permission was made within the time limited for the taking of an appeal as of right.[3] This postulates that permission was needlessly granted, but concludes that since the appeal is here it should be proceeded with just as if properly taken as of right.

The taking of an appeal, or the making of a motion for leave to appeal, requires the dual procedure of serving the notice on the adverse party and filing it with the clerk. If the party takes one of those steps on time but omits the other, she can be allowed an extension of time to do the other. Any of the courts involved can grant this extension: the original court, the appellate court, or even the intermediate appellate court when the case is stepping from one appellate tribunal to another.[4]

An extension of time may be secured if the attorney for the would-be appellant becomes in some fashion disabled,[5] but not if the attorney has merely been voluntarily discharged by the client.[6] Time may also be extended to allow for substitution of a party when something happens to require it.[7] It must be shown that the attorney's disability or the substitution-requiring event occurred before the appeal time expired.

Having dutifully set forth the several exceptions, we can now stress the great rigidity of the time for taking an appeal, or for moving for leave to take an appeal. The two major obduracies of civil practice attend the period:

it is (1) a statute of limitations that cannot be extended except upon the narrow grounds stated, and (2) the passing of the period is additionally deemed to divest the appellate court of jurisdiction.[8] This jurisdiction is of the most austere kind, moreover—subject matter jurisdiction—so that not even mutual consent of the parties can reopen the door once the passing of the time period has closed it.[9] The appellate court and its personnel, without waiting for the adverse party's initiative, often sift through notices of appeal and motions for leave to appeal and any other papers before them for any evidence of untimeliness, and, for that matter, any other jurisdictional defect, dismissing appeals and motions when they find one. Sometimes the court will merely raise the issue, rather than raise and dispose of it sua sponte, eliciting the parties' address to the matter in correspondence through the clerk.

A defect in mere form, as where the caption is imperfect or where the judgment or order being appealed is not accurately described in the notice of appeal, may be ignored by the appellate court "when the interests of justice so demand",[10] which presumably means when no one would be prejudiced by the error, as where the other side knew what was intended.

Prematurity of the appeal is also an ignorable defect if by the time the defect is called to the court's attention the appeal would lie.[11] This can occur when, for example, an overzealous appellant has taken an appeal before waiting to be served with the appealable paper and notice of its entry, or, indeed, where he has not even waited for the paper to be entered. An appellant in that league doubtless subscribes to Emerson's view that nothing

---

2. See Park East Corp. v. Whalen, 38 N.Y.2d 559, 381 N.Y.S.2d 819, 345 N.E.2d 289 (1976).

3. CPLR 5520(b).

4. CPLR 5520(a). See Gamble v. Gamble, 23 A.D.2d 887, 259 N.Y.S.2d 910 (2d Dep't 1965). In some circumstances, when one party has been timely served with a notice of appeal, the statute may be applied to extend the time to appeal with respect to another party. See Leonard v. Regan, 167 A.D.2d 790, 563 N.Y.S.2d 348 (3d Dep't 1990).

5. See CPLR 5514(b).

6. Siegel v. Obes, 112 A.D.2d 930, 492 N.Y.S.2d 447 (2d Dep't 1985).

7. See CPLR 1022.

8. See, e.g., Curran v. City of Rochester, 50 A.D.2d 1059, 376 N.Y.S.2d 284 (4th Dep't 1975).

9. See Haverstraw Park, Inc. v. Runcible Properties Corp., 33 N.Y.2d 637, 347 N.Y.S.2d 585, 301 N.E.2d 553 (1973).

10. CPLR 5520(c).

11. Id.

great can be accomplished without enthusiasm.

§ 535. Injunctions and Stays

It is recognized that the need to retain status quo in the situations provided for by Article 63 of the CPLR, which supplies the provisional remedies of preliminary injunction and temporary restraining order, may also be felt at the appellate stage of the case. CPLR 5518 therefore allows the appellate division in such situations[1] to entertain applications for the injunctive remedies after an appeal has been taken in the action, or a motion made for leave to appeal, including applications seeking them initially as well as applications to modify or vacate those already granted.

Quite apart from, and in no event to be confused with, the injunctions authorized by Article 63 is the well known stay of enforcement of the judgment pending appeal. Here CPLR 5519 supplies the governing provisions, and in some detail. This category of stay seeks to prevent the respondent—assume the plaintiff is the respondent and the defendant the appellant—from realizing on the judgment or order[2] while an appeal is taking place, the appellant's hope being that the appeal will succeed and get the disposition reversed. If that does happen, but without a stay having been granted, and the judgment has meanwhile been enforced, e.g., a money judgment has been paid through property of the appellant levied on by the sheriff, the appellant will afterwards be put to the trouble of seeking restitution.[3] And the appellant may in the meantime have been divested of valuable property without any guarantee that such restitution as may later be ordered against the respondent will be collectible; the respondent may have squandered the money and become insolvent in the interim. A stay avoids that.

Under subdivision (a) of CPLR 5519, which provides for a stay without a court order, the stay results automatically in several situations. When the appellant is the state or one of its political subdivisions or an officer or agency of either, for example, its mere service of a notice of appeal, or of a paper known as an "affidavit of intention to move for permission to appeal", automatically stays enforcement of any judgment rendered against it.[4] This may not be too important when the state itself is the appellant, at least on a money judgment, because none of the procedures available for its enforcement are available against the state anyway.[5] But it may be of moment when other than a money judgment is involved, or when others in this governmental category are appealing. An inquiry should be made into what government creatures qualify here. Some officials with a colorable claim to governmental status have been held to be beyond it, and therefore not entitled to an automatic stay, including, for example, the senior officials of the New York City Transit Authority.[6]

The state's municipalities—the cities, counties, towns, and villages—are among the major beneficiaries of this automatic stay.

When the stay takes effect, it operates to stay proceedings to "enforce" the judgment or order. To use a simple example, a plaintiff's money judgment against a city can't be enforced after the city takes an appeal from the judgment. But how does the stay operate when an order does no more, for example, than deny a motion to dismiss? There is no uniform view among the several departments. Three of the four hold that only the enforcement of the particular judgment or order is stayed, while the First Department appears to hold that the stay operates to suspend all further proceedings in the action.[7]

---

§ 535

1. The situations in which the injunctive remedies are available are set forth in CPLR 6301. See § 327 above.

2. CPLR 5519 speaks throughout of a "judgment or order". We use the word "judgment" henceforth in this section to embrace both.

3. See CPLR 5523, 5015(d).

4. CPLR 5519(a)(1).

5. CPLR 5207.

6. Ronan v. Levitt, 73 Misc.2d 35, 341 N.Y.S.2d 176 (Sup.Ct., Albany County, 1973).

7. See the lead notes in SPR Issues 20 and 34. The question of what the automatic stay operates on when a municipality or other governmental unit appeals has been a thorny issue. In a concerted effort to meet and resolve the issue, in respect of both stays and injunctions, the Second Department handed down a quartet of cases on

A municipality has been known to take a totally groundless appeal just to secure the automatic stay of CPLR 5519(a)(1), but that has been held a frivolous practice under Rule 130–1 and subject to monetary sanctions.[8]

Administrative agencies are also the beneficiaries of the automatic stay, which generated controversy in licensing situations and produced an amendment to CPLR 5501(a)(1) in 1988 providing that when the license of a small corporation or partnership has been administratively revoked, and the revocation cancelled by the supreme court in an Article 78 proceeding[9] so that the license now revives, the automatic stay of the supreme court judgment that results when the agency takes an appeal exists for only 15 days. At the end of the 15 days the license revives again. If the agency wants the stay extended, so that the license will not be valid while the appeal pends, it must move for a discretionary stay under subdivision (c) of CPLR 5519, which we take up later.

Non-governmental litigants get an automatic stay only if they file a bond or take some other step to secure the respondent. A defendant appealing an ordinary money judgment, for example, gets a stay of enforcement without a court order when she serves a notice of appeal or the "affidavit of intention" described above, but only if she gives an undertaking to pay the judgment in the event it is affirmed or the appeal dismissed.[10] Stays without a court order when other than money judgments are involved, including judgments with specific property as their subject, are also provided for upon meeting certain conditions, such as by

placing personal property in neutral custody during the appeal,[11] or by making and depositing with the clerk an instrument that the judgment calls for.[12] In some of those situations, and in still others, a bond is once again exacted as a condition to an automatic stay.[13]

The bond usually covers only the pendency of the particular appeal, and its obligation dissolves if the appellant prevails. Even a reopening of only the liability question may be considered an appellate success adequate to cancel the bond, notwithstanding retention of the damages figure while liability goes back for a retrial.[14]

If the situation is one in which the defendant (D) has to bond the judgment in order to stay its execution during an appeal, D had best bond it promptly. If D does not, and P has the sheriff levy the judgment, D becomes liable for poundage to the sheriff[15] even if D then does bond the judgment and spares the sheriff all further steps. In one recent case this delay by D, a hospital, cost it $30,000 that it could have saved just by being a few days prompter.[16]

On appeal from a judgment against an insured in an ordinary personal injury action defended by an insurer—whose solvency is assumed—an automatic stay results (to the extent of the insurance policy's coverage but not beyond) when the insurer takes certain prescribed steps.[17] If the judgment exceeds the coverage, however, the insured would have to give a bond to stay enforcement with respect to the balance, unless the insurer opts to furnish a full bond, which it may do.

A special provision applies in medical, dental, and podiatric malpractice actions when the

May 1, 1996, each addressing a different aspect of the question: Pokoik v. Dep't of Health Services, 220 A.D.2d 13, 641 N.Y.S.2d 881; Pickerell v. Town of Huntington, 219 A.D.2d 24, 641 N.Y.S.2d 887; Schwartz v. N.Y.C. Housing Auth., 219 A.D.2d 47, 641 N.Y.S.2d 885; and State of New York v. Town of Haverstraw, 219 A.D.2d 64, 641 N.Y.S.2d 879 (1996). The four cases are treated in the lead note in SPR 44.

8. See Matter of Troy Police Benevolent and Protective Ass'n (City of Troy), 223 A.D.2d 995, 636 N.Y.S.2d 499 (3d Dep't 1996), noted in SPR 41:3.

9. Article 78 is treated beginning with § 557 below.

10. CPLR 5519(a)(2). If the judgment directs the payment of money in installments, paragraph 3 of 5519(a) governs the bond. For all of the undertakings mentioned

in CPLR 5519, as for undertakings generally under the CPLR, Article 25 provides the details.

11. CPLR 5519(a)(4).

12. CPLR 5519(a)(5).

13. See paragraphs 3, 4, and 6 of CPLR 5519(a).

14. See La Rocco v. Federal Ins. Co., 35 N.Y.2d 806, 362 N.Y.S.2d 461, 321 N.E.2d 551 (1974), rev'g 42 A.D.2d 475, 349 N.Y.S.2d 135 (3d Dep't 1973).

15. See CPLR 8012.

16. Thornton v. Montefiore Hospital, 117 A.D.2d 552, 498 N.Y.S.2d 828 (1st Dep't 1986).

17. CPLR 5519(b).

plaintiff has had judgment for more than $1 million. It provides that if an appeal is taken by the defendant and an undertaking is given either for one million dollars or for the amount of the defendant's malpractice insurance policy, whichever is greater, the appellate court must stay enforcement proceedings during the appeal if it finds "a reasonable probability that the judgment may be reversed or determined excessive".[18] The attainment of this stay is that it can enable a bonding of $1 million to stay enforcement of a judgment that may be for much more than that.[19]

In those situations in which an undertaking is exacted as a condition of a stay, the direction is that the undertaking be "given". What constitutes a "giving"? If the appellant tenders it to the respondent, who accepts it and thereupon refrains from attempting to enforce the judgment, that should do the job. If it is tendered and rejected, the appellant can apparently satisfy the requirement, and earn the stay, by filing the undertaking with the clerk.[20] If any enforcement procedure should be taken in violation of a stay that the appellant assumes has taken effect, the appellant should promptly move to vacate whatever step has been taken, preferably with an order to show cause in which an interim and unambiguous stay can be included. The motion is best made to the court of original jurisdiction, since it is there that the enforcement will be attempted.[21]

In any situation in which no provision is made for an automatic stay, the appellant can apply for a court-ordered stay under subdivision (c) of CPLR 5519, which allows the application to be made to the appellate court, to the original court, or even to an intermediate appellate court when the latter's order is being appealed. This stay, which lies entirely in the court's discretion, is of course the one turned to when the automatic stay provisions aren't applicable, but the court's powers are not restricted to those cases. The court under subdivision (c) has power even over the automatic stays, and can vacate, limit, or modify them.[22]

When granted, a discretionary stay can be conditional. One of the more popular conditions is that the appeal be prosecuted promptly.[23] Any relevant factor may be considered by the court in exercising its discretion. The stay will be denied, for example, if the court suspects that the appeal has a dilatory aim. The presumptive merit of the appeal will also be an element.[24]

The stay provision also contemplates the circumstance in which the appellant loses at the first appellate level. It keeps the stay in effect through the next level of appeal, provided that the second appeal is taken, or leave for it is moved for, within five days after the appellant is served with notice of the entry in the first appellate court of the order unsuccessfully determining the appeal there.[25] There is some caselaw suggesting that this automatic second-step stay will not result if the initial stay was granted by court order under CPLR 5519(c) without an undertaking,[26] but this is a questionable conclusion. The provision in point on the second-step stay, CPLR 5519(e), does not purport to distinguish between sources of the original stay. The Court of Appeals appears to be of this view.[27] When the

---

18. CPLR 5519(g), enacted in 1988.

19. See the Commentary on McKinney's CPLR 5519(g).

20. See Rhoades v. Adelman, 145 N.Y.S.2d 766 (Sup. Ct., N.Y.County, 1955).

21. See, e.g., CPLR 5240, the provision authorizing a protective order in any situation involving the enforcement of a money judgment.

22. If the state or other governmental unit is the party favored by the stay, the stay can be altered only by the court to which the appeal is being taken. CPLR 5519(c), (a)(1).

23. See, e.g., Kiamesha Dev. Corp. v. Guild Properties, Inc., 3 N.Y.2d 981, 169 N.Y.S.2d 741, 147 N.E.2d 247 (1957).

24. See Matter of Mott, 123 N.Y.S.2d 603, 608 (Sup. Ct., Oswego County, 1953).

25. CPLR 5519(e). Similar protections are set forth when leave to appeal is needed.

26. See DFI Communications, Inc. v. Greenberg, 55 A.D.2d 887, 391 N.Y.S.2d 8 (1st Dep't 1977).

27. After the DFI holding by the appellate division, id., that the CPLR 5519(c) stay would not continue through the second stage, the appellant moved the Court of Appeals for a stay. The court denied it as "unnecessary", which could only mean that in its view the earlier stay did continue, contrary to the appellate division's view. See DFI Communications, Inc. v. Greenberg, 41 N.Y.2d 1017, 395 N.Y.S.2d 639, 363 N.E.2d 1384 (1977).

further appeal is one that requires a motion for leave, and leave is granted, any stay applicable during the pendency of the motion continues until five days after the appeal is determined; when leave is denied, it continues until five days after the movant is served with the order of denial with notice of entry.[28]

E. PERFECTING THE APPEAL

Table of Sections

Sec.

§ 536. "Perfecting" the Appeal, Introductory

After the appeal has been formally taken, whether of right or after an order granting permission has been entered, a record of the case has to be put together. If the appeal is from an order, or from a judgment rendered without testimony in open court, such as one resulting from a dismissal under CPLR 3211 or summary judgment under CPLR 3212, there will ordinarily have been no open-court testimony and therefore no stenographic transcript to secure. This will eliminate one of the main expenses of the appellate process. But if there has been a trial or hearing, a transcript will be needed, and the ordering of it is one of the first steps in what is loosely called "perfecting" the appeal, which consists of ordering and securing a transcript, drawing up a record, writing, serving and filing the briefs, getting the case onto the appellate court's calendar for argument, and, finally, arguing and submitting the case.

It is primarily on the initiative of the appellant that the appeal gets perfected. The burden is on the one initiating the appellate process to secure the transcript and put together a record. The respondent's main job is to see that the record also contains everything she may wish to rely on; other than that, the respondent's attention will be directed to drawing her brief, principally a defensive activity designed to answer the appellant's points and sustain the lower court's doings.

Article 55 turns its attention to the "perfection" phase of the appellate process starting with CPLR 5525, which concerns the transcript. It then attends to the record (CPLR 5526) or a statement in lieu of it (CPLR 5527), to the briefs (CPLR 5528, 5529, and 5530), and to a few other incidentals. One who consults Article 55 for the first time may be surprised to find nothing about the argument of the case, about how one brings it on, or about the time allowed for it. Nor will anything be found about such basic matters as motion days in the court, should the need to make a motion arise; or about pre-argument conferences, if there should be such a practice in a given court. The lawyer should note that these items come almost exclusively from the rules of the particular appellate court, and to note further that the rules in this respect are not uniform. Perhaps the most important fact to absorb is that even those parts of the perfection phase that the CPLR does speak to, such as the record and the briefs, are themselves so heavily addressed in the individual rules of court that in some instances a CPLR provision may seem almost to be eclipsed. This is not to suggest that the CPLR has lost sovereignty; it is merely to acknowledge an unusually potent regent, and any appellate practitioner can vouch that in perfecting an appeal the rules of court are surely that.

In the few sections following, therefore, as the perfection process builds around the CPLR, references to rules of court will be more frequent. This will have the effect, not of extending the discourse, but of curtailing it. The matters involved are mechanical; little is to be gained by repeating step-by-step procedures first outlined by the CPLR and then expanded by an individual court's rules. Calling attention to these provisions rather than repeating them will be our mission. Citations of rules will be mainly to those of the appellate divisions, with occasional reference to the rules of the Court of Appeals. The practitioner must

---

28. CPLR 5519(e)(i) and (ii).

also keep in mind that each of these courts is the sole proprietor of its own rules and can change them on short notice. Our rule citations are therefore only samples, and calling attention to them, or to illustrative ones among them, is intended only to narrow the lawyer's research, never to substitute for it.[1]

Both the CPLR and the rules have many time restrictions on perfecting the appeal, but these are not applied as rigidly as the time for taking the appeal in the first place. This is something of a paradox. The taking of the appeal is among the easiest and quickest steps in practice, yet the failure to take it within the prescribed time is fatal: the court lacks power to grant discretionary extensions. The perfection process, on the other hand, is time consuming and expensive, but the time periods applicable to it are not rigid, and can be extended. Notwithstanding this, the frequent willingness of lawyers to delay whenever they are given to understand that delay may be forgiven has prompted an occasional tightening up on these requirements, and an occasional warning.[2] The lawyer planning anything less than strict adherence to the time limits placed on the perfection steps by local rules of court had better make inquiry about what the consequences of a time lapse will be: attitudes differ from time to time and from court to court. A little check into the local status of strictness will be worthwhile. The grapevine should advise, if rules or recent cases do not. Adherence to the letter will of course obviate the inquiry, but some lawyers feel that there is tradition to be honored. They may not wish to jeopardize their credentials with unseemly diligence! Yet diligence does have its rewards, as may be

detected by looking at the other side of the coin. If the local attitude is strict, or the lapse serious, the result can be a dismissal of the appeal for want of prosecution—a result just as devastating on appeal as it is at trial level. It is in effect a forfeiture on the merits. It is significant enough, in any event, to warrant a separate section later on.[3]

There are several different ways recognized or at least allowed by the CPLR for getting together the record of the case or the parts of it needed for appellate review. The appellate divisions, in fact, have culled from Article 55 three alternative methods. Each court has, to one extent or another, promulgated rules designed to implement them. These will be elaborated later,[4] but we can list them briefly now:

One is the procedure of coming up on a full record—the most expensive means but only an optional one.[5] A second is known as the "Appendix System", whereby an appendix to the brief (or to each brief) contains what is needed from the record without multiple reproductions of the whole record.[6] The third is an agreed statement instead of a record, the least expensive method but also apparently the least used because it requires the kind of agreement between lawyers that the adversary system does not foster.[7] Treatment of these topics and the other constituents of the perfection process are the function of the next few sections.

Practitioners on their way to the Court of Appeals should be aware at the very outset that the Court of Appeals has a procedure, entitled "Sua Sponte Examination of Merits", that can nip the perfection process right in the

---

§ 536

1. Finding the courts' rules is not the burden it once was. Law libraries have the official compilation, which is Title 22 of the New York Code of Rules and Regulations, and McKinney's Consolidated Laws publishes all of them together in a soft cover pamphlet, "McKinney's New York Rules of Court", recompiled and distributed annually.

2. See, for example, the statement of the clerk of the Court of Appeals, advising that thenceforth extensions in conjunction with appeals to the Court of Appeals would be granted only upon a showing of "extraordinary circumstances". N.Y.Law Journal, December 3, 1973, p.1, cols. 3–4.

3. See § 542 below.

4. See §§ 538 and 539 below.

5. See Rules 600.5(c) (First Department), 670.9(a) (Second Department), 800.4(a) (Third Department), 1000.4(a) (Fourth Department). CPLR 5528(a)(5) authorizes this full-record method at appellate division option.

6. CPLR 5528(a)(5); Rules 600.5(a) (First Department), 670.9(b) (Second Department), 800.4(b) (Third Department), 1000.4(d) (Fourth Department). The appendix method may be made mandatory in designated instances by court rule. See, e.g., Rule 500.6, a Court of Appeals rule.

7. CPLR 5527; Rules 600.5(b) (First Department), 670.9(c) (Second Department), 800.4(d) (Third Department), 1000.4(c) (Fourth Department).

bud. It enables the court to examine the merits of "selected cases, on its own motion, by an expedited procedure". Rule 500.4 of the Court of Appeals rules elaborates the procedure and the obligations of the parties when the court invokes it. The selection of a case for this special treatment is often triggered by something about it that suggests to the court at the outset, often from the jurisdictional statement itself,[8] that it may be disposed of expeditiously.[9] Parties are advised by the clerk if their case is selected for this treatment. A case so selected may be detoured from the usual "perfection" route, and will be if the court does decide that the merits can be disposed of without putting the case through the usual perfection process. It will not be, however, if the court terminates the summary consideration, in which event the clerk advises the parties and a new perfection schedule is set.[10]

§ 537. The Transcript

A transcript is the typed-out manuscript of testimony and other colloquy of a trial or hearing, taken down verbatim by the court stenographer (also called court reporter) in her minutes. Appeal from a final judgment after a trial usually needs a transcript; so does an appeal from an order in the infrequent instances in which it was not decided on papers alone but required an open-court hearing. The average order involves no live testimony and hence needs no transcript. The procedure for getting the transcript, needed as part of an appellate record or for a brief's appendix, is set forth in CPLR 5525. The appellant, within the time to appeal, serves the court stenographer

with a request for the transcript and deposits the necessary fee.[1]

The parties can stipulate that only a portion of the minutes be transcribed;[2] it may result in quite a saving if they do, but, absent their mutual agreement, a transcription of the whole is required. It has been held that the court is without power to require a resisting party to accept less.[3] If less is feasible, both sides should be receptive to a stipulation. The transcript is expensive,[4] and the loser may end up paying for all of it as a disbursement.[5] If the parties can unite on a single factual statement of the whole case, they can forego a transcript altogether and prosecute the appeal on a "statement in lieu of record on appeal", but this, as already noted,[6] is apparently asking too much of the adversary system. A statement of this kind is not often the appeal method used.

After the transcript has been drawn up, the court stenographer serves two copies of it on the appellant who ordered it, or as many copies as have otherwise been ordered,[7] whereupon the appellant can review it and propose changes in it to conform with his recollection. The appellant then serves a copy of the transcript and proposed changes on the respondent, who reviews it and proposes her own changes. Hopefully they can resolve disputes and come up with a settled transcript without court aid. If they can't, they must follow a prescribed procedure for having the court settle the transcript,[8] which it is the court's duty to do.[9] A procedure is also set forth whereby the transcript will be deemed settled if a respondent who has been served with it does not respond within a certain time.[10] Certification of the transcript in that instance is by the

---

8. See § 531 above.

9. The word "summarily" had been used in the rule but conveyed a wrong impression and was struck out in an amendment that took effect on March 8, 1989.

10. See Rule 500.4(g).

§ 537

1. CPLR 5525(a).

2. CPLR 5525(b).

3. See Perry v. Tauro, 21 A.D.2d 804, 250 N.Y.S.2d 898 (2d Dep't 1964).

4. See CPLR 8002.

5. CPLR 8301(a)(12). See Sterling Optical Co. v. University of the State of New York, 56 Misc.2d 54, 287 N.Y.S.2d 961 (Sup.Ct., Albany County, 1968).

6. See § 536 above. The statement is authorized by CPLR 5527 and is one of the three distinct methods of prosecuting an appeal.

7. CPLR 5525(a).

8. CPLR 5525(c)(1).

9. See Wahrhaftig v. Space Design Group, Inc., 28 A.D.2d 940, 281 N.Y.S.2d 500 (3d Dep't 1967).

10. CPLR 5525(c)(2), (3).

stenographer,[11] otherwise it is certified by the parties together or by the court.[12] In any instance, a stipulation by the parties will be gladly received in place of certification.[13]

When the transcript is settled by one means or another and there is no agreement between the parties working things out otherwise, the appellant usually ends up with both copies of the transcript. The appellant's next prescribed obligation with respect to it is when he serves his brief on the respondent: the appellant must at that time either serve a copy of the transcript on the respondent or else file it with the clerk of the trial court.[14] The former is preferable because it saves the respondent the trouble of having to consult the transcript at the courthouse (which can be a distance away), so it amounts to a courtesy as well, but there is nothing in the CPLR to preclude the clerk from letting the respondent borrow and remove the filed copy if the appellant has opted for the filing rather than the service.

Court rules can vary the time requirements stated by CPLR 5525 or require that only a single transcript be prepared, and in that case the single copy will have to do service for all parties.[15]

If there has been testimony but no transcript, a procedure is set up whereby the appellant can get together a statement of the proceedings from "the best available sources, including his recollection", and serve it on the respondent. Both sides can then either work out its terms, or present it to the court for settlement.[16]

If the appellant relies in any measure on proceedings at the trial itself, which will al-most invariably be the case on an appeal from a judgment or from an order made after a testimonial hearing, the transcript will be a key item. If it is deficient, or if an unsettled transcript is so replete with errors and omissions as to be uncorrectable, or if no stenographer was used and no transcript is available and the parties' statement is undependable, the court may simply throw up its hands and remand the case for a whole new trial.[17] Or, while the appellate court has the power to permit defects in the transcript to be remedied and can grant a continuance for the purpose, it may not be disposed to review the case at all if no transcript or statement is submitted; it may simply deem itself to have "no alternative but to accept the findings of the trial court" and affirm.[18]

We will assume that the transcript, or statement, is now ready for use on the appeal. How it is used is the subject of the next two sections.

§ 538. The Record

The content and form of the record on appeal are prescribed by CPLR 5526, but the rules of the particular appellate court will usually be found to address the subject as well, sometimes adding a few items.[1]

On appeal from a final judgment, the record contains the notice of appeal, the judgment-roll,[2] a settled transcript if there was testimony,[3] any relevant exhibits used below, copies of all reviewable orders,[4] and any opinions written in the case. On an appeal from an order or from an interlocutory judgment, the record consists of the notice of appeal, the order or

---

11. CPLR 5525(c)(2).

12. CPLR 5525(c)(1).

13. CPLR 5532.

14. CPLR 5525(c)(1).

15. CPLR 5525(a), (e). See, e.g., Rules 600.5(f) (First Department) and 800.6(a) (Third Department).

16. CPLR 5525(d). This is derived from what is presently Rule 10(c) of the Federal Rules of Appellate Procedure.

17. See Ernest LL v. Rosemary LL, 50 A.D.2d 706, 375 N.Y.S.2d 495 (3d Dep't 1975).

18. See, e.g., Hayden v. Sclafani, 45 A.D.2d 942, 359 N.Y.S.2d 324 (2d Dep't 1974). Alternatively, a "dismissal"

---

of the appeal may be the outcome in such a situation. For most purposes the difference would be academic.

§ 538

1. See Rules 600.10 (First Department); 670.10 (Second Department); 800.5(a) (Third Department); 1000.4 (Fourth Department). The Court of Appeals' rules allow for the use there of the record used in the appellate division. See Rule 500.5.

2. CPLR 5017(b). See § 419 above.

3. If no stenographic transcript was made, a statement of the proceedings may be used. CPLR 5525(d).

4. CPLR 5501(a) determines which prior orders are reviewable. See § 530 above.

judgment being appealed, a transcript if there is one, the papers and exhibits on which the order or judgment is based, and any opinions in the case. All papers printed or reproduced must be on paper 11 x 8½ inches.[5]

The appellant, who puts together the record on appeal, must include in it all of the "papers and other exhibits upon which the judgment or order was founded".[6] The appellant may not put the record together selectively, including only materials favorable to his own side while omitting matter favorable to the other.[7]

The record must be adequate for appellate review of whatever it is that is being questioned. Even a stipulation by all parties, approving the record, will not earn appellate review if the record is found inadequate. The appeal in such a case is likely to be stricken from the appellate calendar, if already on it, with, at best, leave to remedy the defects and move to restore the case.[8]

A cross-appellant, i.e., a party also appealing but serving a notice of appeal after another party has already served one, should not assume that the whole burden of putting the record together is on the first appellant. The particular court's rules should be checked into about this. In one case, for example, when a cross-appellant, without the main appellant's consent and in violation of a court rule, merely included a copy of the notice of cross-appeal in his brief and tried to use only the record furnished by the main appellant, the cross-appeal was dismissed.[9]

Although a deficient record will impede or altogether prevent appellate review, especially when the deficiencies are in the transcript

discussed in the prior section, on the other side is the rule that records and materials not offered or received in evidence at the trial are improper to include on the appeal, either in the record, in the briefs, or anywhere else.[10] Even the inclusion of an affidavit not properly part of the record below has been "severely condemned", with a warning that "counsel do not help their cases by attaching to briefs matters dehors the record".[11] Such matters will ordinarily be disregarded by the appellate court, permitted neither to buttress nor to weaken the case as the record shows it.

It is provided by CPLR 5530(a) that the appellant shall file the record on appeal with the appellate court when he files his briefs,[12] and all of this is done, according to that provision, within 20 days after the transcript is settled.[13] The respondent then has 15 days in which to file and serve her briefs, manifesting the ungenerosity of these time allotments. On the face of things, the respondent, whose defensive posture on the appeal mandates that she review the appellant's brief carefully before drawing her own, has only 15 days to do that, and to write her own brief, and to get everything reproduced and filed; and, in the bargain, it may be that she does not even have a copy of the transcript, which may have been filed with the clerk instead of being served on her, the option being the appellant's under CPLR 5525(c) if the parties don't otherwise agree. CPLR 5525(e) recognizes this problem, however, by authorizing the appellate divisions to vary these time requirements in their own departments, and the rules adopted pursuant to this authority do indeed supply different time limitations.[14] The lesson, once again, is

---

5. CPLR 5526.

6. CPLR 5526.

7. See 2001 Real Estate v. Campeau Corp., 148 A.D.2d 315, 538 N.Y.S.2d 531 (1st Dep't 1989).

8. See Guarnacci v. Ferguson, 29 A.D.2d 839, 287 N.Y.S.2d 471 (4th Dep't 1968).

9. Kapchan v. Kapchan, 104 A.D.2d 358, 478 N.Y.S.2d 689 (2d Dep't 1984).

10. See Ro–Stan Equities, Inc. v. Schechter, 44 A.D.2d 577, 353 N.Y.S.2d 224 (2d Dep't 1974).

11. Terner v. Terner, 44 A.D.2d 702, 354 N.Y.S.2d 161, 162 (2d Dep't 1974).

12. On appeals from lower courts, the clerk forwards the record to the appellate court. See § 1704 in the New York City Civil Court Act and in the Uniform District, City, and Justice court acts (McKinney's Vol. 29A, Parts 2 and 3).

13. When cross-appeals are taken, i.e., both sides are dissatisfied and are appealing, the plaintiff gets the appellant status in the appellate court; or, where an appeal is from one appellate court to another, the appellant in the lower one keeps that status in the higher one. CPLR 5530(b).

14. See, e.g., Rule 800.9, the Third Department rule. The Court of Appeals has also addressed these matters in its rules. See Rules 500.5, 500.7.

not to rely solely on the CPLR for these matters, but to consult the rules, or the appellate clerk if the rules are not clear. Some departments, while not rigidly applying the CPLR time limits, may set an outside time of their own for concluding the appeal, which the Court of Appeals has also done.[15] All courts of course reserve to themselves the power to enlarge time on a case by case basis, but one may be stricter than another and a party not adhering to the letter of the time requirements should ascertain local indulgence in advance.

The printing of the record is not required. It may be reproduced by offset printing, mimeographing, or any other method of reproduction offering clear black on white copy on paper 11 x 8½ inches.[16] Indeed, the use of printing, when found unreasonable and unnecessary by the court, may result in denying the printing expense as a disbursement, even if the offender is a successful appellant. In one case, for example, the appellant went to a printing expense of $800 to appeal a $450 judgment—a cost found in context to be "profligate" and denied by the court as a disbursement.[17]

How many copies of the record will be needed? This is determined almost entirely by individual court rule and will depend also on the method of appeal being used. The appellant opting to come up on a full record[18] is burdened with reproducing many copies.[19] If instead the appellant elects the appendix system,[20] only a single copy of the record, usually the original itself, is filed with the appellate court. This again is to be found in the rules of court. When it is the original record which, unreproduced, is to leave the trial court and go to the appellate court, the responsibility for

transmitting it may be placed by rule on the clerk instead of the parties.[21] When the record is filed with the appellate court, it is accompanied by a statement describing the case and containing the several data listed in CPLR 5531, including a statement of the method of appeal being used.[22]

Lost in the course of the foregoing discussion is the third appellate method: the "statement in lieu of record on appeal" offered by CPLR 5527. This can be used only when the questions raised on the appeal "can be determined without an examination" of the record, and when all parties are able to unite on a single statement, which may include portions of the transcript or other items in the record. But if the controversy between the parties is one on which they can now, after trial, draw an agreed statement, it is likely to be one on which they could have used the peaceful procedures of CPLR 3222—the "action on submitted facts"[23]—to bring their controversy to court in the first place, dispensing with adversary procedures altogether. Hence it is not likely that a dispute not amenable to such a mutual statement at the outset will suddenly become so after the bruising ordeal of a trial. But CPLR 5527 is optimistic. It briefly sets forth the statement's requirements, and if the parties can find enough common ground, not to resolve their controversy, but just to enunciate it together, they will find savings in exploiting it.

If the CPLR 5527 statement is used, it is submitted to the trial court for correction and approval. As approved, the statement is by itself the record on appeal and is printed as a joint appendix.[24]

---

15. Rule 500.9.

16. The basic permission for these alternatives is in CPLR 5529(a)(1), directed to briefs and appendices, but under court rules it may apply as well to the record when the record is to be reproduced. See, e.g., Rule 600.10, the First Department rule.

17. Society of the New York Hosp. v. Mogensen, 81 Misc.2d 1089, 1090, 370 N.Y.S.2d 354, 355 (App.T., 1st Dep't, 1975). Involved there was Section 1705 of the New York City Civil Court Act, but the disbursement denial was built mainly around CPLR 8301(a)(12), allowing only "reasonable and necessary expenses" as a disbursement, which makes the Society case relevant in other courts as well.

18. The full record is one of the three alternative appellate routes. See § 536 above.

19. See, e.g., Rule 670.9, the Second Department rule.

20. Since the "appendix" is appended to the brief, it is treated in the next section.

21. See, e.g., Rule 600.5(a), the First Department rule.

22. CPLR 5531(7).

23. See § 304 above.

24. See CPLR 5528(d), discussed in the next section. CPLR 5527 specifically says that the statement "shall be printed", but its Article 55 context would appear to allow the alternatives of offset printing or mimeographing or

The statement must be adequate for appellate review. The parties' agreement can no more force the court to work with an inadequate statement than it can compel a review on an inadequate record.[25]

§ 539. The Briefs and Appendices

Three provisions are concerned with the briefs and appendices. CPLR 5528 governs their content, 5529 their form, and 5530 their filing and service. Again, of course, court rules play a major role, the CPLR in several instances expressly inviting the rules to vary things as they choose.[1] Subdivisions (a) and (b) of CPLR 5528 provide for the contents of the briefs and appendices of the appellant and respondent, respectively; the rules then confirm, add to, or otherwise elaborate the list.[2] The major item meriting attention here is the appendix.

The appendix method is one of the three set forth by the CPLR and recognized by the appellate divisions.[3] A second is the appeal on a full record. This one requires multiple reproductions of the record and is too costly in some cases, measured by the stakes involved. The third is CPLR 5527's statement in lieu of a record, the most desirable method but also the least used because of its requirement, difficult to implement, that the parties agree on almost everything to be presented to the appellate court.

When an appendix is used, the rules of court usually require that only a single copy of the full record, or only the original, be filed with the appellate court. The one copy is kept available for the appellate judges for reference if the appendices should prove inadequate, or if

for any reason a judge should want to consult the record proper.

The appendix, contained in the brief or bound separately, selectively reproduces only "such parts of the record ... as are necessary to consider the questions involved".[4] If it does its job properly it will give the appellate court everything needed for review, thus obviating reference to the record itself. Such is the function of an appendix. An appendix properly compiled by the appellant and included in her brief will make it unnecessary for the respondent to include any at all in his. This is because the appellant is required to include in her appendix not only the part of the record relevant to her side, but also "those parts the appellant reasonably assumes will be relied upon by the respondent".[5] Whatever appeal method is used, it is "highly unprofessional" for the appellant to include only materials favorable to her own side and omit matter favorable to the other. An appellant who did that in one case was scolded by the appellate division, the practice "deplored", and the summary judgment that had been granted against the appellant in the trial court unanimously affirmed.[6] If the respondent finds the appendix contained in the appellant's brief inadequate, he adds an appendix to his own brief, to contain only such additional parts as are necessary for his side.[7] The parties can in the alternative agree on a single appendix, called a "joint appendix", which when used is filed with the appellant's brief.[8]

The contents of appendices, as well as of the briefs themselves, should also be checked against local rule requirements.[9]

---

xeroxing, etc., as is allowed for an appendix itself. See CPLR 5529(a)(1).

25. See Guarnacci v. Ferguson, 29 A.D.2d 839, 287 N.Y.S.2d 471 (4th Dep't 1968).

§ 539

1. See, e.g., CPLR 5528(a)(5), 5530(c).

2. See, e.g., Rules 600.10(c), (d), the First Department rules.

3. See § 536 above.

4. CPLR 5528(a)(5).

5. Id.

6. 2001 Real Estate v. Campeau Corp., 148 A.D.2d 315, 538 N.Y.S.2d 531 (1st Dep't 1989). The appellant was

"only interested in having this court examine fully its own arguments", the court remarked, and the respondent "was compelled to submit its own extensive supplemental record", which was about three times the size of the one the appellant handed in.

7. CPLR 5528(b).

8. CPLR 5528(d). When the full record rather than the appendix method is used, each judge gets a copy of the complete record, and each party's brief, instead of reproducing any part of the record, cites as need be to the relevant portions of it.

9. See, e.g., Rule 670.10(c), the Second Department rule. A Court of Appeals rule allows the use there of the appendix used in the appellate division if it is otherwise in

In order to encourage use of the appendix method without inviting unreasonably lengthy appendices compiled in an excess of caution, the Court of Appeals has held that an outright affirmance should not be visited on a case solely because its appendix is inadequate; that the proper course is to require a further appendix or to dismiss the appeal unless an adequate appendix is filed within a set time. It held so in E.P. Reynolds, Inc. v. Nager Electric Company,[10] acknowledging that the appendix in the case was inadequate. It was about 13 pages in length, extracted from a trial transcript of over 950 pages, and it sought reversal on the ground of the insufficiency of the evidence, a ground that may require consultation of the whole record.

If testimony is included in the appendix, it should be set forth in the order of its transcript appearance, not in some different sequence, such as in the alphabetical order of the witnesses' names. The appendix may contain an alphabetical index, of course, but the testimony itself should be in the chronological order of its giving. Anything else is likely to be found unacceptable.[11] The courts sometimes have occasion to note "an increasing tendency ... to disregard the requirements prescribed for the use of the appendix method and to submit appendices which are inadequate and incomplete", holding this to be an abuse of the system and an intolerable imposition on appellate courts.[12] Non-compliance can also bear costs sanctions.[13]

The foregoing is not to suggest that the appellate court insist on perfect appendices. The court does have a copy of the whole record before it and any judge wishing to can visit the clerk's office, or have the record sent up by the clerk, to check out such things as the

appendix may have inadvertently omitted. The Advisory Committee took note of this possibility,[14] but it is a recourse to be indulged only as an appellate favor when the appendix has been compiled with reasonable competence and diligence, not as a substitute for one thrown together haphazardly.

The form of briefs and appendices is in CPLR 5529, and in much detail. Briefs and appendices do not require printing. Offset printing, mimeographing, xeroxing, or any other competent black on white method of reproduction[15] on 11 x 8½-inch paper suffices.[16] What was mentioned in the prior section, in discussing the record, holds true also for the briefs and appendices: a voluntary printing when the economic significance of the case puts the expense out of proportion may be disallowed as a disbursement even to a successful appellant, and may be publicly castigated as "profligate".[17]

The time for the service and filing of the briefs and appendices, and the number of copies required, is the subject of CPLR 5530, whose subdivision (c) invites the individual rules of the appellate courts to modify the CPLR 5530 requirements at will, which some rules do.[18]

When leave to appeal is required, as it is with the Court of Appeals most often and with lower appellate courts occasionally,[19] the motion for leave will involve the record and may entail, along with motion papers, a set of briefs.[20] Since the would-be appellant must convince the appellate court of the merits of the grievances, and the opposing party (the potential respondent) is obliged to refute them, the briefs pro and con take on the content and form of an outright appeal. They should; the applicant on that motion cannot

conformity with Court of Appeals requirements. See Rule 500.6.

10. 17 N.Y.2d 51, 268 N.Y.S.2d 15, 215 N.E.2d 339 (1966).

11. See, e.g., Kimberly–Clark Corp. v. Power Auth., 35 A.D.2d 330, 316 N.Y.S.2d 68 (4th Dep't 1970).

12. Lo Gerfo v. Lo Gerfo, 30 A.D.2d 156, 158, 290 N.Y.S.2d 1005, 1007 (2d Dep't 1968).

13. CPLR 5528(e). See O'Rourke v. Long, 41 N.Y.2d 219, 391 N.Y.S.2d 553, 359 N.E.2d 1347 (1976).

14. See 2d Rep.Leg.Doc. (1958) No. 13, p. 350.

15. See CPLR 5529(a)(1).

16. CPLR 5529(a)(3).

17. See Society of New York Hosp. v. Mogensen, 81 Misc.2d 1089, 370 N.Y.S.2d 354 (App.T., 1st Dep't, 1975).

18. See, e.g., Rule 800.9(a), the Third Department rule.

19. See CPLR 5602, 5701(c), 5703(a).

20. See, e.g., Rule 500.11, the Court of Appeals rule.

safely save a thing for the appeal proper, because there will be no appeal proper if the brief does not convince the court to grant leave. When leave is forthcoming—the great majority of motions for leave to appeal are denied—the parties are then confronted with the appeal itself, and in that situation they often ask what, if anything, their appeal briefs should contain, which their permission briefs did not. If they did their jobs right, the answer is: not much. The appeal briefs can iron out rough spots in the earlier ones, but the lawyer should not be concerned that their substance is virtually the same. Indeed, if anything of true substance appears only in the appeal brief, having been overlooked in the earlier motion brief, the movant may be considered lucky that the motion was granted without it. And a respondent in that position may well wonder whether, had the point been included in the papers resisting the motion, leave to appeal might have been denied.

Unlike the federal courts,[21] New York does not impose a uniform arbitrary limit on the size of briefs, but individual appellate courts are free to devise limits if they wish. Oversized briefs are not often a problem, but they do appear from time to time and can face the embarrassment of appellate censure. The Court of Appeals, in a rare address to the problem, condemned a 284-page brief for its useless redundancies, irrelevancies, and aimlessness.[22] Pithiness is not merely admired by the appellate courts; it is likely to be far more effective than prolixity.

§ 540. Calendar Practice and the Argument

On the question of appealability, the constitution and the statutes have the say. The same is true of scope of review. The early procedural steps of taking the appeal are also largely dictated by statute, but as the perfection stage is reached—securing the transcript and putting together the record and briefs—statute begins to share power with individual rules of court. Now, arriving at calendar practice in the appellate courts, statute leaves the stage and the court rules become virtually the whole cast. At trial level, calendar practice is largely under the governance of the rules; at appellate level, it is almost entirely so. Our mission here will be to call attention to the several steps still left in perfecting the appeal, and to cite at least a sample rule at each juncture.

The first question is how to get on the court's calendar. The practice will differ from court to court, perhaps entailing the filing of a "note of issue"[1] or some other procedure.[2] The rules will also determine how the parties are notified of when the case comes on for argument and how much time will be allowed for it,[3] and relevant instruction if there is to be, or if there is required to be, a submission without argument. In the Court of Appeals, for example, although appeals are argued orally, motions for leave to appeal ordinarily are not.[4]

In some departments there are what are denominated the "Enumerated" and "Non–Enumerated" calendars. These are just lists of judgments and orders coming under one category or the other; the ones the appellate division deems the more important are listed as "Enumerated" and the more pedestrian the "Non–Enumerated".[5] The consequence of the difference is that appeals in the "Enumerated" category, or most of them, usually get more time for oral argument.[6] In other departments there may be rules that perform an equivalent role in different terminology.[7]

In some departments there is a requirement of a "preargument conference" to take place in designated cases—a procedure designed to make another attempt at restricting the issues and possibly securing settlement, akin to the

---

21. See Rule 28(g) of the Federal Rules of Appellate Procedure.

22. See Slater v. Gallman, 38 N.Y.2d 1, 377 N.Y.S.2d 448, 339 N.E.2d 863 (1975).

§ 540

1. See, e.g., Rule 600.11 (First Department).

2. See, e.g., Rule 500.8 (Court of Appeals).

3. See, e.g., Rule 670.19 (Second Department).

4. See Rule 500.11(g).

5. See, e.g., Rule 600.4 (First Department).

6. See Rule 600.11(f) (First Department).

7. See, e.g., Rule 1000.11, the Fourth Department rule.

purpose of the pretrial conference at trial level.[8] The appellate divisions that have adopted such procedures take them quite seriously and will not suffer a disregard of their requirements. When a conference was duly set up under the Second Department rule, for example, and the respondents' attorney did not attend it, the court, under a provision authorizing sanctions,[9] refused to consider the respondents' brief.[10]

One of the few phases of appellate calendar practice that the CPLR does address is the preference, but the address is terse. CPLR 5521 states that "preferences in the hearing of an appeal may be granted in the discretion of the court to which the appeal is taken". It sets no standard, however, leaving it entirely to the individual courts. Some of the courts have rules that speak to the matter,[11] but even the absence of a governing rule does not seem to make a great deal of difference. The court can grant a preference whenever on a sui generis basis the facts warrant it. We can analogize here to the discretionary grounds on which special preferences are granted at trial level,[12] but the appellate preference is not the coveted prize that the one at trial level is. An appellate court abreast of its calendar may sometimes have more trouble keeping the parties moving than vice-versa.

For all calendar matters, the attorneys should consult the rules, and for what the rules don't cover they should consult the clerk. The clerk's staff will usually be found courteous and willing to help as well as knowledgeable. And if the clerk wants things done a certain way, the lawyer should not be quick to see the contrary in the applicable statutes or rules. The matter can be discussed, but when it comes to calendar practice, the odds in a contest between the law and the clerk are with the clerk.

F. INCIDENTAL APPELLATE PRACTICE

Table of Sections

Sec.
541. Motions in Appellate Courts.
542. Dismissal of Appeal for Want of Prosecution.

§ 541. Motions in Appellate Courts

One does not usually associate a "motion" with the appellate process, except perhaps the motion for leave to appeal, but there are a number of occasions when relief sought from an appellate court, sometimes incidental and sometimes final, is sought by motion. If a stipulation between the parties cannot resolve an incidental dispute, for example, or a stipulation is not sufficient, it will usually take a motion to resolve it—as where an enlargement of time after a certain point in the appellate process has by rule been made to require court approval.[1] The rule of thumb about motions in an appellate court can be derived from the motion practice at trial level: any incidental order that the court has the power to make can be moved for by any interested party.

Several of the things already met require a motion. The provisional remedy of injunction does, and the motion for it can be made during the appellate stage of the litigation.[2] The appellate court is an alternative motion forum (the trial court the other) for a stay of enforcement during an appeal when the stay requires a motion, which it does when an automatic stay is not available.[3]

Most of the motions that appear in the appellate courts are during the appellate process itself, that is, after the appeal has been taken but before it has been decided. The main one before that time is the motion for permission to appeal, made by the aspiring appellant. One seen after that time is the motion to reargue

---

8. See, e.g., Rule 670.4, the Second Department rule. See also § 374 for the analogy to the pretrial conference at trial level.

9. Rule 670.4(b).

10. Romanelli v. Associated Marble Industry, Inc., 365 N.Y.S.2d 264 (2d Dep't 1975).

11. See, e.g., Rule 600.12, the First Department rule.

12. CPLR 3403(a)(3). See § 373 above.

§ 541

1. See, e.g., Rule 670.8(d), the Second Department rule.

2. CPLR 5518.

3. CPLR 5519(c).

made by the appellate loser. These are such key motions in appellate practice, in fact, that special rules will often be found directed to them. The Court of Appeals rule on motions devotes much of its attention, in fact, to the motion for leave to appeal,[4] and to one extent or another all of the appellate divisions regulate that motion. The same is true of the motion to reargue, treated in a later section.[5]

On the mechanics and procedural incidentals of motion practice, the appellate rules again must be the first resort. There will usually be something in point,[6] and if the applicable rule has all the answers, inquiry need go no further. If it does not, one may then consult the CPLR's general article on motion practice, Article 22. If on a given occasion it does not seem to fit—it is devised with courts or original jurisdiction principally in mind—there is nothing for it but to call the clerk.

§ 542. Dismissal of Appeal for Want of Prosecution

The ultimate penalty for failing to bring the appeal to fruition is a dismissal for want of prosecution, the appellate equivalent of a trial-level dismissal on the same ground and every bit as serious. When the time for the taking of a required step passes without the taking, the appeal starts to become ripe for such a dismissal. Most appellate courts, recognizing the bar's need for clear guidance on the matter, have rules directed to dismissals and calendar strikings of this kind.[1] A motion to dismiss is supplied, and the rules may also contain an automatic dismissal for a given omission. An appellate court can, moreover, direct a dismissal sua sponte—a prospect all the more likely when the court has already granted an extension and it has been abused.[2]

If the court does not keep surveillance on its cases, and the respondent is not particularly vigilant, the appeal may hang around for years without getting perfected, but the absence of sua sponte action by the court or early motion initiative by the respondent is no guarantee that a long delayed case is going to sneak through to a disposition on the merits. The court may entertain a dismissal request on the argument of the appeal itself, and grant the dismissal instead of reaching the merits.[3]

The court can, and often does, grant a dismissal motion conditionally, the condition being that the appellant will serve and file the required papers and otherwise perfect the appeal within a stated time, but the appellant's lawyer cannot safely assume that this will always be the result. As has been noted several times already, attitudes on these matters may differ from court to court, or from time to time in the same court, and the indulgence of one moment may become the impatience of another. The lawyer uninitiated in these fluctuations would do well to read Tonkonogy v. Jaffin,[4] which acknowledges prior laxity and warns that the reins are again being tightened. It also stresses the appellant's obligations when faced with a motion to dismiss for want of prosecution. As a category of default, opposition to the motion requires (1) reasons satisfactorily explaining the delay and (2) affidavits averring the merits of the appeal. The lawyer ready to subscribe to the letter of the court's requirements is relieved of having to look into whether the local temper is in a cycle of generosity or sternness. The dilatory lawyer, by contrast, may find himself spending more time on that line of inquiry than on the appeal.

The motion to dismiss an appeal for want of prosecution is addressed to the sound discretion of the court,[5] and the appellant who would stay in court should address that discretion with something substantial.

---

4. Rule 500.11(d).

5. See § 544 below.

6. On motion practice generally, see Rules 500.11 (Court of Appeals), 600.2(a) (First Department), 670.5 (Second Department), 800.2(a) (Third Department), 1000.13 (Fourth Department).

§ 542

1. See, e.g., Rule 500.9, the Court of Appeals rule.

2. See, e.g., Eller v. Eller, 44 A.D.2d 582, 353 N.Y.S.2d 244 (2d Dep't 1974).

3. See, e.g., Weingrad & Weingrad v. Kevelson, 44 A.D.2d 523, 353 N.Y.S.2d 216 (1st Dep't 1974).

4. 21 A.D.2d 264, 249 N.Y.S.2d 934 (1st Dep't 1964).

5. Id.

This category of dismissal may carry even greater consequences than a want of prosecution dismissal does in the trial court. In the trial court, it is not deemed a dismissal on the merits, so that if the original statute of limitations on the claim is still alive it can be sued on again without meeting the defense of res judicata.[6] But it has been held that dismissal of an appeal for want of prosecution does act as a disposition on the merits—the merits just as they were found below. So held a divided Court of Appeals in Bray v. Cox,[7] in which an earlier appellate division order had been appealed and the appeal dismissed for non-prosecution. The case then went back to trial and another appeal was taken, this one from the final judgment. The appellant then sought to raise in the Court of Appeals the same point presented on the prior—the dismissed—appeal. The Court held that the dismissal acted as a bar to all questions that were presented but never reached on the earlier appeal.

A close look at the *Bray* case shows quite a forfeiture. As was noted earlier, New York is unusually generous in its allowance of the interlocutory appeal.[8] The party aggrieved by a nonfinal determination has the option of taking it up for review with an immediate appeal, or in some cases of waiting for final judgment and, if it's unfavorable, appealing the judgment and getting the old order reviewed as part of it.[9] The party who elects the immediate appeal and then lets it lapse forfeits both avenues of review and is stuck forever with the determination that aggrieved him. Here is how one appellate division sums up the impact of the *Bray* case:

Where a party appeals from an intermediate order, thereafter abandons the appeal for failure to perfect, and the appeal is then dismissed by an appellate court, the party is estopped for reasons of judicial economy from seeking review of issues which could have been raised on the appeal from the intermediate order....[10]

G. CONCLUDING THE APPEAL

Table of Sections

§ 543.   Disposition of Appeal

The appellate court will direct whatever result is warranted by its review of the appeal's merits. Subdivision (a) of CPLR 5522 provides that the appellate court may "reverse, affirm, or modify, wholly or in part, any judgment, or order before it, as to any party", and that it shall "render a final determination or, where necessary or proper, remit to another court for further proceedings". The appellate court, in other words, may, within its powers of review, do whatever it thinks has to be done.

If the reviewing court is the appellate division, whose powers are coextensive with the trial court's, it can order a new trial in a money action unless the plaintiff stipulates to take less in damages or the defendant stipulates to pay more—the devices commonly known as "remittitur" and "additur", treated elsewhere.[1]

If restitution in conjunction with the result is called for, as where a levy has gone forward against the property of the defendant and the case is afterwards reversed and the judgment overturned on the appeal, the court can direct it.[2] So can the trial court itself when a judg-

---

6. See § 375 above.

7. 38 N.Y.2d 350, 379 N.Y.S.2d 803, 342 N.E.2d 575 (1976).

8. See § 526 above.

9. See § 530 above.

10. Montalvo v. Nel Taxi Corp., 114 A.D.2d 494, 494 N.Y.S.2d 406 (2d Dep't 1985). D had previously appealed an order denying a motion to vacate his default in answering. He let the appeal lapse and it was dismissed. When judgment was later entered against him after inquest, D

appealed the judgment and tried to get the old default order overturned as part of it. He did not succeed.

§ 543

1. See § 407 above. Subdivision (b) of CPLR 5522 requires the appellate division, upon rendering an additur or remittitur, to list the factors it considered. This category of "remittitur" should not be confused with the one (treated in § 545, below) that merely connotes the sending back of a case from an appellate court to a lower court.

2. CPLR 5523.

ment's vacatur is called to its attention.[3] When the record before the appellate court is complete and nothing is to be gained by a new trial, the court's disposition will be an order directing final judgment, or in the case of the Court of Appeals perhaps an order, after determining the law, remitting the case to the appellate division for findings of fact. If the record is insufficient for final judgment, even if it affects only damages, further proceedings will be needed, and these will take whatever form the appellate order of disposition directs.[4]

On an appeal in a case involving an indemnity claim asserted by way of a cross-claim between co-defendants or a third-party claim against an impleaded defendant, it has generally been understood that if the main judgment that P has against D is overturned, the overturning must carry down as well a third-party judgment that D has against co-defendant X or third-party defendant X for indemnification or contribution to D in respect of P's claim, even if X has not appealed.[5] That should still be the rule when the thing to be indemnified—P's main claim—is the claim that falls. How can an indemnification claim running only in favor of D against X to indemnify D for what D has to pay P be retained under any circumstances when D has paid P nothing, and will not have to?

Now consider this situation. P fell on a sidewalk and sued C, a city, and G, a garage, winning against both. Only C appealed. On appeal it was held that there was no defect in the sidewalk, a holding that should have let G off, too, and would have, had G appealed. But G did not appeal. Does G get the advantage of co-defendant C's victory? The Court of Appeals in Hecht v. City of New York[6] said no: the non-appealing G may not have the fruits of the victory of appellant C. G thus ended up facing

a liability alone—C is apparently out even as an indemnitor or contributor—for something for which the precaution of an appeal, and perhaps just the copying of C's briefs, would have released G altogether.

The lesson to every party in a case in which some adverse party has appealed is to project all possible results of the appeal and, if any of them can affect the client's interest adversely, take an appeal as a precaution.[7] If the 30–day period for an original appeal has expired, there will still be the 10–day period for a cross-appeal measured from the other party's service of its notice of appeal.[8]

How should *Hecht* play out in a clear-cut indemnification situation? There, as noted above, a third-party defendant (the indemnitor) will be given the benefit of an appellate victory by the main defendant (the indemnitee). But what of the converse, in which the third-party defendant is the successful appellant and the defendant the party that failed to appeal. *Hecht* would suggest that the defendant could not be given the advantage of the third-party defendant's victory, but the matter isn't clear.

The Court of Appeals has not reconciled its cases[9], and especially in view of criticism of the *Hecht* decision as too strict,[10] some attorneys may disregard *Hecht* and refrain from appealing in analogous situations in which caution suggests that a losing party, otherwise content not to appeal, should reconsider if some other losing party appeals.[11]

The Second Circuit decision in Hegger v. Green[12] is an even starker example of the consequences of failing to appeal in a multi-defendant case. P brought a wrongful death claim against hospital H and doctor D and got

3. See CPLR 5015(d).

4. See, e.g., Frenchman & Sweet, Inc. v. Philco Discount Corp., 21 A.D.2d 180, 249 N.Y.S.2d 611 (4th Dep't 1964).

5. See, e.g., Salerno v. New York Cent. R. R., 21 A.D.2d 850, 251 N.Y.S.2d 394 (4th Dep't 1964).

6. 60 N.Y.2d 57, 467 N.Y.S.2d 187, 454 N.E.2d 527 (1983).

7. See the discussion of the Hecht case in the lead note in New York State Law Digest No. 285.

8. CPLR 5513(c). The special 10-day period is designed for just such a situation.

9. See and compare Sharrow v. Dick Corp., 86 N.Y.2d 54, 629 N.Y.S.2d 980, 653 N.E.2d 1150 (1995).

10. See Newman, Appellate Practice, N.Y. Law Journal (October 20, 1983).

11. See the discussions in New York State Law Digest No. 427 and SPR 27:3.

12. 646 F.2d 22 (2d Cir.1981).

a half-million dollar verdict. There was some reduction for contributory fault on the decedent's part, and an apportionment of fault between H and D. D's total liability under the original judgment, after considering all things including potential contribution from H, was some $96,000. D did not appeal, but P and H did. P convinced the appellate court that there had been no contributory fault and hence that no deduction was permissible for it. H convinced the appellate court that H was not at fault at all. D did not convince the appellate court of anything because D did not appeal and was not there to state his case. The result was that D's exposure, $96,000 before the appeal, was more than $500,000 after it.[13]

A lawyer with a client so situated who fails to preserve the client's standing before the appellate court with a proper appeal had best have a carefully considered reason for standing pat, or an ample malpractice policy.

The different powers of review of the Court of Appeals and the appellate division, the Court of Appeals being restricted to law questions while the appellate division can review the facts as well, have created certain problems on Court of Appeals review. In formulating its dispositive order, the Court of Appeals is helped by knowing whether the appellate division has based its determination on the law, on the facts, or on both. To that end the appellate division is required in several common instances to state in its order precisely what it has done in that respect.[14] After it has disposed of any questions of law, the Court of Appeals is then better situated to determine what to do with the case, e.g., direct final judgment because no facts remain to be reviewed, remand to the appellate division to review facts not previously reviewed, remand to the trial court for a retrial because that is what the appellate division says it would have done on the facts if it should be found to be in

error on the law, etc. Absent such specific indications from the appellate division as to how it has disposed of the facts, the Court of Appeals is required to presume that the appellate division has not considered the facts,[15] which becomes relevant if the Court of Appeals disposition is one of reversal or modification. If in that situation it appears that the appellate division has not considered the facts, whether because it has said as much or because its silence on the matter has invoked the presumption, the Court of Appeals must remit the case to the appellate division for consideration of the facts raised[16] in an instance in which it might otherwise have been able to direct a final judgment and bring the case to an end.

Whenever the Court of Appeals has before it an appeal on certified questions submitted by the appellate division,[17] the court does not simply answer the questions and send back the answers; it is also required to direct entry of the appropriate judgment or order,[18] i.e., to dispose of the case just as it would on any appeal.

Another point of interplay between the two courts concerns the fact that a final determination in the appellate division is appealable to the Court of Appeals of right if there are two dissenting justices in the appellate division,[19] for which reason the latter's order determining an appeal must state whether there are any dissents.[20]

An opinion is not required from the appellate court and it is therefore in the court's discretion, and in the discretion of each judge or justice, whether to write one. But if the case is one of reversal or modification and no opinion is written, the appellate court must at least "briefly state the grounds of its decision".[21]

---

13. The Hegger case is treated in the lead note in New York State Law Digest No. 259.

14. See CPLR 5712(b),(c).

15. CPLR 5612(a).

16. CPLR 5613.

17. See CPLR 5713.

18. CPLR 5614.

19. CPLR 5601(a).

20. CPLR 5712(a).

21. CPLR 5522(a). For a brief time, between 1975 and 1977, this was also required when the decision was an affirmance. See Commentary C5522:3 on McKinney's CPLR 5522.

§ 544. Reargument

The party who lost the appeal can move to reargue it, which implies an ability to convince the court that it overlooked something or misapprehended the law or the facts, which in turn explains why the great majority of reargument motions are denied. Good chance or not, it is the loser's last one, and the magnetism of a last hurrah is for many a loser irresistible. The number of reargument motions is therefore substantial and for that reason almost all courts have a rule directed to them. The attorney considering such a motion should check carefully into any time limitations the local rule may impose on a motion to reargue.[1]

Also important to take note of here is the general rule, previously met at trial level but relevant on appeal as well, that a motion to reargue may not be permitted to take advantage of changes in the law occurring after the court has handed down its decision, unless the time in which to appeal that decision, or to take a further appeal from it, is still open.[2] This is a necessary adjunct of the rule that "there must be an end to lawsuits and the time to take an appeal cannot forever be extended".[3]

The motion to reargue, which involves no new proof or points—and sometimes a court rule will explicitly preclude reargument motions from raising new points[4]—must be distinguished from the situation in which new proof has been discovered and is felt to be sufficient to change the result of the case. The expedient for the presentation of the new matter is not a motion to reargue in the appellate court, but a motion in the trial court under CPLR 5015(a)(2) to vacate the judgment or order and rehear the issue or try the case anew.

Because the vast majority of reargument motions are denied, one may even say that it is almost futile to move to reargue, especially in the Court of Appeals. When the case is not even one for an appeal as of right, moreover, but requires leave, and leave has been moved for and denied, the chance of obtaining permission to reargue the motion for leave stands on an even lower level of likelihood. That's nevertheless what a defendant sought in Intercontinental Credit Corp. v. Roth.[5] What he found, instead, in addition to the predictable denial of the motion for leave to reargue the motion for leave, was $5000 worth of sanctions under Part 130-1 of the Rules: one $2500 allotment debited to him, and one to his lawyer.

§ 545. Remittitur

The determination of the appellate court is embodied in an order, which is entered in the office of the appellate court's clerk.[1] If further proceedings are contemplated, a copy of the order, together with the appellate record, is remitted to the clerk of the court required to conduct such further proceedings.[2] That would usually be the court of original jurisdiction, as where a new trial has been ordered. But it can instead be an appellate court, as where the Court of Appeals, determining issues of law, remits the case to the appellate division for a review of the facts if there has not yet been one.[3] If no further proceedings are called for, as where the appellate determination is final, the case gets remitted to the original court, whose clerk enters the appellate order and any judgment it may call for.[4]

---

§ 544

1. See, e.g., Rule 500.11(g), the Court of Appeals rule.

2. See § 254 above.

3. Matter of Huie, 20 N.Y.2d 568, 572, 285 N.Y.S.2d 610, 612, 232 N.E.2d 642, 644 (1967).

4. The Court of Appeals rule, Rule 500.11(g), can again serve as the example.

5. 78 N.Y.2d 306, 574 N.Y.S.2d 528, 579 N.E.2d 688 (1991).

§ 545

1. CPLR 5524(a).

2. CPLR 5524(b). This "remittitur" merely means the return of a case to the court it came from, either for further proceedings or for final judgment. It is to be distinguished from the word as used in its "addituritur-remittitur" context, where it implies a reduction of damages for excessiveness. See § 407 above.

3. See CPLR 5613.

4. CPLR 5524(b).

If further proceedings are required, they should be conducted in conformity with the intentions of the appellate court as embodied in the order. If there has been an opinion in the case that sheds any light on intentions, it may of course be consulted as well. In the average case further proceedings will require nothing very unusual: a retrial on all or some issues, a reassessment of damages, new findings by a judge or referee, etc. If perfect implementation of the appellate order has been rendered impossible by changed conditions—an occurrence more likely to appear when equitable relief is involved but not frequent even in that case—the trial court should adapt its proceedings to implement the appellate order as nearly as may be. The Court of Appeals has said that "adapting relief to the exigencies of new conditions ... is not nullification, but enforcement."[5]

If there should be any need to correct a remittitur, i.e., the appellate order accompanying the record on its trip back to the lower court, as where the order does not accurately reflect the appellate disposition intended, a motion to amend the remittitur should be made to the appellate court from which it comes. No other court is authorized to effect such an amendment. It may also happen that the losing party wants to take the case to the U.S. Supreme Court, which may be permissible if a federal right is involved.[6] If the order and the opinion do not make clear the involvement of a federal issue, an amendment of the order of remittitur can be sought from the appellate court to clarify whether a federal issue was passed on.

On rare occasions an appellate remittitur will go lost, as it did in Fry v. Village of Tarrytown.[7] Saying that "for this court to proceed, a copy of the remittitur must be entered in the ... Clerk's Office", the court held itself to be without jurisdiction to take further proceedings, denying a request for them "without prejudice to renewal after the filing of the remittitur". If the remittitur can't be located, an application can ordinarily be made to the appellate court for a new one.

---

5. Rudiger v. Coleman, 228 N.Y. 225, 233, 126 N.E. 723, 726 (1920).

6. 28 U.S.C.A. § 1257. The route to the U.S. Supreme Court from a state court today is by petition for a writ of certiorari exclusively. A 1988 amendment eliminated the appeal of right. See the Commentary on the 1988 Revision in 28 U.S.C.A. § 1257.

7. 176 Misc.2d 275, 671 N.Y.S.2d 633 (Sup.Ct., Westchester County, 1998).

Chapter Twenty

SPECIAL PROCEEDINGS

Analysis

---

§ 546. Special Proceedings, Introductory

The purpose of this chapter is to cover the "special proceeding", an expeditious device available in certain instances.

The first segment will discuss special proceedings generally, including a detailed treatment of Article 4 of the CPLR, whose purpose is to supply a central repository of governing rules for special proceedings. The next will treat the Article 78 proceeding, whose principal function is to supply judicial review of administrative determinations. It is among the most important and frequently used procedures in practice today. The same may be said of the summary proceeding—the device whereby the landlord-tenant dispute, for either rent or repossession, goes to court. The summary proceeding is the final item in this chapter.

THE SPECIAL PROCEEDING, IN GENERAL

§ 547. The "Special Proceeding", Described

A special proceeding is a quick and inexpensive way to implement a right. It is as plenary as an action, culminating in a judgment, but is brought on with the ease, speed, and economy of a mere motion. Combining the best of both worlds, the special proceeding is of course preferable to the ordinary action, but it may be used only when explicitly authorized by law in a particular case. The rule is that it takes an ordinary action to prosecute a right "except where prosecution in the form of a special proceeding is authorized".[1]

When a given procedure is authorized for both an action and a special proceeding, the CPLR mentions only the "action", because the action is defined to include a special proceeding.[2]

Statutes authorizing special proceedings abound, both in and out of the CPLR. Some of the special proceedings authorized by the CPLR itself and already met in this book are the proceeding to settle an infant's claim,[3] the proceeding by an attaching plaintiff against a garnishee to compel the garnishee to deliver property to the levying sheriff,[4] and the several supplied for the enforcement of a money judgment.[5] Some to be studied shortly are the Article 78 proceeding[6] and those supplied for testing the arbitrability of a dispute or the validity of an arbitral award.[7] A special proceeding is also used in the supreme court to determine matters relating to a trust.[8]

Outside the CPLR are many other statutes authorizing special proceedings. These may be found in various parts, likely and unlikely, of the consolidated laws. One of the likely ones is the well-known summary proceeding to recover the possession of real property,[9] taken up later.[10] Although the principal device for determining and punishing a contempt of court today is a mere motion, there may still be occasions to use a special proceeding for it.[11]

The legislature has authorized a special proceeding for the litigation of many other categories of dispute. Its speed has made it appropriate to test election squabbles, for example, especially pre-election challenges carried on under the pressure of an approaching election day.[12] A special need for a procedure quicker than a ponderous action presumably underlies most if not all of the legislative enactments

---

§ 547

1. CPLR 103(b).

2. CPLR 105(b). Procedure in special proceedings is treated in § 550 below.

3. CPLR 1207. See § 200 above.

4. CPLR 6214(d). See § 321 above.

5. CPLR 5225(b), 5227, 5239. See §§ 510 and 521 above.

6. See § 557 et seq., below.

7. See § 591 below.

8. CPLR 7701.

9. RPAPL Article 7.

10. See § 571 et seq., below.

11. See § 484 above.

12. See Election Law Article 16 generally and § 16–116 in particular.

that allow the proceeding. It is permitted, for example, as the means to get a dangerous dog destroyed or securely confined,[13] or to have a person declared an incapacitated person and have a guardian appointed for him,[14] where the need to act fast is plain.

Whether the legislative motive in allowing a special proceeding in a given instance is plain or not, its availability is always good news to the petitioner,[15] the person with the claim. It will spare the petitioner the burdensome trappings of an ordinary action and permit the application to be brought on promptly.

There is no formula for determining when a special proceeding is permissible. Whatever the theoretical purpose may be for authorizing a special proceeding, the legislature has allowed it rather arbitrarily. The would-be petitioner must therefore ascertain that there is statutory authority for bringing a special proceeding instead of an action. Absent such authorization, the rule is that the case must be prosecuted in the form of an ordinary action.

There are a few exceptions. Sometimes when an application has to be made and there's no procedural guidance for it, the courts have directed that the device of the special proceeding be used. They've done this with the application for leave to file a late notice of claim,[16] for example, and with the application for pre-action disclosure.[17]

What happens when a petitioner mistakenly brings a special proceeding when it is not authorized; when a regular action should have been brought instead? There used to be a dismissal for this defect, but no longer. If the defect is the only one—jurisdiction having been duly acquired over the parties—the remedy is for the court to convert the case to an action. New York no longer tolerates a dis-

missal for this relatively innocent error.[18] The conversion is effected by the court's ordering the process and pleadings in the proceeding to be deemed the process and pleadings in an action, the case to be henceforth treated as having been properly brought. The court may prescribe any other conversion steps it deems appropriate. If there are several claims or counterclaims or cross-claims present in a given case, for example, some of which should be actions and others special proceedings, the court may sever any that should be prosecuted in different form and direct that it proceed accordingly.[19]

Conversely, an action for relief that should have been sought in a special proceeding may be converted to one. But when the mistake made by the petitioner is not in bringing an action when a proceeding is proper, but in attempting to "appeal" the objectionable determination, a simple conversion can't help. The reason is that jurisdiction of the other side must be obtained, and while the procedures of an action include the jurisdiction-getting service of process,[20] an appeal does not. Hence a dismissal may be the result,[21] without prejudice to the commencement of a proceeding. Time, however, can run out in the interim, which makes the statute of limitations in special proceedings a sensitive issue. It is the next topic.

§ 548. Statute of Limitations in Special Proceedings

In most categories of special proceeding, problems of timeliness seldom arise. This is probably because the special proceeding has been primarily designed by the legislature for situations calling for speed and dispatch, and it would be especially perverse for the petition-

---

13. Agric. & Mark.L. § 121.

14. Ment.Hyg.L. § 78.03.

15. Parties to the special proceeding are petitioner and respondent instead of plaintiff and defendant. See § 551 below.

16. See Billone v. Town of Huntington, 188 A.D.2d 526, 591 N.Y.S.2d 437 (2d Dep't 1992).

17. See Robinson v. Government of Malaysia, 174 Misc.2d 560, 664 N.Y.S.2d 907 (Sup.Ct., N.Y.County, 1997).

18. See CPLR 103(c).

19. See CPLR 407.

20. See § 553 below.

21. See Common Council of the City of Gloversville v. Town Board of the Town of Johnstown, 144 A.D.2d 90, 536 N.Y.S.2d 881 (1989).

er, the one who presumably needs the relief quickly, to let it ride for any time at all, much less for a time adequate to raise a limitations' problem. When the problem does arise, it is primarily in a case in which the allotted period is unusually short. It is only four months, for example, in the Article 78 proceeding,[1] and only 20 days in the proceeding to test the arbitrability of a dispute after arbitration has been demanded.[2] As one may expect, therefore, those are two special proceedings that raise limitations' issues often. In other categories with time limitations as short or even shorter, however, time problems may appear less frequently simply because of the principals' continuous alertness to the need for judicial relief. This is notably the case in nomination and election disputes, where, despite very short limitations,[3] issues of timeliness are relatively infrequent because the parties will usually have their attorneys perched on the courthouse steps.

In yet other categories of special proceeding, the barrier of time may seem altogether absent, for a combination of reasons. The summary proceeding, the prolific device for the landlord-tenant dispute, for example, involves claims that usually spring from contract and which therefore earn a six-year period of limitations.[4] On top of that is the relief: the landlord seeks in the proceeding either rent or the premises, and the landlord who waits six years for that has not been a notable drain on judicial attention.

The first question to ask is: where does one find the statute of limitations applicable to a given special proceeding? The most likely place is the statute that expressly authorizes the proceeding; it is in any event the first place to look.[5] If there is nothing about time there or in any other provision specifically devised for the particular proceeding,[6] it would be governed, at the outer limit, by the six-year residual provision applicable to ordinary actions not having a specific period.[7] If the relief demanded sounds in equity, such as where it consists of an injunction or like direction, the petitioner must also guard against the sui generis defense of laches.[8] One seeking to have a dangerous dog destroyed, for example, should not bring the proceeding several years after the animal's bite if in the interim it has won prizes for gentleness.

The filing of the notice of petition and petition constitutes the moment of commencement of the proceeding for statute of limitations purposes. When an order to show cause is used instead, as it may be,[9] the filing of the order to show cause marks commencement. Before 1992, when the filing system was adopted for use in the supreme and county courts, it was the service of these papers that marked commencement, not their filing.[10] The interplay of the filing and service requirements, which can of course affect the statute of limitations, are treated later.[11]

§ 549. Venue in Special Proceedings

The proper venue of a special proceeding must be found in the provision that authorizes the particular special proceeding, either expressly or inferentially. CPLR 506(a), which is addressed to the venue of special proceedings "generally" and which may therefore be assumed to set the proper venue, does no such thing. All it does is take whatever county the special statute offers as proper venue in the given instance and authorizes the proceeding to be brought in that county or any other

---

§ 548

1. CPLR 217(1). The Article 78 proceeding is the subject of more detailed study later. See § 566.

2. CPLR 7503(c). See § 593, below, in the arbitration chapter (Practitioner's Edition).

3. See Article 16 of the Election Law.

4. CPLR 213(2).

5. CPLR 7503(c) and some of the sections in Article 16 of the Election Law are examples of statutes that authorize special proceedings and also stipulate time limits.

6. The statute of limitations for an Article 78 proceeding, for example, although not contained in Article 78 itself, is contained in another statute, CPLR 217(1), explicitly addressed to it.

7. CPLR 213(1), 101, 103(b).

8. The laches doctrine is discussed in § 36 above.

9. See § 553 below.

10. See Matter of Fernandez, 130 A.D.2d 657, 515 N.Y.S.2d 588 (2d Dep't 1987).

11. See §§ 550 and 553 below.

"within the judicial district", just as occurs with the venue of ordinary motions.[1] It was in fact an analogy to motion practice and to the similarity the procedure in a special proceeding bears to it that prompted the Advisory Committee to offer these alternatives.[2]

The point is that one must find the initially proper county of venue in or through the statute supplying the particular proceeding.[3] That statute will usually be found to resolve the venue question. The special proceeding to settle an infant's claim, for example, is brought in the county in which an action could have been brought had there been no settlement.[4] A special proceeding in aid of the ·enforcement of a money judgment is brought where the respondent lives or works,[5] and one to compel arbitration is brought where the agreement requiring arbitration specifies or in other counties listed in the applicable statute when the agreement is silent.[6] Those are CPLR provisions authorizing special proceedings. Statutes outside the CPLR that authorize special proceedings may also be found to dictate venue.[7]

Once the county of proper venue is found from the special statute, CPLR 506(a) can operate on it, authorizing venue in any other county in the same judicial district. CPLR 506(a) and its alternatives will not be applicable, however, if the law authorizing the given proceeding has "otherwise prescribed". Precisely what qualifies as an "otherwise" prescription is not clear. If the authorizing law sets down a proper venue county, but without language indicating that it is to be the only proper one, presumably CPLR 506(a) can be allowed to supply its alternatives. Any specific limiting language, however, indicating that the

venue set is the only one authorized, should trigger the "otherwise" clause of CPLR 506(a) and withhold the alternatives. The matter is not terribly important, because even a wrong guess will lead to a mere change of venue to the county the court deems the proper one.[8] The same provision that declares that the selection of a wrong venue is not a jurisdictional defect in an action should apply to a special proceeding as well.[9]

This is especially comforting when one encounters a statute authorizing a special proceeding without any indications at all about venue. Where should the proceeding be brought in such a case? Following through on the CPLR's direction to apply the CPLR in general to any proceeding not having a specific provision addressed to the given procedural matter at hand,[10] the petitioner can presumably borrow for the proceeding the venue instructions that CPLR 503 offers in detail for actions. The county of residence of either party would then be proper venue.[11]

Note that CPLR 506(a), in authorizing venue "in any county within the judicial district where the proceeding is triable", appears to address itself only to the supreme court. It is that court with which Article 5 of the CPLR is preoccupied; the quoted provision is in fact borrowed from the venue provision applicable to motion practice in the supreme court,[12] not in other courts. But this borrowing overlooks that although the supreme court is the proper forum for many, and perhaps even most, special proceedings, it is not the exclusive forum for all of them. The proceeding to destroy a dog, for example, is authorized and usually brought in the lower courts, including the town and village courts.[13] The ubiquitous sum-

---

§ 549

1. See CPLR 2212(a).

2. See Fin.Rep.Advy.Comm., Adv.Draft (Ed. Thompson Co. Jan. 4, 1961), p. A–162, afterwards embodied in 5th Rep.Leg.Doc. (1961) No. 15, p. 74.

3. CPLR 506(b) supplies the venue for the Article 78 proceeding and is separately studied later. See § 565.

4. CPLR 1207.

5. CPLR 5221(a).

6. CPLR 7502(a).

7. See, e.g., Ment.Hyg.L. § 78.03(b).

8. CPLR 511. Those parts of CPLR 511 supplying the special "demand" procedure for changing the venue of an action, however (see § 123 above), are not feasible to apply in a special proceeding and should not be used there.

9. CPLR 509, 101, 103(b).

10. CPLR 103(b).

11. See CPLR 503(a).

12. CPLR 2212(a).

13. See Agric. & Mark.L. § 121, specifying a "municipal judge or justice".

mary proceeding to recover the possession of real property, a species of special proceeding, is almost invariably allotted to the lowest court of civil jurisdiction servicing the area in which the real property is located.[14] Even some of the CPLR's own provisions authorizing special proceedings confer jurisdiction on courts other than the supreme court.[15] Whenever that is so, and the proceeding is being brought in other than the supreme court, the alternatives of CPLR 506(a) would likely be irrelevant and should therefore be deemed inapplicable.

§ 550. Procedure in Special Proceedings

Article 4 of the CPLR governs the special proceeding and is the main source of procedural guidance for it. But it is not the sole source. The first place to look for any procedural instruction for a given special proceeding is in the provision that authorizes it. Some authorizing provisions are so replete with instruction that little or no recourse to Article 4 of the CPLR is needed. An example is the summary proceeding to recover possession of real property under RPAPL Article 7, for which recourse to the CPLR is rarely necessary. Another is the Article 78 proceeding. Also recognizing the numerous cases it sponsors, Article 78 supplies its basic procedures independently of Article 4, to which an Article 78 proceeding therefore turns only on occasion.

Both of these articles, for the very reason of their frequency and importance in practice, are studied individually later.[1] Most statutes authorizing special proceedings do only that, however, leaving procedure to the guidance of CPLR Article 4, sometimes entirely and sometimes with only one or two variations dictated by the authorizing statute, perhaps addressed to such issues as how or upon whom to serve the initiatory papers.[2] To whatever extent it

purports to speak to a given procedure, the authorizing statute governs to the exclusion of Article 4. The progression of governance in special proceedings, therefore, is (1) the authorizing statute, (2) Article 4 of the CPLR, and (3) the CPLR in general. Since Article 4 usually has all that is needed, reference to the CPLR at large is not frequent.

The mission of the next few sections is to examine the procedures prescribed by Article 4, the very existence of which now frees the legislature to authorize a special proceeding for any given purpose without having to devise procedure afresh when it does. The special problems met in special proceedings because of the adoption of the "filing" system for commencing cases in the supreme and county courts are treated in the section on "Bringing the Proceeding".[3]

§ 551. Parties to Special Proceedings

The one who brings the special proceeding is called the "petitioner", and the one it is brought against is called the "respondent"; they are the equivalent of the plaintiff and defendant in an ordinary action.[1] Since most special proceedings involve adversaries, the great majority have respondents. On occasion there may be no adverse party, however, such as may happen with a special proceeding to dispose of an infant's or incompetent's real property. There the question of whether there shall be notice to anyone at all is left to the court's discretion.[2] Most authorizing statutes that require notice of the proceeding to be given "as directed by the court",[3] or be served upon "such persons"[4] or "such other persons"[5] as the court may direct, or involve similar judicial discretion, contemplate that the court will be consulted at the very outset for a determination of who the adversaries are, or who shall be given notice of the proceeding

---

14. See § 572 below.

15. See, e.g., CPLR 1207, 5221(a).

§ 550

1. See § 571 et seq. (summary proceedings) and § 557 et seq. (Article 78 proceedings) below.

2. See, e.g., CPLR 1207, 7503(c).

3. Section 553 below.

§ 551

1. CPLR 401.

2. See, e.g., RPAPL 1721.

3. E.g., CPLR 1207.

4. E.g., Elec.L. § 16–116.

5. E.g., CPLR 5239.

in any event. In these instances the thing to do is bring the proceeding on with an order to show cause—one of the options for commencing a special proceeding[6]—which will enable the court to handle the matter. If the court finds that the application is of interest to no one but the petitioner, as in a proceeding for a change of name sought by a competent adult,[7] it can dispense with notice altogether. When it does so, it can proceed with the petition forthwith—there is no one to notify—and even determine it on the merits summarily if the papers are adequate.[8]

The party-joining devices available without leave of court in an ordinary action after its commencement, such as impleader under CPLR 1007 and the joinder of additional parties on a counterclaim or cross-claim under CPLR 3019(d), are available only by leave of court in a special proceeding.[9] The idea is to prevent an adverse party from using those devices to delay a special proceeding, leaving it to the court to determine whether the joinder is appropriate. As long as court leave is secured, any of the panoply of joinder devices can be used, including intervention and interpleader in addition to those just mentioned.

§ 552. Pleadings in Special Proceedings

The initial pleading in a special proceeding is the "petition", the equivalent of the complaint in an action, and it must in general comply with the requirements applicable to a complaint.[1] CPLR 3013, the core provision applicable to the complaint, applies as well to the petition in a special proceeding.[2] Any pleading direction contained in the statute authorizing the particular special proceeding would of course apply to it. By listing specific requirements, the authorizing statute is able to control more directly the information deemed rel-

evant to the dispute involved in the given proceeding.[3] Absent a pleading instruction in the authorizing statute, the petition need only comply with the usual (and liberal) CPLR demands. And unlike the complaint in an action, the petition in a special proceeding is usually accompanied by affidavits, and because these supply much more detail than a pleading does, the presence of affidavits often reduces dependence on the pleadings. The sufficiency of a pleading in a special proceeding, in fact, should be measured by the supporting affidavits as well as by the pleading itself; the affidavits can be taken as supplying any gaps otherwise discernible in the pleading.

The responsive pleading is an "answer", just as it is in an action, but CPLR 402 requires an answer only "where there is an adverse party", recognizing, as discussed in the prior section, that some special proceedings have none. If there is no adverse party, i.e., the proceeding is being brought ex parte, the petition must state whether any prior application was made for similar relief and, if so, what happened on it, why is this petition being brought anew, etc. This recognizes that when there is no adverse party, there is no one to balance the petitioner's one-sided presentation. This is analogous to the requirement imposed on a party making an ex parte motion in an ordinary action.[4]

The answer may contain a counterclaim, and presumably it may contain a cross-claim if there should be multiple respondents. It is clear that the interposition of a counterclaim or cross-claim against a party and nonparty together, which requires the joinder of the nonparty, requires court leave.[5] Some caselaw suggests that leave is required even for a cross-claim being used against one already a

6. See § 553 below.

7. See Civ.Rts.L. § 62.

8. When the proceeding is ex parte, an interesting question of appealability arises if the relief sought by the petitioner should be denied. See § 526 above.

9. CPLR 401.

§ 552

1. CPLR 402.

2. See Boll v. Shanly, 34 A.D.2d 875, 310 N.Y.S.2d 847 (3d Dep't 1970).

3. See, e.g., Ment.Hyg.L. § 78.03(c).

4. See CPLR 2217(b).

5. See § 551 above.

party,[6] but that should not be a problem. If the court finds that for one reason or another the cross-claim should not be heard in the present proceeding, it can sever it.[7]

A counterclaim must be replied to, just as it must be in an action, but a cross-claim needs an answer only if the pleading containing it demands one.[8] But note that in an action, an answer without a counterclaim may not be voluntarily replied to (court leave is required), while in a special proceeding the petitioner may serve a reply to new matter contained in an answer even though the answer asserts no counterclaim.[9] Any further pleadings require court leave, just as in an action.[10]

§ 553. Bringing the Proceeding

CPLR 403 supplies the procedure for the commencement of the proceeding. Since the procedure is analogous to the making of a motion within an action, the reader may find it profitable, for comparison purposes, to review motion mechanics at this point.[1]

The petitioner brings the special proceeding on by filing with the clerk of the court a notice of petition, which specifies the time and place of the hearing and enumerates the supporting affidavits that accompany the petition,[2] along with the petition itself. The notice of petition is process, the counterpart of the summons in an action. The petition is the pleading, the counterpart of the action's complaint, and it must be filed together with the notice of petition and the supporting affidavits.[3] This is in

contrast to an action, where it is permissible to file the summons initially with just a notice instead of a pleading.[4] A Request for Judicial Intervention (RJI) must also accompany the initiatory papers.[5] Filing an RJI identifies the case at the very outset and gets it assigned to a judge.[6]

After the papers are filed, they must be served. In a "service" court, which means the state's lower courts,[7] the service of the initiatory papers marks commencement for statute of limitations purposes. In the supreme and county courts, it's their filing that marks it. All discussion hereafter assumes that the special proceeding is being brought in the supreme court and that it is the filing of the initiatory papers that formally commences the proceeding.

Just as the summons and complaint in an ordinary action must be served on the defendant within a set period after their filing, so must the notice of petition and petition be served on the respondent within a set period after their filing. With the action, the period for service is 120 days, and it starts at the filing itself.[8] With the special proceeding, the period for service is whatever is left of the applicable statute of limitations plus 15 days.[9] This is needlessly convoluted, but it is best here to clarify rather than condemn. The time element must be negotiated carefully because it quickly becomes intermeshed with the statute of limitations, and the statute of limita-

---

6. See Balaban v. Phillips, 138 Misc.2d 990, 526 N.Y.S.2d 347 (Civ.Ct., N.Y.County, 1988).

7. CPLR 603.

8. See CPLR 3011.

9. CPLR 402.

10. CPLR 402, 3011.

§ 553

1. See § 247 above.

2. CPLR 403(a).

3. CPLR 403(b). The mere notice, which CPLR 305(b) permits to be used (instead of a complaint) with a summons at the outset of an action, see § 60 above, is not an available alternative in a special proceeding. See Lebow v. Village of Lansing Planning Board, 151 A.D.2d 865, 542 N.Y.S.2d 840 (3d Dep't 1989).

4. CPLR 305(b), 3012(a). See § 231 above.

5. See, e.g., Uniform Rule 202.6, the rule applicable in the supreme and county courts. The official form prescribed for the RJI is reprinted in § 77C above.

6. See § 77B above. Uniform Rule 202.8(b), which governs the making of a motion in a case not yet assigned to a judge, has a detailed procedural prescription for a motion, which Uniform Rule 202.9 borrows to apply to a special proceeding.

7. The New York City Civil Court and the district, city, town, and village courts.

8. See § 63 above.

9. See CPLR 306–b. The actual language of the statute is that if the applicable statute of limitations is four months or less, the 15–day provision applies. Because most proceedings are in that range—the Article 78 proceeding, for example, has a four-month statute of limitations under CPLR 217—we just assume in this discussion that the 15–day provision is the applicable one.

tions in a special proceeding is usually a short one.[10]

The legislation that originally introduced the filing system into supreme and county court practice in 1992 required not only that service be made before the expiration of the 15–day period, but that proof of service also be secured and filed within that time, and with a failure to file it bringing about an automatic dismissal of the proceeding.[11] These gratuitous technicalities produced chaos.[12] When the absurdity of so absolutely mandating the filing of proof of service before the 15th day became apparent, the requirement was eliminated. This occurred in an amendment of CPLR 306–b that took effect on January 1, 1998. It now suffices that the papers be served before the 15–day period expires, without regard to proof of service, which no longer plays a jurisdictional role.

Under the amendment, the proceeding may be dismissed if the papers are not served before the 15th day expires, but the dismissal is not automatic. It must be granted by the court, and may be granted only on motion of the respondent. Most importantly, the court can extend the 15–day period "upon good cause shown or in the interest of justice".[13]

The hearing or "return" day may not be set for earlier than the 8th day after the papers are served. The answer and its supporting affidavits must then be served at least two days before the return day, which raises the same problem met with motions: answering papers served at that time, since they are usually served by mail, will not reach the petitioner before the return day. The problem here is avoided the same way it is in motion practice. Instead of using a minimum 8–day notice period, the petitioner can give at least 12 days notice, i.e., set a return day at least 12 days away from the time the initiatory papers

are served. The petitioner who does that can then demand, in the notice of petition, that the respondent's answering papers be served at least 7 days before the return day.[14] This helps assure receipt of the papers in advance of the hearing. The petitioner's reply in that instance, if there is to be a reply, must be served at least one day before the return day.

These time provisions apply to almost all special proceedings. Occasionally a given category of proceeding will have its own time requirements, such as the Article 78 proceeding and the summary proceeding to recover possession of real property.[15] Special time provisions applicable to an individual proceeding of course supersede the general provisions contained in Article 4 of the CPLR.

Recognizing that it has the same jurisdiction-getting function that a summons has in an action, the statute requires that the notice of petition and its accompanying papers be served in the same manner as a summons.[16] This means that the simple mail method widely used for intra-action motions[17] is not available to commence a special proceeding; that service is instead governed by CPLR 308 and the other statutes on service of process. Any of the prescribed methods contained in CPLR 308 may be used, but it is usually preferable to use the personal delivery method of 308(1). The deliver-and-mail method of 308(2) and the affix-and-mail method of 308(4), since both postpone "completion" of service until 10 days after proof of service is filed, can become sticky to apply in a special proceeding. For the same reason, it is awkward, if not perilous, to try to use the mail method of CPLR 312–a in a special proceeding, although CPLR 312–a explicitly applies to it.[18]

But there is an alternative for service of the special proceeding papers, not available in an

---

10. See § 548 above.

11. See subdivision (a) of the old CPLR 306–b, which was in effect until January 1, 1998.

12. These were chronicled in this writer's Practice Review beginning in April 1993, and were prolific enough to require almost monthly tracking.

13. See § 63, above, discussing these provisions in the context of an action, where they have similar application.

14. CPLR 403(b). The analogous provision for motions is CPLR 2214(b).

15. See §§ 567 and 573, et seq., below.

16. CPLR 403(c).

17. CPLR 2103(b)(2).

18. The difficulty of trying to use CPLR 312–a for service in a special proceeding is discussed in § 76A above.

action: the special proceeding, like a motion, may be brought on by an order to show cause instead of by an ordinary notice of petition.[19] It is the order to show cause alternative that holds the answer to many a service dilemma. Whenever difficulty arises in making personal delivery of the papers, or any other problem appears of the kind that in motion practice would prompt a show cause application instead of an ordinary notice of motion, the petitioner need merely exploit the show cause method to start the proceeding. In the order to show cause the judge can direct as to method of service, time of return (abbreviating the otherwise applicable notice minimums), etc.[20]

The use of an unauthorized method without an order to show cause, at least when the papers are shown to have been actually received, has sometimes been sustained on the theory that since an order to show cause could have authorized the method at the outset, it can be sustained by a kind of nunc pro tunc order afterwards.[21] This is not a universal view, however,[22] and since we are dealing here with jurisdiction-getting papers, careless petitioners are courting trouble when they devise methods of their own in the hope of securing judicial approval for them later.

There are some occasions when an order to show cause, ordinarily a help, can instead become a hindrance. It may not be a good idea to resort to the order to show cause procedure near the end of the statute of limitations, for example. The order to show cause requires finding a judge to sign the order and that may consume some time. An ordinary notice of petition, on the other hand, can be filed without preliminary judicial input, formally commencing the action then and there and satisfying the statute of limitations. A classic illustration of how the order to show cause can hurt rather than help may be seen in Krenzer v. Town of Caledonia, Zoning Board of Appeals,[23] in which an inability to find a judge at the last minute resulted in the expiration of the statute of limitations before an order to show cause could be signed.

If the order to show cause is used at the outset, it is best that the copy filed be an executed one, i.e., one that the judge has already signed. Some thoughtful caselaw suggests that an unexecuted one can start things off as long as the executed one is filed later,[24] but the cautious petitioner should see to it that the later filing of the executed copy is also within the applicable statute of limitations.[25]

If, in conjunction with the special proceeding, the petitioner should require either a temporary restraining order or a stay—devices that of course require a judge—the petitioner can use the order to show cause procedure just for the restraining order or stay, while filing an ordinary notice of petition to bring on the proceeding itself: its filing will immediately toll the statute of limitations.[26]

In the common practice of preparing a notice of petition, the lawyer may encounter difficulty in setting a return day because it is likely at this early stage that no judge has yet been assigned to the case. (That, indeed, is the reason for requiring that the filing of the initiatory papers also include an RJI.) Without a judge's input, it is often impossible to set a "firm" return day, since the actual day of the hearing will largely depend on the judge's own calendar preferences. A thoughtful practitioner might therefore think it appropriate to omit a return day altogether, at least at the outset, but this is not the place for thoughtfulness of that kind. It has been held that a return day must be included and that its omission is a

---

19. CPLR 403(d).

20. The advantages of the show cause application are many. See § 248 above.

21. See, e.g., Fagenson v. First–York 86th Street Corp., 73 Misc.2d 1069, 343 N.Y.S.2d 774 (Sup.Ct., N.Y.County, 1973).

22. See Graffagnino v. M.V.A.I.C., 48 Misc.2d 441, 264 N.Y.S.2d 483 (Sup.Ct., N.Y.County, 1965).

23. 167 Misc.2d 708, 634 N.Y.S.2d 927 (Sup.Ct., Monroe County, 1995), aff'd 233 A.D.2d 882, 649 N.Y.S.2d 863 (4th Dep't 1996).

24. Allens Creek etc. v. County of Monroe etc., Sup.Ct., Monroe, March 12, 1998 (Index No. 98/767; Fisher, J.).

25. See the discussion of the Allens Creek case in SPR 70:2, and the lead note in SPR 77, entitled "problem of inadequate time for service after filing special proceeding; availability of extension of time".

26. See the discussion in SPR 62:2

jurisdictional defect,[27] even though the return day may have to be changed after a judge is assigned.

Apparently the best bet is to set a return day satisfactory to statutory notice requirements, even if it appears inevitable that the date selected will be postponed after a judge is assigned.[28] Of course the day set must be a proper one; setting an improper return day, such as a weekend or holiday, is likely to be held a jurisdictional defect.[29]

§ 554. Motions in Special Proceedings

The profusion of motion practice seen in actions has no counterpart in special proceedings for the very reason that the proceeding itself is analogous to a motion and is designed to go to hearing and determination promptly. It is permissible, however, to make a motion in a special proceeding, but if the motion is to be made before the return day of the proceeding itself, it must be made returnable at the same time.[1] A respondent who has a formal legal objection to the proceeding, for example, like want of jurisdiction, can move to dismiss based on it.[2] But alternatively, all the respondent need do is incorporate the objection as a defense in the answer and supply proof of it in the supporting affidavits. The court will consider it just as thoroughly as had it been raised by motion. Since a motion, in other words, is just a device to speed a point to the court's attention, the proceeding itself, replete with an oncoming return day, offers all the context needed to get the objection ruled on quickly.

Then when would a motion be appropriate? It may prove helpful when the purpose is to raise and secure the adjudication of a thresh-

old defense whose favorable determination will altogether obviate an answer on the merits, and when by the nature of the case an answer on the merits would be a time-consuming procedure. Defenses like want of jurisdiction, statute of limitations, and res judicata, for example, and others equally separable from the merits, may put a summary end to the proceeding.

If the dismissal motion is unsuccessful, the court may permit the respondent to answer, CPLR 404(a) so providing and supplying also the time for the service of an answer and a procedure for the petitioner to re-notice the hearing on the merits. While it is usual for the court to allow the respondent to answer on the merits if a legal objection, such as a threshold defense, fails, it is not automatic. If the court determines that an answer can add nothing, for whatever reasons unique to the case, it can in its discretion deny leave to answer,[3] which means in effect that the petitioner wins on the merits.

Since any motion made by the respondent in advance of the proceeding's return day (as most motions in special proceedings are) must be made returnable on that day, there will often be too little time to enable the petitioner to respond to the motion. Problems on this score have no clear solution and must be left to the court to resolve on a case by case basis. If it seems reasonable in the particular case, keeping always in mind that expedition is a prime aim of a special proceeding, the court can of course grant an adjournment to enable the petitioner to meet the motion. One court, pondering the matter, concluded that an "ad hoc adjournment procedure appears to be the

27. See Civil Service Employees Ass'n v. Albrecht, 180 A.D.2d 183, 584 N.Y.S.2d 206 (3d Dep't 1992), involving an Article 78 proceeding. The same court appeared to take a different view in Sears, Roebuck & Co. v. Board of Assessors of Town of Union, 182 A.D.2d 970, 582 N.Y.S.2d 566 (3d Dep't 1992), involving a proceeding seeking review of a real property tax assessment. According to a Fourth Department view expressed in Travis v. N.Y. State Dep't of Envir. Conserv., 185 A.D.2d 714, 585 N.Y.S.2d 929 (1992), not even an amendment may be allowed to insert a date because its initial omission is so basically jurisdictional.

28. See SPR 3:1 for extended discussion of the problem of setting a return day in a special proceeding.

29. See Adamba Imports Int'l, Inc. v. Polytrade Int'l, Inc., N.Y. Law Journal, July 10, 1997, p.26, col.6 (Sup.Ct., N.Y.County; McMahon, J.) (digested in SPR 59:2), noting a departmental conflict on the point.

§ 554

1. CPLR 406.

2. CPLR 404(a).

3. See, e.g., Matter of Dodge, 25 N.Y.2d 273, 303 N.Y.S.2d 847, 250 N.E.2d 849 (1969).

only option available to the court".[4]

When the answer to a petition contains new matter, the petitioner can respond to it in a reply or, again, with a motion, this one denominated a motion to strike the new matter.[5]

There is some authority under pre-CPLR law to the effect that a party can raise a legal objection by oral motion on the return day,[6] but that is not a sound practice. The same authority confirms that the movant's contention must in any event be supported in the papers already submitted to the court, and it takes little effort to draw and serve a page or two in addition, including one formally denominated a "notice of motion", announcing that a formal motion application is being made.

CPLR 405 supplies a few corrective motions in special proceeding practice. Either party can move to correct a defect in the record, and either can make against a pleading the same corrective motions available in an action.[7] These corrective motions, for which special procedural instruction is set forth,[8] are not frequent. Pleading defects in special proceeding context are even less significant than in an action—and today they have a diminished role even in an action—because each party's pleading rests also on supporting papers, for the most part detailed affidavits, and these can be looked at to cure pleading defects.

§ 555. Disclosure in Special Proceedings

Recognizing that among the main purposes of a special proceeding are speed and economy, the disclosure devices, so pervasively relied on in an action—and for the most part available there by mere notices served between parties—are available in a special proceeding only

by leave of court. And it takes good cause to invoke judicial discretion to allow disclosure. The only disclosure device excepted from the leave requirement, and therefore available by mere notice even in a special proceeding, is the notice to admit contained in CPLR 3123.[1]

A bill of particulars, which is not a disclosure device but an amplification of a pleading, has for that reason been held available on mere demand in a special proceeding.[2] Considering again, however, that in a special proceeding detail comes from affidavits supporting the pleadings, a bill of particulars should rarely be needed, or allowed. While not a disclosure device as such, the bill of particulars entails steps akin to one and should not be allowed to become a standard practice because, like the disclosure devices, it would detour the mission the legislature has in mind for the special proceeding.

The requirement of leave of court for the disclosure devices does not apply in the surrogate's court, even though its regular business is carried on in a series of special proceedings, or in the special proceeding relating to an express trust under Article 77 of the CPLR, which is brought in the supreme court.[3] Article 31 of the CPLR applies there on its own terms, making most of the disclosure devices available there without preliminary leave of court.

§ 556. Hearing and Disposition of Special Proceeding

Each party furnishes to the court all papers it has served in the proceeding. Any papers needed for the determination but not already in the court's possession are to be furnished by the petitioner. If the respondent has a needed

---

4. Goldman v. McCord, 120 Misc.2d 754, 466 N.Y.S.2d 584 (Civ.Ct., N.Y. County, 1983).

5. CPLR 404(b).

6. See Rockwell v. Morris, 12 A.D.2d 272, 211 N.Y.S.2d 25 (1st Dep't), aff'd 10 N.Y.2d 721, 219 N.Y.S.2d 268, 176 N.E.2d 836 (1961).

7. CPLR 405(a). See CPLR 3024(a),(b).

8. CPLR 405(b),(c).

§ 555

1. CPLR 408. Recognizing the imminence of the proceeding's return day, and that the admissions are usually

sought for use upon it, CPLR 408 sets forth shorter time requirements for the notice to admit than are applicable in an action under CPLR 3123, the CPLR's principal notice to admit statute.

2. See, e.g., Western Printing & Lithographing Co. v. McCandlish, 55 Misc.2d 607, 286 N.Y.S.2d 59 (Sup.Ct., Dutchess County, 1967).

3. CPLR 408.

paper, the petitioner can require its production at the hearing by including with the petition a notice to that effect. The papers furnished to the court ordinarily go into the court's permanent file.[1]

If no triable issues are raised and the papers before the court are adequate for a determination, the court is required to make the determination summarily. This is analogous to what the court does on an ordinary summary judgment motion within an action. The court's powers on such a motion have for that reason been made applicable to the determination of the proceeding.[2]

If any triable issue of fact arises, precluding a summary disposition, the statute directs that it be tried "forthwith", and by jury if a jury would otherwise be required.[3] The "forthwith" is a relative word, connoting only that the matter should be tried as soon as practicable under all the circumstances, with the judge considering the urgency of the cause in the context of other exigencies that may have even higher priority. In any event, a special preference for the trial is the least the court should grant the case under the "forthwith" direction.

Whether a jury trial is demandable depends of course on what kind of a proceeding is involved. The relief for which trial by jury is centrally authorized by the CPLR[4] does not very often appear in special proceeding context, but if it should, or if there is some specific statutory conferral of the right of trial by jury in a given proceeding,[5] the court must give the parties a chance to demand a jury.[6]

The special proceeding culminates in a "judgment", just as an action does,[7] determining the rights of the parties.[8] The judgment is usually a final one, but it can be made interlocutory if the court contemplates a need for some subsequent step. In one case, for instance, where the court rendered a judgment requiring a party to appoint an arbitrator, the court noted that the party's failure to appoint one would justify the court's doing so in that party's behalf; that a further application could be made to the court for such relief if it should become necessary; and that the judgment now being rendered would be deemed merely an interlocutory one in order to facilitate the follow-up relief.[9]

§ 556

1. CPLR 409(a).

2. CPLR 409(b).

3. CPLR 410.

4. See CPLR 4101(1), (2).

5. See, e.g., Ment.Hyg.L. § 81.11(f) (incompetency proceeding); RPAPL § 745 (summary proceeding to recover realty).

6. CPLR 410.

7. Prior to the CPLR a special proceeding ended in what was called a "final order". See, e.g., Civ.Prac.Act § 1300.

8. CPLR 411.

9. Miller v. Ives, 79 Misc.2d 184, 359 N.Y.S.2d 640 (Sup.Ct., N.Y.County, 1974).

Part II

THE ARTICLE 78 PROCEEDING

A. INTRODUCTORY

§ 557. Article 78 Proceeding, Introductory

The Article 78 proceeding supersedes the common law writs of mandamus, prohibition, and certiorari to review, supplying in replacement of all three of them a uniform device for challenging the activities of an administrative agency in court. The administrative agency is the major device today for the conduct of government, the unit through which regulation reaches down to the people on an individual basis. The difficulty of delineating the writs sharply is what produced the Article 78 proceeding.

While the Article 78 proceeding has occasional uses against other than administrative agencies—it is available even against judges in certain instances—the administrative agency is its primary target. In our bureaucratic age, this means that the Article 78 proceeding is among the most popular and important devices in practice. A volume of the state reports would feel presumptuous on its library shelf if it did not offer a handsome number of Article 78 cases on its pages. So broad and general is the proceeding's grasp that it does not even purport to name the agencies it takes in. It refers to its target as every "body or officer", which it defines as "every court, tribunal, board, corporation, officer, or other person, or aggregation of persons, whose action may be affected" by an Article 78 proceeding.[1] Any of those bodies or persons who would ever have been "affected" by any of the three superseded writs is today subject to Article 78.

The proceeding first went onto the books in 1937 as Article 78 of the Civil Practice Act, the CPLR's predecessor. The proper lines of each of the three old writs had become blurred over the years as the courts sought to apply the writs to ever expanding varieties of administrative action. Also expanding, therefore, were instances in which applicants inadvertently sought the wrong writ altogether. One proceeding designed to do the job of all three of the writs would, it was felt, spare the bar this recurring mistake.[2]

For the most part it did, but only procedurally. For the purpose of getting into court it was sufficient just to bring an "Article 78" proceeding without identifying which of the three predecessor writs would earlier have done the job. But when the court got around to deciding the merits of the proceeding, it found that the substantive reach of the earlier writs was still germane. The new device had paved the way to the courthouse but had not altered the function of the court after arrival. Each old writ was designed to remedy a different grievance, and, despite Article 78's smoother access to the court, "the nature of the alleged grievance [still] determines ... the form of the hearing before the court to which the aggrieved party is entitled, the questions to be determined at such hearing, and the relief which the court has power to grant".[3]

---

§ 557

1. CPLR 7802(a). In a few instances, notably those involving determinations of the Unemployment Insurance Appeal Board and the Workers' Compensation Board, Article 78 is not used; the route is direct appeal, and the appeal goes to the Appellate Division of the Third Department. See Labor L. § 624; Workers' Comp.L. § 23.

2. See 3d Jud.Council Rep. (1937) 129, 172.

3. Newbrand v. City of Yonkers, 285 N.Y. 164, 174–5, 33 N.E.2d 75, 80 (1941).

Only the mechanics were facilitated, but that was gift enough. Dependence on the proceeding became so heavy and the "Article 78" caption in the Civil Practice Act so firmly ensconced in the bar's affections, that the Advisory Committee thought it best not to part the proceeding from its title. Hence, when it devised the CPLR, the committee saw to it that the successor provisions were situated in the same-numbered article slot they had in the old Civil Practice Act: Article 78.

Since the collective scope and extent of the three writs still dictate the scope and extent of permissible judicial review under Article 78, as will be manifest in ensuing sections which discuss the questions the court may ask and answer in an Article 78 proceeding, judicial opinions often open with a statement that this is an Article 78 proceeding "in the nature of" certiorari, mandamus, or prohibition—whatever it is—thus narrowing for the reader the expected terrain of the inquiry.

Briefly stated, the basic function of each of the three writs (and the aggregate function of Article 78) is not hard to set down on paper. Certiorari reviews an administrative determination taken after a judicial-type, or, as it is often described, "quasi judicial", hearing. Mandamus compels action admitting of no discretion and so clearly required as to be merely ministerial. And prohibition prevents a body from exceeding its jurisdiction. If every Article 78 proceeding fell squarely within one of those three categories, the article would be much less of a study than it is. But Article 78 does not have such clear sailing. Nor did its predecessor writs in their later years. Many cases straddle the line between categories, or hover near their outer fringes. These are the ones that caused lingering problems for Article 78. But with the new device in hand, the courts met and managed them all.

CPLR 7803, which prescribes the scope of Article 78 review, does so in the form of a list of questions. It provides that the only questions that may be raised in an Article 78 proceeding are:

1. whether the body or officer failed to perform a duty enjoined upon it by law;

2. whether the body or officer proceeded, is proceeding or is about to proceed without or in excess of jurisdiction;

3. whether a determination was made in violation of lawful procedure, was affected by an error of law or was arbitrary and capricious or an abuse of discretion, including abuse of discretion as to the measure or mode of penalty or discipline imposed; or

4. whether a determination made as a result of a hearing held, and at which evidence was taken [this is the "quasi judicial" hearing], pursuant to direction by law is, on the entire record, supported by substantial evidence.

The first, second, and fourth of the listed questions pertain distinctly to but one of the old writs: number 1 is the old mandamus question, number 2 the prohibition question, and number 4 the certiorari question. That leaves number 3, which is actually several questions, and these are the ones often found in the cloudy areas between the writs instead of at the sunny center of any one of them. The best way to compartmentalize a study is to do each old writ in a separate section, integrating in each the CPLR 7803 question that pertains to it. The next three sections are thus captioned after the three writs and respectively cover questions 1, 2, and 4 of CPLR 7803, along with the relevant parts of question 3. Then a fourth section, entitled the "mandamus-certiorari borderline", the major problem area, will cover what remains to be said of question 3.

The very process of reviewing administrative action necessarily entails an occasional look into an agency's internal workings, but that is just an incidental function of Article 78, not its main aim. The article builds a path from the agency to the courthouse, and its preoccupation is with judicial supervision rather than with the agency's inside workings, which are governed by the State Administrative Procedure Act (SAPA). That act, which became effective in September 1976, supplies for the first time in New York a uniform set of instructions for administrative procedure in and before the state's numerous agencies. Its articles address rule making[4] and adjudicatory proceedings,[5] with a special one on licenses and their revocation.[6]

While SAPA is the supplier of the internals of the administrative process, Article 78 is its judicial supervisor, the vent through which light and air expose and refresh the dank milieu of that ubiquitous and indispensable phenomenon of our civilization: the administrative agency. Regulator, investigator, prosecutor, defender, jury, judge, and scourge, by turns or together, the blessings of the administrative agency are many, but mixed. It is Article 78 that makes it tolerable. Not only by laying a red carpet to the courthouse door to review agency action, but by dictating the scope of that review, Article 78 is itself a kind of Administrative Law lesson. Hence, while our aim is only to determine the function of the courts in watch-dogging the administrative process, what ensues in the next handful of sections may occasionally go into the process itself. The overlapping is unavoidable, but it will be kept to a minimum. After those few sections will come the mechanics of the Article 78 proceeding, which are a quicker study.

B.　SCOPE OF THE PROCEEDING

Table of Sections

4.　Article 2.

5.　Article 3.

6.　Article 4.

§ 558

1.　CPLR 7803(1).

2.　See Hudson v. Nehill, 25 Misc.2d 1025, 206 N.Y.S.2d 918 (Sup.Ct., Rensselaer County, 1960).

3.　Posner v. Levitt, 37 A.D.2d 331, 325 N.Y.S.2d 519 (3d Dep't 1971).

4.　It was in fact an improper attempt to invoke Article 78 to affect executive action that brought about a Court of

§ 558.　Mandamus

The first of the permissible questions that may be raised in an Article 78 proceeding is "whether the body or officer failed to perform a duty enjoined upon it by law".[1] This is from the old writ of mandamus. An Article 78 proceeding in the nature of mandamus is used to compel the performance of a duty that is merely ministerial in nature and involves no exercise of judgment or discretion. It is allowable, for example, to compel election officials to issue absentee ballots to voters entitled to them, there being nothing but the ministerial act of sending them the ballots,[2] but not to compel the comptroller to bring an action to test the legality of the state budget because whether to do so involves his judgment and discretion.[3] This judgment-and-discretion exclusion is what keeps Article 78 from being used to compel most categories of executive action: the demonstration that the activity entails any substantial discretion removes any mandamus possibility, whatever other remedy may be appropriate.[4] Mandamus is designed to require the performance of a positive duty, not a discretionary one. The right to that duty's performance must therefore be free of reasonable doubt or controversy.[5]

Even money payable by a public official can be ordered paid through an Article 78 proceeding in the nature of mandamus if the duty to pay is indisputable. Indeed, the proceeding serves as the enforcement device to collect unpaid judgments rendered against governmental units, including municipalities. Nor is a judgment needed in order to manifest that the obligation to pay is clear enough to justify mandamus; an undisputed agreement can offer the needed certainty.[6]

Appeals discourse on the line between "political" and "justiciable" issues, the former being beyond judicial review altogether. See New York State Inspection, Security and Law Enforcement Employees v. Cuomo, 64 N.Y.2d 233, 485 N.Y.S.2d 719, 475 N.E.2d 90 (1984), and § 136 above.

5.　Petz v. Property Clerk of the 68th Squad, 149 N.Y.S.2d 179 (Sup.Ct., Kings County, 1956).

6.　See, e.g., Fehlhaber Corp. v. O'Hara, 53 A.D.2d 746, 384 N.Y.S.2d 270 (3d Dep't 1976). As to whether Article 78 in the nature of mandamus can exact money from the state without a formal action in the court of claims, see State Division of Human Rights v. New York State De-

The exclusion of mandamus from the realm of executive (as opposed to merely administrative) activity is clearest when the issues involved are public rather than private. Thus, Article 78 will not be allowed to compel a mayor to fill a judicial vacancy, even though that is clearly a mayoral function.[7] But it is the remedy when sought to implement a discretion-free right asserted against an administrator or agency. In the civil service area, for example, if the petitioner in taking an examination shows that an answer he furnished is as good as the one the respondents selected, and demonstrates this clearly enough to leave no room for a contrary view, he is entitled to a mandamus direction that his answer is good.[8] In Article 78 context, this merely means a judgment directing that the answer be accepted and that the examination be regraded accordingly. Examples of Article 78 in the nature of mandamus and its vast range of uses can fill a book, as indeed they almost do: the small-print annotations on CPLR 7801 and 7803 in McKinney's Consolidated Laws of New York run for many pages, with a myriad of illustrations. They are an ideal start for a lawyer stepping into the realm, a reservoir of suggestions and analogies.

Article 78 in the nature of mandamus is also available against corporations, private as well as public, because corporations derive their charter and existence from state law and therefore take on a quasi-governmental status, at least for the purpose of a mandamus-type remedy. But as with all mandamus cases, the remedy lies only when the right to it is clear and involves no arguable discretion. A common and acceptable example is a proceeding against corporate officials to compel them, at the behest of an appropriate petitioner, to permit an inspection of corporate books and records.[9]

The categories of corporation that are subject to Article 78 proceedings run the whole gamut, as long as the right to what is sought is so clear as to fall into the realm of the merely ministerial. The corporation need not be on the one hand wholly commercial nor on the other strictly governmental. Both kinds are included along with in-between ones as well. Incorporated universities and like non-commercial entities, for example, are subject to Article 78. But the article does not apply to a partnership[10] or unincorporated association[11] or to like creatures not owing their status to the state.[12] Unincorporated labor unions are in that category, and therefore escape Article 78 proceedings.[13] But the erroneous use of Article 78 against one not subject to it is not as serious today as it once was: as long as a substantive right is asserted, the worst that will happen is a conversion of the proceeding into an action.[14]

While most often used against agencies and bodies corporate, Article 78 in the nature of mandamus has some uses against a court or, more specifically, a judge. It can be used, for example, to compel the judge to render a decision, as where the judge has failed to do so within a statutorily allotted time, but it cannot dictate what that decision will be, which is a matter of judicial judgment and discretion.[15] The merits of a judicial decision are utterly beyond a mandamus-type review although, as will be seen, Article 78 in the nature of prohibition may sometimes be used to overturn a

partment of Correctional Services, 90 A.D.2d 51, 456 N.Y.S.2d 63 (2d Dep't 1982).

7. Blaikie v. Wagner, 46 Misc.2d 441, 259 N.Y.S.2d 890 (Sup.Ct., N.Y.County, 1965).

8. See Dolan v. Krone, 16 N.Y.2d 917, 264 N.Y.S.2d 703, 212 N.E.2d 155 (1965).

9. See, e.g., Morris v. Pepsi–Cola Co., 21 A.D.2d 651, 249 N.Y.S.2d 565 (1st Dep't 1964).

10. Two Eleven Co. v. Harrison, 66 Misc.2d 245, 319 N.Y.S.2d 897 (Sup.Ct., N.Y.County, 1971).

11. See Weidenfeld v. Keppler, 84 App.Div. 235, 82 N.Y.Supp. 634 (1st Dep't), aff'd 176 N.Y. 562, 68 N.E. 1125 (1903).

12. There is some indication, however, that even an unincorporated creature will be subject to a mandamus-type remedy if, while it does not have the entity status of a corporation, it is nonetheless formed pursuant to statutory direction. See Importers' & Exporters' Ins. Co. v. Rhoades, 239 N.Y. 420, 146 N.E. 648 (1925).

13. See, e.g., Phalen v. Theatrical Protective Union No. 1, 22 N.Y.2d 34, 290 N.Y.S.2d 881, 238 N.E.2d 295 (1968).

14. CPLR 103(c). See § 563 below.

15. See, e.g., Briggs v. Lauman, 21 A.D.2d 734, 250 N.Y.S.2d 126 (3d Dep't 1964).

decision in extraordinary situations.[16] An exception to this, in which Article 78 has been explicitly authorized to challenge and review a judicial determination, is a determination summarily punishing a contempt committed in the court's presence.[17]

Action strictly legislative rather than administrative is also beyond the reach of Article 78. A legislative body cannot be mandamused in regard to anything within its prerogative. This applies not only to the state legislature itself, but to municipal legislatures as well. Thus a resolution by the New York City Board of Estimate adopting a map change cannot be reviewed under Article 78.[18] Even the order of an administrative agency, if wholly legislative in character, may for that reason fall beyond Article 78, such as when the agency is performing a legislatively delegated rate-fixing function.[19]

The uses of Article 78 were expanded by the State Administrative Procedure Act (SAPA), which took effect in 1976. The article was made available to secure judicial review of rules promulgated by an agency.[20] Another part of the SAPA enables a person to secure a declaratory ruling from an agency as to whether a given statute or rule, within the agency's jurisdiction to enforce, applies to that person or to a designated property or state of facts, and authorizes the use of Article 78 to review the ruling.[21]

The general utility of Article 78 is implicitly acknowledged whenever the proceeding is extended to some new purpose. Under the Freedom of Information Law, for example, which seeks to increase public access to governmental records,[22] a denial of access is made reviewable under Article 78.[23]

Is any one of these last few items a "mandamus" use being made of Article 78? It would be if there were no discretion involved. Is it Article 78 in the nature of "certiorari"? It would be if a full-fledged hearing were required before the application could be denied, because, as will be seen, certiorari is a review based on a full record after a quasi-judicial hearing. What happens when there is some element of discretion allotted to the agency, but that no hearing is required, thus putting the case beyond the clear grasp of either category? That is one of the situations that still straddles the line between the two old writs. Article 78's grand favor is that it admits the thing to court astride the dividing line, although there may be some trouble later when the court has to decide just how much it can review.[24]

That mandamus is designed to require the performance of a positive duty rather than a discretionary one does not exclude mandamus from every scene that involves some exercise of discretion. When there is a clear duty to perform a given act, the fact that some exercise of discretion must be made in the course of performing it does not prevent a court from entertaining mandamus to see that the act is performed. The Court of Appeals clarified this in Natural Resources Defense Council, Inc. v.

---

16. See § 559 below.

17. CPLR 7801(2). See Kahn v. Backer, 21 A.D.2d 171, 249 N.Y.S.2d 572 (1st Dep't 1964). Out-of-court contempt (such as for disobedience of an injunction), proved in a contempt proceeding and punished by the court after a hearing, is not within this provision and not subject to Article 78 review.

18. See Porter Flushing Realty Co. v. New York City Planning Commission, 21 A.D.2d 864, 251 N.Y.S.2d 125 (1st Dep't 1964). In zoning matters especially, the line is hard to draw between administrative and quasi-administrative decisions on the one hand, justifying Article 78 review, and genuine legislative activities on the other, precluding Article 78 review. See Bar Harbour Shopping Center, Inc. v. Andrews, 23 Misc.2d 894, 196 N.Y.S.2d 856 (Sup.Ct., Nassau County, 1959). If the act is legislative, a test of its validity must technically be sought in a declaratory judgment action. Today, however, the mistaking of

the remedy is cured by a mere procedural conversion into proper form. Todd Mart v. Town Board of Town of Webster, 49 A.D.2d 12, 370 N.Y.S.2d 683 (4th Dep't 1975). See § 563 below.

19. See, e.g., Lakeland Water District v. Onondaga County Water Authority, 24 N.Y.2d 400, 301 N.Y.S.2d 1, 248 N.E.2d 855 (1969). The case indicates that if a hearing had been statutorily required, Article 78 might be appropriate for review. But in that case it would be Article 78 in the nature of certiorari, not mandamus. See § 560 below.

20. SAPA § 205.

21. SAPA § 204.

22. Pb.Off.L. §§ 84–90.

23. Pb.Off.L. § 89(4)(b).

24. See § 561 below.

New York City Department of Sanitation,[25] in which a city sanitation department was required by law to set up a recycling program and mandamus was brought by a public interest group to make it do so. The use of the word "may" at many points in the enabling act permitted diverse exercises of discretion to be made by the department in carrying out this mandate, but, held the court, the fact that exercises of discretion lie along the way does not prevent the courts from making sure the department takes the trip.

It must be noted that although "mandamus" as such is usually thought of as a device designed exclusively to compel something, it has evolved another and equally important function: that of merely reviewing administrative action without necessarily compelling a particular act. In this respect—another one responsible for muddying the waters between the two writs—it resembles certiorari. But certiorari is technically applicable only when there is a hearing required by law, when the record produced at the hearing is the sole basis on which the determination can rest, and when the so called "substantial evidence" rule is the review standard.[26] When the hearing need not be of the plenary quasi-judicial kind but merely an opportunity for the petitioner to supply the agency what evidence she wishes, when the agency can in the particular situation consider evidence not produced at the "hearing" but coming to the agency's knowledge through other channels, and when judicial review is not limited to the substantial evidence test, it cannot technically be certiorari.[27] It is technically "mandamus" on those facts, but mandamus to "review" rather than the more common mandamus to "compel".

In one case, for example, a petitioner was denied a liquor license on two grounds: (1) he failed to supply assurances that he would operate a restaurant on the premises and (2) the area already had sufficient licensees. The court in an Article 78 proceeding found that his

assurances were sufficient and that the first ground was therefore an inadequate basis for refusing a license. The second ground was found supportable, however, and so the court could not "compel" the issuance of the license. But nor could it approve a refusal: the refusal was based on two grounds and the agency might not wish to refuse if limited—as it would now be limited as a result of the court's decision—to but one of the grounds. That was for the agency to decide, and so the matter was remitted to the agency.[28]

This was a good example of mandamus to "review", and the presence in the case of an element of discretion was yet another factor that kept the case out of the "compel" category. Actually, the case is an example of Article 78's eschewal of labels. Were it merely a question of going into court, we could forget distinctions altogether. Article 78 gets all of these things into the courtroom without a caption. Once there, however, the old distinctions may hang on: they determine which of the four questions enumerated in CPLR 7803 will control the judicial inquiry. With mandamus to "compel", question 1 of CPLR 7803 is the inquiry. With mandamus to "review", question 3 is.[29] When all the requisites of "certiorari" are present, number 4 supplies the controlling question.[30]

The doctrine of the exhaustion of administrative remedies, embodied in the requirement of CPLR 7801(1) that the determination be "final" before being subject to an Article 78 proceeding, applies to mandamus to review. It means that if there are further (and reasonable) administrative steps available to secure a change in the result, the party must pursue them before going to court. The finality requirement applies as well to certiorari, but in either instance caselaw clarifies that if it is plain that pursuit of further administrative relief would be futile, it will be dispensed with

---

25. 83 N.Y.2d 215, 608 N.Y.S.2d 957, 630 N.E.2d 653 (1994), noted in New York State Law Digest No. 414.

26. See CPLR 7803(4).

27. See 125 Bar Corp. v. State Liquor Authority, 24 N.Y.2d 174, 299 N.Y.S.2d 194, 247 N.E.2d 157 (1969).

28. Rochester Colony, Inc. v. Hostetter, 19 A.D.2d 250, 241 N.Y.S.2d 210 (4th Dep't 1963).

29. See § 561 below.

30. See § 560 below.

and an Article 78 proceeding will be deemed ripe.[31]

The courts are also sensitive, of course, to guard against the invocation of judicial jurisdiction for controversies not yet ripe at all. This is not a problem when the Article 78 proceeding is in the nature of certiorari or mandamus to review, i.e., where a determination has already been made and it is merely a question of having to take further steps before pursuing a judicial remedy. But it can appear in something like a mandamus to compel, such as where the petitioner, insisting that he is entitled to something from the respondent, was never refused it because he never asked for it. Thus, where petitioner sought a certain phone service but did not ask the phone company for it, the court found an Article 78 proceeding, predicated on an anticipatory refusal by the company, premature and dismissed it.[32] This is consistent with the exhaustion doctrine.

§ 559. Prohibition

Question 2 listed in CPLR 7803 as a permissible one for an Article 78 proceeding is "whether the body or officer proceeded, is proceeding or is about to proceed without or in excess of jurisdiction". This is from the old writ of prohibition. A judge before whom the Article 78 proceeding comes will often identify it, at the outset of an opinion, as one "in the nature of prohibition".

Article 78 in the nature of prohibition appears against judges more often than the other categories do. This is because prohibition does not lie against strictly administrative action, but only against judicial and quasi-judicial action.[1] When brought against an administrative official, the latter must therefore be shown to be exceeding jurisdiction in some quasi-judicial capacity. If the official's activity is strictly administrative, it is technically "mandamus" that the petitioner is seeking, whether to compel favorable action at the outset or to review unfavorable action already taken.

It is often said that prohibition is available only to forestall rather than review action,[2] but that statement, like almost every other facile statement about the old writs, can be misleading. Quasi-judicial activity taken without jurisdiction does not become valid merely because it has already gone to a determination. If the taker lacked jurisdiction at the outset and would at that time have been subject to prohibition, he is just as subject to it, and his determination just as subject to annulment, in a prohibition proceeding brought afterwards. If these distinctions seem hard to digest, we can remind ourselves once again that at least for the purpose of getting into court one need not identify the "nature" of what is sought at all. One need only label it an Article 78 proceeding.

Prohibition is an extraordinary remedy, available at best only as a matter of judicial discretion and not as a matter of right. Given an extraordinary showing, however, such as a potential violation of the double jeopardy rule,[3] or that the respondent lacks jurisdiction on the very face of the complaint brought before him, prohibition will issue to enjoin even a criminal action.[4] While courts are naturally loath to restrain exercises of jurisdiction by another court, they will do so when the latter, by the very exercise, threatens fundamental constitutional rights. Prohibition has issued, for example, to prevent the seizure of an allegedly obscene film when the proceedings were

31. See, e.g., Kurk v. Medical Society, 46 Misc.2d 790, 260 N.Y.S.2d 520 (Sup.Ct., Queens County, 1965), rev'd on other grounds 24 A.D.2d 897, 264 N.Y.S.2d 859 (2d Dep't), aff'd 18 N.Y.2d 928, 276 N.Y.S.2d 1007, 223 N.E.2d 499 (1966).

32. See Rubano v. New York Tel. Co., 43 Misc.2d 149, 250 N.Y.S.2d 373 (Sup.Ct., Westchester County, 1964).

§ 559

1. See, e.g., Dobler v. Kaplan, 27 Misc.2d 15, 211 N.Y.S.2d 96 (Sup.Ct., Suffolk County, 1961), aff'd 29 Misc.2d 294, 220 N.Y.S.2d 701 (1961).

2. See, e.g., Bradford v. Helman, 24 A.D.2d 937, 264 N.Y.S.2d 930 (1st Dep't 1965).

3. See Di Lorenzo v. Murtagh, 36 N.Y.2d 306, 367 N.Y.S.2d 761, 327 N.E.2d 805 (1975).

4. See, e.g., Powell v. Criminal Court, 44 Misc.2d 838, 255 N.Y.S.2d 1 (Sup.Ct., N.Y.County, 1964).

found to have inadequate procedural safeguards under the First Amendment.[5]

The use of prohibition must always be related to a want of jurisdiction, or at least to an exercise of power so excessive as to be its equivalent, and whether the threatened excess is sufficiently extraordinary to trigger the device is sometimes hard to tell. In one case, for example, applications had been made to vacate two convictions, one on the ground that the defendant was under age and the other on the ground that he did not have counsel. The latter was held to be a defect so basic that the trial court itself retained jurisdiction to vacate the conviction on motion, and, jurisdiction being present, prohibition would not lie to stop it. The other, that based on age, was found not to be of such a fundamental kind; the trial court thus lacked power to vacate the conviction on that ground and prohibition lay to prevent its attempting to.[6]

Niceties of this kind are hard to apply, and are perhaps even undetectable until a court has passed on the particular ground. Indeed, the Court of Appeals has candidly held that the "magnitude" of the issue may be the key factor. So it said in Lee v. County Court of Erie County,[7] reaffirming what it had occasion to point out before: that Article 78 in the nature of prohibition is available not only to restrain an unwarranted assumption of jurisdiction, but also to stop a court from exceeding its "powers" in a case in which it concededly has jurisdiction. Theoretical standards like that are elusive to the attorney who has to apply them in practice. Translating them into the practical means that the advocate's burden is to establish the situation as truly extraordinary.

What is truly "extraordinary"? If we may analogize, it may be akin to the "special circumstances" rule applied in New York in the forum non conveniens area. When a case has no New York contacts with either the parties or the subject matter, the courts insist on some good reason for entertaining the action.[8] So with prohibition: show some special reason why a court should prevent a case from even starting, some unique factor explaining why the case should not go forward at all and why an attack should not be postponed until after judgment. The violation of fundamental constitutional rights by the very fact that the petitioner must endure a trial is one such special circumstance, already mentioned. Another is the unavailability, or in any event the manifest inadequacy in the particular case, of the ordinary process of appeal. Prohibition has therefore become a kind of review route when the usual appellate door is closed, but only in very special circumstances. A mere showing that a determination is unappealable will by no means suffice.[9] Nor can prohibition be turned to by one who, though having an appeal available, has let the time for taking it lapse.[10] It is not available merely to correct substantive or procedural errors of the trial court, no matter how grievous. Only when the court threatens to act in excess of its "powers" may prohibition be turned to, and among the factors the court will consider in determining whether a court's powers have been exceeded are the gravity of the harm to the petitioner, the capacity of a later appeal to undo the harm, and the efficacy of other channels of redress.[11] Where, for example, the petitioner has a strong claim of want of jurisdiction or "excess" of powers against a court, and would, if compelled to pursue other remedies, remain incarcerated in the interim, the extraordinary case for prohibition is at hand.[12] The petitioner's burden is to convince the prohibition court that the other court is guilty of an arro-

---

5. See Milonas v. Schwalb, 65 Misc.2d 1042, 319 N.Y.S.2d 327 (Sup.Ct., N.Y.County, 1971).

6. See Hogan v. Court of General Sessions, 296 N.Y. 1, 68 N.E.2d 849 (1946). The case was precipitated by earlier restrictions on criminal vacatur motions, apparently since removed. See CPL 440.10.

7. 27 N.Y.2d 432, 318 N.Y.S.2d 705, 267 N.E.2d 452 (1971).

8. See § 28 above.

9. See Nigrone v. Murtagh, 36 N.Y.2d 421, 369 N.Y.S.2d 75, 330 N.E.2d 45 (1975).

10. Roberts v. County Court, 39 A.D.2d 246, 333 N.Y.S.2d 882 (4th Dep't 1972), aff'd 34 N.Y.2d 246, 356 N.Y.S.2d 853, 313 N.E.2d 335 (1974).

11. See La Rocca v. Lane, 37 N.Y.2d 575, 376 N.Y.S.2d 93, 338 N.E.2d 606 (1975).

12. Id.

gation of power if not of an outright want of jurisdiction.

If its extraordinary elements are otherwise present, the remedy of prohibition is not limited to criminal cases. It can be used, for example, when the petitioner, a corporation, can show that being compelled to go through a civil trial would constitute an undue burden on its interstate commerce. Suppose, for example, that the petitioner is a defendant in such an action and has moved to dismiss based on the commerce objection. The motion is denied. It can appeal the order of denial to the appellate division. If it does and the order is affirmed, however, the order will be nonfinal, which may preclude further appeal to the New York Court of Appeals.[13] It has been held that a petitioner in that situation may bring a separate prohibition proceeding; that being put through a trial may unduly disrupt its commerce; and that this suffices to make the case extraordinary enough to invoke prohibition.[14] It boils down to a matter of judicial discretion and to how much the petitioner can show to invoke it. The petitioner must show either that there is no other remedy at all, or that all the others are inadequate.[15] Instead of merely demonstrating error in respect of but a part of the case, the petitioner should show that the abuse consists in entertaining the case at all.[16]

The requirement of finality, important as a condition precedent to certiorari and sometimes to mandamus as well,[17] is not applicable to prohibition. This recognizes that with prohibition the defect under attack is a want of subject matter jurisdiction or an exercise of power so excessive as to be its counterpart, which presumably authorizes an attack at any juncture.[18]

An Article 78 proceeding in the nature of prohibition is brought in the supreme court, except when aimed at a justice of that court or a judge of the county court, in which case it is commenced in the appellate division.[19]

§ 560. Certiorari

Question 4 on the list of questions that CPLR 7803 allows in an Article 78 proceeding is "whether a determination made as a result of a hearing held, and at which evidence was taken, pursuant to direction by law is, on the entire record, supported by substantial evidence". This is from the old writ of certiorari to review.[1] The fact that the determination results from a required evidentiary hearing is what invokes the certiorari remedy and with it the substantial evidence criterion. If there is no requirement for a hearing, or the hearing permitted in the particular situation is not of the plenary evidentiary ("quasi judicial") kind, the review standards will be those of mandamus. The practical difference is discussed in the next section.

Although the hearing must be one required by law, it is not necessary that the requirement be express; an implied one is enough, and one will be implied whenever the agency's exercise of a statutory power can adversely affect a substantial right of the petitioner. Thus, where the prospect was the revocation of the petitioner's hack license, a hearing requirement was implied from a silent statute.[2]

---

13. See CPLR 5601(a).

14. See Baltimore Mail S.S. Co. v. Fawcett, 269 N.Y. 379, 199 N.E. 628, cert. den. 298 U.S. 675, 56 S.Ct. 939, 80 L.Ed. 1396 (1936).

15. Schuyler v. State University, 31 A.D.2d 273, 297 N.Y.S.2d 368 (3d Dep't 1969).

16. See State v. King, 36 N.Y.2d 59, 364 N.Y.S.2d 879, 324 N.E.2d 351 (1975).

17. CPLR 7801(1).

18. See Civil Service Employees Ass'n v. Helsby, 31 A.D.2d 325, 297 N.Y.S.2d 813 (3d Dep't), aff'd 24 N.Y.2d 993, 302 N.Y.S.2d 822 (1969).

19. CPLR 506(a). See § 565 below.

§ 560

1. Another certiorari, this one to inquire into detention, is set forth in Article 70 of the CPLR. See CPLR 7001. It is seldom heard from today, having been replaced verbally, if not actually, by the writ of habeas corpus. It was technically the writ used when an inquiry into detention was sought without having the detained person immediately produced, a kind of habeas corpus without the corpus. This is still permissible, see CPLR 7003(a), but in either instance the procedure is a special proceeding under Article 70 of the CPLR, and in neither should the proceeding be confused with the certiorari-to-review purpose of an Article 78 proceeding.

2. See Hecht v. Monaghan, 307 N.Y. 461, 121 N.E.2d 421 (1954).

If neither a right nor a statutory hearing requirement is present, however, any "hearing" voluntarily tendered to the petitioner is a matter of grace rather than a requirement of law and hence not reviewable under the certiorari standard.[3] It will still be Article 78 that brings the case to court, but the review standard will be taken from subdivision 3 of CPLR 7803, generally associated with mandamus to review, and not subdivision 4, the certiorari standard.

The hearing required must be of the judicial or quasi-judicial kind,[4] the kind that the State Administrative Procedure Act (SAPA) defines as one "in which a determination of the legal rights, duties or privileges of named parties thereto is required by law to be made only on a record and after an opportunity for a hearing".[5] The SAPA calls it an "adjudicatory proceeding", and supplies for it a central repository of requirements applicable to all agencies.[6] The hearing that the SAPA calls "adjudicatory" is what the older caselaw means by "judicial or quasi-judicial", and the determination resulting from it is therefore reviewable by certiorari. In present Article 78 parlance, this means that its review is under the substantial evidence standard of CPLR 7803(4), which works out well: it's the same standard the SAPA itself adopts for its adjudicatory proceedings.[7]

When an adjudicatory hearing is required, even a quasi-legislative determination like a rate-making order involving a public utility has been held to qualify for certiorari under Article 78.[8]

Another characteristic of the certiorari case, and a natural concomitant of the substantial evidence rule, is that the determination cannot be based on anything outside the record and will be overturned if it is.[9] When less than a quasi-judicial hearing is permitted, on the other hand, and the review is therefore through mandamus instead of certiorari, matter outside the record, such as data gathered by the agency's own investigators, may form part of the basis for the decision.[10]

The "substantial evidence" test replaces the old "legal residuum" standard, a largely unworkable one, and is roughly analogous to the standard used by the courts in setting aside a jury verdict because the evidence does not support it.[11] The real measure, whatever the wording, is whether the determination strikes the court as rational on the record.[12]

Except for the rules of privileged communications, which must be observed in quasi-judicial hearings before administrative agencies, the rules of evidence are not binding in such hearings.[13] The main entry through this open door is hearsay, but it has been held that "substantial" reliance on hearsay will not be acceptable and that a determination unduly dependent on it will not be upheld if it has the effect of undermining a party's right to cross-examine witnesses.[14] Since the SAPA recognizes the right of cross-examination in administrative "adjudicatory" (i.e., quasi-judicial) proceedings,[15] this rule against undue dependence on hearsay subsists.

The requirement of finality ordinarily applies to a determination sought to be reviewed by certiorari. In familiar administrative parlance, this is known as the doctrine of the exhaustion of administrative remedies: the los-

---

3. See London Sporting Club, Inc. v. Helfand, 3 Misc.2d 431, 152 N.Y.S.2d 819 (Sup.Ct., N.Y. County, 1956), aff'd 6 A.D.2d 775, 175 N.Y.S.2d 152 (1st Dep't 1958).

4. Testa v. Wickham, 51 Misc.2d 968, 274 N.Y.S.2d 421 (Sup.Ct., Albany County, 1966), aff'd 28 A.D.2d 780, 280 N.Y.S.2d 829 (3d Dep't 1967).

5. SAPA § 102(3).

6. SAPA Article 3, §§ 301–307.

7. See SAPA § 306(1).

8. See Lakeland Water District v. Onondaga County Water Authority, 24 N.Y.2d 400, 301 N.Y.S.2d 1, 248 N.E.2d 855 (1969).

9. Simpson v. Wolansky, 38 N.Y.2d 391, 380 N.Y.S.2d 630, 343 N.E.2d 274 (1975).

10. See 125 Bar Corp. v. State Liquor Auth., 24 N.Y.2d 174, 299 N.Y.S.2d 194, 247 N.E.2d 157 (1969).

11. See Testa v. Wickham, 51 Misc.2d 968, 274 N.Y.S.2d 421 (Sup.Ct., Albany County, 1966), aff'd 28 A.D.2d 780, 280 N.Y.S.2d 829 (3d Dep't 1967).

12. Pell v. Board of Education, 34 N.Y.2d 222, 356 N.Y.S.2d 833, 313 N.E.2d 321 (1974). See § 561 below.

13. SAPA § 306(1).

14. See Erdman v. Ingraham, 28 A.D.2d 5, 280 N.Y.S.2d 865 (1st Dep't 1967).

15. SAPA § 306(3).

er must pursue an appellate route within the agency, if one is available, before turning to the courts with an Article 78 proceeding.[16] The doctrine has some application in mandamus, too, but in either situation it is applied pragmatically: where, despite the availability of an internal administrative appeal, it is plain on the facts of the particular case that pursuing the appeal would be futile, an Article 78 proceeding will be deemed ripe enough.[17]

> The Court of Appeals has held ... that the exhaustion rule is not inflexible and need not be followed when the action is challenged as either unconstitutional or outside of a grant of power, when resort to an administrative remedy would be futile or when its pursuit would cause irreparable injury....[18]

When the applicable remedy is mandamus to review, the agency has already acted and the act is the thing to be reviewed. An analogous situation, usually involving mandamus to compel—as opposed to either certiorari or mandamus to review—is where the agency has not acted because the petitioner has not asked it to. There an Article 78 proceeding may be dismissed for prematurity,[19] a result at home with the exhaustion doctrine if not a precise example of it.

§ 561. Mandamus–Certiorari Borderline

Since questions 1, 2, and 4 on CPLR 7803's list each has a clear antecedent among the old writs, they were treated first and number 3 saved for last. Number 3 lists several questions that may be presented in an Article 78 proceeding. These are the nomads that have not found a stable domicile within any one of the writs, the migrants that seem to criss-cross the common frontier of mandamus and certiorari and make things hard for the census taker. Compelled to allot each of them to but a single writ, we would most often have to give them to mandamus; but clearly, as we shall see, they sometimes belong to certiorari. For a few lingering reasons, some already discussed and some to come, and in spite of the alleged fusion of all the writs into the singular Article 78 proceeding, it does become necessary on occasion to pinpoint the category. From the nature of the questions set forth in CPLR 7803(3), the only one of the three writs not in the present contest is prohibition.

The questions that subdivision 3 lists as permissible in an Article 78 proceeding are these:

> whether a determination was made in violation of lawful procedure, was affected by an error of law or was arbitrary and capricious or an abuse of discretion, including abuse of discretion as to the measure or mode of penalty or discipline imposed....

The last item, judicial review of a penalty or discipline imposed by an agency, is reserved for the next section. The rest of subdivision 3 we take up here.

Any substantial violation of applicable procedure is a basis for overturning an administrative determination, without regard to whether the category is mandamus or certiorari. A "procedural" violation will most often be concerned with some aspect of the hearing. The ultimate example of it would be the failure to grant any hearing at all, when one is required. This is so whether the hearing required is the full quasi-judicial one seen in the certiorari category, or something less, which would allocate it to mandamus.[1] With the quasi-judicial proceeding, the one the State Administrative Procedure Act calls an "adjudicatory proceeding" and for which its Article 3 prescribes procedure in some detail, a substantial violation of one of the prescribed procedures would constitute a "violation of lawful procedure" as contemplated by CPLR 7803(3).

16. See CPLR 7801(1).

17. See the discussion in § 558 above.

18. Caso v. New York State Public High School Athletic Ass'n, 78 A.D.2d 41, 434 N.Y.S.2d 60 (4th Dep't 1980).

19. See, e.g., Rubano v. N. Y. Tel. Co., 43 Misc.2d 149, 250 N.Y.S.2d 373 (Sup.Ct., Westchester County, 1964).

§ 561

1. See George v. Fiore, 62 Misc.2d 429, 308 N.Y.S.2d 744 (Sup.Ct., Erie County, 1970).

Denying a party the right to cross-examine a witness,[2] or basing a finding of fact on something outside the record,[3] would be prime examples.

Subdivision 3's listing of an "error of law" as a permissible question is in one sense superfluous. If it means an error in procedure, it is covered by the first item, just noted. If it means an error of substance, it is covered by almost everything else listed in CPLR 7803. Whether a determination is arbitrary and capricious or an abuse of discretion, for example, which are other questions set forth in subdivision 3, or is supported by "substantial evidence", the test contained in of subdivision 4, are all questions of law or in any event so intertwined with the legal issues in the case that they would cover and preserve review for whatever legal conclusions they depend on.

The same is true of the broadly phrased mandamus and prohibition questions appearing in subdivisions 1 and 2 of CPLR 7803. If for any reason these broad review standards should not be found adequate in a given case to secure review of the legal issue involved, and the amenability of the issue to judicial review must stand or fall on its own, the "error of law" caption can be relied on to take it up. A disputed construction of some provision in the agency's enabling act, for example, or of some other statute or rule applicable to the case, would always find a way to review under the "error of law" banner, if nothing else.

Whether the determination is "arbitrary and capricious"—one of the best known phrases in administrative law—has been the subject of much discourse. It is the "arbitrary and capricious" test, rather than the "substantial evidence" test of subdivision 4, that applies when the determination is not required to be based on a full evidentiary hearing, i.e., the quasi-judicial hearing or what the State Administrative Procedure Act calls the "adjudicatory" hearing. This is another way of saying that the "arbitrary and capricious" test is a phenomenon of mandamus, not certiorari, to which the "substantial evidence" test belongs.[4]

What is arbitrary and capricious? It is action taken "without sound basis in reason and ... without regard to the facts".[5] Whether the facts on which the determination is based were adduced at a hearing or otherwise, the determination is "arbitrary and capricious" if the court finds that the conclusion drawn from them, or the administrative action taken based on them, is untenable as a matter of law.

The arbitrary and capricious test is usually associated with mandamus to review rather than mandamus to compel, in case the reader sees a difference. The fact that mandamus to compel covers the question listed in subdivision 1 of CPLR 7803, "whether the body or officer failed to perform a duty enjoined upon it by law", suggests inferentially that any mandamus-type case reached by subdivision 3 is necessarily some other kind of mandamus. But this is an illusion, too. Intermixing is frequent, and conceptually feasible. If there was a duty "enjoined ... by law" under subdivision 1, for example, the failure to perform it would also be "arbitrary and capricious" under subdivision 3. This kind of overlap offers no difficulty. The writ referenced in either case is mandamus.

A more interesting question is the extent to which the "arbitrary and capricious" test of subdivision 3, which is mandamus, differs from the "substantial evidence" test of subdivision 4, which is certiorari. Article 78 does not cancel the need to categorize, remember; it merely postpones it until after the case is safely in court. By virtue of the very fact that subdivisions 3 and 4 supply different tests, the need presumably arises once again to determine whether the case is a mandamus case for

---

2. SAPA § 306(3).

3. SAPA § 302(3).

4. See Colton v. Berman, 21 N.Y.2d 322, 287 N.Y.S.2d 647, 234 N.E.2d 679 (1967). The arbitrary and capricious test was also the one adopted by the Court of Appeals to apply to the judicial review of an award in compulsory arbitration. See Caso v. Coffey, 41 N.Y.2d 153, 391

N.Y.S.2d 88, 359 N.E.2d 683 (1976), treated in § 603 below. The scope of review of an award in the more common voluntary arbitration is more restrictive. See § 602 below.

5. Pell v. Board of Education, 34 N.Y.2d 222, 231, 356 N.Y.S.2d 833, 839, 313 N.E.2d 321, 325 (1974).

application of the "arbitrary and capricious" standard of subdivision 3, or a certiorari case for application of the "substantial evidence" test of subdivision 4.

It is submitted that the tests are indistinguishable. A decision found to be "arbitrary and capricious" cannot be said to be supported by "substantial evidence". And a decision found unsupported by "substantial evidence" is necessarily "arbitrary and capricious". The Court of Appeals appears to have acknowledged that there is no difference. It has held that "rationality is what is reviewed under both the substantial evidence rule and the arbitrary and capricious standard".[6] A decision failing either test as irrational, in other words, must necessarily fail the other test as well.

It helps to have this Court of Appeals acknowledgment on the books. It relieves a judge from having to hunt out the invisible niceties once thought to differentiate the tests. For the purpose of determining how the tests differ, it tells the judge that they really do not differ at all; that in this respect there is nothing to pick between subdivisions 3 and 4.

For yet other purposes, alas, there is still a need to pick. A certiorari case under subdivision 4 gets transferred to the appellate division for initial determination,[7] while a mandamus case under subdivision 3 gets heard in first instance in the supreme court. Thus, just as we are about to assure ourselves that there is no longer a need to identify precisely whether the case is mandamus or certiorari, we find an arbitrary statute which, by directing different levels of initial review, perpetuates the ungratifying need to continue to categorize with punctilio.[8]

The "abuse of discretion" is yet another basis, and a presumably separate basis, for overturning the determination. Discretion is the power to reach any of several decisions within certain confines. Only a decision beyond those confines constitutes an "abuse" of discretion such as a court will overturn, but

the courts are of course the ultimate judge of the confines. If the administrative decision is within the outer limits of discretion, a court will not substitute its judgment for the agency's: as long as the agency's determination is within the borders of discretion as perceived by the court, it qualifies as a question of fact.[9] But when it passes those borders it becomes an "abuse", and an abuse of discretion is a question of law. "Abuse of discretion" is yet another separately verbalized review standard under subdivision 3 of CPLR 7803.

An "abuse of discretion", legally and lexicographically, is just another way of defining something that is "arbitrary and capricious".[10] But since "arbitrary and capricious" can also describe a decision wanting in "substantial evidence", the "substantial evidence" test must be the same as the "abuse of discretion" test, and each would have to be the same as the other. If singled out and instructed to describe how the CPLR distinguishes it, each of these tests could reply in the manner of a Marx Brothers routine, "It thinks I look alike!"

In its context in CPLR 7803(3), the "abuse of discretion" test appears to offer a basis for determining the adequacy of fact findings distinct from the "arbitrary and capricious" and "substantial evidence" tests. It is not limited, in other words, to measuring whether an administratively imposed penalty or discipline is sustainable. The caselaw, however, suggests that the penalty and discipline category is indeed the principal sphere of influence of the "abuse of discretion" standard. Its operation in that realm, of great practical significance because of the judicial reins it puts on agency-imposed punishments, is the subject of the next section.

§ 562. Judicial Review of Penalty or Discipline

After authorizing review of whether there has been an "abuse of discretion", CPLR

---

6. Id.

7. CPLR 7804(g). See § 568 below.

8. For a few other lingering purposes, too, there remains a need to categorize. See §§ 566 and 569 below.

9. See Angelo J. Martone & Son, Inc. v. County of Nassau, 42 Misc.2d 804, 249 N.Y.S.2d 353 (Sup.Ct., Nassau County, 1964).

10. See Douglas v. Miller, 55 Misc.2d 303, 285 N.Y.S.2d 174 (Sup.Ct., Westchester County, 1967), aff'd 31 A.D.2d 889, 298 N.Y.S.2d 911 (2d Dep't 1969).

7803(3) adds the phrase "including abuse of discretion as to the measure or mode of penalty or discipline imposed". This explicitly overrules the earlier notion that the courts lack power to review punishments administratively imposed.[1] Today, in fact, the courts have come to scrutinize quite closely alleged administrative excesses in the imposition of penalties, and cases claiming such excesses are perhaps the most frequent setting for the appearance of the abuse of discretion standard.

The question often if not always appears in a certiorari context, because an administratively imposed punishment or forfeiture will usually be imposed only after there has been a full quasi-judicial hearing. This in turn means that the official review standard is the "substantial evidence" test of subdivision 4, and yet it is subdivision 3 that contains the authority for the court to review alleged excesses in any punishment imposed, further establishing subdivision 3 as a kind of catchall. The courts have no trouble with this. They test the adequacy of the agency's fact findings by the substantial evidence test of subdivision 4 and the measure of the punishment by the abuse of discretion test of subdivision 3.[2] Sometimes the courts will even be found using the word "arbitrary" or some other mandamus-type language to describe the punishment imposed by the agency,[3] but on closer analysis it will more likely be a certiorari situation. The distinction retains significance, as already mentioned and to be returned to yet again,[4] because it determines whether the supreme court can pass on the issues initially or must transfer the case straight away to the appellate division.[5]

The standard by which the courts gauge whether a given punishment constitutes an abuse of discretion was articulated in Stolz v. Board of Regents this way:

> We believe that, reasonably construed, the statute authorizes us to set aside a determination by an administrative agency, only if the measure of punishment or discipline imposed is so disproportionate to the offense, in the light of all the circumstances, as to be shocking to one's sense of fairness.[6]

"One's" sense of fairness is obviously the court's sense of fairness. Although administrative punishment will be upheld when within the range of what the court deems fair,[7] judicial alteration of the punishment is not infrequent when the court finds that the agency has left the range. Sometimes the change is the result of the court's rejection of some of the underlying findings. In one case, for example, after some administrative findings had been rejected by the court, a civil service pharmacist's dismissal was cancelled and a mere 15-day suspension substituted as the maximum warranted by the findings left over.[8] In other instances the court may adopt the agency's findings in full but differ on the punishment they support, as in one case in which the court rejected an agency decision revoking a realtor's license and imposed instead a short suspension, despite full affirmance of the agency's findings of his "untrustworthiness".[9] In these instances the court is substituting in place of the agency's higher penalty a lower one that the court feels to be the highest permissible as a matter of law. The court is treating the matter as in effect a question of law, which every "exercise" of discretion becomes when it goes so far afield—as the court defines the field—that it spills over into an "abuse".

The fact that a suspension or like punishment has already been suffered, and its term

§ 562

1. See, e.g., Sagos v. O'Connell, 301 N.Y. 212, 93 N.E.2d 644 (1950).

2. See, e.g., Pomilio v. Lee, 21 A.D.2d 299, 250 N.Y.S.2d 339 (4th Dep't 1964).

3. See, e.g., Shander v. Allen, 28 A.D.2d 1150, 284 N.Y.S.2d 142 (3d Dep't 1967), aff'd 24 N.Y.2d 974, 302 N.Y.S.2d 599, 250 N.E.2d 81 (1969).

4. See § 568 below.

5. See CPLR 7804(g), treated in § 568 below.

6. 4 A.D.2d 361, 364, 165 N.Y.S.2d 179, 182 (3d Dep't 1957).

7. See, e.g., Walker v. Murphy, 15 N.Y.2d 650, 255 N.Y.S.2d 869, 204 N.E.2d 201 (1964).

8. Pomilio v. Lee, 21 A.D.2d 299, 250 N.Y.S.2d 339 (4th Dep't 1964).

9. Ancis v. Lomenzo, 31 A.D.2d 615, 295 N.Y.S.2d 784 (1st Dep't 1968).

ended, is not necessarily ground for refusing an Article 78 proceeding to review it. The proceeding may be allowed in order to cleanse the record and remove the odium that can otherwise adhere to the petitioner.[10]

§ 563. Overstepping Outer Borders of Article 78

While the Article 78 proceeding may be used today for any category of relief formerly available under any of the three old writs of mandamus, prohibition, or certiorari, it will sometimes happen that the relief the petitioner seeks does not identify with any of the three writs and is beyond the purview of Article 78 altogether. The result in that case used to be a dismissal. Today, as long as a legally cognizable claim is stated and the proper parties are before the court, the result will be a simple conversion from proceeding to action—the action that should have been brought in the first place.[1] This is a boon to the petitioner who has mistaken her remedy. It spares the need to sue anew and it measures the timeliness of the case, for limitations' purposes, from the moment of commencement of the proceeding.

This shows that the lines separating the old writs now contained within Article 78 are not the only muddy ones; the line that purports to define the outer limits of Article 78 will also blur from time to time. While Article 78 may be proper, for example, to determine whether a statute has been applied in a constitutional manner, it may not be used to test whether the statute is constitutional on its face, for which the declaratory judgment action has been held the proper remedy.[2] The line is sometimes hard to draw, and for one who wishes to raise both objections it may be impossible. It is comforting to know that as long as the parties are right and personal jurisdiction has been obtained over them, the worst

that will visit a wrong guess as to form will be a procedural conversion.

While in most special proceedings the notice time for the hearing can be as short as eight days,[3] in the Article 78 proceeding it is ordinarily at least 20 days,[4] which makes it more analogous to the time a defendant has to respond to a summons in an action.[5] Hence, when the court proposes to convert an Article 78 proceeding into an action, the respondent cannot even complain about short notice. And even if there were a time differential, the defect could be met with an extension of the responding time rather than a refusal to convert.

The availability of simple conversion into proper form can be credited with encouraging the courts, at least in cases close to Article 78's outer limits, to abandon altogether a search for the line and just get on with the merits,[6] a healthy accomplishment. But the petitioner must demonstrate some kind of right. A failure to do at least that will still result in a dismissal. In this respect a careful examination of Article 78 and all of its old writ categories will often aid the lawyer in determining whether the client even has an enforcible right, or is really looking for some special privilege or concession not available at all.[7] It may also happen that a remedy has been lodged exclusively in administrative channels without provision for judicial review. That, too, although an infrequent phenomenon today, will result in a dismissal.[8]

C. PROCEDURAL BASICS

Table of Sections

---

10. See, e.g., Leo Newman's Theatre Ticket Office, Inc. v. DiCarlo, 46 Misc.2d 549, 260 N.Y.S.2d 221 (Sup.Ct., N.Y. County, 1965).

§ 563

1. CPLR 103(c). See § 4 above.

2. See Kovarsky v. Housing and Dev. Admin., 31 N.Y.2d 184, 335 N.Y.S.2d 383, 286 N.E.2d 882 (1972).

3. CPLR 403(b).

4. See § 567 below.

5. See CPLR 320(a), 3012(a).

6. See, e.g., Albany Medical Center Hospital v. Breslin, 47 Misc.2d 208, 262 N.Y.S.2d 285 (Sup.Ct., Albany County, 1965).

7. See, e.g., Irving v. Finger Lakes State Parks Commission, 12 Misc.2d 1087, 174 N.Y.S.2d 291 (Sup.Ct., Schuyler County, 1958).

8. See, e.g., Werfel v. Agresta, 36 N.Y.2d 624, 370 N.Y.S.2d 881, 331 N.E.2d 668 (1975).

§ 564.   Parties in Article 78 Proceeding

CPLR 7802 addresses the subject of parties to an Article 78 proceeding. It is additional to CPLR 401, which defines the parties in special proceedings generally.[1] The person aggrieved by the administrative result and who brings the proceeding is called, as in special proceedings in general, the petitioner.

The opposing party may occasionally contest the petitioner's "standing to sue", a loose caption designed to preclude litigation at the behest of a person who has no personal stake in the outcome different from that of any other citizen.[2] The "standing" barrier is not a high one in New York, however. The Court of Appeals has indicated that the right to challenge administrative action should be enlarged rather than diminished.[3] But since a "standing to sue" issue is as likely as not to involve administrative activity, the lawyer should at least be mindful of it in conjunction with Article 78. The subject of standing was treated in the "Parties" chapter earlier.[4]

Turning to the respondent, CPLR 7802(a) provides that the "body or officer" against which (or whom) an Article 78 proceeding may be maintained "includes every court, tribunal, board, corporation, officer, or other person, or aggregation of persons, whose action may be affected by a proceeding under this article". The main entry under this sweeping caption is of course the administrative agency, but executive and judicial personnel are also included as long as a clear case for Article 78 relief can be made out against them. The applicability of Article 78 to private corporations, commercial

and otherwise, occurs primarily when the relief sought is in the nature of mandamus. This was also treated earlier.[5]

The respondent is usually designated by name, but there is authority to use the official title of the respondent's office instead, subject always to the court's power to require names to be added.[6] If the petitioner's right subsists, it is also permissible to maintain the proceeding against a person whose term of office has expired.[7] When the respondent is an individual sued in his official capacity and dies or otherwise ceases to hold office, the proceeding can be continued against his successor. If the official title was used, without designation of names, it is not even necessary to effect a substitution.[8] This suggests that if the petitioner did use the name of the individual respondent, a substitution order is required in order to insert the name of the successor. Quite often this is not done, however, and since the official title is also included in the caption, the proceeding is merely deemed to be against the office and the case goes through to judgment on the merits, which is as things ought to be.

The initial papers determine who the parties are. After the proceeding is commenced, the joinder, impleader, or interpleader of any other party requires a court order, as is true of special proceedings in general.[9] If the court determines that any other person has an interest in the proceeding, whether on the petitioner's or the respondent's side, it can require that such person be notified, and it can can allow intervention by interested persons at any time.[10] It has been held, in fact, that while intervention still requires a court order,[11] the court's power to permit intervention is even

§ 564

  1.   See § 551 above.

  2.   See, e.g., Blaikie v. Wagner, 46 Misc.2d 441, 259 N.Y.S.2d 890 (Sup.Ct., N.Y. County, 1965), holding that a citizen-taxpayer-resident of New York City has no standing to compel the mayor to fill judicial vacancies.

  3.   See Dairylea Cooperative, Inc. v. Walkley, 38 N.Y.2d 6, 377 N.Y.S.2d 451, 339 N.E.2d 865 (1975).

  4.   See § 136 above.

  5.   See § 558 above.

  6.   CPLR 1023.

  7.   CPLR 7802(b). The successor in office may also be joined.

  8.   CPLR 1019.

  9.   CPLR 401.

  10.   CPLR 7802(d); Elinor Homes Co. v. St. Lawrence, 113 A.D.2d 25, 494 N.Y.S.2d 889 (2d Dep't 1985).

  11.   CPLR 401, 1012, 1013.

broader in an Article 78 proceeding than in an action.[12]

A justice, judge, referee, or judicial hearing officer is sometimes the respondent in an Article 78 proceeding, as has been seen.[13] If the grievance arises out of an action or proceeding pending before the respondent, the petitioner is required to designate as additional respondents all of the parties to that pending action or proceeding and to serve copies of all of the Article 78 papers on them. These are the special requirements of subdivision (i) of CPLR 7804. The judicial respondent, J, does not have to appear in the Article 78 proceeding, unless the court otherwise directs. If J elects not to appear, the other parties are notified of this and the results of the Article 78 proceeding bind J. If J does elect to appear, she is entitled to be represented by the attorney general. One of the statute's hopes is that the other parties to the underlying case, now joined as respondents, will conduct the defense in the Article 78 proceeding, thereby obviating an appearance by the judge and his representation by the attorney general.

§ 565. Venue of Article 78 Proceeding

The venue of an Article 78 proceeding is supplied by CPLR 506(b), which permits it to be brought

> in any county within the judicial district where the respondent made the determination complained of or refused to perform the duty specifically enjoined upon him by law, or where the proceedings were brought or taken in the course of which the matter sought to be restrained originated, or where the material events otherwise took place, or

where the principal office of the respondent is located....

The range is broad, and all the broader because one of the additional venue options afforded motions within an action[1] is afforded the Article 78 proceeding as well: it can be brought not only in a county answering to one of the above descriptions, but, as the opening language evinces, in any other county in the same judicial district. Although this permits some forum shopping, its primary justification is that it offers the petitioner convenient alternatives when a supreme court session is not being held in one of the described counties. Except for certain instances in which it must be initiated in the appellate division, which we will see in a moment, an Article 78 proceeding belongs jurisdictionally to the supreme court alone.[2] CPLR 506(b) tells us what counties within the supreme court the proceeding may be brought in.

The remedy for a wrong venue in an Article 78 proceeding is the same as in an action: a mere change of venue to the right county.[3] A change of venue would also be permissible on the so-called "discretionary" grounds: to secure an impartial trial when a proper county would not be able to offer one or to serve the convenience of material witnesses.[4]

As also happens in an action, a failure to object to improper venue is a waiver of the objection.[5] The ensuing judgment on the merits is valid.[6]

When an Article 78 proceeding is brought against a justice of the supreme court or a judge of a county court, it is initiated in the appellate division,[7] one of the few instances in which the appellate division exercises original jurisdiction. This recognizes the incongruity of

<hr />

12. See, e.g., Helms v. Diamond, 76 Misc.2d 253, 349 N.Y.S.2d 917 (Sup.Ct., Schenectady County, 1973).

13. See § 558 above.

§ 565

1. See CPLR 2212(a).

2. CPLR 7804(b).

3. CPLR 510(1). See Franklin National Bank v. Superintendent of Banks, 40 Misc.2d 315, 243 N.Y.S.2d 214 (Sup.Ct., Nassau County, 1963). CPLR 511, which governs the procedure for a change of venue, should also govern in

an Article 78 proceeding to the extent feasible, but the special "demand" procedure that subdivision (b) of CPLR 511 sets up for a change of venue in an action (see § 123 above) is mechanically awkward in a special proceeding and should not be used there.

4. CPLR 510(2),(3). See § 124 above.

5. See Hvac and Sprinkler Contractors Ass'n, Inc. v. State Univ. Constr. Fund, 80 Misc.2d 1047, 364 N.Y.S.2d 422 (Sup.Ct., Nassau County, 1975).

6. CPLR 509.

7. CPLR 506(b)(1).

allowing one supreme court justice to review another's activity. For this purpose judges of the county court,[8] especially because they exercise plenary jurisdiction of felonies, are deemed to be on an equal plane with the supreme court and can also be subjected to Article 78 only in the appellate division. If some other person, such as a district attorney, must also be included as a respondent, it has been held permissible to include that person in the proceeding brought in the appellate division, but the converse is not permissible; the presence of some other person as a respondent does not enable the whole proceeding to be brought in the supreme court.[9]

A special provision in subdivision (b) of CPLR 506 authorizes venue only in the supreme court in Albany County, the seat of government, if the proceeding is against certain governmental respondents, including the commissioner of education, the tax commissioner, the comptroller, and some half dozen others enumerated in the statute.[10] This list supersedes the more generous list of venue alternatives contained in the opening language of subdivision (a), quoted above and applicable to other respondents. Even the provision authorizing venue in any other county in the same judicial district appears to be inapplicable to the respondents enumerated in subdivision (b), leaving Albany County as the sole proper venue.[11] There is no need to raise this to the level of a jurisdictional issue, however. Should the proceeding be brought and entertained in the supreme court in a county other than Albany without objection to venue, the court there should be able to dispose of it on the merits.

§ 566. Statute of Limitations in Article 78 Proceeding

The statute of limitations in an Article 78 proceeding is short. It is four months, supplied and governed by CPLR 217(1), whose treatment we have reserved until now. CPLR 217(1) provides that the four months start to run when

> the determination to be reviewed becomes final and binding upon the petitioner ... or after the respondent's refusal, upon the demand of the petitioner ... to perform its duty....

The first one, which measures the four months from the time the determination "becomes final", is generally the starting point for an Article 78 proceeding in the nature of certiorari, while the second one, measured from the respondent's refusal to perform its duty after demand has been duly made, is the usual one for an Article 78 proceeding in the nature of mandamus, but the lines to neither one can be described as straight and unwavering. The lawyer may note here yet another instance in which distinctions between the old writs subsist despite Article 78's embrace of them all.[1] When the consequence attending a wrong guess is a limitations' dismissal, the practitioner should not be guessing at all. The petitioner with any doubt at all should bring the proceeding fast and leave to the scholars the pinpointing of which writ is involved and which technical starting time goes with it. The judges themselves will disagree on whether a given Article 78 proceeding smacks of one writ or the other, with the result that each would start the four months from a different moment.[2]

The "determination" of which CPLR 217(1) speaks, and whose moment of finality starts the four months, applies not only to what is strictly speaking "certiorari", where the determination follows a quasi-judicial hearing mandated by law, but also to "mandamus to re-

---

8. CPLR 506(b)(1) also refers to the court of "general sessions", which entertained the felonies in New York County prior to September 1, 1962, but was abolished on that date and superseded by the supreme court. Const. Art. VI, § 35(a). This reference is now superfluous.

9. Pollak v. Mogavero, 114 A.D.2d 640, 494 N.Y.S.2d 476 (3d Dep't 1985).

10. CPLR 506(b)(2).

11. CPLR 506(a). See Posner v. Rockefeller, 33 A.D.2d 683, 305 N.Y.S.2d 852 (1st Dep't 1969), aff'd 25 N.Y.2d 720, 307 N.Y.S.2d 224, 255 N.E.2d 563 (1969).

§ 566

1. See 2d Rep.Leg.Doc. (1958) No. 13, p. 394.

2. See, e.g., Colodney v. New York Coffee & Sugar Exch., 2 N.Y.2d 149, 157 N.Y.S.2d 573, 138 N.E.2d 810 (1956) (majority and dissenting opinions).

view", where an administrative determination involves discretion but does not require a plenary hearing. The involvement of discretion, therefore, is one strong indicator that the "final determination" moment starts the four months.[3] But it is not always a certain one.[4] Another test, equally well known, is to ask whether what the petitioner seeks is something to which she has a clear legal right—that is, something of a mere ministerial nature—for if the thing demanded is not of that kind, the case will stay in the "review" category and the "final determination" will remain the trigger. (If it is of that kind, it will be the refusal after demand that starts the four months.) This is so whether or not the determination followed a hearing of the judicial or quasi-judicial kind, or an informal hearing, or no hearing at all. Where, for example, petitioners, liquor licensees, sought to annul a license issued by the state liquor authority to one who would be competing with the petitioners, the four months ran from the date of issuance of the license; it was held to be "final and binding" at that time.[5] Since the issuance of a liquor license rested in the discretion of the respondent, the proceeding, whether analogized to certiorari or to mandamus, was one for "review" within the meaning of CPLR 217(1) and the four months thus ran from the time the determination became final and binding.

Once the determination has reached that stage, the four months start to run and the "petitioner cannot, by renewing the application, extend the limitation" because that would enable the petitioner to "toll the statute ad infinitum, and make an absurdity" of it.[6]

The lawyer who is not very happy with some of these distinctions can find company among hosts of other lawyers who are listed as petitioners' counsel in Article 78 cases dismissed as untimely. Close divisions even on appellate benches in these matters[7] attest to the difficulty of drawing the right line, and they seem to be a steady progression. In Waterside Associates v. New York State Department of Environmental Conservation,[8] for example, the petitioner wanted the respondent, the environmental conservation department, to stop designating areas of a certain parcel as wetlands and made a permit application that it hoped would start a process to accomplish that. The respondent would not process the application and sent a form letter saying so. Was this the "refusal" that would trigger the four months of an Article 78 proceeding? Four judges said yes and three judges said no. Whatever the stakes, all was lost by a single vote, and in the highest tribunal of the state. And it was lost not on some great matter of public policy, some profound issue that tries men's souls, but on a dispute over the moment that starts the four-month period for bringing an Article 78 proceeding against an administrative agency.[9]

If the would-be petitioner arrives at the lawyer's office with enough time left under all measures, the lawyer should consider herself twice blessed—once for the client and once for his punctuality—and fly to court. The only time the attorney can be excused for a late suit is when the client arrives too late in the first place.

When the case is clearly a mandamus-to-compel one, and the four-month measure is

---

3. Alliano v. Adams, 2 A.D.2d 532, 157 N.Y.S.2d 119 (1st Dep't 1956), aff'd 3 N.Y.2d 801, 166 N.Y.S.2d 4, 144 N.E.2d 645 (1957).

4. See and compare Foy v. Brennan, 285 App.Div. 669, 140 N.Y.S.2d 132 (1st Dep't 1955).

5. Cohen v. State Liquor Authority, 25 A.D.2d 773, 269 N.Y.S.2d 525 (2d Dep't 1966).

6. Mallen v. Morton, 199 Misc. 805, 811, 99 N.Y.S.2d 521, 528–9 (Sup.Ct., N.Y.County, 1950).

7. See, e.g., Owners Committee on Electric Rates, Inc. v. Public Service Commission, 150 A.D.2d 45, 545 N.Y.S.2d 416 (3d Dep't 1989), rev'd 76 N.Y.2d 779, 559 N.Y.S.2d 957 (1990).

8. 72 N.Y.2d 1009, 534 N.Y.S.2d 915, 531 N.E.2d 636 (1988).

9. The Waterside case and the dilemma of determining the starting time of the Article 78 statute of limitations is the subject of the lead note in New York State Law Digest No. 354. In another case that never reached the merits and in which the hapless petitioner had to deal with not one agency, but three, the four-month period for Article 78 review was apparently held to run from the time the petitioner failed to furnish papers to one agency that it had already furnished to another of them. See Essex County v. Zagata, 91 N.Y.2d 447, 672 N.Y.S.2d 281 (1998), treated in the lead note in New York State Law Digest No. 463.

from demand and refusal, another thing the courts look out for is a delayed demand. Postponing the demand would obviously be an easy way for a petitioner to avoid the limitation, and so the laches doctrine also gets invoked here.[10] Where the petitioner was removed from office, for example, and without excuse delayed a demand for reinstatement, his proceeding was dismissed for laches.[11] Of course, if a reasonably diligent petitioner is not aware of the facts that would prompt him to make the demand, his delay in making it is excusable and laches will not be applied.[12]

Up to now we have been talking about certiorari and mandamus. A word should be said about prohibition. With prohibition, the very applicability of the four-month statute of limitations of CPLR 217(1) is questionable. It has from time to time been applied to an Article 78 proceeding in the nature of prohibition,[13] but since the proceeding in such an instance is one that implies a lack of jurisdiction on the part of the respondent—a defect that would presumably be a continuing one—it can be argued that the four months may be measured from any point during the jurisdiction's continued exercise. That would be so, in any event, when the objection is addressed strictly to the respondent's lack of subject matter jurisdiction, the traditional arena of prohibition. But the writ's function (and Article 78's function as its successor) has been extended to that ill-defined realm, previously discussed, in which jurisdiction exists but "power" is exceeded.[14] The petitioner objecting to this exercise of "power" would do well, at least until we have a further clarification of the matter, to commence the proceeding within four months of its first perceived exercise.

CPLR 217(1) also addresses the disabilities of infancy and insanity, should the petitioner be under either disability when the four months are set to begin. It permits the court in such an instance to extend the four months for a period of up to two years.

The moment of the claim's interposition for limitations' purposes is when the petition and notice of petition are filed in court. When an order to show cause is used to bring on the proceeding, as the statute allows,[15] the filing of the order to show cause marks interposition. The service of these initiatory papers must then be effected within whatever is left of the applicable statute of limitations plus 15 days, the exotic formula supplied by CPLR 306–b, the statute at the heart of the filing system for commencing actions in the supreme and county courts, adopted in 1992. The interplay of the filing and service requirements under this system, which affect the statute of limitations and can be demanding, is treated in depth in the section on special proceedings generally.[16]

CPLR 7804(c), which governs the service of the initial papers in an Article 78 proceeding, adds the requirement that when the respondent is a state body or officer (as opposed to one at municipal level, for example), service must also be made on the attorney general through a prescribed procedure. If service is timely made on the respondent but late on the attorney general, however, it has been held that all is preserved. The reason is that the purpose of this provision is to assure a defense by the attorney general if the named respondent does not have separate counsel,[17] not to make the attorney general the party.[18] Conversely, however, and for the same reason, timely service on the attorney general is not a substitute for timely service on the named respondent, and where the latter was served late the proceeding was dismissed under the statute of limitations.[19]

---

10. See Austin v. Board of Higher Education, 5 N.Y.2d 430, 186 N.Y.S.2d 1, 158 N.E.2d 681 (1959).

11. Peruzzin v. Test, 282 App.Div. 550, 125 N.Y.S.2d 353 (4th Dep't 1953).

12. O'Connell v. Kern, 287 N.Y. 297, 39 N.E.2d 246 (1942).

13. See, e.g., Feldman v. Matthews, 32 Misc.2d 996, 223 N.Y.S.2d 604 (Sup.Ct., Monroe County, 1962).

14. See § 559 above.

15. CPLR 7804(c). See § 567 below.

16. See § 553 above.

17. See Commentary C2214:30 on the analogous provision of McKinney's CPLR 2214.

18. Chem–Trol Pollution Services, Inc. v. Ingraham, 42 A.D.2d 192, 345 N.Y.S.2d 714 (4th Dep't 1973).

19. Cohen v. State Tax Commission, 51 A.D.2d 79, 378 N.Y.S.2d 507 (3d Dep't 1976).

One final note is also a note of warning. CPLR 217(1) defers to any statute that requires that a given Article 78 proceeding be brought in less than four months. Review of a village board of appeals in a zoning matter, for example, gets only 30 days from the decision's filing with the village clerk,[20] and there are other similar examples.[21] The lawyer dealing with any municipal, governmental or quasi-governmental body should, upon losing a decision, make the applicable statute of limitations the first point of research. If there is nothing specific addressed to the particular proceeding, the four months of CPLR 217(1) will apply. Special sensitivity to time issues must be exercised in election cases, where, for obvious reasons, the time in which to bring remedial proceedings is short.[22] Furthermore, if the time for its bringing has expired, the petitioner cannot, by labeling the proceeding one under Article 78 instead of under the Election Law, secure the former's more favorable four-month period.[23]

D. MECHANICS

Table of Sections

§ 567. Bringing the Proceeding

The procedure for commencing the Article 78 proceeding is similar to that applicable to special proceedings in general, but Article 78 prefers its own statement for certain particulars, setting them forth in CPLR 7804(c).

The technical moment of the commencement of the proceeding for statute of limitations purposes, as noted in the prior section and elaborated in the section on special proceedings generally,[1] is the filing of the initiatory papers. We turn here to what those papers are in an Article 78 proceeding.

The notice of petition and petition, including supporting affidavits, are the initiatory papers, but the return day cannot be set for earlier than the 20th day after service, in contrast to the 8–day minimum applicable to special proceedings generally.[2] The respondent's answer must be served at least 5 days before the return day, and the petitioner who would then serve a reply must do so at least 1 day before. Setting the return day for earlier than the 20th day has sometimes been held a jurisdictional defect,[3] but more recently it has been said that "short notice should be excused unless the error is substantial or it causes prejudice".[4] Under that view, it would be incumbent on the respondent to show "that the defect prevented it from adequately responding" to the claim,[5] which a mistake of only a day or a few days is not likely to do. If the petitioner is really pressed for time, however, it would be safer to bring the proceeding on by order to show cause, which can set an earlier return than the otherwise required 20 days.

The alternative of the order to show cause procedure is available for the Article 78 proceeding just as it is for special proceedings

---

20. Vill.L. § 7–712–c.

21. A list of others appears in 2d Rep.Leg.Doc. (1958) No. 13, p.550. The list needs updating, but even a current one is no substitute for specific inquiry in the individual case when the statute of limitations is hovering about.

22. See the several proceedings supplied by Article 16 of the Election Law.

23. See Mansfield v. Epstein, 5 N.Y.2d 70, 180 N.Y.S.2d 33, 154 N.E.2d 368 (1958); Murray v. Lord, 46 A.D.2d 721, 361 N.Y.S.2d 96 (4th Dep't) aff'd 35 N.Y.2d 737, 361 N.Y.S.2d 909, 320 N.E.2d 644 (1974).

§ 567

1. See § 553 above.

2. CPLR 403(b).

3. See, e.g., Dickerson v. Jensen, 33 A.D.2d 890, 307 N.Y.S.2d 559 (4th Dep't 1969).

4. Marmo v. Department of Environmental Conservation, 134 A.D.2d 260, 520 N.Y.S.2d 442 (2d Dep't 1987). See also Bloeth v. Marks, 20 A.D.2d 372, 247 N.Y.S.2d 410 (1st Dep't 1964), involving a pro se petitioner, and Griswald v. Village of Penn Yan, 244 A.D.2d 950, 665 N.Y.S.2d 177 (4th Dep't 1997).

5. Szklowin v. Planning Board of Town of Blooming Grove, 115 Misc.2d 1045, 455 N.Y.S.2d 70 (Sup.Ct., Orange County, 1982).

generally[6] and for motions in actions.[7] Its availability would suggest that, at worst, the remedy when an ordinary notice of petition is used with fewer than 20 days notice is for the court simply to award more time, putting the return day off as needed.

Whether an order to show cause or a regular notice of petition is used, the petitioner must remember that when the respondent is a body or officer of the state rather than of a municipal or other level, service must also be made on the attorney general.[8]

Labeling the papers a notice of motion instead of a notice of petition has also been held harmless error,[9] but it can lead to some confusion in the clerk's office. A motion has the context of a pending action with an index number already assigned, while an Article 78 proceeding is an independent application and requires its own index number and the payment of a fee for it. As with special proceedings in general, the papers initiating an Article 78 proceeding must be accompanied by a Request for Judicial Intervention (RJI),[10] which gets the case assigned to a judge.[11]

Pending its decision on the merits, the court can stay the enforcement of the determination and any further proceedings by the respondent, imposing conditions as it sees fit.[12] It can do this on either the motion of a party or on its own motion. The value of a stay, which gives the aggrieved person some breathing space while a court looks into the administrative activity, can be attested to by many lawyers. One way of seeking it is by opting to bring the proceeding on by order to show cause and by requesting that the court include a stay in the order.[13]

Pleadings in an Article 78 proceeding are much the same as in any proceeding, with only a few variations. They must be verified, for example,[14] but the consequence of a failure to verify should be no greater in the proceeding than it is in an action.[15] There is even authority, especially when prompt objection is not made, for disregarding the defect altogether.[16] Since the pleadings are usually accompanied by sworn affidavits, which set forth the facts more abundantly, an absence of a formal verification of the pleadings is not likely to be prejudicial.

Another pleading variation in an Article 78 proceeding is that a reply is mandatory not only when the respondent's answer contains a counterclaim, but also when there is "new matter in the answer or where the accuracy of proceedings annexed to the answer is disputed".[17] A reply is technically required, in other words, if the petitioner wants to dispute the correctness of the administrative record.

If there is a record, as there often is—and it is often voluminous—and the court does not already have it, it is the respondent's obligation to furnish it to the court, which the respondent does by filing with the answer "a certified transcript of the record of the proceedings".[18] This is no mean attainment: without the statutory imposition of this burden on the respondent many a petitioner would be in no position to press forward with an Article 78 proceeding. The court can also direct the respondent to supply any omissions in the rec-

---

6. CPLR 403(d).

7. CPLR 2214(d).

8. CPLR 7804(c).

9. Marmo v. Department of Environmental Conservation, note 4, above.

10. See § 553 above.

11. This requirement comes from the Uniform Rules. The relevant rules here are UR 202.6, 202.8(b), and 202.9, applicable in the supreme and county courts. The official RJI form is reprinted in § 77C above.

12. CPLR 7805.

13. In this connection, however, the practitioner must bear in mind the restriction imposed by CPLR 6313(a). It precludes the issuance of a temporary restraining order

against "a public officer, board or municipal corporation" if the effect of it is "to restrain the performance of statutory duties." See § 330 above.

14. CPLR 7804(d).

15. See § 235 above.

16. See Ferro v. Lavine, 46 A.D.2d 313, 362 N.Y.S.2d 591 (3d Dep't 1974).

17. CPLR 7804(d). In other special proceedings a reply is optional even in these situations. See CPLR 402.

18. CPLR 7804(e). It has been held that this applies only to the Article 78 proceeding itself, however. It does not require the furnishing of a transcript during the various administrative stages that precede the commencement of the proceeding. Rivera v. Smith, 137 A.D.2d 281, 528 N.Y.S.2d 930 (3d Dep't 1988).

ord. If no record is filed at all, the court may take such remedial steps as it deems fit, including a dismissal of the respondent's answer with leave to serve a new one with a record annexed to it.[19]

If the respondent has "an objection in point of law" to the petition, CPLR 7804(f) gives the respondent the option of including it as a defense in the answer or making a motion to dismiss based on it. This was intended to draw a limited analogy to an action; the "objections" intended for this alternative treatment are of the kind listed in CPLR 3211(a),[20] and more particularly those on the CPLR 3211(a) list that do not go to the merits and thus make possible a disposition that may spare the court the effort of having to reach the merits at all.[21] Objections of want of jurisdiction and the statute of limitations are perhaps the most common examples.

When taken by motion, the motion must be noticed "within the time allowed for answer". Since the answering time is 20 days, this gives the respondent enough time to notice a motion, but just barely. The motion must be made returnable at the same time and place as the Article 78 proceeding is, as set in the notice of petition.[22]

The statute says that if the motion is denied, the court "shall" permit the respondent to answer,[23] but this, too, envisions that the motion has addressed only a specific defense and thus poses no occasion for a treatment of the whole record on the merits. The courts frown on the making of a motion by a respondent on the presumably narrow ground of a single defense while at the same time putting in on the motion all of the evidence the respondent has on the merits and asking that it

be allowed to serve an answer if the motion is denied. It amounts to the respondent's attempt to get two bites at the apple. "The statute does not contemplate successive hearings on issues of fact, at least unless the court finds some good reason for so ordering."[24]

But what remedy? The statute does say, after all, that the court "shall" permit an answer if the motion is denied, not merely that it "may" do so. While there is some indication that the difference was intended,[25] if it is plain from all the papers that the respondent has nothing with which to answer and that further proceedings would be wasteful, the court should not prolong the petitioner's agony. It should be able to close the case out with a judgment. Some courts lean in that direction, especially when the issues are of law rather than of fact and require no trial.[26] Others suggest that the court may invoke CPLR 3211(c) and treat the motion as one for summary judgment, notifying the parties to submit any additional proof they may have, thereby obviating yet another court hearing.

> It is difficult to see what appropriate purpose is served by permitting the denial of the motion to be followed by an answer that raises no new factual or legal issue....[27]

If the motion is denied and the court does allow an answer, CPLR 7804(f) provides for the time within which the respondent must serve the answer and for the petitioner's time for re-noticing the hearing.

§ 568. Hearing and Determination; Transfer to Appellate Division

The Article 78 proceeding is brought in the supreme court.[1] The supreme court will ordi-

---

19. See Occhino v. Hostetter, 21 A.D.2d 744, 250 N.Y.S.2d 120 (4th Dep't 1964).

20. See § 257 above; 4th Rep.Leg.Doc. (1960) No. 20, p. 181.

21. Hop–Wah v. Coughlin, 118 A.D.2d 275, 504 N.Y.S.2d 806 (3d Dep't 1986), rev'd on other grounds 69 N.Y.2d 791, 513 N.Y.S.2d 115, 505 N.E.2d 625 (1987).

22. CPLR 406.

23. CPLR 7804(f). This is in contrast to CPLR 404(a), applicable to special proceedings in general, which provides only that the court "may" permit an answer in that situation.

24. R. Bernstein Co. v. Popolizio, 97 A.D.2d 735, 468 N.Y.S.2d 888 (1st Dep't 1983).

25. See 5th Rep.Leg.Doc. (1961), p. 755.

26. See, e.g., DeVito v. Nyquist, 56 A.D.2d 159, 391 N.Y.S.2d 747 (3d Dep't), aff'd 43 N.Y.2d 681, 401 N.Y.S.2d 25, 371 N.E.2d 788 (1977).

27. 230 Tenants Corp. v. Board of Standards and Appeals, 101 A.D.2d 53, 474 N.Y.S.2d 498 (1st Dep't 1984).

§ 568

1. CPLR 7804(b). If the proceeding is against a supreme court justice or a county court judge, it is brought initially in the appellate division. CPLR 506(b)(1). There narily dispose of the whole case, but with a big proviso. CPLR 7804(g) provides that if the "substantial evidence" question[2] is raised

> the court shall first dispose of such other objections as could terminate the proceeding, including but not limited to lack of jurisdiction, statute of limitations and res judicata, without reaching the substantial evidence issue. If the determination of the other objections does not terminate the proceeding, the court shall make an order directing that it be transferred for disposition to . . . the appellate division. . . .

The mere presence of the substantial evidence question, which means that the proceeding is one in the nature of "certiorari", will trigger this transfer requirement if some other objection does not terminate the proceeding. And the procedure is just that—a transfer, not an appeal.

The reason for the transfer is partly historical and partly a recognition that a "substantial evidence" review of an administrative record is analogous to an appellate review of a court-made record and for that reason merits quick deposit before the appellate tribunal.[3]

The reason for not allowing the petitioner to initiate the proceeding in the appellate division, requiring instead that it be commenced in the supreme court and the supreme court determine whether to transfer it, is to enable the supreme court to rule on potentially dispositive issues that may obviate consideration of the substantial evidence question. The several such issues listed are illustrative only. The objections intended are perhaps best taken to be the same as those intended by the phrase "objections in point of law" as used in

CPLR 7804(f), discussed in the prior section: threshold objections that are capable of disposing of the case without reaching the merits, like a number of the objections listed in CPLR 3211(a) for use in actions.[4]

There is some suggestion, however, that any legal issue separate from the substantial evidence question—which is itself a question of law—can qualify as an objection that the trial-level judge can pass on, even though not necessarily of the CPLR 3211(a) variety, such as in one case where the question of law was who among certain categories of persons was responsible for a certain tax.[5]

If the substantial evidence question is in the case, and the connected issue is tied in with the merits and would logically be passed on in the course of applying the substantial evidence criterion, the issue should not be passed on by the supreme court but left to the appellate division.[6] One can argue interminably on this matter,[7] but evasive as a sharp definition of "objections" may seem, the price of guessing wrong is not very high.

Before a 1990 amendment that produced the language quoted above, the statement of CPLR 7804(g) was that the supreme court "may" pass on the objections before sending the case up, suggesting that it did not have to; that it could just leave the whole case to the appellate division. Some justices, for example, disposed of only such clear-cut merits-avoiding objections as lack of jurisdiction and the statute of limitations, as the 1990 amendment now specifically invites. It was not of great moment, however, because CPLR 7804(g) went on to provide, as it still does, that "when the proceeding comes before it, whether by appeal or

---

are some rare exceptions in which an Article 78 proceeding is initiated in the appellate division instead of the supreme court, such as one to review a decision of the tax appeals tribunal, which goes directly to the Third Department Appellate Division. See Tax Law § 2016.

2. CPLR 7803(4).

3. See 2d Rep.Leg.Doc. (1958) No. 13, p.402. In some instances, special statutes supersede this transfer requirement and mandate that special term dispose of all the issues initially, including the substantial evidence question. This is notably so of zoning and land use cases. See Gen.City L. § 82(1)(c); Town L. § 267–c(1); Village L. § 7–712–c(1).

4. See Hop–Wah v. Coughlin, 118 A.D.2d 275, 504 N.Y.S.2d 806 (3d Dep't 1986), rev'd on other grounds 69 N.Y.2d 791, 513 N.Y.S.2d 115, 505 N.E.2d 625 (1987).

5. See Komp v. State Tax Commission, 56 Misc.2d 824, 290 N.Y.S.2d 297 (Sup.Ct., Albany County, 1968).

6. See, e.g., Dan's Living Room, Ltd. v. State of New York Liquor Auth., 31 A.D.2d 799, 298 N.Y.S.2d 291 (1st Dep't), aff'd 25 N.Y.2d 759, 303 N.Y.S.2d 513, 250 N.E.2d 574 (1969).

7. The transfer-up provision of CPLR 7804(g) is the subject of the lead note in New York State Law Digest No. 235.

transfer, the appellate division shall dispose of all issues in the proceeding".

If the supreme court has already disposed of some issues, therefore, the appellate division, when the case gets transferred up, can simply conduct an appellate-type review of those issues while making the initial review of the substantial evidence question. Note, however, that the presence of the substantial evidence question requires a transfer of the whole case to the appellate division, and that a transfer is more expeditious than an appeal.

The requirement of transfer when a substantial evidence issue is presented, i.e., in a "certiorari" case, is a principal source of the continuing necessity to pinpoint which old writ the Article 78 proceeding involves. If, for example, the case is really a mandamus situation and involves the "arbitrary and capricious" standard, it should be kept at special term and the whole of it initially decided there. What happens, then, when the lower court incorrectly deems it a certiorari situation involving the "substantial evidence" test and sends it up? This has happened, and can happen frequently, but the courts have made their peace with the problem. The appellate division can just keep the case and decide all of it on the merits even if it should not have been transferred.[8] The Court of Appeals has upheld the appellate division's power to do this.[9]

The converse can also occur: the proceeding may be an authentic certiorari case and invoke the "substantial evidence" test requiring a transfer up, but be erroneously deemed a mandamus case and kept and decided by the supreme court applying the "arbitrary and capricious" standard. On subsequent appeal, the appellate division can just disregard the supreme court disposition, and, treating the case as having been properly transferred up in the first place, dispose of all of the issues, including the substantial evidence issue, de novo.[10]

The transfer purpose has perpetuated arguments about what makes a case a "certiorari" one (transferable) or a "mandamus" one (nontransferable). One court may say, for example, that it turns on whether a hearing is required by law regardless of the kind of hearing it is,[11] while another may hold that it turns on the kind of hearing it is regardless of whether required or not.[12] One case tries to distinguish the other, not, it is submitted, with much success. The only saving factor is the flexibility that the appellate courts have built into the realm. As frequent as errors may be—nisi prius judges keeping cases that should be transferred or transferring cases that should be kept—the appellate court, however it gets the case, seems willing to dispose of it on the merits. Nor need there be any apprehension that so generous a reaction will prompt a party to seek an undue advantage. An error in this connection, after all, is an error by the supreme court justice, not by the petitioner's attorney, who must in any event commence the proceeding in the supreme court.

§ 569. Trial of Issue of Fact in Article 78 Proceeding

Most Article 78 proceedings are resolved on papers alone. Rarely does an Article 78 proceeding present an issue of fact requiring a trial, but CPLR 7804(h) recognizes that it does happen from time to time and provides that "if a triable issue of fact is raised ... it shall be tried forthwith". When the Article 78 proceeding is essentially a mandamus one, for example, and there was no hearing conducted before the agency and hence no transcript to review, it may not be possible to determine from the papers alone whether the administrative activity was arbitrary and capricious. In such an instance, a determination of the facts on which the activity—such as the denial of a license—depends will sometimes require a tri-

---

8. See Pauling v. Smith, 46 A.D.2d 759, 361 N.Y.S.2d 16 (1st Dep't 1974).

9. Matter of 125 Bar Corp. v. State Liquor Auth., 24 N.Y.2d 174, 299 N.Y.S.2d 194, 247 N.E.2d 157 (1969).

10. See Daigle v. State Liquor Auth., 35 A.D.2d 901, 315 N.Y.S.2d 706 (3d Dep't 1970).

11. See, e.g., Metropolitan Theater Ticket Agents Guild, Inc. v. DiCarlo, 48 Misc.2d 208, 264 N.Y.S.2d 650 (Sup.Ct., N.Y.County, 1965).

12. See, e.g., Consolidated Edison Co. v. Kretchmer, 68 Misc.2d 545, 327 N.Y.S.2d 375 (Sup.Ct., Kings County, 1971).

al.[1] In a certiorari situation, on the other hand, which implies that there was a full hearing that developed all the facts, the court's function is to determine whether the findings and conclusions are supported by substantial evidence in the record. Here, therefore, the appearance of factual disputes requiring a trial by the court should be still less frequent.[2]

Whatever the frequency, if an issue of fact does arise, is it triable by jury? CPLR 7804(h) does not say, and CPLR 410, which governs special proceedings in general and to which we should be able to turn for aid, offers none. It merely says that the court must give the parties an opportunity to demand a jury "if" the issues are so triable. It just begs the question.

If the Article 78 proceeding is in the nature of mandamus, there is apparently a right to trial by jury of issues of fact,[3] and a constitutional one at that.[4] There is some suggestion that a jury trial may also be required to try issues of fact arising in certiorari, but the problem seems to have arisen so infrequently that the conclusion is tenuous at best.[5] A court faced with the problem and doubtful as to whether a jury is required would do well to impanel one anyway, as it has the power to do.[6]

It is generally agreed that an issue of fact arising in an Article 78 proceeding in the nature of prohibition, which will occasionally

happen, is not triable by jury,[7] apparently for the reason that prohibition tests jurisdiction and jurisdictional issues are traditionally resolved by the court.

CPLR 7804(h)'s direction that a triable issue of fact arising in an Article 78 proceeding be tried "forthwith" does not mean that everything in sight must be deferred to it. It means in essence that the case is entitled to a special trial preference.[8] How special the preference is must of course depend on the exigencies of the particular case and the other preferred cases standing on the court's calendar. CPLR 7804(h) also recognizes that the proceeding may have been initiated in the appellate division, as it is when it is brought against a supreme court justice or a county court judge.[9] It provides that if the triable issue of fact arises before the appellate division, it can be ordered tried either by a referee or by a trial term of the supreme court, the matter being remitted for that purpose. But the remission is only temporary: the verdict, report, or decision rendered after the trial is returned to the appellate division, and the latter renders the judgment in the case.[10]

§ 570. Judgment and Enforcement in Article 78 Proceeding

The Article 78 proceeding culminates in a "judgment", as all special proceedings do today.[1] CPLR 7806 provides in part that

§ 569

1. See, e.g., Yetta's Rest., Inc. v. State Liquor Auth., 47 Misc.2d 436, 262 N.Y.S.2d 743 (Sup.Ct., N.Y. County, 1965). The court must of course be circumspect here. It should not, in the review context of Article 78, try any fact issue that it is the agency's function to dispose of. The court's function is merely to determine whether the agency's finding is supportable, perhaps remanding to the agency for a hearing or for a further hearing if it appears that a key fact is at issue and has not yet been tried. As the Yetta's case manifests, here is another elusive line on the Article 78 field.

2. See Rochester Colony, Inc. v. Hostetter, 19 A.D.2d 250, 241 N.Y.S.2d 210 (4th Dep't 1963).

3. See People ex rel. Desiderio v. Connolly, 212 A.D. 102, 207 N.Y.Supp. 525 (4th Dep't 1925); Arnold v. Dumpson, 78 Misc.2d 703, 356 N.Y.S.2d 784 (Sup.Ct., N.Y. County, 1974).

4. See 3d Ann.Jud. Council Rep. (1937) 169.

5. Id., at 188, which states its conclusion hedgingly but is cited and relied on in turn in 2d Rep.Leg.Doc. (1958) No. 13, p.404.

6. CPLR 4212. It can qualify as only an "advisory" jury, but the difference between that and a jury of right vanishes if the judge happens to agree with the verdict. See § 381 above.

7. See 3d Jud. Council Rep. (1937) p.167.

8. See Mulligan v. Lackey, 33 A.D.2d 991, 307 N.Y.S.2d 371 (4th Dep't 1970).

9. See CPLR 506(b)(1).

10. CPLR 7804(h) refers to an "order" to be made in the case but should also be construed, if the need arises, to include the "judgment" that formally terminates an Article 78 proceeding today. CPLR 7806.

§ 570

1. CPLR 411. When reading older cases, which refer to a "final order", one should keep in mind that under prior law, Civ.Prac.Act § 1300, the "final order" was the culmination of a special proceeding and served as the equivalent of the "judgment" used today.

the judgment may grant the petitioner the relief to which he is entitled, or may dismiss the proceeding either on the merits or with leave to renew. If the proceeding was brought to review a determination, the judgment may annul or confirm the determination in whole or in part, or modify it, and may direct or prohibit specified action by the respondent.

In that statement, a good deal more detailed for the Article 78 proceeding than the counterpart provision is for judgments in an action,[2] the legislature is merely assuring that the court has the requisite power to render any judgment appropriate to the case. If the record is complete enough to enable the court to render a final judgment on the merits, it will do that; if the case entails a correction of errors and requires further proceedings by the respondent, the correction will be made and back will go the case. Although not expressly listed, a remand to the agency for further proceedings is very much a part of the court's power.

The power to modify a determination, included in CPLR 7806, includes the power to reduce a punishment meted out as part of the administrative process. This was at one time precluded; the court's power was limited to canceling the punishment or penalty, if deemed necessary, with a remand of the case to the agency to fix a different one. Today the court can do it all. The power to review abuses of discretion "as to the measure or mode of penalty or discipline", expressly conferred by CPLR 7803(3),[3] is deemed to carry, as a logical concomitant, the power to reduce a punishment down to what the court finds to be the maximum permissible, should the agency have gone too far.[4]

The power to "direct or prohibit" specified action is explicit in the statute. A judgment in

an Article 78 proceeding that embodies those directions, or, indeed, any other directions needed to secure to the petitioner the Article 78 relief ordered, is enforcible by contempt proceedings.[5] Since many of these directions amount in effect to injunctions, it is reasonably clear today that even outright injunctive relief, if appropriate, is available in an Article 78 proceeding.[6] Although one occasionally hears repeated the older view that it is not,[7] the better view would have to be that it is, at least in cases near the borders of Article 78 itself, i.e., in cases seeking relief arguably if not clearly within the scope of any of the three old writs of mandamus, prohibition, or certiorari. The line between the writs on one side and the injunction on the other is yet another obscure one.[8] The CPLR attitude, that even if the line is identified in a given case it should result in nothing worse than a conversion from wrong form (proceeding) to right form (action),[9] buttresses the view that if it is not clearly perceptible, the form brought should be kept and the relief shaped to the case without further regard to form.

Finally, there is the matter of whether money damages may be awarded in an Article 78 proceeding. CPLR 7806 assumes that they may be, but provides that

> any restitution or damages granted to the petitioner must be incidental to the primary relief sought by the petitioner, and must be such as he might otherwise recover on the same set of facts in a separate action or proceeding suable in the supreme court against the same body or officer in its or his official capacity.

This provision, not added to CPLR 7806 until the last of the legislative reports preceding adoption of the CPLR,[10] allows damages, but only on a combination of narrow grounds.

---

2. CPLR 5011.

3. This provision comes from § 1296(5–a) of the Civil Practice Act, which took effect in 1955.

4. See Mitthauer v. Patterson, 8 N.Y.2d 37, 201 N.Y.S.2d 321, 167 N.E.2d 731 (1960). The use of Article 78 to review and alter administrative punishment and discipline was the subject of separate treatment earlier. See § 562.

5. CPLR 5104, Jud.L. §§ 750, 753.

6. See Policemen's Benevolent Ass'n v. Board of Trustees, 21 A.D.2d 693, 250 N.Y.S.2d 523 (2d Dep't 1964).

7. E.g. Teuch v. Murphy, 45 Misc.2d 81, 256 N.Y.S.2d 25 (Sup.Ct., N.Y. County, 1965).

8. See 3d Jud.Council Rep. (1937) at 157–9.

9. CPLR 103(c).

10. See 6th Rep.Leg.Doc. (1962) No. 8, p.677.

The first requirement is that the relief be "incidental" to the primary relief sought in the Article 78 proceeding. The Court of Appeals held in Gross v. Perales[11] that money is incidental if a grant of the relief that is the primary aim of the Article 78 proceeding would make it a "statutory duty" of the respondent to pay the petitioner the sum sought.

The facts of the *Gross* case can illustrate. The petitioner, P, was a city agency providing public assistance benefits to individuals, and the respondent, R, the state department that oversaw the program and had to reimburse P for a segment of the payments. Regulations required P to terminate or reduce benefits under certain circumstances and R audited P to determine compliance. P fulfilled the requirements of all statutes and rules, but R also applied "internal audit guidelines" that imposed more stringent requirements of which P had no notice, docking P $20 million in reimbursements for not fulfilling them. The court held R's action arbitrary and capricious, set the action aside, and directed R to pay the $20 million as "incidental" relief.

Setting aside an administrative determination as arbitrary and capricious is the primary stuff of Article 78, the court said, and since the setting aside in this case made it obligatory for R to reimburse P the sum withheld, the money was just an incident and the statute was satisfied. There was nothing else for a court to determine.

The second requirement of CPLR 7806 is a showing that damages would lie if sought in a separate supreme court action against the same respondent, which appears to be just a way of ascertaining whether the respondent would be amenable to a money suit in the supreme court. The Court of Appeals in *Gross*

found in CPLR 7806 an intention to let the supreme court entertain the whole proceeding.[12] This would pose no problem if the respondent were a municipal agency, but a problem of immunity looms up if the respondent, as a state agency, qualifies as the alter ego of the state, for the reason that while the state has of course waived sovereign immunity in behalf of itself and those entities that qualify as its alter egos, it has done so only for suit in the court of claims.[13] Under the *Gross* decision, it would seem that the waiver now extends jurisdiction to the supreme court as well when the damages sought are incidental to a legitimate Article 78 proceeding.

If the money damages, as "incidental" to the proceeding, may be included there, the logical next question is, *must* they be? Is there a waiver if they are not, so that a separate suit for the damages later can be defeated with the res judicata or "splitting" doctrine[14]? The New York Court of Appeals will have to answer that question. Until it does, Article 78 petitioners are perhaps best advised to include in the proceeding whatever damages can possibly be deemed "incidental" to it. Prior to the *Gross* case, the U.S. Second Circuit had to answer the waiver question in a case seeking damages for a civil rights violation.[15] The plaintiff had previously brought an Article 78 proceeding in the state court involving the same dispute but did not include there the claim for money damages. The court said there was no waiver and sustained the claim.[16]

If a damages award is made as part of an Article 78 judgment, that part would be enforcible, as would any money judgment, by the procedures of Article 52 of the CPLR.[17] Con-

---

11. 72 N.Y.2d 231, 532 N.Y.S.2d 68 , 527 N.E.2d 1205 (1988).

12. Citing the bill jacket of the 1962 law that enacted CPLR 7806, the court says that all the legislature intended to do with the "incidental" damages language was immunize the state "from paying consequential damages in cases where a state agency improperly denied, revoked or suspended a petitioner's license".

13. Cf. Burgos v. State, 40 Misc.2d 971, 244 N.Y.S.2d 479 (Ct.Cl. 1963), decided before CPLR 7806 became effective.

14. See § 220 above.

15. 42 U.S.C.A. § 1983.

16. See Finkelstein v. Capuano, a/k/a Davidson v. Capuano, 792 F.2d 275 (2d Cir.1986), discussed in the lead note in New York State Law Digest No. 319.

17. See CPLR 5101.

tempt would then be the enforcement device only for the non-money parts of the judgment.[18]

18.   See CPLR 5104.

Part III

THE SUMMARY PROCEEDING

A. PURPOSE AND SCOPE

Table of Sections

§ 571. The RPAPL and the Summary Proceeding; a Perspective

In an endeavor to avoid encumbering the CPLR with provisions directed only to real property actions—of which numerous had evolved over the years—the old Civil Practice Act's formidable allotment of these provisions was transferred into a separate compilation called the Real Property Actions and Proceedings Law, commonly known and officially citable as RPAPL.[1] It became effective at the same time as the CPLR, on September 1, 1963, and its contents are a mixed bag. Essentially, it contains what may best be described as supplementary provisions for some of the real property actions. The CPLR still governs in those actions, the mission of the RPAPL being principally to supply detail for only certain aspects of some of them.

The RPAPL will usually address matters too important to deprive of statutory guidance but too intimately associated with but a single kind of action to deserve space in the CPLR, whose domain is litigation in general. The action to foreclose a mortgage is an illustration. A regular entry in annual litigation in New York, it is governed by the CPLR; but certain parts of it need more intimate regulation, and these get it from the RPAPL. Among other things in the RPAPL article on the fore-

closure action,[2] for example, we find additional instruction on the post-judgment devices of a "surplus money" proceeding (when the foreclosure sale satisfies the mortgage debt and leaves something over),[3] and a "deficiency" proceeding (when the foreclosure sale produces insufficient to pay the mortgage debt),[4] both of which are traditionally associated with the mortgage foreclosure action. Another example is the partition action, whose primary need for special instruction is also at the judgment and enforcement stage, to which the RPAPL article in point[5] therefore devotes the bulk of its attention.

The real property proceeding that comes closest to having a complete statement in the RPAPL—complete enough to require little reference to the CPLR or any other law, although it periodically requires some—is the Summary Proceeding to Recover Possession of Real Property. That's its formal name, but it is equally well known by any of several other common names, such as "landlord-tenant" (or "L & T"), "dispossess", and perhaps others. It is best to call it simply a "summary proceeding", which relates it immediately to its statutory source, Article 7 of the RPAPL, the article that creates and governs the proceeding and which, because of the profusion of summary proceedings, accounts by itself for almost as much citation and use as all the rest of the RPAPL put together. The summary proceeding is a category of special proceeding and is often referred to as such,[6] which means that reference may be had to Article 4 of the CPLR for procedural detail when needed. It is not often needed.

---

§ 571

1. See RPAPL § 101.
2. RPAPL Article 13.
3. See RPAPL §§ 1355, 1361–1362.

4. RPAPL § 1371.
5. RPAPL Article 9.
6. See, e.g., RPAPL § 701.

The summary proceeding is the landlord versus tenant device that seeks dispossession for the tenant's non-payment of rent or for the tenant's holding over after the expiration of the lease term. It also serves as the rent-collecting device when the tenant is in default; dispossession confronts the tenant unless the rent is paid. It is designed only to test the immediate right of possession of real property, including apartments in multiple dwellings. In urban areas, as may be suspected, summary proceedings involving apartments are the most common of all.

The summary proceeding does not try title, for which any of several other actions are available, including principally the common law ejectment action and in some situations the statutory action called an Action to Compel the Determination of a Claim to Real Property.[7] When title is at issue, the remedy is a plenary action, not a summary proceeding. The label, of course, is not the key. The liberal rules of pleading and practice applicable to actions in general presumably apply here as well, which should mean that as long as the petitioner has pleaded the requisite facts and identified the relief sought, a change from the one thing (an adjudication of the right of possession) to the other (an adjudication of where title lies) should be permissible. But two major factors deny the summary proceeding those liberal principles and prevent it from being converted into a title tester or otherwise detoured from its immediate mission of adjudicating the right to immediate possession.

The first is that the summary proceeding is brought in the lowest court of civil jurisdiction locally available, and most of the lower courts lack subject matter jurisdiction of title questions. The second is that the proceeding's purpose "is to afford a means of obtaining a swift determination of disputes between landlord and tenant as to the right of possession".[8] This purpose would be undone by permitting the proceeding to determine title because it would open the door to a distracting array of issues. Hence, while the summary proceeding is the offshoot of the common law action of ejectment, which as ultimately evolved tried issues of both title and possession,[9] the summary proceeding was introduced to offer a more expeditious method only for the possession segment[10] and the courts have been sensitive to keep it on track. The absence of any demand for possession, in fact, prevents the case from qualifying as a summary proceeding and from enjoying its procedural advantages.[11]

Title questions can and sometimes do arise in summary proceedings by way of defense, posing problems that come in for discussion later.[12]

Summary proceedings appear in great numbers annually; in the New York City Civil Court alone, which handles just about all of them for New York City, the annual number is several hundred thousand. The following sections cover the jurisdiction and scope of the summary proceeding, the mechanics of its bringing and adjudication, the judgment it produces, and the steps that go into the enforcement of the judgment.

The summary proceeding, as supplied by Article 7 of the RPAPL and used throughout the state, should not be confused with the special proceeding supplied by Article 7A of the RPAPL.[13] Article 7A, applicable only in New York City and several of its surrounding counties,[14] is a unique procedure that may be invoked by a minimum of one-third of the tenants in a multiple dwelling when conditions dangerous to health and safety exist. It is designed to earmark rents to abate those conditions.

---

7. RPAPL Article 15; see Porcher v. Frueauff, 82 N.Y.S.2d 10 (Sup.Ct., N.Y. County, 1948), aff'd 276 App. Div. 997, 95 N.Y.S.2d 603 (1st Dep't 1950).

8. Lincoln Square Apartments, Section I, Inc. v. Davis, 58 Misc.2d 292, 294, 295 N.Y.S.2d 358, 361 (N.Y.C.Civ.Ct. 1968), aff'd 64 Misc.2d 859, 316 N.Y.S.2d 130 (App.T., 1st Dep't, 1969).

9. See Pernell v. Southall Realty, 416 U.S. 363, 94 S.Ct. 1723, 40 L.Ed.2d 198 (1974).

10. See, e.g., City of New York v. Betancourt, 79 Misc.2d 907, 362 N.Y.S.2d 728 (App.T., 1st Dep't, 1974).

11. See Atherton v. 21 East 92d Street, 149 A.D.2d 354, 539 N.Y.S.2d 933 (1st Dep't 1989).

12. See § 576 below.

13. Sections 769–782.

14. See RPAPL § 769(1).

§ 572. Summary Proceeding; Jurisdiction and Scope

Jurisdiction of the summary proceeding is lodged by statute in the county courts, the New York City Civil Court, and the district, city, town, and village courts.[1] It is also, of course, in the jurisdiction of the supreme court, but seldom brought there. The policy of the law is to have the summary proceeding brought in the lowest court of civil jurisdiction serving the geographical area in which the real property is situated. Hence, if the proceeding is brought in the supreme court, it will likely be transferred to the appropriate lower court[2] unless there is some special reason for keeping it.

Outside New York City, jurisdiction of the proceeding will usually be shared by the county court and the lower court serving the realty's municipality. In that event, the choice of forum is ordinarily with the petitioner. The lawyer should look into this question on a local basis. While all town and village courts, for example, have jurisdiction of the proceeding,[3] in some of those courts there may simply be no local tradition for invoking it—it sometimes boils down to nothing more than that—and the county court has to be turned to instead.

In New York City, the simple summary proceeding is often not so simple. Because of the city's unique housing problems, a special housing part was authorized for the court by § 110 of the New York City Civil Court Act, with summary proceeding jurisdiction for residential properties and a variety of equitable powers.[4] Rules of the court require that summary proceedings involving residential property be brought in the housing part.[5]

The landlord is the usual petitioner in a summary proceeding but there are a number of others who may bring the proceeding in certain instances. RPAPL § 721 contains the list. A representative, attorney, or agent of the landlord may maintain the proceeding for the landlord, and even verify the initiating petition, but the landlord must be the named petitioner.[6] Upon that authority the manager of a multiple dwelling often prosecutes the proceeding in the landlord's behalf. A law enforcement agency can also bring the proceeding when the premises are being used for an unlawful purpose.[7] In New York City, certain not-for-profit corporations and tenant associations may also be allowed to maintain the proceeding.[8]

Although the proceeding lies in some instances when there is no landlord-tenant relationship,[9] in the great majority of cases the landlord-tenant relationship is the one involved, and when it is a statute lists the grounds on which the proceeding may be based.[10] Two of the listed grounds dominate the annual rolls of the summary proceeding.

The first is commonly known as the "holdover" proceeding, in which the lease term has expired and the landlord does not want to renew.[11] This ground is of course unavailable in areas of the state in which rent control or rent stabilization is in force in the particular premises. This is most notably the case in New York City. In a controlled or stabilized apartment, as long as the tenant pays the legal rent and behaves, the tenancy continues; it does not depend on a lease and admits of only such rent increases as the law periodically permits.

The second ground, and the reigning monarch of summary proceeding grounds, is the

---

§ 572

1. RPAPL § 701(1). See also § 204 in each of the uniform acts: the New York City Civil Court Act and the Uniform District, City, and Justice court acts (McKinney's Vol. 29A, Parts 2 and 3).

2. See N.Y.Const. Art. VI, § 19(a).

3. UJCA § 204.

4. The rules of the housing part, an important concomitant of § 110, are in Uniform Rule 208.43.

5. See Uniform Rule 208.42, which also elaborates the procedure to be followed and includes forms.

6. RPAPL § 741. Prior to 1977, the representative could even be the named petitioner, a permission discontinued by an amendment of RPAPL § 721 during that year.

7. RPAPL § 721(8). For the grounds that make occupancy unlawful, see RPAPL § 715.

8. See RPAPL § 721(11).

9. See RPAPL § 713.

10. RPAPL § 711.

11. RPAPL § 711(1).

non-payment of rent. As long as the rent sought is not beyond what the law permits, this ground is of course available whether the premises are rent controlled or stabilized or not.[12]

If the ground on which the claim of repossession is based is not among those recognized for a summary proceeding, the remedy will usually have to be an action, such as one in ejectment, brought in a court with plenary jurisdiction of real property actions. Ejectment, often used to determine claims of title, is also available to test claims of possession that do not fall within the purview of a summary proceeding. Even claims that do can be tested by ejectment instead of a summary proceeding if the claimant wishes. The summary proceeding is not an exclusive device, but because of its great speed and simplicity it is almost always preferred if it is available.

As strictly a possessory device, the summary proceeding may include a claim for rent but may not include any other claim, such as one for property damage.[13]

In rent-regulated areas of the state, where dispossession is unavailable except on narrow grounds as long as the tenant pays the applicable rent, a landlord anxious to secure repossession would sometimes allow rent payments to accrue until they reached a sum the landlord figured the tenant could not pay. Only then would the landlord bring the summary proceeding—having foregone suit as each payment fell due—in the hope that the tenant's inability to get up the total sum would result in a summary dispossession (and a reletting at a higher rent). The tenants involved were usually poor, often too much in need of basics to be glibly accused of having only themselves to

blame for not setting rent payments aside. Caselaw ultimately held that in instances like this, while the landlord retains a money claim against the tenant for all of the accrued rent and can sue for it in any court of competent monetary jurisdiction, the landlord forfeits the right to dispossess the tenant for the non-payment. It was at first held that the summary proceeding, with its dispossession prospect, would not lie in these situations for any part of the accrued rents,[14] but this approach was later modified to bar dispossessory relief only as to the "stale" part.[15] The stale part has sometimes been taken to be anything more than three months of accumulated rent, but not uniformly so.[16] This "staleness" rule, a kind of presumption,[17] means that the summary proceeding can be "brought" for everything, but that in respect of arrears considered stale the proceeding will be treated as an ordinary action. A single final judgment will issue calling for dispossession if the current segment (the sum due for the most recent few months) is not paid, but authorizing enforcement only in the manner of a money judgment for the rest.[18] If it is shown that there was good cause for the delay on the particular facts, or that the landlord's conduct was not intended to "lure" the tenant into some kind of trap, the staleness rule may not apply and the summary proceeding and its dispossession remedy will lie for all of the rent.[19]

B. MECHANICS

Table of Sections

---

12. RPAPL § 711(2). Note the requirement that a rent demand with at least three days' notice be served on the tenant, and that the service be in the same manner prescribed for service of the summary proceeding papers themselves. For service, see RPAPL § 735, treated in § 575 below.

13. See Allyn v. Markowitz, 83 Misc.2d 250, 373 N.Y.S.2d 293 (Rockland County Ct. 1975).

14. See Gramford Realty Corp. v. Valentin, 71 Misc.2d 784, 337 N.Y.S.2d 160 (N.Y.C.Civ.Ct. 1972).

15. City of New York v. Betancourt, 79 Misc.2d 907, 362 N.Y.S.2d 728 (App.T., 1st Dep't, 1974); 1560–80 Pel-

ham Pkwy. Ass'n v. Errico, 177 Misc.2d 947, 678 N.Y.S.2d 860 (App.T., 1st Dep't, 1998).

16. See 269 Associates v. Yerkes, 113 Misc.2d 450, 449 N.Y.S.2d 593 (Civ.Ct., N.Y. County, 1982).

17. See Antillean Holding Co. v. Lindley, 76 Misc.2d 1044, 352 N.Y.S.2d 557 (N.Y.C.Civ.Ct. 1973).

18. City of New York v. Betancourt, note 15, above.

19. See the discussions of the staleness rule in Greenburger v. Leary, 119 Misc.2d 358, 462 N.Y.S.2d 996 (N.Y.C.Civ.Ct., N.Y.County, 1983), and Marriott v. Shaw, 151 Misc.2d 938, 574 N.Y.S.2d 477 (N.Y.C.Civ.Ct., Kings County, 1991).

§ 573. Notice of Petition in Summary Proceeding

The summary proceeding is commenced by the service of a notice of petition and a petition. In a court outside New York City, the notice of petition, which is the initiatory process (the equivalent of a summons in an action), may be issued by the clerk, by a judge of the court, or by the petitioner's attorney;[1] the option of having the attorney issue it does not apply in the New York City Civil Court, where summary proceedings in New York City are brought. There the issuer must be either the clerk or a judge.[2]

The notice of petition specifies the time and place of the hearing and requires the respondent to answer and assert defenses at that time or be barred from asserting them anywhere.[3] Before setting a hearing day, the lawyer should check the court's rules or with the clerk. Since courts with light calendars do not sit every day, the petitioner must be sure to pick out a day when the court does have a session. In multi-judge courts, moreover, which do sit daily, there may be special parts of the court in which the summary proceeding has to be made returnable. The New York City Civil Court, for example, has a profusion of housing parts,[4] which can occupy a number of rooms and judges. Place of return and the precise time of it are administratively determined; if there is doubt, these requirements should be ascertained through the clerk's office.

The minimum return time for the hearing is 5 days, so that the proceeding cannot be made returnable earlier than the 5th day after the service of the notice of petition and petition. There is also a maximum limit: it cannot be made returnable more than 12 days after the service. The issuer of the notice of petition must therefore pick out a return day that falls between the 5th and 12th day after service,[5] and the respondent must answer on that day, which means that the petitioner may not be advised of any defense until the hearing on the return day. The petitioner who gives at least 8 days notice of petition, however, can require the respondent to serve an answer at least 3 days before the return day,[6] thus assuring at least a little advance notice of a defense.[7]

If the rules so provide in a particular court, a special set of initiatory procedures becomes applicable in a summary proceeding for the non-payment of rent—not applicable to the holdover or any other ground—the gist of which requires the respondent to answer before the clerk within 5 days.[8] The clerk then sets a hearing day only if the respondent answers,[9] and the judge renders a default judgment if the respondent does not.[10] Since many non-payment proceedings result in a default, this procedure makes it unnecessary for such cases to be processed through the hearing calendar on the return day. The petitioner must inquire into whether the rules of a particular court have adopted this alternative.[11]

The petitioner should follow the time requirements to the letter, since the courts in summary proceedings are more prone to visit

---

§ 573

1. RPAPL § 731(1). It may not be issued by a petitioner appearing pro se.

2. N.Y.C.Civ.Ct.Act. § 401(c).

3. RPAPL § 731(2). For a sample form of a notice of petition, see the official one contained in the rules of the New York City Civil Court, Uniform Rule 208.42(b).

4. See N.Y.C.Civ.Ct.Act § 110 and Uniform Rule 208.43, the rule implementing it.

5. RPAPL § 733(1).

6. RPAPL § 743.

7. For a sample form using this alternative, see the official one contained in the rules of the district courts, Uniform Rule 212.42.

8. RPAPL § 732(1).

9. RPAPL § 732(2).

10. RPAPL § 732(3).

11. The New York City Civil Court rules, for example, have adopted it. See Uniform Rule 208.42(d).

jurisdictional consequences on defects. Even giving the respondent more notice than required—setting the return day, for example, on the 16th day following service rather than on one falling between the 5th and 12th days—has been held a jurisdictional defect requiring dismissal.[12] Defects in the caption will not necessarily prove fatal today, at least if not shown to have actually prejudiced the respondent, but even cases so holding remind the petitioner that the procedural requirements of the summary proceeding are strictly construed in favor of the respondent.[13] The petitioner who takes that warning to heart will be the better off for it. Later sections further illustrate the tendency to treat as jurisdictional defects those which in other contexts might prove innocent and ignorable irregularities.

As is true of the special proceeding in general,[14] so of the summary proceeding as well: it can be commenced by an order to show cause instead of a notice of petition,[15] but some special reason should be demonstrated to justify the show cause procedure.

§ 574. Petition in Summary Proceeding

The contents of the petition are set forth in RPAPL § 741. They include allegations of the petitioner's and respondent's interests in the premises and their relationship to one another, a description of the premises, the facts on which the proceeding is based, and the relief sought. The relief can include a judgment for rent, or, if no set rent is applicable for the period involved or part of it, the fair value of the use or occupation of the premises for that period. If the proceeding is based on nonpayment of rent, or on any other ground requiring that notice of some kind be formally given before commencement of the proceeding,[1] the petition should allege that the notice

requirement has been fulfilled. Additional requirements may come from the rules of court. In New York City, for example, where registration statements have to be filed for multiple dwellings and must designate natural persons as managing agents, the petition must allege the proper filing of such a statement.[2]

There is a tendency in the summary proceeding—and perhaps more there than anywhere else—to be strict about all requirements, including those of pleadings. So, for example, where the petitioner had duly served on the respondent a notice to quit, as required in order to terminate a month to month tenancy,[3] and had even alleged in the petition that notice was served "in the manner provided for by law" but did not include the facts about the service, the defect was held so basic that it could not even lend itself to an amendment. The court dismissed the petition, even going to some lengths to do so.[4] When a fact exists, however, and the only defect is an unprejudicial omission to allege it in a pleading, it borders on the unthinkable in general practice to impose on so innocent an omission the ultimate penalty of a dismissal: the cure is a simple amendment. There appears to be no reason why, as long as the defect is not prejudicial, it cannot also be the cure in a summary proceeding. Indeed, some caselaw has specifically held that the pleadings in a summary proceeding should be analogized to those in an action and therefore be given the benefit of CPLR 3026, which directs a liberal construction and instructs that unprejudicial defects be ignored.[5] And the appellate division, noting a trend towards treating summary proceedings "the same as any other type of civil case", has approved the line of cases that "refuse to consider de minimis variations from strict compliance as jurisdictional defects".[6]

---

12. See Garrison v. Abrams, 57 Misc.2d 417, 293 N.Y.S.2d 52 (Rockland County Ct. 1965).

13. See, e.g., Presidential Management Co. v. Farley, 78 Misc.2d 610, 359 N.Y.S.2d 424 (App.T., 2d & 11th Districts, 1974).

14. CPLR 403(d).

15. RPAPL § 733(2).

§ 574

1. See, e.g., RPAPL § 711(2).

2. See Uniform Rule 208.42(g).

3. Real Prop.L. § 232–a.

4. See Margolies v. Lawrence, 67 Misc.2d 468, 324 N.Y.S.2d 418 (N.Y.C.Civ.Ct. 1971).

5. See Bay West Realty Co. v. Christy, 61 Misc.2d 853, 310 N.Y.S.2d 346 (N.Y.C.Civ.Ct. 1969).

The petition must be verified.[7] The mechanics of the verification, because absent from the RPAPL, come from the CPLR.[8] The general rule is that the one bringing the proceeding, i.e., the named petitioner,[9] should be the one verifying the petition.[10] An exception is made when the proceeding is being prosecuted for the landlord by a representative, an attorney, or an agent, who may verify in the landlord's place if the requirements of CPLR 3020(d)[11] have been satisfied,[12] such as where the agent has personal knowledge of the facts. Defects in respect of verification—which in actions are often ignored because not prejudicial[13]—have sometimes, rightly or wrongly, resulted in a jurisdictional dismissal in a summary proceeding.[14]

§ 575. Service in Summary Proceeding

Service marks the commencement of a summary proceeding. Legislation in 1992 that adopted filing as the method for commencing actions in the supreme and county courts[1] does not apply in the state's lower courts: the New York City Civil Court, the district courts (there are district courts in Nassau and Suffolk counties), or in the numerous city, town, and village courts throughout the state.[2] In those courts, service continues to mark commencement,[3] and since most summary proceedings are brought in the lower courts, service will continue to mark commencement of almost all summary proceedings.

A further clarification in that regard was made in a 1994 amendment of § 731 of the RPAPL, addressed to the rare situation in which a summary proceeding is brought in one of the "filing" courts.

Section 731 is the main provision on service in a summary proceeding, whose initiatory papers are the notice of petition and petition. Until the 1994 amendment, § 731 provided that the proceeding shall be commenced by the service of those papers. The amendment strikes out language purporting to say which act marks commencement and now speaks only about the proceeding being "commenced by petition and a notice of petition", without specifying either filing or service as the actual commencement moment. This leaves in charge whatever system is applicable in the particular court. In the supreme or county court, it will be the filing of the initiatory papers that marks commencement; in the lower courts it will continue to be their service that marks it, which of course means that in the great majority of summary proceedings service will continue to be the starting point of the proceeding.

What about the methods of service? While CPLR 308 applies to the methods of service in other special proceedings,[4] service in a summary proceeding is governed by RPAPL § 735 with instructions largely independent of CPLR 308. The petition and notice of petition are served together.

Personal delivery to the respondent is one method, and the best one if the petitioner can manage it, because, as will be seen in a moment, it clearly supports a judgment not only for dispossession, but for rent as well.

As an alternative, the service can be made by delivering copies to a person of suitable age and discretion who resides or is employed at the premises sought to be recovered; or if,

6. Lanz v. Lifrieri, 104 A.D.2d 400, 401, 478 N.Y.S.2d 722, 723 (2d Dep't 1984).

7. RPAPL § 741.

8. See CPLR 3020–3023.

9. The list of those who may bring the proceeding is in RPAPL § 721.

10. See 46 Downing Street Corp. v. Loren, 67 Misc.2d 737, 324 N.Y.S.2d 932 (N.Y.C.Civ.Ct. 1971).

11. See § 233 above.

12. See RPAPL § 741.

13. See State v. McMahon, 78 Misc.2d 388, 356 N.Y.S.2d 933 (Sup.Ct., Albany County, 1974).

14. Dismissal was the result, for example, in the 46 Downing case cited in note 10 above.

§ 575

1. See CPLR 304.

2. See § 400 in each of the court acts that govern the enumerated courts: the New York City Civil, Uniform District, Uniform City, and Uniform Justice court acts.

3. In the supreme and county courts the filing system applies in both actions and special proceedings. For its application in special proceedings, see §§ 550 and 553 above.

4. See CPLR 403(c).

"upon reasonable application", admittance cannot be secured or such person found there, the service can be made by affixing the copies to a conspicuous part of the premises or placing a copy under the entrance door. When either this "delivery", "affixing", or "placing" alternative is used, mailing is required as an additional step within one day afterwards. In fact, two mailings are required, one by registered or certified mail and one by regular first class mail.[5] The mailing is not required when personal delivery to the respondent is the method used.

A periodic question is, what qualifies under RPAPL § 735 as a "reasonable application" to gain admittance in order to serve a person at the premises before resorting to the alternative method of "conspicuous" service? It is akin, but not the same, as the effort needed to make service under paragraphs 1 or 2 of CPLR 308 before using the affixing provision of paragraph 4 of that statute. There the requirement is a showing of "due diligence" in trying to use paragraphs 1 and 2.[6] The requirement under RPAPL § 735 has been described as "less",[7] but it may not be a great deal less. It has been held that one attempt at service on a weekday afternoon does not suffice,[8] unless the process server "could reasonably expect someone to be at home", which is not the case when the single service is attempted during hours "when most people are at work".[9] A service attempt outside the usual 9 a.m. to 5 p.m. working hours, Monday through Friday, has a better chance of being sustained.[10]

Although any of the service methods, properly effected, will suffice for a judgment of dispossession, there is a problem when the petitioner is seeking a rent judgment as well. It has been held by some courts that in order for rent to be included in the judgment the service must also be shown to satisfy the service requirements applicable to an ordinary money action.[11] Personal delivery to the respondent satisfies that requirement,[12] and hence of course supports a rent judgment. Other service methods that would satisfy for in personam jurisdiction in a money action, such as service on a corporate respondent by means of serving the secretary of state, have also been held to support a rent judgment.[13] But other methods, although sufficient to support a money judgment in an ordinary money action under CPLR 308, may be held insufficient for a rent judgment by this line of cases.[14] Without such service, they see the judgment as resting on only an in rem foundation, not an in personam one.

The RPAPL § 735 alternative of deliver-and-mail is today analogous to the deliver-and-mail method of CPLR 308(2), which gives personal jurisdiction in an action without any need to show a prior effort at personal delivery under CPLR 308(1). Insofar as mechanics alone are involved, therefore, a deliver-plus-mail service under RPAPL § 735 should also support a rent judgment.[15] But CPLR 308(2) requires a filing of proof of service and delays "completion" of service—which starts the responding time running—until 20 days after that. Applying that aspect of CPLR 308(2)

---

5. The details as to place of mailing are supplied by subdivisions (a) and (b) of RPAPL § 735(1). The additional requirement of a mailing when personal delivery has not been made is not just a prudent legislative mandate; it is a constitutional precaution. See Greene v. Lindsey, 456 U.S. 444, 102 S.Ct. 1874, 72 L.Ed.2d 249 (1982).

6. See § 74 above.

7. Brooklyn Heights Realty Co. v. Gliwa, 92 A.D.2d 602, 459 N.Y.S.2d 793 (2d Dep't 1983).

8. See Eight Associates v. Hynes, 102 A.D.2d 746, 476 N.Y.S.2d 881 (1st Dep't 1984), aff'd 65 N.Y.2d 739, 492 N.Y.S.2d 15, 481 N.E.2d 555 (1985).

9. Brooklyn Heights Realty Co. v. Gliwa, note 7 above.

10. See Metropolitan Life Ins. Co. v. Scharpf, 124 Misc.2d 1096, 478 N.Y.S.2d 567 (N.Y.C.Civ.Ct., N.Y. County, 1984).

11. See, e.g., 1405 Realty Corp. v. Napier, 68 Misc.2d 793, 328 N.Y.S.2d 44 (N.Y.C.Civ.Ct., Bronx County, 1971).

12. See CPLR 308(1).

13. See Leven v. Browne's Business School, Inc., 71 Misc.2d 842, 337 N.Y.S.2d 307 (Dist.Ct., Nassau County, 1972).

14. See Treiman and Feder, Default Money Judgments in Summary Proceedings, N.Y. Law Journal, July 30, 1985, page 1.

15. On this view, an affix-and-mail service under RPAPL § 735 apparently would not, however, unless it is demonstrated that the other methods proved unavailing despite diligent effort. It would be the analogue of CPLR 308(4), which does not offer personal jurisdiction unless diligence is shown in attempting previously listed methods.

would usually show that the return day set in the summary proceeding is too early, i.e., that the notice time is insufficient. Some courts have cited that factor as a reason for denying a rent judgment in non-personal delivery cases.[16]

It can be argued that these distinctions are unwarranted.[17] Nothing prevents the legislature from stipulating a shorter notice period for rent in a summary proceeding than it requires for a money claim in an action, as long as each procedure satisfies due process. The legislature has expressly authorized a rent judgment in a summary proceeding,[18] as well as the awarding of repossession, and has drawn the service requirements in RPAPL § 735 without distinguishing between them based on method of service.

Decisions nevertheless continue to draw the distinction[19] and deny the rent judgment.[20] A separate action for the rent, with proper service, is of course permissible, but it is often economically unjustifiable for the landlord to pursue it, as pointed out in a justice court decision in 1998 rejecting the distinction.[21]

Mandatory filing applies in a summary proceeding. If the method of service is personal delivery to the respondent, the petition and notice of petition, or order to show cause if that is used, must be filed with proof of service within 3 days after the delivery. The service is deemed complete upon the delivery itself, however, and the adequacy of the return day's notice time is measured from then, not from the time of filing. That is not so when one of the alternative service methods of RPAPL § 735 is used. All the alternatives include a

mailing, the filing must be made within 3 days after the mailing, and it is the filing that constitutes "completion" and measures whether the return time affords the required notice.[22]

A failure to file within the allotted time may be a jurisdictional defect. It has been held to be jurisdictional if the summary proceeding is brought in the county court,[23] but in the lower courts the availability of a nunc pro tunc order to allow late filing[24] has been cited as a reason for not holding the matter jurisdictional.[25] Addressing hypertechnical arguments like these, met so often in summary proceedings, the appellate division said in 1984 in Lanz v. Lifrieri[26] that

> [w]e adopt the reasoning of a recent trend of cases which treat summary proceedings the same way as any other type of civil case and which refuse to consider *de minimis* variations from strict compliance as jurisdictional defects.

Strict compliance is still strongly advocated in some quarters,[27] and in order to avoid technical problems that have any potential at all for undoing jurisdiction, summary proceeding petitioners make a point of serving the papers just so, mailing them right on the heels of serving and filing promptly after service, often on the same or the following day. It is sound practice.

§ 576. Answer and Defenses in Summary Proceeding

The respondent must answer. As in actions, a failure to answer is a default. The require-

---

16. See, e.g., Fairhaven Apts. No. 6, Inc. v. Dolan, 72 Misc.2d 590, 339 N.Y.S.2d 787 (Dist.Ct., Suffolk County, 1972).

17. See the Treiman and Feder article, note 14 above.

18. RPAPL § 741(5).

19. See, e.g., Oppenheim v. Spike, 107 Misc.2d 55, 437 N.Y.S.2d 826 (App.T., 1st Dep't, 1980).

20. 16 Lincoln Square Assocs. v. Amrep Corp., 129 Misc.2d 697, 493 N.Y.S.2d 692 (N.Y.C.Civ.Ct., N.Y. County, 1985).

21. See Fleming v. Flanagan, 680 N.Y.S.2d 427 (Just. Ct., Town of Ramapo, Rockland County, 1998).

22. RPAPL § 735(2).

23. See Shields v. Benderson Dev. Co., 76 Misc.2d 322, 350 N.Y.S.2d 549 (Monroe County Court 1973).

24. See § 411 in the New York City Civil Court Act and in the Uniform District, City, and Justice court acts (McKinney's Vol. 29A, Parts 2 and 3), but note that the late filing starts the responding time anew.

25. See Metropolitan Transp. Auth. v. Terminal Drago Shine Stands, 119 Misc.2d 10, 462 N.Y.S.2d 758 (N.Y.C.Civ.Ct., N.Y. County, 1983), noting a conflict on the point.

26. 104 A.D.2d 400, 401, 478 N.Y.S.2d 722, 723 (2d Dep't).

27. See Wendt and Benjamin, Service of Process under Section 735 of the RPAPL, N.Y. State Bar Journal, April 1988, p.38.

ments come from RPAPL § 743. The petitioner who has given at least 8 days notice of the proceeding can demand, in the notice of petition, that the respondent answer at least 3 days before the return day. The answer can be oral or written. If oral, the respondent appears and answers before the clerk, who jots the substance of it down on the petition; if written, the respondent must "serve" the answer within the required time. Some courts' rules have expanded this to require two steps: that the respondent file the original of the answer with the clerk and serve a copy on the petitioner's lawyer.[1] In either instance the respondent is also required to show up for the hearing on the return day.

If the petitioner does not take advantage of the right to require an answer at least 3 days before the return day, the respondent need not answer until the return day itself, at which time the answer can be oral or in writing. Again, if it is oral, the clerk writes the gist of it on the petition.

The reader is again reminded that the rules of the court can vary these requirements when the ground of the proceeding is the non-payment of rent, adopting instead the procedures of RPAPL § 732 (which does not apply to other grounds), as the New York City Civil Court has done in its rules. Under RPAPL § 732, the notice of petition is made returnable before the clerk instead of the court and requires the respondent to answer before the clerk "within" 5 days instead of "at" a specified time.[2] If the respondent does answer, the clerk fixes a hearing date and notifies the parties by mail.[3] If the respondent does not answer, the clerk refers the matter to a judge, who renders a default judgment for the petitioner.[4]

When RPAPL § 732 is used, the notice of petition must advise the respondent of these requirements.[5] Whether the statute applies in a given court is determined in the court's rules.[6] The advantage of RPAPL § 732, when it does apply, is that it enables the proceeding to go through to a default judgment without appearing on the court's calendar and therefore without requiring any party's appearance on the return day.

Despite that objective, some judges of the New York City Civil Court were nevertheless requiring an inquest before allowing entry of the default judgment. That was held impermissible in Brusco v. Braun,[7] in which the Court of Appeals said that the petitioner is entitled to the default judgment as a matter of right in this situation and need face no inquest.

RPAPL § 743 provides that "[t]he answer may contain any legal or equitable defense, or counterclaim". There is some question today, because of this provision, as to whether a lease clause purporting to preclude a counterclaim in a summary proceeding is valid.[8] Even on the assumption that it is not, and that a counterclaim technically lies, the courts are not disposed to entertain a counterclaim unless it has a direct relationship to the question of whether the landlord is entitled to possession, i.e., where, though labeled a "counterclaim", it amounts at least in part to a defense. The theory of this approach is that the summary proceeding, whose mission is a speedy disposition of the issue of possession in landlord-tenant matters, would otherwise be sidetracked. Its implementation consists in severing any counterclaim not found to have such direct bearing.[9]

§ 576

1. See, e.g., Uniform Rule 208.42(c), the rule applicable in the New York City Civil Court.

2. RPAPL § 732(1).

3. RPAPL § 732(2).

4. RPAPL § 732(3).

5. RPAPL § 732(4).

6. See, e.g., Uniform Rule 208.42(d), the rule adopting it for the New York City Civil Court.

7. 84 N.Y.2d 674, 621 N.Y.S.2d 291, 645 N.E.2d 724 (1994). The case is treated in New York State Law Digest No. 421.

8. See Steinberg v. Carreras, 77 Misc.2d 774, 357 N.Y.S.2d 369 (App.T., 1st Dep't, 1974, concurring opinion), noting the implicit overruling, by Levine v. Ehrenberg, N.Y.L.J. June 11, 1973, p. 18, col. 2 (App.T., 1st Dep't), of Orlowsky v. East House Enterprises, Inc., 32 Misc.2d 664, 228 N.Y.S.2d 19 (App.T., 1st Dep't, 1961), which had upheld the waiver.

9. See Great Park Corp. v. Goldberger, 41 Misc.2d 988, 246 N.Y.S.2d 810 (N.Y.C.Civ.Ct. 1964).

Adopting this reasoning, it has been held that a counterclaim for personal injuries should be severed as a matter of law, i.e., that it would be an abuse of discretion not to sever it,[10] but that the court can in its discretion retain and hear a counterclaim based on the reduced value of the tenancy for a failure to supply heat[11] or make repairs.[12] Even in the latter situations, however, while discretion exists to keep and hear the claim, it can still be exercised to sever it instead, and the claim will be severed if the court finds that its entertainment within the summary proceeding will unfairly prolong the adjudication of the possessory right whose processing the summary proceeding was designed to expedite.

Counterclaims aside, any defense the respondent has may be asserted, i.e., anything destructive of the petitioner's claim of entitlement to possession. If non-payment is the proceeding's basis, for example, a showing of payment, even if the payment was made after the proceeding was brought, is a good defense, although the petitioner in that situation will be entitled to costs.[13] Similarly, in a holdover proceeding, a showing that the lease was duly renewed, or that the premises are rent controlled and require no lease renewal, are good defenses.

What is to be done if the defense of title is interposed, i.e., when the respondent contends that he has title to the premises, or that the petitioner has not. The interposition of a title defense is fortunately rare, but it does happen. Whenever it does, it is an embarrassment: the summary proceeding will often be found in a lower court that lacks subject matter jurisdiction of title questions and which could not adjudicate one even if raised before the court in a plenary action. Some courts have indicated that the issue of title cannot be raised in a summary proceeding at all, by way of defense of otherwise, and that if such an issue exists between the parties the one asserting title ought to commence a plenary action to determine it in a court of competent jurisdiction.[14]

The separate action is a good idea, and is the ultimate resolution of the problem, but the view that a title defense may not be interposed in a summary proceeding is by no means universal. Other courts have assumed that the defense may be used, noting that its interposition does not divest the court of jurisdiction.[15] Indeed, the very question of whether the petitioner is the respondent's landlord may turn on an issue of title, as where a complicated arrangement raises an issue of whether the petitioner is an owner and the respondent his tenant, or the petitioner a mortgagee and the respondent in fact his mortgagor.[16] In a given instance it may even be hard to discern that what is being passed on is, in fact, a title issue.

The courts' response to the problem, if one troubles to read between the lines, attends the judgment stage of the proceeding. As has been seen, the courts merely deny res judicata or collateral estoppel effect to an adjudication purporting, in a summary proceeding, to decide title.[17] With the estoppel effect restricted, the court in the summary proceeding is free to make whatever incidental address to the title issue seems necessary to dispose of the immediate right of possession. In so doing the court does not inadvertently foreclose the title question altogether; it remains open for a plenary test in the supreme court or some other court at a later time.[18]

§ 577. Incidental Procedure in Summary Proceeding

It is the aspiration of the summary proceeding to go to adjudication on the return day,

---

10. Tankoos–Yarmon Hotels, Inc. v. Smith, 58 Misc.2d 1072, 299 N.Y.S.2d 937 (App.T., 1st Dep't, 1968).

11. See Steinberg v. Carreras, note 8 above.

12. See Packer v. Di Misa, 67 Misc.2d 433, 324 N.Y.S.2d 150 (Dist.Ct., Suffolk County, 1971), stressing the distinction between personal injury and property damage.

13. See § 579 below.

14. See Mahshie v. Dooley, 48 Misc.2d 1098, 266 N.Y.S.2d 661 (Sup.Ct., Onondaga County, 1965).

15. See, e.g., Mohar Realty Co. v. Smith, 46 Misc.2d 849, 260 N.Y.S.2d 685 (App.T., 2d Dep't, 1965).

16. See, e.g., O'Frias v. Melton, 32 A.D.2d 1046, 303 N.Y.S.2d 785 (2d Dep't 1969), aff'd 27 N.Y.2d 638, 313 N.Y.S.2d 765, 261 N.E.2d 670 (1970).

17. See § 469 above.

18. See § 579 below.

and to do so summarily. It would be inconsistent with that aim to allow use of the disclosure devices, which pervade the pretrial stage of an action, or even a bill of particulars and the minor skirmishes it invites. Both are discouraged in the summary proceeding, but instead of an absolute ban against them the courts appear to have evolved a rule that they may be permitted in special circumstances.[1] Disclosure proceedings would need a court order in any event, as they do by statute in special proceedings generally.[2] An order should also be required for a bill of particulars. The courts have to be stingy with both, lest the proceeding lose its "summary" character and hence its function.

What about motion practice? The CPLR's main dismissal motion, CPLR 3211 with its diverse grounds, has been held applicable in a summary proceeding, as has the summary judgment provision, CPLR 3212,[3] but both are consistent with the purpose of the summary proceeding, coming, in fact, from CPLR Article 32, entitled "Accelerated Judgment". Other motions, including nondispositive motions, have also been entertained.[4]

As to the time for the making and return of the motion, CPLR 406, which is the motion provision applicable to special proceedings in general, has been held applicable to the summary proceeding. CPLR 406 requires that if the motion is made before the proceeding's hearing day, it must be made returnable at the same time and place. Making it returnable at that time, no matter when the motion papers are served, apparently satisfies this requirement, even though it may afford "little or, indeed, no notice if it is made returnable at the same time as the petition", as one court observed when only one day's notice of motion was given. The same court, lamenting the de-

lays that motion practice entails in proceedings that are supposed to be "summary", held that when more time is needed to respond, the cure for the extremely short notice that CPLR 406 makes possible is an adjournment, tailored to the exigencies of the particular case.[5]

A question of additional parties occasionally arises, especially as to whether third-party practice (impleader) is permissible in a summary proceeding. Here, again, the rule applicable to special proceedings in general must be remembered. It provides that after the proceeding is commenced, impleader requires an order of the court.[6] Under prior law, which lacked such a provision, impleader was held altogether barred from a summary proceeding.[7] It would perhaps be best to retain such a rule. Indeed, some courts, by holding CPLR 401 inapplicable to a summary proceeding,[8] suggest that such a restrictive rule has been retained.

Seldom can a summary proceeding be justifiably held up while the respondent uses the petitioner's proceeding for his own dispute with his own respondent. This is so even when the links are such as would clearly justify impleader in an action. Where, for example, L brings a non-payment summary proceeding against T, his tenant, who has sublet to S, who has not paid T, T might justify the impleader of S were the context an ordinary money action. But to allow T the impleader of S in a summary proceeding brought by L would deny L the expeditious possessory remedy. L should not be deprived of both the rent and the premises while T, whose reletting was at his own risk, does battle with his subtenant.

In several non-payment cases in which the respondent-tenant was in need of welfare assistance, the respondent endeavored to implead the welfare official. An appellate court

---

§ 577

1. See, e.g., Steer Inn Realty Corp. v. Bowen, 52 Misc.2d 963, 277 N.Y.S.2d 231 (Dist.Ct., Suffolk County, 1967).

2. CPLR 408. See McQueen v. Grinker, 158 A.D.2d 355, 551 N.Y.S.2d 493 (1st Dep't 1990).

3. See Metropolitan Life Ins. Co. v. Carroll, 43 Misc.2d 639, 251 N.Y.S.2d 693 (App.T., 1st Dep't, 1964).

4. Some of these are listed in Goldman v. McCord, 120 Misc.2d 754, 466 N.Y.S.2d 584 (N.Y.C.Civ.Ct., N.Y. County, 1983).

5. Id.

6. CPLR 401.

7. See Edaviel Corp. v. Boykin, 205 Misc. 622, 129 N.Y.S.2d 149 (App.T., 1st Dep't, 1954).

8. See Zytelny v. Lodge, N.Y.L.J. Feb. 5, 1975, p. 17, col. 1 (App.T., 2d & 11th Districts).

held that the impleader should not be sustained;[9] that the tenant's remedy is an Article 78 proceeding against the official.[10] Other cases have allowed the impleader.[11] The justification for impleader against a welfare department is the respondent's need of money to pay the rent, a situation not many steps away from allowing the impleader of anyone who may be indebted to the respondent. In one case, in fact, respondent impleaded the Veterans Administration for benefit payments not yet received, but the court rejected it. Even under the New York City Civil Court Act's special "housing part" statute,[12] which applied in that case and which supplies additional procedural flexibility, the court found an insufficient relationship between the landlord's claim and the tenant's claim over.[13] Whatever the motivations for allowing the impleader, it is bound to conflict with the summary nature of the proceeding.[14] The courts remain in conflict on whether to allow it.[15]

There is also a strong rule against staying a summary proceeding, or removing it for such as a consolidation or joint trial with some proceeding in the supreme court or some other superior court.[16] The rule should apply even when a plenary action has been commenced to test a title issue relevant to the summary proceeding. Any other rule can encourage an imaginative respondent to commence such a collateral action just to delay the summary proceeding. If the title issue is genuine and the lower court in the summary proceeding lacks the jurisdiction to adjudicate it, the collateral action to test title can of course be brought, and should be, but the summary proceeding need not be stayed in deference to it. The proceeding can go forward, doing the best it can to determine the right to immediate possession—the function of the summary proceeding—without undue concern with what happens in the title action, which can adjudicate title free of any impediment from the res judicata doctrine or anything else emanating from the summary proceeding. Indeed, even a title action commenced after final judgment has been rendered in the summary proceeding can, if commenced promptly, avoid estoppel consequences that might otherwise come out of the summary proceeding.[17]

§ 578. Trial of Summary Proceeding

Summary as the summary proceeding may be, a genuine issue as to any fact on which the proceeding depends, unresolvable on the papers or from the argument of the parties on the return day, will necessitate a trial. RPAPL § 745(1) provides that the trial shall be by the court "unless, at the time the petition is noticed to be heard, a party demands a trial by jury", thus clearly conferring the right to trial by jury.[1] One does not often see trial by jury in summary proceedings, however. The reason is the lease: it will usually be found to waive the right to trial by jury, and the waiver has been upheld[2] notwithstanding that in the usual landlord-tenant relationship the lease amounts to an adhesion contract.[3] Insofar as any lease

---

9. Id.

10. If speed is required, as it usually is, the Article 78 proceeding can be brought on by order to show cause, CPLR 7804(c), with the papers stressing the pendency of the summary proceeding.

11. See Blackman v. Walker, 65 Misc.2d 138, 316 N.Y.S.2d 930 (Dist.Ct., Nassau County, 1970); Sessa v. Blakney, 71 Misc.2d 432, 336 N.Y.S.2d 149 (Yonkers City Court 1972).

12. CCA § 110.

13. Marcy Realty Co. v. Glassy, 79 Misc.2d 925, 361 N.Y.S.2d 802 (N.Y.C.Civ.Ct. 1974). The court also noted that the Veterans Administration, since a federal creature, is not subject to state impleader.

14. See the discussion in Balaban v. Phillips, 138 Misc.2d 990, 526 N.Y.S.2d 347 (Civ.Ct., N.Y.County, 1988).

15. See Manhattan Plaza, Inc. v. Snyder, 107 Misc.2d 470, 435 N.Y.S.2d 449 (N.Y.C.Civ.Ct., N.Y. County, 1980).

16. See Cohen v. Goldfein, 100 A.D.2d 795, 474 N.Y.S.2d 519 (1st Dep't 1984).

17. RPAPL § 747(2). See § 579 below.

§ 578

1. The right has constitutional origins, since the summary proceeding is the offspring of ejectment, a common law action. See, e.g., Pernell v. Southall Realty, 416 U.S. 363, 94 S.Ct. 1723, 40 L.Ed.2d 198 (1974); N.Y.Const., Art. I, § 2.

2. See, e.g., Avenue Assocs., Inc. v. Buxbaum, 83 Misc.2d 719, 373 N.Y.S.2d 814 (App.T., 1st Dep't, 1975).

3. It was on the "adhesion" principle that the lower court in the Avenue case, later reversed by the appellate term, id., voided the waiver.

provision purports to waive trial by jury on a cause of action for personal injuries or property damages between the parties, however, the waiver is void by statute.[4] That leaves trial by jury intact for those claims, but for the summary proceeding relief of repossession and rent the waiver remains valid.

Given the huge number of summary proceedings brought annually, there is some natural apprehension of what additional disaster would afflict court calendars if the lease waiver were voided and trial by jury were to become the standard mode of trial in a summary proceeding. Since a decidedly preponderant majority of summary proceedings involve no issue of fact, they would lend themselves to the summary judgment procedure,[5] which is available in a summary proceeding.[6] Its use, were a lease waiver of trial by jury to be voided, might then have to be turned to as a calendar-saving device.

If on the return day a trial appears necessary (whether or not it is to be by jury), the request for a jury is by demand made on the return day itself.

The court can order adjournments of the trial on consent of all parties or on a showing that any party requires more time to procure needed witnesses, generally restricted to 10-day periods.

A special provision governs adjournments in New York City, limiting adjournments in some circumstances and requiring interim rent deposits in others.[7]

§ 579. Judgment in Summary Proceeding

The summary proceeding culminates in a "judgment", just as any special proceeding does.[1] If on the return day the judge determines that there is no issue of fact, judgment will be ordered summarily. If there is a triable issue, final judgment will abide a trial. In either instance the judgment will include costs, but only those expressly allowed by statute, which may be only nominal.[2] The actual expenses of the petitioner are not the measure of costs.

The judgment for a successful petitioner awards possession of the premises, with the dispossession of the respondent, if required, to be carried out through a warrant, treated in the next section. If rent was also demanded, and personam jurisdiction secured sufficient to support it,[3] the judgment will include it. If the respondent's occupancy covers a period during which no set rent was due, the court can award the fair value of the use and occupancy of the premises for that period, as long as the notice of petition duly demands it.[4] The rent part of the judgment can be in whatever sum is warranted; it is not arbitrarily limited by the monetary restrictions applicable to ordinary money actions in the court, and this is so right down to the justice courts.[5] If rent was due but was not included in the judgment, statute authorizes a separate money action to recover it.[6] A separate action should of course be permissible if the jurisdiction secured in the proceeding, while sufficient for dispossession, was found insufficient to ground a money judgment. In many if not most instances the sums involved make further proceedings economically unjustifiable, however, and the petitioner simply absorbs the loss.

The judgment will be entered in such books as the court maintains for recording the steps in a summary proceeding. Even if it contains a money award, the judgment will not necessarily be entered and docketed as a money judgment unless a rule of court so provides or a

---

4. Real Prop.L. § 259–c.

5. See Pernell v. Southall Realty, note 1, above.

6. See Metropolitan Life Ins. Co. v. Carroll, 43 Misc.2d 639, 251 N.Y.S.2d 693 (App.T., 1st Dep't, 1964).

7. See RPAPL § 745(2).

§ 579

1. RPAPL § 747(1). Under old Civil Practice Act § 1430, it culminated in a "final order".

2. See §§ 1903 and 1911 in the New York City Civil Court Act and in the Uniform District, Uniform City, and Uniform Justice court acts, McKinney's Vol. 29A, Parts 2 and 3.

3. See § 575 above.

4. RPAPL § 741(5).

5. See § 204 in each of the four uniform acts cited in note 2 above.

6. See RPAPL § 749(3).

court order so directs.[7] This is designed to avoid the administrative burden of automatically recording on the money-judgment ledgers every summary proceeding judgment purporting to award rent—especially since many of them are not enforced. But the petitioner insisting on enforcement is entitled to it, and if the clerk will not voluntarily docket the judgment as a money judgment when the petitioner requests it, the court can be applied to for an order so directing. If the petitioner is in earnest about seeking enforcement, the clerk should docket the judgment without insisting on an order.

The res judicata and collateral estoppel effects of a summary proceeding judgment were discussed elsewhere.[8] In this connection attention should be called once again to RPAPL § 747(2), which concerns the case in which a party may need "affirmative equitable relief" in respect of the premises involved but be unable to get it in the summary proceeding because of the particular court's limited jurisdiction. The statute provides that if a separate action for such relief is commenced within 60 days after entry of the summary proceeding judgment, the latter will not act as a bar, suggesting of course that postponing such separate suit more than the 60 days will. If any title issue arose in the summary proceeding and could not be adjudicated there, or even where the summary proceeding judge purported to resolve a title issue as a necessary part of adjudicating the right to immediate possession, the party aggrieved by the title determination should bring a plenary action to test it in a court of competent jurisdiction and would be wise to do so no later than the 60 days allowed by RPAPL § 747(2).

§ 580. Enforcement in Summary Proceeding; Warrant and Stay

When a final judgment is rendered for the petitioner, the court issues a warrant directed to the court's enforcement officer (sheriff, marshal, or constable) directing the officer to restore the petitioner to possession. The statute, RPAPL § 749(1), says that the court "shall" issue the warrant, and this, holds the Court of Appeals, is mandatory language. Some judges of the civil court in New York City had been staying the issuance of the warrant "as a matter of personal policy preference", a practice the court overturned in Mennella v. Lopez–Torres.[1]

Before executing the warrant the officer must give 72 hours notice to the persons in occupancy, served in the same manner as the notice of petition itself is.[2] Execution of the warrant may take place only during daylight hours.[3] The petitioner's hope, of course, is that the respondent will vacate peaceably, thereby obviating resort to an enforcement officer.

If a breaking-in is required, it must be the enforcement officer who does it.[4] The officer can secure the company of a local police officer if any breach of the peace is anticipated. The petitioner's next hope is that if a forcible entry is required, it will at least reveal vacant premises. If there is property of the tenant inside, the landlord will likely incur expense in moving it out, usually through the enforcement officer, who may have to hire a moving crew in such circumstances. The tenant is ultimately responsible for these expenses, but the necessity of further proceedings to collect them generally discourages the collection effort.

A summary proceeding remains pending not merely until judgment time, but until the execution of the warrant, which is subject to a judicial stay up to that moment.[5] There are several things to note about a stay:

If the summary proceeding was for the nonpayment of rent, the tenant can effect a stay of

---

7. RPAPL § 747(4).

8. See § 469 above.

§ 580

1. 91 N.Y.2d 474, 672 N.Y.S.2d 834 (1998). The case is summarized in New York State Law Digest No. 461.

2. RPAPL § 749(2). Service of the notice of petition is governed by RPAPL § 735. See § 575 above.

3. RPAPL § 749(2).

4. For an illustration of the mechanics of enforcing a warrant in a summary proceeding, see Regan v. Tally Ho Trucking Co., 103 Misc.2d 269, 425 N.Y.S.2d 725 (N.Y.C.Civ.Ct., Bronx County, 1980).

5. See 203 E. 13th Street Corp. v. Lechycky, 67 Misc.2d 451, 324 N.Y.S.2d 560 (App.T., 1st Dep't, 1971).

the warrant merely by depositing into court the amount of rent due plus costs—which the clerk or judge pays over to the landlord upon demand—and in this instance the stay amounts in effect to a cancellation of the whole proceeding. This applies statewide, and while the statute in point, RPAPL § 751(1), authorizes a stay at any time before a warrant is "issued",[6] another and more general one, RPAPL § 749(3), allows it even after issuance and up to the point of the warrant's "execution".

The pre-issuance stay of RPAPL § 751(1) is almost an automatic thing, coming about upon the deposit of the proper sum for rent and costs. The post-issuance stay of RPAPL § 749(3) is not automatic. It requires an exercise of judicial discretion, as the appellate division had occasion to note in New York City Housing Authority v. Torres.[7] The court said that the 1975 amendment of RPAPL § 749(3) to permit vacatur of the warrant means to permit vacatur only "for good cause shown". It was held that a mere showing of inability to get the money to pay the rent is not good cause for vacatur, especially, as in *Torres*, where the tenant is guilty of dilatory conduct and the excuses tendered are found "unworthy of belief".[8]

Because of the time element in this situation, the stay will frequently be sought by order to show cause, a procedure that can stay the warrant at the very threshold of its execution. While it may be the practice of some enforcement officers to hold up the execution of the warrant merely upon being informed, even if only by phone by the respondent's attorney, that a stay has been issued, it has been held that the officer is "not obligated to stop the eviction unless and until … served with a copy of a valid order containing a valid stay".[9]

If the judgment emanates from a summary proceeding based not on a failure to pay the rent, but on a holding over after the expiration of the term, and the premises are residential, a distinction is made between New York City and elsewhere. If the premises are in the city, which generally means the proceeding was brought in the New York City Civil Court, a special provision, RPAPL § 753, governs the stay. If the tenant attests that he cannot find equivalent premises in the neighborhood or would otherwise be subject to hardship if evicted, the court can stay issuance of the warrant for up to six months.[10] It grants the stay, however, only on condition that the tenant deposits with the court the rent—or the court-fixed value of reasonable use and occupation—for the period of the stay.[11] Often the court will allow the stay in spurts of several weeks at a time, or a month or two, building up to the six months, rather than award the whole six-month period in one order. The purpose is to spur the tenant's efforts to seek housing elsewhere, requiring fresh application for continuance of the stay from time to time. The stay provision is unwaivable by lease or otherwise.[12]

For residential premises outside New York City there used to be a similar statute for staying a warrant in a holdover proceeding,[13] but it lost effect in 1967. This would at first blush suggest that a stay in that situation is not authorized at all, but it has been held that since the lower courts that entertain summary proceedings outside New York City have by statute the general power to stay their proceedings,[14] this general power is source enough

---

6. Special stay provisions govern when the landlord has been guilty of a constructive eviction of the tenant by failing to make repairs, RPAPL § 755, or pay utilities, RPAPL § 756.

7. 61 A.D.2d 681, 403 N.Y.S.2d 527 (1st Dep't 1978).

8. For a special provision governing in New York City, see RPAPL § 747(a).

9. Regan v. Tally Ho Trucking Co., note 4 above.

10. RPAPL § 753(1).

11. RPAPL § 753(2).

12. RPAPL § 753(5). The stay is not allowable in certain instances when the premises are sought for demo-

lition or the tenant is found objectionable. See RPAPL § 753(3).

13. RPAPL § 751(4). It was limited to four months instead of the six applicable in New York City under the still effective RPAPL § 753(1).

14. See §§ 212 and 2102 in the Uniform District, Uniform City, and Uniform Justice court acts, and CPLR 2201. The New York City Civil Court Act has similar §§ 212 and 2102, from which a general stay power can be extracted when needed. The cited court acts are in McKinney's Vol. 29A, Parts 2 and 3.

to stay the warrant in a holdover summary proceeding.[15] In view of the legislative history, however, the stay should not exceed the period previously allowed by statute, which was four months for residential premises outside New York City.

The same general source can supply a stay when commercial premises are involved, in any part of the state, there being no special statutes applicable to them. However, since a commercial need is not in quite the same league as a residential one, the courts are more circumspect about the granting of a stay.

Another provision with a narrow but key mission is subdivision 4 of RPAPL § 753, added in 1982 in response to a problem arising in 1968 as a result of First National Stores, Inc. v. Yellowstone Shopping Center, Inc.,[16] the case that made necessary what is still known as a "Yellowstone injunction". It is a short saga.

A typical lease provision enables the landlord (L) to notify the tenant (T) of conduct deemed to be a breach of the lease, giving T a stated time period in which to cure the breach. If T contends he is not in breach, and a court test is necessary, T has a dilemma. T must be sure that the cure period is extended while the test pends, else, if and when T should lose on the point, it will likely be too late to cure the breach and T will lose the lease, as the *Yellowstone* court confirmed in a case involving a commercial tenancy. The court said that the courts are "powerless" to revive the lease in such circumstances. Because of *Yellowstone*, a tenant so situated often had to solve the dilemma by seeking a judicial restraining order, a "Yellowstone" injunction, extending the cure period. And because of equity restrictions on the lower courts, where summary proceedings are brought, the tenant usually had to do this with an action brought in the supreme court.

To obviate this, with its burdensome effect on judicial calendars, at least in the case of residential leases in New York City where the problem was felt most acutely, the legislature in 1982 added a subdivision (4) to RPAPL § 753 requiring the summary proceeding court (in New York City that would of course be the Civil Court), should it hold against T in such a breach-of-the-lease case, to grant a post-judgment stay of the eviction warrant for 10 days, during which time T is allowed to cure the breach. In a test of the new statute, the Court of Appeals held that if T does cure the breach within that time, the lease revives.[17] Hence a separate action, so as to get a pendente lite injunction to keep the lease alive, is unnecessary.

The provision applies only in New York City, however, and only in residential summary proceedings. This should be a warning to those representing holdover residential tenants outside New York City, or commercial tenants anywhere, of the continued need to apply collaterally for Yellowstone injunctions in connection with pending summary proceedings involving arguments about what conduct does or does not constitute a breach of the lease.[18]

As long as the method of service that was used to commence the proceeding secured personal jurisdiction, as mentioned in the prior section, the money part of a judgment rendered in a summary proceeding can be enforced as well as the dispossession part. The money part is enforced in the same manner as an ordinary money judgment, but a special provision in the lower court acts provides that if the judgment emanates from a nonpayment proceeding and the premises are the tenant's residence, no levy shall be made on the tenant's property within the 24–hour period following execution of the warrant, i.e., the dispossession of the tenant.[19] This protection is

15. See Fulton Redevelopment Co. v. Kendall, 68 Misc.2d 813, 327 N.Y.S.2d 956 (Sup.Ct., Westchester County, 1971).

16. 21 N.Y.2d 630, 290 N.Y.S.2d 721, 237 N.E.2d 868 (1968).

17. Post v. 120 East End Avenue Corp., 62 N.Y.2d 19, 475 N.Y.S.2d 821, 464 N.E.2d 125 (1984).

18. See, e.g., TSS–Seedman's, Inc. v. Elota Realty Co., 72 N.Y.2d 1024, 534 N.Y.S.2d 925, 531 N.E.2d 646 (1988).

19. See § 1507 in each of the uniform acts cited in note 13 above.

a special one built into the lower court acts for residential tenants. It is not designed for application to commercial tenancies.[20]

20. An exception is where the judgment is that of a city court outside New York City, where the 24-hour immunity applies to commercial as well as to residential premises. Section 1507 in the Uniform City Court Act does not contain the residential limitation contained in the counterpart sections of the other lower court acts cited in note 14 above.

Chapter Twenty–One

SMALL CLAIMS

§ 581. Small Claims, Generally

A "small claim" in official parlance is any money claim up to a stated figure—$3000 at the present time—for which a quick and untechnical procedure is supplied. The procedure bears little resemblance to either an action or special proceeding,[1] lacking even the reduced formalities applicable to the latter, for which reason we have given it a separate chapter. The "Small Claims Court" may be the only contact many people will ever have with the court system.

One of the main aims of the small claim is to spare all sides the expense of an attorney. Lawyers can and do appear from time to time in small claims. While it's not frequent, all lawyers ought to know the few things there are to know about them. It will equip them to guide a person to the court and to advise of what few steps are needed for preparation, even if the lawyer is not involved in the preparation and will not be appearing in any part of the proceedings.

The small claims procedure comes not from the CPLR, but from the court acts of those lower courts that have a small claims part. In New York City, the civil court has it; in Nassau County and in the western part of Suffolk County (the part having a district court), the district courts have it; city courts have it in cities outside New York City; and the town and village courts (collectively, the justice courts) have it in their respective municipalities. Although often referred to as the "Small Claims Court", it is not a separate court at all. It is merely one of the functions of the lower courts just enumerated. Its wholly informal procedures are supplied by Article 18 of their court acts, four of them. The quartet, with their abbreviations parenthesized for further reference, are (1) the New York City Civil Court Act (CCA); (2) the Uniform District Court Act (UDCA); (3) the Uniform City Court Act (UCCA), applicable to all city courts outside New York City; and (4) the Uniform Justice Court Act (UJCA), applicable to the town and village courts outside New York City and areas having a district court.

Article 18 in each of the four acts contains the jurisdictional requirements applicable to the small claim as well as its basic procedural outlines, but it leaves detail to the courts' individual rules.[2] Our concentration here will be on the statutory outline with occasional illustrative references to the rules, most of which may be found in McKinney's "New York Court Rules" pamphlet, updated and republished annually. While the small claims

---

§ 581

1. The Small Claim under discussion here must be distinguished from the "Alternative Method of Dispute Resolution by Arbitration", authorized by CPLR 3405 and governed in detail by Part 28 of the Rules of the Chief Judge. CPLR 3405 procedure is sometimes referred to as

"court-annexed arbitration". It is separately treated in § 585B below.

2. See § 1802 in each of the four acts in McKinney's Vol. 29A: the CCA, UDCA, and UCCA in Part 3, and the UJCA in Part 2.

rules applicable in the several courts are similar, there having been consultation among their drafters, there are separate ones for the New York City Civil Court,[3] the district courts,[4] the city courts,[5] and the town and village (justice) courts.[6] In addition to filling procedural interstices, the rules will often be found to supply administrative information about the times and places for holding small claims sessions. If data about sessions is needed and not available in the rules, the clerk (or the judge if the court has no clerk) should be consulted. In the New York City Civil Court the well-known system of having "arbitrators" (lawyers volunteering their services) hear and determine small claims, upon the parties' consent, comes from the rules.[7]

The procedure is available only for a money claim. The small claims part can't award equitable relief, such as specific performance or the like,[8] although it does have the power to condition its money judgment in ways that may smack of equity.[9] The present ceiling on the money claim (the legislature alters it from time to time) is $3000 in all of the courts with small claims parts. Also required for a small claim is that the defendant have either residence, office, or regular employment in the area serviced by the court. More specifically, if the small claim is brought in the New York City Civil Court, the defendant must have one of the specified contacts with New York City;[10] in a district court, with one of the court's districts in the county;[11] in a city court, with the county in which the court sits;[12] and in a town or village court, with the particular town

or village.[13] This requirement is designed to prevent undue inconvenience to a defendant called upon to defend a small claim. If none of the contacts exists but the defendant appears and defends without raising the objection, it should be deemed waived; in this sense the requirement is not one of subject matter jurisdiction. If it is raised, however, small claims treatment is precluded, notwithstanding that the defendant may be amenable to jurisdiction in an ordinary action in the court.

The parties usually appear pro se in a small claims proceeding, but either party may appear by attorney if desired. If both sides should appear by attorney, however, the rules of a given court may preclude use of the small claims procedure and convert the case into an ordinary civil action.[14]

On the theory that a corporation, partnership, or association, because of presumed wealth and access to counsel, does not require and should therefore not impose on the small claims part, statute provides that a claim belonging to any such creature may not be brought in the regular small claims part of the court. Nor may this barrier be avoided by an assignment to a natural person: the same statute denies the regular small claims part to an assignee.[15] All of these entities and creatures can be defendants on a small claim, of course, but even in that humble context they have to appear by attorney, except for certain small or closed corporations which, as a result of 1976 legislation, can appear by a shareholder or

---

3. Uniform Rule 208.41.

4. Uniform Rule 212.41.

5. Uniform Rule 210.41.

6. Uniform Rule 214.10.

7. Uniform Rule 208.41(n). These arbitrators have no direct connection with extra-judicial arbitration, governed by Article 75 of the CPLR and studied in the next chapter, although one occasionally sees some part of Article 75 cited in connection with the review of a small claims arbitration.

8. See Scott v. Dale Carpet Cleaning Inc., 120 Misc.2d 118, 465 N.Y.S.2d 680 (N.Y.C.Civ.Ct. 1983).

9. See the discussion and illustration in § 583 below.

10. CCA § 1801.

11. UDCA § 1801.

12. UCCA § 1801. This will sometimes give the small claims part of a city court a greater geographical scope than the conventional part of the court has under the contact requirements of § 213 of the Uniform City Court Act. See § 21, above, and Azzato v. Renne, 123 Misc.2d 609, 474 N.Y.S.2d 220 (Oswego City Court 1984).

13. UJCA § 1801.

14. See, e.g., Uniform Rule 208.41(f), the rule applicable in the New York City Civil Court.

15. See CCA, UDCA, UCCA and UJCA § 1809(1). The section also bars a subrogated insurer from using the small claims part of the court by suing in the name of its insured. Municipal and certain other public corporations are excluded from this exception, and may use the small claims part. Because of an omission from UDCA § 1809(1) of any reference to the association or partnership, those creatures can bring small claims in district courts.

officer.[16]

This barrier against the use of the regular small claims part by commercial claimants has been a long tradition, and remains in effect for Article 18 and the regular small claims part that Article 18 supplies. But the barrier, always a source of complaint from commercial interests, earned legislative attention in 1987 with the enactment[17] of a special small claims article numbered 18–A and entitled "Commercial Claims". It creates for the New York City Civil Court and for the district and city courts (but not for the town and village courts) a "commercial" small claims part for the use of claimants that are corporations, partnerships, or associations. It is maintained distinct from the regular small claims court and is separately treated below in § 585A. Discussion in this chapter until that section is reached is addressed only to the regular small claims part as governed by Article 18 of the lower court acts.

Although the formal procedure of litigation is dispensed with on a small claim, the "substantive law" of the state applies.[18] It is tempered, however, by the instruction that the small claim is to do "substantial justice" within the framework of the substantive law. This guidepost is set forth for the conduct of the hearing[19] as well as for the ultimate test: the criterion for appellate review.[20] What is apparently meant is that the substantive law can be flexed a bit as long as it is not broken off entirely. We return to this point in a few later sections.[21]

As has already been noted, the small claims part is devised for the money action only. It cannot entertain a claim for equitable relief. A few curious cases have denied the use of the small claims part to a claim that seeks only money but is found by the court to present an essentially equitable cause of action. In one case, for example, a divided appellate division found that although the plaintiff wanted only

a money judgment, he was seeking it from a trust fund. The court held that this requires a preliminary determination of whether the claimant is a legitimate beneficiary of the trust, and that this means in turn that the claim is in essence an equitable one unusable in the small claims part.[22] This is an unfortunate result. If a plaintiff, whatever the "equitable" relief he may pursue, converts his claim into money terms and sets an economic value on it within the maximum of the small claims part, it ill behooves a court to deny the claimant use of that part by forcing the claim into some kind of equitable mold. It turns tradition on its ear. While equity will stay its hand if there is an adequate remedy at law, the instant situation is the converse—it rejects a law claim because it perceives a remedy in equity—and is especially gratuitous in small claims context. Whether "legal" or "equitable", the claim is too small to be worth litigating anywhere else. Closing the small claims door thus closes the whole courthouse, a denial of access premised on a technical distinction at war with the very concept of a "small claims" part. Ironically, a rejection of jurisdiction on this ground would probably not occur to nonlawyer town and village justices, who hold the small claims parts in rural areas. They know too little of law to be guilty of this kind of injustice.

Finally, small claims is an alternative procedure, not an exclusive one. A plaintiff with a money claim within small claims jurisdiction may, if he chooses, bring an ordinary action on it.[23]

§ 582. Commencement and Hearing of Small Claim; Incidental Procedure

No summons service or pleadings are required for a small claim. The claimant or someone in the claimant's behalf merely goes

---

16. See CCA, UDCA, UCCA and UJCA § 1809(2); CPLR 321(a).

17. L.1987, c.653.

18. CCA, UDCA, UCCA, and UJCA §§ 1802, 1804.

19. Id., § 1804.

20. Id., § 1807. See § 584, below, for discussion of appellate review of a small claim.

21. See §§ 582 and 584.

22. Hellman v. Ploss, 46 A.D.2d 658, 359 N.Y.S.2d 823 (2d Dep't 1974).

23. CCA, UDCA, UCCA and UJCA § 1802.

to the clerk and orally relates the claim, paying a nominal fee plus mailing costs. The clerk writes out a brief statement of the claim and records it on the books kept for small claims. The clerk also sets a day, time, and place for the hearing. A notice of it, containing the statement of the claim as written up by the clerk, is then sent to the defendant both by ordinary mail and by certified mail with return receipt requested.[1] The mail is addressed to the defendant's residence if it is within the court's area and known to the claimant, or to the defendant's place of business or employment within the area if the defendant resides outside of it or at a place unknown to the claimant. (It will be recalled that local contacts of this kind are jurisdictional requirements.[2])

These basic steps for commencing a small claim are prescribed by statute,[3] but they are much elaborated in the rules.[4] The rules will often be found to prescribe the notice and to require that it advise of the need to bring in witnesses, warn of the consequences of default, and other related things. They usually contain, in fact, the form to be used for a small claim, which leaves the claimant, or the clerk who is helping the claimant, with only the blanks to fill in. The clerk is required to furnish the small claims parties, including the claimant upon first presenting the small claim, a brochure describing the jurisdiction and procedure of the small claims part.[5]

The sessions at which small claims will be heard are determined administratively. As might be expected, the courts with more business have regular sessions while some of the smaller courts have sessions only periodically. The clerk will advise of all these matters on recording the cause of action when the claimant first comes in. At least one evening small claims session a month is mandated by stat-

ute,[6] unless a particular court is administratively exempted from this requirement. Some of the courts have regular evening sessions, sparing the parties loss of work time and otherwise suiting their convenience.

When the parties show up on the return day—or night—the case comes on before a judge, who proceeds promptly with the hearing. In some courts, notably the New York City Civil Court, local lawyers serve as "arbitrators" and hear and decide small claims cases if the parties consent,[7] which they usually do.

The hearing official (judge or arbitrator) is directed by statute "to do substantial justice between the parties according to the rules of substantive law", and formal court procedure is not applicable. With the exception of the rules governing privileged communications and communications with a person now deceased,[8] neither are the rules of evidence.[9] A statute explicitly facilitates the claimant's proof, particularly in property damage and most particularly automobile property damage cases, by admitting into evidence estimates instead of paid bills in certain circumstances.[10]

Pretrial disclosure is available in a small claims action only by court order and only upon a showing of special circumstances.[11] Caselaw has applied a like rule to the bill of particulars.[12] It should take special circumstances indeed to allow either; either will usually be found to impede the small claim unjustifiably. In the great majority of cases all development of the facts should be at the hearing itself. Any other conclusion would undermine the purpose of the small claims part. One case in which pretrial disclosure was directed involved tape recordings of conversa-

---

§ 582

1. CCA, UDCA, UCCA, and UJCA § 1803.

2. See § 581 above.

3. CCA, UDCA, UCCA, and UJCA § 1803.

4. The Small Claims provisions are in Uniform Rules 208.41 for the New York City Civil Court, 212.41 for the district courts, 210.41 for the city courts, and 214.10 for the town and village courts.

5. CCA, UDCA, UCCA, and UJCA § 1803.

6. Id. § 1802.

7. See Uniform Rule 208.41(n).

8. CPLR 4519.

9. CCA, UDCA, UCCA, and UJCA § 1804.

10. Id.

11. Id.

12. See Selman v. Appel's Garage & Service Station, 73 Misc.2d 581, 342 N.Y.S.2d 385 (Long Beach City Court 1973).

tions between the claimant and the defendant, presumably on the very subject matter of the dispute. The court found this an appropriate exception for which to order pretrial disclosure, but even in this instance it required only a discovery of the recordings, which did not involve the kind of expense or delay that a deposition (for example) would entail.[13]

The regular provisions of the court act—those outside the small claims article, Article 18—and for that matter the provisions of the CPLR itself, are applicable in small claims to the extent "not in conflict" with the small claims article,[14] but it is seldom if ever necessary to resort to those other provisions and ordinarily quite inconsistent to do so in the small claims part. Motion practice is of course discouraged.[15] One procedure recognized as occasionally appropriate is impleader, as where the defendant has a legitimate basis on which to hold another responsible in whole or in part for what the claimant is seeking of the defendant. The rules may be found to cover this, applying the small claims' notice procedures to the bringing in of the additional party.[16]

The applicable statutes contemplate that minutes will be taken of a small claims hearing,[17] but a special provision applicable in certain city courts expressly authorizes the taking of minutes "mechanically",[18] which means by tape recording or the like. The parties can presumably waive the requirement that minutes be kept, and upon mutual agreement they can choose whatever recording means they agree on. In the New York City Civil Court, for example, when the parties consent to have an "arbitrator" hear the claim under the court's

rules, they waive the keeping of minutes altogether: the rules provide that no record of proceedings before an arbitrator need be kept.[19]

A small claim is subject to the bar of the statute of limitations, which qualifies as a matter of "substance" within the intendment of the small claims article. It has been said that any other conclusion would be inconsistent with the "important public policy of giving repose to human affairs".[20] The time the claim is deemed interposed for limitations' purposes is when the claimant files the claim and pays the required fee, not when the defendant receives the notice.[21]

It has also been held that the service of a notice of claim on a municipality, pursuant to Gen.Mun.L. § 50–e, is required even on a small claim.[22]

Issue occasionally arises about what satisfies as "substantial justice". In one case, for example, a homeowner sued a city for damages caused by a water main break. The claimant proved no negligence, however, as would have been her burden in an ordinary action, but the court awarded her judgment anyway, holding that in a factual situation like this a rule of strict liability is more appropriate on a small claim. The appellate court, upholding the result but rejecting the "strict liability" determination, purported to find negligence against one of the defendants, thus enabling the claimant to keep the judgment.[23] Had the appellate court not been able to make that "negligence" finding, one suspects that it might have approved the result anyway, notwithstanding the

---

13. Dorfman v. Bell, 86 Misc.2d 359, 381 N.Y.S.2d 983 (Dist.Ct., Nassau County, 1976).

14. CCA, UDCA, UCCA, and UJCA § 1804.

15. See Weiner v. Tel Aviv Car and Limousine Serv., Ltd., 141 Misc.2d 339, 533 N.Y.S.2d 372 (N.Y.C.Civ.Ct. 1988), tracing the history of the small claims part.

16. See, e.g., Uniform Rule 210.41(j), applicable in the city courts.

17. CCA, UDCA, UCCA, and UJCA § 1802.

18. UCCA § 1802.

19. Uniform Rule 208.41(n)(3).

20. Cerio v. Charles Plumbing & Heating, Inc., 87 A.D.2d 972, 972, 450 N.Y.S.2d 90, 91 (4th Dep't 1982).

21. Ryder v. Tannenbaum, 130 Misc.2d 42, 494 N.Y.S.2d 950 (N.Y.C. Civ.Ct., Kings County, 1985), aff'd 137 Misc.2d 326, 524 N.Y.S.2d 321 (App.T., 2d & 11th Dists., 1987).

22. Ragosto v. Triborough Bridge etc., 173 Misc.2d 560, 663 N.Y.S.2d 462 (App.Term, 1st Dep't, 1997). A thoroughgoing review of this issue appears in Schneider v. Town of Orangetown, 171 Misc.2d 497, 655 N.Y.S.2d 720 (Town of Clarkstown, Rockland County, 1997) (noted in SPR 65:3), aff'd 175 Misc.2d 899, 673 N.Y.S.2d 281 (App. T., 2d Dep't, 1998).

23. Bierman v. Consolidated Edison Co. of New York, 66 Misc.2d 237, 320 N.Y.S.2d 331 (App.T., 1st Dep't, 1970), modifying 60 Misc.2d 497, 302 N.Y.S.2d 696 (N.Y.C.Civ.Ct. 1969).

"strict liability" basis on which it rested. A contrary holding would mean that a small claimant, in order to prove a case for limited damage caused by something like a break in a water main—a circumstance pregnant with the suggestion if not the proof of municipal fault—would have to go to much trouble and expense to establish fault. Such an expense would likely exceed the value of the claim and would, again, undermine the function of the small claims part.

We see from the foregoing that an occasional conflict will arise between the "substantial justice" that the statutes want done on a small claim and the "substantive law" that the same statutes also want applied. The legislative hope is that both will harmonize, but it is often unattainable. It would seem, when conflict is at hand or when the technical rule of law is not clear, that giving "substantial justice" the stronger role will result in something more in tune with the purpose of the small claim. On this point there is debate, however, some devoted students of the subject arguing that small claims judges, and even the arbitrators who hear small claims in the New York City Civil Court, "must strictly follow substantive law when deciding the merits of a claim".[24]

That is of course the ideal, and perhaps a few strides towards its attainment can be made when the judge or arbitrator is a lawyer, but what of the numerous town and village courts whose judges are not lawyers? With no lawyers representing the parties and no lawyer on the bench, one must ask how the substantive law can be applied at all, much less "strictly". Even before lawyer judges and lawyer arbitrators, the requirement to apply the substantive law strictly when there are no attorneys present to argue the law would put on the small claims judge the same duties

imposed on a Court of Appeals judge to whom talented and well paid attorneys argue the law in cases with high stakes, and for whom two law clerks offer ready research assistance and counsel.

Whatever the restrictions may be on applying the "substantial justice" criterion to the substantive adjudication of the small claim, it is easily applied to cure procedural omissions, including even those that affect the area of "parties" and which in an ordinary action would likely constitute jurisdictional defects. In one case, for example, a mother brought her son's personal injury small claim without even naming him as a party, but the appellate court, noting that the defendant knew who was seeking what and that it was just a matter of properly channeling the recovery, sustained it.[25] A similar approach was taken when the claimant died before the small claim proceeding was concluded. The general CPLR rule is that when a party dies, nothing further can be done affecting the decedent until a personal representative is appointed in the surrogate's court and the representative so appointed is then substituted for the decedent in the pending action.[26] It was held that no such formality need be indulged in a small claim; that the spouse or next of kin can just step in and take over for the decedent.[27]

There is ordinarily no formal or even written answer in small claims procedure. The defendant simply shows up on the return day and states her position orally, including such defenses as she may have.

The defendant can of course counterclaim, but only for a sum that is itself within the small claims ceiling. The defendant seeking to counterclaim should, within five days of receiving notice of the small claim, file a statement of the counterclaim.[28] If the defendant's coun-

24. See Lebovits, Small Claims Courts Offer Prompt Adjudication Based on Substantive Law, 70 New York State Bar Journal 6, 9 (Dec. 1998).

25. Buonomo v. Stalker, 40 A.D.2d 733, 336 N.Y.S.2d 687 (3d Dep't 1972).

26. CPLR 1015.

27. Bogart v. Imports of Wantagh, 142 Misc.2d 105, 536 N.Y.S.2d 391 (Long Beach City Court 1988).

28. See 1803(c) in each of the lower court acts, added in 1996. This is designed to give the small claims plaintiff early warning of a counterclaim so that the plaintiff will not be surprised, or even intimidated into withdrawing the small claim, by its sudden interposition at the hearing itself. There appears to be little penalty, however, if the defendant fails to act within the prescribed time. See SPR 47:2.

terclaim exceeds the small claims limit, it must be brought as a separate claim in the regular part of the court, or in some other court of competent jurisdiction.[29] A counterclaim in excess of the applicable figure is not "permitted", which apparently means that it must be dismissed in its entirety, without prejudice. The defendant can of course agree to reduce the counterclaim to the small claims figure, but that would amount to the defendant's waiver of the balance.

If the main claim and counterclaim are related, as they almost always are, the defendant who brings the would-be counterclaim as a separate claim in the regular part of the court may seek to remove and consolidate or jointly try the small claim with it, but the courts are justifiably hesitant so to impede a small claim. They do so only when there is sufficient presumptive merit to the defendant's claim to make it appropriate and fair to delay the small claim so as to have it heard together with the counterclaim.[30] One court ordered such a removal but struck a balance by imposing a hefty condition to "accord full protection to both parties". The small claim was for $1300 for defective services. The defendant's claim was for $3450 as the balance due for those services. The defendant brought separate suit for the $3450 in the regular part of the court and moved for the joint trial. The condition for getting it: that the defendant stipulate to have both claims tried "under the more flexible procedural rules and 'substantial justice' standard applicable to Small Claims".[31]

The simple relatedness of claims simultaneously pending in the regular and small claims parts of a court is never a ground for the removal of the small claim, else many a property damage aspect of a tort would be impeded for years by being transferred for consolidation to the regular part of the court, or to some other court, in which the personal injury aspect is pending. Hence, where P sued D for personal injuries in the regular part of the court and moved to have D's small claim against P for property damage consolidated, the motion was denied.[32] Res judicata, as we shall see,[33] is not the problem: no part of the adjudication made on the property damage small claim is binding on the personal injury claim, despite potentially inconsistent findings.[34] Delay of the small claim is the problem, and the courts are sensitive to it.

It may be permissible to remove a small claim to federal court. If despite its small sum the claim arises under federal law, for example, and could have been sued on originally in a U.S. district court, it can be removed there by the defendant.[35] That was done in one case, for example, where the amount involved was only $44.40, presumably for some special reason, probably the involvement of an important precedent for which the defendant wanted the input of a federal court.[36]

There is no trial by jury of a small claim. It is tried either by a judge or in some courts, as already noted, by lawyers who act as arbitrators and to whom the parties consent. A claimant waives the right to trial by jury by bringing a small claim. The defendant does not waive it, however, and can demand a jury if so disposed—it is a constitutional right because the claim is for money only.[37] The defendant makes the demand by filing it with the court before the day set for the hearing, accompanying it with an affidavit specifying the triable issues, the fee for trial by jury in the particular court, and a $50 bond (or cash deposit in place

---

29. CCA, UDCA, UCCA, and UJCA § 1805(c). There is no longer an automatic transfer of a small claim to the regular part of the court merely upon the defendant's interposition of a counterclaim in excess of the small claims ceiling, as there was prior to a 1979 amendment of § 1805.

30. See Fordham Rent A Car Corp. v. Hyman, 109 Misc.2d 176, 439 N.Y.S.2d 793 (N.Y.C.Civ.Ct., Bronx County, 1981).

31. Victoria Kitchens, Inc. v. Leiner, 138 Misc.2d 556, 524 N.Y.S.2d 1019 (N.Y.C.Civ.Ct., Queens County, 1988).

32. See, e.g., Credle v. Alvarez, N.Y. Law Journal, Oct. 28, 1963, p. 16, col. 2 (Sup.Ct., Kings County, per Wecht, J.).

33. See § 585 below.

34. See Czora v. Ahrens, 74 Misc.2d 601, 344 N.Y.S.2d 621 (Erie County Court 1973).

35. See 28 U.S.C.A. § 1441(a).

36. Mungin v. Pittston Stevedoring Corp., E.D.N.Y., Jan. 7, 1974, No. 73–C–1050.

37. See § 377 above.

of it) for the payment of costs if they should be awarded against the defendant.[38]

By the imposition of these requirements it is hoped that the defendant will forego the jury demand and let the case remain a small claim. If the defendant does carry out these requirements, the case is transferred to the regular part of the court, where it gets a preference and is tried by jury. There are yet other ostensible deterrents. If the plaintiff prevails on that trial she can be awarded an additional $25 costs,[39] but it has been held that a winning defendant does not get costs at all.[40]

§ 583. Small Claim Judgment and Enforcement

Whether rendered forthwith or at a later time—quite often the judge or arbitrator decides the case immediately but prefers to postpone revelation of the result until the parties are out of one another's company—the judgment emanating from a small claims proceeding is in most respects the same as one coming from an ordinary money action.[1] There is a special provision, however, that requires that all unsatisfied small claims judgments be indexed "alphabetically and chronologically" under the defendant's name.[2] This is designed to facilitate the securing of information about evasive small claims judgment debtors.

A small claims money judgment, like any other, can make use of any of the enforcement devices supplied by Article 52 of the CPLR. The problem, of course, is that the judgment is usually for so modest a sum that any substantial effort generated by enforcement can easily prove economically unfeasible in both time and money. Certainly a procedure designed to spare the claimant the cost of a lawyer in bringing the proceeding should not be undone by requiring the claimant to retain a lawyer

for enforcement after the claimant has won. But that has often proved to be the case. Some of the enforcement devices require legal expertise, and the more evasive the debtor the greater the need to resort to the more sophisticated enforcement devices, such as disclosure proceedings, delivery orders, installment payment orders, and the like. These involve effort and expense unreasonable to impose on a small claimant.

The legislature has turned some attention to the problem in recent years. One remedy is that the claimant may not have to pay the sheriff enforcement fees in advance, as an ordinary judgment creditor has to do when delivering an execution.[3] Another is that the clerk must assist the claimant with information subpoenas to help uncover data about the defendant's property.[4] Still another provides for a treble damages action (including an attorney's fee) against a defendant against whom there are at least three unsatisfied small claims judgments outstanding, and the only recognized defense is inability to pay.[5] If the unsatisfied claim arose out of the defendant's business, the court is required to advise the attorney general about the failure to pay, and if it is a licensed business, to advise the licensing authority as well,[6] all with a view to encouraging the defendant to pay under threat of business sanctions: the failure of a licensed business to pay a small claims judgment is deemed a basis for revoking or suspending its license.[7]

The brochure that the clerk is required to furnish small claimants must also advise that they, too, can notify the defendant's licensing or certifying authority (should there be one) if a judgment for the claimant is unsatisfied or if

---

38. CCA, UDCA, UCCA, and UJCA § 1806.

39. Id.

40. De Nicola v. Pallas, 82 Misc.2d 156, 368 N.Y.S.2d 762 (Utica City Court 1975).

§ 583

1. For costs and security for costs in a small claims proceeding, see the discussion in Meister v. Engine Trans. Corp., 138 Misc.2d 880, 525 N.Y.S.2d 785 (N.Y.C.Civ.Ct. 1988).

2. CCA, UDCA, UCCA, and UJCA § 1811(c).

3. See CPLR 8011(b)(2).

4. See § 509 above.

5. See CCA, UDCA, UCCA, and UJCA § 1812.

6. Id.

7. CCA, UDCA, UCCA, and UJCA §§ 1813(b).

there is any fraud or equivalent wrongdoing in the defendant's practices.[8]

The legislature has also manifested impatience with defendants who try to avoid their obligations by playing name games. Section 1814 of the lower court acts permits the case to proceed against the defendant in whatever name it uses, mandates an inquiry into names at the merits hearing, and permits amendments to insert correct names even after judgment. A nunc pro tunc order can be made to effect a name correction in all prior papers— the summons, decision, and judgment included—and to permit an enforcement step to proceed as if the defendant had been properly designated all the while. In Bruna v. National Westminster Bank, USA,[9] for example, when P paid D some $1200 for windows (which were never furnished), D had P make the check payable to Mr. Window, Inc., apparently some kind of alter ego of D, although technically they were separate and distinct entities. They were operated as a unit, however, and the fact that ownership was not entirely in common did not pose a barrier for § 1814, under which the court opened Mr. Window right up and offered access to its bank account.

A significant point that emerges from the *Bruna* case is that while it may take a battery of cannon to pierce a corporate veil at the higher reaches of litigation, at the small claims level § 1814 appears to do the job with just a pop gun.

As pointed out earlier, the small claims procedure is addressed to money claims alone,[10] and money is therefore what the judgment awards. Specific performance and other kinds of equitable relief as such are not permissible,[11] but a special statute added in 1985 permits the court to "condition the entry of judgment upon such terms as the court shall deem proper".[12] The legislature considers this a necessary power to implement its instruction that the small claims procedure accomplish "substantial justice".

This power to condition can have a variety of uses. If, for example, the claimant is suing to recover the price paid for an item now claimed defective, and the claimant still has the item, the court can condition a money judgment for the price on the claimant's returning the item. It has many times been argued that without explicit power to "condition" the judgment, the small claims court can do nothing more than render a money judgment or dismiss the claim. That was always an unnecessarily rigid approach, ignoring the "substantial justice" aim of small claims practice, which is its major theme. Conditioning the judgment in this fashion does not necessarily entail the court's invocation of equity powers and the contempt remedy that backs them. If the court is convinced, for example, that requiring the claimant to return the chattel may result in the defendant's getting it without paying the judgment, the court can require the defendant to pay the judgment first, or order the chattel deposited with the court, to be turned over to the defendant only upon a showing that the claimant's judgment has been paid.

If the judgment imposing the condition was the work of an arbitrator instead of a judge, and some kind of follow-up application is needed in connection with the condition, the application can be made to the court if it is not feasible to get it back into the hands of the arbitrator.

There have been cases denying all small claims relief to a claimant who sued for money by purporting to perceive the case as one in "equity" and then dismissing it—a small case with no viable economic access to a regular part of the court—for want of equitable powers in the small claims part.[13] This "conditioning" provision is a path away from at least some of these awkward "equitable" remold-

---

8. See CCA, UDCA, UCCA, and UJCA § 1803, and the McKinney's Commentaries on Civil Court Act § 1803.

9. 138 Misc.2d 548, 524 N.Y.S.2d 1009 (N.Y.C.Civ.Ct., Queens County, 1988).

10. See § 581 above.

11. See Scott v. Dale Carpet Cleaning Inc., 120 Misc.2d 118, 465 N.Y.S.2d 680 (N.Y.C.Civ.Ct. 1983).

12. Subdivision (a) of CCA, UDCA, UCCA, and UJCA § 1805.

13. See, e.g., Hellman v. Ploss, 46 A.D.2d 658, 359 N.Y.S.2d 823 (2d Dep't 1974), discussed in § 581.

ings, which are in effect only a special way of denying equity. The amendment is clearly an expansion of the court's powers, and with the substantial justice theme still playing loud in the background, it may be found to house a few answers the small claims part has long needed.

The defendant who can pay the judgment but for reasons of obstinacy, rancor, animus, or whatever, refuses to, should read carefully the case of House v. Lalor,[14] where a flat refusal to pay a $350 judgment, forcing the plaintiff to levy execution, brought about the forfeiture of the defendant's $185,000 equity in a cooperative apartment.

§ 584. Appeal of Small Claim

The loser on a small claims judgment can appeal, but as a rule only for cases tried before a judge. The rules may provide that agreeing to go before an arbitrator instead of a judge, a common practice in several courts, will carry with it a waiver of the right to appeal. The rules of the court should be checked for this.[1]

Some cases operating under such a rule have held that while it will waive a regular appeal, agreeing to arbitrate does not prevent the court from entertaining an application to vacate the award under CPLR 7511, the provision applicable to the judicial review of conventional arbitration awards.[2] One such case is Rymer v. Leider,[3] a decision of the New York City Civil Court. The proposition is doubtful, but the court's use of the CPLR 7511 review standard was circumspect in *Rymer*, denying the motion to vacate. The court would not entertain mere errors of law or fact as vacatur grounds, citing instead the more serious flaws that CPLR 7511 addresses, such as corruption and partiality. (None of that was shown in *Rymer*.) Should there be something like bias in

the case, some kind of way to bring this to judicial attention would seem necessary, and perhaps CPLR 7511 holds the key. Suppose, for example, it is discovered that the arbitrator concealed a blood relationship to the winning claimant. It would seem imperative that there be some procedure for raising the matter and undoing the decision, and the CPLR 7511 vacatur grounds may indeed be the most logical route.

In a judge-tried case, appeal does lie, but the only ground for appellate review is the same standard—"substantial justice ... according to the rules and principles of substantive law"[4] —applicable at the small claims hearing itself.[5] An appeal goes the same route as one from an ordinary judgment of the court—to the same appellate court and by the same basic procedures.[6]

Some kind of transcription of the proceeding, at least when it has been tried before a judge,[7] will usually be available, but even if it should not be, an appeal may still be taken. When there is no transcript, CPLR 5525(d) permits the appellant to serve a statement of the proceedings "from the best available sources, including his recollection". Finding this "tailor-made" for a small claims appeal, the court held in Glass v. Regency Park Assoc.,[8] that a small claims appellant is not entitled to a new trial just to generate a transcript. The case was decided under the Uniform City Court Act, however, whose § 1802 explicitly authorizes the taking of minutes by means other than stenography in some city courts, and in *Glass* they had been so taken (by tape recording). A counterpart provision does not exist under § 1802 of the other three lower court acts, which may at first suggest that the absence of minutes can require a new trial at the loser's insistence in the other courts, un-

---

14. 119 Misc.2d 193, 462 N.Y.S.2d 772 (Sup.Ct., N.Y. County, 1983).

§ 584

1. See, e.g., Uniform Rule 208.41(n), the rule applicable in the New York City Civil Court.

2. See § 602 below.

3. 122 Misc.2d 873, 471 N.Y.S.2d 733 (1983).

4. CCA, UDCA, UCCA, and UJCA § 1807.

5. Id., § 1804.

6. Id., Article 17 generally and § 1704 in particular.

7. See CCA, UDCA, UCCA, and UJCA § 1802. Agreeing to arbitrate may also mean, under the rules, that there will be no record kept of the proceedings. See, e.g., Uniform Rule 212.41(m), the rule applicable in the district courts.

8. 100 Misc.2d 179, 418 N.Y.S.2d 870 (White Plains City Court 1979).

less perhaps a waiver can be spelled out. The appellant, however, even if entitled to a stenographic transcript, can take the appeal without it, invoking CPLR 5525(d).[9]

"Substantial justice" within the framework of the "substantive law", the appellate review standard, is no more sharply defined at the appellate level than it is at the nisi prius hearing, but since the statutory guidepost is similarly verbalized at both levels, the standard, whatever it is, is the same. One case that may be helpful is Blair v. Five Points Shopping Plaza, Inc.,[10] an appellate division address to the issue. It holds that the lower court decision will not be overturned merely because the appellate panel would have done otherwise on the facts; that the result should strike the senses as "shocking" before it is set aside. That may be just a substitution of one phrase for another, but some phrases may prove more helpful than others. In the area of judicial review of administrative action, for example, there are the "arbitrary and capricious", "abuse of discretion" and "substantial evidence" standards.[11] Perhaps one or a combination of those would be analogous. Before being overturned, the small claims result should at least be as bad as, if not worse than, an administrative decision that would be overturned in an Article 78 proceeding.

§ 585. Res Judicata as Applied to Small Claim

Section 1808 in each of the lower courts' small claims articles states that a small claims judgment "may be pleaded as res judicata only as to the amount involved in the particular action and shall not otherwise be deemed an adjudication of any fact at issue or found therein in any other action or court."[1] The language means to reassure all sides to the

small claim that it will carry no unexpected consequences beyond the matter at issue. The provision was not intended to divest the small claims judgment of its "claim preclusion" effect, which is the more technical meaning of "res judicata" today, but rather of its "collateral estoppel" or "issue preclusion" use.[2] Whether or not that distinction can withstand all tests, it seems to pass a few of them nicely.

It has been held, for example, that if P loses the small claim suit to D, the loss precludes P from suing D for the same thing again even in the regular part of the court.[3] The attempt to duplicate the claim in full made it a "res judicata" ("claim preclusion") situation, and we may assume that the second action would have been barred even had it asked for more money than was involved in the small claims action, notwithstanding the technical language of the statute. Although the statute says there is no "res judicata" in that instance, the court in effect held that there is, and indeed there must be. How else would a claim prosecuted as a small claim be laid to rest?

But suppose that P sues D in the small claims part for recovery of a $100 down payment on a suit of clothes purchased from D, and wins. Then D sues P to recover the price of the suit, $236. This was an actual case. The court allowed the second action, holding that it was not precluded by the first. It then found for D for the $236 in the second action. The court gave effect to the earlier small claims action by deducting the $100 found there for P, resulting in a net judgment in the second action of $136 for D.[4] Since the claim on which D sued in the second action was not the same as P's claim against D in the small claims proceeding, although they both of course involved common issues—Was the clothing as

9. Compare § 1704 in the Uniform Justice Court Act, applicable in the town and village courts. It anticipates the absence of a transcript and enlists the aid of the clerk in putting together a descriptive statement. See the McKinney's Commentary on UJCA § 1704.

10. 51 A.D.2d 167, 379 N.Y.S.2d 532 (3d Dep't 1976).

11. See CPLR 7803(3), (4); § 561 above.

§ 585

1. CCA, UDCA, UCCA, and UJCA § 1808.

2. For the distinctions between res judicata and collateral estoppel and other related doctrines, see § 443 above.

3. Rosen v. Parking Garage, 40 Misc.2d 178, 242 N.Y.S.2d 677 (N.Y.C.Civ.Ct. 1963).

4. Roland Meledandri Inc. v. Kirtz, N.Y.C.Civ.Ct., N.Y.County, Index No. 183301–67, Dec. 7, 1967 (per Gittleson, J.). By allowing the small claims judgment as an offset, the case illustrates what § 1808 means when it makes the small claims adjudication res judicata "only as to the amount involved" in the small claim.

warranted? Had P paid for it? How much was he supposed to pay? Who breached the contract?—the relevant doctrine was collateral estoppel (issue preclusion) and did not apply. Hence, if an owner-driver of a car gets a small claims judgment for property damage from the other car, the findings implicit in the judgment will not be binding, either way, in a later action between the same parties for personal injuries. There, again, the relevant doctrine is collateral estoppel, and it does not apply to a small claims judgment.[5]

Even if the collateral estoppel doctrine itself applied in the small claims part, moreover, its impact would often be avoided under the so-called "full and fair opportunity" test. Under that test, the court, in determining the estoppel impact of a prior decision, can consider among other things the size of the claim and the court it came from.[6]

When res judicata (claim preclusion) is the relevant doctrine, however, as it is when the claim is the same, it is applicable notwithstanding the statutory language. It has even been applied to a counterclaim voluntarily interposed in a small claims action, for example. The counterclaimant was held bound by the result and was precluded from relitigating the same claim later,[7] yet a further example of the courts' efforts to make sense of § 1808's purpose if not of its language.[8] Although the door must be left open to variations when unique facts warrant it, as they often do in the res judicata arena, this general approach of construing § 1808 to deny issue preclusion (collateral estoppel) effect to a small claims judgment while allowing it claim preclusion effect seems reasonable. A more rigid construction would likely divest the small claims judgment of any capacity to end even the dispute directly at issue.

The small claims part has from time to time been used to harass a defendant with repetitious suits on the same dispute despite the claimant's prior losses. This can of course be done in the regular part of the court as well, but it is particularly easy in small claims procedure because it is so inexpensive. A statute, § 1810 in the lower court acts, was passed to meet the problem. It says that when the clerk believes the claimant is using the small claims part for oppression or harassment, the clerk can require the claimant to seek court leave before proceeding. It is just a safeguard, empowering the clerk not to preclude the suit but only to refer the matter to a judge.[9] In one case in which a claimant had continually brought claims on the same cause against various United Nations personnel as "agent" of her estranged husband, the court refused an "injunction" barring her from suing, but did direct the clerk to refuse to accept further small claims applications from her.[10]

§ 585A. "Commercial" Small Claims Part

The legislature in 1987 enacted a new and additional Small Claims article in the New York City Civil Court Act, the Uniform District Court Act, and the Uniform City Court Act, designed to stand alongside the original Small Claims article (Article 18). The new one is numbered 18–A, and each of its sections, most of which are similar if not identical to their counterparts in Article 18, has the same number but with a hyphen and an "A" after it.[1] The basic purpose of the new Article 18–A is to create a small claims part for the use of claimants that are corporations, partnerships, or associations. (Article 18 itself denies the use

---

5. See the discussion in Royster v. Consolidated Edison, 114 Misc.2d 529, 452 N.Y.S.2d 146 (N.Y.C.Civ.Ct. 1982).

6. See § 467 above.

7. 64 West Park Avenue Corp. v. Parlong Realty Corp., 77 Misc.2d 1019, 354 N.Y.S.2d 342 (Sup.Ct., Nassau County, 1974).

8. Section 1808 was carried over without substantial change from § 186 of the old New York City Municipal Court Code.

9. CCA, UDCA, UCCA, and UJCA § 1810.

10. Menon v. Weil, 66 Misc.2d 114, 320 N.Y.S.2d 405 (N.Y.C.Civ.Ct. 1971).

§ 585A

1. Article 18–A was not included in the Uniform Justice Court Act and hence does not apply at all in the town and village courts.

of the small claims part to such claimants.[2])

Under the definition contained in § 1801-A, a claim is "commercial" not based on its subject matter, but merely because the claimant is a corporation, partnership, or association, which we can conveniently refer to in this section as an "entity". The claim itself need not be "commercial" in nature, e.g., arise via contract; as long as the claimant is an entity, even a tort claim will presumably fit under Article 18-A. This seems to be corroborated by § 1804-A, whose reference to the facilitated proof permitted for "repairs"—which is based on the original § 1804[3]—suggests the tort of property damage, for which that reference was originally designed (notably in automobile cases).

Under Article 18-A, certain assignees may also bring the claim.[4]

It is required that the claimant have its "principal" office in New York State.[5] It must also be shown that the defendant has a local residential or business contact: for the civil court, with the city; for a city court, with the county in which the city is located; and for the district court, with the "municipality".[6]

The ceiling for commercial small claims jurisdiction is the same as that set for the regular small claims part under Article 18, presently $3000.[7]

Article 18-A can be read to require that the "commercial" small claims part be an entirely distinct one, separate from the regular small claims part set up by Article 18 for natural person claimants. There should still be some leeway, however, in the chief administrator's

broad administrative arsenal, to coordinate or even fuse the two. One judge sitting in one room should be able to handle both categories of small claim, either during different hours or even during the same hours. If these "commercial" claimants turn out in numbers deemed great enough to inundate the natural person claimants, the problem can be recognized and dealt with administratively, perhaps only then mandating entirely separate parts, etc.

Indeed, in some of the city courts there may be only one or two judges sitting, which suggests the awkwardness of reading this new article to require distinct parts even when there are not the judicial personnel to staff them.

A safety valve, or in any event something intended to have that effect, against an inundation of "commercial" small claims is the restriction that no entity bring more than five such small claims per month.[8]

§ 585B. Court–Annexed Arbitration of Claims Under Stated Sums

Quite apart from "Small Claims" as governed by Article 18 of the quartet of lower court acts,[1] just treated,[2] and distinct as well from the conventional out-of-court arbitration governed by Article 75 of the CPLR to be treated below,[3] is the system known as the Alternative Method of Dispute Resolution by Arbitration. It is authorized by CPLR 3405 and governed in detail by Part 28 of the Rules of the Chief Judge.[4] We can refer to it as

---

2. See CCA § 1809.

3. See § 582 above.

4. See § 1809-A.

5. Section 1801-A.

6. Id. The district court reference to "municipality" may have been intended to require that the contact be with the particular district sued in (compare UDCA § 1801 in the regular small claims article), but it is more logically read to refer to the county, which is also defined as a "municipality" for some purposes. See, e.g., Gen. Mun.L. § 2.

7. See § 1801-A in the New York City Civil and in the Uniform District and City court acts. Uniform City Court Act § 1801-A, which provides that if a given city court has basic monetary jurisdiction of less than $1000, the com-

mercial claims jurisdiction shall be deemed reduced to that figure, is irrelevant: an amendment of UCCA § 202 that took effect in 1991 made all of the city courts' monetary jurisdiction uniform.

8. See § 1803-A.

§ 585B

1. The New York City Civil Court Act (CCA), the Uniform District Court Act (UDCA), the Uniform City Court Act (UCCA), and the Uniform Justice Court Act (UJCA).

2. See §§ 581–585A.

3. See Chapter 22, below, consisting of §§ 586–609.

4. Part 28 presently consists of Rules 28.1 through 28.16.

"court-annexed arbitration" to give it a title that can distinguish it from the other procedures.[5]

Court-annexed arbitration is a set of procedures designed for the hearing of money cases that fall beyond the small claims jurisdiction[6] but are still under a designated higher figure, which is presently $10,000 for cases brought in the New York City Civil Court and $6000 for cases brought in other courts.[7] The procedure applies only in courts designated by the chief administrator, which can be any of the usual courts of civil jurisdiction except the town and village courts.[8] Whether the procedure applies in any given court is up to the chief administrator and must be ascertained by individual inquiry.

The procedure requires that the determination of claims not exceeding the applicable figure be by arbitrators, the arbitrators appointed by a commissioner who has been designated to serve the particular county.[9] When it applies, the arbitration is mandatory. A party cannot refuse it. But the loser in the arbitration is allowed to demand a trial de novo in court, in which the whole claim is heard afresh and the arbitration award disregarded. It is the conferral of this trial de novo right that preserves the procedure's constitutionality (the right to trial by jury is the principal right involved),[10] but the right is encumbered with monetary burdens, including the obligation to pay—with no right of recovery back—the fees of the arbitration panel,[11] which in a fashion amounts to a penalty imposed on a person for asserting the right to trial by jury.

It may seem idle to require arbitration and then let the loser go to court as if arbitration never took place, but statistically the loser has accepted the result in a high enough percentage of the cases to make the procedure a saving, and in the view of the courts' administrators, a success.

Generally speaking the case is commenced in the usual way and goes through the usual pre-trial procedures. The difference is that when the note of issue, or, in the lower courts, the notice of trial[12] is filed, the case goes on the arbitration calendar instead of on the regular trial calendar.[13] If the main claim is subject to court-annexed arbitration, any counterclaim or cross-claim interposed in the action is also submitted to the arbitration, and in this instance without regard to the amount of the counterclaim or cross-claim.[14]

It has been held that the parties cannot waive the arbitration procedure; that a trial de novo is available only after the arbitration proceedings have been concluded; that the procedure is so obligatory that a court can declare a mistrial sua sponte upon discovering that a case before it should have been but was not submitted to the court-annexed arbitration procedure; and that the court even at this belated stage can place the case on the arbitration calendar.[15] But it has also been held that the submission to arbitration is not irrevocable if it afterwards develops that the value of the plaintiff's claim exceeds the court-annexed arbitration ceiling. It has been held, for example, that the usual motion under CPLR 325(b) may be made by the plaintiff to the supreme court to raise the demand as it stands in the original complaint in the lower court and remove the case to a higher court,[16] and that a granting of the motion will take the case out of the arbitration.[17]

---

5. The federal courts have a similar device with higher monetary reaches. See 28 U.S.C.A. §§ 651–658.

6. The small claims ceiling is presently $3000. See § 581 above.

7. See CPLR 3405, added to the CPLR in 1978. It was previously subdivision 10 of Judiciary Law § 213, which was repealed in conjunction with the 1978 overhaul of judicial administration.

8. See Rule 28.2.

9. Rules 28.3–28.5.

10. Chase v. Scalici, 97 A.D.2d 25, 468 N.Y.S.2d 365 (2d Dep't 1983).

11. Rule 28.12(c).

12. See, e.g., N.Y.C.Civ.Ct.Act § 1301.

13. See Rule 28.2(e).

14. Rule 28.2(d).

15. National Instrument Co. v. Hortigro, Inc., 121 Misc.2d 1077, 469 N.Y.S.2d 566 (Dist.Ct., Nassau County, 1983).

16. See § 25 above.

17. Petropol v. Shahid, 115 A.D.2d 820, 495 N.Y.S.2d 778 (3d Dep't 1985).

If there are several claims in the case, each of them for the applicable ceiling or less when measured individually, all are subject to court-annexed arbitration.[18]

Submission to the court-annexed arbitration procedure can also be made on a voluntary basis. The rule calls this a submission by stipulation. Stipulated arbitration is not restricted to the otherwise applicable maximum nor even to the court's overall monetary limitations.[19]

Most of the cases coming before the courts with an objection to court-annexed arbitration have concerned some phase of the trial de novo procedure. The loser in the arbitration who is bent on having it overturned must seek the trial de novo by filing the demand with the clerk and serving it on the other parties within 30 days after being served with notice that the award has been filed in court.[20] The 30-day period is jurisdictional, as it is with the taking of an appeal in conventional practice. Hence, while the omission of one of the steps—filing or serving—can be excused, the omission of both steps within the requisite time cannot be excused and will result in a forfeiture of the right to a trial de novo.[21]

The making of a timely demand for a trial de novo by any party is in effect made in behalf of all, so that the party who has demanded it cannot afterwards withdraw the demand without the consent of the other parties.[22]

A trial de novo may not be demanded by a party in default.[23] Indeed, a defaulting party is not even entitled to notice of the arbitration hearing itself.[24]

Motions relating to court-annexed arbitration proceedings are made to the court.[25] Among the recognized motions is one to vacate an award. The rule that authorizes it[26] also sets forth the grounds for vacating the award. These are modeled on the vacatur grounds listed in CPLR 7511(b) for vacating conventional arbitration awards.[27]

A judgment may be entered on an award made in court-annexed arbitration without going through the confirmation procedures spelled out in CPLR 7510,[28] which apply only to conventional arbitration.[29]

The use of the court-annexed arbitration system in the Rochester City Court, in Monroe County, one of the first places in which it was established, led to the routine practice of transferring ordinary small claims—claims for less than $3000—to the regular part of the court, where it would then be subjected to arbitration under this special system and then in turn subjected to a trial de novo at the behest of the loser. This was an outright denial of the use of the small claims parts and the practice was invalidated in Lortz v. Lortz.[30]

---

18. Ferber v. Schultz, 104 Misc.2d 1009, 429 N.Y.S.2d 861 (N.Y.C.Civ.Ct. 1980).

19. Rule 28.2(c).

20. Rule 28.12.

21. Chase v. Scalici, 97 A.D.2d 25, 468 N.Y.S.2d 365 (2d Dep't 1983).

22. Transcontinental Music Corp. v. Gallo, 67 A.D.2d 750, 412 N.Y.S.2d 219 (3d Dep't 1979).

23. Rule 28.12.

24. Statom v. Lumbermens Mutual Cas. Co., 106 Misc.2d 442, 431 N.Y.S.2d 875 (App.T., 1st Dep't, 1980).

25. Rule 28.14.

26. Rule 28.13.

27. See § 602 below.

28. See § 601 below.

29. See Zampella v. Plaza at Latham Ass'n, 69 A.D.2d 957, 416 N.Y.S.2d 89 (3d Dep't 1979).

30. 162 Misc.2d 539, 616 N.Y.S.2d 876 (Monroe County Court 1994). See the discussion in SPR 25:3.

Chapter Twenty–Two

ARBITRATION

Analysis

A. IN GENERAL

Table of Sections

§ 586. Arbitration, a Perspective

Arbitration is a form of dispute resolution almost wholly independent of the court system. What links exist are few and occur mainly at the outset, when the courts may be called on to determine whether arbitration is required, and at the end, when they may be asked to confirm the award made in the arbitration or conduct a limited review of it. The in-between period belongs to the arbitrators and the courts do not interfere.[1]

Arbitration is usually voluntary—historically it was almost entirely so—coming about by a contract between the parties, but more recently it has been made compulsory or semi-compulsory in certain instances. The main area from which arbitration sprang was commercial. The business community manifested a preference for its advantages as outweighing its shortcomings. Thus, what is still often referred to as "commercial arbitration" soon became the principal context in which the large body of law surrounding the arbitral process developed.

The outweighing of pros over cons ultimately impressed more than the business community, and today arbitration is a process well known in nearly all phases of labor-management relations, blue-collar, white-collar and governmental; is becoming a standard device in parts of the tort realm, notably under uninsured motorist endorsements and the no-fault law; has made inroads into family disputes; and, expanding past the borders of state and nation alike, is becoming a trusted tool in international commerce.

In arbitration, the dispute is resolved by a person or persons of the parties' choosing, either by drawing up a submission of an existing controversy or by incorporating into a contract a clause agreeing to submit all future controversies arising out of the contract. Before 1920, such an agreement for future arbitration would not be enforced; despite it, a party could just refuse to arbitrate, remitting the aggrieved person to the usual court action for relief, or to an action for damages for

---

§ 586

1. Nationwide Mutual Ins. Co. v. Miller, 95 A.D.2d 961, 464 N.Y.S.2d 291 (3d Dep't 1983).

violating the agreement to arbitrate.[2] If the parties did follow through on their agreement, however, going through the arbitration to the point of award, the courts did enforce the award. This was known as common-law arbitration. Although it continues to be an available alternative,[3] it has been almost totally eclipsed by the much more efficient statutory arbitration, now found in Article 75 of the CPLR.

New York has been a lively participant in the change of attitude towards arbitration. Prior to 1920, an agreement to submit a dispute to arbitration was deemed an attempt to oust the courts of their jurisdiction and was held void as against public policy.[4] In that year New York law was amended to recognize and enforce agreements to arbitrate disputes, present or future.[5] In 1921 the Civil Practice Act, the CPLR's predecessor, was amended to reflect those changes,[6] and in the same year the Court of Appeals sustained the new scheme. Rejecting a constitutional attack, the court noted that an agreement to arbitrate neither unlawfully deprives litigants of access to the supreme court nor divests them of the constitutional right to trial by jury because these rights are waivable and the agreement to arbitrate waives them.[7] From that moment on, New York became and has remained an enthusiastic supporter of the arbitral process.[8] Indeed, the most influential organization in the field, at state, national, and even international level, the American Arbitration Association, is headquartered in New York City.[9]

In 1937, a consolidation of the arbitration provisions took place,[10] and this put them into such good shape that even years later the revisers who produced the CPLR still deemed them "basically sound", noted that they had even become the model for other states, and carried the gist of them forward into the CPLR, which took effect in 1963, with little change.[11]

Since the beginning of the 1920s it has thus been New York's policy "to interfere as little as possible with the freedom of consenting parties" to arbitrate their disputes. When they agree to that method "they in effect select their own forum. Their quest is . . . for a non-judicial tribunal that will arrive at a private and practical determination with maximum dispatch and minimum expense."[12] And today not only do the courts not interfere with an agreement to arbitrate; they have become the means of enforcing it, staying their own proceedings if brought in violation of the agreement and thereby "compelling" arbitration, through procedures to be taken up in this chapter.

The advantages of arbitration are many. In addition to speed, economy, and privacy—no regularly augmented court records to tell the world what's happening—the parties can select as their arbitrator a specialist in their particular commercial (or other) field, thereby exploiting his experience and expertise. This enables custom and usage to be made a prime ingredient in the decisional process in a given commercial, industrial, or other specialized field, and more meaningfully than can be accomplished in court. Even when custom and usage is made admissible before a judge in litigation, as under the Uniform Commercial Code,[13] the judge can decide what it is only through what experts have testified to in court, and each side is likely to produce an

---

2. See, e.g., Thomas W. Finucane Co. v. Board of Ed., 190 N.Y. 76, 82 N.E. 737 (1907).

3. Hellman v. Wolbrom, 31 A.D.2d 477, 298 N.Y.S.2d 540 (1st Dep't 1969).

4. Meacham v. Jamestown, F. & C.R. Co., 211 N.Y. 346, 105 N.E. 653 (1914).

5. L.1920, c. 275.

6. Civ.Prac.Act § 1448 et seq.

7. Berkovitz v. Arbib & Houlberg, 230 N.Y. 261, 130 N.E. 288 (1921).

8. See Gilbert v. Burnstine, 255 N.Y. 348, 174 N.E. 706 (1931).

9. The address of the AAA is 140 West 51st Street, New York, NY 10020–1203. Information about the availability of their facilities and services and the procedures to be applied in their arbitrations may be secured by mail to that address.

10. See 17th Jud.Council Rep. (1951) 213, 233.

11. See 2d Rep.Leg.Doc. (1958) No. 13, p. 130.

12. Siegel v. Lewis, 40 N.Y.2d 687, 689, 389 N.Y.S.2d 800, 801, 358 N.E.2d 484, 485 (1976).

13. See, e.g., U.C.C. §§ 2–202, 2–208.

expert tilting custom and usage its own way. Even the most able judge can be hoodwinked in this manner, whereas the wool will not be so lightly drawn over the eyes of one with a career in the field. It has even been held that the arbitrator can decide a case based on his own knowledge alone,[14] which is so impermissible in litigation that a judge with any personal knowledge of a case is for that reason alone disqualified from hearing it.

In contrast with litigation, arbitration is informal. Litigation has two major offerings: the substantive law and the procedural law of the state. Neither is applicable in arbitration. Arbitrators fashion their own substantive law, and only "complete irrationality" will find the courts interfering,[15] which is just another way of saying that an award in arbitration may be overturned on only a few narrow grounds—these contained in CPLR 7511(b) and taken up in detail later[16]—and an error of law is not among them. Nor is an error of fact. Except for the few grounds listed, the courts will not scrutinize an award.

The arbitrator's findings must be so beside the mark as to amount to bias before a court will intercede, an infrequent result. In a wrongful death arbitration arising under the MVAIC endorsement of an automobile liability policy,[17] for example, an award of $500 was upheld even though it came to only a fraction of the funeral expenses alone, to say nothing of what loss of earnings might total for the decedent, a young father of two. The court nevertheless rejected the accusation of bias. The decedent had first struck an abutment before being struck, in turn, by a hit-and-run vehicle, and there was room to find that the principal cause of the death was the decedent's own conduct, with but a pittance of responsibility imputed to the second driver.[18] In a jury verdict delivered in court, the findings would have been rejected as a compromise,[19] but in the arbitration award they were beyond review, the product of neither irrationality nor bias. Compromise, in fact, instead of a rigid attempt to affix the labels of right and wrong, is another of arbitration's major offerings.

So inapplicable are the formal rules of law that even when the arbitrator states that he is applying a given law, and then misapplies it, the award will not be upset.[20]

Except for a few basic guarantees, such as the right to be heard and to be represented by counsel at the arbitration, the procedural law of the state, including the rules of evidence, is also inapplicable to arbitration.[21]

A party intent on speed, informality, economy, privacy, and expertise, or any combination of those advantages, does well to choose arbitration; one who wants the substantive law of the state applied, or some advantage that procedure offers (such as use of the pretrial disclosure devices or the protections of a given exclusionary rule of evidence), will of course prefer litigation. Which to choose? Many factors must be considered. If the controversy already exists when the question of whether to select arbitration arises, a more astute appraisal can be made by each party of which mode of resolution to select. If either refuses arbitration, litigation is of course the only path open. Both sides must agree to arbitration.

---

14.   Siegel v. Lewis, note 12, above.

15.   Lentine v. Fundaro, 29 N.Y.2d 382, 328 N.Y.S.2d 418, 278 N.E.2d 633 (1972).

16.   See § 602.

17.   See Ins.L. § 3420(f)(1). MVAIC stands for the Motor Vehicle Accident Indemnification Corporation and the cited statute provides for its endorsement in liability policies.

18.   Torano v. Motor Vehicle Acc. Indemnification Corp., 19 A.D.2d 356, 243 N.Y.S.2d 434 (1st Dep't 1963), aff'd 15 N.Y.2d 882, 258 N.Y.S.2d 418, 206 N.E.2d 353 (1965).

19.   That would have been so, in any event, under the New York rule of contributory negligence applicable at the time, which barred a plaintiff negligent in any degree from

any recovery at all. Under the comparative negligence rule, CPLR 1411–1413, applicable to accidents occurring after September 1, 1975, a verdict of this kind could be sustained on the basis of only a small percentage of fault being attributed to the other car.

20.   Associated Teachers of Huntington, Inc. v. Board of Ed., 33 N.Y.2d 229, 351 N.Y.S.2d 670, 306 N.E.2d 791 (1973).

21.   See Professional Staff Congress/City University of New York v. Board of Higher Ed., 39 N.Y.2d 319, 383 N.Y.S.2d 592, 347 N.E.2d 918 (1976). For discussion of the procedures applicable to the arbitration, see § 597 below.

The more difficult choice comes in determining whether to include in a contract an agreement to arbitrate future controversies. Here each party must anticipate the kinds of disputes likely to arise and which mode will serve it better in their resolution. If both decide on arbitration, into the contract goes the arbitration clause. Indeed, it is this category—contracting for arbitration in advance of the dispute—to which the arbitral process traces most of its business today. The primary teacher of which mode to turn to is experience. One approaching for the first time the question of whether to commit a client to arbitration should inquire of others in the area about the advantages and even the likely results of arbitration. Because in many important fields arbitration is much the favored method, the novice need only poke around in the field for a while to determine when to use what.

Arbitration is a procedure wholly out of court. It is not, as it used to be, a "special proceeding", but an entirely extra-judicial procedure. The special proceeding is one of the means used, however, to raise in court such questions as whether arbitration is required and what if anything must be arbitrated (these being known as the threshold questions). It is also the expedient for getting the award confirmed into judgment after the arbitration is concluded. These are procedural matters elaborated later in this chapter.[22]

Arbitration is available today under CPLR 7501 "without regard to the justiciable character of the controversy". This language is designed at least in part to assure the availability of the arbitral process in labor disputes for such matters as "rates of pay, wages, hours of employment" and the like.[23] These are usually matters of negotiation[24] and not the kind of business that a court handles, which is what "justiciable" means. Dispensing with the "justiciable" criterion avoids the problem by permitting arbitration of these issues, incidentally pointing up the special utility of arbitration in the labor area.

Liberating arbitration from the "justiciable" requirement also reinforces caselaw, predating the CPLR, which allows the courts, by way of confirming an arbitral award, to give judgment for equitable relief that the courts could not entertain in an original litigation, such as for the specific performance of a personal services or construction contract.[25]

It has even been held that a merely "advisory arbitration", i.e., one not binding on the parties but whose result they agree to "consider", is permissible under this provision,[26] but such an "award", if that it be, may be too elusive to confirm into a judgment.[27] One may even wonder what is gained by such a transmutation, since an unenforcible judgment is not much better than an unenforcible award.

An arbitrator is not restricted to the relief requested by the parties. Arbitrators' powers are analogous to those of a chancellor in equity and they can shape the relief they deem appropriate accordingly. So, for example, an arbitration brought only to strike defamatory matter from a dismissed teacher's file can go further and order her temporary reinstatement.[28]

Extrajudicial arbitration under Article 75 of the CPLR should not be confused with other procedures or devices making use of what may be called "arbitration". In the Small Claims parts of some of the lower courts, for example, such as the New York City Civil Court, volunteer lawyers who serve with the parties' consent as judges are called "arbitrators", but

---

22. See § 591.

23. See 2d Rep.Leg.Doc. (1958) No. 13, p. 132.

24. When these matters go to arbitration after an impasse, labor parlance calls it "interest" arbitration, in which the arbitrators actually write a contract for the parties. This is in contrast with the more usual situation, in which a dispute under an existing agreement is arbitrated—which is called "grievance" arbitration in labor terminology.

25. These situations are reviewed under the "public policy" caption in the next section.

26. See Board of Ed. of Central School Dist. No. 1 v. Cracovia, 36 A.D.2d 851, 321 N.Y.S.2d 496 (2d Dep't 1971).

27. See Schwartz v. North Salem Board of Ed., 65 Misc.2d 472, 318 N.Y.S.2d 774 (Sup.Ct., Westchester County, 1971).

28. Board of Ed. v. Bellmore–Merrick United Secondary Teachers, Inc., 39 N.Y.2d 167, 383 N.Y.S.2d 242, 347 N.E.2d 603 (1976).

have little to do with Article 75 and the conventional arbitral process.[29]

Equally unrelated to Article 75 is the court-annexed arbitration, a semi-compulsory kind used within the court system for money claims not exceeding a certain figure. It was at first inaugurated on an experimental basis in some lower courts as a way to expedite the disposition of cases too big for the Small Claims part but still of modest dimension.[30] It is now standardized under CPLR 3405, but it applies in a given court only if so directed by the court's administrators. The procedure is officially denominated the "Alternative Method of Dispute Resolution by Arbitration", and is implemented by rules.[31] We refer to it here as "semi-compulsory" because "compulsory", while often heard, is misleading: the losing party in a CPLR 3405 arbitration can disregard the award and secure a full trial de novo in court,[32] which is surely not the loser's right with the usual consensual arbitration that occupies Article 75 (and this chapter). Nor should this in-court category of what is sometimes described as "compulsory" arbitration be confused with the use of compulsory arbitration in the area of labor relations, where by statute a collective bargaining impasse may have to be submitted to binding arbitration without the mutual assent of the parties.[33]

Yet another "arbitration" category is that authorized by CPLR 3045, enacted in 1986. It applies in medical malpractice actions and seeks to encourage the use of arbitration to resolve damages issues. Under CPLR 3045, a defendant who concedes liability can ask the plaintiff to arbitrate damages. If the plaintiff agrees, arbitration takes place under the procedures of Article 75–A, called "Health Care Arbitration".[34]

These other categories have been mentioned only to distinguish them from the broad realm of out-of-court arbitration governed by Article 75 and studied in this chapter.

Arbitration falls under the caption of Alternative Dispute Resolution, or ADR, in present day terminology, a caption under which it may be found even in law school curricula. What makes it "alternative" is that it is alternative to litigation. All other alternatives to litigation also fall under the ADR caption, like "mediation", which differs from arbitration in that arbitration binds the parties while mediation does not.

At the end of this chapter we will compare the New York Arbitration Act (Article 75 of the CPLR) with the Federal Arbitration Act,[35] the valuation or appraisal proceeding,[36] and the Simplified Procedure for Court Determination of Disputes (an unsuccessful effort to get back into court some of the commercial business lost over the years to arbitration).[37]

While it may be said in general that arbitration is available for any category of dispute and for any kind of issue, there are a few notable exceptions in which "public policy" precludes arbitration. That's the next topic.

§ 587. "Public Policy" as Barring Arbitration

CPLR 7501 authorizes arbitration for "any controversy" and does not purport to set any limits. Caselaw has set some, however, drawing up over the years a small roster of subjects whose release from the grip of the courts would violate "public policy". So, for example, it was held that "New York's antitrust law represents a public policy of the first magnitude" and therefore "should not be left within the purview of commercial arbitration", whatever the choice of forum expressed by the parties.[1] So too, for another example, it has been held that the issue of whether a contract

---

29. See § 582 above.

30. See Bayer v. Ras, 71 Misc.2d 464, 336 N.Y.S.2d 261 (Monroe County Court 1972).

31. See Part 28 of the Rules of the Chief Judge.

32. See § 585B, above, which treats this CPLR 3405 category of arbitration.

33. See § 603 below.

34. CPLR 7550 through 7565.

35. Title 9 of the U.S. Code. See § 607 below.

36. CPLR 7601. See § 608 below.

37. CPLR 3031–3037. See § 609 below.

§ 587

1. Aimcee Wholesale Corp. v. Tomar Products, Inc., 21 N.Y.2d 621, 626, 289 N.Y.S.2d 968, 971 (1968).

is usurious cannot be taken from the courts, else the usurer could, with its unequal bargaining power, exact of the "necessitous borrower" a submission both to arbitration and to the usurer's choice of arbitrators, and by that means to the usury itself.[2] The liquidation of insolvent insurance companies, the awarding of punitive damages, and violations of the criminal law are other matters held non-arbitrable under the public policy caption.[3]

Determining which subjects or issues stand behind this "public policy" barrier was not hard to do at the outset, because only "a small number of problems have been recognized as so interlaced with strong public policy considerations that they have been placed beyond the reach of the arbitrators' discretion".[4] But as dependence on arbitration has grown, the public policy barrier has also expanded. Paradoxically, in fact, it has been both expanding and contracting: the courts sometimes seem to weave back and forth in trying to draw a public policy line.

It is not mere "public policy" that builds the barrier, but something more. It has to be a "public policy of the first magnitude",[5] or at least a "strong" public policy.[6] This is for the reason that "public policy" taken alone is uninstructive. A state's public policy is its law, whether constitutional, statutory, decisional, or otherwise. But to apply so obvious and simple a definition would bar arbitration altogether, because presumably a first principle of the arbitral process is that the substantive law does not apply to it. Until the courts formulate a test specifically for the arbitration process, perhaps we can borrow Judge Cardozo's public policy test as enunciated in a different context in Loucks v. Standard Oil Co. of New York,[7] a conflict of laws setting.

The question in *Loucks* was whether a New York court, in a case having contacts with another state as well as New York, would apply the other state's law to an issue before it. Involved was the general rule that one state will not apply another's law if doing so would offend the forum's "public policy". One of the arguments was that any foreign law that differs in content from the forum's, on whatever issue, must necessarily violate the forum's public policy. Realizing that such a standard would result in a forum's refusal ever to apply any foreign law at all, an untenable result in a modern world and especially in a federal society, the New York Court of Appeals rejected this narrow a definition and held that before foreign law is rejected it would have to be shown to "violate some fundamental principle of justice, some prevalent conception of good morals, some deep-rooted tradition of the common weal".[8]

If application of that test to arbitrability does not offer a sharp line, it at least clarifies that it will be only a "deep-rooted" public policy that will exclude an issue from the arbitral process. That would be so, in any event, if both sides have bargaining power and have chosen arbitration with their eyes open.

In the family law area, public policy becomes involved when a separation agreement purports to authorize arbitration of certain issues. Arbitration has been allowed for money matters, but issues of custody and visitation do not have clear sailing. Some courts suggest that arbitration is permissible at least for an initial determination of those issues, the court reserving a power of complete review and even disregard of the award if it is found to be detrimental to the child's interests,[9] but others

---

2. Durst v. Abrash, 22 A.D.2d 39, 253 N.Y.S.2d 351 (1st Dep't 1964), aff'd 17 N.Y.2d 445, 266 N.Y.S.2d 806 (1965). The public policy barrier falls, however, and the arbitration even of a usury issue may be allowed to arbitration, if the arbitration is sought by the borrower, who is presumably the weaker of the parties. Rosenblum v. Steiner, 43 N.Y.2d 896, 403 N.Y.S.2d 716 (1978).

3. See Garrity v. Lyle Stuart, Inc., 40 N.Y.2d 354, 386 N.Y.S.2d 831, 353 N.E.2d 793 (1976); Mendelsohn v. A & D Catering Corp., 100 A.D.2d 209, 473 N.Y.S.2d 481 (2d Dep't 1984).

4. Associated Teachers of Huntington, Inc. v. Board of Ed., 33 N.Y.2d 229, 235, 351 N.Y.S.2d 670, 675, 306 N.E.2d 791, 795 (1973).

5. Aimcee Wholesale Corp. v. Tomar Products, Inc., note 1, above.

6. Associated Teachers of Huntington, Inc. v. Board of Ed., note 4, above.

7. 224 N.Y. 99, 120 N.E. 198 (1918).

8. 224 N.Y. at 111, 120 N.E. at 202.

9. See, e.g., Sheets v. Sheets, 22 A.D.2d 176, 254 N.Y.S.2d 320 (1st Dep't 1964).

reject this two-step process and hold that under their parens patriae relationship, the courts' obligations to the child are primary and cannot be deferred to arbitration at all.[10] They point out that since even those courts that allow arbitration of custody and visitation do so subject to plenary judicial review and even a hearing de novo, allowing arbitration at all is only postponing the inevitable and hence a waste of time, expense and effort.[11] Under the *Loucks* standard, in other words, judicial control of child custody—children being traditionally wards of the court—is too "deep-rooted" to be abandoned to arbitration.

In some instances the judges may be closely divided about what violates a "strong public policy". The imposition of punitive or exemplary damages is concededly a delicate matter, for example, and has been held to be beyond arbitration.[12] Yet an agreement fixing damages at three times a stated figure for each day of a contract's violation has been upheld by a divided Court of Appeals,[13] the majority stressing that the field involved was collective bargaining, where arbitration is especially favored, and that the rights of no third persons were involved.

Distribution of a decedent's estate and such connected matters as the probate of a will and the determination of intestate shares and the rights of creditors in an estate have been held non-arbitrable,[14] although it would seem permissible to arbitrate a clearly delineated existing dispute between given persons notwithstanding some relationship to a decedent's estate. There need not be a sweeping prohibition if at root there lies just a private dispute over money.

The old rule that arbitration could not be allowed to entertain anything that would be beyond the general understanding of what a court is competent to handle was responsible for a few taboos, but these were left behind when CPLR 7501 authorized arbitration "without regard to the justiciable character of the controversy".[15] When the old rule was in effect, it was contrary to public policy to let an arbitrator do what a court could not, but this is no longer so. The breakdown of this barrier began even before the CPLR arrived. In Staklinski v. Pyramid Electric Co., for example,[16] which involved a contract authorizing arbitrators to resolve disputes under a personal services arrangement and expressly empowered them to award specific performance, if called for, an award was made directing an employer to reinstate its production and engineering manager. When judicial confirmation of the award was sought, it was resisted on the ground that public policy precludes the courts from compelling an employer to retain the services of one of its officials. The court nevertheless upheld the award, noting that the parties agreed to this remedy and that this made it permissible in arbitration notwithstanding that it might be barred in litigation.

Shortly after that, the same rule was applied to authorize confirmation of an award granting specific performance of a construction contract, the court rejecting the argument—however successful it might have been in an ordinary action in equity—that it would involve the courts in superintending a complex agreement.[17]

Another illustration is the case involving what might be described as the internal busi-

10. See, e.g., Glauber v. Glauber, 192 A.D.2d 94, 600 N.Y.S.2d 740 (2d Dep't 1993).

11. See Nestel v. Nestel, 38 A.D.2d 942, 331 N.Y.S.2d 241 (2d Dep't 1972).

12. See, e.g., Garrity v. Lyle Stuart, Inc., 40 N.Y.2d 354, 386 N.Y.S.2d 831, 353 N.E.2d 793 (1976). When choice of law issues supervene in a situation involving several states and an interplay between the federal and New York arbitration acts, the New York restriction on an arbitral award of punitive damages may be circumvented and the arbitrator allowed to award punitive damages after all. See Mastrobuono v. Shearson Lehman Hutton, Inc., 514 U.S. 52, 115 S.Ct. 1212, 131 L.Ed.2d 76 (1995),

and its discussion in the lead note in New York State Law Digest No. 423.

13. Matter of Associated General Contractors, New York State Chapter, Inc., 36 N.Y.2d 957, 373 N.Y.S.2d 555, 335 N.E.2d 859 (1975). The vote was 4–3.

14. See In re Jacobovitz' Will, 58 Misc.2d 330, 295 N.Y.S.2d 527 (Surr.Ct., Nassau County, 1968).

15. See § 586 above.

16. 6 N.Y.2d 159, 188 N.Y.S.2d 541, 160 N.E.2d 78 (1959).

17. Grayson–Robinson Stores v. Iris Constr. Corp., 8 N.Y.2d 133, 202 N.Y.S.2d 303, 168 N.E.2d 377 (1960).

ness and management of a corporation. As long as the dispute it involves is susceptible of determination without requiring an ongoing corporate supervision by either arbitrators (initially) or courts (ultimately), arbitration may be allowed, especially in the case of the closed corporation.[18]

The "illegality" of a contract, as exemplified by the usury issue previously mentioned,[19] would of course be a "public policy" violation of the kind that bars arbitration,[20] but the mere contention that performance would be illegal will not suffice to suspend arbitration or "it would be the rare arbitration agreement that could not be nullified" by the contention alone. Hence, as long as the agreement is on its face lawful and calls for lawful performance, arbitration will not be refused merely because a party contends that a refusal to perform would offend the law in some way.[21] When the agreement is valid on its face, the one resisting arbitration on public policy grounds has the burden of demonstrating how that policy is violated.[22] The court should be able to discern the public policy violation without engaging in extended fact-finding or legal analysis.[23]

Although it is best to treat the policy issue as a so-called "threshold" one, i.e., to raise it at the outset by an application to stay arbitration[24] and thus prevent arbitration from taking place at all, some courts have held that it would even be permissible to entertain the issue after arbitration has taken place, as by an application to vacate the award or by way of resisting an application to confirm it.[25] A

genuine public policy objection is available at either terminal of the arbitration.[26] The Court of Appeals has said that if the public policy barrier may be in the picture but it is not clear at the threshold stage of arbitration, and that relief of a type to invoke the public policy objection is not the only relief possible, the case can be let through to an award. The award may settle on relief acceptable to public policy standards, and if it does the policy problem is avoided. If objectionable relief is awarded, on the other hand, the public policy issue can now be raised by an application to vacate the award or by way of resisting an application to confirm it.[27]

Public policy has its other side, too. In some areas, far from barring arbitration, it embraces the arbitral process almost with relief. This is notably the case in the labor area, where the Court of Appeals has said that "arbitration is so preferable a means of settling labor disputes that it can be said that public policy impels its use".[28]

A difficulty with this seemingly fervent embrace of arbitration is that it is not consistent; the courts are often ambivalent. Their ardor can appear in a labor dispute in the public sector in two different guises, on the one hand applauding the arbitral process for general use, but on the other precluding it from addressing a particular issue. Cohoes City School District v. Cohoes Teachers Association[29] is an example. It was a dispute between a teachers' union and a local school board, very much a labor dispute in the public sector, where the

18. See, e.g., Vogel v. Lewis, 25 A.D.2d 212, 268 N.Y.S.2d 237 (1st Dep't 1966), aff'd 19 N.Y.2d 589, 278 N.Y.S.2d 236, 224 N.E.2d 738 (1967).

19. Durst v. Abrash, 22 A.D.2d 39, 253 N.Y.S.2d 351 (1st Dep't 1964).

20. Nyack Board of Ed. v. Nyack Teachers Ass'n, 77 Misc.2d 116, 352 N.Y.S.2d 973 (Sup.Ct., Rockland County, 1974).

21. National Eqpt. Rental Ltd. v. American Pecco Corp., 28 N.Y.2d 639, 641, 320 N.Y.S.2d 248, 249, 269 N.E.2d 37, 38 (1971).

22. Schachter v. Lester Witte & Co., 52 A.D.2d 121, 383 N.Y.S.2d 316 (1st Dep't 1976), aff'd 41 N.Y.2d 1067, 396 N.Y.S.2d 175, 364 N.E.2d 840 (1977).

23. Matter of Sprinzen, 46 N.Y.2d 623, 415 N.Y.S.2d 974, 389 N.E.2d 456 (1979).

24. The mechanics of raising issues of arbitrability are treated later. See § 591.

25. See Meyers v. Kinney Motors, Inc., 32 A.D.2d 266, 301 N.Y.S.2d 171 (1st Dep't 1969).

26. Hirsch v. Hirsch, 37 N.Y.2d 312, 372 N.Y.S.2d 71, 333 N.E.2d 371 (1975).

27. See Port Washington Union Free School Dist. v. Port Washington Teachers Ass'n, 45 N.Y.2d 411, 408 N.Y.S.2d 453, 380 N.E.2d 280 (1978).

28. Associated Teachers of Huntington, Inc. v. Board of Ed., 33 N.Y.2d 229, 236, 351 N.Y.S.2d 670, 676, 306 N.E.2d 791, 796 (1973).

29. 40 N.Y.2d 774, 390 N.Y.S.2d 53, 358 N.E.2d 878 (1976).

courts have been plainly supportive of arbitration.[30] But the issue here was whether a board could cede to arbitration its power to determine a teacher's tenure after a probationary period. The court held that public policy precludes delegation of that issue, finding it "inescapably implicit" in the applicable statutes[31] that the issue be withheld from the arbitral process, whatever enthusiasm arbitration may excite for the realm in general.[32]

In a later case the Court of Appeals similarly voided, as against public policy, a provision in a collective bargaining agreement purporting to preclude a school board from inspecting a teacher's personnel files, permanently staying arbitration of the issue.[33] What appeared for a while to be a key case in the area, and perhaps an initial reference point, was Acting Superintendent of Schools of Liverpool Central School Dist. v. United Liverpool Faculty Ass'n,[34] in which the court would not allow arbitration of a dispute involving a teacher firing under a clause in a collective bargaining agreement. The basis was that the clause was ambiguous on whether the present dispute was within its terms. The court discussed the terms and purported to set a standard for determining whether a given employer-employee dispute in the public sector will be barred from arbitration by the public policy doctrine, but the court itself appeared to have some difficulty in applying the standard in similar cases afterwards. In South Colonie Central School District v. Longo, for example,[35] decided hardly a month after *Liverpool*, the court upheld arbitration of a similar issue. And a few months later still, the court handed down Binghamton Civil Service Forum v. City of Binghamton,[36] a case that makes it very difficult for courts to know where to draw the "public policy" line.

The court in *Binghamton* held that public policy was not violated by an arbitrator's overturning a mayor's dismissal of a municipal employee who had admitted bribery. If there is any substance at all in the notion that "public policy" can at some point tie an arbitrator's hands, it would seem that those hands should have been tied in the *Binghamton* case. If arbitration can prevent a mayor from firing a corrupt employee, it is difficult to understand how conduct manifestly less offensive can offend the sensibilities of "public policy"—as it is often found to do—and bar arbitration.

The court afterwards held in Matter of Blackburne,[37] a firing case involving the federal Hatch Act, that arbitration was barred by public policy because the agency involved was getting federal funds and that if it should fail to fire the employee for a violation of the act, the funding would be lost.

Are these decisions consistent? The court reached the conclusion it did in *Binghamton* because, it said, there was no specific state statute mandating dismissal and it was therefore open to the parties to leave the ultimate decision of the issue to an arbitrator. In another case less than a year later, Port Jefferson Station Teachers Ass'n v. Brookhaven–Comsewogue Union Free School Dist.,[38] the court said that "[o]nly when the award contravenes a strong public policy, almost invariably involving an important constitutional or statutory duty or responsibility, may it be set aside" on the public policy ground. "Incantations of 'public policy'", noted the court, "may not be advanced to overturn every arbitration award that impairs the flexibility of management" of a public entity.

A very specific constitutional or statutory statement on the matter at issue would always help determine what public policy would

30. Associated Teachers of Huntington, Inc. v. Board of Ed., note 28 above.

31. Educ.L. §§ 2501, 2509(2) & (7), 2573, 3012–3013, 6206; Civ.Serv.L. § 200 et seq.

32. 40 N.Y.2d at 778, 390 N.Y.S.2d at 56, 358 N.E.2d at 881.

33. Board of Education, Great Neck, U.F.S.D. v. Areman, 41 N.Y.2d 527, 394 N.Y.S.2d 143, 362 N.E.2d 943 (1977).

34. 42 N.Y.2d 509, 399 N.Y.S.2d 189, 369 N.E.2d 746 (1977).

35. 43 N.Y.2d 136, 400 N.Y.S.2d 798, 371 N.E.2d 516 (1977).

36. 44 N.Y.2d 23, 403 N.Y.S.2d 482, 374 N.E.2d 380 (1978).

37. 87 N.Y.2d 660, 642 N.Y.S.2d 160 (1996).

38. 45 N.Y.2d 898, 899, 411 N.Y.S.2d 1, 2 (1978).

say about submitting an issue to arbitration, but is it a sine qua non? Are there not matters that can be discerned as touching public policy without specific enumeration? Must a statute say specifically that a mayor can fire a corrupt employee before the mayor's right to do so can be cancelled by an arbitrator? Is it not "inescapably implicit"—the phrase the Court of Appeals used in the *Cohoes* case[39]—that the power to fire a corrupt employee is among a mayor's powers?

Sometimes the undoing of public policy through undue deference to arbitration can be the by-product of a procedural tangle in which the undoing process is just not clearly enough perceived. That may be what occurred in Harris v. Shearson Hayden Stone, Inc.,[40] discussed in the treatment of class actions earlier.[41] That was the case in which a brokerage house "floated" remittances to commodities customers, i.e., drew checks on distant banks to prolong collection (thereby prolonging as well the broker's retention of the high interest payable in the meantime). Class status for the aggrieved customers was rejected because all of them had signed contracts containing arbitration agreements. Having consented to arbitration, they were held to have waived the right to litigate and with it the right to bring a class action. But there is a public policy underlying the class action as well: that of seeing to it that a wrongdoer does not escape liability for a massive wrong to a great number of people merely because the economic interest of each would not support an individual action. That public policy was undermined by reading the

general arbitration commitment—contained in what amounted to adhesion contracts in the *Harris* case—to bar a class action. The dissent in *Harris* would have given the class action at least a start,[42] and, it is submitted, better implemented the several competing public policies involved.

§ 588. The Agreement to Arbitrate

Arbitration requires a written agreement, whether to submit a present controversy to arbitration or to submit a future one to arbitration, and the commitment to arbitrate is normally undertaken by both sides.[1] Some appellate division decisions had held that an arbitration clause giving only one side the right to elect arbitration would not be enforced for want of mutuality,[2] but the Court of Appeals held otherwise on that point in Sablosky v. Edward S. Gordon Co.[3] Stressing the benefits of arbitration and its emergence during the 1970s and 1980s "as a preferred method for the settlement of many controversies", the court held that as long as there is consideration for the overall contract, a provision giving only one side the call on whether a dispute goes to arbitration will be upheld.[4]

Except in the few instances when arbitration has been made mandatory or the right to demand it has been conferred by statute as an option on only one side,[5] the agreement is the source of the arbitrator's jurisdiction as well as that of the courts to enforce the obligation to arbitrate and to enter a judgment on the

---

39. Note 29 above.

40. 82 A.D.2d 87, 441 N.Y.S.2d 70 (1st Dep't 1981), aff'd 56 N.Y.2d 627, 450 N.Y.S.2d 482, 435 N.E.2d 1097 (1982).

41. See § 142 above.

42. The dissent's suggestions are noted in the discussion of the Harris case in § 142 above.

§ 588

1. CPLR 7501. An exception is compulsory arbitration, such as mandated between insurers under the no-fault law under 5105 of the Insurance Law. Compulsory arbitration is discussed in § 603 below.

2. See, e.g., Firedoor Corp. of America, Inc. v. R. K. & A. Jones, Inc., 47 A.D.2d 878, 366 N.Y.S.2d 443 (1st Dep't 1975).

3. 73 N.Y.2d 133, 538 N.Y.S.2d 513, 535 N.E.2d 643 (1989).

4. The employer, a brokerage firm in the Sablosky case, got the choice of forum option under a contract with one of its sales persons. The employee's arguments of unconscionability and adhesion contract were rejected.

5. Under the no-fault law applicable in the tort realm, for example, an insurer is required to give a claimant the option to seek certain benefits through arbitration but does not retain that option for itself. See Ins.L. § 5106(b). This provision was attacked for lacking mutuality, but it was held to violate nothing in the federal constitution. See Country–Wide Insurance Co. v. Harnett, 426 F.Supp. 1030 (S.D.N.Y.), aff'd 431 U.S. 934, 97 S.Ct. 2644, 53 L.Ed.2d 252 (1977).

award.[6]

To assure New York jurisdiction, it is best that the agreement specify New York as the place of the arbitration or otherwise authorize proceedings in New York. The choice of specific venue can be left to the arbitrator, however, such as by merely including in the agreement a reference to the arbitrator's own rules, should there be any with a venue direction. The standard arbitration clause of the American Arbitration Association ("AAA"), which has an extensive set of rules, is an example. AAA rules authorize the AAA to set the locale of the arbitration whenever the agreement is silent.[7]

A rule like that should ordinarily give the New York courts such jurisdiction as they need to compel the arbitration, i.e., to compel the parties to submit to arbitration at a locale selected by the AAA. If the AAA has not yet set a locale when the New York court's jurisdiction is invoked and the agreement does not specify New York, a showing of any New York contacts with the subject of the dispute or with the parties should suffice to confirm New York jurisdiction. Since we are assuming that a proceeding to test arbitrability has been brought in a New York court, we will also assume that there exist some New York contacts with the case to account for its New York presence. Indeed, the statute in point, CPLR 7502(a), seems to authorize New York jurisdiction to compel arbitration without any stated New York contacts at all, but a showing of at least a minimal New York nexus—sufficient in any event to justify the limited exercise of judicial jurisdiction needed to get the arbitration started (or stopped)—will avoid due process objections.[8]

If New York has a relationship to the parties or the transaction at issue, spelling out a basis

for a New York court's entertainment of arbitrability should not be hard. But on many occasions the New York courts have been called on to resolve arbitration-related questions arising in cases having almost all of their contacts with other states. This often occurs in the securities industry, for example, and has been addressed by lower courts in cases involving customer/broker contracts—cases that had virtually all of their roots outside New York but in which the customer contract called for arbitration before the NYSE (New York Stock Exchange) or the NASD (the National Association of Securities Dealers), both of which have their arbitration machinery, or at least their arbitration start-up machinery, in New York. Does a contract stipulation to NYSE or NASD arbitration alone suffice to permit a New York court to entertain threshold issues, i.e., an application to stay the arbitration, or compel it, or decide a time-related issue connected with it? The matter has yet to be definitively resolved by the Court of Appeals and in the meantime the caselaw is in conflict.[9]

Since so much can be accomplished when one is aware of potential problems in time to guard against them in the agreement itself, another thing the drafter might consider is whether the transaction on which the client is about to embark touches a state or nation not congenial to arbitration. If it does, the drafter can put into the contract not only a clause stipulating to arbitration in New York, but one directing that New York law be applied to all issues of arbitrability wherever they may be deemed to arise.[10]

The agreement to arbitrate "must be clear and direct, and must not depend upon implication, inveiglement or subtlety". Where a buyer sent an order form and the seller an acknowledgment form, only the latter having an arbitration clause—the buyer's form saying he is

---

6. CPLR 7501.

7. See the Commercial Arbitration Rules of the American Arbitration Association.

8. More detailed discussion of jurisdiction and venue is in § 591 below.

9. See Merrill Lynch v. Lauer, 49 F.3d 323 (7th Cir. 1995), and Merrill Lynch v. McLeod, 208 A.D.2d 81, 622 N.Y.S.2d 954 (1st Dep't 1995), and their discussion in the lead note in New York State Law Digest No. 423.

10. This will not guarantee that a jurisdiction hostile to arbitration—if that is where a question of arbitrability arises—will subordinate its laws to New York's. It may label the issue as exclusively "procedural" and apply its own rules automatically. But neither will the clause do any harm. See Quigley, Convention on Foreign Arbitral Awards, 58 A.B.A.J. 821 (1972).

bound only by what he signs but the seller's form saying the buyer's silence accepts the seller's terms—the court analogized this to the irresistible force meeting the immovable object and held the agreement too ambiguous to enforce.[11] This is a recurring issue in the textiles industry especially. The Court of Appeals held in Marlene Industries Corp. v. Carnac Textiles, Inc.[12] that a merchant may not rely on the small print in a document as a source of an arbitration commitment after sending the document as a confirmation of an oral agreement of sale; that it must be shown that both sides expressly assented to the arbitration commitment. Noting that arbitration waives the substantive and procedural law of the state, the court in Marlene says that "it would be unfair to infer such a significant waiver on the basis of anything less than a clear indication of intent".[13]

But there are many ways to agree. The agreement can be indirect as long as it is clear. Being a member of a group, such as a union, whose by-laws require arbitration of given disputes, or making a contract with such a group agreeing to be bound by its rules, can satisfy as the necessary "agreement".[14] If a contract with an arbitration clause is made by an organization to which an individual belongs and to which he cedes the right to contract in his behalf, he is bound by the arbitral process even though he did not individually accede to the contract and is in fact opposed to it. This is, again, an indispensable rule in the labor field, where any other conclusion would prevent any collective result from binding individual balkers.[15]

In a case that distinguishes Marlene, the Court of Appeals held that signing one confirmation form containing an arbitration clause will submit the signer to arbitrate under subsequent confirmation forms of the same series.[16] And when a sale is brokered, the broker's notes may commit both parties to arbitration with neither signing:

> [S]everal recent decisions by the New York Court of Appeals hold that when a sale of goods is negotiated by a broker who sends sales notes containing an arbitration clause to both parties, the broker is deemed to act for both parties. Although the parties do not expressly agree to arbitration and do not sign the broker's notes, the "buyer and seller nonetheless are bound to arbitrate in accordance with those documents when they merely retain them and proceed with the transaction".[17]

While the agreement must be "written", there is no requirement that it be signed.[18] It is sufficient if other proof exists that it is the agreement of the parties.[19]

A mere reference in a contract between A and B, which has no arbitration clause, to a contract between B and C, which has, will not require arbitration of disputes between A and B.[20] But when the parties' dealings have reference to their own earlier contracts, arbitration obligations can be traced back even if some of the links are oral. Hence an oral extension of an earlier written contract containing an arbitration clause also extends the clause.[21] Conversely, an oral agreement of sale, later confirmed by delivery of a purchase order containing the clause, at least between parties having a history of dealings in an in-

11. Application of Doughboy Industries, Inc., 17 A.D.2d 216, 220, 233 N.Y.S.2d 488, 493 (1st Dep't 1962).

12. 45 N.Y.2d 327, 408 N.Y.S.2d 410, 380 N.E.2d 239 (1978).

13. The Marlene case is the subject of a lead note in New York State Law Digest No. 226.

14. In re Willard Alexander, Inc., 31 N.Y.2d 270, 338 N.Y.S.2d 609, 290 N.E.2d 813 (1972).

15. See Antinore v. State, 49 A.D.2d 6, 371 N.Y.S.2d 213 (4th Dep't 1975), aff'd 40 N.Y.2d 921, 389 N.Y.S.2d 576, 358 N.E.2d 268 (1976).

16. Ernest J. Michel & Co. v. Anabasis Trade, Inc., 50 N.Y.2d 951, 431 N.Y.S.2d 459, 409 N.E.2d 933 (1980).

17. Graniteville Co. v. Star Knits of Cal., Inc., 680 F.Supp. 587 (S.D.N.Y.1988), quoting from Itoman (U.S.A.), Inc. v. Daewoo Corp., 68 N.Y.2d 925, 510 N.Y.S.2d 74, 502 N.E.2d 989 (1986).

18. Crawford v. Merrill Lynch, 35 N.Y.2d 291, 361 N.Y.S.2d 140, 319 N.E.2d 408 (1974).

19. Helen Whiting, Inc. v. Trojan Textile Corp., 307 N.Y. 360, 121 N.E.2d 367 (1954).

20. Hadjioannou v. Avramides, 40 N.Y.2d 929, 389 N.Y.S.2d 833, 358 N.E.2d 516 (1976).

21. Acadia Company v. Edlitz, 7 N.Y.2d 348, 197 N.Y.S.2d 457, 165 N.E.2d 411 (1960).

dustry whose custom is shown to do things this way, validates the obligation to arbitrate.[22] All the more clearly, of course, a written agreement without an arbitration clause but supplemental to a basic agreement containing one, especially when both are simultaneously executed and the relationship is plain, will extend the clause to disputes under the supplemental agreement.[23]

An assignee succeeding to the rights of an assignor may avail herself of an arbitration clause in the contract,[24] and is ordinarily bound by it.[25]

Municipalities and other governmental units can be bound by an arbitration commitment,[26] as can even the state itself.[27]

The arbitration clause can be broad or narrow. A "broad" one requires all disputes under the agreement to be arbitrated; a "narrow" one designates only specific issues for arbitration. An example of a broad clause is the AAA's standard one recommended for inclusion in commercial contracts, requiring submission to AAA arbitration of "any controversy or claim arising out of or relating to this contract, or the breach thereof".[28] Except for issues of the making of the contract and the timeliness of the claim, which are questions for the courts to answer,[29] a broad arbitration clause requires that virtually every other issue be submitted to the arbitrators. This means all disputes "logically connected with the agreement",[30] and it even leaves to the arbitrators

the decision of whether the contract has been terminated[31] or whether to terminate it now.[32] A broad clause may even be held to authorize the arbitrator to consider disputes existing before the agreement, at least when there is some connection between them and the subject matter of the present agreement.[33]

A narrow clause is potentially the more litigious because it involves the court in determining whether a given dispute is within the reduced scope of arbitration contemplated. Hence, where a liability insurance policy calls for arbitration only of issues of liability or damages, an issue of coverage, i.e., whether the policy applies in a given situation at all, is beyond arbitration altogether and must be heard and determined by a court.[34]

Analogous to a narrow clause is one that calls for arbitration of an issue only when a certain preliminary fact exists. This constitutes a condition precedent to arbitration and it is the court's job to determine whether the condition has been met. For example, where arbitration of the rental value of premises was called for only if a public taking occurred and if the taking did not "substantially interfere" with the conduct of a certain business, the court had to decide those issues before arbitration of the value issue could be ordered.[35]

Notwithstanding the narrowness of the arbitration clause, a voluntary submission by the parties, at the arbitration itself, of matters not

22. S. Kornblum Metals Co. v. Intsel Corp., 38 N.Y.2d 376, 379 N.Y.S.2d 826, 342 N.E.2d 591 (1976).

23. Dimson v. Elghanayan, 26 A.D.2d 442, 275 N.Y.S.2d 178 (1st Dep't 1966), rev'd on other grounds 19 N.Y.2d 316, 280 N.Y.S.2d 97, 227 N.E.2d 10 (1967).

24. S & L Vending Corp. v. 52 Thompkins Ave. Restaurant, 26 A.D.2d 935, 274 N.Y.S.2d 697 (2d Dep't 1966).

25. Blum's Inc. v. Ferro Union Corp., 36 A.D.2d 584, 318 N.Y.S.2d 414 (1st Dep't), aff'd 29 N.Y.2d 689, 325 N.Y.S.2d 418, 274 N.E.2d 751 (1971).

26. See Village of Brockport v. County of Monroe Pure Waters Div., 75 A.D.2d 483, 429 N.Y.S.2d 931 (4th Dep't 1980), aff'd 54 N.Y.2d 678, 442 N.Y.S.2d 510, 425 N.E.2d 898 (1981).

27. See Dormitory Auth. of the State of N.Y. v. Span Elec. Corp., 18 N.Y.2d 114, 271 N.Y.S.2d 983, 218 N.E.2d 693 (1966).

28. See the Commercial Arbitration Rules brochure of the American Arbitration Association.

29. See § 589 below.

30. Blum Folding Paper Box Co. v. Friedlander, 27 N.Y.2d 35, 38, 313 N.Y.S.2d 375, 377, 261 N.E.2d 382, 383 (1970).

31. Popular Publications, Inc. v. McCall Corp., 36 A.D.2d 927, 321 N.Y.S.2d 308 (1st Dep't 1971).

32. Coler v. GCA Corp., 39 A.D.2d 656, 331 N.Y.S.2d 938 (1st Dep't), aff'd 31 N.Y.2d 775, 339 N.Y.S.2d 104, 291 N.E.2d 385 (1972).

33. See Board of Education, Union Free School District No. 7 v. Great Neck Teachers Ass'n, 69 Misc.2d 1061, 332 N.Y.S.2d 326 (Sup.Ct., Nassau County), aff'd 40 A.D.2d 950, 338 N.Y.S.2d 400 (2d Dep't 1972).

34. See Vanguard Ins. Co. v. Polchlopek, 18 N.Y.2d 376, 275 N.Y.S.2d 515, 222 N.E.2d 383 (1966).

35. See Humble Oil & Refining Co. v. Civitano, 32 A.D.2d 670, 300 N.Y.S.2d 795 (2d Dep't 1969). Conditions precedent to arbitration are further elaborated in § 589 below.

within the clause, or for that matter not within the agreement at all, constitutes a waiver of arbitral limitations and an undertaking to be bound by what the arbitrator does with those issues.[36]

It may happen that a clause submits to arbitration only "questions of fact, as distinguished from questions of law", which the clause did in Instructional Television Corp. v. National Broadcasting Co.[37] The court had an interesting and helpful resolution in that situation. It held that the arbitrator should find the facts and then make a submission of the findings to the court pursuant to CPLR 3222.[38] The court would then apply the law and dispose of the whole case accordingly.

B. THRESHOLD QUESTIONS

Table of Sections

§ 589. Questions for Court; Arbitrability; "Separability"

There are normally only two issues a court can entertain when arbitration is in the picture. The first is the obvious question of whether the dispute is arbitrable, which can embrace such constituent issues as whether a valid agreement to arbitrate was made and complied with or whether, if the arbitration clause is a narrow one, the particular dispute is within it.[1] The second is whether the arbitration was timely sought, i.e., the statute of limitations, which in New York is generally a question for the court rather than for the arbitrators.[2] It has also been held that whether an issue has already been resolved by a prior arbitration—a question of res judicata—is also for the court to decide,[3] for which one justifying theory may be that if the matter has already been decided, there is nothing for any arbitration to handle. These are familiarly known as the "threshold" questions. If a threshold issue is properly raised, the arbitration cannot go forward unless and until it is resolved, and resolved in favor of arbitration.

The limitations question raises some special problems and is separately treated.[4] So are the mechanics of raising a threshold question.[5] The elements that make up "arbitrability" itself are the subject here.

Various elements go into it. The most obvious question is whether the party against whom arbitration is sought has committed itself to arbitration in the requisite writing. Since almost the whole arbitration process as well as the court's power to require it is jurisdictionally traceable to the contract, a showing that there is no contract will void arbitration and leave all issues, whatever they may be, to the courts. In this respect, however, we meet the so-called "separability" doctrine, adopted in New York in 1973 in Weinrott v. Carp.[6] It has to do with attempts to avoid arbitration by making technical attacks on the agreement containing the arbitration clause.

There are some objections to the contract that will necessarily void the whole of it, including the obligation to arbitrate. Duress or fraud in the execution will do it. A showing that the paper was signed at gunpoint, for example, or misrepresented to be just a chain letter praising springtime, will infiltrate every corner of the contract, voiding the arbitration

---

36. See United Buying Service International Corp. v. United Buying Svc. of Northeastern New York, Inc., 38 A.D.2d 75, 327 N.Y.S.2d 7 (1st Dep't 1971), aff'd 30 N.Y.2d 822, 334 N.Y.S.2d 911, 286 N.E.2d 284 (1972).

37. 45 A.D.2d 1004, 357 N.Y.S.2d 915, 916 (2d Dep't 1974).

38. The procedure under CPLR 3222 dispenses with pleadings and all of the other accouterments of an adversary action. See § 304 above.

§ 589

1. CPLR 7503(a).

2. CPLR 7502(b). This is in contrast with the Federal Arbitration Act, which leaves timeliness questions to the arbitrators. See § 607 below.

3. City of Rochester v. AFSCME, Local 1635, 54 A.D.2d 257, 388 N.Y.S.2d 489 (4th Dep't 1976). For further discussion of how the res judicata doctrine can appear in arbitration context, see § 598 below.

4. See § 590 below.

5. See § 591 below.

6. 32 N.Y.2d 190, 344 N.Y.S.2d 848, 298 N.E.2d 42 (1973).

clause along with everything else. But such defects are academic fodder. The objection that one actually sees raised as a way of getting out from under an agreement to arbitrate is that the party, although fully aware he was signing a contract, was inveigled into signing it on false premises—the ubiquitous objection of "fraud in the inducement". It is upon this that the *Weinrott* case works the "separability" doctrine, which applies when the arbitration clause is a broad one. The doctrine's theory is that whatever the motivations that led the party to make this bargain, the one item in the contract to which the party subscribed with eyes open is its arbitration clause. Thus, unless the fraudulent inducement can be demonstrated to touch the arbitration clause itself, the party's agreement to arbitrate will be deemed voluntary, sufficing to turn all the rest of the case over to the arbitrator—including the charge of fraud in respect of all the rest of the contract. To that extent the arbitration provision of the contract is "separable". If, so separated, the inducement charge cannot be shown to touch it directly, the party is remitted to the arbitrator for any other plaints under the contract. The "valid agreement" whose making CPLR 7503(a) authorizes the court to determine has been construed, in short, to mean "a valid agreement to arbitrate". By segregating the arbitration provision and testing its validity independently, it can be deemed valid "even if the substantive portions of the contract were induced by fraud".[7]

The courts were at least partly motivated in reaching for this separability rule by their experience with the law in its earlier state, which made the inducement issue easy to raise. Merely raising it often postponed arbitration indefinitely as the issue "laboriously worked its way through the New York court system".[8] This was of course at war with arbitration, a primary aim of which is expedition.

The separability doctrine had already been adopted by the U.S. Supreme Court for application under the Federal Arbitration Act,[9] which had had a similar experience with the problem.[10] Under both the federal and New York acts today the notion that anything affecting the "validity" of the contract must necessarily affect the arbitration clause as well is rejected. It is a question of intent, and if an intent can be spelled out sufficient to validate at least the arbitration provision in the contract, the arbitrator herself can be given the power to determine the validity of everything else.

A similar separability rule has since been applied to "duress" in the inducement as well. A claim of "economic duress" has the same potential for dilatory mischief as "fraud". Hence the matter, under a broad clause, should be left to the arbitrator.[11] Whether a similar separation can be worked out under a narrow clause will of course depend on its particular phraseology.

To some, it is theoretically awkward for an arbitrator, who needs a valid contract before she has power, to exercise the power needed to validate the contract. But it is quite analogous to a court finding that it has jurisdiction in a case, which courts do all the time. There has even been invented the doctrine of "jurisdiction to determine jurisdiction",[12] from which a court can draw just that mite of power sufficient to say whether it has power over the case in general. Hence there is nothing really unique about the separability doctrine.

Consistent with it, arbitrators, under broad arbitrability clauses, have been allowed to take a number of other steps affecting the viability of the contract that gives them the power. The issue of the "mutuality" of the contract can illustrate: its absence might void the contract in a court, and yet the issue will be left to the

---

7. Id. at 198, 344 N.Y.S.2d at 855, 298 N.E.2d at 47.

8. Id. at 199, 344 N.Y.S.2d at 856, 298 N.E.2d at 47.

9. See Prima Paint Corp. v. Flood & Conklin Mfg. Co., 388 U.S. 395, 87 S.Ct. 1801, 18 L.Ed.2d 1270 (1967); see also Robert Lawrence Co. v. Devonshire Fabrics, Inc., 271 F.2d 402 (2d Cir.1959). For a discussion of the federal act and its comparison with New York's, see § 607 below.

10. See Aksen, Prima Paint v. Flood & Conklin—What Does It mean?, 43 St. John's L.Rev. 1 (1968).

11. See Candid Productions, Inc. v. SFM Media Service Corp., 51 A.D.2d 943, 381 N.Y.S.2d 280 (1st Dep't 1976).

12. See, e.g., United States v. United Mine Workers of America, 330 U.S. 258, 67 S.Ct. 677, 91 L.Ed. 884 (1947).

arbitrators if the clause is broad. So held Exercycle Corporation v. Maratta,[13] a herald of the *Weinrott* case and the separability doctrine. It is further instructive to note the four categories of "exceptions" that *Exercycle* listed in 1961, in which the courts do intervene to bar an arbitration. Much has happened since that list was compiled, and half of it has not survived.

The first listed exception is fraud or duress rendering the agreement voidable. Today under *Weinrott* and its progeny the issues of fraud or duress in the inducement are left to the arbitrator.

The second is where there is no bona fide dispute between the parties—i.e., that the claim is frivolous. This was known as the *Cutler-Hammer* rule, after the case that applied it.[14] It has been overruled by the second sentence of CPLR 7501, which provides that "the court shall not consider whether the claim with respect to which arbitration is sought is tenable, or otherwise pass upon the merits of the dispute". Even frivolity today is left for the arbitrators to decide; the Court of Appeals has said that "a claim need not be tenable in order to be arbitrable".[15] Down went the second item on the *Exercycle* list.

The third is where the performance sought in the demand for arbitration is prohibited by statute. This is the "public policy" objection, discussed earlier,[16] which survives and may even be said to be expanding in proportion to the expansion of arbitration itself.

The fourth and final exception listed in *Exercycle* is where a condition precedent to the arbitration has not been carried out. This ordinarily continues to be a matter for the court to decide,[17] which gives *Exercycle* a 50% batting

average today—its first two exceptions gone by the boards but the second two still up.

An illustration of where a condition precedent must be fulfilled before an obligation to arbitrate arises is sometimes met in the tort sphere today, where arbitration is relatively new. Whether a given tortfeasor is insured, for example, as in an uninsured motorist case, may have to be decided by a court before arbitration can be ordered of issues of liability and damages.[18]

The issue of whether a condition precedent has been satisfied is for the court to decide only if it is clear that a condition precedent exists. If the issue is *whether* it does, and this turns, as it likely will, on a construction of the contract, the matter will be left to the arbitrator. In that situation, in fact, the arbitrator will also be allowed to decide if the condition—should she determine that there is one—has been fulfilled.[19]

The Court of Appeals has endeavored to set down a kind of formula for determining who as between court and arbitrator determines whether a condition precedent to arbitration has been fulfilled. It said in United Nations Development Corp. v. Norkin Plumbing Co.[20] that a distinction must first be made between statutory and contractual conditions precedent. The statutory one is for the court to decide. With the contractual one, a further examination must be made into whether the arbitration clause is broad or narrow. If it is narrow, which evinces an intent not to have arbitration resolve everything, i.e., it shows an intent to restrict arbitration to stated issues, satisfaction of a condition precedent will usually be for the court to decide. But with a broad arbitration clause, compliance will ordinarily be for the arbitration to resolve unless the

13. 9 N.Y.2d 329, 214 N.Y.S.2d 353, 174 N.E.2d 463 (1961).

14. International Ass'n of Machinists v. Cutler–Hammer, Inc., 297 N.Y. 519, 74 N.E.2d 464 (1947).

15. Nationwide General Ins. Co. v. Investors Ins. Co. of America, 37 N.Y.2d 91, 96, 371 N.Y.S.2d 463, 467, 332 N.E.2d 333, 336 (1975).

16. See § 587.

17. See Opan Realty Corp. v. Pedrone, 36 N.Y.2d 943, 373 N.Y.S.2d 549, 335 N.E.2d 854 (1975).

18. See, e.g., Matter of Motor Vehicle Accident Indemnification Corp. v. Malone, 16 N.Y.2d 1027, 265 N.Y.S.2d 906, 213 N.E.2d 316 (1965).

19. Pearl Street Development Corp. v. Conduit and Foundation Corp., 41 N.Y.2d 167, 391 N.Y.S.2d 98, 359 N.E.2d 693 (1976).

20. 45 N.Y.2d 358, 408 N.Y.S.2d 424, 380 N.E.2d 253 (1978).

contract "expressly" makes compliance with a given requirement of the contract a condition precedent, in which event the court rather than the arbitrator gets the question.

The court must also look into the purpose of the condition precedent, to see whether the condition is still relevant. In one case involving a construction contract, for example,[21] the contract called for arbitration, but it segregated issues involving the progress of the work and required that these issues be first submitted to the project's architect for resolution. Two years after the project's completion, an issue arose about whether the owner's delays had damaged the contractor. Since the purpose of the submission to the architect was to avoid delays in the work, the fact that the project was now completed manifested that a delay in the progress of the work would no longer be threatened by a submission of the case to arbitration. Arbitration was therefore ordered, including arbitration of the condition precedent issue.[22]

Consistent with the separability doctrine, as applied to the contract's initial validity, is the arbitrator's power to undo the contract at later stages without simultaneously undoing his own power to undo. Under a broad clause, therefore, the arbitrator can rescind the contract,[23] or reform it,[24] or find that it has been terminated[25] or abandoned.[26] It is no more necessary that a court determine every issue of the contract's continuance than it is for a court to determine every issue of its initial validity.

A variation on the "separability" theme occurred in Primex International Corp. v. Wal–Mart Stores, Inc.,[27] in which, over a period of several years, W and B made three contracts, in each of which B was to act as a buyer for W, which owned a chain of stores. The first two contracts had an arbitration clause; the third didn't. W later sued B in a court action for cheating in transactions falling under all three contract periods, contending that arbitration was not required because the last contract abrogated the arbitration clause. The Court of Appeals rejected the argument, holding that merely because the third contract had a "merger" clause, superseding the substantive provisions of the earlier contracts, this would not affect the arbitration clause in the earlier contracts without a specific indication of intent to do so, and that was lacking here. The court remanded the case to have the various disputed transactions parsed, with those falling under the first two contracts to be left to arbitration and with the court allowed to entertain only the claims arising under the third contract.

A question of arbitrability can arise in connection with a counterclaim or any other claim among the parties. The threshold questions can be addressed to the claim in whatever form it appears, and resolved accordingly.[28] It is also possible that while one claim is legitimately before the arbitrators, the claimant may, by way of amendment, seek to interpose yet another—a matter reserved for later treatment.[29]

§ 590. Statute of Limitations as Applied to Arbitration

As a general rule, the same statute of limitations applicable to a litigable claim is applicable to an arbitrable one. And as shown in the prior section, under New York law the question of the timeliness of an arbitration is in general for the court to decide. When a timeliness issue arises, it is usually with respect to a dispute arising under a contract agreeing to

---

21. County of Rockland v. Primiano Constr. Co., 51 N.Y.2d 1, 431 N.Y.S.2d 478, 409 N.E.2d 951 (1980).

22. Id.

23. See Coler v. GCA Corp., 39 A.D.2d 656, 331 N.Y.S.2d 938 (1st Dep't 1972).

24. See SCM Corp. v. Fisher Park Lane Co., 40 N.Y.2d 788, 390 N.Y.S.2d 398, 358 N.E.2d 1024 (1976).

25. See Popular Publications, Inc. v. McCall Corp., 36 A.D.2d 927, 321 N.Y.S.2d 308 (1st Dep't 1971).

26. See R.H. Macy & Co., Inc. v. National Sleep Products, Inc., 39 N.Y.2d 268, 383 N.Y.S.2d 562, 347 N.E.2d 887 (1976).

27. 89 N.Y.2d 594, 657 N.Y.S.2d 385 (1997).

28. See, e.g., Aimcee Wholesale Corp. v. Tomar Products, 21 N.Y.2d 621, 289 N.Y.S.2d 968, 237 N.E.2d 223 (1968).

29. See § 599 below.

arbitrate a future controversy[1] and the situation is one in which one side is seeking arbitration and the other resisting it. In that instance, the party seeking arbitration serves on the other side a "demand for arbitration" or a "notice of intention to arbitrate". The claim is deemed interposed upon that service.[2]

The "demand" is met in several contexts, mainly under CPLR 7503(c), which is also the abode of the "notice of intention to arbitrate". CPLR 7503(c) enables a party seeking arbitration to compel the other side to promptly raise any objections it may have to arbitration or else be deemed to have waived them. This is a key juncture of judicial involvement in compelling arbitration and is studied in depth later.[3] For the moment we merely note that CPLR 7503(c) authorizes service of the "demand" or "notice" either in the manner of a summons or by mail (registered or certified), and that when mail is used the claim is apparently deemed interposed, and the statute of limitations tolled, when the mail is posted rather than when it is received.[4]

Although the general rule is that the applicable period will be culled from the same body of statutes that govern in an action, it has been recognized that a rigid search for the appropriate period can in a given case force the claim into an inflexible legal mold—most periods of limitation are determined by the nature of the substantive claim asserted—and that this can frustrate the arbitral process, which is designed to escape that kind of rigidity. The major pronouncement on the point is Paver & Wildfoerster v. Catholic High School Association,[5] in which the Court of Appeals held that the courts should not, in statute of limitations guise, bind the case to the technical rules of law that arbitration is designed to avoid; that a court should hold an otherwise arbitrable claim time barred only if the claim "on no view of the facts could survive a time-bar in any kind of action at law".[6] If, in other words, several alternative theories can reasonably or perhaps only colorably be cited in support of the claim, and any of them carries a limitation period still alive, the courts should sustain the claim as timely, at least to the extent of sending the whole case off to arbitration and letting the arbitrator take it from there, the timeliness question included.

In *Paver*, the claim was against an architect for property damage sounding in both contract (which in an action gets six years[7]) and tort (which in an action gets three years[8]), a situation troublesome in litigation[9] but whose trouble, it was felt, should not be inflicted on arbitrators, too. The court said that the purpose of CPLR 7502(b), the provision governing statute of limitations issues in arbitration, is "to bar stale claims, not to fragmentize claims into legal categories, the very categories from which arbitration frees those who choose arbitration as their mode of dispute determination".[10]

If a period of limitations comes from the agreement of the parties instead of from a statute (which would be the case if the agreement stipulates a shorter period than the statute does), the issue of timeliness is for the arbitrator rather than the courts.[11] The rea-

---

§ 590

1. When a submission is being made of an existing controversy, the less frequent circumstance, the submission "is deemed to embrace all issues of fact and law with reference to the controversies submitted" to arbitration, and this is deemed to embrace as well a question of timeliness. It is hence for the arbitrators to decide timeliness questions if they should arise in that context. Cohen v. Cohen, 17 A.D.2d 279, 233 N.Y.S.2d 787 (1st Dep't 1962).

2. CPLR 7502(b).

3. See § 593 below.

4. See Knickerbocker Ins. Co. v. Gilbert, 28 N.Y.2d 57, 66, 320 N.Y.S.2d 12, 18, 268 N.E.2d 758, 763 (1971). The cautious plaintiff would do best to act early enough so that the mail is also received within the applicable period.

5. 38 N.Y.2d 669, 382 N.Y.S.2d 22, 345 N.E.2d 565 (1976).

6. Id. at 678, 382 N.Y.S.2d at 27, 345 N.E.2d at 570.

7. CPLR 213(2).

8. CPLR 214(4).

9. See the distinction made in Paver, 38 N.Y.2d at 676, 382 N.Y.S.2d at 26, 345 N.E.2d at 569, of Sosnow v. Paul, 36 N.Y.2d 780, 369 N.Y.S.2d 693, 330 N.E.2d 643 (1975), aff'g 43 A.D.2d 978, 352 N.Y.S.2d 502 (2d Dep't 1974).

10. 38 N.Y.2d at 677, 382 N.Y.S.2d at 26, 345 N.E.2d at 570.

11. City School District of the City of Poughkeepsie v. Poughkeepsie Public School Teachers Ass'n, Inc., 35 N.Y.2d 599, 364 N.Y.S.2d 492, 324 N.E.2d 144 (1974).

soning is that a provision contained in the agreement involves a construction of the agreement and is best left to the arbitrator.[12] In this connection it should be stressed that the agreement, if it would set its own time limit, should set a reasonable one. CPLR 7502(b) adopts Article 2 of the CPLR as the criterion of timeliness, and while CPLR 201 allows a writing to set a period shorter than the otherwise applicable statutory one, caselaw holds that the period stipulated must be reasonable. If it is unreasonable, it will be disregarded, leaving the statutory one in charge,[13] but the issue of reasonableness should be brought to the court's attention and preserved as an objection. In one case an arbitration was barred because it was not brought within a stipulated five-day period, while an action on the claim was barred because it was arbitrable. All doors were closed, in other words, because of the time barrier—which was so short, however, that the court hinted strongly that it would have been disregarded as unreasonably harsh had an unreasonableness issue been raised and preserved.[14]

If a limitations objection is not raised in court, it may be presented to the arbitrator, whose ruling on it will then be accorded the same respect the merits are.[15]

An entirely separate limitations question is this: what happens when an arbitration is timely commenced but the claim is ultimately, and after a substantial interim, found not arbitrable? For purposes of the ordinary action that is now to be brought, the whole period of the arbitrability test is deemed to toll—stop the running of—the statute of limitations, thus helping assure the timeliness of the later action.[16]

Near the end of this chapter a comparison is made between the Federal Arbitration Act and New York's.[17] One of the things to take note of there is that under the federal act all timeliness questions go to the arbitrator. Another is that it may well happen that because of the subject matter involved, the arbitrability of an issue appearing in a New York action will be governed by the federal act. When that happens, all timeliness issues, whether statutory or contractual, are for the arbitrator,[18] while if the New York act is found to govern, some of them may be for the court.[19]

C.   COURT APPLICATIONS

Table of Sections

§ 591.   Court Applications Generally; Form; Venue

There are several issues the courts may pass on in conjunction with the arbitral process. We have already noted that the "threshold" questions are in this category—the issues of whether the dispute is arbitrable and whether the arbitration has been sought within the applicable period of limitations. Other occasions on which court involvement may become necessary appear after the arbitration has gone to award, and include applications to confirm, vacate, or modify the award.[1] CPLR 7502(a) prescribes the form that all of these applications are required to take, and supplies the venue for them.

It may happen that an arbitration-related issue will arise in a pending action, such as

---

12. See Long Island Lumber Co. v. Martin, 15 N.Y.2d 380, 259 N.Y.S.2d 142, 207 N.E.2d 190 (1965).

13. See § 39 above.

14. See River Brand Rice Mills, Inc. v. Latrobe Brewing Co., 305 N.Y. 36, 110 N.E.2d 545 (1953).

15. CPLR 7502(b).

16. CPLR 204(b). See the end of § 592 below.

17. See § 607.

18. See A/S J. Ludwig Mowinckels Rederi v. Dow Chemical Co., 25 N.Y.2d 576, 307 N.Y.S.2d 660, 255 N.E.2d 774 (1970).

19. See § 589; Smith Barney v. Luckie, 85 N.Y.2d 193, 623 N.Y.S.2d 800 (1995), discussed in the lead note in New York State Law Digest No. 423.

§ 591

1. See § 601 below.

where the aggrieved person, in disregard of an obligation to arbitrate, brings an ordinary action on the claim. In that instance the action itself furnishes context enough for a court application to compel arbitration, and so it takes the form of an ordinary motion made within the action.[2] An advantage in this situation is that the motion papers can be served, as in any action, by ordinary mail addressed to the parties' attorneys.[3]

The granting of a motion to compel arbitration results only in a stay of the action, not a dismissal.[4] A dismissal of an action brought in violation of an obligation to arbitrate does not occur until the arbitration has gone to an award. Only at that point does a dismissal motion on this ground lie.[5]

When no action is pending—the more frequent situation—the first court application connected with the arbitrable controversy, if court involvement is necessary, takes the form of a special proceeding. Should any further application to the court be necessary in connection with the dispute, the indication of CPLR 7502(a) is that it should take the form of a motion made within that proceeding, but the Court of Appeals held in Solkav v. Besicorp Group Inc.,[6] at least in respect of a post-award application to confirm the award, that a separate special proceeding is needed.[7]

If any specific procedures are prescribed for the special proceeding, as in some of the steps set forth in CPLR 7503 to be met in upcoming sections, they of course govern. In the absence of special directions, the general provisions of Article 4 govern procedure in the special proceeding.[8]

The venue of the special proceeding is also governed by CPLR 7502(a).[9] The statute seems to contemplate that the special proceeding may be brought in any court, but in practice it

is almost invariably brought in the supreme court.[10] We will assume that the proceeding is to be brought in the supreme court and the inquiry will be into the proper county of venue.

If the agreement selects a county, it will ordinarily be accepted as proper venue. If the agreement is silent, proper venue is the county where any one of the parties resides or does business. If the arbitration has already taken place, as is the case when the proceeding is brought to confirm or vacate an award, a further venue alternative is the county where the arbitration has already been held. These are a generous assortment, and the choice is presumably the petitioner's—the one who brings the special proceeding. But even if the list in a given instance proves expansive, and offers a variety of venue choices, the petitioner should choose a venue appropriate to the case. The courts do not look with favor on applications in counties far removed from where the arbitration is to take place.[11] The proceeding might also be subjected to a change of venue, but, while this is permissible,[12] it is not a popular remedy because it delays the prompt determination of arbitrability questions.

If there is no proper county of venue by any of the criteria set forth above, liberal though the list be, CPLR 7502(a) has in store its most generous gesture of all: it permits the proceeding to be brought "in any county". As one may guess, dependence on this presumably limitless generosity is not frequent. If the case is one in which the agreement does not fix a New York venue and no party at all has a residential or business contact with New York, it is not likely that the New York courts will be called on to aid the arbitration.

---

2. CPLR 7503(a), 7502(a).

3. See CPLR 2103(b).

4. CPLR 7503(a). See American Reserve Ins. Co. v. China Ins. Co., 297 N.Y. 322, 79 N.E.2d 425 (1948).

5. CPLR 3211(a)(5).

6. 91 N.Y.2d 482, 672 N.Y.S.2d 838 (1998).

7. See the discussion of the Solkav case in the lead note in New York State Law Digest No. 462.

8. See § 550 et seq., above.

9. The venue referred to here is that of a court application, not of the arbitration itself, whose venue is generally left to the arbitrator to decide. See § 597 below.

10. The jurisdiction of other courts to entertain the proceeding is discussed in § 606 below.

11. See Bauer v. Motor Vehicle Accident Indem. Corp., 31 A.D.2d 239, 296 N.Y.S.2d 675 (4th Dep't 1969).

12. See CPLR 510, 511, 103(b).

Even though CPLR 7502(a) offers the proceeding a venue, it does not insulate it from a forum non conveniens dismissal, for which there is precedent even in the arbitrability context.[13] Some special circumstances should be shown in that situation—as must be shown in an ordinary action when it is seemingly devoid of New York contacts[14]—before the court exercises jurisdiction.

All of this discussion of venue assumes that the court has personal jurisdiction over the respondent against whom the proceeding is brought. In determining whether it has, the court should be able to apply the same jurisdictional principles that govern in an action—including longarm jurisdiction under CPLR 302 and any other basis that would avail in an action. This is not often a problem. Presumably, if no party has a residential or business nexus with the state, the agreement itself will specify New York as the situs of the arbitration or subscribe to rules that would permit the arbitrator to, and that by itself should suffice as a kind of consensual submission to the jurisdiction of a New York court to determine arbitrability issues. And it would supply personal jurisdiction. The Court of Appeals has also noted the question of whether rem jurisdiction, such as the quasi in rem use of an attachment of the respondent's property, would be jurisdictionally available to support a special proceeding to compel arbitration, but did not pass on it.[15]

Perhaps the most common context posing the issue of where the New York court system gets its jurisdiction when the parties and the transaction in the particular case have had almost all of their contacts with other states is in controversies within the securities industry. The matter is a thorny one still in need of definitive resolution by the Court of Appeals.[16] Keep in mind that we have merely assumed the jurisdiction here, concentrating instead on the less challenging issue of proper venue within the system.

There are several contexts for raising the threshold questions of arbitrability and timeliness. The plaintiff who wants arbitration can bring a proceeding to compel it. Alternatively, she can throw the initiative onto the other side, the party opposing arbitration, and require that party to bring a proceeding to determine arbitrability. Another possibility is that the plaintiff may be the one resisting arbitration, in which case she may just bring an ordinary action on the claim, ignoring the agreement to arbitrate, which will require the defendant to act. In each of these situations the procedural steps vary, but there are steps available in all contexts. The ensuing sections study the variations.

§ 592. Applying to Compel or Stay Arbitration; CPLR 7503(a) and (b)

CPLR 7503, a key provision in the New York law of arbitration, contemplates three different situations: subdivision (a) is the application to "compel" arbitration; subdivision (b) is the application to "stay" it; and subdivision (c), entitled "notice of intention to arbitrate", is the provision whereby the party seeking arbitration can throw onto the other side the burden of applying to the court to determine arbitrability. Subdivision (c), in other words, is a way of requiring that the party resisting arbitration promptly make an application under subdivision (b). The ultimate purpose of all three provisions is the same: to secure from the court a determination of whether arbitration is required, i.e., of the so-called "threshold" questions. Subdivision (c), a prolific generator of caselaw, is taken up separately in the next section. The present section addresses the rest of CPLR 7503.

In several situations a party may wish to compel arbitration under subdivision (a). If P, the party with a grievance, wants it arbitrated, but the other side, D, has indicated that he will not submit to arbitration, subdivision (a)

---

13. See Hadjioannou v. Avramides, 40 N.Y.2d 929, 389 N.Y.S.2d 833, 358 N.E.2d 516 (1976).

14. See § 28 above.

15. Hadjioannou v. Avramides, note 13, above. Quasi in rem jurisdiction is treated in § 104, above. For further

discussion of jurisdictional bases for a New York proceeding to test arbitrability, see § 588, above.

16. See the discussion in the lead note in New York State Law Digest No. 423.

authorizes P to take the initiative and bring a court proceeding to compel arbitration. P does not have to; P can simply initiate the arbitration and proceed with it. But if P does that, and D does not participate in the arbitration, any award P gets will be insecure for the reason that when P applies to confirm the award, D will be permitted to resist it by showing that arbitration was not called for in the first place.[1] In other words, the threshold questions remain available to D when P, foregoing an early test of arbitrability, just proceeds with arbitration and D does not participate in it.

If P does bring a proceeding to compel arbitration, however, and prevails in it, D's failure to participate in the arbitration is at his own risk. In that situation, D is foreclosed from later resisting the award based on the threshold questions: D is bound by the determination that the dispute was arbitrable.[2] Yet another alternative for P in this situation, to be elaborated in the next section, is to serve a notice of intention to arbitrate on D under subdivision (c) and shift the onus of a court proceeding to him.

Another variation on the theme is this: P may not be the one with a grievance. D may be the one with a claim, but suppose that, in disregard of the obligation to arbitrate, D has brought an ordinary action on her claim against P. P's remedy in that situation is also under subdivision (a): P applies to "compel" arbitration. If the application is granted, it automatically operates as a stay of D's action. Here, since a pending action furnishes appropriate context for the application, it takes the form of a mere motion to compel arbitration rather than an independent special proceeding.[3]

The notion that the court will "compel" the arbitration can be misleading. Although even the caption of subdivision (a) is "application to compel arbitration", it does not give rise to the usual court "injunction" one might expect when "compel" is the word used. Nor does it have to. In the present situation, for example, a successful application by P to "compel" arbitration accomplishes its goal when it results in an automatic stay of D's action. D in the present example is the one with a grievance, and if D does not voluntarily turn now to the arbitral process, she will simply find herself with no remedy at all, a situation that P is likely to find congenial. In this situation, in other words, P does not really want to compel arbitration; he merely wants to preclude litigation.[4] So effective is the stay of the action, as a way of getting the one who brought it to pursue her remedy in arbitration instead, that it has even been held improper for the court, in its dispositive order, to grant leave to move to vacate the stay if the arbitration is not timely sought. If D, who brought the now-stayed action, does not want to pursue arbitration, it is no skin off P's nose. It would be awkward to require P, who as the defendant in D's action successfully brought on the application to "compel" arbitration, to initiate the arbitration and lay out what might be a substantial filing fee, when it is D, not P, who fancies that she has a dispute needing resolution.[5]

The remedy for an action brought in contravention of a commitment to arbitrate is merely a stay of it, not a dismissal, which does not occur until an award is made.[6] This "stay" result of CPLR 7503(a) has been held to put a freeze on the action at whatever point it has reached. The Court of Appeals held in American Reserve Insurance Co. v. China Insurance Co.[7] that even an attachment of the defendant's assets secured in the action remains in effect with whatever it has accomplished at the moment the stay is entered, but stressed that should the plaintiff fail to proceed to arbitration, thereby keeping the defendant's assets

---

§ 592

1. CPLR 7511(b)(2). See § 602 below.

2. Compare paragraph 1 of CPLR 7511(b) with paragraph 2. See § 602 below.

3. CPLR 7503(a), 7502(a).

4. See Marillo v. Shearson Hayden Stone Inc., 159 A.D.2d 1012, 552 N.Y.S.2d 730 (4th Dep't 1990).

5. See Adelphi Enterprises, Inc. v. Mirpa, Inc., 33 A.D.2d 1019, 307 N.Y.S.2d 978 (2d Dep't 1970).

6. CPLR 3211(a)(5).

7. 297 N.Y. 322, 79 N.E.2d 425 (1948).

attached in the stayed action indefinitely, the defendant could apply to the court for an order vacating the attachment "in its discretion".[8]

If the action brought in violation of an agreement to arbitrate is brought outside New York, it will of course be beyond the power of a New York court to affect it with a simple stay. In that instance, as long as New York is the place agreed on for arbitration, the court can issue an outright injunction enjoining the violating party—the plaintiff in the foreign action—from proceeding with it. This recognizes that a refusal to grant such an injunction would enable a party to avoid the agreement to arbitrate through the simple expedient of bringing an action elsewhere.[9] There is some indication, however, that if the contract's calling for arbitration in New York is the state's sole nexus with the case—all other contacts, including even the residence of the witnesses, being with a sister state or foreign country— an injunction precluding maintenance of an action in that place may be denied on forum non conveniens grounds without prejudice to applying, there, to compel arbitration.[10] If the New York court has jurisdiction of the foreign plaintiff, however, as apparently it has (or the stage even for a mere conveniens objection would not be set), perhaps it would be more consistent with the purpose of arbitration to entertain the application, enjoining the action and compelling arbitration if arbitrability is found, and leaving it to the arbitrator, when he determines where the arbitration itself is to take place,[11] to assess the conveniens factor. An arguable issue of whether a party agreed to conduct an arbitration in New York, in other words, may reasonably be held to supply at

least sufficient nexus to neutralize the conveniens objection and get the arbitrability question to prompt adjudication in a New York court.

Everything said above is built around subdivision (a) of CPLR 7503, the application to compel arbitration. Subdivision (b) is the application to stay the arbitration. Here the one against whom a claim is asserted—the potential defendant in an action—maintains that it is litigable, not arbitrable. Under subdivision (b), he takes the initiative of bringing the threshold questions to court with a special proceeding to stay arbitration.[12] Two situations should be recognized.

In the first, P, the party with a claim, has gone ahead with arbitration. D, the adverse party who contends that the dispute is not arbitrable, has been notified of the arbitration by a general demand or other informal procedure. Now D has two alternatives. The first is that D can bring a threshold proceeding under subdivision (b) to stay the arbitration and get an early determination of arbitrability in time to participate in the arbitration if the stay is not granted. The second alternative—available only if D does not participate in the arbitration[13]—is to save the threshold objections to interpose by way of resisting an award, should there be one, when judicial confirmation of it is sought later. The latter course is really not advisable because if D loses on those issues when they are raised so belatedly, D will have forfeited the right to participate in the arbitration on the merits. It is entirely up to D, though. D does have the option, in this first

---

8. Id. at 327, 79 N.E.2d at 427. An interesting point about the American Reserve case is that at the time of its decision, an attachment was not available even in conjunction with an already pending arbitration. A 1985 amendment adding subdivision (c) to CPLR 7502 makes it available, however, see § 599 below, giving the determination of the American Reserve case even a stronger base now than it had when decided.

9. See H. M. Hamilton & Co., Inc. v. American Home Assurance Co., 21 A.D.2d 500, 251 N.Y.S.2d 215 (1st Dep't), aff'd 15 N.Y.2d 595, 255 N.Y.S.2d 262, 203 N.E.2d 649 (1964).

10. See AAACON Auto Transport, Inc. v. Feldman, 77 Misc.2d 120, 353 N.Y.S.2d 851 (Sup.Ct., N.Y. County, 1973).

11. CPLR 7506(b). See § 597 below.

12. Remember that when the special proceeding is brought in the supreme court, it is the filing of the initiatory papers, not their service, that marks commencement of the proceeding, the service to follow. Procedure in special proceedings generally is discussed in § 550 above, and the application of the filing system in special proceedings is more specifically treated in § 553 above. The system's actual application in an arbitrability case (the Newkirk case) can be seen in § 593 following.

13. CPLR 7511(b)(2). See § 602 below.

situation we are discussing, of saving the threshold objections until the end.

In yet another situation, it becomes *mandatory* for D to bring the proceeding to stay arbitration because here D does not have the option of saving the threshold objections for later. This is the situation, perhaps the most common one, in which P exploits the formal procedures of subdivision (c) of CPLR 7503, throwing the burden of bringing the proceeding onto D. The procedures of subdivision (c) are taken up in the next section.

The party who would stay the arbitration must note that the arbitration is not stayed merely upon the bringing of a special proceeding or the making of a motion for a stay, as happened under prior law (where the making of the application worked an automatic stay). Under the CPLR, the arbitration will not be in any wise impeded until a stay is granted by a court. The arbitration can therefore go forward while the CPLR 7503(b) application for a stay is pending. In Ahern Painting Contractors, Inc. v. District Council,[14] for example, it did go forward, producing an award of more than $28,000 by default, which the court confirmed. The court hinted that if a copy of the petition in the stay proceeding had at least been served on the arbitrator, or a request for an adjournment had been addressed to him, the result might have been otherwise. In practice, arbitrators so advised will usually postpone the arbitration voluntarily. If a given arbitrator will not, the applicant can seek the stay from the court with an order to show cause,[15] asking the court to include in the order a temporary stay and seeing to it that a copy of the order is promptly served on the arbitrator as well as the other parties.

The temporary stay included in the order to show cause operates from the moment it is served until the court can hear and dispose of the application that the order brings on. If the application to stay arbitration is then granted,

a regular CPLR 7503(b) stay will take over, barring arbitration (but permitting litigation of the claim if the claimant wants to sue); if it is denied, arbitration can proceed and litigation will be barred.

There may even be occasion for a court to invoke its general stay powers under CPLR 2201, independent of CPLR 7503(a), in order to stay an action in deference to arbitration. In one case, for example,[16] in which employee E sued employer R to recover wages, R maintained that the action should be stayed because R had a contract with E's union requiring the arbitration of the claim. CPLR 7503(a) was deemed unavailable as the source of the stay, however, because it authorizes a stay only when issued to "compel" arbitration, and arbitration could not be compelled in this case: it could not be compelled against the employee because he was not a party to the arbitration-requiring contract with R (the union was), nor could it be compelled against the union because it was not a party to the action. Yet it was inappropriate to let the action proceed in violation of the union/employer contract, by which E was bound. The court's answer: a stay of the action under the court's general stay power conferred by CPLR 2201.[17]

Two final points. One on the statute of limitations and one on preserving an arbitrability determination for an appeal.

The period during which arbitrability questions are being determined by the courts is not part of the running of the statute of limitations applicable to an action if, upon an ultimate holding that the dispute is not arbitrable, litigation becomes necessary. The tolled period runs from the time an initial "demand" for arbitration is served[18] until a "final determination" is made that there is no requirement to arbitrate. A toll under this provision, however, cannot extend the time in which to commence an action to more than one year from that determination.[19]

---

14. 141 A.D.2d 791, 530 N.Y.S.2d 21 (2d Dep't 1988).

15. CPLR 403(d), 2214(d).

16. Heimlich v. Charlton Lithographing, Inc., 103 Misc.2d 741, 428 N.Y.S.2d 127 (Sup.Ct., N.Y. County, 1979).

17. See § 255 above.

18. For discussion of what a "demand" for arbitration is, see § 593 following.

Between this and the prior section we have noted several contexts in which a question of arbitrability can arise. Whatever the context, if the order directs arbitration and the aggrieved person wants the order reviewed, it should be appealed forthwith. Going ahead with the arbitration and then trying to get the order reviewed as part of an appeal from a judgment confirming an unfavorable award on the merits will not work. An order compelling arbitration has been held to be a final one by the Court of Appeals,[20] and this holds consequences under the statute governing the scope of review on appeal. The statute, CPLR 5501(a)(1),[21] preserves for review as part of a final judgment only a nonfinal order that necessarily affects the judgment. An order compelling arbitration affects the judgment, but it is a final order when made and therefore does not qualify for the delayed review permissible only for nonfinal orders.[22]

Those resisting an arbitration and wishing to preserve their objections at every level must also attend to some perhaps unexpected procedural detail. The Court of Appeals held in Commerce and Indus. Ins. Co. v. Nester[23] that if the application to stay arbitration is denied and arbitration is directed to proceed, the resister must be sure to appeal the order of denial to the appellate division and then, most importantly, seek from the appellate division, pending the appeal, a stay of the supreme court's order directing the arbitration to go forward. If the resister participates in the arbitration without having asked for that stay, all objections to the arbitration will be deemed waived.[24]

§ 593. Notice of Intention to Arbitrate; CPLR 7503(c)

When P, the party with a claim, wants it arbitrated, and D, the other party, contends or is likely to contend that the dispute is not arbitrable, P's favorite device is the "notice of intention to arbitrate" under CPLR 7503(c), which we will henceforth simply call a notice.[1] When P serves such a notice on D, it requires D to raise any arbitrability objections within 20 days afterwards, or waive them. CPLR 7503(c) has some important detail and there is much caselaw on several parts of it. The practitioner relying on CPLR 7503(c) should be prepared to carry out its requirements punctiliously, whichever side of the arbitrability controversy the client may be on.[2]

The notice must specify the agreement along with the name and address of the party serving the notice, whom we will call P. It is also customary, if P is represented by counsel, to state counsel's name, address, etc., as well. The notice must then recite that unless D applies to the court within 20 days to stay the arbitration, D shall be precluded from raising the threshold objections either of arbitrability or of timeliness. This 20–day period was held to be a statute of limitations in Jonathan Logan, Inc. v. Stillwater Worsted Mills, Inc.,[3]

19. CPLR 204(b).

20. Flanagan v. Prudential–Bache Securities, Inc., 67 N.Y.2d 500, 504 N.Y.S.2d 82, 495 N.E.2d 345 (1986).

21. See § 530 above.

22. See Matter of Morrow, 135 A.D.2d 931, 522 N.Y.S.2d 333 (3d Dep't 1987).

23. 90 N.Y.2d 255, 660 N.Y.S.2d 366 (1997).

24. See the discussion of Nester in the lead note in New York State Law Digest No. 451.

§ 593

1. It is also referred to by CPLR 7503(c) as a simple "demand" for arbitration. Whatever its title, it should carefully carry out the requirements of CPLR 7503(c) if it would impose on its recipient the requirements of this provision. It is not clear whether a "demand" for arbitration not carrying out the requirements of CPLR 7503(c)

can nonetheless qualify as a "demand" at least for the purpose of measuring the interposition of the claim for limitations' purposes under CPLR 7502(b). To be on the safe side it is wisest to use, even for this purpose, the formal notice of intention to arbitrate under CPLR 7503(c).

2. When the party to the arbitration agreement is deceased or incompetent, the requirements of this provision and of arbitration generally are carried on through the personal representative or committee. CPLR 7512. A controversy involving an incompetent or conservatee may not be submitted to arbitration except by court order, and with the exception of arbitrations involving uninsured and underinsured motorist claims, the same applies to controversies involving infants. CPLR 1209.

3. 31 A.D.2d 208, 295 N.Y.S.2d 853 (1st Dep't 1968), aff'd on opinion below 24 N.Y.2d 898, 301 N.Y.S.2d 636, 249 N.E.2d 477 (1969). The case was decided when the applicable period was only 10 days. The holding endures causing a complete forfeiture of the right to question arbitrability even if it is missed by only a day.[4] The holding and the rigidity it has given to CPLR 7503(c) account for much of the caselaw on it. As a statute of limitations, and one of the shortest on record to boot, the 20–day period cannot be extended by the courts under CPLR 2004—which authorizes discretionary extensions of time for almost all other things in civil procedure[5]—even for good cause shown.[6] This stiffness has caused the courts to demand precision on both sides.

First, on P's side. P may serve the notice either in the same manner as a summons or by registered or certified mail with return receipt requested.[7] It has been held that the use of ordinary mail voids the notice and relieves D from having to apply within the 20 days.[8] D is similarly relieved when the notice fails to specify the time period, or to warn D that an omission to apply results in a bar of arbitrability objections,[9] or when the notice erroneously offers D fewer than the required 20 days,[10] or omits P's address, or P's attorney's address if the attorney is serving the notice. In this last instance, the court said that a party using a statute that can sharply curtail the rights of another must itself toe the line closely.[11]

Since it is such an advantage to P, the party who is seeking arbitration, to throw off onto D, the side resisting it, the burden of making a court application to determine whether arbitration is required (and, in the bargain, with only a 20–day period in which to act), P should take care not to forfeit the advantage with sharp practice. Disguising the notice will void it. In Nationwide Mut. Ins. Co. v. Monroe,[12] for

example, the notice was folded into quarters, its lettering facing down, and was stapled to the back of the 11th of 18 documents, just a mite more obvious than had it been inscribed on the inner gauze layer of a band-aid. It was ineffective to limit D's time and what would otherwise have been a late application was held timely.

As for D's side, D being the one on whom the notice was served and who must now apply for the stay of arbitration within the 20 days, caselaw has recognized the rigors of treating so short a period as one of unextendable limitation and has therefore, along with a few amendments, endeavored to abate some of them. The period remains one of limitation, having been pronounced so to acknowledge that any other rule would encourage laxness and defeat the expeditious aims of arbitration, but its edges have been softened. D's obligation within the 20 days is to commence a special proceeding to stay arbitration, but CPLR 7503(c) authorizes commencement of the proceeding by serving the initiatory papers[13] either in the same manner as a summons or by registered or certified mail with return receipt requested—the same methods offered to P when P serves the notice in the first place. It was held in Knickerbocker Ins. Co. v. Gilbert,[14] moreover, that D's 20 days start not when P posts the notice, but when D actually receives it, an obvious advantage to D.[15]

At the other terminal is another advantage to D: all D has to do is post the special proceeding papers on or before the 20th day and the time requirement will be satisfied even

and today governs the 20–day period, adopted by a 1973 amendment.

4. See, e.g., Raisler Corp. v. N. Y. City Housing Auth., 32 N.Y.2d 274, 344 N.Y.S.2d 917, 298 N.E.2d 91 (1973).

5. See § 6 above.

6. See Sisters of Charity of Saint Vincent De Paul v. Boegel and Allodi, 32 A.D.2d 818, 302 N.Y.S.2d 462 (2d Dep't 1969).

7. CPLR 7503(c).

8. Jefferson v. Government Employees Ins. Co., 48 A.D.2d 855, 368 N.Y.S.2d 573 (2d Dep't 1975).

9. See Herzberg v. Motor Veh. Acc. Indem. Corp., 42 Misc.2d 790, 249 N.Y.S.2d 588 (Sup.Ct., Kings County, 1964).

10. Sleepy Hollow etc. v. De Angelis, 51 A.D.2d 267, 380 N.Y.S.2d 815 (3d Dep't 1976).

11. Allstate Ins. Co. v. Neithardt, 24 A.D.2d 941, 265 N.Y.S.2d 128 (1st Dep't 1965).

12. 75 A.D.2d 765, 427 N.Y.S.2d 822 (1st Dep't 1980).

13. These are the usual notice of petition and petition with supporting affidavits. CPLR 403(b).

14. 28 N.Y.2d 57, 66, 320 N.Y.S.2d 12, 18, 268 N.E.2d 758, 763 (1971).

15. The Knickerbocker case also indicates, however, that for statute of limitations purposes, P will be deemed to have commenced the arbitration upon the posting of the notice of intention rather than upon D's receipt of it, an advantage to P.

though P may not receive them until some days later.[16] This is a codification of another point enunciated in the *Knickerbocker* case. Note, however, that the five days added to time periods measured from mail service within an action[17] do not append to the 20 days of CPLR 7503(c). They apply only to interlocutory papers within an action or proceeding, and no action or proceeding is yet pending when the notice of intention of CPLR 7503(c) is served.[18]

The posting of the special proceeding papers must be by the registered or certified method. The use of ordinary mail is a jurisdictional defect,[19] just as it is when the plaintiff uses it for the initial notice,[20] and can result in a dismissal of the proceeding.[21] Finally, if P has used a lawyer to serve the notice of intention and the lawyer's name is on the notice, D may serve the special proceeding papers on P's lawyer instead of on P.[22]

These are a few of the concessions made to D in light of the great brevity of this unique period of limitation. It was worse when it started out. It was in fact a 10–day period when first construed as a statute of limitations.[23] A major concession was the 1973 amendment of CPLR 7503(c) extending it to 20. So short a period opened the door to some fanciful abuses, such as serving the notice of intention on a large corporate party at an office wholly irrelevant to the particular case in the hope that before the notice could filter back to an appropriate office the time to stay arbitration would have expired. This ploy was rejected.[24] A party serving the notice of inten-

tion at an office clearly unrelated to the business at hand, especially when background dealings have been conducted with the more appropriate office, should be estopped from pleading the time limitation of CPLR 7503(c). It is akin to dressing the notice in some kind of camouflage, as was unsuccessfully attempted in the *Nationwide* case,[25] where estoppel could also account for the result.

An estoppel question has also arisen in several CPLR 7503(c) cases in which the party serving the notice of intention expressly extended his adversary's time to apply to stay arbitration. The courts are divided on the issue of whether to estop a party who has offered such an extension from relying on the 20–day notice of CPLR 7503(c).[26]

The better view is that the estoppel should lie. It would not be unique to 7503(c) cases, having precedent in the statute of limitations sphere generally.[27] But suggesting that the estoppel lies is not to advise the would-be arbitration-stayer to rely on the extension. It is better to commence the stay proceeding within the 20–day period without regard to the professed willingness of the other side to grant extensions of time, perhaps just applying the proffered extensions to periodic postponements of the proceeding's return day rather than to its commencement.

A failure to comply with the 20–day period of CPLR 7503(c) can result not only in conceding arbitrability, but also in forfeiting participation in the choice of the organization that is to conduct the arbitration.

---

16. CPLR 7503(c).

17. See CPLR 2103(b)(2).

18. See Monarch Ins. Co. v. Pollack, 32 A.D.2d 819, 302 N.Y.S.2d 432 (2d Dep't 1969).

19. Yak Taxi, Inc. v. Teke, 41 N.Y.2d 1020, 395 N.Y.S.2d 627, 363 N.E.2d 1372 (1977). Perhaps if an order to show cause were used to commence the proceeding, see CPLR 403(d), it could direct service by ordinary mail. See Allstate Ins. Co. v. Carrillo, 69 Misc.2d 350, 329 N.Y.S.2d 985 (Sup.Ct., Westchester County, 1972). For the time being it seems the safer course not to depend on ordinary mail.

20. See note 8, above, and text at that point.

21. See J.P.L. Inc. v. L & A Music Co., 112 A.D.2d 230, 491 N.Y.S.2d 446 (2d Dep't 1985).

22. CPLR 7503(c). This is yet another codification of one of the holdings of the Knickerbocker case.

23. See Jonathan Logan, Inc. v. Stillwater Worsted Mills, Inc., 31 A.D.2d 208, 295 N.Y.S.2d 853 (1st Dep't 1968), aff'd on opinion below 24 N.Y.2d 898, 301 N.Y.S.2d 636, 249 N.E.2d 477 (1969).

24. See Empire Mutual Ins. Co. v. Levy, 35 A.D.2d 916, 316 N.Y.S.2d 24 (1st Dep't 1970).

25. Note 12 above.

26. See, e.g., Allstate Ins. Co. v. Carrillo, 69 Misc.2d 350, 329 N.Y.S.2d 985 (Sup.Ct., Westchester County, 1972), allowing the estoppel, and General Accident Fire and Life Assur. Corp. v. Cerretto, 60 Misc.2d 216, 303 N.Y.S.2d 223 (Sup.Ct., Monroe County, 1969), holding that neither the court nor the parties can extend the time.

27. See § 56 above.

Perhaps it is the combination of the rigors built by both the legislature and the courts into the 20–day period of CPLR 7503(c) that produced Matarasso v. Continental Casualty Co.[28] in 1982, which holds that if the parties "never agreed to arbitrate", i.e., if there is no arbitration commitment between them at all, the 20–day limit of CPLR 7503(c) will not apply. In our view, however, the party facing the 20–day wire (that would be the party resisting arbitration) in the face of any kind of notice purporting to allege an arbitrability commitment in any way, shape, or form may find it the better part of valor to meet the deadline anyway. Whether the case is a "never agreed to" situation of a kind to dissolve the 20–day limit is itself a question tied up with the merits of the application. No one reading the diverse and often irreconcilable cases on what constitutes a valid commitment to arbitrate[29] would want to predict what will satisfy a court as a never-agreed-to-at-all case.[30]

Commencing a special proceeding to stay arbitration does not itself work a stay.[31] If the exigencies are such that D requires a stay even while the special proceeding pends, D should seek to commence the proceeding with an order to show cause[32] instead of a regular notice of petition. The court can be asked to include an interim stay in the order. If D is faced with the 20–day period of CPLR 7503(c), however, and would bring the proceeding on by the show cause method, D should see to it that the order is both secured and served within the requisite 20 days. Getting the order within the period but serving it beyond, even though service is carried out precisely as the court has directed in the order to show cause itself, is not sufficient and will forfeit the right to con-

test arbitrability, as happened in the very case that pronounced the time period a statute of limitations.[33]

The practitioner should also keep in mind that the actual moment that commences a special proceeding in the supreme court is the filing of the initiatory papers, not their service.[34] Hence, in addition to carrying out the special service requirements of CPLR 7503(c), the attorney should make sure that the papers are filed in court prior to their service, and, indeed, that an index number is secured and affixed to the papers so that the papers bear the number when they are served. There is also a short time limit, following the filing, in which service has to be made.[35]

Because the filing system was adopted only in 1992, and the key cases on CPLR 7503(c) were all decided before then, none had occasion to address how the filing system would interplay with the already demanding service requirements of CPLR 7503(c). Since the statute of limitations is on the line in these situations, and an especially short one at that, oversights in applying these requirements can have unfortunate consequences.[36] Practitioners negotiating with CPLR 7503(c) may find it helpful to first review the section[37] on how the filing system works in special proceedings.

Although it is rare to see any of these arbitration-connected special proceedings in a lower court, some of them can be brought there.[38] It is therefore important to remember that the lower courts remain "service" courts, i.e., courts in which an action or proceeding is commenced by service of the initiatory papers, not their filing. Again for the reason that the statute of limitations may be involved, practi-

28.   56 N.Y.2d 264, 451 N.Y.S.2d 703, 436 N.E.2d 1305.

29.   See § 588 above.

30.   See the lead note on this subject in New York State Law Digest No. 272.

31.   See Central Gen. Hosp. v. Local 1115 Nursing Home, 61 Misc.2d 447, 305 N.Y.S.2d 948 (Sup.Ct., Nassau County, 1969).

32.   The order to show cause alternative offered for special proceedings in general, CPLR 403(d), is also available for proceedings contemplated by CPLR 7503.

33.   Jonathan Logan, Inc. v. Stillwater Worsted Mills, Inc., note 3, above.

34.   The legislation that adopted the filing system for commencing actions in the supreme and county courts applies in special proceedings, CPLR 304, which include the special proceeding of CPLR 7503(c) to test arbitrability.

35.   See CPLR 306–b.

36.   An early example of this is Newkirk Pub., Inc. v. L & A Music Co., Sup.Ct., N.Y.County (Index No. 18269/92, Nov. 20, 1992, Evans, J.).

37.   Section 53 above.

38.   See § 606 below.

tioners must gauge their procedures accordingly if the special proceeding is to be brought, or has been, in a lower court, such as the New York City Civil Court.

CPLR 7503(c) is clear in its requirements and, as the caselaw manifests, rigid. One served with the CPLR 7503(c) notice is required to raise the arbitrability questions in a promptly commenced special proceeding. The party cannot forego the proceeding and preserve the objections by other means.[39]

§ 594. Trial of Threshold Question

Whenever a triable issue is raised about whether there is an obligation to arbitrate or the arbitration was timely sought, the court is directed to try it "forthwith".[1] This evinces a legislative intention to expedite the arbitral process, but the "forthwith" here, as elsewhere,[2] is a relative word, merely calling for a special preference for the trial. Disputes about whether the arbitration-requiring instrument is the one agreed to, or received, are the kind that occasionally require a trial.[3] Also, when a condition precedent to arbitration must be carried out, such as the giving of notice within a certain time, it will qualify as a threshold question requiring prompt trial if it presents an issue of fact.[4] The dispute must be genuine, and arguments of this kind, at least relative to the overall quantity of consensual arbitrations, are rare. Fortunately so; they apparently require a trial by jury.

Although there has been some suggestion, not altogether clear, that not every triable issue affecting arbitrability is jury triable,[5] later caselaw manifests that a jury trial is required (if demanded) in respect of an issue of whether a party has made an agreement to arbitrate,[6] or otherwise bound itself to the arbitral process.[7] If the underlying dispute between the parties is over money, as it usually is, and would be triable by jury if it were the subject of an ordinary action, as it would be,[8] a jury should be demandable to determine a genuine issue of arbitrability for the reason that a finding on the issue dictates whether the party stays in court and gets a jury or goes to arbitration and forfeits it.

§ 595. Waiver of Arbitration

The party who contends that a dispute is arbitrable and wants the matter laid to rest by a court should pursue one of the CPLR 7503 methods to determine arbitrability, as treated in the prior sections. Clear-cut and direct, they guard against an inadvertent waiver of the right to arbitrate.

If the party asserting a claim is the one who wants arbitration, she should apply to compel arbitration under CPLR 7503(a) or make the other side apply to stay arbitration by using a notice of intention to arbitrate under CPLR 7503(c), either of which will earn a quick determination.

Bringing an ordinary action on the claim is inconsistent with an assertion that the claim is arbitrable and is therefore a waiver of arbitration by the plaintiff, the party suing.[1] The

39. There is some caselaw suggesting otherwise, however. See, e.g., Incorporated Village of Lynbrook v. Lynbrook Police Benevolent Ass'n, Inc., 87 Misc.2d 57, 385 N.Y.S.2d 484 (Sup.Ct., Nassau County, 1976).

§ 594

1. CPLR 7503(a).

2. See CPLR 7804(h) ("forthwith") and 3211(c) ("immediate"), discussed in §§ 569 and 271, above.

3. See Wander Iron Works, Inc.v. Wilaka Const. Co., 38 A.D.2d 529, 326 N.Y.S.2d 673 (1st Dep't 1971).

4. See Motor Vehicle Accident Indemnification Corp. v. Stein, 23 A.D.2d 526, 255 N.Y.S.2d 483 (4th Dep't 1965).

5. See, e.g., Andolina v. Motor Vehicle Acc. Indem. Corp., 23 A.D.2d 958, 259 N.Y.S.2d 938 (4th Dep't 1965).

6. See S. Kornblum Metals Co. v. Intsel Corp., 38 N.Y.2d 376, 379 N.Y.S.2d 826, 342 N.E.2d 591 (1976); RLC Electronics, Inc. v. American Electronics Laboratories, Inc., 39 A.D.2d 757, 332 N.Y.S.2d 119 (2d Dep't 1972).

7. See Anthony Drugs of Bethpage, Inc. v. Local 1199 Drug and Hospital Union, AFL–CIO, 34 A.D.2d 788, 311 N.Y.S.2d 622 (2d Dep't 1970).

8. CPLR 4101(1); N.Y.Const. Art. I, § 2.

§ 595

1. See Manitt Construction Corp. v. J. S. Plumbing & Heating Corp., 50 Misc.2d 502, 270 N.Y.S.2d 716 (Sup.Ct., Queens County, 1966). There is authority, however, that resorting to the courts on one claim will not waive arbitrability of an entirely separate one even if both arise from a common agreement. See Denihan v. Denihan, 34 N.Y.2d 307, 357 N.Y.S.2d 454, 313 N.E.2d 759 (1974).

defendant in that situation, if he maintains the claim is arbitrable and wants arbitration, should move under CPLR 7503(a) to compel arbitration. The motion is made in the action and its granting results in a stay of the action, thus compelling the plaintiff to go to arbitration, or nowhere. A defendant in that position should not participate in the action on the merits. He should not even serve an answer; the motion to compel should be the defendant's sole step. A defendant concerned that the time it takes to bring the motion on will cause the answering time to expire and put him in default can bring the motion on by order to show cause, asking the court to include in it an extension of the time to answer—which can probably be obtained from the plaintiff by stipulation anyway. There is some suggestion that as long as the answering time is still open, so is the defendant's time to demand arbitration. It has been held, for example, that waiting 18 months, resulting from a series of extensions of the time to answer, will not necessarily make the demand untimely.[2] But a different conclusion may be drawn if the defendant in the interim participates in some way on the merits.

If the defendant does answer, it has been held that the answer will not waive the right to arbitrate if it includes arbitrability as a defense, but it is also clear that going beyond that step, such as by taking the plaintiff's deposition or otherwise becoming involved on the merits, will bring the waiver.[3]

The above is concerned with waiving the right to arbitrate, which can come about by bringing or participating in an action on the claim. It is not to be confused with the converse: waiving litigation by participating in the arbitration. The party resisting arbitration

will also find her remedies in CPLR 7503. Prior sections, in fact, were addressed in large measure to the resister's tools, one of which is the application to stay arbitration under CPLR 7503(b). Just as the party urging arbitrability cannot participate in an action on the merits, so the party urging that the claim is litigable should not—until a court determines that arbitration is required—participate in the arbitration on the merits. Participation will waive the right to litigate even when the participator purports to "reserve" the right to contest arbitrability.[4] For this purpose, merely writing a letter to the arbitrator asserting an evidentiary objection or contesting the arbitrator's power to issue a subpoena may qualify as merits participation sufficient to work the waiver.[5]

When P brings an action against D in violation of an agreement to arbitrate, P waives arbitration but not litigation. D does not waive arbitration, of course, unless he participates in the action, and can insist on arbitrating the claim, using the remedy of a motion to compel arbitration under CPLR 7503(a). P's suit in effect gives D a choice of forums, which is not a bad position for D to be in: D can now insist on arbitration, or ignore arbitration and litigate. But D cannot have things both ways. D cannot stop P's court action on the ground that it is arbitrable while also resisting arbitration on the ground that P's very commencement of a court action waived it. That would be having one's cake and eating it too.[6]

Bringing a court action for the purpose of securing an order of attachment in conjunction with an arbitrable controversy has been deemed a waiver of the right to insist on arbitration,[7] but that was when the use of the provisional remedies was absolutely precluded

2. See City Trade & Industries, Ltd. v. New Central Jute Mills Co., 25 N.Y.2d 49, 302 N.Y.S.2d 557, 250 N.E.2d 52 (1969).

3. See De Sapio v. Kohlmeyer, 35 N.Y.2d 402, 362 N.Y.S.2d 843, 321 N.E.2d 770 (1974).

4. See Hodges International, Inc. v. Rembrandt Fabrics, Ltd., 44 A.D.2d 77, 353 N.Y.S.2d 462 (1st Dep't 1974).

5. Unicon Management Corp. v. Pavcrete Constr. Corp., 23 A.D.2d 837, 259 N.Y.S.2d 598 (1st Dep't 1965).

6. But see Sowalskie v. Cohoes Housing Auth., Inc., 69 Misc.2d 665, 330 N.Y.S.2d 481 (Sup.Ct., Albany County,

1968), allowing D to accomplish just that. The authorities relied on there, River Brand Rice Mills, Inc. v. Latrobe Brewing Co., 305 N.Y. 36, 110 N.E.2d 545 (1953), and Duke Laboratories, Inc. v. Lutz, 9 Misc.2d 779, 168 N.Y.S.2d 998 (Sup.Ct., N.Y.County, 1957), are distinguishable because they found arbitration barred by the applicable statute of limitations, which does not appear to be the case in Sowalskie. See Sommer v. Quarant Contracting, Inc., 40 A.D.2d 95, 337 N.Y.S.2d 957 (1st Dep't 1972).

7. Hadjioannou v. Avramides, 40 N.Y.2d 929, 389 N.Y.S.2d 833, 358 N.E.2d 516 (1976).

in conjunction with an arbitration. That changed in 1985 with the addition of subdivision (c) to CPLR 7502, making the provisional remedies of attachment and injunction available from a court in conjunction with an arbitration.[8] Today, therefore, it is of course clear that making a court application, not to litigate the claim in court but just to secure the court's issuance of the attachment or injunction, would not be a waiver of the right to arbitrate.

D. THE ARBITRATION

Table of Sections

§ 596. The Arbitrator

The parties choose their arbitrator or arbitrators, naming designated persons in their agreement or reserving the right to name them when a dispute arises, or simply providing for arbitration pursuant to the rules of a given organization and leaving the appointment of the arbitrator to the rules. The Commercial Arbitration Rules of the American Arbitration Association ("AAA"), for example, supply the requisite guideposts, authorizing the parties to name and appoint an arbitrator directly or to eliminate from a list of AAA-designated persons those who are unacceptable and leave it to the AAA to select an arbitrator from those remaining.

The CPLR is delighted to leave all of these matters to the parties and to the arbitration forum they have chosen. It is only when the parties fail to agree on an arbitrator or on a method for the arbitrator's selection, or when the one designated fails to act, or in similar situations, that the parties may turn to the court for the appointment of an arbitrator.[1]

The number of arbitrators is also up to the parties. One or three is the usual preference. The AAA rules provide that when the agreement does not specify how many, there shall be one. Opting for three, popularly called tripartite arbitration, usually means that each party chooses one arbitrator and the two chosen select a third. Only the third need be neutral. It is expected, and today acknowledged, that each of the other two will be partisan. Although an individual party may not act as his own arbitrator in this tripartite process, a corporate or association officer or the equivalent can be the organization's arbitrator.[2]

One of the grounds on which to vacate an award is the partiality of the arbitrator—in tripartite arbitration the partiality of the neutral member.[3] Presumably the arbitration forum itself will resolve any problem of partisanship. To the extent that the court is to become involved with the issue at all, its involvement should take place after an award has been made, either upon an application to vacate the award or by way of resisting the winner's effort to confirm it.[4] It has been suggested that the courts may not even have the power to disqualify an arbitrator in advance of the arbitration proceedings,[5] but in an appropriate case judicial intervention can probably be secured.[6]

Disqualification for bias, such as an arbitrator's relationship of some kind to a party or one of the parties' lawyers in the case, whether through blood, business, society, or otherwise, direct or indirect, is usually limited to where the relationship is unknown to the other party in time to raise the objection. A party aware of the relationship, even one as close as

---

8. See § 599 below.

§ 596

1. See CPLR 7504.

2. See Astoria Medical Group v. Health Ins. Plan of Greater New York, 11 N.Y.2d 128, 227 N.Y.S.2d 401, 182 N.E.2d 85 (1962).

3. See CPLR 7511(b)(1)(ii).

4. Applications to vacate awards and the grounds recognized for vacatur are discussed in § 602 below.

5. See Siegel v. Lewis, 40 N.Y.2d 687, 389 N.Y.S.2d 800, 358 N.E.2d 484 (1976).

6. See Astoria Medical Group v. Health Ins. Plan of Greater New York, note 2, above.

an employer-employee or attorney-client relationship, who continues the arbitration despite it, may well be held to have waived the objection.[7] The courts are justifiably suspicious that the aware party may be playing two hands, hoping for a favorable result on the one hand but keeping a trump card in the other.

Actual bias, if demonstrable, will undo an award; it is not deemed waived. But the presumptive prejudice born of a disqualifying relationship is waivable, and one who proceeds with actual or constructive knowledge of it, and without objecting to it, waives it.[8] Even if the overall circumstances are not such as would bar confirmation of the award, however, the courts have no praise for an arbitration that permits an arbitrator with an arguably disqualifying relationship to sit.[9]

It is clear that the arbitrator can decide the case on his own knowledge. Indeed, it may be that very knowledge or experience or expertise that the parties are out to exploit when they designate the particular arbitrator.[10] This is yet another contrast to litigation, where any personal knowledge on the part of the judge is deemed to affect objectivity and to require the judge's disqualification.

In view of the foregoing, is it conceivable that an employee of one of the parties could be designated the arbitrator? A contract calling for precisely that, and in unequivocal terms— and between parties with obvious bargaining power (no adhesion contract this)—was upheld by the Court of Appeals in Westinghouse Elec. Corp. v. New York City Transit Auth.,[11] an ugly situation in which one can only conclude that the big corporate loser bit off more than it could chew by signing a contract with so one-sided a dispute-resolution clause. The case involved a multi-million dollar contract between Westinghouse (W) and a municipal transit authority (T), with a provision making E, one of

T's employees, the sole adjudicator of all disputes between the parties. Worse than that: E was also involved in the parties' dealings, and of course on T's side. When a dispute arose and W brought the dispute before E, E, as expected, decided the dispute in favor of his employer, T. W then took the decision to court for review, where it was upheld.

Distasteful as the result may seem, it is somewhat sweetened by the special provision the contract contained for judicial review: it called for review, not by the standards of Article 75 of the CPLR, which ordinarily governs the review of arbitration awards and is narrow,[12] but by those of Article 78, which governs the review of administrative determinations and is broader.[13] Here the contract explicitly recited that E's determination could be rejected if found "arbitrary, capricious or [so] grossly erroneous [as] to evidence bad faith", a standard roughly paralleling that set forth for certain Article 78 proceedings.[14] That the applicable review criterion is broader under Article 78 than under Article 75 was comforting only in a relative sense, however. Even under Article 78 standards, the courts can't do a real laying-on of hands because the fact-finding process is with E. No de novo hearing of the facts takes place in court. All the court has before it is whatever record was made before the arbitrator, who, as the party's employee in the *Westinghouse* case, could be expected to find all key facts in favor of his employer.[15] It's just a matter of determining which side of the bread the butter is on.

§ 597. The Arbitration Hearing

When we arrive at the arbitration hearing itself, the CPLR naturally becomes sketchy. While much involved at the outset, when questions of arbitrability are raised, and perhaps even more involved at the end, when confirma-

---

7. Siegel v. Lewis, note 5, above.

8. Milliken Woolens, Inc. v. Weber Knit Sportswear, Inc., 11 A.D.2d 166, 202 N.Y.S.2d 431 (1st Dep't 1960), aff'd 9 N.Y.2d 878, 216 N.Y.S.2d 696, 175 N.E.2d 826 (1961).

9. See Baar & Beards, Inc. v. Oleg Cassini, Inc., 37 A.D.2d 106, 322 N.Y.S.2d 462 (1st Dep't 1971).

10. See Siegel v. Lewis, note 5, above.

11. 82 N.Y.2d 47, 603 N.Y.S.2d 404, 623 N.E.2d 531 (1993).

12. See § 602 below.

13. See §§ 558–563 above.

14. See CPLR 7803(3).

15. See the discussion of the Westinghouse case in New York State Law Digest No. 408.

tion or vacatur of the award is sought, the CPLR recognizes that the in-between is the arbitration proper. This is almost entirely the business of the arbitrators—the core of what the courts defer to when arbitration rather than litigation has been selected. Our business here, therefore, is to set forth only the few things the CPLR does have to prescribe for the hearing,[1] and it is noteworthy that even these few are for the most part waivable.[2] The reader who wants a broad procedural perspective of the arbitration itself should consult a compilation like the American Arbitration Association's Commercial Arbitration Rules, which is the end product of long experience. The procedural questions likely to occur to the reader as we embark on the CPLR guidelines—and they are only that—are much more likely to find answers in the rules.

Each arbitrator is required to take an oath to hear and decide the case fairly.[3] All of the arbitrators (if there are more than one) conduct the hearing, but it takes only a majority of them to "determine any question and render an award".[4] Ordinarily no proof can be taken if any one of the arbitrators is absent, but their conference, before making an award, however desirable it may be to have it conducted in one another's presence, can be by other means, even by telephone.[5]

Each party has the absolute right to be represented by an attorney at the arbitration and can assert this right at any time. This is the one procedural right the statute makes unwaivable.[6] In one case, for example,[7] in which P was dissatisfied with an arbitration award made by a committee of a dental society and sued D for dental malpractice in court, D moved to dismiss the action on the ground that the claim had gone through to an award. It was found, however, that in order for P to obtain the arbitration, P was required to sign a submission form that included a waiver of counsel, so P had no lawyer at the arbitration. This was held to void the award, which therefore could not stand as a basis on which to dismiss the action.[8]

The arbitrator has the power to administer oaths,[9] but it has been held that the swearing of witnesses is not required.[10] The parties are of course entitled to be heard, to present evidence, and to call and cross-examine witnesses.[11] Should subpoenas be necessary, any arbitrator or attorney of record of a party can issue them.[12] If a duly notified party does not appear, the arbitrator can hear and determine the case on the evidence of the parties who do.[13]

Although an arbitrator may not in general exclude pertinent evidence,[14] the usual evidentiary rules applicable in court are waived in arbitration.[15] This can go pretty far. Accepting into evidence a detective agency report that disparaged a party's character, for example, and narrated all manner of hearsay gossip about her, was held inadequate basis to reject an award, albeit by a closely divided Court of Appeals.[16] A case like that is near the line of

§ 597

1. These come mainly from CPLR 7506.

2. See CPLR 7506(f).

3. CPLR 7506(a).

4. CPLR 7506(e).

5. See Artie Shaw Presents, Inc. v. Snyder, 46 A.D.2d 867, 362 N.Y.S.2d 158 (1st Dep't 1974).

6. CPLR 7506(d), (f).

7. Sartiano v. Becker, 119 A.D.2d 656, 501 N.Y.S.2d 94 (2d Dep't 1986).

8. See CPLR 3211(a)(5), discussed in § 263 above. While the action may not be dismissed in that circumstance, may it be stayed under CPLR 7503(a) so that arbitration can be compelled, a fresh arbitration now to take place but with counsel permitted? The point was noted but left open in Nastasi v. Artenberg, 130 A.D.2d 469, 515 N.Y.S.2d 52 (2d Dep't 1987).

9. CPLR 7505.

10. Kozlowski v. Seville Syndicate, Inc., 64 Misc.2d 109, 314 N.Y.S.2d 439 (Sup.Ct., N.Y.County, 1970).

11. CPLR 7506(c).

12. CPLR 7505, 2302(a).

13. CPLR 7506(c).

14. See Gervant v. New England Fire Ins. Co., 306 N.Y. 393, 118 N.E.2d 574 (1954). The arbitrary exclusion of material evidence may subject the arbitrator to a charge of misconduct, a ground for vacating the award. See § 602 below.

15. See Professional Staff Congress/CUNY v. Board of Higher Education, 39 N.Y.2d 319, 383 N.Y.S.2d 592, 347 N.E.2d 918 (1976).

16. Brill v. Muller Bros., Inc., 13 N.Y.2d 776, 242 N.Y.S.2d 69, 192 N.E.2d 34 (1963).

"misconduct", however, and if found to rise to that level in a given case can bring about a vacatur of the award.[17]

CPLR 3102(c) permits an application to the court for an order directing disclosure in aid of arbitration, but the courts are hesitant to allow it. They find it inconsistent to allow the time-consuming processes of litigation's pretrial disclosure devices to interfere with the expeditious aims of arbitration.[18] It has therefore been generally understood to require very special circumstances before court aid will be offered for this purpose,[19] although one occasionally sees cases that seem to take a more liberal view of it. Document discovery has been allowed, for example, on a court's mere finding, not elaborated, that the documents are needed "to present a proper case".[20] Presumably the court will have to be satisfied not only that the documents are needed, but that judicial intervention is the only way for the party to the arbitration to get them. If any more generous approach than that is taken, the courts might find themselves applied to for disclosure in aid of arbitration as a matter of course, a result that would disserve the courts and arbitration both.

Should need arise, the arbitrator should be able, by one means or another, to secure for the parties such preliminary disclosure as he deems necessary[21] consistent with an expeditious arbitration. The party in need of disclosure should inquire into the rules, or even the unwritten practices, of the arbitrator. Under American Arbitration Association rules, for example, a "pre-hearing conference" can be requested, which can include "an exchange of information". Or, even without relying on a rule, the party seeking disclosure can simply write a letter to the arbitrator describing the disclosure need and asking that disclosure be directed in advance of the hearing. If the direction issues, it can prove productive for the simple tactical reason that a party would rarely want to risk offending the arbitrator by refusing it.

If push comes to shove, however, practitioners must note there is caselaw holding that it is "firmly established" that arbitrators can't order the parties to an arbitration "to engage in disclosure proceedings".[22] While practically speaking an arbitrator should be able to generate a kind of limited pretrial disclosure, if that fails then perhaps now the party can make out the "exceptional" case needed for judicially ordered disclosure in aid of arbitration.

The time and place of the arbitration hearing is left to the arbitrator, whose only stated obligation is to give the parties at least 8 days notice of it in writing, either personally or by registered or certified mail.[23] When the rules of an established arbitration unit are adopted, using again the example of the American Arbitration Association, they will usually be found to address these matters in more detail. Since the CPLR contemplates leaving the place of arbitration entirely to the arbitrators, there is no provision for judicial intervention in the matter. Indeed, the courts have even been said to be "without power" to change the venue of an arbitration when there is no suggestion that there has been bad faith in setting it.[24]

The arbitrator can adjourn the hearing as need be,[25] and of course has all the related incidental powers to grant additional time to prepare briefs and memos, secure witnesses,

17. See CPLR 7511(b)(1)(i), treated in § 602 below.

18. Katz v. Burkin, 3 A.D.2d 238, 160 N.Y.S.2d 159 (1st Dep't 1957).

19. See Motor Vehicle Accident Indemnification Corp. v. McCabe, 19 A.D.2d 349, 243 N.Y.S.2d 495 (1st Dep't 1963).

20. See, e.g., Hendler & Murray, P.C. v. Lambert, 127 A.D.2d 820, 511 N.Y.S.2d 941 (2d Dep't 1987).

21. See Motor Vehicle Accident Indemnification Corp. v. McCabe, note 19, above. See also Hooper v. Motor Veh.

Accid. Indem. Corp., 42 Misc.2d 446, 248 N.Y.S.2d 255 (Sup.Ct., N.Y.County, 1963).

22. Goldsborough v. N.Y. State Dep't of Correc'l Services, 217 A.D.2d 546, 628 N.Y.S.2d 813 (2d Dep't 1995). See the discussion of the Goldsborough case in SPR 52:4.

23. CPLR 7506(b).

24. See D.M.C. Constr. Corp. v. A. Leo Nash Steel Corp., 41 N.Y.2d 855, 393 N.Y.S.2d 709, 362 N.E.2d 260 (1977), reversing on the dissenting opinion below 51 A.D.2d 1040, 381 N.Y.S.2d 325 (2d Dep't 1976).

25. CPLR 7506(b).

and the like, and even to allow these time extensions ex parte.[26]

While there is no set time for commencing the arbitration hearing, a situation that has been criticized as an "aberration" in our law,[27] the court may, on application of a party, direct the arbitrator to proceed to a hearing and determination promptly.[28] In a situation in which a dispute arises about whether the arbitration is governed by the federal or New York arbitration statutes, a finding that the New York provisions apply enables the court to speed the arbitration along, a power found not to exist under the federal provisions.[29]

A likely advantage of selecting arbitration through an organization set up for it, in addition to securing a set of rules to which the parties can quickly turn for the few procedural questions that have to be asked and answered, is the availability of facilities for the arbitration. Little is needed physically, other than a room with a table and a few chairs and perhaps a blackboard or other graphic aid. But when the services of a stenographer—whether a record is to be kept is up to the parties—or interpreter or other such person are required, the parties may find the organization prepared to offer them promptly.

§ 598. Impleader and Consolidation in Arbitration

Assume that P properly commences an arbitration of a money claim against D, there being an agreement to arbitrate between them, but that D maintains that X is liable to D for all or part of what P may recover of D, i.e., the situation which in court enables D to implead X without further ado.[1] An impediment in arbitration is that unless D and X have their own agreement to arbitrate, D cannot bring X into the arbitration. And if D cannot implead X, D is just as unlikely to be allowed to use the litigation precursor of impleader, a vouching-in notice.[2] Denied these remedies, D would apparently have to bring an ordinary indemnity action against X, should P's arbitration go to award against D and D pay it, and in that action it would be open to X to dispute not only his indemnification relationship to D, but also the validity of P's claim against D—the thing to be indemnified—because the award would not be binding on X.

This is one of the drawbacks of the arbitral process. One in the potential position of D should, when he first considers agreeing to arbitration, contemplate whether there is any likelihood of an indemnification situation arising and, if there is, try to get all potentially involved persons to agree to arbitration together.

It may not even be sufficient if one in D's position does have an arbitration agreement with X, unless it stipulates that D can work that arbitration in with arbitral claims brought against D by others. D will not be helped, for example, if P, seeking arbitration on one side, and X, against whom D seeks arbitration on the other, will not agree to the same arbitrator or arbitrators, unless the courts are willing to attenuate the traditional right of arbitrator selection in deference to the obvious advantages of consolidation—which may be happening and which we return to later in this section.

A lot of foresight is necessary in order to work out in advance an arbitration agreement that contemplates and provides for the joinder of additional parties, but when it is present it does a good job. An example is Raisler Corp. v. N.Y. City Housing Authority,[3] in which the authority so drafted its contracts that it was able, when brought into arbitration by one contractor, to bring in another who signed a

26. Sweet Associates, Inc. v. Central Sch. Dist. No. 3, 21 A.D.2d 726, 250 N.Y.S.2d 98 (3d Dep't 1964).

27. See the dissenting opinion in Glen Creations, Inc. v. Cotra Corp., 39 A.D.2d 866, 867, 333 N.Y.S.2d 232, 233 (1st Dep't 1972).

28. CPLR 7506(b).

29. See Salvano v. Merrill Lynch, 85 N.Y.2d 173, 623 N.Y.S.2d 790, 647 N.E.2d 1298 (1995), discussed in the lead note in New York State Law Digest No. 423. A

comparison of the federal and New York arbitration acts appears in § 607 below.

§ 598

1. CPLR 1007. See § 155 et seq., above.

2. For vouching-in, see § 168 above.

3. 32 N.Y.2d 274, 344 N.Y.S.2d 917, 298 N.E.2d 91 (1973).

similar contract and to require it to participate in the selection of common arbitrators. Once all parties are before the arbitrator, incidentally, the arbitrator is empowered to make awards directly between parties who initially had no mutual contract to arbitrate.

An analogous situation is where the P v. D claim is in ordinary litigation, but D has a contract with X requiring arbitration of all claims, and with a clause broad enough to take in indemnity claims as well. X may not be deprived of his contractual right to arbitrate in this instance, either, and it is not necessarily an excuse that the underlying claim for which indemnity is sought is in litigation and not subject to arbitration.[4] D's remedy is to try to introduce into the arbitration with X whatever judgment P gets against D in court. While it is the general rule that the procedural and substantive law does not bind an arbitrator— which suggests that if the arbitrator ignores the litigation result there is nothing a court can do about it—an exception may be emerging when it is the res judicata doctrine that seeks arbitral recognition. But as we shall see, the res judicata doctrine itself may pose barriers when the parties are not the same. There is, after all, the basic rule that one not a party to a proceeding cannot be bound by anything it adjudicates.[5]

It has been held that whether an issue has already been decided by a prior arbitration is for a court and not an arbitrator to decide, and this rule has been applied both when the issue was the effect of a prior arbitration on a subsequent litigation[6] or on a subsequent arbitration.[7] While it may be relatively easy to apply these rules when the parties are the same in both rounds, complications arise when

the parties are not the same—when the doctrine being applied is not the "claim preclusion" aspect of the res judicata doctrine, but the collateral estoppel or "issue preclusion" aspect.[8] In the situation we address here the parties are not the same, and that is the root of the problem. Can res judicata do its work here? Are there any other remedies?

Some states have statutes that allow an arbitration to be stayed between one set of parties based on the pendency of related litigation between another set[9]—often, of course, one party is a member of each set—but New York has not. In the absence of such a statute, is there any way out for a person (M) caught in the middle with an arbitration commitment with one party (A) but only the prospect of litigation with another (L) involved in some phase of the same dispute but not obliged to arbitrate? The answer appears to be maybe. The prospect of a cure is much strengthened if the parties to the arbitration agreement give some anticipatory attention to the problem in the contract.

M's dilemma is that there may be inconsistent determinations of his responsibilities and liabilities between the arbitration with A and the litigation with L. A major case illustrates that there is something that M can do, or at least try to do, to avoid the problem. HRH Constr. Corp. v. Bethlehem Steel Corp.,[10] decided in 1978, shows the problem and its potential resolutions.

The case involved the construction industry, where problems of this kind have been found to arise frequently. The basic fact pattern involved a general contractor as M, the one caught in the middle. M had no arbitration agreement with the owner (L), who, when a

---

4. See Greene Steel & Wire Co. v. F. W. Hartmann & Co., Inc., 235 N.Y.S.2d 238 (Sup.Ct., Kings County, 1962), aff'd 20 A.D.2d 683, 247 N.Y.S.2d 1008 (2d Dep't 1964).

5. See § 458 above.

6. See Rembrandt Industries, Inc. v. Hodges International, Inc., 38 N.Y.2d 502, 381 N.Y.S.2d 451, 344 N.E.2d 383 (1976). This is really just the general issue of whether an arbitration award is entitled to res judicata effect, which, as previously noted, it is. See § 456 above.

7. See, e.g., City of Rochester v. AFSCME, Local 1635, 54 A.D.2d 257, 388 N.Y.S.2d 489 (4th Dep't 1976), citing and relying on the Rembrandt case.

8. For the differences, see § 443 above.

9. See, e.g., § 1281.2(c) of California's Civil Procedure Code, a key statute involved in the U.S. Supreme Court case of Volt Information Sciences, Inc. v. Board of Trustees of the Leland Stanford Junior University, 489 U.S. 468, 109 S.Ct. 1248, 103 L.Ed.2d 488 (1989), discussed in § 607 below.

10. 45 N.Y.2d 675, 412 N.Y.S.2d 366, 384 N.E.2d 1289.

dispute arose, therefore brought an ordinary action against M. Contending that whatever L was complaining about was the responsibility of a subcontractor, A, M wanted to implead A. But between M and A there was an arbitration commitment. M had apparently anticipated the problem, however, and it was provided in the M–A contract that if owner L should sue M for anything arguably the fault of A, M could implead A into the court action despite the commitment to arbitrate.

It was also provided that if any issue should arise in an arbitration between M and A, which issue had previously been adjudicated in a litigation between L and M, those litigated issues shall be "determinative and conclusive" between M and A in the arbitration.

The Court of Appeals found the language of the contract inadequate to divest A of its arbitration right so as to subject A to impleader into the litigation merely because L sued M. It said this would be an "aberrational result", but it did leave the door open to such a possibility if the parties use "unmistakable language" of such an intent. The obvious lesson to parties who are considering a contract with an arbitration clause and who can anticipate anything like the present dilemma is to use such "unmistakable" language in the contract. If one in the position of M has sufficient bargaining power in a particular transaction, it would not be amiss for M to cite the *HRH* case at the point in the contract where the subject clause is to be inserted, and thereupon use words saying specifically that the impleader barred in *HRH* is precisely what is sought to be secured here.

Although the impleader possibility was frustrated in the *HRH* case, the attempt to have findings made in the litigation between M and L bind in the arbitration involving M and A succeeded. The court found the contract language in this respect to constitute "a directive as to how the dispute in question shall be resolved in arbitration".

From one point of view this could be regarded as a violation of CPLR 7511(b), which restricts the scope of judicial review. It could be taken as an attempt to expand the judicial review standard by permitting the courts to scan the award to make sure the substantive law, in this case the doctrine of collateral estoppel (issue preclusion), has been followed. But an answer to that is this: the stipulation to have the litigation result bind in the arbitration can be deemed to put each litigated issue beyond the arbitrator's power to address afresh. The arbitrator who nevertheless addresses it can then be said to have "exceeded his power", which does fit one of the narrow review grounds applicable to an arbitration award.[11]

An alternative supporting rationale for the *HRH* result is that when the parties (M and A here) agree in their contract that any issue decided in a specified litigation (that between L and M here) shall bind in the M–A arbitration, they are narrowing the arbitration clause so as to exclude that issue from the commitment to arbitrate if and when the issue is decided in a court case. Hence, even if the arbitration clause itself is a broad one, the added statement about the binding nature of the litigation will just be deemed to narrow it pro rata.[12]

Even when litigation is not in the picture, the attempt to consolidate two or more arbitration proceedings raises issues. While arbitration is not itself either an action or a special proceeding—so as to subject it to the usual procedures of the CPLR in general and CPLR 602, the consolidation provision, in particular—a judicial power to order the consolidation of separate arbitrations, when common issues warrant it, has been spelled out from the general language of CPLR 7501. In providing that a written agreement to arbitrate "confers jurisdiction on the courts of the state to enforce it", CPLR 7501 has been held to include a general power to regulate other matters that

---

11. See paragraph (1)(iii) of CPLR 7511(b), treated in § 602 below.

12. The HRH case and the problems discussed here are the subject of a lead note in New York State Law Digest No. 233.

can be said to relate to "enforcement" as well, one of them being the power to consolidate.[13]

But stating that the power exists is not to suggest that it is easy to apply. Even if A's separate agreements with X and with Y each have an arbitration clause, can X and Y be compelled to arbitrate with each other merely because of common issues which in the courts could support consolidation? One of the parties may not be willing to have his liabilities heard along with the other's. Even were the court to skirt that issue, it would face the still more formidable one that neither set of parties is willing to submit to the other's choice of arbitrators. The barrier is absent when the separate pairs, A and X on the one side, A and Y on the other, consent to the same arbitrators,[14] but perhaps consent is not necessary today. The Court of Appeals has indicated that it prefers the consolidation of arbitrations when both arise out of "a commonality of context", and the court ordered consolidation in such an instance while even conceding that it may thereby dilute a given party's participation in selecting arbitrators.[15] Permitting such dilution would of course abate a major obstacle to the consolidation of separate arbitrations.

§ 599. Provisional and Other Incidental Remedies in Arbitration

A 1985 amendment adding subdivision (c) to CPLR 7502 made the provisional remedies of attachment and preliminary injunction available for use in conjunction with an arbitration, but only if it is shown that the award to which the applicant may be entitled may be rendered ineffectual without such provisional relief.

The application for the remedy is made to the supreme court in the county where the arbitration is pending. If the arbitration has not yet been commenced, the proper venue is a county specified in subdivision (a) of CPLR 7502, the provision that sets the venue for arbitration-connected court applications in general.[1] Articles 62 and 63 of the CPLR, which govern the attachment and injunction remedies in a court action, also apply here, but with the proviso that the sole ground for their grant is the standard noted above.[2]

As to the attachment, one early view of CPLR 7502(c) was that at least one of the grounds listed in CPLR 6201 as a prerequisite for an attachment[3] must also be satisfied before the remedy is granted in connection with an arbitration,[4] but that view was rejected by the appellate division in Drexel Burnham Lambert Inc. v. Ruebsamen,[5] noting that CPLR 7502(c) "unequivocally specifies" that the only ground that has to be met is that the award may be rendered ineffectual if the remedy is withheld. There are of course supervening constitutional requirements that confine the provisional remedies,[6] but these can be met without also insisting that one of the statutory grounds of CPLR 6201 be satisfied. CPLR 6201 does not exhaust the constitutional premises for issuing an attachment, and as long as the applicant satisfies the burden of proof and the other side is given proper notice and an opportunity to oppose the attachment,

---

13. See Chariot Textiles Corp. v. Wannalancit Textile Co., 18 N.Y.2d 793, 275 N.Y.S.2d 382 (1966), rev'g on dissenting opinion in 21 A.D.2d 762, 763, 250 N.Y.S.2d 493, 494 (1st Dep't 1964).

14. See Vigo Steamship Corp. v. Marship Corp. of Monrovia, 26 N.Y.2d 157, 309 N.Y.S.2d 165, 257 N.E.2d 624 (1970); Symphony Fabrics Corp. v. Bernson Silk Mills, Inc., 16 A.D.2d 473, 229 N.Y.S.2d 200 (1st Dep't 1962), aff'd 12 N.Y.2d 409, 240 N.Y.S.2d 23, 190 N.E.2d 418 (1963). See generally Finkelstein, Consolidation of Arbitration Proceedings by the Courts, N.Y. Law Journal, October 14, 1969, p.1.

15. See County of Sullivan v. Edward L. Nezelek, Inc., 42 N.Y.2d 123, 397 N.Y.S.2d 371, 366 N.E.2d 72 (1977), ordering consolidation where there were separate and different parties and two separate but related contracts. The court indicated that the parties to a given contract

can expressly preclude consolidation, if they choose to, by so providing in the agreement.

§ 599

1. See § 591 above.

2. The other two provisional remedies, the receivership of Article 64 of the CPLR and the lis pendens of Article 65, and the provisional-like remedy of the order to seize a chattel of Article 71, are not included in the authorization of CPLR 7502(c).

3. See § 314 above.

4. See Continental Chartering and Brokerage, Inc. v. T.J. Stevenson and Co., 678 F.Supp. 58 (S.D.N.Y.1987).

5. 139 A.D.2d 323, 531 N.Y.S.2d 547 (1st Dep't 1988).

6. See §§ 307, 315, and 338, above.

the CPLR 7502(c) "rendered ineffectual" standard should suffice on its own.

A divided Court of Appeals held in Cooper v. Ateliers de la Motobecane, S.A.,[7] that an attachment is not available in commercial arbitrations subject to the "Convention on the Recognition and Enforcement of Foreign Arbitral Awards", a treaty to which the United States is a party. The decision has been held by other courts to continue to bar attachments in treaty-governed cases despite the intervening adoption of CPLR 7502(c),[8] but the point seems worthy of reconsideration by the Court of Appeals in view of the policy underlying the statute.

As to the injunction, the question arose whether, in addition to the statutory "rendered ineffectual" requirement, the applicant must also meet the usual equity requirements applicable to injunctive relief. Answering yes, a court said in Saferstein v. Wendy,[9] that the applicant must show "[1] a likelihood of success on the merits, [2] irreparable injury if relief is withheld and [3] a balance in his favor of the equities". On the first point, the court notes the restrictive powers of review the court has over arbitral awards and holds that the "success on the merits" inquiry can go no further than determine whether the arbitration clause embraces the relief demanded. In *Saferstein* the clause was broad and clearly embraced the relief sought, which was reformation of an agreement for the development and manufacture of a product.[10] (The applicant wanted the injunction to stop termination of the agreement pending the arbitration.) The irreparable injury element was also met, the court noting that on the facts money damages would be speculative at best and hence not adequate to protect the applicant, a factor also affecting the third element, a balancing of the equities. The balance here, including a bond exacted of the applicant to protect the other side, was found to favor the preliminary injunction, which the court granted.

The chief use for an injunction in connection with an arbitration should be at the outset, before the arbitration is even under way. CPLR 7502(c)'s authorization of a preliminary injunction, which covers the pendency of the proceeding itself, should carry with it the temporary restraining order, an integral part of Article 63,[11] the CPLR's preliminary injunction article, thus enabling an applicant on a proper showing to secure relief through an order to show cause even before the preliminary injunction application comes on for a hearing.[12] Once the arbitration is under way, injunctive relief can be sought from the arbitrator. Arbitrators can issue permanent injunctions,[13] and this should carry with it the power to issue preliminary injunctions and temporary restraining orders[14] if the arbitrator is in the picture early enough.

Just a brief historical note. Before 1985, New York law on the use of the provisional remedies in connection with arbitrations was ambivalent. The principal source of authority for the use of a provisional remedy in an arbitrable case prior to 1985 was American Reserve Ins. Co. v. China Ins. Co.,[15] and even that case approached the subject on a tangent. The court held that an attachment, even though granted in an action brought in violation of an arbitration agreement, was subject to nothing more than a stay, just as the action itself is subject to a stay in deference to arbitration. It was authority, therefore, not for issuing an attachment in conjunction with an arbitration, but for just letting it stand if it had already been issued in the action. CPLR

---

7. 57 N.Y.2d 408, 456 N.Y.S.2d 728, 442 N.E.2d 1239 (1982), discussed in a lead note in New York State Law Digest No. 277.

8. See Drexel Burnham Lambert Inc. v. Ruebsamen, note 5, above.

9. 137 Misc.2d 1032, 523 N.Y.S.2d 725 (Sup.Ct., N.Y. County, 1987).

10. The product involved was a "lice comb", probably some kind of minuscule device used by the fastidious to keep their lice well groomed.

11. See CPLR 6313.

12. See § 330 above.

13. See Sprinzen v. Nomberg, 46 N.Y.2d 623, 415 N.Y.S.2d 974, 389 N.E.2d 456 (1979).

14. See J. Brooks Securities, Inc. v. Vanderbilt Securities, Inc., 126 Misc.2d 875, 484 N.Y.S.2d 472 (Sup.Ct., N.Y. County, 1985).

15. 297 N.Y. 322, 79 N.E.2d 425 (1948).

7502(c) is of course direct authority for the issuance of an arbitration-connected attachment today.

What about other procedures? Amendments in the course of arbitration, such as to add further claims, are generally left to the arbitrators. At least this is so when the matter sought to be added is closely enough related to the claims already in arbitration to be deemed embraced within the original arbitration demand. There is indication, however, that should a party attempt to interpose a wholly distinct claim during the arbitration, the other side, treating it as an independent matter altogether, may get a separate determination of its arbitrability with a prompt court application for a stay.[16] That would seem a viable prospect only where the agreement involves a narrow arbitration clause, however, or where the new dispute has no connection at all to the agreement.

The availability of disclosure proceedings within or in conjunction with arbitration was treated earlier.[17]

Needless to say, the calendar and trial practices of litigation are irrelevant to the arbitral process.

§ 600.   The Award

Arbitration culminates in an "award". In a case with multiple arbitrators, only a majority is needed; the award need not be unanimous.[1] If a party defaults, there will be no summary default as such. A party's failure to appear is not deemed an admission.[2] The arbitrator may determine the controversy on whatever evidence is offered by those who appear.[3]

The award must be in writing and must be signed and affirmed by the arbitrators making it,[4] but it need not state reasons or, if figures are included, the calculations supporting them.[5] The award is satisfactory as long as it is "final and definite";[6] arbitrators are not required to set forth their underlying findings.[7] A party who would raise in court one of the narrow grounds for vacating or modifying an award can show the requisite facts, through affidavits or otherwise, in the papers bringing or resisting a special proceeding to confirm, modify, or vacate the award, procedures we turn to in the following sections.

The award must be made within such time as the agreement stipulates, or, absent agreement, within such time as a court may order. The parties can extend the time otherwise provided. A failure to object in writing to the lateness of the award waives the objection.[8]

The award can include the arbitrators' expenses and fees, which the court can disallow or reduce if found excessive.[9] The award does not ordinarily include attorneys' fees unless the agreement expressly provides for them[10] or a special statute allows them.[11]

The arbitrator delivers a copy of the award to each party in the manner provided in the agreement, or, in the absence of such a provision, by personal delivery or by registered or certified mail with return receipt requested.[12] If ordinary mail is authorized by the arbitration rules of an organization specified by the

16.   See Davis, Brody & Wisniewski v. Temple Emanu–El of East Meadow, 49 Misc.2d 1067, 268 N.Y.S.2d 954 (Sup.Ct., Suffolk County, 1966), aff'd 27 A.D.2d 842, 277 N.Y.S.2d 860 (2d Dep't 1967).

17.   See § 597.

§ 600

1.   CPLR 7506(e).

2.   See 2d Rep.Leg.Doc. (1958) No.13, p.140.

3.   CPLR 7506(c).

4.   CPLR 7507. As to what an "affirmation" is, see CPLR 2106. A procedure for award by confession is set forth in CPLR 7508.

5.   See Bay Ridge Medical Group, v. Health Ins. Plan of Greater N.Y., 22 A.D.2d 807, 254 N.Y.S.2d 616 (2d Dep't 1964).

6.   CPLR 7511(b)(1)(iii).

7.   Colletti v. Mesh, 23 A.D.2d 245, 260 N.Y.S.2d 130 (1st Dep't), aff'd 17 N.Y.2d 460, 266 N.Y.S.2d 814, 213 N.E.2d 894 (1965).

8.   CPLR 7507.

9.   CPLR 7513.

10.   See Koenigsberg v. Zinn, 51 A.D.2d 929, 381 N.Y.S.2d 248 (1st Dep't 1976).

11.   See, e.g., Kamakazi Music Corp. v. Robbins Music Corp., 684 F.2d 228 (2d Cir.1982), involving the federal copyright law.

12.   CPLR 7507.

parties in their agreement, the parties will be deemed to have adopted that method.[13] Even if that is not the case, the use of ordinary mail will not necessarily invalidate the delivery.[14]

The arbitrator has the power to modify the award after rendering it, but a party must apply for the modification in writing and on notice to the other parties within 20 days after the award has been delivered. The other parties then have 10 days, from receipt of the notice, within which to serve on the arbitrator and the other parties a written objection to the modification. The arbitrator then has 30 days in which to dispose of the application to modify.[15] The grounds for modification by the arbitrator are the same as those listed in CPLR 7511(c), which governs when a modification of an award is sought from the court. They are treated later.[16]

After the award has been delivered, any party can apply to the court to confirm, vacate, or modify it. There is a year in which to apply to confirm,[17] but only 90 days in which to apply to vacate or modify.[18] The period in each instance is measured from the delivery of the award to the applicant.

E. CONVERTING AWARD INTO JUDGMENT

Table of Sections

§ 601.　Confirmation of Award

The winner of the award who gets complete satisfaction from the loser voluntarily may find scant incentive for bothering with the further step of "confirming" it, which means getting a formal court judgment entered on it. But the CPLR provides for such a conversion, and it is perhaps best that the winner make it a habit to get the award confirmed into a judgment. It usually takes only a special proceeding to accomplish this, and it holds certain fringe benefits. Once the award is confirmed into a judgment, all of the enforcement of judgment remedies become available for it. Further, while the award is itself entitled to res judicata treatment, on closer scrutiny one may discover that it is sometimes not the award, but rather a judgment entered on the award, that is so treated.[1]

There is only one year, measured from delivery of the award, in which to apply to confirm it,[2] and the year is in every sense a statute of limitations.[3]

There are other paths to confirmation besides the winner's direct application for it. Any party can apply, within 90 days from the delivery of the award, to vacate or modify it.[4] If the court denies either motion, it confirms the award; if it grants a motion to modify, it

13. The Commercial Arbitration Rules of the American Arbitration Association, for example, authorize ordinary mail.

14. See Kozlowski v. Seville Syndicate, Inc., 64 Misc.2d 109, 314 N.Y.S.2d 439 (Sup.Ct., N.Y. County, 1970).

15. CPLR 7509.

16. See § 604.

17. CPLR 7510, 215(5).

18. CPLR 7511(a).

§ 601

1. See, e.g., Bird v. Meadow Gold Products Corp., 60 Misc.2d 212, 302 N.Y.S.2d 701 (Sup.Ct., Kings County, 1969), citing Springs Cotton Mills v. Buster Boy Suit Co., 275 A.D. 196, 88 N.Y.S.2d 295 (1st Dep't), aff'd 300 N.Y. 586, 89 N.E.2d 877 (1949).

2. CPLR 7510, 215(5).

3. See Belli v. Matthew Bender & Co., 24 A.D.2d 72, 263 N.Y.S.2d 846 (1st Dep't 1965). The confirmation standards and procedures discussed in this and the ensuing sections apply to the usual Article 75 arbitration and should not be confused with the court-annexed arbitration known as the "Alternative Method of Dispute Resolution by Arbitration" treated in § 585B above. It has been held that a judgment may be entered on an award in the latter category without going through the confirmation procedures spelled out in CPLR 7510. See Zampella v. Plaza at Latham Ass'n, 69 A.D.2d 957, 416 N.Y.S.2d 89 (3d Dep't 1979).

4. CPLR 7511(a).

confirms the award as modified.[5] If the arbitrator has rendered an award but then "clarified" it with a "supplemental" award, the 90 days to modify has been held to run from the supplemental award.[6]

It is apparently not mandatory that the losing party make an affirmative application to vacate or modify. The loser, by way of opposing a motion to confirm, which can be made any time within a year, can interpose whatever vacatur or modification grounds he may have, and can do this even though the 90 days in which to make an independent application to vacate or modify have expired.[7]

Whatever the nature of the application—whether to confirm, vacate, or modify—it will usually take the form of a special proceeding. It does so when no prior application has been made to the court in respect of this particular arbitration. While not a unanimous view, it was for a long time assumed that if there was a prior related application, such as at the outset where a special proceeding was brought to test arbitrability and arbitration was directed, the later post-award application could take the form of a motion, captioned in that earlier proceeding.[8] The Court of Appeals rejected that idea in Solkav v. Besicorp Group Inc.,[9] holding that confirmation of the award must be sought in a new special proceeding.[10]

Practitioners bringing proceedings to confirm, vacate, or modify an award should note carefully the procedures for the special proceedings that they entail. The filing of the initiatory papers in the proceeding marks its commencement for statute of limitations purposes and there is then a limited additional time for the service of the papers.[11]

Any party who would for whatever reason seek an appellate review of the award must see to it that a judgment or order is first rendered at trial level, whether confirming, vacating, or modifying, because the award itself is not appealable.[12]

There is precedent for a New York court to confirm an arbitration award made outside the state, assuming that New York has the requisite jurisdiction over the parties,[13] but it is more usual for the winner to secure that confirmation at home, i.e., get the award confirmed into a judgment there and then seek to convert the judgment into a New York judgment.

The several contexts from which a confirmation can emerge—direct application or opposition to an application to vacate or modify (subjects to which we next turn)—are applications made against the other parties to the arbitration, not against the arbitrators, who are neither necessary nor proper parties. This is a conspicuous distinction between a proceeding brought in respect of an arbitral award under Article 75 of the CPLR and one brought to review an administrative determination under Article 78.[14]

§ 602. Application to Vacate Award; Scope of Review

Perhaps the best insights into the differences between litigation and arbitration come from a study of the application to vacate the award. The narrowness of the vacatur grounds, which are listed in CPLR 7511(b)(1), a generator of much caselaw, manifest how much more is left to the final and unreview-

---

5. CPLR 7511(e). For detailed treatment of the applications to vacate or modify, see §§ 602 and 604, below.

6. Leombruno v. City of Glens Falls, 110 A.D.2d 996, 488 N.Y.S.2d 284 (3d Dep't 1985). The arbitrator's time to modify the award is itself limited, see § 600 above. Presumably, whatever "clarification" the arbitrator came up with in the Leombruno case was within his jurisdiction and within the proper time for exercising it.

7. See 2d Rep.Leg.Doc. (1958) No.13, p.144.

8. CPLR 7502(a). See, e.g., Solartechnik v. Besicorp Group Inc., 227 A.D.2d 94, 652 N.Y.S.2d 654 (3d Dep't 1997),

9. 91 N.Y.2d 482, 672 N.Y.S.2d 838 (1998).

10. See the discussion of Solkav in the lead note in New York State Law Digest No. 462. It has been suggested that the court on the initial application might reserve jurisdiction for post-award steps, but that has some unsuspected risks for the winner of the award. See the lead note in SPR 73:3.

11. See the discussion of special proceedings generally in § 553 above, and the reference to them in the specific context of arbitration towards the end of § 593 above.

12. CPLR 5701.

13. See Swan v. Sit'N Chat Restaurant, Inc., 43 A.D.2d 949, 352 N.Y.S.2d 31 (2d Dep't 1974).

14. See § 603 below.

able determination of an arbitrator than to a trial judge in litigation or even to an agency in the administrative process.

It is at this moment, in fact, that a party who chose arbitration may develop some second thoughts about it. Too late. The courts do not review arbitral awards for errors of fact or law, as would be permissible on an appeal from a judgment. The question of whether the arbitrator was right or wrong is not for the courts.[1] As we have already noted, neither the substantive law of the state nor even the rules of evidence bind the arbitrator, so that an error the arbitrator makes in respect of either is unreviewable.[2] The award is subject to review only on the few narrow grounds allowed by the legislature under CPLR 7511(b)(1). This section takes up those grounds. Their study, incidentally, can as well be entitled "scope of review", which is precisely what one is looking at when inquiring into the judicially cognizable grounds for overturning an award.

A few introductory points. A distinction is made between a party who was duly notified of the arbitration or who participated in it, and one who neither participated nor had notice. The first is restricted to the vacatur grounds listed in CPLR 7511(b)(1); the second may also raise on the vacatur motion any of the threshold questions, i.e., arbitrability and timeliness,[3] because not given an earlier opportunity to raise them.

Technically, under the language of CPLR 7511(b)(1), the party limited to the usual vacatur grounds is the one who participated in the arbitration or was served with a "notice of intention to arbitrate", the well-known device of CPLR 7503(c). It may happen, however, that the arbitration got under way through P's successful application against D under CPLR 7503(a) to compel arbitration. Should D then have failed to participate in the arbitration, he should still be deemed restricted to the (b)(1) vacatur grounds, that is, he should be barred

from raising the threshold questions even though he escapes the precise language of CPLR 7511(b)(1). Since D had a chance to raise those questions in the earlier "compel" proceeding, it would be inappropriate to let him raise them again on a vacatur application.

A second point concerns time limits. As the prior section mentioned, the applicant has 90 days from delivery of the award in which to apply to vacate it. It is incumbent on the party opposing that application to show that the 90 days has expired,[4] which is just another way of saying once again that untimeliness is an affirmative defense.

For reference purposes as we treat the several vacatur grounds, it is best to set them down verbatim at the outset. As numbered in CPLR 7511(b)(1), they are:

(i) corruption, fraud or misconduct in procuring the award; or

(ii) partiality of an arbitrator appointed as a neutral, except where the award was by confession; or

(iii) an arbitrator, or agency or person making the award exceeded his power or so imperfectly executed it that a final and definite award upon the subject matter submitted was not made; or

(iv) failure to follow the procedure of this article, unless the party applying to vacate the award continued with the arbitration with notice of the defect and without objection.

Any evidence of fraud or collusion between an arbitrator and a party would of course constitute corruption or misconduct under subparagraph (i), but the defect need not be as flagrant as that. An unreasonable refusal to adjourn the hearing, for example, resulting in a party's inability to secure needed evidence,

---

§ 602

1. See Colletti v. Mesh, 23 A.D.2d 245, 260 N.Y.S.2d 130 (1st Dep't), aff'd 17 N.Y.2d 460, 266 N.Y.S.2d 814, 213 N.E.2d 894 (1965).

2. See Raisler Corp. v. N.Y.C. Hsg. Auth., 32 N.Y.2d 274, 344 N.Y.S.2d 917, 298 N.E.2d 91 (1973).

3. CPLR 7511(b)(2).

4. See Ganser v. N.Y. Tel. Co., 39 A.D.2d 653, 331 N.Y.S.2d 914 (1st Dep't 1972).

has been held to qualify as misconduct.[5] So is a refusal to hear pertinent and material evidence, unless the evidence is excluded by the agreement itself, as happened in one case in which the agreement was found to import confidence to certain discussions.[6]

Nor need the misconduct be intentional. An arbitrator's statements misleading a party into not submitting evidence, with the arbitrator afterwards citing that very omission as part of the rationale of the award, has been deemed misconduct.[7]

Under subparagraph (ii), the "partiality" ground to which some reference was had earlier,[8] the stress in tripartite arbitration is on the neutral arbitrator, since partisanship is recognized and permitted today for the other two.[9] Relationship of one kind or another to a party is the most frequent objection here, but the relationship alone is less often the disqualifying factor than the failure to reveal it. The major burden of disclosure falls on the arbitrator. It is incumbent on the arbitrator to reveal all facts relevant to possible bias on his part, which enables each side to judge for itself whether it wants the arbitrator disqualified for potential bias. Thus, where a business relationship was revealed but the extent of it was not, the award was vacated, the Court of Appeals calling for "maximum prehearing disclosure" on the issue.[10] The time for the revelation of these facts is in advance of the arbitration, of course. A party who, with knowledge of an arguably disqualifying relationship, nonetheless assents to the arbitrator is more likely than not to have waived the objection altogether. Even appellate cases that allow a post-award attack on the ground of relationship are likely to involve a dissent if the party knew the basic facts in advance.[11]

Judges do not welcome post-award plaints about prejudice from a party who should have made the objection early and stuck by it; they always suspect that the party would have commended the same arbitrator for magnanimous objectivity had the award gone in his favor.

Subparagraph (iii) has also been a source of some disagreement among the judges, who have not been able to draw a sharp line between what belongs within the sacrosanct sphere of the merits and what goes so far beyond them as to constitute an "excess" of power and hence a ground to vacate. The excess standard is not so difficult to minister when the arbitration clause is narrow, applying only to designated issues and thereby putting all others beyond arbitration. But when the arbitration clause is a broad one, calling for arbitration of everything, an attempt to denominate something an "excess" will have some rough sailing. Granite Worsted Mills v. Aronson Cowen, Ltd.[12] is an example, the Court of Appeals dividing 4–3 in it. The clause in that case was a broad one, but one of the substantive provisions in the contract excluded consequential damages and the arbitrator nonetheless awarded them. The majority found this to be an excess of power and vacated the award. The minority were of the view that the arbitrator was doing nothing more than interpreting the agreement and that his error in this regard, if error it was, was beyond judicial scrutiny.

The minority position was more in tune with the purpose of arbitration and better fitted to the strict channels of CPLR 7511. And, indeed, it was destined to prevail as a statement of the law. The Court of Appeals in

---

5. See Woodco Mfg. Corp. v. G.R. & R. Mfg., Inc., 51 A.D.2d 631, 378 N.Y.S.2d 504 (3d Dep't 1976).

6. See Professional Staff Congress/CUNY v. Board of Higher Ed., 39 N.Y.2d 319, 383 N.Y.S.2d 592, 347 N.E.2d 918 (1976).

7. See Lewis v. County of Suffolk, 70 A.D.2d 107, 419 N.Y.S.2d 680 (2d Dep't 1979).

8. See § 596 above.

9. See Astoria Medical Group v. Health Ins. Plan of Greater N.Y., 11 N.Y.2d 128, 227 N.Y.S.2d 401, 182 N.E.2d 85 (1962).

10. See J.P. Stevens & Co. v. Rytex Corp., 34 N.Y.2d 123, 128, 356 N.Y.S.2d 278, 282, 312 N.E.3d 466, 469 (1974).

11. See, e.g., Baar & Beards, Inc. v. Oleg Cassini, Inc., 37 A.D.2d 106, 322 N.Y.S.2d 462 (1st Dep't 1971) rev'd 30 N.Y.2d 649, 331 N.Y.S.2d 670 (1972).

12. 25 N.Y.2d 451, 306 N.Y.S.2d 934, 255 N.E.2d 168 (1969).

Silverman v. Benmor Coats, Inc.[13] overruled the *Granite Worsted* decision, holding that to exclude a particular substantive issue from arbitration, the arbitration clause itself must enumerate "the subjects intended to be put beyond the arbitrator's reach". If the argument is over the substantive agreement at large and whether the arbitrator properly construed it, instead of with respect to the arbitration clause itself and its specific enumeration of issues, the award will be upheld as beyond the court's power to review.

Other decisional address to an "excess of power" has held that it exists only when the arbitrators give the provisions in dispute "a completely irrational construction", in effect making a new contract for the parties.[14] The courts have long been at home with the "completely irrational" criterion. They often manage to uphold an award even though there is substantive language in the contract itself that can be deemed to exclude part of it.[15] Even the award in the now-overruled *Granite Worsted* case could have been upheld had it just been subjected to the "irrational" test, as the majority in that case itself conceded. They acknowledged that the arbitrator might have found the contract provision that precluded consequential damages unconscionable, for example, which would have been a rational ground for rejecting it. Their protest was that the award did not say as much. But that in turn seems to disregard the caselaw holding that the award does not have to; that the award need state neither findings nor reasons.[16] There is not even a requirement that minutes be kept of arbitral proceedings; nor is it even permissible as a rule for the arbitrator to submit an affidavit in support of his award.[17] Venerable caselaw holds, in fact, that

every presumption and intendment is in favor of an award's validity and only if "it affirmatively appears, either upon the face of the award or by extrinsic evidence that the arbitrators exceeded their authority", will the award be overturned.[18]

Another part of subparagraph (iii) authorizes vacatur of the award if the arbitrator "so imperfectly executed it that a final and definite award" was not made. The underlying policy of this provision is to have the whole existing dispute determined at once and embodied in one award. If there is indication that something still remains to be done—and it requires clear evidence to convince the court on this point, too—the matter will usually be remitted to the arbitrator with instructions to take the still-needed steps. Thus, where an arbitral submission required that a figure be reduced by a certain formula and the arbitrator had not done that, the award failed of both finality and definiteness and was vacated and the matter remitted.[19]

The Court of Appeals held in Meisels v. Uhr[20] that an award doesn't lack finality merely because the arbitrators retain jurisdiction of possible future disputes. In that case the court found that the retention of jurisdiction concerned "only potential disputes that might arise", and that this did not divest the award already made of its finality.

A failure to follow a procedure prescribed by Article 75 is made a vacatur basis by subparagraph (iv), unless the point is waived. Most of the procedures of the hearing, for example, as embodied in CPLR 7506,[21] are waivable.[22] One that is not waivable is the right to an attor-

---

13. 61 N.Y.2d 299, 473 N.Y.S.2d 774, 461 N.E.2d 1261 (1984).

14. See National Cash Register Co. v. Wilson, 8 N.Y.2d 377, 208 N.Y.S.2d 951, 171 N.E.2d 302 (1960). The excess of power provision of CPLR 7511(b)(1)(iii) is also the source through which the Court of Appeals has extruded an administrative review standard for compulsory arbitration cases, a matter irrelevant to the voluntary arbitration we concentrate on here and deferred for that reason to the next section.

15. See, e.g., Swartz v. Swartz, 49 A.D.2d 254, 374 N.Y.S.2d 857 (4th Dep't 1975).

16. See § 600 above.

17. See Dahlke v. X–L–O Automotive Accessories, Inc., 40 A.D.2d 666, 337 N.Y.S.2d 86 (1st Dep't 1972).

18. Hiscock v. Harris, 74 N.Y. 108, 112–23 (1878).

19. Biscardi v. Maryland Cas. Co., 40 A.D.2d 610, 335 N.Y.S.2d 941 (2d Dep't 1972).

20. 79 N.Y.2d 526, 583 N.Y.S.2d 951, 593 N.E.2d 1359 (1992).

21. See § 597 above.

22. CPLR 7506(f).

ney,[23] and any activity that has the effect of divesting a party of that right would be an example of a procedural defect entitling the party to a vacatur of the award under subparagraph (iv).

Near the outset of this chapter a section was devoted to the "public policy" realm—a discussion of several areas in which public policy requires that the courts keep full rein on a subject, thus totally precluding the submission of anything to arbitration. Those areas, few that they be, are carved out by caselaw. It is common to raise the public policy objection, should it be present, at the outset, treating it as a threshold question and seeking a stay of arbitration with it. But, as earlier noted,[24] the objection is so pervasive that it is available after arbitration as well as before. Although not expressly listed as a vacatur ground in CPLR 7511(b)(1), therefore, "public policy" is for all practical purposes an addition to that list and may be treated as such.[25]

Upon vacating an award in whole or in part, the court may, if appropriate, direct a rehearing by the arbitrators, or simply strike such part of the award as is impermissible and confirm the rest.[26] It amounts to a pro tanto vacatur.[27]

Since the arbitral process has also been made available, at the claimant's option, under the state's so-called "no-fault" law in personal injury cases,[28] the lawyer should note a unique procedure applicable there, adopted in 1977.[29] The award made by the arbitrator is first reviewed by a "master arbitrator" under internal procedures promulgated or approved by the superintendent of insurance and not re-

stricted to the grounds of CPLR 7511. The decision of the master arbitrator may then be reviewed, and upon that review Article 75 of the CPLR and the limited review grounds of CPLR 7511 do apply.[30] The rationale of the no-fault award, for example, while "a matter of primary concern to a master arbitrator, is of no moment to the court" and cannot be reviewed by it.[31] The Court of Appeals, enumerating the master arbitrator's review powers in *Petrofsky v. Allstate Ins. Co.*,[32] holds that while broader than the review powers of the court, they do not include a de novo trial of the facts. Finding the master arbitrator in *Petrofsky* to have "engaged in extensive factual review, making independent findings of fact", the court vacated the award and reinstated the original arbitrator's.

The no-fault procedure can be termed semiconsensual, since it is available only at the claimant's option. Compulsory arbitration, the next step along this line, is in a class by itself and gets separate housing in the next section.

§ 603. Scope of Review in Compulsory Arbitration

New York's first substantial contact with the problem of whether to apply the usual arbitration scope of review, as embodied in CPLR 7511, to awards emanating from arbitration not felt to be of the usual voluntary type, was in the tort area in cases involving an uninsured motorist or hit-and-run driver or the like. Under a clause contained in the insurance policy, an injured insured person gets protection in these instances from her own insurer. Coverage like this came onto the scene in the late 1950s.[1] The insurance indus-

---

23. CPLR 7506(d),(f).

24. See § 587.

25. See Meyers v. Kinney Motors, Inc., 32 A.D.2d 266, 301 N.Y.S.2d 171 (1st Dep't 1969).

26. CPLR 7511(d).

27. See Wolff & Munier, Inc. v. Diesel Constr. Co., 41 A.D.2d 618, 340 N.Y.S.2d 455 (1st Dep't 1973).

28. The formal name of the "no-fault" law is the Comprehensive Motor Vehicle Insurance Reparations Act. Ins.L. § 5101. It covers §§ 5101–5108 of the Insurance Law. The provision requiring the insurer to offer the claimant the option of arbitration is in § 5106(b).

29. L.1977, c. 892, § 13.

30. Ins.L. § 5106(c). This provision further directs that if the master arbitrator's award is $5000 or more,

excluding interest and attorney's fees—which may be included in the award upon the authority of § 5106(a)—either the insurer or the claimant may bring an ordinary court action to adjudicate the claim de novo, which cancels the award entirely.

31. Petition of Carty, 149 A.D.2d 328, 539 N.Y.S.2d 374 (1st Dep't 1989).

32. 54 N.Y.2d 207, 445 N.Y.S.2d 77, 429 N.E.2d 755 (1981).

§ 603

1. See Aksen, Arbitration of Automobile Accident Cases, 1 Conn.L.Rev. 70, 73 (1968).

try and its government overseers opted to have disputes between insured and insurer in this category arbitrated instead of litigated, the insurance policy itself containing the clause requiring it.[2] Since the policy is a contract, the resulting arbitration can technically be called voluntary, but recognizing that the contract is strictly a take-it-or-leave-it proposition, the courts have had some trouble treating it as a merely voluntary undertaking. Thus, dissenting in a case involving such an endorsement, Chief Judge Desmond protested that the arbitration it called for was not of the "conventional, consensual" kind and should therefore not be restricted to the usual, and narrow, scope of review applicable to totally voluntary arbitration.[3] But if not that standard, what other?

It was not the tort category that brought the matter to a head in cases involving compulsory arbitration, but the labor realm. One of the landmarks was Mount St. Mary's Hospital v. Catherwood,[4] decided in 1970, involving the validity of a labor law provision[5] that mandated the arbitration of disputes in cases involving nonprofit hospitals and their employees. The Court of Appeals sustained the legislation, but it recognized potential problems of due process if parties in a compulsory arbitration were held to the same restrictive standards of judicial review imposed on the parties to a voluntary arbitration. (In voluntary arbitration, the doctrine of waiver can be credited with—or blamed for—all variations.) The court therefore altered the scope of review in compulsory arbitration. Using the "excess of power" standard of CPLR 7511(b)(1)(iii) as its touchstone, the court expanded it to hold that it "includes review in the case of compulsory arbitration (but only in such case) of whether the award is supported by evidence or other basis in reason".[6]

While it was now reasonably clear that an Article 78 standard was being imported, which of them—Article 78 has several—was it to be? Was it the "arbitrary and capricious" test of CPLR 7803(3)? The "substantial evidence" rule of CPLR 7803(4)? Some other? And what of the mechanics of the process? Would Article 78 apply in its entirety for review of compulsory arbitral awards, or would Article 75 continue to supply the procedure, with only the review criterion borrowed from Article 78?

These problems were addressed by the Court of Appeals in Caso v. Coffey,[7] at the end of 1976. It is only the Article 78 review standard that gets imported. The procedures of Article 75 supply everything else. Since the essential procedure under each article is a special proceeding, at first blush there seems little to choose from. But there is this significant accomplishment: with Article 75 controlling procedure, it is clear that the proceeding is to be brought against the adverse parties only and not, as might have happened had Article 78 been adopted, against the arbitrators themselves.

Finally, which of the Article 78 standards is to be used? The Court of Appeals in *Caso* adopted the "arbitrary and capricious" standard of CPLR 7803(3), but offered as alternatives the word "rational" and the phrase "plausible basis". The court specifically said that it was not using the "substantial evidence" test, although conceding that it, too, would meet a "rationality" standard.

If this sounds familiar, it is because the law subjects us to the same exercise of sameness within the confines of Article 78 itself. In the study of Article 78, we had occasion to compare its several different review standards and concluded that they are essentially the same, the "abuse of discretion" test, in fact, being yet another entry in those earlier sweepstakes[8]

---

2. An example of the policy endorsement appears in Rosenbaum v. American Surety Co. of N.Y., 11 N.Y.2d 310, 229 N.Y.S.2d 375, 183 N.E.2d 667 (1962).

3. See the dissenting opinion in Torano v. M.V.A.I.C., 15 N.Y.2d 882, 883, 258 N.Y.S.2d 418, 419, 206 N.E.2d 353 (1965).

4. 26 N.Y.2d 493, 311 N.Y.S.2d 863, 260 N.E.2d 508 (1970).

5. Labor L. § 716.

6. 26 N.Y.2d at 508, 311 N.Y.S.2d at 875, 260 N.E.2d at 516.

7. 41 N.Y.2d 153, 391 N.Y.S.2d 88, 359 N.E.2d 683.

8. See § 561.

and a successful competitor for sameness. We may now add "plausible basis". And lest the *Caso* decision be assumed to have differentiated the "substantial evidence" test, we may note that the substantial evidence test was the one applied by the lower court in *Caso*,[9] which was affirmed!

All of the above has to do with appellate review of the overall record in these cases. What about the review of individual questions of law? In the usual consensual arbitration, errors of law are generally unreviewable, again on the theory that the parties surrendered the technical rules of substantive law by opting for the more flexible approaches of arbitration. But what about an arbitration that is the product not of option, but of compulsion, which makes it much more difficult to insulate errors of law from judicial review? The no-fault realm, another species of compulsory arbitration, became the arena for the resolution of that question. It did not take long for the courts to acknowledge that it is one thing to hold that volunteering for arbitration waives judicial review even of issues of law, but quite another to spell out a waiver when the arbitration is compulsory. The most extended treatment of the matter is the Second Department's Shand v. Aetna Ins. Co.,[10] which tried to reconcile a series of Court of Appeals cases and in doing so reached the conclusion that as long as there is a rational basis for the arbitrator's decision, the decision is beyond judicial review whether it poses issues of fact or issues of law. The issue of law involved in *Shand* was which of two categories of insurer was to cover a certain automobile injury. The court, even though it found the arbitrator's selection "certainly questionable", held that it was "not so irrational as to require vacatur".

Apparently in the realization that such an approach would make every no-fault arbitrator a court of last resort on legal as well as factual issues, other departments did not follow suit.

They held that if the no-fault arbitrator's error is one of law, it is subject to judicial review.[11] The Second Department itself appeared to make peace with the issue, too. In subsequent cases it appeared to review issues of law in compulsory arbitration contexts as part of the overall standard that the *Shand* case had articulated in this language:

> The test thus applicable for review of no-fault arbitrations where error of law is in issue is essentially similar to that utilized for review of quasi-legislative determinations—whether *any* reasonable hypothesis can be found to support the questioned interpretation.

In Massapequa General Hospital v. Travelers Insurance Co.,[12] for example, the issue was whether the arbitrator had violated a regulation in the way he awarded interest on the claim—a question of law. The court did find a violation, and based on it concluded that there was no reasonable hypothesis "to explain the arbitrator's failure to observe and apply the applicable insurance regulations". The court interpreted the regulation, in other words, and overturned the offending part of the award accordingly—just as any court would do with any issue of law.

One may conclude that whatever the verbal formula used by the courts in reviewing compulsory arbitration awards, if the court perceives a given error as one of law, it manages to review it. If it were otherwise, the *Shand* observation would surely come home to roost: that every arbitrator in every compulsory arbitration would amount to a legislature. That's sometimes what happens in voluntary arbitration, but there the parties asked for it.

§ 604. Application to Modify Award

CPLR 7511(c) sets forth the grounds on which the court can modify an arbitration award. It can be modified if:

---

9. 53 A.D.2d 373, 385 N.Y.S.2d 593 (2d Dep't 1976).

10. 74 A.D.2d 442, 428 N.Y.S.2d 462 (2d Dep't 1980). The case is the subject of the lead note in New York State Law Digest No. 250.

11. See, e.g., Karmilowicz v. Allstate Ins. Co., 77 A.D.2d 131, 432 N.Y.S.2d 698 (1st Dep't 1980); Trans-

america Ins. Co. v. Lumbermen's Cas. Ins. Co., 77 A.D.2d 5, 432 N.Y.S.2d 269 (3d Dep't 1980); and Brunner v. Allstate Ins. Co., 79 A.D.2d 491, 437 N.Y.S.2d 199 (4th Dep't 1981).

12. 104 A.D.2d 638, 480 N.Y.S.2d 18 (2d Dep't 1984).

1. there was a miscalculation of figures or a mistake in the description of any person, thing or property referred to in the award; or

2. the arbitrators have awarded upon a matter not submitted to them and the award may be corrected without affecting the merits of the decision upon the issues submitted; or

3. the award is imperfect in a matter of form, not affecting the merits of the controversy.

The mistake will qualify as a mere "miscalculation" so as to permit modification under paragraph 1 if it is so plain as to permit a mere ministerial correction. Where an insurer's liability was limited to a stated figure by statute, for example, and the combined award to the parties exceeded it, the court reduced it down to the maximum.[1] Similarly, when an award plainly contains a duplicative item of damages the court will by way of modification strike it.[2]

Paragraph 2 enables the court to retain an award on an arbitrable matter while striking out anything awarded on a matter not arbitrable—a situation of course more likely to arise when the arbitration clause is narrow. If the parties permit the arbitration to proceed with an unsubmitted matter without objection, however, they may be held to have conceded its arbitrability and waived the right to invoke this provision.[3]

If the court grants the application and modifies the award, it will then confirm the award as modified.[4]

The time in which to apply to the court for the modification, as elaborated earlier,[5] is the 90–day period following delivery of the award to the applicant.[6]

The party seeking modification may be able to apply to the arbitrator for it without having to go to court.[7] The procedure for that was also discussed earlier.[8] The grounds are the same.

§ 605. Judgment on Award

When an award is confirmed, either in full or as modified, a judgment is entered on it.[1] The judgment-roll, consisting of the basic papers in the case,[2] is then filed with the clerk of the court.[3] At this moment the award becomes the equivalent of an ordinary judgment rendered after a court trial, for several purposes.

One is the enforcement of the judgment. Usually the award and its confirmatory judgment is for money, which enables it to use the arsenal of enforcement devices in Article 52 of the CPLR. The docketing procedures will also apply,[4] as will those whereby the judgment is to become a lien on real property[5] or personal property.[6] If the award is for equitable relief, the judgment will embody that, too,[7] making the contempt penalties available.[8]

The award will now be entitled to res judicata treatment as well. It would probably get that treatment even without conversion into a judgment,[9] but the further step enhances the prospect.[10]

The statute providing for the entry of a judgment on the award, CPLR 7514(a), states

---

§ 604

1. See Mancini v. Allstate Ins. Co., 38 A.D.2d 602, 328 N.Y.S.2d 563 (2d Dep't 1971).

2. See Miller v. Cosmopolitan Mutual Ins. Co., 33 A.D.2d 917, 307 N.Y.S.2d 592 (2d Dep't 1970).

3. See Aigen v. Giannone, 49 A.D.2d 562, 370 N.Y.S.2d 186 (2d Dep't 1975).

4. CPLR 7511(e).

5. See § 601.

6. CPLR 7511(a).

7. See CPLR 7509.

8. See § 600.

§ 605

1. CPLR 7514(a).

2. These are listed in CPLR 7514(b).

3. CPLR 5017(a).

4. CPLR 5018.

5. CPLR 5203.

6. CPLR 5234.

7. See, e.g., Bradigan v. Bishop Homes, Inc., 20 A.D.2d 966, 249 N.Y.S.2d 1018 (4th Dep't 1964).

8. CPLR 5104.

9. See § 456 above.

10. See Seetransport etc. v. Navimpex etc., 29 F.3d 79 (2d Cir.1994), discussed in SPR 26:3.

that the entry shall be made upon the "confirmation" of the award. Actually, a "judgment" will be the usual outcome whatever the disposition, since it is the paper in which a special proceeding culminates[11] and the special proceeding is the usual post-award vehicle. Hence, even a vacatur of the award, if that is what the special proceeding decides on, should be embodied in a judgment, which can even be true of a disposition remanding the case to the arbitrators for further proceedings. It would be that or an "order", in any event. The point takes on significance for appellate purposes, since in New York practice a judgment or order is appealable,[12] but an "award" is not.

Although the confirmation turns the award into a judgment for many purposes, it does not do so for all purposes, such as those of CPLR 5015(a), which supplies the grounds on which a judgment may be vacated. CPLR 5015(a) does not as a rule apply to an arbitration award or to a judgment entered on one. So, for example, a losing party who afterwards finds new evidence that would authorize a motion to vacate the judgment and secure a new trial on the ground of newly discovered evidence if the judgment were the ordinary product of litigation,[13] will be without a remedy. Since the court cannot sift the original evidence before the arbitrator, it is in no position to gauge the impact that new evidence would have. The motion therefore does not lie.[14] Nor is there as yet a procedure for reopening the award before the arbitrator in a case like this. It is one of the drawbacks of arbitrating.[15] If the later discovered evidence reveals a bribe of an arbitrator or something else that would have been a ground for vacating or modifying the award under CPLR 7511,[16] as opposed to evidence that goes merely to the merits of the award (which the court could not have reviewed earlier anyway), it should be permissible for the court to vacate the judgment for the purpose

of vacating the award. Conduct of that kind should be regarded as undermining the jurisdictional foundation on which the award rests.

§ 606. Involvement of Courts Other than Supreme Court

CPLR 7501 authorizes "the courts of the state" to enforce arbitration agreements and enter judgment on awards. Were nothing else in the picture, that would apparently mean all courts of civil jurisdiction.[1] In practice, however, it is almost always the supreme court to which parties turn with arbitrability or enforcement questions. The involvement of other courts is rare. The supreme court is accustomed to handling arbitrability and connected enforcement questions even when the sums involved in a given dispute are within the jurisdiction of lower courts. This is of course in contrast to ordinary money actions brought in the supreme court that could have been brought in a lower court. In such ordinary litigation there are tools that can get the case transferred down,[2] implementing a statewide policy of keeping out of the supreme court cases that can be litigated in lower courts. That policy has not been extended to matters arising under Article 75, however, and the supreme court does not transfer down to lower courts either arbitrability questions or enforcement of award questions raised in special proceedings brought before the supreme court.

The statewide habit of using the supreme court almost exclusively for these matters may have caused the bar to overlook that for at least some phases of the arbitral process some of the lower courts do have jurisdiction. The New York City Civil Court, for example, can entertain the threshold question of arbitrability if it arises within an action duly brought in and pending before it. But absent such a pending action it cannot entertain arbitrability questions. Thus, when a special proceeding

11. CPLR 411.
12. See CPLR 5701.
13. CPLR 5015(a)(2).
14. Central General Hospital v. Hanover Ins. Co., 49 N.Y.2d 950, 428 N.Y.S.2d 881, 406 N.E.2d 739 (1980).
15. See Mole v. Queen Ins. Co. of America, 14 A.D.2d 1, 217 N.Y.S.2d 330 (4th Dep't 1961).

16. See §§ 602 and 604 above.

§ 606

1. CPLR 101.
2. See §§ 26 and 27 above.

must be brought to test the arbitrability of a given dispute, the civil court cannot entertain it. It has jurisdiction, however, of a proceeding to confirm an already rendered award as long as the relief awarded is within the civil court's subject matter jurisdiction.[3] The same conclusions apply to the district courts of Nassau and Suffolk counties.[4] The city courts of the state can enter a judgment on an arbitral award if it is for relief within their subject matter jurisdiction, but cannot entertain arbitrability questions.[5] The town and village courts have no jurisdiction of any phase of the process. If an action is brought there in which a genuine issue of the dispute's arbitrability is raised, the town or village justice is restricted to staying the action while an arbitrability test is resolved in some other court.[6]

The courts just treated each have a statute addressing their arbitration-connected powers. A county court, which has not, has been held to be without jurisdiction of arbitrability questions, at least when brought in the form of a special proceeding in a case exceeding its subject matter jurisdiction.[7] Were an action duly brought in the county court within its jurisdiction, however, and were an arbitrability issue to arise in it, the court should be deemed possessed of sufficient power to entertain and dispose of a motion to compel arbitration.[8]

The supreme court's availability for these issues, whatever the nature or scope of the controversy, has made it unnecessary to make nice jurisdictional allotments among the lower courts. The paucity of caselaw on problems like this reflects as much.

F. RELATED PROCEDURES COMPARED

Table of Sections

§ 607. Federal Arbitration Act Compared

Chapter 1 of Title 9 of the United States Code contains the United States Arbitration Act, which governs arbitrability questions to the exclusion of state arbitration law whenever the matter involved qualifies as a "maritime" transaction or one involving interstate or foreign "commerce".[1] Those categories are broad, and on the face of things it would appear necessary in many cases to determine just where the federal act stops and the New York act starts.[2] We have been largely spared that inquiry in many cases, however, not because the "maritime" and "commerce" lines are sharp, but because the similarities between the federal and New York acts so outweigh their differences that in most cases the result of an arbitrability inquiry is the same under

---

3. See N.Y.C.Civ.Ct.Act. § 206.

4. Unif.Dist.Ct.Act § 206.

5. Unif.City Ct.Act § 206. But see D–Lion Co. v. United Excavating & Paving, Inc., 41 Misc.2d 56, 245 N.Y.S.2d 418 (Nassau County Dist. Ct. 1963), which can be viewed as authority to permit a city court to entertain an arbitrability question raised within a pending city court action. The case so held in respect of a district court when the Uniform District Court Act offered no greater instruction on the matter than the Uniform City Court Act does now.

6. Unif.Just.Ct.Act. § 206.

7. See Columbia Memorial Hospital v. McFarland Builders Inc., 74 Misc.2d 870, 344 N.Y.S.2d 63 (Columbia County Court 1973).

8. CPLR 7503(a), 7502(a).

§ 607

1. 9 U.S.C.A. § 1, part of Chapter 1 of Title 9, which is the Federal Arbitration Act. Chapter 2 of the title, §§ 201–208, contains the legislation implementing the arbitration

of commercial disputes in international commerce called for by a treaty the United States subscribes to and which binds in both federal and state courts. The treaty is known as the Convention on the Recognition and Enforcement of Foreign Arbitral Awards, which is also the caption Congress has given the implementing legislation in Chapter 2 of Title 9. For the transactions that fall under Chapter 2 as international, see 9 U.S.C.A. § 202.

2. Section 1 of 9 U.S.C.A. defines "maritime transactions" and "commerce", and lists certain excepted categories, but whether the definitions are met in a given case can of course be a close question. An example of a "maritime" transaction that invokes the federal act is A/S J. Ludwig Mowinckels Rederi v. Dow Chemical Co., 25 N.Y.2d 576, 307 N.Y.S.2d 660, 255 N.E.2d 774 (1970). An illustration of one involving interstate "commerce" is Sears Roebuck and Co. v. Glenwal Co., 325 F.Supp. 86 (S.D.N.Y.1970), aff'd on opinion below 442 F.2d 1350 (2d Cir.1971).

either act. Both acts qualify as enthusiastic supporters of arbitration.

The procedure to compel arbitration under the federal act is by "petition" for an "order" directing arbitration, which comes down to what amounts to a motion.[3] The petition and supporting papers may be served on other parties in the manner provided in the Federal Rules of Civil Procedure.[4] If the proceeding is one to confirm, vacate, or modify an award, i.e., a post-award application, procedure and the territorial scope of process for getting into court is further elaborated in the federal act.[5] If a genuine issue of fact arises as to arbitrability, it is to be tried "summarily".[6]

The application to compel arbitration may be brought in the locale specified in the agreement as the arbitration situs. Although sometimes viewed as mere venue, this is really more of a predicate for personal jurisdiction: the court in the contract-selected venue, especially when it is not the domicile or residence of the party against whom the proceeding to compel arbitration is brought, must trace its jurisdiction of that person to the agreement itself. If jurisdiction is present, the remaining requirement is to see that notice is given. This can be satisfied by any method comporting with due process. If the agreement adopts the arbitration procedures of an organization like the American Arbitration Association, for example, whose rules authorize ordinary mail, that method suffices.[7] Indeed, if the agreement is altogether silent about locale, but adopts organizational rules that provide for it—the

AAA rules again being the prime example—the organization will be permitted to set the situs of the arbitration (and through it the venue of judicial proceedings needed to compel arbitration[8]) as well as provide for the service of papers, including process.[9]

If an ordinary action is brought on a claim alleged to be arbitrable under the federal act, the arbitrability question should be raised, as it is under the New York act, by a motion to stay the action. If the motion succeeds, a stay suspends the action and the parties are remitted to arbitration,[10] even to arbitration in a foreign country if the agreement so provides.[11]

There are a number of other similarities. The same "separability" doctrine, i.e., the rationale that leaves to the arbitrators the question of whether the arbitration-requiring contract was induced by fraud unless the fraud can be shown to infect the arbitration clause itself, applies under the federal act. The doctrine's federal pronouncement,[12] in fact, preceded its New York adoption.[13] One also finds federal areas of sensitivity in which public policy precludes arbitration,[14] again a phenomenon paralleling New York's reaction to certain subjects.[15]

The time period for applying to confirm an award is the same under both acts: one year.[16] For applying to vacate or modify the award, the period is also the same, as least approximately: three months under the federal act,[17] 90 days under New York's.[18] In one of the

---

3. 9 U.S.C.A. §§ 4, 6.

4. 9 U.S.C.A. § 4. For service of process and its territorial scope in these situations, see AAACON Auto Transport, Inc. v. Teafatiller, 334 F.Supp. 1042 (S.D.N.Y.1971).

5. See 9 U.S.C.A. §§ 9, 12.

6. 9 U.S.C.A. § 4.

7. See Lawn v. Franklin, 328 F.Supp. 791 (S.D.N.Y. 1971).

8. See Reed & Martin, Inc. v. Westinghouse Electric Corp., 439 F.2d 1268 (2d Cir.1971). This is true of New York arbitration law as well. See §§ 588 and 591 above.

9. See Burger Chef Systems, Inc. v. Baldwin Inc., 365 F.Supp. 1229 (S.D.N.Y.1973).

10. 9 U.S.C.A. §§ 3, 6.

11. See Scherk v. Alberto–Culver Co., 417 U.S. 506, 94 S.Ct. 2449, 41 L.Ed.2d 270 (1974).

12. Prima Paint Corp. v. Flood & Conklin Mfg. Co., 388 U.S. 395, 87 S.Ct., 1801, 18 L.Ed.2d 1270 (1967).

13. See § 589 above.

14. Until recently, for example, there had been a broad policy against the arbitration of issues involving violations of the securities laws, see, e.g., Greater Continental Corp. v. Schechter, 422 F.2d 1100 (2d Cir.1970), but the U.S. Supreme Court changed course on that and now allows the arbitration of claims under the securities acts of both 1933 and 1934 as well as in some other areas that had previously been deemed too sensitive. See Rodriguez de Quijas v. Shearson/American Express, 490 U.S. 477, 109 S.Ct. 1917, 104 L.Ed.2d 526 (1989).

15. See § 587 above.

16. 9 U.S.C.A. § 9; CPLR 7510.

17. 9 U.S.C.A. § 12.

18. CPLR 7511(a).

incidentals of applying the three-month period there is a substantial difference, however, of which the practitioner should take note. Under New York law, although the loser in arbitration has only 90 days for a vacatur application if she initiates the application, if she saves the application to use in opposition to the winner's motion to confirm, for which the winner has a year, the loser also gets that year for the vacatur application.[19] The Second Circuit held in Florasynth, Inc. v. Pickholz,[20] however, that that is not the rule under the federal act, even though the federal act is modeled on New York's. The result is that a loser who lets the 90 days pass, saving a vacatur request to interpose against a confirmation application, had better be sure that the arbitration is governed by the New York act, not the federal act. In *Florasynth*, where the federal act was applied, the arbitration loser was too late with the vacatur request.

The grounds supplied for vacating[21] or modifying[22] an award are substantially similar, and under both acts the process culminates in a judgment confirming the award as is or as modified.[23]

There are several differences between the federal and New York acts that occasionally require a judge to determine precisely which act governs. One difference concerns the statute of limitations. Under the New York act, the timeliness of an arbitrable claim is determined by the court, i.e., it is one of the threshold questions,[24] while under the federal act an issue of timeliness is left to the arbitrator.[25]

A second difference involves CPLR 7503(c), the provision whereby the party seeking arbitration can throw onto his adversary, the one resisting it, the burden of bringing a judicial proceeding to test arbitrability—and severely restrict the resister's time for doing so. The federal act has no precise counterpart. CPLR 7503(c) is invoked, it will be recalled, and the resister is limited to 20 days within which to apply to stay arbitration, when the seeker of arbitration serves on the resister a "demand" or "notice of intention to arbitrate" containing the warnings listed in CPLR 7503(c), including a specification of the 20–day restriction.[26] What happens when the demand or notice is used in an instance not clearly governed by the New York act? The recipient really has little choice: he must resolve every doubt in favor of applying the New York law, and make the application to test arbitrability within the 20 days. If the recipient of the notice does that, and the case should turn out to be governed by the federal act after all, he has lost nothing but a bit of breath on the way to the courthouse. But if the recipient of the notice lets more than 20 days pass and the New York act is ultimately found to be the one applicable, the right to contest arbitrability will have been forfeited. And even if the federal act applies, there is authority to the effect that the New York 20–day period still governs.[27]

These are procedural differences. Sometimes there's a strikingly substantive difference. Under the state act, for example, arbitrators can't award punitive damages.[28] Under the federal act, the indications are that they can.[29]

---

19. See § 601 above.

20. 750 F.2d 171 (2d Cir.1984).

21. See 9 U.S.C.A. § 10; CPLR 7511(b).

22. See 9 U.S.C.A. § 11; CPLR 7511(c).

23. 9 U.S.C.A. § 13; CPLR 7514.

24. CPLR 7502(b), 7503(a). See § 590 above.

25. See A/S J. Ludwig Mowinckels Rederi v. Dow Chemical Co., 25 N.Y.2d 576, 307 N.Y.S.2d 660, 255 N.E.2d 774, cert. denied 398 U.S. 939, 90 S.Ct. 1844, 26 L.Ed.2d 272 (1970).

26. See § 593 above, elaborating the CPLR 7503(c) procedures.

27. The issue is in conflict at the moment. CPLR 7503(c) does not apply by its own terms, and was held inapplicable in AAACON Auto Transport, Inc. v. Newman,

77 Misc.2d 1069, 356 N.Y.S.2d 171 (Sup.Ct., N.Y. County, 1974). But a later case, City of Long Beach v. Catalyst Waste-to-Energy Corp. of Long Beach, 144 Misc.2d 119, 543 N.Y.S.2d 1013 (Sup.Ct., N.Y.County, 1988), reaches the conclusion that it does apply, by indirection. The U.S. Supreme Court directs that when a federal claim has no accompanying statute of limitations, the forum state's period as applied to an analogous claim should be used. See § 615 below. The analogy here, holds the Long Beach case, is the 20–day statute of limitations of CPLR 7503(c).

28. See § 587 above.

29. So a number of federal cases have held, although the view is not unanimous. See "Report on Punitive Damages in Commercial Arbitration", Committee on Arbitration, Commercial and Federal Litigation Section, New York State Bar Association (Dec. 1989). The U.S. Supreme Court has not yet resolved the issue.

At this point the reader may be tempted to ask how the two acts can ever be confused. Is the choice of act not wholly dependent on the choice of forum? Is an arbitration act not a mere procedural law, so that a New York court will apply only the New York act and a federal court only the federal act? The answer to these questions is No, and a clear No at that. It is the nature of the transaction that determines which act applies. This is so regardless of the court in which the arbitrability question may arise. If the transaction is within the "maritime" or "commerce" realm embraced by the federal act, that act governs notwithstanding that the issue may arise in a state court action or proceeding.

Many a case within the "commerce" criterion of the federal act is within the subject matter jurisdiction of a state court; so is many a "maritime" case, under the saving-to-suitors clause of the jurisdictional statute that governs admiralty cases in the federal courts.[30] If in any such case an arbitrability question is raised, the federal act must be looked to for the answer.[31] Conversely, a case may appear in a federal court well within its jurisdiction but not involve either a "maritime" or "commerce" subject, as will often occur when diversity of citizenship accounts for federal subject matter jurisdiction in the case.[32] In that instance the federal court looks to the arbitration act of the forum state for the resolution of arbitrability questions, the federal act being of its own terms inapplicable.[33] But if the transaction does fall under the "maritime" or "commerce" standard, even the diversity case in the federal court must apply the federal instead of the state arbitration act.[34]

From the foregoing it can be seen that the federal act does not confer jurisdiction on a court—either state or federal—to hear any case; it merely provides that if subject matter jurisdiction is otherwise present and the case presents a transaction reached by the federal act, the federal act governs arbitrability. In this respect the Federal Arbitration Act is treated as a "substantive" rather than "procedural" statute, having been accorded that treatment, notwithstanding its predominantly procedural mission, because "arbitration ... substantially affects the cause of action".[35]

A further interplay relevant to a New York practice study appears when it is sought to remove to the federal court a proceeding to stay arbitration commenced in a New York court under the New York act. The case of Sears Roebuck and Co. v. Glenwal Co.[36] can illustrate:

S (seeking arbitration) served on R (resisting it) a notice of intention to arbitrate under CPLR 7503(c), and R, as required, promptly brought a special proceeding against S to stay the arbitration. S wanted to remove the proceeding to the federal court on the basis of diversity of citizenship. Since the general rule is that only a defendant is authorized to effect a removal,[37] the question was whether S was a "defendant" for this purpose. It was held that S was; that his notice served on R was not itself a proceeding, but merely required R to commence one; and that when R did, against S, S was in that context a defendant and thereby entitled to remove the case, thus giving the arbitrability questions—whichever act might govern them—to the federal court to decide. There proved to be no need, however, to decide which act governed the arbitrability questions; as so often happens, the two acts were the same in respect of the particular issue involved. The case nicely illustrates how the questions of jurisdiction and arbitrability must be separated, and how the question of

---

30. 28 U.S.C.A. § 1333.

31. See, e.g., A/S J. Ludwig Mowinckels Rederi v. Dow Chemical Co., 25 N.Y.2d 576, 307 N.Y.S.2d 660, 255 N.E.2d 774 (1970).

32. See 28 U.S.C.A. § 1332.

33. See Bernhardt v. Polygraphic Co. of America, 350 U.S. 198, 76 S.Ct. 273, 100 L.Ed. 199 (1956); Kochery, The Enforcement of Arbitration Agreements in the Federal Courts: Erie v. Tompkins, 39 Cornell L.Q. 74 (1953).

34. See Robert Lawrence Co. v. Devonshire Fabric, Inc., 271 F.2d 402 (2d Cir.1959).

35. Bernhardt v. Polygraphic Co. of America, 350 U.S. 198, 203, 76 S.Ct. 273, 276, 100 L.Ed. 199 (1956).

36. 325 F.Supp. 86 (S.D.N.Y.1970), aff'd on opinion below 442 F.2d 1350 (2d Cir.1971).

37. See 28 U.S.C.A. § 1441(a).

which act applies to an issue does not depend on which court gets the question.

Suppose that the transaction, because of its nature, would be governed by the federal act, but that the contract between the parties itself stipulates to the application of state law. That happened, for example, in Cone Mills Corp. v. August F. Nielsen Co.,[38] in which the federal act presumably governed because the transaction involved interstate commerce. The court held that if the federal act is applicable by its terms, then it must be applied despite a clause in the contract stipulating to the application of the state act (in this case the New York act). It is not clear, however, that the federal act requires that degree of deference. The U.S. Supreme Court appeared more deferential to the parties' choice—to the parties' choice of law in general if not a choice of the state arbitration act in particular—in Volt Information Sciences, Inc. v. Board of Trustees of the Leland Stanford Junior University,[39] which involved an interstate commerce transaction. The contract in Volt had an arbitration clause, presumably governed by the federal arbitration act, but it also had a choice of law clause calling for the application of the law of the place where the project involved was "located". That was California. Under California law, an otherwise required arbitration between two parties can be stayed if there is a related litigation pending in the courts that also involves other parties and the others are not bound to arbitrate.[40] Under the federal act, the arbitration is not subject to such a stay.[41] A divided Supreme Court held the voluntary choice of California law permissible; the choice was neither precluded by nor did it undermine the federal act.

While it is plain from Volt that the federal act may be subordinated to state law through the inclusion of a choice of law clause alongside an arbitration clause, it is not clear that a state court would be precluded from deferring to the federal act in such a case if it chose to.

In other words, if state law is made applicable through the choice of law clause, the state court that decides what the "state law" is might just hold that under state law a choice of law clause will not be permitted to preempt arbitration law emanating from the federal act if the federal act is otherwise applicable.

Perhaps the root of the problem is the incongruity of including in a contract both an arbitration clause—and even a broad arbitration clause—as well as a substantive choice of law provision. Those who want the substantive law applied to their case should not be giving it to arbitration. Parties making themselves aware of the problems involved in Volt and like cases should try to anticipate some of the possibilities that may arise in their own situations and perhaps, if they still want arbitration, draw the arbitration clause more narrowly. If they want to cover the contingency of being "caught in the middle", for example, with an arbitration commitment with one party but with only the prospect of litigation with another party involved in some phase of the same dispute but not obliged to arbitrate, they can provide for that in the contract with specific instructions.[42] They should not leave it to spacious clauses calling for arbitration in one breath and choice of law in another. If the two are not inherently contradictions, they can, as Volt manifests, be read as such.

When the situation involves not only the competing elements of the federal and state arbitration acts but also touches on several states and thus additionally poses choice of law questions about which state's law will govern what, complications expand and the results become unpredictable, as manifest in Mastrobuono v. Shearson Lehman Hutton, Inc.[43] In Mastrobuono, an FAA-governed arbitration in the securities realm had been brought in Illinois and the award included punitive damages. The contract, however, had a choice of law clause choosing New York law, and because

---

38. 90 A.D.2d 31, 455 N.Y.S.2d 625 (1st Dep't 1982).

39. 489 U.S. 468, 109 S.Ct. 1248, 103 L.Ed.2d 488 (1989).

40. See § 1281.2(c) of California's Civil Procedure Code.

41. New York arbitration law is the same as the federal on this point. See § 598 above.

42. See § 598 above.

43. 514 U.S. 52, 115 S.Ct. 1212, 131 L.Ed.2d 76 (1995).

under New York law an arbitrator is not authorized to allow punitive damages the lower federal courts that reviewed the award disallowed the punitive damages. The U.S. Supreme Court reversed, holding that the lower courts had improperly read the arbitration and choice of law clauses in the contract. Through a choice of law tangle the court sustained the arbitrator's power to award punitive damages.[44]

New York's rule barring arbitrators from awarding them[45] is deemed nothing short of a benediction by brokerage houses, and it more than anything else accounts for (1) the frequent appearance of New York choice of law clauses alongside choice of arbitration clauses in securities-related contracts, and (2) some of the more interesting cases involving competition between the federal and state arbitration acts.

§ 608. Valuation or Appraisal Proceeding

If the parties agree that a question of "valuation, appraisal or other issue or controversy" shall be determined by a person named or selected by a prescribed means, CPLR 7601 authorizes a special proceeding to implement the agreement. Appraisal of this kind is useful in many contexts, mainly in a commercial or other contract setting, to evaluate an asset, a business, a loss, or any other property or property right, tangible or intangible, if the parties cannot come to one mind on its worth.[1]

Appraisal as contemplated by CPLR 7601 differs from arbitration in a number of ways, addressed in detail by the Court of Appeals in Matter of Delmar Box Co.[2] Arbitration usually disposes of the entire controversy between the parties and culminates in an award and a judgment confirming it. Appraisal addresses a specific issue; the overall controversy between

the parties, if it subsists, is litigated as an ordinary action, the appraisal to be binding on the parties within it. The appraisal is also a less formal procedure. The parties may supply the appraiser with such data or argument as they wish, but the appraiser need not (as an arbitrator must) conduct an evidentiary hearing on notice. Hence an appraiser takes no oath. He is in effect a private person whose judgment on a stipulated issue the parties agree to accept as binding.

More than one appraiser can be selected. Akin to tripartite arbitration, the agreement can call for each side to appoint an appraiser and for the two thus selected to appoint a third, often called in this context an "umpire", as illustrated in the insurance policy involved in the *Delmar* case.

There are several remedies when an appraisal agreement is not carried out. The first and most prominent is a special proceeding for specific performance of it, which CPLR 7601 authorizes in terms. The proceeding is governed by the procedures of Article 4 of the CPLR. An alternative also offered by CPLR 7601 is enforcement of the agreement as if it were one to arbitrate. The drawback of so proceeding, however, is that it invokes the procedures of Article 75 of the CPLR, which suggests that this option is appropriate only in special circumstances. While much less formal than litigation, the procedures of arbitration are nonetheless more rigid than those ordinarily applicable to an appraisal.

There are other remedies as well.[3] If the plaintiff in an action, for example, has failed to honor an appraisal agreement in respect of a given issue, the action may be dismissed as premature or stayed pending the appraisal; or, if the defendant is the recalcitrant one, the plaintiff can simply litigate the issue within

---

44. There are a number of other issues in the case. See the discussion in the lead note in New York State Law Digest No. 423.

45. See § 587, note 12, above.

§ 608

1. An extensive study of the appraisal procedure, including its background in New York Law, appears in the

1958 Report of the Law Revision Commission (Leg.Doc. No.65) at p. 385.

2. 309 N.Y. 60, 127 N.E.2d 808 (1955).

3. See 4th Rep.Leg.Doc. (1960) No. 20, p. 62.

the action and let the court decide it.[4]

When the occasion arises for judicial review of an appraisal, an analogy is drawn to the standards used on an arbitration. Hence, while a mere error of law or fact is not a ground for rejecting the appraisal, something qualifying as "misconduct"[5] is, such as a refusal to entertain pertinent evidence.[6] A difference, however, is that if an arbitration award is set aside, the result is arbitration de novo, while when an appraisal fails the court just makes the appraisal itself.[7]

While a proceeding can be brought under CPLR 7601 to compel specific performance of an appraisal agreement, the appraisal once made does not ordinarily go through another proceeding to "confirm" it, as an arbitration award does.[8] It just stands by for use in whatever action or proceeding between the parties may be necessary to resolve their controversy.[9] If things go right, in fact, the result of the appraisal should either resolve the parties' dispute or else find a place in evidence in an action or proceeding, pending or potential. But suppose that there is no pending action to which the appraisal is relevant; that the appraisal is the sole issue between the parties, and that it needs some kind of judicial confirmation.

The Court of Appeals met the problem in Matter of Penn Central Corp. (Conrail),[10] and held that if need be, a special proceeding may be brought to "confirm" the appraisal. Two carriers in *Penn Central* owned land and sold it, agreeing to escrow the purchase money pending an appraisal to determine the share of each. Then one of the parties refused to honor the appraisal and the other needed some way to get it confirmed. CPLR 7601 on its face would not help because it is designed to get

the appraisal going, not to confirm its outcome. The court in *Penn Central* interpolated the right to bring a special proceeding to obtain a judicial confirmation of the appraisal.

§ 609. Simplified Procedure for Court Determination of Disputes; CPLR 3031–3037

Last in our treatment, and apparently last as well in the affections of the New York bar, is the "Simplified Procedure" supplied by 3031 through 3037 of the CPLR. It was an effort of the late 1950s to get back into the courts some of the commercial business that had turned to arbitration.[1] It has not succeeded. Arbitration has since expanded in popularity, spreading over even into the tort realm, while the Simplified Procedure has languished at the brink of atrophy. It has no substantial body of case-law.

What the Simplified Procedure offers is a chance to keep the substantive law—in arbitration the substantive law does not apply—while facilitating procedure. It does away with summons service, among other things to be noted, contemplating the mere filing of a statement. The parties opt for the Simplified Procedure in the same way they do for arbitration: by a written submission of a present controversy[2] or by a written contract agreeing to use the procedure for future controversies.[3]

In the submission of a present controversy, the parties draw up a statement signed by them and their attorneys "specifying plainly and concisely the claims and defenses between the parties and the relief requested". They file this with the clerk along with a note of issue.[4] The case is then put right on the calendar for

---

4. Matter of Delmar Box Co., note 2, above.

5. See CPLR 7511(b)(1)(i).

6. See Gervant v. New England Fire Ins. Co., 306 N.Y. 393, 118 N.E.2d 574 (1954).

7. See Clark v. Kraftco Corp., 323 F.Supp. 358 (S.D.N.Y.1971).

8. CPLR 7510, 7514.

9. The standard fire insurance policy in New York prescribes an appraisal procedure, Ins.L. § 3404, and a special statutory direction for judicial aid is applicable for its implementation. See Ins.L. § 3408, to which CPLR 7601 explicitly defers.

10. 56 N.Y.2d 120, 451 N.Y.S.2d 62, 436 N.E.2d 512 (1982).

§ 609

1. For the history of this procedure, see Commentary C3031:3 on McKinney's CPLR 3031.

2. CPLR 3031, 3032.

3. CPLR 3033, 3034.

4. CPLR 3031, 3036(6).

what is hoped will be an expeditious determination.

In the future-controversy case, it is anticipated that the parties will do likewise when a dispute arises. But if either resists, the other can file her own statement of the claim and ask the court to settle its terms. This is done with a motion.[5] By providing that the court shall determine the manner of service of the motion papers, the applicable rule[6] in effect requires that the motion be brought on by order to show cause.[7]

The submission of an existing controversy can be made to any court having jurisdiction of the subject matter of the dispute.[8] A contract calling for application of the Simplified Procedure to a future dispute, however, is limited to the supreme court.[9] Whenever the supreme court is involved, its usual venue rules[10] are applicable.[11]

If there is any substantial dispute about the making of the contract containing the agreement to use the Simplified Procedure, it must be tried, and by jury if one is demanded.[12] This is analogous to the "threshold" questions of arbitration, to which yet another parallel can be drawn. It will be recalled that any claim that a contract containing an arbitration clause was induced by fraud will be left to the arbitrator unless it is shown that the fraud induced the arbitration clause itself. This is the "separability" doctrine studied earlier.[13] It has been in effect extended to the Simplified Procedure: it has been held that unless the alleged fraud is shown to have induced the clause agreeing to the Simplified Procedure,

the latter will apply and the whole case will be determined under it.[14]

If an ordinary action is brought in violation of an agreement to submit the claim through the Simplified Procedure, the action may be stayed,[15] thereby remitting the plaintiff to the Simplified Procedure method if he would pursue his claim at all. This is again analogous to the arbitration process.[16]

There is an occasional tendency to confuse the Simplified Procedure with the Action on Submitted Facts contained in CPLR 3222. The latter's main difference is that it involves no dispute on the facts; it presents to the court an agreed statement of facts calling only for an application of the law. The Simplified Procedure, like arbitration itself, can involve triable issues of fact as well as of law.[17]

Under the Simplified Procedure, trial is by the court. Trial by jury is waived.[18]

The ways in which procedure is facilitated are listed in CPLR 3036. The rules of evidence do not apply, except for those governing privileged communications.[19] Provision is made for the securing of expert testimony if deemed advisable by the court.[20] The court can allow amendment of statements. It is also authorized, on motion of any party or on its own motion, to permit pretrial disclosure—apparently through the entire range of the disclosure devices of Article 31 of the CPLR.[21]

A note of issue may be filed by either side after the statement is ready, whether made ready by mutual agreement or by court settlement, and prompt trial is provided for. No formal statement of readiness, however, such as must usually accompany the note of issue

---

5. CPLR 3034.

6. CPLR 3034(2).

7. See discussion in Commentary C3034:2 on McKinney's CPLR 3034.

8. CPLR 3031, 101. See also § 910 in the New York City Civil Court Act and in the Uniform District, City, and Justice court acts, McKinney's Vol. 29A, Parts 2 and 3.

9. CPLR 3033(1).

10. CPLR Article 5.

11. CPLR 3036(8).

12. CPLR 3034(3).

13. See § 589.

14. See Bawi U. S. Center, Inc. v. Joe Brand, Inc., 55 A.D.2d 870, 390 N.Y.S.2d 118 (1st Dep't 1977).

15. CPLR 3036(3).

16. For a comparison of the Simplified Procedure and arbitration, see Commentary C3031:4 on McKinney's CPLR 3031.

17. The Simplified Procedure is distinguished from the action on submitted facts and from yet other procedures in Commentary C3031:6 on McKinney's CPLR 3031.

18. CPLR 3031, 3033(1).

19. CPLR 3036(1).

20. CPLR 3036(2).

21. CPLR 3036(5).

under court rules in an ordinary action (attesting to the completion of pretrial procedures),[22] is needed under the Simplified Procedure.[23]

While purporting at many junctures to facilitate procedure, which is indeed its sole attraction, the Simplified Procedure provides, in CPLR 3036(1), for what may be responsible for its undoing. It states that the rules of procedure "shall be dispensed with" but immediately adds: "unless the court shall otherwise direct". It thereby empowers a judge, with but a wave of the hand, and apparently without an explanation to anyone, to cancel out summarily the sole advantage of the Simplified Procedure. Whatever the propensity of the judges to do this—and what few cases there are on this device evince no such inclination at all—the mere existence of this power may be one of the factors accountable for the unpopularity of the Simplified Procedure. A party bent on securing the ease and speed of arbitration is not likely to be enticed away from it with a promise that can be broken at will.

Like an ordinary action, a case under the Simplified Procedure culminates in a final judgment.[24] Costs and disbursements are awardable in the court's discretion,[25] and upon entry of the judgment it becomes enforcible in the same way as any other of like kind.[26]

Appeal lies from the final judgment, but interlocutory orders made during the course of the dispute may not be appealed as of right, notwithstanding that they would be appealable in an ordinary action. Their separate appeal requires leave of the trial or appellate court. But they may be reviewed on an appeal from the final judgment.[27]

The substantive law of the state of course governs on the appeal, as it does in all phases of a Simplified Procedure case, and in this lies its principal contrast to arbitration. Review of an arbitration award is not measured by its fidelity to the substantive law, and the award can be vacated on only a few narrow grounds.[28] The substantial evidence test of CPLR 7803(4), on the other hand, applicable in an Article 78 proceeding in the nature of certiorari to review an administrative determination,[29] has been borrowed by the Simplified Procedure as the standard for appellate review of the trial judge's fact findings.[30]

Although designed primarily to lure the commercial dispute back into the courts, the Simplified Procedure is not restricted to that category. It is apparently available for any subject matter, including tort,[31] but it has made no headway anywhere.

---

22. See § 370 above.

23. CPLR 3036(6).

24. Provision is also made for a default judgment. CPLR 3036(4).

25. CPLR 3036(9).

26. CPLR 3036(8).

27. CPLR 3037. An order determining whether the Simplified Procedure is applicable, e.g., whether a contract agreeing to it was made, is an exception and may be appealed of right.

28. See § 602 above.

29. See §§ 560–561 above.

30. CPLR 3037.

31. See 5th Jud.Conf.Rep. (1960) 96, 103.

Chapter Twenty–Three

FEDERAL PRACTICE REVIEWED AND COMPARED: PARALLELS AND PITFALLS

Analysis

A. FEDERAL PRACTICE, INTRODUCTORY

Table of Sections

§ 610. A Brief Comparison of New York and Federal Practice; Introductory

The purpose of this chapter is to compare and more particularly contrast the basic features of federal civil practice and their New York practice counterparts, with a special accent on differences that can make trouble if overlooked. The treatment is necessarily selective; this is not to be a text on federal practice, nor even a basic primer. It is primarily an enumeration of distinctions designed for lawyers versed in New York practice who are considering whether to bring a federal action,

who are defending a federal action, or who, defending a case brought in a state court, are considering whether (and how) to remove the case to a federal court. It is also aimed at the lawyer in the opposite category: the lawyer expert in federal practice but less familiar with New York state practice who wants to review the more prominent differences between the two. The approach will be akin to that used in comparing the New York and federal arbitration acts earlier.[1]

Some states have adopted the Federal Rules of Civil Procedure (FRCP[2]), right down to the numbering, just adding to or subtracting from each provision as need be to supplement procedure and to meet differences in jurisdiction or in local need. In states like that, lawyers who are conversant with federal practice can find the state equivalent of a familiar federal rule just by checking the same-numbered rule in the state practice.

§ 610

1. See § 607 above.

2. The Federal Rules of Civil Procedure will be abbreviated to FRCP throughout this chapter.

New York lawyers do not get that break. Although there are many provisions in the New York Civil Practice Law and Rules (CPLR) that have been modeled in some measure on the FRCP, most of the CPLR has not been. The New York CPLR is an independent formulation, and not even in the sequence of its subjects, much less in their numbering, does it offer an analogy to the FRCP. And of course there are several key missions that the state practice act must carry out which the FRCP sidesteps entirely by merely adopting state practice. With one casual sweep of an adoptive phrase here and there, for example, the FRCP relieves itself of having to provide for longarm jurisdiction.[3] There are also the verbiage-demanding provisional remedies,[4] and the broad range of supplementary proceedings for the enforcement of judgments,[5] to say nothing of the state's law of time limitations, which the FRCP does not address at all but which federal practice often ends up adopting by other routes, and not just in cases predicated on diversity of citizenship.[6] These are weighty and hard-working occupants of the state's practice act, and the frequent support they lend to federal practice has enabled the FRCP to guard its diet and maintain a slim and snappy figure.

So there are some points in common between the two practices simply through the dependence of federal law on state law, but, alas, only some.

In each subject treated an effort has been made to cite the basic federal provisions in point. These will usually be the Federal Rules of Civil Procedure, but in a number of instances references will be to federal statutes, notably to Title 28 of the United States Code, the judiciary article. It is by statute that both the district courts[7] and the courts of appeals in the

federal system[8] are established, and of course statutes supply the basic instructions on their subject matter jurisdiction and its exercise.

The accent will be on pitfalls: points of difference in which an assumption from the wrong practice can prove fatal on some key matter, like jurisdiction, timeliness, choice of forum, and the like. Often a brief foundation will be laid for a subject solely for the purpose of highlighting some sensitive disparity.

A few fundamentals are appropriate background. New York state is part of the federal Second Circuit, which it shares with Connecticut and Vermont.[9] The state is divided into four districts, by the compass: the Northern, Western, Southern, and Eastern districts.[10] The counties that make up each district are also set by statute,[11] and Congress does change the makeup of the districts from time to time. Columbia, Greene, and Ulster counties, for example, relatively rural, had been in the Southern District, in which they mixed with the heavily urban New York and Bronx counties and the suburban Westchester and Rockland counties, among others, until 1978, when they were shifted to the Northern District, blending there with a much less urban and suburban mixture. The difference can be a substantial factor in considering, among other things, whether to choose a federal or state forum in a case whose subject matter can produce divergent views between urban and rural jurors. This element, in fact, is one of the important ones on the list of choice of forum factors set forth below.[12]

While the principal governing tool in federal civil practice is of course the FRCP,[13] it is not the only one. Some matters dictated by statute have been explicitly barred from governance by rule. One such is the setting of venue:[14] selecting the district in which a federal civil

---

3. See § 626 below.

4. See § 640 below.

5. See § 641 below.

6. See § 615 below.

7. 28 U.S.C.A., Chapter 5.

8. 28 U.S.C.A., Chapter 3.

9. 28 U.S.C.A. § 41.

10. 28 U.S.C.A. § 112.

11. Id.

12. See § 616.

13. A separate compilation, the Federal Rules of Appellate Procedure (FRAP), governs appeals in the federal courts.

14. See FRCP Rule 82. The subject matter jurisdiction of the federal courts is of course set by statute and may not be varied by the rules.

action must be brought is left strictly to statute.[15]

Supplementing the Federal Rules of Civil Procedure are the local rules that each district is empowered to enact for itself, consistent, of course, with the FRCP,[16] and many federal district judges have on top of that their own rules. These tend to govern the kinds of details the judge would be able to dictate as a matter of discretion on a case by case basis in any event, but that is not always so. For a long time, for example, some of the judges had a rule requiring that a party obtain permission from the judge before making a motion. This was a controversial matter that created resentment among many members of the bar, and yet for years such rules remained in effect, unreviewed by the Court of Appeals. Then in 1987, in Richardson Greenshields Securities, Inc. v. Lau,[17] the matter finally squeezed through to appellate review and the Court of Appeals for the Second Circuit rejected the preliminary permission requirement. It held that "a court has no power to prevent a party from filing pleadings, motions or appeals" authorized by the FRCP. The court did not reject a requirement for the "conferencing" of motions—a requirement some judges have that the party first seek to confer with the court and opposing counsel to see whether the issue can be resolved without a motion—but it cautioned that the judge "must conduct such conferences promptly upon the request of the moving party", especially when it is shown that "time is of the essence, as in Richardson, where a statute of limitations concern was raised". There, the court admonishes, "the judge must either conduct a conference immediately or permit the motion to be filed without a conference".[18]

The Richardson case also illustrates the stark difference between federal and New York practice on the appealability of interlocutory (nonfinal) dispositions.[19]

The importance of the courts' and judges' own rules cannot be stressed enough in any address to federal civil practice, especially in the kind of treatment being undertaken here, where the picture of each federal scene is painted in broad strokes and detail has to be omitted. Only a few district court rules will be cited, and these only by way of occasionally illustrating the kind of thing the rules cover. Every lawyer considering whether to bring a case in, or remove a case to, a federal court should study the particular district court's rules, and should do so before acting. Additionally, after the action is commenced in or removed to a federal court and the case is assigned to a particular judge, the lawyer should promptly obtain a copy of any rules the judge may have adopted and examine them carefully.

Another point that a lawyer unfamiliar with federal practice should be aware of is the role of the court of appeals on the federal scene. Conflicts can and do arise among New York's four appellate divisions, the state's intermediate appellate courts, but they do not last very long. The New York Court of Appeals is disposed to intervene with dispatch to resolve them. For that and other reasons conflicts among the state appellate courts occur with nothing like the frequency of conflicts among the federal circuits. Commentators trying to keep abreast of the whole federal scene often have to review not one practice, but a dozen. Not until Congress or the U.S. Supreme Court intervenes is a conflict among circuits likely to be resolved, and because of the statistical unlikelihood of getting to the U.S. Supreme Court—even to resolve a conflict among circuits—the conflict can endure for years. In that interim, the court of appeals for the local circuit rules the roost. "Get me a Second Circuit case!" is usually the theme that researchers in the U.S. attorney's office and in federal litigation departments march to.

What a district court does may ultimately face review in the court of appeals, but it has

---

15. See § 617 below.

16. FRCP Rule 83.

17. 825 F.2d 647.

18. For New York's treatment of the same problem, see Goldheart International Ltd. v. Vulcan Constr. Corp., 124 A.D.2d 507, 508 N.Y.S.2d 182 (1st Dep't 1986).

19. See § 642 and item 9 on the list of choice of forum factors in § 616 below.

precious little prospect of going beyond. Hence the pragmatic theme just sounded. In view of the federal restrictions on the interlocutory appeal, moreover, many procedural determinations have little chance of being reviewed even at court of appeals level, especially in matters of everyday procedure. The sky in a United States district court action is therefore the court of appeals. Going beyond that is like breaking through the sky to get to heaven.

Among the more striking differences between federal and New York civil practice are those met at the very outset, when the action is commenced. Here a mistake can mean a loss of jurisdiction and a dismissal. If the statute of limitations has expired, the dismissal may mean the complete forfeiture of the case. The action's commencement will therefore be done in some detail.[20] Preliminary to that will be an overview of the federal courts' subject matter jurisdiction and related topics,[21] and a brief treatment of the statute of limitations in federal practice.[22] When the lawyer has a choice of forum between federal and state courts, many factors go into the choice. A separate section, which turns out to be the longest in this book, lists those factors.[23]

The treatment comprises only a few dozen sections and the reader can get a quick perspective of it by scanning the section headings listed at the outset of this chapter.

B. SUBJECT MATTER JURISDICTION

Table of Sections

---

20. See § 621 et seq., below.
21. See §§ 611–614 below.
22. See § 615 below.
23. See § 616 below.

§ 611

1. See § 8 above.
2. Two excepted categories are claims against the state, which are the exclusive province of the New York Court of Claims, and matters that are within the exclusive jurisdiction of the federal courts. See § 12 above.

§ 611. Subject Matter Jurisdiction in the Federal Courts

In a New York practice course in a law school curriculum, only a small fraction of time is allotted to subject matter jurisdiction. It is just a matter of listing the jurisdiction of the various courts, which goes quickly. The course is built mainly around the New York Supreme Court, the state's principal trial court, and one of the features of the supreme court's subject matter jurisdiction is probably the factor that accounts for the few problems met and the very few cases generated on the topic of subject matter jurisdiction in New York practice: in New York, the supreme court is a court of general jurisdiction.[1] Whatever original jurisdiction any court in the New York state system has, the supreme court shares it,[2] and a defect in subject matter jurisdiction in New York practice usually results in nothing more serious than a transfer of the case from the wrong court to the right court.[3]

There is no such "sharing" court in the federal system. We address in this chapter the national system of federal courts,[4] and there is no court of "general" jurisdiction among them. All of them, from the U.S. Supreme Court on down, are courts of limited jurisdiction. One may even say *severely* limited jurisdiction, and the limitations originate in the federal constitution itself.[5] The primary obligation of a federal courts course in a law school curriculum, therefore, is to study the limitations, and it is an extensive study. It accounts for the greater allotment of attention to subject matter jurisdiction in a federal than in a New York practice course[6] and, coordi-

---

3. See § 24 above.

4. By "national" courts we mean to exclude the internal courts of the District of Columbia and the territories, for which Congress can create courts of "general" jurisdiction. Reference in this chapter is to the courts set up within the states in general, and New York in particular.

5. Article III, § 2.

6. The jurisdiction of the United States district courts is the main topic of this chapter. Federal appellate jurisdiction is treated in § 642 below.

nately, the increased attention that must be given by the practitioner to determining subject matter jurisdiction before attempting to invoke it in the federal system. In this chapter, however, the purpose is to stress contrasts and warn of pitfalls, and in that context federal subject matter jurisdiction serves as mere background. Hence the topic that usually preoccupies the federal courts course in law school gets only a thumbnail sketch here, injected principally if not solely as a framework for some practical problem. Many of these practical points earn little attention in an academic curriculum, on the other hand, or none at all, so this chapter is really a trade-off in which the giant of academia—subject matter jurisdiction—is just a dwarf, outlined in this section in a brief stroke and trotted out from time to time in other sections only for its role in some predicament.

There is also the phenomenon in federal practice of plaintiffs bringing doubtful cases into the district court. One does not see that happening with courts of limited jurisdiction in state practice. The reason is that as far as general civil practice in money actions is concerned—and the money action is of course the predominant category of action in both systems—one finds many levels of monetary restriction in the courts of limited jurisdiction in the state system, but in all of them the restriction is a maximum, not a minimum.[7] When a plaintiff invokes the jurisdiction of a lower court in the state system, the plaintiff is conceding that the value of the case does not exceed the court's jurisdiction. In the diversity action in a federal district court, on the other hand, where one also finds a monetary qualification, presently $75,000, the sum is not a ceiling, but a floor:[8] the case has to be worth *more* than $75,000 to invoke the federal diversity jurisdiction. Since plaintiffs are implicitly prone to inflate the value they put on their

cases, cases suspect about their monetary worth are a more frequent event in federal practice.

Under the diversity statute,[9] the diversity must be "complete"—the citizenship of each plaintiff must differ from that of each defendant on the claim,[10] although citizenships among those on one side can be the same. And "citizenship" equates with the state concept of domicile, not mere residence: to be a "citizen" of a given state for diversity purposes a person must be, in addition to a citizen of the United States, a domiciliary of a particular state.[11] A person who is not a citizen of the United States is an alien, and an alien, while provided for in the diversity statute, is not treated quite the same as a citizen.

A corporation is deemed a citizen of its state of incorporation, which is easy to determine, as well as the state in which it has its "principal place of business",[12] which can sometimes be hard to determine. An unincorporated association is not treated as an entity at all for diversity purposes, which means that each of its members must have citizenship different from all those on the other side of the litigation.[13] The same applies with partnerships. All the partners' citizenships must be counted, including limited partners,[14] decreasing the likelihood of diversity and hence the prospect of federal subject matter jurisdiction.

Dispute is frequent on these and like matters, with plaintiffs attempting to bring many doubtful cases under the diversity jurisdiction and with defendants generating a stream of motions to dismiss; or, in removal cases, conversely, with defendants attempting to bring many doubtful cases under the diversity jurisdiction and with plaintiffs generating a stream of motions, this time not to dismiss, but to remand the case to the state court.[15] These

---

7. See §§ 19–22 above.

8. 28 U.S.C.A. § 1332.

9. Id.

10. Strawbridge v. Curtiss, 7 U.S. (1 Cranch) 267, 2 L.Ed. 435 (1806).

11. See Williamson v. Osenton, 232 U.S. 619, 34 S.Ct. 442, 58 L.Ed. 758 (1914).

12. 28 U.S.C.A. § 1332(c).

13. United Steelworkers of America v. R.H. Bouligny, Inc., 382 U.S. 145, 86 S.Ct. 272, 15 L.Ed.2d 217 (1965).

14. Carden v. Arkoma Associates, 494 U.S. 185, 110 S.Ct. 1015, 108 L.Ed.2d 157 (1990).

15. See § 619 below.

disputes produce masses of caselaw on subject matter jurisdiction, and swell the study.

For historical reasons, the federal courts lack jurisdiction of matrimonial actions and of family disputes in general.[16] And while they can and do, under the diversity statute, entertain plenary actions between representatives of a decedent's estate and third persons with no direct connection to the estate, they lack jurisdiction of matters involving the internals of an estate's administration, such as probate, will contests, accountings, and the like.[17] Elements from these excluded areas sometimes crop up obliquely in an otherwise legitimate federal action, and the battle of subject matter jurisdiction resumes (and the caselaw expands).

Under the most numerous category of subject matter jurisdiction in the federal courts, the so-called "federal question" case in which jurisdiction is based on the claim's arising under federal law, the caselaw is just as massive. When does a case "arise under" federal law? Is it sufficient that there is some federal issue in the case? Can the federal issue be injected by way of counterclaim, or defense, or is it restricted to the main claim?

In many of the federal question categories, jurisdiction of the subject matter may have been conferred on the federal courts exclusively. In others there may be nothing purporting to make the jurisdiction exclusive, in which event it is concurrent with the state courts and the plaintiff has a choice of forum, at least at the outset. In many such cases the relevant statute is not clear. If the case is brought in a state court, what is clear is that a dispute on the issue is going to arise, along with more caselaw on subject matter jurisdiction.

The list goes on and on, and the subject, like the universe, is always expanding, commandeering, in contrast to the New York state side

of things, a disproportionate segment of the attention of the federal courts.

Subject matter jurisdiction, a rigid concept in New York practice,[18] is no less so in federal practice. The general rule is that subject matter jurisdiction cannot be conferred by consent, laches, waiver, estoppel, or anything else, except Congress acting within the confines of the constitution.[19] An objection to subject matter jurisdiction, moreover, can be raised at any time, and either by motion of a party or by the court sua sponte.[20] What happens, then, when the plaintiff sues in a federal court in New York believing that there is federal jurisdiction, but the court disagrees and dismisses it, and the dismissal is affirmed on appeal (or no appeal is taken)? If the original statute of limitations has now expired, will there be any time extension so that the action can now be brought in a New York state court?

As long as the defect in the federal court was one of subject matter rather than personal jurisdiction, New York awards the case the six months of CPLR 205(a) for a new action.[21] The cautious plaintiff who does not want to chance a New York change of heart on that score might consider the doubtfulness of federal jurisdiction a good reason for foregoing a federal action and suing in a state court instead, especially if the statute of limitations is closing in.[22]

And if the state court to which the plaintiff intends to turn if dismissed from the federal court is that of a state other than New York, the question of whether there will be a new time period awarded for the action is entirely a matter of that state's law. It may not have as generous a saving statute as CPLR 205(a).

Whatever the basis of subject matter jurisdiction may be in the federal action—federal

---

16. See Barber v. Barber, 62 U.S. (21 How.) 582, 16 L.Ed. 226 (1858); Ex Parte Burrus, 136 U.S. 586, 10 S.Ct. 850, 34 L.Ed. 500 (1890).

17. See, e.g., Sutton v. English, 246 U.S. 199, 38 S.Ct. 254, 62 L.Ed. 664 (1918); Broderick's Will, 88 U.S. (21 Wall.) 503, 22 L.Ed. 599 (1875).

18. See § 8 above.

19. See Owen Equipment & Erection Co. v. Kroger, 437 U.S. 365, 98 S.Ct. 2396, 57 L.Ed.2d 274 (1978).

20. FRCP Rule 12(h)(3).

21. See Dyer v. Cahan, 150 A.D.2d 172, 540 N.Y.S.2d 785 (1st Dep't 1989). A defect in personal jurisdiction does not get the extension. See § 52 above.

22. See item 18 on the list of choice of forum factors in § 616 below.

question,[23] diversity of citizenship,[24] admiralty,[25] or any other—it must be pleaded in the complaint.[26] It is usually pleaded in the opening paragraph of the complaint in a federal civil action, and an official form[27] prescribes the precise terminology for alleging it. If there is subject matter jurisdiction but it has not been pleaded, or has been pleaded improperly, an amendment is of course permissible.[28] In New York practice, while it is also true that an objection to subject matter jurisdiction may be raised at any time,[29] there is no requirement that the jurisdiction be pleaded in the complaint.

§ 612. "Case or Controversy" Requirement; Justiciability, Standing, Ripeness, Mootness, Etc.

Under the caption of "Standing to Sue" treated earlier in its New York practice context,[1] a number of elements were mentioned that touch on the "justiciability" of a case. By "justiciability" is meant the features that make it appropriate for the judicial branch of government to handle the case, as opposed to the "political" branches—the executive and legislative. Connected with justiciability if not subsumed under it are several other related topics, including standing, ripeness, mootness, and yet other things.

The earlier discussion was designed to assure the reader with more federal than state court experience that this family of subjects is seen in New York practice as well, but with nothing like the frequency with which one finds them in federal practice. At the converse juncture that we reach here, where we confront primarily the New York lawyer turning to federal practice, the reassurance of the earlier section becomes the warning of the present one.

Cases from the U.S. Supreme Court on the subject matter jurisdiction of the federal courts often address issues met under captions like "standing", "political question", "ripeness", "mootness", "advisory opinion", and perhaps yet other things. Some of these can be deemed species of the genus "justiciability", a word used to gather in all matters competent for the judiciary to pass on under our system of jurisprudence. The word's most active function, though, is its negative one: it bars the courts from entertaining any issue not appropriate to the judicial function, i.e., not "justiciable".

The "justiciability" concept comes from Section 2 of Article III of the federal constitution, which sets forth the outer limits of the federal courts' subject matter jurisdiction. Each of the jurisdictional grants on that list is preceded either by the word "cases" or the word "controversies", meaning that whatever the subject is, the courts can entertain it only if it arises in the context of a "case" or a "controversy".[2]

One can see readily enough how that bars the federal courts from rendering an "advisory opinion". If the court's opinion is only "advisory", it is not the court that is resolving the "case" or "controversy". Through somewhat more complex channels, the same "case" or "controversy" criteria account for the other entries on the list of complex cases considering subject matter jurisdiction. Here we have to be forgiven for some condensation, but condensation is indispensable in setting forth background.

Most of us remember from our law school course on federal jurisdiction the many cases, often hard to reconcile, on "standing to sue". If the court finds that the plaintiff in a case lacks a direct enough interest in its outcome,

---

23. See 28 U.S.C.A. § 1331, known as the general federal question statute because it supplies federal subject matter jurisdiction in all actions "arising under the Constitution, laws, or treaties of the United States". It no longer has, as it once did, any monetary qualifications.

24. 28 U.S.C.A. § 1332, with a more-than-$75,000 amount in controversy requirement.

25. 28 U.S.C.A. § 1333.

26. FRCP Rule 8(a).

27. Official Form 2 appended to the Federal Rules of Civil Procedure.

28. 28 U.S.C.A. § 1653.

29. CPLR 3211(a)(2), (e).

§ 612

1. See § 136.

2. Aetna Life Ins. Co. v. Haworth, 300 U.S. 227, 57 S.Ct. 461, 81 L.Ed. 617 (1937).

the plaintiff is said to lack "standing", and if the plaintiff lacks standing then in that plaintiff's hands there is no "case" or "controversy". A federal action purporting to present such a "case" therefore has to be dismissed for want of subject matter jurisdiction. A 1923 landmark on that point is Frothingham v. Mellon,[3] precluding an action by a taxpayer to test the constitutionality of a federal spending measure. The difficulties of *Frothingham's* "standing" doctrine can be seen in the distinction made of the case more than 40 years later in Flast v. Cohen,[4] an extensive discourse on the standing issue, which sustained such an action when the spending measure under attack was alleged to violate the establishment clause. Both cases involved what we have come to call a "taxpayer" suit.

"Ripeness" and "mootness" are similar labels that can dismiss an action as not being a proper "case" or "controversy". "Ripeness" dismisses the case because it is not yet ready: whatever the threat of which the plaintiff complains, it is not yet near enough at hand to warrant judicial intervention.[5] "Mootness" can work a like dismissal at the other end: the plaintiff's interest, genuine enough at the outset, has been mooted by some later event, like a change of status, the divestiture of an interest, the mere passing of time, etc.[6] In both situations, the "case" or "controversy" standard is violated and a dismissal is the result.

The more important cases on these issues from the U.S. Supreme Court are often the media through which philosophical shifts can be felt in the changing membership of the court from generation to generation, from decade to decade, and even from year to year.

"Justiciability" as an issue is often met in cases concerning the separation of powers, as where the courts are asked to do something more properly left to the executive or legislative branches of government. Here, too, especially at the highest judicial level, a judge's

philosophical view of the judicial function plays a major role. In drawing the line, the so-called "activist" judge would give the judiciary a wider role; an advocate of "judicial restraint" would defer more to the other branches. When such deference appears, and a case is dismissed for a want of "justiciability", one may hear the case described as involving a "political" question, best left to one of the other branches of government.[7]

And so it goes, and so perhaps it will always go as long as reasonable minds may differ about these fundamental issues. An unfortunate aspect of the subject is that federal judges at both district and circuit level are sometimes hard pressed to divine the U.S. Supreme Court's current disposition of mind on one of these fundamental points, which increases the likelihood of an appeal, disagreement among the judges along the way, and unpredictability of result.

This is not to suggest that these "case" or "controversy" doctrines are a constant friction in federal practice. They are not met all that often, but whatever their frequency on the calendars of the federal courts, they are found there more often than in New York practice, and their appearance occurs more often than not in cases in which the plaintiff is out to make some new law.

In the federal courts the "case" or "controversy" requirement of the federal constitution accounts for these topics. Their counterparts in state practice do not have as specific a genesis. It was said in New York State Inspection, Security and Law Enforcement Employees v. Cuomo[8] that in New York they arise "by implication" from the tripartite separation of powers and from the limitations traditionally associated with the judicial branch of government.

The advisory opinion that is barred from both systems should not be confused with the declaratory judgment. The declaratory judg-

3. 262 U.S. 447, 43 S.Ct. 597, 67 L.Ed. 1078.

4. 392 U.S. 83, 88 S.Ct. 1942, 20 L.Ed.2d 947 (1968).

5. See, e.g., United Public Workers v. Mitchell, 330 U.S. 75, 67 S.Ct. 556, 91 L.Ed. 754 (1947).

6. See, e.g., Golden v. Zwickler, 394 U.S. 103, 89 S.Ct. 956, 22 L.Ed.2d 113 (1969).

7. See the discussion in Baker v. Carr, 369 U.S. 186, 82 S.Ct. 691, 7 L.Ed.2d 663 (1962).

8. 64 N.Y.2d 233, 485 N.Y.S.2d 719, 475 N.E.2d 90 (1984).

ment is available in the federal courts as it is in the New York courts,[9] and the discussion of the declaratory judgment earlier in its New York practice niche[10] can in large measure be applied to the federal declaratory judgment as well. A point to take special note of on the federal side, however, is a certain measure of continuing suspicion that the declaratory action may be used to circumvent restrictions on subject matter jurisdiction, which it may not be allowed to do. The statute in point[11] makes a declaratory judgment available in a federal court only "[i]n a case of actual controversy within its jurisdiction", language designed to assure that subject matter jurisdiction must be shown to exist without regard to the declaratory form in which the plaintiff casts the action.[12] There is no precisely comparable language in New York's declaratory judgment statute,[13] but the New York provision accomplishes the same thing (avoiding the implication that the device may be used as a jurisdiction expander) by conferring broad jurisdiction of the declaratory judgment device only on the supreme court. In New York, the supreme court has "general" jurisdiction and therefore does not confront the rigors of subject matter jurisdiction that confine the federal courts.[14]

The "actual controversy" language of the federal statute is a reminder that the device will not support an advisory opinion. (The federal constitution imposes the restriction, so the statute is only a reminder.) The comparable language that puts across the same idea under the New York statute is the requirement that the declaration be sought only in a "justiciable controversy".[15]

§ 613. The Abstention Doctrines

Just a few words on this subject, which can easily fill a small tome. In several situations in

federal practice, a federal court may refuse to entertain the jurisdiction it concededly has in a case—of both subject matter and parties— and elect to leave the matter to the state courts instead. These instances have come to be known as the "abstention" doctrines, and there are several of them. An application of one of the abstention doctrines will either dismiss or stay the federal action, compelling the plaintiff to turn to the state court, either for the whole case or for a particular issue. When abstention is visited on a case, it will always prove costly in time, money, and energy.[1] A plaintiff may therefore wish to consider, before invoking federal jurisdiction, whether the case poses any abstention possibility at all. It is a relatively infrequent happening, but if the possibility is present it is another item that should be added to the list of choice of forum factors.[2]

The first category is "Pullman" abstention, after Railroad Commission of Texas v. Pullman Co,[3] which started things off in 1941. In this category, a federal constitutional test is sought of a state law and the state law is unclear. The federal court in the "Pullman" class stays the action so that the plaintiff can bring a state court action to secure a definitive interpretation of the state law from the state courts. The interpretation may avoid the federal issue, which is the *Pullman* doctrine's ultimate hope. If it does not, the plaintiff may return to the federal court and move to vacate the stay and go on with the constitutional test.

The procedural steps to be followed in implementing *Pullman* abstention were not clear. There was even a risk that the state court would seize and decide the federal constitutional issue, barring the plaintiff, through

---

9. See 28 U.S.C.A. §§ 2201, 2202.

10. See § 436 et seq., above.

11. 28 U.S.C.A. § 2201.

12. See Skelly Oil Co. v. Phillips Petroleum Co., 339 U.S. 667, 70 S.Ct. 876, 94 L.Ed. 1194 (1950).

13. CPLR 3001.

14. See § 611 above.

15. CPLR 3001. See § 436 above. An exception to the restriction on the advisory opinion in New York is the

power explicitly conferred by the state constitution on the New York Court of Appeals to answer questions of New York law put by certain other courts. See § 528A above.

§ 613

1. See the delays met in Spencer Motor Serv., Inc. v. O'Connor, 340 U.S. 602, 71 S.Ct. 508, 95 L.Ed. 573 (1951), before the case was finally decided on the merits.

2. See item 18 on the list of choice of forum factors in § 616 below.

3. 312 U.S. 496, 61 S.Ct. 643, 85 L.Ed. 971.

the res judicata doctrine, from having the federal court address it, as the plaintiff preferred. Things reached a point of such confusion that the U.S. Supreme Court was moved to do an unusual thing. In England v. Louisiana State Board of Medical Examiners,[4] the court offered a detailed formula for just what the plaintiff has to do and just how far the plaintiff has to go in submitting the matter to the state court without running afoul of the res judicata doctrine.

Pullman abstention results in a stay of the federal action, anticipating a possible return of the plaintiff after the state test is over. Other categories of abstention bring an outright dismissal of the federal action. Notable among these are a number of cases from which one can spell out a fervent federal wish to avoid becoming the review forum for state administrative determinations, by way of either original federal jurisdiction or through removal from a state court,[5] a line of abstention distinct from *Pullman* and its simple aim of avoiding unnecessary constitutional determinations. This line started with Burford v. Sun Oil Co.[6] in 1943. There are sundry others. They are reviewed and contrasted by the Second Circuit in Law Enforcement Insurance Co. v. Corcoran.[7] A report by the Committee on Federal Courts of the New York State Bar Association[8] also reviews them, including the related line of cases starting with Younger v. Harris[9] in 1971, and with a special accent on the application of the abstention doctrines as they are applied in the Second Circuit.

If abstention is a significant possibility, it may be politic to forego federal jurisdiction altogether. But if the plaintiff nevertheless opts for a federal court in New York and the action is timely, there should be no statute of limitations problem if the action is then dis-

missed under one of the abstention doctrines, even if the applicable statute of limitations has by that time expired. An abstention dismissal is not on the merits and does not qualify as a neglect to prosecute or as a voluntary dismissal. Those are the exceptions enumerated in CPLR 205(a), the statute that allows six months from an earlier nonmerits dismissal for commencement of a new action.[10] The case should therefore earn the CPLR 205(a) extension in which to start the action anew in a New York state court.

If the New York Court of Appeals certification procedure, which permits certain courts to submit questions of New York law to the New York Court of Appeals for an advisory ruling,[11] were available to a U.S. district court, it could constitute a significant alternative to abstention of the *Pullman* kind. But the procedure is not available to the U.S. district courts. It is available to the federal courts of appeals, however, and even if delayed until that level its application can be a time saver.[12]

§ 614. Supplemental Jurisdiction

In our federal system, a plaintiff who has a federal claim against a defendant will often find that the same wrongful conduct has given rise to a claim under state law as well. They may be separate claims, or they may merely be different "counts" or "grounds" or "theories" in support of what is essentially a single claim. Each can be sued on in its own court system, of course, but that creates duplication and waste. If jurisdiction of the federal claim has not been conferred exclusively on the federal courts, both claims can be brought in the state court. More to the point in this section, where the assumption will be that there is no diversity of citizenship between the parties to serve as an alternative ground for federal jurisdic-

---

4. 375 U.S. 411, 84 S.Ct. 461, 11 L.Ed.2d 440 (1964).

5. See, e.g., Lucchese v. Carboni, 22 F.Supp.2d 256 (S.D.N.Y.1998), and Greenberg v. Veteran, 710 F.Supp. 962 (S.D.N.Y.), rev'd 889 F.2d 418 (2d Cir. 1989), remanding a CPLR Article 78 proceeding that had been removed from state court on the ostensible basis of a federal question.

6. 319 U.S. 315, 63 S.Ct. 1098, 87 L.Ed. 1424.

7. 807 F.2d 38 (2d Cir.1986).

8. The Abstention Doctrine: The Consequences of Federal Court Deference to State Court Proceedings, August 30, 1988.

9. 401 U.S. 37, 91 S.Ct. 746, 27 L.Ed.2d 669.

10. See § 52 above.

11. See § 528A above.

12. See the discussion in the lead note in New York State Law Digest No. 329.

tion, is whether the plaintiff can bring both claims in the federal court.

Under the doctrine of "supplemental" jurisdiction, the plaintiff usually can. The doctrine permits a federal court to entertain a state claim of which it would otherwise lack subject matter jurisdiction when it is joined with a related federal claim, the two arising out of the same event or connected series of events. This used to be called "pendent" jurisdiction, arising as a caselaw doctrine[1] and going under that name for decades before being codified under the name of "supplemental jurisdiction" in § 1367 of Title 28, enacted in 1990. Under this doctrine, the federal claim acts as the equivalent of a jurisdictional crutch. In the constitutional sense, the relatedness of the two claims makes both of them part of the same constitutional "case".

A separate but analogous doctrine was known as "ancillary jurisdiction", also a caselaw creation, this one designed originally (and still primarily but not exclusively) for the use of defendants in diversity of citizenship cases. It enables a party to interpose a claim against one having the same citizenship as itself based upon the claim's relationship to another claim in the same action between other parties who do have diverse citizenship. This "ancillary" jurisdiction doctrine has also been merged into § 1367's "supplemental" jurisdiction. Because it is best understood after the subjects of joinder of parties and claims are treated, the "ancillary" aspect of supplemental jurisdiction will be deferred until then.[2]

If the federal court hears both claims and disposes of all on the merits, the result is of course res judicata.[3] But the federal court, in various situations in which the state claim has to depend on supplemental jurisdiction, has discretion to dismiss the state claim without reaching its merits.[4] It can be hard in some cases to discern whether the federal court has done that, or whether it has in fact decided the merits of the state claim. Sometimes the state court views it one way and a federal court, afterwards trying to clarify the matter, views it another.[5] But as long as the final view is that the disposition did not reach the merits, a new action can be commenced on the state claim in the state court.

Suppose, however, that the original statute of limitations has by now expired? Subdivision (d) of § 1367 answers the problem by extending the statute of limitations until 30 days after the federal dismissal, unless state law provides a longer time, which New York in fact does: the six-month period that CPLR 205(a) offers for a new action after the non-merits dismissal of an earlier one[6] has been held to apply in this situation,[7] some six times more generous a gift than the federal statute's 30 days.

When it was known as the "pendent" jurisdiction doctrine, it was held by the U.S. Supreme Court to support jurisdiction in federal question cases only of a state claim asserted between the same persons who were named parties to the federal claim. If the state claim in a multi-party case ran against a person who was not also subject to the federal claim, the court held that the doctrine would not support the state claim against that person. This had come to be known in the lower courts as "pendent party jurisdiction", but the U.S. Supreme Court rejected it. It first did so in 1976 in Aldinger v. Howard,[8] and then in 1989 held

§ 614

1. See United Mine Workers v. Gibbs, 383 U.S. 715, 86 S.Ct. 1130, 16 L.Ed.2d 218 (1966), in which "pendent" jurisdiction was given its most generous construction.

2. See §§ 630 and 632 below.

3. See § 469 above.

4. These situations are now enumerated in subdivision (c) of § 1367 and are discussed at length in the Practice Commentary on 28 U.S.C.A. § 1367.

5. See, e.g., McLearn v. Cowen & Co. in the New York Court of Appeals, 48 N.Y.2d 696, 422 N.Y.S.2d 60, 397

N.E.2d 750 (1979), followed by the same case in the Second Circuit in 660 F.2d 845 (2d Cir.1981). Both courts were divided. The case is discussed in more detail in § 469, above, and is the subject of a lead note in New York State Law Digest No. 240 and a follow up summary in Digest 265.

6. See § 52 above.

7. See, e.g., Kleinberger v. Town of Sharon, 116 A.D.2d 367, 501 N.Y.S.2d 746 (3d Dep't 1986).

8. 427 U.S. 1, 96 S.Ct. 2413, 49 L.Ed.2d 276.

in Finley v. United States[9] that the doctrine would not even be acceptable to support the state claim when the federal claim lies exclusively in federal jurisdiction, thus making it impossible for the plaintiff to bring both claims together in either a federal or state court.

Subdivision (a) of § 1367 overruled both cases and allows this kind of jurisdiction. Shall it now be called "supplemental party jurisdiction"? By whatever name, an example of it under § 1367 appears in Klein v. Goetzmann.[10]

The doctrine is primarily an incident of subject matter jurisdiction, but there has been some effort to extend it to the area of personal jurisdiction as well. Suppose, for example, that the plaintiff under a federal statute can make nationwide service of process with respect to the federal claim,[11] but has no basis for doing so on the state claim, such as where the state claim does not invoke a state longarm statute that might authorize extrastate service.[12] May the nationwide service applicable to the federal claim also be used for the state claim? This has come to be known as "pendent personal jurisdiction" and has some support in the cases.[13] If the doctrine is needed but held unavailable, the plaintiff's only alternative may be to bring suit, in either a state or federal court (or both), in the state in which all the needed defendants will be amenable to personal jurisdiction. If no single state qualifies, multiple suits may again be necessary. Here the plaintiff had best have checked the statute of limitation provisions of the state turned to. That state will not necessarily apply New York's statute of limitations.

An attempt to get the U.S. Supreme Court to go beyond § 1367 and adopt a kind of "pendent appellate jurisdiction" was rejected in Swint v. Chambers County Comm'n,[14] in which some defendants and an agency moved

in the district court for summary judgment, which was denied. Under caselaw, the individual defendants could appeal but the agency couldn't.[15] The U.S. Supreme Court would not allow the agency a free appellate ride on the coattails of the individual defendants.

C. CHOOSING THE FORUM

Table of Sections

§ 615. The Federal Statute of Limitations

State-court practitioners will usually find in their state statutes specific lists of what periods apply to what actions. Congress has never made that effort on the federal scene. The statute of limitations in federal practice, even though it carries the same potential for destroying a case as in state practice, is therefore a more elusive subject. At the risk of oversimplification, the following few points may be noted.

The statute of limitations in federal practice depends first on what the basis of subject matter jurisdiction is in the action. If it is diversity of citizenship, state law must be looked to for the applicable statute of limitations. That's the rule of the leading case of Guaranty Trust Co. v. York,[1] holding that the point is governed by Erie R.R. Co. v. Tompkins.[2] This is so notwithstanding that for many purposes the statute of limitations is deemed "procedural" while *Erie* is supposed to point to state law only for "substantive" is-

---

9. 490 U.S. 545, 109 S.Ct. 2003, 104 L.Ed.2d 593.

10. 810 F.Supp. 417 (N.D.N.Y.1993).

11. For discussion of the extraterritorial bases of personal jurisdiction in the federal courts, see § 626 below.

12. The federal courts use the longarm statutes of the forum state under the adoptive provision of FRCP Rule 4(k)(1)(A), also discussed in § 626 below.

13. See, e.g., In re Penn Central Securities, 338 F.Supp. 436 (E.D.Pa.1972), aff'd 484 F.2d 553 (3d Cir.

1973); International Controls Corp. v. Vesco, 593 F.2d 166 (2d Cir.1979).

14. 514 U.S. 35, 115 S.Ct. 1203, 131 L.Ed.2d 60 (1995).

15. See the summary of the case in SPR 37:4.

§ 615

1. 326 U.S. 99, 65 S.Ct. 1464, 89 L.Ed. 2079 (1945).

2. 304 U.S. 64, 58 S.Ct. 817, 82 L.Ed. 1188 (1938).

sues.[3] It must also be remembered that this resort to state law in a diversity case has been carried right down to a determination of the moment that the action is deemed commenced, as held in Walker v. Armco Steel Corp.[4] The line of a limitations inquiry in a diversity case, therefore, although it leads to state law, is in any event a straight one.

In a nondiversity case, however, and especially in the "arising under" (federal question) case, the line may be elusive. If the federal statute that supplies the substantive cause of action has a limitations period to go with it, that period of course governs. But a "void which is commonplace in federal statutory law", as the U.S. Supreme Court acknowledged in Board of Regents v. Tomanio,[5] exists when no federal statute supplies a time period for the particular federal claim. In that instance, says *Tomanio*, the applicable period is "the state law of limitations governing an analogous cause of action". This sends the lawyer looking to state law for state counterparts to the federal claim, which can of course be troublesome. In one instance, for example, involving one of the most sensitive of all federal claims—the civil rights claim of 42 U.S.C.A. § 1983—a New York trial court, a New York appellate court, and a federal court of appeals each reached a different conclusion on what statute of limitations to borrow.[6] The fact that the federal court of appeals was one of the entrants would seem to have settled the matter, except that there was a fourth source heard from shortly afterwards—the U.S. Supreme Court—which went still another way, and that settled it,[7] until the court offered still another clarification a few years later[8]—all of this just to determine what statute to apply to one category of federal claim!

In reaching for an analogous claim in state law, so as to "borrow" the state statute of limitations that applies to it, the federal court must bear in mind the policies underlying the federal claim being sued on so as "to assure that the importation of state law will not frustrate or interfere with the implementation of national policies".[9] It may even be more appropriate in some cases, the court said in DelCostello v. International Brotherhood of Teamsters,[10] to borrow time periods "drawn from federal law—either express limitations periods from related federal statutes, or such alternatives as laches". In West v. Conrail,[11] for example, the court borrowed a time period from the National Labor Relations Act for a claim in the labor area that did not have a time period of its own, and in Agency Holding Corp. v. Malley–Duff & Associates, Inc.,[12] it borrowed for RICO claims the statute of limitations found in another federal statute (the Clayton Act) instead of requiring reference to state law.

Laches is not ordinarily an appropriate standard to use when the relief being sought on the federal claim is legal as opposed to equitable in nature. The laches doctrine is a flexible one applied in equity cases when the relief sought is of the traditional "equity" category, i.e., relief that lies in the court's discretion. It is a sui generis phenomenon requiring a showing of the plaintiff's unreasonable delay on the facts of the particular case coupled with a showing that the defendant was in fact prejudiced by the delay.[13] It would be appropriate to apply where the claim sued on is federal, lacks an accompanying statute of limitations, and authorizes equitable relief. But while in that instance laches rather than a state statute of limitations would apply, state law is some-

---

3. See item 10 on the list of choice of forum factors in § 616 below.

4. 446 U.S. 740, 100 S.Ct. 1978, 64 L.Ed.2d 659 (1980), discussed in § 625, below, and in Commentary C4–37 on FRCP Rule 4 in 28 U.S.C.A.

5. 446 U.S. 478, 483, 100 S.Ct. 1790, 1794–95, 64 L.Ed.2d 440, 447 (1980).

6. See the lead note in New York State Law Digest No. 264.

7. Wilson v. Garcia, 471 U.S. 261, 105 S.Ct. 1938, 85 L.Ed.2d 254 (1985).

8. Owens v. Okure, 488 U.S. 235, 109 S.Ct. 573, 102 L.Ed.2d 594 (1989).

9. Occidental Life Ins. Co. v. EEOC, 432 U.S. 355, 367, 97 S.Ct. 2447, 2455, 53 L.Ed.2d 402, 412 (1977).

10. 462 U.S. 151, 162, 103 S.Ct. 2281, 2284, 76 L.Ed.2d 476, 487 (1983).

11. 481 U.S. 35, 107 S.Ct. 1538, 95 L.Ed.2d 32 (1987).

12. 483 U.S. 143, 107 S.Ct. 2759, 97 L.Ed.2d 121 (1987).

13. See § 36 above.

times peeked at, as part of the laches inquiry, just to see what others in the neighborhood think an appropriate time period is for the particular claim.

Laches is generally the doctrine applied for timeliness measures in admiralty actions—another category of federal subject matter jurisdiction—absent a period prescribed in a special maritime-realm statute supplying the particular claim sued on, like the Jones Act or some other that contains a period of limitations and can offer a handy analogy. Using the analogizing technique described in the *DelCostello* case, for example, the Supreme Court found in McAllister v. Magnolia Petroleum Co.[14] that the Jones Act itself offered the needed statute of limitations for an unseaworthiness claim, an admiralty category of action that has no time period of its own.

The difficulties met in trying to borrow a state time period to apply in a federal action not dependent on diversity of citizenship for subject matter jurisdiction could have been avoided and the subject made academic—reserved for historians—under a statute that Congress was considering in 1990. The proposed statute would have adopted a uniform statute of limitations for all federal claims not having one of their own. Congress instead adopted a hybrid that perpetuates the need to make these state-law analogies in non-diversity cases.

The statute adopted, § 1658 of Title 28, took effect December 1, 1990. In it Congress purported at last to adopt a "general" statute of limitations—a four-year period—for federal question cases. But the statute goes hardly anywhere. It applies only to "a civil action arising under an Act of Congress enacted after the date of the enactment of this section", which means that it applies only to claims recognized by statutes adopted after December 1, 1990. The myriad of claims recognized by statutes adopted before that date are not covered by § 1658 and thus continue—when the statute that created the claim does not contain an accompanying statute of limitations—to grope for analogies in state law.

It would take decades if not generations before newly created claims could accumulate in numbers that might compete with the mass of previously recognized claims that lack—and of course still lack—a statute of limitations. Those claims, the very ones that created the outcry for a general statute of limitations,[15] are the ones that don't get it from § 1658. Section 1658 sets itself smartly on the starting line, in other words, only to fall flat on its face with its first step.[16]

A plaintiff who has technically missed the statute of limitations in respect of a claim for failing to join it in the original complaint, or for failing to designate the defendant properly, or for yet other reasons, may try to correct the matter with an amendment in the hope that the matter now added will be allowed to "relate back" to an earlier time, such as the time the claim in the original pleading was deemed interposed, and thus avoid the bar of the statute. New York has such a provision in CPLR 203(f), treated earlier.[17] So has federal practice, in FRCP Rule 15(c), which makes itself at least as generous by allowing the relation back if (1) state law supplies the statute of limitations in the case and would allow the relation back, or if (2), regardless of state law, the matter in the proposed amendment arises out of the transaction or occurrence set forth in the original pleading.[18]

---

14. 357 U.S. 221, 78 S.Ct. 1201, 2 L.Ed.2d 1272 (1958).

15. In Sentry Corp. v. Harris, 802 F.2d 229, 246 (7th Cir.1986), for example, after treating several of the sticky problems caused by the absence of a uniform federal statute of limitations, especially in respect of tolling provisions, the court said that "[w]e join the growing number of commentators and courts who have called upon Congress to eliminate these complex cases, that do much to consume the time and energies of judges but that do little to advance the cause of justice, by enacting federal limitations periods for all federal causes of action".

16. Section 1658 and the specifics of what it does and doesn't do are the subject of the Practice Commentary on 28 U.S.C.A. § 1658.

17. See § 49 above.

18. This generous approach is the result of an amendment of Rule 15(c), discussed at length in Siegel, The Recent (Dec. 1, 1991) Changes in the Federal Rules of Civil Procedure, 142 F.R.D. 359, 362 (1992).

The "relation back" rule is a category of "tolling" provision. Practitioners are aware of a variety of other tolling provisions that are often found under state law. These are provisions that suspend the running of the statute of limitations on a variety of contingencies.[19] Do these state tolls apply in federal practice? They do in diversity cases under the *Erie/Guaranty Trust/Walker* trio. They do not apply, however, in federal actions in which Congress has supplied a specific statute of limitations,[20] but they may apply in federal actions in which a state statute of limitations is being applied by analogy for want of a specific federal period.[21]

When is the action deemed commenced for statute of limitations purposes? In federal practice, the rule is that the filing of the complaint commences the action.[22] As of 1992, the filing of the summons and complaint also marks commencement of a supreme court action in New York.[23] This New York turn to filing instead of service as the moment of commencement avoids a problem that existed before 1992, when service marked commencement in the supreme court. The problem would arise in a district court action based on diversity of citizenship. What would the moment of commencement be? The U.S. Supreme Court held in the *Walker* case, mentioned above, that the *Erie* doctrine must govern the issue and that it must therefore be whatever state law provides. This meant that the diversity plaintiff who filed the action within the statute of limitations but then made service afterwards would be time barred in New York. With the 1992 adoption of filing to mark commencement in the supreme court, such an action would be timely and the issue should no longer arise.[24]

As in New York practice, the statute of limitations is an affirmative defense for the defendant to plead and prove.[25]

The procedural incidents and the time for service of the summons and complaint following their filing, including differences between federal and New York practice, are treated in a later section.[26]

§ 616. Choice of Forum Factors

We draw here a check list of some of the various factors that go into deciding which, as between a federal and New York court, is best for the case at hand. The plaintiff's lawyer who is about to bring suit must consider these things before suing; the defendant's lawyer whose client has been sued in a state court must consider these things in deciding whether to remove the case to the federal court. The assumption, of course, is that jurisdiction of the controversy is concurrent, as it always is when there is diversity of citizenship between the parties and as it may often be, even in the absence of diversity, when the claim arises under federal law. In the latter situation, the "federal question" case, jurisdiction will be concurrent unless Congress has conferred it on the federal courts exclusively.[1] Jurisdiction is often concurrent even in admiralty cases under the well known "saving to suitors" clause of the admiralty jurisdiction statute.[2]

The purpose here is not to resolve the various factors, but merely to list them. And the list is by no means exhaustive. Nor is it set forth with any kind of priority in mind. In any given situation one factor may loom larger than another, or a unique consideration may appear to point the direction. Here we list only

---

19. See §§ 50–56 above.

20. See Burnett v. N.Y. Central R.R. Co., 380 U.S. 424, 85 S.Ct. 1050, 13 L.Ed.2d 941 (1965).

21. Note the DelCostello case on this matter, too, note 10 above, and see, e.g., Whitmore v. City of New York, 541 F.Supp. 564 (E.D.N.Y.1982).

22. FRCP Rule 3.

23. CPLR 304.

24. While service continues to mark commencement in New York's lower courts, see § 63 above, it is the practice

in the supreme court, as the state's court of general jurisdiction, to which Walker looks for determining when an action is commenced in state practice.

25. FRCP Rule 8(c). The several ways of interposing a statute of limitations defense are discussed in SPR 65:4, stressing the practice in the Second Circuit.

26. See § 625 below.

§ 616

1. See § 611, above, on subject matter jurisdiction.

2. 28 U.S.C.A. § 1333.

general factors, and with no special sequence intended.

1. Who Chooses the Forum?

The question may seem facetious. Is it not always the plaintiff who chooses the forum? In situations of concurrent federal/state jurisdiction, the answer is no. If the plaintiff opts for state jurisdiction, the defendant will often be able to remove the case to federal court. The choice of forum in that instance shifts, and it becomes the defendant who must sift the choice of forum factors before deciding whether to remove. The plaintiff, realizing this, may sometimes be able to thwart removal.[3] The factors that go into choosing a forum must be screened by both sides.

2. Lawyer's Familiarity with Forum.

It often happens that attorneys will choose a forum based principally if not exclusively on their own familiarity with its practice. That is of course a factor, but it is only one factor. It may be in the client's best interest that the other forum be chosen, for any of the various reasons that appear on a choice of forum list.

3. Factors Concerning Judges.

A number of factors concerning the judges in the two systems are of course on the list, and to many lawyers these are its main occupants. To whatever extent information is available about them—and when they have been on the bench for a while the information becomes common knowledge—lawyers sift it carefully, concerned about the judges' quality, independence, compassion, expertise in the subject matter of the particular case, integrity, individual reputation, and so forth.

Some ingredients are system-wide in scope, such as in the method by which the judges are selected, which can influence the bar's perception of the judges' independence and insulation from political influence. In New York, for example, trial judges are elected or appointed for terms of varying lengths, up to 14 years.

Under the federal constitution, the federal judges have life tenure.[4]

There are significant differences in the way judges function in the two systems, despite many similarities. The judge in a federal jury trial will usually be found to have, or in any event to be exercising, a greater role at the trial in such things as marshaling the evidence, and in eliciting requests to charge at early stages of the trial, pursuant to Rule 51 of the Federal Rules of Civil Procedure. A New York statute, CPLR 4110–b, adopted in 1973 and modeled on Rule 51, contains similar directions about the charge but does not appear to have gained much momentum in New York practice.[5] This may make a difference to a trial lawyer, but it should also be kept in mind that any individual judge in either court system can, despite the prevalent practice in the court at large, take a more or less active role than expected and thus reduce the significance of this factor. This is especially so in New York in multi-judge courts, where the Individual Assignment System is in effect and where there is therefore no way to determine which judge is going to get the case.

One also hears from time to time of federal judges who will sometimes vary the sequence of summation in jury trials, allowing the plaintiff to sum up first (the defendant traditionally goes first), the defendant going next, and the plaintiff then being allowed the last word by way of rebuttal.

Elements like these, including the reputation of individual judges, must be localized. They can qualify as choice of forum factors only in areas in which judges serve or have been assigned to only a particular geographical area so that the judge who will get the case can be discerned in advance. That is usually impossible to predict in a multi-judge county or district.

4. Factors Concerning Juries.

If the case is triable by jury, a basic factor will be the standards and methods by which jurors are empaneled. There is much to consid-

---

3. Removal is the subject of § 619 below.

4. Article III, § 1.

5. See the Commentary on McKinney's CPLR 4110–b.

er in this category, notably in the geographical unit from which the jurors are selected. In an action in the supreme court in the state system, the unit is the county; in an action in the federal district court, the unit is the district. If the attitudes of the differing populations of those areas in a given case are known (or knowable—more and more consideration is being given to these matters in current trial practice), they may rise to the top of the list of choice of forum factors in the particular case. If the case is essentially one between property owners on one side and property renters on the other, for example, the more urban jury array will be disposed to see things through a tenant's eyes, while the more the mix is diluted with suburban and rural jurors, the more sensitivity will there be to the owner's views.

If a large sum of money is involved, lawyers traditionally try to avoid the rural in favor of the urban area, where juries are reputedly more generous. A graphic example of this occurred in Schimansky v. Nelson,[6] treated earlier.[7] P had brought a wrongful death action in a state court in a rural county, realizing only after the case was at an advanced stage that federal jurisdiction was available, and, at the time, in the Southern District, which includes Manhattan and the Bronx and generous attitudes about money. P was allowed to discontinue the New York action so as to be able to bring it in the federal court.

A federal civil jury must be unanimous unless the parties stipulate otherwise,[8] while in New York practice a 5/6ths vote suffices.[9] This gives an individual juror a complete veto power in federal but not in state practice, which is a consideration to trial lawyers.

The voir dire in federal practice is conducted by the judge; in New York practice, by the lawyers with the judge rarely present.[10] Some lawyers prefer to do the voir dire questioning on their own; others, that the judge do it, especially when the opposing attorney—if it is known in advance who the opposing attorney is likely to be—is known for contentiousness.

5.   Geography.

The lawyer familiar with the venue rules in both systems[11] knows how significant a role geography can play. The layout of the four federal districts in New York often makes it a factor in choosing between a federal and state forum. If the federal district is a large one in area, choosing federal instead of state jurisdiction may mean a good deal more travel for some of the parties than were the action brought in the supreme court. If the plaintiff has a choice, for example, between St. Lawrence County in the state system, at the northeast corner of the state just below Canada, and the federal Northern District that embraces it, which has courthouses in several counties but all of them far from St. Lawrence, it is clear what kind of a trip a lawyer and client face when a motion or conference is on in the federal court and they live in St. Lawrence County. It may be only a few miles, however— or only a few blocks—to the local courthouse if the action is brought in the supreme court.

Convenience to the plaintiff—and inconvenience to the defendant—are calculated by plaintiffs when they choose a forum. Conversely, convenience to the defendant and inconvenience to the plaintiff are calculated by defendants when they are sued in the state court and have the option of removing the case to the federal court. Speed (or slowness) of access to the judge is often part of choice of forum planning.

6.   Calendar Conditions.

How up to date the courts are with their calendars is a key determinant in choosing a forum. Some thought should always be given to local calendar conditions. Plaintiffs are usually the ones in search of speed, and defendants, especially defendants with the removal option in hand, often consider how best they

---

6.   50 A.D.2d 634, 374 N.Y.S.2d 771 (3d Dep't 1975).

7.   See § 297 above.

8.   FRCP Rule 48

9.   CPLR 4113(a).

10.   See § 392 above.

11.   Venue in the supreme court in New York is the subject of §§ 116–125 above. Federal venue is treated in § 617 below.

can delay the case. What either must do to implement this element depends entirely on local conditions. In some places the federal courts may be more up to date on their civil calendars; in others, the state courts.

7. Forum Non Conveniens Risks.

If a plaintiff wants the case litigated in New York, in whatever court, the plaintiff is not likely to be happy if the case is visited with a forum non conveniens dismissal or transfer. Attorneys must therefore be familiar with the conveniens rules in both systems. While the ingredients that go into a conveniens test are similar between the two, they are not the same. And the disposition of the case, should a conveniens objection be sustained, may be strikingly different. The successful application of a forum non conveniens objection in New York state practice dismisses the action, for example, while in the federal court it will usually just transfer it.[12]

8. Impact of Choice of Forum Clause.

This is connected with the forum non conveniens doctrine. If it is shown in an action in New York that the parties, as in a contract, have opted for the jurisdiction of but a single place, and that place is not New York, is the New York court, state or federal, obliged to dismiss the action, or at least transfer it? The New York courts are not obliged to do either,[13] and the U.S. Supreme Court held in Stewart Organization, Inc. v. Ricoh Corp.[14] that neither are the federal courts. But there are still differences, and in at least one category of case— the big commercial case—the difference can be pronounced because of a special set of New York statutes[15] that erases the forum non conveniens doctrine as a source of dismissal under certain circumstances.

One of those statutes is intended to assure that if the parties to a commercial case involving more than $1 million want a New York

court to hear the case, and stipulate to both New York judicial jurisdiction and to an application of New York law to govern the substantive issues in the case, the stipulation will be binding: it will confer jurisdiction despite the absence of other New York contacts and will even overcome a forum non conveniens objection that might otherwise lie. That instruction would probably be followed to the letter in a New York state court action, assuring retention of the case if brought there, but the U.S. Supreme Court held in *Stewart* that a forum selection clause remains at most but one of many factors for a federal court to consider in determining whether to uphold a conveniens objection. Hence the fact that a contract between the parties stipulates to one forum alone, while it may be deemed conclusive under state law, cannot supersede a federal court's discretion even in a diversity action, where state law may have to be resorted to for a variety of other things.

This can of course influence a plaintiff with a commercial claim having the requisite elements to bring it in a New York instead of a federal court, just as it will influence the defendant, if bent on getting the case out of New York altogether, to remove it to the federal court and have a go at a conveniens objection there.[16]

Defendants who are sued in a New York court under a contract containing those stipulations and who want to keep the case in New York but also want a federal forum, had best recall the maxim about not being able to have one's cake and eat it, too. If they do not try to remove the case, the stipulation will bind and the case will stay in New York, where they want it, but in a state court. If they remove it to the federal court, the stipulation will not bind and the case may be subjected to a conveniens disposition, taking it out of New York altogether.

---

12. See the brief discussion of the federal forum non conveniens rules in § 618 below. The New York counterparts are discussed in §§ 28 and 29 above.

13. The New York forum non conveniens doctrine is treated in § 28 above.

14. 487 U.S. 22, 108 S.Ct. 2239, 101 L.Ed.2d 22 (1988).

15. CPLR 327(b) and §§ 5–1401 and 5–1402 of the General Obligations Law. See § 28 above.

16. The interplay of these factors is explored in Youngblood, Forum–Selection Clauses in New York Affected by High Court's Decision, N.Y. Law Journal, July 1, 1988.

9. Appellate Differences

A final judgment is appealable to the first tier appellate court in either system, but it is well known that the appeal from a nonfinal order, while freely available in New York practice,[17] is almost entirely unavailable in federal practice, which tends to foreclose all appellate review until a final judgment has been rendered.[18] Lawyers contemplating the need, or just wanting the option, of appellate review of individual dispositions in the pretrial phase of the action will tend towards a New York court. Those who want the case to ride to final judgment without piecemeal review, willing to forego it for themselves and anxious to deny it to the other side, will lean towards the federal court.

The appellate division in New York possesses and exercises a broader power of review over supreme court dispositions than the federal court of appeals does over the district courts, at least in matters of discretion. The federal appellate court overturns a district judge's finding of fact only when it finds it to have been "clearly erroneous",[19] while in New York the appellate division is more prone merely to substitute its own discretion for that of the trial judge even if the court does not find an "abuse" of discretion as such. This plays a special role in money actions, and most notably in tort actions that include an award for pain and suffering. The appellate division is more likely, with the "additur" or "remittitur" devices,[20] to alter the sum set by the lower court for damages than a federal court of appeals is, and lawyers representing plaintiffs in tort actions often cite that as a factor pointing to the federal court.

10. Substantive Law Differences?

This element tends to play a role only with lawyers with extended experience in both court systems.

On the face of things, there should be no difference between the two systems in what substantive law is applied to the case. If the basis of subject matter jurisdiction is that the claim arises under federal law, the applicable law should be the federal law for the substantive issues whichever court the case may be brought in. The same is true of a case dependent on the admiralty or maritime jurisdiction, which is governed by the so-called general maritime law as periodically adjusted by Congress.

On the diversity side, while the federal court will of course be following its own rules of procedure, the doctrine of Erie v. Tompkins[21] is a reasonably solid assurance that the federal court will be applying the law of the forum state to all substantive issues in the case, including choice of law rules if the action involves the law of two or more states.[22] But here we meet one of the most elusive borderlines in the law: the one that presumes to separate "substance" from "procedure". Hence the *Erie* assurance is not absolute. Even with respect to a rule of evidence whose impact may be most substantial, for example, and which appears to differ between state and federal court enough to invoke the *Erie* doctrine, a federal court may still apply its own rule and its doing so can make a difference.[23]

Whatever the category of an issue in the case, if it is perceived to be a key one and it appears that the two systems would apply different rules to its resolution, the difference has to be considered by the forum-choosing lawyer.

11. Rules of Evidence.

Having touched on the subject of evidence, we can expand on it slightly. In the federal courts, the evidentiary guideposts are largely codified into the Federal Rules of Evidence. On the New York side, there are several dozen statutes,[24] but much more is left to caselaw, or,

---

17. See § 526 above.

18. See § 642 below.

19. See FRCP Rule 52(a).

20. See § 407 above.

21. 304 U.S. 64, 58 S.Ct. 817, 82 L.Ed. 1188 (1938).

22. See Day and Zimmerman, Inc. v. Challoner, 423 U.S. 3, 96 S.Ct. 167, 46 L.Ed.2d 3 (1975).

23. See the lead note in New York State Law Digest No. 263.

24. CPLR Article 45.

to hear some practitioners describe it, to the judges' intuitions, especially in respect of hearsay evidence. Other lawyers do not see such a difference, but here, again, only a lawyer with an extended trial experience in both systems is in a position to do justice to this factor on a choice of forum list. Lawyers who prefer a more extensive code will tend to the federal courts.[25]

While the subject of "evidence" is generally deemed to include the rules about privileged communications, privileges differ from the mass of other rules of evidence. Most rules of evidence are designed only to find the best route to the truth. The rules about privileged communications are willing to obscure the truth, if need be, in order to sanctify certain relationships (doctor/patient, husband/wife, lawyer/client, etc.). At least in diversity of citizenship cases, the federal courts apply the state law of privileged communications, recognizing the delicate state policies that would be undermined if the rule were otherwise.[26]

12. Scope of Process.

There will be instances in which the geographical reach of the summons will differ between the two systems, but this is minimized by Rule 4(k)(1)(A) of the Federal Rules of Civil Procedure, which adopts for federal use the same extraterritorial bases of jurisdiction recognized in the forum state's courts.[27] It is a factor, however, whenever extraterritorial jurisdiction is doubtful and the system selected will have to make do without it. Personal service in the absence of an extraterritorial basis will be limited to the geographical borders of the state in both systems, but with a mild extension in the federal system under what is known as the "100 mile bulge". It is probably more of a consideration for defendants contemplating removal to a federal court than for plaintiffs about to sue there because

the "bulge" provision is applicable mainly to the joinder of additional parties after the plaintiff's original roster of defendants is complete.[28]

In a number of situations, Congress has by statute allowed nationwide summons service in certain cases. Most of these are categories of federal question jurisdiction, but an example of it in a diversity of citizenship context is the device known as federal statutory interpleader. In interpleader, a stakeholder stuck between conflicting claimants to the same money or property is able to protect itself from double liability by making the claimants litigate their claims in the same court. There is a problem, of course, when not all of the conflicting claimants are subject to jurisdiction in the same court. Under federal statutory interpleader, Congress has allowed nationwide service of the federal summons in certain circumstances in an attempt to meet the problem, and it of course offers a special advantage in the federal court.[29]

On subpoena service, geographical reach is a factor relevant whenever a key witness is not within obvious reach of the court's process. There the advantage is usually on the federal side. A New York state court subpoena may not be served outside the state.[30] There are instances in which a federal subpoena may.[31]

13. Compulsory Counterclaim Rule.

All counterclaims are "permissive" in New York practice. The defendant can interpose a claim against the plaintiff as a counterclaim or, even if it is related to the main claim, withhold it and sue on it in a separate action.[32] The defendant cannot do that in federal practice, which has a compulsory counterclaim rule.[33] By suing in a federal court, a plaintiff may be able to compel the defendant to interpose as a counterclaim any claim arising out of

---

25. A New York evidence code, recommended by the New York Law Revision Commission, has been proposed for New York but the legislature has yet to adopt it.

26. See Rule 501 of the Federal Rules of Evidence.

27. See § 626 below.

28. See FRCP Rule 4(k)(1)(B), also discussed in § 626, below.

29. See § 154 above.

30. See § 383 above.

31. See FRCP Rule 45.

32. The doctrine of collateral estoppel will sometimes make this "permissive" counterclaim notion an illusion, however. See § 224 above.

33. FRCP Rule 13(a). See § 632 below.

the transaction on which the plaintiff's claim is based, thereby denying the defendant an independent choice of forum on the counterclaim.

14. Temporary Restraining Order Practice.

In both systems, a preliminary injunction is available to keep status quo during the pendency of certain actions, and in both systems a temporary restraining order (TRO) is available as a device to keep status quo while the preliminary injunction application comes on for a contested hearing.[34] But lawyers versed primarily in federal practice, and more often than not those representing defendants, suggest that the TRO is granted too casually by New York judges. They find the federal judges more circumspect, often even requiring that notice of a TRO be given to the opposing party, sometimes by telephone right from the judge's chambers, by no means a common practice with state judges. An amendment to require such notice of a TRO in New York practice as well has been proposed annually to the legislature for decades, but has yet to pass.

How this figures as a possible choice of forum factor is difficult to gauge. If the plaintiff wants the TRO immediately, presumably it points to the New York courts for the action. If the defendant opposes it, and is sued in a New York court and can remove the case to the federal court, removal will be the defendant's course, but it is quite likely that whatever TRO is destined to issue in the case will already have issued in the state court before removal (and the TRO of course retains its validity during the removal process[35]).

15. Procedural Differences.

Several of the items already enumerated are clearly "procedural" elements, but a separate caption might be made of procedural matters in general, since any lawyer who has tried cases in both systems can point to any number of perceived differences, general or specific, and count them as choice of forum factors. This is therefore a Pandora's Box of elements that may matter to lawyers who know both systems well.

There are numerous subcategories of procedure and any given lawyer in any given kind of case may prefer the procedure of one system over another for a variety of reasons, some objective and some not.

A prominent example is in the disclosure devices, where, liberal as disclosure has become under the New York CPLR, it is still more restrictive than its federal counterpart. Interrogatories under the Federal Rules of Civil Procedure, for example, do not have the fetters that they have under the CPLR,[36] and play a larger role in federal practice.

Disclosure from a nonparty witness is also freely available on the federal side, often prompting a plaintiff's lawyer to put this at or near the top of the list of choice of forum factors if pretrial testimony from a key but reluctant witness is needed. While a number of efforts have been made to remove the hobbles from nonparty disclosure in New York, there remain impediments in the requirements of the applicable statute[37] and in the attitudes of some of the state judges.

These are only sample items. Lawyers versed in both systems have their own catalogs.

16. Court–Annexed Arbitration.

A form of compulsory or at least semi-compulsory arbitration is in effect in some measure in both court systems for money claims at the lower reaches of jurisdiction, but "lower reaches" has a different meaning in each. In the New York system, court-annexed arbitration is widespread but is capped at $10,000 in some courts, $6000 in others.[38] In the federal courts, the sums are much higher,[39] and partic-

---

34. FRCP Rule 65; CPLR Article 63.

35. See §§ 619 and 640 below.

36. See § 361 above and § 638 below.

37. See CPLR 3101(a)(4); Dioguardi v. St. John's Riverside Hospital, 144 A.D.2d 333, 533 N.Y.S.2d 915 (2d Dep't 1988); and § 345 above.

38. See CPLR 3405; § 585B above.

39. See 28 U.S.C.A. § 658, part of the several sections governing court-annexed arbitration in the federal courts, §§ 651–658, which are the subject of Practice Commentaries in 28 U.S.C.A.

ipation in the system is left to local option.[40] The lawyer favorably disposed to the arbitration system can select a court in which it applies. Conversely, the lawyer who wants to avoid the arbitration process and assure the litigation of the case can choose a court accordingly.

17. Differences in Enforcing Judgments and Orders.

A section later on briefly lists federal enforcement provisions,[41] and a whole chapter has already been devoted to state enforcement procedures.[42] Lawyers involved in the enforcement stage of litigation, or who have at least had some experience with it from time to time, may have a preference between the office of the federal marshal, who enforces federal process, and the sheriff, or, in New York City, the sheriff or city marshals, who enforce New York state process. The actual steps used in enforcing the common money judgment do not differ substantially between the two systems, however, principally because the federal rules adopt the state practice in respect of most of the enforcement devices.[43]

If enforcement is not likely to be needed, as where the defendant is clearly solvent or the liability sued on is covered by insurance, this will of course not be a factor.

The plaintiff's lawyer should give special thought to enforcement when planning an injunction action, or any other that sounds in equity and may require use of the contempt remedy. The contempt remedy has teeth in both systems, but some of the teeth in the New York system are soft, especially—ironically—on the criminal as opposed to civil contempt side.[44] On the federal side the teeth may be fangs, and the incentive to obedience keen, a matter also noted in the treatment of enforcement, below.[45]

18. Doubtfulness of Subject Matter Jurisdiction.

If subject matter jurisdiction in the federal action is doubtful, that is a good reason for choosing a state forum, or in any event an important factor to consider, especially if the expiration of the applicable statute of limitations is drawing near. It was previously pointed out that a dismissal for want of subject matter jurisdiction by a federal court in New York entitles the plaintiff to the six months of CPLR 205(a) in which to commence a new action, but that this generous statute applies only if the second action is brought in a New York state court. We thus added the admonition that if it is to the courts of some other state that the plaintiff will now have to turn, the plaintiff had better have noted the law of limitations of that state.[46] We repeat the warning here as a significant factor in a choice of forum inquiry.

If the case is of a nature to possibly invoke one of the abstention doctrines, which can result in a dismissal or a stay despite the presence of all necessary jurisdiction,[47] that, too, should be considered in weighing a choice of forum.

19. Court Environment and Dignity.

It will happen in some parts of the system, for a variety of reasons ranging from the pressure of a court's calendars to the adequacy of its physical facilities and staffing, that there is an appreciable difference in environment between state and federal court. Lawyers report this as a significant choice of forum element, more commonly cited in urban areas.

20. Privacy.

As compared to out-of-court arbitration, which includes insulation from public view—privacy—as one of its attractions,[48] litigation is an open book. But the federal book is more

---

40. See, for example, the plan for court-annexed arbitration in the Eastern District of New York, presently embodied in Appendix F of the Southern and Eastern District Rules.

41. See § 641 below.

42. See § 476 et seq.

43. See § 641 below.

44. See § 482 above.

45. See § 641.

46. See § 611 above.

47. See § 613 above.

48. See § 586 above.

open than the New York book, and some lawyers occasionally cite this as a choice of forum factor, pro or con. In federal practice, the mandatory filing system is in effect. Every paper served on a party in federal practice must be filed with the court "within a reasonable time after service",[49] which exposes the case step by step to the public media. New York does not follow the mandatory filing system,[50] offering at least a bit more privacy— although nothing stops either party from filing any paper in the case at any time.

21.   Last Minute Considerations.

As noted earlier,[51] there was until 1992 a difference between the federal district court and the New York supreme court in the determination of the moment that an action is deemed commenced for statute of limitations purposes: in the federal court it was filing; in the supreme court it was service. When that was so, some lawyers who were down to the wire might decide on the federal court merely because a filing could be accomplished readily while service was perceived to pose some problem. It is almost always inexcusable for a lawyer to cut things so close that all other choice of forum factors have to be sacrificed to one as narrow as that, but the matter should now be academic. With New York's adoption of the "filing" system for use in the supreme court in 1992, filing is the commencement moment in both systems.

22.   Sanctions.

The New York courts as of the 1980s adopted sanctions provisions to punish frivolous litigation practices. Attention was devoted to this earlier.[52] But the New York rule, albeit without a monetary ceiling on a costs assessment, has a $10,000 maximum on a punitive

levy, while there is no ceiling at all on the federal counterpart, Rule 11 of the Federal Rules of Civil Procedure. Sanctions have gone up to the hundreds of thousands under Rule 11 and it is obviously the more powerful deterrent to frivolity[53]—but also, many have argued, to advocacy. It imposes a heavy burden on the attorney to see to it that there is something substantial to the client's case, and a protestation of good faith in believing what the client had to say will not avail. The Second Circuit has held that after the 1983 amendment of Rule 11 it does not suffice for an attorney's self-protection to show "that he personally was unaware of the groundless nature of an argument or claim"; that Rule 11 "explicitly and unambiguously imposes an affirmative duty on each attorney to conduct a reasonable inquiry into the viability of a pleading [and, it is safe to add, just about every other paper] before it is signed"; and that "[s]imply put, subjective good faith no longer provides the safe harbor it once did".[54]

A "safe-harbor" provision, or in any event what is commonly known as that, was afterwards inserted into Rule 11 with the requirement that a motion for sanctions first be served on the alleged offender and not filed in court earlier than 21 days after that, the three weeks intended to give the alleged offender a chance to withdraw the objectionable paper without facing any sanctions at all.[55]

Those with a choice of forum who anticipate frivolous conduct on the other side may want to gauge the deterrent value of each of the two systems' sanction rules and choose accordingly. On the federal side, incidentally, Rule 11 is not alone; there are several other sources of sanctions and attorney's fees.[56]

---

49.   FRCP Rule 5(d). See § 633 below.

50.   See § 77, above, comparing the state and federal systems in this regard.

51.   Section 615.

52.   See § 414A above.

53.   See the Advisory Committee notes on the 1983 amendment of Rule 11.

54.   Eastway Constr. Corp. v. City of New York, 762 F.2d 243, 253 (2d Cir.1985).

55.   This was part of the 1993 amendment of Rule 11, extensively treated in an accompanying Advisory Committee note which may be found following Rule 11 in 28 U.S.C.A.

56.   See the listing and discussion in Oliveri v. Thompson, 803 F.2d 1265 (2d Cir.1986). Note also that Rule 11 does not apply at all to discovery procedure, which has its own sanctions provisions. See § 639 below.

* * *

As we said at the start, the list can go on and on. Each lawyer can doubtless add several elements from personal experience. There is no natural end to a list like this, but the one drawn here should in any event call attention to just how much there is to consider in choosing between a federal and New York forum.

§ 617. Venue in Federal Courts

Just as it does in New York practice, the topic of venue in federal practice presupposes the existence of both subject matter and personal jurisdiction and simply determines which unit of the court the case is to be brought in. The unit in the supreme court in New York practice is the county.[1] The unit in the U.S. district courts is the district.[2] Venue in New York is largely but not entirely keyed to the residence of the parties.[3] Residence also plays a role in the federal courts,[4] but alongside other venue bases.

The principal federal venue statute is § 1391 of Title 28, with a number of subdivisions. We do here only the basics.

When jurisdiction is grounded on diversity of citizenship, proper venue is dictated by subdivision (a); when anything else is the ground for subject matter jurisdiction, venue is dictated by subdivision (b). The two subdivisions are almost identical, but not quite. In both categories, venue may be laid in the district of any defendant's residence as long as all defendants reside in the same state. So provides paragraph (1) of each of the two subdivisions.[5]

Alternatively, under paragraph (2) of each, venue may be laid in "a judicial district in which a substantial part of the events or omissions giving rise to the claim occurred" or where "a substantial part of property that is the subject of the action is situated".

The "events or omissions" clause should be emphasized. It is based on the same kinds of contacts that support "longarm" jurisdiction,[6] so that it will generally be so that as long as longarm jurisdiction is available in a given district, venue will also be proper in that district. This may overlap paragraph (3) in each of the two subdivisions.

Paragraph (3) in each of them is the same in that the paragraph can't be invoked unless the options of paragraphs (1) and (2) of subdivision (a) prove unavailing. But in another respect paragraph (3) is not the same. Under subdivision (a), the diversity provision, paragraph (3) permits venue in "a judicial district in which any defendant is subject to personal jurisdiction at the time the action is commenced". When personal jurisdiction is based on "longarm" contacts, as just noted, paragraph (2) will usually suffice, so that paragraph (3) in this instance will often be superfluous. But paragraph (3) would support venue in a district when any defendant is subject to jurisdiction there on a basis other than longarm jurisdiction, such as when the defendant is an individual served with process while physically present in the district.

Under subdivision (b), governing in federal question cases, the venue alternative offered by paragraph (3) is the district in which any defendant may be "found". It is not clear how this "found" requirement is intended to differ from the "subject to personal jurisdiction" requirement of subdivision (a)'s paragraph 3.[7]

Venue in cases with corporate parties is a bit more involved. If the plaintiff is the corporation, it presumably has to follow the venue prescriptions of subdivisions (a) and (b). But if

---

§ 617

1. See § 116 above.

2. 28 U.S.C.A. § 1391.

3. CPLR 503.

4. In federal practice "residence", on which venue may be based, must always be distinguished from the "citizenship" that premises the diversity of citizenship requirement in the area of subject matter jurisdiction. "Citizenship" is more analogous to the state concept of "domicile". See § 611 above.

5. Note that neither provision authorizes venue in the plaintiff's own district of residence, as subdivision (a) did allow before its amendment in the Judicial Improvements Act of 1990 (Pub.L. 101–650).

6. See § 84 above.

7. Both subdivisions are compared and contrasted in the Commentaries on 28 U.S.C.A. § 1391, which also note the 1990 amendment of subdivision (e), governing venue when the United States or one of its agencies or employees is a defendant.

the defendant is a corporation, the plaintiff's choice of venue expands. For venue purposes, the corporate defendant is deemed a resident of (and may be sued in) any district in which it is amenable to personal jurisdiction; and if it is subject to jurisdiction throughout the state, as where it is doing or is qualified to do business throughout the state, it is deemed a resident of any district with which its contacts, measured in that district alone, would subject it to personal jurisdiction.[8]

Any district is proper venue in an action against an alien,[9] and there are special provisions governing actions against a federal officer or agency[10] and against a foreign state.[11]

Those are the general venue instructions. If a special statute supplies venue in a given category of case, the special statute governs. In federal statutory interpleader, for example, proper venue is any district in which any of the claimants resides.[12]

If venue is set in an improper district, the federal court can "dismiss, or if it be in the interest of justice, transfer" the action to a proper district.[13] The fact that an improper venue can dismiss the action in federal practice is of course in contrast with New York supreme court practice, where the almost universal rule is that the setting of venue in an improper county brings on nothing worse than a change of venue to a proper county.[14] The procedure for objecting to venue consequently varies between federal and New York practice.

The procedure for objecting to venue in state practice was treated earlier.[15] The federal procedure is for the defendant either to move to dismiss for improper venue,[16] or to include improper venue as a defense in the answer. The making of a motion to dismiss on some other ground without including the venue objection will waive it; or, if no motion is made,

the failure to include the venue objection in the original answer or in an amendment made of it as of course[17] will waive it.[18] This is analogous to the consequence spelled out in New York practice for the failure to raise a timely objection to personal jurisdiction,[19] but in federal practice it applies to that and to a venue objection as well.

§ 618. Forum Non Conveniens Doctrine in Federal Courts

The forum non conveniens doctrine, which at one time brought about, as it still does in New York practice, a dismissal of the action without prejudice to suit elsewhere,[1] is almost entirely superseded in federal practice by § 1404(a) of Title 28, under which a transfer to a more appropriate district—anywhere in the federal system—is directed, not a dismissal. A New York state court can work only within its own confines, and if the more appropriate forum is outside the state the court's only option is to dismiss or perhaps stay the New York action so that it can then be recommenced in the other place. The nationwide federal system has broader options, and transfer is the one preferred.

Section 1404(a), the transfer statute, is based on the assumption that venue has been set in a proper district but that another district, equally proper, is preferable. Section 1404(a) must be distinguished from § 1406(a), the "wrong venue" statute discussed in the prior section, whose premise is that the venue has been initially set in an improper district.

Another contrast, then, between federal and New York practice is that as a general rule the forum non conveniens doctrine in New York dismisses the action, while in the federal system it merely transfers it to another district. If

---

8. 28 U.S.C.A. § 1391(c).

9. 28 U.S.C.A. § 1391(d).

10. 28 U.S.C.A. § 1391(e).

11. 28 U.S.C.A. § 1391(f).

12. 28 U.S.C.A. § 1397.

13. See 28 U.S.C.A. § 1406(a), sometimes referred to as the "wrong venue" statute to distinguish it from § 1404(a), the transfer statute considered in § 618 below.

14. See § 116 above.

15. See §§ 123–125.

16. FRCP Rule 12(b)(3).

17. See FRCP Rule 15(a).

18. FRCP Rule 12(h)(1).

19. See § 274 above.

§ 618

1. See § 28 above.

the decidedly more appropriate place for the action is a court in a foreign country, however, as where the claim arose there and the contacts that that nation has with the case predominate, a dismissal is still permissible consistent with § 1404(a).[2] A dismissal without prejudice to commencement of the action in a state court is also allowed under some of the abstention doctrines,[3] which are themselves a kind of "conveniens" phenomenon.

The criterion for transfer under § 1404(a) is that "the convenience of parties and witnesses" and "the interest of justice" will be better served in the other district, and the balance must tip substantially to the proposed transferee district before a transfer will be ordered. The court also sifts a number of other factors in determining this.[4]

Section 1404(a) also requires a showing that the proposed transferee district is one in which the action "might have been brought", which means two things: (1) the district would be a proper venue for the action under the venue statutes, and (2) the defendant would be amenable to personal jurisdiction there. Both conditions must be met without regard to any professed willingness on the part of the defendant to waive them.[5]

For purposes of the *Erie* doctrine on choice of substantive law in diversity actions,[6] a transfer under § 1404(a) has been held to be just a change of courtrooms, not a change of law. Hence the law to which the transferee court must refer, whenever state law becomes relevant under *Erie*, is the law of the state in which the action was originally commenced, not the law of the state containing the district court to which it has been transferred.[7] This is

so even when it is the plaintiff who has moved for the transfer. A divided U.S. Supreme Court so held even when it was shown that the plaintiff deliberately sued in the inappropriate district to obtain a certain choice of law advantage, and it let the plaintiff keep the advantage.[8]

§ 619. Removal

If the action is within the concurrent jurisdiction of both the federal and state courts, and the plaintiff chooses the state court, the defendant often has the option of removing the action to the federal court. The opportunity to remove the case is in fact the element that makes the list of choice of forum factors, discussed earlier,[1] a tactically important matter to defendants as well as plaintiffs.

The requirements of subject matter jurisdiction for removal are largely the same as for original jurisdiction. The general rule is that a case that would be within the original jurisdiction of the district court is removable to it when brought in a state court. So prescribes § 1441(a) of Title 28, the principal removal provision.[2]

A federal question case is removable without reference to the citizenship of any party, but when diversity of citizenship is the removal basis there is an important limitation. Even though there is complete diversity in the case, it may not be removed if any of the defendants is a citizen (i.e., domiciliary) of the state in which the action was brought.[3] This is consistent with the rationale of diversity jurisdiction, which is to protect the outsider from local prejudice: when the outsider sues in the defen-

---

2. See, e.g., Piper Aircraft Co. v. Reyno, 454 U.S. 235, 102 S.Ct. 252, 70 L.Ed.2d 419 (1981).

3. See § 613 above.

4. See Gulf Oil Corp. v. Gilbert, 330 U.S. 501, 67 S.Ct. 839, 91 L.Ed. 1055 (1947).

5. See Hoffman v. Blaski, 363 U.S. 335, 80 S.Ct. 1084, 4 L.Ed.2d 1254 (1960).

6. Erie v. Tompkins, 304 U.S. 64, 58 S.Ct. 817, 82 L.Ed. 1188 (1938).

7. Van Dusen v. Barrack, 376 U.S. 612, 84 S.Ct. 805, 11 L.Ed.2d 945 (1964).

8. See Ferens v. John Deere Co., 494 U.S. 516, 110 S.Ct. 1274, 108 L.Ed.2d 443 (1990).

§ 619

1. See § 616.

2. There are of course some exceptions, in which removal is precluded by statute. See, for example, 28 U.S.C.A. § 1445(c), precluding the removal of workers' compensation cases. For the removability of certain admiralty claims, should they be brought in state court under the "saving to suitors" clause of 28 U.S.C.A. § 1333, see Gonsalves v. Amoco Shipping Co., 733 F.2d 1020 (2d Cir.1984).

3. 28 U.S.C.A. § 1441(b).

dant's own state courts, the defendant has no grievance. There is obviously a tactical weapon here for the plaintiff. While the general postulate in the removal area is that the ultimate choice of forum is with the defendant, the plaintiff can re-secure the choice in some cases. If the plaintiff has the option of joining or omitting a given defendant, as is often so of commercial actions and almost invariably so of tort cases, the inclusion of an arguably liable defendant whose citizenship is the same as the plaintiff's can tie all the defendants' hands and prevent the removal.

If there are several defendants on the claim, the general rule is that all must join in removing it: any defendant refusing to remove spoils the removal for the other defendants.[4]

The removal is made to the district court of the district in which the state court is sitting. That's the proper district of venue in a removed action.[5] The venue requirements applicable to original actions[6] do not apply in removed actions, but the transfer statute[7] does. Once the case is removed, therefore, it is subject to transfer to another district just as if originally commenced in the federal court.

A statute with a checkered history, subdivision (c) of § 1441, provides that if there are several claims—several entirely separate claims and not just different counts or theories in support of but a single claim[8]—and any one of them would be removable if sued on alone, the defendants on that claim can remove it and if they do the whole case gets removed, including the nonremovable claims. The latter can be retained or remanded, in the district court's discretion. If there is essentially but one claim, but with different theories or counts in support, and one of them is a federal

one to which the others, arising under state law, can be deemed "supplemental" within the meaning of 28 U.S.C.A. § 1367,[9] the whole case is removable under subdivision (a) of § 1441 without having to depend on subdivision (c).[10]

The fact that in federal question cases the doctrine of supplemental jurisdiction makes subdivision (a) by itself an adequate "take along" provision puts subdivision (c) into a kind of limbo. A 1990 amendment made subdivision (c) inapplicable in diversity of citizenship cases, where it seemed to serve best, reducing the situation to this: subdivision (c) now functions chiefly if not only in federal question cases, where it is rarely needed, while having lost its function in diversity cases, where it did offer some jurisdictional aid from time to time.[11]

The time to remove is tight. The defendant(s) must remove the case within 30 days after being served with "the initial pleading" in the state court action.[12] This has been found to hold some special pitfalls for New York state court defendants. The complaint in a New York action of course qualifies as an "initial pleading" that will start the 30 days, but in some New York state court cases a defendant waiting for the complaint may find that the removal period has already come and gone, with the consequent forfeiture of federal jurisdiction. This is of course traceable to the option a plaintiff has in New York practice, in a supreme or county court action, of starting the action with a brief "notice" instead of a regular complaint.[13] A number of federal cases have held that when the notice is used, it is the notice that starts the 30-day removal period, not the complaint, which comes in later.

---

4. See Chicago, R.I. & P. Ry. Co. v. Martin, 178 U.S. 245, 20 S.Ct. 854, 44 L.Ed. 1055 (1900).

5. 28 U.S.C.A. §§ 1441(a), 1446(a).

6. See § 617 above.

7. 28 U.S.C.A. § 1404(a). See § 618 above.

8. For the differences on this score, see American Fire & Cas. Co. v. Finn, 341 U.S. 6, 71 S.Ct. 534, 95 L.Ed. 702 (1951), decided when subdivision (c) could also function in diversity cases, which, as the text shortly demonstrates, it no longer does.

9. See § 614 above.

10. In that instance, the dropping of the federal claim after the removal gives the district court discretion either to dismiss or remand the pendent state claim, with a decided preference for remand, especially if it would spare the plaintiff a statute of limitations or other procedural barrier. See Carnegie–Mellon Univ. v. Cohill, 484 U.S. 343, 108 S.Ct. 614, 98 L.Ed.2d 720 (1988).

11. There is an extensive Commentary on the 1990 amendment in 28 U.S.C.A. § 1441.

12. 28 U.S.C.A. § 1446(b).

13. CPLR 305(b). See § 60 above.

That is notably the case when diversity of citizenship is the basis for federal subject matter jurisdiction: since the complaint in a New York state court action does not have to say anything about the parties' citizenship, it offers no more data than the notice would on the subject of citizenship and hence the notice is reasonably held to be the starting point for the 30 days. If the removal is sought in a federal question case, however, presumably the plaintiff should be able to wait for the complaint to come in before considering removal, but it is probably best even in that case to treat the notice—if it is used by the plaintiff to start the action—as the starting point for the 30 days if it gives any hint at all that the claim being asserted is a federal one.[14]

In Jones Chemicals, Inc. v. Distribution Architects Int'l,[15] for example, the arguable basis of federal jurisdiction was the diversity of citizenship of the parties. The defendants were served with a summons and CPLR 305(b) notice setting forth some information that reflected on the possible removability of the case—the plaintiff's residence, the names of co-defendants, etc.—but not enough to make federal jurisdiction certain. The defendants were nevertheless held subject to the 30–day removal period, the court holding that they had a duty to investigate promptly so as to be able to act within the 30 days.[16]

Some corporate defendants with inefficient bureaucracies can find themselves in perpetual forfeit of federal jurisdiction if they do not set up a system for getting summonses and their accompanying papers—in New York practice, a notice or complaint—into the hands of their lawyers promptly, so that a possible removal to federal court can be considered, and can be considered on time.

If the case is not removable at the outset but becomes so later in the course of its state court travels, as by an amendment adding a federal claim or dropping a nondiverse party, the 30 days in which to remove start anew from the service of the "amended pleading, motion, order or other paper" first manifesting removability.[17]

The procedure for removal is in § 1446. No permission of either the federal or state court is required. The defendants who want to remove simply do it. They just file with the clerk of the district court of the local district a notice of removal[18] signed pursuant to Rule 11 of the Federal Rules of Civil Procedure, which makes monetary sanctions applicable if the removal is totally baseless.[19] The notice sets forth the jurisdictional grounds relied on for the removal. The old requirement that a bond accompany the removal papers was eliminated in 1988 legislation.[20]

Accompanying the notice must be "all process, pleadings, and orders" already served on the defendant in the state court action.[21]

"Promptly after the filing" of the papers with the district court, the defendants must serve written notice of the removal on all parties to the action[22] and file a copy of the removal notice with the state court clerk. It is the filing of the notice with the state court clerk that technically marks the removal moment, an important one to pinpoint in order to make the line between the discontinuance of

---

14. Consecutive lead notes in New York State Law Digest Nos. 342 and 343 go into these matters in more detail.

15. 786 F.Supp. 310 (W.D.N.Y.1992).

16. The lead note in New York State Law Digest No. 392 is built around the Jones case. See also the note on the time for removal in SPR 77:3.

17. 28 U.S.C.A. § 1446(b). A one year cut-off, however, measured from the commencement of the action, applies when the newly established basis is diversity of citizenship. This is the result of a 1988 amendment, discussed in the Commentary on § 1446 in 28 U.S.C.A.

18. Section 1446(a). It used to be called a "petition" and had to be verified, but was changed to a mere "notice" in 1988 legislation.

19. Rule 11 is noted in §§ 631 and 633, below, and in item 22 on the list of choice of forum factors in § 616 above.

20. The bond requirement was in the old subdivision (d) of § 1446, which was repealed. See the Commentary on the 1988 Revision of § 1446 in 28 U.S.C.A.

21. Section 1446(a).

22. The statute so providing, 28 U.S.C.A. § 1446(d), speaks of serving only "adverse" parties, but all parties other than those joining in the removal notice should be served, adverse or not.

state court jurisdiction and the onset of federal court jurisdiction as clear and as clean as possible.

A district court decision, Lomaglio Assocs. Inc. v. LBK Marketing Corp.,[23] suggests that a defendant removing an action to federal court waives any objection that the defendant might have had to personal jurisdiction, but the law appears to be to the contrary. Indeed, one of the very purposes of removal may be to have the federal court dispose of the objection.[24]

By allowing the defendant to remove the case with no prior leave whatever, the statute makes the defendant the initial judge of removability. The ultimate judge, of course, is the federal judge. The way the propriety of the removal is tested by the plaintiff or other objecting party is by motion to the federal court, after removal, to remand the case.

An application to remand can be based on the invalidity of the removal ground, or on a defect in the removal procedure. If the ground is the want of federal subject matter jurisdiction, the motion to remand of course lies at any time. But if it is based on some procedural defect, such as the lateness of the removal, the remand motion in the federal court is itself time limited: it must be made within 30 days after the filing of the notice of removal.[25] For this purpose, a remand in a case involving a "supplemental" claim—previously known as a "pendent"[26] or "ancillary"[27] claim—on the ground that the claim on which it depended for jurisdiction has been disposed of, is not deemed procedural and is not subject to the 30–day time limit.[28]

A remand order is not as a rule appealable.[29] The general purpose of this is to make each district judge the final judge of removability.[30] But in extraordinary cases review of a remand order has been allowed, sometimes through the mandamus process,[31] as in one case, for example, where a district judge remanded the case because he thought his calendars were already too heavy.[32] That is not a remand ground.

Procedure after removal is governed by several statutes[33] and by a key provision with an unlikely location, Rule 81(c) of the Federal Rules of Civil Procedure. The case proceeds as if it had been commenced in the federal court. No repleading is required. And whatever occurred in the state court before removal remains valid and in full force in the federal court until duly altered.[34] This is especially important in a case in which one of the provisional remedies has issued before removal, such as an attachment or injunction. They remain intact until modified by the federal court.[35] With respect to perhaps the most tense and sensitive of these devices, the temporary restraining order (TRO), however, the plaintiff must keep in mind that when a case with an outstanding TRO is removed, the TRO now becomes subject to the time limiting provisions of the applicable federal rule, which is Rule 65 of the Federal Rules of Civil Procedure, measured from the time of removal, and it is that rule which will govern all further proceedings with respect to the injunction.[36]

FRCP Rule 81(c) answers questions about pleadings in removed cases, and the time for filing them, if the pleadings are not already in

---

23. 876 F.Supp. 41 (S.D.N.Y.1995).

24. See the discussion in SPR 32:4.

25. 28 U.S.C.A. § 1447(c). The actual language of § 1447(c) is that the 30–day time limit applies to "any defect other than lack of subject matter jurisdiction", language used in a 1996 amendment and thought to be a mere clarification but itself posing some unanticipated problems. See the Commentary on the 1996 revision of § 1447(c) in 28 U.S.C.A. § 1447.

26. See § 614 above.

27. Ancillary jurisdiction is discussed in §§ 632 and 634 below.

28. See the Commentary on § 1447 in 28 U.S.C.A.

29. 28 U.S.C.A. § 1447(d).

30. And of course an order denying remand is not appealable for the reason that it is an interlocutory order. See § 642 below.

31. Mandamus is also briefly discussed in § 642 below.

32. Thermtron Products, Inc. v. Hermansdorfer, 423 U.S. 336, 96 S.Ct. 584, 46 L.Ed.2d 542 (1976).

33. 28 U.S.C.A. §§ 1447–1450.

34. See 28 U.S.C.A. § 1450.

35. Id.

36. See Granny Goose Foods, Inc. v. Brotherhood of Teamsters, 415 U.S. 423, 94 S.Ct. 1113, 39 L.Ed.2d 435 (1974), and the further discussion of this point in § 640 below.

when removal occurs. And it contains important instructions on preserving the right to trial by jury in removed actions. In federal practice, trial by jury is demanded by requesting it in a pleading,[37] while in New York practice it is demanded in or shortly after the filing of the note of issue.[38] If the pleadings are already in when the case is removed, Rule 81(c) prescribes the steps for a party's demanding a trial by jury in the federal court. If the pleading is not put in until after removal, each party wanting trial by jury should demand it in the pleading served after removal. And because of the New York practice of allowing commencement of the action with a mere notice instead of a complaint, it is quite possible that neither the complaint nor answer will have yet been served when the case is removed.

D. FORMS

Table of Sections

Sec.
620. Forms in Federal Courts.

§ 620. Forms in Federal Courts

There is an appendix of forms annexed to the Federal Rules of Civil Procedure, numbering just about three dozen. These, like the New York counterparts that are largely modeled on them,[1] are "sufficient under the rules"[2] at whatever junctures they become relevant. Also like their New York parallels, they are "intended to indicate the simplicity and brevity of statement which the rules contemplate".[3]

There is a form for the summons (Form 1), and for the allegation of jurisdiction that goes into the complaint (Form 2).[4] There is then a progression of example forms of complaint in sundry actions, and forms for a variety of other procedural items, including answers, motions, several kinds of notices, the judgment or decision, etc. The forms for use at the appellate stage of proceedings, including the notice of appeal itself, are part of a briefer appendix of forms annexed to the Federal Rules of Appellate Procedure.[5]

The forms are primarily illustrative, not intended to be confining. Adjustments that add clarity to the purpose at hand are welcome, keeping in mind the theme of "simplicity and brevity". The rules of the particular court (and even of the particular judge) may also be profitably perused for anything they may say about forms.[6] The much more prolific form books published commercially, while not official in the sense of being presumptively proper, as the official forms are, are still useful tools that are a good source of ideas for the lawyer (and a good source of income for the publisher). If they are used, the lawyer should not hesitate to modify them, by way of addition, subtraction, or other adjustment that tailors them more perfectly to the purpose at hand.

E. COMMENCEMENT AND PERSONAL JURISDICTION

Table of Sections

Sec.
621. Commencing a Federal Action; Introductory.
622. Personal Jurisdiction: An Overview of Federal Rule 4.
623. The Federal Summons and Its Issuance.
624. Methods of Service in Federal Practice.
625. Time Limits on Federal Summons Service; Interplay With Statute of Limitations.
626. Bases for Extraterritorial Jurisdiction in Federal Courts.
627. Rem Jurisdiction in the Federal Courts.

37. See § 631 below.

38. See § 369 above.

§ 620

1. See § 7 above.

2. See FRCP Rule 84.

3. Id.

4. See § 611 above.

5. Federal appellate practice is briefly discussed in § 642 below.

6. The court rules are recompiled and updated annually by McKinney's in a softcover entitled New York Rules of Court, State and Federal. A compendium of the rules of the individual federal judges, compiled by the Section on Commercial and Federal Litigation of the New York State Bar Association, has been published and is available through the Association.

§ 621. Commencing a Federal Action; Introductory

Overall, there are probably more similarities than there are differences between federal and New York state practice, but some of the areas of difference tend to hold special pitfalls. A mistake in commencing the action, for example, can let in the plaintiff's most potent enemy, the statute of limitations, and yet it is at the commencement stage that one perceives some of the most substantial differences between procedure in the federal and New York courts.

Rule 4 of the Federal Rules of Civil Procedure governs the subject of personal jurisdiction in federal civil practice, doing there, in a single rule, the job it takes almost all of Article 3 of the CPLR to accomplish in the New York courts. Under its caption, "Summons", Rule 4 governs the summons in all its particulars: form, method of service, place of service, amenability to service, time of service, etc. This makes it the key instruction in federal practice on the commencement of a civil action, and worthy of a few sections of close attention. The section immediately following offers an overview of Rule 4 and the few after that go into several of its key components.

Paradoxically, it is Rule 3, not Rule 4, that bears the caption "Commencement of Action". But Rule 3 contains only a single sentence, "[a] civil action is commenced by filing a complaint with the court", and in practical terms the "commencement" of a civil action involves a whole congeries of requirements, of which the filing of the complaint is only the first. It is the summons and its service that really determines how the case gets under way, and it is Rule 4 that governs the summons and its service. Hence it is far more accurate to re-member that Rules 3 and 4 together govern the commencement of the action, and that Rule 4 has a good deal more to say about the subject than Rule 3 has.

Against the line or two of type that Rule 3 occupies are the more than 150 that make up Rule 4. That ratio speaks worlds about the relative demands that the two rules make on the lawyer's attention. Add in the fact that the moment of commencement is all bound up with the statute of limitations, and the lesson is at hand: as demanding as Rule 4 may be, a mistake in its use can be fatal. Lawyers with mistakes inside them are advised to save them for other places. The ensuing treatment of the rule is designed to give the lawyer a broad perspective of its demands and a word of warning at its more dangerous pitfalls.

The rule has no small number of pitfalls. Indeed, in some instances even a lawyer with an intimate knowledge of Rule 4 can get tripped up, as in a case based on diversity of citizenship, where, for a statute of limitations measure, neither Rule 3 nor Rule 4 governs. State law does, but nothing on the face of either rule warns of that because it comes from caselaw.[1] Points like that will be stressed.

§ 622. Personal Jurisdiction: An Overview of Federal Rule 4

Rule 4 was completely recast and extensively altered effective December 1, 1993. The subject allotment of its several subdivisions is briefly this:[1]

Subdivision (a) of Rule 4 governs the form of the summons and lists its contents.

Subdivision (b) addresses the issuance of the summons.

Subdivision (c) prescribes who may serve the summons.

Subdivision (d) introduces the procedure, new with the December 1, 1993 amendment,

---

§ 621

1. See § 625 below.

§ 622

1. A comprehensive treatment of the amended rule appears in the Commentary on Rule 4 in 28 U.S.C.A., in two articles in 151 F.R.D. 441 and 152 F.R.D. 249, and in a seven-part series from Issue 12 through Issue 18 of Siegel's Practice Review.

whereby the plaintiff may seek a waiver of service from the defendant.

Subdivisions (e) through (j) supply the various methods of service.

Subdivision (k) governs the geographical area within which the federal summons may be served.

Subdivision (*l*) governs proof of service.

Subdivision (m), to which we will pay special attention, governs the time within which service must be made following the filing of the complaint. This subdivision is much involved in the interplay between Rule 4 and the statute of limitations.

Subdivision (n) governs rem jurisdiction in the federal courts.

§ 623. The Federal Summons and Its Issuance

In New York practice the summons may be issued by the plaintiff's lawyer.[1] In federal practice the clerk issues it. So provides subdivision (a) of Rule 4, unchanged in this respect by the 1993 amendment. Under subdivision (c)(1), responsibility for the service of the summons is on the plaintiff's attorney, in common with New York practice.

The initial step for the plaintiff in a federal civil action is to draft the complaint and obtain and fill out a form of summons. The plaintiff then files the complaint with the court, opening a file of the case, and, ordinarily, presenting the summons to the clerk at that time to have the clerk sign and seal it. If the summons presented to the clerk is properly filled out, the clerk takes the above steps and returns a copy of the summons to the plaintiff to go about having it served. The contents of the summons are listed in Rule 4(a). There is an official form for it.[2]

As a result of the 1993 amendment of Rule 4, which introduces in subdivision (d) a procedure whereby the plaintiff can seek a waiver of service from the defendant, it should not be

necessary to present a summons to the clerk at the same time the complaint is presented for filing. (Waiver papers sent to the defendant, while they must include a complaint, need not contain a summons.) Some clerks have been insisting on it anyway, and it does no harm. The summons can just be held back by the plaintiff until—if a waiver request is used and a waiver does not materialize—conventional service becomes necessary. And under subdivision (b) of Rule 4, if the summons is not presented to the clerk initially, it can be presented for issuance later.

Among the things the summons must set forth under Rule 4(a) is the defendant's answering time, which in federal practice is the basic 20 days supplied by Rule 12(a) of the Federal Rules of Civil Procedure. The 20 become 60 when service is made on a federal officer or agency[3] or on a foreign nation or one of its instrumentalities.[4] When the plaintiff uses the waiver of service request and the defendant furnishes the waiver, the answering time is 60 days (90 if the waiver request was addressed to the defendant outside the country).

The court can allow amendment of the summons at any time,[5] and will ordinarily do so if no prejudice can be shown. A good example is where the summons has designated the wrong person as the defendant and it would now be too late for a new action if the plaintiff had to start over. In that situation the plaintiff's case is effectively dead unless the summons can be amended to substitute the intended defendant. Is the amendment permissible? It is, if the intended defendant knew of the suit in time. Suppose, for example, that the defendant is a partnership but that the plaintiff, unaware of this, sued it as a corporation (or vice versa), a not uncommon situation in litigation. If the court can conclude that the intended defendant knew of the suit within the applicable period of limitations and knew further that it was the intended party, the amendment,

---

§ 623

1. See § 60 above.

2. See Form 1 in the FRCP's appendix of forms.

3. Rule 12(a)(3).

4. See 28 U.S.C.A. § 1608(d).

5. Rule 4(a).

which in this instance is the equivalent of an order of substitution, may be allowed.[6]

In these situations, in which the statute of limitations is on the scene—which makes them the most delicate of all amendment cases—Rule 15(c) of the Federal Rules is implicated, governing the relation back of amendments. When an amendment is allowed to "relate back" to an earlier time, statute of limitations consequences are avoided.[7]

The summons and complaint are served together in federal practice, while in New York practice in the supreme and county courts under CPLR 305(b) the plaintiff has the alternative of serving a mere notice with the summons, the complaint to follow later under a demand procedure pursuant to CPLR 3012(b).[8] There is no such option on the federal side. When the summons is served, the complaint goes with it.

When a waiver of service is requested under subdivision (d) of Rule 4, the complaint but not the summons is included with the papers sent. While the sending of the waiver request need not be by a process server, a process server must be used if conventional service is made, whether initially or after a futile attempt to secure a waiver. Any nonparty 18 or over may serve process.[9]

§ 624. Methods of Service in Federal Practice

The methods of service in Rule 4 are contained in subdivisions (e) through (j), and there are always a number of connected issues that march alongside the service methods. They pose a broad range of questions, any one of which, improperly answered, can lead to a dismissal and the barrier of the statute of limitations. We can touch on only a few matters here.[1]

The categories of defendant governed by each of the subdivisions on service are

Subdivision (e): Service on individuals in U.S.

Subdivision (f): Service on individuals outside U.S.

Subdivision (g): Service on infants and incompetents.

Subdivision (h): Service on corporations and associations, etc.

Subdivision (i): Service on U.S. and its agencies.

Subdivision (j): Service on state and foreign governmental units.

We'll make just a few observations about each of them, highlighting trouble spots.

For about a decade, a common method of service was the ordinary first-class mail method contained in subdivision (c)(2)(C)(ii) of the pre–1993 Rule 4, introduced in a 1983 amendment but completely abrogated a decade later in the 1993 amendment, which adopted the waiver of service provision in its place. Lawyers should be alert to that short-lived but active provision. The caselaw on it during the years between 1983 and 1993 was prolific. Much of that caselaw is academic today, but some remains viable, of course depending on the extent of the change in the rule provision affected.

In respect of the time allowed for service, for example, factors previously applicable to the superseded mail methods may now apply to the newly adopted waiver procedure. As elaborated below,[2] there is a 120–day period following the filing of the complaint in which to make service. Subdivision (m) of the amended Rule 4 so provides. When the waiver procedure of subdivision (d) is used, the time that it uses up comes out of the 120 days allowed by subdivision (m), which means that the time left to

6. See Hirsch v. Bruchhausen, 284 F.2d 783 (2d Cir. 1960). For the New York rule in point, see § 65 above.

7. See the discussion of relation back in § 615 above.

8. See § 60 above.

9. The time allowed for service is discussed in § 625 below. The methods of service and who does the serving are discussed in § 624, immediately following.

§ 624

1. More expansive treatment on all of these provisions may be found in the Commentaries on Rule 4 in 28 U.S.C.A.

2. See § 625.

make conventional service if the defendant does not oblige with a waiver will be steadily diminishing. The plaintiff's lawyer must be alert to this.

As in New York practice, a process server may be any person 18 or over and not a party. Marshals used to do the serving in federal practice, but they were taken out of the business in the 1983 amendment, except in a few instances.[3] One of these is where the court specifically directs the marshal to make the service, as when trouble of some kind is expected.

Allowing service by private process servers gives the plaintiff closer control over the service ritual, but it carries an onus with it. The plaintiff's attorney has been made responsible for proper summons service,[4] and the process server's mistakes are laid at the plaintiff's door. While the plaintiff was not entirely relieved of responsibility for the marshals' omissions when the marshals did the serving, defendants were much more hesitant to contest service and contests were in fact less frequent than they have proved to be under amended Rule 4.

Subdivision (e)(2) of Rule 4 contains the more traditional methods of service, including the well-known method of

> delivering a copy of the summons and of the complaint to the individual personally or by leaving copies thereof at the individual's dwelling house or usual place of abode with some person of suitable age and discretion then residing therein....

This provision is similar to CPLR 308(2) in New York practice,[5] which is modeled on it, but it is not the same. Under the federal provision, for example, the person of suitable age must be shown to be residing at the premises, a requirement not imposed in the New York counterpart. And there is an additional requirement of a mailing under CPLR 308(2) which the federal provision does not have. The lawyer cannot assume identicalness without

checking, and it is often a more demanding task to compare two similar provisions than to contrast two starkly different ones.

Subdivisions (e) and (f) apply to individual defendants who are of age and competent, subdivision (e) governing service within the United States and its territories and subdivision (f) governing service beyond.

Subdivision (g), directed to service on infants and incompetents and recognizing the interest that their domiciles have in their protection, sets forth no special federal prescription for service; it merely adopts the methods applicable in the state in which service is "made".

Subdivisions (h) and (i) are devoted to supplying methods of serving, and to identifying the proper persons to serve in behalf of, various categories of defendants, like corporations, associations, partnerships, the United States, federal and state agencies and officials, etc. Subdivision (j)(2) does the same when one of the states of the United States or their municipalities and agencies is a defendant. A statute governs service on foreign nations and their instrumentalities;[6] Rule 4(j)(1) merely calls attention to it.

Service on foreign nations and their agencies should not be confused with service on a foreign national—an alien or alien corporation—which is governed by subdivision (e) or (f) of Rule 4, depending on where the service is made. Subdivision (f) also takes note of the "Convention on the Service Abroad of Judicial and Extrajudicial Documents in Civil or Commercial Matters", commonly known as the "Hague Convention". The convention is a treaty binding in federal and state courts alike.[7] It provides that whatever conditions have been imposed by the nation in which process is being served must be fulfilled. Some nations may require an accompanying translation, for example, or forbid service by a given method, such as mail. All such bind the plaintiff. But the convention and its requirements

---

3. See Rule 4(c)(2).

4. Rule 4(c)(1).

5. See § 72 above.

6. 28 U.S.C.A. § 1608.

7. The convention is set out following Rule 4 in 28 U.S.C.A.

apply only when the service actually has to take place in the foreign nation, and on that front there is better news for plaintiffs.

If the defendant, although an alien, is amenable to local jurisdiction through physical presence or an agent anywhere in the country, or through longarm jurisdiction that authorizes service on a defendant absent from the forum state to be made in another American state where the defendant does have a presence, then service can be made domestically—i.e., within the United States—and the requirements of the convention become irrelevant. The U.S. Supreme Court, addressing this issue in 1988 in Volkswagenwerk A.G. v. Schlunk,[8] held that if domestic service is available, then the Hague Convention does not apply and its more demanding requirements need not be met.

In the *Schlunk* case, an action for wrongful death alleged to have been caused by defects in one of the defendant corporation's cars, the service was made on a German corporation through service on its wholly owned American subsidiary as authorized by Illinois law. The Supreme Court said that this was permissible because it is forum law—the local longarm statute and its concomitant notions of amenability to service—that determines the issue of service. All the convention says is that it applies when there is "occasion to transmit" a document abroad, but it does not prescribe the circumstances that create the "occasion". In *Schlunk*, because under Illinois law the defendant was amenable to domestic service, there was no "occasion" to make service abroad.

For service on most categories of defendant, service by a method authorized by state law is available as an alternative. State law methods are allowed, for example, by subdivision (e)(1) for service on individual defendants and by subdivision (h)(1) for service on corporations and associations, in each instance permitting resort to the law of either the forum state or the state of service. If New York is either state, that would mean the adoption of CPLR

308(5) and 311(b), which allow court-invented service if some sticky problem should arise that needs a little preliminary judicial help.[9]

Proof of service, which is governed by Rule 4(*l*), consists of an affidavit from the process server, or a certificate from the marshal if the marshal did the serving. When the waiver procedure of Rule 4(d) is used, and works, the plaintiff files the waiver with the clerk,[10] which serves roughly the same function as proof of service.

§ 625. Time Limits on Federal Summons Service; Interplay With Statute of Limitations

Before 1983, federal practice had no arbitrary time limit on summons service after the filing of the complaint. A kind of due diligence standard was applied, and it was applied flexibly. As long as the delay in service was not outrageous, the courts were disposed to respond to tardiness issues by allowing late service. The question the courts preferred to ask was whether service could yet be made, or be made right.[1] This was a healthy attitude, but it was probably due mainly to the fact that the federal marshals were the main process servers, which supported a tacit if not explicit presumption that things were proceeding reasonably.

With the removal of the marshal as the general process server in federal practice—the main purpose of Rule 4's 1983 amendment—it was thought advisable to put some kind of stated cap on the time for serving the summons. The 1983 amendment did that by adopting a 120–day time period measured from the complaint's filing, and the 1993 amendment, in subdivision (m), retains this 120–day restriction. That's four months, and it would seem ample, but given the vagaries of litigation it can run out fast. And if in general the 120 days is generous, its very generosity may prove plaintiffs' undoing, lulling them into casualness until the bell is about to ring. If the

---

8. 486 U.S. 694, 108 S.Ct. 2104, 100 L.Ed.2d 722.

9. See §§ 70 and 75 above.

10. Rule 4(d)(4).

§ 625

1. See, e.g., Grammenos v. Lemos, 457 F.2d 1067 (2d Cir.1972).

period lapses when the statute of limitations is near at hand, the result can be disaster.

The 120–day period is not absolute. It can be enlarged. But this requires a court order, which presumably requires a showing of "good cause" why service was not made on time. Subdivision (m) is ambiguous about that, also allowing the court to extend the time even if good cause is not shown.[2] The plaintiff who doesn't effect service on time is of course safer by being able to satisfy a "good cause" showing. And for several reasons, psychology among them, the plaintiff aware that an enlargement of time may be needed does best to take the initiative of moving for it within the 120–day period, instead of saving the request for use in opposition to a dismissal motion made after the period has expired.

It is impossible to draw a line between what will and what will not suffice as "good cause" for a time extension. Cases around the country go all over the place[3] and the plaintiff who does not have some powerful reason, such as the defendant's deliberate evasion of process, is asking for trouble. And it may not even matter that the 120 days has not been missed by much. In one case that reached the Second Circuit, for example, it appears to have been missed by only a matter of days, but the excuse offered by the plaintiff was that he had made a "minimal miscalculation", to which the court made a minimal response: "This excuse does not hold water."[4]

Much depends on the discretion of the district judge, and if there is any room for upholding the judge's exercise of discretion the court of appeals is likely to uphold it. Two different judges can react to the same "excuse" differently, and because of the broad range of deference shown the district judges by the courts of appeal in matters of discretion, this can of course mean that the case will live or die based simply on the luck of the draw when the case is first assigned to a judge.

A dismissal for failure to effect service during the 120 days, or for making service improperly if that should be the dismissal ground, ordinarily requires a motion. If the motion is made by the defendant, it must of course be on notice to the plaintiff. If the court is disposed to dismiss sua sponte, which it can do under subdivision (m), the court itself must assure that the plaintiff has notice of its proposed action. Note that in New York practice the court can't dismiss on this ground sua sponte; a motion by the defendant is required.[5]

If the dismissal is granted, it is "without prejudice".[6] This means that it is not on the merits and that the claim cannot be met with the defense of res judicata should it be sued on anew. But if the statute of limitations has meanwhile expired, it will be the limitations defense that greets a new action, which will make the case just as dead as a disposition on the merits, and with much less trouble for the defendant. Hence it is to be noted once again that it is the statute of limitations, almost exclusively, that gives subdivision (m) its tension.

It is important that the lawyer, and most particularly the New York lawyer, understand the interplay of the 120–day period of Rule 4(m) and the operation of the statute of limitations.

Under Rule 3 of the Federal Rules of Civil Procedure, the formal "commencement" of a federal action occurs when the complaint is filed. For limitations purposes, the summons issued at that time but served later is deemed to relate back to the complaint's filing. Thus, if the complaint is filed on or before the last day of the applicable statute of limitations, whatever the period may be,[7] the action is timely even if the summons is served later (but of course within the 120-day period following filing). That's the general rule in all but diversity of citizenship cases, where the demands are greater, as will be seen in a moment.

---

2. See the note in SPR 34:4.

3. See Commentary C4–41 on Rule 4 in 28 U.S.C.A.

4. Yosef v. Passamaquoddy Tribe, 876 F.2d 283, 287 (2d Cir.1989).

5. See § 63 above.

6. Rule 4(m)

7. The federal statute of limitations is briefly discussed in § 615.

Taking a closer look, precisely how does the 120–day period figure with respect to the statute of limitations? Assume throughout that the complaint is filed on the last day for commencing the action. If the summons is served within the 120 days following, the service should relate back to the complaint's filing without difficulty. If it is not served within the 120 days, but the 120–day period is enlarged by the court, the enlargement should supply the needed link back to the complaint's filing, and there, too, the action should be preserved as timely. If no extension is granted, the result will be a dismissal, and it will now be too late to sue over. It should therefore be plain to all lawyers that playing loose with the 120 days after having delayed suit until the eve of the expiration of the statute of limitations can easily have fatal consequences. Plaintiffs who manage to file the complaint just under the wire will have to atone with punctilio now for the laxity of which they were guilty before.

If the action is based on diversity of citizenship, the New York plaintiff must double the precautions: in the diversity case, Federal Rule 3 does not govern the moment of "commencement" for limitations' purposes. State law does, under the *Erie* doctrine,[8] as the U.S. Supreme Court explicitly held on this point in *Walker v. Armco Steel Corp.*[9] But to which New York court should we look to determine when an action is deemed commenced in the New York courts—the supreme court, in which filing marks commencement (just as in federal practice), or some lower court, in which service may mark commencement?[10] The analogy is almost certainly to be to the New York supreme court, the state's court of general jurisdiction, but the diversity plaintiff does herself no harm by not only filing the complaint within the applicable statute of limitations, but also seeing to it that the summons is actually served on the defendant before the statute expires.

The plaintiff intent on using the waiver procedure of subdivision (d) of Rule 4 must keep an especially sharp eye on subdivision (m)'s 120–day requirement. The waiver procedure has its own time requirements. The defendant has at least 30 days in which to return the waiver[11] and the plaintiff must resort to some other method if the defendant decides not to return it. Those 30 days come out of subdivision (m)'s overall 120–day allotment. The plaintiff who would use the waiver procedure must therefore not dally. Waiting a month or two before using it, and another month for the waiver's return, only then turning to a conventional service method when the waiver does not materialize, will leave a plaintiff with precious little remaining of the 120–day period for service. This is one of those junctures at which the warning to Leave Time for Trouble must be at the forefront of all planning.[12]

There are several ways of interposing a statute of limitations defense when the defendant has one.[13]

§ 626. Bases for Extraterritorial Jurisdiction in Federal Courts

Subdivision (k) of Rule 4 determines the territorial scope of the federal summons. The basic unit for the service of a summons in a federal civil action is the state in which the federal court sits, a conclusion that comes about indirectly, through clause (A) of subdivision (k)(1).

Under subdivision (f) of the pre–1993 version of Rule 4, there was a specific provision making the state the basic unit within which a federal summons could be served. The subdivision also recited a few narrow instances in which the service could be made within 100 miles of the federal courthouse even if it passed the state line,[1] but full extraterritorial service was permissible only when a federal or forum state statute or rule explicitly permitted

---

8. Erie R.R. Co. v. Tompkins, 304 U.S. 64, 58 S.Ct. 817, 82 L.Ed. 1188 (1938).

9. 446 U.S. 740, 100 S.Ct. 1978, 64 L.Ed.2d 659 (1980).

10. See §§ 45, 60, and 63 above.

11. See Commentary C4–18 on Rule 4 in 28 U.S.C.A.

12. See § 231A above.

13. See the discussion in SPR 65:4, stressing the practice in the Second Circuit.

§ 626

1. This is the "100–mile bulge" provision, which is continued under the present rule in subdivision (k)(1)(B).

it. That was the instruction of old subdivision (e).

The rules are essentially still the same, but through a different route. And in one instance, set forth in subdivision (k)(2) of the current Rule 4, the national contacts of the defendant have been made a basis for extraterritorial jurisdiction even when the defendant's contacts do not suffice to support the jurisdiction of any individual state. Subdivision (k)(2) is a far reaching innovation, literally and figuratively, and has been made a separately captioned subtopic further on in this section.

The point about the state being the basic unit for service is made obliquely in Rule 4. Subdivision (k)(1)(A) adopts for use in federal actions all of the provisions that forum state law provide for the geographical reach of state process, and it is from that provision that we must also, today, draw the conclusion that the state is always available as a basic unit for the service of federal process. Since as a general rule the states have traditionally upheld personal jurisdiction upon no greater a showing than that the defendant was served with the summons while physically within the state—which we can call "transient" jurisdiction—the forum state will continue to serve as a permissible area for the service of a federal summons as well.

When subdivision (k)(1)(A) adopts state bases for extraterritorial personal jurisdiction—state "longarm" statutes and rules—it does so regardless of the basis on which subject matter jurisdiction may rest in the action. Many lawyers looking to state law to resolve an issue in a federal action automatically assume that they are doing so under the constraints of the *Erie* doctrine, which is seen mainly in diversity cases. But this provision of Rule 4 adopts state extraterritorial bases for personal jurisdiction regardless of the basis on which subject matter jurisdiction may rest, including the federal question ("arising under") case, the admiralty case, and the case in which the United States

is a party, as well as the diversity of citizenship case.

The "corporate presence" test that subjects corporations to local jurisdiction, finding them present in the state and therefore amenable to process whenever they are doing regular business in the state,[2] also applies in the federal courts, through caselaw if not through Rule 4(k)(1)(A). It was held by an en banc Second Circuit in a landmark case, Arrowsmith v. United Press Int'l, 320 F.2d 219 (2d Cir.1963), that the test used to determine whether the corporation is "doing business" should be the test the state uses; that there should not be a separate "federal" test, at least in diversity cases. In federal question cases the point is not so well settled.[3]

The summons may of course be served outside the state whenever a federal statute so authorizes (as many federal statutes do in a variety of cases). The rule provision so stating[4] is just a reminder about the existence of such statutes.

The jurisdictional bases supplied by subdivision (k) apply to all instances of summons service, not just to the plaintiff's initial service on the defendant. They apply, for example, to service in third-party practice under Rule 14 and to service made on a person being joined as an additional party under Rule 19.

Whenever a state court exercises extraterritorial jurisdiction, there is of course a constitutional test to be met. The test is measured by the demands of the due process clause of the 14th Amendment, which every exercise of longarm jurisdiction in a state court must satisfy. This is the well known "minimum contacts" test of the line of cases begun by the U.S. Supreme Court's *International Shoe* decision in 1945.[5] A federal court using a state longarm statute uses the same test—the 14th Amendment test. But what constitutional standard applies when extrastate jurisdiction is based on a federal statute or rule, such as one purporting to allow nationwide service?

2.   See § 82, above, for New York's corporate presence test.

3.   See Commentary C4–36 on Rule 4 in 28 U.S.C.A.

4.   Subdivision (k)(1)(D) of Rule 4.

5.   See § 84 above.

Is it a 5th Amendment test? Is it sufficient to show that the defendant has had adequate contacts with any part of the country, even if the action is pending in a district far from the place of contacts? The U.S. Supreme Court appeared to assume so in Omni Capital Int'l v. Rudolf Wolff & Co.,[6] and an affirmative ought to be the answer, but the court sidestepped actual decision of the question in *Omni* and there is disagreement on the point in the lower courts.[7] There are always the federal venue and change of venue rules to guard against undue inconvenience if, while there is technically jurisdiction, it is found that the action would be more conveniently tried elsewhere.[8]

Apart from nationwide service as authorized by federal statutes, and apart as well from adopted state longarm statutes allowing service anywhere, is the so-called "100–mile bulge" provision contained in subdivision (k)(1)(B). The bulge area is a 100–mile radius of the courthouse, measured on a straight line, i.e., by air miles, or "as the crow flies".[9] Subdivision (k)(1)(B) permits service of the summons to be made anywhere within that circle even if it crosses state lines, as long as it does not go beyond the country. This permission for bulge service is in addition to whatever other bases may be available to permit extraterritorial service, such as under a federal statute or under a state longarm statute applicable under other parts of Rule 4(k). Because such statutes are quite often available, and are usually more generous in their geographical stretch than subdivision (k)(1)(B)'s modest bulge is, the bulge proves superfluous in most cases.

The bulge has diminished utility for the additional reason that it is not available for the plaintiff to use at the outset of an action. The plaintiff cannot plan an action with the idea of naming someone a defendant for whom "bulge" service is needed; the bulge applies only in the instances delineated in subdivision

(k)(1)(B), and initial use by the plaintiff is not among them. Bulge service is available against third-party defendants impleaded under Rule 14,[10] which is perhaps its most valuable use, and in several other instances involving the joinder of additional parties.[11]

The New General Federal "Longarm" Statute: Subdivision (k)(2)

An innovation under the 1993 revision of Rule 4 is paragraph (2) of subdivision (k). It operates when the defendant has had contacts with the nation as a whole sufficient to support jurisdiction along the lines of a "longarm" inquiry, but when there is no federal statute authorizing nationwide service in the case through clause (D) of paragraph (1) nor any state statute that could validly authorize jurisdiction through clause (A) of that paragraph because the contacts with no single state by themselves suffice to invoke it.

Subdivision (k)(2) dissolves all sovereign lines in such a case and allows the service of the federal summons anywhere at all—state, nation, or beyond.

It offers this jurisdiction only to claims arising under federal law. It does not support jurisdiction if the claim is based on state or foreign law, although the doctrine of supplemental jurisdiction may help for such a claim if there is otherwise a federal claim present.[12]

Subdivision (k)(2) is a kind of general longarm statute akin to those that some states have adopted, like California, whose statute[13] authorizes extraterritorial jurisdiction whenever its exercise would be consistent with the requirements of due process in the particular case. The U.S. Supreme Court in its 1987 *Omni* case, cited earlier, was invited to establish such general longarm authority for the federal courts through the decisional route, but rejected the invitation. Subdivision (k)(2) now in effect adopts by rule what the Supreme

6. 484 U.S. 97, 108 S.Ct. 404, 98 L.Ed.2d 415 (1987).

7. See Commentary C4–34 on Rule 4 in 28 U.S.C.A.

8. See §§ 617 and 618 above.

9. Surface routes with their bends and curves do not have to be considered. See, e.g., Pillsbury Co. v. Delta Boat & Barge Rental, Inc., 72 F.R.D. 630 (E.D.La.1976).

10. See § 630 below.

11. See Commentary C4–31 on Rule 4 in 28 U.S.C.A.

12. See the discussion of supplemental jurisdiction on this point in Commentary C4–35 on Rule 4 in 28 U.S.C.A. and in SPR 16:2.

13. Cal.Code Civ.Proc. § 410.10.

Court refused to do through the common law process in *Omni*.

Jurisdiction under subdivision (k)(2) is available only when it is shown that the defendant "is not subject to the jurisdiction of the courts of general jurisdiction of any state". This means that the availability of jurisdiction in any state court at all can become a bone of contention.[14] In Warn v. M/Y Maridome,[15] for example, a case involving a yacht accident off Greece, the yacht owner was doing an overall U.S. business sufficient to support personal jurisdiction in the United States under Rule 4(k)(2), but up came a showing that the contacts with one state—Virginia—sufficed for an exercise of jurisdiction by that state. That by itself cancelled the use of Rule 4(k)(2), precluding venue elsewhere in a federal court.[16]

It is not just the usual "contacts" jurisdiction that will fall within the embrace of subdivision (k)(2), i.e., a case in which the claim is shown to have arisen out of acts in the United States for which the defendant is responsible. If service is made somewhere in the country on a defendant servable anywhere within national borders, jurisdiction should be just as available against that person as were he served within the borders of a particular state in a state court action, and without reference to the activities out of which the claim arose. This is the continuing notion of physical presence (within the borders of the territory serviced by the court) as a basis for jurisdiction in its own right.

It should also be permissible to use the defendant's U.S. citizenship as a basis upon which to subject the defendant to federal jurisdiction even if the claim has no local contacts and the defendant is living abroad at the time of service. Just as domicile in a state would constitutionally support a state court's power to subject the domiciliary to local jurisdiction of a state court through extrastate service even if there's nothing else in the case that would do it, then so, too, should U.S. citizenship support a federal court's power to subject a U.S. citizen to the jurisdiction of a federal court through extranational service, on the authority of subdivision (k)(2) of Rule 4, as long as the claim arises under federal law and as long as there appears to be no state that authorizes jurisdiction under subdivision (k)(1)(A).

That's going to the constitutional limit, and that's where subdivision (k)(2) says it wants to go.

This aspect of subdivision (k)(2)'s potential should prove especially helpful when a federal statute authorizes service anywhere in the country in the particular category of case. It would presumably be subdivision (k)(1)(D) that would govern in that case—the provision that refers to such statutes. But suppose also that the federal statute in point does not appear to allow service outside the country even though it could constitutionally do so on the facts. Subdivision (k)(2) would leap in and allow service on the citizen/defendant in the foreign country of her present sojourn, whether the specific federal statute in point elects to go that far or not.[17]

In view of this broad reach for federal process service under subdivision (k)(2) in nondiversity cases, instances may increase in which jurisdiction is technically present but its exercise would be unduly burdensome in the particular case. The venue rules and the forum non conveniens doctrine must be depended on to avoid undue inconvenience in those circumstances.

§ 627. Rem Jurisdiction in the Federal Courts

The treatment of rem jurisdiction undertaken earlier—divided into the subcategories of (1) strictly in rem, (2) in rem, and (3) quasi in rem[1]—is relevant as well to federal jurisdic-

---

14. See Commentary C4–35 on Rule 4 in 28 U.S.C.A.

15. 961 F.Supp. 1357 (S.D.Cal.1997).

16. See the discussion of the Warn case in SPR 62:4.

17. These other possibilities are treated in more depth in Commentary C4–35 on Rule 4 in 28 U.S.C.A. and in SPR 16:1–2.

§ 627

1. See § 101 et seq., above.

tion, including the diminution in the use of quasi in rem jurisdiction brought about by the *Shaffer* case.[2]

Federal practice makes use of all of these categories to one degree or another, to whatever extent they are still used in this age of expanded personal jurisdiction.[3] The subject is governed by subdivision (n) of Rule 4.

Paragraph (1) of subdivision (n) merely notes that particular federal statutes may pertain to the issue of rem jurisdiction and leaves the matter to them.

The principal federal statute on rem jurisdiction is § 1655 of Title 28, which offers a broad range of jurisdiction, principally in the second category listed above. Section 1655 goes even further than its caption suggests. Its caption is "Lien Enforcement", but as its abundant caselaw manifests, § 1655 offers rem jurisdiction in a broad range of "in rem" actions, not just "lien" cases. It is less needed today than during the earlier years of its long history, for the obvious reason of the expansion of "longarm" personal jurisdiction, heavily exploited in federal practice through Rule 4(k).[4]

Quite often today, for example, when it can be shown that a case affects local property, which is the § 1655 predicate, it is also likely that the case will have had local contacts of the kind that support longarm jurisdiction and will be the subject of a state longarm statute giving full personam jurisdiction in the action. And when outright personam jurisdiction is available, on a longarm or any other basis, the need to depend on any category of rem jurisdiction declines, if, indeed, it does not disappear altogether.

Section 1655 nevertheless remains alive and well, and gainfully employed. It should be used unhesitatingly by any plaintiff who finds some benefit from its provisions. As a perusal of the statute quickly reveals, it has some advantages, such as in method of notice, but it also has some disadvantages, such as in the delay it entails in finalizing a judgment if personal notice has not been given. The plaintiff's lawyer with a choice of using the rem jurisdiction of § 1655 or a personam basis imported from state law through Rule 4(k) should appraise the advantages of each alternative and choose accordingly.

If § 1655 offers a federal court the jurisdiction it needs in categories 1 and 2, is there any authority for using the quasi in rem jurisdiction of category 3? There is, and that is where paragraph (2) of subdivision (n) comes in. It adopts for use in the federal courts state bases of rem and quasi in rem jurisdiction.[5]

Many states have attachment or like statutes exploiting quasi in rem jurisdiction. Before 1963, if such an action were commenced in a state court, it could be removed to a federal court by the defendant whenever there was a removal basis as a matter of federal subject matter jurisdiction, and many such quasi in rem actions found their way into the federal courts through this removal route. But there was no authority permitting the use of such jurisdiction as a basis on which to commence an action in a federal court originally. Since 1963, and now under Rule 4(n)(2), there is. The rule also adopts forum state law for the procedures to be used in securing the quasi in rem jurisdiction, which in New York means following the instructions of Article 62 of the CPLR, the attachment article.[6]

The addition of quasi in rem jurisdiction to the federal arsenal was a substantial achievement in 1963, reflecting the frequent reliance put on this category of jurisdiction over the years, but the gift was to be enjoyed for little more than a decade. In 1977, in the *Shaffer* case,[7] the U.S. Supreme Court, in a reconsid-

---

2. Shaffer v. Heitner, 433 U.S. 186, 97 S.Ct. 2569, 53 L.Ed.2d 683. See § 104 above.

3. In the admiralty and maritime realm, the federal courts make special use of rem jurisdiction, and particularly its "strictly in rem" category, which has been traditionally employed in admiralty cases. See the special Supplemental Rules for Certain Admiralty and Maritime Claims appended to the Federal Rules of Civil Procedure.

4. See § 626 above.

5. See Commentary C4–42 on the revised Rule 4 in 28 U.S.C.A.

6. The use in federal practice of the order of attachment, a provisional remedy, is discussed in § 640 below.

7. Shaffer v. Heitner, 433 U.S. 186, 97 S.Ct. 2569, 53 L.Ed.2d 683.

ered application of the due process clause, drastically reduced this category of jurisdiction in all cases and this of course affected its use in the contexts of both original and removal jurisdiction.[8]

Should a given case find any way to squeeze itself under any of the few quasi in rem possibilities constitutionally surviving under state law today, paragraph (2) of Rule 4(n) still permits its exploitation in a federal court, and there are, indeed, examples of its continuing use.[9]

§ 628. Raising and Preserving a Jurisdictional Objection

Rule 12 of the Federal Rules of Civil Procedure governs the raising of jurisdictional objections in the federal courts. If the objection is to subject matter jurisdiction, it can be raised at any time and in any form, pursuant to Rule 12(h)(3). This is not true of an objection to personal jurisdiction, however, where procedure is tighter, and raising an objection to personal jurisdiction is the subject of this section.

The objection may consist of the absence of a jurisdictional basis, of some defect in the summons, or of insufficient service of the summons. Rule 12(b) assigns three separate numbers to them—numbers (2), (4), and (5)—a bit less economical in this respect than its New York counterpart in CPLR 3211(a), where all three are covered in but one paragraph (paragraph 8). Whichever of the three it may be, all go to personal jurisdiction, and if the objection is good it can bring on a dismissal.

Rule 12(b) gives the defendant the option of interposing the objection either in a motion to dismiss or as a defense in the answer. If the defendant wants a prompt adjudication, the Rule 12 dismissal motion should be her procedure. If the defendant wants for any reason to preserve the objection for later adjudication, perhaps in the tactical hope of winning a favorable outcome on the point when it would

clearly be too late for the plaintiff to bring a new action, the defendant's step is to include the objection as a defense in the answer. The New York lawyer can see the parallel in these things to state practice under CPLR 3211, which is in some measure modeled on Rule 12.

A defendant making any Rule 12 motion on any ground must see that any objection he may have to personal jurisdiction is included in the motion, or the objection is lost. A special waiver provision, embodied in subdivisions (g) and (h)(1) of Rule 12, so provides. It is designed to discourage the defendant's waste of the court's time on a Rule 12 motion on other grounds while withholding a jurisdictional objection that has been available all the while. Hence the defendant can safely use the defense-in-the-answer route for an objection to personal jurisdiction only if she makes no Rule 12 motion at all—again analogous to New York practice under CPLR 3211(e).[1]

If the defendant uses the answer route but then changes her mind and wants a pretrial adjudication of the jurisdictional point after all, the time for a Rule 12(b) motion will likely have expired. In that situation, the defendant can raise the point with a summary judgment motion under Rule 56.[2] It is somewhat awkward—summary judgment is technically designed to dispose of a case on its merits—but Rule 12(d) dictates that jurisdictional objections (among others) be disposed of "before trial on application of any party", and the name of the "application" that brings the matter to judicial attention is of secondary importance. Although denominated a "summary judgment" motion in this scenario, its granting will have the impact—and the res judicata effect should the point ever arise—of disposing only of the jurisdictional issue, not the merits.

The warning to the New York state court plaintiff, about being wary of a defendant who takes a jurisdictional objection by way of an-

---

8. See § 104 above.

9. See, e.g., Intermeat v. American Poultry, Inc., 575 F.2d 1017 (2d Cir.1978).

§ 628

1. See § 274 above.

2. This, too, is permissible in New York practice. See § 283 above.

swer instead of by motion,[3] applies to the federal plaintiff as well. The defendant may be pursuing the defense-in-the-answer alternative in order to postpone the jurisdictional adjudication, and the defendant's reason for postponing it should be the plaintiff's reason for accelerating it. If there is anything to the objection, especially if it is of the curable variety (such as a defect in the summons or in the mechanics of its service), the plaintiff should try to have the matter disposed of forthwith. The principal tool for doing this is a motion to strike the jurisdictional defense pursuant to Rule 12(f).[4] The motion will of course succeed if the court is convinced that the jurisdictional defense is groundless as a matter of law. But even if it depends on the resolution of a factual issue, the plaintiff can now—as the defendant did above—cite Rule 12(d), which evinces Rule 12's preference for early adjudication of jurisdictional matters. Under it, the court can order a preliminary hearing of the issue of fact. But the same rule, 12(d), also gives the court discretion to defer the issue until the trial if it sees fit.

If the jurisdictional objection does depend on only a factual issue, such as whether the mechanics of service were just so, and there is yet time to serve again before the statute of limitations expires, fresh service, or even a new action, may be the plaintiff's best course. The federal plaintiff must be even warier than the New York plaintiff when the particular objection that the defendant has taken by answer is the defense of improper service. In New York, that defense has a life of only 60 days: the defendant must move for judgment on it within 60 days after serving the answer, or waive it.[5] No such time restriction exists in federal practice, so the defense can stand in the answer indefinitely, increasing the likelihood that the statute of limitations will expire before the defense can be adjudicated, with obvious consequences for the plaintiff if the defense should be sustained.

It may happen that the jurisdictional issue will require discovery proceedings. The defendant may contend, however, that discovery, too, requires personal jurisdiction and that not even discovery can proceed until jurisdiction has been sustained. The U.S. Supreme Court has rejected that proposition, holding that the simple fact of the defendant's appearance to raise the jurisdictional objection is a sufficient turn of the jurisdictional wheel to allow for the limited discovery needed for full resolution of the jurisdictional point.[6]

§ 629. Vacating Defaults in Federal Court

If the defendant is in default for nonappearance—the category of default relevant to a treatment of Rule 4—and the plaintiff is adamant in holding him to it, the defendant's remedy is to move to vacate the default under Rule 55(c) or Rule 60(b). Generally speaking, Rule 55(c) governs if no judgment has yet been entered, Rule 60(b)(1) (principally its "excusable neglect" category) if one has. Under Rule 55(c), the application to set aside the default has no set time limit but should be made with reasonable diligence simply to avoid laches being added in as an element. Under Rule 60(b)(1), an additional requirement is that the motion to vacate be made within a year after the judgment is taken.

There is a strong policy in federal practice, as there is in New York state practice, to have every case adjudicated on its merits. The logical adjunct of this policy is a liberal attitude about vacating defaults.

Rule 55(c) permits a default to be set aside for "good cause", but the phrase in this context does not have the same history it has in Rule 4(m) and may be less intimidating than it sounds. In Rule 4(m), it is concerned with a plaintiff's default in failing to effect summons service on time. Rule 55(c), on the other hand, is concerned primarily if not exclusively with a defendant's default. While purporting to oppose laxity from any source in litigation, the

---

3. See § 269 above.

4. The New York analog is CPLR 3211(b).

5. CPLR 3211(e). See the discussion in SPR 50:3.

6. See Insurance Corp. of Ireland, Ltd. v. Compagnie des Bauxites de Guinee, 456 U.S. 694, 102 S.Ct. 2099, 72 L.Ed.2d 492 (1982).

courts generally find a defendant's default more excusable than a plaintiff's for the obvious reason that the show is the plaintiff's and the plaintiff's failure to keep it rolling is therefore all the more perverse. Practically speaking, this has generated a more indulgent attitude towards defendants' defaults. The standard applied to gauge "good cause" under Rule 55(c), for example, was described by the Second Circuit in Meehan v. Snow[1] as "lenient" and was held to depend on "whether the default was willful, whether setting it aside would prejudice the adversary, and whether a meritorious defense is presented". The fact of the different treatment is worth noting, but it gives defendants no guarantee. There is still a large dose of discretion that goes into determining whether to set aside a default, and different judges apply it in different ways.

The requirement about demonstrating a defense is premised on the proposition that if the defendant cannot make a prima facie showing of a reasonable position on the merits, then a default judgment is as good as any other to make the case go away. An affidavit of merits should therefore accompany all applications that seek to open a default to let the defendant defend the case on the merits.

The court can impose conditions on the vacatur, and is likely to if the other side is faultless and has been put to trouble and expense because of the default. This is true of both Rule 55(c) and Rule 60(b), the FRCP's chief provision on vacating judgments. The latter, in fact, states explicitly that the court can impose "such terms as are just".

It is self-evidently preferable to seek vacatur of the default before a judgment has been entered on it. The weight of a judgment added to the fact of the default makes the onus of lifting it greater. The Rule 60(b) standard used for vacating a judgment has been held to be more "rigorous" than the Rule 55(c) standard used when merely setting aside a default.[2]

If the default was based on the defendant's not being notified of the action, i.e., a failure of summons service, or if for any other reason the defendant claims a want of personal jurisdiction and the default has gone to judgment, the motion to vacate should be based on clause (4) of Rule 60(b), that "the judgment is void". If it is based exclusively on that ground, an affidavit of merits need not be included.[3] But lest the court disagree about that, defendants should hedge their bets by including in the alternative a request under clause (1) to open the default. If clause (4) prevails, the action may of course be dismissed. But if it does not, clause (1) can come into play, the court directing merely that the default be opened and the defendant permitted to defend on the merits. Because the latter prospect depends also on a paper showing of a valid defense, an affidavit of merits should of course accompany an application made in the alternative in this fashion. It is a healthy convention in any practice.[4]

F. PARTIES, PLEADINGS, AND PAPERS

Table of Sections

§ 630. Parties in Federal Practice

The rules about the joinder of parties in federal actions are similar to those that govern in New York. In some instances, the federal rules have even been the model for their New York counterparts.

The rule that addresses which persons should be made parties to the action is Rule 19 of the Federal Rules of Civil Procedure. The New York counterpart is CPLR 1001.[1] As long

---

§ 629

1. 652 F.2d 274, 277 (2d Cir.1981).

2. Id.

3. See Peralta v. Heights Medical Center, Inc., 485 U.S. 80, 108 S.Ct. 896, 99 L.Ed.2d 75 (1988).

4. See the lead note in New York State Law Digest No. 352.

§ 630

1. CPLR 1001 is treated in §§ 131–133 above.

as jurisdiction is available against a person whose joinder would conduce to a more effective judgment, the practice in both systems favors that person's joinder. If jurisdiction is unavailable, a dismissal is technically permissible in either system for the person's nonjoinder, but only after the court considers all possibilities short of that, including conditional dispositions, to see if the action can be maintained without the additional joinder. Both practices frown on dismissals for nonjoinder until judicial imagination in the use of alternatives has been exhausted.[2]

The jurisdictional problem in a diversity of citizenship case on the federal side can of course touch not only personal jurisdiction, as it can in a state action, but on subject matter jurisdiction as well, which rarely happens in state court. Recognizing this, Rule 19(a) requires the investigation of alternatives when the joinder of the person in question is impeded by a want of either kind of jurisdiction.

The "real party in interest" provision in federal practice is Rule 17(a) of the Federal Rules of Civil Procedure, the counterpart of CPLR 1004.[3]

The rules about permissive joinder are also similar.[4] One difference is that when a person who should join as a plaintiff refuses to, New York allows that person to be named and joined as a defendant,[5] while the federal rule allows the person to be made a defendant or in some instances "an involuntary plaintiff".[6]

The misjoinder of a party is an easier matter in both systems. In neither is it a ground for dismissal, and in both the misjoined party can be dropped at any time.[7]

The federal class action rule, Rule 23 of the Federal Rules of Civil Procedure, could be a textbook chapter by itself. We highlight only its jurisdictional requirements.

As noted in the discussion of the New York class action, which is set forth in Article 9 of the CPLR,[8] a number of its ideas were drawn from Rule 23 and in some respects, at least as verbalized in Article 9, made even more expansive. New York caselaw, however, has given the class action little encouragement. The class action in federal practice is a more vibrant force than it is in New York practice, at least in federal question cases.

The class action lost most of its use in diversity actions because of U.S. Supreme Court constructions of the diversity statute:[9] while for the diversity measure itself the court holds that only the citizenship of the representatives, not of the whole class, need be considered,[10] which is an obvious aid to diversity, the court in effect revoked that gift with its construction of the monetary requirement. To meet the monetary requirement, which is currently set at $75,000, the court held that each member of the class must be shown to have at least that much at stake individually; that the claims of individual class members cannot be aggregated to meet the monetary requirement.[11] It then added for good measure that even if one or several of the members do have interests in excess of the monetary minimum, their claims will still not support jurisdiction of the others, such as through some kind of ancillary or pendent—now known as "supplemental"—jurisdiction.[12] It is hard to meet

---

2. See Provident Tradesmens Bank & Tr. Co. v. Patterson, 390 U.S. 102, 119, 88 S.Ct. 733, 743, 19 L.Ed.2d 936, 950 (1968); § 133 above.

3. See § 137 above.

4. FRCP Rule 20, CPLR 1002.

5. CPLR 1001(a).

6. FRCP Rule 19(a).

7. FRCP Rule 21, New York CPLR 1003.

8. See §§ 139–147 above.

9. 28 U.S.C.A. § 1332.

10. Supreme Tribe of Ben Hur v. Cauble, 255 U.S. 356, 41 S.Ct. 338, 65 L.Ed. 673 (1921).

11. Snyder v. Harris, 394 U.S. 332, 89 S.Ct. 1053, 22 L.Ed.2d 319 (1969).

12. Zahn v. International Paper Co., 414 U.S. 291, 94 S.Ct. 505, 38 L.Ed.2d 511 (1973). Pendent jurisdiction is discussed in § 614 above. Ancillary jurisdiction is discussed later in this section and in § 632 below. Both categories were codified in 1990 as supplemental jurisdiction in § 1367 of Title 28. (See the Practice Commentary on 28 U.S.C.A. § 1367.) There is currently a conflict among the federal circuits about whether § 1367 overrules the Zahn case and allows this kind of "free ride" for the claims under the monetary minimum. See Leonhardt v. Western Sugar Co., 160 F.3d 631 (10th Cir.1998), holding that Zahn remains law and finding a majority of district courts also of that view, but citing several circuits going the other way and allowing the free ride.

these monetary requirements for a class action for the obvious reason that individuals with more than $75,000 at stake do not need the class action to help them into court, nor do they want it. They usually prefer to prosecute their actions independently. The class action is primarily a device for those whose monetary interests are too small to make individual prosecution worthwhile.[13] The result is that plaintiffs who have only diversity jurisdiction to rely on as a basis for federal jurisdiction must often today turn to the state courts instead. When the state courts they turn to are New York's, however, the reception is restrained.[14]

There is much kinship in third-party practice (impleader) between the federal and New York courts. Both are generous in the use of this important device. The New York provisions are in CPLR 1007–1011;[15] in federal practice the job is done by one rule, Rule 14 of the Federal Rules of Civil Procedure. The basic purpose of impleader in both systems is to enable a defendant to bring in an indemnitor—one who would have to hold the defendant harmless for all or part of the plaintiff's demand against the defendant. But both allow the joinder of additional claims, at least as long as the indemnity link is present. On the federal side, Rule 18(a) does this explicitly. In New York practice, it required caselaw to get there.[16]

The subject of "contribution" among tortfeasors, studied just after impleader,[17] is as much a substantive subject as a procedural one. Procedurally, contribution can be sought by cross-claim between defendants already joined, but may be sought through the impleader device against one not already joined. To the extent relevant in any federal action, such as a tort action in which jurisdiction is based on diversity of citizenship and the governing law is New York's, the New York rules

of contribution govern substantively but as a general proposition the contribution is sought through the procedural instructions of the Federal Rules.

If the case is in the federal court on diversity grounds, some interesting questions of subject matter jurisdiction arise with impleader. Suppose, for example, that P, a citizen of Vermont, sues D, a citizen of New York. (We assume the monetary requirements are met.) D wants to implead X, also a New York citizen, for indemnification, but there is no diversity on the third-party claim. There does not have to be. The third-party claim gets what is known as "ancillary jurisdiction".

"Ancillary jurisdiction" is akin to the "pendent jurisdiction" noted earlier[18]—both are today codified under 28 U.S.C.A. § 1367 as "supplemental jurisdiction"—but while pendent jurisdiction is relevant mainly to support a plaintiff's state-created claim as "pendent" to one arising under federal law, which made it primarily a feature of the "federal question" category of jurisdiction, ancillary jurisdiction does its main work in supporting jurisdiction of certain claims interposed by other parties than the plaintiff. It is designed to avoid piecemeal litigation. It functions in both federal question and diversity contexts,[19] but because of the merger of both doctrines under the "supplemental" caption there is no need to distinguish the contexts of subject matter jurisdiction in which it arises.

The clearest application of the "ancillary" jurisdiction is on the diversity side, in actions in which there is proper diversity and monetary amount on the main claim but not on a counterclaim or cross-claim.[20]

Ancillary (now supplemental) jurisdiction applies to support jurisdiction of a third-party claim that does not otherwise have it, but it will not supply jurisdiction of a claim that P, the main plaintiff, attempts to assert against X

---

13. See § 139 above.

14. See § 141 above.

15. See §§ 155–168 above.

16. See the discussion of the George Cohen case in § 157 above.

17. See §§ 169–177.

18. See § 614 above.

19. See the Second Circuit's discussion in Federman v. Empire Fire and Marine Ins. Co., 597 F.2d 798 (2d Cir. 1979).

20. The use of ancillary ("supplemental") jurisdiction on counterclaims and cross-claims is noted in § 632 below.

after X has been impleaded by D. As a matter of procedure, P may interpose such a direct claim against the impleaded X,[21] just as P may do in a New York court.[22] But suppose there is no diversity between P and X, as where P of New York sues D of Vermont and D impleads X, also of New York. While P may assert a direct claim against X as a matter of procedure—Rule 14(a) explicitly invites it—the claim will fail for want of subject matter jurisdiction because the U.S. Supreme Court has refused to extend supplemental jurisdiction that far. The court holds that in these diversity contexts the supplemental jurisdiction is primarily a tool for defendants, in court against their will, to facilitate their assertion of claims against others.[23] Hence in diversity cases the doctrine may not be used to support claims by a plaintiff that would not otherwise be able to find subject matter jurisdiction on their own.

The rules for intervention in federal and New York practice are not identical but do have some parallels. As was noted earlier, New York practice divides the subject into intervention as of right and intervention by permission.[24] So do the Federal Rules of Civil Procedure. Subdivision (a) of Rule 24 governs intervention of right, subdivision (b) intervention by leave of court. While defendants seeking to intervene may rely on supplemental jurisdiction if they need it for subject matter jurisdiction, those seeking to intervene as plaintiffs cannot. While the consensus in the federal courts had been that a plaintiff's claim that could satisfy the requirements of intervention of right under Rule 24(a) could rely on ancillary jurisdiction if it needed it, and that only one that had to depend for intervention on the court's discretion under Rule 24(b) could not,[25] § 1367 appears to deny supplemental jurisdiction to intervening plaintiffs

in both categories,[26] making it necessary in each that the proposed plaintiff intervenor independently demonstrate the presence of subject matter jurisdiction on her claim.

The federal provision on interpleader is Rule 22. When the rule is relied on in diversity cases, the usual requirements of the diversity statute apply. The amount in controversy requirement must be met and there must be complete diversity between the stakeholder plaintiff and the defendant claimants. To alleviate the dilemma of a stakeholder unable to satisfy the jurisdiction and venue requirements with respect to all claimants in a single diversity action, Congress enacted a special set of statutes that ease the path of the stakeholder in point of (1) diversity, (2) monetary requirement, (3) scope of process, and (4) venue. These statutes[27] are collectively referred to as "federal statutory interpleader",[28] to distinguish it from an interpleader predicated only on Rule 22, which does not get the quartet of advantages offered by statutory interpleader.

§ 631. Pleadings in Federal Practice

New York practice calls it a "cause of action". Federal terminology favors the simple word "claim". The key provision manifesting the different use in each practice is the motion supplied to dismiss for insufficiency: Rule 12(b)(6) in federal practice, CPLR 3211(a)(7) in New York state practice. As a general rule, the two phrases are the same and may be treated as interchangeable, even though one occasionally hears the suggestion that there is some kind of fundamental difference between them.[1] One basic and delightful difference that all admirers of brevity can acknowledge is that "claim" has less than half the letters and only one fourth the syllables that "cause of action" has, which gives it the advantage hands down.

21. Rule 14(a).

22. See § 164 above.

23. See Owen Equipment & Erection Co. v. Kroger, 437 U.S. 365, 98 S.Ct. 2396, 57 L.Ed.2d 274 (1978).

24. See §§ 178–183 above.

25. For a case that awarded ancillary jurisdiction in both categories of intervention, see United States v. Local 638, 347 F.Supp. 164 (S.D.N.Y.1972).

26. See § 1367(b).

27. 28 U.S.C.A. §§ 1335, 1397, and 2361.

28. They are discussed at the end of the chapter treating New York interpleader. See § 154 above.

§ 631

1. See § 211 above.

It is the word we make use of here, whichever the court system being discussed.

The basic New York pleading requirement contained in CPLR 3013 has its counterpart in Rule 8(a) of the Federal Rules of Civil Procedure. Rule 8(a) wants "a short and plain statement of the claim showing that the pleader is entitled to relief". The CPLR 3013 requirement is that the statement "be sufficiently particular to give the court and parties notice of the transactions, occurrences, or series of transactions or occurrences, intended to be proved and the material elements of each cause of action or defense". The federal rule does not mention "material elements", but a federal pleading should be certain to cover them at least as well as the New York pleading would. How can any plaintiff go comfortably to any court with a pleading that omits some material element of the claim?

In both practices the role of the pleadings has declined as the use of pretrial discovery and disclosure—we use the terms here interchangeably—has increased. In the federal system, disclosure is even more expansive than it is in New York practice,[2] and because of the higher stakes usually involved in federal litigation, especially in commercial cases, the full range of the disclosure devices is used there with greater regularity. The knowledge that in almost all federal actions the disclosure devices are destined to be exploited, and sometimes exploited mercilessly, enables the judges to assume that details of each side's position will be available to the other in the more effective vehicle of disclosure, so that the pleading stage should just present the basics.

There is another side to this coin, however. There is no bill of particulars in federal civil practice, as there is in New York practice. The pleading in federal practice therefore becomes the prime vehicle for the presentation of certain matters—usually those requiring greater specificity under the rules. Special damages, for example, must be pleaded in a federal complaint,[3] while New York practice leaves them to the bill of particulars.[4]

The provision second in command in New York pleading practice, CPLR 3014, imposes several requirements and offers several options that also have federal counterparts, albeit with some differences. CPLR 3014 is the provision that imposes the separate numbering requirement for claims and allegations.[5] Its federal counterpart is Rule 10(b). Rule 10(b) says that separate claims have to be separately numbered only if founded on "separate" transactions, suggesting that different counts or grounds in support of what is really a single "claim" don't have to be. But the common practice in both systems is to use separate numbering in both situations. The repetition of statements common to two or more claims is not necessary. Prior relevant paragraphs can be carried forward merely by referring to them by number.[6] The federal rule does not declare, as CPLR 3014 does, that prior statements are "deemed repeated" without a specific reference back, but even with that option available the New York pleader still prefers the numerical reference method to carry forward prior allegations. It is usually more conducive to clarity, which is the aim in both practices.

A document appended to a pleading is deemed part of it,[7] and it is always best to refer to the writing in the body of the pleading.

The permission that New York CPLR 3014 offers to plead claims or defenses alternatively or hypothetically, and regardless of consistency, was discussed earlier.[8] These are also options in federal practice,[9] and just as useful there.

The specific manner of alleging things in federal pleadings is perhaps best absorbed through a browsing of some of the official forms. There are more than a dozen official

---

2. See §§ 636 and 637 below.

3. FRCP Rule 9(g).

4. See § 238 above.

5. See § 212 above.

6. FRCP Rule 10(c); CPLR 3014.

7. FRCP Rule 10(c) says "a written instrument"; CPLR 3014 says "any writing".

8. See § 214 above.

9. FRCP Rule 8(e).

forms devoted to pleadings in the appendix of forms annexed to the Federal Rules of Civil Procedure, and as was seen with some of the official forms in New York practice earlier,[10] a picture is worth a thousand words.

A jury waiver can result inadvertently if a New York lawyer carries the assumptions of New York practice into a federal court. In New York practice a jury is not demanded until the note of issue stage, which comes long after the pleadings.[11] In federal practice, demanding a jury is important at the pleading stage itself. The demand for the jury can be "indorsed upon" the pleading or made the subject of a written demand served "not later than 10 days after the service of the last pleading directed to [the] issue".[12] A pleader intent on demanding a jury whatever the other side may do should include the demand in the pleading. Ordinarily, the only justification for waiting and using the demand method is where the pleader wants first to see what position the other side is taking on the issues.

Another point about juries that becomes important at the pleading stage in federal practice, especially since the filing of the complaint is what starts a federal action, has to do with the joinder of claims, or in any event with the relief being sought on whatever claim is pleaded. A CPLR provision instructs explicitly that a plaintiff joining legal and equitable demands for relief in respect of a claim or claims arising out of the same transaction waives trial by jury of the legal claim.[13] There is no counterpart in federal practice, and there should therefore be no waiver in that situation.

The rules on the joinder of claims are also similar in the two systems, and liberal. Once the proper links for the joinder of parties are in place, Rule 18(a) of the Federal Rules of Civil Procedure says that any party asserting "an original claim, counterclaim, cross-claim, or third-party claim, may join … as many claims, legal, equitable, or maritime, as the party has against an opposing party". Rule 14(a) expands on that in the impleader context. The New York counterparts, equally generous, are CPLR 601,[14] 1008, and 1009.[15]

In each practice, certain matters are the subject of special pleading requirements. CPLR 3015 and 3016, treated earlier,[16] have the lists of those items in New York practice. The federal counterpart is Rule 9. In either practice, the lists have to be scanned before preparing any pleading just to see whether there is anything on the special list that affects the case. A number of the items exist in common between the two practices.

Pleading with particularity the elements that go into a fraud claim is one example,[17] but the New York courts have been a bit less rigorous in the application of this requirement.[18] This suggests that New York lawyers drafting federal pleadings should toe the line more closely with these special requirements and not assume that their New York experience can be trusted to take them safely through the federal courts.

Conditions precedent are another example, and with another difference. If there are any conditions precedent to the validity of the claim, the federal plaintiff must plead the satisfaction of all of them, at least in general terms.[19] In New York practice, only the satisfaction of a condition precedent imposed by a statute need be pleaded; one imposed by a contract need not be.[20]

The corporate status of any party must be pleaded in New York practice.[21] It need not be in federal practice unless it is relevant to subject matter jurisdiction,[22] as it would be in a case founded on diversity of citizenship. As was pointed out earlier, the basis of the court's subject matter jurisdiction must be pleaded in

---

10. See § 210.

11. See § 369 above.

12. FRCP Rule 38(b).

13. See § 378 above.

14. See § 126 above.

15. See § 164 above.

16. See §§ 215–216 above.

17. FRCP Rule 9(b), CPLR 3016(b).

18. See § 216 above.

19. FRCP Rule 9(c).

20. CPLR 3015(a).

21. CPLR 3015(b).

22. FRCP Rule 9(a).

the complaint in federal practice. There is no counterpart requirement in New York state practice.[23]

The New York provision that imposes the requirement that all papers be signed and that imposes sanctions for frivolous conduct in litigation, Rule 130–1,[24] has a counterpart and is in fact modeled on Rule 11 of the Federal Rules of Civil Procedure. Under Rule 11, the signing constitutes a certification of the paper's integrity "to the best of the [signer's] knowledge" and represents to the court among other things that it is interposed in good faith and is not being used for any "improper purpose".[25] Monetary sanctions under Rule 11, which have no arbitrary cap—compare the $10,000 limit that New York imposes at least on a punitive (as against a compensatory) sanction[26]—may still be imposed, with a punitive or compensatory aim, but an extensive amendment of Rule 11 that took effect on December 1, 1993, re-arranges its aims. The amended rule retains but discourages monetary sanctions, preferring nonmonetary cures, and when monetary penalties are imposed as deterrents the money as a general rule is to be paid into court, not to the opposing party. The court does retain discretion to assess attorney's fees and expenses against the wrongdoer, but only when "warranted for effective deterrence".[27]

Perhaps the main feature of the amendment is what has become known as the "safe harbor" provision, under which a party seeking sanctions serves the sanctions motion on the other side but does not file it in court until 21 days later. The interim is designed to give the other side three weeks in which to withdraw or correct the challenged "paper, claim, defense, contention, allegation, or denial". If the withdrawal or correction occurs, the motion presumably never gets to court.[28]

The amendment also directs that a motion for sanctions be made separately. No more "tack-ons", in which a motion for relief of any of myriad kinds would also contain a demand for sanctions because of the other side's behavior. This produced a mass of "satellite" litigation that often proved unwarranted as well as distracting.

Rule 11 is not applicable to conduct connected with disclosure and discovery,[29] which have their own sanction provisions in Rules 26(g) and 37.

The answer in federal practice has the usual mission of interposing the defendant's denials, defenses, counterclaims, and cross-claims. Denials are governed by Rule 8(b) of the Federal Rules of Civil Procedure, for the most part parallel to CPLR 3018(a). The direct denial of matters known to be false, and the denial of knowledge or information sufficient to form a belief of matters the responder does not know one way or the other, are explicitly covered in the two rules. The denial "upon information and belief"—where the responder has only second-hand knowledge on the basis of which he believes an allegation false—is available in both practices but arises by implication on the federal side.[30]

When the responding party wants to deny only part of an allegation, and admit the rest, it was pointed out in New York practice that the better technique is to single out the matter to be admitted and deny the balance. It avoids an inadvertent admission.[31] In federal practice that technique is expressly prescribed.[32]

A general denial, in which the responding party denies everything, is allowed in both practices, but of course has to be saved for an appropriate case and must always be used in good faith. Rule 8(b) makes that explicit, and Rule 11 of course stands in the wings to give it teeth. General denials should be saved for an-

23. See § 611 above.

24. See § 414A above.

25. Rule 11(b).

26. See § 414A.

27. Rule 11(c)(2). See the extensive Advisory Committee note on the 1993 amendment of Rule 11, following the rule in 28 U.S.C.A.

28. See Rule 11(c)(1)(A).

29. See Rule 11(d).

30. See FRCP Rule 11(b), CPLR 3023.

31. See § 221 above.

32. Rule 8(b).

swers responding to terse complaints. The more extensive the allegations of the complaint, the greater the risk of a charge of bad faith in responding to it with a general denial.

This is not to say that each paragraph of the complaint must be met by a distinct paragraph in the answer, although some practitioners prefer that and it is of course permissible. A common response to several of the complaint's allegations can be handled in one paragraph of the answer, as it is in New York practice,[33] such as by using one paragraph for direct denials, another for denials on information and belief, etc.

Like CPLR 3018(b) in New York practice, FRCP Rule 8(c) has a long list of affirmative defenses that it is the defendant's obligation to plead. The lists are similar, the federal one a bit longer. Anything on the list should be set forth "in short and plain terms".[34] The federal rule does not define what an affirmative defense is, as the New York rule attempts to do,[35] but with or without a definition one can say of both practices that if there is any doubt about whether a given matter can be put into evidence at the trial under the cover of a denial, it should be pleaded as a defense and explicitly denominated as such. The federal forms even illustrate how defenses and denials can be mixed, as long as clarity is not sacrificed.[36]

The relief clauses are governed by parallel provisions, Rule 8(a) in federal practice, CPLR 3017(a) in New York. The complaint should demand whatever relief the plaintiff seeks and the claim supports. In money actions a specific sum can be asked for in the complaint, and of course if a default judgment is sought it is important to be able to show that it was.[37]

The answer in federal practice is filed with the court as well as served on the plaintiff.[38] The time for answering the complaint, discussed earlier,[39] and the time for answering subsequent claims, like counterclaims, cross-claims, and third-party claims, is governed by Federal Rule 12(a).

Amendments of pleadings are governed by similar provisions in the two systems.[40] The most sensitive of the situations involving an amendment, that which seeks to relate an added claim back to an earlier time in the hope of saving it from the bar of the statute of limitations, is treated in an earlier section.[41]

§ 632. Counterclaims and Cross–Claims in Federal Practice

New York does not have a compulsory counterclaim rule. All counterclaims in New York are permissive, whether or not they are related to the plaintiff's claim, at least to the extent that a defendant's failure to interpose it does not waive it. There is still a right to bring a separate action on it.[1] Federal practice differs substantially in this regard. If the counterclaim arises out of the same transaction as the plaintiff's claim, it is a "compulsory" counterclaim and the general rule is that the failure to interpose it waives it.[2]

This risk of waiver suggests that any doubt about whether a counterclaim has the kind of relationship to the main claim that would make it compulsory should be resolved in favor of pleading it instead of suing on it separately. If another action was already pending on the would-be counterclaim when the action was commenced, however, it need not be pleaded as a counterclaim; the pendency of the other action divests the counterclaim of its "compul-

---

33. See § 228 above.

34. Rule 8(b). Form 20 of the official forms appended to the Federal Rules of Civil Procedure illustrates the brevity the rule encourages.

35. See § 223 above.

36. See the "Third Defense" in official form 20.

37. See FRCP Rule 54(c).

38. FRCP Rule 5(d).

39. See § 623 above.

40. See FRCP Rule 15 and CPLR 3025. The New York rules on amendments are in §§ 236 and 237 above.

41. See § 615.

§ 632

1. See § 224 above. As indicated in that section, however, this notion may be illusory because the doctrine of collateral estoppel may make the result of the earlier action binding.

2. FRCP Rule 13(a). See Cummings v. Dresher, 18 N.Y.2d 105, 108, 271 N.Y.S.2d 976, 978, 218 N.E.2d 688, 690 (1966) (concurring opinion of Fuld, J.).

sory" status. The same is true of a related counterclaim that requires for its adjudication third persons who are beyond the court's jurisdiction.[3]

As pointed out earlier in listing the choice of forum factors,[4] the compulsory counterclaim rule can have a tactical advantage to a plaintiff. By suing in a federal court instead of a New York court, which does not have a compulsory counterclaim rule, the plaintiff can compel the defendant to interpose all related claims in the forum the plaintiff has chosen.

Unrelated counterclaims are permissive. The defendant can interpose them or not, and there is no waiver.[5]

All of these rules have to do with procedure only. There may of course be a problem with subject matter jurisdiction. Jurisdiction of the main claim may be based on a federal question, for example, and the counterclaim may not have that or any other predicate for subject matter jurisdiction. Or, if the main claim is based on diversity, which would of course serve the defendant as well, the main claim may satisfy the monetary jurisdiction required by the diversity statute[6] while the counterclaim may not. Here the ancillary jurisdiction doctrine, now codified in 28 U.S.C.A. § 1367 as "supplemental jurisdiction" and discussed earlier,[7] comes into play. If it applies, it supports jurisdiction, as "ancillary" or "supplemental" to the main claim, of a counterclaim that would otherwise lack jurisdiction. Does it apply? It does to a compulsory counterclaim,[8] but not to a merely permissive one, for which the defendant must independently demonstrate a ground for subject matter jurisdiction.[9]

It is the relatedness of the claim that earns it the jurisdictional support, in other words,

and it is for that reason that cross-claims get ancillary jurisdiction, too. In federal practice, a cross-claim may be interposed between co-parties only if it arises out of the transaction that grounds the main claim or some counterclaim in the case.[10] This is in contrast to New York practice, which allows a cross-claim to assert even unrelated claims.[11] The relatedness required of cross-claims as a matter of procedure automatically earns them the supplemental status as a matter of jurisdiction.

A counterclaim or cross-claim should be clearly labeled as such. If there is doubt about whether a given matter is an outright counterclaim or a mere defense, it would seem best to label it as both and to seek in the relief clause whatever relief the pleader deems appropriate. An error of mere labeling is seldom serious, however. "When a party has mistakenly designated a defense as a counterclaim or a counterclaim as a defense, the court on terms, if justice so requires, shall treat the pleading as if there had been a proper designation."[12]

As in New York practice, when a counterclaim or cross-claim exists against a plaintiff or defendant along with some other person not yet a party, that other person can be added as a party on the claim.[13]

§ 633. Papers

The same rules that apply "to captions and other matters of form of pleadings apply to all motions and other papers".[1] Local rules should also be consulted for matters of form.

The mandatory filing system is used in federal practice. With only a few exceptions, every paper served on a party must be filed with the court "within a reasonable time after ser-

---

3. FRCP Rule 13(a).

4. See § 616 above.

5. Rule 13(b).

6. 28 U.S.C.A. § 1332.

7. See § 630 above.

8. See the court's first footnote in Baker v. Gold Seal Liquors, Inc., 417 U.S. 467, 469, 94 S.Ct. 2504, 2506, 41 L.Ed.2d 243, 247 (1974).

9. See Federman v. Empire Fire and Marine Ins. Co., 597 F.2d 798 (2d Cir.1979).

10. Rule 13(g).

11. See § 227 above.

12. FRCP Rule 8(c).

13. See FRCP Rule 13(h). For the New York counterparts, see §§ 224 and 227 above.

§ 633

1. FRCP Rule 7(b)(2). See Rule 10, and § 631 above.

vice".[2] While New York practice may require the filing of papers in designated instances, it has no uniform mandatory filing requirement akin to this federal one.[3]

As to what papers must be served on the other parties, the two practices concur, and in all fundamental particulars: the same papers that would have to be served in a New York action would also have to be served in a federal action, and whatever is served on any party must be served on every party who has appeared.[4]

We are of course referring here to interlocutory papers—the usual run of papers that go back and forth in litigation after jurisdiction has been obtained.

The federal rule about the method of serving interlocutory papers is also akin to New York's. The service is made on the party's attorney and ordinary mail is the principal medium. Service by mail is complete upon the posting.[5] When the paper served requires a response within a stated period and the paper is served by mail, the federal rule adds only three days to the time period[6] as against the five that CPLR 2103(b)(2) adds in New York practice, but for all of these matters of time and method it behooves the lawyer to inquire, and to inquire regularly, into anything in either the rules of the court or of the individual judge that may also be in point.

This is especially important today, when other methods of service gaining favor with lawyers may not yet have achieved recognition in the statutes or rules. Service by facsimile (fax) machine or through an overnight delivery service are prime examples. In 1990 New York adopted statutes on both methods for applica-

tion in the state courts.[7] These of course do not apply in the federal courts, where the rules of the individual courts and judges should be consulted. The Federal Rules of Civil Procedure recognize that individual courts may by local rule permit the electronic filing of papers.[8]

Overnight service, which includes the U.S. Post Office's "express" service, is frequently used now, and as long as there is no argument about the timeliness of the paper's service, or of a response that a paper so served requires, it should not pose problems.[9]

Rule 11 of the Federal Rules of Civil Procedure requires that all papers be signed by at least one of the attorneys of record, and in the attorney's individual name, and makes the attorney a kind of surety for the legitimacy of what is said in the paper. A violation of Rule 11, as noted earlier,[10] can lead to substantial sanctions.

New York litigators are aware of the importance of CPLR 2004 in civil practice, the provision that authorizes the court in its discretion to extend the time for the doing of almost any time-limited act. It has some exceptions, of course, and vital ones at that,[11] but just a few. The federal counterpart, just as important in federal practice, is subdivision (b) of Rule 6, the "enlargement of time" rule.[12] It has the same broad aim and impact as its CPLR counterpart, but it also lists some exceptions. The exceptions listed in Rule 6(b) bar the court from enlarging the time periods applicable to:

—a motion for judgment notwithstanding the verdict; [13]

---

2. FRCP Rule 5(d).

3. See § 77 above.

4. FRCP Rule 5(a). For the New York counterparts, see §§ 202 and 203 above.

5. FRCP Rule 5(b).

6. Rule 6(e).

7. See § 202 above.

8. See Rule 5(e). A report on fax service issued by the Commercial and Federal Litigation Section of the New York State Bar Association, published at page 7 of the New York Law Journal of December 16, 1988, concluded that fax service was permissible under FRCP Rule 5(b).

9. The New York provision on overnight service, CPLR 2103(b)(5), adds only one day to the response period applicable to the paper served, as against the five that get added when mail is used.

10. See § 631.

11. See § 33 above.

12. Subdivision (a) of Rule 6 of the Federal Rules of Civil Procedure contains the instructions for how time periods are computed.

13. FRCP Rule 50(b).

—a motion for a new trial by one against whom judgment notwithstanding the verdict has been granted;[14]

—a motion to amend a judge's findings after a bench trial (a trial by the court without a jury);[15]

—a motion for a new trial;[16]

—a motion to amend a judgment;[17] and

—a motion to vacate a final judgment or order.[18]

Rule 6(b) applies the enlargement power (with the stated exceptions) only to time periods supplied by the Federal Rules of Civil Procedure. For that reason, the two major exceptions that bar a New York judge from granting a discretionary extension of time also amount to exceptions and preclude a discretionary enlargement under the federal rule: the time for commencing an action (the statute of limitations) and the time for taking an appeal. Neither of those time periods come from the Federal Rules of Civil Procedure. The time for commencing an action is dictated by statute,[19] and the time to appeal comes from the Federal Rules of Appellate Procedure, which has its own time and time-extension instructions.[20]

G. MOTIONS

Table of Sections

§ 634. Motion Practice Generally

Motion practice is addressed by the Federal Rules of Civil Procedure, by the rules of the district courts, and often by the individual rules of some of the judges. We set forth here a few basics that come from the FRCP, with only a few references to illustrative district court rules. The admonition appears between every line of every discourse on federal motion practice, however, that practitioners who do not have all of the rules at their fingertips must get them and check them out before undertaking either to make or to respond to a motion.

For a time, some of the individual judges had rules requiring the attorney to get permission from the judge before making a motion, or a particular kind of motion. These generated controversy, but because of the federal policy against interlocutory appeals there was little means for testing the validity of this requirement in the court of appeals. As noted in an earlier section,[1] the Second Circuit finally did get an opportunity to address the matter and held the preliminary-permission requirement invalid in Richardson Greenshields Securities, Inc. v. Lau.[2] While the court did not reject a requirement for the "conferencing" of motions—a requirement that the matter be put to the judge preliminarily to see if the dispute can be resolved without a formal motion—it did say that "the judge must either conduct a conference immediately or permit the motion to be filed without a conference".[3] Some lawyers still report that judges who insist on requiring permission for motions are managing to continue the requirement despite the *Greenshields* case.

The formal prescription for motion practice in the federal courts is found in several rules. Unless the motion is made during a hearing or trial in court, it must be in writing, stating "with particularity the grounds therefor ... and ... the relief or order sought".[4] The rule

---

14. FRCP Rule 50(c)(2).

15. FRCP Rule 52(b).

16. FRCP Rule 59(b),(d).

17. FRCP Rule 59(e).

18. FRCP Rule 60(b).

19. See § 615 above.

20. See Rule 4 of the Federal Rules of Appellate Procedure, briefly discussed in § 642 below.

§ 634

1. See § 610 above.

2. 825 F.2d 647 (2d Cir.1987).

3. Id. at 652.

4. FRCP Rule 7(b)(1).

applicable to the form of pleadings[5] applies to motions as well.[6] A motion must be signed by one of the attorneys of record pursuant to the requirements of Rule 11, which certifies the integrity of the motion.[7]

Rule 6(d) of the Federal Rules of Civil Procedure requires at least five days notice of motion, subject of course to the three-day extension when mail is used,[8] but it is idle to assume that this instruction is the last word on the subject. The matter is often governed by local rules of the district court and may even be addressed and varied in the rules of the individual judges. In rural districts covering large areas, a much longer notice time may be required, for example,[9] but time variations for all or for given motions may be found in the metropolitan districts, too.[10] The Federal Rules of Civil Procedure may itself offer more time for a given category of motion, as it has done, for example, with the motion for summary judgment.[11]

The federal as well as the New York courts' rules are annually recompiled and published in the softcover, "McKinney's New York Rules of Court" pamphlet. The rules of the individual judges have been compiled into a softcover by the Commercial and Federal Litigation Section of the New York State Bar Association, and may also appear periodically in the New York Law Journal. Those and other sources should be checked. If a copy of the judge's rules cannot be found after a reasonable inquiry, a call to the judge's chambers is in order.

When the usual procedures of a notice of motion are for some reason inadequate, as when some emergency requires the motion's hearing and disposition earlier than would otherwise be possible,[12] an order to show cause may be used. The local rules of the court and of the individual judge must also be consulted for any details about show cause applications. The applicant presenting the order to show cause, which is of course tendered ex parte, must always be prepared to show the judge some special reason why an ordinary notice of motion will not do.[13]

Whether oral argument of a motion will be allowed is up to the individual court[14] and must again be determined locally. Local rules should also be examined for details of the form that the order disposing of the motion should take and the procedure for submitting it and getting it entered.[15] In contrast to New York practice, where the prevailing party serves notice of entry along with a copy of the order, in federal practice it is the clerk who is supposed to serve notice of entry (which is done by mail).[16] In some districts, however, this rule may not be consistently applied, or applied at all. A local inquiry must be made to ascertain the practice. Should the order be of the rare variety that can be immediately appealed, the recipient should note that the appeal time in federal practice runs from the entry of the order, and not, as in New York practice, from the service of notice of entry.[17]

§ 635. Dismissal and Summary Judgment Motions; Rules 12 and 56

Rules 12 and 56 of the Federal Rules of Civil Procedure address key motions in federal practice. Rule 56 is the summary judgment motion and we return to it shortly. Rule 12 supplies among other things the major dismissal motion in federal practice, the counterpart of CPLR 3211 but with some significant differences.

---

5. FRCP Rule 10.

6. FRCP Rule 7(b)(2).

7. Rule 7(b)(3). Rule 11 is discussed in § 631 and in the last item on the list of choice of forum factors in § 616, above.

8. FRCP Rule 6(e).

9. Rule 7.1 of the Northern District's rules, for example, presently requires 21 days notice of motion.

10. See, e.g., Rule 6.1 of the Civil Rules in the Southern and Eastern districts.

11. FRCP Rule 56(c).

12. FRCP Rule 6(d).

13. See, e.g., Rule 6.1(d) of the current Civil Rules in the Southern and Eastern districts.

14. See FRCP Rule 78.

15. See, e.g., Rule 6.2 of the Civil Rules of the Southern and Eastern Districts.

16. FRCP Rule 77(d).

17. See Rule 4(a) of the Federal Rules of Appellate Procedure. The New York procedure is treated in § 533 above.

CPLR 3211(a) contains a long list of grounds on which a motion to dismiss can be predicated.[1] Rule 12(b) contains fewer grounds. The seven grounds listed in Rule 12(b) are

(1) lack of subject matter jurisdiction;

(2) lack of personal jurisdiction;

(3) improper venue;

(4) insufficiency of process;

(5) insufficiency of service of process;

(6) failure to state a claim upon which relief can be granted; and

(7) failure to join an indispensable party.

Ground (1) has a parallel in CPLR 3211(a)(2). Grounds (2), (4), and (5) all go to personal jurisdiction and are covered by paragraph 8 of CPLR 3211(a) under the single caption of "jurisdiction of the person". This means that a defense using such general phraseology in New York practice will preserve objections to service as well as objections to basis; that in New York the defendant may even be assuming a risk in being too specific, as occurred in Hatch v. Tran,[2] in which a defendant who pleaded that the complaint wasn't "properly served" (which concerns the method of service) was precluded from afterwards contending that there was no jurisdictional basis (which concerns only the place of service). In federal practice under Rule 12(a), in contrast, specificity is required. In one case, for example, a defendant who interposed the defense of lack of "personal jurisdiction" was held to waive the defense of insufficient service.[3]

Ground (6) with its failure to state a "claim" is essentially the same as CPLR 3211(a)(7) and its failure to state a "cause of action". Ground 7, the failure to join an indis-

pensable party, is the same as CPLR 3211(a)(10).

All of these grounds lend themselves to a pre-answer motion to dismiss in both practices except for ground (3) on the federal list, improper venue, which has no New York counterpart. Improper venue is not a dismissal ground in New York[4] as it is in federal practice,[5] and there is thus no occasion for offering it the New York housing of a dismissal motion.

One important part of CPLR 3211(a) that has no counterpart in Rule 12 is the motion to dismiss based on the pendency of the same claim in some other court.[6] A federal court asked to dismiss or stay a federal action in deference to a pending state court action has no "hard and fast rule" to guide it and must sift through a number of factors.[7]

Most of the other items on the New York CPLR 3211(a) list that are not on the Rule 12(b) list, notably the affirmative defenses listed in paragraph 5 of CPLR 3211(a), can nevertheless lend themselves to a Rule 12(b) dismissal motion, but in a roundabout way. It will be helpful first to consider ground (6) in Rule 12(b), the failure to state a claim.

There is much in common between Rule 12(b)(6) and CPLR 3211(a)(7), the New York motion to dismiss for failure to state a cause of action.[8] Both federal and New York practice authorize the court to treat a dismissal motion as one for summary judgment, as long as notice is given of the court's intention to do this (so that all sides can now submit whatever evidence they may have previously withheld on the assumption that the motion was more narrowly based). But they do it in different terms. The New York rule permits this treatment no matter what ground the CPLR

---

§ 635

1. See §§ 257–268 above.

2. 170 A.D.2d 649, 567 N.Y.S.2d 72 (2d Dep't 1991).

3. See Santos v. State Farm Fire & Cas. Co., 902 F.2d 1092 (2d Cir.1990).

4. See § 116 above.

5. See § 617 above.

6. CPLR 3211(a)(4). It has a substantial caselaw. See § 262 above.

7. See Moses H. Cone Memorial Hospital v. Mercury Constr. Corp., 460 U.S. 1, 103 S.Ct. 927, 74 L.Ed.2d 765 (1983). It may also overlap to some extent one of the "abstention" doctrines, noted in § 613 above. The Mercury case and the pending-elsewhere problem are discussed in the lead note in New York State Law Digest No. 281 (May 1983).

8. The federal "claim" and the state "cause of action" are for practical purposes the same. See § 631 above. "Claim", as we use it here, refers to both.

3211(a) dismissal motion is based on,[9] but it says only that the court "may" treat the dismissal motion as a summary judgment motion. Rule 12(b) refers only to a motion based on paragraph (6), the motion to dismiss for failure to state a claim, and it says that if "matters outside the pleading are presented to and not excluded by the court, the motion shall be treated as one for summary judgment. . . ." The operative federal verb is "shall", as against New York's permissive "may". This has made Rule 12(b)(6) a much more prodigious worker than its New York counterpart, and it is sometimes the route used to raise by a pre-answer motion in a district court some of the other grounds listed in CPLR 3211(a) that do not have literal counterparts in Rule 12(b).

A motion to dismiss based on the statute of limitations, for example, which has no explicit authorization under Rule 12(b), may be treated as a motion for summary judgment on the authority of Rule 12(b) if evidence outside the pleadings is submitted to and considered by the court.[10]

If all the pleadings are in, the movant has the alternative of a motion for "judgment on the pleadings", which the Federal Rules of Civil Procedure offer in Rule 12(c).[11] Rule 12(c) also has a provision requiring the court to treat the motion as one for summary judgment when matters outside the pleadings are presented to and not excluded by the court, and this enables the Rule 12(c) motion for judgment on the pleadings to be used to raise by motion defenses not explicitly listed in Rule 12(b).[12]

Yet another motion possibility for a defense-based dismissal, before or after a responsive pleading has been served—assuming, if such a pleading has been served, that it duly raises and preserves the defense—is a direct motion for summary judgment under Rule 56. The summary judgment can be predicated on the defense as long as the defense is dispositive of the action.[13]

Rule 12(f) supplies a "motion to strike" various things. One is "any insufficient defense", and in this respect it corresponds to CPLR 3211(b)'s motion to dismiss a defense.[14] The other is "redundant, immaterial, impertinent, or scandalous matter", which makes it a corrective (rather than dispositive) motion, similar to but broader than its New York counterpart.[15] Rule 12(e) separately supplies another corrective motion, the motion for a more definite statement. This one is more closely allied to its New York analog[16] and has in common with it that the motion is available only to one required to respond to the objectionable pleading.

In New York practice, an objection to personal jurisdiction may be taken as a defense in the answer only if no prior dismissal motion was made: the making of the motion without joining the jurisdictional objection waives it.[17] The same is true of federal practice, from which this idea comes, but in federal practice the waiver occurs not only with respect to personal jurisdiction—covered in the trio of grounds contained in (2), (4), and (5) of Rule 12(b)—but also with the objection of improper venue, ground (3).[18] The grounds of failure to state a claim or defense or join an indispensable party, and of course the objection to subject matter jurisdiction, may be raised at any time, even at the trial.[19]

The Rule 12 dismissal motion is made within the answering time and before the defen-

---

9. CPLR 3211(c). See § 270 above.

10. See Gluck v. Amicor Inc., 487 F.Supp. 608 (S.D.N.Y.1980).

11. New York had such a rule before the CPLR, but abolished it. CPLR 3211, the motion to dismiss, and CPLR 3212, the motion for summary judgment, between them picked up the slack so effectively that the "judgment on the pleadings" rule has not been missed at all in New York practice.

12. See Falls Riverway Realty, Inc. v. City of Niagara Falls, 754 F.2d 49 (2d Cir.1985).

13. See Holm v. Shilensky, 388 F.2d 54 (2d Cir.1968).

14. The motion is discussed in § 269 above.

15. CPLR 3024(b).

16. CPLR 3024(a).

17. CPLR 3211(e). See § 274 above.

18. Rule 12(g), (h)(1).

19. See Rule 12(h)(2),(3), analogous in this respect to the corresponding grounds under CPLR 3211(a) and (b). See § 274 above.

dant answers. The mere making of the motion extends the answering time,[20] at least with respect to the claim moved against. If there are several claims and the motion is not made against the others, the movant who has not the indulgence of the other side or an enlargement of time from the court can answer the other claims while the motion pends. If the practice of the individual judge is to require the "conferencing" of such motions,[21] an advantage of the conference, if the motion then goes forward, is that it offers the movant an opportunity to have the judge regulate these things.

If the motion is denied, the defendant can serve an answer "within 10 days after notice of the court's action".[22] The Federal Rules make it the clerk's obligation to serve notice of the entry of the order,[23] but because this rule may not be followed in a given district it is always a good idea for a movant to keep abreast of entries through inquiry at the clerk's office.

The summary judgment motion is governed in detail by Rule 56. Its function is essentially the same as that of its New York counterpart, CPLR 3212: not to resolve issues of fact, but to determine whether any genuine issues of fact exist.[24] The summary judgment remedy is no less "drastic" in federal than in state practice. It will ordinarily put an end to the case as effectively as a judgment on the merits and the movant therefore bears the usual "heavy burden of demonstrating the absence of any material issues of fact".[25]

In federal practice, the summary judgment motion does not have to await the joinder of issue, as it does in New York practice under CPLR 3212.[26] But it has in common with its

New York counterpart that it can be addressed to all or part of the case.

H. DISCOVERY

Table of Sections

§ 636. Discovery, In General

Discovery is the preoccupation of federal litigation practice, consuming much of the time and effort of the parties and their lawyers, and—often to their chagrin—of the judges as well. The subject is governed by Rules 26 through 37 of the Federal Rules of Civil Procedure, and it was the federal rules that set the liberal disclosure standards for the country.

Much of the New York disclosure article, Article 31 of the CPLR, is modeled on the federal rules, which continue to exert their influence. A recent example is the longstanding federal practice of requiring the updating of previously made disclosures.[1] New York had no such supplementation requirement but finally adopted one in 1994, when a new subdivision (h), added to CPLR 3101, took effect.[2]

Of course a number of differences remain. In this and the next three sections we paint the federal disclosure picture in broad strokes, concentrating only on the highlights, emphasizing the differences, and omitting details. A New York deposition requires at least 20 days notice, for example,[3] while the federal counterpart provides only for "reasonable notice",[4] and a "request" seeks a document from a party under the federal provision[5] while a "no-

---

20.   FRCP Rule 12(a).

21.   See §§ 610, 634, above.

22.   Rule 12(a).

23.   FRCP Rule 77(d).

24.   See § 278 et seq.

25.   Eastway Constr. Corp. v. City of New York, 762 F.2d 243, 249 (2d Cir.1985).

26.   See § 279 above. The time for the motion in federal practice is governed by subdivisions (a) and (b) of Rule 56.

§ 636

1.   FRCP Rule 26(e).

2.   See § 352A above.

3.   CPLR 3107.

4.   FRCP Rule 30(b)(1).

5.   FRCP Rule 34(a).

tice" does it under the New York provision.[6] Details of that kind are plain on the face of the relevant rules and will not be touched on at all.

That it still takes four sections just for an overview of discovery is some indication of the subject's size. In this section the subject is introduced and a few preliminaries noted. The next three sections handle the criteria for discovery and discuss the matters excluded (§ 637), the various discovery devices (§ 638), and protective orders and sanctions (§ 639). The discovery rules have undergone extensive revision in recent years and there are helpful Advisory Committee notes on the amendments.[7]

New York's Article 31 is captioned "Disclosure", and that's the word New York lawyers usually use to describe the overall subject, with the word "discovery" usually connoting only the device used for document production.[8] The word favored in federal practice to describe the whole subject is "discovery", and that had in fact been the word used in the caption of Rule 26, the opening rule on the subject. A 1993 amendment of Rule 26 changed the caption from "General Provisions Governing Discovery" to add a semicolon and the phrase "Duty of Disclosure", but with the "Disclosure" reserved for the new practice, also introduced in the 1993 amendments, of requiring the furnishing of certain information by the parties without awaiting either a notice or a court order (a practice for which New York has no counterpart). This is known as the "mandatory disclosure" requirement in federal practice.[9] To many federal lawyers the two terms now have different connotations, "disclosure" used for the mandatory disclosures that Rule 26(a) requires and "discovery"

connoting the usual furnishing of information and documents pursuant to notices and court orders.

For a number of matters, some of them fundamental, the practitioner will once again have to turn to the rules of the individual courts and even of the individual judges for guidance. A perusal of the local rules jointly adopted by the Southern and Eastern districts in New York show the wide range of topics that the rules cover in civil procedure generally and for discovery in particular.[10]

The pretrial conference[11] is used in varying degrees by federal judges to get the attorneys before them early to confer on a number of points, enumerated in an expansion of the rule effected by amendments in 1983 and 1993. The failure to cooperate in participating in the pretrial conference or in carrying out orders issuing out of it can invoke sanctions, including money sanctions that contain attorneys' fees.[12]

Rule 26(f), another provision amended in 1993, mandates a "planning" session that the parties are expected to arrange for on their own and in which they are expected to arrange for the mandatory disclosure required by Rule 26(a)(1) as well as "to develop a proposed discovery plan" addressed to items that the rule then enumerates.

In federal practice, all requests, responses, and objections to discovery must be signed by one of the attorneys of record individually. This is a specific requirement of Rule 26(g) and it matches the requirement that Rule 11 imposes on motions and papers generally in federal litigation. The signing is the attorney's certificate that the position taken is tenable. It leads to sanctions if the court finds that it is

---

6. CPLR 3120(a).

7. They are reprinted following the respective rules in the Federal Rules of Civil Procedure segment of 28 U.S.C.A.

8. CPLR 3120.

9. The initial reaction of the New York federal courts to the mandatory disclosure requirement is noted in SPR 12:1. Rule 26(a) itself enables a district court, by rule, to opt out of the mandatory disclosure requirement and to allow a judge to cancel it by order. See § 638 below.

10. The numbering system in the Southern/Eastern districts compilation has been made to parallel the provisions of the Federal Rules of Civil Procedure pertaining to the same subject matter, which has proved a boon to practitioners.

11. FRCP Rule 16.

12. FRCP Rule 16(f).

not.[13]

The equivalent in New York practice came about in 1998 with the general signing requirement adopted by Rule 130–1 for all papers in litigation, and with the sanctions of that rule available for infractions.[14]

§ 637. Discovery Criteria and Excluded Areas

The broad and general criterion in federal practice is stated in FRCP Rule 26(b)(1), authorizing the discovery of

> any matter, not privileged, which is relevant to the subject matter involved in the pending action . . .

with the added remonstrance that

> the information sought need not be admissible at the trial if the information sought appears reasonably calculated to lead to the discovery of admissible evidence.

New York lawyers can recognize this generous standard. It's the one the drafters of the CPLR wanted to include in terms but which the legislature rejected. It applies in New York practice nevertheless, not in the same words— the New York phrase is the more restrictive "material and necessary" standard[1]—but through the construction made of that phrase in 1968 by the New York Court of Appeals in the leading case of Allen v. Crowell–Collier Publishing Co.[2]

It is thus the rule, and a pervasive one in federal practice, that the information sought need not itself be evidence; it is discoverable if it can merely *lead* to the discovery of admissible evidence. Relevancy is the theme, and

there is little in that criterion to offer refuge to one resisting disclosure.

For discovery from a nonparty, relevancy alone does not suffice in New York practice; additional requirements are imposed.[3] There are no such additional requirements imposed in federal practice, and this freer availability of discovery from nonparties is often cited as a factor when a lawyer with a choice of forum chooses a federal forum.[4]

The areas excluded from discovery in federal practice are similar to but not the same as those of New York.

Both systems exempt from discovery all "privileged" matter,[5] which imports for application to pretrial discovery the rules of privileged communication that would exclude the matter at the trial itself. This "privileged" exclusion is virtually absolute.[6] But in that other area of exclusion, materials "prepared in anticipation of litigation", there are some significant differences. Both practices use the quoted phrase to spell out an excluded category distinct from the "privileged" category, and in both practices the exclusion in this instance is only conditional. A showing of "substantial need" and "undue hardship" lifts the immunity and exposes the materials to discovery.[7] But in New York there is a rival category that the "litigation" materials must compete with: the "attorney's work product" of CPLR 3101(c), which has fortunately been underplayed by the New York courts and the system thereby spared what would otherwise have become a perennial thorn in disclosure practice.[8] The concern of the legislature, which is what keeps this separate "attorney's work product" on the books, is that without it the "litigation"

---

13. On Rule 11 sanctions, see § 631 and the last item on the list of choice of forum factors in § 616, above. This special sanction provision of Rule 26(g) is in addition to the general provision on disclosure sanctions, Rule 37, treated in § 639 below.

14. See § 414A above.

§ 637

1. CPLR 3101(a).

2. 21 N.Y.2d 403, 288 N.Y.S.2d 449, 235 N.E.2d 430 (1968). See § 344 above. On other fronts the New York courts did not have to exploit the federal model by using the construction route because the legislature took the initiative. Examples of specific New York adoptions of

federal discovery requirements are those pertaining to the identity of experts: CPLR 3101(d)(1)(i), modeled on what is now FRCP Rule 26(a)(2)(A); and the disclosure of liability insurance applicable in the case, CPLR 3101(f), modeled on what is now Rule 26(a)(1)(D).

3. CPLR 3101(a)(3),(4). See § 345 above.

4. See item 15 on the choice of forum list in § 616 above.

5. FRCP Rule 26(b)(1), CPLR 3101(b).

6. See § 346 above.

7. FRCP Rule 26(b)(3), CPLR 3101(d)(2).

8. See § 347 above.

materials might somehow violate the attorney-client privilege by revealing materials that the attorney's legal efforts have gone into. This apprehension was at all times unwarranted because of the distinct existence of the "privilege" category.

In federal practice, the courts have always been directed to guard against revealing an attorney's "mental impressions, conclusions, opinions or legal theories", should such ever be contained in any writing of which the court is otherwise disposed to allow disclosure, and it is through that instruction that the attorney-client privilege is sheltered. The quoted language, which comes from Hickman v. Taylor,[9] was later codified in FRCP Rule 26(b)(3) and then by New York in CPLR 3101(d)(2). The federal courts remain sensitive against the possible obscuring of the attorney-client privilege in the guise of the "materials" standard, with respect to individual and corporate parties both,[10] and they have found no need of a separate "attorney's work product" category to assist them.

The furnishing of written reports of experts, mandatory in federal practice,[11] is sometimes encumbered with conditions in New York practice,[12] a difference often deplored by federal and sister-state practitioners.

§ 638. The Discovery Devices

Federal practice has the same range of discovery devices that New York practice has. (The New York devices are listed in § 350.) And a simple notice or request is the usual method for bringing on the discovery. Actually, the devices generally come on through the parties' agreement, which is what the federal courts have struggled to encourage, with the agreed terms of a given discovery merely being confirmed in the notice or request. Scheduling

a deposition of an adverse party without at least trying to consult about mutual convenience is a discourtesy in any event.

The Federal Rules of Civil Procedure welcome stipulations by the parties to resolve almost all matters of discovery, even permitting them to "modify" what the rules otherwise require.[1] There are a few exceptions to that, in which the stipulation has to be approved by the court, but even in those instances the approval can occur through the common federal practice of the judge merely indorsing a "so ordered" on the stipulation. Stipulations to resolve discovery matters are usually welcome even for devices purporting to require a court order in first instance, such as the physical or mental examination of a party.[2]

Both federal and New York practice require a court order for initial discovery in only a few instances. An earlier section[3] goes over the New York list in detail. Among the instances requiring a court order in federal practice are the deposing of a prisoner,[4] discovery for the purpose of perpetuating testimony and other evidence before an action is brought,[5] or during the pendency of an appeal,[6] and discovery to aid in foreign litigation.[7] Some of these will be returned to below.

There is no prescribed sequence in the use of the discovery devices, and until recently no arbitrary limit in either New York or federal practice on the number of times a given device could be used, although the court's rules could prescribe a sequence or impose limits, and the court could do so on a case by case basis. The federal court is given explicit power to impose limits on the number and length of federal disclosure items,[8] and the FRCP itself imposes arbitrary limits—subject to court alteration—on the number of depositions[9] and the number

---

9.   329 U.S. 495, 67 S.Ct. 385, 91 L.Ed. 451 (1947).

10.   See Upjohn Co. v. United States, 449 U.S. 383, 101 S.Ct. 677, 66 L.Ed.2d 584 (1981).

11.   See FRCP Rule 26(a)(2).

12.   See §§ 348A and 362 above.

§ 638

1.   FRCP Rule 29.

2.   See FRCP Rule 35.

3.   Section 352.

4.   FRCP Rule 30(a)(2).

5.   FRCP Rule 27(a)(3).

6.   FRCP Rule 27(b).

7.   28 U.S.C.A. § 1782(a).

8.   FRCP Rule 26(b)(2).

9.   Under Rule 30(a)(2)(A), the limit is 10.

of written interrogatories.[10]

The federal requirement to supplement earlier responses[11] had no New York analog until subdivision (h) was added to CPLR 3101 in 1994, imposing a general supplementation requirement in New York practice. The federal rule requires supplementation of prior responses "at appropriate intervals ... if the party learns that in some material respect the information disclosed is incomplete or incorrect".[12] The New York supplementation requirement is discussed in an earlier section.[13]

A notable change made in the federal discovery rules in 1993, and the most controversial, is the introduction of the requirement of mandatory disclosure—disclosure required without a court order or even a demand by the adverse party. This requirement was imposed in an amendment of Rule 26(a)(1); it has no counterpart in New York practice.

Rule 26(a)(1) now says that "a party shall, without awaiting a discovery request, provide to other parties" all of the things contained on the list that then follows. That's just the basic list (there are yet other parts to the rule). The things on the list include (paraphrasing):

(A) the names and addresses of witnesses to relevant "discoverable information";

(B) copies, or descriptions and locations, of all documents and tangibles relevant to the case and possessed or controlled by the party;

(C) damages computations and the materials on which they are based; and

(D) any insurance agreement that may cover all or part of the judgment being sought.

The form of the mandatory disclosure is governed by paragraph (4) of Rule 26(a). Unless the court otherwise directs, the disclosures are to be made "in writing, signed, served, and promptly filed with the court".

None of the things of which Rule 26(a)(1) requires disclosure is unique. Everything listed is disclosable, and has been. What is unique is the rule's requirement that the disclosures be made without awaiting a request.

The mandatory disclosure rule applies "[e]xcept to the extent otherwise ... directed by ... local rule". That's in the very opening clause of Rule 26(a)(1). It gives each district the power to opt out of the rule and to continue disclosure on the usual basis of a party's demand or an order of the court. The rules of each court should be consulted to determine the particular district's position on this matter.[14]

We turn now to the individual federal discovery devices, stressing some points of contrast with their New York counterparts.

As in New York practice, the deposition on oral questions is one of the devices most commonly used.[15] The deposition on written questions is available,[16] but less popular, and for the same reasons that apply in New York practice.[17] Priority, the issue of who takes the other's deposition first, is generally with the defendant in New York practice, as long as the defendant seeks it expeditiously. This is spelled out obliquely by requiring the plaintiff to obtain a court order for another person's deposition if the plaintiff seeks it too soon after the summons has been served.[18] FRCP Rule 30(a)(1) did much the same thing before its 1993 amendment, but the amendment struck the provision so directing and even before the amendment there was not, in local federal practice, as strong an inclination to favor defendants in deposition priority as there is in New York state practice. The matter is sometimes even mentioned as another factor to consider in choosing a forum when there is concurrent federal and state jurisdiction.[19]

---

10. Under Rule 33(a), the limit is 25.

11. Rule 26(e).

12. Rule 26(e)(1).

13. See § 352A above.

14. See, e.g., the opt-out provision in Southern District Rule 26.4.

15. FRCP Rule 30.

16. FRCP Rule 31.

17. See § 359 above.

18. Otherwise the plaintiff needs no court order for a deposition. CPLR 3106(a). See § 354 above.

19. Section 616 contains an extensive list of choice of forum considerations.

In New York practice one often hears the deposition described as an "EBT", for "examination before trial". This terminology, not wholly accurate to begin with for the reason that depositions can take place at other time junctures,[20] is less often heard in federal parlance.

The prescribed means for recording a federal deposition had been by stenography, with the use of other means, such as audio or video tape recording, requiring either the parties' stipulation or a court order. A 1993 amendment permits the party taking the deposition to choose the method, including audio or video tape, subject to a court order directing otherwise.[21] In New York practice, the procedure of videotaping is prescribed by the rules,[22] but the issue of whether a party willing to pay for videotaping can insist on it over the objection of the opposing party is still being explored in the courts.[23]

Deposition by telephone is acknowledged as permissible in federal practice, but only by stipulation or court order.[24] The New York CPLR is silent on the matter but would presumably not preclude a telephone deposition if the parties volunteer for it or the court directs it.

For the deposition of a corporation, partnership, association, or government agency, the two practices appear to differ but the difference may be imaginary. On the federal side it is the corporation or other entity that designates who is to give the deposition in its behalf.[25] On the New York side a rule purports to allow the seeking party to designate the individual agent or employee who is to do the deposing for an adverse corporate party, but it sets forth a procedure whereby the corpora-

tion, through the service of a mere notice, can do the designating itself after all.[26]

Violations of disclosure and discovery requirements in federal practice and the sanctions they face are spread over two rules.[27] New York has a single sanctions provision for disclosure violations.[28]

Both practices provide for the perpetuation of testimony, such as the deposing of a person before an action is brought. While New York covers it in just a phrase included in a general statute,[29] a separate rule and more elaborate procedural instruction attends the matter in federal practice and includes the use of a verified petition to start the perpetuation machinery.[30] There is even a federal provision addressing the perpetuation of testimony while an appeal pends, anticipating that further proceedings may be necessary in the district court.[31] A New York court would have similar powers at the appellate stage, but they would have to be spelled out by implication from other provisions.[32]

Depositions and other discovery needed from sources outside the state, frequent enough in New York practice, are even more frequently encountered in the federal courts because of the greater role they play in national and international litigation. The rules on the federal side therefore tend to be more detailed on the subject than their New York counterparts. Both practices have rules prescribing the persons before whom depositions may be taken within the United States[33] or in a foreign country.[34] Two of the major devices for extrastate discovery, the commission and the letter rogatory, now called in federal practice a "letter of request",[35] are the subject of only a few words in the CPLR and not much more in the Feder-

---

20. See § 354 above.

21. Rule 30(b)(2).

22. See, e.g., Uniform Rule 202.15, applicable in the supreme and county courts.

23. See SPR 3:4.

24. Rule 30(b)(7).

25. FRCP Rule 30(b)(6).

26. CPLR 3106(d). See Commentary C3106:7 on McKinney's CPLR 3106.

27. Rules 26(g) and 37.

28. CPLR 3126.

29. CPLR 3102(c).

30. FRCP Rule 27(a).

31. FRCP Rule 27(b).

32. E.g., CPLR 3102(d), 3103.

33. FRCP Rule 28(a), CPLR 3113(a)(2).

34. FRCP Rule 28(b), CPLR 3113(a)(3).

35. The change was made in a 1993 amendment of Rule 28(b).

al Rules,[36] all procedural detail being left to the parties to work out on their own or for the court to prescribe in an order.

The use of these devices is freer in the federal courts, where it is not necessary to show, when applying for a commission or letter of request, that a conventional deposition would be "impracticable or inconvenient".[37] That kind of showing may be required in a New York court.[38]

The state department's aid can be elicited in the transmittal of a letter of request or letter rogatory,[39] but this is just an option.

The United States has subscribed to a detailed treaty entitled the "Convention on the Taking of Evidence Abroad in Civil or Commercial Matters", commonly known as the Hague Evidence Convention, applicable in both federal and state courts.[40] The convention also supplies procedures for obtaining evidence from abroad, including among other things the device of a letter of request. The parties may of course find the convention helpful, but the U.S. Supreme Court has held that it is not exclusive of the other extrastate discovery devices and it need not necessarily be resorted to before those devices are used. A foreign party within the court's jurisdiction, for example, can still be directed to disclose here materials in that party's control elsewhere.[41]

The federal equivalent of CPLR 3120, allowing discovery of documents and other tangible things and permitting entry onto land for discovery purposes, is Rule 34. Both provisions apply to discovery from parties. The New York rule prescribes a motion procedure for discovery against a nonparty.[42] Until 1991, in federal practice discovery from a nonparty witness

was not available independently of a deposition. It had to be pursued through a separate plenary action. With the adoption of a new Rule 45 of the Federal Rules of Civil Procedure, effective December 1, 1991, a separate action to obtain such discovery is no longer necessary.[43]

On the New York side, too, there has been recent amendment activity on the discovery device. Before 1994, each document sought had to be "specifically designated", while under Federal Rule 34(b) a request for document discovery could be made "by individual item or by category". The difference was pointed out by the First Department in Mendelowitz v. Xerox Corp.,[44] which noted that when discovery demands use words like "all", "all other", or "any and all", a kind of suspicion arose among New York judges that the specificity required by CPLR 3120 was lacking. Effective January 1, 1994, an amendment of CPLR 3120(a) allows discovery in New York practice to be sought by "category" of documents, adopting the federal practice in this respect.[45]

The interrogatories device, governed by Federal Rule 33, is more extensively exploited in the federal courts, to such a degree that there were periodic movements to impose some special limit on the number of interrogatories that could be used. One finally succeeded in late 1993, when a limit of 25 interrogatories was imposed, but with the court empowered to allow more if it sees fit.[46]

Interrogatories under the Federal Rules of Civil Procedure have no built-in restrictions of the kind that appear in their New York counterparts,[47] such as the requirement that in tort actions based on negligence a party must elect

---

36. See CPLR 3108, 3113(a)(3); FRCP Rule 28(b).

37. Rule 28(b).

38. See, e.g., Susan A. v. Steven J.A., 141 A.D.2d 790, 529 N.Y.S.2d 867 (2d Dep't 1988), involving visitation rights in a family dispute, a category in which the New York courts are especially watchful to minimize the expense of litigation. Compare Wiseman v. American Motors Sales Corp., 103 A.D.2d 230, 479 N.Y.S.2d 528 (2d Dep't 1984).

39. See 28 U.S.C.A. § 1781, which recognizes both terms.

40. The convention is set forth following 28 U.S.C.A. § 1781.

41. See Societe Nationale Industrielle Aerospatiale v. U.S. District Court, 482 U.S. 522, 107 S.Ct. 2542, 96 L.Ed.2d 461 (1987).

42. See CPLR 3120(b).

43. See Commentary C45–6 on Rule 45 in the 28 U.S.C.A. set.

44. 169 A.D.2d 300, 573 N.Y.S.2d 548 (1991).

45. See § 362, above, and SPR 9:2.

46. Rule 33(a).

47. CPLR 3130–3134.

between using interrogatories and a deposition.[48]

For physical and mental examinations in New York practice, no court order is required under CPLR 3121. A notice serves. The federal parallel[49] purports to require an order,[50] but in both practices the physical examination is especially the kind of thing the parties must work out by agreement. A "so ordered" on a stipulation is better than making the court work out the details.

The notice to admit of CPLR 3123 has its counterpart in the request for admission of FRCP Rule 36. Both provisions are self-contained instructions on the device, which is probably underused in both systems. Under the federal rule, a party may not object to a request to admit solely on the ground that it poses "a genuine issue"; the rule's preference even in that situation is that the party either deny or state why he can neither admit nor deny. There is no precise analogy for that under the New York provision, but it has been held in New York that matters that constitute "the very dispute of the lawsuit" do not lend themselves to the admission device,[51] and as a practical matter that's true of both systems.

The sanction for a violation of a request to admit in both practices is an order assessing against the wrongdoer the costs of proof of the matter—should the matter be proved—with an attorney's fee included.[52]

In New York practice, the provision for assisting foreign litigation by exacting discovery from local persons is CPLR 3102(e).[53] In federal practice the matter is governed by a statute,[54] but some procedure for it may be found addressed in local rules.

§ 639. Protective Orders and Sanctions

The protective order provision in the CPLR's disclosure article occupies its own section, CPLR 3103, and from that vantage point guards against abuses in the use of any of the disclosure devices.[1] The chief federal counterpart is in Rule 26(c), which bears the "protective orders" caption, but there are also protective order powers enumerated in Rule 26(b)(2). The two between them cover all the grounds, especially in view of the fact that while eight specific types of protective order are set forth in Rule 26(c), they are merely illustrative. They follow the rule's major statement that the court is empowered to make "any order which justice requires to protect a party or person from annoyance, embarrassment, oppression, or undue burden or expense, including one or more" of the eight listed.

In New York practice, the mere making of a motion for a protective order suspends all pending discovery on the matter affected.[2] The federal rules have no counterpart. In federal practice "it is not the filing of . . . a motion that stays the deposition, but rather a court order".[3] If the other side will not agree to suspend the discovery and there is any kind of emergency on the scene that requires a stay, the application for a protective order can be sought by an order to show cause.

In New York, disclosure is also automatically stayed upon the mere making of a motion to dismiss or for summary judgment.[4] Federal practice has no counterpart for this, and federal practitioners who occasionally find themselves in a New York court find the practice an irritant. In federal practice it takes an application to the court to suspend disclosure.[5]

In CPLR disclosure, the enforcement provisions consist chiefly of CPLR 3124 and 3126.

48. See CPLR 3130(1).

49. Rule 35.

50. Rule 35(a).

51. See § 364 above.

52. See FRCP Rule 37(c)(2), CPLR 3123(c).

53. See item 3 on the list in § 352.

54. 28 U.S.C.A. § 1782.

§ 639

1. See § 353 above.

2. CPLR 3103(b).

3. Federal Aviation Admin. v. Landy, 705 F.2d 624 (2d Cir.1983).

4. See CPLR 3214(b). An exception to this is where the dismissal motion is based on improper service, which does not invoke such an automatic suspension.

5. See, e.g., Hachette Distribution, Inc. v. Hudson County News Co., 136 F.R.D. 356 (E.D.N.Y.1991).

Under CPLR 3124, the seeking party is not in quest of sanctions, but only of an order compelling the disclosure that should have been offered without making a motion necessary in the first place.[6] The federal parallel to CPLR 3124 is subdivision (a) of Rule 37, the motion for an order "compelling disclosure or discovery". The use of both terms is designed to assure that the Rule 37 sanctions will be available for the violation of the mandatory disclosure requirement[7] as well as for refusals to comply with the usual discovery devices.[8] Rule 37(a) provides for imposing the expenses of the "compel" motion on the unsuccessful party, with an attorney's fee included,[9] creating a kind of presumption that whoever loses on the motion is the party responsible for generating it. Attempts to adopt a similar presumption in New York practice have not been successful.

It has become the habit in New York practice for a party objecting to another's recalcitrance in respect of disclosure not to stop off at CPLR 3124 to pick up a court order and make another try, but to move for a sanction directly under CPLR 3126 when a notice is disobeyed.[10] This is possible in New York practice because the sanctions of CPLR 3126 are available not only for the disobedience of a court order, but also for the wilful disobedience of a mere notice. Under a 1994 amendment of CPLR 3122, however, there is some doubt about whether a direct invocation of CPLR 3126 and its sanction provisions is available for a violation of CPLR 3120 or 3121, the discovery and physical and mental examination provisions. It is arguable that in those instances an interim stop has to be made at CPLR 3124 for an order directing the discovery or examination first, with a CPLR 3126 visit allowed only afterwards, should the CPLR 3124 order be disobeyed.[11]

On the federal side, under Rule 37(b), sanctions are available only for a failure to comply with an order. A stopover at Rule 37(a) for a court order may therefore be a prerequisite to the invocation of one of the Rule 37(b) sanctions, like a preclusion order or a default judgment, but under Rule 37(a) itself monetary assessments can be made against the party whose conduct comes into question.

In New York, most of the categories of sanction for disclosure offenses are contained in CPLR 3126;[12] subdivision (b) of Rule 37 is its main counterpart.

Among the federal sanctions that may be imposed under Rule 37(b) are the explicit three listed in CPLR 3126: the establishment order, the preclusion order, and the outright default.[13] But in both provisions the list is again merely illustrative, being introduced with the instruction that "the court in which the action is pending may make such orders in regard to the failure as are just ... among others the following...."[14] From the similar language in CPLR 3126 the New York courts have spelled out the remedy most commonly seen in the New York courts today: a second chance given to the recalcitrant party in a conditional order that also includes costs and an attorney's fee. Ironically, an application of one of the three enumerated sanctions, while seen from time to time, is rare.[15] Other subdivisions of Rule 37 cover other specific instances of discovery misconduct.[16]

CPLR 3126 does not list contempt as a sanction against a party; it deems the other remedies, enumerated or implied, sufficient.[17] Treating a party as in contempt for a discovery violation does stand as a federal option against

---

6. See § 366 above.

7. The mandatory disclosure requirement is discussed in § 638 above.

8. See amended Rule 37(a)(2)(A).

9. FRCP Rule 37(a)(4).

10. See § 367 above.

11. See § 366, above, and SPR 10:1–2.

12. There is some overlap, however, with the protective order provision of CPLR 3103, which has also been

found a source of sanctions for some categories of disclosure wrongdoing. See Lipin v. Bender, 193 A.D.2d 424, 597 N.Y.S.2d 340 (1st Dep't 1993), noted in SPR 6:1.

13. See subparagraphs (A), (B), and (C) of Rule 37(b)(2), paralleling subdivisions 1, 2 and 3 of CPLR 3126.

14. FRCP Rule 37(b)(2).

15. See § 367 above.

16. See subdivisions (c) and (d) of Rule 37.

17. See Commentary C3126:4 on McKinney's CPLR 3126.

a party under Rule 37.[18]

In both practices, contempt of court is of course the remedy against a nonparty witness, against whom the other enumerated civil sanctions would not be meaningful. Subpoenas are served on nonparty witnesses to obtain discovery,[19] and these of course ground the contempt remedy, should it prove necessary.

Reasonable expenses and attorney's fees may be assessed against the wrongdoer instead of or in addition to the enumerated civil sanctions. On the federal side this is explicit.[20] On the New York side it is implied.[21]

In New York practice the disclosure sanctions are centralized in CPLR 3126. Only the notice to admit device has its own penalty built in: the penalty of paying the other side's expenses and an attorney's fee.[22] On the federal side, Rule 37 is not alone in authorizing sanctions. Rule 30(g) imposes a money sanction, for example, for a party's failure to attend and go forward at a deposition that he himself set up, or to which he failed to properly subpoena a witness (wasting the other parties' time). And for falsely certifying a discovery request, response, or objection, Rule 26(g) authorizes not only money penalties, but any "appropriate sanction".

I. REMEDIES, ORDERS, AND JUDGMENTS

Table of Sections

§ 640. Provisional Remedies

The four provisional remedies in New York are the attachment, the injunction, the receiv-

ership, and the notice of pendency (lis pendens), governed by Articles 62–65 of the CPLR. Their general purposes and functions were treated earlier.[1] The order to seize a chattel in a replevin action, governed by Article 71 of the CPLR,[2] has features in common with a provisional remedy and is usually considered one for procedural purposes. We will consider it such here.

Some of the New York remedies apply in the federal courts; others have federal counterparts with independent instruction and do not use New York law.

Rule 64 of the Federal Rules of Civil Procedure adopts from state law "all remedies providing for seizure of person or property", and includes among them

> attachment, garnishment, replevin, sequestration, and other corresponding or equivalent remedies, however designated and regardless of whether by state procedure the remedy is ancillary to an action or must be obtained by an independent action.

The attachment[3] and replevin entries on the list make Articles 62 (attachment) and 71 (replevin) of the New York CPLR applicable in the federal court.

One does see Article 71 used in federal actions,[4] but not often, and certainly not as often as Article 62 is used, the order of attachment. One reason is that the attachment applies in money actions, which proliferate in the federal courts as they do in the New York courts, while the action to recover a chattel is less common. Another reason is that even when an action involving a chattel is brought in a federal court, the controversy will almost invariably concern a chattel of far greater value than the run of chattels met in New York replevin actions, and a chattel of great value is likely to

---

18. FRCP Rule 37(b)(2)(D).

19. See CPLR 3106(b), FRCP Rule 30(a).

20. FRCP Rule 37(b)(2).

21. The implication comes from the "such orders . . . as are just" language of CPLR 3126.

22. CPLR 3123(c).

§ 640

1. See § 306 et seq.

2. See § 337 et seq., above.

---

3. A distinct attachment provision, with its own instructions, is the maritime attachment supplied in admiralty actions by Rule B of the supplemental admiralty rules annexed to the Federal Rules of Civil Procedure. See the Advisory Committee's notes on those rules.

4. See, e.g., Honeywell Information Systems, Inc. v. Demographic Systems, Inc., 396 F.Supp. 273 (S.D.N.Y. 1975).

be unique, irreplaceable by mere money. For a unique chattel, equitable relief is available, and when the person seeking the chattel frames the complaint in equity—to put an end to this string of deductions—the provisional remedy that becomes relevant, if any at all does, is the injunction rather than the order to seize a chattel. Hence the infrequent appearance of Article 71 in federal actions.

Turning to the four provisional remedies in their CPLR sequence, and how they or their counterparts fare in the federal courts, the attachment comes first.

Article 62 of the CPLR, in point of procedure the most detailed and demanding of the provisional remedies, applies in the federal courts, supplying the grounds for the attachment[5] and the procedural minutiae as well. As earlier noted and stressed, there are numerous time periods in the attachment article, some of which carry jurisdictional consequences if overlooked.[6] CPLR 6213, for example, provides that when the attachment is granted before service is made, the service must be made within 60 days after the grant or the attachment becomes void.

In New York practice in the supreme court, the filing of the summons and complaint marks commencement of the action;[7] in federal practice, the filing of the complaint marks it.[8] In both practices, the summons and complaint must be served on the defendant within 120 days after the initial filing.[9] The plaintiff securing an attachment must see to service of the summons and complaint within the 60 days after the granting of the attachment regardless of where the 120–day period may stand. If the action has just been filed, for example, the plaintiff, in order to preserve the attachment, will lose just about half of the 120–day time period that would otherwise be available for service. Service made within the 120 days but beyond the 60 days will suffice to

secure jurisdiction of the defendant, but will forfeit the attachment.

Similar diligence should be pursued in fulfilling the other time periods of Article 62. The 90–day period for perfecting the attachment, for example, can carry jurisdictional consequences when missed.[10] Constitutional considerations as well may be exerting pressure when the attachment is initially granted ex parte, thus requiring a prompt follow-up motion on notice.[11]

For the preliminary injunction (the injunction pendente lite), the second of the provisional remedies on the New York list, one does not see the federal courts following the New York provisions, contained in Article 63 of the CPLR. This is in contrast to the attachment. The Federal Rules have their own provision for the preliminary injunction—Rule 65 of the Federal Rules of Civil Procedure—and practice on the preliminary injunction and on its important adjunct, the temporary restraining order, comes from that rule and not from state practice. In common to both practices, of course, is that spelling out a context in which an injunction will even be entertained is not the contribution of any statute or rule; it comes from the massive body of caselaw known as "equity".[12] The requirement of a showing that the plaintiff has no adequate remedy at law, for example, a traditional prerequisite for equitable intervention, is the subject of cases going back centuries. Even phrases included in the statutes and rules themselves, like the "immediate and irreparable injury" standard found in both the federal and New York provisions on the temporary restraining order,[13] are essentially only borrowings from this historic caselaw.

Hence it is also true, and true of both systems, that reported cases involving injunctions continue to be sui generis exercises to determine whether an injunction is warranted on the facts of the particular case. In contrast to

---

5. CPLR 6201.

6. See §§ 318–322 above.

7. See §§ 45, 60, and 63 above.

8. FRCP Rule 3.

9. CPLR 306–b; FRCP Rule 4(m).

10. See § 321 above.

11. See § 315 above.

12. See §§ 327–328 above.

13. FRCP Rule 65(b); CPLR 6301, 6313(a).

cases on attachment, they rarely entail constructions of the governing statutes or rules.

Because of the equitable nature of the injunction, in neither system will it issue if it appears that money damages will make the plaintiff whole.[14]

In both practices the preliminary injunction itself—the device that puts the restraint on the defendant during the entire pendency of the action—must be on notice,[15] and must be bonded.[16] And in both practices the stickiest problem is the restraint sought to cover the brief time that it takes to bring the motion for a preliminary injunction on for a hearing. It is that brief interim that is serviced by the temporary restraining order, or TRO,[17] and practice with respect to the TRO in the federal and New York courts is not the same.

Although in both systems the applicable provision authorizes the granting of the TRO ex parte[18]—its usual housing is an order to show cause bringing on the motion for the preliminary injunction—the federal judges usually insist that at least informal notice be given to the attorney for the defendant, even if only by telephone.[19] The federal rule even requires that the plaintiff's lawyer certify what effort he made to give the other side notice of the TRO and the reasons why notice should be dispensed with.[20]

There are no such specific requirements in New York practice. As already noted on the roster of choice of forum factors,[21] federal practitioners who step only infrequently into the New York courts often complain—for the most part when they are representing defendants—of the relative ease with which a New York state judge will grant a TRO on ex parte papers without any attempt at notice at all. Annual efforts to amend the CPLR to alter

that, and to adopt the federal practice, have so far not succeeded.

It should be observed that this giving of notice to the other side's attorney at the very outset of the action is possible only when the plaintiff's lawyer knows or can ascertain who the defendant's attorney is. In federal practice, and certainly in sizable commercial cases in the federal courts, the lawyers may know about each other because the parties will often have law firms on regular retainer. In the average case met in the state court system there is no such knowledge, and without it the practice of notifying the opposing lawyer of a TRO application is not likely to work. To notify the party instead of the lawyer, on the other hand, has high potential for encouraging conduct of the very kind the TRO is designed to prevent.

If a TRO is granted, it lasts in New York practice until the preliminary injunction hearing. There is no explicit time limit that the court has to put on it, although the statute requires that the preliminary injunction hearing be set for "the earliest possible time",[22] as the federal rule also does. But the federal rule also has a time limit: the TRO cannot survive for more than 10 days unless extended for a like period.[23]

This difference becomes a sensitive point in a New York state court action that has been removed to a federal court while a state-granted TRO is outstanding. Assume that at the moment of removal, the TRO may have several weeks to run under the terms imposed by the state court. Those several weeks will be cut back to the federal 10 days when the case is removed, measured from the removal itself.[24] The plaintiff must be ever alert to this, so as to take whatever steps are necessary to satisfy the now-applicable federal requirements and assure that the TRO does not lapse

---

14. See § 327 above. Jackson Dairy, Inc. v. H.P. Hood & Sons, Inc., 596 F.2d 70 (2d Cir.1979).

15. FRCP Rule 65(a)(1); CPLR 6311(1).

16. FRCP Rule 65(c); CPLR 6312(b).

17. See § 330 above.

18. FRCP Rule 65(b); CPLR 6313.

19. See the Advisory Committees notes on the 1966 amendment of Rule 65.

20. FRCP Rule 65(b).

21. See § 616 above.

22. CPLR 6313(a).

23. FRCP Rule 65(b).

24. See Granny Goose Foods, Inc. v. Brotherhood of Teamsters, 415 U.S. 423, 94 S.Ct. 1113, 39 L.Ed.2d 435 (1974).

before the preliminary injunction hearing comes on. The matter should be brought to the federal court's attention promptly after removal so that a hearing can be set or other steps taken to preserve the TRO.

This alertness in removal cases should extend to all of the provisional remedies. And it should extend as well to the converse situation—that in which the federal law itself has no arbitrary time limit in point, but the state law has. An example is where state law puts an arbitrary time limit on a device, and the time is running when the removal occurs, as can often happen with an attachment, for example. Whatever it is that has to be done during that period—e.g., perfection of a levy of an attachment order within 90 days after the levy is made[25]—should be done within that period even if the case has now arrived in a federal court.

Returning to the injunction device, we note that the furnishing of security (a bond) is mandatory for the preliminary injunction in both systems. For the TRO, however, while the general rule on the federal side is that a bond is mandatory for the TRO as well,[26] and will only rarely be dispensed with, the New York CPLR leaves a bond in connection with a TRO entirely to the court's discretion.[27]

When an application for a preliminary injunction arrives before the court, it will usually be decided on papers alone in New York practice while an actual testimonial hearing frequently occurs in the federal court. This live hearing may duplicate some of the evidence likely to be adduced at the trial itself, of course, so, recognizing the possible duplication, the federal rule allows the court to advance the trial of the action on the merits and consolidate it with the hearing on the injunction application,[28] which can of course amount to quite a preference for the case. And even

without those steps, the federal rule makes part of the record all the evidence put in at the injunction hearing so as to dispense with repeated proof of the same matter if it is tried before the same judge later.

The third of the CPLR-denominated provisional remedies is the provisional receivership of CPLR Article 64. In common with the preliminary injunction, it does not depend on state law for use in a federal court. In respect not only of the procedure applicable to the receivership, but also of the very grounds for appointing a receiver, federal practice has its own provisions. These are found in both statute[29] and rule,[30] and the practitioner must look to those provisions and to the caselaw on them for receivership answers. Article 64 of the CPLR is a negligible commodity in the federal courts.

The same is not true of the notice of pendency, however—the popular "lis pendens" used in real property actions.[31] The Federal Rules of Civil Procedure deliberately omitted a rule on the lis pendens, for the stated reason that "this would appear to be a matter of substantive law affecting state laws of property".[32] That left governance to the doctrine of Erie v. Tompkins,[33] and *Erie* of course dictates the application of state law to the lis pendens in a federal court.[34] After that, Congress explicitly instructed that state law on the lis pendens be followed for federal actions as long as the state system makes its lis pendens provisions available for federal use,[35] which New York does.[36] The result is that Article 65 of the CPLR applies in the federal courts, and when real property in New York state is involved in the federal action the article can of course be quite an aid.

The filing of the lis pendens (with a complaint accompanying it) must be made with the county clerk of the county in which the

---

25. See § 321 above.

26. FRCP Rule 65(c).

27. CPLR 6313(c).

28. FRCP Rule 65(a)(2).

29. 28 U.S.C.A. § 959.

30. FRCP Rule 66.

31. See §§ 334–336 above.

32. See the Advisory Committee note on Rule 64.

33. 304 U.S. 64, 58 S.Ct. 817, 82 L.Ed. 1188 (1938).

34. See Frederick v. Baxter Arms Corp., 39 F.Supp. 609 (E.D.N.Y.1941).

35. 28 U.S.C.A. § 1964.

36. CPLR 6501.

real property is located,[37] for only from that vantage point does it put the world on notice of the plaintiff's pending action. But even though the county clerk's office is a state office, such court applications as have to be made with respect to the lis pendens, such as a motion to cancel it under CPLR 6514, must be made to the federal court in which the action is pending, not to a state court.[38]

Generally speaking, all of these remedies and the provisions that go with them apply in federal actions without regard to the basis on which subject matter jurisdiction rests. They are not limited to diversity of citizenship cases. The provisions of Rule 64, for example, employing state law for attachments, like Rule 4(k)(1)(A) and its embrace of state bases of extraterritorial jurisdiction, do their adopting of state law independently of the *Erie* doctrine.

§ 641. Orders and Judgments; Entry, Vacatur, Enforcement

In highlighting only a few of the more important differences between New York and federal practice, the first thing to note is the different practice in the service of notice of entry of a judgment or order.

In New York practice the prevailing party ordinarily serves the notice of entry.[1] In federal practice, while a party is permitted to serve notice of entry of a judgment or order, the official burden of serving it is on the clerk, at least theoretically.[2] An important corollary is the time to take an appeal, which in New York practice runs from the time the loser is served with the notice of entry.[3] In federal practice the appeal period runs from the time of entry itself, not from the service of the notice of entry.[4] As noted earlier,[5] this may be less important in respect of interlocutory orders in

federal practice, which are usually not appealable anyway,[6] but it is all important when an appeal is sought from the final judgment. In federal practice the loser must keep closer track of anything entered; he cannot sit back and wait to be served with a notice of entry.

For the preparation, form, and mechanics of submitting and entering orders and judgments, local rules should be consulted,[7] and it may sometimes save time if they are consulted first.

A federal judgment can be made a lien against real property, but under New York law, which governs this even for federal court judgments, the judgment has to be docketed with the county clerk's office of the real property county.[8] There was earlier discussion of these docketing procedures, including the procedure for converting a federal judgment into a New York judgment for lien and enforcement purposes.[9]

A key provision in New York practice is CPLR 5015, which supplies the grounds for vacating a judgment or order. The counterpart of CPLR 5015, and in large measure its model, is Rule 60(b) of the Federal Rules of Civil Procedure, a rule frequently relied on. Rule 60(b)'s enumerated grounds for vacating judgments parallel those on the New York list, which were extensively reviewed earlier.[10] Under the federal provision, a paragraph (6) adds a catch-all category, allowing vacatur for "any other reason [than the five previously listed grounds] justifying relief from the operation of the judgment". This may at first suggest that there are more bases under the federal than the New York provision for vacating a judgment, but the New York list is not exhaustive and reasons other than those listed may also

---

37. CPLR 6511(a).

38. See, e.g., Cayuga Indian Nation of New York v. Fox, 544 F.Supp. 542 (N.D.N.Y.1982).

§ 641

1. See §§ 250 and 418 above.

2. FRCP Rule 77(d).

3. See § 533 above.

4. See Rule 4(a) of the Federal Rules of Appellate Procedure.

5. See § 634 above.

6. See § 642 below.

7. See, e.g., Civil Rule 77.1 of the Southern and Eastern district rules.

8. CPLR 5018(b).

9. See § 422 above.

10. See § 426 et seq.

be accepted,[11] making the two practices parallel in this regard as well.

Under the New York provision, only the ground of excusable default carries a specific time limit for the vacatur motion: one year.[12] Under the federal provision, the first three grounds carry a one-year limit: excusable default, newly discovered evidence, and fraud or other misconduct. A reasonable time, measured on a case by case basis, applies to the latter two in New York practice. Under both rules, a vacatur sought on the ground of want of jurisdiction has no time limit at all.

The stay of enforcement of the judgment is governed by Rule 62 of the Federal Rules of Civil Procedure, including provisions for a stay pending appeal, which in New York is governed by CPLR 5519. Rule 62 also allows the alternative of a stay under state law if the judgment has become a lien on the defendant's property.[13]

For the enforcement of money judgments, the CPLR has an extensive set of provisions in Article 52. The chapter on the enforcement of money judgments[14] goes through the many and varied devices that New York enlists in that cause.[15] Most of the chapter applies in the federal courts as well as in the state courts through the skimpy Rule 69 of the Federal Rules of Civil Procedure. After briefly listing a writ of execution as the process to enforce a federal money judgment, Rule 69(a) goes on to adopt the whole panoply of enforcement devices used in the state in which the federal court sits, thereby relieving the federal rules of the burden of legislating on this demanding subject. Says Rule 69(a):

The procedure on execution, in proceedings supplementary to and in aid of a judgment, and in proceedings on and in aid of execution shall be in accordance with the practice

and procedure of the state in which the district court is held.

For discovery in aid of enforcement, for which New York provides in CPLR 5223 and 5224,[16] the rule authorizes the use of either the state devices or the discovery devices of the Federal Rules of Civil Procedure, which can be even more generous than their New York counterparts.[17]

This sweeping adoption of state law for enforcing judgments makes applicable in the federal courts not only the devices themselves but also the state rules about what property is subject to enforcement, who is a proper garnishee, how the judgment is made a lien on real or personal property, and like matters.

As for the execution device itself, it is only one of the devices on the New York list. As "process" of the court, it is issued by the clerk in federal practice and must be delivered for implementation to a federal marshal.[18] To obtain enforcement in other states, a certified copy of the judgment can be filed in another district, which makes the judgment the equivalent of one rendered in that district for enforcement purposes.[19]

The sale of real property on a levy of execution on a New York money judgment is governed by CPLR 5236. That provision governs on a levy of execution on a federal judgment as well. To be distinguished from a sale on execution is a sale of real property sold under a direct order or decree of the court, for which federal law makes special provision.[20]

It is the New York practice for the attorney to issue "process", which includes an execution and a subpoena, while the federal practice is to have the clerk issue them. Under the comprehensive appropriation that Rule 69 makes of state enforcement law, that ought to enable the attorney to do the issuing of the corresponding papers for federal enforcement

---

11. See the Commentary on McKinney's CPLR 5015.

12. The vacating of a default judgment is discussed in § 427 above.

13. Rule 62(f).

14. See § 485 et seq., above.

15. See § 492 et seq., above.

16. See § 509 above.

17. Rule 69(a). Sections 636–639, above, discuss discovery in federal practice.

18. See Rule 4.1, which also prescribes the geographical area within which the process may be served.

19. See 28 U.S.C.A. § 1963.

20. See 28 U.S.C.A. § 2001.

as well, but whether this is permissible has yet to be definitively determined.

Another reason for allowing the attorney to issue the relevant processes is that with just the flick of a paper, a federal judgment can be converted into a New York judgment. All the judgment creditor has to do is obtain a transcript of the federal judgment from the district court clerk and file it with any county clerk in the state. That converts the judgment into the equivalent of a supreme court judgment in the New York system and makes it fully enforcible as such, including the use of the sheriff's office instead of the federal marshal's for the levying of an execution.[21]

As in New York practice, contempt in the federal courts is the remedy for enforcing judgments requiring specific acts, i.e., equity judgments and orders,[22] with a monetary assessment made to carry out whatever mission, punitive or compensatory, is required.[23] Differences in the strength of the contempt remedy, especially in respect of criminal contempt, make the federal equity judgment more potent than its New York counterpart, as earlier noted in the section on choice of forum factors.[24]

J. APPEALS

Table of Sections

Sec.
642. Appeals to the Court of Appeals.

§ 642. Appeals to the Court of Appeals

In both New York and federal practice, the final judgment is appealable: on the state side from the supreme court to the appellate division under CPLR 5701(a)(1), on the federal side from the district court to the court of

appeals for the circuit under 28 U.S.C.A. § 1291.[1] It is in respect of the appeal from a nonfinal disposition (an interlocutory or intermediate order) that the two practices are diametrically opposed: in New York, virtually any such order can be appealed immediately and need not await the final judgment;[2] in federal practice, with only a few exceptions, the interlocutory disposition is not appealable. Of the exceptions, listed in subdivision (a) of § 1292 of Title 28, perhaps the best known is the order affecting an injunction.[3]

This pronounced difference in the two practices makes appealability one of the factors a lawyer considers in choosing a forum.[4]

There is also in federal practice what is known as the "collateral order" doctrine, pronounced in Cohen v. Beneficial Industrial Loan Corp.,[5] under which an order that does not finally dispose of the whole case, but of some right that is "separable from, and collateral to" the main issues in the action, may be treated as a final disposition in its own right and appealed immediately under § 1291. The *Cohen* case sets forth the criteria for measuring whether such a "collateral order" is at hand. Few orders qualify. Absent a definitive precedent already in point, whether an order is "collateral" often triggers a dispute.[6]

In addition to the few exceptions listed in § 1292(a), under which interlocutory orders may be appealed, there are two other procedures that can make possible the appeal of an interlocutory order. One is the so-called "certification" procedure that a district judge can make under subdivision (b) of § 1292; the other is a determination the judge can make under Rule 54(b) of the Federal Rules of Civil

---

21. See § 422 above.

22. FRCP Rule 70.

23. See, e.g., Perfect Fit Industries, Inc. v. Acme Quilting Co., 646 F.2d 800 (2d Cir.1981).

24. See item 17 on the list in § 616 above.

§ 642

1. Under subdivision (c) of 28 U.S.C.A. § 2072, added in 1990, the U.S. Supreme Court, through rules, can define the term "final" as used in § 1291. See the Commentary on 28 U.S.C.A. § 2072.

2. See § 526 above.

3. The Supreme Court can provide, by rule, for interlocutory appeals "not otherwise provided for" in the first four subdivisions of the section. See 28 U.S.C.A. § 1292(e), added in 1992. This permits the court to enlarge the list of appealable interlocutory determinations, but not curtail it. See House Report 102–1006, Part 1 (Oct. 3, 1992), p.18.

4. See item 9 on the list in § 616 above.

5. 337 U.S. 541, 69 S.Ct. 1221. 93 L.Ed. 1528 (1949).

6. See, e.g., Gulfstream Aerospace Corp. v. Mayacamas Corp., 485 U.S. 271, 108 S.Ct. 1133, 99 L.Ed.2d 296 (1988).

Procedure.[7] In both procedures the district judge can set the stage but the court of appeals has the final say as to whether the appeal will in fact be entertained.

For a § 1292(b) certification, the district judge has to find these three things and recite them in the order:

    1. the order involves "a controlling question of law";

    2. there is "substantial ground for a difference of opinion" on it; and

    3. an immediate appeal "may materially advance the ultimate termination of the litigation".

The initial judge of whether those three elements are present is the district judge; the ultimate judge is the court of appeals. The statute provides that it is still in the "discretion" of the court of appeals whether to entertain such an appeal, and the court can refuse to entertain it by disagreeing on any one of the three stated elements.[8] Indeed, it can refuse the appeal for any other reason or for no reason at all.

The procedure for a litigant who does obtain a § 1292(b) certification from a district judge is not to take an appeal yet, but to apply to the court of appeals for leave to appeal. The procedure for doing this is a petition for permission to appeal, and it must be filed within 10 days after the § 1292(b) order is entered in the district court.[9] Procedure in the event the petition is granted is prescribed by rule.[10] If the court of appeals does grant permission, it is not restricted to reviewing only the issue the district judge certified; it can carry its review into other matters as well if so disposed.[11]

Rule 54(b) is designed to solve a problem in cases in which there are multiple claims or parties. If the court renders a final decision on one but not all of the claims, the loser may be in a dilemma. If the decision is not "final" and hence not appealable because it does not dispose of the whole case, it cannot be appealed as a final determination under § 1291; the appeal will have to wait until the whole case is done with, and that may take a long time. If, on the other hand, the decision is final and appealable and the loser does not appeal it now, the time will run out and an appeal will be forfeited. Rule 54(b) is designed to enable the district judge to resolve the problem with a specific finding on the matter. If the judge makes an "express determination that there is no just reason for delay" and an "express direction for the entry of judgment",[12] the loser presumably knows that she can and must appeal now.

The Second Circuit disfavors Rule 54(b) certifications, however, and wants them saved for where there would otherwise be "hardship". The judge is therefore required to explain in the order why the certification is being made. The court has even indicated that it is incumbent on the district judge to "alert the parties to the invocation of Rule 54(b)", and has held that where the judge fails to do that, the appeal time will not be deemed to run from the earlier time, which means that it can be saved for appeal as part of the later, final disposition in the case.[13] This appears to be indulgent of the would-be appellant's dilemma, but in a given case it can lull an aspiring appellant into a false sense of security, making her guess whether or not what the judge has done is a proper Rule 54(b) certification. If it is a proper certification, and no appeal is taken, the right to appeal may be waived.

The propriety of a Rule 54(b) certification, like one made under 1292(b), is reviewable by the court of appeals, which can simply refuse to entertain the appeal.[14]

---

7. This is also referred to frequently as a "certification", so it is important, when using the term, to accompany it with mention of the section or rule relied on.

8. 28 U.S.C.A. § 1292(b).

9. See Rule 5(a) of the Federal Rules of Appellate Procedure. The Second Circuit ordinarily does not take oral argument on these applications. See Rule 5(b)(3) of the Second Circuit Rules.

10. See Rule 5(d) of the Federal Rules of Appellate Procedure.

11. See Capital Temporaries, Inc., of Hartford v. Olsten Corp., 506 F.2d 658 (2d Cir.1974).

12. FRCP Rule 54(b).

13. See Ansam Associates, Inc. v. Cola Petroleum, Ltd., 760 F.2d 442 (2d Cir.1985); Ginett v. Computer Task Group, Inc., 962 F.2d 1085 (2d Cir.1992).

Recognizing appealability difficulties met in class actions over the years, a 1998 amendment that added subdivision (f) to Rule 23 of the Federal Rules of Civil Procedure authorizes the court of appeals in its discretion to permit an appeal from an order that either grants or denies class certification to an action.

Unless one of the above situations is at hand, it is extremely difficult to circumvent the finality requirement and get a nonfinal disposition reviewed in federal practice. But it is not impossible. In certain exceedingly rare situations, a writ of mandamus or some other writ[15] may be sought from the court of appeals to undo a district judge's order. An illustration is in Thermtron Products, Inc. v. Hermansdorfer,[16] where, in disregard of a statute, a district judge remanded a case legitimately removed from a state court on the mere ground that his calendar was congested.[17]

If an order cannot be appealed independently for want of finality, it may be reviewed as part of an appeal from the final judgment later if it presents an issue of law and can be shown to affect the final outcome.[18]

In both court systems, the appellate court will of course review issues of law, but the New York appellate division has greater review powers over issues of fact. It reviews both the law and the facts and in effect stands in the shoes of the trial judge, doing whatever it thinks the trial judge should have done.[19] The federal court of appeals, on the other hand, will overturn an exercise of a district judge's discretion only when it finds this discretion to have been clearly abused. In a jury case, both courts will of course defer to the jury function, but even this deference is relative.[20] Perhaps the difference is most pronounced in a bench trial, where a federal rule provides that the fact findings of a federal judge "shall not be set aside unless clearly erroneous",[21] while in New York "the rule is that the Appellate Division is not so limited, that its authority is as broad as that of the trial court".[22]

The procedure to be followed in taking and perfecting an appeal is governed extensively by the Federal Rules of Appellate Procedure, and the lawyer should of course be alert as well to the rules of the courts of appeals. The Second Circuit has "Rules Supplementing Federal Rules of Appellate Procedure", even numbered to correspond to them.[23] Mentioning just a few fundamentals that get the appeal started and which have to meet tight time requirements: the time in which to appeal is 30 days, it runs from the entry of the judgment or order being appealed and not (as in New York practice) from the service of notice of entry on the appellant,[24] the taking of the appeal consists of filing a notice of appeal with the district court clerk,[25] and that clerk then serves copies of it on the other parties and transmits a copy to the clerk of the court of appeals.[26]

---

14. See Sears, Roebuck & Co. v. Mackey, 351 U.S. 427, 76 S.Ct. 895, 100 L.Ed. 1297 (1956).

15. These come from what is known in federal practice as the "all writs" statute, 28 U.S.C.A. § 1651, which gives all courts the power to issue writs "necessary or appropriate in aid of their respective jurisdictions".

16. 423 U.S. 336, 96 S.Ct. 584, 46 L.Ed.2d 542 (1976).

17. See § 619 above.

18. See Dow Chemical Pacific Ltd. v. Rascator Maritime, S.A., 782 F.2d 329 (2d Cir.1986).

19. See § 529 above.

20. See item 9 on the list of choice of forum factors in § 616 above.

21. FRCP Rule 52(a).

22. Northern Westchester Professional Park Associates v. Town of Bedford, 60 N.Y.2d 492, 470 N.Y.S.2d 350, 458 N.E.2d 809 (1983). See § 529 above.

23. The rules of the courts of appeals are published and updated annually as part of the 28 U.S.C.A. set.

24. Federal Rules of Appellate Procedure, Rule 4(a). Under a 1991 amendment, Rule 4(a)(6) gives the district court some discretion to reopen the appeal time when timely notice of entry is not received in certain narrow circumstances.

25. Id., Rule 3(a).

26. Id., Rule 3(d).

Appendix

RESEARCHING THE LAW OF NEW YORK PRACTICE ON WESTLAW®

Analysis

Section 1. Introduction

New York Practice, Third Edition, provides a strong base for analyzing even the most complex problem involving New York practice. Whether your research requires examination of rules, statutes, case law, expert commentary or other materials, West books and Westlaw are excellent sources of information.

To keep you abreast of current developments, Westlaw provides frequently updated databases. With Westlaw, you have unparalleled legal research resources at your fingertips.

Additional Resources

If you have not previously used Westlaw or have questions not covered in this appendix, see the *Westlaw Reference Manual* or call the West Group Reference Attorneys at 1–800–REF–ATTY (1–

800–733–2889). The West Group Reference Attorneys are trained, licensed attorneys, available 24 hours a day to assist you with your Westlaw search questions.

Section 2.   Westlaw Databases

Each database on Westlaw is assigned an abbreviation called an *identifier*, which you use to access the database. You can find identifiers for all databases in the online Westlaw Directory and in the printed *Westlaw Database Directory*. When you need to know more detailed information about a database, use Scope. Scope contains coverage information, lists of related databases and valuable search tips. To access Scope, click the **Scope** button while in the database.

The following chart lists Westlaw databases that contain information pertaining to New York practice. For a complete list of databases, see the online Westlaw Directory or the printed *Westlaw Database Directory*. Because new information is continually being added to Westlaw, you should also check the Welcome to Westlaw window and the Westlaw Directory for new database information.

Selected Westlaw Databases

Database	Identifier	Coverage
General Case Law		
New York Cases	NY–CS	
Court of Appeals		Begins with 1885
Supreme Court, Appellate Division		Begins with 1896
Supreme Court		Begins with 1888
Miscellaneous courts of record		Begins with 1888
New York State and Federal Cases	NY–CS–ALL	Varies by court
West's North Eastern Reporter®	NE	See dates above
Topical Case Law		
New York Business Organizations Cases	NYBUS–CS	Begins with 1885
New York Civil Rights Cases	NYCIV–CS	Begins with 1885
New York Commercial Law & Contracts Cases	NYCML–CS	Begins with 1885
New York Criminal Justice Cases	NYCJ–CS	Begins with 1885
New York Education Cases	NYED–CS	Begins with 1885
New York Business Energy Cases	NYEN–CS	Begins with 1885
New York Environmental Law Cases	NYENV–CS	Begins with 1885
New York Environment Cases and Administrative Materials	NYENV	Varies by source
New York Estate Planning & Probate Cases	NYEPP–CS	Begins with 1885
New York Family Law Cases	NYFL–CS	Begins with 1885
New York Finance & Banking Cases	NYFIN–CS	Begins with 1885
New York Government Benefits Cases	NYGB–CS	Begins with 1885
New York Government Contracts Cases	NYGC–CS	Begins with 1885
New York Health Law Cases	NYHTH–CS	Begins with 1885
New York Insurance Cases	NYIN–CS	Begins with 1885

Database	Identifier	Coverage
New York Labor & Employment Cases	NYLB–CS	Begins with 1885
New York Legal Ethics & Professional Responsibility Cases	NYETH–CS	Begins with 1885
New York Pension & Retirement Benefits Cases	NYPEN–CS	Begins with 1885
New York Products Liability Cases	NYPL–CS	Begins with 1885
New York Professional Malpractice Cases	NYMAL–CS	Begins with 1885
New York Public Employee Reporter	NY–PER	Begins with 1982
New York Public Utilities Reports	NY–PUR	
Headnotes to cases and administrative decisions from *Public Utilities Reports*		Begins with 1953
Full-text coverage from *Public Utilities Reports*		Begins with 1974
Supplemental coverage from New York Public Service Commission		Begins with 1984
Cases from West National Reporter System		Begins with 1930
New York Real Property Cases	NYRP–CS	Begins with 1885
New York Securities & Blue Sky Law Cases	NYSEC–CS	Begins with 1885
New York Taxation Cases	NYTX–CS	Begins with 1885
New York Taxation Cases and Administrative Materials	NYTAX	Varies by source
New York Tort Law Cases	NYTRT–CS	Begins with 1885
New York Workers' Compensation Cases	NYWC–CS	Begins with 1885
New York Workers' Compensation Law Reporter	NY–WCLR	Begins with 1990
Court Filings		
Court of Appeals of New York–New Filings	NY–NEWAPP	Begins with March 1995
CourtLink Dockets–New York County Clerk Records	NY–CTYCK–DOCK	Begins with November 1985
CourtLink Dockets–New York Judgment Docket and Lien Book Records	NY–JL–DOCK	Varies by county
CourtLink Dockets–New York Supreme Court Civil Cases	NY–SCT–DOCK	Varies by county
Rules and Orders		
New York Court Rules	NY–RULES	Current data
New York Court Orders	NY–ORDERS	Current data
Statutes and Regulations		
New York Statutes–Annotated	NY–ST–ANN	Current data
New York Statutes–Annotated (historical) 1987, 1989–1997	NY–STANNYY (where YY is the last two digits of a year, e.g., NY–STANN95)	Individual year
New York Statutes–Unannotated	NY–ST	Current data

Database	Identifier	Coverage
New York Statutes–General Index	NY–ST–IDX	Current data
New York Legislative Service	NY–LEGIS	Current data
New York Bill Tracking–Summaries and Full Text Combined	NY–BILLS	Current data
New York Administrative Code	NY–ADC	Current data
New York City Administrative Code	NYC–CODE	Current data
New York City Rules and Regulations	NYC–RULES	Current data
New York Regulation Tracking	NY–REGTRK	Current data
New York Environmental, Health and Safety Regulations	ENFLEX–NY	Current data

Administrative and Executive Materials

Database	Identifier	Coverage
New York Attorney General Opinions	NY–AG	Begins with 1977
New York Comptroller Opinions	NY–CPTR	Begins with 1977
New York Department of Health Administrative Review Board	NYDOH–ARB	Begins with 1990
New York Environmental Law Administrative Decisions	NYENV–ADMIN	
New York Department of Environmental Conservation		Begins with 1970
New York Freshwater Wetlands Appeals Board		Begins with December 1976
New York Environmental Records	EDR–NY	Current data
City of New York Commission on Human Rights	NYCCIV–ADMIN	Begins with 1970
New York City Corporation Counsel Opinions	NYC–CCO	Begins with 1980
New York City Taxation Administrative Decisions	NYCTX–ADMIN	
Finance hearing decisions and letter rulings		Begins with 1983
Opinions and determinations		Begins with 1993
New York City Taxation Administrative Guidance	NYCTX–ADG	Begins with 1982
New York Insurance Bulletins	NYIN–BUL	Begins with 1924
New York Public Employee Reporter	NY–PER	Begins with 1982
New York Public Utilities Reports	NY–PUR	
Headnotes to cases and administrative decisions from *Public Utilities Reports*		Begins with 1953
Full-text coverage from *Public Utilities Reports*		Begins with 1974
Supplemental coverage from New York Public Service Commission		Begins with 1984

Cases from West's National Reporter System®		Begins with 1930
New York Taxation Administrative Decisions	NYTX–ADMIN	
Decisions and opinion letters		Begins with 1978
Private letter rulings		Begins with April 1983
New York Taxation Administrative Guidance	NYTX–ADG	
Memoranda		Begins with 1978
Opinions of counsel		Begins with 1960
Stock Allocation Publication List		1995
Re–Insurance Allocation Percentage Listing		1996
New York Workers' Compensation Administrative Decisions	NYWC–ADMIN	Begins with 1985
New York Workers' Compensation Law Reporter	NY–WCLR	Begins with 1990

Ethics Opinions

New York Commission on Judicial Conduct–Disciplinary Opinions	NYETH–DISP	Begins with 1978
New York State Ethics Commission Advisory Opinions	NY–ETH	Begins with 1988
New York Legal Ethics & Professional Responsibility–Ethics Opinions	NYETH–EO	
New York State Bar Association Committee on Professional Ethics		Begins with 1977
New York County Lawyers' Association Committee on Professional Ethics		Begins with December 1979
The Association of the Bar of the City of New York Committee on Professional and Judicial Ethics		Begins with 1986
New York Advisory Committee on Judicial Ethics		Begins with 1987
City of New York Conflicts of Interest Board	NYC–ETH	
Advisory opinions		Begins with 1990
Rules		Current through August 1995

Public Information, Records and Filings

Dun & Bradstreet Business Records Plus–New York	NY–DUNBR	Current data
Executive Affiliation Records	EA–ALL	Current data
Name Availability Records	NA–ALL	Current data
New York Bankruptcy Records	NY–BKR	Varies by county
New York Business Finder Records	NY–BUSFIND	Current data
New York Department of State Corporations & Limited Partnerships	NY–CORP	Current data
New York "Doing Business As" Records	NY–DBA	Begins with January 1990
New York Lawsuit Records	NY–LS	Varies by court
New York Liens Filings	NY–LIENS	Varies by jurisdiction
New York Litigation Preparation Records	NY–LITPREP	Current data

Database	Identifier	Coverage
New York Motor Vehicle Records	NY–DMV	Current data
New York People Finder–Name Tracker Records	NY–PEOPLE	Current data
New York Real Property Assessors' Records	NY–RPA	Varies by county
New York Real Property Asset Transfers	NY–RPT	Varies by county
New York Real Property Refinances	NY–RPR	Varies by county
New York Uniform Commercial Code Records	NY–UCC	Current data
New York UCC, Liens/Civil Judgment Filings	NY–ULJ	Varies by source
Texts, Periodicals and Research Tools		
New York Journals & Law Reviews	NY–JLR	Varies by publication
New York Jurisprudence 2d	NYJUR	Current through November 1998 cumulative supplement
West's® McKinney's® Forms	NY–FORMS	Current data
West's McKinney's Forms–All Forms Indices	NYFORMSIDX–ALL	Current through July 1997
West's McKinney's Forms–Civil Practice Law and Rules Index	NYFORMSIDX–CPLR	Current through July 1997
Insurance Materials		
New York Insurance Statutes, Regulations and Bulletins	NYIN–COMBINED	Varies by source
Annotated New York Insurance Statutes	NYIN–ST	Current data
New York Insurance Administrative Code	NYIN–ADC	Current data
New York Insurance Administrative Code Supplement	NYIN–ADSUPP	Current data
New York Insurance Bulletins	NYIN–BUL	Begins with 1924
New York Insurance Cases	NYIN–CS	Begins with 1885
News, Current Events and Directories		
New York Criminal Law News	NYCLN	Full coverage begins with 1995 (vol. 1995, no. 7)
New York Law Journal	NYLJ	Begins with April 1990
New York News	NYNEWS	Varies by source
New York Papers	NYNP	Varies by source
New York Real Estate Law Reporter	NYRELR	Begins with March 1995
Westlaw State Bulletins–New York	WSB–NY	Current data
West Legal Directory™–New York	WLD–NY	Current data

Section 3.   Retrieving a Document with a Citation: Find and Hypertext Links

3.1   Find

Find is a Westlaw service that allows you to retrieve a document by entering its citation. Find allows you to retrieve documents from anywhere in Westlaw without accessing or changing databases. Find is available for many documents, including rules (state and federal), the *United*

States Code Annotated®, state statutes, case law (state and federal), administrative materials, texts and periodicals.

To use Find, simply access the Find service and type the citation. The following list provides some examples:

To Find This Document	Access Find and Type
Press v. County of Monroe, 50 N.Y.2d 695 (1980)	**50 ny2d 695**
McKinney's C.P.L.R. § 6211	**ny cplr 6211**
N.Y. Codes R. & Regs. tit. 4, § 207.1	**4 nycrr 207.1**

For a complete list of publications that can be retrieved with Find and their abbreviations, consult the Publications list. Click the **Publications** button after accessing Find.

3.2 Hypertext Links

Use hypertext links to move from one location to another on Westlaw. For example, use hypertext links to go directly from the statute, case or law review article you are viewing to a cited statute, case or article; from a headnote to the corresponding text in the opinion; or from an entry in a statutes index database to the full text of the statute.

Section 4. Searching with Natural Language: WIN—Westlaw is Natural

Overview: With WIN, you can retrieve documents by simply describing your issue in plain English. If you are a relatively new Westlaw user, Natural Language searching can make it easier for you to retrieve cases that are on point. If you are an experienced Westlaw user, Natural Language gives you a valuable alternative search method.

When you enter a Natural Language description, Westlaw automatically identifies legal phrases, removes common words and generates variations of terms in your description. Westlaw then searches for the concepts in your description. Concepts may include significant terms, phrases, legal citations or topic and key numbers. Westlaw retrieves the 20 documents that most closely match your description, beginning with the document most likely to match.

4.1 Natural Language Search

Access a database, such as New York Cases (NY–CS). If the Terms and Connectors Query Editor is displayed, click the **Natural Language** tab. In the *Natural Language Description* text box, type a Natural Language description such as the following:

what are the requirements for the application of collateral estoppel

4.2 Next Command

Westlaw displays the 20 documents that most closely match your description, beginning with the document most likely to match. If you want to view additional documents, click your right mouse button and choose **Go to Next 10 Documents** from the pop-up menu.

4.3 Natural Language Browse Commands

Best Mode: To display the best portion (the portion that most closely matches your description) of each document in your search result, click the **Best Section** arrow at the bottom of the window.

Standard Browsing Commands: You can also browse your Natural Language search result using standard Westlaw browsing commands, such as citations list, Locate, page mode and term mode. When you browse your Natural Language search result in term mode, the five portions of each document that are most likely to match your description are displayed.

Section 5. Searching with Terms and Connectors

Overview: With Terms and Connectors searching, you enter a query, which consists of key terms from your issue and connectors specifying the relationship between these terms.

Terms and Connectors searching is useful when you want to retrieve a document for which you know specific details, such as the title or the fact situation. Terms and Connectors searching is also useful when you want to retrieve documents relating to a specific issue. If the Natural Language Description Editor is displayed when you access a database, click the **Terms and Connectors** tab.

5.1 Terms

Plurals and Possessives: Plurals are automatically retrieved when you enter the singular form of a term. This is true for both regular and irregular plurals (e.g., **child** retrieves *children*). If you enter the plural form of a term, you will not retrieve the singular form.

If you enter the nonpossessive form of a term, Westlaw automatically retrieves the possessive form as well. However, if you enter the possessive form, only the possessive form is retrieved.

Automatic Equivalencies: Some terms have alternative forms or equivalencies; for example, 5 and *five* are equivalent terms. Westlaw automatically retrieves equivalent terms. The *Westlaw Reference Manual* contains a list of equivalent terms.

Compound Words, Abbreviations and Acronyms: When a compound word is one of your search terms, use a hyphen to retrieve all forms of the word. For example, the term **cross-claim** retrieves *cross-claim*, *cross claim* and *crossclaim*.

When using an abbreviation or acronym as a search term, place a period after each of the letters to retrieve any of its forms. For example, the term **c.p.l.r.** retrieves *cplr, c.p.l.r., c p l r* and *c. p. l. r.* Note: The abbreviation does *not* retrieve *civil practice law and rules* or *Civ.Prac. Law & Rules*, so remember to add alternative terms to your query such as **"civil practice law"** or **civ.prac.law**.

The Root Expander and the Universal Character: When you use the Terms and Connectors search method, placing the root expander (!) at the end of a root term generates all other terms with that root. For example, adding the ! to the root *discover* in the query

discover! /5 scope

instructs Westlaw to retrieve such terms as *discover, discovered, discoverable* and *discovery*.

The universal character (*) stands for one character and can be inserted in the middle or at the end of a term. For example, the term

withdr*w

will retrieve *withdraw* and *withdrew*. Adding two asterisks to the root *jur*

jur**

instructs Westlaw to retrieve all forms of the root with up to two additional characters. Terms such as *jury* or *juror* are retrieved by this query. However, terms with more than two letters following the root, such as *jurisdiction,* are not retrieved. Plurals are always retrieved, even if more than two letters follow the root.

Phrase Searching: To search for an exact phrase, place it within quotation marks. For example, to search for references to *supplemental jurisdiction,* type **"supplemental jurisdiction"**. When you are using the Terms and Connectors search method, you should use phrase searching only if you are certain that the terms in the phrase will not appear in any other order.

5.2 Alternative Terms

After selecting the terms for your query, consider which alternative terms are necessary. For example, if you are searching for the term *supplemental*, you might also want to search for the terms *ancillary* and *pendent*. You should consider both synonyms and antonyms as alternative terms. You can also use the Westlaw thesaurus to add alternative terms to your query.

5.3 Connectors

After selecting terms and alternative terms for your query, use connectors to specify the relationship that should exist between search terms in your retrieved documents. The connectors are described below:

Use:	To retrieve documents with:	Example:
& (and)	both terms	**diversity & counter-claim**
or (space)	either term or both terms	**abstention abstain* * ***
/p	search terms in the same paragraph	**discovery /p "order for protection"**
/s	search terms in the same sentence	**interplead** /s statut* * ***
+s	the first search term preceding the second within the same sentence	**burden +s prov* * * proof**

Use:	To exclude documents with:	Example:
/n	search terms within "n" terms of each other (where "n" is a number)	**summary /3 judgment**
+n	the first search term preceding the second by "n" terms (where "n" is a number)	**pennoyer +3 neff**
" "	search terms appearing in the same order as in the quotation marks	**"res judicata"**
% (but not)	search terms following the % symbol	**attorney lawyer /5 client /s privileg! % sy,di(work-product)**

5.4 Field Restrictions

Overview: Documents in each Westlaw database consist of several segments, or fields. One field may contain the citation, another the title, another the synopsis and so forth. Not all databases contain the same fields. Also depending on the database, fields with the same name may contain different types of information.

To view a list of fields for a specific database and their contents, see Scope for that database. Note that in some databases not every field is available for every document.

To retrieve only those documents containing your search terms in a specific field, restrict your search to that field. To restrict your search to a specific field, type the field name or abbreviation followed by your search terms enclosed in parentheses. For example, to retrieve a case in the New York Cases database (NY–CS) entitled *Lomando v. Duncan,* search for your terms in the title field (ti):

ti(lomando & duncan)

The fields discussed below are available in Westlaw databases you might use for researching civil procedure issues.

Digest and Synopsis Fields: The digest (di) and synopsis (sy) fields, added to case law databases by West's attorney-editors, summarize the main points of a case. The synopsis field contains a brief description of a case. The digest field contains the topic and headnote fields and includes the complete hierarchy of concepts used by West's editors to classify the headnotes to specific West digest topics and key numbers. Restricting your search to the synopsis and digest fields limits your result to cases in which your terms are related to a major issue in the case.

Consider restricting your search to one or both of these fields if

- you are searching for common terms or terms with more than one meaning, and you need to narrow your search; or

- you cannot narrow your search by using a smaller database.

For example, to retrieve New York cases that discuss the principal place of business in relation to jurisdiction, access the New York Cases database (NY–CS) and type the following query:

sy,di(principal /s place /s business /p jurisdiction)

Headnote Field: The headnote field (he) is part of the digest field, but does not contain topic numbers, hierarchical classification information or key numbers. The headnote field contains a one-sentence summary for each point of law in a case and any supporting citations given by the author of the opinion. A headnote field restriction is useful when you are searching for specific statutory sections or rule numbers. For example, to retrieve headnotes from New York cases that cite C.P.L.R. § 2101(f), access the New York Cases database (NY–CS) and type the following query:

he(2101(f))

Topic Field: The topic field (to) is also part of the digest field. It contains hierarchical classification information, including the West digest topic names and numbers and the key numbers. You should restrict search terms to the topic field in a case law database if

- a digest field search retrieves too many documents; or

- you want to retrieve cases with digest paragraphs classified under more than one topic.

For example, the topic Interpleader has the topic number 222. To retrieve New York cases that discuss attorney fees in interpleader matters, access the New York Cases database (NY–CS) and type a query like the following:

to(222) /p attorney /3 fee

To retrieve cases classified under more than one topic and key number, search for your terms in the topic field. For example, to search for cases discussing remittitur, which may be classified to Appeal and Error (30), Costs (102), Courts (106), Damages (115) or Federal Courts (170b), among other topics, type a query like the following:

to(remittitur)

For a complete list of West digest topics and their corresponding topic numbers, access the Key Number Service: click the **Key Number Service** button or choose **Key Number Service** from the Services menu.

Note: Slip opinions, cases not reported by West and cases from topical services do not contain the digest, headnote and topic fields.

Prelim and Caption Fields: When searching in a database containing statutes, rules or regulations, restrict your search to the prelim (pr) and caption (ca) fields to retrieve documents in which your terms are important enough to appear in a section name or heading. For example, to retrieve New York statutes relating to interpleader actions, access the New York Statutes–Annotated database (NY–ST–ANN) and type the following:

pr,ca(interpleader)

5.5 Date Restrictions

You can use Westlaw to retrieve documents *decided* or *issued* before, after or on a specified date, as well as within a range of dates. The following sample queries contain date restrictions:

da(1999) & amend! /5 complaint pleading

da(aft 1995) & amend! /5 complaint pleading

da(9/26/1998) & amend! /5 complaint pleading

You can also search for documents *added to a database* on or after a specified date, as well as within a range of dates. The following sample queries contain added-date restrictions:

ad(aft 1996) & amend! /5 complaint pleading

ad(aft 2–1–1998 & bef 2–17–1998) & amend! /5 complaint pleading

Section 6.   Searching with Topic and Key Numbers

To retrieve cases that address a specific point of law, use topic and key numbers as your search terms. If you have an on-point case, run a search using the topic and key number from the relevant headnote in an appropriate database to find other cases containing headnotes classified to that topic and key number. For example, to search for state cases containing headnotes classified under topic 267 (Motions) and key number 33 (Quashing or dismissal), access the New York Cases database (NY–CS) and enter the following query:

267k33

For a complete list of West digest topic and key numbers, access the Key Number Service: click the **Key Number Service** button or choose **Key Number Service** from the Services menu.

> Note: Slip opinions, cases not reported by West and cases from topical services do not contain West topic and key numbers.

Section 7.   Verifying Your Research with Citator Services

Overview: A citator service is a tool that helps you ensure that your cases are good law; helps you retrieve cases, legislation or articles that cite a case, rule or statute; and helps you verify that the spelling and format of your citations are correct.

7.1   KeyCite

KeyCite is the citation research service from West Group that integrates all case law on Westlaw. KeyCite helps you trace the history of a case, retrieve a list of all cases and selected secondary sources that cite a case, and track legal issues decided in a case.

KeyCite provides both direct and negative indirect history for any case within the scope of its coverage. The History of the Case window displays a case's direct appellate history and its negative indirect history, which consists of cases outside the direct appellate line that may have a negative impact on its precedential value. The history also includes related references, which are opinions involving the same parties and facts but resolving different issues.

In addition to case history, the Citations to the Case window in KeyCite lists all cases on Westlaw and secondary sources, such as law review articles and ALR® annotations, that cite the decision. These citing references are added to KeyCite as soon as they are added to Westlaw. All citing cases on Westlaw are included in KeyCite—even unpublished opinions.

For citation verification, the KeyCite result provides the case title; parallel citations, including many looseleaf citations; the court of decision; the docket number; and the filing date.

7.2   Westlaw As a Citator

For citations not covered by KeyCite, including persuasive secondary authority such as restatements and treatises, use Westlaw as a citator to retrieve cases that cite your authority.

Using Westlaw as a citator, you can search for documents citing a specific statute, rule, regulation, agency decision or other authority. For example, to retrieve New York cases citing 28 U.S.C.A. § 1334, access the New York Cases database (NY–CS) and type a query like the following:

28 +5 1334

Section 8.   Researching with Westlaw—Examples

8.1   Retrieving Law Review Articles

Recent law review articles are often a good place to begin researching a legal issue because law review articles serve 1) as an excellent introduction to a new topic or review for a stale one, providing terminology to help you formulate a query; 2) as a finding tool for pertinent primary authority, such as rules, statutes and cases; and 3) in some instances, as persuasive secondary authority.

Suppose you need to gain more background information on supplemental jurisdiction.

Solution

- To retrieve law review articles relevant to your issue, access the New York Journals & Law Reviews database (NY–JLR). Using the Natural Language search method, enter a description like the following:

supplemental jurisdiction

- If you have a citation to an article in a specific publication, use Find to retrieve it. For more information on Find, see Section 3.1 of this appendix. For example, to retrieve the article found at 62 Fordham L. Rev. 721, access Find and type

62 fordham l rev 721

- If you know the title of an article but not which journal it appeared in, access the New York Journals & Law Reviews database (NY–JLR) and search for key terms from the title in the title field. For example, to retrieve the article "Upside Down and Inside Out: Appellate Review of Discretion Under the Supplemental Jurisdiction Statute, 28 U.S.C. § 1367," type the following Terms and Connectors query:

ti("upside down" & "inside out")

8.2   Retrieving Rules or Statutes

Suppose you need to retrieve New York rules or statutes dealing with injunctions.

Solution

- Access the New York Statutes–Annotated database (NY–ST–ANN). Search for your terms in the prelim and caption fields using the Terms and Connectors search method:

pr,ca(injunction enjoin!)

- When you know the citation for a specific rule or statute, use Find to retrieve it. For example, to retrieve N.Y. Bus. Corp. Law § 1115, access Find and type

ny bus corp 1115

- To look at surrounding statutory sections, use the Table of Contents service. Click a hypertext link in the prelim or caption field. You can also use Documents in Sequence to retrieve the section following § 1115, even if that following section was not retrieved with your search or Find request. Click your right mouse button and choose **Documents in Sequence** from the pop-up menu.

- When you retrieve a statute on Westlaw, it will contain an Update message if legislation amending or repealing it is available online. To display this legislation, click the hypertext link in the Update message.

Because slip copy versions of laws are added to Westlaw before they contain full editorial enhancements, they are not retrieved with Update. To retrieve slip copy versions of laws, access the United States Public Laws database (US–PL) or a state's legislative service database (XX–LEGIS, where XX is the state's two-letter postal abbreviation). Then type **ci(slip)** and descriptive terms, e.g., **ci(slip) & injunction enjoin!** Slip copy documents are replaced by the editorially enhanced versions within a few working days. Update also does not retrieve legislation that enacts a new statute or covers a topic that will not be incorporated into the statutes. To retrieve this legislation, access US–PL or a legislative service database and enter a query containing terms that describe the new legislation.

8.3 Retrieving Case Law

Suppose you need to retrieve New York case law in which the New York courts discuss vacating a default judgment.

Solution

- Access the New York Cases database (NY–CS). Type a Natural Language description such as the following:

vacating a default judgment

- When you know the citation for a specific case, use Find to retrieve it. (For more information on Find, see Section 3.1 of this appendix.) For example, to retrieve *Luna Baking Co. v. Myerwold*, 69 A.D.2d 832 (1979), access Find and type

69 ad2d 832

- If you find a topic and key number that is on point, run a search using that topic and key number to retrieve additional cases discussing that point of law. For example, to retrieve cases containing headnotes classified under topic 228 (Judgment) and key number 143(3) (Mistake, surprise, or excusable neglect in general), type the following query:

228k143(3)

- To retrieve cases written by a particular judge, add a judge field (ju) restriction to your query. For example, to retrieve cases written by Justice Spain that contain headnotes classified under topic 228 (Judgment), type the following query:

ju(spain) & to(228)

8.4 Using KeyCite

Suppose one of the cases you retrieve in your case law research is *Bruno v. Village of Port Chester*, 430 N.Y.S.2d 13 (1980). You want to determine whether this case is good law and to find other cases that have cited this case.

Solution

- Use KeyCite to retrieve direct history and negative indirect history for *Bruno v. Village of Port Chester*. While viewing the case, click the **KC** button.

- Use KeyCite to display citing references for *Bruno*. From the History of the Case display, click the **Citations** tab.

8.5 Following Recent Developments

As the litigation specialist in your firm, you are expected to keep up with and summarize recent legal developments in New York. How can you do this efficiently?

Solution

One of the easiest ways to stay abreast of recent developments in New York law is by accessing the Westlaw State Bulletins–New York database (WSB–NY). The WSB–NY database contains summaries of recent federal and state judicial, legislative and administrative activities affecting New York law.

- When you access WSB–NY you will automatically retrieve a list of documents added to the database in the last two weeks.

- To read a summary of a document, double-click its entry in the list.

- To view the full text of a document, access Find while viewing its summary.

- To search this database, choose **New Query** from the Research menu. At the Terms and Connectors Query Editor, type your query. For example, to retrieve references discussing federal removal jurisdiction, type a query like the following:

remov! /s jurisdiction

Table of Cases

*

Table of Statutes and CPLR Citations

Table of Court Rules

*

Index

COMPLAINT

See, also, Pleading, generally, this index

Amendments,

Bad complaints, 82

Reply should not be used for, 362

Dismissal for failure to serve, extension of limitations, 69

Form of summons served with, 83

Impleader,

Effect if impleader complaint negates main claim, 258, 259

Service, 254, 255

Limitations of actions,

Dismissal for failure to serve, extension, 69

Interposition of claim, federal practice, 58

Motion to dismiss, failure to serve duly demanded complaint, 418

Names, all parties, 317

Parties, requirement to name all, 317

Preliminary injunction, 502

Service, failure to serve duly demanded complaint, motion to dismiss, 418

Summary judgment in lieu of complaint, 448 et seq.

Summons, form of summons served with, 83

Verification, designated instances, 372

COMPROMISE AND SETTLEMENT

Class actions, 245 et seq.

Contribution, effect of settlement with fewer than all tortfeasors, 288 et seq.

Failure to pay, entry of judgment, 667

Incompetent or incapacitated persons, claims, 314, 315

Infants claims, 314, 315

Joint tort liability adjustment, General Obligations Law, 271

Motion,

Claim of infants or incompetent persons, settlement, 314

Settle order, 404 et seq.

Non-settling tortfeasors, contribution, 291, 292

Notice of claim against public corporation, late service of notice, 36, 37

Offer to compromise, accelerated judgment, 465

Preliminary conferences, 126

Pretrial conferences, 595

Public policy, encouraging settlements, limitations of actions, 50, 718

Statements, disclosure, 537

Stipulations, 323

Vacatur as term of settlement, 719

Verdict, compromise verdict, 646, 647

COMPROMISE VERDICTS

Generally, 646, 647

COMPULSORY ARBITRATION

Arbitration, this index

COMPULSORY COUNTERCLAIM

Defined, federal practice, 354

COMPULSORY REFERENCE

Defined, trial by referee, 612

COMPUTATION

Income execution, computing the 10%, 817 et seq.

Service of papers, time, 318 et seq.

Statute of limitations, 41

COMPUTERS

Personal jurisdiction, internet, 155, 156

CONCEALMENT

Summons, concealment vitiates service, 93

CONCILIATION PROCEEDINGS

Family court jurisdiction, 18

CONCURRENT JURISDICTION

Adoption proceedings, family and surrogate's courts, 19

Supreme court, 15

CONDEMNATION

Appraisal reports, exchange, 526

CONDITIONS

Forum non conveniens dismissal or stay, 31

Judgments, vacation, 699

Orders of court, vacation, 699

CONDITIONS PRECEDENT

Generally, 34 et seq.

Arbitration, 990, 993, 994

General denial forbidden, contractual conditions precedent, 350

Leave to sue, 37

Notice of claim against public corporation, 34 et seq.

Pleading, satisfaction, contractual condition precedent, 337

Statute of limitations, condition precedent category of time period, 40, 41

CONDOMINIUMS

Leviable property right, enforcement of judgments, 789

CONFERENCES

Appeals, preargument conferences, 895, 896

Arbitration, pre-hearing conferences, 1011

Judicial conference, state court administration, 6

Preliminary conferences, 125 et seq.

Pretrial conferences, 594 et seq.

Distinguished from preliminary conferences, 126

CONFESSION OF JUDGMENT

Generally, 461 et seq.

Affidavits, 461 et seq.

Amendment, 463

Collateral estoppel, 464

Effect of, 464

Enforcement, 464

Entry, 464

Filing, 464

Full faith and credit judgment registration procedure, barred from use, 703

Money actions, 461

Res judicata, 464

Vacating, 464, 465

CONFIRMATION MOTION

Advisory jury, move to confirm verdict, time, 618

Arbitration, generally, this index

Attachment, 479, 482

Seizure of chattel, 517

CONFLICTS

Court acts and CPLR, 3

CPLR provisions, statute controls, 3

Statute of limitations, foreign claims, borrowing statute, 75 et seq.

CONFORMING PLEADINGS TO PROOF

Trial motion, 652 et seq.